Profiles
of
Indiana

2010
Second Edition

Profiles
of
Indiana

A UNIVERSAL REFERENCE BOOK

Grey House
Publishing

PUBLISHER: Leslie Mackenzie
EDITORIAL DIRECTOR: Laura Mars
EDITOR: David Garoogian
MARKETING DIRECTOR: Jessica Moody

Grey House Publishing, Inc.
4919 Route 22
Amenia, NY 12501
518.789.8700
FAX 845.373.6390
www.greyhouse.com
e-mail: books @greyhouse.com

ISBN: 978-1-59237-556-1

Table of Contents

Introduction

Welcome to the second edition of *Profiles of Indiana–Facts, Figures & Statistics for 714 Populated Places in Indiana*. As with the other titles in our State Profiles series, we built this work using content from Grey House Publishing's award-winning *Profiles of America*—a 4-volume compilation of data on more than 42,000 places in the United States. We have updated and included the Indiana chapter from *Profiles of America,* and added entire fresh chapters of demographic information and ranking sections, so that *Profiles of Indiana* is the most comprehensive portrait of the state of Indiana ever published.

This second edition provides data on all populated communities and counties in the state of Indiana for which the US Census provides individual statistics. It includes seven major sections that cover everything from **Education** to **Ethnic Backgrounds** to **Climate**. All sections include **Comparative Statistics** or **Rankings**, and full-color **Maps** at the back of the book provide valuable information in a quickly processed, visual format. Here's an overview of each section:

1. Profiles

This section, organized by county, gives detailed profiles of 714 places plus 92 counties, and is based on the 2000 Census. This core Census data has been so extensively updated, however, that nearly 80% of this section has 2010 numbers. In addition, we have added current government statistics and original research, so that these profiles pull together statistical and descriptive information on every Census-recognized place in the state. Major fields of information include:

Geography	*Housing*	*Education*	*Religion*
Ancestry	*Transportation*	*Population*	*Climate*
Economy	*Industry*	*Health*	

In addition to place profiles, this section includes an **Alphabetical Place Index** and **Comparative Statistics** that compare Indiana's 100 largest communities by dozens of data points.

2. Education

This section begins with an *Educational State Profile,* summarizing number of schools, students, diplomas granted and educational dollars spent. Following the state profile are **School District Rankings** on 16 topics ranging from *Teacher/Student Ratios* to *High School Drop-Out Rates*. Following these rankings are *National Assessment of Educational Progress (NAEP)* and *Indiana Statewide Testing for Educational Progress-Plus (ISTEP+)* results.

3. Ancestry

This section provides a detailed look at the ancestral and racial makeup of Indiana. 217 ethnic categories are ranked three ways: 1) by number, based on all places regardless of population; 2) by percent, based on all places regardless of population; 3) by percent, based on places with populations of 10,000 or more. You will discover, for example, that Bloomington has the greatest number of *Afghans* in the state (107), and that 54.3% of the population of Jasper are of *German* ancestry.

4. Hispanic Population

This section defines Indiana's Hispanic population by 23 Hispanic backgrounds from Argentinian to Venezuelan. It ranks each of 15 categories, from Median Age to Median Home Value, by each Hispanic background. For example, you'll see that Muncie has the highest percentage of *Mexicans* who speak English-only at home (70.3%), and that Indianapolis has the highest percentage of *Puerto Ricans* who are four-year college graduates (32.1%).

5. Asian Population

Similar in format to the section on Hispanic Population, this section defines Indiana's Asian population by 21 Asian backgrounds from Bangladeshi to Vietnamese. It ranks each of 14 categories, from Median Age to Median Home Value, by each Asian background. You will learn that *Asian Indians* in Munster have a median household income of $119,134 and that 96.1% of *Chinese* in West Lafayette are high-school graduates.

6. Weather

This important topic is explored in detail in this section, which includes a State Summary, a map of the state's weather stations, and profiles of both National and Cooperative Weather Stations. In addition, you'll find Weather Station Rankings, where you'll see that, over the 30-year recorded period, South Bend Michiana Regional reported the highest annual snowfall in the state with 76.6 inches.

UPDATE This section also includes current Storm data, with the most destructive weather events ranked by both fatalities and property damage, from 1985-2010. Here you will learn that a flash flood caused $100 million in property damage in East Columbus in June 2008 and that an F3 tornado was responsible for 20 fatalities in Evansville in November 2005.

7. Maps

For a more visual point of view, there are 16 full-color maps of Indiana at the back of the book. They provide information on topics such as *Federal Lands and Indian Reservations, Core-Based Statistical Areas and Counties, Population Demographics, Median Age, Income, Median Home Values, Educational Attainment, Congressional Districts,* and the *2008 Presidential Election.*

Note: The extensive **User's Guide** that follows this Introduction is segmented into six sections and examines, in some detail, each data field in the individual profiles and comparative sections for all chapters. It provides sources for all data points and statistical definitions as necessary.

User's Guide: Profiles

Places Covered

All 92 counties.

566 incorporated municipalities. Comprised of 117 cities and 449 towns.

34 census designated places (CDP). The U.S. Bureau of the Census defines a CDP as "a statistical entity, defined for each decennial census according to Census Bureau guidelines, comprising a densely settled concentration of population that is not within an incorporated place, but is locally identified by a name. CDPs are delineated cooperatively by state and local officials and the Census Bureau, following Census Bureau guidelines. Beginning with Census 2000 there are no size limits."

114 unincorporated communities. The communities included have both their own zip code and statistics for their ZIP Code Tabulation Area (ZCTA) available from the Census Bureau. They are referred to as "postal areas." A ZCTA is a statistical entity developed by the Census Bureau to approximate the delivery area for a US Postal Service 5-digit or 3-digit ZIP Code in the US and Puerto Rico. A ZCTA is an aggregation of census blocks that have the same predominant ZIP Code associated with the mailing addresses in the Census Bureau's Master Address File. Thus, the Postal Service's delivery areas have been adjusted to encompass whole census blocks so that the Census Bureau can tabulate census data for the ZCTAs. ZCTAs do not include all ZIP Codes used for mail delivery and therefore do not precisely depict the area within which mail deliveries associated with that ZIP Code occur. Additionally, some areas that are known by a unique name, although they are part of a larger incorporated place, are also included as "postal areas."

Important Notes

- Unincorporated communities that span multiple zip codes are not included in this book.

- In each community profile, only school districts that have schools that are physically located within the community are shown. In addition, statistics for each school district cover the entire district, regardless of the physical location of the schools within the district.

- Special care should be taken when interpreting certain statistics for communities containing large colleges or universities. College students were counted as residents of the area in which they were living while attending college (as they have been since the 1950 census). One effect this may have is skewing the figures for population, income, housing, and educational attainment.

- Some information (e.g. unemployment rates) is available for both counties and individual communities. Other information is available for just counties (e.g. election results), or just individual communities (e.g. local newspapers).

- Some statistical information is available only for larger communities. In addition, the larger places are more apt to have services such as newspapers, airports, school districts, etc.

- For the most complete information on any community, you should also check the entry for the county in which the community is located. In addition, more information and services will be listed under the larger places in the county.

For a more in-depth discussion of geographic areas, please refer to the Census Bureau's Geographic Areas Reference Manual at http://www.census.gov/geo/www/garm.html.

Data Sources

CENSUS 2000

The parts of the data which are from the 2000 Decennial Census are from the following sources: *U.S. Bureau of the Census, Census of Population and Housing, 2000: Summary Files 1 and 3.* Summary File 3 (SF 3) consists of 813 detailed tables of Census 2000 social, economic and housing characteristics compiled from a sample of approximately 19 million housing units (about 1 in 6 households) that received the Census 2000 long-form questionnaire. Summary File 1 (SF 1) contains 286 tables focusing on age, sex, households, families, and housing units. This file presents 100-percent population and housing figures for the total population, for 63 race categories, and for many other race and Hispanic or Latino categories.

Comparing SF 3 Estimates with Corresponding Values in SF 1

As in earlier censuses, the responses from the sample of households reporting on long forms must be weighted to reflect the entire population. Specifically, each responding household represents, on average, six or seven other households who reported using short forms.

One consequence of the weighting procedures is that each estimate based on the long form responses has an associated confidence interval. These confidence intervals are wider (as a percentage of the estimate) for geographic areas with smaller populations and for characteristics that occur less frequently in the area being examined (such as the proportion of people in poverty in a middle-income neighborhood).

In order to release as much useful information as possible, statisticians must balance a number of factors. In particular, for Census 2000, the Bureau of the Census created weighting areas—geographic areas from which about two hundred or more long forms were completed—which are large enough to produce good quality estimates. If smaller weighting areas had been used, the confidence intervals around the estimates would have been significantly wider, rendering many estimates less useful due to their lower reliability.

The disadvantage of using weighting areas this large is that, for smaller geographic areas within them, the estimates of characteristics that are also reported on the short form will not match the counts reported in SF 1. Examples of these characteristics are the total number of people, the number of people reporting specific racial categories, and the number of housing units. The official values for items reported on the short form come from SF 1 and SF 2.

The differences between the long form estimates in SF 3 and values in SF 1 are particularly noticeable for the smallest places, tracts, and block groups. The long form estimates of total population and total housing units in SF 3 will, however, match the SF 1 counts for larger geographic areas such as counties and states, and will be essentially the same for medium and large cities.

SF 1 gives exact numbers even for very small groups and areas, whereas SF 3 gives estimates for small groups and areas such as tracts and small places that are less exact. The goal of SF 3 is to identify large differences among areas or large changes over time. Estimates for small areas and small population groups often do exhibit large changes from one census to the next, so having the capability to measure them is worthwhile.

2010 Estimates and 2015 Projections

Some 2000 Census data has been updated with data provided by Claritas. Founded in 1971, Claritas is the industry leader in applied demography and the preeminent provider of small-area demographic estimates.

Information for Communities

PHYSICAL CHARACTERISTICS

Place Type: Lists the type of place (city, town, village, borough, special city, CDP, township, plantation, gore, district, grant, location, reservation, or postal area). *Source: U.S. Bureau of the Census, Census of Population and Housing, 2000: Summary File 1 and U.S. Postal Service, City State File.*

Land and Water Area: Land and water area in square miles. *Source: U.S. Bureau of the Census, Census of Population and Housing, 2000: Summary File 1.*

Latitude and Longitude: Latitude and longitude in degrees. *Source: U.S. Bureau of the Census, Census of Population and Housing, 2000: Summary File 1.*

Elevation: Elevation in feet. *Source: U.S. Geological Survey, Geographic Names Information System (GNIS).*

HISTORY

History: Historical information. *Source: Columbia University Press, The Columbia Gazetteer of North America; Original research.*

POPULATION

Population: 1990 and 2000 figures are a 100% count of population. 2010 estimates and 2015 projections were provided by Claritas. *Source: Claritas; U.S. Bureau of the Census, Census of Population and Housing, 2000: Summary File 1.*

Population by Race: 2010 estimates includes the U.S. Bureau of the Census categories of White alone; Black alone; Asian alone; and Hispanic of any race. Alone refers to the fact that these figures are not in combination with any other race. 2010 data for American Indian/Alaska Native and Native Hawaiian/Other Pacific Islander was not available.

The concept of race, as used by the Census Bureau, reflects self-identification by people according to the race or races with which they most closely identify. These categories are socio-political constructs and should not be interpreted as being scientific or anthropological in nature. Furthermore, the race categories include both racial and national-origin groups.

- **White.** A person having origins in any of the original peoples of Europe, the Middle East, or North Africa. It includes people who indicate their race as White or report entries such as Irish, German, Italian, Lebanese, Near Easterner, Arab, or Polish.
- **Black or African American.** A person having origins in any of the Black racial groups of Africa. It includes people who indicate their race as Black, African American, or Negro, or provide written entries such as African American, Afro-American, Kenyan, Nigerian, or Haitian.
- **Asian.** A person having origins in any of the original peoples of the Far East, Southeast Asia, or the Indian subcontinent including, for example, Cambodia, China, India, Japan, Korea, Malaysia, Pakistan, the Philippine Islands, Thailand, and Vietnam. It includes Asian Indian, Chinese, Filipino, Korean, Japanese, Vietnamese, and Other Asian.
- **Hispanic.** The data on the Hispanic or Latino population, which was asked of all people, were derived from answers to long-form questionnaire Item 5, and short-form questionnaire Item 7. The terms Spanish, Hispanic origin, and Latino are used interchangeably. Some respondents identify with all three terms, while others may identify with only one of these three specific terms. Hispanics or Latinos who identify with the terms Spanish, Hispanic, or Latino are those who classify themselves in one of the specific Hispanic or Latino categories listed on the questionnaire—Mexican, Puerto Rican, or Cuban—as well as those who indicate that they are other Spanish, Hispanic, or Latino. People who do not identify with one of the specific origins listed on the questionnaire but indicate that they are other Spanish, Hispanic, or Latino are those whose origins are from Spain, the Spanish-speaking countries of Central or South America, the Dominican Republic, or people identifying themselves generally as Spanish, Spanish-American, Hispanic, Hispano, Latino, and so on. All write-in responses to the other Spanish/Hispanic/Latino category were coded. Origin can be viewed as the heritage, nationality group, lineage, or country of birth of the person or the person's parents or ancestors before their arrival in the United States. People who identify their origin as Spanish, Hispanic, or Latino may be of any race.

Population Density: 2010 population estimate divided by the land area in square miles. *Source: Claritas; U.S. Bureau of the Census, Census of Population and Housing, 2000: Summary File 1.*

Average Household Size: Average household size was calculated by dividing the total population by the total number of households. Figures are 2010 estimates. *Source: Claritas.*

Median Age: Figures are 2010 estimates. *Source: Claritas.*

Male/Female Ratio: Number of males per 100 females. Figures are 2010 estimates. *Source: Claritas.*

Marital Status: Percentage of population never married, now married, widowed, or divorced. *Source: U.S. Bureau of the Census, Census of Population and Housing, 2000: Summary File 3.*

The marital status classification refers to the status at the time of enumeration. Data on marital status are tabulated only for the population 15 years old and over. Each person was asked whether they were "Now married," "Widowed," "Divorced," or "Never married." Couples who live together (for example, people in common-law marriages) were able to report the marital status they considered to be the most appropriate.

- **Never married.** Never married includes all people who have never been married, including people whose only marriage(s) was annulled.
- **Now married.** All people whose current marriage has not ended by widowhood or divorce. This category includes people defined as "separated."
- **Widowed.** This category includes widows and widowers who have not remarried.
- **Divorced.** This category includes people who are legally divorced and who have not remarried.

Foreign Born: Percentage of population who were not U.S. citizens at birth. Foreign-born people are those who indicated they were either a U.S. citizen by naturalization or they were not a citizen of the United States. *Source: U.S. Bureau of the Census, Census of Population and Housing, 2000: Summary File 3.*

Ancestry: Largest ancestry groups reported (up to five). Includes multiple ancestries. *Source: U.S. Bureau of the Census, Census of Population and Housing, 2000: Summary File 3.*

The data represent self-classification by people according to the ancestry group or groups with which they most closely identify. Ancestry refers to a person's ethnic origin or descent, "roots," heritage, or the place of birth of the person, the person's parents, or their ancestors before their arrival in the United States. Some ethnic identities, such as Egyptian or Polish, can be traced to geographic areas outside the United States, while other ethnicities such as Pennsylvania German or Cajun evolved in the United States.

The ancestry question was intended to provide data for groups that were not included in the Hispanic origin and race questions. Therefore, although data on all groups are collected, the ancestry data shown in these tabulations are for non-Hispanic and non-race groups. Hispanic and race groups are included in the "Other groups" category for the ancestry tables in these tabulations.

The ancestry question allowed respondents to report one or more ancestry groups, although only the first two were coded. If a response was in terms of a dual ancestry, for example, "Irish English," the person was assigned two codes, in this case one for Irish and another for English. However, in certain cases, multiple responses such as "French Canadian," "Greek Cypriote," and "Scotch Irish" were assigned a single code reflecting their status as unique groups. If a person reported one of these unique groups in addition to another group, for example, "Scotch Irish English," resulting in three terms, that person received one code for the unique group (Scotch-Irish) and another one for the remaining group (English). If a person reported "English Irish French," only English and Irish were coded. Certain combinations of ancestries where the ancestry group is a part of another, such as "German-Bavarian," were coded as a single ancestry using the more specific group (Bavarian). Also, responses such as "Polish-American" or "Italian-American" were coded and tabulated as a single entry (Polish or Italian).

The Census Bureau accepted "American" as a unique ethnicity if it was given alone, with an ambiguous response, or with state names. If the respondent listed any other ethnic identity such as "Italian-American," generally the "American" portion of the response was not coded. However, distinct groups such as "American Indian," "Mexican American," and "African American" were coded and identified separately because they represented groups who considered themselves different from those who reported as "Indian," "Mexican," or "African," respectively.

The data is based on the total number of ancestries reported and coded. Thus, the sum of the counts in this type of presentation is not the total population but the total of all responses.

ECONOMY

Unemployment Rate: May 2010. Includes all civilians age 16 or over who were unemployed and looking for work. *Source: U.S. Department of Labor, Bureau of Labor Statistics, Local Area Unemployment Statistics (http://www.bls.gov/lau/home.htm).*

Total Civilian Labor Force: May 2010. Includes all civilians age 16 or over who were either employed, or unemployed and looking for work. *Source: U.S. Department of Labor, Bureau of Labor Statistics, Local Area Unemployment Statistics (http://www.bls.gov/lau/home.htm).*

Single-Family Building Permits Issued: Building permits issued for new single-family housing units in 2009. *Source: U.S. Census Bureau, Manufacturing and Construction Division (http://www.census.gov/const/www/permitsindex.html).*

Multi-Family Building Permits Issued: Building permits issued for new multi-family housing units in 2009. *Source: U.S. Census Bureau, Manufacturing and Construction Division (http://www.census.gov/const/www/permitsindex.html).*

Statistics on housing units authorized by building permits include housing units issued in local permit-issuing jurisdictions by a building or zoning permit. Not all areas of the country require a building or zoning permit. The statistics only represent those areas that do require a permit. Current surveys indicate that construction is undertaken for all but a very small percentage of housing units authorized by building permits. A major portion typically get under way during the month of permit issuance and most of the remainder begin within the three following months. Because of this lag, the housing unit authorization statistics do not represent the number of units actually put into construction for the period shown, and should therefore not be directly interpreted as "housing starts."

Statistics are based upon reports submitted by local building permit officials in response to a mail survey. They are obtained using Form C-404 const/www/c404.pdf, "Report of New Privately-Owned Residential Building or Zoning Permits Issued." When a report is not received, missing data are either (1) obtained from the Survey of Use of Permits (SUP) which is used to collect information on housing starts, or (2) imputed based on the assumption that the ratio of current month authorizations to those of a year ago should be the same for reporting and non-reporting places.

Employment by Occupation: Percentage of the employed civilian population 16 years and over in management, professional, service, sales, farming, construction, and production occupations. *Source: U.S. Bureau of the Census, Census of Population and Housing, 2000: Summary File 3.*

- **Management** includes management, business, and financial operations occupations:
    Management occupations, except farmers and farm managers
    Farmers and farm managers
    Business and financial operations occupations:
        Business operations specialists
        Financial specialists

- **Professional** includes professional and related occupations:
    Computer and mathematical occupations
    Architecture and engineering occupations:
        Architects, surveyors, cartographers, and engineers
        Drafters, engineering, and mapping technicians
    Life, physical, and social science occupations
    Community and social services occupations
    Legal occupations
    Education, training, and library occupations
    Arts, design, entertainment, sports, and media occupations
    Healthcare practitioners and technical occupations:
        Health diagnosing and treating practitioners and technical occupations
        Health technologists and technicians

- **Service** occupations include:
    Healthcare support occupations
    Protective service occupations:
        Fire fighting, prevention, and law enforcement workers, including supervisors

Other protective service workers, including supervisors
Food preparation and serving related occupations
Building and grounds cleaning and maintenance occupations
Personal care and service occupations

- **Sales** and office occupations include:
  Sales and related occupations
  Office and administrative support occupations

- **Farming,** fishing, and forestry occupations

- **Construction,** extraction, and maintenance occupations include:
  Construction and extraction occupations:
  Supervisors, construction, and extraction workers
  Construction trades workers
  Extraction workers
  Installation, maintenance, and repair occupations

- **Production,** transportation, and material moving occupations include:
  Production occupations
  Transportation and material moving occupations:
  Supervisors, transportation, and material moving workers
  Aircraft and traffic control occupations
  Motor vehicle operators
  Rail, water, and other transportation occupations
  Material moving workers

INCOME

Per Capita Income: Per capita income is the mean income computed for every man, woman, and child in a particular group. It is derived by dividing the total income of a particular group by the total population in that group. Per capita income is rounded to the nearest whole dollar. Figures shown are 2010 estimates. *Source: Claritas.*

Median Household Income: Includes the income of the householder and all other individuals 15 years old and over in the household, whether they are related to the householder or not. The median divides the income distribution into two equal parts: one-half of the cases falling below the median income and one-half above the median. For households, the median income is based on the distribution of the total number of households including those with no income. Median income for households is computed on the basis of a standard distribution and is rounded to the nearest whole dollar. Figures shown are 2010 estimates. *Source: Claritas.*

Average Household Income: Average household income is obtained by dividing total household income by the total number of households. Figures shown are 2010 estimates. *Source: Claritas.*

Percent of Households with Income of $100,000 or more: Figures shown are 2010 estimates. *Source: Claritas.*

Poverty Rate: Percentage of population with income in 1999 below the poverty level. Based on individuals for whom poverty status is determined. Poverty status was determined for all people except institutionalized people, people in military group quarters, people in college dormitories, and unrelated individuals under 15 years old. *Source: U.S. Bureau of the Census, Census of Population and Housing, 2000: Summary File 3.*

The poverty status of families and unrelated individuals in 1999 was determined using 48 thresholds (income cutoffs) arranged in a two-dimensional matrix. The matrix consists of family size (from 1 person to 9 or more people) cross-classified by presence and number of family members under 18 years old (from no children present to 8 or more children present). Unrelated individuals and 2-person families were further differentiated by the age of the reference person (RP) (under 65 years old and 65 years old and over).

To determine a person's poverty status, one compares the person's total family income with the poverty threshold appropriate for that person's family size and composition. If the total income of that person's family is less than the threshold appropriate for that family, then the person is considered poor, together with every member of his or her family. If a person is not living with anyone related by birth, marriage, or adoption, then the person's own income is compared with his or her poverty threshold.

TAXES

Total City Taxes Per Capita: Total city taxes collected divided by the population of the city. *Source: U.S. Bureau of the Census, State and Local Government Finances, 2006-07 (http://www.census.gov/govs/www/estimate.html).*

Taxes include:
- Property Taxes
- Sales and Gross Receipts Taxes
- Federal Customs Duties
- General Sales and Gross Receipts Taxes
- Selective Sales Taxes (alcoholic beverages; amusements; insurance premiums; motor fuels; pari-mutuels; public utilities; tobacco products; other)
- License Taxes (alcoholic beverages; amusements; corporations in general; hunting and fishing; motor vehicles motor vehicle operators; public utilities; occupation and business, NEC; other)
- Income Taxes (individual income; corporation net income; other)
- Death and Gift
- Documentary & Stock Transfer
- Severance
- Taxes, NEC

Total City Property Taxes Per Capita: Total city property taxes collected divided by the population of the city. *Source: U.S. Bureau of the Census, State and Local Government Finances, 2006-07 (http://www.census.gov/govs/www/estimate.html).*

Property Taxes include general property taxes, relating to property as a whole, taxed at a single rate or at classified rates according to the class of property. Property refers to real property (e.g. land and structures) as well as personal property; personal property can be either tangible (e.g. automobiles and boats) or intangible (e.g. bank accounts and stocks and bonds). Special property taxes, levied on selected types of property (e.g. oil and gas properties, house trailers, motor vehicles, and intangibles) and subject to rates not directly related to general property tax rates. Taxes based on income produced by property as a measure of its value on the assessment date.

EDUCATION

Educational Attainment: Figures shown are 2010 estimates and show the percent of population age 25 and over with:

- **High school diploma (including GED) or higher:** includes people whose highest degree is a high school diploma or its equivalent, people who attended college but did not receive a degree, and people who received a college, university, or professional degree.
- **Bachelor's degree or higher**
- **Master's degree or higher:** Master's degrees include the traditional MA and MS degrees and field-specific degrees, such as MSW, MEd, MBA, and MLS. *Source: Claritas.*

School Districts: Lists the name of each school district, the grade range (PK=pre-kindergarten; KG=kindergarten), the student enrollment, and the district headquarters' phone number. In each community profile, only school districts that have schools that are physically located within the community are shown. In addition, statistics for each school district cover the entire district, regardless of the physical location of the schools within the district. *Source: U.S. Department of Education, National Center for Educational Statistics, Directory of Public Elementary and Secondary Education Agencies, 2008-09.*

Four-year Colleges: Lists the name of each four-year college, the type of institution (private or public; for-profit or non-profit; religious affiliation; historically black), the total student enrollment (Fall 2008 estimate), the general telephone number, and the annual tuition (including fees) for full-time, first-time undergraduate students (in-state and out-of-state). *Source: U.S. Department of Education, National Center for Educational Statistics, IPEDS College Data, 2009-10.*

Two-year Colleges: Lists the name of each two-year college, the type of institution (private or public; for-profit or non-profit; religious affiliation; historically black), the total student enrollment (Fall 2008 estimate), the general telephone number, and the annual tuition (including fees) for full-time, first-time undergraduate students (in-state and out-of-state). *Source: U.S. Department of Education, National Center for Educational Statistics, IPEDS College Data, 2009-10.*

Vocational/Technical Schools: Lists the name of each vocational/technical school, the type of institution (private or public; for-profit or non-profit; religious affiliation; historically black), the total student enrollment (Fall 2008 estimate), the general telephone number, and the annual tuition and fees for full-time students. *Source: U.S. Department of Education, National Center for Educational Statistics, IPEDS College Data, 2009-10.*

HOUSING

Homeownership Rate: Percentage of housing units that are owner-occupied. Figures shown are 2010 estimates. *Source: Claritas.*

Median Home Value: Median value of all owner-occupied housing units as reported by the owner. Figures shown are 2010 estimates. *Source: Claritas.*

Median Rent: Median monthly contract rent on specified renter-occupied and specified vacant-for-rent units. Specified renter-occupied and specified vacant-for-rent units exclude 1-family houses on 10 acres or more. Contract rent is the monthly rent agreed to or contracted for, regardless of any furnishings, utilities, fees, meals, or services that may be included. For vacant units, it is the monthly rent asked for the rental unit at the time of enumeration. *Source: U.S. Bureau of the Census, Census of Population and Housing, 2000: Summary File 3.*

Median Age of Housing: Median age of housing was calculated by subtracting median year structure built from 2000 (e.g. if the median year structure built is 1967, the median age of housing in that area is 33 years—2000 minus 1967). Year structure built refers to when the building was first constructed, not when it was remodeled, added to, or converted. For mobile homes, houseboats, RVs, etc, the manufacturer's model year was assumed to be the year built. The data relate to the number of units built during the specified periods that were still in existence at the time of enumeration. *Source: U.S. Bureau of the Census, Census of Population and Housing, 2000: Summary File 3.*

HOSPITALS

Lists the hospital name and the number of licensed beds. *Source: Grey House Publishing, Directory of Hospital Personnel, 2010.*

SAFETY

Violent Crime Rate: Number of violent crimes reported per 10,000 population. Violent crimes include murder, forcible rape, robbery, and aggravated assault. *Source: Federal Bureau of Investigation, Uniform Crime Reports 2008 (http://www.fbi.gov/ucr/ucr.htm).*

Property Crime Rate: Number of property crimes reported per 10,000 population. Property crimes include burglary, larceny-theft, and motor vehicle theft. *Source: Federal Bureau of Investigation, Uniform Crime Reports 2008 (http://www.fbi.gov/ucr/ucr.htm).*

NEWSPAPERS

Lists the name, circulation and news focus of daily and weekly newspapers. Includes newspapers with offices located in the community profiled. *Source: MediaContactsPro 2009*

TRANSPORTATION

Commute to Work: Percentage of workers 16 years old and over that use the following means of transportation to commute to work: car; public transportation; walk; work from home. *Source: U.S. Bureau of the Census, Census of Population and Housing, 2000: Summary File 3.*

The means of transportation data for some areas may show workers using modes of public transportation that are not available in those areas (e.g. subway or elevated riders in a metropolitan area where there actually is no subway or elevated service). This result is largely due to people who worked during the reference week at a location that was different from their usual place of work (such as people away from home on business in an area where subway service was available) and people who used more than one means of transportation each day but whose principal means was unavailable where they lived (e.g. residents of non-metropolitan areas who drove to the fringe of a metropolitan area and took the commuter railroad most of the distance to work).

Travel Time to Work: Travel time to work for workers 16 years old and over. Reported for the following intervals: less than 15 minutes; 15 to 30 minutes; 30 to 45 minutes; 45 to 60 minutes; 60 minutes or more. *Source: U.S. Bureau of the Census, Census of Population and Housing, 2000: Summary File 3.*

Travel time to work refers to the total number of minutes that it usually took the person to get from home to work each day during the reference week. The elapsed time includes time spent waiting for public transportation, picking up passengers in carpools, and time spent in other activities related to getting to work.

Amtrak: Indicates if Amtrak rail or bus service is available. Please note that the cities being served continually change. *Source: National Railroad Passenger Corporation, Amtrak National Timetable, 2010 (www.amtrak.com).*

AIRPORTS

Lists the local airport(s) along with type of service and hub size. *Source: U.S. Department of Transportation, Bureau of Transportation Statistics (http://www.bts.gov).*

ADDITIONAL INFORMATION CONTACTS

The following phone numbers are provided as sources of additional information: Chambers of Commerce; Economic Development Agencies; and Convention & Visitors Bureaus. Efforts have been made to provide the most recent area codes. However, area code changes may have occurred in listed numbers. *Source: Original research.*

Information for Counties

PHYSICAL CHARACTERISTICS

Physical Location: Describes the physical location of the county. *Source: Columbia University Press, The Columbia Gazetteer of North America and original research.*

Land and Water Area: Land and water area in square miles. *Source: U.S. Bureau of the Census, Census of Population and Housing, 2000: Summary File 1.*

Time Zone: Lists the time zone. *Source: Original research.*

Year Organized: Year the county government was organized. *Source: National Association of Counties (www.naco.org).*

County Seat: Lists the county seat. If a county has more than one seat, then both are listed. *Source: National Association of Counties (www.naco.org).*

Metropolitan Area: Indicates the metropolitan area the county is located in. Also lists all the component counties of that metropolitan area. The Office of Management and Budget (OMB) defines metropolitan and micropolitan statistical areas. The most current definitions are as of November 2008. *Source: U.S. Bureau of the Census (http://www.census.gov/population/www/estimates/metrodef.html).*

Climate: Includes all weather stations located within the county. Indicates the station name and elevation as well as the monthly average high and low temperatures, average precipitation, and average snowfall. The period of record is generally 1970-1999, however, certain weather stations contain averages going back as far as 1900. *Source: Grey House Publishing, Weather America: A Thirty-Year Summary of Statistical Weather Data and Rankings, 2001.*

POPULATION

Population: 1990 and 2000 figures are a 100% count of population. 2010 estimates and 2015 projections were provided by Claritas. *Source: Claritas; U.S. Bureau of the Census, Census of Population and Housing, 2000: Summary File 1.*

Population by Race: 2010 estimates includes the U.S. Bureau of the Census categories of White alone; Black alone; Asian alone; and Hispanic of any race. Alone refers to the fact that these figures are not in combination with any other race. 2010 data for American Indian/Alaska Native and Native Hawaiian/Other Pacific Islander was not available.

The concept of race, as used by the Census Bureau, reflects self-identification by people according to the race or races with which they most closely identify. These categories are socio-political constructs and should not be interpreted as being scientific or anthropological in nature. Furthermore, the race categories include both racial and national-origin groups.

- **White.** A person having origins in any of the original peoples of Europe, the Middle East, or North Africa. It includes people who indicate their race as White or report entries such as Irish, German, Italian, Lebanese, Near Easterner, Arab, or Polish.

- **Black or African American.** A person having origins in any of the Black racial groups of Africa. It includes people who indicate their race as Black, African American, or Negro, or provide written entries such as African American, Afro-American, Kenyan, Nigerian, or Haitian.

- **Asian.** A person having origins in any of the original peoples of the Far East, Southeast Asia, or the Indian subcontinent including, for example, Cambodia, China, India, Japan, Korea, Malaysia, Pakistan, the Philippine Islands, Thailand, and Vietnam. It includes Asian Indian, Chinese, Filipino, Korean, Japanese, Vietnamese, and Other Asian.

- **Hispanic.** The data on the Hispanic or Latino population, which was asked of all people, were derived from answers to long-form questionnaire Item 5, and short-form questionnaire Item 7. The terms Spanish, Hispanic origin, and Latino are used interchangeably. Some respondents identify with all three terms, while others may identify with only one of these three specific terms. Hispanics or Latinos who identify with the terms Spanish, Hispanic, or Latino are those who classify themselves in one of the specific Hispanic or Latino categories listed on the questionnaire—Mexican, Puerto Rican, or Cuban—as well as those who indicate that they are other Spanish, Hispanic, or Latino. People who do not identify with one of the specific origins listed on the questionnaire but indicate that they are other Spanish, Hispanic, or Latino are those whose origins are from Spain, the Spanish-speaking countries of Central or South

America, the Dominican Republic, or people identifying themselves generally as Spanish, Spanish-American, Hispanic, Hispano, Latino, and so on. All write-in responses to the other Spanish/Hispanic/Latino category were coded. Origin can be viewed as the heritage, nationality group, lineage, or country of birth of the person or the person's parents or ancestors before their arrival in the United States. People who identify their origin as Spanish, Hispanic, or Latino may be of any race.

Population Density: 2010 population estimate divided by the land area in square miles. *Source: Claritas; U.S. Bureau of the Census, Census of Population and Housing, 2000: Summary File 1.*

Average Household Size: Average household size was calculated by dividing the total population by the total number of households. Figures are 2010 estimates. *Source: Claritas.*

Median Age: Figures are 2010 estimates. *Source: Claritas.*

Male/Female Ratio: Number of males per 100 females. Figures are 2010 estimates. *Source: Claritas.*

RELIGION

Religion: Lists the largest religious groups (up to five) based on the number of adherents divided by the population of the county. Adherents are defined as "all members, including full members, their children and the estimated number of other regular participants who are not considered as communicant, confirmed or full members." The data is based on a study of 149 religious bodies sponsored by the Association of Statisticians of American Religious Bodies. The 149 bodies reported 268,254 congregations and 141,371,963 adherents. *Source: Glenmary Research Center, Religious Congregations & Membership in the United States 2000.*

ECONOMY

Unemployment Rate: May 2010. Includes all civilians age 16 or over who were unemployed and looking for work. *Source: U.S. Department of Labor, Bureau of Labor Statistics, Local Area Unemployment Statistics (http://www.bls.gov/lau/home.htm).*

Total Civilian Labor Force: May 2010. Includes all civilians age 16 or over who were either employed, or unemployed and looking for work. *Source: U.S. Department of Labor, Bureau of Labor Statistics, Local Area Unemployment Statistics (http://www.bls.gov/lau/home.htm).*

Leading Industries: Lists the three largest industries (excluding government) based on the number of employees. *Source: U.S. Bureau of the Census, County Business Patterns 2008 (http://www.census.gov/epcd/cbp/view/cbpview.html).*

Farms: The total number of farms and the total acreage they occupy. *Source: U.S. Department of Agriculture, National Agricultural Statistics Service, 2007 Census of Agriculture (http://www.agcensus.usda.gov).*

Companies that Employ 500 or more persons: The numbers of companies that employ 500 or more persons. Includes private employers only. *Source: U.S. Bureau of the Census, County Business Patterns 2008 (http://www.census.gov/epcd/cbp/view/cbpview.html).*

Companies that Employ 100 - 499 persons: The numbers of companies that employ 100 - 499 persons. Includes private employers only. *Source: U.S. Bureau of the Census, County Business Patterns 2008 (http://www.census.gov/epcd/cbp/view/cbpview.html).*

Companies that Employ 1 - 99 persons: The numbers of companies that employ 1 - 99 persons. Includes private employers only. *Source: U.S. Bureau of the Census, County Business Patterns 2008 (http://www.census.gov/epcd/cbp/view/cbpview.html)*

Black-Owned Businesses: Number of businesses that are majority-owned by a Black or African-American person(s). Majority ownership is defined as having 51 percent or more of the stock or equity in the business. Black or African American is defined as a person having origins in any of the black racial groups of Africa, including those who consider themselves to be "Haitian." *Source: U.S. Bureau of the Census, 2002 Economic Census, Survey of Business Owners: Black-Owned Firms, 2002 (http://www.census.gov/csd/sbo/index.html).*

Asian-Owned Businesses: Number of businesses that are majority-owned by an Asian person(s). Majority ownership is defined as having 51 percent or more of the stock or equity in the business. *Source: U.S. Bureau of the Census, 2002 Economic Census, Survey of Business Owners: Black-Owned Firms, 2002 (http://www.census.gov/csd/sbo/index.html).*

Hispanic-Owned Businesses: Number of businesses that are majority-owned by a person(s) of Hispanic or Latino origin. Majority ownership is defined as having 51 percent or more of the stock or equity in the business. Hispanic or Latino origin is defined as a person of Cuban, Mexican, Puerto Rican, South or Central American, or other Spanish culture or origin, regardless of race. *Source: U.S. Bureau of the Census, 2002 Economic Census, Survey of Business Owners: Hispanic-Owned Firms, 2002 (http://www.census.gov/csd/sbo/index.html).*

Women-Owned Businesses: Number of businesses that are majority-owned by a woman. Majority ownership is defined as having 51 percent or more of the stock or equity in the business. *Source: U.S. Bureau of the Census, 2002 Economic Census, Survey of Business Owners: Women-Owned Firms, 2002 (http://www.census.gov/csd/sbo/index.html).*

The Survey of Business Owners (SBO), formerly known as the Surveys of Minority- and Women-Owned Business Enterprises (SMOBE/SWOBE), provides statistics that describe the composition of U.S. businesses by gender, Hispanic or Latino origin, and race. Additional statistics include owner's age, education level, veteran status, and primary function in the business; family- and home-based businesses; types of customers and workers; and sources of financing for expansion, capital improvements, or start-up. Economic policymakers in federal, state and local governments use the SBO data to understand conditions of business success and failure by comparing census-to-census changes in business performances and by comparing minority-/nonminority- and women-/men-owned businesses.

Retail Sales per Capita: Total dollar amount of estimated retail sales divided by the estimated population of the county in 2010. *Source: Editor & Publisher Market Guide 2010*

Single-Family Building Permits Issued: Building permits issued for new, single-family housing units in 2009. *Source: U.S. Census Bureau, Manufacturing and Construction Division (http://www.census.gov/const/www/permitsindex.html).*

Multi-Family Building Permits Issued: Building permits issued for new, multi-family housing units in 2009. *Source: U.S. Census Bureau, Manufacturing and Construction Division (http://www.census.gov/const/www/permitsindex.html).*

Statistics on housing units authorized by building permits include housing units issued in local permit-issuing jurisdictions by a building or zoning permit. Not all areas of the country require a building or zoning permit. The statistics only represent those areas that do require a permit. Current surveys indicate that construction is undertaken for all but a very small percentage of housing units authorized by building permits. A major portion typically get under way during the month of permit issuance and most of the remainder begin within the three following months. Because of this lag, the housing unit authorization statistics do not represent the number of units actually put into construction for the period shown, and should therefore not be directly interpreted as "housing starts."

Statistics are based upon reports submitted by local building permit officials in response to a mail survey. They are obtained using Form C-404 const/www/c404.pdf, "Report of New Privately-Owned Residential Building or Zoning Permits Issued." When a report is not received, missing data are either (1) obtained from the Survey of Use of Permits (SUP) which is used to collect information on housing starts, or (2) imputed based on the assumption that the ratio of current month authorizations to those of a year ago should be the same for reporting and non-reporting places.

INCOME

Per Capita Income: Per capita income is the mean income computed for every man, woman, and child in a particular group. It is derived by dividing the total income of a particular group by the total population in that group. Per capita income is rounded to the nearest whole dollar. Figures shown are 2010 estimates. *Source: Claritas.*

Median Household Income: Includes the income of the householder and all other individuals 15 years old and over in the household, whether they are related to the householder or not. The median divides the income distribution into two equal parts: one-half of the cases falling below the median income and one-half above the median. For households, the median income is based on the distribution of the total number of households including those with no income. Median income for households is computed on the basis of a standard distribution and is rounded to the nearest whole dollar. Figures shown are 2010 estimates. *Source: Claritas.*

Average Household Income: Average household income is obtained by dividing total household income by the total number of households. Figures shown are 2010 estimates. *Source: Claritas.*

Percent of Households with Income of $100,000 or more: Figures shown are 2010 estimates. *Source: Claritas.*

Poverty Rate: Estimated percentage of population with income in 2008 below the poverty level. *Source: U.S. Bureau of the Census, Small Area Income & Poverty Estimates.*

Bankruptcy Rate: The personal bankruptcy filing rate is the number of bankruptcies per thousand residents in 2009. Personal bankruptcy filings include both Chapter 7 (liquidations) and Chapter 13 (reorganizations) based on the county of residence of the filer. *Source: Federal Deposit Insurance Corporation, Regional Economic Conditions (http://www2.fdic.gov/recon/index.html).*

TAXES

Total County Taxes Per Capita: Total county taxes collected divided by the population of the county. *Source: U.S. Bureau of the Census, State and Local Government Finances, 2006-07 (http://www.census.gov/govs/www/estimate.html).*

Taxes include:
- Property Taxes
- Sales and Gross Receipts Taxes
- Federal Customs Duties
- General Sales and Gross Receipts Taxes
- Selective Sales Taxes (alcoholic beverages; amusements; insurance premiums; motor fuels; pari-mutuels; public utilities; tobacco products; other)
- License Taxes (alcoholic beverages; amusements; corporations in general; hunting and fishing; motor vehicles motor vehicle operators; public utilities; occupation and business, NEC; other)
- Income Taxes (individual income; corporation net income; other)
- Death and Gift
- Documentary & Stock Transfer
- Severance
- Taxes, NEC

Total County Property Taxes Per Capita: Total county property taxes collected divided by the population of the county. *Source: U.S. Bureau of the Census, State and Local Government Finances, 2006-07 (http://www.census.gov/govs/www/estimate.html).*

Property Taxes include general property taxes, relating to property as a whole, taxed at a single rate or at classified rates according to the class of property. Property refers to real property (e.g. land and structures) as well as personal property; personal property can be either tangible (e.g. automobiles and boats) or intangible (e.g. bank accounts and stocks and bonds). Special property taxes, levied on selected types of property (e.g. oil and gas properties, house trailers, motor vehicles, and intangibles) and subject to rates not directly related to general property tax rates. Taxes based on income produced by property as a measure of its value on the assessment date.

EDUCATION

Educational Attainment: Figures shown are 2010 estimates and show the percent of population age 25 and over with:

- **High school diploma (including GED) or higher:** includes people whose highest degree was a high school diploma or its equivalent, people who attended college but did not receive a degree, and people who received a college, university, or professional degree.
- **Bachelor's degree or higher**
- **Master's degree or higher:** Master's degrees include the traditional MA and MS degrees and field-specific degrees, such as MSW, MEd, MBA, and MLS. *Source: Claritas.*

HOUSING

Homeownership Rate: Percentage of housing units that are owner-occupied. Figures shown are 2010 estimates. *Source: Claritas.*

Median Home Value: Median value of all owner-occupied housing units as reported by the owner. Figures shown are 2010 estimates. *Source: Claritas.*

xxii   User's Guide: Profiles

Median Rent: Median monthly contract rent on specified renter-occupied and specified vacant-for-rent units. Specified renter-occupied and specified vacant-for-rent units exclude 1-family houses on 10 acres or more. Contract rent is the monthly rent agreed to or contracted for, regardless of any furnishings, utilities, fees, meals, or services that may be included. For vacant units, it is the monthly rent asked for the rental unit at the time of enumeration. *Source: U.S. Bureau of the Census, 2006-2008 American Community Survey 3-Year Estimates.*

Median Year Structure Built: Year structure built refers to when the building was first constructed, not when it was remodeled, added to, or converted. For mobile homes, houseboats, RVs, etc, the manufacturer's model year was assumed to be the year built. The data relate to the number of units built during the specified periods that were still in existence at the time of enumeration. *Source: U.S. Bureau of the Census, 2006-2008 American Community Survey 3-Year Estimates.*

HEALTH AND VITAL STATISTICS

Birth Rate: Estimated number of births per 10,000 population in 2009. *Source: U.S. Census Bureau, Annual Components of Population Change, July 1, 2008 - July 1 , 2009 (http://www.census.gov/popest/births.html).*

Death Rate: Estimated number of deaths per 10,000 population in 2009. *Source: U.S. Census Bureau, Annual Components of Population Change, July 1, 2008 - July 1 , 2009 (http://www.census.gov/popest/births.html).*

Age-adjusted Cancer Mortality Rate: Number of age-adjusted deaths from cancer per 100,000 population in 2006. Cancer is defined as International Classification of Disease (ICD) codes C00 - D48.9 Neoplasms. *Source: Centers for Disease Control, CDC Wonder (http://wonder.cdc.gov).*

Age-adjusted death rates are weighted averages of the age-specific death rates, where the weights represent a fixed population by age. They are used because the rates of almost all causes of death vary by age. Age adjustment is a technique for "removing" the effects of age from crude rates, so as to allow meaningful comparisons across populations with different underlying age structures. For example, comparing the crude rate of heart disease in New York to that of California is misleading, because the relatively older population in New York will lead to a higher crude death rate, even if the age-specific rates of heart disease in New York and California are the same. For such a comparison, age-adjusted rates would be preferable. Age-adjusted rates should be viewed as relative indexes rather than as direct or actual measures of mortality risk.

Death rates based on counts of twenty or less (≤ 20) are flagged as "Unreliable". Death rates based on fewer than three years of data for counties with populations of less than 100,000 in the 1990 Census counts, are also flagged as "Unreliable" if the number of deaths is five or less (≤ 5).

Air Quality Index: The percentage of days in 2008 the AQI fell into the Good (0-50), Moderate (51-100), Unhealthy for Sensitive Groups (101-150), and Unhealthy (151+) ranges. Data covers January 2008 through December 2008. Counties with less than 90 days of air quality data were excluded. *Source: AirData: Access to Air Pollution Data , U.S. Environmental Protection Agency, Office of Air and Radiation (http://www.epa.gov/air/data/index.html).*

The AQI is an index for reporting daily air quality. It tells you how clean or polluted your air is, and what associated health concerns you should be aware of. The AQI focuses on health effects that can happen within a few hours or days after breathing polluted air. EPA uses the AQI for five major air pollutants regulated by the Clean Air Act: ground-level ozone, particulate matter, carbon monoxide, sulfur dioxide, and nitrogen dioxide. For each of these pollutants, EPA has established national air quality standards to protect against harmful health effects.

The AQI runs from 0 to 500. The higher the AQI value, the greater the level of air pollution and the greater the health danger. For example, an AQI value of 50 represents good air quality and little potential to affect public health, while an AQI value over 300 represents hazardous air quality. An AQI value of 100 generally corresponds to the national air quality standard for the pollutant, which is the level EPA has set to protect public health. So, AQI values below 100 are generally thought of as satisfactory. When AQI values are above 100, air quality is considered to be unhealthy—at first for certain sensitive groups of people, then for everyone as AQI values get higher. Each category corresponds to a different level of health concern. For example, when the AQI for a pollutant is between 51 and 100, the health concern is "Moderate." Here are the six levels of health concern and what they mean:

- "Good" The AQI value for your community is between 0 and 50. Air quality is considered satisfactory and air pollution poses little or no risk.
- "Moderate" The AQI for your community is between 51 and 100. Air quality is acceptable; however, for some pollutants there may be a moderate health concern for a very small number of individuals. For example, people who are unusually sensitive to ozone may experience respiratory symptoms.

- "Unhealthy for Sensitive Groups" Certain groups of people are particularly sensitive to the harmful effects of certain air pollutants. This means they are likely to be affected at lower levels than the general public. For example, children and adults who are active outdoors and people with respiratory disease are at greater risk from exposure to ozone, while people with heart disease are at greater risk from carbon monoxide. Some people may be sensitive to more than one pollutant. When AQI values are between 101 and 150, members of sensitive groups may experience health effects. The general public is not likely to be affected when the AQI is in this range.
- "Unhealthy" AQI values are between 151 and 200. Everyone may begin to experience health effects. Members of sensitive groups may experience more serious health effects.
- "Very Unhealthy" AQI values between 201 and 300 trigger a health alert, meaning everyone may experience more serious health effects.
- "Hazardous" AQI values over 300 trigger health warnings of emergency conditions. The entire population is more likely to be affected.

Number of Physicians: The number of active, non-federal physicians per 10,000 population in 2007. *Source: Area Resource File (ARF). 2008 Release. U.S. Department of Health and Human Services, Health Resources and Services Administration, Bureau of Health Professions, Rockville, MD, June 2009.*

Number of Hospital Beds: The number of hospital beds per 10,000 population in 2006. *Source: Area Resource File (ARF). 2008 Release. U.S. Department of Health and Human Services, Health Resources and Services Administration, Bureau of Health Professions, Rockville, MD, June 2009.*

Number of Hospital Admissions: The number of hospital admissions per 10,000 population in 2006. *Source: Area Resource File (ARF). 2008 Release. U.S. Department of Health and Human Services, Health Resources and Services Administration, Bureau of Health Professions, Rockville, MD, June 2009.*

ELECTIONS

Elections: 2008 Presidential election results. *Source: Dave Leip's Atlas of U.S. Presidential Elections (http://www.uselectionatlas.org).*

NATIONAL AND STATE PARKS

Lists National and State parks located in the area. *Source: U.S. Geological Survey, Geographic Names Information System.*

ADDITIONAL INFORMATION CONTACTS

The following phone numbers are provided as sources of additional information: Chambers of Commerce; Economic Development Agencies; and Convention & Visitors Bureaus. Efforts have been made to provide the most recent area codes. However, area code changes may have occurred in listed numbers. *Source: Original research.*

User's Guide: Education

School District Rankings

Number of Schools: Total number of schools in the district. *Source: U.S. Department of Education, National Center for Education Statistics, Common Core of Data, Public Elementary/Secondary School Universe Survey: School Year 2006-2007.*

Number of Teachers: Teachers are defined as individuals who provide instruction to pre-kindergarten, kindergarten, grades 1 through 12, or ungraded classes, or individuals who teach in an environment other than a classroom setting, and who maintain daily student attendance records. Numbers reported are full-time equivalents (FTE). *Source: U.S. Department of Education, National Center for Education Statistics, Common Core of Data, Local Education Agency (School District) Universe Survey: School Year 2006-2007.*

Number of Students: A student is an individual for whom instruction is provided in an elementary or secondary education program that is not an adult education program and is under the jurisdiction of a school, school system, or other education institution. *Sources: U.S. Department of Education, National Center for Education Statistics, Common Core of Data, Local Education Agency (School District) Universe Survey: School Year 2006-2007 and Public Elementary/Secondary School Universe Survey: School Year 2006-2007*

Individual Education Program (IEP) Students: A written instructional plan for students with disabilities designated as special education students under IDEA-Part B. The written instructional plan includes a statement of present levels of educational performance of a child; statement of annual goals, including short-term instructional objectives; statement of specific educational services to be provided and the extent to which the child will be able to participate in regular educational programs; the projected date for initiation and anticipated duration of services; the appropriate objectives, criteria and evaluation procedures; and the schedules for determining, on at least an annual basis, whether instructional objectives are being achieved. *Source: U.S. Department of Education, National Center for Education Statistics, Common Core of Data, Local Education Agency (School District) Universe Survey: School Year 2006-2007*

English Language Learner (ELL) Students: Formerly referred to as Limited English Proficient (LEP). Students being served in appropriate programs of language assistance (e.g., English as a Second Language, High Intensity Language Training, bilingual education). Does not include pupils enrolled in a class to learn a language other than English. Also Limited-English-Proficient students are individuals who were not born in the United States or whose native language is a language other than English; or individuals who come from environments where a language other than English is dominant; or individuals who are American Indians and Alaskan Natives and who come from environments where a language other than English has had a significant impact on their level of English language proficiency; and who, by reason thereof, have sufficient difficulty speaking, reading, writing, or understanding the English language, to deny such individuals the opportunity to learn successfully in classrooms where the language of instruction is English or to participate fully in our society. *Source: U.S. Department of Education, National Center for Education Statistics, Common Core of Data, Local Education Agency (School District) Universe Survey: School Year 2006-2007*

Migrant Students: A migrant student as defined under federal regulation 34 CFR 200.40: 1) (a) Is younger than 22 (and has not graduated from high school or does not hold a high school equivalency certificate), but (b), if the child is too young to attend school-sponsored educational programs, is old enough to benefit from an organized instructional program; and 2) A migrant agricultural worker or a migrant fisher or has a parent, spouse, or guardian who is a migrant agricultural worker or a migrant fisher; and 3) Performs, or has a parent, spouse, or guardian who performs qualifying agricultural or fishing employment as a principal means of livelihood; and 4) Has moved within the preceding 36 months to obtain or to accompany or join a parent, spouse, or guardian to obtain, temporary or seasonal employment in agricultural or fishing work; and 5) Has moved from one school district to another; or in a state that is comprised of a single school district, has moved from one administrative area to another within such district; or resides in a school district of more than 15,000 square miles, and migrates a distance of 20 miles or more to a temporary residence to engage in a fishing activity. Provision 5 currently applies only to Alaska. *Note: Data covers the 2004-2005 school year. Source: U.S. Department of Education, National Center for Education Statistics, Common Core of Data, Public Elementary/Secondary School Universe Survey: School Year 2006-2007*

Students Eligible for Free Lunch Program: The free lunch program is defined as a program under the National School Lunch Act that provides cash subsidies for free lunches to students based on family size and income criteria. *Source: U.S. Department of Education, National Center for Education Statistics, Common Core of Data, Public Elementary/Secondary School Universe Survey: School Year 2006-2007*

Students Eligible for Reduced-Price Lunch Program: A student who is eligible to participate in the Reduced-Price Lunch Program under the National School Lunch Act. *Source: U.S. Department of Education, National Center for Education Statistics, Common Core of Data, Public Elementary/Secondary School Universe Survey: School Year 2006-2007*

Student/Teacher Ratio: The number of students divided by the number of teachers (FTE). See Number of Students and Number of Teachers above for for information.

Student/Librarian Ratio: The number of students divided by the number of library and media support staff. Library and media support staff are defined as staff members who render other professional library and media services; also includes library aides and those involved in library/media support. Their duties include selecting, preparing, caring for, and making available to instructional staff, equipment, films, filmstrips, transparencies, tapes, TV programs, and similar materials maintained separately or as part of an instructional materials center. Also included are activities in the audio-visual center, TV studio, related-work-study areas, and services provided by audio-visual personnel. Numbers are based on full-time equivalents. *Source: U.S. Department of Education, National Center for Education Statistics, Common Core of Data, Local Education Agency (School District) Universe Survey: School Year 2006-2007.*

Student/Counselor Ratio: The number of students divided by the number of guidance counselors. Guidance counselors are professional staff assigned specific duties and school time for any of the following activities in an elementary or secondary setting: counseling with students and parents; consulting with other staff members on learning problems; evaluating student abilities; assisting students in making educational and career choices; assisting students in personal and social development; providing referral assistance; and/or working with other staff members in planning and conducting guidance programs for students. The state applies its own standards in apportioning the aggregate of guidance counselors/directors into the elementary and secondary level components. Numbers reported are full-time equivalents. *Source: U.S. Department of Education, National Center for Education Statistics, Common Core of Data, Local Education Agency (School District) Universe Survey: School Year 2006-2007.*

Current Spending per Student: Expenditure for Instruction, Support Services, and Other Elementary/Secondary Programs. Includes salaries, employee benefits, purchased services, and supplies, as well as payments made by states on behalf of school districts. Also includes transfers made by school districts into their own retirement system. Excludes expenditure for Non-Elementary/Secondary Programs, debt service, capital outlay, and transfers to other governments or school districts. This item is formally called "Current Expenditures for Public Elementary/Secondary Education."

Instruction: Includes payments from all funds for salaries, employee benefits, supplies, materials, and contractual services for elementary/secondary instruction. It excludes capital outlay, debt service, and interfund transfers for elementary/secondary instruction. Instruction covers regular, special, and vocational programs offered in both the regular school year and summer school. It excludes instructional support activities as well as adult education and community services. Instruction salaries includes salaries for teachers and teacher aides and assistants.

Support Services: Relates to support services functions (series 2000) defined in Financial Accounting for Local and State School Systems (National Center for Education Statistics 2000). Includes payments from all funds for salaries, employee benefits, supplies, materials, and contractual services. It excludes capital outlay, debt service, and interfund transfers. It includes expenditure for the following functions:

- Business/Central/Other Support Services
- General Administration
- Instructional Staff Support
- Operation and Maintenance
- Pupil Support Services
- Pupil Transportation Services
- School Administration
- Nonspecified Support Services

Values shown are dollars per pupil per year. They were calculated by dividing the total dollar amounts by the fall membership. Fall membership is comprised of the total student enrollment on October 1 (or the closest school day to October 1) for all grade levels (including prekindergarten and kindergarten) and ungraded pupils. Membership includes students both present and absent on the measurement day. *Source: U.S. Department of Education, National Center for Education Statistics, Common Core of Data, School District Finance Survey (F-33), Fiscal Year 2007.*

Drop-out Rate: A dropout is a student who was enrolled in school at some time during the previous school year; was not enrolled at the beginning of the current school year; has not graduated from high school or completed a state or district approved educational program; and does not meet any of the following exclusionary conditions: has transferred to another public school district, private school, or state- or district-approved educational program; is temporarily absent due to suspension or school-approved illness; or has died. The values shown cover grades 9 through 12. *Note: Drop-out rates are no longer available to the general public disaggregated by grade, race/ethnicity, and gender at the school district level. Beginning with the 2005–06 school year the CCD is reporting dropout data aggregated from the local education agency (district) level to the state level. This allows data users to compare event dropout rates across states, regions, and other jurisdictions. Source: U.S. Department of Education, National Center for Education Statistics, Common Core of Data, Local Education Agency (School District) Universe Survey Dropout and Completion Data, 2005-2006; U.S. Department of Education, National Center for Education Statistics, Common Core of Data, State Dropout and Completion Data File, 2005-2006*

Average Freshman Graduation Rate (AFGR): The AFGR is the number of regular diploma recipients in a given year divided by the average of the membership in grades 8, 9, and 10, reported 5, 4, and 3 years earlier, respectively. For example, the denominator of the 2005–06 AFGR is the average of the 8th-grade membership in 2001–02, 9th-grade membership in 2002–03, and 10th-grade membership in 2003–04. Ungraded students are prorated into these grades. Averaging these three grades provides an estimate of the number of first-time freshmen in the class of 2002–03 freshmen in order to estimate the on-time graduation rate for 2005–06.

Caution in interpreting the AFGR. Although the AFGR was selected as the best of the available alternatives, several factors make it fall short of a true on-time graduation rate. First, the AFGR does not take into account any imbalances in the number of students moving in and out of the nation or individual states over the high school years. As a result, the averaged freshman class is at best an approximation of the actual number of freshmen, where differences in the rates of transfers, retention, and dropping out in the three grades affect the average. Second, by including all graduates in a specific year, the graduates may include students who repeated a grade in high school or completed high school early and thus are not on-time graduates in that year. *Source: U.S. Department of Education, National Center for Education Statistics, Common Core of Data, Local Education Agency (School District) Universe Survey Dropout and Completion Data, 2005-2006; U.S. Department of Education, National Center for Education Statistics, Common Core of Data, State Dropout and Completion Data File, 2005-2006*

Number of Diploma Recipients: A student who has received a diploma during the previous school year or subsequent summer school. This category includes regular diploma recipients and other diploma recipients. A High School Diploma is a formal document certifying the successful completion of a secondary school program prescribed by the state education agency or other appropriate body. *Note: Diploma counts are no longer available to the general public disaggregated by grade, race/ethnicity, and gender at the school district level. Source: U.S. Department of Education, National Center for Education Statistics, Common Core of Data, Local Education Agency (School District) Universe Survey Dropout and Completion Data, 2005-2006; U.S. Department of Education, National Center for Education Statistics, Common Core of Data, State Dropout and Completion Data File, 2005-2006*

Note: n/a indicates data not available.

State Educational Profile

Please refer to the District Rankings section in the front of this User's Guide for an explanation of data for all items except for the following:

Average Salary: The average salary for classroom teachers in 2009-2010. *Source: National Education Association, Rankings & Estimates: Rankings of the States 2009 and Estimates of School Statistics 2010*

College Entrance Exam Scores:

Scholastic Aptitude Test (SAT). *Note: Data covers the 2009 school year. The College Board strongly discourages the comparison or ranking of states on the basis of SAT scores alone. Source: The College Board, Mean SAT Critical Reading, Mathematics and Writing Scores by State, with Changes for Selected Years*

American College Testing Program (ACT). *ACT, Average ACT Scores by State: Graduating Class 2009*

National Assessment of Educational Progress (NAEP)

The National Assessment of Educational Progress (NAEP), also known as "the Nation's Report Card," is the only nationally representative and continuing assessment of what America's students know and can do in various subject areas. As a result of the "No Child Left Behind" legislation, all states are required to participate in NAEP.

For more information, visit the U.S. Department of Education, National Center for Education Statistics at http://nces.ed.gov/nationsreportcard.

Indiana Statewide Testing for Educational Progress-Plus (ISTEP+)

The Indiana Statewide Testing for Educational Progress-Plus (ISTEP+) measures what students know and are able to do at each grade level in core academic subjects. Based on Indiana's Academic Standards, the test includes English/Language arts in grades 3-8, Science in grades 4 and 6 and Social Studies in grades 5 and 7. For more information, visit the Indiana Department of Education at http://www.doe.in.gov.

User's Guide: Ancestry

Places Covered

The ranking tables are based on **600 places** in Indiana. Places include 566 municipalities and 34 census designated places (CDP). The U.S. Bureau of the Census defines a CDP as "a statistical entity, defined for each decennial census according to Census Bureau guidelines, comprising a densely settled concentration of population that is not within an incorporated place, but is locally identified by a name. CDPs are delineated cooperatively by state and local officials and the Census Bureau, following Census Bureau guidelines. Beginning with Census 2000 there are no size limits."

Source of Data

The ancestries shown in this chapter were compiled from three different sections of the 2000 Census: Race; Hispanic Origin; and Ancestry. While the ancestries are sorted alphabetically for ease-of-use, it's important to note the origin of each piece of data. Data for Race and Hispanic Origin was taken from Summary File 1 (SF1) while Ancestry data was taken from Summary File 3 (SF3). The distinction is important because SF1 contains the 100-percent data, which is the information compiled from the questions asked of all people and about every housing unit. SF3 was compiled from a sample of approximately 19 million housing units (about 1 in 6 households) that received the Census 2000 long-form questionnaire.

Ancestries Based on Race

The data on race were derived from answers to the question on race that was asked of all people. The concept of race, as used by the Census Bureau, reflects self-identification by people according to the race or races with which they most closely identify. These categories are sociopolitical constructs and should not be interpreted as being scientific or anthropological in nature. Furthermore, the race categories include both racial and national-origin groups.

If an individual did not provide a race response, the race or races of the householder or other household members were assigned using specific rules of precedence of household relationship. For example, if race was missing for a natural-born child in the household, then either the race or races of the householder, another natural-born child, or the spouse of the householder were assigned. If race was not reported for anyone in the household, the race or races of a householder in a previously processed household were assigned.

African-American/Black:
   Not Hispanic
   Hispanic
Alaska Native tribes, specified:
   Alaska Athabascan
   Aleut
   Eskimo
   Tlingit-Haida
   All other tribes
Alaska Native tribes, not specified
American Indian or Alaska Native
   tribes, not specified
American Indian tribes, specified:
   Apache
   Blackfeet
   Cherokee
   Cheyenne
   Chickasaw
   Chippewa
   Choctaw
   Colville
   Comanche
   Cree
   Creek
   Crow

Delaware
Houma
Iroquois
Kiowa
Latin American Indians
Lumbee
Menominee
Navajo
Osage
Ottawa
Paiute
Pima
Potawatomi
Pueblo
Puget Sound Salish
Seminole
Shoshone
Sioux
Tohono O'Odham
Ute
Yakama
Yaqui
Yuman
All other tribes

American Indian tribes,
   not specified
Asian:
   Bangladeshi
   Cambodian
   Chinese, except Taiwanese
   Filipino
   Hmong
   Indian
   Indonesian
   Japanese
   Korean
   Laotian
   Malaysian
   Pakistani
   Sri Lankan
   Taiwanese
   Thai
   Vietnamese
   Other Asian, specified
   Other Asian, not specified
Hawaii Native/Pacific Islander:
   Melanesian:
      Fijian
      Other Melanesian

Micronesian:
   Guamanian/Chamorro
   Other Micronesian
Polynesian:
   Native Hawaiian
   Samoan
   Tongan
   Other Polynesian
Other Pacific Islander, specified
Other Pacific Islander,
   not specified
White:
   Not Hispanic
   Hispanic

African American or Black: A person having origins in any of the Black racial groups of Africa. It includes people who indicate their race as "Black, African Am., or Negro," or provide written entries such as African American, Afro American, Kenyan, Nigerian, or Haitian.

American Indian or Alaska Native: A person having origins in any of the original peoples of North and South America (including Central America) and who maintain tribal affiliation or community attachment. It includes people who classified themselves as described below.

American Indian - Includes people who indicated their race as "American Indian," entered the name of an Indian tribe, or reported such entries as Canadian Indian, French American Indian, or Spanish-American Indian.

Respondents who identified themselves as American Indian were asked to report their enrolled or principal tribe. Therefore, tribal data in tabulations reflect the written entries reported on the questionnaires. Some of the entries (for example, Iroquois, Sioux, Colorado River, and Flathead) represent nations or reservations. The information on tribe is based on self identification and therefore does not reflect any designation of federally or state-recognized tribe. Information on American Indian tribes is presented in summary files. The information for Census 2000 is derived from the American Indian Tribal Classification List for the 1990 census that was updated based on a December 1997 Federal Register Notice, entitled "Indian Entities Recognized and Eligible to Receive Service From the United States Bureau of Indian Affairs," Department of the Interior, Bureau of Indian Affairs, issued by the Office of Management and Budget.

Alaska Native - Includes written responses of Eskimos, Aleuts, and Alaska Indians, as well as entries such as Arctic Slope, Inupiat, Yupik, Alutiiq, Egegik, and Pribilovian. The Alaska tribes are the Alaskan Athabascan, Tlingit, and Haida. The information for Census 2000 is based on the American Indian Tribal Classification List for the 1990 census, which was expanded to list the individual Alaska Native Villages when provided as a written response for race.

Asian: A person having origins in any of the original peoples of the Far East, Southeast Asia, or the Indian subcontinent including, for example, Cambodia, China, India, Japan, Korea, Malaysia, Pakistan, the Philippine Islands, Thailand, and Vietnam. It includes "Asian Indian," "Chinese," "Filipino," "Korean," "Japanese," "Vietnamese," and "Other Asian."

Asian Indian - Includes people who indicated their race as "Asian Indian" or identified themselves as Bengalese, Bharat, Dravidian, East Indian, or Goanese.

Chinese - Includes people who indicate their race as "Chinese" or who identify themselves as Cantonese, or Chinese American.

Filipino - Includes people who indicate their race as "Filipino" or who report entries such as Philipino, Philipine, or Filipino American.

Japanese - Includes people who indicate their race as "Japanese" or who report entries such as Nipponese or Japanese American.

Korean - Includes people who indicate their race as "Korean" or who provide a response of Korean American.

Vietnamese - Includes people who indicate their race as "Vietnamese" or who provide a response of Vietnamese American.

Cambodian - Includes people who provide a response such as Cambodian or Cambodia.

Hmong - Includes people who provide a response such as Hmong, Laohmong, or Mong.

Laotian - Includes people who provide a response such as Laotian, Laos, or Lao.

Thai - Includes people who provide a response such as Thai, Thailand, or Siamese.

Other Asian - Includes people who provide a response of Bangladeshi; Bhutanese; Burmese; Indochinese; Indonesian; Iwo Jiman; Madagascar; Malaysian; Maldivian; Nepalese; Okinawan; Pakistani; Singaporean; Sri Lankan; or Other Asian, specified and Other Asian, not specified.

Native Hawaiian or Other Pacific Islander: A person having origins in any of the original peoples of Hawaii, Guam, Samoa, or other Pacific Islands. It includes people who indicate their race as "Native Hawaiian," "Guamanian or Chamorro," "Samoan," and "Other Pacific Islander."

Native Hawaiian - Includes people who indicate their race as "Native Hawaiian" or who identify themselves as "Part Hawaiian" or "Hawaiian."

Guamanian or Chamorro - Includes people who indicate their race as such, including written entries of Chamorro or Guam.

Samoan - Includes people who indicate their race as "Samoan" or who identify themselves as American Samoan or Western Samoan.

Other Pacific Islander - Includes people who provide a write-in response of a Pacific Islander group, such as Carolinian, Chuukese (Trukese), Fijian, Kosraean, Melanesian, Micronesian, Northern Mariana Islander, Palauan, Papua New Guinean, Pohnpeian, Polynesian, Solomon Islander, Tahitian, Tokelauan, Tongan, Yapese, or Pacific Islander, not specified.

White: A person having origins in any of the original peoples of Europe, the Middle East, or North Africa. It includes people who indicate their race as "White" or report entries such as Irish, German, Italian, Lebanese, Near Easterner, Arab, or Polish.

Ancestries Based on Hispanic Origin

Hispanic or Latino:	Salvadoran	Argentinean	Uruguayan
Central American:	Other Central American	Bolivian	Venezuelan
Costa Rican	Cuban	Chilean	Other South American
Guatemalan	Dominican Republic	Colombian	Other Hispanic/Latino
Honduran	Mexican	Ecuadorian	
Nicaraguan	Puerto Rican	Paraguayan	
Panamanian	South American:	Peruvian	

The data on the Hispanic or Latino population were derived from answers to a question that was asked of all people. The terms "Spanish," "Hispanic origin," and "Latino" are used interchangeably. Some respondents identify with all three terms while others may identify with only one of these three specific terms. Hispanics or Latinos who identify with the terms "Spanish," "Hispanic," or "Latino" are those who classify themselves in one of the specific Spanish, Hispanic, or Latino categories listed on the questionnaire ("Mexican," "Puerto Rican," or "Cuban") as well as those who indicate that they are "other Spanish/Hispanic/Latino." People who do not identify with one of the specific origins listed on the questionnaire but indicate that they are "other Spanish, Hispanic, or Latino" are those whose origins are from Spain, the Spanish-speaking countries of Central or South America, the Dominican Republic, or people identifying themselves generally as Spanish, Spanish-American, Hispanic, Hispano, Latino, and so on. All write-in responses to the "other Spanish/Hispanic/Latino" category were coded.

Origin can be viewed as the heritage, nationality group, lineage, or country of birth of the person or the person's parents or ancestors before their arrival in the United States. People who identify their origin as Spanish, Hispanic, or Latino may be of any race.

In all cases where the origin of households, families, or occupied housing units is classified as Spanish, Hispanic, or Latino, the origin of the householder is used. If an individual could not provide a Hispanic origin response, their origin was assigned using specific rules of precedence of household relationship. For example, if origin was missing for a natural-born daughter in the household, then either the origin of the householder, another natural-born child, or spouse of the householder was assigned. If Hispanic origin was not reported for anyone in the household, the Hispanic origin of a householder in a previously processed household with the same race was assigned.

Other Ancestries

Acadian/Cajun	Moroccan	French, except Basque	Scottish
Afghan	Palestinian	French Canadian	Serbian
African, Subsaharan:	Syrian	German	Slavic
African	Other Arab	German Russian	Slovak
Cape Verdean	Armenian	Greek	Slovene
Ethiopian	Assyrian/Chaldean/Syriac	Guyanese	Soviet Union
Ghanian	Australian	Hungarian	Swedish
Kenyan	Austrian	Icelander	Swiss
Liberian	Basque	Iranian	Turkish
Nigerian	Belgian	Irish	Ukrainian
Senegalese	Brazilian	Israeli	United States or American
Sierra Leonean	British	Italian	Welsh
Somalian	Bulgarian	Latvian	West Indian, excluding Hispanic:
South African	Canadian	Lithuanian	Bahamian
Sudanese	Carpatho Rusyn	Luxemburger	Barbadian
Ugandan	Celtic	Macedonian	Belizean
Zairian	Croatian	Maltese	Bermudan
Zimbabwean	Cypriot	New Zealander	British West Indian
Other Subsaharan African	Czech	Northern European	Dutch West Indian
Albanian	Czechoslovakian	Norwegian	Haitian
Alsatian	Danish	Pennsylvania German	Jamaican
Arab:	Dutch	Polish	Trinidadian and
Arab/Arabic	Eastern European	Portuguese	Tobagonian
Egyptian	English	Romanian	U.S. Virgin Islander
Iraqi	Estonian	Russian	West Indian
Jordanian	European	Scandinavian	Other West Indian
Lebanese	Finnish	Scotch-Irish	Yugoslavian

The data on ancestry were derived from answers to long-form questionnaire Item 10, which was asked of a sample of the population. The data represent self-classification by people according to the ancestry group or groups with which they most closely identify. Ancestry refers to a person's ethnic origin or descent, "roots," heritage, or the place of birth of the person, the person's parents, or their ancestors before their arrival in the United States. Some ethnic identities, such as Egyptian or Polish, can be traced to geographic areas outside the United States, while other ethnicities, such as Pennsylvania German or Cajun, evolved in the United States.

The intent of the ancestry question was not to measure the degree of attachment the respondent had to a particular ethnicity. For example, a response of "Irish" might reflect total involvement in an Irish community or only a memory of ancestors several generations removed from the individual. Also, the question was intended to provide data for groups that were not included in the Hispanic origin and race questions. Official Hispanic origin data come from long-form questionnaire Item 5, and official race data come from long-form questionnaire Item 6. Therefore, although data on all groups are collected, the ancestry data shown in these tabulations are for non-Hispanic and non-race groups.

The ancestry question allowed respondents to report one or more ancestry groups, although only the first two were coded. If a response was in terms of a dual ancestry, for example, "Irish English," the person was assigned two codes, in this case one for Irish and another for English. However, in certain cases, multiple responses such as "French Canadian," "Greek Cypriote," and "Scotch Irish" were assigned a single code reflecting their status as unique groups. If a person reported one of these unique groups in addition to another group, for example, "Scotch Irish English," resulting in three terms, that person received one code for the unique group (Scotch-Irish) and another one for the remaining group (English). If a person reported "English Irish French," only English and Irish were coded. Certain combinations of ancestries where the ancestry group is a part of another, such as "German-Bavarian," were coded as a single ancestry using the more specific group (Bavarian). Also, responses such as "Polish-American" or "Italian-American" were coded and tabulated as a single entry (Polish or Italian).

The Census Bureau accepted "American" as a unique ethnicity if it was given alone, with an ambiguous response, or with state names. If the respondent listed any other ethnic identity such as "Italian-American," generally the "American" portion of the response was not coded. However, distinct groups such as "American Indian," "Mexican American," and "African American" were coded and identified separately because they represented groups who considered themselves different from those who reported as "Indian," "Mexican," or "African," respectively.

Census 2000 tabulations on ancestry are presented using two types of data presentations — one using total people as the base, and the other using total responses as the base. This chapter uses total responses as the base and includes the total number of ancestries reported and coded. If a person reported a multiple ancestry such as "French

Danish," that response was counted twice in the tabulations — once in the French category and again in the Danish category. Thus, the sum of the counts in this type of presentation is not the total population but the total of all responses.

An automated coding system was used for coding ancestry in Census 2000. This greatly reduced the potential for error associated with a clerical review. Specialists with knowledge of the subject matter reviewed, edited, coded, and resolved inconsistent or incomplete responses. The code list used in Census 2000, containing over 1,000 categories, reflects the results of the Census Bureau's experience with the 1990 ancestry question, research, and consultation with many ethnic experts. Many decisions were made to determine the classification of responses. These decisions affected the grouping of the tabulated data. For example, the Italian category includes the responses of Sicilian and Tuscan, as well as a number of other responses.

Although some people consider religious affiliation a component of ethnic identity, the ancestry question was not designed to collect any information concerning religion. Thus, if a religion was given as an answer to the ancestry question, it was listed in the "Other groups" category which is not shown in this chapter.

Ancestry should not be confused with a person's place of birth, although a person's place of birth and ancestry may be the same.

Ranking Section

In the ranking section of this chapter, each ancestry has three tables. The first table shows the top 10 places sorted by number (based on all places, regardless of population), the second table shows the top 10 places sorted by percent (based on all places, regardless of population), the third table shows the top 10 places sorted by percent (based on places with populations of 10,000 or more).

Within each table, column one displays the place name, the state, and the county (if a place spans more than one county, the county that holds the majority of the population is shown). Column two displays the number of people reporting each ancestry, and column three is the percent of the total population reporting each ancestry. For tables representing ancestries based on race or Hispanic origin, the 100-percent population figure from SF1 is used to calculate the value in the "%" column. For all other ancestries the sample population figure from SF3 is used to calculate the value in the "%" column.

Alphabetical Ancestry Cross-Reference Guide

Acadian/Cajun
Afghan
African *See African, sub-Saharan: African*
African American/Black
African American/Black: Hispanic
African American/Black: Not Hispanic
African, sub-Saharan
African, sub-Saharan: African
African, sub-Saharan: Cape Verdean
African, sub-Saharan: Ethiopian
African, sub-Saharan: Ghanian
African, sub-Saharan: Kenyan
African, sub-Saharan: Liberian
African, sub-Saharan: Nigerian
African, sub-Saharan: Other
African, sub-Saharan: Senegalese
African, sub-Saharan: Sierra Leonean
African, sub-Saharan: Somalian
African, sub-Saharan: South African
African, sub-Saharan: Sudanese
African, sub-Saharan: Ugandan
African, sub-Saharan: Zairian
African, sub-Saharan: Zimbabwean
Alaska Athabascan *See Alaska Native: Alaska Athabascan*
Alaska Native tribes, not specified
Alaska Native tribes, specified
Alaska Native: Alaska Athabascan
Alaska Native: Aleut
Alaska Native: All other tribes
Alaska Native: Eskimo
Alaska Native: Tlingit-Haida
Albanian
Aleut *See Alaska Native: Aleut*
Alsatian
American *See United States or American*
American Indian or Alaska Native tribes, not specified
American Indian tribes, not specified
American Indian tribes, specified
American Indian: All other tribes
American Indian: Apache
American Indian: Blackfeet
American Indian: Cherokee
American Indian: Cheyenne
American Indian: Chickasaw
American Indian: Chippewa
American Indian: Choctaw
American Indian: Colville
American Indian: Comanche
American Indian: Cree
American Indian: Creek
American Indian: Crow
American Indian: Delaware
American Indian: Houma
American Indian: Iroquois
American Indian: Kiowa
American Indian: Latin American Indians
American Indian: Lumbee
American Indian: Menominee
American Indian: Navajo
American Indian: Osage
American Indian: Ottawa
American Indian: Paiute
American Indian: Pima
American Indian: Potawatomi

American Indian: Pueblo
American Indian: Puget Sound Salish
American Indian: Seminole
American Indian: Shoshone
American Indian: Sioux
American Indian: Tohono O'Odham
American Indian: Ute
American Indian: Yakama
American Indian: Yaqui
American Indian: Yuman
Apache *See American Indian: Apache*
Arab
Arab/Arabic *See Arab: Arab/Arabic*
Arab: Arab/Arabic
Arab: Egyptian
Arab: Iraqi
Arab: Jordanian
Arab: Lebanese
Arab: Moroccan
Arab: Other
Arab: Palestinian
Arab: Syrian
Argentinean *See Hispanic: Argentinean*
Armenian
Asian
Asian: Bangladeshi
Asian: Cambodian
Asian: Chinese, except Taiwanese
Asian: Filipino
Asian: Hmong
Asian: Indian
Asian: Indonesian
Asian: Japanese
Asian: Korean
Asian: Laotian
Asian: Malaysian
Asian: Other Asian, not specified
Asian: Other Asian, specified
Asian: Pakistani
Asian: Sri Lankan
Asian: Taiwanese
Asian: Thai
Asian: Vietnamese
Assyrian/Chaldean/Syriac
Australian
Austrian
Bahamian *See West Indian: Bahamian, excluding Hispanic*
Bangladeshi *See Asian: Bangladeshi*
Barbadian *See West Indian: Barbadian, excluding Hispanic*
Basque
Belgian
Belizean *See West Indian: Belizean, excluding Hispanic*
Bermudan *See West Indian: Bermudan, excluding Hispanic*
Blackfeet *See American Indian: Blackfeet*
Bolivian *See Hispanic: Bolivian*
Brazilian
British
British West Indian *See West Indian: British West Indian, excluding Hispanic*
Bulgarian
Cambodian *See Asian: Cambodian*
Canadian

Cape Verdean *See African, sub-Saharan: Cape Verdean*
Carpatho Rusyn
Celtic
Central American: *See Hispanic: Central American*
Cherokee *See American Indian: Cherokee*
Cheyenne *See American Indian: Cheyenne*
Chickasaw *See American Indian: Chickasaw*
Chilean *See Hispanic: Chilean*
Chinese, except Taiwanese *See Asian: Chinese, except Taiwanese*
Chippewa *See American Indian: Chippewa*
Choctaw *See American Indian: Choctaw*
Colombian *See Hispanic: Colombian*
Colville *See American Indian: Colville*
Comanche *See American Indian: Comanche*
Costa Rican *See Hispanic: Costa Rican*
Cree *See American Indian: Cree*
Creek *See American Indian: Creek*
Croatian
Crow *See American Indian: Crow*
Cuban *See Hispanic: Cuban*
Cypriot
Czech
Czechoslovakian
Danish
Delaware *See American Indian: Delaware*
Dominican Republic *See Hispanic: Dominican Republic*
Dutch
Dutch West Indian *See West Indian: Dutch West Indian, excluding Hispanic*
Eastern European
Ecuadorian *See Hispanic: Ecuadorian*
Egyptian *See Arab: Egyptian*
English
Eskimo *See Alaska Native: Eskimo*
Estonian
Ethiopian *See African, sub-Saharan: Ethiopian*
European
Fijian *See Hawaii Native/Pacific Islander: Fijian*
Filipino *See Asian: Filipino*
Finnish
French Canadian
French, except Basque
German
German Russian
Ghanian *See African, sub-Saharan: Ghanian*
Greek
Guamanian or Chamorro *See Hawaii Native/Pacific Islander: Guamanian or Chamorro*
Guatemalan *See Hispanic: Guatemalan*
Guyanese
Haitian *See West Indian: Haitian, excluding Hispanic*
Hawaii Native/Pacific Islander
Hawaii Native/Pacific Islander: Fijian
Hawaii Native/Pacific Islander: Guamanian or Chamorro
Hawaii Native/Pacific Islander: Melanesian
Hawaii Native/Pacific Islander: Micronesian
Hawaii Native/Pacific Islander: Native Hawaiian

Hawaii Native/Pacific Islander: Other Melanesian
Hawaii Native/Pacific Islander: Other Micronesian
Hawaii Native/Pacific Islander: Other Pacific Islander, not specified
Hawaii Native/Pacific Islander: Other Pacific Islander, specified
Hawaii Native/Pacific Islander: Other Polynesian
Hawaii Native/Pacific Islander: Polynesian
Hawaii Native/Pacific Islander: Samoan
Hawaii Native/Pacific Islander: Tongan
Hispanic or Latino
Hispanic: Argentinean
Hispanic: Bolivian
Hispanic: Central American
Hispanic: Chilean
Hispanic: Colombian
Hispanic: Costa Rican
Hispanic: Cuban
Hispanic: Dominican Republic
Hispanic: Ecuadorian
Hispanic: Guatemalan
Hispanic: Honduran
Hispanic: Mexican
Hispanic: Nicaraguan
Hispanic: Other
Hispanic: Other Central American
Hispanic: Other South American
Hispanic: Panamanian
Hispanic: Paraguayan
Hispanic: Peruvian
Hispanic: Puerto Rican
Hispanic: Salvadoran
Hispanic: South American
Hispanic: Uruguayan
Hispanic: Venezuelan
Hmong *See Asian: Hmong*
Honduran *See Hispanic: Honduran*
Houma *See American Indian: Houma*
Hungarian
Icelander
Indian, American *See American Indian*
Indian, Asian *See Asian: Indian*
Indonesian *See Asian: Indonesian*
Iranian
Iraqi *See Arab: Iraqi*
Irish
Iroquois *See American Indian: Iroquois*
Israeli
Italian
Jamaican *See West Indian: Jamaican, excluding Hispanic*
Japanese *See Asian: Japanese*
Jordanian *See Arab: Jordanian*
Kenyan *See African, sub-Saharan: Kenyan*
Kiowa *See American Indian: Kiowa*
Korean *See Asian: Korean*
Laotian *See Asian: Laotian*
Latin American Indians *See American Indian: Latin American Indians*
Latino *See Hispanic or Latino*
Latvian
Lebanese *See Arab: Lebanese*
Liberian *See African, sub-Saharan: Liberian*
Lithuanian
Lumbee *See American Indian: Lumbee*
Luxemburger
Macedonian
Malaysian *See Asian: Malaysian*
Maltese

Melanesian: *See Hawaii Native/Pacific Islander: Melanesian*
Menominee *See American Indian: Menominee*
Mexican *See Hispanic: Mexican*
Micronesian: *See Hawaii Native/Pacific Islander: Micronesian*
Moroccan *See Arab: Moroccan*
Native Hawaiian *See Hawaii Native/Pacific Islander: Native Hawaiian*
Navajo *See American Indian: Navajo*
New Zealander
Nicaraguan *See Hispanic: Nicaraguan*
Nigerian *See African, sub-Saharan: Nigerian*
Northern European
Norwegian
Osage *See American Indian: Osage*
Ottawa *See American Indian: Ottawa*
Paiute *See American Indian: Paiute*
Pakistani *See Asian: Pakistani*
Palestinian *See Arab: Palestinian*
Panamanian *See Hispanic: Panamanian*
Paraguayan *See Hispanic: Paraguayan*
Pennsylvania German
Peruvian *See Hispanic: Peruvian*
Pima *See American Indian: Pima*
Polish
Polynesian: *See Hawaii Native/Pacific Islander: Polynesian*
Portuguese
Potawatomi *See American Indian: Potawatomi*
Pueblo *See American Indian: Pueblo*
Puerto Rican *See Hispanic: Puerto Rican*
Puget Sound Salish *See American Indian: Puget Sound Salish*
Romanian
Russian
Salvadoran *See Hispanic: Salvadoran*
Samoan *See Hawaii Native/Pacific Islander: Samoan*
Scandinavian
Scotch-Irish
Scottish
Seminole *See American Indian: Seminole*
Senegalese *See African, sub-Saharan: Senegalese*
Serbian
Shoshone *See American Indian: Shoshone*
Sierra Leonean *See African, sub-Saharan: Sierra Leonean*
Sioux *See American Indian: Sioux*
Slavic
Slovak
Slovene
Somalian *See African, sub-Saharan: Somalian*
South African *See African, sub-Saharan: South African*
South American: *See Hispanic: South American*
Soviet Union
Sri Lankan *See Asian: Sri Lankan*
sub-Saharan African *See African, sub-Saharan*
Sudanese *See African, sub-Saharan: Sudanese*
Swedish
Swiss
Syrian *See Arab: Syrian*
Taiwanese *See Asian: Taiwanese*
Thai *See Asian: Thai*
Tlingit-Haida *See Alaska Native: Tlingit-Haida*
Tohono O'Odham *See American Indian: Tohono O'Odham*
Tongan *See Hawaii Native/Pacific Islander: Tongan*

Trinidadian and Tobagonian *See West Indian: Trinidadian and Tobagonian, excluding Hispanic*
Turkish
U.S. Virgin Islander *See West Indian: U.S. Virgin Islander, excluding Hispanic*
Ugandan *See African, sub-Saharan: Ugandan*
Ukrainian
United States or American
Uruguayan *See Hispanic: Uruguayan*
Ute *See American Indian: Ute*
Venezuelan *See Hispanic: Venezuelan*
Vietnamese *See Asian: Vietnamese*
Welsh
West Indian, excluding Hispanic
West Indian: Bahamian, excluding Hispanic
West Indian: Barbadian, excluding Hispanic
West Indian: Belizean, excluding Hispanic
West Indian: Bermudan, excluding Hispanic
West Indian: British West Indian, excluding Hispanic
West Indian: Dutch West Indian, excluding Hispanic
West Indian: Haitian, excluding Hispanic
West Indian: Jamaican, excluding Hispanic
West Indian: Other, excluding Hispanic
West Indian: Trinidadian and Tobagonian, excluding Hispanic
West Indian: U.S. Virgin Islander, excluding Hispanic
West Indian: West Indian, excluding Hispanic
White
White: Hispanic
White: Not Hispanic
Yakama *See American Indian: Yakama*
Yaqui *See American Indian: Yaqui*
Yugoslavian
Yuman *See American Indian: Yuman*
Zairian *See African, sub-Saharan: Zairian*
Zimbabwean *See African, sub-Saharan: Zimbabwean*

User's Guide: Hispanic Population

Places Covered

Ranking tables cover all counties and all places in Indiana with populations of 10,000 or more.

Source of Data

CENSUS 2000

Data for this chapter was derived from following source: *U.S. Bureau of the Census, Census of Population and Housing, 2000: Summary File 4.* Summary File 4 (SF 4) contains sample data, which is the information compiled from the questions asked of a sample (generally 1-in-6) of all people and housing units. Summary File 4 is repeated or iterated for the total population and 335 additional population groups. This chapter focuses on the following 24 population groups:

Hispanic or Latino (of any race)
    Central American
        Costa Rican
        Guatemalan
        Honduran
        Nicaraguan
        Panamanian
        Salvadoran
    Cuban
    Dominican (Dominican Republic)
    Mexican
    Puerto Rican
    South American
        Argentinian
        Bolivian
        Chilean
        Colombian
        Ecuadorian
        Paraguayan
        Peruvian
        Uruguayan
        Venezuelan
    Spaniard
    Other Hispanic or Latino

Please note that the above list only includes Spanish-speaking population groups. Groups such as Brazilian are not classified as Hispanic by the Bureau of the Census because they primarily speak Portugese.

In order for any of the tables for a specific group to be shown in Summary File 4, the data must meet a minimum population threshold. For Summary File 4, all tables are repeated for each race group, American Indian and Alaska Native tribe, and Hispanic or Latino group if the 100-percent count of people of that specific group in a particular geographic area is 100 or more. There also must be 50 or more unweighted people of that specific group in a particular geographic area. For example, if there are 100 or more 100-percent people tabulated as Chilean in County A, and there are 50 or more unweighted people, then all matrices for Chilean are shown in SF 4 for County A.

To maintain confidentiality, the Census Bureau applies statistical procedures that introduce some uncertainty into data for small geographic areas with small population groups. Therefore, tables may contain both sampling and nonsampling error.

In an iterated file such as SF 4, the universes *households, families,* and *occupied housing units* are classified by the race or ethnic group of the householder. In any population table where there is no note, the universe classification is always based on the race or ethnicity of the person. In all housing tables, the universe classification is based on the race or ethnicity of the householder.

Comparing SF 4 Estimates with Corresponding Values in SF 1 and SF 2

As in earlier censuses, the responses from the sample of households reporting on long forms must be weighted to reflect the entire population. Specifically, each responding household represents, on average, six or seven other households who reported using short forms. One consequence of the weighting procedures is that each estimate based on the long form responses has an associated confidence interval. These confidence intervals are wider (as a percentage of the estimate) for geographic areas with smaller populations and for characteristics that occur less frequently in the area being examined (such as the proportion of people in poverty in a middle-income neighborhood). In order to release as much useful information as possible, statisticians must balance a number of factors. In particular, for Census 2000, the Bureau of the Census created weighting areas—geographic areas from which about two hundred or more long forms were completed—which are large enough to produce good quality estimates. If smaller weighting areas had been used, the confidence intervals around the estimates would have been significantly wider, rendering many estimates less useful due to their lower reliability. The disadvantage of using weighting areas this large is that, for smaller geographic areas within them, the estimates of characteristics that are also reported on the short form will not match the counts reported in SF 1 or SF 2. Examples of these characteristics are the total number of people, the number of people reporting specific racial categories, and the number of housing units. The official values for items reported on the short form come from SF 1 and SF 2. The differences between the long form estimates in SF 4 and values in SF 1 or SF 2 are particularly noticeable for the smallest places, tracts, and block groups. The long form estimates of total population and total housing units in SF 4 will, however, match the SF 1 and SF 2 counts for larger geographic areas such as counties and states, and will be essentially the same for medium and large cities. This phenomenon also occurred for the 1990 Census, although in that case, the weighting areas included relatively small places. As a result, the long form estimates matched the short form counts for those places, but the confidence intervals around the estimates of characteristics collected only on the long form were often significantly wider (as a percentage of the estimate). SF 1 gives exact numbers even for very small groups and areas; whereas, SF 4 gives estimates for small groups and areas such as tracts and small places that are less exact. The goal of SF 4 is to identify large differences among areas or large changes over time. Estimates for small areas and small population groups often do exhibit large changes from one census to the next, so having the capability to measure them is worthwhile.

Topics

POPULATION

Total Population: Sample count of total population.

Hispanic Population: The data on the Hispanic or Latino population, which was asked of all people, were derived from answers to long-form questionnaire Item 5, and short-form questionnaire Item 7. The terms "Spanish," "Hispanic origin," and "Latino" are used interchangeably. Some respondents identify with all three terms, while others may identify with only one of these three specific terms. Hispanics or Latinos who identify with the terms "Spanish," "Hispanic," or "Latino" are those who classify themselves in one of the specific Hispanic or Latino categories listed on the questionnaire — "Mexican," "Puerto Rican," or "Cuban" — as well as those who indicate that they are "other Spanish, Hispanic, or Latino." People who do not identify with one of the specific origins listed on the questionnaire but indicate that they are "other Spanish, Hispanic, or Latino" are those whose origins are from Spain, the Spanish-speaking countries of Central or South America, the Dominican Republic, or people identifying themselves generally as Spanish, Spanish-American, Hispanic, Hispano, Latino, and so on. All write-in responses to the "other Spanish/Hispanic/Latino" category were coded. Origin can be viewed as the heritage, nationality group, lineage, or country of birth of the person or the person's parents or ancestors before their arrival in the United States. People who identify their origin as Spanish, Hispanic, or Latino may be of any race.

Population groups whose primary language is not Spanish are not classified as Hispanic by the Bureau of the Census and are not included in this chapter (eg. Brazilian).

AGE

Median Age: Divides the age distribution into two equal parts: one-half of the cases falling below the median age and one-half above the median. Median age is computed on the basis of a single year of age standard distribution.

The data on age, which was asked of all people, were derived from answers to the long-form questionnaire Item 4 and short-form questionnaire Item 6. The age classification is based on the age of the person in complete years as of April 1, 2000. The age of the person usually was derived from their date of birth information. Their reported age was used only when date of birth information was unavailable.

HOUSEHOLD SIZE

Average Household Size: A measure obtained by dividing the number of people in households by the total number of households (or householders). In cases where household members are tabulated by race or Hispanic origin, household members are classified by the race or Hispanic origin of the householder rather than the race or Hispanic origin of each individual. Average household size is rounded to the nearest hundredth.

LANGUAGE SPOKEN AT HOME

English Only: Number and percentage of population 5 years and over who report speaking English-only at home.

Spanish: Number and percentage of population 5 years and over who report speaking Spanish at home.

Language spoken at home data were derived from answers to long-form questionnaire Items 11a and 11b, which were asked of a sample of the population. Data were edited to include in tabulations only the population 5 years old and over. Questions 11a and 11b referred to languages spoken at home in an effort to measure the current use of languages other than English. People who knew languages other than English but did not use them at home or who only used them elsewhere were excluded. Most people who reported speaking a language other than English at home also speak English. The questions did not permit determination of the primary or dominant language of people who spoke both English and another language.

FOREIGN-BORN

Foreign Born: Number and percentage of population who were not U.S. citizens at birth. Foreign-born people are those who indicated they were either a U.S. citizen by naturalization or they were not a citizen of the United States.

Foreign-Born Naturalized Citizens: Number and percentage of population who were not U.S. citizens at birth but became U.S. citizens by naturalization.

The data on place of birth were derived from answers to long-form questionnaire Item 12 which was asked of a sample of the population. Respondents were asked to report the U.S. state, Puerto Rico, U.S. Island Area, or foreign country where they were born. People not reporting a place of birth were assigned the state or country of birth of another family member or their residence 5 years earlier, or were imputed the response of another person with similar characteristics. People born outside the United States were asked to report their place of birth according to current international boundaries. Since numerous changes in boundaries of foreign countries have occurred in the last century, some people may have reported their place of birth in terms of boundaries that existed at the time of their birth or emigration, or in accordance with their own national preference.

EDUCATIONAL ATTAINMENT

High School Graduates: Number and percentage of the population age 25 and over who have a high school diploma or higher. This category includes people whose highest degree was a high school diploma or its equivalent, people who attended college but did not receive a degree, and people who received a college, university, or professional degree. People who reported completing the 12th grade but not receiving a diploma are not high school graduates.

4-Years College Graduates: Number and percentage of the population age 25 and over who have a 4-year college, university, or professional degree.

Data on educational attainment were derived from answers to long-form questionnaire Item 9, which was asked of a sample of the population. Data on attainment are tabulated for the population 25 years old and over.

The order in which degrees were listed on the questionnaire suggested that doctorate degrees were "higher" than professional school degrees, which were "higher" than master's degrees. The question included instructions for people currently enrolled in school to report the level of the previous grade attended or the highest degree received. Respondents who did not report educational attainment or enrollment level were assigned the attainment of a person of the same age, race, Hispanic or Latino origin, occupation and sex, where possible, who resided in the same or a nearby area. Respondents who filled more than one box were edited to the highest level or degree reported.

The question included a response category that allowed respondents to report completing the 12th grade without receiving a high school diploma. It allowed people who received either a high school diploma or the equivalent (Test of General Educational Development—G.E.D.) and did not attend college, to be reported as "high school graduate(s)." The category "Associate degree" included people whose highest degree is an associate degree, which generally requires 2 years of college level work and is either in an occupational program that prepares them for a specific occupation, or an academic program primarily in the arts and sciences. The course work may or may not be transferable to a bachelor's degree. Master's degrees include the traditional MA and MS degrees and field-specific degrees, such as MSW, MEd, MBA, MLS, and MEng. Some examples of professional degrees include medicine, dentistry, chiropractic, optometry, osteopathic medicine, pharmacy, podiatry, veterinary medicine, law, and theology. Vocational and technical training such as barber school training; business, trade, technical, and vocational schools; or other training for a specific trade, are specifically excluded.

INCOME AND POVERTY

Median Household Income (in dollars): Includes the income of the householder and all other individuals 15 years old and over in the household, whether they are related to the householder or not. The median divides the income distribution into two equal parts: one-half of the cases falling below the median income and one-half above the median. For households, the median income is based on the distribution of the total number of households including those with no income. Median income for households is computed on the basis of a standard distribution and is rounded to the nearest whole dollar.

Per Capita Income (in dollars): Per capita income is the mean income computed for every man, woman, and child in a particular group. It is derived by dividing the total income of a particular group by the total population in that group. Per capita income is rounded to the nearest whole dollar.

The data on income in 1999 were derived from answers to long-form questionnaire Items 31 and 32, which were asked of a sample of the population 15 years old and over. "Total income" is the sum of the amounts reported separately for wage or salary income; net self-employment income; interest, dividends, or net rental or royalty income or income from estates and trusts; social security or railroad retirement income; Supplemental Security Income (SSI); public assistance or welfare payments; retirement, survivor, or disability pensions; and all other income.

Receipts from the following sources are not included as income: capital gains, money received from the sale of property (unless the recipient was engaged in the business of selling such property); the value of income "in kind" from food stamps, public housing subsidies, medical care, employer contributions for individuals, etc.; withdrawal of bank deposits; money borrowed; tax refunds; exchange of money between relatives living in the same household; and gifts and lump-sum inheritances, insurance payments, and other types of lump-sum receipts.

The eight types of income reported in the census are defined as follows:

Wage or salary income. Wage or salary income includes total money earnings received for work performed as an employee during the calendar year 1999. It includes wages, salary, armed forces pay, commissions, tips, piece-rate payments, and cash bonuses earned before deductions were made for taxes, bonds, pensions, union dues, etc.

Self-employment income. Self-employment income includes both farm and nonfarm self-employment income. Nonfarm self-employment income includes net money income (gross receipts minus expenses) from one's own business, professional enterprise, or partnership. Gross receipts include the value of all goods sold and services rendered. Expenses include costs of goods purchased, rent, heat, light, power, depreciation charges, wages and salaries paid, business taxes (not personal income taxes), etc. Farm self-employment income includes net money income (gross receipts minus operating expenses) from the operation of a farm by a person on his or her own account, as an owner, renter, or sharecropper. Gross receipts include the value of all products sold, government farm programs, money received from the rental of farm equipment to others, and incidental receipts from the sale of wood, sand, gravel, etc. Operating expenses include cost of feed, fertilizer, seed, and other farming supplies, cash wages paid to farmhands, depreciation charges, cash rent, interest on farm mortgages, farm building repairs, farm taxes (not state and federal personal income taxes), etc. The value of fuel, food, or other farm products used for family living is not included as part of net income.

Interest, dividends, or net rental income. Interest, dividends, or net rental income includes interest on savings or bonds, dividends from stockholdings or membership in associations, net income from rental of property to others and receipts from boarders or lodgers, net royalties, and periodic payments from an estate or trust fund.

Social Security income. Social security income includes social security pensions and survivors benefits, permanent disability insurance payments made by the Social Security Administration prior to deductions for medical insurance, and railroad retirement insurance checks from the U.S. government. Medicare reimbursements are not included.

Supplemental Security Income (SSI). Supplemental Security Income (SSI) is a nationwide U.S. assistance program administered by the Social Security Administration that guarantees a minimum level of income for needy aged, blind, or disabled individuals. The census questionnaire for Puerto Rico asked about the receipt of SSI; however, SSI is not a federally administered program in Puerto Rico. Therefore, it is probably not being interpreted by most respondents as the same as SSI in the United States. The only way a resident of Puerto Rico could have appropriately reported SSI would have been if they lived in the United States at any time during calendar year 1999 and received SSI.

Public assistance income. Public assistance income includes general assistance and Temporary Assistance to Needy Families (TANF). Separate payments received for hospital or other medical care (vendor payments) are excluded. This does not include Supplemental Security Income (SSI).

Retirement income. Retirement income includes: (1) retirement pensions and survivor benefits from a former employer; labor union; or federal, state, or local government; and the U.S. military; (2) income from workers' compensation; disability income from companies or unions; federal, state, or local government; and the U.S. military; (3) periodic receipts from annuities and insurance; and (4) regular income from IRA and KEOGH plans. This does not include social security income.

All other income. All other income includes unemployment compensation, Veterans' Administration (VA) payments, alimony and child support, contributions received periodically from people not living in the household, military family allotments, and other kinds of periodic income other than earnings.

Poverty Status: Number and percentage of population with income in 1999 below the poverty level. Based on individuals for whom poverty status is determined. Poverty status was determined for all people except institutionalized people, people in military group quarters, people in college dormitories, and unrelated individuals under 15 years old.

The poverty status of families and unrelated individuals in 1999 was determined using 48 thresholds (income cutoffs) arranged in a two dimensional matrix. The matrix consists of family size (from 1 person to 9 or more people) cross-classified by presence and number of family members under 18 years old (from no children present to 8 or more children present). Unrelated individuals and 2-person families were further differentiated by the age of the reference person (RP) (under 65 years old and 65 years old and over).

To determine a person's poverty status, one compares the person's total family income with the poverty threshold appropriate for that person's family size and composition. If the total income of that person's family is less than the threshold appropriate for that family, then the person is considered poor, together with every member of his or her family. If a person is not living with anyone related by birth, marriage, or adoption, then the person's own income is compared with his or her poverty threshold.

HOUSING

Homeownership: Number and percentage of housing units that are owner-occupied.

The data on tenure, which was asked at all occupied housing units, were obtained from answers to long-form questionnaire Item 33, and short-form questionnaire Item 2. All occupied housing units are classified as either owner occupied or renter occupied.

A housing unit is owner occupied if the owner or co-owner lives in the unit even if it is mortgaged or not fully paid for. The owner or co-owner must live in the unit and usually is Person 1 on the questionnaire. The unit is "Owned by you or someone in this household with a mortgage or loan" if it is being purchased with a mortgage or some other debt arrangement, such as a deed of trust, trust deed, contract to purchase, land contract, or purchase agreement. The unit is also considered owned with a mortgage if it is built on leased land and there is a mortgage on the unit. Mobile homes occupied by owners with installment loans balances are also included in this category.

Median Gross Rent (in dollars): Median monthly gross rent on specified renter-occupied and specified vacant-for-rent units. Specified renter-occupied and specified vacant-for-rent units exclude 1-family houses on 10 acres or more.

The data on gross rent were obtained from answers to long-form questionnaire Items 45a-d, which were asked on a sample basis. Gross rent is the contract rent plus the estimated average monthly cost of utilities (electricity, gas, water and sewer) and fuels (oil, coal, kerosene, wood, etc.) if these are paid by the renter (or paid for the renter by someone else). Gross rent is intended to eliminate differentials that result from varying practices with respect to the inclusion of utilities and fuels as part of the rental payment. The estimated costs of utilities and fuels are reported on an annual basis but are converted to monthly figures for the tabulations. Renter units occupied without payment of cash rent are shown separately as "No cash rent" in the tabulations.

Housing units that are renter occupied without payment of cash rent are shown separately as "No cash rent" in census data products. The unit may be owned by friends or relatives who live elsewhere and who allow occupancy without charge. Rent-free houses or apartments may be provided to compensate caretakers, ministers, tenant farmers, sharecroppers, or others.

Contract rent is the monthly rent agreed to or contracted for, regardless of any furnishings, utilities, fees, meals, or services that may be included. For vacant units, it is the monthly rent asked for the rental unit at the time of enumeration.

If the contract rent includes rent for a business unit or for living quarters occupied by another household, only that part of the rent estimated to be for the respondent's unit was included. Excluded was any rent paid for additional units or for business premises.

If a renter pays rent to the owner of a condominium or cooperative, and the condominium fee or cooperative carrying charge also is paid by the renter to the owner, the condominium fee or carrying charge was included as rent.

If a renter receives payments from lodgers or roomers who are listed as members of the household, the rent without deduction for any payments received from the lodgers or roomers was to be reported. The respondent was to report the rent agreed to or contracted for even if paid by someone else such as friends or relatives living elsewhere, a church or welfare agency, or the government through subsidies or vouchers.

The median divides the rent distribution into two equal parts: one-half of the cases falling below the median contract rent and one-half above the median. Median contract rents are computed on the basis of a standard distribution and are rounded to the nearest whole dollar. Units reported as "No cash rent" are excluded.

Median Home Value (in dollars): Reported by the owner of specified owner-occupied or specified vacant-for-sale housing units. Specified owner-occupied and specified vacant-for-sale housing units include only 1-family houses on less than 10 acres without a business or medical office on the property. The data for "specified units" exclude mobile homes, houses with a business or medical office, houses on 10 or more acres, and housing units in multi-unit buildings.

The data on value (also referred to as "price asked" for vacant units) were obtained from answers to long-form questionnaire Item 51, which was asked on a sample basis at owner-occupied housing units and units that were being bought, or vacant for sale at the time of enumeration. Value is the respondent's estimate of how much the property (house and lot, mobile home and lot, or condominium unit) would sell for if it were for sale. If the house or mobile home was owned or being bought, but the land on which it sits was not, the respondent was asked to estimate the combined value of the house or mobile home and the land. For vacant units, value was the price asked for the property. Value was tabulated separately for all owner-occupied and vacant-for-sale housing units, owner-occupied and vacant-for-sale mobile homes, and specified owner-occupied and specified vacant-for-sale housing units.

The median divides the value distribution into two equal parts: one-half of the cases falling below the median value of the property (house and lot, mobile home and lot, or condominium unit) and one-half above the median. Median values are computed on the basis of a standard distribution and are rounded to the nearest hundred dollars.

User's Guide: Asian Population

Places Covered

Ranking tables cover all counties and places in Indiana with Asian and/or Native Hawaiian and other Pacific Islander residents.

Source of Data

CENSUS 2000

Data for this chapter was derived from following source: *U.S. Bureau of the Census, Census of Population and Housing, 2000: Summary File 4.* Summary File 4 (SF 4) contains sample data, which is the information compiled from the questions asked of a sample (generally 1-in-6) of all people and housing units. Summary File 4 is repeated or iterated for the total population and 335 additional population groups. This chapter focuses on the following 23 population groups:

Asian
     Asian Indian
     Bangladeshi
     Cambodian
     Chinese (except Taiwanese)
     Filipino
     Hmong
     Indonesian
     Japanese
     Korean
     Laotian
     Malaysian
     Pakistani
     Sri Lankan
     Taiwanese
     Thai
     Vietnamese
Native Hawaiian and Other Pacific Islander
     Fijian
     Guamanian or Chamorro
     Hawaiian, Native
     Samoan
     Tongan

Please note that this chapter only includes people who responded to the question on race by indicating only one race. These people are classified by the Census Bureau as the race *alone* population. For example, respondents reporting a single detailed Asian group, such as Korean or Filipino, would be included in the Asian *alone* population. Respondents reporting more than one detailed Asian group, such as Chinese and Japanese or Asian Indian and Chinese and Vietnamese would also be included in the Asian *alone* population. This is because all of the detailed groups in these example combinations are part of the larger Asian race category. The same criteria apply to the Native Hawaiian and Other Pacific Islander groups.

In order for any of the tables for a specific group to be shown in Summary File 4, the data must meet a minimum population threshold. For Summary File 4, all tables are repeated for each race group, American Indian and Alaska Native tribe, and Hispanic or Latino group if the 100-percent count of people of that specific group in a particular geographic area is 100 or more. There also must be 50 or more unweighted people of that specific group in a particular geographic area. For example, if there are 100 or more 100-percent people tabulated as Korean in County A, and there are 50 or more unweighted people, then all matrices for Korean are shown in SF 4 for County A.

To maintain confidentiality, the Census Bureau applies statistical procedures that introduce some uncertainty into data for small geographic areas with small population groups. Therefore, tables may contain both sampling and nonsampling error.

In an iterated file such as SF 4, the universes *households, families,* and *occupied housing units* are classified by the race or ethnic group of the householder. In any population table where there is no note, the universe classification is always based on the race or ethnicity of the person. In all housing tables, the universe classification is based on the race or ethnicity of the householder.

Comparing SF 4 Estimates with Corresponding Values in SF 1 and SF 2

As in earlier censuses, the responses from the sample of households reporting on long forms must be weighted to reflect the entire population. Specifically, each responding household represents, on average, six or seven other households who reported using short forms. One consequence of the weighting procedures is that each estimate based on the long form responses has an associated confidence interval. These confidence intervals are wider (as a percentage of the estimate) for geographic areas with smaller populations and for characteristics that occur less frequently in the area being examined (such as the proportion of people in poverty in a middle-income neighborhood). In order to release as much useful information as possible, statisticians must balance a number of factors. In particular, for Census 2000, the Bureau of the Census created weighting areas—geographic areas from which about two hundred or more long forms were completed—which are large enough to produce good quality estimates. If smaller weighting areas had been used, the confidence intervals around the estimates would have been significantly wider, rendering many estimates less useful due to their lower reliability. The disadvantage of using weighting areas this large is that, for smaller geographic areas within them, the estimates of characteristics that are also reported on the short form will not match the counts reported in SF 1 or SF 2. Examples of these characteristics are the total number of people, the number of people reporting specific racial categories, and the number of housing units. The official values for items reported on the short form come from SF 1 and SF 2. The differences between the long form estimates in SF 4 and values in SF 1 or SF 2 are particularly noticeable for the smallest places, tracts, and block groups. The long form estimates of total population and total housing units in SF 4 will, however, match the SF 1 and SF 2 counts for larger geographic areas such as counties and states, and will be essentially the same for medium and large cities. This phenomenon also occurred for the 1990 Census, although in that case, the weighting areas included relatively small places. As a result, the long form estimates matched the short form counts for those places, but the confidence intervals around the estimates of characteristics collected only on the long form were often significantly wider (as a percentage of the estimate). SF 1 gives exact numbers even for very small groups and areas; whereas, SF 4 gives estimates for small groups and areas such as tracts and small places that are less exact. The goal of SF 4 is to identify large differences among areas or large changes over time. Estimates for small areas and small population groups often do exhibit large changes from one census to the next, so having the capability to measure them is worthwhile.

Topics

POPULATION

Total Population: Sample count of total population of all races.

Asian Population: A person having origins in any of the original peoples of the Far East, Southeast Asia, or the Indian subcontinent including, for example, Cambodia, China, India, Japan, Korea, Malaysia, Pakistan, the Philippine Islands, Thailand, and Vietnam. It includes Asian Indian, Bangladeshi, Cambodian, Chinese (except Taiwanese), Filipino, Hmong, Indonesian, Japanese, Korean, Laotian, Malaysian, Pakistani, Sri Lankan, Taiwanese, Thai, and Vietnamese.

Native Hawaiian or Other Pacific Islander (NHPI) Population: A person having origins in any of the original peoples of Hawaii, Guam, Samoa, or other Pacific Islands. It includes people who indicate their race as Fijian, Guamanian or Chamorro, Native Hawaiian, Samoan, and Tongan.

The data on race, which was asked of all people, were derived from answers to long-form questionnaire Item 6 and short-form questionnaire Item 8. The concept of race, as used by the Census Bureau, reflects self-identification by people according to the race or races with which they most closely identify. These categories are socio-political constructs and should not be interpreted as being scientific or anthropological in nature. Furthermore, the race categories include both racial and national-origin groups.

If an individual did not provide a race response, the race or races of the householder or other household members were assigned using specific rules of precedence of household relationship. For example, if race was missing for a natural-born child in the household, then either the race or races of the householder, another natural-born child, or the spouse of the householder were assigned. If race was not reported for anyone in the household, the race or races of a householder in a previously processed household were assigned.

AGE

Median Age: Divides the age distribution into two equal parts: one-half of the cases falling below the median age and one-half above the median. Median age is computed on the basis of a single year of age standard distribution.

The data on age, which was asked of all people, were derived from answers to the long-form questionnaire Item 4 and short-form questionnaire Item 6. The age classification is based on the age of the person in complete years as of April 1, 2000. The age of the person usually was derived from their date of birth information. Their reported age was used only when date of birth information was unavailable.

HOUSEHOLD SIZE

Average Household Size: A measure obtained by dividing the number of people in households by the total number of households (or householders). In cases where household members are tabulated by race or Hispanic origin, household members are classified by the race or Hispanic origin of the householder rather than the race or Hispanic origin of each individual. Average household size is rounded to the nearest hundredth.

LANGUAGE SPOKEN AT HOME

English Only: Number and percentage of population 5 years and over who report speaking English-only at home.

Language spoken at home data were derived from answers to long-form questionnaire Items 11a and 11b, which were asked of a sample of the population. Data were edited to include in tabulations only the population 5 years old and over. Questions 11a and 11b referred to languages spoken at home in an effort to measure the current use of languages other than English. People who knew languages other than English but did not use them at home or who only used them elsewhere were excluded. Most people who reported speaking a language other than English at home also speak English. The questions did not permit determination of the primary or dominant language of people who spoke both English and another language.

FOREIGN-BORN

Foreign Born: Number and percentage of population who were not U.S. citizens at birth. Foreign-born people are those who indicated they were either a U.S. citizen by naturalization or they were not a citizen of the United States.

Foreign-Born Naturalized Citizens: Number and percentage of population who were not U.S. citizens at birth but became U.S. citizens by naturalization.

The data on place of birth were derived from answers to long-form questionnaire Item 12 which was asked of a sample of the population. Respondents were asked to report the U.S. state, Puerto Rico, U.S. Island Area, or foreign country where they were born. People not reporting a place of birth were assigned the state or country of birth of another family member or their residence 5 years earlier, or were imputed the response of another person with similar characteristics. People born outside the United States were asked to report their place of birth according to current international boundaries. Since numerous changes in boundaries of foreign countries have occurred in the last century, some people may have reported their place of birth in terms of boundaries that existed at the time of their birth or emigration, or in accordance with their own national preference.

EDUCATIONAL ATTAINMENT

High School Graduates: Number and percentage of the population age 25 and over who have a high school diploma or higher. This category includes people whose highest degree was a high school diploma or its equivalent, people who attended college but did not receive a degree, and people who received a college, university, or professional degree. People who reported completing the 12th grade but not receiving a diploma are not high school graduates.

Four-Year College Graduates: Number and percentage of the population age 25 and over who have a 4-year college, university, or professional degree.

Data on educational attainment were derived from answers to long-form questionnaire Item 9, which was asked of a sample of the population. Data on attainment are tabulated for the population 25 years old and over.

The order in which degrees were listed on the questionnaire suggested that doctorate degrees were "higher" than professional school degrees, which were "higher" than master's degrees. The question included instructions for people currently enrolled in school to report the level of the previous grade attended or the highest degree received.

Respondents who did not report educational attainment or enrollment level were assigned the attainment of a person of the same age, race, Hispanic or Latino origin, occupation and sex, where possible, who resided in the same or a nearby area. Respondents who filled more than one box were edited to the highest level or degree reported.

The question included a response category that allowed respondents to report completing the 12th grade without receiving a high school diploma. It allowed people who received either a high school diploma or the equivalent (Test of General Educational Development—G.E.D.) and did not attend college, to be reported as "high school graduate(s)." The category "Associate degree" included people whose highest degree is an associate degree, which generally requires 2 years of college level work and is either in an occupational program that prepares them for a specific occupation, or an academic program primarily in the arts and sciences. The course work may or may not be transferable to a bachelor's degree. Master's degrees include the traditional MA and MS degrees and field-specific degrees, such as MSW, MEd, MBA, MLS, and MEng. Some examples of professional degrees include medicine, dentistry, chiropractic, optometry, osteopathic medicine, pharmacy, podiatry, veterinary medicine, law, and theology. Vocational and technical training such as barber school training; business, trade, technical, and vocational schools; or other training for a specific trade, are specifically excluded.

INCOME AND POVERTY

Median Household Income (in dollars): Includes the income of the householder and all other individuals 15 years old and over in the household, whether they are related to the householder or not. The median divides the income distribution into two equal parts: one-half of the cases falling below the median income and one-half above the median. For households, the median income is based on the distribution of the total number of households including those with no income. Median income for households is computed on the basis of a standard distribution and is rounded to the nearest whole dollar.

Per Capita Income (in dollars): Per capita income is the mean income computed for every man, woman, and child in a particular group. It is derived by dividing the total income of a particular group by the total population in that group. Per capita income is rounded to the nearest whole dollar.

The data on income in 1999 were derived from answers to long-form questionnaire Items 31 and 32, which were asked of a sample of the population 15 years old and over. "Total income" is the sum of the amounts reported separately for wage or salary income; net self-employment income; interest, dividends, or net rental or royalty income or income from estates and trusts; social security or railroad retirement income; Supplemental Security Income (SSI); public assistance or welfare payments; retirement, survivor, or disability pensions; and all other income.

Receipts from the following sources are not included as income: capital gains, money received from the sale of property (unless the recipient was engaged in the business of selling such property); the value of income "in kind" from food stamps, public housing subsidies, medical care, employer contributions for individuals, etc.; withdrawal of bank deposits; money borrowed; tax refunds; exchange of money between relatives living in the same household; and gifts and lump-sum inheritances, insurance payments, and other types of lump-sum receipts.

The eight types of income reported in the census are defined as follows:

Wage or salary income. Wage or salary income includes total money earnings received for work performed as an employee during the calendar year 1999. It includes wages, salary, armed forces pay, commissions, tips, piece-rate payments, and cash bonuses earned before deductions were made for taxes, bonds, pensions, union dues, etc.

Self-employment income. Self-employment income includes both farm and nonfarm self-employment income. Nonfarm self-employment income includes net money income (gross receipts minus expenses) from one's own business, professional enterprise, or partnership. Gross receipts include the value of all goods sold and services rendered. Expenses include costs of goods purchased, rent, heat, light, power, depreciation charges, wages and salaries paid, business taxes (not personal income taxes), etc. Farm self-employment income includes net money income (gross receipts minus operating expenses) from the operation of a farm by a person on his or her own account, as an owner, renter, or sharecropper. Gross receipts include the value of all products sold, government farm programs, money received from the rental of farm equipment to others, and incidental receipts from the sale of wood, sand, gravel, etc. Operating expenses include cost of feed, fertilizer, seed, and other farming supplies, cash wages paid to farmhands, depreciation charges, cash rent, interest on farm mortgages, farm building repairs, farm taxes (not state and federal personal income taxes), etc. The value of fuel, food, or other farm products used for family living is not included as part of net income.

Interest, dividends, or net rental income. Interest, dividends, or net rental income includes interest on savings or bonds, dividends from stockholdings or membership in associations, net income from rental of property to others and receipts from boarders or lodgers, net royalties, and periodic payments from an estate or trust fund.

Social Security income. Social security income includes social security pensions and survivors benefits, permanent disability insurance payments made by the Social Security Administration prior to deductions for medical insurance, and railroad retirement insurance checks from the U.S. government. Medicare reimbursements are not included.

Supplemental Security Income (SSI). Supplemental Security Income (SSI) is a nationwide U.S. assistance program administered by the Social Security Administration that guarantees a minimum level of income for needy aged, blind, or disabled individuals. The census questionnaire for Puerto Rico asked about the receipt of SSI; however, SSI is not a federally administered program in Puerto Rico. Therefore, it is probably not being interpreted by most respondents as the same as SSI in the United States. The only way a resident of Puerto Rico could have appropriately reported SSI would have been if they lived in the United States at any time during calendar year 1999 and received SSI.

Public assistance income. Public assistance income includes general assistance and Temporary Assistance to Needy Families (TANF). Separate payments received for hospital or other medical care (vendor payments) are excluded. This does not include Supplemental Security Income (SSI).

Retirement income. Retirement income includes: (1) retirement pensions and survivor benefits from a former employer; labor union; or federal, state, or local government; and the U.S. military; (2) income from workers' compensation; disability income from companies or unions; federal, state, or local government; and the U.S. military; (3) periodic receipts from annuities and insurance; and (4) regular income from IRA and KEOGH plans. This does not include social security income.

All other income. All other income includes unemployment compensation, Veterans' Administration (VA) payments, alimony and child support, contributions received periodically from people not living in the household, military family allotments, and other kinds of periodic income other than earnings.

Poverty Status: Number and percentage of population with income in 1999 below the poverty level. Based on individuals for whom poverty status is determined. Poverty status was determined for all people except institutionalized people, people in military group quarters, people in college dormitories, and unrelated individuals under 15 years old.

The poverty status of families and unrelated individuals in 1999 was determined using 48 thresholds (income cutoffs) arranged in a two dimensional matrix. The matrix consists of family size (from 1 person to 9 or more people) cross-classified by presence and number of family members under 18 years old (from no children present to 8 or more children present). Unrelated individuals and 2-person families were further differentiated by the age of the reference person (RP) (under 65 years old and 65 years old and over).

To determine a person's poverty status, one compares the person's total family income with the poverty threshold appropriate for that person's family size and composition. If the total income of that person's family is less than the threshold appropriate for that family, then the person is considered poor, together with every member of his or her family. If a person is not living with anyone related by birth, marriage, or adoption, then the person's own income is compared with his or her poverty threshold.

HOUSING

Homeownership: Number and percentage of housing units that are owner-occupied.

The data on tenure, which was asked at all occupied housing units, were obtained from answers to long-form questionnaire Item 33, and short-form questionnaire Item 2. All occupied housing units are classified as either owner occupied or renter occupied.

A housing unit is owner occupied if the owner or co-owner lives in the unit even if it is mortgaged or not fully paid for. The owner or co-owner must live in the unit and usually is Person 1 on the questionnaire. The unit is "Owned by you or someone in this household with a mortgage or loan" if it is being purchased with a mortgage or some other debt arrangement, such as a deed of trust, trust deed, contract to purchase, land contract, or purchase agreement. The unit is also considered owned with a mortgage if it is built on leased land and there is a mortgage on the unit. Mobile homes occupied by owners with installment loans balances are also included in this category.

Median Gross Rent (in dollars): Median monthly gross rent on specified renter-occupied and specified vacant-for-rent units. Specified renter-occupied and specified vacant-for-rent units exclude 1-family houses on 10 acres or more.

The data on gross rent were obtained from answers to long-form questionnaire Items 45a-d, which were asked on a sample basis. Gross rent is the contract rent plus the estimated average monthly cost of utilities (electricity, gas, water and sewer) and fuels (oil, coal, kerosene, wood, etc.) if these are paid by the renter (or paid for the renter by someone else). Gross rent is intended to eliminate differentials that result from varying practices with respect to the inclusion of utilities and fuels as part of the rental payment. The estimated costs of utilities and fuels are reported on an annual basis but are converted to monthly figures for the tabulations. Renter units occupied without payment of cash rent are shown separately as "No cash rent" in the tabulations.

Housing units that are renter occupied without payment of cash rent are shown separately as "No cash rent" in census data products. The unit may be owned by friends or relatives who live elsewhere and who allow occupancy without charge. Rent-free houses or apartments may be provided to compensate caretakers, ministers, tenant farmers, sharecroppers, or others.

Contract rent is the monthly rent agreed to or contracted for, regardless of any furnishings, utilities, fees, meals, or services that may be included. For vacant units, it is the monthly rent asked for the rental unit at the time of enumeration.

If the contract rent includes rent for a business unit or for living quarters occupied by another household, only that part of the rent estimated to be for the respondent's unit was included. Excluded was any rent paid for additional units or for business premises.

If a renter pays rent to the owner of a condominium or cooperative, and the condominium fee or cooperative carrying charge also is paid by the renter to the owner, the condominium fee or carrying charge was included as rent.

If a renter receives payments from lodgers or roomers who are listed as members of the household, the rent without deduction for any payments received from the lodgers or roomers was to be reported. The respondent was to report the rent agreed to or contracted for even if paid by someone else such as friends or relatives living elsewhere, a church or welfare agency, or the government through subsidies or vouchers.

The median divides the rent distribution into two equal parts: one-half of the cases falling below the median contract rent and one-half above the median. Median contract rents are computed on the basis of a standard distribution and are rounded to the nearest whole dollar. Units reported as "No cash rent" are excluded.

Median Home Value (in dollars): Reported by the owner of specified owner-occupied or specified vacant-for-sale housing units. Specified owner-occupied and specified vacant-for-sale housing units include only 1-family houses on less than 10 acres without a business or medical office on the property. The data for "specified units" exclude mobile homes, houses with a business or medical office, houses on 10 or more acres, and housing units in multi-unit buildings.

The data on value (also referred to as "price asked" for vacant units) were obtained from answers to long-form questionnaire Item 51, which was asked on a sample basis at owner-occupied housing units and units that were being bought, or vacant for sale at the time of enumeration. Value is the respondent's estimate of how much the property (house and lot, mobile home and lot, or condominium unit) would sell for if it were for sale. If the house or mobile home was owned or being bought, but the land on which it sits was not, the respondent was asked to estimate the combined value of the house or mobile home and the land. For vacant units, value was the price asked for the property. Value was tabulated separately for all owner-occupied and vacant-for-sale housing units, owner-occupied and vacant-for-sale mobile homes, and specified owner-occupied and specified vacant-for-sale housing units.

The median divides the value distribution into two equal parts: one-half of the cases falling below the median value of the property (house and lot, mobile home and lot, or condominium unit) and one-half above the median. Median values are computed on the basis of a standard distribution and are rounded to the nearest hundred dollars.

User's Guide: Climate

Inclusion Criteria — How the Data and Stations Were Selected

There were two central goals in the preparation of the climate chapter. The first was to select those data elements which would have the broadest possible use by the greatest range of potential users. For most of the National Weather Service stations there is a substantial quantity and variety of climatological data that is collected, however for the majority of stations the data is more limited. After evaluating the available data set, the editors chose nine temperature measures, five precipitation measures, and heating and cooling degree days — sixteen key data elements that are widely requested and are believed to be of the greatest general interest.

The second goal was to provide data for as many weather stations as possible. Although there are over 10,000 stations in the United States, not every station collects data for both precipitation and temperature, and even among those that do, the data is not always complete for the last thirty years. As the editors used a different methodology than that of NCDC to compute data, a formal data sufficiency criteria was devised and applied to the source tapes in order to select stations for inclusion.

Sources of the Data

The data in the climate chapter is compiled from several sources. The majority comes from the original National Climactic Data Center computer tapes (TD-3220 Summary of Month Co-Operative). This data was used to create the entire table for each Cooperative station and part of each National Weather Service station. The remainder of the data for each NWS station comes from the International Station Meteorological Climate Summary, Version 4.0, September 1996, which is also available from the NCDC.

NCDC has two main classes or types of weather stations; first order stations which are staffed by professional meteorologists and cooperative stations which are staffed by volunteers. In the climate chapter all first order stations operated by the National Weather Service are included, as well as every cooperative station that met our selection criteria.

Potential cautions in using *Weather America*

First, as with any statistical reference work of this type, users need to be aware of the source of the data. The information here comes from NOAA, and it is the most comprehensive and reliable core data available. Although it is the best, it is not perfect. Most weather stations are staffed by volunteers, times of observation sometimes vary, stations occasionally are moved (especially over a thirty year period), equipment is changed or upgraded, and all of these factors affect the uniformity of the data. the climate chapter does not attempt to correct for these factors, and is not intended for either climatologists or atmospheric scientists. Users with concerns about data collection and reporting protocols are both referred to NCDC technical documentation, and also, they are perhaps better served by using the original computer tapes themselves as well.

Second, users need to be aware of the methodology used, which is described later in this User's Guide. Although this methodology has produced fully satisfactory results, it is not directly compatible with other methodologies, hence variances in the results published here and those which appear in other publications will doubtlessly arise.

Third, is the trap of that informal logical fallacy known as "hasty generalization," and its corollaries. This may involve presuming the future will be like the past (specifically, next year will be an average year), or it may involve misunderstanding the limitations of an arithmetic average, but more interestingly, it may involve those mistakes made most innocently by generalizing informally on too broad a basis. As weather is highly localized, the data should be taken in that context. A weather station collects data about climatic conditions at that spot, and that spot may or may not be an effective paradigm for an entire town or area. For example, the weather station in Burlington, Vermont is located at the airport about 3 miles east of the center of town. Most of Burlington is a lot closer to Lake Champlain, and that should mean to a careful user that there could be a significant difference between the temperature readings gathered at the weather station and readings that might be gathered at City Hall downtown. How much would this difference be? How could it be estimated? There are no answers here for these sorts of questions, but it is important for users of this book to raise them for themselves. (It is interesting to note that similar situations abound across the country. For example, compare different readings for the multiple stations in San Francisco, CA or for those around New York City.)

Our source of data has been consistent, so has our methodology. The data has been computed and reported consistently as well. As a result, the the climate chapter should prove valuable to the careful and informed reader.

Weather Station Tables

The weather station tables are grouped by type (National Weather Service and Cooperative) and then arranged alphabetically. The station name is almost always a place name, and is shown here just as it appears in NCDC data. The station name is followed by the county in which the station is located, the elevation of the station (at the time beginning of the thirty year period) and the latitude and longitude.

The National Weather Service Station tables contain 30 data elements which were compiled from two different sources, the International Station Meteorological Climate Summary (ISMCS) and NCDC TD-3220 data tapes. The following 14 elements are from the ISMCS: maximum precipitation, minimum precipitation, maximum 24-hour precipitation, maximum snowfall, maximum 24-hour snowfall, thunderstorm days, foggy days, predominant sky cover, relative humidity (morning and afternoon), dewpoint, wind speed and direction, and maximum wind gust. The remaining 16 elements come from the TD-3220 data tapes. The period of record (POR) for data from the TD-3220 data tapes is 1970-1999. The POR for ISMCS data varies from station to station.

Weather Elements (National Weather Service and Cooperative Stations)

The following elements were compiled by the editor from the NCDC TD-3220 data tapes using a period of record of 1970-1999.

The average temperatures (maximum, minimum, and mean) are the average (see Methodology below) of those temperatures for all available values for a given month. For example, for a given station the average maximum temperature for July is the arithmetic average of all available maximum July temperatures for that station. (Maximum means the highest recorded temperature, minimum means the lowest recorded temperature, and mean means an arithmetic average temperature.)

The extreme maximum temperature is the highest temperature recorded in each month over the period 1970-1999. The extreme minimum temperature is the lowest temperature recorded in each month over the same time period.

The days for maximum temperature and minimum temperature are the average number of days those criteria were met for all available instances. The symbol >= means greater than or equal to, the symbol <= means less than or equal to. For example, for a given station, the number of days the maximum temperature was greater than or equal to 90°F in July, is just an arithmetic average of the number of days in all the available Julys for that station.

Heating and cooling degree days are based on the median temperature for a given day and its variance from 65°F. For example, for a given station if the day's high temperature was 50°F and the day's low temperature was 30°F, the median (midpoint) temperature was 40°F. 40°F is 25 degrees below 65°F, hence on this day there would be 25 heating degree days. The also applies for cooling degree days. For example, for a given station if the day's high temperature was 80°F and the day's low temperature was 70°F, the median (midpoint) temperature was 75°F. 75°F is 10 degrees above 65°F, hence on this day there would be 10 cooling degree days. All heating and/or cooling degree days in a month are summed for the month giving respective totals for each element for that month. These sums for a given month for a given station over the past thirty years are again summed and then arithmetically averaged. It should be noted that the heating and cooling degree days do not cancel each other out. It is possible to have both for a given station in the same month.

Precipitation data is computed the same as heating and cooling degree days. Mean precipitation and mean snowfall are arithmetic averages of cumulative totals for the month. All available values for the thirty year period for a given month for a given station are summed and then divided by the number of values. The same is true for days of greater than or equal to 0.1" and 1.0" of precipitation, and days of greater than or equal to 1.0" of snow depth on the ground. The word trace appears for precipitation and snowfall amounts that are too small to measure.

Finally, remember that all values presented in the tables and the rankings are averages of available data (see Methodology below) for that specific data element for the last thirty years (1970-1999).

Weather Elements (National Weather Service Stations Only)

The following elements were taken directly from the International Station Meteorological Climate Summary. The periods of records vary per station.

Maximum precipitation, minimum precipitation, maximum 24-hour precipitation, maximum snowfall, maximum 24-hour snowfall, thunderstorm days, foggy days, relative humidity (morning and afternoon), dewpoint, prevailing wind speed and direction, and maximum wind gust are all self-explanatory.

The word trace appears for precipitation and snowfall amounts that are too small to measure.

Predominant sky cover contains four possible entries: CLR (clear); SCT (scattered); BRK (broken); and OVR (overcast).

How Cooperative Stations Were Selected

The basic criteria is that a station must have data for temperature, precipitation, heating and cooling degree days of sufficient quantity in order to create a meaningful average. More specifically, the definition of sufficiency here has two parts. First, there must be 22 values for a given data element (with the exception of cooling degree days which required only 14 values in order to be considered sufficient- more about this later), and second, eight of the sixteen elements included in the table must pass this sufficiency test. For example, in regard to average maximum temperature (the first element on every data table), a given station needs to have a value for every month of at least 22 of the last thirty years in order to meet the criteria, and, in addition, every station included must have at least eight of the sixteen elements at least this minimal level of completeness in order to fulfill the criteria. By using this procedure, 3,933 stations met these requirements and are included here.

Methodology

The following discussion applies only to data compiled from the NCDC TD-3220 data tapes.

the climate chapter is based on an arithmetic average of all available data for a specific data element at a given station. For example, the average maximum daily high temperature during July for Pontiac, MI was abstracted from NCDC source tapes for the thirty Julys, starting in July, 1970 and ending in July, 1999. These thirty figures were then summed and divided by thirty to produce an arithmetic average. As might be expected, there were not thirty values for every data element on every table. For a variety of reasons, NCDC data is sometimes incomplete. Thus the following standards were established.

For those data elements where there were 26-30 values, the data was taken to be essentially complete and an average was computed. For data elements where there were 22-25 values, the data was taken as being partly complete but still valid enough to use to compute an average. Such averages are shown in **bold italic** type to indicate that there was less than 26 values. For the few data elements where there were not even 22 values, no average was computed and 'na' appears in the space. If any of the twelve months for a given data element reported a value of 'na', no annual average was computed and the annual average was reported as 'na' as well.

This procedure was followed for 15 of the 16 data elements. The one exception is cooling degree days. The collection of this data began in 1980 so the following standards were adopted: for those data elements where there were 17-20 values, the data was taken to be essentially complete and an average was computed. For data elements where there were 14-16 values, the data was taken as being partly complete but still valid enough to use to compute an average. Such averages are shown in **bold italic** type to indicate that there was 14-16 values. For the few data elements where there were not even 14 values, no average was computed and 'na' appears in the space. If any of the twelve months for a given data element reported a value of 'na', no annual average was computed and the annual average was reported as 'na' as well.

Thus the basic computational methodology of the climate chapter is to provide an arithmetic average. Because of this, such a pure arithmetic average is somewhat different from the special type of average (called a "normal") which NCDC procedures produces and appears in federal publications.

Perhaps the best outline of the contrasting normalization methodology is found in the following paragraph (which appears as part of an NCDC technical document titled, CLIM81 1961-1990 NORMALS TD-9641 prepared by Lewis France of NCDC in May, 1992):

Normals have been defined as the arithmetic mean of a climatological element computed over a long time period. International agreements eventually led to the decision that the appropriate time period would be three consecutive decades (Guttman, 1989). The data record should be consistent (have no changes in location, instruments, observation practices, etc.; these are identified here as "exposure changes") and have no missing values so a normal will reflect the actual average climatic conditions. If any significant exposure changes have occurred, the data record is said to be "inhomogeneous," and the normal may not reflect a true climatic average. Such data need to be adjusted to remove the nonclimatic inhomogeneities. The resulting (adjusted) record is then said to be "homogeneous." If no exposure changes have occurred at a station, the normal is calculated simply by averaging the appropriate 30 values from the 1961-1990 record.

In the main, there are two "inhomogeneities" that NCDC is correcting for with normalization: adjusting for variances in time of day of observation (at the so-called First Order stations data is based on midnight to midnight observation times and this practice is not necessarily followed at cooperative stations which are staffed by volunteers), and second, estimating data that is either missing or incongruent.

A long discussion of the normalization process is not required here but a short note concerning comparative results of the two methodologies is appropriate.

When the editors first started compiling the climate chapter a concern arose because the normalization process would not be replicated: would our methodology produce strikingly different results than NCDC's? To allay concerns, results of the two processes were compared for the time period normalized results are available (1961-1990). In short, what was found was that the answer to this question is no. Never-the-less, users should be aware that because of both the time period covered (1970-1999) and the methodology used, data in the climate chapter is not compatible with data from other sources.

Adams County

Located in eastern Indiana; bounded on the east by Ohio. Covers a land area of 339.36 square miles, a water area of 0.57 square miles, and is located in the Eastern Time Zone. The county was founded in 1835. County seat is Decatur.

Adams County is part of the Decatur, IN Micropolitan Statistical Area. The entire metro area includes: Adams County, IN

Weather Station: Berne   Elevation: 859 feet

	Jan	Feb	Mar	Apr	May	Jun	Jul	Aug	Sep	Oct	Nov	Dec
High	32	37	48	61	72	81	85	83	76	64	50	38
Low	17	21	30	40	50	60	64	62	55	43	34	24
Precip	2.1	2.1	2.9	3.8	3.8	4.4	4.1	3.6	3.0	2.6	3.2	2.7
Snow	9.4	7.2	4.4	1.1	0.0	0.0	0.0	0.0	0.0	0.4	2.1	6.1

High and Low temperatures in degrees Fahrenheit; Precipitation and Snow in inches

Population: 31,105 (1990); 33,625 (2000); 34,132 (2010); 34,249 (2015 projected); Race: 96.8% White, 0.4% Black, 0.2% Asian, 2.6% Other, 3.4% Hispanic of any race (2010); Density: 100.6 persons per square mile (2010); Average household size: 2.75 (2010); Median age: 33.8 (2010); Males per 100 females: 98.6 (2010).
Religion: Five largest groups: 14.3% Catholic Church, 11.6% Lutheran Church—Missouri Synod, 8.0% The United Methodist Church, 8.0% Old Order Amish Church, 4.5% United Church of Christ (2000).
Economy: Unemployment rate: 9.8% (5/2010); Total civilian labor force: 16,142 (5/2010); Leading industries: 40.0% manufacturing; 12.8% health care and social assistance; 12.8% retail trade (2008); Farms: 1,315 totaling 182,490 acres (2007); Companies that employ 500 or more persons: 3 (2008); Companies that employ 100 to 499 persons: 21 (2008); Companies that employ less than 100 persons: 734 (2008); Black-owned businesses: n/a (2002); Hispanic-owned businesses: n/a (2002); Asian-owned businesses: n/a (2002); Women-owned businesses: 999 (2002); Retail sales per capita: $14,484 (2010). Single-family building permits issued: 46 (2009); Multi-family building permits issued: 0 (2009).
Income: Per capita income: $19,406 (2010); Median household income: $44,536 (2010); Average household income: $53,803 (2010); Percent of households with income of $100,000 or more: 9.8% (2010); Poverty rate: 12.7% (2008); Bankruptcy rate: 5.75% (2009).
Taxes: Total county taxes per capita: $262 (2007); County property taxes per capita: $189 (2007).
Education: Percent of population age 25 and over with: High school diploma (including GED) or higher: 82.1% (2010); Bachelor's degree or higher: 11.9% (2010); Master's degree or higher: 3.5% (2010).
Housing: Homeownership rate: 77.6% (2010); Median home value: $108,277 (2010); Median contract rent: $438 per month (2006-2008 3-year est.); Median year structure built: 1967 (2006-2008 3-year est.).
Health: Birth rate: 191.8 per 10,000 population (2009); Death rate: 93.1 per 10,000 population (2009); Age-adjusted cancer mortality rate: 170.9 deaths per 100,000 population (2006); Number of physicians: 5.0 per 10,000 population (2007); Hospital beds: 14.8 per 10,000 population (2006); Hospital admissions: 693.4 per 10,000 population (2006).
Elections: 2008 Presidential election results: 36.5% Obama, 62.2% McCain, 0.0% Nader
National and State Parks: Limberlost State Memorial
Additional Information Contacts
Adams County Government . . . . (219) 724-5315
    http://www.co.adams.in.us
Berne Chamber of Commerce . . . . (260) 589-8080
    http://www.bernein.com
City of Berne . . . . (260) 589-8526
    http://www.cityofberne.com
City of Decatur . . . . (260) 724-7171
    http://www.decaturin.org
Decatur Chamber of Commerce . . . . (260) 724-2604
    http://www.decaturchamber.org

Adams County Communities

BERNE (city). Covers a land area of 1.799 square miles and a water area of 0 square miles. Located at 40.65° N. Lat; 84.95° W. Long. Elevation is 843 feet.
History: Mennonite immigrants from Berne, Switzerland, settled here in 1852 and named Berne for their former home. The Mennonite Book Concern was established here in 1882.

Population: 3,747 (1990); 4,150 (2000); 4,056 (2010); 4,007 (2015 projected); Race: 96.4% White, 0.7% Black, 0.1% Asian, 2.8% Other, 2.3% Hispanic of any race (2010); Density: 2,255.0 persons per square mile (2010); Average household size: 2.51 (2010); Median age: 35.7 (2010); Males per 100 females: 93.2 (2010); Marriage status: 17.8% never married, 64.9% now married, 11.3% widowed, 6.0% divorced (2000); Foreign born: 1.9% (2000); Ancestry (includes multiple ancestries): 28.7% German, 28.0% Swiss, 10.0% Irish, 7.7% United States or American, 5.5% Other groups (2000).
Economy: Single-family building permits issued: 3 (2009); Multi-family building permits issued: 0 (2009); Employment by occupation: 11.5% management, 18.6% professional, 15.4% services, 23.2% sales, 1.6% farming, 6.6% construction, 23.0% production (2000).
Income: Per capita income: $16,809 (2010); Median household income: $34,337 (2010); Average household income: $42,998 (2010); Percent of households with income of $100,000 or more: 4.6% (2010); Poverty rate: 3.6% (2000).
Taxes: Total city taxes per capita: $185 (2007); City property taxes per capita: $160 (2007).
Education: Percent of population age 25 and over with: High school diploma (including GED) or higher: 81.3% (2010); Bachelor's degree or higher: 17.7% (2010); Master's degree or higher: 4.9% (2010).
School District(s)
South Adams Schools (PK-12)
    2008-09 Enrollment: 1,414 . . . . (260) 589-3133
Housing: Homeownership rate: 69.2% (2010); Median home value: $86,751 (2010); Median contract rent: $348 per month (2000); Median year structure built: 1963 (2000).
Safety: Violent crime rate: 0.0 per 10,000 population; Property crime rate: 129.6 per 10,000 population (2008).
Newspapers: Berne Tri-Weekly News (Community news; Circulation 2,500)
Transportation: Commute to work: 93.5% car, 0.0% public transportation, 3.2% walk, 1.9% work from home (2000); Travel time to work: 66.7% less than 15 minutes, 20.6% 15 to 30 minutes, 4.1% 30 to 45 minutes, 4.0% 45 to 60 minutes, 4.6% 60 minutes or more (2000)
Additional Information Contacts
Berne Chamber of Commerce . . . . (260) 589-8080
    http://www.bernein.com
City of Berne . . . . (260) 589-8526
    http://www.cityofberne.com

DECATUR (city). County seat. Covers a land area of 4.923 square miles and a water area of 0.006 square miles. Located at 40.83° N. Lat; 84.92° W. Long. Elevation is 801 feet.
History: Decatur was named for Stephen Decatur, American naval hero. Novelist Gene Stratton Porter (1868-1924) lived here for three years.
Population: 9,160 (1990); 9,528 (2000); 9,425 (2010); 9,277 (2015 projected); Race: 94.7% White, 0.7% Black, 0.3% Asian, 4.4% Other, 7.0% Hispanic of any race (2010); Density: 1,914.4 persons per square mile (2010); Average household size: 2.35 (2010); Median age: 37.1 (2010); Males per 100 females: 96.5 (2010); Marriage status: 22.5% never married, 56.5% now married, 8.1% widowed, 12.8% divorced (2000); Foreign born: 1.9% (2000); Ancestry (includes multiple ancestries): 32.4% German, 12.0% Other groups, 9.9% United States or American, 8.6% Irish, 8.0% English (2000).
Economy: Single-family building permits issued: 6 (2009); Multi-family building permits issued: 0 (2009); Employment by occupation: 8.8% management, 13.2% professional, 16.8% services, 20.3% sales, 0.1% farming, 10.3% construction, 30.5% production (2000).
Income: Per capita income: $21,320 (2010); Median household income: $42,057 (2010); Average household income: $50,345 (2010); Percent of households with income of $100,000 or more: 8.3% (2010); Poverty rate: 7.7% (2000).
Taxes: Total city taxes per capita: $348 (2007); City property taxes per capita: $249 (2007).
Education: Percent of population age 25 and over with: High school diploma (including GED) or higher: 86.0% (2010); Bachelor's degree or higher: 11.3% (2010); Master's degree or higher: 3.3% (2010).
School District(s)
North Adams Community Schools (PK-12)
    2008-09 Enrollment: 2,156 . . . . (260) 724-7146
Housing: Homeownership rate: 70.3% (2010); Median home value: $91,660 (2010); Median contract rent: $327 per month (2000); Median year structure built: 1958 (2000).

Hospitals: Adams County Memorial Hospital (87 beds)
Safety: Violent crime rate: 8.4 per 10,000 population; Property crime rate: 92.8 per 10,000 population (2008).
Newspapers: Decatur Daily Democrat (Local news; Circulation 6,300)
Transportation: Commute to work: 93.3% car, 0.2% public transportation, 2.0% walk, 2.4% work from home (2000); Travel time to work: 57.3% less than 15 minutes, 16.1% 15 to 30 minutes, 14.7% 30 to 45 minutes, 7.7% 45 to 60 minutes, 4.3% 60 minutes or more (2000)
Additional Information Contacts
City of Decatur . . . . (260) 724-7171
   http://www.decaturin.org
Decatur Chamber of Commerce . . . . (260) 724-2604
   http://www.decaturchamber.org

GENEVA (town). Covers a land area of 1.148 square miles and a water area of 0.126 square miles. Located at 40.59° N. Lat; 84.96° W. Long. Elevation is 850 feet.
History: Geneva was the home of novelist Gene Stratton Porter from 1893 to 1913. Her books were set in the Limberlost Swamps here.
Population: 1,345 (1990); 1,368 (2000); 1,303 (2010); 1,275 (2015 projected); Race: 97.5% White, 0.7% Black, 0.3% Asian, 1.5% Other, 1.2% Hispanic of any race (2010); Density: 1,135.4 persons per square mile (2010); Average household size: 2.31 (2010); Median age: 36.4 (2010); Males per 100 females: 98.0 (2010); Marriage status: 20.6% never married, 57.4% now married, 7.6% widowed, 14.3% divorced (2000); Foreign born: 0.8% (2000); Ancestry (includes multiple ancestries): 25.9% German, 10.3% United States or American, 9.4% English, 9.1% Irish, 7.3% Other groups (2000).
Economy: Employment by occupation: 5.9% management, 11.1% professional, 12.8% services, 21.6% sales, 0.9% farming, 11.2% construction, 36.6% production (2000).
Income: Per capita income: $20,202 (2010); Median household income: $37,500 (2010); Average household income: $46,910 (2010); Percent of households with income of $100,000 or more: 5.9% (2010); Poverty rate: 11.9% (2000).
Taxes: Total city taxes per capita: $395 (2007); City property taxes per capita: $257 (2007).
Education: Percent of population age 25 and over with: High school diploma (including GED) or higher: 83.0% (2010); Bachelor's degree or higher: 11.2% (2010); Master's degree or higher: 2.3% (2010).
School District(s)
South Adams Schools (PK-12)
   2008-09 Enrollment: 1,414 . . . . (260) 589-3133
Housing: Homeownership rate: 68.6% (2010); Median home value: $83,750 (2010); Median contract rent: $251 per month (2000); Median year structure built: 1962 (2000).
Transportation: Commute to work: 96.3% car, 0.4% public transportation, 1.2% walk, 0.9% work from home (2000); Travel time to work: 36.9% less than 15 minutes, 37.2% 15 to 30 minutes, 14.5% 30 to 45 minutes, 3.0% 45 to 60 minutes, 8.3% 60 minutes or more (2000)

MONROE (town). Covers a land area of 0.480 square miles and a water area of 0 square miles. Located at 40.74° N. Lat; 84.94° W. Long. Elevation is 823 feet.
Population: 763 (1990); 734 (2000); 732 (2010); 729 (2015 projected); Race: 98.2% White, 0.0% Black, 0.0% Asian, 1.8% Other, 1.9% Hispanic of any race (2010); Density: 1,525.1 persons per square mile (2010); Average household size: 2.88 (2010); Median age: 33.1 (2010); Males per 100 females: 102.8 (2010); Marriage status: 18.2% never married, 66.9% now married, 5.8% widowed, 9.1% divorced (2000); Foreign born: 0.0% (2000); Ancestry (includes multiple ancestries): 35.4% German, 12.6% United States or American, 12.4% Swiss, 11.5% Other groups, 5.7% English (2000).
Economy: Employment by occupation: 5.9% management, 15.4% professional, 12.9% services, 20.8% sales, 0.5% farming, 12.9% construction, 31.5% production (2000).
Income: Per capita income: $16,956 (2010); Median household income: $46,642 (2010); Average household income: $48,642 (2010); Percent of households with income of $100,000 or more: 3.9% (2010); Poverty rate: 4.0% (2000).
Taxes: Total city taxes per capita: $216 (2007); City property taxes per capita: $140 (2007).
Education: Percent of population age 25 and over with: High school diploma (including GED) or higher: 84.2% (2010); Bachelor's degree or higher: 11.7% (2010); Master's degree or higher: 3.4% (2010).

School District(s)
Adams Central Community Schools (KG-12)
   2008-09 Enrollment: 1,154 . . . . (260) 692-6193
Housing: Homeownership rate: 85.4% (2010); Median home value: $112,216 (2010); Median contract rent: $310 per month (2000); Median year structure built: 1956 (2000).
Transportation: Commute to work: 93.2% car, 0.5% public transportation, 1.9% walk, 3.3% work from home (2000); Travel time to work: 52.5% less than 15 minutes, 22.6% 15 to 30 minutes, 6.2% 30 to 45 minutes, 15.3% 45 to 60 minutes, 3.4% 60 minutes or more (2000)

Allen County

Located in northeastern Indiana; bounded on the east by Ohio; crossed by the St. Joseph, St. Marys, and Maumee Rivers. Covers a land area of 657.25 square miles, a water area of 2.85 square miles, and is located in the Eastern Time Zone. The county was founded in 1823. County seat is Fort Wayne.

Allen County is part of the Fort Wayne, IN Metropolitan Statistical Area. The entire metro area includes: Allen County, IN; Wells County, IN; Whitley County, IN

Weather Station: Fort Wayne Baer Field									Elevation: 790 feet		
	Jan	Feb	Mar	Apr	May	Jun	Jul	Aug	Sep	Oct	Nov	Dec
High	31	35	47	60	72	81	85	82	76	63	49	37
Low	16	19	29	39	50	59	63	61	53	42	33	23
Precip	2.0	1.9	2.9	3.7	3.7	3.8	3.7	3.5	2.8	2.7	3.0	2.7
Snow	9.9	7.7	4.6	1.2	tr	tr	0.0	tr	0.0	0.5	3.0	7.9

High and Low temperatures in degrees Fahrenheit; Precipitation and Snow in inches

Population: 300,836 (1990); 331,849 (2000); 353,710 (2010); 361,998 (2015 projected); Race: 80.8% White, 11.5% Black, 1.9% Asian, 5.8% Other, 6.3% Hispanic of any race (2010); Density: 538.2 persons per square mile (2010); Average household size: 2.51 (2010); Median age: 36.1 (2010); Males per 100 females: 96.7 (2010).
Religion: Five largest groups: 17.4% Catholic Church, 7.7% Lutheran Church—Missouri Synod, 4.5% The United Methodist Church, 3.8% Evangelical Lutheran Church in America, 1.5% Christian Churches and Churches of Christ (2000).
Economy: Unemployment rate: 10.0% (5/2010); Total civilian labor force: 176,075 (5/2010); Leading industries: 17.7% manufacturing; 16.0% health care and social assistance; 12.7% retail trade (2008); Farms: 1,649 totaling 254,136 acres (2007); Companies that employ 500 or more persons: 20 (2008); Companies that employ 100 to 499 persons: 275 (2008); Companies that employ less than 100 persons: 9,172 (2008); Black-owned businesses: 1,074 (2002); Hispanic-owned businesses: n/a (2002); Asian-owned businesses: 545 (2002); Women-owned businesses: 6,250 (2002); Retail sales per capita: $14,633 (2010). Single-family building permits issued: 655 (2009); Multi-family building permits issued: 60 (2009).
Income: Per capita income: $24,508 (2010); Median household income: $48,455 (2010); Average household income: $62,094 (2010); Percent of households with income of $100,000 or more: 14.7% (2010); Poverty rate: 11.5% (2008); Bankruptcy rate: 8.17% (2009).
Taxes: Total county taxes per capita: $277 (2007); County property taxes per capita: $231 (2007).
Education: Percent of population age 25 and over with: High school diploma (including GED) or higher: 88.2% (2010); Bachelor's degree or higher: 26.0% (2010); Master's degree or higher: 8.3% (2010).
Housing: Homeownership rate: 71.5% (2010); Median home value: $106,475 (2010); Median contract rent: $500 per month (2006-2008 3-year est.); Median year structure built: 1970 (2006-2008 3-year est.)
Health: Birth rate: 150.4 per 10,000 population (2009); Death rate: 76.4 per 10,000 population (2009); Age-adjusted cancer mortality rate: 182.2 deaths per 100,000 population (2006); Air Quality Index: 60.3% good, 39.3% moderate, 0.3% unhealthy for sensitive individuals, 0.0% unhealthy (percent of days in 2008); Number of physicians: 22.6 per 10,000 population (2007); Hospital beds: 50.9 per 10,000 population (2006); Hospital admissions: 1,830.9 per 10,000 population (2006).
Elections: 2008 Presidential election results: 47.4% Obama, 51.8% McCain, 0.1% Nader
Additional Information Contacts
Allen County Government . . . . (219) 449-3155
   http://www.co.allen.in.us
City of Fort Wayne . . . . (260) 427-1221
   http://www.ci.ft-wayne.in.us

City of New Haven . . . . (260) 748-7000
   http://www.newhavenin.org
Greater Fort Wayne Chamber of Commerce . . . . (260) 424-1435
   http://www.fwchamber.org
New Haven Chamber of Commerce . . . . (260) 749-4484
   http://www.newhavenchamber.org
Town of Grabill . . . . (260) 627-5227
   http://www.grabill.net

Allen County Communities

FORT WAYNE (city). County seat. Covers a land area of 78.952
square miles and a water area of 0.169 square miles. Located at 41.07° N.
Lat; 85.12° W. Long. Elevation is 810 feet.
History: The first fort at the site of Fort Wayne was Fort Miami, established
in the 1680's by the French. Another stockade was built by Anthony Wayne
in 1794. By 1819 a trading post and gristmill were started and more settlers
appeared. When Allen County was organized in 1824, Fort Wayne was
named as county seat. It was incorporated in 1829. The building of the
Wabash & Erie Canal between 1832 and 1840 was a boost for Fort
Wayne's economy. Fort Wayne may have claims to the first baseball game
played under the lights at its League Park, where in 1883 an arc-lighting
system illuminated the field for a game between a professional team from
Quincy, Illinois, and a team of students from a Fort Wayne college.
Population: 205,671 (1990); 205,727 (2000); 200,606 (2010); 199,029
(2015 projected); Race: 71.4% White, 18.5% Black, 2.0% Asian, 8.1%
Other, 9.2% Hispanic of any race (2010); Density: 2,540.8 persons per
square mile (2010); Average household size: 2.37 (2010); Median age:
35.4 (2010); Males per 100 females: 95.3 (2010); Marriage status: 30.3%
never married, 49.5% now married, 7.3% widowed, 12.9% divorced (2000);
Foreign born: 4.9% (2000); Ancestry (includes multiple ancestries): 27.5%
German, 24.9% Other groups, 10.5% Irish, 7.6% English, 7.0% United
States or American (2000).
Economy: Unemployment rate: 10.7% (5/2010); Total civilian labor force:
124,564 (5/2010); Single-family building permits issued: 86 (2009);
Multi-family building permits issued: 20 (2009); Employment by occupation:
10.4% management, 18.3% professional, 14.8% services, 27.9% sales,
0.1% farming, 8.1% construction, 20.4% production (2000).
Income: Per capita income: $20,360 (2010); Median household income:
$39,804 (2010); Average household income: $48,890 (2010); Percent of
households with income of $100,000 or more: 7.8% (2010); Poverty rate:
12.5% (2000).
Taxes: Total city taxes per capita: $495 (2007); City property taxes per
capita: $288 (2007).
Education: Percent of population age 25 and over with: High school
diploma (including GED) or higher: 85.6% (2010); Bachelor's degree or
higher: 22.2% (2010); Master's degree or higher: 7.0% (2010).

School District(s)
East Allen County Schools (PK-12)
   2008-09 Enrollment: 10,209 . . . . (260) 446-0100
Fort Wayne Community Schools (PK-12)
   2008-09 Enrollment: 31,419 . . . . (260) 467-2025
IN Department of Correction (05-12)
   2008-09 Enrollment: 793 . . . . (317) 233-3111
Imagine Master Academy (KG-07)
   2008-09 Enrollment: 677 . . . . (260) 420-8395
Imagine Master on Broadway (KG-05)
   2008-09 Enrollment: 400 . . . . (260) 420-8395
M S D Southwest Allen County (PK-12)
   2008-09 Enrollment: 6,811 . . . . (260) 431-2010
Northwest Allen County Schools (KG-12)
   2008-09 Enrollment: 6,310 . . . . (260) 637-3155
Timothy L Johnson Academy (KG-05)
   2008-09 Enrollment: 205 . . . . (260) 441-8727

Four-year College(s)
Brown Mackie College-Fort Wayne (Private, For-profit)
   Fall 2008 Enrollment: 212 . . . . (260) 484-4400
   2009-10 Tuition: In-state $13,488; Out-of-state $13,488
Concordia Theological Seminary (Private, Not-for-profit, Lutheran Church -
Missouri Synod)
   Fall 2008 Enrollment: 382 . . . . (260) 452-2100
ITT Technical Institute-Fort Wayne (Private, For-profit)
   Fall 2008 Enrollment: 618 . . . . (260) 497-6200
   2009-10 Tuition: In-state $17,148; Out-of-state $17,148

Indiana Business College-Ft Wayne (Private, For-profit)
   Fall 2008 Enrollment: 499 . . . . (260) 471-7667
   2009-10 Tuition: In-state $11,535; Out-of-state $11,535
Indiana Institute of Technology (Private, Not-for-profit)
   Fall 2008 Enrollment: 3,653 . . . . (800) 937-2448
   2009-10 Tuition: In-state $21,400; Out-of-state $21,400
Indiana University-Purdue University-Fort Wayne (Public)
   Fall 2008 Enrollment: 12,338 . . . . (260) 481-6100
   2009-10 Tuition: In-state $6,233; Out-of-state $14,829
International Business College (Private, For-profit)
   Fall 2008 Enrollment: 629 . . . . (260) 459-4500
   2009-10 Tuition: In-state $12,760; Out-of-state $12,760
Trine University-Fort Wayne Campus (Private, Not-for-profit)
   Fall 2008 Enrollment: 200 . . . . (260) 483-4949
   2009-10 Tuition: In-state $7,152; Out-of-state $7,152
University of Saint Francis-Ft Wayne (Private, Not-for-profit, Roman
Catholic)
   Fall 2008 Enrollment: 2,112 . . . . (260) 399-7700
   2009-10 Tuition: In-state $21,760; Out-of-state $21,760
Two-year College(s)
Ivy Tech Community College-Northeast (Public)
   Fall 2008 Enrollment: 7,871 . . . . (260) 482-9171
   2009-10 Tuition: In-state $3,090; Out-of-state $6,306
Masters of Cosmetology College (Private, For-profit)
   Fall 2008 Enrollment: 97 . . . . (260) 747-6667
Vocational/Technical School(s)
Ravenscroft Beauty College (Private, For-profit)
   Fall 2008 Enrollment: 225 . . . . (260) 486-8868
   2009-10 Tuition: $9,800
Rudae's School of Beauty Culture (Private, For-profit)
   Fall 2008 Enrollment: 157 . . . . (260) 483-2466
   2009-10 Tuition: $9,900
Housing: Homeownership rate: 61.0% (2010); Median home value:
$84,571 (2010); Median contract rent: $415 per month (2000); Median year
structure built: 1962 (2000).
Hospitals: Dupont Hospital (131 beds); Lutheran Hospital of Indiana (435
beds); Parkview Behavioral Health (107 beds); Parkview Memorial Hospital
(656 beds); Parkview North Hospital (42 beds); St. Joseph Hospital (191
beds); VA Northern Indiana Health Care System - Fort Wayne Campus
(243 beds)
Safety: Violent crime rate: 32.5 per 10,000 population; Property crime rate:
410.6 per 10,000 population (2008).
Newspapers: El Mexicano Newspaper (Local news; Circulation 10,000);
Fort Wayne Business Journal (Local news); Frost Illustrated (Local news;
Circulation 9,000); Greater Fort Wayne Business Weekly (Local news); Ink
(Local news; Circulation 9,500); The Journal Gazette (Local news;
Circulation 117,777); The News-Sentinel (Local news; Circulation 31,213);
Today's Catholic (Regional news; Circulation 16,575)
Transportation: Commute to work: 94.0% car, 1.2% public transportation,
2.1% walk, 2.0% work from home (2000); Travel time to work: 32.7% less
than 15 minutes, 48.9% 15 to 30 minutes, 12.3% 30 to 45 minutes, 2.7%
45 to 60 minutes, 3.3% 60 minutes or more (2000)
Additional Information Contacts
City of Fort Wayne . . . . (260) 427-1221
   http://www.ci.ft-wayne.in.us
Greater Fort Wayne Chamber of Commerce . . . . (260) 424-1435
   http://www.fwchamber.org

GRABILL (town). Covers a land area of 0.617 square miles and a water
area of 0 square miles. Located at 41.21° N. Lat; 84.96° W. Long.
Elevation is 817 feet.
Population: 888 (1990); 1,113 (2000); 1,114 (2010); 1,124 (2015
projected); Race: 96.7% White, 0.2% Black, 0.2% Asian, 3.0% Other, 1.0%
Hispanic of any race (2010); Density: 1,806.7 persons per square mile
(2010); Average household size: 2.83 (2010); Median age: 30.3 (2010);
Males per 100 females: 93.7 (2010); Marriage status: 23.5% never married,
62.0% now married, 5.3% widowed, 9.3% divorced (2000); Foreign born:
2.3% (2000); Ancestry (includes multiple ancestries): 38.1% German,
10.6% English, 10.1% Irish, 7.3% Other groups, 5.2% French (except
Basque) (2000).
Economy: Employment by occupation: 8.9% management, 13.8%
professional, 12.6% services, 26.9% sales, 0.7% farming, 11.3%
construction, 25.8% production (2000).
Income: Per capita income: $19,934 (2010); Median household income:
$50,439 (2010); Average household income: $56,580 (2010); Percent of

households with income of $100,000 or more: 9.4% (2010); Poverty rate: 8.2% (2000).

Taxes: Total city taxes per capita: $264 (2007); City property taxes per capita: $170 (2007).

Education: Percent of population age 25 and over with: High school diploma (including GED) or higher: 83.2% (2010); Bachelor's degree or higher: 19.8% (2010); Master's degree or higher: 4.3% (2010).

Housing: Homeownership rate: 83.0% (2010); Median home value: $111,378 (2010); Median contract rent: $349 per month (2000); Median year structure built: 1981 (2000).

Newspapers: East Allen Courier (Community news; Circulation 7,100)

Transportation: Commute to work: 92.0% car, 0.7% public transportation, 3.1% walk, 3.8% work from home (2000); Travel time to work: 33.6% less than 15 minutes, 39.2% 15 to 30 minutes, 21.9% 30 to 45 minutes, 2.4% 45 to 60 minutes, 2.9% 60 minutes or more (2000)

Additional Information Contacts

Town of Grabill . . . . (260) 627-5227
    http://www.grabill.net

HARLAN (unincorporated postal area, zip code 46743). Covers a land area of 16.232 square miles and a water area of 0 square miles. Located at 41.21° N. Lat; 84.85° W. Long. Elevation is 784 feet.

Population: 1,183 (2000); Race: 99.4% White, 0.0% Black, 0.0% Asian, 0.6% Other, 0.0% Hispanic of any race (2000); Density: 72.9 persons per square mile (2000); Age: 25.2% under 18, 15.1% over 64 (2000); Marriage status: 24.1% never married, 65.4% now married, 4.0% widowed, 6.5% divorced (2000); Foreign born: 0.0% (2000); Ancestry (includes multiple ancestries): 26.1% German, 11.1% United States or American, 10.9% English, 6.3% Other groups, 5.2% French (except Basque) (2000).

Economy: Employment by occupation: 14.6% management, 10.6% professional, 9.0% services, 24.0% sales, 1.3% farming, 13.5% construction, 27.0% production (2000).

Income: Per capita income: $19,923 (2000); Median household income: $47,798 (2000); Poverty rate: 2.8% (2000).

Education: Percent of population age 25 and over with: High school diploma (including GED) or higher: 82.7% (2000); Bachelor's degree or higher: 14.1% (2000).

School District(s)

East Allen County Schools (PK-12)
    2008-09 Enrollment: 10,209 . . . . (260) 446-0100

Housing: Homeownership rate: 86.0% (2000); Median home value: $111,500 (2000); Median contract rent: $421 per month (2000); Median year structure built: 1960 (2000).

Transportation: Commute to work: 94.4% car, 0.0% public transportation, 1.1% walk, 4.5% work from home (2000); Travel time to work: 23.0% less than 15 minutes, 44.7% 15 to 30 minutes, 20.8% 30 to 45 minutes, 9.1% 45 to 60 minutes, 2.3% 60 minutes or more (2000)

HOAGLAND (unincorporated postal area, zip code 46745). Covers a land area of 17.536 square miles and a water area of 0 square miles. Located at 40.95° N. Lat; 85.00° W. Long. Elevation is 823 feet.

History: Laid out 1872.

Population: 1,606 (2000); Race: 98.5% White, 0.0% Black, 1.5% Asian, 0.0% Other, 0.8% Hispanic of any race (2000); Density: 91.6 persons per square mile (2000); Age: 29.6% under 18, 12.2% over 64 (2000); Marriage status: 23.4% never married, 67.3% now married, 4.7% widowed, 4.6% divorced (2000); Foreign born: 1.8% (2000); Ancestry (includes multiple ancestries): 57.1% German, 10.8% Irish, 10.2% United States or American, 6.4% French (except Basque), 4.4% Swiss (2000).

Economy: Employment by occupation: 14.2% management, 17.1% professional, 13.3% services, 24.2% sales, 0.0% farming, 8.3% construction, 23.0% production (2000).

Income: Per capita income: $19,818 (2000); Median household income: $56,034 (2000); Poverty rate: 3.5% (2000).

Education: Percent of population age 25 and over with: High school diploma (including GED) or higher: 87.6% (2000); Bachelor's degree or higher: 15.5% (2000).

School District(s)

East Allen County Schools (PK-12)
    2008-09 Enrollment: 10,209 . . . . (260) 446-0100

Housing: Homeownership rate: 90.6% (2000); Median home value: $102,600 (2000); Median contract rent: $375 per month (2000); Median year structure built: 1970 (2000).

Transportation: Commute to work: 91.9% car, 0.0% public transportation, 1.3% walk, 5.6% work from home (2000); Travel time to work: 13.6% less

than 15 minutes, 50.2% 15 to 30 minutes, 34.3% 30 to 45 minutes, 1.2% 45 to 60 minutes, 0.7% 60 minutes or more (2000)

HUNTERTOWN (town). Covers a land area of 1.626 square miles and a water area of 0 square miles. Located at 41.22° N. Lat; 85.16° W. Long. Elevation is 837 feet.

History: Settled 1830s.

Population: 1,502 (1990); 1,771 (2000); 2,150 (2010); 2,254 (2015 projected); Race: 96.4% White, 1.0% Black, 1.3% Asian, 1.3% Other, 1.3% Hispanic of any race (2010); Density: 1,322.6 persons per square mile (2010); Average household size: 2.69 (2010); Median age: 37.4 (2010); Males per 100 females: 96.9 (2010); Marriage status: 19.6% never married, 64.3% now married, 4.9% widowed, 11.2% divorced (2000); Foreign born: 1.0% (2000); Ancestry (includes multiple ancestries): 36.0% German, 9.0% United States or American, 9.0% Irish, 8.7% English, 7.1% Other groups (2000).

Economy: Employment by occupation: 13.9% management, 15.9% professional, 13.5% services, 23.7% sales, 0.0% farming, 11.0% construction, 22.0% production (2000).

Income: Per capita income: $28,606 (2010); Median household income: $70,166 (2010); Average household income: $77,043 (2010); Percent of households with income of $100,000 or more: 25.9% (2010); Poverty rate: 4.2% (2000).

Taxes: Total city taxes per capita: $176 (2007); City property taxes per capita: $37 (2007).

Education: Percent of population age 25 and over with: High school diploma (including GED) or higher: 94.0% (2010); Bachelor's degree or higher: 27.5% (2010); Master's degree or higher: 9.8% (2010).

School District(s)

Northwest Allen County Schools (KG-12)
    2008-09 Enrollment: 6,310 . . . . (260) 637-3155

Housing: Homeownership rate: 84.2% (2010); Median home value: $144,064 (2010); Median contract rent: $521 per month (2000); Median year structure built: 1975 (2000).

Transportation: Commute to work: 95.5% car, 0.0% public transportation, 0.8% walk, 2.8% work from home (2000); Travel time to work: 21.6% less than 15 minutes, 45.6% 15 to 30 minutes, 24.4% 30 to 45 minutes, 3.5% 45 to 60 minutes, 4.9% 60 minutes or more (2000)

LEO (unincorporated postal area, zip code 46765). Aka Leo-Cedarville. Covers a land area of 10.898 square miles and a water area of 0.028 square miles. Located at 41.22° N. Lat; 85.02° W. Long. Elevation is 791 feet.

History: Laid out 1849.

Population: 3,948 (2000); Race: 97.0% White, 0.1% Black, 0.0% Asian, 2.9% Other, 0.9% Hispanic of any race (2000); Density: 362.3 persons per square mile (2000); Age: 31.8% under 18, 10.7% over 64 (2000); Marriage status: 20.5% never married, 70.7% now married, 4.8% widowed, 4.0% divorced (2000); Foreign born: 0.8% (2000); Ancestry (includes multiple ancestries): 39.8% German, 10.9% English, 9.6% United States or American, 6.7% French (except Basque), 6.4% Irish (2000).

Economy: Employment by occupation: 15.4% management, 20.2% professional, 7.8% services, 28.0% sales, 0.0% farming, 7.3% construction, 21.3% production (2000).

Income: Per capita income: $22,688 (2000); Median household income: $67,011 (2000); Poverty rate: 2.3% (2000).

Education: Percent of population age 25 and over with: High school diploma (including GED) or higher: 90.4% (2000); Bachelor's degree or higher: 26.2% (2000).

School District(s)

East Allen County Schools (PK-12)
    2008-09 Enrollment: 10,209 . . . . (260) 446-0100

Housing: Homeownership rate: 92.5% (2000); Median home value: $131,100 (2000); Median contract rent: $590 per month (2000); Median year structure built: 1976 (2000).

Transportation: Commute to work: 96.5% car, 0.0% public transportation, 0.2% walk, 3.2% work from home (2000); Travel time to work: 17.1% less than 15 minutes, 60.9% 15 to 30 minutes, 17.6% 30 to 45 minutes, 2.3% 45 to 60 minutes, 2.1% 60 minutes or more (2000)

LEO-CEDARVILLE (town). Aka Leo. Covers a land area of 3.733 square miles and a water area of 0.136 square miles. Located at 41.21° N. Lat; 85.01° W. Long. Elevation is 797 feet.

History: Leo-Cedarville was formed by the incorporation of the villages of Leo and Cedarville into a town in the mid-1990s in a defensive move

against the rapidly expanding Fort Wayne, whose city limits currently sit five miles from the town.
Population: 2,039 (1990); 2,782 (2000); 3,371 (2010); 3,578 (2015 projected); Race: 97.3% White, 0.3% Black, 0.7% Asian, 1.7% Other, 0.8% Hispanic of any race (2010); Density: 902.9 persons per square mile (2010); Average household size: 2.97 (2010); Median age: 35.6 (2010); Males per 100 females: 98.3 (2010); Marriage status: 21.3% never married, 70.0% now married, 3.8% widowed, 4.9% divorced (2000); Foreign born: 1.5% (2000); Ancestry (includes multiple ancestries): 39.8% German, 11.0% English, 8.6% United States or American, 6.4% Irish, 4.6% Dutch (2000).
Economy: Employment by occupation: 16.4% management, 18.9% professional, 9.8% services, 28.1% sales, 0.0% farming, 6.8% construction, 20.0% production (2000).
Income: Per capita income: $29,789 (2010); Median household income: $80,400 (2010); Average household income: $88,662 (2010); Percent of households with income of $100,000 or more: 32.7% (2010); Poverty rate: 1.2% (2000).
Taxes: Total city taxes per capita: $240 (2007); City property taxes per capita: $96 (2007).
Education: Percent of population age 25 and over with: High school diploma (including GED) or higher: 94.1% (2010); Bachelor's degree or higher: 31.7% (2010); Master's degree or higher: 8.9% (2010).
Housing: Homeownership rate: 91.1% (2010); Median home value: $169,515 (2010); Median contract rent: $491 per month (2000); Median year structure built: 1974 (2000).
Transportation: Commute to work: 97.5% car, 0.0% public transportation, 0.4% walk, 1.8% work from home (2000); Travel time to work: 20.8% less than 15 minutes, 54.9% 15 to 30 minutes, 20.0% 30 to 45 minutes, 1.9% 45 to 60 minutes, 2.5% 60 minutes or more (2000)

MONROEVILLE (town).
Covers a land area of 0.751 square miles and a water area of 0 square miles. Located at 40.97° N. Lat; 84.86° W. Long. Elevation is 787 feet.
History: Settled 1841, incorporated 1865.
Population: 1,308 (1990); 1,236 (2000); 1,464 (2010); 1,566 (2015 projected); Race: 94.7% White, 0.2% Black, 0.1% Asian, 5.1% Other, 4.4% Hispanic of any race (2010); Density: 1,949.4 persons per square mile (2010); Average household size: 2.59 (2010); Median age: 35.5 (2010); Males per 100 females: 94.4 (2010); Marriage status: 23.3% never married, 58.1% now married, 8.5% widowed, 10.0% divorced (2000); Foreign born: 0.8% (2000); Ancestry (includes multiple ancestries): 38.9% German, 12.5% Irish, 9.2% United States or American, 8.5% Other groups, 7.8% French (except Basque) (2000).
Economy: Employment by occupation: 7.2% management, 11.5% professional, 13.6% services, 20.6% sales, 0.0% farming, 15.0% construction, 32.1% production (2000).
Income: Per capita income: $20,315 (2010); Median household income: $46,703 (2010); Average household income: $53,078 (2010); Percent of households with income of $100,000 or more: 8.9% (2010); Poverty rate: 10.0% (2000).
Taxes: Total city taxes per capita: $353 (2007); City property taxes per capita: $260 (2007).
Education: Percent of population age 25 and over with: High school diploma (including GED) or higher: 88.4% (2010); Bachelor's degree or higher: 13.6% (2010); Master's degree or higher: 3.9% (2010).
School District(s)
East Allen County Schools (PK-12)
    2008-09 Enrollment: 10,209 . . . . (260) 446-0100
Housing: Homeownership rate: 84.2% (2010); Median home value: $96,173 (2010); Median contract rent: $315 per month (2000); Median year structure built: 1959 (2000).
Newspapers: Monroeville News (Community news; Circulation 1,250)
Transportation: Commute to work: 91.9% car, 0.4% public transportation, 5.1% walk, 2.3% work from home (2000); Travel time to work: 21.7% less than 15 minutes, 37.3% 15 to 30 minutes, 28.7% 30 to 45 minutes, 4.5% 45 to 60 minutes, 7.9% 60 minutes or more (2000)

NEW HAVEN (city).
Covers a land area of 8.151 square miles and a water area of 0.004 square miles. Located at 41.06° N. Lat; 85.02° W. Long. Elevation is 758 feet.
History: New Haven was settled when the Wabash & Erie Canal was built. Its first residents, who came from New England, named it for the city in Connecticut.

Population: 12,280 (1990); 12,406 (2000); 12,825 (2010); 13,278 (2015 projected); Race: 96.5% White, 0.7% Black, 0.4% Asian, 2.5% Other, 2.7% Hispanic of any race (2010); Density: 1,573.4 persons per square mile (2010); Average household size: 2.47 (2010); Median age: 38.2 (2010); Males per 100 females: 98.0 (2010); Marriage status: 23.2% never married, 58.0% now married, 6.5% widowed, 12.2% divorced (2000); Foreign born: 1.7% (2000); Ancestry (includes multiple ancestries): 37.6% German, 11.7% Irish, 11.2% United States or American, 10.2% English, 9.1% Other groups (2000).
Economy: Employment by occupation: 10.5% management, 13.1% professional, 14.4% services, 27.1% sales, 0.0% farming, 10.3% construction, 24.6% production (2000).
Income: Per capita income: $22,106 (2010); Median household income: $46,310 (2010); Average household income: $54,468 (2010); Percent of households with income of $100,000 or more: 8.6% (2010); Poverty rate: 6.6% (2000).
Taxes: Total city taxes per capita: $385 (2007); City property taxes per capita: $245 (2007).
Education: Percent of population age 25 and over with: High school diploma (including GED) or higher: 87.0% (2010); Bachelor's degree or higher: 15.0% (2010); Master's degree or higher: 4.1% (2010).
School District(s)
East Allen County Schools (PK-12)
    2008-09 Enrollment: 10,209 . . . . (260) 446-0100
Housing: Homeownership rate: 79.7% (2010); Median home value: $86,376 (2010); Median contract rent: $418 per month (2000); Median year structure built: 1966 (2000).
Safety: Violent crime rate: 9.5 per 10,000 population; Property crime rate: 270.8 per 10,000 population (2008).
Newspapers: Allen County Times (Community news; Circulation 5,000)
Transportation: Commute to work: 95.0% car, 0.1% public transportation, 1.2% walk, 3.0% work from home (2000); Travel time to work: 36.9% less than 15 minutes, 46.0% 15 to 30 minutes, 12.2% 30 to 45 minutes, 1.9% 45 to 60 minutes, 3.0% 60 minutes or more (2000)
Additional Information Contacts
City of New Haven . . . . (260) 748-7000
    http://www.newhavenin.org
New Haven Chamber of Commerce . . . . (260) 749-4484
    http://www.newhavenchamber.org

WOODBURN (city).
Aka Shirley City. Covers a land area of 0.918 square miles and a water area of 0 square miles. Located at 41.12° N. Lat; 84.85° W. Long. Elevation is 751 feet.
History: Laid out 1865. Until 1936, called Shirley City.
Population: 1,504 (1990); 1,579 (2000); 1,834 (2010); 1,947 (2015 projected); Race: 97.5% White, 0.3% Black, 0.0% Asian, 2.2% Other, 3.3% Hispanic of any race (2010); Density: 1,998.4 persons per square mile (2010); Average household size: 2.65 (2010); Median age: 32.1 (2010); Males per 100 females: 98.9 (2010); Marriage status: 21.9% never married, 59.3% now married, 5.6% widowed, 13.2% divorced (2000); Foreign born: 0.6% (2000); Ancestry (includes multiple ancestries): 42.7% German, 10.9% Irish, 6.8% United States or American, 6.6% French (except Basque), 5.8% English (2000).
Economy: Employment by occupation: 7.8% management, 12.4% professional, 14.8% services, 27.8% sales, 0.6% farming, 14.7% construction, 21.9% production (2000).
Income: Per capita income: $21,339 (2010); Median household income: $48,477 (2010); Average household income: $56,662 (2010); Percent of households with income of $100,000 or more: 8.8% (2010); Poverty rate: 5.8% (2000).
Taxes: Total city taxes per capita: $176 (2007); City property taxes per capita: $73 (2007).
Education: Percent of population age 25 and over with: High school diploma (including GED) or higher: 86.3% (2010); Bachelor's degree or higher: 12.5% (2010); Master's degree or higher: 2.4% (2010).
School District(s)
East Allen County Schools (PK-12)
    2008-09 Enrollment: 10,209 . . . . (260) 446-0100
Housing: Homeownership rate: 77.0% (2010); Median home value: $84,274 (2010); Median contract rent: $379 per month (2000); Median year structure built: 1977 (2000).
Transportation: Commute to work: 95.1% car, 0.0% public transportation, 3.3% walk, 0.9% work from home (2000); Travel time to work: 21.6% less than 15 minutes, 39.3% 15 to 30 minutes, 28.8% 30 to 45 minutes, 5.8% 45 to 60 minutes, 4.5% 60 minutes or more (2000)

YODER (unincorporated postal area, zip code 46798). Covers a land area of 20.927 square miles and a water area of 0.013 square miles. Located at 40.94° N. Lat; 85.23° W. Long. Elevation is 810 feet.

Population: 1,872 (2000); Race: 97.9% White, 0.0% Black, 0.4% Asian, 1.7% Other, 2.3% Hispanic of any race (2000); Density: 89.5 persons per square mile (2000); Age: 27.8% under 18, 8.1% over 64 (2000); Marriage status: 20.9% never married, 64.8% now married, 5.7% widowed, 8.7% divorced (2000); Foreign born: 1.8% (2000); Ancestry (includes multiple ancestries): 42.6% German, 13.1% Irish, 10.8% United States or American, 10.5% English, 10.0% Other groups (2000).

Economy: Employment by occupation: 9.7% management, 13.3% professional, 10.1% services, 27.3% sales, 0.0% farming, 11.2% construction, 28.3% production (2000).

Income: Per capita income: $20,389 (2000); Median household income: $49,500 (2000); Poverty rate: 3.5% (2000).

Education: Percent of population age 25 and over with: High school diploma (including GED) or higher: 85.4% (2000); Bachelor's degree or higher: 10.5% (2000).

Housing: Homeownership rate: 94.0% (2000); Median home value: $94,100 (2000); Median contract rent: $519 per month (2000); Median year structure built: 1974 (2000).

Transportation: Commute to work: 97.4% car, 0.0% public transportation, 0.2% walk, 2.4% work from home (2000); Travel time to work: 28.8% less than 15 minutes, 49.3% 15 to 30 minutes, 14.1% 30 to 45 minutes, 4.0% 45 to 60 minutes, 3.7% 60 minutes or more (2000)

Bartholomew County

Located in south central Indiana; drained by the East Fork of the White River. Covers a land area of 406.84 square miles, a water area of 2.52 square miles, and is located in the Eastern Time Zone. The county was founded in 1821. County seat is Columbus.

Bartholomew County is part of the Columbus, IN Metropolitan Statistical Area. The entire metro area includes: Bartholomew County, IN

Weather Station: Columbus										Elevation: 620 feet	
	Jan	Feb	Mar	Apr	May	Jun	Jul	Aug	Sep	Oct	Nov	Dec
High	36	41	52	64	74	82	86	85	79	67	53	42
Low	19	22	31	41	51	61	65	62	54	42	34	25
Precip	2.6	2.5	3.7	4.5	4.5	3.4	4.0	3.8	3.0	2.8	3.7	3.1
Snow	5.1	3.5	1.9	tr	tr	0.0	0.0	0.0	0.0	tr	0.5	2.1

High and Low temperatures in degrees Fahrenheit; Precipitation and Snow in inches

Population: 63,657 (1990); 71,435 (2000); 76,312 (2010); 78,427 (2015 projected); Race: 91.4% White, 2.1% Black, 3.1% Asian, 3.3% Other, 4.5% Hispanic of any race (2010); Density: 187.6 persons per square mile (2010); Average household size: 2.51 (2010); Median age: 38.7 (2010); Males per 100 females: 97.5 (2010).

Religion: Five largest groups: 8.6% Christian Churches and Churches of Christ, 8.4% Lutheran Church—Missouri Synod, 7.7% Catholic Church, 7.7% The United Methodist Church, 5.7% American Baptist Churches in the USA (2000).

Economy: Unemployment rate: 9.3% (5/2010); Total civilian labor force: 37,127 (5/2010); Leading industries: 29.1% manufacturing; 12.2% health care and social assistance; 11.7% retail trade (2008); Farms: 668 totaling 166,356 acres (2007); Companies that employ 500 or more persons: 12 (2008); Companies that employ 100 to 499 persons: 61 (2008); Companies that employ less than 100 persons: 1,853 (2008); Black-owned businesses: n/a (2002); Hispanic-owned businesses: n/a (2002); Asian-owned businesses: n/a (2002); Women-owned businesses: 1,585 (2002); Retail sales per capita: $14,105 (2010). Single-family building permits issued: 125 (2009); Multi-family building permits issued: 0 (2009).

Income: Per capita income: $25,938 (2010); Median household income: $52,604 (2010); Average household income: $65,143 (2010); Percent of households with income of $100,000 or more: 17.0% (2010); Poverty rate: 10.6% (2008); Bankruptcy rate: 5.45% (2009).

Taxes: Total county taxes per capita: $321 (2007); County property taxes per capita: $131 (2007).

Education: Percent of population age 25 and over with: High school diploma (including GED) or higher: 88.9% (2010); Bachelor's degree or higher: 27.7% (2010); Master's degree or higher: 11.9% (2010).

Housing: Homeownership rate: 75.5% (2010); Median home value: $130,815 (2010); Median contract rent: $565 per month (2006-2008 3-year est.); Median year structure built: 1971 (2006-2008 3-year est.)

Health: Birth rate: 142.6 per 10,000 population (2009); Death rate: 89.9 per 10,000 population (2009); Age-adjusted cancer mortality rate: 206.6 deaths per 100,000 population (2006); Number of physicians: 21.0 per 10,000 population (2007); Hospital beds: 31.8 per 10,000 population (2006); Hospital admissions: 1,286.6 per 10,000 population (2006).

Elections: 2008 Presidential election results: 43.7% Obama, 55.0% McCain, 0.1% Nader

Additional Information Contacts

Bartholomew County Government. . . . . (812) 376-2510
http://www.bartholomewco.com
City of Columbus . . . . (812) 376-2510
http://www.columbus.in.gov
Columbus Area Chamber of Commerce . . . . (812) 379-4457
http://www.columbusareachamber.com

Bartholomew County Communities

CLIFFORD (town). Covers a land area of 0.100 square miles and a water area of 0 square miles. Located at 39.28° N. Lat; 85.87° W. Long. Elevation is 659 feet.

Population: 308 (1990); 291 (2000); 307 (2010); 318 (2015 projected); Race: 96.1% White, 0.0% Black, 0.0% Asian, 3.9% Other, 1.0% Hispanic of any race (2010); Density: 3,058.8 persons per square mile (2010); Average household size: 2.58 (2010); Median age: 36.4 (2010); Males per 100 females: 99.4 (2010); Marriage status: 22.7% never married, 57.1% now married, 6.9% widowed, 13.3% divorced (2000); Foreign born: 0.0% (2000); Ancestry (includes multiple ancestries): 22.5% United States or American, 17.0% German, 8.5% Irish, 8.1% English, 7.7% Other groups (2000).

Economy: Employment by occupation: 5.6% management, 6.5% professional, 8.9% services, 29.8% sales, 0.0% farming, 23.4% construction, 25.8% production (2000).

Income: Per capita income: $29,854 (2010); Median household income: $68,561 (2010); Average household income: $80,378 (2010); Percent of households with income of $100,000 or more: 23.5% (2010); Poverty rate: 15.1% (2000).

Taxes: Total city taxes per capita: $272 (2007); City property taxes per capita: $272 (2007).

Education: Percent of population age 25 and over with: High school diploma (including GED) or higher: 92.3% (2010); Bachelor's degree or higher: 13.9% (2010); Master's degree or higher: 7.2% (2010).

Housing: Homeownership rate: 82.4% (2010); Median home value: $131,081 (2010); Median contract rent: $413 per month (2000); Median year structure built: 1959 (2000).

Transportation: Commute to work: 96.8% car, 0.0% public transportation, 3.2% walk, 0.0% work from home (2000); Travel time to work: 23.4% less than 15 minutes, 57.3% 15 to 30 minutes, 12.9% 30 to 45 minutes, 3.2% 45 to 60 minutes, 3.2% 60 minutes or more (2000)

COLUMBUS (city). County seat. Covers a land area of 25.948 square miles and a water area of 0.425 square miles. Located at 39.21° N. Lat; 85.91° W. Long. Elevation is 630 feet.

History: Columbus was settled by General John Tipton, John Lindsay, and Luke Bonesteel in 1820, and was called Tiptonia. In 1821 General Tipton offered land for a county seat if the new town were named for him. The county commissioners accepted the land, but named the town Columbus.

Population: 34,728 (1990); 39,059 (2000); 40,773 (2010); 41,395 (2015 projected); Race: 87.5% White, 3.0% Black, 5.0% Asian, 4.5% Other, 5.6% Hispanic of any race (2010); Density: 1,571.3 persons per square mile (2010); Average household size: 2.40 (2010); Median age: 39.0 (2010); Males per 100 females: 94.7 (2010); Marriage status: 20.5% never married, 59.8% now married, 6.7% widowed, 13.0% divorced (2000); Foreign born: 5.5% (2000); Ancestry (includes multiple ancestries): 21.9% German, 15.8% United States or American, 12.9% Other groups, 11.3% English, 10.3% Irish (2000).

Economy: Unemployment rate: 10.4% (5/2010); Total civilian labor force: 19,308 (5/2010); Employment by occupation: 12.9% management, 22.2% professional, 12.2% services, 23.3% sales, 0.1% farming, 6.4% construction, 22.9% production (2000).

Income: Per capita income: $26,716 (2010); Median household income: $49,147 (2010); Average household income: $64,043 (2010); Percent of households with income of $100,000 or more: 16.8% (2010); Poverty rate: 8.1% (2000).

Taxes: Total city taxes per capita: $384 (2007); City property taxes per capita: $376 (2007).

Education: Percent of population age 25 and over with: High school diploma (including GED) or higher: 89.1% (2010); Bachelor's degree or higher: 33.1% (2010); Master's degree or higher: 14.7% (2010).

School District(s)

Bartholomew Con School Corp (PK-12)

    2008-09 Enrollment: 11,146 . . . . (812) 376-4220

Flat Rock-Hawcreek School Corp (PK-12)

    2008-09 Enrollment: 1,028 . . . . (812) 546-2000

Two-year College(s)

Indiana Business College-Columbus (Private, For-profit)

    Fall 2008 Enrollment: 240 . . . . (812) 379-9000

    2009-10 Tuition: In-state $11,535; Out-of-state $11,535

Ivy Tech Community College-Columbus (Public)

    Fall 2008 Enrollment: 3,240. . . . . (812) 372-9925

    2009-10 Tuition: In-state $3,090; Out-of-state $6,306

Housing: Homeownership rate: 67.4% (2010); Median home value: $131,358 (2010); Median contract rent: $488 per month (2000); Median year structure built: 1968 (2000).

Hospitals: Behavioral Healthcare of Columbus Hospital (70 beds); Columbus Regional Hospital (225 beds)

Safety: Violent crime rate: 11.5 per 10,000 population; Property crime rate: 495.9 per 10,000 population (2008).

Newspapers: The Columbus Republic (Local news; Circulation 22,500)

Transportation: Commute to work: 94.5% car, 0.5% public transportation, 1.6% walk, 2.1% work from home (2000); Travel time to work: 59.8% less than 15 minutes, 26.8% 15 to 30 minutes, 6.1% 30 to 45 minutes, 3.4% 45 to 60 minutes, 3.9% 60 minutes or more (2000)

Additional Information Contacts

City of Columbus . . . . (812) 376-2510

    http://www.columbus.in.gov

Columbus Area Chamber of Commerce . . . . (812) 379-4457

    http://www.columbusareachamber.com

ELIZABETHTOWN (town).

Covers a land area of 0.252 square miles and a water area of 0 square miles. Located at 39.13° N. Lat; 85.81° W. Long. Elevation is 636 feet.

Population: 497 (1990); 391 (2000); 416 (2010); 427 (2015 projected); Race: 95.4% White, 1.0% Black, 0.0% Asian, 3.6% Other, 9.4% Hispanic of any race (2010); Density: 1,652.2 persons per square mile (2010); Average household size: 2.67 (2010); Median age: 39.9 (2010); Males per 100 females: 103.9 (2010); Marriage status: 17.7% never married, 61.0% now married, 6.6% widowed, 14.8% divorced (2000); Foreign born: 1.3% (2000); Ancestry (includes multiple ancestries): 18.8% United States or American, 14.5% Other groups, 11.2% German, 6.6% Irish, 5.1% English (2000).

Economy: Single-family building permits issued: 1 (2009); Multi-family building permits issued: 0 (2009); Employment by occupation: 6.8% management, 5.1% professional, 14.2% services, 22.7% sales, 0.0% farming, 18.8% construction, 32.4% production (2000).

Income: Per capita income: $22,961 (2010); Median household income: $50,000 (2010); Average household income: $59,343 (2010); Percent of households with income of $100,000 or more: 12.8% (2010); Poverty rate: 12.7% (2000).

Taxes: Total city taxes per capita: $96 (2007); City property taxes per capita: $71 (2007).

Education: Percent of population age 25 and over with: High school diploma (including GED) or higher: 84.7% (2010); Bachelor's degree or higher: 12.5% (2010); Master's degree or higher: 7.3% (2010).

Housing: Homeownership rate: 87.8% (2010); Median home value: $115,541 (2010); Median contract rent: $455 per month (2000); Median year structure built: 1970 (2000).

Transportation: Commute to work: 100.0% car, 0.0% public transportation, 0.0% walk, 0.0% work from home (2000); Travel time to work: 16.5% less than 15 minutes, 54.5% 15 to 30 minutes, 16.5% 30 to 45 minutes, 1.1% 45 to 60 minutes, 11.4% 60 minutes or more (2000)

HARTSVILLE (town).

Covers a land area of 0.332 square miles and a water area of 0 square miles. Located at 39.26° N. Lat; 85.69° W. Long. Elevation is 761 feet.

History: Hartsville was the first location of Hartsville College, founded in 1850 by the United Brethren denomination but moved to Huntington in 1898.

Population: 391 (1990); 376 (2000); 396 (2010); 406 (2015 projected); Race: 99.0% White, 0.0% Black, 0.5% Asian, 0.5% Other, 1.3% Hispanic of any race (2010); Density: 1,191.5 persons per square mile (2010);

Average household size: 2.76 (2010); Median age: 39.5 (2010); Males per 100 females: 104.1 (2010); Marriage status: 23.9% never married, 62.0% now married, 5.6% widowed, 8.5% divorced (2000); Foreign born: 0.0% (2000); Ancestry (includes multiple ancestries): 24.3% United States or American, 19.1% Other groups, 14.1% German, 9.7% English, 8.8% Irish (2000).

Economy: Employment by occupation: 8.9% management, 11.5% professional, 14.7% services, 23.6% sales, 0.0% farming, 10.5% construction, 30.9% production (2000).

Income: Per capita income: $26,986 (2010); Median household income: $68,750 (2010); Average household income: $74,406 (2010); Percent of households with income of $100,000 or more: 23.1% (2010); Poverty rate: 7.7% (2000).

Taxes: Total city taxes per capita: $34 (2007); City property taxes per capita: $29 (2007).

Education: Percent of population age 25 and over with: High school diploma (including GED) or higher: 90.8% (2010); Bachelor's degree or higher: 24.8% (2010); Master's degree or higher: 11.5% (2010).

Housing: Homeownership rate: 88.1% (2010); Median home value: $132,895 (2010); Median contract rent: $268 per month (2000); Median year structure built: 1948 (2000).

Transportation: Commute to work: 97.3% car, 0.0% public transportation, 0.5% walk, 2.2% work from home (2000); Travel time to work: 6.2% less than 15 minutes, 67.4% 15 to 30 minutes, 17.4% 30 to 45 minutes, 1.1% 45 to 60 minutes, 7.9% 60 minutes or more (2000)

HOPE (town).

Covers a land area of 0.954 square miles and a water area of 0 square miles. Located at 39.30° N. Lat; 85.76° W. Long. Elevation is 715 feet.

Population: 2,256 (1990); 2,140 (2000); 2,335 (2010); 2,444 (2015 projected); Race: 98.5% White, 0.5% Black, 0.0% Asian, 1.0% Other, 1.8% Hispanic of any race (2010); Density: 2,446.6 persons per square mile (2010); Average household size: 2.74 (2010); Median age: 36.1 (2010); Males per 100 females: 96.7 (2010); Marriage status: 19.0% never married, 61.2% now married, 9.4% widowed, 10.5% divorced (2000); Foreign born: 0.7% (2000); Ancestry (includes multiple ancestries): 26.7% United States or American, 16.8% German, 10.5% Other groups, 9.0% Irish, 5.5% English (2000).

Economy: Single-family building permits issued: 1 (2009); Multi-family building permits issued: 0 (2009); Employment by occupation: 6.9% management, 12.5% professional, 17.3% services, 21.5% sales, 0.2% farming, 11.3% construction, 30.3% production (2000).

Income: Per capita income: $19,819 (2010); Median household income: $49,034 (2010); Average household income: $54,374 (2010); Percent of households with income of $100,000 or more: 7.9% (2010); Poverty rate: 11.0% (2000).

Taxes: Total city taxes per capita: $88 (2007); City property taxes per capita: $85 (2007).

Education: Percent of population age 25 and over with: High school diploma (including GED) or higher: 85.9% (2010); Bachelor's degree or higher: 15.2% (2010); Master's degree or higher: 5.8% (2010).

School District(s)

Flat Rock-Hawcreek School Corp (PK-12)

    2008-09 Enrollment: 1,028 . . . . (812) 546-2000

Housing: Homeownership rate: 78.4% (2010); Median home value: $106,304 (2010); Median contract rent: $450 per month (2000); Median year structure built: 1961 (2000).

Newspapers: Hope Star-Journal (Community news; Circulation 2,000)

Transportation: Commute to work: 94.5% car, 0.8% public transportation, 1.2% walk, 2.2% work from home (2000); Travel time to work: 18.5% less than 15 minutes, 51.4% 15 to 30 minutes, 17.7% 30 to 45 minutes, 5.1% 45 to 60 minutes, 7.3% 60 minutes or more (2000)

JONESVILLE (town).

Covers a land area of 0.129 square miles and a water area of 0 square miles. Located at 39.06° N. Lat; 85.89° W. Long. Elevation is 594 feet.

History: Laid out 1851.

Population: 246 (1990); 220 (2000); 236 (2010); 243 (2015 projected); Race: 97.0% White, 2.1% Black, 0.0% Asian, 0.8% Other, 0.4% Hispanic of any race (2010); Density: 1,825.6 persons per square mile (2010); Average household size: 2.65 (2010); Median age: 38.9 (2010); Males per 100 females: 103.4 (2010); Marriage status: 14.6% never married, 62.2% now married, 8.6% widowed, 14.6% divorced (2000); Foreign born: 0.0% (2000); Ancestry (includes multiple ancestries): 19.4% English, 16.8% Irish,

16.8% Other groups, 16.4% German, 15.5% United States or American (2000).
Economy: Employment by occupation: 5.6% management, 11.2% professional, 18.7% services, 33.6% sales, 0.0% farming, 0.0% construction, 30.8% production (2000).
Income: Per capita income: $28,366 (2010); Median household income: $74,219 (2010); Average household income: $74,972 (2010); Percent of households with income of $100,000 or more: 27.0% (2010); Poverty rate: 4.7% (2000).
Taxes: Total city taxes per capita: $220 (2007); City property taxes per capita: $151 (2007).
Education: Percent of population age 25 and over with: High school diploma (including GED) or higher: 85.1% (2010); Bachelor's degree or higher: 20.8% (2010); Master's degree or higher: 7.1% (2010).
Housing: Homeownership rate: 86.5% (2010); Median home value: $133,000 (2010); Median contract rent: $400 per month (2000); Median year structure built: 1956 (2000).
Transportation: Commute to work: 100.0% car, 0.0% public transportation, 0.0% walk, 0.0% work from home (2000); Travel time to work: 19.2% less than 15 minutes, 64.4% 15 to 30 minutes, 16.3% 30 to 45 minutes, 0.0% 45 to 60 minutes, 0.0% 60 minutes or more (2000)

TAYLORSVILLE (CDP). Covers a land area of 1.045 square miles and a water area of 0 square miles. Located at 39.29° N. Lat; 85.94° W. Long. Elevation is 653 feet.
History: Laid out 1849.
Population: 1,076 (1990); 936 (2000); 822 (2010); 772 (2015 projected); Race: 95.1% White, 2.3% Black, 0.0% Asian, 2.6% Other, 2.6% Hispanic of any race (2010); Density: 786.4 persons per square mile (2010); Average household size: 2.59 (2010); Median age: 38.7 (2010); Males per 100 females: 101.0 (2010); Marriage status: 16.7% never married, 66.5% now married, 4.5% widowed, 12.3% divorced (2000); Foreign born: 0.0% (2000); Ancestry (includes multiple ancestries): 26.8% German, 15.7% Irish, 11.8% United States or American, 8.2% English, 6.7% Other groups (2000).
Economy: Employment by occupation: 4.2% management, 13.7% professional, 12.0% services, 18.8% sales, 0.0% farming, 10.9% construction, 40.4% production (2000).
Income: Per capita income: $17,773 (2010); Median household income: $41,762 (2010); Average household income: $46,356 (2010); Percent of households with income of $100,000 or more: 6.6% (2010); Poverty rate: 9.2% (2000).
Education: Percent of population age 25 and over with: High school diploma (including GED) or higher: 74.8% (2010); Bachelor's degree or higher: 8.0% (2010); Master's degree or higher: 3.9% (2010).
School District(s)
Bartholomew Con School Corp (PK-12)
    2008-09 Enrollment: 11,146 . . . . (812) 376-4220
Housing: Homeownership rate: 81.7% (2010); Median home value: $111,198 (2010); Median contract rent: $194 per month (2000); Median year structure built: 1964 (2000).
Transportation: Commute to work: 90.0% car, 2.2% public transportation, 0.0% walk, 5.1% work from home (2000); Travel time to work: 32.6% less than 15 minutes, 57.6% 15 to 30 minutes, 2.1% 30 to 45 minutes, 2.6% 45 to 60 minutes, 5.2% 60 minutes or more (2000)

Benton County

Located in western Indiana; bounded on the west by Illinois. Covers a land area of 406.31 square miles, a water area of 0.09 square miles, and is located in the Eastern Time Zone. The county was founded in 1840. County seat is Fowler.

Benton County is part of the Lafayette, IN Metropolitan Statistical Area. The entire metro area includes: Benton County, IN; Carroll County, IN; Tippecanoe County, IN

Population: 9,441 (1990); 9,421 (2000); 8,706 (2010); 8,360 (2015 projected); Race: 94.7% White, 1.1% Black, 0.1% Asian, 4.1% Other, 4.1% Hispanic of any race (2010); Density: 21.4 persons per square mile (2010); Average household size: 2.56 (2010); Median age: 40.0 (2010); Males per 100 females: 98.0 (2010).
Religion: Five largest groups: 34.6% Catholic Church, 11.2% The United Methodist Church, 10.6% Christian Churches and Churches of Christ, 2.9% Evangelical Lutheran Church in America, 2.8% Southern Baptist Convention (2000).

Economy: Unemployment rate: 9.5% (5/2010); Total civilian labor force: 4,174 (5/2010); Leading industries: 25.6% manufacturing; 14.2% retail trade; 12.0% wholesale trade (2008); Farms: 399 totaling 270,810 acres (2007); Companies that employ 500 or more persons: 0 (2008); Companies that employ 100 to 499 persons: 0 (2008); Companies that employ less than 100 persons: 213 (2008); Black-owned businesses: n/a (2002); Hispanic-owned businesses: n/a (2002); Asian-owned businesses: n/a (2002); Women-owned businesses: 168 (2002); Retail sales per capita: $11,515 (2010). Single-family building permits issued: 12 (2009); Multi-family building permits issued: 0 (2009).
Income: Per capita income: $20,966 (2010); Median household income: $47,500 (2010); Average household income: $54,234 (2010); Percent of households with income of $100,000 or more: 10.1% (2010); Poverty rate: 10.4% (2008); Bankruptcy rate: 4.86% (2009).
Taxes: Total county taxes per capita: $327 (2007); County property taxes per capita: $189 (2007).
Education: Percent of population age 25 and over with: High school diploma (including GED) or higher: 89.8% (2010); Bachelor's degree or higher: 13.5% (2010); Master's degree or higher: 4.2% (2010).
Housing: Homeownership rate: 74.6% (2010); Median home value: $84,328 (2010); Median contract rent: $n/a per month (2006-2008 3-year est.); Median year structure built: n/a (2006-2008 3-year est.)
Health: Birth rate: 138.2 per 10,000 population (2009); Death rate: 96.4 per 10,000 population (2009); Age-adjusted cancer mortality rate: 219.3 deaths per 100,000 population (2006); Number of physicians: 3.4 per 10,000 population (2007); Hospital beds: 0.0 per 10,000 population (2006); Hospital admissions: 0.0 per 10,000 population (2006).
Elections: 2008 Presidential election results: 41.0% Obama, 57.2% McCain, 0.0% Nader
Additional Information Contacts
Benton County Government . . . . (765) 884-0930
    http://www.in.gov/mylocal/benton_county.htm
Town of Fowler . . . . (765) 884-0570
    http://www.townoffowler.com

Benton County Communities

AMBIA (town). Covers a land area of 0.146 square miles and a water area of 0 square miles. Located at 40.49° N. Lat; 87.51° W. Long. Elevation is 732 feet.
Population: 248 (1990); 197 (2000); 164 (2010); 153 (2015 projected); Race: 89.0% White, 1.8% Black, 0.0% Asian, 9.1% Other, 15.2% Hispanic of any race (2010); Density: 1,124.6 persons per square mile (2010); Average household size: 2.65 (2010); Median age: 42.5 (2010); Males per 100 females: 100.0 (2010); Marriage status: 14.8% never married, 75.6% now married, 6.7% widowed, 3.0% divorced (2000); Foreign born: 4.1% (2000); Ancestry (includes multiple ancestries): 43.3% Other groups, 14.9% German, 12.4% United States or American, 7.2% English, 5.2% Irish (2000).
Economy: Employment by occupation: 10.7% management, 9.3% professional, 5.3% services, 21.3% sales, 0.0% farming, 14.7% construction, 38.7% production (2000).
Income: Per capita income: $20,254 (2010); Median household income: $45,500 (2010); Average household income: $52,742 (2010); Percent of households with income of $100,000 or more: 6.5% (2010); Poverty rate: 0.5% (2000).
Taxes: Total city taxes per capita: $81 (2007); City property taxes per capita: $81 (2007).
Education: Percent of population age 25 and over with: High school diploma (including GED) or higher: 92.9% (2010); Bachelor's degree or higher: 8.9% (2010); Master's degree or higher: 0.9% (2010).
Housing: Homeownership rate: 83.9% (2010); Median home value: $76,667 (2010); Median contract rent: $375 per month (2000); Median year structure built: before 1940 (2000).
Transportation: Commute to work: 88.0% car, 0.0% public transportation, 8.0% walk, 4.0% work from home (2000); Travel time to work: 15.3% less than 15 minutes, 36.1% 15 to 30 minutes, 16.7% 30 to 45 minutes, 12.5% 45 to 60 minutes, 19.4% 60 minutes or more (2000)

BOSWELL (town). Covers a land area of 0.474 square miles and a water area of 0 square miles. Located at 40.51° N. Lat; 87.38° W. Long. Elevation is 755 feet.
Population: 767 (1990); 827 (2000); 768 (2010); 734 (2015 projected); Race: 88.0% White, 1.3% Black, 0.1% Asian, 10.5% Other, 13.9% Hispanic of any race (2010); Density: 1,618.9 persons per square mile

(2010); Average household size: 2.53 (2010); Median age: 38.3 (2010); Males per 100 females: 91.5 (2010); Marriage status: 23.2% never married, 50.7% now married, 12.1% widowed, 14.0% divorced (2000); Foreign born: 1.5% (2000); Ancestry (includes multiple ancestries): 17.8% United States or American, 17.1% Other groups, 16.2% German, 14.9% Irish, 10.4% English (2000).

Economy: Employment by occupation: 6.0% management, 8.7% professional, 22.3% services, 21.5% sales, 0.3% farming, 8.7% construction, 32.6% production (2000).

Income: Per capita income: $18,119 (2010); Median household income: $41,066 (2010); Average household income: $46,180 (2010); Percent of households with income of $100,000 or more: 6.6% (2010); Poverty rate: 8.3% (2000).

Taxes: Total city taxes per capita: $168 (2007); City property taxes per capita: $168 (2007).

Education: Percent of population age 25 and over with: High school diploma (including GED) or higher: 80.8% (2010); Bachelor's degree or higher: 11.3% (2010); Master's degree or higher: 5.5% (2010).

School District(s)

Benton Community School Corp (KG-12)

   2008-09 Enrollment: 1,836 . . . . (765) 884-0850

Housing: Homeownership rate: 78.9% (2010); Median home value: $72,321 (2010); Median contract rent: $353 per month (2000); Median year structure built: 1942 (2000).

Newspapers: Boswell Enterprise (Community news; Circulation 400)

Transportation: Commute to work: 88.2% car, 0.0% public transportation, 3.4% walk, 6.2% work from home (2000); Travel time to work: 37.0% less than 15 minutes, 28.1% 15 to 30 minutes, 17.0% 30 to 45 minutes, 12.8% 45 to 60 minutes, 5.1% 60 minutes or more (2000)

EARL PARK (town).

Covers a land area of 0.943 square miles and a water area of 0 square miles. Located at 40.68° N. Lat; 87.41° W. Long. Elevation is 807 feet.

History: Laid out 1872.

Population: 443 (1990); 485 (2000); 438 (2010); 416 (2015 projected); Race: 96.6% White, 0.5% Black, 0.2% Asian, 2.7% Other, 4.1% Hispanic of any race (2010); Density: 464.7 persons per square mile (2010); Average household size: 2.62 (2010); Median age: 40.3 (2010); Males per 100 females: 91.3 (2010); Marriage status: 24.3% never married, 47.0% now married, 18.0% widowed, 10.7% divorced (2000); Foreign born: 0.0% (2000); Ancestry (includes multiple ancestries): 27.4% German, 13.7% Irish, 9.0% French (except Basque), 8.4% Other groups, 8.2% English (2000).

Economy: Single-family building permits issued: 0 (2009); Multi-family building permits issued: 0 (2009); Employment by occupation: 12.4% management, 11.4% professional, 6.4% services, 24.8% sales, 1.5% farming, 14.4% construction, 29.2% production (2000).

Income: Per capita income: $17,405 (2010); Median household income: $37,045 (2010); Average household income: $46,667 (2010); Percent of households with income of $100,000 or more: 4.5% (2010); Poverty rate: 10.4% (2000).

Taxes: Total city taxes per capita: $116 (2007); City property taxes per capita: $63 (2007).

Education: Percent of population age 25 and over with: High school diploma (including GED) or higher: 87.5% (2010); Bachelor's degree or higher: 7.8% (2010); Master's degree or higher: 2.7% (2010).

Housing: Homeownership rate: 71.2% (2010); Median home value: $85,172 (2010); Median contract rent: $364 per month (2000); Median year structure built: 1941 (2000).

Transportation: Commute to work: 92.0% car, 0.0% public transportation, 2.0% walk, 3.5% work from home (2000); Travel time to work: 44.6% less than 15 minutes, 33.7% 15 to 30 minutes, 8.3% 30 to 45 minutes, 12.4% 45 to 60 minutes, 1.0% 60 minutes or more (2000)

FOWLER (town).

County seat. Covers a land area of 1.395 square miles and a water area of 0.006 square miles. Located at 40.61° N. Lat; 87.31° W. Long. Elevation is 823 feet.

History: Laid out 1872.

Population: 2,348 (1990); 2,415 (2000); 2,199 (2010); 2,100 (2015 projected); Race: 95.7% White, 1.7% Black, 0.1% Asian, 2.5% Other, 1.6% Hispanic of any race (2010); Density: 1,575.8 persons per square mile (2010); Average household size: 2.42 (2010); Median age: 40.4 (2010); Males per 100 females: 97.6 (2010); Marriage status: 18.4% never married, 60.1% now married, 10.1% widowed, 11.4% divorced (2000); Foreign born: 0.0% (2000); Ancestry (includes multiple ancestries): 29.0% German,

13.3% United States or American, 12.5% Irish, 12.0% Other groups, 8.4% French (except Basque) (2000).

Economy: Single-family building permits issued: 6 (2009); Multi-family building permits issued: 0 (2009); Employment by occupation: 13.8% management, 12.7% professional, 13.3% services, 27.1% sales, 0.0% farming, 10.1% construction, 23.1% production (2000).

Income: Per capita income: $22,536 (2010); Median household income: $49,276 (2010); Average household income: $56,650 (2010); Percent of households with income of $100,000 or more: 12.3% (2010); Poverty rate: 5.8% (2000).

Taxes: Total city taxes per capita: $219 (2007); City property taxes per capita: $152 (2007).

Education: Percent of population age 25 and over with: High school diploma (including GED) or higher: 91.0% (2010); Bachelor's degree or higher: 15.5% (2010); Master's degree or higher: 6.6% (2010).

Housing: Homeownership rate: 72.5% (2010); Median home value: $79,940 (2010); Median contract rent: $330 per month (2000); Median year structure built: 1950 (2000).

Newspapers: Benton Review (Community news; Circulation 3,400)

Transportation: Commute to work: 95.3% car, 0.4% public transportation, 2.0% walk, 2.4% work from home (2000); Travel time to work: 45.8% less than 15 minutes, 18.7% 15 to 30 minutes, 20.4% 30 to 45 minutes, 10.1% 45 to 60 minutes, 4.9% 60 minutes or more (2000)

Additional Information Contacts

Town of Fowler . . . . (765) 884-0570
  http://www.townoffowler.com

OTTERBEIN (town).

Covers a land area of 0.572 square miles and a water area of 0 square miles. Located at 40.48° N. Lat; 87.09° W. Long. Elevation is 705 feet.

History: Laid out 1872.

Population: 1,291 (1990); 1,312 (2000); 1,392 (2010); 1,418 (2015 projected); Race: 97.3% White, 0.3% Black, 0.1% Asian, 2.2% Other, 1.1% Hispanic of any race (2010); Density: 2,431.6 persons per square mile (2010); Average household size: 2.63 (2010); Median age: 35.6 (2010); Males per 100 females: 98.3 (2010); Marriage status: 21.2% never married, 58.4% now married, 8.4% widowed, 12.1% divorced (2000); Foreign born: 0.3% (2000); Ancestry (includes multiple ancestries): 22.9% German, 12.6% United States or American, 11.7% Irish, 9.1% Other groups, 7.0% English (2000).

Economy: Employment by occupation: 9.8% management, 9.3% professional, 19.2% services, 21.9% sales, 0.6% farming, 10.7% construction, 28.5% production (2000).

Income: Per capita income: $23,674 (2010); Median household income: $53,876 (2010); Average household income: $62,358 (2010); Percent of households with income of $100,000 or more: 14.9% (2010); Poverty rate: 6.9% (2000).

Taxes: Total city taxes per capita: $117 (2007); City property taxes per capita: $108 (2007).

Education: Percent of population age 25 and over with: High school diploma (including GED) or higher: 91.6% (2010); Bachelor's degree or higher: 20.5% (2010); Master's degree or higher: 5.6% (2010).

School District(s)

Benton Community School Corp (KG-12)

   2008-09 Enrollment: 1,836 . . . . (765) 884-0850

Housing: Homeownership rate: 71.5% (2010); Median home value: $107,609 (2010); Median contract rent: $433 per month (2000); Median year structure built: 1958 (2000).

Transportation: Commute to work: 93.2% car, 0.5% public transportation, 0.8% walk, 4.4% work from home (2000); Travel time to work: 27.5% less than 15 minutes, 48.1% 15 to 30 minutes, 18.8% 30 to 45 minutes, 3.7% 45 to 60 minutes, 1.9% 60 minutes or more (2000)

OXFORD (town).

Covers a land area of 0.513 square miles and a water area of 0 square miles. Located at 40.52° N. Lat; 87.25° W. Long. Elevation is 738 feet.

History: In 1896 in Oxford a racehorse named Dan Patch was born, and brought a measure of fame to the town for the records he set. For a time, Oxford was the seat of Benton County.

Population: 1,273 (1990); 1,271 (2000); 1,148 (2010); 1,090 (2015 projected); Race: 95.6% White, 0.9% Black, 0.0% Asian, 3.6% Other, 1.6% Hispanic of any race (2010); Density: 2,236.4 persons per square mile (2010); Average household size: 2.51 (2010); Median age: 42.2 (2010); Males per 100 females: 95.9 (2010); Marriage status: 18.1% never married, 56.0% now married, 14.1% widowed, 11.8% divorced (2000); Foreign born:

0.4% (2000); Ancestry (includes multiple ancestries): 20.9% German, 16.7% United States or American, 10.9% Irish, 6.3% Other groups, 6.1% English (2000).
Economy: Employment by occupation: 6.3% management, 13.5% professional, 16.4% services, 22.9% sales, 1.5% farming, 13.2% construction, 26.2% production (2000).
Income: Per capita income: $22,125 (2010); Median household income: $49,815 (2010); Average household income: $55,111 (2010); Percent of households with income of $100,000 or more: 8.9% (2010); Poverty rate: 5.1% (2000).
Taxes: Total city taxes per capita: $153 (2007); City property taxes per capita: $148 (2007).
Education: Percent of population age 25 and over with: High school diploma (including GED) or higher: 89.0% (2010); Bachelor's degree or higher: 14.4% (2010); Master's degree or higher: 1.6% (2010).

School District(s)

Benton Community School Corp (KG-12)
    2008-09 Enrollment: 1,836 . . . . (765) 884-0850
Housing: Homeownership rate: 76.7% (2010); Median home value: $86,071 (2010); Median contract rent: $319 per month (2000); Median year structure built: 1952 (2000).
Transportation: Commute to work: 94.5% car, 0.5% public transportation, 3.1% walk, 1.5% work from home (2000); Travel time to work: 31.0% less than 15 minutes, 28.7% 15 to 30 minutes, 26.2% 30 to 45 minutes, 10.2% 45 to 60 minutes, 3.9% 60 minutes or more (2000)

Blackford County

Located in eastern Indiana; drained by the Salamonie River. Covers a land area of 165.10 square miles, a water area of 0.31 square miles, and is located in the Eastern Time Zone. The county was founded in 1838. County seat is Hartford City.

Weather Station: Hartford City 4 ESE   Elevation: 941 feet

	Jan	Feb	Mar	Apr	May	Jun	Jul	Aug	Sep	Oct	Nov	Dec
High	31	36	47	60	71	80	83	81	75	63	49	37
Low	15	19	29	39	50	59	63	60	53	42	33	22
Precip	1.9	2.0	2.8	3.4	3.7	4.5	4.1	4.1	2.8	2.4	3.3	2.6
Snow	7.6	6.0	3.5	1.0	tr	0.0	0.0	0.0	0.0	0.4	1.6	5.9

High and Low temperatures in degrees Fahrenheit; Precipitation and Snow in inches

Population: 14,067 (1990); 14,048 (2000); 12,937 (2010); 12,335 (2015 projected); Race: 97.5% White, 0.5% Black, 0.2% Asian, 1.8% Other, 0.9% Hispanic of any race (2010); Density: 78.4 persons per square mile (2010); Average household size: 2.36 (2010); Median age: 41.6 (2010); Males per 100 females: 98.8 (2010).
Religion: Five largest groups: 8.5% The United Methodist Church, 5.9% Catholic Church, 3.4% Church of the Nazarene, 3.1% Christian Church (Disciples of Christ), 2.6% Evangelical Lutheran Church in America (2000).
Economy: Unemployment rate: 12.1% (5/2010); Total civilian labor force: 6,728 (5/2010); Leading industries: 44.8% manufacturing; 11.7% health care and social assistance; 11.3% retail trade (2008); Farms: 250 totaling 84,626 acres (2007); Companies that employ 500 or more persons: 0 (2008); Companies that employ 100 to 499 persons: 7 (2008); Companies that employ less than 100 persons: 267 (2008); Black-owned businesses: n/a (2002); Hispanic-owned businesses: n/a (2002); Asian-owned businesses: n/a (2002); Women-owned businesses: 307 (2002); Retail sales per capita: $10,308 (2010). Single-family building permits issued: 3 (2009); Multi-family building permits issued: 0 (2009).
Income: Per capita income: $19,215 (2010); Median household income: $38,783 (2010); Average household income: $45,480 (2010); Percent of households with income of $100,000 or more: 5.3% (2010); Poverty rate: 13.9% (2008); Bankruptcy rate: 7.64% (2009).
Taxes: Total county taxes per capita: $306 (2007); County property taxes per capita: $210 (2007).
Education: Percent of population age 25 and over with: High school diploma (including GED) or higher: 85.4% (2010); Bachelor's degree or higher: 10.9% (2010); Master's degree or higher: 3.7% (2010).
Housing: Homeownership rate: 77.6% (2010); Median home value: $78,347 (2010); Median contract rent: $n/a per month (2006-2008 3-year est.); Median year structure built: n/a (2006-2008 3-year est.)
Health: Birth rate: 101.9 per 10,000 population (2009); Death rate: 123.4 per 10,000 population (2009); Age-adjusted cancer mortality rate: 162.5 deaths per 100,000 population (2006); Number of physicians: 6.8 per 10,000 population (2007); Hospital beds: 11.3 per 10,000 population (2006); Hospital admissions: 476.8 per 10,000 population (2006).

Elections: 2008 Presidential election results: 49.2% Obama, 49.4% McCain, 0.1% Nader
Additional Information Contacts
Blackford County Government. . . . . (765) 348-1620
    http://www.blackfordcounty.com
City of Hartford City . . . . (765) 348-1116
    http://www.hartfordcity.net

Blackford County Communities

HARTFORD CITY (city). County seat. Covers a land area of 3.721 square miles and a water area of 0.006 square miles. Located at 40.45° N. Lat; 85.36° W. Long. Elevation is 919 feet.
History: Settled 1832, laid out 1839.
Population: 6,987 (1990); 6,928 (2000); 6,264 (2010); 5,920 (2015 projected); Race: 97.5% White, 0.3% Black, 0.3% Asian, 1.9% Other, 0.9% Hispanic of any race (2010); Density: 1,683.3 persons per square mile (2010); Average household size: 2.30 (2010); Median age: 41.0 (2010); Males per 100 females: 92.9 (2010); Marriage status: 18.9% never married, 59.4% now married, 9.4% widowed, 12.3% divorced (2000); Foreign born: 0.2% (2000); Ancestry (includes multiple ancestries): 15.1% German, 14.0% United States or American, 10.2% Other groups, 8.8% Irish, 7.6% English (2000).
Economy: Employment by occupation: 5.8% management, 13.1% professional, 14.6% services, 21.3% sales, 0.2% farming, 9.1% construction, 36.0% production (2000).
Income: Per capita income: $18,094 (2010); Median household income: $35,437 (2010); Average household income: $41,408 (2010); Percent of households with income of $100,000 or more: 3.0% (2010); Poverty rate: 10.4% (2000).
Taxes: Total city taxes per capita: $237 (2007); City property taxes per capita: $199 (2007).
Education: Percent of population age 25 and over with: High school diploma (including GED) or higher: 84.4% (2010); Bachelor's degree or higher: 12.0% (2010); Master's degree or higher: 4.6% (2010).

School District(s)

Blackford County Schools (PK-12)
    2008-09 Enrollment: 2,133 . . . . (765) 348-7550
Housing: Homeownership rate: 74.0% (2010); Median home value: $68,887 (2010); Median contract rent: $312 per month (2000); Median year structure built: 1954 (2000).
Hospitals: Blackford Community Hospital (65 beds)
Safety: Violent crime rate: 15.9 per 10,000 population; Property crime rate: 337.5 per 10,000 population (2008).
Newspapers: Hartford City News-Times (Local news; Circulation 2,200); Market Basket (Community news; Circulation 13,500)
Transportation: Commute to work: 93.7% car, 0.0% public transportation, 1.8% walk, 3.4% work from home (2000); Travel time to work: 51.4% less than 15 minutes, 18.1% 15 to 30 minutes, 20.2% 30 to 45 minutes, 5.3% 45 to 60 minutes, 4.9% 60 minutes or more (2000)
Additional Information Contacts
City of Hartford City . . . . (765) 348-1116
    http://www.hartfordcity.net

MONTPELIER (city). Covers a land area of 1.097 square miles and a water area of 0 square miles. Located at 40.55° N. Lat; 85.28° W. Long. Elevation is 869 feet.
History: Settled 1836, laid out 1837, incorporated 1937.
Population: 1,917 (1990); 1,929 (2000); 1,769 (2010); 1,688 (2015 projected); Race: 97.2% White, 0.3% Black, 0.0% Asian, 2.5% Other, 1.6% Hispanic of any race (2010); Density: 1,612.1 persons per square mile (2010); Average household size: 2.35 (2010); Median age: 38.0 (2010); Males per 100 females: 98.5 (2010); Marriage status: 16.3% never married, 56.8% now married, 9.2% widowed, 17.7% divorced (2000); Foreign born: 0.0% (2000); Ancestry (includes multiple ancestries): 19.7% German, 11.2% Irish, 10.2% United States or American, 6.9% English, 5.9% Other groups (2000).
Economy: Employment by occupation: 6.8% management, 8.3% professional, 12.1% services, 16.4% sales, 1.2% farming, 11.6% construction, 43.7% production (2000).
Income: Per capita income: $18,337 (2010); Median household income: $38,385 (2010); Average household income: $43,101 (2010); Percent of households with income of $100,000 or more: 4.9% (2010); Poverty rate: 9.5% (2000).

Taxes: Total city taxes per capita: $176 (2007); City property taxes per capita: $156 (2007).

Education: Percent of population age 25 and over with: High school diploma (including GED) or higher: 82.1% (2010); Bachelor's degree or higher: 7.4% (2010); Master's degree or higher: 3.0% (2010).

School District(s)

Blackford County Schools (PK-12)

   2008-09 Enrollment: 2,133 . . . . (765) 348-7550

Housing: Homeownership rate: 70.7% (2010); Median home value: $67,600 (2010); Median contract rent: $279 per month (2000); Median year structure built: 1952 (2000).

Newspapers: Montpelier Herald (Community news; Circulation 407)

Transportation: Commute to work: 93.6% car, 0.0% public transportation, 3.4% walk, 2.7% work from home (2000); Travel time to work: 31.6% less than 15 minutes, 32.9% 15 to 30 minutes, 19.8% 30 to 45 minutes, 7.4% 45 to 60 minutes, 8.3% 60 minutes or more (2000)

SHAMROCK LAKES (town). Covers a land area of 0.268 square miles and a water area of 0.051 square miles. Located at 40.41° N. Lat; 85.42° W. Long. Elevation is 883 feet.

Population: 209 (1990); 168 (2000); 142 (2010); 130 (2015 projected); Race: 99.3% White, 0.0% Black, 0.0% Asian, 0.7% Other, 1.4% Hispanic of any race (2010); Density: 529.4 persons per square mile (2010); Average household size: 2.45 (2010); Median age: 48.6 (2010); Males per 100 females: 108.8 (2010); Marriage status: 18.8% never married, 68.4% now married, 3.0% widowed, 9.8% divorced (2000); Foreign born: 0.0% (2000); Ancestry (includes multiple ancestries): 30.8% English, 17.3% German, 16.7% Irish, 12.8% United States or American, 5.1% Swiss (2000).

Economy: Employment by occupation: 8.9% management, 40.0% professional, 2.2% services, 25.6% sales, 2.2% farming, 4.4% construction, 16.7% production (2000).

Income: Per capita income: $24,324 (2010); Median household income: $56,250 (2010); Average household income: $60,819 (2010); Percent of households with income of $100,000 or more: 15.5% (2010); Poverty rate: 2.6% (2000).

Taxes: Total city taxes per capita: $151 (2007); City property taxes per capita: $132 (2007).

Education: Percent of population age 25 and over with: High school diploma (including GED) or higher: 90.9% (2010); Bachelor's degree or higher: 16.4% (2010); Master's degree or higher: 5.5% (2010).

Housing: Homeownership rate: 91.4% (2010); Median home value: $107,813 (2010); Median contract rent: $450 per month (2000); Median year structure built: 1967 (2000).

Transportation: Commute to work: 100.0% car, 0.0% public transportation, 0.0% walk, 0.0% work from home (2000); Travel time to work: 20.5% less than 15 minutes, 39.8% 15 to 30 minutes, 19.3% 30 to 45 minutes, 3.4% 45 to 60 minutes, 17.0% 60 minutes or more (2000)

Boone County

Located in central Indiana; drained by Sugar and Raccoon Creeks and the Eel River. Covers a land area of 422.85 square miles, a water area of 0.42 square miles, and is located in the Eastern Time Zone. The county was founded in 1830. County seat is Lebanon.

Boone County is part of the Indianapolis-Carmel, IN Metropolitan Statistical Area. The entire metro area includes: Boone County, IN; Brown County, IN; Hamilton County, IN; Hancock County, IN; Hendricks County, IN; Johnson County, IN; Marion County, IN; Morgan County, IN; Putnam County, IN; Shelby County, IN

Weather Station: Whitestown										Elevation: 935 feet	
	Jan	Feb	Mar	Apr	May	Jun	Jul	Aug	Sep	Oct	Nov	Dec
High	33	39	50	63	74	83	86	84	78	66	51	39
Low	16	20	29	40	50	59	63	60	53	42	33	23
Precip	2.4	2.3	3.4	3.9	4.5	4.1	4.6	3.5	3.0	3.0	3.7	3.0
Snow	9.1	6.0	3.0	0.3	0.0	0.0	0.0	0.0	0.0	0.3	1.0	5.7

High and Low temperatures in degrees Fahrenheit; Precipitation and Snow in inches

Population: 38,147 (1990); 46,107 (2000); 56,605 (2010); 61,313 (2015 projected); Race: 95.0% White, 1.5% Black, 1.5% Asian, 2.0% Other, 2.0% Hispanic of any race (2010); Density: 133.9 persons per square mile (2010); Average household size: 2.63 (2010); Median age: 37.0 (2010); Males per 100 females: 96.4 (2010).

Religion: Five largest groups: 10.0% Catholic Church, 6.4% The United Methodist Church, 5.9% Presbyterian Church (U.S.A.), 5.0% Christian Church (Disciples of Christ), 4.8% Christian Churches and Churches of Christ (2000).

Economy: Unemployment rate: 7.8% (5/2010); Total civilian labor force: 27,411 (5/2010); Leading industries: 14.5% health care and social assistance; 11.2% manufacturing; 10.3% retail trade (2008); Farms: 582 totaling 222,706 acres (2007); Companies that employ 500 or more persons: 2 (2008); Companies that employ 100 to 499 persons: 26 (2008); Companies that employ less than 100 persons: 1,373 (2008); Black-owned businesses: n/a (2002); Hispanic-owned businesses: n/a (2002); Asian-owned businesses: n/a (2002); Women-owned businesses: 1,165 (2002); Retail sales per capita: $9,275 (2010). Single-family building permits issued: 260 (2009); Multi-family building permits issued: 8 (2009).

Income: Per capita income: $32,494 (2010); Median household income: $63,627 (2010); Average household income: $86,214 (2010); Percent of households with income of $100,000 or more: 26.0% (2010); Poverty rate: 6.4% (2008); Bankruptcy rate: 6.25% (2009).

Taxes: Total county taxes per capita: $268 (2007); County property taxes per capita: $114 (2007).

Education: Percent of population age 25 and over with: High school diploma (including GED) or higher: 92.0% (2010); Bachelor's degree or higher: 37.0% (2010); Master's degree or higher: 15.0% (2010).

Housing: Homeownership rate: 80.3% (2010); Median home value: $152,412 (2010); Median contract rent: $613 per month (2006-2008 3-year est.); Median year structure built: 1976 (2006-2008 3-year est.)

Health: Birth rate: 138.0 per 10,000 population (2009); Death rate: 79.6 per 10,000 population (2009); Age-adjusted cancer mortality rate: 192.1 deaths per 100,000 population (2006); Air Quality Index: 83.2% good, 16.8% moderate, 0.0% unhealthy for sensitive individuals, 0.0% unhealthy (percent of days in 2008); Number of physicians: 42.0 per 10,000 population (2007); Hospital beds: 9.1 per 10,000 population (2006); Hospital admissions: 394.9 per 10,000 population (2006).

Elections: 2008 Presidential election results: 36.5% Obama, 62.3% McCain, 0.0% Nader

Additional Information Contacts

Boone County Government . . . . (765) 482-2940

   http://www.bccn.boone.in.us

City of Lebanon . . . . (765) 482-1218

   http://www.cityoflebanon.org

Lebanon Chamber of Commerce. . . . . (765) 482-1320

   http://www.boonechamber.org

Town of Zionsville . . . . (317) 873-5410

   http://www.zionsville-in.gov

Zionsville Chamber of Commerce . . . . (317) 873-3836

   http://www.zionsvillechamber.org

Boone County Communities

ADVANCE (town). Covers a land area of 0.625 square miles and a water area of 0 square miles. Located at 39.99° N. Lat; 86.61° W. Long. Elevation is 928 feet.

Population: 587 (1990); 562 (2000); 666 (2010); 720 (2015 projected); Race: 97.4% White, 0.6% Black, 0.2% Asian, 1.8% Other, 1.5% Hispanic of any race (2010); Density: 1,065.0 persons per square mile (2010); Average household size: 2.72 (2010); Median age: 36.7 (2010); Males per 100 females: 97.6 (2010); Marriage status: 15.5% never married, 65.1% now married, 5.7% widowed, 13.8% divorced (2000); Foreign born: 0.0% (2000); Ancestry (includes multiple ancestries): 15.2% German, 13.3% Irish, 13.3% Other groups, 10.1% United States or American, 6.7% English (2000).

Economy: Employment by occupation: 8.1% management, 13.9% professional, 11.5% services, 28.8% sales, 1.4% farming, 16.3% construction, 20.0% production (2000).

Income: Per capita income: $30,660 (2010); Median household income: $67,188 (2010); Average household income: $85,143 (2010); Percent of households with income of $100,000 or more: 28.2% (2010); Poverty rate: 6.9% (2000).

Taxes: Total city taxes per capita: $218 (2007); City property taxes per capita: $106 (2007).

Education: Percent of population age 25 and over with: High school diploma (including GED) or higher: 87.9% (2010); Bachelor's degree or higher: 18.4% (2010); Master's degree or higher: 6.3% (2010).

Housing: Homeownership rate: 84.1% (2010); Median home value: $127,778 (2010); Median contract rent: $442 per month (2000); Median year structure built: before 1940 (2000).

Transportation: Commute to work: 95.3% car, 0.0% public transportation, 0.7% walk, 3.4% work from home (2000); Travel time to work: 14.3% less than 15 minutes, 39.9% 15 to 30 minutes, 24.1% 30 to 45 minutes, 16.4% 45 to 60 minutes, 5.2% 60 minutes or more (2000)

JAMESTOWN (town). Covers a land area of 0.516 square miles and a water area of 0 square miles. Located at 39.92° N. Lat; 86.62° W. Long. Elevation is 951 feet.

History: Jamestown developed as a stop on the stagecoach route, and later as a station on the New York Central Railroad.

Population: 792 (1990); 886 (2000); 1,058 (2010); 1,141 (2015 projected); Race: 98.7% White, 0.4% Black, 0.0% Asian, 0.9% Other, 1.3% Hispanic of any race (2010); Density: 2,051.0 persons per square mile (2010); Average household size: 2.42 (2010); Median age: 38.3 (2010); Males per 100 females: 95.9 (2010); Marriage status: 18.6% never married, 65.6% now married, 5.9% widowed, 9.9% divorced (2000); Foreign born: 0.0% (2000); Ancestry (includes multiple ancestries): 27.3% German, 18.3% English, 14.6% United States or American, 13.2% Irish, 9.9% Other groups (2000).

Economy: Single-family building permits issued: 0 (2009); Multi-family building permits issued: 0 (2009); Employment by occupation: 10.2% management, 15.0% professional, 17.8% services, 25.0% sales, 0.2% farming, 12.2% construction, 19.8% production (2000).

Income: Per capita income: $29,518 (2010); Median household income: $59,821 (2010); Average household income: $72,157 (2010); Percent of households with income of $100,000 or more: 20.8% (2010); Poverty rate: 7.8% (2000).

Taxes: Total city taxes per capita: $88 (2007); City property taxes per capita: $85 (2007).

Education: Percent of population age 25 and over with: High school diploma (including GED) or higher: 88.0% (2010); Bachelor's degree or higher: 18.5% (2010); Master's degree or higher: 9.0% (2010).

School District(s)
Western Boone Co Com Sch Dist (PK-12)
    2008-09 Enrollment: 1,923 . . . . (765) 482-6333

Housing: Homeownership rate: 77.6% (2010); Median home value: $122,774 (2010); Median contract rent: $422 per month (2000); Median year structure built: 1953 (2000).

Transportation: Commute to work: 93.9% car, 0.0% public transportation, 4.5% walk, 1.6% work from home (2000); Travel time to work: 17.2% less than 15 minutes, 32.5% 15 to 30 minutes, 28.4% 30 to 45 minutes, 16.4% 45 to 60 minutes, 5.6% 60 minutes or more (2000)

LEBANON (city). County seat. Covers a land area of 7.283 square miles and a water area of 0 square miles. Located at 40.05° N. Lat; 86.47° W. Long. Elevation is 938 feet.

History: Named for the Biblical mountain of cedars, although the trees in the area are primarily hickory trees. Lebanon received its biblical name because the forests surrounding it reminded one of its founders of the Cedars of Lebanon. Lebanon was the home of Samuel M. Ralston (1857-1925), governor of Indiana and U.S. senator.

Population: 12,526 (1990); 14,222 (2000); 15,320 (2010); 15,948 (2015 projected); Race: 95.4% White, 1.2% Black, 1.1% Asian, 2.3% Other, 2.8% Hispanic of any race (2010); Density: 2,103.7 persons per square mile (2010); Average household size: 2.35 (2010); Median age: 35.3 (2010); Males per 100 females: 94.5 (2010); Marriage status: 20.6% never married, 57.9% now married, 9.1% widowed, 12.4% divorced (2000); Foreign born: 1.2% (2000); Ancestry (includes multiple ancestries): 22.9% German, 14.6% United States or American, 12.0% Irish, 11.0% English, 10.4% Other groups (2000).

Economy: Single-family building permits issued: 3 (2009); Multi-family building permits issued: 8 (2009); Employment by occupation: 8.9% management, 13.3% professional, 19.2% services, 26.8% sales, 0.0% farming, 10.4% construction, 21.4% production (2000).

Income: Per capita income: $24,997 (2010); Median household income: $48,665 (2010); Average household income: $59,123 (2010); Percent of households with income of $100,000 or more: 11.7% (2010); Poverty rate: 7.1% (2000).

Taxes: Total city taxes per capita: $344 (2007); City property taxes per capita: $157 (2007).

Education: Percent of population age 25 and over with: High school diploma (including GED) or higher: 88.6% (2010); Bachelor's degree or higher: 22.4% (2010); Master's degree or higher: 7.8% (2010).

School District(s)
Lebanon Community School Corp (KG-12)
    2008-09 Enrollment: 3,517 . . . . (765) 482-0380

Housing: Homeownership rate: 69.0% (2010); Median home value: $101,596 (2010); Median contract rent: $429 per month (2000); Median year structure built: 1967 (2000).

Hospitals: Witham Memorial Hospital (80 beds)

Newspapers: The Lebanon Reporter (Community news; Circulation 6,000)

Transportation: Commute to work: 95.0% car, 0.1% public transportation, 1.4% walk, 2.7% work from home (2000); Travel time to work: 42.9% less than 15 minutes, 23.1% 15 to 30 minutes, 25.1% 30 to 45 minutes, 5.9% 45 to 60 minutes, 3.0% 60 minutes or more (2000)

Additional Information Contacts
City of Lebanon . . . . (765) 482-1218
    http://www.cityoflebanon.org
Lebanon Chamber of Commerce . . . . (765) 482-1320
    http://www.boonechamber.org

THORNTOWN (town). Covers a land area of 0.571 square miles and a water area of 0 square miles. Located at 40.12° N. Lat; 86.60° W. Long. Elevation is 856 feet.

History: Thorntown was called Keewaskee, meaning "place of thorns," when a trading post was established here by Jesuit missionaries. Thorntown was platted in 1829 by Cornelius Westfall.

Population: 1,552 (1990); 1,562 (2000); 1,775 (2010); 1,888 (2015 projected); Race: 96.2% White, 0.3% Black, 0.2% Asian, 3.4% Other, 2.9% Hispanic of any race (2010); Density: 3,109.2 persons per square mile (2010); Average household size: 2.60 (2010); Median age: 36.8 (2010); Males per 100 females: 98.3 (2010); Marriage status: 17.3% never married, 61.2% now married, 7.3% widowed, 14.1% divorced (2000); Foreign born: 0.5% (2000); Ancestry (includes multiple ancestries): 17.8% United States or American, 17.0% German, 9.2% Irish, 8.5% English, 7.7% Other groups (2000).

Economy: Single-family building permits issued: 4 (2009); Multi-family building permits issued: 0 (2009); Employment by occupation: 6.7% management, 7.6% professional, 19.9% services, 25.1% sales, 1.0% farming, 15.4% construction, 24.3% production (2000).

Income: Per capita income: $25,838 (2010); Median household income: $55,333 (2010); Average household income: $67,122 (2010); Percent of households with income of $100,000 or more: 16.4% (2010); Poverty rate: 6.6% (2000).

Taxes: Total city taxes per capita: $163 (2007); City property taxes per capita: $77 (2007).

Education: Percent of population age 25 and over with: High school diploma (including GED) or higher: 87.8% (2010); Bachelor's degree or higher: 9.5% (2010); Master's degree or higher: 3.6% (2010).

School District(s)
Western Boone Co Com Sch Dist (PK-12)
    2008-09 Enrollment: 1,923 . . . . (765) 482-6333

Housing: Homeownership rate: 81.4% (2010); Median home value: $117,019 (2010); Median contract rent: $405 per month (2000); Median year structure built: 1948 (2000).

Transportation: Commute to work: 90.4% car, 0.4% public transportation, 4.6% walk, 2.7% work from home (2000); Travel time to work: 27.2% less than 15 minutes, 39.9% 15 to 30 minutes, 17.5% 30 to 45 minutes, 11.9% 45 to 60 minutes, 3.5% 60 minutes or more (2000)

ULEN (town). Covers a land area of 0.063 square miles and a water area of 0 square miles. Located at 40.06° N. Lat; 86.46° W. Long. Elevation is 942 feet.

Population: 50 (1990); 123 (2000); 168 (2010); 177 (2015 projected); Race: 97.6% White, 0.6% Black, 0.6% Asian, 1.2% Other, 0.6% Hispanic of any race (2010); Density: 2,659.2 persons per square mile (2010); Average household size: 2.08 (2010); Median age: 42.9 (2010); Males per 100 females: 76.8 (2010); Marriage status: 16.7% never married, 82.1% now married, 0.0% widowed, 1.2% divorced (2000); Foreign born: 0.0% (2000); Ancestry (includes multiple ancestries): 46.7% German, 33.3% English, 17.1% Dutch, 13.3% Irish, 9.5% Italian (2000).

Economy: Employment by occupation: 22.0% management, 36.6% professional, 0.0% services, 24.4% sales, 0.0% farming, 9.8% construction, 7.3% production (2000).

Income: Per capita income: $34,401 (2010); Median household income: $47,500 (2010); Average household income: $75,461 (2010); Percent of households with income of $100,000 or more: 23.7% (2010); Poverty rate: 0.0% (2000).
Taxes: Total city taxes per capita: $208 (2007); City property taxes per capita: $200 (2007).
Education: Percent of population age 25 and over with: High school diploma (including GED) or higher: 90.4% (2010); Bachelor's degree or higher: 33.6% (2010); Master's degree or higher: 15.2% (2010).
Housing: Homeownership rate: 72.4% (2010); Median home value: $146,053 (2010); Median contract rent: $n/a per month (2000); Median year structure built: before 1940 (2000).
Transportation: Commute to work: 100.0% car, 0.0% public transportation, 0.0% walk, 0.0% work from home (2000); Travel time to work: 48.7% less than 15 minutes, 25.6% 15 to 30 minutes, 17.9% 30 to 45 minutes, 7.7% 45 to 60 minutes, 0.0% 60 minutes or more (2000)

WHITESTOWN (town). Covers a land area of 0.255 square miles and a water area of 0 square miles. Located at 39.99° N. Lat; 86.34° W. Long. Elevation is 938 feet.
History: Laid out 1851.
Population: 476 (1990); 471 (2000); 667 (2010); 745 (2015 projected); Race: 97.0% White, 0.4% Black, 1.3% Asian, 1.2% Other, 1.2% Hispanic of any race (2010); Density: 2,611.2 persons per square mile (2010); Average household size: 2.61 (2010); Median age: 38.6 (2010); Males per 100 females: 104.0 (2010); Marriage status: 21.0% never married, 56.0% now married, 5.8% widowed, 17.2% divorced (2000); Foreign born: 0.9% (2000); Ancestry (includes multiple ancestries): 24.7% United States or American, 17.4% German, 13.6% English, 10.9% Irish, 7.7% Other groups (2000).
Economy: Employment by occupation: 8.7% management, 11.4% professional, 17.7% services, 27.2% sales, 0.0% farming, 15.0% construction, 20.1% production (2000).
Income: Per capita income: $26,219 (2010); Median household income: $58,451 (2010); Average household income: $67,539 (2010); Percent of households with income of $100,000 or more: 12.5% (2010); Poverty rate: 7.3% (2000).
Taxes: Total city taxes per capita: $204 (2007); City property taxes per capita: $194 (2007).
Education: Percent of population age 25 and over with: High school diploma (including GED) or higher: 84.7% (2010); Bachelor's degree or higher: 16.2% (2010); Master's degree or higher: 6.4% (2010).
School District(s)
Zionsville Community Schools (PK-12)
 2008-09 Enrollment: 5,355 . . . . (317) 873-2858
Housing: Homeownership rate: 85.5% (2010); Median home value: $138,542 (2010); Median contract rent: $570 per month (2000); Median year structure built: before 1940 (2000).
Transportation: Commute to work: 91.1% car, 0.0% public transportation, 2.4% walk, 5.7% work from home (2000); Travel time to work: 20.2% less than 15 minutes, 57.5% 15 to 30 minutes, 20.2% 30 to 45 minutes, 1.3% 45 to 60 minutes, 0.9% 60 minutes or more (2000)

ZIONSVILLE (town). Covers a land area of 5.800 square miles and a water area of 0.066 square miles. Located at 39.95° N. Lat; 86.26° W. Long. Elevation is 843 feet.
History: On his way to his inauguration in Washington in 1861, Abraham Lincoln spoke from the back of a train in Zionsville, saying, "I would like to spend more time here, but there is an event to take place in Washington which cannot start until I get there."
Population: 7,014 (1990); 8,775 (2000); 10,263 (2010); 11,154 (2015 projected); Race: 92.8% White, 2.0% Black, 3.4% Asian, 1.7% Other, 2.1% Hispanic of any race (2010); Density: 1,769.4 persons per square mile (2010); Average household size: 2.77 (2010); Median age: 38.5 (2010); Males per 100 females: 93.5 (2010); Marriage status: 17.0% never married, 70.8% now married, 4.1% widowed, 8.1% divorced (2000); Foreign born: 2.5% (2000); Ancestry (includes multiple ancestries): 24.3% German, 15.4% English, 12.3% United States or American, 10.1% Irish, 5.2% Scottish (2000).
Economy: Single-family building permits issued: 60 (2009); Multi-family building permits issued: 0 (2009); Employment by occupation: 31.0% management, 25.6% professional, 7.7% services, 25.5% sales, 0.0% farming, 6.9% construction, 3.3% production (2000).
Income: Per capita income: $45,471 (2010); Median household income: $92,284 (2010); Average household income: $128,584 (2010); Percent of

households with income of $100,000 or more: 46.5% (2010); Poverty rate: 4.0% (2000).
Taxes: Total city taxes per capita: $275 (2007); City property taxes per capita: $235 (2007).
Education: Percent of population age 25 and over with: High school diploma (including GED) or higher: 96.9% (2010); Bachelor's degree or higher: 66.5% (2010); Master's degree or higher: 27.1% (2010).
School District(s)
Zionsville Community Schools (PK-12)
 2008-09 Enrollment: 5,355 . . . . (317) 873-2858
Housing: Homeownership rate: 81.6% (2010); Median home value: $276,420 (2010); Median contract rent: $625 per month (2000); Median year structure built: 1981 (2000).
Newspapers: Zionsville Times Sentinel (Community news; Circulation 3,750)
Transportation: Commute to work: 91.8% car, 0.2% public transportation, 1.9% walk, 5.6% work from home (2000); Travel time to work: 27.1% less than 15 minutes, 37.1% 15 to 30 minutes, 30.2% 30 to 45 minutes, 4.2% 45 to 60 minutes, 1.4% 60 minutes or more (2000)
Additional Information Contacts
Town of Zionsville . . . . (317) 873-5410
 http://www.zionsville-in.gov
Zionsville Chamber of Commerce . . . . (317) 873-3836
 http://www.zionsvillechamber.org

Brown County

Located in south central Indiana; drained by Salt Creek and its north fork. Covers a land area of 312.26 square miles, a water area of 4.36 square miles, and is located in the Eastern Time Zone. The county was founded in 1836. County seat is Nashville.

Brown County is part of the Indianapolis-Carmel, IN Metropolitan Statistical Area. The entire metro area includes: Boone County, IN; Brown County, IN; Hamilton County, IN; Hancock County, IN; Hendricks County, IN; Johnson County, IN; Marion County, IN; Morgan County, IN; Putnam County, IN; Shelby County, IN

Population: 14,080 (1990); 14,957 (2000); 14,398 (2010); 13,970 (2015 projected); Race: 96.6% White, 1.0% Black, 0.3% Asian, 2.1% Other, 1.4% Hispanic of any race (2010); Density: 46.1 persons per square mile (2010); Average household size: 2.46 (2010); Median age: 44.8 (2010); Males per 100 females: 100.4 (2010).
Religion: Five largest groups: 7.1% Catholic Church, 6.0% Christian Churches and Churches of Christ, 5.1% American Baptist Churches in the USA, 3.8% The United Methodist Church, 1.7% Church of the Nazarene (2000).
Economy: Unemployment rate: 9.4% (5/2010); Total civilian labor force: 7,336 (5/2010); Leading industries: 22.0% accommodation & food services; 15.9% retail trade; 10.3% construction (2008); Farms: 169 totaling 16,959 acres (2007); Companies that employ 500 or more persons: 0 (2008); Companies that employ 100 to 499 persons: 2 (2008); Companies that employ less than 100 persons: 407 (2008); Black-owned businesses: n/a (2002); Hispanic-owned businesses: n/a (2002); Asian-owned businesses: n/a (2002); Women-owned businesses: 304 (2002); Retail sales per capita: $4,200 (2010). Single-family building permits issued: 166 (2009); Multi-family building permits issued: 0 (2009).
Income: Per capita income: $24,262 (2010); Median household income: $49,201 (2010); Average household income: $59,784 (2010); Percent of households with income of $100,000 or more: 13.4% (2010); Poverty rate: 10.5% (2008); Bankruptcy rate: 5.89% (2009).
Taxes: Total county taxes per capita: $685 (2007); County property taxes per capita: $472 (2007).
Education: Percent of population age 25 and over with: High school diploma (including GED) or higher: 87.4% (2010); Bachelor's degree or higher: 18.9% (2010); Master's degree or higher: 6.7% (2010).
Housing: Homeownership rate: 84.1% (2010); Median home value: $142,299 (2010); Median contract rent: $n/a per month (2006-2008 3-year est.); Median year structure built: n/a (2006-2008 3-year est.)
Health: Birth rate: 70.1 per 10,000 population (2009); Death rate: 94.2 per 10,000 population (2009); Age-adjusted cancer mortality rate: 196.2 deaths per 100,000 population (2006); Number of physicians: 5.4 per 10,000 population (2007); Hospital beds: 0.0 per 10,000 population (2006); Hospital admissions: 0.0 per 10,000 population (2006).
Elections: 2008 Presidential election results: 47.8% Obama, 50.4% McCain, 0.0% Nader

National and State Parks: Brown County State Park; Middle Fork State Wildlife Refuge; TC Steele State Memorial; Yellowwood State Forest

Additional Information Contacts

Brown County Government . . . . (812) 988-7064
  http://www.townofnashville.org

Brown County Communities

NASHVILLE (town). County seat. Covers a land area of 0.950 square miles and a water area of 0.006 square miles. Located at 39.20° N. Lat; 86.23° W. Long. Elevation is 594 feet.

History: Local tradition in Nashville tells of the Liars' Bench on the courthouse lawn which accommodated six tellers of tall and unlikely tales. When a bigger and better story was told by someone standing, one of the seated liars would be pushed off the end of the bench to make room for the bigger liar.

Population: 909 (1990); 825 (2000); 813 (2010); 784 (2015 projected); Race: 96.1% White, 1.2% Black, 0.6% Asian, 2.1% Other, 1.0% Hispanic of any race (2010); Density: 855.9 persons per square mile (2010); Average household size: 2.27 (2010); Median age: 47.6 (2010); Males per 100 females: 95.0 (2010); Marriage status: 18.2% never married, 46.8% now married, 18.6% widowed, 16.4% divorced (2000); Foreign born: 1.9% (2000); Ancestry (includes multiple ancestries): 17.9% German, 15.9% Irish, 12.5% English, 6.8% Other groups, 5.2% French (except Basque) (2000).

Economy: Employment by occupation: 11.7% management, 23.5% professional, 15.5% services, 34.4% sales, 0.0% farming, 5.2% construction, 9.7% production (2000).

Income: Per capita income: $25,586 (2010); Median household income: $46,367 (2010); Average household income: $58,890 (2010); Percent of households with income of $100,000 or more: 12.1% (2010); Poverty rate: 16.5% (2000).

Taxes: Total city taxes per capita: $995 (2007); City property taxes per capita: $726 (2007).

Education: Percent of population age 25 and over with: High school diploma (including GED) or higher: 93.8% (2010); Bachelor's degree or higher: 23.8% (2010); Master's degree or higher: 9.1% (2010).

School District(s)

Brown County School Corporation (PK-12)
  2008-09 Enrollment: 2,197 . . . . (812) 988-6601

Housing: Homeownership rate: 79.3% (2010); Median home value: $157,456 (2010); Median contract rent: $444 per month (2000); Median year structure built: 1963 (2000).

Newspapers: Brown County Democrat (Local news; Circulation 4,800)

Transportation: Commute to work: 86.0% car, 0.0% public transportation, 7.6% walk, 5.0% work from home (2000); Travel time to work: 47.1% less than 15 minutes, 11.7% 15 to 30 minutes, 21.2% 30 to 45 minutes, 6.8% 45 to 60 minutes, 13.2% 60 minutes or more (2000)

Carroll County

Located in northwest central Indiana; crossed by the Wabash River; drained by the Tippecanoe River. Covers a land area of 372.26 square miles, a water area of 2.80 square miles, and is located in the Eastern Time Zone. The county was founded in 1828. County seat is Delphi.

Carroll County is part of the Lafayette, IN Metropolitan Statistical Area. The entire metro area includes: Benton County, IN; Carroll County, IN; Tippecanoe County, IN

Weather Station: Delphi 3 S   Elevation: 669 feet

	Jan	Feb	Mar	Apr	May	Jun	Jul	Aug	Sep	Oct	Nov	Dec
High	33	38	50	63	74	83	86	83	78	66	51	39
Low	17	21	31	40	50	60	63	61	54	43	34	24
Precip	1.9	1.9	3.0	3.6	3.9	3.9	4.2	4.1	3.0	2.7	3.1	2.7
Snow	6.2	4.6	2.5	0.8	tr	0.0	0.0	0.0	0.0	0.2	0.9	5.3

High and Low temperatures in degrees Fahrenheit; Precipitation and Snow in inches

Population: 18,809 (1990); 20,165 (2000); 19,780 (2010); 19,451 (2015 projected); Race: 96.5% White, 0.6% Black, 0.1% Asian, 2.9% Other, 4.0% Hispanic of any race (2010); Density: 53.1 persons per square mile (2010); Average household size: 2.56 (2010); Median age: 40.3 (2010); Males per 100 females: 100.1 (2010).

Religion: Five largest groups: 7.5% The United Methodist Church, 4.8% Presbyterian Church (U.S.A.), 4.6% Christian Churches and Churches of Christ, 4.0% Catholic Church, 3.5% Assemblies of God (2000).

Economy: Unemployment rate: 9.4% (5/2010); Total civilian labor force: 9,555 (5/2010); Leading industries: 10.0% retail trade; 9.7% accommodation & food services; 6.2% health care and social assistance (2008); Farms: 581 totaling 192,334 acres (2007); Companies that employ 500 or more persons: 1 (2008); Companies that employ 100 to 499 persons: 2 (2008); Companies that employ less than 100 persons: 417 (2008); Black-owned businesses: n/a (2002); Hispanic-owned businesses: n/a (2002); Asian-owned businesses: n/a (2002); Women-owned businesses: n/a (2002); Retail sales per capita: $7,474 (2010). Single-family building permits issued: 32 (2009); Multi-family building permits issued: 6 (2009).

Income: Per capita income: $22,138 (2010); Median household income: $48,648 (2010); Average household income: $56,748 (2010); Percent of households with income of $100,000 or more: 11.3% (2010); Poverty rate: 8.5% (2008); Bankruptcy rate: 4.13% (2009).

Taxes: Total county taxes per capita: $264 (2007); County property taxes per capita: $135 (2007).

Education: Percent of population age 25 and over with: High school diploma (including GED) or higher: 87.1% (2010); Bachelor's degree or higher: 13.5% (2010); Master's degree or higher: 4.6% (2010).

Housing: Homeownership rate: 78.5% (2010); Median home value: $95,711 (2010); Median contract rent: $n/a per month (2006-2008 3-year est.); Median year structure built: n/a (2006-2008 3-year est.)

Health: Birth rate: 111.4 per 10,000 population (2009); Death rate: 83.5 per 10,000 population (2009); Age-adjusted cancer mortality rate: 216.5 deaths per 100,000 population (2006); Air Quality Index: 92.3% good, 7.7% moderate, 0.0% unhealthy for sensitive individuals, 0.0% unhealthy (percent of days in 2008); Number of physicians: 4.5 per 10,000 population (2007); Hospital beds: 0.0 per 10,000 population (2006); Hospital admissions: 0.0 per 10,000 population (2006).

Elections: 2008 Presidential election results: 42.8% Obama, 55.6% McCain, 0.0% Nader

Additional Information Contacts

Carroll County Government . . . . (317) 564-3172
  http://www.in.gov/mylocal/carroll_county.htm
City of Delphi . . . . (765) 564-2097
  http://www.cityofdelphi.org
Town of Flora . . . . (574) 967-4844
  http://www.townofflora.org

Carroll County Communities

BRINGHURST (unincorporated postal area, zip code 46913). Covers a land area of 32.909 square miles and a water area of 0 square miles. Located at 40.50° N. Lat; 86.50° W. Long. Elevation is 722 feet.

Population: 1,379 (2000); Race: 98.8% White, 0.7% Black, 0.0% Asian, 0.5% Other, 1.1% Hispanic of any race (2000); Density: 41.9 persons per square mile (2000); Age: 29.1% under 18, 10.1% over 64 (2000); Marriage status: 19.1% never married, 74.7% now married, 2.6% widowed, 3.6% divorced (2000); Foreign born: 0.4% (2000); Ancestry (includes multiple ancestries): 18.8% United States or American, 15.6% German, 13.1% English, 12.5% Other groups, 6.8% Irish (2000).

Economy: Employment by occupation: 6.8% management, 18.8% professional, 12.4% services, 17.9% sales, 0.0% farming, 14.0% construction, 30.0% production (2000).

Income: Per capita income: $19,559 (2000); Median household income: $57,574 (2000); Poverty rate: 5.3% (2000).

Education: Percent of population age 25 and over with: High school diploma (including GED) or higher: 84.6% (2000); Bachelor's degree or higher: 16.5% (2000).

Housing: Homeownership rate: 94.0% (2000); Median home value: $99,500 (2000); Median contract rent: $350 per month (2000); Median year structure built: 1961 (2000).

Transportation: Commute to work: 94.1% car, 0.0% public transportation, 0.7% walk, 3.3% work from home (2000); Travel time to work: 22.3% less than 15 minutes, 33.0% 15 to 30 minutes, 22.8% 30 to 45 minutes, 14.2% 45 to 60 minutes, 7.7% 60 minutes or more (2000)

BURLINGTON (town). Covers a land area of 0.541 square miles and a water area of 0 square miles. Located at 40.48° N. Lat; 86.39° W. Long. Elevation is 784 feet.

History: Burlington was founded in 1832 as a stagecoach and tavern stop on the Michigan Road. It was named for Wyandotte Chief Burlington.

Population: 568 (1990); 444 (2000); 384 (2010); 360 (2015 projected); Race: 98.7% White, 0.0% Black, 0.0% Asian, 1.3% Other, 0.8% Hispanic

of any race (2010); Density: 709.2 persons per square mile (2010); Average household size: 2.27 (2010); Median age: 43.0 (2010); Males per 100 females: 97.9 (2010); Marriage status: 23.4% never married, 50.5% now married, 12.6% widowed, 13.4% divorced (2000); Foreign born: 0.0% (2000); Ancestry (includes multiple ancestries): 18.9% German, 12.8% English, 10.3% Irish, 9.1% United States or American, 7.5% Other groups (2000).

Economy: Employment by occupation: 5.8% management, 11.6% professional, 21.0% services, 13.4% sales, 0.0% farming, 17.4% construction, 30.8% production (2000).

Income: Per capita income: $23,609 (2010); Median household income: $44,519 (2010); Average household income: $54,852 (2010); Percent of households with income of $100,000 or more: 12.4% (2010); Poverty rate: 5.5% (2000).

Taxes: Total city taxes per capita: $305 (2007); City property taxes per capita: $287 (2007).

Education: Percent of population age 25 and over with: High school diploma (including GED) or higher: 92.9% (2010); Bachelor's degree or higher: 13.4% (2010); Master's degree or higher: 4.2% (2010).

Housing: Homeownership rate: 74.0% (2010); Median home value: $91,818 (2010); Median contract rent: $333 per month (2000); Median year structure built: 1957 (2000).

Transportation: Commute to work: 89.9% car, 0.0% public transportation, 8.8% walk, 0.0% work from home (2000); Travel time to work: 30.4% less than 15 minutes, 24.4% 15 to 30 minutes, 42.9% 30 to 45 minutes, 1.4% 45 to 60 minutes, 0.9% 60 minutes or more (2000)

CAMDEN (town). Covers a land area of 0.260 square miles and a water area of <.001 square miles. Located at 40.60° N. Lat; 86.53° W. Long. Elevation is 673 feet.

Population: 611 (1990); 582 (2000); 572 (2010); 563 (2015 projected); Race: 98.6% White, 0.0% Black, 0.0% Asian, 1.4% Other, 0.3% Hispanic of any race (2010); Density: 2,202.2 persons per square mile (2010); Average household size: 2.66 (2010); Median age: 36.4 (2010); Males per 100 females: 96.6 (2010); Marriage status: 18.0% never married, 67.1% now married, 6.6% widowed, 8.3% divorced (2000); Foreign born: 0.0% (2000); Ancestry (includes multiple ancestries): 22.4% United States or American, 18.5% German, 11.3% Irish, 9.4% English, 6.9% Other groups (2000).

Economy: Employment by occupation: 5.0% management, 7.1% professional, 21.1% services, 22.3% sales, 0.9% farming, 13.0% construction, 30.7% production (2000).

Income: Per capita income: $19,992 (2010); Median household income: $46,833 (2010); Average household income: $53,140 (2010); Percent of households with income of $100,000 or more: 8.8% (2010); Poverty rate: 4.2% (2000).

Taxes: Total city taxes per capita: $282 (2007); City property taxes per capita: $258 (2007).

Education: Percent of population age 25 and over with: High school diploma (including GED) or higher: 84.3% (2010); Bachelor's degree or higher: 11.5% (2010); Master's degree or higher: 4.7% (2010).

Housing: Homeownership rate: 82.8% (2010); Median home value: $90,769 (2010); Median contract rent: $318 per month (2000); Median year structure built: before 1940 (2000).

Transportation: Commute to work: 92.7% car, 0.6% public transportation, 3.5% walk, 2.9% work from home (2000); Travel time to work: 32.6% less than 15 minutes, 29.9% 15 to 30 minutes, 18.8% 30 to 45 minutes, 16.1% 45 to 60 minutes, 2.6% 60 minutes or more (2000)

CUTLER (unincorporated postal area, zip code 46920). Covers a land area of 32.669 square miles and a water area of 0 square miles. Located at 40.47° N. Lat; 86.47° W. Long. Elevation is 751 feet.

Population: 1,487 (2000); Race: 99.2% White, 0.0% Black, 0.0% Asian, 0.8% Other, 2.2% Hispanic of any race (2000); Density: 45.5 persons per square mile (2000); Age: 29.1% under 18, 13.4% over 64 (2000); Marriage status: 18.3% never married, 66.5% now married, 6.0% widowed, 9.2% divorced (2000); Foreign born: 0.6% (2000); Ancestry (includes multiple ancestries): 19.8% German, 17.2% United States or American, 11.9% Other groups, 11.0% Irish, 7.9% English (2000).

Economy: Employment by occupation: 8.5% management, 11.9% professional, 13.2% services, 17.3% sales, 0.9% farming, 13.5% construction, 34.7% production (2000).

Income: Per capita income: $23,432 (2000); Median household income: $45,833 (2000); Poverty rate: 3.2% (2000).

Education: Percent of population age 25 and over with: High school diploma (including GED) or higher: 93.7% (2000); Bachelor's degree or higher: 12.9% (2000).

Housing: Homeownership rate: 82.1% (2000); Median home value: $89,000 (2000); Median contract rent: $353 per month (2000); Median year structure built: 1958 (2000).

Transportation: Commute to work: 93.1% car, 0.0% public transportation, 3.3% walk, 3.2% work from home (2000); Travel time to work: 24.4% less than 15 minutes, 28.2% 15 to 30 minutes, 36.9% 30 to 45 minutes, 9.2% 45 to 60 minutes, 1.4% 60 minutes or more (2000)

DELPHI (city). County seat. Covers a land area of 2.557 square miles and a water area of 0 square miles. Located at 40.58° N. Lat; 86.67° W. Long. Elevation is 568 feet.

History: Delphi was named by Samuel Milroy (1780-1845), a member of the State Constitutional Convention of 1816, who sold the first town lots in 1828. Poet James Whitcomb Riley was a resident here.

Population: 2,679 (1990); 3,015 (2000); 2,928 (2010); 2,874 (2015 projected); Race: 89.7% White, 0.4% Black, 0.3% Asian, 9.6% Other, 17.2% Hispanic of any race (2010); Density: 1,145.3 persons per square mile (2010); Average household size: 2.59 (2010); Median age: 38.4 (2010); Males per 100 females: 98.9 (2010); Marriage status: 18.9% never married, 57.0% now married, 10.7% widowed, 13.4% divorced (2000); Foreign born: 10.8% (2000); Ancestry (includes multiple ancestries): 22.6% United States or American, 19.3% German, 14.4% Other groups, 14.1% Irish, 8.6% English (2000).

Economy: Employment by occupation: 6.8% management, 13.8% professional, 18.3% services, 20.7% sales, 0.7% farming, 8.3% construction, 31.4% production (2000).

Income: Per capita income: $18,819 (2010); Median household income: $40,202 (2010); Average household income: $48,555 (2010); Percent of households with income of $100,000 or more: 8.5% (2010); Poverty rate: 13.4% (2000).

Taxes: Total city taxes per capita: $531 (2007); City property taxes per capita: $503 (2007).

Education: Percent of population age 25 and over with: High school diploma (including GED) or higher: 84.8% (2010); Bachelor's degree or higher: 14.6% (2010); Master's degree or higher: 5.5% (2010).

School District(s)

Delphi Community School Corp (KG-12)
    2008-09 Enrollment: 1,664 . . . . (765) 564-2100

Housing: Homeownership rate: 63.7% (2010); Median home value: $88,894 (2010); Median contract rent: $346 per month (2000); Median year structure built: before 1940 (2000).

Transportation: Commute to work: 91.7% car, 0.4% public transportation, 2.7% walk, 3.8% work from home (2000); Travel time to work: 50.5% less than 15 minutes, 19.3% 15 to 30 minutes, 21.7% 30 to 45 minutes, 4.5% 45 to 60 minutes, 4.0% 60 minutes or more (2000)

Additional Information Contacts

City of Delphi . . . . (765) 564-2097
    http://www.cityofdelphi.org

FLORA (town). Covers a land area of 1.032 square miles and a water area of 0 square miles. Located at 40.54° N. Lat; 86.52° W. Long. Elevation is 702 feet.

History: Laid out 1872, incorporated 1898.

Population: 2,179 (1990); 2,227 (2000); 2,003 (2010); 1,933 (2015 projected); Race: 98.1% White, 1.1% Black, 0.0% Asian, 0.8% Other, 1.7% Hispanic of any race (2010); Density: 1,940.4 persons per square mile (2010); Average household size: 2.44 (2010); Median age: 40.8 (2010); Males per 100 females: 89.0 (2010); Marriage status: 19.0% never married, 58.9% now married, 12.2% widowed, 9.9% divorced (2000); Foreign born: 1.4% (2000); Ancestry (includes multiple ancestries): 22.2% German, 18.5% United States or American, 12.0% Irish, 11.6% Other groups, 7.9% English (2000).

Economy: Single-family building permits issued: 0 (2009); Multi-family building permits issued: 0 (2009); Employment by occupation: 8.3% management, 14.0% professional, 15.3% services, 20.8% sales, 0.9% farming, 11.2% construction, 29.3% production (2000).

Income: Per capita income: $20,816 (2010); Median household income: $43,679 (2010); Average household income: $51,478 (2010); Percent of households with income of $100,000 or more: 8.0% (2010); Poverty rate: 6.3% (2000).

Taxes: Total city taxes per capita: $349 (2007); City property taxes per capita: $321 (2007).

Education: Percent of population age 25 and over with: High school diploma (including GED) or higher: 83.4% (2010); Bachelor's degree or higher: 12.1% (2010); Master's degree or higher: 5.7% (2010).

School District(s)

Carroll Consolidated Sch Corp (PK-12)

    2008-09 Enrollment: 1,119 . . . . (574) 967-4113

Housing: Homeownership rate: 70.7% (2010); Median home value: $78,377 (2010); Median contract rent: $328 per month (2000); Median year structure built: 1948 (2000).

Newspapers: Carroll County Comet (Community news; Circulation 5,131)

Transportation: Commute to work: 92.7% car, 0.3% public transportation, 3.9% walk, 2.3% work from home (2000); Travel time to work: 44.9% less than 15 minutes, 15.1% 15 to 30 minutes, 27.9% 30 to 45 minutes, 9.1% 45 to 60 minutes, 3.0% 60 minutes or more (2000)

Additional Information Contacts

Town of Flora . . . . (574) 967-4844

    http://www.townofflora.org

YEOMAN (town). Covers a land area of 0.122 square miles and a water area of 0 square miles. Located at 40.66° N. Lat; 86.72° W. Long. Elevation is 663 feet.

History: Laid out 1880.

Population: 131 (1990); 96 (2000); 89 (2010); 85 (2015 projected); Race: 98.9% White, 0.0% Black, 0.0% Asian, 1.1% Other, 0.0% Hispanic of any race (2010); Density: 729.9 persons per square mile (2010); Average household size: 2.62 (2010); Median age: 41.1 (2010); Males per 100 females: 117.1 (2010); Marriage status: 30.0% never married, 63.7% now married, 0.0% widowed, 6.3% divorced (2000); Foreign born: 3.2% (2000); Ancestry (includes multiple ancestries): 20.2% German, 14.9% United States or American, 12.8% Dutch, 9.6% Irish, 2.1% Other groups (2000).

Economy: Employment by occupation: 27.4% management, 0.0% professional, 14.5% services, 4.8% sales, 0.0% farming, 11.3% construction, 41.9% production (2000).

Income: Per capita income: $22,504 (2010); Median household income: $48,125 (2010); Average household income: $61,397 (2010); Percent of households with income of $100,000 or more: 11.8% (2010); Poverty rate: 2.1% (2000).

Taxes: Total city taxes per capita: $32 (2007); City property taxes per capita: $11 (2007).

Education: Percent of population age 25 and over with: High school diploma (including GED) or higher: 90.3% (2010); Bachelor's degree or higher: 11.3% (2010); Master's degree or higher: 3.2% (2010).

Housing: Homeownership rate: 79.4% (2010); Median home value: $104,167 (2010); Median contract rent: $242 per month (2000); Median year structure built: before 1940 (2000).

Transportation: Commute to work: 100.0% car, 0.0% public transportation, 0.0% walk, 0.0% work from home (2000); Travel time to work: 25.8% less than 15 minutes, 45.2% 15 to 30 minutes, 16.1% 30 to 45 minutes, 9.7% 45 to 60 minutes, 3.2% 60 minutes or more (2000)

Cass County

Located in north central Indiana; intersected by the Wabash River; drained by the Eel River and Deer Creek. Covers a land area of 412.87 square miles, a water area of 2.06 square miles, and is located in the Eastern Time Zone. The county was founded in 1828. County seat is Logansport.

Cass County is part of the Logansport, IN Micropolitan Statistical Area. The entire metro area includes: Cass County, IN

Population: 38,413 (1990); 40,930 (2000); 38,933 (2010); 37,859 (2015 projected); Race: 90.6% White, 1.6% Black, 0.8% Asian, 7.1% Other, 11.8% Hispanic of any race (2010); Density: 94.3 persons per square mile (2010); Average household size: 2.52 (2010); Median age: 38.7 (2010); Males per 100 females: 102.8 (2010).

Religion: Five largest groups: 10.1% Catholic Church, 7.3% The United Methodist Church, 3.4% American Baptist Churches in the USA, 2.5% Christian Churches and Churches of Christ, 2.0% Presbyterian Church (U.S.A.) (2000).

Economy: Unemployment rate: 9.9% (5/2010); Total civilian labor force: 19,489 (5/2010); Leading industries: 32.2% manufacturing; 21.1% health care and social assistance; 11.5% retail trade (2008); Farms: 868 totaling 228,199 acres (2007); Companies that employ 500 or more persons: 3 (2008); Companies that employ 100 to 499 persons: 18 (2008); Companies that employ less than 100 persons: 755 (2008); Black-owned businesses: n/a (2002); Hispanic-owned businesses: n/a (2002); Asian-owned

businesses: n/a (2002); Women-owned businesses: 717 (2002); Retail sales per capita: $11,788 (2010). Single-family building permits issued: 12 (2009); Multi-family building permits issued: 0 (2009).

Income: Per capita income: $21,194 (2010); Median household income: $44,428 (2010); Average household income: $54,191 (2010); Percent of households with income of $100,000 or more: 10.9% (2010); Poverty rate: 11.4% (2008); Bankruptcy rate: 6.10% (2009).

Taxes: Total county taxes per capita: $220 (2007); County property taxes per capita: $114 (2007).

Education: Percent of population age 25 and over with: High school diploma (including GED) or higher: 80.6% (2010); Bachelor's degree or higher: 13.6% (2010); Master's degree or higher: 5.1% (2010).

Housing: Homeownership rate: 73.8% (2010); Median home value: $79,629 (2010); Median contract rent: $436 per month (2006-2008 3-year est.); Median year structure built: 1947 (2006-2008 3-year est.)

Health: Birth rate: 140.0 per 10,000 population (2009); Death rate: 99.1 per 10,000 population (2009); Age-adjusted cancer mortality rate: 201.5 deaths per 100,000 population (2006); Number of physicians: 11.5 per 10,000 population (2007); Hospital beds: 127.2 per 10,000 population (2006); Hospital admissions: 874.8 per 10,000 population (2006).

Elections: 2008 Presidential election results: 44.8% Obama, 53.3% McCain, 0.0% Nader

Additional Information Contacts

Cass County Government . . . . (219) 753-7720

    http://www.co.cass.in.us

City of Logansport . . . . (574) 753-2551

    http://www.cityoflogansport.org

Logansport/Cass County Chamber Of Commerce . . . . (574) 753-6388

    http://www.logan-casschamber.com

Cass County Communities

GALVESTON (town). Covers a land area of 0.567 square miles and a water area of 0 square miles. Located at 40.57° N. Lat; 86.19° W. Long. Elevation is 801 feet.

Population: 1,635 (1990); 1,532 (2000); 1,404 (2010); 1,334 (2015 projected); Race: 98.0% White, 0.4% Black, 0.2% Asian, 1.4% Other, 2.0% Hispanic of any race (2010); Density: 2,477.1 persons per square mile (2010); Average household size: 2.54 (2010); Median age: 39.0 (2010); Males per 100 females: 95.3 (2010); Marriage status: 20.3% never married, 63.4% now married, 5.9% widowed, 10.4% divorced (2000); Foreign born: 0.8% (2000); Ancestry (includes multiple ancestries): 17.9% German, 16.3% United States or American, 12.7% Other groups, 10.3% English, 7.0% Irish (2000).

Economy: Single-family building permits issued: 0 (2009); Multi-family building permits issued: 0 (2009); Employment by occupation: 9.5% management, 14.6% professional, 12.8% services, 24.5% sales, 0.4% farming, 14.1% construction, 24.3% production (2000).

Income: Per capita income: $28,627 (2010); Median household income: $61,691 (2010); Average household income: $73,533 (2010); Percent of households with income of $100,000 or more: 21.9% (2010); Poverty rate: 4.4% (2000).

Taxes: Total city taxes per capita: $139 (2007); City property taxes per capita: $130 (2007).

Education: Percent of population age 25 and over with: High school diploma (including GED) or higher: 89.7% (2010); Bachelor's degree or higher: 14.5% (2010); Master's degree or higher: 5.6% (2010).

School District(s)

Southeastern School Corp (KG-12)

    2008-09 Enrollment: 1,569 . . . . (574) 626-2525

Housing: Homeownership rate: 86.1% (2010); Median home value: $90,602 (2010); Median contract rent: $438 per month (2000); Median year structure built: 1961 (2000).

Transportation: Commute to work: 95.0% car, 0.0% public transportation, 4.4% walk, 0.3% work from home (2000); Travel time to work: 23.4% less than 15 minutes, 60.3% 15 to 30 minutes, 9.8% 30 to 45 minutes, 3.1% 45 to 60 minutes, 3.3% 60 minutes or more (2000)

LOGANSPORT (city). County seat. Covers a land area of 8.260 square miles and a water area of 0.165 square miles. Located at 40.75° N. Lat; 86.36° W. Long. Elevation is 633 feet.

History: Logansport began as a trading post situated at the junction of the Wabash and Eel Rivers. The first permanent settler was Alexander Chamberlain, who built the Log Pioneer Inn in 1828.

Population: 17,525 (1990); 19,684 (2000); 18,761 (2010); 18,254 (2015 projected); Race: 84.7% White, 2.3% Black, 1.3% Asian, 11.6% Other, 21.1% Hispanic of any race (2010); Density: 2,271.2 persons per square mile (2010); Average household size: 2.52 (2010); Median age: 36.9 (2010); Males per 100 females: 104.7 (2010); Marriage status: 24.9% never married, 51.3% now married, 8.8% widowed, 14.9% divorced (2000); Foreign born: 7.1% (2000); Ancestry (includes multiple ancestries): 20.8% German, 14.5% Other groups, 12.8% United States or American, 8.4% Irish, 5.2% English (2000).
Economy: Employment by occupation: 5.1% management, 11.5% professional, 18.1% services, 22.0% sales, 0.5% farming, 9.8% construction, 33.0% production (2000).
Income: Per capita income: $18,988 (2010); Median household income: $39,045 (2010); Average household income: $48,450 (2010); Percent of households with income of $100,000 or more: 7.6% (2010); Poverty rate: 10.1% (2000).
Taxes: Total city taxes per capita: $345 (2007); City property taxes per capita: $301 (2007).
Education: Percent of population age 25 and over with: High school diploma (including GED) or higher: 74.3% (2010); Bachelor's degree or higher: 11.8% (2010); Master's degree or higher: 4.3% (2010).

School District(s)

IN Department of Correction (05-12)
 2008-09 Enrollment: 793 . . . . (317) 233-3111
Logansport Community Sch Corp (PK-12)
 2008-09 Enrollment: 4,303 . . . . (574) 722-2911
Housing: Homeownership rate: 64.0% (2010); Median home value: $67,958 (2010); Median contract rent: $352 per month (2000); Median year structure built: 1941 (2000).
Hospitals: Logansport Memorial Hospital (104 beds); Logansport State Hospital (396 beds)
Safety: Violent crime rate: 10.7 per 10,000 population; Property crime rate: 485.3 per 10,000 population (2008).
Newspapers: Pharos-Tribune (Local news)
Transportation: Commute to work: 92.9% car, 1.9% public transportation, 2.5% walk, 1.4% work from home (2000); Travel time to work: 61.6% less than 15 minutes, 20.0% 15 to 30 minutes, 7.8% 30 to 45 minutes, 5.4% 45 to 60 minutes, 5.2% 60 minutes or more (2000)

Additional Information Contacts

City of Logansport . . . . (574) 753-2551
 http://www.cityoflogansport.org
Logansport/Cass County Chamber Of Commerce . . . . (574) 753-6388
 http://www.logan-casschamber.com

LUCERNE (unincorporated postal area, zip code 46950).

Covers a land area of 29.291 square miles and a water area of 0 square miles. Located at 40.88° N. Lat; 86.38° W. Long. Elevation is 797 feet.
Population: 665 (2000); Race: 100.0% White, 0.0% Black, 0.0% Asian, 0.0% Other, 0.0% Hispanic of any race (2000); Density: 22.7 persons per square mile (2000); Age: 20.1% under 18, 22.6% over 64 (2000); Marriage status: 14.0% never married, 76.6% now married, 7.8% widowed, 1.6% divorced (2000); Foreign born: 0.0% (2000); Ancestry (includes multiple ancestries): 19.4% German, 14.0% English, 6.4% United States or American, 5.1% Other groups, 4.1% Irish (2000).
Economy: Employment by occupation: 16.8% management, 15.2% professional, 10.9% services, 24.8% sales, 5.6% farming, 18.7% construction, 8.0% production (2000).
Income: Per capita income: $21,232 (2000); Median household income: $39,722 (2000); Poverty rate: 3.6% (2000).
Education: Percent of population age 25 and over with: High school diploma (including GED) or higher: 91.5% (2000); Bachelor's degree or higher: 16.1% (2000).
Housing: Homeownership rate: 79.0% (2000); Median home value: $69,200 (2000); Median contract rent: $272 per month (2000); Median year structure built: 1948 (2000).
Transportation: Commute to work: 82.9% car, 4.1% public transportation, 1.9% walk, 7.6% work from home (2000); Travel time to work: 12.9% less than 15 minutes, 55.4% 15 to 30 minutes, 16.1% 30 to 45 minutes, 0.0% 45 to 60 minutes, 15.5% 60 minutes or more (2000)

ONWARD (town).

Covers a land area of 0.087 square miles and a water area of 0 square miles. Located at 40.69° N. Lat; 86.19° W. Long. Elevation is 768 feet.
Population: 63 (1990); 81 (2000); 87 (2010); 89 (2015 projected); Race: 95.4% White, 1.1% Black, 0.0% Asian, 3.4% Other, 4.6% Hispanic of any

race (2010); Density: 1,004.9 persons per square mile (2010); Average household size: 2.72 (2010); Median age: 40.4 (2010); Males per 100 females: 77.6 (2010); Marriage status: 8.2% never married, 77.6% now married, 14.3% widowed, 0.0% divorced (2000); Foreign born: 0.0% (2000); Ancestry (includes multiple ancestries): 27.9% Irish, 11.5% Other groups, 9.8% Scottish, 6.6% United States or American, 6.6% French (except Basque) (2000).
Economy: Employment by occupation: 0.0% management, 0.0% professional, 5.9% services, 29.4% sales, 0.0% farming, 26.5% construction, 38.2% production (2000).
Income: Per capita income: $30,307 (2010); Median household income: $71,875 (2010); Average household income: $81,719 (2010); Percent of households with income of $100,000 or more: 28.1% (2010); Poverty rate: 6.6% (2000).
Taxes: Total city taxes per capita: $73 (2007); City property taxes per capita: $61 (2007).
Education: Percent of population age 25 and over with: High school diploma (including GED) or higher: 89.5% (2010); Bachelor's degree or higher: 19.3% (2010); Master's degree or higher: 3.5% (2010).
Housing: Homeownership rate: 78.1% (2010); Median home value: $113,889 (2010); Median contract rent: $288 per month (2000); Median year structure built: 1969 (2000).
Transportation: Commute to work: 88.2% car, 0.0% public transportation, 0.0% walk, 11.8% work from home (2000); Travel time to work: 13.3% less than 15 minutes, 73.3% 15 to 30 minutes, 0.0% 30 to 45 minutes, 0.0% 45 to 60 minutes, 13.3% 60 minutes or more (2000)

ROYAL CENTER (town).

Covers a land area of 0.501 square miles and a water area of 0 square miles. Located at 40.86° N. Lat; 86.50° W. Long. Elevation is 735 feet.
History: Laid out 1846.
Population: 859 (1990); 832 (2000); 749 (2010); 707 (2015 projected); Race: 98.7% White, 0.1% Black, 0.0% Asian, 1.2% Other, 0.8% Hispanic of any race (2010); Density: 1,494.8 persons per square mile (2010); Average household size: 2.52 (2010); Median age: 38.9 (2010); Males per 100 females: 99.7 (2010); Marriage status: 20.0% never married, 63.2% now married, 10.8% widowed, 6.0% divorced (2000); Foreign born: 0.6% (2000); Ancestry (includes multiple ancestries): 26.3% German, 14.5% United States or American, 12.7% Irish, 8.5% Other groups, 8.4% English (2000).
Economy: Employment by occupation: 8.2% management, 16.6% professional, 16.1% services, 21.7% sales, 0.0% farming, 6.1% construction, 31.3% production (2000).
Income: Per capita income: $22,724 (2010); Median household income: $51,935 (2010); Average household income: $57,685 (2010); Percent of households with income of $100,000 or more: 9.4% (2010); Poverty rate: 4.7% (2000).
Taxes: Total city taxes per capita: $232 (2007); City property taxes per capita: $216 (2007).
Education: Percent of population age 25 and over with: High school diploma (including GED) or higher: 85.6% (2010); Bachelor's degree or higher: 12.5% (2010); Master's degree or higher: 6.9% (2010).

School District(s)

Pioneer Regional School Corp (KG-12)
 2008-09 Enrollment: 1,010 . . . . (574) 643-2605
Housing: Homeownership rate: 82.2% (2010); Median home value: $65,634 (2010); Median contract rent: $328 per month (2000); Median year structure built: 1944 (2000).
Newspapers: Royal Centre Record (Community news; Circulation 1,161)
Transportation: Commute to work: 93.3% car, 0.0% public transportation, 2.9% walk, 2.9% work from home (2000); Travel time to work: 29.2% less than 15 minutes, 51.5% 15 to 30 minutes, 10.4% 30 to 45 minutes, 1.7% 45 to 60 minutes, 7.2% 60 minutes or more (2000)

TWELVE MILE (unincorporated postal area, zip code 46988).

Covers a land area of 26.364 square miles and a water area of 0.006 square miles. Located at 40.87° N. Lat; 86.23° W. Long. Elevation is 801 feet.
Population: 1,104 (2000); Race: 96.3% White, 1.5% Black, 0.0% Asian, 2.2% Other, 0.0% Hispanic of any race (2000); Density: 41.9 persons per square mile (2000); Age: 22.3% under 18, 12.1% over 64 (2000); Marriage status: 20.9% never married, 55.8% now married, 6.9% widowed, 16.4% divorced (2000); Foreign born: 0.0% (2000); Ancestry (includes multiple ancestries): 17.0% German, 12.2% Other groups, 11.6% Irish, 8.0% United States or American, 4.8% English (2000).

Economy: Employment by occupation: 4.3% management, 17.9% professional, 8.5% services, 22.4% sales, 0.0% farming, 15.5% construction, 31.4% production (2000).
Income: Per capita income: $15,559 (2000); Median household income: $36,360 (2000); Poverty rate: 7.0% (2000).
Education: Percent of population age 25 and over with: High school diploma (including GED) or higher: 81.7% (2000); Bachelor's degree or higher: 9.6% (2000).
Housing: Homeownership rate: 78.4% (2000); Median home value: $69,100 (2000); Median contract rent: $198 per month (2000); Median year structure built: 1966 (2000).
Transportation: Commute to work: 90.8% car, 0.0% public transportation, 0.0% walk, 9.2% work from home (2000); Travel time to work: 14.8% less than 15 minutes, 47.7% 15 to 30 minutes, 18.0% 30 to 45 minutes, 5.7% 45 to 60 minutes, 13.8% 60 minutes or more (2000)

WALTON (town). Covers a land area of 0.431 square miles and a water area of 0 square miles. Located at 40.66° N. Lat; 86.24° W. Long. Elevation is 771 feet.
History: Laid out 1852.
Population: 1,062 (1990); 1,069 (2000); 920 (2010); 858 (2015 projected); Race: 91.3% White, 0.1% Black, 0.1% Asian, 8.5% Other, 12.1% Hispanic of any race (2010); Density: 2,132.5 persons per square mile (2010); Average household size: 2.53 (2010); Median age: 41.3 (2010); Males per 100 females: 93.3 (2010); Marriage status: 20.8% never married, 59.9% now married, 9.0% widowed, 10.3% divorced (2000); Foreign born: 12.8% (2000); Ancestry (includes multiple ancestries): 17.9% German, 17.9% Other groups, 11.6% United States or American, 10.7% English, 9.6% Irish (2000).
Economy: Single-family building permits issued: 0 (2009); Multi-family building permits issued: 0 (2009); Employment by occupation: 7.2% management, 16.4% professional, 13.2% services, 22.6% sales, 0.6% farming, 5.8% construction, 34.1% production (2000).
Income: Per capita income: $23,614 (2010); Median household income: $49,338 (2010); Average household income: $59,354 (2010); Percent of households with income of $100,000 or more: 11.0% (2010); Poverty rate: 6.0% (2000).
Taxes: Total city taxes per capita: $175 (2007); City property taxes per capita: $162 (2007).
Education: Percent of population age 25 and over with: High school diploma (including GED) or higher: 77.7% (2010); Bachelor's degree or higher: 18.0% (2010); Master's degree or higher: 7.5% (2010).

School District(s)
Southeastern School Corp (KG-12)
    2008-09 Enrollment: 1,569 . . . . (574) 626-2525
Housing: Homeownership rate: 79.9% (2010); Median home value: $90,247 (2010); Median contract rent: $303 per month (2000); Median year structure built: 1954 (2000).
Transportation: Commute to work: 96.2% car, 0.4% public transportation, 1.6% walk, 0.4% work from home (2000); Travel time to work: 25.3% less than 15 minutes, 50.9% 15 to 30 minutes, 16.0% 30 to 45 minutes, 2.2% 45 to 60 minutes, 5.7% 60 minutes or more (2000)

Clark County

Located in southeastern Indiana; bounded on the southeast by the Ohio River and the Kentucky border; drained by Silver Creek. Covers a land area of 375.04 square miles, a water area of 1.16 square miles, and is located in the Eastern Time Zone. The county was founded in 1801. County seat is Jeffersonville.

Clark County is part of the Louisville/Jefferson County, KY-IN Metropolitan Statistical Area. The entire metro area includes: Clark County, IN; Floyd County, IN; Harrison County, IN; Washington County, IN; Bullitt County, KY; Henry County, KY; Jefferson County, KY; Meade County, KY; Nelson County, KY; Oldham County, KY; Shelby County, KY; Spencer County, KY; Trimble County, KY

Population: 87,777 (1990); 96,472 (2000); 108,825 (2010); 114,417 (2015 projected); Race: 88.5% White, 7.4% Black, 0.8% Asian, 3.3% Other, 3.2% Hispanic of any race (2010); Density: 290.2 persons per square mile (2010); Average household size: 2.37 (2010); Median age: 37.8 (2010); Males per 100 females: 95.9 (2010).
Religion: Five largest groups: 12.7% Catholic Church, 8.4% Southern Baptist Convention, 4.1% The United Methodist Church, 2.8% Christian

Churches and Churches of Christ, 2.2% Christian Church (Disciples of Christ) (2000).
Economy: Unemployment rate: 8.5% (5/2010); Total civilian labor force: 54,122 (5/2010); Leading industries: 18.1% manufacturing; 15.8% retail trade; 11.4% transportation & warehousing (2008); Farms: 585 totaling 86,668 acres (2007); Companies that employ 500 or more persons: 7 (2008); Companies that employ 100 to 499 persons: 79 (2008); Companies that employ less than 100 persons: 2,372 (2008); Black-owned businesses: n/a (2002); Hispanic-owned businesses: n/a (2002); Asian-owned businesses: n/a (2002); Women-owned businesses: 2,171 (2002); Retail sales per capita: $17,016 (2010). Single-family building permits issued: 341 (2009); Multi-family building permits issued: 34 (2009).
Income: Per capita income: $24,104 (2010); Median household income: $46,698 (2010); Average household income: $57,513 (2010); Percent of households with income of $100,000 or more: 12.5% (2010); Poverty rate: 10.8% (2008); Bankruptcy rate: 9.25% (2009).
Taxes: Total county taxes per capita: $284 (2007); County property taxes per capita: $128 (2007).
Education: Percent of population age 25 and over with: High school diploma (including GED) or higher: 84.6% (2010); Bachelor's degree or higher: 17.5% (2010); Master's degree or higher: 6.1% (2010).
Housing: Homeownership rate: 71.0% (2010); Median home value: $119,250 (2010); Median contract rent: $520 per month (2006-2008 3-year est.); Median year structure built: 1976 (2006-2008 3-year est.)
Health: Birth rate: 133.6 per 10,000 population (2009); Death rate: 97.1 per 10,000 population (2009); Age-adjusted cancer mortality rate: 186.0 deaths per 100,000 population (2006); Air Quality Index: 58.3% good, 40.7% moderate, 1.0% unhealthy for sensitive individuals, 0.0% unhealthy (percent of days in 2008); Number of physicians: 14.4 per 10,000 population (2007); Hospital beds: 40.3 per 10,000 population (2006); Hospital admissions: 1,602.8 per 10,000 population (2006).
Elections: 2008 Presidential election results: 46.0% Obama, 53.1% McCain, 0.0% Nader
National and State Parks: Deam Lake State Recreation Area; Falls of the Ohio State Park
Additional Information Contacts
Clark County Government . . . . (812) 285-6200
    http://www.co.clark.in.us
Charlestown Chamber of Commerce. . . . . (812) 256-3422
    http://www.charlestown-in.com
City of Charlestown . . . . (812) 256-3422
    http://www.cityofcharlestown.com
City of Jeffersonville. . . . . (812) 285-6422
    http://www.cityofjeff.net
Clarksville Chamber of Commerce . . . . (812) 945-0266
    http://www.2chambers.com/clarksville,-indiana.htm
Jeffersonville Chamber of Commerce . . . . (812) 285-6244
    http://www.in.gov/judiciary/clark
Town of Clarksville. . . . . (812) 283-1500
    http://town.clarksville.in.us
Town of Sellersburg. . . . . (812) 246-7089
    http://www.sellersburg.org

Clark County Communities

BORDEN (town). Aka New Providence. Covers a land area of 1.111 square miles and a water area of 0 square miles. Located at 38.47° N. Lat; 85.94° W. Long. Elevation is 561 feet.
Population: 434 (1990); 818 (2000); 1,072 (2010); 1,181 (2015 projected); Race: 96.0% White, 0.0% Black, 0.6% Asian, 3.5% Other, 2.8% Hispanic of any race (2010); Density: 965.1 persons per square mile (2010); Average household size: 2.52 (2010); Median age: 37.8 (2010); Males per 100 females: 101.1 (2010); Marriage status: 20.6% never married, 63.8% now married, 4.3% widowed, 11.2% divorced (2000); Foreign born: 0.4% (2000); Ancestry (includes multiple ancestries): 24.9% German, 18.1% United States or American, 13.7% Irish, 11.3% English, 7.6% Other groups (2000).
Economy: Employment by occupation: 7.7% management, 10.5% professional, 14.3% services, 27.0% sales, 0.0% farming, 11.8% construction, 28.7% production (2000).
Income: Per capita income: $24,364 (2010); Median household income: $54,035 (2010); Average household income: $61,706 (2010); Percent of households with income of $100,000 or more: 13.6% (2010); Poverty rate: 11.0% (2000).

Taxes: Total city taxes per capita: $197 (2007); City property taxes per capita: $164 (2007).
Education: Percent of population age 25 and over with: High school diploma (including GED) or higher: 80.0% (2010); Bachelor's degree or higher: 13.5% (2010); Master's degree or higher: 4.0% (2010).

School District(s)
West Clark Community Schools (PK-12)
   2008-09 Enrollment: 3,987 . . . . (812) 246-3375
Housing: Homeownership rate: 85.4% (2010); Median home value: $120,599 (2010); Median contract rent: $363 per month (2000); Median year structure built: 1968 (2000).
Transportation: Commute to work: 95.7% car, 0.5% public transportation, 3.4% walk, 0.0% work from home (2000); Travel time to work: 14.6% less than 15 minutes, 33.8% 15 to 30 minutes, 41.2% 30 to 45 minutes, 4.7% 45 to 60 minutes, 5.6% 60 minutes or more (2000)

CHARLESTOWN (city).
Covers a land area of 2.332 square miles and a water area of 0 square miles. Located at 38.45° N. Lat; 85.66° W. Long. Elevation is 591 feet.
History: Charleston was platted in 1808, and served as the seat of Clark County from 1811 to 1878. In 1940 the E.I. du Pont de Nemours Company built a plant here, followed by the Goodyear Tire and Rubber Company's plant.
Population: 5,954 (1990); 5,993 (2000); 6,473 (2010); 6,787 (2015 projected); Race: 91.1% White, 2.0% Black, 0.2% Asian, 6.7% Other, 7.9% Hispanic of any race (2010); Density: 2,775.8 persons per square mile (2010); Average household size: 2.54 (2010); Median age: 34.6 (2010); Males per 100 females: 95.8 (2010); Marriage status: 23.0% never married, 52.3% now married, 7.9% widowed, 16.8% divorced (2000); Foreign born: 2.7% (2000); Ancestry (includes multiple ancestries): 24.1% United States or American, 13.4% Other groups, 11.4% Irish, 11.3% German, 7.2% English (2000).
Economy: Single-family building permits issued: 16 (2009); Multi-family building permits issued: 0 (2009); Employment by occupation: 8.8% management, 8.6% professional, 20.6% services, 23.8% sales, 0.0% farming, 11.0% construction, 27.2% production (2000).
Income: Per capita income: $19,912 (2010); Median household income: $41,276 (2010); Average household income: $50,908 (2010); Percent of households with income of $100,000 or more: 9.6% (2010); Poverty rate: 19.2% (2000).
Taxes: Total city taxes per capita: $209 (2007); City property taxes per capita: $159 (2007).
Education: Percent of population age 25 and over with: High school diploma (including GED) or higher: 78.7% (2010); Bachelor's degree or higher: 12.9% (2010); Master's degree or higher: 3.6% (2010).

School District(s)
Greater Clark County Schools (PK-12)
   2008-09 Enrollment: 10,997 . . . . (812) 283-0701
Housing: Homeownership rate: 66.1% (2010); Median home value: $105,020 (2010); Median contract rent: $348 per month (2000); Median year structure built: 1959 (2000).
Safety: Violent crime rate: 5.5 per 10,000 population; Property crime rate: 431.6 per 10,000 population (2008).
Newspapers: Charlestown Leader (Community news; Circulation 12,321)
Transportation: Commute to work: 94.3% car, 0.5% public transportation, 1.7% walk, 2.6% work from home (2000); Travel time to work: 25.6% less than 15 minutes, 36.6% 15 to 30 minutes, 23.7% 30 to 45 minutes, 9.3% 45 to 60 minutes, 4.8% 60 minutes or more (2000)
Additional Information Contacts
Charlestown Chamber of Commerce. . . . . (812) 256-3422
   http://www.charlestown-in.com
City of Charlestown . . . . (812) 256-3422
   http://www.cityofcharlestown.com

CLARKSVILLE (town).
Covers a land area of 10.091 square miles and a water area of 0.084 square miles. Located at 38.31° N. Lat; 85.76° W. Long. Elevation is 456 feet.
History: Named for General George Rogers Clark, who founded the town in 1784. Clarksville was founded in 1784 by George Rogers Clark on land given to Clark by the State of Virginia in reward for his military service. Clarksville was the site of the duel between Henry Clay and Humphrey Marshall in which each was wounded.
Population: 21,212 (1990); 21,400 (2000); 21,544 (2010); 21,748 (2015 projected); Race: 87.3% White, 7.3% Black, 1.2% Asian, 4.2% Other, 5.2% Hispanic of any race (2010); Density: 2,134.9 persons per square mile

(2010); Average household size: 2.23 (2010); Median age: 37.9 (2010); Males per 100 females: 93.7 (2010); Marriage status: 23.5% never married, 53.2% now married, 9.4% widowed, 13.9% divorced (2000); Foreign born: 2.9% (2000); Ancestry (includes multiple ancestries): 20.0% German, 13.5% Irish, 12.8% Other groups, 12.8% United States or American, 8.8% English (2000).
Economy: Single-family building permits issued: 14 (2009); Multi-family building permits issued: 2 (2009); Employment by occupation: 9.8% management, 14.5% professional, 14.0% services, 31.4% sales, 0.2% farming, 9.8% construction, 20.3% production (2000).
Income: Per capita income: $22,754 (2010); Median household income: $38,946 (2010); Average household income: $51,037 (2010); Percent of households with income of $100,000 or more: 9.5% (2010); Poverty rate: 8.1% (2000).
Taxes: Total city taxes per capita: $560 (2007); City property taxes per capita: $478 (2007).
Education: Percent of population age 25 and over with: High school diploma (including GED) or higher: 82.1% (2010); Bachelor's degree or higher: 15.5% (2010); Master's degree or higher: 4.9% (2010).

School District(s)
Clarksville Com School Corp (PK-12)
   2008-09 Enrollment: 1,382 . . . . (812) 282-7753
Greater Clark County Schools (PK-12)
   2008-09 Enrollment: 10,997 . . . . (812) 283-0701

Two-year College(s)
PJ's College of Cosmetology (Private, For-profit)
   Fall 2008 Enrollment: 72 . . . . (317) 846-8999
Housing: Homeownership rate: 59.5% (2010); Median home value: $110,032 (2010); Median contract rent: $462 per month (2000); Median year structure built: 1968 (2000).
Newspapers: The Courier-Journal - Indiana Bureau (Regional news)
Transportation: Commute to work: 94.0% car, 0.8% public transportation, 2.0% walk, 2.1% work from home (2000); Travel time to work: 36.7% less than 15 minutes, 45.5% 15 to 30 minutes, 13.6% 30 to 45 minutes, 1.8% 45 to 60 minutes, 2.4% 60 minutes or more (2000)
Additional Information Contacts
Clarksville Chamber of Commerce . . . . (812) 945-0266
   http://www.2chambers.com/clarksville,-indiana.htm
Town of Clarksville. . . . . (812) 283-1500
   http://town.clarksville.in.us

HENRYVILLE (CDP).
Covers a land area of 2.884 square miles and a water area of 0 square miles. Located at 38.54° N. Lat; 85.76° W. Long. Elevation is 518 feet.
Population: 1,183 (1990); 1,545 (2000); 2,072 (2010); 2,292 (2015 projected); Race: 99.2% White, 0.1% Black, 0.1% Asian, 0.6% Other, 0.6% Hispanic of any race (2010); Density: 718.4 persons per square mile (2010); Average household size: 2.56 (2010); Median age: 35.4 (2010); Males per 100 females: 98.1 (2010); Marriage status: 20.2% never married, 63.5% now married, 3.6% widowed, 12.7% divorced (2000); Foreign born: 0.0% (2000); Ancestry (includes multiple ancestries): 21.8% German, 18.2% United States or American, 17.1% Irish, 15.1% English, 4.6% Other groups (2000).
Economy: Employment by occupation: 10.5% management, 12.5% professional, 10.2% services, 26.2% sales, 0.0% farming, 13.5% construction, 27.1% production (2000).
Income: Per capita income: $21,513 (2010); Median household income: $53,648 (2010); Average household income: $55,151 (2010); Percent of households with income of $100,000 or more: 8.8% (2010); Poverty rate: 4.9% (2000).
Education: Percent of population age 25 and over with: High school diploma (including GED) or higher: 87.5% (2010); Bachelor's degree or higher: 16.8% (2010); Master's degree or higher: 5.6% (2010).

School District(s)
West Clark Community Schools (PK-12)
   2008-09 Enrollment: 3,987 . . . . (812) 246-3375
Housing: Homeownership rate: 74.4% (2010); Median home value: $119,223 (2010); Median contract rent: $422 per month (2000); Median year structure built: 1974 (2000).
Transportation: Commute to work: 96.4% car, 0.5% public transportation, 0.0% walk, 1.9% work from home (2000); Travel time to work: 15.6% less than 15 minutes, 34.8% 15 to 30 minutes, 33.0% 30 to 45 minutes, 11.1% 45 to 60 minutes, 5.5% 60 minutes or more (2000)

JEFFERSONVILLE (city). County seat. Covers a land area of 13.581 square miles and a water area of <.001 square miles. Located at 38.29° N. Lat; 85.73° W. Long. Elevation is 446 feet.

History: Jeffersonville was platted in 1802 and named by William Henry Harrison for Thomas Jefferson, who had suggested the plan. The Howard Shipyards were founded in 1834 and influenced the economy of Jeffersonville for a century. The city sustained heavy damage in the 1937 flooding of the Ohio River.

Population: 24,214 (1990); 27,362 (2000); 28,911 (2010); 29,957 (2015 projected); Race: 79.5% White, 15.6% Black, 1.1% Asian, 3.8% Other, 3.1% Hispanic of any race (2010); Density: 2,128.7 persons per square mile (2010); Average household size: 2.24 (2010); Median age: 37.8 (2010); Males per 100 females: 93.8 (2010); Marriage status: 23.8% never married, 54.3% now married, 6.7% widowed, 15.3% divorced (2000); Foreign born: 1.7% (2000); Ancestry (includes multiple ancestries): 19.4% Other groups, 18.9% German, 12.9% United States or American, 12.8% Irish, 8.1% English (2000).

Economy: Unemployment rate: 9.0% (5/2010); Total civilian labor force: 15,399 (5/2010); Single-family building permits issued: 145 (2009); Multi-family building permits issued: 25 (2009); Employment by occupation: 11.1% management, 15.8% professional, 14.9% services, 29.8% sales, 0.0% farming, 8.9% construction, 19.6% production (2000).

Income: Per capita income: $23,465 (2010); Median household income: $43,676 (2010); Average household income: $53,124 (2010); Percent of households with income of $100,000 or more: 10.7% (2010); Poverty rate: 10.1% (2000).

Taxes: Total city taxes per capita: $393 (2007); City property taxes per capita: $279 (2007).

Education: Percent of population age 25 and over with: High school diploma (including GED) or higher: 84.3% (2010); Bachelor's degree or higher: 17.6% (2010); Master's degree or higher: 6.1% (2010).

School District(s)
Greater Clark County Schools (PK-12)
  2008-09 Enrollment: 10,997 . . . . (812) 283-0701
Four-year College(s)
Mid-America College of Funeral Service (Private, Not-for-profit)
  Fall 2008 Enrollment: 77 . . . . (812) 288-8878
  2009-10 Tuition: In-state $9,050; Out-of-state $9,050
Ottawa University-Jeffersonville (Private, Not-for-profit, American Baptist)
  Fall 2008 Enrollment: 108 . . . . (812) 280-7271
  2009-10 Tuition: In-state $9,440; Out-of-state $9,440
Vocational/Technical School(s)
Ideal Beauty Academy (Private, For-profit)
  Fall 2008 Enrollment: 70 . . . . (812) 282-1371
  2009-10 Tuition: $13,725

Housing: Homeownership rate: 63.3% (2010); Median home value: $109,962 (2010); Median contract rent: $405 per month (2000); Median year structure built: 1970 (2000).

Hospitals: Clark Memorial Hospital (241 beds)

Newspapers: The Evening News (Community news; Circulation 14,016)

Transportation: Commute to work: 94.4% car, 1.2% public transportation, 2.1% walk, 1.3% work from home (2000); Travel time to work: 35.9% less than 15 minutes, 46.8% 15 to 30 minutes, 12.6% 30 to 45 minutes, 2.5% 45 to 60 minutes, 2.2% 60 minutes or more (2000)

Additional Information Contacts
City of Jeffersonville. . . . . (812) 285-6422
  http://www.cityofjeff.net
Jeffersonville Chamber of Commerce . . . . (812) 285-6244
  http://www.in.gov/judiciary/clark

MARYSVILLE (unincorporated postal area, zip code 47141). Covers a land area of 32.033 square miles and a water area of 0 square miles. Located at 38.54° N. Lat; 85.60° W. Long. Elevation is 712 feet.

Population: 1,414 (2000); Race: 97.8% White, 0.7% Black, 0.0% Asian, 1.5% Other, 0.3% Hispanic of any race (2000); Density: 44.1 persons per square mile (2000); Age: 26.0% under 18, 12.2% over 64 (2000); Marriage status: 13.3% never married, 71.1% now married, 6.1% widowed, 9.5% divorced (2000); Foreign born: 0.0% (2000); Ancestry (includes multiple ancestries): 26.0% United States or American, 12.1% German, 8.6% Irish, 8.4% English, 7.5% Other groups (2000).

Economy: Employment by occupation: 10.0% management, 12.5% professional, 11.1% services, 23.5% sales, 1.7% farming, 9.8% construction, 31.3% production (2000).

Income: Per capita income: $19,161 (2000); Median household income: $37,750 (2000); Poverty rate: 6.6% (2000).

Education: Percent of population age 25 and over with: High school diploma (including GED) or higher: 73.4% (2000); Bachelor's degree or higher: 10.0% (2000).

Housing: Homeownership rate: 88.8% (2000); Median home value: $96,900 (2000); Median contract rent: $275 per month (2000); Median year structure built: 1975 (2000).

Transportation: Commute to work: 96.7% car, 1.1% public transportation, 0.0% walk, 2.2% work from home (2000); Travel time to work: 10.2% less than 15 minutes, 24.8% 15 to 30 minutes, 32.6% 30 to 45 minutes, 24.8% 45 to 60 minutes, 7.5% 60 minutes or more (2000)

MEMPHIS (CDP). Covers a land area of 2.499 square miles and a water area of 0 square miles. Located at 38.48° N. Lat; 85.76° W. Long. Elevation is 486 feet.

Population: 365 (1990); 400 (2000); 497 (2010); 541 (2015 projected); Race: 97.6% White, 0.0% Black, 0.4% Asian, 2.0% Other, 0.0% Hispanic of any race (2010); Density: 198.9 persons per square mile (2010); Average household size: 2.59 (2010); Median age: 45.0 (2010); Males per 100 females: 101.2 (2010); Marriage status: 13.5% never married, 64.8% now married, 11.6% widowed, 10.1% divorced (2000); Foreign born: 0.0% (2000); Ancestry (includes multiple ancestries): 34.0% German, 25.7% English, 14.5% Irish, 6.5% Swedish, 4.4% United States or American (2000).

Economy: Employment by occupation: 8.3% management, 10.7% professional, 22.0% services, 20.5% sales, 0.0% farming, 11.2% construction, 27.3% production (2000).

Income: Per capita income: $25,427 (2010); Median household income: $53,049 (2010); Average household income: $66,784 (2010); Percent of households with income of $100,000 or more: 15.6% (2010); Poverty rate: 5.9% (2000).

Education: Percent of population age 25 and over with: High school diploma (including GED) or higher: 83.0% (2010); Bachelor's degree or higher: 11.1% (2010); Master's degree or higher: 4.3% (2010).

Housing: Homeownership rate: 90.1% (2010); Median home value: $141,981 (2010); Median contract rent: $414 per month (2000); Median year structure built: 1964 (2000).

Transportation: Commute to work: 96.9% car, 0.0% public transportation, 3.1% walk, 0.0% work from home (2000); Travel time to work: 24.5% less than 15 minutes, 43.4% 15 to 30 minutes, 23.5% 30 to 45 minutes, 8.7% 45 to 60 minutes, 0.0% 60 minutes or more (2000)

NABB (unincorporated postal area, zip code 47147). Covers a land area of 32.001 square miles and a water area of 0.006 square miles. Located at 38.59° N. Lat; 85.53° W. Long. Elevation is 699 feet.

Population: 1,062 (2000); Race: 96.7% White, 2.2% Black, 0.0% Asian, 1.1% Other, 1.1% Hispanic of any race (2000); Density: 33.2 persons per square mile (2000); Age: 27.0% under 18, 9.4% over 64 (2000); Marriage status: 18.5% never married, 65.9% now married, 7.4% widowed, 8.2% divorced (2000); Foreign born: 0.0% (2000); Ancestry (includes multiple ancestries): 25.5% German, 16.0% United States or American, 10.3% English, 10.1% Irish, 5.9% Other groups (2000).

Economy: Employment by occupation: 6.3% management, 12.5% professional, 10.8% services, 30.9% sales, 0.0% farming, 12.0% construction, 27.6% production (2000).

Income: Per capita income: $17,847 (2000); Median household income: $43,958 (2000); Poverty rate: 6.9% (2000).

Education: Percent of population age 25 and over with: High school diploma (including GED) or higher: 86.3% (2000); Bachelor's degree or higher: 7.1% (2000).

Housing: Homeownership rate: 88.1% (2000); Median home value: $73,100 (2000); Median contract rent: $309 per month (2000); Median year structure built: 1958 (2000).

Transportation: Commute to work: 97.6% car, 0.0% public transportation, 0.0% walk, 1.7% work from home (2000); Travel time to work: 12.5% less than 15 minutes, 19.4% 15 to 30 minutes, 37.2% 30 to 45 minutes, 15.6% 45 to 60 minutes, 15.3% 60 minutes or more (2000)

NEW WASHINGTON (CDP). Aka New Otto. Covers a land area of 5.221 square miles and a water area of 0 square miles. Located at 38.56° N. Lat; 85.54° W. Long. Elevation is 719 feet.

Population: 581 (1990); 547 (2000); 656 (2010); 705 (2015 projected); Race: 99.4% White, 0.6% Black, 0.0% Asian, 0.0% Other, 0.0% Hispanic of any race (2010); Density: 125.7 persons per square mile (2010);

Average household size: 2.30 (2010); Median age: 40.1 (2010); Males per 100 females: 86.4 (2010); Marriage status: 18.2% never married, 68.5% now married, 6.0% widowed, 7.3% divorced (2000); Foreign born: 0.0% (2000); Ancestry (includes multiple ancestries): 30.4% German, 17.7% Irish, 15.5% English, 10.6% United States or American, 8.2% Dutch (2000).

Economy: Employment by occupation: 5.5% management, 12.4% professional, 13.4% services, 37.1% sales, 0.0% farming, 12.4% construction, 19.2% production (2000).

Income: Per capita income: $22,720 (2010); Median household income: $41,667 (2010); Average household income: $52,819 (2010); Percent of households with income of $100,000 or more: 12.4% (2010); Poverty rate: 8.2% (2000).

Education: Percent of population age 25 and over with: High school diploma (including GED) or higher: 88.2% (2010); Bachelor's degree or higher: 19.3% (2010); Master's degree or higher: 4.1% (2010).

School District(s)

Greater Clark County Schools (PK-12)
    2008-09 Enrollment: 10,997 . . . . (812) 283-0701

Housing: Homeownership rate: 79.1% (2010); Median home value: $102,155 (2010); Median contract rent: $316 per month (2000); Median year structure built: 1952 (2000).

Transportation: Commute to work: 91.6% car, 0.0% public transportation, 2.1% walk, 4.9% work from home (2000); Travel time to work: 25.1% less than 15 minutes, 14.4% 15 to 30 minutes, 41.3% 30 to 45 minutes, 14.0% 45 to 60 minutes, 5.2% 60 minutes or more (2000)

OAK PARK (CDP).

Covers a land area of 2.234 square miles and a water area of 0.009 square miles. Located at 38.30° N. Lat; 85.69° W. Long. Elevation is 459 feet.

Population: 5,606 (1990); 5,379 (2000); 5,128 (2010); 5,166 (2015 projected); Race: 85.5% White, 11.8% Black, 0.5% Asian, 2.1% Other, 1.0% Hispanic of any race (2010); Density: 2,295.4 persons per square mile (2010); Average household size: 2.48 (2010); Median age: 38.4 (2010); Males per 100 females: 95.4 (2010); Marriage status: 21.0% never married, 63.9% now married, 5.9% widowed, 9.1% divorced (2000); Foreign born: 1.3% (2000); Ancestry (includes multiple ancestries): 25.8% German, 14.7% United States or American, 14.1% Irish, 12.8% Other groups, 10.4% English (2000).

Economy: Employment by occupation: 12.1% management, 21.2% professional, 14.4% services, 26.2% sales, 0.0% farming, 8.4% construction, 17.6% production (2000).

Income: Per capita income: $26,494 (2010); Median household income: $60,514 (2010); Average household income: $65,644 (2010); Percent of households with income of $100,000 or more: 15.5% (2010); Poverty rate: 3.4% (2000).

Education: Percent of population age 25 and over with: High school diploma (including GED) or higher: 91.1% (2010); Bachelor's degree or higher: 25.2% (2010); Master's degree or higher: 9.2% (2010).

Housing: Homeownership rate: 81.2% (2010); Median home value: $130,781 (2010); Median contract rent: $509 per month (2000); Median year structure built: 1971 (2000).

Transportation: Commute to work: 95.3% car, 0.8% public transportation, 0.3% walk, 2.9% work from home (2000); Travel time to work: 25.1% less than 15 minutes, 53.5% 15 to 30 minutes, 16.4% 30 to 45 minutes, 2.7% 45 to 60 minutes, 2.3% 60 minutes or more (2000)

OTISCO (unincorporated postal area, zip code 47163).

Covers a land area of 20.286 square miles and a water area of 0.046 square miles. Located at 38.54° N. Lat; 85.66° W. Long. Elevation is 673 feet.

Population: 1,733 (2000); Race: 98.9% White, 0.8% Black, 0.3% Asian, 0.0% Other, 0.0% Hispanic of any race (2000); Density: 85.4 persons per square mile (2000); Age: 23.6% under 18, 11.7% over 64 (2000); Marriage status: 17.0% never married, 69.8% now married, 3.9% widowed, 9.3% divorced (2000); Foreign born: 0.4% (2000); Ancestry (includes multiple ancestries): 19.0% German, 17.1% United States or American, 12.7% English, 11.0% Irish, 5.7% Other groups (2000).

Economy: Employment by occupation: 8.1% management, 14.8% professional, 10.2% services, 27.0% sales, 0.7% farming, 15.8% construction, 23.4% production (2000).

Income: Per capita income: $18,444 (2000); Median household income: $44,653 (2000); Poverty rate: 2.7% (2000).

Education: Percent of population age 25 and over with: High school diploma (including GED) or higher: 77.9% (2000); Bachelor's degree or higher: 11.8% (2000).

Housing: Homeownership rate: 95.0% (2000); Median home value: $98,800 (2000); Median contract rent: $275 per month (2000); Median year structure built: 1981 (2000).

Transportation: Commute to work: 91.2% car, 0.0% public transportation, 1.8% walk, 5.2% work from home (2000); Travel time to work: 13.6% less than 15 minutes, 30.4% 15 to 30 minutes, 45.1% 30 to 45 minutes, 9.9% 45 to 60 minutes, 1.0% 60 minutes or more (2000)

SELLERSBURG (town).

Covers a land area of 4.005 square miles and a water area of 0.012 square miles. Located at 38.38° N. Lat; 85.75° W. Long. Elevation is 486 feet.

History: Laid out 1846.

Population: 6,023 (1990); 6,071 (2000); 6,346 (2010); 6,520 (2015 projected); Race: 97.9% White, 0.6% Black, 0.3% Asian, 1.2% Other, 1.8% Hispanic of any race (2010); Density: 1,584.4 persons per square mile (2010); Average household size: 2.39 (2010); Median age: 37.9 (2010); Males per 100 females: 92.4 (2010); Marriage status: 18.0% never married, 60.2% now married, 6.7% widowed, 15.1% divorced (2000); Foreign born: 1.2% (2000); Ancestry (includes multiple ancestries): 27.3% German, 17.9% Irish, 12.1% English, 11.7% United States or American, 8.6% Other groups (2000).

Economy: Single-family building permits issued: 4 (2009); Multi-family building permits issued: 5 (2009); Employment by occupation: 8.1% management, 13.8% professional, 14.9% services, 29.7% sales, 0.0% farming, 11.1% construction, 22.4% production (2000).

Income: Per capita income: $22,891 (2010); Median household income: $46,710 (2010); Average household income: $54,851 (2010); Percent of households with income of $100,000 or more: 10.9% (2010); Poverty rate: 5.3% (2000).

Taxes: Total city taxes per capita: $328 (2007); City property taxes per capita: $234 (2007).

Education: Percent of population age 25 and over with: High school diploma (including GED) or higher: 88.6% (2010); Bachelor's degree or higher: 18.6% (2010); Master's degree or higher: 6.4% (2010).

School District(s)

West Clark Community Schools (PK-12)
    2008-09 Enrollment: 3,987 . . . . (812) 246-3375

Two-year College(s)

Ivy Tech Community College-South Central (Public)
    Fall 2008 Enrollment: 4,195. . . . . (812) 246-3301
    2009-10 Tuition: In-state $3,090; Out-of-state $6,306

Housing: Homeownership rate: 80.0% (2010); Median home value: $111,145 (2010); Median contract rent: $392 per month (2000); Median year structure built: 1967 (2000).

Transportation: Commute to work: 97.2% car, 0.8% public transportation, 0.9% walk, 1.0% work from home (2000); Travel time to work: 29.6% less than 15 minutes, 48.8% 15 to 30 minutes, 14.9% 30 to 45 minutes, 2.2% 45 to 60 minutes, 4.4% 60 minutes or more (2000)

Additional Information Contacts

Town of Sellersburg . . . . (812) 246-7089
    http://www.sellersburg.org

UNDERWOOD (unincorporated postal area, zip code 47177).

Covers a land area of 6.332 square miles and a water area of 0.027 square miles. Located at 38.60° N. Lat; 85.76° W. Long. Elevation is 623 feet.

Population: 620 (2000); Race: 100.0% White, 0.0% Black, 0.0% Asian, 0.0% Other, 1.1% Hispanic of any race (2000); Density: 97.9 persons per square mile (2000); Age: 28.9% under 18, 14.4% over 64 (2000); Marriage status: 22.9% never married, 63.1% now married, 5.6% widowed, 8.4% divorced (2000); Foreign born: 0.0% (2000); Ancestry (includes multiple ancestries): 32.1% United States or American, 18.6% German, 16.3% English, 6.0% Other groups, 3.3% Welsh (2000).

Economy: Employment by occupation: 9.4% management, 3.4% professional, 22.1% services, 28.5% sales, 1.9% farming, 12.7% construction, 22.1% production (2000).

Income: Per capita income: $18,229 (2000); Median household income: $42,083 (2000); Poverty rate: 6.3% (2000).

Education: Percent of population age 25 and over with: High school diploma (including GED) or higher: 68.7% (2000); Bachelor's degree or higher: 6.9% (2000).

Housing: Homeownership rate: 95.1% (2000); Median home value: $76,600 (2000); Median contract rent: $175 per month (2000); Median year structure built: 1971 (2000).

Transportation: Commute to work: 100.0% car, 0.0% public transportation, 0.0% walk, 0.0% work from home (2000); Travel time to work: 13.9% less than 15 minutes, 30.9% 15 to 30 minutes, 43.2% 30 to 45 minutes, 6.9% 45 to 60 minutes, 5.0% 60 minutes or more (2000)

UTICA (town). Covers a land area of 0.434 square miles and a water area of 0 square miles. Located at 38.33° N. Lat; 85.65° W. Long. Elevation is 443 feet.
History: Laid out 1816.
Population: 651 (1990); 591 (2000); 719 (2010); 787 (2015 projected); Race: 96.5% White, 2.1% Black, 0.3% Asian, 1.1% Other, 1.3% Hispanic of any race (2010); Density: 1,656.6 persons per square mile (2010); Average household size: 2.21 (2010); Median age: 46.6 (2010); Males per 100 females: 90.7 (2010); Marriage status: 18.5% never married, 63.2% now married, 5.4% widowed, 12.9% divorced (2000); Foreign born: 0.9% (2000); Ancestry (includes multiple ancestries): 20.5% German, 17.9% United States or American, 14.7% Irish, 5.3% English, 4.8% Other groups (2000).
Economy: Single-family building permits issued: 1 (2009); Multi-family building permits issued: 0 (2009); Employment by occupation: 12.3% management, 8.6% professional, 13.3% services, 26.2% sales, 0.3% farming, 14.6% construction, 24.6% production (2000).
Income: Per capita income: $27,675 (2010); Median household income: $46,806 (2010); Average household income: $60,808 (2010); Percent of households with income of $100,000 or more: 13.8% (2010); Poverty rate: 8.1% (2000).
Taxes: Total city taxes per capita: $140 (2007); City property taxes per capita: $117 (2007).
Education: Percent of population age 25 and over with: High school diploma (including GED) or higher: 79.5% (2010); Bachelor's degree or higher: 11.4% (2010); Master's degree or higher: 4.0% (2010).
Housing: Homeownership rate: 81.8% (2010); Median home value: $107,792 (2010); Median contract rent: $456 per month (2000); Median year structure built: 1968 (2000).
Transportation: Commute to work: 93.3% car, 0.0% public transportation, 1.0% walk, 3.0% work from home (2000); Travel time to work: 11.4% less than 15 minutes, 57.8% 15 to 30 minutes, 20.4% 30 to 45 minutes, 3.5% 45 to 60 minutes, 6.9% 60 minutes or more (2000)

Clay County

Located in western Indiana; drained by the Eel River and Small Birch Creek. Covers a land area of 357.62 square miles, a water area of 2.78 square miles, and is located in the Eastern Time Zone. The county was founded in 1825. County seat is Brazil.

Clay County is part of the Terre Haute, IN Metropolitan Statistical Area. The entire metro area includes: Clay County, IN; Sullivan County, IN; Vermillion County, IN; Vigo County, IN

Population: 24,705 (1990); 26,556 (2000); 26,716 (2010); 26,617 (2015 projected); Race: 97.1% White, 0.9% Black, 0.4% Asian, 1.5% Other, 1.0% Hispanic of any race (2010); Density: 74.7 persons per square mile (2010); Average household size: 2.55 (2010); Median age: 38.3 (2010); Males per 100 females: 95.1 (2010).
Religion: Five largest groups: 8.0% The United Methodist Church, 5.4% Christian Churches and Churches of Christ, 4.1% American Baptist Churches in the USA, 3.5% Catholic Church, 3.1% United Church of Christ (2000).
Economy: Unemployment rate: 9.8% (5/2010); Total civilian labor force: 12,566 (5/2010); Leading industries: 27.8% manufacturing; 19.0% retail trade; 12.1% health care and social assistance (2008); Farms: 666 totaling 157,563 acres (2007); Companies that employ 500 or more persons: 1 (2008); Companies that employ 100 to 499 persons: 4 (2008); Companies that employ less than 100 persons: 491 (2008); Black-owned businesses: n/a (2002); Hispanic-owned businesses: n/a (2002); Asian-owned businesses: n/a (2002); Women-owned businesses: 499 (2002); Retail sales per capita: $12,009 (2010). Single-family building permits issued: 9 (2009); Multi-family building permits issued: 0 (2009).
Income: Per capita income: $20,315 (2010); Median household income: $44,251 (2010); Average household income: $52,217 (2010); Percent of households with income of $100,000 or more: 9.5% (2010); Poverty rate: 11.8% (2008); Bankruptcy rate: 8.45% (2009).
Taxes: Total county taxes per capita: $125 (2007); County property taxes per capita: $87 (2007).
Education: Percent of population age 25 and over with: High school diploma (including GED) or higher: 86.5% (2010); Bachelor's degree or higher: 15.3% (2010); Master's degree or higher: 4.7% (2010).

Housing: Homeownership rate: 77.8% (2010); Median home value: $83,959 (2010); Median contract rent: $420 per month (2006-2008 3-year est.); Median year structure built: 1964 (2006-2008 3-year est.)
Health: Birth rate: 125.5 per 10,000 population (2009); Death rate: 111.2 per 10,000 population (2009); Age-adjusted cancer mortality rate: 220.8 deaths per 100,000 population (2006); Number of physicians: 4.9 per 10,000 population (2007); Hospital beds: 9.3 per 10,000 population (2006); Hospital admissions: 351.1 per 10,000 population (2006).
Elections: 2008 Presidential election results: 43.5% Obama, 55.0% McCain, 0.0% Nader
Additional Information Contacts
Clay County Government. . . . . (812) 448-9025
  http://www.claycountyin.gov
Brazil Chamber of Commerce . . . . (812) 448-8457
  http://www.claycountychamber.org
City of Brazil. . . . . (812) 443-2221
  http://www.brazil.in.gov
Town of Clay City. . . . . (812) 939-2345
  http://www.claycity.net

Clay County Communities

BOWLING GREEN (unincorporated postal area, zip code 47833). Covers a land area of 35.048 square miles and a water area of 0 square miles. Located at 39.36° N. Lat; 86.99° W. Long. Elevation is 653 feet.
History: Bowling Green was founded in 1825 on the bluffs along the Eel River. For a time it served as the seat of Clay County.
Population: 953 (2000); Race: 94.6% White, 5.4% Black, 0.0% Asian, 0.0% Other, 0.0% Hispanic of any race (2000); Density: 27.2 persons per square mile (2000); Age: 29.3% under 18, 9.7% over 64 (2000); Marriage status: 22.0% never married, 63.8% now married, 5.3% widowed, 8.9% divorced (2000); Foreign born: 0.0% (2000); Ancestry (includes multiple ancestries): 31.2% United States or American, 18.4% German, 8.3% Irish, 4.3% Scotch-Irish, 3.4% Other groups (2000).
Economy: Employment by occupation: 8.1% management, 6.3% professional, 10.6% services, 26.3% sales, 1.8% farming, 12.6% construction, 34.3% production (2000).
Income: Per capita income: $14,218 (2000); Median household income: $38,676 (2000); Poverty rate: 15.7% (2000).
Education: Percent of population age 25 and over with: High school diploma (including GED) or higher: 71.2% (2000); Bachelor's degree or higher: 7.6% (2000).
Housing: Homeownership rate: 84.2% (2000); Median home value: $71,700 (2000); Median contract rent: $512 per month (2000); Median year structure built: 1973 (2000).
Transportation: Commute to work: 95.7% car, 0.0% public transportation, 0.0% walk, 4.3% work from home (2000); Travel time to work: 12.5% less than 15 minutes, 28.1% 15 to 30 minutes, 25.6% 30 to 45 minutes, 19.4% 45 to 60 minutes, 14.4% 60 minutes or more (2000)

BRAZIL (city). County seat. Covers a land area of 3.341 square miles and a water area of 0.028 square miles. Located at 39.52° N. Lat; 87.12° W. Long. Elevation is 656 feet.
History: Brazil's development was based on its coal mines and clay plants, which manufactured glazed building bricks and tiles. Brazil was named for the country in South America, the name suggested by resident William Stewart who had just read a magazine article about Brazil.
Population: 7,806 (1990); 8,188 (2000); 8,361 (2010); 8,399 (2015 projected); Race: 96.1% White, 1.4% Black, 0.7% Asian, 1.8% Other, 0.9% Hispanic of any race (2010); Density: 2,502.3 persons per square mile (2010); Average household size: 2.38 (2010); Median age: 36.7 (2010); Males per 100 females: 91.4 (2010); Marriage status: 20.1% never married, 55.0% now married, 10.6% widowed, 14.3% divorced (2000); Foreign born: 1.0% (2000); Ancestry (includes multiple ancestries): 21.2% United States or American, 17.4% German, 11.3% English, 10.4% Irish, 6.3% Other groups (2000).
Economy: Single-family building permits issued: 9 (2009); Multi-family building permits issued: 0 (2009); Employment by occupation: 8.6% management, 12.4% professional, 17.7% services, 21.2% sales, 0.3% farming, 9.6% construction, 30.1% production (2000).
Income: Per capita income: $17,602 (2010); Median household income: $34,863 (2010); Average household income: $42,517 (2010); Percent of households with income of $100,000 or more: 6.2% (2010); Poverty rate: 13.2% (2000).

Taxes: Total city taxes per capita: $128 (2007); City property taxes per capita: $124 (2007).

Education: Percent of population age 25 and over with: High school diploma (including GED) or higher: 81.7% (2010); Bachelor's degree or higher: 13.3% (2010); Master's degree or higher: 3.2% (2010).

School District(s)
Clay Community Schools (PK-12)
    2008-09 Enrollment: 4,573 . . . . (812) 443-4461
Housing: Homeownership rate: 64.5% (2010); Median home value: $67,655 (2010); Median contract rent: $291 per month (2000); Median year structure built: 1952 (2000).

Hospitals: St. Vincent Clay Hospital (58 beds)

Safety: Violent crime rate: 93.8 per 10,000 population; Property crime rate: 338.5 per 10,000 population (2008).

Newspapers: Brazil Times (Local news; Circulation 5,200)

Transportation: Commute to work: 94.9% car, 0.0% public transportation, 2.1% walk, 1.9% work from home (2000); Travel time to work: 42.0% less than 15 minutes, 25.0% 15 to 30 minutes, 21.4% 30 to 45 minutes, 4.9% 45 to 60 minutes, 6.8% 60 minutes or more (2000)

Additional Information Contacts
Brazil Chamber of Commerce . . . . (812) 448-8457
    http://www.claycountychamber.org
City of Brazil . . . . (812) 443-2221
    http://www.brazil.in.gov

CARBON (town). Covers a land area of 0.158 square miles and a water area of 0 square miles. Located at 39.59° N. Lat; 87.10° W. Long. Elevation is 689 feet.

Population: 350 (1990); 334 (2000); 310 (2010); 298 (2015 projected); Race: 97.4% White, 1.0% Black, 0.0% Asian, 1.6% Other, 1.3% Hispanic of any race (2010); Density: 1,957.8 persons per square mile (2010); Average household size: 2.63 (2010); Median age: 37.3 (2010); Males per 100 females: 93.8 (2010); Marriage status: 17.3% never married, 67.9% now married, 4.5% widowed, 10.3% divorced (2000); Foreign born: 2.6% (2000); Ancestry (includes multiple ancestries): 19.1% United States or American, 11.8% German, 7.9% Irish, 7.4% Other groups, 2.9% French (except Basque) (2000).

Economy: Employment by occupation: 9.9% management, 3.3% professional, 15.1% services, 19.1% sales, 2.6% farming, 12.5% construction, 37.5% production (2000).

Income: Per capita income: $18,048 (2010); Median household income: $41,346 (2010); Average household income: $47,097 (2010); Percent of households with income of $100,000 or more: 6.8% (2010); Poverty rate: 14.8% (2000).

Taxes: Total city taxes per capita: $21 (2007); City property taxes per capita: $21 (2007).

Education: Percent of population age 25 and over with: High school diploma (including GED) or higher: 86.3% (2010); Bachelor's degree or higher: 12.7% (2010); Master's degree or higher: 5.4% (2010).

Housing: Homeownership rate: 86.4% (2010); Median home value: $81,053 (2010); Median contract rent: $313 per month (2000); Median year structure built: 1954 (2000).

Transportation: Commute to work: 100.0% car, 0.0% public transportation, 0.0% walk, 0.0% work from home (2000); Travel time to work: 17.2% less than 15 minutes, 29.8% 15 to 30 minutes, 23.8% 30 to 45 minutes, 13.2% 45 to 60 minutes, 15.9% 60 minutes or more (2000)

CENTER POINT (town). Aka Centerpoint. Covers a land area of 0.740 square miles and a water area of 0.022 square miles. Located at 39.41° N. Lat; 87.07° W. Long. Elevation is 656 feet.

Population: 278 (1990); 292 (2000); 285 (2010); 283 (2015 projected); Race: 96.8% White, 0.4% Black, 0.4% Asian, 2.5% Other, 0.7% Hispanic of any race (2010); Density: 385.2 persons per square mile (2010); Average household size: 2.69 (2010); Median age: 36.5 (2010); Males per 100 females: 96.6 (2010); Marriage status: 25.1% never married, 56.3% now married, 5.6% widowed, 13.0% divorced (2000); Foreign born: 0.0% (2000); Ancestry (includes multiple ancestries): 20.8% German, 18.7% United States or American, 7.1% English, 5.3% Irish, 3.5% Scotch-Irish (2000).

Economy: Employment by occupation: 13.7% management, 21.4% professional, 20.6% services, 11.5% sales, 0.0% farming, 8.4% construction, 24.4% production (2000).

Income: Per capita income: $22,876 (2010); Median household income: $52,500 (2010); Average household income: $60,361 (2010); Percent of

households with income of $100,000 or more: 13.5% (2010); Poverty rate: 6.6% (2000).

Taxes: Total city taxes per capita: $24 (2007); City property taxes per capita: $24 (2007).

Education: Percent of population age 25 and over with: High school diploma (including GED) or higher: 93.0% (2010); Bachelor's degree or higher: 16.1% (2010); Master's degree or higher: 2.2% (2010).

Housing: Homeownership rate: 83.7% (2010); Median home value: $96,875 (2010); Median contract rent: $242 per month (2000); Median year structure built: 1945 (2000).

Transportation: Commute to work: 92.4% car, 0.0% public transportation, 2.3% walk, 5.3% work from home (2000); Travel time to work: 16.9% less than 15 minutes, 43.5% 15 to 30 minutes, 21.8% 30 to 45 minutes, 4.0% 45 to 60 minutes, 13.7% 60 minutes or more (2000)

CLAY CITY (town). Covers a land area of 0.534 square miles and a water area of 0 square miles. Located at 39.27° N. Lat; 87.11° W. Long. Elevation is 594 feet.

History: Settled 1873, incorporated 1888.

Population: 929 (1990); 1,019 (2000); 925 (2010); 877 (2015 projected); Race: 98.1% White, 0.0% Black, 0.0% Asian, 1.9% Other, 2.3% Hispanic of any race (2010); Density: 1,731.0 persons per square mile (2010); Average household size: 2.31 (2010); Median age: 37.7 (2010); Males per 100 females: 89.9 (2010); Marriage status: 16.2% never married, 61.2% now married, 11.3% widowed, 11.2% divorced (2000); Foreign born: 0.0% (2000); Ancestry (includes multiple ancestries): 22.1% United States or American, 15.6% German, 8.6% Irish, 7.6% Other groups, 6.6% English (2000).

Economy: Employment by occupation: 6.4% management, 11.3% professional, 16.2% services, 27.0% sales, 0.4% farming, 16.4% construction, 22.3% production (2000).

Income: Per capita income: $19,320 (2010); Median household income: $39,113 (2010); Average household income: $44,532 (2010); Percent of households with income of $100,000 or more: 7.0% (2010); Poverty rate: 8.9% (2000).

Taxes: Total city taxes per capita: $85 (2007); City property taxes per capita: $84 (2007).

Education: Percent of population age 25 and over with: High school diploma (including GED) or higher: 83.6% (2010); Bachelor's degree or higher: 14.0% (2010); Master's degree or higher: 2.8% (2010).

School District(s)
Clay Community Schools (PK-12)
    2008-09 Enrollment: 4,573 . . . . (812) 443-4461
Housing: Homeownership rate: 73.6% (2010); Median home value: $68,393 (2010); Median contract rent: $232 per month (2000); Median year structure built: 1949 (2000).

Newspapers: Clay City News (Local news; Circulation 2,000)

Transportation: Commute to work: 93.5% car, 0.0% public transportation, 3.1% walk, 2.6% work from home (2000); Travel time to work: 25.7% less than 15 minutes, 15.4% 15 to 30 minutes, 33.6% 30 to 45 minutes, 17.4% 45 to 60 minutes, 7.8% 60 minutes or more (2000)

Additional Information Contacts
Town of Clay City . . . . (812) 939-2345
    http://www.claycity.net

CORY (unincorporated postal area, zip code 47846). Covers a land area of 34.372 square miles and a water area of 0.146 square miles. Located at 39.37° N. Lat; 87.20° W. Long. Elevation is 630 feet.

Population: 725 (2000); Race: 97.1% White, 0.0% Black, 0.8% Asian, 2.1% Other, 0.0% Hispanic of any race (2000); Density: 21.1 persons per square mile (2000); Age: 27.0% under 18, 18.2% over 64 (2000); Marriage status: 17.8% never married, 61.9% now married, 10.3% widowed, 10.0% divorced (2000); Foreign born: 0.8% (2000); Ancestry (includes multiple ancestries): 19.0% German, 17.1% United States or American, 13.2% English, 11.9% Irish, 7.6% Other groups (2000).

Economy: Employment by occupation: 4.8% management, 8.7% professional, 17.0% services, 33.8% sales, 1.3% farming, 19.3% construction, 15.1% production (2000).

Income: Per capita income: $15,040 (2000); Median household income: $35,625 (2000); Poverty rate: 0.9% (2000).

Education: Percent of population age 25 and over with: High school diploma (including GED) or higher: 96.7% (2000); Bachelor's degree or higher: 8.0% (2000).

Housing: Homeownership rate: 91.4% (2000); Median home value: $93,300 (2000); Median contract rent: $325 per month (2000); Median year structure built: 1970 (2000).
Transportation: Commute to work: 91.0% car, 1.9% public transportation, 0.0% walk, 7.1% work from home (2000); Travel time to work: 8.7% less than 15 minutes, 48.8% 15 to 30 minutes, 28.4% 30 to 45 minutes, 2.1% 45 to 60 minutes, 12.1% 60 minutes or more (2000)

HARMONY (town). Covers a land area of 0.754 square miles and a water area of 0 square miles. Located at 39.53° N. Lat; 87.07° W. Long. Elevation is 719 feet.

History: Harmony was once a prosperous coal-mining town.
Population: 645 (1990); 589 (2000); 547 (2010); 527 (2015 projected); Race: 97.4% White, 0.0% Black, 0.9% Asian, 1.6% Other, 0.2% Hispanic of any race (2010); Density: 725.3 persons per square mile (2010); Average household size: 2.48 (2010); Median age: 39.1 (2010); Males per 100 females: 89.3 (2010); Marriage status: 19.3% never married, 53.4% now married, 11.1% widowed, 16.1% divorced (2000); Foreign born: 0.0% (2000); Ancestry (includes multiple ancestries): 16.6% United States or American, 14.7% German, 9.7% Irish, 9.3% English, 3.7% Other groups (2000).
Economy: Single-family building permits issued: 0 (2009); Multi-family building permits issued: 0 (2009); Employment by occupation: 7.0% management, 12.2% professional, 16.8% services, 29.0% sales, 1.0% farming, 6.6% construction, 27.3% production (2000).
Income: Per capita income: $23,448 (2010); Median household income: $49,477 (2010); Average household income: $56,516 (2010); Percent of households with income of $100,000 or more: 13.1% (2010); Poverty rate: 8.2% (2000).
Taxes: Total city taxes per capita: $56 (2007); City property taxes per capita: $51 (2007).
Education: Percent of population age 25 and over with: High school diploma (including GED) or higher: 89.2% (2010); Bachelor's degree or higher: 16.1% (2010); Master's degree or higher: 5.5% (2010).
Housing: Homeownership rate: 79.2% (2010); Median home value: $85,278 (2010); Median contract rent: $317 per month (2000); Median year structure built: 1957 (2000).
Transportation: Commute to work: 95.8% car, 0.0% public transportation, 1.4% walk, 2.8% work from home (2000); Travel time to work: 46.5% less than 15 minutes, 25.1% 15 to 30 minutes, 21.5% 30 to 45 minutes, 3.3% 45 to 60 minutes, 3.6% 60 minutes or more (2000)

KNIGHTSVILLE (town). Covers a land area of 1.020 square miles and a water area of 0 square miles. Located at 39.52° N. Lat; 87.09° W. Long. Elevation is 653 feet.

Population: 740 (1990); 624 (2000); 619 (2010); 612 (2015 projected); Race: 96.9% White, 1.5% Black, 0.8% Asian, 0.8% Other, 0.2% Hispanic of any race (2010); Density: 606.6 persons per square mile (2010); Average household size: 2.44 (2010); Median age: 43.5 (2010); Males per 100 females: 88.1 (2010); Marriage status: 16.6% never married, 70.8% now married, 6.1% widowed, 6.5% divorced (2000); Foreign born: 0.0% (2000); Ancestry (includes multiple ancestries): 24.4% United States or American, 12.5% English, 12.5% German, 4.7% Irish, 3.8% Other groups (2000).
Economy: Employment by occupation: 9.2% management, 8.4% professional, 11.9% services, 27.6% sales, 1.1% farming, 9.2% construction, 32.6% production (2000).
Income: Per capita income: $23,168 (2010); Median household income: $48,214 (2010); Average household income: $57,633 (2010); Percent of households with income of $100,000 or more: 14.3% (2010); Poverty rate: 5.0% (2000).
Taxes: Total city taxes per capita: $36 (2007); City property taxes per capita: $36 (2007).
Education: Percent of population age 25 and over with: High school diploma (including GED) or higher: 84.1% (2010); Bachelor's degree or higher: 14.6% (2010); Master's degree or higher: 5.8% (2010).
Housing: Homeownership rate: 81.1% (2010); Median home value: $80,690 (2010); Median contract rent: $254 per month (2000); Median year structure built: 1949 (2000).
Transportation: Commute to work: 94.5% car, 0.0% public transportation, 2.7% walk, 2.0% work from home (2000); Travel time to work: 50.2% less than 15 minutes, 25.9% 15 to 30 minutes, 15.1% 30 to 45 minutes, 1.6% 45 to 60 minutes, 7.2% 60 minutes or more (2000)

POLAND (unincorporated postal area, zip code 47868). Covers a land area of 65.362 square miles and a water area of 0.173 square miles. Located at 39.41° N. Lat; 86.90° W. Long. Elevation is 696 feet.

Population: 3,212 (2000); Race: 98.6% White, 0.0% Black, 0.0% Asian, 1.4% Other, 0.0% Hispanic of any race (2000); Density: 49.1 persons per square mile (2000); Age: 26.1% under 18, 14.2% over 64 (2000); Marriage status: 15.2% never married, 67.0% now married, 5.1% widowed, 12.6% divorced (2000); Foreign born: 0.3% (2000); Ancestry (includes multiple ancestries): 19.4% German, 18.6% United States or American, 11.0% Other groups, 10.6% Irish, 7.3% English (2000).
Economy: Employment by occupation: 8.6% management, 10.2% professional, 10.8% services, 23.3% sales, 0.5% farming, 16.7% construction, 29.9% production (2000).
Income: Per capita income: $16,592 (2000); Median household income: $36,321 (2000); Poverty rate: 13.2% (2000).
Education: Percent of population age 25 and over with: High school diploma (including GED) or higher: 74.3% (2000); Bachelor's degree or higher: 7.2% (2000).
Housing: Homeownership rate: 89.2% (2000); Median home value: $79,600 (2000); Median contract rent: $363 per month (2000); Median year structure built: 1976 (2000).
Transportation: Commute to work: 95.9% car, 0.0% public transportation, 0.0% walk, 2.7% work from home (2000); Travel time to work: 6.5% less than 15 minutes, 24.0% 15 to 30 minutes, 23.3% 30 to 45 minutes, 16.7% 45 to 60 minutes, 29.5% 60 minutes or more (2000)

STAUNTON (town). Covers a land area of 0.341 square miles and a water area of 0 square miles. Located at 39.48° N. Lat; 87.18° W. Long. Elevation is 646 feet.

History: Founded 1851.
Population: 592 (1990); 550 (2000); 545 (2010); 540 (2015 projected); Race: 98.2% White, 0.0% Black, 0.2% Asian, 1.7% Other, 1.3% Hispanic of any race (2010); Density: 1,599.3 persons per square mile (2010); Average household size: 2.79 (2010); Median age: 38.1 (2010); Males per 100 females: 98.2 (2010); Marriage status: 21.1% never married, 64.9% now married, 4.2% widowed, 9.8% divorced (2000); Foreign born: 0.5% (2000); Ancestry (includes multiple ancestries): 26.8% German, 20.6% United States or American, 9.9% Irish, 9.0% Other groups, 7.5% English (2000).
Economy: Employment by occupation: 1.9% management, 10.5% professional, 16.0% services, 28.0% sales, 1.6% farming, 7.8% construction, 34.2% production (2000).
Income: Per capita income: $22,622 (2010); Median household income: $58,894 (2010); Average household income: $61,910 (2010); Percent of households with income of $100,000 or more: 13.8% (2010); Poverty rate: 6.5% (2000).
Taxes: Total city taxes per capita: $29 (2007); City property taxes per capita: $27 (2007).
Education: Percent of population age 25 and over with: High school diploma (including GED) or higher: 91.3% (2010); Bachelor's degree or higher: 21.7% (2010); Master's degree or higher: 7.6% (2010).
Housing: Homeownership rate: 86.2% (2010); Median home value: $98,000 (2010); Median contract rent: $368 per month (2000); Median year structure built: 1963 (2000).
Transportation: Commute to work: 95.3% car, 0.0% public transportation, 2.0% walk, 1.2% work from home (2000); Travel time to work: 25.2% less than 15 minutes, 37.6% 15 to 30 minutes, 22.0% 30 to 45 minutes, 7.2% 45 to 60 minutes, 8.0% 60 minutes or more (2000)

Clinton County

Located in central Indiana; drained by Sugar Creek. Covers a land area of 405.10 square miles, a water area of 0.18 square miles, and is located in the Eastern Time Zone. The county was founded in 1830. County seat is Frankfort.

Clinton County is part of the Frankfort, IN Micropolitan Statistical Area. The entire metro area includes: Clinton County, IN

Weather Station: Frankfort Disposal Plant   Elevation: 833 feet

	Jan	Feb	Mar	Apr	May	Jun	Jul	Aug	Sep	Oct	Nov	Dec
High	32	37	49	61	72	81	84	82	77	64	50	38
Low	17	20	30	39	50	59	63	61	54	42	33	23
Precip	2.0	2.0	3.2	3.7	4.1	4.3	4.2	4.0	3.0	2.9	3.4	2.9
Snow	8.0	5.8	3.5	0.6	tr	0.0	0.0	0.0	0.0	0.4	1.1	6.2

High and Low temperatures in degrees Fahrenheit; Precipitation and Snow in inches

Population: 30,974 (1990); 33,866 (2000); 34,239 (2010); 34,328 (2015 projected); Race: 89.3% White, 0.6% Black, 0.3% Asian, 9.8% Other, 14.5% Hispanic of any race (2010); Density: 84.5 persons per square mile (2010); Average household size: 2.62 (2010); Median age: 36.9 (2010); Males per 100 females: 97.1 (2010).
Religion: Five largest groups: 7.3% The United Methodist Church, 6.5% Christian Churches and Churches of Christ, 4.2% Catholic Church, 3.1% Presbyterian Church (U.S.A.), 3.0% Southern Baptist Convention (2000).
Economy: Unemployment rate: 10.1% (5/2010); Total civilian labor force: 16,395 (5/2010); Leading industries: 39.5% manufacturing; 12.9% health care and social assistance; 11.4% retail trade (2008); Farms: 693 totaling 255,314 acres (2007); Companies that employ 500 or more persons: 1 (2008); Companies that employ 100 to 499 persons: 18 (2008); Companies that employ less than 100 persons: 627 (2008); Black-owned businesses: n/a (2002); Hispanic-owned businesses: n/a (2002); Asian-owned businesses: n/a (2002); Women-owned businesses: 482 (2002); Retail sales per capita: $8,477 (2010). Single-family building permits issued: 16 (2009); Multi-family building permits issued: 0 (2009).
Income: Per capita income: $21,233 (2010); Median household income: $47,301 (2010); Average household income: $55,432 (2010); Percent of households with income of $100,000 or more: 11.4% (2010); Poverty rate: 14.5% (2008); Bankruptcy rate: 6.69% (2009).
Taxes: Total county taxes per capita: $225 (2007); County property taxes per capita: $118 (2007).
Education: Percent of population age 25 and over with: High school diploma (including GED) or higher: 79.8% (2010); Bachelor's degree or higher: 13.3% (2010); Master's degree or higher: 4.1% (2010).
Housing: Homeownership rate: 73.5% (2010); Median home value: $99,055 (2010); Median contract rent: $478 per month (2006-2008 3-year est.); Median year structure built: 1950 (2006-2008 3-year est.)
Health: Birth rate: 150.4 per 10,000 population (2009); Death rate: 98.1 per 10,000 population (2009); Age-adjusted cancer mortality rate: 211.2 deaths per 100,000 population (2006); Number of physicians: 5.3 per 10,000 population (2007); Hospital beds: 7.4 per 10,000 population (2006); Hospital admissions: 335.5 per 10,000 population (2006).
Elections: 2008 Presidential election results: 42.8% Obama, 55.8% McCain, 0.0% Nader
Additional Information Contacts
Clinton County Government . . . . (765) 654-5715
   http://www.cityoffrankfort.net
City of Frankfort . . . . (765) 654-5715
   http://www.cityoffrankfort.net
Clinton County Chamber of Commerce . . . . (765) 654-5507
   http://www.ccinchamber.org

Clinton County Communities

COLFAX (town). Covers a land area of 0.362 square miles and a water area of 0 square miles. Located at 40.19° N. Lat; 86.66° W. Long. Elevation is 840 feet.
Population: 757 (1990); 768 (2000); 762 (2010); 760 (2015 projected); Race: 98.4% White, 0.0% Black, 0.1% Asian, 1.4% Other, 3.7% Hispanic of any race (2010); Density: 2,102.3 persons per square mile (2010); Average household size: 2.64 (2010); Median age: 35.2 (2010); Males per 100 females: 99.5 (2010); Marriage status: 22.1% never married, 63.0% now married, 7.4% widowed, 7.5% divorced (2000); Foreign born: 0.3% (2000); Ancestry (includes multiple ancestries): 22.7% German, 12.2% Other groups, 11.2% Irish, 9.8% United States or American, 8.8% English (2000).
Economy: Employment by occupation: 3.6% management, 11.4% professional, 17.8% services, 21.4% sales, 0.0% farming, 10.2% construction, 35.5% production (2000).
Income: Per capita income: $19,833 (2010); Median household income: $47,450 (2010); Average household income: $52,223 (2010); Percent of households with income of $100,000 or more: 8.0% (2010); Poverty rate: 7.8% (2000).
Taxes: Total city taxes per capita: $222 (2007); City property taxes per capita: $187 (2007).
Education: Percent of population age 25 and over with: High school diploma (including GED) or higher: 81.8% (2010); Bachelor's degree or higher: 10.0% (2010); Master's degree or higher: 1.1% (2010).
Housing: Homeownership rate: 78.9% (2010); Median home value: $89,275 (2010); Median contract rent: $229 per month (2000); Median year structure built: before 1940 (2000).

Transportation: Commute to work: 92.3% car, 0.6% public transportation, 2.5% walk, 4.6% work from home (2000); Travel time to work: 15.8% less than 15 minutes, 46.8% 15 to 30 minutes, 25.2% 30 to 45 minutes, 7.4% 45 to 60 minutes, 4.8% 60 minutes or more (2000)

FOREST (unincorporated postal area, zip code 46039). Covers a land area of 27.750 square miles and a water area of 0.014 square miles. Located at 40.36° N. Lat; 86.30° W. Long. Elevation is 879 feet.
Population: 839 (2000); Race: 100.0% White, 0.0% Black, 0.0% Asian, 0.0% Other, 0.0% Hispanic of any race (2000); Density: 30.2 persons per square mile (2000); Age: 22.5% under 18, 15.8% over 64 (2000); Marriage status: 16.5% never married, 63.8% now married, 8.2% widowed, 11.4% divorced (2000); Foreign born: 0.0% (2000); Ancestry (includes multiple ancestries): 25.1% United States or American, 18.7% German, 18.1% Irish, 14.4% English, 5.2% Scotch-Irish (2000).
Economy: Employment by occupation: 5.3% management, 22.1% professional, 5.6% services, 15.7% sales, 4.8% farming, 13.7% construction, 32.7% production (2000).
Income: Per capita income: $22,456 (2000); Median household income: $51,625 (2000); Poverty rate: 10.7% (2000).
Education: Percent of population age 25 and over with: High school diploma (including GED) or higher: 92.1% (2000); Bachelor's degree or higher: 13.4% (2000).
Housing: Homeownership rate: 93.5% (2000); Median home value: $86,700 (2000); Median contract rent: $363 per month (2000); Median year structure built: before 1940 (2000).
Transportation: Commute to work: 96.8% car, 0.0% public transportation, 1.3% walk, 0.0% work from home (2000); Travel time to work: 16.8% less than 15 minutes, 53.9% 15 to 30 minutes, 22.4% 30 to 45 minutes, 1.8% 45 to 60 minutes, 5.0% 60 minutes or more (2000)

FRANKFORT (city). County seat. Covers a land area of 5.142 square miles and a water area of 0 square miles. Located at 40.28° N. Lat; 86.51° W. Long. Elevation is 850 feet.
History: Frankfort was named for Frankfurt am Main, Germany, the home of the grandfather of the Pence brothers who owned the land on which the city was founded. Frankfort developed as the county seat of Clinton County.
Population: 15,154 (1990); 16,662 (2000); 16,506 (2010); 16,387 (2015 projected); Race: 81.5% White, 0.8% Black, 0.3% Asian, 17.4% Other, 26.9% Hispanic of any race (2010); Density: 3,210.2 persons per square mile (2010); Average household size: 2.58 (2010); Median age: 35.2 (2010); Males per 100 females: 96.0 (2010); Marriage status: 22.6% never married, 57.2% now married, 9.3% widowed, 10.9% divorced (2000); Foreign born: 9.0% (2000); Ancestry (includes multiple ancestries): 17.9% Other groups, 16.0% German, 15.0% United States or American, 10.9% Irish, 7.6% English (2000).
Economy: Single-family building permits issued: 2 (2009); Multi-family building permits issued: 0 (2009); Employment by occupation: 6.7% management, 6.5% professional, 12.9% services, 20.8% sales, 1.9% farming, 11.3% construction, 39.9% production (2000).
Income: Per capita income: $17,558 (2010); Median household income: $38,476 (2010); Average household income: $44,693 (2010); Percent of households with income of $100,000 or more: 5.6% (2010); Poverty rate: 11.7% (2000).
Taxes: Total city taxes per capita: $192 (2007); City property taxes per capita: $171 (2007).
Education: Percent of population age 25 and over with: High school diploma (including GED) or higher: 72.4% (2010); Bachelor's degree or higher: 10.3% (2010); Master's degree or higher: 3.2% (2010).
School District(s)
Clinton Prairie School Corp (KG-12)
   2008-09 Enrollment: 999 . . . . (765) 659-1339
Community Schools Of Frankfort (PK-12)
   2008-09 Enrollment: 3,173 . . . . (765) 654-5585
Housing: Homeownership rate: 63.4% (2010); Median home value: $88,126 (2010); Median contract rent: $422 per month (2000); Median year structure built: 1951 (2000).
Hospitals: St. Vincent Frankfort Hospital (25 beds)
Newspapers: Frankfort Times (Local news; Circulation 8,300); The Times (Local news; Circulation 6,400)
Transportation: Commute to work: 93.2% car, 1.0% public transportation, 1.3% walk, 1.4% work from home (2000); Travel time to work: 60.5% less than 15 minutes, 14.1% 15 to 30 minutes, 17.8% 30 to 45 minutes, 6.2% 45 to 60 minutes, 1.5% 60 minutes or more (2000)

Additional Information Contacts
City of Frankfort . . . . (765) 654-5715
   http://www.cityoffrankfort.net
Clinton County Chamber of Commerce . . . . (765) 654-5507
   http://www.ccinchamber.org

KIRKLIN (town).

Covers a land area of 0.323 square miles and a water area of 0 square miles. Located at 40.19° N. Lat; 86.36° W. Long. Elevation is 919 feet.

History: Kirklin was established at the junction of the Michigan Road with a state road. Nathan Kirklin bought the land here in 1828 and built a tavern.

Population: 707 (1990); 766 (2000); 752 (2010); 741 (2015 projected); Race: 92.8% White, 1.5% Black, 0.7% Asian, 5.1% Other, 4.4% Hispanic of any race (2010); Density: 2,327.8 persons per square mile (2010); Average household size: 2.57 (2010); Median age: 36.7 (2010); Males per 100 females: 106.0 (2010); Marriage status: 19.6% never married, 55.9% now married, 7.8% widowed, 16.6% divorced (2000); Foreign born: 1.5% (2000); Ancestry (includes multiple ancestries): 20.6% German, 14.8% Irish, 12.8% United States or American, 10.7% Other groups, 3.7% English (2000).

Economy: Employment by occupation: 5.8% management, 12.3% professional, 9.9% services, 23.7% sales, 1.2% farming, 21.3% construction, 25.7% production (2000).

Income: Per capita income: $25,079 (2010); Median household income: $57,344 (2010); Average household income: $64,334 (2010); Percent of households with income of $100,000 or more: 17.7% (2010); Poverty rate: 12.0% (2000).

Taxes: Total city taxes per capita: $140 (2007); City property taxes per capita: $119 (2007).

Education: Percent of population age 25 and over with: High school diploma (including GED) or higher: 76.5% (2010); Bachelor's degree or higher: 12.4% (2010); Master's degree or higher: 5.7% (2010).

Housing: Homeownership rate: 80.2% (2010); Median home value: $90,656 (2010); Median contract rent: $435 per month (2000); Median year structure built: 1951 (2000).

Transportation: Commute to work: 95.5% car, 0.0% public transportation, 1.8% walk, 2.7% work from home (2000); Travel time to work: 14.7% less than 15 minutes, 28.7% 15 to 30 minutes, 29.7% 30 to 45 minutes, 14.1% 45 to 60 minutes, 12.8% 60 minutes or more (2000)

MICHIGANTOWN (town).

Covers a land area of 0.265 square miles and a water area of 0 square miles. Located at 40.32° N. Lat; 86.39° W. Long. Elevation is 876 feet.

History: Michigantown was founded in 1830 and named for the Michigan Road, for which it served as a stage stop.

Population: 471 (1990); 406 (2000); 360 (2010); 342 (2015 projected); Race: 98.3% White, 0.0% Black, 0.3% Asian, 1.4% Other, 1.4% Hispanic of any race (2010); Density: 1,359.9 persons per square mile (2010); Average household size: 2.67 (2010); Median age: 38.0 (2010); Males per 100 females: 93.5 (2010); Marriage status: 19.7% never married, 60.0% now married, 11.0% widowed, 9.3% divorced (2000); Foreign born: 0.5% (2000); Ancestry (includes multiple ancestries): 22.3% United States or American, 19.5% German, 13.5% Irish, 10.7% French (except Basque), 9.5% Other groups (2000).

Economy: Single-family building permits issued: 0 (2009); Multi-family building permits issued: 0 (2009); Employment by occupation: 7.2% management, 11.3% professional, 22.7% services, 10.8% sales, 1.5% farming, 10.8% construction, 35.6% production (2000).

Income: Per capita income: $25,627 (2010); Median household income: $51,250 (2010); Average household income: $66,111 (2010); Percent of households with income of $100,000 or more: 15.6% (2010); Poverty rate: 5.0% (2000).

Taxes: Total city taxes per capita: $118 (2007); City property taxes per capita: $98 (2007).

Education: Percent of population age 25 and over with: High school diploma (including GED) or higher: 90.9% (2010); Bachelor's degree or higher: 11.9% (2010); Master's degree or higher: 4.1% (2010).

School District(s)

Clinton Central School Corp (KG-12)
   2008-09 Enrollment: 1,044 . . . . (765) 249-2515

Housing: Homeownership rate: 75.6% (2010); Median home value: $92,727 (2010); Median contract rent: $392 per month (2000); Median year structure built: 1941 (2000).

Transportation: Commute to work: 87.3% car, 0.0% public transportation, 10.6% walk, 2.1% work from home (2000); Travel time to work: 30.3% less than 15 minutes, 41.1% 15 to 30 minutes, 17.3% 30 to 45 minutes, 7.6% 45 to 60 minutes, 3.8% 60 minutes or more (2000)

MULBERRY (town).

Covers a land area of 0.588 square miles and a water area of 0 square miles. Located at 40.34° N. Lat; 86.66° W. Long. Elevation is 781 feet.

History: Laid out 1858.

Population: 1,362 (1990); 1,387 (2000); 1,419 (2010); 1,436 (2015 projected); Race: 98.4% White, 0.4% Black, 0.1% Asian, 1.1% Other, 1.1% Hispanic of any race (2010); Density: 2,414.7 persons per square mile (2010); Average household size: 2.57 (2010); Median age: 42.3 (2010); Males per 100 females: 88.9 (2010); Marriage status: 17.5% never married, 61.0% now married, 12.7% widowed, 8.8% divorced (2000); Foreign born: 1.2% (2000); Ancestry (includes multiple ancestries): 20.6% German, 13.7% United States or American, 9.5% Irish, 8.9% English, 6.6% Dutch (2000).

Economy: Employment by occupation: 7.3% management, 16.0% professional, 13.7% services, 22.9% sales, 1.3% farming, 9.5% construction, 29.4% production (2000).

Income: Per capita income: $22,964 (2010); Median household income: $56,690 (2010); Average household income: $60,860 (2010); Percent of households with income of $100,000 or more: 12.6% (2010); Poverty rate: 5.0% (2000).

Taxes: Total city taxes per capita: $84 (2007); City property taxes per capita: $74 (2007).

Education: Percent of population age 25 and over with: High school diploma (including GED) or higher: 85.3% (2010); Bachelor's degree or higher: 14.4% (2010); Master's degree or higher: 5.1% (2010).

Housing: Homeownership rate: 78.4% (2010); Median home value: $118,478 (2010); Median contract rent: $381 per month (2000); Median year structure built: before 1940 (2000).

Transportation: Commute to work: 95.6% car, 0.0% public transportation, 2.0% walk, 2.1% work from home (2000); Travel time to work: 17.9% less than 15 minutes, 59.0% 15 to 30 minutes, 17.9% 30 to 45 minutes, 3.3% 45 to 60 minutes, 1.8% 60 minutes or more (2000)

ROSSVILLE (town).

Covers a land area of 0.516 square miles and a water area of 0 square miles. Located at 40.41° N. Lat; 86.59° W. Long. Elevation is 725 feet.

History: Laid out 1834.

Population: 1,188 (1990); 1,513 (2000); 1,520 (2010); 1,516 (2015 projected); Race: 97.4% White, 1.1% Black, 0.4% Asian, 1.1% Other, 0.7% Hispanic of any race (2010); Density: 2,943.3 persons per square mile (2010); Average household size: 2.64 (2010); Median age: 38.5 (2010); Males per 100 females: 87.4 (2010); Marriage status: 17.6% never married, 69.5% now married, 4.9% widowed, 8.0% divorced (2000); Foreign born: 0.2% (2000); Ancestry (includes multiple ancestries): 23.2% German, 15.6% United States or American, 13.3% English, 9.9% Irish, 4.0% Other groups (2000).

Economy: Employment by occupation: 13.5% management, 13.4% professional, 13.4% services, 24.7% sales, 0.3% farming, 12.4% construction, 22.4% production (2000).

Income: Per capita income: $24,443 (2010); Median household income: $56,811 (2010); Average household income: $62,445 (2010); Percent of households with income of $100,000 or more: 12.7% (2010); Poverty rate: 3.7% (2000).

Taxes: Total city taxes per capita: $92 (2007); City property taxes per capita: $84 (2007).

Education: Percent of population age 25 and over with: High school diploma (including GED) or higher: 84.1% (2010); Bachelor's degree or higher: 15.1% (2010); Master's degree or higher: 4.9% (2010).

School District(s)

Rossville Con School District (KG-12)
   2008-09 Enrollment: 1,038 . . . . (765) 379-2990

Housing: Homeownership rate: 83.6% (2010); Median home value: $117,576 (2010); Median contract rent: $417 per month (2000); Median year structure built: 1964 (2000).

Transportation: Commute to work: 94.4% car, 0.0% public transportation, 1.5% walk, 3.9% work from home (2000); Travel time to work: 17.5% less than 15 minutes, 46.5% 15 to 30 minutes, 29.4% 30 to 45 minutes, 3.6% 45 to 60 minutes, 3.1% 60 minutes or more (2000)

Crawford County

Located in southern Indiana; bounded on the south by the Ohio River and the Kentucky border; drained by the Blue and Little Blue Rivers. Covers a land area of 305.68 square miles, a water area of 3.17 square miles, and is located in the Eastern Time Zone. The county was founded in 1818. County seat is English.

Weather Station: English 4 S Elevation: 508 feet

	Jan	Feb	Mar	Apr	May	Jun	Jul	Aug	Sep	Oct	Nov	Dec
High	41	47	58	68	77	84	88	87	81	70	57	46
Low	21	24	32	41	49	58	63	61	53	41	34	25
Precip	3.5	3.2	4.9	5.0	5.1	4.9	4.2	3.8	3.5	3.3	4.3	4.0
Snow	2.4	na	0.5	tr	0.0	0.0	0.0	0.0	0.0	tr	0.3	0.5

High and Low temperatures in degrees Fahrenheit; Precipitation and Snow in inches

Population: 9,914 (1990); 10,743 (2000); 10,483 (2010); 10,187 (2015 projected); Race: 97.6% White, 0.4% Black, 0.2% Asian, 1.8% Other, 1.3% Hispanic of any race (2010); Density: 34.3 persons per square mile (2010); Average household size: 2.47 (2010); Median age: 39.4 (2010); Males per 100 females: 99.8 (2010).
Religion: Five largest groups: 15.5% Christian Churches and Churches of Christ, 7.0% The United Methodist Church, 5.8% The Wesleyan Church, 2.6% General Association of Regular Baptist Churches, 2.4% The Church of Jesus Christ of Latter-day Saints (
Economy: Unemployment rate: 10.1% (5/2010); Total civilian labor force: 5,451 (5/2010); Leading industries: 15.3% accommodation & food services; 14.8% retail trade; 5.1% manufacturing (2008); Farms: 354 totaling 45,401 acres (2007); Companies that employ 500 or more persons: 0 (2008); Companies that employ 100 to 499 persons: 2 (2008); Companies that employ less than 100 persons: 137 (2008); Black-owned businesses: n/a (2002); Hispanic-owned businesses: n/a (2002); Asian-owned businesses: n/a (2002); Women-owned businesses: n/a (2002); Retail sales per capita: $5,425 (2010). Single-family building permits issued: 0 (2009); Multi-family building permits issued: 0 (2009).
Income: Per capita income: $19,021 (2010); Median household income: $38,991 (2010); Average household income: $47,195 (2010); Percent of households with income of $100,000 or more: 8.1% (2010); Poverty rate: 17.1% (2008); Bankruptcy rate: 8.70% (2009).
Taxes: Total county taxes per capita: $399 (2007); County property taxes per capita: $277 (2007).
Education: Percent of population age 25 and over with: High school diploma (including GED) or higher: 76.5% (2010); Bachelor's degree or higher: 9.1% (2010); Master's degree or higher: 4.3% (2010).
Housing: Homeownership rate: 82.0% (2010); Median home value: $86,719 (2010); Median contract rent: $n/a per month (2006-2008 3-year est.); Median year structure built: n/a (2006-2008 3-year est.)
Health: Birth rate: 103.4 per 10,000 population (2009); Death rate: 109.1 per 10,000 population (2009); Age-adjusted cancer mortality rate: 209.1 deaths per 100,000 population (2006); Number of physicians: 0.0 per 10,000 population (2007); Hospital beds: 0.0 per 10,000 population (2006); Hospital admissions: 0.0 per 10,000 population (2006).
Elections: 2008 Presidential election results: 48.2% Obama, 50.4% McCain, 0.0% Nader
National and State Parks: Hilands Overlook State Park
Additional Information Contacts
Crawford County Government . . . . (812) 338-2565
 http://www.selectcrawfordcounty.com

Crawford County Communities

ALTON (town). Covers a land area of 0.170 square miles and a water area of 0.025 square miles. Located at 38.12° N. Lat; 86.42° W. Long. Elevation is 427 feet.
Population: 57 (1990); 53 (2000); 58 (2010); 55 (2015 projected); Race: 98.3% White, 0.0% Black, 0.0% Asian, 1.7% Other, 0.0% Hispanic of any race (2010); Density: 341.8 persons per square mile (2010); Average household size: 2.42 (2010); Median age: 45.0 (2010); Males per 100 females: 123.1 (2010); Marriage status: 3.3% never married, 66.7% now married, 26.7% widowed, 3.3% divorced (2000); Foreign born: 0.0% (2000); Ancestry (includes multiple ancestries): 30.2% Irish, 16.3% German, 9.3% Dutch, 7.0% French (except Basque), 4.7% English (2000).
Economy: Employment by occupation: 0.0% management, 11.1% professional, 11.1% services, 22.2% sales, 16.7% farming, 0.0% construction, 38.9% production (2000).

Income: Per capita income: $21,414 (2010); Median household income: $38,750 (2010); Average household income: $56,354 (2010); Percent of households with income of $100,000 or more: 12.5% (2010); Poverty rate: 9.3% (2000).
Taxes: Total city taxes per capita: $18 (2007); City property taxes per capita: $0 (2007).
Education: Percent of population age 25 and over with: High school diploma (including GED) or higher: 76.2% (2010); Bachelor's degree or higher: 16.7% (2010); Master's degree or higher: 9.5% (2010).
Housing: Homeownership rate: 83.3% (2010); Median home value: $70,000 (2010); Median contract rent: $n/a per month (2000); Median year structure built: 1956 (2000).
Transportation: Commute to work: 100.0% car, 0.0% public transportation, 0.0% walk, 0.0% work from home (2000); Travel time to work: 22.2% less than 15 minutes, 33.3% 15 to 30 minutes, 22.2% 30 to 45 minutes, 0.0% 45 to 60 minutes, 22.2% 60 minutes or more (2000)

ECKERTY (unincorporated postal area, zip code 47116). Covers a land area of 33.242 square miles and a water area of 0.044 square miles. Located at 38.32° N. Lat; 86.61° W. Long. Elevation is 745 feet.
Population: 854 (2000); Race: 100.0% White, 0.0% Black, 0.0% Asian, 0.0% Other, 1.4% Hispanic of any race (2000); Density: 25.7 persons per square mile (2000); Age: 21.6% under 18, 13.6% over 64 (2000); Marriage status: 20.5% never married, 61.7% now married, 2.9% widowed, 14.8% divorced (2000); Foreign born: 0.1% (2000); Ancestry (includes multiple ancestries): 21.9% Irish, 18.6% German, 16.3% Other groups, 7.1% English, 6.3% United States or American (2000).
Economy: Employment by occupation: 9.7% management, 11.9% professional, 17.8% services, 15.8% sales, 5.9% farming, 11.1% construction, 27.7% production (2000).
Income: Per capita income: $15,721 (2000); Median household income: $41,319 (2000); Poverty rate: 18.9% (2000).
Education: Percent of population age 25 and over with: High school diploma (including GED) or higher: 70.5% (2000); Bachelor's degree or higher: 6.4% (2000).
School District(s)
Crawford Co Com School Corp (KG-12)
 2008-09 Enrollment: 1,682 . . . . (812) 365-2135
Housing: Homeownership rate: 91.5% (2000); Median home value: $63,900 (2000); Median contract rent: $325 per month (2000); Median year structure built: 1977 (2000).
Transportation: Commute to work: 93.3% car, 0.0% public transportation, 0.0% walk, 2.7% work from home (2000); Travel time to work: 7.9% less than 15 minutes, 21.6% 15 to 30 minutes, 44.5% 30 to 45 minutes, 10.9% 45 to 60 minutes, 15.0% 60 minutes or more (2000)

ENGLISH (town). County seat. Covers a land area of 3.052 square miles and a water area of 0 square miles. Located at 38.33° N. Lat; 86.46° W. Long. Elevation is 505 feet.
History: The town of English was laid out in 1839, and grew when it became the county seat in 1893. The town was named for William Hayden English, a U.S. congressman from Indiana.
Population: 850 (1990); 673 (2000); 638 (2010); 610 (2015 projected); Race: 97.6% White, 0.8% Black, 0.3% Asian, 1.3% Other, 0.8% Hispanic of any race (2010); Density: 209.0 persons per square mile (2010); Average household size: 2.32 (2010); Median age: 40.2 (2010); Males per 100 females: 95.7 (2010); Marriage status: 19.1% never married, 50.5% now married, 17.6% widowed, 12.8% divorced (2000); Foreign born: 1.1% (2000); Ancestry (includes multiple ancestries): 26.9% United States or American, 12.2% German, 7.6% English, 5.1% Irish, 4.3% Other groups (2000).
Economy: Single-family building permits issued: 0 (2009); Multi-family building permits issued: 0 (2009); Employment by occupation: 4.8% management, 8.4% professional, 10.0% services, 30.4% sales, 1.2% farming, 9.6% construction, 35.6% production (2000).
Income: Per capita income: $15,920 (2010); Median household income: $31,714 (2010); Average household income: $37,106 (2010); Percent of households with income of $100,000 or more: 4.4% (2010); Poverty rate: 33.9% (2000).
Taxes: Total city taxes per capita: $107 (2007); City property taxes per capita: $74 (2007).
Education: Percent of population age 25 and over with: High school diploma (including GED) or higher: 71.4% (2010); Bachelor's degree or higher: 9.3% (2010); Master's degree or higher: 4.2% (2010).

Crawford Co Com School Corp (KG-12)
    2008-09 Enrollment: 1,682 . . . . (812) 365-2135
Housing: Homeownership rate: 78.4% (2010); Median home value:
$65,806 (2010); Median contract rent: $99 per month (2000); Median year
structure built: 1974 (2000).
Transportation: Commute to work: 95.2% car, 0.0% public transportation,
0.0% walk, 4.0% work from home (2000); Travel time to work: 29.6% less
than 15 minutes, 12.1% 15 to 30 minutes, 21.7% 30 to 45 minutes, 18.8%
45 to 60 minutes, 17.9% 60 minutes or more (2000)

GRANTSBURG (unincorporated postal area, zip code 47123).
Covers a land area of 0.288 square miles and a water area of 0 square
miles. Located at 38.28° N. Lat; 86.46° W. Long. Elevation is 614 feet.
Population: 30 (2000); Race: 100.0% White, 0.0% Black, 0.0% Asian,
0.0% Other, 0.0% Hispanic of any race (2000); Density: 104.2 persons per
square mile (2000); Age: 0.0% under 18, 47.6% over 64 (2000); Marriage
status: 0.0% never married, 47.6% now married, 52.4% widowed, 0.0%
divorced (2000); Foreign born: 0.0% (2000); Ancestry (includes multiple
ancestries): 52.4% United States or American (2000).
Economy: Employment by occupation: 0.0% management, 0.0%
professional, 0.0% services, 100.0% sales, 0.0% farming, 0.0%
construction, 0.0% production (2000).
Income: Per capita income: $7,138 (2000); Median household income:
$4,318 (2000); Poverty rate: 52.4% (2000).
Education: Percent of population age 25 and over with: High school
diploma (including GED) or higher: 52.4% (2000); Bachelor's degree or
higher: 0.0% (2000).
Housing: Homeownership rate: 100.0% (2000); Median home value:
$55,000 (2000); Median contract rent: $n/a per month (2000); Median year
structure built: 1985 (2000).
Transportation: Commute to work: 100.0% car, 0.0% public
transportation, 0.0% walk, 0.0% work from home (2000); Travel time to
work: 0.0% less than 15 minutes, 0.0% 15 to 30 minutes, 100.0% 30 to 45
minutes, 0.0% 45 to 60 minutes, 0.0% 60 minutes or more (2000)

LEAVENWORTH (town). Covers a land area of 0.834 square miles
and a water area of 0.050 square miles. Located at 38.19° N. Lat; 86.34°
W. Long. Elevation is 659 feet.
History: Leavenworth was founded in 1818 and served as Crawford
County's seat from 1843 to 1893. A boat-building industry was established
in 1830 by David Lyon, and Leavenworth became a shipping point on the
Ohio River. The 1937 flooding of the Ohio River destroyed most of the
town, which was rebuilt on the hills behind the original site.
Population: 320 (1990); 353 (2000); 297 (2010); 291 (2015 projected);
Race: 96.6% White, 0.3% Black, 1.0% Asian, 2.0% Other, 2.0% Hispanic
of any race (2010); Density: 356.1 persons per square mile (2010);
Average household size: 2.52 (2010); Median age: 42.2 (2010); Males per
100 females: 96.7 (2010); Marriage status: 25.8% never married, 41.1%
now married, 16.0% widowed, 17.1% divorced (2000); Foreign born: 1.7%
(2000); Ancestry (includes multiple ancestries): 18.3% United States or
American, 9.6% European, 5.8% German, 4.9% English, 3.5% Irish (2000).
Economy: Single-family building permits issued: 0 (2009); Multi-family
building permits issued: 0 (2009); Employment by occupation: 0.9%
management, 12.2% professional, 30.4% services, 11.3% sales, 0.0%
farming, 15.7% construction, 29.6% production (2000).
Income: Per capita income: $21,798 (2010); Median household income:
$45,417 (2010); Average household income: $55,788 (2010); Percent of
households with income of $100,000 or more: 14.4% (2010); Poverty rate:
18.6% (2000).
Taxes: Total city taxes per capita: $68 (2007); City property taxes per
capita: $37 (2007).
Education: Percent of population age 25 and over with: High school
diploma (including GED) or higher: 79.3% (2010); Bachelor's degree or
higher: 5.6% (2010); Master's degree or higher: 3.3% (2010).
School District(s)
Crawford Co Com School Corp (KG-12)
    2008-09 Enrollment: 1,682 . . . . (812) 365-2135
Housing: Homeownership rate: 80.2% (2010); Median home value:
$97,857 (2010); Median contract rent: $183 per month (2000); Median year
structure built: 1959 (2000).
Transportation: Commute to work: 93.9% car, 0.0% public transportation,
3.5% walk, 2.6% work from home (2000); Travel time to work: 33.9% less
than 15 minutes, 28.6% 15 to 30 minutes, 17.0% 30 to 45 minutes, 8.9%
45 to 60 minutes, 11.6% 60 minutes or more (2000)

MARENGO (town). Covers a land area of 0.765 square miles and a
water area of 0 square miles. Located at 38.37° N. Lat; 86.34° W. Long.
Elevation is 597 feet.
History: Marengo grew as a resort village in an area of coldwater springs
and caves. Quarrying was an early industry.
Population: 856 (1990); 829 (2000); 811 (2010); 786 (2015 projected);
Race: 98.4% White, 0.6% Black, 0.0% Asian, 1.0% Other, 1.0% Hispanic
of any race (2010); Density: 1,060.0 persons per square mile (2010);
Average household size: 2.43 (2010); Median age: 36.8 (2010); Males per
100 females: 95.4 (2010); Marriage status: 17.7% never married, 52.3%
now married, 13.1% widowed, 16.9% divorced (2000); Foreign born: 1.0%
(2000); Ancestry (includes multiple ancestries): 14.2% German, 10.9%
Irish, 8.5% United States or American, 7.5% Other groups, 4.7% English
(2000).
Economy: Employment by occupation: 5.7% management, 12.2%
professional, 19.1% services, 22.8% sales, 1.2% farming, 6.5%
construction, 32.5% production (2000).
Income: Per capita income: $14,883 (2010); Median household income:
$33,367 (2010); Average household income: $36,287 (2010); Percent of
households with income of $100,000 or more: 3.0% (2010); Poverty rate:
23.9% (2000).
Taxes: Total city taxes per capita: $79 (2007); City property taxes per
capita: $37 (2007).
Education: Percent of population age 25 and over with: High school
diploma (including GED) or higher: 77.0% (2010); Bachelor's degree or
higher: 4.5% (2010); Master's degree or higher: 2.4% (2010).
School District(s)
Crawford Co Com School Corp (KG-12)
    2008-09 Enrollment: 1,682 . . . . (812) 365-2135
Housing: Homeownership rate: 70.4% (2010); Median home value:
$71,951 (2010); Median contract rent: $263 per month (2000); Median year
structure built: 1959 (2000).
Transportation: Commute to work: 97.5% car, 0.0% public transportation,
0.0% walk, 1.7% work from home (2000); Travel time to work: 23.2% less
than 15 minutes, 19.7% 15 to 30 minutes, 22.3% 30 to 45 minutes, 23.2%
45 to 60 minutes, 11.6% 60 minutes or more (2000)

MILLTOWN (town). Covers a land area of 1.407 square miles and a
water area of 0 square miles. Located at 38.34° N. Lat; 86.27° W. Long.
Elevation is 620 feet.
Population: 917 (1990); 932 (2000); 939 (2010); 932 (2015 projected);
Race: 98.1% White, 0.4% Black, 0.1% Asian, 1.4% Other, 0.6% Hispanic
of any race (2010); Density: 667.2 persons per square mile (2010);
Average household size: 2.55 (2010); Median age: 38.9 (2010); Males per
100 females: 99.4 (2010); Marriage status: 18.1% never married, 61.0%
now married, 5.2% widowed, 15.6% divorced (2000); Foreign born: 0.2%
(2000); Ancestry (includes multiple ancestries): 23.5% German, 15.1%
Irish, 14.8% United States or American, 7.9% Other groups, 7.2% English
(2000).
Economy: Single-family building permits issued: 0 (2009); Multi-family
building permits issued: 0 (2009); Employment by occupation: 9.0%
management, 15.2% professional, 13.7% services, 24.2% sales, 0.9%
farming, 13.9% construction, 23.1% production (2000).
Income: Per capita income: $24,222 (2010); Median household income:
$51,533 (2010); Average household income: $62,459 (2010); Percent of
households with income of $100,000 or more: 14.2% (2010); Poverty rate:
13.5% (2000).
Taxes: Total city taxes per capita: $92 (2007); City property taxes per
capita: $69 (2007).
Education: Percent of population age 25 and over with: High school
diploma (including GED) or higher: 83.6% (2010); Bachelor's degree or
higher: 11.5% (2010); Master's degree or higher: 3.9% (2010).
School District(s)
Crawford Co Com School Corp (KG-12)
    2008-09 Enrollment: 1,682 . . . . (812) 365-2135
Housing: Homeownership rate: 86.1% (2010); Median home value:
$101,266 (2010); Median contract rent: $246 per month (2000); Median
year structure built: 1962 (2000).
Transportation: Commute to work: 97.5% car, 0.0% public transportation,
0.7% walk, 1.8% work from home (2000); Travel time to work: 19.3% less
than 15 minutes, 29.2% 15 to 30 minutes, 22.6% 30 to 45 minutes, 21.2%
45 to 60 minutes, 7.8% 60 minutes or more (2000)

SULPHUR (unincorporated postal area, zip code 47174). Covers a land area of 1.713 square miles and a water area of 0 square miles. Located at 38.21° N. Lat; 86.46° W. Long. Elevation is 712 feet.

History: Sulphur was named for the sulphur springs located nearby. White Sulphur Spring was discovered in the 1860's by men who were drilling for oil. A hotel was built for the visitors who came for the medicinal value of the water, which was also bottled and sold.

Population: 104 (2000); Race: 100.0% White, 0.0% Black, 0.0% Asian, 0.0% Other, 0.0% Hispanic of any race (2000); Density: 60.7 persons per square mile (2000); Age: 27.8% under 18, 6.9% over 64 (2000); Marriage status: 7.7% never married, 55.8% now married, 9.6% widowed, 26.9% divorced (2000); Foreign born: 0.0% (2000); Ancestry (includes multiple ancestries): 40.3% English, 27.8% German, 26.4% Irish, 20.8% United States or American, 13.9% Dutch (2000).

Economy: Employment by occupation: 0.0% management, 10.6% professional, 19.1% services, 42.6% sales, 0.0% farming, 17.0% construction, 10.6% production (2000).

Income: Per capita income: $23,731 (2000); Median household income: $75,406 (2000); Poverty rate: 0.0% (2000).

Education: Percent of population age 25 and over with: High school diploma (including GED) or higher: 100.0% (2000); Bachelor's degree or higher: 31.3% (2000).

Housing: Homeownership rate: 100.0% (2000); Median home value: $n/a (2000); Median contract rent: $n/a per month (2000); Median year structure built: 1994 (2000).

Transportation: Commute to work: 100.0% car, 0.0% public transportation, 0.0% walk, 0.0% work from home (2000); Travel time to work: 0.0% less than 15 minutes, 72.3% 15 to 30 minutes, 10.6% 30 to 45 minutes, 0.0% 45 to 60 minutes, 17.0% 60 minutes or more (2000)

TASWELL (unincorporated postal area, zip code 47175). Covers a land area of 20.554 square miles and a water area of 0.001 square miles. Located at 38.35° N. Lat; 86.55° W. Long. Elevation is 778 feet.

Population: 819 (2000); Race: 100.0% White, 0.0% Black, 0.0% Asian, 0.0% Other, 0.0% Hispanic of any race (2000); Density: 39.8 persons per square mile (2000); Age: 21.6% under 18, 11.2% over 64 (2000); Marriage status: 18.2% never married, 64.1% now married, 7.5% widowed, 10.2% divorced (2000); Foreign born: 0.0% (2000); Ancestry (includes multiple ancestries): 22.7% United States or American, 16.4% English, 13.9% Irish, 9.8% German, 3.8% Other groups (2000).

Economy: Employment by occupation: 8.9% management, 11.2% professional, 3.6% services, 20.0% sales, 0.0% farming, 11.8% construction, 44.4% production (2000).

Income: Per capita income: $33,405 (2000); Median household income: $39,219 (2000); Poverty rate: 8.8% (2000).

Education: Percent of population age 25 and over with: High school diploma (including GED) or higher: 74.0% (2000); Bachelor's degree or higher: 12.4% (2000).

Housing: Homeownership rate: 90.2% (2000); Median home value: $84,000 (2000); Median contract rent: $125 per month (2000); Median year structure built: 1979 (2000).

Transportation: Commute to work: 92.5% car, 0.0% public transportation, 0.0% walk, 5.7% work from home (2000); Travel time to work: 7.7% less than 15 minutes, 23.7% 15 to 30 minutes, 35.5% 30 to 45 minutes, 16.4% 45 to 60 minutes, 16.7% 60 minutes or more (2000)

Daviess County

Located in southwestern Indiana; bounded on the south by the East Fork of the White River, on the west by the West Fork of the White River. Covers a land area of 430.66 square miles, a water area of 6.20 square miles, and is located in the Eastern Time Zone. The county was founded in 1816. County seat is Washington.

Daviess County is part of the Washington, IN Micropolitan Statistical Area. The entire metro area includes: Daviess County, IN

Weather Station: Washington										Elevation: 524 feet		
	Jan	Feb	Mar	Apr	May	Jun	Jul	Aug	Sep	Oct	Nov	Dec
High	39	45	56	67	77	85	88	86	80	69	55	44
Low	23	27	36	45	55	64	68	66	58	47	38	28
Precip	2.7	2.6	4.2	4.2	5.4	4.0	4.9	3.7	2.9	3.2	4.3	3.4
Snow	4.2	3.0	1.8	tr	tr	0.0	0.0	0.0	0.0	tr	0.3	2.2

High and Low temperatures in degrees Fahrenheit; Precipitation and Snow in inches

Population: 27,533 (1990); 29,820 (2000); 30,292 (2010); 30,412 (2015 projected); Race: 96.1% White, 0.6% Black, 0.3% Asian, 3.0% Other, 4.0% Hispanic of any race (2010); Density: 70.3 persons per square mile (2010); Average household size: 2.68 (2010); Median age: 35.3 (2010); Males per 100 females: 99.8 (2010).

Religion: Five largest groups: 14.0% Catholic Church, 9.8% Christian Churches and Churches of Christ, 8.6% The United Methodist Church, 5.1% American Baptist Churches in the USA, 3.9% Old Order Amish Church (2000).

Economy: Unemployment rate: 5.8% (5/2010); Total civilian labor force: 15,266 (5/2010); Leading industries: 19.4% manufacturing; 15.3% retail trade; 13.9% health care and social assistance (2008); Farms: 969 totaling 199,367 acres (2007); Companies that employ 500 or more persons: 2 (2008); Companies that employ 100 to 499 persons: 9 (2008); Companies that employ less than 100 persons: 786 (2008); Black-owned businesses: n/a (2002); Hispanic-owned businesses: n/a (2002); Asian-owned businesses: n/a (2002); Women-owned businesses: 347 (2002); Retail sales per capita: $13,608 (2010). Single-family building permits issued: 8 (2009); Multi-family building permits issued: 0 (2009).

Income: Per capita income: $20,154 (2010); Median household income: $43,578 (2010); Average household income: $54,381 (2010); Percent of households with income of $100,000 or more: 10.0% (2010); Poverty rate: 14.6% (2008); Bankruptcy rate: 3.48% (2009).

Taxes: Total county taxes per capita: $323 (2007); County property taxes per capita: $211 (2007).

Education: Percent of population age 25 and over with: High school diploma (including GED) or higher: 71.9% (2010); Bachelor's degree or higher: 11.3% (2010); Master's degree or higher: 4.7% (2010).

Housing: Homeownership rate: 77.7% (2010); Median home value: $84,198 (2010); Median contract rent: $377 per month (2006-2008 3-year est.); Median year structure built: 1964 (2006-2008 3-year est.)

Health: Birth rate: 168.5 per 10,000 population (2009); Death rate: 95.0 per 10,000 population (2009); Age-adjusted cancer mortality rate: 182.5 deaths per 100,000 population (2006); Air Quality Index: 99.4% good, 0.6% moderate, 0.0% unhealthy for sensitive individuals, 0.0% unhealthy (percent of days in 2008); Number of physicians: 6.6 per 10,000 population (2007); Hospital beds: 23.4 per 10,000 population (2006); Hospital admissions: 902.9 per 10,000 population (2006).

Elections: 2008 Presidential election results: 31.8% Obama, 67.1% McCain, 0.0% Nader

National and State Parks: Glendale State Fish and Wildlife Area

Additional Information Contacts

Daviess County Government . . . . (812) 254-5262
   http://www.daviesscounty.net
City of Washington . . . . (812) 254-5575
   http://www.washingtonin.us
Daviess County Chamber of Commerce . . . . (812) 254-5262
   http://www.daviesscounty.net

Daviess County Communities

ALFORDSVILLE (town). Covers a land area of 0.068 square miles and a water area of 0 square miles. Located at 38.56° N. Lat; 86.94° W. Long. Elevation is 512 feet.

History: Laid out 1845.

Population: 74 (1990); 112 (2000); 117 (2010); 118 (2015 projected); Race: 98.3% White, 0.0% Black, 0.0% Asian, 1.7% Other, 1.7% Hispanic of any race (2010); Density: 1,711.5 persons per square mile (2010); Average household size: 2.79 (2010); Median age: 32.7 (2010); Males per 100 females: 95.0 (2010); Marriage status: 28.0% never married, 62.0% now married, 3.0% widowed, 7.0% divorced (2000); Foreign born: 0.0% (2000); Ancestry (includes multiple ancestries): 29.8% United States or American, 19.4% Other groups, 16.9% German, 3.2% English, 1.6% Welsh (2000).

Economy: Employment by occupation: 6.8% management, 0.0% professional, 6.8% services, 35.6% sales, 0.0% farming, 11.9% construction, 39.0% production (2000).

Income: Per capita income: $19,810 (2010); Median household income: $51,923 (2010); Average household income: $54,821 (2010); Percent of households with income of $100,000 or more: 7.1% (2010); Poverty rate: 18.5% (2000).

Taxes: Total city taxes per capita: $43 (2007); City property taxes per capita: $34 (2007).

Education: Percent of population age 25 and over with: High school diploma (including GED) or higher: 75.7% (2010); Bachelor's degree or higher: 15.7% (2010); Master's degree or higher: 7.1% (2010).
Housing: Homeownership rate: 81.0% (2010); Median home value: $73,333 (2010); Median contract rent: $275 per month (2000); Median year structure built: 1968 (2000).
Transportation: Commute to work: 86.4% car, 0.0% public transportation, 8.5% walk, 5.1% work from home (2000); Travel time to work: 8.9% less than 15 minutes, 48.2% 15 to 30 minutes, 25.0% 30 to 45 minutes, 10.7% 45 to 60 minutes, 7.1% 60 minutes or more (2000)

CANNELBURG (town). Covers a land area of 0.187 square miles and a water area of 0 square miles. Located at 38.66° N. Lat; 86.99° W. Long. Elevation is 525 feet.
Population: 97 (1990); 140 (2000); 136 (2010); 137 (2015 projected); Race: 100.0% White, 0.0% Black, 0.0% Asian, 0.0% Other, 0.7% Hispanic of any race (2010); Density: 726.0 persons per square mile (2010); Average household size: 3.28 (2010); Median age: 30.6 (2010); Males per 100 females: 100.0 (2010); Marriage status: 25.3% never married, 70.3% now married, 1.1% widowed, 3.3% divorced (2000); Foreign born: 0.0% (2000); Ancestry (includes multiple ancestries): 38.8% United States or American, 24.8% German, 7.4% Irish, 5.0% English, 3.3% French (except Basque) (2000).
Economy: Employment by occupation: 14.0% management, 10.5% professional, 15.8% services, 19.3% sales, 0.0% farming, 7.0% construction, 33.3% production (2000).
Income: Per capita income: $14,117 (2010); Median household income: $41,000 (2010); Average household income: $44,188 (2010); Percent of households with income of $100,000 or more: 2.5% (2010); Poverty rate: 14.9% (2000).
Taxes: Total city taxes per capita: $57 (2007); City property taxes per capita: $38 (2007).
Education: Percent of population age 25 and over with: High school diploma (including GED) or higher: 66.7% (2010); Bachelor's degree or higher: 7.7% (2010); Master's degree or higher: 5.1% (2010).
Housing: Homeownership rate: 82.5% (2010); Median home value: $95,000 (2010); Median contract rent: $325 per month (2000); Median year structure built: 1968 (2000).
Transportation: Commute to work: 94.7% car, 0.0% public transportation, 5.3% walk, 0.0% work from home (2000); Travel time to work: 42.1% less than 15 minutes, 35.1% 15 to 30 minutes, 8.8% 30 to 45 minutes, 0.0% 45 to 60 minutes, 14.0% 60 minutes or more (2000)

ELNORA (town). Covers a land area of 0.947 square miles and a water area of 0 square miles. Located at 38.87° N. Lat; 87.08° W. Long. Elevation is 479 feet.
Population: 746 (1990); 721 (2000); 720 (2010); 715 (2015 projected); Race: 97.5% White, 0.0% Black, 0.0% Asian, 2.5% Other, 1.5% Hispanic of any race (2010); Density: 760.7 persons per square mile (2010); Average household size: 2.47 (2010); Median age: 41.2 (2010); Males per 100 females: 104.5 (2010); Marriage status: 20.6% never married, 58.7% now married, 10.1% widowed, 10.6% divorced (2000); Foreign born: 0.3% (2000); Ancestry (includes multiple ancestries): 23.3% German, 19.7% United States or American, 13.7% Irish, 6.0% English, 5.1% Other groups (2000).
Economy: Employment by occupation: 7.2% management, 11.4% professional, 18.6% services, 24.0% sales, 1.9% farming, 12.5% construction, 24.3% production (2000).
Income: Per capita income: $18,340 (2010); Median household income: $32,805 (2010); Average household income: $44,854 (2010); Percent of households with income of $100,000 or more: 7.2% (2010); Poverty rate: 17.6% (2000).
Taxes: Total city taxes per capita: $91 (2007); City property taxes per capita: $76 (2007).
Education: Percent of population age 25 and over with: High school diploma (including GED) or higher: 73.5% (2010); Bachelor's degree or higher: 9.4% (2010); Master's degree or higher: 5.1% (2010).

School District(s)
North Daviess Com Schools (KG-12)
    2008-09 Enrollment: 1,098 . . . . (812) 636-8000
Housing: Homeownership rate: 83.2% (2010); Median home value: $42,391 (2010); Median contract rent: $225 per month (2000); Median year structure built: 1947 (2000).
Transportation: Commute to work: 92.7% car, 0.0% public transportation, 2.3% walk, 3.8% work from home (2000); Travel time to work: 40.8% less

than 15 minutes, 26.0% 15 to 30 minutes, 18.0% 30 to 45 minutes, 6.0% 45 to 60 minutes, 9.2% 60 minutes or more (2000)

MONTGOMERY (town). Covers a land area of 0.241 square miles and a water area of 0 square miles. Located at 38.66° N. Lat; 87.04° W. Long. Elevation is 528 feet.
History: Montgomery grew up around St. Peter's Church which was founded in 1818.
Population: 306 (1990); 368 (2000); 364 (2010); 361 (2015 projected); Race: 99.2% White, 0.0% Black, 0.0% Asian, 0.8% Other, 0.5% Hispanic of any race (2010); Density: 1,511.1 persons per square mile (2010); Average household size: 3.10 (2010); Median age: 30.2 (2010); Males per 100 females: 110.4 (2010); Marriage status: 20.5% never married, 61.6% now married, 8.8% widowed, 9.1% divorced (2000); Foreign born: 0.0% (2000); Ancestry (includes multiple ancestries): 24.7% German, 23.7% Irish, 15.6% United States or American, 11.6% English, 9.4% Other groups (2000).
Economy: Employment by occupation: 7.6% management, 14.2% professional, 7.6% services, 23.7% sales, 2.4% farming, 16.6% construction, 28.0% production (2000).
Income: Per capita income: $19,613 (2010); Median household income: $53,618 (2010); Average household income: $60,769 (2010); Percent of households with income of $100,000 or more: 15.4% (2010); Poverty rate: 10.8% (2000).
Taxes: Total city taxes per capita: $125 (2007); City property taxes per capita: $101 (2007).
Education: Percent of population age 25 and over with: High school diploma (including GED) or higher: 69.0% (2010); Bachelor's degree or higher: 7.1% (2010); Master's degree or higher: 2.9% (2010).
School District(s)
Barr-Reeve Com Schools Inc (KG-12)
    2008-09 Enrollment: 740 . . . . (812) 486-3220
Housing: Homeownership rate: 86.3% (2010); Median home value: $99,524 (2010); Median contract rent: $254 per month (2000); Median year structure built: 1940 (2000).
Transportation: Commute to work: 90.0% car, 0.0% public transportation, 3.8% walk, 6.2% work from home (2000); Travel time to work: 38.8% less than 15 minutes, 24.0% 15 to 30 minutes, 24.5% 30 to 45 minutes, 7.1% 45 to 60 minutes, 5.6% 60 minutes or more (2000)

ODON (town). Covers a land area of 0.943 square miles and a water area of 0.011 square miles. Located at 38.84° N. Lat; 86.99° W. Long. Elevation is 545 feet.
History: Odon grew as a farm town on a site at a spring where George Rogers Clark and his soldiers stopped for water and to hunt buffalo.
Population: 1,475 (1990); 1,376 (2000); 1,403 (2010); 1,418 (2015 projected); Race: 98.6% White, 0.2% Black, 0.2% Asian, 0.9% Other, 1.6% Hispanic of any race (2010); Density: 1,487.0 persons per square mile (2010); Average household size: 2.42 (2010); Median age: 39.2 (2010); Males per 100 females: 96.8 (2010); Marriage status: 16.6% never married, 60.3% now married, 13.2% widowed, 9.8% divorced (2000); Foreign born: 0.0% (2000); Ancestry (includes multiple ancestries): 21.8% German, 16.4% United States or American, 9.9% English, 8.1% Irish, 6.4% Other groups (2000).
Economy: Employment by occupation: 11.6% management, 16.5% professional, 13.6% services, 22.2% sales, 0.2% farming, 10.4% construction, 25.5% production (2000).
Income: Per capita income: $22,712 (2010); Median household income: $45,425 (2010); Average household income: $55,722 (2010); Percent of households with income of $100,000 or more: 10.2% (2010); Poverty rate: 11.1% (2000).
Taxes: Total city taxes per capita: $122 (2007); City property taxes per capita: $89 (2007).
Education: Percent of population age 25 and over with: High school diploma (including GED) or higher: 79.6% (2010); Bachelor's degree or higher: 14.0% (2010); Master's degree or higher: 4.2% (2010).
Housing: Homeownership rate: 77.8% (2010); Median home value: $66,216 (2010); Median contract rent: $238 per month (2000); Median year structure built: 1958 (2000).
Transportation: Commute to work: 93.9% car, 0.0% public transportation, 3.4% walk, 1.1% work from home (2000); Travel time to work: 32.8% less than 15 minutes, 32.2% 15 to 30 minutes, 14.5% 30 to 45 minutes, 12.9% 45 to 60 minutes, 7.6% 60 minutes or more (2000)

PLAINVILLE (town). Covers a land area of 0.330 square miles and a water area of 0 square miles. Located at 38.80° N. Lat; 87.15° W. Long. Elevation is 469 feet.
Population: 444 (1990); 513 (2000); 524 (2010); 528 (2015 projected); Race: 98.1% White, 0.0% Black, 0.2% Asian, 1.7% Other, 3.4% Hispanic of any race (2010); Density: 1,588.6 persons per square mile (2010); Average household size: 2.41 (2010); Median age: 38.0 (2010); Males per 100 females: 99.2 (2010); Marriage status: 14.3% never married, 67.3% now married, 10.6% widowed, 7.8% divorced (2000); Foreign born: 1.4% (2000); Ancestry (includes multiple ancestries): 19.7% United States or American, 18.0% German, 12.2% Irish, 8.9% English, 8.7% Other groups (2000).
Economy: Employment by occupation: 8.7% management, 16.2% professional, 11.8% services, 22.7% sales, 0.4% farming, 13.1% construction, 27.1% production (2000).
Income: Per capita income: $22,871 (2010); Median household income: $51,411 (2010); Average household income: $55,442 (2010); Percent of households with income of $100,000 or more: 8.4% (2010); Poverty rate: 9.8% (2000).
Taxes: Total city taxes per capita: $94 (2007); City property taxes per capita: $80 (2007).
Education: Percent of population age 25 and over with: High school diploma (including GED) or higher: 78.5% (2010); Bachelor's degree or higher: 10.6% (2010); Master's degree or higher: 1.5% (2010).
Housing: Homeownership rate: 80.0% (2010); Median home value: $70,909 (2010); Median contract rent: $231 per month (2000); Median year structure built: 1940 (2000).
Transportation: Commute to work: 96.4% car, 0.0% public transportation, 2.2% walk, 0.9% work from home (2000); Travel time to work: 22.9% less than 15 minutes, 37.2% 15 to 30 minutes, 23.3% 30 to 45 minutes, 3.6% 45 to 60 minutes, 13.0% 60 minutes or more (2000)

WASHINGTON (city). Aka Hyatt. County seat. Covers a land area of 4.734 square miles and a water area of 0.028 square miles. Located at 38.65° N. Lat; 87.17° W. Long. Elevation is 502 feet.
History: Washington was founded by Emmanuel Van Trees, who settled here in 1817 on the site where Fort Flora had been built in 1805. The town developed around the Baltimore & Ohio Railroad shops, and became a trading and industrial center.
Population: 11,177 (1990); 11,380 (2000); 11,422 (2010); 11,411 (2015 projected); Race: 92.5% White, 1.4% Black, 0.4% Asian, 5.8% Other, 8.0% Hispanic of any race (2010); Density: 2,412.9 persons per square mile (2010); Average household size: 2.36 (2010); Median age: 37.8 (2010); Males per 100 females: 94.5 (2010); Marriage status: 20.2% never married, 55.3% now married, 9.6% widowed, 14.9% divorced (2000); Foreign born: 4.0% (2000); Ancestry (includes multiple ancestries): 22.3% United States or American, 20.2% German, 12.3% Irish, 10.6% Other groups, 7.1% English (2000).
Economy: Single-family building permits issued: 8 (2009); Multi-family building permits issued: 0 (2009); Employment by occupation: 6.3% management, 15.2% professional, 16.2% services, 24.6% sales, 0.5% farming, 8.9% construction, 28.3% production (2000).
Income: Per capita income: $20,617 (2010); Median household income: $36,861 (2010); Average household income: $49,341 (2010); Percent of households with income of $100,000 or more: 8.4% (2010); Poverty rate: 14.3% (2000).
Taxes: Total city taxes per capita: $250 (2007); City property taxes per capita: $213 (2007).
Education: Percent of population age 25 and over with: High school diploma (including GED) or higher: 76.2% (2010); Bachelor's degree or higher: 11.3% (2010); Master's degree or higher: 4.9% (2010).
School District(s)
Twin Rivers Career & Tech Ed Area (09-12)
    2008-09 Enrollment: n/a . . . . (812) 882-0801
Washington Com Schools (KG-12)
    2008-09 Enrollment: 2,456 . . . . (812) 254-5536
Housing: Homeownership rate: 67.8% (2010); Median home value: $73,040 (2010); Median contract rent: $281 per month (2000); Median year structure built: 1956 (2000).
Hospitals: Davies County Hospital (120 beds)
Newspapers: Washington Times-Herald (Local news; Circulation 9,512)
Transportation: Commute to work: 96.2% car, 0.3% public transportation, 2.1% walk, 0.3% work from home (2000); Travel time to work: 60.1% less

than 15 minutes, 14.2% 15 to 30 minutes, 12.8% 30 to 45 minutes, 7.4% 45 to 60 minutes, 5.5% 60 minutes or more (2000)
Additional Information Contacts
City of Washington. . . . . (812) 254-5575
    http://www.washingtonin.us
Daviess County Chamber of Commerce . . . . (812) 254-5262
    http://www.daviesscounty.net

DeKalb County

Located in northeastern Indiana; bounded on the east by Ohio; drained by the St. Joseph River and Cedar and Fish Creeks. Covers a land area of 362.88 square miles, a water area of 0.97 square miles, and is located in the Eastern Time Zone. The county was founded in 1835. County seat is Auburn.

DeKalb County is part of the Auburn, IN Micropolitan Statistical Area. The entire metro area includes: DeKalb County, IN

Population: 35,324 (1990); 40,285 (2000); 42,138 (2010); 42,754 (2015 projected); Race: 96.8% White, 0.7% Black, 0.4% Asian, 2.1% Other, 2.2% Hispanic of any race (2010); Density: 116.1 persons per square mile (2010); Average household size: 2.57 (2010); Median age: 37.0 (2010); Males per 100 females: 99.8 (2010).
Religion: Five largest groups: 8.3% Catholic Church, 6.4% The United Methodist Church, 5.5% Christian Churches and Churches of Christ, 2.5% Evangelical Lutheran Church in America, 2.5% Lutheran Church—Missouri Synod (2000).
Economy: Unemployment rate: 10.9% (5/2010); Total civilian labor force: 21,357 (5/2010); Leading industries: 42.4% manufacturing; 9.8% retail trade; 9.0% health care and social assistance (2008); Farms: 1,144 totaling 160,665 acres (2007); Companies that employ 500 or more persons: 1 (2008); Companies that employ 100 to 499 persons: 44 (2008); Companies that employ less than 100 persons: 985 (2008); Black-owned businesses: n/a (2002); Hispanic-owned businesses: n/a (2002); Asian-owned businesses: n/a (2002); Women-owned businesses: n/a (2002); Retail sales per capita: $12,431 (2010). Single-family building permits issued: 51 (2009); Multi-family building permits issued: 0 (2009).
Income: Per capita income: $22,485 (2010); Median household income: $49,312 (2010); Average household income: $58,075 (2010); Percent of households with income of $100,000 or more: 11.0% (2010); Poverty rate: 10.3% (2008); Bankruptcy rate: 7.84% (2009).
Taxes: Total county taxes per capita: $465 (2007); County property taxes per capita: $346 (2007).
Education: Percent of population age 25 and over with: High school diploma (including GED) or higher: 87.8% (2010); Bachelor's degree or higher: 17.7% (2010); Master's degree or higher: 5.7% (2010).
Housing: Homeownership rate: 81.1% (2010); Median home value: $110,261 (2010); Median contract rent: $495 per month (2006-2008 3-year est.); Median year structure built: 1972 (2006-2008 3-year est.)
Health: Birth rate: 135.0 per 10,000 population (2009); Death rate: 85.6 per 10,000 population (2009); Age-adjusted cancer mortality rate: 196.9 deaths per 100,000 population (2006); Number of physicians: 8.1 per 10,000 population (2007); Hospital beds: 11.6 per 10,000 population (2006); Hospital admissions: 472.6 per 10,000 population (2006).
Elections: 2008 Presidential election results: 41.8% Obama, 57.0% McCain, 0.0% Nader
Additional Information Contacts
DeKalb County Government . . . . (219) 925-2362
    http://www.dekalb.in.us
DeKalb County Convention and Visitors Bureau . . . . (260) 927-1499
    http://www.dekalbcvb.org

DeKalb County Communities

ALTONA (town). Covers a land area of 0.252 square miles and a water area of 0 square miles. Located at 41.35° N. Lat; 85.15° W. Long. Elevation is 899 feet.
Population: 187 (1990); 198 (2000); 205 (2010); 206 (2015 projected); Race: 97.6% White, 0.5% Black, 1.0% Asian, 1.0% Other, 0.0% Hispanic of any race (2010); Density: 815.0 persons per square mile (2010); Average household size: 2.59 (2010); Median age: 37.1 (2010); Males per 100 females: 99.0 (2010); Marriage status: 20.2% never married, 51.2% now married, 11.9% widowed, 16.7% divorced (2000); Foreign born: 0.0% (2000); Ancestry (includes multiple ancestries): 26.0% German, 17.5%

English, 14.5% United States or American, 9.5% Irish, 7.5% Other groups (2000).
Economy: Employment by occupation: 0.0% management, 10.1% professional, 14.7% services, 31.2% sales, 0.0% farming, 3.7% construction, 40.4% production (2000).
Income: Per capita income: $23,518 (2010); Median household income: $56,250 (2010); Average household income: $59,051 (2010); Percent of households with income of $100,000 or more: 10.1% (2010); Poverty rate: 12.1% (2000).
Taxes: Total city taxes per capita: $87 (2007); City property taxes per capita: $72 (2007).
Education: Percent of population age 25 and over with: High school diploma (including GED) or higher: 90.6% (2010); Bachelor's degree or higher: 12.9% (2010); Master's degree or higher: 1.4% (2010).
Housing: Homeownership rate: 79.7% (2010); Median home value: $96,667 (2010); Median contract rent: $330 per month (2000); Median year structure built: before 1940 (2000).
Transportation: Commute to work: 94.9% car, 0.0% public transportation, 2.0% walk, 3.1% work from home (2000); Travel time to work: 41.1% less than 15 minutes, 36.8% 15 to 30 minutes, 18.9% 30 to 45 minutes, 1.1% 45 to 60 minutes, 2.1% 60 minutes or more (2000)

ASHLEY (town). Aka Ashley-Hudson. Covers a land area of 0.807 square miles and a water area of 0 square miles. Located at 41.52° N. Lat; 85.06° W. Long. Elevation is 1,001 feet.
Population: 787 (1990); 1,010 (2000); 964 (2010); 937 (2015 projected); Race: 96.5% White, 0.7% Black, 0.2% Asian, 2.6% Other, 2.1% Hispanic of any race (2010); Density: 1,194.5 persons per square mile (2010); Average household size: 2.48 (2010); Median age: 35.6 (2010); Males per 100 females: 101.3 (2010); Marriage status: 25.2% never married, 56.2% now married, 3.7% widowed, 14.9% divorced (2000); Foreign born: 1.5% (2000); Ancestry (includes multiple ancestries): 27.2% German, 11.9% United States or American, 11.7% English, 9.9% Other groups, 6.2% Irish (2000).
Economy: Employment by occupation: 6.8% management, 4.5% professional, 11.6% services, 18.0% sales, 0.0% farming, 9.9% construction, 49.2% production (2000).
Income: Per capita income: $21,086 (2010); Median household income: $45,652 (2010); Average household income: $52,204 (2010); Percent of households with income of $100,000 or more: 7.0% (2010); Poverty rate: 12.8% (2000).
Taxes: Total city taxes per capita: $238 (2007); City property taxes per capita: $180 (2007).
Education: Percent of population age 25 and over with: High school diploma (including GED) or higher: 85.8% (2010); Bachelor's degree or higher: 4.3% (2010); Master's degree or higher: 1.6% (2010).
School District(s)
Dekalb Co Ctl United Sch Dist (PK-12)
    2008-09 Enrollment: 4,050 . . . . (260) 920-1011
Housing: Homeownership rate: 74.7% (2010); Median home value: $97,273 (2010); Median contract rent: $308 per month (2000); Median year structure built: 1962 (2000).
Transportation: Commute to work: 89.1% car, 0.6% public transportation, 4.8% walk, 3.8% work from home (2000); Travel time to work: 41.0% less than 15 minutes, 38.6% 15 to 30 minutes, 14.8% 30 to 45 minutes, 3.1% 45 to 60 minutes, 2.4% 60 minutes or more (2000)
Additional Information Contacts
DeKalb County Convention and Visitors Bureau . . . . (260) 927-1499
    http://www.dekalbcvb.org
Town of Ashley . . . . (260) 587-3182
    http://www.ashley.in.gov

AUBURN (city). County seat. Covers a land area of 6.648 square miles and a water area of 0 square miles. Located at 41.36° N. Lat; 85.05° W. Long. Elevation is 866 feet.
History: Auburn developed as a trading center for the surrounding farmlands, and as the seat of DeKalb County.
Population: 9,989 (1990); 12,074 (2000); 12,913 (2010); 13,218 (2015 projected); Race: 96.2% White, 1.3% Black, 0.5% Asian, 1.9% Other, 2.3% Hispanic of any race (2010); Density: 1,942.4 persons per square mile (2010); Average household size: 2.36 (2010); Median age: 37.2 (2010); Males per 100 females: 94.9 (2010); Marriage status: 20.8% never married, 57.7% now married, 8.1% widowed, 13.4% divorced (2000); Foreign born: 0.5% (2000); Ancestry (includes multiple ancestries): 35.2% German,

14.6% United States or American, 9.6% Irish, 9.3% English, 7.0% Other groups (2000).
Economy: Single-family building permits issued: 21 (2009); Multi-family building permits issued: 0 (2009); Employment by occupation: 10.5% management, 14.7% professional, 9.1% services, 22.0% sales, 0.2% farming, 9.8% construction, 33.7% production (2000).
Income: Per capita income: $23,707 (2010); Median household income: $47,145 (2010); Average household income: $56,789 (2010); Percent of households with income of $100,000 or more: 10.8% (2010); Poverty rate: 5.2% (2000).
Taxes: Total city taxes per capita: $189 (2007); City property taxes per capita: $136 (2007).
Education: Percent of population age 25 and over with: High school diploma (including GED) or higher: 88.4% (2010); Bachelor's degree or higher: 23.8% (2010); Master's degree or higher: 7.4% (2010).
School District(s)
Dekalb Co Ctl United Sch Dist (PK-12)
    2008-09 Enrollment: 4,050 . . . . (260) 920-1011
Housing: Homeownership rate: 75.7% (2010); Median home value: $107,834 (2010); Median contract rent: $409 per month (2000); Median year structure built: 1972 (2000).
Hospitals: Dekalb Memorial Hospital (47 beds)
Safety: Violent crime rate: 7.7 per 10,000 population; Property crime rate: 321.8 per 10,000 population (2008).
Newspapers: Clipper (Local news); Evening Star (Local news; Circulation 8,094); Evening Star Plus (Community news); The Journal Gazette - Northeast Bureau (Regional news)
Transportation: Commute to work: 94.7% car, 0.4% public transportation, 2.7% walk, 1.4% work from home (2000); Travel time to work: 55.6% less than 15 minutes, 26.4% 15 to 30 minutes, 11.8% 30 to 45 minutes, 4.3% 45 to 60 minutes, 1.9% 60 minutes or more (2000)
Additional Information Contacts
City of Auburn . . . . (260) 925-2100
    http://www.chamberinauburn.com
DeKalb County Convention and Visitors Bureau . . . . (260) 927-1499
    http://www.dekalbcvb.org

BUTLER (city). Covers a land area of 1.789 square miles and a water area of 0 square miles. Located at 41.43° N. Lat; 84.87° W. Long. Elevation is 866 feet.
Population: 2,619 (1990); 2,725 (2000); 2,673 (2010); 2,639 (2015 projected); Race: 97.3% White, 0.3% Black, 0.1% Asian, 2.3% Other, 2.5% Hispanic of any race (2010); Density: 1,494.5 persons per square mile (2010); Average household size: 2.58 (2010); Median age: 34.2 (2010); Males per 100 females: 98.0 (2010); Marriage status: 22.0% never married, 59.0% now married, 7.5% widowed, 11.5% divorced (2000); Foreign born: 0.0% (2000); Ancestry (includes multiple ancestries): 21.9% German, 12.2% United States or American, 10.6% Irish, 10.3% Other groups, 7.3% English (2000).
Economy: Employment by occupation: 4.7% management, 7.8% professional, 12.3% services, 17.9% sales, 0.0% farming, 7.6% construction, 49.7% production (2000).
Income: Per capita income: $17,651 (2010); Median household income: $42,185 (2010); Average household income: $45,951 (2010); Percent of households with income of $100,000 or more: 3.4% (2010); Poverty rate: 9.7% (2000).
Taxes: Total city taxes per capita: $170 (2007); City property taxes per capita: $133 (2007).
Education: Percent of population age 25 and over with: High school diploma (including GED) or higher: 77.5% (2010); Bachelor's degree or higher: 9.8% (2010); Master's degree or higher: 3.3% (2010).
School District(s)
Dekalb Co Eastern Com Sch Dist (KG-12)
    2008-09 Enrollment: 1,494 . . . . (260) 868-2125
Housing: Homeownership rate: 72.0% (2010); Median home value: $74,972 (2010); Median contract rent: $369 per month (2000); Median year structure built: 1955 (2000).
Newspapers: Butler Bulletin (Local news; Circulation 1,500)
Transportation: Commute to work: 93.4% car, 0.0% public transportation, 2.3% walk, 2.3% work from home (2000); Travel time to work: 40.2% less than 15 minutes, 34.7% 15 to 30 minutes, 17.2% 30 to 45 minutes, 6.3% 45 to 60 minutes, 1.5% 60 minutes or more (2000)
Additional Information Contacts
Butler Chamber of Commerce . . . . (260) 925-2100
    http://www.chamberinauburn.com

City of Butler . . . . (260) 868-5200
  http://www.butler.in.us

CORUNNA (town).
Covers a land area of 0.174 square miles and a water area of 0 square miles. Located at 41.43° N. Lat; 85.14° W. Long. Elevation is 974 feet.

Population: 241 (1990); 254 (2000); 255 (2010); 257 (2015 projected); Race: 98.0% White, 0.4% Black, 0.0% Asian, 1.6% Other, 2.4% Hispanic of any race (2010); Density: 1,462.1 persons per square mile (2010); Average household size: 2.83 (2010); Median age: 36.5 (2010); Males per 100 females: 114.3 (2010); Marriage status: 26.6% never married, 50.3% now married, 11.6% widowed, 11.6% divorced (2000); Foreign born: 0.0% (2000); Ancestry (includes multiple ancestries): 14.8% German, 12.6% English, 12.2% Irish, 11.3% Other groups, 9.6% United States or American (2000).

Economy: Employment by occupation: 5.6% management, 5.6% professional, 14.8% services, 19.4% sales, 1.9% farming, 11.1% construction, 41.7% production (2000).

Income: Per capita income: $24,828 (2010); Median household income: $53,125 (2010); Average household income: $70,389 (2010); Percent of households with income of $100,000 or more: 24.4% (2010); Poverty rate: 4.8% (2000).

Taxes: Total city taxes per capita: $147 (2007); City property taxes per capita: $108 (2007).

Education: Percent of population age 25 and over with: High school diploma (including GED) or higher: 84.8% (2010); Bachelor's degree or higher: 22.4% (2010); Master's degree or higher: 1.8% (2010).

Housing: Homeownership rate: 88.9% (2010); Median home value: $120,833 (2010); Median contract rent: $213 per month (2000); Median year structure built: before 1940 (2000).

Transportation: Commute to work: 91.7% car, 0.0% public transportation, 3.7% walk, 0.0% work from home (2000); Travel time to work: 29.6% less than 15 minutes, 57.4% 15 to 30 minutes, 4.6% 30 to 45 minutes, 4.6% 45 to 60 minutes, 3.7% 60 minutes or more (2000)

GARRETT (city).
Covers a land area of 3.126 square miles and a water area of 0 square miles. Located at 41.34° N. Lat; 85.13° W. Long. Elevation is 879 feet.

History: Garrett developed around the Baltimore & Ohio Railroad shops and roundhouse, and served the surrounding farms.

Population: 5,533 (1990); 5,803 (2000); 5,667 (2010); 5,585 (2015 projected); Race: 96.8% White, 0.6% Black, 0.6% Asian, 2.0% Other, 2.8% Hispanic of any race (2010); Density: 1,813.0 persons per square mile (2010); Average household size: 2.54 (2010); Median age: 35.7 (2010); Males per 100 females: 97.9 (2010); Marriage status: 18.5% never married, 62.1% now married, 6.9% widowed, 12.5% divorced (2000); Foreign born: 1.4% (2000); Ancestry (includes multiple ancestries): 31.4% German, 16.9% United States or American, 7.7% Other groups, 7.3% Irish, 7.3% English (2000).

Economy: Employment by occupation: 7.9% management, 10.7% professional, 14.9% services, 20.7% sales, 0.0% farming, 8.2% construction, 37.6% production (2000).

Income: Per capita income: $20,447 (2010); Median household income: $46,559 (2010); Average household income: $52,357 (2010); Percent of households with income of $100,000 or more: 6.3% (2010); Poverty rate: 6.0% (2000).

Taxes: Total city taxes per capita: $138 (2007); City property taxes per capita: $106 (2007).

Education: Percent of population age 25 and over with: High school diploma (including GED) or higher: 88.4% (2010); Bachelor's degree or higher: 9.9% (2010); Master's degree or higher: 3.8% (2010).

School District(s)
Garrett-Keyser-Butler Com (KG-12)
  2008-09 Enrollment: 1,785 . . . . (260) 357-3185

Housing: Homeownership rate: 78.9% (2010); Median home value: $88,687 (2010); Median contract rent: $387 per month (2000); Median year structure built: 1942 (2000).

Transportation: Commute to work: 95.7% car, 0.0% public transportation, 1.9% walk, 1.9% work from home (2000); Travel time to work: 49.6% less than 15 minutes, 27.8% 15 to 30 minutes, 15.7% 30 to 45 minutes, 3.7% 45 to 60 minutes, 3.2% 60 minutes or more (2000)

Additional Information Contacts
City of Garrett. . . . . (260) 357-4151
  http://www.garrettindiana.us

SAINT JOE (town).
Covers a land area of 0.283 square miles and a water area of 0 square miles. Located at 41.31° N. Lat; 84.90° W. Long. Elevation is 820 feet.

Population: 465 (1990); 478 (2000); 476 (2010); 471 (2015 projected); Race: 97.3% White, 0.4% Black, 0.0% Asian, 2.3% Other, 2.5% Hispanic of any race (2010); Density: 1,680.6 persons per square mile (2010); Average household size: 2.83 (2010); Median age: 35.2 (2010); Males per 100 females: 106.1 (2010); Marriage status: 23.0% never married, 60.4% now married, 5.7% widowed, 10.9% divorced (2000); Foreign born: 1.0% (2000); Ancestry (includes multiple ancestries): 27.0% United States or American, 22.0% German, 7.5% English, 7.1% Irish, 3.1% Other groups (2000).

Economy: Employment by occupation: 6.4% management, 4.7% professional, 19.6% services, 17.0% sales, 0.0% farming, 6.8% construction, 45.5% production (2000).

Income: Per capita income: $22,118 (2010); Median household income: $51,351 (2010); Average household income: $61,994 (2010); Percent of households with income of $100,000 or more: 13.1% (2010); Poverty rate: 5.5% (2000).

Taxes: Total city taxes per capita: $0 (2007); City property taxes per capita: $0 (2007).

Education: Percent of population age 25 and over with: High school diploma (including GED) or higher: 85.7% (2010); Bachelor's degree or higher: 8.6% (2010); Master's degree or higher: 5.3% (2010).

School District(s)
Dekalb Co Eastern Com Sch Dist (KG-12)
  2008-09 Enrollment: 1,494 . . . . (260) 868-2125

Housing: Homeownership rate: 86.9% (2010); Median home value: $118,056 (2010); Median contract rent: $371 per month (2000); Median year structure built: before 1940 (2000).

Transportation: Commute to work: 95.7% car, 0.0% public transportation, 3.4% walk, 0.9% work from home (2000); Travel time to work: 20.7% less than 15 minutes, 50.0% 15 to 30 minutes, 14.7% 30 to 45 minutes, 7.8% 45 to 60 minutes, 6.9% 60 minutes or more (2000)

SPENCERVILLE (unincorporated postal area, zip code 46788).
Covers a land area of 34.654 square miles and a water area of 0.113 square miles. Located at 41.26° N. Lat; 84.93° W. Long. Elevation is 817 feet.

Population: 2,834 (2000); Race: 97.9% White, 0.0% Black, 1.1% Asian, 1.0% Other, 0.0% Hispanic of any race (2000); Density: 81.8 persons per square mile (2000); Age: 35.5% under 18, 5.7% over 64 (2000); Marriage status: 23.1% never married, 69.0% now married, 2.9% widowed, 5.0% divorced (2000); Foreign born: 1.1% (2000); Ancestry (includes multiple ancestries): 34.1% German, 9.4% Irish, 6.8% English, 5.5% United States or American, 4.3% Other groups (2000).

Economy: Employment by occupation: 9.3% management, 18.5% professional, 9.4% services, 19.0% sales, 0.9% farming, 13.7% construction, 29.2% production (2000).

Income: Per capita income: $17,839 (2000); Median household income: $58,621 (2000); Poverty rate: 7.6% (2000).

Education: Percent of population age 25 and over with: High school diploma (including GED) or higher: 83.2% (2000); Bachelor's degree or higher: 21.1% (2000).

Housing: Homeownership rate: 92.6% (2000); Median home value: $127,900 (2000); Median contract rent: $415 per month (2000); Median year structure built: 1974 (2000).

Transportation: Commute to work: 91.1% car, 0.7% public transportation, 5.5% walk, 0.7% work from home (2000); Travel time to work: 23.2% less than 15 minutes, 35.2% 15 to 30 minutes, 29.8% 30 to 45 minutes, 7.0% 45 to 60 minutes, 4.8% 60 minutes or more (2000)

WATERLOO (town).
Covers a land area of 1.500 square miles and a water area of 0 square miles. Located at 41.43° N. Lat; 85.02° W. Long. Elevation is 906 feet.

Population: 2,081 (1990); 2,200 (2000); 2,139 (2010); 2,094 (2015 projected); Race: 93.1% White, 0.6% Black, 0.2% Asian, 6.1% Other, 5.4% Hispanic of any race (2010); Density: 1,426.0 persons per square mile (2010); Average household size: 2.66 (2010); Median age: 34.7 (2010); Males per 100 females: 106.5 (2010); Marriage status: 20.8% never married, 57.6% now married, 6.8% widowed, 14.8% divorced (2000); Foreign born: 1.4% (2000); Ancestry (includes multiple ancestries): 22.0% German, 13.8% United States or American, 9.1% Other groups, 7.0% Irish, 6.9% English (2000).

Economy: Employment by occupation: 6.3% management, 8.6% professional, 10.4% services, 20.9% sales, 0.1% farming, 7.3% construction, 46.4% production (2000).

Income: Per capita income: $19,997 (2010); Median household income: $46,365 (2010); Average household income: $53,047 (2010); Percent of households with income of $100,000 or more: 8.0% (2010); Poverty rate: 12.4% (2000).

Taxes: Total city taxes per capita: $151 (2007); City property taxes per capita: $115 (2007).

Education: Percent of population age 25 and over with: High school diploma (including GED) or higher: 81.9% (2010); Bachelor's degree or higher: 9.8% (2010); Master's degree or higher: 2.2% (2010).

School District(s)
Dekalb Co Ctl United Sch Dist (PK-12)
   2008-09 Enrollment: 4,050 . . . . (260) 920-1011

Housing: Homeownership rate: 78.4% (2010); Median home value: $84,551 (2010); Median contract rent: $364 per month (2000); Median year structure built: 1948 (2000).

Safety: Violent crime rate: 64.3 per 10,000 population; Property crime rate: 399.8 per 10,000 population (2008).

Transportation: Commute to work: 93.4% car, 0.2% public transportation, 1.3% walk, 2.7% work from home (2000); Travel time to work: 39.4% less than 15 minutes, 44.5% 15 to 30 minutes, 10.6% 30 to 45 minutes, 1.9% 45 to 60 minutes, 3.7% 60 minutes or more (2000); Amtrak: train service available.

Dearborn County

Located in southeastern Indiana; bounded on the east by Ohio, and on the southeast by the Ohio River and the Kentucky border; drained by the Whitewater River. Covers a land area of 305.21 square miles, a water area of 1.84 square miles, and is located in the Eastern Time Zone. The county was founded in 1803. County seat is Lawrenceburg.

Dearborn County is part of the Cincinnati-Middletown, OH-KY-IN Metropolitan Statistical Area. The entire metro area includes: Dearborn County, IN; Franklin County, IN; Ohio County, IN; Boone County, KY; Bracken County, KY; Campbell County, KY; Gallatin County, KY; Grant County, KY; Kenton County, KY; Pendleton County, KY; Brown County, OH; Butler County, OH; Clermont County, OH; Hamilton County, OH; Warren County, OH

Population: 38,835 (1990); 46,109 (2000); 50,606 (2010); 52,397 (2015 projected); Race: 97.3% White, 1.0% Black, 0.5% Asian, 1.3% Other, 0.7% Hispanic of any race (2010); Density: 165.8 persons per square mile (2010); Average household size: 2.65 (2010); Median age: 38.4 (2010); Males per 100 females: 98.4 (2010).

Religion: Five largest groups: 18.7% Catholic Church, 4.6% The United Methodist Church, 4.3% American Baptist Churches in the USA, 3.5% Christian Churches and Churches of Christ, 3.1% Lutheran Church—Missouri Synod (2000).

Economy: Unemployment rate: 9.9% (5/2010); Total civilian labor force: 25,319 (5/2010); Leading industries: 23.3% accommodation & food services; 14.8% manufacturing; 14.5% health care and social assistance (2008); Farms: 564 totaling 65,830 acres (2007); Companies that employ 500 or more persons: 4 (2008); Companies that employ 100 to 499 persons: 12 (2008); Companies that employ less than 100 persons: 1,012 (2008); Black-owned businesses: n/a (2002); Hispanic-owned businesses: n/a (2002); Asian-owned businesses: n/a (2002); Women-owned businesses: 765 (2002); Retail sales per capita: $12,239 (2010). Single-family building permits issued: 84 (2009); Multi-family building permits issued: 12 (2009).

Income: Per capita income: $25,606 (2010); Median household income: $58,115 (2010); Average household income: $68,130 (2010); Percent of households with income of $100,000 or more: 18.4% (2010); Poverty rate: 8.1% (2008); Bankruptcy rate: 6.82% (2009).

Taxes: Total county taxes per capita: $221 (2007); County property taxes per capita: $146 (2007).

Education: Percent of population age 25 and over with: High school diploma (including GED) or higher: 87.6% (2010); Bachelor's degree or higher: 17.6% (2010); Master's degree or higher: 5.8% (2010).

Housing: Homeownership rate: 77.8% (2010); Median home value: $143,986 (2010); Median contract rent: $523 per month (2006-2008 3-year est.); Median year structure built: 1979 (2006-2008 3-year est.)

Health: Birth rate: 133.3 per 10,000 population (2009); Death rate: 83.4 per 10,000 population (2009); Age-adjusted cancer mortality rate: 208.8 deaths

per 100,000 population (2006); Number of physicians: 9.1 per 10,000 population (2007); Hospital beds: 19.7 per 10,000 population (2006); Hospital admissions: 996.8 per 10,000 population (2006).

Elections: 2008 Presidential election results: 32.1% Obama, 67.0% McCain, 0.0% Nader

Additional Information Contacts
Dearborn County Government. . . . . (812) 537-8867
   http://www.dearborncounty.org
City of Aurora. . . . . (812) 926-1777
   http://www.aurora.in.us
City of Greendale. . . . . (812) 926-1777
   http://www.indiantrails.com
City of Lawrenceburg. . . . . (812) 532-3573
   http://www.lawrenceburg-in.com
Dearborn County Chamber of Commerce . . . . (812) 537-0814
   http://www.dearborncountychamber.org

Dearborn County Communities

AURORA (city). Covers a land area of 2.776 square miles and a water area of 0.143 square miles. Located at 39.05° N. Lat; 84.90° W. Long. Elevation is 486 feet.

History: Aurora was founded in 1819 along the Ohio River. Judge Jesse Holman of the Indiana Supreme Court suggested that the town be named for the goddess of the dawn. Aurora was severely damaged in the 1937 flood of the Ohio River.

Population: 3,825 (1990); 3,965 (2000); 3,986 (2010); 3,995 (2015 projected); Race: 98.2% White, 0.3% Black, 0.2% Asian, 1.3% Other, 0.5% Hispanic of any race (2010); Density: 1,435.7 persons per square mile (2010); Average household size: 2.43 (2010); Median age: 37.4 (2010); Males per 100 females: 98.0 (2010); Marriage status: 22.9% never married, 55.2% now married, 7.9% widowed, 13.9% divorced (2000); Foreign born: 1.1% (2000); Ancestry (includes multiple ancestries): 30.5% German, 17.2% United States or American, 12.2% Irish, 11.1% English, 10.4% Other groups (2000).

Economy: Employment by occupation: 7.3% management, 9.7% professional, 23.1% services, 24.3% sales, 0.6% farming, 16.4% construction, 18.5% production (2000).

Income: Per capita income: $19,087 (2010); Median household income: $38,233 (2010); Average household income: $46,034 (2010); Percent of households with income of $100,000 or more: 6.6% (2010); Poverty rate: 10.4% (2000).

Taxes: Total city taxes per capita: $302 (2007); City property taxes per capita: $220 (2007).

Education: Percent of population age 25 and over with: High school diploma (including GED) or higher: 81.0% (2010); Bachelor's degree or higher: 15.2% (2010); Master's degree or higher: 3.3% (2010).

School District(s)
South Dearborn Com School Corp (KG-12)
   2008-09 Enrollment: 3,118 . . . . (812) 926-2090

Housing: Homeownership rate: 55.1% (2010); Median home value: $110,467 (2010); Median contract rent: $429 per month (2000); Median year structure built: 1947 (2000).

Safety: Violent crime rate: 83.5 per 10,000 population; Property crime rate: 221.0 per 10,000 population (2008).

Transportation: Commute to work: 94.2% car, 0.0% public transportation, 1.9% walk, 1.7% work from home (2000); Travel time to work: 40.0% less than 15 minutes, 24.5% 15 to 30 minutes, 17.4% 30 to 45 minutes, 12.0% 45 to 60 minutes, 6.1% 60 minutes or more (2000)

Additional Information Contacts
City of Aurora. . . . . (812) 926-1777
   http://www.aurora.in.us
Dearborn County Chamber of Commerce . . . . (812) 537-0814
   http://www.dearborncountychamber.org

BRIGHT (CDP). Covers a land area of 14.309 square miles and a water area of 0 square miles. Located at 39.21° N. Lat; 84.86° W. Long. Elevation is 922 feet.

History: Bright is a community in Dearborn County, which was formed in 1803. It was named for Dr. Henry Dearborn (DR), an officer in the Revolutionary War and the War of 1812.

Population: 3,863 (1990); 5,405 (2000); 5,951 (2010); 6,072 (2015 projected); Race: 98.0% White, 0.8% Black, 0.1% Asian, 1.1% Other, 0.8% Hispanic of any race (2010); Density: 415.9 persons per square mile (2010); Average household size: 2.97 (2010); Median age: 36.6 (2010);

Males per 100 females: 99.7 (2010); Marriage status: 19.7% never married, 70.3% now married, 2.5% widowed, 7.5% divorced (2000); Foreign born: 1.5% (2000); Ancestry (includes multiple ancestries): 39.4% German, 13.0% United States or American, 10.9% Irish, 10.1% English, 5.5% Other groups (2000).
Economy: Employment by occupation: 14.0% management, 18.4% professional, 6.0% services, 28.7% sales, 0.0% farming, 14.7% construction, 18.2% production (2000).
Income: Per capita income: $28,801 (2010); Median household income: $74,168 (2010); Average household income: $85,364 (2010); Percent of households with income of $100,000 or more: 28.0% (2010); Poverty rate: 1.7% (2000).
Education: Percent of population age 25 and over with: High school diploma (including GED) or higher: 91.7% (2010); Bachelor's degree or higher: 22.7% (2010); Master's degree or higher: 6.3% (2010).
Housing: Homeownership rate: 87.2% (2010); Median home value: $167,666 (2010); Median contract rent: $518 per month (2000); Median year structure built: 1981 (2000).
Transportation: Commute to work: 96.4% car, 1.3% public transportation, 0.3% walk, 2.0% work from home (2000); Travel time to work: 17.6% less than 15 minutes, 26.1% 15 to 30 minutes, 32.0% 30 to 45 minutes, 16.3% 45 to 60 minutes, 8.0% 60 minutes or more (2000)

DILLSBORO (town). Covers a land area of 1.010 square miles and a water area of 0 square miles. Located at 39.01° N. Lat; 85.05° W. Long. Elevation is 869 feet.

Population: 1,428 (1990); 1,436 (2000); 1,477 (2010); 1,544 (2015 projected); Race: 98.4% White, 0.2% Black, 0.2% Asian, 1.2% Other, 1.2% Hispanic of any race (2010); Density: 1,462.2 persons per square mile (2010); Average household size: 2.47 (2010); Median age: 41.5 (2010); Males per 100 females: 92.1 (2010); Marriage status: 20.8% never married, 49.6% now married, 18.8% widowed, 10.8% divorced (2000); Foreign born: 0.6% (2000); Ancestry (includes multiple ancestries): 31.1% German, 13.3% Irish, 11.8% United States or American, 7.5% English, 6.9% Other groups (2000).
Economy: Employment by occupation: 5.2% management, 8.6% professional, 17.5% services, 18.2% sales, 1.2% farming, 14.4% construction, 34.9% production (2000).
Income: Per capita income: $22,341 (2010); Median household income: $46,489 (2010); Average household income: $56,126 (2010); Percent of households with income of $100,000 or more: 11.3% (2010); Poverty rate: 10.5% (2000).
Taxes: Total city taxes per capita: $66 (2007); City property taxes per capita: $62 (2007).
Education: Percent of population age 25 and over with: High school diploma (including GED) or higher: 80.4% (2010); Bachelor's degree or higher: 7.7% (2010); Master's degree or higher: 2.0% (2010).
School District(s)
South Dearborn Com School Corp (KG-12)
    2008-09 Enrollment: 3,118 . . . . (812) 926-2090
Housing: Homeownership rate: 69.8% (2010); Median home value: $122,967 (2010); Median contract rent: $384 per month (2000); Median year structure built: 1970 (2000).
Transportation: Commute to work: 94.9% car, 0.4% public transportation, 0.4% walk, 3.4% work from home (2000); Travel time to work: 23.5% less than 15 minutes, 27.6% 15 to 30 minutes, 23.5% 30 to 45 minutes, 11.8% 45 to 60 minutes, 13.7% 60 minutes or more (2000)

GREENDALE (city). Covers a land area of 6.046 square miles and a water area of 0.035 square miles. Located at 39.12° N. Lat; 84.85° W. Long. Elevation is 528 feet.

History: Greendale became associated with the distilling of whiskey in 1809, when the local manufacture of distilled liquors began. The Joseph E. Seagram Company purchased a plant in Greendale in 1933.
Population: 4,388 (1990); 4,296 (2000); 4,624 (2010); 4,692 (2015 projected); Race: 95.8% White, 1.6% Black, 1.1% Asian, 1.4% Other, 0.5% Hispanic of any race (2010); Density: 764.7 persons per square mile (2010); Average household size: 2.38 (2010); Median age: 41.0 (2010); Males per 100 females: 92.3 (2010); Marriage status: 20.7% never married, 59.7% now married, 8.7% widowed, 10.9% divorced (2000); Foreign born: 0.8% (2000); Ancestry (includes multiple ancestries): 35.7% German, 16.0% Irish, 13.9% United States or American, 10.5% English, 6.2% Other groups (2000).

Economy: Employment by occupation: 10.5% management, 18.3% professional, 15.3% services, 29.8% sales, 0.0% farming, 7.3% construction, 18.8% production (2000).
Income: Per capita income: $28,802 (2010); Median household income: $54,792 (2010); Average household income: $68,572 (2010); Percent of households with income of $100,000 or more: 16.3% (2010); Poverty rate: 5.1% (2000).
Taxes: Total city taxes per capita: $530 (2007); City property taxes per capita: $515 (2007).
Education: Percent of population age 25 and over with: High school diploma (including GED) or higher: 89.5% (2010); Bachelor's degree or higher: 24.1% (2010); Master's degree or higher: 9.3% (2010).
Housing: Homeownership rate: 73.5% (2010); Median home value: $134,412 (2010); Median contract rent: $402 per month (2000); Median year structure built: 1959 (2000).
Safety: Violent crime rate: 32.0 per 10,000 population; Property crime rate: 155.6 per 10,000 population (2008).
Transportation: Commute to work: 95.8% car, 0.0% public transportation, 2.4% walk, 1.2% work from home (2000); Travel time to work: 41.6% less than 15 minutes, 27.2% 15 to 30 minutes, 20.3% 30 to 45 minutes, 5.3% 45 to 60 minutes, 5.6% 60 minutes or more (2000)
Additional Information Contacts
City of Greendale . . . . (812) 926-1777
    http://www.indiantrails.com

GUILFORD (unincorporated postal area, zip code 47022). Aka Kennedy. Covers a land area of 39.872 square miles and a water area of 0 square miles. Located at 39.20° N. Lat; 84.94° W. Long. Elevation is 499 feet.

Population: 3,044 (2000); Race: 98.2% White, 0.0% Black, 0.3% Asian, 1.5% Other, 0.0% Hispanic of any race (2000); Density: 76.3 persons per square mile (2000); Age: 31.0% under 18, 9.3% over 64 (2000); Marriage status: 19.9% never married, 71.3% now married, 2.7% widowed, 6.1% divorced (2000); Foreign born: 0.6% (2000); Ancestry (includes multiple ancestries): 46.3% German, 13.9% United States or American, 12.1% English, 11.9% Irish, 3.9% Other groups (2000).
Economy: Employment by occupation: 19.3% management, 15.1% professional, 15.4% services, 22.4% sales, 0.3% farming, 10.6% construction, 16.9% production (2000).
Income: Per capita income: $20,585 (2000); Median household income: $52,250 (2000); Poverty rate: 2.7% (2000).
Education: Percent of population age 25 and over with: High school diploma (including GED) or higher: 87.0% (2000); Bachelor's degree or higher: 16.8% (2000).
School District(s)
Sunman-Dearborn Com Sch Corp (PK-12)
    2008-09 Enrollment: 4,279 . . . . (812) 623-2291
Housing: Homeownership rate: 91.5% (2000); Median home value: $140,800 (2000); Median contract rent: $426 per month (2000); Median year structure built: 1975 (2000).
Transportation: Commute to work: 91.5% car, 1.2% public transportation, 2.0% walk, 4.3% work from home (2000); Travel time to work: 12.1% less than 15 minutes, 28.8% 15 to 30 minutes, 29.7% 30 to 45 minutes, 16.6% 45 to 60 minutes, 12.7% 60 minutes or more (2000)

HIDDEN VALLEY (CDP). Covers a land area of 4.216 square miles and a water area of 0.300 square miles. Located at 39.16° N. Lat; 84.84° W. Long. Elevation is 548 feet.

History: The community of Hidden Valley and lake of the same name was built by James Jacob Rupel, legendary land developer. Active in the Greater Dayton area and Indiana for over 50 years and the former owner of Centre City Offices and the Carillon House in Downtown Dayton.
Population: 1,868 (1990); 4,417 (2000); 5,039 (2010); 5,254 (2015 projected); Race: 97.2% White, 0.6% Black, 0.6% Asian, 1.6% Other, 1.4% Hispanic of any race (2010); Density: 1,195.3 persons per square mile (2010); Average household size: 2.81 (2010); Median age: 38.5 (2010); Males per 100 females: 100.9 (2010); Marriage status: 16.8% never married, 72.8% now married, 2.1% widowed, 8.2% divorced (2000); Foreign born: 0.7% (2000); Ancestry (includes multiple ancestries): 36.6% German, 17.7% Irish, 10.6% United States or American, 10.3% English, 6.3% Other groups (2000).
Economy: Employment by occupation: 19.0% management, 19.0% professional, 12.4% services, 29.9% sales, 0.0% farming, 9.6% construction, 10.1% production (2000).

Income: Per capita income: $32,116 (2010); Median household income: $79,254 (2010); Average household income: $90,172 (2010); Percent of households with income of $100,000 or more: 32.3% (2010); Poverty rate: 2.8% (2000).
Education: Percent of population age 25 and over with: High school diploma (including GED) or higher: 96.5% (2010); Bachelor's degree or higher: 30.8% (2010); Master's degree or higher: 7.9% (2010).
Housing: Homeownership rate: 93.5% (2010); Median home value: $165,448 (2010); Median contract rent: $923 per month (2000); Median year structure built: 1991 (2000).
Transportation: Commute to work: 94.4% car, 0.0% public transportation, 1.2% walk, 4.4% work from home (2000); Travel time to work: 13.2% less than 15 minutes, 30.9% 15 to 30 minutes, 35.1% 30 to 45 minutes, 13.8% 45 to 60 minutes, 7.0% 60 minutes or more (2000)

LAWRENCEBURG (city). County seat. Covers a land area of 4.900 square miles and a water area of 0.142 square miles. Located at 39.09° N. Lat; 84.85° W. Long. Elevation is 479 feet.

History: Lawrenceburg was founded in 1801 by Captain Samuel C. Vance. It developed as a port on the Ohio River. In 1937 the river flooded the town, reaching a crest of 82.6 feet. Lawrenceburg was the site of the church where Henry Ward Beecher was pastor in 1837.
Population: 4,534 (1990); 4,685 (2000); 4,612 (2010); 4,588 (2015 projected); Race: 92.1% White, 5.5% Black, 0.7% Asian, 1.8% Other, 1.0% Hispanic of any race (2010); Density: 941.2 persons per square mile (2010); Average household size: 2.24 (2010); Median age: 37.3 (2010); Males per 100 females: 92.9 (2010); Marriage status: 28.8% never married, 48.8% now married, 8.3% widowed, 14.1% divorced (2000); Foreign born: 0.5% (2000); Ancestry (includes multiple ancestries): 24.0% German, 19.1% United States or American, 10.3% Other groups, 9.3% Irish, 7.9% English (2000).
Economy: Employment by occupation: 6.8% management, 10.8% professional, 22.8% services, 26.1% sales, 0.0% farming, 9.9% construction, 23.6% production (2000).
Income: Per capita income: $18,520 (2010); Median household income: $32,490 (2010); Average household income: $42,390 (2010); Percent of households with income of $100,000 or more: 7.5% (2010); Poverty rate: 14.9% (2000).
Taxes: Total city taxes per capita: $888 (2007); City property taxes per capita: $884 (2007).
Education: Percent of population age 25 and over with: High school diploma (including GED) or higher: 79.5% (2010); Bachelor's degree or higher: 10.5% (2010); Master's degree or higher: 2.2% (2010).

School District(s)
Lawrenceburg Com School Corp (PK-12)
    2008-09 Enrollment: 1,656 . . . . (812) 537-7201
Sunman-Dearborn Com Sch Corp (PK-12)
    2008-09 Enrollment: 4,279 . . . . (812) 623-2291
Housing: Homeownership rate: 45.5% (2010); Median home value: $106,933 (2010); Median contract rent: $404 per month (2000); Median year structure built: 1969 (2000).
Hospitals: Dearborn County Hospital (144 beds)
Newspapers: Aurora Journal Press (Local news; Circulation 6,230); The Dearborn County Register (Community news; Circulation 7,756); The Marketplace (Community news; Circulation 18,000)
Transportation: Commute to work: 90.7% car, 0.0% public transportation, 7.2% walk, 0.0% work from home (2000); Travel time to work: 38.5% less than 15 minutes, 32.6% 15 to 30 minutes, 15.7% 30 to 45 minutes, 9.1% 45 to 60 minutes, 4.0% 60 minutes or more (2000)
Additional Information Contacts
City of Lawrenceburg . . . . (812) 532-3573
    http://www.lawrenceburg-in.com

MOORES HILL (town). Covers a land area of 0.475 square miles and a water area of 0 square miles. Located at 39.11° N. Lat; 85.08° W. Long. Elevation is 991 feet.

History: Laid out 1838.
Population: 673 (1990); 635 (2000); 707 (2010); 736 (2015 projected); Race: 96.2% White, 0.3% Black, 1.0% Asian, 2.5% Other, 0.8% Hispanic of any race (2010); Density: 1,488.2 persons per square mile (2010); Average household size: 2.86 (2010); Median age: 34.8 (2010); Males per 100 females: 105.5 (2010); Marriage status: 20.1% never married, 66.4% now married, 4.3% widowed, 9.2% divorced (2000); Foreign born: 0.5% (2000); Ancestry (includes multiple ancestries): 28.8% United States or

American, 15.3% German, 9.9% Irish, 8.0% Other groups, 5.7% English (2000).
Economy: Employment by occupation: 2.4% management, 2.4% professional, 14.2% services, 27.3% sales, 0.0% farming, 18.2% construction, 35.6% production (2000).
Income: Per capita income: $18,967 (2010); Median household income: $48,929 (2010); Average household income: $53,158 (2010); Percent of households with income of $100,000 or more: 8.9% (2010); Poverty rate: 17.0% (2000).
Taxes: Total city taxes per capita: $37 (2007); City property taxes per capita: $29 (2007).
Education: Percent of population age 25 and over with: High school diploma (including GED) or higher: 80.3% (2010); Bachelor's degree or higher: 7.4% (2010); Master's degree or higher: 2.0% (2010).

School District(s)
South Dearborn Com School Corp (KG-12)
    2008-09 Enrollment: 3,118 . . . . (812) 926-2090
Housing: Homeownership rate: 78.9% (2010); Median home value: $99,792 (2010); Median contract rent: $388 per month (2000); Median year structure built: 1957 (2000).
Transportation: Commute to work: 96.3% car, 0.0% public transportation, 0.8% walk, 2.4% work from home (2000); Travel time to work: 14.2% less than 15 minutes, 35.0% 15 to 30 minutes, 16.7% 30 to 45 minutes, 15.8% 45 to 60 minutes, 18.3% 60 minutes or more (2000)

SAINT LEON (town). Covers a land area of 7.161 square miles and a water area of 0 square miles. Located at 39.28° N. Lat; 84.96° W. Long. Elevation is 1,010 feet.

Population: 495 (1990); 387 (2000); 560 (2010); 595 (2015 projected); Race: 98.8% White, 0.0% Black, 0.2% Asian, 1.1% Other, 0.0% Hispanic of any race (2010); Density: 78.2 persons per square mile (2010); Average household size: 2.92 (2010); Median age: 38.8 (2010); Males per 100 females: 100.7 (2010); Marriage status: 21.6% never married, 65.5% now married, 7.7% widowed, 5.2% divorced (2000); Foreign born: 0.5% (2000); Ancestry (includes multiple ancestries): 69.4% German, 11.7% United States or American, 6.4% Irish, 4.6% English, 1.5% Scottish (2000).
Economy: Employment by occupation: 9.5% management, 15.3% professional, 16.8% services, 34.7% sales, 1.1% farming, 5.8% construction, 16.8% production (2000).
Income: Per capita income: $26,582 (2010); Median household income: $72,368 (2010); Average household income: $76,966 (2010); Percent of households with income of $100,000 or more: 26.6% (2010); Poverty rate: 8.4% (2000).
Taxes: Total city taxes per capita: $4 (2007); City property taxes per capita: $0 (2007).
Education: Percent of population age 25 and over with: High school diploma (including GED) or higher: 90.9% (2010); Bachelor's degree or higher: 20.1% (2010); Master's degree or higher: 7.2% (2010).

School District(s)
Sunman-Dearborn Com Sch Corp (PK-12)
    2008-09 Enrollment: 4,279 . . . . (812) 623-2291
Housing: Homeownership rate: 89.1% (2010); Median home value: $180,625 (2010); Median contract rent: $242 per month (2000); Median year structure built: 1969 (2000).
Transportation: Commute to work: 92.1% car, 0.0% public transportation, 3.2% walk, 3.7% work from home (2000); Travel time to work: 30.6% less than 15 minutes, 36.1% 15 to 30 minutes, 19.7% 30 to 45 minutes, 8.7% 45 to 60 minutes, 4.9% 60 minutes or more (2000)

WEST HARRISON (town). Covers a land area of 0.091 square miles and a water area of 0.009 square miles. Located at 39.26° N. Lat; 84.82° W. Long. Elevation is 518 feet.

History: West Harrison was founded in 1813. General John Hunt Morgan and his Confederate cavalry raided West Harrison in 1863 before moving on to Ohio.
Population: 318 (1990); 284 (2000); 291 (2010); 292 (2015 projected); Race: 97.9% White, 0.7% Black, 0.3% Asian, 1.0% Other, 0.7% Hispanic of any race (2010); Density: 3,197.2 persons per square mile (2010); Average household size: 2.40 (2010); Median age: 40.0 (2010); Males per 100 females: 99.3 (2010); Marriage status: 34.7% never married, 39.0% now married, 8.0% widowed, 18.3% divorced (2000); Foreign born: 0.0% (2000); Ancestry (includes multiple ancestries): 28.3% German, 18.4% Irish, 7.7% English, 6.3% Other groups, 4.0% United States or American (2000).

Economy: Employment by occupation: 10.7% management, 10.7% professional, 13.2% services, 26.4% sales, 2.5% farming, 17.4% construction, 19.0% production (2000).

Income: Per capita income: $27,742 (2010); Median household income: $54,514 (2010); Average household income: $65,620 (2010); Percent of households with income of $100,000 or more: 17.4% (2010); Poverty rate: 31.6% (2000).

Taxes: Total city taxes per capita: $261 (2007); City property taxes per capita: $258 (2007).

Education: Percent of population age 25 and over with: High school diploma (including GED) or higher: 86.1% (2010); Bachelor's degree or higher: 15.4% (2010); Master's degree or higher: 7.2% (2010).

School District(s)
Sunman-Dearborn Com Sch Corp (PK-12)
    2008-09 Enrollment: 4,279 . . . . (812) 623-2291

Housing: Homeownership rate: 66.9% (2010); Median home value: $136,111 (2010); Median contract rent: $333 per month (2000); Median year structure built: before 1940 (2000).

Transportation: Commute to work: 89.7% car, 1.7% public transportation, 2.6% walk, 3.4% work from home (2000); Travel time to work: 37.5% less than 15 minutes, 19.6% 15 to 30 minutes, 25.9% 30 to 45 minutes, 11.6% 45 to 60 minutes, 5.4% 60 minutes or more (2000)

Decatur County

Located in southeast central Indiana; drained by Flatrock, Small Duck, Clifty, and Sand Creeks. Covers a land area of 372.60 square miles, a water area of 0.81 square miles, and is located in the Eastern Time Zone. The county was founded in 1821. County seat is Greensburg.

Decatur County is part of the Greensburg, IN Micropolitan Statistical Area. The entire metro area includes: Decatur County, IN

Weather Station: Greensburg   Elevation: 935 feet

	Jan	Feb	Mar	Apr	May	Jun	Jul	Aug	Sep	Oct	Nov	Dec
High	35	40	51	63	73	81	85	83	77	65	52	40
Low	19	23	32	42	52	61	65	62	56	44	35	25
Precip	2.5	2.3	3.7	4.4	4.9	4.2	4.1	4.2	3.0	3.1	3.8	3.2
Snow	6.4	4.0	2.8	0.5	tr	0.0	0.0	0.0	0.0	0.2	0.8	3.3

High and Low temperatures in degrees Fahrenheit; Precipitation and Snow in inches

Population: 23,645 (1990); 24,555 (2000); 25,052 (2010); 25,111 (2015 projected); Race: 96.6% White, 0.6% Black, 1.7% Asian, 1.1% Other, 1.1% Hispanic of any race (2010); Density: 67.2 persons per square mile (2010); Average household size: 2.48 (2010); Median age: 36.9 (2010); Males per 100 females: 97.1 (2010).

Religion: Five largest groups: 22.2% Catholic Church, 16.1% American Baptist Churches in the USA, 6.6% The United Methodist Church, 4.1% Christian Churches and Churches of Christ, 2.7% Christian Church (Disciples of Christ) (2000).

Economy: Unemployment rate: 10.5% (5/2010); Total civilian labor force: 13,206 (5/2010); Leading industries: 40.5% manufacturing; 13.4% retail trade; 10.4% health care and social assistance (2008); Farms: 639 totaling 204,702 acres (2007); Companies that employ 500 or more persons: 3 (2008); Companies that employ 100 to 499 persons: 13 (2008); Companies that employ less than 100 persons: 648 (2008); Black-owned businesses: n/a (2002); Hispanic-owned businesses: n/a (2002); Asian-owned businesses: n/a (2002); Women-owned businesses: 357 (2002); Retail sales per capita: $14,663 (2010). Single-family building permits issued: 51 (2009); Multi-family building permits issued: 64 (2009).

Income: Per capita income: $22,475 (2010); Median household income: $46,605 (2010); Average household income: $56,004 (2010); Percent of households with income of $100,000 or more: 10.5% (2010); Poverty rate: 12.3% (2008); Bankruptcy rate: 7.42% (2009).

Taxes: Total county taxes per capita: $334 (2007); County property taxes per capita: $132 (2007).

Education: Percent of population age 25 and over with: High school diploma (including GED) or higher: 84.7% (2010); Bachelor's degree or higher: 14.5% (2010); Master's degree or higher: 5.1% (2010).

Housing: Homeownership rate: 71.6% (2010); Median home value: $114,495 (2010); Median contract rent: $443 per month (2006-2008 3-year est.); Median year structure built: 1969 (2006-2008 3-year est.)

Health: Birth rate: 145.9 per 10,000 population (2009); Death rate: 96.1 per 10,000 population (2009); Age-adjusted cancer mortality rate: 216.9 deaths per 100,000 population (2006); Number of physicians: 6.0 per 10,000

population (2007); Hospital beds: 10.0 per 10,000 population (2006); Hospital admissions: 625.2 per 10,000 population (2006).

Elections: 2008 Presidential election results: 37.1% Obama, 61.5% McCain, 0.0% Nader

National and State Parks: Greenburg Reservoir State Fishing Area

Additional Information Contacts
Decatur County Government . . . . (812) 663-2570
    http://www.decaturcounty.in.gov
City of Greensburg . . . . (812) 663-8582
    http://www.cityofgreensburg.com
Greensburg Chamber of Commerce . . . . (812) 663-2832
    http://www.greensburgchamber.com

Decatur County Communities

GREENSBURG (city). County seat. Covers a land area of 4.794 square miles and a water area of 0.039 square miles. Located at 39.34° N. Lat; 85.48° W. Long. Elevation is 958 feet.

History: Greensburg developed as a residential center.

Population: 9,561 (1990); 10,260 (2000); 10,487 (2010); 10,521 (2015 projected); Race: 94.9% White, 0.8% Black, 2.9% Asian, 1.4% Other, 1.1% Hispanic of any race (2010); Density: 2,187.8 persons per square mile (2010); Average household size: 2.31 (2010); Median age: 36.8 (2010); Males per 100 females: 92.6 (2010); Marriage status: 21.8% never married, 55.6% now married, 8.5% widowed, 14.0% divorced (2000); Foreign born: 3.6% (2000); Ancestry (includes multiple ancestries): 21.0% German, 12.7% United States or American, 9.1% English, 8.7% Other groups, 8.3% Irish (2000).

Economy: Single-family building permits issued: 26 (2009); Multi-family building permits issued: 64 (2009); Employment by occupation: 8.6% management, 13.8% professional, 13.5% services, 20.5% sales, 0.3% farming, 8.2% construction, 35.1% production (2000).

Income: Per capita income: $22,344 (2010); Median household income: $43,009 (2010); Average household income: $52,054 (2010); Percent of households with income of $100,000 or more: 9.1% (2010); Poverty rate: 11.4% (2000).

Taxes: Total city taxes per capita: $418 (2007); City property taxes per capita: $397 (2007).

Education: Percent of population age 25 and over with: High school diploma (including GED) or higher: 83.0% (2010); Bachelor's degree or higher: 15.9% (2010); Master's degree or higher: 5.9% (2010).

School District(s)
Decatur County Com Schools (PK-12)
    2008-09 Enrollment: 2,281 . . . . (812) 663-4595
Greensburg Community Schools (PK-12)
    2008-09 Enrollment: 2,221 . . . . (812) 663-4774

Housing: Homeownership rate: 61.8% (2010); Median home value: $100,410 (2010); Median contract rent: $395 per month (2000); Median year structure built: 1963 (2000).

Hospitals: Decatur County Memorial Hospital (115 beds)

Newspapers: Greensburg Daily News (Local news; Circulation 6,200)

Transportation: Commute to work: 94.7% car, 0.0% public transportation, 2.9% walk, 2.0% work from home (2000); Travel time to work: 75.3% less than 15 minutes, 12.1% 15 to 30 minutes, 6.3% 30 to 45 minutes, 1.9% 45 to 60 minutes, 4.3% 60 minutes or more (2000)

Additional Information Contacts
City of Greensburg . . . . (812) 663-8582
    http://www.cityofgreensburg.com
Greensburg Chamber of Commerce . . . . (812) 663-2832
    http://www.greensburgchamber.com

MILFORD (town). Aka Clifty. Covers a land area of 0.090 square miles and a water area of 0 square miles. Located at 39.35° N. Lat; 85.61° W. Long. Elevation is 843 feet.

History: Laid out 1835.

Population: 126 (1990); 121 (2000); 109 (2010); 111 (2015 projected); Race: 99.1% White, 0.0% Black, 0.0% Asian, 0.9% Other, 0.9% Hispanic of any race (2010); Density: 1,215.3 persons per square mile (2010); Average household size: 2.60 (2010); Median age: 35.9 (2010); Males per 100 females: 101.9 (2010); Marriage status: 21.0% never married, 68.6% now married, 8.6% widowed, 1.9% divorced (2000); Foreign born: 0.0% (2000); Ancestry (includes multiple ancestries): 22.2% United States or American, 21.4% Other groups, 21.4% Irish, 7.9% German, 7.1% English (2000).

Economy: Employment by occupation: 12.0% management, 8.0% professional, 8.0% services, 6.0% sales, 4.0% farming, 20.0% construction, 42.0% production (2000).

Income: Per capita income: $21,877 (2010); Median household income: $52,273 (2010); Average household income: $57,083 (2010); Percent of households with income of $100,000 or more: 9.5% (2010); Poverty rate: 15.9% (2000).

Taxes: Total city taxes per capita: $8 (2007); City property taxes per capita: $0 (2007).

Education: Percent of population age 25 and over with: High school diploma (including GED) or higher: 85.1% (2010); Bachelor's degree or higher: 9.5% (2010); Master's degree or higher: 2.7% (2010).

Housing: Homeownership rate: 76.2% (2010); Median home value: $94,286 (2010); Median contract rent: $416 per month (2000); Median year structure built: 1963 (2000).

Transportation: Commute to work: 100.0% car, 0.0% public transportation, 0.0% walk, 0.0% work from home (2000); Travel time to work: 4.3% less than 15 minutes, 56.5% 15 to 30 minutes, 17.4% 30 to 45 minutes, 6.5% 45 to 60 minutes, 15.2% 60 minutes or more (2000)

MILLHOUSEN (town). Covers a land area of 1.012 square miles and a water area of 0 square miles. Located at 39.21° N. Lat; 85.43° W. Long. Elevation is 896 feet.

History: Settled 1838, plotted 1858.

Population: 151 (1990); 136 (2000); 142 (2010); 142 (2015 projected); Race: 100.0% White, 0.0% Black, 0.0% Asian, 0.0% Other, 0.0% Hispanic of any race (2010); Density: 140.2 persons per square mile (2010); Average household size: 2.58 (2010); Median age: 41.5 (2010); Males per 100 females: 108.8 (2010); Marriage status: 9.9% never married, 68.3% now married, 12.9% widowed, 8.9% divorced (2000); Foreign born: 0.0% (2000); Ancestry (includes multiple ancestries): 46.9% German, 5.4% United States or American, 4.1% English, 2.0% Irish, 1.4% Dutch (2000).

Economy: Employment by occupation: 7.9% management, 17.5% professional, 7.9% services, 20.6% sales, 0.0% farming, 15.9% construction, 30.2% production (2000).

Income: Per capita income: $25,984 (2010); Median household income: $46,029 (2010); Average household income: $69,818 (2010); Percent of households with income of $100,000 or more: 14.5% (2010); Poverty rate: 2.7% (2000).

Taxes: Total city taxes per capita: $83 (2007); City property taxes per capita: $61 (2007).

Education: Percent of population age 25 and over with: High school diploma (including GED) or higher: 86.5% (2010); Bachelor's degree or higher: 12.5% (2010); Master's degree or higher: 1.9% (2010).

Housing: Homeownership rate: 87.3% (2010); Median home value: $138,462 (2010); Median contract rent: $225 per month (2000); Median year structure built: before 1940 (2000).

Transportation: Commute to work: 93.7% car, 0.0% public transportation, 3.2% walk, 3.2% work from home (2000); Travel time to work: 6.6% less than 15 minutes, 57.4% 15 to 30 minutes, 21.3% 30 to 45 minutes, 9.8% 45 to 60 minutes, 4.9% 60 minutes or more (2000)

NEWPOINT (town). Aka New Point. Covers a land area of 0.273 square miles and a water area of 0 square miles. Located at 39.31° N. Lat; 85.32° W. Long.

Population: 296 (1990); 290 (2000); 292 (2010); 294 (2015 projected); Race: 96.6% White, 0.3% Black, 1.0% Asian, 2.1% Other, 3.1% Hispanic of any race (2010); Density: 1,069.2 persons per square mile (2010); Average household size: 2.68 (2010); Median age: 37.4 (2010); Males per 100 females: 111.6 (2010); Marriage status: 16.8% never married, 67.3% now married, 7.1% widowed, 8.8% divorced (2000); Foreign born: 0.0% (2000); Ancestry (includes multiple ancestries): 18.5% German, 11.0% United States or American, 5.5% English, 4.8% Irish, 4.1% European (2000).

Economy: Employment by occupation: 5.3% management, 6.0% professional, 14.7% services, 19.3% sales, 0.0% farming, 6.7% construction, 48.0% production (2000).

Income: Per capita income: $22,585 (2010); Median household income: $56,786 (2010); Average household income: $58,601 (2010); Percent of households with income of $100,000 or more: 10.1% (2010); Poverty rate: 7.3% (2000).

Taxes: Total city taxes per capita: $84 (2007); City property taxes per capita: $59 (2007).

Education: Percent of population age 25 and over with: High school diploma (including GED) or higher: 87.8% (2010); Bachelor's degree or higher: 9.7% (2010); Master's degree or higher: 3.1% (2010).

Housing: Homeownership rate: 81.7% (2010); Median home value: $128,704 (2010); Median contract rent: $373 per month (2000); Median year structure built: before 1940 (2000).

Transportation: Commute to work: 88.4% car, 0.0% public transportation, 6.8% walk, 4.8% work from home (2000); Travel time to work: 31.4% less than 15 minutes, 60.0% 15 to 30 minutes, 4.3% 30 to 45 minutes, 1.4% 45 to 60 minutes, 2.9% 60 minutes or more (2000)

SAINT PAUL (town). Covers a land area of 0.308 square miles and a water area of 0 square miles. Located at 39.42° N. Lat; 85.62° W. Long. Elevation is 856 feet.

Population: 1,067 (1990); 1,022 (2000); 972 (2010); 946 (2015 projected); Race: 98.1% White, 0.1% Black, 0.2% Asian, 1.5% Other, 2.0% Hispanic of any race (2010); Density: 3,152.5 persons per square mile (2010); Average household size: 2.77 (2010); Median age: 33.5 (2010); Males per 100 females: 94.0 (2010); Marriage status: 24.1% never married, 62.8% now married, 3.7% widowed, 9.4% divorced (2000); Foreign born: 0.3% (2000); Ancestry (includes multiple ancestries): 20.6% German, 17.4% United States or American, 13.1% Irish, 10.5% English, 9.1% Other groups (2000).

Economy: Employment by occupation: 5.0% management, 4.6% professional, 15.6% services, 22.9% sales, 0.0% farming, 14.1% construction, 37.8% production (2000).

Income: Per capita income: $20,212 (2010); Median household income: $46,773 (2010); Average household income: $56,403 (2010); Percent of households with income of $100,000 or more: 7.4% (2010); Poverty rate: 9.1% (2000).

Taxes: Total city taxes per capita: $79 (2007); City property taxes per capita: $65 (2007).

Education: Percent of population age 25 and over with: High school diploma (including GED) or higher: 79.1% (2010); Bachelor's degree or higher: 10.1% (2010); Master's degree or higher: 4.1% (2010).

Housing: Homeownership rate: 80.1% (2010); Median home value: $106,928 (2010); Median contract rent: $407 per month (2000); Median year structure built: 1955 (2000).

Transportation: Commute to work: 93.3% car, 0.0% public transportation, 3.9% walk, 2.2% work from home (2000); Travel time to work: 18.6% less than 15 minutes, 56.6% 15 to 30 minutes, 9.4% 30 to 45 minutes, 4.6% 45 to 60 minutes, 10.8% 60 minutes or more (2000)

WESTPORT (town). Covers a land area of 1.326 square miles and a water area of 0.012 square miles. Located at 39.17° N. Lat; 85.57° W. Long. Elevation is 814 feet.

History: Laid out 1836.

Population: 1,607 (1990); 1,515 (2000); 1,396 (2010); 1,337 (2015 projected); Race: 98.7% White, 0.0% Black, 0.1% Asian, 1.2% Other, 0.4% Hispanic of any race (2010); Density: 1,052.9 persons per square mile (2010); Average household size: 2.42 (2010); Median age: 35.5 (2010); Males per 100 females: 93.4 (2010); Marriage status: 21.7% never married, 56.8% now married, 9.1% widowed, 12.4% divorced (2000); Foreign born: 0.6% (2000); Ancestry (includes multiple ancestries): 16.3% German, 14.6% United States or American, 8.3% Irish, 7.9% English, 4.0% Other groups (2000).

Economy: Employment by occupation: 3.6% management, 14.7% professional, 14.7% services, 19.4% sales, 0.3% farming, 10.2% construction, 37.1% production (2000).

Income: Per capita income: $20,425 (2010); Median household income: $43,901 (2010); Average household income: $49,006 (2010); Percent of households with income of $100,000 or more: 6.6% (2010); Poverty rate: 10.5% (2000).

Taxes: Total city taxes per capita: $162 (2007); City property taxes per capita: $128 (2007).

Education: Percent of population age 25 and over with: High school diploma (including GED) or higher: 86.3% (2010); Bachelor's degree or higher: 13.3% (2010); Master's degree or higher: 6.1% (2010).

Housing: Homeownership rate: 75.2% (2010); Median home value: $106,935 (2010); Median contract rent: $317 per month (2000); Median year structure built: 1964 (2000).

Transportation: Commute to work: 95.0% car, 0.0% public transportation, 1.5% walk, 2.2% work from home (2000); Travel time to work: 22.0% less than 15 minutes, 45.5% 15 to 30 minutes, 18.5% 30 to 45 minutes, 6.4% 45 to 60 minutes, 7.6% 60 minutes or more (2000)

Delaware County

Located in eastern Indiana; drained by the Mississinewa River and the West Fork of the White River. Covers a land area of 393.29 square miles, a water area of 2.63 square miles, and is located in the Eastern Time Zone. The county was founded in 1827. County seat is Muncie.

Delaware County is part of the Muncie, IN Metropolitan Statistical Area. The entire metro area includes: Delaware County, IN

Weather Station: Muncie   Elevation: 977 feet

	Jan	Feb	Mar	Apr	May	Jun	Jul	Aug	Sep	Oct	Nov	Dec
High	32	37	48	61	72	81	85	83	77	64	50	38
Low	17	20	30	40	51	60	64	62	54	42	33	23
Precip	2.1	2.2	3.2	3.6	4.1	4.2	3.9	3.4	2.9	2.7	3.3	3.0
Snow	8.4	6.0	3.0	0.5	tr	0.0	0.0	0.0	0.0	0.2	1.2	6.3

High and Low temperatures in degrees Fahrenheit; Precipitation and Snow in inches

Population: 119,659 (1990); 118,769 (2000); 113,800 (2010); 110,579 (2015 projected); Race: 89.9% White, 6.7% Black, 1.0% Asian, 2.4% Other, 1.4% Hispanic of any race (2010); Density: 289.4 persons per square mile (2010); Average household size: 2.28 (2010); Median age: 35.2 (2010); Males per 100 females: 92.6 (2010).
Religion: Five largest groups: 6.0% Catholic Church, 5.9% The United Methodist Church, 2.5% Church of the Nazarene, 1.7% Southern Baptist Convention, 1.3% Christian Church (Disciples of Christ) (2000).
Economy: Unemployment rate: 10.7% (5/2010); Total civilian labor force: 54,687 (5/2010); Leading industries: 25.6% health care and social assistance; 15.6% retail trade; 12.6% manufacturing (2008); Farms: 659 totaling 154,470 acres (2007); Companies that employ 500 or more persons: 4 (2008); Companies that employ 100 to 499 persons: 66 (2008); Companies that employ less than 100 persons: 2,484 (2008); Black-owned businesses: n/a (2002); Hispanic-owned businesses: n/a (2002); Asian-owned businesses: n/a (2002); Women-owned businesses: 2,005 (2002); Retail sales per capita: $14,763 (2010). Single-family building permits issued: 44 (2009); Multi-family building permits issued: 0 (2009).
Income: Per capita income: $21,826 (2010); Median household income: $39,126 (2010); Average household income: $52,222 (2010); Percent of households with income of $100,000 or more: 10.6% (2010); Poverty rate: 17.2% (2008); Bankruptcy rate: 7.09% (2009).
Taxes: Total county taxes per capita: $238 (2007); County property taxes per capita: $194 (2007).
Education: Percent of population age 25 and over with: High school diploma (including GED) or higher: 84.2% (2010); Bachelor's degree or higher: 22.0% (2010); Master's degree or higher: 9.8% (2010).
Housing: Homeownership rate: 68.5% (2010); Median home value: $84,103 (2010); Median contract rent: $500 per month (2006-2008 3-year est.); Median year structure built: 1961 (2006-2008 3-year est.).
Health: Birth rate: 112.9 per 10,000 population (2009); Death rate: 100.4 per 10,000 population (2009); Age-adjusted cancer mortality rate: 230.7 deaths per 100,000 population (2006); Air Quality Index: 84.7% good, 15.3% moderate, 0.0% unhealthy for sensitive individuals, 0.0% unhealthy (percent of days in 2008); Number of physicians: 19.3 per 10,000 population (2007); Hospital beds: 33.4 per 10,000 population (2006); Hospital admissions: 1,475.5 per 10,000 population (2006).
Elections: 2008 Presidential election results: 56.8% Obama, 41.9% McCain, 0.0% Nader
Additional Information Contacts
Delaware County Government . . . . (765) 747-7726
    http://www.co.delware.in.us
City of Muncie . . . . (765) 747-4831
    http://www.cityofmuncie.com
Muncie-Delaware County Chamber of Commerce . . . . (765) 288-6681
    http://www.muncie.com
Town of Yorktown . . . . (765) 759-8521
    http://www.yorktownindiana.org

Delaware County Communities

ALBANY (town). Covers a land area of 1.651 square miles and a water area of 0 square miles. Located at 40.30° N. Lat; 85.23° W. Long. Elevation is 909 feet.
Population: 2,396 (1990); 2,368 (2000); 2,264 (2010); 2,211 (2015 projected); Race: 97.2% White, 0.8% Black, 0.0% Asian, 2.0% Other, 0.4% Hispanic of any race (2010); Density: 1,371.2 persons per square mile (2010); Average household size: 2.35 (2010); Median age: 40.9 (2010);

Males per 100 females: 89.0 (2010); Marriage status: 20.6% never married, 61.1% now married, 7.3% widowed, 10.9% divorced (2000); Foreign born: 0.6% (2000); Ancestry (includes multiple ancestries): 19.7% United States or American, 15.2% German, 11.7% English, 9.9% Other groups, 9.4% Irish (2000).
Economy: Single-family building permits issued: 2 (2009); Multi-family building permits issued: 0 (2009); Employment by occupation: 4.8% management, 8.8% professional, 13.1% services, 29.0% sales, 0.0% farming, 12.1% construction, 32.2% production (2000).
Income: Per capita income: $20,744 (2010); Median household income: $40,058 (2010); Average household income: $48,657 (2010); Percent of households with income of $100,000 or more: 7.8% (2010); Poverty rate: 5.9% (2000).
Taxes: Total city taxes per capita: $79 (2007); City property taxes per capita: $71 (2007).
Education: Percent of population age 25 and over with: High school diploma (including GED) or higher: 90.6% (2010); Bachelor's degree or higher: 9.6% (2010); Master's degree or higher: 4.3% (2010).
School District(s)
Delaware Community School Corp (KG-12)
    2008-09 Enrollment: 2,739 . . . . (765) 284-5074
Housing: Homeownership rate: 77.7% (2010); Median home value: $86,593 (2010); Median contract rent: $323 per month (2000); Median year structure built: 1957 (2000).
Transportation: Commute to work: 94.2% car, 0.0% public transportation, 4.4% walk, 1.0% work from home (2000); Travel time to work: 33.1% less than 15 minutes, 40.0% 15 to 30 minutes, 17.2% 30 to 45 minutes, 2.9% 45 to 60 minutes, 6.8% 60 minutes or more (2000)

DALEVILLE (town). Covers a land area of 1.992 square miles and a water area of 0.020 square miles. Located at 40.12° N. Lat; 85.55° W. Long. Elevation is 912 feet.
History: When Daleville was platted in 1838, it was expected that a canal would be built here. Instead, the railroad came in 1852.
Population: 1,686 (1990); 1,658 (2000); 1,587 (2010); 1,537 (2015 projected); Race: 98.1% White, 0.3% Black, 0.8% Asian, 0.9% Other, 0.9% Hispanic of any race (2010); Density: 796.7 persons per square mile (2010); Average household size: 2.43 (2010); Median age: 39.2 (2010); Males per 100 females: 93.1 (2010); Marriage status: 18.7% never married, 63.4% now married, 7.5% widowed, 10.4% divorced (2000); Foreign born: 0.3% (2000); Ancestry (includes multiple ancestries): 19.8% German, 11.4% Irish, 11.2% United States or American, 8.3% English, 7.0% Other groups (2000).
Economy: Single-family building permits issued: 1 (2009); Multi-family building permits issued: 0 (2009); Employment by occupation: 8.1% management, 14.9% professional, 17.6% services, 26.3% sales, 1.2% farming, 13.2% construction, 18.7% production (2000).
Income: Per capita income: $24,457 (2010); Median household income: $50,342 (2010); Average household income: $59,465 (2010); Percent of households with income of $100,000 or more: 12.5% (2010); Poverty rate: 2.7% (2000).
Taxes: Total city taxes per capita: $8 (2007); City property taxes per capita: $0 (2007).
Education: Percent of population age 25 and over with: High school diploma (including GED) or higher: 87.9% (2010); Bachelor's degree or higher: 18.9% (2010); Master's degree or higher: 7.3% (2010).
School District(s)
Daleville Community Schools (KG-12)
    2008-09 Enrollment: 680 . . . . (765) 378-3329
Housing: Homeownership rate: 81.8% (2010); Median home value: $104,733 (2010); Median contract rent: $433 per month (2000); Median year structure built: 1955 (2000).
Transportation: Commute to work: 97.2% car, 0.3% public transportation, 1.2% walk, 1.2% work from home (2000); Travel time to work: 24.7% less than 15 minutes, 51.3% 15 to 30 minutes, 13.2% 30 to 45 minutes, 5.0% 45 to 60 minutes, 5.9% 60 minutes or more (2000)

EATON (town). Covers a land area of 1.119 square miles and a water area of <.001 square miles. Located at 40.34° N. Lat; 85.35° W. Long. Elevation is 886 feet.
Population: 1,629 (1990); 1,603 (2000); 1,457 (2010); 1,374 (2015 projected); Race: 98.8% White, 0.0% Black, 0.2% Asian, 1.0% Other, 0.8% Hispanic of any race (2010); Density: 1,301.6 persons per square mile (2010); Average household size: 2.47 (2010); Median age: 36.4 (2010); Males per 100 females: 98.2 (2010); Marriage status: 21.1% never married,

59.7% now married, 7.2% widowed, 12.0% divorced (2000); Foreign born: 0.8% (2000); Ancestry (includes multiple ancestries): 20.3% United States or American, 15.5% German, 9.5% Irish, 8.9% English, 8.1% Other groups (2000).

Economy: Single-family building permits issued: 0 (2009); Multi-family building permits issued: 0 (2009); Employment by occupation: 6.1% management, 6.6% professional, 14.3% services, 25.9% sales, 0.1% farming, 15.7% construction, 31.2% production (2000).

Income: Per capita income: $20,082 (2010); Median household income: $39,453 (2010); Average household income: $49,201 (2010); Percent of households with income of $100,000 or more: 7.8% (2010); Poverty rate: 11.1% (2000).

Taxes: Total city taxes per capita: $136 (2007); City property taxes per capita: $136 (2007).

Education: Percent of population age 25 and over with: High school diploma (including GED) or higher: 85.4% (2010); Bachelor's degree or higher: 10.8% (2010); Master's degree or higher: 3.8% (2010).

School District(s)
Delaware Community School Corp (KG-12)
   2008-09 Enrollment: 2,739 . . . . (765) 284-5074

Housing: Homeownership rate: 83.2% (2010); Median home value: $73,402 (2010); Median contract rent: $331 per month (2000); Median year structure built: 1950 (2000).

Transportation: Commute to work: 94.6% car, 0.0% public transportation, 2.1% walk, 2.8% work from home (2000); Travel time to work: 21.1% less than 15 minutes, 48.8% 15 to 30 minutes, 20.4% 30 to 45 minutes, 4.5% 45 to 60 minutes, 5.1% 60 minutes or more (2000)

GASTON (town). Covers a land area of 0.351 square miles and a water area of 0 square miles. Located at 40.31° N. Lat; 85.50° W. Long. Elevation is 886 feet.

Population: 1,033 (1990); 1,010 (2000); 950 (2010); 920 (2015 projected); Race: 98.0% White, 0.4% Black, 0.0% Asian, 1.6% Other, 0.2% Hispanic of any race (2010); Density: 2,709.9 persons per square mile (2010); Average household size: 2.66 (2010); Median age: 38.2 (2010); Males per 100 females: 97.1 (2010); Marriage status: 26.2% never married, 54.1% now married, 4.6% widowed, 15.1% divorced (2000); Foreign born: 0.0% (2000); Ancestry (includes multiple ancestries): 28.5% United States or American, 18.5% German, 6.8% English, 4.9% Irish, 4.0% Other groups (2000).

Economy: Single-family building permits issued: 1 (2009); Multi-family building permits issued: 0 (2009); Employment by occupation: 5.6% management, 18.9% professional, 21.7% services, 16.7% sales, 0.0% farming, 18.3% construction, 18.7% production (2000).

Income: Per capita income: $20,337 (2010); Median household income: $42,500 (2010); Average household income: $54,789 (2010); Percent of households with income of $100,000 or more: 11.1% (2010); Poverty rate: 11.8% (2000).

Taxes: Total city taxes per capita: $159 (2007); City property taxes per capita: $127 (2007).

Education: Percent of population age 25 and over with: High school diploma (including GED) or higher: 75.5% (2010); Bachelor's degree or higher: 11.1% (2010); Master's degree or higher: 4.3% (2010).

School District(s)
Wes-Del Community Schools (KG-12)
   2008-09 Enrollment: 807 . . . . (765) 358-4006

Housing: Homeownership rate: 81.3% (2010); Median home value: $78,261 (2010); Median contract rent: $338 per month (2000); Median year structure built: 1949 (2000).

Transportation: Commute to work: 85.3% car, 0.0% public transportation, 3.3% walk, 4.9% work from home (2000); Travel time to work: 29.3% less than 15 minutes, 36.8% 15 to 30 minutes, 18.8% 30 to 45 minutes, 7.9% 45 to 60 minutes, 7.1% 60 minutes or more (2000)

MUNCIE (city). County seat. Covers a land area of 24.184 square miles and a water area of 0.015 square miles. Located at 40.19° N. Lat; 85.38° W. Long. Elevation is 932 feet.

History: A railroad station and some factories were the impetus for the growth of Muncie, which was platted in 1827 and called Munseytown. Incorporation as a town came in 1847, and by 1865 Muncie was declared a city. About 1887 natural gas wells began to bring many new industries to Muncie. One of these was the Ball Brothers Company, producers of canning jars.

Population: 71,709 (1990); 67,430 (2000); 63,039 (2010); 60,791 (2015 projected); Race: 84.7% White, 10.8% Black, 1.2% Asian, 3.2% Other,

1.9% Hispanic of any race (2010); Density: 2,606.6 persons per square mile (2010); Average household size: 2.17 (2010); Median age: 31.3 (2010); Males per 100 females: 90.9 (2010); Marriage status: 38.0% never married, 42.6% now married, 7.7% widowed, 11.8% divorced (2000); Foreign born: 1.9% (2000); Ancestry (includes multiple ancestries): 17.5% German, 15.3% Other groups, 12.8% United States or American, 9.3% Irish, 9.0% English (2000).

Economy: Unemployment rate: 11.0% (5/2010); Total civilian labor force: 30,007 (5/2010); Single-family building permits issued: 6 (2009); Multi-family building permits issued: 0 (2009); Employment by occupation: 7.3% management, 20.3% professional, 20.4% services, 28.0% sales, 0.2% farming, 6.6% construction, 17.1% production (2000).

Income: Per capita income: $17,007 (2010); Median household income: $29,478 (2010); Average household income: $39,788 (2010); Percent of households with income of $100,000 or more: 5.2% (2010); Poverty rate: 23.1% (2000).

Taxes: Total city taxes per capita: $326 (2007); City property taxes per capita: $299 (2007).

Education: Percent of population age 25 and over with: High school diploma (including GED) or higher: 79.1% (2010); Bachelor's degree or higher: 21.2% (2010); Master's degree or higher: 9.4% (2010).

School District(s)
Burris Laboratory School (KG-12)
   2008-09 Enrollment: 549 . . . . (765) 285-8488
Cowan Community School Corp (KG-12)
   2008-09 Enrollment: 713 . . . . (765) 289-4866
Delaware Community School Corp (KG-12)
   2008-09 Enrollment: 2,739 . . . . (765) 284-5074
Hoosier Academy - Muncie (KG-08)
   2008-09 Enrollment: 77 . . . . (317) 288-9633
IN Acad for Sci Math Humanities (11-12)
   2008-09 Enrollment: 282 . . . . (765) 285-8488
Muncie Community Schools (PK-12)
   2008-09 Enrollment: 7,284 . . . . (765) 747-5205

Four-year College(s)
Ball State University (Public)
   Fall 2008 Enrollment: 20,243 . . . . (765) 289-1241
   2009-10 Tuition: In-state $7,830; Out-of-state $20,398
Indiana Business College-Muncie (Private, For-profit)
   Fall 2008 Enrollment: 268 . . . . (765) 288-8681
   2009-10 Tuition: In-state $11,535; Out-of-state $11,535

Two-year College(s)
Ivy Tech Community College-East Central (Public)
   Fall 2008 Enrollment: 6,915 . . . . (765) 289-2291
   2009-10 Tuition: In-state $3,090; Out-of-state $6,306

Housing: Homeownership rate: 57.6% (2010); Median home value: $62,929 (2010); Median contract rent: $380 per month (2000); Median year structure built: 1956 (2000).

Hospitals: Ball Memorial Hospital (436 beds)

Safety: Violent crime rate: 53.6 per 10,000 population; Property crime rate: 403.6 per 10,000 population (2008).

Newspapers: The Star Press (Local news; Circulation 36,557)

Transportation: Commute to work: 86.8% car, 1.7% public transportation, 7.9% walk, 2.5% work from home (2000); Travel time to work: 56.4% less than 15 minutes, 28.7% 15 to 30 minutes, 7.1% 30 to 45 minutes, 2.8% 45 to 60 minutes, 5.0% 60 minutes or more (2000)

Additional Information Contacts
City of Muncie . . . . (765) 747-4831
   http://www.cityofmuncie.com
Muncie-Delaware County Chamber of Commerce . . . . (765) 288-6681
   http://www.muncie.com

SELMA (town). Covers a land area of 0.848 square miles and area of 0 square miles. Located at 40.19° N. Lat; 85.27° W. Long. Elevation is 1,010 feet.

Population: 800 (1990); 880 (2000); 794 (2010); 745 (2015 projected); Race: 98.0% White, 0.4% Black, 0.0% Asian, 1.6% Other, 0.6% Hispanic of any race (2010); Density: 935.9 persons per square mile (2010); Average household size: 2.43 (2010); Median age: 38.1 (2010); Males per 100 females: 92.3 (2010); Marriage status: 18.3% never married, 67.4% now married, 5.6% widowed, 8.7% divorced (2000); Foreign born: 0.0% (2000); Ancestry (includes multiple ancestries): 20.1% German, 15.5% United States or American, 9.5% English, 9.3% Irish, 9.1% Other groups (2000).

Economy: Single-family building permits issued: 2 (2009); Multi-family building permits issued: 0 (2009); Employment by occupation: 6.1% management, 13.9% professional, 15.8% services, 27.7% sales, 0.0% farming, 10.9% construction, 25.5% production (2000).

Income: Per capita income: $24,092 (2010); Median household income: $51,149 (2010); Average household income: $58,272 (2010); Percent of households with income of $100,000 or more: 11.7% (2010); Poverty rate: 4.7% (2000).

Taxes: Total city taxes per capita: $75 (2007); City property taxes per capita: $74 (2007).

Education: Percent of population age 25 and over with: High school diploma (including GED) or higher: 86.0% (2010); Bachelor's degree or higher: 12.0% (2010); Master's degree or higher: 6.7% (2010).

School District(s)

Liberty-Perry Com School Corp (KG-12)

    2008-09 Enrollment: 1,094 . . . . (765) 282-5615

Housing: Homeownership rate: 81.2% (2010); Median home value: $93,833 (2010); Median contract rent: $378 per month (2000); Median year structure built: 1954 (2000).

Transportation: Commute to work: 97.3% car, 0.0% public transportation, 2.7% walk, 0.0% work from home (2000); Travel time to work: 24.7% less than 15 minutes, 59.3% 15 to 30 minutes, 9.9% 30 to 45 minutes, 1.2% 45 to 60 minutes, 4.8% 60 minutes or more (2000)

YORKTOWN (town). Covers a land area of 3.526 square miles and a water area of 0.061 square miles. Located at 40.17° N. Lat; 85.48° W. Long. Elevation is 902 feet.

Population: 4,769 (1990); 4,785 (2000); 4,830 (2010); 4,702 (2015 projected); Race: 97.3% White, 1.1% Black, 0.2% Asian, 1.4% Other, 0.8% Hispanic of any race (2010); Density: 1,369.8 persons per square mile (2010); Average household size: 2.37 (2010); Median age: 39.5 (2010); Males per 100 females: 91.7 (2010); Marriage status: 17.4% never married, 63.1% now married, 7.7% widowed, 11.8% divorced (2000); Foreign born: 1.0% (2000); Ancestry (includes multiple ancestries): 23.9% German, 16.5% Irish, 11.3% United States or American, 10.7% English, 7.5% Other groups (2000).

Economy: Single-family building permits issued: 11 (2009); Multi-family building permits issued: 0 (2009); Employment by occupation: 13.9% management, 21.2% professional, 17.3% services, 20.5% sales, 0.2% farming, 6.8% construction, 20.0% production (2000).

Income: Per capita income: $29,471 (2010); Median household income: $56,028 (2010); Average household income: $70,235 (2010); Percent of households with income of $100,000 or more: 18.3% (2010); Poverty rate: 4.1% (2000).

Taxes: Total city taxes per capita: $257 (2007); City property taxes per capita: $248 (2007).

Education: Percent of population age 25 and over with: High school diploma (including GED) or higher: 91.5% (2010); Bachelor's degree or higher: 24.0% (2010); Master's degree or higher: 10.3% (2010).

School District(s)

Mt Pleasant Twp Com Sch Corp (KG-12)

    2008-09 Enrollment: 2,251 . . . . (765) 759-2720

Housing: Homeownership rate: 79.7% (2010); Median home value: $96,955 (2010); Median contract rent: $404 per month (2000); Median year structure built: 1967 (2000).

Transportation: Commute to work: 99.3% car, 0.0% public transportation, 0.0% walk, 0.7% work from home (2000); Travel time to work: 38.2% less than 15 minutes, 38.5% 15 to 30 minutes, 8.4% 30 to 45 minutes, 3.3% 45 to 60 minutes, 11.7% 60 minutes or more (2000)

Additional Information Contacts

Town of Yorktown . . . . (765) 759-8521

    http://www.yorktownindiana.org

Dubois County

Located in southwestern Indiana; bounded on the north by the East Fork of the White River; drained by the Patoka River. Covers a land area of 430.09 square miles, a water area of 5.14 square miles, and is located in the Eastern Time Zone. The county was founded in 1817. County seat is Jasper.

Dubois County is part of the Jasper, IN Micropolitan Statistical Area. The entire metro area includes: Dubois County, IN; Pike County, IN

Weather Station: Dubois S Ind. Forage Farm									Elevation: 688 feet		
	Jan	Feb	Mar	Apr	May	Jun	Jul	Aug	Sep	Oct	Nov	Dec
High	37	43	53	65	74	82	86	85	79	67	54	43
Low	20	23	33	43	52	61	65	63	56	44	35	25
Precip	2.9	2.6	4.2	4.7	5.3	4.7	4.4	4.0	3.5	3.3	4.2	3.5
Snow	na	na	na	tr	0.0	0.0	0.0	0.0	0.0	0.2	tr	na

High and Low temperatures in degrees Fahrenheit; Precipitation and Snow in inches

Population: 36,616 (1990); 39,674 (2000); 41,795 (2010); 42,591 (2015 projected); Race: 95.4% White, 0.3% Black, 0.4% Asian, 3.8% Other, 5.3% Hispanic of any race (2010); Density: 97.2 persons per square mile (2010); Average household size: 2.56 (2010); Median age: 38.6 (2010); Males per 100 females: 99.1 (2010).

Religion: Five largest groups: 58.1% Catholic Church, 6.4% Evangelical Lutheran Church in America, 5.2% United Church of Christ, 3.0% Christian Churches and Churches of Christ, 2.9% The United Methodist Church (2000).

Economy: Unemployment rate: 7.1% (5/2010); Total civilian labor force: 21,980 (5/2010); Leading industries: 39.7% manufacturing; 12.0% retail trade; 10.9% health care and social assistance (2008); Farms: 761 totaling 182,175 acres (2007); Companies that employ 500 or more persons: 9 (2008); Companies that employ 100 to 499 persons: 38 (2008); Companies that employ less than 100 persons: 1,280 (2008); Black-owned businesses: n/a (2002); Hispanic-owned businesses: n/a (2002); Asian-owned businesses: n/a (2002); Women-owned businesses: 867 (2002); Retail sales per capita: $21,992 (2010). Single-family building permits issued: 70 (2009); Multi-family building permits issued: 26 (2009).

Income: Per capita income: $25,035 (2010); Median household income: $54,054 (2010); Average household income: $64,736 (2010); Percent of households with income of $100,000 or more: 14.6% (2010); Poverty rate: 7.5% (2008); Bankruptcy rate: 3.92% (2009).

Taxes: Total county taxes per capita: $251 (2007); County property taxes per capita: $125 (2007).

Education: Percent of population age 25 and over with: High school diploma (including GED) or higher: 82.7% (2010); Bachelor's degree or higher: 20.2% (2010); Master's degree or higher: 8.3% (2010).

Housing: Homeownership rate: 78.6% (2010); Median home value: $120,943 (2010); Median contract rent: $412 per month (2006-2008 3-year est.); Median year structure built: 1973 (2006-2008 3-year est.)

Health: Birth rate: 139.5 per 10,000 population (2009); Death rate: 88.4 per 10,000 population (2009); Age-adjusted cancer mortality rate: 168.4 deaths per 100,000 population (2006); Air Quality Index: 67.5% good, 32.5% moderate, 0.0% unhealthy for sensitive individuals, 0.0% unhealthy (percent of days in 2008); Number of physicians: 16.5 per 10,000 population (2007); Hospital beds: 31.4 per 10,000 population (2006); Hospital admissions: 1,463.7 per 10,000 population (2006).

Elections: 2008 Presidential election results: 47.1% Obama, 51.3% McCain, 0.0% Nader

National and State Parks: Lick Fork State Recreation Area

Additional Information Contacts

Dubois County Government. . . . . (812) 481-7000

    http://www.duboiscountyin.org

City of Huntingburg . . . . (812) 683-2211

    http://www.huntingburg.org

City of Jasper . . . . (812) 482-6944

    http://www.jasperindiana.gov

Jasper Chamber of Commerce . . . . (812) 482-6866

    http://www.jasperin.org

Dubois County Communities

BIRDSEYE (town). Covers a land area of 0.642 square miles and a water area of 0 square miles. Located at 38.31° N. Lat; 86.69° W. Long. Elevation is 722 feet.

History: Laid out 1880.

Population: 465 (1990); 465 (2000); 462 (2010); 460 (2015 projected); Race: 98.3% White, 0.0% Black, 0.0% Asian, 1.7% Other, 5.8% Hispanic of any race (2010); Density: 720.1 persons per square mile (2010); Average household size: 2.43 (2010); Median age: 36.9 (2010); Males per 100 females: 104.4 (2010); Marriage status: 17.1% never married, 61.0% now married, 12.3% widowed, 9.7% divorced (2000); Foreign born: 0.0% (2000); Ancestry (includes multiple ancestries): 25.6% United States or American, 20.6% German, 9.9% Other groups, 9.5% English, 7.1% Irish (2000).

Economy: Employment by occupation: 1.0% management, 6.9% professional, 11.3% services, 16.7% sales, 1.0% farming, 18.1% construction, 45.1% production (2000).

Income: Per capita income: $19,946 (2010); Median household income: $46,500 (2010); Average household income: $48,592 (2010); Percent of households with income of $100,000 or more: 5.8% (2010); Poverty rate: 14.0% (2000).

Taxes: Total city taxes per capita: $81 (2007); City property taxes per capita: $40 (2007).

Education: Percent of population age 25 and over with: High school diploma (including GED) or higher: 70.5% (2010); Bachelor's degree or higher: 5.0% (2010); Master's degree or higher: 3.4% (2010).

School District(s)

Southeast Dubois Co Sch Corp (PK-12)
    2008-09 Enrollment: 1,440 . . . . (812) 367-1653

Housing: Homeownership rate: 81.6% (2010); Median home value: $88,846 (2010); Median contract rent: $180 per month (2000); Median year structure built: 1971 (2000).

Transportation: Commute to work: 97.0% car, 0.0% public transportation, 2.0% walk, 1.0% work from home (2000); Travel time to work: 15.5% less than 15 minutes, 42.5% 15 to 30 minutes, 25.0% 30 to 45 minutes, 4.0% 45 to 60 minutes, 13.0% 60 minutes or more (2000)

CELESTINE (unincorporated postal area, zip code 47521). Covers a land area of 17.548 square miles and a water area of 0.010 square miles. Located at 38.38° N. Lat; 86.74° W. Long. Elevation is 594 feet.

Population: 797 (2000); Race: 100.0% White, 0.0% Black, 0.0% Asian, 0.0% Other, 0.0% Hispanic of any race (2000); Density: 45.4 persons per square mile (2000); Age: 29.6% under 18, 5.6% over 64 (2000); Marriage status: 20.5% never married, 71.3% now married, 5.3% widowed, 3.0% divorced (2000); Foreign born: 0.0% (2000); Ancestry (includes multiple ancestries): 60.3% German, 6.8% United States or American, 4.9% Other groups, 3.0% Irish, 2.9% Italian (2000).

Economy: Employment by occupation: 4.2% management, 9.5% professional, 6.8% services, 24.1% sales, 2.5% farming, 16.3% construction, 36.6% production (2000).

Income: Per capita income: $18,503 (2000); Median household income: $56,625 (2000); Poverty rate: 0.0% (2000).

Education: Percent of population age 25 and over with: High school diploma (including GED) or higher: 83.7% (2000); Bachelor's degree or higher: 12.0% (2000).

School District(s)

Northeast Dubois Co Sch Corp (PK-12)
    2008-09 Enrollment: 979 . . . . (812) 678-2781

Housing: Homeownership rate: 100.0% (2000); Median home value: $100,000 (2000); Median contract rent: $n/a per month (2000); Median year structure built: 1980 (2000).

Transportation: Commute to work: 96.8% car, 0.0% public transportation, 0.0% walk, 3.2% work from home (2000); Travel time to work: 19.0% less than 15 minutes, 60.3% 15 to 30 minutes, 13.3% 30 to 45 minutes, 0.0% 45 to 60 minutes, 7.4% 60 minutes or more (2000)

DUBOIS (unincorporated postal area, zip code 47527). Covers a land area of 57.222 square miles and a water area of 0.014 square miles. Located at 38.47° N. Lat; 86.77° W. Long. Elevation is 505 feet.

Population: 1,672 (2000); Race: 100.0% White, 0.0% Black, 0.0% Asian, 0.0% Other, 0.0% Hispanic of any race (2000); Density: 29.2 persons per square mile (2000); Age: 23.9% under 18, 12.8% over 64 (2000); Marriage status: 21.4% never married, 59.7% now married, 6.8% widowed, 12.1% divorced (2000); Foreign born: 0.0% (2000); Ancestry (includes multiple ancestries): 48.5% German, 16.2% United States or American, 11.6% Irish, 4.8% English, 1.8% Scottish (2000).

Economy: Employment by occupation: 9.5% management, 7.2% professional, 5.8% services, 26.9% sales, 7.3% farming, 10.4% construction, 32.9% production (2000).

Income: Per capita income: $17,774 (2000); Median household income: $39,141 (2000); Poverty rate: 3.7% (2000).

Education: Percent of population age 25 and over with: High school diploma (including GED) or higher: 80.1% (2000); Bachelor's degree or higher: 2.8% (2000).

School District(s)

Northeast Dubois Co Sch Corp (PK-12)
    2008-09 Enrollment: 979 . . . . (812) 678-2781

Housing: Homeownership rate: 84.6% (2000); Median home value: $79,400 (2000); Median contract rent: $232 per month (2000); Median year structure built: 1970 (2000).

Transportation: Commute to work: 93.8% car, 0.0% public transportation, 3.3% walk, 2.9% work from home (2000); Travel time to work: 27.1% less than 15 minutes, 42.8% 15 to 30 minutes, 20.7% 30 to 45 minutes, 4.5% 45 to 60 minutes, 4.9% 60 minutes or more (2000)

FERDINAND (town). Covers a land area of 2.238 square miles and a water area of 0 square miles. Located at 38.22° N. Lat; 86.86° W. Long. Elevation is 538 feet.

History: Ferdinand was settled by German Catholics. It was the southern terminus of the Ferdinand Railroad, the shortest steam line in Indiana, with one locomotive making the eight-mile trip north to Huntingburg twice a day.

Population: 2,470 (1990); 2,277 (2000); 2,335 (2010); 2,355 (2015 projected); Race: 98.8% White, 0.0% Black, 0.2% Asian, 0.9% Other, 0.7% Hispanic of any race (2010); Density: 1,043.2 persons per square mile (2010); Average household size: 2.66 (2010); Median age: 39.5 (2010); Males per 100 females: 91.4 (2010); Marriage status: 20.1% never married, 66.7% now married, 7.5% widowed, 5.7% divorced (2000); Foreign born: 0.3% (2000); Ancestry (includes multiple ancestries): 63.7% German, 6.7% United States or American, 6.3% Irish, 4.0% French (except Basque), 3.7% English (2000).

Economy: Single-family building permits issued: 2 (2009); Multi-family building permits issued: 0 (2009); Employment by occupation: 12.3% management, 17.2% professional, 14.3% services, 17.0% sales, 0.2% farming, 8.5% construction, 30.6% production (2000).

Income: Per capita income: $23,282 (2010); Median household income: $56,564 (2010); Average household income: $63,926 (2010); Percent of households with income of $100,000 or more: 14.5% (2010); Poverty rate: 9.9% (2000).

Taxes: Total city taxes per capita: $249 (2007); City property taxes per capita: $172 (2007).

Education: Percent of population age 25 and over with: High school diploma (including GED) or higher: 82.6% (2010); Bachelor's degree or higher: 26.4% (2010); Master's degree or higher: 12.6% (2010).

School District(s)

North Spencer County Sch Corp (PK-12)
    2008-09 Enrollment: 2,102 . . . . (812) 937-2400
Southeast Dubois Co Sch Corp (PK-12)
    2008-09 Enrollment: 1,440 . . . . (812) 367-1653

Housing: Homeownership rate: 84.4% (2010); Median home value: $124,225 (2010); Median contract rent: $329 per month (2000); Median year structure built: 1965 (2000).

Newspapers: Ferdinand News (Community news; Circulation 3,100); Spencer County Leader (Community news; Circulation 2,200)

Transportation: Commute to work: 94.3% car, 0.0% public transportation, 2.1% walk, 3.3% work from home (2000); Travel time to work: 39.3% less than 15 minutes, 42.8% 15 to 30 minutes, 7.9% 30 to 45 minutes, 3.3% 45 to 60 minutes, 6.6% 60 minutes or more (2000)

HOLLAND (town). Covers a land area of 0.350 square miles and a water area of <.001 square miles. Located at 38.24° N. Lat; 87.03° W. Long. Elevation is 528 feet.

Population: 675 (1990); 695 (2000); 638 (2010); 613 (2015 projected); Race: 98.0% White, 0.0% Black, 0.3% Asian, 1.7% Other, 1.9% Hispanic of any race (2010); Density: 1,825.4 persons per square mile (2010); Average household size: 2.55 (2010); Median age: 38.3 (2010); Males per 100 females: 101.9 (2010); Marriage status: 21.2% never married, 59.4% now married, 7.7% widowed, 11.6% divorced (2000); Foreign born: 0.3% (2000); Ancestry (includes multiple ancestries): 59.2% German, 10.3% United States or American, 9.6% Irish, 6.1% English, 3.8% French (except Basque) (2000).

Economy: Employment by occupation: 5.5% management, 12.9% professional, 15.0% services, 24.3% sales, 0.8% farming, 9.8% construction, 31.7% production (2000).

Income: Per capita income: $23,247 (2010); Median household income: $48,611 (2010); Average household income: $59,770 (2010); Percent of households with income of $100,000 or more: 9.2% (2010); Poverty rate: 9.2% (2000).

Taxes: Total city taxes per capita: $135 (2007); City property taxes per capita: $26 (2007).

Education: Percent of population age 25 and over with: High school diploma (including GED) or higher: 89.6% (2010); Bachelor's degree or higher: 17.1% (2010); Master's degree or higher: 12.0% (2010).

School District(s)

Southwest Dubois Co Sch Corp (PK-12)

    2008-09 Enrollment: 1,767 . . . . (812) 683-3971

Housing: Homeownership rate: 85.6% (2010); Median home value: $88,500 (2010); Median contract rent: $221 per month (2000); Median year structure built: 1957 (2000).

Transportation: Commute to work: 90.1% car, 0.0% public transportation, 5.9% walk, 3.5% work from home (2000); Travel time to work: 29.9% less than 15 minutes, 46.0% 15 to 30 minutes, 16.6% 30 to 45 minutes, 4.7% 45 to 60 minutes, 2.8% 60 minutes or more (2000)

HUNTINGBURG (city). Covers a land area of 3.627 square miles and a water area of 0 square miles. Located at 38.29° N. Lat; 86.95° W. Long. Elevation is 489 feet.

History: Huntingburg, settled by German immigrants, developed around clay mines and poettery works.

Population: 5,437 (1990); 5,598 (2000); 5,823 (2010); 5,922 (2015 projected); Race: 86.1% White, 0.2% Black, 0.3% Asian, 13.4% Other, 18.4% Hispanic of any race (2010); Density: 1,605.4 persons per square mile (2010); Average household size: 2.48 (2010); Median age: 38.7 (2010); Males per 100 females: 95.5 (2010); Marriage status: 24.8% never married, 53.1% now married, 9.5% widowed, 12.6% divorced (2000); Foreign born: 7.4% (2000); Ancestry (includes multiple ancestries): 39.8% German, 13.5% Other groups, 12.5% United States or American, 8.0% Irish, 6.2% English (2000).

Economy: Single-family building permits issued: 4 (2009); Multi-family building permits issued: 2 (2009); Employment by occupation: 7.8% management, 10.1% professional, 13.1% services, 22.3% sales, 0.3% farming, 9.2% construction, 37.2% production (2000).

Income: Per capita income: $19,534 (2010); Median household income: $40,679 (2010); Average household income: $49,060 (2010); Percent of households with income of $100,000 or more: 7.0% (2010); Poverty rate: 10.8% (2000).

Taxes: Total city taxes per capita: $322 (2007); City property taxes per capita: $245 (2007).

Education: Percent of population age 25 and over with: High school diploma (including GED) or higher: 71.5% (2010); Bachelor's degree or higher: 15.6% (2010); Master's degree or higher: 6.6% (2010).

School District(s)

Southeast Dubois Co Sch Corp (PK-12)

    2008-09 Enrollment: 1,440 . . . . (812) 367-1653

Southwest Dubois Co Sch Corp (PK-12)

    2008-09 Enrollment: 1,767 . . . . (812) 683-3971

Housing: Homeownership rate: 67.9% (2010); Median home value: $89,864 (2010); Median contract rent: $319 per month (2000); Median year structure built: 1955 (2000).

Newspapers: Huntingburg Press (Community news; Circulation 2,700)

Transportation: Commute to work: 93.9% car, 0.1% public transportation, 3.0% walk, 1.7% work from home (2000); Travel time to work: 51.4% less than 15 minutes, 38.1% 15 to 30 minutes, 4.0% 30 to 45 minutes, 2.4% 45 to 60 minutes, 4.1% 60 minutes or more (2000)

Additional Information Contacts

City of Huntingburg . . . . (812) 683-2211

    http://www.huntingburg.org

JASPER (city). County seat. Covers a land area of 9.224 square miles and a water area of 0.039 square miles. Located at 38.39° N. Lat; 86.93° W. Long. Elevation is 466 feet.

History: Jasper was settled by German Catholics in 1838, on a site where a town had been founded about 20 years earlier. An early industry was desk manufacturing.

Population: 10,695 (1990); 12,100 (2000); 12,671 (2010); 12,833 (2015 projected); Race: 94.2% White, 0.7% Black, 0.9% Asian, 4.2% Other, 6.3% Hispanic of any race (2010); Density: 1,373.7 persons per square mile (2010); Average household size: 2.38 (2010); Median age: 39.3 (2010); Males per 100 females: 98.3 (2010); Marriage status: 23.2% never married, 58.3% now married, 7.3% widowed, 11.2% divorced (2000); Foreign born: 2.8% (2000); Ancestry (includes multiple ancestries): 54.3% German, 11.0% United States or American, 8.4% Irish, 6.7% English, 5.9% Other groups (2000).

Economy: Single-family building permits issued: 26 (2009); Multi-family building permits issued: 24 (2009); Employment by occupation: 12.3% management, 15.1% professional, 12.2% services, 25.8% sales, 0.1% farming, 7.9% construction, 26.7% production (2000).

Income: Per capita income: $27,192 (2010); Median household income: $52,609 (2010); Average household income: $65,711 (2010); Percent of households with income of $100,000 or more: 15.1% (2010); Poverty rate: 5.6% (2000).

Taxes: Total city taxes per capita: $317 (2007); City property taxes per capita: $299 (2007).

Education: Percent of population age 25 and over with: High school diploma (including GED) or higher: 83.5% (2010); Bachelor's degree or higher: 25.0% (2010); Master's degree or higher: 9.8% (2010).

School District(s)

Greater Jasper Con Schs (PK-12)

    2008-09 Enrollment: 3,257 . . . . (812) 482-1801

Housing: Homeownership rate: 70.3% (2010); Median home value: $123,824 (2010); Median contract rent: $380 per month (2000); Median year structure built: 1971 (2000).

Hospitals: Memorial Hospital and Health Care Center (131 beds)

Safety: Violent crime rate: 5.0 per 10,000 population; Property crime rate: 129.6 per 10,000 population (2008).

Newspapers: The Herald (Local news; Circulation 12,600)

Transportation: Commute to work: 96.0% car, 0.1% public transportation, 1.4% walk, 2.1% work from home (2000); Travel time to work: 72.0% less than 15 minutes, 20.0% 15 to 30 minutes, 3.3% 30 to 45 minutes, 1.6% 45 to 60 minutes, 3.0% 60 minutes or more (2000)

Additional Information Contacts

City of Jasper . . . . (812) 482-6944

    http://www.jasperindiana.gov

Jasper Chamber of Commerce . . . . (812) 482-6866

    http://www.jasperin.org

SAINT ANTHONY (unincorporated postal area, zip code 47575). Covers a land area of 21.388 square miles and a water area of 0.019 square miles. Located at 38.31° N. Lat; 86.81° W. Long. Elevation is 545 feet.

Population: 970 (2000); Race: 100.0% White, 0.0% Black, 0.0% Asian, 0.0% Other, 0.0% Hispanic of any race (2000); Density: 45.4 persons per square mile (2000); Age: 25.5% under 18, 7.4% over 64 (2000); Marriage status: 21.7% never married, 59.5% now married, 9.6% widowed, 9.2% divorced (2000); Foreign born: 0.0% (2000); Ancestry (includes multiple ancestries): 57.8% German, 12.9% United States or American, 4.1% Irish, 2.9% French (except Basque), 2.3% Other groups (2000).

Economy: Employment by occupation: 11.5% management, 9.3% professional, 6.7% services, 20.6% sales, 3.9% farming, 14.4% construction, 33.6% production (2000).

Income: Per capita income: $17,837 (2000); Median household income: $42,143 (2000); Poverty rate: 1.3% (2000).

Education: Percent of population age 25 and over with: High school diploma (including GED) or higher: 78.1% (2000); Bachelor's degree or higher: 8.8% (2000).

Housing: Homeownership rate: 92.2% (2000); Median home value: $105,900 (2000); Median contract rent: $275 per month (2000); Median year structure built: 1974 (2000).

Transportation: Commute to work: 91.9% car, 0.0% public transportation, 1.9% walk, 6.2% work from home (2000); Travel time to work: 26.8% less than 15 minutes, 65.7% 15 to 30 minutes, 4.5% 30 to 45 minutes, 0.9% 45 to 60 minutes, 2.1% 60 minutes or more (2000)

SCHNELLVILLE (unincorporated postal area, zip code 47580). Covers a land area of 1.921 square miles and a water area of 0 square miles. Located at 38.34° N. Lat; 86.75° W. Long. Elevation is 653 feet.

Population: 170 (2000); Race: 100.0% White, 0.0% Black, 0.0% Asian, 0.0% Other, 0.0% Hispanic of any race (2000); Density: 88.5 persons per square mile (2000); Age: 25.5% under 18, 23.0% over 64 (2000); Marriage status: 24.4% never married, 55.0% now married, 16.8% widowed, 3.8% divorced (2000); Foreign born: 0.0% (2000); Ancestry (includes multiple ancestries): 57.0% German, 8.5% Dutch, 6.1% Scotch-Irish, 5.5% European, 4.2% Irish (2000).

Economy: Employment by occupation: 4.2% management, 12.5% professional, 0.0% services, 16.7% sales, 7.3% farming, 7.3% construction, 52.1% production (2000).

Income: Per capita income: $19,002 (2000); Median household income: $36,250 (2000); Poverty rate: 0.0% (2000).

Education: Percent of population age 25 and over with: High school diploma (including GED) or higher: 72.4% (2000); Bachelor's degree or higher: 7.3% (2000).

Housing: Homeownership rate: 75.7% (2000); Median home value: $75,800 (2000); Median contract rent: $425 per month (2000); Median year structure built: 1940 (2000).
Transportation: Commute to work: 84.4% car, 0.0% public transportation, 0.0% walk, 7.3% work from home (2000); Travel time to work: 14.6% less than 15 minutes, 50.6% 15 to 30 minutes, 34.8% 30 to 45 minutes, 0.0% 45 to 60 minutes, 0.0% 60 minutes or more (2000)

Elkhart County

Located in northern Indiana; bounded on the north by Michigan; drained by the Elkhart and St. Joseph Rivers. Covers a land area of 463.81 square miles, a water area of 4.03 square miles, and is located in the Eastern Time Zone. The county was founded in 1830. County seat is Goshen.

Elkhart County is part of the Elkhart-Goshen, IN Metropolitan Statistical Area. The entire metro area includes: Elkhart County, IN

Weather Station: Goshen College   Elevation: 872 feet

	Jan	Feb	Mar	Apr	May	Jun	Jul	Aug	Sep	Oct	Nov	Dec
High	31	35	47	60	72	81	84	82	75	62	48	36
Low	17	20	29	39	49	59	63	61	54	43	33	23
Precip	1.8	1.7	2.7	3.4	3.4	4.0	3.5	4.0	3.7	3.0	2.8	2.6
Snow	10.7	8.0	5.0	1.3	tr	0.0	0.0	0.0	0.0	0.4	3.9	8.9

High and Low temperatures in degrees Fahrenheit; Precipitation and Snow in inches

Population: 156,229 (1990); 182,791 (2000); 201,748 (2010); 209,406 (2015 projected); Race: 81.7% White, 5.5% Black, 1.1% Asian, 11.8% Other, 15.0% Hispanic of any race (2010); Density: 435.0 persons per square mile (2010); Average household size: 2.73 (2010); Median age: 34.7 (2010); Males per 100 females: 100.2 (2010).
Religion: Five largest groups: 6.2% Catholic Church, 4.8% Mennonite Church USA, 4.5% The United Methodist Church, 3.0% The Missionary Church, 2.6% Old Order Amish Church (2000).
Economy: Unemployment rate: 13.7% (5/2010); Total civilian labor force: 86,365 (5/2010); Leading industries: 52.3% manufacturing; 8.1% health care and social assistance; 8.1% retail trade (2008); Farms: 1,617 totaling 163,295 acres (2007); Companies that employ 500 or more persons: 28 (2008); Companies that employ 100 to 499 persons: 200 (2008); Companies that employ less than 100 persons: 4,966 (2008); Black-owned businesses: 332 (2002); Hispanic-owned businesses: 191 (2002); Asian-owned businesses: 132 (2002); Women-owned businesses: 4,430 (2002); Retail sales per capita: $15,010 (2010). Single-family building permits issued: 137 (2009); Multi-family building permits issued: 48 (2009).
Income: Per capita income: $22,849 (2010); Median household income: $50,046 (2010); Average household income: $62,440 (2010); Percent of households with income of $100,000 or more: 13.4% (2010); Poverty rate: 12.6% (2008); Bankruptcy rate: 7.84% (2009).
Taxes: Total county taxes per capita: $302 (2007); County property taxes per capita: $165 (2007).
Education: Percent of population age 25 and over with: High school diploma (including GED) or higher: 77.7% (2010); Bachelor's degree or higher: 17.3% (2010); Master's degree or higher: 5.5% (2010).
Housing: Homeownership rate: 72.0% (2010); Median home value: $124,239 (2010); Median contract rent: $587 per month (2006-2008 3-year est.); Median year structure built: 1975 (2006-2008 3-year est.)
Health: Birth rate: 168.6 per 10,000 population (2009); Death rate: 71.7 per 10,000 population (2009); Age-adjusted cancer mortality rate: 191.7 deaths per 100,000 population (2006); Air Quality Index: 75.9% good, 23.6% moderate, 0.5% unhealthy for sensitive individuals, 0.0% unhealthy (percent of days in 2008); Number of physicians: 11.8 per 10,000 population (2007); Hospital beds: 21.4 per 10,000 population (2006); Hospital admissions: 968.9 per 10,000 population (2006).
Elections: 2008 Presidential election results: 43.9% Obama, 55.1% McCain, 0.0% Nader
Additional Information Contacts

Elkhart County Communities

BRISTOL (town). Covers a land area of 2.383 square miles and a water area of 0.113 square miles. Located at 41.72° N. Lat; 85.81° W. Long. Elevation is 748 feet.
Population: 1,133 (1990); 1,382 (2000); 1,641 (2010); 1,755 (2015 projected); Race: 84.1% White, 1.5% Black, 1.8% Asian, 12.6% Other, 13.8% Hispanic of any race (2010); Density: 688.5 persons per square mile (2010); Average household size: 2.56 (2010); Median age: 33.6 (2010); Males per 100 females: 100.9 (2010); Marriage status: 24.3% never married, 58.8% now married, 4.8% widowed, 12.0% divorced (2000); Foreign born: 4.3% (2000); Ancestry (includes multiple ancestries): 31.6% German, 16.8% Other groups, 10.2% Irish, 9.2% United States or American, 7.0% French (except Basque) (2000).
Economy: Employment by occupation: 9.2% management, 8.9% professional, 9.9% services, 29.7% sales, 0.0% farming, 11.0% construction, 31.3% production (2000).
Income: Per capita income: $24,793 (2010); Median household income: $52,823 (2010); Average household income: $63,471 (2010); Percent of households with income of $100,000 or more: 14.5% (2010); Poverty rate: 5.9% (2000).
Taxes: Total city taxes per capita: $509 (2007); City property taxes per capita: $429 (2007).
Education: Percent of population age 25 and over with: High school diploma (including GED) or higher: 82.6% (2010); Bachelor's degree or higher: 15.1% (2010); Master's degree or higher: 3.9% (2010).
School District(s)
Elkhart Community Schools (PK-12)
  2008-09 Enrollment: 13,505 . . . . (574) 262-5516
Middlebury Community Schools (PK-12)
  2008-09 Enrollment: 4,276 . . . . (574) 825-9425
Housing: Homeownership rate: 56.2% (2010); Median home value: $122,892 (2010); Median contract rent: $483 per month (2000); Median year structure built: 1964 (2000).
Transportation: Commute to work: 90.8% car, 0.3% public transportation, 4.4% walk, 3.4% work from home (2000); Travel time to work: 29.1% less than 15 minutes, 51.4% 15 to 30 minutes, 13.4% 30 to 45 minutes, 4.0% 45 to 60 minutes, 2.1% 60 minutes or more (2000)

DUNLAP (CDP). Covers a land area of 4.234 square miles and a water area of 0.006 square miles. Located at 41.63° N. Lat; 85.91° W. Long. Elevation is 774 feet.
Population: 5,625 (1990); 5,887 (2000); 5,974 (2010); 6,083 (2015 projected); Race: 86.5% White, 3.8% Black, 1.6% Asian, 8.1% Other, 9.0% Hispanic of any race (2010); Density: 1,410.9 persons per square mile (2010); Average household size: 2.80 (2010); Median age: 37.4 (2010); Males per 100 females: 99.5 (2010); Marriage status: 20.9% never married, 67.8% now married, 4.1% widowed, 7.2% divorced (2000); Foreign born: 4.6% (2000); Ancestry (includes multiple ancestries): 31.7% German, 12.4% Other groups, 10.3% Irish, 9.5% English, 7.7% United States or American (2000).
Economy: Employment by occupation: 9.6% management, 16.1% professional, 10.2% services, 27.2% sales, 0.0% farming, 6.4% construction, 30.5% production (2000).
Income: Per capita income: $21,703 (2010); Median household income: $54,865 (2010); Average household income: $60,916 (2010); Percent of households with income of $100,000 or more: 12.3% (2010); Poverty rate: 6.1% (2000).
Education: Percent of population age 25 and over with: High school diploma (including GED) or higher: 86.7% (2010); Bachelor's degree or higher: 15.7% (2010); Master's degree or higher: 6.4% (2010).
Housing: Homeownership rate: 86.4% (2010); Median home value: $122,776 (2010); Median contract rent: $561 per month (2000); Median year structure built: 1970 (2000).
Transportation: Commute to work: 95.3% car, 0.4% public transportation, 0.7% walk, 3.1% work from home (2000); Travel time to work: 37.2% less than 15 minutes, 49.5% 15 to 30 minutes, 9.5% 30 to 45 minutes, 2.0% 45 to 60 minutes, 1.8% 60 minutes or more (2000)

ELKHART (city). Covers a land area of 21.365 square miles and a water area of 0.894 square miles. Located at 41.68° N. Lat; 85.96° W. Long. Elevation is 748 feet.

History: Elkhart was named for an island, thought by some to be shaped like an elk's heart, at the place where two rivers meet. The town was platted in 1832 by Dr. Havilah Beardsley. Elkhart grew when the Michigan Southern Railway Company built its shops here in 1870. It was incorporated in 1873. The musical instrument company begun here in 1875 by Charles G. Conn became the largest band instrument manufacturer in the world.

Population: 47,334 (1990); 51,874 (2000); 53,296 (2010); 53,257 (2015 projected); Race: 65.0% White, 14.7% Black, 1.3% Asian, 19.0% Other, 24.2% Hispanic of any race (2010); Density: 2,494.6 persons per square mile (2010); Average household size: 2.61 (2010); Median age: 34.0 (2010); Males per 100 females: 99.1 (2010); Marriage status: 27.8% never married, 50.4% now married, 6.8% widowed, 15.0% divorced (2000); Foreign born: 11.4% (2000); Ancestry (includes multiple ancestries): 30.3% Other groups, 18.7% German, 8.2% Irish, 7.0% United States or American, 6.6% English (2000).

Economy: Unemployment rate: 15.8% (5/2010); Total civilian labor force: 22,040 (5/2010); Single-family building permits issued: 3 (2009); Multi-family building permits issued: 0 (2009); Employment by occupation: 9.2% management, 10.8% professional, 11.4% services, 21.4% sales, 0.3% farming, 7.6% construction, 39.3% production (2000).

Income: Per capita income: $19,542 (2010); Median household income: $39,990 (2010); Average household income: $50,442 (2010); Percent of households with income of $100,000 or more: 8.6% (2010); Poverty rate: 13.6% (2000).

Taxes: Total city taxes per capita: $491 (2007); City property taxes per capita: $406 (2007).

Education: Percent of population age 25 and over with: High school diploma (including GED) or higher: 74.2% (2010); Bachelor's degree or higher: 15.8% (2010); Master's degree or higher: 4.7% (2010).

School District(s)
Baugo Community Schools (KG-12)
    2008-09 Enrollment: 1,949 . . . . (574) 293-8583
Concord Community Schools (KG-12)
    2008-09 Enrollment: 4,667 . . . . (574) 875-5161
Elkhart Community Schools (PK-12)
    2008-09 Enrollment: 13,505 . . . . (574) 262-5516

Four-year College(s)
Associated Mennonite Biblical Seminary (Private, Not-for-profit, Mennonite Church)
    Fall 2008 Enrollment: 146 . . . . (574) 295-3726

Two-year College(s)
Indiana Business College-Elkhart (Private, For-profit)
    Fall 2008 Enrollment: 185 . . . . (574) 522-0397
    2009-10 Tuition: In-state $11,535; Out-of-state $11,535

Housing: Homeownership rate: 57.0% (2010); Median home value: $101,917 (2010); Median contract rent: $474 per month (2000); Median year structure built: 1960 (2000).

Hospitals: Elkhart General Hospital (365 beds)

Safety: Violent crime rate: 39.9 per 10,000 population; Property crime rate: 677.4 per 10,000 population (2008).

Newspapers: South Bend Tribune - Elkhart Bureau (Local news; Circulation 100,000); The Truth (Local news; Circulation 3,000)

Transportation: Commute to work: 93.4% car, 1.3% public transportation, 2.1% walk, 2.1% work from home (2000); Travel time to work: 41.6% less than 15 minutes, 41.0% 15 to 30 minutes, 12.5% 30 to 45 minutes, 2.8% 45 to 60 minutes, 2.2% 60 minutes or more (2000); Amtrak: train service available.

Additional Information Contacts
City of Elkhart. . . . . (574) 522-5272
    http://www.elkhartindiana.org
Greater Elkhart Chamber of Commerce . . . . (574) 293-1531
    http://www.elkhart.org

GOSHEN (city). County seat. Covers a land area of 13.190 square miles and a water area of 0.209 square miles. Located at 41.58° N. Lat; 85.83° W. Long. Elevation is 801 feet.

History: Goshen was established by Mennonite settlers, who in 1894 founded Elkhart Academy which became Goshen College.

Population: 24,885 (1990); 29,383 (2000); 32,009 (2010); 33,336 (2015 projected); Race: 74.1% White, 1.9% Black, 1.2% Asian, 22.8% Other,

32.1% Hispanic of any race (2010); Density: 2,426.8 persons per square mile (2010); Average household size: 2.67 (2010); Median age: 33.9 (2010); Males per 100 females: 103.1 (2010); Marriage status: 25.9% never married, 57.6% now married, 6.9% widowed, 9.6% divorced (2000); Foreign born: 15.8% (2000); Ancestry (includes multiple ancestries): 25.4% German, 23.7% Other groups, 11.2% United States or American, 7.2% Irish, 5.4% Swiss (2000).

Economy: Unemployment rate: 12.7% (5/2010); Total civilian labor force: 13,671 (5/2010); Single-family building permits issued: 12 (2009); Multi-family building permits issued: 0 (2009); Employment by occupation: 9.7% management, 15.1% professional, 12.1% services, 20.0% sales, 0.3% farming, 7.7% construction, 35.1% production (2000).

Income: Per capita income: $21,056 (2010); Median household income: $46,322 (2010); Average household income: $56,993 (2010); Percent of households with income of $100,000 or more: 10.3% (2010); Poverty rate: 9.3% (2000).

Taxes: Total city taxes per capita: $354 (2007); City property taxes per capita: $276 (2007).

Education: Percent of population age 25 and over with: High school diploma (including GED) or higher: 75.2% (2010); Bachelor's degree or higher: 21.4% (2010); Master's degree or higher: 6.7% (2010).

School District(s)
Fairfield Community Schools (KG-12)
    2008-09 Enrollment: 2,090 . . . . (574) 831-2188
Goshen Community Schools (KG-12)
    2008-09 Enrollment: 6,268 . . . . (574) 533-8631
Middlebury Community Schools (PK-12)
    2008-09 Enrollment: 4,276 . . . . (574) 825-9425

Four-year College(s)
Goshen College (Private, Not-for-profit, Mennonite Church)
    Fall 2008 Enrollment: 957 . . . . (574) 535-7000
    2009-10 Tuition: In-state $23,400; Out-of-state $23,400

Housing: Homeownership rate: 63.8% (2010); Median home value: $107,449 (2010); Median contract rent: $436 per month (2000); Median year structure built: 1969 (2000).

Hospitals: Goshen General Hospital (115 beds); Oaklawn Psychiatric Center

Safety: Violent crime rate: 14.0 per 10,000 population; Property crime rate: 398.7 per 10,000 population (2008).

Newspapers: El Puente (Local news; Circulation 6,000); The Goshen News (Local news; Circulation 17,117)

Transportation: Commute to work: 91.9% car, 0.2% public transportation, 3.9% walk, 1.8% work from home (2000); Travel time to work: 46.6% less than 15 minutes, 36.8% 15 to 30 minutes, 12.2% 30 to 45 minutes, 2.2% 45 to 60 minutes, 2.2% 60 minutes or more (2000)

Additional Information Contacts
City of Goshen . . . . (574) 533-8625
    http://www.ci.goshen.in.us
Goshen Chamber of Commerce . . . . (574) 533-2102
    http://www.goshen.org

MIDDLEBURY (town). Covers a land area of 3.398 square miles and a water area of 0.004 square miles. Located at 41.67° N. Lat; 85.70° W. Long. Elevation is 833 feet.

History: Laid out 1835.

Population: 2,489 (1990); 2,956 (2000); 3,480 (2010); 3,693 (2015 projected); Race: 96.8% White, 0.2% Black, 1.0% Asian, 2.0% Other, 0.5% Hispanic of any race (2010); Density: 1,024.0 persons per square mile (2010); Average household size: 2.82 (2010); Median age: 34.3 (2010); Males per 100 females: 100.8 (2010); Marriage status: 18.0% never married, 68.0% now married, 5.6% widowed, 8.4% divorced (2000); Foreign born: 3.3% (2000); Ancestry (includes multiple ancestries): 33.4% German, 14.1% United States or American, 7.5% Irish, 7.2% English, 6.1% Swiss (2000).

Economy: Employment by occupation: 15.8% management, 12.9% professional, 9.1% services, 27.0% sales, 0.0% farming, 11.5% construction, 23.9% production (2000).

Income: Per capita income: $27,722 (2010); Median household income: $61,955 (2010); Average household income: $77,054 (2010); Percent of households with income of $100,000 or more: 20.3% (2010); Poverty rate: 1.7% (2000).

Taxes: Total city taxes per capita: $407 (2007); City property taxes per capita: $329 (2007).

Education: Percent of population age 25 and over with: High school diploma (including GED) or higher: 80.0% (2010); Bachelor's degree or higher: 19.7% (2010); Master's degree or higher: 6.1% (2010).

School District(s)

Middlebury Community Schools (PK-12)

   2008-09 Enrollment: 4,276 . . . . (574) 825-9425

Housing: Homeownership rate: 74.7% (2010); Median home value: $165,268 (2010); Median contract rent: $458 per month (2000); Median year structure built: 1978 (2000).

Transportation: Commute to work: 94.8% car, 0.0% public transportation, 2.5% walk, 2.1% work from home (2000); Travel time to work: 54.8% less than 15 minutes, 29.1% 15 to 30 minutes, 13.1% 30 to 45 minutes, 1.3% 45 to 60 minutes, 1.6% 60 minutes or more (2000)

Additional Information Contacts

Town of Middlebury . . . . (574) 825-1499

   http://www.middleburyin.com

MILLERSBURG (town). Covers a land area of 0.527 square miles and a water area of 0 square miles. Located at 41.52° N. Lat; 85.69° W. Long. Elevation is 886 feet.

History: Laid out 1855.

Population: 889 (1990); 868 (2000); 981 (2010); 1,032 (2015 projected); Race: 98.7% White, 0.2% Black, 0.0% Asian, 1.1% Other, 1.5% Hispanic of any race (2010); Density: 1,860.9 persons per square mile (2010); Average household size: 2.88 (2010); Median age: 31.6 (2010); Males per 100 females: 107.0 (2010); Marriage status: 14.8% never married, 71.1% now married, 4.2% widowed, 9.9% divorced (2000); Foreign born: 0.9% (2000); Ancestry (includes multiple ancestries): 24.4% German, 15.2% United States or American, 10.4% Irish, 6.7% English, 4.8% Other groups (2000).

Economy: Employment by occupation: 9.7% management, 10.3% professional, 12.2% services, 19.1% sales, 0.7% farming, 9.2% construction, 38.9% production (2000).

Income: Per capita income: $20,380 (2010); Median household income: $49,782 (2010); Average household income: $58,864 (2010); Percent of households with income of $100,000 or more: 8.2% (2010); Poverty rate: 4.0% (2000).

Taxes: Total city taxes per capita: $249 (2007); City property taxes per capita: $200 (2007).

Education: Percent of population age 25 and over with: High school diploma (including GED) or higher: 73.1% (2010); Bachelor's degree or higher: 7.9% (2010); Master's degree or higher: 1.8% (2010).

School District(s)

Fairfield Community Schools (KG-12)

   2008-09 Enrollment: 2,090 . . . . (574) 831-2188

Housing: Homeownership rate: 78.3% (2010); Median home value: $106,127 (2010); Median contract rent: $383 per month (2000); Median year structure built: 1966 (2000).

Transportation: Commute to work: 90.3% car, 0.7% public transportation, 2.6% walk, 3.2% work from home (2000); Travel time to work: 28.1% less than 15 minutes, 54.9% 15 to 30 minutes, 11.8% 30 to 45 minutes, 3.6% 45 to 60 minutes, 1.7% 60 minutes or more (2000)

NAPPANEE (city). Covers a land area of 3.689 square miles and a water area of 0 square miles. Located at 41.44° N. Lat; 85.99° W. Long. Elevation is 869 feet.

History: Nappanee grew up along the Baltimore & Ohio Railroad. Furniture manufacturing was an early industry in Nappanee, which was platted in 1874.

Population: 5,683 (1990); 6,710 (2000); 8,053 (2010); 8,659 (2015 projected); Race: 92.4% White, 0.5% Black, 0.6% Asian, 6.5% Other, 8.4% Hispanic of any race (2010); Density: 2,182.9 persons per square mile (2010); Average household size: 2.72 (2010); Median age: 33.0 (2010); Males per 100 females: 100.9 (2010); Marriage status: 23.8% never married, 62.9% now married, 5.4% widowed, 7.9% divorced (2000); Foreign born: 2.6% (2000); Ancestry (includes multiple ancestries): 32.4% German, 13.3% United States or American, 7.7% Other groups, 7.1% Irish, 4.7% English (2000).

Economy: Single-family building permits issued: 3 (2009); Multi-family building permits issued: 0 (2009); Employment by occupation: 8.0% management, 10.3% professional, 12.4% services, 22.6% sales, 0.0% farming, 9.2% construction, 37.7% production (2000).

Income: Per capita income: $22,456 (2010); Median household income: $53,775 (2010); Average household income: $61,121 (2010); Percent of

households with income of $100,000 or more: 11.4% (2010); Poverty rate: 4.6% (2000).

Taxes: Total city taxes per capita: $401 (2007); City property taxes per capita: $328 (2007).

Education: Percent of population age 25 and over with: High school diploma (including GED) or higher: 76.6% (2010); Bachelor's degree or higher: 13.0% (2010); Master's degree or higher: 4.3% (2010).

School District(s)

Wa-Nee Community Schools (KG-12)

   2008-09 Enrollment: 3,127 . . . . (574) 773-3131

Housing: Homeownership rate: 70.3% (2010); Median home value: $101,864 (2010); Median contract rent: $448 per month (2000); Median year structure built: 1966 (2000).

Safety: Violent crime rate: 1.4 per 10,000 population; Property crime rate: 272.2 per 10,000 population (2008).

Newspapers: Advance News (Community news; Circulation 2,800)

Transportation: Commute to work: 93.8% car, 0.0% public transportation, 1.2% walk, 3.0% work from home (2000); Travel time to work: 56.5% less than 15 minutes, 27.6% 15 to 30 minutes, 12.2% 30 to 45 minutes, 3.1% 45 to 60 minutes, 0.5% 60 minutes or more (2000)

Additional Information Contacts

City of Nappanee . . . . (574) 773-2112

   http://www.nappanee.org

NEW PARIS (CDP). Covers a land area of 0.832 square miles and a water area of 0 square miles. Located at 41.50° N. Lat; 85.82° W. Long. Elevation is 810 feet.

History: Laid out 1838.

Population: 1,007 (1990); 1,006 (2000); 1,015 (2010); 1,014 (2015 projected); Race: 96.7% White, 0.0% Black, 0.0% Asian, 3.3% Other, 2.0% Hispanic of any race (2010); Density: 1,220.1 persons per square mile (2010); Average household size: 2.66 (2010); Median age: 36.3 (2010); Males per 100 females: 96.7 (2010); Marriage status: 16.4% never married, 68.1% now married, 8.5% widowed, 7.1% divorced (2000); Foreign born: 2.7% (2000); Ancestry (includes multiple ancestries): 31.1% German, 17.2% United States or American, 10.8% Irish, 10.7% English, 3.6% French (except Basque) (2000).

Economy: Employment by occupation: 11.8% management, 7.1% professional, 9.4% services, 21.7% sales, 0.0% farming, 6.1% construction, 43.9% production (2000).

Income: Per capita income: $20,963 (2010); Median household income: $50,510 (2010); Average household income: $55,700 (2010); Percent of households with income of $100,000 or more: 9.4% (2010); Poverty rate: 5.0% (2000).

Education: Percent of population age 25 and over with: High school diploma (including GED) or higher: 72.2% (2010); Bachelor's degree or higher: 14.3% (2010); Master's degree or higher: 0.2% (2010).

School District(s)

Fairfield Community Schools (KG-12)

   2008-09 Enrollment: 2,090 . . . . (574) 831-2188

Housing: Homeownership rate: 76.4% (2010); Median home value: $110,377 (2010); Median contract rent: $476 per month (2000); Median year structure built: 1955 (2000).

Transportation: Commute to work: 92.7% car, 0.0% public transportation, 1.0% walk, 2.6% work from home (2000); Travel time to work: 54.4% less than 15 minutes, 31.0% 15 to 30 minutes, 11.7% 30 to 45 minutes, 1.7% 45 to 60 minutes, 1.3% 60 minutes or more (2000)

SIMONTON LAKE (CDP). Covers a land area of 3.261 square miles and a water area of 0.413 square miles. Located at 41.74° N. Lat; 85.97° W. Long. Elevation is 787 feet.

Population: 3,172 (1990); 4,053 (2000); 4,475 (2010); 4,638 (2015 projected); Race: 91.7% White, 2.3% Black, 2.6% Asian, 3.4% Other, 4.6% Hispanic of any race (2010); Density: 1,372.4 persons per square mile (2010); Average household size: 2.37 (2010); Median age: 40.3 (2010); Males per 100 females: 100.5 (2010); Marriage status: 20.4% never married, 65.3% now married, 4.7% widowed, 9.6% divorced (2000); Foreign born: 1.1% (2000); Ancestry (includes multiple ancestries): 23.3% German, 10.9% Irish, 10.3% United States or American, 8.9% Other groups, 8.5% Italian (2000).

Economy: Employment by occupation: 14.3% management, 9.9% professional, 13.2% services, 31.6% sales, 0.0% farming, 9.3% construction, 21.6% production (2000).

Income: Per capita income: $29,374 (2010); Median household income: $56,483 (2010); Average household income: $69,500 (2010); Percent of

households with income of $100,000 or more: 17.4% (2010); Poverty rate: 2.8% (2000).

Education: Percent of population age 25 and over with: High school diploma (including GED) or higher: 90.8% (2010); Bachelor's degree or higher: 22.0% (2010); Master's degree or higher: 6.7% (2010).

Housing: Homeownership rate: 72.4% (2010); Median home value: $143,131 (2010); Median contract rent: $493 per month (2000); Median year structure built: 1973 (2000).

Transportation: Commute to work: 97.2% car, 0.0% public transportation, 0.0% walk, 2.8% work from home (2000); Travel time to work: 37.0% less than 15 minutes, 44.3% 15 to 30 minutes, 13.8% 30 to 45 minutes, 1.7% 45 to 60 minutes, 3.2% 60 minutes or more (2000)

WAKARUSA (town). Covers a land area of 2.260 square miles and a water area of 0 square miles. Located at 41.53° N. Lat; 86.01° W. Long. Elevation is 840 feet.

History: Laid out 1852.

Population: 1,786 (1990); 1,618 (2000); 1,860 (2010); 1,951 (2015 projected); Race: 96.0% White, 0.9% Black, 0.3% Asian, 2.8% Other, 1.6% Hispanic of any race (2010); Density: 823.0 persons per square mile (2010); Average household size: 2.60 (2010); Median age: 38.9 (2010); Males per 100 females: 88.3 (2010); Marriage status: 18.2% never married, 59.7% now married, 15.2% widowed, 6.9% divorced (2000); Foreign born: 1.6% (2000); Ancestry (includes multiple ancestries): 34.4% German, 19.0% United States or American, 6.2% Irish, 6.0% Swiss, 5.9% Other groups (2000).

Economy: Employment by occupation: 7.5% management, 16.5% professional, 9.9% services, 29.4% sales, 1.0% farming, 9.9% construction, 25.8% production (2000).

Income: Per capita income: $24,626 (2010); Median household income: $52,232 (2010); Average household income: $66,007 (2010); Percent of households with income of $100,000 or more: 13.4% (2010); Poverty rate: 4.0% (2000).

Taxes: Total city taxes per capita: $525 (2007); City property taxes per capita: $438 (2007).

Education: Percent of population age 25 and over with: High school diploma (including GED) or higher: 83.2% (2010); Bachelor's degree or higher: 14.5% (2010); Master's degree or higher: 5.8% (2010).

School District(s)
Penn-Harris-Madison Sch Corp (KG-12)
   2008-09 Enrollment: 10,459 . . . . (574) 259-7941
Wa-Nee Community Schools (KG-12)
   2008-09 Enrollment: 3,127 . . . . (574) 773-3131

Housing: Homeownership rate: 82.1% (2010); Median home value: $133,761 (2010); Median contract rent: $392 per month (2000); Median year structure built: 1952 (2000).

Newspapers: Wakarusa Tribune (Local news; Circulation 1,400)

Transportation: Commute to work: 90.9% car, 0.0% public transportation, 5.1% walk, 2.6% work from home (2000); Travel time to work: 46.2% less than 15 minutes, 38.2% 15 to 30 minutes, 12.0% 30 to 45 minutes, 1.4% 45 to 60 minutes, 2.2% 60 minutes or more (2000)

Fayette County

Located in eastern Indiana; drained by the Whitewater River. Covers a land area of 214.96 square miles, a water area of 0.16 square miles, and is located in the Eastern Time Zone. The county was founded in 1818. County seat is Connersville.

Fayette County is part of the Connersville, IN Micropolitan Statistical Area. The entire metro area includes: Fayette County, IN

Population: 26,015 (1990); 25,588 (2000); 24,136 (2010); 23,391 (2015 projected); Race: 96.6% White, 1.8% Black, 0.3% Asian, 1.3% Other, 0.9% Hispanic of any race (2010); Density: 112.3 persons per square mile (2010); Average household size: 2.40 (2010); Median age: 39.8 (2010); Males per 100 females: 93.3 (2010).

Religion: Five largest groups: 11.2% Catholic Church, 6.1% The United Methodist Church, 3.6% Southern Baptist Convention, 3.5% Christian Churches and Churches of Christ, 3.3% Independent, Non-Charismatic Churches (2000).

Economy: Unemployment rate: 13.5% (5/2010); Total civilian labor force: 10,060 (5/2010); Leading industries: 26.1% health care and social assistance; 15.8% retail trade; 8.8% accommodation & food services (2008); Farms: 391 totaling 92,505 acres (2007); Companies that employ 500 or more persons: 1 (2008); Companies that employ 100 to 499

persons: 9 (2008); Companies that employ less than 100 persons: 465 (2008); Black-owned businesses: n/a (2002); Hispanic-owned businesses: n/a (2002); Asian-owned businesses: n/a (2002); Women-owned businesses: 224 (2002); Retail sales per capita: $11,885 (2010). Single-family building permits issued: 11 (2009); Multi-family building permits issued: 0 (2009).

Income: Per capita income: $19,693 (2010); Median household income: $39,293 (2010); Average household income: $47,563 (2010); Percent of households with income of $100,000 or more: 7.5% (2010); Poverty rate: 15.2% (2008); Bankruptcy rate: 10.82% (2009).

Taxes: Total county taxes per capita: $370 (2007); County property taxes per capita: $204 (2007).

Education: Percent of population age 25 and over with: High school diploma (including GED) or higher: 76.9% (2010); Bachelor's degree or higher: 8.9% (2010); Master's degree or higher: 4.1% (2010).

Housing: Homeownership rate: 73.6% (2010); Median home value: $87,365 (2010); Median contract rent: $437 per month (2006-2008 3-year est.); Median year structure built: 1959 (2006-2008 3-year est.).

Health: Birth rate: 127.4 per 10,000 population (2009); Death rate: 121.6 per 10,000 population (2009); Age-adjusted cancer mortality rate: 218.8 deaths per 100,000 population (2006); Number of physicians: 7.0 per 10,000 population (2007); Hospital beds: 45.1 per 10,000 population (2006); Hospital admissions: 995.9 per 10,000 population (2006).

Elections: 2008 Presidential election results: 46.4% Obama, 52.0% McCain, 0.0% Nader

Additional Information Contacts
Fayette County Government . . . . (765) 825-8987
   http://www.co.fayette.in.us
City of Connersville . . . . (765) 825-4211
   http://www.connersvillein.gov
Connersville Chamber of Commerce . . . . (765) 825-2561
   http://www.connersvillechamber.com

Fayette County Communities

CONNERSVILLE (city). County seat. Covers a land area of 8.135 square miles and a water area of 0.012 square miles. Located at 39.65° N. Lat; 85.13° W. Long. Elevation is 823 feet.

History: Settlement at Connersville began in 1808 when John Conner established a fur-trading post here. He founded the town of Connersville in 1813 and served as its first sheriff, in addition to operating the gristmill, sawmill, tavern, and store.

Population: 15,855 (1990); 15,411 (2000); 13,898 (2010); 13,177 (2015 projected); Race: 95.5% White, 2.6% Black, 0.3% Asian, 1.7% Other, 1.2% Hispanic of any race (2010); Density: 1,708.5 persons per square mile (2010); Average household size: 2.27 (2010); Median age: 39.1 (2010); Males per 100 females: 89.5 (2010); Marriage status: 19.8% never married, 56.7% now married, 9.5% widowed, 14.0% divorced (2000); Foreign born: 0.6% (2000); Ancestry (includes multiple ancestries): 20.7% United States or American, 12.7% German, 10.1% Irish, 9.4% Other groups, 8.7% English (2000).

Economy: Employment by occupation: 6.5% management, 10.5% professional, 17.7% services, 18.1% sales, 0.0% farming, 8.8% construction, 38.6% production (2000).

Income: Per capita income: $17,683 (2010); Median household income: $33,504 (2010); Average household income: $40,499 (2010); Percent of households with income of $100,000 or more: 4.6% (2010); Poverty rate: 10.5% (2000).

Taxes: Total city taxes per capita: $365 (2007); City property taxes per capita: $329 (2007).

Education: Percent of population age 25 and over with: High school diploma (including GED) or higher: 74.1% (2010); Bachelor's degree or higher: 6.8% (2010); Master's degree or higher: 2.7% (2010).

School District(s)
Fayette County School Corp (PK-12)
   2008-09 Enrollment: 4,239 . . . . (765) 825-2178

Housing: Homeownership rate: 64.4% (2010); Median home value: $75,390 (2010); Median contract rent: $365 per month (2000); Median year structure built: 1951 (2000).

Hospitals: Fayette Memorial Hospital (140 beds)

Newspapers: The Connersville News-Examiner (Local news; Circulation 8,000)

Transportation: Commute to work: 95.5% car, 0.0% public transportation, 2.2% walk, 1.6% work from home (2000); Travel time to work: 55.4% less than 15 minutes, 18.0% 15 to 30 minutes, 11.1% 30 to 45 minutes, 8.3%

45 to 60 minutes, 7.1% 60 minutes or more (2000); Amtrak: train service available.

Additional Information Contacts

City of Connersville . . . . (765) 825-4211
    http://www.connersvillein.gov
Connersville Chamber of Commerce . . . . (765) 825-2561
    http://www.connersvillechamber.com

Floyd County

Located in southern Indiana; hilly region, bounded on the south by the Ohio River and the Kentucky border; drained by tributaries of the Ohio River. Covers a land area of 148.00 square miles, a water area of 0.31 square miles, and is located in the Eastern Time Zone. The county was founded in 1819. County seat is New Albany.

Floyd County is part of the Louisville/Jefferson County, KY-IN Metropolitan Statistical Area. The entire metro area includes: Clark County, IN; Floyd County, IN; Harrison County, IN; Washington County, IN; Bullitt County, KY; Henry County, KY; Jefferson County, KY; Meade County, KY; Nelson County, KY; Oldham County, KY; Shelby County, KY; Spencer County, KY; Trimble County, KY

Population: 64,404 (1990); 70,823 (2000); 74,619 (2010); 76,282 (2015 projected); Race: 91.6% White, 5.2% Black, 0.6% Asian, 2.5% Other, 1.7% Hispanic of any race (2010); Density: 504.2 persons per square mile (2010); Average household size: 2.49 (2010); Median age: 39.2 (2010); Males per 100 females: 93.9 (2010).
Religion: Five largest groups: 20.9% Catholic Church, 15.5% Southern Baptist Convention, 6.9% The United Methodist Church, 5.2% Christian Churches and Churches of Christ, 2.1% Christian Church (Disciples of Christ) (2000).
Economy: Unemployment rate: 8.0% (5/2010); Total civilian labor force: 36,904 (5/2010); Leading industries: 23.7% manufacturing; 19.1% health care and social assistance; 12.6% retail trade (2008); Farms: 279 totaling 23,997 acres (2007); Companies that employ 500 or more persons: 5 (2008); Companies that employ 100 to 499 persons: 36 (2008); Companies that employ less than 100 persons: 1,767 (2008); Black-owned businesses: n/a (2002); Hispanic-owned businesses: n/a (2002); Asian-owned businesses: n/a (2002); Women-owned businesses: 1,993 (2002); Retail sales per capita: $8,942 (2010). Single-family building permits issued: 129 (2009); Multi-family building permits issued: 2 (2009).
Income: Per capita income: $27,077 (2010); Median household income: $54,031 (2010); Average household income: $67,894 (2010); Percent of households with income of $100,000 or more: 19.0% (2010); Poverty rate: 11.4% (2008); Bankruptcy rate: 7.13% (2009).
Taxes: Total county taxes per capita: $223 (2007); County property taxes per capita: $103 (2007).
Education: Percent of population age 25 and over with: High school diploma (including GED) or higher: 87.8% (2010); Bachelor's degree or higher: 21.8% (2010); Master's degree or higher: 7.8% (2010).
Housing: Homeownership rate: 72.5% (2010); Median home value: $142,685 (2010); Median contract rent: $550 per month (2006-2008 3-year est.); Median year structure built: 1971 (2006-2008 3-year est.)
Health: Birth rate: 125.5 per 10,000 population (2009); Death rate: 89.2 per 10,000 population (2009); Age-adjusted cancer mortality rate: 208.9 deaths per 100,000 population (2006); Air Quality Index: 83.0% good, 16.1% moderate, 1.0% unhealthy for sensitive individuals, 0.0% unhealthy (percent of days in 2008); Number of physicians: 18.4 per 10,000 population (2007); Hospital beds: 36.8 per 10,000 population (2006); Hospital admissions: 1,803.3 per 10,000 population (2006).
Elections: 2008 Presidential election results: 44.5% Obama, 54.6% McCain, 0.0% Nader

Additional Information Contacts

Floyd County Government . . . . (812) 948-5466
    http://www.floydcounty.in.gov
City of New Albany . . . . (812) 948-5360
    http://www.cityofnewalbany.com
One Southern Indiana . . . . (812) 945-0266
    http://www.sicc.org
Town of Georgetown . . . . (812) 951-3012
    http://www.georgetown.in.gov

Floyd County Communities

FLOYDS KNOBS (unincorporated postal area, zip code 47119). Covers a land area of 41.579 square miles and a water area of 0.027 square miles. Located at 38.34° N. Lat; 85.89° W. Long. Elevation is 771 feet.
History: James B. Moore of New York built a gristmill here in 1815, and the community called Mooresville grew up around it. Another early industry was the making of beaver top hats. The name was changed in 1843 to honor Colonel Davis Floyd of Jeffersonville. The Knobs part of the name refers to the hills in the area, noted for its strawberry growing.
Population: 9,777 (2000); Race: 99.5% White, 0.1% Black, 0.0% Asian, 0.4% Other, 1.1% Hispanic of any race (2000); Density: 235.1 persons per square mile (2000); Age: 27.6% under 18, 8.9% over 64 (2000); Marriage status: 21.5% never married, 64.4% now married, 4.8% widowed, 9.4% divorced (2000); Foreign born: 0.8% (2000); Ancestry (includes multiple ancestries): 35.7% German, 14.2% Irish, 11.7% United States or American, 11.5% English, 7.6% French (except Basque) (2000).
Economy: Employment by occupation: 17.2% management, 19.8% professional, 10.5% services, 28.0% sales, 0.2% farming, 7.3% construction, 17.0% production (2000).
Income: Per capita income: $29,877 (2000); Median household income: $63,732 (2000); Poverty rate: 2.8% (2000).
Education: Percent of population age 25 and over with: High school diploma (including GED) or higher: 90.0% (2000); Bachelor's degree or higher: 29.2% (2000).

School District(s)

New Albany-Floyd Co Con Sch (PK-12)
    2008-09 Enrollment: 11,837 . . . . (812) 949-4200
Housing: Homeownership rate: 91.6% (2000); Median home value: $141,800 (2000); Median contract rent: $460 per month (2000); Median year structure built: 1976 (2000).
Transportation: Commute to work: 94.1% car, 0.7% public transportation, 0.3% walk, 4.1% work from home (2000); Travel time to work: 21.2% less than 15 minutes, 48.0% 15 to 30 minutes, 23.2% 30 to 45 minutes, 4.6% 45 to 60 minutes, 3.0% 60 minutes or more (2000)

GALENA (CDP). Covers a land area of 2.649 square miles and a water area of 0 square miles. Located at 38.35° N. Lat; 85.94° W. Long. Elevation is 810 feet.
History: Galena was laid out in 1836, when it was called Germantown for the German immigrants who settled here. The Galena Mill, built in 1857, was a steam-powered flour mill.
Population: 1,249 (1990); 1,831 (2000); 1,983 (2010); 2,069 (2015 projected); Race: 97.5% White, 0.6% Black, 0.6% Asian, 1.4% Other, 1.0% Hispanic of any race (2010); Density: 748.5 persons per square mile (2010); Average household size: 2.86 (2010); Median age: 38.4 (2010); Males per 100 females: 97.9 (2010); Marriage status: 18.7% never married, 64.2% now married, 5.6% widowed, 11.4% divorced (2000); Foreign born: 0.7% (2000); Ancestry (includes multiple ancestries): 39.7% German, 17.5% Irish, 11.6% United States or American, 10.7% Other groups, 9.7% English (2000).
Economy: Employment by occupation: 9.5% management, 19.9% professional, 10.9% services, 27.5% sales, 0.8% farming, 14.3% construction, 17.1% production (2000).
Income: Per capita income: $35,695 (2010); Median household income: $80,430 (2010); Average household income: $102,019 (2010); Percent of households with income of $100,000 or more: 36.2% (2010); Poverty rate: 2.9% (2000).
Education: Percent of population age 25 and over with: High school diploma (including GED) or higher: 94.8% (2010); Bachelor's degree or higher: 29.0% (2010); Master's degree or higher: 11.7% (2010).
Housing: Homeownership rate: 91.3% (2010); Median home value: $192,734 (2010); Median contract rent: $558 per month (2000); Median year structure built: 1982 (2000).
Transportation: Commute to work: 93.2% car, 0.0% public transportation, 0.0% walk, 5.3% work from home (2000); Travel time to work: 9.9% less than 15 minutes, 44.6% 15 to 30 minutes, 38.8% 30 to 45 minutes, 5.3% 45 to 60 minutes, 1.5% 60 minutes or more (2000)

GEORGETOWN (town). Covers a land area of 1.792 square miles and a water area of 0.016 square miles. Located at 38.30° N. Lat; 85.97° W. Long. Elevation is 722 feet.
Population: 2,170 (1990); 2,227 (2000); 2,662 (2010); 2,814 (2015 projected); Race: 98.6% White, 0.2% Black, 0.2% Asian, 1.0% Other, 0.6%

Hispanic of any race (2010); Density: 1,485.1 persons per square mile (2010); Average household size: 2.70 (2010); Median age: 39.0 (2010); Males per 100 females: 101.2 (2010); Marriage status: 20.6% never married, 64.1% now married, 4.3% widowed, 11.0% divorced (2000); Foreign born: 0.7% (2000); Ancestry (includes multiple ancestries): 26.2% German, 14.7% Irish, 14.0% United States or American, 11.5% English, 6.7% Other groups (2000).
Economy: Single-family building permits issued: 25 (2009); Multi-family building permits issued: 2 (2009); Employment by occupation: 7.7% management, 19.8% professional, 13.9% services, 24.7% sales, 0.2% farming, 14.9% construction, 18.7% production (2000).
Income: Per capita income: $28,562 (2010); Median household income: $65,052 (2010); Average household income: $77,246 (2010); Percent of households with income of $100,000 or more: 23.6% (2010); Poverty rate: 3.1% (2000).
Taxes: Total city taxes per capita: $83 (2007); City property taxes per capita: $46 (2007).
Education: Percent of population age 25 and over with: High school diploma (including GED) or higher: 91.0% (2010); Bachelor's degree or higher: 16.0% (2010); Master's degree or higher: 5.7% (2010).
School District(s)
New Albany-Floyd Co Con Sch (PK-12)
    2008-09 Enrollment: 11,837 . . . . (812) 949-4200
Housing: Homeownership rate: 90.3% (2010); Median home value: $139,161 (2010); Median contract rent: $398 per month (2000); Median year structure built: 1975 (2000).
Safety: Violent crime rate: 6.6 per 10,000 population; Property crime rate: 69.2 per 10,000 population (2008).
Transportation: Commute to work: 95.5% car, 0.3% public transportation, 1.4% walk, 2.4% work from home (2000); Travel time to work: 11.4% less than 15 minutes, 51.0% 15 to 30 minutes, 31.1% 30 to 45 minutes, 3.7% 45 to 60 minutes, 2.9% 60 minutes or more (2000)
Additional Information Contacts
Town of Georgetown . . . . (812) 951-3012
    http://www.georgetown.in.gov

GREENVILLE (town). Covers a land area of 0.619 square miles and a water area of 0 square miles. Located at 38.37° N. Lat; 85.98° W. Long. Elevation is 827 feet.
History: Greenville was settled in 1807 and laid out in 1816 as a station on the Old Stage Road. A ready supply of white-oak timber led to the town becoming a center for the production of barrels, wine kegs, and wooden clocks.
Population: 545 (1990); 591 (2000); 671 (2010); 710 (2015 projected); Race: 96.9% White, 0.6% Black, 0.6% Asian, 1.9% Other, 1.2% Hispanic of any race (2010); Density: 1,084.2 persons per square mile (2010); Average household size: 2.73 (2010); Median age: 40.0 (2010); Males per 100 females: 98.5 (2010); Marriage status: 19.8% never married, 65.6% now married, 6.5% widowed, 8.2% divorced (2000); Foreign born: 0.2% (2000); Ancestry (includes multiple ancestries): 31.9% German, 16.8% Irish, 12.4% United States or American, 10.6% English, 6.9% French (except Basque) (2000).
Economy: Employment by occupation: 20.5% management, 17.5% professional, 9.9% services, 23.2% sales, 0.0% farming, 9.9% construction, 19.0% production (2000).
Income: Per capita income: $31,989 (2010); Median household income: $70,918 (2010); Average household income: $87,713 (2010); Percent of households with income of $100,000 or more: 33.7% (2010); Poverty rate: 4.0% (2000).
Taxes: Total city taxes per capita: $33 (2007); City property taxes per capita: $12 (2007).
Education: Percent of population age 25 and over with: High school diploma (including GED) or higher: 91.4% (2010); Bachelor's degree or higher: 20.2% (2010); Master's degree or higher: 7.2% (2010).
School District(s)
New Albany-Floyd Co Con Sch (PK-12)
    2008-09 Enrollment: 11,837 . . . . (812) 949-4200
Housing: Homeownership rate: 91.1% (2010); Median home value: $190,323 (2010); Median contract rent: $425 per month (2000); Median year structure built: 1969 (2000).
Transportation: Commute to work: 93.0% car, 0.0% public transportation, 0.0% walk, 5.5% work from home (2000); Travel time to work: 14.0% less than 15 minutes, 52.5% 15 to 30 minutes, 24.8% 30 to 45 minutes, 8.3% 45 to 60 minutes, 0.4% 60 minutes or more (2000)

NEW ALBANY (city). County seat. Covers a land area of 14.625 square miles and a water area of 0.169 square miles. Located at 38.30° N. Lat; 85.82° W. Long. Elevation is 449 feet.
History: New Albany began as a river town, utilizing its location on the Ohio River for shipping and industry. The town was platted in 1813 by three brothers from New York, who named it for the capital of their former home state. New Albany received its city charter in 1838. Shipyards here built many vessels in the mid-1800's, including the "Robert E. Lee" built in 1866 for Captain John W. Cannon.
Population: 38,060 (1990); 37,603 (2000); 36,196 (2010); 35,526 (2015 projected); Race: 87.3% White, 8.6% Black, 0.6% Asian, 3.6% Other, 2.0% Hispanic of any race (2010); Density: 2,474.9 persons per square mile (2010); Average household size: 2.25 (2010); Median age: 39.2 (2010); Males per 100 females: 90.9 (2010); Marriage status: 24.8% never married, 51.9% now married, 8.5% widowed, 14.8% divorced (2000); Foreign born: 1.3% (2000); Ancestry (includes multiple ancestries): 21.7% German, 15.3% Other groups, 14.9% United States or American, 11.7% Irish, 9.1% English (2000).
Economy: Unemployment rate: 9.7% (5/2010); Total civilian labor force: 17,987 (5/2010); Single-family building permits issued: 21 (2009); Multi-family building permits issued: 0 (2009); Employment by occupation: 9.4% management, 16.1% professional, 15.7% services, 28.1% sales, 0.1% farming, 9.9% construction, 20.8% production (2000).
Income: Per capita income: $21,923 (2010); Median household income: $40,237 (2010); Average household income: $49,623 (2010); Percent of households with income of $100,000 or more: 9.2% (2010); Poverty rate: 13.7% (2000).
Taxes: Total city taxes per capita: $316 (2007); City property taxes per capita: $180 (2007).
Education: Percent of population age 25 and over with: High school diploma (including GED) or higher: 82.4% (2010); Bachelor's degree or higher: 17.4% (2010); Master's degree or higher: 6.0% (2010).
School District(s)
Community Montessori Inc (KG-10)
    2008-09 Enrollment: 432 . . . . (812) 948-1000
New Albany-Floyd Co Con Sch (PK-12)
    2008-09 Enrollment: 11,837 . . . . (812) 949-4200
Four-year College(s)
Indiana University-Southeast (Public)
    Fall 2008 Enrollment: 6,482. . . . . (812) 941-2000
    2009-10 Tuition: In-state $5,890; Out-of-state $14,578
Housing: Homeownership rate: 58.2% (2010); Median home value: $117,247 (2010); Median contract rent: $409 per month (2000); Median year structure built: 1959 (2000).
Hospitals: Floyd Memorial Hospital and Health Services (245 beds); Southern Indiana Rehabilitation Hospital (60 beds)
Safety: Violent crime rate: 33.8 per 10,000 population; Property crime rate: 607.6 per 10,000 population (2008).
Newspapers: New Albany Tribune (Local news; Circulation 12,000)
Transportation: Commute to work: 94.2% car, 0.9% public transportation, 2.1% walk, 2.0% work from home (2000); Travel time to work: 36.7% less than 15 minutes, 45.8% 15 to 30 minutes, 12.6% 30 to 45 minutes, 1.7% 45 to 60 minutes, 3.2% 60 minutes or more (2000)
Additional Information Contacts
City of New Albany. . . . . (812) 948-5360
    http://www.cityofnewalbany.com
One Southern Indiana . . . . (812) 945-0266
    http://www.sicc.org

Fountain County
Located in western Indiana; bounded on the west and north by the Wabash River; drained by Coal Creek. Covers a land area of 395.69 square miles, a water area of 2.23 square miles, and is located in the Eastern Time Zone. The county was founded in 1825. County seat is Covington.
Population: 17,808 (1990); 17,954 (2000); 16,911 (2010); 16,335 (2015 projected); Race: 97.5% White, 0.5% Black, 0.5% Asian, 1.5% Other, 1.8% Hispanic of any race (2010); Density: 42.7 persons per square mile (2010); Average household size: 2.50 (2010); Median age: 40.8 (2010); Males per 100 females: 99.0 (2010).
Religion: Five largest groups: 9.1% Christian Churches and Churches of Christ, 7.7% The United Methodist Church, 4.9% Catholic Church, 4.2% New Testament Association of Independent Baptist Churches and other Fundamental Baptist Associations, 2.8% C

Economy: Unemployment rate: 10.5% (5/2010); Total civilian labor force: 9,138 (5/2010); Leading industries: 12.2% retail trade; 8.9% health care and social assistance; 7.9% accommodation & food services (2008); Farms: 503 totaling 188,727 acres (2007); Companies that employ 500 or more persons: 2 (2008); Companies that employ 100 to 499 persons: 4 (2008); Companies that employ less than 100 persons: 343 (2008); Black-owned businesses: n/a (2002); Hispanic-owned businesses: n/a (2002); Asian-owned businesses: n/a (2002); Women-owned businesses: 526 (2002); Retail sales per capita: $12,050 (2010). Single-family building permits issued: 6 (2009); Multi-family building permits issued: 0 (2009).

Income: Per capita income: $21,659 (2010); Median household income: $45,524 (2010); Average household income: $54,409 (2010); Percent of households with income of $100,000 or more: 9.5% (2010); Poverty rate: 11.5% (2008); Bankruptcy rate: 5.80% (2009).

Taxes: Total county taxes per capita: $250 (2007); County property taxes per capita: $145 (2007).

Education: Percent of population age 25 and over with: High school diploma (including GED) or higher: 85.1% (2010); Bachelor's degree or higher: 10.6% (2010); Master's degree or higher: 4.0% (2010).

Housing: Homeownership rate: 76.7% (2010); Median home value: $87,927 (2010); Median contract rent: $n/a per month (2006-2008 3-year est.); Median year structure built: n/a (2006-2008 3-year est.)

Health: Birth rate: 125.2 per 10,000 population (2009); Death rate: 115.7 per 10,000 population (2009); Age-adjusted cancer mortality rate: 190.1 deaths per 100,000 population (2006); Air Quality Index: 95.1% good, 4.9% moderate, 0.0% unhealthy for sensitive individuals, 0.0% unhealthy (percent of days in 2008); Number of physicians: 2.3 per 10,000 population (2007); Hospital beds: 0.0 per 10,000 population (2006); Hospital admissions: 0.0 per 10,000 population (2006).

Elections: 2008 Presidential election results: 41.8% Obama, 56.1% McCain, 0.0% Nader

National and State Parks: Shades State Park

Additional Information Contacts
Fountain County Government . . . . (765) 793-2243
   http://www.co.fountain.in.us
City of Attica. . . . . (765) 762-6767
   http://www.wcchamber.net
Fountain County Government . . . . (800) 457-8283
   http://www.in.gov

Fountain County Communities

ATTICA (city). Covers a land area of 1.517 square miles and a water area of 0 square miles. Located at 40.29° N. Lat; 87.24° W. Long. Elevation is 545 feet.

History: Attica developed in the late 1840's when the Wabash & Erie Canal was extended here. A prominent resident of Attica was Dr. John Evans (1814-1897), a physician who later served as Territorial Governor of Colorado and as a U.S. senator.

Population: 3,461 (1990); 3,491 (2000); 3,209 (2010); 3,093 (2015 projected); Race: 97.3% White, 0.1% Black, 0.2% Asian, 2.4% Other, 2.3% Hispanic of any race (2010); Density: 2,114.8 persons per square mile (2010); Average household size: 2.48 (2010); Median age: 40.2 (2010); Males per 100 females: 95.6 (2010); Marriage status: 18.7% never married, 57.6% now married, 12.6% widowed, 11.1% divorced (2000); Foreign born: 1.4% (2000); Ancestry (includes multiple ancestries): 19.1% United States or American, 14.0% German, 12.0% Irish, 7.3% Other groups, 6.1% English (2000).

Economy: Single-family building permits issued: 1 (2009); Multi-family building permits issued: 0 (2009); Employment by occupation: 5.1% management, 9.1% professional, 19.7% services, 22.3% sales, 0.6% farming, 7.2% construction, 36.0% production (2000).

Income: Per capita income: $19,458 (2010); Median household income: $41,049 (2010); Average household income: $48,878 (2010); Percent of households with income of $100,000 or more: 7.8% (2010); Poverty rate: 11.3% (2000).

Taxes: Total city taxes per capita: $160 (2007); City property taxes per capita: $146 (2007).

Education: Percent of population age 25 and over with: High school diploma (including GED) or higher: 80.0% (2010); Bachelor's degree or higher: 8.0% (2010); Master's degree or higher: 3.5% (2010).

School District(s)
Attica Consolidated Sch Corp (PK-12)
   2008-09 Enrollment: 895 . . . . (765) 762-7000

Housing: Homeownership rate: 67.5% (2010); Median home value: $88,243 (2010); Median contract rent: $324 per month (2000); Median year structure built: 1950 (2000).

Newspapers: Fountain County Neighbor (Community news; Circulation 2,200); The Messenger (Local news; Circulation 2,500)

Transportation: Commute to work: 92.7% car, 0.0% public transportation, 4.4% walk, 1.4% work from home (2000); Travel time to work: 51.2% less than 15 minutes, 12.1% 15 to 30 minutes, 18.2% 30 to 45 minutes, 13.6% 45 to 60 minutes, 4.9% 60 minutes or more (2000)

Additional Information Contacts
City of Attica. . . . . (765) 762-6767
   http://www.wcchamber.net
Fountain County Government . . . . (800) 457-8283
   http://www.in.gov

COVINGTON (city). County seat. Covers a land area of 1.168 square miles and a water area of 0 square miles. Located at 40.14° N. Lat; 87.39° W. Long. Elevation is 564 feet.

History: Covington was laid out in 1826 along the east bank of the Wabash River. A prominent resident was Edward A. Hannegan (1807-1859), U.S. senator and minister to Prussia, where he is said to have dazzled the court. Back home, Hannegan's bid for the presidency was ended when he stabbed his brother-in-law to death.

Population: 2,750 (1990); 2,565 (2000); 2,334 (2010); 2,231 (2015 projected); Race: 96.3% White, 0.9% Black, 1.4% Asian, 1.5% Other, 1.0% Hispanic of any race (2010); Density: 1,998.3 persons per square mile (2010); Average household size: 2.28 (2010); Median age: 44.1 (2010); Males per 100 females: 94.2 (2010); Marriage status: 18.1% never married, 56.0% now married, 15.4% widowed, 10.5% divorced (2000); Foreign born: 1.8% (2000); Ancestry (includes multiple ancestries): 19.4% German, 19.4% United States or American, 9.6% English, 5.6% Irish, 3.0% Other groups (2000).

Economy: Single-family building permits issued: 1 (2009); Multi-family building permits issued: 0 (2009); Employment by occupation: 10.1% management, 15.7% professional, 11.7% services, 27.2% sales, 1.0% farming, 6.8% construction, 27.4% production (2000).

Income: Per capita income: $25,028 (2010); Median household income: $47,992 (2010); Average household income: $57,670 (2010); Percent of households with income of $100,000 or more: 11.6% (2010); Poverty rate: 7.4% (2000).

Taxes: Total city taxes per capita: $137 (2007); City property taxes per capita: $136 (2007).

Education: Percent of population age 25 and over with: High school diploma (including GED) or higher: 87.8% (2010); Bachelor's degree or higher: 14.0% (2010); Master's degree or higher: 4.7% (2010).

School District(s)
Covington Community Sch Corp (PK-12)
   2008-09 Enrollment: 1,001 . . . . (765) 793-4877

Housing: Homeownership rate: 71.5% (2010); Median home value: $90,194 (2010); Median contract rent: $314 per month (2000); Median year structure built: 1956 (2000).

Transportation: Commute to work: 93.3% car, 0.0% public transportation, 3.6% walk, 2.8% work from home (2000); Travel time to work: 41.6% less than 15 minutes, 35.7% 15 to 30 minutes, 11.6% 30 to 45 minutes, 6.7% 45 to 60 minutes, 4.5% 60 minutes or more (2000)

HILLSBORO (town). Aka Hillsborough. Covers a land area of 0.320 square miles and a water area of 0 square miles. Located at 40.10° N. Lat; 87.15° W. Long. Elevation is 705 feet.

History: Early industry in Hillsboro was based on the clay soil used in the manufacture of tiles and bricks.

Population: 536 (1990); 489 (2000); 468 (2010); 452 (2015 projected); Race: 98.7% White, 0.2% Black, 0.2% Asian, 0.9% Other, 1.1% Hispanic of any race (2010); Density: 1,461.9 persons per square mile (2010); Average household size: 2.59 (2010); Median age: 38.9 (2010); Males per 100 females: 101.7 (2010); Marriage status: 17.1% never married, 66.7% now married, 8.0% widowed, 8.3% divorced (2000); Foreign born: 0.9% (2000); Ancestry (includes multiple ancestries): 24.6% German, 14.6% United States or American, 14.3% Irish, 11.8% English, 11.3% Other groups (2000).

Economy: Employment by occupation: 6.6% management, 15.3% professional, 16.6% services, 20.1% sales, 0.0% farming, 6.6% construction, 34.9% production (2000).

Income: Per capita income: $23,772 (2010); Median household income: $55,208 (2010); Average household income: $60,635 (2010); Percent of

households with income of $100,000 or more: 10.5% (2010); Poverty rate: 9.5% (2000).
Taxes: Total city taxes per capita: $73 (2007); City property taxes per capita: $67 (2007).
Education: Percent of population age 25 and over with: High school diploma (including GED) or higher: 90.6% (2010); Bachelor's degree or higher: 17.2% (2010); Master's degree or higher: 6.6% (2010).
Housing: Homeownership rate: 84.0% (2010); Median home value: $91,875 (2010); Median contract rent: $354 per month (2000); Median year structure built: 1941 (2000).
Transportation: Commute to work: 92.0% car, 0.0% public transportation, 6.2% walk, 1.8% work from home (2000); Travel time to work: 32.9% less than 15 minutes, 32.9% 15 to 30 minutes, 20.3% 30 to 45 minutes, 10.4% 45 to 60 minutes, 3.6% 60 minutes or more (2000)

KINGMAN (town). Covers a land area of 0.816 square miles and a water area of 0 square miles. Located at 39.96° N. Lat; 87.27° W. Long. Elevation is 702 feet.
Population: 588 (1990); 538 (2000); 461 (2010); 429 (2015 projected); Race: 98.7% White, 0.0% Black, 0.0% Asian, 1.3% Other, 0.4% Hispanic of any race (2010); Density: 564.8 persons per square mile (2010); Average household size: 2.51 (2010); Median age: 38.8 (2010); Males per 100 females: 103.1 (2010); Marriage status: 23.4% never married, 51.5% now married, 12.3% widowed, 12.8% divorced (2000); Foreign born: 0.6% (2000); Ancestry (includes multiple ancestries): 17.2% German, 9.2% United States or American, 4.9% English, 4.3% Irish, 2.6% Polish (2000).
Economy: Employment by occupation: 2.7% management, 9.0% professional, 13.1% services, 17.6% sales, 1.4% farming, 9.0% construction, 47.1% production (2000).
Income: Per capita income: $14,166 (2010); Median household income: $31,957 (2010); Average household income: $35,285 (2010); Percent of households with income of $100,000 or more: 1.1% (2010); Poverty rate: 16.2% (2000).
Taxes: Total city taxes per capita: $47 (2007); City property taxes per capita: $39 (2007).
Education: Percent of population age 25 and over with: High school diploma (including GED) or higher: 81.0% (2010); Bachelor's degree or higher: 6.6% (2010); Master's degree or higher: 1.9% (2010).
Housing: Homeownership rate: 71.2% (2010); Median home value: $57,667 (2010); Median contract rent: $263 per month (2000); Median year structure built: 1953 (2000).
Transportation: Commute to work: 95.9% car, 0.0% public transportation, 2.7% walk, 0.0% work from home (2000); Travel time to work: 23.5% less than 15 minutes, 37.1% 15 to 30 minutes, 24.0% 30 to 45 minutes, 3.6% 45 to 60 minutes, 11.8% 60 minutes or more (2000)

MELLOTT (town). Covers a land area of 0.157 square miles and a water area of 0 square miles. Located at 40.16° N. Lat; 87.14° W. Long. Elevation is 728 feet.
Population: 222 (1990); 207 (2000); 192 (2010); 186 (2015 projected); Race: 97.9% White, 0.5% Black, 0.5% Asian, 1.0% Other, 2.1% Hispanic of any race (2010); Density: 1,222.3 persons per square mile (2010); Average household size: 2.49 (2010); Median age: 41.6 (2010); Males per 100 females: 93.9 (2010); Marriage status: 8.6% never married, 59.3% now married, 11.1% widowed, 21.0% divorced (2000); Foreign born: 0.0% (2000); Ancestry (includes multiple ancestries): 17.5% United States or American, 14.5% German, 12.3% Other groups, 7.9% English, 6.1% Dutch (2000).
Economy: Employment by occupation: 0.0% management, 9.9% professional, 22.0% services, 3.3% sales, 2.2% farming, 12.1% construction, 50.5% production (2000).
Income: Per capita income: $21,348 (2010); Median household income: $44,500 (2010); Average household income: $50,032 (2010); Percent of households with income of $100,000 or more: 7.8% (2010); Poverty rate: 11.1% (2000).
Taxes: Total city taxes per capita: $10 (2007); City property taxes per capita: $0 (2007).
Education: Percent of population age 25 and over with: High school diploma (including GED) or higher: 89.7% (2010); Bachelor's degree or higher: 11.0% (2010); Master's degree or higher: 5.9% (2010).
Housing: Homeownership rate: 81.8% (2010); Median home value: $77,692 (2010); Median contract rent: $325 per month (2000); Median year structure built: 1970 (2000).
Transportation: Commute to work: 95.6% car, 0.0% public transportation, 0.0% walk, 2.2% work from home (2000); Travel time to work: 18.0% less

than 15 minutes, 33.7% 15 to 30 minutes, 24.7% 30 to 45 minutes, 14.6% 45 to 60 minutes, 9.0% 60 minutes or more (2000)

NEWTOWN (town). Covers a land area of 0.504 square miles and a water area of 0 square miles. Located at 40.20° N. Lat; 87.14° W. Long. Elevation is 725 feet.
Population: 243 (1990); 162 (2000); 127 (2010); 120 (2015 projected); Race: 94.5% White, 0.0% Black, 1.6% Asian, 3.9% Other, 4.7% Hispanic of any race (2010); Density: 251.9 persons per square mile (2010); Average household size: 2.76 (2010); Median age: 37.2 (2010); Males per 100 females: 130.9 (2010); Marriage status: 15.0% never married, 60.9% now married, 5.3% widowed, 18.8% divorced (2000); Foreign born: 0.0% (2000); Ancestry (includes multiple ancestries): 19.9% Irish, 14.5% United States or American, 13.9% German, 7.8% Other groups, 4.2% English (2000).
Economy: Employment by occupation: 11.1% management, 13.9% professional, 22.2% services, 4.2% sales, 0.0% farming, 6.9% construction, 41.7% production (2000).
Income: Per capita income: $23,272 (2010); Median household income: $58,929 (2010); Average household income: $63,261 (2010); Percent of households with income of $100,000 or more: 17.4% (2010); Poverty rate: 8.0% (2000).
Taxes: Total city taxes per capita: $56 (2007); City property taxes per capita: $50 (2007).
Education: Percent of population age 25 and over with: High school diploma (including GED) or higher: 93.8% (2010); Bachelor's degree or higher: 18.5% (2010); Master's degree or higher: 8.6% (2010).
Housing: Homeownership rate: 84.8% (2010); Median home value: $137,500 (2010); Median contract rent: $325 per month (2000); Median year structure built: 1952 (2000).
Transportation: Commute to work: 97.2% car, 0.0% public transportation, 2.8% walk, 0.0% work from home (2000); Travel time to work: 11.1% less than 15 minutes, 29.2% 15 to 30 minutes, 44.4% 30 to 45 minutes, 15.3% 45 to 60 minutes, 0.0% 60 minutes or more (2000)

VEEDERSBURG (town). Covers a land area of 2.716 square miles and a water area of 0 square miles. Located at 40.11° N. Lat; 87.26° W. Long. Elevation is 633 feet.
History: Veedersburg was a brick manufacturing center. The Veedersburg Paver Company furnished the brick for paving the Indianapolis Motor Speedway.
Population: 2,288 (1990); 2,299 (2000); 2,132 (2010); 2,039 (2015 projected); Race: 98.3% White, 0.5% Black, 0.0% Asian, 1.2% Other, 4.6% Hispanic of any race (2010); Density: 784.9 persons per square mile (2010); Average household size: 2.48 (2010); Median age: 40.1 (2010); Males per 100 females: 97.2 (2010); Marriage status: 17.3% never married, 62.3% now married, 7.4% widowed, 13.0% divorced (2000); Foreign born: 0.9% (2000); Ancestry (includes multiple ancestries): 18.8% German, 15.5% United States or American, 10.2% English, 7.1% Irish, 6.9% Other groups (2000).
Economy: Single-family building permits issued: 4 (2009); Multi-family building permits issued: 0 (2009); Employment by occupation: 4.2% management, 12.3% professional, 16.2% services, 15.7% sales, 0.6% farming, 8.9% construction, 42.2% production (2000).
Income: Per capita income: $20,719 (2010); Median household income: $45,359 (2010); Average household income: $51,765 (2010); Percent of households with income of $100,000 or more: 7.7% (2010); Poverty rate: 10.9% (2000).
Taxes: Total city taxes per capita: $179 (2007); City property taxes per capita: $171 (2007).
Education: Percent of population age 25 and over with: High school diploma (including GED) or higher: 83.5% (2010); Bachelor's degree or higher: 7.3% (2010); Master's degree or higher: 3.1% (2010).
School District(s)
Southeast Fountain School Corp (KG-12)
    2008-09 Enrollment: 1,310 . . . . (765) 294-2254
Housing: Homeownership rate: 75.2% (2010); Median home value: $86,644 (2010); Median contract rent: $306 per month (2000); Median year structure built: 1957 (2000).
Transportation: Commute to work: 96.0% car, 0.0% public transportation, 1.6% walk, 1.8% work from home (2000); Travel time to work: 40.2% less than 15 minutes, 21.5% 15 to 30 minutes, 23.6% 30 to 45 minutes, 8.7% 45 to 60 minutes, 6.1% 60 minutes or more (2000)

WALLACE (town). Covers a land area of 0.085 square miles and a water area of 0 square miles. Located at 39.98° N. Lat; 87.14° W. Long. Elevation is 699 feet.

History: Laid out 1832.

Population: 89 (1990); 100 (2000); 90 (2010); 86 (2015 projected); Race: 97.8% White, 0.0% Black, 1.1% Asian, 1.1% Other, 1.1% Hispanic of any race (2010); Density: 1,064.5 persons per square mile (2010); Average household size: 2.65 (2010); Median age: 37.0 (2010); Males per 100 females: 114.3 (2010); Marriage status: 26.8% never married, 59.2% now married, 7.0% widowed, 7.0% divorced (2000); Foreign born: 17.4% (2000); Ancestry (includes multiple ancestries): 25.7% United States or American, 11.0% Other groups, 11.0% German, 6.4% French (except Basque), 6.4% Irish (2000).

Economy: Employment by occupation: 4.5% management, 4.5% professional, 20.5% services, 18.2% sales, 0.0% farming, 9.1% construction, 43.2% production (2000).

Income: Per capita income: $18,094 (2010); Median household income: $44,000 (2010); Average household income: $58,676 (2010); Percent of households with income of $100,000 or more: 5.9% (2010); Poverty rate: 23.4% (2000).

Taxes: Total city taxes per capita: $0 (2007); City property taxes per capita: $0 (2007).

Education: Percent of population age 25 and over with: High school diploma (including GED) or higher: 80.0% (2010); Bachelor's degree or higher: 1.7% (2010); Master's degree or higher: 0.0% (2010).

Housing: Homeownership rate: 79.4% (2010); Median home value: $85,000 (2010); Median contract rent: $275 per month (2000); Median year structure built: before 1940 (2000).

Transportation: Commute to work: 79.5% car, 0.0% public transportation, 18.2% walk, 2.3% work from home (2000); Travel time to work: 32.6% less than 15 minutes, 23.3% 15 to 30 minutes, 39.5% 30 to 45 minutes, 0.0% 45 to 60 minutes, 4.7% 60 minutes or more (2000)

Franklin County

Located in southeastern Indiana; bounded on the east by Ohio; drained by the Whitewater River and its East Fork. Covers a land area of 386.00 square miles, a water area of 5.33 square miles, and is located in the Eastern Time Zone. The county was founded in 1810. County seat is Brookville.

Franklin County is part of the Cincinnati-Middletown, OH-KY-IN Metropolitan Statistical Area. The entire metro area includes: Dearborn County, IN; Franklin County, IN; Ohio County, IN; Boone County, KY; Bracken County, KY; Campbell County, KY; Gallatin County, KY; Grant County, KY; Kenton County, KY; Pendleton County, KY; Brown County, OH; Butler County, OH; Clermont County, OH; Hamilton County, OH; Warren County, OH

Weather Station: Brookville											Elevation: 629 feet	
	Jan	Feb	Mar	Apr	May	Jun	Jul	Aug	Sep	Oct	Nov	Dec
High	36	41	52	64	75	83	87	85	79	67	54	42
Low	17	20	29	38	48	58	62	60	52	40	32	23
Precip	2.8	2.6	3.7	4.0	4.6	4.0	4.3	3.9	2.6	3.0	3.7	3.3
Snow	na	3.8	2.3	0.3	tr	0.0	0.0	0.0	0.0	tr	1.1	2.8

High and Low temperatures in degrees Fahrenheit; Precipitation and Snow in inches

Population: 19,580 (1990); 22,151 (2000); 23,556 (2010); 24,093 (2015 projected); Race: 98.1% White, 0.4% Black, 0.6% Asian, 0.9% Other, 0.7% Hispanic of any race (2010); Density: 61.0 persons per square mile (2010); Average household size: 2.70 (2010); Median age: 38.0 (2010); Males per 100 females: 99.4 (2010).

Religion: Five largest groups: 24.4% Catholic Church, 9.6% Southern Baptist Convention, 9.2% Christian Churches and Churches of Christ, 4.2% The United Methodist Church, 2.2% Evangelical Lutheran Church in America (2000).

Economy: Unemployment rate: 10.5% (5/2010); Total civilian labor force: 11,451 (5/2010); Leading industries: 22.1% health care and social assistance; 14.6% manufacturing; 14.5% accommodation & food services (2008); Farms: 723 totaling 126,322 acres (2007); Companies that employ 500 or more persons: 0 (2008); Companies that employ 100 to 499 persons: 5 (2008); Companies that employ less than 100 persons: 469 (2008); Black-owned businesses: n/a (2002); Hispanic-owned businesses: n/a (2002); Asian-owned businesses: n/a (2002); Women-owned businesses: 230 (2002); Retail sales per capita: $4,367 (2010).

Single-family building permits issued: 48 (2009); Multi-family building permits issued: 0 (2009).

Income: Per capita income: $23,195 (2010); Median household income: $52,455 (2010); Average household income: $62,883 (2010); Percent of households with income of $100,000 or more: 14.4% (2010); Poverty rate: 10.3% (2008); Bankruptcy rate: 5.16% (2009).

Taxes: Total county taxes per capita: $257 (2007); County property taxes per capita: $150 (2007).

Education: Percent of population age 25 and over with: High school diploma (including GED) or higher: 86.0% (2010); Bachelor's degree or higher: 16.6% (2010); Master's degree or higher: 5.7% (2010).

Housing: Homeownership rate: 79.7% (2010); Median home value: $126,130 (2010); Median contract rent: $415 per month (2006-2008 3-year est.); Median year structure built: 1975 (2006-2008 3-year est.)

Health: Birth rate: 135.6 per 10,000 population (2009); Death rate: 90.7 per 10,000 population (2009); Age-adjusted cancer mortality rate: 186.6 deaths per 100,000 population (2006); Number of physicians: 12.5 per 10,000 population (2007); Hospital beds: 0.0 per 10,000 population (2006); Hospital admissions: 0.0 per 10,000 population (2006).

Elections: 2008 Presidential election results: 32.1% Obama, 66.1% McCain, 0.1% Nader

National and State Parks: Mounds State Recreation Area

Additional Information Contacts

Franklin County Government . . . . (765) 647-4985
http://www.franklincounty.in.gov

Franklin County Communities

BATH (unincorporated postal area, zip code 47010). Aka New Bath. Covers a land area of 12.152 square miles and a water area of 0.051 square miles. Located at 39.51° N. Lat; 84.82° W. Long. Elevation is 1,010 feet.

Population: 399 (2000); Race: 95.1% White, 0.0% Black, 0.0% Asian, 4.9% Other, 0.0% Hispanic of any race (2000); Density: 32.8 persons per square mile (2000); Age: 18.1% under 18, 22.6% over 64 (2000); Marriage status: 14.3% never married, 71.7% now married, 4.2% widowed, 9.8% divorced (2000); Foreign born: 1.7% (2000); Ancestry (includes multiple ancestries): 28.9% German, 18.1% Irish, 11.5% United States or American, 6.0% French (except Basque), 4.9% Other groups (2000).

Economy: Employment by occupation: 14.7% management, 7.1% professional, 11.5% services, 23.7% sales, 0.0% farming, 26.3% construction, 16.7% production (2000).

Income: Per capita income: $16,022 (2000); Median household income: $35,139 (2000); Poverty rate: 11.5% (2000).

Education: Percent of population age 25 and over with: High school diploma (including GED) or higher: 75.4% (2000); Bachelor's degree or higher: 17.3% (2000).

Housing: Homeownership rate: 70.3% (2000); Median home value: $78,600 (2000); Median contract rent: $325 per month (2000); Median year structure built: 1961 (2000).

Transportation: Commute to work: 92.1% car, 0.0% public transportation, 0.0% walk, 4.6% work from home (2000); Travel time to work: 37.5% less than 15 minutes, 31.9% 15 to 30 minutes, 21.5% 30 to 45 minutes, 3.5% 45 to 60 minutes, 5.6% 60 minutes or more (2000)

BROOKVILLE (town). County seat. Covers a land area of 1.338 square miles and a water area of 0 square miles. Located at 39.42° N. Lat; 85.01° W. Long. Elevation is 666 feet.

History: Brookville was laid out in 1808 on a site selected by Amos Butler and Jesse Brooks Thomas. They called their settlement Brooksville in honor of Thomas' mother, whose maiden name was Brooks. The "s" was removed when Franklin County was organized a few years later and Brookville became the county seat. Thomas became a U.S. senator from Illinois and was instrumental in the Missouri Compromise of 1820.

Population: 2,675 (1990); 2,652 (2000); 2,551 (2010); 2,497 (2015 projected); Race: 97.6% White, 0.4% Black, 1.4% Asian, 0.6% Other, 0.4% Hispanic of any race (2010); Density: 1,906.9 persons per square mile (2010); Average household size: 2.22 (2010); Median age: 39.7 (2010); Males per 100 females: 90.7 (2010); Marriage status: 19.6% never married, 53.1% now married, 12.9% widowed, 14.4% divorced (2000); Foreign born: 1.1% (2000); Ancestry (includes multiple ancestries): 36.9% German, 12.8% Other groups, 11.0% United States or American, 11.0% Irish, 8.6% English (2000).

Economy: Employment by occupation: 11.8% management, 14.5% professional, 13.4% services, 20.8% sales, 0.0% farming, 8.6% construction, 30.9% production (2000).
Income: Per capita income: $20,005 (2010); Median household income: $33,636 (2010); Average household income: $44,349 (2010); Percent of households with income of $100,000 or more: 7.5% (2010); Poverty rate: 8.0% (2000).
Taxes: Total city taxes per capita: $132 (2007); City property taxes per capita: $91 (2007).
Education: Percent of population age 25 and over with: High school diploma (including GED) or higher: 81.9% (2010); Bachelor's degree or higher: 12.4% (2010); Master's degree or higher: 4.2% (2010).

School District(s)
Franklin County Com Sch Corp (PK-12)
    2008-09 Enrollment: 2,995 . . . . (765) 647-4128
Housing: Homeownership rate: 58.1% (2010); Median home value: $90,786 (2010); Median contract rent: $323 per month (2000); Median year structure built: 1947 (2000).
Newspapers: Brookville American (Local news; Circulation 1,028); Democrat (Community news; Circulation 5,000)
Transportation: Commute to work: 88.7% car, 0.0% public transportation, 8.4% walk, 2.8% work from home (2000); Travel time to work: 50.9% less than 15 minutes, 15.6% 15 to 30 minutes, 18.8% 30 to 45 minutes, 6.5% 45 to 60 minutes, 8.2% 60 minutes or more (2000)

CEDAR GROVE (town). Covers a land area of 0.149 square miles and a water area of 0 square miles. Located at 39.35° N. Lat; 84.93° W. Long. Elevation is 600 feet.

Population: 246 (1990); 185 (2000); 184 (2010); 184 (2015 projected); Race: 99.5% White, 0.0% Black, 0.0% Asian, 0.5% Other, 0.0% Hispanic of any race (2010); Density: 1,233.6 persons per square mile (2010); Average household size: 2.63 (2010); Median age: 39.1 (2010); Males per 100 females: 102.2 (2010); Marriage status: 21.3% never married, 56.7% now married, 10.0% widowed, 12.0% divorced (2000); Foreign born: 0.0% (2000); Ancestry (includes multiple ancestries): 58.8% German, 13.7% United States or American, 11.5% Irish, 6.0% Dutch, 3.8% Italian (2000).
Economy: Employment by occupation: 10.3% management, 15.0% professional, 12.1% services, 17.8% sales, 1.9% farming, 17.8% construction, 25.2% production (2000).
Income: Per capita income: $24,941 (2010); Median household income: $55,556 (2010); Average household income: $71,464 (2010); Percent of households with income of $100,000 or more: 14.3% (2010); Poverty rate: 6.6% (2000).
Taxes: Total city taxes per capita: $195 (2007); City property taxes per capita: $157 (2007).
Education: Percent of population age 25 and over with: High school diploma (including GED) or higher: 86.6% (2010); Bachelor's degree or higher: 11.9% (2010); Master's degree or higher: 2.2% (2010).

School District(s)
Franklin County Com Sch Corp (PK-12)
    2008-09 Enrollment: 2,995 . . . . (765) 647-4128
Housing: Homeownership rate: 80.0% (2010); Median home value: $129,412 (2010); Median contract rent: $365 per month (2000); Median year structure built: before 1940 (2000).
Transportation: Commute to work: 95.3% car, 1.9% public transportation, 1.9% walk, 0.9% work from home (2000); Travel time to work: 25.5% less than 15 minutes, 22.6% 15 to 30 minutes, 23.6% 30 to 45 minutes, 14.2% 45 to 60 minutes, 14.2% 60 minutes or more (2000)

LAUREL (town). Covers a land area of 0.238 square miles and a water area of 0 square miles. Located at 39.50° N. Lat; 85.18° W. Long. Elevation is 725 feet.

History: Laurel was founded in 1836 by James Conwell, who named it for Laurel, Delaware. It began as a farming community, becoming a mill town and shipping center during the canal period.
Population: 544 (1990); 579 (2000); 557 (2010); 548 (2015 projected); Race: 98.2% White, 0.0% Black, 0.0% Asian, 1.8% Other, 1.4% Hispanic of any race (2010); Density: 2,342.1 persons per square mile (2010); Average household size: 2.79 (2010); Median age: 33.8 (2010); Males per 100 females: 101.1 (2010); Marriage status: 23.9% never married, 54.0% now married, 12.1% widowed, 10.0% divorced (2000); Foreign born: 0.0% (2000); Ancestry (includes multiple ancestries): 29.4% United States or American, 7.1% German, 6.4% Other groups, 5.9% Irish, 2.3% English (2000).

Economy: Employment by occupation: 4.8% management, 6.7% professional, 21.0% services, 11.9% sales, 0.0% farming, 11.4% construction, 44.3% production (2000).
Income: Per capita income: $15,069 (2010); Median household income: $40,000 (2010); Average household income: $41,675 (2010); Percent of households with income of $100,000 or more: 2.5% (2010); Poverty rate: 13.6% (2000).
Taxes: Total city taxes per capita: $55 (2007); City property taxes per capita: $48 (2007).
Education: Percent of population age 25 and over with: High school diploma (including GED) or higher: 71.3% (2010); Bachelor's degree or higher: 7.1% (2010); Master's degree or higher: 1.1% (2010).

School District(s)
Franklin County Com Sch Corp (PK-12)
    2008-09 Enrollment: 2,995 . . . . (765) 647-4128
Housing: Homeownership rate: 74.5% (2010); Median home value: $80,400 (2010); Median contract rent: $319 per month (2000); Median year structure built: 1948 (2000).
Transportation: Commute to work: 93.2% car, 0.0% public transportation, 4.9% walk, 2.0% work from home (2000); Travel time to work: 12.9% less than 15 minutes, 12.4% 15 to 30 minutes, 41.3% 30 to 45 minutes, 21.4% 45 to 60 minutes, 11.9% 60 minutes or more (2000)

METAMORA (unincorporated postal area, zip code 47030). Covers a land area of 33.836 square miles and a water area of 0 square miles. Located at 39.42° N. Lat; 85.13° W. Long. Elevation is 719 feet.

History: The community of Metamora developed around the Whitewater Canal, where a number of mills and factories were located.
Population: 1,553 (2000); Race: 99.6% White, 0.1% Black, 0.0% Asian, 0.3% Other, 0.0% Hispanic of any race (2000); Density: 45.9 persons per square mile (2000); Age: 30.1% under 18, 11.4% over 64 (2000); Marriage status: 22.0% never married, 63.1% now married, 5.5% widowed, 9.5% divorced (2000); Foreign born: 0.0% (2000); Ancestry (includes multiple ancestries): 20.3% German, 17.4% United States or American, 8.3% Other groups, 7.6% Irish, 5.9% English (2000).
Economy: Employment by occupation: 9.3% management, 12.1% professional, 7.3% services, 18.7% sales, 0.0% farming, 16.3% construction, 36.3% production (2000).
Income: Per capita income: $15,701 (2000); Median household income: $40,298 (2000); Poverty rate: 8.8% (2000).
Education: Percent of population age 25 and over with: High school diploma (including GED) or higher: 64.0% (2000); Bachelor's degree or higher: 8.7% (2000).
Housing: Homeownership rate: 84.6% (2000); Median home value: $90,400 (2000); Median contract rent: $309 per month (2000); Median year structure built: 1975 (2000).
Transportation: Commute to work: 92.9% car, 0.0% public transportation, 0.7% walk, 3.7% work from home (2000); Travel time to work: 6.6% less than 15 minutes, 21.1% 15 to 30 minutes, 32.0% 30 to 45 minutes, 15.7% 45 to 60 minutes, 24.6% 60 minutes or more (2000)

MOUNT CARMEL (town). Covers a land area of 0.042 square miles and a water area of 0 square miles. Located at 39.40° N. Lat; 84.87° W. Long. Elevation is 1,020 feet.

Population: 108 (1990); 106 (2000); 116 (2010); 121 (2015 projected); Race: 99.1% White, 0.0% Black, 0.0% Asian, 0.9% Other, 0.0% Hispanic of any race (2010); Density: 2,764.3 persons per square mile (2010); Average household size: 2.83 (2010); Median age: 37.7 (2010); Males per 100 females: 110.9 (2010); Marriage status: 21.2% never married, 60.0% now married, 3.5% widowed, 15.3% divorced (2000); Foreign born: 0.0% (2000); Ancestry (includes multiple ancestries): 41.1% German, 12.9% Other groups, 9.7% Irish, 9.7% United States or American, 6.5% Dutch (2000).
Economy: Employment by occupation: 10.9% management, 4.3% professional, 10.9% services, 19.6% sales, 0.0% farming, 21.7% construction, 32.6% production (2000).
Income: Per capita income: $20,611 (2010); Median household income: $51,136 (2010); Average household income: $54,878 (2010); Percent of households with income of $100,000 or more: 7.3% (2010); Poverty rate: 27.0% (2000).
Taxes: Total city taxes per capita: $430 (2007); City property taxes per capita: $327 (2007).
Education: Percent of population age 25 and over with: High school diploma (including GED) or higher: 87.5% (2010); Bachelor's degree or higher: 5.0% (2010); Master's degree or higher: 1.3% (2010).

Housing: Homeownership rate: 82.9% (2010); Median home value: $125,000 (2010); Median contract rent: $425 per month (2000); Median year structure built: before 1940 (2000).
Transportation: Commute to work: 87.0% car, 0.0% public transportation, 2.2% walk, 8.7% work from home (2000); Travel time to work: 23.8% less than 15 minutes, 40.5% 15 to 30 minutes, 11.9% 30 to 45 minutes, 16.7% 45 to 60 minutes, 7.1% 60 minutes or more (2000)

OLDENBURG (town). Covers a land area of 0.416 square miles and a water area of 0 square miles. Located at 39.33° N. Lat; 85.20° W. Long. Elevation is 889 feet.
History: Oldenburg was founded in 1837 by German immigrants. It was once a brick manufacturing center.
Population: 715 (1990); 647 (2000); 635 (2010); 623 (2015 projected); Race: 98.1% White, 0.0% Black, 0.8% Asian, 1.1% Other, 0.5% Hispanic of any race (2010); Density: 1,525.4 persons per square mile (2010); Average household size: 2.67 (2010); Median age: 45.1 (2010); Males per 100 females: 89.6 (2010); Marriage status: 41.9% never married, 46.0% now married, 10.1% widowed, 2.0% divorced (2000); Foreign born: 0.0% (2000); Ancestry (includes multiple ancestries): 64.1% German, 14.8% Irish, 9.2% English, 3.9% United States or American, 3.9% French (except Basque) (2000).
Economy: Employment by occupation: 8.6% management, 21.1% professional, 15.5% services, 22.4% sales, 0.7% farming, 8.9% construction, 23.0% production (2000).
Income: Per capita income: $28,761 (2010); Median household income: $65,854 (2010); Average household income: $80,856 (2010); Percent of households with income of $100,000 or more: 21.3% (2010); Poverty rate: 17.7% (2000).
Taxes: Total city taxes per capita: $69 (2007); City property taxes per capita: $69 (2007).
Education: Percent of population age 25 and over with: High school diploma (including GED) or higher: 94.5% (2010); Bachelor's degree or higher: 36.8% (2010); Master's degree or higher: 23.5% (2010).
Housing: Homeownership rate: 79.6% (2010); Median home value: $157,143 (2010); Median contract rent: $321 per month (2000); Median year structure built: 1952 (2000).
Transportation: Commute to work: 75.3% car, 0.0% public transportation, 14.4% walk, 10.3% work from home (2000); Travel time to work: 69.1% less than 15 minutes, 16.4% 15 to 30 minutes, 5.0% 30 to 45 minutes, 3.4% 45 to 60 minutes, 6.1% 60 minutes or more (2000)

Fulton County

Located in northern Indiana; drained by the Tippecanoe River. Covers a land area of 368.51 square miles, a water area of 2.87 square miles, and is located in the Eastern Time Zone. The county was founded in 1835. County seat is Rochester.

Weather Station: Rochester											Elevation: 767 feet
	Jan	Feb	Mar	Apr	May	Jun	Jul	Aug	Sep	Oct	Nov	Dec
High	30	35	46	59	71	80	84	82	75	63	48	36
Low	14	17	27	37	48	58	62	60	52	40	31	21
Precip	2.0	1.7	2.7	3.9	4.1	4.0	3.9	3.6	3.5	2.9	3.4	2.7
Snow	9.5	8.3	3.8	1.2	0.0	0.0	0.0	0.0	0.0	0.3	2.7	6.7

High and Low temperatures in degrees Fahrenheit; Precipitation and Snow in inches

Population: 18,840 (1990); 20,511 (2000); 20,345 (2010); 20,199 (2015 projected); Race: 95.0% White, 1.0% Black, 0.4% Asian, 3.6% Other, 3.3% Hispanic of any race (2010); Density: 55.2 persons per square mile (2010); Average household size: 2.51 (2010); Median age: 40.0 (2010); Males per 100 females: 97.4 (2010).
Religion: Five largest groups: 9.4% The United Methodist Church, 5.2% Catholic Church, 3.2% American Baptist Churches in the USA, 2.4% New Testament Association of Independent Baptist Churches and other Fundamental Baptist Associations, 2.4% Christ
Economy: Unemployment rate: 10.3% (5/2010); Total civilian labor force: 10,851 (5/2010); Leading industries: 37.4% manufacturing; 15.1% retail trade; 8.4% accommodation & food services (2008); Farms: 639 totaling 184,847 acres (2007); Companies that employ 500 or more persons: 0 (2008); Companies that employ 100 to 499 persons: 11 (2008); Companies that employ less than 100 persons: 464 (2008); Black-owned businesses: n/a (2002); Hispanic-owned businesses: n/a (2002); Asian-owned businesses: n/a (2002); Women-owned businesses: 542 (2002); Retail sales per capita: $11,446 (2010). Single-family building permits issued: 19 (2009); Multi-family building permits issued: 0 (2009).

Income: Per capita income: $21,372 (2010); Median household income: $44,905 (2010); Average household income: $53,852 (2010); Percent of households with income of $100,000 or more: 9.6% (2010); Poverty rate: 12.2% (2008); Bankruptcy rate: 8.70% (2009).
Taxes: Total county taxes per capita: $279 (2007); County property taxes per capita: $146 (2007).
Education: Percent of population age 25 and over with: High school diploma (including GED) or higher: 86.4% (2010); Bachelor's degree or higher: 14.2% (2010); Master's degree or higher: 5.9% (2010).
Housing: Homeownership rate: 77.1% (2010); Median home value: $89,121 (2010); Median contract rent: $431 per month (2006-2008 3-year est.); Median year structure built: 1959 (2006-2008 3-year est.)
Health: Birth rate: 126.3 per 10,000 population (2009); Death rate: 108.1 per 10,000 population (2009); Age-adjusted cancer mortality rate: 256.6 deaths per 100,000 population (2006); Number of physicians: 4.5 per 10,000 population (2007); Hospital beds: 17.3 per 10,000 population (2006); Hospital admissions: 536.5 per 10,000 population (2006).
Elections: 2008 Presidential election results: 41.1% Obama, 57.2% McCain, 0.0% Nader
Additional Information Contacts
Fulton County Government . . . . (574) 223-2912
    http://www.co.fulton.in.us
City of Rochester . . . . (574) 223-2510
    http://www.rochester.in.us

Fulton County Communities

AKRON (town). Covers a land area of 0.455 square miles and a water area of 0 square miles. Located at 41.03° N. Lat; 86.02° W. Long. Elevation is 850 feet.
Population: 1,001 (1990); 1,076 (2000); 994 (2010); 952 (2015 projected); Race: 89.4% White, 0.0% Black, 0.0% Asian, 10.6% Other, 20.1% Hispanic of any race (2010); Density: 2,185.5 persons per square mile (2010); Average household size: 2.78 (2010); Median age: 35.9 (2010); Males per 100 females: 99.2 (2010); Marriage status: 22.4% never married, 58.8% now married, 10.0% widowed, 8.7% divorced (2000); Foreign born: 9.0% (2000); Ancestry (includes multiple ancestries): 22.2% Other groups, 20.2% German, 14.7% United States or American, 10.2% English, 7.8% Irish (2000).
Economy: Single-family building permits issued: 0 (2009); Multi-family building permits issued: 0 (2009); Employment by occupation: 6.5% management, 13.3% professional, 11.2% services, 15.9% sales, 1.6% farming, 4.9% construction, 46.8% production (2000).
Income: Per capita income: $16,957 (2010); Median household income: $41,493 (2010); Average household income: $47,046 (2010); Percent of households with income of $100,000 or more: 5.0% (2010); Poverty rate: 7.6% (2000).
Taxes: Total city taxes per capita: $127 (2007); City property taxes per capita: $118 (2007).
Education: Percent of population age 25 and over with: High school diploma (including GED) or higher: 81.9% (2010); Bachelor's degree or higher: 12.4% (2010); Master's degree or higher: 3.8% (2010).
School District(s)
Tippecanoe Valley School Corp (KG-12)
    2008-09 Enrollment: 2,151 . . . . (574) 353-7741
Housing: Homeownership rate: 74.0% (2010); Median home value: $76,379 (2010); Median contract rent: $325 per month (2000); Median year structure built: before 1940 (2000).
Transportation: Commute to work: 92.9% car, 0.0% public transportation, 6.0% walk, 0.8% work from home (2000); Travel time to work: 34.0% less than 15 minutes, 36.8% 15 to 30 minutes, 20.8% 30 to 45 minutes, 6.0% 45 to 60 minutes, 2.4% 60 minutes or more (2000)

FULTON (town). Covers a land area of 0.181 square miles and a water area of 0 square miles. Located at 40.94° N. Lat; 86.26° W. Long. Elevation is 794 feet.
Population: 371 (1990); 326 (2000); 277 (2010); 256 (2015 projected); Race: 99.6% White, 0.0% Black, 0.0% Asian, 0.4% Other, 0.0% Hispanic of any race (2010); Density: 1,527.6 persons per square mile (2010); Average household size: 2.52 (2010); Median age: 38.1 (2010); Males per 100 females: 93.7 (2010); Marriage status: 24.1% never married, 58.3% now married, 7.1% widowed, 10.5% divorced (2000); Foreign born: 2.4% (2000); Ancestry (includes multiple ancestries): 19.8% German, 18.6% United States or American, 9.6% Irish, 7.8% Dutch, 6.3% English (2000).

Economy: Single-family building permits issued: 0 (2009); Multi-family building permits issued: 0 (2009); Employment by occupation: 4.4% management, 17.6% professional, 9.4% services, 19.5% sales, 0.0% farming, 9.4% construction, 39.6% production (2000).
Income: Per capita income: $25,815 (2010); Median household income: $58,088 (2010); Average household income: $65,227 (2010); Percent of households with income of $100,000 or more: 20.9% (2010); Poverty rate: 2.4% (2000).
Taxes: Total city taxes per capita: $92 (2007); City property taxes per capita: $92 (2007).
Education: Percent of population age 25 and over with: High school diploma (including GED) or higher: 90.2% (2010); Bachelor's degree or higher: 9.8% (2010); Master's degree or higher: 3.8% (2010).
School District(s)
Caston School Corporation (PK-12)
    2008-09 Enrollment: 785 . . . . (574) 857-2035
Housing: Homeownership rate: 89.1% (2010); Median home value: $69,167 (2010); Median contract rent: $388 per month (2000); Median year structure built: before 1940 (2000).
Transportation: Commute to work: 84.2% car, 0.0% public transportation, 8.2% walk, 7.6% work from home (2000); Travel time to work: 28.1% less than 15 minutes, 34.9% 15 to 30 minutes, 24.7% 30 to 45 minutes, 8.2% 45 to 60 minutes, 4.1% 60 minutes or more (2000)

KEWANNA (town). Covers a land area of 0.524 square miles and a water area of 0 square miles. Located at 41.01° N. Lat; 86.41° W. Long. Elevation is 794 feet.
Population: 542 (1990); 614 (2000); 536 (2010); 503 (2015 projected); Race: 97.2% White, 0.6% Black, 0.0% Asian, 2.2% Other, 0.7% Hispanic of any race (2010); Density: 1,022.7 persons per square mile (2010); Average household size: 2.26 (2010); Median age: 42.2 (2010); Males per 100 females: 97.1 (2010); Marriage status: 11.5% never married, 54.2% now married, 19.4% widowed, 14.9% divorced (2000); Foreign born: 1.0% (2000); Ancestry (includes multiple ancestries): 23.8% German, 14.1% Irish, 12.5% English, 12.1% United States or American, 4.5% French (except Basque) (2000).
Economy: Single-family building permits issued: 0 (2009); Multi-family building permits issued: 0 (2009); Employment by occupation: 4.5% management, 10.6% professional, 15.2% services, 16.7% sales, 0.8% farming, 9.8% construction, 42.4% production (2000).
Income: Per capita income: $18,448 (2010); Median household income: $29,677 (2010); Average household income: $42,722 (2010); Percent of households with income of $100,000 or more: 4.2% (2010); Poverty rate: 13.0% (2000).
Taxes: Total city taxes per capita: $119 (2007); City property taxes per capita: $119 (2007).
Education: Percent of population age 25 and over with: High school diploma (including GED) or higher: 85.2% (2010); Bachelor's degree or higher: 9.2% (2010); Master's degree or higher: 3.2% (2010).
Housing: Homeownership rate: 74.7% (2010); Median home value: $55,818 (2010); Median contract rent: $306 per month (2000); Median year structure built: 1943 (2000).
Newspapers: Observer (Local news; Circulation 685)
Transportation: Commute to work: 93.5% car, 0.0% public transportation, 5.0% walk, 0.8% work from home (2000); Travel time to work: 32.9% less than 15 minutes, 38.4% 15 to 30 minutes, 10.1% 30 to 45 minutes, 8.9% 45 to 60 minutes, 9.7% 60 minutes or more (2000)

ROCHESTER (city). Aka Pershing. County seat. Covers a land area of 4.557 square miles and a water area of 1.111 square miles. Located at 41.06° N. Lat; 86.20° W. Long. Elevation is 781 feet.
History: Rochester was founded in 1831 as a trading post, and became a resort town on Lake Manitou.
Population: 6,111 (1990); 6,414 (2000); 6,273 (2010); 6,147 (2015 projected); Race: 94.9% White, 0.9% Black, 0.9% Asian, 3.2% Other, 2.5% Hispanic of any race (2010); Density: 1,376.5 persons per square mile (2010); Average household size: 2.35 (2010); Median age: 41.0 (2010); Males per 100 females: 91.6 (2010); Marriage status: 19.9% never married, 53.2% now married, 11.5% widowed, 15.4% divorced (2000); Foreign born: 1.3% (2000); Ancestry (includes multiple ancestries): 20.4% German, 20.4% United States or American, 12.0% Irish, 8.0% English, 7.6% Other groups (2000).
Economy: Single-family building permits issued: 0 (2009); Multi-family building permits issued: 0 (2009); Employment by occupation: 6.7%

management, 10.2% professional, 13.6% services, 25.2% sales, 0.5% farming, 9.8% construction, 33.9% production (2000).
Income: Per capita income: $20,682 (2010); Median household income: $39,457 (2010); Average household income: $48,999 (2010); Percent of households with income of $100,000 or more: 7.9% (2010); Poverty rate: 11.9% (2000).
Taxes: Total city taxes per capita: $217 (2007); City property taxes per capita: $206 (2007).
Education: Percent of population age 25 and over with: High school diploma (including GED) or higher: 84.6% (2010); Bachelor's degree or higher: 14.0% (2010); Master's degree or higher: 5.7% (2010).
School District(s)
Rochester Community Sch Corp (PK-12)
    2008-09 Enrollment: 1,915 . . . . (574) 223-2159
Housing: Homeownership rate: 67.4% (2010); Median home value: $82,531 (2010); Median contract rent: $384 per month (2000); Median year structure built: 1961 (2000).
Hospitals: Woodlawn Hospital (49 beds)
Newspapers: Rochester Sentinel (Local news; Circulation 11,150); Shopping Guide News (Community news; Circulation 9,300)
Transportation: Commute to work: 94.5% car, 0.0% public transportation, 0.9% walk, 3.8% work from home (2000); Travel time to work: 62.6% less than 15 minutes, 10.0% 15 to 30 minutes, 14.6% 30 to 45 minutes, 3.7% 45 to 60 minutes, 9.1% 60 minutes or more (2000)
Additional Information Contacts
City of Rochester . . . . (574) 223-2510
    http://www.rochester.in.us

Gibson County

Located in southwestern Indiana; bounded on the west by the Wabash River and the Illinois border, and on the north by the White River; also drained by the Patoka and Black Rivers. Covers a land area of 488.78 square miles, a water area of 10.27 square miles, and is located in the Central Time Zone. The county was founded in 1813. County seat is Princeton.

Gibson County is part of the Evansville, IN-KY Metropolitan Statistical Area. The entire metro area includes: Gibson County, IN; Posey County, IN; Vanderburgh County, IN; Warrick County, IN; Henderson County, KY; Webster County, KY

Weather Station: Princeton 1 W									Elevation: 479 feet		
	Jan	Feb	Mar	Apr	May	Jun	Jul	Aug	Sep	Oct	Nov	Dec
High	37	44	55	66	76	85	88	86	80	69	54	43
Low	22	26	35	45	55	64	68	66	58	47	37	27
Precip	2.7	2.8	4.3	4.7	5.1	4.0	4.0	3.8	3.1	3.4	4.4	3.6
Snow	na	3.8	1.0	0.3	0.0	0.0	0.0	0.0	0.0	0.1	0.3	2.1

High and Low temperatures in degrees Fahrenheit; Precipitation and Snow in inches

Population: 31,913 (1990); 32,500 (2000); 32,590 (2010); 32,344 (2015 projected); Race: 95.7% White, 2.1% Black, 0.6% Asian, 1.5% Other, 1.0% Hispanic of any race (2010); Density: 66.7 persons per square mile (2010); Average household size: 2.43 (2010); Median age: 39.6 (2010); Males per 100 females: 97.2 (2010).
Religion: Five largest groups: 18.7% Catholic Church, 7.6% The United Methodist Church, 3.1% Church of the Nazarene, 2.6% Assemblies of God, 2.0% United Church of Christ (2000).
Economy: Unemployment rate: 7.3% (5/2010); Total civilian labor force: 16,144 (5/2010); Leading industries: 10.6% retail trade; 9.8% health care and social assistance; 7.9% administration, support, waste management, remediation services (2008); Farms: 590 totaling 231,082 acres (2007); Companies that employ 500 or more persons: 1 (2008); Companies that employ 100 to 499 persons: 25 (2008); Companies that employ less than 100 persons: 691 (2008); Black-owned businesses: n/a (2002); Hispanic-owned businesses: n/a (2002); Asian-owned businesses: n/a (2002); Women-owned businesses: 455 (2002); Retail sales per capita: $12,079 (2010). Single-family building permits issued: 75 (2009); Multi-family building permits issued: 0 (2009).
Income: Per capita income: $23,462 (2010); Median household income: $48,637 (2010); Average household income: $57,827 (2010); Percent of households with income of $100,000 or more: 12.8% (2010); Poverty rate: 11.9% (2008); Bankruptcy rate: 6.06% (2009).
Taxes: Total county taxes per capita: $348 (2007); County property taxes per capita: $240 (2007).

Education: Percent of population age 25 and over with: High school diploma (including GED) or higher: 87.6% (2010); Bachelor's degree or higher: 14.4% (2010); Master's degree or higher: 4.2% (2010).
Housing: Homeownership rate: 76.4% (2010); Median home value: $88,611 (2010); Median contract rent: $398 per month (2006-2008 3-year est.); Median year structure built: 1969 (2006-2008 3-year est.)
Health: Birth rate: 123.4 per 10,000 population (2009); Death rate: 95.6 per 10,000 population (2009); Age-adjusted cancer mortality rate: 186.6 deaths per 100,000 population (2006); Air Quality Index: 90.8% good, 9.2% moderate, 0.0% unhealthy for sensitive individuals, 0.0% unhealthy (percent of days in 2008); Number of physicians: 7.6 per 10,000 population (2007); Hospital beds: 21.2 per 10,000 population (2006); Hospital admissions: 329.9 per 10,000 population (2006).
Elections: 2008 Presidential election results: 42.8% Obama, 56.0% McCain, 0.0% Nader
Additional Information Contacts
Gibson County Government . . . . (812) 385-5286
   http://www.gibsoncounty-in.gov
City of Princeton. . . . . (812) 385-4428
   http://www.princeton-indiana.com
Gibson County Chamber of Commerce. . . . . (812) 385-2134
   http://www.gibsoncountychamber.org

Gibson County Communities

BUCKSKIN (unincorporated postal area, zip code 47647). Covers a land area of 1.220 square miles and a water area of 0 square miles. Located at 38.21° N. Lat; 87.42° W. Long. Elevation is 459 feet.
Population: 86 (2000); Race: 91.6% White, 0.0% Black, 0.0% Asian, 8.4% Other, 0.0% Hispanic of any race (2000); Density: 70.5 persons per square mile (2000); Age: 10.8% under 18, 38.6% over 64 (2000); Marriage status: 17.6% never married, 9.5% now married, 52.7% widowed, 20.3% divorced (2000); Foreign born: 0.0% (2000); Ancestry (includes multiple ancestries): 72.3% German, 47.0% Irish, 19.3% English, 8.4% Other groups (2000).
Economy: Employment by occupation: 0.0% management, 0.0% professional, 46.4% services, 0.0% sales, 0.0% farming, 25.0% construction, 28.6% production (2000).
Income: Per capita income: $13,642 (2000); Median household income: $30,156 (2000); Poverty rate: 0.0% (2000).
Education: Percent of population age 25 and over with: High school diploma (including GED) or higher: 46.8% (2000); Bachelor's degree or higher: 0.0% (2000).
Housing: Homeownership rate: 84.4% (2000); Median home value: $85,000 (2000); Median contract rent: $275 per month (2000); Median year structure built: before 1940 (2000).
Transportation: Commute to work: 71.4% car, 0.0% public transportation, 0.0% walk, 28.6% work from home (2000); Travel time to work: 0.0% less than 15 minutes, 0.0% 15 to 30 minutes, 60.0% 30 to 45 minutes, 0.0% 45 to 60 minutes, 40.0% 60 minutes or more (2000)

FORT BRANCH (town). Covers a land area of 0.741 square miles and a water area of 0 square miles. Located at 38.24° N. Lat; 87.57° W. Long. Elevation is 449 feet.
History: The town of Fort Branch was named for Old Fort Branch, built in 1811.
Population: 2,447 (1990); 2,320 (2000); 2,445 (2010); 2,471 (2015 projected); Race: 98.0% White, 0.3% Black, 0.4% Asian, 1.2% Other, 0.7% Hispanic of any race (2010); Density: 3,299.7 persons per square mile (2010); Average household size: 2.30 (2010); Median age: 39.4 (2010); Males per 100 females: 96.7 (2010); Marriage status: 20.4% never married, 61.7% now married, 9.4% widowed, 8.5% divorced (2000); Foreign born: 0.4% (2000); Ancestry (includes multiple ancestries): 38.6% German, 11.1% English, 10.9% United States or American, 9.2% Irish, 8.6% Other groups (2000).
Economy: Employment by occupation: 8.7% management, 10.4% professional, 16.3% services, 26.7% sales, 0.2% farming, 9.1% construction, 28.6% production (2000).
Income: Per capita income: $24,506 (2010); Median household income: $48,492 (2010); Average household income: $56,376 (2010); Percent of households with income of $100,000 or more: 12.0% (2010); Poverty rate: 4.4% (2000).
Taxes: Total city taxes per capita: $89 (2007); City property taxes per capita: $63 (2007).

Education: Percent of population age 25 and over with: High school diploma (including GED) or higher: 88.8% (2010); Bachelor's degree or higher: 13.3% (2010); Master's degree or higher: 3.0% (2010).
School District(s)
South Gibson School Corp (PK-12)
   2008-09 Enrollment: 2,040 . . . . (812) 753-4230
Housing: Homeownership rate: 72.3% (2010); Median home value: $98,117 (2010); Median contract rent: $316 per month (2000); Median year structure built: 1956 (2000).
Newspapers: South Gibson Star-Times (Local news; Circulation 2,700)
Transportation: Commute to work: 94.8% car, 0.3% public transportation, 2.0% walk, 2.0% work from home (2000); Travel time to work: 34.6% less than 15 minutes, 30.8% 15 to 30 minutes, 24.6% 30 to 45 minutes, 5.1% 45 to 60 minutes, 4.9% 60 minutes or more (2000)

FRANCISCO (town). Covers a land area of 0.545 square miles and a water area of 0 square miles. Located at 38.33° N. Lat; 87.44° W. Long. Elevation is 472 feet.
History: Francisco developed when the Wabash & Erie Canal was built, and was named for a Spanish laborer on the canal.
Population: 560 (1990); 543 (2000); 549 (2010); 546 (2015 projected); Race: 98.0% White, 1.1% Black, 0.0% Asian, 0.9% Other, 0.2% Hispanic of any race (2010); Density: 1,006.5 persons per square mile (2010); Average household size: 2.47 (2010); Median age: 41.9 (2010); Males per 100 females: 98.9 (2010); Marriage status: 23.0% never married, 53.4% now married, 11.1% widowed, 12.5% divorced (2000); Foreign born: 0.2% (2000); Ancestry (includes multiple ancestries): 22.7% United States or American, 19.4% German, 5.7% Irish, 5.5% English, 4.0% Other groups (2000).
Economy: Employment by occupation: 5.8% management, 10.0% professional, 12.7% services, 26.3% sales, 2.3% farming, 8.1% construction, 34.7% production (2000).
Income: Per capita income: $26,435 (2010); Median household income: $59,583 (2010); Average household income: $64,696 (2010); Percent of households with income of $100,000 or more: 12.6% (2010); Poverty rate: 9.5% (2000).
Taxes: Total city taxes per capita: $77 (2007); City property taxes per capita: $50 (2007).
Education: Percent of population age 25 and over with: High school diploma (including GED) or higher: 91.6% (2010); Bachelor's degree or higher: 9.6% (2010); Master's degree or higher: 3.2% (2010).
School District(s)
East Gibson School Corporation (PK-12)
   2008-09 Enrollment: 996 . . . . (812) 749-4755
Housing: Homeownership rate: 88.3% (2010); Median home value: $83,556 (2010); Median contract rent: $322 per month (2000); Median year structure built: 1948 (2000).
Transportation: Commute to work: 99.6% car, 0.0% public transportation, 0.0% walk, 0.0% work from home (2000); Travel time to work: 22.4% less than 15 minutes, 39.6% 15 to 30 minutes, 23.6% 30 to 45 minutes, 8.4% 45 to 60 minutes, 6.0% 60 minutes or more (2000)

HAUBSTADT (town). Covers a land area of 0.685 square miles and a water area of 0 square miles. Located at 38.20° N. Lat; 87.57° W. Long. Elevation is 472 feet.
Population: 1,524 (1990); 1,529 (2000); 1,494 (2010); 1,464 (2015 projected); Race: 99.5% White, 0.1% Black, 0.0% Asian, 0.5% Other, 0.1% Hispanic of any race (2010); Density: 2,181.0 persons per square mile (2010); Average household size: 2.58 (2010); Median age: 37.8 (2010); Males per 100 females: 104.9 (2010); Marriage status: 18.6% never married, 64.1% now married, 7.1% widowed, 10.2% divorced (2000); Foreign born: 0.1% (2000); Ancestry (includes multiple ancestries): 54.5% German, 11.9% United States or American, 9.2% Irish, 4.2% English, 2.5% Other groups (2000).
Economy: Employment by occupation: 11.8% management, 13.2% professional, 14.5% services, 21.4% sales, 0.0% farming, 14.8% construction, 24.3% production (2000).
Income: Per capita income: $30,547 (2010); Median household income: $66,282 (2010); Average household income: $78,355 (2010); Percent of households with income of $100,000 or more: 21.4% (2010); Poverty rate: 5.7% (2000).
Taxes: Total city taxes per capita: $161 (2007); City property taxes per capita: $116 (2007).

Education: Percent of population age 25 and over with: High school diploma (including GED) or higher: 91.0% (2010); Bachelor's degree or higher: 20.5% (2010); Master's degree or higher: 5.8% (2010).

School District(s)

South Gibson School Corp (PK-12)

    2008-09 Enrollment: 2,040 . . . . (812) 753-4230

Housing: Homeownership rate: 82.9% (2010); Median home value: $130,226 (2010); Median contract rent: $286 per month (2000); Median year structure built: 1970 (2000).

Transportation: Commute to work: 93.0% car, 0.0% public transportation, 1.3% walk, 5.0% work from home (2000); Travel time to work: 28.0% less than 15 minutes, 32.7% 15 to 30 minutes, 31.9% 30 to 45 minutes, 5.4% 45 to 60 minutes, 2.2% 60 minutes or more (2000)

HAZLETON (town). Aka Buena Vista. Covers a land area of 0.342 square miles and a water area of 0 square miles. Located at 38.48° N. Lat; 87.54° W. Long. Elevation is 453 feet.

History: Also spelled Hazelton.

Population: 357 (1990); 288 (2000); 261 (2010); 248 (2015 projected); Race: 96.6% White, 0.8% Black, 0.0% Asian, 2.7% Other, 0.0% Hispanic of any race (2010); Density: 762.1 persons per square mile (2010); Average household size: 2.66 (2010); Median age: 40.7 (2010); Males per 100 females: 100.8 (2010); Marriage status: 25.1% never married, 49.8% now married, 13.2% widowed, 11.9% divorced (2000); Foreign born: 0.0% (2000); Ancestry (includes multiple ancestries): 13.4% German, 10.3% United States or American, 10.0% Irish, 6.2% English, 3.8% Other groups (2000).

Economy: Employment by occupation: 3.4% management, 12.9% professional, 17.2% services, 24.1% sales, 0.0% farming, 12.9% construction, 29.3% production (2000).

Income: Per capita income: $17,701 (2010); Median household income: $41,964 (2010); Average household income: $46,403 (2010); Percent of households with income of $100,000 or more: 4.1% (2010); Poverty rate: 25.9% (2000).

Taxes: Total city taxes per capita: $55 (2007); City property taxes per capita: $34 (2007).

Education: Percent of population age 25 and over with: High school diploma (including GED) or higher: 84.3% (2010); Bachelor's degree or higher: 1.6% (2010); Master's degree or higher: 0.5% (2010).

Housing: Homeownership rate: 88.8% (2010); Median home value: $48,667 (2010); Median contract rent: $195 per month (2000); Median year structure built: before 1940 (2000).

Newspapers: White River News (Community news; Circulation 425)

Transportation: Commute to work: 89.5% car, 0.0% public transportation, 4.4% walk, 3.5% work from home (2000); Travel time to work: 16.4% less than 15 minutes, 32.7% 15 to 30 minutes, 31.8% 30 to 45 minutes, 7.3% 45 to 60 minutes, 11.8% 60 minutes or more (2000)

MACKEY (town). Covers a land area of 0.082 square miles and a water area of 0 square miles. Located at 38.25° N. Lat; 87.39° W. Long. Elevation is 449 feet.

Population: 89 (1990); 142 (2000); 141 (2010); 139 (2015 projected); Race: 97.9% White, 0.7% Black, 0.0% Asian, 1.4% Other, 0.7% Hispanic of any race (2010); Density: 1,709.7 persons per square mile (2010); Average household size: 2.43 (2010); Median age: 40.0 (2010); Males per 100 females: 98.6 (2010); Marriage status: 11.9% never married, 51.2% now married, 15.5% widowed, 21.4% divorced (2000); Foreign born: 0.0% (2000); Ancestry (includes multiple ancestries): 24.1% German, 15.2% United States or American, 7.1% French (except Basque), 7.1% English, 3.6% Dutch (2000).

Economy: Employment by occupation: 4.7% management, 9.3% professional, 11.6% services, 27.9% sales, 4.7% farming, 4.7% construction, 37.2% production (2000).

Income: Per capita income: $19,508 (2010); Median household income: $43,571 (2010); Average household income: $47,931 (2010); Percent of households with income of $100,000 or more: 5.2% (2010); Poverty rate: 8.0% (2000).

Taxes: Total city taxes per capita: $199 (2007); City property taxes per capita: $142 (2007).

Education: Percent of population age 25 and over with: High school diploma (including GED) or higher: 88.7% (2010); Bachelor's degree or higher: 9.3% (2010); Master's degree or higher: 3.1% (2010).

School District(s)

East Gibson School Corporation (PK-12)

    2008-09 Enrollment: 996 . . . . (812) 749-4755

Housing: Homeownership rate: 77.6% (2010); Median home value: $83,333 (2010); Median contract rent: $400 per month (2000); Median year structure built: 1945 (2000).

Transportation: Commute to work: 88.4% car, 0.0% public transportation, 4.7% walk, 4.7% work from home (2000); Travel time to work: 19.5% less than 15 minutes, 29.3% 15 to 30 minutes, 41.5% 30 to 45 minutes, 4.9% 45 to 60 minutes, 4.9% 60 minutes or more (2000)

OAKLAND CITY (city). Covers a land area of 1.100 square miles and a water area of 0 square miles. Located at 38.33° N. Lat; 87.34° W. Long. Elevation is 463 feet.

History: Oakland City developed around Oakland City College, established by the Baptist church in 1891.

Population: 2,810 (1990); 2,588 (2000); 2,507 (2010); 2,467 (2015 projected); Race: 97.4% White, 0.8% Black, 0.3% Asian, 1.5% Other, 2.3% Hispanic of any race (2010); Density: 2,278.9 persons per square mile (2010); Average household size: 2.30 (2010); Median age: 37.6 (2010); Males per 100 females: 91.7 (2010); Marriage status: 26.3% never married, 50.0% now married, 9.1% widowed, 14.6% divorced (2000); Foreign born: 1.7% (2000); Ancestry (includes multiple ancestries): 21.3% German, 13.1% Irish, 11.3% English, 11.0% Other groups, 9.3% United States or American (2000).

Economy: Employment by occupation: 8.1% management, 14.7% professional, 18.0% services, 23.5% sales, 1.0% farming, 10.9% construction, 23.8% production (2000).

Income: Per capita income: $17,864 (2010); Median household income: $37,271 (2010); Average household income: $45,137 (2010); Percent of households with income of $100,000 or more: 7.5% (2010); Poverty rate: 11.9% (2000).

Taxes: Total city taxes per capita: $153 (2007); City property taxes per capita: $124 (2007).

Education: Percent of population age 25 and over with: High school diploma (including GED) or higher: 85.5% (2010); Bachelor's degree or higher: 17.1% (2010); Master's degree or higher: 6.0% (2010).

School District(s)

East Gibson School Corporation (PK-12)

    2008-09 Enrollment: 996 . . . . (812) 749-4755

Gibson-Pike-Warrick Coop (KG-12)

    2008-09 Enrollment: n/a . . . . (812) 354-3627

Four-year College(s)

Oakland City University (Private, Not-for-profit, Baptist)

    Fall 2008 Enrollment: 1,733. . . . . (812) 749-4781

    2009-10 Tuition: In-state $15,410; Out-of-state $15,410

Housing: Homeownership rate: 71.6% (2010); Median home value: $70,552 (2010); Median contract rent: $286 per month (2000); Median year structure built: 1957 (2000).

Safety: Violent crime rate: 11.9 per 10,000 population; Property crime rate: 265.8 per 10,000 population (2008).

Transportation: Commute to work: 86.1% car, 0.7% public transportation, 9.0% walk, 3.0% work from home (2000); Travel time to work: 36.1% less than 15 minutes, 19.2% 15 to 30 minutes, 25.4% 30 to 45 minutes, 15.1% 45 to 60 minutes, 4.1% 60 minutes or more (2000)

OWENSVILLE (town). Covers a land area of 0.496 square miles and a water area of 0 square miles. Located at 38.27° N. Lat; 87.69° W. Long. Elevation is 509 feet.

History: Laid out 1817; incorporated 1881.

Population: 1,069 (1990); 1,322 (2000); 1,347 (2010); 1,345 (2015 projected); Race: 98.0% White, 0.2% Black, 0.1% Asian, 1.6% Other, 1.3% Hispanic of any race (2010); Density: 2,715.7 persons per square mile (2010); Average household size: 2.56 (2010); Median age: 39.9 (2010); Males per 100 females: 98.7 (2010); Marriage status: 14.5% never married, 58.8% now married, 11.3% widowed, 15.4% divorced (2000); Foreign born: 0.5% (2000); Ancestry (includes multiple ancestries): 19.3% German, 14.0% English, 14.0% United States or American, 11.8% Irish, 6.9% Other groups (2000).

Economy: Employment by occupation: 3.6% management, 12.9% professional, 17.4% services, 23.6% sales, 1.3% farming, 10.1% construction, 31.0% production (2000).

Income: Per capita income: $23,430 (2010); Median household income: $55,000 (2010); Average household income: $60,705 (2010); Percent of households with income of $100,000 or more: 13.7% (2010); Poverty rate: 8.9% (2000).

Taxes: Total city taxes per capita: $212 (2007); City property taxes per capita: $152 (2007).

Education: Percent of population age 25 and over with: High school diploma (including GED) or higher: 88.8% (2010); Bachelor's degree or higher: 17.1% (2010); Master's degree or higher: 4.8% (2010).

School District(s)

South Gibson School Corp (PK-12)

    2008-09 Enrollment: 2,040 . . . . (812) 753-4230

Housing: Homeownership rate: 82.6% (2010); Median home value: $79,487 (2010); Median contract rent: $222 per month (2000); Median year structure built: 1960 (2000).

Transportation: Commute to work: 94.5% car, 0.0% public transportation, 1.5% walk, 1.3% work from home (2000); Travel time to work: 25.0% less than 15 minutes, 38.8% 15 to 30 minutes, 17.6% 30 to 45 minutes, 14.7% 45 to 60 minutes, 3.9% 60 minutes or more (2000)

PATOKA (town). Covers a land area of 0.704 square miles and a water area of 0 square miles. Located at 38.40° N. Lat; 87.58° W. Long. Elevation is 436 feet.

History: Patoka was settled in 1789 on the Patoka River, and platted in 1813. It was a stagecoach stop on the Vincennes-Evansville line. The name is of Indian origin meaning "logs on the bottom."

Population: 780 (1990); 749 (2000); 777 (2010); 780 (2015 projected); Race: 97.7% White, 1.5% Black, 0.1% Asian, 0.6% Other, 0.1% Hispanic of any race (2010); Density: 1,104.0 persons per square mile (2010); Average household size: 2.41 (2010); Median age: 41.0 (2010); Males per 100 females: 101.3 (2010); Marriage status: 19.1% never married, 57.6% now married, 7.4% widowed, 15.8% divorced (2000); Foreign born: 0.1% (2000); Ancestry (includes multiple ancestries): 18.5% United States or American, 16.5% German, 12.5% English, 9.3% Other groups, 8.5% Irish (2000).

Economy: Employment by occupation: 5.9% management, 8.1% professional, 14.8% services, 22.7% sales, 0.7% farming, 12.1% construction, 35.7% production (2000).

Income: Per capita income: $24,951 (2010); Median household income: $48,929 (2010); Average household income: $59,472 (2010); Percent of households with income of $100,000 or more: 10.9% (2010); Poverty rate: 10.8% (2000).

Taxes: Total city taxes per capita: $38 (2007); City property taxes per capita: $20 (2007).

Education: Percent of population age 25 and over with: High school diploma (including GED) or higher: 86.0% (2010); Bachelor's degree or higher: 13.5% (2010); Master's degree or higher: 3.3% (2010).

Housing: Homeownership rate: 86.6% (2010); Median home value: $61,563 (2010); Median contract rent: $275 per month (2000); Median year structure built: 1971 (2000).

Transportation: Commute to work: 90.0% car, 0.0% public transportation, 3.6% walk, 4.1% work from home (2000); Travel time to work: 41.0% less than 15 minutes, 27.6% 15 to 30 minutes, 16.6% 30 to 45 minutes, 9.9% 45 to 60 minutes, 4.8% 60 minutes or more (2000)

PRINCETON (city). County seat. Covers a land area of 4.850 square miles and a water area of 0 square miles. Located at 38.35° N. Lat; 87.57° W. Long. Elevation is 499 feet.

History: Princeton was founded in 1814 and named for Captain William Prince. An early industry was Evans Mill, a wool-carding mill which had Abraham Lincoln as a customer in 1827.

Population: 8,418 (1990); 8,175 (2000); 8,213 (2010); 8,151 (2015 projected); Race: 89.5% White, 6.1% Black, 1.6% Asian, 2.7% Other, 1.5% Hispanic of any race (2010); Density: 1,693.4 persons per square mile (2010); Average household size: 2.24 (2010); Median age: 38.7 (2010); Males per 100 females: 91.2 (2010); Marriage status: 21.2% never married, 53.6% now married, 11.5% widowed, 13.7% divorced (2000); Foreign born: 1.6% (2000); Ancestry (includes multiple ancestries): 17.3% German, 16.8% United States or American, 13.2% Irish, 11.7% English, 11.3% Other groups (2000).

Economy: Single-family building permits issued: 1 (2009); Multi-family building permits issued: 0 (2009); Employment by occupation: 6.3% management, 11.4% professional, 24.1% services, 21.8% sales, 0.5% farming, 8.7% construction, 27.2% production (2000).

Income: Per capita income: $20,096 (2010); Median household income: $36,420 (2010); Average household income: $45,353 (2010); Percent of households with income of $100,000 or more: 8.0% (2010); Poverty rate: 15.8% (2000).

Taxes: Total city taxes per capita: $353 (2007); City property taxes per capita: $253 (2007).

Education: Percent of population age 25 and over with: High school diploma (including GED) or higher: 83.9% (2010); Bachelor's degree or higher: 11.5% (2010); Master's degree or higher: 2.1% (2010).

School District(s)

North Gibson School Corp (KG-12)

    2008-09 Enrollment: 2,079 . . . . (812) 385-4851

Housing: Homeownership rate: 62.2% (2010); Median home value: $69,663 (2010); Median contract rent: $313 per month (2000); Median year structure built: 1953 (2000).

Hospitals: Gibson General Hospital (109 beds)

Newspapers: Oakland City Journal (Community news; Circulation 6,000); Princeton Daily Clarion (Local news; Circulation 12,000)

Transportation: Commute to work: 92.9% car, 0.0% public transportation, 4.8% walk, 1.2% work from home (2000); Travel time to work: 56.5% less than 15 minutes, 18.2% 15 to 30 minutes, 12.5% 30 to 45 minutes, 9.4% 45 to 60 minutes, 3.4% 60 minutes or more (2000)

Additional Information Contacts

City of Princeton. . . . . (812) 385-4428

    http://www.princeton-indiana.com

Gibson County Chamber of Commerce. . . . . (812) 385-2134

    http://www.gibsoncountychamber.org

SOMERVILLE (town). Covers a land area of 0.294 square miles and a water area of 0 square miles. Located at 38.27° N. Lat; 87.37° W. Long. Elevation is 469 feet.

Population: 223 (1990); 312 (2000); 304 (2010); 299 (2015 projected); Race: 99.0% White, 0.3% Black, 0.0% Asian, 0.7% Other, 0.3% Hispanic of any race (2010); Density: 1,034.3 persons per square mile (2010); Average household size: 2.60 (2010); Median age: 40.2 (2010); Males per 100 females: 100.0 (2010); Marriage status: 13.3% never married, 70.8% now married, 7.5% widowed, 8.3% divorced (2000); Foreign born: 0.6% (2000); Ancestry (includes multiple ancestries): 15.8% United States or American, 12.6% German, 8.6% English, 3.4% Irish, 2.0% Other groups (2000).

Economy: Employment by occupation: 6.0% management, 9.7% professional, 20.1% services, 16.4% sales, 0.0% farming, 7.5% construction, 40.3% production (2000).

Income: Per capita income: $20,461 (2010); Median household income: $44,722 (2010); Average household income: $53,675 (2010); Percent of households with income of $100,000 or more: 10.3% (2010); Poverty rate: 5.2% (2000).

Taxes: Total city taxes per capita: $16 (2007); City property taxes per capita: $3 (2007).

Education: Percent of population age 25 and over with: High school diploma (including GED) or higher: 87.1% (2010); Bachelor's degree or higher: 13.4% (2010); Master's degree or higher: 3.8% (2010).

Housing: Homeownership rate: 87.2% (2010); Median home value: $82,500 (2010); Median contract rent: $300 per month (2000); Median year structure built: 1956 (2000).

Transportation: Commute to work: 94.6% car, 0.0% public transportation, 1.5% walk, 3.8% work from home (2000); Travel time to work: 10.4% less than 15 minutes, 24.8% 15 to 30 minutes, 43.2% 30 to 45 minutes, 16.8% 45 to 60 minutes, 4.8% 60 minutes or more (2000)

Grant County

Located in east central Indiana; drained by the Mississinewa River. Covers a land area of 414.03 square miles, a water area of 0.81 square miles, and is located in the Eastern Time Zone. The county was founded in 1831. County seat is Marion.

Grant County is part of the Marion, IN Micropolitan Statistical Area. The entire metro area includes: Grant County, IN

Weather Station: Marion 2 N										Elevation: 787 feet	
	Jan	Feb	Mar	Apr	May	Jun	Jul	Aug	Sep	Oct	Nov	Dec
High	32	36	47	60	72	81	85	82	76	64	50	38
Low	16	19	28	38	49	58	63	60	53	41	33	22
Precip	2.1	2.0	3.0	3.7	4.2	3.9	4.7	3.7	2.8	2.6	3.4	2.8
Snow	7.7	6.8	3.2	1.0	0.0	0.0	0.0	0.0	0.0	0.4	1.1	6.0

High and Low temperatures in degrees Fahrenheit; Precipitation and Snow in inches

Population: 74,169 (1990); 73,403 (2000); 67,948 (2010); 65,082 (2015 projected); Race: 88.9% White, 6.7% Black, 0.7% Asian, 3.7% Other, 3.0% Hispanic of any race (2010); Density: 164.1 persons per square mile

(2010); Average household size: 2.36 (2010); Median age: 39.3 (2010); Males per 100 females: 92.2 (2010).

Religion: Five largest groups: 8.6% The Wesleyan Church, 6.5% Southern Baptist Convention, 5.7% Catholic Church, 5.4% The United Methodist Church, 3.2% Christian Church (Disciples of Christ) (2000).

Economy: Unemployment rate: 11.3% (5/2010); Total civilian labor force: 32,663 (5/2010); Leading industries: 20.2% health care and social assistance; 17.5% manufacturing; 12.9% retail trade (2008); Farms: 524 totaling 202,138 acres (2007); Companies that employ 500 or more persons: 6 (2008); Companies that employ 100 to 499 persons: 25 (2008); Companies that employ less than 100 persons: 1,417 (2008); Black-owned businesses: n/a (2002); Hispanic-owned businesses: n/a (2002); Asian-owned businesses: n/a (2002); Women-owned businesses: 1,091 (2002); Retail sales per capita: $12,494 (2010). Single-family building permits issued: 43 (2009); Multi-family building permits issued: 4 (2009).

Income: Per capita income: $19,543 (2010); Median household income: $38,814 (2010); Average household income: $48,740 (2010); Percent of households with income of $100,000 or more: 7.8% (2010); Poverty rate: 17.8% (2008); Bankruptcy rate: 7.59% (2009).

Taxes: Total county taxes per capita: $232 (2007); County property taxes per capita: $170 (2007).

Education: Percent of population age 25 and over with: High school diploma (including GED) or higher: 82.7% (2010); Bachelor's degree or higher: 17.3% (2010); Master's degree or higher: 6.9% (2010).

Housing: Homeownership rate: 69.5% (2010); Median home value: $76,406 (2010); Median contract rent: $425 per month (2006-2008 3-year est.); Median year structure built: 1962 (2006-2008 3-year est.)

Health: Birth rate: 112.4 per 10,000 population (2009); Death rate: 112.8 per 10,000 population (2009); Age-adjusted cancer mortality rate: 206.9 deaths per 100,000 population (2006); Number of physicians: 13.2 per 10,000 population (2007); Hospital beds: 24.2 per 10,000 population (2006); Hospital admissions: 902.1 per 10,000 population (2006).

Elections: 2008 Presidential election results: 42.9% Obama, 55.9% McCain, 0.0% Nader

Additional Information Contacts

Grant County Government . . . . (765) 668-8871
    http://www.grantcounty.net
City of Gas City . . . . (765) 677-3079
    http://www.gascityindiana.com
City of Marion . . . . (765) 662-9931
    http://www.marionindiana.us
Gas City Chamber of Commerce . . . . (765) 674-7545
    http://www.gascity.com
Marion-Grant County Chamber of Commerce . . . . (765) 664-5107
    http://www.marionchamber.org
Town of Upland . . . . (765) 998-2579
    http://www.upland.in.gov

Grant County Communities

FAIRMOUNT (town). Covers a land area of 1.472 square miles and a water area of 0 square miles. Located at 40.41° N. Lat; 85.64° W. Long. Elevation is 863 feet.

History: Fairmount developed around the Wesleyan Camp Meeting Grounds, site of state and national conferences of the Methodist Church.

Population: 3,185 (1990); 2,992 (2000); 2,654 (2010); 2,481 (2015 projected); Race: 97.9% White, 0.3% Black, 0.1% Asian, 1.7% Other, 0.5% Hispanic of any race (2010); Density: 1,803.3 persons per square mile (2010); Average household size: 2.39 (2010); Median age: 40.3 (2010); Males per 100 females: 92.6 (2010); Marriage status: 19.7% never married, 58.1% now married, 9.2% widowed, 13.1% divorced (2000); Foreign born: 0.0% (2000); Ancestry (includes multiple ancestries): 16.6% German, 14.1% United States or American, 12.6% Irish, 8.6% Other groups, 6.4% English (2000).

Economy: Employment by occupation: 8.5% management, 14.8% professional, 18.0% services, 24.1% sales, 1.0% farming, 9.2% construction, 24.5% production (2000).

Income: Per capita income: $21,326 (2010); Median household income: $42,237 (2010); Average household income: $51,147 (2010); Percent of households with income of $100,000 or more: 6.9% (2010); Poverty rate: 9.1% (2000).

Taxes: Total city taxes per capita: $146 (2007); City property taxes per capita: $138 (2007).

Education: Percent of population age 25 and over with: High school diploma (including GED) or higher: 85.0% (2010); Bachelor's degree or higher: 9.8% (2010); Master's degree or higher: 2.9% (2010).

School District(s)

Madison-Grant United Sch Corp (PK-12)
    2008-09 Enrollment: 1,516 . . . . (765) 948-4143

Housing: Homeownership rate: 74.3% (2010); Median home value: $75,155 (2010); Median contract rent: $311 per month (2000); Median year structure built: 1956 (2000).

Safety: Violent crime rate: 25.8 per 10,000 population; Property crime rate: 284.0 per 10,000 population (2008).

Newspapers: News-Sun (Community news; Circulation 4,400)

Transportation: Commute to work: 94.4% car, 0.0% public transportation, 3.9% walk, 0.9% work from home (2000); Travel time to work: 23.6% less than 15 minutes, 48.7% 15 to 30 minutes, 18.0% 30 to 45 minutes, 3.1% 45 to 60 minutes, 6.6% 60 minutes or more (2000)

FOWLERTON (town). Covers a land area of 0.188 square miles and a water area of 0 square miles. Located at 40.41° N. Lat; 85.57° W. Long. Elevation is 879 feet.

Population: 306 (1990); 298 (2000); 262 (2010); 245 (2015 projected); Race: 98.5% White, 0.0% Black, 0.0% Asian, 1.5% Other, 0.4% Hispanic of any race (2010); Density: 1,392.7 persons per square mile (2010); Average household size: 2.50 (2010); Median age: 41.1 (2010); Males per 100 females: 98.5 (2010); Marriage status: 14.7% never married, 67.9% now married, 5.5% widowed, 11.9% divorced (2000); Foreign born: 0.0% (2000); Ancestry (includes multiple ancestries): 35.4% United States or American, 8.6% Other groups, 7.2% German, 5.5% Irish, 3.8% English (2000).

Economy: Employment by occupation: 3.4% management, 7.8% professional, 25.9% services, 26.7% sales, 0.0% farming, 10.3% construction, 25.9% production (2000).

Income: Per capita income: $20,941 (2010); Median household income: $45,658 (2010); Average household income: $49,548 (2010); Percent of households with income of $100,000 or more: 5.7% (2010); Poverty rate: 18.6% (2000).

Taxes: Total city taxes per capita: $56 (2007); City property taxes per capita: $52 (2007).

Education: Percent of population age 25 and over with: High school diploma (including GED) or higher: 84.9% (2010); Bachelor's degree or higher: 11.2% (2010); Master's degree or higher: 5.0% (2010).

Housing: Homeownership rate: 76.2% (2010); Median home value: $77,778 (2010); Median contract rent: $313 per month (2000); Median year structure built: 1962 (2000).

Transportation: Commute to work: 94.7% car, 0.0% public transportation, 0.0% walk, 5.3% work from home (2000); Travel time to work: 14.0% less than 15 minutes, 47.7% 15 to 30 minutes, 21.5% 30 to 45 minutes, 1.9% 45 to 60 minutes, 15.0% 60 minutes or more (2000)

GAS CITY (city). Covers a land area of 3.714 square miles and a water area of 0 square miles. Located at 40.48° N. Lat; 85.60° W. Long. Elevation is 856 feet.

History: Natural gas was discovered here in 1887, giving brief fortune to Gas City. The Owens-Illinois Glass Company Plant was founded here during the gas boom.

Population: 6,369 (1990); 5,940 (2000); 5,622 (2010); 5,410 (2015 projected); Race: 96.4% White, 0.5% Black, 0.1% Asian, 2.9% Other, 1.9% Hispanic of any race (2010); Density: 1,513.6 persons per square mile (2010); Average household size: 2.42 (2010); Median age: 39.9 (2010); Males per 100 females: 91.0 (2010); Marriage status: 19.9% never married, 56.9% now married, 8.8% widowed, 14.3% divorced (2000); Foreign born: 1.0% (2000); Ancestry (includes multiple ancestries): 17.5% German, 15.3% United States or American, 10.0% Irish, 9.5% Other groups, 7.5% English (2000).

Economy: Single-family building permits issued: 9 (2009); Multi-family building permits issued: 0 (2009); Employment by occupation: 8.4% management, 13.7% professional, 13.1% services, 25.5% sales, 0.0% farming, 8.1% construction, 31.2% production (2000).

Income: Per capita income: $19,932 (2010); Median household income: $40,162 (2010); Average household income: $48,522 (2010); Percent of households with income of $100,000 or more: 6.5% (2010); Poverty rate: 10.2% (2000).

Taxes: Total city taxes per capita: $245 (2007); City property taxes per capita: $245 (2007).

Education: Percent of population age 25 and over with: High school diploma (including GED) or higher: 84.2% (2010); Bachelor's degree or higher: 13.1% (2010); Master's degree or higher: 4.7% (2010).

School District(s)
Mississinewa Community School Corp (PK-12)
   2008-09 Enrollment: 2,275 . . . . (765) 674-8528
Housing: Homeownership rate: 74.0% (2010); Median home value: $73,932 (2010); Median contract rent: $379 per month (2000); Median year structure built: 1960 (2000).
Safety: Violent crime rate: 8.8 per 10,000 population; Property crime rate: 305.5 per 10,000 population (2008).
Newspapers: Courier (Community news; Circulation 1,300); Oak Hill Times (Community news; Circulation 1,500); Twin City Journal-Reporter (Community news; Circulation 2,150)
Transportation: Commute to work: 96.0% car, 0.0% public transportation, 1.9% walk, 1.3% work from home (2000); Travel time to work: 39.7% less than 15 minutes, 39.1% 15 to 30 minutes, 10.1% 30 to 45 minutes, 4.3% 45 to 60 minutes, 6.8% 60 minutes or more (2000)
Additional Information Contacts
City of Gas City . . . . (765) 677-3079
   http://www.gascityindiana.com
Gas City Chamber of Commerce . . . . (765) 674-7545
   http://www.gascity.com

JONESBORO (city). Covers a land area of 0.849 square miles and a water area of 0 square miles. Located at 40.47° N. Lat; 85.63° W. Long. Elevation is 853 feet.

History: Jonesboro was founded in 1837 by Obadiah Jones. Its location on the Mississinewa River made it a trading center.
Population: 2,073 (1990); 1,887 (2000); 1,674 (2010); 1,563 (2015 projected); Race: 96.7% White, 0.2% Black, 0.0% Asian, 3.1% Other, 2.2% Hispanic of any race (2010); Density: 1,971.0 persons per square mile (2010); Average household size: 2.40 (2010); Median age: 41.6 (2010); Males per 100 females: 92.4 (2010); Marriage status: 17.0% never married, 62.2% now married, 5.6% widowed, 15.2% divorced (2000); Foreign born: 0.5% (2000); Ancestry (includes multiple ancestries): 17.1% United States or American, 14.7% Other groups, 12.1% German, 7.7% Irish, 6.4% English (2000).
Economy: Employment by occupation: 7.7% management, 9.6% professional, 15.7% services, 18.1% sales, 0.0% farming, 8.8% construction, 40.1% production (2000).
Income: Per capita income: $19,454 (2010); Median household income: $41,961 (2010); Average household income: $46,857 (2010); Percent of households with income of $100,000 or more: 5.3% (2010); Poverty rate: 6.5% (2000).
Taxes: Total city taxes per capita: $97 (2007); City property taxes per capita: $97 (2007).
Education: Percent of population age 25 and over with: High school diploma (including GED) or higher: 82.5% (2010); Bachelor's degree or higher: 11.2% (2010); Master's degree or higher: 3.7% (2010).

School District(s)
Mississinewa Community School Corp (PK-12)
   2008-09 Enrollment: 2,275 . . . . (765) 674-8528
Housing: Homeownership rate: 78.6% (2010); Median home value: $66,111 (2010); Median contract rent: $301 per month (2000); Median year structure built: 1948 (2000).
Transportation: Commute to work: 96.7% car, 0.3% public transportation, 0.8% walk, 1.9% work from home (2000); Travel time to work: 37.1% less than 15 minutes, 42.4% 15 to 30 minutes, 7.9% 30 to 45 minutes, 8.6% 45 to 60 minutes, 4.0% 60 minutes or more (2000)

MARION (city). County seat. Covers a land area of 13.297 square miles and a water area of 0.044 square miles. Located at 40.54° N. Lat; 85.66° W. Long. Elevation is 810 feet.

History: The first settlers came to Marion in 1826. The town was laid out in 1831 and named for General Francis Marion, cavalry officer in the American Revolution. Marion grew rapidly when natural gas and oil were discovered here in the 1880's, but the boom was short-lived. Diversified industry replaced the oil wells.
Population: 32,960 (1990); 31,320 (2000); 28,604 (2010); 27,127 (2015 projected); Race: 80.3% White, 14.1% Black, 0.7% Asian, 4.9% Other, 4.2% Hispanic of any race (2010); Density: 2,151.2 persons per square mile (2010); Average household size: 2.24 (2010); Median age: 38.0 (2010); Males per 100 females: 88.8 (2010); Marriage status: 25.2% never married, 50.7% now married, 10.1% widowed, 14.0% divorced (2000);

Foreign born: 1.8% (2000); Ancestry (includes multiple ancestries): 22.5% Other groups, 13.9% German, 13.6% United States or American, 7.7% English, 7.0% Irish (2000).
Economy: Unemployment rate: 12.8% (5/2010); Total civilian labor force: 13,303 (5/2010); Employment by occupation: 7.0% management, 15.9% professional, 18.7% services, 21.5% sales, 0.1% farming, 7.2% construction, 29.5% production (2000).
Income: Per capita income: $17,764 (2010); Median household income: $32,050 (2010); Average household income: $42,414 (2010); Percent of households with income of $100,000 or more: 6.5% (2010); Poverty rate: 16.9% (2000).
Taxes: Total city taxes per capita: $364 (2007); City property taxes per capita: $357 (2007).
Education: Percent of population age 25 and over with: High school diploma (including GED) or higher: 77.6% (2010); Bachelor's degree or higher: 16.2% (2010); Master's degree or higher: 6.7% (2010).

School District(s)
Dr Robert H Faulkner Academy (KG-05)
   2008-09 Enrollment: 168 . . . . (765) 662-9910
Eastbrook Community Sch Corp (PK-12)
   2008-09 Enrollment: 1,730 . . . . (765) 664-0624
Marion Community Schools (PK-12)
   2008-09 Enrollment: 4,878 . . . . (765) 662-2546
Four-year College(s)
Indiana Wesleyan University (Private, Not-for-profit, Wesleyan)
   Fall 2008 Enrollment: 15,442 . . . . (765) 674-6901
   2009-10 Tuition: In-state $20,496; Out-of-state $20,496
Two-year College(s)
Indiana Business College-Marion (Private, For-profit)
   Fall 2008 Enrollment: 151 . . . . (765) 662-7497
Vocational/Technical School(s)
Marion Community Schools Tucker Career & Technology (Public)
   Fall 2008 Enrollment: 74 . . . . (765) 664-9091
   2009-10 Tuition: $6,750
Housing: Homeownership rate: 58.5% (2010); Median home value: $61,191 (2010); Median contract rent: $343 per month (2000); Median year structure built: 1955 (2000).
Hospitals: Marion General Hospital (191 beds)
Safety: Violent crime rate: 25.9 per 10,000 population; Property crime rate: 519.5 per 10,000 population (2008).
Newspapers: Chronicle-Tribune (Local news; Circulation 19,794); News-Herald (Local news; Circulation 3,250)
Transportation: Commute to work: 88.7% car, 0.9% public transportation, 5.9% walk, 2.7% work from home (2000); Travel time to work: 61.3% less than 15 minutes, 21.4% 15 to 30 minutes, 8.5% 30 to 45 minutes, 3.9% 45 to 60 minutes, 4.9% 60 minutes or more (2000)
Additional Information Contacts
City of Marion . . . . (765) 662-9931
   http://www.marionindiana.us
Marion-Grant County Chamber of Commerce . . . . (765) 664-5107
   http://www.marionchamber.org

MATTHEWS (town). Covers a land area of 0.348 square miles and a water area of 0 square miles. Located at 40.38° N. Lat; 85.49° W. Long. Elevation is 879 feet.

History: Matthews was established in 1833 with a gristmill, sawmill, blacksmith shop, and general store.
Population: 576 (1990); 595 (2000); 472 (2010); 428 (2015 projected); Race: 98.5% White, 0.4% Black, 0.0% Asian, 1.1% Other, 0.2% Hispanic of any race (2010); Density: 1,354.7 persons per square mile (2010); Average household size: 2.36 (2010); Median age: 45.5 (2010); Males per 100 females: 90.3 (2010); Marriage status: 13.3% never married, 71.3% now married, 6.5% widowed, 8.9% divorced (2000); Foreign born: 0.0% (2000); Ancestry (includes multiple ancestries): 22.3% United States or American, 15.3% German, 11.1% Irish, 9.4% English, 8.7% Other groups (2000).
Economy: Employment by occupation: 7.9% management, 18.8% professional, 19.4% services, 13.5% sales, 0.7% farming, 9.2% construction, 30.6% production (2000).
Income: Per capita income: $17,650 (2010); Median household income: $36,429 (2010); Average household income: $41,500 (2010); Percent of households with income of $100,000 or more: 2.0% (2010); Poverty rate: 5.5% (2000).
Taxes: Total city taxes per capita: $113 (2007); City property taxes per capita: $113 (2007).

Education: Percent of population age 25 and over with: High school diploma (including GED) or higher: 86.9% (2010); Bachelor's degree or higher: 10.9% (2010); Master's degree or higher: 1.8% (2010).

School District(s)
Eastbrook Community Sch Corp (PK-12)
   2008-09 Enrollment: 1,730 . . . . (765) 664-0624
Housing: Homeownership rate: 84.5% (2010); Median home value: $81,556 (2010); Median contract rent: $278 per month (2000); Median year structure built: 1958 (2000).
Transportation: Commute to work: 91.6% car, 0.0% public transportation, 4.1% walk, 3.4% work from home (2000); Travel time to work: 22.4% less than 15 minutes, 31.8% 15 to 30 minutes, 33.2% 30 to 45 minutes, 5.9% 45 to 60 minutes, 6.6% 60 minutes or more (2000)

SWAYZEE (town).
Covers a land area of 0.472 square miles and a water area of 0 square miles. Located at 40.50° N. Lat; 85.82° W. Long. Elevation is 860 feet.
Population: 1,087 (1990); 1,011 (2000); 894 (2010); 832 (2015 projected); Race: 95.6% White, 0.7% Black, 0.0% Asian, 3.7% Other, 2.7% Hispanic of any race (2010); Density: 1,893.6 persons per square mile (2010); Average household size: 2.46 (2010); Median age: 42.4 (2010); Males per 100 females: 93.5 (2010); Marriage status: 16.4% never married, 67.1% now married, 7.0% widowed, 9.5% divorced (2000); Foreign born: 0.0% (2000); Ancestry (includes multiple ancestries): 21.4% United States or American, 19.5% German, 12.5% English, 9.7% Irish, 7.7% Other groups (2000).
Economy: Single-family building permits issued: 0 (2009); Multi-family building permits issued: 0 (2009); Employment by occupation: 8.3% management, 17.2% professional, 12.1% services, 21.2% sales, 1.1% farming, 10.6% construction, 29.7% production (2000).
Income: Per capita income: $22,368 (2010); Median household income: $50,931 (2010); Average household income: $55,393 (2010); Percent of households with income of $100,000 or more: 9.4% (2010); Poverty rate: 6.0% (2000).
Taxes: Total city taxes per capita: $94 (2007); City property taxes per capita: $94 (2007).
Education: Percent of population age 25 and over with: High school diploma (including GED) or higher: 88.6% (2010); Bachelor's degree or higher: 14.8% (2010); Master's degree or higher: 5.7% (2010).
School District(s)
Oak Hill United School Corp (KG-12)
   2008-09 Enrollment: 1,483 . . . . (765) 395-3341
Housing: Homeownership rate: 84.8% (2010); Median home value: $88,710 (2010); Median contract rent: $350 per month (2000); Median year structure built: 1956 (2000).
Transportation: Commute to work: 89.9% car, 0.0% public transportation, 7.1% walk, 2.4% work from home (2000); Travel time to work: 24.3% less than 15 minutes, 51.1% 15 to 30 minutes, 12.5% 30 to 45 minutes, 5.3% 45 to 60 minutes, 6.8% 60 minutes or more (2000)

SWEETSER (town).
Covers a land area of 0.975 square miles and a water area of 0.009 square miles. Located at 40.57° N. Lat; 85.76° W. Long. Elevation is 843 feet.
History: Laid out 1871.
Population: 940 (1990); 906 (2000); 938 (2010); 889 (2015 projected); Race: 97.3% White, 0.1% Black, 0.4% Asian, 2.1% Other, 2.1% Hispanic of any race (2010); Density: 962.0 persons per square mile (2010); Average household size: 2.49 (2010); Median age: 44.6 (2010); Males per 100 females: 95.4 (2010); Marriage status: 18.5% never married, 62.8% now married, 8.6% widowed, 10.2% divorced (2000); Foreign born: 0.1% (2000); Ancestry (includes multiple ancestries): 22.2% German, 13.3% English, 12.5% Irish, 10.7% United States or American, 8.4% Other groups (2000).
Economy: Employment by occupation: 5.1% management, 17.3% professional, 9.5% services, 31.5% sales, 0.0% farming, 14.9% construction, 21.7% production (2000).
Income: Per capita income: $22,211 (2010); Median household income: $48,421 (2010); Average household income: $55,782 (2010); Percent of households with income of $100,000 or more: 9.4% (2010); Poverty rate: 5.0% (2000).
Taxes: Total city taxes per capita: $73 (2007); City property taxes per capita: $69 (2007).
Education: Percent of population age 25 and over with: High school diploma (including GED) or higher: 92.2% (2010); Bachelor's degree or higher: 18.7% (2010); Master's degree or higher: 5.9% (2010).

School District(s)
Oak Hill United School Corp (KG-12)
   2008-09 Enrollment: 1,483 . . . . (765) 395-3341
Housing: Homeownership rate: 76.5% (2010); Median home value: $94,231 (2010); Median contract rent: $386 per month (2000); Median year structure built: 1957 (2000).
Transportation: Commute to work: 92.5% car, 0.5% public transportation, 3.3% walk, 3.3% work from home (2000); Travel time to work: 38.2% less than 15 minutes, 44.2% 15 to 30 minutes, 12.4% 30 to 45 minutes, 1.8% 45 to 60 minutes, 3.4% 60 minutes or more (2000)

UPLAND (town).
Covers a land area of 3.932 square miles and a water area of 0.009 square miles. Located at 40.46° N. Lat; 85.50° W. Long. Elevation is 935 feet.
History: Upland was laid out in 1867 when the railroad arrived and a sawmill was built. Many of the early settlers were Quakers.
Population: 3,420 (1990); 3,803 (2000); 3,939 (2010); 4,028 (2015 projected); Race: 92.9% White, 1.5% Black, 2.1% Asian, 3.5% Other, 3.7% Hispanic of any race (2010); Density: 1,001.7 persons per square mile (2010); Average household size: 2.64 (2010); Median age: 21.6 (2010); Males per 100 females: 98.3 (2010); Marriage status: 42.9% never married, 48.8% now married, 5.0% widowed, 3.2% divorced (2000); Foreign born: 1.3% (2000); Ancestry (includes multiple ancestries): 25.7% German, 9.7% English, 8.5% United States or American, 8.2% Irish, 6.9% Other groups (2000).
Economy: Employment by occupation: 6.3% management, 28.7% professional, 23.6% services, 25.1% sales, 0.3% farming, 5.6% construction, 10.5% production (2000).
Income: Per capita income: $10,978 (2010); Median household income: $40,571 (2010); Average household income: $47,698 (2010); Percent of households with income of $100,000 or more: 6.1% (2010); Poverty rate: 14.5% (2000).
Taxes: Total city taxes per capita: $47 (2007); City property taxes per capita: $44 (2007).
Education: Percent of population age 25 and over with: High school diploma (including GED) or higher: 88.7% (2010); Bachelor's degree or higher: 38.2% (2010); Master's degree or higher: 19.1% (2010).
School District(s)
Eastbrook Community Sch Corp (PK-12)
   2008-09 Enrollment: 1,730 . . . . (765) 664-0624
Four-year College(s)
Taylor University (Private, Not-for-profit, Interdenominational)
   Fall 2008 Enrollment: 1,871. . . . . (765) 998-2751
   2009-10 Tuition: In-state $25,396; Out-of-state $25,396
Housing: Homeownership rate: 68.3% (2010); Median home value: $91,456 (2010); Median contract rent: $360 per month (2000); Median year structure built: 1964 (2000).
Transportation: Commute to work: 65.7% car, 0.1% public transportation, 24.2% walk, 7.0% work from home (2000); Travel time to work: 61.4% less than 15 minutes, 25.7% 15 to 30 minutes, 6.4% 30 to 45 minutes, 1.7% 45 to 60 minutes, 4.9% 60 minutes or more (2000)
Additional Information Contacts
Town of Upland . . . . (765) 998-2579
   http://www.upland.in.gov

VAN BUREN (town).
Covers a land area of 0.584 square miles and a water area of 0 square miles. Located at 40.61° N. Lat; 85.50° W. Long. Elevation is 846 feet.
Population: 983 (1990); 935 (2000); 788 (2010); 724 (2015 projected); Race: 97.1% White, 0.1% Black, 0.3% Asian, 2.5% Other, 1.9% Hispanic of any race (2010); Density: 1,348.3 persons per square mile (2010); Average household size: 2.45 (2010); Median age: 38.2 (2010); Males per 100 females: 97.5 (2010); Marriage status: 13.4% never married, 68.3% now married, 7.1% widowed, 11.2% divorced (2000); Foreign born: 0.7% (2000); Ancestry (includes multiple ancestries): 18.5% German, 14.2% Other groups, 11.2% Irish, 7.9% English, 7.0% United States or American (2000).
Economy: Employment by occupation: 7.1% management, 11.8% professional, 15.4% services, 26.2% sales, 0.8% farming, 10.1% construction, 28.7% production (2000).
Income: Per capita income: $19,448 (2010); Median household income: $41,737 (2010); Average household income: $47,383 (2010); Percent of households with income of $100,000 or more: 6.9% (2010); Poverty rate: 9.6% (2000).

Taxes: Total city taxes per capita: $204 (2007); City property taxes per capita: $204 (2007).
Education: Percent of population age 25 and over with: High school diploma (including GED) or higher: 83.6% (2010); Bachelor's degree or higher: 10.8% (2010); Master's degree or higher: 3.6% (2010).

School District(s)
Eastbrook Community Sch Corp (PK-12)
    2008-09 Enrollment: 1,730 . . . . (765) 664-0624
Housing: Homeownership rate: 72.0% (2010); Median home value: $69,054 (2010); Median contract rent: $316 per month (2000); Median year structure built: 1947 (2000).
Transportation: Commute to work: 93.8% car, 0.0% public transportation, 2.8% walk, 3.1% work from home (2000); Travel time to work: 22.1% less than 15 minutes, 52.8% 15 to 30 minutes, 16.3% 30 to 45 minutes, 2.9% 45 to 60 minutes, 5.9% 60 minutes or more (2000)

Greene County

Located in southwestern Indiana; drained by the West Fork of White River and the Eel River. Covers a land area of 541.73 square miles, a water area of 4.18 square miles, and is located in the Eastern Time Zone. The county was founded in 1821. County seat is Bloomfield.

Greene County is part of the Bloomington, IN Metropolitan Statistical Area. The entire metro area includes: Greene County, IN; Monroe County, IN; Owen County, IN

Population: 30,410 (1990); 33,157 (2000); 32,415 (2010); 31,816 (2015 projected); Race: 97.7% White, 0.5% Black, 0.3% Asian, 1.5% Other, 1.1% Hispanic of any race (2010); Density: 59.8 persons per square mile (2010); Average household size: 2.39 (2010); Median age: 40.3 (2010); Males per 100 females: 98.1 (2010).
Religion: Five largest groups: 7.9% Christian Churches and Churches of Christ, 6.3% The United Methodist Church, 6.2% American Baptist Churches in the USA, 2.5% Churches of Christ, 2.5% Catholic Church (2000).
Economy: Unemployment rate: 8.3% (5/2010); Total civilian labor force: 16,198 (5/2010); Leading industries: 20.2% retail trade; 17.9% health care and social assistance; 11.2% accommodation & food services (2008); Farms: 799 totaling 169,750 acres (2007); Companies that employ 500 or more persons: 1 (2008); Companies that employ 100 to 499 persons: 4 (2008); Companies that employ less than 100 persons: 600 (2008); Black-owned businesses: n/a (2002); Hispanic-owned businesses: n/a (2002); Asian-owned businesses: n/a (2002); Women-owned businesses: n/a (2002); Retail sales per capita: $8,634 (2010). Single-family building permits issued: n/a (2009); Multi-family building permits issued: n/a (2009).
Income: Per capita income: $20,745 (2010); Median household income: $40,508 (2010); Average household income: $49,780 (2010); Percent of households with income of $100,000 or more: 9.6% (2010); Poverty rate: 13.7% (2008); Bankruptcy rate: 5.68% (2009).
Taxes: Total county taxes per capita: $278 (2007); County property taxes per capita: $142 (2007).
Education: Percent of population age 25 and over with: High school diploma (including GED) or higher: 83.6% (2010); Bachelor's degree or higher: 11.5% (2010); Master's degree or higher: 5.3% (2010).
Housing: Homeownership rate: 77.3% (2010); Median home value: $83,688 (2010); Median contract rent: $332 per month (2006-2008 3-year est.); Median year structure built: 1971 (2006-2008 3-year est.)
Health: Birth rate: 119.2 per 10,000 population (2009); Death rate: 107.5 per 10,000 population (2009); Age-adjusted cancer mortality rate: 225.1 deaths per 100,000 population (2006); Air Quality Index: 79.3% good, 20.7% moderate, 0.0% unhealthy for sensitive individuals, 0.0% unhealthy (percent of days in 2008); Number of physicians: 3.7 per 10,000 population (2007); Hospital beds: 7.6 per 10,000 population (2006); Hospital admissions: 367.4 per 10,000 population (2006).
Elections: 2008 Presidential election results: 41.9% Obama, 56.4% McCain, 0.0% Nader
Additional Information Contacts
Greene County Government . . . . (812) 384-8532
    http://www.gcindiana.info
City of Linton . . . . (812) 384-8532
    http://www.gcindiana.info
Greene County Chamber of Commerce . . . . (812) 847-4846
    http://www.lintonchamber.org

Greene County Communities

BLOOMFIELD (town). County seat. Covers a land area of 1.381 square miles and a water area of 0 square miles. Located at 39.02° N. Lat; 86.94° W. Long. Elevation is 607 feet.
Population: 2,592 (1990); 2,542 (2000); 2,553 (2010); 2,512 (2015 projected); Race: 95.1% White, 3.0% Black, 0.4% Asian, 1.5% Other, 1.3% Hispanic of any race (2010); Density: 1,849.0 persons per square mile (2010); Average household size: 2.06 (2010); Median age: 41.2 (2010); Males per 100 females: 96.1 (2010); Marriage status: 18.7% never married, 51.7% now married, 12.8% widowed, 16.9% divorced (2000); Foreign born: 1.0% (2000); Ancestry (includes multiple ancestries): 20.9% German, 13.0% English, 11.2% Irish, 10.1% United States or American, 5.1% Other groups (2000).
Economy: Employment by occupation: 6.6% management, 20.6% professional, 11.4% services, 31.3% sales, 0.0% farming, 10.3% construction, 19.9% production (2000).
Income: Per capita income: $21,615 (2010); Median household income: $35,641 (2010); Average household income: $44,002 (2010); Percent of households with income of $100,000 or more: 7.7% (2010); Poverty rate: 16.6% (2000).
Taxes: Total city taxes per capita: $82 (2007); City property taxes per capita: $66 (2007).
Education: Percent of population age 25 and over with: High school diploma (including GED) or higher: 88.2% (2010); Bachelor's degree or higher: 16.3% (2010); Master's degree or higher: 6.6% (2010).
School District(s)
Bloomfield School District (PK-12)
    2008-09 Enrollment: 1,105 . . . . (812) 384-4507
Eastern Greene Schools (PK-12)
    2008-09 Enrollment: 1,334 . . . . (812) 825-5722
Housing: Homeownership rate: 60.4% (2010); Median home value: $77,754 (2010); Median contract rent: $298 per month (2000); Median year structure built: 1957 (2000).
Transportation: Commute to work: 89.5% car, 0.0% public transportation, 6.1% walk, 2.0% work from home (2000); Travel time to work: 32.4% less than 15 minutes, 26.0% 15 to 30 minutes, 21.3% 30 to 45 minutes, 11.7% 45 to 60 minutes, 8.6% 60 minutes or more (2000)
Additional Information Contacts
Greene County Chamber of Commerce . . . . (812) 847-4846
    http://www.lintonchamber.org

JASONVILLE (city). Covers a land area of 1.302 square miles and a water area of <.001 square miles. Located at 39.16° N. Lat; 87.20° W. Long. Elevation is 633 feet.
History: Laid out 1859.
Population: 2,200 (1990); 2,490 (2000); 2,505 (2010); 2,486 (2015 projected); Race: 97.3% White, 0.3% Black, 0.4% Asian, 2.0% Other, 1.7% Hispanic of any race (2010); Density: 1,923.5 persons per square mile (2010); Average household size: 2.46 (2010); Median age: 38.1 (2010); Males per 100 females: 92.1 (2010); Marriage status: 19.3% never married, 54.2% now married, 11.6% widowed, 14.8% divorced (2000); Foreign born: 0.6% (2000); Ancestry (includes multiple ancestries): 20.8% United States or American, 16.9% German, 12.3% Irish, 11.0% Other groups, 8.6% English (2000).
Economy: Employment by occupation: 3.9% management, 11.2% professional, 17.4% services, 14.1% sales, 0.0% farming, 15.5% construction, 37.9% production (2000).
Income: Per capita income: $12,859 (2010); Median household income: $26,257 (2010); Average household income: $31,648 (2010); Percent of households with income of $100,000 or more: 1.5% (2010); Poverty rate: 19.9% (2000).
Taxes: Total city taxes per capita: $85 (2007); City property taxes per capita: $70 (2007).
Education: Percent of population age 25 and over with: High school diploma (including GED) or higher: 77.8% (2010); Bachelor's degree or higher: 5.8% (2010); Master's degree or higher: 0.9% (2010).
School District(s)
M S D Shakamak Schools (PK-12)
    2008-09 Enrollment: 885 . . . . (812) 665-3550
Housing: Homeownership rate: 64.0% (2010); Median home value: $51,911 (2010); Median contract rent: $236 per month (2000); Median year structure built: 1953 (2000).
Newspapers: The Jasonville Independent (Regional news)

Transportation: Commute to work: 92.4% car, 0.0% public transportation, 4.3% walk, 1.2% work from home (2000); Travel time to work: 32.2% less than 15 minutes, 16.5% 15 to 30 minutes, 19.6% 30 to 45 minutes, 18.6% 45 to 60 minutes, 13.1% 60 minutes or more (2000)

LINTON (city). Covers a land area of 2.962 square miles and a water area of 0 square miles. Located at 39.03° N. Lat; 87.16° W. Long. Elevation is 531 feet.

History: Linton developed as a coal-mining town.
Population: 5,814 (1990); 5,774 (2000); 5,687 (2010); 5,632 (2015 projected); Race: 97.1% White, 0.5% Black, 0.5% Asian, 1.9% Other, 1.7% Hispanic of any race (2010); Density: 1,920.3 persons per square mile (2010); Average household size: 2.27 (2010); Median age: 40.8 (2010); Males per 100 females: 91.6 (2010); Marriage status: 16.1% never married, 58.6% now married, 12.9% widowed, 12.4% divorced (2000); Foreign born: 0.7% (2000); Ancestry (includes multiple ancestries): 21.0% United States or American, 14.0% German, 11.9% Irish, 8.2% English, 7.9% Other groups (2000).
Economy: Employment by occupation: 6.7% management, 14.6% professional, 21.2% services, 21.0% sales, 1.0% farming, 13.7% construction, 21.8% production (2000).
Income: Per capita income: $19,613 (2010); Median household income: $35,434 (2010); Average household income: $45,183 (2010); Percent of households with income of $100,000 or more: 7.4% (2010); Poverty rate: 12.3% (2000).
Taxes: Total city taxes per capita: $72 (2007); City property taxes per capita: $62 (2007).
Education: Percent of population age 25 and over with: High school diploma (including GED) or higher: 81.7% (2010); Bachelor's degree or higher: 9.1% (2010); Master's degree or higher: 5.1% (2010).

School District(s)
Greene-Sullivan Sp Ed Coop (KG-12)
    2008-09 Enrollment: n/a . . . . (812) 847-8497
Linton-Stockton School Corp (PK-12)
    2008-09 Enrollment: 1,349 . . . . (812) 847-6020
Housing: Homeownership rate: 69.5% (2010); Median home value: $64,048 (2010); Median contract rent: $274 per month (2000); Median year structure built: 1959 (2000).
Hospitals: Greene County General Hospital (76 beds)
Newspapers: Linton Daily Citizen (Local news; Circulation 4,500)
Transportation: Commute to work: 92.6% car, 0.0% public transportation, 3.7% walk, 2.3% work from home (2000); Travel time to work: 40.5% less than 15 minutes, 19.7% 15 to 30 minutes, 11.8% 30 to 45 minutes, 11.2% 45 to 60 minutes, 16.8% 60 minutes or more (2000)
Additional Information Contacts
City of Linton . . . . (812) 384-8532
    http://www.gcindiana.info

LYONS (town). Covers a land area of 0.865 square miles and a water area of 0 square miles. Located at 38.98° N. Lat; 87.08° W. Long. Elevation is 531 feet.

Population: 753 (1990); 748 (2000); 716 (2010); 695 (2015 projected); Race: 98.6% White, 0.0% Black, 0.4% Asian, 1.0% Other, 0.8% Hispanic of any race (2010); Density: 827.5 persons per square mile (2010); Average household size: 2.44 (2010); Median age: 40.2 (2010); Males per 100 females: 93.0 (2010); Marriage status: 16.6% never married, 62.8% now married, 10.1% widowed, 10.4% divorced (2000); Foreign born: 0.9% (2000); Ancestry (includes multiple ancestries): 18.1% United States or American, 17.2% German, 11.3% English, 9.9% Other groups, 8.1% Irish (2000).
Economy: Employment by occupation: 4.0% management, 17.3% professional, 20.2% services, 22.1% sales, 1.5% farming, 16.9% construction, 18.0% production (2000).
Income: Per capita income: $13,762 (2010); Median household income: $29,902 (2010); Average household income: $35,230 (2010); Percent of households with income of $100,000 or more: 3.3% (2010); Poverty rate: 20.7% (2000).
Taxes: Total city taxes per capita: $80 (2007); City property taxes per capita: $77 (2007).
Education: Percent of population age 25 and over with: High school diploma (including GED) or higher: 75.3% (2010); Bachelor's degree or higher: 6.1% (2010); Master's degree or higher: 2.9% (2010).

School District(s)
White River Valley Sch Dist (KG-12)
    2008-09 Enrollment: 846 . . . . (812) 659-1424

Housing: Homeownership rate: 68.8% (2010); Median home value: $47,959 (2010); Median contract rent: $216 per month (2000); Median year structure built: 1958 (2000).
Transportation: Commute to work: 94.8% car, 0.0% public transportation, 3.0% walk, 1.5% work from home (2000); Travel time to work: 29.1% less than 15 minutes, 31.7% 15 to 30 minutes, 16.6% 30 to 45 minutes, 12.5% 45 to 60 minutes, 10.2% 60 minutes or more (2000)

NEWBERRY (town). Covers a land area of 0.489 square miles and a water area of 0 square miles. Located at 38.92° N. Lat; 87.01° W. Long. Elevation is 551 feet.

History: Laid out 1822.
Population: 207 (1990); 206 (2000); 200 (2010); 194 (2015 projected); Race: 99.0% White, 0.5% Black, 0.0% Asian, 0.5% Other, 0.5% Hispanic of any race (2010); Density: 408.6 persons per square mile (2010); Average household size: 2.44 (2010); Median age: 39.3 (2010); Males per 100 females: 104.1 (2010); Marriage status: 19.2% never married, 57.0% now married, 9.3% widowed, 14.5% divorced (2000); Foreign born: 0.0% (2000); Ancestry (includes multiple ancestries): 26.3% United States or American, 13.4% German, 9.7% French (except Basque), 6.9% Irish, 5.5% Other groups (2000).
Economy: Employment by occupation: 10.5% management, 12.9% professional, 21.0% services, 18.5% sales, 0.8% farming, 11.3% construction, 25.0% production (2000).
Income: Per capita income: $20,871 (2010); Median household income: $38,000 (2010); Average household income: $52,256 (2010); Percent of households with income of $100,000 or more: 13.4% (2010); Poverty rate: 12.9% (2000).
Taxes: Total city taxes per capita: $49 (2007); City property taxes per capita: $34 (2007).
Education: Percent of population age 25 and over with: High school diploma (including GED) or higher: 80.7% (2010); Bachelor's degree or higher: 11.1% (2010); Master's degree or higher: 6.7% (2010).
Housing: Homeownership rate: 86.6% (2010); Median home value: $98,889 (2010); Median contract rent: $139 per month (2000); Median year structure built: 1945 (2000).
Transportation: Commute to work: 98.4% car, 0.0% public transportation, 0.0% walk, 0.0% work from home (2000); Travel time to work: 8.2% less than 15 minutes, 60.7% 15 to 30 minutes, 5.7% 30 to 45 minutes, 16.4% 45 to 60 minutes, 9.0% 60 minutes or more (2000)

OWENSBURG (unincorporated postal area, zip code 47453). Covers a land area of 11.208 square miles and a water area of 0.023 square miles. Located at 38.92° N. Lat; 86.74° W. Long. Elevation is 643 feet.

Population: 533 (2000); Race: 100.0% White, 0.0% Black, 0.0% Asian, 0.0% Other, 1.3% Hispanic of any race (2000); Density: 47.6 persons per square mile (2000); Age: 33.0% under 18, 11.4% over 64 (2000); Marriage status: 9.9% never married, 67.1% now married, 9.6% widowed, 13.4% divorced (2000); Foreign born: 0.0% (2000); Ancestry (includes multiple ancestries): 20.8% United States or American, 13.6% German, 12.9% French (except Basque), 7.7% English, 6.5% Other groups (2000).
Economy: Employment by occupation: 0.0% management, 4.7% professional, 12.4% services, 18.3% sales, 0.0% farming, 37.9% construction, 26.6% production (2000).
Income: Per capita income: $14,454 (2000); Median household income: $27,188 (2000); Poverty rate: 18.3% (2000).
Education: Percent of population age 25 and over with: High school diploma (including GED) or higher: 88.8% (2000); Bachelor's degree or higher: 4.6% (2000).
Housing: Homeownership rate: 86.5% (2000); Median home value: $59,400 (2000); Median contract rent: $325 per month (2000); Median year structure built: 1987 (2000).
Transportation: Commute to work: 100.0% car, 0.0% public transportation, 0.0% walk, 0.0% work from home (2000); Travel time to work: 10.1% less than 15 minutes, 12.4% 15 to 30 minutes, 58.0% 30 to 45 minutes, 10.7% 45 to 60 minutes, 8.9% 60 minutes or more (2000)

SOLSBERRY (unincorporated postal area, zip code 47459). Covers a land area of 58.893 square miles and a water area of 0 square miles. Located at 39.11° N. Lat; 86.74° W. Long. Elevation is 778 feet.

History: Laid out 1848.
Population: 3,477 (2000); Race: 98.8% White, 0.0% Black, 0.0% Asian, 1.2% Other, 0.0% Hispanic of any race (2000); Density: 59.0 persons per square mile (2000); Age: 26.9% under 18, 8.0% over 64 (2000); Marriage status: 17.9% never married, 67.5% now married, 3.5% widowed, 11.1%

divorced (2000); Foreign born: 0.2% (2000); Ancestry (includes multiple ancestries): 15.6% United States or American, 13.6% German, 9.3% Irish, 7.5% English, 5.6% Other groups (2000).
Economy: Employment by occupation: 10.5% management, 12.6% professional, 13.4% services, 18.6% sales, 0.8% farming, 19.6% construction, 24.5% production (2000).
Income: Per capita income: $17,620 (2000); Median household income: $39,389 (2000); Poverty rate: 8.4% (2000).
Education: Percent of population age 25 and over with: High school diploma (including GED) or higher: 78.6% (2000); Bachelor's degree or higher: 12.0% (2000).
Housing: Homeownership rate: 88.5% (2000); Median home value: $84,300 (2000); Median contract rent: $331 per month (2000); Median year structure built: 1981 (2000).
Transportation: Commute to work: 94.4% car, 0.0% public transportation, 2.2% walk, 3.1% work from home (2000); Travel time to work: 10.3% less than 15 minutes, 44.8% 15 to 30 minutes, 34.7% 30 to 45 minutes, 4.1% 45 to 60 minutes, 6.1% 60 minutes or more (2000)

SWITZ CITY (town). Covers a land area of 0.224 square miles and a water area of 0 square miles. Located at 39.03° N. Lat; 87.05° W. Long. Elevation is 620 feet.
History: Switz City grew up around the nearby strip-mining coal fields.
Population: 257 (1990); 311 (2000); 303 (2010); 295 (2015 projected); Race: 96.4% White, 1.3% Black, 0.7% Asian, 1.7% Other, 1.7% Hispanic of any race (2010); Density: 1,351.2 persons per square mile (2010); Average household size: 2.46 (2010); Median age: 37.5 (2010); Males per 100 females: 98.0 (2010); Marriage status: 17.2% never married, 67.6% now married, 5.9% widowed, 9.2% divorced (2000); Foreign born: 0.6% (2000); Ancestry (includes multiple ancestries): 21.8% United States or American, 9.5% German, 8.8% Irish, 6.9% English, 2.2% Other groups (2000).
Economy: Employment by occupation: 10.7% management, 9.4% professional, 17.4% services, 21.5% sales, 0.0% farming, 18.8% construction, 22.1% production (2000).
Income: Per capita income: $20,338 (2010); Median household income: $46,719 (2010); Average household income: $51,954 (2010); Percent of households with income of $100,000 or more: 10.1% (2010); Poverty rate: 10.7% (2010).
Taxes: Total city taxes per capita: $39 (2007); City property taxes per capita: $35 (2007).
Education: Percent of population age 25 and over with: High school diploma (including GED) or higher: 87.5% (2010); Bachelor's degree or higher: 12.5% (2010); Master's degree or higher: 10.5% (2010).
School District(s)
White River Valley Sch Dist (KG-12)
    2008-09 Enrollment: 846 . . . . (812) 659-1424
Housing: Homeownership rate: 79.8% (2010); Median home value: $70,952 (2010); Median contract rent: $318 per month (2000); Median year structure built: 1953 (2000).
Transportation: Commute to work: 97.9% car, 0.0% public transportation, 0.0% walk, 2.1% work from home (2000); Travel time to work: 37.1% less than 15 minutes, 25.2% 15 to 30 minutes, 11.9% 30 to 45 minutes, 15.4% 45 to 60 minutes, 10.5% 60 minutes or more (2000)

WORTHINGTON (town). Covers a land area of 0.807 square miles and a water area of 0 square miles. Located at 39.11° N. Lat; 86.98° W. Long. Elevation is 515 feet.
History: Laid out 1849.
Population: 1,473 (1990); 1,481 (2000); 1,411 (2010); 1,364 (2015 projected); Race: 97.8% White, 0.6% Black, 0.1% Asian, 1.5% Other, 0.3% Hispanic of any race (2010); Density: 1,747.7 persons per square mile (2010); Average household size: 2.25 (2010); Median age: 42.8 (2010); Males per 100 females: 91.2 (2010); Marriage status: 18.4% never married, 54.8% now married, 12.6% widowed, 14.1% divorced (2000); Foreign born: 0.3% (2000); Ancestry (includes multiple ancestries): 19.1% German, 13.4% United States or American, 11.5% Irish, 11.1% English, 6.1% Other groups (2000).
Economy: Employment by occupation: 5.5% management, 16.4% professional, 14.4% services, 18.8% sales, 0.6% farming, 12.7% construction, 31.6% production (2000).
Income: Per capita income: $22,887 (2010); Median household income: $36,188 (2010); Average household income: $48,392 (2010); Percent of households with income of $100,000 or more: 8.8% (2010); Poverty rate: 13.0% (2000).

Taxes: Total city taxes per capita: $48 (2007); City property taxes per capita: $37 (2007).
Education: Percent of population age 25 and over with: High school diploma (including GED) or higher: 82.9% (2010); Bachelor's degree or higher: 14.4% (2010); Master's degree or higher: 7.2% (2010).
School District(s)
White River Valley Sch Dist (KG-12)
    2008-09 Enrollment: 846 . . . . (812) 659-1424
Housing: Homeownership rate: 75.7% (2010); Median home value: $70,000 (2010); Median contract rent: $252 per month (2000); Median year structure built: 1945 (2000).
Newspapers: Worthington Times (Local news; Circulation 800)
Transportation: Commute to work: 94.0% car, 0.3% public transportation, 2.5% walk, 2.3% work from home (2000); Travel time to work: 34.5% less than 15 minutes, 20.8% 15 to 30 minutes, 15.7% 30 to 45 minutes, 12.0% 45 to 60 minutes, 17.0% 60 minutes or more (2000)

Hamilton County

Located in central Indiana; drained by the West Fork of the White River, and by several creeks. Covers a land area of 397.94 square miles, a water area of 4.79 square miles, and is located in the Eastern Time Zone. The county was founded in 1823. County seat is Noblesville.

Hamilton County is part of the Indianapolis-Carmel, IN Metropolitan Statistical Area. The entire metro area includes: Boone County, IN; Brown County, IN; Hamilton County, IN; Hancock County, IN; Hendricks County, IN; Johnson County, IN; Marion County, IN; Morgan County, IN; Putnam County, IN; Shelby County, IN

Population: 108,936 (1990); 182,740 (2000); 283,472 (2010); 328,658 (2015 projected); Race: 89.2% White, 4.2% Black, 3.9% Asian, 2.7% Other, 3.1% Hispanic of any race (2010); Density: 712.3 persons per square mile (2010); Average household size: 2.76 (2010); Median age: 34.1 (2010); Males per 100 females: 97.3 (2010).
Religion: Five largest groups: 20.1% Catholic Church, 4.9% The United Methodist Church, 3.9% Christian Churches and Churches of Christ, 2.1% Evangelical Lutheran Church in America, 1.5% Christian Church (Disciples of Christ) (2000).
Economy: Unemployment rate: 6.9% (5/2010); Total civilian labor force: 139,289 (5/2010); Leading industries: 13.8% retail trade; 12.5% health care and social assistance; 11.0% finance & insurance (2008); Farms: 636 totaling 123,600 acres (2007); Companies that employ 500 or more persons: 13 (2008); Companies that employ 100 to 499 persons: 155 (2008); Companies that employ less than 100 persons: 7,286 (2008); Black-owned businesses: n/a (2002); Hispanic-owned businesses: 194 (2002); Asian-owned businesses: 500 (2002); Women-owned businesses: 6,073 (2002); Retail sales per capita: $14,118 (2010). Single-family building permits issued: 1,353 (2009); Multi-family building permits issued: 829 (2009).
Income: Per capita income: $38,867 (2010); Median household income: $84,421 (2010); Average household income: $107,717 (2010); Percent of households with income of $100,000 or more: 39.2% (2010); Poverty rate: 4.2% (2008); Bankruptcy rate: 5.53% (2009).
Taxes: Total county taxes per capita: $185 (2007); County property taxes per capita: $114 (2007).
Education: Percent of population age 25 and over with: High school diploma (including GED) or higher: 96.4% (2010); Bachelor's degree or higher: 54.3% (2010); Master's degree or higher: 17.0% (2010).
Housing: Homeownership rate: 80.6% (2010); Median home value: $194,679 (2010); Median contract rent: $751 per month (2006-2008 3-year est.); Median year structure built: 1994 (2006-2008 3-year est.)
Health: Birth rate: 153.0 per 10,000 population (2009); Death rate: 43.9 per 10,000 population (2009); Age-adjusted cancer mortality rate: 170.9 deaths per 100,000 population (2006); Air Quality Index: 79.3% good, 19.0% moderate, 1.6% unhealthy for sensitive individuals, 0.0% unhealthy (percent of days in 2008); Number of physicians: 39.5 per 10,000 population (2007); Hospital beds: 17.0 per 10,000 population (2006); Hospital admissions: 788.6 per 10,000 population (2006).
Elections: 2008 Presidential election results: 38.4% Obama, 60.6% McCain, 0.0% Nader
Additional Information Contacts
Hamilton County Government . . . . (317) 776-9719
    http://www.co.hamilton.in.us
Carmel Chamber of Commerce . . . . (317) 846-1049
    http://www.carmelchamber.com

City of Carmel . . . . (317) 571-2400
    http://www.ci.carmel.in.us
City of Noblesville . . . . (317) 776-6328
    http://www.cityofnoblesville.org
Fishers Chamber of Commerce. . . . . (317) 578-0700
    http://www.fisherschamber.com
Hamilton County Convention and Visitors Bureau. . . . . (317) 848-3181
    http://www.hccvb.org
Noblesville Chamber of Commerce . . . . (317) 773-0086
    http://www.noblesvillechamber.com
Town of Cicero. . . . . (317) 984-4900
    http://www.ciceroin.org
Town of Fishers . . . . (317) 595-3140
    http://www.fishers.in.us
Town of Westfield . . . . (317) 804-3020
    http://www.westfield.in.gov
Westfield Chamber of Commerce . . . . (317) 804-3030
    http://www.westfieldchamber.org

Hamilton County Communities

ARCADIA (town). Covers a land area of 0.550 square miles and a water area of 0 square miles. Located at 40.17° N. Lat; 86.02° W. Long. Elevation is 860 feet.

Population: 1,447 (1990); 1,747 (2000); 1,643 (2010); 1,699 (2015 projected); Race: 94.9% White, 0.7% Black, 0.2% Asian, 4.1% Other, 1.8% Hispanic of any race (2010); Density: 2,987.0 persons per square mile (2010); Average household size: 2.74 (2010); Median age: 34.9 (2010); Males per 100 females: 101.1 (2010); Marriage status: 23.8% never married, 59.8% now married, 5.7% widowed, 10.7% divorced (2000); Foreign born: 0.6% (2000); Ancestry (includes multiple ancestries): 15.6% German, 12.4% United States or American, 8.8% Irish, 7.5% English, 5.5% Other groups (2000).

Economy: Single-family building permits issued: 2 (2009); Multi-family building permits issued: 0 (2009); Employment by occupation: 6.0% management, 15.5% professional, 11.8% services, 26.0% sales, 1.1% farming, 19.2% construction, 20.3% production (2000).

Income: Per capita income: $24,435 (2010); Median household income: $61,888 (2010); Average household income: $69,712 (2010); Percent of households with income of $100,000 or more: 18.7% (2010); Poverty rate: 10.5% (2000).

Taxes: Total city taxes per capita: $107 (2007); City property taxes per capita: $98 (2007).

Education: Percent of population age 25 and over with: High school diploma (including GED) or higher: 80.2% (2010); Bachelor's degree or higher: 12.7% (2010); Master's degree or higher: 4.2% (2010).

School District(s)
Hamilton Heights School Corp (PK-12)
    2008-09 Enrollment: 2,238 . . . . (317) 984-3538

Housing: Homeownership rate: 71.9% (2010); Median home value: $118,386 (2010); Median contract rent: $377 per month (2000); Median year structure built: 1958 (2000).

Transportation: Commute to work: 94.8% car, 0.0% public transportation, 3.1% walk, 1.8% work from home (2000); Travel time to work: 22.4% less than 15 minutes, 35.5% 15 to 30 minutes, 22.8% 30 to 45 minutes, 12.7% 45 to 60 minutes, 6.5% 60 minutes or more (2000)

Additional Information Contacts
Hamilton County Convention and Visitors Bureau. . . . . (317) 848-3181
    http://www.hccvb.org

ATLANTA (town). Covers a land area of 0.300 square miles and a water area of 0 square miles. Located at 40.21° N. Lat; 86.02° W. Long. Elevation is 863 feet.

Population: 681 (1990); 761 (2000); 768 (2010); 813 (2015 projected); Race: 93.6% White, 0.1% Black, 0.5% Asian, 5.7% Other, 3.1% Hispanic of any race (2010); Density: 2,557.3 persons per square mile (2010); Average household size: 2.98 (2010); Median age: 32.4 (2010); Males per 100 females: 103.2 (2010); Marriage status: 25.0% never married, 51.9% now married, 10.8% widowed, 12.3% divorced (2000); Foreign born: 0.0% (2000); Ancestry (includes multiple ancestries): 18.7% German, 15.7% Irish, 14.7% English, 12.4% United States or American, 11.9% Other groups (2000).

Economy: Single-family building permits issued: 0 (2009); Multi-family building permits issued: 0 (2009); Employment by occupation: 8.7%

management, 12.3% professional, 19.8% services, 29.6% sales, 0.0% farming, 14.2% construction, 15.4% production (2000).

Income: Per capita income: $20,610 (2010); Median household income: $54,891 (2010); Average household income: $61,826 (2010); Percent of households with income of $100,000 or more: 17.6% (2010); Poverty rate: 7.0% (2000).

Taxes: Total city taxes per capita: $72 (2007); City property taxes per capita: $62 (2007).

Education: Percent of population age 25 and over with: High school diploma (including GED) or higher: 89.4% (2010); Bachelor's degree or higher: 10.0% (2010); Master's degree or higher: 4.9% (2010).

Housing: Homeownership rate: 79.3% (2010); Median home value: $110,985 (2010); Median contract rent: $515 per month (2000); Median year structure built: before 1940 (2000).

Transportation: Commute to work: 91.0% car, 0.0% public transportation, 3.1% walk, 5.1% work from home (2000); Travel time to work: 23.1% less than 15 minutes, 22.3% 15 to 30 minutes, 32.6% 30 to 45 minutes, 14.2% 45 to 60 minutes, 7.7% 60 minutes or more (2000)

CARMEL (city). Covers a land area of 17.812 square miles and a water area of 0.107 square miles. Located at 39.97° N. Lat; 86.10° W. Long. Elevation is 853 feet.

Population: 27,705 (1990); 37,733 (2000); 48,221 (2010); 55,106 (2015 projected); Race: 87.6% White, 3.9% Black, 6.2% Asian, 2.4% Other, 3.1% Hispanic of any race (2010); Density: 2,707.2 persons per square mile (2010); Average household size: 2.73 (2010); Median age: 36.2 (2010); Males per 100 females: 95.7 (2010); Marriage status: 17.9% never married, 70.7% now married, 4.2% widowed, 7.2% divorced (2000); Foreign born: 7.3% (2000); Ancestry (includes multiple ancestries): 28.1% German, 15.1% Irish, 15.0% English, 10.3% Other groups, 7.7% United States or American (2000).

Economy: Unemployment rate: 6.8% (5/2010); Total civilian labor force: 32,899 (5/2010); Single-family building permits issued: 274 (2009); Multi-family building permits issued: 397 (2009); Employment by occupation: 26.7% management, 29.4% professional, 8.1% services, 28.2% sales, 0.1% farming, 3.1% construction, 4.3% production (2000).

Income: Per capita income: $44,123 (2010); Median household income: $91,343 (2010); Average household income: $120,925 (2010); Percent of households with income of $100,000 or more: 45.1% (2010); Poverty rate: 2.5% (2000).

Taxes: Total city taxes per capita: $464 (2007); City property taxes per capita: $405 (2007).

Education: Percent of population age 25 and over with: High school diploma (including GED) or higher: 97.7% (2010); Bachelor's degree or higher: 61.6% (2010); Master's degree or higher: 22.6% (2010).

School District(s)
Carmel Clay Schools (PK-12)
    2008-09 Enrollment: 15,319 . . . . (317) 844-9961
Options Charter School - Carmel (09-12)
    2008-09 Enrollment: 129 . . . . (317) 815-2098

Housing: Homeownership rate: 79.5% (2010); Median home value: $235,826 (2010); Median contract rent: $658 per month (2000); Median year structure built: 1982 (2000).

Hospitals: Clarian North Medical Center; St. Vincent Carmel Hospital (100 beds)

Safety: Violent crime rate: 3.5 per 10,000 population; Property crime rate: 147.0 per 10,000 population (2008).

Newspapers: The Highflyer (Community news; Circulation 68,705)

Transportation: Commute to work: 93.4% car, 0.1% public transportation, 0.9% walk, 5.1% work from home (2000); Travel time to work: 27.8% less than 15 minutes, 37.7% 15 to 30 minutes, 24.2% 30 to 45 minutes, 6.5% 45 to 60 minutes, 3.8% 60 minutes or more (2000)

Additional Information Contacts
Carmel Chamber of Commerce . . . . (317) 846-1049
    http://www.carmelchamber.com
City of Carmel . . . . (317) 571-2400
    http://www.ci.carmel.in.us

CICERO (town). Covers a land area of 1.495 square miles and a water area of 0.433 square miles. Located at 40.12° N. Lat; 86.01° W. Long. Elevation is 833 feet.

History: Cicero, named for a Delaware chief, grew around a Seventh-Day Adventist academy nearby.

Population: 3,667 (1990); 4,303 (2000); 4,586 (2010); 4,962 (2015 projected); Race: 96.0% White, 0.4% Black, 0.5% Asian, 3.1% Other, 2.5%

Hispanic of any race (2010); Density: 3,067.1 persons per square mile (2010); Average household size: 2.50 (2010); Median age: 36.8 (2010); Males per 100 females: 98.7 (2010); Marriage status: 15.7% never married, 62.1% now married, 5.0% widowed, 17.2% divorced (2000); Foreign born: 2.4% (2000); Ancestry (includes multiple ancestries): 26.5% United States or American, 18.5% German, 10.2% English, 9.8% Irish, 3.8% Other groups (2000).

Economy: Employment by occupation: 6.9% management, 25.4% professional, 16.9% services, 31.9% sales, 0.8% farming, 6.5% construction, 11.5% production (2000).

Income: Per capita income: $29,872 (2010); Median household income: $61,498 (2010); Average household income: $74,716 (2010); Percent of households with income of $100,000 or more: 18.4% (2010); Poverty rate: 1.7% (2000).

Taxes: Total city taxes per capita: $216 (2007); City property taxes per capita: $193 (2007).

Education: Percent of population age 25 and over with: High school diploma (including GED) or higher: 95.3% (2010); Bachelor's degree or higher: 31.2% (2010); Master's degree or higher: 12.6% (2010).

Housing: Homeownership rate: 78.4% (2010); Median home value: $136,360 (2010); Median contract rent: $520 per month (2000); Median year structure built: 1978 (2000).

Transportation: Commute to work: 96.2% car, 0.0% public transportation, 1.7% walk, 2.1% work from home (2000); Travel time to work: 25.8% less than 15 minutes, 29.7% 15 to 30 minutes, 24.8% 30 to 45 minutes, 10.5% 45 to 60 minutes, 9.2% 60 minutes or more (2000)

Additional Information Contacts

Town of Cicero. . . . . (317) 984-4900
http://www.ciceroin.org

FISHERS (town). Aka Fishers Station. Covers a land area of 21.690 square miles and a water area of 0.096 square miles. Located at 39.95° N. Lat; 86.01° W. Long. Elevation is 817 feet.

Population: 12,437 (1990); 37,835 (2000); 68,773 (2010); 81,516 (2015 projected); Race: 85.0% White, 7.4% Black, 4.7% Asian, 2.8% Other, 3.7% Hispanic of any race (2010); Density: 3,170.7 persons per square mile (2010); Average household size: 2.71 (2010); Median age: 32.9 (2010); Males per 100 females: 96.1 (2010); Marriage status: 19.0% never married, 70.9% now married, 1.8% widowed, 8.3% divorced (2000); Foreign born: 4.0% (2000); Ancestry (includes multiple ancestries): 29.2% German, 13.3% English, 13.3% Irish, 11.2% Other groups, 7.2% United States or American (2000).

Economy: Unemployment rate: 6.2% (5/2010); Total civilian labor force: 38,988 (5/2010); Single-family building permits issued: 469 (2009); Multi-family building permits issued: 57 (2009); Employment by occupation: 28.2% management, 27.3% professional, 7.2% services, 30.6% sales, 0.1% farming, 2.9% construction, 3.8% production (2000).

Income: Per capita income: $38,168 (2010); Median household income: $85,583 (2010); Average household income: $103,384 (2010); Percent of households with income of $100,000 or more: 38.3% (2010); Poverty rate: 1.8% (2000).

Taxes: Total city taxes per capita: $243 (2007); City property taxes per capita: $163 (2007).

Education: Percent of population age 25 and over with: High school diploma (including GED) or higher: 98.6% (2010); Bachelor's degree or higher: 62.7% (2010); Master's degree or higher: 16.2% (2010).

School District(s)

Hamilton Southeastern Schools (PK-12)
    2008-09 Enrollment: 17,140 . . . . (317) 594-4100

Housing: Homeownership rate: 77.3% (2010); Median home value: $182,390 (2010); Median contract rent: $718 per month (2000); Median year structure built: 1995 (2000).

Safety: Violent crime rate: 3.7 per 10,000 population; Property crime rate: 132.6 per 10,000 population (2008).

Newspapers: Broad Ripple-Glendale Northside (Local news; Circulation 5,300); Carmel Star (Community news); Lawrence Topics (Community news; Circulation 7,637); The Noblesville Ledger (Local news; Circulation 11,776); North Side Topics (Community news; Circulation 19,757)

Transportation: Commute to work: 94.0% car, 0.1% public transportation, 0.4% walk, 4.9% work from home (2000); Travel time to work: 21.5% less than 15 minutes, 40.9% 15 to 30 minutes, 28.3% 30 to 45 minutes, 5.8% 45 to 60 minutes, 3.5% 60 minutes or more (2000)

Additional Information Contacts

Fishers Chamber of Commerce. . . . . (317) 578-0700
http://www.fisherschamber.com

Town of Fishers . . . . (317) 595-3140
http://www.fishers.in.us

NOBLESVILLE (city). County seat. Covers a land area of 17.916 square miles and a water area of 1.150 square miles. Located at 40.05° N. Lat; 86.02° W. Long. Elevation is 771 feet.

History: Named for James Noble, first U.S. Senator from Indiana. Noblesville was founded in 1823 by William Conner who had built a trading post nearby in 1818. Noblesville became the seat of Hamilton County, and Conner became a state senator.

Population: 20,364 (1990); 28,590 (2000); 36,306 (2010); 41,245 (2015 projected); Race: 93.8% White, 2.3% Black, 1.2% Asian, 2.7% Other, 2.8% Hispanic of any race (2010); Density: 2,026.5 persons per square mile (2010); Average household size: 2.65 (2010); Median age: 34.1 (2010); Males per 100 females: 98.9 (2010); Marriage status: 18.7% never married, 67.4% now married, 5.2% widowed, 8.7% divorced (2000); Foreign born: 2.0% (2000); Ancestry (includes multiple ancestries): 27.8% German, 13.8% Irish, 13.4% English, 11.1% United States or American, 7.4% Other groups (2000).

Economy: Unemployment rate: 8.7% (5/2010); Total civilian labor force: 21,946 (5/2010); Single-family building permits issued: 412 (2009); Multi-family building permits issued: 326 (2009); Employment by occupation: 18.4% management, 25.5% professional, 10.3% services, 28.1% sales, 0.1% farming, 7.2% construction, 10.3% production (2000).

Income: Per capita income: $32,239 (2010); Median household income: $68,932 (2010); Average household income: $86,017 (2010); Percent of households with income of $100,000 or more: 28.1% (2010); Poverty rate: 5.4% (2000).

Taxes: Total city taxes per capita: $501 (2007); City property taxes per capita: $374 (2007).

Education: Percent of population age 25 and over with: High school diploma (including GED) or higher: 93.7% (2010); Bachelor's degree or higher: 44.5% (2010); Master's degree or higher: 12.8% (2010).

School District(s)

Carmel Clay Schools (PK-12)
    2008-09 Enrollment: 15,319 . . . . (317) 844-9961
Hamilton Southeastern Schools (PK-12)
    2008-09 Enrollment: 17,140 . . . . (317) 594-4100
Noblesville Schools (PK-12)
    2008-09 Enrollment: 8,779 . . . . (317) 773-3171
Options Charter Sch - Noblesville (09-12)
    2008-09 Enrollment: 135 . . . . (317) 773-8659

Vocational/Technical School(s)

Hair Fashions By Kaye Beauty College (Private, For-profit)
    Fall 2008 Enrollment: 73 . . . . (317) 773-6189
    2009-10 Tuition: $12,600

Housing: Homeownership rate: 75.3% (2010); Median home value: $165,144 (2010); Median contract rent: $548 per month (2000); Median year structure built: 1985 (2000).

Hospitals: Riverview Hospital (161 beds)

Safety: Violent crime rate: 12.9 per 10,000 population; Property crime rate: 227.5 per 10,000 population (2008).

Newspapers: Fishers Sun Herald (Community news; Circulation 7,440); Lawrence Times (Local news; Circulation 7,310); Noblesville Daily Times (Local news; Circulation 400)

Transportation: Commute to work: 93.8% car, 0.2% public transportation, 1.3% walk, 3.9% work from home (2000); Travel time to work: 23.1% less than 15 minutes, 28.5% 15 to 30 minutes, 29.5% 30 to 45 minutes, 13.2% 45 to 60 minutes, 5.7% 60 minutes or more (2000)

Additional Information Contacts

City of Noblesville . . . . (317) 776-6328
http://www.cityofnoblesville.org
Noblesville Chamber of Commerce . . . . (317) 773-0086
http://www.noblesvillechamber.com

SHERIDAN (town). Covers a land area of 1.318 square miles and a water area of 0 square miles. Located at 40.13° N. Lat; 86.22° W. Long. Elevation is 951 feet.

History: Laid out 1860.

Population: 2,292 (1990); 2,520 (2000); 2,772 (2010); 3,045 (2015 projected); Race: 95.7% White, 1.5% Black, 0.2% Asian, 2.5% Other, 1.8% Hispanic of any race (2010); Density: 2,103.6 persons per square mile (2010); Average household size: 2.62 (2010); Median age: 34.7 (2010); Males per 100 females: 90.0 (2010); Marriage status: 23.0% never married, 57.2% now married, 7.6% widowed, 12.2% divorced (2000); Foreign born:

0.8% (2000); Ancestry (includes multiple ancestries): 37.1% United States or American, 12.2% German, 8.3% English, 6.7% Irish, 6.2% Other groups (2000).

Economy: Single-family building permits issued: 5 (2009); Multi-family building permits issued: 26 (2009); Employment by occupation: 12.5% management, 16.5% professional, 14.3% services, 28.1% sales, 1.1% farming, 15.0% construction, 12.6% production (2000).

Income: Per capita income: $18,493 (2010); Median household income: $43,375 (2010); Average household income: $50,170 (2010); Percent of households with income of $100,000 or more: 11.5% (2010); Poverty rate: 5.9% (2000).

Taxes: Total city taxes per capita: $220 (2007); City property taxes per capita: $203 (2007).

Education: Percent of population age 25 and over with: High school diploma (including GED) or higher: 89.6% (2010); Bachelor's degree or higher: 19.0% (2010); Master's degree or higher: 2.2% (2010).

School District(s)

Sheridan Community Schools (PK-12)

    2008-09 Enrollment: 1,152 . . . . (317) 758-4172

Housing: Homeownership rate: 69.7% (2010); Median home value: $124,494 (2010); Median contract rent: $356 per month (2000); Median year structure built: 1954 (2000).

Transportation: Commute to work: 89.7% car, 0.0% public transportation, 3.2% walk, 5.6% work from home (2000); Travel time to work: 26.1% less than 15 minutes, 42.4% 15 to 30 minutes, 15.8% 30 to 45 minutes, 9.4% 45 to 60 minutes, 6.3% 60 minutes or more (2000)

WESTFIELD (town). Covers a land area of 7.629 square miles and a water area of 0.013 square miles. Located at 40.03° N. Lat; 86.12° W. Long. Elevation is 886 feet.

History: Westfield was founded in 1834 by a group of Quakers, and was an important station on the Underground Railroad for slaves fleeing to the north.

Population: 5,121 (1990); 9,293 (2000); 15,774 (2010); 18,445 (2015 projected); Race: 90.6% White, 2.5% Black, 2.6% Asian, 4.3% Other, 4.8% Hispanic of any race (2010); Density: 2,067.7 persons per square mile (2010); Average household size: 2.67 (2010); Median age: 33.8 (2010); Males per 100 females: 97.6 (2010); Marriage status: 20.3% never married, 61.8% now married, 5.2% widowed, 12.7% divorced (2000); Foreign born: 3.7% (2000); Ancestry (includes multiple ancestries): 29.1% German, 15.1% Irish, 13.9% English, 10.9% Other groups, 8.7% United States or American (2000).

Economy: Single-family building permits issued: 182 (2009); Multi-family building permits issued: 23 (2009); Employment by occupation: 18.0% management, 24.2% professional, 10.0% services, 31.4% sales, 0.4% farming, 7.8% construction, 8.1% production (2000).

Income: Per capita income: $33,744 (2010); Median household income: $74,605 (2010); Average household income: $90,512 (2010); Percent of households with income of $100,000 or more: 33.3% (2010); Poverty rate: 4.0% (2000).

Taxes: Total city taxes per capita: $273 (2007); City property taxes per capita: $198 (2007).

Education: Percent of population age 25 and over with: High school diploma (including GED) or higher: 93.9% (2010); Bachelor's degree or higher: 41.7% (2010); Master's degree or higher: 12.7% (2010).

School District(s)

Westfield-Washington Schools (PK-12)

    2008-09 Enrollment: 5,887 . . . . (317) 867-8000

Housing: Homeownership rate: 73.2% (2010); Median home value: $177,591 (2010); Median contract rent: $545 per month (2000); Median year structure built: 1992 (2000).

Safety: Violent crime rate: 9.5 per 10,000 population; Property crime rate: 269.4 per 10,000 population (2008).

Transportation: Commute to work: 95.9% car, 0.5% public transportation, 0.9% walk, 2.1% work from home (2000); Travel time to work: 31.3% less than 15 minutes, 33.2% 15 to 30 minutes, 23.4% 30 to 45 minutes, 8.4% 45 to 60 minutes, 3.7% 60 minutes or more (2000)

Additional Information Contacts

Town of Westfield . . . . (317) 804-3020

    http://www.westfield.in.gov

Westfield Chamber of Commerce . . . . (317) 804-3030

    http://www.westfieldchamber.org

Hancock County

Located in central Indiana; drained by the Big Blue River and by Sugar and Brandywine Creeks. Covers a land area of 306.12 square miles, a water area of 0.61 square miles, and is located in the Eastern Time Zone. The county was founded in 1827. County seat is Greenfield.

Hancock County is part of the Indianapolis-Carmel, IN Metropolitan Statistical Area. The entire metro area includes: Boone County, IN; Brown County, IN; Hamilton County, IN; Hancock County, IN; Hendricks County, IN; Johnson County, IN; Marion County, IN; Morgan County, IN; Putnam County, IN; Shelby County, IN

Weather Station: Greenfield   Elevation: 862 feet

	Jan	Feb	Mar	Apr	May	Jun	Jul	Aug	Sep	Oct	Nov	Dec
High	33	38	50	62	73	82	86	84	78	65	51	39
Low	17	20	30	40	51	60	64	62	55	43	33	23
Precip	2.5	2.4	3.3	4.1	4.7	4.4	5.0	4.0	3.1	3.1	3.9	3.1
Snow	na	na	1.5	0.2	0.0	0.0	0.0	0.0	0.0	tr	0.7	3.0

High and Low temperatures in degrees Fahrenheit; Precipitation and Snow in inches

Population: 45,527 (1990); 55,391 (2000); 69,347 (2010); 75,610 (2015 projected); Race: 94.8% White, 2.9% Black, 0.9% Asian, 1.4% Other, 1.5% Hispanic of any race (2010); Density: 226.5 persons per square mile (2010); Average household size: 2.59 (2010); Median age: 37.1 (2010); Males per 100 females: 97.3 (2010).

Religion: Five largest groups: 9.1% The United Methodist Church, 7.3% Catholic Church, 5.4% Christian Churches and Churches of Christ, 2.3% Church of the Nazarene, 2.1% Southern Baptist Convention (2000).

Economy: Unemployment rate: 8.8% (5/2010); Total civilian labor force: 35,317 (5/2010); Leading industries: 17.9% manufacturing; 12.4% health care and social assistance; 11.9% retail trade (2008); Farms: 686 totaling 171,673 acres (2007); Companies that employ 500 or more persons: 3 (2008); Companies that employ 100 to 499 persons: 20 (2008); Companies that employ less than 100 persons: 1,418 (2008); Black-owned businesses: n/a (2002); Hispanic-owned businesses: n/a (2002); Asian-owned businesses: n/a (2002); Women-owned businesses: 1,099 (2002); Retail sales per capita: $9,626 (2010). Single-family building permits issued: 149 (2009); Multi-family building permits issued: 149 (2009).

Income: Per capita income: $29,667 (2010); Median household income: $63,359 (2010); Average household income: $77,022 (2010); Percent of households with income of $100,000 or more: 23.7% (2010); Poverty rate: 5.7% (2008); Bankruptcy rate: 8.70% (2009).

Taxes: Total county taxes per capita: $275 (2007); County property taxes per capita: $106 (2007).

Education: Percent of population age 25 and over with: High school diploma (including GED) or higher: 90.6% (2010); Bachelor's degree or higher: 25.9% (2010); Master's degree or higher: 9.8% (2010).

Housing: Homeownership rate: 80.4% (2010); Median home value: $148,703 (2010); Median contract rent: $593 per month (2006-2008 3-year est.); Median year structure built: 1981 (2006-2008 3-year est.)

Health: Birth rate: 150.0 per 10,000 population (2009); Death rate: 79.5 per 10,000 population (2009); Age-adjusted cancer mortality rate: 216.5 deaths per 100,000 population (2006); Air Quality Index: 79.9% good, 19.0% moderate, 1.1% unhealthy for sensitive individuals, 0.0% unhealthy (percent of days in 2008); Number of physicians: 15.9 per 10,000 population (2007); Hospital beds: 16.4 per 10,000 population (2006); Hospital admissions: 661.8 per 10,000 population (2006).

Elections: 2008 Presidential election results: 34.7% Obama, 64.3% McCain, 0.0% Nader

Additional Information Contacts

Hancock County Government . . . . (317) 462-1102

    http://www.hancockcoingov.org

City of Greenfield . . . . (317) 477-4300

    http://www.greenfieldin.org

Greenfield Chamber of Commerce . . . . (317) 477-4188

    http://www.greenfieldcc.org

Town of Fortville . . . . (812) 948-4711

    http://floydcounty.in.gov

Hancock County Communities

CHARLOTTESVILLE (unincorporated postal area, zip code 46117). Aka Charlottsvillle. Covers a land area of 10.456 square miles and a water area of 0.005 square miles. Located at 39.80° N. Lat; 85.61° W. Long. Elevation is 942 feet.

Population: 662 (2000); Race: 100.0% White, 0.0% Black, 0.0% Asian, 0.0% Other, 0.0% Hispanic of any race (2000); Density: 63.3 persons per square mile (2000); Age: 27.8% under 18, 13.1% over 64 (2000); Marriage status: 16.5% never married, 72.2% now married, 7.9% widowed, 3.4% divorced (2000); Foreign born: 0.0% (2000); Ancestry (includes multiple ancestries): 26.1% United States or American, 23.7% English, 20.4% Irish, 14.2% German, 4.2% Scottish (2000).
Economy: Employment by occupation: 2.5% management, 6.5% professional, 8.4% services, 37.1% sales, 0.0% farming, 26.8% construction, 18.7% production (2000).
Income: Per capita income: $20,061 (2000); Median household income: $57,583 (2000); Poverty rate: 1.0% (2000).
Education: Percent of population age 25 and over with: High school diploma (including GED) or higher: 80.7% (2000); Bachelor's degree or higher: 7.6% (2000).

School District(s)
Eastern Hancock Co Com Sch Corp (KG-12)
    2008-09 Enrollment: 1,061 . . . . (317) 467-0064
Housing: Homeownership rate: 90.9% (2000); Median home value: $114,300 (2000); Median contract rent: $653 per month (2000); Median year structure built: 1955 (2000).
Transportation: Commute to work: 97.2% car, 0.0% public transportation, 0.0% walk, 2.8% work from home (2000); Travel time to work: 15.5% less than 15 minutes, 38.2% 15 to 30 minutes, 16.8% 30 to 45 minutes, 12.0% 45 to 60 minutes, 17.5% 60 minutes or more (2000)

FORTVILLE (town).
Covers a land area of 1.216 square miles and a water area of 0 square miles. Located at 39.93° N. Lat; 85.84° W. Long. Elevation is 856 feet.
History: Fortville was founded in 1849 by Cephas Fort.
Population: 2,949 (1990); 3,444 (2000); 3,380 (2010); 3,388 (2015 projected); Race: 95.5% White, 1.4% Black, 0.4% Asian, 2.7% Other, 3.7% Hispanic of any race (2010); Density: 2,779.2 persons per square mile (2010); Average household size: 2.40 (2010); Median age: 34.6 (2010); Males per 100 females: 93.9 (2010); Marriage status: 25.1% never married, 53.2% now married, 6.5% widowed, 15.1% divorced (2000); Foreign born: 0.0% (2000); Ancestry (includes multiple ancestries): 21.6% German, 21.2% United States or American, 15.4% Irish, 5.7% Other groups, 5.3% Italian (2000).
Economy: Employment by occupation: 11.9% management, 8.2% professional, 11.6% services, 37.0% sales, 0.0% farming, 10.9% construction, 20.4% production (2000).
Income: Per capita income: $23,172 (2010); Median household income: $46,910 (2010); Average household income: $55,773 (2010); Percent of households with income of $100,000 or more: 11.3% (2010); Poverty rate: 6.5% (2000).
Taxes: Total city taxes per capita: $161 (2007); City property taxes per capita: $129 (2007).
Education: Percent of population age 25 and over with: High school diploma (including GED) or higher: 85.4% (2010); Bachelor's degree or higher: 20.6% (2010); Master's degree or higher: 2.5% (2010).

School District(s)
Hamilton Southeastern Schools (PK-12)
    2008-09 Enrollment: 17,140 . . . . (317) 594-4100
Mt Vernon Community Sch Corp (PK-12)
    2008-09 Enrollment: 3,632 . . . . (317) 485-3100
Housing: Homeownership rate: 67.9% (2010); Median home value: $118,076 (2010); Median contract rent: $393 per month (2000); Median year structure built: 1970 (2000).
Newspapers: Fortville Community Shopper (Local news; Circulation 5,000)
Transportation: Commute to work: 93.3% car, 0.0% public transportation, 3.6% walk, 2.5% work from home (2000); Travel time to work: 15.1% less than 15 minutes, 34.4% 15 to 30 minutes, 31.0% 30 to 45 minutes, 13.6% 45 to 60 minutes, 5.8% 60 minutes or more (2000)
Additional Information Contacts
Town of Fortville. . . . . (812) 948-4711
    http://floydcounty.in.gov

GREENFIELD (city).
County seat. Covers a land area of 8.031 square miles and a water area of 0.039 square miles. Located at 39.79° N. Lat; 85.77° W. Long. Elevation is 883 feet.
History: Named for John Green, an early settler. Greenfield was the birthplace in 1849 of poet James Whitcomb Riley. An early industry here was tomato canning.

Population: 12,256 (1990); 14,600 (2000); 18,057 (2010); 19,763 (2015 projected); Race: 96.4% White, 0.7% Black, 1.3% Asian, 1.7% Other, 1.9% Hispanic of any race (2010); Density: 2,248.4 persons per square mile (2010); Average household size: 2.40 (2010); Median age: 35.7 (2010); Males per 100 females: 94.5 (2010); Marriage status: 19.9% never married, 59.0% now married, 8.6% widowed, 12.5% divorced (2000); Foreign born: 0.9% (2000); Ancestry (includes multiple ancestries): 22.6% German, 13.8% United States or American, 12.7% English, 10.7% Irish, 9.5% Other groups (2000).
Economy: Single-family building permits issued: 35 (2009); Multi-family building permits issued: 147 (2009); Employment by occupation: 10.9% management, 16.4% professional, 15.8% services, 26.5% sales, 0.2% farming, 11.8% construction, 18.5% production (2000).
Income: Per capita income: $25,479 (2010); Median household income: $49,075 (2010); Average household income: $61,305 (2010); Percent of households with income of $100,000 or more: 13.5% (2010); Poverty rate: 4.3% (2000).
Taxes: Total city taxes per capita: $300 (2007); City property taxes per capita: $269 (2007).
Education: Percent of population age 25 and over with: High school diploma (including GED) or higher: 87.3% (2010); Bachelor's degree or higher: 22.7% (2010); Master's degree or higher: 8.2% (2010).

School District(s)
Greenfield-Central Com Schools (PK-12)
    2008-09 Enrollment: 4,701 . . . . (317) 462-4434
Mt Vernon Community Sch Corp (PK-12)
    2008-09 Enrollment: 3,632 . . . . (317) 485-3100
Southern Hancock Co Com Sch Corp (PK-12)
    2008-09 Enrollment: 3,365 . . . . (317) 861-4463
Housing: Homeownership rate: 67.4% (2010); Median home value: $121,247 (2010); Median contract rent: $526 per month (2000); Median year structure built: 1972 (2000).
Hospitals: Hancock Regional Hospital (94 beds)
Safety: Violent crime rate: 6.4 per 10,000 population; Property crime rate: 179.6 per 10,000 population (2008).
Newspapers: Greenfield Daily Reporter (Local news; Circulation 9,287); Hancock County Image (Community news; Circulation 25,000)
Transportation: Commute to work: 95.1% car, 0.3% public transportation, 1.0% walk, 2.6% work from home (2000); Travel time to work: 41.0% less than 15 minutes, 20.3% 15 to 30 minutes, 24.7% 30 to 45 minutes, 10.3% 45 to 60 minutes, 3.7% 60 minutes or more (2000)
Additional Information Contacts
City of Greenfield . . . . (317) 477-4300
    http://www.greenfieldin.org
Greenfield Chamber of Commerce . . . . (317) 477-4188
    http://www.greenfieldcc.org

MCCORDSVILLE (town).
Covers a land area of 3.203 square miles and a water area of 0 square miles. Located at 39.89° N. Lat; 85.92° W. Long. Elevation is 850 feet.
History: Laid out 1865.
Population: 684 (1990); 1,134 (2000); 1,861 (2010); 2,116 (2015 projected); Race: 88.0% White, 9.8% Black, 0.1% Asian, 2.1% Other, 1.1% Hispanic of any race (2010); Density: 581.0 persons per square mile (2010); Average household size: 2.74 (2010); Median age: 37.8 (2010); Males per 100 females: 94.3 (2010); Marriage status: 15.9% never married, 68.0% now married, 7.0% widowed, 9.2% divorced (2000); Foreign born: 0.0% (2000); Ancestry (includes multiple ancestries): 23.4% German, 21.1% Irish, 19.5% United States or American, 17.1% English, 11.5% Other groups (2000).
Economy: Employment by occupation: 25.5% management, 23.5% professional, 9.6% services, 30.2% sales, 0.0% farming, 3.6% construction, 7.6% production (2000).
Income: Per capita income: $32,928 (2010); Median household income: $75,000 (2010); Average household income: $89,926 (2010); Percent of households with income of $100,000 or more: 34.8% (2010); Poverty rate: 0.0% (2000).
Taxes: Total city taxes per capita: $410 (2007); City property taxes per capita: $350 (2007).
Education: Percent of population age 25 and over with: High school diploma (including GED) or higher: 90.7% (2010); Bachelor's degree or higher: 35.9% (2010); Master's degree or higher: 17.9% (2010).

School District(s)
Geist Montessori Academy (01-08)
    2008-09 Enrollment: 103 . . . . (317) 335-1158

Mt Vernon Community Sch Corp (PK-12)
    2008-09 Enrollment: 3,632 . . . . (317) 485-3100
Housing: Homeownership rate: 90.0% (2010); Median home value: $160,377 (2010); Median contract rent: $416 per month (2000); Median year structure built: 1974 (2000).
Transportation: Commute to work: 92.8% car, 0.0% public transportation, 0.8% walk, 6.4% work from home (2000); Travel time to work: 19.8% less than 15 minutes, 37.1% 15 to 30 minutes, 32.7% 30 to 45 minutes, 6.0% 45 to 60 minutes, 4.4% 60 minutes or more (2000)

NEW PALESTINE (town). Covers a land area of 0.750 square miles and a water area of 0 square miles. Located at 39.72° N. Lat; 85.89° W. Long. Elevation is 837 feet.

History: Laid out 1838.
Population: 997 (1990); 1,264 (2000); 1,705 (2010); 1,894 (2015 projected); Race: 96.9% White, 1.6% Black, 0.4% Asian, 1.1% Other, 0.4% Hispanic of any race (2010); Density: 2,273.8 persons per square mile (2010); Average household size: 2.64 (2010); Median age: 38.1 (2010); Males per 100 females: 96.0 (2010); Marriage status: 16.4% never married, 71.0% now married, 5.9% widowed, 6.7% divorced (2000); Foreign born: 0.5% (2000); Ancestry (includes multiple ancestries): 25.4% German, 22.9% United States or American, 12.2% Irish, 11.6% English, 4.1% Other groups (2000).
Economy: Single-family building permits issued: 5 (2009); Multi-family building permits issued: 0 (2009); Employment by occupation: 18.6% management, 14.6% professional, 13.0% services, 25.3% sales, 0.0% farming, 13.0% construction, 15.5% production (2000).
Income: Per capita income: $29,556 (2010); Median household income: $62,621 (2010); Average household income: $77,887 (2010); Percent of households with income of $100,000 or more: 25.7% (2010); Poverty rate: 2.6% (2000).
Taxes: Total city taxes per capita: $147 (2007); City property taxes per capita: $124 (2007).
Education: Percent of population age 25 and over with: High school diploma (including GED) or higher: 93.1% (2010); Bachelor's degree or higher: 20.9% (2010); Master's degree or higher: 8.0% (2010).
School District(s)
Southern Hancock Co Com Sch Corp (PK-12)
    2008-09 Enrollment: 3,365 . . . . (317) 861-4463
Housing: Homeownership rate: 87.6% (2010); Median home value: $156,000 (2010); Median contract rent: $440 per month (2000); Median year structure built: 1966 (2000).
Newspapers: New Palestine Press (Community news; Circulation 25,000)
Transportation: Commute to work: 94.8% car, 0.0% public transportation, 2.1% walk, 3.1% work from home (2000); Travel time to work: 18.9% less than 15 minutes, 35.5% 15 to 30 minutes, 28.2% 30 to 45 minutes, 10.9% 45 to 60 minutes, 6.5% 60 minutes or more (2000)

SHIRLEY (town). Covers a land area of 0.370 square miles and a water area of 0 square miles. Located at 39.89° N. Lat; 85.58° W. Long. Elevation is 1,027 feet.

Population: 817 (1990); 806 (2000); 900 (2010); 954 (2015 projected); Race: 98.7% White, 0.0% Black, 0.6% Asian, 0.8% Other, 0.1% Hispanic of any race (2010); Density: 2,432.1 persons per square mile (2010); Average household size: 2.60 (2010); Median age: 34.2 (2010); Males per 100 females: 97.4 (2010); Marriage status: 22.2% never married, 62.7% now married, 8.7% widowed, 6.5% divorced (2000); Foreign born: 0.4% (2000); Ancestry (includes multiple ancestries): 19.2% German, 11.4% United States or American, 8.2% English, 7.5% Irish, 5.9% Other groups (2000).
Economy: Employment by occupation: 3.2% management, 8.8% professional, 16.0% services, 21.3% sales, 0.0% farming, 21.0% construction, 29.8% production (2000).
Income: Per capita income: $19,950 (2010); Median household income: $43,898 (2010); Average household income: $50,947 (2010); Percent of households with income of $100,000 or more: 8.7% (2010); Poverty rate: 6.3% (2000).
Taxes: Total city taxes per capita: $283 (2007); City property taxes per capita: $206 (2007).
Education: Percent of population age 25 and over with: High school diploma (including GED) or higher: 84.4% (2010); Bachelor's degree or higher: 11.2% (2010); Master's degree or higher: 4.2% (2010).
Housing: Homeownership rate: 82.7% (2010); Median home value: $104,583 (2010); Median contract rent: $296 per month (2000); Median year structure built: before 1940 (2000).

Transportation: Commute to work: 92.9% car, 0.0% public transportation, 0.8% walk, 3.2% work from home (2000); Travel time to work: 22.1% less than 15 minutes, 37.7% 15 to 30 minutes, 13.9% 30 to 45 minutes, 17.5% 45 to 60 minutes, 8.7% 60 minutes or more (2000)

SPRING LAKE (town). Covers a land area of 0.154 square miles and a water area of 0.007 square miles. Located at 39.77° N. Lat; 85.85° W. Long. Elevation is 850 feet.

History: Settled 1884, laid out 1912.
Population: 216 (1990); 262 (2000); 293 (2010); 310 (2015 projected); Race: 96.9% White, 2.4% Black, 0.0% Asian, 0.7% Other, 2.0% Hispanic of any race (2010); Density: 1,898.0 persons per square mile (2010); Average household size: 2.59 (2010); Median age: 39.8 (2010); Males per 100 females: 102.1 (2010); Marriage status: 8.7% never married, 79.5% now married, 3.5% widowed, 8.3% divorced (2000); Foreign born: 0.8% (2000); Ancestry (includes multiple ancestries): 17.5% United States or American, 17.1% German, 9.1% Other groups, 7.6% English, 6.8% Irish (2000).
Economy: Employment by occupation: 10.5% management, 26.1% professional, 11.8% services, 21.6% sales, 0.0% farming, 13.1% construction, 17.0% production (2000).
Income: Per capita income: $34,072 (2010); Median household income: $81,250 (2010); Average household income: $89,115 (2010); Percent of households with income of $100,000 or more: 38.1% (2010); Poverty rate: 2.7% (2000).
Taxes: Total city taxes per capita: $87 (2007); City property taxes per capita: $51 (2007).
Education: Percent of population age 25 and over with: High school diploma (including GED) or higher: 89.4% (2010); Bachelor's degree or higher: 18.8% (2010); Master's degree or higher: 4.3% (2010).
Housing: Homeownership rate: 80.5% (2010); Median home value: $183,929 (2010); Median contract rent: $600 per month (2000); Median year structure built: 1955 (2000).
Transportation: Commute to work: 98.0% car, 0.0% public transportation, 0.0% walk, 2.0% work from home (2000); Travel time to work: 22.3% less than 15 minutes, 45.3% 15 to 30 minutes, 16.9% 30 to 45 minutes, 12.8% 45 to 60 minutes, 2.7% 60 minutes or more (2000)

WILKINSON (town). Covers a land area of 0.216 square miles and a water area of 0 square miles. Located at 39.88° N. Lat; 85.60° W. Long. Elevation is 1,001 feet.

History: Laid out 1883.
Population: 469 (1990); 356 (2000); 430 (2010); 470 (2015 projected); Race: 98.6% White, 0.0% Black, 0.0% Asian, 1.4% Other, 0.5% Hispanic of any race (2010); Density: 1,994.9 persons per square mile (2010); Average household size: 2.42 (2010); Median age: 37.4 (2010); Males per 100 females: 103.8 (2010); Marriage status: 14.0% never married, 66.1% now married, 8.4% widowed, 11.5% divorced (2000); Foreign born: 0.7% (2000); Ancestry (includes multiple ancestries): 20.7% United States or American, 14.8% German, 10.6% Irish, 9.1% English, 3.7% Dutch (2000).
Economy: Single-family building permits issued: 0 (2009); Multi-family building permits issued: 0 (2009); Employment by occupation: 4.0% management, 12.6% professional, 16.7% services, 33.8% sales, 0.0% farming, 13.6% construction, 19.2% production (2000).
Income: Per capita income: $24,239 (2010); Median household income: $55,102 (2010); Average household income: $58,680 (2010); Percent of households with income of $100,000 or more: 15.7% (2010); Poverty rate: 2.5% (2000).
Taxes: Total city taxes per capita: $232 (2007); City property taxes per capita: $159 (2007).
Education: Percent of population age 25 and over with: High school diploma (including GED) or higher: 86.3% (2010); Bachelor's degree or higher: 6.7% (2010); Master's degree or higher: 1.3% (2010).
Housing: Homeownership rate: 80.9% (2010); Median home value: $118,939 (2010); Median contract rent: $385 per month (2000); Median year structure built: 1945 (2000).
Transportation: Commute to work: 93.4% car, 0.0% public transportation, 2.5% walk, 0.0% work from home (2000); Travel time to work: 12.6% less than 15 minutes, 33.8% 15 to 30 minutes, 33.8% 30 to 45 minutes, 11.1% 45 to 60 minutes, 8.6% 60 minutes or more (2000)

Harrison County

Located in southern Indiana; bounded on the east, south, and southwest by the Ohio River and the Kentucky border, and on the west by the Blue River.

Covers a land area of 485.22 square miles, a water area of 1.66 square miles, and is located in the Eastern Time Zone. The county was founded in 1808. County seat is Corydon.

Harrison County is part of the Louisville/Jefferson County, KY-IN Metropolitan Statistical Area. The entire metro area includes: Clark County, IN; Floyd County, IN; Harrison County, IN; Washington County, IN; Bullitt County, KY; Henry County, KY; Jefferson County, KY; Meade County, KY; Nelson County, KY; Oldham County, KY; Shelby County, KY; Spencer County, KY; Trimble County, KY

Population: 29,890 (1990); 34,325 (2000); 37,465 (2010); 38,676 (2015 projected); Race: 97.4% White, 1.0% Black, 0.3% Asian, 1.3% Other, 1.6% Hispanic of any race (2010); Density: 77.2 persons per square mile (2010); Average household size: 2.54 (2010); Median age: 38.8 (2010); Males per 100 females: 98.8 (2010).
Religion: Five largest groups: 18.5% Catholic Church, 12.1% The United Methodist Church, 4.8% Christian Church (Disciples of Christ), 4.1% Southern Baptist Convention, 2.8% Christian Churches and Churches of Christ (2000).
Economy: Unemployment rate: 8.5% (5/2010); Total civilian labor force: 18,850 (5/2010); Leading industries: 17.8% manufacturing; 15.1% retail trade; 14.1% health care and social assistance (2008); Farms: 1,125 totaling 154,998 acres (2007); Companies that employ 500 or more persons: 1 (2008); Companies that employ 100 to 499 persons: 9 (2008); Companies that employ less than 100 persons: 685 (2008); Black-owned businesses: n/a (2002); Hispanic-owned businesses: n/a (2002); Asian-owned businesses: n/a (2002); Women-owned businesses: 1,330 (2002); Retail sales per capita: $11,035 (2010). Single-family building permits issued: 82 (2009); Multi-family building permits issued: 0 (2009).
Income: Per capita income: $24,445 (2010); Median household income: $52,793 (2010); Average household income: $62,248 (2010); Percent of households with income of $100,000 or more: 14.0% (2010); Poverty rate: 9.7% (2008); Bankruptcy rate: 7.87% (2009).
Taxes: Total county taxes per capita: $287 (2007); County property taxes per capita: $131 (2007).
Education: Percent of population age 25 and over with: High school diploma (including GED) or higher: 87.3% (2010); Bachelor's degree or higher: 13.9% (2010); Master's degree or higher: 4.2% (2010).
Housing: Homeownership rate: 85.9% (2010); Median home value: $121,179 (2010); Median contract rent: $496 per month (2006-2008 3-year est.); Median year structure built: 1978 (2006-2008 3-year est.)
Health: Birth rate: 123.5 per 10,000 population (2009); Death rate: 93.7 per 10,000 population (2009); Age-adjusted cancer mortality rate: 196.7 deaths per 100,000 population (2006); Number of physicians: 6.5 per 10,000 population (2007); Hospital beds: 6.8 per 10,000 population (2006); Hospital admissions: 442.6 per 10,000 population (2006).
Elections: 2008 Presidential election results: 40.3% Obama, 58.3% McCain, 0.1% Nader
Additional Information Contacts
Harrison County Government . . . . (812) 738-8241
   http://www.harrisoncounty.in.gov
Chamber of Commerce of Harrison County. . . . . (812) 738-2137
   http://www.harrisonchamber.org

Harrison County Communities

CORYDON (town). County seat. Covers a land area of 1.590 square miles and a water area of 0 square miles. Located at 38.21° N. Lat; 86.12° W. Long. Elevation is 587 feet.
History: Corydon was named by General William Henry Harrison, who owned the land on which the town was platted. Harrison chose the name for the young shepherd in the song "Pastoral Elegy," a favorite of the day. Corydon served as the capital of Indiana for a time, and was the site of the only Civil War battle fought in Indiana. The Battle of Corydon occurred in 1863, when General John Hunt Morgan and his Confederate troops crossed the Ohio River and invaded the town.
Population: 2,733 (1990); 2,715 (2000); 2,695 (2010); 2,736 (2015 projected); Race: 96.1% White, 1.9% Black, 0.2% Asian, 1.9% Other, 2.4% Hispanic of any race (2010); Density: 1,695.5 persons per square mile (2010); Average household size: 2.26 (2010); Median age: 42.3 (2010); Males per 100 females: 89.4 (2010); Marriage status: 20.7% never married, 55.9% now married, 12.2% widowed, 11.2% divorced (2000); Foreign born: 0.2% (2000); Ancestry (includes multiple ancestries): 20.7% German, 13.7% Irish, 13.2% United States or American, 9.0% English, 5.7% Other groups (2000).

Economy: Employment by occupation: 6.2% management, 12.6% professional, 19.6% services, 21.8% sales, 0.8% farming, 11.1% construction, 27.8% production (2000).
Income: Per capita income: $26,110 (2010); Median household income: $45,207 (2010); Average household income: $60,778 (2010); Percent of households with income of $100,000 or more: 14.5% (2010); Poverty rate: 10.3% (2000).
Taxes: Total city taxes per capita: $585 (2007); City property taxes per capita: $223 (2007).
Education: Percent of population age 25 and over with: High school diploma (including GED) or higher: 83.4% (2010); Bachelor's degree or higher: 21.2% (2010); Master's degree or higher: 8.9% (2010).
School District(s)
South Harrison Com Schools (PK-12)
   2008-09 Enrollment: 3,141 . . . . (812) 738-2168
Housing: Homeownership rate: 70.8% (2010); Median home value: $117,371 (2010); Median contract rent: $382 per month (2000); Median year structure built: 1952 (2000).
Hospitals: Harrison County Hospital (68 beds)
Safety: Violent crime rate: 0.0 per 10,000 population; Property crime rate: 141.6 per 10,000 population (2008).
Newspapers: Clarion News (Local news; Circulation 14,939); Corydon Democrat (Local news; Circulation 8,000)
Transportation: Commute to work: 97.3% car, 0.0% public transportation, 1.5% walk, 0.4% work from home (2000); Travel time to work: 47.2% less than 15 minutes, 19.6% 15 to 30 minutes, 25.5% 30 to 45 minutes, 1.7% 45 to 60 minutes, 6.0% 60 minutes or more (2000)
Additional Information Contacts
Chamber of Commerce of Harrison County. . . . . (812) 738-2137
   http://www.harrisonchamber.org

CRANDALL (town). Covers a land area of 0.103 square miles and a water area of 0 square miles. Located at 38.28° N. Lat; 86.06° W. Long. Elevation is 653 feet.
Population: 147 (1990); 131 (2000); 142 (2010); 145 (2015 projected); Race: 97.2% White, 1.4% Black, 0.7% Asian, 0.7% Other, 1.4% Hispanic of any race (2010); Density: 1,383.8 persons per square mile (2010); Average household size: 2.63 (2010); Median age: 40.0 (2010); Males per 100 females: 102.9 (2010); Marriage status: 21.5% never married, 45.9% now married, 8.9% widowed, 23.7% divorced (2000); Foreign born: 0.0% (2000); Ancestry (includes multiple ancestries): 24.2% United States or American, 14.6% Irish, 14.0% English, 12.7% Other groups, 12.1% German (2000).
Economy: Employment by occupation: 9.9% management, 9.9% professional, 12.7% services, 9.9% sales, 0.0% farming, 11.3% construction, 46.5% production (2000).
Income: Per capita income: $27,414 (2010); Median household income: $61,667 (2010); Average household income: $68,704 (2010); Percent of households with income of $100,000 or more: 20.4% (2010); Poverty rate: 9.6% (2000).
Taxes: Total city taxes per capita: $22 (2007); City property taxes per capita: $15 (2007).
Education: Percent of population age 25 and over with: High school diploma (including GED) or higher: 91.8% (2010); Bachelor's degree or higher: 15.5% (2010); Master's degree or higher: 3.1% (2010).
Housing: Homeownership rate: 92.6% (2010); Median home value: $120,833 (2010); Median contract rent: $325 per month (2000); Median year structure built: before 1940 (2000).
Transportation: Commute to work: 100.0% car, 0.0% public transportation, 0.0% walk, 0.0% work from home (2000); Travel time to work: 15.9% less than 15 minutes, 42.0% 15 to 30 minutes, 20.3% 30 to 45 minutes, 13.0% 45 to 60 minutes, 8.7% 60 minutes or more (2000)

DEPAUW (unincorporated postal area, zip code 47115). Covers a land area of 52.186 square miles and a water area of 0 square miles. Located at 38.35° N. Lat; 86.22° W. Long. Elevation is 650 feet.
Population: 2,351 (2000); Race: 98.8% White, 0.0% Black, 0.0% Asian, 1.2% Other, 0.0% Hispanic of any race (2000); Density: 45.1 persons per square mile (2000); Age: 25.1% under 18, 17.0% over 64 (2000); Marriage status: 20.3% never married, 61.5% now married, 8.9% widowed, 9.3% divorced (2000); Foreign born: 0.0% (2000); Ancestry (includes multiple ancestries): 19.7% German, 13.5% United States or American, 8.7% French (except Basque), 8.7% Irish, 8.2% English (2000).

Economy: Employment by occupation: 11.9% management, 16.4% professional, 10.1% services, 22.6% sales, 2.2% farming, 13.8% construction, 22.9% production (2000).
Income: Per capita income: $19,944 (2000); Median household income: $38,597 (2000); Poverty rate: 9.2% (2000).
Education: Percent of population age 25 and over with: High school diploma (including GED) or higher: 78.2% (2000); Bachelor's degree or higher: 12.2% (2000).
Housing: Homeownership rate: 86.9% (2000); Median home value: $79,000 (2000); Median contract rent: $234 per month (2000); Median year structure built: 1974 (2000).
Transportation: Commute to work: 88.7% car, 0.0% public transportation, 1.4% walk, 7.8% work from home (2000); Travel time to work: 26.6% less than 15 minutes, 18.0% 15 to 30 minutes, 25.2% 30 to 45 minutes, 19.1% 45 to 60 minutes, 11.1% 60 minutes or more (2000)

ELIZABETH (town). Covers a land area of 0.137 square miles and a water area of 0 square miles. Located at 38.12° N. Lat; 85.97° W. Long. Elevation is 728 feet.
Population: 124 (1990); 137 (2000); 150 (2010); 156 (2015 projected); Race: 98.7% White, 0.0% Black, 0.0% Asian, 1.3% Other, 0.7% Hispanic of any race (2010); Density: 1,091.8 persons per square mile (2010); Average household size: 2.63 (2010); Median age: 37.9 (2010); Males per 100 females: 108.3 (2010); Marriage status: 16.0% never married, 60.4% now married, 13.2% widowed, 10.4% divorced (2000); Foreign born: 0.0% (2000); Ancestry (includes multiple ancestries): 43.1% United States or American, 19.0% German, 10.9% English, 5.8% Irish, 5.8% Other groups (2000).
Economy: Employment by occupation: 6.7% management, 16.7% professional, 23.3% services, 25.0% sales, 0.0% farming, 1.7% construction, 26.7% production (2000).
Income: Per capita income: $20,339 (2010); Median household income: $45,625 (2010); Average household income: $52,632 (2010); Percent of households with income of $100,000 or more: 7.0% (2010); Poverty rate: 10.2% (2000).
Taxes: Total city taxes per capita: $14 (2007); City property taxes per capita: $7 (2007).
Education: Percent of population age 25 and over with: High school diploma (including GED) or higher: 82.4% (2010); Bachelor's degree or higher: 5.9% (2010); Master's degree or higher: 1.0% (2010).

School District(s)

South Harrison Com Schools (PK-12)
    2008-09 Enrollment: 3,141 . . . . (812) 738-2168
Housing: Homeownership rate: 91.2% (2010); Median home value: $123,077 (2010); Median contract rent: $446 per month (2000); Median year structure built: 1942 (2000).
Transportation: Commute to work: 100.0% car, 0.0% public transportation, 0.0% walk, 0.0% work from home (2000); Travel time to work: 35.0% less than 15 minutes, 3.3% 15 to 30 minutes, 31.7% 30 to 45 minutes, 23.3% 45 to 60 minutes, 6.7% 60 minutes or more (2000)

LACONIA (town). Covers a land area of 0.050 square miles and a water area of 0 square miles. Located at 38.03° N. Lat; 86.08° W. Long. Elevation is 663 feet.
History: Laid out 1816.
Population: 75 (1990); 29 (2000); 59 (2010); 63 (2015 projected); Race: 98.3% White, 0.0% Black, 1.7% Asian, 0.0% Other, 0.0% Hispanic of any race (2010); Density: 1,186.6 persons per square mile (2010); Average household size: 2.57 (2010); Median age: 34.4 (2010); Males per 100 females: 110.7 (2010); Marriage status: 0.0% never married, 23.1% now married, 53.8% widowed, 23.1% divorced (2000); Foreign born: 0.0% (2000); Ancestry (includes multiple ancestries): 50.0% German, 50.0% English, 20.8% United States or American, 16.7% Irish, 8.3% Other groups (2000).
Economy: Employment by occupation: 0.0% management, 0.0% professional, 100.0% services, 0.0% sales, 0.0% farming, 0.0% construction, 0.0% production (2000).
Income: Per capita income: $21,165 (2010); Median household income: $47,500 (2010); Average household income: $50,543 (2010); Percent of households with income of $100,000 or more: 8.7% (2010); Poverty rate: 50.0% (2000).
Taxes: Total city taxes per capita: $0 (2007); City property taxes per capita: $0 (2007).

Education: Percent of population age 25 and over with: High school diploma (including GED) or higher: 86.5% (2010); Bachelor's degree or higher: 13.5% (2010); Master's degree or higher: 5.4% (2010).
Housing: Homeownership rate: 91.3% (2010); Median home value: $112,500 (2010); Median contract rent: $375 per month (2000); Median year structure built: 1962 (2000).
Transportation: Commute to work: 100.0% car, 0.0% public transportation, 0.0% walk, 0.0% work from home (2000); Travel time to work: 0.0% less than 15 minutes, 0.0% 15 to 30 minutes, 0.0% 30 to 45 minutes, 0.0% 45 to 60 minutes, 100.0% 60 minutes or more (2000)

LANESVILLE (town). Covers a land area of 0.402 square miles and a water area of 0 square miles. Located at 38.23° N. Lat; 85.98° W. Long. Elevation is 699 feet.
History: Lanesville was settled in 1792 as a stage stop and trading center for surrounding farms. It was platted in 1817, and named for General Lane, a surveyor who was an early resident.
Population: 598 (1990); 614 (2000); 632 (2010); 638 (2015 projected); Race: 97.5% White, 0.0% Black, 1.3% Asian, 1.3% Other, 0.2% Hispanic of any race (2010); Density: 1,572.2 persons per square mile (2010); Average household size: 2.51 (2010); Median age: 37.9 (2010); Males per 100 females: 93.9 (2010); Marriage status: 22.6% never married, 64.6% now married, 6.3% widowed, 6.5% divorced (2000); Foreign born: 1.6% (2000); Ancestry (includes multiple ancestries): 42.7% German, 18.2% Irish, 14.7% United States or American, 10.5% English, 6.3% Dutch (2000).
Economy: Employment by occupation: 10.2% management, 23.2% professional, 9.8% services, 29.8% sales, 0.0% farming, 8.9% construction, 18.1% production (2000).
Income: Per capita income: $27,839 (2010); Median household income: $61,184 (2010); Average household income: $69,153 (2010); Percent of households with income of $100,000 or more: 18.7% (2010); Poverty rate: 2.1% (2000).
Taxes: Total city taxes per capita: $54 (2007); City property taxes per capita: $30 (2007).
Education: Percent of population age 25 and over with: High school diploma (including GED) or higher: 92.5% (2010); Bachelor's degree or higher: 16.5% (2010); Master's degree or higher: 6.4% (2010).

School District(s)

Lanesville Community School Corp (KG-12)
    2008-09 Enrollment: 667 . . . . (812) 952-2555
Housing: Homeownership rate: 87.6% (2010); Median home value: $136,667 (2010); Median contract rent: $473 per month (2000); Median year structure built: 1968 (2000).
Transportation: Commute to work: 93.2% car, 0.0% public transportation, 1.0% walk, 4.8% work from home (2000); Travel time to work: 11.1% less than 15 minutes, 54.4% 15 to 30 minutes, 27.7% 30 to 45 minutes, 4.1% 45 to 60 minutes, 2.7% 60 minutes or more (2000)

MAUCKPORT (town). Covers a land area of 0.136 square miles and a water area of 0.016 square miles. Located at 38.02° N. Lat; 86.20° W. Long. Elevation is 440 feet.
Population: 95 (1990); 83 (2000); 105 (2010); 111 (2015 projected); Race: 97.1% White, 0.0% Black, 1.0% Asian, 1.9% Other, 1.0% Hispanic of any race (2010); Density: 772.7 persons per square mile (2010); Average household size: 2.50 (2010); Median age: 38.0 (2010); Males per 100 females: 90.9 (2010); Marriage status: 17.3% never married, 37.3% now married, 5.3% widowed, 40.0% divorced (2000); Foreign born: 0.0% (2000); Ancestry (includes multiple ancestries): 9.0% Irish, 9.0% German, 5.6% Other groups, 3.4% United States or American, 2.2% Dutch (2000).
Economy: Employment by occupation: 2.5% management, 5.0% professional, 37.5% services, 15.0% sales, 2.5% farming, 12.5% construction, 25.0% production (2000).
Income: Per capita income: $21,934 (2010); Median household income: $45,714 (2010); Average household income: $49,702 (2010); Percent of households with income of $100,000 or more: 2.4% (2010); Poverty rate: 18.0% (2000).
Taxes: Total city taxes per capita: $35 (2007); City property taxes per capita: $24 (2007).
Education: Percent of population age 25 and over with: High school diploma (including GED) or higher: 82.9% (2010); Bachelor's degree or higher: 10.0% (2010); Master's degree or higher: 7.1% (2010).
Housing: Homeownership rate: 90.5% (2010); Median home value: $95,000 (2010); Median contract rent: $257 per month (2000); Median year structure built: before 1940 (2000).

Transportation: Commute to work: 88.9% car, 0.0% public transportation, 0.0% walk, 2.8% work from home (2000); Travel time to work: 8.6% less than 15 minutes, 48.6% 15 to 30 minutes, 20.0% 30 to 45 minutes, 14.3% 45 to 60 minutes, 8.6% 60 minutes or more (2000)

NEW MIDDLETOWN (town). Covers a land area of 0.042 square miles and a water area of 0 square miles. Located at 38.16° N. Lat; 86.05° W. Long. Elevation is 702 feet.
Population: 66 (1990); 77 (2000); 87 (2010); 90 (2015 projected); Race: 95.4% White, 1.1% Black, 0.0% Asian, 3.4% Other, 1.1% Hispanic of any race (2010); Density: 2,072.1 persons per square mile (2010); Average household size: 2.72 (2010); Median age: 45.4 (2010); Males per 100 females: 148.6 (2010); Marriage status: 26.5% never married, 59.2% now married, 8.2% widowed, 6.1% divorced (2000); Foreign born: 7.8% (2000); Ancestry (includes multiple ancestries): 28.1% United States or American, 17.2% Irish, 17.2% Other groups, 10.9% German, 4.7% Canadian (2000).
Economy: Employment by occupation: 0.0% management, 0.0% professional, 11.8% services, 17.6% sales, 0.0% farming, 29.4% construction, 41.2% production (2000).
Income: Per capita income: $24,761 (2010); Median household income: $61,111 (2010); Average household income: $63,984 (2010); Percent of households with income of $100,000 or more: 15.6% (2010); Poverty rate: 6.3% (2000).
Taxes: Total city taxes per capita: $0 (2007); City property taxes per capita: $0 (2007).
Education: Percent of population age 25 and over with: High school diploma (including GED) or higher: 87.7% (2010); Bachelor's degree or higher: 12.3% (2010); Master's degree or higher: 1.5% (2010).
School District(s)
South Harrison Com Schools (PK-12)
    2008-09 Enrollment: 3,141 . . . . (812) 738-2168
Housing: Homeownership rate: 90.6% (2010); Median home value: $115,625 (2010); Median contract rent: $425 per month (2000); Median year structure built: before 1940 (2000).
Transportation: Commute to work: 100.0% car, 0.0% public transportation, 0.0% walk, 0.0% work from home (2000); Travel time to work: 9.4% less than 15 minutes, 40.6% 15 to 30 minutes, 40.6% 30 to 45 minutes, 9.4% 45 to 60 minutes, 0.0% 60 minutes or more (2000)

NEW SALISBURY (unincorporated postal area, zip code 47161). Aka Corydon Junction. Covers a land area of 23.072 square miles and a water area of 0.021 square miles. Located at 38.31° N. Lat; 86.09° W. Long. Elevation is 728 feet.
History: Laid out 1830.
Population: 3,426 (2000); Race: 99.1% White, 0.0% Black, 0.5% Asian, 0.4% Other, 2.3% Hispanic of any race (2000); Density: 148.5 persons per square mile (2000); Age: 28.9% under 18, 6.1% over 64 (2000); Marriage status: 20.9% never married, 63.7% now married, 4.8% widowed, 10.6% divorced (2000); Foreign born: 2.3% (2000); Ancestry (includes multiple ancestries): 22.7% United States or American, 20.7% German, 11.5% Irish, 8.3% Other groups, 5.4% English (2000).
Economy: Employment by occupation: 11.8% management, 10.8% professional, 10.0% services, 26.2% sales, 0.3% farming, 15.8% construction, 25.1% production (2000).
Income: Per capita income: $19,170 (2000); Median household income: $47,804 (2000); Poverty rate: 9.4% (2000).
Education: Percent of population age 25 and over with: High school diploma (including GED) or higher: 83.6% (2000); Bachelor's degree or higher: 9.4% (2000).
Housing: Homeownership rate: 86.9% (2000); Median home value: $95,300 (2000); Median contract rent: $363 per month (2000); Median year structure built: 1978 (2000).
Transportation: Commute to work: 94.8% car, 0.0% public transportation, 2.0% walk, 3.2% work from home (2000); Travel time to work: 20.3% less than 15 minutes, 28.0% 15 to 30 minutes, 29.0% 30 to 45 minutes, 17.6% 45 to 60 minutes, 5.2% 60 minutes or more (2000)

PALMYRA (town). Covers a land area of 0.928 square miles and a water area of 0.058 square miles. Located at 38.40° N. Lat; 86.11° W. Long. Elevation is 771 feet.
History: Palmyra was founded in 1810 as a farming village.
Population: 650 (1990); 633 (2000); 662 (2010); 673 (2015 projected); Race: 99.1% White, 0.0% Black, 0.2% Asian, 0.8% Other, 0.9% Hispanic of any race (2010); Density: 713.7 persons per square mile (2010); Average household size: 2.51 (2010); Median age: 37.8 (2010); Males per

100 females: 94.1 (2010); Marriage status: 25.3% never married, 56.1% now married, 9.0% widowed, 9.6% divorced (2000); Foreign born: 0.2% (2000); Ancestry (includes multiple ancestries): 32.2% German, 20.3% United States or American, 13.8% English, 8.8% Irish, 6.6% Other groups (2000).
Economy: Employment by occupation: 7.2% management, 13.1% professional, 15.5% services, 30.6% sales, 0.0% farming, 15.1% construction, 18.6% production (2000).
Income: Per capita income: $22,488 (2010); Median household income: $48,953 (2010); Average household income: $56,904 (2010); Percent of households with income of $100,000 or more: 11.9% (2010); Poverty rate: 7.8% (2000).
Taxes: Total city taxes per capita: $63 (2007); City property taxes per capita: $24 (2007).
Education: Percent of population age 25 and over with: High school diploma (including GED) or higher: 82.9% (2010); Bachelor's degree or higher: 10.8% (2010); Master's degree or higher: 1.5% (2010).
School District(s)
North Harrison Com School Corp (KG-12)
    2008-09 Enrollment: 2,324 . . . . (812) 347-2407
Housing: Homeownership rate: 82.7% (2010); Median home value: $119,837 (2010); Median contract rent: $425 per month (2000); Median year structure built: 1965 (2000).
Transportation: Commute to work: 92.4% car, 0.0% public transportation, 5.5% walk, 1.4% work from home (2000); Travel time to work: 15.7% less than 15 minutes, 31.4% 15 to 30 minutes, 36.6% 30 to 45 minutes, 12.2% 45 to 60 minutes, 4.2% 60 minutes or more (2000)

RAMSEY (unincorporated postal area, zip code 47166). Covers a land area of 14.357 square miles and a water area of 0 square miles. Located at 38.31° N. Lat; 86.16° W. Long. Elevation is 705 feet.
Population: 1,245 (2000); Race: 99.6% White, 0.0% Black, 0.0% Asian, 0.4% Other, 0.0% Hispanic of any race (2000); Density: 86.7 persons per square mile (2000); Age: 24.9% under 18, 6.2% over 64 (2000); Marriage status: 18.2% never married, 61.3% now married, 6.3% widowed, 14.2% divorced (2000); Foreign born: 1.1% (2000); Ancestry (includes multiple ancestries): 21.7% German, 14.6% United States or American, 14.5% Irish, 6.9% Other groups, 4.0% French (except Basque) (2000).
Economy: Employment by occupation: 11.2% management, 10.7% professional, 13.7% services, 21.9% sales, 1.0% farming, 11.6% construction, 29.9% production (2000).
Income: Per capita income: $17,202 (2000); Median household income: $49,896 (2000); Poverty rate: 4.6% (2000).
Education: Percent of population age 25 and over with: High school diploma (including GED) or higher: 82.2% (2000); Bachelor's degree or higher: 16.6% (2000).
School District(s)
North Harrison Com School Corp (KG-12)
    2008-09 Enrollment: 2,324 . . . . (812) 347-2407
Housing: Homeownership rate: 87.0% (2000); Median home value: $87,500 (2000); Median contract rent: $423 per month (2000); Median year structure built: 1979 (2000).
Transportation: Commute to work: 95.3% car, 0.0% public transportation, 1.8% walk, 2.9% work from home (2000); Travel time to work: 20.6% less than 15 minutes, 27.1% 15 to 30 minutes, 23.9% 30 to 45 minutes, 18.4% 45 to 60 minutes, 10.1% 60 minutes or more (2000)

Hendricks County

Located in central Indiana; drained by the Eel and Whitelick Rivers and Mill Creek. Covers a land area of 408.39 square miles, a water area of 0.48 square miles, and is located in the Eastern Time Zone. The county was founded in 1823. County seat is Danville.

Hendricks County is part of the Indianapolis-Carmel, IN Metropolitan Statistical Area. The entire metro area includes: Boone County, IN; Brown County, IN; Hamilton County, IN; Hancock County, IN; Hendricks County, IN; Johnson County, IN; Marion County, IN; Morgan County, IN; Putnam County, IN; Shelby County, IN

Population: 75,717 (1990); 104,093 (2000); 142,372 (2010); 159,268 (2015 projected); Race: 91.0% White, 5.0% Black, 1.7% Asian, 2.3% Other, 2.5% Hispanic of any race (2010); Density: 348.6 persons per square mile (2010); Average household size: 2.62 (2010); Median age: 35.4 (2010); Males per 100 females: 100.2 (2010).

Religion: Five largest groups: 11.9% Catholic Church, 9.4% Christian Churches and Churches of Christ, 4.6% The United Methodist Church, 3.7% General Association of Regular Baptist Churches, 2.2% New Testament Association of Independent Baptist Chur

Economy: Unemployment rate: 7.9% (5/2010); Total civilian labor force: 71,430 (5/2010); Leading industries: 18.0% retail trade; 12.2% accommodation & food services; 11.9% transportation & warehousing (2008); Farms: 714 totaling 171,741 acres (2007); Companies that employ 500 or more persons: 8 (2008); Companies that employ 100 to 499 persons: 66 (2008); Companies that employ less than 100 persons: 2,808 (2008); Black-owned businesses: n/a (2002); Hispanic-owned businesses: n/a (2002); Asian-owned businesses: n/a (2002); Women-owned businesses: 2,565 (2002); Retail sales per capita: $12,514 (2010). Single-family building permits issued: 617 (2009); Multi-family building permits issued: 128 (2009).

Income: Per capita income: $28,798 (2010); Median household income: $65,860 (2010); Average household income: $76,396 (2010); Percent of households with income of $100,000 or more: 24.3% (2010); Poverty rate: 5.2% (2008); Bankruptcy rate: 7.11% (2009).

Taxes: Total county taxes per capita: $251 (2007); County property taxes per capita: $90 (2007).

Education: Percent of population age 25 and over with: High school diploma (including GED) or higher: 94.4% (2010); Bachelor's degree or higher: 32.4% (2010); Master's degree or higher: 9.8% (2010).

Housing: Homeownership rate: 81.1% (2010); Median home value: $151,455 (2010); Median contract rent: $718 per month (2006-2008 3-year est.); Median year structure built: 1992 (2006-2008 3-year est.)

Health: Birth rate: 128.3 per 10,000 population (2009); Death rate: 61.3 per 10,000 population (2009); Age-adjusted cancer mortality rate: 170.9 deaths per 100,000 population (2006); Air Quality Index: 90.5% good, 9.5% moderate, 0.0% unhealthy for sensitive individuals, 0.0% unhealthy (percent of days in 2008); Number of physicians: 11.6 per 10,000 population (2007); Hospital beds: 10.8 per 10,000 population (2006); Hospital admissions: 492.5 per 10,000 population (2006).

Elections: 2008 Presidential election results: 37.7% Obama, 61.1% McCain, 0.0% Nader

Additional Information Contacts

Hendricks County Government . . . . (317) 745-9221
   http://www.co.hendricks.in.us
Brownsburg Chamber of Commerce . . . . (317) 852-7885
   http://www.brownsburg.com
Greater Avon Chamber of Commerce . . . . (317) 272-4333
   http://www.avonchamber.org
Plainfield Chamber of Commerce . . . . (317) 839-3800
   http://www.plainfield-in.com
Town of Avon . . . . (317) 272-0948
   http://www.avongov.org
Town of Brownsburg . . . . (317) 852-1120
   http://www.brownsburg.org
Town of Danville . . . . (317) 745-4180
   http://www.danvilleindiana.org
Town of Plainfield. . . . . (317) 839-2561
   http://www.townofplainfield.com

Hendricks County Communities

AMO (town). Covers a land area of 0.610 square miles and a water area of 0 square miles. Located at 39.68° N. Lat; 86.61° W. Long. Elevation is 823 feet.

Population: 475 (1990); 414 (2000); 587 (2010); 666 (2015 projected); Race: 98.8% White, 0.3% Black, 0.2% Asian, 0.7% Other, 0.5% Hispanic of any race (2010); Density: 962.9 persons per square mile (2010); Average household size: 2.68 (2010); Median age: 35.1 (2010); Males per 100 females: 95.7 (2010); Marriage status: 20.6% never married, 55.7% now married, 9.8% widowed, 13.9% divorced (2000); Foreign born: 0.0% (2000); Ancestry (includes multiple ancestries): 40.6% United States or American, 14.6% German, 8.2% English, 6.2% Irish, 3.5% Other groups (2000).

Economy: Employment by occupation: 9.8% management, 13.0% professional, 17.1% services, 31.1% sales, 0.0% farming, 13.0% construction, 16.1% production (2000).

Income: Per capita income: $25,974 (2010); Median household income: $67,813 (2010); Average household income: $70,263 (2010); Percent of households with income of $100,000 or more: 22.4% (2010); Poverty rate: 6.7% (2000).

Taxes: Total city taxes per capita: $26 (2007); City property taxes per capita: $0 (2007).

Education: Percent of population age 25 and over with: High school diploma (including GED) or higher: 92.7% (2010); Bachelor's degree or higher: 15.2% (2010); Master's degree or higher: 3.1% (2010).

School District(s)

Mill Creek Community Sch Corp (PK-12)
   2008-09 Enrollment: 1,621 . . . . (317) 539-9200

Housing: Homeownership rate: 80.8% (2010); Median home value: $144,608 (2010); Median contract rent: $475 per month (2000); Median year structure built: 1945 (2000).

Transportation: Commute to work: 84.3% car, 0.0% public transportation, 6.8% walk, 8.4% work from home (2000); Travel time to work: 18.3% less than 15 minutes, 28.0% 15 to 30 minutes, 20.0% 30 to 45 minutes, 20.0% 45 to 60 minutes, 13.7% 60 minutes or more (2000)

AVON (town). Covers a land area of 6.381 square miles and a water area of 0.012 square miles. Located at 39.76° N. Lat; 86.38° W. Long. Elevation is 833 feet.

History: Avon was incorporated in 1995. Previous town names included Hampton, White Lick, Smootsdale and New Philadelphia. The name Avon was placed on a sign by the railroad company.

Population: 2,450 (1990); 6,248 (2000); 7,606 (2010); 8,618 (2015 projected); Race: 91.2% White, 2.7% Black, 3.0% Asian, 3.1% Other, 3.0% Hispanic of any race (2010); Density: 1,192.0 persons per square mile (2010); Average household size: 2.84 (2010); Median age: 34.4 (2010); Males per 100 females: 99.3 (2010); Marriage status: 15.1% never married, 73.1% now married, 2.7% widowed, 9.0% divorced (2000); Foreign born: 3.6% (2000); Ancestry (includes multiple ancestries): 24.7% German, 13.1% Irish, 13.0% United States or American, 9.8% Other groups, 8.3% English (2000).

Economy: Single-family building permits issued: 159 (2009); Multi-family building permits issued: 0 (2009); Employment by occupation: 19.7% management, 15.6% professional, 10.5% services, 27.2% sales, 0.0% farming, 9.9% construction, 17.1% production (2000).

Income: Per capita income: $30,319 (2010); Median household income: $76,860 (2010); Average household income: $86,010 (2010); Percent of households with income of $100,000 or more: 29.4% (2010); Poverty rate: 2.9% (2000).

Taxes: Total city taxes per capita: $362 (2007); City property taxes per capita: $208 (2007).

Education: Percent of population age 25 and over with: High school diploma (including GED) or higher: 96.3% (2010); Bachelor's degree or higher: 37.6% (2010); Master's degree or higher: 11.0% (2010).

School District(s)

Avon Community School Corp (PK-12)
   2008-09 Enrollment: 8,380 . . . . (317) 272-2920

Housing: Homeownership rate: 92.3% (2010); Median home value: $164,626 (2010); Median contract rent: $701 per month (2000); Median year structure built: 1995 (2000).

Hospitals: Clarian West Medical Center

Newspapers: Hendricks County Flyer (Community news; Circulation 34,000); The Indianapolis Star - Metro West Bureau (Regional news; Circulation 20,000)

Transportation: Commute to work: 97.3% car, 0.3% public transportation, 0.0% walk, 2.1% work from home (2000); Travel time to work: 25.4% less than 15 minutes, 39.6% 15 to 30 minutes, 24.6% 30 to 45 minutes, 6.7% 45 to 60 minutes, 3.8% 60 minutes or more (2000)

Additional Information Contacts

Greater Avon Chamber of Commerce . . . . (317) 272-4333
   http://www.avonchamber.org
Town of Avon . . . . (317) 272-0948
   http://www.avongov.org

BROWNSBURG (town). Covers a land area of 7.320 square miles and a water area of 0 square miles. Located at 39.84° N. Lat; 86.39° W. Long. Elevation is 879 feet.

History: Brownsburg's first settler was James B. Brown, a Kentucky native, who settled in Brown Township in 1824. At the time the area was dense and unbroken wilderness with only hunters and trappers in the area.

Population: 10,095 (1990); 14,520 (2000); 17,700 (2010); 19,435 (2015 projected); Race: 94.4% White, 1.5% Black, 1.6% Asian, 2.5% Other, 2.8% Hispanic of any race (2010); Density: 2,417.9 persons per square mile (2010); Average household size: 2.58 (2010); Median age: 35.0 (2010); Males per 100 females: 95.2 (2010); Marriage status: 17.2% never married,

68.3% now married, 6.1% widowed, 8.4% divorced (2000); Foreign born: 1.9% (2000); Ancestry (includes multiple ancestries): 25.8% German, 17.9% United States or American, 13.4% Irish, 12.5% English, 8.1% Other groups (2000).
Economy: Single-family building permits issued: 124 (2009); Multi-family building permits issued: 0 (2009); Employment by occupation: 15.1% management, 26.7% professional, 7.4% services, 31.2% sales, 0.0% farming, 6.4% construction, 13.2% production (2000).
Income: Per capita income: $30,032 (2010); Median household income: $66,753 (2010); Average household income: $77,731 (2010); Percent of households with income of $100,000 or more: 25.3% (2010); Poverty rate: 2.3% (2000).
Taxes: Total city taxes per capita: $462 (2007); City property taxes per capita: $339 (2007).
Education: Percent of population age 25 and over with: High school diploma (including GED) or higher: 96.4% (2010); Bachelor's degree or higher: 41.7% (2010); Master's degree or higher: 11.6% (2010).
School District(s)
Brownsburg Community Sch Corp (PK-12)
    2008-09 Enrollment: 7,225 . . . . (317) 852-5726
Housing: Homeownership rate: 77.0% (2010); Median home value: $139,286 (2010); Median contract rent: $541 per month (2000); Median year structure built: 1987 (2000).
Safety: Violent crime rate: 13.9 per 10,000 population; Property crime rate: 166.5 per 10,000 population (2008).
Transportation: Commute to work: 95.1% car, 0.3% public transportation, 0.3% walk, 3.0% work from home (2000); Travel time to work: 21.2% less than 15 minutes, 37.4% 15 to 30 minutes, 30.0% 30 to 45 minutes, 7.1% 45 to 60 minutes, 4.3% 60 minutes or more (2000)
Additional Information Contacts
Brownsburg Chamber of Commerce . . . . (317) 852-7885
    http://www.brownsburg.com
Town of Brownsburg . . . . (317) 852-1120
    http://www.brownsburg.org

CLAYTON (town). Covers a land area of 0.497 square miles and a water area of 0 square miles. Located at 39.68° N. Lat; 86.52° W. Long. Elevation is 876 feet.
Population: 610 (1990); 693 (2000); 854 (2010); 945 (2015 projected); Race: 97.8% White, 0.4% Black, 0.0% Asian, 1.9% Other, 2.8% Hispanic of any race (2010); Density: 1,718.7 persons per square mile (2010); Average household size: 2.64 (2010); Median age: 35.0 (2010); Males per 100 females: 98.6 (2010); Marriage status: 16.4% never married, 64.2% now married, 6.2% widowed, 13.1% divorced (2000); Foreign born: 0.0% (2000); Ancestry (includes multiple ancestries): 26.7% United States or American, 14.9% Irish, 14.7% German, 8.4% English, 6.0% Other groups (2000).
Economy: Employment by occupation: 10.5% management, 13.0% professional, 13.6% services, 34.9% sales, 0.6% farming, 13.3% construction, 14.1% production (2000).
Income: Per capita income: $22,953 (2010); Median household income: $53,511 (2010); Average household income: $61,138 (2010); Percent of households with income of $100,000 or more: 10.5% (2010); Poverty rate: 4.9% (2000).
Taxes: Total city taxes per capita: $109 (2007); City property taxes per capita: $90 (2007).
Education: Percent of population age 25 and over with: High school diploma (including GED) or higher: 91.6% (2010); Bachelor's degree or higher: 8.6% (2010); Master's degree or higher: 1.4% (2010).
School District(s)
Mill Creek Community Sch Corp (PK-12)
    2008-09 Enrollment: 1,621 . . . . (317) 539-9200
Housing: Homeownership rate: 85.8% (2010); Median home value: $110,833 (2010); Median contract rent: $619 per month (2000); Median year structure built: before 1940 (2000).
Transportation: Commute to work: 96.1% car, 0.0% public transportation, 1.4% walk, 0.8% work from home (2000); Travel time to work: 13.5% less than 15 minutes, 30.7% 15 to 30 minutes, 32.1% 30 to 45 minutes, 14.6% 45 to 60 minutes, 9.0% 60 minutes or more (2000)

COATESVILLE (town). Covers a land area of 0.664 square miles and a water area of 0 square miles. Located at 39.68° N. Lat; 86.66° W. Long. Elevation is 883 feet.
Population: 504 (1990); 516 (2000); 708 (2010); 800 (2015 projected); Race: 96.8% White, 1.4% Black, 0.0% Asian, 1.8% Other, 0.6% Hispanic

of any race (2010); Density: 1,065.7 persons per square mile (2010); Average household size: 2.68 (2010); Median age: 32.8 (2010); Males per 100 females: 98.9 (2010); Marriage status: 19.2% never married, 61.9% now married, 7.7% widowed, 11.2% divorced (2000); Foreign born: 0.0% (2000); Ancestry (includes multiple ancestries): 18.1% German, 14.7% English, 12.1% United States or American, 10.4% Irish, 6.0% Other groups (2000).
Economy: Employment by occupation: 5.5% management, 10.6% professional, 12.3% services, 26.4% sales, 0.0% farming, 21.3% construction, 23.8% production (2000).
Income: Per capita income: $23,503 (2010); Median household income: $57,589 (2010); Average household income: $62,898 (2010); Percent of households with income of $100,000 or more: 13.3% (2010); Poverty rate: 4.2% (2000).
Taxes: Total city taxes per capita: $147 (2007); City property taxes per capita: $101 (2007).
Education: Percent of population age 25 and over with: High school diploma (including GED) or higher: 92.6% (2010); Bachelor's degree or higher: 18.3% (2010); Master's degree or higher: 2.0% (2010).
Housing: Homeownership rate: 82.6% (2010); Median home value: $141,667 (2010); Median contract rent: $414 per month (2000); Median year structure built: 1950 (2000).
Transportation: Commute to work: 95.3% car, 0.0% public transportation, 0.9% walk, 3.9% work from home (2000); Travel time to work: 12.5% less than 15 minutes, 26.3% 15 to 30 minutes, 23.2% 30 to 45 minutes, 17.4% 45 to 60 minutes, 20.5% 60 minutes or more (2000)

DANVILLE (town). County seat. Covers a land area of 6.126 square miles and a water area of 0.003 square miles. Located at 39.76° N. Lat; 86.51° W. Long. Elevation is 951 feet.
History: Danville was settled in 1824 by Daniel Clark, a justice of the peace, for whom the town was named. In 1878 citizens of Danville carried off the desks, bookcases, and books of Central Normal College at Ladoga, and re-established it in Danville.
Population: 4,837 (1990); 6,418 (2000); 9,045 (2010); 10,155 (2015 projected); Race: 95.6% White, 2.4% Black, 0.7% Asian, 1.3% Other, 2.2% Hispanic of any race (2010); Density: 1,476.6 persons per square mile (2010); Average household size: 2.54 (2010); Median age: 34.7 (2010); Males per 100 females: 98.9 (2010); Marriage status: 21.2% never married, 61.8% now married, 8.2% widowed, 8.8% divorced (2000); Foreign born: 1.6% (2000); Ancestry (includes multiple ancestries): 24.9% United States or American, 15.6% German, 15.2% Irish, 10.8% English, 6.5% Other groups (2000).
Economy: Single-family building permits issued: 14 (2009); Multi-family building permits issued: 80 (2009); Employment by occupation: 8.1% management, 18.7% professional, 13.1% services, 32.2% sales, 1.0% farming, 12.6% construction, 14.4% production (2000).
Income: Per capita income: $28,178 (2010); Median household income: $62,448 (2010); Average household income: $72,586 (2010); Percent of households with income of $100,000 or more: 21.4% (2010); Poverty rate: 2.5% (2000).
Taxes: Total city taxes per capita: $226 (2007); City property taxes per capita: $184 (2007).
Education: Percent of population age 25 and over with: High school diploma (including GED) or higher: 95.1% (2010); Bachelor's degree or higher: 28.8% (2010); Master's degree or higher: 11.1% (2010).
School District(s)
Danville Community School Corp (PK-12)
    2008-09 Enrollment: 2,612 . . . . (317) 745-2212
Housing: Homeownership rate: 71.9% (2010); Median home value: $145,167 (2010); Median contract rent: $467 per month (2000); Median year structure built: 1969 (2000).
Hospitals: Hendricks Regional Health (141 beds)
Safety: Violent crime rate: 8.5 per 10,000 population; Property crime rate: 142.2 per 10,000 population (2008).
Newspapers: Republican (Community news; Circulation 1,360)
Transportation: Commute to work: 93.8% car, 0.0% public transportation, 0.2% walk, 4.8% work from home (2000); Travel time to work: 33.2% less than 15 minutes, 26.9% 15 to 30 minutes, 25.9% 30 to 45 minutes, 10.7% 45 to 60 minutes, 3.3% 60 minutes or more (2000)
Additional Information Contacts
Town of Danville . . . . (317) 745-4180
    http://www.danvilleindiana.org

LIZTON (town). Covers a land area of 0.285 square miles and a water area of 0 square miles. Located at 39.88° N. Lat; 86.54° W. Long. Elevation is 955 feet.

History: The area in which Lizton was established in 1851 was swamp land, but a drainage system converted it into fertile farm land. James Whitcomb Riley wrote about Lizton in his poem, "The Lizton Humorist."

Population: 416 (1990); 372 (2000); 483 (2010); 541 (2015 projected); Race: 97.3% White, 0.6% Black, 0.0% Asian, 2.1% Other, 1.4% Hispanic of any race (2010); Density: 1,692.2 persons per square mile (2010); Average household size: 2.54 (2010); Median age: 35.7 (2010); Males per 100 females: 98.0 (2010); Marriage status: 19.6% never married, 55.6% now married, 5.9% widowed, 18.9% divorced (2000); Foreign born: 2.3% (2000); Ancestry (includes multiple ancestries): 18.7% United States or American, 17.9% German, 10.4% English, 6.5% Irish, 6.2% Italian (2000).

Economy: Single-family building permits issued: 0 (2009); Multi-family building permits issued: 0 (2009); Employment by occupation: 5.3% management, 14.3% professional, 15.9% services, 29.1% sales, 0.0% farming, 14.3% construction, 21.2% production (2000).

Income: Per capita income: $27,077 (2010); Median household income: $56,250 (2010); Average household income: $67,605 (2010); Percent of households with income of $100,000 or more: 16.3% (2010); Poverty rate: 3.1% (2000).

Taxes: Total city taxes per capita: $236 (2007); City property taxes per capita: $166 (2007).

Education: Percent of population age 25 and over with: High school diploma (including GED) or higher: 95.3% (2010); Bachelor's degree or higher: 23.0% (2010); Master's degree or higher: 4.1% (2010).

School District(s)
North West Hendricks Schools (KG-12)
    2008-09 Enrollment: 1,833 . . . . (317) 994-4100

Housing: Homeownership rate: 71.6% (2010); Median home value: $154,054 (2010); Median contract rent: $428 per month (2000); Median year structure built: 1942 (2000).

Transportation: Commute to work: 99.5% car, 0.0% public transportation, 0.0% walk, 0.5% work from home (2000); Travel time to work: 10.9% less than 15 minutes, 44.3% 15 to 30 minutes, 16.9% 30 to 45 minutes, 19.1% 45 to 60 minutes, 8.7% 60 minutes or more (2000)

NORTH SALEM (town). Covers a land area of 0.262 square miles and a water area of 0 square miles. Located at 39.85° N. Lat; 86.64° W. Long. Elevation is 892 feet.

History: Laid out 1835.

Population: 499 (1990); 591 (2000); 793 (2010); 895 (2015 projected); Race: 98.4% White, 0.0% Black, 1.1% Asian, 0.5% Other, 0.5% Hispanic of any race (2010); Density: 3,021.2 persons per square mile (2010); Average household size: 2.59 (2010); Median age: 33.2 (2010); Males per 100 females: 92.5 (2010); Marriage status: 20.3% never married, 56.3% now married, 6.8% widowed, 16.7% divorced (2000); Foreign born: 0.2% (2000); Ancestry (includes multiple ancestries): 22.7% German, 14.9% English, 14.3% Irish, 11.7% United States or American, 9.6% Other groups (2000).

Economy: Employment by occupation: 9.4% management, 14.6% professional, 12.0% services, 31.1% sales, 0.0% farming, 11.6% construction, 21.3% production (2000).

Income: Per capita income: $21,888 (2010); Median household income: $51,705 (2010); Average household income: $56,364 (2010); Percent of households with income of $100,000 or more: 10.8% (2010); Poverty rate: 9.1% (2000).

Taxes: Total city taxes per capita: $212 (2007); City property taxes per capita: $160 (2007).

Education: Percent of population age 25 and over with: High school diploma (including GED) or higher: 90.8% (2010); Bachelor's degree or higher: 16.7% (2010); Master's degree or higher: 5.8% (2010).

School District(s)
North West Hendricks Schools (KG-12)
    2008-09 Enrollment: 1,833 . . . . (317) 994-4100

Housing: Homeownership rate: 79.7% (2010); Median home value: $95,439 (2010); Median contract rent: $429 per month (2000); Median year structure built: before 1940 (2000).

Transportation: Commute to work: 92.2% car, 0.0% public transportation, 3.1% walk, 1.9% work from home (2000); Travel time to work: 21.7% less than 15 minutes, 23.3% 15 to 30 minutes, 26.9% 30 to 45 minutes, 15.4% 45 to 60 minutes, 12.6% 60 minutes or more (2000)

PITTSBORO (town). Covers a land area of 1.527 square miles and a water area of 0 square miles. Located at 39.86° N. Lat; 86.46° W. Long. Elevation is 938 feet.

Population: 1,045 (1990); 1,588 (2000); 2,413 (2010); 2,767 (2015 projected); Race: 96.7% White, 0.5% Black, 0.3% Asian, 2.4% Other, 1.7% Hispanic of any race (2010); Density: 1,580.3 persons per square mile (2010); Average household size: 2.58 (2010); Median age: 32.9 (2010); Males per 100 females: 94.1 (2010); Marriage status: 17.5% never married, 65.9% now married, 7.3% widowed, 9.2% divorced (2000); Foreign born: 0.2% (2000); Ancestry (includes multiple ancestries): 31.6% United States or American, 16.9% German, 9.3% Irish, 6.5% English, 4.1% Other groups (2000).

Economy: Single-family building permits issued: 6 (2009); Multi-family building permits issued: 0 (2009); Employment by occupation: 13.8% management, 18.4% professional, 11.3% services, 31.4% sales, 0.2% farming, 9.9% construction, 15.0% production (2000).

Income: Per capita income: $29,098 (2010); Median household income: $65,837 (2010); Average household income: $75,301 (2010); Percent of households with income of $100,000 or more: 23.2% (2010); Poverty rate: 3.0% (2000).

Taxes: Total city taxes per capita: $248 (2007); City property taxes per capita: $130 (2007).

Education: Percent of population age 25 and over with: High school diploma (including GED) or higher: 96.1% (2010); Bachelor's degree or higher: 31.9% (2010); Master's degree or higher: 8.7% (2010).

School District(s)
North West Hendricks Schools (KG-12)
    2008-09 Enrollment: 1,833 . . . . (317) 994-4100

Housing: Homeownership rate: 81.2% (2010); Median home value: $141,918 (2010); Median contract rent: $514 per month (2000); Median year structure built: 1986 (2000).

Transportation: Commute to work: 94.7% car, 0.2% public transportation, 1.1% walk, 3.2% work from home (2000); Travel time to work: 23.8% less than 15 minutes, 31.5% 15 to 30 minutes, 34.5% 30 to 45 minutes, 6.5% 45 to 60 minutes, 3.7% 60 minutes or more (2000)

PLAINFIELD (town). Covers a land area of 17.981 square miles and a water area of 0.047 square miles. Located at 39.69° N. Lat; 86.38° W. Long. Elevation is 728 feet.

History: Named by Quaker settlers, "the plain people". Plainfield, which called itself the Village of Friendly Folk, developed as the headquarters of the Society of Friends. It was in Plainfield in 1842 that Martin Van Buren, campaigning for the 1844 election, was dumped into a mudhole when his carriage was purposely upset by residents who wanted him to pay attention to the need for road improvements.

Population: 15,796 (1990); 18,396 (2000); 24,109 (2010); 26,619 (2015 projected); Race: 81.0% White, 14.5% Black, 2.0% Asian, 2.4% Other, 3.0% Hispanic of any race (2010); Density: 1,340.8 persons per square mile (2010); Average household size: 2.39 (2010); Median age: 35.2 (2010); Males per 100 females: 111.4 (2010); Marriage status: 22.4% never married, 58.5% now married, 6.3% widowed, 12.8% divorced (2000); Foreign born: 1.5% (2000); Ancestry (includes multiple ancestries): 23.7% German, 17.2% United States or American, 12.0% Irish, 11.9% English, 9.9% Other groups (2000).

Economy: Unemployment rate: 8.5% (5/2010); Total civilian labor force: 13,871 (5/2010); Single-family building permits issued: 102 (2009); Multi-family building permits issued: 48 (2009); Employment by occupation: 11.4% management, 15.5% professional, 14.3% services, 30.5% sales, 0.0% farming, 12.2% construction, 16.1% production (2000).

Income: Per capita income: $25,381 (2010); Median household income: $53,950 (2010); Average household income: $62,913 (2010); Percent of households with income of $100,000 or more: 15.8% (2010); Poverty rate: 5.2% (2000).

Taxes: Total city taxes per capita: $457 (2007); City property taxes per capita: $342 (2007).

Education: Percent of population age 25 and over with: High school diploma (including GED) or higher: 91.7% (2010); Bachelor's degree or higher: 26.5% (2010); Master's degree or higher: 8.7% (2010).

School District(s)
Plainfield Community Sch Corp (PK-12)
    2008-09 Enrollment: 4,586 . . . . (317) 839-2578

Housing: Homeownership rate: 67.4% (2010); Median home value: $143,490 (2010); Median contract rent: $545 per month (2000); Median year structure built: 1977 (2000).

Safety: Violent crime rate: 23.5 per 10,000 population; Property crime rate: 353.0 per 10,000 population (2008).
Newspapers: Westside Flyer (Local news; Circulation 12,000)
Transportation: Commute to work: 93.9% car, 0.0% public transportation, 1.3% walk, 3.2% work from home (2000); Travel time to work: 34.5% less than 15 minutes, 31.9% 15 to 30 minutes, 25.4% 30 to 45 minutes, 5.4% 45 to 60 minutes, 2.9% 60 minutes or more (2000)
Additional Information Contacts
Plainfield Chamber of Commerce . . . . (317) 839-3800
   http://www.plainfield-in.com
Town of Plainfield. . . . . (317) 839-2561
   http://www.townofplainfield.com

STILESVILLE (town). Covers a land area of 0.282 square miles and a water area of 0 square miles. Located at 39.64° N. Lat; 86.63° W. Long. Elevation is 804 feet.

History: Laid out 1828.
Population: 301 (1990); 261 (2000); 359 (2010); 406 (2015 projected); Race: 96.9% White, 0.8% Black, 0.0% Asian, 2.2% Other, 0.8% Hispanic of any race (2010); Density: 1,273.2 persons per square mile (2010); Average household size: 2.46 (2010); Median age: 37.7 (2010); Males per 100 females: 102.8 (2010); Marriage status: 15.2% never married, 65.0% now married, 10.1% widowed, 9.7% divorced (2000); Foreign born: 0.0% (2000); Ancestry (includes multiple ancestries): 22.5% United States or American, 14.0% English, 13.7% German, 11.2% Irish, 8.4% European (2000).
Economy: Employment by occupation: 11.8% management, 9.0% professional, 10.4% services, 20.1% sales, 2.1% farming, 20.8% construction, 25.7% production (2000).
Income: Per capita income: $24,592 (2010); Median household income: $50,000 (2010); Average household income: $60,068 (2010); Percent of households with income of $100,000 or more: 13.7% (2010); Poverty rate: 0.0% (2000).
Taxes: Total city taxes per capita: $110 (2007); City property taxes per capita: $67 (2007).
Education: Percent of population age 25 and over with: High school diploma (including GED) or higher: 89.8% (2010); Bachelor's degree or higher: 18.1% (2010); Master's degree or higher: 5.1% (2010).
Housing: Homeownership rate: 80.8% (2010); Median home value: $140,426 (2010); Median contract rent: $438 per month (2000); Median year structure built: 1952 (2000).
Transportation: Commute to work: 96.5% car, 0.0% public transportation, 0.0% walk, 0.0% work from home (2000); Travel time to work: 15.3% less than 15 minutes, 20.1% 15 to 30 minutes, 36.8% 30 to 45 minutes, 14.6% 45 to 60 minutes, 13.2% 60 minutes or more (2000)

Henry County

Located in eastern Indiana; drained by the Big Blue River, Flatrock and Fall Creeks. Covers a land area of 392.93 square miles, a water area of 1.97 square miles, and is located in the Eastern Time Zone. The county was founded in 1821. County seat is New Castle.

Henry County is part of the New Castle, IN Micropolitan Statistical Area. The entire metro area includes: Henry County, IN

Weather Station: New Castle 4 N									Elevation: 1,062 feet		
	Jan	Feb	Mar	Apr	May	Jun	Jul	Aug	Sep	Oct	Nov	Dec
High	33	37	48	60	72	80	84	82	76	64	50	39
Low	16	19	29	38	48	58	62	60	53	41	32	23
Precip	2.2	2.2	3.0	4.0	4.6	4.6	4.7	3.5	2.8	3.0	3.6	2.8
Snow	na	na	2.2	0.3	tr	0.0	0.0	0.0	0.0	tr	0.8	na

High and Low temperatures in degrees Fahrenheit; Precipitation and Snow in inches

Population: 48,139 (1990); 48,508 (2000); 47,062 (2010); 46,214 (2015 projected); Race: 97.3% White, 1.2% Black, 0.3% Asian, 1.2% Other, 1.0% Hispanic of any race (2010); Density: 119.8 persons per square mile (2010); Average household size: 2.40 (2010); Median age: 41.6 (2010); Males per 100 females: 97.2 (2010).
Religion: Five largest groups: 4.7% Southern Baptist Convention, 4.6% Church of the Nazarene, 4.4% The United Methodist Church, 4.4% Christian Churches and Churches of Christ, 4.3% Christian Church (Disciples of Christ) (2000).
Economy: Unemployment rate: 12.3% (5/2010); Total civilian labor force: 23,245 (5/2010); Leading industries: 22.0% manufacturing; 22.0% health care and social assistance; 15.5% retail trade (2008); Farms: 781 totaling

174,400 acres (2007); Companies that employ 500 or more persons: 2 (2008); Companies that employ 100 to 499 persons: 13 (2008); Companies that employ less than 100 persons: 870 (2008); Black-owned businesses: n/a (2002); Hispanic-owned businesses: n/a (2002); Asian-owned businesses: n/a (2002); Women-owned businesses: 891 (2002); Retail sales per capita: $13,283 (2010). Single-family building permits issued: 18 (2009); Multi-family building permits issued: 0 (2009).
Income: Per capita income: $21,846 (2010); Median household income: $42,897 (2010); Average household income: $53,222 (2010); Percent of households with income of $100,000 or more: 10.9% (2010); Poverty rate: 12.3% (2008); Bankruptcy rate: 9.55% (2009).
Taxes: Total county taxes per capita: $325 (2007); County property taxes per capita: $187 (2007).
Education: Percent of population age 25 and over with: High school diploma (including GED) or higher: 82.6% (2010); Bachelor's degree or higher: 14.1% (2010); Master's degree or higher: 4.4% (2010).
Housing: Homeownership rate: 77.6% (2010); Median home value: $95,629 (2010); Median contract rent: $445 per month (2006-2008 3-year est.); Median year structure built: 1957 (2006-2008 3-year est.)
Health: Birth rate: 114.2 per 10,000 population (2009); Death rate: 114.2 per 10,000 population (2009); Age-adjusted cancer mortality rate: 214.5 deaths per 100,000 population (2006); Air Quality Index: 76.6% good, 23.4% moderate, 0.0% unhealthy for sensitive individuals, 0.0% unhealthy (percent of days in 2008); Number of physicians: 7.5 per 10,000 population (2007); Hospital beds: 22.6 per 10,000 population (2006); Hospital admissions: 728.3 per 10,000 population (2006).
Elections: 2008 Presidential election results: 47.2% Obama, 51.1% McCain, 0.0% Nader
Additional Information Contacts
Henry County Government . . . . (765) 529-6401
   http://www.henryco.net
City of New Castle . . . . (765) 521-6803
   http://www.cityofnewcastle.net
New Castle Chamber of Commerce . . . . (765) 529-5210
   http://www.nchcchamber.com

Henry County Communities

BLOUNTSVILLE (town). Covers a land area of 0.121 square miles and a water area of 0 square miles. Located at 40.06° N. Lat; 85.23° W. Long. Elevation is 1,099 feet.

Population: 155 (1990); 166 (2000); 176 (2010); 181 (2015 projected); Race: 99.4% White, 0.0% Black, 0.0% Asian, 0.6% Other, 2.3% Hispanic of any race (2010); Density: 1,455.7 persons per square mile (2010); Average household size: 2.55 (2010); Median age: 40.8 (2010); Males per 100 females: 95.6 (2010); Marriage status: 7.3% never married, 73.6% now married, 1.8% widowed, 17.3% divorced (2000); Foreign born: 0.0% (2000); Ancestry (includes multiple ancestries): 26.1% United States or American, 19.4% German, 10.6% Other groups, 0.6% English, 0.6% Swiss (2000).
Economy: Employment by occupation: 0.0% management, 6.6% professional, 14.8% services, 9.8% sales, 0.0% farming, 21.3% construction, 47.5% production (2000).
Income: Per capita income: $18,793 (2010); Median household income: $39,500 (2010); Average household income: $50,000 (2010); Percent of households with income of $100,000 or more: 5.8% (2010); Poverty rate: 8.9% (2000).
Taxes: Total city taxes per capita: $500 (2007); City property taxes per capita: $456 (2007).
Education: Percent of population age 25 and over with: High school diploma (including GED) or higher: 88.6% (2010); Bachelor's degree or higher: 8.9% (2010); Master's degree or higher: 2.4% (2010).
Housing: Homeownership rate: 88.4% (2010); Median home value: $85,000 (2010); Median contract rent: $313 per month (2000); Median year structure built: 1942 (2000).
Transportation: Commute to work: 100.0% car, 0.0% public transportation, 0.0% walk, 0.0% work from home (2000); Travel time to work: 0.0% less than 15 minutes, 24.0% 15 to 30 minutes, 54.0% 30 to 45 minutes, 2.0% 45 to 60 minutes, 20.0% 60 minutes or more (2000)

CADIZ (town). Covers a land area of 0.145 square miles and a water area of 0 square miles. Located at 39.95° N. Lat; 85.48° W. Long. Elevation is 1,093 feet.

Population: 202 (1990); 161 (2000); 156 (2010); 154 (2015 projected); Race: 98.1% White, 0.0% Black, 0.6% Asian, 1.3% Other, 0.6% Hispanic

of any race (2010); Density: 1,072.6 persons per square mile (2010); Average household size: 2.74 (2010); Median age: 43.8 (2010); Males per 100 females: 108.0 (2010); Marriage status: 32.5% never married, 48.8% now married, 7.3% widowed, 11.4% divorced (2000); Foreign born: 2.5% (2000); Ancestry (includes multiple ancestries): 26.9% United States or American, 12.5% German, 10.0% Irish, 6.9% French (except Basque), 6.3% Other groups (2000).
Economy: Employment by occupation: 4.8% management, 22.9% professional, 31.3% services, 10.8% sales, 0.0% farming, 10.8% construction, 19.3% production (2000).
Income: Per capita income: $20,135 (2010); Median household income: $44,375 (2010); Average household income: $52,500 (2010); Percent of households with income of $100,000 or more: 5.3% (2010); Poverty rate: 13.1% (2000).
Taxes: Total city taxes per capita: $26 (2007); City property taxes per capita: $13 (2007).
Education: Percent of population age 25 and over with: High school diploma (including GED) or higher: 87.3% (2010); Bachelor's degree or higher: 13.6% (2010); Master's degree or higher: 6.4% (2010).
Housing: Homeownership rate: 86.0% (2010); Median home value: $126,563 (2010); Median contract rent: $306 per month (2000); Median year structure built: 1947 (2000).
Transportation: Commute to work: 100.0% car, 0.0% public transportation, 0.0% walk, 0.0% work from home (2000); Travel time to work: 24.4% less than 15 minutes, 45.1% 15 to 30 minutes, 29.3% 30 to 45 minutes, 1.2% 45 to 60 minutes, 0.0% 60 minutes or more (2000)

DUNREITH (town). Covers a land area of 0.140 square miles and a water area of 0 square miles. Located at 39.80° N. Lat; 85.43° W. Long. Elevation is 1,043 feet.
History: Dunreith developed around the Pennsylvania Railroad station.
Population: 205 (1990); 184 (2000); 178 (2010); 177 (2015 projected); Race: 99.4% White, 0.0% Black, 0.0% Asian, 0.6% Other, 1.7% Hispanic of any race (2010); Density: 1,273.8 persons per square mile (2010); Average household size: 2.34 (2010); Median age: 47.0 (2010); Males per 100 females: 93.5 (2010); Marriage status: 23.6% never married, 58.8% now married, 5.4% widowed, 12.2% divorced (2000); Foreign born: 0.0% (2000); Ancestry (includes multiple ancestries): 31.8% United States or American, 20.0% German, 10.6% English, 7.6% Irish, 5.3% French (except Basque) (2000).
Economy: Employment by occupation: 6.5% management, 19.4% professional, 9.7% services, 30.1% sales, 0.0% farming, 6.5% construction, 28.0% production (2000).
Income: Per capita income: $28,270 (2010); Median household income: $52,500 (2010); Average household income: $65,954 (2010); Percent of households with income of $100,000 or more: 26.3% (2010); Poverty rate: 4.7% (2000).
Taxes: Total city taxes per capita: $29 (2007); City property taxes per capita: $17 (2007).
Education: Percent of population age 25 and over with: High school diploma (including GED) or higher: 82.6% (2010); Bachelor's degree or higher: 9.4% (2010); Master's degree or higher: 0.7% (2010).
Housing: Homeownership rate: 78.9% (2010); Median home value: $110,870 (2010); Median contract rent: $333 per month (2000); Median year structure built: 1944 (2000).
Transportation: Commute to work: 81.6% car, 0.0% public transportation, 13.8% walk, 4.6% work from home (2000); Travel time to work: 26.5% less than 15 minutes, 50.6% 15 to 30 minutes, 0.0% 30 to 45 minutes, 15.7% 45 to 60 minutes, 7.2% 60 minutes or more (2000)

GREENSBORO (town). Covers a land area of 0.122 square miles and a water area of 0 square miles. Located at 39.87° N. Lat; 85.46° W. Long. Elevation is 981 feet.
Population: 204 (1990); 174 (2000); 170 (2010); 167 (2015 projected); Race: 99.4% White, 0.0% Black, 0.0% Asian, 0.6% Other, 0.0% Hispanic of any race (2010); Density: 1,391.5 persons per square mile (2010); Average household size: 2.54 (2010); Median age: 40.9 (2010); Males per 100 females: 107.3 (2010); Marriage status: 14.4% never married, 63.0% now married, 16.4% widowed, 6.2% divorced (2000); Foreign born: 0.0% (2000); Ancestry (includes multiple ancestries): 15.4% United States or American, 8.8% Other groups, 7.7% German, 4.9% English, 4.4% British (2000).
Economy: Employment by occupation: 2.6% management, 3.9% professional, 27.3% services, 19.5% sales, 0.0% farming, 15.6% construction, 31.2% production (2000).

Income: Per capita income: $21,171 (2010); Median household income: $47,500 (2010); Average household income: $56,455 (2010); Percent of households with income of $100,000 or more: 13.4% (2010); Poverty rate: 5.5% (2000).
Taxes: Total city taxes per capita: $49 (2007); City property taxes per capita: $37 (2007).
Education: Percent of population age 25 and over with: High school diploma (including GED) or higher: 83.6% (2010); Bachelor's degree or higher: 15.5% (2010); Master's degree or higher: 1.7% (2010).
Housing: Homeownership rate: 86.6% (2010); Median home value: $123,529 (2010); Median contract rent: $214 per month (2000); Median year structure built: before 1940 (2000).
Transportation: Commute to work: 96.1% car, 0.0% public transportation, 0.0% walk, 3.9% work from home (2000); Travel time to work: 29.7% less than 15 minutes, 33.8% 15 to 30 minutes, 10.8% 30 to 45 minutes, 12.2% 45 to 60 minutes, 13.5% 60 minutes or more (2000)

KENNARD (town). Covers a land area of 0.290 square miles and a water area of 0 square miles. Located at 39.90° N. Lat; 85.51° W. Long. Elevation is 1,040 feet.
Population: 382 (1990); 455 (2000); 403 (2010); 387 (2015 projected); Race: 98.3% White, 0.5% Black, 0.2% Asian, 1.0% Other, 0.5% Hispanic of any race (2010); Density: 1,389.2 persons per square mile (2010); Average household size: 2.62 (2010); Median age: 37.0 (2010); Males per 100 females: 108.8 (2010); Marriage status: 18.4% never married, 60.2% now married, 10.7% widowed, 10.7% divorced (2000); Foreign born: 0.2% (2000); Ancestry (includes multiple ancestries): 16.9% German, 12.9% United States or American, 10.9% Irish, 9.2% Other groups, 8.5% English (2000).
Economy: Employment by occupation: 10.9% management, 9.6% professional, 10.9% services, 24.4% sales, 0.0% farming, 10.3% construction, 34.0% production (2000).
Income: Per capita income: $18,326 (2010); Median household income: $42,241 (2010); Average household income: $47,500 (2010); Percent of households with income of $100,000 or more: 7.1% (2010); Poverty rate: 10.0% (2000).
Taxes: Total city taxes per capita: $70 (2007); City property taxes per capita: $49 (2007).
Education: Percent of population age 25 and over with: High school diploma (including GED) or higher: 82.3% (2010); Bachelor's degree or higher: 11.2% (2010); Master's degree or higher: 4.2% (2010).
School District(s)
C A Beard Memorial School Corp (KG-12)
   2008-09 Enrollment: 1,348 . . . . (765) 345-5101
Housing: Homeownership rate: 85.1% (2010); Median home value: $105,612 (2010); Median contract rent: $338 per month (2000); Median year structure built: 1948 (2000).
Transportation: Commute to work: 94.9% car, 0.0% public transportation, 0.0% walk, 3.8% work from home (2000); Travel time to work: 15.3% less than 15 minutes, 40.0% 15 to 30 minutes, 20.0% 30 to 45 minutes, 10.7% 45 to 60 minutes, 14.0% 60 minutes or more (2000)

KNIGHTSTOWN (town). Covers a land area of 0.710 square miles and a water area of 0 square miles. Located at 39.79° N. Lat; 85.52° W. Long. Elevation is 932 feet.
History: Knightstown was named for John Knight, an engineer who was involved in the construction of the National Road here.
Population: 2,048 (1990); 2,148 (2000); 1,912 (2010); 1,829 (2015 projected); Race: 98.5% White, 0.9% Black, 0.2% Asian, 0.4% Other, 0.3% Hispanic of any race (2010); Density: 2,693.7 persons per square mile (2010); Average household size: 2.38 (2010); Median age: 39.2 (2010); Males per 100 females: 96.5 (2010); Marriage status: 18.5% never married, 57.1% now married, 8.7% widowed, 15.7% divorced (2000); Foreign born: 0.2% (2000); Ancestry (includes multiple ancestries): 24.1% German, 15.9% English, 12.1% Irish, 10.5% United States or American, 10.4% Other groups (2000).
Economy: Single-family building permits issued: 0 (2009); Multi-family building permits issued: 0 (2009); Employment by occupation: 8.5% management, 10.9% professional, 15.8% services, 24.2% sales, 0.8% farming, 10.9% construction, 28.9% production (2000).
Income: Per capita income: $21,818 (2010); Median household income: $41,500 (2010); Average household income: $51,647 (2010); Percent of households with income of $100,000 or more: 8.1% (2010); Poverty rate: 7.1% (2000).

Taxes: Total city taxes per capita: $220 (2007); City property taxes per capita: $143 (2007).
Education: Percent of population age 25 and over with: High school diploma (including GED) or higher: 83.9% (2010); Bachelor's degree or higher: 11.5% (2010); Master's degree or higher: 4.1% (2010).
School District(s)
C A Beard Memorial School Corp (KG-12)
    2008-09 Enrollment: 1,348 . . . . (765) 345-5101
IN State Department Of Health (05-12)
    2008-09 Enrollment: 107 . . . . (317) 233-7102
Housing: Homeownership rate: 73.3% (2010); Median home value: $97,434 (2010); Median contract rent: $319 per month (2000); Median year structure built: before 1940 (2000).
Newspapers: Tri-County Banner-Republican (Local news; Circulation 2,100)
Transportation: Commute to work: 96.2% car, 0.0% public transportation, 2.4% walk, 1.3% work from home (2000); Travel time to work: 25.1% less than 15 minutes, 30.6% 15 to 30 minutes, 16.0% 30 to 45 minutes, 18.8% 45 to 60 minutes, 9.5% 60 minutes or more (2000)

LEWISVILLE (town). Covers a land area of 0.327 square miles and a water area of 0 square miles. Located at 39.80° N. Lat; 85.35° W. Long. Elevation is 1,053 feet.
History: Laid out 1829.
Population: 478 (1990); 395 (2000); 383 (2010); 372 (2015 projected); Race: 97.9% White, 0.0% Black, 0.0% Asian, 2.1% Other, 1.3% Hispanic of any race (2010); Density: 1,169.8 persons per square mile (2010); Average household size: 2.55 (2010); Median age: 41.3 (2010); Males per 100 females: 107.0 (2010); Marriage status: 22.3% never married, 58.6% now married, 6.1% widowed, 13.1% divorced (2000); Foreign born: 1.4% (2000); Ancestry (includes multiple ancestries): 38.6% United States or American, 8.7% Irish, 8.7% German, 6.3% Other groups, 4.1% English (2000).
Economy: Employment by occupation: 6.3% management, 9.8% professional, 17.8% services, 24.1% sales, 1.7% farming, 9.2% construction, 31.0% production (2000).
Income: Per capita income: $29,075 (2010); Median household income: $60,484 (2010); Average household income: $74,933 (2010); Percent of households with income of $100,000 or more: 24.0% (2010); Poverty rate: 8.3% (2000).
Taxes: Total city taxes per capita: $43 (2007); City property taxes per capita: $0 (2007).
Education: Percent of population age 25 and over with: High school diploma (including GED) or higher: 85.5% (2010); Bachelor's degree or higher: 17.1% (2010); Master's degree or higher: 4.5% (2010).
Housing: Homeownership rate: 82.7% (2010); Median home value: $102,778 (2010); Median contract rent: $383 per month (2000); Median year structure built: before 1940 (2000).
Transportation: Commute to work: 90.1% car, 0.0% public transportation, 4.3% walk, 4.3% work from home (2000); Travel time to work: 24.7% less than 15 minutes, 48.1% 15 to 30 minutes, 6.5% 30 to 45 minutes, 13.6% 45 to 60 minutes, 7.1% 60 minutes or more (2000)

MIDDLETOWN (town). Covers a land area of 1.101 square miles and a water area of 0 square miles. Located at 40.05° N. Lat; 85.54° W. Long. Elevation is 978 feet.
History: Laid out 1829.
Population: 2,366 (1990); 2,488 (2000); 2,359 (2010); 2,274 (2015 projected); Race: 98.1% White, 0.8% Black, 0.2% Asian, 0.9% Other, 0.6% Hispanic of any race (2010); Density: 2,143.2 persons per square mile (2010); Average household size: 2.42 (2010); Median age: 40.7 (2010); Males per 100 females: 92.9 (2010); Marriage status: 19.0% never married, 54.3% now married, 10.4% widowed, 16.3% divorced (2000); Foreign born: 0.5% (2000); Ancestry (includes multiple ancestries): 23.3% United States or American, 17.1% German, 10.7% Other groups, 9.7% Irish, 7.1% English (2000).
Economy: Employment by occupation: 6.7% management, 11.7% professional, 17.4% services, 29.7% sales, 0.0% farming, 17.7% construction, 16.8% production (2000).
Income: Per capita income: $21,105 (2010); Median household income: $42,500 (2010); Average household income: $52,353 (2010); Percent of households with income of $100,000 or more: 10.4% (2010); Poverty rate: 8.2% (2000).
Taxes: Total city taxes per capita: $162 (2007); City property taxes per capita: $125 (2007).

Education: Percent of population age 25 and over with: High school diploma (including GED) or higher: 87.1% (2010); Bachelor's degree or higher: 14.4% (2010); Master's degree or higher: 3.7% (2010).
School District(s)
Shenandoah School Corporation (KG-12)
    2008-09 Enrollment: 1,366 . . . . (765) 354-2266
Housing: Homeownership rate: 77.8% (2010); Median home value: $96,357 (2010); Median contract rent: $381 per month (2000); Median year structure built: 1954 (2000).
Newspapers: Middletown News (Local news; Circulation 1,770)
Transportation: Commute to work: 91.9% car, 0.4% public transportation, 2.4% walk, 3.8% work from home (2000); Travel time to work: 25.7% less than 15 minutes, 39.8% 15 to 30 minutes, 12.7% 30 to 45 minutes, 10.2% 45 to 60 minutes, 11.5% 60 minutes or more (2000)

MOORELAND (town). Covers a land area of 0.140 square miles and a water area of 0 square miles. Located at 39.99° N. Lat; 85.25° W. Long. Elevation is 1,138 feet.
History: Mooreland was named for early settler Philip Moore.
Population: 465 (1990); 393 (2000); 342 (2010); 323 (2015 projected); Race: 99.1% White, 0.0% Black, 0.0% Asian, 0.9% Other, 0.6% Hispanic of any race (2010); Density: 2,437.1 persons per square mile (2010); Average household size: 2.67 (2010); Median age: 37.3 (2010); Males per 100 females: 103.6 (2010); Marriage status: 16.0% never married, 67.6% now married, 6.0% widowed, 10.3% divorced (2000); Foreign born: 0.0% (2000); Ancestry (includes multiple ancestries): 15.3% United States or American, 12.0% German, 10.4% English, 10.2% Other groups, 8.9% Irish (2000).
Economy: Employment by occupation: 4.9% management, 8.6% professional, 19.6% services, 20.9% sales, 1.8% farming, 13.5% construction, 30.7% production (2000).
Income: Per capita income: $20,540 (2010); Median household income: $46,364 (2010); Average household income: $52,559 (2010); Percent of households with income of $100,000 or more: 9.4% (2010); Poverty rate: 10.2% (2000).
Taxes: Total city taxes per capita: $70 (2007); City property taxes per capita: $40 (2007).
Education: Percent of population age 25 and over with: High school diploma (including GED) or higher: 75.0% (2010); Bachelor's degree or higher: 10.6% (2010); Master's degree or higher: 3.7% (2010).
Housing: Homeownership rate: 88.3% (2010); Median home value: $93,500 (2010); Median contract rent: $304 per month (2000); Median year structure built: 1940 (2000).
Transportation: Commute to work: 100.0% car, 0.0% public transportation, 0.0% walk, 0.0% work from home (2000); Travel time to work: 10.7% less than 15 minutes, 40.7% 15 to 30 minutes, 30.7% 30 to 45 minutes, 10.7% 45 to 60 minutes, 7.3% 60 minutes or more (2000)

MOUNT SUMMIT (town). Covers a land area of 0.179 square miles and a water area of 0 square miles. Located at 40.00° N. Lat; 85.38° W. Long. Elevation is 1,093 feet.
History: Mount Summit is at one of the highest elevations in Henry County.
Population: 289 (1990); 313 (2000); 390 (2010); 421 (2015 projected); Race: 99.0% White, 0.3% Black, 0.0% Asian, 0.8% Other, 1.3% Hispanic of any race (2010); Density: 2,176.8 persons per square mile (2010); Average household size: 2.55 (2010); Median age: 43.0 (2010); Males per 100 females: 101.0 (2010); Marriage status: 20.5% never married, 64.0% now married, 5.4% widowed, 10.0% divorced (2000); Foreign born: 0.0% (2000); Ancestry (includes multiple ancestries): 16.9% United States or American, 12.0% German, 11.0% Irish, 10.3% Other groups, 6.3% English (2000).
Economy: Employment by occupation: 13.8% management, 12.6% professional, 13.2% services, 22.2% sales, 0.0% farming, 20.4% construction, 18.0% production (2000).
Income: Per capita income: $27,087 (2010); Median household income: $60,197 (2010); Average household income: $71,373 (2010); Percent of households with income of $100,000 or more: 18.3% (2010); Poverty rate: 5.3% (2000).
Taxes: Total city taxes per capita: $20 (2007); City property taxes per capita: $7 (2007).
Education: Percent of population age 25 and over with: High school diploma (including GED) or higher: 91.7% (2010); Bachelor's degree or higher: 19.2% (2010); Master's degree or higher: 6.5% (2010).

Housing: Homeownership rate: 90.2% (2010); Median home value: $118,367 (2010); Median contract rent: $340 per month (2000); Median year structure built: 1950 (2000).
Transportation: Commute to work: 89.7% car, 0.0% public transportation, 7.9% walk, 2.4% work from home (2000); Travel time to work: 37.9% less than 15 minutes, 40.4% 15 to 30 minutes, 9.3% 30 to 45 minutes, 9.3% 45 to 60 minutes, 3.1% 60 minutes or more (2000)

NEW CASTLE (city). County seat. Covers a land area of 5.951 square miles and a water area of 0 square miles. Located at 39.92° N. Lat; 85.36° W. Long. Elevation is 1,070 feet.
History: New Castle was the birthplace in 1867 of Wilbur Wright, who with his brother Orville flew the first heavier-than-air craft in 1903 in North Carolina. New Castle developed as an industrial city.
Population: 18,045 (1990); 17,780 (2000); 16,748 (2010); 16,139 (2015 projected); Race: 95.4% White, 2.5% Black, 0.3% Asian, 1.8% Other, 1.3% Hispanic of any race (2010); Density: 2,814.1 persons per square mile (2010); Average household size: 2.27 (2010); Median age: 41.1 (2010); Males per 100 females: 94.7 (2010); Marriage status: 21.4% never married, 54.1% now married, 10.5% widowed, 13.9% divorced (2000); Foreign born: 0.6% (2000); Ancestry (includes multiple ancestries): 21.9% United States or American, 11.7% German, 9.3% English, 9.2% Other groups, 7.6% Irish (2000).
Economy: Single-family building permits issued: 3 (2009); Multi-family building permits issued: 0 (2009); Employment by occupation: 6.8% management, 14.3% professional, 20.4% services, 21.2% sales, 0.1% farming, 11.0% construction, 26.3% production (2000).
Income: Per capita income: $19,131 (2010); Median household income: $33,158 (2010); Average household income: $44,183 (2010); Percent of households with income of $100,000 or more: 7.4% (2010); Poverty rate: 12.4% (2000).
Taxes: Total city taxes per capita: $239 (2007); City property taxes per capita: $215 (2007).
Education: Percent of population age 25 and over with: High school diploma (including GED) or higher: 76.5% (2010); Bachelor's degree or higher: 13.3% (2010); Master's degree or higher: 4.0% (2010).

School District(s)
Blue River Valley Schools (KG-12)
    2008-09 Enrollment: 742 . . . . (765) 836-4816
New Castle Community Sch Corp (KG-12)
    2008-09 Enrollment: 3,952 . . . . (765) 521-7201
Housing: Homeownership rate: 67.4% (2010); Median home value: $75,301 (2010); Median contract rent: $360 per month (2000); Median year structure built: 1951 (2000).
Hospitals: Henry County Memorial Hospital (107 beds)
Safety: Violent crime rate: 9.9 per 10,000 population; Property crime rate: 862.4 per 10,000 population (2008).
Newspapers: New Castle Courier-Times (Local news; Circulation 18,000)
Transportation: Commute to work: 94.7% car, 0.2% public transportation, 2.7% walk, 1.6% work from home (2000); Travel time to work: 56.7% less than 15 minutes, 14.1% 15 to 30 minutes, 13.4% 30 to 45 minutes, 7.4% 45 to 60 minutes, 8.3% 60 minutes or more (2000)
Additional Information Contacts
City of New Castle . . . . (765) 521-6803
    http://www.cityofnewcastle.net
New Castle Chamber of Commerce . . . . (765) 529-5210
    http://www.nchcchamber.com

SPICELAND (town). Covers a land area of 0.439 square miles and a water area of 0 square miles. Located at 39.83° N. Lat; 85.43° W. Long. Elevation is 1,050 feet.
History: Spiceland was settled in 1828 by a group of Quakers from North Carolina. From Spiceland Academy, founded in 1834, came historian Charles Austin Beard.
Population: 757 (1990); 807 (2000); 695 (2010); 653 (2015 projected); Race: 98.3% White, 0.1% Black, 0.0% Asian, 1.6% Other, 2.2% Hispanic of any race (2010); Density: 1,583.4 persons per square mile (2010); Average household size: 2.46 (2010); Median age: 39.3 (2010); Males per 100 females: 98.6 (2010); Marriage status: 18.2% never married, 65.3% now married, 9.5% widowed, 7.0% divorced (2000); Foreign born: 0.5% (2000); Ancestry (includes multiple ancestries): 20.5% German, 13.2% United States or American, 11.2% English, 6.7% Irish, 5.5% Other groups (2000).

Economy: Employment by occupation: 8.9% management, 14.8% professional, 14.3% services, 19.4% sales, 0.0% farming, 10.5% construction, 32.1% production (2000).
Income: Per capita income: $22,930 (2010); Median household income: $50,192 (2010); Average household income: $56,440 (2010); Percent of households with income of $100,000 or more: 11.7% (2010); Poverty rate: 2.5% (2000).
Taxes: Total city taxes per capita: $64 (2007); City property taxes per capita: $51 (2007).
Education: Percent of population age 25 and over with: High school diploma (including GED) or higher: 85.5% (2010); Bachelor's degree or higher: 14.9% (2010); Master's degree or higher: 2.7% (2010).
Housing: Homeownership rate: 81.6% (2010); Median home value: $99,722 (2010); Median contract rent: $375 per month (2000); Median year structure built: 1942 (2000).
Transportation: Commute to work: 95.2% car, 0.0% public transportation, 2.1% walk, 2.1% work from home (2000); Travel time to work: 37.6% less than 15 minutes, 26.7% 15 to 30 minutes, 9.5% 30 to 45 minutes, 13.9% 45 to 60 minutes, 12.3% 60 minutes or more (2000)

SPRINGPORT (town). Covers a land area of 0.133 square miles and a water area of 0 square miles. Located at 40.04° N. Lat; 85.39° W. Long. Elevation is 1,063 feet.
Population: 194 (1990); 174 (2000); 209 (2010); 224 (2015 projected); Race: 98.6% White, 0.5% Black, 0.0% Asian, 1.0% Other, 0.0% Hispanic of any race (2010); Density: 1,572.4 persons per square mile (2010); Average household size: 2.58 (2010); Median age: 43.3 (2010); Males per 100 females: 120.0 (2010); Marriage status: 19.4% never married, 66.1% now married, 2.4% widowed, 12.1% divorced (2000); Foreign born: 0.0% (2000); Ancestry (includes multiple ancestries): 20.4% German, 16.6% United States or American, 11.5% English, 9.6% Other groups, 8.9% Irish (2000).
Economy: Employment by occupation: 14.3% management, 18.6% professional, 24.3% services, 11.4% sales, 0.0% farming, 10.0% construction, 21.4% production (2000).
Income: Per capita income: $25,560 (2010); Median household income: $56,500 (2010); Average household income: $71,512 (2010); Percent of households with income of $100,000 or more: 14.8% (2010); Poverty rate: 9.6% (2000).
Taxes: Total city taxes per capita: $61 (2007); City property taxes per capita: $43 (2007).
Education: Percent of population age 25 and over with: High school diploma (including GED) or higher: 84.6% (2010); Bachelor's degree or higher: 16.8% (2010); Master's degree or higher: 8.1% (2010).
Housing: Homeownership rate: 91.4% (2010); Median home value: $117,188 (2010); Median contract rent: $317 per month (2000); Median year structure built: before 1940 (2000).
Transportation: Commute to work: 92.9% car, 0.0% public transportation, 4.3% walk, 2.9% work from home (2000); Travel time to work: 10.3% less than 15 minutes, 63.2% 15 to 30 minutes, 5.9% 30 to 45 minutes, 7.4% 45 to 60 minutes, 13.2% 60 minutes or more (2000)

STRAUGHN (town). Covers a land area of 0.140 square miles and a water area of 0 square miles. Located at 39.80° N. Lat; 85.29° W. Long. Elevation is 1,096 feet.
Population: 318 (1990); 263 (2000); 241 (2010); 229 (2015 projected); Race: 99.6% White, 0.4% Black, 0.0% Asian, 0.0% Other, 0.8% Hispanic of any race (2010); Density: 1,724.8 persons per square mile (2010); Average household size: 2.54 (2010); Median age: 41.8 (2010); Males per 100 females: 94.4 (2010); Marriage status: 29.0% never married, 61.1% now married, 7.7% widowed, 2.3% divorced (2000); Foreign born: 0.4% (2000); Ancestry (includes multiple ancestries): 18.5% English, 14.6% German, 10.7% United States or American, 10.7% Irish, 5.0% Dutch (2000).
Economy: Employment by occupation: 9.2% management, 16.9% professional, 16.9% services, 26.2% sales, 2.3% farming, 4.6% construction, 23.8% production (2000).
Income: Per capita income: $20,465 (2010); Median household income: $42,500 (2010); Average household income: $54,342 (2010); Percent of households with income of $100,000 or more: 10.5% (2010); Poverty rate: 15.3% (2000).
Taxes: Total city taxes per capita: $167 (2007); City property taxes per capita: $150 (2007).

Education: Percent of population age 25 and over with: High school diploma (including GED) or higher: 79.9% (2010); Bachelor's degree or higher: 10.6% (2010); Master's degree or higher: 5.6% (2010).

School District(s)

South Henry School Corp (KG-12)

    2008-09 Enrollment: 821 . . . . (765) 987-7882

Housing: Homeownership rate: 86.3% (2010); Median home value: $83,077 (2010); Median contract rent: $99 per month (2000); Median year structure built: before 1940 (2000).

Transportation: Commute to work: 98.5% car, 0.0% public transportation, 1.5% walk, 0.0% work from home (2000); Travel time to work: 24.6% less than 15 minutes, 47.7% 15 to 30 minutes, 16.2% 30 to 45 minutes, 4.6% 45 to 60 minutes, 6.9% 60 minutes or more (2000)

SULPHUR SPRINGS (town). Covers a land area of 0.302 square miles and a water area of 0 square miles. Located at 40.00° N. Lat; 85.44° W. Long. Elevation is 1,063 feet.

History: Laid out 1853.

Population: 257 (1990); 346 (2000); 328 (2010); 319 (2015 projected); Race: 95.7% White, 1.8% Black, 1.2% Asian, 1.2% Other, 0.3% Hispanic of any race (2010); Density: 1,085.5 persons per square mile (2010); Average household size: 2.58 (2010); Median age: 38.9 (2010); Males per 100 females: 89.6 (2010); Marriage status: 14.5% never married, 69.3% now married, 10.5% widowed, 5.7% divorced (2000); Foreign born: 0.0% (2000); Ancestry (includes multiple ancestries): 28.3% United States or American, 19.7% German, 10.8% English, 7.2% Irish, 3.3% Other groups (2000).

Economy: Employment by occupation: 6.8% management, 23.7% professional, 15.8% services, 19.2% sales, 0.0% farming, 13.6% construction, 20.9% production (2000).

Income: Per capita income: $22,215 (2010); Median household income: $46,149 (2010); Average household income: $57,205 (2010); Percent of households with income of $100,000 or more: 13.4% (2010); Poverty rate: 3.9% (2000).

Taxes: Total city taxes per capita: $58 (2007); City property taxes per capita: $43 (2007).

Education: Percent of population age 25 and over with: High school diploma (including GED) or higher: 90.2% (2010); Bachelor's degree or higher: 12.5% (2010); Master's degree or higher: 2.2% (2010).

Housing: Homeownership rate: 90.6% (2010); Median home value: $124,432 (2010); Median contract rent: $335 per month (2000); Median year structure built: 1950 (2000).

Transportation: Commute to work: 94.4% car, 0.0% public transportation, 1.7% walk, 4.0% work from home (2000); Travel time to work: 29.4% less than 15 minutes, 41.8% 15 to 30 minutes, 22.4% 30 to 45 minutes, 3.5% 45 to 60 minutes, 2.9% 60 minutes or more (2000)

Howard County

Located in central Indiana; drained by Wildcat Creek. Covers a land area of 293.07 square miles, a water area of 0.86 square miles, and is located in the Eastern Time Zone. The county was founded in 1844. County seat is Kokomo.

Howard County is part of the Kokomo, IN Metropolitan Statistical Area. The entire metro area includes: Howard County, IN; Tipton County, IN

Weather Station: Kokomo 3 WSW											Elevation: 816 feet	
	Jan	Feb	Mar	Apr	May	Jun	Jul	Aug	Sep	Oct	Nov	Dec
High	30	35	47	60	71	81	84	82	76	64	49	36
Low	14	18	27	37	48	58	62	59	51	40	31	21
Precip	2.5	2.3	3.3	3.9	4.0	3.9	4.5	4.2	3.1	3.1	3.7	3.1
Snow	13.2	10.3	6.1	1.4	tr	0.0	0.0	0.0	0.0	0.4	2.1	9.6

High and Low temperatures in degrees Fahrenheit; Precipitation and Snow in inches

Population: 80,827 (1990); 84,964 (2000); 83,034 (2010); 81,549 (2015 projected); Race: 89.0% White, 6.6% Black, 1.3% Asian, 3.2% Other, 2.1% Hispanic of any race (2010); Density: 283.3 persons per square mile (2010); Average household size: 2.31 (2010); Median age: 39.7 (2010); Males per 100 females: 93.9 (2010).

Religion: Five largest groups: 11.3% Catholic Church, 4.8% The United Methodist Church, 3.8% Christian Churches and Churches of Christ, 2.2% Christian Church (Disciples of Christ), 1.9% Independent, Non-Charismatic Churches (2000).

Economy: Unemployment rate: 12.3% (5/2010); Total civilian labor force: 35,145 (5/2010); Leading industries: 15.9% health care and social

assistance; 15.1% retail trade; 11.9% accommodation & food services (2008); Farms: 601 totaling 162,281 acres (2007); Companies that employ 500 or more persons: 9 (2008); Companies that employ 100 to 499 persons: 23 (2008); Companies that employ less than 100 persons: 1,867 (2008); Black-owned businesses: n/a (2002); Hispanic-owned businesses: n/a (2002); Asian-owned businesses: n/a (2002); Women-owned businesses: 1,467 (2002); Retail sales per capita: $16,689 (2010). Single-family building permits issued: 11 (2009); Multi-family building permits issued: 62 (2009).

Income: Per capita income: $24,628 (2010); Median household income: $46,750 (2010); Average household income: $57,310 (2010); Percent of households with income of $100,000 or more: 12.9% (2010); Poverty rate: 13.3% (2008); Bankruptcy rate: 9.07% (2009).

Taxes: Total county taxes per capita: $238 (2007); County property taxes per capita: $191 (2007).

Education: Percent of population age 25 and over with: High school diploma (including GED) or higher: 85.3% (2010); Bachelor's degree or higher: 19.9% (2010); Master's degree or higher: 8.1% (2010).

Housing: Homeownership rate: 69.1% (2010); Median home value: $99,098 (2010); Median contract rent: $483 per month (2006-2008 3-year est.); Median year structure built: 1965 (2006-2008 3-year est.)

Health: Birth rate: 129.4 per 10,000 population (2009); Death rate: 105.9 per 10,000 population (2009); Age-adjusted cancer mortality rate: 191.9 deaths per 100,000 population (2006); Number of physicians: 14.2 per 10,000 population (2007); Hospital beds: 41.2 per 10,000 population (2006); Hospital admissions: 1,456.5 per 10,000 population (2006).

Elections: 2008 Presidential election results: 46.3% Obama, 52.4% McCain, 0.0% Nader

Additional Information Contacts

Howard County Government . . . . (765) 456-2234
   http://www.co.howard.in.us

City of Kokomo . . . . (765) 456-7370
   http://www.cityofkokomo.org

Kokomo/Howard County Chamber of Commerce . . . . (765) 457-5301
   http://www.kokomochamber.com

Howard County Communities

GREENTOWN (town). Covers a land area of 1.004 square miles and a water area of 0 square miles. Located at 40.47° N. Lat; 85.96° W. Long. Elevation is 840 feet.

History: Greentown was named for Miami Chief Green. It was founded in 1848 by English, German, Scotch, and Dutch immigrants who received the land from the U.S. government.

Population: 2,396 (1990); 2,546 (2000); 2,400 (2010); 2,317 (2015 projected); Race: 97.5% White, 0.5% Black, 0.3% Asian, 1.7% Other, 0.9% Hispanic of any race (2010); Density: 2,389.4 persons per square mile (2010); Average household size: 2.42 (2010); Median age: 40.4 (2010); Males per 100 females: 91.2 (2010); Marriage status: 19.8% never married, 60.1% now married, 8.7% widowed, 11.4% divorced (2000); Foreign born: 0.0% (2000); Ancestry (includes multiple ancestries): 22.0% United States or American, 20.1% German, 12.7% Irish, 8.1% English, 7.2% Other groups (2000).

Economy: Single-family building permits issued: 0 (2009); Multi-family building permits issued: 0 (2009); Employment by occupation: 7.9% management, 14.4% professional, 16.2% services, 27.6% sales, 0.0% farming, 8.8% construction, 25.1% production (2000).

Income: Per capita income: $25,005 (2010); Median household income: $50,926 (2010); Average household income: $61,178 (2010); Percent of households with income of $100,000 or more: 14.1% (2010); Poverty rate: 9.2% (2000).

Taxes: Total city taxes per capita: $124 (2007); City property taxes per capita: $100 (2007).

Education: Percent of population age 25 and over with: High school diploma (including GED) or higher: 91.2% (2010); Bachelor's degree or higher: 14.1% (2010); Master's degree or higher: 5.8% (2010).

School District(s)

Eastern Howard School Corp (PK-12)

    2008-09 Enrollment: 1,312 . . . . (765) 628-3391

Housing: Homeownership rate: 76.4% (2010); Median home value: $120,736 (2010); Median contract rent: $375 per month (2000); Median year structure built: 1963 (2000).

Transportation: Commute to work: 94.9% car, 0.0% public transportation, 2.8% walk, 2.3% work from home (2000); Travel time to work: 29.1% less

than 15 minutes, 53.7% 15 to 30 minutes, 7.4% 30 to 45 minutes, 1.7% 45 to 60 minutes, 8.1% 60 minutes or more (2000)

INDIAN HEIGHTS (CDP). Covers a land area of 0.861 square miles and a water area of 0 square miles. Located at 40.42° N. Lat; 86.11° W. Long. Elevation is 856 feet.

Population: 3,437 (1990); 3,274 (2000); 3,294 (2010); 3,282 (2015 projected); Race: 93.3% White, 3.9% Black, 0.1% Asian, 2.6% Other, 2.9% Hispanic of any race (2010); Density: 3,825.7 persons per square mile (2010); Average household size: 2.59 (2010); Median age: 36.5 (2010); Males per 100 females: 96.1 (2010); Marriage status: 19.3% never married, 61.9% now married, 6.9% widowed, 12.0% divorced (2000); Foreign born: 0.6% (2000); Ancestry (includes multiple ancestries): 22.1% United States or American, 14.4% German, 12.9% Other groups, 10.7% Irish, 10.5% English (2000).
Economy: Employment by occupation: 6.0% management, 8.7% professional, 15.9% services, 25.5% sales, 0.0% farming, 10.3% construction, 33.5% production (2000).
Income: Per capita income: $19,805 (2010); Median household income: $47,175 (2010); Average household income: $51,249 (2010); Percent of households with income of $100,000 or more: 6.9% (2010); Poverty rate: 4.6% (2000).
Education: Percent of population age 25 and over with: High school diploma (including GED) or higher: 84.0% (2010); Bachelor's degree or higher: 8.3% (2010); Master's degree or higher: 1.2% (2010).
Housing: Homeownership rate: 79.3% (2010); Median home value: $75,372 (2010); Median contract rent: $544 per month (2000); Median year structure built: 1963 (2000).
Transportation: Commute to work: 97.9% car, 0.0% public transportation, 0.5% walk, 1.7% work from home (2000); Travel time to work: 44.4% less than 15 minutes, 33.6% 15 to 30 minutes, 11.3% 30 to 45 minutes, 5.6% 45 to 60 minutes, 5.1% 60 minutes or more (2000)

KOKOMO (city). County seat. Covers a land area of 16.196 square miles and a water area of 0.059 square miles. Located at 40.48° N. Lat; 86.13° W. Long. Elevation is 810 feet.

History: Kokomo was platted in 1844. The coming of the railroad in 1853 and the discovery of natural gas in 1886 brought growth to the town. Kokomo was named for a Miami chief.
Population: 45,808 (1990); 46,113 (2000); 44,387 (2010); 43,262 (2015 projected); Race: 84.4% White, 10.3% Black, 1.3% Asian, 4.0% Other, 2.8% Hispanic of any race (2010); Density: 2,740.7 persons per square mile (2010); Average household size: 2.16 (2010); Median age: 38.3 (2010); Males per 100 females: 91.6 (2010); Marriage status: 24.3% never married, 50.8% now married, 8.8% widowed, 16.1% divorced (2000); Foreign born: 2.0% (2000); Ancestry (includes multiple ancestries): 21.2% Other groups, 15.8% German, 15.1% United States or American, 8.8% Irish, 7.7% English (2000).
Economy: Unemployment rate: 13.8% (5/2010); Total civilian labor force: 19,282 (5/2010); Single-family building permits issued: 3 (2009); Multi-family building permits issued: 62 (2009); Employment by occupation: 6.9% management, 16.8% professional, 17.3% services, 21.1% sales, 0.1% farming, 9.7% construction, 28.0% production (2000).
Income: Per capita income: $21,199 (2010); Median household income: $37,585 (2010); Average household income: $46,204 (2010); Percent of households with income of $100,000 or more: 6.6% (2010); Poverty rate: 13.0% (2000).
Taxes: Total city taxes per capita: $486 (2007); City property taxes per capita: $456 (2007).
Education: Percent of population age 25 and over with: High school diploma (including GED) or higher: 81.7% (2010); Bachelor's degree or higher: 17.3% (2010); Master's degree or higher: 6.7% (2010).

School District(s)
Kokomo-Center Twp Con Sch Corp (PK-12)
    2008-09 Enrollment: 6,837 . . . . (765) 455-8000
Northwestern School Corp (KG-12)
    2008-09 Enrollment: 1,631 . . . . (765) 452-3060
Taylor Community School Corp (KG-12)
    2008-09 Enrollment: 1,440 . . . . (765) 453-3035

Four-year College(s)
Indiana University-Kokomo (Public)
    Fall 2008 Enrollment: 2,690. . . . . (765) 453-2000
    2009-10 Tuition: In-state $5,838; Out-of-state $14,527

Two-year College(s)
Ivy Tech Community College-Kokomo (Public)
    Fall 2008 Enrollment: 3,895. . . . . (765) 459-0561
    2009-10 Tuition: In-state $3,090; Out-of-state $6,306

Vocational/Technical School(s)
Rudae's School of Beauty Culture Inc (Private, For-profit)
    Fall 2008 Enrollment: 66 . . . . (800) 466-9744
    2009-10 Tuition: $9,900
Housing: Homeownership rate: 58.7% (2010); Median home value: $80,706 (2010); Median contract rent: $426 per month (2000); Median year structure built: 1957 (2000).
Hospitals: Howard Regional Health System (150 beds); Saint Joseph Hospital (156 beds)
Safety: Violent crime rate: 47.4 per 10,000 population; Property crime rate: 586.3 per 10,000 population (2008).
Newspapers: Kokomo Herald (Local news); Kokomo Tribune (Local news; Circulation 23,323)
Transportation: Commute to work: 94.4% car, 0.5% public transportation, 2.2% walk, 1.8% work from home (2000); Travel time to work: 58.5% less than 15 minutes, 27.8% 15 to 30 minutes, 5.9% 30 to 45 minutes, 3.2% 45 to 60 minutes, 4.7% 60 minutes or more (2000)
Additional Information Contacts
City of Kokomo. . . . . (765) 456-7370
    http://www.cityofkokomo.org
Kokomo/Howard County Chamber of Commerce . . . . (765) 457-5301
    http://www.kokomochamber.com

RUSSIAVILLE (town). Covers a land area of 0.802 square miles and a water area of 0 square miles. Located at 40.41° N. Lat; 86.27° W. Long. Elevation is 843 feet.

History: Laid out 1845.
Population: 1,056 (1990); 1,092 (2000); 1,220 (2010); 1,233 (2015 projected); Race: 98.3% White, 0.4% Black, 0.4% Asian, 0.9% Other, 0.9% Hispanic of any race (2010); Density: 1,520.9 persons per square mile (2010); Average household size: 2.52 (2010); Median age: 36.8 (2010); Males per 100 females: 97.1 (2010); Marriage status: 15.3% never married, 67.2% now married, 7.8% widowed, 9.7% divorced (2000); Foreign born: 0.7% (2000); Ancestry (includes multiple ancestries): 19.8% German, 16.4% United States or American, 13.1% English, 10.0% Other groups, 8.0% Irish (2000).
Economy: Single-family building permits issued: 0 (2009); Multi-family building permits issued: 0 (2009); Employment by occupation: 4.2% management, 15.1% professional, 17.7% services, 21.2% sales, 0.0% farming, 9.7% construction, 32.1% production (2000).
Income: Per capita income: $24,654 (2010); Median household income: $51,425 (2010); Average household income: $62,371 (2010); Percent of households with income of $100,000 or more: 15.3% (2010); Poverty rate: 5.7% (2000).
Taxes: Total city taxes per capita: $232 (2007); City property taxes per capita: $151 (2007).
Education: Percent of population age 25 and over with: High school diploma (including GED) or higher: 88.8% (2010); Bachelor's degree or higher: 12.1% (2010); Master's degree or higher: 4.5% (2010).

School District(s)
Western School Corp (KG-12)
    2008-09 Enrollment: 2,517 . . . . (765) 883-5576
Housing: Homeownership rate: 82.6% (2010); Median home value: $100,954 (2010); Median contract rent: $358 per month (2000); Median year structure built: 1964 (2000).
Transportation: Commute to work: 94.6% car, 0.4% public transportation, 2.2% walk, 2.4% work from home (2000); Travel time to work: 25.6% less than 15 minutes, 47.4% 15 to 30 minutes, 16.4% 30 to 45 minutes, 3.1% 45 to 60 minutes, 7.6% 60 minutes or more (2000)

Huntington County

Located in northeast central Indiana; drained by the Wabash, Salamonie, and Little Rivers. Covers a land area of 382.59 square miles, a water area of 5.35 square miles, and is located in the Eastern Time Zone. The county was founded in 1832. County seat is Huntington.

Huntington County is part of the Huntington, IN Micropolitan Statistical Area. The entire metro area includes: Huntington County, IN

Population: 35,427 (1990); 38,075 (2000); 37,393 (2010); 36,765 (2015 projected); Race: 97.3% White, 0.5% Black, 0.6% Asian, 1.7% Other, 1.2%

Hispanic of any race (2010); Density: 97.7 persons per square mile (2010); Average household size: 2.51 (2010); Median age: 38.8 (2010); Males per 100 females: 94.2 (2010).

Religion: Five largest groups: 13.3% Catholic Church, 7.8% The United Methodist Church, 4.8% The Salvation Army, 4.1% United Church of Christ, 3.8% Christian Churches and Churches of Christ (2000).

Economy: Unemployment rate: 10.7% (5/2010); Total civilian labor force: 19,828 (5/2010); Leading industries: 29.6% manufacturing; 12.9% health care and social assistance; 10.7% retail trade (2008); Farms: 766 totaling 199,070 acres (2007); Companies that employ 500 or more persons: 2 (2008); Companies that employ 100 to 499 persons: 23 (2008); Companies that employ less than 100 persons: 885 (2008); Black-owned businesses: n/a (2002); Hispanic-owned businesses: n/a (2002); Asian-owned businesses: n/a (2002); Women-owned businesses: 779 (2002); Retail sales per capita: $12,742 (2010). Single-family building permits issued: 29 (2009); Multi-family building permits issued: 0 (2009).

Income: Per capita income: $21,811 (2010); Median household income: $46,783 (2010); Average household income: $56,210 (2010); Percent of households with income of $100,000 or more: 10.3% (2010); Poverty rate: 10.8% (2008); Bankruptcy rate: 7.77% (2009).

Taxes: Total county taxes per capita: $282 (2007); County property taxes per capita: $157 (2007).

Education: Percent of population age 25 and over with: High school diploma (including GED) or higher: 87.3% (2010); Bachelor's degree or higher: 15.2% (2010); Master's degree or higher: 5.7% (2010).

Housing: Homeownership rate: 80.7% (2010); Median home value: $94,884 (2010); Median contract rent: $437 per month (2006-2008 3-year est.); Median year structure built: 1955 (2006-2008 3-year est.)

Health: Birth rate: 121.8 per 10,000 population (2009); Death rate: 108.5 per 10,000 population (2009); Age-adjusted cancer mortality rate: 151.0 deaths per 100,000 population (2006); Air Quality Index: 96.7% good, 3.3% moderate, 0.0% unhealthy for sensitive individuals, 0.0% unhealthy (percent of days in 2008); Number of physicians: 9.5 per 10,000 population (2007); Hospital beds: 9.5 per 10,000 population (2006); Hospital admissions: 465.5 per 10,000 population (2006).

Elections: 2008 Presidential election results: 35.7% Obama, 62.9% McCain, 0.0% Nader

National and State Parks: Kil-So-Quah State Recreation Area; Little Turtle State Recreation Area; Markle State Recreation Area; Mount Etna State Recreation Area

Additional Information Contacts

Huntington County Government . . . . (219) 358-4822
   http://www.huntington.in.us
City of Huntington . . . . (260) 356-1400
   http://www.huntington.in.us
Huntington Chamber of Commerce . . . . (219) 356-5300
   http://www.huntington-chamber.com
Huntington County Chamber of Commerce . . . . (260) 356-5300
   http://www.huntington-chamber.com
Town of Andrews . . . . (260) 356-1400
   http://www.huntington.in.us

Huntington County Communities

ANDREWS (town). Covers a land area of 0.496 square miles and a water area of 0 square miles. Located at 40.86° N. Lat; 85.60° W. Long. Elevation is 712 feet.

History: Andrews was the birthplace of educator Ellwood Patterson Cubberley who graduated from Indiana University in 1891 and went on to be president of Vincennes University and instrumental in the early days of Stanford University.

Population: 1,156 (1990); 1,290 (2000); 1,285 (2010); 1,279 (2015 projected); Race: 96.5% White, 0.2% Black, 0.4% Asian, 2.9% Other, 2.3% Hispanic of any race (2010); Density: 2,592.1 persons per square mile (2010); Average household size: 2.65 (2010); Median age: 40.3 (2010); Males per 100 females: 99.5 (2010); Marriage status: 21.3% never married, 57.8% now married, 6.5% widowed, 14.3% divorced (2000); Foreign born: 1.0% (2000); Ancestry (includes multiple ancestries): 20.9% German, 13.8% United States or American, 8.2% Other groups, 7.3% Irish, 6.1% English (2000).

Economy: Employment by occupation: 4.8% management, 6.1% professional, 14.6% services, 11.7% sales, 0.0% farming, 14.1% construction, 48.8% production (2000).

Income: Per capita income: $21,691 (2010); Median household income: $46,466 (2010); Average household income: $59,070 (2010); Percent of

households with income of $100,000 or more: 11.2% (2010); Poverty rate: 8.2% (2000).

Taxes: Total city taxes per capita: $177 (2007); City property taxes per capita: $132 (2007).

Education: Percent of population age 25 and over with: High school diploma (including GED) or higher: 85.2% (2010); Bachelor's degree or higher: 10.3% (2010); Master's degree or higher: 1.9% (2010).

School District(s)

Huntington Co Com Sch Corp (PK-12)
   2008-09 Enrollment: 6,049 . . . . (260) 356-7812

Housing: Homeownership rate: 82.5% (2010); Median home value: $115,625 (2010); Median contract rent: $358 per month (2000); Median year structure built: 1952 (2000).

Transportation: Commute to work: 93.5% car, 0.0% public transportation, 2.5% walk, 1.8% work from home (2000); Travel time to work: 27.2% less than 15 minutes, 40.3% 15 to 30 minutes, 16.2% 30 to 45 minutes, 12.4% 45 to 60 minutes, 3.9% 60 minutes or more (2000)

Additional Information Contacts

Huntington County Chamber of Commerce . . . . (260) 356-5300
   http://www.huntington-chamber.com
Town of Andrews . . . . (260) 356-1400
   http://www.huntington.in.us

HUNTINGTON (city). County seat. Covers a land area of 8.345 square miles and a water area of 0.086 square miles. Located at 40.88° N. Lat; 85.49° W. Long. Elevation is 748 feet.

History: Huntington was named in 1831 for Samuel Huntington, a member of the first Continental Congress. Previous to that the community was known as Wepecheange, meaning "place of flints." Huntington was the home of John R. Kissinger, on whom Dr. Walter Reed experimented with yellow fever tests in 1900 in Cuba.

Population: 17,066 (1990); 17,450 (2000); 16,375 (2010); 15,695 (2015 projected); Race: 97.0% White, 0.6% Black, 0.7% Asian, 1.7% Other, 1.3% Hispanic of any race (2010); Density: 1,962.2 persons per square mile (2010); Average household size: 2.40 (2010); Median age: 35.9 (2010); Males per 100 females: 92.1 (2010); Marriage status: 26.9% never married, 54.5% now married, 6.0% widowed, 12.6% divorced (2000); Foreign born: 1.0% (2000); Ancestry (includes multiple ancestries): 28.5% German, 13.6% United States or American, 9.8% Irish, 7.4% Other groups, 6.6% English (2000).

Economy: Employment by occupation: 8.1% management, 12.2% professional, 16.6% services, 21.5% sales, 0.1% farming, 7.7% construction, 33.9% production (2000).

Income: Per capita income: $19,474 (2010); Median household income: $39,708 (2010); Average household income: $48,724 (2010); Percent of households with income of $100,000 or more: 6.7% (2010); Poverty rate: 8.1% (2000).

Taxes: Total city taxes per capita: $270 (2007); City property taxes per capita: $262 (2007).

Education: Percent of population age 25 and over with: High school diploma (including GED) or higher: 84.0% (2010); Bachelor's degree or higher: 14.2% (2010); Master's degree or higher: 5.6% (2010).

School District(s)

Huntington Co Com Sch Corp (PK-12)
   2008-09 Enrollment: 6,049 . . . . (260) 356-7812

Four-year College(s)

Huntington University (Private, Not-for-profit, United Brethren Church)
   Fall 2008 Enrollment: 1,230 . . . . (260) 356-6000
   2009-10 Tuition: In-state $21,290; Out-of-state $21,290

Housing: Homeownership rate: 73.1% (2010); Median home value: $78,701 (2010); Median contract rent: $401 per month (2000); Median year structure built: 1944 (2000).

Hospitals: Parkview Huntington Hospital (36 beds)

Safety: Violent crime rate: 18.1 per 10,000 population; Property crime rate: 241.9 per 10,000 population (2008).

Newspapers: Huntington County Tab (Community news; Circulation 15,800); Huntington Herald-Press (Local news; Circulation 7,700)

Transportation: Commute to work: 89.5% car, 0.1% public transportation, 5.3% walk, 3.4% work from home (2000); Travel time to work: 56.3% less than 15 minutes, 19.9% 15 to 30 minutes, 15.3% 30 to 45 minutes, 5.7% 45 to 60 minutes, 2.7% 60 minutes or more (2000)

Additional Information Contacts

City of Huntington . . . . (260) 356-1400
   http://www.huntington.in.us

Huntington Chamber of Commerce . . . . (219) 356-5300
　　http://www.huntington-chamber.com

MARKLE (town). Covers a land area of 0.987 square miles and a water area of 0.030 square miles. Located at 40.82° N. Lat; 85.33° W. Long. Elevation is 810 feet.
Population: 1,273 (1990); 1,102 (2000); 1,107 (2010); 1,102 (2015 projected); Race: 98.6% White, 0.5% Black, 0.2% Asian, 0.7% Other, 1.2% Hispanic of any race (2010); Density: 1,121.4 persons per square mile (2010); Average household size: 2.57 (2010); Median age: 38.2 (2010); Males per 100 females: 98.7 (2010); Marriage status: 18.4% never married, 55.2% now married, 12.2% widowed, 14.2% divorced (2000); Foreign born: 0.4% (2000); Ancestry (includes multiple ancestries): 26.9% German, 12.7% English, 11.2% Irish, 9.7% United States or American, 8.6% Other groups (2000).
Economy: Employment by occupation: 11.5% management, 10.0% professional, 11.3% services, 25.3% sales, 0.6% farming, 12.8% construction, 28.5% production (2000).
Income: Per capita income: $22,328 (2010); Median household income: $53,448 (2010); Average household income: $58,721 (2010); Percent of households with income of $100,000 or more: 12.7% (2010); Poverty rate: 6.7% (2000).
Taxes: Total city taxes per capita: $309 (2007); City property taxes per capita: $245 (2007).
Education: Percent of population age 25 and over with: High school diploma (including GED) or higher: 91.0% (2010); Bachelor's degree or higher: 12.1% (2010); Master's degree or higher: 3.9% (2010).
Housing: Homeownership rate: 81.0% (2010); Median home value: $92,078 (2010); Median contract rent: $322 per month (2000); Median year structure built: 1951 (2000).
Transportation: Commute to work: 92.7% car, 0.0% public transportation, 3.7% walk, 2.5% work from home (2000); Travel time to work: 25.6% less than 15 minutes, 44.4% 15 to 30 minutes, 25.0% 30 to 45 minutes, 3.2% 45 to 60 minutes, 1.8% 60 minutes or more (2000)

MOUNT ETNA (town). Covers a land area of 0.082 square miles and a water area of 0 square miles. Located at 40.74° N. Lat; 85.56° W. Long. Elevation is 810 feet.
History: Mount Etna was founded in 1839, and named for Mt. Etna in Sicily.
Population: 111 (1990); 110 (2000); 95 (2010); 97 (2015 projected); Race: 96.8% White, 1.1% Black, 0.0% Asian, 2.1% Other, 1.1% Hispanic of any race (2010); Density: 1,159.9 persons per square mile (2010); Average household size: 2.64 (2010); Median age: 43.8 (2010); Males per 100 females: 97.9 (2010); Marriage status: 21.6% never married, 54.5% now married, 9.1% widowed, 14.8% divorced (2000); Foreign born: 1.9% (2000); Ancestry (includes multiple ancestries): 33.0% German, 22.6% United States or American, 18.9% English, 12.3% Irish, 3.8% Scottish (2000).
Economy: Employment by occupation: 5.7% management, 7.5% professional, 15.1% services, 34.0% sales, 0.0% farming, 5.7% construction, 32.1% production (2000).
Income: Per capita income: $22,520 (2010); Median household income: $52,273 (2010); Average household income: $56,875 (2010); Percent of households with income of $100,000 or more: 8.3% (2010); Poverty rate: 10.7% (2000).
Taxes: Total city taxes per capita: $123 (2007); City property taxes per capita: $38 (2007).
Education: Percent of population age 25 and over with: High school diploma (including GED) or higher: 91.2% (2010); Bachelor's degree or higher: 16.2% (2010); Master's degree or higher: 5.9% (2010).
Housing: Homeownership rate: 88.9% (2010); Median home value: $131,818 (2010); Median contract rent: $n/a per month (2000); Median year structure built: before 1940 (2000).
Transportation: Commute to work: 100.0% car, 0.0% public transportation, 0.0% walk, 0.0% work from home (2000); Travel time to work: 7.5% less than 15 minutes, 66.0% 15 to 30 minutes, 5.7% 30 to 45 minutes, 9.4% 45 to 60 minutes, 11.3% 60 minutes or more (2000)

ROANOKE (town). Covers a land area of 0.623 square miles and a water area of 0 square miles. Located at 40.96° N. Lat; 85.37° W. Long. Elevation is 758 feet.
History: Roanoke was known for the Roanoke Classical Seminary founded in 1861 by Frederick S. Reefy. The emphasis in culture provided by the seminary gave Roanoke the reputation as the Athens of Indiana.

Population: 1,280 (1990); 1,495 (2000); 1,290 (2010); 1,253 (2015 projected); Race: 97.8% White, 0.3% Black, 0.9% Asian, 1.1% Other, 1.1% Hispanic of any race (2010); Density: 2,071.4 persons per square mile (2010); Average household size: 2.51 (2010); Median age: 40.3 (2010); Males per 100 females: 97.5 (2010); Marriage status: 21.1% never married, 64.2% now married, 6.2% widowed, 8.5% divorced (2000); Foreign born: 0.3% (2000); Ancestry (includes multiple ancestries): 40.7% German, 12.6% Irish, 10.9% United States or American, 7.4% English, 5.9% Other groups (2000).
Economy: Employment by occupation: 11.9% management, 15.6% professional, 13.7% services, 20.7% sales, 0.2% farming, 9.7% construction, 28.2% production (2000).
Income: Per capita income: $24,319 (2010); Median household income: $56,163 (2010); Average household income: $61,267 (2010); Percent of households with income of $100,000 or more: 14.5% (2010); Poverty rate: 5.4% (2000).
Taxes: Total city taxes per capita: $165 (2007); City property taxes per capita: $163 (2007).
Education: Percent of population age 25 and over with: High school diploma (including GED) or higher: 91.5% (2010); Bachelor's degree or higher: 19.7% (2010); Master's degree or higher: 8.0% (2010).
　　　　　　　　　　School District(s)
Huntington Co Com Sch Corp (PK-12)
　　2008-09 Enrollment: 6,049 . . . . (260) 356-7812
M S D Southwest Allen County (PK-12)
　　2008-09 Enrollment: 6,811 . . . . (260) 431-2010
Housing: Homeownership rate: 86.7% (2010); Median home value: $116,123 (2010); Median contract rent: $400 per month (2000); Median year structure built: 1968 (2000).
Transportation: Commute to work: 96.8% car, 0.5% public transportation, 2.1% walk, 0.6% work from home (2000); Travel time to work: 31.6% less than 15 minutes, 38.7% 15 to 30 minutes, 23.4% 30 to 45 minutes, 2.7% 45 to 60 minutes, 3.5% 60 minutes or more (2000)

WARREN (town). Covers a land area of 0.912 square miles and a water area of 0 square miles. Located at 40.68° N. Lat; 85.42° W. Long. Elevation is 823 feet.
History: Laid out 1836.
Population: 1,234 (1990); 1,272 (2000); 1,280 (2010); 1,266 (2015 projected); Race: 97.7% White, 0.7% Black, 0.1% Asian, 1.5% Other, 2.1% Hispanic of any race (2010); Density: 1,403.8 persons per square mile (2010); Average household size: 2.45 (2010); Median age: 41.7 (2010); Males per 100 females: 89.9 (2010); Marriage status: 19.7% never married, 60.1% now married, 6.7% widowed, 13.6% divorced (2000); Foreign born: 0.3% (2000); Ancestry (includes multiple ancestries): 28.0% German, 19.0% United States or American, 12.3% English, 9.4% Irish, 5.1% Other groups (2000).
Economy: Employment by occupation: 7.7% management, 11.3% professional, 22.1% services, 16.6% sales, 1.3% farming, 11.1% construction, 29.8% production (2000).
Income: Per capita income: $22,215 (2010); Median household income: $46,560 (2010); Average household income: $55,502 (2010); Percent of households with income of $100,000 or more: 10.4% (2010); Poverty rate: 3.1% (2000).
Taxes: Total city taxes per capita: $230 (2007); City property taxes per capita: $194 (2007).
Education: Percent of population age 25 and over with: High school diploma (including GED) or higher: 88.1% (2010); Bachelor's degree or higher: 13.2% (2010); Master's degree or higher: 4.4% (2010).
　　　　　　　　　　School District(s)
Huntington Co Com Sch Corp (PK-12)
　　2008-09 Enrollment: 6,049 . . . . (260) 356-7812
Housing: Homeownership rate: 81.9% (2010); Median home value: $93,086 (2010); Median contract rent: $343 per month (2000); Median year structure built: before 1940 (2000).
Transportation: Commute to work: 93.1% car, 0.3% public transportation, 4.7% walk, 1.6% work from home (2000); Travel time to work: 36.4% less than 15 minutes, 30.1% 15 to 30 minutes, 22.7% 30 to 45 minutes, 7.0% 45 to 60 minutes, 3.9% 60 minutes or more (2000)

Jackson County

Located in southern Indiana; bounded on the south by the Muscatatuck River; drained by the East Fork of the White River. Covers a land area of 509.31 square miles, a water area of 4.44 square miles, and is located in the Eastern Time Zone. The county was founded in 1815. County seat is Brownstown.

Jackson County is part of the Seymour, IN Micropolitan Statistical Area. The entire metro area includes: Jackson County, IN

Weather Station: Seymour 2 N											Elevation: 567 feet	
	Jan	Feb	Mar	Apr	May	Jun	Jul	Aug	Sep	Oct	Nov	Dec
High	37	42	53	65	74	82	85	84	79	67	54	42
Low	19	22	31	40	51	60	64	61	53	40	33	24
Precip	3.1	2.7	3.8	4.7	4.9	4.0	4.4	4.3	3.0	3.3	4.0	3.4
Snow	na	na	2.3	tr	0.0	0.0	0.0	0.0	0.0	0.2	0.6	1.9

High and Low temperatures in degrees Fahrenheit; Precipitation and Snow in inches

Population: 37,730 (1990); 41,335 (2000); 42,382 (2010); 42,663 (2015 projected); Race: 94.0% White, 0.7% Black, 0.9% Asian, 4.4% Other, 5.4% Hispanic of any race (2010); Density: 83.2 persons per square mile (2010); Average household size: 2.48 (2010); Median age: 38.4 (2010); Males per 100 females: 98.6 (2010).
Religion: Five largest groups: 17.5% Lutheran Church—Missouri Synod, 9.8% Christian Churches and Churches of Christ, 5.4% American Baptist Churches in the USA, 5.2% Church of the Nazarene, 4.4% The United Methodist Church (2000).
Economy: Unemployment rate: 9.6% (5/2010); Total civilian labor force: 21,657 (5/2010); Leading industries: 34.7% manufacturing; 12.5% retail trade; 11.8% health care and social assistance (2008); Farms: 827 totaling 209,293 acres (2007); Companies that employ 500 or more persons: 4 (2008); Companies that employ 100 to 499 persons: 28 (2008); Companies that employ less than 100 persons: 1,036 (2008); Black-owned businesses: n/a (2002); Hispanic-owned businesses: n/a (2002); Asian-owned businesses: n/a (2002); Women-owned businesses: 522 (2002); Retail sales per capita: $12,809 (2010). Single-family building permits issued: 59 (2009); Multi-family building permits issued: 21 (2009).
Income: Per capita income: $22,381 (2010); Median household income: $46,088 (2010); Average household income: $55,732 (2010); Percent of households with income of $100,000 or more: 10.3% (2010); Poverty rate: 10.5% (2008); Bankruptcy rate: 9.46% (2009).
Taxes: Total county taxes per capita: $124 (2007); County property taxes per capita: $71 (2007).
Education: Percent of population age 25 and over with: High school diploma (including GED) or higher: 83.2% (2010); Bachelor's degree or higher: 13.9% (2010); Master's degree or higher: 4.8% (2010).
Housing: Homeownership rate: 72.7% (2010); Median home value: $101,898 (2010); Median contract rent: $491 per month (2006-2008 3-year est.); Median year structure built: 1972 (2006-2008 3-year est.)
Health: Birth rate: 135.0 per 10,000 population (2009); Death rate: 99.6 per 10,000 population (2009); Age-adjusted cancer mortality rate: 223.3 deaths per 100,000 population (2006); Air Quality Index: 83.2% good, 16.3% moderate, 0.5% unhealthy for sensitive individuals, 0.0% unhealthy (percent of days in 2008); Number of physicians: 11.6 per 10,000 population (2007); Hospital beds: 25.7 per 10,000 population (2006); Hospital admissions: 878.6 per 10,000 population (2006).
Elections: 2008 Presidential election results: 42.3% Obama, 56.0% McCain, 0.0% Nader
National and State Parks: Starve Hollow State Beach
Additional Information Contacts
Jackson County Government. . . . . (812) 358-6116
  http://www.seymour.org
City of Seymour . . . . (812) 522-4020
  http://www.seymourcity.com
Seymour Chamber of Commerce . . . . (812) 522-3681
  http://www.seymourchamber.org

Jackson County Communities

BROWNSTOWN (town). County seat. Covers a land area of 1.431 square miles and a water area of 0 square miles. Located at 38.88° N. Lat; 86.04° W. Long. Elevation is 623 feet.
History: Brownstown was founded in 1816 as a farm town and seat of Jackson County.
Population: 3,094 (1990); 2,978 (2000); 2,914 (2010); 2,874 (2015 projected); Race: 98.3% White, 0.2% Black, 0.3% Asian, 1.2% Other, 1.0% Hispanic of any race (2010); Density: 2,035.8 persons per square mile (2010); Average household size: 2.39 (2010); Median age: 39.1 (2010); Males per 100 females: 89.7 (2010); Marriage status: 19.5% never married, 58.3% now married, 8.7% widowed, 13.4% divorced (2000); Foreign born:

1.6% (2000); Ancestry (includes multiple ancestries): 21.4% German, 21.3% United States or American, 9.5% English, 8.8% Irish, 5.3% Other groups (2000).
Economy: Employment by occupation: 8.3% management, 13.8% professional, 15.5% services, 22.0% sales, 0.4% farming, 10.0% construction, 30.0% production (2000).
Income: Per capita income: $20,973 (2010); Median household income: $42,764 (2010); Average household income: $51,419 (2010); Percent of households with income of $100,000 or more: 8.3% (2010); Poverty rate: 11.7% (2000).
Taxes: Total city taxes per capita: $146 (2007); City property taxes per capita: $125 (2007).
Education: Percent of population age 25 and over with: High school diploma (including GED) or higher: 87.7% (2010); Bachelor's degree or higher: 15.2% (2010); Master's degree or higher: 6.3% (2010).
School District(s)
Brownstown Cnt Com Sch Corp (PK-12)
  2008-09 Enrollment: 1,797 . . . . (812) 358-4271
Housing: Homeownership rate: 71.4% (2010); Median home value: $108,169 (2010); Median contract rent: $340 per month (2000); Median year structure built: 1970 (2000).
Newspapers: Banner (Local news; Circulation 3,875)
Transportation: Commute to work: 93.9% car, 0.4% public transportation, 2.2% walk, 2.9% work from home (2000); Travel time to work: 41.2% less than 15 minutes, 35.3% 15 to 30 minutes, 11.0% 30 to 45 minutes, 7.1% 45 to 60 minutes, 5.4% 60 minutes or more (2000)

CROTHERSVILLE (town). Covers a land area of 1.144 square miles and a water area of 0 square miles. Located at 38.79° N. Lat; 85.84° W. Long. Elevation is 558 feet.
Population: 1,808 (1990); 1,570 (2000); 1,412 (2010); 1,354 (2015 projected); Race: 97.7% White, 0.1% Black, 0.6% Asian, 1.6% Other, 2.8% Hispanic of any race (2010); Density: 1,234.1 persons per square mile (2010); Average household size: 2.40 (2010); Median age: 39.2 (2010); Males per 100 females: 96.1 (2010); Marriage status: 18.8% never married, 60.8% now married, 7.3% widowed, 13.0% divorced (2000); Foreign born: 0.4% (2000); Ancestry (includes multiple ancestries): 26.9% United States or American, 14.8% German, 7.8% Irish, 6.2% English, 5.6% Other groups (2000).
Economy: Employment by occupation: 4.3% management, 7.8% professional, 13.0% services, 25.0% sales, 0.5% farming, 7.2% construction, 42.2% production (2000).
Income: Per capita income: $20,266 (2010); Median household income: $39,355 (2010); Average household income: $48,844 (2010); Percent of households with income of $100,000 or more: 9.5% (2010); Poverty rate: 8.8% (2000).
Taxes: Total city taxes per capita: $98 (2007); City property taxes per capita: $81 (2007).
Education: Percent of population age 25 and over with: High school diploma (including GED) or higher: 79.8% (2010); Bachelor's degree or higher: 7.7% (2010); Master's degree or higher: 3.5% (2010).
School District(s)
Crothersville Community Schools (PK-12)
  2008-09 Enrollment: 548 . . . . (812) 793-2601
Housing: Homeownership rate: 76.0% (2010); Median home value: $89,223 (2010); Median contract rent: $327 per month (2000); Median year structure built: 1962 (2000).
Newspapers: Crothersville Times (Community news; Circulation 1,400)
Transportation: Commute to work: 96.3% car, 0.0% public transportation, 1.2% walk, 1.9% work from home (2000); Travel time to work: 23.3% less than 15 minutes, 46.2% 15 to 30 minutes, 21.6% 30 to 45 minutes, 4.8% 45 to 60 minutes, 4.1% 60 minutes or more (2000)

FREETOWN (unincorporated postal area, zip code 47235). Covers a land area of 48.294 square miles and a water area of 0.071 square miles. Located at 38.98° N. Lat; 86.13° W. Long. Elevation is 650 feet.
Population: 1,938 (2000); Race: 98.1% White, 0.4% Black, 0.0% Asian, 1.5% Other, 0.9% Hispanic of any race (2000); Density: 40.1 persons per square mile (2000); Age: 24.1% under 18, 10.0% over 64 (2000); Marriage status: 21.6% never married, 67.9% now married, 3.3% widowed, 7.2% divorced (2000); Foreign born: 0.0% (2000); Ancestry (includes multiple ancestries): 30.8% United States or American, 16.2% German, 9.7% English, 9.1% Other groups, 5.5% Irish (2000).

Economy: Employment by occupation: 14.4% management, 16.4% professional, 6.1% services, 18.6% sales, 1.1% farming, 16.0% construction, 27.4% production (2000).
Income: Per capita income: $19,434 (2000); Median household income: $45,781 (2000); Poverty rate: 6.8% (2000).
Education: Percent of population age 25 and over with: High school diploma (including GED) or higher: 79.9% (2000); Bachelor's degree or higher: 18.2% (2000).

School District(s)
Brownstown Cnt Com Sch Corp (PK-12)
    2008-09 Enrollment: 1,797 . . . . (812) 358-4271
Housing: Homeownership rate: 89.6% (2000); Median home value: $96,600 (2000); Median contract rent: $245 per month (2000); Median year structure built: 1973 (2000).
Transportation: Commute to work: 94.3% car, 2.3% public transportation, 0.0% walk, 2.8% work from home (2000); Travel time to work: 5.7% less than 15 minutes, 36.2% 15 to 30 minutes, 37.3% 30 to 45 minutes, 13.3% 45 to 60 minutes, 7.5% 60 minutes or more (2000)

MEDORA (town). Covers a land area of 0.319 square miles and a water area of 0 square miles. Located at 38.82° N. Lat; 86.17° W. Long. Elevation is 528 feet.
Population: 805 (1990); 565 (2000); 515 (2010); 490 (2015 projected); Race: 98.6% White, 0.0% Black, 0.2% Asian, 1.2% Other, 1.9% Hispanic of any race (2010); Density: 1,616.6 persons per square mile (2010); Average household size: 2.41 (2010); Median age: 37.5 (2010); Males per 100 females: 97.3 (2010); Marriage status: 27.0% never married, 50.6% now married, 12.9% widowed, 9.5% divorced (2000); Foreign born: 0.5% (2000); Ancestry (includes multiple ancestries): 20.3% German, 14.2% United States or American, 11.6% Irish, 8.0% Other groups, 7.5% English (2000).
Economy: Single-family building permits issued: 0 (2009); Multi-family building permits issued: 0 (2009); Employment by occupation: 3.0% management, 6.0% professional, 14.3% services, 18.5% sales, 6.4% farming, 12.1% construction, 39.6% production (2000).
Income: Per capita income: $18,024 (2010); Median household income: $36,563 (2010); Average household income: $43,388 (2010); Percent of households with income of $100,000 or more: 5.6% (2010); Poverty rate: 10.9% (2000).
Taxes: Total city taxes per capita: $80 (2007); City property taxes per capita: $71 (2007).
Education: Percent of population age 25 and over with: High school diploma (including GED) or higher: 76.4% (2010); Bachelor's degree or higher: 6.0% (2010); Master's degree or higher: 4.0% (2010).

School District(s)
Medora Community School Corp (KG-12)
    2008-09 Enrollment: 285 . . . . (812) 966-2210
Housing: Homeownership rate: 82.2% (2010); Median home value: $58,333 (2010); Median contract rent: $342 per month (2000); Median year structure built: 1963 (2000).
Transportation: Commute to work: 91.4% car, 0.8% public transportation, 6.7% walk, 0.0% work from home (2000); Travel time to work: 20.4% less than 15 minutes, 22.7% 15 to 30 minutes, 35.7% 30 to 45 minutes, 10.6% 45 to 60 minutes, 10.6% 60 minutes or more (2000)

NORMAN (unincorporated postal area, zip code 47264). Covers a land area of 99.737 square miles and a water area of 0.149 square miles. Located at 38.96° N. Lat; 86.27° W. Long. Elevation is 869 feet.
Population: 1,428 (2000); Race: 99.7% White, 0.0% Black, 0.0% Asian, 0.3% Other, 0.0% Hispanic of any race (2000); Density: 14.3 persons per square mile (2000); Age: 16.6% under 18, 16.0% over 64 (2000); Marriage status: 13.3% never married, 74.9% now married, 4.3% widowed, 7.4% divorced (2000); Foreign born: 0.0% (2000); Ancestry (includes multiple ancestries): 17.5% United States or American, 14.6% German, 11.4% Irish, 8.7% English, 6.1% Other groups (2000).
Economy: Employment by occupation: 7.4% management, 3.0% professional, 14.1% services, 12.8% sales, 6.0% farming, 20.8% construction, 35.8% production (2000).
Income: Per capita income: $17,232 (2000); Median household income: $35,625 (2000); Poverty rate: 8.1% (2000).
Education: Percent of population age 25 and over with: High school diploma (including GED) or higher: 68.7% (2000); Bachelor's degree or higher: 4.5% (2000).

Housing: Homeownership rate: 89.7% (2000); Median home value: $73,500 (2000); Median contract rent: $248 per month (2000); Median year structure built: 1966 (2000).
Transportation: Commute to work: 95.2% car, 0.0% public transportation, 0.3% walk, 3.2% work from home (2000); Travel time to work: 3.0% less than 15 minutes, 36.7% 15 to 30 minutes, 32.2% 30 to 45 minutes, 19.4% 45 to 60 minutes, 8.6% 60 minutes or more (2000)

SEYMOUR (city). Covers a land area of 10.837 square miles and a water area of 0 square miles. Located at 38.95° N. Lat; 85.89° W. Long. Elevation is 604 feet.
History: Seymour developed as a factory town at the junction of three railroads.
Population: 15,888 (1990); 18,101 (2000); 18,628 (2010); 18,786 (2015 projected); Race: 89.9% White, 1.3% Black, 1.3% Asian, 7.5% Other, 9.8% Hispanic of any race (2010); Density: 1,718.9 persons per square mile (2010); Average household size: 2.40 (2010); Median age: 36.8 (2010); Males per 100 females: 98.1 (2010); Marriage status: 20.9% never married, 57.8% now married, 7.8% widowed, 13.5% divorced (2000); Foreign born: 4.4% (2000); Ancestry (includes multiple ancestries): 23.9% German, 20.1% United States or American, 10.3% Other groups, 8.9% Irish, 6.3% English (2000).
Economy: Single-family building permits issued: 43 (2009); Multi-family building permits issued: 21 (2009); Employment by occupation: 7.6% management, 12.8% professional, 10.4% services, 22.7% sales, 1.0% farming, 10.1% construction, 35.3% production (2000).
Income: Per capita income: $21,170 (2010); Median household income: $42,301 (2010); Average household income: $51,251 (2010); Percent of households with income of $100,000 or more: 7.8% (2010); Poverty rate: 10.0% (2000).
Taxes: Total city taxes per capita: $297 (2007); City property taxes per capita: $253 (2007).
Education: Percent of population age 25 and over with: High school diploma (including GED) or higher: 81.5% (2010); Bachelor's degree or higher: 13.9% (2010); Master's degree or higher: 5.0% (2010).

School District(s)
Seymour Community Schools (PK-12)
    2008-09 Enrollment: 4,111 . . . . (812) 522-3340
Housing: Homeownership rate: 62.2% (2010); Median home value: $88,043 (2010); Median contract rent: $421 per month (2000); Median year structure built: 1968 (2000).
Hospitals: Schneck Medical Center (166 beds)
Safety: Violent crime rate: 49.3 per 10,000 population; Property crime rate: 665.8 per 10,000 population (2008).
Newspapers: The Tribune (Local news; Circulation 1,300)
Transportation: Commute to work: 95.1% car, 0.0% public transportation, 1.8% walk, 1.7% work from home (2000); Travel time to work: 57.4% less than 15 minutes, 25.3% 15 to 30 minutes, 10.3% 30 to 45 minutes, 2.7% 45 to 60 minutes, 4.3% 60 minutes or more (2000)
Additional Information Contacts
City of Seymour . . . . (812) 522-4020
    http://www.seymourcity.com
Seymour Chamber of Commerce . . . . (812) 522-3681
    http://www.seymourchamber.org

VALLONIA (unincorporated postal area, zip code 47281). Covers a land area of 52.840 square miles and a water area of 0.269 square miles. Located at 38.80° N. Lat; 86.09° W. Long. Elevation is 535 feet.
History: Vallonia is on the site of old Fort Vallonia, built in 1805. Vallonia was platted in 1810, and was the first seat of Jackson County.
Population: 1,392 (2000); Race: 99.6% White, 0.0% Black, 0.0% Asian, 0.4% Other, 0.0% Hispanic of any race (2000); Density: 26.3 persons per square mile (2000); Age: 22.9% under 18, 16.3% over 64 (2000); Marriage status: 13.7% never married, 68.0% now married, 7.2% widowed, 11.0% divorced (2000); Foreign born: 0.0% (2000); Ancestry (includes multiple ancestries): 21.6% German, 19.0% United States or American, 10.7% Other groups, 5.5% Irish, 3.9% English (2000).
Economy: Employment by occupation: 12.8% management, 11.3% professional, 6.8% services, 15.4% sales, 4.1% farming, 15.5% construction, 34.1% production (2000).
Income: Per capita income: $16,292 (2000); Median household income: $32,188 (2000); Poverty rate: 6.2% (2000).
Education: Percent of population age 25 and over with: High school diploma (including GED) or higher: 69.8% (2000); Bachelor's degree or higher: 7.2% (2000).

Housing: Homeownership rate: 84.4% (2000); Median home value: $91,600 (2000); Median contract rent: $191 per month (2000); Median year structure built: 1965 (2000).
Transportation: Commute to work: 91.1% car, 0.0% public transportation, 0.0% walk, 7.8% work from home (2000); Travel time to work: 16.8% less than 15 minutes, 39.7% 15 to 30 minutes, 23.2% 30 to 45 minutes, 11.2% 45 to 60 minutes, 9.1% 60 minutes or more (2000)

Jasper County

Located in northwestern Indiana; bounded on the north by the Kankakee River; drained by the Iroquois River. Covers a land area of 559.87 square miles, a water area of 1.36 square miles, and is located in the Central Time Zone. The county was founded in 1835. County seat is Rensselaer.

Jasper County is part of the Chicago-Naperville-Joliet, IL-IN-WI Metropolitan Statistical Area. The entire metro area includes: Chicago-Naperville-Joliet, IL Metropolitan Division (Cook County, IL; DeKalb County, IL; DuPage County, IL; Grundy County, IL; Kane County, IL; Kendall County, IL; McHenry County, IL; Will County, IL); Gary, IN Metropolitan Division (Jasper County, IN; Lake County, IN; Newton County, IN; Porter County, IN); Lake County-Kenosha County, IL-WI Metropolitan Division (Lake County, IL; Kenosha County, WI)

Weather Station: Rensselaer   Elevation: 649 feet

	Jan	Feb	Mar	Apr	May	Jun	Jul	Aug	Sep	Oct	Nov	Dec
High	31	36	47	60	72	81	85	82	76	64	49	36
Low	15	19	29	39	50	60	64	61	53	41	32	21
Precip	2.0	1.7	3.2	3.5	4.3	4.4	3.8	3.5	3.5	3.1	3.2	2.7
Snow	na	na	na	0.3	0.0	0.0	0.0	0.0	0.0	tr	0.5	na

High and Low temperatures in degrees Fahrenheit; Precipitation and Snow in inches

Population: 24,960 (1990); 30,043 (2000); 33,039 (2010); 34,325 (2015 projected); Race: 96.6% White, 0.9% Black, 0.3% Asian, 2.2% Other, 4.2% Hispanic of any race (2010); Density: 59.0 persons per square mile (2010); Average household size: 2.67 (2010); Median age: 36.0 (2010); Males per 100 females: 98.7 (2010).
Religion: Five largest groups: 13.7% Catholic Church, 5.4% The United Methodist Church, 5.2% Reformed Church in America, 4.8% Christian Reformed Church in North America, 2.9% Lutheran Church—Missouri Synod (2000).
Economy: Unemployment rate: 10.0% (5/2010); Total civilian labor force: 15,146 (5/2010); Leading industries: 16.2% manufacturing; 14.9% health care and social assistance; 14.6% retail trade (2008); Farms: 734 totaling 340,339 acres (2007); Companies that employ 500 or more persons: 0 (2008); Companies that employ 100 to 499 persons: 18 (2008); Companies that employ less than 100 persons: 745 (2008); Black-owned businesses: n/a (2002); Hispanic-owned businesses: n/a (2002); Asian-owned businesses: n/a (2002); Women-owned businesses: 497 (2002); Retail sales per capita: $15,196 (2010). Single-family building permits issued: 91 (2009); Multi-family building permits issued: 0 (2009).
Income: Per capita income: $23,311 (2010); Median household income: $53,345 (2010); Average household income: $63,369 (2010); Percent of households with income of $100,000 or more: 14.5% (2010); Poverty rate: 8.9% (2008); Bankruptcy rate: 6.10% (2009).
Taxes: Total county taxes per capita: $292 (2007); County property taxes per capita: $151 (2007).
Education: Percent of population age 25 and over with: High school diploma (including GED) or higher: 86.6% (2010); Bachelor's degree or higher: 15.1% (2010); Master's degree or higher: 4.5% (2010).
Housing: Homeownership rate: 76.6% (2010); Median home value: $126,874 (2010); Median contract rent: $501 per month (2006-2008 3-year est.); Median year structure built: 1979 (2006-2008 3-year est.)
Health: Birth rate: 142.9 per 10,000 population (2009); Death rate: 90.5 per 10,000 population (2009); Age-adjusted cancer mortality rate: 202.5 deaths per 100,000 population (2006); Air Quality Index: 100.0% good, 0.0% moderate, 0.0% unhealthy for sensitive individuals, 0.0% unhealthy (percent of days in 2008); Number of physicians: 7.1 per 10,000 population (2007); Hospital beds: 13.2 per 10,000 population (2006); Hospital admissions: 435.2 per 10,000 population (2006).
Elections: 2008 Presidential election results: 39.2% Obama, 59.6% McCain, 0.1% Nader
Additional Information Contacts
Jasper County Government . . . . (219) 866-4926
   http://www.jaspercountyin.gov

City of Rensselaer . . . . (219) 866-5213
   http://www.cityofrensselaerin.com
Town of De Motte. . . . . (219) 987-3831
   http://www.townofdemotte.com

Jasper County Communities

COLLEGEVILLE (CDP). Covers a land area of 1.290 square miles and a water area of 0 square miles. Located at 40.91° N. Lat; 87.15° W. Long. Elevation is 666 feet.
History: Seat of St. Joseph's College.
Population: 993 (1990); 865 (2000); 924 (2010); 964 (2015 projected); Race: 91.9% White, 5.8% Black, 0.1% Asian, 2.2% Other, 5.0% Hispanic of any race (2010); Density: 716.2 persons per square mile (2010); Average household size: 2.70 (2010); Median age: 23.4 (2010); Males per 100 females: 112.4 (2010); Marriage status: 46.7% never married, 48.3% now married, 4.4% widowed, 0.6% divorced (2000); Foreign born: 0.7% (2000); Ancestry (includes multiple ancestries): 23.7% German, 15.2% Irish, 11.0% Italian, 9.8% Other groups, 6.2% Polish (2000).
Economy: Employment by occupation: 10.4% management, 25.4% professional, 14.1% services, 35.2% sales, 1.4% farming, 3.7% construction, 9.9% production (2000).
Income: Per capita income: $18,539 (2010); Median household income: $56,250 (2010); Average household income: $77,005 (2010); Percent of households with income of $100,000 or more: 25.2% (2010); Poverty rate: 19.5% (2000).
Education: Percent of population age 25 and over with: High school diploma (including GED) or higher: 94.3% (2010); Bachelor's degree or higher: 15.8% (2010); Master's degree or higher: 5.7% (2010).
Housing: Homeownership rate: 78.2% (2010); Median home value: $135,714 (2010); Median contract rent: $575 per month (2000); Median year structure built: 1973 (2000).
Transportation: Commute to work: 59.7% car, 0.0% public transportation, 33.4% walk, 3.2% work from home (2000); Travel time to work: 75.6% less than 15 minutes, 12.5% 15 to 30 minutes, 3.3% 30 to 45 minutes, 8.6% 45 to 60 minutes, 0.0% 60 minutes or more (2000)

DE MOTTE (town). Aka Demotte. Covers a land area of 3.590 square miles and a water area of 0 square miles. Located at 41.19° N. Lat; 87.19° W. Long. Elevation is 669 feet.
Population: 2,518 (1990); 3,234 (2000); 3,845 (2010); 4,104 (2015 projected); Race: 98.5% White, 0.2% Black, 0.1% Asian, 1.2% Other, 2.2% Hispanic of any race (2010); Density: 1,070.9 persons per square mile (2010); Average household size: 2.57 (2010); Median age: 38.5 (2010); Males per 100 females: 94.9 (2010); Marriage status: 20.1% never married, 59.4% now married, 11.3% widowed, 9.2% divorced (2000); Foreign born: 2.4% (2000); Ancestry (includes multiple ancestries): 25.0% German, 19.5% Dutch, 12.5% Irish, 10.4% English, 7.9% Polish (2000).
Economy: Single-family building permits issued: 33 (2009); Multi-family building permits issued: 0 (2009); Employment by occupation: 8.8% management, 16.9% professional, 17.7% services, 16.6% sales, 1.1% farming, 14.3% construction, 24.6% production (2000).
Income: Per capita income: $25,035 (2010); Median household income: $54,967 (2010); Average household income: $64,363 (2010); Percent of households with income of $100,000 or more: 14.1% (2010); Poverty rate: 7.7% (2000).
Taxes: Total city taxes per capita: $179 (2007); City property taxes per capita: $131 (2007).
Education: Percent of population age 25 and over with: High school diploma (including GED) or higher: 85.6% (2010); Bachelor's degree or higher: 17.4% (2010); Master's degree or higher: 5.3% (2010).
Housing: Homeownership rate: 74.6% (2010); Median home value: $141,242 (2010); Median contract rent: $457 per month (2000); Median year structure built: 1979 (2000).
Newspapers: Action Plus Shopper (Community news; Circulation 15,500); Kankakee Valley Post-News (Community news; Circulation 3,220)
Transportation: Commute to work: 93.4% car, 0.6% public transportation, 2.6% walk, 2.0% work from home (2000); Travel time to work: 32.4% less than 15 minutes, 18.0% 15 to 30 minutes, 22.8% 30 to 45 minutes, 16.2% 45 to 60 minutes, 10.6% 60 minutes or more (2000)
Additional Information Contacts
Town of De Motte. . . . . (219) 987-3831
   http://www.townofdemotte.com

FAIR OAKS (unincorporated postal area, zip code 47943). Covers a land area of 60.150 square miles and a water area of 0.024 square miles. Located at 41.07° N. Lat; 87.26° W. Long. Elevation is 702 feet.
Population: 763 (2000); Race: 97.5% White, 0.0% Black, 0.6% Asian, 1.9% Other, 3.8% Hispanic of any race (2000); Density: 12.7 persons per square mile (2000); Age: 29.3% under 18, 7.3% over 64 (2000); Marriage status: 20.8% never married, 69.0% now married, 3.8% widowed, 6.4% divorced (2000); Foreign born: 1.2% (2000); Ancestry (includes multiple ancestries): 21.9% German, 14.6% Dutch, 13.5% United States or American, 13.4% Irish, 6.6% Polish (2000).
Economy: Employment by occupation: 12.9% management, 9.5% professional, 3.7% services, 16.7% sales, 1.2% farming, 13.7% construction, 42.3% production (2000).
Income: Per capita income: $19,114 (2000); Median household income: $47,143 (2000); Poverty rate: 6.1% (2000).
Education: Percent of population age 25 and over with: High school diploma (including GED) or higher: 85.1% (2000); Bachelor's degree or higher: 10.6% (2000).
Housing: Homeownership rate: 72.9% (2000); Median home value: $113,100 (2000); Median contract rent: $409 per month (2000); Median year structure built: 1973 (2000).
Transportation: Commute to work: 85.9% car, 2.1% public transportation, 8.1% walk, 3.9% work from home (2000); Travel time to work: 18.8% less than 15 minutes, 39.7% 15 to 30 minutes, 15.9% 30 to 45 minutes, 17.8% 45 to 60 minutes, 7.8% 60 minutes or more (2000)

REMINGTON (town). Covers a land area of 1.034 square miles and a water area of 0 square miles. Located at 40.76° N. Lat; 87.15° W. Long. Elevation is 735 feet.
History: Laid out 1860.
Population: 1,274 (1990); 1,323 (2000); 1,353 (2010); 1,367 (2015 projected); Race: 97.6% White, 0.9% Black, 1.0% Asian, 0.5% Other, 2.1% Hispanic of any race (2010); Density: 1,308.7 persons per square mile (2010); Average household size: 2.62 (2010); Median age: 36.3 (2010); Males per 100 females: 95.2 (2010); Marriage status: 19.1% never married, 56.7% now married, 9.9% widowed, 14.3% divorced (2000); Foreign born: 0.9% (2000); Ancestry (includes multiple ancestries): 31.1% German, 13.8% Irish, 11.2% English, 9.1% United States or American, 6.4% Other groups (2000).
Economy: Single-family building permits issued: 0 (2009); Multi-family building permits issued: 0 (2009); Employment by occupation: 13.7% management, 10.3% professional, 11.5% services, 21.1% sales, 2.5% farming, 12.1% construction, 28.8% production (2000).
Income: Per capita income: $26,218 (2010); Median household income: $52,694 (2010); Average household income: $68,598 (2010); Percent of households with income of $100,000 or more: 15.1% (2010); Poverty rate: 7.5% (2000).
Taxes: Total city taxes per capita: $266 (2007); City property taxes per capita: $227 (2007).
Education: Percent of population age 25 and over with: High school diploma (including GED) or higher: 91.4% (2010); Bachelor's degree or higher: 16.4% (2010); Master's degree or higher: 4.8% (2010).
School District(s)
Tri-County School Corp (KG-12)
    2008-09 Enrollment: 764 . . . . (219) 279-2418
Housing: Homeownership rate: 67.7% (2010); Median home value: $94,943 (2010); Median contract rent: $386 per month (2000); Median year structure built: 1950 (2000).
Transportation: Commute to work: 92.9% car, 0.0% public transportation, 4.3% walk, 2.1% work from home (2000); Travel time to work: 55.4% less than 15 minutes, 21.8% 15 to 30 minutes, 11.0% 30 to 45 minutes, 4.5% 45 to 60 minutes, 7.2% 60 minutes or more (2000)

RENSSELAER (city). County seat. Covers a land area of 2.901 square miles and a water area of 0.060 square miles. Located at 40.93° N. Lat; 87.15° W. Long. Elevation is 659 feet.
History: Rensselaer was founded in 1837 by James Van Rensselaer, a merchant from New York who operated a gristmill here. Rensselaer soon became a trading center for the surrounding farming community.
Population: 5,104 (1990); 5,294 (2000); 5,408 (2010); 5,449 (2015 projected); Race: 96.0% White, 1.3% Black, 0.3% Asian, 2.3% Other, 4.0% Hispanic of any race (2010); Density: 1,864.1 persons per square mile (2010); Average household size: 2.34 (2010); Median age: 37.1 (2010); Males per 100 females: 91.8 (2010); Marriage status: 21.9% never married,

55.3% now married, 11.5% widowed, 11.2% divorced (2000); Foreign born: 1.9% (2000); Ancestry (includes multiple ancestries): 25.0% German, 11.9% Irish, 11.7% English, 10.8% United States or American, 7.6% Other groups (2000).
Economy: Single-family building permits issued: 10 (2009); Multi-family building permits issued: 0 (2009); Employment by occupation: 9.0% management, 16.3% professional, 15.6% services, 18.6% sales, 0.2% farming, 12.9% construction, 27.4% production (2000).
Income: Per capita income: $22,444 (2010); Median household income: $38,759 (2010); Average household income: $52,654 (2010); Percent of households with income of $100,000 or more: 9.5% (2010); Poverty rate: 10.0% (2000).
Taxes: Total city taxes per capita: $191 (2007); City property taxes per capita: $162 (2007).
Education: Percent of population age 25 and over with: High school diploma (including GED) or higher: 84.7% (2010); Bachelor's degree or higher: 19.1% (2010); Master's degree or higher: 5.7% (2010).
School District(s)
Rensselaer Central School Corp (PK-12)
    2008-09 Enrollment: 1,868 . . . . (219) 866-7822
Four-year College(s)
Saint Josephs College (Private, Not-for-profit, Roman Catholic)
    Fall 2008 Enrollment: 1,076. . . . . (219) 866-6000
    2009-10 Tuition: In-state $24,530; Out-of-state $24,530
Housing: Homeownership rate: 61.8% (2010); Median home value: $96,344 (2010); Median contract rent: $348 per month (2000); Median year structure built: 1951 (2000).
Hospitals: Jasper County Hospital (86 beds)
Newspapers: Brook Reporter (Local news; Circulation 1,000); Morocco Courier (Community news; Circulation 900); Remington Press (Community news; Circulation 1,200); Rensselaer Republican (Regional news; Circulation 3,000); Shoppers News (Community news; Circulation 14,000)
Transportation: Commute to work: 90.9% car, 0.0% public transportation, 5.5% walk, 1.6% work from home (2000); Travel time to work: 69.7% less than 15 minutes, 13.1% 15 to 30 minutes, 4.7% 30 to 45 minutes, 7.7% 45 to 60 minutes, 4.8% 60 minutes or more (2000); Amtrak: train service available.
Additional Information Contacts
City of Rensselaer . . . . (219) 866-5213
    http://www.cityofrensselaerin.com

WHEATFIELD (town). Covers a land area of 0.552 square miles and a water area of 0 square miles. Located at 41.19° N. Lat; 87.05° W. Long. Elevation is 663 feet.
Population: 621 (1990); 772 (2000); 696 (2010); 664 (2015 projected); Race: 90.9% White, 4.6% Black, 0.0% Asian, 4.5% Other, 3.3% Hispanic of any race (2010); Density: 1,260.7 persons per square mile (2010); Average household size: 2.64 (2010); Median age: 31.3 (2010); Males per 100 females: 106.5 (2010); Marriage status: 28.7% never married, 52.9% now married, 6.6% widowed, 11.9% divorced (2000); Foreign born: 0.0% (2000); Ancestry (includes multiple ancestries): 21.1% German, 12.1% United States or American, 11.3% Dutch, 9.6% Irish, 7.8% Polish (2000).
Economy: Single-family building permits issued: 5 (2009); Multi-family building permits issued: 0 (2009); Employment by occupation: 11.2% management, 8.8% professional, 18.9% services, 17.7% sales, 1.5% farming, 21.2% construction, 20.6% production (2000).
Income: Per capita income: $19,287 (2010); Median household income: $47,969 (2010); Average household income: $52,582 (2010); Percent of households with income of $100,000 or more: 7.8% (2010); Poverty rate: 7.5% (2000).
Taxes: Total city taxes per capita: $99 (2007); City property taxes per capita: $75 (2007).
Education: Percent of population age 25 and over with: High school diploma (including GED) or higher: 84.9% (2010); Bachelor's degree or higher: 12.5% (2010); Master's degree or higher: 3.8% (2010).
School District(s)
Kankakee Valley School Corp (KG-12)
    2008-09 Enrollment: 3,553 . . . . (219) 987-4711
Housing: Homeownership rate: 74.1% (2010); Median home value: $108,125 (2010); Median contract rent: $418 per month (2000); Median year structure built: 1961 (2000).
Transportation: Commute to work: 93.1% car, 0.0% public transportation, 4.2% walk, 1.5% work from home (2000); Travel time to work: 36.6% less than 15 minutes, 18.3% 15 to 30 minutes, 22.3% 30 to 45 minutes, 10.7% 45 to 60 minutes, 12.2% 60 minutes or more (2000)

Jay County

Located in eastern Indiana; bounded on the east by Ohio; drained by the Salamonie River. Covers a land area of 383.64 square miles, a water area of 0.18 square miles, and is located in the Eastern Time Zone. The county was founded in 1835. County seat is Portland.

Weather Station: Portland 1 SW   Elevation: 908 feet

	Jan	Feb	Mar	Apr	May	Jun	Jul	Aug	Sep	Oct	Nov	Dec
High	32	36	47	60	71	80	84	82	76	63	50	37
Low	16	18	27	38	49	58	62	60	52	40	32	22
Precip	1.9	1.9	2.6	3.6	3.9	4.1	4.5	3.9	2.7	2.6	3.1	2.5
Snow	6.3	5.8	2.9	0.4	0.0	0.0	0.0	0.0	0.0	0.2	0.7	4.7

High and Low temperatures in degrees Fahrenheit; Precipitation and Snow in inches

Population: 21,502 (1990); 21,806 (2000); 21,366 (2010); 21,047 (2015 projected); Race: 96.2% White, 0.5% Black, 0.7% Asian, 2.6% Other, 2.9% Hispanic of any race (2010); Density: 55.7 persons per square mile (2010); Average household size: 2.54 (2010); Median age: 38.9 (2010); Males per 100 females: 96.8 (2010).
Religion: Five largest groups: 9.4% Catholic Church, 8.1% The United Methodist Church, 5.3% Church of the Nazarene, 3.6% Christian Churches and Churches of Christ, 3.5% New Testament Association of Independent Baptist Churches and other Fundamental
Economy: Unemployment rate: 8.9% (5/2010); Total civilian labor force: 12,115 (5/2010); Leading industries: 42.2% manufacturing; 13.9% health care and social assistance; 10.8% retail trade (2008); Farms: 881 totaling 197,225 acres (2007); Companies that employ 500 or more persons: 1 (2008); Companies that employ 100 to 499 persons: 9 (2008); Companies that employ less than 100 persons: 409 (2008); Black-owned businesses: n/a (2002); Hispanic-owned businesses: n/a (2002); Asian-owned businesses: n/a (2002); Women-owned businesses: n/a (2002); Retail sales per capita: $7,951 (2010). Single-family building permits issued: 18 (2009); Multi-family building permits issued: 60 (2009).
Income: Per capita income: $19,447 (2010); Median household income: $42,542 (2010); Average household income: $49,658 (2010); Percent of households with income of $100,000 or more: 7.2% (2010); Poverty rate: 14.3% (2008); Bankruptcy rate: 7.41% (2009).
Taxes: Total county taxes per capita: $375 (2007); County property taxes per capita: $150 (2007).
Education: Percent of population age 25 and over with: High school diploma (including GED) or higher: 82.9% (2010); Bachelor's degree or higher: 11.1% (2010); Master's degree or higher: 3.4% (2010).
Housing: Homeownership rate: 79.1% (2010); Median home value: $76,778 (2010); Median contract rent: $382 per month (2006-2008 3-year est.); Median year structure built: 1950 (2006-2008 3-year est.)
Health: Birth rate: 141.1 per 10,000 population (2009); Death rate: 100.4 per 10,000 population (2009); Age-adjusted cancer mortality rate: 262.1 deaths per 100,000 population (2006); Number of physicians: 6.6 per 10,000 population (2007); Hospital beds: 16.4 per 10,000 population (2006); Hospital admissions: 554.2 per 10,000 population (2006).
Elections: 2008 Presidential election results: 45.1% Obama, 52.9% McCain, 0.1% Nader
National and State Parks: Limberlost State Game Reserve
Additional Information Contacts
Jay County Government . . . . (260) 726-4951
   http://www.co.jay.in.us
City of Portland . . . . (260) 726-9395
   http://www.thecityofportland.net

Jay County Communities

BRYANT (town). Aka Briant. Covers a land area of 0.303 square miles and a water area of 0 square miles. Located at 40.53° N. Lat; 84.96° W. Long. Elevation is 876 feet.
Population: 299 (1990); 272 (2000); 238 (2010); 222 (2015 projected); Race: 98.7% White, 0.0% Black, 0.0% Asian, 1.3% Other, 0.8% Hispanic of any race (2010); Density: 785.6 persons per square mile (2010); Average household size: 3.09 (2010); Median age: 33.8 (2010); Males per 100 females: 101.7 (2010); Marriage status: 11.0% never married, 72.6% now married, 3.7% widowed, 12.8% divorced (2000); Foreign born: 0.0% (2000); Ancestry (includes multiple ancestries): 34.3% United States or American, 20.9% German, 10.4% Other groups, 9.8% Irish, 6.7% Swiss (2000).
Economy: Single-family building permits issued: 0 (2009); Multi-family building permits issued: 0 (2009); Employment by occupation: 0.0%

management, 1.9% professional, 11.5% services, 18.6% sales, 0.0% farming, 16.7% construction, 51.3% production (2000).
Income: Per capita income: $19,497 (2010); Median household income: $51,705 (2010); Average household income: $62,338 (2010); Percent of households with income of $100,000 or more: 9.1% (2010); Poverty rate: 4.4% (2000).
Taxes: Total city taxes per capita: $103 (2007); City property taxes per capita: $95 (2007).
Education: Percent of population age 25 and over with: High school diploma (including GED) or higher: 80.1% (2010); Bachelor's degree or higher: 7.1% (2010); Master's degree or higher: 0.7% (2010).
School District(s)
Jay School Corp (KG-12)
   2008-09 Enrollment: 3,671 . . . . (260) 726-9341
Housing: Homeownership rate: 89.6% (2010); Median home value: $84,667 (2010); Median contract rent: $308 per month (2000); Median year structure built: before 1940 (2000).
Transportation: Commute to work: 93.3% car, 0.0% public transportation, 2.0% walk, 1.3% work from home (2000); Travel time to work: 49.0% less than 15 minutes, 31.3% 15 to 30 minutes, 15.0% 30 to 45 minutes, 2.0% 45 to 60 minutes, 2.7% 60 minutes or more (2000)

DUNKIRK (city). Covers a land area of 1.125 square miles and a water area of 0 square miles. Located at 40.37° N. Lat; 85.21° W. Long. Elevation is 945 feet.
Population: 2,864 (1990); 2,646 (2000); 2,452 (2010); 2,348 (2015 projected); Race: 97.3% White, 0.3% Black, 1.2% Asian, 1.2% Other, 0.7% Hispanic of any race (2010); Density: 2,179.0 persons per square mile (2010); Average household size: 2.43 (2010); Median age: 40.5 (2010); Males per 100 females: 93.8 (2010); Marriage status: 20.7% never married, 59.6% now married, 8.8% widowed, 10.9% divorced (2000); Foreign born: 0.4% (2000); Ancestry (includes multiple ancestries): 16.9% United States or American, 15.5% German, 9.4% Irish, 7.1% English, 2.7% Other groups (2000).
Economy: Employment by occupation: 4.6% management, 4.7% professional, 16.0% services, 17.7% sales, 0.8% farming, 13.2% construction, 42.9% production (2000).
Income: Per capita income: $17,492 (2010); Median household income: $39,286 (2010); Average household income: $42,954 (2010); Percent of households with income of $100,000 or more: 4.6% (2010); Poverty rate: 10.5% (2000).
Taxes: Total city taxes per capita: $216 (2007); City property taxes per capita: $203 (2007).
Education: Percent of population age 25 and over with: High school diploma (including GED) or higher: 76.5% (2010); Bachelor's degree or higher: 5.9% (2010); Master's degree or higher: 1.5% (2010).
School District(s)
Jay School Corp (KG-12)
   2008-09 Enrollment: 3,671 . . . . (260) 726-9341
Housing: Homeownership rate: 76.2% (2010); Median home value: $54,327 (2010); Median contract rent: $256 per month (2000); Median year structure built: 1945 (2000).
Newspapers: Dunkirk News & Sun (Local news; Circulation 2,000)
Transportation: Commute to work: 96.3% car, 0.0% public transportation, 2.0% walk, 1.3% work from home (2000); Travel time to work: 40.2% less than 15 minutes, 32.3% 15 to 30 minutes, 18.2% 30 to 45 minutes, 3.4% 45 to 60 minutes, 5.8% 60 minutes or more (2000)

PENNVILLE (town). Covers a land area of 0.392 square miles and a water area of 0 square miles. Located at 40.49° N. Lat; 85.14° W. Long. Elevation is 879 feet.
Population: 656 (1990); 706 (2000); 671 (2010); 650 (2015 projected); Race: 99.1% White, 0.0% Black, 0.0% Asian, 0.9% Other, 2.4% Hispanic of any race (2010); Density: 1,710.7 persons per square mile (2010); Average household size: 2.43 (2010); Median age: 39.0 (2010); Males per 100 females: 97.9 (2010); Marriage status: 19.7% never married, 53.7% now married, 5.1% widowed, 21.6% divorced (2000); Foreign born: 0.4% (2000); Ancestry (includes multiple ancestries): 21.5% German, 18.3% United States or American, 5.8% English, 4.6% Other groups, 4.6% Irish (2000).
Economy: Employment by occupation: 3.5% management, 7.0% professional, 12.5% services, 22.0% sales, 0.6% farming, 15.3% construction, 39.0% production (2000).
Income: Per capita income: $18,297 (2010); Median household income: $36,250 (2010); Average household income: $45,127 (2010); Percent of

households with income of $100,000 or more: 6.2% (2010); Poverty rate: 9.4% (2000).

Taxes: Total city taxes per capita: $86 (2007); City property taxes per capita: $64 (2007).

Education: Percent of population age 25 and over with: High school diploma (including GED) or higher: 81.6% (2010); Bachelor's degree or higher: 6.2% (2010); Master's degree or higher: 3.3% (2010).

School District(s)

Jay School Corp (KG-12)
    2008-09 Enrollment: 3,671 . . . . (260) 726-9341

Housing: Homeownership rate: 69.6% (2010); Median home value: $56,444 (2010); Median contract rent: $244 per month (2000); Median year structure built: 1951 (2000).

Transportation: Commute to work: 92.4% car, 0.0% public transportation, 2.0% walk, 5.6% work from home (2000); Travel time to work: 10.1% less than 15 minutes, 52.1% 15 to 30 minutes, 25.5% 30 to 45 minutes, 8.0% 45 to 60 minutes, 4.2% 60 minutes or more (2000)

PORTLAND (city). County seat. Covers a land area of 4.108 square miles and a water area of 0.007 square miles. Located at 40.43° N. Lat; 84.98° W. Long. Elevation is 909 feet.

History: Portland was the birthplace of Elwood Haynes (1857-1925) who invented the first successful clutch-driven automobile.

Population: 6,540 (1990); 6,437 (2000); 6,098 (2010); 5,889 (2015 projected); Race: 93.9% White, 0.8% Black, 0.6% Asian, 4.8% Other, 6.1% Hispanic of any race (2010); Density: 1,484.3 persons per square mile (2010); Average household size: 2.27 (2010); Median age: 40.1 (2010); Males per 100 females: 90.4 (2010); Marriage status: 21.0% never married, 55.8% now married, 10.7% widowed, 12.4% divorced (2000); Foreign born: 3.3% (2000); Ancestry (includes multiple ancestries): 20.0% United States or American, 18.1% German, 9.2% Other groups, 7.9% Irish, 7.5% English (2000).

Economy: Employment by occupation: 7.4% management, 11.2% professional, 13.8% services, 19.5% sales, 0.5% farming, 10.7% construction, 36.9% production (2000).

Income: Per capita income: $19,929 (2010); Median household income: $36,516 (2010); Average household income: $45,491 (2010); Percent of households with income of $100,000 or more: 5.4% (2010); Poverty rate: 9.6% (2000).

Taxes: Total city taxes per capita: $276 (2007); City property taxes per capita: $267 (2007).

Education: Percent of population age 25 and over with: High school diploma (including GED) or higher: 81.4% (2010); Bachelor's degree or higher: 12.5% (2010); Master's degree or higher: 4.0% (2010).

School District(s)

Jay School Corp (KG-12)
    2008-09 Enrollment: 3,671 . . . . (260) 726-9341

Housing: Homeownership rate: 70.7% (2010); Median home value: $71,589 (2010); Median contract rent: $306 per month (2000); Median year structure built: 1945 (2000).

Hospitals: Jay County Hospital (65 beds)

Safety: Violent crime rate: 13.0 per 10,000 population; Property crime rate: 504.6 per 10,000 population (2008).

Newspapers: The Commercial Review (Community news)

Transportation: Commute to work: 93.5% car, 0.3% public transportation, 2.5% walk, 1.7% work from home (2000); Travel time to work: 63.7% less than 15 minutes, 17.6% 15 to 30 minutes, 11.2% 30 to 45 minutes, 5.3% 45 to 60 minutes, 2.2% 60 minutes or more (2000)

Additional Information Contacts

City of Portland . . . . (260) 726-9395
    http://www.thecityofportland.net

REDKEY (town). Aka Red Key. Covers a land area of 0.935 square miles and a water area of 0.005 square miles. Located at 40.35° N. Lat; 85.15° W. Long. Elevation is 961 feet.

Population: 1,383 (1990); 1,427 (2000); 1,368 (2010); 1,337 (2015 projected); Race: 98.7% White, 0.4% Black, 0.1% Asian, 0.9% Other, 1.3% Hispanic of any race (2010); Density: 1,463.7 persons per square mile (2010); Average household size: 2.38 (2010); Median age: 38.1 (2010); Males per 100 females: 96.6 (2010); Marriage status: 21.4% never married, 55.2% now married, 9.4% widowed, 14.0% divorced (2000); Foreign born: 0.0% (2000); Ancestry (includes multiple ancestries): 22.1% United States or American, 13.0% German, 10.9% Irish, 6.7% Other groups, 5.2% English (2000).

Economy: Employment by occupation: 5.4% management, 7.6% professional, 15.1% services, 21.5% sales, 0.5% farming, 13.4% construction, 36.6% production (2000).

Income: Per capita income: $17,856 (2010); Median household income: $39,488 (2010); Average household income: $42,626 (2010); Percent of households with income of $100,000 or more: 4.2% (2010); Poverty rate: 14.0% (2000).

Taxes: Total city taxes per capita: $114 (2007); City property taxes per capita: $88 (2007).

Education: Percent of population age 25 and over with: High school diploma (including GED) or higher: 81.7% (2010); Bachelor's degree or higher: 8.2% (2010); Master's degree or higher: 1.9% (2010).

School District(s)

Jay School Corp (KG-12)
    2008-09 Enrollment: 3,671 . . . . (260) 726-9341

Housing: Homeownership rate: 74.9% (2010); Median home value: $57,699 (2010); Median contract rent: $242 per month (2000); Median year structure built: 1944 (2000).

Transportation: Commute to work: 96.2% car, 0.0% public transportation, 1.5% walk, 1.1% work from home (2000); Travel time to work: 22.6% less than 15 minutes, 37.5% 15 to 30 minutes, 21.2% 30 to 45 minutes, 9.9% 45 to 60 minutes, 8.8% 60 minutes or more (2000)

SALAMONIA (town). Covers a land area of 0.367 square miles and a water area of 0 square miles. Located at 40.38° N. Lat; 84.86° W. Long. Elevation is 971 feet.

Population: 138 (1990); 158 (2000); 149 (2010); 148 (2015 projected); Race: 93.3% White, 0.0% Black, 4.7% Asian, 2.0% Other, 2.7% Hispanic of any race (2010); Density: 405.4 persons per square mile (2010); Average household size: 2.87 (2010); Median age: 37.9 (2010); Males per 100 females: 101.4 (2010); Marriage status: 21.1% never married, 55.8% now married, 12.6% widowed, 10.5% divorced (2000); Foreign born: 0.6% (2000); Ancestry (includes multiple ancestries): 36.6% United States or American, 10.4% German, 6.1% Irish, 4.3% English, 3.7% Other groups (2000).

Economy: Employment by occupation: 1.3% management, 20.0% professional, 13.3% services, 16.0% sales, 2.7% farming, 9.3% construction, 37.3% production (2000).

Income: Per capita income: $16,017 (2010); Median household income: $40,000 (2010); Average household income: $43,221 (2010); Percent of households with income of $100,000 or more: 1.9% (2010); Poverty rate: 16.1% (2000).

Taxes: Total city taxes per capita: $401 (2007); City property taxes per capita: $20 (2007).

Education: Percent of population age 25 and over with: High school diploma (including GED) or higher: 81.8% (2010); Bachelor's degree or higher: 16.2% (2010); Master's degree or higher: 1.0% (2010).

Housing: Homeownership rate: 84.6% (2010); Median home value: $74,545 (2010); Median contract rent: $225 per month (2000); Median year structure built: before 1940 (2000).

Transportation: Commute to work: 94.3% car, 0.0% public transportation, 0.0% walk, 2.9% work from home (2000); Travel time to work: 45.6% less than 15 minutes, 27.9% 15 to 30 minutes, 16.2% 30 to 45 minutes, 2.9% 45 to 60 minutes, 7.4% 60 minutes or more (2000)

Jefferson County

Located in southeastern Indiana; bounded on the south partly by the Ohio River and the Kentucky border; drained by Big Creek. Covers a land area of 361.37 square miles, a water area of 1.58 square miles, and is located in the Eastern Time Zone. The county was founded in 1810. County seat is Madison.

Jefferson County is part of the Madison, IN Micropolitan Statistical Area. The entire metro area includes: Jefferson County, IN

Weather Station: Madison Sewage Plant									Elevation: 459 feet		
	Jan	Feb	Mar	Apr	May	Jun	Jul	Aug	Sep	Oct	Nov	Dec
High	40	46	56	67	76	84	87	86	80	69	56	45
Low	23	26	35	43	53	62	67	65	58	46	37	28
Precip	3.0	2.8	4.3	4.3	4.9	4.3	4.3	4.0	2.9	3.3	3.8	3.6
Snow	5.7	4.2	2.4	tr	tr	0.0	0.0	0.0	0.0	0.1	tr	2.9

High and Low temperatures in degrees Fahrenheit; Precipitation and Snow in inches

Population: 29,797 (1990); 31,705 (2000); 33,055 (2010); 33,535 (2015 projected); Race: 95.6% White, 1.6% Black, 0.7% Asian, 2.1% Other, 1.5%

Hispanic of any race (2010); Density: 91.5 persons per square mile (2010); Average household size: 2.40 (2010); Median age: 39.0 (2010); Males per 100 females: 98.4 (2010).
Religion: Five largest groups: 12.2% American Baptist Churches in the USA, 9.1% Catholic Church, 8.3% Southern Baptist Convention, 5.6% The United Methodist Church, 4.8% Christian Churches and Churches of Christ (2000).
Economy: Unemployment rate: 10.5% (5/2010); Total civilian labor force: 16,150 (5/2010); Leading industries: 30.3% manufacturing; 17.4% health care and social assistance; 14.6% retail trade (2008); Farms: 694 totaling 102,514 acres (2007); Companies that employ 500 or more persons: 4 (2008); Companies that employ 100 to 499 persons: 14 (2008); Companies that employ less than 100 persons: 742 (2008); Black-owned businesses: n/a (2002); Hispanic-owned businesses: n/a (2002); Asian-owned businesses: n/a (2002); Women-owned businesses: 440 (2002); Retail sales per capita: $12,141 (2010). Single-family building permits issued: 55 (2009); Multi-family building permits issued: 0 (2009).
Income: Per capita income: $22,202 (2010); Median household income: $46,844 (2010); Average household income: $55,472 (2010); Percent of households with income of $100,000 or more: 11.7% (2010); Poverty rate: 13.2% (2008); Bankruptcy rate: 7.48% (2009).
Taxes: Total county taxes per capita: $293 (2007); County property taxes per capita: $227 (2007).
Education: Percent of population age 25 and over with: High school diploma (including GED) or higher: 83.9% (2010); Bachelor's degree or higher: 18.1% (2010); Master's degree or higher: 8.3% (2010).
Housing: Homeownership rate: 73.2% (2010); Median home value: $98,225 (2010); Median contract rent: $451 per month (2006-2008 3-year est.); Median year structure built: 1974 (2006-2008 3-year est.)
Health: Birth rate: 114.2 per 10,000 population (2009); Death rate: 96.6 per 10,000 population (2009); Age-adjusted cancer mortality rate: 202.3 deaths per 100,000 population (2006); Number of physicians: 13.6 per 10,000 population (2007); Hospital beds: 79.3 per 10,000 population (2006); Hospital admissions: 1,436.1 per 10,000 population (2006).
Elections: 2008 Presidential election results: 46.4% Obama, 52.3% McCain, 0.0% Nader
National and State Parks: Clifty Falls State Park
Additional Information Contacts
Jefferson County Government . . . . (812) 265-8922
  http://madisonindiana.org
City of Madison . . . . (812) 265-8300
  http://www.madison-in.gov
Madison Chamber of Commerce . . . . (812) 265-3135
  http://www.madisonchamber.org

Jefferson County Communities

BROOKSBURG (town). Covers a land area of 0.110 square miles and a water area of 0.002 square miles. Located at 38.73° N. Lat; 85.24° W. Long. Elevation is 472 feet.
Population: 79 (1990); 74 (2000); 79 (2010); 80 (2015 projected); Race: 94.9% White, 1.3% Black, 0.0% Asian, 3.8% Other, 1.3% Hispanic of any race (2010); Density: 719.0 persons per square mile (2010); Average household size: 2.55 (2010); Median age: 38.9 (2010); Males per 100 females: 107.9 (2010); Marriage status: 7.9% never married, 54.0% now married, 12.7% widowed, 25.4% divorced (2000); Foreign born: 0.0% (2000); Ancestry (includes multiple ancestries): 25.3% Irish, 21.5% Other groups, 13.9% United States or American, 10.1% English, 2.5% Scottish (2000).
Economy: Employment by occupation: 4.8% management, 19.0% professional, 19.0% services, 14.3% sales, 0.0% farming, 21.4% construction, 21.4% production (2000).
Income: Per capita income: $19,950 (2010); Median household income: $43,438 (2010); Average household income: $49,355 (2010); Percent of households with income of $100,000 or more: 6.5% (2010); Poverty rate: 2.5% (2000).
Taxes: Total city taxes per capita: $82 (2007); City property taxes per capita: $14 (2007).
Education: Percent of population age 25 and over with: High school diploma (including GED) or higher: 79.2% (2010); Bachelor's degree or higher: 5.7% (2010); Master's degree or higher: 0.0% (2010).
Housing: Homeownership rate: 83.9% (2010); Median home value: $112,500 (2010); Median contract rent: $225 per month (2000); Median year structure built: before 1940 (2000).

Transportation: Commute to work: 95.2% car, 0.0% public transportation, 4.8% walk, 0.0% work from home (2000); Travel time to work: 19.0% less than 15 minutes, 59.5% 15 to 30 minutes, 11.9% 30 to 45 minutes, 4.8% 45 to 60 minutes, 4.8% 60 minutes or more (2000)

CANAAN (unincorporated postal area, zip code 47224). Covers a land area of 28.808 square miles and a water area of 0.040 square miles. Located at 38.89° N. Lat; 85.21° W. Long. Elevation is 948 feet.
Population: 653 (2000); Race: 99.1% White, 0.9% Black, 0.0% Asian, 0.0% Other, 0.0% Hispanic of any race (2000); Density: 22.7 persons per square mile (2000); Age: 15.6% under 18, 4.5% over 64 (2000); Marriage status: 19.9% never married, 71.0% now married, 0.8% widowed, 8.3% divorced (2000); Foreign born: 0.0% (2000); Ancestry (includes multiple ancestries): 33.6% United States or American, 19.1% German, 10.5% Other groups, 5.1% Irish, 4.9% English (2000).
Economy: Employment by occupation: 3.1% management, 6.4% professional, 23.1% services, 23.7% sales, 2.5% farming, 20.6% construction, 20.6% production (2000).
Income: Per capita income: $17,668 (2000); Median household income: $43,170 (2000); Poverty rate: 8.0% (2000).
Education: Percent of population age 25 and over with: High school diploma (including GED) or higher: 72.7% (2000); Bachelor's degree or higher: 2.9% (2000).
School District(s)
Madison Consolidated Schools (KG-12)
  2008-09 Enrollment: 3,434 . . . . (812) 273-8511
Housing: Homeownership rate: 76.1% (2000); Median home value: $74,700 (2000); Median contract rent: $287 per month (2000); Median year structure built: 1975 (2000).
Transportation: Commute to work: 95.0% car, 0.0% public transportation, 1.7% walk, 3.3% work from home (2000); Travel time to work: 17.9% less than 15 minutes, 35.2% 15 to 30 minutes, 19.9% 30 to 45 minutes, 12.1% 45 to 60 minutes, 15.0% 60 minutes or more (2000)

DEPUTY (unincorporated postal area, zip code 47230). Covers a land area of 42.876 square miles and a water area of 0.169 square miles. Located at 38.80° N. Lat; 85.62° W. Long. Elevation is 627 feet.
Population: 1,776 (2000); Race: 99.3% White, 0.0% Black, 0.0% Asian, 0.7% Other, 0.3% Hispanic of any race (2000); Density: 41.4 persons per square mile (2000); Age: 28.6% under 18, 9.4% over 64 (2000); Marriage status: 15.2% never married, 67.2% now married, 6.4% widowed, 11.2% divorced (2000); Foreign born: 0.3% (2000); Ancestry (includes multiple ancestries): 24.4% United States or American, 9.5% German, 8.2% Irish, 7.3% Other groups, 4.2% English (2000).
Economy: Employment by occupation: 3.7% management, 9.5% professional, 11.7% services, 16.6% sales, 0.8% farming, 20.7% construction, 37.0% production (2000).
Income: Per capita income: $13,405 (2000); Median household income: $32,948 (2000); Poverty rate: 8.2% (2000).
Education: Percent of population age 25 and over with: High school diploma (including GED) or higher: 71.2% (2000); Bachelor's degree or higher: 4.3% (2000).
School District(s)
Madison Consolidated Schools (KG-12)
  2008-09 Enrollment: 3,434 . . . . (812) 273-8511
Housing: Homeownership rate: 89.6% (2000); Median home value: $72,200 (2000); Median contract rent: $338 per month (2000); Median year structure built: 1972 (2000).
Transportation: Commute to work: 98.0% car, 0.0% public transportation, 0.0% walk, 2.0% work from home (2000); Travel time to work: 10.4% less than 15 minutes, 37.2% 15 to 30 minutes, 29.4% 30 to 45 minutes, 13.8% 45 to 60 minutes, 9.2% 60 minutes or more (2000)

DUPONT (town). Aka Du Pont. Covers a land area of 1.026 square miles and a water area of 0 square miles. Located at 38.89° N. Lat; 85.51° W. Long. Elevation is 791 feet.
History: Laid out 1849.
Population: 391 (1990); 392 (2000); 367 (2010); 352 (2015 projected); Race: 97.3% White, 0.8% Black, 0.5% Asian, 1.4% Other, 1.4% Hispanic of any race (2010); Density: 357.8 persons per square mile (2010); Average household size: 2.70 (2010); Median age: 36.8 (2010); Males per 100 females: 105.0 (2010); Marriage status: 22.0% never married, 49.4% now married, 4.6% widowed, 23.9% divorced (2000); Foreign born: 3.4% (2000); Ancestry (includes multiple ancestries): 21.1% German, 17.2%

Other groups, 12.5% United States or American, 11.2% English, 9.9% Irish (2000).

Economy: Employment by occupation: 9.1% management, 17.6% professional, 13.9% services, 16.4% sales, 1.2% farming, 12.1% construction, 29.7% production (2000).

Income: Per capita income: $19,670 (2010); Median household income: $47,132 (2010); Average household income: $52,241 (2010); Percent of households with income of $100,000 or more: 5.2% (2010); Poverty rate: 19.3% (2000).

Taxes: Total city taxes per capita: $224 (2007); City property taxes per capita: $117 (2007).

Education: Percent of population age 25 and over with: High school diploma (including GED) or higher: 79.1% (2010); Bachelor's degree or higher: 6.4% (2010); Master's degree or higher: 5.5% (2010).

School District(s)
Madison Consolidated Schools (KG-12)
     2008-09 Enrollment: 3,434 . . . . (812) 273-8511

Housing: Homeownership rate: 85.2% (2010); Median home value: $74,444 (2010); Median contract rent: $338 per month (2000); Median year structure built: 1954 (2000).

Transportation: Commute to work: 98.8% car, 0.0% public transportation, 1.2% walk, 0.0% work from home (2000); Travel time to work: 10.9% less than 15 minutes, 52.1% 15 to 30 minutes, 19.4% 30 to 45 minutes, 9.1% 45 to 60 minutes, 8.5% 60 minutes or more (2000)

HANOVER (town). Covers a land area of 2.100 square miles and a water area of 0 square miles. Located at 38.71° N. Lat; 85.47° W. Long. Elevation is 784 feet.

History: Hanover developed around Hanover College, founded in 1827 by the Presbyterian denomination as a manual labor academy.

Population: 3,641 (1990); 2,834 (2000); 2,773 (2010); 2,745 (2015 projected); Race: 96.3% White, 1.4% Black, 0.8% Asian, 1.5% Other, 1.9% Hispanic of any race (2010); Density: 1,320.2 persons per square mile (2010); Average household size: 2.54 (2010); Median age: 31.6 (2010); Males per 100 females: 91.0 (2010); Marriage status: 20.4% never married, 58.2% now married, 7.1% widowed, 14.3% divorced (2000); Foreign born: 0.9% (2000); Ancestry (includes multiple ancestries): 20.4% United States or American, 19.7% German, 12.4% Other groups, 10.0% Irish, 9.1% English (2000).

Economy: Single-family building permits issued: 14 (2009); Multi-family building permits issued: 0 (2009); Employment by occupation: 6.9% management, 20.8% professional, 17.0% services, 21.2% sales, 0.0% farming, 13.1% construction, 21.0% production (2000).

Income: Per capita income: $16,922 (2010); Median household income: $43,241 (2010); Average household income: $49,989 (2010); Percent of households with income of $100,000 or more: 8.1% (2010); Poverty rate: 8.5% (2000).

Taxes: Total city taxes per capita: $40 (2007); City property taxes per capita: $33 (2007).

Education: Percent of population age 25 and over with: High school diploma (including GED) or higher: 79.8% (2010); Bachelor's degree or higher: 15.1% (2010); Master's degree or higher: 9.0% (2010).

School District(s)
Southwestern-Jefferson Co Con (PK-12)
     2008-09 Enrollment: 1,357 . . . . (812) 866-6255

Four-year College(s)
Hanover College (Private, Not-for-profit, Presbyterian Church (USA))
     Fall 2008 Enrollment: 926 . . . . (812) 866-7000
     2009-10 Tuition: In-state $26,350; Out-of-state $26,350

Housing: Homeownership rate: 66.6% (2010); Median home value: $77,151 (2010); Median contract rent: $409 per month (2000); Median year structure built: 1973 (2000).

Transportation: Commute to work: 87.7% car, 0.0% public transportation, 7.9% walk, 3.2% work from home (2000); Travel time to work: 42.3% less than 15 minutes, 35.5% 15 to 30 minutes, 8.5% 30 to 45 minutes, 4.5% 45 to 60 minutes, 9.3% 60 minutes or more (2000)

MADISON (city). County seat. Covers a land area of 8.556 square miles and a water area of 0.327 square miles. Located at 38.75° N. Lat; 85.39° W. Long. Elevation is 489 feet.

History: Madison was settled in 1805, and the town was platted in 1809 by Colonel John Paul, a Revolutionary War soldier, who named it for President James Madison. Shipyards flourished here in the 1830's, and by 1850 Madison was the largest city in Indiana. Tobacco was an important part of the economy in the early 1900's.

Population: 12,373 (1990); 12,004 (2000); 12,225 (2010); 12,280 (2015 projected); Race: 94.0% White, 2.6% Black, 0.9% Asian, 2.6% Other, 1.9% Hispanic of any race (2010); Density: 1,428.8 persons per square mile (2010); Average household size: 2.18 (2010); Median age: 42.2 (2010); Males per 100 females: 97.1 (2010); Marriage status: 21.4% never married, 55.4% now married, 9.4% widowed, 13.8% divorced (2000); Foreign born: 1.4% (2000); Ancestry (includes multiple ancestries): 21.5% German, 14.4% United States or American, 11.3% English, 10.6% Irish, 8.8% Other groups (2000).

Economy: Single-family building permits issued: 15 (2009); Multi-family building permits issued: 0 (2009); Employment by occupation: 12.0% management, 18.3% professional, 14.7% services, 24.9% sales, 0.2% farming, 7.8% construction, 22.1% production (2000).

Income: Per capita income: $24,123 (2010); Median household income: $42,113 (2010); Average household income: $54,358 (2010); Percent of households with income of $100,000 or more: 12.5% (2010); Poverty rate: 12.3% (2000).

Taxes: Total city taxes per capita: $379 (2007); City property taxes per capita: $315 (2007).

Education: Percent of population age 25 and over with: High school diploma (including GED) or higher: 85.5% (2010); Bachelor's degree or higher: 24.3% (2010); Master's degree or higher: 10.4% (2010).

School District(s)
Madison Consolidated Schools (KG-12)
     2008-09 Enrollment: 3,434 . . . . (812) 273-8511

Two-year College(s)
Ivy Tech Community College-Southeast (Public)
     Fall 2008 Enrollment: 2,254 . . . . (812) 265-2580
     2009-10 Tuition: In-state $3,090; Out-of-state $6,306

Housing: Homeownership rate: 63.0% (2010); Median home value: $103,929 (2010); Median contract rent: $327 per month (2000); Median year structure built: 1961 (2000).

Hospitals: King's Daughters Hospital (142 beds); Madison State Hospital (150 beds)

Newspapers: Madison Courier (Local news; Circulation 9,876); Madison Weekly Herald (Community news; Circulation 500); RoundAbout Madison (Local news)

Transportation: Commute to work: 92.5% car, 1.1% public transportation, 3.3% walk, 2.1% work from home (2000); Travel time to work: 63.5% less than 15 minutes, 18.6% 15 to 30 minutes, 7.3% 30 to 45 minutes, 4.9% 45 to 60 minutes, 5.6% 60 minutes or more (2000)

Additional Information Contacts
City of Madison . . . . (812) 265-8300
     http://www.madison-in.gov
Madison Chamber of Commerce . . . . (812) 265-3135
     http://www.madisonchamber.org

Jennings County

Located in southeastern Indiana; drained by Vernon, Graham, and Sand Creeks. Covers a land area of 377.22 square miles, a water area of 1.13 square miles, and is located in the Eastern Time Zone. The county was founded in 1816. County seat is Vernon.

Jennings County is part of the North Vernon, IN Micropolitan Statistical Area. The entire metro area includes: Jennings County, IN

Weather Station: North Vernon 1 NW								Elevation: 744 feet			
	Jan	Feb	Mar	Apr	May	Jun	Jul	Aug	Sep	Oct	Nov	Dec
High	39	45	55	67	75	84	87	85	na	68	54	44
Low	21	25	34	43	52	61	65	63	na	45	36	27
Precip	2.3	2.6	3.7	4.5	4.5	3.7	4.4	4.4	2.9	3.2	4.0	3.3
Snow	4.0	2.8	1.7	0.1	tr	0.0	0.0	0.0	0.0	0.0	0.2	na

High and Low temperatures in degrees Fahrenheit; Precipitation and Snow in inches

Population: 23,661 (1990); 27,554 (2000); 28,056 (2010); 28,069 (2015 projected); Race: 96.4% White, 1.1% Black, 0.4% Asian, 2.1% Other, 1.6% Hispanic of any race (2010); Density: 74.4 persons per square mile (2010); Average household size: 2.62 (2010); Median age: 37.3 (2010); Males per 100 females: 98.0 (2010).

Religion: Five largest groups: 13.1% American Baptist Churches in the USA, 9.4% Catholic Church, 4.1% The United Methodist Church, 3.6% Christian Churches and Churches of Christ, 1.4% The Church of Jesus Christ of Latter-day Saints (2000).

Economy: Unemployment rate: 11.0% (5/2010); Total civilian labor force: 14,117 (5/2010); Leading industries: 29.4% manufacturing; 14.3% health care and social assistance; 11.5% retail trade (2008); Farms: 613 totaling 138,331 acres (2007); Companies that employ 500 or more persons: 1 (2008); Companies that employ 100 to 499 persons: 17 (2008); Companies that employ less than 100 persons: 440 (2008); Black-owned businesses: n/a (2002); Hispanic-owned businesses: n/a (2002); Asian-owned businesses: n/a (2002); Women-owned businesses: n/a (2002); Retail sales per capita: $5,610 (2010). Single-family building permits issued: 45 (2009); Multi-family building permits issued: 0 (2009).

Income: Per capita income: $20,441 (2010); Median household income: $45,864 (2010); Average household income: $54,073 (2010); Percent of households with income of $100,000 or more: 9.7% (2010); Poverty rate: 12.3% (2008); Bankruptcy rate: 10.37% (2009).

Taxes: Total county taxes per capita: $242 (2007); County property taxes per capita: $150 (2007).

Education: Percent of population age 25 and over with: High school diploma (including GED) or higher: 80.8% (2010); Bachelor's degree or higher: 8.0% (2010); Master's degree or higher: 2.2% (2010).

Housing: Homeownership rate: 73.1% (2010); Median home value: $86,526 (2010); Median contract rent: $451 per month (2006-2008 3-year est.); Median year structure built: 1981 (2006-2008 3-year est.)

Health: Birth rate: 132.7 per 10,000 population (2009); Death rate: 89.9 per 10,000 population (2009); Age-adjusted cancer mortality rate: 196.5 deaths per 100,000 population (2006); Number of physicians: 2.8 per 10,000 population (2007); Hospital beds: 8.9 per 10,000 population (2006); Hospital admissions: 245.2 per 10,000 population (2006).

Elections: 2008 Presidential election results: 44.9% Obama, 52.9% McCain, 0.0% Nader

National and State Parks: Brush Creek State Fish and Wildlife Area; Crosley State Fish and Wildlife Area; Muscatatuck National Wildlife Refuge; Muscatatuck State Park; Selmier State Forest

Additional Information Contacts

Jennings County Government . . . . (812) 352-3005
 http://www.jenningscounty-in.gov
City of North Vernon . . . . (812) 346-4865
 http://www.jenningsco.org
Jennings County Chamber of Commerce . . . . (812) 346-2339
 http://www.jenningscountychamber.com

Jennings County Communities

BUTLERVILLE (unincorporated postal area, zip code 47223). Covers a land area of 62.492 square miles and a water area of 0.285 square miles. Located at 39.04° N. Lat; 85.49° W. Long. Elevation is 807 feet.

Population: 1,943 (2000); Race: 95.2% White, 1.1% Black, 0.0% Asian, 3.7% Other, 0.0% Hispanic of any race (2000); Density: 31.1 persons per square mile (2000); Age: 23.3% under 18, 10.6% over 64 (2000); Marriage status: 12.0% never married, 73.8% now married, 6.8% widowed, 7.5% divorced (2000); Foreign born: 0.0% (2000); Ancestry (includes multiple ancestries): 14.5% German, 13.1% United States or American, 10.2% English, 9.7% Irish, 2.6% Other groups (2000).

Economy: Employment by occupation: 14.0% management, 5.5% professional, 19.1% services, 20.9% sales, 1.0% farming, 6.6% construction, 32.9% production (2000).

Income: Per capita income: $18,252 (2000); Median household income: $40,379 (2000); Poverty rate: 15.2% (2000).

Education: Percent of population age 25 and over with: High school diploma (including GED) or higher: 68.1% (2000); Bachelor's degree or higher: 5.5% (2000).

Housing: Homeownership rate: 82.6% (2000); Median home value: $76,300 (2000); Median contract rent: $334 per month (2000); Median year structure built: 1964 (2000).

Transportation: Commute to work: 87.2% car, 1.1% public transportation, 2.4% walk, 9.3% work from home (2000); Travel time to work: 24.4% less than 15 minutes, 27.6% 15 to 30 minutes, 28.8% 30 to 45 minutes, 7.7% 45 to 60 minutes, 11.3% 60 minutes or more (2000)

COMMISKEY (unincorporated postal area, zip code 47227). Covers a land area of 44.476 square miles and a water area of 0.118 square miles. Located at 38.87° N. Lat; 85.64° W. Long. Elevation is 696 feet.

Population: 1,370 (2000); Race: 97.9% White, 0.0% Black, 0.5% Asian, 1.6% Other, 2.1% Hispanic of any race (2000); Density: 30.8 persons per square mile (2000); Age: 30.2% under 18, 13.4% over 64 (2000); Marriage status: 16.2% never married, 70.9% now married, 3.5% widowed, 9.3% divorced (2000); Foreign born: 0.4% (2000); Ancestry (includes multiple

ancestries): 18.3% United States or American, 15.2% German, 10.7% Irish, 7.2% Other groups, 4.5% English (2000).

Economy: Employment by occupation: 13.0% management, 13.6% professional, 11.6% services, 13.6% sales, 3.0% farming, 19.7% construction, 25.6% production (2000).

Income: Per capita income: $17,236 (2000); Median household income: $40,610 (2000); Poverty rate: 6.9% (2000).

Education: Percent of population age 25 and over with: High school diploma (including GED) or higher: 72.3% (2000); Bachelor's degree or higher: 10.9% (2000).

School District(s)
Jennings County Schools (PK-12)
 2008-09 Enrollment: 5,195 . . . . (812) 346-4483
Housing: Homeownership rate: 81.5% (2000); Median home value: $89,700 (2000); Median contract rent: $300 per month (2000); Median year structure built: 1977 (2000).

Transportation: Commute to work: 96.6% car, 0.0% public transportation, 0.0% walk, 2.5% work from home (2000); Travel time to work: 3.8% less than 15 minutes, 48.0% 15 to 30 minutes, 31.1% 30 to 45 minutes, 8.1% 45 to 60 minutes, 9.0% 60 minutes or more (2000)

NORTH VERNON (city). Covers a land area of 4.389 square miles and a water area of 0.010 square miles. Located at 39.00° N. Lat; 85.62° W. Long. Elevation is 719 feet.

History: North Vernon was platted in 1854 as a railroad town and trading center.

Population: 5,920 (1990); 6,515 (2000); 6,344 (2010); 6,218 (2015 projected); Race: 95.1% White, 2.0% Black, 0.6% Asian, 2.3% Other, 2.1% Hispanic of any race (2010); Density: 1,445.5 persons per square mile (2010); Average household size: 2.40 (2010); Median age: 35.7 (2010); Males per 100 females: 90.8 (2010); Marriage status: 20.3% never married, 56.5% now married, 9.1% widowed, 14.1% divorced (2000); Foreign born: 0.8% (2000); Ancestry (includes multiple ancestries): 19.0% German, 15.3% United States or American, 10.4% English, 8.6% Other groups, 6.9% Irish (2000).

Economy: Employment by occupation: 8.5% management, 16.5% professional, 15.2% services, 19.9% sales, 1.0% farming, 10.8% construction, 28.1% production (2000).

Income: Per capita income: $20,396 (2010); Median household income: $41,780 (2010); Average household income: $49,402 (2010); Percent of households with income of $100,000 or more: 7.9% (2010); Poverty rate: 11.8% (2000).

Taxes: Total city taxes per capita: $233 (2007); City property taxes per capita: $216 (2007).

Education: Percent of population age 25 and over with: High school diploma (including GED) or higher: 80.4% (2010); Bachelor's degree or higher: 10.4% (2010); Master's degree or higher: 3.5% (2010).

School District(s)
Jennings County Schools (PK-12)
 2008-09 Enrollment: 5,195 . . . . (812) 346-4483
Housing: Homeownership rate: 54.6% (2010); Median home value: $77,156 (2010); Median contract rent: $359 per month (2000); Median year structure built: 1969 (2000).

Hospitals: St. Vincent Jennings Hospital (25 beds)

Safety: Violent crime rate: 15.9 per 10,000 population; Property crime rate: 427.4 per 10,000 population (2008).

Newspapers: Plain Dealer (Regional news; Circulation 6,600); Sun (Local news; Circulation 6,200)

Transportation: Commute to work: 95.9% car, 0.6% public transportation, 1.7% walk, 1.8% work from home (2000); Travel time to work: 58.6% less than 15 minutes, 17.5% 15 to 30 minutes, 17.3% 30 to 45 minutes, 2.7% 45 to 60 minutes, 3.9% 60 minutes or more (2000)

Additional Information Contacts

City of North Vernon . . . . (812) 346-4865
 http://www.jenningsco.org
Jennings County Chamber of Commerce . . . . (812) 346-2339
 http://www.jenningscountychamber.com

PARIS CROSSING (unincorporated postal area, zip code 47270). Covers a land area of 19.361 square miles and a water area of 0.058 square miles. Located at 38.83° N. Lat; 85.71° W. Long. Elevation is 623 feet.

Population: 819 (2000); Race: 98.4% White, 0.0% Black, 0.0% Asian, 1.6% Other, 0.0% Hispanic of any race (2000); Density: 42.3 persons per square mile (2000); Age: 29.0% under 18, 6.3% over 64 (2000); Marriage

status: 11.7% never married, 75.0% now married, 3.3% widowed, 10.0% divorced (2000); Foreign born: 0.0% (2000); Ancestry (includes multiple ancestries): 20.0% German, 17.8% United States or American, 9.8% English, 7.2% Irish, 4.0% Dutch (2000).
Economy: Employment by occupation: 10.8% management, 6.3% professional, 8.0% services, 21.4% sales, 0.0% farming, 20.5% construction, 33.0% production (2000).
Income: Per capita income: $16,066 (2000); Median household income: $35,417 (2000); Poverty rate: 9.1% (2000).
Education: Percent of population age 25 and over with: High school diploma (including GED) or higher: 80.3% (2000); Bachelor's degree or higher: 3.3% (2000).
Housing: Homeownership rate: 86.5% (2000); Median home value: $78,400 (2000); Median contract rent: $275 per month (2000); Median year structure built: 1977 (2000).
Transportation: Commute to work: 100.0% car, 0.0% public transportation, 0.0% walk, 0.0% work from home (2000); Travel time to work: 5.6% less than 15 minutes, 42.8% 15 to 30 minutes, 33.4% 30 to 45 minutes, 12.0% 45 to 60 minutes, 6.2% 60 minutes or more (2000)

SCIPIO (unincorporated postal area, zip code 47273). Covers a land area of 29.239 square miles and a water area of 0.046 square miles. Located at 39.08° N. Lat; 85.73° W. Long. Elevation is 679 feet.
Population: 1,863 (2000); Race: 97.0% White, 0.2% Black, 0.0% Asian, 2.8% Other, 1.7% Hispanic of any race (2000); Density: 63.7 persons per square mile (2000); Age: 29.3% under 18, 8.8% over 64 (2000); Marriage status: 15.0% never married, 70.1% now married, 2.8% widowed, 12.1% divorced (2000); Foreign born: 1.4% (2000); Ancestry (includes multiple ancestries): 21.7% United States or American, 21.4% German, 13.2% Other groups, 9.8% Irish, 8.1% English (2000).
Economy: Employment by occupation: 9.0% management, 8.4% professional, 12.9% services, 23.8% sales, 0.0% farming, 10.7% construction, 35.2% production (2000).
Income: Per capita income: $19,022 (2000); Median household income: $49,400 (2000); Poverty rate: 4.6% (2000).
Education: Percent of population age 25 and over with: High school diploma (including GED) or higher: 86.5% (2000); Bachelor's degree or higher: 5.8% (2000).
School District(s)
Jennings County Schools (PK-12)
    2008-09 Enrollment: 5,195 . . . . (812) 346-4483
Housing: Homeownership rate: 90.2% (2000); Median home value: $85,800 (2000); Median contract rent: $400 per month (2000); Median year structure built: 1971 (2000).
Transportation: Commute to work: 94.4% car, 0.0% public transportation, 2.6% walk, 2.3% work from home (2000); Travel time to work: 15.2% less than 15 minutes, 51.7% 15 to 30 minutes, 28.3% 30 to 45 minutes, 2.6% 45 to 60 minutes, 2.3% 60 minutes or more (2000)

VERNON (town). County seat. Covers a land area of 0.239 square miles and a water area of 0 square miles. Located at 38.98° N. Lat; 85.61° W. Long. Elevation is 663 feet.
History: The land grant that established Vernon in 1815 stipulated that it should be the county seat forever.
Population: 370 (1990); 330 (2000); 322 (2010); 314 (2015 projected); Race: 96.6% White, 2.8% Black, 0.0% Asian, 0.6% Other, 0.3% Hispanic of any race (2010); Density: 1,349.7 persons per square mile (2010); Average household size: 2.47 (2010); Median age: 37.6 (2010); Males per 100 females: 107.7 (2010); Marriage status: 35.3% never married, 39.1% now married, 13.6% widowed, 12.0% divorced (2000); Foreign born: 0.0% (2000); Ancestry (includes multiple ancestries): 15.8% German, 11.5% United States or American, 10.2% Irish, 4.0% French (except Basque), 3.4% Other groups (2000).
Economy: Employment by occupation: 6.6% management, 8.0% professional, 13.9% services, 21.2% sales, 0.0% farming, 11.7% construction, 38.7% production (2000).
Income: Per capita income: $22,932 (2010); Median household income: $44,231 (2010); Average household income: $55,575 (2010); Percent of households with income of $100,000 or more: 12.7% (2010); Poverty rate: 9.5% (2000).
Taxes: Total city taxes per capita: $46 (2007); City property taxes per capita: $22 (2007).
Education: Percent of population age 25 and over with: High school diploma (including GED) or higher: 90.4% (2010); Bachelor's degree or higher: 9.6% (2010); Master's degree or higher: 3.7% (2010).

Housing: Homeownership rate: 73.0% (2010); Median home value: $96,250 (2010); Median contract rent: $388 per month (2000); Median year structure built: before 1940 (2000).
Transportation: Commute to work: 93.1% car, 0.0% public transportation, 2.3% walk, 4.6% work from home (2000); Travel time to work: 28.0% less than 15 minutes, 28.8% 15 to 30 minutes, 22.4% 30 to 45 minutes, 15.2% 45 to 60 minutes, 5.6% 60 minutes or more (2000)

Johnson County

Located in central Indiana; drained by the West Fork of the White River. Covers a land area of 320.19 square miles, a water area of 1.36 square miles, and is located in the Eastern Time Zone. The county was founded in 1822. County seat is Franklin.

Johnson County is part of the Indianapolis-Carmel, IN Metropolitan Statistical Area. The entire metro area includes: Boone County, IN; Brown County, IN; Hamilton County, IN; Hancock County, IN; Hendricks County, IN; Johnson County, IN; Marion County, IN; Morgan County, IN; Putnam County, IN; Shelby County, IN

Weather Station: New Whiteland									Elevation: 784 feet			
	Jan	Feb	Mar	Apr	May	Jun	Jul	Aug	Sep	Oct	Nov	Dec
High	33	38	51	62	73	82	85	83	77	65	51	39
Low	16	19	30	40	51	60	63	61	53	41	32	22
Precip	2.2	2.1	3.6	4.2	4.5	4.0	4.3	3.6	2.9	2.9	4.0	3.1
Snow	na	na	na	0.4	0.0	0.0	0.0	0.0	0.0	0.3	0.4	na

High and Low temperatures in degrees Fahrenheit; Precipitation and Snow in inches

Population: 88,109 (1990); 115,209 (2000); 143,555 (2010); 156,470 (2015 projected); Race: 94.6% White, 1.7% Black, 1.7% Asian, 2.0% Other, 2.4% Hispanic of any race (2010); Density: 448.3 persons per square mile (2010); Average household size: 2.57 (2010); Median age: 36.0 (2010); Males per 100 females: 96.8 (2010).
Religion: Five largest groups: 8.5% Catholic Church, 7.2% Christian Churches and Churches of Christ, 5.1% Independent, Non-Charismatic Churches, 3.0% The United Methodist Church, 2.3% General Association of Regular Baptist Churches (2000).
Economy: Unemployment rate: 8.5% (5/2010); Total civilian labor force: 72,729 (5/2010); Leading industries: 21.8% retail trade; 13.9% manufacturing; 13.8% accommodation & food services (2008); Farms: 585 totaling 142,181 acres (2007); Companies that employ 500 or more persons: 4 (2008); Companies that employ 100 to 499 persons: 58 (2008); Companies that employ less than 100 persons: 2,975 (2008); Black-owned businesses: n/a (2002); Hispanic-owned businesses: n/a (2002); Asian-owned businesses: n/a (2002); Women-owned businesses: 2,206 (2002); Retail sales per capita: $13,312 (2010). Single-family building permits issued: 264 (2009); Multi-family building permits issued: 414 (2009).
Income: Per capita income: $28,106 (2010); Median household income: $61,278 (2010); Average household income: $73,149 (2010); Percent of households with income of $100,000 or more: 21.7% (2010); Poverty rate: 7.4% (2008); Bankruptcy rate: 9.03% (2009).
Taxes: Total county taxes per capita: $415 (2007); County property taxes per capita: $116 (2007).
Education: Percent of population age 25 and over with: High school diploma (including GED) or higher: 90.3% (2010); Bachelor's degree or higher: 25.9% (2010); Master's degree or higher: 8.4% (2010).
Housing: Homeownership rate: 75.7% (2010); Median home value: $137,579 (2010); Median contract rent: $634 per month (2006-2008 3-year est.); Median year structure built: 1984 (2006-2008 3-year est.)
Health: Birth rate: 138.7 per 10,000 population (2009); Death rate: 82.3 per 10,000 population (2009); Age-adjusted cancer mortality rate: 200.9 deaths per 100,000 population (2006); Air Quality Index: 85.0% good, 14.4% moderate, 0.6% unhealthy for sensitive individuals, 0.0% unhealthy (percent of days in 2008); Number of physicians: 14.8 per 10,000 population (2007); Hospital beds: 21.1 per 10,000 population (2006); Hospital admissions: 487.4 per 10,000 population (2006).
Elections: 2008 Presidential election results: 36.7% Obama, 62.1% McCain, 0.0% Nader
National and State Parks: Atterbury State Fish and Wildlife Area
Additional Information Contacts
Johnson County Government . . . . (317) 346-4700
   http://www.co.johnson.in.us
City of Franklin . . . . (317) 736-3609
   http://www.franklin-in.gov

City of Greenwood . . . . (317) 881-8527
  http://www.greenwood.in.gov
Franklin Chamber of Commerce . . . . (317) 736-6334
  http://www.franklincoc.org
Greenwood Chamber of Commerce . . . . (317) 888-4856
  http://www.greenwood-chamber.com
Johnson County Development Corporation . . . . (317) 736-4300
  http://www.jcdc.org
Town of Bargersville . . . . (317) 422-5115
  http://www.townofbargersville.org
Town of Edinburgh. . . . . (812) 526-3512
  http://www.edinburgh.in.us
Town of New Whiteland . . . . (317) 535-9487
  http://www.townofnewwhiteland.com
Town of Whiteland . . . . (317) 535-5531
  http://www.townofwhiteland.com

Johnson County Communities

BARGERSVILLE (town). Covers a land area of 1.092 square miles
and a water area of 0 square miles. Located at 39.52° N. Lat; 86.16° W.
Long. Elevation is 820 feet.
Population: 1,777 (1990); 2,120 (2000); 2,744 (2010); 3,045 (2015
projected); Race: 98.6% White, 0.2% Black, 0.5% Asian, 0.8% Other, 0.5%
Hispanic of any race (2010); Density: 2,512.8 persons per square mile
(2010); Average household size: 2.65 (2010); Median age: 34.2 (2010);
Males per 100 females: 101.5 (2010); Marriage status: 18.1% never
married, 63.2% now married, 4.6% widowed, 14.0% divorced (2000);
Foreign born: 0.6% (2000); Ancestry (includes multiple ancestries): 26.4%
United States or American, 20.3% German, 10.3% Irish, 8.3% English,
7.3% Other groups (2000).
Economy: Single-family building permits issued: 2 (2009); Multi-family
building permits issued: 19 (2009); Employment by occupation: 9.0%
management, 12.1% professional, 14.9% services, 27.2% sales, 0.3%
farming, 16.2% construction, 20.4% production (2000).
Income: Per capita income: $27,080 (2010); Median household income:
$63,884 (2010); Average household income: $71,949 (2010); Percent of
households with income of $100,000 or more: 20.2% (2010); Poverty rate:
4.3% (2000).
Taxes: Total city taxes per capita: $107 (2007); City property taxes per
capita: $101 (2007).
Education: Percent of population age 25 and over with: High school
diploma (including GED) or higher: 91.5% (2010); Bachelor's degree or
higher: 15.1% (2010); Master's degree or higher: 5.0% (2010).
School District(s)
Center Grove Com Sch Corp (PK-12)
  2008-09 Enrollment: 7,564 . . . . (317) 881-9326
Franklin Community School Corp (KG-12)
  2008-09 Enrollment: 5,019 . . . . (317) 738-5800
Housing: Homeownership rate: 77.8% (2010); Median home value:
$123,245 (2010); Median contract rent: $503 per month (2000); Median
year structure built: 1972 (2000).
Safety: Violent crime rate: 14.7 per 10,000 population; Property crime rate:
0.0 per 10,000 population (2008).
Transportation: Commute to work: 96.2% car, 0.0% public transportation,
1.2% walk, 2.6% work from home (2000); Travel time to work: 21.6% less
than 15 minutes, 34.1% 15 to 30 minutes, 26.9% 30 to 45 minutes, 12.0%
45 to 60 minutes, 5.4% 60 minutes or more (2000)
Additional Information Contacts
Johnson County Development Corporation . . . . (317) 736-4300
  http://www.jcdc.org
Town of Bargersville . . . . (317) 422-5115
  http://www.townofbargersville.org

EDINBURGH (town). Covers a land area of 2.843 square miles and a
water area of 0 square miles. Located at 39.35° N. Lat; 85.96° W. Long.
Elevation is 673 feet.
Population: 4,559 (1990); 4,505 (2000); 5,048 (2010); 5,331 (2015
projected); Race: 98.6% White, 0.6% Black, 0.1% Asian, 0.8% Other, 1.9%
Hispanic of any race (2010); Density: 1,775.8 persons per square mile
(2010); Average household size: 2.43 (2010); Median age: 36.2 (2010);
Males per 100 females: 98.0 (2010); Marriage status: 20.0% never married,
58.3% now married, 6.0% widowed, 15.7% divorced (2000); Foreign born:
0.7% (2000); Ancestry (includes multiple ancestries): 15.0% United States

or American, 13.3% English, 11.3% German, 5.8% Other groups, 5.7%
Irish (2000).
Economy: Single-family building permits issued: 3 (2009); Multi-family
building permits issued: 0 (2009); Employment by occupation: 6.7%
management, 5.6% professional, 13.7% services, 20.2% sales, 0.4%
farming, 11.1% construction, 42.4% production (2000).
Income: Per capita income: $17,309 (2010); Median household income:
$36,240 (2010); Average household income: $42,176 (2010); Percent of
households with income of $100,000 or more: 4.5% (2010); Poverty rate:
12.4% (2000).
Taxes: Total city taxes per capita: $426 (2007); City property taxes per
capita: $421 (2007).
Education: Percent of population age 25 and over with: High school
diploma (including GED) or higher: 69.4% (2010); Bachelor's degree or
higher: 4.5% (2010); Master's degree or higher: 1.5% (2010).
School District(s)
Edinburgh Community Sch Corp (PK-12)
  2008-09 Enrollment: 887 . . . . (812) 526-2681
Housing: Homeownership rate: 63.5% (2010); Median home value:
$96,291 (2010); Median contract rent: $395 per month (2000); Median year
structure built: 1963 (2000).
Transportation: Commute to work: 89.4% car, 0.0% public transportation,
6.2% walk, 0.6% work from home (2000); Travel time to work: 49.8% less
than 15 minutes, 30.8% 15 to 30 minutes, 8.6% 30 to 45 minutes, 7.5% 45
to 60 minutes, 3.4% 60 minutes or more (2000)
Additional Information Contacts
Town of Edinburgh. . . . . (812) 526-3512
  http://www.edinburgh.in.us

FRANKLIN (city). County seat. Covers a land area of 11.263 square
miles and a water area of 0 square miles. Located at 39.49° N. Lat; 86.05°
W. Long. Elevation is 725 feet.
History: Named for Benjamin Franklin, American statesman and inventor.
Franklin developed as a shipping center for grain and tomatoes. In 1834
Franklin College was established as the Indiana Baptist Manual Labor
Institute.
Population: 13,593 (1990); 19,463 (2000); 24,389 (2010); 26,560 (2015
projected); Race: 93.7% White, 2.7% Black, 1.0% Asian, 2.5% Other, 2.3%
Hispanic of any race (2010); Density: 2,165.5 persons per square mile
(2010); Average household size: 2.53 (2010); Median age: 34.8 (2010);
Males per 100 females: 92.3 (2010); Marriage status: 23.6% never married,
57.7% now married, 7.8% widowed, 10.9% divorced (2000); Foreign born:
1.5% (2000); Ancestry (includes multiple ancestries): 19.1% German,
13.8% United States or American, 12.3% Irish, 10.8% Other groups, 9.8%
English (2000).
Economy: Single-family building permits issued: 22 (2009); Multi-family
building permits issued: 0 (2009); Employment by occupation: 11.0%
management, 16.7% professional, 14.7% services, 25.0% sales, 0.6%
farming, 11.0% construction, 21.0% production (2000).
Income: Per capita income: $23,289 (2010); Median household income:
$54,045 (2010); Average household income: $61,378 (2010); Percent of
households with income of $100,000 or more: 14.1% (2010); Poverty rate:
7.6% (2000).
Taxes: Total city taxes per capita: $408 (2007); City property taxes per
capita: $398 (2007).
Education: Percent of population age 25 and over with: High school
diploma (including GED) or higher: 86.2% (2010); Bachelor's degree or
higher: 21.3% (2010); Master's degree or higher: 8.4% (2010).
School District(s)
Clark-Pleasant Com School Corp (KG-12)
  2008-09 Enrollment: 5,598 . . . . (317) 535-7579
Franklin Community School Corp (KG-12)
  2008-09 Enrollment: 5,019 . . . . (317) 738-5800
Four-year College(s)
Franklin College (Private, Not-for-profit, American Baptist)
  Fall 2008 Enrollment: 1,153. . . . . (317) 738-8000
  2009-10 Tuition: In-state $23,275; Out-of-state $23,275
Housing: Homeownership rate: 68.6% (2010); Median home value:
$117,207 (2010); Median contract rent: $492 per month (2000); Median
year structure built: 1980 (2000).
Hospitals: Johnson Memorial Hospital (161 beds)
Safety: Violent crime rate: 39.4 per 10,000 population; Property crime rate:
470.4 per 10,000 population (2008).

Newspapers: Daily Journal (Local news; Circulation 18,000); Franklin Challenger (Community news; Circulation 300); Greenwood News (Local news; Circulation 17,000)
Transportation: Commute to work: 94.0% car, 0.2% public transportation, 2.8% walk, 1.4% work from home (2000); Travel time to work: 45.4% less than 15 minutes, 25.0% 15 to 30 minutes, 18.6% 30 to 45 minutes, 7.0% 45 to 60 minutes, 4.0% 60 minutes or more (2000)
Additional Information Contacts
City of Franklin . . . . (317) 736-3609
  http://www.franklin-in.gov
Franklin Chamber of Commerce . . . . (317) 736-6334
  http://www.franklincoc.org

GREENWOOD (city).
Covers a land area of 14.273 square miles and a water area of <.001 square miles. Located at 39.61° N. Lat; 86.11° W. Long. Elevation is 804 feet.
History: Named for Samuel Greenwood who plotted the village in 1872. Greenwood developed as an industrial town with automobile-parts factories and a canning company.
Population: 27,969 (1990); 36,037 (2000); 46,350 (2010); 50,408 (2015 projected); Race: 94.0% White, 1.3% Black, 2.2% Asian, 2.5% Other, 3.3% Hispanic of any race (2010); Density: 3,247.3 persons per square mile (2010); Average household size: 2.34 (2010); Median age: 36.2 (2010); Males per 100 females: 94.5 (2010); Marriage status: 23.1% never married, 58.4% now married, 6.9% widowed, 11.6% divorced (2000); Foreign born: 2.4% (2000); Ancestry (includes multiple ancestries): 24.8% German, 14.6% United States or American, 13.0% Irish, 10.7% English, 7.8% Other groups (2000).
Economy: Unemployment rate: 9.1% (5/2010); Total civilian labor force: 25,858 (5/2010); Single-family building permits issued: 77 (2009); Multi-family building permits issued: 3 (2009); Employment by occupation: 14.9% management, 20.7% professional, 12.0% services, 30.0% sales, 0.1% farming, 10.0% construction, 12.3% production (2000).
Income: Per capita income: $26,657 (2010); Median household income: $52,089 (2010); Average household income: $62,654 (2010); Percent of households with income of $100,000 or more: 16.0% (2010); Poverty rate: 7.0% (2000).
Taxes: Total city taxes per capita: $241 (2007); City property taxes per capita: $235 (2007).
Education: Percent of population age 25 and over with: High school diploma (including GED) or higher: 92.2% (2010); Bachelor's degree or higher: 27.0% (2010); Master's degree or higher: 8.0% (2010).
School District(s)
Center Grove Com Sch Corp (PK-12)
  2008-09 Enrollment: 7,564 . . . . (317) 881-9326
Central Nine Career Center (09-12)
  2008-09 Enrollment: n/a . . . . (317) 888-4401
Clark-Pleasant Com School Corp (KG-12)
  2008-09 Enrollment: 5,598 . . . . (317) 535-7579
Greenwood Community Sch Corp (PK-12)
  2008-09 Enrollment: 3,865 . . . . (317) 889-4060
Housing: Homeownership rate: 64.3% (2010); Median home value: $125,018 (2010); Median contract rent: $528 per month (2000); Median year structure built: 1980 (2000).
Hospitals: Valle Vista Health System (102 beds)
Safety: Violent crime rate: 39.6 per 10,000 population; Property crime rate: 383.3 per 10,000 population (2008).
Newspapers: Greenwood Southside Challenger (Local news; Circulation 1,500); The Indianapolis Star - Metro South Bureau (Regional news)
Transportation: Commute to work: 95.9% car, 0.1% public transportation, 1.7% walk, 1.9% work from home (2000); Travel time to work: 25.7% less than 15 minutes, 37.4% 15 to 30 minutes, 26.9% 30 to 45 minutes, 7.2% 45 to 60 minutes, 2.9% 60 minutes or more (2000)
Additional Information Contacts
City of Greenwood . . . . (317) 881-8527
  http://www.greenwood.in.gov
Greenwood Chamber of Commerce . . . . (317) 888-4856
  http://www.greenwood-chamber.com

NEEDHAM (unincorporated postal area, zip code 46162).
Covers a land area of 11.140 square miles and a water area of 0 square miles. Located at 39.54° N. Lat; 85.95° W. Long. Elevation is 738 feet.
Population: 411 (2000); Race: 100.0% White, 0.0% Black, 0.0% Asian, 0.0% Other, 0.0% Hispanic of any race (2000); Density: 36.9 persons per square mile (2000); Age: 22.6% under 18, 11.3% over 64 (2000); Marriage

status: 37.6% never married, 50.3% now married, 8.2% widowed, 3.9% divorced (2000); Foreign born: 1.9% (2000); Ancestry (includes multiple ancestries): 27.0% English, 14.3% Dutch, 12.7% Other groups, 10.5% German, 6.2% Irish (2000).
Economy: Employment by occupation: 27.5% management, 12.0% professional, 16.5% services, 11.5% sales, 3.0% farming, 16.0% construction, 13.5% production (2000).
Income: Per capita income: $16,440 (2000); Median household income: $55,278 (2000); Poverty rate: 9.9% (2000).
Education: Percent of population age 25 and over with: High school diploma (including GED) or higher: 75.0% (2000); Bachelor's degree or higher: 3.4% (2000).
Housing: Homeownership rate: 79.0% (2000); Median home value: $92,200 (2000); Median contract rent: $193 per month (2000); Median year structure built: 1943 (2000).
Transportation: Commute to work: 79.0% car, 4.0% public transportation, 0.0% walk, 17.0% work from home (2000); Travel time to work: 32.5% less than 15 minutes, 25.9% 15 to 30 minutes, 7.8% 30 to 45 minutes, 12.0% 45 to 60 minutes, 21.7% 60 minutes or more (2000)

NEW WHITELAND (town).
Covers a land area of 1.229 square miles and a water area of 0 square miles. Located at 39.56° N. Lat; 86.09° W. Long. Elevation is 807 feet.
Population: 4,271 (1990); 4,579 (2000); 5,333 (2010); 5,834 (2015 projected); Race: 98.1% White, 0.1% Black, 0.7% Asian, 1.1% Other, 1.5% Hispanic of any race (2010); Density: 4,339.0 persons per square mile (2010); Average household size: 2.80 (2010); Median age: 35.3 (2010); Males per 100 females: 96.6 (2010); Marriage status: 17.9% never married, 69.4% now married, 4.0% widowed, 8.7% divorced (2000); Foreign born: 0.9% (2000); Ancestry (includes multiple ancestries): 24.3% German, 15.6% United States or American, 13.9% Irish, 11.0% English, 8.6% Other groups (2000).
Economy: Single-family building permits issued: 20 (2009); Multi-family building permits issued: 0 (2009); Employment by occupation: 9.8% management, 11.1% professional, 11.4% services, 28.8% sales, 0.0% farming, 16.3% construction, 22.6% production (2000).
Income: Per capita income: $22,429 (2010); Median household income: $57,820 (2010); Average household income: $62,823 (2010); Percent of households with income of $100,000 or more: 11.8% (2010); Poverty rate: 3.0% (2000).
Taxes: Total city taxes per capita: $92 (2007); City property taxes per capita: $86 (2007).
Education: Percent of population age 25 and over with: High school diploma (including GED) or higher: 88.1% (2010); Bachelor's degree or higher: 11.7% (2010); Master's degree or higher: 1.7% (2010).
School District(s)
Clark-Pleasant Com School Corp (KG-12)
  2008-09 Enrollment: 5,598 . . . . (317) 535-7579
Housing: Homeownership rate: 88.2% (2010); Median home value: $99,396 (2010); Median contract rent: $710 per month (2000); Median year structure built: 1964 (2000).
Safety: Violent crime rate: 22.2 per 10,000 population; Property crime rate: 191.4 per 10,000 population (2008).
Transportation: Commute to work: 95.3% car, 0.0% public transportation, 0.4% walk, 2.5% work from home (2000); Travel time to work: 22.0% less than 15 minutes, 31.6% 15 to 30 minutes, 31.4% 30 to 45 minutes, 11.0% 45 to 60 minutes, 4.1% 60 minutes or more (2000)
Additional Information Contacts
Town of New Whiteland . . . . (317) 535-9487
  http://www.townofnewwhiteland.com

NINEVEH (unincorporated postal area, zip code 46164).
Covers a land area of 22.920 square miles and a water area of 0.845 square miles. Located at 39.32° N. Lat; 86.11° W. Long. Elevation is 771 feet.
Population: 4,133 (2000); Race: 97.5% White, 0.4% Black, 0.4% Asian, 1.7% Other, 0.6% Hispanic of any race (2000); Density: 180.3 persons per square mile (2000); Age: 23.1% under 18, 11.5% over 64 (2000); Marriage status: 18.1% never married, 66.7% now married, 5.0% widowed, 10.2% divorced (2000); Foreign born: 0.8% (2000); Ancestry (includes multiple ancestries): 26.9% German, 14.7% Irish, 12.1% English, 7.6% Other groups, 7.0% United States or American (2000).
Economy: Employment by occupation: 11.5% management, 14.3% professional, 11.5% services, 25.5% sales, 0.1% farming, 19.0% construction, 18.2% production (2000).

Income: Per capita income: $20,532 (2000); Median household income: $46,810 (2000); Poverty rate: 7.6% (2000).
Education: Percent of population age 25 and over with: High school diploma (including GED) or higher: 87.2% (2000); Bachelor's degree or higher: 14.0% (2000).
Housing: Homeownership rate: 94.2% (2000); Median home value: $116,300 (2000); Median contract rent: $540 per month (2000); Median year structure built: 1976 (2000).
Transportation: Commute to work: 98.0% car, 0.0% public transportation, 0.0% walk, 2.0% work from home (2000); Travel time to work: 8.1% less than 15 minutes, 31.1% 15 to 30 minutes, 25.4% 30 to 45 minutes, 14.8% 45 to 60 minutes, 20.6% 60 minutes or more (2000)

PRINCES LAKES (town).
Covers a land area of 1.281 square miles and a water area of 0.193 square miles. Located at 39.35° N. Lat; 86.10° W. Long. Elevation is 820 feet.
Population: 1,190 (1990); 1,506 (2000); 1,807 (2010); 1,967 (2015 projected); Race: 94.5% White, 3.5% Black, 0.3% Asian, 1.7% Other, 3.2% Hispanic of any race (2010); Density: 1,410.2 persons per square mile (2010); Average household size: 2.47 (2010); Median age: 40.8 (2010); Males per 100 females: 94.1 (2010); Marriage status: 18.0% never married, 64.5% now married, 4.6% widowed, 12.9% divorced (2000); Foreign born: 0.9% (2000); Ancestry (includes multiple ancestries): 21.9% German, 12.7% Irish, 10.1% English, 9.3% United States or American, 8.5% Other groups (2000).
Economy: Single-family building permits issued: 1 (2009); Multi-family building permits issued: 0 (2009); Employment by occupation: 8.7% management, 14.5% professional, 12.0% services, 23.5% sales, 0.3% farming, 15.8% construction, 25.2% production (2000).
Income: Per capita income: $27,781 (2010); Median household income: $57,488 (2010); Average household income: $68,363 (2010); Percent of households with income of $100,000 or more: 16.2% (2010); Poverty rate: 6.2% (2000).
Taxes: Total city taxes per capita: $98 (2007); City property taxes per capita: $92 (2007).
Education: Percent of population age 25 and over with: High school diploma (including GED) or higher: 89.8% (2010); Bachelor's degree or higher: 17.6% (2010); Master's degree or higher: 4.4% (2010).
Housing: Homeownership rate: 89.5% (2010); Median home value: $138,616 (2010); Median contract rent: $535 per month (2000); Median year structure built: 1963 (2000).
Transportation: Commute to work: 96.1% car, 0.0% public transportation, 0.0% walk, 3.9% work from home (2000); Travel time to work: 10.0% less than 15 minutes, 39.0% 15 to 30 minutes, 22.7% 30 to 45 minutes, 16.5% 45 to 60 minutes, 11.8% 60 minutes or more (2000)

TRAFALGAR (town).
Covers a land area of 1.289 square miles and a water area of 0 square miles. Located at 39.41° N. Lat; 86.15° W. Long. Elevation is 827 feet.
History: Laid out 1850.
Population: 650 (1990); 798 (2000); 1,064 (2010); 1,189 (2015 projected); Race: 93.8% White, 4.5% Black, 0.8% Asian, 0.9% Other, 0.8% Hispanic of any race (2010); Density: 825.6 persons per square mile (2010); Average household size: 2.83 (2010); Median age: 33.3 (2010); Males per 100 females: 98.9 (2010); Marriage status: 19.3% never married, 62.9% now married, 2.5% widowed, 15.3% divorced (2000); Foreign born: 0.2% (2000); Ancestry (includes multiple ancestries): 22.3% German, 12.6% Irish, 11.5% United States or American, 10.5% English, 8.6% Other groups (2000).
Economy: Single-family building permits issued: 6 (2009); Multi-family building permits issued: 32 (2009); Employment by occupation: 8.9% management, 13.1% professional, 10.8% services, 23.9% sales, 0.0% farming, 14.5% construction, 28.8% production (2000).
Income: Per capita income: $24,078 (2010); Median household income: $63,194 (2010); Average household income: $68,108 (2010); Percent of households with income of $100,000 or more: 16.3% (2010); Poverty rate: 8.4% (2000).
Taxes: Total city taxes per capita: $111 (2007); City property taxes per capita: $53 (2007).
Education: Percent of population age 25 and over with: High school diploma (including GED) or higher: 89.8% (2010); Bachelor's degree or higher: 17.0% (2010); Master's degree or higher: 4.9% (2010).
School District(s)
Nineveh-Hensley-Jackson United (PK-12)
    2008-09 Enrollment: 1,840 . . . . (317) 878-2100

Housing: Homeownership rate: 81.6% (2010); Median home value: $136,775 (2010); Median contract rent: $485 per month (2000); Median year structure built: 1983 (2000).
Transportation: Commute to work: 94.6% car, 1.0% public transportation, 3.1% walk, 1.3% work from home (2000); Travel time to work: 22.3% less than 15 minutes, 36.8% 15 to 30 minutes, 20.7% 30 to 45 minutes, 15.5% 45 to 60 minutes, 4.7% 60 minutes or more (2000)

WHITELAND (town).
Covers a land area of 2.272 square miles and a water area of 0 square miles. Located at 39.54° N. Lat; 86.08° W. Long. Elevation is 794 feet.
Population: 2,446 (1990); 3,958 (2000); 5,415 (2010); 6,096 (2015 projected); Race: 97.2% White, 0.3% Black, 0.8% Asian, 1.7% Other, 1.6% Hispanic of any race (2010); Density: 2,383.8 persons per square mile (2010); Average household size: 2.84 (2010); Median age: 33.7 (2010); Males per 100 females: 100.1 (2010); Marriage status: 16.5% never married, 68.5% now married, 2.5% widowed, 12.5% divorced (2000); Foreign born: 0.6% (2000); Ancestry (includes multiple ancestries): 23.3% German, 15.8% United States or American, 14.7% Irish, 13.7% English, 9.3% Other groups (2000).
Economy: Single-family building permits issued: 2 (2009); Multi-family building permits issued: 0 (2009); Employment by occupation: 13.3% management, 15.5% professional, 12.0% services, 27.2% sales, 0.0% farming, 10.2% construction, 21.9% production (2000).
Income: Per capita income: $25,163 (2010); Median household income: $65,390 (2010); Average household income: $71,340 (2010); Percent of households with income of $100,000 or more: 18.8% (2010); Poverty rate: 1.9% (2000).
Taxes: Total city taxes per capita: $68 (2007); City property taxes per capita: $64 (2007).
Education: Percent of population age 25 and over with: High school diploma (including GED) or higher: 93.5% (2010); Bachelor's degree or higher: 20.0% (2010); Master's degree or higher: 4.5% (2010).
School District(s)
Clark-Pleasant Com School Corp (KG-12)
    2008-09 Enrollment: 5,598 . . . . (317) 535-7579
Housing: Homeownership rate: 87.8% (2010); Median home value: $128,092 (2010); Median contract rent: $722 per month (2000); Median year structure built: 1986 (2000).
Transportation: Commute to work: 97.6% car, 0.0% public transportation, 0.0% walk, 1.8% work from home (2000); Travel time to work: 17.0% less than 15 minutes, 41.1% 15 to 30 minutes, 28.8% 30 to 45 minutes, 6.6% 45 to 60 minutes, 6.5% 60 minutes or more (2000)
Additional Information Contacts
Town of Whiteland . . . . (317) 535-5531
    http://www.townofwhiteland.com

Knox County

Located in southwestern Indiana; bounded on the west by the Wabash River and the Illinois border, on the east by the West Fork of the White River, and on the south by the White River. Covers a land area of 515.83 square miles, a water area of 8.22 square miles, and is located in the Eastern Time Zone. The county was founded in 1790. County seat is Vincennes.

Knox County is part of the Vincennes, IN Micropolitan Statistical Area. The entire metro area includes: Knox County, IN

Population: 39,884 (1990); 39,256 (2000); 37,992 (2010); 37,289 (2015 projected); Race: 95.2% White, 2.1% Black, 1.1% Asian, 1.7% Other, 1.1% Hispanic of any race (2010); Density: 73.7 persons per square mile (2010); Average household size: 2.32 (2010); Median age: 38.2 (2010); Males per 100 females: 98.2 (2010).
Religion: Five largest groups: 14.5% Catholic Church, 6.0% The United Methodist Church, 5.0% American Baptist Churches in the USA, 3.9% United Church of Christ, 3.6% Christian Churches and Churches of Christ (2000).
Economy: Unemployment rate: 7.1% (5/2010); Total civilian labor force: 20,323 (5/2010); Leading industries: 25.5% health care and social assistance; 16.6% retail trade; 13.6% manufacturing (2008); Farms: 568 totaling 327,267 acres (2007); Companies that employ 500 or more persons: 1 (2008); Companies that employ 100 to 499 persons: 15 (2008); Companies that employ less than 100 persons: 971 (2008); Black-owned businesses: n/a (2002); Hispanic-owned businesses: n/a (2002); Asian-owned businesses: n/a (2002); Women-owned businesses: 818

(2002); Retail sales per capita: $14,477 (2010). Single-family building permits issued: 34 (2009); Multi-family building permits issued: 0 (2009).

Income: Per capita income: $20,785 (2010); Median household income: $39,660 (2010); Average household income: $50,337 (2010); Percent of households with income of $100,000 or more: 9.9% (2010); Poverty rate: 16.6% (2008); Bankruptcy rate: 5.34% (2009).

Taxes: Total county taxes per capita: $249 (2007); County property taxes per capita: $176 (2007).

Education: Percent of population age 25 and over with: High school diploma (including GED) or higher: 86.0% (2010); Bachelor's degree or higher: 15.1% (2010); Master's degree or higher: 5.7% (2010).

Housing: Homeownership rate: 71.0% (2010); Median home value: $78,740 (2010); Median contract rent: $385 per month (2006-2008 3-year est.); Median year structure built: 1956 (2006-2008 3-year est.)

Health: Birth rate: 122.7 per 10,000 population (2009); Death rate: 117.9 per 10,000 population (2009); Age-adjusted cancer mortality rate: 187.8 deaths per 100,000 population (2006); Air Quality Index: 72.0% good, 28.0% moderate, 0.0% unhealthy for sensitive individuals, 0.0% unhealthy (percent of days in 2008); Number of physicians: 18.2 per 10,000 population (2007); Hospital beds: 61.1 per 10,000 population (2006); Hospital admissions: 2,263.3 per 10,000 population (2006).

Elections: 2008 Presidential election results: 46.1% Obama, 52.6% McCain, 0.0% Nader

National and State Parks: George Rogers Clark National Historical Park; George Rogers Clark State Memorial; White Oak State Fishing Area

Additional Information Contacts

Knox County Government . . . . (812) 885-2521
    http://knoxcountychamber.com
City of Bicknell . . . . (812) 735-3559
    http://www.bicknelldevelopment.com
City of Vincennes . . . . (812) 882-7285
    http://www.vincennes.org
Knox County Chamber of Commerce . . . . (812) 882-6440
    http://www.knoxcountychamber.com
Vincennes Chamber of Commerce . . . . (812) 886-0400
    http://www.vincennescvb.org

Knox County Communities

BICKNELL (city). Covers a land area of 1.524 square miles and a water area of 0 square miles. Located at 38.77° N. Lat; 87.30° W. Long. Elevation is 528 feet.

History: Coal mining began in Bicknell in 1875, and was responsible for the growth of the community. The town was founded by a Bicknell, an ancestor of Ernest P. Bicknell (1862-1930) who directed American Red Cross activities abroad.

Population: 3,364 (1990); 3,378 (2000); 3,127 (2010); 3,015 (2015 projected); Race: 97.6% White, 0.6% Black, 0.2% Asian, 1.6% Other, 0.9% Hispanic of any race (2010); Density: 2,052.1 persons per square mile (2010); Average household size: 2.39 (2010); Median age: 37.8 (2010); Males per 100 females: 89.5 (2010); Marriage status: 19.1% never married, 57.8% now married, 9.0% widowed, 14.0% divorced (2000); Foreign born: 1.7% (2000); Ancestry (includes multiple ancestries): 18.4% United States or American, 15.9% German, 8.7% Irish, 7.2% Other groups, 7.1% English (2000).

Economy: Employment by occupation: 6.3% management, 11.2% professional, 21.2% services, 24.1% sales, 1.0% farming, 12.8% construction, 23.4% production (2000).

Income: Per capita income: $15,898 (2010); Median household income: $28,889 (2010); Average household income: $38,209 (2010); Percent of households with income of $100,000 or more: 5.3% (2010); Poverty rate: 26.3% (2000).

Taxes: Total city taxes per capita: $94 (2007); City property taxes per capita: $71 (2007).

Education: Percent of population age 25 and over with: High school diploma (including GED) or higher: 80.0% (2010); Bachelor's degree or higher: 4.2% (2010); Master's degree or higher: 1.9% (2010).

School District(s)

North Knox School Corp (KG-12)
    2008-09 Enrollment: 1,334 . . . . (812) 735-4434

Housing: Homeownership rate: 70.1% (2010); Median home value: $47,774 (2010); Median contract rent: $272 per month (2000); Median year structure built: 1944 (2000).

Transportation: Commute to work: 92.5% car, 0.0% public transportation, 3.8% walk, 1.1% work from home (2000); Travel time to work: 34.7% less

than 15 minutes, 30.2% 15 to 30 minutes, 23.6% 30 to 45 minutes, 2.4% 45 to 60 minutes, 9.2% 60 minutes or more (2000)

Additional Information Contacts

City of Bicknell . . . . (812) 735-3559
    http://www.bicknelldevelopment.com
Knox County Chamber of Commerce . . . . (812) 882-6440
    http://www.knoxcountychamber.com

BRUCEVILLE (town). Covers a land area of 0.294 square miles and a water area of 0 square miles. Located at 38.75° N. Lat; 87.41° W. Long. Elevation is 554 feet.

History: Bruceville was first settled by Major William Bruce in 1805, who built a fort on his land. The town was founded in 1811. Major Bruce operated a tavern and inn here, and raised his family of 25 children. Abraham Lincoln was a guest of Bruce in 1844.

Population: 471 (1990); 469 (2000); 463 (2010); 455 (2015 projected); Race: 97.8% White, 0.4% Black, 0.0% Asian, 1.7% Other, 1.1% Hispanic of any race (2010); Density: 1,576.8 persons per square mile (2010); Average household size: 2.50 (2010); Median age: 38.5 (2010); Males per 100 females: 93.7 (2010); Marriage status: 21.5% never married, 55.3% now married, 8.5% widowed, 14.7% divorced (2000); Foreign born: 1.1% (2000); Ancestry (includes multiple ancestries): 21.1% United States or American, 15.7% European, 11.3% German, 10.0% Other groups, 5.5% Irish (2000).

Economy: Employment by occupation: 5.8% management, 18.8% professional, 20.2% services, 28.8% sales, 0.0% farming, 6.7% construction, 19.7% production (2000).

Income: Per capita income: $17,673 (2010); Median household income: $37,885 (2010); Average household income: $43,811 (2010); Percent of households with income of $100,000 or more: 5.4% (2010); Poverty rate: 14.0% (2000).

Taxes: Total city taxes per capita: $119 (2007); City property taxes per capita: $101 (2007).

Education: Percent of population age 25 and over with: High school diploma (including GED) or higher: 89.8% (2010); Bachelor's degree or higher: 10.9% (2010); Master's degree or higher: 3.9% (2010).

School District(s)

North Knox School Corp (KG-12)
    2008-09 Enrollment: 1,334 . . . . (812) 735-4434

Housing: Homeownership rate: 87.0% (2010); Median home value: $69,310 (2010); Median contract rent: $288 per month (2000); Median year structure built: before 1940 (2000).

Transportation: Commute to work: 94.2% car, 0.0% public transportation, 1.9% walk, 1.9% work from home (2000); Travel time to work: 25.7% less than 15 minutes, 58.9% 15 to 30 minutes, 6.9% 30 to 45 minutes, 5.4% 45 to 60 minutes, 3.0% 60 minutes or more (2000)

DECKER (town). Covers a land area of 0.262 square miles and a water area of 0.007 square miles. Located at 38.51° N. Lat; 87.52° W. Long. Elevation is 466 feet.

Population: 281 (1990); 283 (2000); 274 (2010); 272 (2015 projected); Race: 99.3% White, 0.7% Black, 0.0% Asian, 0.0% Other, 0.4% Hispanic of any race (2010); Density: 1,046.6 persons per square mile (2010); Average household size: 2.58 (2010); Median age: 39.0 (2010); Males per 100 females: 101.5 (2010); Marriage status: 27.1% never married, 45.7% now married, 8.5% widowed, 18.6% divorced (2000); Foreign born: 0.0% (2000); Ancestry (includes multiple ancestries): 30.7% United States or American, 10.5% German, 10.1% Irish, 6.9% Other groups, 2.2% French (except Basque) (2000).

Economy: Employment by occupation: 5.4% management, 3.2% professional, 22.6% services, 25.8% sales, 3.2% farming, 15.1% construction, 24.7% production (2000).

Income: Per capita income: $19,135 (2010); Median household income: $35,750 (2010); Average household income: $48,514 (2010); Percent of households with income of $100,000 or more: 6.6% (2010); Poverty rate: 21.3% (2000).

Taxes: Total city taxes per capita: $91 (2007); City property taxes per capita: $87 (2007).

Education: Percent of population age 25 and over with: High school diploma (including GED) or higher: 87.4% (2010); Bachelor's degree or higher: 9.3% (2010); Master's degree or higher: 1.1% (2010).

Housing: Homeownership rate: 83.0% (2010); Median home value: $52,222 (2010); Median contract rent: $175 per month (2000); Median year structure built: before 1940 (2000).

Transportation: Commute to work: 100.0% car, 0.0% public transportation, 0.0% walk, 0.0% work from home (2000); Travel time to work: 21.7% less than 15 minutes, 56.5% 15 to 30 minutes, 17.4% 30 to 45 minutes, 4.3% 45 to 60 minutes, 0.0% 60 minutes or more (2000)

EDWARDSPORT (town). Covers a land area of 0.278 square miles and a water area of 0 square miles. Located at 38.81° N. Lat; 87.25° W. Long. Elevation is 502 feet.

History: Edwardsport developed as a docking place for the flatboats on the White River. Later, the Indiana Public Service Company used water power and coal from the nearby strip mines to generate electricity for many parts of southwestern Indiana.

Population: 380 (1990); 363 (2000); 372 (2010); 376 (2015 projected); Race: 96.5% White, 0.3% Black, 0.0% Asian, 3.2% Other, 2.2% Hispanic of any race (2010); Density: 1,337.7 persons per square mile (2010); Average household size: 2.45 (2010); Median age: 41.8 (2010); Males per 100 females: 101.1 (2010); Marriage status: 19.7% never married, 62.4% now married, 10.3% widowed, 7.6% divorced (2000); Foreign born: 0.6% (2000); Ancestry (includes multiple ancestries): 20.6% German, 15.8% Irish, 11.4% English, 10.0% United States or American, 8.6% Other groups (2000).

Economy: Employment by occupation: 11.5% management, 7.7% professional, 15.4% services, 19.2% sales, 3.3% farming, 10.4% construction, 32.4% production (2000).

Income: Per capita income: $24,189 (2010); Median household income: $52,703 (2010); Average household income: $58,865 (2010); Percent of households with income of $100,000 or more: 13.8% (2010); Poverty rate: 20.5% (2000).

Taxes: Total city taxes per capita: $49 (2007); City property taxes per capita: $46 (2007).

Education: Percent of population age 25 and over with: High school diploma (including GED) or higher: 86.9% (2010); Bachelor's degree or higher: 9.7% (2010); Master's degree or higher: 3.4% (2010).

School District(s)

North Knox School Corp (KG-12)
    2008-09 Enrollment: 1,334 . . . . (812) 735-4434
Housing: Homeownership rate: 83.6% (2010); Median home value: $79,000 (2010); Median contract rent: $261 per month (2000); Median year structure built: before 1940 (2000).

Transportation: Commute to work: 96.2% car, 0.0% public transportation, 2.2% walk, 0.0% work from home (2000); Travel time to work: 36.2% less than 15 minutes, 24.3% 15 to 30 minutes, 29.7% 30 to 45 minutes, 4.3% 45 to 60 minutes, 5.4% 60 minutes or more (2000)

MONROE CITY (town). Covers a land area of 0.269 square miles and a water area of 0 square miles. Located at 38.61° N. Lat; 87.35° W. Long. Elevation is 522 feet.

Population: 538 (1990); 548 (2000); 494 (2010); 468 (2015 projected); Race: 99.2% White, 0.2% Black, 0.0% Asian, 0.6% Other, 0.2% Hispanic of any race (2010); Density: 1,838.5 persons per square mile (2010); Average household size: 2.41 (2010); Median age: 41.0 (2010); Males per 100 females: 98.4 (2010); Marriage status: 20.2% never married, 60.5% now married, 8.5% widowed, 10.8% divorced (2000); Foreign born: 0.0% (2000); Ancestry (includes multiple ancestries): 17.3% United States or American, 15.4% German, 10.6% English, 7.6% Irish, 5.4% Other groups (2000).

Economy: Employment by occupation: 7.2% management, 14.0% professional, 11.4% services, 27.1% sales, 2.1% farming, 12.3% construction, 25.8% production (2000).

Income: Per capita income: $25,466 (2010); Median household income: $53,947 (2010); Average household income: $62,010 (2010); Percent of households with income of $100,000 or more: 13.7% (2010); Poverty rate: 7.1% (2000).

Taxes: Total city taxes per capita: $32 (2007); City property taxes per capita: $25 (2007).

Education: Percent of population age 25 and over with: High school diploma (including GED) or higher: 90.6% (2010); Bachelor's degree or higher: 12.6% (2010); Master's degree or higher: 3.5% (2010).

Housing: Homeownership rate: 77.5% (2010); Median home value: $85,143 (2010); Median contract rent: $288 per month (2000); Median year structure built: 1954 (2000).

Transportation: Commute to work: 93.6% car, 0.0% public transportation, 3.0% walk, 3.4% work from home (2000); Travel time to work: 24.3% less than 15 minutes, 43.4% 15 to 30 minutes, 11.9% 30 to 45 minutes, 7.5% 45 to 60 minutes, 12.8% 60 minutes or more (2000)

OAKTOWN (town). Covers a land area of 0.281 square miles and a water area of 0 square miles. Located at 38.87° N. Lat; 87.44° W. Long. Elevation is 472 feet.

History: Laid out 1867.

Population: 691 (1990); 633 (2000); 588 (2010); 565 (2015 projected); Race: 98.1% White, 0.0% Black, 0.2% Asian, 1.7% Other, 2.0% Hispanic of any race (2010); Density: 2,090.4 persons per square mile (2010); Average household size: 2.41 (2010); Median age: 38.8 (2010); Males per 100 females: 95.3 (2010); Marriage status: 23.4% never married, 55.3% now married, 8.9% widowed, 12.4% divorced (2000); Foreign born: 3.1% (2000); Ancestry (includes multiple ancestries): 15.9% United States or American, 15.8% German, 11.1% Other groups, 8.3% English, 4.7% Irish (2000).

Economy: Employment by occupation: 6.7% management, 13.1% professional, 22.9% services, 20.5% sales, 6.4% farming, 9.8% construction, 20.5% production (2000).

Income: Per capita income: $20,229 (2010); Median household income: $39,500 (2010); Average household income: $46,560 (2010); Percent of households with income of $100,000 or more: 9.4% (2010); Poverty rate: 17.6% (2000).

Taxes: Total city taxes per capita: $44 (2007); City property taxes per capita: $38 (2007).

Education: Percent of population age 25 and over with: High school diploma (including GED) or higher: 87.7% (2010); Bachelor's degree or higher: 8.2% (2010); Master's degree or higher: 2.1% (2010).

Housing: Homeownership rate: 78.6% (2010); Median home value: $64,255 (2010); Median contract rent: $225 per month (2000); Median year structure built: 1941 (2000).

Transportation: Commute to work: 89.0% car, 0.0% public transportation, 2.4% walk, 3.1% work from home (2000); Travel time to work: 27.8% less than 15 minutes, 35.2% 15 to 30 minutes, 24.6% 30 to 45 minutes, 6.8% 45 to 60 minutes, 5.7% 60 minutes or more (2000)

SANDBORN (town). Covers a land area of 0.400 square miles and a water area of 0 square miles. Located at 38.89° N. Lat; 87.18° W. Long. Elevation is 479 feet.

Population: 455 (1990); 451 (2000); 455 (2010); 457 (2015 projected); Race: 97.4% White, 0.2% Black, 0.0% Asian, 2.4% Other, 0.4% Hispanic of any race (2010); Density: 1,137.5 persons per square mile (2010); Average household size: 2.29 (2010); Median age: 45.6 (2010); Males per 100 females: 98.7 (2010); Marriage status: 13.8% never married, 69.7% now married, 8.9% widowed, 7.6% divorced (2000); Foreign born: 0.4% (2000); Ancestry (includes multiple ancestries): 22.8% German, 18.2% United States or American, 9.1% Other groups, 9.1% English, 7.6% Irish (2000).

Economy: Employment by occupation: 9.0% management, 18.1% professional, 17.0% services, 17.6% sales, 3.7% farming, 18.1% construction, 16.5% production (2000).

Income: Per capita income: $28,238 (2010); Median household income: $51,603 (2010); Average household income: $65,251 (2010); Percent of households with income of $100,000 or more: 14.6% (2010); Poverty rate: 11.5% (2000).

Taxes: Total city taxes per capita: $79 (2007); City property taxes per capita: $67 (2007).

Education: Percent of population age 25 and over with: High school diploma (including GED) or higher: 82.9% (2010); Bachelor's degree or higher: 8.1% (2010); Master's degree or higher: 4.5% (2010).

Housing: Homeownership rate: 86.4% (2010); Median home value: $62,927 (2010); Median contract rent: $292 per month (2000); Median year structure built: before 1940 (2000).

Transportation: Commute to work: 92.5% car, 0.0% public transportation, 3.8% walk, 3.8% work from home (2000); Travel time to work: 20.1% less than 15 minutes, 26.8% 15 to 30 minutes, 35.8% 30 to 45 minutes, 6.1% 45 to 60 minutes, 11.2% 60 minutes or more (2000)

VINCENNES (city). County seat. Covers a land area of 7.137 square miles and a water area of 0.068 square miles. Located at 38.67° N. Lat; 87.51° W. Long. Elevation is 420 feet.

History: Vincennes had its beginnings about 1732, when Francois Morgane de Vincennes built a fort here. The French flag flew over Vincennes until 1763, when it was ceded to Great Britain by the Treaty of Paris. The American flag replaced the Union Jack in 1779 when George Rogers Clark captured Fort Sackville. Vincennes was the first seat of government for the Indiana Territory created in 1800, with William Henry Harrison as governor.

Population: 20,200 (1990); 18,701 (2000); 17,375 (2010); 16,722 (2015 projected); Race: 92.7% White, 3.7% Black, 1.5% Asian, 2.1% Other, 1.4% Hispanic of any race (2010); Density: 2,434.5 persons per square mile (2010); Average household size: 2.19 (2010); Median age: 35.0 (2010); Males per 100 females: 101.0 (2010); Marriage status: 34.4% never married, 44.7% now married, 9.0% widowed, 11.9% divorced (2000); Foreign born: 1.4% (2000); Ancestry (includes multiple ancestries): 19.9% German, 17.5% United States or American, 8.7% Irish, 8.4% Other groups, 8.3% English (2000).

Economy: Single-family building permits issued: 1 (2009); Multi-family building permits issued: 0 (2009); Employment by occupation: 7.4% management, 17.7% professional, 22.9% services, 27.7% sales, 0.8% farming, 7.4% construction, 16.2% production (2000).

Income: Per capita income: $18,062 (2010); Median household income: $33,049 (2010); Average household income: $42,970 (2010); Percent of households with income of $100,000 or more: 6.9% (2010); Poverty rate: 20.7% (2000).

Taxes: Total city taxes per capita: $324 (2007); City property taxes per capita: $280 (2007).

Education: Percent of population age 25 and over with: High school diploma (including GED) or higher: 84.2% (2010); Bachelor's degree or higher: 15.3% (2010); Master's degree or higher: 6.1% (2010).

School District(s)

South Knox School Corp (KG-12)
  2008-09 Enrollment: 1,168 . . . . (812) 726-4440
Vincennes Community Sch Corp (KG-12)
  2008-09 Enrollment: 2,709 . . . . (812) 882-4844

Four-year College(s)

Vincennes University (Public)
  Fall 2008 Enrollment: 11,590. . . . . (812) 888-8888
  2009-10 Tuition: In-state $4,420; Out-of-state $10,364

Two-year College(s)

Good Samaritan Hospital School of Radiologic Technology (Public)
  Fall 2008 Enrollment: 19 . . . . (812) 885-8011
  2009-10 Tuition: In-state $2,015; Out-of-state $2,015

Vocational/Technical School(s)

Vincennes Beauty College (Private, For-profit)
  Fall 2008 Enrollment: 86 . . . . (812) 882-1086
  2009-10 Tuition: $9,475

Housing: Homeownership rate: 62.2% (2010); Median home value: $71,256 (2010); Median contract rent: $334 per month (2000); Median year structure built: 1953 (2000).

Hospitals: Good Samaritan Hospital (271 beds)

Safety: Violent crime rate: 14.6 per 10,000 population; Property crime rate: 770.3 per 10,000 population (2008).

Newspapers: Vincennes Sun-Commercial (Regional news; Circulation 14,700)

Transportation: Commute to work: 91.2% car, 0.1% public transportation, 6.4% walk, 1.7% work from home (2000); Travel time to work: 69.7% less than 15 minutes, 17.8% 15 to 30 minutes, 6.8% 30 to 45 minutes, 1.9% 45 to 60 minutes, 3.8% 60 minutes or more (2000)

Additional Information Contacts

City of Vincennes. . . . . (812) 882-7285
  http://www.vincennes.org
Vincennes Chamber of Commerce . . . . (812) 886-0400
  http://www.vincennescvb.org

WHEATLAND (town). Covers a land area of 0.414 square miles and a water area of 0 square miles. Located at 38.66° N. Lat; 87.30° W. Long. Elevation is 505 feet.

History: Laid out 1858.

Population: 487 (1990); 504 (2000); 494 (2010); 488 (2015 projected); Race: 98.6% White, 0.0% Black, 0.4% Asian, 1.0% Other, 0.4% Hispanic of any race (2010); Density: 1,194.0 persons per square mile (2010); Average household size: 2.44 (2010); Median age: 41.1 (2010); Males per 100 females: 95.3 (2010); Marriage status: 16.4% never married, 60.2% now married, 6.5% widowed, 16.9% divorced (2000); Foreign born: 1.2% (2000); Ancestry (includes multiple ancestries): 19.5% United States or American, 16.8% German, 12.5% English, 7.0% Scottish, 5.3% Irish (2000).

Economy: Employment by occupation: 6.9% management, 15.7% professional, 14.7% services, 31.8% sales, 1.4% farming, 9.2% construction, 20.3% production (2000).

Income: Per capita income: $29,979 (2010); Median household income: $63,372 (2010); Average household income: $73,366 (2010); Percent of

households with income of $100,000 or more: 20.8% (2010); Poverty rate: 16.3% (2000).

Taxes: Total city taxes per capita: $70 (2007); City property taxes per capita: $63 (2007).

Education: Percent of population age 25 and over with: High school diploma (including GED) or higher: 89.2% (2010); Bachelor's degree or higher: 7.9% (2010); Master's degree or higher: 2.9% (2010).

Housing: Homeownership rate: 78.2% (2010); Median home value: $86,364 (2010); Median contract rent: $275 per month (2000); Median year structure built: 1950 (2000).

Transportation: Commute to work: 90.6% car, 0.0% public transportation, 5.7% walk, 3.8% work from home (2000); Travel time to work: 17.6% less than 15 minutes, 54.9% 15 to 30 minutes, 18.1% 30 to 45 minutes, 3.9% 45 to 60 minutes, 5.4% 60 minutes or more (2000)

Kosciusko County

Located in northern Indiana; drained by the Tippecanoe and Eel Rivers; includes Wawasee and Winona Lakes. Covers a land area of 537.50 square miles, a water area of 16.84 square miles, and is located in the Eastern Time Zone. The county was founded in 1835. County seat is Warsaw.

Kosciusko County is part of the Warsaw, IN Micropolitan Statistical Area. The entire metro area includes: Kosciusko County, IN

Weather Station: Warsaw   Elevation: 807 feet

	Jan	Feb	Mar	Apr	May	Jun	Jul	Aug	Sep	Oct	Nov	Dec
High	31	36	47	59	71	80	83	81	75	63	49	37
Low	15	18	28	38	49	58	62	60	53	42	32	22
Precip	1.8	1.4	2.1	3.5	3.8	4.4	4.0	4.0	3.2	3.3	2.9	2.5
Snow	na	na	na	0.2	0.0	0.0	0.0	0.0	0.0	tr	na	na

High and Low temperatures in degrees Fahrenheit; Precipitation and Snow in inches

Population: 65,294 (1990); 74,057 (2000); 76,628 (2010); 77,371 (2015 projected); Race: 92.5% White, 0.8% Black, 0.8% Asian, 6.0% Other, 7.2% Hispanic of any race (2010); Density: 142.6 persons per square mile (2010); Average household size: 2.57 (2010); Median age: 36.9 (2010); Males per 100 females: 100.6 (2010).

Religion: Five largest groups: 7.1% The United Methodist Church, 6.4% Catholic Church, 4.4% Christian Churches and Churches of Christ, 3.2% Independent, Non-Charismatic Churches, 2.6% The Wesleyan Church (2000).

Economy: Unemployment rate: 9.5% (5/2010); Total civilian labor force: 42,928 (5/2010); Leading industries: 42.4% manufacturing; 10.7% retail trade; 10.3% health care and social assistance (2008); Farms: 1,235 totaling 251,340 acres (2007); Companies that employ 500 or more persons: 11 (2008); Companies that employ 100 to 499 persons: 38 (2008); Companies that employ less than 100 persons: 1,896 (2008); Black-owned businesses: n/a (2002); Hispanic-owned businesses: n/a (2002); Asian-owned businesses: n/a (2002); Women-owned businesses: 927 (2002); Retail sales per capita: $11,103 (2010). Single-family building permits issued: 172 (2009); Multi-family building permits issued: 28 (2009).

Income: Per capita income: $24,279 (2010); Median household income: $51,564 (2010); Average household income: $62,708 (2010); Percent of households with income of $100,000 or more: 13.7% (2010); Poverty rate: 9.0% (2008); Bankruptcy rate: 9.02% (2009).

Taxes: Total county taxes per capita: $156 (2007); County property taxes per capita: $100 (2007).

Education: Percent of population age 25 and over with: High school diploma (including GED) or higher: 81.9% (2010); Bachelor's degree or higher: 19.3% (2010); Master's degree or higher: 6.5% (2010).

Housing: Homeownership rate: 76.8% (2010); Median home value: $121,888 (2010); Median contract rent: $511 per month (2006-2008 3-year est.); Median year structure built: 1972 (2006-2008 3-year est.)

Health: Birth rate: 142.2 per 10,000 population (2009); Death rate: 80.1 per 10,000 population (2009); Age-adjusted cancer mortality rate: 205.7 deaths per 100,000 population (2006); Number of physicians: 7.7 per 10,000 population (2007); Hospital beds: 9.5 per 10,000 population (2006); Hospital admissions: 462.7 per 10,000 population (2006).

Elections: 2008 Presidential election results: 30.6% Obama, 68.0% McCain, 0.0% Nader

National and State Parks: Tri-County State Fish And Game Area

Additional Information Contacts

Kosciusko County Government . . . . (574) 372-2329
  http://www.kcgov.com

City of Warsaw. . . . . (574) 372-9545
    http://www.warsawcity.net
Town of Syracuse . . . . (574) 372-2433
    http://www.kcgov.com
Town of Winona Lake . . . . (574) 267-7581
    http://www.winonalake.net
Warsaw Kosciusko County Chamber of Commerce . . . . . . (574) 267-6311
    http://www.wkchamber.com

Kosciusko County Communities

BURKET (town). Covers a land area of 0.073 square miles and a water
area of 0 square miles. Located at 41.15° N. Lat; 85.96° W. Long.
Elevation is 863 feet.
Population: 200 (1990); 195 (2000); 222 (2010); 230 (2015 projected);
Race: 97.3% White, 0.9% Black, 0.0% Asian, 1.8% Other, 1.4% Hispanic
of any race (2010); Density: 3,056.9 persons per square mile (2010);
Average household size: 2.74 (2010); Median age: 36.2 (2010); Males per
100 females: 113.5 (2010); Marriage status: 26.8% never married, 48.3%
now married, 10.7% widowed, 14.1% divorced (2000); Foreign born: 0.0%
(2000); Ancestry (includes multiple ancestries): 22.1% United States or
American, 20.6% Other groups, 13.6% German, 11.6% Irish, 9.0% Dutch
(2000).
Economy: Employment by occupation: 2.0% management, 9.1%
professional, 17.2% services, 13.1% sales, 0.0% farming, 6.1%
construction, 52.5% production (2000).
Income: Per capita income: $21,368 (2010); Median household income:
$46,250 (2010); Average household income: $57,500 (2010); Percent of
households with income of $100,000 or more: 8.6% (2010); Poverty rate:
11.6% (2000).
Taxes: Total city taxes per capita: $172 (2007); City property taxes per
capita: $99 (2007).
Education: Percent of population age 25 and over with: High school
diploma (including GED) or higher: 89.0% (2010); Bachelor's degree or
higher: 9.0% (2010); Master's degree or higher: 3.4% (2010).
Housing: Homeownership rate: 85.2% (2010); Median home value:
$121,875 (2010); Median contract rent: $275 per month (2000); Median
year structure built: before 1940 (2000).
Transportation: Commute to work: 82.8% car, 0.0% public transportation,
7.1% walk, 9.1% work from home (2000); Travel time to work: 16.7% less
than 15 minutes, 56.7% 15 to 30 minutes, 15.6% 30 to 45 minutes, 8.9%
45 to 60 minutes, 2.2% 60 minutes or more (2000)

CLAYPOOL (town). Covers a land area of 0.361 square miles and a
water area of 0 square miles. Located at 41.12° N. Lat; 85.88° W. Long.
Elevation is 889 feet.
Population: 418 (1990); 311 (2000); 336 (2010); 346 (2015 projected);
Race: 97.6% White, 0.0% Black, 0.0% Asian, 2.4% Other, 0.9% Hispanic
of any race (2010); Density: 931.0 persons per square mile (2010);
Average household size: 2.69 (2010); Median age: 36.5 (2010); Males per
100 females: 101.2 (2010); Marriage status: 22.0% never married, 65.1%
now married, 5.4% widowed, 7.5% divorced (2000); Foreign born: 0.9%
(2000); Ancestry (includes multiple ancestries): 30.0% German, 17.0%
United States or American, 16.1% Irish, 9.1% English, 7.9% Other groups
(2000).
Economy: Employment by occupation: 6.0% management, 4.5%
professional, 14.2% services, 12.7% sales, 0.0% farming, 6.0%
construction, 56.7% production (2000).
Income: Per capita income: $27,945 (2010); Median household income:
$59,659 (2010); Average household income: $76,960 (2010); Percent of
households with income of $100,000 or more: 23.2% (2010); Poverty rate:
9.5% (2000).
Taxes: Total city taxes per capita: $272 (2007); City property taxes per
capita: $272 (2007).
Education: Percent of population age 25 and over with: High school
diploma (including GED) or higher: 71.7% (2010); Bachelor's degree or
higher: 11.0% (2010); Master's degree or higher: 6.4% (2010).
Housing: Homeownership rate: 80.0% (2010); Median home value:
$124,242 (2010); Median contract rent: $367 per month (2000); Median
year structure built: before 1940 (2000).
Transportation: Commute to work: 96.1% car, 0.0% public transportation,
3.1% walk, 0.8% work from home (2000); Travel time to work: 31.5% less
than 15 minutes, 48.0% 15 to 30 minutes, 18.9% 30 to 45 minutes, 0.0%
45 to 60 minutes, 1.6% 60 minutes or more (2000)

ETNA GREEN (town). Covers a land area of 0.470 square miles and
a water area of <.001 square miles. Located at 41.27° N. Lat; 86.04° W.
Long. Elevation is 817 feet.
Population: 599 (1990); 663 (2000); 700 (2010); 719 (2015 projected);
Race: 94.7% White, 0.4% Black, 0.6% Asian, 4.3% Other, 5.9% Hispanic
of any race (2010); Density: 1,490.0 persons per square mile (2010);
Average household size: 2.89 (2010); Median age: 33.2 (2010); Males per
100 females: 102.3 (2010); Marriage status: 30.0% never married, 52.7%
now married, 5.6% widowed, 11.8% divorced (2000); Foreign born: 0.0%
(2000); Ancestry (includes multiple ancestries): 21.4% German, 15.4%
United States or American, 14.2% Irish, 7.3% English, 2.6% Dutch (2000).
Economy: Single-family building permits issued: 0 (2009); Multi-family
building permits issued: 0 (2009); Employment by occupation: 2.0%
management, 12.7% professional, 11.7% services, 23.1% sales, 0.0%
farming, 9.4% construction, 41.1% production (2000).
Income: Per capita income: $19,247 (2010); Median household income:
$46,509 (2010); Average household income: $57,718 (2010); Percent of
households with income of $100,000 or more: 7.5% (2010); Poverty rate:
4.9% (2000).
Taxes: Total city taxes per capita: $98 (2007); City property taxes per
capita: $76 (2007).
Education: Percent of population age 25 and over with: High school
diploma (including GED) or higher: 81.9% (2010); Bachelor's degree or
higher: 12.9% (2010); Master's degree or higher: 2.6% (2010).
Housing: Homeownership rate: 81.3% (2010); Median home value:
$100,833 (2010); Median contract rent: $375 per month (2000); Median
year structure built: 1961 (2000).
Transportation: Commute to work: 85.4% car, 0.0% public transportation,
3.1% walk, 5.8% work from home (2000); Travel time to work: 29.1% less
than 15 minutes, 55.8% 15 to 30 minutes, 11.9% 30 to 45 minutes, 1.4%
45 to 60 minutes, 1.8% 60 minutes or more (2000)

LEESBURG (town). Covers a land area of 0.232 square miles and a
water area of 0 square miles. Located at 41.33° N. Lat; 85.85° W. Long.
Elevation is 850 feet.
History: Laid out 1835.
Population: 584 (1990); 625 (2000); 538 (2010); 500 (2015 projected);
Race: 94.2% White, 0.0% Black, 1.5% Asian, 4.3% Other, 4.1% Hispanic
of any race (2010); Density: 2,315.4 persons per square mile (2010);
Average household size: 2.42 (2010); Median age: 40.7 (2010); Males per
100 females: 102.3 (2010); Marriage status: 15.2% never married, 70.7%
now married, 4.2% widowed, 9.9% divorced (2000); Foreign born: 3.8%
(2000); Ancestry (includes multiple ancestries): 27.1% German, 18.0%
United States or American, 15.9% Other groups, 8.1% Irish, 5.1% Dutch
(2000).
Economy: Employment by occupation: 12.9% management, 8.2%
professional, 11.0% services, 19.9% sales, 0.0% farming, 10.1%
construction, 37.9% production (2000).
Income: Per capita income: $31,002 (2010); Median household income:
$57,258 (2010); Average household income: $74,122 (2010); Percent of
households with income of $100,000 or more: 18.5% (2010); Poverty rate:
5.2% (2000).
Taxes: Total city taxes per capita: $164 (2007); City property taxes per
capita: $136 (2007).
Education: Percent of population age 25 and over with: High school
diploma (including GED) or higher: 89.3% (2010); Bachelor's degree or
higher: 27.8% (2010); Master's degree or higher: 11.8% (2010).
School District(s)
Warsaw Community Schools (KG-12)
    2008-09 Enrollment: 6,944 . . . . (574) 371-5098
Housing: Homeownership rate: 81.5% (2010); Median home value:
$142,647 (2010); Median contract rent: $410 per month (2000); Median
year structure built: 1948 (2000).
Transportation: Commute to work: 93.4% car, 0.0% public transportation,
0.6% walk, 4.7% work from home (2000); Travel time to work: 40.7% less
than 15 minutes, 47.7% 15 to 30 minutes, 7.0% 30 to 45 minutes, 3.3% 45
to 60 minutes, 1.3% 60 minutes or more (2000)

MENTONE (town). Covers a land area of 0.630 square miles and a
water area of 0 square miles. Located at 41.17° N. Lat; 86.03° W. Long.
Elevation is 840 feet.
Population: 930 (1990); 898 (2000); 951 (2010); 977 (2015 projected);
Race: 93.4% White, 0.2% Black, 0.0% Asian, 6.4% Other, 7.8% Hispanic
of any race (2010); Density: 1,508.7 persons per square mile (2010);

Average household size: 2.68 (2010); Median age: 33.1 (2010); Males per 100 females: 94.5 (2010); Marriage status: 23.9% never married, 59.6% now married, 7.8% widowed, 8.7% divorced (2000); Foreign born: 4.5% (2000); Ancestry (includes multiple ancestries): 23.2% German, 15.6% United States or American, 14.3% Other groups, 8.1% Irish, 6.2% English (2000).

Economy: Single-family building permits issued: 2 (2009); Multi-family building permits issued: 0 (2009); Employment by occupation: 6.1% management, 9.0% professional, 16.3% services, 21.9% sales, 2.4% farming, 9.0% construction, 35.3% production (2000).

Income: Per capita income: $21,549 (2010); Median household income: $49,886 (2010); Average household income: $57,761 (2010); Percent of households with income of $100,000 or more: 10.1% (2010); Poverty rate: 6.3% (2000).

Taxes: Total city taxes per capita: $221 (2007); City property taxes per capita: $152 (2007).

Education: Percent of population age 25 and over with: High school diploma (including GED) or higher: 80.5% (2010); Bachelor's degree or higher: 11.7% (2010); Master's degree or higher: 4.7% (2010).

School District(s)
Tippecanoe Valley School Corp (KG-12)
    2008-09 Enrollment: 2,151 . . . . (574) 353-7741

Housing: Homeownership rate: 72.7% (2010); Median home value: $88,070 (2010); Median contract rent: $367 per month (2000); Median year structure built: before 1940 (2000).

Transportation: Commute to work: 86.4% car, 0.0% public transportation, 7.2% walk, 3.0% work from home (2000); Travel time to work: 36.6% less than 15 minutes, 44.0% 15 to 30 minutes, 14.1% 30 to 45 minutes, 3.1% 45 to 60 minutes, 2.3% 60 minutes or more (2000)

MILFORD (town). Covers a land area of 1.079 square miles and a water area of 0.002 square miles. Located at 41.40° N. Lat; 85.84° W. Long. Elevation is 843 feet.

History: Laid out 1836.

Population: 1,388 (1990); 1,550 (2000); 1,558 (2010); 1,550 (2015 projected); Race: 93.3% White, 1.1% Black, 0.3% Asian, 5.3% Other, 9.5% Hispanic of any race (2010); Density: 1,444.2 persons per square mile (2010); Average household size: 2.43 (2010); Median age: 37.1 (2010); Males per 100 females: 94.8 (2010); Marriage status: 17.5% never married, 61.5% now married, 7.3% widowed, 13.8% divorced (2000); Foreign born: 5.4% (2000); Ancestry (includes multiple ancestries): 22.4% German, 18.5% Other groups, 13.6% United States or American, 9.4% Irish, 7.4% English (2000).

Economy: Employment by occupation: 8.3% management, 8.3% professional, 9.9% services, 18.3% sales, 0.3% farming, 13.3% construction, 41.6% production (2000).

Income: Per capita income: $23,313 (2010); Median household income: $46,833 (2010); Average household income: $57,079 (2010); Percent of households with income of $100,000 or more: 11.8% (2010); Poverty rate: 4.0% (2000).

Taxes: Total city taxes per capita: $263 (2007); City property taxes per capita: $197 (2007).

Education: Percent of population age 25 and over with: High school diploma (including GED) or higher: 74.8% (2010); Bachelor's degree or higher: 13.6% (2010); Master's degree or higher: 3.8% (2010).

School District(s)
Wawasee Community School Corp (PK-12)
    2008-09 Enrollment: 3,303 . . . . (574) 457-3188

Housing: Homeownership rate: 69.0% (2010); Median home value: $114,966 (2010); Median contract rent: $377 per month (2000); Median year structure built: 1963 (2000).

Newspapers: The Elkhart City Paper (Regional news; Circulation 28,700); The Elkhart County Paper (Community news; Circulation 33,625); The Kosciusko County Paper (Community news; Circulation 27,100); Mail-Journal (Local news; Circulation 4,000); Paper-Elkhart Edition (Local news; Circulation 27,525); Paper-Goshen Edition (Local news; Circulation 30,660); Senior Life-Allen Edition (Local news; Circulation 27,950); Senior Life-Elkhart/Kosciusko Edition (Local news; Circulation 6,800); Senior Life-Saint Joseph Edition (Local news; Circulation 26,350)

Transportation: Commute to work: 90.8% car, 0.0% public transportation, 5.4% walk, 2.7% work from home (2000); Travel time to work: 45.3% less than 15 minutes, 40.2% 15 to 30 minutes, 8.7% 30 to 45 minutes, 3.4% 45 to 60 minutes, 2.3% 60 minutes or more (2000)

NORTH WEBSTER (town). Covers a land area of 0.717 square miles and a water area of 0 square miles. Located at 41.32° N. Lat; 85.69° W. Long. Elevation is 873 feet.

Population: 982 (1990); 1,067 (2000); 933 (2010); 889 (2015 projected); Race: 97.1% White, 0.6% Black, 0.3% Asian, 1.9% Other, 2.5% Hispanic of any race (2010); Density: 1,301.2 persons per square mile (2010); Average household size: 2.32 (2010); Median age: 40.2 (2010); Males per 100 females: 94.0 (2010); Marriage status: 19.3% never married, 64.1% now married, 7.6% widowed, 9.0% divorced (2000); Foreign born: 1.1% (2000); Ancestry (includes multiple ancestries): 23.4% United States or American, 21.9% German, 9.9% English, 9.2% Other groups, 7.4% Irish (2000).

Economy: Employment by occupation: 9.0% management, 10.9% professional, 9.2% services, 29.2% sales, 0.0% farming, 11.1% construction, 30.6% production (2000).

Income: Per capita income: $26,194 (2010); Median household income: $52,361 (2010); Average household income: $60,223 (2010); Percent of households with income of $100,000 or more: 14.2% (2010); Poverty rate: 6.5% (2000).

Taxes: Total city taxes per capita: $205 (2007); City property taxes per capita: $194 (2007).

Education: Percent of population age 25 and over with: High school diploma (including GED) or higher: 84.9% (2010); Bachelor's degree or higher: 20.8% (2010); Master's degree or higher: 6.2% (2010).

School District(s)
Wawasee Community School Corp (PK-12)
    2008-09 Enrollment: 3,303 . . . . (574) 457-3188

Housing: Homeownership rate: 73.3% (2010); Median home value: $121,739 (2010); Median contract rent: $413 per month (2000); Median year structure built: 1967 (2000).

Transportation: Commute to work: 92.3% car, 0.0% public transportation, 4.3% walk, 2.1% work from home (2000); Travel time to work: 32.7% less than 15 minutes, 41.2% 15 to 30 minutes, 17.5% 30 to 45 minutes, 3.5% 45 to 60 minutes, 5.2% 60 minutes or more (2000)

PIERCETON (town). Covers a land area of 0.915 square miles and a water area of 0 square miles. Located at 41.20° N. Lat; 85.70° W. Long. Elevation is 922 feet.

Population: 1,071 (1990); 695 (2000); 729 (2010); 736 (2015 projected); Race: 95.3% White, 1.4% Black, 1.0% Asian, 2.3% Other, 2.5% Hispanic of any race (2010); Density: 796.5 persons per square mile (2010); Average household size: 2.60 (2010); Median age: 36.1 (2010); Males per 100 females: 97.6 (2010); Marriage status: 20.2% never married, 59.9% now married, 6.6% widowed, 13.2% divorced (2000); Foreign born: 0.0% (2000); Ancestry (includes multiple ancestries): 26.7% German, 23.6% United States or American, 11.4% Other groups, 7.9% Irish, 7.3% English (2000).

Economy: Employment by occupation: 6.7% management, 7.3% professional, 15.1% services, 20.9% sales, 0.0% farming, 9.3% construction, 40.7% production (2000).

Income: Per capita income: $20,165 (2010); Median household income: $48,000 (2010); Average household income: $51,982 (2010); Percent of households with income of $100,000 or more: 7.9% (2010); Poverty rate: 11.9% (2000).

Taxes: Total city taxes per capita: $302 (2007); City property taxes per capita: $220 (2007).

Education: Percent of population age 25 and over with: High school diploma (including GED) or higher: 75.3% (2010); Bachelor's degree or higher: 6.8% (2010); Master's degree or higher: 1.7% (2010).

School District(s)
Whitko Community School Corp (PK-12)
    2008-09 Enrollment: 1,961 . . . . (574) 594-2658

Housing: Homeownership rate: 75.0% (2010); Median home value: $93,810 (2010); Median contract rent: $405 per month (2000); Median year structure built: 1957 (2000).

Transportation: Commute to work: 96.1% car, 0.0% public transportation, 0.6% walk, 3.3% work from home (2000); Travel time to work: 23.7% less than 15 minutes, 55.5% 15 to 30 minutes, 12.8% 30 to 45 minutes, 3.1% 45 to 60 minutes, 5.0% 60 minutes or more (2000)

SIDNEY (town). Covers a land area of 0.130 square miles and a water area of 0.005 square miles. Located at 41.10° N. Lat; 85.74° W. Long. Elevation is 912 feet.

Population: 167 (1990); 168 (2000); 168 (2010); 176 (2015 projected); Race: 97.6% White, 0.0% Black, 0.0% Asian, 2.4% Other, 2.4% Hispanic of any race (2010); Density: 1,291.2 persons per square mile (2010); Average household size: 2.67 (2010); Median age: 41.4 (2010); Males per 100 females: 110.0 (2010); Marriage status: 19.6% never married, 66.4% now married, 5.6% widowed, 8.4% divorced (2000); Foreign born: 1.1% (2000); Ancestry (includes multiple ancestries): 36.8% United States or American, 14.1% Irish, 9.2% German, 8.1% Other groups, 4.3% Swiss (2000).
Economy: Single-family building permits issued: 0 (2009); Multi-family building permits issued: 0 (2009); Employment by occupation: 1.2% management, 5.9% professional, 15.3% services, 30.6% sales, 0.0% farming, 9.4% construction, 37.6% production (2000).
Income: Per capita income: $22,884 (2010); Median household income: $49,063 (2010); Average household income: $58,810 (2010); Percent of households with income of $100,000 or more: 12.7% (2010); Poverty rate: 8.6% (2000).
Taxes: Total city taxes per capita: $134 (2007); City property taxes per capita: $25 (2007).
Education: Percent of population age 25 and over with: High school diploma (including GED) or higher: 75.8% (2010); Bachelor's degree or higher: 10.0% (2010); Master's degree or higher: 2.5% (2010).
Housing: Homeownership rate: 87.3% (2010); Median home value: $107,353 (2010); Median contract rent: $508 per month (2000); Median year structure built: before 1940 (2000).
Transportation: Commute to work: 97.5% car, 0.0% public transportation, 0.0% walk, 2.5% work from home (2000); Travel time to work: 7.7% less than 15 minutes, 76.9% 15 to 30 minutes, 7.7% 30 to 45 minutes, 0.0% 45 to 60 minutes, 7.7% 60 minutes or more (2000)

SILVER LAKE (town). Covers a land area of 0.291 square miles and a water area of 0 square miles. Located at 41.07° N. Lat; 85.89° W. Long. Elevation is 899 feet.

History: Laid out 1859.
Population: 528 (1990); 546 (2000); 543 (2010); 542 (2015 projected); Race: 94.8% White, 0.0% Black, 0.2% Asian, 5.0% Other, 4.6% Hispanic of any race (2010); Density: 1,864.6 persons per square mile (2010); Average household size: 2.54 (2010); Median age: 36.7 (2010); Males per 100 females: 97.5 (2010); Marriage status: 20.7% never married, 62.3% now married, 8.2% widowed, 8.9% divorced (2000); Foreign born: 3.5% (2000); Ancestry (includes multiple ancestries): 21.4% English, 18.6% United States or American, 13.0% German, 10.6% Other groups, 7.7% Irish (2000).
Economy: Employment by occupation: 11.2% management, 9.1% professional, 21.1% services, 17.8% sales, 2.5% farming, 4.1% construction, 34.3% production (2000).
Income: Per capita income: $21,150 (2010); Median household income: $45,333 (2010); Average household income: $53,143 (2010); Percent of households with income of $100,000 or more: 7.9% (2010); Poverty rate: 12.1% (2000).
Taxes: Total city taxes per capita: $195 (2007); City property taxes per capita: $158 (2007).
Education: Percent of population age 25 and over with: High school diploma (including GED) or higher: 75.2% (2010); Bachelor's degree or higher: 9.6% (2010); Master's degree or higher: 3.3% (2010).
Housing: Homeownership rate: 81.3% (2010); Median home value: $95,429 (2010); Median contract rent: $319 per month (2000); Median year structure built: 1949 (2000).
Transportation: Commute to work: 91.9% car, 0.0% public transportation, 5.1% walk, 0.0% work from home (2000); Travel time to work: 25.8% less than 15 minutes, 48.7% 15 to 30 minutes, 15.3% 30 to 45 minutes, 3.8% 45 to 60 minutes, 6.4% 60 minutes or more (2000)

SYRACUSE (town). Covers a land area of 1.609 square miles and a water area of 0.309 square miles. Located at 41.42° N. Lat; 85.75° W. Long. Elevation is 886 feet.

History: Syracuse was settled as a summer resort town on Lakes Syracuse, Wawasee, and Papakeechee.
Population: 2,729 (1990); 3,038 (2000); 2,809 (2010); 2,698 (2015 projected); Race: 93.1% White, 1.2% Black, 0.5% Asian, 5.2% Other, 5.4% Hispanic of any race (2010); Density: 1,746.1 persons per square mile (2010); Average household size: 2.29 (2010); Median age: 40.1 (2010); Males per 100 females: 99.1 (2010); Marriage status: 23.8% never married, 54.6% now married, 6.3% widowed, 15.3% divorced (2000); Foreign born: 1.4% (2000); Ancestry (includes multiple ancestries): 24.2% German,

12.7% Irish, 12.3% Other groups, 10.8% United States or American, 7.7% English (2000).
Economy: Employment by occupation: 8.6% management, 4.7% professional, 14.4% services, 24.3% sales, 0.4% farming, 14.2% construction, 33.5% production (2000).
Income: Per capita income: $28,527 (2010); Median household income: $50,574 (2010); Average household income: $65,993 (2010); Percent of households with income of $100,000 or more: 15.9% (2010); Poverty rate: 5.7% (2000).
Taxes: Total city taxes per capita: $439 (2007); City property taxes per capita: $328 (2007).
Education: Percent of population age 25 and over with: High school diploma (including GED) or higher: 86.3% (2010); Bachelor's degree or higher: 22.4% (2010); Master's degree or higher: 9.3% (2010).
School District(s)
Wawasee Community School Corp (PK-12)
    2008-09 Enrollment: 3,303 . . . . (574) 457-3188
Housing: Homeownership rate: 72.1% (2010); Median home value: $137,010 (2010); Median contract rent: $412 per month (2000); Median year structure built: 1968 (2000).
Transportation: Commute to work: 91.7% car, 0.0% public transportation, 4.8% walk, 1.9% work from home (2000); Travel time to work: 47.7% less than 15 minutes, 36.0% 15 to 30 minutes, 9.8% 30 to 45 minutes, 3.0% 45 to 60 minutes, 3.5% 60 minutes or more (2000)
Additional Information Contacts
Town of Syracuse . . . . (574) 372-2433
    http://www.kcgov.com

WARSAW (city). County seat. Covers a land area of 10.481 square miles and a water area of 1.067 square miles. Located at 41.24° N. Lat; 85.84° W. Long. Elevation is 827 feet.

History: In its name, Warsaw remembers the Polish nationality of Thaddeus Kosciusko (1746-1817), for whom Kosciusko County was named. Kosciusko was an aide to General Washington during the Revolutionary War, in addition to being a Polish national hero.
Population: 11,314 (1990); 12,415 (2000); 12,629 (2010); 12,666 (2015 projected); Race: 87.2% White, 2.0% Black, 1.7% Asian, 9.2% Other, 12.6% Hispanic of any race (2010); Density: 1,205.0 persons per square mile (2010); Average household size: 2.38 (2010); Median age: 36.9 (2010); Males per 100 females: 98.7 (2010); Marriage status: 23.9% never married, 56.5% now married, 7.1% widowed, 12.4% divorced (2000); Foreign born: 7.0% (2000); Ancestry (includes multiple ancestries): 23.0% German, 16.3% Other groups, 12.4% United States or American, 10.3% English, 10.2% Irish (2000).
Economy: Single-family building permits issued: 42 (2009); Multi-family building permits issued: 22 (2009); Employment by occupation: 10.4% management, 13.8% professional, 11.1% services, 25.3% sales, 0.8% farming, 8.5% construction, 30.1% production (2000).
Income: Per capita income: $21,539 (2010); Median household income: $41,506 (2010); Average household income: $52,025 (2010); Percent of households with income of $100,000 or more: 9.1% (2010); Poverty rate: 9.2% (2000).
Taxes: Total city taxes per capita: $542 (2007); City property taxes per capita: $465 (2007).
Education: Percent of population age 25 and over with: High school diploma (including GED) or higher: 79.7% (2010); Bachelor's degree or higher: 20.7% (2010); Master's degree or higher: 7.4% (2010).
School District(s)
Warsaw Community Schools (KG-12)
    2008-09 Enrollment: 6,944 . . . . (574) 371-5098
Housing: Homeownership rate: 59.9% (2010); Median home value: $103,496 (2010); Median contract rent: $412 per month (2000); Median year structure built: 1966 (2000).
Hospitals: Kosciusko Community Hospital (72 beds)
Safety: Violent crime rate: 8.9 per 10,000 population; Property crime rate: 508.0 per 10,000 population (2008).
Newspapers: Times -Union (Local news; Circulation 12,049)
Transportation: Commute to work: 91.6% car, 1.7% public transportation, 2.6% walk, 2.9% work from home (2000); Travel time to work: 62.3% less than 15 minutes, 20.9% 15 to 30 minutes, 9.6% 30 to 45 minutes, 3.8% 45 to 60 minutes, 3.3% 60 minutes or more (2000)
Additional Information Contacts
City of Warsaw. . . . . (574) 372-9545
    http://www.warsawcity.net

Warsaw Kosciusko County Chamber of Commerce . . . . . . (574) 267-6311
    http://www.wkchamber.com

WINONA LAKE (town). Covers a land area of 2.898 square miles
and a water area of 0.350 square miles. Located at 41.22° N. Lat; 85.81°
W. Long. Elevation is 817 feet.

History: Winona Lake is a vacation retreat area. Evangelist Billy Sunday
built a tabernacle here that influenced the character of the town.

Population: 4,223 (1990); 3,987 (2000); 4,092 (2010); 4,116 (2015
projected); Race: 87.4% White, 1.1% Black, 0.9% Asian, 10.6% Other,
11.6% Hispanic of any race (2010); Density: 1,411.9 persons per square
mile (2010); Average household size: 2.64 (2010); Median age: 35.4
(2010); Males per 100 females: 97.7 (2010); Marriage status: 25.9% never
married, 57.3% now married, 7.6% widowed, 9.3% divorced (2000);
Foreign born: 4.0% (2000); Ancestry (includes multiple ancestries): 27.9%
German, 14.5% United States or American, 12.2% English, 8.6% Other
groups, 8.4% Irish (2000).

Economy: Single-family building permits issued: 8 (2009); Multi-family
building permits issued: 0 (2009); Employment by occupation: 10.1%
management, 19.4% professional, 13.7% services, 22.8% sales, 0.0%
farming, 7.5% construction, 26.5% production (2000).

Income: Per capita income: $24,348 (2010); Median household income:
$53,951 (2010); Average household income: $65,879 (2010); Percent of
households with income of $100,000 or more: 14.5% (2010); Poverty rate:
6.7% (2000).

Taxes: Total city taxes per capita: $208 (2007); City property taxes per
capita: $143 (2007).

Education: Percent of population age 25 and over with: High school
diploma (including GED) or higher: 86.8% (2010); Bachelor's degree or
higher: 35.5% (2010); Master's degree or higher: 11.3% (2010).

School District(s)
Warsaw Community Schools (KG-12)
    2008-09 Enrollment: 6,944 . . . . (574) 371-5098
Four-year College(s)
Grace College and Theological Seminary (Private, Not-for-profit, Brethren
Church)
    Fall 2008 Enrollment: 1,509. . . . . (574) 372-5100
    2009-10 Tuition: In-state $21,100; Out-of-state $21,100

Housing: Homeownership rate: 68.7% (2010); Median home value:
$125,740 (2010); Median contract rent: $378 per month (2000); Median
year structure built: 1969 (2000).

Safety: Violent crime rate: 30.6 per 10,000 population; Property crime rate:
126.9 per 10,000 population (2008).

Transportation: Commute to work: 94.5% car, 0.9% public transportation,
1.7% walk, 2.9% work from home (2000); Travel time to work: 54.5% less
than 15 minutes, 29.2% 15 to 30 minutes, 11.9% 30 to 45 minutes, 1.5%
45 to 60 minutes, 3.0% 60 minutes or more (2000)

Additional Information Contacts
Town of Winona Lake . . . . (574) 267-7581
    http://www.winonalake.net

LaGrange County

Located in northeastern Indiana; bounded on the north by Michigan;
drained by the Pigeon and Short Little Elkhart Rivers. Covers a land area of
379.56 square miles, a water area of 7.15 square miles, and is located in
the Eastern Time Zone. The county was founded in 1832. County seat is
LaGrange.

Population: 29,446 (1990); 34,909 (2000); 37,542 (2010); 38,559 (2015
projected); Race: 95.7% White, 0.3% Black, 0.5% Asian, 3.5% Other, 3.9%
Hispanic of any race (2010); Density: 98.9 persons per square mile (2010);
Average household size: 3.06 (2010); Median age: 31.5 (2010); Males per
100 females: 102.4 (2010).

Religion: Five largest groups: 17.2% Old Order Amish Church, 6.1% The
United Methodist Church, 4.6% Mennonite Church USA, 2.3% Christian
Churches and Churches of Christ, 2.0% Catholic Church (2000).

Economy: Unemployment rate: 10.8% (5/2010); Total civilian labor force:
16,888 (5/2010); Leading industries: 53.3% manufacturing; 10.2% retail
trade; 7.2% health care and social assistance (2008); Farms: 1,507 totaling
161,709 acres (2007); Companies that employ 500 or more persons: 1
(2008); Companies that employ 100 to 499 persons: 25 (2008); Companies
that employ less than 100 persons: 784 (2008); Black-owned businesses:
n/a (2002); Hispanic-owned businesses: n/a (2002); Asian-owned
businesses: n/a (2002); Women-owned businesses: n/a (2002); Retail

sales per capita: $8,536 (2010). Single-family building permits issued: 65
(2009); Multi-family building permits issued: 0 (2009).

Income: Per capita income: $19,796 (2010); Median household income:
$51,177 (2010); Average household income: $60,555 (2010); Percent of
households with income of $100,000 or more: 12.2% (2010); Poverty rate:
10.2% (2008); Bankruptcy rate: 6.04% (2009).

Taxes: Total county taxes per capita: $261 (2007); County property taxes
per capita: $120 (2007).

Education: Percent of population age 25 and over with: High school
diploma (including GED) or higher: 56.8% (2010); Bachelor's degree or
higher: 9.5% (2010); Master's degree or higher: 3.0% (2010).

Housing: Homeownership rate: 85.6% (2010); Median home value:
$142,098 (2010); Median contract rent: $518 per month (2006-2008 3-year
est.); Median year structure built: 1976 (2006-2008 3-year est.)

Health: Birth rate: 193.3 per 10,000 population (2009); Death rate: 64.0 per
10,000 population (2009); Age-adjusted cancer mortality rate: 138.6 deaths
per 100,000 population (2006); Number of physicians: 3.5 per 10,000
population (2007); Hospital beds: 6.8 per 10,000 population (2006);
Hospital admissions: 273.2 per 10,000 population (2006).

Elections: 2008 Presidential election results: 38.6% Obama, 60.1%
McCain, 0.0% Nader

National and State Parks: Pigeon River State Fish and Wildlife Area

Additional Information Contacts
LaGrange County Government . . . . (260) 499-6300
    http://www.lagrangecounty.org

LaGrange County Communities

HOWE (unincorporated postal area, zip code 46746). Covers a land area
of 75.122 square miles and a water area of 1.106 square miles. Located at
41.72° N. Lat; 85.39° W. Long. Elevation is 877 feet.

History: Howe was laid out in 1834 on the site of a large apple orchard,
said to have been planted by Johnny Appleseed. First called Lima, Howe
was renamed in 1884 to honor John B. Howe, the founder of Howe School.

Population: 4,106 (2000); Race: 94.1% White, 0.3% Black, 1.1% Asian,
4.5% Other, 7.2% Hispanic of any race (2000); Density: 54.7 persons per
square mile (2000); Age: 27.0% under 18, 11.6% over 64 (2000); Marriage
status: 21.0% never married, 64.8% now married, 5.4% widowed, 8.8%
divorced (2000); Foreign born: 5.4% (2000); Ancestry (includes multiple
ancestries): 23.0% German, 16.3% Other groups, 14.0% United States or
American, 10.1% English, 8.6% Irish (2000).

Economy: Employment by occupation: 10.7% management, 13.5%
professional, 13.0% services, 16.0% sales, 2.0% farming, 8.3%
construction, 36.5% production (2000).

Income: Per capita income: $16,841 (2000); Median household income:
$38,594 (2000); Poverty rate: 7.4% (2000).

Education: Percent of population age 25 and over with: High school
diploma (including GED) or higher: 77.0% (2000); Bachelor's degree or
higher: 14.8% (2000).

School District(s)
Lakeland School Corporation (KG-12)
    2008-09 Enrollment: 2,218 . . . . (260) 499-2400

Housing: Homeownership rate: 80.5% (2000); Median home value:
$92,200 (2000); Median contract rent: $387 per month (2000); Median year
structure built: 1964 (2000).

Transportation: Commute to work: 90.5% car, 1.1% public transportation,
3.6% walk, 2.4% work from home (2000); Travel time to work: 40.0% less
than 15 minutes, 30.0% 15 to 30 minutes, 19.8% 30 to 45 minutes, 5.7%
45 to 60 minutes, 4.5% 60 minutes or more (2000)

LAGRANGE (town). County seat. Covers a land area of 1.699 square
miles and a water area of 0 square miles. Located at 41.64° N. Lat; 85.41°
W. Long. Elevation is 932 feet.

History: LaGrange became the seat of LaGrange County in 1844. The
town was named in 1836 for the Marquis de LaFayette's country residence
near Paris, by the French immigrants who settled here. LaGrange was
incorporated in 1855.

Population: 2,769 (1990); 2,919 (2000); 2,789 (2010); 2,733 (2015
projected); Race: 91.3% White, 0.7% Black, 0.8% Asian, 7.2% Other, 8.8%
Hispanic of any race (2010); Density: 1,641.3 persons per square mile
(2010); Average household size: 2.42 (2010); Median age: 35.4 (2010);
Males per 100 females: 96.3 (2010); Marriage status: 24.3% never married,
53.1% now married, 9.3% widowed, 13.3% divorced (2000); Foreign born:
5.3% (2000); Ancestry (includes multiple ancestries): 19.1% German,

15.3% United States or American, 11.6% Other groups, 8.8% English, 6.5% Irish (2000).

Economy: Employment by occupation: 5.9% management, 10.0% professional, 15.6% services, 18.1% sales, 2.1% farming, 9.2% construction, 39.2% production (2000).

Income: Per capita income: $19,874 (2010); Median household income: $38,297 (2010); Average household income: $47,790 (2010); Percent of households with income of $100,000 or more: 7.4% (2010); Poverty rate: 7.1% (2000).

Taxes: Total city taxes per capita: $311 (2007); City property taxes per capita: $253 (2007).

Education: Percent of population age 25 and over with: High school diploma (including GED) or higher: 72.3% (2010); Bachelor's degree or higher: 13.9% (2010); Master's degree or higher: 4.2% (2010).

School District(s)
Lakeland School Corporation (KG-12)
    2008-09 Enrollment: 2,218 . . . . (260) 499-2400
Prairie Heights Com Sch Corp (KG-12)
    2008-09 Enrollment: 1,591 . . . . (800) 800-9596

Housing: Homeownership rate: 70.6% (2010); Median home value: $102,768 (2010); Median contract rent: $364 per month (2000); Median year structure built: 1954 (2000).

Hospitals: LaGrange Community Hospital (62 beds)

Newspapers: The Crystal Valley Trading Post (Community news; Circulation 25,000); Lagrange News (Community news; Circulation 6,000); Lagrange Standard (Community news; Circulation 6,000); Lagrange-Countian (Community news; Circulation 9,600); Middlebury Independent (Local news; Circulation 1,200)

Transportation: Commute to work: 91.5% car, 0.0% public transportation, 5.1% walk, 2.5% work from home (2000); Travel time to work: 56.9% less than 15 minutes, 26.7% 15 to 30 minutes, 11.0% 30 to 45 minutes, 1.2% 45 to 60 minutes, 4.2% 60 minutes or more (2000)

SHIPSHEWANA (town). Covers a land area of 0.920 square miles and a water area of 0 square miles. Located at 41.67° N. Lat; 85.58° W. Long. Elevation is 892 feet.

History: Shipshewana began as a trading center for Amish farmers in the area.

Population: 600 (1990); 536 (2000); 563 (2010); 574 (2015 projected); Race: 98.2% White, 0.4% Black, 0.2% Asian, 1.2% Other, 1.6% Hispanic of any race (2010); Density: 612.0 persons per square mile (2010); Average household size: 3.33 (2010); Median age: 28.1 (2010); Males per 100 females: 98.2 (2010); Marriage status: 24.1% never married, 59.7% now married, 9.2% widowed, 7.0% divorced (2000); Foreign born: 0.6% (2000); Ancestry (includes multiple ancestries): 25.4% German, 23.9% United States or American, 9.3% Swiss, 6.7% Irish, 5.8% English (2000).

Economy: Employment by occupation: 12.3% management, 7.7% professional, 12.9% services, 28.7% sales, 1.0% farming, 8.1% construction, 29.4% production (2000).

Income: Per capita income: $18,802 (2010); Median household income: $49,224 (2010); Average household income: $62,944 (2010); Percent of households with income of $100,000 or more: 14.8% (2010); Poverty rate: 8.0% (2000).

Taxes: Total city taxes per capita: $1,558 (2007); City property taxes per capita: $695 (2007).

Education: Percent of population age 25 and over with: High school diploma (including GED) or higher: 37.5% (2010); Bachelor's degree or higher: 4.9% (2010); Master's degree or higher: 1.9% (2010).

School District(s)
Westview School Corporation (PK-12)
    2008-09 Enrollment: 2,299 . . . . (260) 768-4404

Housing: Homeownership rate: 80.5% (2010); Median home value: $190,541 (2010); Median contract rent: $399 per month (2000); Median year structure built: 1974 (2000).

Transportation: Commute to work: 80.0% car, 0.3% public transportation, 6.1% walk, 4.8% work from home (2000); Travel time to work: 55.3% less than 15 minutes, 34.2% 15 to 30 minutes, 9.8% 30 to 45 minutes, 0.0% 45 to 60 minutes, 0.7% 60 minutes or more (2000)

TOPEKA (town). Covers a land area of 1.378 square miles and a water area of 0 square miles. Located at 41.53° N. Lat; 85.54° W. Long. Elevation is 925 feet.

History: Laid out 1843.

Population: 937 (1990); 1,159 (2000); 1,121 (2010); 1,090 (2015 projected); Race: 95.0% White, 0.0% Black, 1.7% Asian, 3.3% Other, 2.2%

Hispanic of any race (2010); Density: 813.6 persons per square mile (2010); Average household size: 2.88 (2010); Median age: 30.4 (2010); Males per 100 females: 97.4 (2010); Marriage status: 22.6% never married, 58.6% now married, 4.8% widowed, 14.0% divorced (2000); Foreign born: 3.7% (2000); Ancestry (includes multiple ancestries): 28.0% German, 13.7% United States or American, 10.7% Other groups, 8.8% Irish, 6.7% English (2000).

Economy: Employment by occupation: 5.6% management, 8.4% professional, 12.2% services, 15.2% sales, 0.0% farming, 9.8% construction, 48.8% production (2000).

Income: Per capita income: $19,478 (2010); Median household income: $47,700 (2010); Average household income: $57,050 (2010); Percent of households with income of $100,000 or more: 9.8% (2010); Poverty rate: 9.1% (2000).

Taxes: Total city taxes per capita: $543 (2007); City property taxes per capita: $455 (2007).

Education: Percent of population age 25 and over with: High school diploma (including GED) or higher: 49.0% (2010); Bachelor's degree or higher: 6.7% (2010); Master's degree or higher: 3.2% (2010).

School District(s)
Westview School Corporation (PK-12)
    2008-09 Enrollment: 2,299 . . . . (260) 768-4404

Housing: Homeownership rate: 75.3% (2010); Median home value: $126,485 (2010); Median contract rent: $331 per month (2000); Median year structure built: 1965 (2000).

Transportation: Commute to work: 88.5% car, 0.0% public transportation, 3.2% walk, 3.2% work from home (2000); Travel time to work: 43.4% less than 15 minutes, 38.0% 15 to 30 minutes, 14.0% 30 to 45 minutes, 1.6% 45 to 60 minutes, 3.0% 60 minutes or more (2000)

Lake County

Located in northwestern Indiana; bounded on the north by Lake Michigan, on the west by Illinois, and on the south by the Kankakee River; crossed by the Grand Calumet and Little Calumet Rivers. Covers a land area of 496.98 square miles, a water area of 129.36 square miles, and is located in the Central Time Zone. The county was founded in 1836. County seat is Crown Point.

Lake County is part of the Chicago-Naperville-Joliet, IL-IN-WI Metropolitan Statistical Area. The entire metro area includes: Chicago-Naperville-Joliet, IL Metropolitan Division (Cook County, IL; DeKalb County, IL; DuPage County, IL; Grundy County, IL; Kane County, IL; Kendall County, IL; McHenry County, IL; Will County, IL); Gary, IN Metropolitan Division (Jasper County, IN; Lake County, IN; Newton County, IN; Porter County, IN); Lake County-Kenosha County, IL-WI Metropolitan Division (Lake County, IL; Kenosha County, WI)

Weather Station: Hobart 2 WNW									Elevation: 639 feet			
	Jan	Feb	Mar	Apr	May	Jun	Jul	Aug	Sep	Oct	Nov	Dec
High	32	37	48	60	72	81	85	83	77	65	50	37
Low	15	20	29	38	47	58	63	61	54	43	33	22
Precip	1.9	1.6	2.7	3.6	3.9	4.4	3.5	3.7	3.7	3.0	3.5	2.4
Snow	9.1	7.4	3.2	0.8	tr	0.0	0.0	0.0	0.0	tr	1.1	5.8

High and Low temperatures in degrees Fahrenheit; Precipitation and Snow in inches

Weather Station: Lowell									Elevation: 662 feet			
	Jan	Feb	Mar	Apr	May	Jun	Jul	Aug	Sep	Oct	Nov	Dec
High	30	35	47	60	72	81	84	82	76	64	48	36
Low	13	17	28	37	48	58	62	60	52	40	31	20
Precip	1.8	1.7	3.0	4.2	4.4	4.6	4.0	3.9	3.5	3.1	3.6	2.7
Snow	10.7	9.2	4.0	0.5	tr	0.0	0.0	0.0	0.0	0.2	1.9	6.6

High and Low temperatures in degrees Fahrenheit; Precipitation and Snow in inches

Population: 475,594 (1990); 484,564 (2000); 496,500 (2010); 500,213 (2015 projected); Race: 64.4% White, 25.6% Black, 1.2% Asian, 8.9% Other, 15.1% Hispanic of any race (2010); Density: 999.0 persons per square mile (2010); Average household size: 2.59 (2010); Median age: 37.5 (2010); Males per 100 females: 92.8 (2010).

Religion: Five largest groups: 26.5% Catholic Church, 2.2% Southern Baptist Convention, 1.9% Lutheran Church—Missouri Synod, 1.6% The United Methodist Church, 1.3% Christian Churches and Churches of Christ (2000).

Economy: Unemployment rate: 10.6% (5/2010); Total civilian labor force: 219,997 (5/2010); Leading industries: 17.4% health care and social assistance; 14.8% manufacturing; 14.8% retail trade (2008); Farms: 441

totaling 128,439 acres (2007); Companies that employ 500 or more persons: 27 (2008); Companies that employ 100 to 499 persons: 216 (2008); Companies that employ less than 100 persons: 10,098 (2008); Black-owned businesses: 3,282 (2002); Hispanic-owned businesses: 1,576 (2002); Asian-owned businesses: 688 (2002); Women-owned businesses: 8,460 (2002); Retail sales per capita: $15,026 (2010). Single-family building permits issued: 636 (2009); Multi-family building permits issued: 51 (2009).

Income: Per capita income: $23,820 (2010); Median household income: $49,386 (2010); Average household income: $61,884 (2010); Percent of households with income of $100,000 or more: 15.9% (2010); Poverty rate: 16.7% (2008); Bankruptcy rate: 8.83% (2009).

Taxes: Total county taxes per capita: $405 (2007); County property taxes per capita: $366 (2007).

Education: Percent of population age 25 and over with: High school diploma (including GED) or higher: 86.1% (2010); Bachelor's degree or higher: 18.9% (2010); Master's degree or higher: 6.0% (2010).

Housing: Homeownership rate: 71.2% (2010); Median home value: $121,855 (2010); Median contract rent: $605 per month (2006-2008 3-year est.); Median year structure built: 1963 (2006-2008 3-year est.)

Health: Birth rate: 142.4 per 10,000 population (2009); Death rate: 94.8 per 10,000 population (2009); Age-adjusted cancer mortality rate: 218.8 deaths per 100,000 population (2006); Air Quality Index: 68.1% good, 31.3% moderate, 0.6% unhealthy for sensitive individuals, 0.0% unhealthy (percent of days in 2008); Number of physicians: 16.8 per 10,000 population (2007); Hospital beds: 45.7 per 10,000 population (2006); Hospital admissions: 1,853.6 per 10,000 population (2006).

Elections: 2008 Presidential election results: 66.6% Obama, 32.4% McCain, 0.0% Nader

National and State Parks: Hoosier Prairie State Nature Preserve

Additional Information Contacts

Lake County Government . . . . (219) 755-3200
    http://www.lakecountyin.org/index.jsp
Cedar Lake Chamber of Commerce . . . . (219) 374-6157
    http://www.cedarlakechamber.com
City of Crown Point . . . . (219) 662-3235
    http://www.crownpoint.in.gov
City of East Chicago . . . . (219) 391-8491
    http://www.eastchicago.com
City of Gary . . . . (219) 881-4730
    http://www.gary.in.us
City of Hammond . . . . (219) 853-6346
    http://www.gohammond.com/web
City of Hobart . . . . (219) 942-1940
    http://www.city.hobart.in.us
City of Lake Station . . . . (219) 962-2081
    http://www.lakestation.in.gov
City of Whiting . . . . (219) 659-3100
    http://www.whitingindiana.com
Crown Point Chamber of Commerce . . . . (219) 663-1800
    http://www.crownpointguide.com
Dyer Chamber of Commerce . . . . (219) 865-1045
    http://www.dyerchamberofcommerce.com
East Chicago Chamber of Commerce . . . . (219) 391-8200
    http://www.eastchicago.com
Gary Chamber of Commerce . . . . (219) 885-7407
    http://www.garychamber.com
Griffith Chamber of Commerce . . . . (219) 838-2661
    http://www.griffithchamberofcommerce.com
Hammond Chamber of Commerce . . . . (219) 937-0111
    http://www.downtownhammond.org
Highland Chamber of Commerce . . . . (219) 923-3666
    http://www.highlandchamber.com
Hobart Chamber of Commerce . . . . (219) 942-5774
    http://www.hobartchamber.com
Lake Station Chamber of Commerce . . . . (219) 962-1159
    http://www.2chambers.com
Lowell Chamber of Commerce . . . . (219) 696-9130
    http://www.lowellinchamber.com
Merrillville Chamber of Commerce . . . . (219) 769-8180
    http://www.merrillvillecoc.org
Munster Chamber of Commerce . . . . (219) 836-5549
    http://www.chambermunster.org
Saint John Chamber of Commerce . . . . (219) 365-4686
    http://www.stjohnchamber.com

Schererville Chamber of Commerce . . . . (219) 322-5412
    http://www.46375.org
Town of Cedar Lake . . . . (219) 374-7400
    http://www.cedarlakein.org
Town of Dyer . . . . (219) 865-2421
    http://www.dyeronline.com
Town of Griffith . . . . (219) 924-7500
    http://www.grffith.in.gov
Town of Highland . . . . (219) 838-1080
    http://www.highland.in.gov
Town of Lowell . . . . (219) 696-7794
    http://www.lowell.net
Town of Merrillville . . . . (219) 769-3501
    http://www.merrillville.in.gov
Town of Munster . . . . (219) 836-6900
    http://www.ci.munster.in.us
Town of Saint John . . . . (219) 365-6465
    http://www.saintjohnin.com
Town of Schererville . . . . (219) 322-2211
    http://www.schererville.org
Whiting & Robertsdale Chamber of Commerce . . . . (219) 659-0292
    http://www.whitingindiana.com

Lake County Communities

CEDAR LAKE (town). Covers a land area of 6.791 square miles and a water area of 1.325 square miles. Located at 41.36° N. Lat; 87.43° W. Long. Elevation is 709 feet.

Population: 8,974 (1990); 9,279 (2000); 11,025 (2010); 11,722 (2015 projected); Race: 96.2% White, 0.3% Black, 0.2% Asian, 3.4% Other, 5.1% Hispanic of any race (2010); Density: 1,623.4 persons per square mile (2010); Average household size: 2.69 (2010); Median age: 36.7 (2010); Males per 100 females: 100.9 (2010); Marriage status: 24.1% never married, 60.7% now married, 5.6% widowed, 9.6% divorced (2000); Foreign born: 1.2% (2000); Ancestry (includes multiple ancestries): 28.2% German, 15.4% Irish, 10.1% Polish, 7.6% Other groups, 7.5% English (2000).

Economy: Single-family building permits issued: 62 (2009); Multi-family building permits issued: 0 (2009); Employment by occupation: 6.2% management, 11.6% professional, 13.1% services, 25.9% sales, 0.5% farming, 22.2% construction, 20.6% production (2000).

Income: Per capita income: $24,348 (2010); Median household income: $57,988 (2010); Average household income: $65,544 (2010); Percent of households with income of $100,000 or more: 18.5% (2010); Poverty rate: 6.6% (2000).

Taxes: Total city taxes per capita: $237 (2007); City property taxes per capita: $187 (2007).

Education: Percent of population age 25 and over with: High school diploma (including GED) or higher: 88.6% (2010); Bachelor's degree or higher: 11.3% (2010); Master's degree or higher: 2.5% (2010).

School District(s)

Crown Point Community Sch Corp (PK-12)
    2008-09 Enrollment: 7,417 . . . . (219) 663-3371
Hanover Community School Corp (KG-12)
    2008-09 Enrollment: 1,975 . . . . (219) 374-3500

Housing: Homeownership rate: 78.9% (2010); Median home value: $134,182 (2010); Median contract rent: $473 per month (2000); Median year structure built: 1959 (2000).

Safety: Violent crime rate: 9.2 per 10,000 population; Property crime rate: 290.3 per 10,000 population (2008).

Transportation: Commute to work: 95.1% car, 0.6% public transportation, 1.2% walk, 2.0% work from home (2000); Travel time to work: 20.2% less than 15 minutes, 35.5% 15 to 30 minutes, 22.9% 30 to 45 minutes, 12.6% 45 to 60 minutes, 8.7% 60 minutes or more (2000)

Additional Information Contacts

Cedar Lake Chamber of Commerce . . . . (219) 374-6157
    http://www.cedarlakechamber.com
Town of Cedar Lake . . . . (219) 374-7400
    http://www.cedarlakein.org

CROWN POINT (city). County seat. Covers a land area of 16.620 square miles and a water area of 0.006 square miles. Located at 41.42° N. Lat; 87.35° W. Long. Elevation is 732 feet.

History: Named for Solon Robinson, a settler who was called King of the Squatters. Crown Point was founded by Solon Robinson, who came here from Connecticut in 1834 and built a cabin. Robinson, who served as Lake County's first justice of the peace, built the first courthouse for Lake County when Crown Point was chosen as the county seat. The town was first called Robinson's Prairie; the later name refers to Robinson's nickname of King of the Squatters.

Population: 18,540 (1990); 19,806 (2000); 23,974 (2010); 25,525 (2015 projected); Race: 91.6% White, 3.8% Black, 1.2% Asian, 3.5% Other, 6.1% Hispanic of any race (2010); Density: 1,442.5 persons per square mile (2010); Average household size: 2.44 (2010); Median age: 42.5 (2010); Males per 100 females: 93.1 (2010); Marriage status: 22.8% never married, 59.4% now married, 8.4% widowed, 9.4% divorced (2000); Foreign born: 6.4% (2000); Ancestry (includes multiple ancestries): 26.6% German, 15.4% Irish, 11.7% Polish, 9.1% English, 8.6% Other groups (2000).

Economy: Single-family building permits issued: 102 (2009); Multi-family building permits issued: 0 (2009); Employment by occupation: 11.7% management, 19.7% professional, 14.2% services, 30.4% sales, 0.2% farming, 10.0% construction, 13.9% production (2000).

Income: Per capita income: $30,333 (2010); Median household income: $62,467 (2010); Average household income: $75,457 (2010); Percent of households with income of $100,000 or more: 22.8% (2010); Poverty rate: 3.7% (2000).

Taxes: Total city taxes per capita: $283 (2007); City property taxes per capita: $241 (2007).

Education: Percent of population age 25 and over with: High school diploma (including GED) or higher: 91.4% (2010); Bachelor's degree or higher: 27.0% (2010); Master's degree or higher: 8.7% (2010).

School District(s)
Crown Point Community Sch Corp (PK-12)
    2008-09 Enrollment: 7,417 . . . . (219) 663-3371
Northwest Indiana Spec Ed Coop (KG-12)
    2008-09 Enrollment: 57 . . . . (219) 663-6500

Housing: Homeownership rate: 76.9% (2010); Median home value: $145,256 (2010); Median contract rent: $579 per month (2000); Median year structure built: 1972 (2000).

Hospitals: St. Anthony Medical Center (411 beds)

Safety: Violent crime rate: 4.1 per 10,000 population; Property crime rate: 262.7 per 10,000 population (2008).

Newspapers: Crown Point Star (Community news; Circulation 3,000); Lofs Shopping News (Community news; Circulation 5,000); Lowell Shopping News (Community news; Circulation 6,000)

Transportation: Commute to work: 94.1% car, 1.2% public transportation, 1.9% walk, 2.2% work from home (2000); Travel time to work: 36.9% less than 15 minutes, 22.7% 15 to 30 minutes, 22.5% 30 to 45 minutes, 8.4% 45 to 60 minutes, 9.4% 60 minutes or more (2000)

Additional Information Contacts
City of Crown Point . . . . (219) 662-3235
    http://www.crownpoint.in.gov
Crown Point Chamber of Commerce . . . . (219) 663-1800
    http://www.crownpointguide.com

DYER (town). Covers a land area of 5.960 square miles and a water area of 0 square miles. Located at 41.50° N. Lat; 87.51° W. Long. Elevation is 640 feet.

History: On January 24, 1910, citizens of Dyer decided by a vote of 57 to 35 to incorporate as a town under the laws of the State of Indiana. The Town of Dyer was formally incorporated on February 8, 1910.

Population: 11,403 (1990); 13,895 (2000); 16,412 (2010); 17,315 (2015 projected); Race: 93.0% White, 1.0% Black, 2.5% Asian, 3.5% Other, 6.6% Hispanic of any race (2010); Density: 2,753.6 persons per square mile (2010); Average household size: 2.72 (2010); Median age: 41.0 (2010); Males per 100 females: 93.9 (2010); Marriage status: 20.1% never married, 67.5% now married, 5.8% widowed, 6.6% divorced (2000); Foreign born: 4.9% (2000); Ancestry (includes multiple ancestries): 22.2% German, 21.0% Polish, 17.6% Irish, 10.0% Italian, 9.7% Other groups (2000).

Economy: Single-family building permits issued: 42 (2009); Multi-family building permits issued: 0 (2009); Employment by occupation: 13.5% management, 22.4% professional, 11.0% services, 29.2% sales, 0.1% farming, 11.6% construction, 12.2% production (2000).

Income: Per capita income: $32,788 (2010); Median household income: $73,847 (2010); Average household income: $90,030 (2010); Percent of households with income of $100,000 or more: 31.6% (2010); Poverty rate: 3.4% (2000).

Taxes: Total city taxes per capita: $231 (2007); City property taxes per capita: $194 (2007).

Education: Percent of population age 25 and over with: High school diploma (including GED) or higher: 93.1% (2010); Bachelor's degree or higher: 27.9% (2010); Master's degree or higher: 7.9% (2010).

School District(s)
Lake Central School Corp (PK-12)
    2008-09 Enrollment: 10,042 . . . . (219) 558-2707

Housing: Homeownership rate: 91.6% (2010); Median home value: $168,908 (2010); Median contract rent: $622 per month (2000); Median year structure built: 1978 (2000).

Hospitals: Saint Margaret Mercy Healthcare Centers (794 beds)

Safety: Violent crime rate: 6.3 per 10,000 population; Property crime rate: 236.1 per 10,000 population (2008).

Transportation: Commute to work: 90.4% car, 4.8% public transportation, 0.7% walk, 3.5% work from home (2000); Travel time to work: 19.0% less than 15 minutes, 34.3% 15 to 30 minutes, 23.6% 30 to 45 minutes, 7.0% 45 to 60 minutes, 16.0% 60 minutes or more (2000); Amtrak: train service available.

Additional Information Contacts
Dyer Chamber of Commerce . . . . (219) 865-1045
    http://www.dyerchamberofcommerce.com
Town of Dyer . . . . (219) 865-2421
    http://www.dyeronline.com

EAST CHICAGO (city). Covers a land area of 11.977 square miles and a water area of 3.654 square miles. Located at 41.63° N. Lat; 87.46° W. Long. Elevation is 591 feet.

History: Named for its location east of the city of Chicago. East Chicago was incorporated as a town in 1889. Growth was slow until 1901, when a steel mill was built and work was begun on the Indiana Harbor and Ship Canal. Other industries followed, and East Chicago became an important petroleum refining area.

Population: 33,892 (1990); 32,414 (2000); 29,386 (2010); 28,170 (2015 projected); Race: 36.0% White, 37.9% Black, 0.2% Asian, 25.9% Other, 54.0% Hispanic of any race (2010); Density: 2,453.5 persons per square mile (2010); Average household size: 2.73 (2010); Median age: 31.9 (2010); Males per 100 females: 91.7 (2010); Marriage status: 38.4% never married, 42.8% now married, 8.3% widowed, 10.5% divorced (2000); Foreign born: 14.7% (2000); Ancestry (includes multiple ancestries): 77.6% Other groups, 4.8% Polish, 1.5% German, 1.2% Irish, 0.8% Italian (2000).

Economy: Unemployment rate: 13.8% (5/2010); Total civilian labor force: 9,999 (5/2010); Single-family building permits issued: 69 (2009); Multi-family building permits issued: 0 (2009); Employment by occupation: 5.5% management, 11.7% professional, 21.7% services, 23.8% sales, 0.1% farming, 9.1% construction, 28.0% production (2000).

Income: Per capita income: $14,679 (2010); Median household income: $29,481 (2010); Average household income: $39,936 (2010); Percent of households with income of $100,000 or more: 6.0% (2010); Poverty rate: 24.4% (2000).

Taxes: Total city taxes per capita: $1,444 (2007); City property taxes per capita: $1,438 (2007).

Education: Percent of population age 25 and over with: High school diploma (including GED) or higher: 66.7% (2010); Bachelor's degree or higher: 8.6% (2010); Master's degree or higher: 2.1% (2010).

School District(s)
East Chicago Lighthouse Charter (KG-06)
    2008-09 Enrollment: 292 . . . . (219) 378-7451
East Chicago Urban Enterprise Acad (KG-07)
    2008-09 Enrollment: 382 . . . . (219) 392-3650
School City Of East Chicago (PK-12)
    2008-09 Enrollment: 5,679 . . . . (219) 391-4100

Housing: Homeownership rate: 45.4% (2010); Median home value: $80,067 (2010); Median contract rent: $337 per month (2000); Median year structure built: 1947 (2000).

Hospitals: St. Catherine Hospital of East Chicago (290 beds)

Safety: Violent crime rate: 100.4 per 10,000 population; Property crime rate: 632.0 per 10,000 population (2008).

Transportation: Commute to work: 88.1% car, 3.1% public transportation, 5.6% walk, 1.5% work from home (2000); Travel time to work: 37.3% less than 15 minutes, 35.1% 15 to 30 minutes, 16.5% 30 to 45 minutes, 4.2% 45 to 60 minutes, 6.8% 60 minutes or more (2000)

Additional Information Contacts
City of East Chicago . . . . (219) 391-8491
    http://www.eastchicago.com
East Chicago Chamber of Commerce . . . . (219) 391-8200
    http://www.eastchicago.com

GARY (city). Covers a land area of 50.229 square miles and a water area of 7.015 square miles. Located at 41.58° N. Lat; 87.34° W. Long. Elevation is 600 feet.

History: Named for Judge Elbet H. Gary, chairman of the board of directors of U.S. Steel. The site of Gary was selected by the United States Steel Corporation in 1905 as the location of a new plant, as reported by Judge Elbert H. Gary in the Corporation's annual report. What was at first a work camp was expanded by the Gary Land Company into the city of Gary. Since the area was all sand where no grass would grow, soil had to be imported and trees and shrubs planted. Other industries soon joined the steel company, and Gary's industrial character was fixed.

Population: 116,646 (1990); 102,746 (2000); 93,509 (2010); 89,575 (2015 projected); Race: 10.7% White, 85.0% Black, 0.2% Asian, 4.2% Other, 5.2% Hispanic of any race (2010); Density: 1,861.6 persons per square mile (2010); Average household size: 2.60 (2010); Median age: 33.6 (2010); Males per 100 females: 85.1 (2010); Marriage status: 38.8% never married, 38.4% now married, 9.4% widowed, 13.5% divorced (2000); Foreign born: 1.6% (2000); Ancestry (includes multiple ancestries): 74.3% Other groups, 2.0% United States or American, 1.9% German, 1.7% Irish, 1.3% African (2000).

Economy: Unemployment rate: 11.8% (5/2010); Total civilian labor force: 33,993 (5/2010); Single-family building permits issued: 4 (2009); Multi-family building permits issued: 0 (2009); Employment by occupation: 6.5% management, 14.1% professional, 24.0% services, 26.8% sales, 0.0% farming, 7.3% construction, 21.3% production (2000).

Income: Per capita income: $16,646 (2010); Median household income: $31,221 (2010); Average household income: $43,367 (2010); Percent of households with income of $100,000 or more: 8.2% (2010); Poverty rate: 25.8% (2000).

Taxes: Total city taxes per capita: $779 (2007); City property taxes per capita: $764 (2007).

Education: Percent of population age 25 and over with: High school diploma (including GED) or higher: 79.1% (2010); Bachelor's degree or higher: 11.8% (2010); Master's degree or higher: 4.4% (2010).

School District(s)
21st Century Charter Sch of Gary (KG-12)
    2008-09 Enrollment: 350 . . . . (317) 536-1027
Aspire Charter Academy (KG-05)
    2008-09 Enrollment: 413 . . . . (219) 944-7400
Charter School Of The Dunes (KG-08)
    2008-09 Enrollment: 329 . . . . (219) 939-9690
Gary Community School Corp (PK-12)
    2008-09 Enrollment: 12,729 . . . . (219) 881-5401
Gary Lighthouse Charter School (KG-08)
    2008-09 Enrollment: 676 . . . . (219) 880-1762
Kipp Lead College Prep Charter (05-07)
    2008-09 Enrollment: 209 . . . . (219) 979-9236
Lake Ridge Schools (KG-12)
    2008-09 Enrollment: 2,157 . . . . (219) 838-1819
Thea Bowman Leadership Academy (KG-11)
    2008-09 Enrollment: 1,300 . . . . (312) 226-3355
West Gary Lighthouse Charter (KG-07)
    2008-09 Enrollment: 504 . . . . (219) 977-9583

Four-year College(s)
Indiana University-Northwest (Public)
    Fall 2008 Enrollment: 4,794. . . . . (219) 980-6500
    2009-10 Tuition: In-state $5,919; Out-of-state $15,024

Two-year College(s)
Ivy Tech Community College-Northwest (Public)
    Fall 2008 Enrollment: 5,752. . . . . (219) 981-1111
    2009-10 Tuition: In-state $3,090; Out-of-state $6,306

Vocational/Technical School(s)
Moler Hairstyling College (Private, For-profit)
    Fall 2008 Enrollment: 26 . . . . (219) 944-0960

Housing: Homeownership rate: 56.9% (2010); Median home value: $60,955 (2010); Median contract rent: $361 per month (2000); Median year structure built: 1955 (2000).

Hospitals: Methodist Hospitals-North Lake Campus (469 beds)

Safety: Violent crime rate: 93.0 per 10,000 population; Property crime rate: 433.4 per 10,000 population (2008).

Newspapers: Gary Crusader (Local news; Circulation 36,000)

Transportation: Commute to work: 90.1% car, 4.7% public transportation, 2.5% walk, 1.7% work from home (2000); Travel time to work: 22.0% less than 15 minutes, 44.6% 15 to 30 minutes, 20.0% 30 to 45 minutes, 5.2% 45 to 60 minutes, 8.2% 60 minutes or more (2000)

Additional Information Contacts
City of Gary . . . . (219) 881-4730
    http://www.gary.in.us
Gary Chamber of Commerce. . . . . (219) 885-7407
    http://www.garychamber.com

GRIFFITH (town). Covers a land area of 7.170 square miles and a water area of 0 square miles. Located at 41.53° N. Lat; 87.42° W. Long. Elevation is 630 feet.

History: Named for Benjamin Griffith, a civil engineer for the railroad. Settled c.1854. Incorporated 1904.

Population: 17,026 (1990); 17,334 (2000); 17,606 (2010); 17,720 (2015 projected); Race: 75.1% White, 16.7% Black, 0.8% Asian, 7.4% Other, 12.1% Hispanic of any race (2010); Density: 2,455.6 persons per square mile (2010); Average household size: 2.54 (2010); Median age: 38.1 (2010); Males per 100 females: 93.5 (2010); Marriage status: 26.3% never married, 56.9% now married, 7.0% widowed, 9.8% divorced (2000); Foreign born: 3.1% (2000); Ancestry (includes multiple ancestries): 23.5% German, 20.2% Other groups, 13.7% Polish, 13.3% Irish, 6.3% English (2000).

Economy: Single-family building permits issued: 4 (2009); Multi-family building permits issued: 10 (2009); Employment by occupation: 9.8% management, 16.1% professional, 13.7% services, 30.4% sales, 0.2% farming, 12.0% construction, 17.8% production (2000).

Income: Per capita income: $25,552 (2010); Median household income: $56,038 (2010); Average household income: $64,698 (2010); Percent of households with income of $100,000 or more: 15.8% (2010); Poverty rate: 3.9% (2000).

Taxes: Total city taxes per capita: $336 (2007); City property taxes per capita: $310 (2007).

Education: Percent of population age 25 and over with: High school diploma (including GED) or higher: 92.1% (2010); Bachelor's degree or higher: 17.2% (2010); Master's degree or higher: 3.6% (2010).

School District(s)
Griffith Public Schools (KG-12)
    2008-09 Enrollment: 2,671 . . . . (219) 924-4250

Housing: Homeownership rate: 67.8% (2010); Median home value: $129,797 (2010); Median contract rent: $612 per month (2000); Median year structure built: 1965 (2000).

Safety: Violent crime rate: 24.1 per 10,000 population; Property crime rate: 448.9 per 10,000 population (2008).

Transportation: Commute to work: 93.2% car, 3.3% public transportation, 1.4% walk, 1.5% work from home (2000); Travel time to work: 27.3% less than 15 minutes, 38.7% 15 to 30 minutes, 15.4% 30 to 45 minutes, 5.4% 45 to 60 minutes, 13.2% 60 minutes or more (2000)

Additional Information Contacts
Griffith Chamber of Commerce . . . . (219) 838-2661
    http://www.griffithchamberofcommerce.com
Town of Griffith. . . . . (219) 924-7500
    http://www.grffith.in.gov

HAMMOND (city). Covers a land area of 22.878 square miles and a water area of 1.951 square miles. Located at 41.61° N. Lat; 87.49° W. Long. Elevation is 600 feet.

History: Named for George H. Hammond, a Detroit butcher who adapted the refrigeration boxcar. George H. Hammond, a Detroit butcher, opened a slaughterhouse in what was to become Hammond in 1869, when the refrigerator box was invented by the Davis brothers in Detroit and shipping of dressed beef became possible. Before Hammond was incorporated as a city in 1884, it had been known as Hohman for an early settler, and as State Line for its location on the Indiana-Illinois border. Hammond's slaughterhouse was the beginning of much industry in Hammond.

Population: 84,236 (1990); 83,048 (2000); 75,392 (2010); 72,366 (2015 projected); Race: 61.0% White, 19.6% Black, 0.6% Asian, 18.8% Other, 30.6% Hispanic of any race (2010); Density: 3,295.3 persons per square mile (2010); Average household size: 2.54 (2010); Median age: 35.6 (2010); Males per 100 females: 95.0 (2010); Marriage status: 30.4% never married, 49.7% now married, 8.5% widowed, 11.4% divorced (2000); Foreign born: 7.3% (2000); Ancestry (includes multiple ancestries): 34.7% Other groups, 14.0% German, 12.3% Polish, 11.5% Irish, 4.7% English (2000).

Economy: Unemployment rate: 12.1% (5/2010); Total civilian labor force: 32,507 (5/2010); Single-family building permits issued: 3 (2009);

Multi-family building permits issued: 2 (2009); Employment by occupation: 7.9% management, 12.6% professional, 17.6% services, 28.7% sales, 0.0% farming, 10.9% construction, 22.4% production (2000).

Income: Per capita income: $18,212 (2010); Median household income: $38,841 (2010); Average household income: $46,341 (2010); Percent of households with income of $100,000 or more: 6.9% (2010); Poverty rate: 14.3% (2000).

Taxes: Total city taxes per capita: $614 (2007); City property taxes per capita: $514 (2007).

Education: Percent of population age 25 and over with: High school diploma (including GED) or higher: 81.1% (2010); Bachelor's degree or higher: 13.1% (2010); Master's degree or higher: 3.4% (2010).

School District(s)
School City Of Hammond (PK-12)
  2008-09 Enrollment: 14,679 . . . . (219) 933-2400

Four-year College(s)
Purdue University-Calumet Campus (Public)
  Fall 2008 Enrollment: 9,325. . . . . (219) 989-2400
  2009-10 Tuition: In-state $5,887; Out-of-state $13,174

Two-year College(s)
Kaplan College-Hammond (Private, For-profit)
  Fall 2008 Enrollment: 360 . . . . (219) 844-0100
  2009-10 Tuition: In-state $13,312; Out-of-state $13,312

Housing: Homeownership rate: 64.5% (2010); Median home value: $89,983 (2010); Median contract rent: $439 per month (2000); Median year structure built: 1951 (2000).

Hospitals: St. Margaret Mercy Healthcare Centers (475 beds)

Safety: Violent crime rate: 87.7 per 10,000 population; Property crime rate: 512.6 per 10,000 population (2008).

Newspapers: The Calumet Press (Community news; Circulation 39,000)

Transportation: Commute to work: 90.4% car, 4.6% public transportation, 2.6% walk, 1.5% work from home (2000); Travel time to work: 27.1% less than 15 minutes, 38.4% 15 to 30 minutes, 18.3% 30 to 45 minutes, 7.3% 45 to 60 minutes, 9.0% 60 minutes or more (2000); Amtrak: train service available.

Additional Information Contacts
City of Hammond . . . . (219) 853-6346
  http://www.gohammond.com/web
Hammond Chamber of Commerce . . . . (219) 937-0111
  http://www.downtownhammond.org

HIGHLAND (town). Aka Highlands. Covers a land area of 6.868 square miles and a water area of 0.023 square miles. Located at 41.55° N. Lat; 87.45° W. Long. Elevation is 623 feet.

History: Named origianlly Clough, then for its location on an area of high ground, in 1888. Highland was settled by people of Dutch descent, who established truck-gardening farms in the area.

Population: 23,696 (1990); 23,546 (2000); 23,137 (2010); 22,898 (2015 projected); Race: 91.0% White, 2.5% Black, 1.4% Asian, 5.1% Other, 10.1% Hispanic of any race (2010); Density: 3,368.7 persons per square mile (2010); Average household size: 2.37 (2010); Median age: 42.6 (2010); Males per 100 females: 92.0 (2010); Marriage status: 23.4% never married, 59.7% now married, 8.2% widowed, 8.7% divorced (2000); Foreign born: 4.5% (2000); Ancestry (includes multiple ancestries): 22.5% German, 17.6% Polish, 14.9% Irish, 11.2% Other groups, 9.2% English (2000).

Economy: Single-family building permits issued: 5 (2009); Multi-family building permits issued: 0 (2009); Employment by occupation: 13.0% management, 19.8% professional, 13.0% services, 30.3% sales, 0.0% farming, 9.6% construction, 14.2% production (2000).

Income: Per capita income: $28,952 (2010); Median household income: $59,407 (2010); Average household income: $68,579 (2010); Percent of households with income of $100,000 or more: 17.9% (2010); Poverty rate: 3.0% (2000).

Taxes: Total city taxes per capita: $303 (2007); City property taxes per capita: $277 (2007).

Education: Percent of population age 25 and over with: High school diploma (including GED) or higher: 91.4% (2010); Bachelor's degree or higher: 24.6% (2010); Master's degree or higher: 7.7% (2010).

School District(s)
School Town Of Highland (KG-12)
  2008-09 Enrollment: 3,421 . . . . (219) 922-5615

Vocational/Technical School(s)
Creative Hair Styling Academy Inc (Private, For-profit)
  Fall 2008 Enrollment: 63 . . . . (219) 838-2004
  2009-10 Tuition: $8,100

Housing: Homeownership rate: 78.8% (2010); Median home value: $140,484 (2010); Median contract rent: $626 per month (2000); Median year structure built: 1966 (2000).

Safety: Violent crime rate: 15.9 per 10,000 population; Property crime rate: 397.6 per 10,000 population (2008).

Transportation: Commute to work: 92.4% car, 4.0% public transportation, 1.4% walk, 2.0% work from home (2000); Travel time to work: 33.3% less than 15 minutes, 38.6% 15 to 30 minutes, 13.0% 30 to 45 minutes, 6.3% 45 to 60 minutes, 8.9% 60 minutes or more (2000)

Additional Information Contacts
Highland Chamber of Commerce . . . . (219) 923-3666
  http://www.highlandchamber.com
Town of Highland . . . . (219) 838-1080
  http://www.highland.in.gov

HOBART (city). Covers a land area of 26.215 square miles and a water area of 0.492 square miles. Located at 41.52° N. Lat; 87.26° W. Long. Elevation is 623 feet.

History: Hobart was founded by George Earle, an Englishman who built a home here and named the town for his brother. The town was platted in 1849.

Population: 24,651 (1990); 25,363 (2000); 26,912 (2010); 27,523 (2015 projected); Race: 88.6% White, 2.9% Black, 0.9% Asian, 7.6% Other, 12.4% Hispanic of any race (2010); Density: 1,026.6 persons per square mile (2010); Average household size: 2.50 (2010); Median age: 39.8 (2010); Males per 100 females: 94.1 (2010); Marriage status: 24.0% never married, 57.7% now married, 8.1% widowed, 10.2% divorced (2000); Foreign born: 2.9% (2000); Ancestry (includes multiple ancestries): 23.7% German, 15.5% Irish, 14.0% Other groups, 11.3% Polish, 10.0% English (2000).

Economy: Unemployment rate: 11.4% (5/2010); Total civilian labor force: 13,644 (5/2010); Single-family building permits issued: 14 (2009); Multi-family building permits issued: 0 (2009); Employment by occupation: 9.4% management, 15.9% professional, 14.2% services, 26.9% sales, 0.1% farming, 15.1% construction, 18.5% production (2000).

Income: Per capita income: $25,282 (2010); Median household income: $56,098 (2010); Average household income: $63,293 (2010); Percent of households with income of $100,000 or more: 14.7% (2010); Poverty rate: 4.8% (2000).

Taxes: Total city taxes per capita: $504 (2007); City property taxes per capita: $469 (2007).

Education: Percent of population age 25 and over with: High school diploma (including GED) or higher: 89.0% (2010); Bachelor's degree or higher: 16.7% (2010); Master's degree or higher: 4.9% (2010).

School District(s)
River Forest Community Sch Corp (PK-12)
  2008-09 Enrollment: 1,569 . . . . (219) 962-2909
School City Of Hobart (KG-12)
  2008-09 Enrollment: 3,939 . . . . (219) 942-8885

Two-year College(s)
College of Court Reporting Inc (Private, For-profit)
  Fall 2008 Enrollment: 236 . . . . (219) 942-1459
  2009-10 Tuition: In-state $12,350; Out-of-state $12,350

Housing: Homeownership rate: 81.9% (2010); Median home value: $123,259 (2010); Median contract rent: $539 per month (2000); Median year structure built: 1960 (2000).

Hospitals: Saint Mary's Medical Center

Safety: Violent crime rate: 26.7 per 10,000 population; Property crime rate: 519.9 per 10,000 population (2008).

Transportation: Commute to work: 94.5% car, 1.6% public transportation, 0.9% walk, 2.1% work from home (2000); Travel time to work: 26.4% less than 15 minutes, 40.8% 15 to 30 minutes, 20.6% 30 to 45 minutes, 4.5% 45 to 60 minutes, 7.7% 60 minutes or more (2000)

Additional Information Contacts
City of Hobart. . . . . (219) 942-1940
  http://www.city.hobart.in.us
Hobart Chamber of Commerce . . . . (219) 942-5774
  http://www.hobartchamber.com

LAKE DALECARLIA (CDP).
Covers a land area of 1.420 square miles and a water area of 0.280 square miles. Located at 41.33° N. Lat; 87.40° W. Long. Elevation is 712 feet.

Population: 1,276 (1990); 1,285 (2000); 1,411 (2010); 1,467 (2015 projected); Race: 97.1% White, 0.9% Black, 0.1% Asian, 2.0% Other, 3.2% Hispanic of any race (2010); Density: 993.4 persons per square mile (2010); Average household size: 2.48 (2010); Median age: 41.8 (2010); Males per 100 females: 100.1 (2010); Marriage status: 21.9% never married, 59.5% now married, 9.4% widowed, 9.3% divorced (2000); Foreign born: 4.3% (2000); Ancestry (includes multiple ancestries): 20.2% Irish, 19.4% German, 18.5% Polish, 10.4% Italian, 9.5% English (2000).

Economy: Employment by occupation: 7.9% management, 20.2% professional, 11.7% services, 22.5% sales, 0.0% farming, 19.7% construction, 18.0% production (2000).

Income: Per capita income: $31,041 (2010); Median household income: $67,339 (2010); Average household income: $77,167 (2010); Percent of households with income of $100,000 or more: 24.0% (2010); Poverty rate: 4.1% (2000).

Education: Percent of population age 25 and over with: High school diploma (including GED) or higher: 93.9% (2010); Bachelor's degree or higher: 23.3% (2010); Master's degree or higher: 9.1% (2010).

Housing: Homeownership rate: 91.2% (2010); Median home value: $149,408 (2010); Median contract rent: $390 per month (2000); Median year structure built: 1956 (2000).

Transportation: Commute to work: 96.8% car, 0.0% public transportation, 0.0% walk, 0.0% work from home (2000); Travel time to work: 20.8% less than 15 minutes, 23.3% 15 to 30 minutes, 34.2% 30 to 45 minutes, 9.6% 45 to 60 minutes, 12.1% 60 minutes or more (2000)

LAKE STATION (city).
Covers a land area of 8.297 square miles and a water area of 0.170 square miles. Located at 41.57° N. Lat; 87.26° W. Long. Elevation is 620 feet.

Population: 13,875 (1990); 13,948 (2000); 13,717 (2010); 13,577 (2015 projected); Race: 78.9% White, 1.3% Black, 0.5% Asian, 19.3% Other, 30.2% Hispanic of any race (2010); Density: 1,653.2 persons per square mile (2010); Average household size: 2.68 (2010); Median age: 35.4 (2010); Males per 100 females: 98.9 (2010); Marriage status: 29.0% never married, 52.6% now married, 7.1% widowed, 11.3% divorced (2000); Foreign born: 4.3% (2000); Ancestry (includes multiple ancestries): 25.5% Other groups, 15.9% German, 14.6% Irish, 5.8% United States or American, 5.5% English (2000).

Economy: Single-family building permits issued: 6 (2009); Multi-family building permits issued: 0 (2009); Employment by occupation: 5.7% management, 6.9% professional, 19.1% services, 24.5% sales, 0.3% farming, 18.3% construction, 25.2% production (2000).

Income: Per capita income: $17,670 (2010); Median household income: $40,333 (2010); Average household income: $47,639 (2010); Percent of households with income of $100,000 or more: 6.5% (2010); Poverty rate: 14.6% (2000).

Taxes: Total city taxes per capita: $561 (2007); City property taxes per capita: $550 (2007).

Education: Percent of population age 25 and over with: High school diploma (including GED) or higher: 79.7% (2010); Bachelor's degree or higher: 5.6% (2010); Master's degree or higher: 1.6% (2010).

School District(s)
Lake Station Community Schools (PK-12)
    2008-09 Enrollment: 1,474 . . . . (219) 962-1159
River Forest Community Sch Corp (PK-12)
    2008-09 Enrollment: 1,569 . . . . (219) 962-2909

Housing: Homeownership rate: 80.2% (2010); Median home value: $81,142 (2010); Median contract rent: $437 per month (2000); Median year structure built: 1956 (2000).

Transportation: Commute to work: 95.7% car, 1.1% public transportation, 1.1% walk, 0.8% work from home (2000); Travel time to work: 25.4% less than 15 minutes, 45.4% 15 to 30 minutes, 19.1% 30 to 45 minutes, 4.0% 45 to 60 minutes, 6.1% 60 minutes or more (2000)

Additional Information Contacts
City of Lake Station . . . . (219) 962-2081
    http://www.lakestation.in.gov
Lake Station Chamber of Commerce. . . . . (219) 962-1159
    http://www.2chambers.com

LAKES OF THE FOUR SEASONS (CDP).
Covers a land area of 2.680 square miles and a water area of 0.414 square miles. Located at 41.40° N. Lat; 87.21° W. Long. Elevation is 764 feet.

History: Lakes of the Four Seasons (LOFS) is a private, gated community of about 10,000 residents located half-way between Crown Point and Valparaiso, Indiana. The community has its own private security force, four lakes, an 18 hole championship golf course, parks, playgrounds, athletic fields, tennis courts, beaches, a swimming pool, two restaurants, a clubhouse, and pro-shop. A set of restrictive covenants governs construction, maintenance, and general rules of the community through the POA.

Population: 6,556 (1990); 7,291 (2000); 7,953 (2010); 8,493 (2015 projected); Race: 95.7% White, 0.5% Black, 1.0% Asian, 2.8% Other, 5.0% Hispanic of any race (2010); Density: 2,967.3 persons per square mile (2010); Average household size: 2.85 (2010); Median age: 39.5 (2010); Males per 100 females: 96.1 (2010); Marriage status: 22.1% never married, 68.9% now married, 3.4% widowed, 5.7% divorced (2000); Foreign born: 5.2% (2000); Ancestry (includes multiple ancestries): 28.0% German, 16.0% Irish, 13.8% Polish, 10.8% English, 8.2% Other groups (2000).

Economy: Employment by occupation: 14.4% management, 22.9% professional, 11.1% services, 27.6% sales, 0.0% farming, 10.6% construction, 13.4% production (2000).

Income: Per capita income: $31,449 (2010); Median household income: $79,592 (2010); Average household income: $89,597 (2010); Percent of households with income of $100,000 or more: 30.8% (2010); Poverty rate: 2.6% (2000).

Education: Percent of population age 25 and over with: High school diploma (including GED) or higher: 96.1% (2010); Bachelor's degree or higher: 32.2% (2010); Master's degree or higher: 9.7% (2010).

Housing: Homeownership rate: 96.0% (2010); Median home value: $175,277 (2010); Median contract rent: $858 per month (2000); Median year structure built: 1981 (2000).

Transportation: Commute to work: 96.2% car, 0.0% public transportation, 0.0% walk, 3.8% work from home (2000); Travel time to work: 11.4% less than 15 minutes, 33.3% 15 to 30 minutes, 26.2% 30 to 45 minutes, 14.3% 45 to 60 minutes, 14.8% 60 minutes or more (2000)

LOWELL (town).
Covers a land area of 4.081 square miles and a water area of 0.081 square miles. Located at 41.29° N. Lat; 87.41° W. Long. Elevation is 669 feet.

History: Settled 1849, laid out 1853.

Population: 6,494 (1990); 7,505 (2000); 8,648 (2010); 9,106 (2015 projected); Race: 95.6% White, 0.1% Black, 0.3% Asian, 4.1% Other, 5.5% Hispanic of any race (2010); Density: 2,119.3 persons per square mile (2010); Average household size: 2.70 (2010); Median age: 36.4 (2010); Males per 100 females: 96.8 (2010); Marriage status: 22.2% never married, 63.0% now married, 5.8% widowed, 9.1% divorced (2000); Foreign born: 1.4% (2000); Ancestry (includes multiple ancestries): 32.2% German, 17.1% Irish, 12.0% Polish, 11.3% English, 7.6% Other groups (2000).

Economy: Single-family building permits issued: 41 (2009); Multi-family building permits issued: 0 (2009); Employment by occupation: 10.5% management, 15.7% professional, 13.8% services, 25.7% sales, 0.5% farming, 14.9% construction, 19.0% production (2000).

Income: Per capita income: $24,850 (2010); Median household income: $59,685 (2010); Average household income: $67,006 (2010); Percent of households with income of $100,000 or more: 17.9% (2010); Poverty rate: 6.5% (2000).

Taxes: Total city taxes per capita: $315 (2007); City property taxes per capita: $282 (2007).

Education: Percent of population age 25 and over with: High school diploma (including GED) or higher: 91.7% (2010); Bachelor's degree or higher: 16.3% (2010); Master's degree or higher: 6.0% (2010).

School District(s)
Tri-Creek School Corporation (KG-12)
    2008-09 Enrollment: 3,690 . . . . (219) 696-6661

Housing: Homeownership rate: 80.4% (2010); Median home value: $135,143 (2010); Median contract rent: $487 per month (2000); Median year structure built: 1972 (2000).

Safety: Violent crime rate: 3.6 per 10,000 population; Property crime rate: 169.3 per 10,000 population (2008).

Newspapers: Cedar Lake Journal (Community news; Circulation 5,150); Lowell Tribune (Community news; Circulation 4,564); Northern Star (Community news; Circulation 2,250); South Lake Advertiser (Community news; Circulation 2,650)

Transportation: Commute to work: 95.8% car, 0.5% public transportation, 1.7% walk, 1.6% work from home (2000); Travel time to work: 31.2% less than 15 minutes, 22.2% 15 to 30 minutes, 23.8% 30 to 45 minutes, 11.5% 45 to 60 minutes, 11.2% 60 minutes or more (2000)

Additional Information Contacts

Lowell Chamber of Commerce . . . . (219) 696-9130
   http://www.lowellinchamber.com
Town of Lowell . . . . (219) 696-7794
   http://www.lowell.net

MERRILLVILLE (town).

Covers a land area of 33.283 square miles and a water area of 0.034 square miles. Located at 41.48° N. Lat; 87.33° W. Long. Elevation is 656 feet.

History: Named for Dudley Merrill, a local storekeeper. Merrillville was settled at the place where many smaller trails met with the Sauk Trail.

Population: 27,793 (1990); 30,560 (2000); 34,503 (2010); 35,960 (2015 projected); Race: 54.7% White, 34.7% Black, 2.2% Asian, 8.4% Other, 12.9% Hispanic of any race (2010); Density: 1,036.7 persons per square mile (2010); Average household size: 2.50 (2010); Median age: 39.1 (2010); Males per 100 females: 91.6 (2010); Marriage status: 25.4% never married, 56.8% now married, 8.0% widowed, 9.7% divorced (2000); Foreign born: 7.0% (2000); Ancestry (includes multiple ancestries): 32.7% Other groups, 16.0% German, 10.6% Irish, 9.8% Polish, 5.5% English (2000).

Economy: Unemployment rate: 9.7% (5/2010); Total civilian labor force: 16,382 (5/2010); Single-family building permits issued: 16 (2009); Multi-family building permits issued: 36 (2009); Employment by occupation: 9.7% management, 18.6% professional, 14.3% services, 28.0% sales, 0.1% farming, 9.6% construction, 19.7% production (2000).

Income: Per capita income: $25,703 (2010); Median household income: $56,645 (2010); Average household income: $64,535 (2010); Percent of households with income of $100,000 or more: 15.1% (2010); Poverty rate: 4.3% (2000).

Taxes: Total city taxes per capita: $243 (2007); City property taxes per capita: $217 (2007).

Education: Percent of population age 25 and over with: High school diploma (including GED) or higher: 90.4% (2010); Bachelor's degree or higher: 23.2% (2010); Master's degree or higher: 7.3% (2010).

School District(s)
Merrillville Community School (PK-12)
   2008-09 Enrollment: 7,021 . . . . (219) 650-5300

Four-year College(s)
Brown Mackie College-Merrillville (Private, For-profit)
   Fall 2008 Enrollment: 775 . . . . (219) 769-3321
   2009-10 Tuition: In-state $12,183; Out-of-state $12,183
University of Phoenix-Northwest Indiana Campus (Private, For-profit)
   Fall 2008 Enrollment: n/a . . . . (219) 794-1500
   2009-10 Tuition: In-state $8,808; Out-of-state $8,808

Two-year College(s)
Kaplan College-Merrillville (Private, For-profit)
   Fall 2008 Enrollment: 396 . . . . (219) 947-8400
   2009-10 Tuition: In-state $13,104; Out-of-state $13,104

Vocational/Technical School(s)
Everest College-Merrillville (Private, For-profit)
   Fall 2008 Enrollment: 928 . . . . (219) 756-6811
   2009-10 Tuition: $14,250
Merrillville Beauty College (Private, For-profit)
   Fall 2008 Enrollment: 32 . . . . (219) 769-2232
   2009-10 Tuition: $11,500
Success Schools LLC (Private, For-profit)
   Fall 2008 Enrollment: 95 . . . . (219) 736-9999
   2009-10 Tuition: $14,000

Housing: Homeownership rate: 70.0% (2010); Median home value: $121,062 (2010); Median contract rent: $631 per month (2000); Median year structure built: 1970 (2000).

Hospitals: Methodist Hospitals - Southlake Campus (319 beds)

Safety: Violent crime rate: 15.5 per 10,000 population; Property crime rate: 297.0 per 10,000 population (2008).

Newspapers: Northwest Indiana Catholic (Community news; Circulation 20,000); Post-Tribune (Local news; Circulation 69,561)

Transportation: Commute to work: 94.5% car, 2.1% public transportation, 1.2% walk, 1.5% work from home (2000); Travel time to work: 24.8% less than 15 minutes, 36.5% 15 to 30 minutes, 20.3% 30 to 45 minutes, 6.5% 45 to 60 minutes, 11.9% 60 minutes or more (2000)

Additional Information Contacts

Merrillville Chamber of Commerce . . . . (219) 769-8180
   http://www.merrillvillecoc.org
Town of Merrillville . . . . (219) 769-3501
   http://www.merrillville.in.gov

MUNSTER (town).

Covers a land area of 7.540 square miles and a water area of 0.054 square miles. Located at 41.55° N. Lat; 87.50° W. Long. Elevation is 610 feet.

History: Named for Eldert Munster, who settled here in 1855. Settled 1855.

Population: 19,949 (1990); 21,511 (2000); 22,595 (2010); 22,841 (2015 projected); Race: 89.7% White, 1.8% Black, 5.2% Asian, 3.3% Other, 7.6% Hispanic of any race (2010); Density: 2,996.5 persons per square mile (2010); Average household size: 2.57 (2010); Median age: 45.7 (2010); Males per 100 females: 91.4 (2010); Marriage status: 20.7% never married, 63.6% now married, 9.4% widowed, 6.4% divorced (2000); Foreign born: 7.9% (2000); Ancestry (includes multiple ancestries): 19.5% German, 19.4% Polish, 14.1% Irish, 12.1% Other groups, 8.0% Italian (2000).

Economy: Single-family building permits issued: 29 (2009); Multi-family building permits issued: 0 (2009); Employment by occupation: 15.2% management, 31.1% professional, 9.1% services, 24.4% sales, 0.3% farming, 7.3% construction, 12.6% production (2000).

Income: Per capita income: $36,657 (2010); Median household income: $71,712 (2010); Average household income: $95,041 (2010); Percent of households with income of $100,000 or more: 32.7% (2010); Poverty rate: 4.3% (2000).

Taxes: Total city taxes per capita: $415 (2007); City property taxes per capita: $375 (2007).

Education: Percent of population age 25 and over with: High school diploma (including GED) or higher: 95.3% (2010); Bachelor's degree or higher: 42.5% (2010); Master's degree or higher: 16.4% (2010).

School District(s)
School Town Of Munster (PK-12)
   2008-09 Enrollment: 4,307 . . . . (219) 836-9111

Housing: Homeownership rate: 88.9% (2010); Median home value: $192,788 (2010); Median contract rent: $641 per month (2000); Median year structure built: 1968 (2000).

Hospitals: Community Hospital (354 beds); Heartland Memorial Hospital

Safety: Violent crime rate: 3.2 per 10,000 population; Property crime rate: 238.1 per 10,000 population (2008).

Newspapers: The Times of NW Indiana (Regional news; Circulation 94,565); The Times-Illinois Edition (Regional news); Vidette Times (Local news)

Transportation: Commute to work: 89.7% car, 4.4% public transportation, 1.5% walk, 3.8% work from home (2000); Travel time to work: 32.0% less than 15 minutes, 34.9% 15 to 30 minutes, 13.9% 30 to 45 minutes, 7.3% 45 to 60 minutes, 12.0% 60 minutes or more (2000)

Additional Information Contacts

Munster Chamber of Commerce . . . . (219) 836-5549
   http://www.chambermunster.org
Town of Munster . . . . (219) 836-6900
   http://www.ci.munster.in.us

NEW CHICAGO (town).

Covers a land area of 0.672 square miles and a water area of 0 square miles. Located at 41.55° N. Lat; 87.27° W. Long. Elevation is 636 feet.

History: New Chicago was the home of the United States Electric Carriage Company, which built the first electric buggy in 1898.

Population: 2,090 (1990); 2,063 (2000); 1,994 (2010); 1,951 (2015 projected); Race: 82.3% White, 0.7% Black, 0.4% Asian, 16.6% Other, 23.5% Hispanic of any race (2010); Density: 2,968.6 persons per square mile (2010); Average household size: 2.39 (2010); Median age: 34.7 (2010); Males per 100 females: 94.2 (2010); Marriage status: 25.9% never married, 48.9% now married, 7.6% widowed, 17.6% divorced (2000); Foreign born: 4.7% (2000); Ancestry (includes multiple ancestries): 27.3% Other groups, 17.4% German, 13.0% Irish, 11.7% Polish, 8.7% United States or American (2000).

Economy: Single-family building permits issued: 4 (2009); Multi-family building permits issued: 0 (2009); Employment by occupation: 5.5% management, 10.8% professional, 20.5% services, 22.6% sales, 0.0% farming, 19.5% construction, 21.1% production (2000).

Income: Per capita income: $18,401 (2010); Median household income: $35,943 (2010); Average household income: $44,095 (2010); Percent of households with income of $100,000 or more: 5.3% (2010); Poverty rate: 14.2% (2000).

Taxes: Total city taxes per capita: $104 (2007); City property taxes per capita: $94 (2007).
Education: Percent of population age 25 and over with: High school diploma (including GED) or higher: 75.1% (2010); Bachelor's degree or higher: 4.7% (2010); Master's degree or higher: 1.7% (2010).
Housing: Homeownership rate: 80.6% (2010); Median home value: $50,145 (2010); Median contract rent: $456 per month (2000); Median year structure built: 1962 (2000).
Transportation: Commute to work: 96.5% car, 0.6% public transportation, 0.8% walk, 1.3% work from home (2000); Travel time to work: 23.0% less than 15 minutes, 44.7% 15 to 30 minutes, 20.9% 30 to 45 minutes, 5.7% 45 to 60 minutes, 5.6% 60 minutes or more (2000)

SAINT JOHN (town). Covers a land area of 6.724 square miles and a water area of 0.048 square miles. Located at 41.44° N. Lat; 87.47° W. Long. Elevation is 725 feet.

History: St. John was founded in 1837. It is generally agreed that the Town of St. John had its beginning when John Hack, a German immigrant farmer and his family arrived in 1837, in the area then known asWestern prairie or Prairie West.
Population: 5,656 (1990); 8,382 (2000); 10,616 (2010); 11,684 (2015 projected); Race: 96.2% White, 0.2% Black, 0.7% Asian, 2.9% Other, 5.7% Hispanic of any race (2010); Density: 1,578.8 persons per square mile (2010); Average household size: 2.91 (2010); Median age: 41.6 (2010); Males per 100 females: 99.2 (2010); Marriage status: 18.9% never married, 72.0% now married, 5.7% widowed, 3.4% divorced (2000); Foreign born: 3.3% (2000); Ancestry (includes multiple ancestries): 24.0% German, 23.1% Polish, 17.2% Irish, 12.4% Italian, 8.4% Dutch (2000).
Economy: Single-family building permits issued: 115 (2009); Multi-family building permits issued: 0 (2009); Employment by occupation: 16.7% management, 20.2% professional, 7.8% services, 28.2% sales, 0.0% farming, 14.9% construction, 12.2% production (2000).
Income: Per capita income: $31,406 (2010); Median household income: $81,700 (2010); Average household income: $91,344 (2010); Percent of households with income of $100,000 or more: 35.8% (2010); Poverty rate: 1.7% (2000).
Taxes: Total city taxes per capita: $336 (2007); City property taxes per capita: $293 (2007).
Education: Percent of population age 25 and over with: High school diploma (including GED) or higher: 94.2% (2010); Bachelor's degree or higher: 23.7% (2010); Master's degree or higher: 6.2% (2010).
School District(s)
Lake Central School Corp (PK-12)
    2008-09 Enrollment: 10,042 . . . . (219) 558-2707
Housing: Homeownership rate: 93.4% (2010); Median home value: $198,051 (2010); Median contract rent: $380 per month (2000); Median year structure built: 1989 (2000).
Safety: Violent crime rate: 0.8 per 10,000 population; Property crime rate: 99.4 per 10,000 population (2008).
Transportation: Commute to work: 95.3% car, 2.5% public transportation, 0.8% walk, 1.1% work from home (2000); Travel time to work: 14.7% less than 15 minutes, 31.3% 15 to 30 minutes, 27.1% 30 to 45 minutes, 12.9% 45 to 60 minutes, 13.9% 60 minutes or more (2000)
Additional Information Contacts
Saint John Chamber of Commerce . . . . (219) 365-4686
    http://www.stjohnchamber.com
Town of Saint John . . . . (219) 365-6465
    http://www.saintjohnin.com

SCHERERVILLE (town). Covers a land area of 13.610 square miles and a water area of 0.031 square miles. Located at 41.48° N. Lat; 87.44° W. Long. Elevation is 669 feet.

History: Named for Nicholas Scherer, who plotted the town in 1866. Laid out 1866.
Population: 19,752 (1990); 24,851 (2000); 29,423 (2010); 31,252 (2015 projected); Race: 87.5% White, 2.9% Black, 3.6% Asian, 6.0% Other, 9.5% Hispanic of any race (2010); Density: 2,161.9 persons per square mile (2010); Average household size: 2.57 (2010); Median age: 39.6 (2010); Males per 100 females: 95.3 (2010); Marriage status: 23.0% never married, 62.6% now married, 5.9% widowed, 8.5% divorced (2000); Foreign born: 8.3% (2000); Ancestry (includes multiple ancestries): 22.9% German, 17.3% Polish, 15.1% Irish, 13.0% Other groups, 6.8% English (2000).
Economy: Unemployment rate: 8.0% (5/2010); Total civilian labor force: 15,321 (5/2010); Single-family building permits issued: 15 (2009); Multi-family building permits issued: 0 (2009); Employment by occupation:

14.4% management, 21.2% professional, 12.4% services, 25.9% sales, 0.0% farming, 11.2% construction, 14.9% production (2000).
Income: Per capita income: $33,337 (2010); Median household income: $69,665 (2010); Average household income: $86,778 (2010); Percent of households with income of $100,000 or more: 28.5% (2010); Poverty rate: 3.1% (2000).
Taxes: Total city taxes per capita: $333 (2007); City property taxes per capita: $296 (2007).
Education: Percent of population age 25 and over with: High school diploma (including GED) or higher: 94.4% (2010); Bachelor's degree or higher: 30.8% (2010); Master's degree or higher: 10.6% (2010).
School District(s)
Campagna Academy Charter School (09-12)
    2008-09 Enrollment: 147 . . . . (219) 322-8614
Lake Central School Corp (PK-12)
    2008-09 Enrollment: 10,042 . . . . (219) 558-2707
Vocational/Technical School(s)
Don Roberts School of Hair Design (Private, For-profit)
    Fall 2008 Enrollment: 43 . . . . (219) 864-1600
    2009-10 Tuition: $10,850
Housing: Homeownership rate: 78.4% (2010); Median home value: $174,039 (2010); Median contract rent: $579 per month (2000); Median year structure built: 1982 (2000).
Safety: Violent crime rate: 6.5 per 10,000 population; Property crime rate: 294.7 per 10,000 population (2008).
Transportation: Commute to work: 93.4% car, 2.2% public transportation, 1.4% walk, 2.1% work from home (2000); Travel time to work: 18.2% less than 15 minutes, 37.1% 15 to 30 minutes, 25.1% 30 to 45 minutes, 7.3% 45 to 60 minutes, 12.3% 60 minutes or more (2000)
Additional Information Contacts
Schererville Chamber of Commerce . . . . (219) 322-5412
    http://www.46375.org
Town of Schererville . . . . (219) 322-2211
    http://www.schererville.org

SCHNEIDER (town). Covers a land area of 0.878 square miles and a water area of 0 square miles. Located at 41.18° N. Lat; 87.44° W. Long. Elevation is 636 feet.

Population: 310 (1990); 317 (2000); 319 (2010); 318 (2015 projected); Race: 93.7% White, 0.3% Black, 0.3% Asian, 5.6% Other, 6.0% Hispanic of any race (2010); Density: 363.3 persons per square mile (2010); Average household size: 2.69 (2010); Median age: 39.3 (2010); Males per 100 females: 98.1 (2010); Marriage status: 25.1% never married, 61.8% now married, 5.8% widowed, 7.3% divorced (2000); Foreign born: 1.1% (2000); Ancestry (includes multiple ancestries): 23.8% German, 22.6% Irish, 14.6% Other groups, 13.5% English, 8.9% Italian (2000).
Economy: Single-family building permits issued: 0 (2009); Multi-family building permits issued: 0 (2009); Employment by occupation: 7.2% management, 2.2% professional, 15.9% services, 16.7% sales, 0.0% farming, 27.5% construction, 30.4% production (2000).
Income: Per capita income: $27,105 (2010); Median household income: $65,625 (2010); Average household income: $71,483 (2010); Percent of households with income of $100,000 or more: 22.9% (2010); Poverty rate: 5.9% (2000).
Taxes: Total city taxes per capita: $448 (2007); City property taxes per capita: $441 (2007).
Education: Percent of population age 25 and over with: High school diploma (including GED) or higher: 91.5% (2010); Bachelor's degree or higher: 9.5% (2010); Master's degree or higher: 4.3% (2010).
Housing: Homeownership rate: 85.6% (2010); Median home value: $157,292 (2010); Median contract rent: $330 per month (2000); Median year structure built: 1950 (2000).
Transportation: Commute to work: 96.3% car, 0.0% public transportation, 2.2% walk, 1.5% work from home (2000); Travel time to work: 24.6% less than 15 minutes, 33.6% 15 to 30 minutes, 14.9% 30 to 45 minutes, 14.2% 45 to 60 minutes, 12.7% 60 minutes or more (2000)

WHITING (city). Covers a land area of 1.763 square miles and a water area of 1.519 square miles. Located at 41.67° N. Lat; 87.49° W. Long. Elevation is 587 feet.

History: Whiting was settled by German immigrants. For many years a Standard Oil Company plant, established in 1889, was the major industry.
Population: 5,155 (1990); 5,137 (2000); 5,089 (2010); 5,066 (2015 projected); Race: 82.6% White, 1.1% Black, 1.2% Asian, 15.1% Other, 38.8% Hispanic of any race (2010); Density: 2,886.9 persons per square

mile (2010); Average household size: 2.46 (2010); Median age: 37.8 (2010); Males per 100 females: 92.1 (2010); Marriage status: 31.5% never married, 48.0% now married, 9.3% widowed, 11.3% divorced (2000); Foreign born: 10.8% (2000); Ancestry (includes multiple ancestries): 29.5% Other groups, 18.0% Slovak, 17.1% Polish, 16.1% Irish, 11.5% German (2000).

Economy: Single-family building permits issued: 5 (2009); Multi-family building permits issued: 0 (2009); Employment by occupation: 8.0% management, 16.0% professional, 14.4% services, 27.2% sales, 0.0% farming, 11.8% construction, 22.5% production (2000).

Income: Per capita income: $20,227 (2010); Median household income: $39,185 (2010); Average household income: $49,684 (2010); Percent of households with income of $100,000 or more: 8.7% (2010); Poverty rate: 12.3% (2000).

Taxes: Total city taxes per capita: $1,605 (2007); City property taxes per capita: $1,597 (2007).

Education: Percent of population age 25 and over with: High school diploma (including GED) or higher: 83.7% (2010); Bachelor's degree or higher: 17.7% (2010); Master's degree or higher: 5.6% (2010).

School District(s)

School City Of Hammond (PK-12)
   2008-09 Enrollment: 14,679 . . . . (219) 933-2400
Whiting School City (PK-12)
   2008-09 Enrollment: 915 . . . . (219) 659-0656

Four-year College(s)

Calumet College of Saint Joseph (Private, Not-for-profit, Roman Catholic)
   Fall 2008 Enrollment: 1,213 . . . . (219) 473-7770
   2009-10 Tuition: In-state $13,220; Out-of-state $13,220

Housing: Homeownership rate: 55.4% (2010); Median home value: $115,980 (2010); Median contract rent: $389 per month (2000); Median year structure built: before 1940 (2000).

Safety: Violent crime rate: 16.9 per 10,000 population; Property crime rate: 452.8 per 10,000 population (2008).

Transportation: Commute to work: 86.3% car, 1.8% public transportation, 9.9% walk, 1.7% work from home (2000); Travel time to work: 43.3% less than 15 minutes, 27.5% 15 to 30 minutes, 17.4% 30 to 45 minutes, 6.8% 45 to 60 minutes, 5.0% 60 minutes or more (2000); Amtrak: train service available.

Additional Information Contacts

City of Whiting . . . . (219) 659-3100
   http://www.whitingindiana.com
Whiting & Robertsdale Chamber of Commerce . . . . (219) 659-0292
   http://www.whitingindiana.com

WINFIELD (town). Covers a land area of 12.298 square miles and a water area of 0 square miles. Located at 41.41° N. Lat; 87.26° W. Long. Elevation is 709 feet.

History: The town was incorporated 1993, making it one of newest towns in Indiana. Prior to that time it had been part of Winfield Township as an unincorporated town. Winfield is named for General Winfield Scott.

Population: 1,003 (1990); 2,298 (2000); 4,102 (2010); 4,577 (2015 projected); Race: 93.5% White, 0.4% Black, 1.0% Asian, 5.1% Other, 6.2% Hispanic of any race (2010); Density: 333.5 persons per square mile (2010); Average household size: 2.96 (2010); Median age: 37.8 (2010); Males per 100 females: 96.4 (2010); Marriage status: 19.3% never married, 63.7% now married, 10.7% widowed, 6.3% divorced (2000); Foreign born: 9.0% (2000); Ancestry (includes multiple ancestries): 27.9% German, 12.7% Irish, 12.2% Polish, 9.2% Other groups, 8.0% English (2000).

Economy: Single-family building permits issued: 49 (2009); Multi-family building permits issued: 3 (2009); Employment by occupation: 15.7% management, 20.6% professional, 10.3% services, 27.0% sales, 0.2% farming, 14.2% construction, 12.0% production (2000).

Income: Per capita income: $32,051 (2010); Median household income: $83,106 (2010); Average household income: $97,114 (2010); Percent of households with income of $100,000 or more: 35.2% (2010); Poverty rate: 2.8% (2000).

Taxes: Total city taxes per capita: $196 (2007); City property taxes per capita: $89 (2007).

Education: Percent of population age 25 and over with: High school diploma (including GED) or higher: 90.4% (2010); Bachelor's degree or higher: 27.4% (2010); Master's degree or higher: 8.4% (2010).

Housing: Homeownership rate: 90.7% (2010); Median home value: $203,995 (2010); Median contract rent: $546 per month (2000); Median year structure built: 1995 (2000).

Transportation: Commute to work: 94.3% car, 0.9% public transportation, 0.2% walk, 4.5% work from home (2000); Travel time to work: 15.4% less than 15 minutes, 37.1% 15 to 30 minutes, 23.8% 30 to 45 minutes, 14.4% 45 to 60 minutes, 9.3% 60 minutes or more (2000)

LaPorte County

Located in northwestern Indiana; bounded on the northwest by Lake Michigan, on the north by Michigan, and partly on the south by the Kankakee River. Covers a land area of 598.24 square miles, a water area of 14.80 square miles, and is located in the Central Time Zone. The county was founded in 1832. County seat is La Porte.

LaPorte County is part of the Michigan City-La Porte, IN Metropolitan Statistical Area. The entire metro area includes: LaPorte County, IN

Population: 107,062 (1990); 110,106 (2000); 111,575 (2010); 112,103 (2015 projected); Race: 84.8% White, 10.5% Black, 0.4% Asian, 4.3% Other, 4.6% Hispanic of any race (2010); Density: 186.5 persons per square mile (2010); Average household size: 2.47 (2010); Median age: 38.8 (2010); Males per 100 females: 106.8 (2010).

Religion: Five largest groups: 23.0% Catholic Church, 3.4% Lutheran Church—Missouri Synod, 2.8% Evangelical Lutheran Church in America, 2.8% The United Methodist Church, 2.4% Christian Churches and Churches of Christ (2000).

Economy: Unemployment rate: 11.4% (5/2010); Total civilian labor force: 51,626 (5/2010); Leading industries: 23.3% manufacturing; 16.0% retail trade; 14.1% health care and social assistance (2008); Farms: 869 totaling 256,159 acres (2007); Companies that employ 500 or more persons: 5 (2008); Companies that employ 100 to 499 persons: 48 (2008); Companies that employ less than 100 persons: 2,527 (2008); Black-owned businesses: n/a (2002); Hispanic-owned businesses: n/a (2002); Asian-owned businesses: n/a (2002); Women-owned businesses: n/a (2002); Retail sales per capita: $13,599 (2010). Single-family building permits issued: 114 (2009); Multi-family building permits issued: 24 (2009).

Income: Per capita income: $21,622 (2010); Median household income: $46,183 (2010); Average household income: $55,908 (2010); Percent of households with income of $100,000 or more: 10.9% (2010); Poverty rate: 12.7% (2008); Bankruptcy rate: 6.84% (2009).

Taxes: Total county taxes per capita: $305 (2007); County property taxes per capita: $204 (2007).

Education: Percent of population age 25 and over with: High school diploma (including GED) or higher: 86.0% (2010); Bachelor's degree or higher: 16.2% (2010); Master's degree or higher: 5.3% (2010).

Housing: Homeownership rate: 74.8% (2010); Median home value: $117,854 (2010); Median contract rent: $521 per month (2006-2008 3-year est.); Median year structure built: 1964 (2006-2008 3-year est.)

Health: Birth rate: 122.5 per 10,000 population (2009); Death rate: 95.4 per 10,000 population (2009); Age-adjusted cancer mortality rate: 213.3 deaths per 100,000 population (2006); Air Quality Index: 89.1% good, 10.9% moderate, 0.0% unhealthy for sensitive individuals, 0.0% unhealthy (percent of days in 2008); Number of physicians: 12.1 per 10,000 population (2007); Hospital beds: 36.2 per 10,000 population (2006); Hospital admissions: 1,260.8 per 10,000 population (2006).

Elections: 2008 Presidential election results: 60.2% Obama, 38.2% McCain, 0.1% Nader

National and State Parks: Kingsbury State Fish And Game Area; Kingsbury State Fish and Wildlife Area

Additional Information Contacts

LaPorte County Government . . . . (219) 326-6808
   http://www.laportecounty.org

LaPorte County Communities

HANNA (unincorporated postal area, zip code 46340). Covers a land area of 35.426 square miles and a water area of 0.165 square miles. Located at 41.39° N. Lat; 86.76° W. Long. Elevation is 706 feet.

History: Laid out 1858.

Population: 1,068 (2000); Race: 93.0% White, 1.5% Black, 0.2% Asian, 5.3% Other, 0.0% Hispanic of any race (2000); Density: 30.1 persons per square mile (2000); Age: 24.5% under 18, 14.8% over 64 (2000); Marriage status: 18.1% never married, 70.0% now married, 6.5% widowed, 5.4% divorced (2000); Foreign born: 0.2% (2000); Ancestry (includes multiple ancestries): 35.6% German, 19.5% Irish, 9.2% United States or American, 7.7% Polish, 5.1% English (2000).

Economy: Employment by occupation: 9.6% management, 16.9% professional, 10.0% services, 20.6% sales, 1.4% farming, 19.4% construction, 22.0% production (2000).

Income: Per capita income: $19,064 (2000); Median household income: $48,056 (2000); Poverty rate: 6.3% (2000).

Education: Percent of population age 25 and over with: High school diploma (including GED) or higher: 86.4% (2000); Bachelor's degree or higher: 11.7% (2000).

Housing: Homeownership rate: 90.2% (2000); Median home value: $95,200 (2000); Median contract rent: $377 per month (2000); Median year structure built: 1965 (2000).

Transportation: Commute to work: 86.7% car, 0.0% public transportation, 4.5% walk, 8.8% work from home (2000); Travel time to work: 22.1% less than 15 minutes, 31.8% 15 to 30 minutes, 26.6% 30 to 45 minutes, 16.1% 45 to 60 minutes, 3.4% 60 minutes or more (2000)

KINGSBURY (town). Covers a land area of 0.584 square miles and a water area of 0 square miles. Located at 41.52° N. Lat; 86.70° W. Long. Elevation is 748 feet.

History: Kingsbury developed around the Wabash and the Grand Trunk Railroads in the mid-1800's.

Population: 258 (1990); 229 (2000); 264 (2010); 278 (2015 projected); Race: 94.3% White, 1.1% Black, 0.0% Asian, 4.5% Other, 6.4% Hispanic of any race (2010); Density: 451.7 persons per square mile (2010); Average household size: 2.90 (2010); Median age: 36.8 (2010); Males per 100 females: 103.1 (2010); Marriage status: 23.2% never married, 68.5% now married, 2.4% widowed, 6.0% divorced (2000); Foreign born: 3.8% (2000); Ancestry (includes multiple ancestries): 32.9% German, 13.8% Irish, 9.0% United States or American, 9.0% Polish, 9.0% French (except Basque) (2000).

Economy: Single-family building permits issued: 0 (2009); Multi-family building permits issued: 0 (2009); Employment by occupation: 0.8% management, 8.2% professional, 8.2% services, 29.5% sales, 0.0% farming, 11.5% construction, 41.8% production (2000).

Income: Per capita income: $19,669 (2010); Median household income: $48,125 (2010); Average household income: $60,027 (2010); Percent of households with income of $100,000 or more: 17.6% (2010); Poverty rate: 9.7% (2000).

Taxes: Total city taxes per capita: $47 (2007); City property taxes per capita: $34 (2007).

Education: Percent of population age 25 and over with: High school diploma (including GED) or higher: 89.4% (2010); Bachelor's degree or higher: 18.2% (2010); Master's degree or higher: 6.5% (2010).

Housing: Homeownership rate: 84.6% (2010); Median home value: $133,065 (2010); Median contract rent: $363 per month (2000); Median year structure built: 1951 (2000).

Transportation: Commute to work: 95.9% car, 0.0% public transportation, 3.3% walk, 0.0% work from home (2000); Travel time to work: 32.0% less than 15 minutes, 38.5% 15 to 30 minutes, 19.7% 30 to 45 minutes, 4.9% 45 to 60 minutes, 4.9% 60 minutes or more (2000)

KINGSFORD HEIGHTS (town). Covers a land area of 0.941 square miles and a water area of 0 square miles. Located at 41.48° N. Lat; 86.69° W. Long. Elevation is 725 feet.

Population: 1,486 (1990); 1,453 (2000); 1,405 (2010); 1,385 (2015 projected); Race: 90.6% White, 4.6% Black, 0.1% Asian, 4.6% Other, 2.2% Hispanic of any race (2010); Density: 1,492.7 persons per square mile (2010); Average household size: 2.77 (2010); Median age: 34.9 (2010); Males per 100 females: 97.3 (2010); Marriage status: 21.7% never married, 54.9% now married, 7.1% widowed, 16.3% divorced (2000); Foreign born: 1.0% (2000); Ancestry (includes multiple ancestries): 20.7% United States or American, 19.8% Other groups, 15.6% German, 11.0% Irish, 6.6% Polish (2000).

Economy: Single-family building permits issued: 1 (2009); Multi-family building permits issued: 0 (2009); Employment by occupation: 5.8% management, 4.9% professional, 9.4% services, 21.7% sales, 0.0% farming, 8.9% construction, 49.3% production (2000).

Income: Per capita income: $15,701 (2010); Median household income: $34,491 (2010); Average household income: $43,141 (2010); Percent of households with income of $100,000 or more: 4.1% (2010); Poverty rate: 13.4% (2000).

Taxes: Total city taxes per capita: $79 (2007); City property taxes per capita: $56 (2007).

Education: Percent of population age 25 and over with: High school diploma (including GED) or higher: 81.1% (2010); Bachelor's degree or higher: 7.4% (2010); Master's degree or higher: 1.9% (2010).

School District(s)

Laporte Community School Corp (PK-12)

   2008-09 Enrollment: 6,455 . . . . (219) 362-7056

Housing: Homeownership rate: 74.4% (2010); Median home value: $74,020 (2010); Median contract rent: $409 per month (2000); Median year structure built: 1956 (2000).

Transportation: Commute to work: 98.0% car, 0.4% public transportation, 1.1% walk, 0.5% work from home (2000); Travel time to work: 16.7% less than 15 minutes, 60.1% 15 to 30 minutes, 8.7% 30 to 45 minutes, 8.2% 45 to 60 minutes, 6.3% 60 minutes or more (2000)

LA CROSSE (town). Covers a land area of 0.539 square miles and a water area of 0 square miles. Located at 41.31° N. Lat; 86.89° W. Long. Elevation is 676 feet.

Population: 677 (1990); 561 (2000); 578 (2010); 586 (2015 projected); Race: 97.2% White, 0.2% Black, 0.5% Asian, 2.1% Other, 3.5% Hispanic of any race (2010); Density: 1,071.5 persons per square mile (2010); Average household size: 2.50 (2010); Median age: 40.3 (2010); Males per 100 females: 92.7 (2010); Marriage status: 22.2% never married, 62.8% now married, 5.3% widowed, 9.7% divorced (2000); Foreign born: 0.4% (2000); Ancestry (includes multiple ancestries): 39.1% German, 12.8% Irish, 11.3% English, 10.2% Polish, 6.5% Dutch (2000).

Economy: Single-family building permits issued: 0 (2009); Multi-family building permits issued: 0 (2009); Employment by occupation: 5.4% management, 9.3% professional, 12.8% services, 30.4% sales, 0.8% farming, 14.8% construction, 26.5% production (2000).

Income: Per capita income: $18,677 (2010); Median household income: $40,724 (2010); Average household income: $46,364 (2010); Percent of households with income of $100,000 or more: 4.3% (2010); Poverty rate: 1.5% (2000).

Taxes: Total city taxes per capita: $223 (2007); City property taxes per capita: $185 (2007).

Education: Percent of population age 25 and over with: High school diploma (including GED) or higher: 92.3% (2010); Bachelor's degree or higher: 10.9% (2010); Master's degree or higher: 3.7% (2010).

School District(s)

Dewey Township Schools (KG-12)

   2008-09 Enrollment: 168 . . . . (219) 326-6808

Housing: Homeownership rate: 85.7% (2010); Median home value: $111,446 (2010); Median contract rent: $342 per month (2000); Median year structure built: before 1940 (2000).

Transportation: Commute to work: 99.2% car, 0.0% public transportation, 0.0% walk, 0.8% work from home (2000); Travel time to work: 21.8% less than 15 minutes, 34.1% 15 to 30 minutes, 27.4% 30 to 45 minutes, 9.5% 45 to 60 minutes, 7.1% 60 minutes or more (2000)

LA PORTE (city). County seat. Covers a land area of 11.459 square miles and a water area of 0.711 square miles. Located at 41.60° N. Lat; 86.71° W. Long. Elevation is 814 feet.

History: La Porte was founded in 1830 when the Michigan Road was under construction. Its name is French for "the door," and through La Porte passed much commerce.

Population: 21,701 (1990); 21,621 (2000); 20,754 (2010); 20,369 (2015 projected); Race: 90.7% White, 1.8% Black, 0.4% Asian, 7.1% Other, 9.7% Hispanic of any race (2010); Density: 1,811.1 persons per square mile (2010); Average household size: 2.32 (2010); Median age: 38.3 (2010); Males per 100 females: 94.9 (2010); Marriage status: 22.0% never married, 53.6% now married, 9.5% widowed, 15.0% divorced (2000); Foreign born: 4.2% (2000); Ancestry (includes multiple ancestries): 29.7% German, 12.8% Other groups, 11.8% Irish, 10.9% Polish, 9.3% United States or American (2000).

Economy: Single-family building permits issued: 14 (2009); Multi-family building permits issued: 0 (2009); Employment by occupation: 8.9% management, 13.0% professional, 16.7% services, 21.7% sales, 0.4% farming, 11.0% construction, 28.3% production (2000).

Income: Per capita income: $20,041 (2010); Median household income: $38,998 (2010); Average household income: $47,203 (2010); Percent of households with income of $100,000 or more: 7.0% (2010); Poverty rate: 11.0% (2000).

Taxes: Total city taxes per capita: $325 (2007); City property taxes per capita: $272 (2007).

Education: Percent of population age 25 and over with: High school diploma (including GED) or higher: 85.0% (2010); Bachelor's degree or higher: 15.3% (2010); Master's degree or higher: 5.2% (2010).

School District(s)

IN Department of Correction (05-12)
  2008-09 Enrollment: 793 . . . . (317) 233-3111
Laporte Community School Corp (PK-12)
  2008-09 Enrollment: 6,455 . . . . (219) 362-7056
Renaissance Academy Charter School (KG-08)
  2008-09 Enrollment: 117 . . . . (219) 878-8711

Housing: Homeownership rate: 62.4% (2010); Median home value: $101,424 (2010); Median contract rent: $405 per month (2000); Median year structure built: 1950 (2000).
Hospitals: LaPorte Regional Health System (227 beds)
Safety: Violent crime rate: 22.3 per 10,000 population; Property crime rate: 701.8 per 10,000 population (2008).
Newspapers: LaPorte Herald-Argus (Local news)
Transportation: Commute to work: 93.4% car, 0.5% public transportation, 3.0% walk, 1.2% work from home (2000); Travel time to work: 52.3% less than 15 minutes, 25.0% 15 to 30 minutes, 11.3% 30 to 45 minutes, 6.2% 45 to 60 minutes, 5.2% 60 minutes or more (2000)

Additional Information Contacts

City of La Porte . . . . (219) 362-0151
  http://www.cityoflaporte.com
Greater LaPorte Chamber of Commerce. . . . . (219) 362-3178
  http://www.lpchamber.com

LONG BEACH (town). Covers a land area of 1.042 square miles and a water area of 2.111 square miles. Located at 41.74° N. Lat; 86.85° W. Long. Elevation is 633 feet.

Population: 2,044 (1990); 1,559 (2000); 1,716 (2010); 1,731 (2015 projected); Race: 93.2% White, 3.7% Black, 0.9% Asian, 2.2% Other, 1.4% Hispanic of any race (2010); Density: 1,646.3 persons per square mile (2010); Average household size: 2.11 (2010); Median age: 53.0 (2010); Males per 100 females: 92.4 (2010); Marriage status: 18.3% never married, 68.6% now married, 6.1% widowed, 7.0% divorced (2000); Foreign born: 2.9% (2000); Ancestry (includes multiple ancestries): 41.2% Irish, 27.2% German, 13.4% English, 9.3% Polish, 8.4% Other groups (2000).
Economy: Single-family building permits issued: 6 (2009); Multi-family building permits issued: 0 (2009); Employment by occupation: 30.9% management, 32.8% professional, 7.0% services, 22.0% sales, 0.0% farming, 4.1% construction, 3.2% production (2000).
Income: Per capita income: $41,143 (2010); Median household income: $61,103 (2010); Average household income: $86,431 (2010); Percent of households with income of $100,000 or more: 23.5% (2010); Poverty rate: 0.9% (2000).
Taxes: Total city taxes per capita: $543 (2007); City property taxes per capita: $351 (2007).
Education: Percent of population age 25 and over with: High school diploma (including GED) or higher: 97.5% (2010); Bachelor's degree or higher: 51.4% (2010); Master's degree or higher: 17.3% (2010).
Housing: Homeownership rate: 80.1% (2010); Median home value: $251,546 (2010); Median contract rent: $600 per month (2000); Median year structure built: 1953 (2000).
Transportation: Commute to work: 86.9% car, 4.5% public transportation, 0.9% walk, 5.6% work from home (2000); Travel time to work: 32.7% less than 15 minutes, 29.8% 15 to 30 minutes, 9.5% 30 to 45 minutes, 6.3% 45 to 60 minutes, 21.7% 60 minutes or more (2000)

MICHIANA SHORES (town). Covers a land area of 0.346 square miles and a water area of 0 square miles. Located at 41.75° N. Lat; 86.81° W. Long. Elevation is 610 feet.

Population: 378 (1990); 330 (2000); 340 (2010); 339 (2015 projected); Race: 91.5% White, 0.3% Black, 2.6% Asian, 5.6% Other, 2.9% Hispanic of any race (2010); Density: 982.9 persons per square mile (2010); Average household size: 2.18 (2010); Median age: 50.3 (2010); Males per 100 females: 109.9 (2010); Marriage status: 16.3% never married, 54.4% now married, 9.5% widowed, 19.8% divorced (2000); Foreign born: 10.3% (2000); Ancestry (includes multiple ancestries): 21.7% German, 19.6% Irish, 10.3% Polish, 9.3% Swedish, 8.2% United States or American (2000).
Economy: Single-family building permits issued: 1 (2009); Multi-family building permits issued: 0 (2009); Employment by occupation: 17.1% management, 21.4% professional, 7.1% services, 30.7% sales, 0.0% farming, 7.9% construction, 15.7% production (2000).

Income: Per capita income: $29,019 (2010); Median household income: $50,676 (2010); Average household income: $62,692 (2010); Percent of households with income of $100,000 or more: 16.0% (2010); Poverty rate: 2.5% (2000).
Taxes: Total city taxes per capita: $75 (2007); City property taxes per capita: $54 (2007).
Education: Percent of population age 25 and over with: High school diploma (including GED) or higher: 95.0% (2010); Bachelor's degree or higher: 45.2% (2010); Master's degree or higher: 8.0% (2010).
Housing: Homeownership rate: 91.0% (2010); Median home value: $158,065 (2010); Median contract rent: $538 per month (2000); Median year structure built: 1962 (2000).
Transportation: Commute to work: 91.3% car, 2.9% public transportation, 2.2% walk, 3.6% work from home (2000); Travel time to work: 44.4% less than 15 minutes, 23.3% 15 to 30 minutes, 9.8% 30 to 45 minutes, 2.3% 45 to 60 minutes, 20.3% 60 minutes or more (2000)

MICHIGAN CITY (city). Covers a land area of 19.600 square miles and a water area of 3.517 square miles. Located at 41.70° N. Lat; 86.88° W. Long. Elevation is 627 feet.

History: It was in Michigan City that Daniel Webster made a Fourth of July speech in 1837. The city was founded in 1832 at the northern end of the Michigan Road, on Lake Michigan. From the early 1840's it served as a port for shipping interests and later for a fishing fleet.
Population: 33,822 (1990); 32,900 (2000); 32,541 (2010); 32,174 (2015 projected); Race: 70.6% White, 24.3% Black, 0.4% Asian, 4.8% Other, 4.5% Hispanic of any race (2010); Density: 1,660.3 persons per square mile (2010); Average household size: 2.39 (2010); Median age: 37.0 (2010); Males per 100 females: 105.3 (2010); Marriage status: 28.1% never married, 47.2% now married, 8.6% widowed, 16.1% divorced (2000); Foreign born: 2.1% (2000); Ancestry (includes multiple ancestries): 28.3% Other groups, 20.2% German, 11.1% Polish, 9.8% Irish, 7.2% United States or American (2000).
Economy: Unemployment rate: 11.8% (5/2010); Total civilian labor force: 14,130 (5/2010); Single-family building permits issued: 8 (2009); Multi-family building permits issued: 24 (2009); Employment by occupation: 8.5% management, 12.8% professional, 21.3% services, 25.7% sales, 0.2% farming, 9.3% construction, 22.2% production (2000).
Income: Per capita income: $18,941 (2010); Median household income: $38,183 (2010); Average household income: $47,229 (2010); Percent of households with income of $100,000 or more: 6.9% (2010); Poverty rate: 13.3% (2000).
Taxes: Total city taxes per capita: $520 (2007); City property taxes per capita: $353 (2007).
Education: Percent of population age 25 and over with: High school diploma (including GED) or higher: 82.7% (2010); Bachelor's degree or higher: 15.0% (2010); Master's degree or higher: 5.0% (2010).

School District(s)

Michigan City Area Schools (PK-12)
  2008-09 Enrollment: 6,911 . . . . (219) 873-2000

Four-year College(s)

Brown Mackie College-Michigan City (Private, For-profit)
  Fall 2008 Enrollment: 378 . . . . (219) 877-3100
  2009-10 Tuition: In-state $10,116; Out-of-state $10,116

Housing: Homeownership rate: 63.7% (2010); Median home value: $90,988 (2010); Median contract rent: $411 per month (2000); Median year structure built: 1956 (2000).
Hospitals: St. Anthony Memorial Health Centers (310 beds)
Safety: Violent crime rate: 38.8 per 10,000 population; Property crime rate: 557.9 per 10,000 population (2008).
Newspapers: The News-Dispatch (Community news; Circulation 1,800)
Transportation: Commute to work: 93.2% car, 1.8% public transportation, 2.6% walk, 1.4% work from home (2000); Travel time to work: 54.1% less than 15 minutes, 26.8% 15 to 30 minutes, 8.7% 30 to 45 minutes, 5.5% 45 to 60 minutes, 4.9% 60 minutes or more (2000); Amtrak: train service available.

Additional Information Contacts

City of Michigan City . . . . (219) 873-1410
  http://www.emichigancity.com
Michigan City Area Chamber of Commerce . . . . (219) 874-6221
  http://www.michigancitychamber.com

MILL CREEK (unincorporated postal area, zip code 46365). Covers a land area of 23.309 square miles and a water area of 0.101 square miles. Located at 41.59° N. Lat; 86.53° W. Long.

Population: 1,003 (2000); Race: 100.0% White, 0.0% Black, 0.0% Asian, 0.0% Other, 0.0% Hispanic of any race (2000); Density: 43.0 persons per square mile (2000); Age: 32.6% under 18, 2.8% over 64 (2000); Marriage status: 20.6% never married, 68.0% now married, 4.0% widowed, 7.3% divorced (2000); Foreign born: 0.7% (2000); Ancestry (includes multiple ancestries): 32.5% German, 14.8% Irish, 12.4% Polish, 8.3% United States or American, 8.2% English (2000).
Economy: Employment by occupation: 8.9% management, 18.2% professional, 7.6% services, 21.9% sales, 2.4% farming, 17.7% construction, 23.3% production (2000).
Income: Per capita income: $20,208 (2000); Median household income: $53,125 (2000); Poverty rate: 1.6% (2000).
Education: Percent of population age 25 and over with: High school diploma (including GED) or higher: 90.7% (2000); Bachelor's degree or higher: 15.1% (2000).
Housing: Homeownership rate: 88.3% (2000); Median home value: $110,700 (2000); Median contract rent: $460 per month (2000); Median year structure built: 1975 (2000).
Transportation: Commute to work: 93.5% car, 0.0% public transportation, 2.7% walk, 2.0% work from home (2000); Travel time to work: 22.5% less than 15 minutes, 40.1% 15 to 30 minutes, 26.3% 30 to 45 minutes, 10.1% 45 to 60 minutes, 1.0% 60 minutes or more (2000)

POTTAWATTAMIE PARK (town). Aka Pottawattomie Park.

Covers a land area of 0.251 square miles and a water area of 0 square miles. Located at 41.72° N. Lat; 86.86° W. Long. Elevation is 623 feet.
Population: 281 (1990); 300 (2000); 239 (2010); 239 (2015 projected); Race: 85.4% White, 9.6% Black, 1.7% Asian, 3.3% Other, 2.1% Hispanic of any race (2010); Density: 953.5 persons per square mile (2010); Average household size: 1.93 (2010); Median age: 51.1 (2010); Males per 100 females: 92.7 (2010); Marriage status: 20.4% never married, 66.0% now married, 8.0% widowed, 5.6% divorced (2000); Foreign born: 8.0% (2000); Ancestry (includes multiple ancestries): 28.2% German, 15.3% Other groups, 14.0% English, 7.3% Polish, 6.3% Lebanese (2000).
Economy: Employment by occupation: 19.8% management, 36.6% professional, 8.9% services, 26.7% sales, 0.0% farming, 6.9% construction, 1.0% production (2000).
Income: Per capita income: $32,544 (2010); Median household income: $42,857 (2010); Average household income: $63,811 (2010); Percent of households with income of $100,000 or more: 13.1% (2010); Poverty rate: 8.6% (2000).
Education: Percent of population age 25 and over with: High school diploma (including GED) or higher: 95.9% (2010); Bachelor's degree or higher: 46.9% (2010); Master's degree or higher: 18.4% (2010).
Housing: Homeownership rate: 59.8% (2010); Median home value: $222,917 (2010); Median contract rent: $475 per month (2000); Median year structure built: 1959 (2000).
Transportation: Commute to work: 97.0% car, 2.0% public transportation, 0.0% walk, 1.0% work from home (2000); Travel time to work: 58.2% less than 15 minutes, 15.3% 15 to 30 minutes, 0.0% 30 to 45 minutes, 12.2% 45 to 60 minutes, 14.3% 60 minutes or more (2000)

ROLLING PRAIRIE (unincorporated postal area, zip code 46371).

Covers a land area of 37.421 square miles and a water area of 0.667 square miles. Located at 41.67° N. Lat; 86.60° W. Long. Elevation is 822 feet.
History: The site for Rolling Prairie was chosen in 1831 by Ezekial Provolt, who built a cabin here in 1834. The town was laid out in 1853.
Population: 3,132 (2000); Race: 98.4% White, 0.6% Black, 0.5% Asian, 0.5% Other, 1.1% Hispanic of any race (2000); Density: 83.7 persons per square mile (2000); Age: 24.5% under 18, 11.7% over 64 (2000); Marriage status: 16.9% never married, 63.7% now married, 8.1% widowed, 11.2% divorced (2000); Foreign born: 0.3% (2000); Ancestry (includes multiple ancestries): 31.3% German, 13.7% Irish, 13.2% Polish, 9.0% English, 6.7% United States or American (2000).
Economy: Employment by occupation: 9.0% management, 12.7% professional, 20.3% services, 17.7% sales, 0.9% farming, 13.9% construction, 25.4% production (2000).
Income: Per capita income: $19,422 (2000); Median household income: $50,548 (2000); Poverty rate: 4.1% (2000).
Education: Percent of population age 25 and over with: High school diploma (including GED) or higher: 85.1% (2000); Bachelor's degree or higher: 10.3% (2000).

New Prairie United School Corp (PK-12)
   2008-09 Enrollment: 2,747 . . . . (574) 654-7273
Housing: Homeownership rate: 91.6% (2000); Median home value: $98,700 (2000); Median contract rent: $446 per month (2000); Median year structure built: 1962 (2000).
Transportation: Commute to work: 90.2% car, 1.2% public transportation, 3.5% walk, 4.7% work from home (2000); Travel time to work: 27.1% less than 15 minutes, 45.9% 15 to 30 minutes, 13.9% 30 to 45 minutes, 7.2% 45 to 60 minutes, 5.9% 60 minutes or more (2000)

TRAIL CREEK (town). Covers a land area of 1.218 square miles and

a water area of 0 square miles. Located at 41.69° N. Lat; 86.85° W. Long. Elevation is 627 feet.
Population: 2,463 (1990); 2,296 (2000); 2,099 (2010); 2,140 (2015 projected); Race: 76.1% White, 19.4% Black, 0.3% Asian, 4.2% Other, 2.8% Hispanic of any race (2010); Density: 1,722.9 persons per square mile (2010); Average household size: 2.31 (2010); Median age: 39.3 (2010); Males per 100 females: 85.6 (2010); Marriage status: 13.0% never married, 69.1% now married, 10.6% widowed, 7.3% divorced (2000); Foreign born: 1.6% (2000); Ancestry (includes multiple ancestries): 42.7% German, 25.0% Polish, 13.3% Irish, 11.2% English, 5.5% Other groups (2000).
Economy: Single-family building permits issued: 0 (2009); Multi-family building permits issued: 0 (2009); Employment by occupation: 14.0% management, 20.1% professional, 12.3% services, 26.6% sales, 0.3% farming, 10.8% construction, 15.9% production (2000).
Income: Per capita income: $20,354 (2010); Median household income: $42,244 (2010); Average household income: $48,030 (2010); Percent of households with income of $100,000 or more: 5.8% (2010); Poverty rate: 5.3% (2000).
Taxes: Total city taxes per capita: $181 (2007); City property taxes per capita: $148 (2007).
Education: Percent of population age 25 and over with: High school diploma (including GED) or higher: 88.4% (2010); Bachelor's degree or higher: 17.7% (2010); Master's degree or higher: 5.5% (2010).
Housing: Homeownership rate: 66.3% (2010); Median home value: $113,144 (2010); Median contract rent: $458 per month (2000); Median year structure built: 1961 (2000).
Transportation: Commute to work: 94.9% car, 0.9% public transportation, 0.8% walk, 3.3% work from home (2000); Travel time to work: 60.2% less than 15 minutes, 22.3% 15 to 30 minutes, 8.2% 30 to 45 minutes, 5.0% 45 to 60 minutes, 4.4% 60 minutes or more (2000)

UNION MILLS (unincorporated postal area, zip code 46382). Covers

a land area of 49.412 square miles and a water area of 0.036 square miles. Located at 41.48° N. Lat; 86.77° W. Long. Elevation is 735 feet.
Population: 1,990 (2000); Race: 99.3% White, 0.4% Black, 0.0% Asian, 0.3% Other, 0.0% Hispanic of any race (2000); Density: 40.3 persons per square mile (2000); Age: 27.3% under 18, 13.5% over 64 (2000); Marriage status: 15.1% never married, 71.5% now married, 4.7% widowed, 8.7% divorced (2000); Foreign born: 0.0% (2000); Ancestry (includes multiple ancestries): 38.8% German, 11.7% Irish, 10.8% English, 8.4% United States or American, 6.2% Polish (2000).
Economy: Employment by occupation: 7.7% management, 9.1% professional, 16.5% services, 22.5% sales, 1.8% farming, 18.5% construction, 23.9% production (2000).
Income: Per capita income: $17,184 (2000); Median household income: $41,302 (2000); Poverty rate: 2.4% (2000).
Education: Percent of population age 25 and over with: High school diploma (including GED) or higher: 88.1% (2000); Bachelor's degree or higher: 8.9% (2000).

South Central Com School Corp (PK-12)
   2008-09 Enrollment: 855 . . . . (219) 767-2263
Housing: Homeownership rate: 91.6% (2000); Median home value: $93,300 (2000); Median contract rent: $526 per month (2000); Median year structure built: 1968 (2000).
Transportation: Commute to work: 92.5% car, 0.8% public transportation, 0.8% walk, 5.9% work from home (2000); Travel time to work: 17.7% less than 15 minutes, 47.8% 15 to 30 minutes, 14.4% 30 to 45 minutes, 12.4% 45 to 60 minutes, 7.7% 60 minutes or more (2000)

WANATAH (town). Covers a land area of 1.370 square miles and a water area of 0 square miles. Located at 41.43° N. Lat; 86.89° W. Long. Elevation is 732 feet.

History: Wanatah is named for an Indian chief whose name means "keep knee deep in mud."

Population: 900 (1990); 1,013 (2000); 1,020 (2010); 1,028 (2015 projected); Race: 80.7% White, 15.0% Black, 0.2% Asian, 4.1% Other, 2.9% Hispanic of any race (2010); Density: 744.3 persons per square mile (2010); Average household size: 2.48 (2010); Median age: 38.3 (2010); Males per 100 females: 158.2 (2010); Marriage status: 20.5% never married, 63.1% now married, 6.5% widowed, 9.9% divorced (2000); Foreign born: 0.2% (2000); Ancestry (includes multiple ancestries): 36.8% German, 13.7% Irish, 9.8% English, 8.6% Other groups, 7.8% United States or American (2000).

Economy: Single-family building permits issued: 0 (2009); Multi-family building permits issued: 0 (2009); Employment by occupation: 9.9% management, 11.3% professional, 12.4% services, 26.3% sales, 1.1% farming, 18.2% construction, 20.8% production (2000).

Income: Per capita income: $20,864 (2010); Median household income: $56,977 (2010); Average household income: $64,088 (2010); Percent of households with income of $100,000 or more: 12.9% (2010); Poverty rate: 5.3% (2000).

Taxes: Total city taxes per capita: $209 (2007); City property taxes per capita: $166 (2007).

Education: Percent of population age 25 and over with: High school diploma (including GED) or higher: 82.7% (2010); Bachelor's degree or higher: 12.2% (2010); Master's degree or higher: 4.2% (2010).

School District(s)
Cass Township Schools (KG-08)
    2008-09 Enrollment: 247 . . . . (219) 326-6808

Housing: Homeownership rate: 85.5% (2010); Median home value: $130,189 (2010); Median contract rent: $445 per month (2000); Median year structure built: 1961 (2000).

Transportation: Commute to work: 91.0% car, 0.2% public transportation, 3.4% walk, 4.6% work from home (2000); Travel time to work: 34.4% less than 15 minutes, 32.4% 15 to 30 minutes, 22.4% 30 to 45 minutes, 5.8% 45 to 60 minutes, 5.0% 60 minutes or more (2000)

WESTVILLE (town). Covers a land area of 3.126 square miles and a water area of 0 square miles. Located at 41.54° N. Lat; 86.90° W. Long. Elevation is 794 feet.

History: Settled 1836, laid out 1851.

Population: 5,333 (1990); 2,116 (2000); 2,206 (2010); 2,250 (2015 projected); Race: 96.9% White, 0.6% Black, 0.4% Asian, 2.0% Other, 1.4% Hispanic of any race (2010); Density: 705.8 persons per square mile (2010); Average household size: 2.44 (2010); Median age: 38.8 (2010); Males per 100 females: 99.6 (2010); Marriage status: 22.3% never married, 53.4% now married, 7.0% widowed, 17.2% divorced (2000); Foreign born: 1.2% (2000); Ancestry (includes multiple ancestries): 27.1% German, 16.2% Irish, 9.0% Other groups, 8.7% English, 7.2% United States or American (2000).

Economy: Single-family building permits issued: 12 (2009); Multi-family building permits issued: 0 (2009); Employment by occupation: 7.4% management, 10.0% professional, 15.3% services, 27.6% sales, 0.7% farming, 11.1% construction, 27.8% production (2000).

Income: Per capita income: $23,351 (2010); Median household income: $48,723 (2010); Average household income: $56,931 (2010); Percent of households with income of $100,000 or more: 10.1% (2010); Poverty rate: 6.3% (2000).

Taxes: Total city taxes per capita: $49 (2007); City property taxes per capita: $39 (2007).

Education: Percent of population age 25 and over with: High school diploma (including GED) or higher: 88.5% (2010); Bachelor's degree or higher: 12.6% (2010); Master's degree or higher: 2.4% (2010).

School District(s)
M S D Of New Durham Township (KG-12)
    2008-09 Enrollment: 895 . . . . (219) 785-2239

Four-year College(s)
Purdue University-North Central Campus (Public)
    Fall 2008 Enrollment: 4,245 . . . . (219) 785-5200
    2009-10 Tuition: In-state $6,384; Out-of-state $15,057

Housing: Homeownership rate: 78.2% (2010); Median home value: $101,657 (2010); Median contract rent: $387 per month (2000); Median year structure built: 1978 (2000).

Safety: Violent crime rate: 6.0 per 10,000 population; Property crime rate: 169.0 per 10,000 population (2008).

Newspapers: Regional News (Community news; Circulation 3,000); Westville Indicator (Community news; Circulation 5,200)

Transportation: Commute to work: 96.7% car, 0.9% public transportation, 1.5% walk, 0.4% work from home (2000); Travel time to work: 27.1% less than 15 minutes, 46.2% 15 to 30 minutes, 15.4% 30 to 45 minutes, 6.5% 45 to 60 minutes, 4.9% 60 minutes or more (2000)

Lawrence County

Located in southern Indiana; drained by Salt Creek and the East Fork of the White River. Covers a land area of 448.83 square miles, a water area of 3.24 square miles, and is located in the Eastern Time Zone. The county was founded in 1819. County seat is Bedford.

Lawrence County is part of the Bedford, IN Micropolitan Statistical Area. The entire metro area includes: Lawrence County, IN

Weather Station: Oolitic Purdue Exp. Farm								Elevation: 649 feet			
	Jan	Feb	Mar	Apr	May	Jun	Jul	Aug	Sep	Oct	Nov	Dec
High	37	42	53	64	74	82	86	84	78	67	54	42
Low	18	21	30	40	50	59	64	62	53	41	33	24
Precip	2.7	2.6	3.8	4.6	5.0	3.9	4.4	4.1	2.9	3.3	3.9	3.3
Snow	5.8	3.8	2.7	tr	tr	0.0	0.0	0.0	0.0	tr	0.4	2.6

High and Low temperatures in degrees Fahrenheit; Precipitation and Snow in inches

Population: 42,836 (1990); 45,922 (2000); 45,884 (2010); 45,567 (2015 projected); Race: 97.1% White, 0.6% Black, 0.5% Asian, 1.7% Other, 1.1% Hispanic of any race (2010); Density: 102.2 persons per square mile (2010); Average household size: 2.35 (2010); Median age: 40.8 (2010); Males per 100 females: 95.2 (2010).

Religion: Five largest groups: 8.7% Christian Churches and Churches of Christ, 8.1% American Baptist Churches in the USA, 5.5% Catholic Church, 3.0% Churches of Christ, 3.0% The United Methodist Church (2000).

Economy: Unemployment rate: 11.0% (5/2010); Total civilian labor force: 22,661 (5/2010); Leading industries: 24.0% manufacturing; 21.4% health care and social assistance; 17.8% retail trade (2008); Farms: 820 totaling 134,637 acres (2007); Companies that employ 500 or more persons: 3 (2008); Companies that employ 100 to 499 persons: 14 (2008); Companies that employ less than 100 persons: 892 (2008); Black-owned businesses: n/a (2002); Hispanic-owned businesses: n/a (2002); Asian-owned businesses: n/a (2002); Women-owned businesses: 985 (2002); Retail sales per capita: $10,940 (2010). Single-family building permits issued: 9 (2009); Multi-family building permits issued: 0 (2009).

Income: Per capita income: $21,320 (2010); Median household income: $42,078 (2010); Average household income: $50,632 (2010); Percent of households with income of $100,000 or more: 9.1% (2010); Poverty rate: 14.3% (2008); Bankruptcy rate: 8.21% (2009).

Taxes: Total county taxes per capita: $281 (2007); County property taxes per capita: $166 (2007).

Education: Percent of population age 25 and over with: High school diploma (including GED) or higher: 80.5% (2010); Bachelor's degree or higher: 11.8% (2010); Master's degree or higher: 4.6% (2010).

Housing: Homeownership rate: 76.7% (2010); Median home value: $91,747 (2010); Median contract rent: $400 per month (2006-2008 3-year est.); Median year structure built: 1973 (2006-2008 3-year est.)

Health: Birth rate: 112.8 per 10,000 population (2009); Death rate: 105.8 per 10,000 population (2009); Age-adjusted cancer mortality rate: 186.2 deaths per 100,000 population (2006); Number of physicians: 9.8 per 10,000 population (2007); Hospital beds: 28.4 per 10,000 population (2006); Hospital admissions: 920.1 per 10,000 population (2006).

Elections: 2008 Presidential election results: 38.9% Obama, 59.4% McCain, 0.0% Nader

National and State Parks: Spring Mill State Park

Additional Information Contacts

Lawrence County Government . . . . (812) 275-7543
    http://www.bedfordonline.com/government/lawrence/index.htm
Bedford Area Chamber of Commerce . . . . (812) 275-4493
    http://www.bedfordchamber.com
City of Bedford . . . . (812) 279-6555
    http://www.bedford.in.us
City of Mitchell . . . . (812) 849-3831
    http://www.mitchell-in.gov

Lawrence County Communities

BEDFORD (city). Aka Eureka. County seat. Covers a land area of 11.898 square miles and a water area of 0 square miles. Located at 38.86° N. Lat; 86.49° W. Long. Elevation is 686 feet.

History: Beford developed as the center of a limestone industry, providing stone for such buildings as the Empire State Building and the Chicago Museum of Fine Arts.

Population: 13,817 (1990); 13,768 (2000); 12,908 (2010); 12,450 (2015 projected); Race: 95.5% White, 1.3% Black, 0.8% Asian, 2.3% Other, 1.6% Hispanic of any race (2010); Density: 1,084.8 persons per square mile (2010); Average household size: 2.10 (2010); Median age: 43.9 (2010); Males per 100 females: 87.6 (2010); Marriage status: 19.1% never married, 54.4% now married, 11.9% widowed, 14.6% divorced (2000); Foreign born: 1.1% (2000); Ancestry (includes multiple ancestries): 18.3% United States or American, 12.6% German, 9.8% Irish, 9.1% English, 8.8% Other groups (2000).

Economy: Single-family building permits issued: 8 (2009); Multi-family building permits issued: 0 (2009); Employment by occupation: 8.8% management, 17.3% professional, 18.9% services, 23.3% sales, 0.1% farming, 8.3% construction, 23.3% production (2000).

Income: Per capita income: $20,367 (2010); Median household income: $34,292 (2010); Average household income: $43,648 (2010); Percent of households with income of $100,000 or more: 6.8% (2010); Poverty rate: 11.5% (2000).

Taxes: Total city taxes per capita: $360 (2007); City property taxes per capita: $336 (2007).

Education: Percent of population age 25 and over with: High school diploma (including GED) or higher: 77.7% (2010); Bachelor's degree or higher: 14.5% (2010); Master's degree or higher: 5.4% (2010).

School District(s)

North Lawrence Com Schools (PK-12)
    2008-09 Enrollment: 5,343 . . . . (812) 279-3521

Housing: Homeownership rate: 62.0% (2010); Median home value: $84,307 (2010); Median contract rent: $358 per month (2000); Median year structure built: 1952 (2000).

Hospitals: Bedford Regional Medical Center (49 beds); Dunn Memorial Hospital (137 beds)

Safety: Violent crime rate: 22.3 per 10,000 population; Property crime rate: 415.4 per 10,000 population (2008).

Newspapers: Bedford Times-Mail (Local news; Circulation 14,349)

Transportation: Commute to work: 93.5% car, 1.1% public transportation, 2.5% walk, 1.6% work from home (2000); Travel time to work: 50.8% less than 15 minutes, 16.7% 15 to 30 minutes, 22.9% 30 to 45 minutes, 5.6% 45 to 60 minutes, 3.9% 60 minutes or more (2000)

Additional Information Contacts

Bedford Area Chamber of Commerce . . . . (812) 275-4493
    http://www.bedfordchamber.com
City of Bedford . . . . (812) 279-6555
    http://www.bedford.in.us

HELTONVILLE (unincorporated postal area, zip code 47436). Covers a land area of 43.054 square miles and a water area of 0.010 square miles. Located at 38.97° N. Lat; 86.41° W. Long. Elevation is 653 feet.

Population: 1,232 (2000); Race: 95.3% White, 3.2% Black, 0.7% Asian, 0.8% Other, 0.0% Hispanic of any race (2000); Density: 28.6 persons per square mile (2000); Age: 22.3% under 18, 10.6% over 64 (2000); Marriage status: 17.6% never married, 57.0% now married, 7.2% widowed, 18.1% divorced (2000); Foreign born: 0.6% (2000); Ancestry (includes multiple ancestries): 17.5% United States or American, 9.5% English, 9.1% Irish, 8.5% German, 8.2% Other groups (2000).

Economy: Employment by occupation: 6.5% management, 20.1% professional, 10.3% services, 21.8% sales, 1.0% farming, 10.9% construction, 29.4% production (2000).

Income: Per capita income: $19,392 (2000); Median household income: $40,481 (2000); Poverty rate: 9.0% (2000).

Education: Percent of population age 25 and over with: High school diploma (including GED) or higher: 82.2% (2000); Bachelor's degree or higher: 8.7% (2000).

School District(s)

North Lawrence Com Schools (PK-12)
    2008-09 Enrollment: 5,343 . . . . (812) 279-3521

Housing: Homeownership rate: 87.4% (2000); Median home value: $78,900 (2000); Median contract rent: $363 per month (2000); Median year structure built: 1970 (2000).

Transportation: Commute to work: 98.0% car, 0.0% public transportation, 0.0% walk, 2.0% work from home (2000); Travel time to work: 11.4% less than 15 minutes, 20.9% 15 to 30 minutes, 50.4% 30 to 45 minutes, 7.0% 45 to 60 minutes, 10.4% 60 minutes or more (2000)

MITCHELL (city). Covers a land area of 3.394 square miles and a water area of 0.005 square miles. Located at 38.73° N. Lat; 86.47° W. Long. Elevation is 682 feet.

History: The first settlers came to Mitchell in 1813. The town was platted about 1852 when the Louisville, New Albany, & Salem Railroad came through Lawrence County. The town was named for O.M. Mitchell, a construction engineer for the Ohio & Mississippi Railroad which crossed the original line in 1856.

Population: 4,819 (1990); 4,567 (2000); 4,384 (2010); 4,267 (2015 projected); Race: 97.8% White, 0.4% Black, 0.2% Asian, 1.6% Other, 0.6% Hispanic of any race (2010); Density: 1,291.7 persons per square mile (2010); Average household size: 2.28 (2010); Median age: 39.4 (2010); Males per 100 females: 88.5 (2010); Marriage status: 20.3% never married, 54.7% now married, 11.2% widowed, 13.8% divorced (2000); Foreign born: 0.7% (2000); Ancestry (includes multiple ancestries): 20.1% United States or American, 17.8% English, 13.2% German, 7.2% Irish, 5.2% Other groups (2000).

Economy: Single-family building permits issued: 1 (2009); Multi-family building permits issued: 0 (2009); Employment by occupation: 4.3% management, 9.9% professional, 17.9% services, 20.5% sales, 0.3% farming, 11.2% construction, 35.8% production (2000).

Income: Per capita income: $16,463 (2010); Median household income: $31,978 (2010); Average household income: $38,173 (2010); Percent of households with income of $100,000 or more: 3.1% (2010); Poverty rate: 16.9% (2000).

Taxes: Total city taxes per capita: $612 (2007); City property taxes per capita: $607 (2007).

Education: Percent of population age 25 and over with: High school diploma (including GED) or higher: 72.7% (2010); Bachelor's degree or higher: 6.9% (2010); Master's degree or higher: 2.7% (2010).

School District(s)

Mitchell Community Schools (PK-12)
    2008-09 Enrollment: 2,019 . . . . (812) 849-4481

Housing: Homeownership rate: 67.2% (2010); Median home value: $71,034 (2010); Median contract rent: $308 per month (2000); Median year structure built: 1965 (2000).

Newspapers: Mitchell Tribune (Community news; Circulation 2,800)

Transportation: Commute to work: 94.9% car, 0.3% public transportation, 1.2% walk, 2.0% work from home (2000); Travel time to work: 40.4% less than 15 minutes, 29.3% 15 to 30 minutes, 14.3% 30 to 45 minutes, 8.9% 45 to 60 minutes, 7.2% 60 minutes or more (2000)

Additional Information Contacts

City of Mitchell . . . . (812) 849-3831
    http://www.mitchell-in.gov

OOLITIC (town). Covers a land area of 0.805 square miles and a water area of 0 square miles. Located at 38.89° N. Lat; 86.52° W. Long. Elevation is 600 feet.

History: Oolitic was named for the oolitic texture of the limestone in the quarries that surround it, which provided the town with its early industry.

Population: 1,425 (1990); 1,152 (2000); 1,263 (2010); 1,281 (2015 projected); Race: 98.3% White, 0.0% Black, 0.2% Asian, 1.5% Other, 0.2% Hispanic of any race (2010); Density: 1,569.0 persons per square mile (2010); Average household size: 2.21 (2010); Median age: 40.3 (2010); Males per 100 females: 89.9 (2010); Marriage status: 19.5% never married, 58.0% now married, 7.2% widowed, 15.4% divorced (2000); Foreign born: 0.8% (2000); Ancestry (includes multiple ancestries): 16.4% United States or American, 9.4% Irish, 8.9% English, 8.5% German, 6.4% Other groups (2000).

Economy: Single-family building permits issued: 0 (2009); Multi-family building permits issued: 0 (2009); Employment by occupation: 5.5% management, 14.4% professional, 15.7% services, 22.1% sales, 1.1% farming, 11.4% construction, 29.9% production (2000).

Income: Per capita income: $20,063 (2010); Median household income: $35,121 (2010); Average household income: $44,650 (2010); Percent of households with income of $100,000 or more: 8.0% (2010); Poverty rate: 13.2% (2000).

Taxes: Total city taxes per capita: $111 (2007); City property taxes per capita: $92 (2007).

Education: Percent of population age 25 and over with: High school diploma (including GED) or higher: 83.6% (2010); Bachelor's degree or higher: 11.4% (2010); Master's degree or higher: 6.5% (2010).

School District(s)

North Lawrence Com Schools (PK-12)

    2008-09 Enrollment: 5,343 . . . . (812) 279-3521

Housing: Homeownership rate: 65.0% (2010); Median home value: $88,824 (2010); Median contract rent: $302 per month (2000); Median year structure built: 1963 (2000).

Transportation: Commute to work: 95.2% car, 0.0% public transportation, 1.2% walk, 1.4% work from home (2000); Travel time to work: 42.7% less than 15 minutes, 22.3% 15 to 30 minutes, 23.2% 30 to 45 minutes, 5.2% 45 to 60 minutes, 6.5% 60 minutes or more (2000)

SPRINGVILLE (unincorporated postal area, zip code 47462). Covers a land area of 75.918 square miles and a water area of 0.049 square miles. Located at 38.96° N. Lat; 86.63° W. Long. Elevation is 640 feet.

History: Laid out 1832.

Population: 4,834 (2000); Race: 97.1% White, 0.0% Black, 0.8% Asian, 2.1% Other, 0.2% Hispanic of any race (2000); Density: 63.7 persons per square mile (2000); Age: 24.7% under 18, 10.2% over 64 (2000); Marriage status: 16.7% never married, 68.1% now married, 4.8% widowed, 10.4% divorced (2000); Foreign born: 0.2% (2000); Ancestry (includes multiple ancestries): 16.1% United States or American, 10.6% Irish, 10.4% German, 9.0% Other groups, 5.1% English (2000).

Economy: Employment by occupation: 7.4% management, 14.6% professional, 15.2% services, 18.0% sales, 0.4% farming, 13.8% construction, 30.6% production (2000).

Income: Per capita income: $18,517 (2000); Median household income: $41,930 (2000); Poverty rate: 8.4% (2000).

Education: Percent of population age 25 and over with: High school diploma (including GED) or higher: 76.5% (2000); Bachelor's degree or higher: 7.2% (2000).

School District(s)

North Lawrence Com Schools (PK-12)

    2008-09 Enrollment: 5,343 . . . . (812) 279-3521

Housing: Homeownership rate: 90.1% (2000); Median home value: $81,000 (2000); Median contract rent: $337 per month (2000); Median year structure built: 1977 (2000).

Transportation: Commute to work: 95.5% car, 0.0% public transportation, 0.6% walk, 3.4% work from home (2000); Travel time to work: 13.6% less than 15 minutes, 47.3% 15 to 30 minutes, 27.1% 30 to 45 minutes, 6.3% 45 to 60 minutes, 5.7% 60 minutes or more (2000)

WILLIAMS (unincorporated postal area, zip code 47470). Covers a land area of 75.964 square miles and a water area of 0.137 square miles. Located at 38.84° N. Lat; 86.68° W. Long. Elevation is 574 feet.

Population: 1,691 (2000); Race: 99.3% White, 0.0% Black, 0.0% Asian, 0.7% Other, 0.0% Hispanic of any race (2000); Density: 22.3 persons per square mile (2000); Age: 29.8% under 18, 10.9% over 64 (2000); Marriage status: 20.0% never married, 64.0% now married, 8.5% widowed, 7.6% divorced (2000); Foreign born: 0.7% (2000); Ancestry (includes multiple ancestries): 23.3% United States or American, 19.5% Other groups, 19.4% German, 15.0% Irish, 11.2% English (2000).

Economy: Employment by occupation: 6.7% management, 16.5% professional, 11.8% services, 18.4% sales, 2.4% farming, 11.6% construction, 32.6% production (2000).

Income: Per capita income: $19,183 (2000); Median household income: $36,389 (2000); Poverty rate: 13.3% (2000).

Education: Percent of population age 25 and over with: High school diploma (including GED) or higher: 81.7% (2000); Bachelor's degree or higher: 11.9% (2000).

Housing: Homeownership rate: 85.7% (2000); Median home value: $69,700 (2000); Median contract rent: $250 per month (2000); Median year structure built: 1973 (2000).

Transportation: Commute to work: 93.5% car, 0.0% public transportation, 2.2% walk, 2.3% work from home (2000); Travel time to work: 13.2% less than 15 minutes, 50.9% 15 to 30 minutes, 13.2% 30 to 45 minutes, 14.3% 45 to 60 minutes, 8.5% 60 minutes or more (2000)

Madison County

Located in east central Indiana; drained by the West Fork of the White River and by many creeks. Covers a land area of 452.13 square miles, a water area of 0.78 square miles, and is located in the Eastern Time Zone. The county was founded in 1823. County seat is Anderson.

Madison County is part of the Anderson, IN Metropolitan Statistical Area. The entire metro area includes: Madison County, IN

Weather Station: Anderson Sewage Plant   Elevation: 843 feet

	Jan	Feb	Mar	Apr	May	Jun	Jul	Aug	Sep	Oct	Nov	Dec
High	33	38	49	61	71	80	84	82	75	64	50	38
Low	19	23	31	40	51	60	64	62	54	43	35	24
Precip	2.1	2.3	3.2	3.8	4.1	4.2	4.3	3.3	3.0	2.8	3.7	2.8
Snow	6.6	4.6	2.1	0.2	0.0	0.0	0.0	0.0	0.0	tr	0.7	3.6

High and Low temperatures in degrees Fahrenheit; Precipitation and Snow in inches

Weather Station: Elwood Wastewater Plant   Elevation: 839 feet

	Jan	Feb	Mar	Apr	May	Jun	Jul	Aug	Sep	Oct	Nov	Dec
High	32	37	48	61	72	81	85	83	77	65	51	38
Low	15	19	28	38	48	58	62	59	52	40	32	22
Precip	2.3	1.9	3.0	3.8	4.1	4.3	4.5	3.9	3.2	2.7	3.6	3.0
Snow	na	na	na	tr	0.0	0.0	0.0	0.0	0.0	tr	tr	na

High and Low temperatures in degrees Fahrenheit; Precipitation and Snow in inches

Population: 130,669 (1990); 133,358 (2000); 131,607 (2010); 130,361 (2015 projected); Race: 88.6% White, 8.3% Black, 0.5% Asian, 2.6% Other, 2.4% Hispanic of any race (2010); Density: 291.1 persons per square mile (2010); Average household size: 2.39 (2010); Median age: 39.6 (2010); Males per 100 females: 100.1 (2010).

Religion: Five largest groups: 6.1% Catholic Church, 4.5% The United Methodist Church, 4.2% Church of God (Anderson, Indiana), 3.1% American Baptist Churches in the USA, 2.7% Christian Church (Disciples of Christ) (2000).

Economy: Unemployment rate: 10.9% (5/2010); Total civilian labor force: 62,156 (5/2010); Leading industries: 20.2% health care and social assistance; 15.3% retail trade; 12.3% accommodation & food services (2008); Farms: 870 totaling 217,355 acres (2007); Companies that employ 500 or more persons: 4 (2008); Companies that employ 100 to 499 persons: 42 (2008); Companies that employ less than 100 persons: 2,453 (2008); Black-owned businesses: 238 (2002); Hispanic-owned businesses: 135 (2002); Asian-owned businesses: n/a (2002); Women-owned businesses: 2,281 (2002); Retail sales per capita: $12,394 (2010). Single-family building permits issued: 61 (2009); Multi-family building permits issued: 8 (2009).

Income: Per capita income: $22,676 (2010); Median household income: $44,343 (2010); Average household income: $55,846 (2010); Percent of households with income of $100,000 or more: 12.1% (2010); Poverty rate: 14.6% (2008); Bankruptcy rate: 9.01% (2009).

Taxes: Total county taxes per capita: $280 (2007); County property taxes per capita: $175 (2007).

Education: Percent of population age 25 and over with: High school diploma (including GED) or higher: 86.1% (2010); Bachelor's degree or higher: 16.9% (2010); Master's degree or higher: 6.9% (2010).

Housing: Homeownership rate: 75.5% (2010); Median home value: $88,526 (2010); Median contract rent: $483 per month (2006-2008 3-year est.); Median year structure built: 1962 (2006-2008 3-year est.)

Health: Birth rate: 123.0 per 10,000 population (2009); Death rate: 108.7 per 10,000 population (2009); Age-adjusted cancer mortality rate: 203.1 deaths per 100,000 population (2006); Air Quality Index: 72.1% good, 27.9% moderate, 0.0% unhealthy for sensitive individuals, 0.0% unhealthy (percent of days in 2008); Number of physicians: 11.5 per 10,000 population (2007); Hospital beds: 17.6 per 10,000 population (2006); Hospital admissions: 684.2 per 10,000 population (2006).

Elections: 2008 Presidential election results: 52.6% Obama, 46.0% McCain, 0.1% Nader

National and State Parks: Mounds State Park

Additional Information Contacts

Madison County Government . . . . (765) 641-9470
    http://www.madisoncty.com
Alexandria Monroe Chamber of Commerce . . . . (765) 724-3144
    http://www.alexandriachamber.com
Chamber of Commerce for Anderson & Madison County . . (765) 642-0264
    http://www.andersoninchamber.com
City of Alexandria. . . . . (765) 642-0264
    http://andersoninchamber.com
City of Anderson . . . . (765) 648-6000
    http://www.cityofanderson.com
City of Elwood . . . . (765) 552-5076
    http://www.elwoodindiana.org

Elwood Chamber of Commerce. (765) 552-0180
   http://www.elwoodchamber.org
Town of Chesterfield . . . . (765) 378-3331
   http://www.chesterfield.in.gov
Town of Pendleton. . . . . (765) 778-2173
   http://www.town.pendleton.in.us

Madison County Communities

ALEXANDRIA (city). Covers a land area of 2.712 square miles and a water area of 0 square miles. Located at 40.26° N. Lat; 85.67° W. Long. Elevation is 869 feet.
History: In Alexandria the Johns-Manville Company operated the first rock-wool insulation factory in the world, utilizing the argillaceous limestone found here.
Population: 5,783 (1990); 6,260 (2000); 5,985 (2010); 5,821 (2015 projected); Race: 97.4% White, 0.7% Black, 0.2% Asian, 1.7% Other, 1.4% Hispanic of any race (2010); Density: 2,207.2 persons per square mile (2010); Average household size: 2.49 (2010); Median age: 36.4 (2010); Males per 100 females: 96.9 (2010); Marriage status: 16.7% never married, 63.7% now married, 6.7% widowed, 12.9% divorced (2000); Foreign born: 1.0% (2000); Ancestry (includes multiple ancestries): 19.5% German, 15.1% English, 13.5% Other groups, 10.9% Irish, 5.5% United States or American (2000).
Economy: Single-family building permits issued: 0 (2009); Multi-family building permits issued: 0 (2009); Employment by occupation: 10.5% management, 12.2% professional, 15.0% services, 24.1% sales, 0.0% farming, 12.0% construction, 26.2% production (2000).
Income: Per capita income: $19,964 (2010); Median household income: $41,886 (2010); Average household income: $48,595 (2010); Percent of households with income of $100,000 or more: 5.8% (2010); Poverty rate: 7.0% (2000).
Taxes: Total city taxes per capita: $348 (2007); City property taxes per capita: $250 (2007).
Education: Percent of population age 25 and over with: High school diploma (including GED) or higher: 83.9% (2010); Bachelor's degree or higher: 11.4% (2010); Master's degree or higher: 4.9% (2010).
School District(s)
Alexandria Com School Corp (KG-12)
   2008-09 Enrollment: 1,549 . . . . (765) 724-4496
Two-year College(s)
Alexandria School of Scientific Therapeutics (Private, For-profit)
   Fall 2008 Enrollment: 56 . . . . (765) 724-9152
Housing: Homeownership rate: 70.5% (2010); Median home value: $83,118 (2010); Median contract rent: $400 per month (2000); Median year structure built: 1948 (2000).
Safety: Violent crime rate: 8.6 per 10,000 population; Property crime rate: 414.5 per 10,000 population (2008).
Newspapers: Alexandria Times-Tribune (Community news; Circulation 2,500)
Transportation: Commute to work: 93.6% car, 0.0% public transportation, 1.9% walk, 0.0% work from home (2000); Travel time to work: 33.1% less than 15 minutes, 37.3% 15 to 30 minutes, 12.5% 30 to 45 minutes, 4.8% 45 to 60 minutes, 12.3% 60 minutes or more (2000)
Additional Information Contacts
Alexandria Monroe Chamber of Commerce . . . . (765) 724-3144
   http://www.alexandriachamber.com
City of Alexandria. . . . . (765) 642-0264
   http://andersoninchamber.com

ANDERSON (city). County seat. Covers a land area of 40.047 square miles and a water area of 0.109 square miles. Located at 40.10° N. Lat; 85.68° W. Long. Elevation is 879 feet.
History: Anderson was platted in 1823 and named for Delaware Chief Kikthawenund, who was called Captain Anderson by the settlers. It was incorporated as Andersontown in 1838, and reincorporated as a city in 1865. The discovery of natural gas in 1886 brought industrial development, followed by the automotive industry.
Population: 59,652 (1990); 59,734 (2000); 56,970 (2010); 55,648 (2015 projected); Race: 80.5% White, 15.2% Black, 0.7% Asian, 3.7% Other, 3.6% Hispanic of any race (2010); Density: 1,422.6 persons per square mile (2010); Average household size: 2.26 (2010); Median age: 38.3 (2010); Males per 100 females: 93.1 (2010); Marriage status: 25.3% never married, 50.8% now married, 8.9% widowed, 14.9% divorced (2000); Foreign born: 1.8% (2000); Ancestry (includes multiple ancestries): 18.9%

Other groups, 15.9% United States or American, 14.8% German, 9.0% English, 7.8% Irish (2000).
Economy: Unemployment rate: 11.8% (5/2010); Total civilian labor force: 26,589 (5/2010); Single-family building permits issued: 22 (2009); Multi-family building permits issued: 6 (2009); Employment by occupation: 8.6% management, 14.2% professional, 19.0% services, 26.9% sales, 0.1% farming, 9.5% construction, 21.6% production (2000).
Income: Per capita income: $20,887 (2010); Median household income: $37,063 (2010); Average household income: $48,189 (2010); Percent of households with income of $100,000 or more: 8.1% (2010); Poverty rate: 13.4% (2000).
Taxes: Total city taxes per capita: $282 (2007); City property taxes per capita: $266 (2007).
Education: Percent of population age 25 and over with: High school diploma (including GED) or higher: 83.8% (2010); Bachelor's degree or higher: 16.2% (2010); Master's degree or higher: 6.9% (2010).
School District(s)
Anderson Community School Corp (PK-12)
   2008-09 Enrollment: 9,421 . . . . (765) 641-2028
Anderson Preparatory Academy (06-08)
   2008-09 Enrollment: 235 . . . . (765) 649-8472
Four-year College(s)
Anderson University (Private, Not-for-profit, Church of God)
   Fall 2008 Enrollment: 2,737. . . . . (765) 649-9071
   2009-10 Tuition: In-state $22,910; Out-of-state $22,910
Two-year College(s)
Indiana Business College-Anderson (Private, For-profit)
   Fall 2008 Enrollment: 202 . . . . (765) 644-7514
   2009-10 Tuition: In-state $11,535; Out-of-state $11,535
Vocational/Technical School(s)
Apex Academy of Hair Design Inc (Private, For-profit)
   Fall 2008 Enrollment: 16 . . . . (765) 642-7560
   2009-10 Tuition: $7,600
Housing: Homeownership rate: 65.8% (2010); Median home value: $71,303 (2010); Median contract rent: $400 per month (2000); Median year structure built: 1956 (2000).
Hospitals: Community Hospital of Anderson (132 beds); St. John's Health System (225 beds)
Safety: Violent crime rate: 34.9 per 10,000 population; Property crime rate: 507.4 per 10,000 population (2008).
Newspapers: Herald-Bulletin (Regional news; Circulation 39,937)
Transportation: Commute to work: 92.5% car, 1.0% public transportation, 3.6% walk, 2.4% work from home (2000); Travel time to work: 43.4% less than 15 minutes, 26.8% 15 to 30 minutes, 13.7% 30 to 45 minutes, 9.8% 45 to 60 minutes, 6.4% 60 minutes or more (2000)
Additional Information Contacts
Chamber of Commerce for Anderson & Madison County . . (765) 642-0264
   http://www.andersoninchamber.com
City of Anderson . . . . (765) 648-6000
   http://www.cityofanderson.com

CHESTERFIELD (town). Covers a land area of 1.148 square miles and a water area of 0 square miles. Located at 40.11° N. Lat; 85.59° W. Long. Elevation is 909 feet.
History: The Chesterfield Spiritualist Camp was built here in 1890 by Dr. J. Westerfield and his followers.
Population: 2,730 (1990); 2,969 (2000); 2,788 (2010); 2,699 (2015 projected); Race: 98.1% White, 0.6% Black, 0.3% Asian, 1.0% Other, 2.0% Hispanic of any race (2010); Density: 2,428.8 persons per square mile (2010); Average household size: 2.26 (2010); Median age: 38.7 (2010); Males per 100 females: 91.1 (2010); Marriage status: 21.1% never married, 57.1% now married, 9.2% widowed, 12.6% divorced (2000); Foreign born: 1.4% (2000); Ancestry (includes multiple ancestries): 19.2% United States or American, 13.0% German, 9.8% English, 6.4% Irish, 4.3% Other groups (2000).
Economy: Single-family building permits issued: 0 (2009); Multi-family building permits issued: 0 (2009); Employment by occupation: 6.7% management, 14.2% professional, 16.2% services, 25.6% sales, 0.6% farming, 11.6% construction, 25.1% production (2000).
Income: Per capita income: $21,689 (2010); Median household income: $42,785 (2010); Average household income: $49,699 (2010); Percent of households with income of $100,000 or more: 7.8% (2010); Poverty rate: 5.9% (2000).
Taxes: Total city taxes per capita: $150 (2007); City property taxes per capita: $142 (2007).

Education: Percent of population age 25 and over with: High school diploma (including GED) or higher: 88.7% (2010); Bachelor's degree or higher: 17.0% (2010); Master's degree or higher: 4.7% (2010).
Housing: Homeownership rate: 79.7% (2010); Median home value: $69,094 (2010); Median contract rent: $373 per month (2000); Median year structure built: 1958 (2000).
Safety: Violent crime rate: 14.6 per 10,000 population; Property crime rate: 211.8 per 10,000 population (2008).
Transportation: Commute to work: 95.6% car, 0.0% public transportation, 1.9% walk, 2.1% work from home (2000); Travel time to work: 28.5% less than 15 minutes, 43.5% 15 to 30 minutes, 10.4% 30 to 45 minutes, 10.3% 45 to 60 minutes, 7.3% 60 minutes or more (2000)
Additional Information Contacts
Town of Chesterfield . . . . (765) 378-3331
 http://www.chesterfield.in.gov

COUNTRY CLUB HEIGHTS (town). Covers a land area of 0.306 square miles and a water area of 0 square miles. Located at 40.12° N. Lat; 85.68° W. Long. Elevation is 879 feet.

Population: 112 (1990); 91 (2000); 73 (2010); 68 (2015 projected); Race: 91.8% White, 5.5% Black, 0.0% Asian, 2.7% Other, 2.7% Hispanic of any race (2010); Density: 238.9 persons per square mile (2010); Average household size: 2.35 (2010); Median age: 41.9 (2010); Males per 100 females: 97.3 (2010); Marriage status: 10.5% never married, 77.9% now married, 3.5% widowed, 8.1% divorced (2000); Foreign born: 0.0% (2000); Ancestry (includes multiple ancestries): 19.4% English, 18.3% German, 9.7% Scotch-Irish, 7.5% French (except Basque), 6.5% Irish (2000).
Economy: Employment by occupation: 25.0% management, 40.9% professional, 0.0% services, 29.5% sales, 0.0% farming, 0.0% construction, 4.5% production (2000).
Income: Per capita income: $20,235 (2010); Median household income: $36,250 (2010); Average household income: $59,919 (2010); Percent of households with income of $100,000 or more: 9.7% (2010); Poverty rate: 4.3% (2000).
Taxes: Total city taxes per capita: $264 (2007); City property taxes per capita: $264 (2007).
Education: Percent of population age 25 and over with: High school diploma (including GED) or higher: 84.3% (2010); Bachelor's degree or higher: 15.7% (2010); Master's degree or higher: 7.8% (2010).
Housing: Homeownership rate: 77.4% (2010); Median home value: $66,667 (2010); Median contract rent: $n/a per month (2000); Median year structure built: 1961 (2000).
Transportation: Commute to work: 100.0% car, 0.0% public transportation, 0.0% walk, 0.0% work from home (2000); Travel time to work: 81.8% less than 15 minutes, 9.1% 15 to 30 minutes, 4.5% 30 to 45 minutes, 0.0% 45 to 60 minutes, 4.5% 60 minutes or more (2000)

EDGEWOOD (town). Covers a land area of 0.805 square miles and a water area of 0 square miles. Located at 40.10° N. Lat; 85.73° W. Long. Elevation is 879 feet.

History: Edgewood grew as a residential suburb for employees of the manufacturing plants in nearby Anderson.
Population: 2,069 (1990); 1,988 (2000); 1,916 (2010); 1,865 (2015 projected); Race: 92.9% White, 5.4% Black, 0.2% Asian, 1.5% Other, 0.5% Hispanic of any race (2010); Density: 2,379.5 persons per square mile (2010); Average household size: 2.27 (2010); Median age: 47.4 (2010); Males per 100 females: 93.3 (2010); Marriage status: 13.3% never married, 70.1% now married, 8.1% widowed, 8.5% divorced (2000); Foreign born: 1.5% (2000); Ancestry (includes multiple ancestries): 23.7% German, 17.1% English, 15.5% Irish, 15.0% United States or American, 5.5% Other groups (2000).
Economy: Single-family building permits issued: 0 (2009); Multi-family building permits issued: 2 (2009); Employment by occupation: 16.2% management, 31.6% professional, 6.7% services, 30.2% sales, 0.0% farming, 5.7% construction, 9.5% production (2000).
Income: Per capita income: $35,399 (2010); Median household income: $64,959 (2010); Average household income: $79,891 (2010); Percent of households with income of $100,000 or more: 24.6% (2010); Poverty rate: 1.9% (2000).
Taxes: Total city taxes per capita: $104 (2007); City property taxes per capita: $82 (2007).
Education: Percent of population age 25 and over with: High school diploma (including GED) or higher: 96.5% (2010); Bachelor's degree or higher: 38.1% (2010); Master's degree or higher: 17.7% (2010).

Housing: Homeownership rate: 93.1% (2010); Median home value: $106,438 (2010); Median contract rent: $468 per month (2000); Median year structure built: 1956 (2000).
Transportation: Commute to work: 97.0% car, 0.0% public transportation, 0.0% walk, 2.6% work from home (2000); Travel time to work: 50.0% less than 15 minutes, 29.7% 15 to 30 minutes, 9.7% 30 to 45 minutes, 5.9% 45 to 60 minutes, 4.7% 60 minutes or more (2000)

ELWOOD (city). Covers a land area of 3.550 square miles and a water area of 0 square miles. Located at 40.27° N. Lat; 85.83° W. Long. Elevation is 860 feet.

History: Elwood was the birthplace of Wendell L. Wilkie, presidential nominee in 1940, who lived here until 1919. His speech accepting the nomination was made in Elwood.
Population: 9,767 (1990); 9,737 (2000); 8,976 (2010); 8,599 (2015 projected); Race: 97.9% White, 0.1% Black, 0.2% Asian, 1.9% Other, 2.1% Hispanic of any race (2010); Density: 2,528.8 persons per square mile (2010); Average household size: 2.50 (2010); Median age: 39.0 (2010); Males per 100 females: 96.9 (2010); Marriage status: 17.7% never married, 60.6% now married, 7.0% widowed, 14.6% divorced (2000); Foreign born: 1.3% (2000); Ancestry (includes multiple ancestries): 29.3% United States or American, 17.5% German, 11.1% Irish, 8.8% English, 8.7% Other groups (2000).
Economy: Single-family building permits issued: 2 (2009); Multi-family building permits issued: 0 (2009); Employment by occupation: 6.6% management, 10.8% professional, 16.8% services, 20.6% sales, 0.0% farming, 10.9% construction, 34.2% production (2000).
Income: Per capita income: $17,496 (2010); Median household income: $35,666 (2010); Average household income: $44,386 (2010); Percent of households with income of $100,000 or more: 7.0% (2010); Poverty rate: 15.2% (2000).
Taxes: Total city taxes per capita: $308 (2007); City property taxes per capita: $302 (2007).
Education: Percent of population age 25 and over with: High school diploma (including GED) or higher: 77.7% (2010); Bachelor's degree or higher: 8.0% (2010); Master's degree or higher: 3.4% (2010).
School District(s)
Elwood Community School Corp (PK-12)
 2008-09 Enrollment: 1,786 . . . . (765) 552-9861
Housing: Homeownership rate: 76.4% (2010); Median home value: $73,769 (2010); Median contract rent: $390 per month (2000); Median year structure built: before 1940 (2000).
Hospitals: St. Vincent Mercy Hospital (25 beds)
Safety: Violent crime rate: 6.7 per 10,000 population; Property crime rate: 747.1 per 10,000 population (2008).
Newspapers: Elwood Call-Leader (Community news; Circulation 4,000)
Transportation: Commute to work: 96.3% car, 0.0% public transportation, 2.9% walk, 0.3% work from home (2000); Travel time to work: 49.7% less than 15 minutes, 15.3% 15 to 30 minutes, 20.3% 30 to 45 minutes, 8.9% 45 to 60 minutes, 5.9% 60 minutes or more (2000)
Additional Information Contacts
City of Elwood . . . . (765) 552-5076
 http://www.elwoodindiana.org
Elwood Chamber of Commerce. . . . . (765) 552-0180
 http://www.elwoodchamber.org

FRANKTON (town). Covers a land area of 1.009 square miles and a water area of 0 square miles. Located at 40.22° N. Lat; 85.77° W. Long. Elevation is 837 feet.

Population: 1,795 (1990); 1,905 (2000); 1,802 (2010); 1,784 (2015 projected); Race: 96.6% White, 0.1% Black, 0.4% Asian, 2.9% Other, 2.6% Hispanic of any race (2010); Density: 1,786.0 persons per square mile (2010); Average household size: 2.50 (2010); Median age: 38.4 (2010); Males per 100 females: 97.4 (2010); Marriage status: 20.6% never married, 61.1% now married, 8.1% widowed, 10.2% divorced (2000); Foreign born: 0.7% (2000); Ancestry (includes multiple ancestries): 23.2% English, 20.3% German, 12.5% Irish, 8.2% United States or American, 8.0% Other groups (2000).
Economy: Single-family building permits issued: 0 (2009); Multi-family building permits issued: 0 (2009); Employment by occupation: 8.2% management, 11.9% professional, 17.9% services, 24.1% sales, 0.3% farming, 10.5% construction, 27.0% production (2000).
Income: Per capita income: $22,419 (2010); Median household income: $49,936 (2010); Average household income: $55,860 (2010); Percent of

households with income of $100,000 or more: 11.5% (2010); Poverty rate: 8.1% (2000).
Taxes: Total city taxes per capita: $99 (2007); City property taxes per capita: $61 (2007).
Education: Percent of population age 25 and over with: High school diploma (including GED) or higher: 88.6% (2010); Bachelor's degree or higher: 8.9% (2010); Master's degree or higher: 1.8% (2010).
School District(s)
Frankton-Lapel Community Schs (PK-12)
    2008-09 Enrollment: 2,541 . . . . (765) 734-1261
Housing: Homeownership rate: 88.3% (2010); Median home value: $85,090 (2010); Median contract rent: $377 per month (2000); Median year structure built: 1960 (2000).
Transportation: Commute to work: 97.5% car, 0.0% public transportation, 0.8% walk, 1.1% work from home (2000); Travel time to work: 22.5% less than 15 minutes, 37.9% 15 to 30 minutes, 22.0% 30 to 45 minutes, 9.4% 45 to 60 minutes, 8.2% 60 minutes or more (2000)

INGALLS (town). Covers a land area of 0.686 square miles and a water area of 0 square miles. Located at 39.95° N. Lat; 85.80° W. Long. Elevation is 866 feet.
Population: 889 (1990); 1,168 (2000); 1,101 (2010); 1,070 (2015 projected); Race: 96.1% White, 0.6% Black, 0.3% Asian, 3.0% Other, 1.6% Hispanic of any race (2010); Density: 1,606.0 persons per square mile (2010); Average household size: 2.71 (2010); Median age: 35.9 (2010); Males per 100 females: 103.9 (2010); Marriage status: 19.8% never married, 64.2% now married, 5.3% widowed, 10.7% divorced (2000); Foreign born: 0.4% (2000); Ancestry (includes multiple ancestries): 32.2% United States or American, 12.5% German, 8.5% English, 7.2% Other groups, 6.7% Irish (2000).
Economy: Single-family building permits issued: 1 (2009); Multi-family building permits issued: 0 (2009); Employment by occupation: 10.8% management, 5.0% professional, 15.5% services, 25.4% sales, 0.0% farming, 14.4% construction, 28.9% production (2000).
Income: Per capita income: $22,638 (2010); Median household income: $53,289 (2010); Average household income: $60,425 (2010); Percent of households with income of $100,000 or more: 12.6% (2010); Poverty rate: 5.4% (2000).
Taxes: Total city taxes per capita: $133 (2007); City property taxes per capita: $124 (2007).
Education: Percent of population age 25 and over with: High school diploma (including GED) or higher: 80.9% (2010); Bachelor's degree or higher: 4.4% (2010); Master's degree or higher: 0.7% (2010).
Housing: Homeownership rate: 83.7% (2010); Median home value: $92,281 (2010); Median contract rent: $467 per month (2000); Median year structure built: 1966 (2000).
Transportation: Commute to work: 94.7% car, 0.0% public transportation, 0.4% walk, 2.5% work from home (2000); Travel time to work: 15.2% less than 15 minutes, 26.2% 15 to 30 minutes, 37.4% 30 to 45 minutes, 15.7% 45 to 60 minutes, 5.6% 60 minutes or more (2000)

LAPEL (town). Covers a land area of 0.766 square miles and a water area of 0 square miles. Located at 40.06° N. Lat; 85.84° W. Long. Elevation is 860 feet.
History: Laid out 1876.
Population: 1,942 (1990); 1,855 (2000); 1,833 (2010); 1,766 (2015 projected); Race: 98.5% White, 0.1% Black, 0.1% Asian, 1.3% Other, 0.4% Hispanic of any race (2010); Density: 2,392.8 persons per square mile (2010); Average household size: 2.45 (2010); Median age: 38.2 (2010); Males per 100 females: 94.6 (2010); Marriage status: 20.5% never married, 58.7% now married, 8.2% widowed, 12.6% divorced (2000); Foreign born: 0.5% (2000); Ancestry (includes multiple ancestries): 27.0% United States or American, 18.9% German, 9.5% Irish, 8.3% English, 6.9% Other groups (2000).
Economy: Single-family building permits issued: 1 (2009); Multi-family building permits issued: 0 (2009); Employment by occupation: 9.9% management, 15.4% professional, 13.0% services, 28.3% sales, 0.2% farming, 13.3% construction, 19.9% production (2000).
Income: Per capita income: $20,910 (2010); Median household income: $43,017 (2010); Average household income: $50,821 (2010); Percent of households with income of $100,000 or more: 7.9% (2010); Poverty rate: 5.7% (2000).
Taxes: Total city taxes per capita: $94 (2007); City property taxes per capita: $89 (2007).

Education: Percent of population age 25 and over with: High school diploma (including GED) or higher: 88.9% (2010); Bachelor's degree or higher: 12.4% (2010); Master's degree or higher: 4.0% (2010).
School District(s)
Frankton-Lapel Community Schs (PK-12)
    2008-09 Enrollment: 2,541 . . . . (765) 734-1261
Housing: Homeownership rate: 78.8% (2010); Median home value: $98,395 (2010); Median contract rent: $391 per month (2000); Median year structure built: 1955 (2000).
Newspapers: Lapel Post (Community news; Circulation 850)
Transportation: Commute to work: 96.1% car, 0.0% public transportation, 2.3% walk, 1.3% work from home (2000); Travel time to work: 20.5% less than 15 minutes, 47.1% 15 to 30 minutes, 19.9% 30 to 45 minutes, 7.7% 45 to 60 minutes, 4.7% 60 minutes or more (2000)

MARKLEVILLE (town). Covers a land area of 0.406 square miles and a water area of 0 square miles. Located at 39.98° N. Lat; 85.61° W. Long. Elevation is 951 feet.
History: Laid out 1852.
Population: 412 (1990); 383 (2000); 363 (2010); 354 (2015 projected); Race: 98.9% White, 0.0% Black, 0.0% Asian, 1.1% Other, 0.8% Hispanic of any race (2010); Density: 894.4 persons per square mile (2010); Average household size: 2.75 (2010); Median age: 39.4 (2010); Males per 100 females: 100.6 (2010); Marriage status: 26.0% never married, 59.2% now married, 2.9% widowed, 11.8% divorced (2000); Foreign born: 0.0% (2000); Ancestry (includes multiple ancestries): 31.7% United States or American, 11.5% Irish, 9.9% German, 7.7% Other groups, 7.3% English (2000).
Economy: Employment by occupation: 8.9% management, 10.6% professional, 19.1% services, 23.8% sales, 0.0% farming, 13.5% construction, 24.1% production (2000).
Income: Per capita income: $23,489 (2010); Median household income: $57,353 (2010); Average household income: $64,962 (2010); Percent of households with income of $100,000 or more: 18.2% (2010); Poverty rate: 0.8% (2000).
Taxes: Total city taxes per capita: $128 (2007); City property taxes per capita: $122 (2007).
Education: Percent of population age 25 and over with: High school diploma (including GED) or higher: 95.9% (2010); Bachelor's degree or higher: 23.6% (2010); Master's degree or higher: 8.5% (2010).
Housing: Homeownership rate: 91.7% (2010); Median home value: $101,667 (2010); Median contract rent: $467 per month (2000); Median year structure built: 1949 (2000).
Transportation: Commute to work: 95.9% car, 0.0% public transportation, 3.0% walk, 1.0% work from home (2000); Travel time to work: 14.7% less than 15 minutes, 53.2% 15 to 30 minutes, 18.4% 30 to 45 minutes, 9.6% 45 to 60 minutes, 4.1% 60 minutes or more (2000)

ORESTES (town). Covers a land area of 0.394 square miles and a water area of 0 square miles. Located at 40.27° N. Lat; 85.72° W. Long. Elevation is 873 feet.
Population: 463 (1990); 334 (2000); 265 (2010); 242 (2015 projected); Race: 95.8% White, 0.0% Black, 0.0% Asian, 4.2% Other, 1.5% Hispanic of any race (2010); Density: 673.2 persons per square mile (2010); Average household size: 2.57 (2010); Median age: 39.4 (2010); Males per 100 females: 120.8 (2010); Marriage status: 24.2% never married, 56.0% now married, 4.8% widowed, 15.0% divorced (2000); Foreign born: 0.8% (2000); Ancestry (includes multiple ancestries): 23.5% English, 20.8% United States or American, 14.9% German, 14.3% Irish, 11.1% Other groups (2000).
Economy: Employment by occupation: 2.3% management, 3.5% professional, 14.6% services, 32.2% sales, 0.0% farming, 15.8% construction, 31.6% production (2000).
Income: Per capita income: $21,288 (2010); Median household income: $47,955 (2010); Average household income: $54,782 (2010); Percent of households with income of $100,000 or more: 8.7% (2010); Poverty rate: 3.8% (2000).
Taxes: Total city taxes per capita: $173 (2007); City property taxes per capita: $167 (2007).
Education: Percent of population age 25 and over with: High school diploma (including GED) or higher: 84.6% (2010); Bachelor's degree or higher: 4.4% (2010); Master's degree or higher: 1.1% (2010).
Housing: Homeownership rate: 84.5% (2010); Median home value: $73,889 (2010); Median contract rent: $319 per month (2000); Median year structure built: 1940 (2000).

Transportation: Commute to work: 98.8% car, 0.0% public transportation, 0.0% walk, 1.2% work from home (2000); Travel time to work: 26.7% less than 15 minutes, 29.1% 15 to 30 minutes, 33.9% 30 to 45 minutes, 7.3% 45 to 60 minutes, 3.0% 60 minutes or more (2000)

PENDLETON (town). Covers a land area of 6.705 square miles and a water area of 0.055 square miles. Located at 40.00° N. Lat; 85.74° W. Long. Elevation is 846 feet.

History: Pendleton was the county seat in the 1820's.
Population: 3,273 (1990); 3,873 (2000); 4,226 (2010); 4,361 (2015 projected); Race: 97.9% White, 0.5% Black, 0.4% Asian, 1.2% Other, 0.7% Hispanic of any race (2010); Density: 630.3 persons per square mile (2010); Average household size: 2.47 (2010); Median age: 38.9 (2010); Males per 100 females: 93.8 (2010); Marriage status: 16.5% never married, 60.7% now married, 8.5% widowed, 14.3% divorced (2000); Foreign born: 0.0% (2000); Ancestry (includes multiple ancestries): 17.7% United States or American, 16.8% German, 10.5% English, 4.6% Irish, 4.4% Other groups (2000).
Economy: Single-family building permits issued: 9 (2009); Multi-family building permits issued: 0 (2009); Employment by occupation: 13.8% management, 14.9% professional, 10.3% services, 29.1% sales, 0.0% farming, 10.9% construction, 21.0% production (2000).
Income: Per capita income: $28,900 (2010); Median household income: $63,616 (2010); Average household income: $71,469 (2010); Percent of households with income of $100,000 or more: 24.8% (2010); Poverty rate: 4.1% (2000).
Taxes: Total city taxes per capita: $344 (2007); City property taxes per capita: $323 (2007).
Education: Percent of population age 25 and over with: High school diploma (including GED) or higher: 94.2% (2010); Bachelor's degree or higher: 29.4% (2010); Master's degree or higher: 8.3% (2010).

School District(s)
IN Department of Correction (05-12)
    2008-09 Enrollment: 793 . . . . (317) 233-3111
South Madison Com Sch Corp (PK-12)
    2008-09 Enrollment: 4,177 . . . . (765) 778-2152

Housing: Homeownership rate: 78.9% (2010); Median home value: $131,686 (2010); Median contract rent: $508 per month (2000); Median year structure built: 1957 (2000).
Newspapers: Pendleton Times (Community news; Circulation 2,300)
Transportation: Commute to work: 95.0% car, 0.0% public transportation, 0.0% walk, 5.0% work from home (2000); Travel time to work: 34.6% less than 15 minutes, 30.1% 15 to 30 minutes, 22.9% 30 to 45 minutes, 9.9% 45 to 60 minutes, 2.5% 60 minutes or more (2000)
Additional Information Contacts
Town of Pendleton . . . . (765) 778-2173
    http://www.town.pendleton.in.us

RIVER FOREST (town). Covers a land area of 0.016 square miles and a water area of 0 square miles. Located at 40.11° N. Lat; 85.72° W. Long. Elevation is 873 feet.

Population: 16 (1990); 28 (2000); 20 (2010); 19 (2015 projected); Race: 65.0% White, 30.0% Black, 0.0% Asian, 5.0% Other, 0.0% Hispanic of any race (2010); Density: 1,246.4 persons per square mile (2010); Average household size: 2.50 (2010); Median age: 50.0 (2010); Males per 100 females: 100.0 (2010); Marriage status: 15.0% never married, 85.0% now married, 0.0% widowed, 0.0% divorced (2000); Foreign born: 0.0% (2000); Ancestry (includes multiple ancestries): 69.0% United States or American, 13.8% English, 6.9% French (except Basque), 6.9% Scottish, 6.9% Other groups (2000).
Economy: Employment by occupation: 25.0% management, 0.0% professional, 12.5% services, 62.5% sales, 0.0% farming, 0.0% construction, 0.0% production (2000).
Income: Per capita income: $30,802 (2010); Median household income: $62,500 (2010); Average household income: $68,750 (2010); Percent of households with income of $100,000 or more: 12.5% (2010); Poverty rate: 0.0% (2000).
Taxes: Total city taxes per capita: $222 (2007); City property taxes per capita: $148 (2007).
Education: Percent of population age 25 and over with: High school diploma (including GED) or higher: 92.9% (2010); Bachelor's degree or higher: 21.4% (2010); Master's degree or higher: 7.1% (2010).
Housing: Homeownership rate: 87.5% (2010); Median home value: $95,000 (2010); Median contract rent: $n/a per month (2000); Median year structure built: 1955 (2000).

Transportation: Commute to work: 100.0% car, 0.0% public transportation, 0.0% walk, 0.0% work from home (2000); Travel time to work: 12.5% less than 15 minutes, 50.0% 15 to 30 minutes, 37.5% 30 to 45 minutes, 0.0% 45 to 60 minutes, 0.0% 60 minutes or more (2000)

SUMMITVILLE (town). Covers a land area of 0.539 square miles and a water area of 0 square miles. Located at 40.33° N. Lat; 85.64° W. Long. Elevation is 883 feet.

History: Laid out 1867.
Population: 1,015 (1990); 1,090 (2000); 1,026 (2010); 995 (2015 projected); Race: 99.3% White, 0.5% Black, 0.1% Asian, 0.1% Other, 0.4% Hispanic of any race (2010); Density: 1,904.8 persons per square mile (2010); Average household size: 2.57 (2010); Median age: 37.8 (2010); Males per 100 females: 95.4 (2010); Marriage status: 17.3% never married, 67.3% now married, 6.3% widowed, 9.1% divorced (2000); Foreign born: 0.0% (2000); Ancestry (includes multiple ancestries): 16.2% United States or American, 14.3% German, 10.2% Irish, 9.4% English, 6.6% Other groups (2000).
Economy: Single-family building permits issued: 0 (2009); Multi-family building permits issued: 0 (2009); Employment by occupation: 11.5% management, 12.5% professional, 15.8% services, 19.9% sales, 0.4% farming, 10.2% construction, 29.7% production (2000).
Income: Per capita income: $19,647 (2010); Median household income: $42,147 (2010); Average household income: $52,067 (2010); Percent of households with income of $100,000 or more: 11.1% (2010); Poverty rate: 7.9% (2000).
Taxes: Total city taxes per capita: $135 (2007); City property taxes per capita: $133 (2007).
Education: Percent of population age 25 and over with: High school diploma (including GED) or higher: 81.9% (2010); Bachelor's degree or higher: 10.2% (2010); Master's degree or higher: 3.5% (2010).

School District(s)
Madison-Grant United Sch Corp (PK-12)
    2008-09 Enrollment: 1,516 . . . . (765) 948-4143

Housing: Homeownership rate: 80.9% (2010); Median home value: $75,167 (2010); Median contract rent: $311 per month (2000); Median year structure built: 1948 (2000).
Transportation: Commute to work: 91.5% car, 0.0% public transportation, 4.9% walk, 2.5% work from home (2000); Travel time to work: 20.2% less than 15 minutes, 38.2% 15 to 30 minutes, 27.5% 30 to 45 minutes, 9.5% 45 to 60 minutes, 4.6% 60 minutes or more (2000)

WOODLAWN HEIGHTS (town). Covers a land area of 0.120 square miles and a water area of 0 square miles. Located at 40.11° N. Lat; 85.69° W. Long. Elevation is 866 feet.

Population: 109 (1990); 73 (2000); 65 (2010); 63 (2015 projected); Race: 92.3% White, 3.1% Black, 1.5% Asian, 3.1% Other, 3.1% Hispanic of any race (2010); Density: 540.5 persons per square mile (2010); Average household size: 2.60 (2010); Median age: 44.4 (2010); Males per 100 females: 85.7 (2010); Marriage status: 8.2% never married, 91.8% now married, 0.0% widowed, 0.0% divorced (2000); Foreign born: 0.0% (2000); Ancestry (includes multiple ancestries): 49.1% English, 28.3% German, 13.2% Irish, 13.2% Dutch, 11.3% French (except Basque) (2000).
Economy: Employment by occupation: 45.5% management, 33.3% professional, 0.0% services, 12.1% sales, 0.0% farming, 9.1% construction, 0.0% production (2000).
Income: Per capita income: $30,276 (2010); Median household income: $54,688 (2010); Average household income: $70,000 (2010); Percent of households with income of $100,000 or more: 16.0% (2010); Poverty rate: 5.7% (2000).
Taxes: Total city taxes per capita: $70 (2007); City property taxes per capita: $70 (2007).
Education: Percent of population age 25 and over with: High school diploma (including GED) or higher: 91.1% (2010); Bachelor's degree or higher: 22.2% (2010); Master's degree or higher: 6.7% (2010).
Housing: Homeownership rate: 92.0% (2010); Median home value: $82,000 (2010); Median contract rent: $275 per month (2000); Median year structure built: 1972 (2000).
Transportation: Commute to work: 100.0% car, 0.0% public transportation, 0.0% walk, 0.0% work from home (2000); Travel time to work: 51.5% less than 15 minutes, 24.2% 15 to 30 minutes, 15.2% 30 to 45 minutes, 0.0% 45 to 60 minutes, 9.1% 60 minutes or more (2000)

Marion County

Located in central Indiana; drained by the West Fork of the White River. Covers a land area of 396.25 square miles, a water area of 6.79 square miles, and is located in the Eastern Time Zone. The county was founded in 1821. County seat is Indianapolis.

Marion County is part of the Indianapolis-Carmel, IN Metropolitan Statistical Area. The entire metro area includes: Boone County, IN; Brown County, IN; Hamilton County, IN; Hancock County, IN; Hendricks County, IN; Johnson County, IN; Marion County, IN; Morgan County, IN; Putnam County, IN; Shelby County, IN

Weather Station: Indianapolis Int'l Airport   Elevation: 790 feet

	Jan	Feb	Mar	Apr	May	Jun	Jul	Aug	Sep	Oct	Nov	Dec
High	34	40	51	63	74	82	86	84	78	66	52	40
Low	18	22	32	42	52	62	66	64	56	44	34	25
Precip	2.5	2.4	3.5	3.7	4.3	4.0	4.5	3.7	2.8	2.8	3.6	3.0
Snow	9.2	6.3	3.0	0.4	tr	tr	0.0	tr	0.0	0.4	1.3	5.8

High and Low temperatures in degrees Fahrenheit; Precipitation and Snow in inches

Weather Station: Indianapolis SE Side   Elevation: 843 feet

	Jan	Feb	Mar	Apr	May	Jun	Jul	Aug	Sep	Oct	Nov	Dec
High	34	39	50	62	73	81	85	83	77	65	51	40
Low	18	21	31	41	52	61	65	63	55	43	34	24
Precip	2.0	2.0	3.1	3.8	4.6	4.1	4.9	3.6	2.5	2.8	3.7	2.8
Snow	na	na	0.9	0.1	tr	0.0	0.0	0.0	0.0	0.2	0.2	1.4

High and Low temperatures in degrees Fahrenheit; Precipitation and Snow in inches

Weather Station: Oaklandon Geist Reservoir   Elevation: 793 feet

	Jan	Feb	Mar	Apr	May	Jun	Jul	Aug	Sep	Oct	Nov	Dec
High	33	38	49	62	72	81	84	83	77	65	51	39
Low	17	19	29	39	50	60	64	61	54	42	33	23
Precip	2.3	2.3	3.4	4.0	4.8	4.1	4.7	4.0	3.4	3.1	3.9	3.2
Snow	7.6	5.7	2.8	0.4	0.0	0.0	0.0	0.0	0.0	0.3	0.9	5.4

High and Low temperatures in degrees Fahrenheit; Precipitation and Snow in inches

Population: 797,159 (1990); 860,454 (2000); 885,200 (2010); 892,917 (2015 projected); Race: 66.2% White, 25.7% Black, 1.6% Asian, 6.5% Other, 7.8% Hispanic of any race (2010); Density: 2,233.9 persons per square mile (2010); Average household size: 2.38 (2010); Median age: 36.1 (2010); Males per 100 females: 94.8 (2010).
Religion: Five largest groups: 12.7% Catholic Church, 3.7% The United Methodist Church, 2.9% Christian Churches and Churches of Christ, 2.6% Independent, Non-Charismatic Churches, 2.0% Christian Church (Disciples of Christ) (2000).
Economy: Unemployment rate: 9.7% (5/2010); Total civilian labor force: 449,527 (5/2010); Leading industries: 14.1% health care and social assistance; 10.3% manufacturing; 9.8% retail trade (2008); Farms: 263 totaling 17,233 acres (2007); Companies that employ 500 or more persons: 83 (2008); Companies that employ 100 to 499 persons: 788 (2008); Companies that employ less than 100 persons: 23,318 (2008); Black-owned businesses: 5,822 (2002); Hispanic-owned businesses: 857 (2002); Asian-owned businesses: 1,400 (2002); Women-owned businesses: 16,820 (2002); Retail sales per capita: $16,751 (2010). Single-family building permits issued: 638 (2009); Multi-family building permits issued: 454 (2009).
Income: Per capita income: $25,122 (2010); Median household income: $46,180 (2010); Average household income: $60,544 (2010); Percent of households with income of $100,000 or more: 14.3% (2010); Poverty rate: 16.5% (2008); Bankruptcy rate: 8.46% (2009).
Education: Percent of population age 25 and over with: High school diploma (including GED) or higher: 84.6% (2010); Bachelor's degree or higher: 27.8% (2010); Master's degree or higher: 9.9% (2010).
Housing: Homeownership rate: 60.7% (2010); Median home value: $117,370 (2010); Median contract rent: $575 per month (2006-2008 3-year est.); Median year structure built: 1968 (2006-2008 3-year est.)
Health: Birth rate: 160.4 per 10,000 population (2009); Death rate: 82.0 per 10,000 population (2009); Age-adjusted cancer mortality rate: 210.4 deaths per 100,000 population (2006); Air Quality Index: 58.2% good, 41.3% moderate, 0.5% unhealthy for sensitive individuals, 0.0% unhealthy (percent of days in 2008); Number of physicians: 25.4 per 10,000 population (2007); Hospital beds: 55.2 per 10,000 population (2006); Hospital admissions: 2,112.1 per 10,000 population (2006).
Elections: 2008 Presidential election results: 63.7% Obama, 35.3% McCain, 0.0% Nader
Additional Information Contacts

Marion County Government. . . . . (317) 327-4740
   http://www.indy.gov
City of Beech Grove. . . . . (317) 788-4977
   http://www.beechgrove.com
City of Indianapolis. . . . . (317) 327-4622
   http://www.indygov.org
City of Lawrence . . . . (317) 549-8670
   http://www.cityoflawrence.org
Greater Indianapolis Chamber of Commerce . . . . (317) 464-2222
   http://www.indychamber.com
Indiana Chamber of Commerce. . . . . (317) 264-3110
   http://www.indianachamber.com
Lawrence Chamber of Commerce. . . . . (317) 541-9876
   http://www.lawrencechamberofcommerce.org
Marion/Indianapolis County Government. . . . . (317) 327-4622
   http:www//indygov.org
Speedway Chamber of Commerce . . . . (317) 244-3789
   http://www.in.gov/mylocal
Town of Cumberland . . . . (317) 894-6213
   http://www.town.cumberland.in.us
Town of Speedway . . . . (317) 246-4111
   http://www.townofspeedway.org

Marion County Communities

BEECH GROVE (city). Covers a land area of 4.297 square miles and a water area of 0 square miles. Located at 39.71° N. Lat; 86.09° W. Long. Elevation is 804 feet.
History: Named for the many local beech trees. Incorporated 1906.
Population: 13,663 (1990); 14,880 (2000); 13,625 (2010); 13,217 (2015 projected); Race: 94.2% White, 1.1% Black, 0.9% Asian, 3.8% Other, 4.7% Hispanic of any race (2010); Density: 3,170.5 persons per square mile (2010); Average household size: 2.36 (2010); Median age: 38.4 (2010); Males per 100 females: 90.0 (2010); Marriage status: 25.2% never married, 52.1% now married, 8.4% widowed, 14.4% divorced (2000); Foreign born: 1.7% (2000); Ancestry (includes multiple ancestries): 27.9% German, 20.2% United States or American, 18.8% Irish, 11.8% English, 8.3% Other groups (2000).
Economy: Single-family building permits issued: 0 (2009); Multi-family building permits issued: 0 (2009); Employment by occupation: 8.2% management, 16.8% professional, 15.9% services, 29.1% sales, 0.0% farming, 10.7% construction, 19.3% production (2000).
Income: Per capita income: $23,808 (2010); Median household income: $47,895 (2010); Average household income: $56,451 (2010); Percent of households with income of $100,000 or more: 11.6% (2010); Poverty rate: 6.1% (2000).
Taxes: Total city taxes per capita: $326 (2007); City property taxes per capita: $290 (2007).
Education: Percent of population age 25 and over with: High school diploma (including GED) or higher: 85.4% (2010); Bachelor's degree or higher: 19.6% (2010); Master's degree or higher: 8.1% (2010).
School District(s)
Beech Grove City Schools (PK-12)
   2008-09 Enrollment: 2,311 . . . . (317) 788-4481
Housing: Homeownership rate: 64.7% (2010); Median home value: $109,615 (2010); Median contract rent: $502 per month (2000); Median year structure built: 1963 (2000).
Hospitals: St. Francis Beech Grove (500 beds)
Safety: Violent crime rate: 24.0 per 10,000 population; Property crime rate: 368.5 per 10,000 population (2008).
Newspapers: Perry Township Weekly (Local news; Circulation 24,000); Southside Times (Community news; Circulation 25,000)
Transportation: Commute to work: 93.8% car, 1.4% public transportation, 2.0% walk, 2.3% work from home (2000); Travel time to work: 28.2% less than 15 minutes, 41.0% 15 to 30 minutes, 17.0% 30 to 45 minutes, 3.3% 45 to 60 minutes, 10.5% 60 minutes or more (2000)
Additional Information Contacts
City of Beech Grove. . . . . (317) 788-4977
   http://www.beechgrove.com
Marion/Indianapolis County Government. . . . . (317) 327-4622
   http:www//indygov.org

CAMBY (unincorporated postal area, zip code 46113). Part of the City of Indianapolis. Covers a land area of 17.365 square miles and a water area

of 0.074 square miles. Located at 39.63° N. Lat; 86.31° W. Long. Elevation is 764 feet.
Population: 6,666 (2000); Race: 98.1% White, 0.0% Black, 0.7% Asian, 1.2% Other, 0.0% Hispanic of any race (2000); Density: 383.9 persons per square mile (2000); Age: 26.9% under 18, 10.1% over 64 (2000); Marriage status: 17.3% never married, 67.2% now married, 4.5% widowed, 11.0% divorced (2000); Foreign born: 1.0% (2000); Ancestry (includes multiple ancestries): 21.8% German, 14.9% Irish, 13.4% United States or American, 11.1% Other groups, 8.7% English (2000).
Economy: Single-family building permits issued: 587 (2009); Multi-family building permits issued: 454 (2009); Employment by occupation: 12.7% management, 11.1% professional, 12.6% services, 30.4% sales, 0.5% farming, 17.1% construction, 15.5% production (2000).
Income: Per capita income: $20,324 (2000); Median household income: $52,352 (2000); Poverty rate: 7.0% (2000).
Education: Percent of population age 25 and over with: High school diploma (including GED) or higher: 80.8% (2000); Bachelor's degree or higher: 12.5% (2000).

School District(s)
Mooresville Con School Corp (PK-12)
    2008-09 Enrollment: 4,437 . . . . (317) 831-0950
Housing: Homeownership rate: 89.3% (2000); Median home value: $118,300 (2000); Median contract rent: $460 per month (2000); Median year structure built: 1979 (2000).
Transportation: Commute to work: 96.8% car, 0.0% public transportation, 0.5% walk, 1.6% work from home (2000); Travel time to work: 18.1% less than 15 minutes, 40.9% 15 to 30 minutes, 29.9% 30 to 45 minutes, 6.7% 45 to 60 minutes, 4.3% 60 minutes or more (2000)

CLERMONT (town). Covers a land area of 0.681 square miles and a water area of 0 square miles. Located at 39.81° N. Lat; 86.32° W. Long. Elevation is 833 feet.
History: When Clermont was platted in 1849 it was called Mechanicsburg, but the name was changed in 1855.
Population: 1,678 (1990); 1,477 (2000); 1,589 (2010); 1,697 (2015 projected); Race: 87.5% White, 6.6% Black, 2.7% Asian, 3.2% Other, 3.2% Hispanic of any race (2010); Density: 2,332.1 persons per square mile (2010); Average household size: 2.46 (2010); Median age: 39.3 (2010); Males per 100 females: 98.4 (2010); Marriage status: 24.0% never married, 60.2% now married, 6.6% widowed, 9.2% divorced (2000); Foreign born: 2.4% (2000); Ancestry (includes multiple ancestries): 25.3% German, 15.7% Irish, 12.1% Other groups, 11.5% English, 9.5% United States or American (2000).
Economy: Employment by occupation: 16.7% management, 15.9% professional, 8.6% services, 35.2% sales, 0.0% farming, 11.3% construction, 12.3% production (2000).
Income: Per capita income: $36,546 (2010); Median household income: $73,833 (2010); Average household income: $89,853 (2010); Percent of households with income of $100,000 or more: 28.5% (2010); Poverty rate: 6.8% (2000).
Taxes: Total city taxes per capita: $110 (2007); City property taxes per capita: $110 (2007).
Education: Percent of population age 25 and over with: High school diploma (including GED) or higher: 95.1% (2010); Bachelor's degree or higher: 36.6% (2010); Master's degree or higher: 15.4% (2010).
Housing: Homeownership rate: 88.2% (2010); Median home value: $140,647 (2010); Median contract rent: $607 per month (2000); Median year structure built: 1964 (2000).
Transportation: Commute to work: 97.0% car, 0.0% public transportation, 0.0% walk, 3.0% work from home (2000); Travel time to work: 10.1% less than 15 minutes, 57.5% 15 to 30 minutes, 26.4% 30 to 45 minutes, 2.4% 45 to 60 minutes, 3.7% 60 minutes or more (2000)

CROWS NEST (town). Covers a land area of 0.446 square miles and a water area of 0 square miles. Located at 39.85° N. Lat; 86.17° W. Long. Elevation is 774 feet.
History: Joined Indianapolis in 1970.
Population: 114 (1990); 96 (2000); 70 (2010); 68 (2015 projected); Race: 47.1% White, 50.0% Black, 1.4% Asian, 1.4% Other, 2.9% Hispanic of any race (2010); Density: 156.9 persons per square mile (2010); Average household size: 2.69 (2010); Median age: 35.9 (2010); Males per 100 females: 100.0 (2010); Marriage status: 18.2% never married, 66.2% now married, 0.0% widowed, 15.6% divorced (2000); Foreign born: 0.0% (2000); Ancestry (includes multiple ancestries): 36.9% English, 13.1%

German, 10.7% Swedish, 8.3% Scotch-Irish, 7.1% French (except Basque) (2000).
Economy: Employment by occupation: 42.2% management, 42.2% professional, 0.0% services, 6.7% sales, 0.0% farming, 0.0% construction, 8.9% production (2000).
Income: Per capita income: $38,258 (2010); Median household income: $75,000 (2010); Average household income: $101,154 (2010); Percent of households with income of $100,000 or more: 34.6% (2010); Poverty rate: 0.0% (2000).
Taxes: Total city taxes per capita: $0 (2007); City property taxes per capita: $0 (2007).
Education: Percent of population age 25 and over with: High school diploma (including GED) or higher: 97.6% (2010); Bachelor's degree or higher: 61.0% (2010); Master's degree or higher: 31.7% (2010).
Housing: Homeownership rate: 96.2% (2010); Median home value: $243,750 (2010); Median contract rent: $1,125 per month (2000); Median year structure built: before 1940 (2000).
Transportation: Commute to work: 100.0% car, 0.0% public transportation, 0.0% walk, 0.0% work from home (2000); Travel time to work: 13.3% less than 15 minutes, 86.7% 15 to 30 minutes, 0.0% 30 to 45 minutes, 0.0% 45 to 60 minutes, 0.0% 60 minutes or more (2000)

CUMBERLAND (town). Covers a land area of 1.892 square miles and a water area of 0.035 square miles. Located at 39.78° N. Lat; 85.95° W. Long. Elevation is 853 feet.
History: The Town was officially platted on July 7, 1831 and originally had just six streets. The first Cumberland Post Office was established in 1842.
Population: 5,021 (1990); 5,500 (2000); 5,729 (2010); 5,996 (2015 projected); Race: 78.2% White, 17.1% Black, 1.6% Asian, 3.0% Other, 2.4% Hispanic of any race (2010); Density: 3,028.1 persons per square mile (2010); Average household size: 2.68 (2010); Median age: 37.2 (2010); Males per 100 females: 95.7 (2010); Marriage status: 24.1% never married, 61.7% now married, 4.8% widowed, 9.4% divorced (2000); Foreign born: 2.9% (2000); Ancestry (includes multiple ancestries): 26.4% German, 16.5% Other groups, 11.3% United States or American, 11.3% Irish, 9.7% English (2000).
Economy: Employment by occupation: 15.6% management, 19.0% professional, 10.3% services, 32.8% sales, 0.0% farming, 8.5% construction, 13.8% production (2000).
Income: Per capita income: $30,019 (2010); Median household income: $67,816 (2010); Average household income: $80,587 (2010); Percent of households with income of $100,000 or more: 26.2% (2010); Poverty rate: 6.6% (2000).
Education: Percent of population age 25 and over with: High school diploma (including GED) or higher: 92.9% (2010); Bachelor's degree or higher: 30.5% (2010); Master's degree or higher: 12.9% (2010).
Housing: Homeownership rate: 81.9% (2010); Median home value: $140,261 (2010); Median contract rent: $435 per month (2000); Median year structure built: 1983 (2000).
Transportation: Commute to work: 92.6% car, 1.5% public transportation, 1.3% walk, 3.7% work from home (2000); Travel time to work: 24.4% less than 15 minutes, 40.4% 15 to 30 minutes, 29.2% 30 to 45 minutes, 3.2% 45 to 60 minutes, 2.8% 60 minutes or more (2000)
Additional Information Contacts
Town of Cumberland . . . . (317) 894-6213
    http://www.town.cumberland.in.us

HOMECROFT (town). Covers a land area of 0.232 square miles and a water area of 0 square miles. Located at 39.66° N. Lat; 86.13° W. Long. Elevation is 758 feet.
Population: 772 (1990); 751 (2000); 721 (2010); 694 (2015 projected); Race: 97.5% White, 0.6% Black, 0.7% Asian, 1.2% Other, 3.2% Hispanic of any race (2010); Density: 3,113.9 persons per square mile (2010); Average household size: 2.28 (2010); Median age: 44.1 (2010); Males per 100 females: 95.9 (2010); Marriage status: 20.1% never married, 62.0% now married, 7.5% widowed, 10.3% divorced (2000); Foreign born: 2.0% (2000); Ancestry (includes multiple ancestries): 32.1% German, 13.9% United States or American, 13.0% Irish, 10.4% English, 3.9% Other groups (2000).
Economy: Employment by occupation: 17.7% management, 26.0% professional, 12.2% services, 27.6% sales, 0.0% farming, 6.0% construction, 10.4% production (2000).
Income: Per capita income: $33,509 (2010); Median household income: $65,714 (2010); Average household income: $76,021 (2010); Percent of

households with income of $100,000 or more: 24.1% (2010); Poverty rate: 2.1% (2000).

Taxes: Total city taxes per capita: $87 (2007); City property taxes per capita: $83 (2007).

Education: Percent of population age 25 and over with: High school diploma (including GED) or higher: 91.8% (2010); Bachelor's degree or higher: 33.3% (2010); Master's degree or higher: 12.7% (2010).

Housing: Homeownership rate: 79.1% (2010); Median home value: $135,473 (2010); Median contract rent: $670 per month (2000); Median year structure built: 1948 (2000).

Transportation: Commute to work: 93.7% car, 0.5% public transportation, 1.3% walk, 3.9% work from home (2000); Travel time to work: 26.4% less than 15 minutes, 48.2% 15 to 30 minutes, 18.8% 30 to 45 minutes, 3.0% 45 to 60 minutes, 3.5% 60 minutes or more (2000)

INDIANAPOLIS (special city). County seat. Covers a land area of 361.480 square miles and a water area of 6.678 square miles. Located at 39.79° N. Lat; 86.14° W. Long. Elevation is 715 feet.

History: Settlement began in Indianapolis in 1820, when several families built cabins here and called it Fall Creek. That same year, Fall Creek was selected as the site for Indiana's capital because of its location near the center of the state. The new city was named Indianapolis in 1821; the first legislature met here in 1825. Indianapolis was incorporated as a city in 1847. Henry Ward Beecher, well-known writer, preacher, and brother of Harriet Beecher Stowe, lived in Indianapolis at that time.

Population: 730,993 (1990); 781,870 (2000); 802,032 (2010); 807,668 (2015 projected); Race: 65.3% White, 26.6% Black, 1.6% Asian, 6.6% Other, 7.9% Hispanic of any race (2010); Density: 2,218.7 persons per square mile (2010); Average household size: 2.37 (2010); Median age: 36.1 (2010); Males per 100 females: 95.1 (2010); Marriage status: 31.8% never married, 48.7% now married, 6.4% widowed, 13.1% divorced (2000); Foreign born: 4.6% (2000); Ancestry (includes multiple ancestries): 30.0% Other groups, 16.6% German, 10.2% Irish, 9.3% United States or American, 7.7% English (2000).

Economy: Unemployment rate: 9.7% (5/2010); Total civilian labor force: 411,848 (5/2010); Single-family building permits issued: 587 (2009); Multi-family building permits issued: 454 (2009); Employment by occupation: 13.1% management, 19.6% professional, 14.9% services, 28.3% sales, 0.1% farming, 8.6% construction, 15.2% production (2000).

Income: Per capita income: $24,937 (2010); Median household income: $45,657 (2010); Average household income: $59,953 (2010); Percent of households with income of $100,000 or more: 14.0% (2010); Poverty rate: 11.9% (2000).

Taxes: Total city taxes per capita: $1,185 (2007); City property taxes per capita: $913 (2007).

Education: Percent of population age 25 and over with: High school diploma (including GED) or higher: 84.2% (2010); Bachelor's degree or higher: 27.7% (2010); Master's degree or higher: 9.9% (2010).

School District(s)

Andrew J Brown Academy (KG-08)
    2008-09 Enrollment: 663 . . . . (317) 891-0730
Carmel Clay Schools (PK-12)
    2008-09 Enrollment: 15,319 . . . . (317) 844-9961
Challenge Foundation Academy (KG-05)
    2008-09 Enrollment: 393 . . . . (317) 803-3182
Charles A Tindley Accelerated Schl (06-12)
    2008-09 Enrollment: 404 . . . . (317) 545-1745
Christel House Academy (KG-08)
    2008-09 Enrollment: 416 . . . . (317) 783-4690
Decatur Discovery Academy Inc (07-12)
    2008-09 Enrollment: 186 . . . . (317) 856-0900
Fall Creek Academy (KG-12)
    2008-09 Enrollment: 352 . . . . (317) 536-1027
Flanner House Elementary School (KG-06)
    2008-09 Enrollment: 210 . . . . (317) 925-4231
Fountain Square Academy (05-12)
    2008-09 Enrollment: 206 . . . . (317) 536-1027
Franklin Township Com Sch Corp (PK-12)
    2008-09 Enrollment: 8,828 . . . . (317) 862-2411
Herron Charter (09-12)
    2008-09 Enrollment: 333 . . . . (317) 231-0010
Hoosier Academy - Indianapolis (KG-10)
    2008-09 Enrollment: 295 . . . . (317) 547-1400
Hope Academy (09-12)
    2008-09 Enrollment: 35 . . . . (317) 572-9356

IN Department of Correction (05-12)
    2008-09 Enrollment: 793 . . . . (317) 233-3111
IN Sch for the Blind & Vis Imprd (PK-12)
    2008-09 Enrollment: 153 . . . . (317) 253-1481
Imagine Life Sciences Acad - East (KG-05)
    2008-09 Enrollment: 597 . . . . (317) 292-0061
Indiana Math and Science Academy (06-09)
    2008-09 Enrollment: 230 . . . . (317) 298-0025
Indiana School For The Deaf (PK-12)
    2008-09 Enrollment: 336 . . . . (317) 924-8400
Indianapolis Metropolitan High Sch (09-12)
    2008-09 Enrollment: 342 . . . . (317) 524-4501
Indianapolis Public Schools (PK-12)
    2008-09 Enrollment: 34,050 . . . . (317) 226-4411
Indpls Lighthouse Charter School (PK-08)
    2008-09 Enrollment: 530 . . . . (317) 897-2430
Irvington Community School (KG-11)
    2008-09 Enrollment: 619 . . . . (317) 357-5359
Kipp Indpls College Preparatory (05-08)
    2008-09 Enrollment: 238 . . . . (317) 637-9780
Lawrence Early College Hs For S&T (09-12)
    2008-09 Enrollment: 192 . . . . (317) 964-8080
M S D Decatur Township (KG-12)
    2008-09 Enrollment: 6,342 . . . . (317) 856-5265
M S D Lawrence Township (PK-12)
    2008-09 Enrollment: 16,119 . . . . (317) 423-8200
M S D Perry Township (PK-12)
    2008-09 Enrollment: 14,213 . . . . (317) 789-3700
M S D Pike Township (PK-12)
    2008-09 Enrollment: 10,713 . . . . (317) 293-0393
M S D Warren Township (PK-12)
    2008-09 Enrollment: 12,165 . . . . (317) 869-4300
M S D Washington Township (PK-12)
    2008-09 Enrollment: 10,219 . . . . (317) 845-9400
M S D Wayne Township (PK-12)
    2008-09 Enrollment: 15,384 . . . . (317) 243-8251
Monument Lighthouse Charter School (KG-07)
    2008-09 Enrollment: 401 . . . . (317) 897-2430
Se Neighborhood Sch Of Excellence (KG-06)
    2008-09 Enrollment: 255 . . . . (317) 423-0204
The Indianapolis Project School (KG-06)
    2008-09 Enrollment: 167 . . . . (317) 608-0210

Four-year College(s)

Brown Mackie College-Indianapolis (Private, For-profit)
    Fall 2008 Enrollment: 402 . . . . (317) 554-8301
    2009-10 Tuition: In-state $10,728; Out-of-state $10,728
Butler University (Private, Not-for-profit)
    Fall 2008 Enrollment: 4,438. (317) 940-8000
    2009-10 Tuition: In-state $29,246; Out-of-state $29,246
Christian Theological Seminary (Private, Not-for-profit, Christian Church (Disciples of Christ))
    Fall 2008 Enrollment: 253 . . . . (317) 924-1331
Crossroads Bible College
    Fall 2008 Enrollment: 158 . . . . (317) 352-8736
    2009-10 Tuition: In-state $12,220; Out-of-state $12,220
DeVry University-Indiana (Private, For-profit)
    Fall 2008 Enrollment: 590 . . . . (317) 581-8854
    2009-10 Tuition: In-state $14,592; Out-of-state $14,592
ITT Technical Institute-Indianapolis (Private, For-profit)
    Fall 2008 Enrollment: 4,036. (317) 875-8640
    2009-10 Tuition: In-state $16,374; Out-of-state $16,374
Indiana Business College-Indianapolis (Private, For-profit)
    Fall 2008 Enrollment: 1,889. (317) 264-5656
    2009-10 Tuition: In-state $11,535; Out-of-state $11,535
Indiana University-Purdue University-Indianapolis (Public)
    Fall 2008 Enrollment: 30,300. . . . . (317) 274-5555
    2009-10 Tuition: In-state $7,523; Out-of-state $22,420
Marian College (Private, Not-for-profit, Roman Catholic)
    Fall 2008 Enrollment: 2,143. (317) 955-6000
    2009-10 Tuition: In-state $24,000; Out-of-state $24,000
Martin University (Private, Not-for-profit)
    Fall 2008 Enrollment: 1,236. (317) 543-3235
    2009-10 Tuition: In-state $13,520; Out-of-state $13,520

The Art Institute of Indianapolis (Private, For-profit)
Fall 2008 Enrollment: 824 . . . . (317) 613-4800
2009-10 Tuition: In-state $16,912; Out-of-state $16,912
University of Indianapolis (Private, Not-for-profit, United Methodist)
Fall 2008 Enrollment: 4,829 . . . . (317) 788-3368
2009-10 Tuition: In-state $21,170; Out-of-state $21,170
University of Phoenix-Indianapolis Campus (Private, For-profit)
Fall 2008 Enrollment: 358 . . . . (317) 585-8610
2009-10 Tuition: In-state $9,360; Out-of-state $9,360

Two-year College(s)

Aviation Institute of Maintenance-Indianapolis (Private, For-profit)
Fall 2008 Enrollment: 156 . . . . (317) 243-4519
Indiana Business College-Medical (Private, For-profit)
Fall 2008 Enrollment: 505 . . . . (317) 375-8000
2009-10 Tuition: In-state $11,535; Out-of-state $11,535
Indiana Business College-Northwest (Private, For-profit)
Fall 2008 Enrollment: 304 . . . . (317) 873-6500
2009-10 Tuition: In-state $11,535; Out-of-state $11,535
International Business College-Indianapolis (Private, For-profit)
Fall 2008 Enrollment: 406 . . . . (317) 813-2300
2009-10 Tuition: In-state $13,370; Out-of-state $13,370
Ivy Tech Community College-Central Indiana (Public)
Fall 2008 Enrollment: 16,415 . . . . (317) 921-4800
2009-10 Tuition: In-state $3,090; Out-of-state $6,306
Kaplan College-Indianapolis (Private, For-profit)
Fall 2008 Enrollment: 1,107 . . . . (317) 299-6001
Lincoln College of Technology (Private, For-profit)
Fall 2008 Enrollment: 1,492 . . . . (317) 632-5553
MedTech College (Private, For-profit)
Fall 2008 Enrollment: 618 . . . . (317) 845-0100
2009-10 Tuition: In-state $13,234; Out-of-state $13,234

Vocational/Technical School(s)

Empire Beauty School-Indianapolis (Private, For-profit)
Fall 2008 Enrollment: 164 . . . . (570) 429-4321
2009-10 Tuition: $14,250
Hair Fashions By Kaye Beauty College (Private, For-profit)
Fall 2008 Enrollment: 144 . . . . (317) 576-8000
2009-10 Tuition: $13,600
Honors Beauty College (Private, For-profit)
Fall 2008 Enrollment: 122 . . . . (317) 598-9400
2009-10 Tuition: $12,100
J Everett Light Career Center (Public)
Fall 2008 Enrollment: 58 . . . . (317) 259-5265
2009-10 Tuition: In-state $9,900; Out-of-state $9,900
Regency Beauty Institute (Private, For-profit)
Fall 2008 Enrollment: 122 . . . . (800) 787-6456
2009-10 Tuition: $15,770
Regency Beauty Institute (Private, For-profit)
Fall 2008 Enrollment: 85 . . . . (800) 787-6456
2009-10 Tuition: $15,770
TechSkills-Indianapolis (Private, For-profit)
Fall 2008 Enrollment: 327 . . . . (317) 251-4600

Housing: Homeownership rate: 60.0% (2010); Median home value: $116,575 (2010); Median contract rent: $486 per month (2000); Median year structure built: 1966 (2000).
Hospitals: Community Health Network (1025 beds); Community Hospital North (282 beds); Community Hospital South; Fairbanks Alcohol and Drug Addiction Treatment Center (70 beds); Indiana Heart Hospital (72 beds); Indiana Orthopaedic Hospital; Indiana University Hospital; Larue D. Carter Memorial Hospital (146 beds); Richard L Roudebush VA Medical Center (170 beds); St Vincent Seton Specialty Hospital - Indianapolis (29 beds); St. Francis at Indianapolis; St. Vincent Heart Center of Indiana (80 beds); St. Vincent Indianapolis Hospital (650 beds); St. Vincent Women's Hospital (182 beds); Westview Hospital (116 beds); Wishard Health Services (354 beds)
Safety: Violent crime rate: 120.4 per 10,000 population; Property crime rate: 608.4 per 10,000 population (2008).
Newspapers: The Court and Commercial Record (Community news; Circulation 1,050); The Criterion (Regional news; Circulation 69,900); Cumberland Courier Weekly (Local news; Circulation 12,500); East Side Herald (Community news; Circulation 25,000); Franklin Township Informer (Local news; Circulation 2,800); IBJ Corporation (Local news); Indiana Global (Regional news; Circulation 5,000); The Indianapolis Star - Metro North Bureau (Regional news); The Indianapolis Star (Local news; Circulation 252,041); Indy Info (Regional news); The Journal Gazette -

Indianapolis Bureau (Regional news; Circulation 60,000); Kentucky Jewish Post & Opinion (Regional news); La Ola Latinoamericana; La Voz de Indiana (Local news; Circulation 15,000); Lawrence Township Journal (Local news; Circulation 12,400); Northwest Press (Community news; Circulation 17,160); South Bend Tribune - Indianapolis Bureau (Local news); Spotlight (Community news; Circulation 4,700); West Side Community News (Local news; Circulation 20,000); West Side Messenger (Local news; Circulation 7,000)
Transportation: Commute to work: 92.3% car, 2.4% public transportation, 2.0% walk, 2.5% work from home (2000); Travel time to work: 25.8% less than 15 minutes, 47.6% 15 to 30 minutes, 18.8% 30 to 45 minutes, 3.8% 45 to 60 minutes, 4.0% 60 minutes or more (2000); Amtrak: train service available.
Additional Information Contacts
City of Indianapolis . . . . (317) 327-4622
http://www.indygov.org
Greater Indianapolis Chamber of Commerce . . . . (317) 464-2222
http://www.indychamber.com
Indiana Chamber of Commerce . . . . (317) 264-3110
http://www.indianachamber.com

LAWRENCE (city). Covers a land area of 20.082 square miles and a water area of 0.102 square miles. Located at 39.86° N. Lat; 85.99° W. Long. Elevation is 873 feet.
History: Named for Captain James Lawrence, U.S. Naval officer in the War of 1812. Fort Benjamin Harrison is here.
Population: 26,837 (1990); 38,915 (2000); 45,445 (2010); 48,035 (2015 projected); Race: 68.0% White, 24.5% Black, 1.7% Asian, 5.8% Other, 7.6% Hispanic of any race (2010); Density: 2,263.0 persons per square mile (2010); Average household size: 2.66 (2010); Median age: 34.5 (2010); Males per 100 females: 93.8 (2010); Marriage status: 25.1% never married, 57.6% now married, 4.3% widowed, 13.0% divorced (2000); Foreign born: 5.5% (2000); Ancestry (includes multiple ancestries): 25.5% Other groups, 20.0% German, 12.7% Irish, 10.1% United States or American, 8.5% English (2000).
Economy: Unemployment rate: 8.5% (5/2010); Total civilian labor force: 22,917 (5/2010); Single-family building permits issued: 51 (2009); Multi-family building permits issued: 0 (2009); Employment by occupation: 16.0% management, 20.0% professional, 11.4% services, 31.0% sales, 0.1% farming, 8.7% construction, 12.8% production (2000).
Income: Per capita income: $26,620 (2010); Median household income: $55,793 (2010); Average household income: $70,918 (2010); Percent of households with income of $100,000 or more: 20.5% (2010); Poverty rate: 6.7% (2000).
Taxes: Total city taxes per capita: $263 (2007); City property taxes per capita: $233 (2007).
Education: Percent of population age 25 and over with: High school diploma (including GED) or higher: 88.4% (2010); Bachelor's degree or higher: 29.5% (2010); Master's degree or higher: 9.3% (2010).
Housing: Homeownership rate: 75.6% (2010); Median home value: $122,919 (2010); Median contract rent: $515 per month (2000); Median year structure built: 1982 (2000).
Transportation: Commute to work: 95.8% car, 0.5% public transportation, 0.7% walk, 2.5% work from home (2000); Travel time to work: 20.6% less than 15 minutes, 43.3% 15 to 30 minutes, 26.3% 30 to 45 minutes, 5.6% 45 to 60 minutes, 4.3% 60 minutes or more (2000)
Additional Information Contacts
City of Lawrence . . . . (317) 549-8670
http://www.cityoflawrence.org
Lawrence Chamber of Commerce . . . . (317) 541-9876
http://www.lawrencechamberofcommerce.org

MERIDIAN HILLS (town). Covers a land area of 1.484 square miles and a water area of 0.002 square miles. Located at 39.88° N. Lat; 86.15° W. Long. Elevation is 791 feet.
History: Former municipality, merged with Indianapolis 1970.
Population: 1,728 (1990); 1,713 (2000); 1,687 (2010); 1,684 (2015 projected); Race: 97.2% White, 1.5% Black, 0.5% Asian, 0.8% Other, 0.7% Hispanic of any race (2010); Density: 1,136.8 persons per square mile (2010); Average household size: 2.48 (2010); Median age: 47.1 (2010); Males per 100 females: 97.1 (2010); Marriage status: 14.9% never married, 72.9% now married, 6.3% widowed, 5.9% divorced (2000); Foreign born: 2.1% (2000); Ancestry (includes multiple ancestries): 33.8% German, 18.5% English, 15.1% Irish, 6.1% Italian, 6.1% French (except Basque) (2000).

Economy: Employment by occupation: 29.2% management, 35.6% professional, 3.9% services, 28.7% sales, 0.0% farming, 1.2% construction, 1.3% production (2000).

Income: Per capita income: $62,558 (2010); Median household income: $115,000 (2010); Average household income: $155,026 (2010); Percent of households with income of $100,000 or more: 57.9% (2010); Poverty rate: 0.2% (2000).

Taxes: Total city taxes per capita: $82 (2007); City property taxes per capita: $67 (2007).

Education: Percent of population age 25 and over with: High school diploma (including GED) or higher: 99.1% (2010); Bachelor's degree or higher: 79.3% (2010); Master's degree or higher: 38.3% (2010).

Housing: Homeownership rate: 94.0% (2010); Median home value: $378,148 (2010); Median contract rent: $1,250 per month (2000); Median year structure built: 1955 (2000).

Transportation: Commute to work: 96.7% car, 0.0% public transportation, 0.0% walk, 3.0% work from home (2000); Travel time to work: 25.3% less than 15 minutes, 60.2% 15 to 30 minutes, 10.6% 30 to 45 minutes, 1.1% 45 to 60 minutes, 2.8% 60 minutes or more (2000)

NORTH CROWS NEST (town). Covers a land area of 0.064 square miles and a water area of 0 square miles. Located at 39.86° N. Lat; 86.16° W. Long. Elevation is 781 feet.

Population: 57 (1990); 42 (2000); 34 (2010); 33 (2015 projected); Race: 55.9% White, 44.1% Black, 0.0% Asian, 0.0% Other, 0.0% Hispanic of any race (2010); Density: 529.4 persons per square mile (2010); Average household size: 2.43 (2010); Median age: 31.7 (2010); Males per 100 females: 112.5 (2010); Marriage status: 21.4% never married, 71.4% now married, 0.0% widowed, 7.1% divorced (2000); Foreign born: 0.0% (2000); Ancestry (includes multiple ancestries): 38.1% English, 23.8% Italian, 19.0% German, 19.0% Scottish, 11.9% Serbian (2000).

Economy: Employment by occupation: 25.0% management, 37.5% professional, 0.0% services, 37.5% sales, 0.0% farming, 0.0% construction, 0.0% production (2000).

Income: Per capita income: $43,790 (2010); Median household income: $75,000 (2010); Average household income: $123,571 (2010); Percent of households with income of $100,000 or more: 42.9% (2010); Poverty rate: 0.0% (2000).

Taxes: Total city taxes per capita: $238 (2007); City property taxes per capita: $190 (2007).

Education: Percent of population age 25 and over with: High school diploma (including GED) or higher: 100.0% (2010); Bachelor's degree or higher: 57.9% (2010); Master's degree or higher: 26.3% (2010).

Housing: Homeownership rate: 85.7% (2010); Median home value: $225,000 (2010); Median contract rent: $n/a per month (2000); Median year structure built: before 1940 (2000).

Transportation: Commute to work: 87.5% car, 0.0% public transportation, 12.5% walk, 0.0% work from home (2000); Travel time to work: 50.0% less than 15 minutes, 50.0% 15 to 30 minutes, 0.0% 30 to 45 minutes, 0.0% 45 to 60 minutes, 0.0% 60 minutes or more (2000)

ROCKY RIPPLE (town). Covers a land area of 0.304 square miles and a water area of 0 square miles. Located at 39.84° N. Lat; 86.17° W. Long. Elevation is 705 feet.

Population: 751 (1990); 712 (2000); 620 (2010); 583 (2015 projected); Race: 83.7% White, 12.9% Black, 0.2% Asian, 3.2% Other, 2.3% Hispanic of any race (2010); Density: 2,036.3 persons per square mile (2010); Average household size: 2.20 (2010); Median age: 44.3 (2010); Males per 100 females: 93.1 (2010); Marriage status: 29.0% never married, 52.6% now married, 7.0% widowed, 11.4% divorced (2000); Foreign born: 2.4% (2000); Ancestry (includes multiple ancestries): 29.1% German, 17.2% Irish, 15.2% Other groups, 13.4% English, 8.7% United States or American (2000).

Economy: Employment by occupation: 15.4% management, 23.8% professional, 15.7% services, 24.1% sales, 0.0% farming, 9.2% construction, 11.8% production (2000).

Income: Per capita income: $29,394 (2010); Median household income: $54,870 (2010); Average household income: $65,647 (2010); Percent of households with income of $100,000 or more: 12.4% (2010); Poverty rate: 2.4% (2000).

Taxes: Total city taxes per capita: $27 (2007); City property taxes per capita: $27 (2007).

Education: Percent of population age 25 and over with: High school diploma (including GED) or higher: 85.3% (2010); Bachelor's degree or higher: 36.1% (2010); Master's degree or higher: 13.3% (2010).

Housing: Homeownership rate: 80.5% (2010); Median home value: $107,584 (2010); Median contract rent: $558 per month (2000); Median year structure built: 1952 (2000).

Transportation: Commute to work: 92.0% car, 1.1% public transportation, 1.3% walk, 3.2% work from home (2000); Travel time to work: 22.9% less than 15 minutes, 55.1% 15 to 30 minutes, 14.6% 30 to 45 minutes, 1.7% 45 to 60 minutes, 5.8% 60 minutes or more (2000)

SOUTHPORT (city). Covers a land area of 0.642 square miles and a water area of 0 square miles. Located at 39.66° N. Lat; 86.11° W. Long. Elevation is 748 feet.

History: Laid out 1852.

Population: 1,978 (1990); 1,852 (2000); 1,681 (2010); 1,610 (2015 projected); Race: 91.0% White, 1.8% Black, 1.9% Asian, 5.2% Other, 6.9% Hispanic of any race (2010); Density: 2,619.7 persons per square mile (2010); Average household size: 2.10 (2010); Median age: 38.4 (2010); Males per 100 females: 101.6 (2010); Marriage status: 24.4% never married, 58.8% now married, 7.1% widowed, 9.7% divorced (2000); Foreign born: 3.4% (2000); Ancestry (includes multiple ancestries): 26.8% German, 13.3% United States or American, 12.0% English, 10.8% Other groups, 8.8% Irish (2000).

Economy: Single-family building permits issued: 0 (2009); Multi-family building permits issued: 0 (2009); Employment by occupation: 12.4% management, 17.4% professional, 14.0% services, 25.8% sales, 0.3% farming, 11.9% construction, 18.2% production (2000).

Income: Per capita income: $26,079 (2010); Median household income: $41,240 (2010); Average household income: $54,153 (2010); Percent of households with income of $100,000 or more: 10.4% (2010); Poverty rate: 6.2% (2000).

Taxes: Total city taxes per capita: $103 (2007); City property taxes per capita: $79 (2007).

Education: Percent of population age 25 and over with: High school diploma (including GED) or higher: 86.5% (2010); Bachelor's degree or higher: 22.2% (2010); Master's degree or higher: 7.6% (2010).

Housing: Homeownership rate: 44.5% (2010); Median home value: $123,340 (2010); Median contract rent: $582 per month (2000); Median year structure built: 1962 (2000).

Transportation: Commute to work: 92.7% car, 0.7% public transportation, 0.4% walk, 4.3% work from home (2000); Travel time to work: 20.1% less than 15 minutes, 38.8% 15 to 30 minutes, 33.4% 30 to 45 minutes, 5.1% 45 to 60 minutes, 2.6% 60 minutes or more (2000)

SPEEDWAY (town). Covers a land area of 4.755 square miles and a water area of 0.008 square miles. Located at 39.79° N. Lat; 86.25° W. Long. Elevation is 748 feet.

History: Named for Indianapolis Motor Speedway, located in the city. Speedway, laid out in 1912 by Carl Fisher, James T. Allison, and Frank H. Wheeler, gained fame as the home of the Indianapolis Motor Speedway.

Population: 13,092 (1990); 12,881 (2000); 12,502 (2010); 12,413 (2015 projected); Race: 72.2% White, 17.7% Black, 2.6% Asian, 7.5% Other, 7.6% Hispanic of any race (2010); Density: 2,629.2 persons per square mile (2010); Average household size: 2.09 (2010); Median age: 38.5 (2010); Males per 100 females: 91.1 (2010); Marriage status: 28.6% never married, 47.3% now married, 8.3% widowed, 15.8% divorced (2000); Foreign born: 4.5% (2000); Ancestry (includes multiple ancestries): 22.7% German, 17.5% Other groups, 12.8% Irish, 11.4% English, 10.1% United States or American (2000).

Economy: Single-family building permits issued: 0 (2009); Multi-family building permits issued: 0 (2009); Employment by occupation: 11.8% management, 19.8% professional, 14.8% services, 29.9% sales, 0.2% farming, 6.5% construction, 17.0% production (2000).

Income: Per capita income: $24,429 (2010); Median household income: $43,742 (2010); Average household income: $51,414 (2010); Percent of households with income of $100,000 or more: 9.5% (2010); Poverty rate: 8.8% (2000).

Taxes: Total city taxes per capita: $440 (2007); City property taxes per capita: $381 (2007).

Education: Percent of population age 25 and over with: High school diploma (including GED) or higher: 89.9% (2010); Bachelor's degree or higher: 24.5% (2010); Master's degree or higher: 8.3% (2010).

School District(s)
School Town Of Speedway (KG-12)
　　2008-09 Enrollment: 1,628 . . . . (317) 244-0236

Housing: Homeownership rate: 47.5% (2010); Median home value: $121,755 (2010); Median contract rent: $499 per month (2000); Median year structure built: 1962 (2000).
Safety: Violent crime rate: 47.1 per 10,000 population; Property crime rate: 466.2 per 10,000 population (2008).
Newspapers: The Press (Community news; Circulation 8,700)
Transportation: Commute to work: 92.3% car, 2.2% public transportation, 3.0% walk, 1.4% work from home (2000); Travel time to work: 29.0% less than 15 minutes, 48.4% 15 to 30 minutes, 16.1% 30 to 45 minutes, 2.6% 45 to 60 minutes, 3.9% 60 minutes or more (2000)
Additional Information Contacts
Speedway Chamber of Commerce . . . . (317) 244-3789
  http://www.in.gov/mylocal
Town of Speedway . . . . (317) 246-4111
  http://www.townofspeedway.org

SPRING HILL (town). Covers a land area of 0.110 square miles and a water area of 0 square miles. Located at 39.83° N. Lat; 86.19° W. Long. Elevation is 761 feet.

Population: 112 (1990); 97 (2000); 97 (2010); 97 (2015 projected); Race: 66.0% White, 27.8% Black, 2.1% Asian, 4.1% Other, 2.1% Hispanic of any race (2010); Density: 881.1 persons per square mile (2010); Average household size: 2.06 (2010); Median age: 43.2 (2010); Males per 100 females: 94.0 (2010); Marriage status: 31.5% never married, 54.6% now married, 4.6% widowed, 9.3% divorced (2000); Foreign born: 4.0% (2000); Ancestry (includes multiple ancestries): 13.6% United States or American, 12.8% Greek, 12.0% Irish, 11.2% Italian, 11.2% English (2000).
Economy: Employment by occupation: 8.6% management, 32.1% professional, 13.6% services, 45.7% sales, 0.0% farming, 0.0% construction, 0.0% production (2000).
Income: Per capita income: $32,010 (2010); Median household income: $59,375 (2010); Average household income: $66,915 (2010); Percent of households with income of $100,000 or more: 19.1% (2010); Poverty rate: 10.4% (2000).
Taxes: Total city taxes per capita: $144 (2007); City property taxes per capita: $62 (2007).
Education: Percent of population age 25 and over with: High school diploma (including GED) or higher: 97.4% (2010); Bachelor's degree or higher: 50.0% (2010); Master's degree or higher: 30.3% (2010).
Housing: Homeownership rate: 68.1% (2010); Median home value: $162,500 (2010); Median contract rent: $1,400 per month (2000); Median year structure built: 1982 (2000).
Transportation: Commute to work: 94.3% car, 0.0% public transportation, 0.0% walk, 5.7% work from home (2000); Travel time to work: 9.1% less than 15 minutes, 80.3% 15 to 30 minutes, 10.6% 30 to 45 minutes, 0.0% 45 to 60 minutes, 0.0% 60 minutes or more (2000)

WARREN PARK (town). Covers a land area of 0.450 square miles and a water area of 0 square miles. Located at 39.78° N. Lat; 86.05° W. Long. Elevation is 827 feet.

Population: 1,757 (1990); 1,656 (2000); 1,451 (2010); 1,376 (2015 projected); Race: 88.3% White, 7.0% Black, 1.2% Asian, 3.4% Other, 2.8% Hispanic of any race (2010); Density: 3,227.3 persons per square mile (2010); Average household size: 1.78 (2010); Median age: 49.4 (2010); Males per 100 females: 71.3 (2010); Marriage status: 15.2% never married, 42.6% now married, 27.6% widowed, 14.6% divorced (2000); Foreign born: 3.1% (2000); Ancestry (includes multiple ancestries): 20.5% German, 19.7% Irish, 13.3% English, 12.7% Other groups, 10.7% United States or American (2000).
Economy: Employment by occupation: 13.7% management, 17.5% professional, 11.3% services, 35.4% sales, 0.0% farming, 9.7% construction, 12.4% production (2000).
Income: Per capita income: $24,118 (2010); Median household income: $28,008 (2010); Average household income: $43,152 (2010); Percent of households with income of $100,000 or more: 8.1% (2010); Poverty rate: 6.2% (2000).
Taxes: Total city taxes per capita: $90 (2007); City property taxes per capita: $85 (2007).
Education: Percent of population age 25 and over with: High school diploma (including GED) or higher: 81.8% (2010); Bachelor's degree or higher: 17.0% (2010); Master's degree or higher: 4.7% (2010).
Housing: Homeownership rate: 33.4% (2010); Median home value: $117,292 (2010); Median contract rent: $532 per month (2000); Median year structure built: 1962 (2000).

Transportation: Commute to work: 92.1% car, 1.0% public transportation, 3.8% walk, 2.5% work from home (2000); Travel time to work: 32.0% less than 15 minutes, 44.1% 15 to 30 minutes, 22.1% 30 to 45 minutes, 1.8% 45 to 60 minutes, 0.0% 60 minutes or more (2000)

WILLIAMS CREEK (town). Covers a land area of 0.338 square miles and a water area of 0 square miles. Located at 39.90° N. Lat; 86.14° W. Long. Elevation is 778 feet.

Population: 425 (1990); 413 (2000); 401 (2010); 394 (2015 projected); Race: 98.5% White, 0.2% Black, 0.2% Asian, 1.0% Other, 0.7% Hispanic of any race (2010); Density: 1,185.6 persons per square mile (2010); Average household size: 2.62 (2010); Median age: 47.7 (2010); Males per 100 females: 91.0 (2010); Marriage status: 16.0% never married, 69.0% now married, 5.8% widowed, 9.2% divorced (2000); Foreign born: 1.5% (2000); Ancestry (includes multiple ancestries): 30.5% German, 20.5% English, 18.5% Irish, 6.8% Scotch-Irish, 5.9% Italian (2000).
Economy: Employment by occupation: 36.1% management, 32.7% professional, 5.4% services, 19.8% sales, 0.0% farming, 1.5% construction, 4.5% production (2000).
Income: Per capita income: $75,751 (2010); Median household income: $153,750 (2010); Average household income: $196,536 (2010); Percent of households with income of $100,000 or more: 71.2% (2010); Poverty rate: 1.2% (2000).
Taxes: Total city taxes per capita: $207 (2007); City property taxes per capita: $166 (2007).
Education: Percent of population age 25 and over with: High school diploma (including GED) or higher: 99.6% (2010); Bachelor's degree or higher: 77.8% (2010); Master's degree or higher: 36.4% (2010).
Housing: Homeownership rate: 96.7% (2010); Median home value: $562,500 (2010); Median contract rent: $n/a per month (2000); Median year structure built: 1950 (2000).
Transportation: Commute to work: 92.5% car, 0.0% public transportation, 4.0% walk, 3.5% work from home (2000); Travel time to work: 35.4% less than 15 minutes, 40.6% 15 to 30 minutes, 22.9% 30 to 45 minutes, 1.0% 45 to 60 minutes, 0.0% 60 minutes or more (2000)

WYNNEDALE (town). Covers a land area of 0.167 square miles and a water area of 0 square miles. Located at 39.83° N. Lat; 86.19° W. Long. Elevation is 758 feet.

Population: 269 (1990); 275 (2000); 275 (2010); 274 (2015 projected); Race: 66.2% White, 27.3% Black, 2.9% Asian, 3.6% Other, 1.8% Hispanic of any race (2010); Density: 1,643.6 persons per square mile (2010); Average household size: 2.08 (2010); Median age: 43.5 (2010); Males per 100 females: 88.4 (2010); Marriage status: 21.5% never married, 64.4% now married, 7.8% widowed, 6.3% divorced (2000); Foreign born: 0.0% (2000); Ancestry (includes multiple ancestries): 28.1% Other groups, 24.9% German, 20.4% English, 9.8% Italian, 8.0% Scottish (2000).
Economy: Employment by occupation: 25.2% management, 43.6% professional, 10.4% services, 17.8% sales, 0.0% farming, 0.0% construction, 3.1% production (2000).
Income: Per capita income: $32,010 (2010); Median household income: $58,333 (2010); Average household income: $64,962 (2010); Percent of households with income of $100,000 or more: 18.9% (2010); Poverty rate: 0.9% (2000).
Taxes: Total city taxes per capita: $55 (2007); City property taxes per capita: $44 (2007).
Education: Percent of population age 25 and over with: High school diploma (including GED) or higher: 98.6% (2010); Bachelor's degree or higher: 49.5% (2010); Master's degree or higher: 30.5% (2010).
Housing: Homeownership rate: 68.9% (2010); Median home value: $165,323 (2010); Median contract rent: $n/a per month (2000); Median year structure built: 1959 (2000).
Transportation: Commute to work: 92.6% car, 1.2% public transportation, 0.0% walk, 6.1% work from home (2000); Travel time to work: 32.7% less than 15 minutes, 63.4% 15 to 30 minutes, 3.9% 30 to 45 minutes, 0.0% 45 to 60 minutes, 0.0% 60 minutes or more (2000)

Marshall County

Located in northern Indiana; drained by the Yellow and Tippecanoe River; includes several lakes. Covers a land area of 444.27 square miles, a water area of 5.65 square miles, and is located in the Eastern Time Zone. The county was founded in 1835. County seat is Plymouth.

Marshall County is part of the Plymouth, IN Micropolitan Statistical Area. The entire metro area includes: Marshall County, IN

Population: 42,182 (1990); 45,128 (2000); 46,912 (2010); 47,422 (2015 projected); Race: 93.1% White, 0.8% Black, 0.4% Asian, 5.7% Other, 9.4% Hispanic of any race (2010); Density: 105.6 persons per square mile (2010); Average household size: 2.66 (2010); Median age: 37.0 (2010); Males per 100 females: 99.6 (2010).
Religion: Five largest groups: 10.3% Catholic Church, 7.2% The United Methodist Church, 3.1% United Church of Christ, 3.0% The Wesleyan Church, 2.8% Lutheran Church—Missouri Synod (2000).
Economy: Unemployment rate: 10.3% (5/2010); Total civilian labor force: 23,676 (5/2010); Leading industries: 36.3% manufacturing; 12.8% retail trade; 11.0% health care and social assistance (2008); Farms: 866 totaling 179,016 acres (2007); Companies that employ 500 or more persons: 1 (2008); Companies that employ 100 to 499 persons: 31 (2008); Companies that employ less than 100 persons: 1,075 (2008); Black-owned businesses: n/a (2002); Hispanic-owned businesses: n/a (2002); Asian-owned businesses: n/a (2002); Women-owned businesses: n/a (2002); Retail sales per capita: $12,258 (2010). Single-family building permits issued: 82 (2009); Multi-family building permits issued: 18 (2009).
Income: Per capita income: $22,779 (2010); Median household income: $51,174 (2010); Average household income: $61,190 (2010); Percent of households with income of $100,000 or more: 13.2% (2010); Poverty rate: 9.6% (2008); Bankruptcy rate: 7.04% (2009).
Taxes: Total county taxes per capita: $200 (2007); County property taxes per capita: $150 (2007).
Education: Percent of population age 25 and over with: High school diploma (including GED) or higher: 82.7% (2010); Bachelor's degree or higher: 17.5% (2010); Master's degree or higher: 6.4% (2010).
Housing: Homeownership rate: 78.0% (2010); Median home value: $118,928 (2010); Median contract rent: $501 per month (2006-2008 3-year est.); Median year structure built: 1965 (2006-2008 3-year est.)
Health: Birth rate: 143.5 per 10,000 population (2009); Death rate: 90.0 per 10,000 population (2009); Age-adjusted cancer mortality rate: 185.2 deaths per 100,000 population (2006); Number of physicians: 8.4 per 10,000 population (2007); Hospital beds: 31.1 per 10,000 population (2006); Hospital admissions: 1,006.5 per 10,000 population (2006).
Elections: 2008 Presidential election results: 42.5% Obama, 56.1% McCain, 0.0% Nader
National and State Parks: Menominee State Wetlands
Additional Information Contacts
Marshall County Government . . . . (574) 936-8922
   http://www.co.marshall.in.us
City of Plymouth. . . . . (574) 936-2124
   http://www.plymouthin.com
Marshall County Convention and Visitors Bureau . . . . (574) 936-1882
   http://marshallcountytourism.org
Plymouth Area Chamber of Commerce. . . . . (574) 936-2323
   http://www.plychamber.org
Town of Bourbon . . . . (574) 342-4755
   http://www.bourbon-in.gov
Town of Bremen . . . . (574) 546-2044
   http://www.bremenin.org

Marshall County Communities

ARGOS (town). Covers a land area of 0.678 square miles and a water area of 0 square miles. Located at 41.23° N. Lat; 86.24° W. Long. Elevation is 728 feet.
History: Argos began as a stagecoach stop on the Michigan Road. The name was chosen by Schuyler Colfax, vice-president under the Grant administration.
Population: 1,673 (1990); 1,613 (2000); 1,597 (2010); 1,577 (2015 projected); Race: 98.2% White, 0.6% Black, 0.1% Asian, 1.1% Other, 1.3% Hispanic of any race (2010); Density: 2,354.6 persons per square mile (2010); Average household size: 2.62 (2010); Median age: 34.1 (2010); Males per 100 females: 99.6 (2010); Marriage status: 19.8% never married, 59.9% now married, 7.6% widowed, 12.7% divorced (2000); Foreign born: 0.3% (2000); Ancestry (includes multiple ancestries): 35.0% German, 12.5% Irish, 10.8% English, 9.2% United States or American, 7.7% Other groups (2000).
Economy: Single-family building permits issued: 1 (2009); Multi-family building permits issued: 0 (2009); Employment by occupation: 5.9% management, 10.2% professional, 12.6% services, 23.1% sales, 0.8% farming, 8.4% construction, 39.1% production (2000).

Income: Per capita income: $19,067 (2010); Median household income: $43,359 (2010); Average household income: $49,861 (2010); Percent of households with income of $100,000 or more: 7.0% (2010); Poverty rate: 11.5% (2000).
Taxes: Total city taxes per capita: $188 (2007); City property taxes per capita: $182 (2007).
Education: Percent of population age 25 and over with: High school diploma (including GED) or higher: 85.9% (2010); Bachelor's degree or higher: 14.4% (2010); Master's degree or higher: 5.2% (2010).
School District(s)
Argos Community Schools (KG-12)
   2008-09 Enrollment: 659 . . . . (574) 892-5139
Housing: Homeownership rate: 74.8% (2010); Median home value: $95,690 (2010); Median contract rent: $375 per month (2000); Median year structure built: 1948 (2000).
Transportation: Commute to work: 93.3% car, 0.0% public transportation, 3.6% walk, 2.3% work from home (2000); Travel time to work: 41.8% less than 15 minutes, 32.2% 15 to 30 minutes, 12.5% 30 to 45 minutes, 5.3% 45 to 60 minutes, 8.2% 60 minutes or more (2000)
Additional Information Contacts
Marshall County Convention and Visitors Bureau . . . . (574) 936-1882
   http://marshallcountytourism.org

BOURBON (town). Covers a land area of 1.037 square miles and a water area of 0.004 square miles. Located at 41.29° N. Lat; 86.11° W. Long. Elevation is 843 feet.
Population: 1,723 (1990); 1,691 (2000); 1,831 (2010); 1,851 (2015 projected); Race: 93.4% White, 0.3% Black, 1.0% Asian, 5.3% Other, 8.2% Hispanic of any race (2010); Density: 1,765.3 persons per square mile (2010); Average household size: 2.60 (2010); Median age: 33.7 (2010); Males per 100 females: 94.4 (2010); Marriage status: 23.4% never married, 59.0% now married, 6.0% widowed, 11.6% divorced (2000); Foreign born: 2.9% (2000); Ancestry (includes multiple ancestries): 30.8% German, 14.5% United States or American, 10.7% Other groups, 10.6% Irish, 7.4% English (2000).
Economy: Single-family building permits issued: 1 (2009); Multi-family building permits issued: 0 (2009); Employment by occupation: 4.9% management, 14.2% professional, 12.1% services, 23.3% sales, 0.2% farming, 11.4% construction, 33.9% production (2000).
Income: Per capita income: $20,873 (2010); Median household income: $47,237 (2010); Average household income: $54,619 (2010); Percent of households with income of $100,000 or more: 7.7% (2010); Poverty rate: 5.9% (2000).
Taxes: Total city taxes per capita: $206 (2007); City property taxes per capita: $203 (2007).
Education: Percent of population age 25 and over with: High school diploma (including GED) or higher: 83.2% (2010); Bachelor's degree or higher: 13.6% (2010); Master's degree or higher: 4.2% (2010).
School District(s)
Triton School Corporation (KG-12)
   2008-09 Enrollment: 1,079 . . . . (574) 342-2255
Housing: Homeownership rate: 74.3% (2010); Median home value: $98,070 (2010); Median contract rent: $373 per month (2000); Median year structure built: 1951 (2000).
Newspapers: Bourbon News-Mirror (Community news; Circulation 1,300)
Transportation: Commute to work: 92.7% car, 0.5% public transportation, 4.7% walk, 2.1% work from home (2000); Travel time to work: 36.4% less than 15 minutes, 44.1% 15 to 30 minutes, 9.9% 30 to 45 minutes, 5.3% 45 to 60 minutes, 4.4% 60 minutes or more (2000)
Additional Information Contacts
Town of Bourbon . . . . (574) 342-4755
   http://www.bourbon-in.gov

BREMEN (town). Covers a land area of 2.280 square miles and a water area of 0 square miles. Located at 41.44° N. Lat; 86.14° W. Long. Elevation is 853 feet.
History: Bremen reports that its fire department was the 1882 and 1887 winner of the hose and engine maneuvers at the state championships.
Population: 4,937 (1990); 4,486 (2000); 4,456 (2010); 4,421 (2015 projected); Race: 86.1% White, 0.6% Black, 0.7% Asian, 12.7% Other, 19.7% Hispanic of any race (2010); Density: 1,954.6 persons per square mile (2010); Average household size: 2.63 (2010); Median age: 36.0 (2010); Males per 100 females: 97.1 (2010); Marriage status: 21.3% never married, 63.3% now married, 7.0% widowed, 8.4% divorced (2000); Foreign born: 8.2% (2000); Ancestry (includes multiple ancestries): 33.6%

German, 17.3% Other groups, 9.6% United States or American, 9.4% Irish, 8.2% English (2000).

Economy: Single-family building permits issued: 3 (2009); Multi-family building permits issued: 4 (2009); Employment by occupation: 11.6% management, 14.0% professional, 10.6% services, 16.9% sales, 0.7% farming, 8.6% construction, 37.6% production (2000).

Income: Per capita income: $20,837 (2010); Median household income: $48,739 (2010); Average household income: $55,518 (2010); Percent of households with income of $100,000 or more: 8.8% (2010); Poverty rate: 6.5% (2000).

Taxes: Total city taxes per capita: $306 (2007); City property taxes per capita: $306 (2007).

Education: Percent of population age 25 and over with: High school diploma (including GED) or higher: 79.7% (2010); Bachelor's degree or higher: 14.9% (2010); Master's degree or higher: 5.9% (2010).

School District(s)
Bremen Public Schools (PK-12)
    2008-09 Enrollment: 1,477 . . . . (574) 546-3929

Housing: Homeownership rate: 76.1% (2010); Median home value: $115,448 (2010); Median contract rent: $385 per month (2000); Median year structure built: 1964 (2000).

Hospitals: Community Hospital of Bremen (24 beds)

Safety: Violent crime rate: 2.1 per 10,000 population; Property crime rate: 156.7 per 10,000 population (2008).

Newspapers: Bremen Enquirer (Community news; Circulation 21,000)

Transportation: Commute to work: 93.6% car, 0.0% public transportation, 3.5% walk, 1.8% work from home (2000); Travel time to work: 56.1% less than 15 minutes, 22.6% 15 to 30 minutes, 15.4% 30 to 45 minutes, 3.5% 45 to 60 minutes, 2.4% 60 minutes or more (2000)

Additional Information Contacts
Town of Bremen. . . . . (574) 546-2044
    http://www.bremenin.org

CULVER (town). Covers a land area of 0.785 square miles and a water area of 0 square miles. Located at 41.21° N. Lat; 86.42° W. Long. Elevation is 764 feet.

History: Culver developed as a resort town near Lake Maxinkuckee. It was named for Henry Harrison Culver of St. Louis who founded Culver Military Academy in 1894.

Population: 1,598 (1990); 1,539 (2000); 1,509 (2010); 1,479 (2015 projected); Race: 94.4% White, 1.0% Black, 1.2% Asian, 3.4% Other, 3.8% Hispanic of any race (2010); Density: 1,923.4 persons per square mile (2010); Average household size: 2.34 (2010); Median age: 42.6 (2010); Males per 100 females: 97.3 (2010); Marriage status: 23.8% never married, 53.3% now married, 11.8% widowed, 11.1% divorced (2000); Foreign born: 1.7% (2000); Ancestry (includes multiple ancestries): 31.4% German, 15.5% English, 11.9% Irish, 9.0% United States or American, 7.3% Other groups (2000).

Economy: Single-family building permits issued: 6 (2009); Multi-family building permits issued: 0 (2009); Employment by occupation: 12.4% management, 24.5% professional, 16.4% services, 20.1% sales, 0.7% farming, 9.1% construction, 16.7% production (2000).

Income: Per capita income: $22,162 (2010); Median household income: $42,330 (2010); Average household income: $52,976 (2010); Percent of households with income of $100,000 or more: 10.7% (2010); Poverty rate: 10.4% (2000).

Taxes: Total city taxes per capita: $380 (2007); City property taxes per capita: $370 (2007).

Education: Percent of population age 25 and over with: High school diploma (including GED) or higher: 90.5% (2010); Bachelor's degree or higher: 29.5% (2010); Master's degree or higher: 12.4% (2010).

School District(s)
Culver Community Schools Corp (PK-12)
    2008-09 Enrollment: 1,076 . . . . (574) 842-3364

Housing: Homeownership rate: 76.4% (2010); Median home value: $97,273 (2010); Median contract rent: $323 per month (2000); Median year structure built: 1947 (2000).

Safety: Violent crime rate: 6.7 per 10,000 population; Property crime rate: 140.6 per 10,000 population (2008).

Newspapers: Culver Citizen (Local news; Circulation 1,620)

Transportation: Commute to work: 85.0% car, 0.9% public transportation, 8.4% walk, 4.1% work from home (2000); Travel time to work: 44.3% less than 15 minutes, 27.4% 15 to 30 minutes, 12.6% 30 to 45 minutes, 6.4% 45 to 60 minutes, 9.3% 60 minutes or more (2000)

LA PAZ (town). Aka Lapaz. Covers a land area of 0.515 square miles and a water area of 0 square miles. Located at 41.45° N. Lat; 86.30° W. Long. Elevation is 863 feet.

Population: 619 (1990); 489 (2000); 424 (2010); 398 (2015 projected); Race: 92.7% White, 0.7% Black, 0.0% Asian, 6.6% Other, 3.8% Hispanic of any race (2010); Density: 822.5 persons per square mile (2010); Average household size: 2.34 (2010); Median age: 35.6 (2010); Males per 100 females: 110.9 (2010); Marriage status: 24.3% never married, 52.5% now married, 5.4% widowed, 17.9% divorced (2000); Foreign born: 1.2% (2000); Ancestry (includes multiple ancestries): 32.5% German, 16.9% Other groups, 14.5% United States or American, 7.3% Irish, 4.8% Dutch (2000).

Economy: Employment by occupation: 2.8% management, 5.2% professional, 15.3% services, 26.8% sales, 0.0% farming, 10.1% construction, 39.7% production (2000).

Income: Per capita income: $20,071 (2010); Median household income: $44,527 (2010); Average household income: $46,989 (2010); Percent of households with income of $100,000 or more: 3.3% (2010); Poverty rate: 5.2% (2000).

Taxes: Total city taxes per capita: $172 (2007); City property taxes per capita: $168 (2007).

Education: Percent of population age 25 and over with: High school diploma (including GED) or higher: 85.1% (2010); Bachelor's degree or higher: 4.3% (2010); Master's degree or higher: 3.3% (2010).

Housing: Homeownership rate: 71.8% (2010); Median home value: $84,242 (2010); Median contract rent: $406 per month (2000); Median year structure built: 1952 (2000).

Transportation: Commute to work: 90.5% car, 0.7% public transportation, 3.2% walk, 1.8% work from home (2000); Travel time to work: 33.9% less than 15 minutes, 36.4% 15 to 30 minutes, 22.1% 30 to 45 minutes, 0.0% 45 to 60 minutes, 7.5% 60 minutes or more (2000)

PLYMOUTH (city). County seat. Covers a land area of 6.959 square miles and a water area of 0.015 square miles. Located at 41.34° N. Lat; 86.31° W. Long. Elevation is 797 feet.

History: Plymouth was founded in 1834 as a shipping center and county seat.

Population: 8,666 (1990); 9,840 (2000); 10,476 (2010); 10,707 (2015 projected); Race: 86.5% White, 1.7% Black, 0.5% Asian, 11.3% Other, 22.7% Hispanic of any race (2010); Density: 1,505.4 persons per square mile (2010); Average household size: 2.50 (2010); Median age: 35.1 (2010); Males per 100 females: 97.4 (2010); Marriage status: 23.7% never married, 52.7% now married, 9.6% widowed, 14.0% divorced (2000); Foreign born: 11.7% (2000); Ancestry (includes multiple ancestries): 25.3% German, 20.0% Other groups, 9.4% Irish, 9.3% United States or American, 7.7% English (2000).

Economy: Single-family building permits issued: 27 (2009); Multi-family building permits issued: 0 (2009); Employment by occupation: 6.9% management, 11.3% professional, 13.6% services, 20.4% sales, 0.4% farming, 8.6% construction, 38.7% production (2000).

Income: Per capita income: $19,982 (2010); Median household income: $42,423 (2010); Average household income: $50,865 (2010); Percent of households with income of $100,000 or more: 8.3% (2010); Poverty rate: 13.1% (2000).

Taxes: Total city taxes per capita: $316 (2007); City property taxes per capita: $297 (2007).

Education: Percent of population age 25 and over with: High school diploma (including GED) or higher: 78.9% (2010); Bachelor's degree or higher: 16.3% (2010); Master's degree or higher: 7.1% (2010).

School District(s)
Plymouth Community School Corp (KG-12)
    2008-09 Enrollment: 3,486 . . . . (574) 936-3115

Housing: Homeownership rate: 60.7% (2010); Median home value: $92,129 (2010); Median contract rent: $415 per month (2000); Median year structure built: 1964 (2000).

Hospitals: BHC of Northern Indiana (80 beds); Saint Joseph's Regional Medical Center - Plymouth Campus (58 beds)

Safety: Violent crime rate: 8.1 per 10,000 population; Property crime rate: 409.9 per 10,000 population (2008).

Newspapers: Pilot News (Community news; Circulation 9,400); South Bend Tribune - Plymouth Bureau (Local news; Circulation 100,000)

Transportation: Commute to work: 91.0% car, 0.9% public transportation, 4.2% walk, 2.5% work from home (2000); Travel time to work: 59.1% less

than 15 minutes, 20.6% 15 to 30 minutes, 9.5% 30 to 45 minutes, 5.9% 45 to 60 minutes, 4.9% 60 minutes or more (2000)
Additional Information Contacts
City of Plymouth. . . . . (574) 936-2124
  http://www.plymouthin.com
Plymouth Area Chamber of Commerce . . . . (574) 936-2323
  http://www.plychamber.org

TIPPECANOE (unincorporated postal area, zip code 46570). Covers a land area of 21.095 square miles and a water area of 0.036 square miles. Located at 41.20° N. Lat; 86.12° W. Long. Elevation is 781 feet.

History: Laid out 1882.
Population: 1,053 (2000); Race: 95.4% White, 0.0% Black, 0.0% Asian, 4.6% Other, 3.5% Hispanic of any race (2000); Density: 49.9 persons per square mile (2000); Age: 27.8% under 18, 12.5% over 64 (2000); Marriage status: 19.7% never married, 61.7% now married, 8.7% widowed, 9.9% divorced (2000); Foreign born: 2.7% (2000); Ancestry (includes multiple ancestries): 26.0% German, 15.8% Irish, 11.3% English, 10.4% United States or American, 9.9% Other groups (2000).
Economy: Employment by occupation: 5.2% management, 4.3% professional, 17.5% services, 17.3% sales, 0.5% farming, 13.7% construction, 41.4% production (2000).
Income: Per capita income: $17,102 (2000); Median household income: $40,385 (2000); Poverty rate: 5.4% (2000).
Education: Percent of population age 25 and over with: High school diploma (including GED) or higher: 67.6% (2000); Bachelor's degree or higher: 5.3% (2000).
Housing: Homeownership rate: 87.8% (2000); Median home value: $72,500 (2000); Median contract rent: $267 per month (2000); Median year structure built: 1968 (2000).
Transportation: Commute to work: 91.0% car, 0.9% public transportation, 3.8% walk, 2.4% work from home (2000); Travel time to work: 25.8% less than 15 minutes, 31.1% 15 to 30 minutes, 22.8% 30 to 45 minutes, 6.0% 45 to 60 minutes, 14.2% 60 minutes or more (2000)

Martin County

Located in southwestern Indiana; drained by the Lost River and East Fork of the White River. Covers a land area of 336.14 square miles, a water area of 4.39 square miles, and is located in the Eastern Time Zone. The county was founded in 1820. County seat is Shoals.

Weather Station: Crane Naval Depot											Elevation: 728 feet	
	Jan	Feb	Mar	Apr	May	Jun	Jul	Aug	Sep	Oct	Nov	Dec
High	39	45	56	67	77	84	88	86	81	69	56	45
Low	21	26	34	44	54	62	67	65	58	46	37	27
Precip	3.0	2.7	4.1	5.0	5.5	3.9	4.9	4.0	3.3	3.4	4.2	3.4
Snow	na	na	1.8	tr	0.0	0.0	0.0	0.0	0.0	tr	tr	na

High and Low temperatures in degrees Fahrenheit; Precipitation and Snow in inches

Weather Station: Shoals Hiway 50 Bridge											Elevation: 547 feet	
	Jan	Feb	Mar	Apr	May	Jun	Jul	Aug	Sep	Oct	Nov	Dec
High	37	43	54	66	75	83	87	85	79	68	55	43
Low	19	22	31	40	50	59	64	62	54	42	34	25
Precip	3.0	2.8	4.3	4.6	5.6	4.2	4.7	3.6	3.3	3.3	4.4	3.5
Snow	5.7	4.0	2.8	tr	0.0	0.0	0.0	0.0	0.0	0.1	0.3	2.7

High and Low temperatures in degrees Fahrenheit; Precipitation and Snow in inches

Population: 10,369 (1990); 10,369 (2000); 9,878 (2010); 9,567 (2015 projected); Race: 98.2% White, 0.6% Black, 0.1% Asian, 1.1% Other, 0.7% Hispanic of any race (2010); Density: 29.4 persons per square mile (2010); Average household size: 2.35 (2010); Median age: 41.2 (2010); Males per 100 females: 104.6 (2010).
Religion: Five largest groups: 25.4% Catholic Church, 11.0% The United Methodist Church, 9.8% Christian Churches and Churches of Christ, 3.5% Evangelical Lutheran Church in America, 2.9% Old Order Amish Church (2000).
Economy: Unemployment rate: 7.0% (5/2010); Total civilian labor force: 5,200 (5/2010); Leading industries: 26.4% manufacturing; 17.8% retail trade; 13.5% accommodation & food services (2008); Farms: 278 totaling 61,331 acres (2007); Companies that employ 500 or more persons: 0 (2008); Companies that employ 100 to 499 persons: 2 (2008); Companies that employ less than 100 persons: 177 (2008); Black-owned businesses: n/a (2002); Hispanic-owned businesses: n/a (2002); Asian-owned businesses: n/a (2002); Women-owned businesses: n/a (2002); Retail

sales per capita: $9,457 (2010). Single-family building permits issued: 1 (2009); Multi-family building permits issued: 0 (2009).
Income: Per capita income: $22,367 (2010); Median household income: $45,195 (2010); Average household income: $52,899 (2010); Percent of households with income of $100,000 or more: 9.1% (2010); Poverty rate: 12.9% (2008); Bankruptcy rate: 4.40% (2009).
Taxes: Total county taxes per capita: $218 (2007); County property taxes per capita: $195 (2007).
Education: Percent of population age 25 and over with: High school diploma (including GED) or higher: 80.1% (2010); Bachelor's degree or higher: 9.2% (2010); Master's degree or higher: 4.2% (2010).
Housing: Homeownership rate: 80.2% (2010); Median home value: $75,481 (2010); Median contract rent: $n/a per month (2006-2008 3-year est.); Median year structure built: n/a (2006-2008 3-year est.)
Health: Birth rate: 114.6 per 10,000 population (2009); Death rate: 112.6 per 10,000 population (2009); Age-adjusted cancer mortality rate: 168.7 deaths per 100,000 population (2006); Number of physicians: 4.0 per 10,000 population (2007); Hospital beds: 0.0 per 10,000 population (2006); Hospital admissions: 0.0 per 10,000 population (2006).
Elections: 2008 Presidential election results: 34.8% Obama, 63.7% McCain, 0.0% Nader
National and State Parks: Martin County State Forest; Martin State Forest
Additional Information Contacts
Martin County Government . . . . (812) 295-4093
  http://www.martincountyindianachamberofcommerce.org

Martin County Communities

CRANE (town). Covers a land area of 0.119 square miles and a water area of 0 square miles. Located at 38.89° N. Lat; 86.90° W. Long. Elevation is 610 feet.

Population: 216 (1990); 203 (2000); 183 (2010); 173 (2015 projected); Race: 98.4% White, 0.0% Black, 0.0% Asian, 1.6% Other, 0.5% Hispanic of any race (2010); Density: 1,537.4 persons per square mile (2010); Average household size: 2.38 (2010); Median age: 41.3 (2010); Males per 100 females: 96.8 (2010); Marriage status: 10.5% never married, 65.0% now married, 7.0% widowed, 17.5% divorced (2000); Foreign born: 0.0% (2000); Ancestry (includes multiple ancestries): 16.1% German, 15.0% Irish, 13.0% United States or American, 9.8% English, 9.3% French (except Basque) (2000).
Economy: Employment by occupation: 0.0% management, 18.6% professional, 20.9% services, 17.4% sales, 0.0% farming, 19.8% construction, 23.3% production (2000).
Income: Per capita income: $23,113 (2010); Median household income: $48,026 (2010); Average household income: $55,779 (2010); Percent of households with income of $100,000 or more: 10.4% (2010); Poverty rate: 13.6% (2000).
Taxes: Total city taxes per capita: $100 (2007); City property taxes per capita: $0 (2007).
Education: Percent of population age 25 and over with: High school diploma (including GED) or higher: 91.9% (2010); Bachelor's degree or higher: 11.3% (2010); Master's degree or higher: 6.5% (2010).
Housing: Homeownership rate: 81.8% (2010); Median home value: $82,500 (2010); Median contract rent: $320 per month (2000); Median year structure built: 1951 (2000).
Transportation: Commute to work: 88.8% car, 0.0% public transportation, 4.5% walk, 3.4% work from home (2000); Travel time to work: 38.4% less than 15 minutes, 4.7% 15 to 30 minutes, 12.8% 30 to 45 minutes, 33.7% 45 to 60 minutes, 10.5% 60 minutes or more (2000)

LOOGOOTEE (city). Covers a land area of 1.566 square miles and a water area of 0 square miles. Located at 38.67° N. Lat; 86.91° W. Long. Elevation is 538 feet.

History: Loogootee grew when natural gas was found here in 1899, and several glass factories were established. The town was named for Lowe, an engineer on the first railroad, and Gootee, who owned the land on which the town was built.
Population: 2,904 (1990); 2,741 (2000); 2,637 (2010); 2,555 (2015 projected); Race: 98.3% White, 0.5% Black, 0.4% Asian, 0.9% Other, 0.5% Hispanic of any race (2010); Density: 1,684.1 persons per square mile (2010); Average household size: 2.22 (2010); Median age: 42.4 (2010); Males per 100 females: 100.4 (2010); Marriage status: 20.8% never married, 54.0% now married, 10.8% widowed, 14.4% divorced (2000); Foreign born: 0.6% (2000); Ancestry (includes multiple ancestries): 21.4%

United States or American, 20.1% German, 16.3% Irish, 7.8% English, 5.6% Other groups (2000).

Economy: Single-family building permits issued: 1 (2009); Multi-family building permits issued: 0 (2009); Employment by occupation: 9.2% management, 17.4% professional, 17.3% services, 21.2% sales, 0.0% farming, 13.8% construction, 20.9% production (2000).

Income: Per capita income: $22,996 (2010); Median household income: $41,655 (2010); Average household income: $51,025 (2010); Percent of households with income of $100,000 or more: 8.0% (2010); Poverty rate: 16.4% (2000).

Taxes: Total city taxes per capita: $131 (2007); City property taxes per capita: $108 (2007).

Education: Percent of population age 25 and over with: High school diploma (including GED) or higher: 82.4% (2010); Bachelor's degree or higher: 14.2% (2010); Master's degree or higher: 6.8% (2010).

School District(s)
Loogootee Community Sch Corp (KG-12)
    2008-09 Enrollment: 1,047 . . . . (812) 295-2595

Housing: Homeownership rate: 73.8% (2010); Median home value: $79,178 (2010); Median contract rent: $263 per month (2000); Median year structure built: 1964 (2000).

Newspapers: Loogootee Tribune (Community news; Circulation 3,100)

Transportation: Commute to work: 92.6% car, 0.0% public transportation, 2.7% walk, 4.4% work from home (2000); Travel time to work: 43.6% less than 15 minutes, 20.2% 15 to 30 minutes, 27.5% 30 to 45 minutes, 4.9% 45 to 60 minutes, 3.7% 60 minutes or more (2000)

SHOALS (town). County seat. Covers a land area of 1.801 square miles and a water area of 0.095 square miles. Located at 38.66° N. Lat; 86.79° W. Long. Elevation is 505 feet.

History: Shoals was founded in 1816 and named for the shallow place in the White River that afforded a crossing. The area was known as a haven for moonshiners and bootleggers during prohibition.

Population: 853 (1990); 807 (2000); 741 (2010); 707 (2015 projected); Race: 95.4% White, 2.3% Black, 0.0% Asian, 2.3% Other, 2.7% Hispanic of any race (2010); Density: 411.3 persons per square mile (2010); Average household size: 2.05 (2010); Median age: 44.5 (2010); Males per 100 females: 112.3 (2010); Marriage status: 13.8% never married, 55.3% now married, 13.2% widowed, 17.7% divorced (2000); Foreign born: 0.6% (2000); Ancestry (includes multiple ancestries): 24.1% United States or American, 16.4% Other groups, 10.5% German, 7.4% English, 6.0% Irish (2000).

Economy: Employment by occupation: 9.0% management, 11.2% professional, 23.9% services, 20.1% sales, 0.7% farming, 8.6% construction, 26.5% production (2000).

Income: Per capita income: $19,596 (2010); Median household income: $34,634 (2010); Average household income: $41,746 (2010); Percent of households with income of $100,000 or more: 7.5% (2010); Poverty rate: 20.4% (2000).

Taxes: Total city taxes per capita: $145 (2007); City property taxes per capita: $122 (2007).

Education: Percent of population age 25 and over with: High school diploma (including GED) or higher: 77.1% (2010); Bachelor's degree or higher: 6.4% (2010); Master's degree or higher: 3.7% (2010).

School District(s)
Shoals Community School Corp (PK-12)
    2008-09 Enrollment: 676 . . . . (812) 247-2060

Housing: Homeownership rate: 73.3% (2010); Median home value: $56,061 (2010); Median contract rent: $204 per month (2000); Median year structure built: 1964 (2000).

Newspapers: Shoals News (Local news; Circulation 2,700)

Transportation: Commute to work: 91.8% car, 0.0% public transportation, 4.5% walk, 2.6% work from home (2000); Travel time to work: 41.0% less than 15 minutes, 21.5% 15 to 30 minutes, 21.8% 30 to 45 minutes, 7.3% 45 to 60 minutes, 8.4% 60 minutes or more (2000)

Miami County

Located in north central Indiana; crossed by the Wabash, Mississinewa, and Eel Rivers. Covers a land area of 375.62 square miles, a water area of 1.74 square miles, and is located in the Eastern Time Zone. The county was founded in 1832. County seat is Peru.

Miami County is part of the Peru, IN Micropolitan Statistical Area. The entire metro area includes: Miami County, IN

Population: 36,897 (1990); 36,082 (2000); 35,923 (2010); 35,338 (2015 projected); Race: 91.0% White, 5.1% Black, 0.3% Asian, 3.6% Other, 1.7% Hispanic of any race (2010); Density: 95.6 persons per square mile (2010); Average household size: 2.44 (2010); Median age: 39.3 (2010); Males per 100 females: 122.8 (2010).

Religion: Five largest groups: 7.4% American Baptist Churches in the USA, 6.7% Catholic Church, 5.9% The United Methodist Church, 5.0% Christian Churches and Churches of Christ, 3.3% Lutheran Church—Missouri Synod (2000).

Economy: Unemployment rate: 11.2% (5/2010); Total civilian labor force: 17,094 (5/2010); Leading industries: 30.9% manufacturing; 15.4% health care and social assistance; 11.6% retail trade (2008); Farms: 682 totaling 178,030 acres (2007); Companies that employ 500 or more persons: 2 (2008); Companies that employ 100 to 499 persons: 13 (2008); Companies that employ less than 100 persons: 594 (2008); Black-owned businesses: n/a (2002); Hispanic-owned businesses: n/a (2002); Asian-owned businesses: n/a (2002); Women-owned businesses: 864 (2002); Retail sales per capita: $8,293 (2010). Single-family building permits issued: 10 (2009); Multi-family building permits issued: 0 (2009).

Income: Per capita income: $20,278 (2010); Median household income: $44,411 (2010); Average household income: $52,857 (2010); Percent of households with income of $100,000 or more: 9.4% (2010); Poverty rate: 14.2% (2008); Bankruptcy rate: 7.59% (2009).

Taxes: Total county taxes per capita: $125 (2007); County property taxes per capita: $81 (2007).

Education: Percent of population age 25 and over with: High school diploma (including GED) or higher: 83.9% (2010); Bachelor's degree or higher: 11.3% (2010); Master's degree or higher: 4.0% (2010).

Housing: Homeownership rate: 75.1% (2010); Median home value: $82,885 (2010); Median contract rent: $426 per month (2006-2008 3-year est.); Median year structure built: 1956 (2006-2008 3-year est.)

Health: Birth rate: 114.4 per 10,000 population (2009); Death rate: 88.1 per 10,000 population (2009); Age-adjusted cancer mortality rate: 221.0 deaths per 100,000 population (2006); Number of physicians: 4.9 per 10,000 population (2007); Hospital beds: 6.8 per 10,000 population (2006); Hospital admissions: 416.1 per 10,000 population (2006).

Elections: 2008 Presidential election results: 39.4% Obama, 58.9% McCain, 0.0% Nader

National and State Parks: Frances Slocum State Forest

Additional Information Contacts
Miami County Government . . . . (765) 472-3901
    http://www.miamicountyin.gov
City of Peru . . . . (765) 472-2400
    http://www.cityofperu.org
Peru Chamber of Commerce . . . . (765) 472-1923
    http://miamicochamber.com

Miami County Communities

AMBOY (town). Covers a land area of 0.354 square miles and a water area of 0 square miles. Located at 40.60° N. Lat; 85.92° W. Long. Elevation is 810 feet.

Population: 370 (1990); 360 (2000); 312 (2010); 293 (2015 projected); Race: 97.8% White, 0.3% Black, 0.3% Asian, 1.6% Other, 3.5% Hispanic of any race (2010); Density: 882.1 persons per square mile (2010); Average household size: 2.50 (2010); Median age: 42.4 (2010); Males per 100 females: 110.8 (2010); Marriage status: 14.6% never married, 75.3% now married, 4.5% widowed, 5.6% divorced (2000); Foreign born: 1.7% (2000); Ancestry (includes multiple ancestries): 19.2% German, 13.3% United States or American, 10.5% Other groups, 6.8% Swiss, 6.5% Dutch (2000).

Economy: Employment by occupation: 8.6% management, 16.6% professional, 12.3% services, 28.8% sales, 0.0% farming, 14.1% construction, 19.6% production (2000).

Income: Per capita income: $23,576 (2010); Median household income: $50,446 (2010); Average household income: $59,260 (2010); Percent of households with income of $100,000 or more: 12.0% (2010); Poverty rate: 7.1% (2000).

Taxes: Total city taxes per capita: $113 (2007); City property taxes per capita: $93 (2007).

Education: Percent of population age 25 and over with: High school diploma (including GED) or higher: 83.4% (2010); Bachelor's degree or higher: 9.4% (2010); Master's degree or higher: 3.6% (2010).

Housing: Homeownership rate: 84.8% (2010); Median home value: $87,059 (2010); Median contract rent: $329 per month (2000); Median year structure built: before 1940 (2000).
Transportation: Commute to work: 96.3% car, 0.0% public transportation, 0.0% walk, 2.5% work from home (2000); Travel time to work: 14.5% less than 15 minutes, 34.6% 15 to 30 minutes, 36.5% 30 to 45 minutes, 3.1% 45 to 60 minutes, 11.3% 60 minutes or more (2000)

BUNKER HILL (town). Covers a land area of 0.436 square miles and a water area of 0 square miles. Located at 40.65° N. Lat; 86.10° W. Long. Elevation is 820 feet.

Population: 989 (1990); 987 (2000); 917 (2010); 885 (2015 projected); Race: 95.4% White, 0.7% Black, 0.2% Asian, 3.7% Other, 0.7% Hispanic of any race (2010); Density: 2,102.1 persons per square mile (2010); Average household size: 2.51 (2010); Median age: 37.1 (2010); Males per 100 females: 107.0 (2010); Marriage status: 19.3% never married, 61.2% now married, 5.7% widowed, 13.8% divorced (2000); Foreign born: 2.6% (2000); Ancestry (includes multiple ancestries): 22.7% German, 13.8% English, 12.4% United States or American, 9.0% Irish, 8.4% Other groups (2000).
Economy: Single-family building permits issued: 0 (2009); Multi-family building permits issued: 0 (2009); Employment by occupation: 5.9% management, 7.2% professional, 14.5% services, 26.0% sales, 0.7% farming, 17.4% construction, 28.4% production (2000).
Income: Per capita income: $20,253 (2010); Median household income: $44,609 (2010); Average household income: $50,178 (2010); Percent of households with income of $100,000 or more: 8.5% (2010); Poverty rate: 7.1% (2000).
Taxes: Total city taxes per capita: $173 (2007); City property taxes per capita: $154 (2007).
Education: Percent of population age 25 and over with: High school diploma (including GED) or higher: 89.9% (2010); Bachelor's degree or higher: 17.4% (2010); Master's degree or higher: 7.8% (2010).
School District(s)
Maconaquah School Corp (PK-12)
    2008-09 Enrollment: 2,287 . . . . (765) 689-9131
Housing: Homeownership rate: 73.8% (2010); Median home value: $74,694 (2010); Median contract rent: $290 per month (2000); Median year structure built: 1957 (2000).
Transportation: Commute to work: 94.1% car, 0.0% public transportation, 2.6% walk, 1.7% work from home (2000); Travel time to work: 27.8% less than 15 minutes, 46.6% 15 to 30 minutes, 18.8% 30 to 45 minutes, 0.4% 45 to 60 minutes, 6.4% 60 minutes or more (2000)

CONVERSE (town). Covers a land area of 0.891 square miles and a water area of 0 square miles. Located at 40.58° N. Lat; 85.86° W. Long. Elevation is 830 feet.

Population: 1,158 (1990); 1,137 (2000); 965 (2010); 895 (2015 projected); Race: 96.7% White, 0.2% Black, 0.6% Asian, 2.5% Other, 3.9% Hispanic of any race (2010); Density: 1,083.3 persons per square mile (2010); Average household size: 2.42 (2010); Median age: 40.9 (2010); Males per 100 females: 102.7 (2010); Marriage status: 18.0% never married, 60.7% now married, 9.5% widowed, 11.8% divorced (2000); Foreign born: 0.4% (2000); Ancestry (includes multiple ancestries): 21.8% German, 13.8% United States or American, 9.3% English, 8.7% Irish, 5.9% Other groups (2000).
Economy: Single-family building permits issued: 1 (2009); Multi-family building permits issued: 0 (2009); Employment by occupation: 11.2% management, 17.2% professional, 14.1% services, 23.7% sales, 0.0% farming, 8.1% construction, 25.7% production (2000).
Income: Per capita income: $20,431 (2010); Median household income: $42,390 (2010); Average household income: $49,831 (2010); Percent of households with income of $100,000 or more: 8.0% (2010); Poverty rate: 15.7% (2000).
Taxes: Total city taxes per capita: $273 (2007); City property taxes per capita: $253 (2007).
Education: Percent of population age 25 and over with: High school diploma (including GED) or higher: 85.8% (2010); Bachelor's degree or higher: 17.2% (2010); Master's degree or higher: 4.7% (2010).
School District(s)
Oak Hill United School Corp (KG-12)
    2008-09 Enrollment: 1,483 . . . . (765) 395-3341
Housing: Homeownership rate: 78.2% (2010); Median home value: $82,188 (2010); Median contract rent: $303 per month (2000); Median year structure built: 1952 (2000).

Transportation: Commute to work: 92.3% car, 0.6% public transportation, 5.8% walk, 0.4% work from home (2000); Travel time to work: 22.8% less than 15 minutes, 43.9% 15 to 30 minutes, 27.1% 30 to 45 minutes, 3.0% 45 to 60 minutes, 3.2% 60 minutes or more (2000)

DENVER (town). Covers a land area of 0.233 square miles and a water area of 0 square miles. Located at 40.86° N. Lat; 86.07° W. Long. Elevation is 712 feet.

Population: 504 (1990); 541 (2000); 472 (2010); 442 (2015 projected); Race: 97.9% White, 0.0% Black, 0.0% Asian, 2.1% Other, 0.8% Hispanic of any race (2010); Density: 2,022.4 persons per square mile (2010); Average household size: 2.68 (2010); Median age: 38.5 (2010); Males per 100 females: 111.7 (2010); Marriage status: 21.6% never married, 58.3% now married, 5.7% widowed, 14.4% divorced (2000); Foreign born: 0.0% (2000); Ancestry (includes multiple ancestries): 29.8% German, 13.4% Irish, 12.7% United States or American, 9.7% Other groups, 6.9% English (2000).
Economy: Employment by occupation: 11.3% management, 4.4% professional, 16.0% services, 24.4% sales, 3.3% farming, 5.8% construction, 34.9% production (2000).
Income: Per capita income: $17,424 (2010); Median household income: $37,333 (2010); Average household income: $46,946 (2010); Percent of households with income of $100,000 or more: 4.5% (2010); Poverty rate: 9.5% (2000).
Taxes: Total city taxes per capita: $39 (2007); City property taxes per capita: $35 (2007).
Education: Percent of population age 25 and over with: High school diploma (including GED) or higher: 83.8% (2010); Bachelor's degree or higher: 7.0% (2010); Master's degree or higher: 2.5% (2010).
School District(s)
North Miami Community Schools (PK-12)
    2008-09 Enrollment: 1,098 . . . . (765) 985-3891
Housing: Homeownership rate: 88.6% (2010); Median home value: $76,774 (2010); Median contract rent: $392 per month (2000); Median year structure built: before 1940 (2000).
Transportation: Commute to work: 94.1% car, 0.0% public transportation, 0.0% walk, 5.9% work from home (2000); Travel time to work: 21.3% less than 15 minutes, 56.7% 15 to 30 minutes, 18.1% 30 to 45 minutes, 1.2% 45 to 60 minutes, 2.8% 60 minutes or more (2000)

GRISSOM AFB (CDP). Covers a land area of 4.197 square miles and a water area of 0 square miles. Located at 40.67° N. Lat; 86.15° W. Long.

Population: 4,271 (1990); 1,652 (2000); 1,483 (2010); 1,403 (2015 projected); Race: 88.5% White, 5.9% Black, 0.5% Asian, 5.1% Other, 2.9% Hispanic of any race (2010); Density: 353.3 persons per square mile (2010); Average household size: 2.73 (2010); Median age: 31.1 (2010); Males per 100 females: 110.4 (2010); Marriage status: 24.6% never married, 61.1% now married, 0.6% widowed, 13.8% divorced (2000); Foreign born: 1.2% (2000); Ancestry (includes multiple ancestries): 25.9% German, 18.4% Other groups, 11.3% United States or American, 9.0% Irish, 7.3% English (2000).
Economy: Employment by occupation: 10.5% management, 7.8% professional, 20.6% services, 31.0% sales, 0.0% farming, 6.2% construction, 23.8% production (2000).
Income: Per capita income: $19,639 (2010); Median household income: $52,448 (2010); Average household income: $53,539 (2010); Percent of households with income of $100,000 or more: 5.3% (2010); Poverty rate: 8.9% (2000).
Education: Percent of population age 25 and over with: High school diploma (including GED) or higher: 93.2% (2010); Bachelor's degree or higher: 18.3% (2010); Master's degree or higher: 3.1% (2010).
Housing: Homeownership rate: 20.2% (2010); Median home value: $96,296 (2010); Median contract rent: $547 per month (2000); Median year structure built: 1963 (2000).
Transportation: Commute to work: 98.0% car, 0.0% public transportation, 0.7% walk, 0.7% work from home (2000); Travel time to work: 24.6% less than 15 minutes, 52.2% 15 to 30 minutes, 15.7% 30 to 45 minutes, 3.3% 45 to 60 minutes, 4.1% 60 minutes or more (2000)

MACY (town). Covers a land area of 0.141 square miles and a water area of 0 square miles. Located at 40.96° N. Lat; 86.12° W. Long. Elevation is 850 feet.

History: Laid out 1860.
Population: 218 (1990); 248 (2000); 218 (2010); 203 (2015 projected); Race: 95.0% White, 0.0% Black, 0.0% Asian, 5.0% Other, 3.2% Hispanic

of any race (2010); Density: 1,543.1 persons per square mile (2010); Average household size: 2.79 (2010); Median age: 38.6 (2010); Males per 100 females: 134.4 (2010); Marriage status: 20.2% never married, 73.8% now married, 5.4% widowed, 0.6% divorced (2000); Foreign born: 0.0% (2000); Ancestry (includes multiple ancestries): 21.5% German, 14.6% United States or American, 10.3% Irish, 8.6% English, 5.6% Other groups (2000).

Economy: Employment by occupation: 0.0% management, 16.1% professional, 15.3% services, 22.0% sales, 0.0% farming, 12.7% construction, 33.9% production (2000).

Income: Per capita income: $21,867 (2010); Median household income: $43,125 (2010); Average household income: $60,160 (2010); Percent of households with income of $100,000 or more: 10.3% (2010); Poverty rate: 2.6% (2000).

Taxes: Total city taxes per capita: $80 (2007); City property taxes per capita: $63 (2007).

Education: Percent of population age 25 and over with: High school diploma (including GED) or higher: 86.1% (2010); Bachelor's degree or higher: 10.4% (2010); Master's degree or higher: 2.1% (2010).

Housing: Homeownership rate: 84.6% (2010); Median home value: $86,667 (2010); Median contract rent: $194 per month (2000); Median year structure built: before 1940 (2000).

Transportation: Commute to work: 98.2% car, 0.0% public transportation, 1.8% walk, 0.0% work from home (2000); Travel time to work: 10.7% less than 15 minutes, 63.4% 15 to 30 minutes, 14.3% 30 to 45 minutes, 8.0% 45 to 60 minutes, 3.6% 60 minutes or more (2000)

MEXICO (CDP). Covers a land area of 5.479 square miles and a water area of 0 square miles. Located at 40.82° N. Lat; 86.11° W. Long. Elevation is 702 feet.

History: Mexico was settled largely by German Baptists as a stagecoach stop between Indianapolis and Michigan City.

Population: 1,014 (1990); 984 (2000); 795 (2010); 731 (2015 projected); Race: 98.4% White, 0.1% Black, 0.1% Asian, 1.4% Other, 0.4% Hispanic of any race (2010); Density: 145.1 persons per square mile (2010); Average household size: 2.48 (2010); Median age: 45.7 (2010); Males per 100 females: 113.1 (2010); Marriage status: 21.3% never married, 58.9% now married, 8.9% widowed, 10.9% divorced (2000); Foreign born: 0.0% (2000); Ancestry (includes multiple ancestries): 29.9% German, 18.6% United States or American, 11.7% Dutch, 7.7% Irish, 6.6% Other groups (2000).

Economy: Employment by occupation: 9.8% management, 11.9% professional, 10.7% services, 27.7% sales, 0.0% farming, 12.6% construction, 27.3% production (2000).

Income: Per capita income: $23,260 (2010); Median household income: $53,189 (2010); Average household income: $57,671 (2010); Percent of households with income of $100,000 or more: 6.5% (2010); Poverty rate: 5.1% (2000).

Education: Percent of population age 25 and over with: High school diploma (including GED) or higher: 92.7% (2010); Bachelor's degree or higher: 9.0% (2010); Master's degree or higher: 3.7% (2010).

Housing: Homeownership rate: 86.9% (2010); Median home value: $107,474 (2010); Median contract rent: $286 per month (2000); Median year structure built: 1965 (2000).

Transportation: Commute to work: 94.5% car, 0.0% public transportation, 2.9% walk, 1.6% work from home (2000); Travel time to work: 43.8% less than 15 minutes, 26.6% 15 to 30 minutes, 21.4% 30 to 45 minutes, 4.7% 45 to 60 minutes, 3.5% 60 minutes or more (2000)

PERU (city). Aka Bunker Hill Air Force Base. County seat. Covers a land area of 4.615 square miles and a water area of 0.043 square miles. Located at 40.75° N. Lat; 86.06° W. Long. Elevation is 650 feet.

History: Peru's reputation as the Circus City of the World, serving as winter quarters for many circuses, began in the late 1800's when Ben Wallace started the Hagenbeck-Wallace Circus.

Population: 13,422 (1990); 12,994 (2000); 11,458 (2010); 10,780 (2015 projected); Race: 92.3% White, 2.9% Black, 0.5% Asian, 4.3% Other, 1.8% Hispanic of any race (2010); Density: 2,482.7 persons per square mile (2010); Average household size: 2.29 (2010); Median age: 39.6 (2010); Males per 100 females: 99.1 (2010); Marriage status: 21.4% never married, 53.8% now married, 10.3% widowed, 14.4% divorced (2000); Foreign born: 1.2% (2000); Ancestry (includes multiple ancestries): 20.9% German, 13.2% United States or American, 11.7% Irish, 10.2% Other groups, 7.8% English (2000).

Economy: Single-family building permits issued: 2 (2009); Multi-family building permits issued: 0 (2009); Employment by occupation: 6.7% management, 11.7% professional, 16.4% services, 21.9% sales, 0.4% farming, 9.6% construction, 33.2% production (2000).

Income: Per capita income: $20,344 (2010); Median household income: $35,406 (2010); Average household income: $47,305 (2010); Percent of households with income of $100,000 or more: 7.8% (2010); Poverty rate: 11.8% (2000).

Taxes: Total city taxes per capita: $412 (2007); City property taxes per capita: $347 (2007).

Education: Percent of population age 25 and over with: High school diploma (including GED) or higher: 81.1% (2010); Bachelor's degree or higher: 10.6% (2010); Master's degree or higher: 3.4% (2010).

School District(s)
Maconaquah School Corp (PK-12)
    2008-09 Enrollment: 2,287 . . . . (765) 689-9131
Peru Community Schools (PK-12)
    2008-09 Enrollment: 2,323 . . . . (765) 473-3081

Housing: Homeownership rate: 68.0% (2010); Median home value: $60,812 (2010); Median contract rent: $345 per month (2000); Median year structure built: 1941 (2000).

Hospitals: Dukes Memorial Hospital (158 beds)

Newspapers: Peru Tribune (Local news; Circulation 6,957)

Transportation: Commute to work: 92.0% car, 0.1% public transportation, 3.9% walk, 3.2% work from home (2000); Travel time to work: 55.2% less than 15 minutes, 24.4% 15 to 30 minutes, 10.5% 30 to 45 minutes, 4.2% 45 to 60 minutes, 5.8% 60 minutes or more (2000)

Additional Information Contacts
City of Peru . . . . (765) 472-2400
    http://www.cityofperu.org
Peru Chamber of Commerce . . . . (765) 472-1923
    http://miamicochamber.com

Monroe County

Located in south central Indiana; drained by the West Fork of the White River, and several creeks. Covers a land area of 394.35 square miles, a water area of 16.97 square miles, and is located in the Eastern Time Zone. The county was founded in 1818. County seat is Bloomington.

Monroe County is part of the Bloomington, IN Metropolitan Statistical Area. The entire metro area includes: Greene County, IN; Monroe County, IN; Owen County, IN

Weather Station: Bloomington Indiana Univ.   Elevation: 830 feet

	Jan	Feb	Mar	Apr	May	Jun	Jul	Aug	Sep	Oct	Nov	Dec
High	36	42	52	64	74	82	86	85	78	67	54	42
Low	19	23	32	42	52	62	66	64	56	44	36	25
Precip	2.6	2.6	3.7	4.5	5.1	4.1	4.3	3.9	3.5	3.1	4.0	3.3
Snow	na	na	na	tr	0.0	0.0	0.0	0.0	0.0	0.2	tr	1.6

High and Low temperatures in degrees Fahrenheit; Precipitation and Snow in inches

Population: 108,978 (1990); 120,563 (2000); 130,820 (2010); 135,264 (2015 projected); Race: 88.9% White, 3.3% Black, 4.4% Asian, 3.4% Other, 2.3% Hispanic of any race (2010); Density: 331.7 persons per square mile (2010); Average household size: 2.26 (2010); Median age: 30.0 (2010); Males per 100 females: 97.1 (2010).

Religion: Five largest groups: 10.5% Catholic Church, 4.1% Christian Churches and Churches of Christ, 3.7% The United Methodist Church, 2.0% American Baptist Churches in the USA, 1.7% Churches of Christ (2000).

Economy: Unemployment rate: 7.0% (5/2010); Total civilian labor force: 70,817 (5/2010); Leading industries: 16.4% health care and social assistance; 15.1% retail trade; 14.8% accommodation & food services (2008); Farms: 481 totaling 53,538 acres (2007); Companies that employ 500 or more persons: 6 (2008); Companies that employ 100 to 499 persons: 68 (2008); Companies that employ less than 100 persons: 2,995 (2008); Black-owned businesses: 135 (2002); Hispanic-owned businesses: n/a (2002); Asian-owned businesses: 180 (2002); Women-owned businesses: 3,073 (2002); Retail sales per capita: $12,947 (2010). Single-family building permits issued: 195 (2009); Multi-family building permits issued: 70 (2009).

Income: Per capita income: $22,453 (2010); Median household income: $40,081 (2010); Average household income: $55,236 (2010); Percent of households with income of $100,000 or more: 13.6% (2010); Poverty rate: 20.7% (2008); Bankruptcy rate: 3.61% (2009).

Taxes: Total county taxes per capita: $262 (2007); County property taxes per capita: $188 (2007).

Education: Percent of population age 25 and over with: High school diploma (including GED) or higher: 91.7% (2010); Bachelor's degree or higher: 42.4% (2010); Master's degree or higher: 20.9% (2010).

Housing: Homeownership rate: 55.8% (2010); Median home value: $141,035 (2010); Median contract rent: $601 per month (2006-2008 3-year est.); Median year structure built: 1978 (2006-2008 3-year est.)

Health: Birth rate: 108.6 per 10,000 population (2009); Death rate: 62.2 per 10,000 population (2009); Age-adjusted cancer mortality rate: 165.9 deaths per 100,000 population (2006); Number of physicians: 21.1 per 10,000 population (2007); Hospital beds: 28.0 per 10,000 population (2006); Hospital admissions: 1,242.2 per 10,000 population (2006).

Elections: 2008 Presidential election results: 65.6% Obama, 33.4% McCain, 0.1% Nader

National and State Parks: Allens Creek State Recreation Area; Fairfax State Recreation Area; North Fork State Wildlife Refuge; Paynetown State Recreation Area

Additional Information Contacts

Monroe County Government . . . . (812) 349-2550
http://www.co.monroe.in.us
City of Bloomington . . . . (812) 349-3400
http://bloomington.in.gov
Monroe County Visitors Center . . . . (812) 334-8900
http://www.visitbloomington.com
Town of Ellettsville . . . . (812) 876-3860
http://ellettsville.in.us

Monroe County Communities

BLOOMINGTON (city). County seat. Covers a land area of 19.735 square miles and a water area of 0.199 square miles. Located at 39.16° N. Lat; 86.52° W. Long. Elevation is 771 feet.

History: Bloomington was settled in 1815 and developed around the stone quarries and mills. In 1820 Indiana University was founded here. Bloomington was named by a group of early settlers who enjoyed the many flowers on the hillsides.

Population: 65,260 (1990); 69,291 (2000); 68,802 (2010); 69,056 (2015 projected); Race: 84.0% White, 4.7% Black, 7.1% Asian, 4.2% Other, 3.2% Hispanic of any race (2010); Density: 3,486.3 persons per square mile (2010); Average household size: 2.04 (2010); Median age: 25.7 (2010); Males per 100 females: 95.7 (2010); Marriage status: 60.0% never married, 29.0% now married, 3.5% widowed, 7.5% divorced (2000); Foreign born: 8.1% (2000); Ancestry (includes multiple ancestries): 24.9% German, 15.7% Other groups, 13.3% Irish, 10.9% English, 6.7% United States or American (2000).

Economy: Unemployment rate: 6.9% (5/2010); Total civilian labor force: 38,108 (5/2010); Employment by occupation: 10.8% management, 33.1% professional, 20.0% services, 25.4% sales, 0.1% farming, 4.1% construction, 6.4% production (2000).

Income: Per capita income: $18,714 (2010); Median household income: $28,213 (2010); Average household income: $45,099 (2010); Percent of households with income of $100,000 or more: 10.1% (2010); Poverty rate: 29.6% (2000).

Taxes: Total city taxes per capita: $0 (2007); City property taxes per capita: $0 (2007).

Education: Percent of population age 25 and over with: High school diploma (including GED) or higher: 93.1% (2010); Bachelor's degree or higher: 55.9% (2010); Master's degree or higher: 29.7% (2010).

School District(s)

Monroe County Com Sch Corp (PK-12)
2008-09 Enrollment: 11,025 . . . . (812) 330-7700
Richland-Bean Blossom C S C (PK-12)
2008-09 Enrollment: 2,848 . . . . (812) 876-7100

Four-year College(s)

Indiana University-Bloomington (Public)
Fall 2008 Enrollment: 40,354. . . . . (812) 855-4848
2009-10 Tuition: In-state $8,613; Out-of-state $26,160

Two-year College(s)

Ivy Tech Community College-Bloominton
Fall 2008 Enrollment: 5,385. . . . . (812) 332-1559
2009-10 Tuition: In-state $3,090; Out-of-state $6,306

Vocational/Technical School(s)

Hair Arts Academy (Private, For-profit)
Fall 2008 Enrollment: 35 . . . . (812) 339-1117
2009-10 Tuition: $9,626

Housing: Homeownership rate: 35.5% (2010); Median home value: $144,616 (2010); Median contract rent: $491 per month (2000); Median year structure built: 1974 (2000).

Hospitals: Bloomington Hospital (355 beds)

Safety: Violent crime rate: 37.0 per 10,000 population; Property crime rate: 384.6 per 10,000 population (2008).

Newspapers: Herald-Times (Local news; Circulation 33,000)

Transportation: Commute to work: 76.0% car, 3.0% public transportation, 14.5% walk, 3.3% work from home (2000); Travel time to work: 60.9% less than 15 minutes, 28.6% 15 to 30 minutes, 4.9% 30 to 45 minutes, 1.8% 45 to 60 minutes, 3.8% 60 minutes or more (2000)

Additional Information Contacts

City of Bloomington . . . . (812) 349-3400
http://bloomington.in.gov
Monroe County Visitors Center . . . . (812) 334-8900
http://www.visitbloomington.com

ELLETTSVILLE (town). Covers a land area of 2.155 square miles and a water area of 0 square miles. Located at 39.23° N. Lat; 86.62° W. Long. Elevation is 696 feet.

History: Ellettsville developed around the stone quarries, some of which specialized in fine carving and ornamentation. Ellettsville was platted in 1837 and named for Edward Elletts who had operated a tavern here in the early 1800's.

Population: 3,857 (1990); 5,078 (2000); 6,103 (2010); 6,566 (2015 projected); Race: 95.0% White, 1.7% Black, 1.0% Asian, 2.3% Other, 1.2% Hispanic of any race (2010); Density: 2,832.6 persons per square mile (2010); Average household size: 2.60 (2010); Median age: 33.3 (2010); Males per 100 females: 93.9 (2010); Marriage status: 21.9% never married, 52.4% now married, 6.1% widowed, 19.6% divorced (2000); Foreign born: 1.4% (2000); Ancestry (includes multiple ancestries): 20.0% German, 16.0% United States or American, 13.5% English, 12.2% Other groups, 10.3% Irish (2000).

Economy: Employment by occupation: 11.0% management, 17.5% professional, 14.7% services, 25.7% sales, 0.0% farming, 9.2% construction, 21.8% production (2000).

Income: Per capita income: $20,967 (2010); Median household income: $45,352 (2010); Average household income: $54,671 (2010); Percent of households with income of $100,000 or more: 10.6% (2010); Poverty rate: 9.2% (2000).

Taxes: Total city taxes per capita: $215 (2007); City property taxes per capita: $204 (2007).

Education: Percent of population age 25 and over with: High school diploma (including GED) or higher: 91.9% (2010); Bachelor's degree or higher: 22.4% (2010); Master's degree or higher: 9.1% (2010).

School District(s)

Richland-Bean Blossom C S C (PK-12)
2008-09 Enrollment: 2,848 . . . . (812) 876-7100

Housing: Homeownership rate: 75.4% (2010); Median home value: $125,164 (2010); Median contract rent: $421 per month (2000); Median year structure built: 1977 (2000).

Newspapers: Journal (Local news; Circulation 2,500)

Transportation: Commute to work: 93.4% car, 0.8% public transportation, 2.9% walk, 1.1% work from home (2000); Travel time to work: 27.9% less than 15 minutes, 51.9% 15 to 30 minutes, 13.4% 30 to 45 minutes, 3.1% 45 to 60 minutes, 3.7% 60 minutes or more (2000)

Additional Information Contacts

Town of Ellettsville . . . . (812) 876-3860
http://ellettsville.in.us

STINESVILLE (town). Covers a land area of 0.109 square miles and a water area of 0 square miles. Located at 39.29° N. Lat; 86.65° W. Long. Elevation is 581 feet.

History: Old limestone quarries. Laid out 1855.

Population: 154 (1990); 194 (2000); 224 (2010); 240 (2015 projected); Race: 96.9% White, 0.4% Black, 0.4% Asian, 2.2% Other, 0.4% Hispanic of any race (2010); Density: 2,059.7 persons per square mile (2010); Average household size: 2.73 (2010); Median age: 35.3 (2010); Males per 100 females: 113.3 (2010); Marriage status: 15.1% never married, 59.7% now married, 11.5% widowed, 13.7% divorced (2000); Foreign born: 0.0% (2000); Ancestry (includes multiple ancestries): 35.9% Other groups,

18.0% United States or American, 16.0% German, 9.7% Irish, 6.3% English (2000).
Economy: Employment by occupation: 7.0% management, 14.1% professional, 29.6% services, 18.3% sales, 0.0% farming, 8.5% construction, 22.5% production (2000).
Income: Per capita income: $27,030 (2010); Median household income: $64,286 (2010); Average household income: $77,317 (2010); Percent of households with income of $100,000 or more: 20.7% (2010); Poverty rate: 1.0% (2000).
Taxes: Total city taxes per capita: $63 (2007); City property taxes per capita: $42 (2007).
Education: Percent of population age 25 and over with: High school diploma (including GED) or higher: 92.4% (2010); Bachelor's degree or higher: 12.5% (2010); Master's degree or higher: 4.9% (2010).

School District(s)
Richland-Bean Blossom C S C (PK-12)
   2008-09 Enrollment: 2,848 . . . . (812) 876-7100
Housing: Homeownership rate: 89.0% (2010); Median home value: $130,263 (2010); Median contract rent: $450 per month (2000); Median year structure built: before 1940 (2000).
Transportation: Commute to work: 90.6% car, 0.0% public transportation, 6.3% walk, 3.1% work from home (2000); Travel time to work: 11.3% less than 15 minutes, 37.1% 15 to 30 minutes, 24.2% 30 to 45 minutes, 8.1% 45 to 60 minutes, 19.4% 60 minutes or more (2000)

UNIONVILLE (unincorporated postal area, zip code 47468). Covers a land area of 21.994 square miles and a water area of 1.637 square miles. Located at 39.25° N. Lat; 86.39° W. Long. Elevation is 879 feet.
Population: 1,215 (2000); Race: 99.4% White, 0.0% Black, 0.0% Asian, 0.6% Other, 0.0% Hispanic of any race (2000); Density: 55.2 persons per square mile (2000); Age: 31.6% under 18, 9.5% over 64 (2000); Marriage status: 19.8% never married, 65.2% now married, 7.3% widowed, 7.7% divorced (2000); Foreign born: 6.2% (2000); Ancestry (includes multiple ancestries): 22.3% German, 14.2% United States or American, 13.2% English, 11.9% Irish, 9.6% Other groups (2000).
Economy: Employment by occupation: 18.0% management, 22.9% professional, 5.8% services, 23.4% sales, 0.0% farming, 10.8% construction, 19.1% production (2000).
Income: Per capita income: $18,520 (2000); Median household income: $45,441 (2000); Poverty rate: 12.8% (2000).
Education: Percent of population age 25 and over with: High school diploma (including GED) or higher: 81.9% (2000); Bachelor's degree or higher: 31.2% (2000).

School District(s)
Monroe County Com Sch Corp (PK-12)
   2008-09 Enrollment: 11,025 . . . . (812) 330-7700
Housing: Homeownership rate: 85.5% (2000); Median home value: $116,300 (2000); Median contract rent: $460 per month (2000); Median year structure built: 1973 (2000).
Transportation: Commute to work: 88.6% car, 0.6% public transportation, 5.0% walk, 5.0% work from home (2000); Travel time to work: 8.8% less than 15 minutes, 37.9% 15 to 30 minutes, 25.5% 30 to 45 minutes, 9.7% 45 to 60 minutes, 18.1% 60 minutes or more (2000)

Montgomery County

Located in west central Indiana; drained by Sugar and Raccoon Creeks. Covers a land area of 504.51 square miles, a water area of 0.83 square miles, and is located in the Eastern Time Zone. The county was founded in 1823. County seat is Crawfordsville.

Montgomery County is part of the Crawfordsville, IN Micropolitan Statistical Area. The entire metro area includes: Montgomery County, IN

Population: 34,436 (1990); 37,629 (2000); 37,864 (2010); 37,776 (2015 projected); Race: 94.9% White, 1.0% Black, 0.5% Asian, 3.6% Other, 3.6% Hispanic of any race (2010); Density: 75.1 persons per square mile (2010); Average household size: 2.49 (2010); Median age: 39.1 (2010); Males per 100 females: 100.2 (2010).
Religion: Five largest groups: 11.7% Christian Churches and Churches of Christ, 6.8% The United Methodist Church, 5.3% Catholic Church, 4.4% American Baptist Churches in the USA, 3.6% Christian Church (Disciples of Christ) (2000).
Economy: Unemployment rate: 9.3% (5/2010); Total civilian labor force: 19,745 (5/2010); Leading industries: 42.4% manufacturing; 12.1% retail

trade; 10.4% health care and social assistance (2008); Farms: 745 totaling 301,279 acres (2007); Companies that employ 500 or more persons: 3 (2008); Companies that employ 100 to 499 persons: 16 (2008); Companies that employ less than 100 persons: 866 (2008); Black-owned businesses: n/a (2002); Hispanic-owned businesses: n/a (2002); Asian-owned businesses: n/a (2002); Women-owned businesses: 498 (2002); Retail sales per capita: $11,380 (2010). Single-family building permits issued: 32 (2009); Multi-family building permits issued: 0 (2009).
Income: Per capita income: $23,178 (2010); Median household income: $49,673 (2010); Average household income: $58,888 (2010); Percent of households with income of $100,000 or more: 12.2% (2010); Poverty rate: 11.5% (2008); Bankruptcy rate: 5.72% (2009).
Taxes: Total county taxes per capita: $296 (2007); County property taxes per capita: $201 (2007).
Education: Percent of population age 25 and over with: High school diploma (including GED) or higher: 85.2% (2010); Bachelor's degree or higher: 16.8% (2010); Master's degree or higher: 5.5% (2010).
Housing: Homeownership rate: 74.1% (2010); Median home value: $104,167 (2010); Median contract rent: $454 per month (2006-2008 3-year est.); Median year structure built: 1962 (2006-2008 3-year est.)
Health: Birth rate: 127.0 per 10,000 population (2009); Death rate: 96.1 per 10,000 population (2009); Age-adjusted cancer mortality rate: 201.5 deaths per 100,000 population (2006); Number of physicians: 9.8 per 10,000 population (2007); Hospital beds: 23.1 per 10,000 population (2006); Hospital admissions: 698.8 per 10,000 population (2006).
Elections: 2008 Presidential election results: 39.3% Obama, 59.3% McCain, 0.0% Nader
Additional Information Contacts
Montgomery County Government . . . . (765) 364-6430
   http://www.montgomeryco.net
City of Crawfordsville . . . . (765) 364-5160
   http://www.crawfordsville.net
Crawfordsville Chamber of Commerce . . . . (765) 362-6800
   http://www.crawfordsvillechamber.com

Montgomery County Communities

ALAMO (town). Covers a land area of 0.057 square miles and a water area of 0 square miles. Located at 39.98° N. Lat; 87.05° W. Long. Elevation is 814 feet.
Population: 112 (1990); 137 (2000); 137 (2010); 137 (2015 projected); Race: 97.1% White, 0.7% Black, 0.0% Asian, 2.2% Other, 2.2% Hispanic of any race (2010); Density: 2,388.5 persons per square mile (2010); Average household size: 2.63 (2010); Median age: 37.1 (2010); Males per 100 females: 107.6 (2010); Marriage status: 17.6% never married, 72.1% now married, 0.0% widowed, 10.3% divorced (2000); Foreign born: 6.5% (2000); Ancestry (includes multiple ancestries): 26.9% Other groups, 15.7% United States or American, 12.0% German, 8.3% English, 7.4% Dutch (2000).
Economy: Employment by occupation: 0.0% management, 0.0% professional, 9.4% services, 21.9% sales, 0.0% farming, 18.8% construction, 50.0% production (2000).
Income: Per capita income: $17,694 (2010); Median household income: $40,625 (2010); Average household income: $47,837 (2010); Percent of households with income of $100,000 or more: 9.6% (2010); Poverty rate: 29.6% (2000).
Taxes: Total city taxes per capita: $29 (2007); City property taxes per capita: $22 (2007).
Education: Percent of population age 25 and over with: High school diploma (including GED) or higher: 82.6% (2010); Bachelor's degree or higher: 9.8% (2010); Master's degree or higher: 2.2% (2010).
Housing: Homeownership rate: 82.7% (2010); Median home value: $105,769 (2010); Median contract rent: $417 per month (2000); Median year structure built: 1964 (2000).
Transportation: Commute to work: 86.2% car, 0.0% public transportation, 6.9% walk, 6.9% work from home (2000); Travel time to work: 14.8% less than 15 minutes, 66.7% 15 to 30 minutes, 18.5% 30 to 45 minutes, 0.0% 45 to 60 minutes, 0.0% 60 minutes or more (2000)

CRAWFORDSVILLE (city). County seat. Covers a land area of 8.378 square miles and a water area of 0 square miles. Located at 40.03° N. Lat; 86.89° W. Long. Elevation is 787 feet.
History: Crawfordsville was laid out in 1823 by Major Ambrose Whitlock, and named for Colonel William Crawford of Virginia. A prominent resident

of Crawfordsville was Civil War General Lew Wallace, better known as the author of the novel "Ben Hur."
Population: 13,844 (1990); 15,243 (2000); 14,620 (2010); 14,263 (2015 projected); Race: 90.0% White, 2.0% Black, 0.7% Asian, 7.3% Other, 7.6% Hispanic of any race (2010); Density: 1,745.0 persons per square mile (2010); Average household size: 2.33 (2010); Median age: 37.1 (2010); Males per 100 females: 101.8 (2010); Marriage status: 25.5% never married, 51.6% now married, 9.8% widowed, 13.1% divorced (2000); Foreign born: 2.9% (2000); Ancestry (includes multiple ancestries): 17.4% German, 12.5% Irish, 10.7% United States or American, 10.5% Other groups, 9.1% English (2000).
Economy: Single-family building permits issued: 21 (2009); Multi-family building permits issued: 0 (2009); Employment by occupation: 8.4% management, 14.1% professional, 15.7% services, 23.3% sales, 0.6% farming, 7.7% construction, 30.1% production (2000).
Income: Per capita income: $20,225 (2010); Median household income: $40,144 (2010); Average household income: $49,391 (2010); Percent of households with income of $100,000 or more: 8.3% (2010); Poverty rate: 12.9% (2000).
Taxes: Total city taxes per capita: $337 (2007); City property taxes per capita: $328 (2007).
Education: Percent of population age 25 and over with: High school diploma (including GED) or higher: 80.9% (2010); Bachelor's degree or higher: 16.8% (2010); Master's degree or higher: 5.3% (2010).

School District(s)
Crawfordsville Com Schools (PK-12)
    2008-09 Enrollment: 2,359 . . . . (765) 362-2342
North Montgomery Com Sch Corp (PK-12)
    2008-09 Enrollment: 2,153 . . . . (765) 359-2112
South Montgomery Com Sch Corp (KG-12)
    2008-09 Enrollment: 1,935 . . . . (765) 866-0203

Four-year College(s)
Wabash College (Private, Not-for-profit)
    Fall 2008 Enrollment: 911 . . . . (765) 361-6100
    2009-10 Tuition: In-state $29,750; Out-of-state $29,750
Housing: Homeownership rate: 59.3% (2010); Median home value: $90,285 (2010); Median contract rent: $399 per month (2000); Median year structure built: 1956 (2000).
Hospitals: Saint Clare Medical Center (120 beds)
Safety: Violent crime rate: 19.3 per 10,000 population; Property crime rate: 511.3 per 10,000 population (2008).
Newspapers: Journal Review (Local news; Circulation 10,700); Weekly (Local news; Circulation 5,000)
Transportation: Commute to work: 90.5% car, 0.3% public transportation, 6.2% walk, 2.0% work from home (2000); Travel time to work: 68.3% less than 15 minutes, 15.6% 15 to 30 minutes, 6.2% 30 to 45 minutes, 5.6% 45 to 60 minutes, 4.3% 60 minutes or more (2000); Amtrak: train service available.
Additional Information Contacts
City of Crawfordsville . . . . (765) 364-5160
    http://www.crawfordsville.net
Crawfordsville Chamber of Commerce . . . . (765) 362-6800
    http://www.crawfordsvillechamber.com

DARLINGTON (town). Covers a land area of 0.315 square miles and a water area of 0 square miles. Located at 40.10° N. Lat; 86.77° W. Long. Elevation is 755 feet.
Population: 778 (1990); 854 (2000); 860 (2010); 862 (2015 projected); Race: 99.1% White, 0.0% Black, 0.2% Asian, 0.7% Other, 0.8% Hispanic of any race (2010); Density: 2,725.9 persons per square mile (2010); Average household size: 2.65 (2010); Median age: 36.6 (2010); Males per 100 females: 94.1 (2010); Marriage status: 15.3% never married, 57.0% now married, 12.3% widowed, 15.4% divorced (2000); Foreign born: 0.2% (2000); Ancestry (includes multiple ancestries): 22.5% German, 17.7% Irish, 12.2% English, 7.6% United States or American, 4.9% Other groups (2000).
Economy: Employment by occupation: 5.6% management, 12.2% professional, 11.5% services, 25.3% sales, 0.0% farming, 12.2% construction, 33.2% production (2000).
Income: Per capita income: $21,580 (2010); Median household income: $50,140 (2010); Average household income: $58,154 (2010); Percent of households with income of $100,000 or more: 9.8% (2010); Poverty rate: 7.1% (2000).
Taxes: Total city taxes per capita: $97 (2007); City property taxes per capita: $62 (2007).

Education: Percent of population age 25 and over with: High school diploma (including GED) or higher: 84.1% (2010); Bachelor's degree or higher: 17.2% (2010); Master's degree or higher: 5.2% (2010).
Housing: Homeownership rate: 85.2% (2010); Median home value: $105,469 (2010); Median contract rent: $303 per month (2000); Median year structure built: 1945 (2000).
Transportation: Commute to work: 93.7% car, 0.8% public transportation, 2.6% walk, 2.9% work from home (2000); Travel time to work: 27.5% less than 15 minutes, 44.7% 15 to 30 minutes, 16.2% 30 to 45 minutes, 5.9% 45 to 60 minutes, 5.7% 60 minutes or more (2000)

LADOGA (town). Covers a land area of 0.502 square miles and a water area of 0 square miles. Located at 39.91° N. Lat; 86.79° W. Long. Elevation is 820 feet.
Population: 1,164 (1990); 1,047 (2000); 1,050 (2010); 1,039 (2015 projected); Race: 98.8% White, 0.1% Black, 0.1% Asian, 1.0% Other, 0.7% Hispanic of any race (2010); Density: 2,091.4 persons per square mile (2010); Average household size: 2.63 (2010); Median age: 39.4 (2010); Males per 100 females: 100.8 (2010); Marriage status: 16.6% never married, 67.6% now married, 6.3% widowed, 9.5% divorced (2000); Foreign born: 0.0% (2000); Ancestry (includes multiple ancestries): 16.4% German, 16.2% United States or American, 8.3% Irish, 7.5% English, 5.6% Other groups (2000).
Economy: Employment by occupation: 9.3% management, 10.4% professional, 17.6% services, 22.3% sales, 0.0% farming, 8.1% construction, 32.3% production (2000).
Income: Per capita income: $22,571 (2010); Median household income: $55,867 (2010); Average household income: $58,853 (2010); Percent of households with income of $100,000 or more: 10.3% (2010); Poverty rate: 7.7% (2000).
Taxes: Total city taxes per capita: $82 (2007); City property taxes per capita: $78 (2007).
Education: Percent of population age 25 and over with: High school diploma (including GED) or higher: 84.1% (2010); Bachelor's degree or higher: 15.8% (2010); Master's degree or higher: 5.4% (2010).

School District(s)
South Montgomery Com Sch Corp (KG-12)
    2008-09 Enrollment: 1,935 . . . . (765) 866-0203
Housing: Homeownership rate: 80.4% (2010); Median home value: $114,844 (2010); Median contract rent: $403 per month (2000); Median year structure built: before 1940 (2000).
Transportation: Commute to work: 94.6% car, 0.0% public transportation, 3.3% walk, 1.6% work from home (2000); Travel time to work: 27.4% less than 15 minutes, 41.2% 15 to 30 minutes, 11.4% 30 to 45 minutes, 10.7% 45 to 60 minutes, 9.3% 60 minutes or more (2000)

LINDEN (town). Covers a land area of 0.259 square miles and a water area of 0 square miles. Located at 40.18° N. Lat; 86.90° W. Long. Elevation is 801 feet.
Population: 737 (1990); 700 (2000); 696 (2010); 687 (2015 projected); Race: 97.0% White, 0.9% Black, 0.0% Asian, 2.2% Other, 1.9% Hispanic of any race (2010); Density: 2,688.4 persons per square mile (2010); Average household size: 2.34 (2010); Median age: 41.0 (2010); Males per 100 females: 99.4 (2010); Marriage status: 15.0% never married, 63.6% now married, 8.2% widowed, 13.2% divorced (2000); Foreign born: 0.7% (2000); Ancestry (includes multiple ancestries): 15.0% German, 14.9% United States or American, 7.4% English, 6.9% Irish, 4.5% Other groups (2000).
Economy: Employment by occupation: 6.5% management, 9.7% professional, 18.9% services, 23.9% sales, 0.0% farming, 7.4% construction, 33.6% production (2000).
Income: Per capita income: $21,873 (2010); Median household income: $46,375 (2010); Average household income: $51,120 (2010); Percent of households with income of $100,000 or more: 7.7% (2010); Poverty rate: 5.0% (2000).
Taxes: Total city taxes per capita: $129 (2007); City property taxes per capita: $87 (2007).
Education: Percent of population age 25 and over with: High school diploma (including GED) or higher: 83.4% (2010); Bachelor's degree or higher: 9.5% (2010); Master's degree or higher: 4.0% (2010).
Housing: Homeownership rate: 78.8% (2010); Median home value: $92,000 (2010); Median contract rent: $330 per month (2000); Median year structure built: 1956 (2000).
Transportation: Commute to work: 94.2% car, 0.0% public transportation, 3.0% walk, 2.1% work from home (2000); Travel time to work: 28.8% less

than 15 minutes, 35.3% 15 to 30 minutes, 20.7% 30 to 45 minutes, 4.6% 45 to 60 minutes, 10.5% 60 minutes or more (2000)

NEW MARKET (town). Covers a land area of 0.320 square miles and a water area of 0 square miles. Located at 39.95° N. Lat; 86.92° W. Long. Elevation is 804 feet.
Population: 614 (1990); 659 (2000); 708 (2010); 729 (2015 projected); Race: 98.9% White, 0.0% Black, 0.0% Asian, 1.1% Other, 2.8% Hispanic of any race (2010); Density: 2,212.3 persons per square mile (2010); Average household size: 2.67 (2010); Median age: 39.5 (2010); Males per 100 females: 89.8 (2010); Marriage status: 13.4% never married, 70.1% now married, 6.9% widowed, 9.6% divorced (2000); Foreign born: 1.1% (2000); Ancestry (includes multiple ancestries): 19.0% United States or American, 15.6% German, 8.3% Irish, 6.2% English, 2.6% French (except Basque) (2000).
Economy: Employment by occupation: 5.4% management, 16.7% professional, 9.6% services, 19.2% sales, 0.6% farming, 12.8% construction, 35.6% production (2000).
Income: Per capita income: $23,164 (2010); Median household income: $58,780 (2010); Average household income: $63,283 (2010); Percent of households with income of $100,000 or more: 11.3% (2010); Poverty rate: 0.5% (2000).
Taxes: Total city taxes per capita: $80 (2007); City property taxes per capita: $80 (2007).
Education: Percent of population age 25 and over with: High school diploma (including GED) or higher: 91.8% (2010); Bachelor's degree or higher: 17.8% (2010); Master's degree or higher: 4.7% (2010).
School District(s)
South Montgomery Com Sch Corp (KG-12)
    2008-09 Enrollment: 1,935 . . . . (765) 866-0203
Housing: Homeownership rate: 81.5% (2010); Median home value: $109,091 (2010); Median contract rent: $367 per month (2000); Median year structure built: 1954 (2000).
Transportation: Commute to work: 91.2% car, 0.0% public transportation, 3.6% walk, 5.2% work from home (2000); Travel time to work: 32.8% less than 15 minutes, 46.9% 15 to 30 minutes, 7.9% 30 to 45 minutes, 4.5% 45 to 60 minutes, 7.9% 60 minutes or more (2000)

NEW RICHMOND (town). Covers a land area of 0.179 square miles and a water area of 0 square miles. Located at 40.19° N. Lat; 86.97° W. Long. Elevation is 781 feet.
Population: 328 (1990); 349 (2000); 330 (2010); 317 (2015 projected); Race: 97.9% White, 1.5% Black, 0.0% Asian, 0.6% Other, 0.3% Hispanic of any race (2010); Density: 1,843.8 persons per square mile (2010); Average household size: 2.52 (2010); Median age: 38.7 (2010); Males per 100 females: 97.6 (2010); Marriage status: 16.8% never married, 68.3% now married, 8.4% widowed, 6.5% divorced (2000); Foreign born: 0.0% (2000); Ancestry (includes multiple ancestries): 20.9% German, 9.7% United States or American, 7.7% Irish, 7.4% Other groups, 5.6% English (2000).
Economy: Employment by occupation: 8.6% management, 14.2% professional, 7.4% services, 23.5% sales, 0.0% farming, 11.7% construction, 34.6% production (2000).
Income: Per capita income: $24,478 (2010); Median household income: $57,337 (2010); Average household income: $61,775 (2010); Percent of households with income of $100,000 or more: 12.2% (2010); Poverty rate: 3.8% (2000).
Taxes: Total city taxes per capita: $131 (2007); City property taxes per capita: $125 (2007).
Education: Percent of population age 25 and over with: High school diploma (including GED) or higher: 86.7% (2010); Bachelor's degree or higher: 12.4% (2010); Master's degree or higher: 1.3% (2010).
Housing: Homeownership rate: 82.4% (2010); Median home value: $99,048 (2010); Median contract rent: $308 per month (2000); Median year structure built: 1943 (2000).
Transportation: Commute to work: 94.8% car, 1.3% public transportation, 0.0% walk, 3.9% work from home (2000); Travel time to work: 18.2% less than 15 minutes, 34.5% 15 to 30 minutes, 29.7% 30 to 45 minutes, 8.8% 45 to 60 minutes, 8.8% 60 minutes or more (2000)

NEW ROSS (town). Covers a land area of 0.290 square miles and a water area of 0 square miles. Located at 39.96° N. Lat; 86.71° W. Long. Elevation is 886 feet.
History: New Ross grew as a trading center for surrounding farms.

Population: 331 (1990); 334 (2000); 312 (2010); 301 (2015 projected); Race: 98.7% White, 0.0% Black, 0.0% Asian, 1.3% Other, 0.6% Hispanic of any race (2010); Density: 1,077.2 persons per square mile (2010); Average household size: 2.54 (2010); Median age: 39.0 (2010); Males per 100 females: 103.9 (2010); Marriage status: 11.0% never married, 67.8% now married, 12.3% widowed, 8.9% divorced (2000); Foreign born: 0.6% (2000); Ancestry (includes multiple ancestries): 21.6% German, 14.6% Other groups, 6.7% Scottish, 6.1% United States or American, 5.5% Irish (2000).
Economy: Employment by occupation: 10.6% management, 11.2% professional, 13.7% services, 13.7% sales, 0.0% farming, 21.1% construction, 29.8% production (2000).
Income: Per capita income: $23,525 (2010); Median household income: $50,500 (2010); Average household income: $62,866 (2010); Percent of households with income of $100,000 or more: 15.4% (2010); Poverty rate: 4.9% (2000).
Taxes: Total city taxes per capita: $61 (2007); City property taxes per capita: $55 (2007).
Education: Percent of population age 25 and over with: High school diploma (including GED) or higher: 84.8% (2010); Bachelor's degree or higher: 11.4% (2010); Master's degree or higher: 2.8% (2010).
School District(s)
South Montgomery Com Sch Corp (KG-12)
    2008-09 Enrollment: 1,935 . . . . (765) 866-0203
Housing: Homeownership rate: 87.0% (2010); Median home value: $92,581 (2010); Median contract rent: $336 per month (2000); Median year structure built: before 1940 (2000).
Transportation: Commute to work: 95.6% car, 0.0% public transportation, 3.2% walk, 0.0% work from home (2000); Travel time to work: 16.5% less than 15 minutes, 48.7% 15 to 30 minutes, 23.4% 30 to 45 minutes, 8.9% 45 to 60 minutes, 2.5% 60 minutes or more (2000)

WAVELAND (town). Covers a land area of 0.361 square miles and a water area of 0 square miles. Located at 39.87° N. Lat; 87.04° W. Long. Elevation is 774 feet.
History: Laid out 1835.
Population: 474 (1990); 416 (2000); 414 (2010); 409 (2015 projected); Race: 96.4% White, 0.2% Black, 0.2% Asian, 3.1% Other, 1.7% Hispanic of any race (2010); Density: 1,146.1 persons per square mile (2010); Average household size: 2.56 (2010); Median age: 38.4 (2010); Males per 100 females: 107.0 (2010); Marriage status: 17.8% never married, 64.4% now married, 7.6% widowed, 10.2% divorced (2000); Foreign born: 0.0% (2000); Ancestry (includes multiple ancestries): 20.2% United States or American, 19.3% German, 14.0% Irish, 11.2% English, 5.2% Dutch (2000).
Economy: Employment by occupation: 1.4% management, 17.4% professional, 15.0% services, 18.8% sales, 1.4% farming, 16.0% construction, 30.0% production (2000).
Income: Per capita income: $22,232 (2010); Median household income: $57,727 (2010); Average household income: $57,500 (2010); Percent of households with income of $100,000 or more: 9.3% (2010); Poverty rate: 2.9% (2000).
Taxes: Total city taxes per capita: $46 (2007); City property taxes per capita: $42 (2007).
Education: Percent of population age 25 and over with: High school diploma (including GED) or higher: 84.9% (2010); Bachelor's degree or higher: 13.7% (2010); Master's degree or higher: 5.8% (2010).
School District(s)
South Montgomery Com Sch Corp (KG-12)
    2008-09 Enrollment: 1,935 . . . . (765) 866-0203
Housing: Homeownership rate: 77.8% (2010); Median home value: $85,806 (2010); Median contract rent: $392 per month (2000); Median year structure built: before 1940 (2000).
Transportation: Commute to work: 92.9% car, 0.0% public transportation, 5.2% walk, 1.9% work from home (2000); Travel time to work: 18.9% less than 15 minutes, 50.0% 15 to 30 minutes, 13.6% 30 to 45 minutes, 1.5% 45 to 60 minutes, 16.0% 60 minutes or more (2000)

WAYNETOWN (town). Covers a land area of 0.436 square miles and a water area of 0 square miles. Located at 40.08° N. Lat; 87.06° W. Long. Elevation is 784 feet.
History: Waynetown developed around the tile factories and brick kilns that made use of the clay in the area.
Population: 911 (1990); 909 (2000); 824 (2010); 787 (2015 projected); Race: 98.8% White, 0.1% Black, 0.0% Asian, 1.1% Other, 0.8% Hispanic of any race (2010); Density: 1,890.8 persons per square mile (2010);

Average household size: 2.43 (2010); Median age: 37.1 (2010); Males per 100 females: 98.6 (2010); Marriage status: 17.1% never married, 64.5% now married, 7.6% widowed, 10.8% divorced (2000); Foreign born: 1.1% (2000); Ancestry (includes multiple ancestries): 15.6% United States or American, 15.3% German, 8.2% Irish, 7.6% English, 5.9% Other groups (2000).

Economy: Employment by occupation: 6.9% management, 12.2% professional, 10.4% services, 28.0% sales, 1.1% farming, 8.0% construction, 33.3% production (2000).

Income: Per capita income: $21,177 (2010); Median household income: $48,347 (2010); Average household income: $51,866 (2010); Percent of households with income of $100,000 or more: 7.1% (2010); Poverty rate: 8.6% (2000).

Taxes: Total city taxes per capita: $59 (2007); City property taxes per capita: $55 (2007).

Education: Percent of population age 25 and over with: High school diploma (including GED) or higher: 87.5% (2010); Bachelor's degree or higher: 10.3% (2010); Master's degree or higher: 1.7% (2010).

Housing: Homeownership rate: 79.1% (2010); Median home value: $77,907 (2010); Median contract rent: $306 per month (2000); Median year structure built: 1944 (2000).

Transportation: Commute to work: 91.4% car, 0.5% public transportation, 4.5% walk, 2.9% work from home (2000); Travel time to work: 13.6% less than 15 minutes, 61.7% 15 to 30 minutes, 9.8% 30 to 45 minutes, 7.9% 45 to 60 minutes, 7.0% 60 minutes or more (2000)

WINGATE (town). Covers a land area of 0.275 square miles and a water area of 0 square miles. Located at 40.17° N. Lat; 87.07° W. Long. Elevation is 778 feet.

Population: 286 (1990); 299 (2000); 333 (2010); 345 (2015 projected); Race: 99.4% White, 0.0% Black, 0.3% Asian, 0.3% Other, 1.5% Hispanic of any race (2010); Density: 1,209.5 persons per square mile (2010); Average household size: 2.60 (2010); Median age: 38.9 (2010); Males per 100 females: 99.4 (2010); Marriage status: 18.6% never married, 55.0% now married, 11.4% widowed, 15.0% divorced (2000); Foreign born: 0.0% (2000); Ancestry (includes multiple ancestries): 23.0% United States or American, 6.0% German, 5.7% English, 5.3% Scotch-Irish, 4.7% Other groups (2000).

Economy: Employment by occupation: 0.8% management, 19.2% professional, 13.6% services, 16.0% sales, 0.0% farming, 4.0% construction, 46.4% production (2000).

Income: Per capita income: $19,380 (2010); Median household income: $44,545 (2010); Average household income: $50,352 (2010); Percent of households with income of $100,000 or more: 7.8% (2010); Poverty rate: 22.2% (2000).

Taxes: Total city taxes per capita: $149 (2007); City property taxes per capita: $142 (2007).

Education: Percent of population age 25 and over with: High school diploma (including GED) or higher: 88.4% (2010); Bachelor's degree or higher: 6.2% (2010); Master's degree or higher: 2.2% (2010).

Housing: Homeownership rate: 83.6% (2010); Median home value: $94,706 (2010); Median contract rent: $333 per month (2000); Median year structure built: 1954 (2000).

Transportation: Commute to work: 97.4% car, 0.0% public transportation, 1.7% walk, 0.0% work from home (2000); Travel time to work: 6.8% less than 15 minutes, 45.3% 15 to 30 minutes, 26.5% 30 to 45 minutes, 17.1% 45 to 60 minutes, 4.3% 60 minutes or more (2000)

Morgan County

Located in central Indiana; drained by the West Fork of the White River, Whitelick River, and Camp Creek. Covers a land area of 406.47 square miles, a water area of 2.92 square miles, and is located in the Eastern Time Zone. The county was founded in 1821. County seat is Martinsville.

Morgan County is part of the Indianapolis-Carmel, IN Metropolitan Statistical Area. The entire metro area includes: Boone County, IN; Brown County, IN; Hamilton County, IN; Hancock County, IN; Hendricks County, IN; Johnson County, IN; Marion County, IN; Morgan County, IN; Putnam County, IN; Shelby County, IN

Weather Station: Martinsville 2 SW										Elevation: 606 feet		
	Jan	Feb	Mar	Apr	May	Jun	Jul	Aug	Sep	Oct	Nov	Dec
High	36	41	51	63	73	81	85	84	78	66	53	41
Low	18	21	30	40	49	59	63	61	52	40	33	24
Precip	2.5	2.4	3.5	4.3	4.8	3.9	4.2	4.0	3.1	3.0	3.9	3.0
Snow	6.7	4.8	2.6	tr	0.0	0.0	0.0	0.0	0.0	0.2	0.7	2.7

High and Low temperatures in degrees Fahrenheit; Precipitation and Snow in inches

Population: 55,920 (1990); 66,689 (2000); 71,490 (2010); 73,469 (2015 projected); Race: 97.5% White, 0.8% Black, 0.4% Asian, 1.3% Other, 0.9% Hispanic of any race (2010); Density: 175.9 persons per square mile (2010); Average household size: 2.68 (2010); Median age: 38.3 (2010); Males per 100 females: 99.2 (2010).

Religion: Five largest groups: 5.5% Christian Churches and Churches of Christ, 4.9% Southern Baptist Convention, 4.8% Catholic Church, 4.1% American Baptist Churches in the USA, 3.6% Christian Church (Disciples of Christ) (2000).

Economy: Unemployment rate: 9.4% (5/2010); Total civilian labor force: 36,264 (5/2010); Leading industries: 19.7% retail trade; 17.0% manufacturing; 16.1% health care and social assistance (2008); Farms: 642 totaling 114,136 acres (2007); Companies that employ 500 or more persons: 1 (2008); Companies that employ 100 to 499 persons: 13 (2008); Companies that employ less than 100 persons: 1,231 (2008); Black-owned businesses: n/a (2002); Hispanic-owned businesses: n/a (2002); Asian-owned businesses: n/a (2002); Women-owned businesses: 1,446 (2002); Retail sales per capita: $10,908 (2010). Single-family building permits issued: 75 (2009); Multi-family building permits issued: 2 (2009).

Income: Per capita income: $24,115 (2010); Median household income: $54,993 (2010); Average household income: $64,732 (2010); Percent of households with income of $100,000 or more: 15.8% (2010); Poverty rate: 10.6% (2008); Bankruptcy rate: 9.09% (2009).

Taxes: Total county taxes per capita: $247 (2007); County property taxes per capita: $98 (2007).

Education: Percent of population age 25 and over with: High school diploma (including GED) or higher: 83.6% (2010); Bachelor's degree or higher: 13.5% (2010); Master's degree or higher: 4.3% (2010).

Housing: Homeownership rate: 80.7% (2010); Median home value: $133,124 (2010); Median contract rent: $536 per month (2006-2008 3-year est.); Median year structure built: 1977 (2006-2008 3-year est.)

Health: Birth rate: 126.7 per 10,000 population (2009); Death rate: 83.1 per 10,000 population (2009); Age-adjusted cancer mortality rate: 198.0 deaths per 100,000 population (2006); Air Quality Index: 88.1% good, 11.6% moderate, 0.4% unhealthy for sensitive individuals, 0.0% unhealthy (percent of days in 2008); Number of physicians: 9.0 per 10,000 population (2007); Hospital beds: 25.2 per 10,000 population (2006); Hospital admissions: 697.0 per 10,000 population (2006).

Elections: 2008 Presidential election results: 35.9% Obama, 62.9% McCain, 0.0% Nader

National and State Parks: Bradford Woods State Reservation; Morgan Monroe State Forest

Additional Information Contacts

Morgan County Government . . . . (765) 342-8110
   http://www.martinsvillechamber.com
City of Martinsville . . . . (765) 342-2861
   http://www.martinsville.in.gov
Martinsville Chamber of Commerce. . . . . (765) 342-8110
   http://www.martinsvillechamber.com
Mooresville Chamber of Commerce . . . . (317) 831-6509
   http://www.mooresvillechamber.org
Town of Mooresville. . . . . (317) 831-1608
   http://www.mooresville.org

Morgan County Communities

BETHANY (town). Covers a land area of 0.083 square miles and a water area of 0.011 square miles. Located at 39.53° N. Lat; 86.37° W. Long. Elevation is 650 feet.

Population: 90 (1990); 94 (2000); 91 (2010); 88 (2015 projected); Race: 95.6% White, 0.0% Black, 0.0% Asian, 4.4% Other, 1.1% Hispanic of any race (2010); Density: 1,097.4 persons per square mile (2010); Average household size: 2.76 (2010); Median age: 31.1 (2010); Males per 100 females: 116.7 (2010); Marriage status: 38.6% never married, 43.2% now married, 0.0% widowed, 18.2% divorced (2000); Foreign born: 0.0% (2000); Ancestry (includes multiple ancestries): 30.8% United States or American, 23.1% Other groups, 3.8% Irish, 3.8% Czech, 3.8% German (2000).

Economy: Employment by occupation: 0.0% management, 0.0% professional, 8.0% services, 32.0% sales, 0.0% farming, 40.0% construction, 20.0% production (2000).
Income: Per capita income: $19,450 (2010); Median household income: $48,750 (2010); Average household income: $57,652 (2010); Percent of households with income of $100,000 or more: 12.1% (2010); Poverty rate: 1.9% (2000).
Taxes: Total city taxes per capita: $32 (2007); City property taxes per capita: $32 (2007).
Education: Percent of population age 25 and over with: High school diploma (including GED) or higher: 79.6% (2010); Bachelor's degree or higher: 9.3% (2010); Master's degree or higher: 1.9% (2010).
Housing: Homeownership rate: 75.8% (2010); Median home value: $98,571 (2010); Median contract rent: $400 per month (2000); Median year structure built: before 1940 (2000).
Transportation: Commute to work: 92.0% car, 0.0% public transportation, 0.0% walk, 8.0% work from home (2000); Travel time to work: 0.0% less than 15 minutes, 17.4% 15 to 30 minutes, 39.1% 30 to 45 minutes, 13.0% 45 to 60 minutes, 30.4% 60 minutes or more (2000)

BROOKLYN (town). Covers a land area of 0.777 square miles and a water area of 0.019 square miles. Located at 39.54° N. Lat; 86.37° W. Long. Elevation is 663 feet.
History: A supply of clay near Brooklyn provided the material for the manufacture of drain tile and brick. A brief gold rush took place in the early 1900's at Gold Creek, near Brooklyn.
Population: 1,464 (1990); 1,545 (2000); 1,471 (2010); 1,442 (2015 projected); Race: 96.5% White, 0.2% Black, 0.1% Asian, 3.3% Other, 1.4% Hispanic of any race (2010); Density: 1,893.3 persons per square mile (2010); Average household size: 2.76 (2010); Median age: 35.4 (2010); Males per 100 females: 106.0 (2010); Marriage status: 20.4% never married, 62.7% now married, 6.3% widowed, 10.6% divorced (2000); Foreign born: 0.6% (2000); Ancestry (includes multiple ancestries): 19.3% German, 14.0% United States or American, 12.2% Other groups, 10.6% Irish, 9.5% English (2000).
Economy: Single-family building permits issued: 1 (2009); Multi-family building permits issued: 0 (2009); Employment by occupation: 7.0% management, 10.2% professional, 12.7% services, 28.3% sales, 0.4% farming, 19.3% construction, 22.1% production (2000).
Income: Per capita income: $20,926 (2010); Median household income: $48,864 (2010); Average household income: $58,117 (2010); Percent of households with income of $100,000 or more: 13.0% (2010); Poverty rate: 9.5% (2000).
Taxes: Total city taxes per capita: $98 (2007); City property taxes per capita: $53 (2007).
Education: Percent of population age 25 and over with: High school diploma (including GED) or higher: 81.2% (2010); Bachelor's degree or higher: 9.8% (2010); Master's degree or higher: 2.2% (2010).

School District(s)
M S D Martinsville Schools (PK-12)
    2008-09 Enrollment: 5,470 . . . . (765) 342-6641
Housing: Homeownership rate: 78.5% (2010); Median home value: $100,893 (2010); Median contract rent: $459 per month (2000); Median year structure built: 1975 (2000).
Transportation: Commute to work: 96.0% car, 0.5% public transportation, 0.2% walk, 2.6% work from home (2000); Travel time to work: 17.5% less than 15 minutes, 30.2% 15 to 30 minutes, 37.5% 30 to 45 minutes, 11.8% 45 to 60 minutes, 3.0% 60 minutes or more (2000)

MARTINSVILLE (city). County seat. Covers a land area of 4.464 square miles and a water area of 0.010 square miles. Located at 39.42° N. Lat; 86.42° W. Long. Elevation is 604 feet.
History: Named for John Martin, a member of the board of commissioners who made this city the county seat. Prospectors drilling for gas in Martinsville discovered artesian wells of therapeutic waters, giving the town the nickname of Artesian City.
Population: 12,101 (1990); 11,698 (2000); 11,779 (2010); 11,684 (2015 projected); Race: 97.3% White, 1.1% Black, 0.3% Asian, 1.3% Other, 1.3% Hispanic of any race (2010); Density: 2,638.8 persons per square mile (2010); Average household size: 2.45 (2010); Median age: 37.3 (2010); Males per 100 females: 98.1 (2010); Marriage status: 20.7% never married, 55.1% now married, 9.5% widowed, 14.6% divorced (2000); Foreign born: 0.7% (2000); Ancestry (includes multiple ancestries): 28.0% United States or American, 15.5% German, 11.0% Irish, 8.8% Other groups, 6.8% English (2000).

Economy: Single-family building permits issued: 7 (2009); Multi-family building permits issued: 0 (2009); Employment by occupation: 8.1% management, 11.6% professional, 17.8% services, 23.6% sales, 0.1% farming, 18.8% construction, 19.9% production (2000).
Income: Per capita income: $19,565 (2010); Median household income: $37,993 (2010); Average household income: $48,522 (2010); Percent of households with income of $100,000 or more: 7.4% (2010); Poverty rate: 11.6% (2000).
Taxes: Total city taxes per capita: $247 (2007); City property taxes per capita: $230 (2007).
Education: Percent of population age 25 and over with: High school diploma (including GED) or higher: 74.7% (2010); Bachelor's degree or higher: 12.4% (2010); Master's degree or higher: 5.5% (2010).
School District(s)
M S D Martinsville Schools (PK-12)
    2008-09 Enrollment: 5,470 . . . . (765) 342-6641
Mooresville Con School Corp (PK-12)
    2008-09 Enrollment: 4,437 . . . . (317) 831-0950
Housing: Homeownership rate: 63.4% (2010); Median home value: $97,292 (2010); Median contract rent: $413 per month (2000); Median year structure built: 1962 (2000).
Hospitals: Morgan Hospital Medical Centre (106 beds)
Safety: Violent crime rate: 16.2 per 10,000 population; Property crime rate: 792.0 per 10,000 population (2008).
Newspapers: The Reporter-Times (Local news; Circulation 6,499)
Transportation: Commute to work: 92.5% car, 0.1% public transportation, 3.8% walk, 2.0% work from home (2000); Travel time to work: 47.2% less than 15 minutes, 11.6% 15 to 30 minutes, 17.3% 30 to 45 minutes, 14.2% 45 to 60 minutes, 9.7% 60 minutes or more (2000)
Additional Information Contacts
City of Martinsville . . . . (765) 342-2861
    http://www.martinsville.in.gov
Martinsville Chamber of Commerce. . . . . (765) 342-8110
    http://www.martinsvillechamber.com

MONROVIA (town). Covers a land area of 0.886 square miles and a water area of 0 square miles. Located at 39.57° N. Lat; 86.48° W. Long. Elevation is 801 feet.
History: Laid out 1834.
Population: 654 (1990); 628 (2000); 680 (2010); 704 (2015 projected); Race: 98.5% White, 0.0% Black, 0.0% Asian, 1.5% Other, 1.2% Hispanic of any race (2010); Density: 767.8 persons per square mile (2010); Average household size: 2.70 (2010); Median age: 39.1 (2010); Males per 100 females: 93.7 (2010); Marriage status: 22.5% never married, 59.6% now married, 6.1% widowed, 11.8% divorced (2000); Foreign born: 0.0% (2000); Ancestry (includes multiple ancestries): 26.9% United States or American, 21.1% German, 8.4% Irish, 5.5% Other groups, 4.9% English (2000).
Economy: Single-family building permits issued: 11 (2009); Multi-family building permits issued: 0 (2009); Employment by occupation: 6.8% management, 14.8% professional, 12.8% services, 29.1% sales, 0.6% farming, 16.3% construction, 19.6% production (2000).
Income: Per capita income: $26,315 (2010); Median household income: $56,349 (2010); Average household income: $71,875 (2010); Percent of households with income of $100,000 or more: 15.5% (2010); Poverty rate: 8.6% (2000).
Taxes: Total city taxes per capita: $193 (2007); City property taxes per capita: $55 (2007).
Education: Percent of population age 25 and over with: High school diploma (including GED) or higher: 82.5% (2010); Bachelor's degree or higher: 11.6% (2010); Master's degree or higher: 2.3% (2010).
School District(s)
Monroe-Gregg School District (PK-12)
    2008-09 Enrollment: 1,540 . . . . (317) 996-3720
Housing: Homeownership rate: 82.1% (2010); Median home value: $123,352 (2010); Median contract rent: $441 per month (2000); Median year structure built: 1952 (2000).
Transportation: Commute to work: 92.2% car, 0.0% public transportation, 4.5% walk, 2.7% work from home (2000); Travel time to work: 17.9% less than 15 minutes, 26.9% 15 to 30 minutes, 43.2% 30 to 45 minutes, 11.4% 45 to 60 minutes, 0.6% 60 minutes or more (2000)

MOORESVILLE (town). Covers a land area of 5.536 square miles and a water area of 0.016 square miles. Located at 39.60° N. Lat; 86.36° W. Long. Elevation is 712 feet.

History: Laid out 1824.

Population: 7,302 (1990); 9,273 (2000); 10,658 (2010); 11,321 (2015 projected); Race: 97.6% White, 0.6% Black, 0.6% Asian, 1.2% Other, 0.9% Hispanic of any race (2010); Density: 1,925.2 persons per square mile (2010); Average household size: 2.58 (2010); Median age: 37.2 (2010); Males per 100 females: 93.5 (2010); Marriage status: 20.1% never married, 59.6% now married, 6.9% widowed, 13.4% divorced (2000); Foreign born: 0.3% (2000); Ancestry (includes multiple ancestries): 26.3% United States or American, 22.0% German, 12.9% Irish, 8.1% English, 5.3% Other groups (2000).

Economy: Single-family building permits issued: 14 (2009); Multi-family building permits issued: 2 (2009); Employment by occupation: 10.4% management, 14.1% professional, 15.2% services, 27.6% sales, 0.0% farming, 13.8% construction, 19.0% production (2000).

Income: Per capita income: $24,995 (2010); Median household income: $55,952 (2010); Average household income: $64,799 (2010); Percent of households with income of $100,000 or more: 17.0% (2010); Poverty rate: 4.3% (2000).

Taxes: Total city taxes per capita: $292 (2007); City property taxes per capita: $259 (2007).

Education: Percent of population age 25 and over with: High school diploma (including GED) or higher: 87.0% (2010); Bachelor's degree or higher: 17.1% (2010); Master's degree or higher: 4.1% (2010).

School District(s)
Mooresville Con School Corp (PK-12)
    2008-09 Enrollment: 4,437 . . . . (317) 831-0950

Housing: Homeownership rate: 76.3% (2010); Median home value: $129,155 (2010); Median contract rent: $444 per month (2000); Median year structure built: 1972 (2000).

Hospitals: Saint Francis Hospital - Mooresville (64 beds)

Safety: Violent crime rate: 8.5 per 10,000 population; Property crime rate: 301.2 per 10,000 population (2008).

Newspapers: Times (Local news; Circulation 6,000)

Transportation: Commute to work: 95.0% car, 0.0% public transportation, 1.9% walk, 1.9% work from home (2000); Travel time to work: 29.8% less than 15 minutes, 37.2% 15 to 30 minutes, 24.9% 30 to 45 minutes, 4.5% 45 to 60 minutes, 3.5% 60 minutes or more (2000)

Additional Information Contacts

Mooresville Chamber of Commerce . . . . (317) 831-6509
    http://www.mooresvillechamber.org
Town of Mooresville . . . . (317) 831-1608
    http://www.mooresville.org

MORGANTOWN (town). Covers a land area of 0.382 square miles and a water area of 0 square miles. Located at 39.37° N. Lat; 86.26° W. Long. Elevation is 679 feet.

History: Laid out 1831.

Population: 978 (1990); 964 (2000); 950 (2010); 931 (2015 projected); Race: 96.3% White, 3.3% Black, 0.1% Asian, 0.3% Other, 0.5% Hispanic of any race (2010); Density: 2,485.0 persons per square mile (2010); Average household size: 2.52 (2010); Median age: 37.6 (2010); Males per 100 females: 91.9 (2010); Marriage status: 21.0% never married, 51.8% now married, 17.1% widowed, 10.1% divorced (2000); Foreign born: 0.2% (2000); Ancestry (includes multiple ancestries): 32.6% United States or American, 16.6% Irish, 14.3% German, 12.3% English, 9.3% Other groups (2000).

Economy: Single-family building permits issued: 0 (2009); Multi-family building permits issued: 0 (2009); Employment by occupation: 6.7% management, 6.1% professional, 21.5% services, 25.7% sales, 0.6% farming, 20.0% construction, 19.4% production (2000).

Income: Per capita income: $19,844 (2010); Median household income: $39,762 (2010); Average household income: $51,889 (2010); Percent of households with income of $100,000 or more: 7.5% (2010); Poverty rate: 8.3% (2000).

Taxes: Total city taxes per capita: $171 (2007); City property taxes per capita: $121 (2007).

Education: Percent of population age 25 and over with: High school diploma (including GED) or higher: 72.2% (2010); Bachelor's degree or higher: 6.4% (2010); Master's degree or higher: 2.7% (2010).

School District(s)
Brown County School Corporation (PK-12)
    2008-09 Enrollment: 2,197 . . . . (812) 988-6601

Housing: Homeownership rate: 65.3% (2010); Median home value: $94,697 (2010); Median contract rent: $433 per month (2000); Median year structure built: 1954 (2000).

Transportation: Commute to work: 86.4% car, 0.0% public transportation, 11.0% walk, 2.5% work from home (2000); Travel time to work: 24.2% less than 15 minutes, 25.5% 15 to 30 minutes, 23.5% 30 to 45 minutes, 14.6% 45 to 60 minutes, 12.2% 60 minutes or more (2000)

PARAGON (town). Covers a land area of 0.251 square miles and a water area of 0 square miles. Located at 39.39° N. Lat; 86.56° W. Long. Elevation is 581 feet.

Population: 533 (1990); 663 (2000); 668 (2010); 670 (2015 projected); Race: 99.1% White, 0.0% Black, 0.0% Asian, 0.9% Other, 0.7% Hispanic of any race (2010); Density: 2,660.7 persons per square mile (2010); Average household size: 2.76 (2010); Median age: 34.1 (2010); Males per 100 females: 103.7 (2010); Marriage status: 15.0% never married, 67.3% now married, 5.8% widowed, 11.9% divorced (2000); Foreign born: 0.3% (2000); Ancestry (includes multiple ancestries): 22.3% United States or American, 15.2% German, 12.3% Other groups, 11.7% English, 8.6% Irish (2000).

Economy: Single-family building permits issued: 0 (2009); Multi-family building permits issued: 0 (2009); Employment by occupation: 5.1% management, 2.4% professional, 11.8% services, 15.8% sales, 0.0% farming, 21.9% construction, 43.1% production (2000).

Income: Per capita income: $16,155 (2010); Median household income: $41,346 (2010); Average household income: $44,184 (2010); Percent of households with income of $100,000 or more: 4.5% (2010); Poverty rate: 13.3% (2000).

Taxes: Total city taxes per capita: $80 (2007); City property taxes per capita: $69 (2007).

Education: Percent of population age 25 and over with: High school diploma (including GED) or higher: 73.4% (2010); Bachelor's degree or higher: 2.2% (2010); Master's degree or higher: 0.7% (2010).

School District(s)
M S D Martinsville Schools (PK-12)
    2008-09 Enrollment: 5,470 . . . . (765) 342-6641

Housing: Homeownership rate: 72.7% (2010); Median home value: $86,531 (2010); Median contract rent: $429 per month (2000); Median year structure built: 1956 (2000).

Transportation: Commute to work: 85.4% car, 2.7% public transportation, 9.2% walk, 1.4% work from home (2000); Travel time to work: 22.1% less than 15 minutes, 38.3% 15 to 30 minutes, 12.8% 30 to 45 minutes, 14.8% 45 to 60 minutes, 12.1% 60 minutes or more (2000)

Newton County

Located in northwestern Indiana; bounded on the west by Illinois, and on the north by the Kankakee River; also drained by the Iroquois River. Covers a land area of 401.85 square miles, a water area of 1.68 square miles, and is located in the Central Time Zone. The county was founded in 1857. County seat is Kentland.

Newton County is part of the Chicago-Naperville-Joliet, IL-IN-WI Metropolitan Statistical Area. The entire metro area includes: Chicago-Naperville-Joliet, IL Metropolitan Division (Cook County, IL; DeKalb County, IL; DuPage County, IL; Grundy County, IL; Kane County, IL; Kendall County, IL; McHenry County, IL; Will County, IL); Gary, IN Metropolitan Division (Jasper County, IN; Lake County, IN; Newton County, IN; Porter County, IN); Lake County-Kenosha County, IL-WI Metropolitan Division (Lake County, IL; Kenosha County, WI)

Weather Station: Kentland										Elevation: 692 feet		
	Jan	Feb	Mar	Apr	May	Jun	Jul	Aug	Sep	Oct	Nov	Dec
High	31	37	49	62	74	83	86	84	78	66	50	37
Low	15	19	30	39	50	60	63	61	54	42	33	21
Precip	1.6	1.5	2.8	3.5	4.3	4.3	4.2	3.9	3.6	2.9	3.4	2.6
Snow	7.5	6.8	3.2	0.8	0.0	0.0	0.0	0.0	0.0	0.1	2.0	6.3

High and Low temperatures in degrees Fahrenheit; Precipitation and Snow in inches

Population: 13,551 (1990); 14,566 (2000); 13,845 (2010); 13,437 (2015 projected); Race: 95.9% White, 0.7% Black, 0.4% Asian, 3.0% Other, 3.9% Hispanic of any race (2010); Density: 34.5 persons per square mile (2010); Average household size: 2.65 (2010); Median age: 40.6 (2010); Males per 100 females: 98.0 (2010).

Religion: Five largest groups: 9.1% Catholic Church, 7.5% The United Methodist Church, 3.8% Christian Church (Disciples of Christ), 3.8% American Baptist Churches in the USA, 3.1% Southern Baptist Convention (2000).

Economy: Unemployment rate: 10.3% (5/2010); Total civilian labor force: 6,690 (5/2010); Leading industries: 35.3% manufacturing; 14.7% retail trade; 8.6% accommodation & food services (2008); Farms: 434 totaling 190,432 acres (2007); Companies that employ 500 or more persons: 0 (2008); Companies that employ 100 to 499 persons: 4 (2008); Companies that employ less than 100 persons: 313 (2008); Black-owned businesses: n/a (2002); Hispanic-owned businesses: n/a (2002); Asian-owned businesses: n/a (2002); Women-owned businesses: 276 (2002); Retail sales per capita: $8,311 (2010). Single-family building permits issued: 15 (2009); Multi-family building permits issued: 0 (2009).
Income: Per capita income: $22,010 (2010); Median household income: $50,544 (2010); Average household income: $58,450 (2010); Percent of households with income of $100,000 or more: 11.0% (2010); Poverty rate: 9.7% (2008); Bankruptcy rate: 5.58% (2009).
Taxes: Total county taxes per capita: $406 (2007); County property taxes per capita: $293 (2007).
Education: Percent of population age 25 and over with: High school diploma (including GED) or higher: 83.6% (2010); Bachelor's degree or higher: 10.2% (2010); Master's degree or higher: 3.7% (2010).
Housing: Homeownership rate: 78.7% (2010); Median home value: $116,357 (2010); Median contract rent: $n/a per month (2006-2008 3-year est.); Median year structure built: n/a (2006-2008 3-year est.)
Health: Birth rate: 104.8 per 10,000 population (2009); Death rate: 104.1 per 10,000 population (2009); Age-adjusted cancer mortality rate: 214.1 deaths per 100,000 population (2006); Number of physicians: 2.1 per 10,000 population (2007); Hospital beds: 0.0 per 10,000 population (2006); Hospital admissions: 0.0 per 10,000 population (2006).
Elections: 2008 Presidential election results: 43.4% Obama, 54.6% McCain, 0.1% Nader
National and State Parks: La Salle State Fish and Wildlife Area; Willow Slough State Game Preserve
Additional Information Contacts
Newton County Government . . . . (219) 474-6081
  http://www.newtoncountyin.com/gov_services.htm

Newton County Communities

BROOK (town). Covers a land area of 0.661 square miles and a water area of 0.009 square miles. Located at 40.86° N. Lat; 87.36° W. Long. Elevation is 653 feet.
History: An early industry in Brook was the Hess Manufacturing Company, whose cosmetics line started when a local druggist concocted witch hazel lotion in a copper clothes boiler.
Population: 918 (1990); 1,062 (2000); 999 (2010); 971 (2015 projected); Race: 93.6% White, 0.8% Black, 0.9% Asian, 4.7% Other, 9.2% Hispanic of any race (2010); Density: 1,511.9 persons per square mile (2010); Average household size: 2.62 (2010); Median age: 40.9 (2010); Males per 100 females: 91.4 (2010); Marriage status: 25.1% never married, 61.2% now married, 6.1% widowed, 7.6% divorced (2000); Foreign born: 5.7% (2000); Ancestry (includes multiple ancestries): 15.6% German, 14.1% English, 13.9% United States or American, 12.2% Other groups, 8.4% Irish (2000).
Economy: Single-family building permits issued: 0 (2009); Multi-family building permits issued: 0 (2009); Employment by occupation: 8.2% management, 7.2% professional, 15.4% services, 20.6% sales, 1.0% farming, 11.0% construction, 36.6% production (2000).
Income: Per capita income: $18,189 (2010); Median household income: $43,313 (2010); Average household income: $47,486 (2010); Percent of households with income of $100,000 or more: 6.0% (2010); Poverty rate: 7.9% (2000).
Taxes: Total city taxes per capita: $175 (2007); City property taxes per capita: $134 (2007).
Education: Percent of population age 25 and over with: High school diploma (including GED) or higher: 84.0% (2010); Bachelor's degree or higher: 12.9% (2010); Master's degree or higher: 4.7% (2010).
Housing: Homeownership rate: 73.9% (2010); Median home value: $94,839 (2010); Median contract rent: $317 per month (2000); Median year structure built: before 1940 (2000).
Transportation: Commute to work: 94.6% car, 0.0% public transportation, 2.7% walk, 0.8% work from home (2000); Travel time to work: 33.3% less than 15 minutes, 41.1% 15 to 30 minutes, 12.2% 30 to 45 minutes, 4.5% 45 to 60 minutes, 8.9% 60 minutes or more (2000)

GOODLAND (town). Covers a land area of 0.784 square miles and a water area of 0 square miles. Located at 40.76° N. Lat; 87.29° W. Long. Elevation is 722 feet.
Population: 1,127 (1990); 1,096 (2000); 1,058 (2010); 1,030 (2015 projected); Race: 96.1% White, 0.6% Black, 0.2% Asian, 3.1% Other, 5.2% Hispanic of any race (2010); Density: 1,348.7 persons per square mile (2010); Average household size: 2.65 (2010); Median age: 38.0 (2010); Males per 100 females: 97.0 (2010); Marriage status: 21.8% never married, 56.1% now married, 10.2% widowed, 11.8% divorced (2000); Foreign born: 0.0% (2000); Ancestry (includes multiple ancestries): 29.6% German, 14.3% Irish, 12.2% English, 11.0% United States or American, 7.4% Other groups (2000).
Economy: Single-family building permits issued: 0 (2009); Multi-family building permits issued: 0 (2009); Employment by occupation: 7.8% management, 9.7% professional, 16.3% services, 15.1% sales, 1.2% farming, 13.2% construction, 36.8% production (2000).
Income: Per capita income: $18,158 (2010); Median household income: $43,250 (2010); Average household income: $47,381 (2010); Percent of households with income of $100,000 or more: 5.8% (2010); Poverty rate: 6.2% (2000).
Taxes: Total city taxes per capita: $153 (2007); City property taxes per capita: $152 (2007).
Education: Percent of population age 25 and over with: High school diploma (including GED) or higher: 82.6% (2010); Bachelor's degree or higher: 9.1% (2010); Master's degree or higher: 4.5% (2010).
Housing: Homeownership rate: 71.7% (2010); Median home value: $79,730 (2010); Median contract rent: $353 per month (2000); Median year structure built: 1943 (2000).
Transportation: Commute to work: 91.0% car, 0.0% public transportation, 5.1% walk, 3.1% work from home (2000); Travel time to work: 50.4% less than 15 minutes, 26.6% 15 to 30 minutes, 12.3% 30 to 45 minutes, 6.9% 45 to 60 minutes, 3.8% 60 minutes or more (2000)

KENTLAND (town). County seat. Covers a land area of 1.457 square miles and a water area of 0 square miles. Located at 40.77° N. Lat; 87.44° W. Long. Elevation is 679 feet.
History: Kentland was the birthplace in 1866 of George Ade, Hoosier author, humorist, and playwright. An early industry here was the Whole Milk Cheese Factory.
Population: 1,836 (1990); 1,822 (2000); 1,682 (2010); 1,602 (2015 projected); Race: 97.4% White, 0.4% Black, 0.3% Asian, 1.9% Other, 4.5% Hispanic of any race (2010); Density: 1,154.4 persons per square mile (2010); Average household size: 2.40 (2010); Median age: 42.8 (2010); Males per 100 females: 97.0 (2010); Marriage status: 24.5% never married, 53.8% now married, 9.5% widowed, 12.2% divorced (2000); Foreign born: 2.6% (2000); Ancestry (includes multiple ancestries): 21.5% German, 15.0% Irish, 11.2% English, 10.7% United States or American, 8.6% Other groups (2000).
Economy: Single-family building permits issued: 1 (2009); Multi-family building permits issued: 0 (2009); Employment by occupation: 8.7% management, 12.1% professional, 16.2% services, 22.0% sales, 0.8% farming, 10.1% construction, 30.1% production (2000).
Income: Per capita income: $21,076 (2010); Median household income: $42,051 (2010); Average household income: $50,958 (2010); Percent of households with income of $100,000 or more: 7.3% (2010); Poverty rate: 7.5% (2000).
Taxes: Total city taxes per capita: $193 (2007); City property taxes per capita: $157 (2007).
Education: Percent of population age 25 and over with: High school diploma (including GED) or higher: 89.1% (2010); Bachelor's degree or higher: 16.1% (2010); Master's degree or higher: 7.5% (2010).
School District(s)
South Newton School Corp (PK-12)
    2008-09 Enrollment: 915 . . . . (219) 474-5184
Housing: Homeownership rate: 68.7% (2010); Median home value: $95,745 (2010); Median contract rent: $355 per month (2000); Median year structure built: 1949 (2000).
Newspapers: Newton County Enterprise (Community news; Circulation 2,000)
Transportation: Commute to work: 92.2% car, 0.2% public transportation, 3.9% walk, 2.5% work from home (2000); Travel time to work: 62.3% less than 15 minutes, 20.3% 15 to 30 minutes, 5.9% 30 to 45 minutes, 4.6% 45 to 60 minutes, 7.0% 60 minutes or more (2000)

LAKE VILLAGE (CDP).

Covers a land area of 3.978 square miles and a water area of 0 square miles. Located at 41.13° N. Lat; 87.44° W. Long. Elevation is 659 feet.

History: Lake Village was located on land that had been reclaimed from a swamp. It grew as the center of a farming and goat-raising area.

Population: 780 (1990); 855 (2000); 770 (2010); 734 (2015 projected); Race: 94.7% White, 0.1% Black, 0.4% Asian, 4.8% Other, 3.0% Hispanic of any race (2010); Density: 193.6 persons per square mile (2010); Average household size: 2.77 (2010); Median age: 40.3 (2010); Males per 100 females: 100.0 (2010); Marriage status: 16.3% never married, 55.5% now married, 6.7% widowed, 21.6% divorced (2000); Foreign born: 1.1% (2000); Ancestry (includes multiple ancestries): 24.8% German, 16.1% Irish, 11.8% Polish, 10.7% Other groups, 10.2% United States or American (2000).

Economy: Employment by occupation: 10.5% management, 10.5% professional, 16.2% services, 11.1% sales, 0.0% farming, 22.8% construction, 28.8% production (2000).

Income: Per capita income: $22,072 (2010); Median household income: $53,169 (2010); Average household income: $62,077 (2010); Percent of households with income of $100,000 or more: 10.4% (2010); Poverty rate: 5.2% (2000).

Education: Percent of population age 25 and over with: High school diploma (including GED) or higher: 77.1% (2010); Bachelor's degree or higher: 7.7% (2010); Master's degree or higher: 1.1% (2010).

School District(s)

North Newton School Corp (KG-12)

    2008-09 Enrollment: 1,531 . . . . (219) 285-2228

Housing: Homeownership rate: 83.1% (2010); Median home value: $129,040 (2010); Median contract rent: $381 per month (2000); Median year structure built: 1969 (2000).

Transportation: Commute to work: 94.6% car, 0.0% public transportation, 0.0% walk, 5.4% work from home (2000); Travel time to work: 12.3% less than 15 minutes, 17.8% 15 to 30 minutes, 25.0% 30 to 45 minutes, 27.1% 45 to 60 minutes, 17.8% 60 minutes or more (2000)

MOROCCO (town).

Covers a land area of 0.579 square miles and a water area of 0 square miles. Located at 40.94° N. Lat; 87.45° W. Long. Elevation is 696 feet.

History: The area in which Morocco was sited was once known as Beaver Prairie for the abundance of beaver in the streams.

Population: 1,044 (1990); 1,127 (2000); 1,045 (2010); 1,005 (2015 projected); Race: 97.5% White, 0.8% Black, 0.2% Asian, 1.5% Other, 2.4% Hispanic of any race (2010); Density: 1,805.3 persons per square mile (2010); Average household size: 2.43 (2010); Median age: 40.0 (2010); Males per 100 females: 100.6 (2010); Marriage status: 21.9% never married, 53.8% now married, 13.7% widowed, 10.6% divorced (2000); Foreign born: 0.9% (2000); Ancestry (includes multiple ancestries): 28.0% German, 15.3% Irish, 14.1% English, 10.4% United States or American, 9.5% Other groups (2000).

Economy: Single-family building permits issued: 1 (2009); Multi-family building permits issued: 0 (2009); Employment by occupation: 8.6% management, 14.2% professional, 13.8% services, 18.8% sales, 1.6% farming, 12.8% construction, 30.2% production (2000).

Income: Per capita income: $20,947 (2010); Median household income: $42,849 (2010); Average household income: $51,517 (2010); Percent of households with income of $100,000 or more: 7.9% (2010); Poverty rate: 9.3% (2000).

Taxes: Total city taxes per capita: $120 (2007); City property taxes per capita: $114 (2007).

Education: Percent of population age 25 and over with: High school diploma (including GED) or higher: 82.7% (2010); Bachelor's degree or higher: 12.3% (2010); Master's degree or higher: 5.9% (2010).

School District(s)

North Newton School Corp (KG-12)

    2008-09 Enrollment: 1,531 . . . . (219) 285-2228

Housing: Homeownership rate: 73.3% (2010); Median home value: $101,488 (2010); Median contract rent: $340 per month (2000); Median year structure built: 1944 (2000).

Transportation: Commute to work: 94.4% car, 0.4% public transportation, 1.7% walk, 2.8% work from home (2000); Travel time to work: 37.2% less than 15 minutes, 29.7% 15 to 30 minutes, 12.1% 30 to 45 minutes, 8.9% 45 to 60 minutes, 12.1% 60 minutes or more (2000)

MOUNT AYR (town).

Covers a land area of 0.149 square miles and a water area of 0 square miles. Located at 40.95° N. Lat; 87.29° W. Long. Elevation is 709 feet.

Population: 151 (1990); 147 (2000); 150 (2010); 153 (2015 projected); Race: 100.0% White, 0.0% Black, 0.0% Asian, 0.0% Other, 0.0% Hispanic of any race (2010); Density: 1,003.9 persons per square mile (2010); Average household size: 2.59 (2010); Median age: 41.5 (2010); Males per 100 females: 92.3 (2010); Marriage status: 22.5% never married, 52.5% now married, 13.3% widowed, 11.7% divorced (2000); Foreign born: 0.0% (2000); Ancestry (includes multiple ancestries): 31.6% United States or American, 16.1% German, 11.5% Irish, 10.3% Dutch, 6.9% Italian (2000).

Economy: Single-family building permits issued: 0 (2009); Multi-family building permits issued: 0 (2009); Employment by occupation: 0.0% management, 10.5% professional, 8.4% services, 25.3% sales, 0.0% farming, 8.4% construction, 47.4% production (2000).

Income: Per capita income: $29,716 (2010); Median household income: $64,063 (2010); Average household income: $76,164 (2010); Percent of households with income of $100,000 or more: 19.0% (2010); Poverty rate: 0.0% (2000).

Taxes: Total city taxes per capita: $74 (2007); City property taxes per capita: $74 (2007).

Education: Percent of population age 25 and over with: High school diploma (including GED) or higher: 90.6% (2010); Bachelor's degree or higher: 17.0% (2010); Master's degree or higher: 1.9% (2010).

Housing: Homeownership rate: 70.7% (2010); Median home value: $121,154 (2010); Median contract rent: $425 per month (2000); Median year structure built: before 1940 (2000).

Transportation: Commute to work: 96.8% car, 0.0% public transportation, 0.0% walk, 3.2% work from home (2000); Travel time to work: 19.6% less than 15 minutes, 39.1% 15 to 30 minutes, 16.3% 30 to 45 minutes, 16.3% 45 to 60 minutes, 8.7% 60 minutes or more (2000)

ROSELAWN (CDP).

Covers a land area of 8.119 square miles and a water area of 0 square miles. Located at 41.15° N. Lat; 87.28° W. Long. Elevation is 682 feet.

Population: 3,045 (1990); 3,933 (2000); 4,068 (2010); 4,120 (2015 projected); Race: 95.5% White, 0.6% Black, 0.7% Asian, 3.2% Other, 4.5% Hispanic of any race (2010); Density: 501.2 persons per square mile (2010); Average household size: 2.89 (2010); Median age: 38.0 (2010); Males per 100 females: 101.1 (2010); Marriage status: 18.7% never married, 68.5% now married, 6.4% widowed, 6.3% divorced (2000); Foreign born: 2.8% (2000); Ancestry (includes multiple ancestries): 25.2% German, 13.5% Irish, 12.5% United States or American, 8.1% Other groups, 7.6% English (2000).

Economy: Employment by occupation: 8.3% management, 8.9% professional, 17.3% services, 19.9% sales, 0.9% farming, 20.5% construction, 24.2% production (2000).

Income: Per capita income: $21,839 (2010); Median household income: $56,148 (2010); Average household income: $63,494 (2010); Percent of households with income of $100,000 or more: 12.9% (2010); Poverty rate: 3.9% (2000).

Education: Percent of population age 25 and over with: High school diploma (including GED) or higher: 86.6% (2010); Bachelor's degree or higher: 5.5% (2010); Master's degree or higher: 1.9% (2010).

Housing: Homeownership rate: 92.2% (2010); Median home value: $124,901 (2010); Median contract rent: $388 per month (2000); Median year structure built: 1981 (2000).

Transportation: Commute to work: 94.5% car, 0.0% public transportation, 1.0% walk, 3.4% work from home (2000); Travel time to work: 20.3% less than 15 minutes, 18.4% 15 to 30 minutes, 17.2% 30 to 45 minutes, 22.8% 45 to 60 minutes, 21.3% 60 minutes or more (2000)

Noble County

Located in northeastern Indiana; drained by the Elkhart River; includes many small lakes. Covers a land area of 411.11 square miles, a water area of 6.50 square miles, and is located in the Eastern Time Zone. The county was founded in 1835. County seat is Albion.

Noble County is part of the Kendallville, IN Micropolitan Statistical Area. The entire metro area includes: Noble County, IN

Population: 37,877 (1990); 46,275 (2000); 47,783 (2010); 48,175 (2015 projected); Race: 91.2% White, 0.6% Black, 0.5% Asian, 7.7% Other, 10.9% Hispanic of any race (2010); Density: 116.2 persons per square mile

(2010); Average household size: 2.71 (2010); Median age: 36.0 (2010); Males per 100 females: 102.6 (2010).
Religion: Five largest groups: 7.8% Catholic Church, 7.7% The United Methodist Church, 5.6% Lutheran Church—Missouri Synod, 1.4% Assemblies of God, 1.1% Evangelical Lutheran Church in America (2000).
Economy: Unemployment rate: 12.1% (5/2010); Total civilian labor force: 23,549 (5/2010); Leading industries: 53.5% manufacturing; 10.4% retail trade; 8.4% health care and social assistance (2008); Farms: 1,196 totaling 159,860 acres (2007); Companies that employ 500 or more persons: 1 (2008); Companies that employ 100 to 499 persons: 35 (2008); Companies that employ less than 100 persons: 902 (2008); Black-owned businesses: n/a (2002); Hispanic-owned businesses: n/a (2002); Asian-owned businesses: n/a (2002); Women-owned businesses: 707 (2002); Retail sales per capita: $8,456 (2010). Single-family building permits issued: 72 (2009); Multi-family building permits issued: 0 (2009).
Income: Per capita income: $20,611 (2010); Median household income: $48,018 (2010); Average household income: $56,168 (2010); Percent of households with income of $100,000 or more: 10.5% (2010); Poverty rate: 10.0% (2008); Bankruptcy rate: 8.94% (2009).
Taxes: Total county taxes per capita: $49 (2007); County property taxes per capita: $9 (2007).
Education: Percent of population age 25 and over with: High school diploma (including GED) or higher: 79.8% (2010); Bachelor's degree or higher: 13.5% (2010); Master's degree or higher: 4.7% (2010).
Housing: Homeownership rate: 78.2% (2010); Median home value: $109,894 (2010); Median contract rent: $468 per month (2006-2008 3-year est.); Median year structure built: 1971 (2006-2008 3-year est.)
Health: Birth rate: 145.1 per 10,000 population (2009); Death rate: 82.7 per 10,000 population (2009); Age-adjusted cancer mortality rate: 215.3 deaths per 100,000 population (2006); Number of physicians: 6.1 per 10,000 population (2006); Hospital beds: 6.5 per 10,000 population (2006); Hospital admissions: 356.2 per 10,000 population (2006).
Elections: 2008 Presidential election results: 41.6% Obama, 57.0% McCain, 0.0% Nader
National and State Parks: Chain O'Lakes State Park; Gene Stratton Porter State Memorial
Additional Information Contacts
Noble County Government . . . . (260) 636-2658
　http://www.nobleco.org
City of Kendallville . . . . (260) 347-2452
　http://www.kendallville-in.org
City of Ligonier . . . . (260) 894-4113
　http://www.ligonier-in.org
Kendallville Chamber of Commerce . . . . (260) 347-1554
　http://www.kendallvillechamber.com
Noble County Convention and Visitors Bureau . . . . (260) 599-0060
　http://www.nccvb.org

Noble County Communities

ALBION (town). County seat. Covers a land area of 1.396 square miles and a water area of 0 square miles. Located at 41.39° N. Lat; 85.42° W. Long. Elevation is 955 feet.
History: Albion was first called The Center. The name was changed to Albion about 1845, when the town was successful in its bid to become the new seat of Noble County. Albion was a station on the Underground Railroad, helping slaves to escape to freedom.
Population: 1,919 (1990); 2,284 (2000); 2,410 (2010); 2,454 (2015 projected); Race: 96.6% White, 1.4% Black, 0.1% Asian, 1.9% Other, 1.6% Hispanic of any race (2010); Density: 1,726.8 persons per square mile (2010); Average household size: 2.63 (2010); Median age: 33.5 (2010); Males per 100 females: 112.9 (2010); Marriage status: 26.3% never married, 50.6% now married, 6.0% widowed, 17.1% divorced (2000); Foreign born: 0.6% (2000); Ancestry (includes multiple ancestries): 28.1% German, 13.1% United States or American, 11.0% Other groups, 8.5% Irish, 7.2% English (2000).
Economy: Single-family building permits issued: 1 (2009); Multi-family building permits issued: 0 (2009); Employment by occupation: 6.0% management, 9.3% professional, 13.2% services, 18.0% sales, 0.4% farming, 9.2% construction, 43.8% production (2000).
Income: Per capita income: $19,954 (2010); Median household income: $46,250 (2010); Average household income: $52,415 (2010); Percent of households with income of $100,000 or more: 6.5% (2010); Poverty rate: 4.7% (2000).

Taxes: Total city taxes per capita: $335 (2007); City property taxes per capita: $326 (2007).
Education: Percent of population age 25 and over with: High school diploma (including GED) or higher: 83.7% (2010); Bachelor's degree or higher: 12.6% (2010); Master's degree or higher: 3.5% (2010).
School District(s)
Central Noble Com School Corp (KG-12)
　2008-09 Enrollment: 1,332 . . . . (260) 636-2175
Housing: Homeownership rate: 75.4% (2010); Median home value: $87,407 (2010); Median contract rent: $393 per month (2000); Median year structure built: 1967 (2000).
Safety: Violent crime rate: 0.0 per 10,000 population; Property crime rate: 0.0 per 10,000 population (2008).
Newspapers: Albion New Era (Community news; Circulation 2,000)
Transportation: Commute to work: 94.7% car, 0.4% public transportation, 3.1% walk, 0.6% work from home (2000); Travel time to work: 50.4% less than 15 minutes, 31.1% 15 to 30 minutes, 9.1% 30 to 45 minutes, 3.8% 45 to 60 minutes, 5.6% 60 minutes or more (2000)

AVILLA (town). Covers a land area of 1.367 square miles and a water area of 0 square miles. Located at 41.36° N. Lat; 85.23° W. Long. Elevation is 965 feet.
Population: 1,578 (1990); 2,049 (2000); 2,300 (2010); 2,396 (2015 projected); Race: 97.0% White, 0.3% Black, 0.6% Asian, 2.2% Other, 0.9% Hispanic of any race (2010); Density: 1,682.8 persons per square mile (2010); Average household size: 2.47 (2010); Median age: 37.6 (2010); Males per 100 females: 97.4 (2010); Marriage status: 19.8% never married, 57.6% now married, 12.2% widowed, 10.3% divorced (2000); Foreign born: 1.3% (2000); Ancestry (includes multiple ancestries): 36.1% German, 11.5% Irish, 8.2% United States or American, 6.6% English, 6.2% Other groups (2000).
Economy: Single-family building permits issued: 3 (2009); Multi-family building permits issued: 0 (2009); Employment by occupation: 7.4% management, 12.6% professional, 14.2% services, 19.4% sales, 1.0% farming, 5.8% construction, 39.6% production (2000).
Income: Per capita income: $20,856 (2010); Median household income: $47,300 (2010); Average household income: $53,421 (2010); Percent of households with income of $100,000 or more: 7.9% (2010); Poverty rate: 5.7% (2000).
Taxes: Total city taxes per capita: $217 (2007); City property taxes per capita: $196 (2007).
Education: Percent of population age 25 and over with: High school diploma (including GED) or higher: 86.9% (2010); Bachelor's degree or higher: 11.6% (2010); Master's degree or higher: 2.0% (2010).
School District(s)
East Noble School Corp (PK-12)
　2008-09 Enrollment: 3,911 . . . . (260) 347-2502
Housing: Homeownership rate: 68.8% (2010); Median home value: $113,693 (2010); Median contract rent: $433 per month (2000); Median year structure built: 1978 (2000).
Transportation: Commute to work: 96.1% car, 0.0% public transportation, 2.2% walk, 1.1% work from home (2000); Travel time to work: 39.0% less than 15 minutes, 38.5% 15 to 30 minutes, 15.4% 30 to 45 minutes, 4.2% 45 to 60 minutes, 2.9% 60 minutes or more (2000)
Additional Information Contacts
Noble County Convention and Visitors Bureau . . . . (260) 599-0060
　http://www.nccvb.org

CROMWELL (town). Covers a land area of 0.297 square miles and a water area of 0 square miles. Located at 41.40° N. Lat; 85.61° W. Long. Elevation is 955 feet.
Population: 507 (1990); 452 (2000); 454 (2010); 452 (2015 projected); Race: 82.6% White, 0.0% Black, 0.4% Asian, 17.0% Other, 49.8% Hispanic of any race (2010); Density: 1,530.0 persons per square mile (2010); Average household size: 3.09 (2010); Median age: 28.9 (2010); Males per 100 females: 105.4 (2010); Marriage status: 20.9% never married, 61.0% now married, 7.1% widowed, 11.0% divorced (2000); Foreign born: 1.9% (2000); Ancestry (includes multiple ancestries): 21.5% German, 15.3% Irish, 14.1% Other groups, 13.4% United States or American, 5.5% English (2000).
Economy: Single-family building permits issued: 0 (2009); Multi-family building permits issued: 0 (2009); Employment by occupation: 4.9% management, 4.4% professional, 17.3% services, 20.0% sales, 0.9% farming, 13.8% construction, 38.7% production (2000).

Income: Per capita income: $18,091 (2010); Median household income: $49,700 (2010); Average household income: $57,687 (2010); Percent of households with income of $100,000 or more: 10.2% (2010); Poverty rate: 14.7% (2000).

Taxes: Total city taxes per capita: $218 (2007); City property taxes per capita: $170 (2007).

Education: Percent of population age 25 and over with: High school diploma (including GED) or higher: 67.6% (2010); Bachelor's degree or higher: 9.4% (2010); Master's degree or higher: 4.7% (2010).

Housing: Homeownership rate: 78.2% (2010); Median home value: $73,125 (2010); Median contract rent: $280 per month (2000); Median year structure built: 1947 (2000).

Transportation: Commute to work: 88.7% car, 0.0% public transportation, 5.4% walk, 5.9% work from home (2000); Travel time to work: 39.9% less than 15 minutes, 38.9% 15 to 30 minutes, 13.9% 30 to 45 minutes, 3.4% 45 to 60 minutes, 3.8% 60 minutes or more (2000)

KENDALLVILLE (city).
Covers a land area of 5.088 square miles and a water area of 0.224 square miles. Located at 41.44° N. Lat; 85.26° W. Long. Elevation is 988 feet.

History: Kendallville was settled in 1833 when David Bundle opened a tavern to serve the many travelers that passed this way. When the New York Central Railroad came through in 1857, the village grew. The Flint & Walling Manufacturing Plant was founded here in 1865 as a machine shop, and became a producer of windmills and pumps.

Population: 8,505 (1990); 9,616 (2000); 9,515 (2010); 9,416 (2015 projected); Race: 95.3% White, 0.5% Black, 0.7% Asian, 3.5% Other, 4.6% Hispanic of any race (2010); Density: 1,870.2 persons per square mile (2010); Average household size: 2.46 (2010); Median age: 36.4 (2010); Males per 100 females: 95.1 (2010); Marriage status: 21.9% never married, 54.1% now married, 9.0% widowed, 15.0% divorced (2000); Foreign born: 2.4% (2000); Ancestry (includes multiple ancestries): 25.9% German, 19.0% United States or American, 10.3% Irish, 10.0% Other groups, 9.5% English (2000).

Economy: Single-family building permits issued: 22 (2009); Multi-family building permits issued: 0 (2009); Employment by occupation: 8.0% management, 10.1% professional, 12.9% services, 21.0% sales, 0.4% farming, 10.0% construction, 37.6% production (2000).

Income: Per capita income: $19,556 (2010); Median household income: $41,046 (2010); Average household income: $48,448 (2010); Percent of households with income of $100,000 or more: 6.8% (2010); Poverty rate: 9.9% (2000).

Taxes: Total city taxes per capita: $36 (2007); City property taxes per capita: $0 (2007).

Education: Percent of population age 25 and over with: High school diploma (including GED) or higher: 79.7% (2010); Bachelor's degree or higher: 16.4% (2010); Master's degree or higher: 5.7% (2010).

School District(s)
Dekalb Co Eastern Com Sch Dist (KG-12)
    2008-09 Enrollment: 1,494 . . . . (260) 868-2125
East Noble School Corp (PK-12)
    2008-09 Enrollment: 3,911 . . . . (260) 347-2502
Garrett-Keyser-Butler Com (KG-12)
    2008-09 Enrollment: 1,785 . . . . (260) 357-3185

Housing: Homeownership rate: 70.3% (2010); Median home value: $91,086 (2010); Median contract rent: $361 per month (2000); Median year structure built: 1962 (2000).

Hospitals: Parkview Noble Hospital (66 beds)

Newspapers: The News-Sun (Local news; Circulation 3,271)

Transportation: Commute to work: 93.9% car, 0.1% public transportation, 3.2% walk, 2.1% work from home (2000); Travel time to work: 59.7% less than 15 minutes, 21.7% 15 to 30 minutes, 10.7% 30 to 45 minutes, 4.0% 45 to 60 minutes, 3.9% 60 minutes or more (2000)

Additional Information Contacts
City of Kendallville . . . . (260) 347-2452
    http://www.kendallville-in.org
Kendallville Chamber of Commerce . . . . (260) 347-1554
    http://www.kendallvillechamber.com

KIMMELL (unincorporated postal area, zip code 46760).
Covers a land area of 24.386 square miles and a water area of 0.422 square miles. Located at 41.36° N. Lat; 85.56° W. Long. Elevation is 915 feet.

History: Kimmell achieved a degree of fame as a producer of onions. In 1936 Andrew W. Milnar of Kimmell grew 1,471 bushels of onions on one acre of land.

Population: 1,368 (2000); Race: 99.1% White, 0.0% Black, 0.0% Asian, 0.9% Other, 0.5% Hispanic of any race (2000); Density: 56.1 persons per square mile (2000); Age: 28.7% under 18, 9.0% over 64 (2000); Marriage status: 20.2% never married, 58.6% now married, 15.3% divorced (2000); Foreign born: 0.5% (2000); Ancestry (includes multiple ancestries): 32.5% German, 14.3% United States or American, 12.3% English, 8.2% Irish, 3.5% Dutch (2000).

Economy: Employment by occupation: 9.3% management, 12.3% professional, 7.1% services, 24.8% sales, 3.2% farming, 8.0% construction, 35.2% production (2000).

Income: Per capita income: $18,128 (2000); Median household income: $39,821 (2000); Poverty rate: 2.4% (2000).

Education: Percent of population age 25 and over with: High school diploma (including GED) or higher: 85.0% (2000); Bachelor's degree or higher: 11.2% (2000).

Housing: Homeownership rate: 82.7% (2000); Median home value: $74,000 (2000); Median contract rent: $325 per month (2000); Median year structure built: 1950 (2000).

Transportation: Commute to work: 87.7% car, 0.0% public transportation, 3.8% walk, 8.4% work from home (2000); Travel time to work: 22.5% less than 15 minutes, 39.3% 15 to 30 minutes, 24.5% 30 to 45 minutes, 7.4% 45 to 60 minutes, 6.4% 60 minutes or more (2000)

LAOTTO (unincorporated postal area, zip code 46763). Aka La Otto.
Covers a land area of 24.578 square miles and a water area of 0 square miles. Located at 41.28° N. Lat; 85.22° W. Long. Elevation is 873 feet.

History: Laid out 1871.

Population: 1,684 (2000); Race: 100.0% White, 0.0% Black, 0.0% Asian, 0.0% Other, 0.7% Hispanic of any race (2000); Density: 68.5 persons per square mile (2000); Age: 27.7% under 18, 9.8% over 64 (2000); Marriage status: 19.2% never married, 71.3% now married, 3.4% widowed, 6.1% divorced (2000); Foreign born: 0.4% (2000); Ancestry (includes multiple ancestries): 31.4% German, 15.2% English, 12.8% United States or American, 8.1% Irish, 5.5% French (except Basque) (2000).

Economy: Employment by occupation: 14.0% management, 13.8% professional, 12.3% services, 20.8% sales, 0.6% farming, 12.5% construction, 26.1% production (2000).

Income: Per capita income: $20,062 (2000); Median household income: $48,654 (2000); Poverty rate: 6.1% (2000).

Education: Percent of population age 25 and over with: High school diploma (including GED) or higher: 88.6% (2000); Bachelor's degree or higher: 14.7% (2000).

School District(s)
East Noble School Corp (PK-12)
    2008-09 Enrollment: 3,911 . . . . (260) 347-2502

Housing: Homeownership rate: 91.0% (2000); Median home value: $104,800 (2000); Median contract rent: $398 per month (2000); Median year structure built: 1969 (2000).

Transportation: Commute to work: 87.0% car, 0.0% public transportation, 7.7% walk, 5.3% work from home (2000); Travel time to work: 31.0% less than 15 minutes, 34.4% 15 to 30 minutes, 24.0% 30 to 45 minutes, 4.4% 45 to 60 minutes, 6.2% 60 minutes or more (2000)

LIGONIER (city).
Covers a land area of 2.250 square miles and a water area of 0 square miles. Located at 41.46° N. Lat; 85.59° W. Long. Elevation is 869 feet.

History: Ligonier was settled along the Elkhart River. Many of the early residents were Jewish.

Population: 3,532 (1990); 4,357 (2000); 4,621 (2010); 4,730 (2015 projected); Race: 59.2% White, 0.6% Black, 0.9% Asian, 39.2% Other, 50.8% Hispanic of any race (2010); Density: 2,054.1 persons per square mile (2010); Average household size: 3.20 (2010); Median age: 31.5 (2010); Males per 100 females: 107.1 (2010); Marriage status: 25.8% never married, 55.6% now married, 7.5% widowed, 11.1% divorced (2000); Foreign born: 23.5% (2000); Ancestry (includes multiple ancestries): 35.8% Other groups, 18.3% German, 11.4% United States or American, 7.0% Irish, 6.0% English (2000).

Economy: Single-family building permits issued: 0 (2009); Multi-family building permits issued: 0 (2009); Employment by occupation: 4.2% management, 7.6% professional, 10.5% services, 15.9% sales, 0.9% farming, 6.5% construction, 54.5% production (2000).

Income: Per capita income: $14,142 (2010); Median household income: $38,085 (2010); Average household income: $45,287 (2010); Percent of households with income of $100,000 or more: 4.8% (2010); Poverty rate: 14.3% (2000).

Taxes: Total city taxes per capita: $272 (2007); City property taxes per capita: $228 (2007).
Education: Percent of population age 25 and over with: High school diploma (including GED) or higher: 64.5% (2010); Bachelor's degree or higher: 10.4% (2010); Master's degree or higher: 3.3% (2010).

School District(s)
West Noble School Corporation (PK-12)
    2008-09 Enrollment: 2,581 . . . . (260) 894-3191
Housing: Homeownership rate: 70.6% (2010); Median home value: $86,071 (2010); Median contract rent: $375 per month (2000); Median year structure built: 1960 (2000).
Safety: Violent crime rate: 4.4 per 10,000 population; Property crime rate: 146.1 per 10,000 population (2008).
Newspapers: Ligonier Advance Leader (Community news; Circulation 2,000)
Transportation: Commute to work: 95.0% car, 0.0% public transportation, 0.9% walk, 2.3% work from home (2000); Travel time to work: 48.5% less than 15 minutes, 31.5% 15 to 30 minutes, 14.8% 30 to 45 minutes, 2.6% 45 to 60 minutes, 2.6% 60 minutes or more (2000)
Additional Information Contacts
City of Ligonier. . . . . (260) 894-4113
    http://www.ligonier-in.org

ROME CITY (town).
Covers a land area of 1.193 square miles and a water area of 0.979 square miles. Located at 41.49° N. Lat; 85.36° W. Long. Elevation is 928 feet.
History: Rome City developed when a dam was built across a tributary of the Elkhart River, forming Sylvan Lake. The settlement, which became a resort community, was platted in 1839 and named by the Irish construction workers.
Population: 1,523 (1990); 1,615 (2000); 1,581 (2010); 1,552 (2015 projected); Race: 97.9% White, 0.3% Black, 0.1% Asian, 1.8% Other, 1.2% Hispanic of any race (2010); Density: 1,325.5 persons per square mile (2010); Average household size: 2.66 (2010); Median age: 37.8 (2010); Males per 100 females: 100.1 (2010); Marriage status: 18.1% never married, 64.9% now married, 6.4% widowed, 10.6% divorced (2000); Foreign born: 0.3% (2000); Ancestry (includes multiple ancestries): 23.2% German, 18.6% United States or American, 11.0% Irish, 9.9% Other groups, 7.7% English (2000).
Economy: Single-family building permits issued: 4 (2009); Multi-family building permits issued: 0 (2009); Employment by occupation: 8.7% management, 10.1% professional, 12.4% services, 18.3% sales, 0.3% farming, 8.9% construction, 41.3% production (2000).
Income: Per capita income: $20,601 (2010); Median household income: $45,714 (2010); Average household income: $54,495 (2010); Percent of households with income of $100,000 or more: 9.8% (2010); Poverty rate: 9.3% (2000).
Taxes: Total city taxes per capita: $119 (2007); City property taxes per capita: $99 (2007).
Education: Percent of population age 25 and over with: High school diploma (including GED) or higher: 72.9% (2010); Bachelor's degree or higher: 11.2% (2010); Master's degree or higher: 3.3% (2010).

School District(s)
East Noble School Corp (PK-12)
    2008-09 Enrollment: 3,911 . . . . (260) 347-2502
Housing: Homeownership rate: 76.3% (2010); Median home value: $100,313 (2010); Median contract rent: $419 per month (2000); Median year structure built: 1952 (2000).
Transportation: Commute to work: 95.6% car, 0.6% public transportation, 0.7% walk, 1.3% work from home (2000); Travel time to work: 24.6% less than 15 minutes, 43.4% 15 to 30 minutes, 14.2% 30 to 45 minutes, 11.8% 45 to 60 minutes, 5.9% 60 minutes or more (2000)

WAWAKA (unincorporated postal area, zip code 46794).
Covers a land area of 28.473 square miles and a water area of 0.203 square miles. Located at 41.46° N. Lat; 85.45° W. Long. Elevation is 899 feet.
History: The name Wawaka is of Indian origin meaning "big heron." The town was founded in 1857 when the New York Central Railroad was built through the area.
Population: 1,640 (2000); Race: 98.1% White, 0.0% Black, 1.0% Asian, 0.9% Other, 0.5% Hispanic of any race (2000); Density: 57.6 persons per square mile (2000); Age: 33.8% under 18, 9.1% over 64 (2000); Marriage status: 23.0% never married, 66.1% now married, 2.9% widowed, 8.0% divorced (2000); Foreign born: 1.4% (2000); Ancestry (includes multiple

ancestries): 25.7% German, 15.2% United States or American, 6.4% Irish, 5.6% Other groups, 5.3% English (2000).
Economy: Employment by occupation: 14.9% management, 7.4% professional, 10.4% services, 11.2% sales, 1.1% farming, 12.9% construction, 42.0% production (2000).
Income: Per capita income: $16,489 (2000); Median household income: $49,100 (2000); Poverty rate: 8.7% (2000).
Education: Percent of population age 25 and over with: High school diploma (including GED) or higher: 74.1% (2000); Bachelor's degree or higher: 8.3% (2000).
Housing: Homeownership rate: 91.6% (2000); Median home value: $92,900 (2000); Median contract rent: $378 per month (2000); Median year structure built: 1964 (2000).
Transportation: Commute to work: 92.5% car, 0.0% public transportation, 2.2% walk, 5.3% work from home (2000); Travel time to work: 34.4% less than 15 minutes, 39.2% 15 to 30 minutes, 14.2% 30 to 45 minutes, 5.5% 45 to 60 minutes, 6.7% 60 minutes or more (2000)

WOLCOTTVILLE (town).
Covers a land area of 1.025 square miles and a water area of 0 square miles. Located at 41.52° N. Lat; 85.36° W. Long. Elevation is 942 feet.
History: Wolcottville grew around a gristmill, sawmill, and distillery established by George Wolcott from Connecticut. The number of nearby lakes made Wolcottville a vacation center as well.
Population: 879 (1990); 933 (2000); 984 (2010); 1,003 (2015 projected); Race: 98.2% White, 0.1% Black, 0.3% Asian, 1.4% Other, 1.8% Hispanic of any race (2010); Density: 959.8 persons per square mile (2010); Average household size: 2.55 (2010); Median age: 38.7 (2010); Males per 100 females: 100.0 (2010); Marriage status: 17.5% never married, 60.4% now married, 4.7% widowed, 17.5% divorced (2000); Foreign born: 0.4% (2000); Ancestry (includes multiple ancestries): 20.4% United States or American, 14.3% German, 11.4% Other groups, 7.6% English, 4.2% Irish (2000).
Economy: Employment by occupation: 2.6% management, 6.1% professional, 10.0% services, 14.2% sales, 0.4% farming, 11.4% construction, 55.2% production (2000).
Income: Per capita income: $23,013 (2010); Median household income: $49,308 (2010); Average household income: $58,549 (2010); Percent of households with income of $100,000 or more: 10.6% (2010); Poverty rate: 10.9% (2000).
Taxes: Total city taxes per capita: $180 (2007); City property taxes per capita: $133 (2007).
Education: Percent of population age 25 and over with: High school diploma (including GED) or higher: 75.0% (2010); Bachelor's degree or higher: 9.4% (2010); Master's degree or higher: 3.2% (2010).

School District(s)
Lakeland School Corporation (KG-12)
    2008-09 Enrollment: 2,218 . . . . (260) 499-2400
Prairie Heights Com Sch Corp (KG-12)
    2008-09 Enrollment: 1,591 . . . . (800) 800-9596
Housing: Homeownership rate: 82.4% (2010); Median home value: $130,405 (2010); Median contract rent: $410 per month (2000); Median year structure built: 1957 (2000).
Transportation: Commute to work: 94.4% car, 0.0% public transportation, 3.3% walk, 0.7% work from home (2000); Travel time to work: 18.0% less than 15 minutes, 54.2% 15 to 30 minutes, 17.5% 30 to 45 minutes, 4.9% 45 to 60 minutes, 5.4% 60 minutes or more (2000)

Ohio County

Located in southeastern Indiana; bounded on the east by the Ohio River and the Kentucky border. Covers a land area of 86.72 square miles, a water area of 0.75 square miles, and is located in the Eastern Time Zone. The county was founded in 1844. County seat is Rising Sun.

Ohio County is part of the Cincinnati-Middletown, OH-KY-IN Metropolitan Statistical Area. The entire metro area includes: Dearborn County, IN; Franklin County, IN; Ohio County, IN; Boone County, KY; Bracken County, KY; Campbell County, KY; Gallatin County, KY; Grant County, KY; Kenton County, KY; Pendleton County, KY; Brown County, OH; Butler County, OH; Clermont County, OH; Hamilton County, OH; Warren County, OH

Population: 5,315 (1990); 5,623 (2000); 5,771 (2010); 5,782 (2015 projected); Race: 98.0% White, 1.1% Black, 0.1% Asian, 0.8% Other, 0.6% Hispanic of any race (2010); Density: 66.5 persons per square mile (2010);

Average household size: 2.47 (2010); Median age: 39.3 (2010); Males per 100 females: 97.8 (2010).
Religion: Five largest groups: 10.9% Christian Churches and Churches of Christ, 7.6% American Baptist Churches in the USA, 5.7% The United Methodist Church, 4.2% Evangelical Lutheran Church in America, 3.3% United Church of Christ (2000).
Economy: Unemployment rate: 9.8% (5/2010); Total civilian labor force: 2,923 (5/2010); Leading industries: 6.2% retail trade; 5.4% health care and social assistance; 2.7% other services (except public administration) (2008); Farms: 179 totaling 21,500 acres (2007); Companies that employ 500 or more persons: 1 (2008); Companies that employ 100 to 499 persons: 0 (2008); Companies that employ less than 100 persons: 92 (2008); Black-owned businesses: n/a (2002); Hispanic-owned businesses: n/a (2002); Asian-owned businesses: n/a (2002); Women-owned businesses: n/a (2002); Retail sales per capita: $3,417 (2010). Single-family building permits issued: 8 (2009); Multi-family building permits issued: 0 (2009).
Income: Per capita income: $23,428 (2010); Median household income: $49,795 (2010); Average household income: $58,283 (2010); Percent of households with income of $100,000 or more: 13.2% (2010); Poverty rate: 9.0% (2008); Bankruptcy rate: 9.26% (2009).
Taxes: Total county taxes per capita: $301 (2007); County property taxes per capita: $168 (2007).
Education: Percent of population age 25 and over with: High school diploma (including GED) or higher: 83.8% (2010); Bachelor's degree or higher: 12.3% (2010); Master's degree or higher: 4.4% (2010).
Housing: Homeownership rate: 76.5% (2010); Median home value: $136,988 (2010); Median contract rent: $n/a per month (2006-2008 3-year est.); Median year structure built: n/a (2006-2008 3-year est.)
Health: Birth rate: 110.0 per 10,000 population (2009); Death rate: 81.2 per 10,000 population (2009); Age-adjusted cancer mortality rate: 255.9 (Unreliable) deaths per 100,000 population (2006); Number of physicians: 0.0 per 10,000 population (2007); Hospital beds: 0.0 per 10,000 population (2006); Hospital admissions: 0.0 per 10,000 population (2006).
Elections: 2008 Presidential election results: 39.7% Obama, 58.7% McCain, 0.0% Nader
Additional Information Contacts
Ohio County Government . . . . (812) 438-2062
    http://www.in.gov/mylocal/ohio_county.htm

Ohio County Communities

RISING SUN (city). County seat. Covers a land area of 1.484 square miles and a water area of 0.102 square miles. Located at 38.95° N. Lat; 84.85° W. Long. Elevation is 502 feet.
History: Rising Sun was platted in 1814 along the Ohio River, and grew as a shipping center.
Population: 2,379 (1990); 2,470 (2000); 2,374 (2010); 2,320 (2015 projected); Race: 97.3% White, 1.9% Black, 0.0% Asian, 0.8% Other, 1.0% Hispanic of any race (2010); Density: 1,599.7 persons per square mile (2010); Average household size: 2.30 (2010); Median age: 38.9 (2010); Males per 100 females: 95.7 (2010); Marriage status: 22.4% never married, 57.7% now married, 11.9% widowed, 8.0% divorced (2000); Foreign born: 0.0% (2000); Ancestry (includes multiple ancestries): 22.8% German, 20.1% United States or American, 15.1% Irish, 12.4% English, 4.2% Other groups (2000).
Economy: Single-family building permits issued: 0 (2009); Multi-family building permits issued: 0 (2009); Employment by occupation: 11.5% management, 14.4% professional, 21.9% services, 19.3% sales, 0.9% farming, 9.5% construction, 22.4% production (2000).
Income: Per capita income: $21,803 (2010); Median household income: $41,655 (2010); Average household income: $50,942 (2010); Percent of households with income of $100,000 or more: 10.0% (2010); Poverty rate: 10.3% (2000).
Taxes: Total city taxes per capita: $71 (2007); City property taxes per capita: $66 (2007).
Education: Percent of population age 25 and over with: High school diploma (including GED) or higher: 82.4% (2010); Bachelor's degree or higher: 14.0% (2010); Master's degree or higher: 5.4% (2010).
School District(s)
Rising Sun-Ohio Co Com (KG-12)
    2008-09 Enrollment: 927 . . . . (812) 438-2655
Housing: Homeownership rate: 64.6% (2010); Median home value: $113,609 (2010); Median contract rent: $373 per month (2000); Median year structure built: 1956 (2000).

Newspapers: Ohio County News (Community news; Circulation 579); Rising Sun Recorder (Community news; Circulation 1,673)
Transportation: Commute to work: 90.3% car, 0.0% public transportation, 4.3% walk, 3.6% work from home (2000); Travel time to work: 41.7% less than 15 minutes, 26.1% 15 to 30 minutes, 13.1% 30 to 45 minutes, 12.3% 45 to 60 minutes, 6.8% 60 minutes or more (2000)

Orange County

Located in southern Indiana; drained by the Lick, Lost, and Potoka Rivers. Covers a land area of 399.52 square miles, a water area of 8.68 square miles, and is located in the Eastern Time Zone. The county was founded in 1815. County seat is Paoli.

Weather Station: Paoli   Elevation: 557 feet

	Jan	Feb	Mar	Apr	May	Jun	Jul	Aug	Sep	Oct	Nov	Dec
High	39	45	55	66	76	84	88	86	80	69	55	44
Low	19	22	31	41	51	60	64	62	54	42	33	24
Precip	3.1	2.9	4.5	5.1	5.1	4.2	4.4	4.0	3.3	3.1	4.2	3.5
Snow	na	na	1.3	0.1	0.0	0.0	0.0	0.0	0.0	0.0	0.2	2.4

High and Low temperatures in degrees Fahrenheit; Precipitation and Snow in inches

Population: 18,409 (1990); 19,306 (2000); 19,598 (2010); 19,603 (2015 projected); Race: 97.1% White, 1.0% Black, 0.2% Asian, 1.7% Other, 1.1% Hispanic of any race (2010); Density: 49.1 persons per square mile (2010); Average household size: 2.43 (2010); Median age: 39.0 (2010); Males per 100 females: 96.5 (2010).
Religion: Five largest groups: 12.7% Christian Churches and Churches of Christ, 8.4% American Baptist Churches in the USA, 7.2% The United Methodist Church, 3.0% Catholic Church, 3.0% The Wesleyan Church (2000).
Economy: Unemployment rate: 10.6% (5/2010); Total civilian labor force: 10,424 (5/2010); Leading industries: 18.6% manufacturing; 9.2% health care and social assistance; 8.5% retail trade (2008); Farms: 474 totaling 97,411 acres (2007); Companies that employ 500 or more persons: 3 (2008); Companies that employ 100 to 499 persons: 11 (2008); Companies that employ less than 100 persons: 390 (2008); Black-owned businesses: n/a (2002); Hispanic-owned businesses: n/a (2002); Asian-owned businesses: n/a (2002); Women-owned businesses: n/a (2002); Retail sales per capita: $8,084 (2010). Single-family building permits issued: 10 (2009); Multi-family building permits issued: 16 (2009).
Income: Per capita income: $19,966 (2010); Median household income: $38,228 (2010); Average household income: $48,806 (2010); Percent of households with income of $100,000 or more: 7.9% (2010); Poverty rate: 15.9% (2008); Bankruptcy rate: 7.84% (2009).
Taxes: Total county taxes per capita: $185 (2007); County property taxes per capita: $95 (2007).
Education: Percent of population age 25 and over with: High school diploma (including GED) or higher: 79.9% (2010); Bachelor's degree or higher: 11.0% (2010); Master's degree or higher: 5.1% (2010).
Housing: Homeownership rate: 78.0% (2010); Median home value: $79,183 (2010); Median contract rent: $n/a per month (2006-2008 3-year est.); Median year structure built: n/a (2006-2008 3-year est.)
Health: Birth rate: 123.2 per 10,000 population (2009); Death rate: 107.9 per 10,000 population (2009); Age-adjusted cancer mortality rate: 257.0 deaths per 100,000 population (2006); Number of physicians: 5.6 per 10,000 population (2007); Hospital beds: 12.4 per 10,000 population (2006); Hospital admissions: 307.8 per 10,000 population (2006).
Elections: 2008 Presidential election results: 41.9% Obama, 56.1% McCain, 0.1% Nader
National and State Parks: Hoosier National Forest; Jackson State Recreation Area; Newton-Stewart State Recreation Area; Pioneer Mothers State Wayside; Springs Valley State Fish and Wildlife Area; Tillery Hill State Recreation Area
Additional Information Contacts
Orange County Government . . . . (812) 723-2649
    http://epics.co.orange.in.us/government/index.html
Town of Paoli . . . . (812) 723-3616
    http://indian.hometownlocator.com

Orange County Communities

FRENCH LICK (town). Covers a land area of 1.623 square miles and a water area of 0 square miles. Located at 38.54° N. Lat; 86.61° W. Long. Elevation is 499 feet.

History: French Lick was founded in 1811 on the site of mineral springs where a trading post had been operated by the French in the early 1700's. The French Lick Springs Hotel was opened in 1840 by Dr. William A. Bowles, who not only entertained visitors to the medicinal springs, but marketed the spring water by boiling and bottling it as Pluto Water.
Population: 2,087 (1990); 1,941 (2000); 1,848 (2010); 1,802 (2015 projected); Race: 93.4% White, 4.2% Black, 0.3% Asian, 2.1% Other, 0.4% Hispanic of any race (2010); Density: 1,139.0 persons per square mile (2010); Average household size: 2.21 (2010); Median age: 43.0 (2010); Males per 100 females: 95.3 (2010); Marriage status: 17.4% never married, 55.6% now married, 11.3% widowed, 15.7% divorced (2000); Foreign born: 1.4% (2000); Ancestry (includes multiple ancestries): 18.7% German, 17.9% United States or American, 13.6% Irish, 10.8% Other groups, 6.6% English (2000).
Economy: Single-family building permits issued: 4 (2009); Multi-family building permits issued: 0 (2009); Employment by occupation: 6.1% management, 15.1% professional, 15.4% services, 24.7% sales, 1.0% farming, 4.9% construction, 32.8% production (2000).
Income: Per capita income: $17,324 (2010); Median household income: $31,932 (2010); Average household income: $38,702 (2010); Percent of households with income of $100,000 or more: 4.6% (2010); Poverty rate: 18.7% (2000).
Taxes: Total city taxes per capita: $178 (2007); City property taxes per capita: $177 (2007).
Education: Percent of population age 25 and over with: High school diploma (including GED) or higher: 78.1% (2010); Bachelor's degree or higher: 11.1% (2010); Master's degree or higher: 4.9% (2010).

School District(s)
Springs Valley Com School Corp (KG-12)
    2008-09 Enrollment: 957 . . . . (812) 936-4474
Housing: Homeownership rate: 65.4% (2010); Median home value: $62,917 (2010); Median contract rent: $272 per month (2000); Median year structure built: 1962 (2000).
Newspapers: Springs Valley Herald (Community news; Circulation 3,000)
Transportation: Commute to work: 89.8% car, 0.0% public transportation, 7.2% walk, 3.0% work from home (2000); Travel time to work: 45.0% less than 15 minutes, 20.1% 15 to 30 minutes, 21.4% 30 to 45 minutes, 6.8% 45 to 60 minutes, 6.6% 60 minutes or more (2000)

ORLEANS (town). Covers a land area of 1.568 square miles and a water area of 0 square miles. Located at 38.66° N. Lat; 86.45° W. Long. Elevation is 633 feet.
History: Orleans was founded in 1815 shortly after General Jackson's victory at New Orleans, and the town was named for that event. Orleans developed as an orchard and dairy center.
Population: 2,117 (1990); 2,273 (2000); 2,267 (2010); 2,251 (2015 projected); Race: 97.3% White, 0.7% Black, 0.0% Asian, 2.0% Other, 2.0% Hispanic of any race (2010); Density: 1,445.4 persons per square mile (2010); Average household size: 2.45 (2010); Median age: 35.8 (2010); Males per 100 females: 93.1 (2010); Marriage status: 15.7% never married, 60.2% now married, 11.2% widowed, 12.9% divorced (2000); Foreign born: 0.2% (2000); Ancestry (includes multiple ancestries): 26.0% United States or American, 12.4% German, 11.0% Other groups, 8.2% English, 6.4% Irish (2000).
Economy: Single-family building permits issued: 3 (2009); Multi-family building permits issued: 16 (2009); Employment by occupation: 8.1% management, 5.9% professional, 21.6% services, 21.2% sales, 1.0% farming, 9.3% construction, 32.8% production (2000).
Income: Per capita income: $18,088 (2010); Median household income: $33,933 (2010); Average household income: $44,391 (2010); Percent of households with income of $100,000 or more: 7.3% (2010); Poverty rate: 17.2% (2000).
Taxes: Total city taxes per capita: $185 (2007); City property taxes per capita: $150 (2007).
Education: Percent of population age 25 and over with: High school diploma (including GED) or higher: 84.6% (2010); Bachelor's degree or higher: 8.3% (2010); Master's degree or higher: 2.5% (2010).

School District(s)
Orleans Community Schools (PK-12)
    2008-09 Enrollment: 831 . . . . (812) 865-2688
Housing: Homeownership rate: 72.2% (2010); Median home value: $79,057 (2010); Median contract rent: $280 per month (2000); Median year structure built: 1964 (2000).
Transportation: Commute to work: 95.0% car, 0.0% public transportation, 0.7% walk, 2.8% work from home (2000); Travel time to work: 47.0% less

than 15 minutes, 32.5% 15 to 30 minutes, 7.3% 30 to 45 minutes, 8.7% 45 to 60 minutes, 4.4% 60 minutes or more (2000)

PAOLI (town). County seat. Covers a land area of 3.783 square miles and a water area of 0 square miles. Located at 38.55° N. Lat; 86.46° W. Long. Elevation is 623 feet.
History: The Orange County Courthouse was constructed in 1850 in Paoli, the county seat.
Population: 3,551 (1990); 3,844 (2000); 3,736 (2010); 3,673 (2015 projected); Race: 97.4% White, 0.6% Black, 0.2% Asian, 1.8% Other, 1.7% Hispanic of any race (2010); Density: 987.5 persons per square mile (2010); Average household size: 2.33 (2010); Median age: 39.0 (2010); Males per 100 females: 93.8 (2010); Marriage status: 17.4% never married, 59.9% now married, 9.6% widowed, 13.1% divorced (2000); Foreign born: 2.3% (2000); Ancestry (includes multiple ancestries): 22.7% United States or American, 13.8% German, 12.2% Irish, 10.9% English, 10.5% Other groups (2000).
Economy: Employment by occupation: 7.4% management, 15.8% professional, 15.5% services, 20.1% sales, 0.8% farming, 10.1% construction, 30.5% production (2000).
Income: Per capita income: $17,148 (2010); Median household income: $31,227 (2010); Average household income: $40,759 (2010); Percent of households with income of $100,000 or more: 5.5% (2010); Poverty rate: 15.1% (2000).
Taxes: Total city taxes per capita: $104 (2007); City property taxes per capita: $82 (2007).
Education: Percent of population age 25 and over with: High school diploma (including GED) or higher: 76.1% (2010); Bachelor's degree or higher: 13.8% (2010); Master's degree or higher: 7.3% (2010).

School District(s)
Lost River Career Cooperative (09-12)
    2008-09 Enrollment: n/a . . . . (812) 723-4818
Paoli Community School Corp (PK-12)
    2008-09 Enrollment: 1,613 . . . . (812) 723-4717
South Central Area Special Ed (KG-12)
    2008-09 Enrollment: n/a . . . . (812) 723-2089
Housing: Homeownership rate: 74.0% (2010); Median home value: $64,977 (2010); Median contract rent: $262 per month (2000); Median year structure built: 1966 (2000).
Newspapers: NEWS (Community news; Circulation 3,200); The Orange Countian (Community news; Circulation 10,573); Republican (Community news; Circulation 3,200)
Transportation: Commute to work: 95.1% car, 0.0% public transportation, 2.7% walk, 2.2% work from home (2000); Travel time to work: 56.9% less than 15 minutes, 24.2% 15 to 30 minutes, 10.2% 30 to 45 minutes, 3.1% 45 to 60 minutes, 5.6% 60 minutes or more (2000)
Additional Information Contacts
Town of Paoli. . . . . (812) 723-3616
    http://indian.hometownlocator.com

WEST BADEN SPRINGS (town). Aka West Baden. Covers a land area of 1.069 square miles and a water area of 0 square miles. Located at 38.56° N. Lat; 86.61° W. Long. Elevation is 479 feet.
Population: 705 (1990); 618 (2000); 543 (2010); 510 (2015 projected); Race: 91.9% White, 4.2% Black, 1.1% Asian, 2.8% Other, 5.9% Hispanic of any race (2010); Density: 507.7 persons per square mile (2010); Average household size: 2.27 (2010); Median age: 40.4 (2010); Males per 100 females: 96.7 (2010); Marriage status: 22.6% never married, 59.6% now married, 6.2% widowed, 11.5% divorced (2000); Foreign born: 0.2% (2000); Ancestry (includes multiple ancestries): 30.7% United States or American, 10.1% English, 8.4% German, 6.7% Other groups, 3.4% Irish (2000).
Economy: Single-family building permits issued: 3 (2009); Multi-family building permits issued: 0 (2009); Employment by occupation: 5.0% management, 14.6% professional, 10.7% services, 15.4% sales, 0.0% farming, 13.6% construction, 40.7% production (2000).
Income: Per capita income: $17,674 (2010); Median household income: $35,987 (2010); Average household income: $40,209 (2010); Percent of households with income of $100,000 or more: 4.6% (2010); Poverty rate: 9.7% (2000).
Taxes: Total city taxes per capita: $322 (2007); City property taxes per capita: $243 (2007).
Education: Percent of population age 25 and over with: High school diploma (including GED) or higher: 76.4% (2010); Bachelor's degree or higher: 10.6% (2010); Master's degree or higher: 5.5% (2010).

Housing: Homeownership rate: 72.0% (2010); Median home value: $57,647 (2010); Median contract rent: $259 per month (2000); Median year structure built: 1968 (2000).
Transportation: Commute to work: 98.6% car, 0.0% public transportation, 0.0% walk, 0.7% work from home (2000); Travel time to work: 43.7% less than 15 minutes, 9.4% 15 to 30 minutes, 27.1% 30 to 45 minutes, 13.4% 45 to 60 minutes, 6.5% 60 minutes or more (2000)

Owen County

Located in southwest central Indiana; drained by the West Fork of the White River and Mill Creek. Covers a land area of 385.18 square miles, a water area of 2.65 square miles, and is located in the Eastern Time Zone. The county was founded in 1818. County seat is Spencer.

Owen County is part of the Bloomington, IN Metropolitan Statistical Area. The entire metro area includes: Greene County, IN; Monroe County, IN; Owen County, IN

Weather Station: Spencer — Elevation: 547 feet

	Jan	Feb	Mar	Apr	May	Jun	Jul	Aug	Sep	Oct	Nov	Dec
High	35	41	51	63	73	81	85	84	78	66	52	41
Low	16	19	29	38	48	58	62	60	52	39	31	22
Precip	2.5	2.5	3.8	4.5	5.0	4.6	4.7	4.5	3.2	3.1	4.0	3.3
Snow	5.8	5.0	2.3	0.3	0.0	0.0	0.0	0.0	0.0	tr	0.5	3.0

High and Low temperatures in degrees Fahrenheit; Precipitation and Snow in inches

Population: 17,281 (1990); 21,786 (2000); 22,394 (2010); 22,483 (2015 projected); Race: 97.5% White, 0.6% Black, 0.3% Asian, 1.7% Other, 1.1% Hispanic of any race (2010); Density: 58.1 persons per square mile (2010); Average household size: 2.55 (2010); Median age: 40.2 (2010); Males per 100 females: 98.1 (2010).
Religion: Five largest groups: 5.6% American Baptist Churches in the USA, 4.7% Christian Churches and Churches of Christ, 4.0% The United Methodist Church, 2.3% Independent, Non-Charismatic Churches, 2.2% Church of the Nazarene (2000).
Economy: Unemployment rate: 9.3% (5/2010); Total civilian labor force: 11,647 (5/2010); Leading industries: 47.0% manufacturing; 10.1% health care and social assistance; 9.4% retail trade (2008); Farms: 570 totaling 87,813 acres (2007); Companies that employ 500 or more persons: 2 (2008); Companies that employ 100 to 499 persons: 2 (2008); Companies that employ less than 100 persons: 309 (2008); Black-owned businesses: n/a (2002); Hispanic-owned businesses: n/a (2002); Asian-owned businesses: n/a (2002); Women-owned businesses: n/a (2002); Retail sales per capita: $5,693 (2010). Single-family building permits issued: 41 (2009); Multi-family building permits issued: 0 (2009).
Income: Per capita income: $20,807 (2010); Median household income: $43,784 (2010); Average household income: $53,483 (2010); Percent of households with income of $100,000 or more: 9.7% (2010); Poverty rate: 13.4% (2008); Bankruptcy rate: 6.42% (2009).
Taxes: Total county taxes per capita: $203 (2007); County property taxes per capita: $92 (2007).
Education: Percent of population age 25 and over with: High school diploma (including GED) or higher: 80.9% (2010); Bachelor's degree or higher: 7.4% (2010); Master's degree or higher: 3.6% (2010).
Housing: Homeownership rate: 82.0% (2010); Median home value: $96,546 (2010); Median contract rent: $444 per month (2006-2008 3-year est.); Median year structure built: 1978 (2006-2008 3-year est.)
Health: Birth rate: 104.9 per 10,000 population (2009); Death rate: 98.2 per 10,000 population (2009); Age-adjusted cancer mortality rate: 225.5 deaths per 100,000 population (2006); Number of physicians: 1.8 per 10,000 population (2007); Hospital beds: 0.0 per 10,000 population (2006); Hospital admissions: 0.0 per 10,000 population (2006).
Elections: 2008 Presidential election results: 43.7% Obama, 54.0% McCain, 0.1% Nader
National and State Parks: McCormicks Creek State Park
Additional Information Contacts
Owen County Government . . . . (812) 829-5015
  http://www.owencounty.in.gov

Owen County Communities

COAL CITY (unincorporated postal area, zip code 47427). Covers a land area of 54.586 square miles and a water area of 0.307 square miles. Located at 39.23° N. Lat; 87.03° W. Long. Elevation is 653 feet.
History: Old surface coal mines nearby. Laid out 1875.

Population: 1,091 (2000); Race: 99.0% White, 0.0% Black, 0.0% Asian, 1.0% Other, 0.0% Hispanic of any race (2000); Density: 20.0 persons per square mile (2000); Age: 26.8% under 18, 11.6% over 64 (2000); Marriage status: 14.3% never married, 72.0% now married, 6.7% widowed, 7.0% divorced (2000); Foreign born: 0.0% (2000); Ancestry (includes multiple ancestries): 21.0% German, 17.0% United States or American, 7.8% Irish, 7.0% Other groups, 5.0% English (2000).
Economy: Employment by occupation: 7.3% management, 10.4% professional, 14.4% services, 14.2% sales, 2.2% farming, 15.9% construction, 35.6% production (2000).
Income: Per capita income: $14,313 (2000); Median household income: $33,276 (2000); Poverty rate: 17.5% (2000).
Education: Percent of population age 25 and over with: High school diploma (including GED) or higher: 77.5% (2000); Bachelor's degree or higher: 7.2% (2000).
Housing: Homeownership rate: 92.9% (2000); Median home value: $59,500 (2000); Median contract rent: $305 per month (2000); Median year structure built: 1967 (2000).
Transportation: Commute to work: 87.3% car, 0.0% public transportation, 1.8% walk, 7.6% work from home (2000); Travel time to work: 11.6% less than 15 minutes, 24.6% 15 to 30 minutes, 27.4% 30 to 45 minutes, 22.8% 45 to 60 minutes, 13.6% 60 minutes or more (2000)

FREEDOM (unincorporated postal area, zip code 47431). Covers a land area of 36.485 square miles and a water area of 0.040 square miles. Located at 39.23° N. Lat; 86.88° W. Long. Elevation is 538 feet.
Population: 1,279 (2000); Race: 97.9% White, 1.0% Black, 0.2% Asian, 0.9% Other, 0.0% Hispanic of any race (2000); Density: 35.1 persons per square mile (2000); Age: 26.2% under 18, 14.1% over 64 (2000); Marriage status: 18.9% never married, 62.2% now married, 5.6% widowed, 13.4% divorced (2000); Foreign born: 0.2% (2000); Ancestry (includes multiple ancestries): 31.8% United States or American, 15.2% German, 7.4% English, 7.1% Other groups, 7.0% French (except Basque) (2000).
Economy: Employment by occupation: 5.6% management, 10.6% professional, 17.4% services, 12.9% sales, 0.0% farming, 19.6% construction, 34.0% production (2000).
Income: Per capita income: $13,807 (2000); Median household income: $29,743 (2000); Poverty rate: 9.5% (2000).
Education: Percent of population age 25 and over with: High school diploma (including GED) or higher: 71.0% (2000); Bachelor's degree or higher: 8.4% (2000).
Housing: Homeownership rate: 87.5% (2000); Median home value: $82,100 (2000); Median contract rent: $247 per month (2000); Median year structure built: 1976 (2000).
Transportation: Commute to work: 93.2% car, 0.0% public transportation, 2.6% walk, 3.0% work from home (2000); Travel time to work: 15.0% less than 15 minutes, 31.4% 15 to 30 minutes, 11.7% 30 to 45 minutes, 10.7% 45 to 60 minutes, 31.2% 60 minutes or more (2000)

GOSPORT (town). Covers a land area of 0.383 square miles and a water area of 0 square miles. Located at 39.35° N. Lat; 86.66° W. Long. Elevation is 696 feet.
History: Gosport was laid out in 1829 as a shipping point for trade on the White River.
Population: 767 (1990); 715 (2000); 692 (2010); 678 (2015 projected); Race: 98.6% White, 0.4% Black, 0.1% Asian, 0.9% Other, 2.3% Hispanic of any race (2010); Density: 1,808.5 persons per square mile (2010); Average household size: 2.50 (2010); Median age: 41.7 (2010); Males per 100 females: 97.2 (2010); Marriage status: 19.0% never married, 55.2% now married, 10.6% widowed, 15.1% divorced (2000); Foreign born: 0.3% (2000); Ancestry (includes multiple ancestries): 12.1% United States or American, 11.7% German, 7.8% Irish, 7.4% Other groups, 4.3% English (2000).
Economy: Employment by occupation: 4.8% management, 11.1% professional, 15.9% services, 19.2% sales, 0.0% farming, 9.6% construction, 39.5% production (2000).
Income: Per capita income: $18,851 (2010); Median household income: $38,233 (2010); Average household income: $48,512 (2010); Percent of households with income of $100,000 or more: 8.6% (2010); Poverty rate: 17.2% (2000).
Taxes: Total city taxes per capita: $68 (2007); City property taxes per capita: $42 (2007).
Education: Percent of population age 25 and over with: High school diploma (including GED) or higher: 79.3% (2010); Bachelor's degree or higher: 5.7% (2010); Master's degree or higher: 2.9% (2010).

Spencer-Owen Community Schools (PK-12)
2008-09 Enrollment: 2,976 . . . . (812) 829-2233
Housing: Homeownership rate: 70.4% (2010); Median home value: $88,611 (2010); Median contract rent: $346 per month (2000); Median year structure built: 1947 (2000).
Transportation: Commute to work: 91.5% car, 0.0% public transportation, 6.2% walk, 0.4% work from home (2000); Travel time to work: 17.1% less than 15 minutes, 34.1% 15 to 30 minutes, 25.2% 30 to 45 minutes, 8.5% 45 to 60 minutes, 15.1% 60 minutes or more (2000)

QUINCY (unincorporated postal area, zip code 47456). Covers a land area of 21.676 square miles and a water area of 0.124 square miles. Located at 39.44° N. Lat; 86.73° W. Long. Elevation is 738 feet.
Population: 799 (2000); Race: 99.1% White, 0.0% Black, 0.0% Asian, 0.9% Other, 0.0% Hispanic of any race (2000); Density: 36.9 persons per square mile (2000); Age: 36.3% under 18, 7.2% over 64 (2000); Marriage status: 8.9% never married, 74.5% now married, 5.5% widowed, 11.1% divorced (2000); Foreign born: 0.0% (2000); Ancestry (includes multiple ancestries): 15.3% Irish, 15.1% United States or American, 13.8% German, 7.7% Swedish, 5.2% English (2000).
Economy: Employment by occupation: 5.2% management, 14.0% professional, 16.5% services, 14.9% sales, 0.0% farming, 23.1% construction, 26.2% production (2000).
Income: Per capita income: $16,421 (2000); Median household income: $36,071 (2000); Poverty rate: 12.4% (2000).
Education: Percent of population age 25 and over with: High school diploma (including GED) or higher: 62.6% (2000); Bachelor's degree or higher: 5.0% (2000).
Housing: Homeownership rate: 91.7% (2000); Median home value: $76,200 (2000); Median contract rent: $266 per month (2000); Median year structure built: 1975 (2000).
Transportation: Commute to work: 92.4% car, 0.0% public transportation, 0.0% walk, 5.1% work from home (2000); Travel time to work: 1.5% less than 15 minutes, 34.0% 15 to 30 minutes, 12.1% 30 to 45 minutes, 29.9% 45 to 60 minutes, 22.5% 60 minutes or more (2000)

SPENCER (town). County seat. Covers a land area of 1.264 square miles and a water area of 0 square miles. Located at 39.28° N. Lat; 86.76° W. Long. Elevation is 561 feet.
History: Spencer was a farming, coal mining, and quarrying center named for Captain Spencer of Kentucky, who was killed at the Battle of Tippecanoe. Spencer was the hometown of poets William Herschell (1873-1939) and William Vaughn Moody (1869-1910).
Population: 2,621 (1990); 2,508 (2000); 2,508 (2010); 2,479 (2015 projected); Race: 97.4% White, 0.4% Black, 0.7% Asian, 1.4% Other, 1.0% Hispanic of any race (2010); Density: 1,984.6 persons per square mile (2010); Average household size: 2.35 (2010); Median age: 38.1 (2010); Males per 100 females: 86.6 (2010); Marriage status: 21.9% never married, 50.5% now married, 10.7% widowed, 17.0% divorced (2000); Foreign born: 0.1% (2000); Ancestry (includes multiple ancestries): 17.3% German, 16.6% United States or American, 14.6% Irish, 9.2% English, 8.1% Other groups (2000).
Economy: Single-family building permits issued: 0 (2009); Multi-family building permits issued: 0 (2009); Employment by occupation: 8.1% management, 12.9% professional, 11.0% services, 25.9% sales, 0.5% farming, 11.9% construction, 29.6% production (2000).
Income: Per capita income: $21,509 (2010); Median household income: $42,017 (2010); Average household income: $51,592 (2010); Percent of households with income of $100,000 or more: 9.8% (2010); Poverty rate: 9.5% (2000).
Taxes: Total city taxes per capita: $212 (2007); City property taxes per capita: $149 (2007).
Education: Percent of population age 25 and over with: High school diploma (including GED) or higher: 77.1% (2010); Bachelor's degree or higher: 8.0% (2010); Master's degree or higher: 4.6% (2010).

Spencer-Owen Community Schools (PK-12)
2008-09 Enrollment: 2,976 . . . . (812) 829-2233
Housing: Homeownership rate: 65.2% (2010); Median home value: $88,869 (2010); Median contract rent: $346 per month (2000); Median year structure built: 1959 (2000).
Newspapers: Owen Leader (Community news; Circulation 450); Spencer Evening World (Local news; Circulation 11,000)

Transportation: Commute to work: 92.4% car, 0.0% public transportation, 5.2% walk, 1.9% work from home (2000); Travel time to work: 42.1% less than 15 minutes, 14.6% 15 to 30 minutes, 21.0% 30 to 45 minutes, 6.5% 45 to 60 minutes, 15.8% 60 minutes or more (2000)

Parke County

Located in western Indiana; bounded on the west by the Wabash River; drained by Sugar and Raccoon Creeks. Covers a land area of 444.77 square miles, a water area of 5.32 square miles, and is located in the Eastern Time Zone. The county was founded in 1821. County seat is Rockville.

Weather Station: Rockville   Elevation: 688 feet

	Jan	Feb	Mar	Apr	May	Jun	Jul	Aug	Sep	Oct	Nov	Dec
High	36	42	53	66	76	84	87	85	79	68	53	41
Low	18	22	32	42	52	61	65	62	56	44	35	25
Precip	2.5	2.2	3.7	4.3	4.8	4.1	4.8	4.2	3.2	3.1	4.3	3.5
Snow	5.0	3.3	2.2	0.2	tr	0.0	0.0	0.0	0.0	0.0	0.4	5.2

High and Low temperatures in degrees Fahrenheit; Precipitation and Snow in inches

Population: 15,410 (1990); 17,241 (2000); 17,124 (2010); 16,949 (2015 projected); Race: 94.3% White, 3.8% Black, 0.2% Asian, 1.7% Other, 1.0% Hispanic of any race (2010); Density: 38.5 persons per square mile (2010); Average household size: 2.49 (2010); Median age: 40.3 (2010); Males per 100 females: 85.9 (2010).
Religion: Five largest groups: 11.7% Christian Churches and Churches of Christ, 4.9% The United Methodist Church, 2.9% Friends (Quakers), 2.7% Southern Baptist Convention, 2.4% Christian Church (Disciples of Christ) (2000).
Economy: Unemployment rate: 9.0% (5/2010); Total civilian labor force: 8,282 (5/2010); Leading industries: 24.0% manufacturing; 18.5% retail trade; 18.3% health care and social assistance (2008); Farms: 477 totaling 177,343 acres (2007); Companies that employ 500 or more persons: 0 (2008); Companies that employ 100 to 499 persons: 2 (2008); Companies that employ less than 100 persons: 269 (2008); Black-owned businesses: n/a (2002); Hispanic-owned businesses: n/a (2002); Asian-owned businesses: n/a (2002); Women-owned businesses: n/a (2002); Retail sales per capita: $4,321 (2010). Single-family building permits issued: 22 (2009); Multi-family building permits issued: 0 (2009).
Income: Per capita income: $20,229 (2010); Median household income: $42,486 (2010); Average household income: $53,094 (2010); Percent of households with income of $100,000 or more: 10.4% (2010); Poverty rate: 16.7% (2008); Bankruptcy rate: 6.84% (2009).
Taxes: Total county taxes per capita: $264 (2007); County property taxes per capita: $110 (2007).
Education: Percent of population age 25 and over with: High school diploma (including GED) or higher: 85.1% (2010); Bachelor's degree or higher: 12.2% (2010); Master's degree or higher: 4.6% (2010).
Housing: Homeownership rate: 79.2% (2010); Median home value: $83,294 (2010); Median contract rent: $n/a per month (2006-2008 3-year est.); Median year structure built: n/a (2006-2008 3-year est.)
Health: Birth rate: 114.8 per 10,000 population (2009); Death rate: 88.2 per 10,000 population (2009); Age-adjusted cancer mortality rate: 253.9 deaths per 100,000 population (2006); Number of physicians: 3.5 per 10,000 population (2007); Hospital beds: 0.0 per 10,000 population (2006); Hospital admissions: 0.0 per 10,000 population (2006).
Elections: 2008 Presidential election results: 42.0% Obama, 56.1% McCain, 0.0% Nader
National and State Parks: Raccoon Lake State Recreation Area; Turkey Run State Park
Additional Information Contacts
Parke County Government . . . . (765) 569-5132
http://www.parkecounty.net

Parke County Communities

BLOOMINGDALE (town). Covers a land area of 0.571 square miles and a water area of 0 square miles. Located at 39.83° N. Lat; 87.25° W. Long. Elevation is 643 feet.
Population: 341 (1990); 319 (2000); 303 (2010); 291 (2015 projected); Race: 98.7% White, 0.0% Black, 0.0% Asian, 1.3% Other, 0.7% Hispanic of any race (2010); Density: 530.7 persons per square mile (2010); Average household size: 2.73 (2010); Median age: 34.7 (2010); Males per 100 females: 103.4 (2010); Marriage status: 18.9% never married, 63.8% now married, 7.4% widowed, 9.9% divorced (2000); Foreign born: 0.7%

(2000); Ancestry (includes multiple ancestries): 25.3% German, 22.5% English, 14.7% Irish, 11.6% United States or American, 6.1% French (except Basque) (2000).
Economy: Employment by occupation: 5.7% management, 17.6% professional, 23.3% services, 24.5% sales, 0.0% farming, 8.8% construction, 20.1% production (2000).
Income: Per capita income: $21,248 (2010); Median household income: $46,500 (2010); Average household income: $59,234 (2010); Percent of households with income of $100,000 or more: 15.3% (2010); Poverty rate: 2.0% (2000).
Taxes: Total city taxes per capita: $99 (2007); City property taxes per capita: $61 (2007).
Education: Percent of population age 25 and over with: High school diploma (including GED) or higher: 90.2% (2010); Bachelor's degree or higher: 11.4% (2010); Master's degree or higher: 5.7% (2010).
Housing: Homeownership rate: 83.8% (2010); Median home value: $69,375 (2010); Median contract rent: $250 per month (2000); Median year structure built: before 1940 (2000).
Transportation: Commute to work: 84.6% car, 0.0% public transportation, 12.2% walk, 3.2% work from home (2000); Travel time to work: 46.4% less than 15 minutes, 22.5% 15 to 30 minutes, 9.9% 30 to 45 minutes, 13.2% 45 to 60 minutes, 7.9% 60 minutes or more (2000)

BRIDGETON (unincorporated postal area, zip code 47836). Covers a land area of 2.929 square miles and a water area of 0.006 square miles. Located at 39.64° N. Lat; 87.17° W. Long. Elevation is 564 feet.
History: Covered bridge here and many others in the surrounding area. Laid out 1857.
Population: 126 (2000); Race: 100.0% White, 0.0% Black, 0.0% Asian, 0.0% Other, 0.0% Hispanic of any race (2000); Density: 43.0 persons per square mile (2000); Age: 31.6% under 18, 4.4% over 64 (2000); Marriage status: 18.8% never married, 63.5% now married, 5.9% widowed, 11.8% divorced (2000); Foreign born: 4.4% (2000); Ancestry (includes multiple ancestries): 45.6% Irish, 17.5% French (except Basque), 17.5% Other groups, 11.4% German, 5.3% English (2000).
Economy: Employment by occupation: 18.0% management, 8.2% professional, 41.0% services, 6.6% sales, 8.2% farming, 9.8% construction, 8.2% production (2000).
Income: Per capita income: $11,926 (2000); Median household income: $16,000 (2000); Poverty rate: 45.6% (2000).
Education: Percent of population age 25 and over with: High school diploma (including GED) or higher: 93.2% (2000); Bachelor's degree or higher: 0.0% (2000).
Housing: Homeownership rate: 100.0% (2000); Median home value: $45,700 (2000); Median contract rent: $n/a per month (2000); Median year structure built: 1965 (2000).
Transportation: Commute to work: 100.0% car, 0.0% public transportation, 0.0% walk, 0.0% work from home (2000); Travel time to work: 18.0% less than 15 minutes, 70.5% 15 to 30 minutes, 0.0% 30 to 45 minutes, 11.5% 45 to 60 minutes, 0.0% 60 minutes or more (2000)

MARSHALL (town). Covers a land area of 0.246 square miles and a water area of 0 square miles. Located at 39.84° N. Lat; 87.18° W. Long. Elevation is 702 feet.
History: Covered bridges in area. Laid out 1878.
Population: 379 (1990); 360 (2000); 328 (2010); 315 (2015 projected); Race: 98.5% White, 0.3% Black, 0.0% Asian, 1.2% Other, 0.6% Hispanic of any race (2010); Density: 1,334.2 persons per square mile (2010); Average household size: 2.73 (2010); Median age: 35.0 (2010); Males per 100 females: 96.4 (2010); Marriage status: 24.9% never married, 55.9% now married, 4.6% widowed, 14.6% divorced (2000); Foreign born: 0.0% (2000); Ancestry (includes multiple ancestries): 25.6% United States or American, 12.0% English, 7.6% German, 5.7% Irish, 4.4% Other groups (2000).
Economy: Employment by occupation: 4.4% management, 6.6% professional, 18.1% services, 18.1% sales, 1.1% farming, 9.3% construction, 42.3% production (2000).
Income: Per capita income: $21,248 (2010); Median household income: $46,250 (2010); Average household income: $57,833 (2010); Percent of households with income of $100,000 or more: 13.3% (2010); Poverty rate: 16.7% (2000).
Taxes: Total city taxes per capita: $53 (2007); City property taxes per capita: $48 (2007).

Education: Percent of population age 25 and over with: High school diploma (including GED) or higher: 89.2% (2010); Bachelor's degree or higher: 10.4% (2010); Master's degree or higher: 5.2% (2010).
School District(s)
Turkey Run Community Sch Corp (PK-12)
    2008-09 Enrollment: 618 . . . . (765) 597-2750
Housing: Homeownership rate: 84.2% (2010); Median home value: $69,375 (2010); Median contract rent: $288 per month (2000); Median year structure built: 1949 (2000).
Transportation: Commute to work: 98.3% car, 0.0% public transportation, 1.7% walk, 0.0% work from home (2000); Travel time to work: 36.7% less than 15 minutes, 23.3% 15 to 30 minutes, 28.3% 30 to 45 minutes, 4.4% 45 to 60 minutes, 7.2% 60 minutes or more (2000)

MECCA (town). Covers a land area of 0.402 square miles and a water area of 0 square miles. Located at 39.72° N. Lat; 87.33° W. Long. Elevation is 512 feet.
History: Covered bridges in area. Laid out 1890.
Population: 331 (1990); 355 (2000); 365 (2010); 369 (2015 projected); Race: 97.5% White, 0.5% Black, 0.0% Asian, 1.9% Other, 0.8% Hispanic of any race (2010); Density: 909.0 persons per square mile (2010); Average household size: 2.54 (2010); Median age: 40.4 (2010); Males per 100 females: 92.1 (2010); Marriage status: 25.4% never married, 50.4% now married, 7.0% widowed, 17.2% divorced (2000); Foreign born: 1.5% (2000); Ancestry (includes multiple ancestries): 13.7% German, 13.7% Irish, 9.1% Other groups, 5.8% United States or American, 4.9% English (2000).
Economy: Employment by occupation: 4.2% management, 7.2% professional, 22.9% services, 18.1% sales, 1.2% farming, 6.0% construction, 40.4% production (2000).
Income: Per capita income: $18,033 (2010); Median household income: $42,200 (2010); Average household income: $46,972 (2010); Percent of households with income of $100,000 or more: 3.5% (2010); Poverty rate: 8.6% (2000).
Taxes: Total city taxes per capita: $132 (2007); City property taxes per capita: $124 (2007).
Education: Percent of population age 25 and over with: High school diploma (including GED) or higher: 86.8% (2010); Bachelor's degree or higher: 8.9% (2010); Master's degree or higher: 5.0% (2010).
Housing: Homeownership rate: 85.2% (2010); Median home value: $66,364 (2010); Median contract rent: $311 per month (2000); Median year structure built: 1960 (2000).
Transportation: Commute to work: 95.1% car, 0.0% public transportation, 3.1% walk, 1.9% work from home (2000); Travel time to work: 32.1% less than 15 minutes, 35.8% 15 to 30 minutes, 21.4% 30 to 45 minutes, 5.7% 45 to 60 minutes, 5.0% 60 minutes or more (2000)

MONTEZUMA (town). Covers a land area of 0.618 square miles and a water area of 0 square miles. Located at 39.79° N. Lat; 87.37° W. Long. Elevation is 509 feet.
History: When the Wabash & Erie Canal was completed in 1848, Montezuma became a commercial center on the Wabash River. Montezuma was settled by Samuel Hill in 1821, and named for the Aztec emperor of Mexico.
Population: 1,174 (1990); 1,179 (2000); 1,092 (2010); 1,044 (2015 projected); Race: 95.2% White, 2.7% Black, 0.2% Asian, 1.9% Other, 0.9% Hispanic of any race (2010); Density: 1,767.3 persons per square mile (2010); Average household size: 2.46 (2010); Median age: 37.5 (2010); Males per 100 females: 98.2 (2010); Marriage status: 21.4% never married, 54.2% now married, 8.8% widowed, 15.7% divorced (2000); Foreign born: 0.5% (2000); Ancestry (includes multiple ancestries): 22.7% United States or American, 17.9% German, 9.6% Irish, 5.5% Other groups, 5.2% English (2000).
Economy: Single-family building permits issued: 0 (2009); Multi-family building permits issued: 0 (2009); Employment by occupation: 6.6% management, 6.6% professional, 18.8% services, 25.1% sales, 2.4% farming, 16.2% construction, 24.2% production (2000).
Income: Per capita income: $17,080 (2010); Median household income: $35,268 (2010); Average household income: $41,633 (2010); Percent of households with income of $100,000 or more: 5.4% (2010); Poverty rate: 20.1% (2000).
Taxes: Total city taxes per capita: $72 (2007); City property taxes per capita: $61 (2007).

Education: Percent of population age 25 and over with: High school diploma (including GED) or higher: 87.0% (2010); Bachelor's degree or higher: 5.7% (2010); Master's degree or higher: 1.2% (2010).

School District(s)

Southwest Parke Com Sch Corp (KG-12)

   2008-09 Enrollment: 917 . . . . (765) 569-2073

Housing: Homeownership rate: 76.9% (2010); Median home value: $55,488 (2010); Median contract rent: $296 per month (2000); Median year structure built: 1952 (2000).

Transportation: Commute to work: 94.3% car, 0.0% public transportation, 1.2% walk, 1.0% work from home (2000); Travel time to work: 35.5% less than 15 minutes, 33.0% 15 to 30 minutes, 18.0% 30 to 45 minutes, 4.4% 45 to 60 minutes, 9.1% 60 minutes or more (2000)

ROCKVILLE (town). County seat. Covers a land area of 1.437 square miles and a water area of 0 square miles. Located at 39.76° N. Lat; 87.22° W. Long. Elevation is 712 feet.

History: Joseph A. Wright, a governor of Indiana, began his law practice in Rockville.

Population: 2,752 (1990); 2,765 (2000); 2,672 (2010); 2,620 (2015 projected); Race: 96.9% White, 0.9% Black, 0.3% Asian, 1.9% Other, 1.2% Hispanic of any race (2010); Density: 1,859.7 persons per square mile (2010); Average household size: 2.15 (2010); Median age: 42.1 (2010); Males per 100 females: 86.6 (2010); Marriage status: 20.3% never married, 52.7% now married, 14.5% widowed, 12.4% divorced (2000); Foreign born: 0.8% (2000); Ancestry (includes multiple ancestries): 20.1% German, 16.0% United States or American, 11.6% English, 9.3% Irish, 7.2% Other groups (2000).

Economy: Single-family building permits issued: 2 (2009); Multi-family building permits issued: 0 (2009); Employment by occupation: 7.3% management, 15.4% professional, 23.8% services, 25.7% sales, 0.6% farming, 8.3% construction, 19.0% production (2000).

Income: Per capita income: $22,306 (2010); Median household income: $35,858 (2010); Average household income: $49,987 (2010); Percent of households with income of $100,000 or more: 8.2% (2010); Poverty rate: 15.4% (2000).

Taxes: Total city taxes per capita: $168 (2007); City property taxes per capita: $161 (2007).

Education: Percent of population age 25 and over with: High school diploma (including GED) or higher: 85.9% (2010); Bachelor's degree or higher: 16.1% (2010); Master's degree or higher: 4.7% (2010).

School District(s)

Rockville Community School Corp (PK-12)

   2008-09 Enrollment: 908 . . . . (765) 569-5582

Housing: Homeownership rate: 64.1% (2010); Median home value: $80,769 (2010); Median contract rent: $263 per month (2000); Median year structure built: 1955 (2000).

Newspapers: Parke County Sentinel (Community news; Circulation 4,500)

Transportation: Commute to work: 89.5% car, 0.0% public transportation, 4.0% walk, 5.3% work from home (2000); Travel time to work: 54.8% less than 15 minutes, 15.8% 15 to 30 minutes, 18.1% 30 to 45 minutes, 5.8% 45 to 60 minutes, 5.6% 60 minutes or more (2000)

ROSEDALE (town). Covers a land area of 0.397 square miles and a water area of 0 square miles. Located at 39.62° N. Lat; 87.28° W. Long. Elevation is 535 feet.

History: Settled c.1819.

Population: 783 (1990); 750 (2000); 709 (2010); 685 (2015 projected); Race: 99.2% White, 0.6% Black, 0.0% Asian, 0.3% Other, 0.4% Hispanic of any race (2010); Density: 1,787.2 persons per square mile (2010); Average household size: 2.55 (2010); Median age: 35.7 (2010); Males per 100 females: 92.1 (2010); Marriage status: 21.7% never married, 59.0% now married, 9.2% widowed, 10.1% divorced (2000); Foreign born: 0.3% (2000); Ancestry (includes multiple ancestries): 21.6% United States or American, 15.3% English, 14.1% German, 8.8% Irish, 5.2% Other groups (2000).

Economy: Employment by occupation: 6.0% management, 13.9% professional, 12.9% services, 29.0% sales, 0.6% farming, 10.1% construction, 27.4% production (2000).

Income: Per capita income: $19,588 (2010); Median household income: $44,545 (2010); Average household income: $49,766 (2010); Percent of households with income of $100,000 or more: 6.1% (2010); Poverty rate: 14.0% (2000).

Taxes: Total city taxes per capita: $59 (2007); City property taxes per capita: $57 (2007).

Education: Percent of population age 25 and over with: High school diploma (including GED) or higher: 91.2% (2010); Bachelor's degree or higher: 9.8% (2010); Master's degree or higher: 4.3% (2010).

School District(s)

Southwest Parke Com Sch Corp (KG-12)

   2008-09 Enrollment: 917 . . . . (765) 569-2073

Housing: Homeownership rate: 82.7% (2010); Median home value: $71,481 (2010); Median contract rent: $217 per month (2000); Median year structure built: before 1940 (2000).

Transportation: Commute to work: 96.8% car, 0.0% public transportation, 2.3% walk, 0.0% work from home (2000); Travel time to work: 18.8% less than 15 minutes, 40.3% 15 to 30 minutes, 27.3% 30 to 45 minutes, 10.1% 45 to 60 minutes, 3.6% 60 minutes or more (2000)

Perry County

Located in southern Indiana; bounded on the south and partly on the east by the Ohio River and the Kentucky border; drained by the Anderson River. Covers a land area of 381.39 square miles, a water area of 4.95 square miles, and is located in the Central Time Zone. The county was founded in 1814. County seat is Tell City.

Weather Station: Tell City   Elevation: 396 feet

	Jan	Feb	Mar	Apr	May	Jun	Jul	Aug	Sep	Oct	Nov	Dec
High	40	45	55	67	76	84	88	87	81	69	56	45
Low	23	26	35	44	54	63	68	66	59	46	37	29
Precip	3.2	3.2	4.6	4.9	5.1	4.3	4.6	3.7	3.3	3.2	4.1	4.0
Snow	4.4	2.6	0.7	0.1	0.0	0.0	0.0	0.0	0.0	0.0	0.4	1.0

High and Low temperatures in degrees Fahrenheit; Precipitation and Snow in inches

Population: 19,107 (1990); 18,899 (2000); 18,949 (2010); 18,873 (2015 projected); Race: 96.2% White, 2.5% Black, 0.1% Asian, 1.2% Other, 1.2% Hispanic of any race (2010); Density: 49.7 persons per square mile (2010); Average household size: 2.33 (2010); Median age: 38.8 (2010); Males per 100 females: 116.6 (2010).

Religion: Five largest groups: 33.1% Catholic Church, 4.9% United Church of Christ, 3.8% American Baptist Churches in the USA, 3.3% The United Methodist Church, 2.1% Churches of Christ (2000).

Economy: Unemployment rate: 9.3% (5/2010); Total civilian labor force: 9,574 (5/2010); Leading industries: 36.5% manufacturing; 15.8% health care and social assistance; 15.5% retail trade (2008); Farms: 425 totaling 70,409 acres (2007); Companies that employ 500 or more persons: 1 (2008); Companies that employ 100 to 499 persons: 6 (2008); Companies that employ less than 100 persons: 376 (2008); Black-owned businesses: n/a (2002); Hispanic-owned businesses: n/a (2002); Asian-owned businesses: n/a (2002); Women-owned businesses: n/a (2002); Retail sales per capita: $11,429 (2010). Single-family building permits issued: 29 (2009); Multi-family building permits issued: 0 (2009).

Income: Per capita income: $21,218 (2010); Median household income: $44,058 (2010); Average household income: $52,449 (2010); Percent of households with income of $100,000 or more: 9.3% (2010); Poverty rate: 11.9% (2008); Bankruptcy rate: 7.42% (2009).

Taxes: Total county taxes per capita: $295 (2007); County property taxes per capita: $200 (2007).

Education: Percent of population age 25 and over with: High school diploma (including GED) or higher: 80.3% (2010); Bachelor's degree or higher: 10.3% (2010); Master's degree or higher: 4.6% (2010).

Housing: Homeownership rate: 78.2% (2010); Median home value: $90,680 (2010); Median contract rent: $n/a per month (2006-2008 3-year est.); Median year structure built: n/a (2006-2008 3-year est.)

Health: Birth rate: 124.9 per 10,000 population (2009); Death rate: 98.9 per 10,000 population (2009); Age-adjusted cancer mortality rate: 176.7 deaths per 100,000 population (2006); Air Quality Index: 83.9% good, 15.1% moderate, 1.0% unhealthy for sensitive individuals, 0.0% unhealthy (percent of days in 2008); Number of physicians: 6.3 per 10,000 population (2007); Hospital beds: 13.3 per 10,000 population (2006); Hospital admissions: 724.1 per 10,000 population (2006).

Elections: 2008 Presidential election results: 60.6% Obama, 37.7% McCain, 0.0% Nader

National and State Parks: Ferdinand State Forest; Harrison-Crawford State Forest

Additional Information Contacts

Perry County Government . . . . (812) 547-6427

   http://www.perrycountyin.org

City of Tell City . . . . (812) 547-2349

   http://www.tellcityindiana.com

Perry County Chamber of Commerce . . . . (812) 547-2385
   http://www.perrycountychamber.com

Perry County Communities

BRANCHVILLE (unincorporated postal area, zip code 47514).
Covers a land area of 6.299 square miles and a water area of 0 square miles. Located at 38.13° N. Lat; 86.58° W. Long. Elevation is 433 feet.
Population: 253 (2000); Race: 100.0% White, 0.0% Black, 0.0% Asian, 0.0% Other, 0.0% Hispanic of any race (2000); Density: 40.2 persons per square mile (2000); Age: 40.1% under 18, 7.4% over 64 (2000); Marriage status: 17.8% never married, 69.9% now married, 7.3% widowed, 5.0% divorced (2000); Foreign born: 0.0% (2000); Ancestry (includes multiple ancestries): 33.2% German, 21.4% United States or American, 19.6% English, 13.4% French (except Basque), 13.4% Irish (2000).
Economy: Employment by occupation: 16.4% management, 8.2% professional, 6.7% services, 13.4% sales, 0.0% farming, 13.4% construction, 41.8% production (2000).
Income: Per capita income: $15,241 (2000); Median household income: $52,250 (2000); Poverty rate: 6.2% (2000).
Education: Percent of population age 25 and over with: High school diploma (including GED) or higher: 69.7% (2000); Bachelor's degree or higher: 16.8% (2000).
Housing: Homeownership rate: 100.0% (2000); Median home value: $67,400 (2000); Median contract rent: $n/a per month (2000); Median year structure built: 1975 (2000).
Transportation: Commute to work: 82.8% car, 0.0% public transportation, 0.0% walk, 17.2% work from home (2000); Travel time to work: 18.0% less than 15 minutes, 22.5% 15 to 30 minutes, 27.0% 30 to 45 minutes, 20.7% 45 to 60 minutes, 11.7% 60 minutes or more (2000)

BRISTOW (unincorporated postal area, zip code 47515). Covers a land area of 61.816 square miles and a water area of 0.028 square miles. Located at 38.18° N. Lat; 86.71° W. Long. Elevation is 410 feet.
Population: 1,111 (2000); Race: 99.6% White, 0.0% Black, 0.0% Asian, 0.4% Other, 0.0% Hispanic of any race (2000); Density: 18.0 persons per square mile (2000); Age: 29.2% under 18, 12.7% over 64 (2000); Marriage status: 17.8% never married, 67.5% now married, 3.7% widowed, 11.0% divorced (2000); Foreign born: 0.0% (2000); Ancestry (includes multiple ancestries): 39.0% German, 15.5% United States or American, 6.6% English, 5.9% Irish, 2.1% French (except Basque) (2000).
Economy: Employment by occupation: 8.5% management, 7.1% professional, 11.1% services, 16.0% sales, 0.5% farming, 15.2% construction, 41.6% production (2000).
Income: Per capita income: $16,762 (2000); Median household income: $40,982 (2000); Poverty rate: 6.2% (2000).
Education: Percent of population age 25 and over with: High school diploma (including GED) or higher: 70.6% (2000); Bachelor's degree or higher: 4.1% (2000).
Housing: Homeownership rate: 87.9% (2000); Median home value: $71,000 (2000); Median contract rent: $200 per month (2000); Median year structure built: 1971 (2000).
Transportation: Commute to work: 92.5% car, 0.0% public transportation, 0.0% walk, 7.5% work from home (2000); Travel time to work: 8.5% less than 15 minutes, 41.9% 15 to 30 minutes, 23.4% 30 to 45 minutes, 14.1% 45 to 60 minutes, 12.2% 60 minutes or more (2000)

CANNELTON (city). Covers a land area of 1.482 square miles and a water area of 0.071 square miles. Located at 37.91° N. Lat; 86.74° W. Long. Elevation is 410 feet.
History: Cannelton was founded in 1837 as a coal-mining town and shipping port on the Ohio River.
Population: 1,786 (1990); 1,209 (2000); 1,076 (2010); 1,010 (2015 projected); Race: 98.0% White, 0.3% Black, 0.1% Asian, 1.7% Other, 1.1% Hispanic of any race (2010); Density: 726.2 persons per square mile (2010); Average household size: 2.31 (2010); Median age: 37.4 (2010); Males per 100 females: 106.9 (2010); Marriage status: 24.8% never married, 49.0% now married, 9.5% widowed, 16.7% divorced (2000); Foreign born: 0.2% (2000); Ancestry (includes multiple ancestries): 24.4% German, 14.6% United States or American, 14.1% English, 10.7% Irish, 8.3% Other groups (2000).
Economy: Single-family building permits issued: 1 (2009); Multi-family building permits issued: 0 (2009); Employment by occupation: 7.1% management, 6.4% professional, 18.3% services, 20.5% sales, 0.4% farming, 11.2% construction, 36.1% production (2000).

Income: Per capita income: $21,587 (2010); Median household income: $45,152 (2010); Average household income: $51,369 (2010); Percent of households with income of $100,000 or more: 6.4% (2010); Poverty rate: 16.0% (2000).
Taxes: Total city taxes per capita: $93 (2007); City property taxes per capita: $89 (2007).
Education: Percent of population age 25 and over with: High school diploma (including GED) or higher: 79.0% (2010); Bachelor's degree or higher: 5.7% (2010); Master's degree or higher: 3.3% (2010).
School District(s)
Cannelton City Schools (PK-12)
   2008-09 Enrollment: 294 . . . . (812) 547-2637
Housing: Homeownership rate: 72.8% (2010); Median home value: $78,644 (2010); Median contract rent: $284 per month (2000); Median year structure built: 1955 (2000).
Transportation: Commute to work: 92.6% car, 0.0% public transportation, 3.8% walk, 0.8% work from home (2000); Travel time to work: 48.5% less than 15 minutes, 25.2% 15 to 30 minutes, 13.6% 30 to 45 minutes, 8.1% 45 to 60 minutes, 4.7% 60 minutes or more (2000)

DERBY (unincorporated postal area, zip code 47525). Covers a land area of 34.266 square miles and a water area of 0.074 square miles. Located at 38.03° N. Lat; 86.55° W. Long. Elevation is 449 feet.
Population: 418 (2000); Race: 97.8% White, 0.0% Black, 0.0% Asian, 2.2% Other, 0.0% Hispanic of any race (2000); Density: 12.2 persons per square mile (2000); Age: 26.2% under 18, 6.5% over 64 (2000); Marriage status: 23.3% never married, 65.5% now married, 4.0% widowed, 7.2% divorced (2000); Foreign born: 0.0% (2000); Ancestry (includes multiple ancestries): 23.6% United States or American, 21.0% German, 14.3% Irish, 11.3% English, 8.0% Other groups (2000).
Economy: Employment by occupation: 2.2% management, 14.9% professional, 15.8% services, 18.4% sales, 5.7% farming, 9.6% construction, 33.3% production (2000).
Income: Per capita income: $14,597 (2000); Median household income: $38,333 (2000); Poverty rate: 3.4% (2000).
Education: Percent of population age 25 and over with: High school diploma (including GED) or higher: 86.6% (2000); Bachelor's degree or higher: 13.8% (2000).
Housing: Homeownership rate: 91.0% (2000); Median home value: $65,600 (2000); Median contract rent: $255 per month (2000); Median year structure built: 1980 (2000).
Transportation: Commute to work: 94.5% car, 0.0% public transportation, 1.8% walk, 3.7% work from home (2000); Travel time to work: 6.2% less than 15 minutes, 37.8% 15 to 30 minutes, 25.4% 30 to 45 minutes, 14.4% 45 to 60 minutes, 16.3% 60 minutes or more (2000)

LEOPOLD (unincorporated postal area, zip code 47551). Covers a land area of 44.776 square miles and a water area of 0.011 square miles. Located at 38.12° N. Lat; 86.55° W. Long. Elevation is 725 feet.
Population: 568 (2000); Race: 97.3% White, 0.0% Black, 0.0% Asian, 2.7% Other, 0.0% Hispanic of any race (2000); Density: 12.7 persons per square mile (2000); Age: 19.6% under 18, 9.2% over 64 (2000); Marriage status: 25.3% never married, 61.4% now married, 2.7% widowed, 10.6% divorced (2000); Foreign born: 0.0% (2000); Ancestry (includes multiple ancestries): 28.5% German, 17.2% French (except Basque), 15.3% United States or American, 11.5% Irish, 6.8% English (2000).
Economy: Employment by occupation: 8.9% management, 19.0% professional, 15.2% services, 14.6% sales, 0.0% farming, 8.2% construction, 34.2% production (2000).
Income: Per capita income: $17,196 (2000); Median household income: $37,500 (2000); Poverty rate: 8.3% (2000).
Education: Percent of population age 25 and over with: High school diploma (including GED) or higher: 84.1% (2000); Bachelor's degree or higher: 11.1% (2000).
School District(s)
Perry Central Com Schools Corp (PK-12)
   2008-09 Enrollment: 1,163 . . . . (812) 843-5576
Housing: Homeownership rate: 92.5% (2000); Median home value: $76,400 (2000); Median contract rent: $375 per month (2000); Median year structure built: 1976 (2000).
Transportation: Commute to work: 93.7% car, 1.3% public transportation, 1.3% walk, 3.8% work from home (2000); Travel time to work: 15.5% less than 15 minutes, 27.3% 15 to 30 minutes, 19.4% 30 to 45 minutes, 16.8% 45 to 60 minutes, 21.1% 60 minutes or more (2000)

ROME (unincorporated postal area, zip code 47574). Covers a land area of 12.940 square miles and a water area of 0 square miles. Located at 37.93° N. Lat; 86.56° W. Long. Elevation is 410 feet.
Population: 167 (2000); Race: 100.0% White, 0.0% Black, 0.0% Asian, 0.0% Other, 0.0% Hispanic of any race (2000); Density: 12.9 persons per square mile (2000); Age: 16.7% under 18, 17.6% over 64 (2000); Marriage status: 14.1% never married, 76.8% now married, 4.0% widowed, 5.1% divorced (2000); Foreign born: 2.8% (2000); Ancestry (includes multiple ancestries): 38.0% German, 10.2% Other groups, 8.3% Italian, 6.5% French (except Basque), 6.5% Scottish (2000).
Economy: Employment by occupation: 11.8% management, 0.0% professional, 11.8% services, 29.4% sales, 0.0% farming, 0.0% construction, 47.1% production (2000).
Income: Per capita income: $13,219 (2000); Median household income: $27,188 (2000); Poverty rate: 14.8% (2000).
Education: Percent of population age 25 and over with: High school diploma (including GED) or higher: 70.0% (2000); Bachelor's degree or higher: 0.0% (2000).
Housing: Homeownership rate: 90.4% (2000); Median home value: $20,700 (2000); Median contract rent: $n/a per month (2000); Median year structure built: 1976 (2000).
Transportation: Commute to work: 82.4% car, 0.0% public transportation, 0.0% walk, 17.6% work from home (2000); Travel time to work: 25.0% less than 15 minutes, 41.1% 15 to 30 minutes, 17.9% 30 to 45 minutes, 16.1% 45 to 60 minutes, 0.0% 60 minutes or more (2000)

SAINT CROIX (unincorporated postal area, zip code 47576). Covers a land area of 29.809 square miles and a water area of 0.671 square miles. Located at 38.19° N. Lat; 86.60° W. Long. Elevation is 725 feet.
Population: 462 (2000); Race: 100.0% White, 0.0% Black, 0.0% Asian, 0.0% Other, 0.0% Hispanic of any race (2000); Density: 15.5 persons per square mile (2000); Age: 18.1% under 18, 17.5% over 64 (2000); Marriage status: 19.2% never married, 70.6% now married, 6.2% widowed, 4.0% divorced (2000); Foreign born: 0.0% (2000); Ancestry (includes multiple ancestries): 35.8% German, 14.0% Irish, 13.5% United States or American, 8.1% French (except Basque), 7.8% English (2000).
Economy: Employment by occupation: 7.0% management, 17.1% professional, 17.1% services, 26.7% sales, 2.1% farming, 8.0% construction, 21.9% production (2000).
Income: Per capita income: $16,913 (2000); Median household income: $38,250 (2000); Poverty rate: 7.8% (2000).
Education: Percent of population age 25 and over with: High school diploma (including GED) or higher: 78.9% (2000); Bachelor's degree or higher: 15.0% (2000).
Housing: Homeownership rate: 87.0% (2000); Median home value: $77,500 (2000); Median contract rent: $304 per month (2000); Median year structure built: 1973 (2000).
Transportation: Commute to work: 94.7% car, 0.0% public transportation, 0.0% walk, 3.2% work from home (2000); Travel time to work: 9.4% less than 15 minutes, 26.5% 15 to 30 minutes, 39.8% 30 to 45 minutes, 18.2% 45 to 60 minutes, 6.1% 60 minutes or more (2000)

TELL CITY (city). County seat. Covers a land area of 4.557 square miles and a water area of 0.051 square miles. Located at 37.95° N. Lat; 86.76° W. Long. Elevation is 420 feet.
History: Tell City was settled in 1857 by a group of Swiss immigrants, and named for the legendary Swiss hero William Tell. An early industry was furniture making.
Population: 8,167 (1990); 7,845 (2000); 7,530 (2010); 7,320 (2015 projected); Race: 97.9% White, 0.6% Black, 0.3% Asian, 1.2% Other, 1.6% Hispanic of any race (2010); Density: 1,652.3 persons per square mile (2010); Average household size: 2.16 (2010); Median age: 42.0 (2010); Males per 100 females: 94.7 (2010); Marriage status: 19.9% never married, 56.5% now married, 9.8% widowed, 13.7% divorced (2000); Foreign born: 0.2% (2000); Ancestry (includes multiple ancestries): 27.0% German, 11.9% United States or American, 11.8% Irish, 8.5% English, 5.7% French (except Basque) (2000).
Economy: Single-family building permits issued: 4 (2009); Multi-family building permits issued: 0 (2009); Employment by occupation: 6.1% management, 13.2% professional, 16.5% services, 23.6% sales, 0.0% farming, 10.7% construction, 30.0% production (2000).
Income: Per capita income: $22,565 (2010); Median household income: $38,228 (2010); Average household income: $48,866 (2010); Percent of

households with income of $100,000 or more: 9.0% (2010); Poverty rate: 11.2% (2000).
Taxes: Total city taxes per capita: $258 (2007); City property taxes per capita: $169 (2007).
Education: Percent of population age 25 and over with: High school diploma (including GED) or higher: 78.6% (2010); Bachelor's degree or higher: 12.3% (2010); Master's degree or higher: 5.8% (2010).
School District(s)
Tell City-Troy Twp School Corp (PK-12)
    2008-09 Enrollment: 1,568 . . . . (812) 547-3300
Housing: Homeownership rate: 69.6% (2010); Median home value: $87,719 (2010); Median contract rent: $301 per month (2000); Median year structure built: 1961 (2000).
Hospitals: Perry County Memorial Hospital
Safety: Violent crime rate: 8.0 per 10,000 population; Property crime rate: 252.7 per 10,000 population (2008).
Newspapers: Perry County News (Local news; Circulation 8,000)
Transportation: Commute to work: 94.7% car, 0.4% public transportation, 1.6% walk, 1.4% work from home (2000); Travel time to work: 56.3% less than 15 minutes, 18.2% 15 to 30 minutes, 12.3% 30 to 45 minutes, 7.6% 45 to 60 minutes, 5.6% 60 minutes or more (2000)
Additional Information Contacts
City of Tell City. . . . . (812) 547-2349
    http://www.tellcityindiana.com
Perry County Chamber of Commerce . . . . (812) 547-2385
    http://www.perrycountychamber.com

TROY (town). Covers a land area of 0.314 square miles and a water area of 0 square miles. Located at 37.99° N. Lat; 86.79° W. Long. Elevation is 472 feet.
History: Troy was founded by families from Virginia. It served as the seat of Perry County until 1818.
Population: 522 (1990); 392 (2000); 373 (2010); 365 (2015 projected); Race: 99.7% White, 0.0% Black, 0.0% Asian, 0.3% Other, 0.8% Hispanic of any race (2010); Density: 1,187.9 persons per square mile (2010); Average household size: 2.41 (2010); Median age: 39.8 (2010); Males per 100 females: 106.1 (2010); Marriage status: 26.7% never married, 49.1% now married, 8.8% widowed, 15.4% divorced (2000); Foreign born: 0.0% (2000); Ancestry (includes multiple ancestries): 30.2% German, 21.9% Irish, 12.8% United States or American, 12.1% French (except Basque), 11.6% Other groups (2000).
Economy: Single-family building permits issued: 0 (2009); Multi-family building permits issued: 0 (2009); Employment by occupation: 5.2% management, 5.2% professional, 14.5% services, 16.8% sales, 0.0% farming, 16.8% construction, 41.6% production (2000).
Income: Per capita income: $21,315 (2010); Median household income: $44,000 (2010); Average household income: $51,201 (2010); Percent of households with income of $100,000 or more: 9.1% (2010); Poverty rate: 19.6% (2000).
Taxes: Total city taxes per capita: $83 (2007); City property taxes per capita: $52 (2007).
Education: Percent of population age 25 and over with: High school diploma (including GED) or higher: 81.1% (2010); Bachelor's degree or higher: 10.2% (2010); Master's degree or higher: 4.2% (2010).
Housing: Homeownership rate: 84.4% (2010); Median home value: $78,462 (2010); Median contract rent: $260 per month (2000); Median year structure built: 1961 (2000).
Transportation: Commute to work: 97.0% car, 0.0% public transportation, 2.4% walk, 0.0% work from home (2000); Travel time to work: 43.2% less than 15 minutes, 14.8% 15 to 30 minutes, 18.3% 30 to 45 minutes, 16.0% 45 to 60 minutes, 7.7% 60 minutes or more (2000)

Pike County

Located in southwestern Indiana; bounded on the north by the White River; drained by the Patoka River. Covers a land area of 336.18 square miles, a water area of 4.91 square miles, and is located in the Eastern Time Zone. The county was founded in 1816. County seat is Petersburg.

Pike County is part of the Jasper, IN Micropolitan Statistical Area. The entire metro area includes: Dubois County, IN; Pike County, IN

Population: 12,509 (1990); 12,837 (2000); 12,525 (2010); 12,306 (2015 projected); Race: 98.4% White, 0.6% Black, 0.2% Asian, 0.9% Other, 0.9% Hispanic of any race (2010); Density: 37.3 persons per square mile (2010);

Average household size: 2.45 (2010); Median age: 41.0 (2010); Males per 100 females: 100.8 (2010).

Religion: Five largest groups: 8.8% The United Methodist Church, 2.5% Catholic Church, 2.5% American Baptist Churches in the USA, 2.2% Christian Churches and Churches of Christ, 2.1% Church of the Nazarene (2000).

Economy: Unemployment rate: 8.3% (5/2010); Total civilian labor force: 5,912 (5/2010); Leading industries: 13.5% health care and social assistance; 10.9% retail trade; 7.4% accommodation & food services (2008); Farms: 334 totaling 73,612 acres (2007); Companies that employ 500 or more persons: 0 (2008); Companies that employ 100 to 499 persons: 4 (2008); Companies that employ less than 100 persons: 185 (2008); Black-owned businesses: n/a (2002); Hispanic-owned businesses: n/a (2002); Asian-owned businesses: n/a (2002); Women-owned businesses: n/a (2002); Retail sales per capita: $4,818 (2010). Single-family building permits issued: 21 (2009); Multi-family building permits issued: 0 (2009).

Income: Per capita income: $20,864 (2010); Median household income: $43,692 (2010); Average household income: $51,566 (2010); Percent of households with income of $100,000 or more: 8.9% (2010); Poverty rate: 10.9% (2008); Bankruptcy rate: 6.81% (2009).

Taxes: Total county taxes per capita: $190 (2007); County property taxes per capita: $182 (2007).

Education: Percent of population age 25 and over with: High school diploma (including GED) or higher: 81.1% (2010); Bachelor's degree or higher: 9.0% (2010); Master's degree or higher: 3.9% (2010).

Housing: Homeownership rate: 81.5% (2010); Median home value: $71,148 (2010); Median contract rent: $n/a per month (2006-2008 3-year est.); Median year structure built: n/a (2006-2008 3-year est.)

Health: Birth rate: 121.5 per 10,000 population (2009); Death rate: 124.0 per 10,000 population (2009); Age-adjusted cancer mortality rate: 180.2 deaths per 100,000 population (2006); Air Quality Index: 100.0% good, 0.0% moderate, 0.0% unhealthy for sensitive individuals, 0.0% unhealthy (percent of days in 2008); Number of physicians: 1.6 per 10,000 population (2007); Hospital beds: 0.0 per 10,000 population (2006); Hospital admissions: 0.0 per 10,000 population (2006).

Elections: 2008 Presidential election results: 44.8% Obama, 53.4% McCain, 0.0% Nader

National and State Parks: Patoka State Fish and Wildlife Area; Pike State Forest

Additional Information Contacts
Pike County Government. . . . . (812) 354-8448
    http://www.in.gov/mylocal/pike_county.htm

Pike County Communities

OTWELL (unincorporated postal area, zip code 47564). Covers a land area of 38.002 square miles and a water area of 0.228 square miles. Located at 38.47° N. Lat; 87.09° W. Long. Elevation is 499 feet.

History: Old surface mines.

Population: 1,418 (2000); Race: 98.7% White, 0.0% Black, 0.4% Asian, 0.9% Other, 0.0% Hispanic of any race (2000); Density: 37.3 persons per square mile (2000); Age: 29.9% under 18, 15.1% over 64 (2000); Marriage status: 16.9% never married, 68.7% now married, 8.3% widowed, 6.1% divorced (2000); Foreign born: 0.9% (2000); Ancestry (includes multiple ancestries): 23.8% German, 22.3% United States or American, 11.2% English, 10.1% Irish, 6.4% French (except Basque) (2000).

Economy: Employment by occupation: 9.3% management, 15.2% professional, 8.5% services, 17.6% sales, 0.8% farming, 13.0% construction, 35.6% production (2000).

Income: Per capita income: $17,579 (2000); Median household income: $36,974 (2000); Poverty rate: 5.7% (2000).

Education: Percent of population age 25 and over with: High school diploma (including GED) or higher: 77.2% (2000); Bachelor's degree or higher: 11.8% (2000).

School District(s)
Pike County School Corp (PK-12)
    2008-09 Enrollment: 2,045 . . . . (812) 354-8731

Housing: Homeownership rate: 84.8% (2000); Median home value: $65,300 (2000); Median contract rent: $200 per month (2000); Median year structure built: 1976 (2000).

Transportation: Commute to work: 94.2% car, 0.0% public transportation, 0.6% walk, 4.2% work from home (2000); Travel time to work: 26.9% less than 15 minutes, 53.2% 15 to 30 minutes, 14.6% 30 to 45 minutes, 1.4% 45 to 60 minutes, 3.9% 60 minutes or more (2000)

PETERSBURG (city). Aka Hosmer. County seat. Covers a land area of 1.464 square miles and a water area of 0 square miles. Located at 38.49° N. Lat; 87.28° W. Long. Elevation is 482 feet.

History: Laid out 1817, incorporated 1924.

Population: 2,449 (1990); 2,570 (2000); 2,371 (2010); 2,269 (2015 projected); Race: 97.8% White, 1.2% Black, 0.0% Asian, 0.9% Other, 0.5% Hispanic of any race (2010); Density: 1,619.4 persons per square mile (2010); Average household size: 2.30 (2010); Median age: 43.7 (2010); Males per 100 females: 97.3 (2010); Marriage status: 20.4% never married, 55.3% now married, 12.0% widowed, 12.3% divorced (2000); Foreign born: 0.6% (2000); Ancestry (includes multiple ancestries): 16.3% United States or American, 14.4% German, 9.8% Irish, 9.8% English, 3.8% Other groups (2000).

Economy: Employment by occupation: 6.8% management, 15.2% professional, 18.2% services, 16.8% sales, 1.9% farming, 8.0% construction, 33.1% production (2000).

Income: Per capita income: $19,131 (2010); Median household income: $37,063 (2010); Average household income: $45,662 (2010); Percent of households with income of $100,000 or more: 6.6% (2010); Poverty rate: 11.6% (2000).

Taxes: Total city taxes per capita: $74 (2007); City property taxes per capita: $73 (2007).

Education: Percent of population age 25 and over with: High school diploma (including GED) or higher: 74.9% (2010); Bachelor's degree or higher: 8.0% (2010); Master's degree or higher: 3.6% (2010).

School District(s)
Pike County School Corp (PK-12)
    2008-09 Enrollment: 2,045 . . . . (812) 354-8731

Housing: Homeownership rate: 70.3% (2010); Median home value: $61,667 (2010); Median contract rent: $246 per month (2000); Median year structure built: 1962 (2000).

Newspapers: Press-Dispatch (Community news; Circulation 5,475)

Transportation: Commute to work: 94.1% car, 0.0% public transportation, 2.9% walk, 2.1% work from home (2000); Travel time to work: 46.2% less than 15 minutes, 21.6% 15 to 30 minutes, 17.8% 30 to 45 minutes, 8.9% 45 to 60 minutes, 5.5% 60 minutes or more (2000)

SPURGEON (town). Covers a land area of 0.175 square miles and a water area of 0 square miles. Located at 38.25° N. Lat; 87.25° W. Long. Elevation is 502 feet.

History: Laid out 1860.

Population: 149 (1990); 227 (2000); 242 (2010); 246 (2015 projected); Race: 97.5% White, 0.8% Black, 0.0% Asian, 1.7% Other, 0.8% Hispanic of any race (2010); Density: 1,385.0 persons per square mile (2010); Average household size: 2.44 (2010); Median age: 39.2 (2010); Males per 100 females: 98.4 (2010); Marriage status: 17.1% never married, 68.6% now married, 10.9% widowed, 3.4% divorced (2000); Foreign born: 3.2% (2000); Ancestry (includes multiple ancestries): 22.5% German, 12.6% United States or American, 11.7% Irish, 8.1% Other groups, 6.3% English (2000).

Economy: Employment by occupation: 2.1% management, 15.6% professional, 15.6% services, 30.2% sales, 2.1% farming, 2.1% construction, 32.3% production (2000).

Income: Per capita income: $24,459 (2010); Median household income: $54,924 (2010); Average household income: $60,152 (2010); Percent of households with income of $100,000 or more: 14.1% (2010); Poverty rate: 4.1% (2000).

Taxes: Total city taxes per capita: $50 (2007); City property taxes per capita: $46 (2007).

Education: Percent of population age 25 and over with: High school diploma (including GED) or higher: 79.4% (2010); Bachelor's degree or higher: 8.5% (2010); Master's degree or higher: 1.8% (2010).

Housing: Homeownership rate: 86.9% (2010); Median home value: $87,273 (2010); Median contract rent: $225 per month (2000); Median year structure built: before 1940 (2000).

Transportation: Commute to work: 92.6% car, 0.0% public transportation, 0.0% walk, 7.4% work from home (2000); Travel time to work: 3.4% less than 15 minutes, 20.7% 15 to 30 minutes, 52.9% 30 to 45 minutes, 23.0% 45 to 60 minutes, 0.0% 60 minutes or more (2000)

STENDAL (unincorporated postal area, zip code 47585). Covers a land area of 37.225 square miles and a water area of 0.415 square miles. Located at 38.26° N. Lat; 87.14° W. Long. Elevation is 610 feet.

Population: 473 (2000); Race: 90.1% White, 0.0% Black, 9.9% Asian, 0.0% Other, 0.0% Hispanic of any race (2000); Density: 12.7 persons per square mile (2000); Age: 17.5% under 18, 17.0% over 64 (2000); Marriage status: 28.4% never married, 63.2% now married, 6.4% widowed, 1.9% divorced (2000); Foreign born: 2.8% (2000); Ancestry (includes multiple ancestries): 30.3% German, 17.5% United States or American, 12.6% Other groups, 9.0% English, 6.9% Norwegian (2000).
Economy: Employment by occupation: 13.0% management, 6.0% professional, 13.9% services, 17.1% sales, 3.2% farming, 15.7% construction, 31.0% production (2000).
Income: Per capita income: $17,624 (2000); Median household income: $48,594 (2000); Poverty rate: 3.7% (2000).
Education: Percent of population age 25 and over with: High school diploma (including GED) or higher: 64.4% (2000); Bachelor's degree or higher: 10.3% (2000).
Housing: Homeownership rate: 100.0% (2000); Median home value: $71,300 (2000); Median contract rent: $n/a per month (2000); Median year structure built: 1977 (2000).
Transportation: Commute to work: 94.4% car, 0.0% public transportation, 0.0% walk, 5.6% work from home (2000); Travel time to work: 10.8% less than 15 minutes, 43.1% 15 to 30 minutes, 27.9% 30 to 45 minutes, 8.8% 45 to 60 minutes, 9.3% 60 minutes or more (2000)

VELPEN (unincorporated postal area, zip code 47590). Covers a land area of 40.595 square miles and a water area of 0.183 square miles. Located at 38.35° N. Lat; 87.10° W. Long. Elevation is 492 feet.
Population: 747 (2000); Race: 100.0% White, 0.0% Black, 0.0% Asian, 0.0% Other, 0.0% Hispanic of any race (2000); Density: 18.4 persons per square mile (2000); Age: 29.1% under 18, 8.0% over 64 (2000); Marriage status: 24.0% never married, 63.0% now married, 3.5% widowed, 9.5% divorced (2000); Foreign born: 0.8% (2000); Ancestry (includes multiple ancestries): 26.8% German, 26.4% United States or American, 13.1% Other groups, 4.9% English, 4.4% French (except Basque) (2000).
Economy: Employment by occupation: 4.2% management, 8.3% professional, 6.1% services, 27.2% sales, 3.3% farming, 17.5% construction, 33.3% production (2000).
Income: Per capita income: $17,467 (2000); Median household income: $35,813 (2000); Poverty rate: 3.5% (2000).
Education: Percent of population age 25 and over with: High school diploma (including GED) or higher: 78.1% (2000); Bachelor's degree or higher: 3.6% (2000).
Housing: Homeownership rate: 80.4% (2000); Median home value: $65,000 (2000); Median contract rent: $211 per month (2000); Median year structure built: 1978 (2000).
Transportation: Commute to work: 96.4% car, 1.7% public transportation, 1.9% walk, 0.0% work from home (2000); Travel time to work: 12.2% less than 15 minutes, 53.3% 15 to 30 minutes, 15.3% 30 to 45 minutes, 3.9% 45 to 60 minutes, 15.3% 60 minutes or more (2000)

WINSLOW (town). Covers a land area of 0.644 square miles and a water area of 0 square miles. Located at 38.38° N. Lat; 87.21° W. Long. Elevation is 443 feet.
History: Winslow developed as a coal-mining town
Population: 875 (1990); 881 (2000); 741 (2010); 683 (2015 projected); Race: 97.6% White, 0.0% Black, 0.8% Asian, 1.6% Other, 3.0% Hispanic of any race (2010); Density: 1,149.9 persons per square mile (2010); Average household size: 2.37 (2010); Median age: 38.7 (2010); Males per 100 females: 99.7 (2010); Marriage status: 20.8% never married, 53.1% now married, 9.6% widowed, 16.5% divorced (2000); Foreign born: 0.1% (2000); Ancestry (includes multiple ancestries): 18.0% United States or American, 14.9% German, 14.2% Irish, 13.4% Other groups, 12.3% English (2000).
Economy: Employment by occupation: 6.7% management, 10.6% professional, 22.7% services, 15.5% sales, 0.8% farming, 10.3% construction, 33.3% production (2000).
Income: Per capita income: $19,132 (2010); Median household income: $37,318 (2010); Average household income: $45,184 (2010); Percent of households with income of $100,000 or more: 7.7% (2010); Poverty rate: 13.5% (2000).
Taxes: Total city taxes per capita: $161 (2007); City property taxes per capita: $135 (2007).
Education: Percent of population age 25 and over with: High school diploma (including GED) or higher: 81.1% (2010); Bachelor's degree or higher: 8.0% (2010); Master's degree or higher: 2.9% (2010).

School District(s)
Pike County School Corp (PK-12)
    2008-09 Enrollment: 2,045 . . . . (812) 354-8731
Housing: Homeownership rate: 74.4% (2010); Median home value: $58,649 (2010); Median contract rent: $213 per month (2000); Median year structure built: 1942 (2000).
Transportation: Commute to work: 93.1% car, 0.5% public transportation, 4.0% walk, 1.3% work from home (2000); Travel time to work: 20.6% less than 15 minutes, 29.7% 15 to 30 minutes, 27.3% 30 to 45 minutes, 15.5% 45 to 60 minutes, 7.0% 60 minutes or more (2000)

Porter County

Located in northwestern Indiana; bounded on the north by Lake Michigan, and on the south by the Kankakee River; drained by the Little Calumet and Grand Calumet Rivers. Covers a land area of 418.11 square miles, a water area of 103.50 square miles, and is located in the Central Time Zone. The county was founded in 1835. County seat is Valparaiso.

Porter County is part of the Chicago-Naperville-Joliet, IL-IN-WI Metropolitan Statistical Area. The entire metro area includes: Chicago-Naperville-Joliet, IL Metropolitan Division (Cook County, IL; DeKalb County, IL; DuPage County, IL; Grundy County, IL; Kane County, IL; Kendall County, IL; McHenry County, IL; Will County, IL); Gary, IN Metropolitan Division (Jasper County, IN; Lake County, IN; Newton County, IN; Porter County, IN); Lake County-Kenosha County, IL-WI Metropolitan Division (Lake County, IL; Kenosha County, WI)

Weather Station: Valparaiso Waterworks — Elevation: 797 feet

	Jan	Feb	Mar	Apr	May	Jun	Jul	Aug	Sep	Oct	Nov	Dec
High	30	36	47	60	71	80	83	81	75	63	49	36
Low	15	19	29	38	49	58	63	61	54	43	33	22
Precip	2.1	1.8	3.0	3.7	3.9	4.5	3.9	3.9	3.8	3.2	3.6	2.8
Snow	11.8	9.2	5.7	1.1	tr	0.0	0.0	0.0	0.0	0.2	3.2	8.6

High and Low temperatures in degrees Fahrenheit; Precipitation and Snow in inches

Weather Station: Wanatah 2 WNW — Elevation: 734 feet

	Jan	Feb	Mar	Apr	May	Jun	Jul	Aug	Sep	Oct	Nov	Dec
High	30	35	46	58	70	80	83	81	75	63	48	36
Low	13	18	27	37	48	58	61	59	51	40	31	20
Precip	1.6	1.6	2.8	3.6	3.7	4.3	4.2	3.7	3.8	2.9	3.4	2.5
Snow	13.5	10.9	6.4	1.2	tr	0.0	0.0	0.0	0.0	0.3	3.3	8.9

High and Low temperatures in degrees Fahrenheit; Precipitation and Snow in inches

Population: 128,932 (1990); 146,798 (2000); 165,040 (2010); 172,946 (2015 projected); Race: 91.7% White, 3.3% Black, 1.1% Asian, 4.0% Other, 7.2% Hispanic of any race (2010); Density: 394.7 persons per square mile (2010); Average household size: 2.54 (2010); Median age: 37.5 (2010); Males per 100 females: 97.4 (2010).
Religion: Five largest groups: 20.8% Catholic Church, 3.4% Lutheran Church—Missouri Synod, 2.6% The United Methodist Church, 2.3% Evangelical Lutheran Church in America, 1.7% Church of the Nazarene (2000).
Economy: Unemployment rate: 8.6% (5/2010); Total civilian labor force: 80,771 (5/2010); Leading industries: 17.8% manufacturing; 14.7% retail trade; 13.5% health care and social assistance (2008); Farms: 517 totaling 115,047 acres (2007); Companies that employ 500 or more persons: 4 (2008); Companies that employ 100 to 499 persons: 74 (2008); Companies that employ less than 100 persons: 3,541 (2008); Black-owned businesses: n/a (2002); Hispanic-owned businesses: 377 (2002); Asian-owned businesses: 167 (2002); Women-owned businesses: 2,782 (2002); Retail sales per capita: $11,019 (2010). Single-family building permits issued: 249 (2009); Multi-family building permits issued: 46 (2009).
Income: Per capita income: $28,798 (2010); Median household income: $62,119 (2010); Average household income: $74,239 (2010); Percent of households with income of $100,000 or more: 21.0% (2010); Poverty rate: 8.7% (2008); Bankruptcy rate: 8.22% (2009).
Taxes: Total county taxes per capita: $166 (2007); County property taxes per capita: $142 (2007).
Education: Percent of population age 25 and over with: High school diploma (including GED) or higher: 91.8% (2010); Bachelor's degree or higher: 24.5% (2010); Master's degree or higher: 7.7% (2010).
Housing: Homeownership rate: 77.0% (2010); Median home value: $142,511 (2010); Median contract rent: $640 per month (2006-2008 3-year est.); Median year structure built: 1977 (2006-2008 3-year est.).
Health: Birth rate: 122.8 per 10,000 population (2009); Death rate: 74.4 per 10,000 population (2009); Age-adjusted cancer mortality rate: 185.4 deaths

per 100,000 population (2006); Air Quality Index: 88.1% good, 11.6% moderate, 0.3% unhealthy for sensitive individuals, 0.0% unhealthy (percent of days in 2008); Number of physicians: 15.7 per 10,000 population (2007); Hospital beds: 17.0 per 10,000 population (2006); Hospital admissions: 768.3 per 10,000 population (2006).

Elections: 2008 Presidential election results: 53.0% Obama, 45.8% McCain, 0.1% Nader

National and State Parks: Indiana Dunes National Lakeshore; Indiana Dunes State Park

Additional Information Contacts

Porter County Government . . . . (219) 926-2255
   http://www.northwestindiana.com

Chesterton-Duneland Chamber of Commerce . . . . (219) 926-5513
   http://www.chestertonchamber.org

City of Portage . . . . (219) 762-7784
   http://www.ci.portage.in.us

City of Valparaiso . . . . (219) 462-1161
   http://www.ci.valparaiso.in.us

Greater Valparaiso Chamber of Commerce . . . . (219) 462-1105
   http://www.valparaisochamber.org

Portage Chamber of Commerce . . . . (219) 762-3300
   http://www.portageinchamber.com

Town of Chesterton . . . . (219) 926-1641
   http://www.chesterton.net

Town of Hebron . . . . (219) 996-4641
   http://www.visithebron.org

Town of Porter . . . . (219) 926-2771
   http://www.townofporter.com

Porter County Communities

BEVERLY SHORES

BEVERLY SHORES (town). Covers a land area of 3.577 square miles and a water area of 2.269 square miles. Located at 41.68° N. Lat; 86.98° W. Long. Elevation is 620 feet.

Population: 622 (1990); 708 (2000); 744 (2010); 762 (2015 projected); Race: 95.6% White, 2.2% Black, 0.5% Asian, 1.7% Other, 0.4% Hispanic of any race (2010); Density: 208.0 persons per square mile (2010); Average household size: 2.00 (2010); Median age: 53.9 (2010); Males per 100 females: 110.2 (2010); Marriage status: 26.0% never married, 58.6% now married, 6.6% widowed, 8.7% divorced (2000); Foreign born: 9.5% (2000); Ancestry (includes multiple ancestries): 28.0% German, 18.5% Irish, 14.7% Lithuanian, 7.7% English, 7.4% Polish (2000).

Economy: Single-family building permits issued: 1 (2009); Multi-family building permits issued: 0 (2009); Employment by occupation: 23.2% management, 29.0% professional, 11.0% services, 22.7% sales, 0.0% farming, 5.5% construction, 8.6% production (2000).

Income: Per capita income: $54,236 (2010); Median household income: $72,656 (2010); Average household income: $108,656 (2010); Percent of households with income of $100,000 or more: 35.2% (2010); Poverty rate: 4.9% (2000).

Taxes: Total city taxes per capita: $488 (2007); City property taxes per capita: $437 (2007).

Education: Percent of population age 25 and over with: High school diploma (including GED) or higher: 97.0% (2010); Bachelor's degree or higher: 59.4% (2010); Master's degree or higher: 24.2% (2010).

Housing: Homeownership rate: 85.2% (2010); Median home value: $286,111 (2010); Median contract rent: $538 per month (2000); Median year structure built: 1962 (2000).

Transportation: Commute to work: 77.4% car, 11.7% public transportation, 0.8% walk, 9.3% work from home (2000); Travel time to work: 12.3% less than 15 minutes, 29.9% 15 to 30 minutes, 15.2% 30 to 45 minutes, 7.9% 45 to 60 minutes, 34.6% 60 minutes or more (2000)

BURNS HARBOR

BURNS HARBOR (town). Aka Westport. Covers a land area of 6.834 square miles and a water area of 0.079 square miles. Located at 41.61° N. Lat; 87.12° W. Long. Elevation is 610 feet.

Population: 581 (1990); 766 (2000); 1,020 (2010); 1,131 (2015 projected); Race: 92.4% White, 1.5% Black, 0.8% Asian, 5.4% Other, 9.1% Hispanic of any race (2010); Density: 149.2 persons per square mile (2010); Average household size: 2.38 (2010); Median age: 38.0 (2010); Males per 100 females: 99.2 (2010); Marriage status: 19.3% never married, 63.7% now married, 3.1% widowed, 13.8% divorced (2000); Foreign born: 2.2% (2000); Ancestry (includes multiple ancestries): 21.1% Irish, 20.7% German, 11.8% Other groups, 11.0% English, 6.8% United States or American (2000).

Economy: Single-family building permits issued: 14 (2009); Multi-family building permits issued: 0 (2009); Employment by occupation: 5.7% management, 8.4% professional, 21.2% services, 19.8% sales, 0.0% farming, 16.9% construction, 27.9% production (2000).

Income: Per capita income: $30,575 (2010); Median household income: $61,968 (2010); Average household income: $72,150 (2010); Percent of households with income of $100,000 or more: 21.5% (2010); Poverty rate: 6.3% (2000).

Taxes: Total city taxes per capita: $681 (2007); City property taxes per capita: $573 (2007).

Education: Percent of population age 25 and over with: High school diploma (including GED) or higher: 91.8% (2010); Bachelor's degree or higher: 22.0% (2010); Master's degree or higher: 5.7% (2010).

Housing: Homeownership rate: 80.8% (2010); Median home value: $122,727 (2010); Median contract rent: $571 per month (2000); Median year structure built: 1960 (2000).

Safety: Violent crime rate: 17.8 per 10,000 population; Property crime rate: 383.2 per 10,000 population (2008).

Transportation: Commute to work: 91.9% car, 0.5% public transportation, 3.7% walk, 2.0% work from home (2000); Travel time to work: 37.7% less than 15 minutes, 27.9% 15 to 30 minutes, 17.1% 30 to 45 minutes, 5.0% 45 to 60 minutes, 12.3% 60 minutes or more (2000)

CHESTERTON

CHESTERTON (town). Covers a land area of 8.513 square miles and a water area of 0.113 square miles. Located at 41.60° N. Lat; 87.05° W. Long. Elevation is 640 feet.

History: Chesterton was first incorporated on October 5, 1869, ending the use of the former name, Calumet.

Population: 9,592 (1990); 10,488 (2000); 11,906 (2010); 12,502 (2015 projected); Race: 94.1% White, 1.6% Black, 1.6% Asian, 2.6% Other, 5.0% Hispanic of any race (2010); Density: 1,398.6 persons per square mile (2010); Average household size: 2.47 (2010); Median age: 38.0 (2010); Males per 100 females: 97.5 (2010); Marriage status: 23.9% never married, 58.5% now married, 6.6% widowed, 10.9% divorced (2000); Foreign born: 2.2% (2000); Ancestry (includes multiple ancestries): 25.6% German, 19.4% Irish, 12.0% English, 10.2% Polish, 9.7% Other groups (2000).

Economy: Single-family building permits issued: 14 (2009); Multi-family building permits issued: 6 (2009); Employment by occupation: 15.4% management, 24.8% professional, 16.9% services, 24.2% sales, 0.2% farming, 10.9% construction, 13.7% production (2000).

Income: Per capita income: $30,098 (2010); Median household income: $60,968 (2010); Average household income: $74,920 (2010); Percent of households with income of $100,000 or more: 20.9% (2010); Poverty rate: 4.3% (2000).

Taxes: Total city taxes per capita: $315 (2007); City property taxes per capita: $224 (2007).

Education: Percent of population age 25 and over with: High school diploma (including GED) or higher: 94.3% (2010); Bachelor's degree or higher: 27.7% (2010); Master's degree or higher: 9.4% (2010).

School District(s)

Duneland School Corporation (KG-12)
   2008-09 Enrollment: 5,866 . . . . (219) 983-3600

Housing: Homeownership rate: 70.6% (2010); Median home value: $145,260 (2010); Median contract rent: $563 per month (2000); Median year structure built: 1971 (2000).

Safety: Violent crime rate: 8.6 per 10,000 population; Property crime rate: 274.4 per 10,000 population (2008).

Newspapers: Chesterton Tribune (Local news; Circulation 6,000)

Transportation: Commute to work: 92.7% car, 2.7% public transportation, 1.7% walk, 2.3% work from home (2000); Travel time to work: 36.3% less than 15 minutes, 31.3% 15 to 30 minutes, 17.6% 30 to 45 minutes, 6.3% 45 to 60 minutes, 8.6% 60 minutes or more (2000)

Additional Information Contacts

Chesterton-Duneland Chamber of Commerce . . . . (219) 926-5513
   http://www.chestertonchamber.org

Town of Chesterton . . . . (219) 926-1641
   http://www.chesterton.net

DUNE ACRES

DUNE ACRES (town). Covers a land area of 2.137 square miles and a water area of 1.380 square miles. Located at 41.64° N. Lat; 87.08° W. Long. Elevation is 627 feet.

Population: 265 (1990); 213 (2000); 284 (2010); 315 (2015 projected); Race: 93.0% White, 2.1% Black, 0.7% Asian, 4.2% Other, 7.7% Hispanic of any race (2010); Density: 132.9 persons per square mile (2010); Average household size: 2.37 (2010); Median age: 41.1 (2010); Males per

100 females: 97.2 (2010); Marriage status: 12.4% never married, 77.5% now married, 3.4% widowed, 6.7% divorced (2000); Foreign born: 8.3% (2000); Ancestry (includes multiple ancestries): 24.9% German, 19.2% English, 17.1% Irish, 8.8% Polish, 8.8% Scottish (2000).
Economy: Single-family building permits issued: 1 (2009); Multi-family building permits issued: 0 (2009); Employment by occupation: 17.1% management, 47.6% professional, 3.8% services, 23.8% sales, 0.0% farming, 3.8% construction, 3.8% production (2000).
Income: Per capita income: $34,341 (2010); Median household income: $63,889 (2010); Average household income: $80,271 (2010); Percent of households with income of $100,000 or more: 24.2% (2010); Poverty rate: 0.0% (2000).
Taxes: Total city taxes per capita: $804 (2007); City property taxes per capita: $773 (2007).
Education: Percent of population age 25 and over with: High school diploma (including GED) or higher: 94.9% (2010); Bachelor's degree or higher: 33.0% (2010); Master's degree or higher: 10.2% (2010).
Housing: Homeownership rate: 81.7% (2010); Median home value: $145,652 (2010); Median contract rent: $1,500 per month (2000); Median year structure built: 1961 (2000).
Transportation: Commute to work: 81.9% car, 2.9% public transportation, 0.0% walk, 15.2% work from home (2000); Travel time to work: 20.2% less than 15 minutes, 30.3% 15 to 30 minutes, 14.6% 30 to 45 minutes, 18.0% 45 to 60 minutes, 16.9% 60 minutes or more (2000)

HEBRON (town). Covers a land area of 1.549 square miles and a water area of 0 square miles. Located at 41.32° N. Lat; 87.20° W. Long. Elevation is 709 feet.
Population: 3,237 (1990); 3,596 (2000); 4,085 (2010); 4,243 (2015 projected); Race: 93.8% White, 1.3% Black, 0.6% Asian, 4.3% Other, 6.5% Hispanic of any race (2010); Density: 2,637.2 persons per square mile (2010); Average household size: 2.48 (2010); Median age: 33.8 (2010); Males per 100 females: 94.2 (2010); Marriage status: 24.7% never married, 56.1% now married, 8.7% widowed, 10.5% divorced (2000); Foreign born: 1.8% (2000); Ancestry (includes multiple ancestries): 27.5% German, 17.7% Irish, 14.2% Polish, 12.2% Other groups, 7.6% English (2000).
Economy: Single-family building permits issued: 1 (2009); Multi-family building permits issued: 0 (2009); Employment by occupation: 6.8% management, 16.5% professional, 12.2% services, 30.5% sales, 0.0% farming, 17.0% construction, 17.0% production (2000).
Income: Per capita income: $23,124 (2010); Median household income: $52,711 (2010); Average household income: $57,286 (2010); Percent of households with income of $100,000 or more: 10.5% (2010); Poverty rate: 4.2% (2000).
Taxes: Total city taxes per capita: $114 (2007); City property taxes per capita: $103 (2007).
Education: Percent of population age 25 and over with: High school diploma (including GED) or higher: 92.3% (2010); Bachelor's degree or higher: 13.0% (2010); Master's degree or higher: 3.2% (2010).

School District(s)
M S D Boone Township (KG-12)
    2008-09 Enrollment: 1,112 . . . . (219) 996-4771
Porter Township School Corp (KG-12)
    2008-09 Enrollment: 1,642 . . . . (219) 477-4933
Housing: Homeownership rate: 71.2% (2010); Median home value: $116,015 (2010); Median contract rent: $485 per month (2000); Median year structure built: 1977 (2000).
Transportation: Commute to work: 96.1% car, 0.4% public transportation, 1.7% walk, 0.9% work from home (2000); Travel time to work: 19.7% less than 15 minutes, 35.0% 15 to 30 minutes, 19.7% 30 to 45 minutes, 13.0% 45 to 60 minutes, 12.6% 60 minutes or more (2000)
Additional Information Contacts
Town of Hebron . . . . (219) 996-4641
    http://www.visithebron.org

KOUTS (town). Covers a land area of 1.116 square miles and a water area of 0 square miles. Located at 41.31° N. Lat; 87.02° W. Long. Elevation is 682 feet.
History: Laid out 1864.
Population: 1,643 (1990); 1,698 (2000); 2,086 (2010); 2,244 (2015 projected); Race: 96.9% White, 0.9% Black, 0.1% Asian, 2.1% Other, 2.7% Hispanic of any race (2010); Density: 1,869.8 persons per square mile (2010); Average household size: 2.43 (2010); Median age: 35.9 (2010); Males per 100 females: 99.8 (2010); Marriage status: 20.0% never married, 62.3% now married, 7.0% widowed, 10.7% divorced (2000); Foreign born:

0.7% (2000); Ancestry (includes multiple ancestries): 41.5% German, 14.4% Irish, 9.7% English, 7.7% United States or American, 6.8% Polish (2000).
Economy: Single-family building permits issued: 5 (2009); Multi-family building permits issued: 0 (2009); Employment by occupation: 10.2% management, 20.5% professional, 11.7% services, 21.8% sales, 0.0% farming, 13.0% construction, 22.9% production (2000).
Income: Per capita income: $24,256 (2010); Median household income: $55,506 (2010); Average household income: $59,386 (2010); Percent of households with income of $100,000 or more: 11.2% (2010); Poverty rate: 3.2% (2000).
Taxes: Total city taxes per capita: $234 (2007); City property taxes per capita: $227 (2007).
Education: Percent of population age 25 and over with: High school diploma (including GED) or higher: 93.4% (2010); Bachelor's degree or higher: 18.8% (2010); Master's degree or higher: 2.8% (2010).
School District(s)
East Porter County School Corp (KG-12)
    2008-09 Enrollment: 2,320 . . . . (219) 766-2214
Housing: Homeownership rate: 81.0% (2010); Median home value: $132,468 (2010); Median contract rent: $465 per month (2000); Median year structure built: 1966 (2000).
Transportation: Commute to work: 96.0% car, 0.6% public transportation, 2.4% walk, 0.6% work from home (2000); Travel time to work: 23.7% less than 15 minutes, 40.5% 15 to 30 minutes, 16.4% 30 to 45 minutes, 11.2% 45 to 60 minutes, 8.3% 60 minutes or more (2000)

OGDEN DUNES (town). Aka Wickliffe. Covers a land area of 0.730 square miles and a water area of 0.712 square miles. Located at 41.62° N. Lat; 87.19° W. Long. Elevation is 610 feet.
History: In 1916, on the site that became Ogden Dunes, a woman was found living alone and avoiding contact with other people. The newspapers called her Diana of the Dunes, and many stories were told about her.
Population: 1,499 (1990); 1,313 (2000); 1,172 (2010); 1,111 (2015 projected); Race: 97.3% White, 1.0% Black, 0.1% Asian, 1.6% Other, 2.6% Hispanic of any race (2010); Density: 1,605.2 persons per square mile (2010); Average household size: 2.24 (2010); Median age: 51.9 (2010); Males per 100 females: 100.0 (2010); Marriage status: 16.7% never married, 66.8% now married, 7.6% widowed, 8.9% divorced (2000); Foreign born: 3.4% (2000); Ancestry (includes multiple ancestries): 20.6% German, 16.7% Irish, 14.8% English, 10.2% Polish, 6.7% Italian (2000).
Economy: Single-family building permits issued: 2 (2009); Multi-family building permits issued: 0 (2009); Employment by occupation: 24.9% management, 35.6% professional, 7.9% services, 20.9% sales, 0.0% farming, 4.1% construction, 6.5% production (2000).
Income: Per capita income: $51,616 (2010); Median household income: $81,171 (2010); Average household income: $115,163 (2010); Percent of households with income of $100,000 or more: 38.6% (2010); Poverty rate: 4.1% (2000).
Taxes: Total city taxes per capita: $464 (2007); City property taxes per capita: $309 (2007).
Education: Percent of population age 25 and over with: High school diploma (including GED) or higher: 98.1% (2010); Bachelor's degree or higher: 55.4% (2010); Master's degree or higher: 21.3% (2010).
Housing: Homeownership rate: 92.4% (2010); Median home value: $260,582 (2010); Median contract rent: $835 per month (2000); Median year structure built: 1960 (2000).
Transportation: Commute to work: 88.2% car, 6.2% public transportation, 0.0% walk, 5.0% work from home (2000); Travel time to work: 14.0% less than 15 minutes, 32.8% 15 to 30 minutes, 25.3% 30 to 45 minutes, 8.5% 45 to 60 minutes, 19.4% 60 minutes or more (2000)

PORTAGE (city). Covers a land area of 25.456 square miles and a water area of 1.970 square miles. Located at 41.58° N. Lat; 87.18° W. Long. Elevation is 636 feet.
History: Named for Portage, Ohio. A new port, accommodating ocean vessels, began operating here in the early 1970s (Burns International Harbor). Incorporated 1959.
Population: 30,561 (1990); 33,496 (2000); 37,616 (2010); 39,259 (2015 projected); Race: 86.5% White, 5.3% Black, 0.8% Asian, 7.5% Other, 13.7% Hispanic of any race (2010); Density: 1,477.7 persons per square mile (2010); Average household size: 2.53 (2010); Median age: 36.4 (2010); Males per 100 females: 95.8 (2010); Marriage status: 23.5% never married, 55.7% now married, 8.2% widowed, 12.6% divorced (2000); Foreign born: 3.0% (2000); Ancestry (includes multiple ancestries): 22.0%

German, 18.3% Other groups, 15.3% Irish, 8.8% English, 8.6% Polish (2000).

Economy: Unemployment rate: 9.7% (5/2010); Total civilian labor force: 17,802 (5/2010); Single-family building permits issued: 33 (2009); Multi-family building permits issued: 0 (2009); Employment by occupation: 7.9% management, 12.8% professional, 16.8% services, 23.5% sales, 0.0% farming, 15.7% construction, 23.2% production (2000).

Income: Per capita income: $23,896 (2010); Median household income: $54,071 (2010); Average household income: $60,731 (2010); Percent of households with income of $100,000 or more: 13.1% (2010); Poverty rate: 7.5% (2000).

Taxes: Total city taxes per capita: $286 (2007); City property taxes per capita: $262 (2007).

Education: Percent of population age 25 and over with: High school diploma (including GED) or higher: 87.3% (2010); Bachelor's degree or higher: 12.0% (2010); Master's degree or higher: 2.8% (2010).

School District(s)

Portage Township Schools (KG-12)
    2008-09 Enrollment: 8,476 . . . . (219) 762-6511

Housing: Homeownership rate: 72.4% (2010); Median home value: $118,030 (2010); Median contract rent: $516 per month (2000); Median year structure built: 1975 (2000).

Safety: Violent crime rate: 46.9 per 10,000 population; Property crime rate: 396.3 per 10,000 population (2008).

Newspapers: The Times - Portage Bureau (Local news)

Transportation: Commute to work: 96.2% car, 1.3% public transportation, 0.4% walk, 1.2% work from home (2000); Travel time to work: 27.8% less than 15 minutes, 38.3% 15 to 30 minutes, 21.8% 30 to 45 minutes, 5.0% 45 to 60 minutes, 7.1% 60 minutes or more (2000)

Additional Information Contacts

City of Portage . . . . (219) 762-7784
    http://www.ci.portage.in.us
Portage Chamber of Commerce . . . . (219) 762-3300
    http://www.portageinchamber.com

PORTER (town). Covers a land area of 6.304 square miles and a water area of 0.305 square miles. Located at 41.62° N. Lat; 87.07° W. Long. Elevation is 640 feet.

History: Laid out 1855.

Population: 3,116 (1990); 4,972 (2000); 6,328 (2010); 6,939 (2015 projected); Race: 92.1% White, 3.1% Black, 0.9% Asian, 3.9% Other, 8.1% Hispanic of any race (2010); Density: 1,003.9 persons per square mile (2010); Average household size: 2.47 (2010); Median age: 36.8 (2010); Males per 100 females: 97.1 (2010); Marriage status: 24.5% never married, 55.7% now married, 5.4% widowed, 14.5% divorced (2000); Foreign born: 2.4% (2000); Ancestry (includes multiple ancestries): 25.3% German, 16.9% Irish, 11.8% English, 11.7% Polish, 8.5% Other groups (2000).

Economy: Single-family building permits issued: 8 (2009); Multi-family building permits issued: 0 (2009); Employment by occupation: 11.5% management, 17.9% professional, 13.8% services, 26.9% sales, 0.0% farming, 15.1% construction, 14.8% production (2000).

Income: Per capita income: $32,398 (2010); Median household income: $61,812 (2010); Average household income: $80,470 (2010); Percent of households with income of $100,000 or more: 23.2% (2010); Poverty rate: 6.5% (2000).

Taxes: Total city taxes per capita: $455 (2007); City property taxes per capita: $334 (2007).

Education: Percent of population age 25 and over with: High school diploma (including GED) or higher: 93.0% (2010); Bachelor's degree or higher: 28.9% (2010); Master's degree or higher: 8.3% (2010).

School District(s)

Duneland School Corporation (KG-12)
    2008-09 Enrollment: 5,866 . . . . (219) 983-3600

Housing: Homeownership rate: 74.4% (2010); Median home value: $136,287 (2010); Median contract rent: $563 per month (2000); Median year structure built: 1969 (2000).

Transportation: Commute to work: 88.1% car, 7.5% public transportation, 2.1% walk, 1.5% work from home (2000); Travel time to work: 34.2% less than 15 minutes, 28.5% 15 to 30 minutes, 15.1% 30 to 45 minutes, 5.1% 45 to 60 minutes, 17.1% 60 minutes or more (2000)

Additional Information Contacts

Town of Porter . . . . (219) 926-2771
    http://www.townofporter.com

SOUTH HAVEN (CDP). Covers a land area of 1.244 square miles and a water area of 0 square miles. Located at 41.54° N. Lat; 87.13° W. Long. Elevation is 653 feet.

Population: 6,174 (1990); 5,619 (2000); 5,660 (2010); 5,700 (2015 projected); Race: 95.2% White, 1.2% Black, 0.3% Asian, 3.3% Other, 8.5% Hispanic of any race (2010); Density: 4,548.2 persons per square mile (2010); Average household size: 2.85 (2010); Median age: 35.2 (2010); Males per 100 females: 96.3 (2010); Marriage status: 23.9% never married, 60.3% now married, 5.0% widowed, 10.8% divorced (2000); Foreign born: 0.9% (2000); Ancestry (includes multiple ancestries): 22.0% German, 18.6% Irish, 11.5% English, 11.3% Other groups, 9.5% United States or American (2000).

Economy: Employment by occupation: 5.3% management, 10.6% professional, 23.4% services, 23.2% sales, 0.0% farming, 13.0% construction, 24.5% production (2000).

Income: Per capita income: $22,858 (2010); Median household income: $61,504 (2010); Average household income: $65,162 (2010); Percent of households with income of $100,000 or more: 14.4% (2010); Poverty rate: 5.8% (2000).

Education: Percent of population age 25 and over with: High school diploma (including GED) or higher: 89.1% (2010); Bachelor's degree or higher: 8.6% (2010); Master's degree or higher: 0.6% (2010).

Housing: Homeownership rate: 79.6% (2010); Median home value: $95,784 (2010); Median contract rent: $557 per month (2000); Median year structure built: 1967 (2000).

Transportation: Commute to work: 96.9% car, 0.9% public transportation, 1.3% walk, 0.7% work from home (2000); Travel time to work: 26.1% less than 15 minutes, 43.4% 15 to 30 minutes, 17.2% 30 to 45 minutes, 5.9% 45 to 60 minutes, 7.4% 60 minutes or more (2000)

TOWN OF PINES (town). Covers a land area of 2.276 square miles and a water area of 0 square miles. Located at 41.68° N. Lat; 86.94° W. Long. Elevation is 627 feet.

Population: 789 (1990); 798 (2000); 879 (2010); 918 (2015 projected); Race: 95.1% White, 0.1% Black, 0.2% Asian, 4.6% Other, 3.6% Hispanic of any race (2010); Density: 386.1 persons per square mile (2010); Average household size: 2.32 (2010); Median age: 43.7 (2010); Males per 100 females: 106.8 (2010); Marriage status: 23.4% never married, 56.3% now married, 5.6% widowed, 14.7% divorced (2000); Foreign born: 2.1% (2000); Ancestry (includes multiple ancestries): 28.4% German, 14.9% United States or American, 12.3% Other groups, 10.2% Irish, 9.7% Polish (2000).

Economy: Single-family building permits issued: 0 (2009); Multi-family building permits issued: 0 (2009); Employment by occupation: 6.0% management, 9.3% professional, 14.6% services, 25.8% sales, 0.0% farming, 19.5% construction, 24.8% production (2000).

Income: Per capita income: $25,745 (2010); Median household income: $50,147 (2010); Average household income: $59,987 (2010); Percent of households with income of $100,000 or more: 13.2% (2010); Poverty rate: 8.7% (2000).

Taxes: Total city taxes per capita: $170 (2007); City property taxes per capita: $77 (2007).

Education: Percent of population age 25 and over with: High school diploma (including GED) or higher: 80.3% (2010); Bachelor's degree or higher: 8.2% (2010); Master's degree or higher: 2.7% (2010).

Housing: Homeownership rate: 72.8% (2010); Median home value: $94,366 (2010); Median contract rent: $434 per month (2000); Median year structure built: 1959 (2000).

Transportation: Commute to work: 90.6% car, 2.2% public transportation, 0.0% walk, 4.6% work from home (2000); Travel time to work: 43.7% less than 15 minutes, 32.0% 15 to 30 minutes, 11.7% 30 to 45 minutes, 7.1% 45 to 60 minutes, 5.6% 60 minutes or more (2000)

VALPARAISO (city). County seat. Covers a land area of 10.904 square miles and a water area of 0.085 square miles. Located at 41.47° N. Lat; 87.05° W. Long. Elevation is 794 feet.

History: Named for the city in Chile, near which Captain David Porter fought in the War of 1812. Valparaiso was sited on the Old Sauk Trail. In 1859 the Valparaiso Male and Female College was founded here by the Methodist Church. The College, purchased by the Lutheran Church in 1925, became Valparaiso University.

Population: 24,568 (1990); 27,428 (2000); 28,611 (2010); 29,136 (2015 projected); Race: 88.8% White, 5.9% Black, 1.8% Asian, 3.5% Other, 5.5% Hispanic of any race (2010); Density: 2,623.9 persons per square mile

(2010); Average household size: 2.22 (2010); Median age: 35.4 (2010); Males per 100 females: 93.6 (2010); Marriage status: 31.5% never married, 50.4% now married, 7.5% widowed, 10.6% divorced (2000); Foreign born: 4.1% (2000); Ancestry (includes multiple ancestries): 32.9% German, 16.2% Irish, 11.9% English, 9.2% Polish, 8.9% Other groups (2000).
Economy: Unemployment rate: 8.4% (5/2010); Total civilian labor force: 15,193 (5/2010); Single-family building permits issued: 50 (2009); Multi-family building permits issued: 40 (2009); Employment by occupation: 11.4% management, 26.9% professional, 14.4% services, 26.5% sales, 0.0% farming, 9.2% construction, 11.7% production (2000).
Income: Per capita income: $26,657 (2010); Median household income: $51,705 (2010); Average household income: $64,128 (2010); Percent of households with income of $100,000 or more: 15.9% (2010); Poverty rate: 9.1% (2000).
Taxes: Total city taxes per capita: $365 (2007); City property taxes per capita: $327 (2007).
Education: Percent of population age 25 and over with: High school diploma (including GED) or higher: 93.5% (2010); Bachelor's degree or higher: 37.1% (2010); Master's degree or higher: 12.2% (2010).

School District(s)

Duneland School Corporation (KG-12)
    2008-09 Enrollment: 5,866 . . . . (219) 983-3600
East Porter County School Corp (KG-12)
    2008-09 Enrollment: 2,320 . . . . (219) 766-2214
Portage Township Schools (KG-12)
    2008-09 Enrollment: 8,476 . . . . (219) 762-6511
Porter County Education Services (KG-12)
    2008-09 Enrollment: n/a . . . . (219) 464-9607
Porter Township School Corp (KG-12)
    2008-09 Enrollment: 1,642 . . . . (219) 477-4933
Union Township School Corp (KG-12)
    2008-09 Enrollment: 1,719 . . . . (219) 759-2531
Valparaiso Community Schools (KG-12)
    2008-09 Enrollment: 6,416 . . . . (219) 531-3000

Four-year College(s)

Valparaiso University (Private, Not-for-profit, Lutheran Church in America)
    Fall 2008 Enrollment: 3,975. . . . . (219) 464-5000
    2009-10 Tuition: In-state $28,320; Out-of-state $28,320

Vocational/Technical School(s)

Don Roberts Beauty School (Private, For-profit)
    Fall 2008 Enrollment: 68 . . . . (219) 462-5189
    2009-10 Tuition: $8,770

Housing: Homeownership rate: 57.0% (2010); Median home value: $141,885 (2010); Median contract rent: $548 per month (2000); Median year structure built: 1971 (2000).
Hospitals: Porter Memorial Health System (402 beds)
Safety: Violent crime rate: 34.1 per 10,000 population; Property crime rate: 289.0 per 10,000 population (2008).
Newspapers: Post-Tribune - Valparaiso Bureau (Local news); The Times - Valparaiso Bureau (Local news)
Transportation: Commute to work: 87.3% car, 0.7% public transportation, 7.8% walk, 2.9% work from home (2000); Travel time to work: 48.8% less than 15 minutes, 24.5% 15 to 30 minutes, 14.7% 30 to 45 minutes, 6.4% 45 to 60 minutes, 5.6% 60 minutes or more (2000).
Additional Information Contacts
City of Valparaiso. . . . . (219) 462-1161
    http://www.ci.valparaiso.in.us
Greater Valparaiso Chamber of Commerce . . . . (219) 462-1105
    http://www.valparaisochamber.org

Posey County

Located in southwestern Indiana; bounded on the west by the Wabash River and the Illinois border, and on the south by the Ohio River and the Kentucky border; drained by Big Creek. Covers a land area of 408.50 square miles, a water area of 10.95 square miles, and is located in the Central Time Zone. The county was founded in 1814. County seat is Mount Vernon.

Posey County is part of the Evansville, IN-KY Metropolitan Statistical Area. The entire metro area includes: Gibson County, IN; Posey County, IN; Vanderburgh County, IN; Warrick County, IN; Henderson County, KY; Webster County, KY

Weather Station: Mount Vernon   Elevation: 419 feet

	Jan	Feb	Mar	Apr	May	Jun	Jul	Aug	Sep	Oct	Nov	Dec
High	39	44	55	66	76	85	88	87	81	69	56	44
Low	22	26	35	45	55	64	68	65	58	46	37	28
Precip	3.2	3.0	4.7	4.5	5.4	3.9	4.2	3.0	2.8	3.0	4.3	3.7
Snow	4.5	3.8	2.3	0.4	0.0	0.0	0.0	0.0	0.0	0.1	0.4	2.2

High and Low temperatures in degrees Fahrenheit; Precipitation and Snow in inches

Population: 25,968 (1990); 27,061 (2000); 25,886 (2010); 25,148 (2015 projected); Race: 97.1% White, 1.2% Black, 0.3% Asian, 1.3% Other, 0.8% Hispanic of any race (2010); Density: 63.4 persons per square mile (2010); Average household size: 2.58 (2010); Median age: 41.5 (2010); Males per 100 females: 100.2 (2010).
Religion: Five largest groups: 20.8% Catholic Church, 8.0% The United Methodist Church, 6.9% United Church of Christ, 3.3% Southern Baptist Convention, 2.8% Assemblies of God (2000).
Economy: Unemployment rate: 7.7% (5/2010); Total civilian labor force: 12,920 (5/2010); Leading industries: 21.9% transportation & warehousing; 19.9% manufacturing; 11.5% retail trade (2008); Farms: 438 totaling 204,004 acres (2007); Companies that employ 500 or more persons: 0 (2008); Companies that employ 100 to 499 persons: 11 (2008); Companies that employ less than 100 persons: 513 (2008); Black-owned businesses: n/a (2002); Hispanic-owned businesses: n/a (2002); Asian-owned businesses: n/a (2002); Women-owned businesses: 615 (2002); Retail sales per capita: $8,657 (2010). Single-family building permits issued: 36 (2009); Multi-family building permits issued: 0 (2009).
Income: Per capita income: $25,329 (2010); Median household income: $56,841 (2010); Average household income: $65,746 (2010); Percent of households with income of $100,000 or more: 18.0% (2010); Poverty rate: 10.1% (2008); Bankruptcy rate: 4.69% (2009).
Taxes: Total county taxes per capita: $295 (2007); County property taxes per capita: $290 (2007).
Education: Percent of population age 25 and over with: High school diploma (including GED) or higher: 87.7% (2010); Bachelor's degree or higher: 16.6% (2010); Master's degree or higher: 5.2% (2010).
Housing: Homeownership rate: 82.8% (2010); Median home value: $113,552 (2010); Median contract rent: $419 per month (2006-2008 3-year est.); Median year structure built: 1971 (2006-2008 3-year est.)
Health: Birth rate: 98.1 per 10,000 population (2009); Death rate: 79.2 per 10,000 population (2009); Age-adjusted cancer mortality rate: 221.4 deaths per 100,000 population (2006); Air Quality Index: 91.0% good, 8.4% moderate, 0.6% unhealthy for sensitive individuals, 0.0% unhealthy (percent of days in 2008); Number of physicians: 3.0 per 10,000 population (2007); Hospital beds: 0.0 per 10,000 population (2006); Hospital admissions: 0.0 per 10,000 population (2006).
Elections: 2008 Presidential election results: 45.6% Obama, 53.3% McCain, 0.0% Nader
National and State Parks: Angel Mounds State Memorial; Harmonie State Park; New Harmony State Memorial; The Labyrinth State Memorial
Additional Information Contacts
Posey County Government . . . . (812) 838-3317
    http://www.mountvernon.in.gov
City of Mount Vernon . . . . (812) 838-3317
    http://www.mountvernon.in.gov

Posey County Communities

CYNTHIANA (town). Covers a land area of 0.402 square miles and a water area of 0 square miles. Located at 38.18° N. Lat; 87.70° W. Long. Elevation is 472 feet.
Population: 669 (1990); 693 (2000); 621 (2010); 586 (2015 projected); Race: 98.7% White, 0.0% Black, 0.3% Asian, 1.0% Other, 0.5% Hispanic of any race (2010); Density: 1,545.9 persons per square mile (2010); Average household size: 2.65 (2010); Median age: 39.3 (2010); Males per 100 females: 94.1 (2010); Marriage status: 19.9% never married, 63.3% now married, 6.6% widowed, 10.3% divorced (2000); Foreign born: 0.7% (2000); Ancestry (includes multiple ancestries): 28.7% German, 18.5% United States or American, 14.3% Other groups, 10.9% Irish, 5.6% English (2000).
Economy: Employment by occupation: 5.7% management, 7.8% professional, 15.1% services, 17.6% sales, 0.5% farming, 14.6% construction, 38.6% production (2000).
Income: Per capita income: $21,214 (2010); Median household income: $50,410 (2010); Average household income: $56,944 (2010); Percent of households with income of $100,000 or more: 6.4% (2010); Poverty rate: 9.7% (2000).

Taxes: Total city taxes per capita: $75 (2007); City property taxes per capita: $65 (2007).
Education: Percent of population age 25 and over with: High school diploma (including GED) or higher: 85.3% (2010); Bachelor's degree or higher: 10.6% (2010); Master's degree or higher: 2.2% (2010).
Housing: Homeownership rate: 82.5% (2010); Median home value: $82,174 (2010); Median contract rent: $275 per month (2000); Median year structure built: 1950 (2000).
Transportation: Commute to work: 93.9% car, 0.0% public transportation, 1.1% walk, 5.0% work from home (2000); Travel time to work: 21.7% less than 15 minutes, 33.0% 15 to 30 minutes, 32.2% 30 to 45 minutes, 11.0% 45 to 60 minutes, 2.0% 60 minutes or more (2000)

GRIFFIN (town).

Covers a land area of 0.068 square miles and a water area of 0 square miles. Located at 38.20° N. Lat; 87.91° W. Long. Elevation is 387 feet.
History: Laid out 1881.
Population: 171 (1990); 160 (2000); 159 (2010); 156 (2015 projected); Race: 98.7% White, 0.0% Black, 0.6% Asian, 0.6% Other, 0.0% Hispanic of any race (2010); Density: 2,348.5 persons per square mile (2010); Average household size: 2.41 (2010); Median age: 46.4 (2010); Males per 100 females: 101.3 (2010); Marriage status: 13.6% never married, 55.2% now married, 17.6% widowed, 13.6% divorced (2000); Foreign born: 0.0% (2000); Ancestry (includes multiple ancestries): 13.8% German, 13.8% United States or American, 9.0% Irish, 5.5% British, 2.8% European (2000).
Economy: Employment by occupation: 1.5% management, 7.4% professional, 10.3% services, 33.8% sales, 0.0% farming, 11.8% construction, 35.3% production (2000).
Income: Per capita income: $26,817 (2010); Median household income: $59,722 (2010); Average household income: $65,720 (2010); Percent of households with income of $100,000 or more: 16.7% (2010); Poverty rate: 17.9% (2000).
Taxes: Total city taxes per capita: $64 (2007); City property taxes per capita: $38 (2007).
Education: Percent of population age 25 and over with: High school diploma (including GED) or higher: 82.4% (2010); Bachelor's degree or higher: 6.7% (2010); Master's degree or higher: 2.5% (2010).
Housing: Homeownership rate: 86.4% (2010); Median home value: $75,000 (2010); Median contract rent: $300 per month (2000); Median year structure built: 1945 (2000).
Transportation: Commute to work: 97.1% car, 2.9% public transportation, 0.0% walk, 0.0% work from home (2000); Travel time to work: 11.8% less than 15 minutes, 17.6% 15 to 30 minutes, 39.7% 30 to 45 minutes, 19.1% 45 to 60 minutes, 11.8% 60 minutes or more (2000)

MOUNT VERNON (city).

County seat. Covers a land area of 2.463 square miles and a water area of 0.066 square miles. Located at 37.93° N. Lat; 87.89° W. Long. Elevation is 400 feet.
History: Mount Vernon, founded in 1805 by Irish trader Andrew McFadden, was first called McFadden's Landing. The name was changed in 1816.
Population: 7,433 (1990); 7,478 (2000); 6,886 (2010); 6,574 (2015 projected); Race: 94.2% White, 3.8% Black, 0.5% Asian, 1.5% Other, 1.0% Hispanic of any race (2010); Density: 2,795.7 persons per square mile (2010); Average household size: 2.38 (2010); Median age: 41.1 (2010); Males per 100 females: 94.9 (2010); Marriage status: 17.9% never married, 59.8% now married, 9.6% widowed, 12.7% divorced (2000); Foreign born: 1.0% (2000); Ancestry (includes multiple ancestries): 28.1% German, 12.9% United States or American, 11.9% English, 11.1% Irish, 8.2% Other groups (2000).
Economy: Employment by occupation: 10.6% management, 20.4% professional, 15.0% services, 24.0% sales, 0.7% farming, 8.4% construction, 20.9% production (2000).
Income: Per capita income: $22,961 (2010); Median household income: $44,265 (2010); Average household income: $55,413 (2010); Percent of households with income of $100,000 or more: 13.4% (2010); Poverty rate: 12.5% (2000).
Taxes: Total city taxes per capita: $268 (2007); City property taxes per capita: $255 (2007).
Education: Percent of population age 25 and over with: High school diploma (including GED) or higher: 84.6% (2010); Bachelor's degree or higher: 15.0% (2010); Master's degree or higher: 5.0% (2010).

School District(s)

M S D Mount Vernon (PK-12)
    2008-09 Enrollment: 2,438 . . . . (812) 838-4471
Housing: Homeownership rate: 71.5% (2010); Median home value: $91,108 (2010); Median contract rent: $325 per month (2000); Median year structure built: 1964 (2000).
Newspapers: Mount Vernon Democrat (Community news; Circulation 3,500); The Posey Advantage (Community news; Circulation 9,500)
Transportation: Commute to work: 94.0% car, 0.0% public transportation, 2.6% walk, 3.0% work from home (2000); Travel time to work: 54.9% less than 15 minutes, 17.1% 15 to 30 minutes, 18.1% 30 to 45 minutes, 5.8% 45 to 60 minutes, 4.1% 60 minutes or more (2000)
Additional Information Contacts
City of Mount Vernon . . . . (812) 838-3317
    http://www.mountvernon.in.gov

NEW HARMONY (town).

Covers a land area of 0.635 square miles and a water area of 0.009 square miles. Located at 38.12° N. Lat; 87.93° W. Long. Elevation is 381 feet.
History: New Harmony was the site of two social experiments. In 1815 the Rappites, a religious group of Germans from Pennsylvania, founded the village of Harmonie, trying to create a society based on cooperative living. After ten years their hard work had created a prosperous town out of the wilderness, but also created discontent. They sold the village to Robert Owen, a Welsh philanthropist and social reformer whose dream was to found a communal society. Owen called his community New Harmony. The experiment as Owen envisioned it was a failure within two years, but New Harmony continued to be an intellectual center.
Population: 846 (1990); 916 (2000); 863 (2010); 833 (2015 projected); Race: 98.0% White, 0.0% Black, 0.6% Asian, 1.4% Other, 1.0% Hispanic of any race (2010); Density: 1,358.1 persons per square mile (2010); Average household size: 2.14 (2010); Median age: 48.1 (2010); Males per 100 females: 91.4 (2010); Marriage status: 17.7% never married, 55.5% now married, 16.8% widowed, 10.0% divorced (2000); Foreign born: 0.8% (2000); Ancestry (includes multiple ancestries): 20.5% German, 15.6% English, 7.5% Irish, 7.4% United States or American, 5.4% Other groups (2000).
Economy: Single-family building permits issued: 0 (2009); Multi-family building permits issued: 0 (2009); Employment by occupation: 11.7% management, 19.4% professional, 22.0% services, 17.9% sales, 0.0% farming, 7.3% construction, 21.8% production (2000).
Income: Per capita income: $22,943 (2010); Median household income: $34,388 (2010); Average household income: $50,078 (2010); Percent of households with income of $100,000 or more: 9.1% (2010); Poverty rate: 12.4% (2000).
Taxes: Total city taxes per capita: $109 (2007); City property taxes per capita: $96 (2007).
Education: Percent of population age 25 and over with: High school diploma (including GED) or higher: 82.0% (2010); Bachelor's degree or higher: 19.6% (2010); Master's degree or higher: 9.6% (2010).

School District(s)

New Harmony Town & Twp Con Sch (PK-12)
    2008-09 Enrollment: 169 . . . . (812) 682-4401
Housing: Homeownership rate: 74.4% (2010); Median home value: $92,500 (2010); Median contract rent: $310 per month (2000); Median year structure built: 1942 (2000).
Transportation: Commute to work: 83.9% car, 0.0% public transportation, 9.0% walk, 6.3% work from home (2000); Travel time to work: 45.6% less than 15 minutes, 21.2% 15 to 30 minutes, 20.1% 30 to 45 minutes, 10.2% 45 to 60 minutes, 2.9% 60 minutes or more (2000)

POSEYVILLE (town).

Covers a land area of 0.664 square miles and a water area of 0 square miles. Located at 38.16° N. Lat; 87.78° W. Long. Elevation is 440 feet.
Population: 1,127 (1990); 1,187 (2000); 1,138 (2010); 1,104 (2015 projected); Race: 98.2% White, 0.4% Black, 0.0% Asian, 1.4% Other, 0.1% Hispanic of any race (2010); Density: 1,714.4 persons per square mile (2010); Average household size: 2.63 (2010); Median age: 40.7 (2010); Males per 100 females: 102.1 (2010); Marriage status: 18.9% never married, 60.2% now married, 10.8% widowed, 10.1% divorced (2000); Foreign born: 0.2% (2000); Ancestry (includes multiple ancestries): 35.6% German, 14.1% United States or American, 10.5% Irish, 9.0% English, 5.6% Other groups (2000).

Economy: Employment by occupation: 13.1% management, 14.7% professional, 12.3% services, 23.2% sales, 0.0% farming, 15.3% construction, 21.5% production (2000).
Income: Per capita income: $25,888 (2010); Median household income: $55,740 (2010); Average household income: $68,706 (2010); Percent of households with income of $100,000 or more: 19.5% (2010); Poverty rate: 5.2% (2000).
Taxes: Total city taxes per capita: $151 (2007); City property taxes per capita: $143 (2007).
Education: Percent of population age 25 and over with: High school diploma (including GED) or higher: 88.3% (2010); Bachelor's degree or higher: 11.9% (2010); Master's degree or higher: 5.1% (2010).

School District(s)
M S D North Posey Co Schools (PK-12)
    2008-09 Enrollment: 1,364 . . . . (812) 874-2243
Housing: Homeownership rate: 83.1% (2010); Median home value: $88,305 (2010); Median contract rent: $285 per month (2000); Median year structure built: 1956 (2000).
Newspapers: Posey County News (Community news; Circulation 4,800)
Transportation: Commute to work: 95.0% car, 0.3% public transportation, 2.2% walk, 1.2% work from home (2000); Travel time to work: 41.3% less than 15 minutes, 17.7% 15 to 30 minutes, 27.8% 30 to 45 minutes, 7.9% 45 to 60 minutes, 5.3% 60 minutes or more (2000)

WADESVILLE (unincorporated postal area, zip code 47638). Covers a land area of 50.665 square miles and a water area of 0.015 square miles. Located at 38.08° N. Lat; 87.78° W. Long. Elevation is 479 feet.
Population: 3,444 (2000); Race: 99.4% White, 0.0% Black, 0.0% Asian, 0.6% Other, 0.3% Hispanic of any race (2000); Density: 68.0 persons per square mile (2000); Age: 29.4% under 18, 8.6% over 64 (2000); Marriage status: 19.0% never married, 69.5% now married, 3.8% widowed, 7.8% divorced (2000); Foreign born: 0.2% (2000); Ancestry (includes multiple ancestries): 40.1% German, 12.7% United States or American, 11.9% English, 9.5% Irish, 6.8% Other groups (2000).
Economy: Employment by occupation: 13.2% management, 19.3% professional, 8.2% services, 23.6% sales, 0.4% farming, 14.8% construction, 20.4% production (2000).
Income: Per capita income: $20,263 (2000); Median household income: $51,103 (2000); Poverty rate: 5.3% (2000).
Education: Percent of population age 25 and over with: High school diploma (including GED) or higher: 88.0% (2000); Bachelor's degree or higher: 16.1% (2000).

School District(s)
M S D North Posey Co Schools (PK-12)
    2008-09 Enrollment: 1,364 . . . . (812) 874-2243
Housing: Homeownership rate: 83.1% (2000); Median home value: $102,700 (2000); Median contract rent: $303 per month (2000); Median year structure built: 1972 (2000).
Transportation: Commute to work: 92.4% car, 0.0% public transportation, 2.0% walk, 4.6% work from home (2000); Travel time to work: 15.2% less than 15 minutes, 45.1% 15 to 30 minutes, 32.2% 30 to 45 minutes, 3.8% 45 to 60 minutes, 3.7% 60 minutes or more (2000)

Pulaski County

Located in northwestern Indiana; drained by the Tippecanoe River. Covers a land area of 433.68 square miles, a water area of 0.89 square miles, and is located in the Eastern Time Zone. The county was founded in 1835. County seat is Winamac.

Weather Station: Winamac 2 SSE   Elevation: 688 feet

	Jan	Feb	Mar	Apr	May	Jun	Jul	Aug	Sep	Oct	Nov	Dec
High	31	36	48	61	72	80	84	81	75	63	49	37
Low	14	18	28	39	50	59	63	61	53	42	32	21
Precip	1.9	1.6	2.8	3.7	3.8	4.1	3.9	3.8	3.4	3.0	3.1	2.5
Snow	8.5	5.3	3.2	1.2	tr	0.0	0.0	0.0	0.0	0.1	2.1	5.4

High and Low temperatures in degrees Fahrenheit; Precipitation and Snow in inches

Population: 12,643 (1990); 13,755 (2000); 13,677 (2010); 13,539 (2015 projected); Race: 96.5% White, 1.4% Black, 0.5% Asian, 1.7% Other, 1.9% Hispanic of any race (2010); Density: 31.5 persons per square mile (2010); Average household size: 2.56 (2010); Median age: 39.2 (2010); Males per 100 females: 101.5 (2010).
Religion: Five largest groups: 17.9% Catholic Church, 5.6% The United Methodist Church, 5.5% Christian Churches and Churches of Christ, 4.3%

Christian Church (Disciples of Christ), 3.5% Lutheran Church—Missouri Synod (2000).
Economy: Unemployment rate: 8.4% (5/2010); Total civilian labor force: 7,128 (5/2010); Leading industries: 34.6% manufacturing; 17.4% health care and social assistance; 12.6% retail trade (2008); Farms: 552 totaling 232,240 acres (2007); Companies that employ 500 or more persons: 1 (2008); Companies that employ 100 to 499 persons: 4 (2008); Companies that employ less than 100 persons: 343 (2008); Black-owned businesses: n/a (2002); Hispanic-owned businesses: n/a (2002); Asian-owned businesses: n/a (2002); Women-owned businesses: 212 (2002); Retail sales per capita: $8,298 (2010). Single-family building permits issued: 18 (2009); Multi-family building permits issued: 0 (2009).
Income: Per capita income: $21,056 (2010); Median household income: $43,159 (2010); Average household income: $54,150 (2010); Percent of households with income of $100,000 or more: 10.2% (2010); Poverty rate: 12.9% (2008); Bankruptcy rate: 6.06% (2009).
Taxes: Total county taxes per capita: $454 (2007); County property taxes per capita: $218 (2007).
Education: Percent of population age 25 and over with: High school diploma (including GED) or higher: 84.7% (2010); Bachelor's degree or higher: 10.8% (2010); Master's degree or higher: 3.2% (2010).
Housing: Homeownership rate: 79.5% (2010); Median home value: $95,103 (2010); Median contract rent: $n/a per month (2006-2008 3-year est.); Median year structure built: n/a (2006-2008 3-year est.)
Health: Birth rate: 121.2 per 10,000 population (2009); Death rate: 119.0 per 10,000 population (2009); Age-adjusted cancer mortality rate: 213.9 deaths per 100,000 population (2006); Number of physicians: 5.1 per 10,000 population (2007); Hospital beds: 18.1 per 10,000 population (2006); Hospital admissions: 558.3 per 10,000 population (2006).
Elections: 2008 Presidential election results: 41.3% Obama, 56.8% McCain, 0.1% Nader
National and State Parks: Winamac State Fish and Wildlife Area
Additional Information Contacts
Pulaski County Government . . . . (574) 946-3313
    http://www.pulaskionline.org

Pulaski County Communities

FRANCESVILLE (town). Covers a land area of 0.306 square miles and a water area of 0 square miles. Located at 40.98° N. Lat; 86.88° W. Long. Elevation is 679 feet.
Population: 897 (1990); 905 (2000); 897 (2010); 885 (2015 projected); Race: 98.2% White, 0.1% Black, 0.1% Asian, 1.6% Other, 1.8% Hispanic of any race (2010); Density: 2,928.6 persons per square mile (2010); Average household size: 2.65 (2010); Median age: 39.2 (2010); Males per 100 females: 98.5 (2010); Marriage status: 21.3% never married, 59.0% now married, 8.9% widowed, 10.7% divorced (2000); Foreign born: 0.1% (2000); Ancestry (includes multiple ancestries): 36.5% German, 16.0% Irish, 11.8% Other groups, 7.9% United States or American, 7.2% French (except Basque) (2000).
Economy: Single-family building permits issued: 0 (2009); Multi-family building permits issued: 0 (2009); Employment by occupation: 8.1% management, 13.8% professional, 13.1% services, 21.8% sales, 3.5% farming, 8.7% construction, 31.0% production (2000).
Income: Per capita income: $21,560 (2010); Median household income: $51,197 (2010); Average household income: $57,409 (2010); Percent of households with income of $100,000 or more: 8.5% (2010); Poverty rate: 4.2% (2000).
Taxes: Total city taxes per capita: $111 (2007); City property taxes per capita: $96 (2007).
Education: Percent of population age 25 and over with: High school diploma (including GED) or higher: 87.8% (2010); Bachelor's degree or higher: 11.5% (2010); Master's degree or higher: 5.1% (2010).

School District(s)
West Central School Corp (KG-12)
    2008-09 Enrollment: 894 . . . . (219) 567-9161
Housing: Homeownership rate: 80.5% (2010); Median home value: $107,530 (2010); Median contract rent: $319 per month (2000); Median year structure built: 1944 (2000).
Newspapers: Francesville Tribune (Community news; Circulation 900)
Transportation: Commute to work: 91.5% car, 0.4% public transportation, 4.0% walk, 2.7% work from home (2000); Travel time to work: 44.2% less than 15 minutes, 22.0% 15 to 30 minutes, 20.1% 30 to 45 minutes, 5.5% 45 to 60 minutes, 8.2% 60 minutes or more (2000)

MEDARYVILLE (town). Covers a land area of 0.456 square miles and a water area of 0 square miles. Located at 41.08° N. Lat; 86.88° W. Long. Elevation is 689 feet.
Population: 689 (1990); 565 (2000); 571 (2010); 568 (2015 projected); Race: 88.8% White, 8.2% Black, 0.0% Asian, 3.0% Other, 4.0% Hispanic of any race (2010); Density: 1,253.6 persons per square mile (2010); Average household size: 2.63 (2010); Median age: 36.3 (2010); Males per 100 females: 122.2 (2010); Marriage status: 18.7% never married, 60.4% now married, 8.1% widowed, 12.8% divorced (2000); Foreign born: 0.5% (2000); Ancestry (includes multiple ancestries): 31.2% German, 12.1% Irish, 9.5% United States or American, 8.5% Other groups, 6.9% English (2000).
Economy: Employment by occupation: 4.6% management, 3.1% professional, 11.6% services, 15.4% sales, 3.1% farming, 10.0% construction, 52.1% production (2000).
Income: Per capita income: $15,658 (2010); Median household income: $39,464 (2010); Average household income: $42,578 (2010); Percent of households with income of $100,000 or more: 4.7% (2010); Poverty rate: 4.9% (2000).
Taxes: Total city taxes per capita: $240 (2007); City property taxes per capita: $205 (2007).
Education: Percent of population age 25 and over with: High school diploma (including GED) or higher: 81.8% (2010); Bachelor's degree or higher: 3.0% (2010); Master's degree or higher: 1.3% (2010).
Housing: Homeownership rate: 87.0% (2010); Median home value: $79,259 (2010); Median contract rent: $360 per month (2000); Median year structure built: 1947 (2000).
Transportation: Commute to work: 86.3% car, 0.0% public transportation, 8.2% walk, 2.3% work from home (2000); Travel time to work: 28.4% less than 15 minutes, 30.8% 15 to 30 minutes, 17.6% 30 to 45 minutes, 5.6% 45 to 60 minutes, 17.6% 60 minutes or more (2000)

MONTEREY (town). Covers a land area of 0.171 square miles and a water area of 0 square miles. Located at 41.15° N. Lat; 86.48° W. Long. Elevation is 722 feet.
History: Laid out 1849.
Population: 230 (1990); 231 (2000); 220 (2010); 213 (2015 projected); Race: 91.8% White, 3.2% Black, 2.3% Asian, 2.7% Other, 2.7% Hispanic of any race (2010); Density: 1,289.0 persons per square mile (2010); Average household size: 2.64 (2010); Median age: 37.8 (2010); Males per 100 females: 103.7 (2010); Marriage status: 19.3% never married, 61.3% now married, 6.6% widowed, 12.7% divorced (2000); Foreign born: 0.0% (2000); Ancestry (includes multiple ancestries): 34.6% German, 12.3% Irish, 10.3% United States or American, 7.0% Polish, 6.6% Other groups (2000).
Economy: Employment by occupation: 18.3% management, 8.3% professional, 23.9% services, 18.3% sales, 4.6% farming, 11.0% construction, 15.6% production (2000).
Income: Per capita income: $23,349 (2010); Median household income: $39,375 (2010); Average household income: $60,934 (2010); Percent of households with income of $100,000 or more: 14.5% (2010); Poverty rate: 14.5% (2000).
Taxes: Total city taxes per capita: $128 (2007); City property taxes per capita: $110 (2007).
Education: Percent of population age 25 and over with: High school diploma (including GED) or higher: 85.5% (2010); Bachelor's degree or higher: 8.6% (2010); Master's degree or higher: 2.0% (2010).
School District(s)
Culver Community Schools Corp (PK-12)
    2008-09 Enrollment: 1,076 . . . . (574) 842-3364
Housing: Homeownership rate: 81.9% (2010); Median home value: $83,333 (2010); Median contract rent: $310 per month (2000); Median year structure built: before 1940 (2000).
Transportation: Commute to work: 88.1% car, 0.0% public transportation, 9.2% walk, 2.8% work from home (2000); Travel time to work: 33.0% less than 15 minutes, 33.0% 15 to 30 minutes, 18.9% 30 to 45 minutes, 7.5% 45 to 60 minutes, 7.5% 60 minutes or more (2000)

STAR CITY (CDP). Covers a land area of 1.056 square miles and a water area of 0 square miles. Located at 40.97° N. Lat; 86.55° W. Long. Elevation is 719 feet.
History: Laid out 1859.
Population: 350 (1990); 377 (2000); 355 (2010); 343 (2015 projected); Race: 99.2% White, 0.0% Black, 0.0% Asian, 0.8% Other, 0.8% Hispanic

of any race (2010); Density: 336.2 persons per square mile (2010); Average household size: 2.73 (2010); Median age: 38.5 (2010); Males per 100 females: 95.1 (2010); Marriage status: 20.4% never married, 73.4% now married, 0.0% widowed, 6.2% divorced (2000); Foreign born: 0.0% (2000); Ancestry (includes multiple ancestries): 33.1% German, 18.3% Irish, 15.1% English, 8.1% United States or American, 3.8% French (except Basque) (2000).
Economy: Employment by occupation: 0.0% management, 8.3% professional, 17.6% services, 9.8% sales, 6.4% farming, 13.7% construction, 44.1% production (2000).
Income: Per capita income: $19,100 (2010); Median household income: $44,615 (2010); Average household income: $52,865 (2010); Percent of households with income of $100,000 or more: 10.0% (2010); Poverty rate: 0.0% (2000).
Education: Percent of population age 25 and over with: High school diploma (including GED) or higher: 89.3% (2010); Bachelor's degree or higher: 9.1% (2010); Master's degree or higher: 4.1% (2010).
Housing: Homeownership rate: 82.3% (2010); Median home value: $82,727 (2010); Median contract rent: $272 per month (2000); Median year structure built: before 1940 (2000).
Transportation: Commute to work: 95.1% car, 0.0% public transportation, 0.0% walk, 4.9% work from home (2000); Travel time to work: 52.6% less than 15 minutes, 21.6% 15 to 30 minutes, 22.7% 30 to 45 minutes, 0.0% 45 to 60 minutes, 3.1% 60 minutes or more (2000)

WINAMAC (town). County seat. Covers a land area of 1.291 square miles and a water area of 0 square miles. Located at 41.05° N. Lat; 86.60° W. Long. Elevation is 709 feet.
History: Winamac was founded in 1835 along the Tippecanoe River, and was named for Potawatomi Chief Winamac.
Population: 2,262 (1990); 2,418 (2000); 2,371 (2010); 2,327 (2015 projected); Race: 96.5% White, 1.4% Black, 0.3% Asian, 1.8% Other, 1.8% Hispanic of any race (2010); Density: 1,836.1 persons per square mile (2010); Average household size: 2.27 (2010); Median age: 42.2 (2010); Males per 100 females: 92.3 (2010); Marriage status: 21.6% never married, 48.0% now married, 15.0% widowed, 15.4% divorced (2000); Foreign born: 1.5% (2000); Ancestry (includes multiple ancestries): 33.5% German, 12.1% Irish, 9.4% United States or American, 9.2% English, 7.8% Other groups (2000).
Economy: Single-family building permits issued: 0 (2009); Multi-family building permits issued: 0 (2009); Employment by occupation: 10.3% management, 15.7% professional, 13.3% services, 21.0% sales, 0.6% farming, 8.0% construction, 31.1% production (2000).
Income: Per capita income: $22,615 (2010); Median household income: $40,963 (2010); Average household income: $52,449 (2010); Percent of households with income of $100,000 or more: 10.2% (2010); Poverty rate: 8.2% (2000).
Taxes: Total city taxes per capita: $135 (2007); City property taxes per capita: $118 (2007).
Education: Percent of population age 25 and over with: High school diploma (including GED) or higher: 84.3% (2010); Bachelor's degree or higher: 16.1% (2010); Master's degree or higher: 4.3% (2010).
School District(s)
Eastern Pulaski Com Sch Corp (PK-12)
    2008-09 Enrollment: 1,277 . . . . (574) 946-4010
Housing: Homeownership rate: 70.5% (2010); Median home value: $86,408 (2010); Median contract rent: $319 per month (2000); Median year structure built: 1953 (2000).
Hospitals: Pulaski Memorial Hospital (29 beds)
Newspapers: The Independent (Local news; Circulation 10,300); Pulaski County Journal (Community news; Circulation 3,600)
Transportation: Commute to work: 95.9% car, 0.0% public transportation, 2.9% walk, 1.3% work from home (2000); Travel time to work: 63.1% less than 15 minutes, 17.9% 15 to 30 minutes, 12.3% 30 to 45 minutes, 2.4% 45 to 60 minutes, 4.3% 60 minutes or more (2000)

Putnam County

Located in central Indiana; drained by the Eel River. Covers a land area of 480.31 square miles, a water area of 2.27 square miles, and is located in the Eastern Time Zone. The county was founded in 1821. County seat is Greencastle.

Putnam County is part of the Indianapolis-Carmel, IN Metropolitan Statistical Area. The entire metro area includes: Boone County, IN; Brown

County, IN; Hamilton County, IN; Hancock County, IN; Hendricks County, IN; Johnson County, IN; Marion County, IN; Morgan County, IN; Putnam County, IN; Shelby County, IN

Weather Station: Greencastle 1 SE   Elevation: 859 feet

	Jan	Feb	Mar	Apr	May	Jun	Jul	Aug	Sep	Oct	Nov	Dec
High	34	40	51	63	74	82	86	84	78	66	52	39
Low	17	22	31	42	52	61	65	63	56	44	34	24
Precip	2.4	2.5	3.7	3.8	4.7	4.2	5.2	4.2	3.2	3.1	3.9	3.1
Snow	9.3	6.5	3.6	0.5	tr	0.0	0.0	0.0	0.0	0.2	1.5	5.7

High and Low temperatures in degrees Fahrenheit; Precipitation and Snow in inches

Population: 30,315 (1990); 36,019 (2000); 37,333 (2010); 37,693 (2015 projected); Race: 93.6% White, 3.5% Black, 0.8% Asian, 2.1% Other, 1.5% Hispanic of any race (2010); Density: 77.7 persons per square mile (2010); Average household size: 2.52 (2010); Median age: 36.2 (2010); Males per 100 females: 111.8 (2010).

Religion: Five largest groups: 5.7% Christian Church (Disciples of Christ), 5.4% Christian Churches and Churches of Christ, 4.3% The United Methodist Church, 4.1% American Baptist Churches in the USA, 2.9% Catholic Church (2000).

Economy: Unemployment rate: 9.5% (5/2010); Total civilian labor force: 16,951 (5/2010); Leading industries: 22.2% manufacturing; 14.9% health care and social assistance; 10.1% retail trade (2008); Farms: 843 totaling 168,446 acres (2007); Companies that employ 500 or more persons: 4 (2008); Companies that employ 100 to 499 persons: 10 (2008); Companies that employ less than 100 persons: 704 (2008); Black-owned businesses: n/a (2002); Hispanic-owned businesses: n/a (2002); Asian-owned businesses: n/a (2002); Women-owned businesses: 701 (2002); Retail sales per capita: $5,984 (2010). Single-family building permits issued: 42 (2009); Multi-family building permits issued: 0 (2009).

Income: Per capita income: $21,032 (2010); Median household income: $47,279 (2010); Average household income: $57,605 (2010); Percent of households with income of $100,000 or more: 12.6% (2010); Poverty rate: 11.7% (2008); Bankruptcy rate: 8.62% (2009).

Taxes: Total county taxes per capita: $223 (2007); County property taxes per capita: $117 (2007).

Education: Percent of population age 25 and over with: High school diploma (including GED) or higher: 84.8% (2010); Bachelor's degree or higher: 16.1% (2010); Master's degree or higher: 6.6% (2010).

Housing: Homeownership rate: 75.5% (2010); Median home value: $112,897 (2010); Median contract rent: $494 per month (2006-2008 3-year est.); Median year structure built: 1969 (2006-2008 3-year est.)

Health: Birth rate: 114.8 per 10,000 population (2009); Death rate: 85.5 per 10,000 population (2009); Age-adjusted cancer mortality rate: 200.8 deaths per 100,000 population (2006); Number of physicians: 5.7 per 10,000 population (2007); Hospital beds: 6.8 per 10,000 population (2006); Hospital admissions: 463.8 per 10,000 population (2006).

Elections: 2008 Presidential election results: 43.2% Obama, 55.2% McCain, 0.0% Nader

National and State Parks: Owen-Putnam State Forest; Richard Lieber State Park

Additional Information Contacts
Putnam County Government . . . . (765) 653-2648
   http://www.co.putnam.in.us
City of Greencastle . . . . (765) 653-3100
   http://www.gogreencastle.com
Cloverdale Chamber of Commerce . . . . (765) 795-3993
   http://www.cloverdale.in.us/Chamber/index.htm
Greater Greencastle Chamber of Commerce . . . . (765) 653-4517
   http://www.gogreencastle.com
Town of Cloverdale . . . . (765) 795-6033
   http://www.cloverdale.in.us

Putnam County Communities

BAINBRIDGE (town). Covers a land area of 0.378 square miles and a water area of 0 square miles. Located at 39.76° N. Lat; 86.81° W. Long. Elevation is 925 feet.

Population: 682 (1990); 743 (2000); 706 (2010); 681 (2015 projected); Race: 98.2% White, 0.3% Black, 0.4% Asian, 1.1% Other, 0.7% Hispanic of any race (2010); Density: 1,867.0 persons per square mile (2010); Average household size: 2.56 (2010); Median age: 37.6 (2010); Males per 100 females: 97.8 (2010); Marriage status: 21.0% never married, 62.5% now married, 4.2% widowed, 12.3% divorced (2000); Foreign born: 1.5% (2000); Ancestry (includes multiple ancestries): 21.5% German, 20.1%

United States or American, 12.5% English, 12.0% Irish, 9.4% Other groups (2000).

Economy: Employment by occupation: 10.3% management, 8.1% professional, 14.1% services, 21.4% sales, 0.5% farming, 16.3% construction, 29.3% production (2000).

Income: Per capita income: $20,157 (2010); Median household income: $46,042 (2010); Average household income: $51,576 (2010); Percent of households with income of $100,000 or more: 5.4% (2010); Poverty rate: 5.5% (2000).

Taxes: Total city taxes per capita: $165 (2007); City property taxes per capita: $144 (2007).

Education: Percent of population age 25 and over with: High school diploma (including GED) or higher: 87.2% (2010); Bachelor's degree or higher: 12.4% (2010); Master's degree or higher: 3.6% (2010).

School District(s)
North Putnam Community Schools (PK-12)
   2008-09 Enrollment: 1,856 . . . . (765) 522-6218

Housing: Homeownership rate: 74.3% (2010); Median home value: $100,385 (2010); Median contract rent: $414 per month (2000); Median year structure built: 1954 (2000).

Transportation: Commute to work: 96.3% car, 0.8% public transportation, 1.1% walk, 1.1% work from home (2000); Travel time to work: 14.6% less than 15 minutes, 27.8% 15 to 30 minutes, 21.8% 30 to 45 minutes, 20.6% 45 to 60 minutes, 15.2% 60 minutes or more (2000)

CLOVERDALE (town). Covers a land area of 3.481 square miles and a water area of 0.065 square miles. Located at 39.51° N. Lat; 86.80° W. Long. Elevation is 814 feet.

Population: 1,710 (1990); 2,243 (2000); 2,201 (2010); 2,170 (2015 projected); Race: 97.0% White, 0.5% Black, 0.1% Asian, 2.3% Other, 1.1% Hispanic of any race (2010); Density: 632.3 persons per square mile (2010); Average household size: 2.54 (2010); Median age: 38.2 (2010); Males per 100 females: 97.4 (2010); Marriage status: 22.8% never married, 57.0% now married, 7.6% widowed, 12.6% divorced (2000); Foreign born: 1.0% (2000); Ancestry (includes multiple ancestries): 21.2% German, 16.3% United States or American, 11.6% Irish, 7.8% English, 6.7% Other groups (2000).

Economy: Single-family building permits issued: 0 (2009); Multi-family building permits issued: 0 (2009); Employment by occupation: 7.2% management, 8.0% professional, 22.0% services, 25.5% sales, 0.0% farming, 13.6% construction, 23.6% production (2000).

Income: Per capita income: $20,872 (2010); Median household income: $45,739 (2010); Average household income: $53,444 (2010); Percent of households with income of $100,000 or more: 8.9% (2010); Poverty rate: 7.4% (2000).

Taxes: Total city taxes per capita: $154 (2007); City property taxes per capita: $118 (2007).

Education: Percent of population age 25 and over with: High school diploma (including GED) or higher: 83.2% (2010); Bachelor's degree or higher: 10.6% (2010); Master's degree or higher: 5.7% (2010).

School District(s)
Cloverdale Community Schools (PK-12)
   2008-09 Enrollment: 1,400 . . . . (765) 795-4664

Housing: Homeownership rate: 72.3% (2010); Median home value: $91,081 (2010); Median contract rent: $376 per month (2000); Median year structure built: 1979 (2000).

Newspapers: Hoosier Topics (Community news; Circulation 17,500)

Transportation: Commute to work: 92.3% car, 0.5% public transportation, 2.0% walk, 4.9% work from home (2000); Travel time to work: 28.0% less than 15 minutes, 31.6% 15 to 30 minutes, 16.5% 30 to 45 minutes, 13.3% 45 to 60 minutes, 10.7% 60 minutes or more (2000)

Additional Information Contacts
Cloverdale Chamber of Commerce . . . . (765) 795-3993
   http://www.cloverdale.in.us/Chamber/index.htm
Town of Cloverdale . . . . (765) 795-6033
   http://www.cloverdale.in.us

FILLMORE (town). Covers a land area of 1.903 square miles and a water area of 0 square miles. Located at 39.67° N. Lat; 86.75° W. Long. Elevation is 846 feet.

History: Laid out 1837.

Population: 497 (1990); 545 (2000); 517 (2010); 501 (2015 projected); Race: 97.1% White, 0.6% Black, 0.2% Asian, 2.1% Other, 1.7% Hispanic of any race (2010); Density: 271.7 persons per square mile (2010); Average household size: 2.65 (2010); Median age: 37.6 (2010); Males per

100 females: 98.1 (2010); Marriage status: 16.3% never married, 72.2% now married, 4.6% widowed, 6.8% divorced (2000); Foreign born: 0.0% (2000); Ancestry (includes multiple ancestries): 19.0% United States or American, 12.0% Irish, 11.6% German, 9.3% Other groups, 3.4% French (except Basque) (2000).

Economy: Employment by occupation: 5.3% management, 8.2% professional, 27.5% services, 16.8% sales, 0.8% farming, 15.6% construction, 25.8% production (2000).

Income: Per capita income: $20,678 (2010); Median household income: $39,500 (2010); Average household income: $54,192 (2010); Percent of households with income of $100,000 or more: 8.2% (2010); Poverty rate: 8.0% (2000).

Taxes: Total city taxes per capita: $45 (2007); City property taxes per capita: $37 (2007).

Education: Percent of population age 25 and over with: High school diploma (including GED) or higher: 83.2% (2010); Bachelor's degree or higher: 6.4% (2010); Master's degree or higher: 2.1% (2010).

School District(s)
South Putnam Community Schools (PK-12)
    2008-09 Enrollment: 1,301 . . . . (765) 653-3119

Housing: Homeownership rate: 84.1% (2010); Median home value: $113,000 (2010); Median contract rent: $375 per month (2000); Median year structure built: 1951 (2000).

Transportation: Commute to work: 97.1% car, 0.0% public transportation, 0.0% walk, 2.1% work from home (2000); Travel time to work: 21.5% less than 15 minutes, 35.2% 15 to 30 minutes, 21.5% 30 to 45 minutes, 14.6% 45 to 60 minutes, 7.3% 60 minutes or more (2000)

GREENCASTLE (city). County seat. Covers a land area of 5.299 square miles and a water area of 0.047 square miles. Located at 39.64° N. Lat; 86.85° W. Long. Elevation is 853 feet.

History: Indiana Asbury University, which later became DePauw University, was founded in 1837 in Greencastle by the Methodist Episcopal Church.

Population: 9,208 (1990); 9,880 (2000); 10,203 (2010); 10,313 (2015 projected); Race: 92.7% White, 2.8% Black, 2.1% Asian, 2.5% Other, 1.7% Hispanic of any race (2010); Density: 1,925.6 persons per square mile (2010); Average household size: 2.28 (2010); Median age: 28.9 (2010); Males per 100 females: 91.5 (2010); Marriage status: 30.3% never married, 51.3% now married, 9.2% widowed, 9.3% divorced (2000); Foreign born: 2.2% (2000); Ancestry (includes multiple ancestries): 20.5% German, 13.3% United States or American, 12.2% Irish, 12.1% Other groups, 10.2% English (2000).

Economy: Single-family building permits issued: 9 (2009); Multi-family building permits issued: 0 (2009); Employment by occupation: 5.9% management, 20.6% professional, 17.1% services, 25.0% sales, 0.0% farming, 6.7% construction, 24.8% production (2000).

Income: Per capita income: $18,827 (2010); Median household income: $39,091 (2010); Average household income: $52,727 (2010); Percent of households with income of $100,000 or more: 10.6% (2010); Poverty rate: 9.8% (2000).

Taxes: Total city taxes per capita: $301 (2007); City property taxes per capita: $176 (2007).

Education: Percent of population age 25 and over with: High school diploma (including GED) or higher: 86.0% (2010); Bachelor's degree or higher: 25.3% (2010); Master's degree or higher: 9.1% (2010).

School District(s)
Area 30 Career Center Edu Inter (09-12)
    2008-09 Enrollment: n/a . . . . (765) 653-3515
Greencastle Community Sch Corp (PK-12)
    2008-09 Enrollment: 2,056 . . . . (765) 653-9771
South Putnam Community Schools (PK-12)
    2008-09 Enrollment: 1,301 . . . . (765) 653-3119

Four-year College(s)
DePauw University (Private, Not-for-profit, United Methodist)
    Fall 2008 Enrollment: 2,298. (765) 658-4800
    2009-10 Tuition: In-state $33,250; Out-of-state $33,250

Housing: Homeownership rate: 55.7% (2010); Median home value: $97,809 (2010); Median contract rent: $377 per month (2000); Median year structure built: 1959 (2000).

Hospitals: Putnam County Hospital (85 beds)

Newspapers: Greencastle Indiana Banner-Graphic (Local news; Circulation 5,580)

Transportation: Commute to work: 80.9% car, 0.0% public transportation, 16.6% walk, 0.9% work from home (2000); Travel time to work: 71.8% less

than 15 minutes, 12.0% 15 to 30 minutes, 6.0% 30 to 45 minutes, 3.4% 45 to 60 minutes, 6.7% 60 minutes or more (2000)

Additional Information Contacts
City of Greencastle . . . . (765) 653-3100
    http://www.gogreencastle.com
Greater Greencastle Chamber of Commerce . . . . (765) 653-4517
    http://www.gogreencastle.com

REELSVILLE (unincorporated postal area, zip code 46171). Covers a land area of 38.867 square miles and a water area of 0.073 square miles. Located at 39.52° N. Lat; 86.96° W. Long. Elevation is 676 feet.

Population: 1,679 (2000); Race: 98.3% White, 1.1% Black, 0.0% Asian, 0.6% Other, 0.0% Hispanic of any race (2000); Density: 43.2 persons per square mile (2000); Age: 27.5% under 18, 15.6% over 64 (2000); Marriage status: 15.7% never married, 68.9% now married, 7.1% widowed, 8.2% divorced (2000); Foreign born: 0.0% (2000); Ancestry (includes multiple ancestries): 22.5% German, 17.3% Other groups, 11.0% Irish, 9.3% English, 5.7% United States or American (2000).

Economy: Employment by occupation: 15.6% management, 11.4% professional, 11.9% services, 18.7% sales, 0.9% farming, 15.6% construction, 26.1% production (2000).

Income: Per capita income: $16,740 (2000); Median household income: $40,847 (2000); Poverty rate: 8.1% (2000).

Education: Percent of population age 25 and over with: High school diploma (including GED) or higher: 75.6% (2000); Bachelor's degree or higher: 9.8% (2000).

School District(s)
South Putnam Community Schools (PK-12)
    2008-09 Enrollment: 1,301 . . . . (765) 653-3119

Housing: Homeownership rate: 93.8% (2000); Median home value: $84,700 (2000); Median contract rent: $275 per month (2000); Median year structure built: 1968 (2000).

Transportation: Commute to work: 92.4% car, 0.0% public transportation, 0.6% walk, 4.0% work from home (2000); Travel time to work: 15.2% less than 15 minutes, 33.4% 15 to 30 minutes, 16.6% 30 to 45 minutes, 12.6% 45 to 60 minutes, 22.1% 60 minutes or more (2000)

ROACHDALE (town). Covers a land area of 0.510 square miles and a water area of 0 square miles. Located at 39.85° N. Lat; 86.80° W. Long. Elevation is 840 feet.

History: Laid out 1879.

Population: 909 (1990); 975 (2000); 887 (2010); 849 (2015 projected); Race: 98.8% White, 0.3% Black, 0.0% Asian, 0.9% Other, 0.0% Hispanic of any race (2010); Density: 1,737.8 persons per square mile (2010); Average household size: 2.56 (2010); Median age: 36.8 (2010); Males per 100 females: 97.6 (2010); Marriage status: 19.0% never married, 60.0% now married, 9.1% widowed, 11.9% divorced (2000); Foreign born: 0.0% (2000); Ancestry (includes multiple ancestries): 16.7% United States or American, 12.6% Irish, 11.0% German, 9.9% English, 7.0% Other groups (2000).

Economy: Single-family building permits issued: 0 (2009); Multi-family building permits issued: 0 (2009); Employment by occupation: 7.1% management, 9.1% professional, 16.4% services, 21.3% sales, 0.0% farming, 13.3% construction, 32.7% production (2000).

Income: Per capita income: $22,174 (2010); Median household income: $49,043 (2010); Average household income: $57,153 (2010); Percent of households with income of $100,000 or more: 15.0% (2010); Poverty rate: 12.6% (2000).

Taxes: Total city taxes per capita: $173 (2007); City property taxes per capita: $166 (2007).

Education: Percent of population age 25 and over with: High school diploma (including GED) or higher: 80.4% (2010); Bachelor's degree or higher: 12.6% (2010); Master's degree or higher: 4.6% (2010).

School District(s)
North Putnam Community Schools (PK-12)
    2008-09 Enrollment: 1,856 . . . . (765) 522-6218

Housing: Homeownership rate: 74.3% (2010); Median home value: $97,206 (2010); Median contract rent: $316 per month (2000); Median year structure built: 1947 (2000).

Transportation: Commute to work: 92.6% car, 0.5% public transportation, 1.8% walk, 5.2% work from home (2000); Travel time to work: 27.1% less than 15 minutes, 24.9% 15 to 30 minutes, 26.1% 30 to 45 minutes, 10.7% 45 to 60 minutes, 11.2% 60 minutes or more (2000)

RUSSELLVILLE (town). Covers a land area of 0.199 square miles and a water area of 0 square miles. Located at 39.85° N. Lat; 86.98° W. Long. Elevation is 820 feet.

History: Laid out 1828.

Population: 336 (1990); 340 (2000); 325 (2010); 317 (2015 projected); Race: 97.5% White, 0.0% Black, 0.6% Asian, 1.8% Other, 2.5% Hispanic of any race (2010); Density: 1,637.1 persons per square mile (2010); Average household size: 2.56 (2010); Median age: 37.3 (2010); Males per 100 females: 101.9 (2010); Marriage status: 10.7% never married, 62.9% now married, 15.4% widowed, 11.0% divorced (2000); Foreign born: 0.0% (2000); Ancestry (includes multiple ancestries): 30.9% United States or American, 10.2% Irish, 8.8% German, 7.5% Other groups, 4.4% English (2000).

Economy: Employment by occupation: 5.8% management, 7.8% professional, 13.6% services, 18.2% sales, 1.3% farming, 16.2% construction, 37.0% production (2000).

Income: Per capita income: $17,834 (2010); Median household income: $40,114 (2010); Average household income: $46,417 (2010); Percent of households with income of $100,000 or more: 5.5% (2010); Poverty rate: 6.1% (2000).

Taxes: Total city taxes per capita: $61 (2007); City property taxes per capita: $61 (2007).

Education: Percent of population age 25 and over with: High school diploma (including GED) or higher: 81.3% (2010); Bachelor's degree or higher: 7.7% (2010); Master's degree or higher: 0.5% (2010).

Housing: Homeownership rate: 81.1% (2010); Median home value: $85,385 (2010); Median contract rent: $238 per month (2000); Median year structure built: before 1940 (2000).

Transportation: Commute to work: 97.4% car, 0.0% public transportation, 1.3% walk, 1.3% work from home (2000); Travel time to work: 19.3% less than 15 minutes, 43.3% 15 to 30 minutes, 17.3% 30 to 45 minutes, 12.0% 45 to 60 minutes, 8.0% 60 minutes or more (2000)

Randolph County

Located in eastern Indiana; bounded on the east by Ohio; drained by the Mississinewa and Whitewater Rivers and the West Fork of the White River; includes the highest point in Indiana (1,240 ft). Covers a land area of 452.83 square miles, a water area of 0.39 square miles, and is located in the Eastern Time Zone. The county was founded in 1818. County seat is Winchester.

Weather Station: Farmland 5 NNW   Elevation: 964 feet

	Jan	Feb	Mar	Apr	May	Jun	Jul	Aug	Sep	Oct	Nov	Dec
High	32	37	47	60	71	80	84	82	76	64	50	38
Low	15	18	27	38	49	59	62	59	52	40	32	22
Precip	1.9	1.8	2.7	3.5	4.0	4.4	4.4	3.6	2.9	2.7	3.2	2.6
Snow	8.1	6.2	4.0	0.7	tr	0.0	0.0	0.0	0.0	0.2	1.3	5.2

High and Low temperatures in degrees Fahrenheit; Precipitation and Snow in inches

Weather Station: Winchester Airport 3E   Elevation: 1,108 feet

	Jan	Feb	Mar	Apr	May	Jun	Jul	Aug	Sep	Oct	Nov	Dec
High	32	36	47	60	71	80	83	81	76	63	49	38
Low	16	19	29	39	50	60	63	61	54	43	33	23
Precip	1.8	1.6	2.9	3.7	4.1	4.3	4.3	3.5	2.7	2.7	3.2	2.8
Snow	5.1	4.9	2.7	0.3	tr	0.0	tr	0.0	0.0	tr	0.6	2.7

High and Low temperatures in degrees Fahrenheit; Precipitation and Snow in inches

Population: 27,148 (1990); 27,401 (2000); 25,618 (2010); 24,697 (2015 projected); Race: 96.7% White, 0.6% Black, 0.3% Asian, 2.4% Other, 2.3% Hispanic of any race (2010); Density: 56.6 persons per square mile (2010); Average household size: 2.43 (2010); Median age: 41.1 (2010); Males per 100 females: 96.2 (2010).

Religion: Five largest groups: 6.0% The United Methodist Church, 4.7% Christian Church (Disciples of Christ), 3.8% Catholic Church, 3.6% Friends (Quakers), 3.4% Church of the Nazarene (2000).

Economy: Unemployment rate: 11.0% (5/2010); Total civilian labor force: 12,961 (5/2010); Leading industries: 38.9% manufacturing; 12.3% retail trade; 11.7% health care and social assistance (2008); Farms: 784 totaling 231,784 acres (2007); Companies that employ 500 or more persons: 0 (2008); Companies that employ 100 to 499 persons: 8 (2008); Companies that employ less than 100 persons: 499 (2008); Black-owned businesses: n/a (2002); Hispanic-owned businesses: n/a (2002); Asian-owned businesses: n/a (2002); Women-owned businesses: 442 (2002); Retail

sales per capita: $8,265 (2010). Single-family building permits issued: 16 (2009); Multi-family building permits issued: 0 (2009).

Income: Per capita income: $20,682 (2010); Median household income: $41,628 (2010); Average household income: $50,299 (2010); Percent of households with income of $100,000 or more: 7.5% (2010); Poverty rate: 13.5% (2008); Bankruptcy rate: 6.93% (2009).

Taxes: Total county taxes per capita: $337 (2007); County property taxes per capita: $211 (2007).

Education: Percent of population age 25 and over with: High school diploma (including GED) or higher: 83.4% (2010); Bachelor's degree or higher: 9.1% (2010); Master's degree or higher: 4.4% (2010).

Housing: Homeownership rate: 78.2% (2010); Median home value: $77,602 (2010); Median contract rent: $383 per month (2006-2008 3-year est.); Median year structure built: 1950 (2006-2008 3-year est.)

Health: Birth rate: 116.4 per 10,000 population (2009); Death rate: 106.2 per 10,000 population (2009); Age-adjusted cancer mortality rate: 259.2 deaths per 100,000 population (2006); Number of physicians: 5.8 per 10,000 population (2007); Hospital beds: 9.6 per 10,000 population (2006); Hospital admissions: 419.3 per 10,000 population (2006).

Elections: 2008 Presidential election results: 44.8% Obama, 53.6% McCain, 0.0% Nader

Additional Information Contacts

Randolph County Government . . . . (800) 905-0514
    http://www.roamrandolph.org
City of Union City . . . . (765) 584-3266
    http://www.randolph-county.org
City of Winchester . . . . (765) 584-1056
    http://www.winchesterindiana.us

Randolph County Communities

FARMLAND (town). Covers a land area of 0.502 square miles and a water area of 0 square miles. Located at 40.18° N. Lat; 85.12° W. Long. Elevation is 1,037 feet.

History: Farmland was settled as a trading town for the surrounding farming area.

Population: 1,397 (1990); 1,456 (2000); 1,310 (2010); 1,248 (2015 projected); Race: 97.9% White, 0.0% Black, 0.0% Asian, 2.1% Other, 0.2% Hispanic of any race (2010); Density: 2,607.5 persons per square mile (2010); Average household size: 2.45 (2010); Median age: 39.0 (2010); Males per 100 females: 92.1 (2010); Marriage status: 19.1% never married, 62.9% now married, 7.8% widowed, 10.2% divorced (2000); Foreign born: 0.3% (2000); Ancestry (includes multiple ancestries): 16.4% German, 16.2% United States or American, 11.3% Irish, 10.9% English, 7.5% Other groups (2000).

Economy: Employment by occupation: 7.2% management, 13.4% professional, 15.8% services, 23.3% sales, 0.3% farming, 11.7% construction, 28.2% production (2000).

Income: Per capita income: $21,278 (2010); Median household income: $43,814 (2010); Average household income: $51,400 (2010); Percent of households with income of $100,000 or more: 7.1% (2010); Poverty rate: 6.5% (2000).

Taxes: Total city taxes per capita: $207 (2007); City property taxes per capita: $202 (2007).

Education: Percent of population age 25 and over with: High school diploma (including GED) or higher: 85.8% (2010); Bachelor's degree or higher: 8.7% (2010); Master's degree or higher: 3.8% (2010).

Housing: Homeownership rate: 81.8% (2010); Median home value: $72,750 (2010); Median contract rent: $280 per month (2000); Median year structure built: 1952 (2000).

Transportation: Commute to work: 92.3% car, 0.0% public transportation, 4.2% walk, 3.5% work from home (2000); Travel time to work: 22.0% less than 15 minutes, 36.9% 15 to 30 minutes, 29.1% 30 to 45 minutes, 3.7% 45 to 60 minutes, 8.3% 60 minutes or more (2000)

LOSANTVILLE (town). Aka Bronson. Covers a land area of 0.177 square miles and a water area of 0 square miles. Located at 40.02° N. Lat; 85.18° W. Long. Elevation is 1,132 feet.

History: Also called Bronson.

Population: 253 (1990); 280 (2000); 243 (2010); 226 (2015 projected); Race: 96.7% White, 0.4% Black, 0.0% Asian, 2.9% Other, 0.8% Hispanic of any race (2010); Density: 1,375.4 persons per square mile (2010); Average household size: 2.51 (2010); Median age: 42.1 (2010); Males per 100 females: 104.2 (2010); Marriage status: 12.9% never married, 68.2% now married, 7.5% widowed, 11.4% divorced (2000); Foreign born: 0.0%

(2000); Ancestry (includes multiple ancestries): 14.4% United States or American, 12.8% Irish, 7.0% English, 5.0% Other groups, 3.4% German (2000).

Economy: Employment by occupation: 5.3% management, 13.2% professional, 17.5% services, 23.7% sales, 2.6% farming, 19.3% construction, 18.4% production (2000).

Income: Per capita income: $21,574 (2010); Median household income: $47,500 (2010); Average household income: $56,598 (2010); Percent of households with income of $100,000 or more: 10.3% (2010); Poverty rate: 15.8% (2000).

Taxes: Total city taxes per capita: $109 (2007); City property taxes per capita: $101 (2007).

Education: Percent of population age 25 and over with: High school diploma (including GED) or higher: 82.9% (2010); Bachelor's degree or higher: 6.5% (2010); Master's degree or higher: 2.9% (2010).

Housing: Homeownership rate: 88.7% (2010); Median home value: $74,667 (2010); Median contract rent: $353 per month (2000); Median year structure built: before 1940 (2000).

Transportation: Commute to work: 92.2% car, 0.0% public transportation, 2.6% walk, 0.9% work from home (2000); Travel time to work: 23.5% less than 15 minutes, 27.0% 15 to 30 minutes, 39.1% 30 to 45 minutes, 5.2% 45 to 60 minutes, 5.2% 60 minutes or more (2000)

LYNN (town).

Covers a land area of 0.564 square miles and a water area of 0 square miles. Located at 40.04° N. Lat; 84.94° W. Long. Elevation is 1,181 feet.

History: Lynn was established in 1847. The arrival of the railroad in 1852 brought a period of prosperity.

Population: 1,205 (1990); 1,143 (2000); 994 (2010); 929 (2015 projected); Race: 96.0% White, 0.3% Black, 0.7% Asian, 3.0% Other, 0.4% Hispanic of any race (2010); Density: 1,763.0 persons per square mile (2010); Average household size: 2.42 (2010); Median age: 39.2 (2010); Males per 100 females: 96.1 (2010); Marriage status: 21.3% never married, 57.9% now married, 8.9% widowed, 11.9% divorced (2000); Foreign born: 0.0% (2000); Ancestry (includes multiple ancestries): 15.7% United States or American, 15.4% German, 12.0% English, 9.7% Irish, 9.1% Other groups (2000).

Economy: Employment by occupation: 5.4% management, 12.0% professional, 16.6% services, 18.3% sales, 0.6% farming, 8.3% construction, 38.8% production (2000).

Income: Per capita income: $21,269 (2010); Median household income: $43,438 (2010); Average household income: $50,976 (2010); Percent of households with income of $100,000 or more: 9.3% (2010); Poverty rate: 10.2% (2000).

Taxes: Total city taxes per capita: $167 (2007); City property taxes per capita: $132 (2007).

Education: Percent of population age 25 and over with: High school diploma (including GED) or higher: 83.4% (2010); Bachelor's degree or higher: 6.1% (2010); Master's degree or higher: 3.0% (2010).

School District(s)

Randolph Southern School Corp (KG-12)
    2008-09 Enrollment: 603 . . . . (765) 874-1181

Housing: Homeownership rate: 78.5% (2010); Median home value: $80,541 (2010); Median contract rent: $290 per month (2000); Median year structure built: 1943 (2000).

Transportation: Commute to work: 90.5% car, 0.0% public transportation, 6.9% walk, 2.2% work from home (2000); Travel time to work: 36.0% less than 15 minutes, 35.0% 15 to 30 minutes, 22.5% 30 to 45 minutes, 1.3% 45 to 60 minutes, 5.1% 60 minutes or more (2000)

MODOC (town).

Covers a land area of 0.118 square miles and a water area of 0 square miles. Located at 40.04° N. Lat; 85.12° W. Long. Elevation is 1,175 feet.

Population: 218 (1990); 225 (2000); 197 (2010); 183 (2015 projected); Race: 97.0% White, 0.0% Black, 0.0% Asian, 3.0% Other, 1.0% Hispanic of any race (2010); Density: 1,670.6 persons per square mile (2010); Average household size: 2.53 (2010); Median age: 43.6 (2010); Males per 100 females: 105.2 (2010); Marriage status: 17.9% never married, 59.3% now married, 9.3% widowed, 13.6% divorced (2000); Foreign born: 0.0% (2000); Ancestry (includes multiple ancestries): 18.6% United States or American, 9.5% Irish, 6.0% German, 6.0% Scotch-Irish, 2.5% British (2000).

Economy: Employment by occupation: 6.0% management, 6.0% professional, 14.5% services, 18.1% sales, 0.0% farming, 9.6% construction, 45.8% production (2000).

Income: Per capita income: $21,574 (2010); Median household income: $47,188 (2010); Average household income: $53,301 (2010); Percent of households with income of $100,000 or more: 9.0% (2010); Poverty rate: 14.6% (2000).

Taxes: Total city taxes per capita: $132 (2007); City property taxes per capita: $132 (2007).

Education: Percent of population age 25 and over with: High school diploma (including GED) or higher: 81.9% (2010); Bachelor's degree or higher: 4.9% (2010); Master's degree or higher: 2.1% (2010).

School District(s)

Union School Corporation (KG-12)
    2008-09 Enrollment: 448 . . . . (765) 853-5464

Housing: Homeownership rate: 88.5% (2010); Median home value: $72,500 (2010); Median contract rent: $242 per month (2000); Median year structure built: before 1940 (2000).

Transportation: Commute to work: 90.4% car, 0.0% public transportation, 6.0% walk, 3.6% work from home (2000); Travel time to work: 13.8% less than 15 minutes, 37.5% 15 to 30 minutes, 23.8% 30 to 45 minutes, 13.8% 45 to 60 minutes, 11.3% 60 minutes or more (2000)

PARKER CITY (town).

Covers a land area of 0.579 square miles and a water area of 0 square miles. Located at 40.19° N. Lat; 85.20° W. Long. Elevation is 1,040 feet.

History: Parker City was settled as a center for trading for the nearby farming communities.

Population: 1,323 (1990); 1,416 (2000); 1,279 (2010); 1,211 (2015 projected); Race: 99.3% White, 0.1% Black, 0.1% Asian, 0.5% Other, 0.5% Hispanic of any race (2010); Density: 2,207.5 persons per square mile (2010); Average household size: 2.41 (2010); Median age: 43.5 (2010); Males per 100 females: 91.2 (2010); Marriage status: 17.9% never married, 60.9% now married, 7.8% widowed, 13.4% divorced (2000); Foreign born: 0.5% (2000); Ancestry (includes multiple ancestries): 19.7% United States or American, 17.4% German, 10.2% English, 8.4% Irish, 5.3% Other groups (2000).

Economy: Employment by occupation: 8.7% management, 15.5% professional, 19.4% services, 25.2% sales, 0.0% farming, 9.3% construction, 21.9% production (2000).

Income: Per capita income: $19,609 (2010); Median household income: $40,580 (2010); Average household income: $47,817 (2010); Percent of households with income of $100,000 or more: 7.6% (2010); Poverty rate: 12.8% (2000).

Taxes: Total city taxes per capita: $109 (2007); City property taxes per capita: $86 (2007).

Education: Percent of population age 25 and over with: High school diploma (including GED) or higher: 83.3% (2010); Bachelor's degree or higher: 11.8% (2010); Master's degree or higher: 6.4% (2010).

School District(s)

Monroe Central School Corp (KG-12)
    2008-09 Enrollment: 1,006 . . . . (765) 468-6868

Housing: Homeownership rate: 82.1% (2010); Median home value: $76,020 (2010); Median contract rent: $311 per month (2000); Median year structure built: 1957 (2000).

Transportation: Commute to work: 92.4% car, 0.0% public transportation, 4.9% walk, 1.6% work from home (2000); Travel time to work: 19.7% less than 15 minutes, 52.5% 15 to 30 minutes, 17.4% 30 to 45 minutes, 4.3% 45 to 60 minutes, 6.0% 60 minutes or more (2000)

RIDGEVILLE (town).

Covers a land area of 0.590 square miles and a water area of 0 square miles. Located at 40.29° N. Lat; 85.02° W. Long. Elevation is 997 feet.

History: Settled 1817, laid out 1837, incorporated 1868.

Population: 872 (1990); 843 (2000); 776 (2010); 744 (2015 projected); Race: 99.7% White, 0.0% Black, 0.0% Asian, 0.3% Other, 0.3% Hispanic of any race (2010); Density: 1,315.8 persons per square mile (2010); Average household size: 2.46 (2010); Median age: 38.2 (2010); Males per 100 females: 101.0 (2010); Marriage status: 18.0% never married, 62.6% now married, 6.6% widowed, 12.8% divorced (2000); Foreign born: 1.2% (2000); Ancestry (includes multiple ancestries): 14.8% German, 13.1% United States or American, 10.1% English, 7.9% Irish, 7.8% Other groups (2000).

Economy: Employment by occupation: 7.0% management, 7.7% professional, 8.5% services, 23.4% sales, 0.5% farming, 17.9% construction, 35.0% production (2000).

Income: Per capita income: $17,950 (2010); Median household income: $39,254 (2010); Average household income: $44,098 (2010); Percent of

households with income of $100,000 or more: 3.5% (2010); Poverty rate: 8.3% (2000).
Taxes: Total city taxes per capita: $132 (2007); City property taxes per capita: $109 (2007).
Education: Percent of population age 25 and over with: High school diploma (including GED) or higher: 78.9% (2010); Bachelor's degree or higher: 4.8% (2010); Master's degree or higher: 0.8% (2010).
School District(s)
Randolph Central School Corp (PK-12)
　　2008-09 Enrollment: 1,766 . . . . (765) 584-1401
Housing: Homeownership rate: 79.1% (2010); Median home value: $53,973 (2010); Median contract rent: $262 per month (2000); Median year structure built: before 1940 (2000).
Transportation: Commute to work: 91.4% car, 0.5% public transportation, 4.7% walk, 2.5% work from home (2000); Travel time to work: 25.3% less than 15 minutes, 39.6% 15 to 30 minutes, 16.7% 30 to 45 minutes, 10.1% 45 to 60 minutes, 8.3% 60 minutes or more (2000)

SARATOGA (town). Covers a land area of 0.264 square miles and a water area of 0 square miles. Located at 40.23° N. Lat; 84.91° W. Long. Elevation is 1,053 feet.
History: Laid out 1875.
Population: 266 (1990); 288 (2000); 263 (2010); 251 (2015 projected); Race: 98.5% White, 0.8% Black, 0.0% Asian, 0.8% Other, 2.3% Hispanic of any race (2010); Density: 996.2 persons per square mile (2010); Average household size: 2.68 (2010); Median age: 39.0 (2010); Males per 100 females: 103.9 (2010); Marriage status: 16.5% never married, 63.6% now married, 7.4% widowed, 12.6% divorced (2000); Foreign born: 1.0% (2000); Ancestry (includes multiple ancestries): 35.8% United States or American, 9.4% German, 8.0% Irish, 6.3% Other groups, 5.6% English (2000).
Economy: Employment by occupation: 1.4% management, 6.3% professional, 19.6% services, 17.5% sales, 0.0% farming, 7.7% construction, 47.6% production (2000).
Income: Per capita income: $22,595 (2010); Median household income: $54,630 (2010); Average household income: $58,724 (2010); Percent of households with income of $100,000 or more: 10.2% (2010); Poverty rate: 6.9% (2000).
Taxes: Total city taxes per capita: $137 (2007); City property taxes per capita: $126 (2007).
Education: Percent of population age 25 and over with: High school diploma (including GED) or higher: 81.8% (2010); Bachelor's degree or higher: 7.4% (2010); Master's degree or higher: 4.5% (2010).
Housing: Homeownership rate: 81.6% (2010); Median home value: $84,615 (2010); Median contract rent: $310 per month (2000); Median year structure built: before 1940 (2000).
Transportation: Commute to work: 81.6% car, 0.0% public transportation, 12.8% walk, 2.8% work from home (2000); Travel time to work: 54.0% less than 15 minutes, 30.7% 15 to 30 minutes, 8.8% 30 to 45 minutes, 2.2% 45 to 60 minutes, 4.4% 60 minutes or more (2000)

UNION CITY (city). Covers a land area of 1.815 square miles and a water area of 0.007 square miles. Located at 40.20° N. Lat; 84.81° W. Long. Elevation is 1,125 feet.
History: Union City was formed straddling the state line with Ohio. Isaac Pusey Gray, governor of Indiana from 1885-1889, lived here.
Population: 3,690 (1990); 3,622 (2000); 3,249 (2010); 3,077 (2015 projected); Race: 88.6% White, 2.7% Black, 0.3% Asian, 8.3% Other, 8.6% Hispanic of any race (2010); Density: 1,789.6 persons per square mile (2010); Average household size: 2.24 (2010); Median age: 38.7 (2010); Males per 100 females: 93.7 (2010); Marriage status: 18.9% never married, 56.6% now married, 9.3% widowed, 15.2% divorced (2000); Foreign born: 2.8% (2000); Ancestry (includes multiple ancestries): 25.2% United States or American, 23.3% German, 12.4% Other groups, 11.5% Irish, 6.6% English (2000).
Economy: Employment by occupation: 7.7% management, 5.3% professional, 15.6% services, 20.2% sales, 1.5% farming, 7.4% construction, 42.2% production (2000).
Income: Per capita income: $16,570 (2010); Median household income: $29,773 (2010); Average household income: $37,422 (2010); Percent of households with income of $100,000 or more: 2.8% (2010); Poverty rate: 19.7% (2000).
Taxes: Total city taxes per capita: $409 (2007); City property taxes per capita: $303 (2007).

Education: Percent of population age 25 and over with: High school diploma (including GED) or higher: 77.9% (2010); Bachelor's degree or higher: 6.9% (2010); Master's degree or higher: 3.2% (2010).
School District(s)
Randolph Eastern School Corp (PK-12)
　　2008-09 Enrollment: 990 . . . . (765) 964-4994
Housing: Homeownership rate: 68.6% (2010); Median home value: $57,143 (2010); Median contract rent: $310 per month (2000); Median year structure built: 1949 (2000).
Transportation: Commute to work: 92.9% car, 0.0% public transportation, 4.2% walk, 2.3% work from home (2000); Travel time to work: 44.6% less than 15 minutes, 29.7% 15 to 30 minutes, 15.4% 30 to 45 minutes, 4.4% 45 to 60 minutes, 5.8% 60 minutes or more (2000)
Additional Information Contacts
City of Union City . . . . (765) 584-3266
　　http://www.randolph-county.org

WINCHESTER (city). County seat. Covers a land area of 3.102 square miles and a water area of <.001 square miles. Located at 40.17° N. Lat; 84.97° W. Long. Elevation is 1,089 feet.
History: Winchester developed as a grain and livestock shipping center, and as the seat of Randolph County.
Population: 5,286 (1990); 5,037 (2000); 4,514 (2010); 4,274 (2015 projected); Race: 96.8% White, 0.5% Black, 0.8% Asian, 1.8% Other, 2.8% Hispanic of any race (2010); Density: 1,455.2 persons per square mile (2010); Average household size: 2.20 (2010); Median age: 43.3 (2010); Males per 100 females: 90.5 (2010); Marriage status: 18.3% never married, 57.2% now married, 10.1% widowed, 14.4% divorced (2000); Foreign born: 0.4% (2000); Ancestry (includes multiple ancestries): 20.3% United States or American, 18.3% German, 9.6% English, 7.3% Irish, 3.9% Other groups (2000).
Economy: Employment by occupation: 7.7% management, 15.1% professional, 19.9% services, 17.3% sales, 0.6% farming, 10.4% construction, 29.0% production (2000).
Income: Per capita income: $20,740 (2010); Median household income: $33,871 (2010); Average household income: $45,923 (2010); Percent of households with income of $100,000 or more: 6.4% (2010); Poverty rate: 15.0% (2000).
Taxes: Total city taxes per capita: $347 (2007); City property taxes per capita: $292 (2007).
Education: Percent of population age 25 and over with: High school diploma (including GED) or higher: 81.8% (2010); Bachelor's degree or higher: 9.6% (2010); Master's degree or higher: 3.9% (2010).
School District(s)
Randolph Central School Corp (PK-12)
　　2008-09 Enrollment: 1,766 . . . . (765) 584-1401
Housing: Homeownership rate: 68.9% (2010); Median home value: $70,470 (2010); Median contract rent: $258 per month (2000); Median year structure built: 1943 (2000).
Hospitals: St. Vincent Randolph Hospital (25 beds)
Safety: Violent crime rate: 26.2 per 10,000 population; Property crime rate: 583.9 per 10,000 population (2008).
Newspapers: The News-Gazette (Local news; Circulation 12,072)
Transportation: Commute to work: 92.8% car, 0.0% public transportation, 4.8% walk, 1.1% work from home (2000); Travel time to work: 57.7% less than 15 minutes, 15.6% 15 to 30 minutes, 15.3% 30 to 45 minutes, 5.4% 45 to 60 minutes, 5.9% 60 minutes or more (2000)
Additional Information Contacts
City of Winchester . . . . (765) 584-1056
　　http://www.winchesterindiana.us

Ripley County

Located in southeastern Indiana; drained by Laughery and Graham Creeks. Covers a land area of 446.36 square miles, a water area of 1.55 square miles, and is located in the Eastern Time Zone. The county was founded in 1816. County seat is Versailles.
Population: 24,616 (1990); 26,523 (2000); 27,469 (2010); 27,684 (2015 projected); Race: 97.3% White, 0.5% Black, 0.5% Asian, 1.8% Other, 1.5% Hispanic of any race (2010); Density: 61.5 persons per square mile (2010); Average household size: 2.60 (2010); Median age: 37.7 (2010); Males per 100 females: 98.4 (2010).
Religion: Five largest groups: 34.7% Catholic Church, 11.8% American Baptist Churches in the USA, 8.4% Evangelical Lutheran Church in

America, 6.3% The United Methodist Church, 4.9% Christian Churches and Churches of Christ (2000).

Economy: Unemployment rate: 10.2% (5/2010); Total civilian labor force: 14,452 (5/2010); Leading industries: 30.2% manufacturing; 10.7% retail trade; 9.1% health care and social assistance (2008); Farms: 873 totaling 159,017 acres (2007); Companies that employ 500 or more persons: 2 (2008); Companies that employ 100 to 499 persons: 12 (2008); Companies that employ less than 100 persons: 645 (2008); Black-owned businesses: n/a (2002); Hispanic-owned businesses: n/a (2002); Asian-owned businesses: n/a (2002); Women-owned businesses: 573 (2002); Retail sales per capita: $11,429 (2010). Single-family building permits issued: 66 (2009); Multi-family building permits issued: 2 (2009).

Income: Per capita income: $22,728 (2010); Median household income: $51,420 (2010); Average household income: $59,597 (2010); Percent of households with income of $100,000 or more: 12.9% (2010); Poverty rate: 10.4% (2008); Bankruptcy rate: 8.19% (2009).

Taxes: Total county taxes per capita: $617 (2007); County property taxes per capita: $215 (2007).

Education: Percent of population age 25 and over with: High school diploma (including GED) or higher: 84.5% (2010); Bachelor's degree or higher: 15.0% (2010); Master's degree or higher: 5.5% (2010).

Housing: Homeownership rate: 78.2% (2010); Median home value: $131,263 (2010); Median contract rent: $426 per month (2006-2008 3-year est.); Median year structure built: 1976 (2006-2008 3-year est.)

Health: Birth rate: 140.0 per 10,000 population (2009); Death rate: 101.4 per 10,000 population (2009); Age-adjusted cancer mortality rate: 218.9 deaths per 100,000 population (2006); Number of physicians: 4.0 per 10,000 population (2007); Hospital beds: 21.5 per 10,000 population (2006); Hospital admissions: 609.7 per 10,000 population (2006).

Elections: 2008 Presidential election results: 34.4% Obama, 63.9% McCain, 0.0% Nader

National and State Parks: Versailles State Park

Additional Information Contacts
Ripley County Government . . . . (812) 689-6115
   http://www.ripleycounty.com
Batesville Area Chamber of Commerce. . . . . (812) 934-3101
   http://www.batesvillein.com
City of Batesville . . . . (812) 933-6101
   http://www.batesvillein.com

Ripley County Communities

BATESVILLE (city). Covers a land area of 5.822 square miles and a water area of 0.066 square miles. Located at 39.29° N. Lat; 85.22° W. Long. Elevation is 971 feet.

History: Batesville was settled by German immigrants, and developed as a furniture manufacturing center.

Population: 5,359 (1990); 6,033 (2000); 6,432 (2010); 6,560 (2015 projected); Race: 96.2% White, 0.4% Black, 1.2% Asian, 2.2% Other, 1.7% Hispanic of any race (2010); Density: 1,104.7 persons per square mile (2010); Average household size: 2.57 (2010); Median age: 38.0 (2010); Males per 100 females: 94.9 (2010); Marriage status: 20.7% never married, 62.4% now married, 7.6% widowed, 9.3% divorced (2000); Foreign born: 0.6% (2000); Ancestry (includes multiple ancestries): 50.1% German, 11.3% Irish, 9.1% English, 8.6% United States or American, 4.3% Other groups (2000).

Economy: Single-family building permits issued: 11 (2009); Multi-family building permits issued: 0 (2009); Employment by occupation: 11.5% management, 22.0% professional, 11.5% services, 25.4% sales, 0.2% farming, 6.0% construction, 23.5% production (2000).

Income: Per capita income: $26,942 (2010); Median household income: $57,939 (2010); Average household income: $70,946 (2010); Percent of households with income of $100,000 or more: 19.1% (2010); Poverty rate: 3.5% (2000).

Taxes: Total city taxes per capita: $181 (2007); City property taxes per capita: $175 (2007).

Education: Percent of population age 25 and over with: High school diploma (including GED) or higher: 90.6% (2010); Bachelor's degree or higher: 27.3% (2010); Master's degree or higher: 9.5% (2010).

School District(s)
Batesville Community Sch Corp (PK-12)
   2008-09 Enrollment: 2,049 . . . . (812) 934-2194

Housing: Homeownership rate: 72.2% (2010); Median home value: $143,842 (2010); Median contract rent: $434 per month (2000); Median year structure built: 1970 (2000).

Hospitals: Margaret Mary Community Hospital (79 beds)

Safety: Violent crime rate: 9.3 per 10,000 population; Property crime rate: 148.0 per 10,000 population (2008).

Newspapers: Herald-Tribune (Community news; Circulation 4,000)

Transportation: Commute to work: 92.0% car, 0.0% public transportation, 3.1% walk, 4.8% work from home (2000); Travel time to work: 67.9% less than 15 minutes, 13.4% 15 to 30 minutes, 5.2% 30 to 45 minutes, 5.6% 45 to 60 minutes, 7.9% 60 minutes or more (2000)

Additional Information Contacts
Batesville Area Chamber of Commerce. . . . . (812) 934-3101
   http://www.batesvillein.com
City of Batesville . . . . (812) 933-6101
   http://www.batesvillein.com

CROSS PLAINS (unincorporated postal area, zip code 47017). Covers a land area of 15.567 square miles and a water area of 0.078 square miles. Located at 38.93° N. Lat; 85.19° W. Long. Elevation is 961 feet.

Population: 484 (2000); Race: 100.0% White, 0.0% Black, 0.0% Asian, 0.0% Other, 0.0% Hispanic of any race (2000); Density: 31.1 persons per square mile (2000); Age: 23.3% under 18, 22.8% over 64 (2000); Marriage status: 16.6% never married, 53.4% now married, 21.2% widowed, 8.9% divorced (2000); Foreign born: 0.0% (2000); Ancestry (includes multiple ancestries): 25.5% German, 15.5% United States or American, 4.8% English, 3.8% Dutch, 3.8% Irish (2000).

Economy: Employment by occupation: 5.2% management, 21.1% professional, 13.4% services, 26.3% sales, 0.0% farming, 12.9% construction, 21.1% production (2000).

Income: Per capita income: $16,376 (2000); Median household income: $36,023 (2000); Poverty rate: 4.0% (2000).

Education: Percent of population age 25 and over with: High school diploma (including GED) or higher: 79.5% (2000); Bachelor's degree or higher: 9.4% (2000).

Housing: Homeownership rate: 93.8% (2000); Median home value: $90,300 (2000); Median contract rent: $196 per month (2000); Median year structure built: 1958 (2000).

Transportation: Commute to work: 100.0% car, 0.0% public transportation, 0.0% walk, 0.0% work from home (2000); Travel time to work: 21.6% less than 15 minutes, 37.6% 15 to 30 minutes, 21.1% 30 to 45 minutes, 12.4% 45 to 60 minutes, 7.2% 60 minutes or more (2000)

FRIENDSHIP (unincorporated postal area, zip code 47021). Covers a land area of 0.473 square miles and a water area of 0 square miles. Located at 38.96° N. Lat; 85.14° W. Long. Elevation is 633 feet.

Population: 49 (2000); Race: 100.0% White, 0.0% Black, 0.0% Asian, 0.0% Other, 0.0% Hispanic of any race (2000); Density: 103.5 persons per square mile (2000); Age: 39.7% under 18, 7.9% over 64 (2000); Marriage status: 9.5% never married, 45.2% now married, 23.8% widowed, 21.4% divorced (2000); Foreign born: 0.0% (2000); Ancestry (includes multiple ancestries): 54.0% German, 23.8% English, 22.2% Other groups, 22.2% Scotch-Irish, 7.9% Italian (2000).

Economy: Employment by occupation: 15.2% management, 12.1% professional, 0.0% services, 42.4% sales, 0.0% farming, 0.0% construction, 30.3% production (2000).

Income: Per capita income: $14,056 (2000); Median household income: $43,092 (2000); Poverty rate: 17.5% (2000).

Education: Percent of population age 25 and over with: High school diploma (including GED) or higher: 63.2% (2000); Bachelor's degree or higher: 0.0% (2000).

Housing: Homeownership rate: 66.7% (2000); Median home value: $59,200 (2000); Median contract rent: $375 per month (2000); Median year structure built: before 1940 (2000).

Transportation: Commute to work: 100.0% car, 0.0% public transportation, 0.0% walk, 0.0% work from home (2000); Travel time to work: 15.2% less than 15 minutes, 12.1% 15 to 30 minutes, 0.0% 30 to 45 minutes, 0.0% 45 to 60 minutes, 72.7% 60 minutes or more (2000)

HOLTON (town). Covers a land area of 1.794 square miles and a water area of 0 square miles. Located at 39.07° N. Lat; 85.38° W. Long. Elevation is 909 feet.

Population: 451 (1990); 407 (2000); 420 (2010); 422 (2015 projected); Race: 99.0% White, 0.0% Black, 0.2% Asian, 0.7% Other, 1.0% Hispanic of any race (2010); Density: 234.1 persons per square mile (2010); Average household size: 2.69 (2010); Median age: 37.7 (2010); Males per 100 females: 102.9 (2010); Marriage status: 19.9% never married, 59.5%

now married, 5.3% widowed, 15.3% divorced (2000); Foreign born: 0.0% (2000); Ancestry (includes multiple ancestries): 21.4% United States or American, 13.0% German, 6.3% English, 5.3% Irish, 4.3% Other groups (2000).

Economy: Employment by occupation: 6.1% management, 12.1% professional, 23.7% services, 15.7% sales, 1.5% farming, 14.6% construction, 26.3% production (2000).

Income: Per capita income: $22,179 (2010); Median household income: $52,632 (2010); Average household income: $58,429 (2010); Percent of households with income of $100,000 or more: 17.3% (2010); Poverty rate: 22.6% (2000).

Taxes: Total city taxes per capita: $148 (2007); City property taxes per capita: $128 (2007).

Education: Percent of population age 25 and over with: High school diploma (including GED) or higher: 80.8% (2010); Bachelor's degree or higher: 15.0% (2010); Master's degree or higher: 5.9% (2010).

Housing: Homeownership rate: 82.1% (2010); Median home value: $125,714 (2010); Median contract rent: $361 per month (2000); Median year structure built: 1946 (2000).

Transportation: Commute to work: 98.0% car, 0.0% public transportation, 0.0% walk, 1.5% work from home (2000); Travel time to work: 29.0% less than 15 minutes, 29.5% 15 to 30 minutes, 22.3% 30 to 45 minutes, 7.8% 45 to 60 minutes, 11.4% 60 minutes or more (2000)

MILAN (town). Covers a land area of 1.901 square miles and a water area of 0.034 square miles. Located at 39.12° N. Lat; 85.13° W. Long. Elevation is 991 feet.

History: Laid out 1854.

Population: 1,578 (1990); 1,816 (2000); 1,690 (2010); 1,626 (2015 projected); Race: 97.0% White, 1.1% Black, 0.4% Asian, 1.5% Other, 0.5% Hispanic of any race (2010); Density: 888.9 persons per square mile (2010); Average household size: 2.58 (2010); Median age: 36.9 (2010); Males per 100 females: 96.7 (2010); Marriage status: 21.9% never married, 51.1% now married, 13.0% widowed, 14.0% divorced (2000); Foreign born: 0.1% (2000); Ancestry (includes multiple ancestries): 31.0% German, 16.7% United States or American, 12.2% Irish, 10.7% Other groups, 9.2% English (2000).

Economy: Employment by occupation: 4.1% management, 11.4% professional, 19.2% services, 17.9% sales, 0.2% farming, 10.1% construction, 37.1% production (2000).

Income: Per capita income: $20,873 (2010); Median household income: $48,558 (2010); Average household income: $54,689 (2010); Percent of households with income of $100,000 or more: 10.1% (2010); Poverty rate: 9.0% (2000).

Taxes: Total city taxes per capita: $64 (2007); City property taxes per capita: $48 (2007).

Education: Percent of population age 25 and over with: High school diploma (including GED) or higher: 83.0% (2010); Bachelor's degree or higher: 12.2% (2010); Master's degree or higher: 5.4% (2010).

School District(s)
Milan Community Schools (KG-12)
    2008-09 Enrollment: 1,289 . . . . (812) 654-2365

Housing: Homeownership rate: 73.4% (2010); Median home value: $110,032 (2010); Median contract rent: $390 per month (2000); Median year structure built: 1960 (2000).

Transportation: Commute to work: 95.2% car, 0.0% public transportation, 1.9% walk, 2.4% work from home (2000); Travel time to work: 21.5% less than 15 minutes, 33.2% 15 to 30 minutes, 20.1% 30 to 45 minutes, 12.5% 45 to 60 minutes, 12.8% 60 minutes or more (2000)

NAPOLEON (town). Covers a land area of 0.188 square miles and a water area of 0 square miles. Located at 39.20° N. Lat; 85.32° W. Long. Elevation is 965 feet.

History: Laid out 1820.

Population: 238 (1990); 238 (2000); 251 (2010); 256 (2015 projected); Race: 97.2% White, 1.6% Black, 0.4% Asian, 0.8% Other, 1.2% Hispanic of any race (2010); Density: 1,335.3 persons per square mile (2010); Average household size: 2.69 (2010); Median age: 38.1 (2010); Males per 100 females: 84.6 (2010); Marriage status: 18.7% never married, 66.3% now married, 9.3% widowed, 5.7% divorced (2000); Foreign born: 1.7% (2000); Ancestry (includes multiple ancestries): 59.3% German, 19.5% United States or American, 12.6% Irish, 10.0% Other groups, 4.3% English (2000).

Economy: Employment by occupation: 13.6% management, 6.8% professional, 11.0% services, 20.3% sales, 0.0% farming, 5.1% construction, 43.2% production (2000).

Income: Per capita income: $26,069 (2010); Median household income: $62,500 (2010); Average household income: $68,629 (2010); Percent of households with income of $100,000 or more: 18.3% (2010); Poverty rate: 11.3% (2000).

Taxes: Total city taxes per capita: $26 (2007); City property taxes per capita: $21 (2007).

Education: Percent of population age 25 and over with: High school diploma (including GED) or higher: 88.2% (2010); Bachelor's degree or higher: 4.3% (2010); Master's degree or higher: 1.2% (2010).

Housing: Homeownership rate: 83.9% (2010); Median home value: $134,615 (2010); Median contract rent: $338 per month (2000); Median year structure built: 1960 (2000).

Transportation: Commute to work: 71.2% car, 1.7% public transportation, 20.3% walk, 6.8% work from home (2000); Travel time to work: 33.6% less than 15 minutes, 57.3% 15 to 30 minutes, 6.4% 30 to 45 minutes, 2.7% 45 to 60 minutes, 0.0% 60 minutes or more (2000)

OSGOOD (town). Covers a land area of 1.299 square miles and a water area of 0.031 square miles. Located at 39.12° N. Lat; 85.29° W. Long. Elevation is 984 feet.

History: Laid out 1857.

Population: 1,739 (1990); 1,669 (2000); 1,674 (2010); 1,663 (2015 projected); Race: 97.7% White, 1.4% Black, 0.1% Asian, 0.8% Other, 1.4% Hispanic of any race (2010); Density: 1,288.8 persons per square mile (2010); Average household size: 2.43 (2010); Median age: 37.5 (2010); Males per 100 females: 95.3 (2010); Marriage status: 18.7% never married, 58.8% now married, 10.9% widowed, 11.6% divorced (2000); Foreign born: 0.4% (2000); Ancestry (includes multiple ancestries): 25.2% German, 14.6% United States or American, 13.7% Irish, 9.5% Other groups, 6.8% English (2000).

Economy: Employment by occupation: 7.4% management, 5.8% professional, 16.4% services, 18.2% sales, 0.4% farming, 10.3% construction, 41.5% production (2000).

Income: Per capita income: $18,827 (2010); Median household income: $42,328 (2010); Average household income: $46,183 (2010); Percent of households with income of $100,000 or more: 5.2% (2010); Poverty rate: 11.0% (2000).

Taxes: Total city taxes per capita: $111 (2007); City property taxes per capita: $88 (2007).

Education: Percent of population age 25 and over with: High school diploma (including GED) or higher: 79.1% (2010); Bachelor's degree or higher: 9.1% (2010); Master's degree or higher: 1.6% (2010).

School District(s)
Jac-Cen-Del Community Sch Corp (KG-12)
    2008-09 Enrollment: 915 . . . . (812) 689-4114

Housing: Homeownership rate: 68.9% (2010); Median home value: $98,293 (2010); Median contract rent: $296 per month (2000); Median year structure built: 1956 (2000).

Transportation: Commute to work: 92.1% car, 0.4% public transportation, 6.2% walk, 1.3% work from home (2000); Travel time to work: 34.2% less than 15 minutes, 24.7% 15 to 30 minutes, 28.7% 30 to 45 minutes, 4.5% 45 to 60 minutes, 7.9% 60 minutes or more (2000)

SUNMAN (town). Covers a land area of 1.014 square miles and a water area of 0 square miles. Located at 39.23° N. Lat; 85.09° W. Long. Elevation is 1,020 feet.

History: Laid out 1856.

Population: 777 (1990); 805 (2000); 755 (2010); 725 (2015 projected); Race: 91.5% White, 0.0% Black, 0.0% Asian, 8.5% Other, 8.5% Hispanic of any race (2010); Density: 744.5 persons per square mile (2010); Average household size: 2.49 (2010); Median age: 33.7 (2010); Males per 100 females: 98.2 (2010); Marriage status: 27.4% never married, 50.1% now married, 9.9% widowed, 12.6% divorced (2000); Foreign born: 3.3% (2000); Ancestry (includes multiple ancestries): 40.0% German, 13.2% United States or American, 12.0% Other groups, 11.9% Irish, 5.7% English (2000).

Economy: Employment by occupation: 5.6% management, 8.9% professional, 12.6% services, 22.8% sales, 0.5% farming, 19.6% construction, 29.8% production (2000).

Income: Per capita income: $20,990 (2010); Median household income: $46,080 (2010); Average household income: $52,162 (2010); Percent of

households with income of $100,000 or more: 9.9% (2010); Poverty rate: 9.6% (2000).

Taxes: Total city taxes per capita: $236 (2007); City property taxes per capita: $203 (2007).

Education: Percent of population age 25 and over with: High school diploma (including GED) or higher: 77.3% (2010); Bachelor's degree or higher: 11.0% (2010); Master's degree or higher: 3.0% (2010).

School District(s)

Sunman-Dearborn Com Sch Corp (PK-12)

    2008-09 Enrollment: 4,279 . . . . (812) 623-2291

Housing: Homeownership rate: 66.7% (2010); Median home value: $114,516 (2010); Median contract rent: $332 per month (2000); Median year structure built: 1970 (2000).

Transportation: Commute to work: 90.6% car, 0.0% public transportation, 7.2% walk, 1.7% work from home (2000); Travel time to work: 32.5% less than 15 minutes, 30.2% 15 to 30 minutes, 21.5% 30 to 45 minutes, 11.9% 45 to 60 minutes, 4.0% 60 minutes or more (2000)

VERSAILLES (town). County seat. Covers a land area of 1.526 square miles and a water area of 0 square miles. Located at 39.06° N. Lat; 85.25° W. Long. Elevation is 965 feet.

History: Versailles was founded in 1818 as a farming center. General John Morgan and his men came to Versailles in 1863 and looted the office of the county treasurer.

Population: 1,791 (1990); 1,784 (2000); 1,790 (2010); 1,782 (2015 projected); Race: 98.5% White, 0.5% Black, 0.1% Asian, 0.8% Other, 0.4% Hispanic of any race (2010); Density: 1,172.8 persons per square mile (2010); Average household size: 2.34 (2010); Median age: 38.1 (2010); Males per 100 females: 88.0 (2010); Marriage status: 20.3% never married, 56.8% now married, 9.2% widowed, 13.7% divorced (2000); Foreign born: 0.6% (2000); Ancestry (includes multiple ancestries): 23.1% German, 12.6% United States or American, 11.2% English, 9.0% Irish, 6.2% Other groups (2000).

Economy: Employment by occupation: 7.9% management, 15.6% professional, 17.2% services, 22.2% sales, 0.0% farming, 8.1% construction, 28.9% production (2000).

Income: Per capita income: $21,316 (2010); Median household income: $41,960 (2010); Average household income: $50,450 (2010); Percent of households with income of $100,000 or more: 9.5% (2010); Poverty rate: 8.7% (2000).

Taxes: Total city taxes per capita: $140 (2007); City property taxes per capita: $133 (2007).

Education: Percent of population age 25 and over with: High school diploma (including GED) or higher: 84.8% (2010); Bachelor's degree or higher: 17.5% (2010); Master's degree or higher: 7.1% (2010).

School District(s)

South Ripley Com Sch Corp (KG-12)

    2008-09 Enrollment: 1,304 . . . . (812) 689-6282

Southeastern Career Center (09-12)

    2008-09 Enrollment: n/a . . . . (812) 689-5253

Housing: Homeownership rate: 68.7% (2010); Median home value: $107,081 (2010); Median contract rent: $338 per month (2000); Median year structure built: 1964 (2000).

Newspapers: Osgood Journal (Community news); Spotlight-Advertiser (Community news); Versailles Republican (Community news; Circulation 5,000)

Transportation: Commute to work: 91.4% car, 0.4% public transportation, 2.8% walk, 5.1% work from home (2000); Travel time to work: 38.1% less than 15 minutes, 22.4% 15 to 30 minutes, 27.2% 30 to 45 minutes, 5.1% 45 to 60 minutes, 7.3% 60 minutes or more (2000)

Rush County

Located in east central Indiana; drained by the Big Blue River and Flatrock Creek. Covers a land area of 408.28 square miles, a water area of 0.34 square miles, and is located in the Eastern Time Zone. The county was founded in 1821. County seat is Rushville.

Weather Station: Rushville Sewage Plant   Elevation: 958 feet

	Jan	Feb	Mar	Apr	May	Jun	Jul	Aug	Sep	Oct	Nov	Dec
High	33	39	49	62	73	81	84	83	77	65	51	39
Low	16	19	29	39	50	59	63	60	53	41	32	23
Precip	2.6	2.5	3.2	4.2	4.9	4.2	4.5	3.5	2.9	2.9	3.6	3.1
Snow	5.7	4.4	2.0	0.3	tr	0.0	0.0	0.0	0.0	0.3	0.6	2.8

High and Low temperatures in degrees Fahrenheit; Precipitation and Snow in inches

Population: 18,129 (1990); 18,261 (2000); 17,094 (2010); 16,400 (2015 projected); Race: 96.7% White, 0.9% Black, 0.6% Asian, 1.8% Other, 0.9% Hispanic of any race (2010); Density: 41.9 persons per square mile (2010); Average household size: 2.53 (2010); Median age: 40.4 (2010); Males per 100 females: 96.7 (2010).

Religion: Five largest groups: 9.8% Catholic Church, 9.7% Christian Churches and Churches of Christ, 8.0% Christian Church (Disciples of Christ), 6.6% The United Methodist Church, 5.2% Southern Baptist Convention (2000).

Economy: Unemployment rate: 9.4% (5/2010); Total civilian labor force: 9,414 (5/2010); Leading industries: 12.0% retail trade; 11.3% health care and social assistance; 11.0% construction (2008); Farms: 607 totaling 216,890 acres (2007); Companies that employ 500 or more persons: 0 (2008); Companies that employ 100 to 499 persons: 8 (2008); Companies that employ less than 100 persons: 389 (2008); Black-owned businesses: n/a (2002); Hispanic-owned businesses: n/a (2002); Asian-owned businesses: n/a (2002); Women-owned businesses: n/a (2002); Retail sales per capita: $10,286 (2009). Single-family building permits issued: 12 (2009); Multi-family building permits issued: 0 (2009).

Income: Per capita income: $21,889 (2010); Median household income: $46,471 (2010); Average household income: $55,820 (2010); Percent of households with income of $100,000 or more: 11.8% (2010); Poverty rate: 10.9% (2008); Bankruptcy rate: 8.70% (2009).

Taxes: Total county taxes per capita: $267 (2007); County property taxes per capita: $145 (2007).

Education: Percent of population age 25 and over with: High school diploma (including GED) or higher: 84.4% (2010); Bachelor's degree or higher: 11.2% (2010); Master's degree or higher: 3.2% (2010).

Housing: Homeownership rate: 72.8% (2010); Median home value: $119,869 (2010); Median contract rent: $n/a per month (2006-2008 3-year est.); Median year structure built: n/a (2006-2008 3-year est.)

Health: Birth rate: 111.8 per 10,000 population (2009); Death rate: 106.6 per 10,000 population (2009); Age-adjusted cancer mortality rate: 220.9 deaths per 100,000 population (2006); Number of physicians: 4.6 per 10,000 population (2007); Hospital beds: 14.3 per 10,000 population (2006); Hospital admissions: 412.3 per 10,000 population (2006).

Elections: 2008 Presidential election results: 42.3% Obama, 56.0% McCain, 0.0% Nader

Additional Information Contacts

Rush County Government . . . . (765) 932-5451

    http://www.rushcounty.in.gov

City of Rushville . . . . (765) 932-2672

    http://www.cityofrushville.in.gov

Rush County Communities

ARLINGTON (unincorporated postal area, zip code 46104). Covers a land area of 29.822 square miles and a water area of 0.032 square miles. Located at 39.64° N. Lat; 85.60° W. Long. Elevation is 922 feet.

History: Arlington was established around a stone quarry.

Population: 1,124 (2000); Race: 98.5% White, 0.0% Black, 0.0% Asian, 1.5% Other, 0.0% Hispanic of any race (2000); Density: 37.7 persons per square mile (2000); Age: 30.5% under 18, 12.6% over 64 (2000); Marriage status: 15.9% never married, 68.9% now married, 8.2% widowed, 6.9% divorced (2000); Foreign born: 0.0% (2000); Ancestry (includes multiple ancestries): 20.1% German, 17.0% United States or American, 15.5% Irish, 7.9% English, 4.2% Other groups (2000).

Economy: Employment by occupation: 16.7% management, 15.6% professional, 18.7% services, 11.6% sales, 1.3% farming, 6.2% construction, 29.8% production (2000).

Income: Per capita income: $16,479 (2000); Median household income: $36,550 (2000); Poverty rate: 2.5% (2000).

Education: Percent of population age 25 and over with: High school diploma (including GED) or higher: 84.9% (2000); Bachelor's degree or higher: 15.0% (2000).

School District(s)

Rush County Schools (PK-12)

    2008-09 Enrollment: 2,696 . . . . (765) 932-4186

Housing: Homeownership rate: 86.8% (2000); Median home value: $69,200 (2000); Median contract rent: $429 per month (2000); Median year structure built: before 1940 (2000).

Transportation: Commute to work: 95.2% car, 0.8% public transportation, 1.3% walk, 2.7% work from home (2000); Travel time to work: 23.9% less than 15 minutes, 33.6% 15 to 30 minutes, 23.2% 30 to 45 minutes, 10.6% 45 to 60 minutes, 8.9% 60 minutes or more (2000)

CARTHAGE (town). Covers a land area of 0.574 square miles and a water area of 0 square miles. Located at 39.73° N. Lat; 85.57° W. Long. Elevation is 876 feet.

Population: 853 (1990); 928 (2000); 796 (2010); 736 (2015 projected); Race: 96.9% White, 0.0% Black, 0.0% Asian, 3.1% Other, 2.1% Hispanic of any race (2010); Density: 1,386.4 persons per square mile (2010); Average household size: 2.51 (2010); Median age: 39.4 (2010); Males per 100 females: 98.0 (2010); Marriage status: 17.3% never married, 65.6% now married, 7.1% widowed, 10.0% divorced (2000); Foreign born: 0.1% (2000); Ancestry (includes multiple ancestries): 19.9% United States or American, 16.7% German, 13.6% Irish, 12.2% English, 5.0% Other groups (2000).

Economy: Employment by occupation: 8.3% management, 6.0% professional, 15.4% services, 23.5% sales, 0.5% farming, 16.4% construction, 30.0% production (2000).

Income: Per capita income: $23,793 (2010); Median household income: $52,022 (2010); Average household income: $60,087 (2010); Percent of households with income of $100,000 or more: 16.4% (2010); Poverty rate: 7.2% (2000).

Taxes: Total city taxes per capita: $20 (2007); City property taxes per capita: $3 (2007).

Education: Percent of population age 25 and over with: High school diploma (including GED) or higher: 80.9% (2010); Bachelor's degree or higher: 6.8% (2010); Master's degree or higher: 1.1% (2010).

School District(s)

C A Beard Memorial School Corp (KG-12)

    2008-09 Enrollment: 1,348 . . . . (765) 345-5101

Housing: Homeownership rate: 71.9% (2010); Median home value: $102,941 (2010); Median contract rent: $365 per month (2000); Median year structure built: before 1940 (2000).

Transportation: Commute to work: 93.3% car, 0.0% public transportation, 4.1% walk, 2.6% work from home (2000); Travel time to work: 17.3% less than 15 minutes, 29.9% 15 to 30 minutes, 16.8% 30 to 45 minutes, 20.2% 45 to 60 minutes, 15.8% 60 minutes or more (2000)

FALMOUTH (unincorporated postal area, zip code 46127). Covers a land area of 22.286 square miles and a water area of 0 square miles. Located at 39.71° N. Lat; 85.32° W. Long. Elevation is 1,070 feet.

Population: 374 (2000); Race: 100.0% White, 0.0% Black, 0.0% Asian, 0.0% Other, 0.0% Hispanic of any race (2000); Density: 16.8 persons per square mile (2000); Age: 22.9% under 18, 23.5% over 64 (2000); Marriage status: 13.0% never married, 59.7% now married, 6.0% widowed, 21.3% divorced (2000); Foreign born: 0.0% (2000); Ancestry (includes multiple ancestries): 67.0% United States or American, 6.9% English, 6.6% Irish, 1.7% German (2000).

Economy: Employment by occupation: 15.8% management, 7.2% professional, 11.8% services, 9.2% sales, 7.9% farming, 15.1% construction, 32.9% production (2000).

Income: Per capita income: $14,315 (2000); Median household income: $27,150 (2000); Poverty rate: 6.6% (2000).

Education: Percent of population age 25 and over with: High school diploma (including GED) or higher: 75.9% (2000); Bachelor's degree or higher: 5.0% (2000).

Housing: Homeownership rate: 80.6% (2000); Median home value: $87,500 (2000); Median contract rent: $382 per month (2000); Median year structure built: before 1940 (2000).

Transportation: Commute to work: 100.0% car, 0.0% public transportation, 0.0% walk, 0.0% work from home (2000); Travel time to work: 16.4% less than 15 minutes, 33.6% 15 to 30 minutes, 46.7% 30 to 45 minutes, 3.3% 45 to 60 minutes, 0.0% 60 minutes or more (2000)

GLENWOOD (town). Covers a land area of 0.173 square miles and a water area of 0 square miles. Located at 39.62° N. Lat; 85.30° W. Long. Elevation is 1,089 feet.

Population: 285 (1990); 318 (2000); 306 (2010); 298 (2015 projected); Race: 97.7% White, 1.0% Black, 0.0% Asian, 1.3% Other, 0.3% Hispanic of any race (2010); Density: 1,770.5 persons per square mile (2010); Average household size: 2.61 (2010); Median age: 42.0 (2010); Males per 100 females: 100.0 (2010); Marriage status: 18.7% never married, 64.8% now married, 4.8% widowed, 11.7% divorced (2000); Foreign born: 0.0% (2000); Ancestry (includes multiple ancestries): 42.9% United States or American, 14.0% German, 9.7% Irish, 4.2% Other groups, 3.9% English (2000).

Economy: Employment by occupation: 10.7% management, 4.5% professional, 15.2% services, 20.5% sales, 0.0% farming, 6.3% construction, 42.9% production (2000).

Income: Per capita income: $21,312 (2010); Median household income: $47,614 (2010); Average household income: $53,526 (2010); Percent of households with income of $100,000 or more: 6.0% (2010); Poverty rate: 14.5% (2000).

Taxes: Total city taxes per capita: $110 (2007); City property taxes per capita: $107 (2007).

Education: Percent of population age 25 and over with: High school diploma (including GED) or higher: 89.6% (2010); Bachelor's degree or higher: 9.4% (2010); Master's degree or higher: 2.4% (2010).

School District(s)

Fayette County School Corp (PK-12)

    2008-09 Enrollment: 4,239 . . . . (765) 825-2178

Housing: Homeownership rate: 81.2% (2010); Median home value: $120,714 (2010); Median contract rent: $338 per month (2000); Median year structure built: before 1940 (2000).

Transportation: Commute to work: 94.6% car, 0.0% public transportation, 5.4% walk, 0.0% work from home (2000); Travel time to work: 32.1% less than 15 minutes, 27.7% 15 to 30 minutes, 21.4% 30 to 45 minutes, 12.5% 45 to 60 minutes, 6.3% 60 minutes or more (2000)

MANILLA (unincorporated postal area, zip code 46150). Covers a land area of 26.940 square miles and a water area of 0.009 square miles. Located at 39.56° N. Lat; 85.61° W. Long. Elevation is 906 feet.

Population: 928 (2000); Race: 98.3% White, 0.0% Black, 0.0% Asian, 1.7% Other, 1.7% Hispanic of any race (2000); Density: 34.4 persons per square mile (2000); Age: 25.6% under 18, 19.0% over 64 (2000); Marriage status: 16.7% never married, 63.1% now married, 11.0% widowed, 9.2% divorced (2000); Foreign born: 1.2% (2000); Ancestry (includes multiple ancestries): 23.3% German, 10.0% United States or American, 9.4% Irish, 9.4% Other groups, 6.7% English (2000).

Economy: Employment by occupation: 9.0% management, 8.8% professional, 9.9% services, 22.5% sales, 2.9% farming, 22.3% construction, 24.5% production (2000).

Income: Per capita income: $18,098 (2000); Median household income: $42,159 (2000); Poverty rate: 6.1% (2000).

Education: Percent of population age 25 and over with: High school diploma (including GED) or higher: 82.9% (2000); Bachelor's degree or higher: 13.4% (2000).

Housing: Homeownership rate: 86.4% (2000); Median home value: $65,500 (2000); Median contract rent: $425 per month (2000); Median year structure built: 1942 (2000).

Transportation: Commute to work: 92.8% car, 3.7% public transportation, 0.0% walk, 3.5% work from home (2000); Travel time to work: 19.3% less than 15 minutes, 42.7% 15 to 30 minutes, 13.0% 30 to 45 minutes, 7.7% 45 to 60 minutes, 17.3% 60 minutes or more (2000)

MILROY (unincorporated postal area, zip code 46156). Covers a land area of 40.307 square miles and a water area of 0.038 square miles. Located at 39.48° N. Lat; 85.47° W. Long. Elevation is 961 feet.

History: Laid out 1830.

Population: 1,575 (2000); Race: 100.0% White, 0.0% Black, 0.0% Asian, 0.0% Other, 0.4% Hispanic of any race (2000); Density: 39.1 persons per square mile (2000); Age: 30.1% under 18, 8.5% over 64 (2000); Marriage status: 22.0% never married, 60.1% now married, 8.2% widowed, 9.6% divorced (2000); Foreign born: 0.5% (2000); Ancestry (includes multiple ancestries): 29.6% United States or American, 23.9% German, 12.1% Irish, 4.8% Other groups, 4.6% English (2000).

Economy: Employment by occupation: 9.1% management, 3.8% professional, 11.1% services, 16.7% sales, 1.4% farming, 16.9% construction, 41.0% production (2000).

Income: Per capita income: $14,936 (2000); Median household income: $37,448 (2000); Poverty rate: 10.6% (2000).

Education: Percent of population age 25 and over with: High school diploma (including GED) or higher: 72.5% (2000); Bachelor's degree or higher: 1.0% (2000).

School District(s)

Rush County Schools (PK-12)

    2008-09 Enrollment: 2,696 . . . . (765) 932-4186

Housing: Homeownership rate: 72.9% (2000); Median home value: $75,600 (2000); Median contract rent: $353 per month (2000); Median year structure built: 1948 (2000).

Transportation: Commute to work: 87.7% car, 0.3% public transportation, 4.6% walk, 7.4% work from home (2000); Travel time to work: 24.3% less than 15 minutes, 40.2% 15 to 30 minutes, 10.2% 30 to 45 minutes, 7.4% 45 to 60 minutes, 17.9% 60 minutes or more (2000)

RUSHVILLE (city). County seat. Covers a land area of 2.246 square miles and a water area of 0 square miles. Located at 39.61° N. Lat; 85.44° W. Long. Elevation is 958 feet.

History: Rushville was founded in 1822 and named for Benjamin F. Rush, a Revolutionary War soldier and a signer of the Declaration of Independence.

Population: 5,690 (1990); 5,995 (2000); 5,467 (2010); 5,178 (2015 projected); Race: 95.0% White, 2.1% Black, 1.5% Asian, 1.4% Other, 0.7% Hispanic of any race (2010); Density: 2,433.7 persons per square mile (2010); Average household size: 2.34 (2010); Median age: 41.5 (2010); Males per 100 females: 89.0 (2010); Marriage status: 19.5% never married, 54.9% now married, 9.7% widowed, 15.9% divorced (2000); Foreign born: 0.6% (2000); Ancestry (includes multiple ancestries): 30.1% United States or American, 17.5% German, 10.8% Other groups, 10.5% English, 10.2% Irish (2000).

Economy: Employment by occupation: 6.1% management, 8.1% professional, 14.5% services, 20.1% sales, 0.4% farming, 9.3% construction, 41.5% production (2000).

Income: Per capita income: $19,605 (2010); Median household income: $35,306 (2010); Average household income: $46,687 (2010); Percent of households with income of $100,000 or more: 7.8% (2010); Poverty rate: 11.0% (2000).

Taxes: Total city taxes per capita: $379 (2007); City property taxes per capita: $350 (2007).

Education: Percent of population age 25 and over with: High school diploma (including GED) or higher: 79.1% (2010); Bachelor's degree or higher: 10.0% (2010); Master's degree or higher: 3.0% (2010).

School District(s)

Rush County Schools (PK-12)

     2008-09 Enrollment: 2,696 . . . . (765) 932-4186

Housing: Homeownership rate: 62.3% (2010); Median home value: $110,840 (2010); Median contract rent: $333 per month (2000); Median year structure built: before 1940 (2000).

Hospitals: Rush Memorial Hospital (15 beds)

Safety: Violent crime rate: 9.9 per 10,000 population; Property crime rate: 298.9 per 10,000 population (2008).

Newspapers: Rushville Republican (Regional news; Circulation 4,400); Rushville Telegram (Community news; Circulation 300)

Transportation: Commute to work: 92.4% car, 1.0% public transportation, 3.0% walk, 2.7% work from home (2000); Travel time to work: 50.0% less than 15 minutes, 16.0% 15 to 30 minutes, 18.3% 30 to 45 minutes, 7.1% 45 to 60 minutes, 8.6% 60 minutes or more (2000)

Additional Information Contacts

City of Rushville . . . . (765) 932-2672

     http://www.cityofrushville.in.gov

Saint Joseph County

Located in northern Indiana; bounded on the north by Michigan; drained by the St. Joseph, Yellow, and Kankakee Rivers. Covers a land area of 457.34 square miles, a water area of 3.63 square miles, and is located in the Eastern Time Zone. The county was founded in 1830. County seat is South Bend.

Saint Joseph County is part of the South Bend-Mishawaka, IN-MI Metropolitan Statistical Area. The entire metro area includes: St. Joseph County, IN; Cass County, MI

Weather Station: South Bend Michiana Regional										Elevation: 770 feet		
	Jan	Feb	Mar	Apr	May	Jun	Jul	Aug	Sep	Oct	Nov	Dec
High	31	35	46	59	71	80	83	81	74	62	48	36
Low	17	20	29	39	49	59	63	62	54	43	34	23
Precip	2.2	2.0	2.9	3.7	3.5	4.1	3.8	4.0	3.9	3.3	3.4	3.1
Snow	22.9	15.5	9.2	2.0	tr	tr	tr	tr	tr	0.5	7.7	18.8

High and Low temperatures in degrees Fahrenheit; Precipitation and Snow in inches

Population: 247,056 (1990); 265,559 (2000); 267,430 (2010); 267,214 (2015 projected); Race: 80.0% White, 11.9% Black, 1.7% Asian, 6.4% Other, 6.6% Hispanic of any race (2010); Density: 584.8 persons per square mile (2010); Average household size: 2.49 (2010); Median age: 36.1 (2010); Males per 100 females: 94.0 (2010).

Religion: Five largest groups: 23.8% Catholic Church, 3.8% The United Methodist Church, 1.6% Evangelical Lutheran Church in America, 1.1% Presbyterian Church (U.S.A.), 1.1% Assemblies of God (2000).

Economy: Unemployment rate: 11.4% (5/2010); Total civilian labor force: 124,979 (5/2010); Leading industries: 14.9% health care and social assistance; 14.0% manufacturing; 12.6% retail trade (2008); Farms: 712 totaling 178,674 acres (2007); Companies that employ 500 or more persons: 16 (2008); Companies that employ 100 to 499 persons: 190 (2008); Companies that employ less than 100 persons: 6,025 (2008); Black-owned businesses: 672 (2002); Hispanic-owned businesses: 277 (2002); Asian-owned businesses: 285 (2002); Women-owned businesses: 4,843 (2002); Retail sales per capita: $14,934 (2010). Single-family building permits issued: 212 (2009); Multi-family building permits issued: 49 (2009).

Income: Per capita income: $22,749 (2010); Median household income: $45,865 (2010); Average household income: $58,785 (2010); Percent of households with income of $100,000 or more: 13.3% (2010); Poverty rate: 14.6% (2008); Bankruptcy rate: 6.10% (2009).

Taxes: Total county taxes per capita: $331 (2007); County property taxes per capita: $278 (2007).

Education: Percent of population age 25 and over with: High school diploma (including GED) or higher: 85.5% (2010); Bachelor's degree or higher: 26.4% (2010); Master's degree or higher: 10.2% (2010).

Housing: Homeownership rate: 71.8% (2010); Median home value: $106,031 (2010); Median contract rent: $581 per month (2006-2008 3-year est.); Median year structure built: 1963 (2006-2008 3-year est.)

Health: Birth rate: 141.9 per 10,000 population (2009); Death rate: 87.4 per 10,000 population (2009); Age-adjusted cancer mortality rate: 201.6 deaths per 100,000 population (2006); Air Quality Index: 79.5% good, 20.5% moderate, 0.0% unhealthy for sensitive individuals, 0.0% unhealthy (percent of days in 2008); Number of physicians: 22.3 per 10,000 population (2007); Hospital beds: 38.3 per 10,000 population (2006); Hospital admissions: 1,655.9 per 10,000 population (2006).

Elections: 2008 Presidential election results: 58.0% Obama, 41.0% McCain, 0.0% Nader

National and State Parks: Potato Creek State Park

Additional Information Contacts

Saint Joseph County Government . . . . (574) 235-9635

     http://www.stjosephcountyindiana.com

Chamber of Commerce of St. Joseph County . . . . (574) 234-0051

     http://www.sjchamber.org

City of Mishawaka . . . . (574) 258-1616

     http://www.mishawakacity.com

City of South Bend . . . . (574) 235-9216

     http://www.ci.south-bend.in.us

Granger Chamber of Commerce . . . . (574) 234-0051

     http://www.sjchamber.org

Mishawaka Chamber of Commerce. . . . . (574) 234-0051

     http://www.sjchamber.org

Town of Walkerton . . . . (574) 586-3711

     http://www.walkerton.org

Saint Joseph County Communities

GEORGETOWN (CDP). Covers a land area of 1.940 square miles and a water area of 0.009 square miles. Located at 41.72° N. Lat; 86.22° W. Long. Elevation is 728 feet.

History: The first settlements in the were established as fur trading posts. The first westerner to make permanent settlement was Pierre Frieschutz Navarre in 1820. Navarre arrived on behalf of the American Fur Company.

Population: 3,993 (1990); 4,497 (2000); 4,518 (2010); 4,461 (2015 projected); Race: 82.7% White, 9.1% Black, 3.9% Asian, 4.2% Other, 4.2% Hispanic of any race (2010); Density: 2,328.9 persons per square mile (2010); Average household size: 2.24 (2010); Median age: 38.2 (2010); Males per 100 females: 95.9 (2010); Marriage status: 28.0% never married, 57.3% now married, 7.1% widowed, 7.6% divorced (2000); Foreign born: 4.7% (2000); Ancestry (includes multiple ancestries): 31.6% German, 17.2% Irish, 14.2% Other groups, 12.3% Polish, 7.5% English (2000).

Economy: Employment by occupation: 14.3% management, 35.7% professional, 12.3% services, 24.7% sales, 0.0% farming, 4.6% construction, 8.2% production (2000).

Income: Per capita income: $29,311 (2010); Median household income: $58,601 (2010); Average household income: $65,735 (2010); Percent of households with income of $100,000 or more: 17.1% (2010); Poverty rate: 10.2% (2000).

Education: Percent of population age 25 and over with: High school diploma (including GED) or higher: 94.9% (2010); Bachelor's degree or higher: 43.7% (2010); Master's degree or higher: 15.4% (2010).
Housing: Homeownership rate: 58.5% (2010); Median home value: $135,392 (2010); Median contract rent: $628 per month (2000); Median year structure built: 1975 (2000).
Transportation: Commute to work: 98.5% car, 0.2% public transportation, 0.4% walk, 0.6% work from home (2000); Travel time to work: 39.3% less than 15 minutes, 44.9% 15 to 30 minutes, 8.3% 30 to 45 minutes, 3.2% 45 to 60 minutes, 4.2% 60 minutes or more (2000)

GRANGER (CDP). Covers a land area of 26.219 square miles and a water area of 0.001 square miles. Located at 41.73° N. Lat; 86.14° W. Long. Elevation is 801 feet.
Population: 20,143 (1990); 28,284 (2000); 29,257 (2010); 29,323 (2015 projected); Race: 92.3% White, 2.3% Black, 3.4% Asian, 2.0% Other, 1.6% Hispanic of any race (2010); Density: 1,115.9 persons per square mile (2010); Average household size: 2.99 (2010); Median age: 38.8 (2010); Males per 100 females: 96.2 (2010); Marriage status: 17.8% never married, 75.1% now married, 3.0% widowed, 4.1% divorced (2000); Foreign born: 4.5% (2000); Ancestry (includes multiple ancestries): 28.1% German, 16.9% Irish, 11.4% English, 10.9% Polish, 7.6% Other groups (2000).
Economy: Employment by occupation: 22.5% management, 28.2% professional, 8.4% services, 28.2% sales, 0.0% farming, 4.6% construction, 8.0% production (2000).
Income: Per capita income: $37,460 (2010); Median household income: $92,456 (2010); Average household income: $112,534 (2010); Percent of households with income of $100,000 or more: 44.0% (2010); Poverty rate: 1.4% (2000).
Education: Percent of population age 25 and over with: High school diploma (including GED) or higher: 96.6% (2010); Bachelor's degree or higher: 52.5% (2010); Master's degree or higher: 20.7% (2010).
School District(s)
Penn-Harris-Madison Sch Corp (KG-12)
    2008-09 Enrollment: 10,459 . . . . (574) 259-7941
Housing: Homeownership rate: 94.7% (2010); Median home value: $184,833 (2010); Median contract rent: $985 per month (2000); Median year structure built: 1984 (2000).
Transportation: Commute to work: 95.5% car, 0.2% public transportation, 0.8% walk, 3.3% work from home (2000); Travel time to work: 26.7% less than 15 minutes, 53.2% 15 to 30 minutes, 13.8% 30 to 45 minutes, 3.4% 45 to 60 minutes, 3.0% 60 minutes or more (2000)
Additional Information Contacts
Granger Chamber of Commerce . . . . (574) 234-0051
    http://www.sjchamber.org

GULIVOIRE PARK (CDP). Covers a land area of 1.373 square miles and a water area of 0 square miles. Located at 41.61° N. Lat; 86.24° W. Long. Elevation is 846 feet.
Population: 2,662 (1990); 2,974 (2000); 2,950 (2010); 2,937 (2015 projected); Race: 96.4% White, 1.4% Black, 0.7% Asian, 1.6% Other, 1.5% Hispanic of any race (2010); Density: 2,148.0 persons per square mile (2010); Average household size: 2.40 (2010); Median age: 44.1 (2010); Males per 100 females: 95.6 (2010); Marriage status: 18.2% never married, 65.9% now married, 8.3% widowed, 7.6% divorced (2000); Foreign born: 1.4% (2000); Ancestry (includes multiple ancestries): 29.6% German, 17.9% Polish, 11.8% Irish, 11.3% Hungarian, 8.9% English (2000).
Economy: Employment by occupation: 13.9% management, 14.7% professional, 9.6% services, 29.2% sales, 0.0% farming, 13.3% construction, 19.3% production (2000).
Income: Per capita income: $24,974 (2010); Median household income: $55,660 (2010); Average household income: $59,922 (2010); Percent of households with income of $100,000 or more: 14.3% (2010); Poverty rate: 3.9% (2000).
Education: Percent of population age 25 and over with: High school diploma (including GED) or higher: 89.5% (2010); Bachelor's degree or higher: 24.5% (2010); Master's degree or higher: 8.2% (2010).
Housing: Homeownership rate: 95.2% (2010); Median home value: $118,255 (2010); Median contract rent: $475 per month (2000); Median year structure built: 1960 (2000).
Transportation: Commute to work: 97.6% car, 0.0% public transportation, 0.5% walk, 1.9% work from home (2000); Travel time to work: 29.0% less than 15 minutes, 58.2% 15 to 30 minutes, 7.7% 30 to 45 minutes, 3.0% 45 to 60 minutes, 2.1% 60 minutes or more (2000)

INDIAN VILLAGE (town). Covers a land area of 0.097 square miles and a water area of 0 square miles. Located at 41.71° N. Lat; 86.23° W. Long. Elevation is 725 feet.
Population: 142 (1990); 144 (2000); 135 (2010); 128 (2015 projected); Race: 92.6% White, 2.2% Black, 0.7% Asian, 4.4% Other, 3.0% Hispanic of any race (2010); Density: 1,397.1 persons per square mile (2010); Average household size: 2.39 (2010); Median age: 36.3 (2010); Males per 100 females: 90.1 (2010); Marriage status: 26.1% never married, 54.6% now married, 5.9% widowed, 13.4% divorced (2000); Foreign born: 2.9% (2000); Ancestry (includes multiple ancestries): 42.9% German, 21.4% Irish, 13.6% Polish, 10.7% Austrian, 7.9% Swiss (2000).
Economy: Employment by occupation: 10.3% management, 36.8% professional, 11.8% services, 25.0% sales, 0.0% farming, 5.9% construction, 10.3% production (2000).
Income: Per capita income: $25,675 (2010); Median household income: $48,125 (2010); Average household income: $62,143 (2010); Percent of households with income of $100,000 or more: 17.9% (2010); Poverty rate: 4.3% (2000).
Taxes: Total city taxes per capita: $36 (2007); City property taxes per capita: $7 (2007).
Education: Percent of population age 25 and over with: High school diploma (including GED) or higher: 63.9% (2010); Bachelor's degree or higher: 26.8% (2010); Master's degree or higher: 12.4% (2010).
Housing: Homeownership rate: 71.4% (2010); Median home value: $93,846 (2010); Median contract rent: $825 per month (2000); Median year structure built: 1960 (2000).
Transportation: Commute to work: 92.6% car, 0.0% public transportation, 0.0% walk, 2.9% work from home (2000); Travel time to work: 50.0% less than 15 minutes, 37.9% 15 to 30 minutes, 9.1% 30 to 45 minutes, 0.0% 45 to 60 minutes, 3.0% 60 minutes or more (2000)

LAKEVILLE (town). Covers a land area of 0.524 square miles and a water area of 0 square miles. Located at 41.52° N. Lat; 86.27° W. Long. Elevation is 843 feet.
Population: 687 (1990); 567 (2000); 555 (2010); 548 (2015 projected); Race: 95.5% White, 0.2% Black, 0.0% Asian, 4.3% Other, 3.2% Hispanic of any race (2010); Density: 1,059.6 persons per square mile (2010); Average household size: 2.13 (2010); Median age: 40.2 (2010); Males per 100 females: 90.1 (2010); Marriage status: 27.6% never married, 40.0% now married, 12.1% widowed, 20.3% divorced (2000); Foreign born: 0.0% (2000); Ancestry (includes multiple ancestries): 28.0% German, 19.0% Irish, 7.0% United States or American, 6.3% Other groups, 5.4% Belgian (2000).
Economy: Employment by occupation: 10.7% management, 5.0% professional, 17.7% services, 20.1% sales, 0.0% farming, 13.7% construction, 32.8% production (2000).
Income: Per capita income: $20,790 (2010); Median household income: $35,000 (2010); Average household income: $44,413 (2010); Percent of households with income of $100,000 or more: 7.7% (2010); Poverty rate: 13.6% (2000).
Taxes: Total city taxes per capita: $70 (2007); City property taxes per capita: $70 (2007).
Education: Percent of population age 25 and over with: High school diploma (including GED) or higher: 81.6% (2010); Bachelor's degree or higher: 11.3% (2010); Master's degree or higher: 2.5% (2010).
School District(s)
Union-North United School Corp (KG-12)
    2008-09 Enrollment: 1,286 . . . . (574) 784-8141
Housing: Homeownership rate: 70.8% (2010); Median home value: $86,667 (2010); Median contract rent: $338 per month (2000); Median year structure built: 1946 (2000).
Transportation: Commute to work: 94.6% car, 1.4% public transportation, 2.7% walk, 0.7% work from home (2000); Travel time to work: 20.1% less than 15 minutes, 51.5% 15 to 30 minutes, 16.7% 30 to 45 minutes, 6.1% 45 to 60 minutes, 5.5% 60 minutes or more (2000)

MISHAWAKA (city). Covers a land area of 15.711 square miles and a water area of 0.336 square miles. Located at 41.66° N. Lat; 86.17° W. Long. Elevation is 719 feet.
History: Mishawaka, situated along the St. Joseph River, developed around the Mishawaka Woolen and Rubber Manufacturing Company plant where felt, rubberboots, and raincoats were produced. Mishawaka was named for the daughter of Shawnee Chief Elkhart.

Population: 43,810 (1990); 46,557 (2000); 46,991 (2010); 46,791 (2015 projected); Race: 89.2% White, 4.6% Black, 1.7% Asian, 4.6% Other, 4.0% Hispanic of any race (2010); Density: 2,990.9 persons per square mile (2010); Average household size: 2.25 (2010); Median age: 36.5 (2010); Males per 100 females: 91.6 (2010); Marriage status: 29.8% never married, 48.0% now married, 8.2% widowed, 14.0% divorced (2000); Foreign born: 4.4% (2000); Ancestry (includes multiple ancestries): 27.2% German, 14.0% Irish, 12.1% Other groups, 9.4% Polish, 8.1% English (2000).

Economy: Unemployment rate: 11.5% (5/2010); Total civilian labor force: 25,343 (5/2010); Single-family building permits issued: 32 (2009); Multi-family building permits issued: 0 (2009); Employment by occupation: 11.1% management, 16.1% professional, 15.5% services, 29.0% sales, 0.1% farming, 8.2% construction, 20.1% production (2000).

Income: Per capita income: $20,949 (2010); Median household income: $39,394 (2010); Average household income: $47,730 (2010); Percent of households with income of $100,000 or more: 7.3% (2010); Poverty rate: 9.9% (2000).

Taxes: Total city taxes per capita: $593 (2007); City property taxes per capita: $535 (2007).

Education: Percent of population age 25 and over with: High school diploma (including GED) or higher: 84.1% (2010); Bachelor's degree or higher: 20.3% (2010); Master's degree or higher: 6.6% (2010).

School District(s)
Penn-Harris-Madison Sch Corp (KG-12)
    2008-09 Enrollment: 10,459 . . . . (574) 259-7941
School City Of Mishawaka (PK-12)
    2008-09 Enrollment: 5,483 . . . . (574) 254-4537

Four-year College(s)
Bethel College (Private, Not-for-profit, Missionary Church Inc)
    Fall 2008 Enrollment: 2,075. . . . . (574) 259-8511
    2009-10 Tuition: In-state $21,578; Out-of-state $21,578
Trine University-South Bend Campus (Private, Not-for-profit)
    Fall 2008 Enrollment: 78 . . . . (574) 243-0500
    2009-10 Tuition: In-state $7,152; Out-of-state $7,152

Housing: Homeownership rate: 59.5% (2010); Median home value: $90,294 (2010); Median contract rent: $461 per month (2000); Median year structure built: 1966 (2000).

Hospitals: St. Joseph Regional Medical Center - Mishawaka (125 beds)

Safety: Violent crime rate: 38.0 per 10,000 population; Property crime rate: 699.8 per 10,000 population (2008).

Newspapers: Mishawaka Enterprise (Community news; Circulation 2,100); South Bend Tribune - Mishawaka Bureau (Local news)

Transportation: Commute to work: 93.9% car, 1.0% public transportation, 3.2% walk, 1.3% work from home (2000); Travel time to work: 36.6% less than 15 minutes, 44.8% 15 to 30 minutes, 12.1% 30 to 45 minutes, 2.3% 45 to 60 minutes, 4.2% 60 minutes or more (2000)

Additional Information Contacts
City of Mishawaka . . . . (574) 258-1616
    http://www.mishawakacity.com
Mishawaka Chamber of Commerce. . . . . (574) 234-0051
    http://www.sjchamber.org

NEW CARLISLE (town). Covers a land area of 1.835 square miles and a water area of 0 square miles. Located at 41.70° N. Lat; 86.50° W. Long. Elevation is 810 feet.

History: New Carlisle was founded in 1835 and named for its founder, Richard R. Carlisle, who was an adventurer. The town became a trading center for the surrounding farm lands.

Population: 1,492 (1990); 1,505 (2000); 1,751 (2010); 1,840 (2015 projected); Race: 96.7% White, 1.0% Black, 0.1% Asian, 2.2% Other, 2.2% Hispanic of any race (2010); Density: 954.4 persons per square mile (2010); Average household size: 2.47 (2010); Median age: 39.5 (2010); Males per 100 females: 85.5 (2010); Marriage status: 22.8% never married, 56.2% now married, 8.5% widowed, 12.5% divorced (2000); Foreign born: 0.8% (2000); Ancestry (includes multiple ancestries): 31.3% German, 14.0% Polish, 13.1% Irish, 12.0% English, 5.6% United States or American (2000).

Economy: Single-family building permits issued: 5 (2009); Multi-family building permits issued: 0 (2009); Employment by occupation: 10.5% management, 14.7% professional, 17.4% services, 25.3% sales, 0.3% farming, 11.1% construction, 20.7% production (2000).

Income: Per capita income: $20,899 (2010); Median household income: $46,568 (2010); Average household income: $52,357 (2010); Percent of households with income of $100,000 or more: 8.8% (2010); Poverty rate: 6.6% (2000).

Taxes: Total city taxes per capita: $334 (2007); City property taxes per capita: $290 (2007).

Education: Percent of population age 25 and over with: High school diploma (including GED) or higher: 88.3% (2010); Bachelor's degree or higher: 15.8% (2010); Master's degree or higher: 5.7% (2010).

School District(s)
New Prairie United School Corp (PK-12)
    2008-09 Enrollment: 2,747 . . . . (574) 654-7273

Housing: Homeownership rate: 74.6% (2010); Median home value: $116,892 (2010); Median contract rent: $364 per month (2000); Median year structure built: 1953 (2000).

Transportation: Commute to work: 95.9% car, 0.0% public transportation, 3.1% walk, 0.6% work from home (2000); Travel time to work: 32.2% less than 15 minutes, 39.3% 15 to 30 minutes, 17.7% 30 to 45 minutes, 6.0% 45 to 60 minutes, 4.8% 60 minutes or more (2000)

NORTH LIBERTY (town). Covers a land area of 0.749 square miles and a water area of 0 square miles. Located at 41.53° N. Lat; 86.43° W. Long. Elevation is 732 feet.

History: Laid out 1836.

Population: 1,406 (1990); 1,402 (2000); 1,503 (2010); 1,507 (2015 projected); Race: 96.7% White, 0.7% Black, 0.1% Asian, 2.5% Other, 0.5% Hispanic of any race (2010); Density: 2,007.5 persons per square mile (2010); Average household size: 2.45 (2010); Median age: 33.9 (2010); Males per 100 females: 93.4 (2010); Marriage status: 20.3% never married, 58.4% now married, 8.9% widowed, 12.4% divorced (2000); Foreign born: 0.8% (2000); Ancestry (includes multiple ancestries): 27.3% German, 16.9% Irish, 13.1% Polish, 9.3% United States or American, 8.6% English (2000).

Economy: Employment by occupation: 8.2% management, 18.9% professional, 12.3% services, 23.3% sales, 0.0% farming, 11.6% construction, 25.7% production (2000).

Income: Per capita income: $21,076 (2010); Median household income: $45,071 (2010); Average household income: $51,497 (2010); Percent of households with income of $100,000 or more: 9.5% (2010); Poverty rate: 10.1% (2000).

Taxes: Total city taxes per capita: $255 (2007); City property taxes per capita: $217 (2007).

Education: Percent of population age 25 and over with: High school diploma (including GED) or higher: 85.4% (2010); Bachelor's degree or higher: 13.4% (2010); Master's degree or higher: 5.0% (2010).

School District(s)
John Glenn School Corporation (KG-12)
    2008-09 Enrollment: 1,824 . . . . (574) 586-3129

Housing: Homeownership rate: 70.3% (2010); Median home value: $103,125 (2010); Median contract rent: $392 per month (2000); Median year structure built: 1947 (2000).

Safety: Violent crime rate: 14.9 per 10,000 population; Property crime rate: 59.7 per 10,000 population (2008).

Transportation: Commute to work: 93.1% car, 0.0% public transportation, 2.8% walk, 2.9% work from home (2000); Travel time to work: 27.3% less than 15 minutes, 30.1% 15 to 30 minutes, 30.0% 30 to 45 minutes, 8.8% 45 to 60 minutes, 3.9% 60 minutes or more (2000)

NOTRE DAME (unincorporated postal area, zip code 46556). Covers a land area of 0.570 square miles and a water area of 0.031 square miles. Located at 41.59° N. Lat; 86.29° W. Long.

Population: 6,747 (2000); Race: 89.1% White, 2.7% Black, 1.9% Asian, 6.3% Other, 6.6% Hispanic of any race (2000); Density: 11,836.8 persons per square mile (2000); Age: 0.4% under 18, 1.4% over 64 (2000); Marriage status: 82.1% never married, 17.8% now married, 0.1% widowed, 0.0% divorced (2000); Foreign born: 2.2% (2000); Ancestry (includes multiple ancestries): 38.6% Irish, 29.6% German, 15.7% Italian, 13.7% Other groups, 10.5% Polish (2000).

Economy: Employment by occupation: 5.0% management, 37.2% professional, 20.4% services, 33.4% sales, 0.0% farming, 0.5% construction, 3.5% production (2000).

Income: Per capita income: $4,448 (2000); Median household income: $26,250 (2000); Poverty rate: 26.4% (2000).

Education: Percent of population age 25 and over with: High school diploma (including GED) or higher: 98.4% (2000); Bachelor's degree or higher: 87.4% (2000).

Four-year College(s)

Holy Cross College (Private, Not-for-profit, Roman Catholic)
　Fall 2008 Enrollment: 499 . . . . (574) 239-8400
　2009-10 Tuition: In-state $18,700; Out-of-state $18,700
Saint Mary's College (Private, Not-for-profit, Roman Catholic)
　Fall 2008 Enrollment: 1,628. . . . . (574) 284-4000
　2009-10 Tuition: In-state $29,616; Out-of-state $29,616
University of Notre Dame (Private, Not-for-profit, Roman Catholic)
　Fall 2008 Enrollment: 11,731. (574) 631-5000
　2009-10 Tuition: In-state $38,477; Out-of-state $38,477
Housing: Homeownership rate: 0.0% (2000); Median home value: $n/a (2000); Median contract rent: $99 per month (2000); Median year structure built: 1950 (2000).
Transportation: Commute to work: 7.2% car, 0.0% public transportation, 82.9% walk, 5.6% work from home (2000); Travel time to work: 88.3% less than 15 minutes, 9.8% 15 to 30 minutes, 0.9% 30 to 45 minutes, 0.6% 45 to 60 minutes, 0.3% 60 minutes or more (2000)

OSCEOLA (town).

Covers a land area of 1.366 square miles and a water area of 0.009 square miles. Located at 41.66° N. Lat; 86.07° W. Long. Elevation is 738 feet.
Population: 2,067 (1990); 1,859 (2000); 1,919 (2010); 1,934 (2015 projected); Race: 95.5% White, 1.7% Black, 1.2% Asian, 1.6% Other, 1.8% Hispanic of any race (2010); Density: 1,405.2 persons per square mile (2010); Average household size: 2.64 (2010); Median age: 38.8 (2010); Males per 100 females: 99.1 (2010); Marriage status: 24.7% never married, 58.1% now married, 5.2% widowed, 12.0% divorced (2000); Foreign born: 1.9% (2000); Ancestry (includes multiple ancestries): 25.9% German, 14.6% Irish, 12.7% United States or American, 9.0% English, 6.5% Polish (2000).
Economy: Employment by occupation: 9.5% management, 10.0% professional, 12.9% services, 24.9% sales, 0.0% farming, 15.2% construction, 27.6% production (2000).
Income: Per capita income: $21,334 (2010); Median household income: $50,592 (2010); Average household income: $56,364 (2010); Percent of households with income of $100,000 or more: 9.5% (2010); Poverty rate: 3.7% (2000).
Taxes: Total city taxes per capita: $116 (2007); City property taxes per capita: $83 (2007).
Education: Percent of population age 25 and over with: High school diploma (including GED) or higher: 82.8% (2010); Bachelor's degree or higher: 15.1% (2010); Master's degree or higher: 4.5% (2010).

School District(s)

Penn-Harris-Madison Sch Corp (KG-12)
　2008-09 Enrollment: 10,459 . . . . (574) 259-7941
Housing: Homeownership rate: 81.8% (2010); Median home value: $101,429 (2010); Median contract rent: $554 per month (2000); Median year structure built: 1953 (2000).
Transportation: Commute to work: 95.6% car, 0.0% public transportation, 1.3% walk, 2.5% work from home (2000); Travel time to work: 29.0% less than 15 minutes, 52.5% 15 to 30 minutes, 13.9% 30 to 45 minutes, 2.6% 45 to 60 minutes, 1.9% 60 minutes or more (2000)

ROSELAND (town).

Covers a land area of 0.389 square miles and a water area of 0 square miles. Located at 41.71° N. Lat; 86.25° W. Long. Elevation is 728 feet.
History: Wild roses that grew in the countryside were the inspiration for the name of Roseland. In 1855 St. Mary's College was founded here by the Roman Catholic Church as a sister institution to Notre Dame University.
Population: 706 (1990); 1,809 (2000); 1,722 (2010); 1,712 (2015 projected); Race: 91.8% White, 1.2% Black, 1.4% Asian, 5.6% Other, 5.0% Hispanic of any race (2010); Density: 4,431.6 persons per square mile (2010); Average household size: 2.06 (2010); Median age: 21.3 (2010); Males per 100 females: 18.5 (2010); Marriage status: 66.9% never married, 25.8% now married, 2.7% widowed, 4.6% divorced (2000); Foreign born: 3.1% (2000); Ancestry (includes multiple ancestries): 23.8% German, 20.7% Irish, 14.5% Polish, 10.6% Other groups, 6.0% Italian (2000).
Economy: Employment by occupation: 5.5% management, 16.9% professional, 12.6% services, 46.1% sales, 0.0% farming, 5.9% construction, 13.1% production (2000).
Income: Per capita income: $10,600 (2010); Median household income: $41,818 (2010); Average household income: $55,160 (2010); Percent of households with income of $100,000 or more: 10.9% (2010); Poverty rate: 5.7% (2000).

Taxes: Total city taxes per capita: $457 (2007); City property taxes per capita: $369 (2007).
Education: Percent of population age 25 and over with: High school diploma (including GED) or higher: 83.2% (2010); Bachelor's degree or higher: 18.7% (2010); Master's degree or higher: 8.7% (2010).
Housing: Homeownership rate: 65.4% (2010); Median home value: $82,128 (2010); Median contract rent: $396 per month (2000); Median year structure built: 1949 (2000).
Transportation: Commute to work: 44.5% car, 1.1% public transportation, 51.1% walk, 2.0% work from home (2000); Travel time to work: 74.7% less than 15 minutes, 19.0% 15 to 30 minutes, 2.7% 30 to 45 minutes, 1.2% 45 to 60 minutes, 2.3% 60 minutes or more (2000)

SOUTH BEND (city).

County seat. Covers a land area of 38.684 square miles and a water area of 0.427 square miles. Located at 41.67° N. Lat; 86.25° W. Long. Elevation is 692 feet.
History: South Bend was founded in 1823 by Alexis Coquillard, who called it Big St. Joseph Station. The location at a bend of the St. Joseph River caused settlers to refer to their community as The Bend, and in 1830 the Post Office officially named it South Bend. Early industries in South Bend were the Studebaker blacksmith and wagon shop which later became an automobile manufacturer, and the Oliver Chilled Plow Works, which used a process for chilling and hardening steel to increase its uses.
Population: 106,787 (1990); 107,789 (2000); 103,620 (2010); 101,440 (2015 projected); Race: 62.0% White, 25.6% Black, 1.5% Asian, 11.0% Other, 12.2% Hispanic of any race (2010); Density: 2,678.6 persons per square mile (2010); Average household size: 2.48 (2010); Median age: 34.9 (2010); Males per 100 females: 93.3 (2010); Marriage status: 32.0% never married, 47.7% now married, 8.4% widowed, 11.8% divorced (2000); Foreign born: 6.4% (2000); Ancestry (includes multiple ancestries): 32.7% Other groups, 17.6% German, 10.7% Polish, 10.5% Irish, 5.9% English (2000).
Economy: Unemployment rate: 13.1% (5/2010); Total civilian labor force: 45,021 (5/2010); Employment by occupation: 9.8% management, 18.3% professional, 16.9% services, 25.6% sales, 0.1% farming, 7.2% construction, 22.0% production (2000).
Income: Per capita income: $18,770 (2010); Median household income: $36,200 (2010); Average household income: $47,031 (2010); Percent of households with income of $100,000 or more: 7.6% (2010); Poverty rate: 16.7% (2000).
Taxes: Total city taxes per capita: $546 (2007); City property taxes per capita: $519 (2007).
Education: Percent of population age 25 and over with: High school diploma (including GED) or higher: 80.8% (2010); Bachelor's degree or higher: 22.5% (2010); Master's degree or higher: 9.3% (2010).

School District(s)

IN Department of Correction (05-12)
　2008-09 Enrollment: 793 . . . . (317) 233-3111
South Bend Community Sch Corp (PK-12)
　2008-09 Enrollment: 21,434 . . . . (574) 283-8000
Veritas Academy (KG-08)
　2008-09 Enrollment: 162 . . . . (574) 287-3230

Four-year College(s)

Brown Mackie College-South Bend (Private, For-profit)
　Fall 2008 Enrollment: 823 . . . . (574) 237-0774
　2009-10 Tuition: In-state $9,966; Out-of-state $9,966
ITT Technical Institute-South Bend (Private, For-profit)
　Fall 2008 Enrollment: 195 . . . . (574) 247-8300
　2009-10 Tuition: In-state $17,148; Out-of-state $17,148
Indiana University-South Bend (Public)
　Fall 2008 Enrollment: 7,712 . . . . (574) 520-4872
　2009-10 Tuition: In-state $6,015; Out-of-state $15,712

Two-year College(s)

Ivy Tech Community College-Northcentral (Public)
　Fall 2008 Enrollment: 6,189. (574) 289-7001
　2009-10 Tuition: In-state $3,090; Out-of-state $6,306
Housing: Homeownership rate: 64.8% (2010); Median home value: $79,399 (2010); Median contract rent: $447 per month (2000); Median year structure built: 1952 (2000).
Hospitals: Memorial Hospital of South Bend (526 beds); Saint Joseph's Regional Medical Center (339 beds)
Safety: Violent crime rate: 79.1 per 10,000 population; Property crime rate: 672.6 per 10,000 population (2008).
Newspapers: South Bend Tribune (Local news; Circulation 91,862); Tri-County News (Regional news; Circulation 1,000)

Transportation: Commute to work: 91.8% car, 2.7% public transportation, 2.1% walk, 2.4% work from home (2000); Travel time to work: 40.3% less than 15 minutes, 41.0% 15 to 30 minutes, 12.6% 30 to 45 minutes, 2.6% 45 to 60 minutes, 3.4% 60 minutes or more (2000); Amtrak: train service available.

Additional Information Contacts

Chamber of Commerce of St. Joseph County . . . . (574) 234-0051
   http://www.sjchamber.org
City of South Bend . . . . (574) 235-9216
   http://www.ci.south-bend.in.us

WALKERTON (town). Covers a land area of 1.735 square miles and a water area of 0 square miles. Located at 41.46° N. Lat; 86.48° W. Long. Elevation is 722 feet.

History: Walkerton was known as one of the largest peppermint-growing centers in the country.

Population: 2,185 (1990); 2,274 (2000); 2,449 (2010); 2,526 (2015 projected); Race: 90.2% White, 0.7% Black, 0.4% Asian, 8.6% Other, 10.3% Hispanic of any race (2010); Density: 1,411.5 persons per square mile (2010); Average household size: 2.75 (2010); Median age: 34.7 (2010); Males per 100 females: 93.1 (2010); Marriage status: 24.2% never married, 53.8% now married, 8.3% widowed, 13.7% divorced (2000); Foreign born: 2.3% (2000); Ancestry (includes multiple ancestries): 26.5% German, 17.8% Irish, 10.6% Other groups, 7.8% English, 7.6% United States or American (2000).

Economy: Single-family building permits issued: 0 (2009); Multi-family building permits issued: 0 (2009); Employment by occupation: 6.7% management, 18.1% professional, 15.3% services, 24.6% sales, 0.5% farming, 12.7% construction, 22.1% production (2000).

Income: Per capita income: $17,970 (2010); Median household income: $42,222 (2010); Average household income: $49,419 (2010); Percent of households with income of $100,000 or more: 7.1% (2010); Poverty rate: 14.5% (2000).

Taxes: Total city taxes per capita: $253 (2007); City property taxes per capita: $244 (2007).

Education: Percent of population age 25 and over with: High school diploma (including GED) or higher: 79.9% (2010); Bachelor's degree or higher: 16.6% (2010); Master's degree or higher: 7.2% (2010).

School District(s)

John Glenn School Corporation (KG-12)
   2008-09 Enrollment: 1,824 . . . . (574) 586-3129
Housing: Homeownership rate: 68.0% (2010); Median home value: $97,434 (2010); Median contract rent: $348 per month (2000); Median year structure built: 1954 (2000).

Safety: Violent crime rate: 82.9 per 10,000 population; Property crime rate: 308.8 per 10,000 population (2008).

Newspapers: Walkerton Independent News (Local news; Circulation 2,400)

Transportation: Commute to work: 88.5% car, 0.0% public transportation, 6.5% walk, 3.9% work from home (2000); Travel time to work: 38.5% less than 15 minutes, 20.4% 15 to 30 minutes, 22.8% 30 to 45 minutes, 13.2% 45 to 60 minutes, 5.1% 60 minutes or more (2000)

Additional Information Contacts

Town of Walkerton . . . . (574) 586-3711
   http://www.walkerton.org

Scott County

Located in southeastern Indiana; bounded on the north by the Muscatatuck River, and drained by its tributaries. Covers a land area of 190.39 square miles, a water area of 2.34 square miles, and is located in the Eastern Time Zone. The county was founded in 1820. County seat is Scottsburg.

Scott County is part of the Scottsburg, IN Micropolitan Statistical Area. The entire metro area includes: Scott County, IN

Weather Station: Scottsburg									Elevation: 547 feet		
	Jan	Feb	Mar	Apr	May	Jun	Jul	Aug	Sep	Oct	Nov	Dec
High	38	44	54	66	75	84	87	86	80	68	55	44
Low	20	23	32	42	52	61	65	63	55	42	34	25
Precip	3.0	2.7	4.2	4.4	4.7	4.2	4.3	4.3	3.0	3.0	3.6	3.3
Snow	5.1	4.8	3.7	0.1	0.0	0.0	0.0	0.0	0.0	0.1	0.5	2.4

High and Low temperatures in degrees Fahrenheit; Precipitation and Snow in inches

Population: 20,991 (1990); 22,960 (2000); 23,643 (2010); 23,737 (2015 projected); Race: 97.8% White, 0.4% Black, 0.2% Asian, 1.5% Other, 1.3%

Hispanic of any race (2010); Density: 124.2 persons per square mile (2010); Average household size: 2.49 (2010); Median age: 37.6 (2010); Males per 100 females: 97.8 (2010).

Religion: Five largest groups: 18.0% Christian Churches and Churches of Christ, 13.2% American Baptist Churches in the USA, 3.1% Church of God (Cleveland, Tennessee), 3.0% The United Methodist Church, 2.9% Catholic Church (2000).

Economy: Unemployment rate: 11.4% (5/2010); Total civilian labor force: 11,492 (5/2010); Leading industries: 33.0% manufacturing; 16.6% retail trade; 15.5% health care and social assistance (2008); Farms: 394 totaling 62,041 acres (2007); Companies that employ 500 or more persons: 1 (2008); Companies that employ 100 to 499 persons: 14 (2008); Companies that employ less than 100 persons: 432 (2008); Black-owned businesses: n/a (2002); Hispanic-owned businesses: n/a (2002); Asian-owned businesses: n/a (2002); Women-owned businesses: 344 (2002); Retail sales per capita: $11,950 (2010). Single-family building permits issued: 13 (2009); Multi-family building permits issued: 8 (2009).

Income: Per capita income: $19,632 (2010); Median household income: $40,195 (2010); Average household income: $48,981 (2010); Percent of households with income of $100,000 or more: 8.6% (2010); Poverty rate: 16.4% (2008); Bankruptcy rate: 9.27% (2009).

Taxes: Total county taxes per capita: $262 (2007); County property taxes per capita: $146 (2007).

Education: Percent of population age 25 and over with: High school diploma (including GED) or higher: 74.5% (2010); Bachelor's degree or higher: 11.2% (2010); Master's degree or higher: 3.6% (2010).

Housing: Homeownership rate: 74.9% (2010); Median home value: $91,546 (2010); Median contract rent: $485 per month (2006-2008 3-year est.); Median year structure built: 1977 (2006-2008 3-year est.)

Health: Birth rate: 118.1 per 10,000 population (2009); Death rate: 110.5 per 10,000 population (2009); Age-adjusted cancer mortality rate: 283.6 deaths per 100,000 population (2006); Number of physicians: 4.2 per 10,000 population (2007); Hospital beds: 10.6 per 10,000 population (2006); Hospital admissions: 606.3 per 10,000 population (2006).

Elections: 2008 Presidential election results: 48.1% Obama, 50.1% McCain, 0.0% Nader

Additional Information Contacts

Scott County Government . . . . (812) 752-8420
   http://www.scottcountyin.com
City of Scottsburg . . . . (812) 752-4343
   http://www.cityofscottsburg.com
Scott County Chamber of Commerce . . . . (812) 752-4080
   http://www.scottchamber.org
Town of Austin . . . . (812) 752-3339
   http://www.greatscottindiana.com

Scott County Communities

AUSTIN (town). Covers a land area of 2.427 square miles and a water area of 0 square miles. Located at 38.74° N. Lat; 85.80° W. Long. Elevation is 558 feet.

History: The Morgan Packing Company plant established the community of Austin as a canning center.

Population: 4,577 (1990); 4,724 (2000); 4,602 (2010); 4,523 (2015 projected); Race: 96.9% White, 1.0% Black, 0.3% Asian, 1.7% Other, 1.5% Hispanic of any race (2010); Density: 1,896.1 persons per square mile (2010); Average household size: 2.52 (2010); Median age: 34.9 (2010); Males per 100 females: 95.8 (2010); Marriage status: 21.0% never married, 56.9% now married, 7.5% widowed, 14.7% divorced (2000); Foreign born: 0.8% (2000); Ancestry (includes multiple ancestries): 21.3% United States or American, 8.5% Other groups, 7.3% German, 6.6% Irish, 3.4% English (2000).

Economy: Single-family building permits issued: 2 (2009); Multi-family building permits issued: 0 (2009); Employment by occupation: 4.6% management, 6.5% professional, 16.4% services, 16.3% sales, 0.5% farming, 10.5% construction, 45.1% production (2000).

Income: Per capita income: $15,494 (2010); Median household income: $32,033 (2010); Average household income: $39,033 (2010); Percent of households with income of $100,000 or more: 5.0% (2010); Poverty rate: 19.1% (2000).

Taxes: Total city taxes per capita: $147 (2007); City property taxes per capita: $132 (2007).

Education: Percent of population age 25 and over with: High school diploma (including GED) or higher: 64.1% (2010); Bachelor's degree or higher: 6.5% (2010); Master's degree or higher: 1.8% (2010).

School District(s)

Scott County School District 1 (KG-12)

2008-09 Enrollment: 1,384 . . . . (812) 794-8750

Housing: Homeownership rate: 64.4% (2010); Median home value: $71,103 (2010); Median contract rent: $344 per month (2000); Median year structure built: 1965 (2000).

Transportation: Commute to work: 96.1% car, 0.9% public transportation, 2.2% walk, 0.4% work from home (2000); Travel time to work: 42.4% less than 15 minutes, 22.0% 15 to 30 minutes, 21.3% 30 to 45 minutes, 9.5% 45 to 60 minutes, 4.8% 60 minutes or more (2000)

Additional Information Contacts

Scott County Chamber of Commerce . . . . (812) 752-4080
  http://www.scottchamber.org
Town of Austin . . . . (812) 752-3339
  http://www.greatscottindiana.com

LEXINGTON (unincorporated postal area, zip code 47138). Covers a land area of 75.189 square miles and a water area of 0.487 square miles. Located at 38.67° N. Lat; 85.61° W. Long. Elevation is 630 feet.

History: Founded c.1811.

Population: 4,270 (2000); Race: 98.2% White, 1.1% Black, 0.4% Asian, 0.3% Other, 0.4% Hispanic of any race (2000); Density: 56.8 persons per square mile (2000); Age: 26.3% under 18, 9.5% over 64 (2000); Marriage status: 18.6% never married, 64.8% now married, 5.1% widowed, 11.4% divorced (2000); Foreign born: 0.7% (2000); Ancestry (includes multiple ancestries): 22.6% United States or American, 17.7% German, 9.8% Irish, 9.2% Other groups, 8.7% English (2000).

Economy: Employment by occupation: 4.0% management, 12.3% professional, 15.2% services, 20.3% sales, 0.7% farming, 12.4% construction, 35.2% production (2000).

Income: Per capita income: $15,748 (2000); Median household income: $39,891 (2000); Poverty rate: 11.3% (2000).

Education: Percent of population age 25 and over with: High school diploma (including GED) or higher: 74.5% (2000); Bachelor's degree or higher: 7.4% (2000).

School District(s)

Scott County School District 2 (PK-12)

2008-09 Enrollment: 2,884 . . . . (812) 752-8946

Housing: Homeownership rate: 86.7% (2000); Median home value: $91,300 (2000); Median contract rent: $340 per month (2000); Median year structure built: 1975 (2000).

Transportation: Commute to work: 95.8% car, 0.5% public transportation, 0.3% walk, 2.6% work from home (2000); Travel time to work: 15.0% less than 15 minutes, 43.1% 15 to 30 minutes, 21.6% 30 to 45 minutes, 12.6% 45 to 60 minutes, 7.8% 60 minutes or more (2000)

SCOTTSBURG (city). County seat. Covers a land area of 4.804 square miles and a water area of 0.011 square miles. Located at 38.68° N. Lat; 85.77° W. Long. Elevation is 564 feet.

History: Laid out 1871.

Population: 5,556 (1990); 6,040 (2000); 5,774 (2010); 5,632 (2015 projected); Race: 97.4% White, 0.5% Black, 0.2% Asian, 1.9% Other, 1.6% Hispanic of any race (2010); Density: 1,201.8 persons per square mile (2010); Average household size: 2.21 (2010); Median age: 37.4 (2010); Males per 100 females: 91.7 (2010); Marriage status: 20.8% never married, 53.3% now married, 9.3% widowed, 16.6% divorced (2000); Foreign born: 0.1% (2000); Ancestry (includes multiple ancestries): 24.4% United States or American, 14.7% German, 11.5% Irish, 8.9% Other groups, 8.8% English (2000).

Economy: Employment by occupation: 11.2% management, 13.0% professional, 15.7% services, 22.0% sales, 0.5% farming, 7.9% construction, 29.6% production (2000).

Income: Per capita income: $19,453 (2010); Median household income: $34,353 (2010); Average household income: $43,470 (2010); Percent of households with income of $100,000 or more: 7.1% (2010); Poverty rate: 15.5% (2000).

Taxes: Total city taxes per capita: $291 (2007); City property taxes per capita: $285 (2007).

Education: Percent of population age 25 and over with: High school diploma (including GED) or higher: 75.2% (2010); Bachelor's degree or higher: 13.7% (2010); Master's degree or higher: 4.4% (2010).

School District(s)

Scott County School District 2 (PK-12)

2008-09 Enrollment: 2,884 . . . . (812) 752-8946

Housing: Homeownership rate: 61.4% (2010); Median home value: $87,349 (2010); Median contract rent: $432 per month (2000); Median year structure built: 1969 (2000).

Hospitals: Scott Memorial Hospital (90 beds)

Safety: Violent crime rate: 67.4 per 10,000 population; Property crime rate: 611.2 per 10,000 population (2008).

Newspapers: Austin Chronicle (Community news; Circulation 1,500); Giveaway (Local news; Circulation 16,687); Scott County Journal (Community news; Circulation 3,700)

Transportation: Commute to work: 94.9% car, 0.3% public transportation, 2.4% walk, 1.4% work from home (2000); Travel time to work: 55.7% less than 15 minutes, 11.2% 15 to 30 minutes, 19.1% 30 to 45 minutes, 8.3% 45 to 60 minutes, 5.8% 60 minutes or more (2000)

Additional Information Contacts

City of Scottsburg . . . . (812) 752-4343
  http://www.cityofscottsburg.com

Shelby County

Located in central Indiana; drained by the Big Blue River. Covers a land area of 412.64 square miles, a water area of 0.47 square miles, and is located in the Eastern Time Zone. The county was founded in 1821. County seat is Shelbyville.

Shelby County is part of the Indianapolis-Carmel, IN Metropolitan Statistical Area. The entire metro area includes: Boone County, IN; Brown County, IN; Hamilton County, IN; Hancock County, IN; Hendricks County, IN; Johnson County, IN; Marion County, IN; Morgan County, IN; Putnam County, IN; Shelby County, IN

Population: 40,307 (1990); 43,445 (2000); 44,458 (2010); 44,798 (2015 projected); Race: 95.4% White, 1.0% Black, 1.1% Asian, 2.5% Other, 3.0% Hispanic of any race (2010); Density: 107.7 persons per square mile (2010); Average household size: 2.52 (2010); Median age: 38.7 (2010); Males per 100 females: 100.0 (2010).

Religion: Five largest groups: 9.1% Catholic Church, 7.8% American Baptist Churches in the USA, 6.4% The United Methodist Church, 3.3% Christian Churches and Churches of Christ, 1.5% Christian Church (Disciples of Christ) (2000).

Economy: Unemployment rate: 9.2% (5/2010); Total civilian labor force: 22,926 (5/2010); Leading industries: 35.4% manufacturing; 12.9% health care and social assistance; 10.9% retail trade (2008); Farms: 636 totaling 205,432 acres (2007); Companies that employ 500 or more persons: 5 (2008); Companies that employ 100 to 499 persons: 24 (2008); Companies that employ less than 100 persons: 900 (2008); Black-owned businesses: n/a (2002); Hispanic-owned businesses: n/a (2002); Asian-owned businesses: n/a (2002); Women-owned businesses: 931 (2002); Retail sales per capita: $12,055 (2010). Single-family building permits issued: 37 (2009); Multi-family building permits issued: 15 (2009).

Income: Per capita income: $25,128 (2010); Median household income: $52,166 (2010); Average household income: $63,939 (2010); Percent of households with income of $100,000 or more: 16.1% (2010); Poverty rate: 10.8% (2008); Bankruptcy rate: 8.05% (2009).

Taxes: Total county taxes per capita: $311 (2007); County property taxes per capita: $159 (2007).

Education: Percent of population age 25 and over with: High school diploma (including GED) or higher: 86.9% (2010); Bachelor's degree or higher: 15.0% (2010); Master's degree or higher: 4.1% (2010).

Housing: Homeownership rate: 74.9% (2010); Median home value: $116,495 (2010); Median contract rent: $523 per month (2006-2008 3-year est.); Median year structure built: 1966 (2006-2008 3-year est.)

Health: Birth rate: 127.2 per 10,000 population (2009); Death rate: 92.8 per 10,000 population (2009); Age-adjusted cancer mortality rate: 187.8 deaths per 100,000 population (2006); Air Quality Index: 81.5% good, 18.5% moderate, 0.0% unhealthy for sensitive individuals, 0.0% unhealthy (percent of days in 2008); Number of physicians: 5.2 per 10,000 population (2007); Hospital beds: 14.2 per 10,000 population (2006); Hospital admissions: 673.2 per 10,000 population (2006).

Elections: 2008 Presidential election results: 39.8% Obama, 58.8% McCain, 0.0% Nader

Additional Information Contacts

Shelby County Government . . . . (317) 392-6330
  http://www.co.shelby.in.us
City of Shelbyville . . . . (317) 392-5103
  http://www.cityofshelbyvillein.com

Shelby County Chamber of Commerce . . . . (317) 398-6647
  http://www.shelbychamber.net

Shelby County Communities

BOGGSTOWN (unincorporated postal area, zip code 46110). Covers a land area of 12.724 square miles and a water area of 0 square miles. Located at 39.56° N. Lat; 85.92° W. Long. Elevation is 761 feet.
Population: 501 (2000); Race: 100.0% White, 0.0% Black, 0.0% Asian, 0.0% Other, 0.0% Hispanic of any race (2000); Density: 39.4 persons per square mile (2000); Age: 33.6% under 18, 11.1% over 64 (2000); Marriage status: 18.5% never married, 75.5% now married, 3.2% widowed, 2.9% divorced (2000); Foreign born: 0.0% (2000); Ancestry (includes multiple ancestries): 27.4% German, 17.7% United States or American, 15.0% French (except Basque), 13.9% Irish, 10.5% Other groups (2000).
Economy: Employment by occupation: 12.7% management, 25.4% professional, 0.0% services, 20.5% sales, 4.6% farming, 24.0% construction, 12.7% production (2000).
Income: Per capita income: $18,661 (2000); Median household income: $44,861 (2000); Poverty rate: 16.5% (2000).
Education: Percent of population age 25 and over with: High school diploma (including GED) or higher: 87.5% (2000); Bachelor's degree or higher: 16.8% (2000).
Housing: Homeownership rate: 72.8% (2000); Median home value: $155,900 (2000); Median contract rent: $409 per month (2000); Median year structure built: before 1940 (2000).
Transportation: Commute to work: 100.0% car, 0.0% public transportation, 0.0% walk, 0.0% work from home (2000); Travel time to work: 13.5% less than 15 minutes, 52.8% 15 to 30 minutes, 13.1% 30 to 45 minutes, 16.3% 45 to 60 minutes, 4.4% 60 minutes or more (2000)

FAIRLAND (CDP). Covers a land area of 3.470 square miles and a water area of 0.016 square miles. Located at 39.58° N. Lat; 85.86° W. Long. Elevation is 771 feet.
Population: 1,348 (1990); 1,276 (2000); 1,310 (2010); 1,326 (2015 projected); Race: 96.7% White, 0.0% Black, 0.4% Asian, 2.9% Other, 1.7% Hispanic of any race (2010); Density: 377.5 persons per square mile (2010); Average household size: 2.70 (2010); Median age: 37.1 (2010); Males per 100 females: 98.2 (2010); Marriage status: 32.7% never married, 44.2% now married, 9.9% widowed, 13.2% divorced (2000); Foreign born: 0.4% (2000); Ancestry (includes multiple ancestries): 31.7% United States or American, 22.1% German, 12.7% Other groups, 10.4% Irish, 7.0% English (2000).
Economy: Employment by occupation: 13.9% management, 10.2% professional, 11.9% services, 18.7% sales, 1.3% farming, 15.0% construction, 29.0% production (2000).
Income: Per capita income: $22,714 (2010); Median household income: $52,692 (2010); Average household income: $61,224 (2010); Percent of households with income of $100,000 or more: 15.2% (2010); Poverty rate: 10.3% (2000).
Education: Percent of population age 25 and over with: High school diploma (including GED) or higher: 85.9% (2010); Bachelor's degree or higher: 11.5% (2010); Master's degree or higher: 5.5% (2010).
School District(s)
Northwestern Con School Corp (PK-12)
  2008-09 Enrollment: 1,582 . . . . (317) 835-7461
Housing: Homeownership rate: 86.0% (2010); Median home value: $96,800 (2010); Median contract rent: $450 per month (2000); Median year structure built: 1963 (2000).
Transportation: Commute to work: 91.7% car, 0.0% public transportation, 1.0% walk, 3.3% work from home (2000); Travel time to work: 13.8% less than 15 minutes, 44.7% 15 to 30 minutes, 23.3% 30 to 45 minutes, 12.7% 45 to 60 minutes, 5.5% 60 minutes or more (2000)

FLAT ROCK (unincorporated postal area, zip code 47234). Covers a land area of 36.032 square miles and a water area of 0 square miles. Located at 39.37° N. Lat; 85.78° W. Long. Elevation is 689 feet.
Population: 1,441 (2000); Race: 98.7% White, 0.0% Black, 0.0% Asian, 1.3% Other, 0.0% Hispanic of any race (2000); Density: 40.0 persons per square mile (2000); Age: 24.3% under 18, 12.2% over 64 (2000); Marriage status: 21.9% never married, 67.9% now married, 4.3% widowed, 5.9% divorced (2000); Foreign born: 2.7% (2000); Ancestry (includes multiple ancestries): 24.6% United States or American, 18.7% German, 8.1% Irish, 7.9% English, 2.6% Other groups (2000).

Economy: Employment by occupation: 18.0% management, 9.1% professional, 6.1% services, 20.6% sales, 3.0% farming, 13.2% construction, 30.0% production (2000).
Income: Per capita income: $17,966 (2000); Median household income: $41,230 (2000); Poverty rate: 5.4% (2000).
Education: Percent of population age 25 and over with: High school diploma (including GED) or higher: 80.3% (2000); Bachelor's degree or higher: 9.4% (2000).
Housing: Homeownership rate: 80.5% (2000); Median home value: $84,600 (2000); Median contract rent: $331 per month (2000); Median year structure built: 1942 (2000).
Transportation: Commute to work: 96.3% car, 0.0% public transportation, 0.6% walk, 2.3% work from home (2000); Travel time to work: 15.3% less than 15 minutes, 58.6% 15 to 30 minutes, 10.4% 30 to 45 minutes, 6.7% 45 to 60 minutes, 9.1% 60 minutes or more (2000)

FOUNTAINTOWN (unincorporated postal area, zip code 46130). Covers a land area of 26.502 square miles and a water area of 0 square miles. Located at 39.68° N. Lat; 85.83° W. Long. Elevation is 850 feet.
Population: 2,219 (2000); Race: 100.0% White, 0.0% Black, 0.0% Asian, 0.0% Other, 0.4% Hispanic of any race (2000); Density: 83.7 persons per square mile (2000); Age: 30.7% under 18, 6.7% over 64 (2000); Marriage status: 23.7% never married, 64.3% now married, 4.8% widowed, 7.2% divorced (2000); Foreign born: 0.4% (2000); Ancestry (includes multiple ancestries): 32.5% German, 23.1% Irish, 15.0% English, 10.7% United States or American, 5.3% Polish (2000).
Economy: Employment by occupation: 17.6% management, 10.5% professional, 9.7% services, 29.7% sales, 0.0% farming, 16.2% construction, 16.3% production (2000).
Income: Per capita income: $24,238 (2000); Median household income: $63,500 (2000); Poverty rate: 2.6% (2000).
Education: Percent of population age 25 and over with: High school diploma (including GED) or higher: 91.0% (2000); Bachelor's degree or higher: 19.1% (2000).
Housing: Homeownership rate: 84.4% (2000); Median home value: $118,200 (2000); Median contract rent: $405 per month (2000); Median year structure built: 1970 (2000).
Transportation: Commute to work: 93.6% car, 0.0% public transportation, 2.1% walk, 4.4% work from home (2000); Travel time to work: 11.9% less than 15 minutes, 38.8% 15 to 30 minutes, 31.5% 30 to 45 minutes, 11.7% 45 to 60 minutes, 6.1% 60 minutes or more (2000)

MORRISTOWN (town). Covers a land area of 0.958 square miles and a water area of 0 square miles. Located at 39.67° N. Lat; 85.69° W. Long. Elevation is 833 feet.
History: Laid out 1828.
Population: 1,087 (1990); 1,133 (2000); 1,149 (2010); 1,150 (2015 projected); Race: 98.3% White, 0.0% Black, 0.2% Asian, 1.6% Other, 1.4% Hispanic of any race (2010); Density: 1,198.9 persons per square mile (2010); Average household size: 2.51 (2010); Median age: 36.2 (2010); Males per 100 females: 92.1 (2010); Marriage status: 21.9% never married, 55.0% now married, 11.1% widowed, 12.0% divorced (2000); Foreign born: 0.4% (2000); Ancestry (includes multiple ancestries): 22.4% German, 19.9% United States or American, 13.0% Irish, 11.7% Other groups, 11.1% English (2000).
Economy: Single-family building permits issued: 0 (2009); Multi-family building permits issued: 15 (2009); Employment by occupation: 6.7% management, 10.1% professional, 21.6% services, 19.4% sales, 0.4% farming, 12.5% construction, 29.3% production (2000).
Income: Per capita income: $22,661 (2010); Median household income: $45,727 (2010); Average household income: $56,595 (2010); Percent of households with income of $100,000 or more: 12.5% (2010); Poverty rate: 5.5% (2000).
Taxes: Total city taxes per capita: $164 (2007); City property taxes per capita: $142 (2007).
Education: Percent of population age 25 and over with: High school diploma (including GED) or higher: 88.1% (2010); Bachelor's degree or higher: 7.4% (2010); Master's degree or higher: 3.6% (2010).
School District(s)
Shelby Eastern Schools (PK-12)
  2008-09 Enrollment: 1,508 . . . . (765) 544-2246
Housing: Homeownership rate: 76.1% (2010); Median home value: $86,481 (2010); Median contract rent: $375 per month (2000); Median year structure built: 1956 (2000).

Transportation: Commute to work: 92.6% car, 0.2% public transportation, 3.7% walk, 1.0% work from home (2000); Travel time to work: 35.8% less than 15 minutes, 26.0% 15 to 30 minutes, 15.2% 30 to 45 minutes, 16.7% 45 to 60 minutes, 6.3% 60 minutes or more (2000)

SHELBYVILLE (city). County seat. Covers a land area of 8.873 square miles and a water area of 0.106 square miles. Located at 39.52° N. Lat; 85.77° W. Long. Elevation is 764 feet.

History: Shelbyville was laid out in 1822 and named for the first governor of Kentucky. Shelbyville was the home of Vice President Thomas A. Hendricks (1819-1885).

Population: 15,890 (1990); 17,951 (2000); 18,205 (2010); 18,296 (2015 projected); Race: 92.5% White, 1.9% Black, 1.9% Asian, 3.7% Other, 4.8% Hispanic of any race (2010); Density: 2,051.7 persons per square mile (2010); Average household size: 2.35 (2010); Median age: 37.0 (2010); Males per 100 females: 98.4 (2010); Marriage status: 23.8% never married, 53.0% now married, 7.4% widowed, 15.7% divorced (2000); Foreign born: 2.8% (2000); Ancestry (includes multiple ancestries): 25.5% German, 23.1% United States or American, 10.7% Irish, 9.8% Other groups, 6.3% English (2000).

Economy: Single-family building permits issued: 4 (2009); Multi-family building permits issued: 0 (2009); Employment by occupation: 9.2% management, 13.3% professional, 15.6% services, 21.8% sales, 0.1% farming, 9.2% construction, 30.7% production (2000).

Income: Per capita income: $21,969 (2010); Median household income: $43,297 (2010); Average household income: $52,779 (2010); Percent of households with income of $100,000 or more: 9.4% (2010); Poverty rate: 9.1% (2000).

Taxes: Total city taxes per capita: $302 (2007); City property taxes per capita: $296 (2007).

Education: Percent of population age 25 and over with: High school diploma (including GED) or higher: 83.8% (2010); Bachelor's degree or higher: 13.7% (2010); Master's degree or higher: 3.3% (2010).

School District(s)

Blue River Career Programs (09-12)
    2008-09 Enrollment: n/a . . . . (317) 392-4191
Blue River Special Ed Coop (PK-12)
    2008-09 Enrollment: n/a . . . . (317) 398-4468
Shelbyville Central Schools (KG-12)
    2008-09 Enrollment: 3,947 . . . . (317) 392-2505
Southwestern Con Sch Shelby Co (KG-12)
    2008-09 Enrollment: 735 . . . . (317) 729-5746

Housing: Homeownership rate: 62.2% (2010); Median home value: $95,499 (2010); Median contract rent: $461 per month (2000); Median year structure built: 1957 (2000).

Hospitals: Major Hospital (89 beds)

Newspapers: Shelbyville News (Community news)

Transportation: Commute to work: 92.7% car, 0.2% public transportation, 3.0% walk, 1.7% work from home (2000); Travel time to work: 61.8% less than 15 minutes, 15.0% 15 to 30 minutes, 11.5% 30 to 45 minutes, 7.4% 45 to 60 minutes, 4.3% 60 minutes or more (2000)

Additional Information Contacts

City of Shelbyville. . . . . (317) 392-5103
    http://www.cityofshelbyvillein.com
Shelby County Chamber of Commerce . . . . (317) 398-6647
    http://www.shelbychamber.net

WALDRON (unincorporated postal area, zip code 46182). Covers a land area of 35.820 square miles and a water area of 0.021 square miles. Located at 39.45° N. Lat; 85.67° W. Long. Elevation is 823 feet.

History: Laid out 1854.

Population: 1,971 (2000); Race: 97.6% White, 0.0% Black, 0.0% Asian, 2.4% Other, 0.4% Hispanic of any race (2000); Density: 55.0 persons per square mile (2000); Age: 28.5% under 18, 17.0% over 64 (2000); Marriage status: 11.4% never married, 67.8% now married, 6.6% widowed, 14.3% divorced (2000); Foreign born: 0.0% (2000); Ancestry (includes multiple ancestries): 32.1% German, 17.2% United States or American, 12.0% Irish, 10.2% English, 3.8% Other groups (2000).

Economy: Employment by occupation: 11.7% management, 10.1% professional, 11.9% services, 24.4% sales, 0.0% farming, 13.4% construction, 28.5% production (2000).

Income: Per capita income: $18,073 (2000); Median household income: $41,524 (2000); Poverty rate: 7.2% (2000).

Education: Percent of population age 25 and over with: High school diploma (including GED) or higher: 82.2% (2000); Bachelor's degree or higher: 11.0% (2000).

School District(s)

Shelby Eastern Schools (PK-12)
    2008-09 Enrollment: 1,508 . . . . (765) 544-2246

Housing: Homeownership rate: 83.0% (2000); Median home value: $88,400 (2000); Median contract rent: $388 per month (2000); Median year structure built: 1947 (2000).

Transportation: Commute to work: 95.0% car, 0.0% public transportation, 4.1% walk, 0.0% work from home (2000); Travel time to work: 30.8% less than 15 minutes, 48.7% 15 to 30 minutes, 10.0% 30 to 45 minutes, 9.6% 45 to 60 minutes, 0.8% 60 minutes or more (2000)

Spencer County

Located in southwestern Indiana; bounded on the south by the Ohio River and the Kentucky border; drained by the Anderson River and Little Pigeon Creek. Covers a land area of 398.69 square miles, a water area of 2.55 square miles, and is located in the Central Time Zone. The county was founded in 1818. County seat is Rockport.

Weather Station: Saint Meinrad   Elevation: 508 feet

	Jan	Feb	Mar	Apr	May	Jun	Jul	Aug	Sep	Oct	Nov	Dec
High	40	47	57	68	77	84	87	86	81	70	57	46
Low	23	27	36	45	53	62	66	65	58	46	37	28
Precip	3.1	3.0	4.4	4.7	4.7	4.1	4.7	3.8	3.3	3.0	4.0	3.7
Snow	3.8	2.8	1.4	tr	0.0	0.0	0.0	0.0	0.0	tr	0.1	1.6

High and Low temperatures in degrees Fahrenheit; Precipitation and Snow in inches

Population: 19,490 (1990); 20,391 (2000); 20,011 (2010); 19,667 (2015 projected); Race: 96.9% White, 0.8% Black, 0.2% Asian, 2.1% Other, 2.3% Hispanic of any race (2010); Density: 50.2 persons per square mile (2010); Average household size: 2.60 (2010); Median age: 41.1 (2010); Males per 100 females: 101.9 (2010).

Religion: Five largest groups: 22.3% Catholic Church, 10.3% The United Methodist Church, 4.7% American Baptist Churches in the USA, 3.9% Southern Baptist Convention, 3.5% Christian Churches and Churches of Christ (2000).

Economy: Unemployment rate: 8.1% (5/2010); Total civilian labor force: 10,941 (5/2010); Leading industries: 26.3% manufacturing; 17.2% retail trade; 6.5% health care and social assistance (2008); Farms: 632 totaling 150,244 acres (2007); Companies that employ 500 or more persons: 1 (2008); Companies that employ 100 to 499 persons: 8 (2008); Companies that employ less than 100 persons: 413 (2008); Black-owned businesses: n/a (2002); Hispanic-owned businesses: n/a (2002); Asian-owned businesses: n/a (2002); Women-owned businesses: 365 (2002); Retail sales per capita: $7,789 (2010). Single-family building permits issued: 37 (2009); Multi-family building permits issued: 0 (2009).

Income: Per capita income: $23,219 (2010); Median household income: $52,961 (2010); Average household income: $61,130 (2010); Percent of households with income of $100,000 or more: 14.6% (2010); Poverty rate: 9.3% (2008); Bankruptcy rate: 6.40% (2009).

Taxes: Total county taxes per capita: $446 (2007); County property taxes per capita: $229 (2007).

Education: Percent of population age 25 and over with: High school diploma (including GED) or higher: 87.0% (2010); Bachelor's degree or higher: 17.2% (2010); Master's degree or higher: 6.9% (2010).

Housing: Homeownership rate: 83.4% (2010); Median home value: $107,674 (2010); Median contract rent: $338 per month (2006-2008 3-year est.); Median year structure built: 1978 (2006-2008 3-year est.)

Health: Birth rate: 114.3 per 10,000 population (2009); Death rate: 96.8 per 10,000 population (2009); Age-adjusted cancer mortality rate: 186.5 deaths per 100,000 population (2006); Air Quality Index: 73.9% good, 26.1% moderate, 0.0% unhealthy for sensitive individuals, 0.0% unhealthy (percent of days in 2008); Number of physicians: 3.0 per 10,000 population (2007); Hospital beds: 0.0 per 10,000 population (2006); Hospital admissions: 0.0 per 10,000 population (2006).

Elections: 2008 Presidential election results: 49.5% Obama, 49.1% McCain, 0.0% Nader

National and State Parks: Lincoln Boyhood National Memorial; Lincoln State Park; Nancy Hanks Lincoln State Memorial; Spencer County State Forest

Additional Information Contacts

Spencer County Government . . . . (812) 649-2242
    http://www.spencerco.org

Spencer County Communities

CHRISNEY (town). Covers a land area of 0.366 square miles and a water area of 0 square miles. Located at 38.01° N. Lat; 87.03° W. Long. Elevation is 469 feet.
Population: 511 (1990); 544 (2000); 500 (2010); 477 (2015 projected); Race: 97.2% White, 0.6% Black, 0.0% Asian, 2.2% Other, 0.6% Hispanic of any race (2010); Density: 1,364.8 persons per square mile (2010); Average household size: 2.56 (2010); Median age: 39.0 (2010); Males per 100 females: 94.6 (2010); Marriage status: 14.3% never married, 60.4% now married, 12.3% widowed, 13.0% divorced (2000); Foreign born: 0.4% (2000); Ancestry (includes multiple ancestries): 20.9% United States or American, 17.5% German, 17.0% Other groups, 11.7% English, 9.6% Irish (2000).
Economy: Employment by occupation: 5.0% management, 11.6% professional, 11.6% services, 24.5% sales, 0.0% farming, 10.0% construction, 37.3% production (2000).
Income: Per capita income: $24,283 (2010); Median household income: $56,686 (2010); Average household income: $62,603 (2010); Percent of households with income of $100,000 or more: 14.4% (2010); Poverty rate: 15.1% (2000).
Taxes: Total city taxes per capita: $84 (2007); City property taxes per capita: $65 (2007).
Education: Percent of population age 25 and over with: High school diploma (including GED) or higher: 89.4% (2010); Bachelor's degree or higher: 10.3% (2010); Master's degree or higher: 3.0% (2010).
School District(s)
North Spencer County Sch Corp (PK-12)
    2008-09 Enrollment: 2,102 . . . . (812) 937-2400
Housing: Homeownership rate: 77.9% (2010); Median home value: $84,516 (2010); Median contract rent: $306 per month (2000); Median year structure built: 1948 (2000).
Transportation: Commute to work: 97.5% car, 0.0% public transportation, 0.8% walk, 1.7% work from home (2000); Travel time to work: 17.6% less than 15 minutes, 42.1% 15 to 30 minutes, 17.6% 30 to 45 minutes, 15.9% 45 to 60 minutes, 6.9% 60 minutes or more (2000)

DALE (town). Covers a land area of 1.529 square miles and a water area of 0 square miles. Located at 38.16° N. Lat; 86.98° W. Long. Elevation is 466 feet.
History: Dale was named for Robert Dale Owen, who founded the colony at New Harmony.
Population: 1,705 (1990); 1,568 (2000); 1,472 (2010); 1,417 (2015 projected); Race: 90.4% White, 1.2% Black, 0.1% Asian, 8.4% Other, 12.6% Hispanic of any race (2010); Density: 962.6 persons per square mile (2010); Average household size: 2.52 (2010); Median age: 40.0 (2010); Males per 100 females: 95.7 (2010); Marriage status: 18.4% never married, 58.2% now married, 9.1% widowed, 14.4% divorced (2000); Foreign born: 7.9% (2000); Ancestry (includes multiple ancestries): 30.9% German, 14.5% Other groups, 9.5% English, 9.3% Irish, 7.8% United States or American (2000).
Economy: Single-family building permits issued: 1 (2009); Multi-family building permits issued: 0 (2009); Employment by occupation: 4.0% management, 10.2% professional, 11.6% services, 20.7% sales, 1.1% farming, 10.0% construction, 42.5% production (2000).
Income: Per capita income: $21,264 (2010); Median household income: $50,414 (2010); Average household income: $54,198 (2010); Percent of households with income of $100,000 or more: 7.4% (2010); Poverty rate: 4.5% (2000).
Taxes: Total city taxes per capita: $120 (2007); City property taxes per capita: $116 (2007).
Education: Percent of population age 25 and over with: High school diploma (including GED) or higher: 81.5% (2010); Bachelor's degree or higher: 12.5% (2010); Master's degree or higher: 6.7% (2010).
School District(s)
North Spencer County Sch Corp (PK-12)
    2008-09 Enrollment: 2,102 . . . . (812) 937-2400
Housing: Homeownership rate: 73.0% (2010); Median home value: $83,441 (2010); Median contract rent: $291 per month (2000); Median year structure built: 1971 (2000).
Transportation: Commute to work: 96.4% car, 0.0% public transportation, 2.3% walk, 1.3% work from home (2000); Travel time to work: 37.7% less than 15 minutes, 33.1% 15 to 30 minutes, 19.7% 30 to 45 minutes, 5.6% 45 to 60 minutes, 3.9% 60 minutes or more (2000)

EVANSTON (unincorporated postal area, zip code 47531). Covers a land area of 24.974 square miles and a water area of 0.020 square miles. Located at 38.05° N. Lat; 86.82° W. Long. Elevation is 413 feet.
Population: 715 (2000); Race: 100.0% White, 0.0% Black, 0.0% Asian, 0.0% Other, 0.0% Hispanic of any race (2000); Density: 28.6 persons per square mile (2000); Age: 22.4% under 18, 10.1% over 64 (2000); Marriage status: 14.9% never married, 75.6% now married, 4.3% widowed, 5.2% divorced (2000); Foreign born: 1.0% (2000); Ancestry (includes multiple ancestries): 31.9% German, 12.1% English, 10.5% Irish, 9.8% United States or American, 3.7% French (except Basque) (2000).
Economy: Employment by occupation: 7.5% management, 10.4% professional, 5.2% services, 31.0% sales, 0.0% farming, 18.0% construction, 27.8% production (2000).
Income: Per capita income: $17,945 (2000); Median household income: $45,682 (2000); Poverty rate: 2.7% (2000).
Education: Percent of population age 25 and over with: High school diploma (including GED) or higher: 84.7% (2000); Bachelor's degree or higher: 10.3% (2000).
Housing: Homeownership rate: 100.0% (2000); Median home value: $75,600 (2000); Median contract rent: $n/a per month (2000); Median year structure built: 1968 (2000).
Transportation: Commute to work: 90.7% car, 0.0% public transportation, 2.6% walk, 4.1% work from home (2000); Travel time to work: 10.0% less than 15 minutes, 47.1% 15 to 30 minutes, 18.4% 30 to 45 minutes, 13.3% 45 to 60 minutes, 11.2% 60 minutes or more (2000)

GENTRYVILLE (town). Covers a land area of 0.389 square miles and a water area of 0 square miles. Located at 38.10° N. Lat; 87.03° W. Long. Elevation is 410 feet.
History: Abraham Lincoln was a clerk in the store of James Gentry, one of the first merchants in Gentryville and the man for whom the town was named.
Population: 277 (1990); 262 (2000); 247 (2010); 238 (2015 projected); Race: 97.6% White, 0.0% Black, 0.4% Asian, 2.0% Other, 1.2% Hispanic of any race (2010); Density: 635.5 persons per square mile (2010); Average household size: 2.68 (2010); Median age: 41.3 (2010); Males per 100 females: 107.6 (2010); Marriage status: 29.2% never married, 64.1% now married, 0.0% widowed, 6.7% divorced (2000); Foreign born: 0.8% (2000); Ancestry (includes multiple ancestries): 32.4% United States or American, 21.2% Other groups, 19.6% German, 10.4% English, 6.0% Irish (2000).
Economy: Single-family building permits issued: 0 (2009); Multi-family building permits issued: 0 (2009); Employment by occupation: 4.4% management, 6.2% professional, 24.8% services, 16.8% sales, 0.0% farming, 18.6% construction, 29.2% production (2000).
Income: Per capita income: $22,128 (2010); Median household income: $56,667 (2010); Average household income: $60,163 (2010); Percent of households with income of $100,000 or more: 10.9% (2010); Poverty rate: 9.6% (2000).
Taxes: Total city taxes per capita: $69 (2007); City property taxes per capita: $65 (2007).
Education: Percent of population age 25 and over with: High school diploma (including GED) or higher: 80.5% (2010); Bachelor's degree or higher: 13.0% (2010); Master's degree or higher: 7.7% (2010).
Housing: Homeownership rate: 92.4% (2010); Median home value: $104,412 (2010); Median contract rent: $238 per month (2000); Median year structure built: 1973 (2000).
Transportation: Commute to work: 96.5% car, 0.0% public transportation, 0.0% walk, 1.8% work from home (2000); Travel time to work: 28.8% less than 15 minutes, 27.9% 15 to 30 minutes, 18.0% 30 to 45 minutes, 21.6% 45 to 60 minutes, 3.6% 60 minutes or more (2000)

GRANDVIEW (town). Aka Grand View. Covers a land area of 0.957 square miles and a water area of 0 square miles. Located at 37.93° N. Lat; 86.98° W. Long. Elevation is 394 feet.
History: Grandview was named for its location on a bluff which afforded a view for five miles up and down the river.
Population: 789 (1990); 696 (2000); 684 (2010); 671 (2015 projected); Race: 96.8% White, 1.9% Black, 0.3% Asian, 1.0% Other, 0.1% Hispanic of any race (2010); Density: 714.9 persons per square mile (2010); Average household size: 2.54 (2010); Median age: 40.7 (2010); Males per 100 females: 102.4 (2010); Marriage status: 19.0% never married, 61.7% now married, 5.6% widowed, 13.7% divorced (2000); Foreign born: 0.0% (2000); Ancestry (includes multiple ancestries): 31.8% United States or

American, 17.9% German, 6.2% English, 5.6% Irish, 4.9% Other groups (2000).

Economy: Single-family building permits issued: 0 (2009); Multi-family building permits issued: 0 (2009); Employment by occupation: 3.6% management, 6.9% professional, 27.5% services, 19.6% sales, 0.6% farming, 9.7% construction, 32.0% production (2000).

Income: Per capita income: $21,119 (2010); Median household income: $46,357 (2010); Average household income: $54,043 (2010); Percent of households with income of $100,000 or more: 11.5% (2010); Poverty rate: 12.0% (2000).

Taxes: Total city taxes per capita: $96 (2007); City property taxes per capita: $73 (2007).

Education: Percent of population age 25 and over with: High school diploma (including GED) or higher: 83.5% (2010); Bachelor's degree or higher: 5.0% (2010); Master's degree or higher: 2.1% (2010).

Housing: Homeownership rate: 79.2% (2010); Median home value: $84,194 (2010); Median contract rent: $278 per month (2000); Median year structure built: 1969 (2000).

Transportation: Commute to work: 96.9% car, 0.0% public transportation, 0.6% walk, 2.5% work from home (2000); Travel time to work: 32.3% less than 15 minutes, 22.5% 15 to 30 minutes, 29.1% 30 to 45 minutes, 11.1% 45 to 60 minutes, 5.1% 60 minutes or more (2000)

LAMAR (unincorporated postal area, zip code 47550). Covers a land area of 37.740 square miles and a water area of 0.106 square miles. Located at 38.07° N. Lat; 86.92° W. Long. Elevation is 410 feet.

Population: 772 (2000); Race: 100.0% White, 0.0% Black, 0.0% Asian, 0.0% Other, 0.0% Hispanic of any race (2000); Density: 20.5 persons per square mile (2000); Age: 28.1% under 18, 7.9% over 64 (2000); Marriage status: 28.5% never married, 60.5% now married, 3.0% widowed, 8.1% divorced (2000); Foreign born: 0.0% (2000); Ancestry (includes multiple ancestries): 28.4% German, 18.9% United States or American, 7.3% Irish, 6.9% English, 6.8% Other groups (2000).

Economy: Employment by occupation: 5.1% management, 18.9% professional, 15.6% services, 18.7% sales, 1.0% farming, 18.3% construction, 22.5% production (2000).

Income: Per capita income: $15,386 (2000); Median household income: $44,013 (2000); Poverty rate: 17.3% (2000).

Education: Percent of population age 25 and over with: High school diploma (including GED) or higher: 77.4% (2000); Bachelor's degree or higher: 12.8% (2000).

School District(s)
North Spencer County Sch Corp (PK-12)

    2008-09 Enrollment: 2,102 . . . . (812) 937-2400

Housing: Homeownership rate: 92.5% (2000); Median home value: $90,400 (2000); Median contract rent: $307 per month (2000); Median year structure built: 1969 (2000).

Transportation: Commute to work: 96.1% car, 0.0% public transportation, 0.6% walk, 3.3% work from home (2000); Travel time to work: 21.0% less than 15 minutes, 25.8% 15 to 30 minutes, 32.4% 30 to 45 minutes, 13.3% 45 to 60 minutes, 7.4% 60 minutes or more (2000)

LINCOLN CITY (unincorporated postal area, zip code 47552). Covers a land area of 3.977 square miles and a water area of 0.090 square miles. Located at 38.11° N. Lat; 86.99° W. Long. Elevation is 436 feet.

History: Lincoln City was platted in 1872 on land that had been part of the farm of Thomas Lincoln, father of Abraham Lincoln, who settled here in 1816 when Abe was seven years old.

Population: 177 (2000); Race: 100.0% White, 0.0% Black, 0.0% Asian, 0.0% Other, 0.0% Hispanic of any race (2000); Density: 44.5 persons per square mile (2000); Age: 31.0% under 18, 8.6% over 64 (2000); Marriage status: 19.6% never married, 75.0% now married, 5.4% widowed, 0.0% divorced (2000); Foreign born: 0.0% (2000); Ancestry (includes multiple ancestries): 31.0% German, 14.2% United States or American, 10.7% English (2000).

Economy: Employment by occupation: 9.6% management, 35.1% professional, 16.0% services, 0.0% sales, 0.0% farming, 17.0% construction, 22.3% production (2000).

Income: Per capita income: $15,027 (2000); Median household income: $40,833 (2000); Poverty rate: 0.0% (2000).

Education: Percent of population age 25 and over with: High school diploma (including GED) or higher: 70.0% (2000); Bachelor's degree or higher: 14.6% (2000).

School District(s)
North Spencer County Sch Corp (PK-12)

    2008-09 Enrollment: 2,102 . . . . (812) 937-2400

Housing: Homeownership rate: 100.0% (2000); Median home value: $68,100 (2000); Median contract rent: $n/a per month (2000); Median year structure built: 1963 (2000).

Transportation: Commute to work: 81.9% car, 0.0% public transportation, 0.0% walk, 18.1% work from home (2000); Travel time to work: 46.8% less than 15 minutes, 24.7% 15 to 30 minutes, 20.8% 30 to 45 minutes, 7.8% 45 to 60 minutes, 0.0% 60 minutes or more (2000)

RICHLAND (unincorporated postal area, zip code 47634). Covers a land area of 51.242 square miles and a water area of 0.056 square miles. Located at 37.93° N. Lat; 87.19° W. Long.

Population: 2,530 (2000); Race: 98.1% White, 0.0% Black, 1.1% Asian, 0.8% Other, 0.0% Hispanic of any race (2000); Density: 49.4 persons per square mile (2000); Age: 26.0% under 18, 13.4% over 64 (2000); Marriage status: 19.2% never married, 59.4% now married, 7.5% widowed, 13.8% divorced (2000); Foreign born: 1.0% (2000); Ancestry (includes multiple ancestries): 22.4% German, 18.0% United States or American, 12.6% Irish, 8.7% Other groups, 8.0% English (2000).

Economy: Employment by occupation: 4.6% management, 10.0% professional, 17.5% services, 28.6% sales, 2.4% farming, 14.2% construction, 22.6% production (2000).

Income: Per capita income: $16,523 (2000); Median household income: $37,987 (2000); Poverty rate: 3.5% (2000).

Education: Percent of population age 25 and over with: High school diploma (including GED) or higher: 82.3% (2000); Bachelor's degree or higher: 7.3% (2000).

School District(s)
South Spencer County Sch Corp (PK-12)

    2008-09 Enrollment: 1,443 . . . . (812) 649-2591

Housing: Homeownership rate: 87.8% (2000); Median home value: $75,300 (2000); Median contract rent: $286 per month (2000); Median year structure built: 1967 (2000).

Transportation: Commute to work: 94.4% car, 0.6% public transportation, 0.0% walk, 4.6% work from home (2000); Travel time to work: 15.2% less than 15 minutes, 31.3% 15 to 30 minutes, 28.3% 30 to 45 minutes, 16.9% 45 to 60 minutes, 8.3% 60 minutes or more (2000)

ROCKPORT (city). County seat. Covers a land area of 1.172 square miles and a water area of 0.019 square miles. Located at 37.88° N. Lat; 87.05° W. Long. Elevation is 440 feet.

History: Rockport was first settled by Daniel Grass in 1807. The Lincoln family, and especially Abraham Lincoln, were visitors in Rockport when they lived 16 miles north. John Pitcher, a Rockport attorney, was a friend of Abe's who allowed him to use his extensive library of law, history, and fiction.

Population: 2,316 (1990); 2,160 (2000); 1,896 (2010); 1,783 (2015 projected); Race: 95.7% White, 2.4% Black, 0.4% Asian, 1.6% Other, 1.8% Hispanic of any race (2010); Density: 1,618.3 persons per square mile (2010); Average household size: 2.46 (2010); Median age: 41.8 (2010); Males per 100 females: 94.1 (2010); Marriage status: 20.7% never married, 57.6% now married, 12.8% widowed, 8.8% divorced (2000); Foreign born: 0.0% (2000); Ancestry (includes multiple ancestries): 23.9% German, 14.9% Irish, 13.0% United States or American, 8.8% Other groups, 6.6% English (2000).

Economy: Single-family building permits issued: 1 (2009); Multi-family building permits issued: 0 (2009); Employment by occupation: 3.1% management, 13.6% professional, 20.0% services, 24.3% sales, 0.3% farming, 12.9% construction, 25.9% production (2000).

Income: Per capita income: $18,928 (2010); Median household income: $38,686 (2010); Average household income: $46,951 (2010); Percent of households with income of $100,000 or more: 8.1% (2010); Poverty rate: 14.9% (2000).

Taxes: Total city taxes per capita: $244 (2007); City property taxes per capita: $185 (2007).

Education: Percent of population age 25 and over with: High school diploma (including GED) or higher: 85.1% (2010); Bachelor's degree or higher: 16.3% (2010); Master's degree or higher: 6.9% (2010).

School District(s)
South Spencer County Sch Corp (PK-12)

    2008-09 Enrollment: 1,443 . . . . (812) 649-2591

Housing: Homeownership rate: 71.4% (2010); Median home value: $85,729 (2010); Median contract rent: $279 per month (2000); Median year structure built: 1961 (2000).
Newspapers: Spencer County Journal-Democrat (Community news; Circulation 5,500)
Transportation: Commute to work: 93.1% car, 0.0% public transportation, 3.8% walk, 1.5% work from home (2000); Travel time to work: 38.1% less than 15 minutes, 25.6% 15 to 30 minutes, 18.5% 30 to 45 minutes, 10.3% 45 to 60 minutes, 7.5% 60 minutes or more (2000)

SAINT MEINRAD (unincorporated postal area, zip code 47577). Covers a land area of 22.356 square miles and a water area of 0.052 square miles. Located at 38.16° N. Lat; 86.81° W. Long. Elevation is 443 feet.
History: The community of St. Meinrad grew up near the St. Meinrad Abbey, founded in 1854 by Benedictine Fathers and named for a ninth-century Swiss hermit. The massive sandstone Abbey Church dominated the village.
Population: 1,131 (2000); Race: 100.0% White, 0.0% Black, 0.0% Asian, 0.0% Other, 0.0% Hispanic of any race (2000); Density: 50.6 persons per square mile (2000); Age: 23.8% under 18, 16.1% over 64 (2000); Marriage status: 24.5% never married, 59.7% now married, 9.5% widowed, 6.3% divorced (2000); Foreign born: 0.0% (2000); Ancestry (includes multiple ancestries): 55.2% German, 14.0% United States or American, 6.1% Irish, 2.2% French (except Basque), 2.0% Other groups (2000).
Economy: Employment by occupation: 7.2% management, 10.4% professional, 6.8% services, 24.8% sales, 2.5% farming, 4.3% construction, 43.9% production (2000).
Income: Per capita income: $15,074 (2000); Median household income: $39,653 (2000); Poverty rate: 19.4% (2000).
Education: Percent of population age 25 and over with: High school diploma (including GED) or higher: 75.9% (2000); Bachelor's degree or higher: 12.1% (2000).

Four-year College(s)
Saint Meinrad School of Theology (Private, Not-for-profit, Roman Catholic)
　Fall 2008 Enrollment: 187 . . . . (812) 357-6611
Housing: Homeownership rate: 85.0% (2000); Median home value: $71,600 (2000); Median contract rent: $132 per month (2000); Median year structure built: 1963 (2000).
Transportation: Commute to work: 88.6% car, 0.0% public transportation, 5.4% walk, 4.8% work from home (2000); Travel time to work: 35.4% less than 15 minutes, 28.7% 15 to 30 minutes, 26.5% 30 to 45 minutes, 4.6% 45 to 60 minutes, 4.8% 60 minutes or more (2000)

SANTA CLAUS (town). Covers a land area of 5.183 square miles and a water area of 0.384 square miles. Located at 38.11° N. Lat; 86.92° W. Long. Elevation is 463 feet.
History: Santa Claus was laid out in 1846. The suggested name of Santa Fe was rejected by the post office, and Santa Claus was suggested as a joke, since it was near Christmas. The name served to bring hundreds of letters through the Santa Claus post office each December, where Jim Martin, postmaster from 1897 to 1935, played Santa Claus.
Population: 927 (1990); 2,041 (2000); 2,199 (2010); 2,256 (2015 projected); Race: 98.4% White, 0.0% Black, 0.5% Asian, 1.1% Other, 1.1% Hispanic of any race (2010); Density: 424.3 persons per square mile (2010); Average household size: 2.72 (2010); Median age: 38.8 (2010); Males per 100 females: 102.1 (2010); Marriage status: 16.0% never married, 75.0% now married, 3.0% widowed, 6.1% divorced (2000); Foreign born: 0.8% (2000); Ancestry (includes multiple ancestries): 46.3% German, 13.6% English, 9.9% Irish, 8.5% United States or American, 6.4% Other groups (2000).
Economy: Single-family building permits issued: 6 (2009); Multi-family building permits issued: 0 (2009); Employment by occupation: 22.6% management, 23.0% professional, 7.2% services, 23.3% sales, 0.2% farming, 4.2% construction, 19.5% production (2000).
Income: Per capita income: $29,029 (2010); Median household income: $66,872 (2010); Average household income: $78,863 (2010); Percent of households with income of $100,000 or more: 24.0% (2010); Poverty rate: 1.2% (2000).
Taxes: Total city taxes per capita: $208 (2007); City property taxes per capita: $153 (2007).
Education: Percent of population age 25 and over with: High school diploma (including GED) or higher: 93.1% (2010); Bachelor's degree or higher: 33.7% (2010); Master's degree or higher: 12.2% (2010).

Housing: Homeownership rate: 89.6% (2010); Median home value: $142,382 (2010); Median contract rent: $615 per month (2000); Median year structure built: 1991 (2000).
Transportation: Commute to work: 96.9% car, 0.4% public transportation, 0.6% walk, 2.0% work from home (2000); Travel time to work: 30.4% less than 15 minutes, 27.5% 15 to 30 minutes, 27.6% 30 to 45 minutes, 7.7% 45 to 60 minutes, 6.9% 60 minutes or more (2000)

Starke County

Located in northwestern Indiana; bounded on the northwest by the Kankakee River; drained by the Yellow River. Covers a land area of 309.31 square miles, a water area of 3.00 square miles, and is located in the Central Time Zone. The county was founded in 1835. County seat is Knox.
Population: 22,747 (1990); 23,556 (2000); 23,780 (2010); 23,833 (2015 projected); Race: 96.4% White, 0.6% Black, 0.3% Asian, 2.7% Other, 3.1% Hispanic of any race (2010); Density: 76.9 persons per square mile (2010); Average household size: 2.61 (2010); Median age: 38.8 (2010); Males per 100 females: 97.2 (2010).
Religion: Five largest groups: 6.6% Catholic Church, 5.7% Lutheran Church—Missouri Synod, 2.5% The United Methodist Church, 1.2% Assemblies of God, 1.1% New Testament Association of Independent Baptist Churches and other Fundamental Baptist Associ
Economy: Unemployment rate: 11.8% (5/2010); Total civilian labor force: 10,911 (5/2010); Leading industries: 26.1% manufacturing; 23.8% retail trade; 14.8% health care and social assistance (2008); Farms: 640 totaling 153,651 acres (2007); Companies that employ 500 or more persons: 0 (2008); Companies that employ 100 to 499 persons: 3 (2008); Companies that employ less than 100 persons: 342 (2008); Black-owned businesses: n/a (2002); Hispanic-owned businesses: n/a (2002); Asian-owned businesses: n/a (2002); Women-owned businesses: n/a (2002); Retail sales per capita: $6,744 (2010). Single-family building permits issued: 59 (2009); Multi-family building permits issued: 0 (2009).
Income: Per capita income: $19,430 (2010); Median household income: $41,830 (2010); Average household income: $50,676 (2010); Percent of households with income of $100,000 or more: 8.2% (2010); Poverty rate: 15.4% (2008); Bankruptcy rate: 8.03% (2009).
Taxes: Total county taxes per capita: $233 (2007); County property taxes per capita: $199 (2007).
Education: Percent of population age 25 and over with: High school diploma (including GED) or higher: 77.2% (2010); Bachelor's degree or higher: 9.6% (2010); Master's degree or higher: 3.2% (2010).
Housing: Homeownership rate: 79.7% (2010); Median home value: $96,437 (2010); Median contract rent: $399 per month (2006-2008 3-year est.); Median year structure built: 1970 (2006-2008 3-year est.)
Health: Birth rate: 145.3 per 10,000 population (2009); Death rate: 110.9 per 10,000 population (2009); Age-adjusted cancer mortality rate: 245.3 deaths per 100,000 population (2006); Number of physicians: 5.6 per 10,000 population (2007); Hospital beds: 21.0 per 10,000 population (2006); Hospital admissions: 563.3 per 10,000 population (2006).
Elections: 2008 Presidential election results: 50.5% Obama, 47.3% McCain, 0.0% Nader
National and State Parks: Bass Lake State Beach; Kaukakee State Fish and Wildlife Area
Additional Information Contacts
Starke County Government . . . . (574) 772-9107
　http://www.stark.in.us
City of Knox . . . . (574) 772-3032
　http://www.cityofknox.net

Starke County Communities

BASS LAKE (CDP). Covers a land area of 9.150 square miles and a water area of 2.139 square miles. Located at 41.23° N. Lat; 86.58° W. Long. Elevation is 715 feet.
Population: 1,104 (1990); 1,249 (2000); 1,450 (2010); 1,481 (2015 projected); Race: 96.2% White, 1.0% Black, 0.7% Asian, 2.1% Other, 1.4% Hispanic of any race (2010); Density: 158.5 persons per square mile (2010); Average household size: 2.60 (2010); Median age: 41.2 (2010); Males per 100 females: 98.1 (2010); Marriage status: 16.0% never married, 66.2% now married, 7.1% widowed, 10.7% divorced (2000); Foreign born: 5.2% (2000); Ancestry (includes multiple ancestries): 36.5% German, 18.9% Irish, 18.6% Polish, 9.0% Other groups, 8.1% English (2000).

Economy: Employment by occupation: 14.0% management, 11.7% professional, 12.2% services, 22.8% sales, 0.0% farming, 13.8% construction, 25.5% production (2000).
Income: Per capita income: $22,032 (2010); Median household income: $48,824 (2010); Average household income: $57,419 (2010); Percent of households with income of $100,000 or more: 10.6% (2010); Poverty rate: 14.7% (2000).
Education: Percent of population age 25 and over with: High school diploma (including GED) or higher: 80.6% (2010); Bachelor's degree or higher: 10.1% (2010); Master's degree or higher: 3.6% (2010).
Housing: Homeownership rate: 85.8% (2010); Median home value: $98,411 (2010); Median contract rent: $396 per month (2000); Median year structure built: 1965 (2000).
Transportation: Commute to work: 98.2% car, 0.0% public transportation, 0.0% walk, 1.8% work from home (2000); Travel time to work: 28.5% less than 15 minutes, 22.0% 15 to 30 minutes, 16.4% 30 to 45 minutes, 7.1% 45 to 60 minutes, 26.0% 60 minutes or more (2000)

GROVERTOWN (unincorporated postal area, zip code 46531). Covers a land area of 23.807 square miles and a water area of 0.009 square miles. Located at 41.35° N. Lat; 86.51° W. Long. Elevation is 725 feet.
Population: 1,335 (2000); Race: 95.4% White, 0.0% Black, 0.0% Asian, 4.6% Other, 4.8% Hispanic of any race (2000); Density: 56.1 persons per square mile (2000); Age: 24.0% under 18, 12.6% over 64 (2000); Marriage status: 24.5% never married, 62.1% now married, 4.7% widowed, 8.8% divorced (2000); Foreign born: 4.0% (2000); Ancestry (includes multiple ancestries): 20.6% Irish, 14.7% United States or American, 12.2% German, 11.1% Polish, 9.7% Other groups (2000).
Economy: Employment by occupation: 5.7% management, 9.5% professional, 11.3% services, 18.8% sales, 0.0% farming, 17.5% construction, 37.3% production (2000).
Income: Per capita income: $18,485 (2000); Median household income: $41,765 (2000); Poverty rate: 7.9% (2000).
Education: Percent of population age 25 and over with: High school diploma (including GED) or higher: 69.0% (2000); Bachelor's degree or higher: 5.4% (2000).
Housing: Homeownership rate: 86.1% (2000); Median home value: $92,800 (2000); Median contract rent: $321 per month (2000); Median year structure built: 1974 (2000).
Transportation: Commute to work: 92.0% car, 0.0% public transportation, 1.3% walk, 6.7% work from home (2000); Travel time to work: 30.7% less than 15 minutes, 29.9% 15 to 30 minutes, 20.3% 30 to 45 minutes, 8.8% 45 to 60 minutes, 10.4% 60 minutes or more (2000)

HAMLET (town). Covers a land area of 0.965 square miles and a water area of 0.009 square miles. Located at 41.38° N. Lat; 86.58° W. Long. Elevation is 705 feet.
History: Hamlet was sited at the crossing of the Pennsylvania and New York Central Railroads. It was platted in 1863 by John Hamlet, for whom it was named, and soon became a shipping center.
Population: 789 (1990); 820 (2000); 770 (2010); 744 (2015 projected); Race: 98.3% White, 0.1% Black, 0.0% Asian, 1.6% Other, 1.6% Hispanic of any race (2010); Density: 797.7 persons per square mile (2010); Average household size: 2.59 (2010); Median age: 35.9 (2010); Males per 100 females: 101.6 (2010); Marriage status: 17.3% never married, 64.0% now married, 5.6% widowed, 13.1% divorced (2000); Foreign born: 1.0% (2000); Ancestry (includes multiple ancestries): 27.8% German, 14.9% Irish, 13.3% United States or American, 7.5% Other groups, 6.4% English (2000).
Economy: Single-family building permits issued: 0 (2009); Multi-family building permits issued: 0 (2009); Employment by occupation: 8.5% management, 6.3% professional, 15.4% services, 19.7% sales, 2.6% farming, 12.8% construction, 34.8% production (2000).
Income: Per capita income: $17,490 (2010); Median household income: $37,833 (2010); Average household income: $44,015 (2010); Percent of households with income of $100,000 or more: 4.0% (2010); Poverty rate: 17.3% (2000).
Taxes: Total city taxes per capita: $229 (2007); City property taxes per capita: $181 (2007).
Education: Percent of population age 25 and over with: High school diploma (including GED) or higher: 77.7% (2010); Bachelor's degree or higher: 4.2% (2010); Master's degree or higher: 1.4% (2010).

Oregon-Davis School Corp (KG-12)
    2008-09 Enrollment: 722 . . . . (574) 867-2111
Housing: Homeownership rate: 77.8% (2010); Median home value: $78,293 (2010); Median contract rent: $386 per month (2000); Median year structure built: 1953 (2000).
Transportation: Commute to work: 95.9% car, 0.6% public transportation, 0.3% walk, 2.4% work from home (2000); Travel time to work: 32.0% less than 15 minutes, 43.8% 15 to 30 minutes, 10.6% 30 to 45 minutes, 5.1% 45 to 60 minutes, 8.5% 60 minutes or more (2000)

KNOX (city). County seat. Covers a land area of 3.928 square miles and a water area of 0 square miles. Located at 41.29° N. Lat; 86.62° W. Long. Elevation is 712 feet.
History: Knox developed as a trading center for the surrounding farmlands.
Population: 3,720 (1990); 3,721 (2000); 3,862 (2010); 3,882 (2015 projected); Race: 95.6% White, 0.3% Black, 0.6% Asian, 3.5% Other, 3.9% Hispanic of any race (2010); Density: 983.2 persons per square mile (2010); Average household size: 2.38 (2010); Median age: 38.3 (2010); Males per 100 females: 91.4 (2010); Marriage status: 21.1% never married, 52.7% now married, 11.0% widowed, 15.2% divorced (2000); Foreign born: 4.6% (2000); Ancestry (includes multiple ancestries): 20.7% German, 13.8% Irish, 13.1% United States or American, 10.4% Other groups, 8.6% English (2000).
Economy: Single-family building permits issued: 9 (2009); Multi-family building permits issued: 0 (2009); Employment by occupation: 6.7% management, 12.5% professional, 14.0% services, 17.4% sales, 0.5% farming, 9.0% construction, 39.8% production (2000).
Income: Per capita income: $17,390 (2010); Median household income: $30,311 (2010); Average household income: $41,415 (2010); Percent of households with income of $100,000 or more: 6.5% (2010); Poverty rate: 15.5% (2000).
Taxes: Total city taxes per capita: $326 (2007); City property taxes per capita: $255 (2007).
Education: Percent of population age 25 and over with: High school diploma (including GED) or higher: 73.6% (2010); Bachelor's degree or higher: 11.9% (2010); Master's degree or higher: 2.8% (2010).

Knox Community School Corp (KG-12)
    2008-09 Enrollment: 2,015 . . . . (574) 772-1600
Knox Beauty College (Private, For-profit)
    Fall 2008 Enrollment: 59 . . . . (574) 772-5500
    2009-10 Tuition: $4,435
Housing: Homeownership rate: 65.5% (2010); Median home value: $77,580 (2010); Median contract rent: $325 per month (2000); Median year structure built: 1958 (2000).
Hospitals: Starke Memorial Hospital (53 beds)
Newspapers: Leader (Community news; Circulation 4,400)
Transportation: Commute to work: 94.2% car, 0.0% public transportation, 4.6% walk, 0.4% work from home (2000); Travel time to work: 57.7% less than 15 minutes, 8.9% 15 to 30 minutes, 19.5% 30 to 45 minutes, 4.3% 45 to 60 minutes, 9.5% 60 minutes or more (2000)
Additional Information Contacts
City of Knox . . . . (574) 772-3032
    http://www.cityofknox.net

KOONTZ LAKE (CDP). Covers a land area of 3.385 square miles and a water area of 0.503 square miles. Located at 41.41° N. Lat; 86.48° W. Long. Elevation is 735 feet.
Population: 1,615 (1990); 1,554 (2000); 1,693 (2010); 1,736 (2015 projected); Race: 97.6% White, 0.2% Black, 0.1% Asian, 2.1% Other, 1.9% Hispanic of any race (2010); Density: 500.1 persons per square mile (2010); Average household size: 2.37 (2010); Median age: 43.5 (2010); Males per 100 females: 99.2 (2010); Marriage status: 23.5% never married, 61.6% now married, 7.5% widowed, 7.4% divorced (2000); Foreign born: 2.5% (2000); Ancestry (includes multiple ancestries): 29.2% German, 17.7% Irish, 12.8% United States or American, 8.8% Polish, 7.8% Other groups (2000).
Economy: Employment by occupation: 9.0% management, 9.5% professional, 11.5% services, 22.3% sales, 0.0% farming, 15.0% construction, 32.7% production (2000).
Income: Per capita income: $22,070 (2010); Median household income: $40,846 (2010); Average household income: $52,651 (2010); Percent of

households with income of $100,000 or more: 7.2% (2010); Poverty rate: 7.7% (2000).
Education: Percent of population age 25 and over with: High school diploma (including GED) or higher: 79.6% (2010); Bachelor's degree or higher: 7.5% (2010); Master's degree or higher: 4.4% (2010).
Housing: Homeownership rate: 83.5% (2010); Median home value: $92,342 (2010); Median contract rent: $406 per month (2000); Median year structure built: 1959 (2000).
Transportation: Commute to work: 95.9% car, 0.0% public transportation, 0.0% walk, 3.4% work from home (2000); Travel time to work: 38.6% less than 15 minutes, 24.8% 15 to 30 minutes, 12.6% 30 to 45 minutes, 10.4% 45 to 60 minutes, 13.6% 60 minutes or more (2000)

NORTH JUDSON (town).

Covers a land area of 0.920 square miles and a water area of 0 square miles. Located at 41.21° N. Lat; 86.77° W. Long. Elevation is 712 feet.
History: Laid out 1861.
Population: 1,582 (1990); 1,675 (2000); 1,597 (2010); 1,549 (2015 projected); Race: 96.2% White, 0.3% Black, 0.0% Asian, 3.4% Other, 7.2% Hispanic of any race (2010); Density: 1,735.4 persons per square mile (2010); Average household size: 2.59 (2010); Median age: 34.0 (2010); Males per 100 females: 90.6 (2010); Marriage status: 19.1% never married, 56.8% now married, 11.3% widowed, 12.7% divorced (2000); Foreign born: 2.3% (2000); Ancestry (includes multiple ancestries): 21.4% German, 14.8% Other groups, 13.0% Irish, 10.7% United States or American, 6.1% Polish (2000).
Economy: Single-family building permits issued: 2 (2009); Multi-family building permits issued: 0 (2009); Employment by occupation: 7.6% management, 12.6% professional, 17.4% services, 20.3% sales, 0.3% farming, 15.2% construction, 26.6% production (2000).
Income: Per capita income: $18,950 (2010); Median household income: $40,752 (2010); Average household income: $48,793 (2010); Percent of households with income of $100,000 or more: 8.1% (2010); Poverty rate: 12.7% (2000).
Taxes: Total city taxes per capita: $285 (2007); City property taxes per capita: $277 (2007).
Education: Percent of population age 25 and over with: High school diploma (including GED) or higher: 78.8% (2010); Bachelor's degree or higher: 12.2% (2010); Master's degree or higher: 2.8% (2010).

School District(s)
North Judson-San Pierre Sch Corp (KG-12)
    2008-09 Enrollment: 1,356 . . . . (574) 896-2155
Housing: Homeownership rate: 69.4% (2010); Median home value: $93,750 (2010); Median contract rent: $327 per month (2000); Median year structure built: 1946 (2000).
Transportation: Commute to work: 96.0% car, 0.0% public transportation, 2.0% walk, 2.0% work from home (2000); Travel time to work: 30.0% less than 15 minutes, 25.7% 15 to 30 minutes, 14.7% 30 to 45 minutes, 14.6% 45 to 60 minutes, 15.1% 60 minutes or more (2000)

SAN PIERRE (CDP).

Covers a land area of 0.142 square miles and a water area of 0 square miles. Located at 41.19° N. Lat; 86.89° W. Long. Elevation is 699 feet.
Population: 175 (1990); 156 (2000); 163 (2010); 164 (2015 projected); Race: 97.5% White, 0.6% Black, 0.0% Asian, 1.8% Other, 1.2% Hispanic of any race (2010); Density: 1,149.5 persons per square mile (2010); Average household size: 2.45 (2010); Median age: 50.5 (2010); Males per 100 females: 96.4 (2010); Marriage status: 49.0% never married, 18.1% now married, 14.8% widowed, 18.1% divorced (2000); Foreign born: 0.0% (2000); Ancestry (includes multiple ancestries): 26.3% United States or American, 13.1% German, 8.1% French (except Basque), 5.0% Dutch (2000).
Economy: Employment by occupation: 0.0% management, 19.0% professional, 15.2% services, 13.9% sales, 0.0% farming, 12.7% construction, 39.2% production (2000).
Income: Per capita income: $20,959 (2010); Median household income: $50,000 (2010); Average household income: $54,353 (2010); Percent of households with income of $100,000 or more: 10.3% (2010); Poverty rate: 0.0% (2000).
Education: Percent of population age 25 and over with: High school diploma (including GED) or higher: 78.1% (2010); Bachelor's degree or higher: 14.8% (2010); Master's degree or higher: 5.5% (2010).
Housing: Homeownership rate: 82.8% (2010); Median home value: $90,909 (2010); Median contract rent: $425 per month (2000); Median year structure built: 1953 (2000).

Transportation: Commute to work: 91.1% car, 0.0% public transportation, 8.9% walk, 0.0% work from home (2000); Travel time to work: 54.4% less than 15 minutes, 0.0% 15 to 30 minutes, 38.0% 30 to 45 minutes, 7.6% 45 to 60 minutes, 0.0% 60 minutes or more (2000)

Steuben County

Located in northeastern Indiana; bounded on the north by Michigan, and on the east by Ohio; drained by Pigeon Creek; includes several lakes. Covers a land area of 308.72 square miles, a water area of 13.76 square miles, and is located in the Eastern Time Zone. The county was founded in 1835. County seat is Angola.

Steuben County is part of the Angola, IN Micropolitan Statistical Area. The entire metro area includes: Steuben County, IN

Weather Station: Angola									Elevation: 1,007 feet			
	Jan	Feb	Mar	Apr	May	Jun	Jul	Aug	Sep	Oct	Nov	Dec
High	29	33	43	57	69	78	82	80	73	61	47	35
Low	14	15	24	35	47	56	61	59	51	39	30	20
Precip	2.0	1.8	2.7	3.5	4.0	3.7	3.9	3.9	3.4	2.7	3.2	2.7
Snow	10.4	7.8	4.2	0.7	tr	0.0	0.0	0.0	0.0	0.3	2.2	8.0

High and Low temperatures in degrees Fahrenheit; Precipitation and Snow in inches

Population: 27,446 (1990); 33,214 (2000); 33,329 (2010); 33,128 (2015 projected); Race: 96.0% White, 0.6% Black, 0.6% Asian, 2.7% Other, 3.0% Hispanic of any race (2010); Density: 108.0 persons per square mile (2010); Average household size: 2.49 (2010); Median age: 38.2 (2010); Males per 100 females: 102.6 (2010).
Religion: Five largest groups: 5.1% The United Methodist Church, 5.1% Catholic Church, 2.8% The Missionary Church, 2.8% Christian Churches and Churches of Christ, 2.2% Lutheran Church—Missouri Synod (2000).
Economy: Unemployment rate: 11.5% (5/2010); Total civilian labor force: 16,704 (5/2010); Leading industries: 32.3% manufacturing; 17.1% retail trade; 10.4% accommodation & food services (2008); Farms: 719 totaling 106,393 acres (2007); Companies that employ 500 or more persons: 1 (2008); Companies that employ 100 to 499 persons: 22 (2008); Companies that employ less than 100 persons: 982 (2008); Black-owned businesses: n/a (2002); Hispanic-owned businesses: n/a (2002); Asian-owned businesses: n/a (2002); Women-owned businesses: 665 (2002); Retail sales per capita: $18,240 (2010). Single-family building permits issued: 74 (2009); Multi-family building permits issued: 0 (2009).
Income: Per capita income: $22,930 (2010); Median household income: $48,145 (2010); Average household income: $58,159 (2010); Percent of households with income of $100,000 or more: 10.7% (2010); Poverty rate: 9.2% (2008); Bankruptcy rate: 8.65% (2009).
Taxes: Total county taxes per capita: $206 (2007); County property taxes per capita: $80 (2007).
Education: Percent of population age 25 and over with: High school diploma (including GED) or higher: 90.3% (2010); Bachelor's degree or higher: 17.5% (2010); Master's degree or higher: 6.7% (2010).
Housing: Homeownership rate: 77.0% (2010); Median home value: $124,138 (2010); Median contract rent: $509 per month (2006-2008 3-year est.); Median year structure built: 1979 (2006-2008 3-year est.)
Health: Birth rate: 123.3 per 10,000 population (2009); Death rate: 84.3 per 10,000 population (2009); Age-adjusted cancer mortality rate: 192.5 deaths per 100,000 population (2006); Number of physicians: 6.0 per 10,000 population (2007); Hospital beds: 7.4 per 10,000 population (2006); Hospital admissions: 297.1 per 10,000 population (2006).
Elections: 2008 Presidential election results: 44.4% Obama, 54.2% McCain, 0.0% Nader
National and State Parks: Cedar Lake Marsh State Fish and Wildlife Area; Marsh Lake Wetlands State Fish and Wildlife Area; Pokagon State Park
Additional Information Contacts
Steuben County Government . . . . (260) 668-1000
    http://www.co.steuben.in.us
Angola Area Chamber of Commerce. . . . . (260) 665-3512
    http://www.angolachamber.org
City of Angola. . . . . (260) 665-2514
    http://www.angolain.org

Steuben County Communities

ANGOLA (city). County seat. Covers a land area of 4.229 square miles and a water area of 0.015 square miles. Located at 41.63° N. Lat; 85.00° W. Long. Elevation is 1,063 feet.
Population: 6,502 (1990); 7,344 (2000); 7,282 (2010); 7,302 (2015 projected); Race: 92.0% White, 1.2% Black, 1.6% Asian, 5.1% Other, 5.6% Hispanic of any race (2010); Density: 1,721.7 persons per square mile (2010); Average household size: 2.36 (2010); Median age: 34.2 (2010); Males per 100 females: 104.0 (2010); Marriage status: 29.9% never married, 49.8% now married, 8.1% widowed, 12.2% divorced (2000); Foreign born: 2.3% (2000); Ancestry (includes multiple ancestries): 27.0% German, 11.5% English, 9.6% United States or American, 9.1% Irish, 8.7% Other groups (2000).
Economy: Single-family building permits issued: 14 (2009); Multi-family building permits issued: 0 (2009); Employment by occupation: 7.6% management, 21.1% professional, 14.3% services, 22.6% sales, 0.0% farming, 5.9% construction, 28.5% production (2000).
Income: Per capita income: $19,460 (2010); Median household income: $40,481 (2010); Average household income: $48,435 (2010); Percent of households with income of $100,000 or more: 6.2% (2010); Poverty rate: 10.5% (2000).
Taxes: Total city taxes per capita: $320 (2007); City property taxes per capita: $272 (2007).
Education: Percent of population age 25 and over with: High school diploma (including GED) or higher: 88.0% (2010); Bachelor's degree or higher: 22.4% (2010); Master's degree or higher: 9.2% (2010).

School District(s)
M S D Steuben County (KG-12)
    2008-09 Enrollment: 3,139 . . . . (260) 665-2854

Four-year College(s)
Trine University (Private, Not-for-profit)
    Fall 2008 Enrollment: 1,451 . . . . (260) 665-4100
    2009-10 Tuition: In-state $24,200; Out-of-state $24,200
Housing: Homeownership rate: 55.5% (2010); Median home value: $104,190 (2010); Median contract rent: $414 per month (2000); Median year structure built: 1972 (2000).
Hospitals: Cameron Memorial Community Hospital (25 beds)
Safety: Violent crime rate: 10.1 per 10,000 population; Property crime rate: 582.3 per 10,000 population (2008).
Newspapers: Herald-Republican (Community news; Circulation 4,474)
Transportation: Commute to work: 91.8% car, 0.7% public transportation, 5.1% walk, 1.1% work from home (2000); Travel time to work: 66.0% less than 15 minutes, 21.2% 15 to 30 minutes, 5.8% 30 to 45 minutes, 2.3% 45 to 60 minutes, 4.8% 60 minutes or more (2000)
Additional Information Contacts
Angola Area Chamber of Commerce . . . . (260) 665-3512
    http://www.angolachamber.org
City of Angola . . . . (260) 665-2514
    http://www.angolain.org

CLEAR LAKE (town). Covers a land area of 1.045 square miles and a water area of 1.313 square miles. Located at 41.73° N. Lat; 84.84° W. Long. Elevation is 1,047 feet.
Population: 267 (1990); 244 (2000); 261 (2010); 269 (2015 projected); Race: 97.7% White, 0.0% Black, 0.8% Asian, 1.5% Other, 1.1% Hispanic of any race (2010); Density: 249.7 persons per square mile (2010); Average household size: 2.44 (2010); Median age: 45.3 (2010); Males per 100 females: 105.5 (2010); Marriage status: 13.7% never married, 72.6% now married, 6.9% widowed, 6.9% divorced (2000); Foreign born: 0.0% (2000); Ancestry (includes multiple ancestries): 50.4% German, 16.4% English, 9.1% Irish, 9.1% United States or American, 8.4% French (except Basque) (2000).
Economy: Employment by occupation: 22.1% management, 14.8% professional, 18.8% services, 24.8% sales, 0.0% farming, 6.7% construction, 12.8% production (2000).
Income: Per capita income: $19,918 (2010); Median household income: $46,250 (2010); Average household income: $50,280 (2010); Percent of households with income of $100,000 or more: 5.6% (2010); Poverty rate: 4.4% (2000).
Taxes: Total city taxes per capita: $275 (2007); City property taxes per capita: $233 (2007).
Education: Percent of population age 25 and over with: High school diploma (including GED) or higher: 93.0% (2010); Bachelor's degree or higher: 16.6% (2010); Master's degree or higher: 7.5% (2010).

Housing: Homeownership rate: 87.9% (2010); Median home value: $173,077 (2010); Median contract rent: $381 per month (2000); Median year structure built: 1955 (2000).
Transportation: Commute to work: 95.2% car, 0.0% public transportation, 2.8% walk, 2.1% work from home (2000); Travel time to work: 33.1% less than 15 minutes, 34.5% 15 to 30 minutes, 4.2% 30 to 45 minutes, 11.3% 45 to 60 minutes, 16.9% 60 minutes or more (2000)

FREMONT (town). Covers a land area of 2.226 square miles and a water area of 0.006 square miles. Located at 41.73° N. Lat; 84.93° W. Long. Elevation is 1,056 feet.
Population: 1,498 (1990); 1,696 (2000); 1,642 (2010); 1,603 (2015 projected); Race: 97.6% White, 0.3% Black, 0.1% Asian, 2.0% Other, 2.7% Hispanic of any race (2010); Density: 737.7 persons per square mile (2010); Average household size: 2.62 (2010); Median age: 35.6 (2010); Males per 100 females: 92.0 (2010); Marriage status: 22.4% never married, 54.6% now married, 6.2% widowed, 16.7% divorced (2000); Foreign born: 1.8% (2000); Ancestry (includes multiple ancestries): 28.8% German, 10.7% Other groups, 10.7% English, 9.5% United States or American, 6.9% Irish (2000).
Economy: Employment by occupation: 8.0% management, 9.8% professional, 13.1% services, 24.5% sales, 0.0% farming, 8.0% construction, 36.6% production (2000).
Income: Per capita income: $19,660 (2010); Median household income: $44,590 (2010); Average household income: $51,510 (2010); Percent of households with income of $100,000 or more: 8.3% (2010); Poverty rate: 7.3% (2000).
Taxes: Total city taxes per capita: $181 (2007); City property taxes per capita: $132 (2007).
Education: Percent of population age 25 and over with: High school diploma (including GED) or higher: 89.3% (2010); Bachelor's degree or higher: 17.8% (2010); Master's degree or higher: 2.5% (2010).

School District(s)
Fremont Community Schools (KG-12)
    2008-09 Enrollment: 1,172 . . . . (260) 495-5005
Housing: Homeownership rate: 77.2% (2010); Median home value: $99,438 (2010); Median contract rent: $406 per month (2000); Median year structure built: 1977 (2000).
Transportation: Commute to work: 93.1% car, 1.0% public transportation, 4.4% walk, 1.5% work from home (2000); Travel time to work: 57.2% less than 15 minutes, 27.5% 15 to 30 minutes, 7.2% 30 to 45 minutes, 4.2% 45 to 60 minutes, 3.9% 60 minutes or more (2000)

HAMILTON (town). Covers a land area of 1.656 square miles and a water area of 0.359 square miles. Located at 41.53° N. Lat; 84.91° W. Long. Elevation is 900 feet.
History: Hamilton was called Enterprise when it was founded in 1836 at a site that provided water power. The town was incorporated in 1914.
Population: 1,022 (1990); 1,233 (2000); 1,256 (2010); 1,250 (2015 projected); Race: 98.6% White, 0.2% Black, 0.1% Asian, 1.1% Other, 1.0% Hispanic of any race (2010); Density: 758.4 persons per square mile (2010); Average household size: 2.47 (2010); Median age: 40.7 (2010); Males per 100 females: 98.7 (2010); Marriage status: 18.8% never married, 59.3% now married, 8.7% widowed, 13.2% divorced (2000); Foreign born: 0.2% (2000); Ancestry (includes multiple ancestries): 30.8% German, 11.4% English, 11.3% Irish, 10.0% United States or American, 5.8% Other groups (2000).
Economy: Employment by occupation: 8.2% management, 10.7% professional, 11.4% services, 24.6% sales, 0.0% farming, 12.9% construction, 32.2% production (2000).
Income: Per capita income: $23,512 (2010); Median household income: $48,833 (2010); Average household income: $57,638 (2010); Percent of households with income of $100,000 or more: 11.0% (2010); Poverty rate: 9.2% (2000).
Education: Percent of population age 25 and over with: High school diploma (including GED) or higher: 89.1% (2010); Bachelor's degree or higher: 13.3% (2010); Master's degree or higher: 6.2% (2010).

School District(s)
Hamilton Community Schools (KG-12)
    2008-09 Enrollment: 543 . . . . (260) 488-2513
Housing: Homeownership rate: 81.3% (2010); Median home value: $126,327 (2010); Median contract rent: $342 per month (2000); Median year structure built: 1971 (2000).
Newspapers: NEWS (Community news; Circulation 800)

Transportation: Commute to work: 94.4% car, 0.3% public transportation, 1.6% walk, 3.2% work from home (2000); Travel time to work: 34.1% less than 15 minutes, 42.9% 15 to 30 minutes, 11.8% 30 to 45 minutes, 7.8% 45 to 60 minutes, 3.5% 60 minutes or more (2000)

HUDSON (town). Covers a land area of 0.819 square miles and a water area of 0 square miles. Located at 41.53° N. Lat; 85.08° W. Long. Elevation is 991 feet.
Population: 520 (1990); 596 (2000); 526 (2010); 490 (2015 projected); Race: 96.0% White, 0.0% Black, 0.0% Asian, 4.0% Other, 1.7% Hispanic of any race (2010); Density: 642.6 persons per square mile (2010); Average household size: 2.73 (2010); Median age: 33.8 (2010); Males per 100 females: 103.1 (2010); Marriage status: 22.6% never married, 58.8% now married, 3.3% widowed, 15.4% divorced (2000); Foreign born: 3.6% (2000); Ancestry (includes multiple ancestries): 28.0% German, 14.4% United States or American, 14.3% Other groups, 8.9% English, 3.9% Irish (2000).
Economy: Employment by occupation: 5.6% management, 6.5% professional, 7.2% services, 17.4% sales, 0.0% farming, 12.8% construction, 50.5% production (2000).
Income: Per capita income: $21,397 (2010); Median household income: $49,438 (2010); Average household income: $57,422 (2010); Percent of households with income of $100,000 or more: 6.2% (2010); Poverty rate: 4.3% (2000).
Taxes: Total city taxes per capita: $226 (2007); City property taxes per capita: $214 (2007).
Education: Percent of population age 25 and over with: High school diploma (including GED) or higher: 85.9% (2010); Bachelor's degree or higher: 7.7% (2010); Master's degree or higher: 4.5% (2010).
Housing: Homeownership rate: 85.0% (2010); Median home value: $86,538 (2010); Median contract rent: $436 per month (2000); Median year structure built: before 1940 (2000).
Transportation: Commute to work: 93.4% car, 0.9% public transportation, 0.6% walk, 4.4% work from home (2000); Travel time to work: 41.8% less than 15 minutes, 37.8% 15 to 30 minutes, 10.9% 30 to 45 minutes, 6.3% 45 to 60 minutes, 3.3% 60 minutes or more (2000)

ORLAND (town). Covers a land area of 0.665 square miles and a water area of 0 square miles. Located at 41.73° N. Lat; 85.17° W. Long. Elevation is 955 feet.
History: Laid out 1838.
Population: 361 (1990); 341 (2000); 316 (2010); 304 (2015 projected); Race: 98.4% White, 0.0% Black, 0.3% Asian, 1.3% Other, 0.3% Hispanic of any race (2010); Density: 475.2 persons per square mile (2010); Average household size: 2.47 (2010); Median age: 41.7 (2010); Males per 100 females: 105.2 (2010); Marriage status: 24.1% never married, 48.9% now married, 8.5% widowed, 18.5% divorced (2000); Foreign born: 1.1% (2000); Ancestry (includes multiple ancestries): 32.6% German, 12.6% Irish, 11.5% United States or American, 9.0% English, 4.4% Dutch (2000).
Economy: Employment by occupation: 5.0% management, 10.6% professional, 11.3% services, 25.6% sales, 0.0% farming, 13.1% construction, 34.4% production (2000).
Income: Per capita income: $26,397 (2010); Median household income: $54,878 (2010); Average household income: $63,125 (2010); Percent of households with income of $100,000 or more: 13.3% (2010); Poverty rate: 7.9% (2000).
Taxes: Total city taxes per capita: $273 (2007); City property taxes per capita: $227 (2007).
Education: Percent of population age 25 and over with: High school diploma (including GED) or higher: 90.8% (2010); Bachelor's degree or higher: 12.2% (2010); Master's degree or higher: 1.7% (2010).
Housing: Homeownership rate: 85.2% (2010); Median home value: $99,583 (2010); Median contract rent: $308 per month (2000); Median year structure built: before 1940 (2000).
Transportation: Commute to work: 94.4% car, 0.0% public transportation, 3.8% walk, 1.9% work from home (2000); Travel time to work: 25.5% less than 15 minutes, 49.0% 15 to 30 minutes, 11.5% 30 to 45 minutes, 6.4% 45 to 60 minutes, 7.6% 60 minutes or more (2000)

PLEASANT LAKE (unincorporated postal area, zip code 46779). Covers a land area of 34.863 square miles and a water area of 0.656 square miles. Located at 41.57° N. Lat; 85.03° W. Long. Elevation is 978 feet.
History: The community of Pleasant Lake was named for the nearby lake, which was called Nipcondish, meaning "pleasant waters," by the Indians.

Population: 2,191 (2000); Race: 98.5% White, 0.0% Black, 0.4% Asian, 1.1% Other, 0.7% Hispanic of any race (2000); Density: 62.8 persons per square mile (2000); Age: 27.1% under 18, 12.7% over 64 (2000); Marriage status: 25.1% never married, 60.1% now married, 4.5% widowed, 10.3% divorced (2000); Foreign born: 0.9% (2000); Ancestry (includes multiple ancestries): 20.3% German, 12.0% United States or American, 10.4% English, 9.7% Other groups, 7.4% Irish (2000).
Economy: Employment by occupation: 10.9% management, 6.9% professional, 14.5% services, 26.8% sales, 0.6% farming, 15.8% construction, 24.6% production (2000).
Income: Per capita income: $19,893 (2000); Median household income: $41,992 (2000); Poverty rate: 6.1% (2000).
Education: Percent of population age 25 and over with: High school diploma (including GED) or higher: 84.6% (2000); Bachelor's degree or higher: 10.0% (2000).
School District(s)
M S D Steuben County (KG-12)
    2008-09 Enrollment: 3,139 . . . . (260) 665-2854
Housing: Homeownership rate: 84.5% (2000); Median home value: $88,800 (2000); Median contract rent: $418 per month (2000); Median year structure built: 1971 (2000).
Transportation: Commute to work: 95.6% car, 0.7% public transportation, 1.4% walk, 2.3% work from home (2000); Travel time to work: 40.4% less than 15 minutes, 41.5% 15 to 30 minutes, 9.7% 30 to 45 minutes, 4.2% 45 to 60 minutes, 4.2% 60 minutes or more (2000)

Sullivan County

Located in southwestern Indiana; bounded on the west by the Wabash River and the Illinois border; drained by Busseron and Maria Creeks. Covers a land area of 447.20 square miles, a water area of 6.85 square miles, and is located in the Eastern Time Zone. The county was founded in 1816. County seat is Sullivan.

Sullivan County is part of the Terre Haute, IN Metropolitan Statistical Area. The entire metro area includes: Clay County, IN; Sullivan County, IN; Vermillion County, IN; Vigo County, IN

Population: 18,993 (1990); 21,751 (2000); 21,261 (2010); 20,902 (2015 projected); Race: 93.4% White, 4.6% Black, 0.2% Asian, 1.8% Other, 1.0% Hispanic of any race (2010); Density: 47.5 persons per square mile (2010); Average household size: 2.46 (2010); Median age: 38.2 (2010); Males per 100 females: 117.2 (2010).
Religion: Five largest groups: 8.1% Christian Churches and Churches of Christ, 7.0% American Baptist Churches in the USA, 6.7% The United Methodist Church, 3.8% Churches of Christ, 2.2% Southern Baptist Convention (2000).
Economy: Unemployment rate: 9.8% (5/2010); Total civilian labor force: 8,694 (5/2010); Leading industries: 17.7% health care and social assistance; 17.6% retail trade; 15.8% manufacturing (2008); Farms: 447 totaling 177,368 acres (2007); Companies that employ 500 or more persons: 0 (2008); Companies that employ 100 to 499 persons: 4 (2008); Companies that employ less than 100 persons: 367 (2008); Black-owned businesses: n/a (2002); Hispanic-owned businesses: n/a (2002); Asian-owned businesses: n/a (2002); Women-owned businesses: n/a (2002); Retail sales per capita: $8,218 (2010). Single-family building permits issued: 2 (2009); Multi-family building permits issued: 0 (2009).
Income: Per capita income: $20,239 (2010); Median household income: $42,123 (2010); Average household income: $52,030 (2010); Percent of households with income of $100,000 or more: 9.8% (2010); Poverty rate: 15.2% (2008); Bankruptcy rate: 7.63% (2009).
Taxes: Total county taxes per capita: $235 (2007); County property taxes per capita: $220 (2007).
Education: Percent of population age 25 and over with: High school diploma (including GED) or higher: 87.6% (2010); Bachelor's degree or higher: 15.5% (2010); Master's degree or higher: 4.7% (2010).
Housing: Homeownership rate: 80.4% (2010); Median home value: $68,573 (2010); Median contract rent: $366 per month (2006-2008 3-year est.); Median year structure built: 1964 (2006-2008 3-year est.)
Health: Birth rate: 105.4 per 10,000 population (2009); Death rate: 114.4 per 10,000 population (2009); Age-adjusted cancer mortality rate: 243.7 deaths per 100,000 population (2006); Number of physicians: 4.2 per 10,000 population (2007); Hospital beds: 11.7 per 10,000 population (2006); Hospital admissions: 650.0 per 10,000 population (2006).
Elections: 2008 Presidential election results: 48.8% Obama, 49.5% McCain, 0.0% Nader

National and State Parks: Greene-Sullivan State Forest
Additional Information Contacts
Sullivan County Government . . . . (812) 398-4924
    http://www.sullivancountyin.us
City of Sullivan . . . . (812) 268-6077
    http://sullivancountyindiana.us

Sullivan County Communities

CARLISLE (town). Covers a land area of 0.537 square miles and a
water area of 0 square miles. Located at 38.96° N. Lat; 87.40° W. Long.
Elevation is 482 feet.
History: Carlisle was settled in 1803 on land granted to Samuel
Ledgerwood for services to the U.S. government. Its early industry was
coal mining.
Population: 621 (1990); 2,660 (2000); 2,678 (2010); 2,666 (2015
projected); Race: 69.5% White, 25.8% Black, 0.2% Asian, 4.5% Other,
2.5% Hispanic of any race (2010); Density: 4,987.0 persons per square
mile (2010); Average household size: 2.52 (2010); Median age: 34.3
(2010); Males per 100 females: 344.9 (2010); Marriage status: 46.3%
never married, 30.5% now married, 5.0% widowed, 18.2% divorced (2000);
Foreign born: 0.0% (2000); Ancestry (includes multiple ancestries): 19.7%
Other groups, 10.8% German, 9.0% United States or American, 7.0% Irish,
4.6% English (2000).
Economy: Employment by occupation: 4.3% management, 18.4%
professional, 22.7% services, 17.1% sales, 1.0% farming, 13.7%
construction, 22.7% production (2000).
Income: Per capita income: $16,711 (2010); Median household income:
$49,224 (2010); Average household income: $57,963 (2010); Percent of
households with income of $100,000 or more: 11.0% (2010); Poverty rate:
13.4% (2000).
Taxes: Total city taxes per capita: $112 (2007); City property taxes per
capita: $105 (2007).
Education: Percent of population age 25 and over with: High school
diploma (including GED) or higher: 83.5% (2010); Bachelor's degree or
higher: 9.1% (2010); Master's degree or higher: 1.5% (2010).
School District(s)
Southwest School Corp (PK-12)
    2008-09 Enrollment: 1,734 . . . . (812) 268-6311
Housing: Homeownership rate: 81.9% (2010); Median home value:
$59,551 (2010); Median contract rent: $294 per month (2000); Median year
structure built: before 1940 (2000).
Transportation: Commute to work: 95.3% car, 0.0% public transportation,
2.2% walk, 2.5% work from home (2000); Travel time to work: 41.7% less
than 15 minutes, 20.7% 15 to 30 minutes, 20.7% 30 to 45 minutes, 9.2%
45 to 60 minutes, 7.7% 60 minutes or more (2000)

DUGGER (town). Covers a land area of 0.582 square miles and a water
area of 0 square miles. Located at 39.07° N. Lat; 87.26° W. Long.
Elevation is 577 feet.
Population: 881 (1990); 955 (2000); 947 (2010); 932 (2015 projected);
Race: 98.9% White, 0.0% Black, 0.0% Asian, 1.1% Other, 1.0% Hispanic
of any race (2010); Density: 1,627.3 persons per square mile (2010);
Average household size: 2.42 (2010); Median age: 41.3 (2010); Males per
100 females: 98.5 (2010); Marriage status: 21.5% never married, 57.2%
now married, 9.0% widowed, 12.4% divorced (2000); Foreign born: 0.0%
(2000); Ancestry (includes multiple ancestries): 11.2% United States or
American, 10.7% Other groups, 9.7% German, 8.5% English, 6.6% Irish
(2000).
Economy: Employment by occupation: 3.7% management, 21.0%
professional, 20.3% services, 22.0% sales, 0.5% farming, 11.2%
construction, 21.3% production (2000).
Income: Per capita income: $19,152 (2010); Median household income:
$40,933 (2010); Average household income: $46,758 (2010); Percent of
households with income of $100,000 or more: 5.9% (2010); Poverty rate:
7.8% (2000).
Taxes: Total city taxes per capita: $70 (2007); City property taxes per
capita: $70 (2007).
Education: Percent of population age 25 and over with: High school
diploma (including GED) or higher: 90.3% (2010); Bachelor's degree or
higher: 10.8% (2010); Master's degree or higher: 3.4% (2010).
School District(s)
Northeast School Corp (PK-12)
    2008-09 Enrollment: 1,495 . . . . (812) 383-5761

Housing: Homeownership rate: 85.7% (2010); Median home value:
$56,234 (2010); Median contract rent: $225 per month (2000); Median year
structure built: 1942 (2000).
Transportation: Commute to work: 96.6% car, 0.0% public transportation,
1.2% walk, 2.2% work from home (2000); Travel time to work: 26.5% less
than 15 minutes, 32.8% 15 to 30 minutes, 16.4% 30 to 45 minutes, 11.3%
45 to 60 minutes, 13.0% 60 minutes or more (2000)

FAIRBANKS (unincorporated postal area, zip code 47849). Covers a
land area of 24.176 square miles and a water area of 0.072 square miles.
Located at 39.19° N. Lat; 87.54° W. Long. Elevation is 551 feet.
History: The community of Fairbanks was named for Lt. Fairbanks who
was killed near here in 1812, while escorting a wagonload of supplies to
Fort Harrison.
Population: 415 (2000); Race: 100.0% White, 0.0% Black, 0.0% Asian,
0.0% Other, 0.0% Hispanic of any race (2000); Density: 17.2 persons per
square mile (2000); Age: 26.4% under 18, 18.7% over 64 (2000); Marriage
status: 5.1% never married, 87.3% now married, 5.7% widowed, 2.0%
divorced (2000); Foreign born: 0.0% (2000); Ancestry (includes multiple
ancestries): 17.1% English, 11.4% Other groups, 8.4% United States or
American, 7.5% German, 7.0% Irish (2000).
Economy: Employment by occupation: 3.6% management, 9.9%
professional, 18.2% services, 29.7% sales, 0.0% farming, 25.0%
construction, 13.5% production (2000).
Income: Per capita income: $17,100 (2000); Median household income:
$39,583 (2000); Poverty rate: 14.9% (2000).
Education: Percent of population age 25 and over with: High school
diploma (including GED) or higher: 83.5% (2000); Bachelor's degree or
higher: 14.0% (2000).
Housing: Homeownership rate: 87.2% (2000); Median home value:
$56,700 (2000); Median contract rent: $288 per month (2000); Median year
structure built: 1963 (2000).
Transportation: Commute to work: 100.0% car, 0.0% public
transportation, 0.0% walk, 0.0% work from home (2000); Travel time to
work: 0.0% less than 15 minutes, 36.5% 15 to 30 minutes, 28.1% 30 to 45
minutes, 16.9% 45 to 60 minutes, 18.5% 60 minutes or more (2000)

FARMERSBURG (town). Covers a land area of 0.726 square miles
and a water area of 0 square miles. Located at 39.25° N. Lat; 87.38° W.
Long. Elevation is 564 feet.
History: Farmersburg developed as a supply center for the surrounding
farming community.
Population: 1,209 (1990); 1,180 (2000); 999 (2010); 921 (2015 projected);
Race: 96.9% White, 0.1% Black, 0.4% Asian, 2.6% Other, 0.9% Hispanic
of any race (2010); Density: 1,376.9 persons per square mile (2010);
Average household size: 2.39 (2010); Median age: 38.1 (2010); Males per
100 females: 97.0 (2010); Marriage status: 22.4% never married, 54.3%
now married, 9.0% widowed, 14.4% divorced (2000); Foreign born: 1.1%
(2000); Ancestry (includes multiple ancestries): 17.5% United States or
American, 14.8% German, 13.8% English, 10.0% Irish, 7.0% Other groups
(2000).
Economy: Employment by occupation: 10.8% management, 14.8%
professional, 19.4% services, 25.3% sales, 1.1% farming, 9.5%
construction, 19.0% production (2000).
Income: Per capita income: $19,649 (2010); Median household income:
$38,800 (2010); Average household income: $46,739 (2010); Percent of
households with income of $100,000 or more: 7.0% (2010); Poverty rate:
11.0% (2000).
Taxes: Total city taxes per capita: $44 (2007); City property taxes per
capita: $38 (2007).
Education: Percent of population age 25 and over with: High school
diploma (including GED) or higher: 88.1% (2010); Bachelor's degree or
higher: 19.0% (2010); Master's degree or higher: 6.7% (2010).
School District(s)
Northeast School Corp (PK-12)
    2008-09 Enrollment: 1,495 . . . . (812) 383-5761
Housing: Homeownership rate: 81.9% (2010); Median home value:
$67,582 (2010); Median contract rent: $335 per month (2000); Median year
structure built: 1959 (2000).
Transportation: Commute to work: 97.0% car, 0.0% public transportation,
1.3% walk, 1.7% work from home (2000); Travel time to work: 21.8% less
than 15 minutes, 36.2% 15 to 30 minutes, 31.3% 30 to 45 minutes, 6.8%
45 to 60 minutes, 4.0% 60 minutes or more (2000)

HYMERA (town). Covers a land area of 0.703 square miles and a water area of 0 square miles. Located at 39.18° N. Lat; 87.30° W. Long. Elevation is 525 feet.

History: Hymera was platted in 1870 and named Pittsburg, after coal was discovered nearby. Postmaster John Badders changed the name to High Mary, referring to his daughter, and the name was later shortened to Hymera.

Population: 771 (1990); 833 (2000); 823 (2010); 811 (2015 projected); Race: 98.5% White, 0.1% Black, 0.1% Asian, 1.2% Other, 0.7% Hispanic of any race (2010); Density: 1,170.3 persons per square mile (2010); Average household size: 2.55 (2010); Median age: 37.6 (2010); Males per 100 females: 104.7 (2010); Marriage status: 23.0% never married, 55.4% now married, 14.0% widowed, 7.5% divorced (2000); Foreign born: 0.0% (2000); Ancestry (includes multiple ancestries): 19.4% United States or American, 11.9% English, 11.4% German, 7.5% Irish, 4.1% Other groups (2000).

Economy: Employment by occupation: 4.3% management, 7.7% professional, 20.7% services, 21.9% sales, 0.0% farming, 15.1% construction, 30.2% production (2000).

Income: Per capita income: $18,651 (2010); Median household income: $38,523 (2010); Average household income: $47,601 (2010); Percent of households with income of $100,000 or more: 7.8% (2010); Poverty rate: 17.2% (2000).

Taxes: Total city taxes per capita: $164 (2007); City property taxes per capita: $147 (2007).

Education: Percent of population age 25 and over with: High school diploma (including GED) or higher: 86.2% (2010); Bachelor's degree or higher: 17.6% (2010); Master's degree or higher: 6.3% (2010).

School District(s)
Northeast School Corp (PK-12)
    2008-09 Enrollment: 1,495 . . . . (812) 383-5761

Housing: Homeownership rate: 86.3% (2010); Median home value: $68,605 (2010); Median contract rent: $189 per month (2000); Median year structure built: 1943 (2000).

Transportation: Commute to work: 94.9% car, 0.3% public transportation, 3.8% walk, 1.0% work from home (2000); Travel time to work: 18.3% less than 15 minutes, 27.2% 15 to 30 minutes, 25.0% 30 to 45 minutes, 14.7% 45 to 60 minutes, 14.7% 60 minutes or more (2000)

MEROM (town). Covers a land area of 0.361 square miles and a water area of 0 square miles. Located at 39.05° N. Lat; 87.56° W. Long. Elevation is 548 feet.

History: From 1817 to 1842 Merom was the seat of Sullivan County and a shipping center. The name, which means "high ground along the waters," reflects Merom's location on a bluff of the Wabash River.

Population: 250 (1990); 294 (2000); 296 (2010); 291 (2015 projected); Race: 99.0% White, 0.3% Black, 0.0% Asian, 0.7% Other, 0.0% Hispanic of any race (2010); Density: 819.2 persons per square mile (2010); Average household size: 2.62 (2010); Median age: 40.3 (2010); Males per 100 females: 97.3 (2010); Marriage status: 21.9% never married, 65.3% now married, 5.0% widowed, 7.9% divorced (2000); Foreign born: 0.3% (2000); Ancestry (includes multiple ancestries): 17.2% United States or American, 13.5% German, 11.9% Irish, 9.6% Other groups, 9.2% English (2000).

Economy: Employment by occupation: 8.8% management, 10.4% professional, 8.8% services, 16.0% sales, 1.6% farming, 12.0% construction, 42.4% production (2000).

Income: Per capita income: $22,197 (2010); Median household income: $52,917 (2010); Average household income: $60,199 (2010); Percent of households with income of $100,000 or more: 11.5% (2010); Poverty rate: 14.5% (2000).

Taxes: Total city taxes per capita: $62 (2007); City property taxes per capita: $48 (2007).

Education: Percent of population age 25 and over with: High school diploma (including GED) or higher: 92.9% (2010); Bachelor's degree or higher: 15.7% (2010); Master's degree or higher: 3.8% (2010).

Housing: Homeownership rate: 86.7% (2010); Median home value: $76,667 (2010); Median contract rent: $333 per month (2000); Median year structure built: before 1940 (2000).

Transportation: Commute to work: 90.9% car, 0.0% public transportation, 7.4% walk, 0.0% work from home (2000); Travel time to work: 25.6% less than 15 minutes, 46.3% 15 to 30 minutes, 3.3% 30 to 45 minutes, 17.4% 45 to 60 minutes, 7.4% 60 minutes or more (2000)

SHELBURN (town). Covers a land area of 0.658 square miles and a water area of 0 square miles. Located at 39.18° N. Lat; 87.39° W. Long. Elevation is 541 feet.

History: Shelburn was founded in 1818. Growth was seen when the first coal mine was established in 1868.

Population: 1,147 (1990); 1,268 (2000); 1,307 (2010); 1,319 (2015 projected); Race: 97.7% White, 0.2% Black, 0.2% Asian, 1.9% Other, 0.3% Hispanic of any race (2010); Density: 1,985.3 persons per square mile (2010); Average household size: 2.43 (2010); Median age: 36.1 (2010); Males per 100 females: 95.7 (2010); Marriage status: 18.5% never married, 54.4% now married, 8.9% widowed, 18.2% divorced (2000); Foreign born: 0.2% (2000); Ancestry (includes multiple ancestries): 18.0% United States or American, 13.0% English, 11.3% German, 10.2% Irish, 6.4% Other groups (2000).

Economy: Employment by occupation: 7.0% management, 9.8% professional, 20.5% services, 17.9% sales, 1.1% farming, 15.8% construction, 27.9% production (2000).

Income: Per capita income: $18,140 (2010); Median household income: $35,995 (2010); Average household income: $43,771 (2010); Percent of households with income of $100,000 or more: 7.3% (2010); Poverty rate: 18.0% (2000).

Taxes: Total city taxes per capita: $55 (2007); City property taxes per capita: $47 (2007).

Education: Percent of population age 25 and over with: High school diploma (including GED) or higher: 86.0% (2010); Bachelor's degree or higher: 10.7% (2010); Master's degree or higher: 2.9% (2010).

School District(s)
Northeast School Corp (PK-12)
    2008-09 Enrollment: 1,495 . . . . (812) 383-5761

Housing: Homeownership rate: 78.2% (2010); Median home value: $56,078 (2010); Median contract rent: $230 per month (2000); Median year structure built: 1961 (2000).

Transportation: Commute to work: 92.8% car, 0.0% public transportation, 2.1% walk, 2.7% work from home (2000); Travel time to work: 31.1% less than 15 minutes, 28.3% 15 to 30 minutes, 21.7% 30 to 45 minutes, 12.7% 45 to 60 minutes, 6.2% 60 minutes or more (2000)

SULLIVAN (city). County seat. Covers a land area of 1.916 square miles and a water area of 0 square miles. Located at 39.09° N. Lat; 87.40° W. Long. Elevation is 528 feet.

History: Sullivan was laid out in 1842 as the seat of Sullivan County, which was moved from Merom to the more central location. The early economy of Sullivan was based on coal mining.

Population: 4,658 (1990); 4,617 (2000); 4,457 (2010); 4,312 (2015 projected); Race: 98.1% White, 0.3% Black, 0.3% Asian, 1.3% Other, 0.8% Hispanic of any race (2010); Density: 2,326.6 persons per square mile (2010); Average household size: 2.28 (2010); Median age: 40.1 (2010); Males per 100 females: 86.7 (2010); Marriage status: 17.8% never married, 50.1% now married, 16.8% widowed, 15.3% divorced (2000); Foreign born: 0.0% (2000); Ancestry (includes multiple ancestries): 14.5% United States or American, 13.1% English, 12.7% German, 10.7% Other groups, 9.6% Irish (2000).

Economy: Single-family building permits issued: 2 (2009); Multi-family building permits issued: 0 (2009); Employment by occupation: 6.3% management, 14.4% professional, 21.0% services, 26.1% sales, 0.0% farming, 12.1% construction, 20.1% production (2000).

Income: Per capita income: $21,141 (2010); Median household income: $36,607 (2010); Average household income: $48,191 (2010); Percent of households with income of $100,000 or more: 8.9% (2010); Poverty rate: 16.6% (2000).

Taxes: Total city taxes per capita: $170 (2007); City property taxes per capita: $159 (2007).

Education: Percent of population age 25 and over with: High school diploma (including GED) or higher: 87.9% (2010); Bachelor's degree or higher: 18.0% (2010); Master's degree or higher: 6.7% (2010).

School District(s)
Rural Community Schools Inc (KG-08)
    2008-09 Enrollment: 148 . . . . (812) 382-4500
Southwest School Corp (PK-12)
    2008-09 Enrollment: 1,734 . . . . (812) 268-6311

Housing: Homeownership rate: 67.9% (2010); Median home value: $65,376 (2010); Median contract rent: $253 per month (2000); Median year structure built: 1948 (2000).

Hospitals: Sullivan County Community Hospital

Safety: Violent crime rate: 4.5 per 10,000 population; Property crime rate: 125.4 per 10,000 population (2008).

Newspapers: Sullivan Daily Times (Regional news; Circulation 4,800)

Transportation: Commute to work: 94.6% car, 0.0% public transportation, 2.5% walk, 1.7% work from home (2000); Travel time to work: 45.0% less than 15 minutes, 24.5% 15 to 30 minutes, 15.5% 30 to 45 minutes, 8.4% 45 to 60 minutes, 6.6% 60 minutes or more (2000)

Additional Information Contacts

City of Sullivan . . . . (812) 268-6077
http://sullivancountyindiana.us

Switzerland County

Located in southeastern Indiana; bounded on the east and south by the Ohio River and the Kentucky border. Covers a land area of 221.18 square miles, a water area of 2.34 square miles, and is located in the Eastern Time Zone. The county was founded in 1814. County seat is Vevay.

Weather Station: Vevay   Elevation: 469 feet

	Jan	Feb	Mar	Apr	May	Jun	Jul	Aug	Sep	Oct	Nov	Dec
High	40	46	57	68	77	85	88	87	80	69	56	45
Low	23	25	34	42	52	61	66	64	57	45	36	28
Precip	3.1	2.9	4.1	4.3	4.7	4.6	3.8	3.9	3.1	3.1	3.6	3.7
Snow	6.5	5.1	3.3	0.1	tr	0.0	0.0	0.0	0.0	0.3	0.6	2.7

High and Low temperatures in degrees Fahrenheit; Precipitation and Snow in inches

Population: 7,738 (1990); 9,065 (2000); 9,754 (2010); 9,979 (2015 projected); Race: 98.1% White, 0.7% Black, 0.1% Asian, 1.1% Other, 1.1% Hispanic of any race (2010); Density: 44.1 persons per square mile (2010); Average household size: 2.57 (2010); Median age: 38.6 (2010); Males per 100 females: 101.3 (2010).

Religion: Five largest groups: 13.4% American Baptist Churches in the USA, 5.1% Christian Churches and Churches of Christ, 3.4% The United Methodist Church, 1.7% Old Order Amish Church, 1.6% Catholic Church (2000).

Economy: Unemployment rate: 7.5% (5/2010); Total civilian labor force: 5,711 (5/2010); Leading industries: 7.6% health care and social assistance; 4.7% retail trade; 3.3% other services (except public administration) (2008); Farms: 374 totaling 47,461 acres (2007); Companies that employ 500 or more persons: 1 (2008); Companies that employ 100 to 499 persons: 1 (2008); Companies that employ less than 100 persons: 126 (2008); Black-owned businesses: n/a (2002); Hispanic-owned businesses: n/a (2002); Asian-owned businesses: n/a (2002); Women-owned businesses: n/a (2002); Retail sales per capita: $3,411 (2010). Single-family building permits issued: 44 (2009); Multi-family building permits issued: 0 (2009).

Income: Per capita income: $21,653 (2010); Median household income: $45,761 (2010); Average household income: $55,803 (2010); Percent of households with income of $100,000 or more: 10.1% (2010); Poverty rate: 16.3% (2008); Bankruptcy rate: 6.47% (2009).

Taxes: Total county taxes per capita: $293 (2007); County property taxes per capita: $159 (2007).

Education: Percent of population age 25 and over with: High school diploma (including GED) or higher: 77.6% (2010); Bachelor's degree or higher: 8.2% (2010); Master's degree or higher: 3.3% (2010).

Housing: Homeownership rate: 76.7% (2010); Median home value: $123,191 (2010); Median contract rent: $n/a per month (2006-2008 3-year est.); Median year structure built: n/a (2006-2008 3-year est.)

Health: Birth rate: 116.8 per 10,000 population (2009); Death rate: 100.3 per 10,000 population (2009); Age-adjusted cancer mortality rate: 181.6 (Unreliable) deaths per 100,000 population (2006); Number of physicians: 0.0 per 10,000 population (2007); Hospital beds: 0.0 per 10,000 population (2006); Hospital admissions: 0.0 per 10,000 population (2006).

Elections: 2008 Presidential election results: 45.0% Obama, 53.3% McCain, 0.0% Nader

Additional Information Contacts

Switzerland County Government . . . . (800) 435-5688
http://www.vevayin.com

Switzerland County Communities

BENNINGTON (unincorporated postal area, zip code 47011). Covers a land area of 26.942 square miles and a water area of 0.067 square miles. Located at 38.84° N. Lat; 85.07° W. Long. Elevation is 889 feet.

Population: 674 (2000); Race: 100.0% White, 0.0% Black, 0.0% Asian, 0.0% Other, 0.0% Hispanic of any race (2000); Density: 25.0 persons per square mile (2000); Age: 36.8% under 18, 9.2% over 64 (2000); Marriage

status: 23.7% never married, 66.1% now married, 3.9% widowed, 6.2% divorced (2000); Foreign born: 0.0% (2000); Ancestry (includes multiple ancestries): 36.0% German, 13.4% Irish, 11.9% United States or American, 3.0% Swiss, 2.2% Other groups (2000).

Economy: Employment by occupation: 9.6% management, 16.9% professional, 11.1% services, 9.9% sales, 0.0% farming, 16.6% construction, 36.0% production (2000).

Income: Per capita income: $12,270 (2000); Median household income: $28,676 (2000); Poverty rate: 32.6% (2000).

Education: Percent of population age 25 and over with: High school diploma (including GED) or higher: 73.0% (2000); Bachelor's degree or higher: 14.4% (2000).

Housing: Homeownership rate: 83.7% (2000); Median home value: $74,600 (2000); Median contract rent: $192 per month (2000); Median year structure built: 1976 (2000).

Transportation: Commute to work: 92.0% car, 0.0% public transportation, 2.2% walk, 4.1% work from home (2000); Travel time to work: 11.3% less than 15 minutes, 34.2% 15 to 30 minutes, 20.3% 30 to 45 minutes, 18.6% 45 to 60 minutes, 15.6% 60 minutes or more (2000)

FLORENCE (unincorporated postal area, zip code 47020). Covers a land area of 22.617 square miles and a water area of 0 square miles. Located at 38.81° N. Lat; 84.94° W. Long. Elevation is 476 feet.

Population: 1,037 (2000); Race: 100.0% White, 0.0% Black, 0.0% Asian, 0.0% Other, 1.4% Hispanic of any race (2000); Density: 45.9 persons per square mile (2000); Age: 27.1% under 18, 10.0% over 64 (2000); Marriage status: 19.5% never married, 61.4% now married, 8.3% widowed, 10.8% divorced (2000); Foreign born: 0.0% (2000); Ancestry (includes multiple ancestries): 27.7% United States or American, 15.9% German, 8.1% Other groups, 6.1% Irish, 5.0% English (2000).

Economy: Employment by occupation: 8.4% management, 6.1% professional, 17.0% services, 17.6% sales, 0.0% farming, 22.2% construction, 28.7% production (2000).

Income: Per capita income: $25,455 (2000); Median household income: $40,859 (2000); Poverty rate: 10.1% (2000).

Education: Percent of population age 25 and over with: High school diploma (including GED) or higher: 58.7% (2000); Bachelor's degree or higher: 3.8% (2000).

Housing: Homeownership rate: 80.4% (2000); Median home value: $87,300 (2000); Median contract rent: $429 per month (2000); Median year structure built: 1982 (2000).

Transportation: Commute to work: 95.7% car, 0.0% public transportation, 2.2% walk, 2.2% work from home (2000); Travel time to work: 12.4% less than 15 minutes, 31.6% 15 to 30 minutes, 23.4% 30 to 45 minutes, 16.6% 45 to 60 minutes, 16.0% 60 minutes or more (2000)

PATRIOT (town). Covers a land area of 0.223 square miles and a water area of 0.038 square miles. Located at 38.83° N. Lat; 84.82° W. Long. Elevation is 472 feet.

History: Suffered during flood of 1937. Laid out 1820.

Population: 201 (1990); 202 (2000); 211 (2010); 215 (2015 projected); Race: 96.2% White, 1.9% Black, 0.0% Asian, 1.9% Other, 2.4% Hispanic of any race (2010); Density: 947.1 persons per square mile (2010); Average household size: 2.80 (2010); Median age: 40.2 (2010); Males per 100 females: 111.0 (2010); Marriage status: 34.4% never married, 48.6% now married, 8.7% widowed, 8.2% divorced (2000); Foreign born: 0.0% (2000); Ancestry (includes multiple ancestries): 41.5% United States or American, 17.0% German, 11.3% English, 9.4% Irish, 6.1% Other groups (2000).

Economy: Employment by occupation: 4.3% management, 10.8% professional, 14.0% services, 17.2% sales, 0.0% farming, 9.7% construction, 44.1% production (2000).

Income: Per capita income: $22,292 (2010); Median household income: $56,500 (2010); Average household income: $59,867 (2010); Percent of households with income of $100,000 or more: 14.7% (2010); Poverty rate: 10.4% (2010).

Taxes: Total city taxes per capita: $21 (2007); City property taxes per capita: $21 (2007).

Education: Percent of population age 25 and over with: High school diploma (including GED) or higher: 78.5% (2010); Bachelor's degree or higher: 6.0% (2010); Master's degree or higher: 0.7% (2010).

Housing: Homeownership rate: 78.7% (2010); Median home value: $116,071 (2010); Median contract rent: $346 per month (2000); Median year structure built: 1954 (2000).

Transportation: Commute to work: 85.7% car, 0.0% public transportation, 9.9% walk, 0.0% work from home (2000); Travel time to work: 25.3% less than 15 minutes, 19.8% 15 to 30 minutes, 18.7% 30 to 45 minutes, 7.7% 45 to 60 minutes, 28.6% 60 minutes or more (2000)

VEVAY (town). County seat. Covers a land area of 1.481 square miles and a water area of 0.054 square miles. Located at 38.74° N. Lat; 85.07° W. Long. Elevation is 482 feet.

History: Vevay was founded in 1801 by Swiss immigrants, who planted vineyards and became known for their fine wines. Vevay was the birthplace of Edward Eggleston, author of "The Hoosier Schoolmaster."

Population: 1,536 (1990); 1,735 (2000); 2,044 (2010); 2,062 (2015 projected); Race: 98.1% White, 0.6% Black, 0.1% Asian, 1.1% Other, 1.6% Hispanic of any race (2010); Density: 1,379.9 persons per square mile (2010); Average household size: 2.23 (2010); Median age: 40.5 (2010); Males per 100 females: 91.0 (2010); Marriage status: 24.0% never married, 48.6% now married, 9.7% widowed, 17.7% divorced (2000); Foreign born: 1.5% (2000); Ancestry (includes multiple ancestries): 19.2% United States or American, 12.5% Other groups, 12.4% German, 9.6% Irish, 7.1% English (2000).

Economy: Employment by occupation: 9.5% management, 13.2% professional, 22.4% services, 18.9% sales, 0.0% farming, 11.8% construction, 24.1% production (2000).

Income: Per capita income: $20,260 (2010); Median household income: $33,811 (2010); Average household income: $45,805 (2010); Percent of households with income of $100,000 or more: 7.6% (2010); Poverty rate: 15.1% (2000).

Taxes: Total city taxes per capita: $172 (2007); City property taxes per capita: $98 (2007).

Education: Percent of population age 25 and over with: High school diploma (including GED) or higher: 79.6% (2010); Bachelor's degree or higher: 10.3% (2010); Master's degree or higher: 5.3% (2010).

School District(s)

Switzerland County School Corp (PK-12)

    2008-09 Enrollment: 1,499 . . . . (812) 427-2611

Housing: Homeownership rate: 62.4% (2010); Median home value: $114,943 (2010); Median contract rent: $298 per month (2000); Median year structure built: 1957 (2000).

Newspapers: Reveille Enterprise (Community news; Circulation 3,000); Switzerland Democrat (Local news; Circulation 600)

Transportation: Commute to work: 88.6% car, 0.3% public transportation, 7.8% walk, 2.0% work from home (2000); Travel time to work: 48.7% less than 15 minutes, 14.0% 15 to 30 minutes, 19.9% 30 to 45 minutes, 7.0% 45 to 60 minutes, 10.5% 60 minutes or more (2000)

Tippecanoe County

Located in west central Indiana; crossed by the Wabash River; drained by the Tippecanoe River. Covers a land area of 499.79 square miles, a water area of 3.28 square miles, and is located in the Eastern Time Zone. The county was founded in 1826. County seat is Lafayette.

Tippecanoe County is part of the Lafayette, IN Metropolitan Statistical Area. The entire metro area includes: Benton County, IN; Carroll County, IN; Tippecanoe County, IN

Weather Station: Lafayette 8 S										Elevation: 731 feet	
	Jan	Feb	Mar	Apr	May	Jun	Jul	Aug	Sep	Oct	Nov	Dec
High	31	37	48	61	72	81	85	83	77	65	50	37
Low	15	19	29	39	50	59	63	61	53	42	32	22
Precip	1.8	1.7	3.0	3.5	4.1	4.2	4.0	3.7	2.8	2.5	3.0	2.5
Snow	7.5	4.6	2.6	0.7	tr	0.0	0.0	0.0	0.0	0.5	0.8	5.1

High and Low temperatures in degrees Fahrenheit; Precipitation and Snow in inches

Weather Station: West Lafayette 6 NW										Elevation: 702 feet	
	Jan	Feb	Mar	Apr	May	Jun	Jul	Aug	Sep	Oct	Nov	Dec
High	31	36	48	60	72	81	84	82	77	64	50	37
Low	15	19	29	39	50	60	63	61	53	42	32	22
Precip	1.8	1.5	2.9	3.8	4.2	4.1	4.0	3.7	3.1	2.8	3.1	2.4
Snow	7.4	4.8	2.4	0.7	0.0	0.0	0.0	0.0	0.0	0.2	1.0	5.0

High and Low temperatures in degrees Fahrenheit; Precipitation and Snow in inches

Weather Station: West Lafayette Purdue Univ. Arpt.										Elevation: 597 feet	
	Jan	Feb	Mar	Apr	May	Jun	Jul	Aug	Sep	Oct	Nov	Dec
High	32	37	49	62	73	83	86	84	77	65	50	38
Low	16	20	31	40	50	60	64	63	55	43	34	24
Precip	1.7	1.5	3.0	3.7	3.8	4.1	3.9	3.9	2.9	2.4	3.0	2.5
Snow	7.2	4.8	2.1	0.6	tr	0.0	0.0	0.0	0.0	0.3	0.9	5.7

High and Low temperatures in degrees Fahrenheit; Precipitation and Snow in inches

Population: 130,598 (1990); 148,955 (2000); 167,458 (2010); 175,810 (2015 projected); Race: 85.5% White, 3.6% Black, 5.3% Asian, 5.5% Other, 7.5% Hispanic of any race (2010); Density: 335.1 persons per square mile (2010); Average household size: 2.40 (2010); Median age: 29.1 (2010); Males per 100 females: 107.0 (2010).

Religion: Five largest groups: 13.1% Catholic Church, 4.0% The United Methodist Church, 2.9% Presbyterian Church (U.S.A.), 1.8% Lutheran Church—Missouri Synod, 1.3% Independent, Charismatic Churches (2000).

Economy: Unemployment rate: 9.0% (5/2010); Total civilian labor force: 79,166 (5/2010); Leading industries: 22.4% manufacturing; 15.4% retail trade; 14.7% health care and social assistance (2008); Farms: 757 totaling 218,301 acres (2007); Companies that employ 500 or more persons: 11 (2008); Companies that employ 100 to 499 persons: 84 (2008); Companies that employ less than 100 persons: 3,269 (2008); Black-owned businesses: n/a (2002); Hispanic-owned businesses: n/a (2002); Asian-owned businesses: 206 (2002); Women-owned businesses: 2,429 (2002); Retail sales per capita: $13,869 (2010). Single-family building permits issued: 409 (2009); Multi-family building permits issued: 27 (2009).

Income: Per capita income: $22,648 (2010); Median household income: $43,672 (2010); Average household income: $57,754 (2010); Percent of households with income of $100,000 or more: 13.6% (2010); Poverty rate: 18.2% (2008); Bankruptcy rate: 3.86% (2009).

Taxes: Total county taxes per capita: $215 (2007); County property taxes per capita: $132 (2007).

Education: Percent of population age 25 and over with: High school diploma (including GED) or higher: 90.0% (2010); Bachelor's degree or higher: 36.5% (2010); Master's degree or higher: 16.2% (2010).

Housing: Homeownership rate: 56.7% (2010); Median home value: $123,272 (2010); Median contract rent: $584 per month (2006-2008 3-year est.); Median year structure built: 1975 (2006-2008 3-year est.)

Health: Birth rate: 134.7 per 10,000 population (2009); Death rate: 62.8 per 10,000 population (2009); Age-adjusted cancer mortality rate: 205.2 deaths per 100,000 population (2006); Air Quality Index: 72.2% good, 27.5% moderate, 0.3% unhealthy for sensitive individuals, 0.0% unhealthy (percent of days in 2008); Number of physicians: 20.2 per 10,000 population (2007); Hospital beds: 32.5 per 10,000 population (2006); Hospital admissions: 1,234.8 per 10,000 population (2006).

Elections: 2008 Presidential election results: 55.0% Obama, 43.5% McCain, 0.1% Nader

Additional Information Contacts

Tippecanoe County Government . . . . (765) 423-9326
    http://www.co.tippecanoe.in.us
City of Lafayette . . . . (765) 807-1021
    http://www.lafayette.in.gov
City of West Lafayette . . . . (765) 775-5100
    http://www.city.west-lafayette.in.us
Lafayette-West Lafayette Chamber of Commerce . . . . (765) 742-4044
    http://www.lafayettechamber.com
Tippecanoe County Government . . . . (765) 423-9326
    http://www.county.tippecanoe.in.us
Town of Battle Ground . . . . (765) 567-2603
    http://battleground.in.gov
West Lafayette Chamber of Commerce . . . . (765) 742-4044
    http://www.lafayettechamber.com

Tippecanoe County Communities

BATTLE GROUND (town). Covers a land area of 1.148 square miles and a water area of 0 square miles. Located at 40.50° N. Lat; 86.84° W. Long. Elevation is 587 feet.

History: A memorial park marks scene of the Battle of Tippecanoe (1811) between Native Americans and U.S. soldiers under Gen. W. H. Harrison.

Population: 1,290 (1990); 1,323 (2000); 1,521 (2010); 1,613 (2015 projected); Race: 97.6% White, 0.2% Black, 0.2% Asian, 2.0% Other, 2.0% Hispanic of any race (2010); Density: 1,325.0 persons per square mile (2010); Average household size: 2.67 (2010); Median age: 35.8 (2010); Males per 100 females: 99.3 (2010); Marriage status: 22.4% never married,

62.5% now married, 3.6% widowed, 11.5% divorced (2000); Foreign born: 1.0% (2000); Ancestry (includes multiple ancestries): 34.7% German, 16.6% Irish, 11.5% English, 8.1% Other groups, 7.3% United States or American (2000).

Economy: Employment by occupation: 14.3% management, 21.2% professional, 17.7% services, 20.5% sales, 0.9% farming, 7.1% construction, 18.3% production (2000).

Income: Per capita income: $21,777 (2010); Median household income: $48,388 (2010); Average household income: $58,169 (2010); Percent of households with income of $100,000 or more: 13.9% (2010); Poverty rate: 5.0% (2000).

Taxes: Total city taxes per capita: $115 (2007); City property taxes per capita: $104 (2007).

Education: Percent of population age 25 and over with: High school diploma (including GED) or higher: 93.4% (2010); Bachelor's degree or higher: 22.5% (2010); Master's degree or higher: 7.6% (2010).

School District(s)

Tippecanoe School Corp (KG-12)
   2008-09 Enrollment: 11,686 . . . . (765) 474-2481

Housing: Homeownership rate: 84.9% (2010); Median home value: $134,049 (2010); Median contract rent: $430 per month (2000); Median year structure built: 1973 (2000).

Transportation: Commute to work: 94.4% car, 0.0% public transportation, 2.0% walk, 3.3% work from home (2000); Travel time to work: 23.8% less than 15 minutes, 60.2% 15 to 30 minutes, 11.0% 30 to 45 minutes, 1.9% 45 to 60 minutes, 3.1% 60 minutes or more (2000).

Additional Information Contacts

Tippecanoe County Government . . . . (765) 423-9326
   http://www.county.tippecanoe.in.us
Town of Battle Ground . . . . (765) 567-2603
   http://battleground.in.gov

CLARKS HILL (town). Covers a land area of 0.275 square miles and a water area of 0 square miles. Located at 40.24° N. Lat; 86.72° W. Long. Elevation is 820 feet.

Population: 716 (1990); 680 (2000); 828 (2010); 904 (2015 projected); Race: 97.9% White, 0.0% Black, 0.1% Asian, 1.9% Other, 1.3% Hispanic of any race (2010); Density: 3,013.0 persons per square mile (2010); Average household size: 2.83 (2010); Median age: 29.7 (2010); Males per 100 females: 94.8 (2010); Marriage status: 15.3% never married, 69.4% now married, 4.3% widowed, 11.1% divorced (2000); Foreign born: 0.6% (2000); Ancestry (includes multiple ancestries): 29.0% United States or American, 13.1% Irish, 8.4% German, 7.1% Other groups, 4.8% English (2000).

Economy: Employment by occupation: 3.8% management, 7.2% professional, 19.2% services, 18.5% sales, 1.4% farming, 17.5% construction, 32.5% production (2000).

Income: Per capita income: $17,350 (2010); Median household income: $44,955 (2010); Average household income: $49,403 (2010); Percent of households with income of $100,000 or more: 6.5% (2010); Poverty rate: 10.1% (2000).

Taxes: Total city taxes per capita: $89 (2007); City property taxes per capita: $65 (2007).

Education: Percent of population age 25 and over with: High school diploma (including GED) or higher: 76.6% (2010); Bachelor's degree or higher: 3.6% (2010); Master's degree or higher: 1.1% (2010).

Housing: Homeownership rate: 72.0% (2010); Median home value: $89,512 (2010); Median contract rent: $380 per month (2000); Median year structure built: 1957 (2000).

Safety: Violent crime rate: 14.5 per 10,000 population; Property crime rate: 72.6 per 10,000 population (2008).

Transportation: Commute to work: 98.6% car, 0.0% public transportation, 0.7% walk, 0.7% work from home (2000); Travel time to work: 9.9% less than 15 minutes, 56.0% 15 to 30 minutes, 22.3% 30 to 45 minutes, 4.3% 45 to 60 minutes, 7.4% 60 minutes or more (2000).

DAYTON (town). Covers a land area of 1.038 square miles and a water area of 0 square miles. Located at 40.37° N. Lat; 86.76° W. Long. Elevation is 676 feet.

Population: 996 (1990); 1,120 (2000); 1,299 (2010); 1,397 (2015 projected); Race: 97.2% White, 0.2% Black, 0.1% Asian, 2.5% Other, 2.8% Hispanic of any race (2010); Density: 1,251.7 persons per square mile (2010); Average household size: 2.71 (2010); Median age: 30.5 (2010); Males per 100 females: 95.0 (2010); Marriage status: 22.5% never married, 59.7% now married, 4.1% widowed, 13.8% divorced (2000); Foreign born:

0.8% (2000); Ancestry (includes multiple ancestries): 25.1% German, 14.4% United States or American, 9.2% Irish, 8.6% Other groups, 5.9% English (2000).

Economy: Employment by occupation: 8.9% management, 13.1% professional, 12.9% services, 26.4% sales, 0.4% farming, 8.9% construction, 29.5% production (2000).

Income: Per capita income: $24,474 (2010); Median household income: $56,633 (2010); Average household income: $65,797 (2010); Percent of households with income of $100,000 or more: 13.8% (2010); Poverty rate: 7.9% (2000).

Taxes: Total city taxes per capita: $109 (2007); City property taxes per capita: $109 (2007).

Education: Percent of population age 25 and over with: High school diploma (including GED) or higher: 89.7% (2010); Bachelor's degree or higher: 18.7% (2010); Master's degree or higher: 4.9% (2010).

School District(s)

Tippecanoe School Corp (KG-12)
   2008-09 Enrollment: 11,686 . . . . (765) 474-2481

Housing: Homeownership rate: 75.8% (2010); Median home value: $124,510 (2010); Median contract rent: $446 per month (2000); Median year structure built: 1975 (2000).

Transportation: Commute to work: 95.2% car, 0.0% public transportation, 1.9% walk, 2.0% work from home (2000); Travel time to work: 35.2% less than 15 minutes, 50.0% 15 to 30 minutes, 10.6% 30 to 45 minutes, 2.3% 45 to 60 minutes, 1.9% 60 minutes or more (2000)

LAFAYETTE (city). County seat. Covers a land area of 20.095 square miles and a water area of 0 square miles. Located at 40.41° N. Lat; 86.87° W. Long. Elevation is 692 feet.

History: Lafayette was founded in 1824 by William Digby, and named for the Marquis de Lafayette. Lafayette was an early shipping center along the Wabash River. It was from Lafayette that the balloon carrying the first airmail in the U.S. was launched. The flight failed to reach its destination and the mail continued on by train.

Population: 49,671 (1990); 56,397 (2000); 59,719 (2010); 61,420 (2015 projected); Race: 83.7% White, 5.2% Black, 1.4% Asian, 9.7% Other, 14.2% Hispanic of any race (2010); Density: 2,971.8 persons per square mile (2010); Average household size: 2.28 (2010); Median age: 32.8 (2010); Males per 100 females: 100.3 (2010); Marriage status: 30.6% never married, 50.9% now married, 6.5% widowed, 12.1% divorced (2000); Foreign born: 7.9% (2000); Ancestry (includes multiple ancestries): 21.7% German, 17.5% Other groups, 11.7% United States or American, 11.5% Irish, 9.3% English (2000).

Economy: Unemployment rate: 10.5% (5/2010); Total civilian labor force: 32,872 (5/2010); Single-family building permits issued: 80 (2009); Multi-family building permits issued: 0 (2009); Employment by occupation: 9.0% management, 20.8% professional, 16.7% services, 24.1% sales, 0.3% farming, 8.0% construction, 21.2% production (2000).

Income: Per capita income: $21,163 (2010); Median household income: $38,667 (2010); Average household income: $48,378 (2010); Percent of households with income of $100,000 or more: 7.4% (2010); Poverty rate: 12.1% (2000).

Taxes: Total city taxes per capita: $388 (2007); City property taxes per capita: $301 (2007).

Education: Percent of population age 25 and over with: High school diploma (including GED) or higher: 85.8% (2010); Bachelor's degree or higher: 26.9% (2010); Master's degree or higher: 10.2% (2010).

School District(s)

Beacon Academy (07-11)
   2008-09 Enrollment: 29 . . . . (765) 543-7808
Lafayette School Corporation (KG-12)
   2008-09 Enrollment: 7,320 . . . . (765) 771-6000
New Community School (KG-08)
   2008-09 Enrollment: 140 . . . . (765) 420-9617
Tippecanoe School Corp (KG-12)
   2008-09 Enrollment: 11,686 . . . . (765) 474-2481

Two-year College(s)

Indiana Business College-Lafayette (Private, For-profit)
   Fall 2008 Enrollment: 290 . . . . (765) 447-9550
   2009-10 Tuition: In-state $11,535; Out-of-state $11,535
Ivy Tech Community College-Lafayette (Public)
   Fall 2008 Enrollment: 6,685 . . . . (765) 269-5000
   2009-10 Tuition: In-state $3,090; Out-of-state $6,306

Saint Elizabeth School of Nursing (Private, Not-for-profit, Roman Catholic)
Fall 2008 Enrollment: 188 . . . . (765) 423-6400
2009-10 Tuition: In-state $15,700; Out-of-state $15,700

Vocational/Technical School(s)

Lafayette Beauty Academy (Private, For-profit)
Fall 2008 Enrollment: 70 . . . . (765) 742-0068
2009-10 Tuition: $7,500

Housing: Homeownership rate: 51.6% (2010); Median home value: $95,759 (2010); Median contract rent: $491 per month (2000); Median year structure built: 1963 (2000).

Hospitals: St. Elizabeth Medical Center (375 beds); St. Elizabeth Regional Health (263 beds); Wabash Valley Hospital

Safety: Violent crime rate: 50.8 per 10,000 population; Property crime rate: 468.8 per 10,000 population (2008).

Newspapers: The Catholic Moment (Regional news; Circulation 27,253); Journal & Courier en Español (Local news); The Journal & Courier (Local news; Circulation 36,788); Lafayette Leader (Community news; Circulation 5,500); Lafayette Magazine (Regional news; Circulation 10,000)

Transportation: Commute to work: 92.3% car, 1.8% public transportation, 2.4% walk, 2.2% work from home (2000); Travel time to work: 51.7% less than 15 minutes, 36.4% 15 to 30 minutes, 6.1% 30 to 45 minutes, 1.7% 45 to 60 minutes, 4.2% 60 minutes or more (2000); Amtrak: train service available.

Additional Information Contacts

City of Lafayette . . . . (765) 807-1021
http://www.lafayette.in.gov
Lafayette-West Lafayette Chamber of Commerce . . . . (765) 742-4044
http://www.lafayettechamber.com

ROMNEY (unincorporated postal area, zip code 47981). Covers a land area of 38.107 square miles and a water area of 0 square miles. Located at 40.24° N. Lat; 86.91° W. Long. Elevation is 738 feet.

History: Founded c.1831.

Population: 786 (2000); Race: 100.0% White, 0.0% Black, 0.0% Asian, 0.0% Other, 0.0% Hispanic of any race (2000); Density: 20.6 persons per square mile (2000); Age: 34.4% under 18, 12.3% over 64 (2000); Marriage status: 11.9% never married, 66.2% now married, 9.8% widowed, 12.1% divorced (2000); Foreign born: 0.0% (2000); Ancestry (includes multiple ancestries): 22.2% United States or American, 20.7% English, 12.4% German, 11.2% Scottish, 7.0% Dutch (2000).

Economy: Employment by occupation: 16.3% management, 12.5% professional, 16.9% services, 18.7% sales, 0.0% farming, 10.8% construction, 24.8% production (2000).

Income: Per capita income: $19,936 (2000); Median household income: $46,932 (2000); Poverty rate: 1.7% (2000).

Education: Percent of population age 25 and over with: High school diploma (including GED) or higher: 90.5% (2000); Bachelor's degree or higher: 17.9% (2000).

Housing: Homeownership rate: 75.0% (2000); Median home value: $113,700 (2000); Median contract rent: $368 per month (2000); Median year structure built: 1957 (2000).

Transportation: Commute to work: 84.5% car, 0.0% public transportation, 5.5% walk, 7.6% work from home (2000); Travel time to work: 22.1% less than 15 minutes, 41.6% 15 to 30 minutes, 34.4% 30 to 45 minutes, 1.9% 45 to 60 minutes, 0.0% 60 minutes or more (2000)

SHADELAND (town). Covers a land area of 27.132 square miles and a water area of 0.232 square miles. Located at 40.36° N. Lat; 86.94° W. Long. Elevation is 620 feet.

History: Laid out 1824.

Population: 1,674 (1990); 1,682 (2000); 1,816 (2010); 1,895 (2015 projected); Race: 96.1% White, 0.4% Black, 1.8% Asian, 1.7% Other, 4.7% Hispanic of any race (2010); Density: 66.9 persons per square mile (2010); Average household size: 2.74 (2010); Median age: 36.5 (2010); Males per 100 females: 110.4 (2010); Marriage status: 26.2% never married, 64.3% now married, 3.9% widowed, 5.5% divorced (2000); Foreign born: 0.9% (2000); Ancestry (includes multiple ancestries): 25.7% German, 13.9% United States or American, 12.3% English, 10.4% Irish, 6.0% Dutch (2000).

Economy: Employment by occupation: 10.4% management, 15.2% professional, 14.9% services, 26.8% sales, 1.3% farming, 13.5% construction, 17.8% production (2000).

Income: Per capita income: $25,045 (2010); Median household income: $59,426 (2010); Average household income: $68,625 (2010); Percent of households with income of $100,000 or more: 17.4% (2010); Poverty rate: 3.1% (2000).

Taxes: Total city taxes per capita: $108 (2007); City property taxes per capita: $79 (2007).

Education: Percent of population age 25 and over with: High school diploma (including GED) or higher: 85.8% (2010); Bachelor's degree or higher: 19.2% (2010); Master's degree or higher: 6.5% (2010).

Housing: Homeownership rate: 81.3% (2010); Median home value: $138,728 (2010); Median contract rent: $438 per month (2000); Median year structure built: 1968 (2000).

Transportation: Commute to work: 92.3% car, 1.0% public transportation, 0.7% walk, 4.3% work from home (2000); Travel time to work: 22.1% less than 15 minutes, 60.1% 15 to 30 minutes, 13.3% 30 to 45 minutes, 2.5% 45 to 60 minutes, 1.9% 60 minutes or more (2000)

WEST LAFAYETTE (city). Covers a land area of 5.513 square miles and a water area of 0.010 square miles. Located at 40.44° N. Lat; 86.91° W. Long. Elevation is 614 feet.

History: Purdue University was founded in 1874 in West Lafayette.

Population: 26,691 (1990); 28,778 (2000); 29,770 (2010); 30,306 (2015 projected); Race: 79.2% White, 3.3% Black, 14.1% Asian, 3.4% Other, 3.9% Hispanic of any race (2010); Density: 5,399.5 persons per square mile (2010); Average household size: 2.20 (2010); Median age: 24.2 (2010); Males per 100 females: 130.3 (2010); Marriage status: 62.5% never married, 31.6% now married, 3.1% widowed, 2.8% divorced (2000); Foreign born: 13.3% (2000); Ancestry (includes multiple ancestries): 26.7% German, 17.0% Other groups, 12.2% Irish, 11.5% English, 5.9% Polish (2000).

Economy: Unemployment rate: 6.6% (5/2010); Total civilian labor force: 13,718 (5/2010); Single-family building permits issued: 72 (2009); Multi-family building permits issued: 23 (2009); Employment by occupation: 9.7% management, 43.0% professional, 16.9% services, 20.6% sales, 1.1% farming, 2.6% construction, 6.0% production (2000).

Income: Per capita income: $19,942 (2010); Median household income: $25,656 (2010); Average household income: $49,172 (2010); Percent of households with income of $100,000 or more: 13.2% (2010); Poverty rate: 38.3% (2000).

Taxes: Total city taxes per capita: $313 (2007); City property taxes per capita: $253 (2007).

Education: Percent of population age 25 and over with: High school diploma (including GED) or higher: 95.9% (2010); Bachelor's degree or higher: 70.1% (2010); Master's degree or higher: 38.5% (2010).

School District(s)

Tippecanoe School Corp (KG-12)
2008-09 Enrollment: 11,686 . . . . (765) 474-2481
West Lafayette Com School Corp (KG-12)
2008-09 Enrollment: 2,062 . . . . (765) 746-1641

Four-year College(s)

Purdue University-Main Campus (Public)
Fall 2008 Enrollment: 41,433. . . . . (765) 494-4600
2009-10 Tuition: In-state $8,638; Out-of-state $25,118

Housing: Homeownership rate: 31.1% (2010); Median home value: $153,425 (2010); Median contract rent: $542 per month (2000); Median year structure built: 1975 (2000).

Safety: Violent crime rate: 20.7 per 10,000 population; Property crime rate: 183.9 per 10,000 population (2008).

Transportation: Commute to work: 74.0% car, 1.9% public transportation, 19.3% walk, 2.7% work from home (2000); Travel time to work: 62.1% less than 15 minutes, 29.9% 15 to 30 minutes, 4.1% 30 to 45 minutes, 1.3% 45 to 60 minutes, 2.6% 60 minutes or more (2000)

Additional Information Contacts

City of West Lafayette . . . . (765) 775-5100
http://www.city.west-lafayette.in.us
West Lafayette Chamber of Commerce . . . . (765) 742-4044
http://www.lafayettechamber.com

WESTPOINT (unincorporated postal area, zip code 47992). Aka West Point. Covers a land area of 36.562 square miles and a water area of 0.162 square miles. Located at 40.31° N. Lat; 87.04° W. Long. Elevation is 673 feet.

History: The community of Westpoint was laid out in 1833 as a stagecoach stop between Lafayette and Attica.

Population: 1,328 (2000); Race: 96.9% White, 2.6% Black, 0.0% Asian, 0.5% Other, 0.4% Hispanic of any race (2000); Density: 36.3 persons per square mile (2000); Age: 28.4% under 18, 14.2% over 64 (2000); Marriage status: 17.5% never married, 67.5% now married, 4.8% widowed, 10.2% divorced (2000); Foreign born: 0.0% (2000); Ancestry (includes multiple

ancestries): 21.5% German, 12.3% Other groups, 11.8% Irish, 9.8% English, 9.4% United States or American (2000).
Economy: Employment by occupation: 6.1% management, 14.7% professional, 15.6% services, 29.2% sales, 2.2% farming, 9.3% construction, 22.9% production (2000).
Income: Per capita income: $22,300 (2000); Median household income: $58,611 (2000); Poverty rate: 1.6% (2000).
Education: Percent of population age 25 and over with: High school diploma (including GED) or higher: 87.1% (2000); Bachelor's degree or higher: 16.9% (2000).
Housing: Homeownership rate: 91.9% (2000); Median home value: $96,000 (2000); Median contract rent: $454 per month (2000); Median year structure built: 1961 (2000).
Transportation: Commute to work: 94.0% car, 0.0% public transportation, 0.0% walk, 6.0% work from home (2000); Travel time to work: 6.8% less than 15 minutes, 52.8% 15 to 30 minutes, 31.0% 30 to 45 minutes, 2.8% 45 to 60 minutes, 6.6% 60 minutes or more (2000)

Tipton County

Located in central Indiana; drained by Cicero and Turkey Creeks. Covers a land area of 260.39 square miles, a water area of 0.02 square miles, and is located in the Eastern Time Zone. The county was founded in 1844. County seat is Tipton.

Tipton County is part of the Kokomo, IN Metropolitan Statistical Area. The entire metro area includes: Howard County, IN; Tipton County, IN

Population: 16,119 (1990); 16,577 (2000); 15,783 (2010); 15,286 (2015 projected); Race: 97.4% White, 0.4% Black, 0.5% Asian, 1.7% Other, 1.8% Hispanic of any race (2010); Density: 60.6 persons per square mile (2010); Average household size: 2.48 (2010); Median age: 41.8 (2010); Males per 100 females: 97.2 (2010).
Religion: Five largest groups: 9.2% Catholic Church, 8.8% Christian Churches and Churches of Christ, 6.9% Christian Church (Disciples of Christ), 4.9% The United Methodist Church, 3.5% The Wesleyan Church (2000).
Economy: Unemployment rate: 10.5% (5/2010); Total civilian labor force: 7,089 (5/2010); Leading industries: 30.6% manufacturing; 16.2% health care and social assistance; 12.0% retail trade (2008); Farms: 458 totaling 165,875 acres (2007); Companies that employ 500 or more persons: 0 (2008); Companies that employ 100 to 499 persons: 7 (2008); Companies that employ less than 100 persons: 322 (2008); Black-owned businesses: n/a (2002); Hispanic-owned businesses: n/a (2002); Asian-owned businesses: n/a (2002); Women-owned businesses: 346 (2002); Retail sales per capita: $9,501 (2010). Single-family building permits issued: 8 (2009); Multi-family building permits issued: 0 (2009).
Income: Per capita income: $26,210 (2010); Median household income: $56,767 (2010); Average household income: $65,021 (2010); Percent of households with income of $100,000 or more: 17.9% (2010); Poverty rate: 8.7% (2008); Bankruptcy rate: 6.13% (2009).
Taxes: Total county taxes per capita: $387 (2007); County property taxes per capita: $180 (2007).
Education: Percent of population age 25 and over with: High school diploma (including GED) or higher: 88.1% (2010); Bachelor's degree or higher: 13.3% (2010); Master's degree or higher: 4.5% (2010).
Housing: Homeownership rate: 78.9% (2010); Median home value: $91,716 (2010); Median contract rent: $n/a per month (2006-2008 3-year est.); Median year structure built: n/a (2006-2008 3-year est.)
Health: Birth rate: 119.6 per 10,000 population (2009); Death rate: 98.2 per 10,000 population (2009); Age-adjusted cancer mortality rate: 194.8 deaths per 100,000 population (2006); Number of physicians: 7.5 per 10,000 population (2007); Hospital beds: 46.5 per 10,000 population (2006); Hospital admissions: 1,019.0 per 10,000 population (2006).
Elections: 2008 Presidential election results: 41.5% Obama, 56.9% McCain, 0.0% Nader
Additional Information Contacts
Tipton County Government . . . . (765) 675-4165
   http://www.tiptonguide.com/city_offices.asp
City of Tipton . . . . (765) 675-2795
   http://www.tiptonguide.com

Tipton County Communities

KEMPTON (town). Covers a land area of 0.163 square miles and a water area of 0 square miles. Located at 40.28° N. Lat; 86.23° W. Long. Elevation is 919 feet.
Population: 378 (1990); 380 (2000); 439 (2010); 459 (2015 projected); Race: 97.7% White, 0.0% Black, 0.2% Asian, 2.1% Other, 1.4% Hispanic of any race (2010); Density: 2,698.4 persons per square mile (2010); Average household size: 2.63 (2010); Median age: 40.3 (2010); Males per 100 females: 102.3 (2010); Marriage status: 19.4% never married, 65.1% now married, 5.3% widowed, 10.2% divorced (2000); Foreign born: 0.8% (2000); Ancestry (includes multiple ancestries): 19.6% German, 15.1% United States or American, 7.8% English, 6.3% Other groups, 5.5% Irish (2000).
Economy: Single-family building permits issued: 0 (2009); Multi-family building permits issued: 0 (2009); Employment by occupation: 3.1% management, 13.0% professional, 12.4% services, 13.7% sales, 2.5% farming, 12.4% construction, 42.9% production (2000).
Income: Per capita income: $23,592 (2010); Median household income: $52,083 (2010); Average household income: $64,027 (2010); Percent of households with income of $100,000 or more: 10.8% (2010); Poverty rate: 4.5% (2000).
Taxes: Total city taxes per capita: $117 (2007); City property taxes per capita: $89 (2007).
Education: Percent of population age 25 and over with: High school diploma (including GED) or higher: 88.3% (2010); Bachelor's degree or higher: 12.4% (2010); Master's degree or higher: 1.0% (2010).
Housing: Homeownership rate: 82.0% (2010); Median home value: $92,581 (2010); Median contract rent: $320 per month (2000); Median year structure built: before 1940 (2000).
Transportation: Commute to work: 96.9% car, 0.0% public transportation, 1.3% walk, 0.6% work from home (2000); Travel time to work: 9.5% less than 15 minutes, 41.1% 15 to 30 minutes, 22.8% 30 to 45 minutes, 12.0% 45 to 60 minutes, 14.6% 60 minutes or more (2000)

SHARPSVILLE (town). Covers a land area of 0.221 square miles and a water area of 0 square miles. Located at 40.37° N. Lat; 86.08° W. Long. Elevation is 879 feet.
History: Laid out 1850.
Population: 771 (1990); 618 (2000); 526 (2010); 483 (2015 projected); Race: 95.8% White, 1.3% Black, 1.0% Asian, 1.9% Other, 2.7% Hispanic of any race (2010); Density: 2,379.2 persons per square mile (2010); Average household size: 2.74 (2010); Median age: 38.5 (2010); Males per 100 females: 103.1 (2010); Marriage status: 20.3% never married, 63.4% now married, 7.3% widowed, 9.1% divorced (2000); Foreign born: 1.2% (2000); Ancestry (includes multiple ancestries): 18.6% United States or American, 17.4% German, 11.3% English, 7.9% Other groups, 5.8% Irish (2000).
Economy: Employment by occupation: 6.3% management, 9.3% professional, 13.8% services, 22.7% sales, 0.0% farming, 10.8% construction, 37.2% production (2000).
Income: Per capita income: $30,940 (2010); Median household income: $78,378 (2010); Average household income: $87,266 (2010); Percent of households with income of $100,000 or more: 33.3% (2010); Poverty rate: 2.8% (2000).
Taxes: Total city taxes per capita: $162 (2007); City property taxes per capita: $126 (2007).
Education: Percent of population age 25 and over with: High school diploma (including GED) or higher: 88.7% (2010); Bachelor's degree or higher: 11.9% (2010); Master's degree or higher: 4.6% (2010).
School District(s)
Northern Com Sch Tipton Co (PK-12)
   2008-09 Enrollment: 1,004 . . . . (765) 963-2585
Housing: Homeownership rate: 85.9% (2010); Median home value: $85,667 (2010); Median contract rent: $438 per month (2000); Median year structure built: 1951 (2000).
Transportation: Commute to work: 98.1% car, 0.0% public transportation, 0.0% walk, 1.9% work from home (2000); Travel time to work: 28.2% less than 15 minutes, 50.2% 15 to 30 minutes, 11.2% 30 to 45 minutes, 8.1% 45 to 60 minutes, 2.3% 60 minutes or more (2000)

TIPTON (city). County seat. Covers a land area of 1.852 square miles and a water area of 0 square miles. Located at 40.28° N. Lat; 86.04° W. Long. Elevation is 869 feet.
History: Laid out 1839.

Population: 5,356 (1990); 5,251 (2000); 4,422 (2010); 4,069 (2015 projected); Race: 97.0% White, 0.4% Black, 0.9% Asian, 1.7% Other, 2.4% Hispanic of any race (2010); Density: 2,387.3 persons per square mile (2010); Average household size: 2.26 (2010); Median age: 42.0 (2010); Males per 100 females: 90.5 (2010); Marriage status: 18.4% never married, 55.5% now married, 12.2% widowed, 13.9% divorced (2000); Foreign born: 1.2% (2000); Ancestry (includes multiple ancestries): 26.9% United States or American, 16.3% German, 10.0% English, 8.8% Irish, 6.0% Other groups (2000).
Economy: Single-family building permits issued: 0 (2009); Multi-family building permits issued: 0 (2009); Employment by occupation: 8.6% management, 10.1% professional, 22.7% services, 22.2% sales, 1.5% farming, 12.1% construction, 22.8% production (2000).
Income: Per capita income: $23,398 (2010); Median household income: $46,264 (2010); Average household income: $52,906 (2010); Percent of households with income of $100,000 or more: 11.4% (2010); Poverty rate: 7.2% (2000).
Taxes: Total city taxes per capita: $615 (2007); City property taxes per capita: $529 (2007).
Education: Percent of population age 25 and over with: High school diploma (including GED) or higher: 84.1% (2010); Bachelor's degree or higher: 12.8% (2010); Master's degree or higher: 3.5% (2010).
School District(s)
Tipton Community School Corp (PK-12)
    2008-09 Enrollment: 1,843 . . . . (765) 675-2147
Housing: Homeownership rate: 70.0% (2010); Median home value: $79,151 (2010); Median contract rent: $401 per month (2000); Median year structure built: 1949 (2000).
Hospitals: Tipton County Memorial Hospital (102 beds)
Safety: Violent crime rate: 15.9 per 10,000 population; Property crime rate: 372.1 per 10,000 population (2008).
Newspapers: Tipton Tribune (Local news; Circulation 5,000)
Transportation: Commute to work: 95.4% car, 0.0% public transportation, 3.3% walk, 0.8% work from home (2000); Travel time to work: 46.5% less than 15 minutes, 23.4% 15 to 30 minutes, 20.8% 30 to 45 minutes, 7.8% 45 to 60 minutes, 1.6% 60 minutes or more (2000)
Additional Information Contacts
City of Tipton . . . . (765) 675-2795
    http://www.tiptonguide.com

WINDFALL CITY (town). Aka Windfall. Covers a land area of 0.291 square miles and a water area of 0 square miles. Located at 40.36° N. Lat; 85.95° W. Long. Elevation is 863 feet.
Population: 779 (1990); 712 (2000); 595 (2010); 545 (2015 projected); Race: 98.7% White, 0.0% Black, 0.0% Asian, 1.3% Other, 2.0% Hispanic of any race (2010); Density: 2,042.7 persons per square mile (2010); Average household size: 2.45 (2010); Median age: 39.4 (2010); Males per 100 females: 100.3 (2010); Marriage status: 15.8% never married, 68.3% now married, 9.2% widowed, 6.7% divorced (2000); Foreign born: 0.0% (2000); Ancestry (includes multiple ancestries): 16.6% United States or American, 14.0% German, 10.2% Other groups, 8.0% Irish, 6.0% English (2000).
Economy: Single-family building permits issued: 0 (2009); Multi-family building permits issued: 0 (2009); Employment by occupation: 7.0% management, 9.3% professional, 16.8% services, 17.4% sales, 0.0% farming, 11.3% construction, 38.3% production (2000).
Income: Per capita income: $24,605 (2010); Median household income: $48,807 (2010); Average household income: $61,019 (2010); Percent of households with income of $100,000 or more: 14.4% (2010); Poverty rate: 9.7% (2000).
Taxes: Total city taxes per capita: $0 (2007); City property taxes per capita: $0 (2007).
Education: Percent of population age 25 and over with: High school diploma (including GED) or higher: 80.9% (2010); Bachelor's degree or higher: 4.0% (2010); Master's degree or higher: 2.5% (2010).
Housing: Homeownership rate: 81.5% (2010); Median home value: $64,783 (2010); Median contract rent: $336 per month (2000); Median year structure built: 1955 (2000).
Transportation: Commute to work: 97.1% car, 0.0% public transportation, 2.4% walk, 0.0% work from home (2000); Travel time to work: 20.9% less than 15 minutes, 47.9% 15 to 30 minutes, 19.1% 30 to 45 minutes, 7.1% 45 to 60 minutes, 5.0% 60 minutes or more (2000)

Union County

Located in eastern Indiana; bounded on the east by Ohio; drained by the East Fork of the Whitewater River. Covers a land area of 161.55 square miles, a water area of 3.70 square miles, and is located in the Eastern Time Zone. The county was founded in 1821. County seat is Liberty.
Population: 6,976 (1990); 7,349 (2000); 7,147 (2010); 7,026 (2015 projected); Race: 97.4% White, 1.1% Black, 0.2% Asian, 1.3% Other, 0.8% Hispanic of any race (2010); Density: 44.2 persons per square mile (2010); Average household size: 2.57 (2010); Median age: 40.2 (2010); Males per 100 females: 97.8 (2010).
Religion: Five largest groups: 11.6% The United Methodist Church, 8.3% Catholic Church, 6.3% Christian Churches and Churches of Christ, 3.4% New Testament Association of Independent Baptist Churches and other Fundamental Baptist Associations, 3.1%
Economy: Unemployment rate: 10.0% (5/2010); Total civilian labor force: 3,655 (5/2010); Leading industries: 22.7% retail trade; 14.6% health care and social assistance; 8.5% accommodation & food services (2008); Farms: 233 totaling 73,249 acres (2007); Companies that employ 500 or more persons: 0 (2008); Companies that employ 100 to 499 persons: 1 (2008); Companies that employ less than 100 persons: 119 (2008); Black-owned businesses: n/a (2002); Hispanic-owned businesses: n/a (2002); Asian-owned businesses: n/a (2002); Women-owned businesses: 180 (2002); Retail sales per capita: $6,466 (2010). Single-family building permits issued: 7 (2009); Multi-family building permits issued: 0 (2009).
Income: Per capita income: $22,171 (2010); Median household income: $45,106 (2010); Average household income: $56,393 (2010); Percent of households with income of $100,000 or more: 11.6% (2010); Poverty rate: 11.9% (2008); Bankruptcy rate: 9.62% (2009).
Taxes: Total county taxes per capita: $446 (2007); County property taxes per capita: $229 (2007).
Education: Percent of population age 25 and over with: High school diploma (including GED) or higher: 84.5% (2010); Bachelor's degree or higher: 11.6% (2010); Master's degree or higher: 3.4% (2010).
Housing: Homeownership rate: 74.1% (2010); Median home value: $116,471 (2010); Median contract rent: $n/a per month (2006-2008 3-year est.); Median year structure built: n/a (2006-2008 3-year est.)
Health: Birth rate: 130.7 per 10,000 population (2009); Death rate: 98.0 per 10,000 population (2009); Age-adjusted cancer mortality rate: 238.0 deaths per 100,000 population (2006); Number of physicians: 7.0 per 10,000 population (2007); Hospital beds: 0.0 per 10,000 population (2006); Hospital admissions: 0.0 per 10,000 population (2006).
Elections: 2008 Presidential election results: 36.6% Obama, 61.6% McCain, 0.1% Nader
National and State Parks: Whitewater State Park
Additional Information Contacts
Union County Government . . . . (765) 458-5464
    http://www.union-county.lib.in.us

Union County Communities

BROWNSVILLE (unincorporated postal area, zip code 47325). Covers a land area of 25.762 square miles and a water area of 0 square miles. Located at 39.68° N. Lat; 85.02° W. Long. Elevation is 791 feet.
Population: 775 (2000); Race: 95.3% White, 0.0% Black, 3.3% Asian, 1.4% Other, 0.0% Hispanic of any race (2000); Density: 30.1 persons per square mile (2000); Age: 26.1% under 18, 8.0% over 64 (2000); Marriage status: 8.9% never married, 83.8% now married, 0.9% widowed, 6.4% divorced (2000); Foreign born: 1.0% (2000); Ancestry (includes multiple ancestries): 19.4% United States or American, 15.1% German, 9.1% Irish, 8.0% English, 5.0% Other groups (2000).
Economy: Employment by occupation: 18.2% management, 9.5% professional, 12.6% services, 12.3% sales, 0.0% farming, 13.5% construction, 33.8% production (2000).
Income: Per capita income: $43,652 (2000); Median household income: $45,735 (2000); Poverty rate: 14.9% (2000).
Education: Percent of population age 25 and over with: High school diploma (including GED) or higher: 75.5% (2000); Bachelor's degree or higher: 8.9% (2000).
Housing: Homeownership rate: 85.6% (2000); Median home value: $77,400 (2000); Median contract rent: $313 per month (2000); Median year structure built: 1972 (2000).
Transportation: Commute to work: 93.1% car, 0.0% public transportation, 1.6% walk, 5.3% work from home (2000); Travel time to work: 8.6% less

than 15 minutes, 50.0% 15 to 30 minutes, 22.8% 30 to 45 minutes, 9.6% 45 to 60 minutes, 8.9% 60 minutes or more (2000)

LIBERTY (town). County seat. Covers a land area of 0.871 square miles and a water area of 0 square miles. Located at 39.63° N. Lat; 84.92° W. Long. Elevation is 984 feet.

History: Liberty was the home from 1824 to 1843 of Ambrose Burnside who achieved military distinction during the Civil War, and later served as governor of Rhode Island and as a U.S. senator.

Population: 2,113 (1990); 2,061 (2000); 1,904 (2010); 1,824 (2015 projected); Race: 96.7% White, 1.5% Black, 0.2% Asian, 1.6% Other, 1.1% Hispanic of any race (2010); Density: 2,186.3 persons per square mile (2010); Average household size: 2.28 (2010); Median age: 41.2 (2010); Males per 100 females: 89.6 (2010); Marriage status: 20.1% never married, 54.2% now married, 11.4% widowed, 14.3% divorced (2000); Foreign born: 0.8% (2000); Ancestry (includes multiple ancestries): 26.0% United States or American, 13.7% German, 8.0% Irish, 6.9% English, 6.1% Other groups (2000).

Economy: Employment by occupation: 9.6% management, 12.8% professional, 19.5% services, 27.1% sales, 0.0% farming, 11.4% construction, 19.7% production (2000).

Income: Per capita income: $17,953 (2010); Median household income: $34,866 (2010); Average household income: $40,879 (2010); Percent of households with income of $100,000 or more: 4.2% (2010); Poverty rate: 11.0% (2000).

Taxes: Total city taxes per capita: $204 (2007); City property taxes per capita: $199 (2007).

Education: Percent of population age 25 and over with: High school diploma (including GED) or higher: 81.2% (2010); Bachelor's degree or higher: 10.1% (2010); Master's degree or higher: 3.0% (2010).

School District(s)
Union Co/Clg Corner Joint Sch Dist (PK-12)
    2008-09 Enrollment: 1,617 . . . . (765) 458-7471

Housing: Homeownership rate: 64.6% (2010); Median home value: $95,789 (2010); Median contract rent: $325 per month (2000); Median year structure built: 1950 (2000).

Newspapers: Liberty Herald (Community news; Circulation 3,000); Union County Review (Community news; Circulation 3,000)

Transportation: Commute to work: 89.6% car, 0.0% public transportation, 6.3% walk, 2.8% work from home (2000); Travel time to work: 36.9% less than 15 minutes, 39.8% 15 to 30 minutes, 14.9% 30 to 45 minutes, 3.7% 45 to 60 minutes, 4.7% 60 minutes or more (2000)

WEST COLLEGE CORNER (town). Covers a land area of 0.263 square miles and a water area of 0 square miles. Located at 39.56° N. Lat; 84.81° W. Long. Elevation is 988 feet.

Population: 686 (1990); 634 (2000); 555 (2010); 516 (2015 projected); Race: 97.5% White, 0.0% Black, 0.2% Asian, 2.3% Other, 0.4% Hispanic of any race (2010); Density: 2,110.1 persons per square mile (2010); Average household size: 2.71 (2010); Median age: 33.5 (2010); Males per 100 females: 105.6 (2010); Marriage status: 17.4% never married, 64.5% now married, 6.3% widowed, 11.8% divorced (2000); Foreign born: 0.8% (2000); Ancestry (includes multiple ancestries): 22.6% German, 21.8% United States or American, 15.6% Irish, 10.5% English, 5.1% Other groups (2000).

Economy: Employment by occupation: 6.5% management, 7.8% professional, 24.2% services, 22.9% sales, 0.0% farming, 18.8% construction, 19.8% production (2000).

Income: Per capita income: $20,103 (2010); Median household income: $44,415 (2010); Average household income: $54,305 (2010); Percent of households with income of $100,000 or more: 11.2% (2010); Poverty rate: 16.1% (2000).

Taxes: Total city taxes per capita: $84 (2007); City property taxes per capita: $61 (2007).

Education: Percent of population age 25 and over with: High school diploma (including GED) or higher: 82.5% (2010); Bachelor's degree or higher: 6.3% (2010); Master's degree or higher: 1.2% (2010).

Housing: Homeownership rate: 64.9% (2010); Median home value: $87,727 (2010); Median contract rent: $321 per month (2000); Median year structure built: 1959 (2000).

Transportation: Commute to work: 91.5% car, 0.0% public transportation, 4.9% walk, 3.5% work from home (2000); Travel time to work: 46.9% less than 15 minutes, 29.7% 15 to 30 minutes, 7.7% 30 to 45 minutes, 4.8% 45 to 60 minutes, 11.0% 60 minutes or more (2000)

Vanderburgh County

Located in southwestern Indiana; bounded on the south by the Ohio River and the Kentucky border; drained by Pigeon Creek. Covers a land area of 234.57 square miles, a water area of 1.16 square miles, and is located in the Central Time Zone. The county was founded in 1818. County seat is Evansville.

Vanderburgh County is part of the Evansville, IN-KY Metropolitan Statistical Area. The entire metro area includes: Gibson County, IN; Posey County, IN; Vanderburgh County, IN; Warrick County, IN; Henderson County, KY; Webster County, KY

Weather Station: Evansville Museum   Elevation: 377 feet

	Jan	Feb	Mar	Apr	May	Jun	Jul	Aug	Sep	Oct	Nov	Dec
High	40	47	58	69	78	87	90	88	82	70	57	46
Low	24	28	38	47	56	65	69	67	60	48	39	30
Precip	2.8	3.3	4.7	4.7	4.9	3.9	4.2	3.3	3.2	3.1	4.5	3.7
Snow	4.9	3.5	2.6	0.5	tr	0.0	0.0	0.0	0.0	tr	0.3	2.0

High and Low temperatures in degrees Fahrenheit; Precipitation and Snow in inches

Weather Station: Evansville Regional Airport   Elevation: 380 feet

	Jan	Feb	Mar	Apr	May	Jun	Jul	Aug	Sep	Oct	Nov	Dec
High	39	45	56	67	77	86	89	87	81	69	56	45
Low	23	27	36	45	55	64	68	66	58	45	37	28
Precip	2.8	2.9	4.4	4.7	5.0	4.1	3.7	3.1	2.9	3.0	4.1	3.5
Snow	4.7	4.1	2.5	0.4	tr	tr	0.0	0.0	tr	0.2	0.4	2.5

High and Low temperatures in degrees Fahrenheit; Precipitation and Snow in inches

Population: 165,058 (1990); 171,922 (2000); 175,057 (2010); 175,372 (2015 projected); Race: 88.0% White, 8.5% Black, 1.1% Asian, 2.4% Other, 1.3% Hispanic of any race (2010); Density: 746.3 persons per square mile (2010); Average household size: 2.30 (2010); Median age: 37.8 (2010); Males per 100 females: 91.1 (2010).

Religion: Five largest groups: 18.3% Catholic Church, 11.2% Southern Baptist Convention, 4.3% United Church of Christ, 4.2% The United Methodist Church, 1.9% Lutheran Church—Missouri Synod (2000).

Economy: Unemployment rate: 8.6% (5/2010); Total civilian labor force: 89,060 (5/2010); Leading industries: 16.8% health care and social assistance; 12.4% retail trade; 12.0% manufacturing (2008); Farms: 335 totaling 71,927 acres (2007); Companies that employ 500 or more persons: 20 (2008); Companies that employ 100 to 499 persons: 156 (2008); Companies that employ less than 100 persons: 4,929 (2008); Black-owned businesses: 315 (2002); Hispanic-owned businesses: n/a (2002); Asian-owned businesses: 126 (2002); Women-owned businesses: 3,238 (2002); Retail sales per capita: $18,547 (2010). Single-family building permits issued: 191 (2009); Multi-family building permits issued: 72 (2009).

Income: Per capita income: $24,216 (2010); Median household income: $43,056 (2010); Average household income: $57,077 (2010); Percent of households with income of $100,000 or more: 12.2% (2010); Poverty rate: 16.9% (2008); Bankruptcy rate: 6.36% (2009).

Taxes: Total county taxes per capita: $305 (2007); County property taxes per capita: $207 (2007).

Education: Percent of population age 25 and over with: High school diploma (including GED) or higher: 86.4% (2010); Bachelor's degree or higher: 21.2% (2010); Master's degree or higher: 7.4% (2010).

Housing: Homeownership rate: 65.6% (2010); Median home value: $99,986 (2010); Median contract rent: $490 per month (2006-2008 3-year est.); Median year structure built: 1961 (2006-2008 3-year est.)

Health: Birth rate: 135.8 per 10,000 population (2009); Death rate: 105.6 per 10,000 population (2009); Age-adjusted cancer mortality rate: 207.4 deaths per 100,000 population (2006); Air Quality Index: 65.9% good, 33.1% moderate, 1.0% unhealthy for sensitive individuals, 0.0% unhealthy (percent of days in 2008); Number of physicians: 25.9 per 10,000 population (2007); Hospital beds: 73.5 per 10,000 population (2006); Hospital admissions: 2,184.5 per 10,000 population (2006).

Elections: 2008 Presidential election results: 50.8% Obama, 48.3% McCain, 0.0% Nader

Additional Information Contacts

Vanderburgh County Government. . . . . (812) 435-5160
    http://www.vanderburghgov.org
Chamber of Commerce of Southwest Indiana . . . . (812) 425-8147
    http://www.evansvillechamber.com
City of Evansville . . . . (812) 436-4992
    http://www.evansvillegov.org

Vanderburgh County Communities

DARMSTADT (town). Covers a land area of 4.721 square miles and a water area of 0.018 square miles. Located at 38.09° N. Lat; 87.57° W. Long. Elevation is 479 feet.

History: Established 1860.

Population: 1,346 (1990); 1,313 (2000); 1,425 (2010); 1,500 (2015 projected); Race: 98.5% White, 0.4% Black, 0.2% Asian, 0.8% Other, 0.7% Hispanic of any race (2010); Density: 301.9 persons per square mile (2010); Average household size: 2.61 (2010); Median age: 44.9 (2010); Males per 100 females: 97.6 (2010); Marriage status: 18.6% never married, 71.7% now married, 5.0% widowed, 4.7% divorced (2000); Foreign born: 0.0% (2000); Ancestry (includes multiple ancestries): 43.7% German, 13.4% English, 11.6% United States or American, 10.6% Irish, 3.6% French (except Basque) (2000).

Economy: Employment by occupation: 16.0% management, 20.1% professional, 13.5% services, 22.7% sales, 0.9% farming, 12.3% construction, 14.5% production (2000).

Income: Per capita income: $39,874 (2010); Median household income: $81,071 (2010); Average household income: $104,606 (2010); Percent of households with income of $100,000 or more: 35.4% (2010); Poverty rate: 1.1% (2000).

Taxes: Total city taxes per capita: $59 (2007); City property taxes per capita: $43 (2007).

Education: Percent of population age 25 and over with: High school diploma (including GED) or higher: 93.1% (2010); Bachelor's degree or higher: 29.0% (2010); Master's degree or higher: 12.9% (2010).

Housing: Homeownership rate: 90.6% (2010); Median home value: $169,898 (2010); Median contract rent: $431 per month (2000); Median year structure built: 1963 (2000).

Transportation: Commute to work: 94.3% car, 0.3% public transportation, 0.8% walk, 4.3% work from home (2000); Travel time to work: 24.6% less than 15 minutes, 56.8% 15 to 30 minutes, 14.6% 30 to 45 minutes, 3.1% 45 to 60 minutes, 1.0% 60 minutes or more (2000)

EVANSVILLE (city). County seat. Covers a land area of 40.704 square miles and a water area of 0.059 square miles. Located at 37.97° N. Lat; 87.55° W. Long. Elevation is 387 feet.

History: Colonel Hugh McGary established a ferry at this spot on the Ohio River in 1812, and a village called McGary's Ferry grew up around it. McGary sold part of his holdings to General Robert Evans in 1818. When the community was designated as the seat of the new Vanderburgh County, it was named Evansville. The town had a good inland harbor, and soon became a transportation hub. It was chartered as a city in 1848.

Population: 126,272 (1990); 121,582 (2000); 114,593 (2010); 111,463 (2015 projected); Race: 84.3% White, 11.8% Black, 0.9% Asian, 2.9% Other, 1.6% Hispanic of any race (2010); Density: 2,815.3 persons per square mile (2010); Average household size: 2.19 (2010); Median age: 37.8 (2010); Males per 100 females: 90.1 (2010); Marriage status: 26.5% never married, 49.8% now married, 8.4% widowed, 15.3% divorced (2000); Foreign born: 1.6% (2000); Ancestry (includes multiple ancestries): 24.6% German, 15.8% Other groups, 10.7% United States or American, 10.4% Irish, 9.1% English (2000).

Economy: Unemployment rate: 9.5% (5/2010); Total civilian labor force: 57,656 (5/2010); Single-family building permits issued: 37 (2009); Multi-family building permits issued: 35 (2009); Employment by occupation: 9.2% management, 15.8% professional, 17.3% services, 28.6% sales, 0.1% farming, 9.0% construction, 19.9% production (2000).

Income: Per capita income: $20,779 (2010); Median household income: $35,984 (2010); Average household income: $46,457 (2010); Percent of households with income of $100,000 or more: 6.8% (2010); Poverty rate: 13.7% (2000).

Taxes: Total city taxes per capita: $393 (2007); City property taxes per capita: $310 (2007).

Education: Percent of population age 25 and over with: High school diploma (including GED) or higher: 83.8% (2010); Bachelor's degree or higher: 17.9% (2010); Master's degree or higher: 5.9% (2010).

School District(s)

Evansville-Vanderburgh Sch Corp (PK-12)
    2008-09 Enrollment: 22,274 . . . . (812) 435-8477
Joshua Academy (KG-05)
    2008-09 Enrollment: 217 . . . . (812) 401-6300
Signature School Inc (09-12)
    2008-09 Enrollment: 301 . . . . (812) 421-1820

Four-year College(s)

Indiana Business College-Evansville (Private, For-profit)
    Fall 2008 Enrollment: 265 . . . . (812) 476-6000
    2009-10 Tuition: In-state $11,535; Out-of-state $11,535
University of Evansville (Private, Not-for-profit, United Methodist)
    Fall 2008 Enrollment: 2,742. . . . . (812) 488-2000
    2009-10 Tuition: In-state $26,756; Out-of-state $26,756
University of Southern Indiana (Public)
    Fall 2008 Enrollment: 10,126. . . . . (812) 464-8600
    2009-10 Tuition: In-state $5,474; Out-of-state $12,755

Two-year College(s)

Ivy Tech Community College-Southwest (Public)
    Fall 2008 Enrollment: 5,351. . . . . (812) 426-2865
    2009-10 Tuition: In-state $3,090; Out-of-state $6,306

Vocational/Technical School(s)

Rogers Academy of Hair Design (Private, For-profit)
    Fall 2008 Enrollment: 126 . . . . (812) 429-0110
    2009-10 Tuition: $9,500

Housing: Homeownership rate: 58.3% (2010); Median home value: $83,970 (2010); Median contract rent: $370 per month (2000); Median year structure built: 1954 (2000).

Hospitals: Deaconess Cross Pointe (60 beds); Deaconess Hospital (400 beds); Evansville Psychiatric Children Center (28 beds); Evansville State Hospital; HealthSouth Deaconess Rehabilitation Hospital (80 beds); St. Mary's Medical Center (564 beds)

Safety: Violent crime rate: 40.0 per 10,000 population; Property crime rate: 469.8 per 10,000 population (2008).

Newspapers: Evansville Courier & Press (Community news; Circulation 74,000); The Message (Regional news; Circulation 5,200)

Transportation: Commute to work: 92.5% car, 1.7% public transportation, 3.2% walk, 1.8% work from home (2000); Travel time to work: 43.3% less than 15 minutes, 42.7% 15 to 30 minutes, 8.0% 30 to 45 minutes, 2.3% 45 to 60 minutes, 3.7% 60 minutes or more (2000)

Additional Information Contacts
Chamber of Commerce of Southwest Indiana . . . . (812) 425-8147
    http://www.evansvillechamber.com
City of Evansville . . . . (812) 436-4992
    http://www.evansvillegov.org

HIGHLAND (CDP). Covers a land area of 2.300 square miles and a water area of 0.004 square miles. Located at 38.04° N. Lat; 87.56° W. Long. Elevation is 482 feet.

History: The area of Highland was almost entirely under water before it was first settled in 1848. Only a high sand ridge stood above the water. People referred to this area as 'Highlands.'.

Population: 3,508 (1990); 4,107 (2000); 3,948 (2010); 4,045 (2015 projected); Race: 97.6% White, 0.8% Black, 0.8% Asian, 0.8% Other, 0.5% Hispanic of any race (2010); Density: 1,716.2 persons per square mile (2010); Average household size: 2.65 (2010); Median age: 41.0 (2010); Males per 100 females: 92.2 (2010); Marriage status: 18.8% never married, 69.8% now married, 5.8% widowed, 5.6% divorced (2000); Foreign born: 2.5% (2000); Ancestry (includes multiple ancestries): 41.7% German, 16.7% Irish, 16.3% English, 12.2% United States or American, 5.4% Other groups (2000).

Economy: Employment by occupation: 15.0% management, 22.3% professional, 8.1% services, 33.9% sales, 0.0% farming, 5.3% construction, 15.4% production (2000).

Income: Per capita income: $31,814 (2010); Median household income: $75,483 (2010); Average household income: $83,733 (2010); Percent of households with income of $100,000 or more: 26.0% (2010); Poverty rate: 0.7% (2000).

Education: Percent of population age 25 and over with: High school diploma (including GED) or higher: 94.7% (2010); Bachelor's degree or higher: 31.5% (2010); Master's degree or higher: 13.2% (2010).

Housing: Homeownership rate: 93.4% (2010); Median home value: $153,475 (2010); Median contract rent: $595 per month (2000); Median year structure built: 1982 (2000).

Transportation: Commute to work: 98.7% car, 0.0% public transportation, 0.3% walk, 1.1% work from home (2000); Travel time to work: 28.1% less than 15 minutes, 55.2% 15 to 30 minutes, 11.0% 30 to 45 minutes, 3.1% 45 to 60 minutes, 2.6% 60 minutes or more (2000)

MELODY HILL (CDP). Covers a land area of 1.361 square miles and a water area of 0.007 square miles. Located at 38.02° N. Lat; 87.51° W. Long. Elevation is 427 feet.

History:.

Population: 2,932 (1990); 3,066 (2000); 2,984 (2010); 2,954 (2015 projected); Race: 95.4% White, 1.8% Black, 1.3% Asian, 1.5% Other, 1.0% Hispanic of any race (2010); Density: 2,191.8 persons per square mile (2010); Average household size: 2.54 (2010); Median age: 41.9 (2010); Males per 100 females: 94.1 (2010); Marriage status: 16.3% never married, 71.9% now married, 5.4% widowed, 6.5% divorced (2000); Foreign born: 2.8% (2000); Ancestry (includes multiple ancestries): 40.9% German, 14.3% Irish, 12.0% English, 11.1% United States or American, 9.3% Other groups (2000).

Economy: Employment by occupation: 13.5% management, 20.3% professional, 10.5% services, 36.0% sales, 0.6% farming, 2.6% construction, 16.7% production (2000).

Income: Per capita income: $28,849 (2010); Median household income: $64,625 (2010); Average household income: $73,142 (2010); Percent of households with income of $100,000 or more: 20.6% (2010); Poverty rate: 1.1% (2000).

Education: Percent of population age 25 and over with: High school diploma (including GED) or higher: 94.3% (2010); Bachelor's degree or higher: 28.8% (2010); Master's degree or higher: 11.6% (2010).

Housing: Homeownership rate: 92.9% (2010); Median home value: $130,115 (2010); Median contract rent: $491 per month (2000); Median year structure built: 1970 (2000).

Transportation: Commute to work: 97.6% car, 0.0% public transportation, 0.0% walk, 2.4% work from home (2000); Travel time to work: 43.8% less than 15 minutes, 45.2% 15 to 30 minutes, 6.6% 30 to 45 minutes, 0.6% 45 to 60 minutes, 3.8% 60 minutes or more (2000)

Vermillion County

Located in western Indiana; bounded on the west by Illinois, and on the east by the Wabash River; drained by the Vermilion River. Covers a land area of 256.89 square miles, a water area of 3.05 square miles, and is located in the Eastern Time Zone. The county was founded in 1824. County seat is Newport.

Vermillion County is part of the Terre Haute, IN Metropolitan Statistical Area. The entire metro area includes: Clay County, IN; Sullivan County, IN; Vermillion County, IN; Vigo County, IN

Population: 16,773 (1990); 16,788 (2000); 16,116 (2010); 15,680 (2015 projected); Race: 97.3% White, 1.0% Black, 0.1% Asian, 1.6% Other, 1.2% Hispanic of any race (2010); Density: 62.7 persons per square mile (2010); Average household size: 2.41 (2010); Median age: 41.1 (2010); Males per 100 females: 96.6 (2010).

Religion: Five largest groups: 6.8% Catholic Church, 6.7% The United Methodist Church, 4.9% American Baptist Churches in the USA, 4.0% Christian Churches and Churches of Christ, 2.1% The Church of Jesus Christ of Latter-day Saints (2000).

Economy: Unemployment rate: 12.0% (5/2010); Total civilian labor force: 7,799 (5/2010); Leading industries: 21.7% manufacturing; 14.7% retail trade; 10.9% accommodation & food services (2008); Farms: 293 totaling 132,353 acres (2007); Companies that employ 500 or more persons: 1 (2008); Companies that employ 100 to 499 persons: 10 (2008); Companies that employ less than 100 persons: 264 (2008); Black-owned businesses: n/a (2002); Hispanic-owned businesses: n/a (2002); Asian-owned businesses: n/a (2002); Women-owned businesses: 344 (2002); Retail sales per capita: $13,187 (2010). Single-family building permits issued: 16 (2009); Multi-family building permits issued: 0 (2009).

Income: Per capita income: $22,434 (2010); Median household income: $42,972 (2010); Average household income: $54,350 (2010); Percent of households with income of $100,000 or more: 10.5% (2010); Poverty rate: 12.2% (2008); Bankruptcy rate: 7.45% (2009).

Taxes: Total county taxes per capita: $389 (2007); County property taxes per capita: $369 (2007).

Education: Percent of population age 25 and over with: High school diploma (including GED) or higher: 85.5% (2010); Bachelor's degree or higher: 11.7% (2010); Master's degree or higher: 3.9% (2010).

Housing: Homeownership rate: 78.4% (2010); Median home value: $71,069 (2010); Median contract rent: $n/a per month (2006-2008 3-year est.); Median year structure built: n/a (2006-2008 3-year est.)

Health: Birth rate: 125.5 per 10,000 population (2009); Death rate: 141.0 per 10,000 population (2009); Age-adjusted cancer mortality rate: 184.7 deaths per 100,000 population (2006); Number of physicians: 2.4 per 10,000 population (2007); Hospital beds: 15.3 per 10,000 population (2006); Hospital admissions: 778.4 per 10,000 population (2006).

Elections: 2008 Presidential election results: 56.1% Obama, 42.2% McCain, 0.1% Nader

Additional Information Contacts

Vermillion County Government . . . . (765) 492-5300
  http://www.vermilliongov.us
City of Clinton. . . . . (765) 832-9880
  http://www.clinton.in.gov

Vermillion County Communities

CAYUGA (town). Covers a land area of 1.002 square miles and a water area of 0 square miles. Located at 39.94° N. Lat; 87.46° W. Long. Elevation is 505 feet.

Population: 1,264 (1990); 1,109 (2000); 1,045 (2010); 1,008 (2015 projected); Race: 97.9% White, 0.3% Black, 0.1% Asian, 1.7% Other, 1.2% Hispanic of any race (2010); Density: 1,043.0 persons per square mile (2010); Average household size: 2.37 (2010); Median age: 40.0 (2010); Males per 100 females: 100.6 (2010); Marriage status: 19.9% never married, 60.7% now married, 10.3% widowed, 9.1% divorced (2000); Foreign born: 0.2% (2000); Ancestry (includes multiple ancestries): 25.3% United States or American, 13.0% German, 10.7% English, 9.2% Irish, 5.1% Other groups (2000).

Economy: Single-family building permits issued: 1 (2009); Multi-family building permits issued: 0 (2009); Employment by occupation: 4.0% management, 10.6% professional, 19.7% services, 16.5% sales, 0.6% farming, 15.9% construction, 32.7% production (2000).

Income: Per capita income: $17,840 (2010); Median household income: $33,063 (2010); Average household income: $42,443 (2010); Percent of households with income of $100,000 or more: 5.7% (2010); Poverty rate: 9.9% (2000).

Taxes: Total city taxes per capita: $175 (2007); City property taxes per capita: $129 (2007).

Education: Percent of population age 25 and over with: High school diploma (including GED) or higher: 84.4% (2010); Bachelor's degree or higher: 6.6% (2010); Master's degree or higher: 2.7% (2010).

School District(s)
North Vermillion Com Sch Corp (KG-12)
  2008-09 Enrollment: 769 . . . . (765) 492-4033

Housing: Homeownership rate: 85.9% (2010); Median home value: $64,024 (2010); Median contract rent: $275 per month (2000); Median year structure built: 1956 (2000).

Newspapers: Herald News (Community news; Circulation 800)

Transportation: Commute to work: 94.5% car, 0.0% public transportation, 3.7% walk, 1.4% work from home (2000); Travel time to work: 35.3% less than 15 minutes, 24.0% 15 to 30 minutes, 27.7% 30 to 45 minutes, 8.3% 45 to 60 minutes, 4.8% 60 minutes or more (2000)

CLINTON (city). Covers a land area of 2.244 square miles and a water area of 0.018 square miles. Located at 39.66° N. Lat; 87.40° W. Long. Elevation is 492 feet.

History: Clinton was laid out along the Wabash River in 1829, and named for DeWitt Clinton (1769-1828), governor of New York. Clinton developed as a coal-mining town.

Population: 5,040 (1990); 5,126 (2000); 4,730 (2010); 4,519 (2015 projected); Race: 96.8% White, 1.2% Black, 0.1% Asian, 1.9% Other, 1.4% Hispanic of any race (2010); Density: 2,108.0 persons per square mile (2010); Average household size: 2.32 (2010); Median age: 40.1 (2010); Males per 100 females: 86.4 (2010); Marriage status: 20.3% never married, 51.7% now married, 15.3% widowed, 12.7% divorced (2000); Foreign born: 1.3% (2000); Ancestry (includes multiple ancestries): 16.5% German, 12.4% Irish, 12.1% English, 11.3% Italian, 10.0% Other groups (2000).

Economy: Single-family building permits issued: 2 (2009); Multi-family building permits issued: 0 (2009); Employment by occupation: 5.6% management, 13.9% professional, 21.4% services, 22.1% sales, 0.0% farming, 11.4% construction, 25.6% production (2000).

Income: Per capita income: $18,302 (2010); Median household income: $35,450 (2010); Average household income: $43,031 (2010); Percent of households with income of $100,000 or more: 5.7% (2010); Poverty rate: 12.5% (2000).

Taxes: Total city taxes per capita: $144 (2007); City property taxes per capita: $128 (2007).

Education: Percent of population age 25 and over with: High school diploma (including GED) or higher: 82.1% (2010); Bachelor's degree or higher: 10.9% (2010); Master's degree or higher: 3.8% (2010).

School District(s)

South Vermillion Com Sch Corp (KG-12)

    2008-09 Enrollment: 2,042 . . . . (765) 832-2426

Housing: Homeownership rate: 66.9% (2010); Median home value: $56,676 (2010); Median contract rent: $248 per month (2000); Median year structure built: before 1940 (2000).

Hospitals: West Central Community Hospital

Safety: Violent crime rate: 27.0 per 10,000 population; Property crime rate: 201.4 per 10,000 population (2008).

Newspapers: Clintonian (Local news; Circulation 5,483); The Daily Clintonian (Local news; Circulation 5,483)

Transportation: Commute to work: 93.1% car, 0.5% public transportation, 3.0% walk, 2.4% work from home (2000); Travel time to work: 39.4% less than 15 minutes, 36.0% 15 to 30 minutes, 19.0% 30 to 45 minutes, 4.0% 45 to 60 minutes, 1.7% 60 minutes or more (2000)

Additional Information Contacts

City of Clinton. . . . . (765) 832-9880

    http://www.clinton.in.gov

DANA (town). Covers a land area of 0.294 square miles and a water area of 0 square miles. Located at 39.80° N. Lat; 87.49° W. Long. Elevation is 640 feet.

History: Ernie Pyle State Memorial.

Population: 612 (1990); 662 (2000); 574 (2010); 532 (2015 projected); Race: 94.6% White, 3.0% Black, 0.3% Asian, 2.1% Other, 3.7% Hispanic of any race (2010); Density: 1,955.6 persons per square mile (2010); Average household size: 2.55 (2010); Median age: 37.7 (2010); Males per 100 females: 95.2 (2010); Marriage status: 11.3% never married, 69.1% now married, 6.8% widowed, 12.9% divorced (2000); Foreign born: 2.6% (2000); Ancestry (includes multiple ancestries): 26.4% United States or American, 19.8% German, 11.2% Other groups, 8.2% Irish, 7.0% English (2000).

Economy: Single-family building permits issued: 0 (2009); Multi-family building permits issued: 0 (2009); Employment by occupation: 10.0% management, 10.7% professional, 16.3% services, 19.6% sales, 3.0% farming, 15.2% construction, 25.2% production (2000).

Income: Per capita income: $18,243 (2010); Median household income: $40,125 (2010); Average household income: $46,667 (2010); Percent of households with income of $100,000 or more: 5.3% (2010); Poverty rate: 9.9% (2000).

Taxes: Total city taxes per capita: $91 (2007); City property taxes per capita: $78 (2007).

Education: Percent of population age 25 and over with: High school diploma (including GED) or higher: 86.6% (2010); Bachelor's degree or higher: 5.7% (2010); Master's degree or higher: 2.2% (2010).

Housing: Homeownership rate: 82.2% (2010); Median home value: $67,632 (2010); Median contract rent: $353 per month (2000); Median year structure built: before 1940 (2000).

Transportation: Commute to work: 91.7% car, 0.0% public transportation, 5.7% walk, 0.8% work from home (2000); Travel time to work: 25.9% less than 15 minutes, 40.7% 15 to 30 minutes, 19.8% 30 to 45 minutes, 10.6% 45 to 60 minutes, 3.0% 60 minutes or more (2000)

FAIRVIEW PARK (town). Covers a land area of 0.905 square miles and a water area of 0 square miles. Located at 39.68° N. Lat; 87.41° W. Long. Elevation is 512 feet.

History: Laid out 1902.

Population: 1,446 (1990); 1,496 (2000); 1,473 (2010); 1,442 (2015 projected); Race: 94.3% White, 1.6% Black, 0.0% Asian, 4.1% Other, 2.3% Hispanic of any race (2010); Density: 1,627.0 persons per square mile (2010); Average household size: 2.30 (2010); Median age: 42.2 (2010); Males per 100 females: 97.2 (2010); Marriage status: 18.5% never married, 64.5% now married, 5.9% widowed, 11.1% divorced (2000); Foreign born: 0.6% (2000); Ancestry (includes multiple ancestries): 18.6% United States or American, 16.5% German, 11.3% English, 10.6% Italian, 9.3% Irish (2000).

Economy: Employment by occupation: 8.1% management, 14.7% professional, 17.3% services, 28.2% sales, 0.3% farming, 13.2% construction, 18.2% production (2000).

Income: Per capita income: $24,138 (2010); Median household income: $41,048 (2010); Average household income: $55,090 (2010); Percent of households with income of $100,000 or more: 13.4% (2010); Poverty rate: 10.1% (2000).

Taxes: Total city taxes per capita: $87 (2007); City property taxes per capita: $83 (2007).

Education: Percent of population age 25 and over with: High school diploma (including GED) or higher: 89.4% (2010); Bachelor's degree or higher: 11.5% (2010); Master's degree or higher: 4.2% (2010).

Housing: Homeownership rate: 73.6% (2010); Median home value: $84,545 (2010); Median contract rent: $356 per month (2000); Median year structure built: 1971 (2000).

Transportation: Commute to work: 96.4% car, 0.3% public transportation, 0.9% walk, 2.1% work from home (2000); Travel time to work: 40.6% less than 15 minutes, 31.4% 15 to 30 minutes, 19.5% 30 to 45 minutes, 2.8% 45 to 60 minutes, 5.7% 60 minutes or more (2000)

HILLSDALE (unincorporated postal area, zip code 47854). Covers a land area of 33.968 square miles and a water area of 0.010 square miles. Located at 39.82° N. Lat; 87.41° W. Long. Elevation is 620 feet.

Population: 961 (2000); Race: 94.2% White, 0.6% Black, 1.2% Asian, 4.0% Other, 0.0% Hispanic of any race (2000); Density: 28.3 persons per square mile (2000); Age: 25.4% under 18, 10.3% over 64 (2000); Marriage status: 14.2% never married, 67.3% now married, 5.9% widowed, 12.6% divorced (2000); Foreign born: 0.9% (2000); Ancestry (includes multiple ancestries): 18.4% German, 15.0% Other groups, 12.7% United States or American, 11.6% English, 9.1% Irish (2000).

Economy: Employment by occupation: 12.9% management, 9.9% professional, 13.8% services, 16.3% sales, 0.0% farming, 21.1% construction, 26.0% production (2000).

Income: Per capita income: $25,532 (2000); Median household income: $43,542 (2000); Poverty rate: 3.5% (2000).

Education: Percent of population age 25 and over with: High school diploma (including GED) or higher: 88.7% (2000); Bachelor's degree or higher: 12.3% (2000).

Housing: Homeownership rate: 90.2% (2000); Median home value: $72,900 (2000); Median contract rent: $282 per month (2000); Median year structure built: 1965 (2000).

Transportation: Commute to work: 97.6% car, 0.0% public transportation, 1.7% walk, 0.0% work from home (2000); Travel time to work: 30.6% less than 15 minutes, 29.0% 15 to 30 minutes, 26.4% 30 to 45 minutes, 8.8% 45 to 60 minutes, 5.2% 60 minutes or more (2000)

NEWPORT (town). County seat. Covers a land area of 0.809 square miles and a water area of 0 square miles. Located at 39.88° N. Lat; 87.40° W. Long. Elevation is 528 feet.

Population: 627 (1990); 578 (2000); 558 (2010); 545 (2015 projected); Race: 96.6% White, 1.3% Black, 0.5% Asian, 1.6% Other, 1.3% Hispanic of any race (2010); Density: 690.0 persons per square mile (2010); Average household size: 2.46 (2010); Median age: 41.0 (2010); Males per 100 females: 116.3 (2010); Marriage status: 17.5% never married, 50.1% now married, 14.1% widowed, 18.2% divorced (2000); Foreign born: 0.9% (2000); Ancestry (includes multiple ancestries): 33.6% United States or American, 9.9% German, 4.5% Irish, 4.3% English, 2.5% Other groups (2000).

Economy: Single-family building permits issued: 0 (2009); Multi-family building permits issued: 0 (2009); Employment by occupation: 10.6% management, 5.1% professional, 20.0% services, 22.1% sales, 1.3% farming, 13.2% construction, 27.7% production (2000).

Income: Per capita income: $22,824 (2010); Median household income: $47,300 (2010); Average household income: $56,523 (2010); Percent of households with income of $100,000 or more: 8.2% (2010); Poverty rate: 9.1% (2000).

Taxes: Total city taxes per capita: $57 (2007); City property taxes per capita: $45 (2007).

Education: Percent of population age 25 and over with: High school diploma (including GED) or higher: 86.0% (2010); Bachelor's degree or higher: 12.0% (2010); Master's degree or higher: 4.8% (2010).

Housing: Homeownership rate: 82.3% (2010); Median home value: $76,538 (2010); Median contract rent: $257 per month (2000); Median year structure built: 1943 (2000).

Transportation: Commute to work: 88.5% car, 0.9% public transportation, 7.5% walk, 1.3% work from home (2000); Travel time to work: 37.7% less than 15 minutes, 29.1% 15 to 30 minutes, 13.5% 30 to 45 minutes, 12.6% 45 to 60 minutes, 7.2% 60 minutes or more (2000)

PERRYSVILLE (town). Covers a land area of 0.252 square miles and a water area of 0 square miles. Located at 40.05° N. Lat; 87.43° W. Long. Elevation is 538 feet.

Population: 443 (1990); 502 (2000); 443 (2010); 415 (2015 projected); Race: 98.2% White, 0.0% Black, 0.2% Asian, 1.6% Other, 0.0% Hispanic

of any race (2010); Density: 1,760.9 persons per square mile (2010); Average household size: 2.33 (2010); Median age: 40.7 (2010); Males per 100 females: 100.5 (2010); Marriage status: 15.6% never married, 61.8% now married, 5.8% widowed, 16.8% divorced (2000); Foreign born: 0.2% (2000); Ancestry (includes multiple ancestries): 22.2% United States or American, 12.8% English, 8.2% German, 6.2% Other groups, 5.4% Dutch (2000).

Economy: Employment by occupation: 8.6% management, 7.8% professional, 16.3% services, 18.8% sales, 0.0% farming, 9.0% construction, 39.6% production (2000).

Income: Per capita income: $15,532 (2010); Median household income: $32,297 (2010); Average household income: $36,329 (2010); Percent of households with income of $100,000 or more: 2.6% (2010); Poverty rate: 9.2% (2000).

Taxes: Total city taxes per capita: $59 (2007); City property taxes per capita: $53 (2007).

Education: Percent of population age 25 and over with: High school diploma (including GED) or higher: 83.0% (2010); Bachelor's degree or higher: 7.2% (2010); Master's degree or higher: 2.0% (2010).

Housing: Homeownership rate: 72.1% (2010); Median home value: $68,065 (2010); Median contract rent: $277 per month (2000); Median year structure built: 1948 (2000).

Transportation: Commute to work: 95.9% car, 1.2% public transportation, 1.7% walk, 0.4% work from home (2000); Travel time to work: 22.4% less than 15 minutes, 49.0% 15 to 30 minutes, 19.1% 30 to 45 minutes, 5.8% 45 to 60 minutes, 3.7% 60 minutes or more (2000)

UNIVERSAL (town). Covers a land area of 0.284 square miles and a water area of 0 square miles. Located at 39.62° N. Lat; 87.45° W. Long. Elevation is 581 feet.

History: Laid out 1911.

Population: 392 (1990); 419 (2000); 407 (2010); 400 (2015 projected); Race: 97.8% White, 1.7% Black, 0.0% Asian, 0.5% Other, 0.5% Hispanic of any race (2010); Density: 1,435.2 persons per square mile (2010); Average household size: 2.45 (2010); Median age: 39.6 (2010); Males per 100 females: 98.5 (2010); Marriage status: 23.7% never married, 58.3% now married, 4.2% widowed, 13.8% divorced (2000); Foreign born: 0.0% (2000); Ancestry (includes multiple ancestries): 18.5% German, 12.3% Italian, 10.6% Other groups, 10.2% Irish, 10.2% English (2000).

Economy: Employment by occupation: 6.9% management, 15.5% professional, 10.6% services, 22.4% sales, 0.4% farming, 20.4% construction, 23.7% production (2000).

Income: Per capita income: $24,319 (2010); Median household income: $48,421 (2010); Average household income: $59,940 (2010); Percent of households with income of $100,000 or more: 12.0% (2010); Poverty rate: 9.3% (2000).

Taxes: Total city taxes per capita: $9 (2007); City property taxes per capita: $0 (2007).

Education: Percent of population age 25 and over with: High school diploma (including GED) or higher: 86.4% (2010); Bachelor's degree or higher: 13.9% (2010); Master's degree or higher: 4.8% (2010).

Housing: Homeownership rate: 88.0% (2010); Median home value: $77,778 (2010); Median contract rent: $306 per month (2000); Median year structure built: before 1940 (2000).

Transportation: Commute to work: 100.0% car, 0.0% public transportation, 0.0% walk, 0.0% work from home (2000); Travel time to work: 30.7% less than 15 minutes, 43.7% 15 to 30 minutes, 17.2% 30 to 45 minutes, 5.0% 45 to 60 minutes, 3.4% 60 minutes or more (2000)

Vigo County

Located in western Indiana; bounded on the west by Illinois; crossed by the Wabash River; drained by Honey Creek. Covers a land area of 403.29 square miles, a water area of 7.17 square miles, and is located in the Eastern Time Zone. The county was founded in 1818. County seat is Terre Haute.

Vigo County is part of the Terre Haute, IN Metropolitan Statistical Area. The entire metro area includes: Clay County, IN; Sullivan County, IN; Vermillion County, IN; Vigo County, IN

Weather Station: Terre Haute Indiana State										Elevation: 505 feet		
	Jan	Feb	Mar	Apr	May	Jun	Jul	Aug	Sep	Oct	Nov	Dec
High	35	40	52	64	75	83	87	85	79	68	53	41
Low	17	21	32	42	52	61	65	63	55	43	33	23
Precip	2.2	2.5	3.7	4.2	4.4	4.0	4.4	3.8	3.0	2.8	3.7	3.1
Snow	na	na	1.6	tr	0.0	0.0	0.0	0.0	0.0	0.0	0.5	2.2

High and Low temperatures in degrees Fahrenheit; Precipitation and Snow in inches

Population: 106,107 (1990); 105,848 (2000); 106,315 (2010); 106,202 (2015 projected); Race: 88.7% White, 7.0% Black, 1.6% Asian, 2.6% Other, 1.6% Hispanic of any race (2010); Density: 263.6 persons per square mile (2010); Average household size: 2.32 (2010); Median age: 35.8 (2010); Males per 100 females: 101.5 (2010).

Religion: Five largest groups: 8.8% Catholic Church, 4.9% The United Methodist Church, 2.8% Christian Churches and Churches of Christ, 2.4% American Baptist Churches in the USA, 1.7% Assemblies of God (2000).

Economy: Unemployment rate: 11.0% (5/2010); Total civilian labor force: 50,201 (5/2010); Leading industries: 19.0% health care and social assistance; 18.5% manufacturing; 15.5% retail trade (2008); Farms: 518 totaling 121,454 acres (2007); Companies that employ 500 or more persons: 9 (2008); Companies that employ 100 to 499 persons: 67 (2008); Companies that employ less than 100 persons: 2,542 (2008); Black-owned businesses: n/a (2002); Hispanic-owned businesses: n/a (2002); Asian-owned businesses: 231 (2002); Women-owned businesses: 1,458 (2002); Retail sales per capita: $28,745 (2010). Single-family building permits issued: 97 (2009); Multi-family building permits issued: 6 (2009).

Income: Per capita income: $20,516 (2010); Median household income: $38,217 (2010); Average household income: $50,432 (2010); Percent of households with income of $100,000 or more: 9.6% (2010); Poverty rate: 19.7% (2008); Bankruptcy rate: 7.15% (2009).

Taxes: Total county taxes per capita: $304 (2007); County property taxes per capita: $207 (2007).

Education: Percent of population age 25 and over with: High school diploma (including GED) or higher: 84.4% (2010); Bachelor's degree or higher: 21.0% (2010); Master's degree or higher: 9.6% (2010).

Housing: Homeownership rate: 66.1% (2010); Median home value: $81,812 (2010); Median contract rent: $453 per month (2006-2008 3-year est.); Median year structure built: 1958 (2006-2008 3-year est.)

Health: Birth rate: 124.9 per 10,000 population (2009); Death rate: 104.9 per 10,000 population (2009); Age-adjusted cancer mortality rate: 203.9 deaths per 100,000 population (2006); Air Quality Index: 71.5% good, 28.5% moderate, 0.0% unhealthy for sensitive individuals, 0.0% unhealthy (percent of days in 2008); Number of physicians: 23.9 per 10,000 population (2007); Hospital beds: 54.7 per 10,000 population (2006); Hospital admissions: 2,218.7 per 10,000 population (2006).

Elections: 2008 Presidential election results: 57.3% Obama, 41.5% McCain, 0.0% Nader

Additional Information Contacts

Vigo County Government.	(812) 462-3211
http://www.vigocounty.org	
City of Terre Haute.	(812) 232-3375
http://www.terrehaute.in.gov	
Greater Terre Haute Chamber of Commerce	(812) 232-2391
http://www.terrehautechamber.com	

Vigo County Communities

LEWIS (unincorporated postal area, zip code 47858). Covers a land area of 37.772 square miles and a water area of 0.039 square miles. Located at 39.25° N. Lat; 87.23° W. Long. Elevation is 610 feet.

Population: 694 (2000); Race: 96.1% White, 0.0% Black, 0.8% Asian, 3.1% Other, 0.0% Hispanic of any race (2000); Density: 18.4 persons per square mile (2000); Age: 25.6% under 18, 15.8% over 64 (2000); Marriage status: 14.3% never married, 71.5% now married, 4.7% widowed, 9.4% divorced (2000); Foreign born: 0.8% (2000); Ancestry (includes multiple ancestries): 29.2% German, 14.0% English, 11.3% Irish, 9.2% Other groups, 5.9% Italian (2000).

Economy: Employment by occupation: 15.3% management, 2.2% professional, 19.3% services, 26.5% sales, 0.0% farming, 11.5% construction, 25.2% production (2000).

Income: Per capita income: $18,312 (2000); Median household income: $34,489 (2000); Poverty rate: 1.5% (2000).

Education: Percent of population age 25 and over with: High school diploma (including GED) or higher: 86.3% (2000); Bachelor's degree or higher: 14.6% (2000).

Housing: Homeownership rate: 94.1% (2000); Median home value: $86,500 (2000); Median contract rent: $125 per month (2000); Median year structure built: 1973 (2000).
Transportation: Commute to work: 83.2% car, 0.0% public transportation, 0.0% walk, 16.8% work from home (2000); Travel time to work: 15.4% less than 15 minutes, 23.2% 15 to 30 minutes, 37.5% 30 to 45 minutes, 10.1% 45 to 60 minutes, 13.9% 60 minutes or more (2000)

NORTH TERRE HAUTE (CDP). Covers a land area of 3.578 square miles and a water area of 0 square miles. Located at 39.53° N. Lat; 87.36° W. Long. Elevation is 495 feet.

History: The Markle Mill was built in 1816 on the banks of Otter Creek, near the site of North Terre Haute, and the town developed around it.
Population: 4,472 (1990); 4,606 (2000); 4,219 (2010); 4,076 (2015 projected); Race: 95.1% White, 3.2% Black, 0.4% Asian, 1.3% Other, 1.7% Hispanic of any race (2010); Density: 1,179.1 persons per square mile (2010); Average household size: 2.36 (2010); Median age: 36.6 (2010); Males per 100 females: 105.6 (2010); Marriage status: 21.3% never married, 57.1% now married, 7.4% widowed, 14.2% divorced (2000); Foreign born: 0.9% (2000); Ancestry (includes multiple ancestries): 19.7% German, 14.9% United States or American, 11.7% Irish, 10.5% English, 6.2% Other groups (2000).
Economy: Employment by occupation: 6.0% management, 15.0% professional, 17.8% services, 30.4% sales, 0.0% farming, 9.4% construction, 21.4% production (2000).
Income: Per capita income: $17,376 (2010); Median household income: $35,865 (2010); Average household income: $41,767 (2010); Percent of households with income of $100,000 or more: 4.6% (2010); Poverty rate: 9.6% (2000).
Education: Percent of population age 25 and over with: High school diploma (including GED) or higher: 85.4% (2010); Bachelor's degree or higher: 12.7% (2010); Master's degree or higher: 4.6% (2010).
Housing: Homeownership rate: 71.8% (2010); Median home value: $78,773 (2010); Median contract rent: $344 per month (2000); Median year structure built: 1965 (2000).
Transportation: Commute to work: 97.5% car, 0.0% public transportation, 0.0% walk, 1.7% work from home (2000); Travel time to work: 34.7% less than 15 minutes, 47.6% 15 to 30 minutes, 10.4% 30 to 45 minutes, 1.1% 45 to 60 minutes, 6.2% 60 minutes or more (2000)

PIMENTO (unincorporated postal area, zip code 47866). Covers a land area of 17.602 square miles and a water area of 0.090 square miles. Located at 39.29° N. Lat; 87.31° W. Long. Elevation is 600 feet.

Population: 412 (2000); Race: 100.0% White, 0.0% Black, 0.0% Asian, 0.0% Other, 0.0% Hispanic of any race (2000); Density: 23.4 persons per square mile (2000); Age: 21.6% under 18, 23.9% over 64 (2000); Marriage status: 27.9% never married, 65.7% now married, 5.4% widowed, 1.1% divorced (2000); Foreign born: 1.1% (2000); Ancestry (includes multiple ancestries): 22.6% German, 19.4% English, 11.6% Irish, 6.8% Other groups, 4.8% Welsh (2000).
Economy: Employment by occupation: 9.0% management, 19.5% professional, 19.5% services, 16.2% sales, 0.0% farming, 15.2% construction, 20.5% production (2000).
Income: Per capita income: $24,021 (2000); Median household income: $47,625 (2000); Poverty rate: 1.6% (2000).
Education: Percent of population age 25 and over with: High school diploma (including GED) or higher: 91.5% (2000); Bachelor's degree or higher: 9.7% (2000).
Housing: Homeownership rate: 90.5% (2000); Median home value: $75,000 (2000); Median contract rent: $466 per month (2000); Median year structure built: 1964 (2000).
Transportation: Commute to work: 84.3% car, 0.0% public transportation, 4.8% walk, 9.5% work from home (2000); Travel time to work: 10.0% less than 15 minutes, 71.6% 15 to 30 minutes, 14.2% 30 to 45 minutes, 4.2% 45 to 60 minutes, 0.0% 60 minutes or more (2000)

RILEY (town). Covers a land area of 0.092 square miles and a water area of 0 square miles. Located at 39.39° N. Lat; 87.30° W. Long. Elevation is 564 feet.

History: Riley, first known as Lockport, developed around a coal mine.
Population: 232 (1990); 160 (2000); 167 (2010); 166 (2015 projected); Race: 98.2% White, 0.6% Black, 0.0% Asian, 1.2% Other, 1.2% Hispanic of any race (2010); Density: 1,824.2 persons per square mile (2010); Average household size: 2.53 (2010); Median age: 38.9 (2010); Males per 100 females: 101.2 (2010); Marriage status: 12.3% never married, 68.9%

now married, 9.4% widowed, 9.4% divorced (2000); Foreign born: 0.0% (2000); Ancestry (includes multiple ancestries): 46.2% United States or American, 26.2% German, 9.0% Irish, 6.9% Dutch, 3.4% English (2000).
Economy: Employment by occupation: 17.2% management, 5.2% professional, 24.1% services, 27.6% sales, 0.0% farming, 10.3% construction, 15.5% production (2000).
Income: Per capita income: $27,672 (2010); Median household income: $60,938 (2010); Average household income: $69,318 (2010); Percent of households with income of $100,000 or more: 19.7% (2010); Poverty rate: 12.0% (2000).
Taxes: Total city taxes per capita: $110 (2007); City property taxes per capita: $77 (2007).
Education: Percent of population age 25 and over with: High school diploma (including GED) or higher: 92.7% (2010); Bachelor's degree or higher: 29.1% (2010); Master's degree or higher: 13.6% (2010).

School District(s)
Vigo County School Corp (PK-12)
    2008-09 Enrollment: 15,971 . . . . (812) 462-4216
Housing: Homeownership rate: 81.8% (2010); Median home value: $134,615 (2010); Median contract rent: $358 per month (2000); Median year structure built: 1960 (2000).
Transportation: Commute to work: 100.0% car, 0.0% public transportation, 0.0% walk, 0.0% work from home (2000); Travel time to work: 25.5% less than 15 minutes, 69.1% 15 to 30 minutes, 5.5% 30 to 45 minutes, 0.0% 45 to 60 minutes, 0.0% 60 minutes or more (2000)

SAINT MARY OF THE WOODS (unincorporated postal area, zip code 47876). Covers a land area of 0.042 square miles and a water area of 0 square miles. Located at 39.43° N. Lat; 87.41° W. Long. Elevation is 564 feet.

Population: 427 (2000); Race: 98.1% White, 1.9% Black, 0.0% Asian, 0.0% Other, 0.0% Hispanic of any race (2000); Density: 10,166.7 persons per square mile (2000); Age: 0.0% under 18, 55.5% over 64 (2000); Marriage status: 78.0% never married, 20.9% now married, 1.2% widowed, 0.0% divorced (2000); Foreign born: 1.4% (2000); Ancestry (includes multiple ancestries): 34.8% German, 19.5% Irish, 6.7% Polish, 3.2% Dutch, 3.2% Other groups (2000).
Economy: Employment by occupation: 4.6% management, 10.1% professional, 44.0% services, 36.7% sales, 4.6% farming, 0.0% construction, 0.0% production (2000).
Income: Per capita income: $5,353 (2000); Median household income: $0 (2000); Poverty rate: 0.0% (2000).
Education: Percent of population age 25 and over with: High school diploma (including GED) or higher: 95.3% (2000); Bachelor's degree or higher: 93.4% (2000).

Four-year College(s)
Saint Mary-of-the-Woods College (Private, Not-for-profit, Roman Catholic)
    Fall 2008 Enrollment: 1,580. . . . . (812) 535-5151
    2009-10 Tuition: In-state $23,060; Out-of-state $23,060
Housing: Homeownership rate: 0.0% (2000); Median home value: $n/a (2000); Median contract rent: $n/a per month (2000); Median year structure built: n/a (2000).
Transportation: Commute to work: 12.6% car, 0.0% public transportation, 82.5% walk, 0.0% work from home (2000); Travel time to work: 87.4% less than 15 minutes, 12.6% 15 to 30 minutes, 0.0% 30 to 45 minutes, 0.0% 45 to 60 minutes, 0.0% 60 minutes or more (2000)

SEELYVILLE (town). Covers a land area of 0.862 square miles and a water area of 0.010 square miles. Located at 39.49° N. Lat; 87.26° W. Long. Elevation is 584 feet.

History: Seelyville was established as a mining center.
Population: 1,090 (1990); 1,182 (2000); 1,118 (2010); 1,107 (2015 projected); Race: 98.0% White, 0.9% Black, 0.4% Asian, 0.7% Other, 0.7% Hispanic of any race (2010); Density: 1,297.2 persons per square mile (2010); Average household size: 2.42 (2010); Median age: 38.5 (2010); Males per 100 females: 102.9 (2010); Marriage status: 22.2% never married, 58.0% now married, 5.7% widowed, 14.2% divorced (2000); Foreign born: 0.3% (2000); Ancestry (includes multiple ancestries): 20.3% United States or American, 19.4% German, 13.7% Irish, 10.3% English, 4.4% Other groups (2000).
Economy: Employment by occupation: 6.6% management, 14.7% professional, 17.5% services, 28.1% sales, 0.0% farming, 12.4% construction, 20.8% production (2000).
Income: Per capita income: $27,442 (2010); Median household income: $56,548 (2010); Average household income: $66,887 (2010); Percent of

households with income of $100,000 or more: 17.6% (2010); Poverty rate: 7.4% (2000).

Taxes: Total city taxes per capita: $82 (2007); City property taxes per capita: $67 (2007).

Education: Percent of population age 25 and over with: High school diploma (including GED) or higher: 88.9% (2010); Bachelor's degree or higher: 20.7% (2010); Master's degree or higher: 9.6% (2010).

Housing: Homeownership rate: 77.0% (2010); Median home value: $92,712 (2010); Median contract rent: $382 per month (2000); Median year structure built: 1959 (2000).

Transportation: Commute to work: 96.5% car, 0.0% public transportation, 0.0% walk, 2.8% work from home (2000); Travel time to work: 20.3% less than 15 minutes, 62.8% 15 to 30 minutes, 8.8% 30 to 45 minutes, 4.6% 45 to 60 minutes, 3.4% 60 minutes or more (2000)

TERRE HAUTE (city). County seat. Covers a land area of 31.238 square miles and a water area of 0.864 square miles. Located at 39.47° N. Lat; 87.39° W. Long. Elevation is 499 feet.

History: Terre Haute's name, meaning "high land," was given to it by French traders in the early 1700's. The city itself was established in 1816 by the Terre Haute Town Company, a group of Indiana and Kentucky businessmen. It was soon selected as the seat of Vigo County, and was incorporated as a town in 1832. Coal mining was the major industry in Terre Haute after 1875. It's reputation as a "union town" was influenced in part by Eugene V. Debs who lived and worked here.

Population: 60,970 (1990); 59,614 (2000); 59,334 (2010); 58,956 (2015 projected); Race: 83.8% White, 11.4% Black, 1.4% Asian, 3.5% Other, 2.1% Hispanic of any race (2010); Density: 1,899.4 persons per square mile (2010); Average household size: 2.25 (2010); Median age: 33.5 (2010); Males per 100 females: 103.4 (2010); Marriage status: 32.8% never married, 45.7% now married, 8.9% widowed, 12.5% divorced (2000); Foreign born: 2.1% (2000); Ancestry (includes multiple ancestries): 18.7% German, 15.2% Other groups, 13.1% United States or American, 10.6% Irish, 9.6% English (2000).

Economy: Unemployment rate: 11.7% (5/2010); Total civilian labor force: 27,127 (5/2010); Single-family building permits issued: 26 (2009); Multi-family building permits issued: 6 (2009); Employment by occupation: 8.5% management, 20.0% professional, 20.5% services, 28.6% sales, 0.2% farming, 6.9% construction, 15.2% production (2000).

Income: Per capita income: $17,937 (2010); Median household income: $32,278 (2010); Average household income: $43,649 (2010); Percent of households with income of $100,000 or more: 6.8% (2010); Poverty rate: 19.2% (2000).

Taxes: Total city taxes per capita: $486 (2007); City property taxes per capita: $386 (2007).

Education: Percent of population age 25 and over with: High school diploma (including GED) or higher: 81.7% (2010); Bachelor's degree or higher: 19.6% (2010); Master's degree or higher: 9.0% (2010).

School District(s)
Covered Bridge Spec Ed Dist (KG-12)
    2008-09 Enrollment: n/a . . . . (812) 462-4030
Vigo County School Corp (PK-12)
    2008-09 Enrollment: 15,971 . . . . (812) 462-4216
Four-year College(s)
Indiana Business College-Terre Haute (Private, For-profit)
    Fall 2008 Enrollment: 275 . . . . (812) 877-2100
    2009-10 Tuition: In-state $11,535; Out-of-state $11,535
Indiana State University (Public)
    Fall 2008 Enrollment: 10,457 . . . . (812) 237-6311
    2009-10 Tuition: In-state $7,426; Out-of-state $16,002
Rose-Hulman Institute of Technology (Private, Not-for-profit)
    Fall 2008 Enrollment: 1,923 . . . . (812) 877-1511
    2009-10 Tuition: In-state $37,360; Out-of-state $37,360
Two-year College(s)
Ivy Tech Community College-Wabash Valley (Public)
    Fall 2008 Enrollment: 5,666 . . . . (812) 299-1121
    2009-10 Tuition: In-state $3,090; Out-of-state $6,306
Vocational/Technical School(s)
J Michael Harrold Beauty Academy (Private, For-profit)
    Fall 2008 Enrollment: 51 . . . . (812) 232-8334
    2009-10 Tuition: $10,305

Housing: Homeownership rate: 58.3% (2010); Median home value: $69,131 (2010); Median contract rent: $353 per month (2000); Median year structure built: 1946 (2000).

Hospitals: Hamilton Center (16 beds); Terre Haute Regional Hospital (278 beds); Union Hospital

Safety: Violent crime rate: 26.3 per 10,000 population; Property crime rate: 846.9 per 10,000 population (2008).

Newspapers: Tribune Star (Local news; Circulation 29,979)

Transportation: Commute to work: 89.7% car, 0.5% public transportation, 6.7% walk, 1.8% work from home (2000); Travel time to work: 53.5% less than 15 minutes, 34.3% 15 to 30 minutes, 6.7% 30 to 45 minutes, 2.1% 45 to 60 minutes, 3.4% 60 minutes or more (2000)

Additional Information Contacts
City of Terre Haute. . . . . (812) 232-3375
    http://www.terrehaute.in.gov
Greater Terre Haute Chamber of Commerce . . . . (812) 232-2391
    http://www.terrehautechamber.com

WEST TERRE HAUTE (town). Covers a land area of 0.756 square miles and a water area of 0 square miles. Located at 39.46° N. Lat; 87.44° W. Long. Elevation is 469 feet.

History: West Terre Haute began as a coal-mining town.

Population: 2,601 (1990); 2,330 (2000); 2,156 (2010); 2,075 (2015 projected); Race: 96.4% White, 0.0% Black, 0.8% Asian, 2.7% Other, 0.6% Hispanic of any race (2010); Density: 2,852.2 persons per square mile (2010); Average household size: 2.53 (2010); Median age: 34.7 (2010); Males per 100 females: 96.4 (2010); Marriage status: 23.8% never married, 52.6% now married, 9.9% widowed, 13.8% divorced (2000); Foreign born: 0.4% (2000); Ancestry (includes multiple ancestries): 19.6% United States or American, 11.1% Other groups, 10.4% German, 9.7% Irish, 4.7% English (2000).

Economy: Employment by occupation: 2.1% management, 9.0% professional, 22.0% services, 26.0% sales, 0.0% farming, 19.6% construction, 21.2% production (2000).

Income: Per capita income: $14,475 (2010); Median household income: $30,510 (2010); Average household income: $36,703 (2010); Percent of households with income of $100,000 or more: 3.4% (2010); Poverty rate: 20.7% (2000).

Taxes: Total city taxes per capita: $147 (2007); City property taxes per capita: $132 (2007).

Education: Percent of population age 25 and over with: High school diploma (including GED) or higher: 69.8% (2010); Bachelor's degree or higher: 5.4% (2010); Master's degree or higher: 1.9% (2010).

School District(s)
Vigo County School Corp (PK-12)
    2008-09 Enrollment: 15,971 . . . . (812) 462-4216
Housing: Homeownership rate: 68.5% (2010); Median home value: $45,977 (2010); Median contract rent: $288 per month (2000); Median year structure built: 1944 (2000).

Transportation: Commute to work: 92.2% car, 0.0% public transportation, 3.5% walk, 2.8% work from home (2000); Travel time to work: 34.2% less than 15 minutes, 49.9% 15 to 30 minutes, 9.6% 30 to 45 minutes, 3.3% 45 to 60 minutes, 3.0% 60 minutes or more (2000)

Wabash County

Located in northeast central Indiana; drained by the Wabash, Eel, Salamonie, and Mississinewa Rivers. Covers a land area of 413.17 square miles, a water area of 7.90 square miles, and is located in the Eastern Time Zone. The county was founded in 1832. County seat is Wabash.

Wabash County is part of the Wabash, IN Micropolitan Statistical Area. The entire metro area includes: Wabash County, IN

Population: 35,069 (1990); 34,960 (2000); 32,340 (2010); 30,918 (2015 projected); Race: 96.7% White, 0.6% Black, 0.5% Asian, 2.2% Other, 1.4% Hispanic of any race (2010); Density: 78.3 persons per square mile (2010); Average household size: 2.43 (2010); Median age: 41.0 (2010); Males per 100 females: 94.4 (2010).

Religion: Five largest groups: 9.3% The United Methodist Church, 8.4% Christian Churches and Churches of Christ, 7.3% Catholic Church, 4.4% Church of the Brethren, 2.5% Evangelical Lutheran Church in America (2000).

Economy: Unemployment rate: 10.3% (5/2010); Total civilian labor force: 16,996 (5/2010); Leading industries: 27.9% manufacturing; 18.6% health care and social assistance; 13.6% retail trade (2008); Farms: 850 totaling 200,689 acres (2007); Companies that employ 500 or more persons: 2 (2008); Companies that employ 100 to 499 persons: 19 (2008); Companies that employ less than 100 persons: 760 (2008); Black-owned businesses:

n/a (2002); Hispanic-owned businesses: n/a (2002); Asian-owned businesses: n/a (2002); Women-owned businesses: 1,185 (2002); Retail sales per capita: $11,998 (2010). Single-family building permits issued: 34 (2009); Multi-family building permits issued: 0 (2009).

Income: Per capita income: $21,847 (2010); Median household income: $46,503 (2010); Average household income: $54,962 (2010); Percent of households with income of $100,000 or more: 10.0% (2010); Poverty rate: 12.0% (2008); Bankruptcy rate: 8.41% (2009).

Taxes: Total county taxes per capita: $334 (2007); County property taxes per capita: $128 (2007).

Education: Percent of population age 25 and over with: High school diploma (including GED) or higher: 84.8% (2010); Bachelor's degree or higher: 17.6% (2010); Master's degree or higher: 6.2% (2010).

Housing: Homeownership rate: 77.0% (2010); Median home value: $94,166 (2010); Median contract rent: $405 per month (2006-2008 3-year est.); Median year structure built: 1957 (2006-2008 3-year est.)

Health: Birth rate: 110.6 per 10,000 population (2009); Death rate: 122.9 per 10,000 population (2009); Age-adjusted cancer mortality rate: 193.1 deaths per 100,000 population (2006); Number of physicians: 7.6 per 10,000 population (2007); Hospital beds: 15.0 per 10,000 population (2006); Hospital admissions: 252.7 per 10,000 population (2006).

Elections: 2008 Presidential election results: 39.3% Obama, 59.4% McCain, 0.0% Nader

National and State Parks: Doranew Holland State Recreation Area; Frances Slocum State Recreation Area; Hogback Ridge State Recreation Area; Lost Bridge State Recreation Area; Miami State Recreation Area; Mount Hope State Recreation Area; Pearson Mill State Recreation Area; Red Bridge State Recreation Area; Salamonie River State Forest

Additional Information Contacts

Wabash County Government . . . . (260) 563-0661
   http://www.wabashcounty85.us
City of Wabash . . . . (260) 563-4171
   http://www.cityofwabash.com
Town of North Manchester . . . . (260) 982-9800
   http://www.nmanchester.org
Wabash Chamber of Commerce . . . . (260) 563-1168
   http://www.wabashchamber.org

Wabash County Communities

LA FONTAINE (town). Covers a land area of 0.612 square miles and a water area of 0 square miles. Located at 40.67° N. Lat; 85.72° W. Long. Elevation is 801 feet.

Population: 902 (1990); 900 (2000); 794 (2010); 748 (2015 projected); Race: 95.8% White, 0.5% Black, 0.4% Asian, 3.3% Other, 2.3% Hispanic of any race (2010); Density: 1,297.0 persons per square mile (2010); Average household size: 2.27 (2010); Median age: 45.2 (2010); Males per 100 females: 92.3 (2010); Marriage status: 18.4% never married, 60.2% now married, 11.7% widowed, 9.6% divorced (2000); Foreign born: 0.0% (2000); Ancestry (includes multiple ancestries): 25.3% German, 19.4% United States or American, 10.4% Other groups, 9.4% Irish, 8.3% English (2000).

Economy: Employment by occupation: 7.4% management, 15.6% professional, 12.9% services, 21.6% sales, 0.5% farming, 5.8% construction, 36.2% production (2000).

Income: Per capita income: $22,045 (2010); Median household income: $48,885 (2010); Average household income: $54,159 (2010); Percent of households with income of $100,000 or more: 6.3% (2010); Poverty rate: 3.8% (2000).

Taxes: Total city taxes per capita: $127 (2007); City property taxes per capita: $111 (2007).

Education: Percent of population age 25 and over with: High school diploma (including GED) or higher: 87.3% (2010); Bachelor's degree or higher: 11.0% (2010); Master's degree or higher: 3.6% (2010).

School District(s)

M S D Wabash County Schools (PK-12)
   2008-09 Enrollment: 2,492 . . . . (260) 563-8050

Housing: Homeownership rate: 77.8% (2010); Median home value: $76,143 (2010); Median contract rent: $273 per month (2000); Median year structure built: before 1940 (2000).

Transportation: Commute to work: 94.3% car, 2.0% public transportation, 2.2% walk, 0.5% work from home (2000); Travel time to work: 21.0% less than 15 minutes, 58.8% 15 to 30 minutes, 14.8% 30 to 45 minutes, 1.0% 45 to 60 minutes, 4.4% 60 minutes or more (2000)

LAGRO (town). Covers a land area of 0.598 square miles and a water area of 0.007 square miles. Located at 40.83° N. Lat; 85.72° W. Long. Elevation is 705 feet.

History: The Wabash & Erie Canal was the impetus for the settlement of Lagro, named for an Indian chief, Les Gros.

Population: 496 (1990); 454 (2000); 401 (2010); 375 (2015 projected); Race: 98.0% White, 0.0% Black, 0.2% Asian, 1.7% Other, 0.5% Hispanic of any race (2010); Density: 670.1 persons per square mile (2010); Average household size: 2.66 (2010); Median age: 40.4 (2010); Males per 100 females: 104.6 (2010); Marriage status: 17.2% never married, 67.7% now married, 5.5% widowed, 9.5% divorced (2000); Foreign born: 0.0% (2000); Ancestry (includes multiple ancestries): 32.7% United States or American, 12.7% German, 9.7% Other groups, 7.2% Irish, 5.7% English (2000).

Economy: Employment by occupation: 3.6% management, 5.2% professional, 23.8% services, 9.3% sales, 0.0% farming, 15.5% construction, 42.5% production (2000).

Income: Per capita income: $20,338 (2010); Median household income: $48,542 (2010); Average household income: $54,073 (2010); Percent of households with income of $100,000 or more: 7.3% (2010); Poverty rate: 6.5% (2000).

Taxes: Total city taxes per capita: $118 (2007); City property taxes per capita: $100 (2007).

Education: Percent of population age 25 and over with: High school diploma (including GED) or higher: 79.9% (2010); Bachelor's degree or higher: 13.4% (2010); Master's degree or higher: 2.6% (2010).

Housing: Homeownership rate: 89.4% (2010); Median home value: $91,875 (2010); Median contract rent: $319 per month (2000); Median year structure built: 1945 (2000).

Transportation: Commute to work: 100.0% car, 0.0% public transportation, 0.0% walk, 0.0% work from home (2000); Travel time to work: 23.4% less than 15 minutes, 58.0% 15 to 30 minutes, 8.0% 30 to 45 minutes, 4.8% 45 to 60 minutes, 5.9% 60 minutes or more (2000)

NORTH MANCHESTER (town). Covers a land area of 3.607 square miles and a water area of 0 square miles. Located at 41.00° N. Lat; 85.77° W. Long. Elevation is 771 feet.

History: Among the early residents in North Manchester was a group of Dunkers, members of a religious sect founded in Germany in 1708. Thomas R. Marshall, Vice President of the United States under Woodrow Wilson, was born in North Manchester.

Population: 6,474 (1990); 6,260 (2000); 5,725 (2010); 5,436 (2015 projected); Race: 94.8% White, 1.4% Black, 1.0% Asian, 2.7% Other, 2.1% Hispanic of any race (2010); Density: 1,587.2 persons per square mile (2010); Average household size: 2.22 (2010); Median age: 39.5 (2010); Males per 100 females: 80.9 (2010); Marriage status: 25.9% never married, 53.4% now married, 12.0% widowed, 8.7% divorced (2000); Foreign born: 0.9% (2000); Ancestry (includes multiple ancestries): 30.4% German, 12.2% United States or American, 9.3% Irish, 8.3% English, 4.6% Other groups (2000).

Economy: Single-family building permits issued: 1 (2009); Multi-family building permits issued: 0 (2009); Employment by occupation: 9.7% management, 19.5% professional, 18.1% services, 24.2% sales, 1.4% farming, 4.7% construction, 22.4% production (2000).

Income: Per capita income: $19,617 (2010); Median household income: $43,182 (2010); Average household income: $50,493 (2010); Percent of households with income of $100,000 or more: 7.4% (2010); Poverty rate: 8.7% (2000).

Taxes: Total city taxes per capita: $216 (2007); City property taxes per capita: $188 (2007).

Education: Percent of population age 25 and over with: High school diploma (including GED) or higher: 87.3% (2010); Bachelor's degree or higher: 30.9% (2010); Master's degree or higher: 13.1% (2010).

School District(s)

Manchester Community Schools (PK-12)
   2008-09 Enrollment: 1,533 . . . . (260) 982-7518

Four-year College(s)

Manchester College (Private, Not-for-profit, Church of Brethren)
   Fall 2008 Enrollment: 1,145 . . . . (260) 982-5000
   2009-10 Tuition: In-state $23,790; Out-of-state $23,790

Housing: Homeownership rate: 67.7% (2010); Median home value: $96,942 (2010); Median contract rent: $326 per month (2000); Median year structure built: 1954 (2000).

Safety: Violent crime rate: 29.1 per 10,000 population; Property crime rate: 253.6 per 10,000 population (2008).
Newspapers: News-Journal (Community news; Circulation 2,200)
Transportation: Commute to work: 84.3% car, 0.0% public transportation, 11.7% walk, 3.0% work from home (2000); Travel time to work: 62.5% less than 15 minutes, 15.7% 15 to 30 minutes, 14.2% 30 to 45 minutes, 5.8% 45 to 60 minutes, 1.8% 60 minutes or more (2000)
Additional Information Contacts
Town of North Manchester. . . . . (260) 982-9800
　http://www.nmanchester.org

ROANN (town).
Covers a land area of 0.180 square miles and a water area of 0 square miles. Located at 40.91° N. Lat; 85.92° W. Long. Elevation is 755 feet.
History: Laid out 1853.
Population: 447 (1990); 400 (2000); 326 (2010); 299 (2015 projected); Race: 95.1% White, 0.0% Black, 0.6% Asian, 4.3% Other, 0.9% Hispanic of any race (2010); Density: 1,814.5 persons per square mile (2010); Average household size: 2.51 (2010); Median age: 42.2 (2010); Males per 100 females: 96.4 (2010); Marriage status: 20.1% never married, 62.8% now married, 8.1% widowed, 9.0% divorced (2000); Foreign born: 0.0% (2000); Ancestry (includes multiple ancestries): 26.9% German, 16.5% English, 11.7% Irish, 5.1% United States or American, 4.1% Other groups (2000).
Economy: Employment by occupation: 9.0% management, 5.8% professional, 6.3% services, 24.2% sales, 2.2% farming, 6.7% construction, 45.7% production (2000).
Income: Per capita income: $24,430 (2010); Median household income: $55,102 (2010); Average household income: $65,538 (2010); Percent of households with income of $100,000 or more: 13.8% (2010); Poverty rate: 9.5% (2000).
Taxes: Total city taxes per capita: $147 (2007); City property taxes per capita: $147 (2007).
Education: Percent of population age 25 and over with: High school diploma (including GED) or higher: 81.0% (2010); Bachelor's degree or higher: 9.1% (2010); Master's degree or higher: 5.2% (2010).
Housing: Homeownership rate: 85.4% (2010); Median home value: $78,571 (2010); Median contract rent: $341 per month (2000); Median year structure built: before 1940 (2000).
Transportation: Commute to work: 98.1% car, 0.0% public transportation, 1.9% walk, 0.0% work from home (2000); Travel time to work: 7.0% less than 15 minutes, 67.9% 15 to 30 minutes, 20.5% 30 to 45 minutes, 4.7% 45 to 60 minutes, 0.0% 60 minutes or more (2000)

URBANA (unincorporated postal area, zip code 46990).
Covers a land area of 30.034 square miles and a water area of 0.031 square miles. Located at 40.89° N. Lat; 85.74° W. Long. Elevation is 791 feet.
History: Laid out 1854.
Population: 851 (2000); Race: 100.0% White, 0.0% Black, 0.0% Asian, 0.0% Other, 0.0% Hispanic of any race (2000); Density: 28.3 persons per square mile (2000); Age: 33.5% under 18, 8.2% over 64 (2000); Marriage status: 13.2% never married, 78.2% now married, 4.1% widowed, 4.5% divorced (2000); Foreign born: 0.0% (2000); Ancestry (includes multiple ancestries): 23.1% German, 9.0% United States or American, 7.7% English, 4.1% Irish, 3.8% Scotch-Irish (2000).
Economy: Employment by occupation: 21.7% management, 10.0% professional, 9.0% services, 26.4% sales, 2.4% farming, 5.7% construction, 24.8% production (2000).
Income: Per capita income: $16,664 (2000); Median household income: $46,063 (2000); Poverty rate: 5.6% (2000).
Education: Percent of population age 25 and over with: High school diploma (including GED) or higher: 94.1% (2000); Bachelor's degree or higher: 22.9% (2000).
Housing: Homeownership rate: 87.7% (2000); Median home value: $82,000 (2000); Median contract rent: $406 per month (2000); Median year structure built: before 1940 (2000).
Transportation: Commute to work: 84.4% car, 0.0% public transportation, 4.0% walk, 8.2% work from home (2000); Travel time to work: 35.1% less than 15 minutes, 40.3% 15 to 30 minutes, 4.6% 30 to 45 minutes, 9.5% 45 to 60 minutes, 10.5% 60 minutes or more (2000)

WABASH (city).
County seat. Covers a land area of 8.903 square miles and a water area of 0.249 square miles. Located at 40.80° N. Lat; 85.82° W. Long. Elevation is 712 feet.

History: Its location along the Wabash River gave the town of Wabash its name, which comes from the Indian "oubache," meaning "water over white stones." The Wabash & Erie Canal was completed through this area in 1835, bringing Irish immigrants as canal workers.
Population: 12,381 (1990); 11,743 (2000); 10,516 (2010); 9,888 (2015 projected); Race: 96.3% White, 0.4% Black, 0.6% Asian, 2.7% Other, 1.7% Hispanic of any race (2010); Density: 1,181.1 persons per square mile (2010); Average household size: 2.30 (2010); Median age: 40.5 (2010); Males per 100 females: 92.4 (2010); Marriage status: 23.0% never married, 54.3% now married, 9.5% widowed, 13.2% divorced (2000); Foreign born: 1.2% (2000); Ancestry (includes multiple ancestries): 22.8% German, 12.4% United States or American, 12.1% English, 10.5% Irish, 8.1% Other groups (2000).
Economy: Single-family building permits issued: 7 (2009); Multi-family building permits issued: 0 (2009); Employment by occupation: 8.4% management, 11.7% professional, 15.0% services, 24.7% sales, 0.6% farming, 7.2% construction, 32.5% production (2000).
Income: Per capita income: $20,644 (2010); Median household income: $38,119 (2010); Average household income: $47,964 (2010); Percent of households with income of $100,000 or more: 7.0% (2010); Poverty rate: 9.3% (2000).
Taxes: Total city taxes per capita: $484 (2007); City property taxes per capita: $475 (2007).
Education: Percent of population age 25 and over with: High school diploma (including GED) or higher: 82.2% (2010); Bachelor's degree or higher: 14.6% (2010); Master's degree or higher: 4.7% (2010).
School District(s)
Heartland Career Center (09-12)
　2008-09 Enrollment: n/a . . . . (260) 563-7481
M S D Wabash County Schools (PK-12)
　2008-09 Enrollment: 2,492 . . . . (260) 563-8050
Wabash City Schools (KG-12)
　2008-09 Enrollment: 1,415 . . . . (260) 563-2151
Housing: Homeownership rate: 69.6% (2010); Median home value: $79,652 (2010); Median contract rent: $333 per month (2000); Median year structure built: 1951 (2000).
Hospitals: Wabash County Hospital (25 beds)
Safety: Violent crime rate: 19.5 per 10,000 population; Property crime rate: 199.7 per 10,000 population (2008).
Newspapers: Paper (Local news; Circulation 16,225); The Paper of Wabash County (Local news; Circulation 16,225); Wabash Plain Dealer (Local news; Circulation 7,000)
Transportation: Commute to work: 95.3% car, 0.2% public transportation, 1.9% walk, 1.9% work from home (2000); Travel time to work: 65.1% less than 15 minutes, 17.3% 15 to 30 minutes, 10.0% 30 to 45 minutes, 3.4% 45 to 60 minutes, 4.2% 60 minutes or more (2000)
Additional Information Contacts
City of Wabash. . . . . (260) 563-4171
　http://www.cityofwabash.com
Wabash Chamber of Commerce . . . . (260) 563-1168
　http://www.wabashchamber.org

Warren County

Located in western Indiana; bounded on the west by Illinois, and on the southeast by the Wabash River. Covers a land area of 364.88 square miles, a water area of 1.72 square miles, and is located in the Eastern Time Zone. The county was founded in 1827. County seat is Williamsport.
Population: 8,176 (1990); 8,419 (2000); 8,549 (2010); 8,544 (2015 projected); Race: 98.2% White, 0.3% Black, 0.4% Asian, 1.1% Other, 1.1% Hispanic of any race (2010); Density: 23.4 persons per square mile (2010); Average household size: 2.52 (2010); Median age: 40.6 (2010); Males per 100 females: 101.2 (2010).
Religion: Five largest groups: 19.5% Christian Churches and Churches of Christ, 9.6% The United Methodist Church, 5.3% Independent, Non-Charismatic Churches, 2.8% Catholic Church, 2.2% Church of the Nazarene (2000).
Economy: Unemployment rate: 8.8% (5/2010); Total civilian labor force: 4,887 (5/2010); Leading industries: 10.0% wholesale trade; 4.9% construction; 3.0% accommodation & food services (2008); Farms: 391 totaling 195,930 acres (2007); Companies that employ 500 or more persons: 0 (2008); Companies that employ 100 to 499 persons: 3 (2008); Companies that employ less than 100 persons: 124 (2008); Black-owned businesses: n/a (2002); Hispanic-owned businesses: n/a (2002); Asian-owned businesses: n/a (2002); Women-owned businesses: 198

(2002); Retail sales per capita: $4,383 (2010). Single-family building permits issued: 16 (2009); Multi-family building permits issued: 0 (2009).
Income: Per capita income: $23,856 (2010); Median household income: $52,673 (2010); Average household income: $60,656 (2010); Percent of households with income of $100,000 or more: 13.1% (2010); Poverty rate: 8.8% (2008); Bankruptcy rate: 5.16% (2009).
Taxes: Total county taxes per capita: $371 (2007); County property taxes per capita: $251 (2007).
Education: Percent of population age 25 and over with: High school diploma (including GED) or higher: 88.9% (2010); Bachelor's degree or higher: 14.5% (2010); Master's degree or higher: 5.1% (2010).
Housing: Homeownership rate: 80.0% (2010); Median home value: $101,244 (2010); Median contract rent: $n/a per month (2006-2008 3-year est.); Median year structure built: n/a (2006-2008 3-year est.)
Health: Birth rate: 102.5 per 10,000 population (2009); Death rate: 115.4 per 10,000 population (2009); Age-adjusted cancer mortality rate: 206.7 deaths per 100,000 population (2006); Number of physicians: 1.2 per 10,000 population (2007); Hospital beds: 18.6 per 10,000 population (2006); Hospital admissions: 747.7 per 10,000 population (2006).
Elections: 2008 Presidential election results: 43.9% Obama, 54.2% McCain, 0.0% Nader
Additional Information Contacts
Warren County Government . . . . (765) 762-3510
    http://warrenadvantage.com

Warren County Communities

PINE VILLAGE (town). Covers a land area of 0.126 square miles and a water area of 0 square miles. Located at 40.45° N. Lat; 87.25° W. Long. Elevation is 692 feet.
Population: 133 (1990); 255 (2000); 258 (2010); 258 (2015 projected); Race: 99.2% White, 0.0% Black, 0.0% Asian, 0.8% Other, 0.8% Hispanic of any race (2010); Density: 2,055.4 persons per square mile (2010); Average household size: 2.41 (2010); Median age: 41.0 (2010); Males per 100 females: 96.9 (2010); Marriage status: 24.8% never married, 51.8% now married, 7.1% widowed, 16.4% divorced (2000); Foreign born: 1.6% (2000); Ancestry (includes multiple ancestries): 18.1% United States or American, 17.3% Irish, 16.1% German, 10.2% English, 6.3% Other groups (2000).
Economy: Employment by occupation: 15.9% management, 6.9% professional, 9.0% services, 19.3% sales, 2.1% farming, 11.7% construction, 35.2% production (2000).
Income: Per capita income: $24,594 (2010); Median household income: $47,981 (2010); Average household income: $57,009 (2010); Percent of households with income of $100,000 or more: 12.1% (2010); Poverty rate: 7.1% (2000).
Taxes: Total city taxes per capita: $181 (2007); City property taxes per capita: $149 (2007).
Education: Percent of population age 25 and over with: High school diploma (including GED) or higher: 88.8% (2010); Bachelor's degree or higher: 15.1% (2010); Master's degree or higher: 7.3% (2010).
School District(s)
M S D Warren County (KG-12)
    2008-09 Enrollment: 1,276 . . . . (765) 762-3364
Housing: Homeownership rate: 77.6% (2010); Median home value: $99,231 (2010); Median contract rent: $380 per month (2000); Median year structure built: before 1940 (2000).
Transportation: Commute to work: 84.9% car, 0.0% public transportation, 5.5% walk, 4.8% work from home (2000); Travel time to work: 22.3% less than 15 minutes, 25.9% 15 to 30 minutes, 33.8% 30 to 45 minutes, 10.1% 45 to 60 minutes, 7.9% 60 minutes or more (2000)

STATE LINE CITY (town). Aka State Line. Covers a land area of 0.135 square miles and a water area of 0 square miles. Located at 40.19° N. Lat; 87.52° W. Long. Elevation is 725 feet.
Population: 192 (1990); 141 (2000); 155 (2010); 160 (2015 projected); Race: 96.8% White, 0.6% Black, 1.9% Asian, 0.6% Other, 0.0% Hispanic of any race (2010); Density: 1,150.9 persons per square mile (2010); Average household size: 2.50 (2010); Median age: 44.8 (2010); Males per 100 females: 106.7 (2010); Marriage status: 26.5% never married, 65.5% now married, 5.3% widowed, 2.7% divorced (2000); Foreign born: 0.0% (2000); Ancestry (includes multiple ancestries): 26.1% Irish, 23.9% German, 9.0% English, 6.7% United States or American, 4.5% Other groups (2000).

Economy: Employment by occupation: 1.6% management, 10.9% professional, 14.1% services, 29.7% sales, 0.0% farming, 9.4% construction, 34.4% production (2000).
Income: Per capita income: $26,254 (2010); Median household income: $61,667 (2010); Average household income: $68,952 (2010); Percent of households with income of $100,000 or more: 17.7% (2010); Poverty rate: 3.7% (2000).
Taxes: Total city taxes per capita: $165 (2007); City property taxes per capita: $151 (2007).
Education: Percent of population age 25 and over with: High school diploma (including GED) or higher: 94.7% (2010); Bachelor's degree or higher: 18.4% (2010); Master's degree or higher: 5.3% (2010).
Housing: Homeownership rate: 90.3% (2010); Median home value: $121,429 (2010); Median contract rent: $275 per month (2000); Median year structure built: 1955 (2000).
Transportation: Commute to work: 86.4% car, 3.4% public transportation, 0.0% walk, 10.2% work from home (2000); Travel time to work: 37.7% less than 15 minutes, 47.2% 15 to 30 minutes, 1.9% 30 to 45 minutes, 0.0% 45 to 60 minutes, 13.2% 60 minutes or more (2000)

WEST LEBANON (town). Covers a land area of 0.616 square miles and a water area of 0 square miles. Located at 40.27° N. Lat; 87.38° W. Long. Elevation is 712 feet.
History: Laid out 1830.
Population: 826 (1990); 793 (2000); 792 (2010); 788 (2015 projected); Race: 98.0% White, 0.0% Black, 0.4% Asian, 1.6% Other, 1.6% Hispanic of any race (2010); Density: 1,285.5 persons per square mile (2010); Average household size: 2.56 (2010); Median age: 39.3 (2010); Males per 100 females: 102.6 (2010); Marriage status: 18.9% never married, 58.8% now married, 6.9% widowed, 15.4% divorced (2000); Foreign born: 0.4% (2000); Ancestry (includes multiple ancestries): 16.1% German, 11.4% United States or American, 11.2% Other groups, 8.6% Irish, 8.2% English (2000).
Economy: Employment by occupation: 6.9% management, 11.1% professional, 12.0% services, 16.9% sales, 0.6% farming, 16.0% construction, 36.6% production (2000).
Income: Per capita income: $26,024 (2010); Median household income: $53,860 (2010); Average household income: $67,613 (2010); Percent of households with income of $100,000 or more: 15.5% (2010); Poverty rate: 8.1% (2000).
Taxes: Total city taxes per capita: $98 (2007); City property taxes per capita: $92 (2007).
Education: Percent of population age 25 and over with: High school diploma (including GED) or higher: 87.1% (2010); Bachelor's degree or higher: 15.7% (2010); Master's degree or higher: 6.5% (2010).
School District(s)
M S D Warren County (KG-12)
    2008-09 Enrollment: 1,276 . . . . (765) 762-3364
Housing: Homeownership rate: 79.0% (2010); Median home value: $99,583 (2010); Median contract rent: $237 per month (2000); Median year structure built: 1960 (2000).
Transportation: Commute to work: 96.3% car, 0.0% public transportation, 0.6% walk, 2.0% work from home (2000); Travel time to work: 38.8% less than 15 minutes, 31.5% 15 to 30 minutes, 13.2% 30 to 45 minutes, 9.4% 45 to 60 minutes, 7.1% 60 minutes or more (2000)

WILLIAMSPORT (town). County seat. Covers a land area of 1.053 square miles and a water area of 0 square miles. Located at 40.28° N. Lat; 87.29° W. Long. Elevation is 659 feet.
History: The land on which Williamsport was founded was owned by General William Henry Harrison. A spur of the Wabash & Erie Canal was built to Williamsport, giving an early boost to commerce and bringing the nickname of Side Cut City.
Population: 1,807 (1990); 1,935 (2000); 1,847 (2010); 1,804 (2015 projected); Race: 99.0% White, 0.3% Black, 0.2% Asian, 0.5% Other, 0.5% Hispanic of any race (2010); Density: 1,754.8 persons per square mile (2010); Average household size: 2.38 (2010); Median age: 39.6 (2010); Males per 100 females: 94.0 (2010); Marriage status: 18.6% never married, 58.0% now married, 13.1% widowed, 10.3% divorced (2000); Foreign born: 0.3% (2000); Ancestry (includes multiple ancestries): 18.4% United States or American, 16.4% German, 8.5% English, 6.5% Irish, 6.1% Other groups (2000).
Economy: Employment by occupation: 7.1% management, 12.7% professional, 16.6% services, 21.0% sales, 1.1% farming, 8.1% construction, 33.5% production (2000).

Income: Per capita income: $23,316 (2010); Median household income: $50,064 (2010); Average household income: $57,244 (2010); Percent of households with income of $100,000 or more: 10.5% (2010); Poverty rate: 5.4% (2000).
Taxes: Total city taxes per capita: $121 (2007); City property taxes per capita: $104 (2007).
Education: Percent of population age 25 and over with: High school diploma (including GED) or higher: 84.7% (2010); Bachelor's degree or higher: 8.0% (2010); Master's degree or higher: 3.0% (2010).

School District(s)
M S D Warren County (KG-12)
    2008-09 Enrollment: 1,276 . . . . (765) 762-3364
Housing: Homeownership rate: 71.1% (2010); Median home value: $87,889 (2010); Median contract rent: $330 per month (2000); Median year structure built: 1959 (2000).
Hospitals: St Vincent Williamsport (16 beds)
Newspapers: Review-Republican (Community news; Circulation 3,700)
Transportation: Commute to work: 95.3% car, 0.0% public transportation, 2.0% walk, 1.9% work from home (2000); Travel time to work: 52.4% less than 15 minutes, 14.3% 15 to 30 minutes, 12.3% 30 to 45 minutes, 14.6% 45 to 60 minutes, 6.4% 60 minutes or more (2000)

Warrick County

Located in southwestern Indiana; bounded on the south by the Ohio River and the Kentucky border. Covers a land area of 384.07 square miles, a water area of 6.79 square miles, and is located in the Central Time Zone. The county was founded in 1813. County seat is Boonville.

Warrick County is part of the Evansville, IN-KY Metropolitan Statistical Area. The entire metro area includes: Gibson County, IN; Posey County, IN; Vanderburgh County, IN; Warrick County, IN; Henderson County, KY; Webster County, KY

Population: 44,920 (1990); 52,383 (2000); 58,654 (2010); 61,381 (2015 projected); Race: 96.1% White, 1.5% Black, 1.1% Asian, 1.3% Other, 1.3% Hispanic of any race (2010); Density: 152.7 persons per square mile (2010); Average household size: 2.58 (2010); Median age: 39.0 (2010); Males per 100 females: 97.2 (2010).
Religion: Five largest groups: 13.2% Catholic Church, 6.3% The United Methodist Church, 4.9% Southern Baptist Convention, 3.1% United Church of Christ, 1.8% Christian Churches and Churches of Christ (2000).
Economy: Unemployment rate: 7.3% (5/2010); Total civilian labor force: 29,962 (5/2010); Leading industries: 19.1% health care and social assistance; 11.5% retail trade; 9.7% construction (2008); Farms: 413 totaling 109,932 acres (2007); Companies that employ 500 or more persons: 3 (2008); Companies that employ 100 to 499 persons: 12 (2008); Companies that employ less than 100 persons: 1,114 (2008); Black-owned businesses: n/a (2002); Hispanic-owned businesses: n/a (2002); Asian-owned businesses: n/a (2002); Women-owned businesses: 1,263 (2002); Retail sales per capita: $5,963 (2010). Single-family building permits issued: 172 (2009); Multi-family building permits issued: 2 (2009).
Income: Per capita income: $28,690 (2010); Median household income: $62,111 (2010); Average household income: $74,762 (2010); Percent of households with income of $100,000 or more: 22.0% (2010); Poverty rate: 7.7% (2008); Bankruptcy rate: 6.15% (2009).
Taxes: Total county taxes per capita: $234 (2007); County property taxes per capita: $183 (2007).
Education: Percent of population age 25 and over with: High school diploma (including GED) or higher: 91.2% (2010); Bachelor's degree or higher: 24.7% (2010); Master's degree or higher: 9.7% (2010).
Housing: Homeownership rate: 82.6% (2010); Median home value: $131,099 (2010); Median contract rent: $565 per month (2006-2008 3-year est.); Median year structure built: 1979 (2006-2008 3-year est.)
Health: Birth rate: 124.7 per 10,000 population (2009); Death rate: 86.5 per 10,000 population (2009); Age-adjusted cancer mortality rate: 211.2 deaths per 100,000 population (2006); Air Quality Index: 89.8% good, 9.9% moderate, 0.4% unhealthy for sensitive individuals, 0.0% unhealthy (percent of days in 2008); Number of physicians: 31.0 per 10,000 population (2007); Hospital beds: 18.9 per 10,000 population (2006); Hospital admissions: 903.7 per 10,000 population (2006).
Elections: 2008 Presidential election results: 43.0% Obama, 55.9% McCain, 0.0% Nader
Additional Information Contacts
Warrick County Government . . . . (812) 897-6160
    http://www.warrickcounty.gov

City of Boonville . . . . (812) 897-6543
    http://www.cityofboonevilleindiana.com
Town of Chandler . . . . (812) 925-6882
    http://www.townofchandler.org
Town of Newburgh . . . . (812) 853-3578
    http://www.newburgh.org
Warrick County Department Economic Development . . . . . (812) 858-3555
    http://www.warick-edd.org

Warrick County Communities

BOONVILLE (city). County seat. Covers a land area of 2.947 square miles and a water area of 0.018 square miles. Located at 38.04° N. Lat; 87.27° W. Long. Elevation is 423 feet.
History: Boonville was laid out in 1818 as a coal-mining and farming center at a place where several wagon trails crossed. It was named for Jesse Boon, the father of Ratliff Boon who was the first treasurer of Warrick County, the first state representative from Warrick County in 1816, and a representative in Congress from 1825-1839.
Population: 6,893 (1990); 6,834 (2000); 6,835 (2010); 6,863 (2015 projected); Race: 98.2% White, 0.6% Black, 0.1% Asian, 1.1% Other, 0.8% Hispanic of any race (2010); Density: 2,319.3 persons per square mile (2010); Average household size: 2.39 (2010); Median age: 38.1 (2010); Males per 100 females: 91.9 (2010); Marriage status: 20.9% never married, 56.2% now married, 13.5% widowed, 9.4% divorced (2000); Foreign born: 0.4% (2000); Ancestry (includes multiple ancestries): 21.3% German, 20.3% United States or American, 9.5% Irish, 6.7% English, 5.0% Other groups (2000).
Economy: Single-family building permits issued: 0 (2009); Multi-family building permits issued: 0 (2009); Employment by occupation: 8.1% management, 15.2% professional, 16.5% services, 24.7% sales, 0.4% farming, 15.1% construction, 20.0% production (2000).
Income: Per capita income: $20,607 (2010); Median household income: $42,462 (2010); Average household income: $49,690 (2010); Percent of households with income of $100,000 or more: 8.6% (2010); Poverty rate: 9.2% (2000).
Taxes: Total city taxes per capita: $349 (2007); City property taxes per capita: $210 (2007).
Education: Percent of population age 25 and over with: High school diploma (including GED) or higher: 85.2% (2010); Bachelor's degree or higher: 15.5% (2010); Master's degree or higher: 7.1% (2010).

School District(s)
Warrick County School Corp (KG-12)
    2008-09 Enrollment: 9,647 . . . . (812) 897-0400
Housing: Homeownership rate: 71.5% (2010); Median home value: $87,335 (2010); Median contract rent: $358 per month (2000); Median year structure built: 1958 (2000).
Hospitals: St. Mary's Warrick Hospital (25 beds)
Safety: Violent crime rate: 0.0 per 10,000 population; Property crime rate: 269.6 per 10,000 population (2008).
Newspapers: Boonville Standard (Community news; Circulation 4,465); The Warrick East (Community news; Circulation 4,453); The Warrick West Shopper (Community news)
Transportation: Commute to work: 95.9% car, 0.3% public transportation, 1.8% walk, 1.4% work from home (2000); Travel time to work: 40.4% less than 15 minutes, 21.7% 15 to 30 minutes, 26.3% 30 to 45 minutes, 8.0% 45 to 60 minutes, 3.6% 60 minutes or more (2000)
Additional Information Contacts
City of Boonville . . . . (812) 897-6543
    http://www.cityofbooneyilleindiana.com
Warrick County Department Economic Development . . . . . (812) 858-3555
    http://www.warick-edd.org

CHANDLER (town). Covers a land area of 1.689 square miles and a water area of 0 square miles. Located at 38.04° N. Lat; 87.36° W. Long. Elevation is 413 feet.
Population: 3,239 (1990); 3,094 (2000); 2,891 (2010); 2,867 (2015 projected); Race: 98.1% White, 0.7% Black, 0.1% Asian, 1.2% Other, 0.9% Hispanic of any race (2010); Density: 1,711.7 persons per square mile (2010); Average household size: 2.54 (2010); Median age: 37.3 (2010); Males per 100 females: 98.1 (2010); Marriage status: 20.3% never married, 62.0% now married, 6.6% widowed, 11.0% divorced (2000); Foreign born: 0.2% (2000); Ancestry (includes multiple ancestries): 16.7% German, 13.1% United States or American, 10.6% Irish, 9.3% English, 6.3% Other groups (2000).

Economy: Single-family building permits issued: 8 (2009); Multi-family building permits issued: 0 (2009); Employment by occupation: 3.4% management, 4.5% professional, 19.5% services, 28.2% sales, 0.7% farming, 14.7% construction, 28.9% production (2000).
Income: Per capita income: $21,600 (2010); Median household income: $47,716 (2010); Average household income: $55,397 (2010); Percent of households with income of $100,000 or more: 8.5% (2010); Poverty rate: 14.1% (2000).
Taxes: Total city taxes per capita: $120 (2007); City property taxes per capita: $77 (2007).
Education: Percent of population age 25 and over with: High school diploma (including GED) or higher: 81.9% (2010); Bachelor's degree or higher: 6.5% (2010); Master's degree or higher: 1.9% (2010).

School District(s)

Warrick County School Corp (KG-12)
    2008-09 Enrollment: 9,647 . . . . (812) 897-0400
Housing: Homeownership rate: 81.4% (2010); Median home value: $78,475 (2010); Median contract rent: $328 per month (2000); Median year structure built: 1966 (2000).
Transportation: Commute to work: 96.1% car, 0.0% public transportation, 1.8% walk, 0.5% work from home (2000); Travel time to work: 20.2% less than 15 minutes, 49.0% 15 to 30 minutes, 21.4% 30 to 45 minutes, 4.4% 45 to 60 minutes, 5.0% 60 minutes or more (2000)
Additional Information Contacts
Town of Chandler. . . . . (812) 925-6882
    http://www.townofchandler.org

ELBERFELD (town). Covers a land area of 0.310 square miles and a water area of 0 square miles. Located at 38.16° N. Lat; 87.44° W. Long. Elevation is 453 feet.

Population: 692 (1990); 636 (2000); 774 (2010); 836 (2015 projected); Race: 99.5% White, 0.0% Black, 0.1% Asian, 0.4% Other, 0.4% Hispanic of any race (2010); Density: 2,495.7 persons per square mile (2010); Average household size: 2.57 (2010); Median age: 40.2 (2010); Males per 100 females: 103.1 (2010); Marriage status: 19.8% never married, 61.8% now married, 7.1% widowed, 11.2% divorced (2000); Foreign born: 0.3% (2000); Ancestry (includes multiple ancestries): 37.5% German, 18.4% United States or American, 9.3% Irish, 8.8% English, 7.4% Other groups (2000).
Economy: Employment by occupation: 6.3% management, 11.7% professional, 19.5% services, 27.6% sales, 0.6% farming, 14.1% construction, 20.1% production (2000).
Income: Per capita income: $24,701 (2010); Median household income: $51,599 (2010); Average household income: $61,827 (2010); Percent of households with income of $100,000 or more: 11.6% (2010); Poverty rate: 4.2% (2000).
Taxes: Total city taxes per capita: $124 (2007); City property taxes per capita: $68 (2007).
Education: Percent of population age 25 and over with: High school diploma (including GED) or higher: 90.4% (2010); Bachelor's degree or higher: 12.6% (2010); Master's degree or higher: 4.8% (2010).

School District(s)

Warrick County School Corp (KG-12)
    2008-09 Enrollment: 9,647 . . . . (812) 897-0400
Housing: Homeownership rate: 82.7% (2010); Median home value: $116,053 (2010); Median contract rent: $266 per month (2000); Median year structure built: 1954 (2000).
Transportation: Commute to work: 93.7% car, 0.3% public transportation, 1.8% walk, 3.6% work from home (2000); Travel time to work: 14.0% less than 15 minutes, 42.4% 15 to 30 minutes, 35.2% 30 to 45 minutes, 4.4% 45 to 60 minutes, 4.0% 60 minutes or more (2000)

LYNNVILLE (town). Covers a land area of 1.707 square miles and a water area of 0.229 square miles. Located at 38.20° N. Lat; 87.31° W. Long. Elevation is 463 feet.

Population: 640 (1990); 781 (2000); 1,053 (2010); 1,161 (2015 projected); Race: 98.9% White, 0.0% Black, 0.2% Asian, 0.9% Other, 0.0% Hispanic of any race (2010); Density: 616.8 persons per square mile (2010); Average household size: 2.33 (2010); Median age: 40.6 (2010); Males per 100 females: 105.3 (2010); Marriage status: 18.0% never married, 61.4% now married, 8.6% widowed, 12.0% divorced (2000); Foreign born: 0.0% (2000); Ancestry (includes multiple ancestries): 25.2% United States or American, 15.7% German, 13.4% Irish, 10.3% English, 7.6% Other groups (2000).

Economy: Employment by occupation: 5.7% management, 12.5% professional, 18.8% services, 21.4% sales, 0.6% farming, 14.0% construction, 27.1% production (2000).
Income: Per capita income: $23,055 (2010); Median household income: $48,036 (2010); Average household income: $53,628 (2010); Percent of households with income of $100,000 or more: 8.6% (2010); Poverty rate: 8.0% (2000).
Taxes: Total city taxes per capita: $82 (2007); City property taxes per capita: $50 (2007).
Education: Percent of population age 25 and over with: High school diploma (including GED) or higher: 88.2% (2010); Bachelor's degree or higher: 12.1% (2010); Master's degree or higher: 7.3% (2010).

School District(s)

Warrick County School Corp (KG-12)
    2008-09 Enrollment: 9,647 . . . . (812) 897-0400
Housing: Homeownership rate: 79.9% (2010); Median home value: $95,870 (2010); Median contract rent: $287 per month (2000); Median year structure built: 1967 (2000).
Transportation: Commute to work: 98.2% car, 0.0% public transportation, 1.2% walk, 0.6% work from home (2000); Travel time to work: 16.6% less than 15 minutes, 25.6% 15 to 30 minutes, 37.3% 30 to 45 minutes, 14.5% 45 to 60 minutes, 6.0% 60 minutes or more (2000)

NEWBURGH (town). Aka House Estates. Covers a land area of 1.358 square miles and a water area of 0.002 square miles. Located at 37.94° N. Lat; 87.40° W. Long. Elevation is 394 feet.

History: Settled 1803, laid out 1818.
Population: 3,189 (1990); 3,088 (2000); 2,841 (2010); 2,749 (2015 projected); Race: 94.8% White, 2.4% Black, 1.2% Asian, 1.5% Other, 1.1% Hispanic of any race (2010); Density: 2,092.7 persons per square mile (2010); Average household size: 2.27 (2010); Median age: 40.0 (2010); Males per 100 females: 95.5 (2010); Marriage status: 18.8% never married, 61.1% now married, 7.4% widowed, 12.6% divorced (2000); Foreign born: 1.3% (2000); Ancestry (includes multiple ancestries): 29.6% German, 14.9% Irish, 14.4% English, 11.7% United States or American, 6.1% Other groups (2000).
Economy: Single-family building permits issued: 3 (2009); Multi-family building permits issued: 0 (2009); Employment by occupation: 16.6% management, 19.7% professional, 17.1% services, 26.4% sales, 0.0% farming, 4.9% construction, 15.2% production (2000).
Income: Per capita income: $35,023 (2010); Median household income: $58,333 (2010); Average household income: $80,066 (2010); Percent of households with income of $100,000 or more: 22.7% (2010); Poverty rate: 2.5% (2000).
Taxes: Total city taxes per capita: $201 (2007); City property taxes per capita: $135 (2007).
Education: Percent of population age 25 and over with: High school diploma (including GED) or higher: 94.5% (2010); Bachelor's degree or higher: 38.6% (2010); Master's degree or higher: 11.6% (2010).

School District(s)

Warrick County School Corp (KG-12)
    2008-09 Enrollment: 9,647 . . . . (812) 897-0400

Four-year College(s)

ITT Technical Institute-Newburgh (Private, For-profit)
    Fall 2008 Enrollment: 442 . . . . (812) 858-1600
    2009-10 Tuition: In-state $17,148; Out-of-state $17,148
Trinity College of the Bible and Trinity Theological Seminary (Private, Not-for-profit)
    Fall 2008 Enrollment: 5,518. . . . . (812) 853-0611
Housing: Homeownership rate: 68.2% (2010); Median home value: $138,834 (2010); Median contract rent: $346 per month (2000); Median year structure built: 1966 (2000).
Hospitals: Women's Hospital
Newspapers: Newburgh-Chandler Register (Community news; Circulation 2,736)
Transportation: Commute to work: 97.3% car, 0.0% public transportation, 1.1% walk, 1.6% work from home (2000); Travel time to work: 24.9% less than 15 minutes, 56.8% 15 to 30 minutes, 11.7% 30 to 45 minutes, 3.7% 45 to 60 minutes, 2.9% 60 minutes or more (2000)
Additional Information Contacts
Town of Newburgh. . . . . (812) 853-3578
    http://www.newburgh.org

TENNYSON (town). Covers a land area of 0.251 square miles and a water area of 0 square miles. Located at 38.08° N. Lat; 87.11° W. Long. Elevation is 407 feet.

Population: 267 (1990); 290 (2000); 412 (2010); 459 (2015 projected); Race: 99.3% White, 0.2% Black, 0.0% Asian, 0.5% Other, 0.5% Hispanic of any race (2010); Density: 1,641.0 persons per square mile (2010); Average household size: 2.77 (2010); Median age: 35.0 (2010); Males per 100 females: 102.0 (2010); Marriage status: 28.4% never married, 48.3% now married, 9.0% widowed, 14.4% divorced (2000); Foreign born: 0.0% (2000); Ancestry (includes multiple ancestries): 17.9% German, 15.4% United States or American, 10.9% English, 7.0% Irish, 6.3% Other groups (2000).

Economy: Employment by occupation: 8.4% management, 4.2% professional, 22.7% services, 8.4% sales, 0.0% farming, 18.5% construction, 37.8% production (2000).

Income: Per capita income: $22,742 (2010); Median household income: $59,451 (2010); Average household income: $62,768 (2010); Percent of households with income of $100,000 or more: 10.7% (2010); Poverty rate: 16.8% (2000).

Taxes: Total city taxes per capita: $60 (2007); City property taxes per capita: $47 (2007).

Education: Percent of population age 25 and over with: High school diploma (including GED) or higher: 81.7% (2010); Bachelor's degree or higher: 6.0% (2010); Master's degree or higher: 0.0% (2010).

School District(s)

Warrick County School Corp (KG-12)

   2008-09 Enrollment: 9,647 . . . . (812) 897-0400

Housing: Homeownership rate: 79.9% (2010); Median home value: $94,375 (2010); Median contract rent: $181 per month (2000); Median year structure built: 1969 (2000).

Transportation: Commute to work: 86.6% car, 0.0% public transportation, 4.2% walk, 5.9% work from home (2000); Travel time to work: 8.0% less than 15 minutes, 30.4% 15 to 30 minutes, 36.6% 30 to 45 minutes, 15.2% 45 to 60 minutes, 9.8% 60 minutes or more (2000)

Washington County

Located in southern Indiana; bounded on the north by the Muscatatuck River and the East Fork of the White River; drained by the Blue and Lost Rivers. Covers a land area of 514.42 square miles, a water area of 2.12 square miles, and is located in the Eastern Time Zone. The county was founded in 1813. County seat is Salem.

Washington County is part of the Louisville/Jefferson County, KY-IN Metropolitan Statistical Area. The entire metro area includes: Clark County, IN; Floyd County, IN; Harrison County, IN; Washington County, IN; Bullitt County, KY; Henry County, KY; Jefferson County, KY; Meade County, KY; Nelson County, KY; Oldham County, KY; Shelby County, KY; Spencer County, KY; Trimble County, KY

Weather Station: Salem										Elevation: 797 feet		
	Jan	Feb	Mar	Apr	May	Jun	Jul	Aug	Sep	Oct	Nov	Dec
High	39	45	55	67	76	84	87	86	80	69	55	44
Low	22	25	33	42	52	61	65	63	56	44	36	27
Precip	3.2	2.9	4.3	4.7	5.1	3.9	4.4	3.5	2.9	2.9	4.0	3.9
Snow	5.7	5.6	3.4	0.2	0.0	0.0	0.0	0.0	0.0	0.2	0.5	2.4

High and Low temperatures in degrees Fahrenheit; Precipitation and Snow in inches

Population: 23,717 (1990); 27,223 (2000); 28,055 (2010); 28,262 (2015 projected); Race: 98.0% White, 0.5% Black, 0.3% Asian, 1.2% Other, 1.0% Hispanic of any race (2010); Density: 54.5 persons per square mile (2010); Average household size: 2.57 (2010); Median age: 38.3 (2010); Males per 100 females: 100.6 (2010).

Religion: Five largest groups: 13.8% Christian Churches and Churches of Christ, 7.4% American Baptist Churches in the USA, 5.9% Churches of Christ, 4.2% The United Methodist Church, 3.8% Christian Church (Disciples of Christ) (2000).

Economy: Unemployment rate: 9.3% (5/2010); Total civilian labor force: 13,550 (5/2010); Leading industries: 33.0% manufacturing; 15.7% retail trade; 14.7% health care and social assistance (2008); Farms: 893 totaling 199,942 acres (2007); Companies that employ 500 or more persons: 0 (2008); Companies that employ 100 to 499 persons: 9 (2008); Companies that employ less than 100 persons: 479 (2008); Black-owned businesses: n/a (2002); Hispanic-owned businesses: n/a (2002); Asian-owned businesses: n/a (2002); Women-owned businesses: 586 (2002); Retail

sales per capita: $8,880 (2010). Single-family building permits issued: 30 (2009); Multi-family building permits issued: 4 (2009).

Income: Per capita income: $19,691 (2010); Median household income: $41,741 (2010); Average household income: $50,586 (2010); Percent of households with income of $100,000 or more: 8.0% (2010); Poverty rate: 13.9% (2008); Bankruptcy rate: 10.24% (2009).

Taxes: Total county taxes per capita: $227 (2007); County property taxes per capita: $122 (2007).

Education: Percent of population age 25 and over with: High school diploma (including GED) or higher: 79.9% (2010); Bachelor's degree or higher: 9.9% (2010); Master's degree or higher: 4.4% (2010).

Housing: Homeownership rate: 77.2% (2010); Median home value: $92,856 (2010); Median contract rent: $329 per month (2006-2008 3-year est.); Median year structure built: 1976 (2006-2008 3-year est.)

Health: Birth rate: 121.9 per 10,000 population (2009); Death rate: 101.0 per 10,000 population (2009); Age-adjusted cancer mortality rate: 218.7 deaths per 100,000 population (2006); Number of physicians: 5.7 per 10,000 population (2007); Hospital beds: 12.6 per 10,000 population (2006); Hospital admissions: 382.5 per 10,000 population (2006).

Elections: 2008 Presidential election results: 40.4% Obama, 57.7% McCain, 0.0% Nader

National and State Parks: Clark State Forest; Jackson-Washington State Forest

Additional Information Contacts

Washington County Government . . . . (812) 883-5748
   http://www.washingtoncountyindiana.com
City of Salem . . . . (812) 883-4264
   http://www.cityofsalemin.com

Washington County Communities

CAMPBELLSBURG (town). Covers a land area of 0.978 square miles and a water area of 0 square miles. Located at 38.65° N. Lat; 86.26° W. Long. Elevation is 827 feet.

Population: 606 (1990); 578 (2000); 577 (2010); 574 (2015 projected); Race: 97.9% White, 0.0% Black, 0.0% Asian, 2.1% Other, 0.9% Hispanic of any race (2010); Density: 590.2 persons per square mile (2010); Average household size: 2.47 (2010); Median age: 35.6 (2010); Males per 100 females: 107.6 (2010); Marriage status: 29.4% never married, 49.8% now married, 11.9% widowed, 8.9% divorced (2000); Foreign born: 0.0% (2000); Ancestry (includes multiple ancestries): 15.1% United States or American, 11.1% English, 8.4% Other groups, 7.8% Irish, 7.3% German (2000).

Economy: Employment by occupation: 3.3% management, 11.4% professional, 13.8% services, 8.1% sales, 1.6% farming, 14.6% construction, 47.2% production (2000).

Income: Per capita income: $17,565 (2010); Median household income: $33,214 (2010); Average household income: $43,942 (2010); Percent of households with income of $100,000 or more: 6.4% (2010); Poverty rate: 15.3% (2000).

Taxes: Total city taxes per capita: $19 (2007); City property taxes per capita: $2 (2007).

Education: Percent of population age 25 and over with: High school diploma (including GED) or higher: 78.0% (2010); Bachelor's degree or higher: 8.6% (2010); Master's degree or higher: 6.0% (2010).

School District(s)

West Washington School Corp (KG-12)

   2008-09 Enrollment: 896 . . . . (812) 755-4872

Housing: Homeownership rate: 68.4% (2010); Median home value: $72,632 (2010); Median contract rent: $258 per month (2000); Median year structure built: 1960 (2000).

Transportation: Commute to work: 95.0% car, 0.0% public transportation, 4.2% walk, 0.8% work from home (2000); Travel time to work: 32.6% less than 15 minutes, 44.1% 15 to 30 minutes, 8.9% 30 to 45 minutes, 6.4% 45 to 60 minutes, 8.1% 60 minutes or more (2000)

FREDERICKSBURG (town). Covers a land area of 1.003 square miles and a water area of 0 square miles. Located at 38.43° N. Lat; 86.19° W. Long. Elevation is 614 feet.

History: Fredericksburg was settled in 1805 and became a toll station on the plank road between New Albany and Vincennes. Many of the settlers here were Quakers who built the Lick Creek Friends Church in 1815.

Population: 75 (1990); 92 (2000); 96 (2010); 97 (2015 projected); Race: 94.8% White, 3.1% Black, 0.0% Asian, 2.1% Other, 2.1% Hispanic of any race (2010); Density: 95.7 persons per square mile (2010); Average household size: 2.67 (2010); Median age: 41.0 (2010); Males per 100 females: 113.3 (2010); Marriage status: 23.9% never married, 47.7% now married, 5.7% widowed, 22.7% divorced (2000); Foreign born: 0.0% (2000); Ancestry (includes multiple ancestries): 17.3% United States or American, 13.3% French (except Basque), 12.2% German, 11.2% Irish, 11.2% Other groups (2000).

Economy: Employment by occupation: 7.7% management, 0.0% professional, 15.4% services, 20.5% sales, 0.0% farming, 25.6% construction, 30.8% production (2000).

Income: Per capita income: $14,490 (2010); Median household income: $33,333 (2010); Average household income: $35,069 (2010); Percent of households with income of $100,000 or more: 0.0% (2010); Poverty rate: 23.5% (2000).

Taxes: Total city taxes per capita: $32 (2007); City property taxes per capita: $32 (2007).

Education: Percent of population age 25 and over with: High school diploma (including GED) or higher: 80.3% (2010); Bachelor's degree or higher: 8.5% (2010); Master's degree or higher: 2.8% (2010).

Housing: Homeownership rate: 83.3% (2010); Median home value: $100,000 (2010); Median contract rent: $361 per month (2000); Median year structure built: 1957 (2000).

Transportation: Commute to work: 97.3% car, 0.0% public transportation, 0.0% walk, 2.7% work from home (2000); Travel time to work: 0.0% less than 15 minutes, 19.4% 15 to 30 minutes, 55.6% 30 to 45 minutes, 25.0% 45 to 60 minutes, 0.0% 60 minutes or more (2000)

HARDINSBURG (town).
Covers a land area of 2.039 square miles and a water area of 0 square miles. Located at 38.46° N. Lat; 86.27° W. Long. Elevation is 689 feet.

History: Laid out 1838.

Population: 322 (1990); 244 (2000); 223 (2010); 224 (2015 projected); Race: 98.7% White, 0.4% Black, 0.0% Asian, 0.9% Other, 1.8% Hispanic of any race (2010); Density: 109.4 persons per square mile (2010); Average household size: 2.65 (2010); Median age: 37.3 (2010); Males per 100 females: 102.7 (2010); Marriage status: 18.6% never married, 59.0% now married, 7.7% widowed, 14.8% divorced (2000); Foreign born: 0.0% (2000); Ancestry (includes multiple ancestries): 17.1% Irish, 14.7% German, 13.5% Polish, 12.7% English, 11.9% United States or American (2000).

Economy: Employment by occupation: 8.3% management, 12.5% professional, 5.2% services, 21.9% sales, 0.0% farming, 14.6% construction, 37.5% production (2000).

Income: Per capita income: $23,337 (2010); Median household income: $45,000 (2010); Average household income: $67,202 (2010); Percent of households with income of $100,000 or more: 16.7% (2010); Poverty rate: 13.9% (2000).

Taxes: Total city taxes per capita: $16 (2007); City property taxes per capita: $16 (2007).

Education: Percent of population age 25 and over with: High school diploma (including GED) or higher: 79.7% (2010); Bachelor's degree or higher: 7.8% (2010); Master's degree or higher: 3.3% (2010).

Housing: Homeownership rate: 83.3% (2010); Median home value: $96,000 (2010); Median contract rent: $355 per month (2000); Median year structure built: 1946 (2000).

Transportation: Commute to work: 92.7% car, 3.1% public transportation, 0.0% walk, 2.1% work from home (2000); Travel time to work: 9.6% less than 15 minutes, 19.1% 15 to 30 minutes, 44.7% 30 to 45 minutes, 12.8% 45 to 60 minutes, 13.8% 60 minutes or more (2000)

LITTLE YORK (town).
Covers a land area of 0.977 square miles and a water area of 0 square miles. Located at 38.70° N. Lat; 85.90° W. Long. Elevation is 548 feet.

History: Laid out 1831.

Population: 155 (1990); 185 (2000); 192 (2010); 195 (2015 projected); Race: 97.9% White, 0.5% Black, 0.0% Asian, 1.6% Other, 0.0% Hispanic of any race (2010); Density: 196.5 persons per square mile (2010); Average household size: 2.74 (2010); Median age: 37.1 (2010); Males per 100 females: 102.1 (2010); Marriage status: 20.0% never married, 71.7% now married, 2.8% widowed, 5.5% divorced (2000); Foreign born: 0.0% (2000); Ancestry (includes multiple ancestries): 15.6% United States or American, 14.5% German, 6.9% English, 5.2% Irish, 5.2% Other groups (2000).

Economy: Employment by occupation: 11.3% management, 12.3% professional, 11.3% services, 19.8% sales, 1.9% farming, 1.9% construction, 41.5% production (2000).

Income: Per capita income: $19,034 (2010); Median household income: $46,667 (2010); Average household income: $51,179 (2010); Percent of households with income of $100,000 or more: 5.7% (2010); Poverty rate: 4.6% (2000).

Taxes: Total city taxes per capita: $5 (2007); City property taxes per capita: $5 (2007).

Education: Percent of population age 25 and over with: High school diploma (including GED) or higher: 83.2% (2010); Bachelor's degree or higher: 8.0% (2010); Master's degree or higher: 4.0% (2010).

Housing: Homeownership rate: 81.4% (2010); Median home value: $84,167 (2010); Median contract rent: $505 per month (2000); Median year structure built: 1959 (2000).

Transportation: Commute to work: 94.1% car, 0.0% public transportation, 2.0% walk, 2.0% work from home (2000); Travel time to work: 42.0% less than 15 minutes, 35.0% 15 to 30 minutes, 14.0% 30 to 45 minutes, 5.0% 45 to 60 minutes, 4.0% 60 minutes or more (2000)

LIVONIA (town).
Covers a land area of 1.045 square miles and a water area of 0 square miles. Located at 38.55° N. Lat; 86.27° W. Long. Elevation is 787 feet.

History: Laid out 1819.

Population: 159 (1990); 112 (2000); 111 (2010); 111 (2015 projected); Race: 95.5% White, 3.6% Black, 0.0% Asian, 0.9% Other, 0.0% Hispanic of any race (2010); Density: 106.3 persons per square mile (2010); Average household size: 2.71 (2010); Median age: 37.3 (2010); Males per 100 females: 101.8 (2010); Marriage status: 35.4% never married, 54.9% now married, 4.9% widowed, 4.9% divorced (2000); Foreign born: 0.0% (2000); Ancestry (includes multiple ancestries): 14.6% United States or American, 9.7% German, 7.8% Irish, 6.8% English, 4.9% Other groups (2000).

Economy: Single-family building permits issued: 0 (2009); Multi-family building permits issued: 0 (2009); Employment by occupation: 5.1% management, 13.6% professional, 22.0% services, 16.9% sales, 3.4% farming, 8.5% construction, 30.5% production (2000).

Income: Per capita income: $21,810 (2010); Median household income: $43,750 (2010); Average household income: $55,000 (2010); Percent of households with income of $100,000 or more: 7.3% (2010); Poverty rate: 11.2% (2000).

Taxes: Total city taxes per capita: $18 (2007); City property taxes per capita: $18 (2007).

Education: Percent of population age 25 and over with: High school diploma (including GED) or higher: 78.1% (2010); Bachelor's degree or higher: 8.2% (2010); Master's degree or higher: 5.5% (2010).

Housing: Homeownership rate: 82.9% (2010); Median home value: $107,143 (2010); Median contract rent: $275 per month (2000); Median year structure built: 1961 (2000).

Transportation: Commute to work: 89.8% car, 3.4% public transportation, 6.8% walk, 0.0% work from home (2000); Travel time to work: 27.1% less than 15 minutes, 28.8% 15 to 30 minutes, 11.9% 30 to 45 minutes, 15.3% 45 to 60 minutes, 16.9% 60 minutes or more (2000)

NEW PEKIN (town).
Aka Pekin. Covers a land area of 2.335 square miles and a water area of 0.035 square miles. Located at 38.50° N. Lat; 86.01° W. Long. Elevation is 712 feet.

Population: 1,085 (1990); 1,334 (2000); 1,252 (2010); 1,206 (2015 projected); Race: 98.2% White, 0.2% Black, 0.0% Asian, 1.6% Other, 1.6% Hispanic of any race (2010); Density: 536.2 persons per square mile (2010); Average household size: 2.49 (2010); Median age: 37.3 (2010); Males per 100 females: 98.1 (2010); Marriage status: 21.7% never married, 57.8% now married, 5.3% widowed, 15.2% divorced (2000); Foreign born: 0.8% (2000); Ancestry (includes multiple ancestries): 14.2% United States or American, 12.2% Other groups, 10.7% German, 10.3% Irish, 6.5% English (2000).

Economy: Employment by occupation: 3.4% management, 7.1% professional, 18.1% services, 16.1% sales, 1.5% farming, 13.6% construction, 40.2% production (2000).

Income: Per capita income: $17,101 (2010); Median household income: $35,500 (2010); Average household income: $42,734 (2010); Percent of households with income of $100,000 or more: 4.4% (2010); Poverty rate: 17.1% (2000).

Taxes: Total city taxes per capita: $65 (2007); City property taxes per capita: $63 (2007).

Education: Percent of population age 25 and over with: High school diploma (including GED) or higher: 72.1% (2010); Bachelor's degree or higher: 6.1% (2010); Master's degree or higher: 2.5% (2010).

Housing: Homeownership rate: 64.1% (2010); Median home value: $71,139 (2010); Median contract rent: $312 per month (2000); Median year structure built: 1975 (2000).
Transportation: Commute to work: 93.1% car, 0.0% public transportation, 3.0% walk, 2.0% work from home (2000); Travel time to work: 24.9% less than 15 minutes, 26.8% 15 to 30 minutes, 23.7% 30 to 45 minutes, 15.9% 45 to 60 minutes, 8.8% 60 minutes or more (2000)

PEKIN (unincorporated postal area, zip code 47165). Aka New Pekin. Covers a land area of 77.457 square miles and a water area of 0.160 square miles. Located at 38.51° N. Lat; 86.01° W. Long. Elevation is 685 feet.
Population: 5,825 (2000); Race: 98.1% White, 0.1% Black, 0.1% Asian, 1.7% Other, 1.5% Hispanic of any race (2000); Density: 75.2 persons per square mile (2000); Age: 27.9% under 18, 9.1% over 64 (2000); Marriage status: 18.7% never married, 65.1% now married, 4.7% widowed, 11.4% divorced (2000); Foreign born: 0.5% (2000); Ancestry (includes multiple ancestries): 20.5% German, 13.3% Irish, 12.8% United States or American, 9.5% Other groups, 8.4% English (2000).
Economy: Employment by occupation: 8.8% management, 15.5% professional, 13.1% services, 20.8% sales, 1.8% farming, 11.9% construction, 28.1% production (2000).
Income: Per capita income: $16,551 (2000); Median household income: $40,149 (2000); Poverty rate: 9.1% (2000).
Education: Percent of population age 25 and over with: High school diploma (including GED) or higher: 78.1% (2000); Bachelor's degree or higher: 10.7% (2000).

School District(s)
East Washington School Corp (KG-12)
    2008-09 Enrollment: 1,716 . . . . (812) 967-3926
Housing: Homeownership rate: 82.7% (2000); Median home value: $81,500 (2000); Median contract rent: $296 per month (2000); Median year structure built: 1978 (2000).
Newspapers: Banner-Gazette (Local news; Circulation 16,500); Washington County Edition (Local news; Circulation 10,000)
Transportation: Commute to work: 94.5% car, 0.7% public transportation, 0.6% walk, 3.1% work from home (2000); Travel time to work: 14.4% less than 15 minutes, 20.9% 15 to 30 minutes, 32.7% 30 to 45 minutes, 21.7% 45 to 60 minutes, 10.3% 60 minutes or more (2000)

SALEM (city). County seat. Covers a land area of 3.890 square miles and a water area of 0.017 square miles. Located at 38.60° N. Lat; 86.09° W. Long. Elevation is 751 feet.
History: Salem was founded in 1814 and named for Salem, North Carolina, the former home of the wife of the county surveyor. John Hay, statesman, diplomat, poet, and historian, was born in 1838 in Salem. In 1863 Salem was burned and looted by General Morgan and his raiders.
Population: 5,982 (1990); 6,172 (2000); 6,350 (2010); 6,390 (2015 projected); Race: 98.4% White, 0.0% Black, 0.4% Asian, 1.2% Other, 0.4% Hispanic of any race (2010); Density: 1,632.6 persons per square mile (2010); Average household size: 2.32 (2010); Median age: 39.7 (2010); Males per 100 females: 92.3 (2010); Marriage status: 20.8% never married, 54.8% now married, 10.7% widowed, 13.7% divorced (2000); Foreign born: 0.9% (2000); Ancestry (includes multiple ancestries): 17.0% United States or American, 13.9% German, 11.0% English, 8.6% Irish, 7.1% Other groups (2000).
Economy: Single-family building permits issued: 2 (2009); Multi-family building permits issued: 4 (2009); Employment by occupation: 7.5% management, 12.7% professional, 17.7% services, 19.3% sales, 0.7% farming, 8.4% construction, 33.7% production (2000).
Income: Per capita income: $17,874 (2010); Median household income: $33,352 (2010); Average household income: $41,164 (2010); Percent of households with income of $100,000 or more: 4.3% (2010); Poverty rate: 11.6% (2000).
Taxes: Total city taxes per capita: $324 (2007); City property taxes per capita: $272 (2007).
Education: Percent of population age 25 and over with: High school diploma (including GED) or higher: 77.5% (2010); Bachelor's degree or higher: 10.6% (2010); Master's degree or higher: 5.0% (2010).

School District(s)
Salem Community Schools (KG-12)
    2008-09 Enrollment: 2,125 . . . . (812) 883-4437
Housing: Homeownership rate: 66.9% (2010); Median home value: $78,127 (2010); Median contract rent: $326 per month (2000); Median year structure built: 1960 (2000).

Hospitals: Washington County Memorial Hospital (70 beds)
Safety: Violent crime rate: 7.7 per 10,000 population; Property crime rate: 29.1 per 10,000 population (2008).
Newspapers: The Salem Democrat (Community news; Circulation 6,500); The Salem Leader (Community news; Circulation 6,500); Your Ad-Vantage (Local news; Circulation 10,500)
Transportation: Commute to work: 94.0% car, 0.2% public transportation, 3.5% walk, 1.3% work from home (2000); Travel time to work: 56.4% less than 15 minutes, 17.4% 15 to 30 minutes, 8.9% 30 to 45 minutes, 10.5% 45 to 60 minutes, 6.8% 60 minutes or more (2000)
Additional Information Contacts
City of Salem . . . . (812) 883-4264
    http://www.cityofsalemin.com

SALTILLO (town). Covers a land area of 1.163 square miles and a water area of 0 square miles. Located at 38.66° N. Lat; 86.29° W. Long. Elevation is 820 feet.
Population: 117 (1990); 107 (2000); 109 (2010); 108 (2015 projected); Race: 98.2% White, 0.0% Black, 0.0% Asian, 1.8% Other, 0.9% Hispanic of any race (2010); Density: 93.7 persons per square mile (2010); Average household size: 2.48 (2010); Median age: 36.8 (2010); Males per 100 females: 101.9 (2010); Marriage status: 17.6% never married, 65.9% now married, 7.7% widowed, 8.8% divorced (2000); Foreign born: 0.0% (2000); Ancestry (includes multiple ancestries): 25.0% United States or American, 12.9% German, 11.2% Other groups, 5.2% English, 0.9% Irish (2000).
Economy: Employment by occupation: 4.3% management, 15.2% professional, 19.6% services, 15.2% sales, 0.0% farming, 8.7% construction, 37.0% production (2000).
Income: Per capita income: $17,565 (2010); Median household income: $35,000 (2010); Average household income: $42,159 (2010); Percent of households with income of $100,000 or more: 6.8% (2010); Poverty rate: 12.1% (2000).
Taxes: Total city taxes per capita: $0 (2007); City property taxes per capita: $0 (2007).
Education: Percent of population age 25 and over with: High school diploma (including GED) or higher: 77.8% (2010); Bachelor's degree or higher: 6.9% (2010); Master's degree or higher: 5.6% (2010).
Housing: Homeownership rate: 68.2% (2010); Median home value: $74,286 (2010); Median contract rent: $275 per month (2000); Median year structure built: 1976 (2000).
Transportation: Commute to work: 100.0% car, 0.0% public transportation, 0.0% walk, 0.0% work from home (2000); Travel time to work: 23.9% less than 15 minutes, 37.0% 15 to 30 minutes, 13.0% 30 to 45 minutes, 13.0% 45 to 60 minutes, 13.0% 60 minutes or more (2000)

Wayne County

Located in eastern Indiana; bounded on the east by Ohio; drained by the Whitewater River and its East Fork. Covers a land area of 403.57 square miles, a water area of 0.78 square miles, and is located in the Eastern Time Zone. The county was founded in 1810. County seat is Richmond.

Wayne County is part of the Richmond, IN Micropolitan Statistical Area. The entire metro area includes: Wayne County, IN

Weather Station: Cambridge City 3 N   Elevation: 997 feet

	Jan	Feb	Mar	Apr	May	Jun	Jul	Aug	Sep	Oct	Nov	Dec
High	33	38	49	61	71	80	83	82	76	64	51	39
Low	15	18	28	37	48	57	61	59	51	39	31	22
Precip	2.4	2.3	3.4	4.2	4.8	4.4	4.2	3.5	2.8	2.8	3.5	3.0
Snow	7.2	5.4	3.5	0.5	tr	0.0	0.0	0.0	0.0	0.1	1.1	4.0

High and Low temperatures in degrees Fahrenheit; Precipitation and Snow in inches

Weather Station: Richmond Water Works   Elevation: 1,013 feet

	Jan	Feb	Mar	Apr	May	Jun	Jul	Aug	Sep	Oct	Nov	Dec
High	34	39	50	62	73	81	85	83	77	64	51	40
Low	17	20	30	39	49	58	62	60	53	41	33	24
Precip	2.5	2.3	3.2	3.9	4.3	4.2	3.8	3.6	2.5	3.1	3.3	2.9
Snow	6.7	4.7	2.4	0.7	tr	0.0	0.0	0.0	0.0	0.2	0.9	3.1

High and Low temperatures in degrees Fahrenheit; Precipitation and Snow in inches

Population: 71,951 (1990); 71,097 (2000); 67,248 (2010); 65,034 (2015 projected); Race: 91.1% White, 5.0% Black, 0.6% Asian, 3.3% Other, 2.2% Hispanic of any race (2010); Density: 166.6 persons per square mile (2010); Average household size: 2.37 (2010); Median age: 40.5 (2010); Males per 100 females: 92.3 (2010).

Religion: Five largest groups: 7.7% Catholic Church, 5.2% The United Methodist Church, 4.3% Christian Churches and Churches of Christ, 3.7% Southern Baptist Convention, 3.3% Evangelical Lutheran Church in America (2000).

Economy: Unemployment rate: 11.4% (5/2010); Total civilian labor force: 33,272 (5/2010); Leading industries: 24.5% manufacturing; 18.4% health care and social assistance; 14.7% retail trade (2008); Farms: 894 totaling 164,117 acres (2007); Companies that employ 500 or more persons: 5 (2008); Companies that employ 100 to 499 persons: 44 (2008); Companies that employ less than 100 persons: 1,598 (2008); Black-owned businesses: n/a (2002); Hispanic-owned businesses: n/a (2002); Asian-owned businesses: n/a (2002); Women-owned businesses: 1,141 (2002); Retail sales per capita: $15,274 (2010). Single-family building permits issued: 29 (2009); Multi-family building permits issued: 0 (2009).

Income: Per capita income: $21,296 (2010); Median household income: $41,398 (2010); Average household income: $51,458 (2010); Percent of households with income of $100,000 or more: 9.4% (2010); Poverty rate: 17.2% (2008); Bankruptcy rate: 6.79% (2009).

Taxes: Total county taxes per capita: $353 (2007); County property taxes per capita: $147 (2007).

Education: Percent of population age 25 and over with: High school diploma (including GED) or higher: 82.4% (2010); Bachelor's degree or higher: 15.8% (2010); Master's degree or higher: 6.2% (2010).

Housing: Homeownership rate: 69.2% (2010); Median home value: $91,929 (2010); Median contract rent: $448 per month (2006-2008 3-year est.); Median year structure built: 1956 (2006-2008 3-year est.)

Health: Birth rate: 126.4 per 10,000 population (2009); Death rate: 112.8 per 10,000 population (2009); Age-adjusted cancer mortality rate: 236.5 deaths per 100,000 population (2006); Air Quality Index: 100.0% good, 0.0% moderate, 0.0% unhealthy for sensitive individuals, 0.0% unhealthy (percent of days in 2008); Number of physicians: 17.2 per 10,000 population (2007); Hospital beds: 79.5 per 10,000 population (2006); Hospital admissions: 1,827.9 per 10,000 population (2006).

Elections: 2008 Presidential election results: 47.0% Obama, 50.8% McCain, 0.0% Nader

Additional Information Contacts

Wayne County Government . . . . (765) 973-9220
   http://www.co.wayne.in.us
City of Richmond . . . . (765) 983-7232
   http://www.richmondindiana.gov
Richmond Chamber of Commerce . . . . (765) 962-1511
   http://www.rwchamber.org

Wayne County Communities

BOSTON (town). Covers a land area of 0.211 square miles and a water area of 0 square miles. Located at 39.74° N. Lat; 84.85° W. Long. Elevation is 1,132 feet.

Population: 159 (1990); 177 (2000); 173 (2010); 170 (2015 projected); Race: 98.8% White, 0.6% Black, 0.0% Asian, 0.6% Other, 0.6% Hispanic of any race (2010); Density: 819.5 persons per square mile (2010); Average household size: 2.51 (2010); Median age: 47.1 (2010); Males per 100 females: 86.0 (2010); Marriage status: 18.2% never married, 70.8% now married, 0.6% widowed, 10.4% divorced (2000); Foreign born: 0.0% (2000); Ancestry (includes multiple ancestries): 26.8% German, 25.8% United States or American, 21.7% Irish, 9.1% English, 4.0% Other groups (2000).

Economy: Employment by occupation: 13.0% management, 8.7% professional, 9.6% services, 21.7% sales, 0.0% farming, 14.8% construction, 32.2% production (2000).

Income: Per capita income: $33,154 (2010); Median household income: $64,375 (2010); Average household income: $87,065 (2010); Percent of households with income of $100,000 or more: 23.2% (2010); Poverty rate: 2.5% (2000).

Taxes: Total city taxes per capita: $52 (2007); City property taxes per capita: $12 (2007).

Education: Percent of population age 25 and over with: High school diploma (including GED) or higher: 88.1% (2010); Bachelor's degree or higher: 24.6% (2010); Master's degree or higher: 7.9% (2010).

Housing: Homeownership rate: 88.4% (2010); Median home value: $142,647 (2010); Median contract rent: $242 per month (2000); Median year structure built: before 1940 (2000).

Transportation: Commute to work: 92.9% car, 2.7% public transportation, 2.7% walk, 0.0% work from home (2000); Travel time to work: 34.5% less than 15 minutes, 48.7% 15 to 30 minutes, 5.3% 30 to 45 minutes, 2.7% 45 to 60 minutes, 8.8% 60 minutes or more (2000)

CAMBRIDGE CITY (town). Covers a land area of 1.045 square miles and a water area of 0 square miles. Located at 39.81° N. Lat; 85.17° W. Long. Elevation is 935 feet.

History: Founded in 1836 as a depot on the Whitewater Canal, Cambridge City was a shipping center for Indianapolis merchants for a time.

Population: 2,110 (1990); 2,121 (2000); 2,089 (2010); 2,055 (2015 projected); Race: 98.9% White, 0.7% Black, 0.1% Asian, 0.3% Other, 1.3% Hispanic of any race (2010); Density: 2,000.0 persons per square mile (2010); Average household size: 2.29 (2010); Median age: 40.8 (2010); Males per 100 females: 89.9 (2010); Marriage status: 20.1% never married, 55.1% now married, 10.9% widowed, 13.8% divorced (2000); Foreign born: 0.2% (2000); Ancestry (includes multiple ancestries): 18.0% United States or American, 17.5% German, 9.1% Irish, 7.6% English, 6.1% Other groups (2000).

Economy: Single-family building permits issued: 0 (2009); Multi-family building permits issued: 0 (2009); Employment by occupation: 9.6% management, 12.7% professional, 14.7% services, 25.4% sales, 0.8% farming, 11.4% construction, 25.5% production (2000).

Income: Per capita income: $21,305 (2010); Median household income: $41,000 (2010); Average household income: $48,632 (2010); Percent of households with income of $100,000 or more: 7.7% (2010); Poverty rate: 8.6% (2000).

Taxes: Total city taxes per capita: $232 (2007); City property taxes per capita: $172 (2007).

Education: Percent of population age 25 and over with: High school diploma (including GED) or higher: 83.0% (2010); Bachelor's degree or higher: 15.0% (2010); Master's degree or higher: 6.8% (2010).

School District(s)

Western Wayne Schools (PK-12)
   2008-09 Enrollment: 1,188 . . . . (765) 478-5375

Housing: Homeownership rate: 65.1% (2010); Median home value: $89,078 (2010); Median contract rent: $323 per month (2000); Median year structure built: before 1940 (2000).

Newspapers: Western Wayne News (Community news; Circulation 2,650)

Transportation: Commute to work: 92.9% car, 0.0% public transportation, 3.8% walk, 1.9% work from home (2000); Travel time to work: 40.7% less than 15 minutes, 32.7% 15 to 30 minutes, 15.8% 30 to 45 minutes, 4.4% 45 to 60 minutes, 6.4% 60 minutes or more (2000)

CENTERVILLE (town). Covers a land area of 1.002 square miles and a water area of 0 square miles. Located at 39.81° N. Lat; 84.99° W. Long. Elevation is 1,010 feet.

History: Centerville was once the seat of Wayne County. It reluctantly gave up the county records to Richmond on August 14, 1873, when shots were fired into the jail where the Centerville citizens had barricaded themselves and the records.

Population: 2,415 (1990); 2,427 (2000); 2,271 (2010); 2,191 (2015 projected); Race: 97.7% White, 0.3% Black, 0.3% Asian, 1.8% Other, 1.9% Hispanic of any race (2010); Density: 2,265.9 persons per square mile (2010); Average household size: 2.44 (2010); Median age: 39.4 (2010); Males per 100 females: 86.8 (2010); Marriage status: 17.4% never married, 59.2% now married, 10.4% widowed, 13.0% divorced (2000); Foreign born: 0.4% (2000); Ancestry (includes multiple ancestries): 22.9% United States or American, 19.7% German, 10.0% Irish, 9.3% English, 6.4% Other groups (2000).

Economy: Single-family building permits issued: 3 (2009); Multi-family building permits issued: 0 (2009); Employment by occupation: 10.7% management, 14.5% professional, 19.8% services, 23.5% sales, 0.0% farming, 9.2% construction, 22.3% production (2000).

Income: Per capita income: $20,000 (2010); Median household income: $42,056 (2010); Average household income: $50,679 (2010); Percent of households with income of $100,000 or more: 7.6% (2010); Poverty rate: 6.7% (2000).

Taxes: Total city taxes per capita: $186 (2007); City property taxes per capita: $175 (2007).

Education: Percent of population age 25 and over with: High school diploma (including GED) or higher: 87.1% (2010); Bachelor's degree or higher: 11.8% (2010); Master's degree or higher: 4.3% (2010).

School District(s)

Centerville-Abington Com Schs (PK-12)
   2008-09 Enrollment: 1,627 . . . . (765) 855-3475

Housing: Homeownership rate: 74.2% (2010); Median home value: $101,506 (2010); Median contract rent: $411 per month (2000); Median year structure built: 1954 (2000).
Transportation: Commute to work: 90.5% car, 0.5% public transportation, 4.8% walk, 3.7% work from home (2000); Travel time to work: 31.3% less than 15 minutes, 51.8% 15 to 30 minutes, 8.9% 30 to 45 minutes, 1.9% 45 to 60 minutes, 6.1% 60 minutes or more (2000)

DUBLIN (town). Covers a land area of 0.538 square miles and a water area of 0 square miles. Located at 39.81° N. Lat; 85.20° W. Long. Elevation is 1,050 feet.
History: Located on the Old National Road, Dublin was the site of The Maples, a tavern built in 1825.
Population: 802 (1990); 697 (2000); 548 (2010); 495 (2015 projected); Race: 99.5% White, 0.0% Black, 0.0% Asian, 0.5% Other, 1.6% Hispanic of any race (2010); Density: 1,018.2 persons per square mile (2010); Average household size: 2.66 (2010); Median age: 37.3 (2010); Males per 100 females: 90.3 (2010); Marriage status: 19.9% never married, 66.7% now married, 7.0% widowed, 6.3% divorced (2000); Foreign born: 0.0% (2000); Ancestry (includes multiple ancestries): 19.6% United States or American, 14.5% German, 7.6% Irish, 5.7% Other groups, 5.0% English (2000).
Economy: Single-family building permits issued: 0 (2009); Multi-family building permits issued: 0 (2009); Employment by occupation: 7.7% management, 13.6% professional, 13.9% services, 25.1% sales, 0.0% farming, 8.0% construction, 31.7% production (2000).
Income: Per capita income: $16,528 (2010); Median household income: $36,579 (2010); Average household income: $45,133 (2010); Percent of households with income of $100,000 or more: 7.3% (2010); Poverty rate: 13.9% (2000).
Taxes: Total city taxes per capita: $188 (2007); City property taxes per capita: $182 (2007).
Education: Percent of population age 25 and over with: High school diploma (including GED) or higher: 76.3% (2010); Bachelor's degree or higher: 9.0% (2010); Master's degree or higher: 5.6% (2010).
Housing: Homeownership rate: 82.5% (2010); Median home value: $78,049 (2010); Median contract rent: $378 per month (2000); Median year structure built: before 1940 (2000).
Transportation: Commute to work: 95.7% car, 0.0% public transportation, 2.1% walk, 1.2% work from home (2000); Travel time to work: 30.1% less than 15 minutes, 32.9% 15 to 30 minutes, 24.8% 30 to 45 minutes, 8.4% 45 to 60 minutes, 3.7% 60 minutes or more (2000)

EAST GERMANTOWN (town). Aka Pershing. Covers a land area of 0.127 square miles and a water area of 0 square miles. Located at 39.81° N. Lat; 85.13° W. Long. Elevation is 951 feet.
Population: 372 (1990); 243 (2000); 187 (2010); 169 (2015 projected); Race: 98.9% White, 1.1% Black, 0.0% Asian, 0.0% Other, 1.1% Hispanic of any race (2010); Density: 1,472.3 persons per square mile (2010); Average household size: 2.42 (2010); Median age: 40.4 (2010); Males per 100 females: 87.0 (2010); Marriage status: 11.3% never married, 63.7% now married, 11.3% widowed, 13.8% divorced (2000); Foreign born: 4.4% (2000); Ancestry (includes multiple ancestries): 44.1% United States or American, 10.5% German, 10.0% Other groups, 7.9% Irish, 3.9% English (2000).
Economy: Single-family building permits issued: 0 (2009); Multi-family building permits issued: 0 (2009); Employment by occupation: 5.3% management, 16.8% professional, 11.6% services, 15.8% sales, 0.0% farming, 7.4% construction, 43.2% production (2000).
Income: Per capita income: $20,619 (2010); Median household income: $44,474 (2010); Average household income: $53,333 (2010); Percent of households with income of $100,000 or more: 9.7% (2010); Poverty rate: 15.3% (2000).
Taxes: Total city taxes per capita: $39 (2007); City property taxes per capita: $4 (2007).
Education: Percent of population age 25 and over with: High school diploma (including GED) or higher: 83.6% (2010); Bachelor's degree or higher: 11.7% (2010); Master's degree or higher: 3.9% (2010).
Housing: Homeownership rate: 79.2% (2010); Median home value: $90,000 (2010); Median contract rent: $400 per month (2000); Median year structure built: 1944 (2000).
Transportation: Commute to work: 89.5% car, 0.0% public transportation, 5.3% walk, 2.1% work from home (2000); Travel time to work: 40.9% less than 15 minutes, 40.9% 15 to 30 minutes, 12.9% 30 to 45 minutes, 3.2% 45 to 60 minutes, 2.2% 60 minutes or more (2000)

ECONOMY (town). Covers a land area of 0.097 square miles and a water area of 0 square miles. Located at 39.97° N. Lat; 85.08° W. Long. Elevation is 1,152 feet.
History: Economy was the site in 1936 of Dr. James R. King's experiment in cooperative medical care, the Economy Mutual Health Association.
Population: 151 (1990); 200 (2000); 201 (2010); 200 (2015 projected); Race: 97.0% White, 0.0% Black, 1.0% Asian, 2.0% Other, 0.5% Hispanic of any race (2010); Density: 2,073.0 persons per square mile (2010); Average household size: 2.75 (2010); Median age: 40.7 (2010); Males per 100 females: 109.4 (2010); Marriage status: 16.4% never married, 66.4% now married, 5.5% widowed, 11.6% divorced (2000); Foreign born: 2.1% (2000); Ancestry (includes multiple ancestries): 24.7% German, 20.6% United States or American, 19.1% Irish, 7.7% English, 5.7% French (except Basque) (2000).
Economy: Employment by occupation: 0.0% management, 6.4% professional, 14.1% services, 41.0% sales, 2.6% farming, 9.0% construction, 26.9% production (2000).
Income: Per capita income: $20,601 (2010); Median household income: $47,115 (2010); Average household income: $56,712 (2010); Percent of households with income of $100,000 or more: 19.2% (2010); Poverty rate: 16.0% (2000).
Taxes: Total city taxes per capita: $82 (2007); City property taxes per capita: $61 (2007).
Education: Percent of population age 25 and over with: High school diploma (including GED) or higher: 92.0% (2010); Bachelor's degree or higher: 24.1% (2010); Master's degree or higher: 7.3% (2010).
Housing: Homeownership rate: 87.7% (2010); Median home value: $127,778 (2010); Median contract rent: $260 per month (2000); Median year structure built: before 1940 (2000).
Transportation: Commute to work: 93.4% car, 0.0% public transportation, 5.3% walk, 0.0% work from home (2000); Travel time to work: 7.9% less than 15 minutes, 64.5% 15 to 30 minutes, 22.4% 30 to 45 minutes, 2.6% 45 to 60 minutes, 2.6% 60 minutes or more (2000)

FOUNTAIN CITY (town). Covers a land area of 0.263 square miles and a water area of 0 square miles. Located at 39.95° N. Lat; 84.92° W. Long. Elevation is 1,102 feet.
History: Fountain was incorporated as Newport in 1834, but the name was changed to Fountain City when water from an underground lake was found to rise to the surface when pipes were sunk to it. Fountain City was a major station on the Underground Railroad of freedom for fugitive slaves.
Population: 748 (1990); 735 (2000); 661 (2010); 624 (2015 projected); Race: 97.4% White, 0.6% Black, 0.5% Asian, 1.5% Other, 0.0% Hispanic of any race (2010); Density: 2,514.0 persons per square mile (2010); Average household size: 2.48 (2010); Median age: 40.6 (2010); Males per 100 females: 97.3 (2010); Marriage status: 21.9% never married, 58.8% now married, 8.7% widowed, 10.6% divorced (2000); Foreign born: 0.3% (2000); Ancestry (includes multiple ancestries): 18.9% German, 16.9% United States or American, 16.7% Other groups, 11.9% Irish, 7.9% English (2000).
Economy: Single-family building permits issued: 0 (2009); Multi-family building permits issued: 0 (2009); Employment by occupation: 5.9% management, 16.7% professional, 14.7% services, 24.3% sales, 0.0% farming, 11.0% construction, 27.4% production (2000).
Income: Per capita income: $20,992 (2010); Median household income: $42,636 (2010); Average household income: $52,246 (2010); Percent of households with income of $100,000 or more: 9.4% (2010); Poverty rate: 8.8% (2000).
Taxes: Total city taxes per capita: $147 (2007); City property taxes per capita: $104 (2007).
Education: Percent of population age 25 and over with: High school diploma (including GED) or higher: 80.9% (2010); Bachelor's degree or higher: 10.8% (2010); Master's degree or higher: 7.2% (2010).
School District(s)
Northeastern Wayne Schools (PK-12)
   2008-09 Enrollment: 1,075 . . . . (765) 847-2821
Housing: Homeownership rate: 78.2% (2010); Median home value: $89,375 (2010); Median contract rent: $355 per month (2000); Median year structure built: 1952 (2000).
Transportation: Commute to work: 91.1% car, 0.0% public transportation, 1.4% walk, 3.7% work from home (2000); Travel time to work: 25.6% less than 15 minutes, 63.1% 15 to 30 minutes, 4.8% 30 to 45 minutes, 1.2% 45 to 60 minutes, 5.4% 60 minutes or more (2000)

GREENS FORK (town). Covers a land area of 0.151 square miles and a water area of 0 square miles. Located at 39.89° N. Lat; 85.04° W. Long. Elevation is 1,010 feet.

History: Laid out 1818.

Population: 430 (1990); 371 (2000); 361 (2010); 354 (2015 projected); Race: 96.7% White, 0.8% Black, 0.0% Asian, 2.5% Other, 0.6% Hispanic of any race (2010); Density: 2,396.4 persons per square mile (2010); Average household size: 2.73 (2010); Median age: 41.0 (2010); Males per 100 females: 101.7 (2010); Marriage status: 29.8% never married, 52.9% now married, 5.2% widowed, 12.1% divorced (2000); Foreign born: 0.0% (2000); Ancestry (includes multiple ancestries): 17.2% English, 16.4% German, 14.8% United States or American, 10.4% Irish, 6.8% Other groups (2000).

Economy: Single-family building permits issued: 0 (2009); Multi-family building permits issued: 0 (2009); Employment by occupation: 4.9% management, 7.6% professional, 25.0% services, 23.4% sales, 0.0% farming, 8.2% construction, 31.0% production (2000).

Income: Per capita income: $21,404 (2010); Median household income: $52,083 (2010); Average household income: $57,841 (2010); Percent of households with income of $100,000 or more: 9.8% (2010); Poverty rate: 8.2% (2000).

Taxes: Total city taxes per capita: $147 (2007); City property taxes per capita: $124 (2007).

Education: Percent of population age 25 and over with: High school diploma (including GED) or higher: 83.7% (2010); Bachelor's degree or higher: 15.0% (2010); Master's degree or higher: 4.9% (2010).

Housing: Homeownership rate: 83.3% (2010); Median home value: $106,757 (2010); Median contract rent: $363 per month (2000); Median year structure built: before 1940 (2000).

Transportation: Commute to work: 98.4% car, 0.0% public transportation, 0.0% walk, 1.6% work from home (2000); Travel time to work: 18.2% less than 15 minutes, 49.7% 15 to 30 minutes, 19.3% 30 to 45 minutes, 5.0% 45 to 60 minutes, 7.7% 60 minutes or more (2000)

HAGERSTOWN (town). Covers a land area of 1.386 square miles and a water area of 0 square miles. Located at 39.91° N. Lat; 85.16° W. Long. Elevation is 1,040 feet.

Population: 1,835 (1990); 1,768 (2000); 1,638 (2010); 1,571 (2015 projected); Race: 98.8% White, 0.1% Black, 0.2% Asian, 0.9% Other, 0.4% Hispanic of any race (2010); Density: 1,182.2 persons per square mile (2010); Average household size: 2.30 (2010); Median age: 40.3 (2010); Males per 100 females: 90.9 (2010); Marriage status: 18.6% never married, 60.4% now married, 11.1% widowed, 10.0% divorced (2000); Foreign born: 0.0% (2000); Ancestry (includes multiple ancestries): 22.7% German, 16.6% United States or American, 12.2% English, 10.3% Irish, 8.7% Other groups (2000).

Economy: Single-family building permits issued: 0 (2009); Multi-family building permits issued: 0 (2009); Employment by occupation: 8.1% management, 16.5% professional, 14.9% services, 29.8% sales, 0.3% farming, 12.1% construction, 18.2% production (2000).

Income: Per capita income: $23,370 (2010); Median household income: $44,494 (2010); Average household income: $53,673 (2010); Percent of households with income of $100,000 or more: 8.6% (2010); Poverty rate: 1.8% (2000).

Taxes: Total city taxes per capita: $270 (2007); City property taxes per capita: $242 (2007).

Education: Percent of population age 25 and over with: High school diploma (including GED) or higher: 91.1% (2010); Bachelor's degree or higher: 17.6% (2010); Master's degree or higher: 5.9% (2010).

School District(s)

Nettle Creek School Corp (PK-12)

    2008-09 Enrollment: 1,214 . . . . (765) 489-4543

Housing: Homeownership rate: 75.4% (2010); Median home value: $91,463 (2010); Median contract rent: $307 per month (2000); Median year structure built: 1945 (2000).

Safety: Violent crime rate: 6.1 per 10,000 population; Property crime rate: 258.0 per 10,000 population (2008).

Transportation: Commute to work: 92.5% car, 0.0% public transportation, 4.6% walk, 1.1% work from home (2000); Travel time to work: 33.8% less than 15 minutes, 35.7% 15 to 30 minutes, 16.9% 30 to 45 minutes, 4.8% 45 to 60 minutes, 8.8% 60 minutes or more (2000)

MILTON (town). Covers a land area of 0.271 square miles and a water area of 0 square miles. Located at 39.78° N. Lat; 85.15° W. Long. Elevation is 928 feet.

Population: 634 (1990); 611 (2000); 603 (2010); 589 (2015 projected); Race: 98.8% White, 0.0% Black, 0.0% Asian, 1.2% Other, 0.2% Hispanic of any race (2010); Density: 2,221.8 persons per square mile (2010); Average household size: 2.54 (2010); Median age: 41.0 (2010); Males per 100 females: 97.1 (2010); Marriage status: 19.3% never married, 58.7% now married, 6.0% widowed, 16.0% divorced (2000); Foreign born: 0.3% (2000); Ancestry (includes multiple ancestries): 22.3% United States or American, 11.4% German, 9.1% Irish, 5.1% English, 4.6% Other groups (2000).

Economy: Employment by occupation: 4.3% management, 9.3% professional, 18.0% services, 18.7% sales, 0.0% farming, 12.7% construction, 37.0% production (2000).

Income: Per capita income: $20,713 (2010); Median household income: $45,255 (2010); Average household income: $52,595 (2010); Percent of households with income of $100,000 or more: 9.3% (2010); Poverty rate: 11.3% (2000).

Taxes: Total city taxes per capita: $99 (2007); City property taxes per capita: $83 (2007).

Education: Percent of population age 25 and over with: High school diploma (including GED) or higher: 81.0% (2010); Bachelor's degree or higher: 10.5% (2010); Master's degree or higher: 5.4% (2010).

Housing: Homeownership rate: 80.6% (2010); Median home value: $78,276 (2010); Median contract rent: $320 per month (2000); Median year structure built: before 1940 (2000).

Transportation: Commute to work: 89.4% car, 0.0% public transportation, 4.4% walk, 2.7% work from home (2000); Travel time to work: 36.8% less than 15 minutes, 30.5% 15 to 30 minutes, 20.7% 30 to 45 minutes, 5.6% 45 to 60 minutes, 6.3% 60 minutes or more (2000)

MOUNT AUBURN (town). Covers a land area of 0.222 square miles and a water area of 0.009 square miles. Located at 39.81° N. Lat; 85.19° W. Long. Elevation is 984 feet.

Population: 138 (1990); 75 (2000); 70 (2010); 67 (2015 projected); Race: 100.0% White, 0.0% Black, 0.0% Asian, 0.0% Other, 0.0% Hispanic of any race (2010); Density: 315.2 persons per square mile (2010); Average household size: 2.59 (2010); Median age: 36.7 (2010); Males per 100 females: 62.8 (2010); Marriage status: 3.4% never married, 91.5% now married, 3.4% widowed, 1.7% divorced (2000); Foreign born: 0.0% (2000); Ancestry (includes multiple ancestries): 27.4% United States or American, 11.3% Irish, 3.2% Swiss, 3.2% Scotch-Irish, 1.6% English (2000).

Economy: Employment by occupation: 20.8% management, 8.3% professional, 0.0% services, 25.0% sales, 0.0% farming, 20.8% construction, 25.0% production (2000).

Income: Per capita income: $24,652 (2010); Median household income: $60,417 (2010); Average household income: $75,278 (2010); Percent of households with income of $100,000 or more: 18.5% (2010); Poverty rate: 3.2% (2000).

Taxes: Total city taxes per capita: $81 (2007); City property taxes per capita: $81 (2007).

Education: Percent of population age 25 and over with: High school diploma (including GED) or higher: 86.0% (2010); Bachelor's degree or higher: 14.0% (2010); Master's degree or higher: 4.7% (2010).

Housing: Homeownership rate: 85.2% (2010); Median home value: $103,571 (2010); Median contract rent: $425 per month (2000); Median year structure built: before 1940 (2000).

Transportation: Commute to work: 100.0% car, 0.0% public transportation, 0.0% walk, 0.0% work from home (2000); Travel time to work: 40.9% less than 15 minutes, 36.4% 15 to 30 minutes, 0.0% 30 to 45 minutes, 0.0% 45 to 60 minutes, 22.7% 60 minutes or more (2000)

RICHMOND (city). County seat. Covers a land area of 23.215 square miles and a water area of 0.060 square miles. Located at 39.83° N. Lat; 84.89° W. Long. Elevation is 981 feet.

History: Richmond was founded in 1805 by soldiers who had been with George Rogers Clark at the capture of Fort Sackville. They were joined by other settlers, many of them Quakers who founded Earlham College in 1847. Richmond was known for its greenhouses and rose cultivation, including the Richmond Rose hybrid developed in 1905.

Population: 39,829 (1990); 39,124 (2000); 36,445 (2010); 35,008 (2015 projected); Race: 85.6% White, 8.6% Black, 0.9% Asian, 4.9% Other, 3.4% Hispanic of any race (2010); Density: 1,569.9 persons per square mile

(2010); Average household size: 2.24 (2010); Median age: 39.1 (2010); Males per 100 females: 89.7 (2010); Marriage status: 24.5% never married, 53.1% now married, 8.9% widowed, 13.6% divorced (2000); Foreign born: 2.4% (2000); Ancestry (includes multiple ancestries): 17.9% German, 14.4% Other groups, 13.6% United States or American, 10.1% Irish, 8.7% English (2000).

Economy: Unemployment rate: 11.3% (5/2010); Total civilian labor force: 17,123 (5/2010); Single-family building permits issued: 15 (2009); Multi-family building permits issued: 0 (2009); Employment by occupation: 8.5% management, 15.4% professional, 17.0% services, 25.2% sales, 0.3% farming, 8.0% construction, 25.7% production (2000).

Income: Per capita income: $19,940 (2010); Median household income: $34,633 (2010); Average household income: $46,059 (2010); Percent of households with income of $100,000 or more: 7.5% (2010); Poverty rate: 15.7% (2000).

Taxes: Total city taxes per capita: $335 (2007); City property taxes per capita: $301 (2007).

Education: Percent of population age 25 and over with: High school diploma (including GED) or higher: 78.7% (2010); Bachelor's degree or higher: 15.4% (2010); Master's degree or higher: 5.8% (2010).

School District(s)

Galileo Charter School (KG-06)
   2008-09 Enrollment: 270 . . . . (765) 983-3709
Richmond Community Schools (PK-12)
   2008-09 Enrollment: 5,542 . . . . (765) 973-3300

Four-year College(s)

Bethany Theological Seminary (Private, Not-for-profit, Church of Brethren)
   Fall 2008 Enrollment: 55 . . . . (765) 983-1800
Earlham College (Private, Not-for-profit, Friends)
   Fall 2008 Enrollment: 1,336 . . . . (765) 983-1200
   2009-10 Tuition: In-state $35,164; Out-of-state $35,164
Indiana University-East (Public)
   Fall 2008 Enrollment: 2,447 . . . . (765) 973-8200
   2009-10 Tuition: In-state $5,801; Out-of-state $14,957

Two-year College(s)

Ivy Tech Community College-Whitewater (Public)
   Fall 2008 Enrollment: 2,601 . . . . (765) 966-2656
   2009-10 Tuition: In-state $3,090; Out-of-state $6,306

Vocational/Technical School(s)

David Demuth Institute of Cosmetology (Private, For-profit)
   Fall 2008 Enrollment: 54 . . . . (765) 935-7964
   2009-10 Tuition: $9,150
PJ's College of Cosmetology (Private, For-profit)
   Fall 2008 Enrollment: 36 . . . . (317) 846-8999
   2009-10 Tuition: $14,600

Housing: Homeownership rate: 59.6% (2010); Median home value: $80,394 (2010); Median contract rent: $364 per month (2000); Median year structure built: 1951 (2000).

Hospitals: Reid Hospital and Health Care Services (233 beds); Richmond State Hospital (312 beds)

Safety: Violent crime rate: 41.6 per 10,000 population; Property crime rate: 464.4 per 10,000 population (2008).

Newspapers: Palladium-Item (Local news; Circulation 21,000)

Transportation: Commute to work: 91.8% car, 1.0% public transportation, 4.0% walk, 1.7% work from home (2000); Travel time to work: 62.1% less than 15 minutes, 26.8% 15 to 30 minutes, 6.1% 30 to 45 minutes, 1.7% 45 to 60 minutes, 3.3% 60 minutes or more (2000)

Additional Information Contacts

City of Richmond . . . . (765) 983-7232
   http://www.richmondindiana.gov
Richmond Chamber of Commerce . . . . (765) 962-1511
   http://www.rwchamber.org

SPRING GROVE (town). Covers a land area of 0.317 square miles and a water area of 0 square miles. Located at 39.84° N. Lat; 84.89° W. Long. Elevation is 981 feet.

Population: 514 (1990); 386 (2000); 358 (2010); 349 (2015 projected); Race: 91.9% White, 3.6% Black, 1.1% Asian, 3.4% Other, 0.6% Hispanic of any race (2010); Density: 1,128.5 persons per square mile (2010); Average household size: 2.23 (2010); Median age: 51.4 (2010); Males per 100 females: 77.2 (2010); Marriage status: 14.1% never married, 57.6% now married, 17.8% widowed, 10.6% divorced (2000); Foreign born: 1.5% (2000); Ancestry (includes multiple ancestries): 17.2% English, 15.5% German, 12.1% United States or American, 11.9% Irish, 6.6% Other groups (2000).

Economy: Single-family building permits issued: 0 (2009); Multi-family building permits issued: 0 (2009); Employment by occupation: 11.7% management, 29.2% professional, 9.1% services, 23.4% sales, 0.0% farming, 8.4% construction, 18.2% production (2000).

Income: Per capita income: $25,579 (2010); Median household income: $52,574 (2010); Average household income: $60,876 (2010); Percent of households with income of $100,000 or more: 12.4% (2010); Poverty rate: 10.1% (2000).

Taxes: Total city taxes per capita: $112 (2007); City property taxes per capita: $101 (2007).

Education: Percent of population age 25 and over with: High school diploma (including GED) or higher: 87.0% (2010); Bachelor's degree or higher: 23.5% (2010); Master's degree or higher: 11.2% (2010).

Housing: Homeownership rate: 73.0% (2010); Median home value: $115,000 (2010); Median contract rent: $493 per month (2000); Median year structure built: 1953 (2000).

Transportation: Commute to work: 92.9% car, 0.0% public transportation, 1.3% walk, 5.8% work from home (2000); Travel time to work: 73.1% less than 15 minutes, 18.6% 15 to 30 minutes, 2.1% 30 to 45 minutes, 4.8% 45 to 60 minutes, 1.4% 60 minutes or more (2000)

WEBSTER (unincorporated postal area, zip code 47392). Covers a land area of 0.064 square miles and a water area of 0 square miles. Located at 39.90° N. Lat; 84.94° W. Long. Elevation is 1,060 feet.

Population: 68 (2000); Race: 100.0% White, 0.0% Black, 0.0% Asian, 0.0% Other, 0.0% Hispanic of any race (2000); Density: 1,055.1 persons per square mile (2000); Age: 10.2% under 18, 51.0% over 64 (2000); Marriage status: 18.4% never married, 73.5% now married, 0.0% widowed, 8.2% divorced (2000); Foreign born: 0.0% (2000); Ancestry (includes multiple ancestries): 20.4% English, 20.4% Irish, 10.2% German, 10.2% Dutch (2000).

Economy: Employment by occupation: 0.0% management, 0.0% professional, 0.0% services, 0.0% sales, 0.0% farming, 40.0% construction, 60.0% production (2000).

Income: Per capita income: $8,847 (2000); Median household income: $28,750 (2000); Poverty rate: 0.0% (2000).

Education: Percent of population age 25 and over with: High school diploma (including GED) or higher: 77.3% (2000); Bachelor's degree or higher: 0.0% (2000).

Housing: Homeownership rate: 100.0% (2000); Median home value: $71,000 (2000); Median contract rent: $n/a per month (2000); Median year structure built: before 1940 (2000).

Transportation: Commute to work: 100.0% car, 0.0% public transportation, 0.0% walk, 0.0% work from home (2000); Travel time to work: 0.0% less than 15 minutes, 100.0% 15 to 30 minutes, 0.0% 30 to 45 minutes, 0.0% 45 to 60 minutes, 0.0% 60 minutes or more (2000)

WHITEWATER (town). Covers a land area of 0.080 square miles and a water area of 0 square miles. Located at 39.94° N. Lat; 84.83° W. Long. Elevation is 1,129 feet.

Population: 93 (1990); 78 (2000); 78 (2010); 76 (2015 projected); Race: 100.0% White, 0.0% Black, 0.0% Asian, 0.0% Other, 0.0% Hispanic of any race (2010); Density: 976.0 persons per square mile (2010); Average household size: 2.60 (2010); Median age: 46.9 (2010); Males per 100 females: 122.9 (2010); Marriage status: 18.4% never married, 55.1% now married, 4.1% widowed, 22.4% divorced (2000); Foreign born: 0.0% (2000); Ancestry (includes multiple ancestries): 28.3% Irish, 25.0% German, 10.0% English, 3.3% United States or American, 3.3% Dutch (2000).

Economy: Employment by occupation: 0.0% management, 0.0% professional, 12.5% services, 15.6% sales, 0.0% farming, 21.9% construction, 50.0% production (2000).

Income: Per capita income: $22,004 (2010); Median household income: $53,125 (2010); Average household income: $57,417 (2010); Percent of households with income of $100,000 or more: 10.0% (2010); Poverty rate: 6.7% (2000).

Taxes: Total city taxes per capita: $0 (2007); City property taxes per capita: $0 (2007).

Education: Percent of population age 25 and over with: High school diploma (including GED) or higher: 84.7% (2010); Bachelor's degree or higher: 13.6% (2010); Master's degree or higher: 5.1% (2010).

Housing: Homeownership rate: 86.7% (2010); Median home value: $113,636 (2010); Median contract rent: $183 per month (2000); Median year structure built: 1950 (2000).

Transportation: Commute to work: 100.0% car, 0.0% public transportation, 0.0% walk, 0.0% work from home (2000); Travel time to work: 18.8% less than 15 minutes, 68.8% 15 to 30 minutes, 6.3% 30 to 45 minutes, 0.0% 45 to 60 minutes, 6.3% 60 minutes or more (2000)

WILLIAMSBURG (unincorporated postal area, zip code 47393). Covers a land area of 35.675 square miles and a water area of 0 square miles. Located at 39.95° N. Lat; 84.99° W. Long. Elevation is 1,060 feet.
Population: 1,562 (2000); Race: 99.0% White, 0.4% Black, 0.3% Asian, 0.3% Other, 1.7% Hispanic of any race (2000); Density: 43.8 persons per square mile (2000); Age: 25.7% under 18, 18.4% over 64 (2000); Marriage status: 19.2% never married, 74.4% now married, 1.9% widowed, 4.5% divorced (2000); Foreign born: 0.6% (2000); Ancestry (includes multiple ancestries): 25.7% United States or American, 12.0% English, 10.4% Irish, 7.8% German, 6.1% Other groups (2000).
Economy: Employment by occupation: 9.8% management, 12.3% professional, 17.9% services, 25.9% sales, 1.6% farming, 11.0% construction, 21.5% production (2000).
Income: Per capita income: $16,632 (2000); Median household income: $40,750 (2000); Poverty rate: 7.0% (2000).
Education: Percent of population age 25 and over with: High school diploma (including GED) or higher: 81.0% (2000); Bachelor's degree or higher: 9.2% (2000).
Housing: Homeownership rate: 87.2% (2000); Median home value: $83,900 (2000); Median contract rent: $216 per month (2000); Median year structure built: 1961 (2000).
Transportation: Commute to work: 95.2% car, 0.0% public transportation, 0.0% walk, 4.3% work from home (2000); Travel time to work: 24.9% less than 15 minutes, 62.1% 15 to 30 minutes, 5.4% 30 to 45 minutes, 5.1% 45 to 60 minutes, 2.6% 60 minutes or more (2000)

Wells County

Located in eastern Indiana; drained by the Wabash and Salamonie Rivers. Covers a land area of 369.96 square miles, a water area of 0.45 square miles, and is located in the Eastern Time Zone. The county was founded in 1835. County seat is Bluffton.

Wells County is part of the Fort Wayne, IN Metropolitan Statistical Area. The entire metro area includes: Allen County, IN; Wells County, IN; Whitley County, IN

Weather Station: Bluffton 1 N									Elevation: 823 feet		
	Jan	Feb	Mar	Apr	May	Jun	Jul	Aug	Sep	Oct	Nov	Dec
High	30	35	46	59	71	80	84	81	75	63	48	37
Low	15	17	28	38	49	59	62	60	52	41	32	22
Precip	2.1	1.8	2.6	3.3	4.1	3.8	4.0	3.6	3.0	2.5	3.1	2.7
Snow	8.4	7.1	3.7	1.1	0.0	0.0	tr	0.0	0.0	0.2	1.8	5.6

High and Low temperatures in degrees Fahrenheit; Precipitation and Snow in inches

Population: 25,948 (1990); 27,600 (2000); 28,034 (2010); 28,083 (2015 projected); Race: 97.7% White, 0.4% Black, 0.3% Asian, 1.6% Other, 1.9% Hispanic of any race (2010); Density: 75.8 persons per square mile (2010); Average household size: 2.56 (2010); Median age: 39.3 (2010); Males per 100 females: 98.2 (2010).
Religion: Five largest groups: 17.8% Catholic Church, 8.8% The United Methodist Church, 7.9% Apostolic Christian Church of America, Inc., 3.5% The Wesleyan Church, 3.3% Evangelical Lutheran Church in America (2000).
Economy: Unemployment rate: 9.0% (5/2010); Total civilian labor force: 14,206 (5/2010); Leading industries: 26.1% manufacturing; 13.5% health care and social assistance; 12.8% wholesale trade (2008); Farms: 701 totaling 194,602 acres (2007); Companies that employ 500 or more persons: 2 (2008); Companies that employ 100 to 499 persons: 19 (2008); Companies that employ less than 100 persons: 632 (2008); Black-owned businesses: n/a (2002); Hispanic-owned businesses: n/a (2002); Asian-owned businesses: n/a (2002); Women-owned businesses: 398 (2002); Retail sales per capita: $7,247 (2010). Single-family building permits issued: 34 (2009); Multi-family building permits issued: 0 (2009).
Income: Per capita income: $22,181 (2010); Median household income: $49,023 (2010); Average household income: $57,225 (2010); Percent of households with income of $100,000 or more: 11.1% (2010); Poverty rate: 8.6% (2008); Bankruptcy rate: 8.23% (2009).
Taxes: Total county taxes per capita: $247 (2007); County property taxes per capita: $111 (2007).

Education: Percent of population age 25 and over with: High school diploma (including GED) or higher: 89.0% (2010); Bachelor's degree or higher: 14.5% (2010); Master's degree or higher: 5.4% (2010).
Housing: Homeownership rate: 78.4% (2010); Median home value: $97,638 (2010); Median contract rent: $443 per month (2006-2008 3-year est.); Median year structure built: 1961 (2006-2008 3-year est.)
Health: Birth rate: 127.0 per 10,000 population (2009); Death rate: 93.2 per 10,000 population (2009); Age-adjusted cancer mortality rate: 162.4 deaths per 100,000 population (2006); Number of physicians: 12.2 per 10,000 population (2007); Hospital beds: 28.4 per 10,000 population (2006); Hospital admissions: 982.3 per 10,000 population (2006).
Elections: 2008 Presidential election results: 33.7% Obama, 65.1% McCain, 0.0% Nader
National and State Parks: Ouabache State Park
Additional Information Contacts
Wells County Government . . . . (260) 824-6479
   http://www.wellscounty.org
City of Bluffton . . . . (260) 824-1520
   http://www.ci.bluffton.in.us
Wells County Chamber of Commerce . . . . (260) 824-0510
   http://www.blufftonwellschamber.com

Wells County Communities

BLUFFTON (city). County seat. Covers a land area of 6.610 square miles and a water area of 0.007 square miles. Located at 40.73° N. Lat; 85.17° W. Long. Elevation is 827 feet.
History: Established in the mid-1800's, Bluffton was built on the bluffs overlooking the Wabash River.
Population: 9,509 (1990); 9,536 (2000); 9,033 (2010); 8,855 (2015 projected); Race: 96.3% White, 0.9% Black, 0.4% Asian, 2.4% Other, 3.5% Hispanic of any race (2010); Density: 1,366.6 persons per square mile (2010); Average household size: 2.30 (2010); Median age: 38.7 (2010); Males per 100 females: 92.8 (2010); Marriage status: 21.1% never married, 55.9% now married, 9.9% widowed, 13.1% divorced (2000); Foreign born: 1.1% (2000); Ancestry (includes multiple ancestries): 27.4% German, 10.8% United States or American, 10.3% Other groups, 8.7% Irish, 8.1% English (2000).
Economy: Employment by occupation: 8.7% management, 14.7% professional, 15.7% services, 23.7% sales, 0.7% farming, 9.0% construction, 27.5% production (2000).
Income: Per capita income: $21,601 (2010); Median household income: $40,534 (2010); Average household income: $50,705 (2010); Percent of households with income of $100,000 or more: 8.5% (2010); Poverty rate: 9.0% (2000).
Taxes: Total city taxes per capita: $207 (2007); City property taxes per capita: $170 (2007).
Education: Percent of population age 25 and over with: High school diploma (including GED) or higher: 83.3% (2010); Bachelor's degree or higher: 13.9% (2010); Master's degree or higher: 5.4% (2010).
School District(s)
M S D Bluffton-Harrison (KG-12)
   2008-09 Enrollment: 1,397 . . . . (260) 824-2620
Northern Wells Com Schools (PK-12)
   2008-09 Enrollment: 2,555 . . . . (260) 622-4125
Housing: Homeownership rate: 66.7% (2010); Median home value: $75,878 (2010); Median contract rent: $342 per month (2000); Median year structure built: 1960 (2000).
Hospitals: Bluffton Regional Medical Center (79 beds); Caylor-Nickel Clinic, P.C. (99 beds)
Safety: Violent crime rate: 2.1 per 10,000 population; Property crime rate: 305.4 per 10,000 population (2008).
Newspapers: Bluffton News-Banner (Community news; Circulation 5,500)
Transportation: Commute to work: 92.6% car, 0.0% public transportation, 4.2% walk, 2.6% work from home (2000); Travel time to work: 62.0% less than 15 minutes, 18.9% 15 to 30 minutes, 11.7% 30 to 45 minutes, 4.7% 45 to 60 minutes, 2.8% 60 minutes or more (2000)
Additional Information Contacts
City of Bluffton . . . . (260) 824-1520
   http://www.ci.bluffton.in.us
Wells County Chamber of Commerce . . . . (260) 824-0510
   http://www.blufftonwellschamber.com

CRAIGVILLE (unincorporated postal area, zip code 46731). Covers a land area of 15.391 square miles and a water area of 0 square miles. Located at 40.79° N. Lat; 85.09° W. Long. Elevation is 850 feet.

Population: 651 (2000); Race: 100.0% White, 0.0% Black, 0.0% Asian, 0.0% Other, 3.9% Hispanic of any race (2000); Density: 42.3 persons per square mile (2000); Age: 34.8% under 18, 13.0% over 64 (2000); Marriage status: 16.6% never married, 79.3% now married, 3.1% widowed, 1.0% divorced (2000); Foreign born: 1.1% (2000); Ancestry (includes multiple ancestries): 44.0% German, 10.0% English, 9.9% Swiss, 4.7% Other groups, 4.0% United States or American (2000).

Economy: Employment by occupation: 15.3% management, 17.7% professional, 4.9% services, 32.4% sales, 0.0% farming, 5.2% construction, 24.5% production (2000).

Income: Per capita income: $21,627 (2000); Median household income: $61,579 (2000); Poverty rate: 3.9% (2000).

Education: Percent of population age 25 and over with: High school diploma (including GED) or higher: 84.9% (2000); Bachelor's degree or higher: 19.1% (2000).

Housing: Homeownership rate: 91.8% (2000); Median home value: $118,200 (2000); Median contract rent: $500 per month (2000); Median year structure built: 1941 (2000).

Transportation: Commute to work: 92.7% car, 0.0% public transportation, 0.0% walk, 7.3% work from home (2000); Travel time to work: 35.0% less than 15 minutes, 32.3% 15 to 30 minutes, 28.1% 30 to 45 minutes, 3.0% 45 to 60 minutes, 1.7% 60 minutes or more (2000)

KEYSTONE (unincorporated postal area, zip code 46759). Covers a land area of 29.208 square miles and a water area of 0 square miles. Located at 40.59° N. Lat; 85.17° W. Long. Elevation is 860 feet.

Population: 765 (2000); Race: 89.6% White, 0.0% Black, 0.0% Asian, 10.4% Other, 1.7% Hispanic of any race (2000); Density: 26.2 persons per square mile (2000); Age: 32.8% under 18, 13.5% over 64 (2000); Marriage status: 16.0% never married, 69.5% now married, 8.9% widowed, 5.6% divorced (2000); Foreign born: 2.0% (2000); Ancestry (includes multiple ancestries): 21.1% German, 18.4% United States or American, 12.2% Other groups, 5.6% Irish, 2.9% Scottish (2000).

Economy: Employment by occupation: 5.6% management, 13.6% professional, 11.5% services, 27.2% sales, 1.9% farming, 5.4% construction, 34.9% production (2000).

Income: Per capita income: $14,501 (2000); Median household income: $39,750 (2000); Poverty rate: 3.9% (2000).

Education: Percent of population age 25 and over with: High school diploma (including GED) or higher: 88.2% (2000); Bachelor's degree or higher: 10.3% (2000).

Housing: Homeownership rate: 83.1% (2000); Median home value: $91,500 (2000); Median contract rent: $278 per month (2000); Median year structure built: 1952 (2000).

Transportation: Commute to work: 91.3% car, 0.0% public transportation, 0.0% walk, 7.0% work from home (2000); Travel time to work: 27.7% less than 15 minutes, 48.6% 15 to 30 minutes, 12.3% 30 to 45 minutes, 7.8% 45 to 60 minutes, 3.5% 60 minutes or more (2000)

LIBERTY CENTER (unincorporated postal area, zip code 46766). Covers a land area of 16.638 square miles and a water area of 0.026 square miles. Located at 40.70° N. Lat; 85.29° W. Long. Elevation is 850 feet.

Population: 631 (2000); Race: 95.2% White, 0.0% Black, 3.6% Asian, 1.2% Other, 0.0% Hispanic of any race (2000); Density: 37.9 persons per square mile (2000); Age: 25.7% under 18, 10.2% over 64 (2000); Marriage status: 16.0% never married, 68.5% now married, 6.5% widowed, 9.0% divorced (2000); Foreign born: 2.6% (2000); Ancestry (includes multiple ancestries): 30.0% German, 14.7% United States or American, 8.7% Other groups, 8.6% English, 4.0% Czech (2000).

Economy: Employment by occupation: 9.0% management, 10.1% professional, 10.1% services, 27.0% sales, 2.2% farming, 10.4% construction, 31.2% production (2000).

Income: Per capita income: $18,316 (2000); Median household income: $50,625 (2000); Poverty rate: 10.0% (2000).

Education: Percent of population age 25 and over with: High school diploma (including GED) or higher: 91.5% (2000); Bachelor's degree or higher: 14.2% (2000).

Housing: Homeownership rate: 83.0% (2000); Median home value: $70,000 (2000); Median contract rent: $375 per month (2000); Median year structure built: before 1940 (2000).

Transportation: Commute to work: 92.6% car, 1.1% public transportation, 2.6% walk, 1.7% work from home (2000); Travel time to work: 27.3% less than 15 minutes, 55.2% 15 to 30 minutes, 8.7% 30 to 45 minutes, 6.7% 45 to 60 minutes, 2.0% 60 minutes or more (2000)

OSSIAN (town). Covers a land area of 1.492 square miles and a water area of 0 square miles. Located at 40.88° N. Lat; 85.16° W. Long. Elevation is 840 feet.

History: Laid out 1850.

Population: 2,582 (1990); 2,943 (2000); 3,025 (2010); 3,017 (2015 projected); Race: 98.0% White, 0.4% Black, 0.3% Asian, 1.3% Other, 1.3% Hispanic of any race (2010); Density: 2,026.9 persons per square mile (2010); Average household size: 2.49 (2010); Median age: 36.7 (2010); Males per 100 females: 96.0 (2010); Marriage status: 20.1% never married, 61.1% now married, 8.6% widowed, 10.1% divorced (2000); Foreign born: 0.9% (2000); Ancestry (includes multiple ancestries): 31.8% German, 12.6% English, 10.6% United States or American, 9.0% Irish, 5.3% Other groups (2000).

Economy: Employment by occupation: 7.8% management, 17.9% professional, 12.7% services, 26.6% sales, 0.3% farming, 10.2% construction, 24.5% production (2000).

Income: Per capita income: $22,518 (2010); Median household income: $50,470 (2010); Average household income: $56,021 (2010); Percent of households with income of $100,000 or more: 9.1% (2010); Poverty rate: 4.4% (2000).

Taxes: Total city taxes per capita: $118 (2007); City property taxes per capita: $95 (2007).

Education: Percent of population age 25 and over with: High school diploma (including GED) or higher: 90.8% (2010); Bachelor's degree or higher: 16.6% (2010); Master's degree or higher: 6.2% (2010).

School District(s)
Northern Wells Com Schools (PK-12)
    2008-09 Enrollment: 2,555 . . . . (260) 622-4125
Housing: Homeownership rate: 74.7% (2010); Median home value: $88,607 (2010); Median contract rent: $413 per month (2000); Median year structure built: 1974 (2000).

Newspapers: Ossian Journal (Community news; Circulation 600); Sunriser News (Community news; Circulation 12,483)

Transportation: Commute to work: 95.8% car, 0.6% public transportation, 0.0% walk, 3.1% work from home (2000); Travel time to work: 27.3% less than 15 minutes, 46.8% 15 to 30 minutes, 20.8% 30 to 45 minutes, 2.7% 45 to 60 minutes, 2.4% 60 minutes or more (2000)

PONETO (town). Covers a land area of 0.115 square miles and a water area of 0 square miles. Located at 40.65° N. Lat; 85.22° W. Long. Elevation is 850 feet.

Population: 236 (1990); 240 (2000); 257 (2010); 266 (2015 projected); Race: 98.8% White, 0.0% Black, 0.4% Asian, 0.8% Other, 0.0% Hispanic of any race (2010); Density: 2,225.7 persons per square mile (2010); Average household size: 2.76 (2010); Median age: 39.7 (2010); Males per 100 females: 100.8 (2010); Marriage status: 13.5% never married, 74.8% now married, 8.4% widowed, 3.2% divorced (2000); Foreign born: 0.0% (2000); Ancestry (includes multiple ancestries): 25.9% German, 14.6% United States or American, 8.0% English, 8.0% Other groups, 3.8% Polish (2000).

Economy: Employment by occupation: 7.6% management, 4.2% professional, 16.0% services, 19.3% sales, 1.7% farming, 15.1% construction, 36.1% production (2000).

Income: Per capita income: $22,312 (2010); Median household income: $51,136 (2010); Average household income: $59,728 (2010); Percent of households with income of $100,000 or more: 10.9% (2010); Poverty rate: 5.2% (2000).

Taxes: Total city taxes per capita: $81 (2007); City property taxes per capita: $68 (2007).

Education: Percent of population age 25 and over with: High school diploma (including GED) or higher: 93.7% (2010); Bachelor's degree or higher: 11.4% (2010); Master's degree or higher: 4.6% (2010).

School District(s)
Southern Wells Com Schools (KG-12)
    2008-09 Enrollment: 789 . . . . (765) 728-5537
Housing: Homeownership rate: 91.3% (2010); Median home value: $116,000 (2010); Median contract rent: $375 per month (2000); Median year structure built: 1944 (2000).

Transportation: Commute to work: 94.1% car, 0.0% public transportation, 3.4% walk, 2.5% work from home (2000); Travel time to work: 29.3% less

than 15 minutes, 51.7% 15 to 30 minutes, 11.2% 30 to 45 minutes, 5.2% 45 to 60 minutes, 2.6% 60 minutes or more (2000)

UNIONDALE (town). Covers a land area of 0.216 square miles and a water area of 0.001 square miles. Located at 40.82° N. Lat; 85.24° W. Long. Elevation is 814 feet.
History: Laid out 1883.
Population: 308 (1990); 277 (2000); 282 (2010); 282 (2015 projected); Race: 99.6% White, 0.0% Black, 0.0% Asian, 0.4% Other, 0.0% Hispanic of any race (2010); Density: 1,304.1 persons per square mile (2010); Average household size: 2.74 (2010); Median age: 38.9 (2010); Males per 100 females: 108.9 (2010); Marriage status: 22.7% never married, 57.6% now married, 8.6% widowed, 11.1% divorced (2000); Foreign born: 0.0% (2000); Ancestry (includes multiple ancestries): 41.2% German, 15.8% English, 15.0% Irish, 6.2% United States or American, 6.2% French (except Basque) (2000).
Economy: Employment by occupation: 16.4% management, 14.7% professional, 9.5% services, 25.0% sales, 0.0% farming, 19.0% construction, 15.5% production (2000).
Income: Per capita income: $22,157 (2010); Median household income: $54,327 (2010); Average household income: $59,782 (2010); Percent of households with income of $100,000 or more: 11.7% (2010); Poverty rate: 2.3% (2000).
Taxes: Total city taxes per capita: $55 (2007); City property taxes per capita: $44 (2007).
Education: Percent of population age 25 and over with: High school diploma (including GED) or higher: 93.2% (2010); Bachelor's degree or higher: 15.3% (2010); Master's degree or higher: 8.4% (2010).
Housing: Homeownership rate: 88.3% (2010); Median home value: $95,714 (2010); Median contract rent: $413 per month (2000); Median year structure built: before 1940 (2000).
Transportation: Commute to work: 95.7% car, 0.0% public transportation, 2.6% walk, 1.7% work from home (2000); Travel time to work: 17.7% less than 15 minutes, 46.0% 15 to 30 minutes, 27.4% 30 to 45 minutes, 8.8% 45 to 60 minutes, 0.0% 60 minutes or more (2000)

VERA CRUZ (town). Covers a land area of 0.087 square miles and a water area of 0 square miles. Located at 40.70° N. Lat; 85.07° W. Long. Elevation is 823 feet.
History: Laid out 1848.
Population: 60 (1990); 55 (2000); 62 (2010); 63 (2015 projected); Race: 98.4% White, 0.0% Black, 0.0% Asian, 1.6% Other, 0.0% Hispanic of any race (2010); Density: 715.9 persons per square mile (2010); Average household size: 2.95 (2010); Median age: 40.0 (2010); Males per 100 females: 93.8 (2010); Marriage status: 21.2% never married, 54.5% now married, 18.2% widowed, 6.1% divorced (2000); Foreign born: 0.0% (2000); Ancestry (includes multiple ancestries): 29.2% German, 20.8% Irish, 16.7% United States or American, 4.2% French (except Basque), 4.2% English (2000).
Economy: Employment by occupation: 0.0% management, 23.1% professional, 0.0% services, 15.4% sales, 23.1% farming, 15.4% construction, 23.1% production (2000).
Income: Per capita income: $21,662 (2010); Median household income: $52,500 (2010); Average household income: $74,167 (2010); Percent of households with income of $100,000 or more: 19.0% (2010); Poverty rate: 0.0% (2000).
Taxes: Total city taxes per capita: $19 (2007); City property taxes per capita: $19 (2007).
Education: Percent of population age 25 and over with: High school diploma (including GED) or higher: 82.5% (2010); Bachelor's degree or higher: 12.5% (2010); Master's degree or higher: 2.5% (2010).
Housing: Homeownership rate: 85.7% (2010); Median home value: $160,000 (2010); Median contract rent: $400 per month (2000); Median year structure built: before 1940 (2000).
Transportation: Commute to work: 100.0% car, 0.0% public transportation, 0.0% walk, 0.0% work from home (2000); Travel time to work: 61.5% less than 15 minutes, 38.5% 15 to 30 minutes, 0.0% 30 to 45 minutes, 0.0% 45 to 60 minutes, 0.0% 60 minutes or more (2000)

ZANESVILLE (town). Covers a land area of 0.746 square miles and a water area of 0 square miles. Located at 40.91° N. Lat; 85.28° W. Long. Elevation is 810 feet.
Population: 585 (1990); 602 (2000); 655 (2010); 674 (2015 projected); Race: 98.2% White, 0.0% Black, 0.8% Asian, 1.1% Other, 0.8% Hispanic of any race (2010); Density: 877.6 persons per square mile (2010);

Average household size: 2.82 (2010); Median age: 40.4 (2010); Males per 100 females: 96.7 (2010); Marriage status: 17.2% never married, 70.5% now married, 1.6% widowed, 10.7% divorced (2000); Foreign born: 0.5% (2000); Ancestry (includes multiple ancestries): 45.7% German, 13.1% Irish, 10.5% Other groups, 9.8% Dutch, 7.6% English (2000).
Economy: Employment by occupation: 9.6% management, 14.4% professional, 12.2% services, 24.9% sales, 0.0% farming, 8.8% construction, 30.0% production (2000).
Income: Per capita income: $25,645 (2010); Median household income: $67,254 (2010); Average household income: $71,929 (2010); Percent of households with income of $100,000 or more: 21.1% (2010); Poverty rate: 4.9% (2000).
Education: Percent of population age 25 and over with: High school diploma (including GED) or higher: 91.7% (2010); Bachelor's degree or higher: 16.1% (2010); Master's degree or higher: 4.7% (2010).
Housing: Homeownership rate: 90.5% (2010); Median home value: $128,571 (2010); Median contract rent: $395 per month (2000); Median year structure built: 1971 (2000).
Transportation: Commute to work: 92.9% car, 0.0% public transportation, 5.1% walk, 0.9% work from home (2000); Travel time to work: 28.4% less than 15 minutes, 44.8% 15 to 30 minutes, 19.0% 30 to 45 minutes, 4.3% 45 to 60 minutes, 3.4% 60 minutes or more (2000)

White County

Located in northwestern Indiana; bounded on the east by the Tippecanoe River; drained by the Tippecanoe River. Covers a land area of 505.24 square miles, a water area of 3.56 square miles, and is located in the Eastern Time Zone. The county was founded in 1834. County seat is Monticello.
Population: 23,265 (1990); 25,267 (2000); 23,634 (2010); 22,795 (2015 projected); Race: 92.8% White, 0.4% Black, 0.3% Asian, 6.5% Other, 8.2% Hispanic of any race (2010); Density: 46.8 persons per square mile (2010); Average household size: 2.56 (2010); Median age: 40.9 (2010); Males per 100 females: 97.1 (2010).
Religion: Five largest groups: 7.0% The United Methodist Church, 6.4% Catholic Church, 5.1% American Baptist Churches in the USA, 4.1% Christian Church (Disciples of Christ), 2.5% Lutheran Church—Missouri Synod (2000).
Economy: Unemployment rate: 10.1% (5/2010); Total civilian labor force: 12,426 (5/2010); Leading industries: 30.4% manufacturing; 17.5% retail trade; 12.6% health care and social assistance (2008); Farms: 646 totaling 318,110 acres (2007); Companies that employ 500 or more persons: 0 (2008); Companies that employ 100 to 499 persons: 13 (2008); Companies that employ less than 100 persons: 664 (2008); Black-owned businesses: n/a (2002); Hispanic-owned businesses: n/a (2002); Asian-owned businesses: n/a (2002); Women-owned businesses: 486 (2002); Retail sales per capita: $14,751 (2010); Single-family building permits issued: 45 (2009); Multi-family building permits issued: 0 (2009).
Income: Per capita income: $20,930 (2010); Median household income: $46,039 (2010); Average household income: $53,743 (2010); Percent of households with income of $100,000 or more: 8.8% (2010); Poverty rate: 11.4% (2008); Bankruptcy rate: 5.55% (2009).
Taxes: Total county taxes per capita: $324 (2007); County property taxes per capita: $207 (2007).
Education: Percent of population age 25 and over with: High school diploma (including GED) or higher: 84.8% (2010); Bachelor's degree or higher: 11.9% (2010); Master's degree or higher: 4.0% (2010).
Housing: Homeownership rate: 75.9% (2010); Median home value: $101,391 (2010); Median contract rent: $485 per month (2006-2008 3-year est.); Median year structure built: 1969 (2006-2008 3-year est.).
Health: Birth rate: 133.0 per 10,000 population (2009); Death rate: 116.0 per 10,000 population (2009); Age-adjusted cancer mortality rate: 269.8 deaths per 100,000 population (2006); Number of physicians: 4.6 per 10,000 population (2007); Hospital beds: 10.4 per 10,000 population (2006); Hospital admissions: 499.7 per 10,000 population (2006).
Elections: 2008 Presidential election results: 44.9% Obama, 53.2% McCain, 0.1% Nader
Additional Information Contacts
White County Government. . . . . (574) 583-7755
   http://www.whitecountyindiana.us
City of Monticello . . . . (574) 583-5712
   http://www.monticelloin.gov

White County Communities

BROOKSTON (town). Covers a land area of 0.593 square miles and a water area of 0 square miles. Located at 40.60° N. Lat; 86.86° W. Long. Elevation is 682 feet.
Population: 1,804 (1990); 1,717 (2000); 1,490 (2010); 1,393 (2015 projected); Race: 98.2% White, 0.1% Black, 0.2% Asian, 1.5% Other, 2.3% Hispanic of any race (2010); Density: 2,512.9 persons per square mile (2010); Average household size: 2.43 (2010); Median age: 39.3 (2010); Males per 100 females: 95.3 (2010); Marriage status: 20.1% never married, 61.6% now married, 5.9% widowed, 12.4% divorced (2000); Foreign born: 0.5% (2000); Ancestry (includes multiple ancestries): 26.0% German, 14.6% United States or American, 12.7% English, 12.0% Irish, 8.4% Other groups (2000).
Economy: Employment by occupation: 9.5% management, 14.9% professional, 14.2% services, 25.8% sales, 0.0% farming, 11.2% construction, 24.3% production (2000).
Income: Per capita income: $21,803 (2010); Median household income: $47,179 (2010); Average household income: $53,185 (2010); Percent of households with income of $100,000 or more: 7.3% (2010); Poverty rate: 5.2% (2000).
Taxes: Total city taxes per capita: $89 (2007); City property taxes per capita: $74 (2007).
Education: Percent of population age 25 and over with: High school diploma (including GED) or higher: 90.7% (2010); Bachelor's degree or higher: 16.0% (2010); Master's degree or higher: 4.4% (2010).
School District(s)
Frontier School Corporation (KG-12)
    2008-09 Enrollment: 824 . . . . (219) 984-5009
Housing: Homeownership rate: 77.2% (2010); Median home value: $96,740 (2010); Median contract rent: $415 per month (2000); Median year structure built: 1964 (2000).
Transportation: Commute to work: 95.2% car, 0.2% public transportation, 1.1% walk, 3.0% work from home (2000); Travel time to work: 12.8% less than 15 minutes, 56.5% 15 to 30 minutes, 23.2% 30 to 45 minutes, 1.7% 45 to 60 minutes, 5.7% 60 minutes or more (2000)

BUFFALO (CDP). Covers a land area of 2.385 square miles and a water area of 0.164 square miles. Located at 40.88° N. Lat; 86.74° W. Long. Elevation is 669 feet.
Population: 512 (1990); 672 (2000); 597 (2010); 555 (2015 projected); Race: 98.3% White, 0.0% Black, 0.0% Asian, 1.7% Other, 2.3% Hispanic of any race (2010); Density: 250.3 persons per square mile (2010); Average household size: 2.63 (2010); Median age: 39.5 (2010); Males per 100 females: 103.8 (2010); Marriage status: 19.8% never married, 61.5% now married, 7.1% widowed, 11.5% divorced (2000); Foreign born: 0.0% (2000); Ancestry (includes multiple ancestries): 36.0% United States or American, 15.4% Irish, 13.2% German, 8.1% Other groups, 7.3% English (2000).
Economy: Employment by occupation: 10.4% management, 12.7% professional, 24.3% services, 19.1% sales, 3.6% farming, 14.3% construction, 15.5% production (2000).
Income: Per capita income: $19,322 (2010); Median household income: $43,958 (2010); Average household income: $51,013 (2010); Percent of households with income of $100,000 or more: 7.9% (2010); Poverty rate: 10.5% (2000).
Education: Percent of population age 25 and over with: High school diploma (including GED) or higher: 83.0% (2010); Bachelor's degree or higher: 4.7% (2010); Master's degree or higher: 1.7% (2010).
School District(s)
North White School Corp (PK-12)
    2008-09 Enrollment: 985 . . . . (219) 253-6618
Housing: Homeownership rate: 85.5% (2010); Median home value: $97,021 (2010); Median contract rent: $466 per month (2000); Median year structure built: 1975 (2000).
Transportation: Commute to work: 91.2% car, 0.0% public transportation, 3.6% walk, 5.2% work from home (2000); Travel time to work: 8.8% less than 15 minutes, 44.1% 15 to 30 minutes, 29.8% 30 to 45 minutes, 5.5% 45 to 60 minutes, 11.8% 60 minutes or more (2000)

BURNETTSVILLE (town). Covers a land area of 0.739 square miles and a water area of 0 square miles. Located at 40.76° N. Lat; 86.59° W. Long. Elevation is 712 feet.
Population: 401 (1990); 373 (2000); 350 (2010); 334 (2015 projected); Race: 98.3% White, 0.0% Black, 0.0% Asian, 1.7% Other, 2.0% Hispanic of any race (2010); Density: 473.5 persons per square mile (2010); Average household size: 2.52 (2010); Median age: 40.7 (2010); Males per 100 females: 107.1 (2010); Marriage status: 14.6% never married, 65.4% now married, 8.8% widowed, 11.2% divorced (2000); Foreign born: 0.0% (2000); Ancestry (includes multiple ancestries): 15.9% German, 15.1% United States or American, 8.2% English, 7.7% Irish, 6.3% Italian (2000).
Economy: Employment by occupation: 9.3% management, 15.2% professional, 13.7% services, 26.0% sales, 0.0% farming, 6.9% construction, 28.9% production (2000).
Income: Per capita income: $24,427 (2010); Median household income: $54,514 (2010); Average household income: $65,414 (2010); Percent of households with income of $100,000 or more: 13.7% (2010); Poverty rate: 9.0% (2000).
Taxes: Total city taxes per capita: $14 (2007); City property taxes per capita: $11 (2007).
Education: Percent of population age 25 and over with: High school diploma (including GED) or higher: 92.3% (2010); Bachelor's degree or higher: 8.5% (2010); Master's degree or higher: 1.6% (2010).
School District(s)
Twin Lakes School Corp (PK-12)
    2008-09 Enrollment: 2,599 . . . . (574) 583-7211
Housing: Homeownership rate: 83.5% (2010); Median home value: $82,857 (2010); Median contract rent: $315 per month (2000); Median year structure built: before 1940 (2000).
Transportation: Commute to work: 84.7% car, 1.5% public transportation, 9.4% walk, 0.5% work from home (2000); Travel time to work: 22.8% less than 15 minutes, 56.9% 15 to 30 minutes, 10.4% 30 to 45 minutes, 6.4% 45 to 60 minutes, 3.5% 60 minutes or more (2000)

CHALMERS (town). Covers a land area of 0.250 square miles and a water area of 0 square miles. Located at 40.66° N. Lat; 86.86° W. Long. Elevation is 712 feet.
Population: 525 (1990); 513 (2000); 484 (2010); 469 (2015 projected); Race: 98.1% White, 0.0% Black, 0.0% Asian, 1.9% Other, 2.3% Hispanic of any race (2010); Density: 1,939.5 persons per square mile (2010); Average household size: 2.72 (2010); Median age: 39.5 (2010); Males per 100 females: 94.4 (2010); Marriage status: 24.3% never married, 58.5% now married, 7.8% widowed, 9.4% divorced (2000); Foreign born: 1.2% (2000); Ancestry (includes multiple ancestries): 29.5% German, 19.0% United States or American, 12.6% English, 10.6% Irish, 8.8% Dutch (2000).
Economy: Employment by occupation: 7.9% management, 9.0% professional, 15.8% services, 30.8% sales, 0.0% farming, 4.5% construction, 32.0% production (2000).
Income: Per capita income: $23,047 (2010); Median household income: $57,000 (2010); Average household income: $62,978 (2010); Percent of households with income of $100,000 or more: 12.9% (2010); Poverty rate: 3.6% (2000).
Taxes: Total city taxes per capita: $306 (2007); City property taxes per capita: $306 (2007).
Education: Percent of population age 25 and over with: High school diploma (including GED) or higher: 89.5% (2010); Bachelor's degree or higher: 16.1% (2010); Master's degree or higher: 6.5% (2010).
School District(s)
Frontier School Corporation (KG-12)
    2008-09 Enrollment: 824 . . . . (219) 984-5009
Housing: Homeownership rate: 83.1% (2010); Median home value: $99,412 (2010); Median contract rent: $375 per month (2000); Median year structure built: before 1940 (2000).
Transportation: Commute to work: 91.1% car, 0.8% public transportation, 3.1% walk, 3.5% work from home (2000); Travel time to work: 15.2% less than 15 minutes, 32.8% 15 to 30 minutes, 44.8% 30 to 45 minutes, 4.0% 45 to 60 minutes, 3.2% 60 minutes or more (2000)

IDAVILLE (unincorporated postal area, zip code 47950). Covers a land area of 36.650 square miles and a water area of 0 square miles. Located at 40.79° N. Lat; 86.65° W. Long. Elevation is 715 feet.
Population: 854 (2000); Race: 94.6% White, 0.0% Black, 2.1% Asian, 3.3% Other, 3.3% Hispanic of any race (2000); Density: 23.3 persons per square mile (2000); Age: 32.3% under 18, 7.4% over 64 (2000); Marriage status: 22.5% never married, 45.9% now married, 10.9% widowed, 20.7% divorced (2000); Foreign born: 2.1% (2000); Ancestry (includes multiple ancestries): 20.7% German, 14.3% United States or American, 8.5% Other groups, 7.4% Irish, 4.8% Italian (2000).

Economy: Employment by occupation: 12.8% management, 5.3% professional, 7.7% services, 19.4% sales, 1.4% farming, 13.0% construction, 40.3% production (2000).
Income: Per capita income: $21,381 (2000); Median household income: $42,256 (2000); Poverty rate: 3.3% (2000).
Education: Percent of population age 25 and over with: High school diploma (including GED) or higher: 88.0% (2000); Bachelor's degree or higher: 5.3% (2000).
Housing: Homeownership rate: 84.4% (2000); Median home value: $73,500 (2000); Median contract rent: $365 per month (2000); Median year structure built: before 1940 (2000).
Transportation: Commute to work: 98.8% car, 0.0% public transportation, 0.0% walk, 1.2% work from home (2000); Travel time to work: 23.9% less than 15 minutes, 45.6% 15 to 30 minutes, 18.7% 30 to 45 minutes, 7.5% 45 to 60 minutes, 4.4% 60 minutes or more (2000)

MONON (town). Covers a land area of 0.562 square miles and a water area of 0 square miles. Located at 40.86° N. Lat; 86.88° W. Long. Elevation is 682 feet.
History: Laid out 1853, incorporated 1879.
Population: 1,612 (1990); 1,733 (2000); 1,508 (2010); 1,410 (2015 projected); Race: 77.9% White, 0.0% Black, 0.2% Asian, 21.9% Other, 24.8% Hispanic of any race (2010); Density: 2,683.5 persons per square mile (2010); Average household size: 2.79 (2010); Median age: 37.2 (2010); Males per 100 females: 99.5 (2010); Marriage status: 25.3% never married, 55.9% now married, 8.4% widowed, 10.5% divorced (2000); Foreign born: 13.2% (2000); Ancestry (includes multiple ancestries): 21.1% Other groups, 16.5% German, 13.4% United States or American, 8.9% Irish, 4.7% English (2000).
Economy: Employment by occupation: 3.4% management, 7.7% professional, 11.5% services, 18.2% sales, 4.4% farming, 8.3% construction, 46.4% production (2000).
Income: Per capita income: $15,752 (2010); Median household income: $37,206 (2010); Average household income: $43,817 (2010); Percent of households with income of $100,000 or more: 5.4% (2010); Poverty rate: 16.4% (2000).
Taxes: Total city taxes per capita: $169 (2007); City property taxes per capita: $114 (2007).
Education: Percent of population age 25 and over with: High school diploma (including GED) or higher: 78.5% (2010); Bachelor's degree or higher: 7.1% (2010); Master's degree or higher: 1.6% (2010).
School District(s)
North White School Corp (PK-12)
    2008-09 Enrollment: 985 . . . . (219) 253-6618
Housing: Homeownership rate: 67.5% (2010); Median home value: $70,920 (2010); Median contract rent: $330 per month (2000); Median year structure built: 1954 (2000).
Newspapers: The News & Review (Community news; Circulation 1,650)
Transportation: Commute to work: 88.7% car, 0.7% public transportation, 6.4% walk, 2.4% work from home (2000); Travel time to work: 38.7% less than 15 minutes, 32.4% 15 to 30 minutes, 12.0% 30 to 45 minutes, 10.7% 45 to 60 minutes, 6.1% 60 minutes or more (2000)

MONTICELLO (city). County seat. Covers a land area of 2.795 square miles and a water area of 0.215 square miles. Located at 40.74° N. Lat; 86.76° W. Long. Elevation is 679 feet.
History: Monticello was established as a resort town on the Tippecanoe River. When the Indiana Hydroelectric Power Company built dams across the river in 1923 and 1925, several lakes were formed which provided recreation sites.
Population: 5,244 (1990); 5,723 (2000); 4,945 (2010); 4,620 (2015 projected); Race: 87.1% White, 0.8% Black, 0.8% Asian, 11.3% Other, 16.0% Hispanic of any race (2010); Density: 1,769.5 persons per square mile (2010); Average household size: 2.39 (2010); Median age: 41.3 (2010); Males per 100 females: 90.5 (2010); Marriage status: 20.2% never married, 52.5% now married, 15.4% widowed, 11.9% divorced (2000); Foreign born: 6.6% (2000); Ancestry (includes multiple ancestries): 20.3% German, 18.2% Other groups, 11.8% United States or American, 10.4% English, 7.1% Irish (2000).
Economy: Employment by occupation: 6.3% management, 14.6% professional, 12.5% services, 19.8% sales, 0.0% farming, 7.8% construction, 38.9% production (2000).
Income: Per capita income: $18,332 (2010); Median household income: $38,237 (2010); Average household income: $44,107 (2010); Percent of

households with income of $100,000 or more: 4.5% (2010); Poverty rate: 8.1% (2000).
Taxes: Total city taxes per capita: $350 (2007); City property taxes per capita: $297 (2007).
Education: Percent of population age 25 and over with: High school diploma (including GED) or higher: 79.7% (2010); Bachelor's degree or higher: 11.6% (2010); Master's degree or higher: 3.8% (2010).
School District(s)
Twin Lakes School Corp (PK-12)
    2008-09 Enrollment: 2,599 . . . . (574) 583-7211
Housing: Homeownership rate: 61.4% (2010); Median home value: $89,650 (2010); Median contract rent: $438 per month (2000); Median year structure built: 1965 (2000).
Hospitals: White County Memorial Hospital (25 beds)
Safety: Violent crime rate: 5.7 per 10,000 population; Property crime rate: 385.1 per 10,000 population (2008).
Newspapers: Monticello Herald-Journal (Local news; Circulation 5,600)
Transportation: Commute to work: 91.3% car, 0.0% public transportation, 5.8% walk, 2.8% work from home (2000); Travel time to work: 61.2% less than 15 minutes, 13.6% 15 to 30 minutes, 12.4% 30 to 45 minutes, 9.8% 45 to 60 minutes, 2.9% 60 minutes or more (2000)
Additional Information Contacts
City of Monticello . . . . (574) 583-5712
    http://www.monticelloin.gov

NORWAY (CDP). Covers a land area of 0.889 square miles and a water area of 0.064 square miles. Located at 40.78° N. Lat; 86.76° W. Long. Elevation is 636 feet.
Population: 353 (1990); 437 (2000); 422 (2010); 410 (2015 projected); Race: 94.8% White, 0.0% Black, 0.0% Asian, 5.2% Other, 9.7% Hispanic of any race (2010); Density: 474.5 persons per square mile (2010); Average household size: 2.59 (2010); Median age: 44.8 (2010); Males per 100 females: 96.3 (2010); Marriage status: 20.8% never married, 41.6% now married, 12.4% widowed, 25.2% divorced (2000); Foreign born: 0.0% (2000); Ancestry (includes multiple ancestries): 30.9% German, 23.0% United States or American, 9.8% Irish, 8.5% English, 6.7% Other groups (2000).
Economy: Employment by occupation: 22.6% management, 3.1% professional, 25.2% services, 10.2% sales, 3.1% farming, 8.4% construction, 27.4% production (2000).
Income: Per capita income: $21,786 (2010); Median household income: $48,500 (2010); Average household income: $56,667 (2010); Percent of households with income of $100,000 or more: 11.1% (2010); Poverty rate: 19.5% (2000).
Education: Percent of population age 25 and over with: High school diploma (including GED) or higher: 84.6% (2010); Bachelor's degree or higher: 12.7% (2010); Master's degree or higher: 4.6% (2010).
Housing: Homeownership rate: 80.2% (2010); Median home value: $114,865 (2010); Median contract rent: $413 per month (2000); Median year structure built: 1956 (2000).
Transportation: Commute to work: 92.5% car, 3.5% public transportation, 0.0% walk, 0.0% work from home (2000); Travel time to work: 58.0% less than 15 minutes, 14.6% 15 to 30 minutes, 11.1% 30 to 45 minutes, 13.7% 45 to 60 minutes, 2.7% 60 minutes or more (2000)

REYNOLDS (town). Covers a land area of 0.528 square miles and a water area of 0 square miles. Located at 40.75° N. Lat; 86.87° W. Long. Elevation is 699 feet.
Population: 528 (1990); 547 (2000); 507 (2010); 490 (2015 projected); Race: 91.3% White, 0.0% Black, 0.2% Asian, 8.5% Other, 8.7% Hispanic of any race (2010); Density: 960.4 persons per square mile (2010); Average household size: 2.79 (2010); Median age: 35.7 (2010); Males per 100 females: 100.4 (2010); Marriage status: 23.5% never married, 62.8% now married, 5.6% widowed, 8.1% divorced (2000); Foreign born: 6.9% (2000); Ancestry (includes multiple ancestries): 23.0% German, 20.6% Other groups, 10.6% United States or American, 8.3% English, 6.5% Irish (2000).
Economy: Employment by occupation: 4.9% management, 10.5% professional, 14.2% services, 32.4% sales, 0.0% farming, 10.5% construction, 27.5% production (2000).
Income: Per capita income: $21,971 (2010); Median household income: $55,455 (2010); Average household income: $61,250 (2010); Percent of households with income of $100,000 or more: 11.5% (2010); Poverty rate: 4.6% (2000).

Taxes: Total city taxes per capita: $92 (2007); City property taxes per capita: $77 (2007).
Education: Percent of population age 25 and over with: High school diploma (including GED) or higher: 82.7% (2010); Bachelor's degree or higher: 12.3% (2010); Master's degree or higher: 6.3% (2010).

School District(s)
North White School Corp (PK-12)
   2008-09 Enrollment: 985 . . . . (219) 253-6618
Housing: Homeownership rate: 73.1% (2010); Median home value: $87,838 (2010); Median contract rent: $366 per month (2000); Median year structure built: 1955 (2000).
Transportation: Commute to work: 96.3% car, 0.0% public transportation, 0.8% walk, 1.2% work from home (2000); Travel time to work: 40.3% less than 15 minutes, 26.1% 15 to 30 minutes, 24.4% 30 to 45 minutes, 6.3% 45 to 60 minutes, 2.9% 60 minutes or more (2000)

WOLCOTT (town). Covers a land area of 0.536 square miles and a water area of 0 square miles. Located at 40.75° N. Lat; 87.04° W. Long. Elevation is 715 feet.
History: Laid out 1861.
Population: 983 (1990); 989 (2000); 975 (2010); 960 (2015 projected); Race: 96.5% White, 1.9% Black, 0.0% Asian, 1.5% Other, 1.0% Hispanic of any race (2010); Density: 1,820.6 persons per square mile (2010); Average household size: 2.64 (2010); Median age: 37.6 (2010); Males per 100 females: 93.5 (2010); Marriage status: 16.8% never married, 62.3% now married, 11.3% widowed, 9.6% divorced (2000); Foreign born: 1.2% (2000); Ancestry (includes multiple ancestries): 32.8% German, 19.2% Other groups, 16.1% Irish, 13.0% English, 11.9% United States or American (2000).
Economy: Employment by occupation: 11.1% management, 10.6% professional, 16.9% services, 19.2% sales, 2.1% farming, 10.6% construction, 29.4% production (2000).
Income: Per capita income: $21,282 (2010); Median household income: $48,732 (2010); Average household income: $55,723 (2010); Percent of households with income of $100,000 or more: 8.9% (2010); Poverty rate: 8.4% (2000).
Taxes: Total city taxes per capita: $180 (2007); City property taxes per capita: $155 (2007).
Education: Percent of population age 25 and over with: High school diploma (including GED) or higher: 86.7% (2010); Bachelor's degree or higher: 16.6% (2010); Master's degree or higher: 3.5% (2010).

School District(s)
Tri-County School Corp (KG-12)
   2008-09 Enrollment: 764 . . . . (219) 279-2418
Housing: Homeownership rate: 74.1% (2010); Median home value: $94,688 (2010); Median contract rent: $345 per month (2000); Median year structure built: 1951 (2000).
Newspapers: Wolcott Enterprise (Community news; Circulation 900)
Transportation: Commute to work: 92.9% car, 0.0% public transportation, 3.0% walk, 1.3% work from home (2000); Travel time to work: 59.0% less than 15 minutes, 13.3% 15 to 30 minutes, 16.6% 30 to 45 minutes, 6.8% 45 to 60 minutes, 4.4% 60 minutes or more (2000)

Whitley County

Located in northeastern Indiana; drained by the Eel River. Covers a land area of 335.52 square miles, a water area of 2.38 square miles, and is located in the Eastern Time Zone. The county was founded in 1835. County seat is Columbia City.

Whitley County is part of the Fort Wayne, IN Metropolitan Statistical Area. The entire metro area includes: Allen County, IN; Wells County, IN; Whitley County, IN

Weather Station: Columbia City   Elevation: 849 feet

	Jan	Feb	Mar	Apr	May	Jun	Jul	Aug	Sep	Oct	Nov	Dec
High	31	35	46	59	71	80	83	81	75	62	48	36
Low	14	17	27	37	48	57	61	59	51	40	31	21
Precip	2.1	1.8	2.9	3.8	3.6	4.3	3.9	3.5	3.6	2.9	3.3	2.8
Snow	9.4	7.4	4.1	1.0	tr	0.0	0.0	0.0	0.0	0.3	2.1	7.2

High and Low temperatures in degrees Fahrenheit; Precipitation and Snow in inches

Population: 27,651 (1990); 30,707 (2000); 32,952 (2010); 33,783 (2015 projected); Race: 97.5% White, 0.5% Black, 0.4% Asian, 1.6% Other, 1.2% Hispanic of any race (2010); Density: 98.2 persons per square mile (2010);

Average household size: 2.51 (2010); Median age: 38.3 (2010); Males per 100 females: 99.7 (2010).
Religion: Five largest groups: 8.6% Catholic Church, 7.8% The United Methodist Church, 4.5% Churches of God, General Conference, 3.9% Lutheran Church—Missouri Synod, 3.2% Evangelical Lutheran Church in America (2000).
Economy: Unemployment rate: 10.2% (5/2010); Total civilian labor force: 17,326 (5/2010); Leading industries: 42.7% manufacturing; 14.5% retail trade; 10.4% health care and social assistance (2008); Farms: 809 totaling 137,082 acres (2007); Companies that employ 500 or more persons: 1 (2008); Companies that employ 100 to 499 persons: 22 (2008); Companies that employ less than 100 persons: 679 (2008); Black-owned businesses: n/a (2002); Hispanic-owned businesses: n/a (2002); Asian-owned businesses: n/a (2002); Women-owned businesses: 678 (2002); Retail sales per capita: $11,313 (2010). Single-family building permits issued: 75 (2009); Multi-family building permits issued: 60 (2009).
Income: Per capita income: $24,853 (2010); Median household income: $52,814 (2010); Average household income: $62,649 (2010); Percent of households with income of $100,000 or more: 14.1% (2010); Poverty rate: 7.5% (2008); Bankruptcy rate: 10.62% (2009).
Taxes: Total county taxes per capita: $277 (2007); County property taxes per capita: $145 (2007).
Education: Percent of population age 25 and over with: High school diploma (including GED) or higher: 88.8% (2010); Bachelor's degree or higher: 16.9% (2010); Master's degree or higher: 4.6% (2010).
Housing: Homeownership rate: 83.7% (2010); Median home value: $118,656 (2010); Median contract rent: $423 per month (2006-2008 3-year est.); Median year structure built: 1972 (2006-2008 3-year est.)
Health: Birth rate: 132.1 per 10,000 population (2009); Death rate: 88.9 per 10,000 population (2009); Age-adjusted cancer mortality rate: 226.1 deaths per 100,000 population (2006); Number of physicians: 6.1 per 10,000 population (2007); Hospital beds: 37.4 per 10,000 population (2006); Hospital admissions: 573.1 per 10,000 population (2006).
Elections: 2008 Presidential election results: 38.6% Obama, 60.1% McCain, 0.0% Nader
Additional Information Contacts
Whitley County Government . . . . (260) 248-3140
   http://www.whitleygov.com
City of Columbia City . . . . (260) 248-5100
   http://www.columbiacity.net

Whitley County Communities

CHURUBUSCO (town). Covers a land area of 0.888 square miles and a water area of 0 square miles. Located at 41.23° N. Lat; 85.32° W. Long. Elevation is 899 feet.
History: Churubusco got its name from a Mexican town where American forces won a battle during the war with Mexico.
Population: 1,830 (1990); 1,666 (2000); 1,823 (2010); 1,845 (2015 projected); Race: 97.7% White, 0.1% Black, 0.4% Asian, 1.8% Other, 1.1% Hispanic of any race (2010); Density: 2,053.6 persons per square mile (2010); Average household size: 2.49 (2010); Median age: 37.7 (2010); Males per 100 females: 95.4 (2010); Marriage status: 29.0% never married, 50.9% now married, 10.6% widowed, 9.5% divorced; Foreign born: 0.9% (2000); Ancestry (includes multiple ancestries): 33.6% German, 14.2% Irish, 11.5% United States or American, 5.8% English, 4.3% Other groups (2000).
Economy: Single-family building permits issued: 2 (2009); Multi-family building permits issued: 22 (2009); Employment by occupation: 7.0% management, 12.5% professional, 15.3% services, 25.9% sales, 0.6% farming, 8.4% construction, 30.3% production (2000).
Income: Per capita income: $24,866 (2010); Median household income: $51,081 (2010); Average household income: $62,064 (2010); Percent of households with income of $100,000 or more: 14.0% (2010); Poverty rate: 4.9% (2000).
Taxes: Total city taxes per capita: $198 (2007); City property taxes per capita: $165 (2007).
Education: Percent of population age 25 and over with: High school diploma (including GED) or higher: 90.3% (2010); Bachelor's degree or higher: 13.5% (2010); Master's degree or higher: 4.2% (2010).

School District(s)
Smith-Green Community Schools (PK-12)
   2008-09 Enrollment: 1,249 . . . . (260) 693-2007

Housing: Homeownership rate: 82.7% (2010); Median home value: $92,263 (2010); Median contract rent: $377 per month (2000); Median year structure built: 1956 (2000).
Newspapers: Churubusco News (Community news; Circulation 2,300)
Transportation: Commute to work: 90.5% car, 0.2% public transportation, 5.8% walk, 3.1% work from home (2000); Travel time to work: 28.4% less than 15 minutes, 45.1% 15 to 30 minutes, 18.2% 30 to 45 minutes, 4.6% 45 to 60 minutes, 3.7% 60 minutes or more (2000)

COLUMBIA CITY (city). County seat. Covers a land area of 5.205 square miles and a water area of 0 square miles. Located at 41.15° N. Lat; 85.48° W. Long. Elevation is 860 feet.

History: Columbia City was the home of Thomas Riley Marshall (1854-1925), Vice-President under Woodrow Wilson, governor of Indiana from 1909-1913, and author of the statement, "What this country really needs is a good five-cent cigar." Also from Columbia City was historical novelist Lloyd C. Douglas, who was born here in 1877.
Population: 6,322 (1990); 7,077 (2000); 7,797 (2010); 8,075 (2015 projected); Race: 97.1% White, 0.9% Black, 0.3% Asian, 1.7% Other, 1.4% Hispanic of any race (2010); Density: 1,497.9 persons per square mile (2010); Average household size: 2.28 (2010); Median age: 36.6 (2010); Males per 100 females: 94.1 (2010); Marriage status: 20.0% never married, 54.9% now married, 9.4% widowed, 15.7% divorced (2000); Foreign born: 1.1% (2000); Ancestry (includes multiple ancestries): 33.5% German, 11.0% United States or American, 8.5% English, 7.9% Irish, 6.3% Other groups (2000).
Economy: Single-family building permits issued: 25 (2009); Multi-family building permits issued: 35 (2009); Employment by occupation: 9.8% management, 12.6% professional, 14.6% services, 24.7% sales, 0.3% farming, 9.4% construction, 28.5% production (2000).
Income: Per capita income: $22,059 (2010); Median household income: $42,382 (2010); Average household income: $50,571 (2010); Percent of households with income of $100,000 or more: 7.2% (2010); Poverty rate: 6.4% (2000).
Taxes: Total city taxes per capita: $194 (2007); City property taxes per capita: $170 (2007).
Education: Percent of population age 25 and over with: High school diploma (including GED) or higher: 86.9% (2010); Bachelor's degree or higher: 16.2% (2010); Master's degree or higher: 4.6% (2010).
School District(s)
Whitley Co Cons Schools (PK-12)
    2008-09 Enrollment: 3,615 . . . . (260) 244-5771
Housing: Homeownership rate: 72.8% (2010); Median home value: $95,574 (2010); Median contract rent: $361 per month (2000); Median year structure built: 1963 (2000).
Hospitals: Parkview Whitley Hospital (45 beds)
Safety: Violent crime rate: 10.8 per 10,000 population; Property crime rate: 199.8 per 10,000 population (2008).
Newspapers: Post & Mail (Local news; Circulation 4,800)
Transportation: Commute to work: 94.9% car, 0.3% public transportation, 1.0% walk, 2.1% work from home (2000); Travel time to work: 50.2% less than 15 minutes, 21.4% 15 to 30 minutes, 19.7% 30 to 45 minutes, 6.9% 45 to 60 minutes, 1.8% 60 minutes or more (2000)
Additional Information Contacts
City of Columbia City . . . . (260) 248-5100
    http://www.columbiacity.net

LARWILL (town). Covers a land area of 0.223 square miles and a water area of 0 square miles. Located at 41.17° N. Lat; 85.62° W. Long. Elevation is 961 feet.

History: Laid out 1854.
Population: 219 (1990); 282 (2000); 293 (2010); 300 (2015 projected); Race: 98.0% White, 0.7% Black, 0.0% Asian, 1.4% Other, 0.7% Hispanic of any race (2010); Density: 1,316.4 persons per square mile (2010); Average household size: 2.69 (2010); Median age: 35.7 (2010); Males per 100 females: 107.8 (2010); Marriage status: 21.8% never married, 56.4% now married, 9.5% widowed, 12.3% divorced (2000); Foreign born: 0.0% (2000); Ancestry (includes multiple ancestries): 18.9% United States or American, 18.3% German, 8.2% Irish, 6.0% Other groups, 1.3% English (2000).
Economy: Employment by occupation: 8.5% management, 14.0% professional, 8.5% services, 6.2% sales, 0.0% farming, 10.9% construction, 51.9% production (2000).
Income: Per capita income: $22,626 (2010); Median household income: $55,833 (2010); Average household income: $61,644 (2010); Percent of

households with income of $100,000 or more: 15.7% (2010); Poverty rate: 10.7% (2000).
Taxes: Total city taxes per capita: $99 (2007); City property taxes per capita: $96 (2007).
Education: Percent of population age 25 and over with: High school diploma (including GED) or higher: 87.8% (2010); Bachelor's degree or higher: 8.5% (2010); Master's degree or higher: 0.0% (2010).
School District(s)
Whitko Community School Corp (PK-12)
    2008-09 Enrollment: 1,961 . . . . (574) 594-2658
Housing: Homeownership rate: 86.1% (2010); Median home value: $113,393 (2010); Median contract rent: $342 per month (2000); Median year structure built: before 1940 (2000).
Transportation: Commute to work: 92.1% car, 0.0% public transportation, 0.0% walk, 1.6% work from home (2000); Travel time to work: 29.0% less than 15 minutes, 36.3% 15 to 30 minutes, 8.9% 30 to 45 minutes, 10.5% 45 to 60 minutes, 15.3% 60 minutes or more (2000)

SOUTH WHITLEY (town). Covers a land area of 0.735 square miles and a water area of 0 square miles. Located at 41.08° N. Lat; 85.62° W. Long. Elevation is 801 feet.

History: Laid out 1837.
Population: 1,501 (1990); 1,782 (2000); 1,841 (2010); 1,888 (2015 projected); Race: 98.7% White, 0.8% Black, 0.1% Asian, 0.5% Other, 0.5% Hispanic of any race (2010); Density: 2,503.4 persons per square mile (2010); Average household size: 2.35 (2010); Median age: 35.7 (2010); Males per 100 females: 97.3 (2010); Marriage status: 20.6% never married, 56.7% now married, 8.4% widowed, 14.3% divorced (2000); Foreign born: 0.2% (2000); Ancestry (includes multiple ancestries): 31.9% German, 13.0% United States or American, 7.1% English, 6.8% Other groups, 6.2% Irish (2000).
Economy: Single-family building permits issued: 2 (2009); Multi-family building permits issued: 3 (2009); Employment by occupation: 6.8% management, 11.7% professional, 13.5% services, 19.5% sales, 0.3% farming, 10.1% construction, 38.0% production (2000).
Income: Per capita income: $22,478 (2010); Median household income: $41,844 (2010); Average household income: $53,526 (2010); Percent of households with income of $100,000 or more: 10.4% (2010); Poverty rate: 8.2% (2000).
Taxes: Total city taxes per capita: $101 (2007); City property taxes per capita: $95 (2007).
Education: Percent of population age 25 and over with: High school diploma (including GED) or higher: 85.9% (2010); Bachelor's degree or higher: 14.9% (2010); Master's degree or higher: 4.0% (2010).
School District(s)
Whitko Community School Corp (PK-12)
    2008-09 Enrollment: 1,961 . . . . (574) 594-2658
Housing: Homeownership rate: 76.5% (2010); Median home value: $88,961 (2010); Median contract rent: $318 per month (2000); Median year structure built: 1951 (2000).
Safety: Violent crime rate: 0.0 per 10,000 population; Property crime rate: 80.7 per 10,000 population (2008).
Newspapers: Tribune-News (Community news; Circulation 1,540)
Transportation: Commute to work: 93.4% car, 0.0% public transportation, 4.7% walk, 1.4% work from home (2000); Travel time to work: 38.4% less than 15 minutes, 26.9% 15 to 30 minutes, 17.8% 30 to 45 minutes, 10.9% 45 to 60 minutes, 6.0% 60 minutes or more (2000)

TRI-LAKES (CDP). Covers a land area of 35.160 square miles and a water area of 0.898 square miles. Located at 41.22° N. Lat; 85.47° W. Long. Elevation is 938 feet.

Population: 3,299 (1990); 3,925 (2000); 3,963 (2010); 3,956 (2015 projected); Race: 97.5% White, 0.4% Black, 0.9% Asian, 1.2% Other, 1.1% Hispanic of any race (2010); Density: 112.7 persons per square mile (2010); Average household size: 2.50 (2010); Median age: 41.5 (2010); Males per 100 females: 106.8 (2010); Marriage status: 16.2% never married, 68.2% now married, 4.1% widowed, 11.5% divorced (2000); Foreign born: 0.5% (2000); Ancestry (includes multiple ancestries): 28.6% German, 13.6% United States or American, 9.7% Irish, 9.3% English, 6.4% Other groups (2000).
Economy: Employment by occupation: 14.6% management, 17.7% professional, 10.4% services, 24.5% sales, 1.1% farming, 13.2% construction, 18.5% production (2000).
Income: Per capita income: $27,646 (2010); Median household income: $62,099 (2010); Average household income: $69,401 (2010); Percent of

households with income of $100,000 or more: 19.3% (2010); Poverty rate: 1.8% (2000).

Education: Percent of population age 25 and over with: High school diploma (including GED) or higher: 92.0% (2010); Bachelor's degree or higher: 21.8% (2010); Master's degree or higher: 7.5% (2010).

Housing: Homeownership rate: 89.1% (2010); Median home value: $156,736 (2010); Median contract rent: $421 per month (2000); Median year structure built: 1964 (2000).

Transportation: Commute to work: 97.7% car, 0.0% public transportation, 0.6% walk, 1.6% work from home (2000); Travel time to work: 26.9% less than 15 minutes, 24.2% 15 to 30 minutes, 31.6% 30 to 45 minutes, 13.0% 45 to 60 minutes, 4.3% 60 minutes or more (2000);

CDP = Census Designated Place

CDP = Census Designated Place

CDP = Census Designated Place

CDP = Census Designated Place

W

Y

Z

CDP = Census Designated Place

Comparative
Statistics

Population

Place	1990	2000	2010 Estimate	2015 Projection
Anderson city *Madison Co.*	59,652	59,734	56,970	55,648
Angola city *Steuben Co.*	6,502	7,344	7,282	7,302
Auburn city *DeKalb Co.*	9,989	12,074	12,913	13,218
Avon town *Hendricks Co.*	2,450	6,248	7,606	8,618
Batesville city *Ripley Co.*	5,359	6,033	6,432	6,560
Bedford city *Lawrence Co.*	13,817	13,768	12,908	12,450
Beech Grove city *Marion Co.*	13,663	14,880	13,625	13,217
Bloomington city *Monroe Co.*	65,260	69,291	68,802	69,056
Bluffton city *Wells Co.*	9,509	9,536	9,033	8,855
Boonville city *Warrick Co.*	6,893	6,834	6,835	6,863
Brazil city *Clay Co.*	7,806	8,188	8,361	8,399
Brownsburg town *Hendricks Co.*	10,095	14,520	17,700	19,435
Carmel city *Hamilton Co.*	27,705	37,733	48,221	55,106
Cedar Lake town *Lake Co.*	8,974	9,279	11,025	11,722
Charlestown city *Clark Co.*	5,954	5,993	6,473	6,787
Chesterton town *Porter Co.*	9,592	10,488	11,906	12,502
Clarksville town *Clark Co.*	21,212	21,400	21,544	21,748
Columbia City city *Whitley Co.*	6,322	7,077	7,797	8,075
Columbus city *Bartholomew Co.*	34,728	39,059	40,773	41,395
Connersville city *Fayette Co.*	15,855	15,411	13,898	13,177
Crawfordsville city *Montgomery Co.*	13,844	15,243	14,620	14,263
Crown Point city *Lake Co.*	18,540	19,806	23,974	25,525
Danville town *Hendricks Co.*	4,837	6,418	9,045	10,155
Decatur city *Adams Co.*	9,160	9,528	9,425	9,277
Dyer town *Lake Co.*	11,403	13,895	16,412	17,315
East Chicago city *Lake Co.*	33,892	32,414	29,386	28,170
Elkhart city *Elkhart Co.*	47,334	51,874	53,296	53,257
Elwood city *Madison Co.*	9,767	9,737	8,976	8,599
Evansville city *Vanderburgh Co.*	126,272	121,582	114,593	111,463
Fishers town *Hamilton Co.*	12,437	37,835	68,773	81,516
Fort Wayne city *Allen Co.*	205,671	205,727	200,606	199,029
Frankfort city *Clinton Co.*	15,154	16,662	16,506	16,387
Franklin city *Johnson Co.*	13,593	19,463	24,389	26,560
Gary city *Lake Co.*	116,646	102,746	93,509	89,575
Goshen city *Elkhart Co.*	24,885	29,383	32,009	33,336
Granger CDP *Saint Joseph Co.*	20,143	28,284	29,257	29,323
Greencastle city *Putnam Co.*	9,208	9,880	10,203	10,313
Greenfield city *Hancock Co.*	12,256	14,600	18,057	19,763
Greensburg city *Decatur Co.*	9,561	10,260	10,487	10,521
Greenwood city *Johnson Co.*	27,969	36,037	46,350	50,408
Griffith town *Lake Co.*	17,026	17,334	17,606	17,720
Hammond city *Lake Co.*	84,236	83,048	75,392	72,366
Highland town *Lake Co.*	23,696	23,546	23,137	22,898
Hobart city *Lake Co.*	24,651	25,363	26,912	27,523
Huntington city *Huntington Co.*	17,066	17,450	16,375	15,695
Indianapolis special city *Marion Co.*	730,993	781,870	802,032	807,668
Jasper city *Dubois Co.*	10,695	12,100	12,671	12,833
Jeffersonville city *Clark Co.*	24,214	27,362	28,911	29,957
Kendallville city *Noble Co.*	8,505	9,616	9,515	9,416
Kokomo city *Howard Co.*	45,808	46,113	44,387	43,262

Place	1990	2000	2010 Estimate	2015 Projection
La Porte city *LaPorte Co.*	21,701	21,621	20,754	20,369
Lafayette city *Tippecanoe Co.*	49,671	56,397	59,719	61,420
Lake Station city *Lake Co.*	13,875	13,948	13,717	13,577
Lakes of the Four Seasons CDP *Lake Co.*	6,556	7,291	7,953	8,493
Lawrence city *Marion Co.*	26,837	38,915	45,445	48,035
Lebanon city *Boone Co.*	12,526	14,222	15,320	15,948
Logansport city *Cass Co.*	17,525	19,684	18,761	18,254
Lowell town *Lake Co.*	6,494	7,505	8,648	9,106
Madison city *Jefferson Co.*	12,373	12,004	12,225	12,280
Marion city *Grant Co.*	32,960	31,320	28,604	27,127
Martinsville city *Morgan Co.*	12,101	11,698	11,779	11,684
Merrillville town *Lake Co.*	27,793	30,560	34,503	35,960
Michigan City city *LaPorte Co.*	33,822	32,900	32,541	32,174
Mishawaka city *Saint Joseph Co.*	43,810	46,557	46,991	46,791
Mooresville town *Morgan Co.*	7,302	9,273	10,658	11,321
Mount Vernon city *Posey Co.*	7,433	7,478	6,886	6,574
Muncie city *Delaware Co.*	71,709	67,430	63,039	60,791
Munster town *Lake Co.*	19,949	21,511	22,595	22,841
Nappanee city *Elkhart Co.*	5,683	6,710	8,053	8,659
New Albany city *Floyd Co.*	38,060	37,603	36,196	35,526
New Castle city *Henry Co.*	18,045	17,780	16,748	16,139
New Haven city *Allen Co.*	12,280	12,406	12,825	13,278
Noblesville city *Hamilton Co.*	20,364	28,590	36,306	41,245
North Vernon city *Jennings Co.*	5,920	6,515	6,344	6,218
Peru city *Miami Co.*	13,422	12,994	11,458	10,780
Plainfield town *Hendricks Co.*	15,796	18,396	24,109	26,619
Plymouth city *Marshall Co.*	8,666	9,840	10,476	10,707
Portage city *Porter Co.*	30,561	33,496	37,616	39,259
Porter town *Porter Co.*	3,116	4,972	6,328	6,939
Princeton city *Gibson Co.*	8,418	8,175	8,213	8,151
Richmond city *Wayne Co.*	39,829	39,124	36,445	35,008
Rochester city *Fulton Co.*	6,111	6,414	6,273	6,147
Saint John town *Lake Co.*	5,656	8,382	10,616	11,684
Salem city *Washington Co.*	5,982	6,172	6,350	6,390
Schererville town *Lake Co.*	19,752	24,851	29,423	31,252
Sellersburg town *Clark Co.*	6,023	6,071	6,346	6,520
Seymour city *Jackson Co.*	15,888	18,101	18,628	18,786
Shelbyville city *Shelby Co.*	15,890	17,951	18,205	18,296
South Bend city *Saint Joseph Co.*	106,787	107,789	103,620	101,440
Speedway town *Marion Co.*	13,092	12,881	12,502	12,413
Tell City city *Perry Co.*	8,167	7,845	7,530	7,320
Terre Haute city *Vigo Co.*	60,970	59,614	59,334	58,956
Valparaiso city *Porter Co.*	24,568	27,428	28,611	29,136
Vincennes city *Knox Co.*	20,200	18,701	17,375	16,722
Wabash city *Wabash Co.*	12,381	11,743	10,516	9,888
Warsaw city *Kosciusko Co.*	11,314	12,415	12,629	12,666
Washington city *Daviess Co.*	11,177	11,380	11,422	11,411
West Lafayette city *Tippecanoe Co.*	26,691	28,778	29,770	30,306
Westfield town *Hamilton Co.*	5,121	9,293	15,774	18,445
Zionsville town *Boone Co.*	7,014	8,775	10,263	11,154

Physical Characteristics

Place	Density (persons per square mile)	Land Area (square miles)	Water Area (square miles)	Elevation (feet)
Anderson city *Madison Co.*	1,422.6	40.05	0.11	879
Angola city *Steuben Co.*	1,721.7	4.23	0.02	1,063
Auburn city *DeKalb Co.*	1,942.4	6.65	0.00	866
Avon town *Hendricks Co.*	1,192.0	6.38	0.01	833
Batesville city *Ripley Co.*	1,104.7	5.82	0.07	971
Bedford city *Lawrence Co.*	1,084.8	11.90	0.00	686
Beech Grove city *Marion Co.*	3,170.5	4.30	0.00	804
Bloomington city *Monroe Co.*	3,486.3	19.73	0.20	771
Bluffton city *Wells Co.*	1,366.6	6.61	0.01	827
Boonville city *Warrick Co.*	2,319.3	2.95	0.02	423
Brazil city *Clay Co.*	2,502.3	3.34	0.03	656
Brownsburg town *Hendricks Co.*	2,417.9	7.32	0.00	879
Carmel city *Hamilton Co.*	2,707.2	17.81	0.11	853
Cedar Lake town *Lake Co.*	1,623.4	6.79	1.32	709
Charlestown city *Clark Co.*	2,775.8	2.33	0.00	591
Chesterton town *Porter Co.*	1,398.6	8.51	0.11	640
Clarksville town *Clark Co.*	2,134.9	10.09	0.08	456
Columbia City city *Whitley Co.*	1,497.9	5.21	0.00	860
Columbus city *Bartholomew Co.*	1,571.3	25.95	0.42	630
Connersville city *Fayette Co.*	1,708.5	8.13	0.01	823
Crawfordsville city *Montgomery Co.*	1,745.0	8.38	0.00	787
Crown Point city *Lake Co.*	1,442.5	16.62	0.01	732
Danville town *Hendricks Co.*	1,476.6	6.13	0.00	951
Decatur city *Adams Co.*	1,914.4	4.92	0.01	801
Dyer town *Lake Co.*	2,753.6	5.96	0.00	640
East Chicago city *Lake Co.*	2,453.5	11.98	3.65	591
Elkhart city *Elkhart Co.*	2,494.6	21.36	0.89	748
Elwood city *Madison Co.*	2,528.8	3.55	0.00	860
Evansville city *Vanderburgh Co.*	2,815.3	40.70	0.06	387
Fishers town *Hamilton Co.*	3,170.7	21.69	0.10	817
Fort Wayne city *Allen Co.*	2,540.8	78.95	0.17	810
Frankfort city *Clinton Co.*	3,210.2	5.14	0.00	850
Franklin city *Johnson Co.*	2,165.5	11.26	0.00	725
Gary city *Lake Co.*	1,861.6	50.23	7.01	600
Goshen city *Elkhart Co.*	2,426.8	13.19	0.21	801
Granger CDP *Saint Joseph Co.*	1,115.9	26.22	0.00	801
Greencastle city *Putnam Co.*	1,925.6	5.30	0.05	853
Greenfield city *Hancock Co.*	2,248.4	8.03	0.04	883
Greensburg city *Decatur Co.*	2,187.8	4.79	0.04	958
Greenwood city *Johnson Co.*	3,247.3	14.27	0.00	804
Griffith town *Lake Co.*	2,455.6	7.17	0.00	630
Hammond city *Lake Co.*	3,295.3	22.88	1.95	600
Highland town *Lake Co.*	3,368.7	6.87	0.02	623
Hobart city *Lake Co.*	1,026.6	26.21	0.49	623
Huntington city *Huntington Co.*	1,962.2	8.35	0.09	748
Indianapolis special city *Marion Co.*	2,218.7	361.48	6.68	715
Jasper city *Dubois Co.*	1,373.7	9.22	0.04	466
Jeffersonville city *Clark Co.*	2,128.7	13.58	0.00	446
Kendallville city *Noble Co.*	1,870.2	5.09	0.22	988
Kokomo city *Howard Co.*	2,740.7	16.20	0.06	810

Place	Density (persons per square mile)	Land Area (square miles)	Water Area (square miles)	Elevation (feet)
La Porte city *LaPorte Co.*	1,811.1	11.46	0.71	814
Lafayette city *Tippecanoe Co.*	2,971.8	20.09	0.00	692
Lake Station city *Lake Co.*	1,653.2	8.30	0.17	620
Lakes of the Four Seasons CDP *Lake Co.*	2,967.3	2.68	0.41	764
Lawrence city *Marion Co.*	2,263.0	20.08	0.10	873
Lebanon city *Boone Co.*	2,103.7	7.28	0.00	938
Logansport city *Cass Co.*	2,271.2	8.26	0.16	633
Lowell town *Lake Co.*	2,119.3	4.08	0.08	669
Madison city *Jefferson Co.*	1,428.8	8.56	0.33	489
Marion city *Grant Co.*	2,151.2	13.30	0.04	810
Martinsville city *Morgan Co.*	2,638.8	4.46	0.01	604
Merrillville town *Lake Co.*	1,036.7	33.28	0.03	656
Michigan City city *LaPorte Co.*	1,660.3	19.60	3.52	627
Mishawaka city *Saint Joseph Co.*	2,990.9	15.71	0.34	719
Mooresville town *Morgan Co.*	1,925.2	5.54	0.02	712
Mount Vernon city *Posey Co.*	2,795.7	2.46	0.07	400
Muncie city *Delaware Co.*	2,606.6	24.18	0.01	932
Munster town *Lake Co.*	2,996.5	7.54	0.05	610
Nappanee city *Elkhart Co.*	2,182.9	3.69	0.00	869
New Albany city *Floyd Co.*	2,474.9	14.63	0.17	449
New Castle city *Henry Co.*	2,814.1	5.95	0.00	1,070
New Haven city *Allen Co.*	1,573.4	8.15	0.00	758
Noblesville city *Hamilton Co.*	2,026.5	17.92	1.15	771
North Vernon city *Jennings Co.*	1,445.5	4.39	0.01	719
Peru city *Miami Co.*	2,482.7	4.62	0.04	650
Plainfield town *Hendricks Co.*	1,340.8	17.98	0.05	728
Plymouth city *Marshall Co.*	1,505.4	6.96	0.01	797
Portage city *Porter Co.*	1,477.7	25.46	1.97	636
Porter town *Porter Co.*	1,003.9	6.30	0.30	640
Princeton city *Gibson Co.*	1,693.4	4.85	0.00	499
Richmond city *Wayne Co.*	1,569.9	23.21	0.06	981
Rochester city *Fulton Co.*	1,376.5	4.56	1.11	781
Saint John town *Lake Co.*	1,578.8	6.72	0.05	725
Salem city *Washington Co.*	1,632.6	3.89	0.02	751
Schererville town *Lake Co.*	2,161.9	13.61	0.03	669
Sellersburg town *Clark Co.*	1,584.4	4.01	0.01	486
Seymour city *Jackson Co.*	1,718.9	10.84	0.00	604
Shelbyville city *Shelby Co.*	2,051.7	8.87	0.11	764
South Bend city *Saint Joseph Co.*	2,678.6	38.68	0.43	692
Speedway town *Marion Co.*	2,629.2	4.75	0.01	748
Tell City city *Perry Co.*	1,652.3	4.56	0.05	420
Terre Haute city *Vigo Co.*	1,899.4	31.24	0.86	499
Valparaiso city *Porter Co.*	2,623.9	10.90	0.08	794
Vincennes city *Knox Co.*	2,434.5	7.14	0.07	420
Wabash city *Wabash Co.*	1,181.1	8.90	0.25	712
Warsaw city *Kosciusko Co.*	1,205.0	10.48	1.07	827
Washington city *Daviess Co.*	2,412.9	4.73	0.03	502
West Lafayette city *Tippecanoe Co.*	5,399.5	5.51	0.01	614
Westfield town *Hamilton Co.*	2,067.7	7.63	0.01	886
Zionsville town *Boone Co.*	1,769.4	5.80	0.07	843

NOTE: Population Density figures as of 2010; Land Area and Water Area figures as of 2000.

Population by Race/Hispanic Origin

Place	White[1] (%)	Black[1] (%)	Asian[1] (%)	Other (%)	Hispanic[2] (%)
Anderson city *Madison Co.*	80.5	15.2	0.7	3.7	3.6
Angola city *Steuben Co.*	92.0	1.2	1.6	5.1	5.6
Auburn city *DeKalb Co.*	96.2	1.3	0.5	1.9	2.3
Avon town *Hendricks Co.*	91.2	2.7	3.0	3.1	3.0
Batesville city *Ripley Co.*	96.2	0.4	1.2	2.2	1.7
Bedford city *Lawrence Co.*	95.5	1.3	0.8	2.3	1.6
Beech Grove city *Marion Co.*	94.2	1.1	0.9	3.8	4.7
Bloomington city *Monroe Co.*	84.0	4.7	7.1	4.2	3.2
Bluffton city *Wells Co.*	96.3	0.9	0.4	2.4	3.5
Boonville city *Warrick Co.*	98.2	0.6	0.1	1.1	0.8
Brazil city *Clay Co.*	96.1	1.4	0.7	1.8	0.9
Brownsburg town *Hendricks Co.*	94.4	1.5	1.6	2.5	2.8
Carmel city *Hamilton Co.*	87.6	3.9	6.2	2.4	3.1
Cedar Lake town *Lake Co.*	96.2	0.3	0.2	3.4	5.1
Charlestown city *Clark Co.*	91.1	2.0	0.2	6.7	7.9
Chesterton town *Porter Co.*	94.1	1.6	1.6	2.6	5.0
Clarksville town *Clark Co.*	87.3	7.3	1.2	4.2	5.2
Columbia City city *Whitley Co.*	97.1	0.9	0.3	1.7	1.4
Columbus city *Bartholomew Co.*	87.5	3.0	5.0	4.5	5.6
Connersville city *Fayette Co.*	95.5	2.6	0.3	1.7	1.2
Crawfordsville city *Montgomery Co.*	90.0	2.0	0.7	7.3	7.6
Crown Point city *Lake Co.*	91.6	3.8	1.2	3.5	6.1
Danville town *Hendricks Co.*	95.6	2.4	0.7	1.3	2.2
Decatur city *Adams Co.*	94.7	0.7	0.3	4.4	7.0
Dyer town *Lake Co.*	93.0	1.0	2.5	3.5	6.6
East Chicago city *Lake Co.*	36.0	37.9	0.2	25.9	54.0
Elkhart city *Elkhart Co.*	65.0	14.7	1.3	19.0	24.2
Elwood city *Madison Co.*	97.9	0.1	0.2	1.9	2.1
Evansville city *Vanderburgh Co.*	84.3	11.8	0.9	2.9	1.6
Fishers town *Hamilton Co.*	85.0	7.4	4.7	2.8	3.7
Fort Wayne city *Allen Co.*	71.4	18.5	2.0	8.1	9.2
Frankfort city *Clinton Co.*	81.5	0.8	0.3	17.4	26.9
Franklin city *Johnson Co.*	93.7	2.7	1.0	2.5	2.3
Gary city *Lake Co.*	10.7	85.0	0.2	4.2	5.2
Goshen city *Elkhart Co.*	74.1	1.9	1.2	22.8	32.1
Granger CDP *Saint Joseph Co.*	92.3	2.3	3.4	2.0	1.6
Greencastle city *Putnam Co.*	92.7	2.8	2.1	2.5	1.7
Greenfield city *Hancock Co.*	96.4	0.7	1.3	1.7	1.9
Greensburg city *Decatur Co.*	94.9	0.8	2.9	1.4	1.1
Greenwood city *Johnson Co.*	94.0	1.3	2.2	2.5	3.3
Griffith town *Lake Co.*	75.1	16.7	0.8	7.4	12.1
Hammond city *Lake Co.*	61.0	19.6	0.6	18.8	30.6
Highland town *Lake Co.*	91.0	2.5	1.4	5.1	10.1
Hobart city *Lake Co.*	88.6	2.9	0.9	7.6	12.4
Huntington city *Huntington Co.*	97.0	0.6	0.7	1.7	1.3
Indianapolis special city *Marion Co.*	65.3	26.6	1.6	6.6	7.9
Jasper city *Dubois Co.*	94.2	0.7	0.9	4.2	6.3
Jeffersonville city *Clark Co.*	79.5	15.6	1.1	3.8	3.1
Kendallville city *Noble Co.*	95.3	0.5	0.7	3.5	4.6
Kokomo city *Howard Co.*	84.4	10.3	1.3	4.0	2.8

Place	White[1] (%)	Black[1] (%)	Asian[1] (%)	Other (%)	Hispanic[2] (%)
La Porte city *LaPorte Co.*	90.7	1.8	0.4	7.1	9.7
Lafayette city *Tippecanoe Co.*	83.7	5.2	1.4	9.7	14.2
Lake Station city *Lake Co.*	78.9	1.3	0.5	19.3	30.2
Lakes of the Four Seasons CDP *Lake Co.*	95.7	0.5	1.0	2.8	5.0
Lawrence city *Marion Co.*	68.0	24.5	1.7	5.8	7.6
Lebanon city *Boone Co.*	95.4	1.2	1.1	2.3	2.8
Logansport city *Cass Co.*	84.7	2.3	1.3	11.6	21.1
Lowell town *Lake Co.*	95.6	0.1	0.3	4.1	5.5
Madison city *Jefferson Co.*	94.0	2.6	0.9	2.6	1.9
Marion city *Grant Co.*	80.3	14.1	0.7	4.9	4.2
Martinsville city *Morgan Co.*	97.3	1.1	0.3	1.3	1.3
Merrillville town *Lake Co.*	54.7	34.7	2.2	8.4	12.9
Michigan City city *LaPorte Co.*	70.6	24.3	0.4	4.8	4.5
Mishawaka city *Saint Joseph Co.*	89.2	4.6	1.7	4.6	4.0
Mooresville town *Morgan Co.*	97.6	0.6	0.6	1.2	0.9
Mount Vernon city *Posey Co.*	94.2	3.8	0.5	1.5	1.0
Muncie city *Delaware Co.*	84.7	10.8	1.2	3.2	1.9
Munster town *Lake Co.*	89.7	1.8	5.2	3.3	7.6
Nappanee city *Elkhart Co.*	92.4	0.5	0.6	6.5	8.4
New Albany city *Floyd Co.*	87.3	8.6	0.6	3.6	2.0
New Castle city *Henry Co.*	95.4	2.5	0.3	1.8	1.3
New Haven city *Allen Co.*	96.5	0.7	0.4	2.5	2.7
Noblesville city *Hamilton Co.*	93.8	2.3	1.2	2.7	2.8
North Vernon city *Jennings Co.*	95.1	2.0	0.6	2.3	2.1
Peru city *Miami Co.*	92.3	2.9	0.5	4.3	1.8
Plainfield town *Hendricks Co.*	81.0	14.5	2.0	2.4	3.0
Plymouth city *Marshall Co.*	86.5	1.7	0.5	11.3	22.7
Portage city *Porter Co.*	86.5	5.3	0.8	7.5	13.7
Porter town *Porter Co.*	92.1	3.1	0.9	3.9	8.1
Princeton city *Gibson Co.*	89.5	6.1	1.6	2.7	1.5
Richmond city *Wayne Co.*	85.6	8.6	0.9	4.9	3.4
Rochester city *Fulton Co.*	94.9	0.9	0.9	3.2	2.5
Saint John town *Lake Co.*	96.2	0.2	0.7	2.9	5.7
Salem city *Washington Co.*	98.4	0.0	0.4	1.2	0.4
Schererville town *Lake Co.*	87.5	2.9	3.6	6.0	9.5
Sellersburg town *Clark Co.*	97.9	0.6	0.3	1.2	1.8
Seymour city *Jackson Co.*	89.9	1.3	1.3	7.5	9.8
Shelbyville city *Shelby Co.*	92.5	1.9	1.9	3.7	4.8
South Bend city *Saint Joseph Co.*	62.0	25.6	1.5	11.0	12.2
Speedway town *Marion Co.*	72.2	17.7	2.6	7.5	7.6
Tell City city *Perry Co.*	97.9	0.6	0.3	1.2	1.6
Terre Haute city *Vigo Co.*	83.8	11.4	1.4	3.5	2.1
Valparaiso city *Porter Co.*	88.8	5.9	1.8	3.5	5.5
Vincennes city *Knox Co.*	92.7	3.7	1.5	2.1	1.4
Wabash city *Wabash Co.*	96.3	0.4	0.6	2.7	1.7
Warsaw city *Kosciusko Co.*	87.2	2.0	1.7	9.2	12.6
Washington city *Daviess Co.*	92.5	1.4	0.4	5.8	8.0
West Lafayette city *Tippecanoe Co.*	79.2	3.3	14.1	3.4	3.9
Westfield town *Hamilton Co.*	90.6	2.5	2.6	4.3	4.8
Zionsville town *Boone Co.*	92.8	2.0	3.4	1.7	2.1

NOTE: Data as of 2010; (1) Figures do not include multiple race combinations; (2) Persons of Hispanic Origin may be of any race

Avg. Household Size, Median Age, Male/Female Ratio & Foreign Born

Place	Average Household Size (persons)	Median Age (years)	Male/Female Ratio (males per 100 females)	Foreign Born (%)
Anderson city *Madison Co.*	2.37	38.3	93.1	1.8
Angola city *Steuben Co.*	2.60	34.2	104.0	2.3
Auburn city *DeKalb Co.*	2.42	37.2	94.9	0.5
Avon town *Hendricks Co.*	2.84	34.4	99.3	3.6
Batesville city *Ripley Co.*	2.64	38.0	94.9	0.6
Bedford city *Lawrence Co.*	2.19	43.9	87.6	1.1
Beech Grove city *Marion Co.*	2.45	38.4	90.0	1.7
Bloomington city *Monroe Co.*	2.54	25.7	95.7	8.1
Bluffton city *Wells Co.*	2.38	38.7	92.8	1.1
Boonville city *Warrick Co.*	2.44	38.1	91.9	0.4
Brazil city *Clay Co.*	2.44	36.7	91.4	1.0
Brownsburg town *Hendricks Co.*	2.61	35.0	95.2	1.9
Carmel city *Hamilton Co.*	2.76	36.2	95.7	7.3
Cedar Lake town *Lake Co.*	2.70	36.7	100.9	1.2
Charlestown city *Clark Co.*	2.56	34.6	95.8	2.7
Chesterton town *Porter Co.*	2.50	38.0	97.5	2.2
Clarksville town *Clark Co.*	2.29	37.9	93.7	2.9
Columbia City city *Whitley Co.*	2.34	36.6	94.1	1.1
Columbus city *Bartholomew Co.*	2.45	39.0	94.7	5.5
Connersville city *Fayette Co.*	2.34	39.1	89.5	0.6
Crawfordsville city *Montgomery Co.*	2.51	37.1	101.8	2.9
Crown Point city *Lake Co.*	2.53	42.5	93.1	6.4
Danville town *Hendricks Co.*	2.67	34.7	98.9	1.6
Decatur city *Adams Co.*	2.40	37.1	96.5	1.9
Dyer town *Lake Co.*	2.77	41.0	93.9	4.9
East Chicago city *Lake Co.*	2.75	31.9	91.7	14.7
Elkhart city *Elkhart Co.*	2.65	34.0	99.1	11.4
Elwood city *Madison Co.*	2.54	39.0	96.9	1.3
Evansville city *Vanderburgh Co.*	2.29	37.8	90.1	1.6
Fishers town *Hamilton Co.*	2.71	32.9	96.1	4.0
Fort Wayne city *Allen Co.*	2.44	35.4	95.3	4.9
Frankfort city *Clinton Co.*	2.70	35.2	96.0	9.0
Franklin city *Johnson Co.*	2.79	34.8	92.3	1.5
Gary city *Lake Co.*	2.62	33.6	85.1	1.6
Goshen city *Elkhart Co.*	2.80	33.9	103.1	15.8
Granger CDP *Saint Joseph Co.*	3.01	38.8	96.2	4.5
Greencastle city *Putnam Co.*	3.04	28.9	91.5	2.2
Greenfield city *Hancock Co.*	2.43	35.7	94.5	0.9
Greensburg city *Decatur Co.*	2.37	36.8	92.6	3.6
Greenwood city *Johnson Co.*	2.37	36.2	94.5	2.4
Griffith town *Lake Co.*	2.54	38.1	93.5	3.1
Hammond city *Lake Co.*	2.56	35.6	95.0	7.3
Highland town *Lake Co.*	2.37	42.6	92.0	4.5
Hobart city *Lake Co.*	2.53	39.8	94.1	2.9
Huntington city *Huntington Co.*	2.57	35.9	92.1	1.0
Indianapolis special city *Marion Co.*	2.43	36.1	95.1	4.6
Jasper city *Dubois Co.*	2.45	39.3	98.3	2.8
Jeffersonville city *Clark Co.*	2.30	37.8	93.8	1.7
Kendallville city *Noble Co.*	2.51	36.4	95.1	2.4
Kokomo city *Howard Co.*	2.20	38.3	91.6	2.0

Place	Average Household Size (persons)	Median Age (years)	Male/Female Ratio (males per 100 females)	Foreign Born (%)
La Porte city *LaPorte Co.*	2.39	38.3	94.9	4.2
Lafayette city *Tippecanoe Co.*	2.30	32.8	100.3	7.9
Lake Station city *Lake Co.*	2.70	35.4	98.9	4.3
Lakes of the Four Seasons CDP *Lake Co.*	2.85	39.5	96.1	5.2
Lawrence city *Marion Co.*	2.67	34.5	93.8	5.5
Lebanon city *Boone Co.*	2.39	35.3	94.5	1.2
Logansport city *Cass Co.*	2.61	36.9	104.7	7.1
Lowell town *Lake Co.*	2.73	36.4	96.8	1.4
Madison city *Jefferson Co.*	2.31	42.2	97.1	1.4
Marion city *Grant Co.*	2.50	38.0	88.8	1.8
Martinsville city *Morgan Co.*	2.53	37.3	98.1	0.7
Merrillville town *Lake Co.*	2.55	39.1	91.6	7.0
Michigan City city *LaPorte Co.*	2.60	37.0	105.3	2.1
Mishawaka city *Saint Joseph Co.*	2.32	36.5	91.6	4.4
Mooresville town *Morgan Co.*	2.62	37.2	93.5	0.3
Mount Vernon city *Posey Co.*	2.43	41.1	94.9	1.0
Muncie city *Delaware Co.*	2.42	31.3	90.9	1.9
Munster town *Lake Co.*	2.60	45.7	91.4	7.9
Nappanee city *Elkhart Co.*	2.74	33.0	100.9	2.6
New Albany city *Floyd Co.*	2.30	39.2	90.9	1.3
New Castle city *Henry Co.*	2.44	41.1	94.7	0.6
New Haven city *Allen Co.*	2.48	38.2	98.0	1.7
Noblesville city *Hamilton Co.*	2.69	34.1	98.9	2.0
North Vernon city *Jennings Co.*	2.45	35.7	90.8	0.8
Peru city *Miami Co.*	2.46	39.6	99.1	1.2
Plainfield town *Hendricks Co.*	2.64	35.2	111.4	1.5
Plymouth city *Marshall Co.*	2.57	35.1	97.4	11.7
Portage city *Porter Co.*	2.56	36.4	95.8	3.0
Porter town *Porter Co.*	2.48	36.8	97.1	2.4
Princeton city *Gibson Co.*	2.33	38.7	91.2	1.6
Richmond city *Wayne Co.*	2.37	39.1	89.7	2.4
Rochester city *Fulton Co.*	2.39	41.0	91.6	1.3
Saint John town *Lake Co.*	2.91	41.6	99.2	3.3
Salem city *Washington Co.*	2.41	39.7	92.3	0.9
Schererville town *Lake Co.*	2.62	39.6	95.3	8.3
Sellersburg town *Clark Co.*	2.43	37.9	92.4	1.2
Seymour city *Jackson Co.*	2.44	36.8	98.1	4.4
Shelbyville city *Shelby Co.*	2.43	37.0	98.4	2.8
South Bend city *Saint Joseph Co.*	2.55	34.9	93.3	6.4
Speedway town *Marion Co.*	2.12	38.5	91.1	4.5
Tell City city *Perry Co.*	2.23	42.0	94.7	0.2
Terre Haute city *Vigo Co.*	2.61	33.5	103.4	2.1
Valparaiso city *Porter Co.*	2.46	35.4	93.6	4.1
Vincennes city *Knox Co.*	2.46	35.0	101.0	1.4
Wabash city *Wabash Co.*	2.39	40.5	92.4	1.2
Warsaw city *Kosciusko Co.*	2.55	36.9	98.7	7.0
Washington city *Daviess Co.*	2.43	37.8	94.5	4.0
West Lafayette city *Tippecanoe Co.*	2.63	24.2	130.3	13.3
Westfield town *Hamilton Co.*	2.70	33.8	97.6	3.7
Zionsville town *Boone Co.*	2.87	38.5	93.5	2.5

NOTE: Average Household Size, Median Age, and Male/Female Ratio figures as of 2010. Foreign Born figures as of 2000.

Five Largest Ancestry Groups

Place	Group 1	Group 2	Group 3	Group 4	Group 5
Anderson city *Madison Co.*	Other (18.9%)	American (15.9%)	German (14.8%)	English (9.0%)	Irish (7.8%)
Angola city *Steuben Co.*	German (27.0%)	English (11.5%)	American (9.6%)	Irish (9.1%)	Other (8.7%)
Auburn city *DeKalb Co.*	German (35.2%)	American (14.6%)	Irish (9.6%)	English (9.3%)	Other (7.0%)
Avon town *Hendricks Co.*	German (24.7%)	Irish (13.1%)	American (13.0%)	Other (9.8%)	English (8.3%)
Batesville city *Ripley Co.*	German (50.1%)	Irish (11.3%)	English (9.1%)	American (8.6%)	Other (4.3%)
Bedford city *Lawrence Co.*	American (18.3%)	German (12.6%)	Irish (9.8%)	English (9.1%)	Other (8.8%)
Beech Grove city *Marion Co.*	German (27.9%)	American (20.2%)	Irish (18.8%)	English (11.8%)	Other (8.3%)
Bloomington city *Monroe Co.*	German (24.9%)	Other (15.7%)	Irish (13.3%)	English (10.9%)	American (6.7%)
Bluffton city *Wells Co.*	German (27.4%)	American (10.8%)	Other (10.3%)	Irish (8.7%)	English (8.1%)
Boonville city *Warrick Co.*	German (21.3%)	American (20.3%)	Irish (9.5%)	English (6.7%)	Other (5.0%)
Brazil city *Clay Co.*	American (21.2%)	German (17.4%)	English (11.3%)	Irish (10.4%)	Other (6.3%)
Brownsburg town *Hendricks Co.*	German (25.8%)	American (17.9%)	Irish (13.4%)	English (12.5%)	Other (8.1%)
Carmel city *Hamilton Co.*	German (28.1%)	Irish (15.1%)	English (15.0%)	Other (10.3%)	American (7.7%)
Cedar Lake town *Lake Co.*	German (28.2%)	Irish (15.4%)	Polish (10.1%)	Other (7.6%)	English (7.5%)
Charlestown city *Clark Co.*	American (24.1%)	Other (13.4%)	Irish (11.4%)	German (11.3%)	English (7.2%)
Chesterton town *Porter Co.*	German (25.6%)	Irish (19.4%)	English (12.0%)	Polish (10.2%)	Other (9.7%)
Clarksville town *Clark Co.*	German (20.0%)	Irish (13.5%)	Other (12.8%)	American (12.8%)	English (8.8%)
Columbia City city *Whitley Co.*	German (33.5%)	American (11.0%)	English (8.5%)	Irish (7.9%)	Other (6.3%)
Columbus city *Bartholomew Co.*	German (21.9%)	American (15.8%)	Other (12.9%)	English (11.3%)	Irish (10.3%)
Connersville city *Fayette Co.*	American (20.7%)	German (12.7%)	Irish (10.1%)	Other (9.4%)	English (8.7%)
Crawfordsville city *Montgomery Co.*	German (17.4%)	Irish (12.5%)	American (10.7%)	Other (10.5%)	English (9.1%)
Crown Point city *Lake Co.*	German (26.6%)	Irish (15.4%)	Polish (11.7%)	English (9.1%)	Other (8.6%)
Danville town *Hendricks Co.*	American (24.9%)	German (15.6%)	Irish (15.2%)	English (10.8%)	Other (6.5%)
Decatur city *Adams Co.*	German (32.4%)	Other (12.0%)	American (9.9%)	Irish (8.6%)	English (8.0%)
Dyer town *Lake Co.*	German (22.2%)	Polish (21.0%)	Irish (17.6%)	Italian (10.0%)	Other (9.7%)
East Chicago city *Lake Co.*	Other (77.6%)	Polish (4.8%)	German (1.5%)	Irish (1.2%)	Italian (0.8%)
Elkhart city *Elkhart Co.*	Other (30.3%)	German (18.7%)	Irish (8.2%)	American (7.0%)	English (6.6%)
Elwood city *Madison Co.*	American (29.3%)	German (17.5%)	Irish (11.1%)	English (8.8%)	Other (8.7%)
Evansville city *Vanderburgh Co.*	German (24.6%)	Other (15.8%)	American (10.7%)	Irish (10.4%)	English (9.1%)
Fishers town *Hamilton Co.*	German (29.2%)	English (13.3%)	Irish (13.3%)	Other (11.2%)	American (7.2%)
Fort Wayne city *Allen Co.*	German (27.5%)	Other (24.9%)	Irish (10.5%)	English (7.6%)	American (7.0%)
Frankfort city *Clinton Co.*	Other (17.9%)	German (16.0%)	American (15.0%)	Irish (10.9%)	English (7.6%)
Franklin city *Johnson Co.*	German (19.1%)	American (13.8%)	Irish (12.3%)	Other (10.8%)	English (9.8%)
Gary city *Lake Co.*	Other (74.3%)	American (2.0%)	German (1.9%)	Irish (1.7%)	African (1.3%)
Goshen city *Elkhart Co.*	German (25.4%)	Other (23.7%)	American (11.2%)	Irish (7.2%)	Swiss (5.4%)
Granger CDP *Saint Joseph Co.*	German (28.1%)	Irish (16.9%)	English (11.4%)	Polish (10.9%)	Other (7.6%)
Greencastle city *Putnam Co.*	German (20.5%)	American (13.3%)	Irish (12.2%)	Other (12.1%)	English (10.2%)
Greenfield city *Hancock Co.*	German (22.6%)	American (13.8%)	English (12.7%)	Irish (10.7%)	Other (9.5%)
Greensburg city *Decatur Co.*	German (21.0%)	American (12.7%)	English (9.1%)	Other (8.7%)	Irish (8.3%)
Greenwood city *Johnson Co.*	German (24.8%)	American (14.6%)	Irish (13.0%)	English (10.7%)	Other (7.8%)
Griffith town *Lake Co.*	German (23.5%)	Other (20.2%)	Polish (13.7%)	Irish (13.3%)	English (6.3%)
Hammond city *Lake Co.*	Other (34.7%)	German (14.0%)	Polish (12.3%)	Irish (11.5%)	English (4.7%)
Highland town *Lake Co.*	German (22.5%)	Polish (17.6%)	Irish (14.9%)	Other (11.2%)	English (9.2%)
Hobart city *Lake Co.*	German (23.7%)	Irish (15.5%)	Other (14.0%)	Polish (11.3%)	English (10.0%)
Huntington city *Huntington Co.*	German (28.5%)	American (13.6%)	Irish (9.8%)	Other (7.4%)	English (6.6%)
Indianapolis special city *Marion Co.*	Other (30.0%)	German (16.6%)	Irish (10.2%)	American (9.3%)	English (7.7%)
Jasper city *Dubois Co.*	German (54.3%)	American (11.0%)	Irish (8.4%)	English (6.7%)	Other (5.9%)
Jeffersonville city *Clark Co.*	Other (19.4%)	German (18.9%)	American (12.9%)	Irish (12.8%)	English (8.1%)
Kendallville city *Noble Co.*	German (25.9%)	American (19.0%)	Irish (10.3%)	Other (10.0%)	English (9.5%)
Kokomo city *Howard Co.*	Other (21.2%)	German (15.8%)	American (15.1%)	Irish (8.8%)	English (7.7%)

Place	Group 1	Group 2	Group 3	Group 4	Group 5
La Porte city *LaPorte Co.*	German (29.7%)	Other (12.8%)	Irish (11.8%)	Polish (10.9%)	American (9.3%)
Lafayette city *Tippecanoe Co.*	German (21.7%)	Other (17.5%)	American (11.7%)	Irish (11.5%)	English (9.3%)
Lake Station city *Lake Co.*	Other (25.5%)	German (15.9%)	Irish (14.6%)	American (5.8%)	English (5.5%)
Lakes of the Four Seasons CDP *Lake Co.*	German (28.0%)	Irish (16.0%)	Polish (13.8%)	English (10.8%)	Other (8.2%)
Lawrence city *Marion Co.*	Other (25.5%)	German (20.0%)	Irish (12.7%)	American (10.1%)	English (8.5%)
Lebanon city *Boone Co.*	German (22.9%)	American (14.6%)	Irish (12.0%)	English (11.0%)	Other (10.4%)
Logansport city *Cass Co.*	German (20.8%)	Other (14.5%)	American (12.8%)	Irish (8.4%)	English (5.2%)
Lowell town *Lake Co.*	German (32.2%)	Irish (17.1%)	Polish (12.0%)	English (11.3%)	Other (7.6%)
Madison city *Jefferson Co.*	German (21.5%)	American (14.4%)	English (11.3%)	Irish (10.6%)	Other (8.8%)
Marion city *Grant Co.*	Other (22.5%)	German (13.9%)	American (13.6%)	English (7.7%)	Irish (7.0%)
Martinsville city *Morgan Co.*	American (28.0%)	German (15.5%)	Irish (11.0%)	Other (8.8%)	English (6.8%)
Merrillville town *Lake Co.*	Other (32.7%)	German (16.0%)	Irish (10.6%)	Polish (9.8%)	English (5.5%)
Michigan City city *LaPorte Co.*	Other (28.3%)	German (20.2%)	Polish (11.1%)	Irish (9.8%)	American (7.2%)
Mishawaka city *Saint Joseph Co.*	German (27.2%)	Irish (14.0%)	Other (12.1%)	Polish (9.4%)	English (8.1%)
Mooresville town *Morgan Co.*	American (26.3%)	German (22.0%)	Irish (12.9%)	English (8.1%)	Other (5.3%)
Mount Vernon city *Posey Co.*	German (28.1%)	American (12.9%)	English (11.9%)	Irish (11.1%)	Other (8.2%)
Muncie city *Delaware Co.*	German (17.5%)	Other (15.3%)	American (12.8%)	Irish (9.3%)	English (9.0%)
Munster town *Lake Co.*	German (19.5%)	Polish (19.4%)	Irish (14.1%)	Other (12.1%)	Italian (8.0%)
Nappanee city *Elkhart Co.*	German (32.4%)	American (13.3%)	Other (7.7%)	Irish (7.1%)	English (4.7%)
New Albany city *Floyd Co.*	German (21.7%)	Other (15.3%)	American (14.9%)	Irish (11.7%)	English (9.1%)
New Castle city *Henry Co.*	American (21.9%)	German (11.7%)	English (9.3%)	Other (9.2%)	Irish (7.6%)
New Haven city *Allen Co.*	German (37.6%)	Irish (11.7%)	American (11.2%)	English (10.2%)	Other (9.1%)
Noblesville city *Hamilton Co.*	German (27.8%)	Irish (13.8%)	English (13.4%)	American (11.1%)	Other (7.4%)
North Vernon city *Jennings Co.*	German (19.0%)	American (15.3%)	English (10.4%)	Other (8.6%)	Irish (6.9%)
Peru city *Miami Co.*	German (20.9%)	American (13.2%)	Irish (11.7%)	Other (10.2%)	English (7.8%)
Plainfield town *Hendricks Co.*	German (23.7%)	American (17.2%)	Irish (12.0%)	English (11.9%)	Other (9.9%)
Plymouth city *Marshall Co.*	German (25.3%)	Other (20.0%)	Irish (9.4%)	American (9.3%)	English (7.7%)
Portage city *Porter Co.*	German (22.0%)	Other (18.3%)	Irish (15.3%)	English (8.8%)	Polish (8.6%)
Porter town *Porter Co.*	German (25.3%)	Irish (16.9%)	English (11.8%)	Polish (11.7%)	Other (8.5%)
Princeton city *Gibson Co.*	German (17.3%)	American (16.8%)	Irish (13.2%)	English (11.7%)	Other (11.3%)
Richmond city *Wayne Co.*	German (17.9%)	Other (14.4%)	American (13.6%)	Irish (10.1%)	English (8.7%)
Rochester city *Fulton Co.*	German (20.4%)	American (20.4%)	Irish (12.0%)	English (8.0%)	Other (7.6%)
Saint John town *Lake Co.*	German (24.0%)	Polish (23.1%)	Irish (17.2%)	Italian (12.4%)	Dutch (8.4%)
Salem city *Washington Co.*	American (17.0%)	German (13.9%)	English (11.0%)	Irish (8.6%)	Other (7.1%)
Schererville town *Lake Co.*	German (22.9%)	Polish (17.3%)	Irish (15.1%)	Other (13.0%)	English (6.8%)
Sellersburg town *Clark Co.*	German (27.3%)	Irish (17.9%)	English (12.1%)	American (11.7%)	Other (8.6%)
Seymour city *Jackson Co.*	German (23.9%)	American (20.1%)	Other (10.3%)	Irish (8.9%)	English (6.3%)
Shelbyville city *Shelby Co.*	German (25.5%)	American (23.1%)	Irish (10.7%)	Other (9.8%)	English (6.3%)
South Bend city *Saint Joseph Co.*	Other (32.7%)	German (17.6%)	Polish (10.7%)	Irish (10.5%)	English (5.9%)
Speedway town *Marion Co.*	German (22.7%)	Other (17.5%)	Irish (12.8%)	English (11.4%)	American (10.1%)
Tell City city *Perry Co.*	German (27.0%)	American (11.9%)	Irish (11.8%)	English (8.5%)	French (5.7%)
Terre Haute city *Vigo Co.*	German (18.7%)	Other (15.2%)	American (13.1%)	Irish (10.6%)	English (9.6%)
Valparaiso city *Porter Co.*	German (32.9%)	Irish (16.2%)	English (11.9%)	Polish (9.2%)	Other (8.9%)
Vincennes city *Knox Co.*	German (19.9%)	American (17.5%)	Irish (8.7%)	Other (8.4%)	English (8.3%)
Wabash city *Wabash Co.*	German (22.8%)	American (12.4%)	English (12.1%)	Irish (10.5%)	Other (8.1%)
Warsaw city *Kosciusko Co.*	German (23.0%)	Other (16.3%)	American (12.4%)	English (10.3%)	Irish (10.2%)
Washington city *Daviess Co.*	American (22.3%)	German (20.2%)	Irish (12.3%)	Other (10.6%)	English (7.1%)
West Lafayette city *Tippecanoe Co.*	German (26.7%)	Other (17.0%)	Irish (12.2%)	English (11.5%)	Polish (5.9%)
Westfield town *Hamilton Co.*	German (29.1%)	Irish (15.1%)	English (13.9%)	Other (10.9%)	American (8.7%)
Zionsville town *Boone Co.*	German (24.3%)	English (15.4%)	American (12.3%)	Irish (10.1%)	Scottish (5.2%)

NOTE: Data as of 2000; "Other" includes Hispanic and race groups; "French" excludes Basque; Please refer to the Explanation of Data for more information.

Marriage Status

Place	Never Married (%)	Now Married (%)	Widowed (%)	Divorced (%)
Anderson city *Madison Co.*	25.3	50.8	8.9	14.9
Angola city *Steuben Co.*	29.9	49.8	8.1	12.2
Auburn city *DeKalb Co.*	20.8	57.7	8.1	13.4
Avon town *Hendricks Co.*	15.1	73.1	2.7	9.0
Batesville city *Ripley Co.*	20.7	62.4	7.6	9.3
Bedford city *Lawrence Co.*	19.1	54.4	11.9	14.6
Beech Grove city *Marion Co.*	25.2	52.1	8.4	14.4
Bloomington city *Monroe Co.*	60.0	29.0	3.5	7.5
Bluffton city *Wells Co.*	21.1	55.9	9.9	13.1
Boonville city *Warrick Co.*	20.9	56.2	13.5	9.4
Brazil city *Clay Co.*	20.1	55.0	10.6	14.3
Brownsburg town *Hendricks Co.*	17.2	68.3	6.1	8.4
Carmel city *Hamilton Co.*	17.9	70.7	4.2	7.2
Cedar Lake town *Lake Co.*	24.1	60.7	5.6	9.6
Charlestown city *Clark Co.*	23.0	52.3	7.9	16.8
Chesterton town *Porter Co.*	23.9	58.5	6.6	10.9
Clarksville town *Clark Co.*	23.5	53.2	9.4	13.9
Columbia City city *Whitley Co.*	20.0	54.9	9.4	15.7
Columbus city *Bartholomew Co.*	20.5	59.8	6.7	13.0
Connersville city *Fayette Co.*	19.8	56.7	9.5	14.0
Crawfordsville city *Montgomery Co.*	25.5	51.6	9.8	13.1
Crown Point city *Lake Co.*	22.8	59.4	8.4	9.4
Danville town *Hendricks Co.*	21.2	61.8	8.2	8.8
Decatur city *Adams Co.*	22.5	56.5	8.1	12.8
Dyer town *Lake Co.*	20.1	67.5	5.8	6.6
East Chicago city *Lake Co.*	38.4	42.8	8.3	10.5
Elkhart city *Elkhart Co.*	27.8	50.4	6.8	15.0
Elwood city *Madison Co.*	17.7	60.6	7.0	14.6
Evansville city *Vanderburgh Co.*	26.5	49.8	8.4	15.3
Fishers town *Hamilton Co.*	19.0	70.9	1.8	8.3
Fort Wayne city *Allen Co.*	30.3	49.5	7.3	12.9
Frankfort city *Clinton Co.*	22.6	57.2	9.3	10.9
Franklin city *Johnson Co.*	23.6	57.7	7.8	10.9
Gary city *Lake Co.*	38.8	38.4	9.4	13.5
Goshen city *Elkhart Co.*	25.9	57.6	6.9	9.6
Granger CDP *Saint Joseph Co.*	17.8	75.1	3.0	4.1
Greencastle city *Putnam Co.*	30.3	51.3	9.2	9.3
Greenfield city *Hancock Co.*	19.9	59.0	8.6	12.5
Greensburg city *Decatur Co.*	21.8	55.6	8.5	14.0
Greenwood city *Johnson Co.*	23.1	58.4	6.9	11.6
Griffith town *Lake Co.*	26.3	56.9	7.0	9.8
Hammond city *Lake Co.*	30.4	49.7	8.5	11.4
Highland town *Lake Co.*	23.4	59.7	8.2	8.7
Hobart city *Lake Co.*	24.0	57.7	8.1	10.2
Huntington city *Huntington Co.*	26.9	54.5	6.0	12.6
Indianapolis special city *Marion Co.*	31.8	48.7	6.4	13.1
Jasper city *Dubois Co.*	23.2	58.3	7.3	11.2
Jeffersonville city *Clark Co.*	23.8	54.3	6.7	15.3
Kendallville city *Noble Co.*	21.9	54.1	9.0	15.0
Kokomo city *Howard Co.*	24.3	50.8	8.8	16.1

Place	Never Married (%)	Now Married (%)	Widowed (%)	Divorced (%)
La Porte city *LaPorte Co.*	22.0	53.6	9.5	15.0
Lafayette city *Tippecanoe Co.*	30.6	50.9	6.5	12.1
Lake Station city *Lake Co.*	29.0	52.6	7.1	11.3
Lakes of the Four Seasons CDP *Lake Co.*	22.1	68.9	3.4	5.7
Lawrence city *Marion Co.*	25.1	57.6	4.3	13.0
Lebanon city *Boone Co.*	20.6	57.9	9.1	12.4
Logansport city *Cass Co.*	24.9	51.3	8.8	14.9
Lowell town *Lake Co.*	22.2	63.0	5.8	9.1
Madison city *Jefferson Co.*	21.4	55.4	9.4	13.8
Marion city *Grant Co.*	25.2	50.7	10.1	14.0
Martinsville city *Morgan Co.*	20.7	55.1	9.5	14.6
Merrillville town *Lake Co.*	25.4	56.8	8.0	9.7
Michigan City city *LaPorte Co.*	28.1	47.2	8.6	16.1
Mishawaka city *Saint Joseph Co.*	29.8	48.0	8.2	14.0
Mooresville town *Morgan Co.*	20.1	59.6	6.9	13.4
Mount Vernon city *Posey Co.*	17.9	59.8	9.6	12.7
Muncie city *Delaware Co.*	38.0	42.6	7.7	11.8
Munster town *Lake Co.*	20.7	63.6	9.4	6.4
Nappanee city *Elkhart Co.*	23.8	62.9	5.4	7.9
New Albany city *Floyd Co.*	24.8	51.9	8.5	14.8
New Castle city *Henry Co.*	21.4	54.1	10.5	13.9
New Haven city *Allen Co.*	23.2	58.0	6.5	12.2
Noblesville city *Hamilton Co.*	18.7	67.4	5.2	8.7
North Vernon city *Jennings Co.*	20.3	56.5	9.1	14.1
Peru city *Miami Co.*	21.4	53.8	10.3	14.4
Plainfield town *Hendricks Co.*	22.4	58.5	6.3	12.8
Plymouth city *Marshall Co.*	23.7	52.7	9.6	14.0
Portage city *Porter Co.*	23.5	55.7	8.2	12.6
Porter town *Porter Co.*	24.5	55.7	5.4	14.5
Princeton city *Gibson Co.*	21.2	53.6	11.5	13.7
Richmond city *Wayne Co.*	24.5	53.1	8.9	13.6
Rochester city *Fulton Co.*	19.9	53.2	11.5	15.4
Saint John town *Lake Co.*	18.9	72.0	5.7	3.4
Salem city *Washington Co.*	20.8	54.8	10.7	13.7
Schererville town *Lake Co.*	23.0	62.6	5.9	8.5
Sellersburg town *Clark Co.*	18.0	60.2	6.7	15.1
Seymour city *Jackson Co.*	20.9	57.8	7.8	13.5
Shelbyville city *Shelby Co.*	23.8	53.0	7.4	15.7
South Bend city *Saint Joseph Co.*	32.0	47.7	8.4	11.8
Speedway town *Marion Co.*	28.6	47.3	8.3	15.8
Tell City city *Perry Co.*	19.9	56.5	9.8	13.7
Terre Haute city *Vigo Co.*	32.8	45.7	8.9	12.5
Valparaiso city *Porter Co.*	31.5	50.4	7.5	10.6
Vincennes city *Knox Co.*	34.4	44.7	9.0	11.9
Wabash city *Wabash Co.*	23.0	54.3	9.5	13.2
Warsaw city *Kosciusko Co.*	23.9	56.5	7.1	12.4
Washington city *Daviess Co.*	20.2	55.3	9.6	14.9
West Lafayette city *Tippecanoe Co.*	62.5	31.6	3.1	2.8
Westfield town *Hamilton Co.*	20.3	61.8	5.2	12.7
Zionsville town *Boone Co.*	17.0	70.8	4.1	8.1

NOTE: Data as of 2000

Employment and Building Permits Issued

Place	Unemployment Rate (%)	Total Civilian Labor Force	Single-Family Building Permits	Multi-Family Building Permits
Anderson city *Madison Co.*	11.8	26,589	22	6
Angola city *Steuben Co.*	n/a	n/a	14	0
Auburn city *DeKalb Co.*	n/a	n/a	21	0
Avon town *Hendricks Co.*	n/a	n/a	159	0
Batesville city *Ripley Co.*	n/a	n/a	11	0
Bedford city *Lawrence Co.*	n/a	n/a	8	0
Beech Grove city *Marion Co.*	n/a	n/a	0	0
Bloomington city *Monroe Co.*	6.9	38,108	n/a	n/a
Bluffton city *Wells Co.*	n/a	n/a	n/a	n/a
Boonville city *Warrick Co.*	n/a	n/a	0	0
Brazil city *Clay Co.*	n/a	n/a	9	0
Brownsburg town *Hendricks Co.*	n/a	n/a	124	0
Carmel city *Hamilton Co.*	6.8	32,899	274	397
Cedar Lake town *Lake Co.*	n/a	n/a	62	0
Charlestown city *Clark Co.*	n/a	n/a	16	0
Chesterton town *Porter Co.*	n/a	n/a	14	6
Clarksville town *Clark Co.*	n/a	n/a	14	2
Columbia City city *Whitley Co.*	n/a	n/a	25	35
Columbus city *Bartholomew Co.*	10.4	19,308	n/a	n/a
Connersville city *Fayette Co.*	n/a	n/a	n/a	n/a
Crawfordsville city *Montgomery Co.*	n/a	n/a	21	0
Crown Point city *Lake Co.*	n/a	n/a	102	0
Danville town *Hendricks Co.*	n/a	n/a	14	80
Decatur city *Adams Co.*	n/a	n/a	6	0
Dyer town *Lake Co.*	n/a	n/a	42	0
East Chicago city *Lake Co.*	13.8	9,999	69	0
Elkhart city *Elkhart Co.*	15.8	22,040	3	0
Elwood city *Madison Co.*	n/a	n/a	2	0
Evansville city *Vanderburgh Co.*	9.5	57,656	37	35
Fishers town *Hamilton Co.*	6.2	38,988	469	57
Fort Wayne city *Allen Co.*	10.7	124,564	86	20
Frankfort city *Clinton Co.*	n/a	n/a	2	0
Franklin city *Johnson Co.*	n/a	n/a	22	0
Gary city *Lake Co.*	11.8	33,993	4	0
Goshen city *Elkhart Co.*	12.7	13,671	12	0
Granger CDP *Saint Joseph Co.*	n/a	n/a	n/a	n/a
Greencastle city *Putnam Co.*	n/a	n/a	9	0
Greenfield city *Hancock Co.*	n/a	n/a	35	147
Greensburg city *Decatur Co.*	n/a	n/a	26	64
Greenwood city *Johnson Co.*	9.1	25,858	77	3
Griffith town *Lake Co.*	n/a	n/a	4	10
Hammond city *Lake Co.*	12.1	32,507	3	2
Highland town *Lake Co.*	n/a	n/a	5	0
Hobart city *Lake Co.*	11.4	13,644	14	0
Huntington city *Huntington Co.*	n/a	n/a	n/a	n/a
Indianapolis special city *Marion Co.*	9.7	411,848	587	454
Jasper city *Dubois Co.*	n/a	n/a	26	24
Jeffersonville city *Clark Co.*	9.0	15,399	145	25
Kendallville city *Noble Co.*	n/a	n/a	22	0
Kokomo city *Howard Co.*	13.8	19,282	3	62

Place	Unemployment Rate (%)	Total Civilian Labor Force	Single-Family Building Permits	Multi-Family Building Permits
La Porte city *LaPorte Co.*	n/a	n/a	14	0
Lafayette city *Tippecanoe Co.*	10.5	32,872	80	0
Lake Station city *Lake Co.*	n/a	n/a	6	0
Lakes of the Four Seasons CDP *Lake Co.*	n/a	n/a	n/a	n/a
Lawrence city *Marion Co.*	8.5	22,917	51	0
Lebanon city *Boone Co.*	n/a	n/a	3	8
Logansport city *Cass Co.*	n/a	n/a	n/a	n/a
Lowell town *Lake Co.*	n/a	n/a	41	0
Madison city *Jefferson Co.*	n/a	n/a	15	0
Marion city *Grant Co.*	12.8	13,303	n/a	n/a
Martinsville city *Morgan Co.*	n/a	n/a	7	0
Merrillville town *Lake Co.*	9.7	16,382	16	36
Michigan City city *LaPorte Co.*	11.8	14,130	8	24
Mishawaka city *Saint Joseph Co.*	11.5	25,343	32	0
Mooresville town *Morgan Co.*	n/a	n/a	14	2
Mount Vernon city *Posey Co.*	n/a	n/a	n/a	n/a
Muncie city *Delaware Co.*	11.0	30,007	6	0
Munster town *Lake Co.*	n/a	n/a	29	0
Nappanee city *Elkhart Co.*	n/a	n/a	3	0
New Albany city *Floyd Co.*	9.7	17,987	21	0
New Castle city *Henry Co.*	n/a	n/a	3	0
New Haven city *Allen Co.*	n/a	n/a	n/a	n/a
Noblesville city *Hamilton Co.*	8.7	21,946	412	326
North Vernon city *Jennings Co.*	n/a	n/a	n/a	n/a
Peru city *Miami Co.*	n/a	n/a	2	0
Plainfield town *Hendricks Co.*	8.5	13,871	102	48
Plymouth city *Marshall Co.*	n/a	n/a	27	0
Portage city *Porter Co.*	9.7	17,802	33	0
Porter town *Porter Co.*	n/a	n/a	8	0
Princeton city *Gibson Co.*	n/a	n/a	1	0
Richmond city *Wayne Co.*	11.3	17,123	15	0
Rochester city *Fulton Co.*	n/a	n/a	0	0
Saint John town *Lake Co.*	n/a	n/a	115	0
Salem city *Washington Co.*	n/a	n/a	2	4
Schererville town *Lake Co.*	8.0	15,321	15	0
Sellersburg town *Clark Co.*	n/a	n/a	4	5
Seymour city *Jackson Co.*	n/a	n/a	43	21
Shelbyville city *Shelby Co.*	n/a	n/a	4	0
South Bend city *Saint Joseph Co.*	13.1	45,021	n/a	n/a
Speedway town *Marion Co.*	n/a	n/a	0	0
Tell City city *Perry Co.*	n/a	n/a	4	0
Terre Haute city *Vigo Co.*	11.7	27,127	26	6
Valparaiso city *Porter Co.*	8.4	15,193	50	40
Vincennes city *Knox Co.*	n/a	n/a	1	0
Wabash city *Wabash Co.*	n/a	n/a	7	0
Warsaw city *Kosciusko Co.*	n/a	n/a	42	22
Washington city *Daviess Co.*	n/a	n/a	8	0
West Lafayette city *Tippecanoe Co.*	6.6	13,718	72	23
Westfield town *Hamilton Co.*	n/a	n/a	182	23
Zionsville town *Boone Co.*	n/a	n/a	60	0

NOTE: Unemployment Rate and Civilian Labor Force as of May 2010; Building permit data covers 2009; n/a not available.

Employment by Occupation

Place	Sales (%)	Prof. (%)	Mgmt (%)	Svcs (%)	Prod. (%)	Constr. (%)
Anderson city *Madison Co.*	26.9	14.2	8.6	19.0	21.6	9.5
Angola city *Steuben Co.*	22.6	21.1	7.6	14.3	28.5	5.9
Auburn city *DeKalb Co.*	22.0	14.7	10.5	9.1	33.7	9.8
Avon town *Hendricks Co.*	27.2	15.6	19.7	10.5	17.1	9.9
Batesville city *Ripley Co.*	25.4	22.0	11.5	11.5	23.5	6.0
Bedford city *Lawrence Co.*	23.3	17.3	8.8	18.9	23.3	8.3
Beech Grove city *Marion Co.*	29.1	16.8	8.2	15.9	19.3	10.7
Bloomington city *Monroe Co.*	25.4	33.1	10.8	20.0	6.4	4.1
Bluffton city *Wells Co.*	23.7	14.7	8.7	15.7	27.5	9.0
Boonville city *Warrick Co.*	24.7	15.2	8.1	16.5	20.0	15.1
Brazil city *Clay Co.*	21.2	12.4	8.6	17.7	30.1	9.6
Brownsburg town *Hendricks Co.*	31.2	26.7	15.1	7.4	13.2	6.4
Carmel city *Hamilton Co.*	28.2	29.4	26.7	8.1	4.3	3.1
Cedar Lake town *Lake Co.*	25.9	11.6	6.2	13.1	20.6	22.2
Charlestown city *Clark Co.*	23.8	8.6	8.8	20.6	27.2	11.0
Chesterton town *Porter Co.*	24.2	24.8	15.4	10.9	13.7	10.9
Clarksville town *Clark Co.*	31.4	14.5	9.8	14.0	20.3	9.8
Columbia City city *Whitley Co.*	24.7	12.6	9.8	14.6	28.5	9.4
Columbus city *Bartholomew Co.*	23.3	22.2	12.9	12.2	22.9	6.4
Connersville city *Fayette Co.*	18.1	10.5	6.5	17.7	38.6	8.8
Crawfordsville city *Montgomery Co.*	23.3	14.1	8.4	15.7	30.1	7.7
Crown Point city *Lake Co.*	30.4	19.7	11.7	14.2	13.9	10.0
Danville town *Hendricks Co.*	32.2	18.7	8.1	13.1	14.4	12.6
Decatur city *Adams Co.*	20.3	13.2	8.8	16.8	30.5	10.3
Dyer town *Lake Co.*	29.2	22.4	13.5	11.0	12.2	11.6
East Chicago city *Lake Co.*	23.8	11.7	5.5	21.7	28.0	9.1
Elkhart city *Elkhart Co.*	21.4	10.8	9.2	11.4	39.3	7.6
Elwood city *Madison Co.*	20.6	10.8	6.6	16.8	34.2	10.9
Evansville city *Vanderburgh Co.*	28.6	15.8	9.2	17.3	19.9	9.0
Fishers town *Hamilton Co.*	30.6	27.3	28.2	7.2	3.8	2.9
Fort Wayne city *Allen Co.*	27.9	18.3	10.4	14.8	20.4	8.1
Frankfort city *Clinton Co.*	20.8	6.5	6.7	12.9	39.9	11.3
Franklin city *Johnson Co.*	25.0	16.7	11.0	14.7	21.0	11.0
Gary city *Lake Co.*	26.8	14.1	6.5	24.0	21.3	7.3
Goshen city *Elkhart Co.*	20.0	15.1	9.7	12.1	35.1	7.7
Granger CDP *Saint Joseph Co.*	28.2	28.2	22.5	8.4	8.0	4.6
Greencastle city *Putnam Co.*	25.0	20.6	5.9	17.1	24.8	6.7
Greenfield city *Hancock Co.*	26.5	16.4	10.9	15.8	18.5	11.8
Greensburg city *Decatur Co.*	20.5	13.8	8.6	13.5	35.1	8.2
Greenwood city *Johnson Co.*	30.0	20.7	14.9	12.0	12.3	10.0
Griffith town *Lake Co.*	30.4	16.1	9.8	13.7	17.8	12.0
Hammond city *Lake Co.*	28.7	12.6	7.9	17.6	22.4	10.9
Highland town *Lake Co.*	30.3	19.8	13.0	13.0	14.2	9.6
Hobart city *Lake Co.*	26.9	15.9	9.4	14.2	18.5	15.1
Huntington city *Huntington Co.*	21.5	12.2	8.1	16.6	33.9	7.7
Indianapolis special city *Marion Co.*	28.3	19.6	13.1	14.9	15.2	8.6
Jasper city *Dubois Co.*	25.8	15.1	12.3	12.2	26.7	7.9
Jeffersonville city *Clark Co.*	29.8	15.8	11.1	14.9	19.6	8.9
Kendallville city *Noble Co.*	21.0	10.1	8.0	12.9	37.6	10.0
Kokomo city *Howard Co.*	21.1	16.8	6.9	17.3	28.0	9.7

Place	Sales (%)	Prof. (%)	Mgmt (%)	Svcs (%)	Prod. (%)	Constr. (%)
La Porte city *LaPorte Co.*	21.7	13.0	8.9	16.7	28.3	11.0
Lafayette city *Tippecanoe Co.*	24.1	20.8	9.0	16.7	21.2	8.0
Lake Station city *Lake Co.*	24.5	6.9	5.7	19.1	25.2	18.3
Lakes of the Four Seasons CDP *Lake Co.*	27.6	22.9	14.4	11.1	13.4	10.6
Lawrence city *Marion Co.*	31.0	20.0	16.0	11.4	12.8	8.7
Lebanon city *Boone Co.*	26.8	13.3	8.9	19.2	21.4	10.4
Logansport city *Cass Co.*	22.0	11.5	5.1	18.1	33.0	9.8
Lowell town *Lake Co.*	25.7	15.7	10.5	13.8	19.0	14.9
Madison city *Jefferson Co.*	24.9	18.3	12.0	14.7	22.1	7.8
Marion city *Grant Co.*	21.5	15.9	7.0	18.7	29.5	7.2
Martinsville city *Morgan Co.*	23.6	11.6	8.1	17.8	19.9	18.8
Merrillville town *Lake Co.*	28.0	18.6	9.7	14.3	19.7	9.6
Michigan City city *LaPorte Co.*	25.7	12.8	8.5	21.3	22.2	9.3
Mishawaka city *Saint Joseph Co.*	29.0	16.1	11.1	15.5	20.1	8.2
Mooresville town *Morgan Co.*	27.6	14.1	10.4	15.2	19.0	13.8
Mount Vernon city *Posey Co.*	24.0	20.4	10.6	15.0	20.9	8.4
Muncie city *Delaware Co.*	28.0	20.3	7.3	20.4	17.1	6.6
Munster town *Lake Co.*	24.4	31.1	15.2	9.1	12.6	7.3
Nappanee city *Elkhart Co.*	22.6	10.3	8.0	12.4	37.7	9.2
New Albany city *Floyd Co.*	28.1	16.1	9.4	15.7	20.8	9.9
New Castle city *Henry Co.*	21.2	14.3	6.8	20.4	26.3	11.0
New Haven city *Allen Co.*	27.1	13.1	10.5	14.4	24.6	10.3
Noblesville city *Hamilton Co.*	28.1	25.5	18.4	10.3	10.3	7.2
North Vernon city *Jennings Co.*	19.9	16.5	8.5	15.2	28.1	10.8
Peru city *Miami Co.*	21.9	11.7	6.7	16.4	33.2	9.6
Plainfield town *Hendricks Co.*	30.5	15.5	11.4	14.3	16.1	12.2
Plymouth city *Marshall Co.*	20.4	11.3	6.9	13.6	38.7	8.6
Portage city *Porter Co.*	23.5	12.8	7.9	16.8	23.2	15.7
Porter town *Porter Co.*	26.9	17.9	11.5	13.8	14.8	15.1
Princeton city *Gibson Co.*	21.8	11.4	6.3	24.1	27.2	8.7
Richmond city *Wayne Co.*	25.2	15.4	8.5	17.0	25.7	8.0
Rochester city *Fulton Co.*	25.2	10.2	6.7	13.6	33.9	9.8
Saint John town *Lake Co.*	28.2	20.2	16.7	7.8	12.2	14.9
Salem city *Washington Co.*	19.3	12.7	7.5	17.7	33.7	8.4
Schererville town *Lake Co.*	25.9	21.2	14.4	12.4	14.9	11.2
Sellersburg town *Clark Co.*	29.7	13.8	8.1	14.9	22.4	11.1
Seymour city *Jackson Co.*	22.7	12.8	7.6	10.4	35.3	10.1
Shelbyville city *Shelby Co.*	21.8	13.3	9.2	15.6	30.7	9.2
South Bend city *Saint Joseph Co.*	25.6	18.3	9.8	16.9	22.0	7.2
Speedway town *Marion Co.*	29.9	19.8	11.8	14.8	17.0	6.5
Tell City city *Perry Co.*	23.6	13.2	6.1	16.5	30.0	10.7
Terre Haute city *Vigo Co.*	28.6	20.0	8.5	20.5	15.2	6.9
Valparaiso city *Porter Co.*	26.5	26.9	11.4	14.4	11.7	9.2
Vincennes city *Knox Co.*	27.7	17.7	7.4	22.9	16.2	7.4
Wabash city *Wabash Co.*	24.7	11.7	8.4	15.0	32.5	7.2
Warsaw city *Kosciusko Co.*	25.3	13.8	10.4	11.1	30.1	8.5
Washington city *Daviess Co.*	24.6	15.2	6.3	16.2	28.3	8.9
West Lafayette city *Tippecanoe Co.*	20.6	43.0	9.7	16.9	6.0	2.6
Westfield town *Hamilton Co.*	31.4	24.2	18.0	10.0	8.1	7.8
Zionsville town *Boone Co.*	25.5	25.6	31.0	7.7	3.3	6.9

NOTE: Data as of 2000

Educational Attainment

| Place | Percent of Population 25 Years and Over with: | | |
	High School Diploma including Equivalency	Bachelor's Degree or Higher	Masters's Degree or Higher
Anderson city *Madison Co.*	83.8	16.2	6.9
Angola city *Steuben Co.*	88.0	22.4	9.2
Auburn city *DeKalb Co.*	88.4	23.8	7.4
Avon town *Hendricks Co.*	96.3	37.6	11.0
Batesville city *Ripley Co.*	90.6	27.3	9.5
Bedford city *Lawrence Co.*	77.7	14.5	5.4
Beech Grove city *Marion Co.*	85.4	19.6	8.1
Bloomington city *Monroe Co.*	93.1	55.9	29.7
Bluffton city *Wells Co.*	83.3	13.9	5.4
Boonville city *Warrick Co.*	85.2	15.5	7.1
Brazil city *Clay Co.*	81.7	13.3	3.2
Brownsburg town *Hendricks Co.*	96.4	41.7	11.6
Carmel city *Hamilton Co.*	97.7	61.6	22.6
Cedar Lake town *Lake Co.*	88.6	11.3	2.5
Charlestown city *Clark Co.*	78.7	12.9	3.6
Chesterton town *Porter Co.*	94.3	27.7	9.4
Clarksville town *Clark Co.*	82.1	15.5	4.9
Columbia City city *Whitley Co.*	86.9	16.2	4.6
Columbus city *Bartholomew Co.*	89.1	33.1	14.7
Connersville city *Fayette Co.*	74.1	6.8	2.7
Crawfordsville city *Montgomery Co.*	80.9	16.8	5.3
Crown Point city *Lake Co.*	91.4	27.0	8.7
Danville town *Hendricks Co.*	95.1	28.8	11.1
Decatur city *Adams Co.*	86.0	11.3	3.3
Dyer town *Lake Co.*	93.1	27.9	7.9
East Chicago city *Lake Co.*	66.7	8.6	2.1
Elkhart city *Elkhart Co.*	74.2	15.8	4.7
Elwood city *Madison Co.*	77.7	8.0	3.4
Evansville city *Vanderburgh Co.*	83.8	17.9	5.9
Fishers town *Hamilton Co.*	98.6	62.7	16.2
Fort Wayne city *Allen Co.*	85.6	22.2	7.0
Frankfort city *Clinton Co.*	72.4	10.3	3.2
Franklin city *Johnson Co.*	86.2	21.3	8.4
Gary city *Lake Co.*	79.1	11.8	4.4
Goshen city *Elkhart Co.*	75.2	21.4	6.7
Granger CDP *Saint Joseph Co.*	96.6	52.5	20.7
Greencastle city *Putnam Co.*	86.0	25.3	9.1
Greenfield city *Hancock Co.*	87.3	22.7	8.2
Greensburg city *Decatur Co.*	83.0	15.9	5.9
Greenwood city *Johnson Co.*	92.2	27.0	8.0
Griffith town *Lake Co.*	92.1	17.2	3.6
Hammond city *Lake Co.*	81.1	13.1	3.4
Highland town *Lake Co.*	91.4	24.6	7.7
Hobart city *Lake Co.*	89.0	16.7	4.9
Huntington city *Huntington Co.*	84.0	14.2	5.6
Indianapolis special city *Marion Co.*	84.2	27.7	9.9
Jasper city *Dubois Co.*	83.5	25.0	9.8
Jeffersonville city *Clark Co.*	84.3	17.6	6.1
Kendallville city *Noble Co.*	79.7	16.4	5.7
Kokomo city *Howard Co.*	81.7	17.3	6.7

Place	Percent of Population 25 Years and Over with:		
	High School Diploma including Equivalency	Bachelor's Degree or Higher	Masters's Degree or Higher
La Porte city *LaPorte Co.*	85.0	15.3	5.2
Lafayette city *Tippecanoe Co.*	85.8	26.9	10.2
Lake Station city *Lake Co.*	79.7	5.6	1.6
Lakes of the Four Seasons CDP *Lake Co.*	96.1	32.2	9.7
Lawrence city *Marion Co.*	88.4	29.5	9.3
Lebanon city *Boone Co.*	88.6	22.4	7.8
Logansport city *Cass Co.*	74.3	11.8	4.3
Lowell town *Lake Co.*	91.7	16.3	6.0
Madison city *Jefferson Co.*	85.5	24.3	10.4
Marion city *Grant Co.*	77.6	16.2	6.7
Martinsville city *Morgan Co.*	74.7	12.4	5.5
Merrillville town *Lake Co.*	90.4	23.2	7.3
Michigan City city *LaPorte Co.*	82.7	15.0	5.0
Mishawaka city *Saint Joseph Co.*	84.1	20.3	6.6
Mooresville town *Morgan Co.*	87.0	17.1	4.1
Mount Vernon city *Posey Co.*	84.6	15.0	5.0
Muncie city *Delaware Co.*	79.1	21.2	9.4
Munster town *Lake Co.*	95.3	42.5	16.4
Nappanee city *Elkhart Co.*	76.6	13.0	4.3
New Albany city *Floyd Co.*	82.4	17.4	6.0
New Castle city *Henry Co.*	76.5	13.3	4.0
New Haven city *Allen Co.*	87.0	15.0	4.1
Noblesville city *Hamilton Co.*	93.7	44.5	12.8
North Vernon city *Jennings Co.*	80.4	10.4	3.5
Peru city *Miami Co.*	81.1	10.6	3.4
Plainfield town *Hendricks Co.*	91.7	26.5	8.7
Plymouth city *Marshall Co.*	78.9	16.3	7.1
Portage city *Porter Co.*	87.3	12.0	2.8
Porter town *Porter Co.*	93.0	28.9	8.3
Princeton city *Gibson Co.*	83.9	11.5	2.1
Richmond city *Wayne Co.*	78.7	15.4	5.8
Rochester city *Fulton Co.*	84.6	14.0	5.7
Saint John town *Lake Co.*	94.2	23.7	6.2
Salem city *Washington Co.*	77.5	10.6	5.0
Schererville town *Lake Co.*	94.4	30.8	10.6
Sellersburg town *Clark Co.*	88.6	18.6	6.4
Seymour city *Jackson Co.*	81.5	13.9	5.0
Shelbyville city *Shelby Co.*	83.8	13.7	3.3
South Bend city *Saint Joseph Co.*	80.8	22.5	9.3
Speedway town *Marion Co.*	89.9	24.5	8.3
Tell City city *Perry Co.*	78.6	12.3	5.8
Terre Haute city *Vigo Co.*	81.7	19.6	9.0
Valparaiso city *Porter Co.*	93.5	37.1	12.2
Vincennes city *Knox Co.*	84.2	15.3	6.1
Wabash city *Wabash Co.*	82.2	14.6	4.7
Warsaw city *Kosciusko Co.*	79.7	20.7	7.4
Washington city *Daviess Co.*	76.2	11.3	4.9
West Lafayette city *Tippecanoe Co.*	95.9	70.1	38.5
Westfield town *Hamilton Co.*	93.9	41.7	12.7
Zionsville town *Boone Co.*	96.9	66.5	27.1

NOTE: Data as of 2010

Income and Poverty

Place	Average Household Income ($)	Median Household Income ($)	Per Capita Income ($)	Households w/$100,000+ Income (%)	Poverty Rate[1] (%)
Anderson city *Madison Co.*	48,189	37,063	20,887	8.1	13.4
Angola city *Steuben Co.*	48,435	40,481	19,460	6.2	10.5
Auburn city *DeKalb Co.*	56,789	47,145	23,707	10.8	5.2
Avon town *Hendricks Co.*	86,010	76,860	30,319	29.4	2.9
Batesville city *Ripley Co.*	70,946	57,939	26,942	19.1	3.5
Bedford city *Lawrence Co.*	43,648	34,292	20,367	6.8	11.5
Beech Grove city *Marion Co.*	56,451	47,895	23,808	11.6	6.1
Bloomington city *Monroe Co.*	45,099	28,213	18,714	10.1	29.6
Bluffton city *Wells Co.*	50,705	40,534	21,601	8.5	9.0
Boonville city *Warrick Co.*	49,690	42,462	20,607	8.6	9.2
Brazil city *Clay Co.*	42,517	34,863	17,602	6.2	13.2
Brownsburg town *Hendricks Co.*	77,731	66,753	30,032	25.3	2.3
Carmel city *Hamilton Co.*	120,925	91,343	44,123	45.1	2.5
Cedar Lake town *Lake Co.*	65,544	57,988	24,348	18.5	6.6
Charlestown city *Clark Co.*	50,908	41,276	19,912	9.6	19.2
Chesterton town *Porter Co.*	74,920	60,968	30,098	20.9	4.3
Clarksville town *Clark Co.*	51,037	38,946	22,754	9.5	8.1
Columbia City city *Whitley Co.*	50,571	42,382	22,059	7.2	6.4
Columbus city *Bartholomew Co.*	64,043	49,147	26,716	16.8	8.1
Connersville city *Fayette Co.*	40,499	33,504	17,683	4.6	10.5
Crawfordsville city *Montgomery Co.*	49,391	40,144	20,225	8.3	12.9
Crown Point city *Lake Co.*	75,457	62,467	30,333	22.8	3.7
Danville town *Hendricks Co.*	72,586	62,448	28,178	21.4	2.5
Decatur city *Adams Co.*	50,345	42,057	21,320	8.3	7.7
Dyer town *Lake Co.*	90,030	73,847	32,788	31.6	3.4
East Chicago city *Lake Co.*	39,936	29,481	14,679	6.0	24.4
Elkhart city *Elkhart Co.*	50,442	39,990	19,542	8.6	13.6
Elwood city *Madison Co.*	44,386	35,666	17,496	7.0	15.2
Evansville city *Vanderburgh Co.*	46,457	35,984	20,779	6.8	13.7
Fishers town *Hamilton Co.*	103,384	85,583	38,168	38.3	1.8
Fort Wayne city *Allen Co.*	48,890	39,804	20,360	7.8	12.5
Frankfort city *Clinton Co.*	44,693	38,476	17,558	5.6	11.7
Franklin city *Johnson Co.*	61,378	54,045	23,289	14.1	7.6
Gary city *Lake Co.*	43,367	31,221	16,646	8.2	25.8
Goshen city *Elkhart Co.*	56,993	46,322	21,056	10.3	9.3
Granger CDP *Saint Joseph Co.*	112,534	92,456	37,460	44.0	1.4
Greencastle city *Putnam Co.*	52,727	39,091	18,827	10.6	9.8
Greenfield city *Hancock Co.*	61,305	49,075	25,479	13.5	4.3
Greensburg city *Decatur Co.*	52,054	43,009	22,344	9.1	11.4
Greenwood city *Johnson Co.*	62,654	52,089	26,657	16.0	7.0
Griffith town *Lake Co.*	64,698	56,038	25,552	15.8	3.9
Hammond city *Lake Co.*	46,341	38,841	18,212	6.9	14.3
Highland town *Lake Co.*	68,579	59,407	28,952	17.9	3.0
Hobart city *Lake Co.*	63,293	56,098	25,282	14.7	4.8
Huntington city *Huntington Co.*	48,724	39,708	19,474	6.7	8.1
Indianapolis special city *Marion Co.*	59,953	45,657	24,937	14.0	11.9
Jasper city *Dubois Co.*	65,711	52,609	27,192	15.1	5.6
Jeffersonville city *Clark Co.*	53,124	43,676	23,465	10.7	10.1
Kendallville city *Noble Co.*	48,448	41,046	19,556	6.8	9.9
Kokomo city *Howard Co.*	46,204	37,585	21,199	6.6	13.0

Place	Average Household Income ($)	Median Household Income ($)	Per Capita Income ($)	Households w/$100,000+ Income (%)	Poverty Rate[1] (%)
La Porte city *LaPorte Co.*	47,203	38,998	20,041	7.0	11.0
Lafayette city *Tippecanoe Co.*	48,378	38,667	21,163	7.4	12.1
Lake Station city *Lake Co.*	47,639	40,333	17,670	6.5	14.6
Lakes of the Four Seasons CDP *Lake Co.*	89,597	79,592	31,449	30.8	2.6
Lawrence city *Marion Co.*	70,918	55,793	26,620	20.5	6.7
Lebanon city *Boone Co.*	59,123	48,665	24,997	11.7	7.1
Logansport city *Cass Co.*	48,450	39,045	18,988	7.6	10.1
Lowell town *Lake Co.*	67,006	59,685	24,850	17.9	6.5
Madison city *Jefferson Co.*	54,358	42,113	24,123	12.5	12.3
Marion city *Grant Co.*	42,414	32,050	17,764	6.5	16.9
Martinsville city *Morgan Co.*	48,522	37,993	19,565	7.4	11.6
Merrillville town *Lake Co.*	64,535	56,645	25,703	15.1	4.3
Michigan City city *LaPorte Co.*	47,229	38,183	18,941	6.9	13.3
Mishawaka city *Saint Joseph Co.*	47,730	39,394	20,949	7.3	9.9
Mooresville town *Morgan Co.*	64,799	55,952	24,995	17.0	4.3
Mount Vernon city *Posey Co.*	55,413	44,265	22,961	13.4	12.5
Muncie city *Delaware Co.*	39,788	29,478	17,007	5.2	23.1
Munster town *Lake Co.*	95,041	71,712	36,657	32.7	4.3
Nappanee city *Elkhart Co.*	61,121	53,775	22,456	11.4	4.6
New Albany city *Floyd Co.*	49,623	40,237	21,923	9.2	13.7
New Castle city *Henry Co.*	44,183	33,158	19,131	7.4	12.4
New Haven city *Allen Co.*	54,468	46,310	22,106	8.6	6.6
Noblesville city *Hamilton Co.*	86,017	68,932	32,239	28.1	5.4
North Vernon city *Jennings Co.*	49,402	41,780	20,396	7.9	11.8
Peru city *Miami Co.*	47,305	35,406	20,344	7.8	11.8
Plainfield town *Hendricks Co.*	62,913	53,950	25,381	15.8	5.2
Plymouth city *Marshall Co.*	50,865	42,423	19,982	8.3	13.1
Portage city *Porter Co.*	60,731	54,071	23,896	13.1	7.5
Porter town *Porter Co.*	80,470	61,812	32,398	23.2	6.5
Princeton city *Gibson Co.*	45,353	36,420	20,096	8.0	15.8
Richmond city *Wayne Co.*	46,059	34,633	19,940	7.5	15.7
Rochester city *Fulton Co.*	48,999	39,457	20,682	7.9	11.9
Saint John town *Lake Co.*	91,344	81,700	31,406	35.8	1.7
Salem city *Washington Co.*	41,164	33,352	17,874	4.3	11.6
Schererville town *Lake Co.*	86,778	69,665	33,337	28.5	3.1
Sellersburg town *Clark Co.*	54,851	46,710	22,891	10.9	5.3
Seymour city *Jackson Co.*	51,251	42,301	21,170	7.8	10.0
Shelbyville city *Shelby Co.*	52,779	43,297	21,969	9.4	9.1
South Bend city *Saint Joseph Co.*	47,031	36,200	18,770	7.6	16.7
Speedway town *Marion Co.*	51,414	43,742	24,429	9.5	8.8
Tell City city *Perry Co.*	48,866	38,228	22,565	9.0	11.2
Terre Haute city *Vigo Co.*	43,649	32,278	17,937	6.8	19.2
Valparaiso city *Porter Co.*	64,128	51,705	26,657	15.9	9.1
Vincennes city *Knox Co.*	42,970	33,049	18,062	6.9	20.7
Wabash city *Wabash Co.*	47,964	38,119	20,644	7.0	9.3
Warsaw city *Kosciusko Co.*	52,025	41,506	21,539	9.1	9.2
Washington city *Daviess Co.*	49,341	36,861	20,617	8.4	14.3
West Lafayette city *Tippecanoe Co.*	49,172	25,656	19,942	13.2	38.3
Westfield town *Hamilton Co.*	90,512	74,605	33,744	33.3	4.0
Zionsville town *Boone Co.*	128,584	92,284	45,471	46.5	4.0

NOTE: Data as of 2010 except for Poverty Rate which is from 2000; (1) Percentage of population with income below the poverty level

Taxes

Place	Total City Taxes Per Capita ($)	City Property Taxes Per Capita ($)
Anderson city *Madison Co.*	282	266
Angola city *Steuben Co.*	320	272
Auburn city *DeKalb Co.*	189	136
Avon town *Hendricks Co.*	362	208
Batesville city *Ripley Co.*	181	175
Bedford city *Lawrence Co.*	360	336
Beech Grove city *Marion Co.*	326	290
Bloomington city *Monroe Co.*	0	0
Bluffton city *Wells Co.*	207	170
Boonville city *Warrick Co.*	349	210
Brazil city *Clay Co.*	128	124
Brownsburg town *Hendricks Co.*	462	339
Carmel city *Hamilton Co.*	464	405
Cedar Lake town *Lake Co.*	237	187
Charlestown city *Clark Co.*	209	159
Chesterton town *Porter Co.*	315	224
Clarksville town *Clark Co.*	560	478
Columbia City city *Whitley Co.*	194	170
Columbus city *Bartholomew Co.*	384	376
Connersville city *Fayette Co.*	365	329
Crawfordsville city *Montgomery Co.*	337	328
Crown Point city *Lake Co.*	283	241
Danville town *Hendricks Co.*	226	184
Decatur city *Adams Co.*	348	249
Dyer town *Lake Co.*	231	194
East Chicago city *Lake Co.*	1,444	1,438
Elkhart city *Elkhart Co.*	491	406
Elwood city *Madison Co.*	308	302
Evansville city *Vanderburgh Co.*	393	310
Fishers town *Hamilton Co.*	243	163
Fort Wayne city *Allen Co.*	495	288
Frankfort city *Clinton Co.*	192	171
Franklin city *Johnson Co.*	408	398
Gary city *Lake Co.*	779	764
Goshen city *Elkhart Co.*	354	276
Granger CDP *Saint Joseph Co.*	n/a	n/a
Greencastle city *Putnam Co.*	301	176
Greenfield city *Hancock Co.*	300	269
Greensburg city *Decatur Co.*	418	397
Greenwood city *Johnson Co.*	241	235
Griffith town *Lake Co.*	336	310
Hammond city *Lake Co.*	614	514
Highland town *Lake Co.*	303	277
Hobart city *Lake Co.*	504	469
Huntington city *Huntington Co.*	270	262
Indianapolis special city *Marion Co.*	1,185	913
Jasper city *Dubois Co.*	317	299
Jeffersonville city *Clark Co.*	393	279
Kendallville city *Noble Co.*	36	0
Kokomo city *Howard Co.*	486	456

Place	Total City Taxes Per Capita ($)	City Property Taxes Per Capita ($)
La Porte city *LaPorte Co.*	325	272
Lafayette city *Tippecanoe Co.*	388	301
Lake Station city *Lake Co.*	561	550
Lakes of the Four Seasons CDP *Lake Co.*	n/a	n/a
Lawrence city *Marion Co.*	263	233
Lebanon city *Boone Co.*	344	157
Logansport city *Cass Co.*	345	301
Lowell town *Lake Co.*	315	282
Madison city *Jefferson Co.*	379	315
Marion city *Grant Co.*	364	357
Martinsville city *Morgan Co.*	247	230
Merrillville town *Lake Co.*	243	217
Michigan City city *LaPorte Co.*	520	353
Mishawaka city *Saint Joseph Co.*	593	535
Mooresville town *Morgan Co.*	292	259
Mount Vernon city *Posey Co.*	268	255
Muncie city *Delaware Co.*	326	299
Munster town *Lake Co.*	415	375
Nappanee city *Elkhart Co.*	401	328
New Albany city *Floyd Co.*	316	180
New Castle city *Henry Co.*	239	215
New Haven city *Allen Co.*	385	245
Noblesville city *Hamilton Co.*	501	374
North Vernon city *Jennings Co.*	233	216
Peru city *Miami Co.*	412	347
Plainfield town *Hendricks Co.*	457	342
Plymouth city *Marshall Co.*	316	297
Portage city *Porter Co.*	286	262
Porter town *Porter Co.*	455	334
Princeton city *Gibson Co.*	353	253
Richmond city *Wayne Co.*	335	301
Rochester city *Fulton Co.*	217	206
Saint John town *Lake Co.*	336	293
Salem city *Washington Co.*	324	272
Schererville town *Lake Co.*	333	296
Sellersburg town *Clark Co.*	328	234
Seymour city *Jackson Co.*	297	253
Shelbyville city *Shelby Co.*	302	296
South Bend city *Saint Joseph Co.*	546	519
Speedway town *Marion Co.*	440	381
Tell City city *Perry Co.*	258	169
Terre Haute city *Vigo Co.*	486	386
Valparaiso city *Porter Co.*	365	327
Vincennes city *Knox Co.*	324	280
Wabash city *Wabash Co.*	484	475
Warsaw city *Kosciusko Co.*	542	465
Washington city *Daviess Co.*	250	213
West Lafayette city *Tippecanoe Co.*	313	253
Westfield town *Hamilton Co.*	273	198
Zionsville town *Boone Co.*	275	235

NOTE: Data as of 2007.

Housing

Place	Homeownership Rate (%)	Median Home Value ($)	Median Year Structure Built	Median Rent ($/month)
Anderson city *Madison Co.*	65.8	71,303	1956	400
Angola city *Steuben Co.*	55.5	104,190	1972	414
Auburn city *DeKalb Co.*	75.7	107,834	1972	409
Avon town *Hendricks Co.*	92.3	164,626	1995	701
Batesville city *Ripley Co.*	72.2	143,842	1970	434
Bedford city *Lawrence Co.*	62.0	84,307	1952	358
Beech Grove city *Marion Co.*	64.7	109,615	1963	502
Bloomington city *Monroe Co.*	35.5	144,616	1974	491
Bluffton city *Wells Co.*	66.7	75,878	1960	342
Boonville city *Warrick Co.*	71.5	87,335	1958	358
Brazil city *Clay Co.*	64.5	67,655	1952	291
Brownsburg town *Hendricks Co.*	77.0	139,286	1987	541
Carmel city *Hamilton Co.*	79.5	235,826	1982	658
Cedar Lake town *Lake Co.*	78.9	134,182	1959	473
Charlestown city *Clark Co.*	66.1	105,020	1959	348
Chesterton town *Porter Co.*	70.6	145,260	1971	563
Clarksville town *Clark Co.*	59.5	110,032	1968	462
Columbia City city *Whitley Co.*	72.8	95,574	1963	361
Columbus city *Bartholomew Co.*	67.4	131,358	1968	488
Connersville city *Fayette Co.*	64.4	75,390	1951	365
Crawfordsville city *Montgomery Co.*	59.3	90,285	1956	399
Crown Point city *Lake Co.*	76.9	145,256	1972	579
Danville town *Hendricks Co.*	71.9	145,167	1969	467
Decatur city *Adams Co.*	70.3	91,660	1958	327
Dyer town *Lake Co.*	91.6	168,908	1978	622
East Chicago city *Lake Co.*	45.4	80,067	1947	337
Elkhart city *Elkhart Co.*	57.0	101,917	1960	474
Elwood city *Madison Co.*	76.4	73,769	before 1940	390
Evansville city *Vanderburgh Co.*	58.3	83,970	1954	370
Fishers town *Hamilton Co.*	77.3	182,390	1995	718
Fort Wayne city *Allen Co.*	61.0	84,571	1962	415
Frankfort city *Clinton Co.*	63.4	88,126	1951	422
Franklin city *Johnson Co.*	68.6	117,207	1980	492
Gary city *Lake Co.*	56.9	60,955	1955	361
Goshen city *Elkhart Co.*	63.8	107,449	1969	436
Granger CDP *Saint Joseph Co.*	94.7	184,833	1984	985
Greencastle city *Putnam Co.*	55.7	97,809	1959	377
Greenfield city *Hancock Co.*	67.4	121,247	1972	526
Greensburg city *Decatur Co.*	61.8	100,410	1963	395
Greenwood city *Johnson Co.*	64.3	125,018	1980	528
Griffith town *Lake Co.*	67.8	129,797	1965	612
Hammond city *Lake Co.*	64.5	89,983	1951	439
Highland town *Lake Co.*	78.8	140,484	1966	626
Hobart city *Lake Co.*	81.9	123,259	1960	539
Huntington city *Huntington Co.*	73.1	78,701	1944	401
Indianapolis special city *Marion Co.*	60.0	116,575	1966	486
Jasper city *Dubois Co.*	70.3	123,824	1971	380
Jeffersonville city *Clark Co.*	63.3	109,962	1970	405
Kendallville city *Noble Co.*	70.3	91,086	1962	361
Kokomo city *Howard Co.*	58.7	80,706	1957	426

Place	Homeownership Rate (%)	Median Home Value ($)	Median Year Structure Built	Median Rent ($/month)
La Porte city *LaPorte Co.*	62.4	101,424	1950	405
Lafayette city *Tippecanoe Co.*	51.6	95,759	1963	491
Lake Station city *Lake Co.*	80.2	81,142	1956	437
Lakes of the Four Seasons CDP *Lake Co.*	96.0	175,277	1981	858
Lawrence city *Marion Co.*	75.6	122,919	1982	515
Lebanon city *Boone Co.*	69.0	101,596	1967	429
Logansport city *Cass Co.*	64.0	67,958	1941	352
Lowell town *Lake Co.*	80.4	135,143	1972	487
Madison city *Jefferson Co.*	63.0	103,929	1961	327
Marion city *Grant Co.*	58.5	61,191	1955	343
Martinsville city *Morgan Co.*	63.4	97,292	1962	413
Merrillville town *Lake Co.*	70.0	121,062	1970	631
Michigan City city *LaPorte Co.*	63.7	90,988	1956	411
Mishawaka city *Saint Joseph Co.*	59.5	90,294	1966	461
Mooresville town *Morgan Co.*	76.3	129,155	1972	444
Mount Vernon city *Posey Co.*	71.5	91,108	1964	325
Muncie city *Delaware Co.*	57.6	62,929	1956	380
Munster town *Lake Co.*	88.9	192,788	1968	641
Nappanee city *Elkhart Co.*	70.3	101,864	1966	448
New Albany city *Floyd Co.*	58.2	117,247	1959	409
New Castle city *Henry Co.*	67.4	75,301	1951	360
New Haven city *Allen Co.*	79.7	86,376	1966	418
Noblesville city *Hamilton Co.*	75.3	165,144	1985	548
North Vernon city *Jennings Co.*	54.6	77,156	1969	359
Peru city *Miami Co.*	68.0	60,812	1941	345
Plainfield town *Hendricks Co.*	67.4	143,490	1977	545
Plymouth city *Marshall Co.*	60.7	92,129	1964	415
Portage city *Porter Co.*	72.4	118,030	1975	516
Porter town *Porter Co.*	74.4	136,287	1969	563
Princeton city *Gibson Co.*	62.2	69,663	1953	313
Richmond city *Wayne Co.*	59.6	80,394	1951	364
Rochester city *Fulton Co.*	67.4	82,531	1961	384
Saint John town *Lake Co.*	93.4	198,051	1989	380
Salem city *Washington Co.*	66.9	78,127	1960	326
Schererville town *Lake Co.*	78.4	174,039	1982	579
Sellersburg town *Clark Co.*	80.0	111,145	1967	392
Seymour city *Jackson Co.*	62.2	88,043	1968	421
Shelbyville city *Shelby Co.*	62.2	95,499	1957	461
South Bend city *Saint Joseph Co.*	64.8	79,399	1952	447
Speedway town *Marion Co.*	47.5	121,755	1962	499
Tell City city *Perry Co.*	69.6	87,719	1961	301
Terre Haute city *Vigo Co.*	58.3	69,131	1946	353
Valparaiso city *Porter Co.*	57.0	141,885	1971	548
Vincennes city *Knox Co.*	62.2	71,256	1953	334
Wabash city *Wabash Co.*	69.6	79,652	1951	333
Warsaw city *Kosciusko Co.*	59.9	103,496	1966	412
Washington city *Daviess Co.*	67.8	73,040	1956	281
West Lafayette city *Tippecanoe Co.*	31.1	153,425	1975	542
Westfield town *Hamilton Co.*	73.2	177,591	1992	545
Zionsville town *Boone Co.*	81.6	276,420	1981	625

NOTE: Homeownership Rate and Median Home Value as of 2010; Median Rent and Median Age of Housing as of 2000.

Commute to Work

Place	Automobile (%)	Public Transportation (%)	Walk (%)	Work from Home (%)
Anderson city *Madison Co.*	92.5	1.0	3.6	2.4
Angola city *Steuben Co.*	91.8	0.7	5.1	1.1
Auburn city *DeKalb Co.*	94.7	0.4	2.7	1.4
Avon town *Hendricks Co.*	97.3	0.3	0.0	2.1
Batesville city *Ripley Co.*	92.0	0.0	3.1	4.8
Bedford city *Lawrence Co.*	93.5	1.1	2.5	1.6
Beech Grove city *Marion Co.*	93.8	1.4	2.0	2.3
Bloomington city *Monroe Co.*	76.0	3.0	14.5	3.3
Bluffton city *Wells Co.*	92.6	0.0	4.2	2.6
Boonville city *Warrick Co.*	95.9	0.3	1.8	1.4
Brazil city *Clay Co.*	94.9	0.0	2.1	1.9
Brownsburg town *Hendricks Co.*	95.1	0.3	0.3	3.0
Carmel city *Hamilton Co.*	93.4	0.1	0.9	5.1
Cedar Lake town *Lake Co.*	95.1	0.6	1.2	2.0
Charlestown city *Clark Co.*	94.3	0.5	1.7	2.6
Chesterton town *Porter Co.*	92.7	2.7	1.7	2.3
Clarksville town *Clark Co.*	94.0	0.8	2.0	2.1
Columbia City city *Whitley Co.*	94.9	0.3	1.0	2.1
Columbus city *Bartholomew Co.*	94.5	0.5	1.6	2.1
Connersville city *Fayette Co.*	95.5	0.0	2.2	1.6
Crawfordsville city *Montgomery Co.*	90.5	0.3	6.2	2.0
Crown Point city *Lake Co.*	94.1	1.2	1.9	2.2
Danville town *Hendricks Co.*	93.8	0.0	0.2	4.8
Decatur city *Adams Co.*	93.3	0.2	2.0	2.4
Dyer town *Lake Co.*	90.4	4.8	0.7	3.5
East Chicago city *Lake Co.*	88.1	3.1	5.6	1.5
Elkhart city *Elkhart Co.*	93.4	1.3	2.1	2.1
Elwood city *Madison Co.*	96.3	0.0	2.9	0.3
Evansville city *Vanderburgh Co.*	92.5	1.7	3.2	1.8
Fishers town *Hamilton Co.*	94.0	0.1	0.4	4.9
Fort Wayne city *Allen Co.*	94.0	1.2	2.1	2.0
Frankfort city *Clinton Co.*	93.2	1.0	1.3	1.4
Franklin city *Johnson Co.*	94.0	0.2	2.8	1.4
Gary city *Lake Co.*	90.1	4.7	2.5	1.7
Goshen city *Elkhart Co.*	91.9	0.2	3.9	1.8
Granger CDP *Saint Joseph Co.*	95.5	0.2	0.8	3.3
Greencastle city *Putnam Co.*	80.9	0.0	16.6	0.9
Greenfield city *Hancock Co.*	95.1	0.3	1.0	2.6
Greensburg city *Decatur Co.*	94.7	0.0	2.9	2.0
Greenwood city *Johnson Co.*	95.9	0.1	1.7	1.9
Griffith town *Lake Co.*	93.2	3.3	1.4	1.5
Hammond city *Lake Co.*	90.4	4.6	2.6	1.5
Highland town *Lake Co.*	92.4	4.0	1.4	2.0
Hobart city *Lake Co.*	94.5	1.6	0.9	2.1
Huntington city *Huntington Co.*	89.5	0.1	5.3	3.4
Indianapolis special city *Marion Co.*	92.3	2.4	2.0	2.5
Jasper city *Dubois Co.*	96.0	0.1	1.4	2.1
Jeffersonville city *Clark Co.*	94.4	1.2	2.1	1.3
Kendallville city *Noble Co.*	93.9	0.1	3.2	2.1
Kokomo city *Howard Co.*	94.4	0.5	2.2	1.8

Place	Automobile (%)	Public Transportation (%)	Walk (%)	Work from Home (%)
La Porte city *LaPorte Co.*	93.4	0.5	3.0	1.2
Lafayette city *Tippecanoe Co.*	92.3	1.8	2.4	2.2
Lake Station city *Lake Co.*	95.7	1.1	1.1	0.8
Lakes of the Four Seasons CDP *Lake Co.*	96.2	0.0	0.0	3.8
Lawrence city *Marion Co.*	95.8	0.5	0.7	2.5
Lebanon city *Boone Co.*	95.0	0.1	1.4	2.7
Logansport city *Cass Co.*	92.9	1.9	2.5	1.4
Lowell town *Lake Co.*	95.8	0.5	1.7	1.6
Madison city *Jefferson Co.*	92.5	1.1	3.3	2.1
Marion city *Grant Co.*	88.7	0.9	5.9	2.7
Martinsville city *Morgan Co.*	92.5	0.1	3.8	2.0
Merrillville town *Lake Co.*	94.5	2.1	1.2	1.5
Michigan City city *LaPorte Co.*	93.2	1.8	2.6	1.4
Mishawaka city *Saint Joseph Co.*	93.9	1.0	3.2	1.3
Mooresville town *Morgan Co.*	95.0	0.0	1.9	1.9
Mount Vernon city *Posey Co.*	94.0	0.0	2.6	3.0
Muncie city *Delaware Co.*	86.8	1.7	7.9	2.5
Munster town *Lake Co.*	89.7	4.4	1.5	3.8
Nappanee city *Elkhart Co.*	93.8	0.0	1.2	3.0
New Albany city *Floyd Co.*	94.2	0.9	2.1	2.0
New Castle city *Henry Co.*	94.7	0.2	2.7	1.6
New Haven city *Allen Co.*	95.0	0.1	1.2	3.0
Noblesville city *Hamilton Co.*	93.8	0.2	1.3	3.9
North Vernon city *Jennings Co.*	95.9	0.6	1.7	1.8
Peru city *Miami Co.*	92.0	0.1	3.9	3.2
Plainfield town *Hendricks Co.*	93.9	0.0	1.3	3.2
Plymouth city *Marshall Co.*	91.0	0.9	4.2	2.5
Portage city *Porter Co.*	96.2	1.3	0.4	1.2
Porter town *Porter Co.*	88.1	7.5	2.1	1.5
Princeton city *Gibson Co.*	92.9	0.0	4.8	1.2
Richmond city *Wayne Co.*	91.8	1.0	4.0	1.7
Rochester city *Fulton Co.*	94.5	0.0	0.9	3.8
Saint John town *Lake Co.*	95.3	2.5	0.8	1.1
Salem city *Washington Co.*	94.0	0.2	3.5	1.3
Schererville town *Lake Co.*	93.4	2.2	1.4	2.1
Sellersburg town *Clark Co.*	97.2	0.8	0.9	1.0
Seymour city *Jackson Co.*	95.1	0.0	1.8	1.7
Shelbyville city *Shelby Co.*	92.7	0.2	3.0	1.7
South Bend city *Saint Joseph Co.*	91.8	2.7	2.1	2.4
Speedway town *Marion Co.*	92.3	2.2	3.0	1.4
Tell City city *Perry Co.*	94.7	0.4	1.6	1.4
Terre Haute city *Vigo Co.*	89.7	0.5	6.7	1.8
Valparaiso city *Porter Co.*	87.3	0.7	7.8	2.9
Vincennes city *Knox Co.*	91.2	0.1	6.4	1.7
Wabash city *Wabash Co.*	95.3	0.2	1.9	1.9
Warsaw city *Kosciusko Co.*	91.6	1.7	2.6	2.9
Washington city *Daviess Co.*	96.2	0.3	2.1	0.3
West Lafayette city *Tippecanoe Co.*	74.0	1.9	19.3	2.7
Westfield town *Hamilton Co.*	95.9	0.5	0.9	2.1
Zionsville town *Boone Co.*	91.8	0.2	1.9	5.6

NOTE: Data as of 2000

Travel Time to Work

Place	Less than 15 Minutes (%)	15 to 30 Minutes (%)	30 to 45 Minutes (%)	45 to 60 Minutes (%)	60 Minutes or More (%)
Anderson city *Madison Co.*	43.4	26.8	13.7	9.8	6.4
Angola city *Steuben Co.*	66.0	21.2	5.8	2.3	4.8
Auburn city *DeKalb Co.*	55.6	26.4	11.8	4.3	1.9
Avon town *Hendricks Co.*	25.4	39.6	24.6	6.7	3.8
Batesville city *Ripley Co.*	67.9	13.4	5.2	5.6	7.9
Bedford city *Lawrence Co.*	50.8	16.7	22.9	5.6	3.9
Beech Grove city *Marion Co.*	28.2	41.0	17.0	3.3	10.5
Bloomington city *Monroe Co.*	60.9	28.6	4.9	1.8	3.8
Bluffton city *Wells Co.*	62.0	18.9	11.7	4.7	2.8
Boonville city *Warrick Co.*	40.4	21.7	26.3	8.0	3.6
Brazil city *Clay Co.*	42.0	25.0	21.4	4.9	6.8
Brownsburg town *Hendricks Co.*	21.2	37.4	30.0	7.1	4.3
Carmel city *Hamilton Co.*	27.8	37.7	24.2	6.5	3.8
Cedar Lake town *Lake Co.*	20.2	35.5	22.9	12.6	8.7
Charlestown city *Clark Co.*	25.6	36.6	23.7	9.3	4.8
Chesterton town *Porter Co.*	36.3	31.3	17.6	6.3	8.6
Clarksville town *Clark Co.*	36.7	45.5	13.6	1.8	2.4
Columbia City city *Whitley Co.*	50.2	21.4	19.7	6.9	1.8
Columbus city *Bartholomew Co.*	59.8	26.8	6.1	3.4	3.9
Connersville city *Fayette Co.*	55.4	18.0	11.1	8.3	7.1
Crawfordsville city *Montgomery Co.*	68.3	15.6	6.2	5.6	4.3
Crown Point city *Lake Co.*	36.9	22.7	22.5	8.4	9.4
Danville town *Hendricks Co.*	33.2	26.9	25.9	10.7	3.3
Decatur city *Adams Co.*	57.3	16.1	14.7	7.7	4.3
Dyer town *Lake Co.*	19.0	34.3	23.6	7.0	16.0
East Chicago city *Lake Co.*	37.3	35.1	16.5	4.2	6.8
Elkhart city *Elkhart Co.*	41.6	41.0	12.5	2.8	2.2
Elwood city *Madison Co.*	49.7	15.3	20.3	8.9	5.9
Evansville city *Vanderburgh Co.*	43.3	42.7	8.0	2.3	3.7
Fishers town *Hamilton Co.*	21.5	40.9	28.3	5.8	3.5
Fort Wayne city *Allen Co.*	32.7	48.9	12.3	2.7	3.3
Frankfort city *Clinton Co.*	60.5	14.1	17.8	6.2	1.5
Franklin city *Johnson Co.*	45.4	25.0	18.6	7.0	4.0
Gary city *Lake Co.*	22.0	44.6	20.0	5.2	8.2
Goshen city *Elkhart Co.*	46.6	36.8	12.2	2.2	2.2
Granger CDP *Saint Joseph Co.*	26.7	53.2	13.8	3.4	3.0
Greencastle city *Putnam Co.*	71.8	12.0	6.0	3.4	6.7
Greenfield city *Hancock Co.*	41.0	20.3	24.7	10.3	3.7
Greensburg city *Decatur Co.*	75.3	12.1	6.3	1.9	4.3
Greenwood city *Johnson Co.*	25.7	37.4	26.9	7.2	2.9
Griffith town *Lake Co.*	27.3	38.7	15.4	5.4	13.2
Hammond city *Lake Co.*	27.1	38.4	18.3	7.3	9.0
Highland town *Lake Co.*	33.3	38.6	13.0	6.3	8.9
Hobart city *Lake Co.*	26.4	40.8	20.6	4.5	7.7
Huntington city *Huntington Co.*	56.3	19.9	15.3	5.7	2.7
Indianapolis special city *Marion Co.*	25.8	47.6	18.8	3.8	4.0
Jasper city *Dubois Co.*	72.0	20.0	3.3	1.6	3.0
Jeffersonville city *Clark Co.*	35.9	46.8	12.6	2.5	2.2
Kendallville city *Noble Co.*	59.7	21.7	10.7	4.0	3.9
Kokomo city *Howard Co.*	58.5	27.8	5.9	3.2	4.7

Place	Less than 15 Minutes (%)	15 to 30 Minutes (%)	30 to 45 Minutes (%)	45 to 60 Minutes (%)	60 Minutes or More (%)
La Porte city *LaPorte Co.*	52.3	25.0	11.3	6.2	5.2
Lafayette city *Tippecanoe Co.*	51.7	36.4	6.1	1.7	4.2
Lake Station city *Lake Co.*	25.4	45.4	19.1	4.0	6.1
Lakes of the Four Seasons CDP *Lake Co.*	11.4	33.3	26.2	14.3	14.8
Lawrence city *Marion Co.*	20.6	43.3	26.3	5.6	4.3
Lebanon city *Boone Co.*	42.9	23.1	25.1	5.9	3.0
Logansport city *Cass Co.*	61.6	20.0	7.8	5.4	5.2
Lowell town *Lake Co.*	31.2	22.2	23.8	11.5	11.2
Madison city *Jefferson Co.*	63.5	18.6	7.3	4.9	5.6
Marion city *Grant Co.*	61.3	21.4	8.5	3.9	4.9
Martinsville city *Morgan Co.*	47.2	11.6	17.3	14.2	9.7
Merrillville town *Lake Co.*	24.8	36.5	20.3	6.5	11.9
Michigan City city *LaPorte Co.*	54.1	26.8	8.7	5.5	4.9
Mishawaka city *Saint Joseph Co.*	36.6	44.8	12.1	2.3	4.2
Mooresville town *Morgan Co.*	29.8	37.2	24.9	4.5	3.5
Mount Vernon city *Posey Co.*	54.9	17.1	18.1	5.8	4.1
Muncie city *Delaware Co.*	56.4	28.7	7.1	2.8	5.0
Munster town *Lake Co.*	32.0	34.9	13.9	7.3	12.0
Nappanee city *Elkhart Co.*	56.5	27.6	12.2	3.1	0.5
New Albany city *Floyd Co.*	36.7	45.8	12.6	1.7	3.2
New Castle city *Henry Co.*	56.7	14.1	13.4	7.4	8.3
New Haven city *Allen Co.*	36.9	46.0	12.2	1.9	3.0
Noblesville city *Hamilton Co.*	23.1	28.5	29.5	13.2	5.7
North Vernon city *Jennings Co.*	58.6	17.5	17.3	2.7	3.9
Peru city *Miami Co.*	55.2	24.4	10.5	4.2	5.8
Plainfield town *Hendricks Co.*	34.5	31.9	25.4	5.4	2.9
Plymouth city *Marshall Co.*	59.1	20.6	9.5	5.9	4.9
Portage city *Porter Co.*	27.8	38.3	21.8	5.0	7.1
Porter town *Porter Co.*	34.2	28.5	15.1	5.1	17.1
Princeton city *Gibson Co.*	56.5	18.2	12.5	9.4	3.4
Richmond city *Wayne Co.*	62.1	26.8	6.1	1.7	3.3
Rochester city *Fulton Co.*	62.6	10.0	14.6	3.7	9.1
Saint John town *Lake Co.*	14.7	31.3	27.1	12.9	13.9
Salem city *Washington Co.*	56.4	17.4	8.9	10.5	6.8
Schererville town *Lake Co.*	18.2	37.1	25.1	7.3	12.3
Sellersburg town *Clark Co.*	29.6	48.8	14.9	2.2	4.4
Seymour city *Jackson Co.*	57.4	25.3	10.3	2.7	4.3
Shelbyville city *Shelby Co.*	61.8	15.0	11.5	7.4	4.3
South Bend city *Saint Joseph Co.*	40.3	41.0	12.6	2.6	3.4
Speedway town *Marion Co.*	29.0	48.4	16.1	2.6	3.9
Tell City city *Perry Co.*	56.3	18.2	12.3	7.6	5.6
Terre Haute city *Vigo Co.*	53.5	34.3	6.7	2.1	3.4
Valparaiso city *Porter Co.*	48.8	24.5	14.7	6.4	5.6
Vincennes city *Knox Co.*	69.7	17.8	6.8	1.9	3.8
Wabash city *Wabash Co.*	65.1	17.3	10.0	3.4	4.2
Warsaw city *Kosciusko Co.*	62.3	20.9	9.6	3.8	3.3
Washington city *Daviess Co.*	60.1	14.2	12.8	7.4	5.5
West Lafayette city *Tippecanoe Co.*	62.1	29.9	4.1	1.3	2.6
Westfield town *Hamilton Co.*	31.3	33.2	23.4	8.4	3.7
Zionsville town *Boone Co.*	27.1	37.1	30.2	4.2	1.4

NOTE: Data as of 2000

Crime

Place	Violent Crime Rate (crimes per 10,000 population)	Property Crime Rate (crimes per 10,000 population)
Anderson city *Madison Co.*	34.9	507.4
Angola city *Steuben Co.*	10.1	582.3
Auburn city *DeKalb Co.*	7.7	321.8
Avon town *Hendricks Co.*	n/a	n/a
Batesville city *Ripley Co.*	9.3	148.0
Bedford city *Lawrence Co.*	22.3	415.4
Beech Grove city *Marion Co.*	24.0	368.5
Bloomington city *Monroe Co.*	37.0	384.6
Bluffton city *Wells Co.*	2.1	305.4
Boonville city *Warrick Co.*	0.0	269.6
Brazil city *Clay Co.*	93.8	338.5
Brownsburg town *Hendricks Co.*	13.9	166.5
Carmel city *Hamilton Co.*	3.5	147.0
Cedar Lake town *Lake Co.*	9.2	290.3
Charlestown city *Clark Co.*	5.5	431.6
Chesterton town *Porter Co.*	8.6	274.4
Clarksville town *Clark Co.*	n/a	n/a
Columbia City city *Whitley Co.*	10.8	199.8
Columbus city *Bartholomew Co.*	11.5	495.9
Connersville city *Fayette Co.*	n/a	n/a
Crawfordsville city *Montgomery Co.*	19.3	511.3
Crown Point city *Lake Co.*	4.1	262.7
Danville town *Hendricks Co.*	8.5	142.2
Decatur city *Adams Co.*	8.4	92.8
Dyer town *Lake Co.*	6.3	236.1
East Chicago city *Lake Co.*	100.4	632.0
Elkhart city *Elkhart Co.*	39.9	677.4
Elwood city *Madison Co.*	6.7	747.1
Evansville city *Vanderburgh Co.*	40.0	469.8
Fishers town *Hamilton Co.*	3.7	132.6
Fort Wayne city *Allen Co.*	32.5	410.6
Frankfort city *Clinton Co.*	n/a	n/a
Franklin city *Johnson Co.*	39.4	470.4
Gary city *Lake Co.*	93.0	433.4
Goshen city *Elkhart Co.*	14.0	398.7
Granger CDP *Saint Joseph Co.*	n/a	n/a
Greencastle city *Putnam Co.*	n/a	n/a
Greenfield city *Hancock Co.*	6.4	179.6
Greensburg city *Decatur Co.*	n/a	n/a
Greenwood city *Johnson Co.*	39.6	383.3
Griffith town *Lake Co.*	24.1	448.9
Hammond city *Lake Co.*	87.7	512.6
Highland town *Lake Co.*	15.9	397.6
Hobart city *Lake Co.*	26.7	519.9
Huntington city *Huntington Co.*	18.1	241.9
Indianapolis special city *Marion Co.*	120.4	608.4
Jasper city *Dubois Co.*	5.0	129.6
Jeffersonville city *Clark Co.*	n/a	n/a
Kendallville city *Noble Co.*	n/a	n/a
Kokomo city *Howard Co.*	47.4	586.3

Place	Violent Crime Rate (crimes per 10,000 population)	Property Crime Rate (crimes per 10,000 population)
La Porte city *LaPorte Co.*	22.3	701.8
Lafayette city *Tippecanoe Co.*	50.8	468.8
Lake Station city *Lake Co.*	n/a	n/a
Lakes of the Four Seasons CDP *Lake Co.*	n/a	n/a
Lawrence city *Marion Co.*	n/a	n/a
Lebanon city *Boone Co.*	n/a	n/a
Logansport city *Cass Co.*	10.7	485.3
Lowell town *Lake Co.*	3.6	169.3
Madison city *Jefferson Co.*	n/a	n/a
Marion city *Grant Co.*	25.9	519.5
Martinsville city *Morgan Co.*	16.2	792.0
Merrillville town *Lake Co.*	15.5	297.0
Michigan City city *LaPorte Co.*	38.8	557.9
Mishawaka city *Saint Joseph Co.*	38.0	699.8
Mooresville town *Morgan Co.*	8.5	301.2
Mount Vernon city *Posey Co.*	n/a	n/a
Muncie city *Delaware Co.*	53.6	403.6
Munster town *Lake Co.*	3.2	238.1
Nappanee city *Elkhart Co.*	1.4	272.2
New Albany city *Floyd Co.*	33.8	607.6
New Castle city *Henry Co.*	9.9	862.4
New Haven city *Allen Co.*	9.5	270.8
Noblesville city *Hamilton Co.*	12.9	227.5
North Vernon city *Jennings Co.*	15.9	427.4
Peru city *Miami Co.*	n/a	n/a
Plainfield town *Hendricks Co.*	23.5	353.0
Plymouth city *Marshall Co.*	8.1	409.9
Portage city *Porter Co.*	46.9	396.3
Porter town *Porter Co.*	n/a	n/a
Princeton city *Gibson Co.*	n/a	n/a
Richmond city *Wayne Co.*	41.6	464.4
Rochester city *Fulton Co.*	n/a	n/a
Saint John town *Lake Co.*	0.8	99.4
Salem city *Washington Co.*	7.7	29.1
Schererville town *Lake Co.*	6.5	294.7
Sellersburg town *Clark Co.*	n/a	n/a
Seymour city *Jackson Co.*	49.3	665.8
Shelbyville city *Shelby Co.*	n/a	n/a
South Bend city *Saint Joseph Co.*	79.1	672.6
Speedway town *Marion Co.*	47.1	466.2
Tell City city *Perry Co.*	8.0	252.7
Terre Haute city *Vigo Co.*	26.3	846.9
Valparaiso city *Porter Co.*	34.1	289.0
Vincennes city *Knox Co.*	14.6	770.3
Wabash city *Wabash Co.*	19.5	199.7
Warsaw city *Kosciusko Co.*	8.9	508.0
Washington city *Daviess Co.*	n/a	n/a
West Lafayette city *Tippecanoe Co.*	20.7	183.9
Westfield town *Hamilton Co.*	9.5	269.4
Zionsville town *Boone Co.*	n/a	n/a

NOTE: Data as of 2008.

Education

Indiana Public School Educational Profile

Category	Value	Category	Value
Schools *(2006-2007)*	1,969	**Diploma Recipients** *(2005-2006)*	57,920
Instructional Level		White, Non-Hispanic	49,885
Primary	1,146	Black, Non-Hispanic	5,140
Middle	347	Asian/Pacific Islander, Non-Hispanic	804
High	347	American Indian/Alaskan Native, Non-Hisp.	138
Other/Not Reported	129	Hispanic	1,953
Curriculum		**High School Drop-out Rate** (%) *(2005-2006)*	2.9
Regular	1,877	White, Non-Hispanic	2.5
Special Education	42	Black, Non-Hispanic	5.0
Vocational	28	Asian/Pacific Islander, Non-Hispanic	1.7
Alternative	22	American Indian/Alaskan Native, Non-Hisp.	3.4
Type		Hispanic	4.8
Magnet	25	**Staff** *(2006-2007)*	
Charter	37	Teachers	61,315.0
Title I Eligible	797	Average Salary ($) *(2009-2010)*	49,986
School-wide Title I	200	Librarians/Media Specialists	955.0
Students *(2006-2007)*	1,045,940	Guidance Counselors	1,893.0
Gender (%)		**Ratios** *(2006-2007)*	
Male	51.4	Student/Teacher Ratio	17.1 to 1
Female	48.6	Student/Librarian Ratio	1,095.2 to 1
Race/Ethnicity (%)		Student/Counselor Ratio	552.5 to 1
White, Non-Hispanic	76.8	**Current Expenditures** *($ per student in FY 2007)*	9,080
Black, Non-Hispanic	12.2	Instruction	5,445
Asian/Pacific Islander	1.3	Support Services	3,244
American Indian/Alaskan Native	0.3	**College Entrance Exam Scores** *(2009)*	
Hispanic	6.1	SAT Reasoning Test™	
Classification (%)		Participation Rate (%)	63
Individual Education Program (IEP)	17.1	Mean SAT Critical Reading Score	496
Migrant *(2005-2006)*	n/a	Mean SAT Writing Score	480
English Language Learner (ELL)	4.1	Mean SAT Math Score	507
Eligible for Free Lunch Program	29.4	American College Testing Program (ACT)	
Eligible for Reduced-Price Lunch Program	8.1	Participation Rate (%)	24
Average Freshman Grad. Rate (%) *(2005-2006)*	73.3	Average Composite Score	22.2
White, Non-Hispanic	76.1	Average English Score	21.6
Black, Non-Hispanic	55.2	Average Math Score	22.4
Asian/Pacific Islander, Non-Hispanic	96.6	Average Reading Score	22.6
American Indian/Alaskan Native, Non-Hisp.	68.0	Average Science Score	21.6
Hispanic	68.0		

Note: *For an explanation of data, please refer to the User's Guide in the front of the book*

Number of Schools

Rank	Number	District Name	City
1	79	Indianapolis Public Schools	Indianapolis
2	54	Fort Wayne Community Schools	Fort Wayne
3	42	Evansville-Vanderburgh Sch Corp	Evansville
4	38	South Bend Community Sch Corp	South Bend
5	29	Gary Community School Corp	Gary
5	29	Vigo County School Corp	Terre Haute
7	22	School City of Hammond	Hammond
8	21	Monroe County Com Sch Corp	Bloomington
9	20	Elkhart Community Schools	Elkhart
9	20	Greater Clark County Schools	Jeffersonville
11	19	East Allen County Schools	New Haven
11	19	M S D Warren Township	Indianapolis
11	19	New Albany-Floyd County Con Sch	New Albany
14	18	Anderson Community School Corp	Anderson
14	18	Hamilton Southeastern Schools	Fishers
14	18	M S D Lawrence Township	Indianapolis
14	18	M S D Perry Township	Indianapolis
18	17	Carmel Clay Schools	Carmel
18	17	Kokomo-Center Twp Con Sch Corp	Kokomo
18	17	Tippecanoe School Corp	Lafayette
21	16	Bartholomew Con School Corp	Columbus
21	16	M S D Wayne Township	Indianapolis
21	16	Muncie Community Schools	Muncie
21	16	North Lawrence Com Schools	Bedford
25	15	Michigan City Area Schools	Michigan City
25	15	Penn-Harris-Madison Sch Corp	Mishawaka
25	15	Richmond Community School Corp	Richmond
25	15	Warrick County School Corp	Boonville
29	14	M S D Washington Twp	Indianapolis
30	13	M S D Pike Township	Indianapolis
30	13	Marion Community Schools	Marion
32	12	Fayette County School Corp	Connersville
32	12	Lafayette School Corporation	Lafayette
32	12	Valparaiso Community Schools	Valparaiso
35	11	Huntington County Com Sch Corp	Huntington
35	11	Laporte Community School Corp	Laporte
35	11	M S D Martinsville Schools	Martinsville
35	11	Portage Township Schools	Portage
35	11	School City of Mishawaka	Mishawaka
40	10	Clay Community Schools	Knightsville
40	10	Goshen Community Schools	Goshen
40	10	Jay School Corp	Portland
40	10	Jennings County Schools	North Vernon
40	10	Lake Central School Corp	Saint John
40	10	New Castle Community Sch Corp	New Castle
40	10	Northwest Allen County Schools	Fort Wayne
40	10	School City of East Chicago	East Chicago
40	10	Warsaw Community Schools	Warsaw
49	9	Avon Community School Corp	Avon
49	9	Center Grove Com Sch Corp	Greenwood
49	9	Crown Point Community Sch Corp	Crown Point
49	9	Duneland School Corporation	Chesterton
49	9	Franklin Township Com Sch Corp	Indianapolis
49	9	Logansport Community Sch Corp	Logansport
49	9	M S D Decatur Township	Indianapolis
49	9	M S D Southwest Allen County	Fort Wayne
49	9	Madison Consolidated Schools	Madison
49	9	Noblesville Schools	Noblesville
49	9	South Harrison Com Schools	Corydon
60	8	Brownsburg Community Sch Corp	Brownsburg
60	8	East Noble School Corp	Kendallville
60	8	Greenfield-Central Com Schools	Greenfield
60	8	M S D Wabash County Schools	Wabash
60	8	Merrillville Community School	Merrillville
60	8	Westfield-Washington Schools	Westfield
60	8	Zionsville Community Schools	Zionsville
67	7	Clark-Pleasant Com School Corp	Whiteland
67	7	Crawfordsville Com Schools	Crawfordsville
67	7	Franklin Community School Corp	Franklin
67	7	Mooresville Con School Corp	Mooresville
67	7	Plymouth Community School Corp	Plymouth
67	7	Richland-Bean Blossom CSC	Ellettsville
67	7	Seymour Community Schools	Seymour
67	7	Sunman-Dearborn Com Sch Corp	Sunman
67	7	Vincennes Community Sch Corp	Vincennes
67	7	West Clark Community Schools	Sellersburg
77	6	Brown County School Corporation	Nashville
77	6	Community Schools of Frankfort	Frankfort
77	6	Concord Community Schools	Elkhart
77	6	Crawford County Com School Corp	Marengo
77	6	Dekalb County Central United SD	Waterloo
77	6	Delaware Community School Corp	Muncie
77	6	East Porter County School Corp	Kouts
77	6	Eastbrook Community Sch Corp	Marion
77	6	Greater Jasper Con Schs	Jasper
77	6	Greenwood Community Sch Corp	Greenwood
77	6	Griffith Public Schools	Griffith
77	6	Lebanon Community School Corp	Lebanon
77	6	M S D Mount Vernon	Mount Vernon
77	6	M S D Steuben County	Angola
77	6	Middlebury Community Schools	Middlebury
77	6	Mount Vernon Community Sch Corp	Fortville
77	6	North Spencer County Sch Corp	Lincoln City
77	6	Northeast School Corp	Hymera
77	6	Plainfield Community Sch Corp	Plainfield
77	6	Rush County Schools	Rushville
77	6	School City of Hobart	Hobart
77	6	School Town of Highland	Highland
77	6	School Town of Munster	Munster
77	6	School Town of Speedway	Speedway
77	6	Scott County SD 2	Scottsburg
77	6	South Dearborn Com School Corp	Aurora
77	6	South Montgomery Com Sch Corp	New Market
77	6	Spencer-Owen Community Schools	Spencer
77	6	Twin Lakes School Corp	Monticello
77	6	Washington Com Schools Inc	Washington
77	6	Whitley County Cons Schools	Columbia City
108	5	Baugo Community Schools	Elkhart
108	5	Beech Grove City Schools	Beech Grove
108	5	Blackford County Schools	Hartford City
108	5	Brownstown Cnt Com Sch Corp	Brownstown
108	5	Elwood Community School Corp	Elwood
108	5	Franklin County Com Sch Corp	Brookville
108	5	Greencastle Community Sch Corp	Greencastle
108	5	Kankakee Valley School Corp	Wheatfield
108	5	Lake Ridge Schools	Gary
108	5	Lakeland School Corporation	Lagrange
108	5	Madison-Grant United Sch Corp	Fairmount
108	5	Mississinewa Community School Corp	Gas City
108	5	New Prairie United School Corp	New Carlisle
108	5	North Adams Community Schools	Decatur
108	5	North Montgomery Com Sch Corp	Crawfordsville
108	5	North Putnam Community Schools	Bainbridge
108	5	Oak Hill United School Corp	Converse
108	5	Peru Community Schools	Peru
108	5	Pike County School Corp	Petersburg
108	5	Randolph Central School Corp	Winchester
108	5	Shelbyville Central Schools	Shelbyville
108	5	South Madison Com Sch Corp	Pendleton
108	5	South Vermillion Com Sch Corp	Clinton
108	5	Southern Hancock Co CS Corp	New Palestine
108	5	Tri-Creek School Corp	Lowell
108	5	Wa-Nee Community Schools	Nappanee
108	5	Wawasee Community School Corp	Syracuse
108	5	Westview School Corporation	Topeka
136	4	Batesville Community Sch Corp	Batesville
136	4	Benton Community School Corp	Fowler
136	4	Centerville-Abington Com Schs	Centerville
136	4	Danville Community School Corp	Danville
136	4	Decatur County Com Schools	Greensburg
136	4	Dekalb County Eastern Com SD	Butler
136	4	Delphi Community School Corp	Delphi
136	4	Fairfield Community Schools	Goshen
136	4	Frankton-Lapel Community Schs	Anderson
136	4	Garrett-Keyser-Butler Com	Garrett
136	4	Hamilton Heights School Corp	Arcadia
136	4	Hanover Community School Corp	Cedar Lake
136	4	John Glenn School Corporation	Walkerton
136	4	Lawrenceburg Com School Corp	Lawrenceburg
136	4	Maconaquah School Corp	Bunker Hill
136	4	Mill Creek Community Sch Corp	Clayton
136	4	Mitchell Community Schools	Mitchell
136	4	Mount Pleasant Twp Com Sch Corp	Yorktown
136	4	Nineveh-Hensley-Jackson United	Trafalgar
136	4	North Gibson School Corp	Princeton
136	4	North Harrison Com School Corp	Ramsey
136	4	North Newton School Corp	Morocco
136	4	North West Hendricks Schools	Lizton
136	4	Northern Wells Com Schools	Ossian
136	4	Northwestern School Corp	Kokomo
136	4	Porter Township School Corp	Valparaiso
136	4	Prairie Heights Com Sch Corp	Lagrange
136	4	Rensselaer Central School Corp	Rensselaer
136	4	Rochester Community Sch Corp	Rochester
136	4	Salem Community Schools	Salem
136	4	Shelby Eastern Schools	Shelbyville
136	4	South Gibson School Corp	Fort Branch
136	4	Southwest Dubois County Sch Corp	Huntingburg
136	4	Southwest School Corp	Sullivan
136	4	Switzerland County School Corp	Vevay
136	4	Tippecanoe Valley School Corp	Akron
136	4	Union County College Corner JSD	Liberty
136	4	Union Township School Corp	Valparaiso
136	4	West Noble School Corporation	Ligonier
136	4	Western School Corp	Russiaville
136	4	Whitko Community School Corp	Pierceton
177	3	Alexandria Com School Corp	Alexandria
177	3	East Washington School Corp	Pekin
177	3	Greensburg Community Schools	Greensburg
177	3	Knox Community School Corp	Knox
177	3	Manchester Community Schools	N Manchester
177	3	Northwestern Con School Corp	Fairland
177	3	Southeastern School Corp	Walton
177	3	Tell City-Troy Twp School Corp	Tell City
177	3	Tipton Community School Corp	Tipton
177	3	West Lafayette Com School Corp	West Lafayette
177	3	Western Boone County Com SD	Thorntown
188	2	Paoli Community School Corp	Paoli

Number of Teachers

Rank	Number	District Name	City
1	2,434.0	Indianapolis Public Schools	Indianapolis
2	1,874.0	Fort Wayne Community Schools	Fort Wayne
3	1,424.0	Evansville-Vanderburgh Sch Corp	Evansville
4	1,261.0	South Bend Community Sch Corp	South Bend
5	1,008.0	Vigo County School Corp	Terre Haute
6	898.0	M S D Lawrence Township	Indianapolis
7	882.0	M S D Wayne Township	Indianapolis
8	866.0	Carmel Clay Schools	Carmel
9	852.0	Gary Community School Corp	Gary
10	832.0	M S D Perry Township	Indianapolis
11	830.0	School City of Hammond	Hammond
12	828.0	Elkhart Community Schools	Elkhart
13	798.0	Hamilton Southeastern Schools	Fishers
14	693.0	M S D Warren Township	Indianapolis
15	676.0	Greater Clark County Schools	Jeffersonville
16	671.0	Monroe County Com Sch Corp	Bloomington
17	670.0	New Albany-Floyd County Con Sch	New Albany
18	615.0	Tippecanoe School Corp	Lafayette
19	610.0	Anderson Community School Corp	Anderson
20	605.0	Bartholomew Con School Corp	Columbus
21	600.0	M S D Pike Township	Indianapolis
22	594.0	M S D Washington Twp	Indianapolis
23	558.0	East Allen County Schools	New Haven
24	521.0	Muncie Community Schools	Muncie
25	501.0	Lake Central School Corp	Saint John
26	495.0	Kokomo-Center Twp Con Sch Corp	Kokomo
27	492.0	Warrick County School Corp	Boonville
28	491.0	Lafayette School Corporation	Lafayette
29	451.0	Penn-Harris-Madison Sch Corp	Mishawaka
30	427.0	Noblesville Schools	Noblesville
31	422.0	Franklin Township Com Sch Corp	Indianapolis
32	405.0	Portage Township Schools	Portage
33	402.0	Goshen Community Schools	Goshen
34	400.0	Michigan City Area Schools	Michigan City
35	393.0	Laporte Community School Corp	Laporte
36	389.0	Center Grove Com Sch Corp	Greenwood
37	388.0	Avon Community School Corp	Avon
38	382.0	Brownsburg Community Sch Corp	Brownsburg
39	378.0	Warsaw Community Schools	Warsaw
40	376.0	Huntington County Com Sch Corp	Huntington
41	374.0	Richmond Community School Corp	Richmond
41	374.0	School City of East Chicago	East Chicago
41	374.0	School City of Mishawaka	Mishawaka
44	373.0	M S D Southwest Allen County	Fort Wayne
45	343.0	Greenfield-Central Com Schools	Greenfield
46	342.0	Logansport Community Sch Corp	Logansport
47	338.0	North Lawrence Com Schools	Bedford
48	337.0	Merrillville Community School	Merrillville
49	332.0	Marion Community Schools	Marion
50	323.0	M S D Decatur Township	Indianapolis
51	320.0	Northwest Allen County Schools	Fort Wayne
52	316.0	M S D Martinsville Schools	Martinsville
53	314.0	Crown Point Community Sch Corp	Crown Point
54	309.0	Jennings County Schools	North Vernon
54	309.0	Valparaiso Community Schools	Valparaiso
56	302.0	Westfield-Washington Schools	Westfield
57	288.0	New Castle Community Sch Corp	New Castle
58	287.0	Zionsville Community Schools	Zionsville
59	272.0	Duneland School Corporation	Chesterton
60	268.0	Concord Community Schools	Elkhart
61	267.0	Clay Community Schools	Knightsville
62	260.0	Franklin Community School Corp	Franklin

Note: This section only includes districts with 1,500 or more students; All categories are ranked from high to low

63	256.0	Clark-Pleasant Com School Corp	Whiteland
63	256.0	Fayette County School Corp	Connersville
65	249.0	Mooresville Con School Corp	Mooresville
66	237.0	East Noble School Corp	Kendallville
67	232.0	Jay School Corp	Portland
68	223.0	Seymour Community Schools	Seymour
68	223.0	Sunman-Dearborn Com Sch Corp	Sunman
70	215.0	Whitley County Cons Schools	Columbia City
71	214.0	Lebanon Community School Corp	Lebanon
71	214.0	School Town of Munster	Munster
73	213.0	Plainfield Community Sch Corp	Plainfield
74	207.0	Middlebury Community Schools	Middlebury
75	201.0	Community Schools of Frankfort	Frankfort
75	201.0	Vincennes Community Sch Corp	Vincennes
77	200.0	Dekalb County Central United SD	Waterloo
78	199.0	West Clark Community Schools	Sellersburg
79	196.0	Madison Consolidated Schools	Madison
79	196.0	South Harrison Com Schools	Corydon
81	194.0	South Madison Com Sch Corp	Pendleton
82	193.0	Wawasee Community School Corp	Syracuse
83	191.0	Greenwood Community Sch Corp	Greenwood
84	189.0	Wa-Nee Community Schools	Nappanee
85	188.0	Greater Jasper Con Schs	Jasper
85	188.0	Spencer-Owen Community Schools	Spencer
87	187.0	Shelbyville Central Schools	Shelbyville
88	183.0	Mount Vernon Community Sch Corp	Fortville
89	182.0	School City of Hobart	Hobart
90	177.0	Kankakee Valley School Corp	Wheatfield
90	177.0	M S D Wabash County Schools	Wabash
92	175.0	South Dearborn Com School Corp	Aurora
93	172.0	Plymouth Community School Corp	Plymouth
93	172.0	Richland-Bean Blossom CSC	Ellettsville
95	165.0	M S D Steuben County	Angola
96	164.0	Delaware Community School Corp	Muncie
96	164.0	M S D Mount Vernon	Mount Vernon
96	164.0	Rush County Schools	Rushville
99	159.0	Crawfordsville Com Schools	Crawfordsville
99	159.0	Scott County SD 2	Scottsburg
101	157.0	Southern Hancock Co CS Corp	New Palestine
102	156.0	School Town of Highland	Highland
103	155.0	Tri-Creek School Corp	Lowell
104	154.0	Franklin County Com Sch Corp	Brookville
105	152.0	Brown County School Corporation	Nashville
105	152.0	North Putnam Community Schools	Bainbridge
107	151.0	Northern Wells Com Schools	Ossian
107	151.0	West Noble School Corporation	Ligonier
109	148.0	Maconaquah School Corp	Bunker Hill
110	147.0	Peru Community Schools	Peru
110	147.0	Twin Lakes School Corp	Monticello
112	142.0	Blackford County Schools	Hartford City
113	141.0	Lakeland School Corporation	Lagrange
113	141.0	New Prairie United School Corp	New Carlisle
113	141.0	Washington Com Schools Inc	Washington
116	138.0	Mount Pleasant Twp Com Sch Corp	Yorktown
117	136.0	Western School Corp	Russiaville
118	135.0	Benton Community School Corp	Fowler
118	135.0	Frankton-Lapel Community Schs	Anderson
118	135.0	Mississinewa Community School Corp	Gas City
121	134.0	Danville Community School Corp	Danville
122	132.0	Union County College Corner JSD	Liberty
123	131.0	Decatur County Com Schools	Greensburg
123	131.0	North Adams Community Schools	Decatur
125	130.0	Griffith Public Schools	Griffith
125	130.0	South Montgomery Com Sch Corp	New Market
125	130.0	Westview School Corporation	Topeka
128	127.0	North Montgomery Com Sch Corp	Crawfordsville
128	127.0	North Spencer County Sch Corp	Lincoln City
128	127.0	Pike County School Corp	Petersburg
128	127.0	South Vermillion Com Sch Corp	Clinton
132	126.0	Dekalb County Eastern Com SD	Butler
133	125.0	Greensburg Community Schools	Greensburg
134	124.0	Elwood Community School Corp	Elwood
135	123.0	Beech Grove City Schools	Beech Grove
136	121.0	Hamilton Heights School Corp	Arcadia
137	120.0	North Gibson School Corp	Princeton
137	120.0	North Harrison Com School Corp	Ramsey
139	119.0	East Porter County School Corp	Kouts
140	118.0	Lake Ridge Schools	Gary
141	116.0	Batesville Community Sch Corp	Batesville
141	116.0	Tippecanoe Valley School Corp	Akron
141	116.0	West Lafayette Com School Corp	West Lafayette
144	115.0	Tipton Community School Corp	Tipton
145	112.0	Randolph Central School Corp	Winchester
145	112.0	Southwest School Corp	Sullivan
147	111.0	Garrett-Keyser-Butler Com	Garrett
148	110.0	Western Boone County Com SD	Thorntown
149	109.0	Fairfield Community Schools	Goshen
149	109.0	Rensselaer Central School Corp	Rensselaer
149	109.0	Salem Community Schools	Salem
152	108.0	Mitchell Community Schools	Mitchell
153	107.0	Whitko Community School Corp	Pierceton
154	106.0	Eastbrook Community Sch Corp	Marion
154	106.0	Greencastle Community Sch Corp	Greencastle
156	104.0	Nineveh-Hensley-Jackson United	Trafalgar
157	103.0	Northwestern School Corp	Kokomo
158	102.0	Rochester Community Sch Corp	Rochester
159	100.0	Knox Community School Corp	Knox
160	99.0	Prairie Heights Com Sch Corp	Lagrange
161	98.0	Centerville-Abington Com Schs	Centerville
161	98.0	Madison-Grant United Sch Corp	Fairmount
161	98.0	North Newton School Corp	Morocco
161	98.0	North West Hendricks Schools	Lizton
161	98.0	South Gibson School Corp	Fort Branch
166	97.0	Baugo Community Schools	Elkhart
167	96.0	Brownstown Cnt Com Sch Corp	Brownstown
167	96.0	Mill Creek Community Sch Corp	Clayton
169	95.0	School Town of Speedway	Speedway
170	92.0	Alexandria Com School Corp	Alexandria
170	92.0	Crawford County Com School Corp	Marengo
170	92.0	Lawrenceburg Com School Corp	Lawrenceburg
170	92.0	Paoli Community School Corp	Paoli
170	92.0	Southwest Dubois County Sch Corp	Huntingburg
175	91.0	Northeast School Corp	Hymera
175	91.0	Union Township School Corp	Valparaiso
177	90.0	John Glenn School Corporation	Walkerton
177	90.0	Oak Hill United School Corp	Converse
177	90.0	Southeastern School Corp	Walton
177	90.0	Switzerland County School Corp	Vevay
181	89.0	Delphi Community School Corp	Delphi
181	89.0	Shelby Eastern Schools	Shelbyville
183	88.0	East Washington School Corp	Pekin
184	85.0	Hanover Community School Corp	Cedar Lake
185	82.0	Manchester Community Schools	N Manchester
186	81.0	Tell City-Troy Twp School Corp	Tell City
187	80.0	Porter Township School Corp	Valparaiso
188	78.0	Northwestern Con School Corp	Fairland

Number of Students

Rank	Number	District Name	City
1	37,057	Indianapolis Public Schools	Indianapolis
2	31,884	Fort Wayne Community Schools	Fort Wayne
3	22,190	Evansville-Vanderburgh Sch Corp	Evansville
4	21,769	South Bend Community Sch Corp	South Bend
5	16,431	Vigo County School Corp	Terre Haute
6	16,138	M S D Lawrence Township	Indianapolis
7	15,315	Hamilton Southeastern Schools	Fishers
8	14,731	Gary Community School Corp	Gary
9	14,713	M S D Wayne Township	Indianapolis
10	14,680	Carmel Clay Schools	Carmel
11	14,511	School City of Hammond	Hammond
12	14,204	M S D Perry Township	Indianapolis
13	13,666	Elkhart Community Schools	Elkhart
14	12,483	M S D Warren Township	Indianapolis
15	11,923	New Albany-Floyd County Con Sch	New Albany
16	11,263	Tippecanoe School Corp	Lafayette
17	11,090	Bartholomew Con School Corp	Columbus
18	11,034	Monroe County Com Sch Corp	Bloomington
19	10,768	Greater Clark County Schools	Jeffersonville
20	10,662	M S D Pike Township	Indianapolis
21	10,599	Penn-Harris-Madison Sch Corp	Mishawaka
22	10,426	M S D Washington Twp	Indianapolis
23	10,228	East Allen County Schools	New Haven
24	10,101	Anderson Community School Corp	Anderson
25	9,728	Lake Central School Corp	Saint John
26	9,590	Warrick County School Corp	Boonville
27	8,404	Portage Township Schools	Portage
28	8,334	Noblesville Schools	Noblesville
29	8,292	Franklin Township Com Sch Corp	Indianapolis
30	7,785	Avon Community School Corp	Avon
31	7,762	Muncie Community Schools	Muncie
32	7,426	Lafayette School Corporation	Lafayette
33	7,361	Center Grove Com Sch Corp	Greenwood
34	7,173	Merrillville Community School	Merrillville
35	7,079	Michigan City Area Schools	Michigan City
36	7,005	Kokomo-Center Twp Con Sch Corp	Kokomo
37	7,004	Crown Point Community Sch Corp	Crown Point
38	6,956	Brownsburg Community Sch Corp	Brownsburg
39	6,931	Warsaw Community Schools	Warsaw
40	6,612	M S D Southwest Allen County	Fort Wayne
41	6,538	Laporte Community School Corp	Laporte
42	6,248	Valparaiso Community Schools	Valparaiso
43	6,235	Goshen Community Schools	Goshen
44	6,232	Huntington County Com Sch Corp	Huntington
45	6,035	Northwest Allen County Schools	Fort Wayne
46	6,026	School City of East Chicago	East Chicago
47	5,954	M S D Decatur Township	Indianapolis
48	5,815	Duneland School Corporation	Chesterton
49	5,716	Richmond Community School Corp	Richmond
50	5,682	School City of Mishawaka	Mishawaka
51	5,675	M S D Martinsville Schools	Martinsville
52	5,428	Westfield-Washington Schools	Westfield
53	5,390	North Lawrence Com Schools	Bedford
54	5,289	Jennings County Schools	North Vernon
55	5,252	Marion Community Schools	Marion
56	5,169	Clark-Pleasant Com School Corp	Whiteland
57	4,954	Zionsville Community Schools	Zionsville
58	4,913	Franklin Community School Corp	Franklin
59	4,764	Concord Community Schools	Elkhart
60	4,661	Clay Community Schools	Knightsville
61	4,655	Greenfield-Central Com Schools	Greenfield
62	4,469	Mooresville Con School Corp	Mooresville
63	4,417	Sunman-Dearborn Com Sch Corp	Sunman
64	4,392	School Town of Munster	Munster
65	4,310	Logansport Community Sch Corp	Logansport
66	4,281	Plainfield Community Sch Corp	Plainfield
67	4,187	Fayette County School Corp	Connersville
68	4,160	Middlebury Community Schools	Middlebury
69	4,153	Dekalb County Central United SD	Waterloo
70	4,028	South Madison Com Sch Corp	Pendleton
71	4,025	Seymour Community Schools	Seymour
72	4,017	New Castle Community Sch Corp	New Castle
73	3,880	Greenwood Community Sch Corp	Greenwood
74	3,879	Jay School Corp	Portland
75	3,872	East Noble School Corp	Kendallville
76	3,858	Shelbyville Central Schools	Shelbyville
77	3,818	School City of Hobart	Hobart
78	3,794	West Clark Community Schools	Sellersburg
79	3,695	Tri-Creek School Corp	Lowell
80	3,631	Whitley County Cons Schools	Columbia City
81	3,529	Lebanon Community School Corp	Lebanon
82	3,526	Plymouth Community School Corp	Plymouth
83	3,511	Kankakee Valley School Corp	Wheatfield
84	3,483	Mount Vernon Community Sch Corp	Fortville
85	3,481	Wawasee Community School Corp	Syracuse
86	3,474	Madison Consolidated Schools	Madison
87	3,447	School Town of Highland	Highland
88	3,385	Southern Hancock Co CS Corp	New Palestine
89	3,320	Community Schools of Frankfort	Frankfort
90	3,311	Wa-Nee Community Schools	Nappanee
91	3,212	South Harrison Com Schools	Corydon
92	3,175	Greater Jasper Con Schs	Jasper
93	3,121	Spencer-Owen Community Schools	Spencer
94	3,065	Franklin County Com Sch Corp	Brookville
95	3,026	M S D Steuben County	Angola
96	2,974	South Dearborn Com School Corp	Aurora
97	2,926	Scott County SD 2	Scottsburg
98	2,835	Richland-Bean Blossom CSC	Ellettsville
99	2,803	Delaware Community School Corp	Muncie
100	2,794	Vincennes Community Sch Corp	Vincennes
101	2,777	New Prairie United School Corp	New Carlisle
102	2,739	Griffith Public Schools	Griffith
103	2,656	Rush County Schools	Rushville
104	2,641	West Noble School Corporation	Ligonier
105	2,614	Twin Lakes School Corp	Monticello
106	2,586	Northern Wells Com Schools	Ossian
107	2,582	M S D Wabash County Schools	Wabash
108	2,567	Danville Community School Corp	Danville
109	2,547	Western School Corp	Russiaville
110	2,539	M S D Mount Vernon	Mount Vernon
111	2,433	Washington Com Schools Inc	Washington
112	2,425	Maconaquah School Corp	Bunker Hill
113	2,411	Frankton-Lapel Community Schs	Anderson
114	2,397	Crawfordsville Com Schools	Crawfordsville
115	2,354	Beech Grove City Schools	Beech Grove
116	2,306	Lake Ridge Schools	Gary
117	2,300	Peru Community Schools	Peru
118	2,297	Mount Pleasant Twp Com Sch Corp	Yorktown
119	2,293	Brown County School Corporation	Nashville
119	2,293	Decatur County Com Schools	Greensburg
121	2,280	North Harrison Com School Corp	Ramsey
122	2,275	Lakeland School Corporation	Lagrange
123	2,259	North Spencer County Sch Corp	Lincoln City
124	2,258	Blackford County Schools	Hartford City
125	2,255	Westview School Corporation	Topeka
126	2,246	Mississinewa Community School Corp	Gas City
127	2,227	East Porter County School Corp	Kouts

Note: This section only includes districts with 1,500 or more students; All categories are ranked from high to low

128	2,224	Hamilton Heights School Corp	Arcadia
129	2,219	North Montgomery Com Sch Corp	Crawfordsville
130	2,211	Tippecanoe Valley School Corp	Akron
131	2,187	North Adams Community Schools	Decatur
132	2,169	Greensburg Community Schools	Greensburg
133	2,158	Salem Community Schools	Salem
134	2,112	Mitchell Community Schools	Mitchell
135	2,106	Pike County School Corp	Petersburg
136	2,094	Fairfield Community Schools	Goshen
137	2,092	North Gibson School Corp	Princeton
138	2,040	South Vermillion Com Sch Corp	Clinton
139	2,039	Knox Community School Corp	Knox
140	2,019	Greencastle Community Sch Corp	Greencastle
141	2,001	West Lafayette Com School Corp	West Lafayette
142	1,997	Whitko Community School Corp	Pierceton
143	1,995	South Montgomery Com Sch Corp	New Market
144	1,985	Batesville Community Sch Corp	Batesville
145	1,967	South Gibson School Corp	Fort Branch
146	1,948	Benton Community School Corp	Fowler
147	1,947	Rochester Community Sch Corp	Rochester
148	1,927	North Putnam Community Schools	Bainbridge
149	1,916	Western Boone County Com SD	Thorntown
150	1,911	Elwood Community School Corp	Elwood
151	1,888	Baugo Community Schools	Elkhart
152	1,854	Nineveh-Hensley-Jackson United	Trafalgar
152	1,854	Tipton Community School Corp	Tipton
154	1,841	Rensselaer Central School Corp	Rensselaer
155	1,839	Southwest Dubois County Sch Corp	Huntingburg
156	1,836	Brownstown Cnt Com Sch Corp	Brownstown
157	1,818	John Glenn School Corporation	Walkerton
158	1,809	Crawford County Com School Corp	Marengo
159	1,792	Hanover Community School Corp	Cedar Lake
160	1,787	Southwest School Corp	Sullivan
161	1,782	Eastbrook Community Sch Corp	Marion
162	1,775	North West Hendricks Schools	Lizton
163	1,734	Prairie Heights Com Sch Corp	Lagrange
164	1,733	East Washington School Corp	Pekin
165	1,729	Randolph Central School Corp	Winchester
166	1,719	Garrett-Keyser-Butler Com	Garrett
167	1,698	Centerville-Abington Com Schs	Centerville
168	1,693	Union Township School Corp	Valparaiso
169	1,683	Mill Creek Community Sch Corp	Clayton
170	1,667	Northwestern School Corp	Kokomo
171	1,651	Union County College Corner JSD	Liberty
172	1,649	Delphi Community School Corp	Delphi
173	1,647	Paoli Community School Corp	Paoli
174	1,643	Porter Township School Corp	Valparaiso
175	1,629	Alexandria Com School Corp	Alexandria
176	1,627	Lawrenceburg Com School Corp	Lawrenceburg
176	1,627	School Town of Speedway	Speedway
178	1,617	Tell City-Troy Twp School Corp	Tell City
179	1,616	North Newton School Corp	Morocco
180	1,607	Southeastern School Corp	Walton
181	1,592	Switzerland County School Corp	Vevay
182	1,571	Northwestern Con School Corp	Fairland
183	1,570	Shelby Eastern Schools	Shelbyville
184	1,556	Madison-Grant United Sch Corp	Fairmount
185	1,552	Manchester Community Schools	N Manchester
186	1,524	Northeast School Corp	Hymera
187	1,509	Oak Hill United School Corp	Converse
188	1,507	Dekalb County Eastern Com SD	Butler

Male Students

Rank	Percent	District Name	City
1	54.2	Lakeland School Corporation	Lagrange
2	53.9	Brown County School Corporation	Nashville
2	53.9	Union County College Corner JSD	Liberty
4	53.5	Tipton Community School Corp	Tipton
5	53.2	Decatur County Com Schools	Greensburg
5	53.2	East Washington School Corp	Pekin
5	53.2	Mitchell Community Schools	Mitchell
5	53.2	Paoli Community School Corp	Paoli
5	53.2	Westview School Corporation	Topeka
10	52.9	Dekalb County Eastern Com SD	Butler
10	52.9	Delaware Community School Corp	Muncie
10	52.9	Greencastle Community Sch Corp	Greencastle
13	52.8	Southeastern School Corp	Walton
14	52.7	Anderson Community School Corp	Anderson
14	52.7	Brownstown Cnt Com Sch Corp	Brownstown
14	52.7	Greenfield-Central Com Schools	Greenfield
14	52.7	Logansport Community Sch Corp	Logansport
14	52.7	M S D Martinsville Schools	Martinsville
14	52.7	M S D Mount Vernon	Mount Vernon
14	52.7	Northern Wells Com Schools	Ossian
14	52.7	Warrick County School Corp	Boonville
14	52.7	Western Boone County Com SD	Thorntown
23	52.6	Benton Community School Corp	Fowler
23	52.6	New Castle Community Sch Corp	New Castle
23	52.6	Washington Com Schools Inc	Washington
26	52.5	North Putnam Community Schools	Bainbridge
26	52.5	Richland-Bean Blossom CSC	Ellettsville
26	52.5	Vincennes Community Sch Corp	Vincennes
29	52.4	Hanover Community School Corp	Cedar Lake
29	52.4	Plymouth Community School Corp	Plymouth
29	52.4	Rochester Community Sch Corp	Rochester
32	52.3	Dekalb County Central United SD	Waterloo
33	52.2	John Glenn School Corporation	Walkerton
33	52.2	Michigan City Area Schools	Michigan City
33	52.2	North Newton School Corp	Morocco
33	52.2	School City of Hammond	Hammond
33	52.2	Tri-Creek School Corp	Lowell
38	52.1	Centerville-Abington Com Schs	Centerville
38	52.1	Crawfordsville Com Schools	Crawfordsville
38	52.1	Lake Central School Corp	Saint John
38	52.1	North Lawrence Com Schools	Bedford
38	52.1	Rensselaer Central School Corp	Rensselaer
38	52.1	Shelbyville Central Schools	Shelbyville
44	52.0	Bartholomew Con School Corp	Columbus
44	52.0	Batesville Community Sch Corp	Batesville
44	52.0	Merrillville Community School	Merrillville
44	52.0	North Harrison Com School Corp	Ramsey
44	52.0	Switzerland Central School Corp	Vevay
44	52.0	Tell City-Troy Twp School Corp	Tell City
50	51.9	Crawford County Com School Corp	Marengo
50	51.9	Lawrenceburg Com School Corp	Lawrenceburg
50	51.9	New Prairie United School Corp	New Carlisle
50	51.9	Northwestern School Corp	Kokomo
50	51.9	Plainfield Community Sch Corp	Plainfield
50	51.9	Shelby Eastern Schools	Shelbyville
56	51.8	Beech Grove City Schools	Beech Grove
56	51.8	Center Grove Com Sch Corp	Greenwood
56	51.8	Delphi Community School Corp	Delphi
56	51.8	M S D Washington Twp	Indianapolis
56	51.8	School Town of Munster	Munster
56	51.8	South Madison Com Sch Corp	Pendleton
62	51.7	Greater Clark County Schools	Jeffersonville
62	51.7	Hamilton Heights School Corp	Arcadia
62	51.7	Jay School Corp	Portland
62	51.7	M S D Wabash County Schools	Wabash
62	51.7	Northwestern Con School Corp	Fairland
62	51.7	Portage Township Schools	Portage
62	51.7	School Town of Speedway	Speedway
62	51.7	South Harrison Com Schools	Corydon
62	51.7	Southwest School Corp	Sullivan
62	51.7	Vigo County School Corp	Terre Haute
62	51.7	West Noble School Corporation	Ligonier
73	51.6	Duneland School Corporation	Chesterton
73	51.6	Fayette County School Corp	Connersville
73	51.6	Knox Community School Corp	Knox
73	51.6	Manchester Community Schools	N Manchester
73	51.6	Muncie Community Schools	Muncie
73	51.6	Nineveh-Hensley-Jackson United	Trafalgar
73	51.6	Noblesville Schools	Noblesville
73	51.6	Sunman-Dearborn Com Sch Corp	Sunman
73	51.6	Warsaw Community Schools	Warsaw
73	51.6	Zionsville Community Schools	Zionsville
83	51.5	Greensburg Community Schools	Greensburg
83	51.5	M S D Warren Township	Indianapolis
83	51.5	North West Hendricks Schools	Lizton
83	51.5	Randolph Central School Corp	Winchester
83	51.5	Richmond Community School Corp	Richmond
83	51.5	Westfield-Washington Schools	Westfield
89	51.4	Danville Community School Corp	Danville
89	51.4	North Adams Community Schools	Decatur
89	51.4	Northeast School Corp	Hymera
89	51.4	Seymour Community Schools	Seymour
89	51.4	South Vermillion Com Sch Corp	Clinton
89	51.4	Union Township School Corp	Valparaiso
95	51.3	Blackford County Schools	Hartford City
95	51.3	East Allen County Schools	New Haven
95	51.3	Elwood Community School Corp	Elwood
95	51.3	Fort Wayne Community Schools	Fort Wayne
95	51.3	Goshen Community Schools	Goshen
95	51.3	Jennings County Schools	North Vernon
95	51.3	Laporte Community School Corp	Laporte
95	51.3	Lebanon Community School Corp	Lebanon
95	51.3	Mississinewa Community School Corp	Gas City
95	51.3	Oak Hill United School Corp	Converse
95	51.3	South Bend Community Sch Corp	South Bend
95	51.3	South Dearborn Com School Corp	Aurora
107	51.2	Brownsburg Community Sch Corp	Brownsburg
107	51.2	Concord Community Schools	Elkhart
107	51.2	Huntington County Com Sch Corp	Huntington
107	51.2	Indianapolis Public Schools	Indianapolis
107	51.2	M S D Lawrence Township	Indianapolis
107	51.2	Monroe County Com Sch Corp	Bloomington
107	51.2	North Gibson School Corp	Princeton
107	51.2	Porter Township School Corp	Valparaiso
107	51.2	Rush County Schools	Rushville
107	51.2	Wa-Nee Community Schools	Nappanee
107	51.2	West Clark Community Schools	Sellersburg
118	51.1	Baugo Community Schools	Elkhart
118	51.1	Crown Point Community Sch Corp	Crown Point
118	51.1	Elkhart Community Schools	Elkhart
118	51.1	Evansville-Vanderburgh Sch Corp	Evansville
118	51.1	Franklin Community School Corp	Franklin
118	51.1	Franklin County Com Sch Corp	Brookville
118	51.1	Lafayette School Corporation	Lafayette
118	51.1	M S D Perry Township	Indianapolis
118	51.1	M S D Southwest Allen County	Fort Wayne
118	51.1	Madison-Grant United Sch Corp	Fairmount
118	51.1	Mount Vernon Community Sch Corp	Fortville
118	51.1	Scott County SD 2	Scottsburg
118	51.1	Tippecanoe Valley School Corp	Akron
118	51.1	West Lafayette Com School Corp	West Lafayette
132	51.0	M S D Steuben County	Angola
132	51.0	M S D Wayne Township	Indianapolis
132	51.0	New Albany-Floyd County Con Sch	New Albany
132	51.0	South Montgomery Com Sch Corp	New Market
132	51.0	Tippecanoe School Corp	Lafayette
132	51.0	Wawasee Community School Corp	Syracuse
132	51.0	Western School Corp	Russiaville
139	50.9	Community Schools of Frankfort	Frankfort
139	50.9	Lake Ridge Schools	Gary
139	50.9	Spencer-Owen Community Schools	Spencer
142	50.8	Alexandria Com School Corp	Alexandria
142	50.8	Carmel Clay Schools	Carmel
142	50.8	East Porter County School Corp	Kouts
142	50.8	Eastbrook Community Sch Corp	Marion
142	50.8	Franklin Township Com Sch Corp	Indianapolis
142	50.8	Hamilton Southeastern Schools	Fishers
142	50.8	Kokomo-Center Twp Con Sch Corp	Kokomo
142	50.8	M S D Decatur Township	Indianapolis
142	50.8	Mount Pleasant Twp Com Sch Corp	Yorktown
142	50.8	Penn-Harris-Madison Sch Corp	Mishawaka
142	50.8	Salem Community Schools	Salem
153	50.7	Greenwood Community Sch Corp	Greenwood
153	50.7	Kankakee Valley School Corp	Wheatfield
153	50.7	Mill Creek Community Sch Corp	Clayton
153	50.7	School City of Mishawaka	Mishawaka
153	50.7	School Town of Highland	Highland
153	50.7	Southern Hancock Co CS Corp	New Palestine
159	50.6	Avon Community School Corp	Avon
159	50.6	Marion Community Schools	Marion
161	50.5	Peru Community Schools	Peru
161	50.5	Prairie Heights Com Sch Corp	Lagrange
161	50.5	School City of Hobart	Hobart
161	50.5	Valparaiso Community Schools	Valparaiso
161	50.5	Whitko Community School Corp	Pierceton
161	50.5	Whitley County Cons Schools	Columbia City
167	50.4	Maconaquah School Corp	Bunker Hill
167	50.4	Mooresville Con School Corp	Mooresville
167	50.4	North Montgomery Com Sch Corp	Crawfordsville
170	50.3	Greater Jasper Con Schs	Jasper
170	50.3	Middlebury Community Schools	Middlebury
172	50.1	Clark-Pleasant Com School Corp	Whiteland
172	50.1	Frankton-Lapel Community Schs	Anderson
172	50.1	M S D Pike Township	Indianapolis
172	50.1	Madison Consolidated Schools	Madison
172	50.1	Northwest Allen County Schools	Fort Wayne
172	50.1	School City of East Chicago	East Chicago
178	49.9	South Gibson School Corp	Fort Branch
179	49.8	Gary Community School Corp	Gary
179	49.8	North Spencer County Sch Corp	Lincoln City
179	49.8	Twin Lakes School Corp	Monticello
182	49.7	Fairfield Community Schools	Goshen
183	49.6	Clay Community Schools	Knightsville
183	49.6	Pike County School Corp	Petersburg
185	49.3	East Noble School Corp	Kendallville
186	49.0	Southwest Dubois County Sch Corp	Huntingburg
187	48.9	Griffith Public Schools	Griffith
188	47.7	Garrett-Keyser-Butler Com	Garrett

Note: This section only includes districts with 1,500 or more students; All categories are ranked from high to low

Female Students

Rank	Percent	District Name	City
1	52.3	Garrett-Keyser-Butler Com	Garrett
2	51.1	Griffith Public Schools	Griffith
3	51.0	Southwest Dubois County Sch Corp	Huntingburg
4	50.7	East Noble School Corp	Kendallville
5	50.4	Clay Community Schools	Knightsville
5	50.4	Pike County School Corp	Petersburg
7	50.3	Fairfield Community Schools	Goshen
8	50.2	Gary Community School Corp	Gary
8	50.2	North Spencer County Sch Corp	Lincoln City
8	50.2	Twin Lakes School Corp	Monticello
11	50.1	South Gibson School Corp	Fort Branch
12	49.9	Clark-Pleasant Com School Corp	Whiteland
12	49.9	Frankton-Lapel Community Schs	Anderson
12	49.9	M S D Pike Township	Indianapolis
12	49.9	Madison Consolidated Schools	Madison
12	49.9	Northwest Allen County Schools	Fort Wayne
12	49.9	School City of East Chicago	East Chicago
18	49.7	Greater Jasper Con Schs	Jasper
18	49.7	Middlebury Community Schools	Middlebury
20	49.6	Maconaquah School Corp	Bunker Hill
20	49.6	Mooresville Con School Corp	Mooresville
20	49.6	North Montgomery Com Sch Corp	Crawfordsville
23	49.5	Peru Community Schools	Peru
23	49.5	Prairie Heights Com Sch Corp	Lagrange
23	49.5	School City of Hobart	Hobart
23	49.5	Valparaiso Community Schools	Valparaiso
23	49.5	Whitko Community School Corp	Pierceton
23	49.5	Whitley County Cons Schools	Columbia City
29	49.4	Avon Community School Corp	Avon
29	49.4	Marion Community Schools	Marion
31	49.3	Greenwood Community Sch Corp	Greenwood
31	49.3	Kankakee Valley School Corp	Wheatfield
31	49.3	Mill Creek Community Sch Corp	Clayton
31	49.3	School City of Mishawaka	Mishawaka
31	49.3	School Town of Highland	Highland
31	49.3	Southern Hancock Co CS Corp	New Palestine
37	49.2	Alexandria Com School Corp	Alexandria
37	49.2	Carmel Clay Schools	Carmel
37	49.2	East Porter County School Corp	Kouts
37	49.2	Eastbrook Community Sch Corp	Marion
37	49.2	Franklin Township Com Sch Corp	Indianapolis
37	49.2	Hamilton Southeastern Schools	Fishers
37	49.2	Kokomo-Center Twp Con Sch Corp	Kokomo
37	49.2	M S D Decatur Township	Indianapolis
37	49.2	Mount Pleasant Twp Com Sch Corp	Yorktown
37	49.2	Penn-Harris-Madison Sch Corp	Mishawaka
37	49.2	Salem Community Schools	Salem
48	49.1	Community Schools of Frankfort	Frankfort
48	49.1	Lake Ridge Schools	Gary
48	49.1	Spencer-Owen Community Schools	Spencer
51	49.0	M S D Steuben County	Angola
51	49.0	M S D Wayne Township	Indianapolis
51	49.0	New Albany-Floyd County Con Sch	New Albany
51	49.0	South Montgomery Com Sch Corp	New Market
51	49.0	Tippecanoe School Corp	Lafayette
51	49.0	Wawasee Community School Corp	Syracuse
51	49.0	Western School Corp	Russiaville
58	48.9	Baugo Community Schools	Elkhart
58	48.9	Crown Point Community Sch Corp	Crown Point
58	48.9	Elkhart Community Schools	Elkhart
58	48.9	Evansville-Vanderburgh Sch Corp	Evansville
58	48.9	Franklin Community School Corp	Franklin
58	48.9	Franklin County Com Sch Corp	Brookville
58	48.9	Lafayette School Corporation	Lafayette
58	48.9	M S D Perry Township	Indianapolis
58	48.9	M S D Southwest Allen County	Fort Wayne
58	48.9	Madison-Grant United Sch Corp	Fairmount
58	48.9	Mount Vernon Community Sch Corp	Fortville
58	48.9	Scott County SD 2	Scottsburg
58	48.9	Tippecanoe Valley School Corp	Akron
58	48.9	West Lafayette Com School Corp	West Lafayette
72	48.8	Brownsburg Community Sch Corp	Brownsburg
72	48.8	Concord Community Schools	Elkhart
72	48.8	Huntington County Com Sch Corp	Huntington
72	48.8	Indianapolis Public Schools	Indianapolis
72	48.8	M S D Lawrence Township	Indianapolis
72	48.8	Monroe County Com Sch Corp	Bloomington
72	48.8	North Gibson School Corp	Princeton
72	48.8	Porter Township School Corp	Valparaiso
72	48.8	Rush County Schools	Rushville
72	48.8	Wa-Nee Community Schools	Nappanee
72	48.8	West Clark Community Schools	Sellersburg
83	48.7	Blackford County Schools	Hartford City
83	48.7	East Allen County Schools	New Haven
83	48.7	Elwood Community School Corp	Elwood
83	48.7	Fort Wayne Community Schools	Fort Wayne
83	48.7	Goshen Community Schools	Goshen
83	48.7	Jennings County Schools	North Vernon
83	48.7	Laporte Community School Corp	Laporte
83	48.7	Lebanon Community School Corp	Lebanon
83	48.7	Mississinewa Community School Corp	Gas City
83	48.7	Oak Hill United School Corp	Converse
83	48.7	South Bend Community Sch Corp	South Bend
83	48.7	South Dearborn Com School Corp	Aurora
95	48.6	Danville Community School Corp	Danville
95	48.6	North Adams Community Schools	Decatur
95	48.6	Northeast School Corp	Hymera
95	48.6	Seymour Community Schools	Seymour
95	48.6	South Vermillion Com Sch Corp	Clinton
95	48.6	Union Township School Corp	Valparaiso
101	48.5	Greensburg Community Schools	Greensburg
101	48.5	M S D Warren Township	Indianapolis
101	48.5	North West Hendricks Schools	Lizton
101	48.5	Randolph Central School Corp	Winchester
101	48.5	Richmond Community School Corp	Richmond
101	48.5	Westfield-Washington Schools	Westfield
107	48.4	Duneland School Corporation	Chesterton
107	48.4	Fayette County School Corp	Connersville
107	48.4	Knox Community School Corp	Knox
107	48.4	Manchester Community Schools	N Manchester
107	48.4	Muncie Community Schools	Muncie
107	48.4	Nineveh-Hensley-Jackson United	Trafalgar
107	48.4	Noblesville Schools	Noblesville
107	48.4	Sunman-Dearborn Com Sch Corp	Sunman
107	48.4	Warsaw Community Schools	Warsaw
107	48.4	Zionsville Community Schools	Zionsville
117	48.3	Greater Clark County Schools	Jeffersonville
117	48.3	Hamilton Heights School Corp	Arcadia
117	48.3	Jay School Corp	Portland
117	48.3	M S D Wabash County Schools	Wabash
117	48.3	Northwestern Con School Corp	Fairland
117	48.3	Portage Township Schools	Portage
117	48.3	School Town of Speedway	Speedway
117	48.3	South Harrison Com Schools	Corydon
117	48.3	Southwest School Corp	Sullivan
117	48.3	Vigo County School Corp	Terre Haute
117	48.3	West Noble School Corporation	Ligonier
128	48.2	Beech Grove City Schools	Beech Grove
128	48.2	Center Grove Com Sch Corp	Greenwood
128	48.2	Delphi Community School Corp	Delphi
128	48.2	M S D Washington Twp	Indianapolis
128	48.2	School Town of Munster	Munster
128	48.2	South Madison Com Sch Corp	Pendleton
134	48.1	Crawford County Com School Corp	Marengo
134	48.1	Lawrenceburg Com School Corp	Lawrenceburg
134	48.1	New Prairie United School Corp	New Carlisle
134	48.1	Northwestern School Corp	Kokomo
134	48.1	Plainfield Community Sch Corp	Plainfield
134	48.1	Shelby Eastern Schools	Shelbyville
140	48.0	Bartholomew Con School Corp	Columbus
140	48.0	Batesville Community Sch Corp	Batesville
140	48.0	Merrillville Community School	Merrillville
140	48.0	North Harrison Com School Corp	Ramsey
140	48.0	Switzerland County School Corp	Vevay
140	48.0	Tell City-Troy Twp School Corp	Tell City
146	47.9	Centerville-Abington Com Schs	Centerville
146	47.9	Crawfordsville Com Schools	Crawfordsville
146	47.9	Lake Central School Corp	Saint John
146	47.9	North Lawrence Com Schools	Bedford
146	47.9	Rensselaer Central School Corp	Rensselaer
146	47.9	Shelbyville Central Schools	Shelbyville
152	47.8	John Glenn School Corporation	Walkerton
152	47.8	Michigan City Area Schools	Michigan City
152	47.8	North Newton School Corp	Morocco
152	47.8	School City of Hammond	Hammond
152	47.8	Tri-Creek School Corp	Lowell
157	47.7	Dekalb County Central United SD	Waterloo
158	47.6	Hanover Community School Corp	Cedar Lake
158	47.6	Plymouth Community School Corp	Plymouth
158	47.6	Rochester Community Sch Corp	Rochester
161	47.5	North Putnam Community Schools	Bainbridge
161	47.5	Richland-Bean Blossom CSC	Ellettsville
161	47.5	Vincennes Community Sch Corp	Vincennes
164	47.4	Benton Community School Corp	Fowler
164	47.4	New Castle Community Sch Corp	New Castle
164	47.4	Washington Com Schools Inc	Washington
167	47.3	Anderson Community School Corp	Anderson
167	47.3	Brownstown Cnt Com Sch Corp	Brownstown
167	47.3	Greenfield-Central Com Schools	Greenfield
167	47.3	Logansport Community Sch Corp	Logansport
167	47.3	M S D Martinsville Schools	Martinsville
167	47.3	M S D Mount Vernon	Mount Vernon
167	47.3	Northern Wells Com Schools	Ossian
167	47.3	Warrick County School Corp	Boonville
167	47.3	Western Boone County Com SD	Thorntown
176	47.2	Southeastern School Corp	Walton
177	47.1	Dekalb County Eastern Com SD	Butler
177	47.1	Delaware Community School Corp	Muncie
177	47.1	Greencastle Community Sch Corp	Greencastle
180	46.8	Decatur County Com Schools	Greensburg
180	46.8	East Washington School Corp	Pekin
180	46.8	Mitchell Community Schools	Mitchell
180	46.8	Paoli Community School Corp	Paoli
180	46.8	Westview School Corporation	Topeka
185	46.5	Tipton Community School Corp	Tipton
186	46.1	Brown County School Corporation	Nashville
186	46.1	Union County College Corner JSD	Liberty
188	45.8	Lakeland School Corporation	Lagrange

Individual Education Program Students

Rank	Percent	District Name	City
1	26.0	Kokomo-Center Twp Con Sch Corp	Kokomo
1	26.0	M S D Mount Vernon	Mount Vernon
3	25.8	Benton Community School Corp	Fowler
4	24.5	Richmond Community School Corp	Richmond
5	24.2	Madison Consolidated Schools	Madison
6	23.5	Randolph Central School Corp	Winchester
7	23.4	Muncie Community Schools	Muncie
8	23.3	South Bend Community Sch Corp	South Bend
9	23.2	Washington Com Schools Inc	Washington
10	23.1	Jennings County Schools	North Vernon
11	22.6	Lafayette School Corporation	Lafayette
11	22.6	North Gibson School Corp	Princeton
11	22.6	Southwest School Corp	Sullivan
14	22.5	New Castle Community Sch Corp	New Castle
15	22.1	South Madison Com Sch Corp	Pendleton
16	22.0	Vigo County School Corp	Terre Haute
17	21.9	Rensselaer Central School Corp	Rensselaer
18	21.8	Evansville-Vanderburgh Sch Corp	Evansville
19	21.7	North Putnam Community Schools	Bainbridge
20	21.5	Lebanon Community School Corp	Lebanon
21	21.4	Clay Community Schools	Knightsville
22	21.2	South Dearborn Com School Corp	Aurora
23	21.1	Pike County School Corp	Petersburg
24	20.9	Greenfield-Central Com Schools	Greenfield
25	20.3	South Montgomery Com Sch Corp	New Market
26	20.2	Spencer-Owen Community Schools	Spencer
27	20.0	Jay School Corp	Portland
27	20.0	Warrick County School Corp	Boonville
29	19.8	Shelbyville Central Schools	Shelbyville
30	19.7	Anderson Community School Corp	Anderson
30	19.7	Union County College Corner JSD	Liberty
32	19.6	Blackford County Schools	Hartford City
33	19.4	Indianapolis Public Schools	Indianapolis
33	19.4	Northeast School Corp	Hymera
35	19.3	Crawfordsville Com Schools	Crawfordsville
35	19.3	Greater Clark County Schools	Jeffersonville
35	19.3	Greencastle Community Sch Corp	Greencastle
35	19.3	Hamilton Heights School Corp	Arcadia
39	19.2	Delaware Community School Corp	Muncie
39	19.2	Mitchell Community Schools	Mitchell
39	19.2	North Lawrence Com Schools	Bedford
42	19.1	Baugo Community Schools	Elkhart
42	19.1	Brown County School Corporation	Nashville
42	19.1	Fort Wayne Community Schools	Fort Wayne
45	19.0	Elwood Community School Corp	Elwood
46	18.9	Michigan City Area Schools	Michigan City
47	18.7	School City of Mishawaka	Mishawaka
48	18.6	Garrett-Keyser-Butler Com	Garrett
49	18.5	New Albany-Floyd County Con Sch	New Albany
49	18.5	Paoli Community School Corp	Paoli
51	18.4	Scott County SD 2	Scottsburg
52	18.3	Eastbrook Community Sch Corp	Marion
52	18.3	M S D Decatur Township	Indianapolis
52	18.3	Richland-Bean Blossom CSC	Ellettsville
55	18.1	South Harrison Com Schools	Corydon
56	18.0	Frankton-Lapel Community Schs	Anderson
56	18.0	Maconaquah School Corp	Bunker Hill
58	17.9	North Newton School Corp	Morocco
58	17.9	South Gibson School Corp	Fort Branch
60	17.8	Tipton Community School Corp	Tipton
61	17.7	Sunman-Dearborn Com Sch Corp	Sunman
62	17.6	M S D Warren Township	Indianapolis

Note: This section only includes districts with 1,500 or more students; All categories are ranked from high to low

62	17.6	Marion Community Schools	Marion
62	17.6	Mount Pleasant Twp Com Sch Corp	Yorktown
62	17.6	Switzerland County School Corp	Vevay
66	17.5	Vincennes Community Sch Corp	Vincennes
67	17.4	Goshen Community Schools	Goshen
67	17.4	Seymour Community Schools	Seymour
67	17.4	Zionsville Community Schools	Zionsville
70	17.3	Mount Vernon Community Sch Corp	Fortville
70	17.3	School Town of Speedway	Speedway
72	17.2	Crawford County Com School Corp	Marengo
72	17.2	East Porter County School Corp	Kouts
72	17.2	Fayette County School Corp	Connersville
72	17.2	Noblesville Schools	Noblesville
76	17.1	Elkhart Community Schools	Elkhart
76	17.1	Franklin Community School Corp	Franklin
76	17.1	M S D Wabash County Schools	Wabash
79	17.0	Brownstown Cnt Com Sch Corp	Brownstown
79	17.0	Lawrenceburg Com School Corp	Lawrenceburg
79	17.0	North Harrison Com School Corp	Ramsey
79	17.0	Southern Hancock Co CS Corp	New Palestine
83	16.9	Kankakee Valley School Corp	Wheatfield
83	16.9	Mill Creek Community Sch Corp	Clayton
83	16.9	Shelby Eastern Schools	Shelbyville
86	16.8	Union Township School Corp	Valparaiso
87	16.7	Decatur County Com Schools	Greensburg
87	16.7	East Noble School Corp	Kendallville
87	16.7	Franklin County Com Sch Corp	Brookville
87	16.7	Greensburg Community Schools	Greensburg
87	16.7	Huntington County Com Sch Corp	Huntington
87	16.7	Western Boone County Com SD	Thorntown
93	16.6	Lake Central School Corp	Saint John
93	16.6	Northwestern School Corp	Kokomo
93	16.6	South Vermillion Com Sch Corp	Clinton
93	16.6	Western School Corp	Russiaville
97	16.5	Dekalb County Eastern Com SD	Butler
97	16.5	Mississinewa Community School Corp	Gas City
97	16.5	Westfield-Washington Schools	Westfield
100	16.4	Madison-Grant United Sch Corp	Fairmount
101	16.3	Duneland School Corporation	Chesterton
101	16.3	Northern Wells Com Schools	Ossian
101	16.3	Peru Community Schools	Peru
104	16.2	North Adams Community Schools	Decatur
104	16.2	North Montgomery Com Sch Corp	Crawfordsville
104	16.2	Tippecanoe Valley School Corp	Akron
107	16.1	Delphi Community School Corp	Delphi
108	16.0	Northwestern Con School Corp	Fairland
109	15.9	Monroe County Com Sch Corp	Bloomington
110	15.8	Prairie Heights Com Sch Corp	Lagrange
110	15.8	Tippecanoe School Corp	Lafayette
112	15.7	M S D Wayne Township	Indianapolis
112	15.7	Portage Township Schools	Portage
112	15.7	School City of East Chicago	East Chicago
115	15.5	M S D Pike Township	Indianapolis
115	15.5	M S D Southwest Allen County	Fort Wayne
117	15.4	School Town of Munster	Munster
118	15.3	Dekalb County Central United SD	Waterloo
118	15.3	Wa-Nee Community Schools	Nappanee
120	15.2	M S D Lawrence Township	Indianapolis
120	15.2	M S D Martinsville Schools	Martinsville
120	15.2	Southeastern School Corp	Walton
120	15.2	Southwest Dubois County Sch Corp	Huntingburg
120	15.2	Twin Lakes School Corp	Monticello
125	15.1	Beech Grove City Schools	Beech Grove
125	15.1	East Washington School Corp	Pekin
125	15.1	Whitko Community School Corp	Pierceton
128	15.0	Alexandria Com School Corp	Alexandria
128	15.0	Bartholomew Con School Corp	Columbus
128	15.0	Franklin Township Com Sch Corp	Indianapolis
128	15.0	M S D Washington Twp	Indianapolis
128	15.0	Oak Hill United School Corp	Converse
128	15.0	Warsaw Community Schools	Warsaw
134	14.9	Avon Community School Corp	Avon
134	14.9	M S D Perry Township	Indianapolis
134	14.9	Plainfield Community Sch Corp	Plainfield
134	14.9	School City of Hammond	Hammond
138	14.8	Hamilton Southeastern Schools	Fishers
139	14.7	Batesville Community Sch Corp	Batesville
139	14.7	Concord Community Schools	Elkhart
139	14.7	Hanover Community School Corp	Cedar Lake
142	14.5	East Allen County Schools	New Haven
142	14.5	Lakeland School Corporation	Lagrange
142	14.5	Middlebury Community Schools	Middlebury
142	14.5	Salem Community Schools	Salem
146	14.4	Community Schools of Frankfort	Frankfort
146	14.4	Gary Community School Corp	Gary
148	14.2	West Lafayette Com School Corp	West Lafayette
149	14.0	Nineveh-Hensley-Jackson United	Trafalgar
149	14.0	North West Hendricks Schools	Lizton
149	14.0	Penn-Harris-Madison Sch Corp	Mishawaka
149	14.0	Valparaiso Community Schools	Valparaiso
149	14.0	Wawasee Community School Corp	Syracuse
149	14.0	West Clark Community Schools	Sellersburg
155	13.9	Manchester Community Schools	N Manchester
156	13.8	Clark-Pleasant Com School Corp	Whiteland
156	13.8	Fairfield Community Schools	Goshen
156	13.8	Lake Ridge Schools	Gary
156	13.8	Logansport Community Sch Corp	Logansport
156	13.8	Whitley County Cons Schools	Columbia City
161	13.7	Center Grove Com Sch Corp	Greenwood
162	13.5	Knox Community School Corp	Knox
162	13.5	North Spencer County Sch Corp	Lincoln City
164	13.3	Greenwood Community Sch Corp	Greenwood
164	13.3	John Glenn School Corporation	Walkerton
166	13.2	Griffith Public Schools	Griffith
166	13.2	Tell City-Troy Twp School Corp	Tell City
168	13.1	Rush County Schools	Rushville
168	13.1	Tri-Creek School Corp	Lowell
170	12.9	M S D Steuben County	Angola
170	12.9	Mooresville Con School Corp	Mooresville
172	12.5	Laporte Community School Corp	Laporte
172	12.5	Merrillville Community School	Merrillville
172	12.5	Northwest Allen County Schools	Fort Wayne
172	12.5	Plymouth Community School Corp	Plymouth
176	12.4	Brownsburg Community Sch Corp	Brownsburg
177	12.3	Carmel Clay Schools	Carmel
178	12.2	Centerville-Abington Com Schs	Centerville
179	11.7	Crown Point Community Sch Corp	Crown Point
180	11.6	Porter Township School Corp	Valparaiso
180	11.6	Rochester Community Sch Corp	Rochester
182	11.5	Danville Community School Corp	Danville
182	11.5	School Town of Highland	Highland
184	11.4	West Noble School Corporation	Ligonier
185	11.3	Greater Jasper Con Schs	Jasper
186	11.2	New Prairie United School Corp	New Carlisle
186	11.2	School City of Hobart	Hobart
188	10.8	Westview School Corporation	Topeka

English Language Learner Students

Rank	Percent	District Name	City
1	29.6	West Noble School Corporation	Ligonier
2	27.8	Goshen Community Schools	Goshen
3	26.6	Westview School Corporation	Topeka
4	25.7	Community Schools of Frankfort	Frankfort
5	18.7	Logansport Community Sch Corp	Logansport
6	17.5	Elkhart Community Schools	Elkhart
7	16.6	Concord Community Schools	Elkhart
8	15.0	School City of Hammond	Hammond
9	14.1	Lafayette School Corporation	Lafayette
10	13.0	M S D Pike Township	Indianapolis
11	11.9	Warsaw Community Schools	Warsaw
12	11.5	Fairfield Community Schools	Goshen
12	11.5	School City of East Chicago	East Chicago
14	11.4	Lakeland School Corporation	Lagrange
15	10.9	Plymouth Community School Corp	Plymouth
16	10.2	M S D Wayne Township	Indianapolis
17	9.9	M S D Washington Twp	Indianapolis
18	9.7	Indianapolis Public Schools	Indianapolis
18	9.7	South Bend Community Sch Corp	South Bend
20	9.6	Wa-Nee Community Schools	Nappanee
21	9.5	Southwest Dubois County Sch Corp	Huntingburg
22	8.9	School Town of Speedway	Speedway
23	7.8	Twin Lakes School Corp	Monticello
24	7.6	Middlebury Community Schools	Middlebury
25	7.5	M S D Lawrence Township	Indianapolis
26	7.3	Seymour Community Schools	Seymour
27	6.6	West Lafayette Com School Corp	West Lafayette
28	6.5	Greater Jasper Con Schs	Jasper
28	6.5	Washington Com Schools Inc	Washington
30	6.4	Crawfordsville Com Schools	Crawfordsville
31	6.0	Bartholomew Con School Corp	Columbus
32	5.6	M S D Perry Township	Indianapolis
33	5.4	Shelbyville Central Schools	Shelbyville
33	5.4	Wawasee Community School Corp	Syracuse
35	5.3	Delphi Community School Corp	Delphi
35	5.3	Fort Wayne Community Schools	Fort Wayne
37	5.1	Kankakee Valley School Corp	Wheatfield
38	5.0	M S D Warren Township	Indianapolis
38	5.0	Tippecanoe School Corp	Lafayette
40	4.5	Westfield-Washington Schools	Westfield
41	4.3	School Town of Highland	Highland
42	4.2	Monroe County Com Sch Corp	Bloomington
43	4.1	Clark-Pleasant Com School Corp	Whiteland
44	4.0	Avon Community School Corp	Avon
45	3.9	Lake Ridge Schools	Gary
46	3.8	Laporte Community School Corp	Laporte
46	3.8	Tippecanoe Valley School Corp	Akron
48	3.7	M S D Steuben County	Angola
49	3.5	Franklin Township Com Sch Corp	Indianapolis
49	3.5	Hamilton Southeastern Schools	Fishers
51	3.2	Greater Clark County Schools	Jeffersonville
52	3.1	Greenwood Community Sch Corp	Greenwood
53	3.0	Brownsburg Community Sch Corp	Brownsburg
53	3.0	East Noble School Corp	Kendallville
53	3.0	Richmond Community School Corp	Richmond
53	3.0	Southeastern School Corp	Walton
57	2.8	East Allen County Schools	New Haven
58	2.7	Jay School Corp	Portland
58	2.7	North Spencer County Sch Corp	Lincoln City
60	2.6	Marion Community Schools	Marion
60	2.6	New Prairie United School Corp	New Carlisle
60	2.6	Noblesville Schools	Noblesville
63	2.5	Portage Township Schools	Portage
64	2.3	Crown Point Community Sch Corp	Crown Point
64	2.3	Elwood Community School Corp	Elwood
64	2.3	Michigan City Area Schools	Michigan City
64	2.3	North Newton School Corp	Morocco
64	2.3	Penn-Harris-Madison Sch Corp	Mishawaka
69	2.2	Merrillville Community School	Merrillville
69	2.2	School City of Hobart	Hobart
69	2.2	Valparaiso Community Schools	Valparaiso
72	1.9	Carmel Clay Schools	Carmel
72	1.9	Lake Central School Corp	Saint John
72	1.9	M S D Decatur Township	Indianapolis
72	1.9	Maconaquah School Corp	Bunker Hill
76	1.8	Franklin Community School Corp	Franklin
76	1.8	Greensburg Community Schools	Greensburg
76	1.8	North Adams Community Schools	Decatur
76	1.8	Rensselaer Central School Corp	Rensselaer
80	1.7	Anderson Community School Corp	Anderson
80	1.7	New Albany-Floyd County Con Sch	New Albany
80	1.7	West Clark Community Schools	Sellersburg
83	1.6	Griffith Public Schools	Griffith
83	1.6	Northwest Allen County Schools	Fort Wayne
83	1.6	Plainfield Community Sch Corp	Plainfield
86	1.5	School City of Mishawaka	Mishawaka
87	1.4	M S D Southwest Allen County	Fort Wayne
88	1.3	Evansville-Vanderburgh Sch Corp	Evansville
88	1.3	Garrett-Keyser-Butler Com	Garrett
88	1.3	Hanover Community School Corp	Cedar Lake
88	1.3	Mount Vernon Community Sch Corp	Fortville
88	1.3	Prairie Heights Com Sch Corp	Lagrange
88	1.3	Warrick County School Corp	Boonville
94	1.2	Beech Grove City Schools	Beech Grove
94	1.2	Dekalb County Central United SD	Waterloo
94	1.2	Lebanon Community School Corp	Lebanon
94	1.2	Manchester Community Schools	N Manchester
98	1.1	John Glenn School Corporation	Walkerton
98	1.1	Kokomo-Center Twp Con Sch Corp	Kokomo
98	1.1	Madison Consolidated Schools	Madison
98	1.1	School Town of Munster	Munster
102	1.0	Greencastle Community Sch Corp	Greencastle
102	1.0	Lawrenceburg Com School Corp	Lawrenceburg
102	1.0	Northwestern School Corp	Kokomo
105	0.9	Batesville Community Sch Corp	Batesville
105	0.9	Jennings County Schools	North Vernon
105	0.9	North Gibson School Corp	Princeton
105	0.9	Western School Corp	Russiaville
109	0.8	Muncie Community Schools	Muncie
109	0.8	Randolph Central School Corp	Winchester
109	0.8	Rush County Schools	Rushville
109	0.8	Tri-Creek School Corp	Lowell
109	0.8	Vigo County School Corp	Terre Haute
109	0.8	Vincennes Community Sch Corp	Vincennes
115	0.7	Alexandria Com School Corp	Alexandria
115	0.7	Center Grove Com Sch Corp	Greenwood
115	0.7	M S D Mount Vernon	Mount Vernon
115	0.7	North Montgomery Com Sch Corp	Crawfordsville
115	0.7	South Harrison Com Schools	Corydon
115	0.7	Whitko Community School Corp	Pierceton
121	0.6	Brownstown Cnt Com Sch Corp	Brownstown
121	0.6	Knox Community School Corp	Knox
121	0.6	Northern Wells Com Schools	Ossian
121	0.6	Porter Township School Corp	Valparaiso
121	0.6	Salem Community Schools	Salem
121	0.6	South Madison Com Sch Corp	Pendleton
121	0.6	Zionsville Community Schools	Zionsville

Note: This section only includes districts with 1,500 or more students; All categories are ranked from high to low

128	0.5	Centerville-Abington Com Schs	Centerville
128	0.5	Danville Community School Corp	Danville
128	0.5	Duneland School Corporation	Chesterton
128	0.5	Mill Creek Community Sch Corp	Clayton
128	0.5	Scott County SD 2	Scottsburg
128	0.5	Tell City-Troy Twp School Corp	Tell City
128	0.5	Union Township School Corp	Valparaiso
128	0.5	Whitley County Cons Schools	Columbia City
136	0.4	Baugo Community Schools	Elkhart
136	0.4	Eastbrook Community Sch Corp	Marion
136	0.4	Huntington County Com Sch Corp	Huntington
136	0.4	Mississinewa Community School Corp	Gas City
136	0.4	Mooresville Con School Corp	Mooresville
136	0.4	Northwestern Con School Corp	Fairland
136	0.4	Sunman-Dearborn Com Sch Corp	Sunman
136	0.4	Union County College Corner JSD	Liberty
144	0.3	Benton Community School Corp	Fowler
144	0.3	Blackford County Schools	Hartford City
144	0.3	Clay Community Schools	Knightsville
144	0.3	Crawford County Com School Corp	Marengo
144	0.3	Dekalb County Eastern Com SD	Butler
144	0.3	Frankton-Lapel Community Schs	Anderson
144	0.3	Greenfield-Central Com Schools	Greenfield
144	0.3	Hamilton Heights School Corp	Arcadia
144	0.3	New Castle Community Sch Corp	New Castle
144	0.3	North West Hendricks Schools	Lizton
144	0.3	South Gibson School Corp	Fort Branch
144	0.3	South Montgomery Com Sch Corp	New Market
144	0.3	Southwest School Corp	Sullivan
157	0.2	Decatur County Com Schools	Greensburg
157	0.2	East Porter County School Corp	Kouts
157	0.2	East Washington School Corp	Pekin
157	0.2	M S D Martinsville Schools	Martinsville
157	0.2	North Harrison Com School Corp	Ramsey
157	0.2	Oak Hill United School Corp	Converse
157	0.2	Peru Community Schools	Peru
157	0.2	Pike County School Corp	Petersburg
157	0.2	Rochester Community Sch Corp	Rochester
157	0.2	Switzerland County School Corp	Vevay
157	0.2	Tipton Community School Corp	Tipton
168	0.1	Fayette County School Corp	Connersville
168	0.1	Gary Community School Corp	Gary
168	0.1	M S D Wabash County Schools	Wabash
168	0.1	Richland-Bean Blossom CSC	Ellettsville
168	0.1	Shelby Eastern Schools	Shelbyville
168	0.1	South Dearborn Com School Corp	Aurora
174	0.0	Brown County School Corporation	Nashville
174	0.0	Delaware Community School Corp	Muncie
174	0.0	Franklin County Com Sch Corp	Brookville
174	0.0	Madison-Grant United Sch Corp	Fairmount
174	0.0	Northeast School Corp	Hymera
174	0.0	Paoli Community School Corp	Paoli
174	0.0	South Vermillion Com Sch Corp	Clinton
174	0.0	Southern Hancock Co CS Corp	New Palestine
174	0.0	Spencer-Owen Community Schools	Spencer
174	0.0	Western Boone County Com SD	Thorntown
n/a	n/a	Mitchell Community Schools	Mitchell
n/a	n/a	Mount Pleasant Twp Com Sch Corp	Yorktown
n/a	n/a	Nineveh-Hensley-Jackson United	Trafalgar
n/a	n/a	North Lawrence Com Schools	Bedford
n/a	n/a	North Putnam Community Schools	Bainbridge

Migrant Students

Rank	Percent	District Name	City
n/a	n/a	Alexandria Com School Corp	Alexandria
n/a	n/a	Anderson Community School Corp	Anderson
n/a	n/a	Avon Community School Corp	Avon
n/a	n/a	Bartholomew Con School Corp	Columbus
n/a	n/a	Batesville Community Sch Corp	Batesville
n/a	n/a	Baugo Community Schools	Elkhart
n/a	n/a	Beech Grove City Schools	Beech Grove
n/a	n/a	Benton Community School Corp	Fowler
n/a	n/a	Blackford County Schools	Hartford City
n/a	n/a	Brown County School Corporation	Nashville
n/a	n/a	Brownsburg Community Sch Corp	Brownsburg
n/a	n/a	Brownstown Cnt Com Sch Corp	Brownstown
n/a	n/a	Carmel Clay Schools	Carmel
n/a	n/a	Center Grove Com Sch Corp	Greenwood
n/a	n/a	Centerville-Abington Com Schs	Centerville
n/a	n/a	Clark-Pleasant Com School Corp	Whiteland
n/a	n/a	Clay Community Schools	Knightsville
n/a	n/a	Community Schools of Frankfort	Frankfort
n/a	n/a	Concord Community Schools	Elkhart
n/a	n/a	Crawford County Com School Corp	Marengo
n/a	n/a	Crawfordsville Com Schools	Crawfordsville
n/a	n/a	Crown Point Community Sch Corp	Crown Point
n/a	n/a	Danville Community School Corp	Danville
n/a	n/a	Decatur County Com Schools	Greensburg
n/a	n/a	Dekalb County Central United SD	Waterloo
n/a	n/a	Dekalb County Eastern Com SD	Butler
n/a	n/a	Delaware Community School Corp	Muncie
n/a	n/a	Delphi Community School Corp	Delphi
n/a	n/a	Duneland School Corporation	Chesterton
n/a	n/a	East Allen County Schools	New Haven
n/a	n/a	East Noble School Corp	Kendallville
n/a	n/a	East Porter County School Corp	Kouts
n/a	n/a	East Washington School Corp	Pekin
n/a	n/a	Eastbrook Community Sch Corp	Marion
n/a	n/a	Elkhart Community Schools	Elkhart
n/a	n/a	Elwood Community School Corp	Elwood
n/a	n/a	Evansville-Vanderburgh Sch Corp	Evansville
n/a	n/a	Fairfield Community Schools	Goshen
n/a	n/a	Fayette County School Corp	Connersville
n/a	n/a	Fort Wayne Community Schools	Fort Wayne
n/a	n/a	Franklin Community School Corp	Franklin
n/a	n/a	Franklin County Com Sch Corp	Brookville
n/a	n/a	Franklin Township Com Sch Corp	Indianapolis
n/a	n/a	Frankton-Lapel Community Schs	Anderson
n/a	n/a	Garrett-Keyser-Butler Com	Garrett
n/a	n/a	Gary Community School Corp	Gary
n/a	n/a	Goshen Community Schools	Goshen
n/a	n/a	Greater Clark County Schools	Jeffersonville
n/a	n/a	Greater Jasper Con Schs	Jasper
n/a	n/a	Greencastle Community Sch Corp	Greencastle
n/a	n/a	Greenfield-Central Com Schools	Greenfield
n/a	n/a	Greensburg Community Schools	Greensburg
n/a	n/a	Greenwood Community Sch Corp	Greenwood
n/a	n/a	Griffith Public Schools	Griffith
n/a	n/a	Hamilton Heights School Corp	Arcadia
n/a	n/a	Hamilton Southeastern Schools	Fishers
n/a	n/a	Hanover Community School Corp	Cedar Lake
n/a	n/a	Huntington County Com Sch Corp	Huntington
n/a	n/a	Indianapolis Public Schools	Indianapolis
n/a	n/a	Jay School Corp	Portland
n/a	n/a	Jennings County Schools	North Vernon
n/a	n/a	John Glenn School Corporation	Walkerton
n/a	n/a	Kankakee Valley School Corp	Wheatfield
n/a	n/a	Knox Community School Corp	Knox
n/a	n/a	Kokomo-Center Twp Con Sch Corp	Kokomo
n/a	n/a	Lafayette School Corporation	Lafayette
n/a	n/a	Lake Central School Corp	Saint John
n/a	n/a	Lake Ridge Schools	Gary
n/a	n/a	Lakeland School Corporation	Lagrange
n/a	n/a	Laporte Community School Corp	Laporte
n/a	n/a	Lawrenceburg Com School Corp	Lawrenceburg
n/a	n/a	Lebanon Community School Corp	Lebanon
n/a	n/a	Logansport Community Sch Corp	Logansport
n/a	n/a	M S D Decatur Township	Indianapolis
n/a	n/a	M S D Lawrence Township	Indianapolis
n/a	n/a	M S D Martinsville Schools	Martinsville
n/a	n/a	M S D Mount Vernon	Mount Vernon
n/a	n/a	M S D Perry Township	Indianapolis
n/a	n/a	M S D Pike Township	Indianapolis
n/a	n/a	M S D Southwest Allen County	Fort Wayne
n/a	n/a	M S D Steuben County	Angola
n/a	n/a	M S D Wabash County Schools	Wabash
n/a	n/a	M S D Warren Township	Indianapolis
n/a	n/a	M S D Washington Twp	Indianapolis
n/a	n/a	M S D Wayne Township	Indianapolis
n/a	n/a	Maconaquah School Corp	Bunker Hill
n/a	n/a	Madison Consolidated Schools	Madison
n/a	n/a	Madison-Grant United Sch Corp	Fairmount
n/a	n/a	Manchester Community Schools	N Manchester
n/a	n/a	Marion Community Schools	Marion
n/a	n/a	Merrillville Community School	Merrillville
n/a	n/a	Michigan City Area Schools	Michigan City
n/a	n/a	Middlebury Community Schools	Middlebury
n/a	n/a	Mill Creek Community Sch Corp	Clayton
n/a	n/a	Mississinewa Community School Corp	Gas City
n/a	n/a	Mitchell Community Schools	Mitchell
n/a	n/a	Monroe County Com Sch Corp	Bloomington
n/a	n/a	Mooresville Con School Corp	Mooresville
n/a	n/a	Mount Pleasant Twp Com Sch Corp	Yorktown
n/a	n/a	Mount Vernon Community Sch Corp	Fortville
n/a	n/a	Muncie Community Schools	Muncie
n/a	n/a	New Albany-Floyd County Con Sch	New Albany
n/a	n/a	New Castle Community Sch Corp	New Castle
n/a	n/a	New Prairie United School Corp	New Carlisle
n/a	n/a	Nineveh-Hensley-Jackson United	Trafalgar
n/a	n/a	Noblesville Schools	Noblesville
n/a	n/a	North Adams Community Schools	Decatur
n/a	n/a	North Gibson School Corp	Princeton
n/a	n/a	North Harrison Com School Corp	Ramsey
n/a	n/a	North Lawrence Com Schools	Bedford
n/a	n/a	North Montgomery Com Sch Corp	Crawfordsville
n/a	n/a	North Newton School Corp	Morocco
n/a	n/a	North Putnam Community Schools	Bainbridge
n/a	n/a	North Spencer County Sch Corp	Lincoln City
n/a	n/a	North West Hendricks Schools	Lizton
n/a	n/a	Northeast School Corp	Hymera
n/a	n/a	Northern Wells Com Schools	Ossian
n/a	n/a	Northwest Allen County Schools	Fort Wayne
n/a	n/a	Northwestern Con School Corp	Fairland
n/a	n/a	Northwestern School Corp	Kokomo
n/a	n/a	Oak Hill United School Corp	Converse
n/a	n/a	Paoli Community School Corp	Paoli
n/a	n/a	Penn-Harris-Madison Sch Corp	Mishawaka
n/a	n/a	Peru Community Schools	Peru
n/a	n/a	Pike County School Corp	Petersburg
n/a	n/a	Plainfield Community Sch Corp	Plainfield
n/a	n/a	Plymouth Community School Corp	Plymouth
n/a	n/a	Portage Township Schools	Portage
n/a	n/a	Porter Township School Corp	Valparaiso
n/a	n/a	Prairie Heights Com Sch Corp	Lagrange
n/a	n/a	Randolph Central School Corp	Winchester
n/a	n/a	Rensselaer Central School Corp	Rensselaer
n/a	n/a	Richland-Bean Blossom CSC	Ellettsville
n/a	n/a	Richmond Community School Corp	Richmond
n/a	n/a	Rochester Community Sch Corp	Rochester
n/a	n/a	Rush County Schools	Rushville
n/a	n/a	Salem Community Schools	Salem
n/a	n/a	School City of East Chicago	East Chicago
n/a	n/a	School City of Hammond	Hammond
n/a	n/a	School City of Hobart	Hobart
n/a	n/a	School City of Mishawaka	Mishawaka
n/a	n/a	School Town of Highland	Highland
n/a	n/a	School Town of Munster	Munster
n/a	n/a	School Town of Speedway	Speedway
n/a	n/a	Scott County SD 2	Scottsburg
n/a	n/a	Seymour Community Schools	Seymour
n/a	n/a	Shelby Eastern Schools	Shelbyville
n/a	n/a	Shelbyville Central Schools	Shelbyville
n/a	n/a	South Bend Community Sch Corp	South Bend
n/a	n/a	South Dearborn Com School Corp	Aurora
n/a	n/a	South Gibson School Corp	Fort Branch
n/a	n/a	South Harrison Com Schools	Corydon
n/a	n/a	South Madison Com Sch Corp	Pendleton
n/a	n/a	South Montgomery Com Sch Corp	New Market
n/a	n/a	South Vermillion Com Sch Corp	Clinton
n/a	n/a	Southeastern School Corp	Walton
n/a	n/a	Southern Hancock Co CS Corp	New Palestine
n/a	n/a	Southwest Dubois County Sch Corp	Huntingburg
n/a	n/a	Southwest School Corp	Sullivan
n/a	n/a	Spencer-Owen Community Schools	Spencer
n/a	n/a	Sunman-Dearborn Com Sch Corp	Sunman
n/a	n/a	Switzerland County School Corp	Vevay
n/a	n/a	Tell City-Troy Twp School Corp	Tell City
n/a	n/a	Tippecanoe School Corp	Lafayette
n/a	n/a	Tippecanoe Valley School Corp	Akron
n/a	n/a	Tipton Community School Corp	Tipton
n/a	n/a	Tri-Creek School Corp	Lowell
n/a	n/a	Twin Lakes School Corp	Monticello
n/a	n/a	Union County College Corner JSD	Liberty
n/a	n/a	Union Township School Corp	Valparaiso
n/a	n/a	Valparaiso Community Schools	Valparaiso
n/a	n/a	Vigo County School Corp	Terre Haute
n/a	n/a	Vincennes Community Sch Corp	Vincennes
n/a	n/a	Wa-Nee Community Schools	Nappanee
n/a	n/a	Warrick County School Corp	Boonville
n/a	n/a	Warsaw Community Schools	Warsaw
n/a	n/a	Washington Com Schools Inc	Washington
n/a	n/a	Wawasee Community School Corp	Syracuse
n/a	n/a	West Clark Community Schools	Sellersburg
n/a	n/a	West Lafayette Com School Corp	West Lafayette
n/a	n/a	West Noble School Corporation	Ligonier
n/a	n/a	Western Boone County Com SD	Thorntown
n/a	n/a	Western School Corp	Russiaville
n/a	n/a	Westfield-Washington Schools	Westfield
n/a	n/a	Westview School Corporation	Topeka
n/a	n/a	Whitko Community School Corp	Pierceton
n/a	n/a	Whitley County Cons Schools	Columbia City
n/a	n/a	Zionsville Community Schools	Zionsville

Note: This section only includes districts with 1,500 or more students; All categories are ranked from high to low

Students Eligible for Free Lunch

Rank	Percent	District Name	City
1	80.4	School City of East Chicago	East Chicago
2	72.7	Indianapolis Public Schools	Indianapolis
3	63.0	Gary Community School Corp	Gary
4	62.6	Lake Ridge Schools	Gary
5	56.1	South Bend Community Sch Corp	South Bend
6	56.0	School City of Hammond	Hammond
7	51.2	Michigan City Area Schools	Michigan City
8	48.5	Muncie Community Schools	Muncie
9	48.1	M S D Wayne Township	Indianapolis
10	47.5	Fort Wayne Community Schools	Fort Wayne
11	47.4	Marion Community Schools	Marion
12	47.3	Richmond Community School Corp	Richmond
13	46.2	Community Schools of Frankfort	Frankfort
14	45.9	Elkhart Community Schools	Elkhart
15	44.5	Anderson Community School Corp	Anderson
16	42.7	Kokomo-Center Twp Con Sch Corp	Kokomo
17	42.5	Elwood Community School Corp	Elwood
18	42.0	Fayette County School Corp	Connersville
19	41.2	West Noble School Corporation	Ligonier
20	40.8	Vincennes Community Sch Corp	Vincennes
21	40.3	Lafayette School Corporation	Lafayette
22	40.1	M S D Decatur Township	Indianapolis
23	39.7	Logansport Community Sch Corp	Logansport
24	39.5	Evansville-Vanderburgh Sch Corp	Evansville
25	39.3	Goshen Community Schools	Goshen
26	39.2	Crawford County Com School Corp	Marengo
27	37.8	M S D Warren Township	Indianapolis
27	37.8	Washington Com Schools Inc	Washington
29	37.5	Knox Community School Corp	Knox
30	36.5	Vigo County School Corp	Terre Haute
31	36.3	Crawfordsville Com Schools	Crawfordsville
32	35.6	School City of Mishawaka	Mishawaka
33	35.4	New Castle Community Sch Corp	New Castle
34	34.9	M S D Perry Township	Indianapolis
35	34.7	Peru Community Schools	Peru
36	34.5	Mississinewa Community School Corp	Gas City
37	33.8	Blackford County Schools	Hartford City
38	33.7	M S D Washington Twp	Indianapolis
39	33.6	Paoli Community School Corp	Paoli
40	33.3	Greater Clark County Schools	Jeffersonville
41	32.8	Beech Grove City Schools	Beech Grove
41	32.8	East Washington School Corp	Pekin
43	32.6	Jennings County Schools	North Vernon
44	32.2	School Town of Speedway	Speedway
45	32.1	Madison Consolidated Schools	Madison
46	31.9	Northeast School Corp	Hymera
47	31.5	Plymouth Community School Corp	Plymouth
48	31.3	M S D Pike Township	Indianapolis
48	31.3	South Vermillion Com Sch Corp	Clinton
50	30.8	Alexandria Com School Corp	Alexandria
51	30.7	Scott County SD 2	Scottsburg
52	30.6	Southwest School Corp	Sullivan
53	30.5	New Albany-Floyd County Con Sch	New Albany
54	30.1	Salem Community Schools	Salem
54	30.1	Shelbyville Central Schools	Shelbyville
54	30.1	Spencer-Owen Community Schools	Spencer
57	29.9	M S D Lawrence Township	Indianapolis
58	29.8	Switzerland County School Corp	Vevay
59	29.5	Mitchell Community Schools	Mitchell
60	29.4	Jay School Corp	Portland
60	29.4	Randolph Central School Corp	Winchester
62	29.3	North Gibson School Corp	Princeton
63	29.0	Concord Community Schools	Elkhart
64	28.9	Merrillville Community School	Merrillville
65	28.3	Clay Community Schools	Knightsville
66	28.1	M S D Steuben County	Angola
67	27.4	Laporte Community School Corp	Laporte
68	27.2	Portage Township Schools	Portage
69	27.0	Tell City-Troy Twp School Corp	Tell City
70	26.9	Seymour Community Schools	Seymour
71	26.5	Greensburg Community Schools	Greensburg
72	26.3	M S D Martinsville Schools	Martinsville
73	26.1	Delphi Community School Corp	Delphi
73	26.1	Warsaw Community Schools	Warsaw
75	26.0	Garrett-Keyser-Butler Com	Garrett
76	25.9	East Allen County Schools	New Haven
76	25.9	Tippecanoe Valley School Corp	Akron
78	25.6	Maconaquah School Corp	Bunker Hill
79	25.4	Lakeland School Corporation	Lagrange
79	25.4	South Harrison Com Schools	Corydon
79	25.4	Twin Lakes School Corp	Monticello
82	25.3	Rochester Community Sch Corp	Rochester
83	24.8	Franklin Community School Corp	Franklin
84	24.7	Bartholomew Con School Corp	Columbus
84	24.7	Madison-Grant United Sch Corp	Fairmount
86	24.5	School City of Hobart	Hobart
87	24.4	Rush County Schools	Rushville
88	24.0	Franklin County Com Sch Corp	Brookville
89	23.8	Manchester Community Schools	N Manchester
90	23.6	Brown County School Corporation	Nashville
91	23.4	Monroe County Com Sch Corp	Bloomington
92	23.2	Wawasee Community School Corp	Syracuse
93	23.1	East Noble School Corp	Kendallville
94	23.0	Rensselaer Central School Corp	Rensselaer
95	22.9	Benton Community School Corp	Fowler
95	22.9	Lawrenceburg Com School Corp	Lawrenceburg
95	22.9	Union County College Corner JSD	Liberty
98	22.7	Greencastle Community Sch Corp	Greencastle
99	22.6	North Lawrence Com Schools	Bedford
100	22.4	Lebanon Community School Corp	Lebanon
101	22.1	M S D Mount Vernon	Mount Vernon
101	22.1	North Newton School Corp	Morocco
101	22.1	Pike County School Corp	Petersburg
104	22.0	Dekalb County Eastern Com SD	Butler
105	21.9	North Harrison Com School Corp	Ramsey
106	21.8	North Putnam Community Schools	Bainbridge
107	21.6	Clark-Pleasant Com School Corp	Whiteland
108	21.4	North Adams Community Schools	Decatur
108	21.4	South Dearborn Com School Corp	Aurora
110	21.2	John Glenn School Corporation	Walkerton
111	20.9	Greenwood Community Sch Corp	Greenwood
112	20.6	M S D Wabash County Schools	Wabash
113	20.1	Brownstown Cnt Com Sch Corp	Brownstown
113	20.1	Prairie Heights Com Sch Corp	Lagrange
113	20.1	Richland-Bean Blossom CSC	Ellettsville
116	19.8	Eastbrook Community Sch Corp	Marion
117	19.6	Delaware Community School Corp	Muncie
118	19.5	Dekalb County Central United SD	Waterloo
118	19.5	Griffith Public Schools	Griffith
118	19.5	Southwest Dubois County Sch Corp	Huntingburg
121	19.1	Kankakee Valley School Corp	Wheatfield
122	19.0	West Clark Community Schools	Sellersburg
123	18.6	Huntington County Com Sch Corp	Huntington
124	18.4	Decatur County Com Schools	Greensburg
125	18.3	South Montgomery Com Sch Corp	New Market
126	18.1	North Montgomery Com Sch Corp	Crawfordsville
127	17.8	Baugo Community Schools	Elkhart
128	17.7	Mooresville Con School Corp	Mooresville
128	17.7	Whitko Community School Corp	Pierceton
130	17.5	Oak Hill United School Corp	Converse
131	17.1	Tippecanoe School Corp	Lafayette
132	16.5	Centerville-Abington Com Schs	Centerville
133	16.2	Shelby Eastern Schools	Shelbyville
133	16.2	Wa-Nee Community Schools	Nappanee
135	16.1	Western School Corp	Russiaville
136	16.0	Franklin Township Com Sch Corp	Indianapolis
136	16.0	Greenfield-Central Com Schools	Greenfield
138	15.7	Tipton Community School Corp	Tipton
139	15.5	Westview School Corporation	Topeka
140	15.4	Southeastern School Corp	Walton
141	15.3	New Prairie United School Corp	New Carlisle
141	15.3	Northwestern Con School Corp	Fairland
143	15.2	Warrick County School Corp	Boonville
144	14.9	Frankton-Lapel Community Schs	Anderson
145	14.5	North Spencer County Sch Corp	Lincoln City
146	14.4	Valparaiso Community Schools	Valparaiso
147	14.2	Northern Wells Com Schools	Ossian
148	14.1	Duneland School Corporation	Chesterton
149	14.0	Hamilton Heights School Corp	Arcadia
149	14.0	Hanover Community School Corp	Cedar Lake
151	13.5	Western Boone County Com SD	Thorntown
152	13.2	Plainfield Community Sch Corp	Plainfield
152	13.2	South Madison Com Sch Corp	Pendleton
154	13.1	Mount Pleasant Twp Com Sch Corp	Yorktown
155	13.0	Greater Jasper Con Schs	Jasper
156	12.5	Middlebury Community Schools	Middlebury
157	12.4	Whitley County Cons Schools	Columbia City
158	11.7	Crown Point Community Sch Corp	Crown Point
159	11.4	Tri-Creek School Corp	Lowell
160	11.3	Nineveh-Hensley-Jackson United	Trafalgar
161	10.6	Mill Creek Community Sch Corp	Clayton
162	10.5	Penn-Harris-Madison Sch Corp	Mishawaka
163	10.4	Danville Community School Corp	Danville
163	10.4	South Gibson School Corp	Fort Branch
165	10.0	Sunman-Dearborn Com Sch Corp	Sunman
166	9.9	Avon Community School Corp	Avon
167	9.5	Westfield-Washington Schools	Westfield
168	9.3	Mount Vernon Community Sch Corp	Fortville
169	9.0	Batesville Community Sch Corp	Batesville
169	9.0	Noblesville Schools	Noblesville
171	8.9	Porter Township School Corp	Valparaiso
172	8.7	Brownsburg Community Sch Corp	Brownsburg
172	8.7	Fairfield Community Schools	Goshen
172	8.7	Northwestern School Corp	Kokomo
172	8.7	Union Township School Corp	Valparaiso
176	8.2	East Porter County School Corp	Kouts
177	7.5	Lake Central School Corp	Saint John
178	7.2	West Lafayette Com School Corp	West Lafayette
179	7.1	School Town of Highland	Highland
180	6.7	Southern Hancock Co CS Corp	New Palestine
181	6.5	Northwest Allen County Schools	Fort Wayne
182	6.4	North West Hendricks Schools	Lizton
183	5.4	Hamilton Southeastern Schools	Fishers
184	4.9	School Town of Munster	Munster
185	4.8	M S D Southwest Allen County	Fort Wayne
186	3.8	Center Grove Com Sch Corp	Greenwood
187	3.6	Carmel Clay Schools	Carmel
188	2.7	Zionsville Community Schools	Zionsville

Students Eligible for Reduced-Price Lunch

Rank	Percent	District Name	City
1	15.8	West Noble School Corporation	Ligonier
2	13.9	Crawford County Com School Corp	Marengo
2	13.9	M S D Warren Township	Indianapolis
4	13.8	Northeast School Corp	Hymera
5	13.5	School City of Mishawaka	Mishawaka
6	12.8	Peru Community Schools	Peru
7	12.6	Westview School Corporation	Topeka
8	12.3	Pike County School Corp	Petersburg
8	12.3	Prairie Heights Com Sch Corp	Lagrange
10	12.2	Manchester Community Schools	N Manchester
11	12.1	Clay Community Schools	Knightsville
11	12.1	Jay School Corp	Portland
11	12.1	Paoli Community School Corp	Paoli
14	12.0	Community Schools of Frankfort	Frankfort
14	12.0	M S D Wayne Township	Indianapolis
16	11.8	Goshen Community Schools	Goshen
16	11.8	Madison Consolidated Schools	Madison
16	11.8	Mississinewa Community School Corp	Gas City
19	11.7	Knox Community School Corp	Knox
19	11.7	North Putnam Community Schools	Bainbridge
19	11.7	Portage Township Schools	Portage
22	11.5	Lake Ridge Schools	Gary
23	11.4	Richmond Community School Corp	Richmond
24	11.2	Union County College Corner JSD	Liberty
25	11.1	Clark-Pleasant Com School Corp	Whiteland
25	11.1	Concord Community Schools	Elkhart
27	10.9	Garrett-Keyser-Butler Com	Garrett
27	10.9	Jennings County Schools	North Vernon
27	10.9	School City of Hammond	Hammond
30	10.8	Greater Clark County Schools	Jeffersonville
30	10.8	North Gibson School Corp	Princeton
32	10.7	Lakeland School Corporation	Lagrange
33	10.6	East Washington School Corp	Pekin
33	10.6	Evansville-Vanderburgh Sch Corp	Evansville
33	10.6	Merrillville Community School	Merrillville
33	10.6	Switzerland County School Corp	Vevay
37	10.5	Blackford County Schools	Hartford City
37	10.5	Elkhart Community Schools	Elkhart
37	10.5	North Montgomery Com Sch Corp	Crawfordsville
37	10.5	Warsaw Community Schools	Warsaw
41	10.3	Logansport Community Sch Corp	Logansport
41	10.3	Tippecanoe Valley School Corp	Akron
43	10.2	Indianapolis Public Schools	Indianapolis
44	10.1	Greensburg Community Schools	Greensburg
44	10.1	South Harrison Com Schools	Corydon
44	10.1	Spencer-Owen Community Schools	Spencer
44	10.1	Twin Lakes School Corp	Monticello
48	10.0	Lafayette School Corporation	Lafayette
49	9.9	Beech Grove City Schools	Beech Grove
49	9.9	Decatur County Com Schools	Greensburg
49	9.9	East Noble School Corp	Kendallville
49	9.9	Huntington County Com Sch Corp	Huntington
49	9.9	Maconaquah School Corp	Bunker Hill
49	9.9	North Harrison Com School Corp	Ramsey
55	9.8	Salem Community Schools	Salem
56	9.7	Vigo County School Corp	Terre Haute
57	9.6	South Vermillion Com Sch Corp	Clinton
57	9.6	West Clark Community Schools	Sellersburg
59	9.5	Brown County School Corporation	Nashville
59	9.5	M S D Washington Twp	Indianapolis
59	9.5	Randolph Central School Corp	Winchester

Note: This section only includes districts with 1,500 or more students; All categories are ranked from high to low

62	9.4	Benton Community School Corp	Fowler
62	9.4	M S D Pike Township	Indianapolis
62	9.4	Plymouth Community School Corp	Plymouth
62	9.4	Vincennes Community Sch Corp	Vincennes
66	9.3	Shelbyville Central Schools	Shelbyville
66	9.3	Southwest School Corp	Sullivan
68	9.2	Washington Com Schools Inc	Washington
69	9.1	Fort Wayne Community Schools	Fort Wayne
69	9.1	M S D Lawrence Township	Indianapolis
69	9.1	M S D Perry Township	Indianapolis
69	9.1	Northern Wells Com Schools	Ossian
69	9.1	Rochester Community Sch Corp	Rochester
74	9.0	Anderson Community School Corp	Anderson
74	9.0	Scott County SD 2	Scottsburg
74	9.0	Southeastern School Corp	Walton
77	8.9	Brownstown Cnt Com Sch Corp	Brownstown
77	8.9	Laporte Community School Corp	Laporte
77	8.9	North Lawrence Com Schools	Bedford
80	8.8	Elwood Community School Corp	Elwood
80	8.8	John Glenn School Corporation	Walkerton
82	8.7	Dekalb County Central United SD	Waterloo
83	8.6	Eastbrook Community Sch Corp	Marion
83	8.6	Madison-Grant United Sch Corp	Fairmount
83	8.6	Southwest Dubois County Sch Corp	Huntingburg
86	8.5	Alexandria Com School Corp	Alexandria
86	8.5	Crawfordsville Com Schools	Crawfordsville
86	8.5	Franklin County Com Sch Corp	Brookville
86	8.5	Greencastle Community Sch Corp	Greencastle
86	8.5	Michigan City Area Schools	Michigan City
86	8.5	Muncie Community Schools	Muncie
86	8.5	Tipton Community School Corp	Tipton
86	8.5	Wa-Nee Community Schools	Nappanee
86	8.5	Wawasee Community School Corp	Syracuse
95	8.4	Kokomo-Center Twp Con Sch Corp	Kokomo
95	8.4	M S D Martinsville Schools	Martinsville
95	8.4	Rensselaer Central School Corp	Rensselaer
95	8.4	Whitko Community School Corp	Pierceton
99	8.3	Dekalb County Eastern Com SD	Butler
99	8.3	Kankakee Valley School Corp	Wheatfield
99	8.3	M S D Steuben County	Angola
102	8.2	Centerville-Abington Com Schs	Centerville
103	8.1	Bartholomew Con School Corp	Columbus
104	8.0	Baugo Community Schools	Elkhart
104	8.0	Franklin Township Com Sch Corp	Indianapolis
104	8.0	North Adams Community Schools	Decatur
104	8.0	Rush County Schools	Rushville
108	7.9	East Allen County Schools	New Haven
108	7.9	New Castle Community Sch Corp	New Castle
108	7.9	North Newton School Corp	Morocco
108	7.9	Seymour Community Schools	Seymour
112	7.8	Delaware Community School Corp	Muncie
112	7.8	Lebanon Community School Corp	Lebanon
112	7.8	M S D Decatur Township	Indianapolis
112	7.8	School Town of Speedway	Speedway
116	7.7	Fayette County School Corp	Connersville
116	7.7	Tell City-Troy Twp School Corp	Tell City
118	7.6	Frankton-Lapel Community Schs	Anderson
118	7.6	New Prairie United School Corp	New Carlisle
120	7.5	Mitchell Community Schools	Mitchell
120	7.5	School City of Hobart	Hobart
122	7.4	Fairfield Community Schools	Goshen
122	7.4	Marion Community Schools	Marion
122	7.4	Plainfield Community Sch Corp	Plainfield
125	7.2	Warrick County School Corp	Boonville
126	7.1	North Spencer County Sch Corp	Lincoln City
126	7.1	South Madison Com Sch Corp	Pendleton
128	7.0	Delphi Community School Corp	Delphi
128	7.0	Franklin Community School Corp	Franklin
128	7.0	Middlebury Community Schools	Middlebury
128	7.0	Western Boone County Com SD	Thorntown
132	6.9	Greenfield-Central Com Schools	Greenfield
132	6.9	Monroe County Com Sch Corp	Bloomington
132	6.9	Northwestern Con School Corp	Fairland
132	6.9	School City of East Chicago	East Chicago
132	6.9	Whitley County Cons Schools	Columbia City
137	6.8	Danville Community School Corp	Danville
137	6.8	Richland-Bean Blossom CSC	Ellettsville
139	6.7	South Gibson School Corp	Fort Branch
140	6.5	North West Hendricks Schools	Lizton
141	6.4	Hamilton Heights School Corp	Arcadia
141	6.4	Mount Pleasant Twp Com Sch Corp	Yorktown
143	6.3	Mooresville Con School Corp	Mooresville
143	6.3	South Montgomery Com Sch Corp	New Market
145	6.2	Greenwood Community Sch Corp	Greenwood
145	6.2	Mount Vernon Community Sch Corp	Fortville
145	6.2	South Bend Community Sch Corp	South Bend
148	6.1	M S D Mount Vernon	Mount Vernon
149	5.9	Griffith Public Schools	Griffith
149	5.9	Tippecanoe School Corp	Lafayette
151	5.8	Brownsburg Community Sch Corp	Brownsburg
152	5.6	Greater Jasper Con Schs	Jasper
152	5.6	Mill Creek Community Sch Corp	Clayton
154	5.5	Avon Community School Corp	Avon
154	5.5	Batesville Community Sch Corp	Batesville
156	5.2	School Town of Highland	Highland
157	5.1	Shelby Eastern Schools	Shelbyville
157	5.1	Union Township School Corp	Valparaiso
159	5.0	Nineveh-Hensley-Jackson United	Trafalgar
160	4.9	New Albany-Floyd County Con Sch	New Albany
161	4.8	South Dearborn Com School Corp	Aurora
161	4.8	Valparaiso Community Schools	Valparaiso
163	4.7	East Porter County School Corp	Kouts
163	4.7	Noblesville Schools	Noblesville
163	4.7	Penn-Harris-Madison Sch Corp	Mishawaka
166	4.4	Oak Hill United School Corp	Converse
167	4.3	Duneland School Corporation	Chesterton
168	4.2	Crown Point Community Sch Corp	Crown Point
168	4.2	Lawrenceburg Com School Corp	Lawrenceburg
168	4.2	M S D Wabash County Schools	Wabash
171	3.9	Porter Township School Corp	Valparaiso
171	3.9	School Town of Munster	Munster
173	3.8	Sunman-Dearborn Com Sch Corp	Sunman
174	3.7	Tri-Creek School Corp	Lowell
175	3.6	Northwest Allen County Schools	Fort Wayne
175	3.6	Western School Corp	Russiaville
175	3.6	Westfield-Washington Schools	Westfield
178	3.5	Southern Hancock Co CS Corp	New Palestine
179	3.2	Hanover Community School Corp	Cedar Lake
179	3.2	Lake Central School Corp	Saint John
181	2.6	M S D Southwest Allen County	Fort Wayne
182	2.5	Hamilton Southeastern Schools	Fishers
182	2.5	Northwestern School Corp	Kokomo
184	2.4	West Lafayette Com School Corp	West Lafayette
185	2.2	Gary Community School Corp	Gary
186	1.9	Carmel Clay Schools	Carmel
187	1.7	Center Grove Com Sch Corp	Greenwood
188	1.0	Zionsville Community Schools	Zionsville

Student/Teacher Ratio

(number of students per teacher)

Rank	Number	District Name	City
1	10.9	Benton Community School Corp	Fowler
2	12.0	Dekalb County Eastern Com SD	Butler
3	12.5	Union County College Corner JSD	Liberty
4	12.6	Logansport Community Sch Corp	Logansport
5	12.7	North Putnam Community Schools	Bainbridge
6	13.6	Greenfield-Central Com Schools	Greenfield
7	13.9	New Castle Community Sch Corp	New Castle
7	13.9	Vincennes Community Sch Corp	Vincennes
9	14.2	Kokomo-Center Twp Con Sch Corp	Kokomo
10	14.3	School City of Mishawaka	Mishawaka
11	14.6	M S D Wabash County Schools	Wabash
12	14.9	Muncie Community Schools	Muncie
13	15.1	Brown County School Corporation	Nashville
13	15.1	Crawfordsville Com Schools	Crawfordsville
13	15.1	Lafayette School Corporation	Lafayette
13	15.1	Richmond Community School Corp	Richmond
17	15.2	Indianapolis Public Schools	Indianapolis
18	15.3	South Montgomery Com Sch Corp	New Market
19	15.4	Elwood Community School Corp	Elwood
19	15.4	Randolph Central School Corp	Winchester
21	15.5	Garrett-Keyser-Butler Com	Garrett
21	15.5	Goshen Community Schools	Goshen
21	15.5	M S D Mount Vernon	Mount Vernon
24	15.6	Evansville-Vanderburgh Sch Corp	Evansville
24	15.6	Peru Community Schools	Peru
26	15.8	Marion Community Schools	Marion
26	15.8	North Lawrence Com Schools	Bedford
28	15.9	Blackford County Schools	Hartford City
28	15.9	Greater Clark County Schools	Jeffersonville
28	15.9	Madison-Grant United Sch Corp	Fairmount
31	16.0	Southwest School Corp	Sullivan
32	16.1	Lakeland School Corporation	Lagrange
32	16.1	School City of East Chicago	East Chicago
32	16.1	South Vermillion Com Sch Corp	Clinton
32	16.1	Tipton Community School Corp	Tipton
36	16.2	Northwestern School Corp	Kokomo
36	16.2	Rush County Schools	Rushville
38	16.3	East Noble School Corp	Kendallville
38	16.3	Vigo County School Corp	Terre Haute
40	16.4	Fayette County School Corp	Connersville
40	16.4	Maconaquah School Corp	Bunker Hill
40	16.4	Monroe County Com Sch Corp	Bloomington
40	16.4	South Harrison Com Schools	Corydon
44	16.5	Community Schools of Frankfort	Frankfort
44	16.5	Elkhart Community Schools	Elkhart
44	16.5	Lebanon Community School Corp	Lebanon
44	16.5	North Newton School Corp	Morocco
44	16.5	Richland-Bean Blossom CSC	Ellettsville
49	16.6	Anderson Community School Corp	Anderson
49	16.6	Huntington County Com Sch Corp	Huntington
49	16.6	Laporte Community School Corp	Laporte
49	16.6	M S D Wayne Township	Indianapolis
49	16.6	Mississinewa Community School Corp	Gas City
49	16.6	Mount Pleasant Twp Com Sch Corp	Yorktown
49	16.6	Pike County School Corp	Petersburg
49	16.6	Spencer-Owen Community Schools	Spencer
57	16.7	Jay School Corp	Portland
57	16.7	North Adams Community Schools	Decatur
57	16.7	Northeast School Corp	Hymera
60	16.8	Carmel Clay Schools	Carmel
60	16.8	Eastbrook Community Sch Corp	Marion
60	16.8	M S D Perry Township	Indianapolis
60	16.8	Oak Hill United School Corp	Converse
64	16.9	Greater Jasper Con Schs	Jasper
64	16.9	Rensselaer Central School Corp	Rensselaer
64	16.9	Whitley County Cons Schools	Columbia City
67	17.0	Fort Wayne Community Schools	Fort Wayne
67	17.0	South Dearborn Com School Corp	Aurora
69	17.1	Batesville Community Sch Corp	Batesville
69	17.1	Delaware Community School Corp	Muncie
69	17.1	Jennings County Schools	North Vernon
69	17.1	Northern Wells Com Schools	Ossian
69	17.1	School Town of Speedway	Speedway
74	17.3	Centerville-Abington Com Schs	Centerville
74	17.3	Gary Community School Corp	Gary
74	17.3	South Bend Community Sch Corp	South Bend
74	17.3	Washington Com Schools Inc	Washington
74	17.3	West Lafayette Com School Corp	West Lafayette
74	17.3	Westview School Corporation	Topeka
74	17.3	Zionsville Community Schools	Zionsville
81	17.4	Greensburg Community Schools	Greensburg
81	17.4	North Gibson School Corp	Princeton
81	17.4	Western Boone County Com SD	Thorntown
84	17.5	Clay Community Schools	Knightsville
84	17.5	Decatur County Com Schools	Greensburg
84	17.5	Mill Creek Community Sch Corp	Clayton
84	17.5	North Montgomery Com Sch Corp	Crawfordsville
84	17.5	Prairie Heights Com Sch Corp	Lagrange
84	17.5	School City of Hammond	Hammond
84	17.5	Wa-Nee Community Schools	Nappanee
84	17.5	West Noble School Corporation	Ligonier
92	17.6	M S D Washington Twp	Indianapolis
92	17.6	Shelby Eastern Schools	Shelbyville
94	17.7	Alexandria Com School Corp	Alexandria
94	17.7	Lawrenceburg Com School Corp	Lawrenceburg
94	17.7	M S D Southwest Allen County	Fort Wayne
94	17.7	Madison Consolidated Schools	Madison
94	17.7	Michigan City Area Schools	Michigan City
94	17.7	Switzerland County School Corp	Vevay
100	17.8	Concord Community Schools	Elkhart
100	17.8	M S D Pike Township	Indianapolis
100	17.8	New Albany-Floyd County Con Sch	New Albany
100	17.8	Nineveh-Hensley-Jackson United	Trafalgar
100	17.8	North Spencer County Sch Corp	Lincoln City
100	17.8	Twin Lakes School Corp	Monticello
106	17.9	Frankton-Lapel Community Schs	Anderson
106	17.9	Mooresville Con School Corp	Mooresville
106	17.9	Paoli Community School Corp	Paoli
106	17.9	Southeastern School Corp	Walton
110	18.0	M S D Lawrence Township	Indianapolis
110	18.0	M S D Martinsville Schools	Martinsville
110	18.0	M S D Warren Township	Indianapolis
110	18.0	Seymour Community Schools	Seymour
110	18.0	Wawasee Community School Corp	Syracuse
110	18.0	Westfield-Washington Schools	Westfield
116	18.1	North West Hendricks Schools	Lizton
117	18.2	Brownsburg Community Sch Corp	Brownsburg
117	18.2	East Allen County Schools	New Haven
119	18.3	Bartholomew Con School Corp	Columbus
119	18.3	M S D Steuben County	Angola
119	18.3	Tippecanoe School Corp	Lafayette
119	18.3	Warsaw Community Schools	Warsaw
123	18.4	Hamilton Heights School Corp	Arcadia
123	18.4	M S D Decatur Township	Indianapolis
123	18.4	Scott County SD 2	Scottsburg

Note: This section only includes districts with 1,500 or more students; All categories are ranked from high to low

126	18.5	Delphi Community School Corp	Delphi
127	18.6	Union Township School Corp	Valparaiso
128	18.7	East Porter County School Corp	Kouts
128	18.7	Western School Corp	Russiaville
128	18.7	Whitko Community School Corp	Pierceton
131	18.9	Center Grove Com Sch Corp	Greenwood
131	18.9	Franklin Community School Corp	Franklin
131	18.9	Manchester Community Schools	N Manchester
131	18.9	Northwest Allen County Schools	Fort Wayne
135	19.0	Greencastle Community Sch Corp	Greencastle
135	19.0	Mount Vernon Community Sch Corp	Fortville
135	19.0	North Harrison Com School Corp	Ramsey
138	19.1	Beech Grove City Schools	Beech Grove
138	19.1	Brownstown Cnt Com Sch Corp	Brownstown
138	19.1	Rochester Community Sch Corp	Rochester
138	19.1	Tippecanoe Valley School Corp	Akron
138	19.1	West Clark Community Schools	Sellersburg
143	19.2	Danville Community School Corp	Danville
143	19.2	Fairfield Community Schools	Goshen
143	19.2	Hamilton Southeastern Schools	Fishers
146	19.4	Lake Central School Corp	Saint John
147	19.5	Baugo Community Schools	Elkhart
147	19.5	Lake Ridge Schools	Gary
147	19.5	Noblesville Schools	Noblesville
147	19.5	Warrick County School Corp	Boonville
151	19.6	Franklin Township Com Sch Corp	Indianapolis
151	19.6	Mitchell Community Schools	Mitchell
153	19.7	Crawford County Com School Corp	Marengo
153	19.7	East Washington School Corp	Pekin
153	19.7	New Prairie United School Corp	New Carlisle
156	19.8	Kankakee Valley School Corp	Wheatfield
156	19.8	Salem Community Schools	Salem
156	19.8	Sunman-Dearborn Com Sch Corp	Sunman
159	19.9	Franklin County Com Sch Corp	Brookville
160	20.0	Southwest Dubois County Sch Corp	Huntingburg
160	20.0	Tell City-Troy Twp School Corp	Tell City
162	20.1	Avon Community School Corp	Avon
162	20.1	Middlebury Community Schools	Middlebury
162	20.1	Northwestern Con School Corp	Fairland
162	20.1	Plainfield Community Sch Corp	Plainfield
162	20.1	South Gibson School Corp	Fort Branch
167	20.2	Clark-Pleasant Com School Corp	Whiteland
167	20.2	John Glenn School Corporation	Walkerton
167	20.2	Valparaiso Community Schools	Valparaiso
170	20.3	Greenwood Community Sch Corp	Greenwood
171	20.4	Knox Community School Corp	Knox
172	20.5	Plymouth Community School Corp	Plymouth
172	20.5	Porter Township School Corp	Valparaiso
172	20.5	School Town of Munster	Munster
175	20.6	Shelbyville Central Schools	Shelbyville
176	20.8	Dekalb County Central United SD	Waterloo
176	20.8	Portage Township Schools	Portage
176	20.8	South Madison Com Sch Corp	Pendleton
179	21.0	School City of Hobart	Hobart
180	21.1	Griffith Public Schools	Griffith
180	21.1	Hanover Community School Corp	Cedar Lake
182	21.3	Merrillville Community School	Merrillville
183	21.4	Duneland School Corporation	Chesterton
184	21.6	Southern Hancock Co CS Corp	New Palestine
185	22.1	School Town of Highland	Highland
186	22.3	Crown Point Community Sch Corp	Crown Point
187	23.5	Penn-Harris-Madison Sch Corp	Mishawaka
188	23.8	Tri-Creek School Corp	Lowell

Student/Librarian Ratio

(number of students per librarian)

Rank	Number	District Name	City
1	435.1	Richmond Community School Corp	Richmond
2	479.4	Crawfordsville Com Schools	Crawfordsville
3	512.0	Tippecanoe School Corp	Lafayette
4	526.1	Gary Community School Corp	Gary
5	528.6	Duneland School Corporation	Chesterton
6	549.7	Delphi Community School Corp	Delphi
7	554.1	Jay School Corp	Portland
8	566.6	Vigo County School Corp	Terre Haute
9	573.0	Garrett-Keyser-Butler Com	Garrett
10	606.3	Maconaquah School Corp	Bunker Hill
11	613.0	Southwest Dubois County Sch Corp	Huntingburg
12	615.7	Logansport Community Sch Corp	Logansport
13	618.0	Nineveh-Hensley-Jackson United	Trafalgar
13	618.0	Tipton Community School Corp	Tipton
15	634.8	M S D Mount Vernon	Mount Vernon
16	638.7	Western Boone County Com SD	Thorntown
17	642.3	North Putnam Community Schools	Bainbridge
18	649.0	Rochester Community Sch Corp	Rochester
19	661.7	Batesville Community Sch Corp	Batesville
20	664.0	Rush County Schools	Rushville
21	673.0	Greencastle Community Sch Corp	Greencastle
22	675.1	Lafayette School Corporation	Lafayette
23	678.5	Westfield-Washington Schools	Westfield
24	679.7	Knox Community School Corp	Knox
25	680.0	South Vermillion Com Sch Corp	Clinton
26	689.6	Monroe County Com Sch Corp	Bloomington
27	699.2	Indianapolis Public Schools	Indianapolis
28	704.0	Mitchell Community Schools	Mitchell
29	719.3	Salem Community Schools	Salem
30	723.0	Greensburg Community Schools	Greensburg
31	752.7	Blackford County Schools	Hartford City
32	753.0	North Spencer County Sch Corp	Lincoln City
33	753.5	Dekalb County Eastern Com SD	Butler
34	760.0	North Harrison Com School Corp	Ramsey
35	762.0	Northeast School Corp	Hymera
36	763.7	School City of Hammond	Hammond
37	776.8	Clay Community Schools	Knightsville
38	778.0	Madison-Grant United Sch Corp	Fairmount
39	785.0	Shelby Eastern Schools	Shelbyville
40	785.5	Northwestern Con School Corp	Fairland
41	802.0	M S D Washington Twp	Indianapolis
42	805.6	South Madison Com Sch Corp	Pendleton
43	813.5	Lawrenceburg Com School Corp	Lawrenceburg
43	813.5	School Town of Speedway	Speedway
45	814.5	Alexandria Com School Corp	Alexandria
46	821.5	Porter Township School Corp	Valparaiso
47	823.5	Paoli Community School Corp	Paoli
48	830.0	Community Schools of Frankfort	Frankfort
49	833.4	Noblesville Schools	Noblesville
50	833.5	Northwestern School Corp	Kokomo
51	849.0	Centerville-Abington Com Schs	Centerville
52	850.8	Hamilton Southeastern Schools	Fishers
53	856.2	Plainfield Community Sch Corp	Plainfield
54	858.1	Carmel Clay Schools	Carmel
55	862.4	Muncie Community Schools	Muncie
56	864.5	Randolph Central School Corp	Winchester
57	865.0	Avon Community School Corp	Avon
58	866.5	East Washington School Corp	Pekin
59	868.5	Madison Consolidated Schools	Madison
60	869.5	Brownsburg Community Sch Corp	Brownsburg
61	875.4	M S D Perry Township	Indianapolis
62	877.8	Kankakee Valley School Corp	Wheatfield
63	880.3	West Noble School Corporation	Ligonier
64	882.3	Lebanon Community School Corp	Lebanon
65	883.4	Sunman-Dearborn Com Sch Corp	Sunman
66	887.5	North West Hendricks Schools	Lizton
67	888.5	M S D Pike Township	Indianapolis
68	891.0	Eastbrook Community Sch Corp	Marion
69	896.0	Hanover Community School Corp	Cedar Lake
70	907.8	Whitley County Cons Schools	Columbia City
71	909.0	John Glenn School Corporation	Walkerton
72	918.0	Brownstown Cnt Com Sch Corp	Brownstown
73	934.3	Delaware Community School Corp	Muncie
74	945.0	Richland-Bean Blossom CSC	Ellettsville
75	948.5	West Clark Community Schools	Sellersburg
76	949.3	M S D Lawrence Township	Indianapolis
77	955.5	Elwood Community School Corp	Elwood
78	968.0	East Noble School Corp	Kendallville
79	1,000.5	West Lafayette Com School Corp	West Lafayette
80	1,021.7	Franklin County Com Sch Corp	Brookville
81	1,044.9	M S D Wayne Township	Indianapolis
82	1,046.0	North Gibson School Corp	Princeton
83	1,058.3	Greater Jasper Con Schs	Jasper
84	1,093.5	North Adams Community Schools	Decatur
85	1,103.7	Wa-Nee Community Schools	Nappanee
86	1,105.5	Tippecanoe Valley School Corp	Akron
87	1,109.5	North Montgomery Com Sch Corp	Crawfordsville
88	1,112.0	Hamilton Heights School Corp	Arcadia
89	1,113.5	East Porter County School Corp	Kouts
90	1,122.3	Anderson Community School Corp	Anderson
91	1,123.0	Mississinewa Community School Corp	Gas City
92	1,128.3	Southern Hancock Co CS Corp	New Palestine
93	1,134.8	M S D Warren Township	Indianapolis
94	1,145.7	South Bend Community Sch Corp	South Bend
95	1,146.5	Brown County School Corporation	Nashville
95	1,146.5	Decatur County Com Schools	Greensburg
97	1,150.0	Peru Community Schools	Peru
98	1,161.0	Mount Vernon Community Sch Corp	Fortville
99	1,167.5	Kokomo-Center Twp Con Sch Corp	Kokomo
100	1,177.0	Beech Grove City Schools	Beech Grove
101	1,179.8	Michigan City Area Schools	Michigan City
102	1,190.8	M S D Decatur Township	Indianapolis
103	1,196.4	Greater Clark County Schools	Jeffersonville
104	1,216.5	Washington Com Schools Inc	Washington
105	1,246.4	Huntington County Com Sch Corp	Huntington
106	1,283.5	Danville Community School Corp	Danville
107	1,291.0	M S D Wabash County Schools	Wabash
108	1,307.0	Twin Lakes School Corp	Monticello
109	1,382.0	Franklin Township Com Sch Corp	Indianapolis
110	1,384.3	Dekalb County Central United SD	Waterloo
111	1,397.0	Vincennes Community Sch Corp	Vincennes
112	1,400.7	Portage Township Schools	Portage
113	1,418.8	M S D Martinsville Schools	Martinsville
114	1,463.0	Scott County SD 2	Scottsburg
115	1,472.2	Center Grove Com Sch Corp	Greenwood
116	1,475.0	Benton Community School Corp	Fowler
117	1,487.0	South Dearborn Com School Corp	Aurora
118	1,489.7	Mooresville Con School Corp	Mooresville
119	1,508.8	Northwest Allen County Schools	Fort Wayne
120	1,509.0	Oak Hill United School Corp	Converse
121	1,513.0	M S D Steuben County	Angola
122	1,552.0	Manchester Community Schools	N Manchester
123	1,560.5	Spencer-Owen Community Schools	Spencer
124	1,562.0	Valparaiso Community Schools	Valparaiso
125	1,584.3	Bartholomew Con School Corp	Columbus
126	1,592.0	Switzerland County School Corp	Vevay
127	1,598.3	Warrick County School Corp	Boonville
128	1,607.0	Southeastern School Corp	Walton
129	1,617.0	Tell City-Troy Twp School Corp	Tell City
130	1,634.5	Laporte Community School Corp	Laporte
131	1,651.0	Union County College Corner JSD	Liberty
132	1,651.3	Zionsville Community Schools	Zionsville
133	1,653.0	M S D Southwest Allen County	Fort Wayne
134	1,683.0	Mill Creek Community Sch Corp	Clayton
135	1,692.0	East Allen County Schools	New Haven
136	1,723.5	School Town of Highland	Highland
137	1,732.8	Warsaw Community Schools	Warsaw
138	1,734.0	Prairie Heights Com Sch Corp	Lagrange
139	1,740.5	Wawasee Community School Corp	Syracuse
140	1,763.0	Plymouth Community School Corp	Plymouth
141	1,787.0	Southwest School Corp	Sullivan
142	1,793.3	Merrillville Community School	Merrillville
143	1,809.0	Crawford County Com School Corp	Marengo
144	1,841.0	Rensselaer Central School Corp	Rensselaer
145	1,888.0	Baugo Community Schools	Elkhart
146	1,909.0	School City of Hobart	Hobart
147	1,929.0	Shelbyville Central Schools	Shelbyville
148	1,940.0	Greenwood Community Sch Corp	Greenwood
149	1,967.0	South Gibson School Corp	Fort Branch
150	1,987.2	New Albany-Floyd County Con Sch	New Albany
151	1,995.0	South Montgomery Com Sch Corp	New Market
152	2,008.5	New Castle Community Sch Corp	New Castle
153	2,008.7	School City of East Chicago	East Chicago
154	2,012.5	Seymour Community Schools	Seymour
155	2,080.0	Middlebury Community Schools	Middlebury
156	2,093.5	Fayette County School Corp	Connersville
157	2,094.0	Fairfield Community Schools	Goshen
158	2,106.0	Pike County School Corp	Petersburg
159	2,196.0	School Town of Munster	Munster
160	2,255.0	Westview School Corporation	Topeka
161	2,275.0	Lakeland School Corporation	Lagrange
162	2,297.0	Mount Pleasant Twp Com Sch Corp	Yorktown
163	2,306.0	Lake Ridge Schools	Gary
164	2,327.5	Greenfield-Central Com Schools	Greenfield
165	2,382.0	Concord Community Schools	Elkhart
166	2,547.0	Western School Corp	Russiaville
167	2,584.5	Clark-Pleasant Com School Corp	Whiteland
168	2,586.0	Northern Wells Com Schools	Ossian
169	2,644.5	Jennings County Schools	North Vernon
170	2,672.0	School City of Mishawaka	Mishawaka
171	2,677.0	North Lawrence Com Schools	Bedford
172	2,733.2	Elkhart Community Schools	Elkhart
173	2,739.0	Griffith Public Schools	Griffith
174	2,777.0	New Prairie United School Corp	New Carlisle
175	3,117.5	Goshen Community Schools	Goshen
176	3,242.7	Lake Central School Corp	Saint John
177	3,502.0	Crown Point Community Sch Corp	Crown Point
178	3,695.0	Tri-Creek School Corp	Lowell
179	4,913.0	Franklin Community School Corp	Franklin
180	5,252.0	Marion Community Schools	Marion
181	7,396.7	Evansville-Vanderburgh Sch Corp	Evansville
182	10,599.0	Penn-Harris-Madison Sch Corp	Mishawaka
183	31,884.0	Fort Wayne Community Schools	Fort Wayne
n/a	n/a	Frankton-Lapel Community Schs	Anderson
n/a	n/a	North Newton School Corp	Morocco
n/a	n/a	South Harrison Com Schools	Corydon
n/a	n/a	Union Township School Corp	Valparaiso
n/a	n/a	Whitko Community School Corp	Pierceton

Note: This section only includes districts with 1,500 or more students; All categories are ranked from high to low

Student/Counselor Ratio

(number of students per counselor)

Rank	Number	District Name	City
1	273.4	North Adams Community Schools	Decatur
2	288.2	Randolph Central School Corp	Winchester
3	295.0	Benton Community School Corp	Fowler
4	321.8	Michigan City Area Schools	Michigan City
5	323.3	Northern Wells Com Schools	Ossian
6	327.4	Gary Community School Corp	Gary
7	336.2	M S D Steuben County	Angola
8	336.5	Greencastle Community Sch Corp	Greencastle
9	340.7	New Albany-Floyd County Con Sch	New Albany
10	342.4	Crawfordsville Com Schools	Crawfordsville
11	343.8	Garrett-Keyser-Butler Com	Garrett
12	346.6	East Washington School Corp	Pekin
13	353.9	Zionsville Community Schools	Zionsville
14	356.9	South Harrison Com Schools	Corydon
15	363.6	John Glenn School Corporation	Walkerton
16	366.6	Huntington County Com Sch Corp	Huntington
17	367.3	M S D Southwest Allen County	Fort Wayne
18	368.2	Rensselaer Central School Corp	Rensselaer
19	369.8	North Montgomery Com Sch Corp	Crawfordsville
20	370.8	Tipton Community School Corp	Tipton
21	373.4	Twin Lakes School Corp	Monticello
22	377.6	Baugo Community Schools	Elkhart
23	377.8	Jennings County Schools	North Vernon
24	379.2	Lakeland School Corporation	Lagrange
25	382.2	Decatur County Com Schools	Greensburg
26	384.3	Lake Ridge Schools	Gary
27	385.4	North Putnam Community Schools	Bainbridge
28	386.8	Wawasee Community School Corp	Syracuse
29	388.1	Muncie Community Schools	Muncie
30	392.5	Shelby Eastern Schools	Shelbyville
31	397.0	Batesville Community Sch Corp	Batesville
32	399.0	South Montgomery Com Sch Corp	New Market
33	399.4	Whitko Community School Corp	Pierceton
34	400.4	Delaware Community School Corp	Muncie
35	402.3	Northwest Allen County Schools	Fort Wayne
36	406.8	Lawrenceburg Com School Corp	Lawrenceburg
37	410.8	Porter Township School Corp	Valparaiso
38	412.3	Delphi Community School Corp	Delphi
39	413.9	Wa-Nee Community Schools	Nappanee
40	415.3	Dekalb County Central United SD	Waterloo
41	415.7	Goshen Community Schools	Goshen
42	416.0	Middlebury Community Schools	Middlebury
43	417.5	Westfield-Washington Schools	Westfield
44	418.0	Scott County SD 2	Scottsburg
45	420.8	Mill Creek Community Sch Corp	Clayton
46	430.2	East Noble School Corp	Kendallville
47	430.3	M S D Wabash County Schools	Wabash
48	433.5	Prairie Heights Com Sch Corp	Lagrange
49	437.6	Hamilton Southeastern Schools	Fishers
50	442.2	Tippecanoe Valley School Corp	Akron
51	443.8	North West Hendricks Schools	Lizton
52	444.8	Hamilton Heights School Corp	Arcadia
53	445.5	Eastbrook Community Sch Corp	Marion
54	450.5	Tippecanoe School Corp	Lafayette
55	451.6	Blackford County Schools	Hartford City
56	453.9	Whitley County Cons Schools	Columbia City
57	456.0	North Harrison Com School Corp	Ramsey
58	459.0	Brownstown Cnt Com Sch Corp	Brownstown
59	460.1	Center Grove Com Sch Corp	Greenwood
60	462.3	Evansville-Vanderburgh Sch Corp	Evansville
61	463.5	Nineveh-Hensley-Jackson United	Trafalgar
62	464.1	Lafayette School Corporation	Lafayette
63	479.0	Western Boone County Com SD	Thorntown
64	482.3	Shelbyville Central Schools	Shelbyville
65	485.0	Maconaquah School Corp	Bunker Hill
66	486.6	Avon Community School Corp	Avon
67	490.8	Sunman-Dearborn Com Sch Corp	Sunman
68	491.3	Franklin Community School Corp	Franklin
69	492.4	School Town of Highland	Highland
70	496.5	M S D Washington Twp	Indianapolis
71	496.9	Brownsburg Community Sch Corp	Brownsburg
72	500.3	West Lafayette Com School Corp	West Lafayette
73	501.6	Kankakee Valley School Corp	Wheatfield
74	502.3	Dekalb County Eastern Com SD	Butler
75	502.9	Laporte Community School Corp	Laporte
76	507.8	M S D Mount Vernon	Mount Vernon
77	509.8	Knox Community School Corp	Knox
78	510.0	South Vermillion Com Sch Corp	Clinton
79	510.8	Franklin County Com Sch Corp	Brookville
80	516.9	Clark-Pleasant Com School Corp	Whiteland
81	517.3	Manchester Community Schools	N Manchester
82	518.7	Madison-Grant United Sch Corp	Fairmount
83	520.9	Noblesville Schools	Noblesville
84	523.0	North Gibson School Corp	Princeton
85	523.4	Fayette County School Corp	Connersville
86	523.5	Fairfield Community Schools	Goshen
87	528.0	Mitchell Community Schools	Mitchell
88	528.6	Duneland School Corporation	Chesterton
89	529.3	Concord Community Schools	Elkhart
90	530.7	Switzerland County School Corp	Vevay
91	534.3	East Allen County Schools	New Haven
92	538.4	Greater Clark County Schools	Jeffersonville
93	538.7	North Newton School Corp	Morocco
94	539.0	Tell City-Troy Twp School Corp	Tell City
95	542.3	Greensburg Community Schools	Greensburg
95	542.3	School Town of Speedway	Speedway
97	549.0	Paoli Community School Corp	Paoli
98	552.8	Franklin Township Com Sch Corp	Indianapolis
99	553.3	Community Schools of Frankfort	Frankfort
100	554.5	Bartholomew Con School Corp	Columbus
101	555.7	Northwestern School Corp	Kokomo
102	558.6	Mooresville Con School Corp	Mooresville
103	561.5	Mississinewa Community School Corp	Gas City
104	564.2	Southern Hancock Co CS Corp	New Palestine
105	564.8	North Spencer County Sch Corp	Lincoln City
106	566.0	Centerville-Abington Com Schs	Centerville
107	567.0	Richland-Bean Blossom CSC	Ellettsville
108	567.4	M S D Warren Township	Indianapolis
109	570.1	Indianapolis Public Schools	Indianapolis
110	574.3	Mount Pleasant Twp Com Sch Corp	Yorktown
111	575.0	Peru Community Schools	Peru
112	579.0	Madison Consolidated Schools	Madison
113	580.5	Mount Vernon Community Sch Corp	Fortville
114	582.6	Clay Community Schools	Knightsville
115	586.8	Vigo County School Corp	Terre Haute
116	588.2	Lebanon Community School Corp	Lebanon
117	592.3	M S D Pike Township	Indianapolis
118	595.7	Southwest School Corp	Sullivan
119	597.3	Hanover Community School Corp	Cedar Lake
120	624.2	Spencer-Owen Community Schools	Spencer
121	630.6	M S D Martinsville Schools	Martinsville
122	634.3	Carmel Clay Schools	Carmel
123	636.8	Kokomo-Center Twp Con Sch Corp	Kokomo
123	636.8	Western School Corp	Russiaville
125	637.0	Elwood Community School Corp	Elwood
126	641.8	Danville Community School Corp	Danville
127	649.0	Rochester Community Sch Corp	Rochester
128	660.3	West Noble School Corporation	Ligonier
129	664.0	Rush County Schools	Rushville
130	668.0	School City of Mishawaka	Mishawaka
131	669.3	North Lawrence Com Schools	Bedford
132	669.5	New Castle Community Sch Corp	New Castle
133	670.8	Seymour Community Schools	Seymour
134	673.4	Anderson Community School Corp	Anderson
135	689.6	Monroe County Com Sch Corp	Bloomington
136	696.6	M S D Wayne Township	Indianapolis
137	698.5	Vincennes Community Sch Corp	Vincennes
138	702.0	Pike County School Corp	Petersburg
139	705.2	Plymouth Community School Corp	Plymouth
140	706.6	Penn-Harris-Madison Sch Corp	Mishawaka
141	707.0	Richmond Community School Corp	Richmond
142	718.3	Logansport Community Sch Corp	Logansport
143	719.3	Elkhart Community Schools	Elkhart
144	725.6	School City of Hammond	Hammond
145	732.0	School Town of Munster	Munster
146	733.5	M S D Lawrence Township	Indianapolis
147	737.7	Warrick County School Corp	Boonville
148	742.3	East Porter County School Corp	Kouts
149	750.3	Marion Community Schools	Marion
150	754.5	Oak Hill United School Corp	Converse
151	758.8	West Clark Community Schools	Sellersburg
152	762.0	Northeast School Corp	Hymera
153	763.6	School City of Hobart	Hobart
154	764.3	Brown County School Corporation	Nashville
155	775.8	Greenfield-Central Com Schools	Greenfield
155	775.8	Jay School Corp	Portland
157	776.0	Greenwood Community Sch Corp	Greenwood
158	781.0	Valparaiso Community Schools	Valparaiso
159	784.7	Beech Grove City Schools	Beech Grove
160	785.5	Northwestern Con School Corp	Fairland
161	803.5	Southeastern School Corp	Walton
162	803.7	Frankton-Lapel Community Schs	Anderson
163	805.6	South Madison Com Sch Corp	Pendleton
164	806.3	South Bend Community Sch Corp	South Bend
165	810.7	Lake Central School Corp	Saint John
166	811.0	Washington Com Schools Inc	Washington
167	814.5	Alexandria Com School Corp	Alexandria
168	825.5	Union County College Corner JSD	Liberty
169	850.6	M S D Decatur Township	Indianapolis
170	856.2	Plainfield Community Sch Corp	Plainfield
171	860.9	School City of East Chicago	East Chicago
172	875.4	M S D Perry Township	Indianapolis
173	904.5	Crawford County Com School Corp	Marengo
174	913.0	Griffith Public Schools	Griffith
175	919.5	Southwest Dubois County Sch Corp	Huntingburg
176	923.8	Tri-Creek School Corp	Lowell
177	925.7	New Prairie United School Corp	New Carlisle
178	933.8	Portage Township Schools	Portage
179	990.1	Warsaw Community Schools	Warsaw
180	991.3	South Dearborn Com School Corp	Aurora
181	996.4	Fort Wayne Community Schools	Fort Wayne
182	1,058.3	Greater Jasper Con Schs	Jasper
183	1,079.0	Salem Community Schools	Salem
184	1,127.5	Westview School Corporation	Topeka
185	1,167.3	Crown Point Community Sch Corp	Crown Point
186	1,195.5	Merrillville Community School	Merrillville
187	1,693.0	Union Township School Corp	Valparaiso
188	1,967.0	South Gibson School Corp	Fort Branch

Current Expenditures per Student

Rank	Dollars	District Name	City
1	13,577	Anderson Community School Corp	Anderson
2	12,725	Dekalb County Eastern Com SD	Butler
3	12,136	School City of East Chicago	East Chicago
4	11,649	Muncie Community Schools	Muncie
5	11,635	Indianapolis Public Schools	Indianapolis
6	11,032	Gary Community School Corp	Gary
7	11,022	North Putnam Community Schools	Bainbridge
8	10,932	Lake Ridge Schools	Gary
9	10,921	M S D Washington Twp	Indianapolis
10	10,827	South Bend Community Sch Corp	South Bend
11	10,656	Kokomo-Center Twp Con Sch Corp	Kokomo
12	10,573	School City of Mishawaka	Mishawaka
13	10,495	Logansport Community Sch Corp	Logansport
14	10,449	Greater Jasper Con Schs	Jasper
15	10,388	Lafayette School Corporation	Lafayette
16	10,233	M S D Mount Vernon	Mount Vernon
17	9,996	M S D Wayne Township	Indianapolis
18	9,901	Evansville-Vanderburgh Sch Corp	Evansville
19	9,893	Crawfordsville Com Schools	Crawfordsville
20	9,832	Fort Wayne Community Schools	Fort Wayne
21	9,749	Elkhart Community Schools	Elkhart
22	9,677	Garrett-Keyser-Butler Com	Garrett
23	9,660	M S D Pike Township	Indianapolis
24	9,632	Richmond Community School Corp	Richmond
25	9,596	Goshen Community Schools	Goshen
26	9,590	Union County College Corner JSD	Liberty
27	9,567	North Newton School Corp	Morocco
28	9,457	Jay School Corp	Portland
29	9,445	Marion Community Schools	Marion
30	9,444	Tell City-Troy Twp School Corp	Tell City
31	9,399	Greater Clark County Schools	Jeffersonville
32	9,379	M S D Perry Township	Indianapolis
33	9,358	New Castle Community Sch Corp	New Castle
34	9,315	Michigan City Area Schools	Michigan City
35	9,272	Westview School Corporation	Topeka
36	9,250	M S D Lawrence Township	Indianapolis
37	9,221	Madison Consolidated Schools	Madison
38	9,137	M S D Wabash County Schools	Wabash
39	9,123	Maconaquah School Corp	Bunker Hill
40	9,079	Brown County School Corporation	Nashville
41	9,067	Southwest Dubois County Sch Corp	Huntingburg
42	8,980	Lawrenceburg Com School Corp	Lawrenceburg
43	8,961	Fayette County School Corp	Connersville
44	8,919	M S D Southwest Allen County	Fort Wayne
45	8,912	Bartholomew Con School Corp	Columbus
45	8,912	Clark-Pleasant Com School Corp	Whiteland
47	8,910	Greenfield-Central Com Schools	Greenfield
48	8,884	Laporte Community School Corp	Laporte
49	8,882	Southwest School Corp	Sullivan
50	8,877	North Lawrence Com Schools	Bedford
51	8,841	Prairie Heights Com Sch Corp	Lagrange
52	8,839	Vincennes Community Sch Corp	Vincennes
53	8,815	Benton Community School Corp	Fowler
54	8,804	M S D Warren Township	Indianapolis
55	8,801	West Lafayette Com School Corp	West Lafayette
56	8,775	Monroe County Com Sch Corp	Bloomington
57	8,756	New Albany-Floyd County Con Sch	New Albany
58	8,752	School City of Hammond	Hammond
59	8,730	South Montgomery Com Sch Corp	New Market
60	8,715	West Noble School Corporation	Ligonier
61	8,713	Wawasee Community School Corp	Syracuse

Note: This section only includes districts with 1,500 or more students; All categories are ranked from high to low

62	8,615	East Allen County Schools	New Haven
63	8,583	Crawford County Com School Corp	Marengo
64	8,554	Duneland School Corporation	Chesterton
65	8,546	Blackford County Schools	Hartford City
66	8,465	Madison-Grant United Sch Corp	Fairmount
67	8,455	Switzerland County School Corp	Vevay
68	8,447	Valparaiso Community Schools	Valparaiso
69	8,399	Spencer-Owen Community Schools	Spencer
70	8,395	Sunman-Dearborn Com Sch Corp	Sunman
71	8,380	Dekalb County Central United SD	Waterloo
72	8,377	Pike County School Corp	Petersburg
73	8,349	Northwestern School Corp	Kokomo
74	8,334	Carmel Clay Schools	Carmel
75	8,322	East Noble School Corp	Kendallville
76	8,315	Whitley County Cons Schools	Columbia City
77	8,296	Elwood Community School Corp	Elwood
78	8,242	North Gibson School Corp	Princeton
79	8,230	Seymour Community Schools	Seymour
80	8,224	Union Township School Corp	Valparaiso
81	8,208	North Spencer County Sch Corp	Lincoln City
82	8,204	Northeast School Corp	Hymera
83	8,178	North Adams Community Schools	Decatur
84	8,085	Concord Community Schools	Elkhart
85	8,061	Greencastle Community Sch Corp	Greencastle
86	8,054	South Madison Com Sch Corp	Pendleton
87	8,053	Zionsville Community Schools	Zionsville
88	8,043	Paoli Community School Corp	Paoli
89	8,027	Wa-Nee Community Schools	Nappanee
90	8,023	South Harrison Com Schools	Corydon
91	8,021	Tippecanoe Valley School Corp	Akron
92	7,995	Community Schools of Frankfort	Frankfort
93	7,994	Griffith Public Schools	Griffith
94	7,988	Knox Community School Corp	Knox
95	7,968	M S D Steuben County	Angola
96	7,967	North West Hendricks Schools	Lizton
97	7,963	Baugo Community Schools	Elkhart
98	7,957	Twin Lakes School Corp	Monticello
99	7,910	North Harrison Com School Corp	Ramsey
100	7,893	East Washington School Corp	Pekin
101	7,873	Lakeland School Corporation	Lagrange
102	7,860	School Town of Munster	Munster
103	7,856	South Dearborn Com School Corp	Aurora
104	7,844	Richland-Bean Blossom CSC	Ellettsville
105	7,839	Peru Community Schools	Peru
106	7,827	Huntington County Com Sch Corp	Huntington
107	7,826	Mitchell Community Schools	Mitchell
108	7,790	Centerville-Abington Com Schs	Centerville
109	7,787	Oak Hill United School Corp	Converse
110	7,781	M S D Decatur Township	Indianapolis
111	7,777	North Montgomery Com Sch Corp	Crawfordsville
112	7,768	Penn-Harris-Madison Sch Corp	Mishawaka
113	7,762	Vigo County School Corp	Terre Haute
114	7,751	Brownstown Cnt Com Sch Corp	Brownstown
115	7,736	Lake Central School Corp	Saint John
116	7,732	Rush County Schools	Rushville
117	7,716	Mississinewa Community School Corp	Gas City
118	7,691	Warsaw Community Schools	Warsaw
119	7,688	Lebanon Community School Corp	Lebanon
120	7,686	Westfield-Washington Schools	Westfield
121	7,668	School Town of Highland	Highland
122	7,660	Brownsburg Community Sch Corp	Brownsburg
123	7,653	Whitko Community School Corp	Pierceton
124	7,642	M S D Martinsville Schools	Martinsville
125	7,590	Beech Grove City Schools	Beech Grove
126	7,576	South Vermillion Com Sch Corp	Clinton
127	7,557	Rensselaer Central School Corp	Rensselaer
128	7,542	School Town of Speedway	Speedway
129	7,533	Washington Com Schools Inc	Washington
130	7,527	South Gibson School Corp	Fort Branch
131	7,520	Merrillville Community School	Merrillville
132	7,491	Franklin Township Com Sch Corp	Indianapolis
133	7,477	Clay Community Schools	Knightsville
134	7,474	Portage Township Schools	Portage
135	7,446	Hamilton Heights School Corp	Arcadia
136	7,441	Avon Community School Corp	Avon
137	7,428	Decatur County Com Schools	Greensburg
138	7,424	Greensburg Community Schools	Greensburg
139	7,410	Shelby Eastern Schools	Shelbyville
140	7,408	Scott County SD 2	Scottsburg
141	7,388	Mount Pleasant Twp Com Sch Corp	Yorktown
142	7,377	Eastbrook Community Sch Corp	Marion
143	7,370	Delaware Community School Corp	Muncie
144	7,357	Western Boone County Com SD	Thorntown
145	7,353	Fairfield Community Schools	Goshen
146	7,335	Batesville Community Sch Corp	Batesville
147	7,334	Mount Vernon Community Sch Corp	Fortville
148	7,332	Tipton Community School Corp	Tipton
149	7,326	Southeastern School Corp	Walton
150	7,323	Alexandria Com School Corp	Alexandria
151	7,310	Rochester Community Sch Corp	Rochester
152	7,308	Shelbyville Central Schools	Shelbyville
153	7,293	Randolph Central School Corp	Winchester
154	7,286	Franklin County Com Sch Corp	Brookville
154	7,286	Northwest Allen County Schools	Fort Wayne
156	7,279	Middlebury Community Schools	Middlebury
157	7,266	Center Grove Com Sch Corp	Greenwood
158	7,252	Jennings County Schools	North Vernon
159	7,238	Danville Community School Corp	Danville
160	7,178	Kankakee Valley School Corp	Wheatfield
161	7,168	Northern Wells Com Schools	Ossian
162	7,165	Greenwood Community Sch Corp	Greenwood
163	7,143	East Porter County School Corp	Kouts
164	7,142	Mill Creek Community Sch Corp	Clayton
165	7,081	Nineveh-Hensley-Jackson United	Trafalgar
166	7,061	Plainfield Community Sch Corp	Plainfield
167	7,039	Mooresville Con School Corp	Mooresville
168	7,012	Manchester Community Schools	N Manchester
169	7,008	Porter Township School Corp	Valparaiso
170	6,997	Delphi Community School Corp	Delphi
171	6,969	Tippecanoe School Corp	Lafayette
172	6,952	Tri-Creek School Corp	Lowell
173	6,948	Warrick County School Corp	Boonville
174	6,903	Hanover Community School Corp	Cedar Lake
175	6,897	Plymouth Community School Corp	Plymouth
176	6,892	Salem Community Schools	Salem
177	6,889	Hamilton Southeastern Schools	Fishers
178	6,880	West Clark Community Schools	Sellersburg
179	6,858	Frankton-Lapel Community Schs	Anderson
180	6,814	John Glenn School Corporation	Walkerton
181	6,765	Franklin Community School Corp	Franklin
182	6,733	School City of Hobart	Hobart
183	6,659	Noblesville Schools	Noblesville
184	6,563	New Prairie United School Corp	New Carlisle
185	6,552	Northwestern Con School Corp	Fairland
186	6,464	Crown Point Community Sch Corp	Crown Point
187	6,340	Western School Corp	Russiaville
188	6,253	Southern Hancock Co CS Corp	New Palestine

Number of Diploma Recipients

Rank	Number	District Name	City
1	1,699	Fort Wayne Community Schools	Fort Wayne
2	1,288	Evansville-Vanderburgh Sch Corp	Evansville
3	1,260	Indianapolis Public Schools	Indianapolis
4	1,051	South Bend Community Sch Corp	South Bend
5	1,003	M S D Lawrence Township	Indianapolis
6	891	Vigo County School Corp	Terre Haute
7	865	Carmel Clay Schools	Carmel
8	711	M S D Warren Township	Indianapolis
9	680	M S D Washington Twp	Indianapolis
10	671	Penn-Harris-Madison Sch Corp	Mishawaka
11	668	M S D Wayne Township	Indianapolis
12	666	M S D Perry Township	Indianapolis
13	652	Gary Community School Corp	Gary
14	651	New Albany-Floyd County Con Sch	New Albany
15	634	Hamilton Southeastern Schools	Fishers
16	630	Warrick County School Corp	Boonville
17	625	Monroe County Com Sch Corp	Bloomington
18	607	Bartholomew Con School Corp	Columbus
19	602	East Allen County Schools	New Haven
20	598	Tippecanoe School Corp	Lafayette
21	575	Lake Central School Corp	Saint John
22	551	Elkhart Community Schools	Elkhart
23	510	Center Grove Com Sch Corp	Greenwood
24	505	Anderson Community School Corp	Anderson
24	505	School City of Hammond	Hammond
26	491	Greater Clark County Schools	Jeffersonville
27	480	Crown Point Community Sch Corp	Crown Point
28	478	M S D Pike Township	Indianapolis
29	471	Portage Township Schools	Portage
30	468	Valparaiso Community Schools	Valparaiso
31	454	M S D Southwest Allen County	Fort Wayne
32	424	Noblesville Schools	Noblesville
33	421	Merrillville Community School	Merrillville
34	400	Huntington County Com Sch Corp	Huntington
35	399	Brownsburg Community Sch Corp	Brownsburg
36	392	Lafayette School Corporation	Lafayette
37	390	Avon Community School Corp	Avon
38	376	Warsaw Community Schools	Warsaw
39	365	Muncie Community Schools	Muncie
40	360	Laporte Community School Corp	Laporte
41	352	Northwest Allen County Schools	Fort Wayne
42	333	Franklin Township Com Sch Corp	Indianapolis
43	330	Kokomo-Center Twp Con Sch Corp	Kokomo
44	325	School Town of Munster	Munster
45	324	Duneland School Corporation	Chesterton
46	320	Michigan City Area Schools	Michigan City
47	304	Mooresville Con School Corp	Mooresville
48	298	M S D Martinsville Schools	Martinsville
49	295	Zionsville Community Schools	Zionsville
50	294	Sunman-Dearborn Com Sch Corp	Sunman
51	293	Goshen Community Schools	Goshen
52	287	M S D Decatur Township	Indianapolis
52	287	North Lawrence Com Schools	Bedford
54	282	Concord Community Schools	Elkhart
55	278	Dekalb County Central United SD	Waterloo
55	278	Greenfield-Central Com Schools	Greenfield
57	271	Clay Community Schools	Knightsville
58	270	Whitley County Cons Schools	Columbia City
59	259	Westfield-Washington Schools	Westfield
60	256	School City of Mishawaka	Mishawaka
61	254	Greater Jasper Con Schs	Jasper
62	250	East Noble School Corp	Kendallville
63	247	Plainfield Community Sch Corp	Plainfield
64	243	Richmond Community School Corp	Richmond
65	242	Middlebury Community Schools	Middlebury
66	241	School City of Hobart	Hobart
67	239	Clark-Pleasant Com School Corp	Whiteland
67	239	Logansport Community Sch Corp	Logansport
69	238	West Clark Community Schools	Sellersburg
70	237	Jennings County Schools	North Vernon
70	237	Seymour Community Schools	Seymour
72	233	Franklin Community School Corp	Franklin
73	232	Greenwood Community Sch Corp	Greenwood
74	231	New Castle Community Sch Corp	New Castle
75	230	Marion Community Schools	Marion
75	230	School Town of Highland	Highland
77	227	Southern Hancock Co CS Corp	New Palestine
77	227	Tri-Creek School Corp	Lowell
79	222	South Dearborn Com School Corp	Aurora
79	222	South Harrison Com Schools	Corydon
81	215	Plymouth Community School Corp	Plymouth
82	203	M S D Mount Vernon	Mount Vernon
82	203	South Madison Com Sch Corp	Pendleton
84	202	School City of East Chicago	East Chicago
85	201	Wawasee Community School Corp	Syracuse
86	197	M S D Steuben County	Angola
86	197	Shelbyville Central Schools	Shelbyville
88	195	Madison Consolidated Schools	Madison
89	194	Franklin County Com Sch Corp	Brookville
90	191	Jay School Corp	Portland
91	190	Lebanon Community School Corp	Lebanon
92	189	Delaware Community School Corp	Muncie
93	187	New Prairie United School Corp	New Carlisle
94	185	Northern Wells Com Schools	Ossian
94	185	Wa-Nee Community Schools	Nappanee
96	184	Fayette County School Corp	Connersville
97	182	North Adams Community Schools	Decatur
98	178	Mount Vernon Community Sch Corp	Fortville
99	175	North Spencer County Sch Corp	Lincoln City
99	175	Vincennes Community Sch Corp	Vincennes
101	174	Richland-Bean Blossom CSC	Ellettsville
101	174	Western School Corp	Russiaville
103	172	Kankakee Valley School Corp	Wheatfield
103	172	M S D Wabash County Schools	Wabash
105	165	Spencer-Owen Community Schools	Spencer
106	162	West Lafayette Com School Corp	West Lafayette
107	158	Danville Community School Corp	Danville
107	158	Mount Pleasant Twp Com Sch Corp	Yorktown
109	154	North Harrison Com School Corp	Ramsey
110	152	Griffith Public Schools	Griffith
111	150	Frankton-Lapel Community Schs	Anderson
111	150	Hamilton Heights School Corp	Arcadia
111	150	Peru Community Schools	Peru
114	147	East Porter County School Corp	Kouts
115	145	Brown County School Corporation	Nashville
115	145	Community Schools of Frankfort	Frankfort
117	142	Rush County Schools	Rushville
117	142	South Montgomery Com Sch Corp	New Market
117	142	Tippecanoe Valley School Corp	Akron
120	141	Crawfordsville Com Schools	Crawfordsville
121	140	West Noble School Corporation	Ligonier
122	138	South Gibson School Corp	Fort Branch
123	135	Maconaquah School Corp	Bunker Hill
123	135	Twin Lakes School Corp	Monticello
125	132	Scott County SD 2	Scottsburg
126	131	Blackford County Schools	Hartford City

Note: This section only includes districts with 1,500 or more students; All categories are ranked from high to low

127	130	Nineveh-Hensley-Jackson United	Trafalgar
127	130	Western Boone County Com SD	Thorntown
129	129	Centerville-Abington Com Schs	Centerville
129	129	Mississinewa Community School Corp	Gas City
131	128	Batesville Community Sch Corp	Batesville
131	128	Decatur County Com Schools	Greensburg
131	128	Salem Community Schools	Salem
131	128	Washington Com Schools Inc	Washington
135	127	Benton Community School Corp	Fowler
136	126	Greensburg Community Schools	Greensburg
137	125	North Gibson School Corp	Princeton
137	125	Whitko Community School Corp	Pierceton
139	124	Fairfield Community Schools	Goshen
140	123	Elwood Community School Corp	Elwood
140	123	Hanover Community School Corp	Cedar Lake
140	123	North Montgomery Com Sch Corp	Crawfordsville
140	123	Prairie Heights Com Sch Corp	Lagrange
144	122	Delphi Community School Corp	Delphi
144	122	John Glenn School Corporation	Walkerton
144	122	Lakeland School Corporation	Lagrange
147	121	Greencastle Community Sch Corp	Greencastle
148	119	Pike County School Corp	Petersburg
149	117	North Putnam Community Schools	Bainbridge
150	116	Beech Grove City Schools	Beech Grove
151	114	Tipton Community School Corp	Tipton
151	114	Union Township School Corp	Valparaiso
153	113	Northwestern School Corp	Kokomo
153	113	Porter Township School Corp	Valparaiso
153	113	Southwest School Corp	Sullivan
156	112	Mitchell Community Schools	Mitchell
156	112	Randolph Central School Corp	Winchester
158	111	South Vermillion Com Sch Corp	Clinton
159	110	Madison-Grant United Sch Corp	Fairmount
159	110	Manchester Community Schools	N Manchester
161	109	Southeastern School Corp	Walton
162	108	North Newton School Corp	Morocco
163	107	Baugo Community Schools	Elkhart
163	107	Rochester Community Sch Corp	Rochester
163	107	Tell City-Troy Twp School Corp	Tell City
166	106	East Washington School Corp	Pekin
167	105	Lake Ridge Schools	Gary
167	105	Southwest Dubois County Sch Corp	Huntingburg
169	104	Rensselaer Central School Corp	Rensselaer
170	103	Crawford County Com School Corp	Marengo
170	103	Northwestern Con School Corp	Fairland
172	102	Eastbrook Community Sch Corp	Marion
172	102	Knox Community School Corp	Knox
174	99	Alexandria Com School Corp	Alexandria
174	99	Garrett-Keyser-Butler Com	Garrett
176	97	Oak Hill United School Corp	Converse
177	96	North West Hendricks Schools	Lizton
178	95	Brownstown Cnt Com Sch Corp	Brownstown
178	95	Paoli Community School Corp	Paoli
180	93	Lawrenceburg Com School Corp	Lawrenceburg
181	91	Shelby Eastern Schools	Shelbyville
182	89	Union County College Corner JSD	Liberty
183	88	Dekalb County Eastern Com SD	Butler
183	88	Westview School Corporation	Topeka
185	87	Mill Creek Community Sch Corp	Clayton
186	86	School Town of Speedway	Speedway
187	78	Switzerland County School Corp	Vevay
188	75	Northeast School Corp	Hymera

High School Drop-out Rate

Rank	Percent	District Name	City
1	9.9	Indianapolis Public Schools	Indianapolis
2	9.7	Lake Ridge Schools	Gary
3	9.2	School City of East Chicago	East Chicago
4	8.0	Richmond Community School Corp	Richmond
4	8.0	South Bend Community Sch Corp	South Bend
6	7.6	Anderson Community School Corp	Anderson
7	6.7	Marion Community Schools	Marion
8	6.5	Seymour Community Schools	Seymour
9	6.0	Elkhart Community Schools	Elkhart
9	6.0	M S D Martinsville Schools	Martinsville
11	5.8	South Vermillion Com Sch Corp	Clinton
12	5.7	Southwest School Corp	Sullivan
13	5.6	Kankakee Valley School Corp	Wheatfield
14	5.4	M S D Steuben County	Angola
15	5.3	Alexandria Com School Corp	Alexandria
15	5.3	M S D Wayne Township	Indianapolis
17	5.2	Lafayette School Corporation	Lafayette
17	5.2	West Noble School Corporation	Ligonier
19	5.0	Monroe County Com Sch Corp	Bloomington
19	5.0	Twin Lakes School Corp	Monticello
21	4.9	Beech Grove City Schools	Beech Grove
21	4.9	Portage Township Schools	Portage
23	4.8	Decatur County Com Schools	Greensburg
24	4.7	North Gibson School Corp	Princeton
24	4.7	Paoli Community School Corp	Paoli
26	4.6	Crawford County Com School Corp	Marengo
27	4.5	Concord Community Schools	Elkhart
27	4.5	Greenfield-Central Com Schools	Greenfield
27	4.5	Lakeland School Corporation	Lagrange
27	4.5	Madison-Grant United Sch Corp	Fairmount
31	4.4	Franklin County Com Sch Corp	Brookville
31	4.4	M S D Pike Township	Indianapolis
31	4.4	North Newton School Corp	Morocco
31	4.4	Washington Com Schools Inc	Washington
35	4.3	Fayette County School Corp	Connersville
35	4.3	Whitko Community School Corp	Pierceton
37	4.2	Jay School Corp	Portland
37	4.2	Mitchell Community Schools	Mitchell
37	4.2	Rochester Community Sch Corp	Rochester
37	4.2	Wa-Nee Community Schools	Nappanee
41	4.1	Delphi Community School Corp	Delphi
41	4.1	Franklin Community School Corp	Franklin
41	4.1	New Castle Community Sch Corp	New Castle
44	4.0	Eastbrook Community Sch Corp	Marion
44	4.0	Garrett-Keyser-Butler Com	Garrett
46	3.9	M S D Warren Township	Indianapolis
46	3.9	Salem Community Schools	Salem
48	3.7	North Adams Community Schools	Decatur
48	3.7	Rensselaer Central School Corp	Rensselaer
50	3.6	Tippecanoe Valley School Corp	Akron
51	3.5	Baugo Community Schools	Elkhart
51	3.5	Mooresville Con School Corp	Mooresville
51	3.5	Vigo County School Corp	Terre Haute
54	3.4	Delaware Community School Corp	Muncie
54	3.4	North Montgomery Com Sch Corp	Crawfordsville
54	3.4	Northwestern Con School Corp	Fairland
54	3.4	Peru Community Schools	Peru
54	3.4	School Town of Highland	Highland
59	3.3	East Washington School Corp	Pekin
59	3.3	Switzerland County School Corp	Vevay
59	3.3	Wawasee Community School Corp	Syracuse
62	3.2	Fort Wayne Community Schools	Fort Wayne
62	3.2	Greencastle Community Sch Corp	Greencastle
62	3.2	South Dearborn Com School Corp	Aurora
62	3.2	Tell City-Troy Twp School Corp	Tell City
66	3.1	Blackford County Schools	Hartford City
66	3.1	Crawfordsville Com Schools	Crawfordsville
66	3.1	Knox Community School Corp	Knox
66	3.1	Middlebury Community Schools	Middlebury
66	3.1	Plymouth Community School Corp	Plymouth
66	3.1	Scott County SD 2	Scottsburg
66	3.1	Shelbyville Central Schools	Shelbyville
73	3.0	Logansport Community Sch Corp	Logansport
73	3.0	Michigan City Area Schools	Michigan City
75	2.9	Clay Community Schools	Knightsville
75	2.9	Franklin Township Com Sch Corp	Indianapolis
75	2.9	Northeast School Corp	Hymera
75	2.9	Westview School Corporation	Topeka
79	2.8	Batesville Community Sch Corp	Batesville
79	2.8	Manchester Community Schools	N Manchester
79	2.8	Mount Vernon Community Sch Corp	Fortville
79	2.8	North Harrison Com School Corp	Ramsey
79	2.8	School City of Hammond	Hammond
79	2.8	Western School Corp	Russiaville
79	2.8	Westfield-Washington Schools	Westfield
86	2.7	Center Grove Com Sch Corp	Greenwood
86	2.7	M S D Lawrence Township	Indianapolis
88	2.6	Jennings County Schools	North Vernon
88	2.6	Noblesville Schools	Noblesville
88	2.6	North Putnam Community Schools	Bainbridge
88	2.6	School City of Hobart	Hobart
92	2.4	Dekalb County Central United SD	Waterloo
92	2.4	Greater Clark County Schools	Jeffersonville
92	2.4	Griffith Public Schools	Griffith
92	2.4	Pike County School Corp	Petersburg
92	2.4	Southeastern School Corp	Walton
92	2.4	Vincennes Community Sch Corp	Vincennes
92	2.4	Warrick County School Corp	Boonville
99	2.3	Brown County School Corporation	Nashville
100	2.2	Muncie Community Schools	Muncie
100	2.2	Oak Hill United School Corp	Converse
102	2.1	Community Schools of Frankfort	Frankfort
102	2.1	John Glenn School Corporation	Walkerton
102	2.1	Prairie Heights Com Sch Corp	Lagrange
102	2.1	Shelby Eastern Schools	Shelbyville
106	2.0	Dekalb County Eastern Com SD	Butler
106	2.0	Elwood Community School Corp	Elwood
106	2.0	Goshen Community Schools	Goshen
106	2.0	Lake Central School Corp	Saint John
106	2.0	School City of Mishawaka	Mishawaka
106	2.0	South Harrison Com Schools	Corydon
112	1.9	East Noble School Corp	Kendallville
112	1.9	Greenwood Community Sch Corp	Greenwood
112	1.9	Mill Creek Community Sch Corp	Clayton
112	1.9	Northern Wells Com Schools	Ossian
112	1.9	Whitley County Cons Schools	Columbia City
117	1.8	Avon Community School Corp	Avon
117	1.8	Brownsburg Community Sch Corp	Brownsburg
117	1.8	Lawrenceburg Com School Corp	Lawrenceburg
117	1.8	M S D Decatur Township	Indianapolis
117	1.8	New Albany-Floyd County Con Sch	New Albany
117	1.8	Randolph Central School Corp	Winchester
117	1.8	Rush County Schools	Rushville
124	1.7	Danville Community School Corp	Danville
124	1.7	North Spencer County Sch Corp	Lincoln City
124	1.7	Tippecanoe School Corp	Lafayette
127	1.6	Bartholomew Con School Corp	Columbus
127	1.6	Fairfield Community Schools	Goshen
127	1.6	M S D Mount Vernon	Mount Vernon
127	1.6	Mississinewa Community School Corp	Gas City
127	1.6	Mount Pleasant Twp Com Sch Corp	Yorktown
132	1.5	East Allen County Schools	New Haven
132	1.5	M S D Wabash County Schools	Wabash
132	1.5	North Lawrence Com Schools	Bedford
132	1.5	South Madison Com Sch Corp	Pendleton
136	1.4	Huntington County Com Sch Corp	Huntington
136	1.4	M S D Washington Twp	Indianapolis
136	1.4	Plainfield Community Sch Corp	Plainfield
136	1.4	South Montgomery Com Sch Corp	New Market
136	1.4	Tipton Community School Corp	Tipton
141	1.3	Crown Point Community Sch Corp	Crown Point
141	1.3	East Porter County School Corp	Kouts
141	1.3	Gary Community School Corp	Gary
141	1.3	Porter Township School Corp	Valparaiso
141	1.3	West Clark Community Schools	Sellersburg
146	1.2	Frankton-Lapel Community Schs	Anderson
146	1.2	Hamilton Heights School Corp	Arcadia
146	1.2	Kokomo-Center Twp Con Sch Corp	Kokomo
146	1.2	North West Hendricks Schools	Lizton
146	1.2	School Town of Speedway	Speedway
151	1.1	Nineveh-Hensley-Jackson United	Trafalgar
151	1.1	Richland-Bean Blossom CSC	Ellettsville
151	1.1	South Gibson School Corp	Fort Branch
151	1.1	Union Township School Corp	Valparaiso
155	1.0	M S D Southwest Allen County	Fort Wayne
156	0.9	M S D Perry Township	Indianapolis
156	0.9	Penn-Harris-Madison Sch Corp	Mishawaka
158	0.8	Greater Jasper Con Schs	Jasper
158	0.8	Merrillville Community School	Merrillville
158	0.8	New Prairie United School Corp	New Carlisle
158	0.8	Spencer-Owen Community Schools	Spencer
158	0.8	Sunman-Dearborn Com Sch Corp	Sunman
158	0.8	Western Boone County Com SD	Thorntown
164	0.7	Brownstown Cnt Com Sch Corp	Brownstown
164	0.7	Hanover Community School Corp	Cedar Lake
164	0.7	Northwestern School Corp	Kokomo
164	0.7	Southern Hancock Co CS Corp	New Palestine
168	0.6	Clark-Pleasant Com School Corp	Whiteland
168	0.6	Lebanon Community School Corp	Lebanon
168	0.6	West Lafayette Com School Corp	West Lafayette
171	0.5	Carmel Clay Schools	Carmel
172	0.4	Hamilton Southeastern Schools	Fishers
172	0.4	Valparaiso Community Schools	Valparaiso
174	0.3	Duneland School Corporation	Chesterton
174	0.3	Laporte Community School Corp	Laporte
176	0.1	Evansville-Vanderburgh Sch Corp	Evansville
177	0.0	Maconaquah School Corp	Bunker Hill
177	0.0	Madison Consolidated Schools	Madison
177	0.0	Zionsville Community Schools	Zionsville
n/a	n/a	Benton Community School Corp	Fowler
n/a	n/a	Centerville-Abington Com Schs	Centerville
n/a	n/a	Greensburg Community Schools	Greensburg
n/a	n/a	Northwest Allen County Schools	Fort Wayne
n/a	n/a	School Town of Munster	Munster
n/a	n/a	Southwest Dubois County Sch Corp	Huntingburg
n/a	n/a	Tri-Creek School Corp	Lowell
n/a	n/a	Union County College Corner JSD	Liberty
n/a	n/a	Warsaw Community Schools	Warsaw

Note: This section only includes districts with 1,500 or more students; All categories are ranked from high to low

Average Freshman Graduation Rate

Rank	Percent	District Name	City
1	100.0	School Town of Munster	Munster
1	100.0	Union Township School Corp	Valparaiso
3	99.8	East Porter County School Corp	Kouts
4	96.5	Batesville Community Sch Corp	Batesville
5	95.3	Hanover Community School Corp	Cedar Lake
6	95.2	Crown Point Community Sch Corp	Crown Point
7	94.2	Zionsville Community Schools	Zionsville
8	94.1	North Spencer County Sch Corp	Lincoln City
9	93.1	Northwestern Con School Corp	Fairland
10	92.6	M S D Southwest Allen County	Fort Wayne
11	92.1	Avon Community School Corp	Avon
12	91.9	Whitley County Cons Schools	Columbia City
13	91.7	Danville Community School Corp	Danville
13	91.7	Western School Corp	Russiaville
15	90.9	Southern Hancock Co CS Corp	New Palestine
16	90.7	Mooresville Con School Corp	Mooresville
16	90.7	Valparaiso Community Schools	Valparaiso
18	90.4	Porter Township School Corp	Valparaiso
19	89.9	West Lafayette Com School Corp	West Lafayette
20	89.4	Dekalb County Central United SD	Waterloo
20	89.4	M S D Mount Vernon	Mount Vernon
22	89.1	South Gibson School Corp	Fort Branch
23	88.9	Carmel Clay Schools	Carmel
23	88.9	Hamilton Southeastern Schools	Fishers
25	88.4	Noblesville Schools	Noblesville
26	88.1	Northwest Allen County Schools	Fort Wayne
27	87.9	Clark-Pleasant Com School Corp	Whiteland
27	87.9	Greater Jasper Con Schs	Jasper
29	87.2	Southwest Dubois County Sch Corp	Huntingburg
30	86.7	Brownsburg Community Sch Corp	Brownsburg
30	86.7	Frankton-Lapel Community Schs	Anderson
30	86.7	North Adams Community Schools	Decatur
33	86.5	Plymouth Community School Corp	Plymouth
34	86.3	Mount Pleasant Twp Com Sch Corp	Yorktown
35	86.2	Penn-Harris-Madison Sch Corp	Mishawaka
36	85.4	Prairie Heights Com Sch Corp	Lagrange
37	85.0	New Prairie United School Corp	New Carlisle
37	85.0	Northwestern School Corp	Kokomo
39	84.8	Sunman-Dearborn Com Sch Corp	Sunman
40	84.7	School Town of Highland	Highland
41	84.6	Tippecanoe School Corp	Lafayette
42	84.5	Franklin County Com Sch Corp	Brookville
43	84.4	Westfield-Washington Schools	Westfield
44	84.3	West Clark Community Schools	Sellersburg
45	84.2	South Dearborn Com School Corp	Aurora
46	83.8	Northern Wells Com Schools	Ossian
47	83.6	Fairfield Community Schools	Goshen
47	83.6	Mount Vernon Community Sch Corp	Fortville
49	83.4	Center Grove Com Sch Corp	Greenwood
50	83.3	Plainfield Community Sch Corp	Plainfield
51	83.2	John Glenn School Corporation	Walkerton
51	83.2	Lake Central School Corp	Saint John
53	83.0	Centerville-Abington Com Schs	Centerville
53	83.0	South Montgomery Com Sch Corp	New Market
55	82.6	Warrick County School Corp	Boonville
56	82.5	North West Hendricks Schools	Lizton
57	82.4	Greenfield-Central Com Schools	Greenfield
58	82.3	Nineveh-Hensley-Jackson United	Trafalgar
59	82.1	Southwest School Corp	Sullivan
60	81.8	School City of Hobart	Hobart
61	81.7	Greenwood Community Sch Corp	Greenwood
61	81.7	Hamilton Heights School Corp	Arcadia
63	81.5	Middlebury Community Schools	Middlebury
63	81.5	North Montgomery Com Sch Corp	Crawfordsville
65	81.2	Richland-Bean Blossom CSC	Ellettsville
66	81.1	Tri-Creek School Corp	Lowell
67	80.6	Mississinewa Community School Corp	Gas City
68	80.4	Delaware Community School Corp	Muncie
69	80.2	Merrillville Community School	Merrillville
69	80.2	Western Boone County Com SD	Thorntown
71	80.1	South Harrison Com Schools	Corydon
72	79.9	Tipton Community School Corp	Tipton
73	79.7	M S D Warren Township	Indianapolis
73	79.7	Wa-Nee Community Schools	Nappanee
75	79.6	Garrett-Keyser-Butler Com	Garrett
75	79.6	North Newton School Corp	Morocco
77	79.5	Madison-Grant United Sch Corp	Fairmount
77	79.5	Manchester Community Schools	N Manchester
79	79.2	Delphi Community School Corp	Delphi
80	79.1	Blackford County Schools	Hartford City
81	78.7	North Gibson School Corp	Princeton
81	78.7	North Harrison Com School Corp	Ramsey
83	78.5	East Allen County Schools	New Haven
84	78.3	Randolph Central School Corp	Winchester
85	78.1	Baugo Community Schools	Elkhart
86	78.0	M S D Lawrence Township	Indianapolis
87	77.6	Benton Community School Corp	Fowler
87	77.6	Griffith Public Schools	Griffith
89	77.5	Greensburg Community Schools	Greensburg
89	77.5	Portage Township Schools	Portage
91	77.4	South Madison Com Sch Corp	Pendleton
92	77.3	M S D Steuben County	Angola
93	77.2	Tippecanoe Valley School Corp	Akron
93	77.2	Warsaw Community Schools	Warsaw
95	76.8	Kankakee Valley School Corp	Wheatfield
96	76.6	Huntington County Com Sch Corp	Huntington
96	76.6	North Putnam Community Schools	Bainbridge
98	76.5	M S D Washington Twp	Indianapolis
99	76.4	Southeastern School Corp	Walton
100	76.3	East Washington School Corp	Pekin
101	76.2	Logansport Community Sch Corp	Logansport
101	76.2	Oak Hill United School Corp	Converse
101	76.2	Whitko Community School Corp	Pierceton
104	75.9	Crawford County Com School Corp	Marengo
104	75.9	Monroe County Com Sch Corp	Bloomington
106	75.6	Brownstown Cnt Com Sch Corp	Brownstown
106	75.6	New Castle Community Sch Corp	New Castle
108	75.4	Decatur County Com Schools	Greensburg
109	74.8	New Albany-Floyd County Con Sch	New Albany
110	74.7	Duneland School Corporation	Chesterton
111	74.6	Concord Community Schools	Elkhart
111	74.6	Dekalb County Eastern Com SD	Butler
113	74.5	Tell City-Troy Twp School Corp	Tell City
114	74.0	M S D Martinsville Schools	Martinsville
115	73.8	East Noble School Corp	Kendallville
115	73.8	Pike County School Corp	Petersburg
115	73.8	Seymour Community Schools	Seymour
118	73.7	Eastbrook Community Sch Corp	Marion
119	73.5	Evansville-Vanderburgh Sch Corp	Evansville
120	73.4	Union County College Corner JSD	Liberty
121	73.1	Salem Community Schools	Salem
122	72.9	Peru Community Schools	Peru
122	72.9	School Town of Speedway	Speedway
124	72.8	Bartholomew Con School Corp	Columbus
124	72.8	Rochester Community Sch Corp	Rochester
126	72.6	Mitchell Community Schools	Mitchell
126	72.6	Rensselaer Central School Corp	Rensselaer
128	72.4	Vincennes Community Sch Corp	Vincennes
128	72.4	Washington Com Schools Inc	Washington
130	72.1	Brown County School Corporation	Nashville
131	72.0	Paoli Community School Corp	Paoli
132	71.9	Greencastle Community Sch Corp	Greencastle
133	71.6	Franklin Township Com Sch Corp	Indianapolis
133	71.6	Maconaquah School Corp	Bunker Hill
135	71.5	Franklin Community School Corp	Franklin
135	71.5	Lebanon Community School Corp	Lebanon
137	71.1	Mill Creek Community Sch Corp	Clayton
138	70.9	West Noble School Corporation	Ligonier
139	70.8	Vigo County School Corp	Terre Haute
139	70.8	Wawasee Community School Corp	Syracuse
141	70.7	Elwood Community School Corp	Elwood
142	70.5	Lawrenceburg Com School Corp	Lawrenceburg
143	70.1	M S D Wabash County Schools	Wabash
144	70.0	Lakeland School Corporation	Lagrange
145	69.6	South Vermillion Com Sch Corp	Clinton
146	69.5	Crawfordsville Com Schools	Crawfordsville
147	69.4	North Lawrence Com Schools	Bedford
148	69.3	Spencer-Owen Community Schools	Spencer
149	69.2	Madison Consolidated Schools	Madison
150	69.1	Fort Wayne Community Schools	Fort Wayne
151	68.9	Clay Community Schools	Knightsville
152	68.6	Alexandria Com School Corp	Alexandria
152	68.6	Laporte Community School Corp	Laporte
152	68.6	Rush County Schools	Rushville
155	68.1	Jay School Corp	Portland
156	67.8	Scott County SD 2	Scottsburg
157	66.9	Shelby Eastern Schools	Shelbyville
158	66.4	M S D Decatur Township	Indianapolis
159	66.2	Westview School Corporation	Topeka
160	65.5	Lafayette School Corporation	Lafayette
160	65.5	Shelbyville Central Schools	Shelbyville
162	65.1	Kokomo-Center Twp Con Sch Corp	Kokomo
162	65.1	M S D Perry Township	Indianapolis
164	65.0	Northeast School Corp	Hymera
165	64.9	M S D Pike Township	Indianapolis
165	64.9	Twin Lakes School Corp	Monticello
167	64.8	Goshen Community Schools	Goshen
168	64.0	Greater Clark County Schools	Jeffersonville
169	63.4	M S D Wayne Township	Indianapolis
170	62.9	Knox Community School Corp	Knox
171	61.5	Community Schools of Frankfort	Frankfort
171	61.5	Fayette County School Corp	Connersville
173	60.5	Switzerland County School Corp	Vevay
174	60.3	Beech Grove City Schools	Beech Grove
174	60.3	Marion Community Schools	Marion
174	60.3	Michigan City Area Schools	Michigan City
177	60.1	Jennings County Schools	North Vernon
178	60.0	South Bend Community Sch Corp	South Bend
179	57.7	Anderson Community School Corp	Anderson
180	57.1	School City of Mishawaka	Mishawaka
181	55.5	Elkhart Community Schools	Elkhart
182	55.0	Muncie Community Schools	Muncie
183	54.5	Lake Ridge Schools	Gary
184	53.1	School City of Hammond	Hammond
185	49.0	Gary Community School Corp	Gary
185	49.0	Richmond Community School Corp	Richmond
187	48.6	School City of East Chicago	East Chicago
188	40.4	Indianapolis Public Schools	Indianapolis

Note: This section only includes districts with 1,500 or more students; All categories are ranked from high to low

Indiana
Grade 4
Public Schools

The Nation's Report Card — Mathematics 2009
Snapshot State Report

Overall Results

- In 2009, the average score of fourth-grade students in Indiana was 243. This was higher than the average score of 239 for public school students in the nation.
- The average score for students in Indiana in 2009 (243) was lower than their average score in 2007 (245) and was higher than their average score in 1992 (221).
- In 2009, the score gap between students in Indiana at the 75th percentile and students at the 25th percentile was 34 points. This performance gap was not significantly different from that of 1992 (38 points).
- The percentage of students in Indiana who performed at or above the NAEP *Proficient* level was 42 percent in 2009. This percentage was smaller than that in 2007 (46 percent) and was greater than that in 1992 (16 percent).
- The percentage of students in Indiana who performed at or above the NAEP *Basic* level was 87 percent in 2009. This percentage ' was not significantly different from that in 2007 (89 percent) and ' was greater than that in 1992 (60 percent). '

Achievement-Level Percentages and Average Score Results

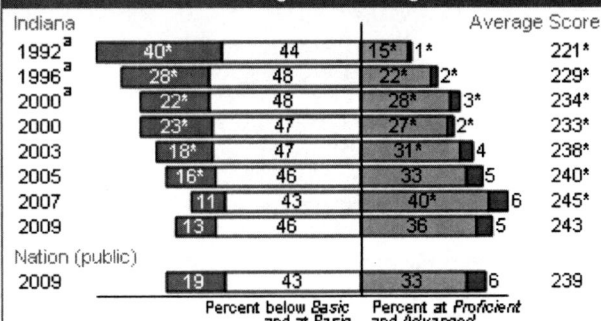

Indiana				Average Score
1992[a]	40*	44	15* 1*	221*
1996[a]	28*	48	22* 2*	229*
2000[a]	22*	48	28* 3*	234*
2000	23*	47	27* 2*	233*
2003	18*	47	31* 4	238*
2005	16*	46	33 5	240*
2007	11	43	40* 6	245*
2009	13	46	36 5	243
Nation (public)				
2009	19	43	33 6	239

Percent below *Basic* and at *Basic*   Percent at *Proficient* and *Advanced*

■ Below *Basic* □ *Basic* ▨ *Proficient* ■ *Advanced*

* Significantly different (*p* < .05) from state's results in 2009.
[a] Accommodations not permitted.
NOTE: Detail may not sum to totals because of rounding.

Compare the Average Score in 2009 to Other States/Jurisdictions

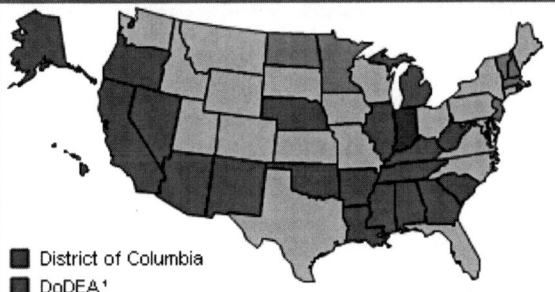

■ District of Columbia
■ DoDEA[1]

[1] Department of Defense Education Activity schools (domestic and overseas).

In 2009, the average score in Indiana was
- lower than those in 6 states/jurisdictions
- higher than those in 24 states/jurisdictions
- not significantly different from those in 21 states/jurisdictions

Compare the Average Score to Nation (public)

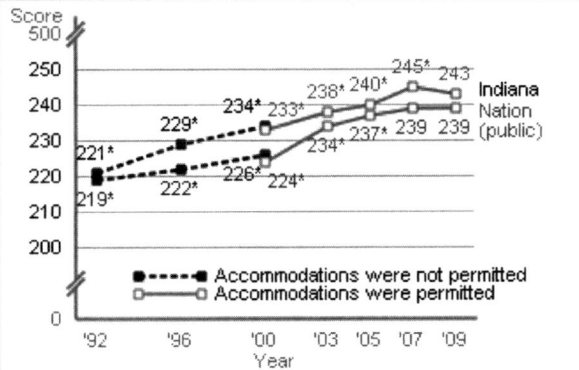

●----● Accommodations were not permitted
○——○ Accommodations were permitted

* Significantly different (*p* < .05) from 2009.

Results for Student Groups in 2009

Reporting Groups	Percent of students	Avg. score	Percentages at or above		Percent at Advanced
			Basic	*Proficient*	
Gender '					
Male 51		243	87	42	6
Female	49	242	88	41	4
Race/Ethnicity					
White 76		247	91	48	6
Black 11		222	66	13	#
Hispanic 7		230	77	23	2
Asian/Pacific Islander	2	‡	‡	‡	‡
American Indian/Alaska Native	#	‡	‡	‡	‡
National School Lunch Program '					
Eligible 45		232	78	26	2
Not eligible	55	251	94	54	9

Rounds to zero.   ‡ Reporting standards not met.

NOTE: Detail may not sum to totals because of rounding, and because the "Information not available" category for the National School Lunch Program, which provides free/reduced-price lunches, and the "Unclassified" category for race/ethnicity are not displayed.

Score Gaps for Student Groups

- In 2009, male students in Indiana had an average score that was not significantly different from that of female students. This performance gap was not significantly different from that in 1992 (3 points). '
- In 2009, Black students had an average score that was 24 points lower than that of White students. This performance gap was not significantly different from that in 1992 (29 points).
- In 2009, Hispanic students had an average score that was 16 points lower than that of White students. Data are not ' reported for Hispanic students in 1992, because reporting standards were not met.
- In 2009, students who were eligible for free/reduced-price school lunch, an indicator of poverty, had an average score that was 18 points lower than that of students who were not eligible for free/reduced-price school lunch. This performance gap was not significantly different from that in 1996 (23 points).

NOTE: Statistical comparisons are calculated on the basis of unrounded scale scores or percentages.

The Nation's Report Card Reading 2009 State Snapshot Report

Indiana
Grade 4
Public Schools

Overall Results

- In 2009, the average score of fourth-grade students in Indiana was 223. This was higher than the average score of 220 for public school students in the nation.
- The average score for students in Indiana in 2009 (223) was not significantly different from their average score in 2007 (222) and was not significantly different from their average score in 1992 (221).
- In 2009, the score gap between students in Indiana at the 75th percentile and students at the 25th percentile was 43 points. This performance gap was not significantly different from that of 1992 (41 points).
- The percentage of students in Indiana who performed at or above the NAEP *Proficient* level was 34 percent in 2009. This percentage was not significantly different from that in 2007 (33 percent) and was not significantly different from that in 1992 (30 percent).
- The percentage of students in Indiana who performed at or above the NAEP *Basic* level was 70 percent in 2009. This percentage was not significantly different from that in 2007 (68 percent) and was not significantly different from that in 1992 (68 percent).

Achievement Level Percentages and Average Score Results

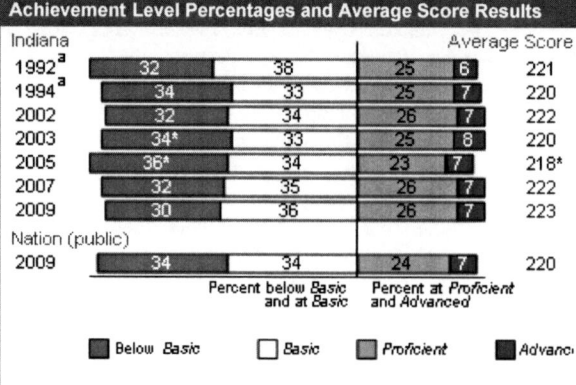

* Significantly different ($p < .05$) from state's results in 2009.
a Accommodations not permitted.

NOTE: Detail may not sum to totals because of rounding.

Compare the Average Score in 2009 to Other States/Jurisdictions

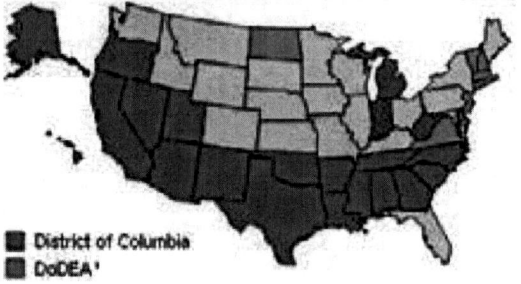

' Department of Defense Education Activity schools (domestic and overseas).

In 2009, the average score in Indiana was
- lower than those in 9 states/jurisdictions
- higher than those in 21 states/jurisdictions
- not significantly different from those in 21 states/jurisdictions

Average Scores for State/Jurisdiction and Nation (public)

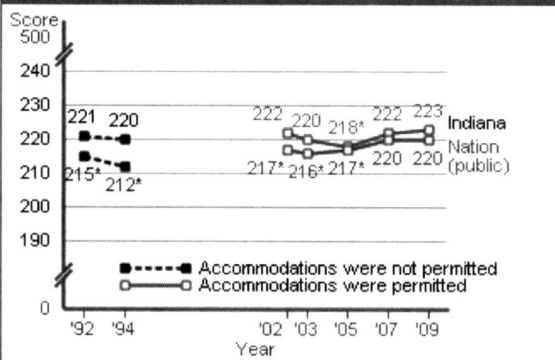

* Significantly different ($p < .05$) from 2009.

Results for Student Groups in 2009

Reporting Groups	Percent of students	Avg. score	Percentages at or above Basic	Proficient	Percent at Advanced
Gender					
Male	51	218	65	29	6
Female	49	227	75	38	8
Race/Ethnicity					
White	77	227	75	38	9
Black	11	206	51	15	2
Hispanic	6	203	50	15	2
Asian/Pacific Islander	1	‡	‡	‡	‡
American Indian/Alaska Native	#	‡	‡	‡	‡
National School Lunch Program					
Eligible	44	210	57	20	2
Not eligible	56	232	80	45	11

Rounds to zero. ‡ Reporting standards not met.

NOTE: Detail may not sum to totals because of rounding, and because the "Information not available" category for the National School Lunch Program, which provides free/reduced-price lunches, and the "Unclassified" category for race/ethnicity are not displayed.

Score Gaps for Student Groups

- In 2009, female students in Indiana had an average score that was higher than that of male students.
- In 2009, Black students had an average score that was 21 points lower than that of White students. This performance gap was not significantly different from that in 1992 (25 points).
- In 2009, Hispanic students had an average score that was 24 points lower than that of White students. Data are not reported for Hispanic students in 1992, because reporting standards were not met.
- In 2009, students who were eligible for free/reduced-price school lunch, an indicator of low income, had an average score that was 22 points lower than that of students who were not eligible for free/reduced-price school lunch. This performance gap was not significantly different from that in 2002 (23 points).

NOTE: Statistical comparisons are calculated on the basis of unrounded scale scores or percentages.
SOURCE: U.S. Department of Education, Institute of Education Sciences, National Center for Education Statistics, National Assessment of Educational Progress (NAEP), various years, 1992–2009 Reading Assessments.

The writing assessment of the National Assessment of Educational Progress (NAEP) measures narrative, informative, and persuasive writing–three purposes identified in the NAEP framework. The NAEP writing scale ranges from 0 to 300.

Overall Writing Results for Indiana

- The average scale score for fourth-grade students in Indiana was 154.
- Indiana's average score (154) was not found to be significantly different[1] from that of the nation's public schools (153).
- Students' average scale scores in Indiana were higher than those in 24 jurisdictions[2], not significantly different from those in 16 jurisdictions, and lower than those in 7 jurisdictions.
- The percentage of students who performed at or above the NAEP *Proficient* level was 26 percent. The percentage of students who performed at or above the *Basic* level was 88 percent.

Student Percentage at Each Achievement Level

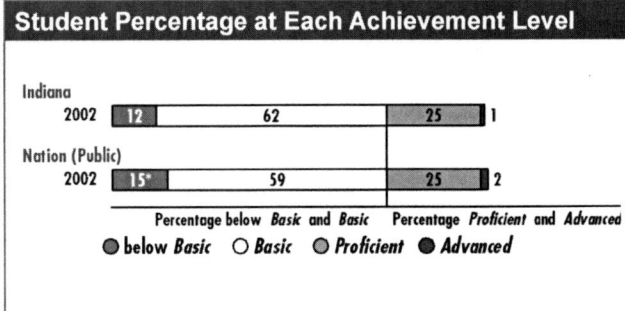

Performance of NAEP Reporting Groups in Indiana

Reporting groups	Percentage of students	Average Score	Below *Basic*	*Basic*	*Proficient*	*Advanced*
Male	50	144	18	65	16	#
Female	50	163	7 ↓	58	33	3
White	80	157 ↓	11	61 ↑	27	2 ↓
Black	13	138	22	66	11	#
Hispanic	4	144	21	62	17	#
Asian/Pacific Islander	1	---	---	---	---	---
American Indian/Alaska Native	1	---	---	---	---	---
Free/reduced-priced school lunch						
Eligible	33	141	21	65	14	#
Not eligible	60	160 ↓	9	60 ↑	29 ↓	2 ↓
Information not available	7	167 ↑	6 ↓	55	37	2

Average Score Gaps Between Selected Groups

- Female students in Indiana had an average score that was higher than that of male students (19 points). This performance gap was not significantly different from that of the Nation (18 points).
- White students had an average score that was higher than that of Black students (18 points). This performance gap was not significantly different from that of the Nation (20 points).
- White students had an average score that was higher than that of Hispanic students (13 points). This performance gap was not significantly different from that of the Nation (19 points).
- Students who were not eligible for free/reduced-price school lunch had an average score that was higher than that of students who were eligible (18 points). This performance gap was not significantly different from that of the Nation (22 points).

Writing Scale Scores at Selected Percentiles

Scale Score Distribution

	25th Percentile	50th Percentile	75th Percentile
Indiana	*131* ↑	*154*	*177*
Nation (Public)	*128*	*153*	*178*

An examination of scores at different percentiles on the 0-300 NAEP writing scale at each grade indicates how well students at lower, middle, and higher levels of the distribution performed. For example, the data above shows that 75 percent of students in public schools nationally scored below *178*, while 75 percent of students in Indiana scored below *177*.

Percentage rounds to zero.
* Significantly different from Indiana.
--- Reporting standards not met; sample size insufficient to permit a reliable estimate.
↑ Significantly higher than, ↓ lower than appropriate subgroup in the nation (public).
[1] Comparisons (higher/lower/not different) are based on statistical tests. The .05 level was used for testing statistical significance.
[2] "Jurisdictions" includes participating states and other jurisdictions (such as Guam or the District of Columbia).
NOTE: Detail may not sum to totals because of rounding. Score gaps are calculated based on differences between unrounded average scale scores.
Visit http://nces.ed.gov/nationsreportcard/states/ for additional results and detailed information.
SOURCE: U.S. Department of Education, Institute of Education Sciences, National Center for Education Statistics, National Assessment of Educational Progress (NAEP), 2002 Writing Assessment.

The National Assessment of Educational Progress (NAEP) assesses science in two major dimensions: Fields of Science (Earth, Physical, and Life) and Knowing and Doing Science (Conceptual Understanding, Scientific Investigation, and Practical Reasoning). The NAEP science scale ranges from 0 to 300. Scales are created separately for each grade.

Overall Science Results for Indiana

- In 2005, the average scale score for fourth-grade students in Indiana was 152. This was not significantly different from their average score in 2000 (154).[1]
- Indiana's average score (152) in 2005 was higher than that of the nation's public schools (149).
- Of the 44 states and one jurisdiction that participated in the 2005 fourth-grade assessment, students' average scale score in Indiana was higher than those in 15 jurisdictions, not significantly different from those in 11 jurisdictions, and lower than those in 18 jurisdictions.[2]
- The percentage of students in Indiana who performed at or above the NAEP *Proficient* level was 27 percent in 2005. This percentage was not significantly different from that in 2000 (32 percent).
- The percentage of students in Indiana who performed at or above the NAEP *Basic* level was 70 percent in 2005. This percentage was not significantly different from that in 2000 (74 percent).

Student Percentages at NAEP Achievement Levels

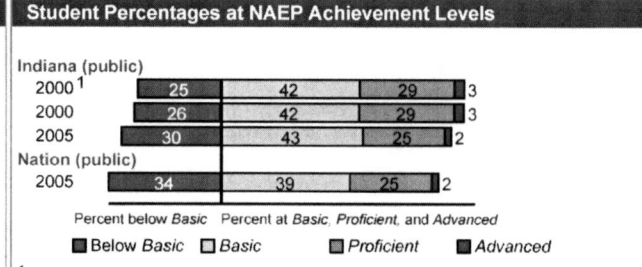

Percent below *Basic*   Percent at *Basic*, *Proficient*, and *Advanced*

■ Below *Basic*   □ *Basic*   ▨ *Proficient*   ■ *Advanced*

[1] Accommodations were not permitted for this assessment.

NOTE: The NAEP grade 4 science achievement levels correspond to the following scale points: Below *Basic*, 137 or lower; *Basic*, 138–169; *Proficient*, 170–204; *Advanced*, 205 or above.

Performance of NAEP Reporting Groups in Indiana: 2005

Reporting groups	Percent of students	Average score	Percent below *Basic*	Percent of students at or above *Basic*	*Proficient*	Percent *Advanced*
Male	50	153	29	71	29	3
Female	50	150	31	69	25	1
White	74↓	158	20	80	33	2
Black	16↑	126	67	33	5	#
Hispanic	5	138	54	46	13	1
Asian/Pacific Islander	1	‡	‡	‡	‡	‡
American Indian/Alaska Native	#	‡	‡	‡	‡	‡
Eligible for free/reduced-price school lunch	42↑	139	46	54	13	#
Not eligible for free/reduced-price school lunch	57	161	18	82	38	3

Average Score Gaps Between Selected Groups

- In 2005, male students in Indiana had an average score that was higher than that of female students by 3 points. In 2000, there was no significant difference between the average score of male and female students.
- In 2005, Black students had an average score that was lower than that of White students by 32 points. In 2000, the average score for Black students was lower than that of White students by 32 points.
- In 2005, Hispanic students had an average score that was lower than that of White students by 21 points. Data are not reported for Hispanic students in 2000, because reporting standards were not met. Therefore, the performance gap results are not reported.
- In 2005, students who were eligible for free/reduced-price school lunch, an indicator of poverty, had an average score that was lower than that of students who were not eligible for free/reduced-price school lunch by 21 points. In 2000, the average score for students who were eligible for free/reduced-price school lunch was lower than the score of those not eligible by 24 points.
- In 2005, the score gap between students at the 75th percentile and students at the 25th percentile was 38 points. In 2000, the score gap between students at the 75th percentile and students at the 25th percentile was 38 points.

Science Scale Scores at Selected Percentiles

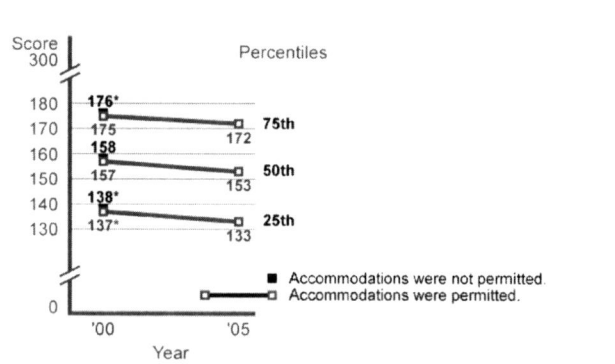

Scores at selected percentiles on the NAEP science scale indicate how well students at lower, middle, and higher levels performed.

The estimate rounds to zero.   ‡ Reporting standards not met.

* Significantly different from 2005.   ↑ Significantly higher than 2000. ↓ Significantly lower than 2000.

[1] Comparisons (higher/lower/not different) are based on statistical tests. The .05 level was used for testing statistical significance. Comparisons across jurisdictions and comparisons with the nation or within a jurisdiction across years may be affected by differences in exclusion rates for students with disabilities (SD) and English language learners (ELL). The exclusion rates for SD and ELL in Indiana were 2 percent and 1 percent in 2005, respectively. Statistical comparisons are calculated on the basis of unrounded scale scores or percentages.

[2] "Jurisdiction" refers to states and the Department of Defense Education Activity schools.

NOTE: Detail may not sum to totals because of rounding and because the "Information not available" category for free/reduced-price school lunch and the "Unclassifed" category for race/ethnicity are not displayed. Visit http://nces.ed.gov/nationsreportcard/states/ for additional results and detailed information.

SOURCE: U.S. Department of Education, Institute of Education Sciences, National Center for Education Statistics, National Assessment of Educational Progress (NAEP), 2000 and 2005 Science Assessments.

 NATIONAL CENTER FOR EDUCATION STATISTICS Institute of Education Sciences

 The Nation's Report Card Mathematics 2009 Snapshot State Report

Indiana
Grade 8
Public Schools

Overall Results

- In 2009, the average score of eighth-grade students in Indiana was 287. This was higher than the average score of 282 for public school students in the nation.
- The average score for students in Indiana in 2009 (287) was not significantly different from their average score in 2007 (285) and was higher than their average score in 1990 (267).
- In 2009, the score gap between students in Indiana at the 75th percentile and students at the 25th percentile was 44 points. This performance gap was not significantly different from that of 1990 (44 points).
- The percentage of students in Indiana who performed at or above the NAEP *Proficient* level was 36 percent in 2009. This percentage was not significantly different from that in 2007 (35 percent) and was greater than that in 1990 (17 percent). '
- The percentage of students in Indiana who performed at or above the NAEP *Basic* level was 78 percent in 2009. This percentage was not significantly different from that in 2007 (76 percent) and ' was greater than that in 1990 (56 percent). '

Achievement-Level Percentages and Average Score Results

Indiana		Average Score
1990[a]	44* / 40 / 14* / 3*	267*
1992[a]	40* / 40 / 17* / 3*	270*
1996[a]	32* / 44 / 21* / 3*	276*
2000[a]	24 / 45 / 26 / 5*	283*
2000	26 / 44 / 24* / 5*	281*
2003	26* / 43 / 25* / 5*	281*
2005	26* / 44 / 25* / 5*	282*
2007	24 / 41 / 28 / 7	285
2009	22 / 42 / 29 / 7	287
Nation (public)		
2009	29 / 39 / 25 / 7	282

Percent below *Basic* and at *Basic* / Percent at *Proficient* and *Advanced*

■ Below *Basic* □ *Basic* ▨ *Proficient* ■ *Advanced*

* Significantly different (*p* < .05) from state's results in 2009. '
a Accommodations not permitted. '
NOTE: Detail may not sum to totals because of rounding. '

Compare the Average Score in 2009 to Other States/Jurisdictions

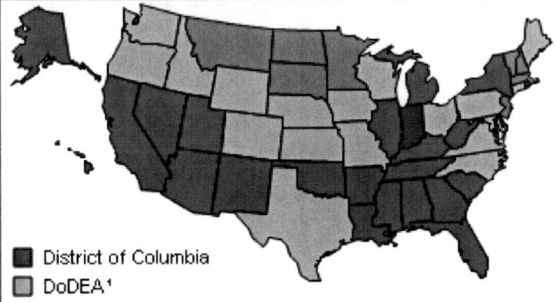

■ District of Columbia
▨ DoDEA[1]

[1] Department of Defense Education Activity schools (domestic and overseas).

In 2009, the average score in **Indiana** was
- lower than those in 8 states/jurisdictions
- higher than those in 24 states/jurisdictions
- not significantly different from those in 19 states/jurisdictions

Compare the Average Score to Nation (public)

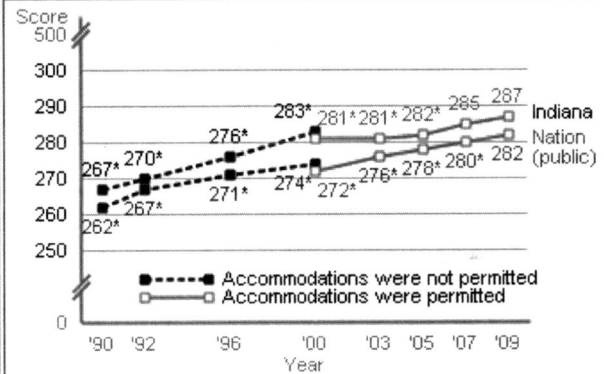

- - - ■ Accommodations were not permitted
—□— Accommodations were permitted

* Significantly different (*p* < .05) from 2009.

Results for Student Groups in 2009

Reporting Groups	Percent of students	Avg. score	Percentages at or above Basic	Proficient	Percent at Advanced
Gender '					
Male 50		288	79	39	8
Female	50	285	76	34	7
Race/Ethnicity					
White 76		291	83	41	8
Black 12		266	54	14	1
Hispanic 7		273	64	19	2
Asian/Pacific Islander	2	‡	‡	‡	‡
American Indian/Alaska Native	#	‡	‡	‡	‡
National School Lunch Program '					
Eligible 37		273	64	21	2
Not eligible	63	295	86	45	10

Rounds to zero.   ‡ Reporting standards not met.

NOTE: Detail may not sum to totals because of rounding, and because the "Information not available" category for the National School Lunch Program, which provides free/reduced-price lunches, and the "Unclassified" category for race/ethnicity are not displayed.

Score Gaps for Student Groups

- In 2009, male students in Indiana had an average score that was not significantly different from that of female students. This performance gap was not significantly different from that in 1990 (5 points). '
- In 2009, Black students had an average score that was 25 points lower than that of White students. This performance gap was not significantly different from that in 1990 (28 points).
- In 2009, Hispanic students had an average score that was 18 points lower than that of White students. Data are not ' reported for Hispanic students in 1990, because reporting standards were not met.
- In 2009, students who were eligible for free/reduced-price school lunch, an indicator of poverty, had an average score that was 22 points lower than that of students who were not eligible for free/reduced-price school lunch. This performance gap was not significantly different from that in 1996 (25 points).

NOTE: Statistical comparisons are calculated on the basis of unrounded scale scores or percentages.

Indiana
Grade 8
Public Schools

The Nation's Report Card — Reading 2009 — State Snapshot Report

Overall Results

- In 2009, the average score of eighth-grade students in Indiana was 266. This was higher than the average score of 262 for public school students in the nation.
- The average score for students in Indiana in 2009 (266) was not significantly different from their average score in 2007 (264) and was not significantly different from their average score in 2002 (265).
- In 2009, the score gap between students in Indiana at the 75th percentile and students at the 25th percentile was 40 points. This performance gap was not significantly different from that of 2002 (42 points).
- The percentage of students in Indiana who performed at or above the NAEP *Proficient* level was 32 percent in 2009. This percentage was not significantly different from that in 2007 (31 percent) and was not significantly different from that in 2002 (32 percent).
- The percentage of students in Indiana who performed at or above the NAEP *Basic* level was 79 percent in 2009. This percentage was not significantly different from that in 2007 (76 percent) and was not significantly different from that in 2002 (77 percent).

Achievement-Level Percentages and Average Score Results

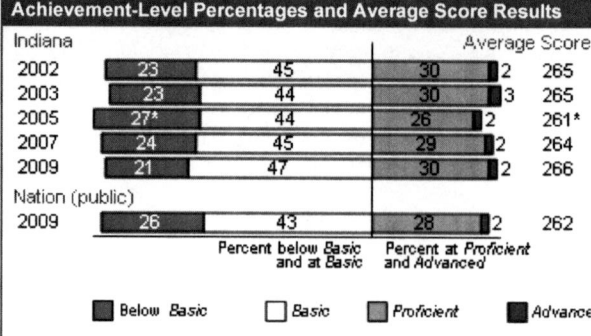

Indiana				Average Score
2002	23	45	30	2	265
2003	23	44	30	3	265
2005	27*	44	26	2	261*
2007	24	45	29	2	264
2009	21	47	30	2	266
Nation (public)				
2009	26	43	28	2	262

Percent below *Basic* and at *Basic*   Percent at *Proficient* and *Advanced*

■ Below *Basic*   □ *Basic*   ▨ *Proficient*   ■ *Advance*

* Significantly different (*p* < .05) from state's results in 2009.

NOTE: Detail may not sum to totals because of rounding.

Compare the Average Score in 2009 to Other States/Jurisdictions

■ District of Columbia
■ DoDEA[1]

[1] Department of Defense Education Activity schools (domestic and overseas).

In 2009, the average score in **Indiana** was
- lower than those in 11 states/jurisdictions
- higher than those in 20 states/jurisdictions
- not significantly different from those in 20 states/jurisdictions

Average Scores for State/Jurisdiction and Nation (public)

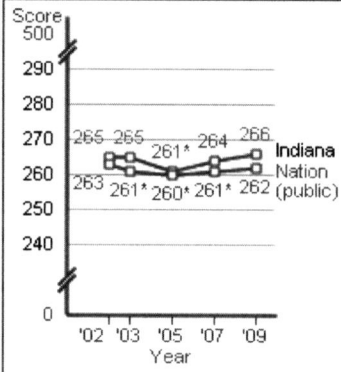

Indiana: 265, 265, 261*, 264, 266
Nation (public): 263, 261*, 260*, 261*, 262

Year: '02 '03 '05 '07 '09

* Significantly different (*p* < .05) from 2009.

Results for Student Groups in 2009

Reporting Groups	Percent of students	Avg. score	Percentages at or above Basic	Percentages at or above Proficient	Percent at Advanced
Gender					
Male	50	263	76	29	2
Female	50	269	82	35	3
Race/Ethnicity					
White	76	269	83	36	3
Black	12	250	60	15	#
Hispanic	6	251	66	15	#
Asian/Pacific Islander	1	‡	‡	‡	‡
American Indian/Alaska Native	#	‡	‡	‡	‡
National School Lunch Program					
Eligible	37	254	68	18	#
Not eligible	63	273	85	40	3

\# Rounds to zero.   ‡ Reporting standards not met.

NOTE: Detail may not sum to totals because of rounding, and because the "Information not available" category for the National School Lunch Program, which provides free/reduced-price lunches, and the "Unclassified" category for race/ethnicity are not displayed.

Score Gaps for Student Groups

- In 2009, female students in Indiana had an average score that was higher than that of male students.
- In 2009, Black students had an average score that was 19 points lower than that of White students. This performance gap was not significantly different from that in 2002 (20 points).
- In 2009, Hispanic students had an average score that was 18 points lower than that of White students. Data are not reported for Hispanic students in 2002, because reporting standards were not met.
- In 2009, students who were eligible for free/reduced-price school lunch, an indicator of low income, had an average score that was 18 points lower than that of students who were not eligible for free/reduced-price school lunch. This performance gap was not significantly different from that in 2002 (16 points).

NOTE: Statistical comparisons are calculated on the basis of unrounded scale scores or percentages.

Indiana
Grade 8
Public Schools

NCES 2008-470IN8   State Snapshot Report

The National Assessment of Educational Progress (NAEP) assesses writing for three purposes identified in the NAEP framework: narrative, informative, and persuasive. The NAEP writing scale ranges from 0 to 300.

Overall Writing Results for Indiana

- In 2007, the average scale score for eighth-grade students in Indiana was 155. This was higher than their average score in 2002 (150).[1]
- Indiana's average score (155) in 2007 was not significantly different from that of the nation's public schools (154).
- Of the 45 states and one other jurisdiction that participated in the 2007 eighth-grade assessment, students' average scale score in Indiana was higher than those in 13 jurisdictions, not significantly different from those in 21 jurisdictions, and lower than those in 11 jurisdictions.[2]
- The percentage of students in Indiana who performed at or above the NAEP *Proficient* level was 30 percent in 2007. This percentage was not significantly different from that in 2002 (26 percent).
- The percentage of students in Indiana who performed at or above the NAEP *Basic* level was 89 percent in 2007. This percentage was greater than that in 2002 (85 percent).

Percentages at NAEP Achievement Levels and Average Score

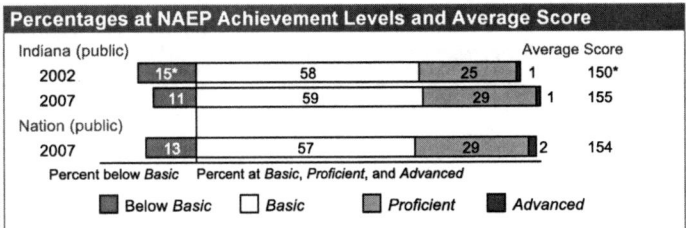

NOTE: The NAEP grade 8 writing achievement levels correspond to the following scale points: Below *Basic*, 113 or lower; *Basic*, 114–172; *Proficient*, 173–223; *Advanced*, 224 or above.

Performance of NAEP Reporting Groups in Indiana: 2007

Reporting groups	Percent of students	Average score	Percent below *Basic*	Percent of students at or above Basic	*Proficient*	Percent *Advanced*
Male	50	144↑	16↓	84↑	17	#
Female	50	165	5	95	42	1
White	78↓	158↑	9↓	91↑	33	1
Black	12	140↑	18↓	82↑	12	#
Hispanic	6↑	139	22	78	18	#
Asian/Pacific Islander	1	‡	‡	‡	‡	‡
American Indian/Alaska Native	#	‡	‡	‡	‡	‡
Eligible for National School Lunch Program	35↑	142	18	82	17	#
Not eligible for National School Lunch Program	65	161↑	7↓	93↑	37	1

Average Score Gaps Between Selected Groups

- In 2007, male students in Indiana had an average score that was lower than that of female students by 22 points. This performance gap was not significantly different from that of 2002 (24 points).
- In 2007, Black students had an average score that was lower than that of White students by 18 points. This performance gap was not significantly different from that of 2002 (27 points).
- In 2007, Hispanic students had an average score that was lower than that of White students by 19 points. Data are not reported for Hispanic students in 2002, because reporting standards were not met. Therefore, the performance gap results are not reported.
- In 2007, students who were eligible for free/reduced-price school lunch, an indicator of poverty, had an average score that was lower than that of students who were not eligible for free/reduced-price school lunch by 19 points. This performance gap was not significantly different from that of 2002 (17 points).
- In 2007, the score gap between students at the 75th percentile and students at the 25th percentile was 42 points. This performance gap was not significantly different from that of 2002 (47 points).

Writing Scores at Selected Percentiles in Indiana

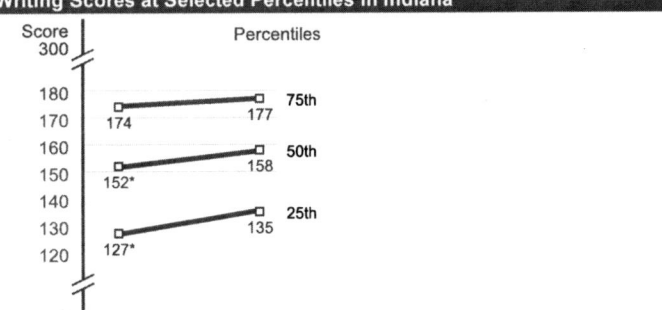

NOTE: Scores at selected percentiles on the NAEP writing scale indicate how well students at lower, middle, and higher levels performed.

Rounds to zero.
‡ Reporting standards not met.
* Significantly different from 2007.
↑ Significantly higher than 2002. ↓ Significantly lower than 2002.
[1] Comparisons (higher/lower/narrower/wider/not different) are based on statistical tests. The .05 level with appropriate adjustments for multiple comparisons was used for testing statistical significance. Statistical comparisons are calculated on the basis of unrounded scale scores or percentages. Comparisons across jurisdictions and comparisons with the nation or within a jurisdiction across years may be affected by differences in exclusion rates for students with disabilities (SD) and English language learners (ELL). The exclusion rates for SD and ELL in Indiana were 3 percent and 1 percent in 2007, respectively. For more information on NAEP significance testing, see http://nces.ed.gov/nationsreportcard/writing/interpret-results.asp#statistical.
[2] "Jurisdiction" refers to states, the District of Columbia, and the Department of Defense Education Activity schools.
NOTE: Detail may not sum to totals because of rounding and because the "Information not available" category for the National School Lunch Program, which provides free and reduced-price lunches, and the "Unclassified" category for race/ethnicity are not displayed. Visit http://nces.ed.gov/nationsreportcard/states/ for additional results and detailed information.
SOURCE: U.S. Department of Education, Institute of Education Sciences, National Center for Education Statistics, National Assessment of Educational Progress (NAEP), 2002 and 2007 Writing Assessments.

The Nation's Report Card

State **Science** 2005

Indiana
Grade 8
Public Schools

Snapshot Report

NCES 2006-467IN8

The National Assessment of Educational Progress (NAEP) assesses science in two major dimensions: Fields of Science (Earth, Physical, and Life) and Knowing and Doing Science (Conceptual Understanding, Scientific Investigation, and Practical Reasoning). The NAEP science scale ranges from 0 to 300. Scales are created separately for each grade.

Overall Science Results for Indiana

- In 2005, the average scale score for eighth-grade students in Indiana was 150. This was lower than their average score in 2000 (154), and was not significantly different from their average score in 1996 (153).[1]

- Indiana's average score (150) in 2005 was higher than that of the nation's public schools (147).

- Of the 44 states and one jurisdiction that participated in the 2005 eighth-grade assessment, students' average scale score in Indiana was higher than those in 18 jurisdictions, not significantly different from those in 8 jurisdictions, and lower than those in 18 jurisdictions.[2]

- The percentage of students in Indiana who performed at or above the NAEP *Proficient* level was 29 percent in 2005. This percentage was not significantly different from that in 2000 (33 percent), and was not significantly different from that in 1996 (30 percent).

- The percentage of students in Indiana who performed at or above the NAEP *Basic* level was 62 percent in 2005. This percentage was not significantly different from that in 2000 (66 percent), and was not significantly different from that in 1996 (65 percent).

Student Percentages at NAEP Achievement Levels

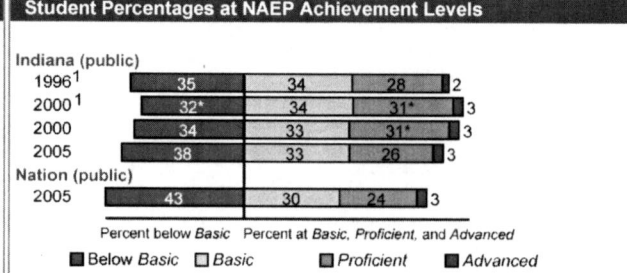

Percent below *Basic*   Percent at *Basic, Proficient,* and *Advanced*

■ Below *Basic*   □ *Basic*   ■ *Proficient*   ■ *Advanced*

[1] Accommodations were not permitted for this assessment.

NOTE: The NAEP grade 8 science achievement levels correspond to the following scale points: Below *Basic*, 142 or lower; *Basic*, 143–169; *Proficient*, 170–207; *Advanced*, 208 or above.

Performance of NAEP Reporting Groups in Indiana: 2005

Reporting groups	Percent of students	Average score	Percent below *Basic*	Percent of students at or above *Basic*	Percent of students at or above *Proficient*	Percent *Advanced*
Male	49	154	34	66	33	4
Female	51	147↓	41	59	25↓	2
White	80	156	30	70	34	3
Black	13	119	77	23	4	#
Hispanic	4	131	65	35	10	#
Asian/Pacific Islander	1	‡	‡	‡	‡	‡
American Indian/Alaska Native	#	‡	‡	‡	‡	‡
Eligible for free/reduced-price school lunch	36↑	135	58	42	15	1
Not eligible for free/reduced-price school lunch	62	159	27	73	37	4

Average Score Gaps Between Selected Groups

- In 2005, male students in Indiana had an average score that was higher than that of female students by 7 points. In 1996, there was no significant difference between the average score of male and female students.

- In 2005, Black students had an average score that was lower than that of White students by 37 points. In 1996, the average score for Black students was lower than that of White students by 32 points.

- In 2005, Hispanic students had an average score that was lower than that of White students by 25 points. Data are not reported for Hispanic students in 1996, because reporting standards were not met. Therefore, the performance gap results are not reported.

- In 2005, students who were eligible for free/reduced-price school lunch, an indicator of poverty, had an average score that was lower than that of students who were not eligible for free/reduced-price school lunch by 24 points. In 1996, the average score for students who were eligible for free/reduced-price school lunch was lower than the score of those not eligible by 22 points.

- In 2005, the score gap between students at the 75th percentile and students at the 25th percentile was 44 points. In 1996, the score gap between students at the 75th percentile and students at the 25th percentile was 41 points.

Science Scale Scores at Selected Percentiles

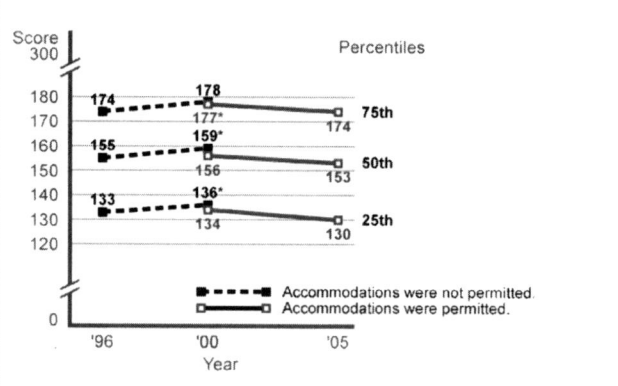

Scores at selected percentiles on the NAEP science scale indicate how well students at lower, middle, and higher levels performed.

The estimate rounds to zero.   ‡ Reporting standards not met.

* Significantly different from 2005.   ↑ Significantly higher than 2000. ↓ Significantly lower than 2000.

[1] Comparisons (higher/lower/not different) are based on statistical tests. The .05 level was used for testing statistical significance. Comparisons across jurisdictions and comparisons with the nation or within a jurisdiction across years may be affected by differences in exclusion rates for students with disabilities (SD) and English language learners (ELL). The exclusion rates for SD and ELL in Indiana were 2 percent and 1 percent in 2005, respectively. Statistical comparisons are calculated on the basis of unrounded scale scores or percentages.

[2] "Jurisdiction" refers to states and the Department of Defense Education Activity schools.

NOTE: Detail may not sum to totals because of rounding and because the "Information not available" category for free/reduced-price school lunch and the "Unclassifed" category for race/ethnicity are not displayed. Visit http://nces.ed.gov/nationsreportcard/states/ for additional results and detailed information.

SOURCE: U.S. Department of Education, Institute of Education Sciences, National Center for Education Statistics, National Assessment of Educational Progress (NAEP), 1996, 2000, and 2005 Science Assessments.

Disaggregation Summary

Test/Report Information		Report Filters			
Test Administration	**ISTEP Spring 2010**	Corp/Diocese	**All Corps/Dioceses**	Subject	**English/language arts**
Test Program	**Public Schools**	School	**All Schools**		
Today's Date	**6-8-2010**	Grade	**3rd Grade**		

Embargo Notice

All "State" level data and any "State" reports accessible via the INORS system are embargoed and cannot be publicly shared until the Indiana Department of Education formally announces the release of the Spring 2010 ISTEP+ results.

English/language arts Students	Total Number of Students	Pass +		Pass		Total Passing		Did Not Pass		Undetermined		Mean/Median Scale Score	Standard Deviation
		N	%	N	%	N	%	N	%	N	%		
All Students	**81201**	**9899**	**12**	**54187**	**67**	**64086**	**79**	**15130**	**19**	**1985**	**2**	**459.7/461.0**	**59.8**
General Education													
TOTAL General Education	69339	9358	13	48276	70	57634	83	10133	15	1572	2	466.5/465.8	54.8
Special Education													
With Accommodations	6376	79	1	2286	36	2365	37	3700	58	311	5	392.3/401.4	71.1
Without Accommodations	5486	462	8	3625	66	4087	74	1297	24	102	2	449.8/451.9	58.3
TOTAL Special Education	11862	541	5	5911	50	6452	54	4997	42	413	3	419.3/425.8	71.4
Limited English Proficiency													
With Accommodations	3878	33	1	2153	56	2186	56	1567	40	125	3	417.7/424.4	53.3
Without Accommodations	1479	37	3	961	65	998	67	371	25	110	7	438.4/442.6	49.1
TOTAL Limited English Proficiency	5357	70	1	3114	58	3184	59	1938	36	235	4	423.2/429.0	53.0
Non-Limited English Proficiency													
With Accommodations	6322	93	1	2394	38	2487	39	3513	56	322	5	395.9/404.4	71.2
Without Accommodations	69522	9736	14	48679	70	58415	84	9679	14	1428	2	468.0/467.4	54.6
TOTAL Non-Limited English Proficiency	75844	9829	13	51073	67	60902	80	13192	17	1750	2	462.2/463.5	59.5
Gender													
Male	41394	4070	10	27347	66	31417	76	8935	22	1042	3	452.9/456.3	60.8
Female	39656	5827	15	26813	68	32640	82	6175	16	841	2	466.7/466.1	57.9
No valid information	151	2	1	27	18	29	19	20	13	102	68	422.8/436.0	68.7
SES													
Paid Lunch	39071	7471	19	27147	69	34618	89	3849	10	604	2	479.1/479.1	55.3
Free or Reduced Lunch	41758	2421	6	26945	65	29366	70	11234	27	1158	3	441.3/444.7	58.0
No valid information	372	7	2	95	26	102	27	47	13	223	60	430.9/437.0	65.4
Ethnicity													
American Indian or Alaskan Native	209	17	8	136	65	153	73	48	23	8	4	446.0/449.0	58.8
Black (Not of Hispanic Origin)	10043	357	4	6020	60	6377	63	3368	34	298	3	430.0/433.9	57.8
Asian or Pacific Islander	1413	309	22	814	58	1123	79	183	13	107	8	476.5/477.0	71.7
Hispanic	6568	281	4	4076	62	4357	66	2020	31	191	3	435.1/438.1	55.7

Produced: 6/8/2010 12:52 PM

White (Not of Hispanic Origin)	58273	8500	15	40112	69	48612	83	8569	15	1092	2	467.7/468.7	57.8
Multiracial	4381	429	10	2954	67	3383	77	900	21	98	2	452.8/454.2	60.1
No valid information	314	6	2	75	24	81	26	42	13	191	61	432.3/437.0	62.2
Migrant	15	0	0	13	87	13	87	2	13	0	0	438.5/441.0	31.9

The cut score of Pass is 417. The cut score of Pass+ is 521. Lowest/Highest Scale Score for English/language arts is 120-780.

Subtotal numbers are rounded within each category. Adding subtotals may not result in exactly 100%.

Report Purpose

This report describes group achievement for selected reporting populations.

Report Legend

N: Number of students

%: Percent of students

■I Report Privacy Notice

Student information is protected by Family Educational Rights and Privacy Act, the Individuals with Disabilities Education Act, and other federal and state laws.

Disaggregation Summary

Test/Report Information		Report Filters			
Test Administration	**ISTEP Spring 2010**	Corp/Diocese	**All Corps/Dioceses**	Subject	**Mathematics**
Test Program	**Public Schools**	School	**All Schools**		
Today's Date	**6-8-2010**	Grade	**3rd Grade**		

┌─ **Embargo Notice** ───┐
All "State" level data and any "State" reports accessible via the INORS system are embargoed and cannot be publicly shared until the Indiana Department of Education formally announces the release of the Spring 2010 ISTEP+ results.
└──┘

Mathematics Students	Total Number of Students	Pass + N	%	Pass N	%	Total Passing N	%	Did Not Pass N	%	Undetermined N	%	Mean/Median Scale Score	Standard Deviation
All Students	**81201**	**19282**	**24**	**41988**	**52**	**61270**	**75**	**18228**	**22**	**1703**	**2**	462.7/465.9	73.0
General Education													
TOTAL General Education	69339	17734	26	36713	53	54447	79	13511	19	1381	2	468.7/471.1	70.0
Special Education													
With Accommodations	6338	384	6	2363	37	2747	43	3360	53	231	4	401.2/403.2	76.4
Without Accommodations	5524	1164	21	2912	53	4076	74	1357	25	91	2	456.4/458.8	73.1
TOTAL Special Education	11862	1548	13	5275	44	6823	58	4717	40	322	3	427.2/430.3	79.8
Limited English Proficiency													
With Accommodations	3933	377	10	1911	49	2288	58	1554	40	91	2	426.0/429.3	70.7
Without Accommodations	1424	190	13	793	56	983	69	414	29	27	2	444.4/447.4	67.8
TOTAL Limited English Proficiency	5357	567	11	2704	50	3271	61	1968	37	118	2	430.9/434.2	70.4
Non-Limited English Proficiency													
With Accommodations	6284	416	7	2418	38	2834	45	3205	51	245	4	404.6/406.9	76.7
Without Accommodations	69560	18299	26	36866	53	55165	79	13055	19	1340	2	470.3/472.7	69.8
TOTAL Non-Limited English Proficiency	75844	18715	25	39284	52	57999	76	16260	21	1585	2	464.9/468.2	72.6
Gender													
Male	41394	10480	25	21263	51	31743	77	8800	21	851	2	465.7/469.2	74.1
Female	39656	8797	22	20702	52	29499	74	9407	24	750	2	459.6/462.5	71.6
No valid information	151	5	3	23	15	28	19	21	14	102	68	416.5/424.0	76.3
SES													
Paid Lunch	39071	13306	34	20319	52	33625	86	4940	13	506	1	485.9/487.9	67.8
Free or Reduced Lunch	41758	5963	14	21585	52	27548	66	13232	32	978	2	440.9/444.3	70.9
No valid information	372	13	3	84	23	97	26	56	15	219	59	424.5/437.0	75.0
Ethnicity													
American Indian or Alaskan Native	209	30	14	113	54	143	68	59	28	7	3	447.8/456.5	68.1
Black (Not of Hispanic Origin)	10043	931	9	4476	45	5407	54	4355	43	281	3	420.7/421.7	72.5
Asian or Pacific Islander	1413	618	44	547	39	1165	82	200	14	48	3	495.5/504.5	85.8
Hispanic	6568	891	14	3368	51	4259	65	2165	33	144	2	439.2/441.6	70.1

White (Not of Hispanic Origin)	58273	15963	27	31133	53	47096	81	10223	18	954	2	472.7/475.6	69.6
Multiracial	4381	836	19	2280	52	3116	71	1182	27	83	2	451.3/454.3	72.3
No valid information	314	13	4	71	23	84	27	44	14	186	59	428.1/436.3	72.4
Migrant	15	2	13	9	60	11	73	4	27	0	0	444.7/438.0	56.7

The cut score of Pass is 413. The cut score of Pass+ is 513. Lowest/Highest Scale Score for Mathematics is 140-735.

Subtotal numbers are rounded within each category. Adding subtotals may not result in exactly 100%.

Report Purpose

This report describes group achievement for selected reporting populations.

Report Legend

N: Number of students

%: Percent of students

Report Privacy Notice

Student information is protected by Family Educational Rights and Privacy Act, the Individuals with Disabilities Education Act, and other federal and state laws.

Disaggregation Summary

Test/Report Information		Report Filters			
Test Administration	**ISTEP Spring 2010**	Corp/Diocese	**All Corps/Dioceses**	Subject	**English/language arts**
Test Program	**Public Schools**	School	**All Schools**		
Today's Date	**6-14-2010**	Grade	**4th Grade**		

Embargo Notice

All "State" level data and any "State" reports accessible via the INORS system are embargoed and cannot be publicly shared until the Indiana Department of Education formally announces the release of the Spring 2010 ISTEP+ results.

English/language arts Students	Total Number of Students	Pass +		Pass		Total Passing		Did Not Pass		Undetermined		Mean/Median Scale Score	Standard Deviation
		N	%	N	%	N	%	N	%	N	%		
All Students	**78870**	**11243**	**14**	**49643**	**63**	**60886**	**77**	**15995**	**20**	**1989**	**3**	**478.5/482.0**	**60.2**
General Education													
TOTAL General Education	67433	10625	16	44564	66	55189	82	10849	16	1395	2	485.8/487.3	54.3
Special Education													
With Accommodations	7360	122	2	2550	35	2672	36	4209	57	479	7	412.4/420.0	72.0
Without Accommodations	4077	496	12	2529	62	3025	74	937	23	115	3	472.7/475.4	60.1
TOTAL Special Education	11437	618	5	5079	44	5697	50	5146	45	594	5	434.4/440.3	73.8
Limited English Proficiency													
With Accommodations	3089	30	1	1568	51	1598	52	1372	44	119	4	434.1/441.2	57.8
Without Accommodations	1259	53	4	764	61	817	65	325	26	117	9	457.9/460.3	47.1
TOTAL Limited English Proficiency	4348	83	2	2332	54	2415	56	1697	39	236	5	440.7/446.6	56.0
Non-Limited English Proficiency													
With Accommodations	7420	138	2	2726	37	2864	39	4086	55	470	6	416.1/422.7	71.7
Without Accommodations	67102	11022	16	44585	66	55607	83	10212	15	1283	2	487.5/489.0	53.9
TOTAL Non-Limited English Proficiency	74522	11160	15	47311	63	58471	78	14298	19	1753	2	480.7/484.2	59.7
Gender													
Male	40181	5090	13	24772	62	29862	74	9214	23	1105	3	473.4/478.0	61.9
Female	38494	6148	16	24836	65	30984	80	6755	18	755	2	484.0/486.0	57.8
No valid information	195	5	3	35	18	40	21	26	13	129	66	446.8/453.0	67.6
SES													
Paid Lunch	38939	8684	22	25464	65	34148	88	4235	11	556	1	498.3/499.9	54.7
Free or Reduced Lunch	39564	2546	6	24089	61	26635	67	11689	30	1240	3	458.9/463.7	58.8
No valid information	367	13	4	90	25	103	28	71	19	193	53	445.0/453.7	73.8
Ethnicity													
American Indian or Alaskan Native	205	24	12	124	60	148	72	52	25	5	2	470.3/473.5	59.3
Black (Not of Hispanic Origin)	9738	339	3	5405	56	5744	59	3696	38	298	3	446.1/450.6	57.3
Asian or Pacific Islander	1356	306	23	742	55	1048	77	200	15	108	8	493.9/498.3	71.5
Hispanic	5753	314	5	3498	61	3812	66	1778	31	163	3	456.0/460.1	56.6

White (Not of Hispanic Origin)	57474	9797	17	37243	65	47040	82	9310	16	1124	2	486.4/489.7	58.3
Multiracial	4017	452	11	2553	64	3005	75	899	22	113	3	472.6/476.5	58.1
No valid information	327	11	3	78	24	89	27	60	18	178	54	445.1/455.7	74.8
Migrant	12	0	0	11	92	11	92	1	8	0	0	462.8/462.0	29.6

The cut score of Pass is 437. The cut score of Pass+ is 535. Lowest/Highest Scale Score for English/language arts is 140-800.

Subtotal numbers are rounded within each category. Adding subtotals may not result in exactly 100%.

Report Purpose

This report describes group achievement for selected reporting populations.

Report Legend

N: Number of students

%: Percent of students

Report Privacy Notice

Student information is protected by Family Educational Rights and Privacy Act, the Individuals with Disabilities Education Act, and other federal and state laws.

Disaggregation Summary

Test/Report Information		Report Filters			
Test Administration	**ISTEP Spring 2010**	Corp/Diocese	**All Corps/Dioceses**	Subject	**Mathematics**
Test Program	**Public Schools**	School	**All Schools**		
Today's Date	**6-14-2010**	Grade	**4th Grade**		

Embargo Notice

All "State" level data and any "State" reports accessible via the INORS system are embargoed and cannot be publicly shared until the Indiana Department of Education formally announces the release of the Spring 2010 ISTEP+ results.

Mathematics Students	Total Number of Students	Pass + N	Pass + %	Pass N	Pass %	Total Passing N	Total Passing %	Did Not Pass N	Did Not Pass %	Undetermined N	Undetermined %	Mean/Median Scale Score	Standard Deviation
All Students	**78870**	**17153**	**22**	**42145**	**53**	**59298**	**75**	**17888**	**23**	**1684**	**2**	491.2/492.1	69.8
General Education													
TOTAL General Education	67433	15918	24	37056	55	52974	79	13252	20	1207	2	496.9/497.0	67.5
Special Education													
With Accommodations	7330	417	6	2910	40	3327	45	3627	49	376	5	438.8/441.3	69.0
Without Accommodations	4107	818	20	2179	53	2997	73	1009	25	101	2	487.7/488.8	70.5
TOTAL Special Education	11437	1235	11	5089	44	6324	55	4636	41	477	4	456.7/457.7	73.4
Limited English Proficiency													
With Accommodations	3149	244	8	1529	49	1773	56	1298	41	78	2	452.4/456.5	68.2
Without Accommodations	1199	157	13	694	58	851	71	327	27	21	2	476.3/477.1	65.9
TOTAL Limited English Proficiency	4348	401	9	2223	51	2624	60	1625	37	99	2	459.0/462.2	68.4
Non-Limited English Proficiency													
With Accommodations	7392	448	6	3030	41	3478	47	3544	48	370	5	441.3/443.9	68.5
Without Accommodations	67130	16304	24	36892	55	53196	79	12719	19	1215	2	498.6/498.6	67.2
TOTAL Non-Limited English Proficiency	74522	16752	22	39922	54	56674	76	16263	22	1585	2	493.1/493.8	69.4
Gender													
Male	40181	9047	23	21077	52	30124	75	9163	23	894	2	491.8/492.8	71.1
Female	38494	8095	21	21035	55	29130	76	8703	23	661	2	490.6/491.5	68.3
No valid information	195	11	6	33	17	44	23	22	11	129	66	470.2/469.5	78.0
SES													
Paid Lunch	38939	12310	32	21253	55	33563	86	4904	13	472	1	513.6/512.4	65.3
Free or Reduced Lunch	39564	4822	12	20810	53	25632	65	12911	33	1021	3	469.0/471.3	66.8
No valid information	367	21	6	82	22	103	28	73	20	191	52	456.1/457.4	75.5
Ethnicity													
American Indian or Alaskan Native	205	35	17	102	50	137	67	61	30	7	3	478.6/479.5	69.4
Black (Not of Hispanic Origin)	9738	657	7	4501	46	5158	53	4319	44	261	3	448.2/451.8	67.0
Asian or Pacific Islander	1356	527	39	578	43	1105	81	224	17	27	2	516.8/521.5	88.6
Hispanic	5753	702	12	3137	55	3839	67	1793	31	121	2	470.3/472.1	65.2

White (Not of Hispanic Origin)	57474	14546	25	31590	55	46136	80	10347	18	991	2	500.8/500.7	66.8
Multiracial	4017	665	17	2173	54	2838	71	1078	27	101	3	480.6/482.3	67.7
No valid information	327	21	6	64	20	85	26	66	20	176	54	457.9/457.0	77.0
Migrant	12	1	8	6	50	7	58	5	42	0	0	466.3/476.0	47.3

The cut score of Pass is 445. The cut score of Pass+ is 541. Lowest/Highest Scale Score for Mathematics is 185-750.
Subtotal numbers are rounded within each category. Adding subtotals may not result in exactly 100%.

Report Purpose
This report describes group achievement for selected reporting populations.

Report Legend
N: Number of students
%: Percent of students

▪▮ Report Privacy Notice
Student information is protected by Family Educational Rights and Privacy Act, the Individuals with Disabilities Education Act, and other federal and state laws.

Disaggregation Summary

Test/Report Information		Report Filters			
Test Administration	**ISTEP Spring 2010**	Corp/Diocese	**All Corps/Dioceses**	Subject	**Science**
Test Program	**Public Schools**	School	**All Schools**		
Today's Date	**6-14-2010**	Grade	**4th Grade**		

Embargo Notice

All "State" level data and any "State" reports accessible via the INORS system are embargoed and cannot be publicly shared until the Indiana Department of Education formally announces the release of the Spring 2010 ISTEP+ results.

Science Students	Total Number of Students	Pass +		Pass		Total Passing		Did Not Pass		Undetermined		Mean/Median Scale Score	Standard Deviation
		N	%	N	%	N	%	N	%	N	%		
All Students	**78870**	**18732**	**24**	**40425**	**51**	**59157**	**75**	**18068**	**23**	**1645**	**2**	497.9/499.7	55.5
General Education													
TOTAL General Education	67433	17304	26	35493	53	52797	78	13393	20	1243	2	502.3/503.4	53.2
Special Education													
With Accommodations	7165	499	7	2804	39	3303	46	3552	50	310	4	457.6/460.3	59.5
Without Accommodations	4272	929	22	2128	50	3057	72	1123	26	92	2	494.3/495.7	56.7
TOTAL Special Education	11437	1428	12	4932	43	6360	56	4675	41	402	4	471.5/473.8	61.1
Limited English Proficiency													
With Accommodations	2971	128	4	1439	48	1567	53	1331	45	73	2	458.5/465.9	57.6
Without Accommodations	1377	124	9	767	56	891	65	456	33	30	2	477.0/477.7	47.5
TOTAL Limited English Proficiency	4348	252	6	2206	51	2458	57	1787	41	103	2	464.4/470.0	55.3
Non-Limited English Proficiency													
With Accommodations	7219	544	8	2941	41	3485	48	3428	47	306	4	460.5/463.1	59.0
Without Accommodations	67303	17936	27	35278	52	53214	79	12853	19	1236	2	504.0/505.2	52.7
TOTAL Non-Limited English Proficiency	74522	18480	25	38219	51	56699	76	16281	22	1542	2	499.8/501.7	54.9
Gender													
Male	40181	10212	25	19734	49	29946	75	9356	23	879	2	498.7/501.0	57.7
Female	38494	8514	22	20658	54	29172	76	8685	23	637	2	497.0/498.5	53.0
No valid information	195	6	3	33	17	39	20	27	14	129	66	473.9/484.0	58.7
SES													
Paid Lunch	38939	13744	35	19941	51	33685	87	4824	12	430	1	516.7/517.4	50.3
Free or Reduced Lunch	39564	4966	13	20405	52	25371	64	13169	33	1024	3	479.2/481.8	54.0
No valid information	367	22	6	79	22	101	28	75	20	191	52	466.5/472.5	68.3
Ethnicity													
American Indian or Alaskan Native	205	41	20	107	52	148	72	53	26	4	2	489.4/496.5	64.0
Black (Not of Hispanic Origin)	9738	510	5	4222	43	4732	49	4730	49	276	3	459.0/462.5	53.8
Asian or Pacific Islander	1356	449	33	599	44	1048	77	280	21	28	2	501.5/512.5	74.8
Hispanic	5753	550	10	3192	55	3742	65	1890	33	121	2	477.1/480.2	50.2

White (Not of Hispanic Origin)	57474	16453	29	30119	52	46572	81	9959	17	943	2	507.1/508.5	52.2
Multiracial	4017	707	18	2119	53	2826	70	1094	27	97	2	489.1/491.3	52.9
No valid information	327	22	7	67	20	89	27	62	19	176	54	470.1/475.3	61.7
Migrant	12	1	8	8	67	9	75	3	25	0	0	476.0/469.5	41.6

The cut score of Pass is 463. The cut score of Pass+ is 535. Lowest/Highest Scale Score for Science is 200-750.

Subtotal numbers are rounded within each category. Adding subtotals may not result in exactly 100%.

Report Purpose

This report describes group achievement for selected reporting populations.

Report Legend

N: Number of students

%: Percent of students

Report Privacy Notice

Student information is protected by Family Educational Rights and Privacy Act, the Individuals with Disabilities Education Act, and other federal and state laws.

Disaggregation Summary

Test/Report Information		Report Filters			
Test Administration	**ISTEP Spring 2010**	Corp/Diocese	**All Corps/Dioceses**	Subject	**English/language arts**
Test Program	**Public Schools**	School	**All Schools**		
Today's Date	**6-8-2010**	Grade	**5th Grade**		

Embargo Notice

All "State" level data and any "State" reports accessible via the INORS system are embargoed and cannot be publicly shared until the Indiana Department of Education formally announces the release of the Spring 2010 ISTEP+ results.

English/language arts Students	Total Number of Students	Pass +		Pass		Total Passing		Did Not Pass		Undetermined		Mean/Median Scale Score	Standard Deviation
		N	%	N	%	N	%	N	%	N	%		
All Students	**77575**	**11127**	**14**	**43987**	**57**	**55114**	**71**	**20666**	**27**	**1795**	**2**	495.8/498.2	54.8
General Education													
TOTAL General Education	66651	10687	16	40383	61	51070	77	14399	22	1182	2	503.1/503.4	49.6
Special Education													
With Accommodations	7931	80	1	2004	25	2084	26	5344	67	503	6	433.8/437.9	58.7
Without Accommodations	2993	360	12	1600	53	1960	65	923	31	110	4	488.6/491.0	55.6
TOTAL Special Education	10924	440	4	3604	33	4044	37	6267	57	613	6	449.1/452.6	62.9
Limited English Proficiency													
With Accommodations	2599	47	2	987	38	1034	40	1444	56	121	5	453.4/458.2	52.8
Without Accommodations	1213	43	4	584	48	627	52	495	41	91	8	470.8/473.6	47.0
TOTAL Limited English Proficiency	3812	90	2	1571	41	1661	44	1939	51	212	6	458.8/463.3	51.7
Non-Limited English Proficiency													
With Accommodations	8056	100	1	2206	27	2306	29	5249	65	501	6	437.1/441.2	58.8
Without Accommodations	65707	10937	17	40210	61	51147	78	13478	21	1082	2	504.7/504.8	49.1
TOTAL Non-Limited English Proficiency	73763	11037	15	42416	58	53453	72	18727	25	1583	2	497.6/500.0	54.3
Gender													
Male	39312	4607	12	21581	55	26188	67	12104	31	1020	3	488.6/492.1	55.4
Female	38157	6516	17	22383	59	28899	76	8546	22	712	2	503.1/504.1	53.2
No valid information	106	4	4	23	22	27	25	16	15	63	59	485.4/486.3	48.3
SES													
Paid Lunch	39167	8523	22	23777	61	32300	82	6335	16	532	1	512.7/513.1	51.1
Free or Reduced Lunch	38097	2594	7	20125	53	22719	60	14254	37	1124	3	478.2/482.0	52.9
No valid information	311	10	3	85	27	95	31	77	25	139	45	473.9/479.5	49.6
Ethnicity													
American Indian or Alaskan Native	197	19	10	117	59	136	69	51	26	10	5	492.2/498.7	51.8
Black (Not of Hispanic Origin)	9520	370	4	4453	47	4823	51	4398	46	299	3	467.5/470.6	50.9
Asian or Pacific Islander	1285	387	30	561	44	948	74	242	19	95	7	514.5/519.1	76.4
Hispanic	5589	355	6	2858	51	3213	57	2209	40	167	3	476.0/478.7	52.0

White (Not of Hispanic Origin)	57001	9555	17	33836	59	43391	76	12605	22	1005	2	502.4/504.4	53.2
Multiracial	3738	433	12	2087	56	2520	67	1122	30	96	3	489.0/491.1	54.0
No valid information	245	8	3	75	31	83	34	39	16	123	50	486.4/488.5	44.3
Migrant	14	0	0	5	36	5	36	8	57	1	7	452.5/443.0	55.8

The cut score of Pass is 468. The cut score of Pass+ is 548. Lowest/Highest Scale Score for English/language arts is 160-820.

Subtotal numbers are rounded within each category. Adding subtotals may not result in exactly 100%.

Report Purpose

This report describes group achievement for selected reporting populations.

Report Legend

N: Number of students

%: Percent of students

Report Privacy Notice

Student information is protected by Family Educational Rights and Privacy Act, the Individuals with Disabilities Education Act, and other federal and state laws.

Disaggregation Summary

Test/Report Information		Report Filters			
Test Administration	**ISTEP Spring 2010**	Corp/Diocese	**All Corps/Dioceses**	Subject	**Mathematics**
Test Program	**Public Schools**	School	**All Schools**		
Today's Date	**6-8-2010**	Grade	**5th Grade**		

Embargo Notice

All "State" level data and any "State" reports accessible via the INORS system are embargoed and cannot be publicly shared until the Indiana Department of Education formally announces the release of the Spring 2010 ISTEP+ results.

Mathematics Students	Total Number of Students	Pass +		Pass		Total Passing		Did Not Pass		Undetermined		Mean/Median Scale Score	Standard Deviation
		N	%	N	%	N	%	N	%	N	%		
All Students	**77575**	**21376**	**28**	**40967**	**53**	**62343**	**80**	**13635**	**18**	**1597**	**2**	**519.5/521.7**	**69.0**
General Education													
TOTAL General Education	66651	20123	30	36144	54	56267	84	9271	14	1113	2	526.8/527.4	65.0
Special Education													
With Accommodations	7944	484	6	3294	41	3778	48	3765	47	401	5	458.0/462.7	70.7
Without Accommodations	2980	769	26	1529	51	2298	77	599	20	83	3	514.1/517.6	70.8
TOTAL Special Education	10924	1253	11	4823	44	6076	56	4364	40	484	4	473.6/478.0	75.0
Limited English Proficiency													
With Accommodations	2659	296	11	1417	53	1713	64	869	33	77	3	483.3/490.2	67.3
Without Accommodations	1153	160	14	677	59	837	73	296	26	20	2	497.5/500.4	64.5
TOTAL Limited English Proficiency	3812	456	12	2094	55	2550	67	1165	31	97	3	487.6/493.3	66.7
Non-Limited English Proficiency													
With Accommodations	8068	536	7	3411	42	3947	49	3719	46	402	5	460.3/465.1	70.7
Without Accommodations	65695	20384	31	35462	54	55846	85	8751	13	1098	2	528.4/528.8	64.8
TOTAL Non-Limited English Proficiency	73763	20920	28	38873	53	59793	81	12470	17	1500	2	521.2/523.2	68.7
Gender													
Male	39312	11190	28	20440	52	31630	80	6813	17	869	2	520.9/522.7	70.3
Female	38157	10179	27	20501	54	30680	80	6811	18	666	2	518.1/520.7	67.5
No valid information	106	7	7	26	25	33	31	11	10	62	58	497.9/507.0	72.4
SES													
Paid Lunch	39167	14911	38	19991	51	34902	89	3780	10	485	1	539.9/539.1	65.5
Free or Reduced Lunch	38097	6442	17	20873	55	27315	72	9807	26	975	3	498.4/503.1	66.1
No valid information	311	23	7	103	33	126	41	48	15	137	44	487.1/494.0	69.2
Ethnicity													
American Indian or Alaskan Native	197	49	25	98	50	147	75	43	22	7	4	508.5/510.3	75.0
Black (Not of Hispanic Origin)	9520	1026	11	4868	51	5894	62	3352	35	274	3	480.7/486.6	67.9
Asian or Pacific Islander	1285	657	51	425	33	1082	84	166	13	37	3	556.1/559.9	96.9
Hispanic	5589	993	18	3128	56	4121	74	1346	24	122	2	501.5/505.1	63.9

White (Not of Hispanic Origin)	57001	17834	31	30325	53	48159	84	7898	14	944	2	527.7/528.8	66.0
Multiracial	3738	798	21	2042	55	2840	76	806	22	92	2	508.8/511.5	68.5
No valid information	245	19	8	81	33	100	41	24	10	121	49	498.9/501.3	62.6
Migrant	14	0	0	8	57	8	57	5	36	1	7	458.9/507.0	86.8

The cut score of Pass is 463. The cut score of Pass+ is 556. Lowest/Highest Scale Score for Mathematics is 245-775.

Subtotal numbers are rounded within each category. Adding subtotals may not result in exactly 100%.

Report Purpose

This report describes group achievement for selected reporting populations.

Report Legend

N: Number of students

%: Percent of students

Report Privacy Notice

Student information is protected by Family Educational Rights and Privacy Act, the Individuals with Disabilities Education Act, and other federal and state laws.

Disaggregation Summary

Test/Report Information		Report Filters			
Test Administration	**ISTEP Spring 2010**	Corp/Diocese	**All Corps/Dioceses**	Subject	**Social Studies**
Test Program	**Public Schools**	School	**All Schools**		
Today's Date	**6-8-2010**	Grade	**5th Grade**		

Embargo Notice

All "State" level data and any "State" reports accessible via the INORS system are embargoed and cannot be publicly shared until the Indiana Department of Education formally announces the release of the Spring 2010 ISTEP+ results.

Social Studies Students	Total Number of Students	Pass +		Pass		Total Passing		Did Not Pass		Undetermined		Mean/Median Scale Score	Standard Deviation
		N	%	N	%	N	%	N	%	N	%		
All Students	**77575**	**15026**	**19**	**34536**	**45**	**49562**	**64**	**26497**	**34**	**1516**	**2**	**502.7/504.0**	**58.1**
General Education													
TOTAL General Education	66651	14182	21	31155	47	45337	68	20248	30	1066	2	508.4/509.0	55.2
Special Education													
With Accommodations	5462	204	4	1428	26	1632	30	3547	65	283	5	454.7/457.6	59.0
Without Accommodations	5462	640	12	1953	36	2593	47	2702	49	167	3	479.3/480.7	64.1
TOTAL Special Education	10924	844	8	3381	31	4225	39	6249	57	450	4	467.1/468.6	62.9
Limited English Proficiency													
With Accommodations	2199	51	2	689	31	740	34	1391	63	68	3	460.8/466.0	53.0
Without Accommodations	1613	83	5	641	40	724	45	852	53	37	2	475.6/477.9	49.0
TOTAL Limited English Proficiency	3812	134	4	1330	35	1464	38	2243	59	105	3	467.1/470.9	51.8
Non-Limited English Proficiency													
With Accommodations	5572	227	4	1551	28	1778	32	3507	63	287	5	457.4/460.4	59.5
Without Accommodations	68191	14665	22	31655	46	46320	68	20747	30	1124	2	508.2/509.4	56.0
TOTAL Non-Limited English Proficiency	73763	14892	20	33206	45	48098	65	24254	33	1411	2	504.5/506.0	57.8
Gender													
Male	39312	8516	22	17097	43	25613	65	12845	33	854	2	505.3/507.2	60.0
Female	38157	6504	17	17422	46	23926	63	13632	36	599	2	500.0/501.2	56.0
No valid information	106	6	6	17	16	23	22	20	19	63	59	489.0/488.0	60.7
SES													
Paid Lunch	39167	11491	29	19029	49	30520	78	8214	21	433	1	522.7/523.5	54.1
Free or Reduced Lunch	38097	3520	9	15438	41	18958	50	18193	48	946	2	482.0/483.7	54.8
No valid information	311	15	5	69	22	84	27	90	29	137	44	478.9/480.4	54.3
Ethnicity													
American Indian or Alaskan Native	197	33	17	96	49	129	65	62	31	6	3	499.9/505.8	57.2
Black (Not of Hispanic Origin)	9520	443	5	3061	32	3504	37	5727	60	289	3	465.7/467.3	53.8
Asian or Pacific Islander	1285	432	34	488	38	920	72	325	25	40	3	517.8/524.9	77.8
Hispanic	5589	479	9	2331	42	2810	50	2650	47	129	2	482.7/484.2	52.5

White (Not of Hispanic Origin)	57001	13079	23	26916	47	39995	70	16168	28	838	1	511.0/512.4	55.9
Multiracial	3738	548	15	1584	42	2132	57	1514	41	92	2	493.4/494.3	56.4
No valid information	245	12	5	60	24	72	29	51	21	122	50	489.5/491.7	50.8
Migrant	14	3	21	2	14	5	36	8	57	1	7	472.3/465.0	69.2

The cut score of Pass is 483. The cut score of Pass+ is 550. Lowest/Highest Scale Score for Social Studies is 220-760.

Subtotal numbers are rounded within each category. Adding subtotals may not result in exactly 100%.

Report Purpose

This report describes group achievement for selected reporting populations.

Report Legend

N: Number of students

%: Percent of students

Report Privacy Notice

Student information is protected by Family Educational Rights and Privacy Act, the Individuals with Disabilities Education Act, and other federal and state laws.

Disaggregation Summary

Test/Report Information		Report Filters			
Test Administration	**ISTEP Spring 2010**	Corp/Diocese	**All Corps/Dioceses**	Subject	**English/language arts**
Test Program	**Public Schools**	School	**All Schools**		
Today's Date	**6-8-2010**	Grade	**6th Grade**		

Embargo Notice

All "State" level data and any "State" reports accessible via the INORS system are embargoed and cannot be publicly shared until the Indiana Department of Education formally announces the release of the Spring 2010 ISTEP+ results.

English/language arts Students	Total Number of Students	Pass +		Pass		Total Passing		Did Not Pass		Undetermined		Mean/Median Scale Score	Standard Deviation
		N	%	N	%	N	%	N	%	N	%		
All Students	**77865**	**15527**	**20**	**40770**	**52**	**56297**	**72**	**19457**	**25**	**2111**	**3**	521.9/523.1	73.0
General Education													
TOTAL General Education	67407	15150	22	37589	56	52739	78	13160	20	1508	2	532.3/531.4	67.0
Special Education													
With Accommodations	8544	136	2	2223	26	2359	28	5673	66	512	6	440.5/442.8	68.4
Without Accommodations	1914	241	13	958	50	1199	63	624	33	91	5	504.2/505.6	70.6
TOTAL Special Education	10458	377	4	3181	30	3558	34	6297	60	603	6	452.3/452.9	73.1
Limited English Proficiency													
With Accommodations	2112	41	2	708	34	749	35	1250	59	113	5	457.6/461.7	63.2
Without Accommodations	1140	54	5	513	45	567	50	467	41	106	9	483.0/484.6	63.8
TOTAL Limited English Proficiency	3252	95	3	1221	38	1316	40	1717	53	219	7	466.3/468.9	64.5
Non-Limited English Proficiency													
With Accommodations	8619	168	2	2384	28	2552	30	5551	64	516	6	443.8/445.8	69.2
Without Accommodations	65994	15264	23	37165	56	52429	79	12189	18	1376	2	534.3/533.3	66.2
TOTAL Non-Limited English Proficiency	74613	15432	21	39549	53	54981	74	17740	24	1892	3	524.2/525.6	72.4
Gender													
Male	39425	5722	15	20665	52	26387	67	11884	30	1154	3	508.6/511.9	71.8
Female	38334	9797	26	20085	52	29882	78	7554	20	898	2	535.5/535.1	71.6
No valid information	106	8	8	20	19	28	26	19	18	59	56	492.1/507.0	91.8
SES													
Paid Lunch	40141	11449	29	22028	55	33477	83	6041	15	623	2	543.8/543.9	68.7
Free or Reduced Lunch	37440	4064	11	18694	50	22758	61	13350	36	1332	4	498.0/499.7	69.8
No valid information	284	14	5	48	17	62	22	66	23	156	55	479.4/473.8	80.0
Ethnicity													
American Indian or Alaskan Native	213	27	13	126	59	153	72	50	23	10	5	514.8/519.0	62.5
Black (Not of Hispanic Origin)	9413	700	7	4339	46	5039	54	4009	43	365	4	486.5/486.8	66.5
Asian or Pacific Islander	1213	402	33	495	41	897	74	220	18	96	8	543.9/552.4	93.6
Hispanic	5382	551	10	2628	49	3179	59	2009	37	194	4	496.1/497.0	68.3

White (Not of Hispanic Origin)	57896	13267	23	31262	54	44529	77	12177	21	1190	2	530.0/531.5	71.6
Multiracial	3517	567	16	1877	53	2444	69	948	27	125	4	514.3/517.3	71.8
No valid information	231	13	6	43	19	56	24	44	19	131	57	491.5/488.5	77.0
Migrant	13	1	8	6	46	7	54	6	46	0	0	501.5/483.0	99.2

The cut score of Pass is 478. The cut score of Pass+ is 579. Lowest/Highest Scale Score for English/language arts is 180-850.

Subtotal numbers are rounded within each category. Adding subtotals may not result in exactly 100%.

Report Purpose

This report describes group achievement for selected reporting populations.

Report Legend

N: Number of students

%: Percent of students

Report Privacy Notice

Student information is protected by Family Educational Rights and Privacy Act, the Individuals with Disabilities Education Act, and other federal and state laws.

Disaggregation Summary

Test/Report Information		Report Filters			
Test Administration	**ISTEP Spring 2010**	Corp/Diocese	**All Corps/Dioceses**	Subject	**Mathematics**
Test Program	**Public Schools**	School	**All Schools**		
Today's Date	**6-8-2010**	Grade	**6th Grade**		

Embargo Notice

All "State" level data and any "State" reports accessible via the INORS system are embargoed and cannot be publicly shared until the Indiana Department of Education formally announces the release of the Spring 2010 ISTEP+ results.

Mathematics Students	Total Number of Students	Pass + N	Pass + %	Pass N	Pass %	Total Passing N	Total Passing %	Did Not Pass N	Did Not Pass %	Undetermined N	Undetermined %	Mean/Median Scale Score	Standard Deviation
All Students	**77865**	**13548**	**17**	**46080**	**59**	**59628**	**77**	**16410**	**21**	**1827**	**2**	**532.9/534.6**	**64.9**
General Education													
TOTAL General Education	67407	13050	19	41684	62	54734	81	11320	17	1353	2	540.6/540.8	60.8
Special Education													
With Accommodations	8525	221	3	3298	39	3519	41	4605	54	401	5	472.7/476.4	65.3
Without Accommodations	1933	277	14	1098	57	1375	71	485	25	73	4	524.5/526.6	66.6
TOTAL Special Education	10458	498	5	4396	42	4894	47	5090	49	474	5	482.4/484.8	68.6
Limited English Proficiency													
With Accommodations	2163	82	4	1063	49	1145	53	941	44	77	4	489.0/494.1	64.1
Without Accommodations	1089	80	7	662	61	742	68	323	30	24	2	510.8/513.6	60.9
TOTAL Limited English Proficiency	3252	162	5	1725	53	1887	58	1264	39	101	3	496.4/500.7	63.9
Non-Limited English Proficiency													
With Accommodations	8609	252	3	3409	40	3661	43	4543	53	405	5	474.8/478.5	65.6
Without Accommodations	66004	13134	20	40946	62	54080	82	10603	16	1321	2	542.1/542.2	60.3
TOTAL Non-Limited English Proficiency	74613	13386	18	44355	59	57741	77	15146	20	1726	2	534.5/536.1	64.5
Gender													
Male	39425	7105	18	22916	58	30021	76	8433	21	971	2	533.2/535.3	66.4
Female	38334	6438	17	23136	60	29574	77	7963	21	797	2	532.6/533.9	63.4
No valid information	106	5	5	28	26	33	31	14	13	59	56	510.1/516.0	63.8
SES													
Paid Lunch	40141	10374	26	24361	61	34735	87	4860	12	546	1	553.0/553.5	61.1
Free or Reduced Lunch	37440	3170	8	21652	58	24822	66	11488	31	1130	3	511.2/514.3	61.8
No valid information	284	4	1	67	24	71	25	62	22	151	53	485.8/496.0	63.9
Ethnicity													
American Indian or Alaskan Native	213	31	15	132	62	163	77	42	20	8	4	530.3/526.6	60.9
Black (Not of Hispanic Origin)	9413	427	5	4958	53	5385	57	3685	39	343	4	495.9/499.8	61.8
Asian or Pacific Islander	1213	513	42	488	40	1001	83	183	15	29	2	569.3/573.6	90.7
Hispanic	5382	433	8	3222	60	3655	68	1577	29	150	3	512.9/516.5	59.7

White (Not of Hispanic Origin)	57896	11708	20	35167	61	46875	81	9968	17	1053	2	540.7/542.2	62.6
Multiracial	3517	431	12	2061	59	2492	71	909	26	116	3	521.1/523.7	63.2
No valid information	231	5	2	52	23	57	25	46	20	128	55	493.5/497.7	59.8
Migrant	13	0	0	7	54	7	54	6	46	0	0	502.4/515.0	61.0

The cut score of Pass is 487. The cut score of Pass+ is 590. Lowest/Highest Scale Score for Mathematics is 290-790.

Subtotal numbers are rounded within each category. Adding subtotals may not result in exactly 100%.

Report Purpose

This report describes group achievement for selected reporting populations.

Report Legend

N: Number of students

%: Percent of students

Report Privacy Notice

Student information is protected by Family Educational Rights and Privacy Act, the Individuals with Disabilities Education Act, and other federal and state laws.

Disaggregation Summary

Test/Report Information		Report Filters			
Test Administration	**ISTEP Spring 2010**	Corp/Diocese	**All Corps/Dioceses**	Subject	**Science**
Test Program	**Public Schools**	School	**All Schools**		
Today's Date	**6-8-2010**	Grade	**6th Grade**		

Embargo Notice

All "State" level data and any "State" reports accessible via the INORS system are embargoed and cannot be publicly shared until the Indiana Department of Education formally announces the release of the Spring 2010 ISTEP+ results.

Science Students	Total Number of Students	Pass + N	Pass + %	Pass N	Pass %	Total Passing N	Total Passing %	Did Not Pass N	Did Not Pass %	Undetermined N	Undetermined %	Mean/Median Scale Score	Standard Deviation
All Students	**77865**	**13773**	**18**	**31034**	**40**	**44807**	**58**	**31122**	**40**	**1936**	**2**	497.1/499.9	61.0
General Education													
TOTAL General Education	67407	13159	20	28574	42	41733	62	24190	36	1484	2	503.8/505.1	56.4
Special Education													
With Accommodations	8409	280	3	1733	21	2013	24	5999	71	397	5	444.3/452.0	69.2
Without Accommodations	2049	334	16	727	35	1061	52	933	46	55	3	487.6/493.2	67.4
TOTAL Special Education	10458	614	6	2460	24	3074	29	6932	66	452	4	452.9/458.9	71.0
Limited English Proficiency													
With Accommodations	2083	24	1	345	17	369	18	1633	78	81	4	434.5/447.8	71.5
Without Accommodations	1169	44	4	314	27	358	31	776	66	35	3	458.6/465.1	62.3
TOTAL Limited English Proficiency	3252	68	2	659	20	727	22	2409	74	116	4	443.2/453.8	69.3
Non-Limited English Proficiency													
With Accommodations	8473	305	4	1850	22	2155	25	5911	70	407	5	447.3/454.6	68.7
Without Accommodations	66140	13400	20	28525	43	41925	63	22802	34	1413	2	505.9/506.9	55.0
TOTAL Non-Limited English Proficiency	74613	13705	18	30375	41	44080	59	28713	38	1820	2	499.4/501.9	59.6
Gender													
Male	39425	7619	19	15709	40	23328	59	15062	38	1035	3	498.7/503.0	63.6
Female	38334	6147	16	15310	40	21457	56	16035	42	842	2	495.5/496.9	58.2
No valid information	106	7	7	15	14	22	21	25	24	59	56	473.4/473.0	65.2
SES													
Paid Lunch	40141	10587	26	18242	45	28829	72	10703	27	609	2	517.0/518.0	54.4
Free or Reduced Lunch	37440	3179	8	12761	34	15940	43	20325	54	1175	3	475.6/479.8	60.5
No valid information	284	7	2	31	11	38	13	94	33	152	54	450.9/452.0	65.1
Ethnicity													
American Indian or Alaskan Native	213	36	17	78	37	114	54	90	42	9	4	495.6/494.8	55.6
Black (Not of Hispanic Origin)	9413	320	3	2229	24	2549	27	6511	69	353	4	455.4/460.5	59.1
Asian or Pacific Islander	1213	371	31	427	35	798	66	379	31	36	3	504.9/521.4	95.7
Hispanic	5382	342	6	1710	32	2052	38	3181	59	149	3	469.1/474.2	61.3

White (Not of Hispanic Origin)	57896	12239	21	25231	44	37470	65	19294	33	1132	2	506.8/508.7	56.6
Multiracial	3517	458	13	1331	38	1789	51	1601	46	127	4	488.2/490.9	59.6
No valid information	231	7	3	28	12	35	15	66	29	130	56	462.4/459.7	58.9
Migrant	13	0	0	6	46	6	46	7	54	0	0	478.8/478.0	53.7

The cut score of Pass is 488. The cut score of Pass+ is 549. Lowest/Highest Scale Score for Science is 200-765.

Subtotal numbers are rounded within each category. Adding subtotals may not result in exactly 100%.

Report Purpose

This report describes group achievement for selected reporting populations.

Report Legend

N: Number of students

%: Percent of students

■ Report Privacy Notice

Student information is protected by Family Educational Rights and Privacy Act, the Individuals with Disabilities Education Act, and other federal and state laws.

Disaggregation Summary

Test/Report Information		Report Filters				
Test Administration	**ISTEP Spring 2010**	Corp/Diocese	**All Corps/Dioceses**	Subject	**English/language arts**	
Test Program	**Public Schools**	School	**All Schools**			
Today's Date	**6-8-2010**	Grade	**7th Grade**			

Embargo Notice

All "State" level data and any "State" reports accessible via the INORS system are embargoed and cannot be publicly shared until the Indiana Department of Education formally announces the release of the Spring 2010 ISTEP+ results.

English/language arts Students	Total Number of Students	Pass +		Pass		Total Passing		Did Not Pass		Undetermined		Mean/Median Scale Score	Standard Deviation
		N	%	N	%	N	%	N	%	N	%		
All Students	**78382**	**12445**	**16**	**43943**	**56**	**56388**	**72**	**19567**	**25**	**2427**	**3**	533.2/534.3	54.8
General Education													
TOTAL General Education	67871	12215	18	40920	60	53135	78	13040	19	1696	2	541.3/540.6	50.1
Special Education													
With Accommodations	9062	102	1	2295	25	2397	26	6015	66	650	7	472.1/472.4	50.8
Without Accommodations	1449	128	9	728	50	856	59	512	35	81	6	516.6/517.8	54.1
TOTAL Special Education	10511	230	2	3023	29	3253	31	6527	62	731	7	478.3/477.9	53.5
Limited English Proficiency													
With Accommodations	1901	18	1	650	34	668	35	1103	58	130	7	482.1/487.1	52.3
Without Accommodations	1070	25	2	509	48	534	50	436	41	100	9	503.0/506.5	48.2
TOTAL Limited English Proficiency	2971	43	1	1159	39	1202	40	1539	52	230	8	489.5/494.5	51.8
Non-Limited English Proficiency													
With Accommodations	9120	122	1	2433	27	2555	28	5918	65	647	7	474.4/474.6	51.2
Without Accommodations	66291	12280	19	40351	61	52631	79	12110	18	1550	2	542.8/541.9	49.4
TOTAL Non-Limited English Proficiency	75411	12402	16	42784	57	55186	73	18028	24	2197	3	534.9/535.9	54.2
Gender													
Male	39438	4880	12	21558	55	26438	67	11700	30	1300	3	524.8/527.0	55.2
Female	38811	7562	19	22360	58	29922	77	7845	20	1044	3	541.8/541.4	53.0
No valid information	133	3	2	25	19	28	21	22	17	83	62	501.4/507.0	54.8
SES													
Paid Lunch	41969	9883	24	24895	59	34778	83	6402	15	789	2	549.9/549.9	51.6
Free or Reduced Lunch	36087	2552	7	18952	53	21504	60	13095	36	1488	4	513.5/515.5	51.9
No valid information	326	10	3	96	29	106	33	70	21	150	46	507.4/509.5	52.6
Ethnicity													
American Indian or Alaskan Native	219	23	11	127	58	150	68	63	29	6	3	525.9/527.0	52.0
Black (Not of Hispanic Origin)	9322	401	4	4421	47	4822	52	4039	43	461	5	504.2/505.4	49.2
Asian or Pacific Islander	1173	361	31	502	43	863	74	220	19	90	8	549.6/557.1	77.5
Hispanic	5241	331	6	2825	54	3156	60	1873	36	212	4	514.0/516.2	51.0

	N	N	%	N	%	N	%	N	%	N	%		
White (Not of Hispanic Origin)	58918	10876	18	34139	58	45015	76	12464	21	1439	2	539.4/540.4	53.7
Multiracial	3280	449	14	1876	57	2325	71	860	26	95	3	529.2/530.3	52.2
No valid information	229	4	2	53	23	57	25	48	21	124	54	497.2/504.0	56.1
Migrant	10	0	0	4	40	4	40	4	40	2	20	478.6/490.5	64.2

The cut score of Pass is 501. The cut score of Pass+ is 584. Lowest/Highest Scale Score for English/language arts is 210-870.

Subtotal numbers are rounded within each category. Adding subtotals may not result in exactly 100%.

Report Purpose

This report describes group achievement for selected reporting populations.

Report Legend

N: Number of students

%: Percent of students

■ Report Privacy Notice

Student information is protected by Family Educational Rights and Privacy Act, the Individuals with Disabilities Education Act, and other federal and state laws.

Disaggregation Summary

Test/Report Information		Report Filters			
Test Administration	**ISTEP Spring 2010**	Corp/Diocese	**All Corps/Dioceses**	Subject	**Mathematics**
Test Program	**Public Schools**	School	**All Schools**		
Today's Date	**6-8-2010**	Grade	**7th Grade**		

Embargo Notice

All "State" level data and any "State" reports accessible via the INORS system are embargoed and cannot be publicly shared until the Indiana Department of Education formally announces the release of the Spring 2010 ISTEP+ results.

Mathematics Students	Total Number of Students	Pass +		Pass		Total Passing		Did Not Pass		Undetermined		Mean/Median Scale Score	Standard Deviation
		N	%	N	%	N	%	N	%	N	%		
All Students	**78382**	**18165**	**23**	**38938**	**50**	**57103**	**73**	**19100**	**24**	**2179**	**3**	553.3/556.1	72.7
General Education													
TOTAL General Education	67871	17577	26	35418	52	52995	78	13340	20	1536	2	562.4/563.3	67.8
Special Education													
With Accommodations	9070	349	4	2842	31	3191	35	5314	59	565	6	484.8/488.6	72.4
Without Accommodations	1441	239	17	678	47	917	64	446	31	78	5	538.4/541.7	74.4
TOTAL Special Education	10511	588	6	3520	33	4108	39	5760	55	643	6	492.2/495.4	75.0
Limited English Proficiency													
With Accommodations	1947	116	6	776	40	892	46	979	50	76	4	501.4/506.6	72.6
Without Accommodations	1024	82	8	523	51	605	59	402	39	17	2	519.1/523.7	67.7
TOTAL Limited English Proficiency	2971	198	7	1299	44	1497	50	1381	46	93	3	507.6/513.8	71.4
Non-Limited English Proficiency													
With Accommodations	9123	389	4	2931	32	3320	36	5239	57	564	6	487.1/490.4	72.6
Without Accommodations	66288	17578	27	34708	52	52286	79	12480	19	1522	2	564.0/564.8	67.2
TOTAL Non-Limited English Proficiency	75411	17967	24	37639	50	55606	74	17719	23	2086	3	555.1/557.8	72.2
Gender													
Male	39438	9382	24	19324	49	28706	73	9579	24	1153	3	553.6/556.7	74.5
Female	38811	8779	23	19591	50	28370	73	9496	24	945	2	553.0/555.5	70.9
No valid information	133	4	3	23	17	27	20	25	19	81	61	510.5/515.0	65.6
SES													
Paid Lunch	41969	13867	33	21281	51	35148	84	6082	14	739	2	575.7/576.5	67.6
Free or Reduced Lunch	36087	4279	12	17572	49	21851	61	12937	36	1299	4	526.9/531.7	69.6
No valid information	326	19	6	85	26	104	32	81	25	141	43	515.6/520.3	72.9
Ethnicity													
American Indian or Alaskan Native	219	46	21	107	49	153	70	61	28	5	2	545.4/543.5	72.4
Black (Not of Hispanic Origin)	9322	609	7	3878	42	4487	48	4392	47	443	5	506.9/511.4	69.3
Asian or Pacific Islander	1173	532	45	420	36	952	81	188	16	33	3	592.8/595.4	96.8
Hispanic	5241	641	12	2623	50	3264	62	1818	35	159	3	529.0/533.8	68.7

Produced: 6/8/2010 4:44 PM

White (Not of Hispanic Origin)	58918	15754	27	30168	51	45922	78	11656	20	1340	2	562.4/564.7	69.7
Multiracial	3280	577	18	1690	52	2267	69	932	28	81	2	543.4/545.4	69.6
No valid information	229	6	3	52	23	58	25	53	23	118	52	504.3/513.5	68.3
Migrant	10	0	0	4	40	4	40	4	40	2	20	500.9/511.0	66.5

The cut score of Pass is 511. The cut score of Pass+ is 603. Lowest/Highest Scale Score for Mathematics is 315-810.

Subtotal numbers are rounded within each category. Adding subtotals may not result in exactly 100%.

Report Purpose

This report describes group achievement for selected reporting populations.

Report Legend

N: Number of students

%: Percent of students

■ Report Privacy Notice

Student information is protected by Family Educational Rights and Privacy Act, the Individuals with Disabilities Education Act, and other federal and state laws.

Disaggregation Summary

Test/Report Information		Report Filters			
Test Administration	**ISTEP Spring 2010**	Corp/Diocese	**All Corps/Dioceses**	Subject	**Social Studies**
Test Program	**Public Schools**	School	**All Schools**		
Today's Date	**6-8-2010**	Grade	**7th Grade**		

Embargo Notice

All "State" level data and any "State" reports accessible via the INORS system are embargoed and cannot be publicly shared until the Indiana Department of Education formally announces the release of the Spring 2010 ISTEP+ results.

Social Studies Students	Total Number of Students	Pass +		Pass		Total Passing		Did Not Pass		Undetermined		Mean/Median Scale Score	Standard Deviation
		N	%	N	%	N	%	N	%	N	%		
All Students	**78382**	**18864**	**24**	**31010**	**40**	**49874**	**64**	**26174**	**33**	**2334**	**3**	505.1/507.5	59.4
General Education													
TOTAL General Education	67871	18125	27	28649	42	46774	69	19408	29	1689	2	512.3/513.4	54.8
Special Education													
With Accommodations	5742	279	5	1177	20	1456	25	3952	69	334	6	450.6/453.0	62.4
Without Accommodations	4769	460	10	1184	25	1644	34	2814	59	311	7	464.0/465.9	68.3
TOTAL Special Education	10511	739	7	2361	22	3100	29	6766	64	645	6	456.6/458.3	65.4
Limited English Proficiency													
With Accommodations	1595	46	3	395	25	441	28	1080	68	74	5	450.9/459.1	65.0
Without Accommodations	1376	81	6	499	36	580	42	759	55	37	3	470.6/477.0	58.1
TOTAL Limited English Proficiency	2971	127	4	894	30	1021	34	1839	62	111	4	460.1/467.8	62.6
Non-Limited English Proficiency													
With Accommodations	5720	313	5	1229	21	1542	27	3844	67	334	6	452.8/454.9	63.1
Without Accommodations	69691	18424	26	28887	41	47311	68	20491	29	1889	3	511.1/512.7	56.0
TOTAL Non-Limited English Proficiency	75411	18737	25	30116	40	48853	65	24335	32	2223	3	506.8/509.1	58.5
Gender													
Male	39438	10704	27	15014	38	25718	65	12478	32	1242	3	508.3/511.8	62.2
Female	38811	8155	21	15980	41	24135	62	13666	35	1010	3	501.9/503.6	56.1
No valid information	133	5	4	16	12	21	16	30	23	82	62	462.8/474.0	73.7
SES													
Paid Lunch	41969	14422	34	17929	43	32351	77	8818	21	800	2	524.0/525.3	53.4
Free or Reduced Lunch	36087	4419	12	13020	36	17439	48	17254	48	1394	4	482.8/485.8	58.2
No valid information	326	23	7	61	19	84	26	102	31	140	43	471.1/476.0	68.7
Ethnicity													
American Indian or Alaskan Native	219	42	19	86	39	128	58	85	39	6	3	493.4/498.0	61.9
Black (Not of Hispanic Origin)	9322	699	7	2769	30	3468	37	5401	58	453	5	467.0/471.3	60.4
Asian or Pacific Islander	1173	520	44	355	30	875	75	256	22	42	4	523.5/537.3	88.1
Hispanic	5241	636	12	1987	38	2623	50	2452	47	166	3	484.2/487.7	56.7

White (Not of Hispanic Origin)	58918	16298	28	24454	42	40752	69	16709	28	1457	2	512.8/514.6	55.9
Multiracial	3280	659	20	1323	40	1982	60	1207	37	91	3	499.4/501.6	56.8
No valid information	229	10	4	36	16	46	20	64	28	119	52	464.8/473.5	69.9
Migrant	10	0	0	3	30	3	30	5	50	2	20	473.4/466.0	44.4

The cut score of Pass is 486. The cut score of Pass+ is 545. Lowest/Highest Scale Score for Social Studies is 240-760.

Subtotal numbers are rounded within each category. Adding subtotals may not result in exactly 100%.

Report Purpose

This report describes group achievement for selected reporting populations.

Report Legend

N: Number of students

%: Percent of students

■ı Report Privacy Notice

Student information is protected by Family Educational Rights and Privacy Act, the Individuals with Disabilities Education Act, and other federal and state laws.

Disaggregation Summary

Test/Report Information		Report Filters			
Test Administration	**ISTEP Spring 2010**	Corp/Diocese	**All Corps/Dioceses**	Subject	**English/language arts**
Test Program	**Public Schools**	School	**All Schools**		
Today's Date	**6-8-2010**	Grade	**8th Grade**		

Embargo Notice

All "State" level data and any "State" reports accessible via the INORS system are embargoed and cannot be publicly shared until the Indiana Department of Education formally announces the release of the Spring 2010 ISTEP+ results.

English/language arts Students	Total Number of Students	Pass +		Pass		Total Passing		Did Not Pass		Undetermined		Mean/Median Scale Score	Standard Deviation
		N	%	N	%	N	%	N	%	N	%		
All Students	**79308**	**7893**	**10**	**46723**	**59**	**54616**	**69**	**21031**	**27**	**3661**	**5**	544.0/544.4	70.5
General Education													
TOTAL General Education	69129	7797	11	44137	64	51934	75	14324	21	2871	4	554.6/552.2	64.2
Special Education													
With Accommodations	8840	43	0	1921	22	1964	22	6174	70	702	8	462.5/465.2	64.9
Without Accommodations	1339	53	4	665	50	718	54	533	40	88	7	512.6/517.4	71.2
TOTAL Special Education	10179	96	1	2586	25	2682	26	6707	66	790	8	469.2/470.8	67.9
Limited English Proficiency													
With Accommodations	1749	6	0	480	27	486	28	1113	64	150	9	470.7/480.3	63.9
Without Accommodations	965	11	1	400	41	411	43	461	48	93	10	499.5/504.0	58.6
TOTAL Limited English Proficiency	2714	17	1	880	32	897	33	1574	58	243	9	480.9/489.4	63.6
Non-Limited English Proficiency													
With Accommodations	8976	60	1	2101	23	2161	24	6103	68	712	8	466.0/468.2	66.0
Without Accommodations	67618	7816	12	43742	65	51558	76	13354	20	2706	4	556.3/553.8	63.3
TOTAL Non-Limited English Proficiency	76594	7876	10	45843	60	53719	70	19457	25	3418	4	546.1/546.3	69.7
Gender													
Male	40307	2753	7	22279	55	25032	62	13262	33	2013	5	530.3/532.4	70.2
Female	38860	5137	13	24422	63	29559	76	7748	20	1553	4	558.1/556.3	68.0
No valid information	141	3	2	22	16	25	18	21	15	95	67	512.4/516.5	74.6
SES													
Paid Lunch	43910	6527	15	28697	65	35224	80	7319	17	1367	3	564.5/563.2	66.6
Free or Reduced Lunch	35004	1354	4	17927	51	19281	55	13619	39	2104	6	517.7/520.4	66.5
No valid information	394	12	3	99	25	111	28	93	24	190	48	513.1/517.0	73.1
Ethnicity													
American Indian or Alaskan Native	216	18	8	119	55	137	63	60	28	19	9	535.4/535.7	71.0
Black (Not of Hispanic Origin)	9421	224	2	4121	44	4345	46	4339	46	737	8	506.1/507.5	62.6
Asian or Pacific Islander	1195	263	22	611	51	874	73	220	18	101	8	566.8/572.5	97.7
Hispanic	5182	186	4	2735	53	2921	56	1978	38	283	5	517.6/521.3	65.1

White (Not of Hispanic Origin)	59979	6963	12	37361	62	44324	74	13467	22	2188	4	552.0/552.3	69.0
Multiracial	3024	232	8	1720	57	1952	65	907	30	165	5	535.7/535.3	68.1
No valid information	291	7	2	56	19	63	22	60	21	168	58	513.7/515.0	72.1
Migrant	12	0	0	9	75	9	75	3	25	0	0	512.1/530.0	48.3

The cut score of Pass is 508. The cut score of Pass+ is 627. Lowest/Highest Scale Score for English/language arts is 230-890.

Subtotal numbers are rounded within each category. Adding subtotals may not result in exactly 100%.

Report Purpose

This report describes group achievement for selected reporting populations.

Report Legend

N: Number of students

%: Percent of students

■ı Report Privacy Notice

Student information is protected by Family Educational Rights and Privacy Act, the Individuals with Disabilities Education Act, and other federal and state laws.

Disaggregation Summary

Test/Report Information		Report Filters			
Test Administration	**ISTEP Spring 2010**	Corp/Diocese	**All Corps/Dioceses**	Subject	**Mathematics**
Test Program	**Public Schools**	School	**All Schools**		
Today's Date	**6-8-2010**	Grade	**8th Grade**		

Embargo Notice

All "State" level data and any "State" reports accessible via the INORS system are embargoed and cannot be publicly shared until the Indiana Department of Education formally announces the release of the Spring 2010 ISTEP+ results.

Mathematics Students	Total Number of Students	Pass +		Pass		Total Passing		Did Not Pass		Undetermined		Mean/Median Scale Score	Standard Deviation
		N	%	N	%	N	%	N	%	N	%		
All Students	**79308**	**13329**	**17**	**43905**	**55**	**57234**	**72**	**18849**	**24**	**3225**	**4**	578.2/581.3	70.6
General Education													
TOTAL General Education	69129	13002	19	40265	58	53267	77	13274	19	2588	4	587.2/588.1	65.1
Special Education													
With Accommodations	8822	194	2	2958	34	3152	36	5100	58	570	6	509.1/515.3	73.6
Without Accommodations	1357	133	10	682	50	815	60	475	35	67	5	554.6/561.0	74.9
TOTAL Special Education	10179	327	3	3640	36	3967	39	5575	55	637	6	515.2/521.3	75.4
Limited English Proficiency													
With Accommodations	1796	56	3	727	40	783	44	917	51	96	5	522.8/530.5	70.1
Without Accommodations	918	51	6	457	50	508	55	375	41	35	4	545.3/545.9	61.1
TOTAL Limited English Proficiency	2714	107	4	1184	44	1291	48	1292	48	131	5	530.4/536.5	68.0
Non-Limited English Proficiency													
With Accommodations	8952	232	3	3096	35	3328	37	5042	56	582	7	511.9/518.3	73.9
Without Accommodations	67642	12990	19	39625	59	52615	78	12515	19	2512	4	588.6/589.5	64.6
TOTAL Non-Limited English Proficiency	76594	13222	17	42721	56	55943	73	17557	23	3094	4	579.8/583.0	70.1
Gender													
Male	40307	7062	18	21741	54	28803	71	9796	24	1708	4	577.8/582.0	72.9
Female	38860	6259	16	22146	57	28405	73	9032	23	1423	4	578.6/580.7	68.2
No valid information	141	8	6	18	13	26	18	21	15	94	67	541.1/545.0	86.9
SES													
Paid Lunch	43910	10892	25	25575	58	36467	83	6245	14	1198	3	599.6/601.6	65.0
Free or Reduced Lunch	35004	2420	7	18238	52	20658	59	12503	36	1843	5	550.8/555.9	67.9
No valid information	394	17	4	92	23	109	28	101	26	184	47	537.1/542.5	75.6
Ethnicity													
American Indian or Alaskan Native	216	28	13	111	51	139	64	59	27	18	8	565.1/566.7	75.8
Black (Not of Hispanic Origin)	9421	304	3	3986	42	4290	46	4427	47	704	7	530.1/535.3	67.1
Asian or Pacific Islander	1195	485	41	480	40	965	81	176	15	54	5	618.3/625.8	88.7
Hispanic	5182	380	7	2814	54	3194	62	1766	34	222	4	553.4/558.5	66.4

White (Not of Hispanic Origin)	59979	11759	20	34817	58	46576	78	11497	19	1906	3	587.5/590.2	67.3
Multiracial	3024	358	12	1647	54	2005	66	862	29	157	5	566.1/567.2	69.0
No valid information	291	15	5	50	17	65	22	62	21	164	56	534.8/541.0	76.7
Migrant	12	1	8	7	58	8	67	4	33	0	0	540.9/544.5	65.7

The cut score of Pass is 537. The cut score of Pass+ is 641. Lowest/Highest Scale Score for Mathematics is 340-830.

Subtotal numbers are rounded within each category. Adding subtotals may not result in exactly 100%.

Report Purpose

This report describes group achievement for selected reporting populations.

Report Legend

N: Number of students

%: Percent of students

■I Report Privacy Notice

Student information is protected by Family Educational Rights and Privacy Act, the Individuals with Disabilities Education Act, and other federal and state laws.

Ancestry

Acadian/Cajun

Top 10 Places Sorted by Number
Based on all places, regardless of population

Place	Number	%
Indianapolis (cons. city) Marion County	31	<0.01
Cicero (town) Hamilton County	26	0.65
South Bend (city) Saint Joseph County	23	0.02
Fort Wayne (city) Allen County	20	0.01
West Lafayette (city) Tippecanoe County	15	0.05
Knox (city) Starke County	13	0.34
Greenville (town) Floyd County	12	1.94
La Porte (city) La Porte County	10	0.05
Merrillville (town) Lake County	8	0.03
Borden (town) Clark County	7	0.77

Top 10 Places Sorted by Percent
Based on all places, regardless of population

Place	Number	%
Greenville (town) Floyd County	12	1.94
Borden (town) Clark County	7	0.77
Cicero (town) Hamilton County	26	0.65
Knox (city) Starke County	13	0.34
Dugger (town) Sullivan County	2	0.21
Middlebury (town) Elkhart County	5	0.17
South Whitley (town) Whitley County	2	0.11
Batesville (city) Ripley County	6	0.10
New Whiteland (town) Johnson County	3	0.06
West Lafayette (city) Tippecanoe County	15	0.05

Top 10 Places Sorted by Percent
Based on places with populations of 10,000 or more

Place	Number	%
West Lafayette (city) Tippecanoe County	15	0.05
La Porte (city) La Porte County	10	0.05
Merrillville (town) Lake County	8	0.03
South Bend (city) Saint Joseph County	23	0.02
Fort Wayne (city) Allen County	20	0.01
Indianapolis (cons. city) Marion County	31	<0.01

Afghan

Top 10 Places Sorted by Number
Based on all places, regardless of population

Place	Number	%
Bloomington (city) Monroe County	107	0.15
Merrillville (town) Lake County	30	0.10
Indianapolis (cons. city) Marion County	22	<0.01
Dyer (town) Lake County	21	0.15
West Lafayette (city) Tippecanoe County	18	0.06
Roselawn (cdp) Jasper County	5	0.13
Kokomo (city) Howard County	5	0.01

Top 10 Places Sorted by Percent
Based on all places, regardless of population

Place	Number	%
Bloomington (city) Monroe County	107	0.15
Dyer (town) Lake County	21	0.15
Roselawn (cdp) Jasper County	5	0.13
Merrillville (town) Lake County	30	0.10
West Lafayette (city) Tippecanoe County	18	0.06
Kokomo (city) Howard County	5	0.01
Indianapolis (cons. city) Marion County	22	<0.01

Top 10 Places Sorted by Percent
Based on places with populations of 10,000 or more

Place	Number	%
Bloomington (city) Monroe County	107	0.15
Dyer (town) Lake County	21	0.15
Merrillville (town) Lake County	30	0.10
West Lafayette (city) Tippecanoe County	18	0.06

Kokomo (city) Howard County	5	0.01
Indianapolis (cons. city) Marion County	22	<0.01

African American/Black

Top 10 Places Sorted by Number
Based on all places, regardless of population

Place	Number	%
Indianapolis (cons. city) Marion County	206,148	26.37
Gary (city) Lake County	87,604	85.26
Fort Wayne (city) Allen County	38,079	18.51
South Bend (city) Saint Joseph County	28,114	26.08
Evansville (city) Vanderburgh County	14,192	11.67
Hammond (city) Lake County	12,699	15.29
East Chicago (city) Lake County	11,942	36.84
Anderson (city) Madison County	9,366	15.68
Michigan City (city) La Porte County	9,122	27.73
Elkhart (city) Elkhart County	8,295	15.99

Top 10 Places Sorted by Percent
Based on all places, regardless of population

Place	Number	%
Gary (city) Lake County	87,604	85.26
East Chicago (city) Lake County	11,942	36.84
Wynnedale (town) Marion County	91	33.09
Carlisle (town) Sullivan County	880	33.08
Michigan City (city) La Porte County	9,122	27.73
Indianapolis (cons. city) Marion County	206,148	26.37
South Bend (city) Saint Joseph County	28,114	26.08
Merrillville (town) Lake County	7,202	23.57
Fort Wayne (city) Allen County	38,079	18.51
Pottawattamie Park (town) La Porte County	51	17.00

Top 10 Places Sorted by Percent
Based on places with populations of 10,000 or more

Place	Number	%
Gary (city) Lake County	87,604	85.26
East Chicago (city) Lake County	11,942	36.84
Michigan City (city) La Porte County	9,122	27.73
Indianapolis (cons. city) Marion County	206,148	26.37
South Bend (city) Saint Joseph County	28,114	26.08
Merrillville (town) Lake County	7,202	23.57
Fort Wayne (city) Allen County	38,079	18.51
Marion (city) Grant County	5,266	16.81
Lawrence (city) Marion County	6,387	16.41
Elkhart (city) Elkhart County	8,295	15.99

African American/Black: Not Hispanic

Top 10 Places Sorted by Number
Based on all places, regardless of population

Place	Number	%
Indianapolis (cons. city) Marion County	204,455	26.15
Gary (city) Lake County	86,704	84.39
Fort Wayne (city) Allen County	37,523	18.24
South Bend (city) Saint Joseph County	27,670	25.67
Evansville (city) Vanderburgh County	14,092	11.59
Hammond (city) Lake County	12,326	14.84
East Chicago (city) Lake County	11,531	35.57
Anderson (city) Madison County	9,294	15.56
Michigan City (city) La Porte County	8,999	27.35
Elkhart (city) Elkhart County	8,166	15.74

Top 10 Places Sorted by Percent
Based on all places, regardless of population

Place	Number	%
Gary (city) Lake County	86,704	84.39
East Chicago (city) Lake County	11,531	35.57
Wynnedale (town) Marion County	91	33.09
Carlisle (town) Sullivan County	880	33.08
Michigan City (city) La Porte County	8,999	27.35
Indianapolis (cons. city) Marion County	204,455	26.15

South Bend (city) Saint Joseph County	27,670	25.67
Merrillville (town) Lake County	7,086	23.19
Fort Wayne (city) Allen County	37,523	18.24
Pottawattamie Park (town) La Porte County	51	17.00

Top 10 Places Sorted by Percent
Based on places with populations of 10,000 or more

Place	Number	%
Gary (city) Lake County	86,704	84.39
East Chicago (city) Lake County	11,531	35.57
Michigan City (city) La Porte County	8,999	27.35
Indianapolis (cons. city) Marion County	204,455	26.15
South Bend (city) Saint Joseph County	27,670	25.67
Merrillville (town) Lake County	7,086	23.19
Fort Wayne (city) Allen County	37,523	18.24
Marion (city) Grant County	5,195	16.59
Lawrence (city) Marion County	6,296	16.18
Elkhart (city) Elkhart County	8,166	15.74

African American/Black: Hispanic

Top 10 Places Sorted by Number
Based on all places, regardless of population

Place	Number	%
Indianapolis (cons. city) Marion County	1,693	0.22
Gary (city) Lake County	900	0.88
Fort Wayne (city) Allen County	556	0.27
South Bend (city) Saint Joseph County	444	0.41
East Chicago (city) Lake County	411	1.27
Hammond (city) Lake County	373	0.45
Elkhart (city) Elkhart County	129	0.25
Michigan City (city) La Porte County	123	0.37
Merrillville (town) Lake County	116	0.38
Evansville (city) Vanderburgh County	100	0.08

Top 10 Places Sorted by Percent
Based on all places, regardless of population

Place	Number	%
West Baden Springs (town) Orange County	8	1.29
East Chicago (city) Lake County	411	1.27
Gary (city) Lake County	900	0.88
Dale (town) Spencer County	13	0.83
Hammond (city) Lake County	373	0.45
Gosport (town) Owen County	3	0.42
South Bend (city) Saint Joseph County	444	0.41
Macy (town) Miami County	1	0.40
Ligonier (city) Noble County	17	0.39
Merrillville (town) Lake County	116	0.38

Top 10 Places Sorted by Percent
Based on places with populations of 10,000 or more

Place	Number	%
East Chicago (city) Lake County	411	1.27
Gary (city) Lake County	900	0.88
Hammond (city) Lake County	373	0.45
South Bend (city) Saint Joseph County	444	0.41
Merrillville (town) Lake County	116	0.38
Michigan City (city) La Porte County	123	0.37
Lake Station (city) Lake County	39	0.28
Fort Wayne (city) Allen County	556	0.27
Elkhart (city) Elkhart County	129	0.25
Lawrence (city) Marion County	91	0.23

African, sub-Saharan

Top 10 Places Sorted by Number
Based on all places, regardless of population

Place	Number	%
Indianapolis (cons. city) Marion County	8,665	1.11
Gary (city) Lake County	1,517	1.48
Fort Wayne (city) Allen County	1,379	0.67
South Bend (city) Saint Joseph County	1,284	1.20

Notes: (cdp) census designated place; Refer to the User's Guide in the front of the book for more detailed information.

Place	Number	%
Elkhart (city) Elkhart County	656	1.27
Terre Haute (city) Vigo County	464	0.78
Anderson (city) Madison County	438	0.73
Bloomington (city) Monroe County	424	0.61
Merrillville (town) Lake County	342	1.11
Mishawaka (city) Saint Joseph County	320	0.68

Top 10 Places Sorted by Percent
Based on all places, regardless of population

Place	Number	%
Carlisle (town) Sullivan County	54	2.12
Clermont (town) Marion County	27	1.84
Economy (town) Wayne County	3	1.55
Gary (city) Lake County	1,517	1.48
Elkhart (city) Elkhart County	656	1.27
South Bend (city) Saint Joseph County	1,284	1.20
Indianapolis (cons. city) Marion County	8,665	1.11
Merrillville (town) Lake County	342	1.11
Rockport (city) Spencer County	22	1.02
Jeffersonville (city) Clark County	278	1.01

Top 10 Places Sorted by Percent
Based on places with populations of 10,000 or more

Place	Number	%
Gary (city) Lake County	1,517	1.48
Elkhart (city) Elkhart County	656	1.27
South Bend (city) Saint Joseph County	1,284	1.20
Indianapolis (cons. city) Marion County	8,665	1.11
Merrillville (town) Lake County	342	1.11
Jeffersonville (city) Clark County	278	1.01
Terre Haute (city) Vigo County	464	0.78
Michigan City (city) La Porte County	253	0.77
Anderson (city) Madison County	438	0.73
East Chicago (city) Lake County	234	0.72

African, Subsaharan: African

Top 10 Places Sorted by Number
Based on all places, regardless of population

Place	Number	%
Indianapolis (cons. city) Marion County	6,845	0.87
Gary (city) Lake County	1,372	1.34
Fort Wayne (city) Allen County	1,111	0.54
South Bend (city) Saint Joseph County	994	0.93
Elkhart (city) Elkhart County	586	1.13
Anderson (city) Madison County	350	0.59
Terre Haute (city) Vigo County	333	0.56
Mishawaka (city) Saint Joseph County	237	0.51
East Chicago (city) Lake County	234	0.72
Jeffersonville (city) Clark County	221	0.80

Top 10 Places Sorted by Percent
Based on all places, regardless of population

Place	Number	%
Carlisle (town) Sullivan County	54	2.12
Clermont (town) Marion County	27	1.84
Economy (town) Wayne County	3	1.55
Gary (city) Lake County	1,372	1.34
Elkhart (city) Elkhart County	586	1.13
Rockport (city) Spencer County	22	1.02
South Bend (city) Saint Joseph County	994	0.93
Oak Park (cdp) Clark County	48	0.89
Wynnedale (town) Marion County	3	0.89
Indianapolis (cons. city) Marion County	6,845	0.87

Top 10 Places Sorted by Percent
Based on places with populations of 10,000 or more

Place	Number	%
Gary (city) Lake County	1,372	1.34
Elkhart (city) Elkhart County	586	1.13
South Bend (city) Saint Joseph County	994	0.93
Indianapolis (cons. city) Marion County	6,845	0.87

Place	Number	%
Jeffersonville (city) Clark County	221	0.80
East Chicago (city) Lake County	234	0.72
Michigan City (city) La Porte County	204	0.62
Anderson (city) Madison County	350	0.59
Terre Haute (city) Vigo County	333	0.56
Fort Wayne (city) Allen County	1,111	0.54

African, Subsaharan: Cape Verdean

Top 10 Places Sorted by Number
Based on all places, regardless of population

Place	Number	%
Indianapolis (cons. city) Marion County	74	0.01
New Albany (city) Floyd County	29	0.08
West Lafayette (city) Tippecanoe County	10	0.03
Patoka (town) Gibson County	1	0.12

Top 10 Places Sorted by Percent
Based on all places, regardless of population

Place	Number	%
Patoka (town) Gibson County	1	0.12
New Albany (city) Floyd County	29	0.08
West Lafayette (city) Tippecanoe County	10	0.03
Indianapolis (cons. city) Marion County	74	0.01

Top 10 Places Sorted by Percent
Based on places with populations of 10,000 or more

Place	Number	%
New Albany (city) Floyd County	29	0.08
West Lafayette (city) Tippecanoe County	10	0.03
Indianapolis (cons. city) Marion County	74	0.01

African, Subsaharan: Ethiopian

Top 10 Places Sorted by Number
Based on all places, regardless of population

Place	Number	%
Indianapolis (cons. city) Marion County	493	0.06
Bloomington (city) Monroe County	75	0.11
Lawrence (city) Marion County	58	0.15
Fort Wayne (city) Allen County	54	0.03
Jeffersonville (city) Clark County	25	0.09
Merrillville (town) Lake County	25	0.08
Lafayette (city) Tippecanoe County	15	0.03
Carmel (city) Hamilton County	12	0.03
Speedway (town) Marion County	9	0.07
Oakland City (city) Gibson County	7	0.27

Top 10 Places Sorted by Percent
Based on all places, regardless of population

Place	Number	%
Oakland City (city) Gibson County	7	0.27
Dayton (town) Tippecanoe County	2	0.18
Lawrence (city) Marion County	58	0.15
Bloomington (city) Monroe County	75	0.11
Jeffersonville (city) Clark County	25	0.09
Alexandria (city) Madison County	6	0.09
Merrillville (town) Lake County	25	0.08
Speedway (town) Marion County	9	0.07
Indianapolis (cons. city) Marion County	493	0.06
Seymour (city) Jackson County	7	0.04

Top 10 Places Sorted by Percent
Based on places with populations of 10,000 or more

Place	Number	%
Lawrence (city) Marion County	58	0.15
Bloomington (city) Monroe County	75	0.11
Jeffersonville (city) Clark County	25	0.09
Merrillville (town) Lake County	25	0.08
Speedway (town) Marion County	9	0.07
Indianapolis (cons. city) Marion County	493	0.06

Place	Number	%
Seymour (city) Jackson County	7	0.04
Fort Wayne (city) Allen County	54	0.03
Lafayette (city) Tippecanoe County	15	0.03
Carmel (city) Hamilton County	12	0.03

African, Subsaharan: Ghanian

Top 10 Places Sorted by Number
Based on all places, regardless of population

Place	Number	%
Merrillville (town) Lake County	101	0.33
Gary (city) Lake County	71	0.07
Mishawaka (city) Saint Joseph County	39	0.08
Indianapolis (cons. city) Marion County	34	<0.01
Bloomington (city) Monroe County	11	0.02
South Bend (city) Saint Joseph County	8	0.01
Elkhart (city) Elkhart County	7	0.01
Lawrence (city) Marion County	6	0.02

Top 10 Places Sorted by Percent
Based on all places, regardless of population

Place	Number	%
Merrillville (town) Lake County	101	0.33
Mishawaka (city) Saint Joseph County	39	0.08
Gary (city) Lake County	71	0.07
Bloomington (city) Monroe County	11	0.02
Lawrence (city) Marion County	6	0.02
South Bend (city) Saint Joseph County	8	0.01
Elkhart (city) Elkhart County	7	0.01
Indianapolis (cons. city) Marion County	34	<0.01

Top 10 Places Sorted by Percent
Based on places with populations of 10,000 or more

Place	Number	%
Merrillville (town) Lake County	101	0.33
Mishawaka (city) Saint Joseph County	39	0.08
Gary (city) Lake County	71	0.07
Bloomington (city) Monroe County	11	0.02
Lawrence (city) Marion County	6	0.02
South Bend (city) Saint Joseph County	8	0.01
Elkhart (city) Elkhart County	7	0.01
Indianapolis (cons. city) Marion County	34	<0.01

African, Subsaharan: Kenyan

Top 10 Places Sorted by Number
Based on all places, regardless of population

Place	Number	%
South Bend (city) Saint Joseph County	84	0.08
Franklin (city) Johnson County	51	0.26
Indianapolis (cons. city) Marion County	36	<0.01
Anderson (city) Madison County	24	0.04
Huntington (city) Huntington County	22	0.13
Elkhart (city) Elkhart County	22	0.04
Muncie (city) Delaware County	21	0.03
Mishawaka (city) Saint Joseph County	13	0.03
Bloomington (city) Monroe County	12	0.02
Richmond (city) Wayne County	8	0.02

Top 10 Places Sorted by Percent
Based on all places, regardless of population

Place	Number	%
Franklin (city) Johnson County	51	0.26
Huntington (city) Huntington County	22	0.13
South Bend (city) Saint Joseph County	84	0.08
Anderson (city) Madison County	24	0.04
Elkhart (city) Elkhart County	22	0.04
Muncie (city) Delaware County	21	0.03
Mishawaka (city) Saint Joseph County	13	0.03
Bloomington (city) Monroe County	12	0.02
Richmond (city) Wayne County	8	0.02
Lawrence (city) Marion County	6	0.02

Notes: (cdp) census designated place; Refer to the User's Guide in the front of the book for more detailed information.

Top 10 Places Sorted by Percent
Based on places with populations of 10,000 or more

Place	Number	%
Franklin (city) Johnson County	51	0.26
Huntington (city) Huntington County	22	0.13
South Bend (city) Saint Joseph County	84	0.08
Anderson (city) Madison County	24	0.04
Elkhart (city) Elkhart County	22	0.04
Muncie (city) Delaware County	21	0.03
Mishawaka (city) Saint Joseph County	13	0.03
Bloomington (city) Monroe County	12	0.02
Richmond (city) Wayne County	8	0.02
Lawrence (city) Marion County	6	0.02

African, Subsaharan: Liberian

Top 10 Places Sorted by Number
Based on all places, regardless of population

Place	Number	%
Indianapolis (cons. city) Marion County	213	0.03
South Bend (city) Saint Joseph County	46	0.04
Anderson (city) Madison County	45	0.08
Gary (city) Lake County	30	0.03
Jeffersonville (city) Clark County	19	0.07
Terre Haute (city) Vigo County	10	0.02
Oakland City (city) Gibson County	5	0.19

Top 10 Places Sorted by Percent
Based on all places, regardless of population

Place	Number	%
Oakland City (city) Gibson County	5	0.19
Anderson (city) Madison County	45	0.08
Jeffersonville (city) Clark County	19	0.07
South Bend (city) Saint Joseph County	46	0.04
Indianapolis (cons. city) Marion County	213	0.03
Gary (city) Lake County	30	0.03
Terre Haute (city) Vigo County	10	0.02

Top 10 Places Sorted by Percent
Based on places with populations of 10,000 or more

Place	Number	%
Anderson (city) Madison County	45	0.08
Jeffersonville (city) Clark County	19	0.07
South Bend (city) Saint Joseph County	46	0.04
Indianapolis (cons. city) Marion County	213	0.03
Gary (city) Lake County	30	0.03
Terre Haute (city) Vigo County	10	0.02

African, Subsaharan: Nigerian

Top 10 Places Sorted by Number
Based on all places, regardless of population

Place	Number	%
Indianapolis (cons. city) Marion County	524	0.07
Terre Haute (city) Vigo County	92	0.15
Fort Wayne (city) Allen County	81	0.04
Merrillville (town) Lake County	65	0.21
Granger (cdp) Saint Joseph County	54	0.19
Dyer (town) Lake County	49	0.35
Michigan City (city) La Porte County	44	0.13
Gary (city) Lake County	43	0.04
Hammond (city) Lake County	37	0.04
Chesterton (town) Porter County	35	0.34

Top 10 Places Sorted by Percent
Based on all places, regardless of population

Place	Number	%
Dyer (town) Lake County	49	0.35
Chesterton (town) Porter County	35	0.34
Roseland (town) Saint Joseph County	4	0.22
Merrillville (town) Lake County	65	0.21

Place	Number	%
Granger (cdp) Saint Joseph County	54	0.19
Terre Haute (city) Vigo County	92	0.15
Rocky Ripple (town) Marion County	1	0.14
Michigan City (city) La Porte County	44	0.13
Valparaiso (city) Porter County	23	0.08
Clarksville (town) Clark County	18	0.08

Top 10 Places Sorted by Percent
Based on places with populations of 10,000 or more

Place	Number	%
Dyer (town) Lake County	49	0.35
Chesterton (town) Porter County	35	0.34
Merrillville (town) Lake County	65	0.21
Granger (cdp) Saint Joseph County	54	0.19
Terre Haute (city) Vigo County	92	0.15
Michigan City (city) La Porte County	44	0.13
Valparaiso (city) Porter County	23	0.08
Clarksville (town) Clark County	18	0.08
Indianapolis (cons. city) Marion County	524	0.07
West Lafayette (city) Tippecanoe County	20	0.07

African, Subsaharan: Senegalese

Top 10 Places Sorted by Number
Based on all places, regardless of population

Place	Number	%
Indianapolis (cons. city) Marion County	8	<0.01
Bloomington (city) Monroe County	7	0.01

Top 10 Places Sorted by Percent
Based on all places, regardless of population

Place	Number	%
Bloomington (city) Monroe County	7	0.01
Indianapolis (cons. city) Marion County	8	<0.01

Top 10 Places Sorted by Percent
Based on places with populations of 10,000 or more

Place	Number	%
Bloomington (city) Monroe County	7	0.01
Indianapolis (cons. city) Marion County	8	<0.01

African, Subsaharan: Sierra Leonean

Top 10 Places Sorted by Number
Based on all places, regardless of population

Place	Number	%
Indianapolis (cons. city) Marion County	89	0.01
West Lafayette (city) Tippecanoe County	5	0.02
Terre Haute (city) Vigo County	5	0.01

Top 10 Places Sorted by Percent
Based on all places, regardless of population

Place	Number	%
West Lafayette (city) Tippecanoe County	5	0.02
Indianapolis (cons. city) Marion County	89	0.01
Terre Haute (city) Vigo County	5	0.01

Top 10 Places Sorted by Percent
Based on places with populations of 10,000 or more

Place	Number	%
West Lafayette (city) Tippecanoe County	5	0.02
Indianapolis (cons. city) Marion County	89	0.01
Terre Haute (city) Vigo County	5	0.01

African, Subsaharan: Somalian

Top 10 Places Sorted by Number
Based on all places, regardless of population

Place	Number	%
Carmel (city) Hamilton County	32	0.08
Fort Wayne (city) Allen County	16	0.01
Bloomington (city) Monroe County	12	0.02
Indianapolis (cons. city) Marion County	6	<0.01

Top 10 Places Sorted by Percent
Based on all places, regardless of population

Place	Number	%
Carmel (city) Hamilton County	32	0.08
Bloomington (city) Monroe County	12	0.02
Fort Wayne (city) Allen County	16	0.01
Indianapolis (cons. city) Marion County	6	<0.01

Top 10 Places Sorted by Percent
Based on places with populations of 10,000 or more

Place	Number	%
Carmel (city) Hamilton County	32	0.08
Bloomington (city) Monroe County	12	0.02
Fort Wayne (city) Allen County	16	0.01
Indianapolis (cons. city) Marion County	6	<0.01

African, Subsaharan: South African

Top 10 Places Sorted by Number
Based on all places, regardless of population

Place	Number	%
Indianapolis (cons. city) Marion County	106	0.01
Bloomington (city) Monroe County	45	0.07
Columbus (city) Bartholomew County	44	0.11
Kendallville (city) Noble County	17	0.18
Vincennes (city) Knox County	16	0.09
South Bend (city) Saint Joseph County	15	0.01
Schererville (town) Lake County	13	0.05
Lawrence (city) Marion County	12	0.03
Jeffersonville (city) Clark County	8	0.03
Fort Wayne (city) Allen County	7	<0.01

Top 10 Places Sorted by Percent
Based on all places, regardless of population

Place	Number	%
Kendallville (city) Noble County	17	0.18
Columbus (city) Bartholomew County	44	0.11
Vincennes (city) Knox County	16	0.09
Bloomington (city) Monroe County	45	0.07
Schererville (town) Lake County	13	0.05
Lawrence (city) Marion County	12	0.03
Jeffersonville (city) Clark County	8	0.03
Clarksville (town) Clark County	6	0.03
Michigan City (city) La Porte County	5	0.02
Indianapolis (cons. city) Marion County	106	0.01

Top 10 Places Sorted by Percent
Based on places with populations of 10,000 or more

Place	Number	%
Columbus (city) Bartholomew County	44	0.11
Vincennes (city) Knox County	16	0.09
Bloomington (city) Monroe County	45	0.07
Schererville (town) Lake County	13	0.05
Lawrence (city) Marion County	12	0.03
Jeffersonville (city) Clark County	8	0.03
Clarksville (town) Clark County	6	0.03
Michigan City (city) La Porte County	5	0.02
Indianapolis (cons. city) Marion County	106	0.01
South Bend (city) Saint Joseph County	15	0.01

Notes: (cdp) census designated place; Refer to the User's Guide in the front of the book for more detailed information.

African, Subsaharan: Sudanese

Top 10 Places Sorted by Number
Based on all places, regardless of population

Place	Number	%
Fort Wayne (city) Allen County	36	0.02
Indianapolis (cons. city) Marion County	22	<0.01
Decatur (city) Adams County	17	0.18
Evansville (city) Vanderburgh County	8	0.01
Walton (town) Cass County	4	0.38
Avilla (town) Noble County	3	0.15

Top 10 Places Sorted by Percent
Based on all places, regardless of population

Place	Number	%
Walton (town) Cass County	4	0.38
Decatur (city) Adams County	17	0.18
Avilla (town) Noble County	3	0.15
Fort Wayne (city) Allen County	36	0.02
Evansville (city) Vanderburgh County	8	0.01
Indianapolis (cons. city) Marion County	22	<0.01

Top 10 Places Sorted by Percent
Based on places with populations of 10,000 or more

Place	Number	%
Fort Wayne (city) Allen County	36	0.02
Evansville (city) Vanderburgh County	8	0.01
Indianapolis (cons. city) Marion County	22	<0.01

African, Subsaharan: Ugandan

Top 10 Places Sorted by Number
Based on all places, regardless of population

Place	Number	%
Indianapolis (cons. city) Marion County	19	<0.01
Shadeland (town) Tippecanoe County	5	0.29
Valparaiso (city) Porter County	5	0.02

Top 10 Places Sorted by Percent
Based on all places, regardless of population

Place	Number	%
Shadeland (town) Tippecanoe County	5	0.29
Valparaiso (city) Porter County	5	0.02
Indianapolis (cons. city) Marion County	19	<0.01

Top 10 Places Sorted by Percent
Based on places with populations of 10,000 or more

Place	Number	%
Valparaiso (city) Porter County	5	0.02
Indianapolis (cons. city) Marion County	19	<0.01

African, Subsaharan: Zairian

Top 10 Places Sorted by Number
Based on all places, regardless of population

Place	Number	%
Terre Haute (city) Vigo County	18	0.03

Top 10 Places Sorted by Percent
Based on all places, regardless of population

Place	Number	%
Terre Haute (city) Vigo County	18	0.03

Top 10 Places Sorted by Percent
Based on places with populations of 10,000 or more

Place	Number	%
Terre Haute (city) Vigo County	18	0.03

African, Subsaharan: Zimbabwean

Top 10 Places Sorted by Number
Based on all places, regardless of population

Place	Number	%
Indianapolis (cons. city) Marion County	35	<0.01
South Bend (city) Saint Joseph County	14	0.01
Fort Wayne (city) Allen County	10	<0.01
Mishawaka (city) Saint Joseph County	8	0.02
Jeffersonville (city) Clark County	5	0.02

Top 10 Places Sorted by Percent
Based on all places, regardless of population

Place	Number	%
Mishawaka (city) Saint Joseph County	8	0.02
Jeffersonville (city) Clark County	5	0.02
South Bend (city) Saint Joseph County	14	0.01
Indianapolis (cons. city) Marion County	35	<0.01
Fort Wayne (city) Allen County	10	<0.01

Top 10 Places Sorted by Percent
Based on places with populations of 10,000 or more

Place	Number	%
Mishawaka (city) Saint Joseph County	8	0.02
Jeffersonville (city) Clark County	5	0.02
South Bend (city) Saint Joseph County	14	0.01
Indianapolis (cons. city) Marion County	35	<0.01
Fort Wayne (city) Allen County	10	<0.01

African, Subsaharan: Other

Top 10 Places Sorted by Number
Based on all places, regardless of population

Place	Number	%
Indianapolis (cons. city) Marion County	161	0.02
South Bend (city) Saint Joseph County	112	0.10
Fort Wayne (city) Allen County	64	0.03
Lawrence (city) Marion County	32	0.08
Bloomington (city) Monroe County	27	0.04
Mishawaka (city) Saint Joseph County	23	0.05
West Lafayette (city) Tippecanoe County	22	0.08
Kokomo (city) Howard County	17	0.04
Crawfordsville (city) Montgomery County	15	0.10
Anderson (city) Madison County	10	0.02

Top 10 Places Sorted by Percent
Based on all places, regardless of population

Place	Number	%
Avilla (town) Noble County	5	0.25
Woodburn (city) Allen County	4	0.25
Jasonville (city) Greene County	4	0.16
South Bend (city) Saint Joseph County	112	0.10
Crawfordsville (city) Montgomery County	15	0.10
Lawrence (city) Marion County	32	0.08
West Lafayette (city) Tippecanoe County	22	0.08
Mishawaka (city) Saint Joseph County	23	0.05
Bloomington (city) Monroe County	27	0.04
Kokomo (city) Howard County	17	0.04

Top 10 Places Sorted by Percent
Based on places with populations of 10,000 or more

Place	Number	%
South Bend (city) Saint Joseph County	112	0.10
Crawfordsville (city) Montgomery County	15	0.10
Lawrence (city) Marion County	32	0.08
West Lafayette (city) Tippecanoe County	22	0.08
Mishawaka (city) Saint Joseph County	23	0.05
Bloomington (city) Monroe County	27	0.04
Kokomo (city) Howard County	17	0.04
Fort Wayne (city) Allen County	64	0.03
Schererville (town) Lake County	7	0.03

Indianapolis (cons. city) Marion County	161	0.02

Alaska Native tribes, specified

Top 10 Places Sorted by Number
Based on all places, regardless of population

Place	Number	%
Indianapolis (cons. city) Marion County	38	<0.01
Winfield (town) Lake County	6	0.26
Shelbyville (city) Shelby County	6	0.03
Lafayette (city) Tippecanoe County	6	0.01
Fort Wayne (city) Allen County	6	<0.01
Simonton Lake (cdp) Elkhart County	5	0.12
South Bend (city) Saint Joseph County	5	<0.01
Bloomington (city) Monroe County	4	0.01
Terre Haute (city) Vigo County	4	0.01
Cannelton (city) Perry County	3	0.25

Top 10 Places Sorted by Percent
Based on all places, regardless of population

Place	Number	%
Winfield (town) Lake County	6	0.26
Cannelton (city) Perry County	3	0.25
Walton (town) Cass County	2	0.19
Elnora (town) Daviess County	1	0.14
Simonton Lake (cdp) Elkhart County	5	0.12
Union City (city) Randolph County	2	0.06
Crothersville (town) Jackson County	1	0.06
Pittsboro (town) Hendricks County	1	0.06
Ellettsville (town) Monroe County	2	0.04
Brookville (town) Franklin County	1	0.04

Top 10 Places Sorted by Percent
Based on places with populations of 10,000 or more

Place	Number	%
Shelbyville (city) Shelby County	6	0.03
Seymour (city) Jackson County	3	0.02
Warsaw (city) Kosciusko County	2	0.01
Lafayette (city) Tippecanoe County	6	0.01
Bloomington (city) Monroe County	4	0.01
Terre Haute (city) Vigo County	4	0.01
Elkhart (city) Elkhart County	3	0.01
Highland (town) Lake County	3	0.01
Jeffersonville (city) Clark County	3	0.01
La Porte (city) La Porte County	3	0.01

Alaska Native: Alaska Athabascan

Top 10 Places Sorted by Number
Based on all places, regardless of population

Place	Number	%
Indianapolis (cons. city) Marion County	5	<0.01
South Bend (city) Saint Joseph County	4	<0.01
North Vernon (city) Jennings County	2	0.03
Richmond (city) Wayne County	2	0.01
Seymour (city) Jackson County	2	0.01
Muncie (city) Delaware County	2	<0.01
Elnora (town) Daviess County	1	0.14
Aurora (city) Dearborn County	1	0.03
Franklin (city) Johnson County	1	0.01
Lebanon (city) Boone County	1	0.01

Top 10 Places Sorted by Percent
Based on all places, regardless of population

Place	Number	%
Elnora (town) Daviess County	1	0.14
North Vernon (city) Jennings County	2	0.03
Aurora (city) Dearborn County	1	0.03
Richmond (city) Wayne County	2	0.01
Seymour (city) Jackson County	2	0.01
Franklin (city) Johnson County	1	0.01
Lebanon (city) Boone County	1	0.01

Notes: (cdp) census designated place; Refer to the User's Guide in the front of the book for more detailed information.

New Castle (city) Henry County	1	0.01
Indianapolis (cons. city) Marion County	5	<0.01
South Bend (city) Saint Joseph County	4	<0.01

Top 10 Places Sorted by Percent
Based on places with populations of 10,000 or more

Place	Number	%
Richmond (city) Wayne County	2	0.01
Seymour (city) Jackson County	2	0.01
Franklin (city) Johnson County	1	0.01
Lebanon (city) Boone County	1	0.01
New Castle (city) Henry County	1	0.01
Indianapolis (cons. city) Marion County	5	<0.01
South Bend (city) Saint Joseph County	4	<0.01
Muncie (city) Delaware County	2	<0.01
Anderson (city) Madison County	1	<0.01
Bloomington (city) Monroe County	1	<0.01

Alaska Native: Aleut

Top 10 Places Sorted by Number
Based on all places, regardless of population

Place	Number	%
Indianapolis (cons. city) Marion County	8	<0.01
Cannelton (city) Perry County	3	0.25
Highland (town) Lake County	3	0.01
La Porte (city) La Porte County	3	0.01
Ellettsville (town) Monroe County	2	0.04
Walton (town) Cass County	1	0.09
Crothersville (town) Jackson County	1	0.06
Simonton Lake (cdp) Elkhart County	1	0.02
Auburn (city) De Kalb County	1	0.01
Martinsville (city) Morgan County	1	0.01

Top 10 Places Sorted by Percent
Based on all places, regardless of population

Place	Number	%
Cannelton (city) Perry County	3	0.25
Walton (town) Cass County	1	0.09
Crothersville (town) Jackson County	1	0.06
Ellettsville (town) Monroe County	2	0.04
Simonton Lake (cdp) Elkhart County	1	0.02
Highland (town) Lake County	3	0.01
La Porte (city) La Porte County	3	0.01
Auburn (city) De Kalb County	1	0.01
Martinsville (city) Morgan County	1	0.01
Seymour (city) Jackson County	1	0.01

Top 10 Places Sorted by Percent
Based on places with populations of 10,000 or more

Place	Number	%
Highland (town) Lake County	3	0.01
La Porte (city) La Porte County	3	0.01
Auburn (city) De Kalb County	1	0.01
Martinsville (city) Morgan County	1	0.01
Seymour (city) Jackson County	1	0.01
Warsaw (city) Kosciusko County	1	0.01
Indianapolis (cons. city) Marion County	8	<0.01
Columbus (city) Bartholomew County	1	<0.01
Fort Wayne (city) Allen County	1	<0.01
Gary (city) Lake County	1	<0.01

Alaska Native: Eskimo

Top 10 Places Sorted by Number
Based on all places, regardless of population

Place	Number	%
Indianapolis (cons. city) Marion County	16	<0.01
Shelbyville (city) Shelby County	6	0.03
Simonton Lake (cdp) Elkhart County	4	0.10
West Lafayette (city) Tippecanoe County	3	0.01
Bloomington (city) Monroe County	3	<0.01

Union City (city) Randolph County	2	0.06
Jeffersonville (city) Clark County	2	0.01
Portage (city) Porter County	2	0.01
Elkhart (city) Elkhart County	2	<0.01
Fort Wayne (city) Allen County	2	<0.01

Top 10 Places Sorted by Percent
Based on all places, regardless of population

Place	Number	%
Simonton Lake (cdp) Elkhart County	4	0.10
Union City (city) Randolph County	2	0.06
Pittsboro (town) Hendricks County	1	0.06
Brookville (town) Franklin County	1	0.04
Shelbyville (city) Shelby County	6	0.03
Melody Hill (cdp) Vanderburgh County	1	0.03
Winona Lake (town) Kosciusko County	1	0.03
West Lafayette (city) Tippecanoe County	3	0.01
Jeffersonville (city) Clark County	2	0.01
Portage (city) Porter County	2	0.01

Top 10 Places Sorted by Percent
Based on places with populations of 10,000 or more

Place	Number	%
Shelbyville (city) Shelby County	6	0.03
West Lafayette (city) Tippecanoe County	3	0.01
Jeffersonville (city) Clark County	2	0.01
Portage (city) Porter County	2	0.01
Crawfordsville (city) Montgomery County	1	0.01
Franklin (city) Johnson County	1	0.01
Indianapolis (cons. city) Marion County	16	<0.01
Bloomington (city) Monroe County	3	<0.01
Elkhart (city) Elkhart County	2	<0.01
Fort Wayne (city) Allen County	2	<0.01

Alaska Native: Tlingit-Haida

Top 10 Places Sorted by Number
Based on all places, regardless of population

Place	Number	%
Indianapolis (cons. city) Marion County	7	<0.01
Winfield (town) Lake County	6	0.26
Lafayette (city) Tippecanoe County	5	<0.01
Fort Wayne (city) Allen County	2	<0.01
Terre Haute (city) Vigo County	2	<0.01
Walton (town) Cass County	1	0.09
Crown Point (city) Lake County	1	0.01
Griffith (town) Lake County	1	0.01
Huntington (city) Huntington County	1	0.01
Warsaw (city) Kosciusko County	1	0.01

Top 10 Places Sorted by Percent
Based on all places, regardless of population

Place	Number	%
Winfield (town) Lake County	6	0.26
Walton (town) Cass County	1	0.09
Lafayette (city) Tippecanoe County	5	0.01
Crown Point (city) Lake County	1	0.01
Griffith (town) Lake County	1	0.01
Huntington (city) Huntington County	1	0.01
Warsaw (city) Kosciusko County	1	0.01
Indianapolis (cons. city) Marion County	7	<0.01
Fort Wayne (city) Allen County	2	<0.01
Terre Haute (city) Vigo County	2	<0.01

Top 10 Places Sorted by Percent
Based on places with populations of 10,000 or more

Place	Number	%
Lafayette (city) Tippecanoe County	5	0.01
Crown Point (city) Lake County	1	0.01
Griffith (town) Lake County	1	0.01
Huntington (city) Huntington County	1	0.01
Warsaw (city) Kosciusko County	1	0.01

Indianapolis (cons. city) Marion County	7	<0.01
Fort Wayne (city) Allen County	2	<0.01
Terre Haute (city) Vigo County	2	<0.01
Hammond (city) Lake County	1	<0.01
Merrillville (town) Lake County	1	<0.01

Alaska Native: All other tribes

Top 10 Places Sorted by Number
Based on all places, regardless of population

Place	Number	%
Indianapolis (cons. city) Marion County	2	<0.01
Jeffersonville (city) Clark County	1	<0.01

Top 10 Places Sorted by Percent
Based on all places, regardless of population

Place	Number	%
Indianapolis (cons. city) Marion County	2	<0.01
Jeffersonville (city) Clark County	1	<0.01

Top 10 Places Sorted by Percent
Based on places with populations of 10,000 or more

Place	Number	%
Indianapolis (cons. city) Marion County	2	<0.01
Jeffersonville (city) Clark County	1	<0.01

Alaska Native tribes, not specified

Top 10 Places Sorted by Number
Based on all places, regardless of population

Place	Number	%
Indianapolis (cons. city) Marion County	3	<0.01
La Paz (town) Marshall County	1	0.20
Van Buren (town) Grant County	1	0.11
Cedar Lake (town) Lake County	1	0.01
Chesterton (town) Porter County	1	0.01
Seymour (city) Jackson County	1	0.01
Vincennes (city) Knox County	1	0.01
Elkhart (city) Elkhart County	1	<0.01
Lafayette (city) Tippecanoe County	1	<0.01
Marion (city) Grant County	1	<0.01

Top 10 Places Sorted by Percent
Based on all places, regardless of population

Place	Number	%
La Paz (town) Marshall County	1	0.20
Van Buren (town) Grant County	1	0.11
Cedar Lake (town) Lake County	1	0.01
Chesterton (town) Porter County	1	0.01
Seymour (city) Jackson County	1	0.01
Vincennes (city) Knox County	1	0.01
Indianapolis (cons. city) Marion County	3	<0.01
Elkhart (city) Elkhart County	1	<0.01
Lafayette (city) Tippecanoe County	1	<0.01
Marion (city) Grant County	1	<0.01

Top 10 Places Sorted by Percent
Based on places with populations of 10,000 or more

Place	Number	%
Chesterton (town) Porter County	1	0.01
Seymour (city) Jackson County	1	0.01
Vincennes (city) Knox County	1	0.01
Indianapolis (cons. city) Marion County	3	<0.01
Elkhart (city) Elkhart County	1	<0.01
Lafayette (city) Tippecanoe County	1	<0.01
Marion (city) Grant County	1	<0.01
Michigan City (city) La Porte County	1	<0.01

Notes: (cdp) census designated place; Refer to the User's Guide in the front of the book for more detailed information.

American Indian or Alaska Native, not specified

Top 10 Places Sorted by Number
Based on all places, regardless of population

Place	Number	%
Indianapolis (cons. city) Marion County	2,039	0.26
Fort Wayne (city) Allen County	590	0.29
South Bend (city) Saint Joseph County	394	0.37
Gary (city) Lake County	342	0.33
Hammond (city) Lake County	289	0.35
Terre Haute (city) Vigo County	255	0.43
Evansville (city) Vanderburgh County	253	0.21
Bloomington (city) Monroe County	214	0.31
Anderson (city) Madison County	195	0.33
Elkhart (city) Elkhart County	175	0.34

Top 10 Places Sorted by Percent
Based on all places, regardless of population

Place	Number	%
Alamo (town) Montgomery County	8	5.84
Michiana Shores (town) La Porte County	9	2.73
Pine Village (town) Warren County	5	1.96
Kempton (town) Tipton County	6	1.58
Brooksburg (town) Jefferson County	1	1.35
Sidney (town) Kosciusko County	2	1.19
Gentryville (town) Spencer County	3	1.15
Lynn (town) Randolph County	13	1.14
Reynolds (town) White County	6	1.10
Montpelier (city) Blackford County	20	1.04

Top 10 Places Sorted by Percent
Based on places with populations of 10,000 or more

Place	Number	%
East Chicago (city) Lake County	151	0.47
Terre Haute (city) Vigo County	255	0.43
Michigan City (city) La Porte County	128	0.39
Lake Station (city) Lake County	55	0.39
Warsaw (city) Kosciusko County	48	0.39
South Bend (city) Saint Joseph County	394	0.37
Peru (city) Miami County	48	0.37
Griffith (town) Lake County	62	0.36
Hammond (city) Lake County	289	0.35
Elkhart (city) Elkhart County	175	0.34

Albanian

Top 10 Places Sorted by Number
Based on all places, regardless of population

Place	Number	%
Bloomington (city) Monroe County	88	0.13
Indianapolis (cons. city) Marion County	37	<0.01
Roselawn (cdp) Jasper County	26	0.66
Greenwood (city) Johnson County	21	0.06
Fort Wayne (city) Allen County	19	0.01
Munster (town) Lake County	16	0.07
Anderson (city) Madison County	14	0.02
Muncie (city) Delaware County	12	0.02
Hobart (city) Lake County	9	0.04
Merrillville (town) Lake County	8	0.03

Top 10 Places Sorted by Percent
Based on all places, regardless of population

Place	Number	%
Roselawn (cdp) Jasper County	26	0.66
Huntertown (town) Allen County	6	0.34
Ogden Dunes (town) Porter County	2	0.15
Bloomington (city) Monroe County	88	0.13
Oak Park (cdp) Clark County	7	0.13
Munster (town) Lake County	16	0.07
Greenwood (city) Johnson County	21	0.06
Hobart (city) Lake County	9	0.04

| **Merrillville** (town) Lake County | 8 | 0.03 |
| **Anderson** (city) Madison County | 14 | 0.02 |

Top 10 Places Sorted by Percent
Based on places with populations of 10,000 or more

Place	Number	%
Bloomington (city) Monroe County	88	0.13
Munster (town) Lake County	16	0.07
Greenwood (city) Johnson County	21	0.06
Hobart (city) Lake County	9	0.04
Merrillville (town) Lake County	8	0.03
Anderson (city) Madison County	14	0.02
Muncie (city) Delaware County	12	0.02
Fort Wayne (city) Allen County	19	0.01
Evansville (city) Vanderburgh County	7	0.01
Kokomo (city) Howard County	6	0.01

Alsatian

Top 10 Places Sorted by Number
Based on all places, regardless of population

Place	Number	%
Indianapolis (cons. city) Marion County	50	0.01
Goshen (city) Elkhart County	31	0.11
Fort Wayne (city) Allen County	24	0.01
Evansville (city) Vanderburgh County	19	0.02
Terre Haute (city) Vigo County	16	0.03
West Lafayette (city) Tippecanoe County	10	0.03
Bloomington (city) Monroe County	10	0.01
Beech Grove (city) Marion County	9	0.06
Mount Vernon (city) Posey County	6	0.08
Wabash (city) Wabash County	6	0.05

Top 10 Places Sorted by Percent
Based on all places, regardless of population

Place	Number	%
Straughn (town) Henry County	2	0.71
Grabill (town) Allen County	3	0.27
Woodburn (city) Allen County	4	0.25
Goshen (city) Elkhart County	31	0.11
Huntertown (town) Allen County	2	0.11
Mount Vernon (city) Posey County	6	0.08
Beech Grove (city) Marion County	9	0.06
Wabash (city) Wabash County	6	0.05
Terre Haute (city) Vigo County	16	0.03
West Lafayette (city) Tippecanoe County	10	0.03

Top 10 Places Sorted by Percent
Based on places with populations of 10,000 or more

Place	Number	%
Goshen (city) Elkhart County	31	0.11
Beech Grove (city) Marion County	9	0.06
Wabash (city) Wabash County	6	0.05
Terre Haute (city) Vigo County	16	0.03
West Lafayette (city) Tippecanoe County	10	0.03
Evansville (city) Vanderburgh County	19	0.02
Hobart (city) Lake County	6	0.02
Indianapolis (cons. city) Marion County	50	0.01
Fort Wayne (city) Allen County	24	0.01
Bloomington (city) Monroe County	10	0.01

American Indian tribes, specified

Top 10 Places Sorted by Number
Based on all places, regardless of population

Place	Number	%
Indianapolis (cons. city) Marion County	2,995	0.38
Fort Wayne (city) Allen County	1,159	0.56
South Bend (city) Saint Joseph County	736	0.68
Evansville (city) Vanderburgh County	467	0.38
Hammond (city) Lake County	459	0.55
Elkhart (city) Elkhart County	372	0.72

Gary (city) Lake County	342	0.33
Mishawaka (city) Saint Joseph County	337	0.72
Lafayette (city) Tippecanoe County	312	0.55
Bloomington (city) Monroe County	304	0.44

Top 10 Places Sorted by Percent
Based on all places, regardless of population

Place	Number	%
Newtown (town) Fountain County	6	3.70
Lake Village (cdp) Newton County	28	3.27
Burns Harbor (town) Porter County	22	2.87
Andrews (town) Huntington County	31	2.40
Brooklyn (town) Morgan County	36	2.33
Leesburg (town) Kosciusko County	13	2.08
Peru (city) Miami County	261	2.01
Sandborn (town) Knox County	9	2.00
Monon (town) White County	32	1.85
Modoc (town) Randolph County	4	1.78

Top 10 Places Sorted by Percent
Based on places with populations of 10,000 or more

Place	Number	%
Peru (city) Miami County	261	2.01
Wabash (city) Wabash County	142	1.21
Elkhart (city) Elkhart County	372	0.72
Mishawaka (city) Saint Joseph County	337	0.72
Marion (city) Grant County	222	0.71
Lake Station (city) Lake County	99	0.71
South Bend (city) Saint Joseph County	736	0.68
New Haven (city) Allen County	78	0.63
Kokomo (city) Howard County	284	0.62
Huntington (city) Huntington County	107	0.61

American Indian: Apache

Top 10 Places Sorted by Number
Based on all places, regardless of population

Place	Number	%
Indianapolis (cons. city) Marion County	104	0.01
Fort Wayne (city) Allen County	27	0.01
Anderson (city) Madison County	17	0.03
Evansville (city) Vanderburgh County	15	0.01
South Bend (city) Saint Joseph County	15	0.01
Elkhart (city) Elkhart County	14	0.03
Hammond (city) Lake County	13	0.02
Bloomington (city) Monroe County	12	0.02
Valparaiso (city) Porter County	11	0.04
Portage (city) Porter County	10	0.03

Top 10 Places Sorted by Percent
Based on all places, regardless of population

Place	Number	%
Claypool (town) Kosciusko County	3	0.96
Milltown (town) Harrison County	4	0.43
Beverly Shores (town) Porter County	2	0.28
Cayuga (town) Vermillion County	3	0.27
Star City (cdp) Pulaski County	1	0.27
Universal (town) Vermillion County	1	0.24
Odon (town) Daviess County	3	0.22
Fairview Park (town) Vermillion County	3	0.20
Churubusco (town) Whitley County	3	0.18
Silver Lake (town) Kosciusko County	1	0.18

Top 10 Places Sorted by Percent
Based on places with populations of 10,000 or more

Place	Number	%
Peru (city) Miami County	6	0.05
Valparaiso (city) Porter County	11	0.04
Huntington (city) Huntington County	7	0.04
Lake Station (city) Lake County	5	0.04
Anderson (city) Madison County	17	0.03
Elkhart (city) Elkhart County	14	0.03

Notes: (cdp) census designated place; Refer to the User's Guide in the front of the book for more detailed information.

Place	Number	%
Portage (city) Porter County	10	0.03
Marion (city) Grant County	8	0.03
Franklin (city) Johnson County	6	0.03
Munster (town) Lake County	6	0.03

American Indian: Blackfeet

Top 10 Places Sorted by Number
Based on all places, regardless of population

Place	Number	%
Indianapolis (cons. city) Marion County	224	0.03
Fort Wayne (city) Allen County	70	0.03
South Bend (city) Saint Joseph County	47	0.04
Elkhart (city) Elkhart County	33	0.06
Gary (city) Lake County	29	0.03
Evansville (city) Vanderburgh County	28	0.02
Kokomo (city) Howard County	27	0.06
Terre Haute (city) Vigo County	26	0.04
Anderson (city) Madison County	25	0.04
Michigan City (city) La Porte County	21	0.06

Top 10 Places Sorted by Percent
Based on all places, regardless of population

Place	Number	%
Lizton (town) Hendricks County	2	0.54
Milton (town) Wayne County	3	0.49
Nashville (town) Brown County	4	0.48
Hudson (town) Steuben County	2	0.34
Mecca (town) Parke County	1	0.28
Fairview Park (town) Vermillion County	4	0.27
Burns Harbor (town) Porter County	2	0.26
Elizabethtown (town) Bartholomew County	1	0.26
Lewisville (town) Henry County	1	0.25
Michigantown (town) Clinton County	1	0.25

Top 10 Places Sorted by Percent
Based on places with populations of 10,000 or more

Place	Number	%
Peru (city) Miami County	12	0.09
Madison (city) Jefferson County	11	0.09
Lake Station (city) Lake County	11	0.08
Elkhart (city) Elkhart County	33	0.06
Kokomo (city) Howard County	27	0.06
Michigan City (city) La Porte County	21	0.06
Mishawaka (city) Saint Joseph County	21	0.05
Marion (city) Grant County	15	0.05
Jeffersonville (city) Clark County	14	0.05
Valparaiso (city) Porter County	14	0.05

American Indian: Cherokee

Top 10 Places Sorted by Number
Based on all places, regardless of population

Place	Number	%
Indianapolis (cons. city) Marion County	1,375	0.18
Fort Wayne (city) Allen County	418	0.20
South Bend (city) Saint Joseph County	274	0.25
Evansville (city) Vanderburgh County	259	0.21
Hammond (city) Lake County	205	0.25
Gary (city) Lake County	168	0.16
Lafayette (city) Tippecanoe County	163	0.29
Muncie (city) Delaware County	158	0.23
Anderson (city) Madison County	147	0.25
Elkhart (city) Elkhart County	143	0.28

Top 10 Places Sorted by Percent
Based on all places, regardless of population

Place	Number	%
Brooklyn (town) Morgan County	29	1.88
Newtown (town) Fountain County	3	1.85
Modoc (town) Randolph County	4	1.78
Burns Harbor (town) Porter County	12	1.57

Place	Number	%
Mauckport (town) Harrison County	1	1.20
Springport (town) Henry County	2	1.15
West College Corner (town) Union County	7	1.10
Clifford (town) Bartholomew County	3	1.03
La Paz (town) Marshall County	5	1.02
Andrews (town) Huntington County	13	1.01

Top 10 Places Sorted by Percent
Based on places with populations of 10,000 or more

Place	Number	%
Lake Station (city) Lake County	45	0.32
Lafayette (city) Tippecanoe County	163	0.29
Kokomo (city) Howard County	133	0.29
Marion (city) Grant County	92	0.29
Elkhart (city) Elkhart County	143	0.28
Bedford (city) Lawrence County	38	0.28
New Haven (city) Allen County	35	0.28
Richmond (city) Wayne County	106	0.27
Mishawaka (city) Saint Joseph County	123	0.26
New Albany (city) Floyd County	96	0.26

American Indian: Cheyenne

Top 10 Places Sorted by Number
Based on all places, regardless of population

Place	Number	%
Indianapolis (cons. city) Marion County	11	<0.01
Gary (city) Lake County	6	0.01
Kokomo (city) Howard County	6	0.01
Terre Haute (city) Vigo County	6	0.01
Fort Wayne (city) Allen County	6	<0.01
Hammond (city) Lake County	5	0.01
Merrillville (town) Lake County	4	0.01
Evansville (city) Vanderburgh County	4	<0.01
Stilesville (town) Hendricks County	3	1.15
Mishawaka (city) Saint Joseph County	3	0.01

Top 10 Places Sorted by Percent
Based on all places, regardless of population

Place	Number	%
Stilesville (town) Hendricks County	3	1.15
Montpelier (city) Blackford County	2	0.10
Greentown (town) Howard County	2	0.08
Paoli (town) Orange County	2	0.05
Rising Sun (city) Ohio County	1	0.04
Danville (town) Hendricks County	2	0.03
Monticello (city) White County	2	0.03
Bremen (town) Marshall County	1	0.02
Ellettsville (town) Monroe County	1	0.02
Garrett (city) De Kalb County	1	0.02

Top 10 Places Sorted by Percent
Based on places with populations of 10,000 or more

Place	Number	%
Gary (city) Lake County	6	0.01
Kokomo (city) Howard County	6	0.01
Terre Haute (city) Vigo County	6	0.01
Hammond (city) Lake County	5	0.01
Merrillville (town) Lake County	4	0.01
Mishawaka (city) Saint Joseph County	3	0.01
Crawfordsville (city) Montgomery County	1	0.01
Dyer (town) Lake County	1	0.01
Franklin (city) Johnson County	1	0.01
Griffith (town) Lake County	1	0.01

American Indian: Chickasaw

Top 10 Places Sorted by Number
Based on all places, regardless of population

Place	Number	%
Indianapolis (cons. city) Marion County	11	<0.01
Anderson (city) Madison County	7	0.01

Place	Number	%
South Bend (city) Saint Joseph County	7	0.01
Brownsburg (town) Hendricks County	4	0.03
Highland (town) Lake County	4	0.02
Evansville (city) Vanderburgh County	4	<0.01
Martinsville (city) Morgan County	3	0.03
Plainfield (town) Hendricks County	3	0.02
Bloomington (city) Monroe County	3	<0.01
Hartsville (town) Bartholomew County	2	0.53

Top 10 Places Sorted by Percent
Based on all places, regardless of population

Place	Number	%
Hartsville (town) Bartholomew County	2	0.53
Bruceville (town) Knox County	1	0.21
Oolitic (town) Lawrence County	2	0.17
West Baden Springs (town) Orange County	1	0.16
Town of Pines (town) Porter County	1	0.13
Hamlet (town) Starke County	1	0.12
Mulberry (town) Clinton County	1	0.07
Odon (town) Daviess County	1	0.07
Ellettsville (town) Monroe County	2	0.04
Dunkirk (city) Jay County	1	0.04

Top 10 Places Sorted by Percent
Based on places with populations of 10,000 or more

Place	Number	%
Brownsburg (town) Hendricks County	4	0.03
Martinsville (city) Morgan County	3	0.03
Highland (town) Lake County	4	0.02
Plainfield (town) Hendricks County	3	0.02
Anderson (city) Madison County	7	0.01
South Bend (city) Saint Joseph County	7	0.01
Michigan City (city) La Porte County	2	0.01
Crawfordsville (city) Montgomery County	1	0.01
Franklin (city) Johnson County	1	0.01
Peru (city) Miami County	1	0.01

American Indian: Chippewa

Top 10 Places Sorted by Number
Based on all places, regardless of population

Place	Number	%
Indianapolis (cons. city) Marion County	84	0.01
Fort Wayne (city) Allen County	67	0.03
South Bend (city) Saint Joseph County	28	0.03
Hammond (city) Lake County	19	0.02
Evansville (city) Vanderburgh County	16	0.01
Bremen (town) Marshall County	13	0.29
Goshen (city) Elkhart County	13	0.04
Mishawaka (city) Saint Joseph County	13	0.03
Michigan City (city) La Porte County	12	0.04
Portage (city) Porter County	12	0.04

Top 10 Places Sorted by Percent
Based on all places, regardless of population

Place	Number	%
Napoleon (town) Ripley County	3	1.26
Gentryville (town) Spencer County	2	0.76
Wheatland (town) Knox County	3	0.60
Camden (town) Carroll County	2	0.34
Bremen (town) Marshall County	13	0.29
Burns Harbor (town) Porter County	2	0.26
Amo (town) Hendricks County	1	0.24
Arcadia (town) Hamilton County	4	0.23
Sandborn (town) Knox County	1	0.22
North Liberty (town) Saint Joseph County	3	0.21

Top 10 Places Sorted by Percent
Based on places with populations of 10,000 or more

Place	Number	%
Chesterton (town) Porter County	7	0.07
New Haven (city) Allen County	6	0.05

Notes: (cdp) census designated place; Refer to the User's Guide in the front of the book for more detailed information.

Place	Number	%
Goshen (city) Elkhart County	13	0.04
Michigan City (city) La Porte County	12	0.04
Portage (city) Porter County	12	0.04
Noblesville (city) Hamilton County	11	0.04
Highland (town) Lake County	9	0.04
Vincennes (city) Knox County	7	0.04
Peru (city) Miami County	5	0.04
Fort Wayne (city) Allen County	67	0.03

American Indian: Choctaw

Top 10 Places Sorted by Number
Based on all places, regardless of population

Place	Number	%
Indianapolis (cons. city) Marion County	72	0.01
South Bend (city) Saint Joseph County	43	0.04
Fort Wayne (city) Allen County	25	0.01
Hammond (city) Lake County	19	0.02
Kokomo (city) Howard County	15	0.03
Mishawaka (city) Saint Joseph County	15	0.03
Richmond (city) Wayne County	14	0.04
Lafayette (city) Tippecanoe County	13	0.02
Gary (city) Lake County	13	0.01
Bloomington (city) Monroe County	10	0.01

Top 10 Places Sorted by Percent
Based on all places, regardless of population

Place	Number	%
Hartsville (town) Bartholomew County	2	0.53
Hudson (town) Steuben County	3	0.50
Memphis (cdp) Clark County	2	0.50
Chrisney (town) Spencer County	2	0.37
Lake Village (cdp) Newton County	2	0.23
Dugger (town) Sullivan County	2	0.21
Long Beach (town) La Porte County	3	0.19
Walton (town) Cass County	2	0.19
Matthews (town) Grant County	1	0.17
Newport (town) Vermillion County	1	0.17

Top 10 Places Sorted by Percent
Based on places with populations of 10,000 or more

Place	Number	%
South Bend (city) Saint Joseph County	43	0.04
Richmond (city) Wayne County	14	0.04
Washington (city) Daviess County	5	0.04
Kokomo (city) Howard County	15	0.03
Mishawaka (city) Saint Joseph County	15	0.03
Michigan City (city) La Porte County	9	0.03
Jeffersonville (city) Clark County	8	0.03
Schererville (town) Lake County	8	0.03
Griffith (town) Lake County	6	0.03
Hammond (city) Lake County	19	0.02

American Indian: Colville

Top 10 Places Sorted by Number
Based on all places, regardless of population

Place	Number	%
Speedway (town) Marion County	2	0.02
Kokomo (city) Howard County	2	<0.01
Cicero (town) Hamilton County	1	0.02

Top 10 Places Sorted by Percent
Based on all places, regardless of population

Place	Number	%
Speedway (town) Marion County	2	0.02
Cicero (town) Hamilton County	1	0.02
Kokomo (city) Howard County	2	<0.01

Top 10 Places Sorted by Percent
Based on places with populations of 10,000 or more

Place	Number	%
Speedway (town) Marion County	2	0.02
Kokomo (city) Howard County	2	<0.01

American Indian: Comanche

Top 10 Places Sorted by Number
Based on all places, regardless of population

Place	Number	%
Indianapolis (cons. city) Marion County	18	<0.01
Fort Wayne (city) Allen County	7	<0.01
Kokomo (city) Howard County	5	0.01
Culver (town) Marshall County	4	0.26
Dunlap (cdp) Elkhart County	4	0.07
Marion (city) Grant County	4	0.01
Elkhart (city) Elkhart County	3	0.01
Goshen (city) Elkhart County	3	0.01
Evansville (city) Vanderburgh County	3	<0.01
Gary (city) Lake County	3	<0.01

Top 10 Places Sorted by Percent
Based on all places, regardless of population

Place	Number	%
Cynthiana (town) Posey County	2	0.29
Culver (town) Marshall County	4	0.26
North Webster (town) Kosciusko County	1	0.09
Hamilton (town) Steuben County	1	0.08
Dunlap (cdp) Elkhart County	4	0.07
Henryville (cdp) Clark County	1	0.06
Roseland (town) Saint Joseph County	1	0.06
Greentown (town) Howard County	1	0.04
Leo-Cedarville (town) Allen County	1	0.04
Salem (city) Washington County	1	0.02

Top 10 Places Sorted by Percent
Based on places with populations of 10,000 or more

Place	Number	%
Kokomo (city) Howard County	5	0.01
Marion (city) Grant County	4	0.01
Elkhart (city) Elkhart County	3	0.01
Goshen (city) Elkhart County	3	0.01
New Albany (city) Floyd County	2	0.01
New Castle (city) Henry County	2	0.01
Noblesville (city) Hamilton County	2	0.01
Beech Grove (city) Marion County	1	0.01
Frankfort (city) Clinton County	1	0.01
Franklin (city) Johnson County	1	0.01

American Indian: Cree

Top 10 Places Sorted by Number
Based on all places, regardless of population

Place	Number	%
Fort Wayne (city) Allen County	12	0.01
Terre Haute (city) Vigo County	10	0.02
Lake Village (cdp) Newton County	8	0.94
Evansville (city) Vanderburgh County	7	0.01
Indianapolis (cons. city) Marion County	7	<0.01
Gary (city) Lake County	6	0.01
New Haven (city) Allen County	5	0.04
Mishawaka (city) Saint Joseph County	5	0.01
South Bend (city) Saint Joseph County	5	<0.01
Knox (city) Starke County	3	0.08

Top 10 Places Sorted by Percent
Based on all places, regardless of population

Place	Number	%
Lake Village (cdp) Newton County	8	0.94
Rockport (city) Spencer County	2	0.09

Place	Number	%
McCordsville (town) Hancock County	1	0.09
Knox (city) Starke County	3	0.08
Clinton (city) Vermillion County	3	0.06
Churubusco (town) Whitley County	1	0.06
New Haven (city) Allen County	5	0.04
Dunkirk (city) Jay County	1	0.04
Attica (city) Fountain County	1	0.03
Terre Haute (city) Vigo County	10	0.02

Top 10 Places Sorted by Percent
Based on places with populations of 10,000 or more

Place	Number	%
New Haven (city) Allen County	5	0.04
Terre Haute (city) Vigo County	10	0.02
Beech Grove (city) Marion County	3	0.02
Frankfort (city) Clinton County	3	0.02
Madison (city) Jefferson County	2	0.02
Fort Wayne (city) Allen County	12	0.01
Evansville (city) Vanderburgh County	7	0.01
Gary (city) Lake County	6	0.01
Mishawaka (city) Saint Joseph County	5	0.01
Clarksville (town) Clark County	2	0.01

American Indian: Creek

Top 10 Places Sorted by Number
Based on all places, regardless of population

Place	Number	%
Indianapolis (cons. city) Marion County	31	<0.01
Hammond (city) Lake County	11	0.01
Gary (city) Lake County	10	0.01
Fort Wayne (city) Allen County	8	<0.01
Noblesville (city) Hamilton County	7	0.02
South Bend (city) Saint Joseph County	6	0.01
Granger (cdp) Saint Joseph County	5	0.02
Marion (city) Grant County	4	0.01
Richmond (city) Wayne County	4	0.01
Corydon (town) Harrison County	3	0.11

Top 10 Places Sorted by Percent
Based on all places, regardless of population

Place	Number	%
Wolcott (town) White County	2	0.20
Holland (town) Dubois County	1	0.14
Bourbon (town) Marshall County	2	0.12
Corydon (town) Harrison County	3	0.11
French Lick (town) Orange County	2	0.10
Dayton (town) Tippecanoe County	1	0.09
Lynn (town) Randolph County	1	0.09
Andrews (town) Huntington County	1	0.08
Parker City (town) Randolph County	1	0.07
Huntingburg (city) Dubois County	2	0.04

Top 10 Places Sorted by Percent
Based on places with populations of 10,000 or more

Place	Number	%
Noblesville (city) Hamilton County	7	0.02
Granger (cdp) Saint Joseph County	5	0.02
Hammond (city) Lake County	11	0.01
Gary (city) Lake County	10	0.01
South Bend (city) Saint Joseph County	6	0.01
Marion (city) Grant County	4	0.01
Richmond (city) Wayne County	4	0.01
Highland (town) Lake County	3	0.01
Lafayette (city) Tippecanoe County	3	0.01
Merrillville (town) Lake County	3	0.01

Notes: (cdp) census designated place; Refer to the User's Guide in the front of the book for more detailed information.

American Indian: Crow

Top 10 Places Sorted by Number
Based on all places, regardless of population

Place	Number	%
Indianapolis (cons. city) Marion County	12	<0.01
Monon (town) White County	8	0.46
Seymour (city) Jackson County	4	0.02
Hobart (city) Lake County	2	0.01
New Castle (city) Henry County	2	0.01
Lafayette (city) Tippecanoe County	2	<0.01
Muncie (city) Delaware County	2	<0.01
Coatesville (town) Hendricks County	1	0.19
Clay City (town) Clay County	1	0.10
Dunkirk (city) Jay County	1	0.04

Top 10 Places Sorted by Percent
Based on all places, regardless of population

Place	Number	%
Monon (town) White County	8	0.46
Coatesville (town) Hendricks County	1	0.19
Clay City (town) Clay County	1	0.10
Dunkirk (city) Jay County	1	0.04
Loogootee (city) Martin County	1	0.04
Seymour (city) Jackson County	4	0.02
Edinburgh (town) Johnson County	1	0.02
Gas City (city) Grant County	1	0.02
Rochester (city) Fulton County	1	0.02
Hobart (city) Lake County	2	0.01

Top 10 Places Sorted by Percent
Based on places with populations of 10,000 or more

Place	Number	%
Seymour (city) Jackson County	4	0.02
Hobart (city) Lake County	2	0.01
New Castle (city) Henry County	2	0.01
Crown Point (city) Lake County	1	0.01
Dyer (town) Lake County	1	0.01
Greensburg (city) Decatur County	1	0.01
Madison (city) Jefferson County	1	0.01
Indianapolis (cons. city) Marion County	12	<0.01
Lafayette (city) Tippecanoe County	2	<0.01
Muncie (city) Delaware County	2	<0.01

American Indian: Delaware

Top 10 Places Sorted by Number
Based on all places, regardless of population

Place	Number	%
Indianapolis (cons. city) Marion County	24	<0.01
Muncie (city) Delaware County	11	0.02
Anderson (city) Madison County	7	0.01
Georgetown (cdp) Saint Joseph County	5	0.11
Gary (city) Lake County	4	<0.01
Rising Sun (city) Ohio County	3	0.12
Granger (cdp) Saint Joseph County	3	0.01
Terre Haute (city) Vigo County	3	0.01
Bryant (town) Jay County	2	0.74
McCordsville (town) Hancock County	2	0.18

Top 10 Places Sorted by Percent
Based on all places, regardless of population

Place	Number	%
Bryant (town) Jay County	2	0.74
McCordsville (town) Hancock County	2	0.18
Worthington (town) Greene County	2	0.14
Clayton (town) Hendricks County	1	0.14
Rising Sun (city) Ohio County	3	0.12
Warren Park (town) Marion County	2	0.12
Georgetown (cdp) Saint Joseph County	5	0.11
Morristown (town) Shelby County	1	0.09
Lake Dalecarlia (cdp) Lake County	1	0.08

Arcadia (town) Hamilton County	1	0.06

Top 10 Places Sorted by Percent
Based on places with populations of 10,000 or more

Place	Number	%
Muncie (city) Delaware County	11	0.02
Anderson (city) Madison County	7	0.01
Granger (cdp) Saint Joseph County	3	0.01
Terre Haute (city) Vigo County	3	0.01
Columbus (city) Bartholomew County	2	0.01
Crown Point (city) Lake County	2	0.01
Bedford (city) Lawrence County	1	0.01
Brownsburg (town) Hendricks County	1	0.01
Dyer (town) Lake County	1	0.01
Lebanon (city) Boone County	1	0.01

American Indian: Houma

Top 10 Places Sorted by Number
Based on all places, regardless of population

Place	Number	%
Indianapolis (cons. city) Marion County	4	<0.01
Richmond (city) Wayne County	1	<0.01

Top 10 Places Sorted by Percent
Based on all places, regardless of population

Place	Number	%
Indianapolis (cons. city) Marion County	4	<0.01
Richmond (city) Wayne County	1	<0.01

Top 10 Places Sorted by Percent
Based on places with populations of 10,000 or more

Place	Number	%
Indianapolis (cons. city) Marion County	4	<0.01
Richmond (city) Wayne County	1	<0.01

American Indian: Iroquois

Top 10 Places Sorted by Number
Based on all places, regardless of population

Place	Number	%
Indianapolis (cons. city) Marion County	65	0.01
Fort Wayne (city) Allen County	26	0.01
Hammond (city) Lake County	16	0.02
Bloomington (city) Monroe County	13	0.02
New Albany (city) Floyd County	12	0.03
Elkhart (city) Elkhart County	9	0.02
Evansville (city) Vanderburgh County	9	0.01
Muncie (city) Delaware County	9	0.01
South Bend (city) Saint Joseph County	9	0.01
Marion (city) Grant County	8	0.03

Top 10 Places Sorted by Percent
Based on all places, regardless of population

Place	Number	%
Topeka (town) La Grange County	4	0.35
Monon (town) White County	4	0.23
Brooklyn (town) Morgan County	3	0.19
Hudson (town) Steuben County	1	0.17
Zanesville (town) Allen County	1	0.17
Nashville (town) Brown County	1	0.12
Spiceland (town) Henry County	1	0.12
Mitchell (city) Lawrence County	4	0.09
Dayton (town) Tippecanoe County	1	0.09
Lynn (town) Randolph County	1	0.09

Top 10 Places Sorted by Percent
Based on places with populations of 10,000 or more

Place	Number	%
Chesterton (town) Porter County	7	0.07

Crawfordsville (city) Montgomery County	6	0.04
New Albany (city) Floyd County	12	0.03
Marion (city) Grant County	8	0.03
Merrillville (town) Lake County	8	0.03
Valparaiso (city) Porter County	7	0.03
Frankfort (city) Clinton County	5	0.03
Huntington (city) Huntington County	5	0.03
Shelbyville (city) Shelby County	5	0.03
Connersville (city) Fayette County	4	0.03

American Indian: Kiowa

Top 10 Places Sorted by Number
Based on all places, regardless of population

Place	Number	%
Indianapolis (cons. city) Marion County	7	<0.01
Huntington (city) Huntington County	3	0.02
Muncie (city) Delaware County	3	<0.01
South Bend (city) Saint Joseph County	3	<0.01
Royal Center (town) Cass County	2	0.24
Carmel (city) Hamilton County	2	0.01
Lebanon (city) Boone County	2	0.01
Fort Wayne (city) Allen County	2	<0.01
Grabill (town) Allen County	1	0.09
Brookville (town) Franklin County	1	0.04

Top 10 Places Sorted by Percent
Based on all places, regardless of population

Place	Number	%
Royal Center (town) Cass County	2	0.24
Grabill (town) Allen County	1	0.09
Brookville (town) Franklin County	1	0.04
Huntington (city) Huntington County	3	0.02
Charlestown (city) Clark County	1	0.02
Rensselaer (city) Jasper County	1	0.02
Carmel (city) Hamilton County	2	0.01
Lebanon (city) Boone County	2	0.01
Columbia City (city) Whitley County	1	0.01
Indianapolis (cons. city) Marion County	7	<0.01

Top 10 Places Sorted by Percent
Based on places with populations of 10,000 or more

Place	Number	%
Huntington (city) Huntington County	3	0.02
Carmel (city) Hamilton County	2	0.01
Lebanon (city) Boone County	2	0.01
Indianapolis (cons. city) Marion County	7	<0.01
Muncie (city) Delaware County	3	<0.01
South Bend (city) Saint Joseph County	3	<0.01
Fort Wayne (city) Allen County	2	<0.01
Anderson (city) Madison County	1	<0.01
Evansville (city) Vanderburgh County	1	<0.01
Goshen (city) Elkhart County	1	<0.01

American Indian: Latin American Indians

Top 10 Places Sorted by Number
Based on all places, regardless of population

Place	Number	%
Indianapolis (cons. city) Marion County	165	0.02
Hammond (city) Lake County	84	0.10
Fort Wayne (city) Allen County	78	0.04
East Chicago (city) Lake County	41	0.13
Elkhart (city) Elkhart County	38	0.07
South Bend (city) Saint Joseph County	36	0.03
Logansport (city) Cass County	27	0.14
Gary (city) Lake County	19	0.02
Bloomington (city) Monroe County	17	0.02
Shelbyville (city) Shelby County	15	0.08

Notes: (cdp) census designated place; Refer to the User's Guide in the front of the book for more detailed information.

Top 10 Places Sorted by Percent
Based on all places, regardless of population

Place	Number	%
Cromwell (town) Noble County	2	0.44
Troy (town) Perry County	1	0.26
Hamlet (town) Starke County	2	0.24
Seelyville (town) Vigo County	2	0.17
English (town) Crawford County	1	0.15
Logansport (city) Cass County	27	0.14
East Chicago (city) Lake County	41	0.13
Huntingburg (city) Dubois County	7	0.13
Bourbon (town) Marshall County	2	0.12
Shirley (town) Hancock County	1	0.12

Top 10 Places Sorted by Percent
Based on places with populations of 10,000 or more

Place	Number	%
Logansport (city) Cass County	27	0.14
East Chicago (city) Lake County	41	0.13
Hammond (city) Lake County	84	0.10
Shelbyville (city) Shelby County	15	0.08
Elkhart (city) Elkhart County	38	0.07
Lake Station (city) Lake County	8	0.06
Warsaw (city) Kosciusko County	8	0.06
Valparaiso (city) Porter County	13	0.05
La Porte (city) La Porte County	10	0.05
Connersville (city) Fayette County	7	0.05

American Indian: Lumbee

Top 10 Places Sorted by Number
Based on all places, regardless of population

Place	Number	%
Indianapolis (cons. city) Marion County	15	<0.01
Evansville (city) Vanderburgh County	10	0.01
Bloomington (city) Monroe County	6	0.01
Fishers (town) Hamilton County	5	0.01
South Bend (city) Saint Joseph County	5	<0.01
Fairview Park (town) Vermillion County	4	0.27
Warsaw (city) Kosciusko County	4	0.03
Batesville (city) Ripley County	3	0.05
Angola (city) Steuben County	3	0.04
Hartford City (city) Blackford County	3	0.04

Top 10 Places Sorted by Percent
Based on all places, regardless of population

Place	Number	%
Clarks Hill (town) Tippecanoe County	2	0.29
Fairview Park (town) Vermillion County	4	0.27
Nashville (town) Brown County	1	0.12
Fairmount (town) Grant County	2	0.07
Monon (town) White County	1	0.06
Roseland (town) Saint Joseph County	1	0.06
Batesville (city) Ripley County	3	0.05
Montpelier (city) Blackford County	1	0.05
Angola (city) Steuben County	3	0.04
Hartford City (city) Blackford County	3	0.04

Top 10 Places Sorted by Percent
Based on places with populations of 10,000 or more

Place	Number	%
Warsaw (city) Kosciusko County	4	0.03
Evansville (city) Vanderburgh County	10	0.01
Bloomington (city) Monroe County	6	0.01
Fishers (town) Hamilton County	5	0.01
Elkhart (city) Elkhart County	3	0.01
Bedford (city) Lawrence County	2	0.01
Jeffersonville (city) Clark County	2	0.01
Portage (city) Porter County	2	0.01
Indianapolis (cons. city) Marion County	15	<0.01
South Bend (city) Saint Joseph County	5	<0.01

American Indian: Menominee

Top 10 Places Sorted by Number
Based on all places, regardless of population

Place	Number	%
South Bend (city) Saint Joseph County	7	0.01
Indianapolis (cons. city) Marion County	7	<0.01
English (town) Crawford County	6	0.89
Hammond (city) Lake County	5	0.01
Plainfield (town) Hendricks County	4	0.02
Nappanee (city) Elkhart County	3	0.04
Highland (town) Lake County	2	0.01
Mishawaka (city) Saint Joseph County	2	<0.01
Plymouth (city) Marshall County	1	0.01
Shelbyville (city) Shelby County	1	0.01

Top 10 Places Sorted by Percent
Based on all places, regardless of population

Place	Number	%
English (town) Crawford County	6	0.89
Nappanee (city) Elkhart County	3	0.04
Plainfield (town) Hendricks County	4	0.02
South Bend (city) Saint Joseph County	7	0.01
Hammond (city) Lake County	5	0.01
Highland (town) Lake County	2	0.01
Plymouth (city) Marshall County	1	0.01
Shelbyville (city) Shelby County	1	0.01
Wabash (city) Wabash County	1	0.01
Indianapolis (cons. city) Marion County	7	<0.01

Top 10 Places Sorted by Percent
Based on places with populations of 10,000 or more

Place	Number	%
Plainfield (town) Hendricks County	4	0.02
South Bend (city) Saint Joseph County	7	0.01
Hammond (city) Lake County	5	0.01
Highland (town) Lake County	2	0.01
Shelbyville (city) Shelby County	1	0.01
Wabash (city) Wabash County	1	0.01
Indianapolis (cons. city) Marion County	7	<0.01
Mishawaka (city) Saint Joseph County	2	<0.01
Elkhart (city) Elkhart County	1	<0.01
Fort Wayne (city) Allen County	1	<0.01

American Indian: Navajo

Top 10 Places Sorted by Number
Based on all places, regardless of population

Place	Number	%
Indianapolis (cons. city) Marion County	66	0.01
Fort Wayne (city) Allen County	14	0.01
Terre Haute (city) Vigo County	10	0.02
Elkhart (city) Elkhart County	9	0.02
Bloomington (city) Monroe County	9	0.01
Dyer (town) Lake County	8	0.06
Merrillville (town) Lake County	8	0.03
Hammond (city) Lake County	8	0.01
Muncie (city) Delaware County	8	0.01
Gary (city) Lake County	7	0.01

Top 10 Places Sorted by Percent
Based on all places, regardless of population

Place	Number	%
Leesburg (town) Kosciusko County	5	0.80
Newpoint (town) Decatur County	1	0.34
Bainbridge (town) Putnam County	2	0.27
Cloverdale (town) Putnam County	4	0.18
Gosport (town) Owen County	1	0.14
Town of Pines (town) Porter County	1	0.13
Borden (town) Clark County	1	0.12
Rockville (town) Parke County	3	0.11
La Fontaine (town) Wabash County	1	0.11

| **Lagrange** (town) La Grange County | 3 | 0.10 |

Top 10 Places Sorted by Percent
Based on places with populations of 10,000 or more

Place	Number	%
Dyer (town) Lake County	8	0.06
Merrillville (town) Lake County	8	0.03
Beech Grove (city) Marion County	5	0.03
Terre Haute (city) Vigo County	10	0.02
Elkhart (city) Elkhart County	9	0.02
Richmond (city) Wayne County	6	0.02
Schererville (town) Lake County	6	0.02
Crown Point (city) Lake County	4	0.02
Griffith (town) Lake County	3	0.02
New Castle (city) Henry County	3	0.02

American Indian: Osage

Top 10 Places Sorted by Number
Based on all places, regardless of population

Place	Number	%
Indianapolis (cons. city) Marion County	20	<0.01
Logansport (city) Cass County	5	0.03
Burns Harbor (town) Porter County	4	0.52
Terre Haute (city) Vigo County	4	0.01
Sheridan (town) Hamilton County	3	0.12
Sullivan (city) Sullivan County	3	0.06
Kokomo (city) Howard County	3	0.01
New Albany (city) Floyd County	3	0.01
Evansville (city) Vanderburgh County	3	<0.01
Fort Wayne (city) Allen County	3	<0.01

Top 10 Places Sorted by Percent
Based on all places, regardless of population

Place	Number	%
Burns Harbor (town) Porter County	4	0.52
Sheridan (town) Hamilton County	3	0.12
Walton (town) Cass County	1	0.09
Lake Dalecarlia (cdp) Lake County	1	0.08
Rockville (town) Parke County	2	0.07
Bristol (town) Elkhart County	1	0.07
Sullivan (city) Sullivan County	3	0.06
Meridian Hills (town) Marion County	1	0.06
Carlisle (town) Sullivan County	1	0.04
Logansport (city) Cass County	5	0.03

Top 10 Places Sorted by Percent
Based on places with populations of 10,000 or more

Place	Number	%
Logansport (city) Cass County	5	0.03
Terre Haute (city) Vigo County	4	0.01
Kokomo (city) Howard County	3	0.01
New Albany (city) Floyd County	3	0.01
Vincennes (city) Knox County	2	0.01
Greenfield (city) Hancock County	1	0.01
Huntington (city) Huntington County	1	0.01
Speedway (town) Marion County	1	0.01
Warsaw (city) Kosciusko County	1	0.01
Indianapolis (cons. city) Marion County	20	<0.01

American Indian: Ottawa

Top 10 Places Sorted by Number
Based on all places, regardless of population

Place	Number	%
Elkhart (city) Elkhart County	8	0.02
Gary (city) Lake County	6	0.01
Indianapolis (cons. city) Marion County	6	<0.01
Lafayette (city) Tippecanoe County	5	0.01
Worthington (town) Greene County	4	0.27
Sandborn (town) Knox County	3	0.67
Fort Wayne (city) Allen County	3	<0.01

Notes: (cdp) census designated place; Refer to the User's Guide in the front of the book for more detailed information.

Grandview (town) Spencer County	2	0.29
Huntertown (town) Allen County	2	0.11
Dunlap (cdp) Elkhart County	2	0.03

Top 10 Places Sorted by Percent
Based on all places, regardless of population

Place	Number	%
Sandborn (town) Knox County	3	0.67
Grandview (town) Spencer County	2	0.29
Worthington (town) Greene County	4	0.27
Pierceton (town) Kosciusko County	1	0.14
Huntertown (town) Allen County	2	0.11
Bristol (town) Elkhart County	1	0.07
Clermont (town) Marion County	1	0.07
Fremont (town) Steuben County	1	0.06
Dunlap (cdp) Elkhart County	2	0.03
Elkhart (city) Elkhart County	8	0.02

Top 10 Places Sorted by Percent
Based on places with populations of 10,000 or more

Place	Number	%
Elkhart (city) Elkhart County	8	0.02
Gary (city) Lake County	6	0.01
Lafayette (city) Tippecanoe County	5	0.01
Columbus (city) Bartholomew County	2	0.01
New Castle (city) Henry County	2	0.01
Griffith (town) Lake County	1	0.01
Lebanon (city) Boone County	1	0.01
New Haven (city) Allen County	1	0.01
Indianapolis (cons. city) Marion County	6	<0.01
Fort Wayne (city) Allen County	3	<0.01

American Indian: Paiute

Top 10 Places Sorted by Number
Based on all places, regardless of population

Place	Number	%
Brazil (city) Clay County	7	0.09
Indianapolis (cons. city) Marion County	3	<0.01
South Bend (city) Saint Joseph County	3	<0.01
Fishers (town) Hamilton County	2	0.01
Converse (town) Miami County	1	0.09
Andrews (town) Huntington County	1	0.08
Highland (cdp) Vanderburgh County	1	0.02
Sullivan (city) Sullivan County	1	0.02
Peru (city) Miami County	1	0.01
Evansville (city) Vanderburgh County	1	<0.01

Top 10 Places Sorted by Percent
Based on all places, regardless of population

Place	Number	%
Brazil (city) Clay County	7	0.09
Converse (town) Miami County	1	0.09
Andrews (town) Huntington County	1	0.08
Highland (cdp) Vanderburgh County	1	0.02
Sullivan (city) Sullivan County	1	0.02
Fishers (town) Hamilton County	2	0.01
Peru (city) Miami County	1	0.01
Indianapolis (cons. city) Marion County	3	<0.01
South Bend (city) Saint Joseph County	3	<0.01
Evansville (city) Vanderburgh County	1	<0.01

Top 10 Places Sorted by Percent
Based on places with populations of 10,000 or more

Place	Number	%
Fishers (town) Hamilton County	2	0.01
Peru (city) Miami County	1	0.01
Indianapolis (cons. city) Marion County	3	<0.01
South Bend (city) Saint Joseph County	3	<0.01
Evansville (city) Vanderburgh County	1	<0.01
Greenwood (city) Johnson County	1	<0.01
Mishawaka (city) Saint Joseph County	1	<0.01

American Indian: Pima

Top 10 Places Sorted by Number
Based on all places, regardless of population

Place	Number	%
Fort Wayne (city) Allen County	6	<0.01
Plainfield (town) Hendricks County	3	0.02
Clarksville (town) Clark County	3	0.01
New Albany (city) Floyd County	2	0.01
Mishawaka (city) Saint Joseph County	2	<0.01
South Bend (city) Saint Joseph County	2	<0.01
Terre Haute (city) Vigo County	2	<0.01
Bright (cdp) Dearborn County	1	0.02
Greenfield (city) Hancock County	1	0.01
Speedway (town) Marion County	1	0.01

Top 10 Places Sorted by Percent
Based on all places, regardless of population

Place	Number	%
Plainfield (town) Hendricks County	3	0.02
Bright (cdp) Dearborn County	1	0.02
Clarksville (town) Clark County	3	0.01
New Albany (city) Floyd County	2	0.01
Greenfield (city) Hancock County	1	0.01
Speedway (town) Marion County	1	0.01
Fort Wayne (city) Allen County	6	<0.01
Mishawaka (city) Saint Joseph County	2	<0.01
South Bend (city) Saint Joseph County	2	<0.01
Terre Haute (city) Vigo County	2	<0.01

Top 10 Places Sorted by Percent
Based on places with populations of 10,000 or more

Place	Number	%
Plainfield (town) Hendricks County	3	0.02
Clarksville (town) Clark County	3	0.01
New Albany (city) Floyd County	2	0.01
Greenfield (city) Hancock County	1	0.01
Speedway (town) Marion County	1	0.01
Fort Wayne (city) Allen County	6	<0.01
Mishawaka (city) Saint Joseph County	2	<0.01
South Bend (city) Saint Joseph County	2	<0.01
Terre Haute (city) Vigo County	2	<0.01
Bloomington (city) Monroe County	1	<0.01

American Indian: Potawatomi

Top 10 Places Sorted by Number
Based on all places, regardless of population

Place	Number	%
South Bend (city) Saint Joseph County	95	0.09
Indianapolis (cons. city) Marion County	56	0.01
Mishawaka (city) Saint Joseph County	30	0.06
Fort Wayne (city) Allen County	23	0.01
Granger (cdp) Saint Joseph County	12	0.04
Lafayette (city) Tippecanoe County	11	0.02
Middlebury (town) Elkhart County	7	0.24
Elkhart (city) Elkhart County	7	0.01
Hammond (city) Lake County	7	0.01
New Whiteland (town) Johnson County	6	0.13

Top 10 Places Sorted by Percent
Based on all places, regardless of population

Place	Number	%
Corunna (town) De Kalb County	1	0.39
Reynolds (town) White County	2	0.37
La Crosse (town) La Porte County	2	0.36
Vernon (town) Jennings County	1	0.30
Grandview (town) Spencer County	2	0.29
Middlebury (town) Elkhart County	7	0.24
Osceola (town) Saint Joseph County	3	0.16
Hamilton (town) Steuben County	2	0.16
Shelburn (town) Sullivan County	2	0.16
New Whiteland (town) Johnson County	6	0.13

Top 10 Places Sorted by Percent
Based on places with populations of 10,000 or more

Place	Number	%
South Bend (city) Saint Joseph County	95	0.09
Mishawaka (city) Saint Joseph County	30	0.06
Granger (cdp) Saint Joseph County	12	0.04
Griffith (town) Lake County	5	0.03
Plainfield (town) Hendricks County	5	0.03
Beech Grove (city) Marion County	4	0.03
Lafayette (city) Tippecanoe County	11	0.02
Lawrence (city) Marion County	6	0.02
Merrillville (town) Lake County	6	0.02
Highland (town) Lake County	5	0.02

American Indian: Pueblo

Top 10 Places Sorted by Number
Based on all places, regardless of population

Place	Number	%
Indianapolis (cons. city) Marion County	31	<0.01
New Albany (city) Floyd County	6	0.02
West Lafayette (city) Tippecanoe County	6	0.02
Fort Wayne (city) Allen County	6	<0.01
Hartford City (city) Blackford County	5	0.07
Hobart (city) Lake County	5	0.02
Waynetown (town) Montgomery County	4	0.44
Rensselaer (city) Jasper County	4	0.08
Crawfordsville (city) Montgomery County	4	0.03
Martinsville (city) Morgan County	4	0.03

Top 10 Places Sorted by Percent
Based on all places, regardless of population

Place	Number	%
Waynetown (town) Montgomery County	4	0.44
Rensselaer (city) Jasper County	4	0.08
Hartford City (city) Blackford County	5	0.07
Crawfordsville (city) Montgomery County	4	0.03
Martinsville (city) Morgan County	4	0.03
Peru (city) Miami County	4	0.03
Bluffton (city) Wells County	3	0.03
New Albany (city) Floyd County	6	0.02
West Lafayette (city) Tippecanoe County	6	0.02
Hobart (city) Lake County	5	0.02

Top 10 Places Sorted by Percent
Based on places with populations of 10,000 or more

Place	Number	%
Crawfordsville (city) Montgomery County	4	0.03
Martinsville (city) Morgan County	4	0.03
Peru (city) Miami County	4	0.03
New Albany (city) Floyd County	6	0.02
West Lafayette (city) Tippecanoe County	6	0.02
Hobart (city) Lake County	5	0.02
Connersville (city) Fayette County	3	0.02
Lake Station (city) Lake County	3	0.02
Carmel (city) Hamilton County	2	0.01
Goshen (city) Elkhart County	2	0.01

American Indian: Puget Sound Salish

Top 10 Places Sorted by Number
Based on all places, regardless of population

Place	Number	%
Mishawaka (city) Saint Joseph County	3	0.01
Wabash (city) Wabash County	2	0.02
Indianapolis (cons. city) Marion County	2	<0.01
Franklin (city) Johnson County	1	0.01
Shelbyville (city) Shelby County	1	0.01
Warsaw (city) Kosciusko County	1	0.01
Bloomington (city) Monroe County	1	<0.01

Notes: (cdp) census designated place; Refer to the User's Guide in the front of the book for more detailed information.

Place	Number	%
Greenwood (city) Johnson County	1	<0.01
West Lafayette (city) Tippecanoe County	1	<0.01

Top 10 Places Sorted by Percent
Based on all places, regardless of population

Place	Number	%
Wabash (city) Wabash County	2	0.02
Mishawaka (city) Saint Joseph County	3	0.01
Franklin (city) Johnson County	1	0.01
Shelbyville (city) Shelby County	1	0.01
Warsaw (city) Kosciusko County	1	0.01
Indianapolis (cons. city) Marion County	2	<0.01
Bloomington (city) Monroe County	1	<0.01
Greenwood (city) Johnson County	1	<0.01
West Lafayette (city) Tippecanoe County	1	<0.01

Top 10 Places Sorted by Percent
Based on places with populations of 10,000 or more

Place	Number	%
Wabash (city) Wabash County	2	0.02
Mishawaka (city) Saint Joseph County	3	0.01
Franklin (city) Johnson County	1	0.01
Shelbyville (city) Shelby County	1	0.01
Warsaw (city) Kosciusko County	1	0.01
Indianapolis (cons. city) Marion County	2	<0.01
Bloomington (city) Monroe County	1	<0.01
Greenwood (city) Johnson County	1	<0.01
West Lafayette (city) Tippecanoe County	1	<0.01

American Indian: Seminole

Top 10 Places Sorted by Number
Based on all places, regardless of population

Place	Number	%
Indianapolis (cons. city) Marion County	20	<0.01
Fort Wayne (city) Allen County	12	0.01
South Bend (city) Saint Joseph County	12	0.01
Marion (city) Grant County	7	0.02
Gary (city) Lake County	7	0.01
Terre Haute (city) Vigo County	5	0.01
Lake Station (city) Lake County	4	0.03
Bloomington (city) Monroe County	4	0.01
Lafayette (city) Tippecanoe County	4	0.01
Huntingburg (city) Dubois County	3	0.05

Top 10 Places Sorted by Percent
Based on all places, regardless of population

Place	Number	%
Oolitic (town) Lawrence County	2	0.17
Carlisle (town) Sullivan County	2	0.08
Monon (town) White County	1	0.06
Huntingburg (city) Dubois County	3	0.05
Lake Station (city) Lake County	4	0.03
Aurora (city) Dearborn County	1	0.03
Winona Lake (town) Kosciusko County	1	0.03
Marion (city) Grant County	7	0.02
Griffith (town) Lake County	3	0.02
Wabash (city) Wabash County	2	0.02

Top 10 Places Sorted by Percent
Based on places with populations of 10,000 or more

Place	Number	%
Lake Station (city) Lake County	4	0.03
Marion (city) Grant County	7	0.02
Griffith (town) Lake County	3	0.02
Wabash (city) Wabash County	2	0.02
Fort Wayne (city) Allen County	12	0.01
South Bend (city) Saint Joseph County	12	0.01
Gary (city) Lake County	7	0.01
Terre Haute (city) Vigo County	5	0.01
Bloomington (city) Monroe County	4	0.01
Lafayette (city) Tippecanoe County	4	0.01

American Indian: Shoshone

Top 10 Places Sorted by Number
Based on all places, regardless of population

Place	Number	%
Elkhart (city) Elkhart County	4	0.01
Vincennes (city) Knox County	3	0.02
Evansville (city) Vanderburgh County	3	<0.01
Indianapolis (cons. city) Marion County	3	<0.01
Peru (city) Miami County	2	0.02
Mishawaka (city) Saint Joseph County	2	<0.01
Griffith (town) Lake County	1	0.01
New Castle (city) Henry County	1	0.01
Bloomington (city) Monroe County	1	<0.01
Carmel (city) Hamilton County	1	<0.01

Top 10 Places Sorted by Percent
Based on all places, regardless of population

Place	Number	%
Vincennes (city) Knox County	3	0.02
Peru (city) Miami County	2	0.02
Elkhart (city) Elkhart County	4	0.01
Griffith (town) Lake County	1	0.01
New Castle (city) Henry County	1	0.01
Evansville (city) Vanderburgh County	3	<0.01
Indianapolis (cons. city) Marion County	3	<0.01
Mishawaka (city) Saint Joseph County	2	<0.01
Bloomington (city) Monroe County	1	<0.01
Carmel (city) Hamilton County	1	<0.01

Top 10 Places Sorted by Percent
Based on places with populations of 10,000 or more

Place	Number	%
Vincennes (city) Knox County	3	0.02
Peru (city) Miami County	2	0.02
Elkhart (city) Elkhart County	4	0.01
Griffith (town) Lake County	1	0.01
New Castle (city) Henry County	1	0.01
Evansville (city) Vanderburgh County	3	<0.01
Indianapolis (cons. city) Marion County	3	<0.01
Mishawaka (city) Saint Joseph County	2	<0.01
Bloomington (city) Monroe County	1	<0.01
Carmel (city) Hamilton County	1	<0.01

American Indian: Sioux

Top 10 Places Sorted by Number
Based on all places, regardless of population

Place	Number	%
Indianapolis (cons. city) Marion County	192	0.02
Fort Wayne (city) Allen County	32	0.02
Terre Haute (city) Vigo County	30	0.05
Evansville (city) Vanderburgh County	30	0.02
South Bend (city) Saint Joseph County	24	0.02
Anderson (city) Madison County	21	0.04
Hammond (city) Lake County	21	0.03
Gary (city) Lake County	18	0.02
Elkhart (city) Elkhart County	16	0.03
Bloomington (city) Monroe County	16	0.02

Top 10 Places Sorted by Percent
Based on all places, regardless of population

Place	Number	%
Lake Village (cdp) Newton County	14	1.64
Wheatland (town) Knox County	3	0.60
Camden (town) Carroll County	3	0.52
Crane (town) Martin County	1	0.49
Leesburg (town) Kosciusko County	3	0.48
Fountain City (town) Wayne County	3	0.41
Wanatah (town) La Porte County	4	0.39
West Lebanon (town) Warren County	3	0.38
Poseyville (town) Posey County	4	0.34

Place	Number	%
Eaton (town) Delaware County	5	0.31

Top 10 Places Sorted by Percent
Based on places with populations of 10,000 or more

Place	Number	%
Lake Station (city) Lake County	10	0.07
Griffith (town) Lake County	11	0.06
Beech Grove (city) Marion County	9	0.06
Madison (city) Jefferson County	7	0.06
Terre Haute (city) Vigo County	30	0.05
Vincennes (city) Knox County	9	0.05
Anderson (city) Madison County	21	0.04
Hammond (city) Lake County	21	0.03
Elkhart (city) Elkhart County	16	0.03
Kokomo (city) Howard County	15	0.03

American Indian: Tohono O'Odham

Top 10 Places Sorted by Number
Based on all places, regardless of population

Place	Number	%
Cedar Lake (town) Lake County	4	0.04
Valparaiso (city) Porter County	4	0.01
Franklin (city) Johnson County	3	0.02
Indianapolis (cons. city) Marion County	2	<0.01
Munster (town) Lake County	1	<0.01
Portage (city) Porter County	1	<0.01
South Bend (city) Saint Joseph County	1	<0.01

Top 10 Places Sorted by Percent
Based on all places, regardless of population

Place	Number	%
Cedar Lake (town) Lake County	4	0.04
Franklin (city) Johnson County	3	0.02
Valparaiso (city) Porter County	4	0.01
Indianapolis (cons. city) Marion County	2	<0.01
Munster (town) Lake County	1	<0.01
Portage (city) Porter County	1	<0.01
South Bend (city) Saint Joseph County	1	<0.01

Top 10 Places Sorted by Percent
Based on places with populations of 10,000 or more

Place	Number	%
Franklin (city) Johnson County	3	0.02
Valparaiso (city) Porter County	4	0.01
Indianapolis (cons. city) Marion County	2	<0.01
Munster (town) Lake County	1	<0.01
Portage (city) Porter County	1	<0.01
South Bend (city) Saint Joseph County	1	<0.01

American Indian: Ute

Top 10 Places Sorted by Number
Based on all places, regardless of population

Place	Number	%
Clinton (city) Vermillion County	4	0.08
West Lafayette (city) Tippecanoe County	4	0.01
South Bend (city) Saint Joseph County	4	<0.01
Plainfield (town) Hendricks County	2	0.01
Fort Wayne (city) Allen County	2	<0.01
Indianapolis (cons. city) Marion County	2	<0.01
Chandler (town) Warrick County	1	0.03
Huntington (city) Huntington County	1	0.01
Peru (city) Miami County	1	0.01
Seymour (city) Jackson County	1	0.01

Top 10 Places Sorted by Percent
Based on all places, regardless of population

Place	Number	%
Clinton (city) Vermillion County	4	0.08
Chandler (town) Warrick County	1	0.03

Notes: (cdp) census designated place; Refer to the User's Guide in the front of the book for more detailed information.

Place	Number	%
West Lafayette (city) Tippecanoe County	4	0.01
Plainfield (town) Hendricks County	2	0.01
Huntington (city) Huntington County	1	0.01
Peru (city) Miami County	1	0.01
Seymour (city) Jackson County	1	0.01
South Bend (city) Saint Joseph County	4	<0.01
Fort Wayne (city) Allen County	2	<0.01
Indianapolis (cons. city) Marion County	2	<0.01

Top 10 Places Sorted by Percent
Based on places with populations of 10,000 or more

Place	Number	%
West Lafayette (city) Tippecanoe County	4	0.01
Plainfield (town) Hendricks County	2	0.01
Huntington (city) Huntington County	1	0.01
Peru (city) Miami County	1	0.01
Seymour (city) Jackson County	1	0.01
South Bend (city) Saint Joseph County	4	<0.01
Fort Wayne (city) Allen County	2	<0.01
Indianapolis (cons. city) Marion County	2	<0.01
Fishers (town) Hamilton County	1	<0.01
Mishawaka (city) Saint Joseph County	1	<0.01

American Indian: Yakama

Top 10 Places Sorted by Number
Based on all places, regardless of population

Place	Number	%
Danville (town) Hendricks County	3	0.05
Indianapolis (cons. city) Marion County	3	<0.01
Frankfort (city) Clinton County	1	0.01
Kokomo (city) Howard County	1	<0.01

Top 10 Places Sorted by Percent
Based on all places, regardless of population

Place	Number	%
Danville (town) Hendricks County	3	0.05
Frankfort (city) Clinton County	1	0.01
Indianapolis (cons. city) Marion County	3	<0.01
Kokomo (city) Howard County	1	<0.01

Top 10 Places Sorted by Percent
Based on places with populations of 10,000 or more

Place	Number	%
Frankfort (city) Clinton County	1	0.01
Indianapolis (cons. city) Marion County	3	<0.01
Kokomo (city) Howard County	1	<0.01

American Indian: Yaqui

Top 10 Places Sorted by Number
Based on all places, regardless of population

Place	Number	%
Indianapolis (cons. city) Marion County	4	<0.01
Fort Wayne (city) Allen County	3	<0.01
Merrillville (town) Lake County	2	0.01
Gary (city) Lake County	2	<0.01
South Bend (city) Saint Joseph County	2	<0.01
Winfield (town) Lake County	1	0.04
Bloomington (city) Monroe County	1	<0.01
Jeffersonville (city) Clark County	1	<0.01
Valparaiso (city) Porter County	1	<0.01

Top 10 Places Sorted by Percent
Based on all places, regardless of population

Place	Number	%
Winfield (town) Lake County	1	0.04
Merrillville (town) Lake County	2	0.01
Indianapolis (cons. city) Marion County	4	<0.01
Fort Wayne (city) Allen County	3	<0.01
Gary (city) Lake County	2	<0.01

Place	Number	%
South Bend (city) Saint Joseph County	2	<0.01
Bloomington (city) Monroe County	1	<0.01
Jeffersonville (city) Clark County	1	<0.01
Valparaiso (city) Porter County	1	<0.01

Top 10 Places Sorted by Percent
Based on places with populations of 10,000 or more

Place	Number	%
Merrillville (town) Lake County	2	0.01
Indianapolis (cons. city) Marion County	4	<0.01
Fort Wayne (city) Allen County	3	<0.01
Gary (city) Lake County	2	<0.01
South Bend (city) Saint Joseph County	2	<0.01
Bloomington (city) Monroe County	1	<0.01
Jeffersonville (city) Clark County	1	<0.01
Valparaiso (city) Porter County	1	<0.01

American Indian: Yuman

Top 10 Places Sorted by Number
Based on all places, regardless of population

Place	Number	%
Indianapolis (cons. city) Marion County	6	<0.01
Town of Pines (town) Porter County	2	0.25
Fort Wayne (city) Allen County	1	<0.01

Top 10 Places Sorted by Percent
Based on all places, regardless of population

Place	Number	%
Town of Pines (town) Porter County	2	0.25
Indianapolis (cons. city) Marion County	6	<0.01
Fort Wayne (city) Allen County	1	<0.01

Top 10 Places Sorted by Percent
Based on places with populations of 10,000 or more

Place	Number	%
Indianapolis (cons. city) Marion County	6	<0.01
Fort Wayne (city) Allen County	1	<0.01

American Indian: All other tribes

Top 10 Places Sorted by Number
Based on all places, regardless of population

Place	Number	%
Indianapolis (cons. city) Marion County	343	0.04
Fort Wayne (city) Allen County	301	0.15
Peru (city) Miami County	184	1.42
Wabash (city) Wabash County	105	0.89
South Bend (city) Saint Joseph County	95	0.09
Mishawaka (city) Saint Joseph County	81	0.17
Elkhart (city) Elkhart County	59	0.11
Marion (city) Grant County	55	0.18
Kokomo (city) Howard County	53	0.11
Huntington (city) Huntington County	47	0.27

Top 10 Places Sorted by Percent
Based on all places, regardless of population

Place	Number	%
Newtown (town) Fountain County	3	1.85
Peru (city) Miami County	184	1.42
Andrews (town) Huntington County	14	1.09
Fillmore (town) Putnam County	5	0.92
Wabash (city) Wabash County	105	0.89
Roann (town) Wabash County	3	0.75
Advance (town) Boone County	4	0.71
Denver (town) Miami County	3	0.55
Troy (town) Perry County	2	0.51
Georgetown (cdp) Saint Joseph County	22	0.49

Top 10 Places Sorted by Percent
Based on places with populations of 10,000 or more

Place	Number	%
Peru (city) Miami County	184	1.42
Wabash (city) Wabash County	105	0.89
Huntington (city) Huntington County	47	0.27
Marion (city) Grant County	55	0.18
Mishawaka (city) Saint Joseph County	81	0.17
Fort Wayne (city) Allen County	301	0.15
New Haven (city) Allen County	16	0.13
Lebanon (city) Boone County	17	0.12
Elkhart (city) Elkhart County	59	0.11
Kokomo (city) Howard County	53	0.11

American Indian tribes, not specified

Top 10 Places Sorted by Number
Based on all places, regardless of population

Place	Number	%
Indianapolis (cons. city) Marion County	365	0.05
Fort Wayne (city) Allen County	96	0.05
Hammond (city) Lake County	71	0.09
South Bend (city) Saint Joseph County	56	0.05
Gary (city) Lake County	54	0.05
Anderson (city) Madison County	48	0.08
Lafayette (city) Tippecanoe County	46	0.08
Evansville (city) Vanderburgh County	44	0.04
Terre Haute (city) Vigo County	35	0.06
Muncie (city) Delaware County	32	0.05

Top 10 Places Sorted by Percent
Based on all places, regardless of population

Place	Number	%
Birdseye (town) Dubois County	7	1.51
Bethany (town) Morgan County	1	1.06
Crane (town) Martin County	2	0.99
Linden (town) Montgomery County	5	0.71
Mecca (town) Parke County	2	0.56
Bunker Hill (town) Miami County	5	0.51
Saint Paul (town) Decatur County	5	0.49
North Webster (town) Kosciusko County	5	0.47
Owensville (town) Gibson County	5	0.38
Wynnedale (town) Marion County	1	0.36

Top 10 Places Sorted by Percent
Based on places with populations of 10,000 or more

Place	Number	%
Peru (city) Miami County	23	0.18
Warsaw (city) Kosciusko County	12	0.10
Hammond (city) Lake County	71	0.09
Auburn (city) De Kalb County	11	0.09
Anderson (city) Madison County	48	0.08
Lafayette (city) Tippecanoe County	46	0.08
Speedway (town) Marion County	10	0.08
Portage (city) Porter County	23	0.07
Terre Haute (city) Vigo County	35	0.06
Elkhart (city) Elkhart County	31	0.06

Arab

Top 10 Places Sorted by Number
Based on all places, regardless of population

Place	Number	%
Indianapolis (cons. city) Marion County	1,973	0.25
Michigan City (city) La Porte County	525	1.60
Bloomington (city) Monroe County	403	0.58
South Bend (city) Saint Joseph County	377	0.35
Hammond (city) Lake County	369	0.44
Fort Wayne (city) Allen County	369	0.18
Evansville (city) Vanderburgh County	365	0.30
Terre Haute (city) Vigo County	291	0.49
West Lafayette (city) Tippecanoe County	286	0.99

Notes: (cdp) census designated place; Refer to the User's Guide in the front of the book for more detailed information.

Muncie (city) Delaware County	246	0.36

Top 10 Places Sorted by Percent
Based on all places, regardless of population

Place	Number	%
Pottawattamie Park (town) La Porte County	19	6.31
Topeka (town) La Grange County	31	2.67
Leavenworth (town) Crawford County	9	2.61
Carlisle (town) Sullivan County	56	2.19
Southport (city) Marion County	39	2.00
Gulivoire Park (cdp) Saint Joseph County	57	1.93
Hebron (town) Porter County	60	1.67
Michigan City (city) La Porte County	525	1.60
Saint John (town) Lake County	84	1.00
West Lafayette (city) Tippecanoe County	286	0.99

Top 10 Places Sorted by Percent
Based on places with populations of 10,000 or more

Place	Number	%
Michigan City (city) La Porte County	525	1.60
West Lafayette (city) Tippecanoe County	286	0.99
Carmel (city) Hamilton County	235	0.62
Bloomington (city) Monroe County	403	0.58
Noblesville (city) Hamilton County	167	0.58
Granger (cdp) Saint Joseph County	152	0.54
Highland (town) Lake County	124	0.53
Terre Haute (city) Vigo County	291	0.49
Mishawaka (city) Saint Joseph County	229	0.49
Hammond (city) Lake County	369	0.44

Arab: Arab/Arabic

Top 10 Places Sorted by Number
Based on all places, regardless of population

Place	Number	%
Hammond (city) Lake County	152	0.18
Indianapolis (cons. city) Marion County	151	0.02
Evansville (city) Vanderburgh County	127	0.10
Muncie (city) Delaware County	90	0.13
Highland (town) Lake County	80	0.34
Fort Wayne (city) Allen County	65	0.03
South Bend (city) Saint Joseph County	62	0.06
Lawrence (city) Marion County	58	0.15
Terre Haute (city) Vigo County	53	0.09
Bloomington (city) Monroe County	50	0.07

Top 10 Places Sorted by Percent
Based on all places, regardless of population

Place	Number	%
Topeka (town) La Grange County	29	2.50
Bruceville (town) Knox County	3	0.67
Long Beach (town) La Porte County	10	0.63
Fowler (town) Benton County	15	0.62
Farmersburg (town) Sullivan County	5	0.41
Highland (town) Lake County	80	0.34
Bremen (town) Marshall County	15	0.33
Daleville (town) Delaware County	5	0.31
Wanatah (town) La Porte County	3	0.30
Remington (town) Jasper County	4	0.28

Top 10 Places Sorted by Percent
Based on places with populations of 10,000 or more

Place	Number	%
Highland (town) Lake County	80	0.34
Hammond (city) Lake County	152	0.18
Lawrence (city) Marion County	58	0.15
Muncie (city) Delaware County	90	0.13
East Chicago (city) Lake County	40	0.12
West Lafayette (city) Tippecanoe County	35	0.12
Speedway (town) Marion County	14	0.11
Evansville (city) Vanderburgh County	127	0.10
Merrillville (town) Lake County	32	0.10

Terre Haute (city) Vigo County	53	0.09

Arab: Egyptian

Top 10 Places Sorted by Number
Based on all places, regardless of population

Place	Number	%
Indianapolis (cons. city) Marion County	519	0.07
West Lafayette (city) Tippecanoe County	66	0.23
Saint John (town) Lake County	62	0.74
Bloomington (city) Monroe County	58	0.08
Fishers (town) Hamilton County	53	0.14
Monticello (city) White County	47	0.84
Hammond (city) Lake County	42	0.05
Speedway (town) Marion County	34	0.26
Lakes of the Four Seasons (cdp) Lake County	27	0.37
New Albany (city) Floyd County	25	0.07

Top 10 Places Sorted by Percent
Based on all places, regardless of population

Place	Number	%
Monticello (city) White County	47	0.84
Saint John (town) Lake County	62	0.74
Knightstown (town) Henry County	9	0.42
Lakes of the Four Seasons (cdp) Lake County	27	0.37
Redkey (town) Jay County	5	0.35
Bunker Hill (town) Miami County	3	0.31
Speedway (town) Marion County	34	0.26
West Lafayette (city) Tippecanoe County	66	0.23
Lawrenceburg (city) Dearborn County	9	0.19
Daleville (town) Delaware County	3	0.19

Top 10 Places Sorted by Percent
Based on places with populations of 10,000 or more

Place	Number	%
Speedway (town) Marion County	34	0.26
West Lafayette (city) Tippecanoe County	66	0.23
New Haven (city) Allen County	22	0.18
Dyer (town) Lake County	23	0.17
Fishers (town) Hamilton County	53	0.14
Bloomington (city) Monroe County	58	0.08
Granger (cdp) Saint Joseph County	23	0.08
Crown Point (city) Lake County	16	0.08
Brownsburg (town) Hendricks County	12	0.08
Indianapolis (cons. city) Marion County	519	0.07

Arab: Iraqi

Top 10 Places Sorted by Number
Based on all places, regardless of population

Place	Number	%
Mishawaka (city) Saint Joseph County	93	0.20
Fort Wayne (city) Allen County	20	0.01
Hammond (city) Lake County	16	0.02
Elkhart (city) Elkhart County	13	0.03
Indianapolis (cons. city) Marion County	10	<0.01
Bloomington (city) Monroe County	7	0.01
South Bend (city) Saint Joseph County	7	0.01
Angola (city) Steuben County	6	0.08

Top 10 Places Sorted by Percent
Based on all places, regardless of population

Place	Number	%
Mishawaka (city) Saint Joseph County	93	0.20
Angola (city) Steuben County	6	0.08
Elkhart (city) Elkhart County	13	0.03
Hammond (city) Lake County	16	0.02
Fort Wayne (city) Allen County	20	0.01
Bloomington (city) Monroe County	7	0.01
South Bend (city) Saint Joseph County	7	0.01
Indianapolis (cons. city) Marion County	10	<0.01

Top 10 Places Sorted by Percent
Based on places with populations of 10,000 or more

Place	Number	%
Mishawaka (city) Saint Joseph County	93	0.20
Elkhart (city) Elkhart County	13	0.03
Hammond (city) Lake County	16	0.02
Fort Wayne (city) Allen County	20	0.01
Bloomington (city) Monroe County	7	0.01
South Bend (city) Saint Joseph County	7	0.01
Indianapolis (cons. city) Marion County	10	<0.01

Arab: Jordanian

Top 10 Places Sorted by Number
Based on all places, regardless of population

Place	Number	%
Hammond (city) Lake County	63	0.08
Bloomington (city) Monroe County	33	0.05
West Lafayette (city) Tippecanoe County	28	0.10
South Bend (city) Saint Joseph County	27	0.03
Indianapolis (cons. city) Marion County	26	<0.01
Fort Wayne (city) Allen County	21	0.01
East Chicago (city) Lake County	16	0.05
Noblesville (city) Hamilton County	14	0.05
Michigan City (city) La Porte County	14	0.04
Granger (cdp) Saint Joseph County	9	0.03

Top 10 Places Sorted by Percent
Based on all places, regardless of population

Place	Number	%
Winfield (town) Lake County	4	0.18
West Lafayette (city) Tippecanoe County	28	0.10
Hammond (city) Lake County	63	0.08
Bloomington (city) Monroe County	33	0.05
East Chicago (city) Lake County	16	0.05
Noblesville (city) Hamilton County	14	0.05
Michigan City (city) La Porte County	14	0.04
South Bend (city) Saint Joseph County	27	0.03
Granger (cdp) Saint Joseph County	9	0.03
Highland (town) Lake County	6	0.03

Top 10 Places Sorted by Percent
Based on places with populations of 10,000 or more

Place	Number	%
West Lafayette (city) Tippecanoe County	28	0.10
Hammond (city) Lake County	63	0.08
Bloomington (city) Monroe County	33	0.05
East Chicago (city) Lake County	16	0.05
Noblesville (city) Hamilton County	14	0.05
Michigan City (city) La Porte County	14	0.04
South Bend (city) Saint Joseph County	27	0.03
Granger (cdp) Saint Joseph County	9	0.03
Highland (town) Lake County	6	0.03
Vincennes (city) Knox County	5	0.03

Arab: Lebanese

Top 10 Places Sorted by Number
Based on all places, regardless of population

Place	Number	%
Indianapolis (cons. city) Marion County	563	0.07
Michigan City (city) La Porte County	444	1.35
South Bend (city) Saint Joseph County	147	0.14
Bloomington (city) Monroe County	131	0.19
Carmel (city) Hamilton County	129	0.34
Fort Wayne (city) Allen County	122	0.06
Granger (cdp) Saint Joseph County	80	0.28
Lawrence (city) Marion County	69	0.18
Noblesville (city) Hamilton County	62	0.21
Merrillville (town) Lake County	60	0.20

Notes: (cdp) census designated place; Refer to the User's Guide in the front of the book for more detailed information.

Top 10 Places Sorted by Percent
Based on all places, regardless of population

Place	Number	%
Pottawattamie Park (town) La Porte County	19	6.31
Southport (city) Marion County	39	2.00
Gulivoire Park (cdp) Saint Joseph County	57	1.93
Hebron (town) Porter County	52	1.45
Michigan City (city) La Porte County	444	1.35
Roseland (town) Saint Joseph County	16	0.88
Newburgh (town) Warrick County	28	0.87
Leavenworth (town) Crawford County	3	0.87
Trail Creek (town) La Porte County	14	0.60
Rochester (city) Fulton County	35	0.55

Top 10 Places Sorted by Percent
Based on places with populations of 10,000 or more

Place	Number	%
Michigan City (city) La Porte County	444	1.35
Carmel (city) Hamilton County	129	0.34
Granger (cdp) Saint Joseph County	80	0.28
Clarksville (town) Clark County	48	0.22
Noblesville (city) Hamilton County	62	0.21
Merrillville (town) Lake County	60	0.20
West Lafayette (city) Tippecanoe County	59	0.20
Bloomington (city) Monroe County	131	0.19
Lawrence (city) Marion County	69	0.18
Portage (city) Porter County	55	0.16

Arab: Moroccan

Top 10 Places Sorted by Number
Based on all places, regardless of population

Place	Number	%
Indianapolis (cons. city) Marion County	197	0.03
Muncie (city) Delaware County	57	0.08
Carlisle (town) Sullivan County	55	2.15
Fort Wayne (city) Allen County	48	0.02
Plainfield (town) Hendricks County	14	0.07
Evansville (city) Vanderburgh County	10	0.01
Munster (town) Lake County	9	0.04
Kokomo (city) Howard County	8	0.02
Hope (town) Bartholomew County	7	0.33

Top 10 Places Sorted by Percent
Based on all places, regardless of population

Place	Number	%
Carlisle (town) Sullivan County	55	2.15
Hope (town) Bartholomew County	7	0.33
Muncie (city) Delaware County	57	0.08
Plainfield (town) Hendricks County	14	0.07
Munster (town) Lake County	9	0.04
Indianapolis (cons. city) Marion County	197	0.03
Fort Wayne (city) Allen County	48	0.02
Kokomo (city) Howard County	8	0.02
Evansville (city) Vanderburgh County	10	0.01

Top 10 Places Sorted by Percent
Based on places with populations of 10,000 or more

Place	Number	%
Muncie (city) Delaware County	57	0.08
Plainfield (town) Hendricks County	14	0.07
Munster (town) Lake County	9	0.04
Indianapolis (cons. city) Marion County	197	0.03
Fort Wayne (city) Allen County	48	0.02
Kokomo (city) Howard County	8	0.02
Evansville (city) Vanderburgh County	10	0.01

Arab: Palestinian

Top 10 Places Sorted by Number
Based on all places, regardless of population

Place	Number	%
West Lafayette (city) Tippecanoe County	81	0.28
Evansville (city) Vanderburgh County	60	0.05
Carmel (city) Hamilton County	58	0.15
Portage (city) Porter County	50	0.15
Noblesville (city) Hamilton County	46	0.16
Hammond (city) Lake County	39	0.05
Indianapolis (cons. city) Marion County	33	<0.01
Fishers (town) Hamilton County	31	0.08
Michigan City (city) La Porte County	28	0.09
Bloomington (city) Monroe County	27	0.04

Top 10 Places Sorted by Percent
Based on all places, regardless of population

Place	Number	%
West Lafayette (city) Tippecanoe County	81	0.28
Noblesville (city) Hamilton County	46	0.16
Carmel (city) Hamilton County	58	0.15
Portage (city) Porter County	50	0.15
South Haven (cdp) Porter County	8	0.14
Decatur (city) Adams County	11	0.12
Pittsboro (town) Hendricks County	2	0.12
Highland (town) Lake County	23	0.10
Michigan City (city) La Porte County	28	0.09
Fishers (town) Hamilton County	31	0.08

Top 10 Places Sorted by Percent
Based on places with populations of 10,000 or more

Place	Number	%
West Lafayette (city) Tippecanoe County	81	0.28
Noblesville (city) Hamilton County	46	0.16
Carmel (city) Hamilton County	58	0.15
Portage (city) Porter County	50	0.15
Highland (town) Lake County	23	0.10
Michigan City (city) La Porte County	28	0.09
Fishers (town) Hamilton County	31	0.08
Mishawaka (city) Saint Joseph County	26	0.06
Evansville (city) Vanderburgh County	60	0.05
Hammond (city) Lake County	39	0.05

Arab: Syrian

Top 10 Places Sorted by Number
Based on all places, regardless of population

Place	Number	%
Indianapolis (cons. city) Marion County	346	0.04
Terre Haute (city) Vigo County	188	0.32
Evansville (city) Vanderburgh County	80	0.07
Elkhart (city) Elkhart County	64	0.12
Fort Wayne (city) Allen County	57	0.03
Muncie (city) Delaware County	49	0.07
Bloomington (city) Monroe County	48	0.07
La Porte (city) La Porte County	43	0.20
Hobart (city) Lake County	38	0.15
Noblesville (city) Hamilton County	36	0.12

Top 10 Places Sorted by Percent
Based on all places, regardless of population

Place	Number	%
Sellersburg (town) Clark County	30	0.48
Shipshewana (town) La Grange County	2	0.37
Terre Haute (city) Vigo County	188	0.32
Whiteland (town) Johnson County	12	0.31
Dillsboro (town) Dearborn County	4	0.28
Clermont (town) Marion County	4	0.27
La Porte (city) La Porte County	43	0.20
Melody Hill (cdp) Vanderburgh County	6	0.20
North Terre Haute (cdp) Vigo County	9	0.19

Woodburn (city) Allen County ... 3 ... 0.19

Top 10 Places Sorted by Percent
Based on places with populations of 10,000 or more

Place	Number	%
Terre Haute (city) Vigo County	188	0.32
La Porte (city) La Porte County	43	0.20
Hobart (city) Lake County	38	0.15
Auburn (city) De Kalb County	17	0.14
Elkhart (city) Elkhart County	64	0.12
Noblesville (city) Hamilton County	36	0.12
Warsaw (city) Kosciusko County	15	0.12
Valparaiso (city) Porter County	27	0.10
Granger (cdp) Saint Joseph County	24	0.09
Fishers (town) Hamilton County	32	0.08

Arab: Other

Top 10 Places Sorted by Number
Based on all places, regardless of population

Place	Number	%
Indianapolis (cons. city) Marion County	128	0.02
South Bend (city) Saint Joseph County	84	0.08
Bloomington (city) Monroe County	49	0.07
Dyer (town) Lake County	35	0.25
Crown Point (city) Lake County	27	0.14
Michigan City (city) La Porte County	23	0.07
Saint John (town) Lake County	22	0.26
Fort Wayne (city) Allen County	18	0.01
Evansville (city) Vanderburgh County	17	0.01
Lawrence (city) Marion County	10	0.03

Top 10 Places Sorted by Percent
Based on all places, regardless of population

Place	Number	%
Leavenworth (town) Crawford County	6	1.74
Milford (town) Kosciusko County	6	0.38
Saint John (town) Lake County	22	0.26
Dyer (town) Lake County	35	0.25
Upland (town) Grant County	9	0.23
Ligonier (city) Noble County	8	0.18
Topeka (town) La Grange County	2	0.17
Oaktown (town) Knox County	1	0.16
Crown Point (city) Lake County	27	0.14
Whiting (city) Lake County	7	0.14

Top 10 Places Sorted by Percent
Based on places with populations of 10,000 or more

Place	Number	%
Dyer (town) Lake County	35	0.25
Crown Point (city) Lake County	27	0.14
South Bend (city) Saint Joseph County	84	0.08
Bloomington (city) Monroe County	49	0.07
Michigan City (city) La Porte County	23	0.07
Wabash (city) Wabash County	8	0.07
New Haven (city) Allen County	7	0.06
Lawrence (city) Marion County	10	0.03
Merrillville (town) Lake County	9	0.03
West Lafayette (city) Tippecanoe County	9	0.03

Armenian

Top 10 Places Sorted by Number
Based on all places, regardless of population

Place	Number	%
Fort Wayne (city) Allen County	148	0.07
Indianapolis (cons. city) Marion County	123	0.02
Fishers (town) Hamilton County	55	0.14
Hammond (city) Lake County	55	0.07
Crown Point (city) Lake County	47	0.24
Carmel (city) Hamilton County	45	0.12
Rockville (town) Parke County	42	1.53

Notes: (cdp) census designated place; Refer to the User's Guide in the front of the book for more detailed information.

Place	Number	%
Terre Haute (city) Vigo County	41	0.07
Evansville (city) Vanderburgh County	35	0.03
Lake Station (city) Lake County	34	0.24

Top 10 Places Sorted by Percent
Based on all places, regardless of population

Place	Number	%
Rockville (town) Parke County	42	1.53
Aurora (city) Dearborn County	22	0.56
Georgetown (town) Floyd County	7	0.32
Crown Point (city) Lake County	47	0.24
Lake Station (city) Lake County	34	0.24
Brownstown (town) Jackson County	6	0.20
Roselawn (cdp) Jasper County	7	0.18
Monticello (city) White County	9	0.16
Fishers (town) Hamilton County	55	0.14
Carmel (city) Hamilton County	45	0.12

Top 10 Places Sorted by Percent
Based on places with populations of 10,000 or more

Place	Number	%
Crown Point (city) Lake County	47	0.24
Lake Station (city) Lake County	34	0.24
Fishers (town) Hamilton County	55	0.14
Carmel (city) Hamilton County	45	0.12
Speedway (town) Marion County	16	0.12
Merrillville (town) Lake County	33	0.11
Munster (town) Lake County	24	0.11
Highland (town) Lake County	24	0.10
Hobart (city) Lake County	22	0.09
Noblesville (city) Hamilton County	24	0.08

Asian

Top 10 Places Sorted by Number
Based on all places, regardless of population

Place	Number	%
Indianapolis (cons. city) Marion County	13,902	1.78
Bloomington (city) Monroe County	4,258	6.15
Fort Wayne (city) Allen County	4,003	1.95
West Lafayette (city) Tippecanoe County	3,565	12.39
Carmel (city) Hamilton County	1,813	4.80
South Bend (city) Saint Joseph County	1,722	1.60
Fishers (town) Hamilton County	1,383	3.66
Columbus (city) Bartholomew County	1,369	3.50
Evansville (city) Vanderburgh County	1,167	0.96
Munster (town) Lake County	1,063	4.94

Top 10 Places Sorted by Percent
Based on all places, regardless of population

Place	Number	%
West Lafayette (city) Tippecanoe County	3,565	12.39
Bloomington (city) Monroe County	4,258	6.15
Cromwell (town) Noble County	26	5.75
Munster (town) Lake County	1,063	4.94
Carmel (city) Hamilton County	1,813	4.80
Georgetown (cdp) Saint Joseph County	188	4.18
Michiana Shores (town) La Porte County	13	3.94
Cadiz (town) Henry County	6	3.73
Onward (town) Cass County	3	3.70
Fishers (town) Hamilton County	1,383	3.66

Top 10 Places Sorted by Percent
Based on places with populations of 10,000 or more

Place	Number	%
West Lafayette (city) Tippecanoe County	3,565	12.39
Bloomington (city) Monroe County	4,258	6.15
Munster (town) Lake County	1,063	4.94
Carmel (city) Hamilton County	1,813	4.80
Fishers (town) Hamilton County	1,383	3.66
Columbus (city) Bartholomew County	1,369	3.50
Granger (cdp) Saint Joseph County	876	3.10

Place	Number	%
Schererville (town) Lake County	742	2.99
Lawrence (city) Marion County	882	2.27
Speedway (town) Marion County	289	2.24

Asian: Bangladeshi

Top 10 Places Sorted by Number
Based on all places, regardless of population

Place	Number	%
Indianapolis (cons. city) Marion County	79	0.01
Fort Wayne (city) Allen County	22	0.01
West Lafayette (city) Tippecanoe County	13	0.05
Mishawaka (city) Saint Joseph County	8	0.02
Fishers (town) Hamilton County	7	0.02
Anderson (city) Madison County	6	0.01
Munster (town) Lake County	4	0.02
Bloomington (city) Monroe County	4	0.01
Merrillville (town) Lake County	3	0.01
Columbus (city) Bartholomew County	2	0.01

Top 10 Places Sorted by Percent
Based on all places, regardless of population

Place	Number	%
Arcadia (town) Hamilton County	1	0.06
Kouts (town) Porter County	1	0.06
West Lafayette (city) Tippecanoe County	13	0.05
Mishawaka (city) Saint Joseph County	8	0.02
Fishers (town) Hamilton County	7	0.02
Munster (town) Lake County	4	0.02
Indianapolis (cons. city) Marion County	79	0.01
Fort Wayne (city) Allen County	22	0.01
Anderson (city) Madison County	6	0.01
Bloomington (city) Monroe County	4	0.01

Top 10 Places Sorted by Percent
Based on places with populations of 10,000 or more

Place	Number	%
West Lafayette (city) Tippecanoe County	13	0.05
Mishawaka (city) Saint Joseph County	8	0.02
Fishers (town) Hamilton County	7	0.02
Munster (town) Lake County	4	0.02
Indianapolis (cons. city) Marion County	79	0.01
Fort Wayne (city) Allen County	22	0.01
Anderson (city) Madison County	6	0.01
Bloomington (city) Monroe County	4	0.01
Merrillville (town) Lake County	3	0.01
Columbus (city) Bartholomew County	2	0.01

Asian: Cambodian

Top 10 Places Sorted by Number
Based on all places, regardless of population

Place	Number	%
Indianapolis (cons. city) Marion County	122	0.02
South Bend (city) Saint Joseph County	88	0.08
Elkhart (city) Elkhart County	84	0.16
Goshen (city) Elkhart County	50	0.17
Fort Wayne (city) Allen County	24	0.01
Bristol (town) Elkhart County	14	1.01
Fishers (town) Hamilton County	9	0.02
Mishawaka (city) Saint Joseph County	8	0.02
North Manchester (town) Wabash County	7	0.11
Lawrence (city) Marion County	7	0.02

Top 10 Places Sorted by Percent
Based on all places, regardless of population

Place	Number	%
Bristol (town) Elkhart County	14	1.01
Amboy (town) Miami County	2	0.56
Goshen (city) Elkhart County	50	0.17
Elkhart (city) Elkhart County	84	0.16
Middlebury (town) Elkhart County	4	0.14

Place	Number	%
North Manchester (town) Wabash County	7	0.11
Waterloo (town) De Kalb County	2	0.09
South Bend (city) Saint Joseph County	88	0.08
Porter (town) Porter County	4	0.08
Dunlap (cdp) Elkhart County	4	0.07

Top 10 Places Sorted by Percent
Based on places with populations of 10,000 or more

Place	Number	%
Goshen (city) Elkhart County	50	0.17
Elkhart (city) Elkhart County	84	0.16
South Bend (city) Saint Joseph County	88	0.08
Brownsburg (town) Hendricks County	4	0.03
Wabash (city) Wabash County	4	0.03
Indianapolis (cons. city) Marion County	122	0.02
Fishers (town) Hamilton County	9	0.02
Mishawaka (city) Saint Joseph County	8	0.02
Lawrence (city) Marion County	7	0.02
Michigan City (city) La Porte County	7	0.02

Asian: Chinese, except Taiwanese

Top 10 Places Sorted by Number
Based on all places, regardless of population

Place	Number	%
Indianapolis (cons. city) Marion County	2,461	0.31
West Lafayette (city) Tippecanoe County	1,027	3.57
Bloomington (city) Monroe County	998	1.44
Carmel (city) Hamilton County	691	1.83
Fort Wayne (city) Allen County	397	0.19
Fishers (town) Hamilton County	329	0.87
South Bend (city) Saint Joseph County	322	0.30
Columbus (city) Bartholomew County	261	0.67
Granger (cdp) Saint Joseph County	220	0.78
Evansville (city) Vanderburgh County	219	0.18

Top 10 Places Sorted by Percent
Based on all places, regardless of population

Place	Number	%
Cadiz (town) Henry County	6	3.73
West Lafayette (city) Tippecanoe County	1,027	3.57
Carmel (city) Hamilton County	691	1.83
Bloomington (city) Monroe County	998	1.44
Roseland (town) Saint Joseph County	19	1.05
Cromwell (town) Noble County	4	0.88
Fishers (town) Hamilton County	329	0.87
Monterey (town) Pulaski County	2	0.87
Granger (cdp) Saint Joseph County	220	0.78
Georgetown (cdp) Saint Joseph County	34	0.76

Top 10 Places Sorted by Percent
Based on places with populations of 10,000 or more

Place	Number	%
West Lafayette (city) Tippecanoe County	1,027	3.57
Carmel (city) Hamilton County	691	1.83
Bloomington (city) Monroe County	998	1.44
Fishers (town) Hamilton County	329	0.87
Granger (cdp) Saint Joseph County	220	0.78
Columbus (city) Bartholomew County	261	0.67
Munster (town) Lake County	132	0.61
Greenwood (city) Johnson County	174	0.48
Lafayette (city) Tippecanoe County	208	0.37
Kokomo (city) Howard County	164	0.36

Asian: Filipino

Top 10 Places Sorted by Number
Based on all places, regardless of population

Place	Number	%
Indianapolis (cons. city) Marion County	2,043	0.26
Fort Wayne (city) Allen County	380	0.18
South Bend (city) Saint Joseph County	231	0.21

Notes: (cdp) census designated place; Refer to the User's Guide in the front of the book for more detailed information.

Place	Number	%
Bloomington (city) Monroe County	205	0.30
Munster (town) Lake County	178	0.83
Hammond (city) Lake County	141	0.17
Merrillville (town) Lake County	139	0.45
West Lafayette (city) Tippecanoe County	137	0.48
Evansville (city) Vanderburgh County	136	0.11
Lawrence (city) Marion County	131	0.34

Top 10 Places Sorted by Percent
Based on all places, regardless of population

Place	Number	%
Stinesville (town) Monroe County	6	3.09
Michiana Shores (town) La Porte County	4	1.21
Cromwell (town) Noble County	4	0.88
Munster (town) Lake County	178	0.83
Etna Green (town) Kosciusko County	5	0.75
Bunker Hill (town) Miami County	7	0.71
Grissom AFB (cdp) Miami County	11	0.67
Long Beach (town) La Porte County	10	0.64
Whitestown (town) Boone County	3	0.64
Salamonia (town) Jay County	1	0.63

Top 10 Places Sorted by Percent
Based on places with populations of 10,000 or more

Place	Number	%
Munster (town) Lake County	178	0.83
Schererville (town) Lake County	130	0.52
West Lafayette (city) Tippecanoe County	137	0.48
Merrillville (town) Lake County	139	0.45
Lawrence (city) Marion County	131	0.34
Valparaiso (city) Porter County	92	0.34
Fishers (town) Hamilton County	120	0.32
Dyer (town) Lake County	45	0.32
Highland (town) Lake County	74	0.31
Bloomington (city) Monroe County	205	0.30

Asian: Hmong

Top 10 Places Sorted by Number
Based on all places, regardless of population

Place	Number	%
Indianapolis (cons. city) Marion County	35	<0.01
Westfield (town) Hamilton County	33	0.36
Carmel (city) Hamilton County	23	0.06
Lawrence (city) Marion County	14	0.04
Noblesville (city) Hamilton County	12	0.04
Granger (cdp) Saint Joseph County	11	0.04
Kokomo (city) Howard County	9	0.02
Bloomington (city) Monroe County	5	0.01
Oakland City (city) Gibson County	2	0.08
Fort Wayne (city) Allen County	2	<0.01

Top 10 Places Sorted by Percent
Based on all places, regardless of population

Place	Number	%
Westfield (town) Hamilton County	33	0.36
Oakland City (city) Gibson County	2	0.08
Carmel (city) Hamilton County	23	0.06
Lawrence (city) Marion County	14	0.04
Noblesville (city) Hamilton County	12	0.04
Granger (cdp) Saint Joseph County	11	0.04
Kokomo (city) Howard County	9	0.02
Bloomington (city) Monroe County	5	0.01
Speedway (town) Marion County	1	0.01
Indianapolis (cons. city) Marion County	35	<0.01

Top 10 Places Sorted by Percent
Based on places with populations of 10,000 or more

Place	Number	%
Carmel (city) Hamilton County	23	0.06
Lawrence (city) Marion County	14	0.04
Noblesville (city) Hamilton County	12	0.04

Place	Number	%
Granger (cdp) Saint Joseph County	11	0.04
Kokomo (city) Howard County	9	0.02
Bloomington (city) Monroe County	5	0.01
Speedway (town) Marion County	1	0.01
Indianapolis (cons. city) Marion County	35	<0.01
Fort Wayne (city) Allen County	2	<0.01
Evansville (city) Vanderburgh County	1	<0.01

Asian: Indian

Top 10 Places Sorted by Number
Based on all places, regardless of population

Place	Number	%
Indianapolis (cons. city) Marion County	3,728	0.48
West Lafayette (city) Tippecanoe County	1,027	3.57
Bloomington (city) Monroe County	703	1.01
Fort Wayne (city) Allen County	661	0.32
Munster (town) Lake County	510	2.37
Columbus (city) Bartholomew County	480	1.23
Carmel (city) Hamilton County	459	1.22
South Bend (city) Saint Joseph County	326	0.30
Fishers (town) Hamilton County	316	0.84
Schererville (town) Lake County	312	1.26

Top 10 Places Sorted by Percent
Based on all places, regardless of population

Place	Number	%
West Lafayette (city) Tippecanoe County	1,027	3.57
Munster (town) Lake County	510	2.37
Georgetown (cdp) Saint Joseph County	69	1.53
Michiana Shores (town) La Porte County	5	1.52
Schererville (town) Lake County	312	1.26
Columbus (city) Bartholomew County	480	1.23
Carmel (city) Hamilton County	459	1.22
Bloomington (city) Monroe County	703	1.01
Granger (cdp) Saint Joseph County	283	1.00
Fishers (town) Hamilton County	316	0.84

Top 10 Places Sorted by Percent
Based on places with populations of 10,000 or more

Place	Number	%
West Lafayette (city) Tippecanoe County	1,027	3.57
Munster (town) Lake County	510	2.37
Schererville (town) Lake County	312	1.26
Columbus (city) Bartholomew County	480	1.23
Carmel (city) Hamilton County	459	1.22
Bloomington (city) Monroe County	703	1.01
Granger (cdp) Saint Joseph County	283	1.00
Fishers (town) Hamilton County	316	0.84
Dyer (town) Lake County	109	0.78
Chesterton (town) Porter County	79	0.75

Asian: Indonesian

Top 10 Places Sorted by Number
Based on all places, regardless of population

Place	Number	%
West Lafayette (city) Tippecanoe County	139	0.48
Bloomington (city) Monroe County	105	0.15
Indianapolis (cons. city) Marion County	70	0.01
Fort Wayne (city) Allen County	28	0.01
South Bend (city) Saint Joseph County	19	0.02
Goshen (city) Elkhart County	17	0.06
Lafayette (city) Tippecanoe County	16	0.03
Mishawaka (city) Saint Joseph County	12	0.03
Carmel (city) Hamilton County	9	0.02
Elkhart (city) Elkhart County	8	0.02

Top 10 Places Sorted by Percent
Based on all places, regardless of population

Place	Number	%
West Lafayette (city) Tippecanoe County	139	0.48

Place	Number	%
Pittsboro (town) Hendricks County	3	0.19
Bloomington (city) Monroe County	105	0.15
Leo-Cedarville (town) Allen County	3	0.11
Goshen (city) Elkhart County	17	0.06
Connersville (city) Fayette County	6	0.04
Lafayette (city) Tippecanoe County	16	0.03
Mishawaka (city) Saint Joseph County	12	0.03
Dyer (town) Lake County	4	0.03
Jasper (city) Dubois County	4	0.03

Top 10 Places Sorted by Percent
Based on places with populations of 10,000 or more

Place	Number	%
West Lafayette (city) Tippecanoe County	139	0.48
Bloomington (city) Monroe County	105	0.15
Goshen (city) Elkhart County	17	0.06
Connersville (city) Fayette County	6	0.04
Lafayette (city) Tippecanoe County	16	0.03
Mishawaka (city) Saint Joseph County	12	0.03
Dyer (town) Lake County	4	0.03
Jasper (city) Dubois County	4	0.03
South Bend (city) Saint Joseph County	19	0.02
Carmel (city) Hamilton County	9	0.02

Asian: Japanese

Top 10 Places Sorted by Number
Based on all places, regardless of population

Place	Number	%
Indianapolis (cons. city) Marion County	1,043	0.13
Bloomington (city) Monroe County	422	0.61
Columbus (city) Bartholomew County	327	0.84
West Lafayette (city) Tippecanoe County	294	1.02
Fishers (town) Hamilton County	173	0.46
Fort Wayne (city) Allen County	169	0.08
Seymour (city) Jackson County	168	0.93
Terre Haute (city) Vigo County	145	0.24
Shelbyville (city) Shelby County	142	0.79
Evansville (city) Vanderburgh County	128	0.11

Top 10 Places Sorted by Percent
Based on all places, regardless of population

Place	Number	%
Onward (town) Cass County	3	3.70
Burns Harbor (town) Porter County	8	1.04
West Lafayette (city) Tippecanoe County	294	1.02
Princeton (city) Gibson County	83	1.02
Dupont (town) Jefferson County	4	1.02
Seymour (city) Jackson County	168	0.93
Michiana Shores (town) La Porte County	3	0.91
Columbus (city) Bartholomew County	327	0.84
Clear Lake (town) Steuben County	2	0.82
Shelbyville (city) Shelby County	142	0.79

Top 10 Places Sorted by Percent
Based on places with populations of 10,000 or more

Place	Number	%
West Lafayette (city) Tippecanoe County	294	1.02
Seymour (city) Jackson County	168	0.93
Columbus (city) Bartholomew County	327	0.84
Shelbyville (city) Shelby County	142	0.79
Bloomington (city) Monroe County	422	0.61
Greensburg (city) Decatur County	56	0.55
Fishers (town) Hamilton County	173	0.46
Granger (cdp) Saint Joseph County	98	0.35
Vincennes (city) Knox County	60	0.32
Madison (city) Jefferson County	37	0.31

Notes: (cdp) census designated place; Refer to the User's Guide in the front of the book for more detailed information.

Asian: Korean

Top 10 Places Sorted by Number
Based on all places, regardless of population

Place	Number	%
Indianapolis (cons. city) Marion County	1,385	0.18
Bloomington (city) Monroe County	1,061	1.53
West Lafayette (city) Tippecanoe County	419	1.46
Lawrence (city) Marion County	315	0.81
Fort Wayne (city) Allen County	258	0.13
Carmel (city) Hamilton County	224	0.59
Fishers (town) Hamilton County	194	0.51
Evansville (city) Vanderburgh County	158	0.13
Terre Haute (city) Vigo County	142	0.24
Muncie (city) Delaware County	142	0.21

Top 10 Places Sorted by Percent
Based on all places, regardless of population

Place	Number	%
Bloomington (city) Monroe County	1,061	1.53
West Lafayette (city) Tippecanoe County	419	1.46
Macy (town) Miami County	3	1.21
Lawrence (city) Marion County	315	0.81
North Salem (town) Hendricks County	4	0.68
Salamonia (town) Jay County	1	0.63
Lynn (town) Randolph County	7	0.61
Carmel (city) Hamilton County	224	0.59
Orland (town) Steuben County	2	0.59
Cynthiana (town) Posey County	4	0.58

Top 10 Places Sorted by Percent
Based on places with populations of 10,000 or more

Place	Number	%
Bloomington (city) Monroe County	1,061	1.53
West Lafayette (city) Tippecanoe County	419	1.46
Lawrence (city) Marion County	315	0.81
Carmel (city) Hamilton County	224	0.59
Munster (town) Lake County	116	0.54
Fishers (town) Hamilton County	194	0.51
Granger (cdp) Saint Joseph County	107	0.38
Schererville (town) Lake County	95	0.38
Mishawaka (city) Saint Joseph County	132	0.28
Terre Haute (city) Vigo County	142	0.24

Asian: Laotian

Top 10 Places Sorted by Number
Based on all places, regardless of population

Place	Number	%
Fort Wayne (city) Allen County	335	0.16
Elkhart (city) Elkhart County	124	0.24
Indianapolis (cons. city) Marion County	89	0.01
South Bend (city) Saint Joseph County	54	0.05
Logansport (city) Cass County	29	0.15
Leesburg (town) Kosciusko County	16	2.56
Cumberland (town) Marion County	16	0.29
Ligonier (city) Noble County	14	0.32
Wabash (city) Wabash County	13	0.11
Lafayette (city) Tippecanoe County	13	0.02

Top 10 Places Sorted by Percent
Based on all places, regardless of population

Place	Number	%
Leesburg (town) Kosciusko County	16	2.56
Wakarusa (town) Elkhart County	12	0.74
Ligonier (city) Noble County	14	0.32
Cumberland (town) Marion County	16	0.29
Simonton Lake (cdp) Elkhart County	10	0.25
Elkhart (city) Elkhart County	124	0.24
Winfield (town) Lake County	5	0.22
Bristol (town) Elkhart County	3	0.22
Fort Wayne (city) Allen County	335	0.16

| **Logansport** (city) Cass County | 29 | 0.15 |

Top 10 Places Sorted by Percent
Based on places with populations of 10,000 or more

Place	Number	%
Elkhart (city) Elkhart County	124	0.24
Fort Wayne (city) Allen County	335	0.16
Logansport (city) Cass County	29	0.15
Wabash (city) Wabash County	13	0.11
South Bend (city) Saint Joseph County	54	0.05
Dyer (town) Lake County	5	0.04
New Haven (city) Allen County	5	0.04
Goshen (city) Elkhart County	10	0.03
Richmond (city) Wayne County	10	0.03
Noblesville (city) Hamilton County	8	0.03

Asian: Malaysian

Top 10 Places Sorted by Number
Based on all places, regardless of population

Place	Number	%
Fort Wayne (city) Allen County	77	0.04
West Lafayette (city) Tippecanoe County	60	0.21
Indianapolis (cons. city) Marion County	41	0.01
South Bend (city) Saint Joseph County	39	0.04
Speedway (town) Marion County	31	0.24
Bloomington (city) Monroe County	28	0.04
Terre Haute (city) Vigo County	27	0.05
Angola (city) Steuben County	14	0.19
West Terre Haute (town) Vigo County	7	0.30
Evansville (city) Vanderburgh County	7	0.01

Top 10 Places Sorted by Percent
Based on all places, regardless of population

Place	Number	%
West Terre Haute (town) Vigo County	7	0.30
Speedway (town) Marion County	31	0.24
West Lafayette (city) Tippecanoe County	60	0.21
Angola (city) Steuben County	14	0.19
Bainbridge (town) Putnam County	1	0.13
Danville (town) Hendricks County	4	0.06
Meridian Hills (town) Marion County	1	0.06
Roseland (town) Saint Joseph County	1	0.06
Terre Haute (city) Vigo County	27	0.05
Fort Wayne (city) Allen County	77	0.04

Top 10 Places Sorted by Percent
Based on places with populations of 10,000 or more

Place	Number	%
Speedway (town) Marion County	31	0.24
West Lafayette (city) Tippecanoe County	60	0.21
Terre Haute (city) Vigo County	27	0.05
Fort Wayne (city) Allen County	77	0.04
South Bend (city) Saint Joseph County	39	0.04
Bloomington (city) Monroe County	28	0.04
Indianapolis (cons. city) Marion County	41	0.01
Evansville (city) Vanderburgh County	7	0.01
Mishawaka (city) Saint Joseph County	4	0.01
Carmel (city) Hamilton County	3	0.01

Asian: Pakistani

Top 10 Places Sorted by Number
Based on all places, regardless of population

Place	Number	%
Indianapolis (cons. city) Marion County	389	0.05
Fort Wayne (city) Allen County	87	0.04
West Lafayette (city) Tippecanoe County	79	0.27
Bloomington (city) Monroe County	57	0.08
Schererville (town) Lake County	35	0.14
Plainfield (town) Hendricks County	33	0.18
Munster (town) Lake County	30	0.14

Granger (cdp) Saint Joseph County	30	0.11
Merrillville (town) Lake County	30	0.10
Crown Point (city) Lake County	26	0.13

Top 10 Places Sorted by Percent
Based on all places, regardless of population

Place	Number	%
Dune Acres (town) Porter County	2	0.94
Pottawattamie Park (town) La Porte County	1	0.33
West Lafayette (city) Tippecanoe County	79	0.27
Plainfield (town) Hendricks County	33	0.18
Schererville (town) Lake County	35	0.14
Munster (town) Lake County	30	0.14
Crown Point (city) Lake County	26	0.13
Georgetown (cdp) Saint Joseph County	6	0.13
Speedway (town) Marion County	15	0.12
Oakland City (city) Gibson County	3	0.12

Top 10 Places Sorted by Percent
Based on places with populations of 10,000 or more

Place	Number	%
West Lafayette (city) Tippecanoe County	79	0.27
Plainfield (town) Hendricks County	33	0.18
Schererville (town) Lake County	35	0.14
Munster (town) Lake County	30	0.14
Crown Point (city) Lake County	26	0.13
Speedway (town) Marion County	15	0.12
Granger (cdp) Saint Joseph County	30	0.11
Merrillville (town) Lake County	30	0.10
Chesterton (town) Porter County	10	0.10
Bloomington (city) Monroe County	57	0.08

Asian: Sri Lankan

Top 10 Places Sorted by Number
Based on all places, regardless of population

Place	Number	%
Indianapolis (cons. city) Marion County	37	<0.01
West Lafayette (city) Tippecanoe County	19	0.07
Fort Wayne (city) Allen County	17	0.01
Granger (cdp) Saint Joseph County	12	0.04
Valparaiso (city) Porter County	7	0.03
Merrillville (town) Lake County	6	0.02
Bloomington (city) Monroe County	6	0.01
Beech Grove (city) Marion County	5	0.03
Fishers (town) Hamilton County	5	0.01
Angola (city) Steuben County	3	0.04

Top 10 Places Sorted by Percent
Based on all places, regardless of population

Place	Number	%
Sweetser (town) Grant County	1	0.11
West Lafayette (city) Tippecanoe County	19	0.07
Granger (cdp) Saint Joseph County	12	0.04
Angola (city) Steuben County	3	0.04
Valparaiso (city) Porter County	7	0.03
Beech Grove (city) Marion County	5	0.03
Dunlap (cdp) Elkhart County	2	0.03
Merrillville (town) Lake County	6	0.02
Plainfield (town) Hendricks County	3	0.02
North Manchester (town) Wabash County	1	0.02

Top 10 Places Sorted by Percent
Based on places with populations of 10,000 or more

Place	Number	%
West Lafayette (city) Tippecanoe County	19	0.07
Granger (cdp) Saint Joseph County	12	0.04
Valparaiso (city) Porter County	7	0.03
Beech Grove (city) Marion County	5	0.03
Merrillville (town) Lake County	6	0.02
Plainfield (town) Hendricks County	3	0.02
Fort Wayne (city) Allen County	17	0.01

Notes: (cdp) census designated place; Refer to the User's Guide in the front of the book for more detailed information.

Place	Number	%
Bloomington (city) Monroe County	6	0.01
Fishers (town) Hamilton County	5	0.01
Carmel (city) Hamilton County	3	0.01

Asian: Taiwanese

Top 10 Places Sorted by Number
Based on all places, regardless of population

Place	Number	%
Bloomington (city) Monroe County	113	0.16
West Lafayette (city) Tippecanoe County	105	0.36
Indianapolis (cons. city) Marion County	105	0.01
Carmel (city) Hamilton County	47	0.12
Fort Wayne (city) Allen County	31	0.02
Columbus (city) Bartholomew County	29	0.07
Terre Haute (city) Vigo County	24	0.04
Granger (cdp) Saint Joseph County	19	0.07
South Bend (city) Saint Joseph County	16	0.01
Evansville (city) Vanderburgh County	11	0.01

Top 10 Places Sorted by Percent
Based on all places, regardless of population

Place	Number	%
West Lafayette (city) Tippecanoe County	105	0.36
Roseland (town) Saint Joseph County	6	0.33
Michiana Shores (town) La Porte County	1	0.30
Bloomington (city) Monroe County	113	0.16
Carmel (city) Hamilton County	47	0.12
Columbus (city) Bartholomew County	29	0.07
Granger (cdp) Saint Joseph County	19	0.07
Tipton (city) Tipton County	3	0.06
Terre Haute (city) Vigo County	24	0.04
Clarksville (town) Clark County	8	0.04

Top 10 Places Sorted by Percent
Based on places with populations of 10,000 or more

Place	Number	%
West Lafayette (city) Tippecanoe County	105	0.36
Bloomington (city) Monroe County	113	0.16
Carmel (city) Hamilton County	47	0.12
Columbus (city) Bartholomew County	29	0.07
Granger (cdp) Saint Joseph County	19	0.07
Terre Haute (city) Vigo County	24	0.04
Clarksville (town) Clark County	8	0.04
Munster (town) Lake County	7	0.03
Crawfordsville (city) Montgomery County	4	0.03
Fort Wayne (city) Allen County	31	0.02

Asian: Thai

Top 10 Places Sorted by Number
Based on all places, regardless of population

Place	Number	%
Indianapolis (cons. city) Marion County	213	0.03
Bloomington (city) Monroe County	92	0.13
Fort Wayne (city) Allen County	78	0.04
West Lafayette (city) Tippecanoe County	59	0.21
Crown Point (city) Lake County	31	0.16
South Bend (city) Saint Joseph County	29	0.03
Elkhart (city) Elkhart County	28	0.05
Evansville (city) Vanderburgh County	27	0.02
Muncie (city) Delaware County	25	0.04
Lawrence (city) Marion County	20	0.05

Top 10 Places Sorted by Percent
Based on all places, regardless of population

Place	Number	%
Uniondale (town) Wells County	1	0.36
Larwill (town) Whitley County	1	0.35
Ashley (town) De Kalb County	3	0.30
Pierceton (town) Kosciusko County	2	0.29
Beverly Shores (town) Porter County	2	0.28

Place	Number	%
Marshall (town) Parke County	1	0.28
Grissom AFB (cdp) Miami County	4	0.24
Birdseye (town) Dubois County	1	0.22
West Lafayette (city) Tippecanoe County	59	0.21
Koontz Lake (cdp) Starke County	3	0.19

Top 10 Places Sorted by Percent
Based on places with populations of 10,000 or more

Place	Number	%
West Lafayette (city) Tippecanoe County	59	0.21
Crown Point (city) Lake County	31	0.16
Dyer (town) Lake County	19	0.14
Bloomington (city) Monroe County	92	0.13
Lake Station (city) Lake County	8	0.06
Elkhart (city) Elkhart County	28	0.05
Lawrence (city) Marion County	20	0.05
Marion (city) Grant County	16	0.05
Peru (city) Miami County	7	0.05
Speedway (town) Marion County	6	0.05

Asian: Vietnamese

Top 10 Places Sorted by Number
Based on all places, regardless of population

Place	Number	%
Indianapolis (cons. city) Marion County	1,227	0.16
Fort Wayne (city) Allen County	682	0.33
South Bend (city) Saint Joseph County	262	0.24
Evansville (city) Vanderburgh County	140	0.12
Bloomington (city) Monroe County	121	0.17
Fishers (town) Hamilton County	115	0.30
Lafayette (city) Tippecanoe County	96	0.17
Columbus (city) Bartholomew County	93	0.24
Mishawaka (city) Saint Joseph County	89	0.19
Carmel (city) Hamilton County	80	0.21

Top 10 Places Sorted by Percent
Based on all places, regardless of population

Place	Number	%
Cromwell (town) Noble County	8	1.77
Middlebury (town) Elkhart County	24	0.81
Warren Park (town) Marion County	9	0.54
Gentryville (town) Spencer County	1	0.38
Fort Wayne (city) Allen County	682	0.33
Brownsburg (town) Hendricks County	45	0.31
Fishers (town) Hamilton County	115	0.30
Avon (town) Hendricks County	19	0.30
Georgetown (cdp) Saint Joseph County	13	0.29
Logansport (city) Cass County	55	0.28

Top 10 Places Sorted by Percent
Based on places with populations of 10,000 or more

Place	Number	%
Fort Wayne (city) Allen County	682	0.33
Brownsburg (town) Hendricks County	45	0.31
Fishers (town) Hamilton County	115	0.30
Logansport (city) Cass County	55	0.28
West Lafayette (city) Tippecanoe County	72	0.25
South Bend (city) Saint Joseph County	262	0.24
Columbus (city) Bartholomew County	93	0.24
Seymour (city) Jackson County	40	0.22
Greensburg (city) Decatur County	23	0.22
Carmel (city) Hamilton County	80	0.21

Asian: Other Asian, specified

Top 10 Places Sorted by Number
Based on all places, regardless of population

Place	Number	%
Fort Wayne (city) Allen County	476	0.23
Indianapolis (cons. city) Marion County	119	0.02
Bloomington (city) Monroe County	32	0.05

Place	Number	%
Muncie (city) Delaware County	31	0.05
Evansville (city) Vanderburgh County	13	0.01
Anderson (city) Madison County	11	0.02
Speedway (town) Marion County	10	0.08
Goshen (city) Elkhart County	10	0.03
Westfield (town) Hamilton County	9	0.10
West Lafayette (city) Tippecanoe County	9	0.03

Top 10 Places Sorted by Percent
Based on all places, regardless of population

Place	Number	%
West Harrison (town) Dearborn County	1	0.35
Fort Wayne (city) Allen County	476	0.23
West Terre Haute (town) Vigo County	4	0.17
Westfield (town) Hamilton County	9	0.10
Speedway (town) Marion County	10	0.08
North Manchester (town) Wabash County	5	0.08
Covington (city) Fountain County	2	0.08
Jasper (city) Dubois County	7	0.06
Lawrenceburg (city) Dearborn County	3	0.06
Brookston (town) White County	1	0.06

Top 10 Places Sorted by Percent
Based on places with populations of 10,000 or more

Place	Number	%
Fort Wayne (city) Allen County	476	0.23
Speedway (town) Marion County	10	0.08
Jasper (city) Dubois County	7	0.06
Bloomington (city) Monroe County	32	0.05
Muncie (city) Delaware County	31	0.05
Goshen (city) Elkhart County	10	0.03
West Lafayette (city) Tippecanoe County	9	0.03
Crown Point (city) Lake County	6	0.03
Brownsburg (town) Hendricks County	4	0.03
Indianapolis (cons. city) Marion County	119	0.02

Asian: Other Asian, not specified

Top 10 Places Sorted by Number
Based on all places, regardless of population

Place	Number	%
Indianapolis (cons. city) Marion County	716	0.09
Bloomington (city) Monroe County	296	0.43
Fort Wayne (city) Allen County	279	0.14
South Bend (city) Saint Joseph County	102	0.09
West Lafayette (city) Tippecanoe County	98	0.34
Elkhart (city) Elkhart County	94	0.18
Terre Haute (city) Vigo County	76	0.13
Evansville (city) Vanderburgh County	66	0.05
Fishers (town) Hamilton County	63	0.17
Hammond (city) Lake County	47	0.06

Top 10 Places Sorted by Percent
Based on all places, regardless of population

Place	Number	%
Topeka (town) La Grange County	19	1.64
Cromwell (town) Noble County	6	1.33
Spring Grove (town) Wayne County	2	0.52
Bloomington (city) Monroe County	296	0.43
Bryant (town) Jay County	1	0.37
Warren Park (town) Marion County	6	0.36
West Lafayette (city) Tippecanoe County	98	0.34
Georgetown (cdp) Saint Joseph County	13	0.29
Angola (city) Steuben County	20	0.27
Lynnville (town) Warrick County	2	0.26

Top 10 Places Sorted by Percent
Based on places with populations of 10,000 or more

Place	Number	%
Bloomington (city) Monroe County	296	0.43
West Lafayette (city) Tippecanoe County	98	0.34
Elkhart (city) Elkhart County	94	0.18

Notes: (cdp) census designated place; Refer to the User's Guide in the front of the book for more detailed information.

Fishers (town) Hamilton County	63	0.17
Dyer (town) Lake County	23	0.17
Schererville (town) Lake County	37	0.15
Speedway (town) Marion County	19	0.15
Fort Wayne (city) Allen County	279	0.14
Terre Haute (city) Vigo County	76	0.13
Munster (town) Lake County	28	0.13

Assyrian/Chaldean/Syriac

Top 10 Places Sorted by Number
Based on all places, regardless of population

Place	Number	%
Merrillville (town) Lake County	55	0.18
Hobart (city) Lake County	49	0.19
Bloomington (city) Monroe County	34	0.05
Valparaiso (city) Porter County	16	0.06
Oxford (town) Benton County	11	0.85
Hebron (town) Porter County	11	0.31
Hammond (city) Lake County	11	0.01
Lowell (town) Lake County	10	0.13
Gary (city) Lake County	10	0.01
Munster (town) Lake County	7	0.03

Top 10 Places Sorted by Percent
Based on all places, regardless of population

Place	Number	%
Oxford (town) Benton County	11	0.85
Burns Harbor (town) Porter County	3	0.38
Hebron (town) Porter County	11	0.31
Southport (city) Marion County	5	0.26
Hobart (city) Lake County	49	0.19
Merrillville (town) Lake County	55	0.18
Lowell (town) Lake County	10	0.13
Valparaiso (city) Porter County	16	0.06
Bloomington (city) Monroe County	34	0.05
Munster (town) Lake County	7	0.03

Top 10 Places Sorted by Percent
Based on places with populations of 10,000 or more

Place	Number	%
Hobart (city) Lake County	49	0.19
Merrillville (town) Lake County	55	0.18
Valparaiso (city) Porter County	16	0.06
Bloomington (city) Monroe County	34	0.05
Munster (town) Lake County	7	0.03
Schererville (town) Lake County	7	0.03
Crown Point (city) Lake County	6	0.03
Hammond (city) Lake County	11	0.01
Gary (city) Lake County	10	0.01

Australian

Top 10 Places Sorted by Number
Based on all places, regardless of population

Place	Number	%
Indianapolis (cons. city) Marion County	221	0.03
Noblesville (city) Hamilton County	52	0.18
Mishawaka (city) Saint Joseph County	46	0.10
Bloomington (city) Monroe County	38	0.05
Fort Wayne (city) Allen County	34	0.02
Evansville (city) Vanderburgh County	28	0.03
South Bend (city) Saint Joseph County	27	0.03
La Porte (city) La Porte County	20	0.09
Muncie (city) Delaware County	19	0.03
Lafayette (city) Tippecanoe County	17	0.03

Top 10 Places Sorted by Percent
Based on all places, regardless of population

Place	Number	%
Dublin (town) Wayne County	11	1.50
Middlebury (town) Elkhart County	16	0.56

Leo-Cedarville (town) Allen County	9	0.33
Wakarusa (town) Elkhart County	5	0.31
Meridian Hills (town) Marion County	5	0.29
Gas City (city) Grant County	12	0.20
Westville (town) La Porte County	4	0.19
Noblesville (city) Hamilton County	52	0.18
Sellersburg (town) Clark County	11	0.18
Ellettsville (town) Monroe County	7	0.14

Top 10 Places Sorted by Percent
Based on places with populations of 10,000 or more

Place	Number	%
Noblesville (city) Hamilton County	52	0.18
Lebanon (city) Boone County	15	0.11
Mishawaka (city) Saint Joseph County	46	0.10
La Porte (city) La Porte County	20	0.09
Chesterton (town) Porter County	9	0.09
Plainfield (town) Hendricks County	16	0.08
Shelbyville (city) Shelby County	13	0.07
Bloomington (city) Monroe County	38	0.05
Carmel (city) Hamilton County	16	0.04
Michigan City (city) La Porte County	14	0.04

Austrian

Top 10 Places Sorted by Number
Based on all places, regardless of population

Place	Number	%
Indianapolis (cons. city) Marion County	1,127	0.14
South Bend (city) Saint Joseph County	416	0.39
Fort Wayne (city) Allen County	292	0.14
Bloomington (city) Monroe County	219	0.32
Valparaiso (city) Porter County	169	0.61
Carmel (city) Hamilton County	164	0.43
Hammond (city) Lake County	141	0.17
Terre Haute (city) Vigo County	131	0.22
Schererville (town) Lake County	126	0.51
Dyer (town) Lake County	105	0.76

Top 10 Places Sorted by Percent
Based on all places, regardless of population

Place	Number	%
Indian Village (town) Saint Joseph County	15	10.71
Wallace (town) Fountain County	6	5.50
Dune Acres (town) Porter County	5	2.59
Leesburg (town) Kosciusko County	8	1.32
Mecca (town) Parke County	4	1.22
Kewanna (town) Fulton County	7	1.16
Michiana Shores (town) La Porte County	3	1.07
Saint John (town) Lake County	87	1.04
Crane (town) Martin County	2	1.04
Lowell (town) Lake County	68	0.91

Top 10 Places Sorted by Percent
Based on places with populations of 10,000 or more

Place	Number	%
Dyer (town) Lake County	105	0.76
Valparaiso (city) Porter County	169	0.61
Schererville (town) Lake County	126	0.51
Griffith (town) Lake County	76	0.44
Carmel (city) Hamilton County	164	0.43
Munster (town) Lake County	88	0.41
South Bend (city) Saint Joseph County	416	0.39
Warsaw (city) Kosciusko County	47	0.38
Crown Point (city) Lake County	70	0.36
Highland (town) Lake County	82	0.35

Basque

Top 10 Places Sorted by Number
Based on all places, regardless of population

Place	Number	%
Kokomo (city) Howard County	23	0.05
West Lafayette (city) Tippecanoe County	17	0.06
Anderson (city) Madison County	17	0.03
Noblesville (city) Hamilton County	12	0.04
New Albany (city) Floyd County	12	0.03
Indianapolis (cons. city) Marion County	12	<0.01
Fort Wayne (city) Allen County	8	<0.01
Bloomington (city) Monroe County	7	0.01
Highland (town) Lake County	6	0.03
Ogden Dunes (town) Porter County	4	0.30

Top 10 Places Sorted by Percent
Based on all places, regardless of population

Place	Number	%
Ogden Dunes (town) Porter County	4	0.30
Wakarusa (town) Elkhart County	3	0.19
West Lafayette (city) Tippecanoe County	17	0.06
Kokomo (city) Howard County	23	0.05
Noblesville (city) Hamilton County	12	0.04
Anderson (city) Madison County	17	0.03
New Albany (city) Floyd County	12	0.03
Highland (town) Lake County	6	0.03
Bloomington (city) Monroe County	7	0.01
Indianapolis (cons. city) Marion County	12	<0.01

Top 10 Places Sorted by Percent
Based on places with populations of 10,000 or more

Place	Number	%
West Lafayette (city) Tippecanoe County	17	0.06
Kokomo (city) Howard County	23	0.05
Noblesville (city) Hamilton County	12	0.04
Anderson (city) Madison County	17	0.03
New Albany (city) Floyd County	12	0.03
Highland (town) Lake County	6	0.03
Bloomington (city) Monroe County	7	0.01
Indianapolis (cons. city) Marion County	12	<0.01
Fort Wayne (city) Allen County	8	<0.01

Belgian

Top 10 Places Sorted by Number
Based on all places, regardless of population

Place	Number	%
Mishawaka (city) Saint Joseph County	1,595	3.41
South Bend (city) Saint Joseph County	1,423	1.33
Granger (cdp) Saint Joseph County	607	2.15
Indianapolis (cons. city) Marion County	576	0.07
Bloomington (city) Monroe County	195	0.28
Elkhart (city) Elkhart County	174	0.34
Fort Wayne (city) Allen County	163	0.08
Lawrence (city) Marion County	116	0.30
Fishers (town) Hamilton County	110	0.28
Lafayette (city) Tippecanoe County	101	0.18

Top 10 Places Sorted by Percent
Based on all places, regardless of population

Place	Number	%
Lakeville (town) Saint Joseph County	30	5.38
Mishawaka (city) Saint Joseph County	1,595	3.41
New Carlisle (town) Saint Joseph County	39	2.67
Shamrock Lakes (town) Blackford County	4	2.56
Granger (cdp) Saint Joseph County	607	2.15
Orestes (town) Madison County	7	1.89
Osceola (town) Saint Joseph County	32	1.83
North Liberty (town) Saint Joseph County	23	1.64
La Paz (town) Marshall County	7	1.39
Gulivoire Park (cdp) Saint Joseph County	40	1.36

Notes: (cdp) census designated place; Refer to the User's Guide in the front of the book for more detailed information.

Top 10 Places Sorted by Percent
Based on places with populations of 10,000 or more

Place	Number	%
Mishawaka (city) Saint Joseph County	1,595	3.41
Granger (cdp) Saint Joseph County	607	2.15
South Bend (city) Saint Joseph County	1,423	1.33
Madison (city) Jefferson County	56	0.46
Plainfield (town) Hendricks County	75	0.40
Elkhart (city) Elkhart County	174	0.34
Lawrence (city) Marion County	116	0.30
Bloomington (city) Monroe County	195	0.28
Fishers (town) Hamilton County	110	0.28
Crown Point (city) Lake County	52	0.27

Brazilian

Top 10 Places Sorted by Number
Based on all places, regardless of population

Place	Number	%
Indianapolis (cons. city) Marion County	208	0.03
Bloomington (city) Monroe County	95	0.14
Lawrence (city) Marion County	55	0.14
South Bend (city) Saint Joseph County	31	0.03
Hammond (city) Lake County	28	0.03
Evansville (city) Vanderburgh County	25	0.02
Schererville (town) Lake County	24	0.10
Peru (city) Miami County	23	0.18
Fort Wayne (city) Allen County	21	0.01
La Porte (city) La Porte County	18	0.08

Top 10 Places Sorted by Percent
Based on all places, regardless of population

Place	Number	%
Alamo (town) Montgomery County	7	6.48
Kewanna (town) Fulton County	2	0.33
Syracuse (town) Kosciusko County	6	0.19
Peru (city) Miami County	23	0.18
Cicero (town) Hamilton County	6	0.15
Bloomington (city) Monroe County	95	0.14
Lawrence (city) Marion County	55	0.14
Bluffton (city) Wells County	13	0.13
Warsaw (city) Kosciusko County	15	0.12
Fremont (town) Steuben County	2	0.12

Top 10 Places Sorted by Percent
Based on places with populations of 10,000 or more

Place	Number	%
Peru (city) Miami County	23	0.18
Bloomington (city) Monroe County	95	0.14
Lawrence (city) Marion County	55	0.14
Warsaw (city) Kosciusko County	15	0.12
Schererville (town) Lake County	24	0.10
La Porte (city) La Porte County	18	0.08
Columbus (city) Bartholomew County	18	0.05
Merrillville (town) Lake County	15	0.05
Fishers (town) Hamilton County	16	0.04
Indianapolis (cons. city) Marion County	208	0.03

British

Top 10 Places Sorted by Number
Based on all places, regardless of population

Place	Number	%
Indianapolis (cons. city) Marion County	3,585	0.46
Bloomington (city) Monroe County	798	1.15
Evansville (city) Vanderburgh County	594	0.49
Fort Wayne (city) Allen County	585	0.28
South Bend (city) Saint Joseph County	396	0.37
Columbus (city) Bartholomew County	345	0.88
Carmel (city) Hamilton County	344	0.91
Noblesville (city) Hamilton County	318	1.10
Lafayette (city) Tippecanoe County	281	0.50

| **Anderson** (city) Madison County | 278 | 0.47 |

Top 10 Places Sorted by Percent
Based on all places, regardless of population

Place	Number	%
Griffin (town) Posey County	8	5.52
Greensboro (town) Henry County	8	4.40
Jonesville (town) Bartholomew County	8	3.45
Whitewater (town) Wayne County	2	3.33
Grissom AFB (cdp) Miami County	51	3.06
Wheatfield (town) Jasper County	23	2.94
Carbon (town) Clay County	10	2.94
Modoc (town) Randolph County	5	2.51
Bruceville (town) Knox County	10	2.22
Spring Lake (town) Hancock County	5	1.90

Top 10 Places Sorted by Percent
Based on places with populations of 10,000 or more

Place	Number	%
Frankfort (city) Clinton County	217	1.30
Bloomington (city) Monroe County	798	1.15
Noblesville (city) Hamilton County	318	1.10
Carmel (city) Hamilton County	344	0.91
Speedway (town) Marion County	117	0.91
Columbus (city) Bartholomew County	345	0.88
West Lafayette (city) Tippecanoe County	211	0.73
Griffith (town) Lake County	126	0.73
Chesterton (town) Porter County	74	0.71
Greenwood (city) Johnson County	225	0.63

Bulgarian

Top 10 Places Sorted by Number
Based on all places, regardless of population

Place	Number	%
Indianapolis (cons. city) Marion County	175	0.02
South Bend (city) Saint Joseph County	57	0.05
Bloomington (city) Monroe County	56	0.08
Fort Wayne (city) Allen County	56	0.03
Merrillville (town) Lake County	55	0.18
Hammond (city) Lake County	47	0.06
Columbus (city) Bartholomew County	46	0.12
Roselawn (cdp) Jasper County	32	0.82
Cedar Lake (town) Lake County	32	0.35
Schererville (town) Lake County	31	0.12

Top 10 Places Sorted by Percent
Based on all places, regardless of population

Place	Number	%
Roselawn (cdp) Jasper County	32	0.82
Cedar Lake (town) Lake County	32	0.35
Roseland (town) Saint Joseph County	5	0.28
New Chicago (town) Lake County	5	0.23
Waterloo (town) De Kalb County	5	0.23
Merrillville (town) Lake County	55	0.18
Parker City (town) Randolph County	2	0.14
Winfield (town) Lake County	3	0.13
Columbus (city) Bartholomew County	46	0.12
Schererville (town) Lake County	31	0.12

Top 10 Places Sorted by Percent
Based on places with populations of 10,000 or more

Place	Number	%
Merrillville (town) Lake County	55	0.18
Columbus (city) Bartholomew County	46	0.12
Schererville (town) Lake County	31	0.12
Munster (town) Lake County	23	0.11
West Lafayette (city) Tippecanoe County	30	0.10
Highland (town) Lake County	23	0.10
Griffith (town) Lake County	17	0.10
Crawfordsville (city) Montgomery County	16	0.10
Crown Point (city) Lake County	18	0.09

| **Bloomington** (city) Monroe County | 56 | 0.08 |

Canadian

Top 10 Places Sorted by Number
Based on all places, regardless of population

Place	Number	%
Indianapolis (cons. city) Marion County	873	0.11
Fort Wayne (city) Allen County	428	0.21
South Bend (city) Saint Joseph County	251	0.23
Fishers (town) Hamilton County	201	0.52
Mishawaka (city) Saint Joseph County	173	0.37
Carmel (city) Hamilton County	155	0.41
Bloomington (city) Monroe County	145	0.21
Lakes of the Four Seasons (cdp) Lake County	134	1.83
Hammond (city) Lake County	126	0.15
Goshen (city) Elkhart County	122	0.42

Top 10 Places Sorted by Percent
Based on all places, regardless of population

Place	Number	%
New Middletown (town) Harrison County	3	4.69
Edwardsport (town) Knox County	7	1.94
Denver (town) Miami County	11	1.86
Lakes of the Four Seasons (cdp) Lake County	134	1.83
Porter (town) Porter County	81	1.60
Pottawattamie Park (town) La Porte County	4	1.33
Schneider (town) Lake County	4	1.15
Amboy (town) Miami County	4	1.13
Pennville (town) Jay County	8	1.12
Sidney (town) Kosciusko County	2	1.08

Top 10 Places Sorted by Percent
Based on places with populations of 10,000 or more

Place	Number	%
Fishers (town) Hamilton County	201	0.52
Goshen (city) Elkhart County	122	0.42
Chesterton (town) Porter County	44	0.42
Carmel (city) Hamilton County	155	0.41
Noblesville (city) Hamilton County	113	0.39
Mishawaka (city) Saint Joseph County	173	0.37
Greenfield (city) Hancock County	54	0.37
Valparaiso (city) Porter County	100	0.36
Marion (city) Grant County	100	0.32
Lake Station (city) Lake County	45	0.32

Carpatho Rusyn

Top 10 Places Sorted by Number
Based on all places, regardless of population

Place	Number	%
West Lafayette (city) Tippecanoe County	8	0.03
Bloomington (city) Monroe County	8	0.01
Chesterton (town) Porter County	7	0.07
Hammond (city) Lake County	5	0.01
Etna Green (town) Kosciusko County	2	0.31

Top 10 Places Sorted by Percent
Based on all places, regardless of population

Place	Number	%
Etna Green (town) Kosciusko County	2	0.31
Chesterton (town) Porter County	7	0.07
West Lafayette (city) Tippecanoe County	8	0.03
Bloomington (city) Monroe County	8	0.01
Hammond (city) Lake County	5	0.01

Top 10 Places Sorted by Percent
Based on places with populations of 10,000 or more

Place	Number	%
Chesterton (town) Porter County	7	0.07
West Lafayette (city) Tippecanoe County	8	0.03

Notes: (cdp) census designated place; Refer to the User's Guide in the front of the book for more detailed information.

Bloomington (city) Monroe County	8	0.01
Hammond (city) Lake County	5	0.01

Celtic

Top 10 Places Sorted by Number
Based on all places, regardless of population

Place	Number	%
Indianapolis (cons. city) Marion County	139	0.02
Carmel (city) Hamilton County	33	0.09
Crawfordsville (city) Montgomery County	29	0.19
Lafayette (city) Tippecanoe County	29	0.05
Columbus (city) Bartholomew County	27	0.07
Valparaiso (city) Porter County	24	0.09
Kokomo (city) Howard County	24	0.05
Hammond (city) Lake County	20	0.02
South Bend (city) Saint Joseph County	20	0.02
Corydon (town) Harrison County	17	0.58

Top 10 Places Sorted by Percent
Based on all places, regardless of population

Place	Number	%
Mount Summit (town) Henry County	2	0.66
Wheatland (town) Knox County	3	0.61
Corydon (town) Harrison County	17	0.58
Newburgh (town) Warrick County	11	0.34
Ellettsville (town) Monroe County	17	0.33
Mitchell (city) Lawrence County	14	0.31
Liberty (town) Union County	6	0.30
Beverly Shores (town) Porter County	2	0.30
Princes Lakes (town) Johnson County	3	0.20
Crawfordsville (city) Montgomery County	29	0.19

Top 10 Places Sorted by Percent
Based on places with populations of 10,000 or more

Place	Number	%
Crawfordsville (city) Montgomery County	29	0.19
Carmel (city) Hamilton County	33	0.09
Valparaiso (city) Porter County	24	0.09
Seymour (city) Jackson County	14	0.08
Columbus (city) Bartholomew County	27	0.07
Dyer (town) Lake County	9	0.06
Lafayette (city) Tippecanoe County	29	0.05
Kokomo (city) Howard County	24	0.05
Vincennes (city) Knox County	10	0.05
Peru (city) Miami County	6	0.05

Croatian

Top 10 Places Sorted by Number
Based on all places, regardless of population

Place	Number	%
Hammond (city) Lake County	1,221	1.47
Schererville (town) Lake County	683	2.75
Hobart (city) Lake County	630	2.48
Indianapolis (cons. city) Marion County	545	0.07
Merrillville (town) Lake County	514	1.67
Highland (town) Lake County	509	2.16
Crown Point (city) Lake County	497	2.54
Munster (town) Lake County	446	2.07
Portage (city) Porter County	445	1.33
Griffith (town) Lake County	400	2.31

Top 10 Places Sorted by Percent
Based on all places, regardless of population

Place	Number	%
Ogden Dunes (town) Porter County	54	4.12
Whiting (city) Lake County	189	3.68
Lakes of the Four Seasons (cdp) Lake County	258	3.53
Schererville (town) Lake County	683	2.75
Crown Point (city) Lake County	497	2.54
Hobart (city) Lake County	630	2.48

Griffith (town) Lake County	400	2.31
Highland (town) Lake County	509	2.16
Munster (town) Lake County	446	2.07
Monterey (town) Pulaski County	5	2.06

Top 10 Places Sorted by Percent
Based on places with populations of 10,000 or more

Place	Number	%
Schererville (town) Lake County	683	2.75
Crown Point (city) Lake County	497	2.54
Hobart (city) Lake County	630	2.48
Griffith (town) Lake County	400	2.31
Highland (town) Lake County	509	2.16
Munster (town) Lake County	446	2.07
Merrillville (town) Lake County	514	1.67
Dyer (town) Lake County	218	1.57
Hammond (city) Lake County	1,221	1.47
Portage (city) Porter County	445	1.33

Cypriot

Top 10 Places Sorted by Number
Based on all places, regardless of population

Place	Number	%
Hammond (city) Lake County	35	0.04
Granger (cdp) Saint Joseph County	28	0.10
Indianapolis (cons. city) Marion County	26	<0.01
Greenwood (city) Johnson County	15	0.04
Lafayette (city) Tippecanoe County	8	0.01
Bloomington (city) Monroe County	7	0.01
Lakes of the Four Seasons (cdp) Lake County	6	0.08
West Lafayette (city) Tippecanoe County	4	0.01

Top 10 Places Sorted by Percent
Based on all places, regardless of population

Place	Number	%
Granger (cdp) Saint Joseph County	28	0.10
Lakes of the Four Seasons (cdp) Lake County	6	0.08
Hammond (city) Lake County	35	0.04
Greenwood (city) Johnson County	15	0.04
Lafayette (city) Tippecanoe County	8	0.01
Bloomington (city) Monroe County	7	0.01
West Lafayette (city) Tippecanoe County	4	0.01
Indianapolis (cons. city) Marion County	26	<0.01

Top 10 Places Sorted by Percent
Based on places with populations of 10,000 or more

Place	Number	%
Granger (cdp) Saint Joseph County	28	0.10
Hammond (city) Lake County	35	0.04
Greenwood (city) Johnson County	15	0.04
Lafayette (city) Tippecanoe County	8	0.01
Bloomington (city) Monroe County	7	0.01
West Lafayette (city) Tippecanoe County	4	0.01
Indianapolis (cons. city) Marion County	26	<0.01

Czech

Top 10 Places Sorted by Number
Based on all places, regardless of population

Place	Number	%
Indianapolis (cons. city) Marion County	1,332	0.17
Bloomington (city) Monroe County	347	0.50
Fort Wayne (city) Allen County	341	0.17
Portage (city) Porter County	294	0.88
West Lafayette (city) Tippecanoe County	215	0.74
Schererville (town) Lake County	211	0.85
Hammond (city) Lake County	205	0.25
Evansville (city) Vanderburgh County	204	0.17
Fishers (town) Hamilton County	190	0.49
Crown Point (city) Lake County	181	0.93

Top 10 Places Sorted by Percent
Based on all places, regardless of population

Place	Number	%
Bethany (town) Morgan County	2	3.85
Bass Lake (cdp) Starke County	47	3.68
Mount Ayr (town) Newton County	5	2.87
Alamo (town) Montgomery County	3	2.78
Kingsbury (town) La Porte County	5	2.38
Wanatah (town) La Porte County	24	2.37
North Judson (town) Starke County	33	2.00
Culver (town) Marshall County	29	1.88
Beverly Shores (town) Porter County	11	1.64
Lake Village (cdp) Newton County	13	1.61

Top 10 Places Sorted by Percent
Based on places with populations of 10,000 or more

Place	Number	%
Crown Point (city) Lake County	181	0.93
Portage (city) Porter County	294	0.88
Schererville (town) Lake County	211	0.85
West Lafayette (city) Tippecanoe County	215	0.74
Munster (town) Lake County	150	0.70
Lake Station (city) Lake County	97	0.69
Highland (town) Lake County	135	0.57
Valparaiso (city) Porter County	155	0.56
Granger (cdp) Saint Joseph County	156	0.55
Bloomington (city) Monroe County	347	0.50

Czechoslovakian

Top 10 Places Sorted by Number
Based on all places, regardless of population

Place	Number	%
Indianapolis (cons. city) Marion County	759	0.10
Hammond (city) Lake County	193	0.23
Fort Wayne (city) Allen County	135	0.07
Portage (city) Porter County	131	0.39
Bloomington (city) Monroe County	131	0.19
Fishers (town) Hamilton County	128	0.33
Evansville (city) Vanderburgh County	119	0.10
Hobart (city) Lake County	103	0.41
South Bend (city) Saint Joseph County	101	0.09
Chesterton (town) Porter County	100	0.96

Top 10 Places Sorted by Percent
Based on all places, regardless of population

Place	Number	%
Crows Nest (town) Marion County	2	2.38
Ogden Dunes (town) Porter County	22	1.68
Orestes (town) Madison County	5	1.35
Wilkinson (town) Hancock County	5	1.23
Medaryville (town) Pulaski County	7	1.21
Whiting (city) Lake County	61	1.19
Beverly Shores (town) Porter County	8	1.19
Roseland (town) Saint Joseph County	21	1.16
Mount Ayr (town) Newton County	2	1.15
Michiana Shores (town) La Porte County	3	1.07

Top 10 Places Sorted by Percent
Based on places with populations of 10,000 or more

Place	Number	%
Chesterton (town) Porter County	100	0.96
Hobart (city) Lake County	103	0.41
Highland (town) Lake County	95	0.40
Portage (city) Porter County	131	0.39
Lake Station (city) Lake County	51	0.36
Schererville (town) Lake County	88	0.35
Fishers (town) Hamilton County	128	0.33
Munster (town) Lake County	72	0.33
Valparaiso (city) Porter County	88	0.32
Griffith (town) Lake County	54	0.31

Notes: (cdp) census designated place; Refer to the User's Guide in the front of the book for more detailed information.

Danish

Top 10 Places Sorted by Number
Based on all places, regardless of population

Place	Number	%
Indianapolis (cons. city) Marion County	1,573	0.20
Fort Wayne (city) Allen County	509	0.25
Bloomington (city) Monroe County	263	0.38
Carmel (city) Hamilton County	246	0.65
South Bend (city) Saint Joseph County	230	0.21
Lawrence (city) Marion County	223	0.57
Granger (cdp) Saint Joseph County	178	0.63
West Lafayette (city) Tippecanoe County	163	0.56
Fishers (town) Hamilton County	157	0.40
Valparaiso (city) Porter County	152	0.55

Top 10 Places Sorted by Percent
Based on all places, regardless of population

Place	Number	%
Michiana Shores (town) La Porte County	13	4.63
Woodlawn Heights (town) Madison County	2	3.77
Dune Acres (town) Porter County	5	2.59
Carbon (town) Clay County	7	2.06
Koontz Lake (cdp) Starke County	30	1.95
Simonton Lake (cdp) Elkhart County	69	1.73
Rocky Ripple (town) Marion County	12	1.70
Knox (city) Starke County	53	1.39
Saint John (town) Lake County	112	1.33
Bass Lake (cdp) Starke County	17	1.33

Top 10 Places Sorted by Percent
Based on places with populations of 10,000 or more

Place	Number	%
Crown Point (city) Lake County	137	0.70
Carmel (city) Hamilton County	246	0.65
Granger (cdp) Saint Joseph County	178	0.63
Lawrence (city) Marion County	223	0.57
West Lafayette (city) Tippecanoe County	163	0.56
Valparaiso (city) Porter County	152	0.55
Munster (town) Lake County	119	0.55
Highland (town) Lake County	101	0.43
Noblesville (city) Hamilton County	118	0.41
Fishers (town) Hamilton County	157	0.40

Dutch

Top 10 Places Sorted by Number
Based on all places, regardless of population

Place	Number	%
Indianapolis (cons. city) Marion County	12,223	1.56
Fort Wayne (city) Allen County	3,576	1.74
South Bend (city) Saint Joseph County	1,933	1.81
Lafayette (city) Tippecanoe County	1,874	3.33
Hammond (city) Lake County	1,780	2.14
Evansville (city) Vanderburgh County	1,700	1.39
Highland (town) Lake County	1,598	6.79
Schererville (town) Lake County	1,445	5.82
Elkhart (city) Elkhart County	1,414	2.73
Bloomington (city) Monroe County	1,331	1.92

Top 10 Places Sorted by Percent
Based on all places, regardless of population

Place	Number	%
De Motte (town) Jasper County	631	19.54
Ulen (town) Boone County	18	17.14
Woodlawn Heights (town) Madison County	7	13.21
Yeoman (town) Carroll County	12	12.77
North Crows Nest (town) Marion County	5	11.90
Mexico (cdp) Miami County	128	11.66
Wheatfield (town) Jasper County	88	11.25
Mount Ayr (town) Newton County	18	10.34
Zanesville (town) Allen County	59	9.80

| Universal (town) Vermillion County | 41 | 9.49 |

Top 10 Places Sorted by Percent
Based on places with populations of 10,000 or more

Place	Number	%
Dyer (town) Lake County	1,004	7.25
Highland (town) Lake County	1,598	6.79
Schererville (town) Lake County	1,445	5.82
Griffith (town) Lake County	873	5.04
Munster (town) Lake County	1,083	5.03
Crown Point (city) Lake County	752	3.84
Chesterton (town) Porter County	349	3.34
Lafayette (city) Tippecanoe County	1,874	3.33
Granger (cdp) Saint Joseph County	930	3.29
Brownsburg (town) Hendricks County	441	3.07

Eastern European

Top 10 Places Sorted by Number
Based on all places, regardless of population

Place	Number	%
Indianapolis (cons. city) Marion County	228	0.03
Bloomington (city) Monroe County	188	0.27
Carmel (city) Hamilton County	117	0.31
South Bend (city) Saint Joseph County	104	0.10
Munster (town) Lake County	100	0.46
Dyer (town) Lake County	44	0.32
Valparaiso (city) Porter County	37	0.13
Zionsville (town) Boone County	35	0.41
Muncie (city) Delaware County	25	0.04
Greenwood (city) Johnson County	22	0.06

Top 10 Places Sorted by Percent
Based on all places, regardless of population

Place	Number	%
Meridian Hills (town) Marion County	9	0.52
Burns Harbor (town) Porter County	4	0.51
Williams Creek (town) Marion County	2	0.49
Munster (town) Lake County	100	0.46
Beverly Shores (town) Porter County	3	0.45
Zionsville (town) Boone County	35	0.41
Dyer (town) Lake County	44	0.32
Carmel (city) Hamilton County	117	0.31
Danville (town) Hendricks County	18	0.28
Rocky Ripple (town) Marion County	2	0.28

Top 10 Places Sorted by Percent
Based on places with populations of 10,000 or more

Place	Number	%
Munster (town) Lake County	100	0.46
Dyer (town) Lake County	44	0.32
Carmel (city) Hamilton County	117	0.31
Bloomington (city) Monroe County	188	0.27
Valparaiso (city) Porter County	37	0.13
Chesterton (town) Porter County	13	0.12
South Bend (city) Saint Joseph County	104	0.10
Speedway (town) Marion County	11	0.09
La Porte (city) La Porte County	16	0.07
Greenwood (city) Johnson County	22	0.06

English

Top 10 Places Sorted by Number
Based on all places, regardless of population

Place	Number	%
Indianapolis (cons. city) Marion County	60,562	7.74
Fort Wayne (city) Allen County	15,638	7.59
Evansville (city) Vanderburgh County	11,096	9.10
Bloomington (city) Monroe County	7,525	10.87
South Bend (city) Saint Joseph County	6,274	5.86
Muncie (city) Delaware County	6,095	9.03
Terre Haute (city) Vigo County	5,739	9.64

Carmel (city) Hamilton County	5,656	14.96
Anderson (city) Madison County	5,363	8.99
Lafayette (city) Tippecanoe County	5,235	9.31

Top 10 Places Sorted by Percent
Based on all places, regardless of population

Place	Number	%
Laconia (town) Harrison County	12	50.00
Woodlawn Heights (town) Madison County	26	49.06
North Crows Nest (town) Marion County	16	38.10
Crows Nest (town) Marion County	31	36.90
Ulen (town) Boone County	35	33.33
Shamrock Lakes (town) Blackford County	48	30.77
Memphis (cdp) Clark County	87	25.74
Orestes (town) Madison County	87	23.51
Frankton (town) Madison County	442	23.15
Bloomingdale (town) Parke County	66	22.53

Top 10 Places Sorted by Percent
Based on places with populations of 10,000 or more

Place	Number	%
Carmel (city) Hamilton County	5,656	14.96
Noblesville (city) Hamilton County	3,883	13.41
Fishers (town) Hamilton County	5,197	13.35
Greenfield (city) Hancock County	1,848	12.71
Brownsburg (town) Hendricks County	1,800	12.55
Wabash (city) Wabash County	1,419	12.09
Chesterton (town) Porter County	1,248	11.96
Valparaiso (city) Porter County	3,265	11.87
Plainfield (town) Hendricks County	2,238	11.85
Beech Grove (city) Marion County	1,670	11.76

Estonian

Top 10 Places Sorted by Number
Based on all places, regardless of population

Place	Number	%
Indianapolis (cons. city) Marion County	69	0.01
Fort Wayne (city) Allen County	25	0.01
Wheatfield (town) Jasper County	15	1.92
Warren Park (town) Marion County	10	0.60
Angola (city) Steuben County	10	0.14
Michigan City (city) La Porte County	10	0.03
Bloomington (city) Monroe County	6	0.01

Top 10 Places Sorted by Percent
Based on all places, regardless of population

Place	Number	%
Wheatfield (town) Jasper County	15	1.92
Warren Park (town) Marion County	10	0.60
Angola (city) Steuben County	10	0.14
Michigan City (city) La Porte County	10	0.03
Indianapolis (cons. city) Marion County	69	0.01
Fort Wayne (city) Allen County	25	0.01
Bloomington (city) Monroe County	6	0.01

Top 10 Places Sorted by Percent
Based on places with populations of 10,000 or more

Place	Number	%
Michigan City (city) La Porte County	10	0.03
Indianapolis (cons. city) Marion County	69	0.01
Fort Wayne (city) Allen County	25	0.01
Bloomington (city) Monroe County	6	0.01

European

Top 10 Places Sorted by Number
Based on all places, regardless of population

Place	Number	%
Indianapolis (cons. city) Marion County	6,617	0.85
Fort Wayne (city) Allen County	1,212	0.59

Notes: (cdp) census designated place; Refer to the User's Guide in the front of the book for more detailed information.

Place	Number	%
Bloomington (city) Monroe County	1,085	1.57
Evansville (city) Vanderburgh County	788	0.65
Richmond (city) Wayne County	661	1.69
Muncie (city) Delaware County	555	0.82
Carmel (city) Hamilton County	553	1.46
South Bend (city) Saint Joseph County	542	0.51
Lafayette (city) Tippecanoe County	530	0.94
Fishers (town) Hamilton County	413	1.06

Top 10 Places Sorted by Percent
Based on all places, regardless of population

Place	Number	%
Bruceville (town) Knox County	71	15.74
Leavenworth (town) Crawford County	33	9.57
Stilesville (town) Hendricks County	24	8.42
Knightstown (town) Henry County	162	7.57
Nashville (town) Brown County	43	5.01
Crows Nest (town) Marion County	4	4.76
Edwardsport (town) Knox County	16	4.44
Sheridan (town) Hamilton County	102	4.33
Newpoint (town) Decatur County	12	4.11
Mentone (town) Kosciusko County	34	4.05

Top 10 Places Sorted by Percent
Based on places with populations of 10,000 or more

Place	Number	%
Madison (city) Jefferson County	243	2.01
Richmond (city) Wayne County	661	1.69
Brownsburg (town) Hendricks County	237	1.65
Frankfort (city) Clinton County	270	1.62
Bloomington (city) Monroe County	1,085	1.57
Carmel (city) Hamilton County	553	1.46
Greensburg (city) Decatur County	136	1.32
West Lafayette (city) Tippecanoe County	369	1.27
Franklin (city) Johnson County	231	1.17
Vincennes (city) Knox County	211	1.14

Finnish

Top 10 Places Sorted by Number
Based on all places, regardless of population

Place	Number	%
Indianapolis (cons. city) Marion County	610	0.08
Hammond (city) Lake County	189	0.23
Bloomington (city) Monroe County	178	0.26
Lafayette (city) Tippecanoe County	159	0.28
Fort Wayne (city) Allen County	156	0.08
South Bend (city) Saint Joseph County	125	0.12
West Lafayette (city) Tippecanoe County	106	0.37
Elkhart (city) Elkhart County	103	0.20
Greenwood (city) Johnson County	84	0.23
Portage (city) Porter County	75	0.22

Top 10 Places Sorted by Percent
Based on all places, regardless of population

Place	Number	%
Dune Acres (town) Porter County	5	2.59
State Line City (town) Warren County	2	1.49
Crandall (town) Harrison County	2	1.27
New Ross (town) Montgomery County	4	1.22
Yorktown (town) Delaware County	50	1.03
Knightstown (town) Henry County	21	0.98
Collegeville (cdp) Jasper County	6	0.69
North Judson (town) Starke County	11	0.67
Wheatfield (town) Jasper County	5	0.64
Winslow (town) Pike County	5	0.57

Top 10 Places Sorted by Percent
Based on places with populations of 10,000 or more

Place	Number	%
West Lafayette (city) Tippecanoe County	106	0.37
Plainfield (town) Hendricks County	54	0.29

Place	Number	%
New Haven (city) Allen County	36	0.29
Lafayette (city) Tippecanoe County	159	0.28
Auburn (city) De Kalb County	34	0.28
Bloomington (city) Monroe County	178	0.26
Lake Station (city) Lake County	35	0.25
Granger (cdp) Saint Joseph County	69	0.24
Hobart (city) Lake County	61	0.24
Hammond (city) Lake County	189	0.23

French, except Basque

Top 10 Places Sorted by Number
Based on all places, regardless of population

Place	Number	%
Indianapolis (cons. city) Marion County	15,444	1.97
Fort Wayne (city) Allen County	7,836	3.80
Evansville (city) Vanderburgh County	2,883	2.37
South Bend (city) Saint Joseph County	2,288	2.14
Bloomington (city) Monroe County	1,926	2.78
Hammond (city) Lake County	1,799	2.17
Lafayette (city) Tippecanoe County	1,706	3.03
Terre Haute (city) Vigo County	1,440	2.42
Fishers (town) Hamilton County	1,420	3.65
Mishawaka (city) Saint Joseph County	1,405	3.00

Top 10 Places Sorted by Percent
Based on all places, regardless of population

Place	Number	%
Fredericksburg (town) Washington County	13	13.27
Troy (town) Perry County	48	12.06
Woodlawn Heights (town) Madison County	6	11.32
Michigantown (town) Clinton County	45	10.69
Newberry (town) Greene County	21	9.68
Crane (town) Martin County	18	9.33
Kingsbury (town) La Porte County	19	9.05
Earl Park (town) Benton County	44	9.00
Fowler (town) Benton County	203	8.43
Clear Lake (town) Steuben County	23	8.39

Top 10 Places Sorted by Percent
Based on places with populations of 10,000 or more

Place	Number	%
New Haven (city) Allen County	817	6.60
Vincennes (city) Knox County	773	4.16
Fort Wayne (city) Allen County	7,836	3.80
Fishers (town) Hamilton County	1,420	3.65
Brownsburg (town) Hendricks County	476	3.32
Speedway (town) Marion County	417	3.24
Auburn (city) De Kalb County	387	3.21
Granger (cdp) Saint Joseph County	897	3.18
Washington (city) Daviess County	358	3.17
New Albany (city) Floyd County	1,161	3.11

French Canadian

Top 10 Places Sorted by Number
Based on all places, regardless of population

Place	Number	%
Indianapolis (cons. city) Marion County	2,041	0.26
Fort Wayne (city) Allen County	751	0.36
South Bend (city) Saint Joseph County	542	0.51
Mishawaka (city) Saint Joseph County	433	0.93
Bloomington (city) Monroe County	339	0.49
Hobart (city) Lake County	305	1.20
Evansville (city) Vanderburgh County	294	0.24
Elkhart (city) Elkhart County	278	0.54
Lafayette (city) Tippecanoe County	273	0.49
Muncie (city) Delaware County	227	0.34

Top 10 Places Sorted by Percent
Based on all places, regardless of population

Place	Number	%
Pine Village (town) Warren County	9	3.54
Norway (cdp) White County	15	3.05
Country Club Heights (town) Madison County	2	2.15
Yeoman (town) Carroll County	2	2.13
Westville (town) La Porte County	42	1.99
Roselawn (cdp) Jasper County	73	1.86
West Harrison (town) Dearborn County	5	1.84
Newtown (town) Fountain County	3	1.81
Ingalls (town) Madison County	21	1.74
Greendale (city) Dearborn County	73	1.71

Top 10 Places Sorted by Percent
Based on places with populations of 10,000 or more

Place	Number	%
Hobart (city) Lake County	305	1.20
Crown Point (city) Lake County	219	1.12
Dyer (town) Lake County	146	1.05
Mishawaka (city) Saint Joseph County	433	0.93
La Porte (city) La Porte County	183	0.85
Schererville (town) Lake County	196	0.75
Speedway (town) Marion County	97	0.75
Highland (town) Lake County	171	0.73
Granger (cdp) Saint Joseph County	204	0.72
Portage (city) Porter County	216	0.64

German

Top 10 Places Sorted by Number
Based on all places, regardless of population

Place	Number	%
Indianapolis (cons. city) Marion County	130,045	16.62
Fort Wayne (city) Allen County	56,716	27.54
Evansville (city) Vanderburgh County	29,976	24.60
South Bend (city) Saint Joseph County	18,800	17.56
Bloomington (city) Monroe County	17,244	24.91
Mishawaka (city) Saint Joseph County	12,725	27.19
Lafayette (city) Tippecanoe County	12,226	21.74
Muncie (city) Delaware County	11,825	17.53
Hammond (city) Lake County	11,586	13.95
Fishers (town) Hamilton County	11,383	29.23

Top 10 Places Sorted by Percent
Based on all places, regardless of population

Place	Number	%
Saint Leon (town) Dearborn County	272	69.39
Oldenburg (town) Franklin County	410	64.06
Ferdinand (town) Dubois County	1,449	63.69
Napoleon (town) Ripley County	137	59.31
Holland (town) Dubois County	420	59.15
Cedar Grove (town) Franklin County	107	58.79
Haubstadt (town) Gibson County	837	54.49
Jasper (city) Dubois County	6,497	54.30
Clear Lake (town) Steuben County	138	50.36
Batesville (city) Ripley County	3,035	50.09

Top 10 Places Sorted by Percent
Based on places with populations of 10,000 or more

Place	Number	%
Jasper (city) Dubois County	6,497	54.30
New Haven (city) Allen County	4,658	37.65
Auburn (city) De Kalb County	4,246	35.18
Valparaiso (city) Porter County	9,042	32.88
La Porte (city) La Porte County	6,417	29.71
Fishers (town) Hamilton County	11,383	29.23
Huntington (city) Huntington County	5,017	28.52
Granger (cdp) Saint Joseph County	7,927	28.09
Carmel (city) Hamilton County	10,610	28.07
Beech Grove (city) Marion County	3,961	27.89

Notes: (cdp) census designated place; Refer to the User's Guide in the front of the book for more detailed information.

German Russian

Top 10 Places Sorted by Number
Based on all places, regardless of population

Place	Number	%
Indianapolis (cons. city) Marion County	26	<0.01
Charlestown (city) Clark County	20	0.33
Muncie (city) Delaware County	10	0.01
Crown Point (city) Lake County	9	0.05
Granger (cdp) Saint Joseph County	7	0.02
West Lafayette (city) Tippecanoe County	6	0.02
Fort Wayne (city) Allen County	4	<0.01
Schneider (town) Lake County	3	0.86

Top 10 Places Sorted by Percent
Based on all places, regardless of population

Place	Number	%
Schneider (town) Lake County	3	0.86
Charlestown (city) Clark County	20	0.33
Crown Point (city) Lake County	9	0.05
Granger (cdp) Saint Joseph County	7	0.02
West Lafayette (city) Tippecanoe County	6	0.02
Muncie (city) Delaware County	10	0.01
Indianapolis (cons. city) Marion County	26	<0.01
Fort Wayne (city) Allen County	4	<0.01

Top 10 Places Sorted by Percent
Based on places with populations of 10,000 or more

Place	Number	%
Crown Point (city) Lake County	9	0.05
Granger (cdp) Saint Joseph County	7	0.02
West Lafayette (city) Tippecanoe County	6	0.02
Muncie (city) Delaware County	10	0.01
Indianapolis (cons. city) Marion County	26	<0.01
Fort Wayne (city) Allen County	4	<0.01

Greek

Top 10 Places Sorted by Number
Based on all places, regardless of population

Place	Number	%
Indianapolis (cons. city) Marion County	2,074	0.27
Merrillville (town) Lake County	729	2.37
Fort Wayne (city) Allen County	678	0.33
Hammond (city) Lake County	577	0.69
Crown Point (city) Lake County	509	2.60
Bloomington (city) Monroe County	447	0.65
Schererville (town) Lake County	418	1.68
Portage (city) Porter County	379	1.13
South Bend (city) Saint Joseph County	347	0.32
Hobart (city) Lake County	331	1.30

Top 10 Places Sorted by Percent
Based on all places, regardless of population

Place	Number	%
Spring Hill (town) Marion County	16	12.80
Lake Dalecarlia (cdp) Lake County	67	5.32
Winfield (town) Lake County	79	3.48
Ogden Dunes (town) Porter County	44	3.35
Pottawattamie Park (town) La Porte County	10	3.32
Crown Point (city) Lake County	509	2.60
Schneider (town) Lake County	9	2.58
Merrillville (town) Lake County	729	2.37
Dyer (town) Lake County	326	2.35
Chesterton (town) Porter County	213	2.04

Top 10 Places Sorted by Percent
Based on places with populations of 10,000 or more

Place	Number	%
Crown Point (city) Lake County	509	2.60
Merrillville (town) Lake County	729	2.37
Dyer (town) Lake County	326	2.35
Chesterton (town) Porter County	213	2.04
Schererville (town) Lake County	418	1.68
Munster (town) Lake County	318	1.48
Lake Station (city) Lake County	189	1.35
Hobart (city) Lake County	331	1.30
Highland (town) Lake County	273	1.16
Portage (city) Porter County	379	1.13

Guyanese

Top 10 Places Sorted by Number
Based on all places, regardless of population

Place	Number	%
Merrillville (town) Lake County	25	0.08
Greencastle (city) Putnam County	18	0.19
Indianapolis (cons. city) Marion County	17	<0.01
West Lafayette (city) Tippecanoe County	11	0.04
Hammond (city) Lake County	11	0.01
Evansville (city) Vanderburgh County	2	<0.01

Top 10 Places Sorted by Percent
Based on all places, regardless of population

Place	Number	%
Greencastle (city) Putnam County	18	0.19
Merrillville (town) Lake County	25	0.08
West Lafayette (city) Tippecanoe County	11	0.04
Hammond (city) Lake County	11	0.01
Indianapolis (cons. city) Marion County	17	<0.01
Evansville (city) Vanderburgh County	2	<0.01

Top 10 Places Sorted by Percent
Based on places with populations of 10,000 or more

Place	Number	%
Merrillville (town) Lake County	25	0.08
West Lafayette (city) Tippecanoe County	11	0.04
Hammond (city) Lake County	11	0.01
Indianapolis (cons. city) Marion County	17	<0.01
Evansville (city) Vanderburgh County	2	<0.01

Hawaii Native/Pacific Islander

Top 10 Places Sorted by Number
Based on all places, regardless of population

Place	Number	%
Indianapolis (cons. city) Marion County	818	0.10
Fort Wayne (city) Allen County	195	0.09
South Bend (city) Saint Joseph County	171	0.16
Muncie (city) Delaware County	117	0.17
Bloomington (city) Monroe County	113	0.16
Evansville (city) Vanderburgh County	111	0.09
Hammond (city) Lake County	104	0.13
Elkhart (city) Elkhart County	71	0.14
Lawrence (city) Marion County	58	0.15
Terre Haute (city) Vigo County	55	0.09

Top 10 Places Sorted by Percent
Based on all places, regardless of population

Place	Number	%
Cromwell (town) Noble County	12	2.65
Newtown (town) Fountain County	1	0.62
Sidney (town) Kosciusko County	1	0.60
Springport (town) Henry County	1	0.57
Reynolds (town) White County	3	0.55
La Crosse (town) La Porte County	3	0.53
Hamlet (town) Starke County	4	0.49
Milford (town) Kosciusko County	7	0.45
Modoc (town) Randolph County	1	0.44
Monroeville (town) Allen County	5	0.40

Top 10 Places Sorted by Percent
Based on places with populations of 10,000 or more

Place	Number	%
West Lafayette (city) Tippecanoe County	51	0.18
Muncie (city) Delaware County	117	0.17
South Bend (city) Saint Joseph County	171	0.16
Bloomington (city) Monroe County	113	0.16
Lawrence (city) Marion County	58	0.15
Logansport (city) Cass County	29	0.15
Elkhart (city) Elkhart County	71	0.14
Portage (city) Porter County	48	0.14
Crown Point (city) Lake County	27	0.14
Vincennes (city) Knox County	27	0.14

Hawaii Native/Pacific Islander: Melanesian

Top 10 Places Sorted by Number
Based on all places, regardless of population

Place	Number	%
Indianapolis (cons. city) Marion County	3	<0.01
Muncie (city) Delaware County	3	<0.01
Kentland (town) Newton County	2	0.11
Crawfordsville (city) Montgomery County	1	0.01
Bloomington (city) Monroe County	1	<0.01
Fort Wayne (city) Allen County	1	<0.01
Gary (city) Lake County	1	<0.01
Jeffersonville (city) Clark County	1	<0.01
Terre Haute (city) Vigo County	1	<0.01
Valparaiso (city) Porter County	1	<0.01

Top 10 Places Sorted by Percent
Based on all places, regardless of population

Place	Number	%
Kentland (town) Newton County	2	0.11
Crawfordsville (city) Montgomery County	1	0.01
Indianapolis (cons. city) Marion County	3	<0.01
Muncie (city) Delaware County	3	<0.01
Bloomington (city) Monroe County	1	<0.01
Fort Wayne (city) Allen County	1	<0.01
Gary (city) Lake County	1	<0.01
Jeffersonville (city) Clark County	1	<0.01
Terre Haute (city) Vigo County	1	<0.01
Valparaiso (city) Porter County	1	<0.01

Top 10 Places Sorted by Percent
Based on places with populations of 10,000 or more

Place	Number	%
Crawfordsville (city) Montgomery County	1	0.01
Indianapolis (cons. city) Marion County	3	<0.01
Muncie (city) Delaware County	3	<0.01
Bloomington (city) Monroe County	1	<0.01
Fort Wayne (city) Allen County	1	<0.01
Gary (city) Lake County	1	<0.01
Jeffersonville (city) Clark County	1	<0.01
Terre Haute (city) Vigo County	1	<0.01
Valparaiso (city) Porter County	1	<0.01

Hawaii Native/Pacific Islander: Fijian

Top 10 Places Sorted by Number
Based on all places, regardless of population

Place	Number	%
Indianapolis (cons. city) Marion County	3	<0.01
Kentland (town) Newton County	2	0.11
Jeffersonville (city) Clark County	1	<0.01
Terre Haute (city) Vigo County	1	<0.01
Valparaiso (city) Porter County	1	<0.01

Top 10 Places Sorted by Percent
Based on all places, regardless of population

Place	Number	%
Kentland (town) Newton County	2	0.11
Indianapolis (cons. city) Marion County	3	<0.01
Jeffersonville (city) Clark County	1	<0.01
Terre Haute (city) Vigo County	1	<0.01
Valparaiso (city) Porter County	1	<0.01

Top 10 Places Sorted by Percent
Based on places with populations of 10,000 or more

Place	Number	%
Indianapolis (cons. city) Marion County	3	<0.01
Jeffersonville (city) Clark County	1	<0.01
Terre Haute (city) Vigo County	1	<0.01
Valparaiso (city) Porter County	1	<0.01

Hawaii Native/Pacific Islander: Other Melanesian

Top 10 Places Sorted by Number
Based on all places, regardless of population

Place	Number	%
Muncie (city) Delaware County	3	<0.01
Crawfordsville (city) Montgomery County	1	0.01
Bloomington (city) Monroe County	1	<0.01
Fort Wayne (city) Allen County	1	<0.01
Gary (city) Lake County	1	<0.01

Top 10 Places Sorted by Percent
Based on all places, regardless of population

Place	Number	%
Crawfordsville (city) Montgomery County	1	0.01
Muncie (city) Delaware County	3	<0.01
Bloomington (city) Monroe County	1	<0.01
Fort Wayne (city) Allen County	1	<0.01
Gary (city) Lake County	1	<0.01

Top 10 Places Sorted by Percent
Based on places with populations of 10,000 or more

Place	Number	%
Crawfordsville (city) Montgomery County	1	0.01
Muncie (city) Delaware County	3	<0.01
Bloomington (city) Monroe County	1	<0.01
Fort Wayne (city) Allen County	1	<0.01
Gary (city) Lake County	1	<0.01

Hawaii Native/Pacific Islander: Micronesian

Top 10 Places Sorted by Number
Based on all places, regardless of population

Place	Number	%
Indianapolis (cons. city) Marion County	136	0.02
Fort Wayne (city) Allen County	57	0.03
South Bend (city) Saint Joseph County	30	0.03
Elkhart (city) Elkhart County	28	0.05
Evansville (city) Vanderburgh County	23	0.02
Logansport (city) Cass County	19	0.10
Gary (city) Lake County	15	0.01
Bloomington (city) Monroe County	13	0.02
Hammond (city) Lake County	11	0.01
Westfield (town) Hamilton County	10	0.11

Top 10 Places Sorted by Percent
Based on all places, regardless of population

Place	Number	%
Newtown (town) Fountain County	1	0.62
Sidney (town) Kosciusko County	1	0.60
Hamlet (town) Starke County	4	0.49

Milford (town) Kosciusko County	7	0.45
Bloomingdale (town) Parke County	1	0.31
Hartsville (town) Bartholomew County	1	0.27
Bourbon (town) Marshall County	3	0.18
Westfield (town) Hamilton County	10	0.11
Milan (town) Ripley County	2	0.11
Logansport (city) Cass County	19	0.10

Top 10 Places Sorted by Percent
Based on places with populations of 10,000 or more

Place	Number	%
Logansport (city) Cass County	19	0.10
Elkhart (city) Elkhart County	28	0.05
Washington (city) Daviess County	6	0.05
Crown Point (city) Lake County	8	0.04
Vincennes (city) Knox County	8	0.04
Franklin (city) Johnson County	7	0.04
Fort Wayne (city) Allen County	57	0.03
South Bend (city) Saint Joseph County	30	0.03
Richmond (city) Wayne County	10	0.03
Portage (city) Porter County	9	0.03

Hawaii Native/Pacific Islander: Guamanian or Chamorro

Top 10 Places Sorted by Number
Based on all places, regardless of population

Place	Number	%
Indianapolis (cons. city) Marion County	125	0.02
Fort Wayne (city) Allen County	49	0.02
South Bend (city) Saint Joseph County	29	0.03
Logansport (city) Cass County	19	0.10
Elkhart (city) Elkhart County	16	0.03
Gary (city) Lake County	15	0.01
Evansville (city) Vanderburgh County	14	0.01
Bloomington (city) Monroe County	13	0.02
Hammond (city) Lake County	11	0.01
Westfield (town) Hamilton County	10	0.11

Top 10 Places Sorted by Percent
Based on all places, regardless of population

Place	Number	%
Newtown (town) Fountain County	1	0.62
Sidney (town) Kosciusko County	1	0.60
Hamlet (town) Starke County	4	0.49
Milford (town) Kosciusko County	7	0.45
Bloomingdale (town) Parke County	1	0.31
Hartsville (town) Bartholomew County	1	0.27
Bourbon (town) Marshall County	3	0.18
Westfield (town) Hamilton County	10	0.11
Milan (town) Ripley County	2	0.11
Logansport (city) Cass County	19	0.10

Top 10 Places Sorted by Percent
Based on places with populations of 10,000 or more

Place	Number	%
Logansport (city) Cass County	19	0.10
Washington (city) Daviess County	6	0.05
Crown Point (city) Lake County	8	0.04
Vincennes (city) Knox County	8	0.04
Franklin (city) Johnson County	7	0.04
South Bend (city) Saint Joseph County	29	0.03
Elkhart (city) Elkhart County	16	0.03
Portage (city) Porter County	9	0.03
Jeffersonville (city) Clark County	8	0.03
Lake Station (city) Lake County	4	0.03

Hawaii Native/Pacific Islander: Other Micronesian

Top 10 Places Sorted by Number
Based on all places, regardless of population

Place	Number	%
Elkhart (city) Elkhart County	12	0.02
Indianapolis (cons. city) Marion County	11	<0.01
Evansville (city) Vanderburgh County	9	0.01
Fort Wayne (city) Allen County	8	<0.01
Richmond (city) Wayne County	5	0.01
Goshen (city) Elkhart County	3	0.01
North Manchester (town) Wabash County	2	0.03
West Lafayette (city) Tippecanoe County	2	0.01
Bristol (town) Elkhart County	1	0.07
Wakarusa (town) Elkhart County	1	0.06

Top 10 Places Sorted by Percent
Based on all places, regardless of population

Place	Number	%
Bristol (town) Elkhart County	1	0.07
Wakarusa (town) Elkhart County	1	0.06
North Manchester (town) Wabash County	2	0.03
Fairmount (town) Grant County	1	0.03
Elkhart (city) Elkhart County	12	0.02
Evansville (city) Vanderburgh County	9	0.01
Richmond (city) Wayne County	5	0.01
Goshen (city) Elkhart County	3	0.01
West Lafayette (city) Tippecanoe County	2	0.01
Indianapolis (cons. city) Marion County	11	<0.01

Top 10 Places Sorted by Percent
Based on places with populations of 10,000 or more

Place	Number	%
Elkhart (city) Elkhart County	12	0.02
Evansville (city) Vanderburgh County	9	0.01
Richmond (city) Wayne County	5	0.01
Goshen (city) Elkhart County	3	0.01
West Lafayette (city) Tippecanoe County	2	0.01
Indianapolis (cons. city) Marion County	11	<0.01
Fort Wayne (city) Allen County	8	<0.01
Granger (cdp) Saint Joseph County	1	<0.01
Mishawaka (city) Saint Joseph County	1	<0.01
Muncie (city) Delaware County	1	<0.01

Hawaii Native/Pacific Islander: Polynesian

Top 10 Places Sorted by Number
Based on all places, regardless of population

Place	Number	%
Indianapolis (cons. city) Marion County	323	0.04
South Bend (city) Saint Joseph County	88	0.08
Fort Wayne (city) Allen County	81	0.04
Muncie (city) Delaware County	72	0.11
Evansville (city) Vanderburgh County	57	0.05
Bloomington (city) Monroe County	53	0.08
Hammond (city) Lake County	51	0.06
Lawrence (city) Marion County	35	0.09
Lafayette (city) Tippecanoe County	33	0.06
Richmond (city) Wayne County	29	0.07

Top 10 Places Sorted by Percent
Based on all places, regardless of population

Place	Number	%
Cromwell (town) Noble County	4	0.88
Reynolds (town) White County	3	0.55
La Crosse (town) La Porte County	3	0.53
Monroeville (town) Allen County	5	0.40
Wheatfield (town) Jasper County	3	0.39
Kewanna (town) Fulton County	2	0.33
Schneider (town) Lake County	1	0.32
Switz City (town) Greene County	1	0.32

Notes: (cdp) census designated place; Refer to the User's Guide in the front of the book for more detailed information.

Place	Number	%
Rome City (town) Noble County	5	0.31
Ashley (town) De Kalb County	3	0.30

Top 10 Places Sorted by Percent
Based on places with populations of 10,000 or more

Place	Number	%
Muncie (city) Delaware County	72	0.11
Lawrence (city) Marion County	35	0.09
Washington (city) Daviess County	10	0.09
South Bend (city) Saint Joseph County	88	0.08
Bloomington (city) Monroe County	53	0.08
East Chicago (city) Lake County	25	0.08
Noblesville (city) Hamilton County	24	0.08
Richmond (city) Wayne County	29	0.07
West Lafayette (city) Tippecanoe County	21	0.07
Vincennes (city) Knox County	14	0.07

Hawaii Native/Pacific Islander: Native Hawaiian

Top 10 Places Sorted by Number
Based on all places, regardless of population

Place	Number	%
Indianapolis (cons. city) Marion County	219	0.03
Fort Wayne (city) Allen County	52	0.03
South Bend (city) Saint Joseph County	45	0.04
Muncie (city) Delaware County	42	0.06
Evansville (city) Vanderburgh County	37	0.03
Bloomington (city) Monroe County	25	0.04
Lawrence (city) Marion County	23	0.06
Richmond (city) Wayne County	21	0.05
Lafayette (city) Tippecanoe County	20	0.04
Mishawaka (city) Saint Joseph County	20	0.04

Top 10 Places Sorted by Percent
Based on all places, regardless of population

Place	Number	%
Reynolds (town) White County	3	0.55
Monroeville (town) Allen County	5	0.40
Wheatfield (town) Jasper County	3	0.39
Kewanna (town) Fulton County	2	0.33
Schneider (town) Lake County	1	0.32
Switz City (town) Greene County	1	0.32
Rome City (town) Noble County	5	0.31
Ashley (town) De Kalb County	3	0.30
North Liberty (town) Saint Joseph County	4	0.29
Pierceton (town) Kosciusko County	2	0.29

Top 10 Places Sorted by Percent
Based on places with populations of 10,000 or more

Place	Number	%
Washington (city) Daviess County	9	0.08
Muncie (city) Delaware County	42	0.06
Lawrence (city) Marion County	23	0.06
West Lafayette (city) Tippecanoe County	16	0.06
Brownsburg (town) Hendricks County	9	0.06
Speedway (town) Marion County	8	0.06
Richmond (city) Wayne County	21	0.05
Noblesville (city) Hamilton County	15	0.05
Jeffersonville (city) Clark County	14	0.05
Clarksville (town) Clark County	11	0.05

Hawaii Native/Pacific Islander: Samoan

Top 10 Places Sorted by Number
Based on all places, regardless of population

Place	Number	%
Indianapolis (cons. city) Marion County	96	0.01
South Bend (city) Saint Joseph County	34	0.03
Hammond (city) Lake County	32	0.04
Muncie (city) Delaware County	28	0.04
Fort Wayne (city) Allen County	28	0.01

Place	Number	%
East Chicago (city) Lake County	18	0.06
Bloomington (city) Monroe County	16	0.02
Evansville (city) Vanderburgh County	15	0.01
Lawrence (city) Marion County	12	0.03
Lafayette (city) Tippecanoe County	12	0.02

Top 10 Places Sorted by Percent
Based on all places, regardless of population

Place	Number	%
Cromwell (town) Noble County	3	0.66
La Crosse (town) La Porte County	3	0.53
Dana (town) Vermillion County	2	0.30
Waveland (town) Montgomery County	1	0.24
Ladoga (town) Montgomery County	2	0.19
Cloverdale (town) Putnam County	4	0.18
Elberfeld (town) Warrick County	1	0.16
Dillsboro (town) Dearborn County	2	0.14
Collegeville (cdp) Jasper County	1	0.12
Marengo (town) Crawford County	1	0.12

Top 10 Places Sorted by Percent
Based on places with populations of 10,000 or more

Place	Number	%
East Chicago (city) Lake County	18	0.06
Shelbyville (city) Shelby County	11	0.06
Hammond (city) Lake County	32	0.04
Muncie (city) Delaware County	28	0.04
Schererville (town) Lake County	9	0.04
Vincennes (city) Knox County	8	0.04
Frankfort (city) Clinton County	7	0.04
Crawfordsville (city) Montgomery County	6	0.04
South Bend (city) Saint Joseph County	34	0.03
Lawrence (city) Marion County	12	0.03

Hawaii Native/Pacific Islander: Tongan

Top 10 Places Sorted by Number
Based on all places, regardless of population

Place	Number	%
Elwood (city) Madison County	8	0.08
South Bend (city) Saint Joseph County	7	0.01
Terre Haute (city) Vigo County	7	0.01
Indianapolis (cons. city) Marion County	5	<0.01
Elkhart (city) Elkhart County	4	0.01
Logansport (city) Cass County	3	0.02
Fishers (town) Hamilton County	3	0.01
Kokomo (city) Howard County	3	0.01
West Lafayette (city) Tippecanoe County	1	<0.01

Top 10 Places Sorted by Percent
Based on all places, regardless of population

Place	Number	%
Elwood (city) Madison County	8	0.08
Logansport (city) Cass County	3	0.02
South Bend (city) Saint Joseph County	7	0.01
Terre Haute (city) Vigo County	7	0.01
Elkhart (city) Elkhart County	4	0.01
Fishers (town) Hamilton County	3	0.01
Kokomo (city) Howard County	3	0.01
Indianapolis (cons. city) Marion County	5	<0.01
West Lafayette (city) Tippecanoe County	1	<0.01

Top 10 Places Sorted by Percent
Based on places with populations of 10,000 or more

Place	Number	%
Logansport (city) Cass County	3	0.02
South Bend (city) Saint Joseph County	7	0.01
Terre Haute (city) Vigo County	7	0.01
Elkhart (city) Elkhart County	4	0.01
Fishers (town) Hamilton County	3	0.01
Kokomo (city) Howard County	3	0.01
Indianapolis (cons. city) Marion County	5	<0.01

Place	Number	%
West Lafayette (city) Tippecanoe County	1	<0.01

Hawaii Native/Pacific Islander: Other Polynesian

Top 10 Places Sorted by Number
Based on all places, regardless of population

Place	Number	%
Bloomington (city) Monroe County	12	0.02
Evansville (city) Vanderburgh County	5	<0.01
Indianapolis (cons. city) Marion County	3	<0.01
Charlestown (city) Clark County	2	0.03
Hobart (city) Lake County	2	0.01
Hammond (city) Lake County	2	<0.01
Kokomo (city) Howard County	2	<0.01
Muncie (city) Delaware County	2	<0.01
South Bend (city) Saint Joseph County	2	<0.01
Huntingburg (city) Dubois County	1	0.02

Top 10 Places Sorted by Percent
Based on all places, regardless of population

Place	Number	%
Charlestown (city) Clark County	2	0.03
Bloomington (city) Monroe County	12	0.02
Huntingburg (city) Dubois County	1	0.02
Hobart (city) Lake County	2	0.01
Crown Point (city) Lake County	1	0.01
Dyer (town) Lake County	1	0.01
Logansport (city) Cass County	1	0.01
New Castle (city) Henry County	1	0.01
Warsaw (city) Kosciusko County	1	0.01
Evansville (city) Vanderburgh County	5	<0.01

Top 10 Places Sorted by Percent
Based on places with populations of 10,000 or more

Place	Number	%
Bloomington (city) Monroe County	12	0.02
Hobart (city) Lake County	2	0.01
Crown Point (city) Lake County	1	0.01
Dyer (town) Lake County	1	0.01
Logansport (city) Cass County	1	0.01
New Castle (city) Henry County	1	0.01
Warsaw (city) Kosciusko County	1	0.01
Evansville (city) Vanderburgh County	5	<0.01
Indianapolis (cons. city) Marion County	3	<0.01
Hammond (city) Lake County	2	<0.01

Hawaii Native/Pacific Islander: Other Pacific Islander, specified

Top 10 Places Sorted by Number
Based on all places, regardless of population

Place	Number	%
Indianapolis (cons. city) Marion County	53	0.01
Anderson (city) Madison County	11	0.02
Evansville (city) Vanderburgh County	9	0.01
Muncie (city) Delaware County	5	0.01
New Albany (city) Floyd County	5	0.01
Fort Wayne (city) Allen County	5	<0.01
West Terre Haute (town) Vigo County	4	0.17
Lawrenceburg (city) Dearborn County	3	0.06
Batesville (city) Ripley County	3	0.05
Valparaiso (city) Porter County	3	0.01

Top 10 Places Sorted by Percent
Based on all places, regardless of population

Place	Number	%
West Harrison (town) Dearborn County	1	0.35
West Terre Haute (town) Vigo County	4	0.17
Lawrenceburg (city) Dearborn County	3	0.06
Batesville (city) Ripley County	3	0.05
Loogootee (city) Martin County	1	0.04

Notes: (cdp) census designated place; Refer to the User's Guide in the front of the book for more detailed information.

Place	Number	%
Tell City (city) Perry County	2	0.03
Anderson (city) Madison County	11	0.02
Porter (town) Porter County	1	0.02
Rensselaer (city) Jasper County	1	0.02
Indianapolis (cons. city) Marion County	53	0.01

Top 10 Places Sorted by Percent
Based on places with populations of 10,000 or more

Place	Number	%
Anderson (city) Madison County	11	0.02
Indianapolis (cons. city) Marion County	53	0.01
Evansville (city) Vanderburgh County	9	0.01
Muncie (city) Delaware County	5	0.01
New Albany (city) Floyd County	5	0.01
Valparaiso (city) Porter County	3	0.01
Highland (town) Lake County	2	0.01
Richmond (city) Wayne County	2	0.01
Shelbyville (city) Shelby County	2	0.01
Crown Point (city) Lake County	1	0.01

Hawaii Native/Pacific Islander: Other Pacific Islander, not specified

Top 10 Places Sorted by Number
Based on all places, regardless of population

Place	Number	%
Indianapolis (cons. city) Marion County	303	0.04
South Bend (city) Saint Joseph County	53	0.05
Fort Wayne (city) Allen County	51	0.02
Bloomington (city) Monroe County	45	0.06
Hammond (city) Lake County	42	0.05
Muncie (city) Delaware County	28	0.04
West Lafayette (city) Tippecanoe County	23	0.08
Portage (city) Porter County	22	0.07
Evansville (city) Vanderburgh County	22	0.02
Elkhart (city) Elkhart County	21	0.04

Top 10 Places Sorted by Percent
Based on all places, regardless of population

Place	Number	%
Cromwell (town) Noble County	8	1.77
Springport (town) Henry County	1	0.57
Modoc (town) Randolph County	1	0.44
Lynn (town) Randolph County	4	0.35
Sharpsville (town) Tipton County	2	0.32
Markleville (town) Madison County	1	0.26
Albany (town) Delaware County	5	0.21
Kingsford Heights (town) La Porte County	3	0.21
Bunker Hill (town) Miami County	2	0.20
Lakeville (town) Saint Joseph County	1	0.18

Top 10 Places Sorted by Percent
Based on places with populations of 10,000 or more

Place	Number	%
West Lafayette (city) Tippecanoe County	23	0.08
Portage (city) Porter County	22	0.07
Bloomington (city) Monroe County	45	0.06
South Bend (city) Saint Joseph County	53	0.05
Hammond (city) Lake County	42	0.05
New Haven (city) Allen County	6	0.05
Indianapolis (cons. city) Marion County	303	0.04
Muncie (city) Delaware County	28	0.04
Elkhart (city) Elkhart County	21	0.04
Carmel (city) Hamilton County	15	0.04

Hispanic or Latino

Top 10 Places Sorted by Number
Based on all places, regardless of population

Place	Number	%
Indianapolis (cons. city) Marion County	30,636	3.92
Hammond (city) Lake County	17,473	21.04

Place	Number	%
East Chicago (city) Lake County	16,728	51.61
Fort Wayne (city) Allen County	11,884	5.78
South Bend (city) Saint Joseph County	9,110	8.45
Elkhart (city) Elkhart County	7,678	14.80
Goshen (city) Elkhart County	5,679	19.33
Lafayette (city) Tippecanoe County	5,136	9.11
Gary (city) Lake County	5,065	4.93
Portage (city) Porter County	3,330	9.94

Top 10 Places Sorted by Percent
Based on all places, regardless of population

Place	Number	%
East Chicago (city) Lake County	16,728	51.61
Ligonier (city) Noble County	1,451	33.30
Whiting (city) Lake County	1,313	25.56
Hammond (city) Lake County	17,473	21.04
Lake Station (city) Lake County	2,875	20.61
Goshen (city) Elkhart County	5,679	19.33
Ambia (town) Benton County	35	17.77
Monon (town) White County	299	17.25
New Chicago (town) Lake County	345	16.72
Plymouth (city) Marshall County	1,475	14.99

Top 10 Places Sorted by Percent
Based on places with populations of 10,000 or more

Place	Number	%
East Chicago (city) Lake County	16,728	51.61
Hammond (city) Lake County	17,473	21.04
Lake Station (city) Lake County	2,875	20.61
Goshen (city) Elkhart County	5,679	19.33
Elkhart (city) Elkhart County	7,678	14.80
Frankfort (city) Clinton County	2,255	13.53
Logansport (city) Cass County	2,476	12.58
Portage (city) Porter County	3,330	9.94
Merrillville (town) Lake County	2,950	9.65
Warsaw (city) Kosciusko County	1,144	9.21

Hispanic: Central American

Top 10 Places Sorted by Number
Based on all places, regardless of population

Place	Number	%
Indianapolis (cons. city) Marion County	1,770	0.23
Fort Wayne (city) Allen County	471	0.23
Elkhart (city) Elkhart County	413	0.80
Hammond (city) Lake County	208	0.25
Logansport (city) Cass County	175	0.89
South Bend (city) Saint Joseph County	165	0.15
Huntingburg (city) Dubois County	146	2.61
Lawrence (city) Marion County	113	0.29
Goshen (city) Elkhart County	101	0.34
Lafayette (city) Tippecanoe County	101	0.18

Top 10 Places Sorted by Percent
Based on all places, regardless of population

Place	Number	%
Monon (town) White County	61	3.52
Huntingburg (city) Dubois County	146	2.61
Mentone (town) Kosciusko County	11	1.22
Brook (town) Newton County	12	1.13
Bourbon (town) Marshall County	17	1.01
Logansport (city) Cass County	175	0.89
Elkhart (city) Elkhart County	413	0.80
Gentryville (town) Spencer County	2	0.76
Bremen (town) Marshall County	33	0.74
Plymouth (city) Marshall County	70	0.71

Top 10 Places Sorted by Percent
Based on places with populations of 10,000 or more

Place	Number	%
Logansport (city) Cass County	175	0.89
Elkhart (city) Elkhart County	413	0.80

Place	Number	%
Washington (city) Daviess County	74	0.65
Jasper (city) Dubois County	65	0.54
Goshen (city) Elkhart County	101	0.34
Lawrence (city) Marion County	113	0.29
Frankfort (city) Clinton County	49	0.29
Speedway (town) Marion County	37	0.29
West Lafayette (city) Tippecanoe County	80	0.28
Hammond (city) Lake County	208	0.25

Hispanic: Costa Rican

Top 10 Places Sorted by Number
Based on all places, regardless of population

Place	Number	%
Indianapolis (cons. city) Marion County	56	0.01
Bloomington (city) Monroe County	17	0.02
South Bend (city) Saint Joseph County	12	0.01
West Lafayette (city) Tippecanoe County	10	0.03
Goshen (city) Elkhart County	9	0.03
Mishawaka (city) Saint Joseph County	8	0.02
Hammond (city) Lake County	8	0.01
Fort Wayne (city) Allen County	8	<0.01
Franklin (city) Johnson County	7	0.04
Carmel (city) Hamilton County	5	0.01

Top 10 Places Sorted by Percent
Based on all places, regardless of population

Place	Number	%
Koontz Lake (cdp) Starke County	2	0.13
Shirley (town) Hancock County	1	0.12
Melody Hill (cdp) Vanderburgh County	3	0.10
Upland (town) Grant County	3	0.08
Bremen (town) Marshall County	3	0.07
Franklin (city) Johnson County	7	0.04
Cloverdale (town) Putnam County	1	0.04
West Lafayette (city) Tippecanoe County	10	0.03
Goshen (city) Elkhart County	9	0.03
Avon (town) Hendricks County	2	0.03

Top 10 Places Sorted by Percent
Based on places with populations of 10,000 or more

Place	Number	%
Franklin (city) Johnson County	7	0.04
West Lafayette (city) Tippecanoe County	10	0.03
Goshen (city) Elkhart County	9	0.03
Bloomington (city) Monroe County	17	0.02
Mishawaka (city) Saint Joseph County	8	0.02
Highland (town) Lake County	4	0.02
Indianapolis (cons. city) Marion County	56	0.01
South Bend (city) Saint Joseph County	12	0.01
Hammond (city) Lake County	8	0.01
Carmel (city) Hamilton County	5	0.01

Hispanic: Guatemalan

Top 10 Places Sorted by Number
Based on all places, regardless of population

Place	Number	%
Fort Wayne (city) Allen County	255	0.12
Indianapolis (cons. city) Marion County	250	0.03
Logansport (city) Cass County	84	0.43
Hammond (city) Lake County	83	0.10
Elkhart (city) Elkhart County	66	0.13
Lawrence (city) Marion County	41	0.11
Goshen (city) Elkhart County	34	0.12
South Bend (city) Saint Joseph County	26	0.02
East Chicago (city) Lake County	21	0.06
Washington (city) Daviess County	20	0.18

Notes: (cdp) census designated place; Refer to the User's Guide in the front of the book for more detailed information.

Top 10 Places Sorted by Percent
Based on all places, regardless of population

Place	Number	%
North Judson (town) Starke County	9	0.54
Marengo (town) Crawford County	4	0.48
Logansport (city) Cass County	84	0.43
Taylorsville (cdp) Bartholomew County	4	0.43
Gentryville (town) Spencer County	1	0.38
Cicero (town) Hamilton County	14	0.33
Brook (town) Newton County	3	0.28
Bourbon (town) Marshall County	4	0.24
Washington (city) Daviess County	20	0.18
Westfield (town) Hamilton County	16	0.17

Top 10 Places Sorted by Percent
Based on places with populations of 10,000 or more

Place	Number	%
Logansport (city) Cass County	84	0.43
Washington (city) Daviess County	20	0.18
Elkhart (city) Elkhart County	66	0.13
Fort Wayne (city) Allen County	255	0.12
Goshen (city) Elkhart County	34	0.12
Lawrence (city) Marion County	41	0.11
Frankfort (city) Clinton County	19	0.11
Hammond (city) Lake County	83	0.10
Crawfordsville (city) Montgomery County	13	0.09
Warsaw (city) Kosciusko County	11	0.09

Hispanic: Honduran

Top 10 Places Sorted by Number
Based on all places, regardless of population

Place	Number	%
Indianapolis (cons. city) Marion County	495	0.06
Elkhart (city) Elkhart County	167	0.32
Plymouth (city) Marshall County	68	0.69
Hammond (city) Lake County	57	0.07
East Chicago (city) Lake County	29	0.09
Lawrence (city) Marion County	28	0.07
Fort Wayne (city) Allen County	28	0.01
Bremen (town) Marshall County	23	0.51
Seymour (city) Jackson County	22	0.12
Speedway (town) Marion County	21	0.16

Top 10 Places Sorted by Percent
Based on all places, regardless of population

Place	Number	%
Mentone (town) Kosciusko County	11	1.22
Plymouth (city) Marshall County	68	0.69
Bourbon (town) Marshall County	10	0.59
Bremen (town) Marshall County	23	0.51
Walkerton (town) Saint Joseph County	10	0.44
Straughn (town) Henry County	1	0.38
Elkhart (city) Elkhart County	167	0.32
Dale (town) Spencer County	5	0.32
New Ross (town) Montgomery County	1	0.30
Meridian Hills (town) Marion County	4	0.23

Top 10 Places Sorted by Percent
Based on places with populations of 10,000 or more

Place	Number	%
Elkhart (city) Elkhart County	167	0.32
Speedway (town) Marion County	21	0.16
Seymour (city) Jackson County	22	0.12
East Chicago (city) Lake County	29	0.09
Jasper (city) Dubois County	11	0.09
Hammond (city) Lake County	57	0.07
Lawrence (city) Marion County	28	0.07
Washington (city) Daviess County	8	0.07
Indianapolis (cons. city) Marion County	495	0.06
Goshen (city) Elkhart County	17	0.06

Hispanic: Nicaraguan

Top 10 Places Sorted by Number
Based on all places, regardless of population

Place	Number	%
Indianapolis (cons. city) Marion County	247	0.03
Lawrence (city) Marion County	15	0.04
South Bend (city) Saint Joseph County	15	0.01
Michigan City (city) La Porte County	12	0.04
Bloomington (city) Monroe County	11	0.02
Elkhart (city) Elkhart County	10	0.02
Evansville (city) Vanderburgh County	10	0.01
Hobart (city) Lake County	9	0.04
West Lafayette (city) Tippecanoe County	9	0.03
Griffith (town) Lake County	8	0.05

Top 10 Places Sorted by Percent
Based on all places, regardless of population

Place	Number	%
Sheridan (town) Hamilton County	4	0.16
Gulivoire Park (cdp) Saint Joseph County	3	0.10
Bourbon (town) Marshall County	1	0.06
Griffith (town) Lake County	8	0.05
Lawrence (city) Marion County	15	0.04
Michigan City (city) La Porte County	12	0.04
Hobart (city) Lake County	9	0.04
Lake Station (city) Lake County	6	0.04
Indianapolis (cons. city) Marion County	247	0.03
West Lafayette (city) Tippecanoe County	9	0.03

Top 10 Places Sorted by Percent
Based on places with populations of 10,000 or more

Place	Number	%
Griffith (town) Lake County	8	0.05
Lawrence (city) Marion County	15	0.04
Michigan City (city) La Porte County	12	0.04
Hobart (city) Lake County	9	0.04
Lake Station (city) Lake County	6	0.04
Indianapolis (cons. city) Marion County	247	0.03
West Lafayette (city) Tippecanoe County	9	0.03
Logansport (city) Cass County	6	0.03
Frankfort (city) Clinton County	5	0.03
Bloomington (city) Monroe County	11	0.02

Hispanic: Panamanian

Top 10 Places Sorted by Number
Based on all places, regardless of population

Place	Number	%
Indianapolis (cons. city) Marion County	138	0.02
Fort Wayne (city) Allen County	30	0.01
South Bend (city) Saint Joseph County	18	0.02
West Lafayette (city) Tippecanoe County	16	0.06
Portage (city) Porter County	13	0.04
Lawrence (city) Marion County	13	0.03
Lafayette (city) Tippecanoe County	13	0.02
Bloomington (city) Monroe County	11	0.02
Fishers (town) Hamilton County	10	0.03
Hammond (city) Lake County	10	0.01

Top 10 Places Sorted by Percent
Based on all places, regardless of population

Place	Number	%
Indian Village (town) Saint Joseph County	1	0.69
Orestes (town) Madison County	1	0.30
Brookston (town) White County	5	0.29
Universal (town) Vermillion County	1	0.24
Wolcott (town) White County	2	0.20
Hillsboro (town) Fountain County	1	0.20
Georgetown (town) Floyd County	4	0.18
Reynolds (town) White County	1	0.18
South Whitley (town) Whitley County	3	0.17

Place	Number	%
Leesburg (town) Kosciusko County	1	0.16

Top 10 Places Sorted by Percent
Based on places with populations of 10,000 or more

Place	Number	%
West Lafayette (city) Tippecanoe County	16	0.06
Portage (city) Porter County	13	0.04
Lawrence (city) Marion County	13	0.03
Fishers (town) Hamilton County	10	0.03
Merrillville (town) Lake County	8	0.03
Indianapolis (cons. city) Marion County	138	0.02
South Bend (city) Saint Joseph County	18	0.02
Lafayette (city) Tippecanoe County	13	0.02
Bloomington (city) Monroe County	11	0.02
Mishawaka (city) Saint Joseph County	9	0.02

Hispanic: Salvadoran

Top 10 Places Sorted by Number
Based on all places, regardless of population

Place	Number	%
Indianapolis (cons. city) Marion County	509	0.07
Elkhart (city) Elkhart County	137	0.26
Huntingburg (city) Dubois County	134	2.39
Fort Wayne (city) Allen County	115	0.06
Logansport (city) Cass County	69	0.35
South Bend (city) Saint Joseph County	66	0.06
Monon (town) White County	61	3.52
Lafayette (city) Tippecanoe County	50	0.09
Jasper (city) Dubois County	46	0.38
Washington (city) Daviess County	38	0.33

Top 10 Places Sorted by Percent
Based on all places, regardless of population

Place	Number	%
Monon (town) White County	61	3.52
Huntingburg (city) Dubois County	134	2.39
Brook (town) Newton County	7	0.66
Morocco (town) Newton County	6	0.53
Spurgeon (town) Pike County	1	0.44
Chalmers (town) White County	2	0.39
Jasper (city) Dubois County	46	0.38
Gentryville (town) Spencer County	1	0.38
Logansport (city) Cass County	69	0.35
Washington (city) Daviess County	38	0.33

Top 10 Places Sorted by Percent
Based on places with populations of 10,000 or more

Place	Number	%
Jasper (city) Dubois County	46	0.38
Logansport (city) Cass County	69	0.35
Washington (city) Daviess County	38	0.33
Elkhart (city) Elkhart County	137	0.26
Goshen (city) Elkhart County	33	0.11
Frankfort (city) Clinton County	18	0.11
Lafayette (city) Tippecanoe County	50	0.09
Indianapolis (cons. city) Marion County	509	0.07
Fort Wayne (city) Allen County	115	0.06
South Bend (city) Saint Joseph County	66	0.06

Hispanic: Other Central American

Top 10 Places Sorted by Number
Based on all places, regardless of population

Place	Number	%
Indianapolis (cons. city) Marion County	75	0.01
Fort Wayne (city) Allen County	29	0.01
Elkhart (city) Elkhart County	25	0.05
South Bend (city) Saint Joseph County	11	0.01
East Chicago (city) Lake County	9	0.03
Washington (city) Daviess County	8	0.07
West Lafayette (city) Tippecanoe County	8	0.03

Notes: (cdp) census designated place; Refer to the User's Guide in the front of the book for more detailed information.

Place	Number	%
Hammond (city) Lake County	8	0.01
Lafayette (city) Tippecanoe County	7	0.01
Goshen (city) Elkhart County	6	0.02

Top 10 Places Sorted by Percent
Based on all places, regardless of population

Place	Number	%
Kentland (town) Newton County	3	0.16
Homecroft (town) Marion County	1	0.13
Battle Ground (town) Tippecanoe County	1	0.08
Washington (city) Daviess County	8	0.07
Geneva (town) Adams County	1	0.07
Grissom AFB (cdp) Miami County	1	0.06
Elkhart (city) Elkhart County	25	0.05
Cicero (town) Hamilton County	2	0.05
Ligonier (city) Noble County	2	0.05
New Chicago (town) Lake County	1	0.05

Top 10 Places Sorted by Percent
Based on places with populations of 10,000 or more

Place	Number	%
Washington (city) Daviess County	8	0.07
Elkhart (city) Elkhart County	25	0.05
East Chicago (city) Lake County	9	0.03
West Lafayette (city) Tippecanoe County	8	0.03
Goshen (city) Elkhart County	6	0.02
Logansport (city) Cass County	4	0.02
Indianapolis (cons. city) Marion County	75	0.01
Fort Wayne (city) Allen County	29	0.01
South Bend (city) Saint Joseph County	11	0.01
Hammond (city) Lake County	8	0.01

Hispanic: Cuban

Top 10 Places Sorted by Number
Based on all places, regardless of population

Place	Number	%
Indianapolis (cons. city) Marion County	457	0.06
Fort Wayne (city) Allen County	136	0.07
Hammond (city) Lake County	120	0.14
Terre Haute (city) Vigo County	108	0.18
Gary (city) Lake County	83	0.08
Bloomington (city) Monroe County	79	0.11
Evansville (city) Vanderburgh County	79	0.06
South Bend (city) Saint Joseph County	76	0.07
Lafayette (city) Tippecanoe County	51	0.09
Logansport (city) Cass County	47	0.24

Top 10 Places Sorted by Percent
Based on all places, regardless of population

Place	Number	%
Crandall (town) Harrison County	1	0.76
Gosport (town) Owen County	3	0.42
Grabill (town) Allen County	4	0.36
Upland (town) Grant County	13	0.34
Milltown (town) Harrison County	3	0.32
Roseland (town) Saint Joseph County	5	0.28
Wilkinson (town) Hancock County	1	0.28
Simonton Lake (cdp) Elkhart County	11	0.27
Star City (cdp) Pulaski County	1	0.27
Logansport (city) Cass County	47	0.24

Top 10 Places Sorted by Percent
Based on places with populations of 10,000 or more

Place	Number	%
Logansport (city) Cass County	47	0.24
Terre Haute (city) Vigo County	108	0.18
Hammond (city) Lake County	120	0.14
Bloomington (city) Monroe County	79	0.11
Noblesville (city) Hamilton County	31	0.11
Lafayette (city) Tippecanoe County	51	0.09
East Chicago (city) Lake County	30	0.09

Place	Number	%
Clarksville (town) Clark County	20	0.09
Gary (city) Lake County	83	0.08
Fishers (town) Hamilton County	32	0.08

Hispanic: Dominican Republic

Top 10 Places Sorted by Number
Based on all places, regardless of population

Place	Number	%
Indianapolis (cons. city) Marion County	262	0.03
Fort Wayne (city) Allen County	23	0.01
South Bend (city) Saint Joseph County	22	0.02
Muncie (city) Delaware County	21	0.03
Bloomington (city) Monroe County	20	0.03
Elkhart (city) Elkhart County	15	0.03
Fishers (town) Hamilton County	14	0.04
Terre Haute (city) Vigo County	12	0.02
Goshen (city) Elkhart County	11	0.04
East Chicago (city) Lake County	10	0.03

Top 10 Places Sorted by Percent
Based on all places, regardless of population

Place	Number	%
Versailles (town) Ripley County	3	0.17
Kewanna (town) Fulton County	1	0.16
Ellettsville (town) Monroe County	4	0.08
Oxford (town) Benton County	1	0.08
Westfield (town) Hamilton County	6	0.06
Whiting (city) Lake County	3	0.06
Long Beach (town) La Porte County	1	0.06
Beech Grove (city) Marion County	8	0.05
Princeton (city) Gibson County	4	0.05
South Haven (cdp) Porter County	3	0.05

Top 10 Places Sorted by Percent
Based on places with populations of 10,000 or more

Place	Number	%
Beech Grove (city) Marion County	8	0.05
Fishers (town) Hamilton County	14	0.04
Goshen (city) Elkhart County	11	0.04
Greensburg (city) Decatur County	4	0.04
Indianapolis (cons. city) Marion County	262	0.03
Muncie (city) Delaware County	21	0.03
Bloomington (city) Monroe County	20	0.03
Elkhart (city) Elkhart County	15	0.03
East Chicago (city) Lake County	10	0.03
Michigan City (city) La Porte County	10	0.03

Hispanic: Mexican

Top 10 Places Sorted by Number
Based on all places, regardless of population

Place	Number	%
Indianapolis (cons. city) Marion County	21,053	2.69
Hammond (city) Lake County	13,583	16.36
East Chicago (city) Lake County	12,245	37.78
Fort Wayne (city) Allen County	8,619	4.19
South Bend (city) Saint Joseph County	7,063	6.55
Elkhart (city) Elkhart County	6,174	11.90
Goshen (city) Elkhart County	4,912	16.72
Lafayette (city) Tippecanoe County	4,249	7.53
Gary (city) Lake County	2,958	2.88
Merrillville (town) Lake County	2,041	6.68

Top 10 Places Sorted by Percent
Based on all places, regardless of population

Place	Number	%
East Chicago (city) Lake County	12,245	37.78
Ligonier (city) Noble County	1,370	31.44
Whiting (city) Lake County	1,155	22.48
Goshen (city) Elkhart County	4,912	16.72
Hammond (city) Lake County	13,583	16.36

Place	Number	%
Akron (town) Fulton County	141	13.10
Lake Station (city) Lake County	1,771	12.70
Plymouth (city) Marshall County	1,204	12.24
Elkhart (city) Elkhart County	6,174	11.90
Frankfort (city) Clinton County	1,907	11.45

Top 10 Places Sorted by Percent
Based on places with populations of 10,000 or more

Place	Number	%
East Chicago (city) Lake County	12,245	37.78
Goshen (city) Elkhart County	4,912	16.72
Hammond (city) Lake County	13,583	16.36
Lake Station (city) Lake County	1,771	12.70
Elkhart (city) Elkhart County	6,174	11.90
Frankfort (city) Clinton County	1,907	11.45
Logansport (city) Cass County	1,998	10.15
Warsaw (city) Kosciusko County	966	7.78
Lafayette (city) Tippecanoe County	4,249	7.53
Merrillville (town) Lake County	2,041	6.68

Hispanic: Puerto Rican

Top 10 Places Sorted by Number
Based on all places, regardless of population

Place	Number	%
East Chicago (city) Lake County	3,088	9.53
Hammond (city) Lake County	2,012	2.42
Indianapolis (cons. city) Marion County	1,904	0.24
Gary (city) Lake County	1,453	1.41
Portage (city) Porter County	987	2.95
Lake Station (city) Lake County	798	5.72
Fort Wayne (city) Allen County	533	0.26
Merrillville (town) Lake County	492	1.61
Hobart (city) Lake County	383	1.51
Elkhart (city) Elkhart County	333	0.64

Top 10 Places Sorted by Percent
Based on all places, regardless of population

Place	Number	%
East Chicago (city) Lake County	3,088	9.53
Lake Station (city) Lake County	798	5.72
New Chicago (town) Lake County	89	4.31
Portage (city) Porter County	987	2.95
New Middletown (town) Harrison County	2	2.60
Hammond (city) Lake County	2,012	2.42
Merrillville (town) Lake County	492	1.61
Hobart (city) Lake County	383	1.51
Gary (city) Lake County	1,453	1.41
Edwardsport (town) Knox County	5	1.38

Top 10 Places Sorted by Percent
Based on places with populations of 10,000 or more

Place	Number	%
East Chicago (city) Lake County	3,088	9.53
Lake Station (city) Lake County	798	5.72
Portage (city) Porter County	987	2.95
Hammond (city) Lake County	2,012	2.42
Merrillville (town) Lake County	492	1.61
Hobart (city) Lake County	383	1.51
Gary (city) Lake County	1,453	1.41
Griffith (town) Lake County	180	1.04
Highland (town) Lake County	214	0.91
Goshen (city) Elkhart County	231	0.79

Hispanic: South American

Top 10 Places Sorted by Number
Based on all places, regardless of population

Place	Number	%
Indianapolis (cons. city) Marion County	758	0.10
Fort Wayne (city) Allen County	282	0.14
Bloomington (city) Monroe County	210	0.30

Notes: (cdp) census designated place; Refer to the User's Guide in the front of the book for more detailed information.

Place	Number	%
South Bend (city) Saint Joseph County	187	0.17
West Lafayette (city) Tippecanoe County	146	0.51
Fishers (town) Hamilton County	95	0.25
Lafayette (city) Tippecanoe County	70	0.12
Lawrence (city) Marion County	69	0.18
Mishawaka (city) Saint Joseph County	66	0.14
Elkhart (city) Elkhart County	64	0.12

Top 10 Places Sorted by Percent
Based on all places, regardless of population

Place	Number	%
Roseland (town) Saint Joseph County	10	0.55
West Lafayette (city) Tippecanoe County	146	0.51
Dale (town) Spencer County	8	0.51
Georgetown (cdp) Saint Joseph County	17	0.38
Wynnedale (town) Marion County	1	0.36
Delphi (city) Carroll County	10	0.33
Pittsboro (town) Hendricks County	5	0.31
Bloomington (city) Monroe County	210	0.30
Orestes (town) Madison County	1	0.30
Leavenworth (town) Crawford County	1	0.28

Top 10 Places Sorted by Percent
Based on places with populations of 10,000 or more

Place	Number	%
West Lafayette (city) Tippecanoe County	146	0.51
Bloomington (city) Monroe County	210	0.30
Fishers (town) Hamilton County	95	0.25
Lawrence (city) Marion County	69	0.18
South Bend (city) Saint Joseph County	187	0.17
Jasper (city) Dubois County	20	0.17
Valparaiso (city) Porter County	43	0.16
Munster (town) Lake County	34	0.16
Granger (cdp) Saint Joseph County	42	0.15
Fort Wayne (city) Allen County	282	0.14

Hispanic: Argentinean

Top 10 Places Sorted by Number
Based on all places, regardless of population

Place	Number	%
Indianapolis (cons. city) Marion County	57	0.01
West Lafayette (city) Tippecanoe County	33	0.11
South Bend (city) Saint Joseph County	24	0.02
Bloomington (city) Monroe County	23	0.03
Lafayette (city) Tippecanoe County	22	0.04
Carmel (city) Hamilton County	13	0.03
Fishers (town) Hamilton County	13	0.03
Muncie (city) Delaware County	10	0.01
Dyer (town) Lake County	9	0.06
Merrillville (town) Lake County	9	0.03

Top 10 Places Sorted by Percent
Based on all places, regardless of population

Place	Number	%
Long Beach (town) La Porte County	2	0.13
West Lafayette (city) Tippecanoe County	33	0.11
Roseland (town) Saint Joseph County	2	0.11
Winona Lake (town) Kosciusko County	3	0.08
Lake Dalecarlia (cdp) Lake County	1	0.08
Hidden Valley (cdp) Dearborn County	3	0.07
Leo-Cedarville (town) Allen County	2	0.07
Dyer (town) Lake County	9	0.06
Zionsville (town) Boone County	5	0.06
Lafayette (city) Tippecanoe County	22	0.04

Top 10 Places Sorted by Percent
Based on places with populations of 10,000 or more

Place	Number	%
West Lafayette (city) Tippecanoe County	33	0.11
Dyer (town) Lake County	9	0.06
Lafayette (city) Tippecanoe County	22	0.04

Place	Number	%
Warsaw (city) Kosciusko County	5	0.04
Bloomington (city) Monroe County	23	0.03
Carmel (city) Hamilton County	13	0.03
Fishers (town) Hamilton County	13	0.03
Merrillville (town) Lake County	9	0.03
Valparaiso (city) Porter County	7	0.03
South Bend (city) Saint Joseph County	24	0.02

Hispanic: Bolivian

Top 10 Places Sorted by Number
Based on all places, regardless of population

Place	Number	%
Anderson (city) Madison County	14	0.02
Goshen (city) Elkhart County	12	0.04
Fort Wayne (city) Allen County	10	<0.01
East Chicago (city) Lake County	9	0.03
Indianapolis (cons. city) Marion County	9	<0.01
Merrillville (town) Lake County	6	0.02
South Bend (city) Saint Joseph County	6	0.01
Munster (town) Lake County	5	0.02
Bloomington (city) Monroe County	5	0.01
Columbus (city) Bartholomew County	5	0.01

Top 10 Places Sorted by Percent
Based on all places, regardless of population

Place	Number	%
Shoals (town) Martin County	2	0.25
Melody Hill (cdp) Vanderburgh County	4	0.13
Cumberland (town) Marion County	3	0.05
Goshen (city) Elkhart County	12	0.04
Huntingburg (city) Dubois County	2	0.04
East Chicago (city) Lake County	9	0.03
Dunlap (cdp) Elkhart County	2	0.03
Anderson (city) Madison County	14	0.02
Merrillville (town) Lake County	6	0.02
Munster (town) Lake County	5	0.02

Top 10 Places Sorted by Percent
Based on places with populations of 10,000 or more

Place	Number	%
Goshen (city) Elkhart County	12	0.04
East Chicago (city) Lake County	9	0.03
Anderson (city) Madison County	14	0.02
Merrillville (town) Lake County	6	0.02
Munster (town) Lake County	5	0.02
Bedford (city) Lawrence County	3	0.02
South Bend (city) Saint Joseph County	6	0.01
Bloomington (city) Monroe County	5	0.01
Columbus (city) Bartholomew County	5	0.01
Hammond (city) Lake County	5	0.01

Hispanic: Chilean

Top 10 Places Sorted by Number
Based on all places, regardless of population

Place	Number	%
Indianapolis (cons. city) Marion County	36	<0.01
South Bend (city) Saint Joseph County	19	0.02
Bloomington (city) Monroe County	13	0.02
Fort Wayne (city) Allen County	12	0.01
Granger (cdp) Saint Joseph County	8	0.03
Fishers (town) Hamilton County	7	0.02
Evansville (city) Vanderburgh County	7	0.01
Goshen (city) Elkhart County	6	0.02
Valparaiso (city) Porter County	6	0.02
Roseland (town) Saint Joseph County	5	0.28

Top 10 Places Sorted by Percent
Based on all places, regardless of population

Place	Number	%
Roseland (town) Saint Joseph County	5	0.28

Place	Number	%
Grissom AFB (cdp) Miami County	2	0.12
Georgetown (cdp) Saint Joseph County	4	0.09
De Motte (town) Jasper County	3	0.09
Hamilton (town) Steuben County	1	0.08
Garrett (city) De Kalb County	4	0.07
Cedar Lake (town) Lake County	5	0.05
Whiteland (town) Johnson County	2	0.05
Winona Lake (town) Kosciusko County	2	0.05
Georgetown (town) Floyd County	1	0.04

Top 10 Places Sorted by Percent
Based on places with populations of 10,000 or more

Place	Number	%
Granger (cdp) Saint Joseph County	8	0.03
Crawfordsville (city) Montgomery County	4	0.03
South Bend (city) Saint Joseph County	19	0.02
Bloomington (city) Monroe County	13	0.02
Fishers (town) Hamilton County	7	0.02
Goshen (city) Elkhart County	6	0.02
Valparaiso (city) Porter County	6	0.02
West Lafayette (city) Tippecanoe County	5	0.02
Crown Point (city) Lake County	4	0.02
New Castle (city) Henry County	3	0.02

Hispanic: Colombian

Top 10 Places Sorted by Number
Based on all places, regardless of population

Place	Number	%
Indianapolis (cons. city) Marion County	222	0.03
Fort Wayne (city) Allen County	116	0.06
Bloomington (city) Monroe County	47	0.07
West Lafayette (city) Tippecanoe County	43	0.15
South Bend (city) Saint Joseph County	42	0.04
Fishers (town) Hamilton County	39	0.10
Carmel (city) Hamilton County	22	0.06
Lawrence (city) Marion County	20	0.05
Lafayette (city) Tippecanoe County	20	0.04
Terre Haute (city) Vigo County	17	0.03

Top 10 Places Sorted by Percent
Based on all places, regardless of population

Place	Number	%
Delphi (city) Carroll County	10	0.33
Orestes (town) Madison County	1	0.30
Fortville (town) Hancock County	7	0.20
Moores Hill (town) Dearborn County	1	0.16
West Lafayette (city) Tippecanoe County	43	0.15
Fishers (town) Hamilton County	39	0.10
Jasper (city) Dubois County	12	0.10
Lagrange (town) La Grange County	3	0.10
Avon (town) Hendricks County	5	0.08
Upland (town) Grant County	3	0.08

Top 10 Places Sorted by Percent
Based on places with populations of 10,000 or more

Place	Number	%
West Lafayette (city) Tippecanoe County	43	0.15
Fishers (town) Hamilton County	39	0.10
Jasper (city) Dubois County	12	0.10
Bloomington (city) Monroe County	47	0.07
Fort Wayne (city) Allen County	116	0.06
Carmel (city) Hamilton County	22	0.06
Lawrence (city) Marion County	20	0.05
Goshen (city) Elkhart County	16	0.05
Granger (cdp) Saint Joseph County	13	0.05
Noblesville (city) Hamilton County	13	0.05

Notes: (cdp) census designated place; Refer to the User's Guide in the front of the book for more detailed information.

Hispanic: Ecuadorian

Top 10 Places Sorted by Number
Based on all places, regardless of population

Place	Number	%
Fort Wayne (city) Allen County	81	0.04
Indianapolis (cons. city) Marion County	55	0.01
Bloomington (city) Monroe County	27	0.04
Mishawaka (city) Saint Joseph County	15	0.03
Sellersburg (town) Clark County	10	0.16
Lawrence (city) Marion County	10	0.03
Richmond (city) Wayne County	10	0.03
West Lafayette (city) Tippecanoe County	10	0.03
Dale (town) Spencer County	8	0.51
Munster (town) Lake County	8	0.04

Top 10 Places Sorted by Percent
Based on all places, regardless of population

Place	Number	%
Dale (town) Spencer County	8	0.51
Sellersburg (town) Clark County	10	0.16
Bristol (town) Elkhart County	2	0.14
Dunlap (cdp) Elkhart County	6	0.10
Corydon (town) Harrison County	2	0.07
Cedar Lake (town) Lake County	6	0.06
North Manchester (town) Wabash County	4	0.06
Bourbon (town) Marshall County	1	0.06
Pittsboro (town) Hendricks County	1	0.06
Fort Wayne (city) Allen County	81	0.04

Top 10 Places Sorted by Percent
Based on places with populations of 10,000 or more

Place	Number	%
Fort Wayne (city) Allen County	81	0.04
Bloomington (city) Monroe County	27	0.04
Munster (town) Lake County	8	0.04
Mishawaka (city) Saint Joseph County	15	0.03
Lawrence (city) Marion County	10	0.03
Richmond (city) Wayne County	10	0.03
West Lafayette (city) Tippecanoe County	10	0.03
Fishers (town) Hamilton County	6	0.02
La Porte (city) La Porte County	4	0.02
Logansport (city) Cass County	4	0.02

Hispanic: Paraguayan

Top 10 Places Sorted by Number
Based on all places, regardless of population

Place	Number	%
South Bend (city) Saint Joseph County	6	0.01
Indianapolis (cons. city) Marion County	6	<0.01
Hidden Valley (cdp) Dearborn County	5	0.11
Simonton Lake (cdp) Elkhart County	2	0.05
Fort Wayne (city) Allen County	2	<0.01
Anderson (city) Madison County	1	<0.01
Bloomington (city) Monroe County	1	<0.01
Carmel (city) Hamilton County	1	<0.01
Elkhart (city) Elkhart County	1	<0.01
Fishers (town) Hamilton County	1	<0.01

Top 10 Places Sorted by Percent
Based on all places, regardless of population

Place	Number	%
Hidden Valley (cdp) Dearborn County	5	0.11
Simonton Lake (cdp) Elkhart County	2	0.05
South Bend (city) Saint Joseph County	6	0.01
Indianapolis (cons. city) Marion County	6	<0.01
Fort Wayne (city) Allen County	2	<0.01
Anderson (city) Madison County	1	<0.01
Bloomington (city) Monroe County	1	<0.01
Carmel (city) Hamilton County	1	<0.01
Elkhart (city) Elkhart County	1	<0.01

Place	Number	%
Fishers (town) Hamilton County	1	<0.01

Top 10 Places Sorted by Percent
Based on places with populations of 10,000 or more

Place	Number	%
South Bend (city) Saint Joseph County	6	0.01
Indianapolis (cons. city) Marion County	6	<0.01
Fort Wayne (city) Allen County	2	<0.01
Anderson (city) Madison County	1	<0.01
Bloomington (city) Monroe County	1	<0.01
Carmel (city) Hamilton County	1	<0.01
Elkhart (city) Elkhart County	1	<0.01
Fishers (town) Hamilton County	1	<0.01
Granger (cdp) Saint Joseph County	1	<0.01
Terre Haute (city) Vigo County	1	<0.01

Hispanic: Peruvian

Top 10 Places Sorted by Number
Based on all places, regardless of population

Place	Number	%
Indianapolis (cons. city) Marion County	177	0.02
Bloomington (city) Monroe County	28	0.04
Fort Wayne (city) Allen County	24	0.01
West Lafayette (city) Tippecanoe County	23	0.08
South Bend (city) Saint Joseph County	23	0.02
Hammond (city) Lake County	18	0.02
Valparaiso (city) Porter County	17	0.06
Richmond (city) Wayne County	14	0.04
East Chicago (city) Lake County	13	0.04
Lawrence (city) Marion County	12	0.03

Top 10 Places Sorted by Percent
Based on all places, regardless of population

Place	Number	%
Leavenworth (town) Crawford County	1	0.28
Homecroft (town) Marion County	1	0.13
West Lafayette (city) Tippecanoe County	23	0.08
Centerville (town) Wayne County	2	0.08
Lake Dalecarlia (cdp) Lake County	1	0.08
Corydon (town) Harrison County	2	0.07
Valparaiso (city) Porter County	17	0.06
Franklin (city) Johnson County	11	0.06
Attica (city) Fountain County	2	0.06
Koontz Lake (cdp) Starke County	1	0.06

Top 10 Places Sorted by Percent
Based on places with populations of 10,000 or more

Place	Number	%
West Lafayette (city) Tippecanoe County	23	0.08
Valparaiso (city) Porter County	17	0.06
Franklin (city) Johnson County	11	0.06
Bloomington (city) Monroe County	28	0.04
Richmond (city) Wayne County	14	0.04
East Chicago (city) Lake County	13	0.04
Munster (town) Lake County	9	0.04
Logansport (city) Cass County	7	0.04
Shelbyville (city) Shelby County	7	0.04
Lawrence (city) Marion County	12	0.03

Hispanic: Uruguayan

Top 10 Places Sorted by Number
Based on all places, regardless of population

Place	Number	%
Bloomington (city) Monroe County	9	0.01
Indianapolis (cons. city) Marion County	9	<0.01
Columbus (city) Bartholomew County	5	0.01
West Lafayette (city) Tippecanoe County	4	0.01
Fort Wayne (city) Allen County	3	<0.01
South Bend (city) Saint Joseph County	3	<0.01
Carmel (city) Hamilton County	2	0.01

Place	Number	%
Vincennes (city) Knox County	1	0.01
East Chicago (city) Lake County	1	<0.01
Elkhart (city) Elkhart County	1	<0.01

Top 10 Places Sorted by Percent
Based on all places, regardless of population

Place	Number	%
Bloomington (city) Monroe County	9	0.01
Columbus (city) Bartholomew County	5	0.01
West Lafayette (city) Tippecanoe County	4	0.01
Carmel (city) Hamilton County	2	0.01
Vincennes (city) Knox County	1	0.01
Indianapolis (cons. city) Marion County	9	<0.01
Fort Wayne (city) Allen County	3	<0.01
South Bend (city) Saint Joseph County	3	<0.01
East Chicago (city) Lake County	1	<0.01
Elkhart (city) Elkhart County	1	<0.01

Top 10 Places Sorted by Percent
Based on places with populations of 10,000 or more

Place	Number	%
Bloomington (city) Monroe County	9	0.01
Columbus (city) Bartholomew County	5	0.01
West Lafayette (city) Tippecanoe County	4	0.01
Carmel (city) Hamilton County	2	0.01
Vincennes (city) Knox County	1	0.01
Indianapolis (cons. city) Marion County	9	<0.01
Fort Wayne (city) Allen County	3	<0.01
South Bend (city) Saint Joseph County	3	<0.01
East Chicago (city) Lake County	1	<0.01
Elkhart (city) Elkhart County	1	<0.01

Hispanic: Venezuelan

Top 10 Places Sorted by Number
Based on all places, regardless of population

Place	Number	%
Indianapolis (cons. city) Marion County	152	0.02
South Bend (city) Saint Joseph County	54	0.05
Bloomington (city) Monroe County	47	0.07
Elkhart (city) Elkhart County	33	0.06
Mishawaka (city) Saint Joseph County	29	0.06
Lawrence (city) Marion County	22	0.06
Fort Wayne (city) Allen County	21	0.01
Evansville (city) Vanderburgh County	20	0.02
Fishers (town) Hamilton County	18	0.05
Speedway (town) Marion County	10	0.08

Top 10 Places Sorted by Percent
Based on all places, regardless of population

Place	Number	%
Wynnedale (town) Marion County	1	0.36
Pittsboro (town) Hendricks County	4	0.25
Georgetown (cdp) Saint Joseph County	9	0.20
Speedway (town) Marion County	10	0.08
Bloomington (city) Monroe County	47	0.07
Gulivoire Park (cdp) Saint Joseph County	2	0.07
Elkhart (city) Elkhart County	33	0.06
Mishawaka (city) Saint Joseph County	29	0.06
Lawrence (city) Marion County	22	0.06
South Bend (city) Saint Joseph County	54	0.05

Top 10 Places Sorted by Percent
Based on places with populations of 10,000 or more

Place	Number	%
Speedway (town) Marion County	10	0.08
Bloomington (city) Monroe County	47	0.07
Elkhart (city) Elkhart County	33	0.06
Mishawaka (city) Saint Joseph County	29	0.06
Lawrence (city) Marion County	22	0.06
South Bend (city) Saint Joseph County	54	0.05
Fishers (town) Hamilton County	18	0.05

Notes: (cdp) census designated place; Refer to the User's Guide in the front of the book for more detailed information.

Place	Number	%
West Lafayette (city) Tippecanoe County	10	0.03
Indianapolis (cons. city) Marion County	152	0.02
Evansville (city) Vanderburgh County	20	0.02

Hispanic: Other South American

Top 10 Places Sorted by Number
Based on all places, regardless of population

Place	Number	%
Indianapolis (cons. city) Marion County	35	<0.01
West Lafayette (city) Tippecanoe County	15	0.05
Bloomington (city) Monroe County	10	0.01
Fort Wayne (city) Allen County	7	<0.01
Schererville (town) Lake County	4	0.02
South Bend (city) Saint Joseph County	4	<0.01
Angola (city) Steuben County	3	0.04
Columbus (city) Bartholomew County	3	0.01
Roseland (town) Saint Joseph County	2	0.11
Ellettsville (town) Monroe County	2	0.04

Top 10 Places Sorted by Percent
Based on all places, regardless of population

Place	Number	%
Roseland (town) Saint Joseph County	2	0.11
Mulberry (town) Clinton County	1	0.07
West Lafayette (city) Tippecanoe County	15	0.05
Westville (town) La Porte County	1	0.05
Angola (city) Steuben County	3	0.04
Ellettsville (town) Monroe County	2	0.04
Georgetown (cdp) Saint Joseph County	2	0.04
Yorktown (town) Delaware County	2	0.04
Chesterfield (town) Madison County	1	0.03
Indian Heights (cdp) Howard County	1	0.03

Top 10 Places Sorted by Percent
Based on places with populations of 10,000 or more

Place	Number	%
West Lafayette (city) Tippecanoe County	15	0.05
Schererville (town) Lake County	4	0.02
Bloomington (city) Monroe County	10	0.01
Columbus (city) Bartholomew County	3	0.01
Fishers (town) Hamilton County	2	0.01
Granger (cdp) Saint Joseph County	2	0.01
Lawrence (city) Marion County	2	0.01
Marion (city) Grant County	2	0.01
Shelbyville (city) Shelby County	2	0.01
Greensburg (city) Decatur County	1	0.01

Hispanic: Other

Top 10 Places Sorted by Number
Based on all places, regardless of population

Place	Number	%
Indianapolis (cons. city) Marion County	4,432	0.57
Fort Wayne (city) Allen County	1,820	0.88
Hammond (city) Lake County	1,491	1.80
South Bend (city) Saint Joseph County	1,275	1.18
East Chicago (city) Lake County	1,240	3.83
Elkhart (city) Elkhart County	662	1.28
Gary (city) Lake County	526	0.51
Lafayette (city) Tippecanoe County	466	0.83
Goshen (city) Elkhart County	373	1.27
Portage (city) Porter County	369	1.10

Top 10 Places Sorted by Percent
Based on all places, regardless of population

Place	Number	%
Ambia (town) Benton County	16	8.12
Boswell (town) Benton County	45	5.44
East Chicago (city) Lake County	1,240	3.83
Hardinsburg (town) Washington County	7	2.87
Monticello (city) White County	160	2.80

Place	Number	%
Cromwell (town) Noble County	11	2.43
Monon (town) White County	41	2.37
Lake Station (city) Lake County	282	2.02
Whiting (city) Lake County	94	1.83
Vera Cruz (town) Wells County	1	1.82

Top 10 Places Sorted by Percent
Based on places with populations of 10,000 or more

Place	Number	%
East Chicago (city) Lake County	1,240	3.83
Lake Station (city) Lake County	282	2.02
Hammond (city) Lake County	1,491	1.80
Frankfort (city) Clinton County	254	1.52
Elkhart (city) Elkhart County	662	1.28
Goshen (city) Elkhart County	373	1.27
South Bend (city) Saint Joseph County	1,275	1.18
Portage (city) Porter County	369	1.10
Merrillville (town) Lake County	334	1.09
Logansport (city) Cass County	210	1.07

Hungarian

Top 10 Places Sorted by Number
Based on all places, regardless of population

Place	Number	%
South Bend (city) Saint Joseph County	3,605	3.37
Indianapolis (cons. city) Marion County	2,281	0.29
Hammond (city) Lake County	1,436	1.73
Mishawaka (city) Saint Joseph County	1,428	3.05
Granger (cdp) Saint Joseph County	1,343	4.76
Highland (town) Lake County	846	3.59
Fort Wayne (city) Allen County	803	0.39
Schererville (town) Lake County	694	2.80
Munster (town) Lake County	541	2.51
Griffith (town) Lake County	519	2.99

Top 10 Places Sorted by Percent
Based on all places, regardless of population

Place	Number	%
Gulivoire Park (cdp) Saint Joseph County	333	11.29
Granger (cdp) Saint Joseph County	1,343	4.76
Buffalo (cdp) White County	26	4.04
Highland (town) Lake County	846	3.59
Georgetown (cdp) Saint Joseph County	166	3.57
Indian Village (town) Saint Joseph County	5	3.57
South Bend (city) Saint Joseph County	3,605	3.37
Saint John (town) Lake County	279	3.32
Koontz Lake (cdp) Starke County	51	3.31
Lakeville (town) Saint Joseph County	18	3.23

Top 10 Places Sorted by Percent
Based on places with populations of 10,000 or more

Place	Number	%
Granger (cdp) Saint Joseph County	1,343	4.76
Highland (town) Lake County	846	3.59
South Bend (city) Saint Joseph County	3,605	3.37
Mishawaka (city) Saint Joseph County	1,428	3.05
Griffith (town) Lake County	519	2.99
Schererville (town) Lake County	694	2.80
Munster (town) Lake County	541	2.51
Dyer (town) Lake County	287	2.07
Hobart (city) Lake County	481	1.89
Chesterton (town) Porter County	191	1.83

Icelander

Top 10 Places Sorted by Number
Based on all places, regardless of population

Place	Number	%
Indianapolis (cons. city) Marion County	79	0.01
Columbia City (city) Whitley County	32	0.45
Terre Haute (city) Vigo County	17	0.03

Place	Number	%
Bloomington (city) Monroe County	17	0.02
Jeffersonville (city) Clark County	14	0.05
Granger (cdp) Saint Joseph County	12	0.04
Vincennes (city) Knox County	11	0.06
Portage (city) Porter County	9	0.03
Fishers (town) Hamilton County	9	0.02
Huntington (city) Huntington County	8	0.05

Top 10 Places Sorted by Percent
Based on all places, regardless of population

Place	Number	%
Gosport (town) Owen County	7	1.00
Royal Center (town) Cass County	6	0.71
Columbia City (city) Whitley County	32	0.45
South Whitley (town) Whitley County	5	0.28
Markle (town) Huntington County	1	0.09
Vincennes (city) Knox County	11	0.06
Jeffersonville (city) Clark County	14	0.05
Huntington (city) Huntington County	8	0.05
Avilla (town) Noble County	1	0.05
Granger (cdp) Saint Joseph County	12	0.04

Top 10 Places Sorted by Percent
Based on places with populations of 10,000 or more

Place	Number	%
Vincennes (city) Knox County	11	0.06
Jeffersonville (city) Clark County	14	0.05
Huntington (city) Huntington County	8	0.05
Granger (cdp) Saint Joseph County	12	0.04
Terre Haute (city) Vigo County	17	0.03
Portage (city) Porter County	9	0.03
Bloomington (city) Monroe County	17	0.02
Fishers (town) Hamilton County	9	0.02
Carmel (city) Hamilton County	6	0.02
Indianapolis (cons. city) Marion County	79	0.01

Iranian

Top 10 Places Sorted by Number
Based on all places, regardless of population

Place	Number	%
Indianapolis (cons. city) Marion County	399	0.05
Fort Wayne (city) Allen County	75	0.04
Carmel (city) Hamilton County	72	0.19
Valparaiso (city) Porter County	62	0.23
West Lafayette (city) Tippecanoe County	61	0.21
Westfield (town) Hamilton County	49	0.54
Granger (cdp) Saint Joseph County	47	0.17
Madison (city) Jefferson County	29	0.24
South Bend (city) Saint Joseph County	28	0.03
Lawrence (city) Marion County	26	0.07

Top 10 Places Sorted by Percent
Based on all places, regardless of population

Place	Number	%
Beverly Shores (town) Porter County	7	1.04
Westfield (town) Hamilton County	49	0.54
Cicero (town) Hamilton County	21	0.53
Nashville (town) Brown County	4	0.47
Madison (city) Jefferson County	29	0.24
Valparaiso (city) Porter County	62	0.23
West Lafayette (city) Tippecanoe County	61	0.21
Carmel (city) Hamilton County	72	0.19
Granger (cdp) Saint Joseph County	47	0.17
Wabash (city) Wabash County	20	0.17

Top 10 Places Sorted by Percent
Based on places with populations of 10,000 or more

Place	Number	%
Madison (city) Jefferson County	29	0.24
Valparaiso (city) Porter County	62	0.23
West Lafayette (city) Tippecanoe County	61	0.21

Notes: (cdp) census designated place; Refer to the User's Guide in the front of the book for more detailed information.

Place	Number	%
Carmel (city) Hamilton County	72	0.19
Granger (cdp) Saint Joseph County	47	0.17
Wabash (city) Wabash County	20	0.17
Munster (town) Lake County	19	0.09
Lawrence (city) Marion County	26	0.07
Fishers (town) Hamilton County	25	0.06
Highland (town) Lake County	14	0.06

Irish

Top 10 Places Sorted by Number
Based on all places, regardless of population

Place	Number	%
Indianapolis (cons. city) Marion County	79,838	10.20
Fort Wayne (city) Allen County	21,601	10.49
Evansville (city) Vanderburgh County	12,659	10.39
South Bend (city) Saint Joseph County	11,246	10.51
Hammond (city) Lake County	9,590	11.55
Bloomington (city) Monroe County	9,185	13.27
Mishawaka (city) Saint Joseph County	6,552	14.00
Lafayette (city) Tippecanoe County	6,492	11.54
Terre Haute (city) Vigo County	6,303	10.58
Muncie (city) Delaware County	6,260	9.28

Top 10 Places Sorted by Percent
Based on all places, regardless of population

Place	Number	%
Long Beach (town) La Porte County	649	41.18
Alton (town) Crawford County	13	30.23
Whitewater (town) Wayne County	17	28.33
Onward (town) Cass County	17	27.87
State Line City (town) Warren County	35	26.12
Brooksburg (town) Jefferson County	20	25.32
Montgomery (town) Daviess County	88	23.66
Schneider (town) Lake County	79	22.64
Troy (town) Perry County	87	21.86
Boston (town) Wayne County	43	21.72

Top 10 Places Sorted by Percent
Based on places with populations of 10,000 or more

Place	Number	%
Chesterton (town) Porter County	2,025	19.41
Beech Grove (city) Marion County	2,673	18.82
Dyer (town) Lake County	2,440	17.61
Granger (cdp) Saint Joseph County	4,768	16.89
Valparaiso (city) Porter County	4,453	16.19
Hobart (city) Lake County	3,941	15.52
Crown Point (city) Lake County	3,006	15.36
Portage (city) Porter County	5,132	15.30
Schererville (town) Lake County	3,744	15.08
Carmel (city) Hamilton County	5,692	15.06

Israeli

Top 10 Places Sorted by Number
Based on all places, regardless of population

Place	Number	%
Bloomington (city) Monroe County	107	0.15
Indianapolis (cons. city) Marion County	93	0.01
Mishawaka (city) Saint Joseph County	24	0.05
Westfield (town) Hamilton County	16	0.18
Gary (city) Lake County	9	0.01
De Motte (town) Jasper County	8	0.25
Fort Wayne (city) Allen County	6	<0.01

Top 10 Places Sorted by Percent
Based on all places, regardless of population

Place	Number	%
De Motte (town) Jasper County	8	0.25
Westfield (town) Hamilton County	16	0.18
Bloomington (city) Monroe County	107	0.15
Mishawaka (city) Saint Joseph County	24	0.05

Place	Number	%
Indianapolis (cons. city) Marion County	93	0.01
Gary (city) Lake County	9	0.01
Fort Wayne (city) Allen County	6	<0.01

Top 10 Places Sorted by Percent
Based on places with populations of 10,000 or more

Place	Number	%
Bloomington (city) Monroe County	107	0.15
Mishawaka (city) Saint Joseph County	24	0.05
Indianapolis (cons. city) Marion County	93	0.01
Gary (city) Lake County	9	0.01
Fort Wayne (city) Allen County	6	<0.01

Italian

Top 10 Places Sorted by Number
Based on all places, regardless of population

Place	Number	%
Indianapolis (cons. city) Marion County	17,442	2.23
Fort Wayne (city) Allen County	4,784	2.32
South Bend (city) Saint Joseph County	3,400	3.18
Hammond (city) Lake County	3,016	3.63
Bloomington (city) Monroe County	2,880	4.16
Mishawaka (city) Saint Joseph County	2,352	5.03
Fishers (town) Hamilton County	1,966	5.05
Evansville (city) Vanderburgh County	1,740	1.43
Munster (town) Lake County	1,725	8.02
Granger (cdp) Saint Joseph County	1,679	5.95

Top 10 Places Sorted by Percent
Based on all places, regardless of population

Place	Number	%
North Crows Nest (town) Marion County	10	23.81
Saint John (town) Lake County	1,040	12.39
Universal (town) Vermillion County	53	12.27
Clinton (city) Vermillion County	582	11.34
Spring Hill (town) Marion County	14	11.20
Collegeville (cdp) Jasper County	96	11.05
Fairview Park (town) Vermillion County	161	10.61
Lake Dalecarlia (cdp) Lake County	131	10.41
Dyer (town) Lake County	1,384	9.99
Wynnedale (town) Marion County	33	9.76

Top 10 Places Sorted by Percent
Based on places with populations of 10,000 or more

Place	Number	%
Dyer (town) Lake County	1,384	9.99
Munster (town) Lake County	1,725	8.02
Crown Point (city) Lake County	1,465	7.49
Hobart (city) Lake County	1,630	6.42
Highland (town) Lake County	1,509	6.41
Schererville (town) Lake County	1,557	6.27
Granger (cdp) Saint Joseph County	1,679	5.95
Chesterton (town) Porter County	580	5.56
Valparaiso (city) Porter County	1,527	5.55
Fishers (town) Hamilton County	1,966	5.05

Latvian

Top 10 Places Sorted by Number
Based on all places, regardless of population

Place	Number	%
Indianapolis (cons. city) Marion County	392	0.05
Elkhart (city) Elkhart County	44	0.09
Fishers (town) Hamilton County	43	0.11
Crown Point (city) Lake County	31	0.16
Lafayette (city) Tippecanoe County	26	0.05
Carmel (city) Hamilton County	23	0.06
Muncie (city) Delaware County	22	0.03
Fort Wayne (city) Allen County	22	0.01
Columbus (city) Bartholomew County	21	0.05
Bloomington (city) Monroe County	20	0.03

Top 10 Places Sorted by Percent
Based on all places, regardless of population

Place	Number	%
Beverly Shores (town) Porter County	14	2.08
Lizton (town) Hendricks County	4	1.04
Spring Grove (town) Wayne County	2	0.49
Frankton (town) Madison County	6	0.31
Rocky Ripple (town) Marion County	2	0.28
Warren Park (town) Marion County	4	0.24
Millersburg (town) Elkhart County	2	0.23
Crown Point (city) Lake County	31	0.16
Ellettsville (town) Monroe County	7	0.14
Fishers (town) Hamilton County	43	0.11

Top 10 Places Sorted by Percent
Based on places with populations of 10,000 or more

Place	Number	%
Crown Point (city) Lake County	31	0.16
Fishers (town) Hamilton County	43	0.11
Elkhart (city) Elkhart County	44	0.09
Munster (town) Lake County	14	0.07
Franklin (city) Johnson County	13	0.07
Carmel (city) Hamilton County	23	0.06
Granger (cdp) Saint Joseph County	17	0.06
Huntington (city) Huntington County	10	0.06
Indianapolis (cons. city) Marion County	392	0.05
Lafayette (city) Tippecanoe County	26	0.05

Lithuanian

Top 10 Places Sorted by Number
Based on all places, regardless of population

Place	Number	%
Indianapolis (cons. city) Marion County	875	0.11
Portage (city) Porter County	280	0.83
Schererville (town) Lake County	256	1.03
Hammond (city) Lake County	248	0.30
Fort Wayne (city) Allen County	245	0.12
Hobart (city) Lake County	225	0.89
Highland (town) Lake County	219	0.93
Munster (town) Lake County	215	1.00
South Bend (city) Saint Joseph County	215	0.20
Merrillville (town) Lake County	197	0.64

Top 10 Places Sorted by Percent
Based on all places, regardless of population

Place	Number	%
Beverly Shores (town) Porter County	99	14.73
Michiana Shores (town) La Porte County	19	6.76
Dune Acres (town) Porter County	9	4.66
Lake Dalecarlia (cdp) Lake County	50	3.97
Porter (town) Porter County	126	2.49
Lakes of the Four Seasons (cdp) Lake County	144	1.97
Lowell (town) Lake County	142	1.91
Bass Lake (cdp) Starke County	24	1.88
Burns Harbor (town) Porter County	14	1.79
New Richmond (town) Montgomery County	6	1.77

Top 10 Places Sorted by Percent
Based on places with populations of 10,000 or more

Place	Number	%
Chesterton (town) Porter County	151	1.45
Dyer (town) Lake County	174	1.26
Schererville (town) Lake County	256	1.03
Munster (town) Lake County	215	1.00
Highland (town) Lake County	219	0.93
Hobart (city) Lake County	225	0.89
Crown Point (city) Lake County	175	0.89
Portage (city) Porter County	280	0.83
Granger (cdp) Saint Joseph County	189	0.67
Merrillville (town) Lake County	197	0.64

Notes: (cdp) census designated place; Refer to the User's Guide in the front of the book for more detailed information.

Luxemburger

Top 10 Places Sorted by Number
Based on all places, regardless of population

Place	Number	%
Indianapolis (cons. city) Marion County	99	0.01
Lafayette (city) Tippecanoe County	50	0.09
Munster (town) Lake County	41	0.19
Portage (city) Porter County	37	0.11
Fort Wayne (city) Allen County	23	0.01
Greenfield (city) Hancock County	22	0.15
Mishawaka (city) Saint Joseph County	21	0.04
Bloomington (city) Monroe County	16	0.02
Hammond (city) Lake County	10	0.01
Westfield (town) Hamilton County	9	0.10

Top 10 Places Sorted by Percent
Based on all places, regardless of population

Place	Number	%
Long Beach (town) La Porte County	5	0.32
Beverly Shores (town) Porter County	2	0.30
Kingsford Heights (town) La Porte County	3	0.21
Munster (town) Lake County	41	0.19
Montezuma (town) Parke County	2	0.17
Cannelton (city) Perry County	2	0.16
Greenfield (city) Hancock County	22	0.15
Winona Lake (town) Kosciusko County	6	0.15
Portage (city) Porter County	37	0.11
Knox (city) Starke County	4	0.11

Top 10 Places Sorted by Percent
Based on places with populations of 10,000 or more

Place	Number	%
Munster (town) Lake County	41	0.19
Greenfield (city) Hancock County	22	0.15
Portage (city) Porter County	37	0.11
Lafayette (city) Tippecanoe County	50	0.09
Mishawaka (city) Saint Joseph County	21	0.04
Schererville (town) Lake County	8	0.03
Bloomington (city) Monroe County	16	0.02
West Lafayette (city) Tippecanoe County	7	0.02
Indianapolis (cons. city) Marion County	99	0.01
Fort Wayne (city) Allen County	23	0.01

Macedonian

Top 10 Places Sorted by Number
Based on all places, regardless of population

Place	Number	%
Crown Point (city) Lake County	613	3.13
Merrillville (town) Lake County	466	1.52
Fort Wayne (city) Allen County	432	0.21
Schererville (town) Lake County	384	1.55
Indianapolis (cons. city) Marion County	233	0.03
Hobart (city) Lake County	230	0.91
Winfield (town) Lake County	148	6.52
Portage (city) Porter County	107	0.32
Lake Station (city) Lake County	82	0.59
Valparaiso (city) Porter County	76	0.28

Top 10 Places Sorted by Percent
Based on all places, regardless of population

Place	Number	%
Winfield (town) Lake County	148	6.52
Crown Point (city) Lake County	613	3.13
Boswell (town) Benton County	16	1.89
Schererville (town) Lake County	384	1.55
Merrillville (town) Lake County	466	1.52
Hobart (city) Lake County	230	0.91
Lakes of the Four Seasons (cdp) Lake County	53	0.73
Pottawattamie Park (town) La Porte County	2	0.66
Lake Station (city) Lake County	82	0.59

Cumberland (town) Marion County	28	0.52

Top 10 Places Sorted by Percent
Based on places with populations of 10,000 or more

Place	Number	%
Crown Point (city) Lake County	613	3.13
Schererville (town) Lake County	384	1.55
Merrillville (town) Lake County	466	1.52
Hobart (city) Lake County	230	0.91
Lake Station (city) Lake County	82	0.59
Portage (city) Porter County	107	0.32
Valparaiso (city) Porter County	76	0.28
Highland (town) Lake County	65	0.28
Speedway (town) Marion County	33	0.26
Fort Wayne (city) Allen County	432	0.21

Maltese

Top 10 Places Sorted by Number
Based on all places, regardless of population

Place	Number	%
Mishawaka (city) Saint Joseph County	26	0.06
Indianapolis (cons. city) Marion County	23	<0.01
South Bend (city) Saint Joseph County	18	0.02
West Lafayette (city) Tippecanoe County	12	0.04
Fort Wayne (city) Allen County	10	<0.01
Angola (city) Steuben County	9	0.12
Richmond (city) Wayne County	8	0.02
Gary (city) Lake County	6	0.01
Lafayette (city) Tippecanoe County	5	0.01
Roseland (town) Saint Joseph County	3	0.17

Top 10 Places Sorted by Percent
Based on all places, regardless of population

Place	Number	%
Roseland (town) Saint Joseph County	3	0.17
Topeka (town) La Grange County	2	0.17
Angola (city) Steuben County	9	0.12
Mishawaka (city) Saint Joseph County	26	0.06
West Lafayette (city) Tippecanoe County	12	0.04
South Bend (city) Saint Joseph County	18	0.02
Richmond (city) Wayne County	8	0.02
Gary (city) Lake County	6	0.01
Lafayette (city) Tippecanoe County	5	0.01
Indianapolis (cons. city) Marion County	23	<0.01

Top 10 Places Sorted by Percent
Based on places with populations of 10,000 or more

Place	Number	%
Mishawaka (city) Saint Joseph County	26	0.06
West Lafayette (city) Tippecanoe County	12	0.04
South Bend (city) Saint Joseph County	18	0.02
Richmond (city) Wayne County	8	0.02
Gary (city) Lake County	6	0.01
Lafayette (city) Tippecanoe County	5	0.01
Indianapolis (cons. city) Marion County	23	<0.01
Fort Wayne (city) Allen County	10	<0.01

New Zealander

Top 10 Places Sorted by Number
Based on all places, regardless of population

Place	Number	%
Avon (town) Hendricks County	22	0.38
Indianapolis (cons. city) Marion County	21	<0.01
Bloomington (city) Monroe County	20	0.03
Rochester (city) Fulton County	8	0.13
La Porte (city) La Porte County	7	0.03
West Lafayette (city) Tippecanoe County	7	0.02
Huntington (city) Huntington County	5	0.03
Linden (town) Montgomery County	3	0.42
Montezuma (town) Parke County	2	0.17

Top 10 Places Sorted by Percent
Based on all places, regardless of population

Place	Number	%
Linden (town) Montgomery County	3	0.42
Avon (town) Hendricks County	22	0.38
Montezuma (town) Parke County	2	0.17
Rochester (city) Fulton County	8	0.13
Bloomington (city) Monroe County	20	0.03
La Porte (city) La Porte County	7	0.03
Huntington (city) Huntington County	5	0.03
West Lafayette (city) Tippecanoe County	7	0.02
Indianapolis (cons. city) Marion County	21	<0.01

Top 10 Places Sorted by Percent
Based on places with populations of 10,000 or more

Place	Number	%
Bloomington (city) Monroe County	20	0.03
La Porte (city) La Porte County	7	0.03
Huntington (city) Huntington County	5	0.03
West Lafayette (city) Tippecanoe County	7	0.02
Indianapolis (cons. city) Marion County	21	<0.01

Northern European

Top 10 Places Sorted by Number
Based on all places, regardless of population

Place	Number	%
Indianapolis (cons. city) Marion County	422	0.05
Carmel (city) Hamilton County	126	0.33
Bloomington (city) Monroe County	83	0.12
West Lafayette (city) Tippecanoe County	64	0.22
Columbus (city) Bartholomew County	51	0.13
Fort Wayne (city) Allen County	50	0.02
Griffith (town) Lake County	46	0.27
South Bend (city) Saint Joseph County	43	0.04
Valparaiso (city) Porter County	40	0.15
Fishers (town) Hamilton County	30	0.08

Top 10 Places Sorted by Percent
Based on all places, regardless of population

Place	Number	%
Springport (town) Henry County	10	6.37
Lizton (town) Hendricks County	7	1.81
Williams Creek (town) Marion County	7	1.71
Meridian Hills (town) Marion County	29	1.68
Hagerstown (town) Wayne County	27	1.52
Crane (town) Martin County	2	1.04
Cloverdale (town) Putnam County	19	0.84
Millersburg (town) Elkhart County	6	0.70
Ladoga (town) Montgomery County	6	0.60
Homecroft (town) Marion County	3	0.40

Top 10 Places Sorted by Percent
Based on places with populations of 10,000 or more

Place	Number	%
Carmel (city) Hamilton County	126	0.33
Griffith (town) Lake County	46	0.27
West Lafayette (city) Tippecanoe County	64	0.22
Greenfield (city) Hancock County	26	0.18
Valparaiso (city) Porter County	40	0.15
Speedway (town) Marion County	18	0.14
Columbus (city) Bartholomew County	51	0.13
Bloomington (city) Monroe County	83	0.12
Brownsburg (town) Hendricks County	16	0.11
Frankfort (city) Clinton County	17	0.10

Notes: (cdp) census designated place; Refer to the User's Guide in the front of the book for more detailed information.

Norwegian

Top 10 Places Sorted by Number
Based on all places, regardless of population

Place	Number	%
Indianapolis (cons. city) Marion County	3,756	0.48
Fort Wayne (city) Allen County	1,214	0.59
Bloomington (city) Monroe County	817	1.18
South Bend (city) Saint Joseph County	653	0.61
Carmel (city) Hamilton County	588	1.56
Fishers (town) Hamilton County	509	1.31
Valparaiso (city) Porter County	485	1.76
Evansville (city) Vanderburgh County	479	0.39
Elkhart (city) Elkhart County	474	0.92
Granger (cdp) Saint Joseph County	467	1.65

Top 10 Places Sorted by Percent
Based on all places, regardless of population

Place	Number	%
Greenville (town) Floyd County	29	4.68
Dune Acres (town) Porter County	8	4.15
Spring Hill (town) Marion County	5	4.00
Poneto (town) Wells County	8	3.77
Shirley (town) Hancock County	26	3.27
Upland (town) Grant County	107	2.79
Troy (town) Perry County	11	2.76
Williams Creek (town) Marion County	10	2.44
Gulivoire Park (cdp) Saint Joseph County	68	2.31
Leesburg (town) Kosciusko County	14	2.31

Top 10 Places Sorted by Percent
Based on places with populations of 10,000 or more

Place	Number	%
Valparaiso (city) Porter County	485	1.76
Granger (cdp) Saint Joseph County	467	1.65
La Porte (city) La Porte County	341	1.58
Carmel (city) Hamilton County	588	1.56
Schererville (town) Lake County	373	1.50
Fishers (town) Hamilton County	509	1.31
West Lafayette (city) Tippecanoe County	376	1.30
Warsaw (city) Kosciusko County	159	1.29
Hobart (city) Lake County	321	1.26
Chesterton (town) Porter County	126	1.21

Pennsylvania German

Top 10 Places Sorted by Number
Based on all places, regardless of population

Place	Number	%
Goshen (city) Elkhart County	252	0.86
Indianapolis (cons. city) Marion County	241	0.03
Mishawaka (city) Saint Joseph County	197	0.42
Elkhart (city) Elkhart County	160	0.31
Fort Wayne (city) Allen County	149	0.07
Granger (cdp) Saint Joseph County	131	0.46
South Bend (city) Saint Joseph County	91	0.09
Simonton Lake (cdp) Elkhart County	67	1.68
Portage (city) Porter County	66	0.20
Richmond (city) Wayne County	56	0.14

Top 10 Places Sorted by Percent
Based on all places, regardless of population

Place	Number	%
Topeka (town) La Grange County	34	2.93
Mount Etna (town) Huntington County	3	2.83
Mexico (cdp) Miami County	26	2.37
Millersburg (town) Elkhart County	17	1.99
Clear Lake (town) Steuben County	5	1.82
Whitestown (town) Boone County	9	1.70
Simonton Lake (cdp) Elkhart County	67	1.68
Wheatland (town) Knox County	7	1.43
Cromwell (town) Noble County	6	1.43

Burnettsville (town) White County	5	1.32

Top 10 Places Sorted by Percent
Based on places with populations of 10,000 or more

Place	Number	%
Goshen (city) Elkhart County	252	0.86
Granger (cdp) Saint Joseph County	131	0.46
Mishawaka (city) Saint Joseph County	197	0.42
Elkhart (city) Elkhart County	160	0.31
Wabash (city) Wabash County	35	0.30
Auburn (city) De Kalb County	25	0.21
Portage (city) Porter County	66	0.20
La Porte (city) La Porte County	38	0.18
Brownsburg (town) Hendricks County	26	0.18
Lake Station (city) Lake County	22	0.16

Polish

Top 10 Places Sorted by Number
Based on all places, regardless of population

Place	Number	%
South Bend (city) Saint Joseph County	11,417	10.67
Indianapolis (cons. city) Marion County	10,643	1.36
Hammond (city) Lake County	10,190	12.27
Mishawaka (city) Saint Joseph County	4,403	9.41
Schererville (town) Lake County	4,296	17.31
Munster (town) Lake County	4,173	19.40
Highland (town) Lake County	4,141	17.59
Fort Wayne (city) Allen County	4,107	1.99
Michigan City (city) La Porte County	3,631	11.06
Granger (cdp) Saint Joseph County	3,064	10.86

Top 10 Places Sorted by Percent
Based on all places, regardless of population

Place	Number	%
Trail Creek (town) La Porte County	579	24.97
Saint John (town) Lake County	1,938	23.08
Dyer (town) Lake County	2,903	20.95
Munster (town) Lake County	4,173	19.40
Bass Lake (cdp) Starke County	238	18.62
Lake Dalecarlia (cdp) Lake County	233	18.51
Gulivoire Park (cdp) Saint Joseph County	528	17.90
Highland (town) Lake County	4,141	17.59
Schererville (town) Lake County	4,296	17.31
Whiting (city) Lake County	879	17.11

Top 10 Places Sorted by Percent
Based on places with populations of 10,000 or more

Place	Number	%
Dyer (town) Lake County	2,903	20.95
Munster (town) Lake County	4,173	19.40
Highland (town) Lake County	4,141	17.59
Schererville (town) Lake County	4,296	17.31
Griffith (town) Lake County	2,377	13.71
Hammond (city) Lake County	10,190	12.27
Crown Point (city) Lake County	2,280	11.65
Hobart (city) Lake County	2,862	11.27
Michigan City (city) La Porte County	3,631	11.06
La Porte (city) La Porte County	2,353	10.90

Portuguese

Top 10 Places Sorted by Number
Based on all places, regardless of population

Place	Number	%
Indianapolis (cons. city) Marion County	402	0.05
Fort Wayne (city) Allen County	201	0.10
South Bend (city) Saint Joseph County	97	0.09
Bloomington (city) Monroe County	81	0.12
Muncie (city) Delaware County	72	0.11
Fishers (town) Hamilton County	48	0.12
Mishawaka (city) Saint Joseph County	47	0.10

New Albany (city) Floyd County	45	0.12
Carmel (city) Hamilton County	41	0.11
Lawrence (city) Marion County	40	0.10

Top 10 Places Sorted by Percent
Based on all places, regardless of population

Place	Number	%
Sunman (town) Ripley County	9	1.17
Bainbridge (town) Putnam County	8	1.01
Kingsbury (town) La Porte County	2	0.95
Hardinsburg (town) Washington County	2	0.79
Trafalgar (town) Johnson County	6	0.73
Leo-Cedarville (town) Allen County	14	0.52
Indian Heights (cdp) Howard County	17	0.50
Mentone (town) Kosciusko County	4	0.48
Bourbon (town) Marshall County	8	0.47
Lakes of the Four Seasons (cdp) Lake County	32	0.44

Top 10 Places Sorted by Percent
Based on places with populations of 10,000 or more

Place	Number	%
Chesterton (town) Porter County	31	0.30
Brownsburg (town) Hendricks County	33	0.23
Plainfield (town) Hendricks County	30	0.16
Speedway (town) Marion County	20	0.16
Bloomington (city) Monroe County	81	0.12
Fishers (town) Hamilton County	48	0.12
New Albany (city) Floyd County	45	0.12
Muncie (city) Delaware County	72	0.11
Carmel (city) Hamilton County	41	0.11
New Haven (city) Allen County	13	0.11

Romanian

Top 10 Places Sorted by Number
Based on all places, regardless of population

Place	Number	%
Indianapolis (cons. city) Marion County	1,122	0.14
Hammond (city) Lake County	412	0.50
Fort Wayne (city) Allen County	344	0.17
Hobart (city) Lake County	216	0.85
Munster (town) Lake County	215	1.00
Highland (town) Lake County	197	0.84
Gary (city) Lake County	182	0.18
Schererville (town) Lake County	181	0.73
Bloomington (city) Monroe County	175	0.25
Merrillville (town) Lake County	138	0.45

Top 10 Places Sorted by Percent
Based on all places, regardless of population

Place	Number	%
Lanesville (town) Harrison County	9	1.45
La Paz (town) Marshall County	6	1.19
Kouts (town) Porter County	20	1.18
Wanatah (town) La Porte County	11	1.09
Etna Green (town) Kosciusko County	7	1.07
Knox (city) Starke County	39	1.02
Munster (town) Lake County	215	1.00
Monrovia (town) Morgan County	6	0.95
Beverly Shores (town) Porter County	6	0.89
Hobart (city) Lake County	216	0.85

Top 10 Places Sorted by Percent
Based on places with populations of 10,000 or more

Place	Number	%
Munster (town) Lake County	215	1.00
Hobart (city) Lake County	216	0.85
Highland (town) Lake County	197	0.84
Schererville (town) Lake County	181	0.73
Griffith (town) Lake County	105	0.61
Hammond (city) Lake County	412	0.50
Dyer (town) Lake County	67	0.48

Notes: (cdp) census designated place; Refer to the User's Guide in the front of the book for more detailed information.

Place	Number	%
Merrillville (town) Lake County	138	0.45
Brownsburg (town) Hendricks County	62	0.43
Crown Point (city) Lake County	80	0.41

Russian

Top 10 Places Sorted by Number
Based on all places, regardless of population

Place	Number	%
Indianapolis (cons. city) Marion County	2,954	0.38
Bloomington (city) Monroe County	1,054	1.52
Fort Wayne (city) Allen County	636	0.31
Hammond (city) Lake County	612	0.74
Carmel (city) Hamilton County	541	1.43
Granger (cdp) Saint Joseph County	440	1.56
South Bend (city) Saint Joseph County	402	0.38
Evansville (city) Vanderburgh County	374	0.31
West Lafayette (city) Tippecanoe County	302	1.04
Munster (town) Lake County	294	1.37

Top 10 Places Sorted by Percent
Based on all places, regardless of population

Place	Number	%
Burket (town) Kosciusko County	8	4.02
Beverly Shores (town) Porter County	25	3.72
Lakes of the Four Seasons (cdp) Lake County	225	3.08
McCordsville (town) Hancock County	31	2.94
Orland (town) Steuben County	10	2.74
Crows Nest (town) Marion County	2	2.38
Trail Creek (town) La Porte County	52	2.24
Lake Dalecarlia (cdp) Lake County	28	2.22
Koontz Lake (cdp) Starke County	34	2.21
La Crosse (town) La Porte County	10	1.86

Top 10 Places Sorted by Percent
Based on places with populations of 10,000 or more

Place	Number	%
Granger (cdp) Saint Joseph County	440	1.56
Bloomington (city) Monroe County	1,054	1.52
Carmel (city) Hamilton County	541	1.43
Munster (town) Lake County	294	1.37
West Lafayette (city) Tippecanoe County	302	1.04
Hobart (city) Lake County	264	1.04
Schererville (town) Lake County	259	1.04
Valparaiso (city) Porter County	261	0.95
Merrillville (town) Lake County	262	0.85
Crown Point (city) Lake County	162	0.83

Scandinavian

Top 10 Places Sorted by Number
Based on all places, regardless of population

Place	Number	%
Indianapolis (cons. city) Marion County	621	0.08
Fort Wayne (city) Allen County	166	0.08
Bloomington (city) Monroe County	164	0.24
South Bend (city) Saint Joseph County	108	0.10
Lebanon (city) Boone County	92	0.65
Valparaiso (city) Porter County	76	0.28
Columbus (city) Bartholomew County	71	0.18
Carmel (city) Hamilton County	70	0.19
Noblesville (city) Hamilton County	63	0.22
Hammond (city) Lake County	60	0.07

Top 10 Places Sorted by Percent
Based on all places, regardless of population

Place	Number	%
Millersburg (town) Elkhart County	13	1.52
Greenville (town) Floyd County	9	1.45
Summitville (town) Madison County	14	1.28
Russiaville (town) Howard County	13	1.21
Bunker Hill (town) Miami County	10	1.02

Place	Number	%
La Paz (town) Marshall County	5	0.99
Darlington (town) Montgomery County	7	0.80
Harmony (town) Clay County	4	0.75
New Palestine (town) Hancock County	9	0.72
Lebanon (city) Boone County	92	0.65

Top 10 Places Sorted by Percent
Based on places with populations of 10,000 or more

Place	Number	%
Lebanon (city) Boone County	92	0.65
Dyer (town) Lake County	50	0.36
Valparaiso (city) Porter County	76	0.28
Bloomington (city) Monroe County	164	0.24
Noblesville (city) Hamilton County	63	0.22
West Lafayette (city) Tippecanoe County	57	0.20
Connersville (city) Fayette County	31	0.20
Carmel (city) Hamilton County	70	0.19
Columbus (city) Bartholomew County	71	0.18
Vincennes (city) Knox County	28	0.15

Scotch-Irish

Top 10 Places Sorted by Number
Based on all places, regardless of population

Place	Number	%
Indianapolis (cons. city) Marion County	10,322	1.32
Fort Wayne (city) Allen County	2,167	1.05
Evansville (city) Vanderburgh County	1,674	1.37
Bloomington (city) Monroe County	1,556	2.25
South Bend (city) Saint Joseph County	1,305	1.22
Anderson (city) Madison County	902	1.51
Lafayette (city) Tippecanoe County	862	1.53
Muncie (city) Delaware County	830	1.23
Carmel (city) Hamilton County	781	2.07
Hammond (city) Lake County	763	0.92

Top 10 Places Sorted by Percent
Based on all places, regardless of population

Place	Number	%
Country Club Heights (town) Madison County	9	9.68
Crows Nest (town) Marion County	7	8.33
Wynnedale (town) Marion County	27	7.99
Williams Creek (town) Marion County	28	6.83
Modoc (town) Randolph County	12	6.03
Rocky Ripple (town) Marion County	38	5.40
Wingate (town) Montgomery County	17	5.35
New Richmond (town) Montgomery County	18	5.31
Universal (town) Vermillion County	22	5.09
French Lick (town) Orange County	90	4.78

Top 10 Places Sorted by Percent
Based on places with populations of 10,000 or more

Place	Number	%
Chesterton (town) Porter County	264	2.53
Bloomington (city) Monroe County	1,556	2.25
Portage (city) Porter County	704	2.10
Carmel (city) Hamilton County	781	2.07
Hobart (city) Lake County	520	2.05
Crawfordsville (city) Montgomery County	311	2.04
Madison (city) Jefferson County	243	2.01
Beech Grove (city) Marion County	275	1.94
Greenfield (city) Hancock County	274	1.88
Franklin (city) Johnson County	370	1.87

Scottish

Top 10 Places Sorted by Number
Based on all places, regardless of population

Place	Number	%
Indianapolis (cons. city) Marion County	13,190	1.69
Fort Wayne (city) Allen County	3,423	1.66
Bloomington (city) Monroe County	2,107	3.04

Place	Number	%
Evansville (city) Vanderburgh County	1,678	1.38
South Bend (city) Saint Joseph County	1,224	1.14
Fishers (town) Hamilton County	1,223	3.14
Muncie (city) Delaware County	1,167	1.73
Terre Haute (city) Vigo County	1,145	1.92
Carmel (city) Hamilton County	1,065	2.82
Lafayette (city) Tippecanoe County	1,030	1.83

Top 10 Places Sorted by Percent
Based on all places, regardless of population

Place	Number	%
North Crows Nest (town) Marion County	8	19.05
Onward (town) Cass County	6	9.84
Dune Acres (town) Porter County	17	8.81
Spring Hill (town) Marion County	10	8.00
Wynnedale (town) Marion County	27	7.99
Wheatland (town) Knox County	34	6.97
River Forest (town) Madison County	2	6.90
New Ross (town) Montgomery County	22	6.71
Meridian Hills (town) Marion County	95	5.50
Long Beach (town) La Porte County	86	5.46

Top 10 Places Sorted by Percent
Based on places with populations of 10,000 or more

Place	Number	%
Fishers (town) Hamilton County	1,223	3.14
Bloomington (city) Monroe County	2,107	3.04
Noblesville (city) Hamilton County	865	2.99
Granger (cdp) Saint Joseph County	839	2.97
Valparaiso (city) Porter County	815	2.96
West Lafayette (city) Tippecanoe County	824	2.85
Carmel (city) Hamilton County	1,065	2.82
Beech Grove (city) Marion County	317	2.23
Greenwood (city) Johnson County	794	2.22
Lebanon (city) Boone County	310	2.18

Serbian

Top 10 Places Sorted by Number
Based on all places, regardless of population

Place	Number	%
Schererville (town) Lake County	1,137	4.58
Hammond (city) Lake County	567	0.68
Munster (town) Lake County	479	2.23
Merrillville (town) Lake County	462	1.50
Crown Point (city) Lake County	458	2.34
Hobart (city) Lake County	415	1.63
Indianapolis (cons. city) Marion County	332	0.04
Highland (town) Lake County	298	1.27
Portage (city) Porter County	231	0.69
East Chicago (city) Lake County	220	0.68

Top 10 Places Sorted by Percent
Based on all places, regardless of population

Place	Number	%
North Crows Nest (town) Marion County	5	11.90
Lake Village (cdp) Newton County	59	7.33
Schererville (town) Lake County	1,137	4.58
Ogden Dunes (town) Porter County	48	3.66
Winfield (town) Lake County	63	2.78
Crown Point (city) Lake County	458	2.34
Munster (town) Lake County	479	2.23
Lakes of the Four Seasons (cdp) Lake County	139	1.90
Hobart (city) Lake County	415	1.63
Whitestown (town) Boone County	8	1.51

Top 10 Places Sorted by Percent
Based on places with populations of 10,000 or more

Place	Number	%
Schererville (town) Lake County	1,137	4.58
Crown Point (city) Lake County	458	2.34
Munster (town) Lake County	479	2.23

Notes: (cdp) census designated place; Refer to the User's Guide in the front of the book for more detailed information.

Place	Number	%
Hobart (city) Lake County	415	1.63
Merrillville (town) Lake County	462	1.50
Dyer (town) Lake County	180	1.30
Highland (town) Lake County	298	1.27
Lake Station (city) Lake County	118	0.84
Chesterton (town) Porter County	73	0.70
Portage (city) Porter County	231	0.69

Slavic

Top 10 Places Sorted by Number
Based on all places, regardless of population

Place	Number	%
Indianapolis (cons. city) Marion County	361	0.05
South Bend (city) Saint Joseph County	151	0.14
Hammond (city) Lake County	115	0.14
Fort Wayne (city) Allen County	93	0.05
Zionsville (town) Boone County	53	0.63
Terre Haute (city) Vigo County	49	0.08
Portage (city) Porter County	44	0.13
Bloomington (city) Monroe County	41	0.06
Mishawaka (city) Saint Joseph County	40	0.09
Merrillville (town) Lake County	39	0.13

Top 10 Places Sorted by Percent
Based on all places, regardless of population

Place	Number	%
Burlington (town) Carroll County	6	1.37
Universal (town) Vermillion County	5	1.16
Whitestown (town) Boone County	6	1.13
Monon (town) White County	12	0.68
Winfield (town) Lake County	15	0.66
Zionsville (town) Boone County	53	0.63
Ogden Dunes (town) Porter County	8	0.61
Long Beach (town) La Porte County	9	0.57
Lizton (town) Hendricks County	2	0.52
Plymouth (city) Marshall County	38	0.39

Top 10 Places Sorted by Percent
Based on places with populations of 10,000 or more

Place	Number	%
Dyer (town) Lake County	26	0.19
Chesterton (town) Porter County	19	0.18
South Bend (city) Saint Joseph County	151	0.14
Hammond (city) Lake County	115	0.14
Portage (city) Porter County	44	0.13
Merrillville (town) Lake County	39	0.13
West Lafayette (city) Tippecanoe County	38	0.13
Beech Grove (city) Marion County	18	0.13
Goshen (city) Elkhart County	35	0.12
Warsaw (city) Kosciusko County	15	0.12

Slovak

Top 10 Places Sorted by Number
Based on all places, regardless of population

Place	Number	%
Hammond (city) Lake County	3,259	3.92
Merrillville (town) Lake County	1,025	3.34
Highland (town) Lake County	969	4.12
Whiting (city) Lake County	926	18.03
Munster (town) Lake County	883	4.10
Schererville (town) Lake County	775	3.12
Indianapolis (cons. city) Marion County	743	0.09
Portage (city) Porter County	727	2.17
Hobart (city) Lake County	680	2.68
Crown Point (city) Lake County	668	3.41

Top 10 Places Sorted by Percent
Based on all places, regardless of population

Place	Number	%
Whiting (city) Lake County	926	18.03

Place	Number	%
Spring Hill (town) Marion County	10	8.00
Winfield (town) Lake County	128	5.64
Saint John (town) Lake County	354	4.22
Highland (town) Lake County	969	4.12
Munster (town) Lake County	883	4.10
Hammond (city) Lake County	3,259	3.92
Burns Harbor (town) Porter County	29	3.71
Merom (town) Sullivan County	11	3.63
Crown Point (city) Lake County	668	3.41

Top 10 Places Sorted by Percent
Based on places with populations of 10,000 or more

Place	Number	%
Highland (town) Lake County	969	4.12
Munster (town) Lake County	883	4.10
Hammond (city) Lake County	3,259	3.92
Crown Point (city) Lake County	668	3.41
Merrillville (town) Lake County	1,025	3.34
Schererville (town) Lake County	775	3.12
Griffith (town) Lake County	499	2.88
Chesterton (town) Porter County	282	2.70
Hobart (city) Lake County	680	2.68
Dyer (town) Lake County	311	2.24

Slovene

Top 10 Places Sorted by Number
Based on all places, regardless of population

Place	Number	%
Indianapolis (cons. city) Marion County	734	0.09
Hammond (city) Lake County	125	0.15
Muncie (city) Delaware County	92	0.14
Fort Wayne (city) Allen County	78	0.04
Plainfield (town) Hendricks County	63	0.33
Bloomington (city) Monroe County	60	0.09
Speedway (town) Marion County	59	0.46
Brownsburg (town) Hendricks County	58	0.40
West Lafayette (city) Tippecanoe County	54	0.19
Granger (cdp) Saint Joseph County	43	0.15

Top 10 Places Sorted by Percent
Based on all places, regardless of population

Place	Number	%
Indian Village (town) Saint Joseph County	4	2.86
Southport (city) Marion County	28	1.44
Roseland (town) Saint Joseph County	17	0.94
Long Beach (town) La Porte County	12	0.76
Sulphur Springs (town) Henry County	2	0.55
Owensville (town) Gibson County	7	0.53
Whiting (city) Lake County	25	0.49
Bass Lake (cdp) Starke County	6	0.47
Speedway (town) Marion County	59	0.46
Brownsburg (town) Hendricks County	58	0.40

Top 10 Places Sorted by Percent
Based on places with populations of 10,000 or more

Place	Number	%
Speedway (town) Marion County	59	0.46
Brownsburg (town) Hendricks County	58	0.40
Plainfield (town) Hendricks County	63	0.33
West Lafayette (city) Tippecanoe County	54	0.19
Hammond (city) Lake County	125	0.15
Granger (cdp) Saint Joseph County	43	0.15
Muncie (city) Delaware County	92	0.14
Highland (town) Lake County	30	0.13
Chesterton (town) Porter County	13	0.12
Merrillville (town) Lake County	34	0.11

Soviet Union

Top 10 Places Sorted by Number
Based on all places, regardless of population

Place	Number	%
La Paz (town) Marshall County	6	1.19
Indianapolis (cons. city) Marion County	6	<0.01

Top 10 Places Sorted by Percent
Based on all places, regardless of population

Place	Number	%
La Paz (town) Marshall County	6	1.19
Indianapolis (cons. city) Marion County	6	<0.01

Top 10 Places Sorted by Percent
Based on places with populations of 10,000 or more

Place	Number	%
Indianapolis (cons. city) Marion County	6	<0.01

Swedish

Top 10 Places Sorted by Number
Based on all places, regardless of population

Place	Number	%
Indianapolis (cons. city) Marion County	5,192	0.66
Fort Wayne (city) Allen County	1,779	0.86
South Bend (city) Saint Joseph County	1,364	1.27
Hammond (city) Lake County	1,020	1.23
Bloomington (city) Monroe County	989	1.43
Valparaiso (city) Porter County	983	3.57
Portage (city) Porter County	883	2.63
Mishawaka (city) Saint Joseph County	773	1.65
Schererville (town) Lake County	700	2.82
Granger (cdp) Saint Joseph County	693	2.46

Top 10 Places Sorted by Percent
Based on all places, regardless of population

Place	Number	%
Crows Nest (town) Marion County	9	10.71
Michiana Shores (town) La Porte County	26	9.25
Burns Harbor (town) Porter County	52	6.65
Memphis (cdp) Clark County	22	6.51
Chesterton (town) Porter County	653	6.26
Ogden Dunes (town) Porter County	82	6.25
Pottawattamie Park (town) La Porte County	15	4.98
Bass Lake (cdp) Starke County	62	4.85
Dune Acres (town) Porter County	9	4.66
Porter (town) Porter County	235	4.64

Top 10 Places Sorted by Percent
Based on places with populations of 10,000 or more

Place	Number	%
Chesterton (town) Porter County	653	6.26
Valparaiso (city) Porter County	983	3.57
Munster (town) Lake County	674	3.13
La Porte (city) La Porte County	640	2.96
Schererville (town) Lake County	700	2.82
Dyer (town) Lake County	377	2.72
Portage (city) Porter County	883	2.63
Granger (cdp) Saint Joseph County	693	2.46
Crown Point (city) Lake County	478	2.44
Hobart (city) Lake County	597	2.35

Swiss

Top 10 Places Sorted by Number
Based on all places, regardless of population

Place	Number	%
Indianapolis (cons. city) Marion County	1,939	0.25
Fort Wayne (city) Allen County	1,905	0.93

Notes: (cdp) census designated place; Refer to the User's Guide in the front of the book for more detailed information.

Goshen (city) Elkhart County	1,577	5.38
Berne (city) Adams County	1,184	27.99
Bluffton (city) Wells County	491	5.09
Elkhart (city) Elkhart County	454	0.88
South Bend (city) Saint Joseph County	414	0.39
Decatur (city) Adams County	381	4.03
Bloomington (city) Monroe County	331	0.48
Evansville (city) Vanderburgh County	304	0.25

Top 10 Places Sorted by Percent
Based on all places, regardless of population

Place	Number	%
Berne (city) Adams County	1,184	27.99
Monroe (town) Adams County	91	12.45
Shipshewana (town) La Grange County	50	9.28
Indian Village (town) Saint Joseph County	11	7.86
Amboy (town) Miami County	24	6.78
Bryant (town) Jay County	20	6.73
Geneva (town) Adams County	90	6.52
Middlebury (town) Elkhart County	175	6.08
Wakarusa (town) Elkhart County	95	5.97
Goshen (city) Elkhart County	1,577	5.38

Top 10 Places Sorted by Percent
Based on places with populations of 10,000 or more

Place	Number	%
Goshen (city) Elkhart County	1,577	5.38
New Haven (city) Allen County	138	1.12
Fort Wayne (city) Allen County	1,905	0.93
Elkhart (city) Elkhart County	454	0.88
Auburn (city) De Kalb County	96	0.80
Carmel (city) Hamilton County	294	0.78
West Lafayette (city) Tippecanoe County	226	0.78
Fishers (town) Hamilton County	255	0.65
Crawfordsville (city) Montgomery County	96	0.63
Mishawaka (city) Saint Joseph County	279	0.60

Turkish

Top 10 Places Sorted by Number
Based on all places, regardless of population

Place	Number	%
Indianapolis (cons. city) Marion County	192	0.02
Bloomington (city) Monroe County	121	0.17
Fort Wayne (city) Allen County	65	0.03
Griffith (town) Lake County	58	0.33
Carmel (city) Hamilton County	46	0.12
Muncie (city) Delaware County	39	0.06
Anderson (city) Madison County	38	0.06
West Lafayette (city) Tippecanoe County	36	0.12
East Chicago (city) Lake County	35	0.11
Jasper (city) Dubois County	30	0.25

Top 10 Places Sorted by Percent
Based on all places, regardless of population

Place	Number	%
Kennard (town) Henry County	4	0.92
Cloverdale (town) Putnam County	20	0.89
Griffith (town) Lake County	58	0.33
Meridian Hills (town) Marion County	5	0.29
Highland (cdp) Vanderburgh County	11	0.27
Jasper (city) Dubois County	30	0.25
New Pekin (town) Washington County	3	0.23
Osgood (town) Ripley County	3	0.18
Bloomington (city) Monroe County	121	0.17
Dana (town) Vermillion County	1	0.15

Top 10 Places Sorted by Percent
Based on places with populations of 10,000 or more

Place	Number	%
Griffith (town) Lake County	58	0.33
Jasper (city) Dubois County	30	0.25

Bloomington (city) Monroe County	121	0.17
Huntington (city) Huntington County	23	0.13
Carmel (city) Hamilton County	46	0.12
West Lafayette (city) Tippecanoe County	36	0.12
East Chicago (city) Lake County	35	0.11
Fishers (town) Hamilton County	30	0.08
Chesterton (town) Porter County	7	0.07
Muncie (city) Delaware County	39	0.06

Ukrainian

Top 10 Places Sorted by Number
Based on all places, regardless of population

Place	Number	%
Indianapolis (cons. city) Marion County	924	0.12
Fort Wayne (city) Allen County	341	0.17
Hammond (city) Lake County	307	0.37
Bloomington (city) Monroe County	272	0.39
Mishawaka (city) Saint Joseph County	238	0.51
South Bend (city) Saint Joseph County	196	0.18
Carmel (city) Hamilton County	176	0.47
Schererville (town) Lake County	160	0.64
Munster (town) Lake County	157	0.73
Granger (cdp) Saint Joseph County	143	0.51

Top 10 Places Sorted by Percent
Based on all places, regardless of population

Place	Number	%
Pottawattamie Park (town) La Porte County	12	3.99
Norway (cdp) White County	16	3.25
Hamlet (town) Starke County	16	1.90
Bass Lake (cdp) Starke County	17	1.33
Lakes of the Four Seasons (cdp) Lake County	92	1.26
Woodburn (city) Allen County	18	1.14
Simonton Lake (cdp) Elkhart County	40	1.00
Roselawn (cdp) Jasper County	38	0.97
North Judson (town) Starke County	15	0.91
Burns Harbor (town) Porter County	7	0.90

Top 10 Places Sorted by Percent
Based on places with populations of 10,000 or more

Place	Number	%
Munster (town) Lake County	157	0.73
Schererville (town) Lake County	160	0.64
Mishawaka (city) Saint Joseph County	238	0.51
Granger (cdp) Saint Joseph County	143	0.51
Carmel (city) Hamilton County	176	0.47
West Lafayette (city) Tippecanoe County	129	0.45
Highland (town) Lake County	95	0.40
Bloomington (city) Monroe County	272	0.39
Hammond (city) Lake County	307	0.37
Lake Station (city) Lake County	52	0.37

United States or American

Top 10 Places Sorted by Number
Based on all places, regardless of population

Place	Number	%
Indianapolis (cons. city) Marion County	72,698	9.29
Fort Wayne (city) Allen County	14,422	7.00
Evansville (city) Vanderburgh County	13,067	10.72
Anderson (city) Madison County	9,501	15.93
Muncie (city) Delaware County	8,603	12.75
Terre Haute (city) Vigo County	7,800	13.10
Kokomo (city) Howard County	6,941	15.10
Lafayette (city) Tippecanoe County	6,586	11.71
Columbus (city) Bartholomew County	6,173	15.77
New Albany (city) Floyd County	5,572	14.91

Top 10 Places Sorted by Percent
Based on all places, regardless of population

Place	Number	%
River Forest (town) Madison County	20	68.97
Riley (town) Vigo County	67	46.21
East Germantown (town) Wayne County	101	44.10
Elizabeth (town) Harrison County	59	43.07
Glenwood (town) Rush County	132	42.86
Patriot (town) Switzerland County	88	41.51
Amo (town) Hendricks County	164	40.59
Cannelburg (town) Daviess County	47	38.84
Lewisville (town) Henry County	160	38.55
Sheridan (town) Hamilton County	874	37.11

Top 10 Places Sorted by Percent
Based on places with populations of 10,000 or more

Place	Number	%
Martinsville (city) Morgan County	3,287	27.96
Shelbyville (city) Shelby County	4,092	23.13
Washington (city) Daviess County	2,510	22.26
New Castle (city) Henry County	3,900	21.90
Connersville (city) Fayette County	3,191	20.70
Beech Grove (city) Marion County	2,865	20.18
Seymour (city) Jackson County	3,612	20.06
Bedford (city) Lawrence County	2,541	18.31
Brownsburg (town) Hendricks County	2,565	17.88
Vincennes (city) Knox County	3,242	17.45

Welsh

Top 10 Places Sorted by Number
Based on all places, regardless of population

Place	Number	%
Indianapolis (cons. city) Marion County	5,008	0.64
Fort Wayne (city) Allen County	1,073	0.52
Evansville (city) Vanderburgh County	810	0.66
Bloomington (city) Monroe County	653	0.94
Terre Haute (city) Vigo County	558	0.94
South Bend (city) Saint Joseph County	468	0.44
Anderson (city) Madison County	462	0.77
Muncie (city) Delaware County	438	0.65
Fishers (town) Hamilton County	395	1.01
Elkhart (city) Elkhart County	347	0.67

Top 10 Places Sorted by Percent
Based on all places, regardless of population

Place	Number	%
Fulton (town) Fulton County	15	4.49
Amboy (town) Miami County	13	3.67
Edwardsport (town) Knox County	13	3.61
Little York (town) Washington County	5	2.89
Porter (town) Porter County	141	2.79
Princes Lakes (town) Johnson County	39	2.64
New Washington (cdp) Clark County	14	2.61
Marshall (town) Parke County	10	2.61
Universal (town) Vermillion County	10	2.31
Linden (town) Montgomery County	16	2.26

Top 10 Places Sorted by Percent
Based on places with populations of 10,000 or more

Place	Number	%
Chesterton (town) Porter County	192	1.84
Lebanon (city) Boone County	184	1.29
Crawfordsville (city) Montgomery County	179	1.17
Greenfield (city) Hancock County	168	1.16
Hobart (city) Lake County	268	1.06
Valparaiso (city) Porter County	281	1.02
Fishers (town) Hamilton County	395	1.01
Granger (cdp) Saint Joseph County	280	0.99
Bloomington (city) Monroe County	653	0.94
Terre Haute (city) Vigo County	558	0.94

Notes: (cdp) census designated place; Refer to the User's Guide in the front of the book for more detailed information.

West Indian, excluding Hispanic

Top 10 Places Sorted by Number
Based on all places, regardless of population

Place	Number	%
Indianapolis (cons. city) Marion County	1,306	0.17
Fort Wayne (city) Allen County	383	0.19
Gary (city) Lake County	288	0.28
Hammond (city) Lake County	115	0.14
Lawrence (city) Marion County	102	0.26
South Bend (city) Saint Joseph County	102	0.10
Bloomington (city) Monroe County	81	0.12
Terre Haute (city) Vigo County	55	0.09
Muncie (city) Delaware County	52	0.08
Michigan City (city) La Porte County	48	0.15

Top 10 Places Sorted by Percent
Based on all places, regardless of population

Place	Number	%
Collegeville (cdp) Jasper County	12	1.38
Carlisle (town) Sullivan County	17	0.67
Austin (town) Scott County	26	0.55
Lowell (town) Lake County	29	0.39
Clay City (town) Clay County	4	0.39
Colfax (town) Clinton County	3	0.39
Greendale (city) Dearborn County	15	0.35
Chesterton (town) Porter County	34	0.33
Crothersville (town) Jackson County	5	0.32
Gary (city) Lake County	288	0.28

Top 10 Places Sorted by Percent
Based on places with populations of 10,000 or more

Place	Number	%
Chesterton (town) Porter County	34	0.33
Gary (city) Lake County	288	0.28
Lawrence (city) Marion County	102	0.26
Fort Wayne (city) Allen County	383	0.19
Indianapolis (cons. city) Marion County	1,306	0.17
West Lafayette (city) Tippecanoe County	47	0.16
Michigan City (city) La Porte County	48	0.15
Hammond (city) Lake County	115	0.14
Speedway (town) Marion County	18	0.14
Carmel (city) Hamilton County	48	0.13

West Indian: Bahamian, excluding Hispanic

Top 10 Places Sorted by Number
Based on all places, regardless of population

Place	Number	%
Gary (city) Lake County	41	0.04
Indianapolis (cons. city) Marion County	17	<0.01
Fort Wayne (city) Allen County	7	<0.01
Austin (town) Scott County	6	0.13
Upland (town) Grant County	4	0.10

Top 10 Places Sorted by Percent
Based on all places, regardless of population

Place	Number	%
Austin (town) Scott County	6	0.13
Upland (town) Grant County	4	0.10
Gary (city) Lake County	41	0.04
Indianapolis (cons. city) Marion County	17	<0.01
Fort Wayne (city) Allen County	7	<0.01

Top 10 Places Sorted by Percent
Based on places with populations of 10,000 or more

Place	Number	%
Gary (city) Lake County	41	0.04
Indianapolis (cons. city) Marion County	17	<0.01
Fort Wayne (city) Allen County	7	<0.01

West Indian: Barbadian, excluding Hispanic

Top 10 Places Sorted by Number
Based on all places, regardless of population

Place	Number	%
Chesterton (town) Porter County	34	0.33
Granger (cdp) Saint Joseph County	15	0.05
Indianapolis (cons. city) Marion County	15	<0.01
Fort Wayne (city) Allen County	11	0.01
Richmond (city) Wayne County	7	0.02
Terre Haute (city) Vigo County	7	0.01
Merrillville (town) Lake County	6	0.02

Top 10 Places Sorted by Percent
Based on all places, regardless of population

Place	Number	%
Chesterton (town) Porter County	34	0.33
Granger (cdp) Saint Joseph County	15	0.05
Richmond (city) Wayne County	7	0.02
Merrillville (town) Lake County	6	0.02
Fort Wayne (city) Allen County	11	0.01
Terre Haute (city) Vigo County	7	0.01
Indianapolis (cons. city) Marion County	15	<0.01

Top 10 Places Sorted by Percent
Based on places with populations of 10,000 or more

Place	Number	%
Chesterton (town) Porter County	34	0.33
Granger (cdp) Saint Joseph County	15	0.05
Richmond (city) Wayne County	7	0.02
Merrillville (town) Lake County	6	0.02
Fort Wayne (city) Allen County	11	0.01
Terre Haute (city) Vigo County	7	0.01
Indianapolis (cons. city) Marion County	15	<0.01

West Indian: Belizean, excluding Hispanic

Top 10 Places Sorted by Number
Based on all places, regardless of population

Place	Number	%
Indianapolis (cons. city) Marion County	37	<0.01
Muncie (city) Delaware County	21	0.03
East Chicago (city) Lake County	11	0.03
Elkhart (city) Elkhart County	7	0.01
Fort Wayne (city) Allen County	5	<0.01
Speedway (town) Marion County	4	0.03
Gary (city) Lake County	4	<0.01

Top 10 Places Sorted by Percent
Based on all places, regardless of population

Place	Number	%
Muncie (city) Delaware County	21	0.03
East Chicago (city) Lake County	11	0.03
Speedway (town) Marion County	4	0.03
Elkhart (city) Elkhart County	7	0.01
Indianapolis (cons. city) Marion County	37	<0.01
Fort Wayne (city) Allen County	5	<0.01
Gary (city) Lake County	4	<0.01

Top 10 Places Sorted by Percent
Based on places with populations of 10,000 or more

Place	Number	%
Muncie (city) Delaware County	21	0.03
East Chicago (city) Lake County	11	0.03
Speedway (town) Marion County	4	0.03
Elkhart (city) Elkhart County	7	0.01
Indianapolis (cons. city) Marion County	37	<0.01
Fort Wayne (city) Allen County	5	<0.01
Gary (city) Lake County	4	<0.01

West Indian: Bermudan, excluding Hispanic

Top 10 Places Sorted by Number
Based on all places, regardless of population

Place	Number	%
Hammond (city) Lake County	13	0.02
Merrillville (town) Lake County	11	0.04
Anderson (city) Madison County	9	0.02
South Bend (city) Saint Joseph County	6	0.01

Top 10 Places Sorted by Percent
Based on all places, regardless of population

Place	Number	%
Merrillville (town) Lake County	11	0.04
Hammond (city) Lake County	13	0.02
Anderson (city) Madison County	9	0.02
South Bend (city) Saint Joseph County	6	0.01

Top 10 Places Sorted by Percent
Based on places with populations of 10,000 or more

Place	Number	%
Merrillville (town) Lake County	11	0.04
Hammond (city) Lake County	13	0.02
Anderson (city) Madison County	9	0.02
South Bend (city) Saint Joseph County	6	0.01

West Indian: British West Indian, excluding Hispanic

Top 10 Places Sorted by Number
Based on all places, regardless of population

Place	Number	%
Fort Wayne (city) Allen County	35	0.02
Indianapolis (cons. city) Marion County	19	<0.01
Lawrence (city) Marion County	10	0.03
Greencastle (city) Putnam County	8	0.08
Merrillville (town) Lake County	8	0.03
Hammond (city) Lake County	7	0.01
Gary (city) Lake County	6	0.01
Kokomo (city) Howard County	6	0.01

Top 10 Places Sorted by Percent
Based on all places, regardless of population

Place	Number	%
Greencastle (city) Putnam County	8	0.08
Lawrence (city) Marion County	10	0.03
Merrillville (town) Lake County	8	0.03
Fort Wayne (city) Allen County	35	0.02
Hammond (city) Lake County	7	0.01
Gary (city) Lake County	6	0.01
Kokomo (city) Howard County	6	0.01
Indianapolis (cons. city) Marion County	19	<0.01

Top 10 Places Sorted by Percent
Based on places with populations of 10,000 or more

Place	Number	%
Lawrence (city) Marion County	10	0.03
Merrillville (town) Lake County	8	0.03
Fort Wayne (city) Allen County	35	0.02
Hammond (city) Lake County	7	0.01
Gary (city) Lake County	6	0.01
Kokomo (city) Howard County	6	0.01
Indianapolis (cons. city) Marion County	19	<0.01

Notes: (cdp) census designated place; Refer to the User's Guide in the front of the book for more detailed information.

West Indian: Dutch West Indian, excluding Hispanic

Top 10 Places Sorted by Number
Based on all places, regardless of population

Place	Number	%
Indianapolis (cons. city) Marion County	21	<0.01
Anderson (city) Madison County	13	0.02
North Terre Haute (cdp) Vigo County	9	0.19
Greenwood (city) Johnson County	8	0.02
New Albany (city) Floyd County	7	0.02
Clay City (town) Clay County	4	0.39
Colfax (town) Clinton County	3	0.39
Kouts (town) Porter County	3	0.18
Windfall City (town) Tipton County	1	0.13
Patoka (town) Gibson County	1	0.12

Top 10 Places Sorted by Percent
Based on all places, regardless of population

Place	Number	%
Clay City (town) Clay County	4	0.39
Colfax (town) Clinton County	3	0.39
North Terre Haute (cdp) Vigo County	9	0.19
Kouts (town) Porter County	3	0.18
Windfall City (town) Tipton County	1	0.13
Patoka (town) Gibson County	1	0.12
Anderson (city) Madison County	13	0.02
Greenwood (city) Johnson County	8	0.02
New Albany (city) Floyd County	7	0.02
Indianapolis (cons. city) Marion County	21	<0.01

Top 10 Places Sorted by Percent
Based on places with populations of 10,000 or more

Place	Number	%
Anderson (city) Madison County	13	0.02
Greenwood (city) Johnson County	8	0.02
New Albany (city) Floyd County	7	0.02
Indianapolis (cons. city) Marion County	21	<0.01

West Indian: Haitian, excluding Hispanic

Top 10 Places Sorted by Number
Based on all places, regardless of population

Place	Number	%
Indianapolis (cons. city) Marion County	127	0.02
Fort Wayne (city) Allen County	94	0.05
Gary (city) Lake County	55	0.05
Bloomington (city) Monroe County	48	0.07
Lowell (town) Lake County	29	0.39
Michigan City (city) La Porte County	16	0.05
Speedway (town) Marion County	14	0.11
Munster (town) Lake County	11	0.05
West Lafayette (city) Tippecanoe County	11	0.04
Lafayette (city) Tippecanoe County	11	0.02

Top 10 Places Sorted by Percent
Based on all places, regardless of population

Place	Number	%
Lowell (town) Lake County	29	0.39
Waynetown (town) Montgomery County	2	0.22
Winona Lake (town) Kosciusko County	7	0.18
Speedway (town) Marion County	14	0.11
Bloomington (city) Monroe County	48	0.07
Mooresville (town) Morgan County	5	0.06
Fort Wayne (city) Allen County	94	0.05
Gary (city) Lake County	55	0.05
Michigan City (city) La Porte County	16	0.05
Munster (town) Lake County	11	0.05

Top 10 Places Sorted by Percent
Based on places with populations of 10,000 or more

Place	Number	%
Speedway (town) Marion County	14	0.11
Bloomington (city) Monroe County	48	0.07
Fort Wayne (city) Allen County	94	0.05
Gary (city) Lake County	55	0.05
Michigan City (city) La Porte County	16	0.05
Munster (town) Lake County	11	0.05
West Lafayette (city) Tippecanoe County	11	0.04
Indianapolis (cons. city) Marion County	127	0.02
Lafayette (city) Tippecanoe County	11	0.02
Lawrence (city) Marion County	9	0.02

West Indian: Jamaican, excluding Hispanic

Top 10 Places Sorted by Number
Based on all places, regardless of population

Place	Number	%
Indianapolis (cons. city) Marion County	711	0.09
Fort Wayne (city) Allen County	179	0.09
Gary (city) Lake County	152	0.15
Hammond (city) Lake County	87	0.10
South Bend (city) Saint Joseph County	85	0.08
Carmel (city) Hamilton County	48	0.13
Evansville (city) Vanderburgh County	44	0.04
Terre Haute (city) Vigo County	37	0.06
Lawrence (city) Marion County	32	0.08
Muncie (city) Delaware County	31	0.05

Top 10 Places Sorted by Percent
Based on all places, regardless of population

Place	Number	%
Collegeville (cdp) Jasper County	6	0.69
Austin (town) Scott County	20	0.42
Greendale (city) Dearborn County	15	0.35
Crothersville (town) Jackson County	5	0.32
Cedar Lake (town) Lake County	16	0.17
Covington (city) Fountain County	4	0.16
Gary (city) Lake County	152	0.15
Carmel (city) Hamilton County	48	0.13
Hammond (city) Lake County	87	0.10
Indianapolis (cons. city) Marion County	711	0.09

Top 10 Places Sorted by Percent
Based on places with populations of 10,000 or more

Place	Number	%
Gary (city) Lake County	152	0.15
Carmel (city) Hamilton County	48	0.13
Hammond (city) Lake County	87	0.10
Indianapolis (cons. city) Marion County	711	0.09
Fort Wayne (city) Allen County	179	0.09
South Bend (city) Saint Joseph County	85	0.08
Lawrence (city) Marion County	32	0.08
Jeffersonville (city) Clark County	22	0.08
Terre Haute (city) Vigo County	37	0.06
Fishers (town) Hamilton County	25	0.06

West Indian: Trinidadian and Tobagonian, excluding Hispanic

Top 10 Places Sorted by Number
Based on all places, regardless of population

Place	Number	%
Indianapolis (cons. city) Marion County	170	0.02
Lawrence (city) Marion County	51	0.13
Fort Wayne (city) Allen County	39	0.02
Lafayette (city) Tippecanoe County	28	0.05
Gary (city) Lake County	17	0.02
Hobart (city) Lake County	7	0.03
Collegeville (cdp) Jasper County	6	0.69
Bloomington (city) Monroe County	6	0.01
West Lafayette (city) Tippecanoe County	5	0.02
South Bend (city) Saint Joseph County	4	<0.01

Top 10 Places Sorted by Percent
Based on all places, regardless of population

Place	Number	%
Collegeville (cdp) Jasper County	6	0.69
Spiceland (town) Henry County	2	0.26
Lawrence (city) Marion County	51	0.13
Lafayette (city) Tippecanoe County	28	0.05
Hobart (city) Lake County	7	0.03
Indianapolis (cons. city) Marion County	170	0.02
Fort Wayne (city) Allen County	39	0.02
Gary (city) Lake County	17	0.02
West Lafayette (city) Tippecanoe County	5	0.02
Bloomington (city) Monroe County	6	0.01

Top 10 Places Sorted by Percent
Based on places with populations of 10,000 or more

Place	Number	%
Lawrence (city) Marion County	51	0.13
Lafayette (city) Tippecanoe County	28	0.05
Hobart (city) Lake County	7	0.03
Indianapolis (cons. city) Marion County	170	0.02
Fort Wayne (city) Allen County	39	0.02
Gary (city) Lake County	17	0.02
West Lafayette (city) Tippecanoe County	5	0.02
Bloomington (city) Monroe County	6	0.01
South Bend (city) Saint Joseph County	4	<0.01

West Indian: U.S. Virgin Islander, excluding Hispanic

Top 10 Places Sorted by Number
Based on all places, regardless of population

Place	Number	%
Indianapolis (cons. city) Marion County	41	0.01
Greencastle (city) Putnam County	11	0.11
Lafayette (city) Tippecanoe County	7	0.01
Jeffersonville (city) Clark County	4	0.01

Top 10 Places Sorted by Percent
Based on all places, regardless of population

Place	Number	%
Greencastle (city) Putnam County	11	0.11
Indianapolis (cons. city) Marion County	41	0.01
Lafayette (city) Tippecanoe County	7	0.01
Jeffersonville (city) Clark County	4	0.01

Top 10 Places Sorted by Percent
Based on places with populations of 10,000 or more

Place	Number	%
Indianapolis (cons. city) Marion County	41	0.01
Lafayette (city) Tippecanoe County	7	0.01
Jeffersonville (city) Clark County	4	0.01

West Indian: West Indian, excluding Hispanic

Top 10 Places Sorted by Number
Based on all places, regardless of population

Place	Number	%
Indianapolis (cons. city) Marion County	148	0.02
Columbus (city) Bartholomew County	24	0.06
Michigan City (city) La Porte County	20	0.06
Carlisle (town) Sullivan County	17	0.67
Peru (city) Miami County	16	0.12
West Lafayette (city) Tippecanoe County	15	0.05
Fort Wayne (city) Allen County	13	0.01
Gary (city) Lake County	13	0.01

Notes: (cdp) census designated place; Refer to the User's Guide in the front of the book for more detailed information.

Place		Number	%
Logansport (city) Cass County		9	0.05
Auburn (city) De Kalb County		8	0.07

Top 10 Places Sorted by Percent
Based on all places, regardless of population

Place	Number	%
Carlisle (town) Sullivan County	17	0.67
Peru (city) Miami County	16	0.12
Auburn (city) De Kalb County	8	0.07
Columbus (city) Bartholomew County	24	0.06
Michigan City (city) La Porte County	20	0.06
West Lafayette (city) Tippecanoe County	15	0.05
Logansport (city) Cass County	9	0.05
Indianapolis (cons. city) Marion County	148	0.02
Munster (town) Lake County	5	0.02
Fort Wayne (city) Allen County	13	0.01

Top 10 Places Sorted by Percent
Based on places with populations of 10,000 or more

Place	Number	%
Peru (city) Miami County	16	0.12
Auburn (city) De Kalb County	8	0.07
Columbus (city) Bartholomew County	24	0.06
Michigan City (city) La Porte County	20	0.06
West Lafayette (city) Tippecanoe County	15	0.05
Logansport (city) Cass County	9	0.05
Indianapolis (cons. city) Marion County	148	0.02
Munster (town) Lake County	5	0.02
Fort Wayne (city) Allen County	13	0.01
Gary (city) Lake County	13	0.01

West Indian: Other, excluding Hispanic

Top 10 Places Sorted by Number
Based on all places, regardless of population

Place	Number	%
Marion (city) Grant County	7	0.02

Top 10 Places Sorted by Percent
Based on all places, regardless of population

Place	Number	%
Marion (city) Grant County	7	0.02

Top 10 Places Sorted by Percent
Based on places with populations of 10,000 or more

Place	Number	%
Marion (city) Grant County	7	0.02

White

Top 10 Places Sorted by Number
Based on all places, regardless of population

Place	Number	%
Indianapolis (cons. city) Marion County	550,768	70.44
Fort Wayne (city) Allen County	159,264	77.42
Evansville (city) Vanderburgh County	106,366	87.48
South Bend (city) Saint Joseph County	73,709	68.38
Hammond (city) Lake County	62,135	74.82
Bloomington (city) Monroe County	61,524	88.79
Muncie (city) Delaware County	58,719	87.08
Terre Haute (city) Vigo County	52,448	87.98
Lafayette (city) Tippecanoe County	50,999	90.43
Anderson (city) Madison County	49,736	83.26

Top 10 Places Sorted by Percent
Based on all places, regardless of population

Place	Number	%
New Market (town) Montgomery County	659	100.00
Milton (town) Wayne County	611	100.00
Campbellsburg (town) Washington County	578	100.00

Place		Number	%
Medora (town) Jackson County		565	100.00
Chalmers (town) White County		513	100.00
Perrysville (town) Vermillion County		502	100.00
Lewisville (town) Henry County		395	100.00
Mooreland (town) Henry County		393	100.00
Markleville (town) Madison County		383	100.00
Burnettsville (town) White County		373	100.00

Top 10 Places Sorted by Percent
Based on places with populations of 10,000 or more

Place	Number	%
Martinsville (city) Morgan County	11,600	99.16
Greenfield (city) Hancock County	14,431	98.84
Huntington (city) Huntington County	17,187	98.49
Auburn (city) De Kalb County	11,892	98.49
Lebanon (city) Boone County	13,982	98.31
Greensburg (city) Decatur County	10,080	98.25
Brownsburg (town) Hendricks County	14,263	98.23
New Haven (city) Allen County	12,181	98.19
Bedford (city) Lawrence County	13,451	97.70
Jasper (city) Dubois County	11,816	97.65

White: Not Hispanic

Top 10 Places Sorted by Number
Based on all places, regardless of population

Place	Number	%
Indianapolis (cons. city) Marion County	536,689	68.64
Fort Wayne (city) Allen County	153,635	74.68
Evansville (city) Vanderburgh County	105,476	86.75
South Bend (city) Saint Joseph County	70,206	65.13
Bloomington (city) Monroe County	60,477	87.28
Muncie (city) Delaware County	58,167	86.26
Hammond (city) Lake County	52,917	63.72
Terre Haute (city) Vigo County	51,799	86.89
Anderson (city) Madison County	48,998	82.03
Lafayette (city) Tippecanoe County	48,481	85.96

Top 10 Places Sorted by Percent
Based on all places, regardless of population

Place	Number	%
Perrysville (town) Vermillion County	502	100.00
Lewisville (town) Henry County	395	100.00
Markleville (town) Madison County	383	100.00
Marshall (town) Parke County	360	100.00
Glenwood (town) Rush County	318	100.00
Hazleton (town) Gibson County	288	100.00
Losantville (town) Randolph County	280	100.00
Poneto (town) Wells County	240	100.00
Cedar Grove (town) Franklin County	185	100.00
Little York (town) Washington County	185	100.00

Top 10 Places Sorted by Percent
Based on places with populations of 10,000 or more

Place	Number	%
Martinsville (city) Morgan County	11,515	98.44
Greenfield (city) Hancock County	14,295	97.91
Greensburg (city) Decatur County	10,030	97.76
Huntington (city) Huntington County	17,045	97.68
Brownsburg (town) Hendricks County	14,150	97.45
Lebanon (city) Boone County	13,843	97.34
Auburn (city) De Kalb County	11,752	97.33
Bedford (city) Lawrence County	13,359	97.03
New Haven (city) Allen County	11,998	96.71
Franklin (city) Johnson County	18,812	96.66

White: Hispanic

Top 10 Places Sorted by Number
Based on all places, regardless of population

Place		Number	%
Indianapolis (cons. city) Marion County		14,079	1.80

Place	Number	%
Hammond (city) Lake County	9,218	11.10
East Chicago (city) Lake County	8,428	26.00
Fort Wayne (city) Allen County	5,629	2.74
South Bend (city) Saint Joseph County	3,503	3.25
Elkhart (city) Elkhart County	2,815	5.43
Lafayette (city) Tippecanoe County	2,518	4.46
Gary (city) Lake County	2,239	2.18
Portage (city) Porter County	2,190	6.54
Goshen (city) Elkhart County	2,121	7.22

Top 10 Places Sorted by Percent
Based on all places, regardless of population

Place	Number	%
East Chicago (city) Lake County	8,428	26.00
Whiting (city) Lake County	809	15.75
Hammond (city) Lake County	9,218	11.10
Lake Station (city) Lake County	1,512	10.84
Plymouth (city) Marshall County	839	8.53
Ambia (town) Benton County	16	8.12
Ligonier (city) Noble County	350	8.03
New Chicago (town) Lake County	157	7.61
Akron (town) Fulton County	80	7.43
Goshen (city) Elkhart County	2,121	7.22

Top 10 Places Sorted by Percent
Based on places with populations of 10,000 or more

Place	Number	%
East Chicago (city) Lake County	8,428	26.00
Hammond (city) Lake County	9,218	11.10
Lake Station (city) Lake County	1,512	10.84
Goshen (city) Elkhart County	2,121	7.22
Logansport (city) Cass County	1,296	6.58
Portage (city) Porter County	2,190	6.54
Merrillville (town) Lake County	1,797	5.88
Elkhart (city) Elkhart County	2,815	5.43
Frankfort (city) Clinton County	904	5.43
Hobart (city) Lake County	1,352	5.33

Yugoslavian

Top 10 Places Sorted by Number
Based on all places, regardless of population

Place	Number	%
Indianapolis (cons. city) Marion County	757	0.10
Fort Wayne (city) Allen County	683	0.33
South Bend (city) Saint Joseph County	224	0.21
Hammond (city) Lake County	206	0.25
Hobart (city) Lake County	132	0.52
Brownsburg (town) Hendricks County	123	0.86
Merrillville (town) Lake County	122	0.40
Munster (town) Lake County	115	0.53
Crown Point (city) Lake County	103	0.53
Highland (town) Lake County	79	0.34

Top 10 Places Sorted by Percent
Based on all places, regardless of population

Place	Number	%
Spring Hill (town) Marion County	3	2.40
Boston (town) Wayne County	3	1.52
New Whiteland (town) Johnson County	51	1.08
Brownsburg (town) Hendricks County	123	0.86
Wanatah (town) La Porte County	8	0.79
Berne (city) Adams County	32	0.76
West Harrison (town) Dearborn County	2	0.74
Middlebury (town) Elkhart County	18	0.63
Gosport (town) Owen County	4	0.57
Chesterton (town) Porter County	56	0.54

Top 10 Places Sorted by Percent
Based on places with populations of 10,000 or more

Place	Number	%
Brownsburg (town) Hendricks County	123	0.86

Notes: (cdp) census designated place; Refer to the User's Guide in the front of the book for more detailed information.

Chesterton (town) Porter County	56	0.54
Munster (town) Lake County	115	0.53
Crown Point (city) Lake County	103	0.53
Hobart (city) Lake County	132	0.52
Merrillville (town) Lake County	122	0.40
Highland (town) Lake County	79	0.34
Fort Wayne (city) Allen County	683	0.33
Dyer (town) Lake County	44	0.32
Hammond (city) Lake County	206	0.25

Hispanic Population

Population

Total Population
Top 10 Places Sorted by Number

Place	Number
Indianapolis, IN (cons. city) Marion County	792,217
Fort Wayne, IN (city) Allen County	205,941
Evansville, IN (city) Vanderburgh County	121,877
South Bend, IN (city) Saint Joseph County	107,045
Gary, IN (city) Lake County	102,746
Hammond, IN (city) Lake County	83,048
Bloomington, IN (city) Monroe County	69,229
Muncie, IN (city) Delaware County	67,468
Anderson, IN (city) Madison County	59,636
Terre Haute, IN (city) Vigo County	59,563

Hispanic
Top 10 Places Sorted by Number

Place	Number
Indianapolis, IN (cons. city) Marion County	29,732
Hammond, IN (city) Lake County	17,459
East Chicago, IN (city) Lake County	16,720
Fort Wayne, IN (city) Allen County	11,752
South Bend, IN (city) Saint Joseph County	9,117
Elkhart, IN (city) Elkhart County	8,126
Goshen, IN (city) Elkhart County	5,846
Lafayette, IN (city) Tippecanoe County	5,309
Gary, IN (city) Lake County	4,806
Portage, IN (city) Porter County	3,492

Hispanic
Top 10 Places Sorted by Percent of Total Population

Place	Percent
East Chicago, IN (city) Lake County	51.58
Hammond, IN (city) Lake County	21.02
Goshen, IN (city) Elkhart County	19.96
Lake Station, IN (city) Lake County	19.79
Elkhart, IN (city) Elkhart County	15.72
Frankfort, IN (city) Clinton County	13.93
Logansport, IN (city) Cass County	12.42
Warsaw, IN (city) Kosciusko County	10.93
Portage, IN (city) Porter County	10.41
Lafayette, IN (city) Tippecanoe County	9.44

Argentinian
Top 10 Places Sorted by Number

Place	Number
No places met population threshold.	

Argentinian
Top 10 Places Sorted by Percent of Hispanic Population

Place	Percent
No places met population threshold.	

Argentinian
Top 10 Places Sorted by Percent of Total Population

Place	Percent
No places met population threshold.	

Bolivian
Top 10 Places Sorted by Number

Place	Number
No places met population threshold.	

Bolivian
Top 10 Places Sorted by Percent of Hispanic Population

Place	Percent
No places met population threshold.	

Bolivian
Top 10 Places Sorted by Percent of Total Population

Place	Percent
No places met population threshold.	

Central American
Top 10 Places Sorted by Number

Place	Number
Indianapolis, IN (cons. city) Marion County	1,721

Central American
Top 10 Places Sorted by Percent of Hispanic Population

Place	Percent
Indianapolis, IN (cons. city) Marion County	5.79

Central American
Top 10 Places Sorted by Percent of Total Population

Place	Percent
Indianapolis, IN (cons. city) Marion County	0.22

Chilean
Top 10 Places Sorted by Number

Place	Number
No places met population threshold.	

Chilean
Top 10 Places Sorted by Percent of Hispanic Population

Place	Percent
No places met population threshold.	

Chilean
Top 10 Places Sorted by Percent of Total Population

Place	Percent
No places met population threshold.	

Colombian
Top 10 Places Sorted by Number

Place	Number
No places met population threshold.	

Colombian
Top 10 Places Sorted by Percent of Hispanic Population

Place	Percent
No places met population threshold.	

Colombian
Top 10 Places Sorted by Percent of Total Population

Place	Percent
No places met population threshold.	

Costa Rican
Top 10 Places Sorted by Number

Place	Number
No places met population threshold.	

Costa Rican
Top 10 Places Sorted by Percent of Hispanic Population

Place	Percent
No places met population threshold.	

Costa Rican
Top 10 Places Sorted by Percent of Total Population

Place	Percent
No places met population threshold.	

Cuban
Top 10 Places Sorted by Number

Place	Number
Indianapolis, IN (cons. city) Marion County	543

Cuban
Top 10 Places Sorted by Percent of Hispanic Population

Place	Percent
Indianapolis, IN (cons. city) Marion County	1.83

Cuban
Top 10 Places Sorted by Percent of Total Population

Place	Percent
Indianapolis, IN (cons. city) Marion County	0.07

Dominican
Top 10 Places Sorted by Number

Place	Number
No places met population threshold.	

Dominican
Top 10 Places Sorted by Percent of Hispanic Population

Place	Percent
No places met population threshold.	

Dominican
Top 10 Places Sorted by Percent of Total Population

Place	Percent
No places met population threshold.	

Ecuadorian
Top 10 Places Sorted by Number

Place	Number
No places met population threshold.	

Ecuadorian
Top 10 Places Sorted by Percent of Hispanic Population

Place	Percent
No places met population threshold.	

Ecuadorian
Top 10 Places Sorted by Percent of Total Population

Place	Percent
No places met population threshold.	

Guatemalan
Top 10 Places Sorted by Number

Place	Number
No places met population threshold.	

Guatemalan
Top 10 Places Sorted by Percent of Hispanic Population

Place	Percent
No places met population threshold.	

Guatemalan
Top 10 Places Sorted by Percent of Total Population

Place	Percent
No places met population threshold.	

Honduran
Top 10 Places Sorted by Number

Place	Number
No places met population threshold.	

Notes: Please refer to the User's Guide for an explanation of data; tables include places with populations > 9,999 and reflect only those areas that meet Summary File 4 population thresholds, therefore there may be less than 10 places listed

Honduran
Top 10 Places Sorted by Percent of Hispanic Population

Place	Percent
No places met population threshold.	

Honduran
Top 10 Places Sorted by Percent of Total Population

Place	Percent
No places met population threshold.	

Mexican
Top 10 Places Sorted by Number

Place	Number
Indianapolis, IN (cons. city) Marion County	20,787
Hammond, IN (city) Lake County	14,096
East Chicago, IN (city) Lake County	12,307
Fort Wayne, IN (city) Allen County	8,695
South Bend, IN (city) Saint Joseph County	7,182
Elkhart, IN (city) Elkhart County	6,709
Goshen, IN (city) Elkhart County	5,093
Lafayette, IN (city) Tippecanoe County	4,470
Gary, IN (city) Lake County	2,850
Merrillville, IN (town) Lake County	2,176

Mexican
Top 10 Places Sorted by Percent of Hispanic Population

Place	Percent
Crawfordsville, IN (city) Montgomery County	92.66
Washington, IN (city) Daviess County	90.51
Frankfort, IN (city) Clinton County	90.26
Goshen, IN (city) Elkhart County	87.12
Logansport, IN (city) Cass County	84.46
Lafayette, IN (city) Tippecanoe County	84.20
Elkhart, IN (city) Elkhart County	82.56
Marion, IN (city) Grant County	82.08
Seymour, IN (city) Jackson County	81.31
Hammond, IN (city) Lake County	80.74

Mexican
Top 10 Places Sorted by Percent of Total Population

Place	Percent
East Chicago, IN (city) Lake County	37.97
Goshen, IN (city) Elkhart County	17.39
Hammond, IN (city) Lake County	16.97
Elkhart, IN (city) Elkhart County	12.98
Lake Station, IN (city) Lake County	12.67
Frankfort, IN (city) Clinton County	12.57
Logansport, IN (city) Cass County	10.49
Lafayette, IN (city) Tippecanoe County	7.95
Warsaw, IN (city) Kosciusko County	7.95
Merrillville, IN (town) Lake County	7.09

Nicaraguan
Top 10 Places Sorted by Number

Place	Number
No places met population threshold.	

Nicaraguan
Top 10 Places Sorted by Percent of Hispanic Population

Place	Percent
No places met population threshold.	

Nicaraguan
Top 10 Places Sorted by Percent of Total Population

Place	Percent
No places met population threshold.	

Panamanian
Top 10 Places Sorted by Number

Place	Number
No places met population threshold.	

Panamanian
Top 10 Places Sorted by Percent of Hispanic Population

Place	Percent
No places met population threshold.	

Panamanian
Top 10 Places Sorted by Percent of Total Population

Place	Percent
No places met population threshold.	

Paraguayan
Top 10 Places Sorted by Number

Place	Number
No places met population threshold.	

Paraguayan
Top 10 Places Sorted by Percent of Hispanic Population

Place	Percent
No places met population threshold.	

Paraguayan
Top 10 Places Sorted by Percent of Total Population

Place	Percent
No places met population threshold.	

Peruvian
Top 10 Places Sorted by Number

Place	Number
No places met population threshold.	

Peruvian
Top 10 Places Sorted by Percent of Hispanic Population

Place	Percent
No places met population threshold.	

Peruvian
Top 10 Places Sorted by Percent of Total Population

Place	Percent
No places met population threshold.	

Puerto Rican
Top 10 Places Sorted by Number

Place	Number
East Chicago, IN (city) Lake County	3,067
Indianapolis, IN (cons. city) Marion County	1,974
Hammond, IN (city) Lake County	1,839
Gary, IN (city) Lake County	1,250
Portage, IN (city) Porter County	906
Lake Station, IN (city) Lake County	793
Fort Wayne, IN (city) Allen County	605
Hobart, IN (city) Lake County	480
South Bend, IN (city) Saint Joseph County	476

Puerto Rican
Top 10 Places Sorted by Percent of Hispanic Population

Place	Percent
Lake Station, IN (city) Lake County	28.67
Gary, IN (city) Lake County	26.01
Portage, IN (city) Porter County	25.95
Hobart, IN (city) Lake County	23.32
East Chicago, IN (city) Lake County	18.34
Hammond, IN (city) Lake County	10.53
Indianapolis, IN (cons. city) Marion County	6.64

(continued from Puerto Rican Percent of Hispanic Population)

Place	Percent
South Bend, IN (city) Saint Joseph County	5.22
Fort Wayne, IN (city) Allen County	5.15

Puerto Rican
Top 10 Places Sorted by Percent of Total Population

Place	Percent
East Chicago, IN (city) Lake County	9.46
Lake Station, IN (city) Lake County	5.67
Portage, IN (city) Porter County	2.70
Hammond, IN (city) Lake County	2.21
Hobart, IN (city) Lake County	1.89
Gary, IN (city) Lake County	1.22
South Bend, IN (city) Saint Joseph County	0.44
Fort Wayne, IN (city) Allen County	0.29
Indianapolis, IN (cons. city) Marion County	0.25

Salvadoran
Top 10 Places Sorted by Number

Place	Number
Indianapolis, IN (cons. city) Marion County	457

Salvadoran
Top 10 Places Sorted by Percent of Hispanic Population

Place	Percent
Indianapolis, IN (cons. city) Marion County	1.54

Salvadoran
Top 10 Places Sorted by Percent of Total Population

Place	Percent
Indianapolis, IN (cons. city) Marion County	0.06

South American
Top 10 Places Sorted by Number

Place	Number
Indianapolis, IN (cons. city) Marion County	981

South American
Top 10 Places Sorted by Percent of Hispanic Population

Place	Percent
Indianapolis, IN (cons. city) Marion County	3.30

South American
Top 10 Places Sorted by Percent of Total Population

Place	Percent
Indianapolis, IN (cons. city) Marion County	0.12

Spaniard
Top 10 Places Sorted by Number

Place	Number
No places met population threshold.	

Spaniard
Top 10 Places Sorted by Percent of Hispanic Population

Place	Percent
No places met population threshold.	

Spaniard
Top 10 Places Sorted by Percent of Total Population

Place	Percent
No places met population threshold.	

Uruguayan
Top 10 Places Sorted by Number

Place	Number
No places met population threshold.	

Notes: Please refer to the User's Guide for an explanation of data; tables include places with populations > 9,999 and reflect only those areas that meet Summary File 4 population thresholds, therefore there may be less than 10 places listed

Uruguayan
Top 10 Places Sorted by Percent of Hispanic Population

Place	Percent
No places met population threshold.	

Uruguayan
Top 10 Places Sorted by Percent of Total Population

Place	Percent
No places met population threshold.	

Venezuelan
Top 10 Places Sorted by Number

Place	Number
No places met population threshold.	

Venezuelan
Top 10 Places Sorted by Percent of Hispanic Population

Place	Percent
No places met population threshold.	

Venezuelan
Top 10 Places Sorted by Percent of Total Population

Place	Percent
No places met population threshold.	

Other Hispanic
Top 10 Places Sorted by Number

Place	Number
Indianapolis, IN (cons. city) Marion County	3,503
Fort Wayne, IN (city) Allen County	1,492
Hammond, IN (city) Lake County	1,337
East Chicago, IN (city) Lake County	1,131
South Bend, IN (city) Saint Joseph County	980
Elkhart, IN (city) Elkhart County	726
Gary, IN (city) Lake County	498
Lafayette, IN (city) Tippecanoe County	408

Other Hispanic
Top 10 Places Sorted by Percent of Hispanic Population

Place	Percent
Fort Wayne, IN (city) Allen County	12.70
Indianapolis, IN (cons. city) Marion County	11.78
South Bend, IN (city) Saint Joseph County	10.75
Gary, IN (city) Lake County	10.36
Elkhart, IN (city) Elkhart County	8.93
Lafayette, IN (city) Tippecanoe County	7.69
Hammond, IN (city) Lake County	7.66
East Chicago, IN (city) Lake County	6.76

Other Hispanic
Top 10 Places Sorted by Percent of Total Population

Place	Percent
East Chicago, IN (city) Lake County	3.49
Hammond, IN (city) Lake County	1.61
Elkhart, IN (city) Elkhart County	1.40
South Bend, IN (city) Saint Joseph County	0.92
Lafayette, IN (city) Tippecanoe County	0.73
Fort Wayne, IN (city) Allen County	0.72
Gary, IN (city) Lake County	0.48
Indianapolis, IN (cons. city) Marion County	0.44

Median Age

Total Population
Top 10 Places Sorted by Number

Place	Years
Munster, IN (town) Lake County	43.0
Crown Point, IN (city) Lake County	41.3
Highland, IN (town) Lake County	39.9

	Years
Dyer, IN (town) Lake County	38.4
Schererville, IN (town) Lake County	38.3
Hobart, IN (city) Lake County	38.0
Washington, IN (city) Daviess County	37.7
Merrillville, IN (town) Lake County	37.4
Carmel, IN (city) Hamilton County	37.3
Jeffersonville, IN (city) Clark County	37.1

Hispanic
Top 10 Places Sorted by Number

Place	Years
Crown Point, IN (city) Lake County	33.2
Munster, IN (town) Lake County	30.5
Highland, IN (town) Lake County	30.0
Gary, IN (city) Lake County	29.1
Terre Haute, IN (city) Vigo County	28.0
Schererville, IN (town) Lake County	27.8
Seymour, IN (city) Jackson County	27.7
Merrillville, IN (town) Lake County	27.4
Crawfordsville, IN (city) Montgomery County	27.1
East Chicago, IN (city) Lake County	27.1

Argentinian
Top 10 Places Sorted by Number

Place	Years
No places met population threshold.	

Bolivian
Top 10 Places Sorted by Number

Place	Years
No places met population threshold.	

Central American
Top 10 Places Sorted by Number

Place	Years
Indianapolis, IN (cons. city) Marion County	28.9

Chilean
Top 10 Places Sorted by Number

Place	Years
No places met population threshold.	

Colombian
Top 10 Places Sorted by Number

Place	Years
No places met population threshold.	

Costa Rican
Top 10 Places Sorted by Number

Place	Years
No places met population threshold.	

Cuban
Top 10 Places Sorted by Number

Place	Years
Indianapolis, IN (cons. city) Marion County	26.8

Dominican
Top 10 Places Sorted by Number

Place	Years
No places met population threshold.	

Ecuadorian
Top 10 Places Sorted by Number

Place	Years
No places met population threshold.	

Guatemalan
Top 10 Places Sorted by Number

Place	Years
No places met population threshold.	

Honduran
Top 10 Places Sorted by Number

Place	Years
No places met population threshold.	

Mexican
Top 10 Places Sorted by Number

Place	Years
Crown Point, IN (city) Lake County	33.7
Munster, IN (town) Lake County	33.5
Gary, IN (city) Lake County	29.9
Griffith, IN (town) Lake County	29.3
Michigan City, IN (city) La Porte County	29.3
Highland, IN (town) Lake County	28.5
Schererville, IN (town) Lake County	27.5
Seymour, IN (city) Jackson County	27.5
Crawfordsville, IN (city) Montgomery County	27.3
Dyer, IN (town) Lake County	27.1

Nicaraguan
Top 10 Places Sorted by Number

Place	Years
No places met population threshold.	

Panamanian
Top 10 Places Sorted by Number

Place	Years
No places met population threshold.	

Paraguayan
Top 10 Places Sorted by Number

Place	Years
No places met population threshold.	

Peruvian
Top 10 Places Sorted by Number

Place	Years
No places met population threshold.	

Puerto Rican
Top 10 Places Sorted by Number

Place	Years
East Chicago, IN (city) Lake County	33.0
Gary, IN (city) Lake County	31.6
Lake Station, IN (city) Lake County	31.4
Fort Wayne, IN (city) Allen County	27.6
South Bend, IN (city) Saint Joseph County	26.1
Hammond, IN (city) Lake County	25.0
Indianapolis, IN (cons. city) Marion County	24.8
Portage, IN (city) Porter County	23.9
Hobart, IN (city) Lake County	23.2

Salvadoran
Top 10 Places Sorted by Number

Place	Years
Indianapolis, IN (cons. city) Marion County	28.9

South American
Top 10 Places Sorted by Number

Place	Years
Indianapolis, IN (cons. city) Marion County	30.0

Notes: Please refer to the User's Guide for an explanation of data; tables include places with populations > 9,999 and reflect only those areas that meet Summary File 4 population thresholds, therefore there may be less than 10 places listed

Spaniard
Top 10 Places Sorted by Number

Place	Years
No places met population threshold.	

Uruguayan
Top 10 Places Sorted by Number

Place	Years
No places met population threshold.	

Venezuelan
Top 10 Places Sorted by Number

Place	Years
No places met population threshold.	

Other Hispanic
Top 10 Places Sorted by Number

Place	Years
Indianapolis, IN (cons. city) Marion County	26.8
Lafayette, IN (city) Tippecanoe County	24.3
Fort Wayne, IN (city) Allen County	24.0
Gary, IN (city) Lake County	22.7
South Bend, IN (city) Saint Joseph County	21.8
Elkhart, IN (city) Elkhart County	20.0
Hammond, IN (city) Lake County	18.4
East Chicago, IN (city) Lake County	16.0

Average Household Size

Total Population
Top 10 Places Sorted by Number

Place	Number
Dyer, IN (town) Lake County	2.80
East Chicago, IN (city) Lake County	2.76
Lake Station, IN (city) Lake County	2.75
Carmel, IN (city) Hamilton County	2.72
Fishers, IN (town) Hamilton County	2.71
Gary, IN (city) Lake County	2.66
Noblesville, IN (city) Hamilton County	2.63
Goshen, IN (city) Elkhart County	2.61
Lawrence, IN (city) Marion County	2.61
Munster, IN (town) Lake County	2.61

Hispanic
Top 10 Places Sorted by Number

Place	Number
Goshen, IN (city) Elkhart County	4.59
Washington, IN (city) Daviess County	4.23
Frankfort, IN (city) Clinton County	4.06
Elkhart, IN (city) Elkhart County	3.99
Crawfordsville, IN (city) Montgomery County	3.95
South Bend, IN (city) Saint Joseph County	3.81
Logansport, IN (city) Cass County	3.78
Warsaw, IN (city) Kosciusko County	3.75
Dyer, IN (town) Lake County	3.62
Michigan City, IN (city) La Porte County	3.61

Argentinian
Top 10 Places Sorted by Number

Place	Number
No places met population threshold.	

Bolivian
Top 10 Places Sorted by Number

Place	Number
No places met population threshold.	

Central American
Top 10 Places Sorted by Number

Place	Number
Indianapolis, IN (cons. city) Marion County	3.29

Chilean
Top 10 Places Sorted by Number

Place	Number
No places met population threshold.	

Colombian
Top 10 Places Sorted by Number

Place	Number
No places met population threshold.	

Costa Rican
Top 10 Places Sorted by Number

Place	Number
No places met population threshold.	

Cuban
Top 10 Places Sorted by Number

Place	Number
Indianapolis, IN (cons. city) Marion County	1.94

Dominican
Top 10 Places Sorted by Number

Place	Number
No places met population threshold.	

Ecuadorian
Top 10 Places Sorted by Number

Place	Number
No places met population threshold.	

Guatemalan
Top 10 Places Sorted by Number

Place	Number
No places met population threshold.	

Honduran
Top 10 Places Sorted by Number

Place	Number
No places met population threshold.	

Mexican
Top 10 Places Sorted by Number

Place	Number
Goshen, IN (city) Elkhart County	4.61
Warsaw, IN (city) Kosciusko County	4.37
Frankfort, IN (city) Clinton County	4.35
Columbus, IN (city) Bartholomew County	4.31
Washington, IN (city) Daviess County	4.28
South Bend, IN (city) Saint Joseph County	4.10
Elkhart, IN (city) Elkhart County	4.06
Crawfordsville, IN (city) Montgomery County	3.97
Logansport, IN (city) Cass County	3.84
Lafayette, IN (city) Tippecanoe County	3.80

Nicaraguan
Top 10 Places Sorted by Number

Place	Number
No places met population threshold.	

Panamanian
Top 10 Places Sorted by Number

Place	Number
No places met population threshold.	

Paraguayan
Top 10 Places Sorted by Number

Place	Number
No places met population threshold.	

Peruvian
Top 10 Places Sorted by Number

Place	Number
No places met population threshold.	

Puerto Rican
Top 10 Places Sorted by Number

Place	Number
Hammond, IN (city) Lake County	3.58
Portage, IN (city) Porter County	3.44
Hobart, IN (city) Lake County	3.26
Fort Wayne, IN (city) Allen County	3.05
South Bend, IN (city) Saint Joseph County	3.05
Lake Station, IN (city) Lake County	2.98
Gary, IN (city) Lake County	2.82
East Chicago, IN (city) Lake County	2.76
Indianapolis, IN (cons. city) Marion County	2.51

Salvadoran
Top 10 Places Sorted by Number

Place	Number
Indianapolis, IN (cons. city) Marion County	3.41

South American
Top 10 Places Sorted by Number

Place	Number
Indianapolis, IN (cons. city) Marion County	2.63

Spaniard
Top 10 Places Sorted by Number

Place	Number
No places met population threshold.	

Uruguayan
Top 10 Places Sorted by Number

Place	Number
No places met population threshold.	

Venezuelan
Top 10 Places Sorted by Number

Place	Number
No places met population threshold.	

Other Hispanic
Top 10 Places Sorted by Number

Place	Number
Elkhart, IN (city) Elkhart County	3.88
East Chicago, IN (city) Lake County	3.77
South Bend, IN (city) Saint Joseph County	3.46
Gary, IN (city) Lake County	3.45
Hammond, IN (city) Lake County	3.17
Lafayette, IN (city) Tippecanoe County	3.01
Fort Wayne, IN (city) Allen County	2.85
Indianapolis, IN (cons. city) Marion County	2.73

Notes: Please refer to the User's Guide for an explanation of data; tables include places with populations > 9,999 and reflect only those areas that meet Summary File 4 population thresholds, therefore there may be less than 10 places listed

Language Spoken: English Only

Total Population 5 Years and Over Who Speak English-Only at Home
Top 10 Places Sorted by Number

Place	Number
Indianapolis, IN (cons. city) Marion County	680,564
Fort Wayne, IN (city) Allen County	173,752
Evansville, IN (city) Vanderburgh County	109,760
Gary, IN (city) Lake County	88,200
South Bend, IN (city) Saint Joseph County	86,206
Hammond, IN (city) Lake County	62,066
Muncie, IN (city) Delaware County	60,865
Bloomington, IN (city) Monroe County	58,783
Terre Haute, IN (city) Vigo County	53,514
Anderson, IN (city) Madison County	53,470

Total Population 5 Years and Over Who Speak English-Only at Home
Top 10 Places Sorted by Percent

Place	Percent
Jeffersonville, IN (city) Clark County	96.80
Noblesville, IN (city) Hamilton County	96.30
Evansville, IN (city) Vanderburgh County	96.20
Greenwood, IN (city) Johnson County	96.20
Anderson, IN (city) Madison County	96.18
Clarksville, IN (town) Clark County	96.17
Muncie, IN (city) Delaware County	95.84
Kokomo, IN (city) Howard County	95.75
Terre Haute, IN (city) Vigo County	95.59
Crawfordsville, IN (city) Montgomery County	95.16

Hispanics 5 Years and Over Who Speak English-Only at Home
Top 10 Places Sorted by Number

Place	Number
Indianapolis, IN (cons. city) Marion County	6,937
Hammond, IN (city) Lake County	4,636
Fort Wayne, IN (city) Allen County	3,235
East Chicago, IN (city) Lake County	2,739
Gary, IN (city) Lake County	1,675
Portage, IN (city) Porter County	1,667
South Bend, IN (city) Saint Joseph County	1,574
Hobart, IN (city) Lake County	1,239
Merrillville, IN (town) Lake County	1,177
Lake Station, IN (city) Lake County	1,166

Hispanics 5 Years and Over Who Speak English-Only at Home
Top 10 Places Sorted by Percent

Place	Percent
Muncie, IN (city) Delaware County	66.67
Hobart, IN (city) Lake County	66.22
Munster, IN (town) Lake County	59.78
Schererville, IN (town) Lake County	58.24
Dyer, IN (town) Lake County	57.78
Jeffersonville, IN (city) Clark County	54.88
Evansville, IN (city) Vanderburgh County	53.74
Portage, IN (city) Porter County	53.52
Valparaiso, IN (city) Porter County	51.76
Noblesville, IN (city) Hamilton County	50.12

Argentinians 5 Years and Over Who Speak English-Only at Home
Top 10 Places Sorted by Number

Place	Number
No places met population threshold.	

Argentinians 5 Years and Over Who Speak English-Only at Home
Top 10 Places Sorted by Percent

Place	Percent
No places met population threshold.	

Bolivians 5 Years and Over Who Speak English-Only at Home
Top 10 Places Sorted by Number

Place	Number
No places met population threshold.	

Bolivians 5 Years and Over Who Speak English-Only at Home
Top 10 Places Sorted by Percent

Place	Percent
No places met population threshold.	

Central Americans 5 Years and Over Who Speak English-Only at Home
Top 10 Places Sorted by Number

Place	Number
Indianapolis, IN (cons. city) Marion County	131

Central Americans 5 Years and Over Who Speak English-Only at Home
Top 10 Places Sorted by Percent

Place	Percent
Indianapolis, IN (cons. city) Marion County	7.83

Chileans 5 Years and Over Who Speak English-Only at Home
Top 10 Places Sorted by Number

Place	Number
No places met population threshold.	

Chileans 5 Years and Over Who Speak English-Only at Home
Top 10 Places Sorted by Percent

Place	Percent
No places met population threshold.	

Colombians 5 Years and Over Who Speak English-Only at Home
Top 10 Places Sorted by Number

Place	Number
No places met population threshold.	

Colombians 5 Years and Over Who Speak English-Only at Home
Top 10 Places Sorted by Percent

Place	Percent
No places met population threshold.	

Costa Ricans 5 Years and Over Who Speak English-Only at Home
Top 10 Places Sorted by Number

Place	Number
No places met population threshold.	

Costa Ricans 5 Years and Over Who Speak English-Only at Home
Top 10 Places Sorted by Percent

Place	Percent
No places met population threshold.	

Cubans 5 Years and Over Who Speak English-Only at Home
Top 10 Places Sorted by Number

Place	Number
Indianapolis, IN (cons. city) Marion County	206

Cubans 5 Years and Over Who Speak English-Only at Home
Top 10 Places Sorted by Percent

Place	Percent
Indianapolis, IN (cons. city) Marion County	40.87

Dominicans 5 Years and Over Who Speak English-Only at Home
Top 10 Places Sorted by Number

Place	Number
No places met population threshold.	

Dominicans 5 Years and Over Who Speak English-Only at Home
Top 10 Places Sorted by Percent

Place	Percent
No places met population threshold.	

Ecuadorians 5 Years and Over Who Speak English-Only at Home
Top 10 Places Sorted by Number

Place	Number
No places met population threshold.	

Ecuadorians 5 Years and Over Who Speak English-Only at Home
Top 10 Places Sorted by Percent

Place	Percent
No places met population threshold.	

Guatemalans 5 Years and Over Who Speak English-Only at Home
Top 10 Places Sorted by Number

Place	Number
No places met population threshold.	

Guatemalans 5 Years and Over Who Speak English-Only at Home
Top 10 Places Sorted by Percent

Place	Percent
No places met population threshold.	

Hondurans 5 Years and Over Who Speak English-Only at Home
Top 10 Places Sorted by Number

Place	Number
No places met population threshold.	

Hondurans 5 Years and Over Who Speak English-Only at Home
Top 10 Places Sorted by Percent

Place	Percent
No places met population threshold.	

Mexicans 5 Years and Over Who Speak English-Only at Home
Top 10 Places Sorted by Number

Place	Number
Indianapolis, IN (cons. city) Marion County	4,475
Hammond, IN (city) Lake County	3,689
Fort Wayne, IN (city) Allen County	2,334

Notes: Please refer to the User's Guide for an explanation of data; tables include places with populations > 9,999 and reflect only those areas that meet Summary File 4 population thresholds, therefore there may be less than 10 places listed

Place	Number
East Chicago, IN (city) Lake County	1,967
South Bend, IN (city) Saint Joseph County	1,140
Gary, IN (city) Lake County	1,050
Portage, IN (city) Porter County	1,015
Merrillville, IN (town) Lake County	967
Hobart, IN (city) Lake County	839
Lake Station, IN (city) Lake County	762

Mexicans 5 Years and Over Who Speak English-Only at Home
Top 10 Places Sorted by Percent

Place	Percent
Muncie, IN (city) Delaware County	70.27
Hobart, IN (city) Lake County	69.86
Dyer, IN (town) Lake County	66.15
Bloomington, IN (city) Monroe County	63.48
Munster, IN (town) Lake County	56.87
Portage, IN (city) Porter County	55.89
Schererville, IN (town) Lake County	55.37
Griffith, IN (town) Lake County	55.08
Highland, IN (town) Lake County	54.33
Crown Point, IN (city) Lake County	52.15

Nicaraguans 5 Years and Over Who Speak English-Only at Home
Top 10 Places Sorted by Number

Place	Number
No places met population threshold.	

Nicaraguans 5 Years and Over Who Speak English-Only at Home
Top 10 Places Sorted by Percent

Place	Percent
No places met population threshold.	

Panamanians 5 Years and Over Who Speak English-Only at Home
Top 10 Places Sorted by Number

Place	Number
No places met population threshold.	

Panamanians 5 Years and Over Who Speak English-Only at Home
Top 10 Places Sorted by Percent

Place	Percent
No places met population threshold.	

Paraguayans 5 Years and Over Who Speak English-Only at Home
Top 10 Places Sorted by Number

Place	Number
No places met population threshold.	

Paraguayans 5 Years and Over Who Speak English-Only at Home
Top 10 Places Sorted by Percent

Place	Percent
No places met population threshold.	

Peruvians 5 Years and Over Who Speak English-Only at Home
Top 10 Places Sorted by Number

Place	Number
No places met population threshold.	

Peruvians 5 Years and Over Who Speak English-Only at Home
Top 10 Places Sorted by Percent

Place	Percent
No places met population threshold.	

Puerto Ricans 5 Years and Over Who Speak English-Only at Home
Top 10 Places Sorted by Number

Place	Number
Indianapolis, IN (cons. city) Marion County	687
Hammond, IN (city) Lake County	472
East Chicago, IN (city) Lake County	395
Gary, IN (city) Lake County	381
Portage, IN (city) Porter County	357
Lake Station, IN (city) Lake County	298
Hobart, IN (city) Lake County	238
Fort Wayne, IN (city) Allen County	206
South Bend, IN (city) Saint Joseph County	180

Puerto Ricans 5 Years and Over Who Speak English-Only at Home
Top 10 Places Sorted by Percent

Place	Percent
Hobart, IN (city) Lake County	53.60
South Bend, IN (city) Saint Joseph County	43.80
Portage, IN (city) Porter County	43.54
Fort Wayne, IN (city) Allen County	40.95
Lake Station, IN (city) Lake County	40.43
Indianapolis, IN (cons. city) Marion County	39.57
Gary, IN (city) Lake County	33.87
Hammond, IN (city) Lake County	28.89
East Chicago, IN (city) Lake County	14.02

Salvadorans 5 Years and Over Who Speak English-Only at Home
Top 10 Places Sorted by Number

Place	Number
Indianapolis, IN (cons. city) Marion County	8

Salvadorans 5 Years and Over Who Speak English-Only at Home
Top 10 Places Sorted by Percent

Place	Percent
Indianapolis, IN (cons. city) Marion County	1.77

South Americans 5 Years and Over Who Speak English-Only at Home
Top 10 Places Sorted by Number

Place	Number
Indianapolis, IN (cons. city) Marion County	180

South Americans 5 Years and Over Who Speak English-Only at Home
Top 10 Places Sorted by Percent

Place	Percent
Indianapolis, IN (cons. city) Marion County	21.00

Spaniards 5 Years and Over Who Speak English-Only at Home
Top 10 Places Sorted by Number

Place	Number
No places met population threshold.	

Spaniards 5 Years and Over Who Speak English-Only at Home
Top 10 Places Sorted by Percent

Place	Percent
No places met population threshold.	

Uruguayans 5 Years and Over Who Speak English-Only at Home
Top 10 Places Sorted by Number

Place	Number
No places met population threshold.	

Uruguayans 5 Years and Over Who Speak English-Only at Home
Top 10 Places Sorted by Percent

Place	Percent
No places met population threshold.	

Venezuelans 5 Years and Over Who Speak English-Only at Home
Top 10 Places Sorted by Number

Place	Number
No places met population threshold.	

Venezuelans 5 Years and Over Who Speak English-Only at Home
Top 10 Places Sorted by Percent

Place	Percent
No places met population threshold.	

Other Hispanics 5 Years and Over Who Speak English-Only at Home
Top 10 Places Sorted by Number

Place	Number
Indianapolis, IN (cons. city) Marion County	1,236
Fort Wayne, IN (city) Allen County	536
Hammond, IN (city) Lake County	442
East Chicago, IN (city) Lake County	354
Gary, IN (city) Lake County	194
Lafayette, IN (city) Tippecanoe County	158
South Bend, IN (city) Saint Joseph County	156
Elkhart, IN (city) Elkhart County	122

Other Hispanics 5 Years and Over Who Speak English-Only at Home
Top 10 Places Sorted by Percent

Place	Percent
Lafayette, IN (city) Tippecanoe County	46.06
Gary, IN (city) Lake County	43.50
Indianapolis, IN (cons. city) Marion County	42.26
Fort Wayne, IN (city) Allen County	40.18
Hammond, IN (city) Lake County	38.64
East Chicago, IN (city) Lake County	37.18
Elkhart, IN (city) Elkhart County	19.18
South Bend, IN (city) Saint Joseph County	19.14

Language Spoken: Spanish

Total Population 5 Years and Over Who Speak Spanish at Home
Top 10 Places Sorted by Number

Place	Number
Indianapolis, IN (cons. city) Marion County	29,762
East Chicago, IN (city) Lake County	12,596
Hammond, IN (city) Lake County	11,468
Fort Wayne, IN (city) Allen County	9,276
South Bend, IN (city) Saint Joseph County	7,227
Elkhart, IN (city) Elkhart County	6,834
Goshen, IN (city) Elkhart County	4,832
Lafayette, IN (city) Tippecanoe County	4,516
Gary, IN (city) Lake County	4,308
Frankfort, IN (city) Clinton County	1,945

Notes: Please refer to the User's Guide for an explanation of data; tables include places with populations > 9,999 and reflect only those areas that meet Summary File 4 population thresholds, therefore there may be less than 10 places listed

Total Population 5 Years and Over Who Speak Spanish at Home
Top 10 Places Sorted by Percent

Place	Percent
East Chicago, IN (city) Lake County	42.70
Goshen, IN (city) Elkhart County	17.84
Hammond, IN (city) Lake County	15.01
Elkhart, IN (city) Elkhart County	14.63
Frankfort, IN (city) Clinton County	12.71
Lake Station, IN (city) Lake County	10.82
Logansport, IN (city) Cass County	10.15
Warsaw, IN (city) Kosciusko County	10.08
Lafayette, IN (city) Tippecanoe County	8.64
South Bend, IN (city) Saint Joseph County	7.37

Hispanics 5 Years and Over Who Speak Spanish at Home
Top 10 Places Sorted by Number

Place	Number
Indianapolis, IN (cons. city) Marion County	19,124
East Chicago, IN (city) Lake County	12,226
Hammond, IN (city) Lake County	10,737
Fort Wayne, IN (city) Allen County	6,799
South Bend, IN (city) Saint Joseph County	6,153
Elkhart, IN (city) Elkhart County	6,147
Goshen, IN (city) Elkhart County	4,465
Lafayette, IN (city) Tippecanoe County	3,764
Gary, IN (city) Lake County	2,706
Frankfort, IN (city) Clinton County	1,692

Hispanics 5 Years and Over Who Speak Spanish at Home
Top 10 Places Sorted by Percent

Place	Percent
Washington, IN (city) Daviess County	94.43
Elkhart, IN (city) Elkhart County	89.68
Goshen, IN (city) Elkhart County	89.12
Frankfort, IN (city) Clinton County	87.67
Seymour, IN (city) Jackson County	86.26
Lafayette, IN (city) Tippecanoe County	82.02
Warsaw, IN (city) Kosciusko County	81.76
East Chicago, IN (city) Lake County	81.38
South Bend, IN (city) Saint Joseph County	79.56
Logansport, IN (city) Cass County	79.05

Argentinians 5 Years and Over Who Speak Spanish at Home
Top 10 Places Sorted by Number

Place	Number
No places met population threshold.	

Argentinians 5 Years and Over Who Speak Spanish at Home
Top 10 Places Sorted by Percent

Place	Percent
No places met population threshold.	

Bolivians 5 Years and Over Who Speak Spanish at Home
Top 10 Places Sorted by Number

Place	Number
No places met population threshold.	

Bolivians 5 Years and Over Who Speak Spanish at Home
Top 10 Places Sorted by Percent

Place	Percent
No places met population threshold.	

Central Americans 5 Years and Over Who Speak Spanish at Home
Top 10 Places Sorted by Number

Place	Number
Indianapolis, IN (cons. city) Marion County	1,542

Central Americans 5 Years and Over Who Speak Spanish at Home
Top 10 Places Sorted by Percent

Place	Percent
Indianapolis, IN (cons. city) Marion County	92.17

Chileans 5 Years and Over Who Speak Spanish at Home
Top 10 Places Sorted by Number

Place	Number
No places met population threshold.	

Chileans 5 Years and Over Who Speak Spanish at Home
Top 10 Places Sorted by Percent

Place	Percent
No places met population threshold.	

Colombians 5 Years and Over Who Speak Spanish at Home
Top 10 Places Sorted by Number

Place	Number
No places met population threshold.	

Colombians 5 Years and Over Who Speak Spanish at Home
Top 10 Places Sorted by Percent

Place	Percent
No places met population threshold.	

Costa Ricans 5 Years and Over Who Speak Spanish at Home
Top 10 Places Sorted by Number

Place	Number
No places met population threshold.	

Costa Ricans 5 Years and Over Who Speak Spanish at Home
Top 10 Places Sorted by Percent

Place	Percent
No places met population threshold.	

Cubans 5 Years and Over Who Speak Spanish at Home
Top 10 Places Sorted by Number

Place	Number
Indianapolis, IN (cons. city) Marion County	292

Cubans 5 Years and Over Who Speak Spanish at Home
Top 10 Places Sorted by Percent

Place	Percent
Indianapolis, IN (cons. city) Marion County	57.94

Dominicans 5 Years and Over Who Speak Spanish at Home
Top 10 Places Sorted by Number

Place	Number
No places met population threshold.	

Dominicans 5 Years and Over Who Speak Spanish at Home
Top 10 Places Sorted by Percent

Place	Percent
No places met population threshold.	

Ecuadorians 5 Years and Over Who Speak Spanish at Home
Top 10 Places Sorted by Number

Place	Number
No places met population threshold.	

Ecuadorians 5 Years and Over Who Speak Spanish at Home
Top 10 Places Sorted by Percent

Place	Percent
No places met population threshold.	

Guatemalans 5 Years and Over Who Speak Spanish at Home
Top 10 Places Sorted by Number

Place	Number
No places met population threshold.	

Guatemalans 5 Years and Over Who Speak Spanish at Home
Top 10 Places Sorted by Percent

Place	Percent
No places met population threshold.	

Hondurans 5 Years and Over Who Speak Spanish at Home
Top 10 Places Sorted by Number

Place	Number
No places met population threshold.	

Hondurans 5 Years and Over Who Speak Spanish at Home
Top 10 Places Sorted by Percent

Place	Percent
No places met population threshold.	

Mexicans 5 Years and Over Who Speak Spanish at Home
Top 10 Places Sorted by Number

Place	Number
Indianapolis, IN (cons. city) Marion County	13,754
East Chicago, IN (city) Lake County	9,061
Hammond, IN (city) Lake County	8,747
Elkhart, IN (city) Elkhart County	5,095
Fort Wayne, IN (city) Allen County	5,026
South Bend, IN (city) Saint Joseph County	4,907
Goshen, IN (city) Elkhart County	3,910
Lafayette, IN (city) Tippecanoe County	3,342
Gary, IN (city) Lake County	1,565
Frankfort, IN (city) Clinton County	1,535

Mexicans 5 Years and Over Who Speak Spanish at Home
Top 10 Places Sorted by Percent

Place	Percent
Washington, IN (city) Daviess County	96.24
Seymour, IN (city) Jackson County	94.31
Elkhart, IN (city) Elkhart County	91.28
Goshen, IN (city) Elkhart County	90.15
Warsaw, IN (city) Kosciusko County	89.61
Frankfort, IN (city) Clinton County	88.02
Lafayette, IN (city) Tippecanoe County	87.19
Columbus, IN (city) Bartholomew County	84.17

Notes: Please refer to the User's Guide for an explanation of data; tables include places with populations > 9,999 and reflect only those areas that meet Summary File 4 population thresholds, therefore there may be less than 10 places listed

Place	
Lawrence, IN (city) Marion County	82.05
East Chicago, IN (city) Lake County	81.87

Nicaraguans 5 Years and Over Who Speak Spanish at Home
Top 10 Places Sorted by Number

Place	Number
No places met population threshold.	

Nicaraguans 5 Years and Over Who Speak Spanish at Home
Top 10 Places Sorted by Percent

Place	Percent
No places met population threshold.	

Panamanians 5 Years and Over Who Speak Spanish at Home
Top 10 Places Sorted by Number

Place	Number
No places met population threshold.	

Panamanians 5 Years and Over Who Speak Spanish at Home
Top 10 Places Sorted by Percent

Place	Percent
No places met population threshold.	

Paraguayans 5 Years and Over Who Speak Spanish at Home
Top 10 Places Sorted by Number

Place	Number
No places met population threshold.	

Paraguayans 5 Years and Over Who Speak Spanish at Home
Top 10 Places Sorted by Percent

Place	Percent
No places met population threshold.	

Peruvians 5 Years and Over Who Speak Spanish at Home
Top 10 Places Sorted by Number

Place	Number
No places met population threshold.	

Peruvians 5 Years and Over Who Speak Spanish at Home
Top 10 Places Sorted by Percent

Place	Percent
No places met population threshold.	

Puerto Ricans 5 Years and Over Who Speak Spanish at Home
Top 10 Places Sorted by Number

Place	Number
East Chicago, IN (city) Lake County	2,403
Hammond, IN (city) Lake County	1,162
Indianapolis, IN (cons. city) Marion County	1,018
Gary, IN (city) Lake County	744
Portage, IN (city) Porter County	463
Lake Station, IN (city) Lake County	439
Fort Wayne, IN (city) Allen County	297
South Bend, IN (city) Saint Joseph County	231
Hobart, IN (city) Lake County	197

Puerto Ricans 5 Years and Over Who Speak Spanish at Home
Top 10 Places Sorted by Percent

Place	Percent
East Chicago, IN (city) Lake County	85.30
Hammond, IN (city) Lake County	71.11
Gary, IN (city) Lake County	66.13
Lake Station, IN (city) Lake County	59.57
Fort Wayne, IN (city) Allen County	59.05
Indianapolis, IN (cons. city) Marion County	58.64
Portage, IN (city) Porter County	56.46
South Bend, IN (city) Saint Joseph County	56.20
Hobart, IN (city) Lake County	44.37

Salvadorans 5 Years and Over Who Speak Spanish at Home
Top 10 Places Sorted by Number

Place	Number
Indianapolis, IN (cons. city) Marion County	444

Salvadorans 5 Years and Over Who Speak Spanish at Home
Top 10 Places Sorted by Percent

Place	Percent
Indianapolis, IN (cons. city) Marion County	98.23

South Americans 5 Years and Over Who Speak Spanish at Home
Top 10 Places Sorted by Number

Place	Number
Indianapolis, IN (cons. city) Marion County	669

South Americans 5 Years and Over Who Speak Spanish at Home
Top 10 Places Sorted by Percent

Place	Percent
Indianapolis, IN (cons. city) Marion County	78.06

Spaniards 5 Years and Over Who Speak Spanish at Home
Top 10 Places Sorted by Number

Place	Number
No places met population threshold.	

Spaniards 5 Years and Over Who Speak Spanish at Home
Top 10 Places Sorted by Percent

Place	Percent
No places met population threshold.	

Uruguayans 5 Years and Over Who Speak Spanish at Home
Top 10 Places Sorted by Number

Place	Number
No places met population threshold.	

Uruguayans 5 Years and Over Who Speak Spanish at Home
Top 10 Places Sorted by Percent

Place	Percent
No places met population threshold.	

Venezuelans 5 Years and Over Who Speak Spanish at Home
Top 10 Places Sorted by Number

Place	Number
No places met population threshold.	

Venezuelans 5 Years and Over Who Speak Spanish at Home
Top 10 Places Sorted by Percent

Place	Percent
No places met population threshold.	

Other Hispanics 5 Years and Over Who Speak Spanish at Home
Top 10 Places Sorted by Number

Place	Number
Indianapolis, IN (cons. city) Marion County	1,655
Fort Wayne, IN (city) Allen County	794
Hammond, IN (city) Lake County	690
South Bend, IN (city) Saint Joseph County	659
East Chicago, IN (city) Lake County	598
Elkhart, IN (city) Elkhart County	514
Gary, IN (city) Lake County	252
Lafayette, IN (city) Tippecanoe County	182

Other Hispanics 5 Years and Over Who Speak Spanish at Home
Top 10 Places Sorted by Percent

Place	Percent
South Bend, IN (city) Saint Joseph County	80.86
Elkhart, IN (city) Elkhart County	80.82
East Chicago, IN (city) Lake County	62.82
Hammond, IN (city) Lake County	60.31
Fort Wayne, IN (city) Allen County	59.52
Indianapolis, IN (cons. city) Marion County	56.58
Gary, IN (city) Lake County	56.50
Lafayette, IN (city) Tippecanoe County	53.06

Foreign Born

Total Population
Top 10 Places Sorted by Number

Place	Number
Indianapolis, IN (cons. city) Marion County	36,360
Fort Wayne, IN (city) Allen County	10,187
South Bend, IN (city) Saint Joseph County	6,854
Hammond, IN (city) Lake County	6,034
Elkhart, IN (city) Elkhart County	5,895
Bloomington, IN (city) Monroe County	5,578
East Chicago, IN (city) Lake County	4,781
Goshen, IN (city) Elkhart County	4,613
Lafayette, IN (city) Tippecanoe County	4,450
West Lafayette, IN (city) Tippecanoe County	3,851

Total Population
Top 10 Places Sorted by Percent

Place	Percent
Goshen, IN (city) Elkhart County	15.75
East Chicago, IN (city) Lake County	14.75
West Lafayette, IN (city) Tippecanoe County	13.30
Elkhart, IN (city) Elkhart County	11.40
Frankfort, IN (city) Clinton County	9.05
Schererville, IN (town) Lake County	8.32
Bloomington, IN (city) Monroe County	8.06
Lafayette, IN (city) Tippecanoe County	7.91
Munster, IN (town) Lake County	7.90
Carmel, IN (city) Hamilton County	7.29

Hispanic
Top 10 Places Sorted by Number

Place	Number
Indianapolis, IN (cons. city) Marion County	15,481
Elkhart, IN (city) Elkhart County	4,722
East Chicago, IN (city) Lake County	4,317
Fort Wayne, IN (city) Allen County	4,211
Hammond, IN (city) Lake County	4,158
Goshen, IN (city) Elkhart County	3,928
South Bend, IN (city) Saint Joseph County	3,531

Notes: Please refer to the User's Guide for an explanation of data; tables include places with populations > 9,999 and reflect only those areas that meet Summary File 4 population thresholds, therefore there may be less than 10 places listed

Place	Number
Lafayette, IN (city) Tippecanoe County	3,100
Frankfort, IN (city) Clinton County	1,452
Logansport, IN (city) Cass County	1,136

Hispanic
Top 10 Places Sorted by Percent

Place	Percent
Goshen, IN (city) Elkhart County	67.19
Seymour, IN (city) Jackson County	66.72
Crawfordsville, IN (city) Montgomery County	65.83
Washington, IN (city) Daviess County	65.46
Frankfort, IN (city) Clinton County	62.59
Lafayette, IN (city) Tippecanoe County	58.39
Clarksville, IN (town) Clark County	58.33
Elkhart, IN (city) Elkhart County	58.11
Columbus, IN (city) Bartholomew County	52.36
Indianapolis, IN (cons. city) Marion County	52.07

Argentinian
Top 10 Places Sorted by Number

Place	Number
No places met population threshold.	

Argentinian
Top 10 Places Sorted by Percent

Place	Percent
No places met population threshold.	

Bolivian
Top 10 Places Sorted by Number

Place	Number
No places met population threshold.	

Bolivian
Top 10 Places Sorted by Percent

Place	Percent
No places met population threshold.	

Central American
Top 10 Places Sorted by Number

Place	Number
Indianapolis, IN (cons. city) Marion County	1,441

Central American
Top 10 Places Sorted by Percent

Place	Percent
Indianapolis, IN (cons. city) Marion County	83.73

Chilean
Top 10 Places Sorted by Number

Place	Number
No places met population threshold.	

Chilean
Top 10 Places Sorted by Percent

Place	Percent
No places met population threshold.	

Colombian
Top 10 Places Sorted by Number

Place	Number
No places met population threshold.	

Colombian
Top 10 Places Sorted by Percent

Place	Percent
No places met population threshold.	

Costa Rican
Top 10 Places Sorted by Number

Place	Number
No places met population threshold.	

Costa Rican
Top 10 Places Sorted by Percent

Place	Percent
No places met population threshold.	

Cuban
Top 10 Places Sorted by Number

Place	Number
Indianapolis, IN (cons. city) Marion County	220

Cuban
Top 10 Places Sorted by Percent

Place	Percent
Indianapolis, IN (cons. city) Marion County	40.52

Dominican
Top 10 Places Sorted by Number

Place	Number
No places met population threshold.	

Dominican
Top 10 Places Sorted by Percent

Place	Percent
No places met population threshold.	

Ecuadorian
Top 10 Places Sorted by Number

Place	Number
No places met population threshold.	

Ecuadorian
Top 10 Places Sorted by Percent

Place	Percent
No places met population threshold.	

Guatemalan
Top 10 Places Sorted by Number

Place	Number
No places met population threshold.	

Guatemalan
Top 10 Places Sorted by Percent

Place	Percent
No places met population threshold.	

Honduran
Top 10 Places Sorted by Number

Place	Number
No places met population threshold.	

Honduran
Top 10 Places Sorted by Percent

Place	Percent
No places met population threshold.	

Mexican
Top 10 Places Sorted by Number

Place	Number
Indianapolis, IN (cons. city) Marion County	11,725
Elkhart, IN (city) Elkhart County	4,174
East Chicago, IN (city) Lake County	3,977
Hammond, IN (city) Lake County	3,869
Goshen, IN (city) Elkhart County	3,555
Fort Wayne, IN (city) Allen County	3,371
South Bend, IN (city) Saint Joseph County	2,917
Lafayette, IN (city) Tippecanoe County	2,845
Frankfort, IN (city) Clinton County	1,365
Logansport, IN (city) Cass County	935

Mexican
Top 10 Places Sorted by Percent

Place	Percent
Seymour, IN (city) Jackson County	74.95
Goshen, IN (city) Elkhart County	69.80
Clarksville, IN (town) Clark County	65.67
Frankfort, IN (city) Clinton County	65.19
Crawfordsville, IN (city) Montgomery County	64.03
Washington, IN (city) Daviess County	63.94
Lafayette, IN (city) Tippecanoe County	63.65
Elkhart, IN (city) Elkhart County	62.21
Lawrence, IN (city) Marion County	59.62
Columbus, IN (city) Bartholomew County	57.64

Nicaraguan
Top 10 Places Sorted by Number

Place	Number
No places met population threshold.	

Nicaraguan
Top 10 Places Sorted by Percent

Place	Percent
No places met population threshold.	

Panamanian
Top 10 Places Sorted by Number

Place	Number
No places met population threshold.	

Panamanian
Top 10 Places Sorted by Percent

Place	Percent
No places met population threshold.	

Paraguayan
Top 10 Places Sorted by Number

Place	Number
No places met population threshold.	

Paraguayan
Top 10 Places Sorted by Percent

Place	Percent
No places met population threshold.	

Peruvian
Top 10 Places Sorted by Number

Place	Number
No places met population threshold.	

Peruvian
Top 10 Places Sorted by Percent

Place	Percent
No places met population threshold.	

Puerto Rican
Top 10 Places Sorted by Number

Place	Number
Indianapolis, IN (cons. city) Marion County	78
East Chicago, IN (city) Lake County	63
South Bend, IN (city) Saint Joseph County	22

Notes: Please refer to the User's Guide for an explanation of data; tables include places with populations > 9,999 and reflect only those areas that meet Summary File 4 population thresholds, therefore there may be less than 10 places listed

Fort Wayne, IN (city) Allen County	18
Gary, IN (city) Lake County	17
Hammond, IN (city) Lake County	12
Hobart, IN (city) Lake County	0
Lake Station, IN (city) Lake County	0
Portage, IN (city) Porter County	0

Puerto Rican
Top 10 Places Sorted by Percent

Place	Percent
South Bend, IN (city) Saint Joseph County	4.62
Indianapolis, IN (cons. city) Marion County	3.95
Fort Wayne, IN (city) Allen County	2.98
East Chicago, IN (city) Lake County	2.05
Gary, IN (city) Lake County	1.36
Hammond, IN (city) Lake County	0.65
Hobart, IN (city) Lake County	0.00
Lake Station, IN (city) Lake County	0.00
Portage, IN (city) Porter County	0.00

Salvadoran
Top 10 Places Sorted by Number

Place	Number
Indianapolis, IN (cons. city) Marion County	385

Salvadoran
Top 10 Places Sorted by Percent

Place	Percent
Indianapolis, IN (cons. city) Marion County	84.25

South American
Top 10 Places Sorted by Number

Place	Number
Indianapolis, IN (cons. city) Marion County	708

South American
Top 10 Places Sorted by Percent

Place	Percent
Indianapolis, IN (cons. city) Marion County	72.17

Spaniard
Top 10 Places Sorted by Number

Place	Number
No places met population threshold.	

Spaniard
Top 10 Places Sorted by Percent

Place	Percent
No places met population threshold.	

Uruguayan
Top 10 Places Sorted by Number

Place	Number
No places met population threshold.	

Uruguayan
Top 10 Places Sorted by Percent

Place	Percent
No places met population threshold.	

Venezuelan
Top 10 Places Sorted by Number

Place	Number
No places met population threshold.	

Venezuelan
Top 10 Places Sorted by Percent

Place	Percent
No places met population threshold.	

Other Hispanic
Top 10 Places Sorted by Number

Place	Number
Indianapolis, IN (cons. city) Marion County	1,140
Elkhart, IN (city) Elkhart County	306
South Bend, IN (city) Saint Joseph County	279
Fort Wayne, IN (city) Allen County	266
Hammond, IN (city) Lake County	166
East Chicago, IN (city) Lake County	148
Lafayette, IN (city) Tippecanoe County	121
Gary, IN (city) Lake County	85

Other Hispanic
Top 10 Places Sorted by Percent

Place	Percent
Elkhart, IN (city) Elkhart County	42.15
Indianapolis, IN (cons. city) Marion County	32.54
Lafayette, IN (city) Tippecanoe County	29.66
South Bend, IN (city) Saint Joseph County	28.47
Fort Wayne, IN (city) Allen County	17.83
Gary, IN (city) Lake County	17.07
East Chicago, IN (city) Lake County	13.09
Hammond, IN (city) Lake County	12.42

Foreign-Born Naturalized Citizens

Total Population
Top 10 Places Sorted by Number

Place	Number
Indianapolis, IN (cons. city) Marion County	12,208
Fort Wayne, IN (city) Allen County	3,332
Hammond, IN (city) Lake County	2,918
South Bend, IN (city) Saint Joseph County	2,375
East Chicago, IN (city) Lake County	2,184
Merrillville, IN (town) Lake County	1,366
Bloomington, IN (city) Monroe County	1,328
Carmel, IN (city) Hamilton County	1,251
Schererville, IN (town) Lake County	1,235
Elkhart, IN (city) Elkhart County	1,192

Total Population
Top 10 Places Sorted by Percent

Place	Percent
East Chicago, IN (city) Lake County	6.74
Schererville, IN (town) Lake County	4.97
Munster, IN (town) Lake County	4.78
Merrillville, IN (town) Lake County	4.45
Crown Point, IN (city) Lake County	4.10
Dyer, IN (town) Lake County	3.77
Hammond, IN (city) Lake County	3.51
Carmel, IN (city) Hamilton County	3.31
Highland, IN (town) Lake County	2.92
Goshen, IN (city) Elkhart County	2.66

Hispanic
Top 10 Places Sorted by Number

Place	Number
Indianapolis, IN (cons. city) Marion County	2,633
East Chicago, IN (city) Lake County	1,920
Hammond, IN (city) Lake County	1,749
South Bend, IN (city) Saint Joseph County	878
Fort Wayne, IN (city) Allen County	769
Elkhart, IN (city) Elkhart County	667
Goshen, IN (city) Elkhart County	495
Lafayette, IN (city) Tippecanoe County	472
Gary, IN (city) Lake County	341
Logansport, IN (city) Cass County	222

Hispanic
Top 10 Places Sorted by Percent

Place	Percent
Noblesville, IN (city) Hamilton County	19.18
Warsaw, IN (city) Kosciusko County	14.89
Valparaiso, IN (city) Porter County	13.53
Clarksville, IN (town) Clark County	13.00
Fishers, IN (town) Hamilton County	11.68
East Chicago, IN (city) Lake County	11.48
Jeffersonville, IN (city) Clark County	11.09
Hammond, IN (city) Lake County	10.02
South Bend, IN (city) Saint Joseph County	9.63
Michigan City, IN (city) La Porte County	9.37

Argentinian
Top 10 Places Sorted by Number

Place	Number
No places met population threshold.	

Argentinian
Top 10 Places Sorted by Percent

Place	Percent
No places met population threshold.	

Bolivian
Top 10 Places Sorted by Number

Place	Number
No places met population threshold.	

Bolivian
Top 10 Places Sorted by Percent

Place	Percent
No places met population threshold.	

Central American
Top 10 Places Sorted by Number

Place	Number
Indianapolis, IN (cons. city) Marion County	321

Central American
Top 10 Places Sorted by Percent

Place	Percent
Indianapolis, IN (cons. city) Marion County	18.65

Chilean
Top 10 Places Sorted by Number

Place	Number
No places met population threshold.	

Chilean
Top 10 Places Sorted by Percent

Place	Percent
No places met population threshold.	

Colombian
Top 10 Places Sorted by Number

Place	Number
No places met population threshold.	

Colombian
Top 10 Places Sorted by Percent

Place	Percent
No places met population threshold.	

Notes: Please refer to the User's Guide for an explanation of data; tables include places with populations > 9,999 and reflect only those areas that meet Summary File 4 population thresholds, therefore there may be less than 10 places listed

Costa Rican
Top 10 Places Sorted by Number

Place	Number
No places met population threshold.	

Costa Rican
Top 10 Places Sorted by Percent

Place	Percent
No places met population threshold.	

Cuban
Top 10 Places Sorted by Number

Place	Number
Indianapolis, IN (cons. city) Marion County	149

Cuban
Top 10 Places Sorted by Percent

Place	Percent
Indianapolis, IN (cons. city) Marion County	27.44

Dominican
Top 10 Places Sorted by Number

Place	Number
No places met population threshold.	

Dominican
Top 10 Places Sorted by Percent

Place	Percent
No places met population threshold.	

Ecuadorian
Top 10 Places Sorted by Number

Place	Number
No places met population threshold.	

Ecuadorian
Top 10 Places Sorted by Percent

Place	Percent
No places met population threshold.	

Guatemalan
Top 10 Places Sorted by Number

Place	Number
No places met population threshold.	

Guatemalan
Top 10 Places Sorted by Percent

Place	Percent
No places met population threshold.	

Honduran
Top 10 Places Sorted by Number

Place	Number
No places met population threshold.	

Honduran
Top 10 Places Sorted by Percent

Place	Percent
No places met population threshold.	

Mexican
Top 10 Places Sorted by Number

Place	Number
East Chicago, IN (city) Lake County	1,809
Hammond, IN (city) Lake County	1,638
Indianapolis, IN (cons. city) Marion County	1,433
South Bend, IN (city) Saint Joseph County	679
Elkhart, IN (city) Elkhart County	559
Fort Wayne, IN (city) Allen County	541
Goshen, IN (city) Elkhart County	450
Lafayette, IN (city) Tippecanoe County	415
Gary, IN (city) Lake County	219
Logansport, IN (city) Cass County	206

Mexican
Top 10 Places Sorted by Percent

Place	Percent
Michigan City, IN (city) La Porte County	14.72
East Chicago, IN (city) Lake County	14.70
Clarksville, IN (town) Clark County	13.22
Warsaw, IN (city) Kosciusko County	12.59
Hammond, IN (city) Lake County	11.62
Dyer, IN (town) Lake County	11.56
Logansport, IN (city) Cass County	9.95
Lawrence, IN (city) Marion County	9.70
South Bend, IN (city) Saint Joseph County	9.45
Lafayette, IN (city) Tippecanoe County	9.28

Nicaraguan
Top 10 Places Sorted by Number

Place	Number
No places met population threshold.	

Nicaraguan
Top 10 Places Sorted by Percent

Place	Percent
No places met population threshold.	

Panamanian
Top 10 Places Sorted by Number

Place	Number
No places met population threshold.	

Panamanian
Top 10 Places Sorted by Percent

Place	Percent
No places met population threshold.	

Paraguayan
Top 10 Places Sorted by Number

Place	Number
No places met population threshold.	

Paraguayan
Top 10 Places Sorted by Percent

Place	Percent
No places met population threshold.	

Peruvian
Top 10 Places Sorted by Number

Place	Number
No places met population threshold.	

Peruvian
Top 10 Places Sorted by Percent

Place	Percent
No places met population threshold.	

Puerto Rican
Top 10 Places Sorted by Number

Place	Number
Indianapolis, IN (cons. city) Marion County	38
Gary, IN (city) Lake County	17
East Chicago, IN (city) Lake County	13

Place	Number
Hammond, IN (city) Lake County	6
Fort Wayne, IN (city) Allen County	0
Hobart, IN (city) Lake County	0
Lake Station, IN (city) Lake County	0
Portage, IN (city) Porter County	0
South Bend, IN (city) Saint Joseph County	0

Puerto Rican
Top 10 Places Sorted by Percent

Place	Percent
Indianapolis, IN (cons. city) Marion County	1.93
Gary, IN (city) Lake County	1.36
East Chicago, IN (city) Lake County	0.42
Hammond, IN (city) Lake County	0.33
Fort Wayne, IN (city) Allen County	0.00
Hobart, IN (city) Lake County	0.00
Lake Station, IN (city) Lake County	0.00
Portage, IN (city) Porter County	0.00
South Bend, IN (city) Saint Joseph County	0.00

Salvadoran
Top 10 Places Sorted by Number

Place	Number
Indianapolis, IN (cons. city) Marion County	88

Salvadoran
Top 10 Places Sorted by Percent

Place	Percent
Indianapolis, IN (cons. city) Marion County	19.26

South American
Top 10 Places Sorted by Number

Place	Number
Indianapolis, IN (cons. city) Marion County	294

South American
Top 10 Places Sorted by Percent

Place	Percent
Indianapolis, IN (cons. city) Marion County	29.97

Spaniard
Top 10 Places Sorted by Number

Place	Number
No places met population threshold.	

Spaniard
Top 10 Places Sorted by Percent

Place	Percent
No places met population threshold.	

Uruguayan
Top 10 Places Sorted by Number

Place	Number
No places met population threshold.	

Uruguayan
Top 10 Places Sorted by Percent

Place	Percent
No places met population threshold.	

Venezuelan
Top 10 Places Sorted by Number

Place	Number
No places met population threshold.	

Notes: Please refer to the User's Guide for an explanation of data; tables include places with populations > 9,999 and reflect only those areas that meet Summary File 4 population thresholds, therefore there may be less than 10 places listed

Venezuelan
Top 10 Places Sorted by Percent

Place	Percent
No places met population threshold.	

Other Hispanic
Top 10 Places Sorted by Number

Place	Number
Indianapolis, IN (cons. city) Marion County	327
South Bend, IN (city) Saint Joseph County	100
Fort Wayne, IN (city) Allen County	94
Elkhart, IN (city) Elkhart County	62
East Chicago, IN (city) Lake County	47
Gary, IN (city) Lake County	42
Hammond, IN (city) Lake County	34
Lafayette, IN (city) Tippecanoe County	19

Other Hispanic
Top 10 Places Sorted by Percent

Place	Percent
South Bend, IN (city) Saint Joseph County	10.20
Indianapolis, IN (cons. city) Marion County	9.33
Elkhart, IN (city) Elkhart County	8.54
Gary, IN (city) Lake County	8.43
Fort Wayne, IN (city) Allen County	6.30
Lafayette, IN (city) Tippecanoe County	4.66
East Chicago, IN (city) Lake County	4.16
Hammond, IN (city) Lake County	2.54

High School Graduates

Total Populations 25 Years and Over Who are High School Graduates
Top 10 Places Sorted by Number

Place	Number
Indianapolis, IN (cons. city) Marion County	414,234
Fort Wayne, IN (city) Allen County	106,487
Evansville, IN (city) Vanderburgh County	64,621
South Bend, IN (city) Saint Joseph County	51,839
Gary, IN (city) Lake County	44,925
Hammond, IN (city) Lake County	39,524
Anderson, IN (city) Madison County	30,196
Lafayette, IN (city) Tippecanoe County	29,342
Bloomington, IN (city) Monroe County	28,564
Muncie, IN (city) Delaware County	28,498

Total Populations 25 Years and Over Who are High School Graduates
Top 10 Places Sorted by Percent

Place	Percent
Fishers, IN (town) Hamilton County	98.16
Carmel, IN (city) Hamilton County	97.02
West Lafayette, IN (city) Tippecanoe County	96.25
Munster, IN (town) Lake County	92.95
Schererville, IN (town) Lake County	92.04
Bloomington, IN (city) Monroe County	91.17
Noblesville, IN (city) Hamilton County	90.79
Valparaiso, IN (city) Porter County	90.63
Dyer, IN (town) Lake County	90.26
Griffith, IN (town) Lake County	89.07

Hispanics 25 Years and Over Who are High School Graduates
Top 10 Places Sorted by Number

Place	Number
Indianapolis, IN (cons. city) Marion County	7,924
Hammond, IN (city) Lake County	4,973
East Chicago, IN (city) Lake County	4,593
Fort Wayne, IN (city) Allen County	2,829
South Bend, IN (city) Saint Joseph County	1,691
Gary, IN (city) Lake County	1,393
Elkhart, IN (city) Elkhart County	1,312
Portage, IN (city) Porter County	1,300
Merrillville, IN (town) Lake County	1,270
Lafayette, IN (city) Tippecanoe County	1,086

Hispanics 25 Years and Over Who are High School Graduates
Top 10 Places Sorted by Percent

Place	Percent
Carmel, IN (city) Hamilton County	100.00
West Lafayette, IN (city) Tippecanoe County	100.00
Bloomington, IN (city) Monroe County	90.12
Highland, IN (town) Lake County	85.67
Schererville, IN (town) Lake County	84.21
Fishers, IN (town) Hamilton County	83.45
Dyer, IN (town) Lake County	82.83
Merrillville, IN (town) Lake County	82.68
Griffith, IN (town) Lake County	80.74
Hobart, IN (city) Lake County	80.66

Argentinians 25 Years and Over Who are High School Graduates
Top 10 Places Sorted by Number

Place	Number
No places met population threshold.	

Argentinians 25 Years and Over Who are High School Graduates
Top 10 Places Sorted by Percent

Place	Percent
No places met population threshold.	

Bolivians 25 Years and Over Who are High School Graduates
Top 10 Places Sorted by Number

Place	Number
No places met population threshold.	

Bolivians 25 Years and Over Who are High School Graduates
Top 10 Places Sorted by Percent

Place	Percent
No places met population threshold.	

Central Americans 25 Years and Over Who are High School Graduates
Top 10 Places Sorted by Number

Place	Number
Indianapolis, IN (cons. city) Marion County	623

Central Americans 25 Years and Over Who are High School Graduates
Top 10 Places Sorted by Percent

Place	Percent
Indianapolis, IN (cons. city) Marion County	54.99

Chileans 25 Years and Over Who are High School Graduates
Top 10 Places Sorted by Number

Place	Number
No places met population threshold.	

Chileans 25 Years and Over Who are High School Graduates
Top 10 Places Sorted by Percent

Place	Percent
No places met population threshold.	

Colombians 25 Years and Over Who are High School Graduates
Top 10 Places Sorted by Number

Place	Number
No places met population threshold.	

Colombians 25 Years and Over Who are High School Graduates
Top 10 Places Sorted by Percent

Place	Percent
No places met population threshold.	

Costa Ricans 25 Years and Over Who are High School Graduates
Top 10 Places Sorted by Number

Place	Number
No places met population threshold.	

Costa Ricans 25 Years and Over Who are High School Graduates
Top 10 Places Sorted by Percent

Place	Percent
No places met population threshold.	

Cubans 25 Years and Over Who are High School Graduates
Top 10 Places Sorted by Number

Place	Number
Indianapolis, IN (cons. city) Marion County	282

Cubans 25 Years and Over Who are High School Graduates
Top 10 Places Sorted by Percent

Place	Percent
Indianapolis, IN (cons. city) Marion County	94.63

Dominicans 25 Years and Over Who are High School Graduates
Top 10 Places Sorted by Number

Place	Number
No places met population threshold.	

Dominicans 25 Years and Over Who are High School Graduates
Top 10 Places Sorted by Percent

Place	Percent
No places met population threshold.	

Ecuadorians 25 Years and Over Who are High School Graduates
Top 10 Places Sorted by Number

Place	Number
No places met population threshold.	

Ecuadorians 25 Years and Over Who are High School Graduates
Top 10 Places Sorted by Percent

Place	Percent
No places met population threshold.	

Guatemalans 25 Years and Over Who are High School Graduates
Top 10 Places Sorted by Number

Place	Number
No places met population threshold.	

Notes: Please refer to the User's Guide for an explanation of data; tables include places with populations > 9,999 and reflect only those areas that meet Summary File 4 population thresholds, therefore there may be less than 10 places listed

Guatemalans 25 Years and Over Who are High School Graduates
Top 10 Places Sorted by Percent

Place	Percent
No places met population threshold.	

Hondurans 25 Years and Over Who are High School Graduates
Top 10 Places Sorted by Number

Place	Number
No places met population threshold.	

Hondurans 25 Years and Over Who are High School Graduates
Top 10 Places Sorted by Percent

Place	Percent
No places met population threshold.	

Mexicans 25 Years and Over Who are High School Graduates
Top 10 Places Sorted by Number

Place	Number
Indianapolis, IN (cons. city) Marion County	4,379
Hammond, IN (city) Lake County	3,975
East Chicago, IN (city) Lake County	3,272
Fort Wayne, IN (city) Allen County	1,800
South Bend, IN (city) Saint Joseph County	1,082
Elkhart, IN (city) Elkhart County	1,016
Merrillville, IN (town) Lake County	947
Gary, IN (city) Lake County	886
Goshen, IN (city) Elkhart County	860
Portage, IN (city) Porter County	816

Mexicans 25 Years and Over Who are High School Graduates
Top 10 Places Sorted by Percent

Place	Percent
West Lafayette, IN (city) Tippecanoe County	100.00
Bloomington, IN (city) Monroe County	91.51
Highland, IN (town) Lake County	86.32
Dyer, IN (town) Lake County	85.14
Hobart, IN (city) Lake County	83.97
Merrillville, IN (town) Lake County	83.73
Schererville, IN (town) Lake County	82.40
Griffith, IN (town) Lake County	78.90
Evansville, IN (city) Vanderburgh County	78.66
Valparaiso, IN (city) Porter County	77.54

Nicaraguans 25 Years and Over Who are High School Graduates
Top 10 Places Sorted by Number

Place	Number
No places met population threshold.	

Nicaraguans 25 Years and Over Who are High School Graduates
Top 10 Places Sorted by Percent

Place	Percent
No places met population threshold.	

Panamanians 25 Years and Over Who are High School Graduates
Top 10 Places Sorted by Number

Place	Number
No places met population threshold.	

Panamanians 25 Years and Over Who are High School Graduates
Top 10 Places Sorted by Percent

Place	Percent
No places met population threshold.	

Paraguayans 25 Years and Over Who are High School Graduates
Top 10 Places Sorted by Number

Place	Number
No places met population threshold.	

Paraguayans 25 Years and Over Who are High School Graduates
Top 10 Places Sorted by Percent

Place	Percent
No places met population threshold.	

Peruvians 25 Years and Over Who are High School Graduates
Top 10 Places Sorted by Number

Place	Number
No places met population threshold.	

Peruvians 25 Years and Over Who are High School Graduates
Top 10 Places Sorted by Percent

Place	Percent
No places met population threshold.	

Puerto Ricans 25 Years and Over Who are High School Graduates
Top 10 Places Sorted by Number

Place	Number
East Chicago, IN (city) Lake County	1,027
Indianapolis, IN (cons. city) Marion County	833
Hammond, IN (city) Lake County	633
Gary, IN (city) Lake County	343
Portage, IN (city) Porter County	334
Lake Station, IN (city) Lake County	286
Fort Wayne, IN (city) Allen County	261
South Bend, IN (city) Saint Joseph County	201
Hobart, IN (city) Lake County	190

Puerto Ricans 25 Years and Over Who are High School Graduates
Top 10 Places Sorted by Percent

Place	Percent
Indianapolis, IN (cons. city) Marion County	85.88
South Bend, IN (city) Saint Joseph County	84.10
Hobart, IN (city) Lake County	82.97
Portage, IN (city) Porter County	82.06
Fort Wayne, IN (city) Allen County	81.56
Hammond, IN (city) Lake County	68.95
Lake Station, IN (city) Lake County	65.60
East Chicago, IN (city) Lake County	54.34
Gary, IN (city) Lake County	47.25

Salvadorans 25 Years and Over Who are High School Graduates
Top 10 Places Sorted by Number

Place	Number
Indianapolis, IN (cons. city) Marion County	174

Salvadorans 25 Years and Over Who are High School Graduates
Top 10 Places Sorted by Percent

Place	Percent
Indianapolis, IN (cons. city) Marion County	50.88

South Americans 25 Years and Over Who are High School Graduates
Top 10 Places Sorted by Number

Place	Number
Indianapolis, IN (cons. city) Marion County	526

South Americans 25 Years and Over Who are High School Graduates
Top 10 Places Sorted by Percent

Place	Percent
Indianapolis, IN (cons. city) Marion County	85.81

Spaniards 25 Years and Over Who are High School Graduates
Top 10 Places Sorted by Number

Place	Number
No places met population threshold.	

Spaniards 25 Years and Over Who are High School Graduates
Top 10 Places Sorted by Percent

Place	Percent
No places met population threshold.	

Uruguayans 25 Years and Over Who are High School Graduates
Top 10 Places Sorted by Number

Place	Number
No places met population threshold.	

Uruguayans 25 Years and Over Who are High School Graduates
Top 10 Places Sorted by Percent

Place	Percent
No places met population threshold.	

Venezuelans 25 Years and Over Who are High School Graduates
Top 10 Places Sorted by Number

Place	Number
No places met population threshold.	

Venezuelans 25 Years and Over Who are High School Graduates
Top 10 Places Sorted by Percent

Place	Percent
No places met population threshold.	

Other Hispanics 25 Years and Over Who are High School Graduates
Top 10 Places Sorted by Number

Place	Number
Indianapolis, IN (cons. city) Marion County	1,207
Fort Wayne, IN (city) Allen County	470
Hammond, IN (city) Lake County	304
East Chicago, IN (city) Lake County	221
South Bend, IN (city) Saint Joseph County	172
Gary, IN (city) Lake County	136
Lafayette, IN (city) Tippecanoe County	110
Elkhart, IN (city) Elkhart County	97

Other Hispanics 25 Years and Over Who are High School Graduates
Top 10 Places Sorted by Percent

Place	Percent
Fort Wayne, IN (city) Allen County	67.72
Indianapolis, IN (cons. city) Marion County	64.89
Lafayette, IN (city) Tippecanoe County	62.15

Notes: Please refer to the User's Guide for an explanation of data; tables include places with populations > 9,999 and reflect only those areas that meet Summary File 4 population thresholds, therefore there may be less than 10 places listed

East Chicago, IN (city) Lake County	59.89
Gary, IN (city) Lake County	57.63
Hammond, IN (city) Lake County	57.58
South Bend, IN (city) Saint Joseph County	41.75
Elkhart, IN (city) Elkhart County	32.55

College Graduates

Total Populations 25 Years and Over Who are Four-Year College Graduates
Top 10 Places Sorted by Number

Place	Number
Indianapolis, IN (cons. city) Marion County	130,099
Fort Wayne, IN (city) Allen County	24,897
Bloomington, IN (city) Monroe County	17,174
Fishers, IN (town) Hamilton County	14,672
Carmel, IN (city) Hamilton County	14,369
South Bend, IN (city) Saint Joseph County	13,548
Evansville, IN (city) Vanderburgh County	13,402
Lafayette, IN (city) Tippecanoe County	8,377
Noblesville, IN (city) Hamilton County	7,535
Columbus, IN (city) Bartholomew County	7,144

Total Populations 25 Years and Over Who are Four-Year College Graduates
Top 10 Places Sorted by Percent

Place	Percent
West Lafayette, IN (city) Tippecanoe County	69.69
Fishers, IN (town) Hamilton County	60.15
Carmel, IN (city) Hamilton County	58.41
Bloomington, IN (city) Monroe County	54.82
Noblesville, IN (city) Hamilton County	40.94
Munster, IN (town) Lake County	39.16
Valparaiso, IN (city) Porter County	34.55
Schererville, IN (town) Lake County	29.47
Columbus, IN (city) Bartholomew County	27.61
Lawrence, IN (city) Marion County	26.83

Hispanics 25 Years and Over Who are Four-Year College Graduates
Top 10 Places Sorted by Number

Place	Number
Indianapolis, IN (cons. city) Marion County	2,038
Hammond, IN (city) Lake County	544
Bloomington, IN (city) Monroe County	470
East Chicago, IN (city) Lake County	455
South Bend, IN (city) Saint Joseph County	340
Fort Wayne, IN (city) Allen County	318
Highland, IN (town) Lake County	239
Merrillville, IN (town) Lake County	219
Carmel, IN (city) Hamilton County	206
Fishers, IN (town) Hamilton County	202

Hispanics 25 Years and Over Who are Four-Year College Graduates
Top 10 Places Sorted by Percent

Place	Percent
West Lafayette, IN (city) Tippecanoe County	78.54
Carmel, IN (city) Hamilton County	74.64
Bloomington, IN (city) Monroe County	69.32
Fishers, IN (town) Hamilton County	49.15
Noblesville, IN (city) Hamilton County	36.63
Munster, IN (town) Lake County	29.53
Muncie, IN (city) Delaware County	27.27
Highland, IN (town) Lake County	27.19
Valparaiso, IN (city) Porter County	23.11
Crawfordsville, IN (city) Montgomery County	19.79

Argentinians 25 Years and Over Who are Four-Year College Graduates
Top 10 Places Sorted by Number

Place	Number
No places met population threshold.	

Argentinians 25 Years and Over Who are Four-Year College Graduates
Top 10 Places Sorted by Percent

Place	Percent
No places met population threshold.	

Bolivians 25 Years and Over Who are Four-Year College Graduates
Top 10 Places Sorted by Number

Place	Number
No places met population threshold.	

Bolivians 25 Years and Over Who are Four-Year College Graduates
Top 10 Places Sorted by Percent

Place	Percent
No places met population threshold.	

Central Americans 25 Years and Over Who are Four-Year College Graduates
Top 10 Places Sorted by Number

Place	Number
Indianapolis, IN (cons. city) Marion County	123

Central Americans 25 Years and Over Who are Four-Year College Graduates
Top 10 Places Sorted by Percent

Place	Percent
Indianapolis, IN (cons. city) Marion County	10.86

Chileans 25 Years and Over Who are Four-Year College Graduates
Top 10 Places Sorted by Number

Place	Number
No places met population threshold.	

Chileans 25 Years and Over Who are Four-Year College Graduates
Top 10 Places Sorted by Percent

Place	Percent
No places met population threshold.	

Colombians 25 Years and Over Who are Four-Year College Graduates
Top 10 Places Sorted by Number

Place	Number
No places met population threshold.	

Colombians 25 Years and Over Who are Four-Year College Graduates
Top 10 Places Sorted by Percent

Place	Percent
No places met population threshold.	

Costa Ricans 25 Years and Over Who are Four-Year College Graduates
Top 10 Places Sorted by Number

Place	Number
No places met population threshold.	

Costa Ricans 25 Years and Over Who are Four-Year College Graduates
Top 10 Places Sorted by Percent

Place	Percent
No places met population threshold.	

Cubans 25 Years and Over Who are Four-Year College Graduates
Top 10 Places Sorted by Number

Place	Number
Indianapolis, IN (cons. city) Marion County	121

Cubans 25 Years and Over Who are Four-Year College Graduates
Top 10 Places Sorted by Percent

Place	Percent
Indianapolis, IN (cons. city) Marion County	40.60

Dominicans 25 Years and Over Who are Four-Year College Graduates
Top 10 Places Sorted by Number

Place	Number
No places met population threshold.	

Dominicans 25 Years and Over Who are Four-Year College Graduates
Top 10 Places Sorted by Percent

Place	Percent
No places met population threshold.	

Ecuadorians 25 Years and Over Who are Four-Year College Graduates
Top 10 Places Sorted by Number

Place	Number
No places met population threshold.	

Ecuadorians 25 Years and Over Who are Four-Year College Graduates
Top 10 Places Sorted by Percent

Place	Percent
No places met population threshold.	

Guatemalans 25 Years and Over Who are Four-Year College Graduates
Top 10 Places Sorted by Number

Place	Number
No places met population threshold.	

Guatemalans 25 Years and Over Who are Four-Year College Graduates
Top 10 Places Sorted by Percent

Place	Percent
No places met population threshold.	

Hondurans 25 Years and Over Who are Four-Year College Graduates
Top 10 Places Sorted by Number

Place	Number
No places met population threshold.	

Hondurans 25 Years and Over Who are Four-Year College Graduates
Top 10 Places Sorted by Percent

Place	Percent
No places met population threshold.	

Mexicans 25 Years and Over Who are Four-Year College Graduates
Top 10 Places Sorted by Number

Place	Number
Indianapolis, IN (cons. city) Marion County	820
Hammond, IN (city) Lake County	424
East Chicago, IN (city) Lake County	299

Notes: Please refer to the User's Guide for an explanation of data; tables include places with populations > 9,999 and reflect only those areas that meet Summary File 4 population thresholds, therefore there may be less than 10 places listed

Place	
Merrillville, IN (town) Lake County	170
Bloomington, IN (city) Monroe County	150
Highland, IN (town) Lake County	147
Fort Wayne, IN (city) Allen County	138
Munster, IN (town) Lake County	136
South Bend, IN (city) Saint Joseph County	135
Schererville, IN (town) Lake County	121

Mexicans 25 Years and Over Who are Four-Year College Graduates
Top 10 Places Sorted by Percent

Place	Percent
West Lafayette, IN (city) Tippecanoe County	65.05
Bloomington, IN (city) Monroe County	57.92
Munster, IN (town) Lake County	30.49
Highland, IN (town) Lake County	24.83
Crawfordsville, IN (city) Montgomery County	20.88
Schererville, IN (town) Lake County	18.85
Terre Haute, IN (city) Vigo County	17.14
Valparaiso, IN (city) Porter County	16.10
Merrillville, IN (town) Lake County	15.03
Muncie, IN (city) Delaware County	14.69

Nicaraguans 25 Years and Over Who are Four-Year College Graduates
Top 10 Places Sorted by Number

Place	Number
No places met population threshold.	

Nicaraguans 25 Years and Over Who are Four-Year College Graduates
Top 10 Places Sorted by Percent

Place	Percent
No places met population threshold.	

Panamanians 25 Years and Over Who are Four-Year College Graduates
Top 10 Places Sorted by Number

Place	Number
No places met population threshold.	

Panamanians 25 Years and Over Who are Four-Year College Graduates
Top 10 Places Sorted by Percent

Place	Percent
No places met population threshold.	

Paraguayans 25 Years and Over Who are Four-Year College Graduates
Top 10 Places Sorted by Number

Place	Number
No places met population threshold.	

Paraguayans 25 Years and Over Who are Four-Year College Graduates
Top 10 Places Sorted by Percent

Place	Percent
No places met population threshold.	

Peruvians 25 Years and Over Who are Four-Year College Graduates
Top 10 Places Sorted by Number

Place	Number
No places met population threshold.	

Peruvians 25 Years and Over Who are Four-Year College Graduates
Top 10 Places Sorted by Percent

Place	Percent
No places met population threshold.	

Puerto Ricans 25 Years and Over Who are Four-Year College Graduates
Top 10 Places Sorted by Number

Place	Number
Indianapolis, IN (cons. city) Marion County	311
East Chicago, IN (city) Lake County	137
Hammond, IN (city) Lake County	69
South Bend, IN (city) Saint Joseph County	56
Fort Wayne, IN (city) Allen County	44
Gary, IN (city) Lake County	35
Portage, IN (city) Porter County	33
Hobart, IN (city) Lake County	20
Lake Station, IN (city) Lake County	6

Puerto Ricans 25 Years and Over Who are Four-Year College Graduates
Top 10 Places Sorted by Percent

Place	Percent
Indianapolis, IN (cons. city) Marion County	32.06
South Bend, IN (city) Saint Joseph County	23.43
Fort Wayne, IN (city) Allen County	13.75
Hobart, IN (city) Lake County	8.73
Portage, IN (city) Porter County	8.11
Hammond, IN (city) Lake County	7.52
East Chicago, IN (city) Lake County	7.25
Gary, IN (city) Lake County	4.82
Lake Station, IN (city) Lake County	1.38

Salvadorans 25 Years and Over Who are Four-Year College Graduates
Top 10 Places Sorted by Number

Place	Number
Indianapolis, IN (cons. city) Marion County	12

Salvadorans 25 Years and Over Who are Four-Year College Graduates
Top 10 Places Sorted by Percent

Place	Percent
Indianapolis, IN (cons. city) Marion County	3.51

South Americans 25 Years and Over Who are Four-Year College Graduates
Top 10 Places Sorted by Number

Place	Number
Indianapolis, IN (cons. city) Marion County	342

South Americans 25 Years and Over Who are Four-Year College Graduates
Top 10 Places Sorted by Percent

Place	Percent
Indianapolis, IN (cons. city) Marion County	55.79

Spaniards 25 Years and Over Who are Four-Year College Graduates
Top 10 Places Sorted by Number

Place	Number
No places met population threshold.	

Spaniards 25 Years and Over Who are Four-Year College Graduates
Top 10 Places Sorted by Percent

Place	Percent
No places met population threshold.	

Uruguayans 25 Years and Over Who are Four-Year College Graduates
Top 10 Places Sorted by Number

Place	Number
No places met population threshold.	

Uruguayans 25 Years and Over Who are Four-Year College Graduates
Top 10 Places Sorted by Percent

Place	Percent
No places met population threshold.	

Venezuelans 25 Years and Over Who are Four-Year College Graduates
Top 10 Places Sorted by Number

Place	Number
No places met population threshold.	

Venezuelans 25 Years and Over Who are Four-Year College Graduates
Top 10 Places Sorted by Percent

Place	Percent
No places met population threshold.	

Other Hispanics 25 Years and Over Who are Four-Year College Graduates
Top 10 Places Sorted by Number

Place	Number
Indianapolis, IN (cons. city) Marion County	304
Fort Wayne, IN (city) Allen County	60
Hammond, IN (city) Lake County	40
Lafayette, IN (city) Tippecanoe County	15
South Bend, IN (city) Saint Joseph County	15
East Chicago, IN (city) Lake County	14
Elkhart, IN (city) Elkhart County	9
Gary, IN (city) Lake County	0

Other Hispanics 25 Years and Over Who are Four-Year College Graduates
Top 10 Places Sorted by Percent

Place	Percent
Indianapolis, IN (cons. city) Marion County	16.34
Fort Wayne, IN (city) Allen County	8.65
Lafayette, IN (city) Tippecanoe County	8.47
Hammond, IN (city) Lake County	7.58
East Chicago, IN (city) Lake County	3.79
South Bend, IN (city) Saint Joseph County	3.64
Elkhart, IN (city) Elkhart County	3.02
Gary, IN (city) Lake County	0.00

Median Household Income

Total Population
Top 10 Places Sorted by Number

Place	Dollars
Carmel, IN (city) Hamilton County	81,583
Fishers, IN (town) Hamilton County	75,638
Munster, IN (town) Lake County	63,243
Dyer, IN (town) Lake County	63,045
Noblesville, IN (city) Hamilton County	61,455
Schererville, IN (town) Lake County	59,243
Crown Point, IN (city) Lake County	52,889
Highland, IN (town) Lake County	51,297
Griffith, IN (town) Lake County	50,030
Merrillville, IN (town) Lake County	49,545

Hispanic
Top 10 Places Sorted by Number

Place	Dollars
Carmel, IN (city) Hamilton County	94,226

Notes: Please refer to the User's Guide for an explanation of data; tables include places with populations > 9,999 and reflect only those areas that meet Summary File 4 population thresholds, therefore there may be less than 10 places listed

Place	Dollars
Munster, IN (town) Lake County	75,665
Fishers, IN (town) Hamilton County	72,083
Dyer, IN (town) Lake County	66,346
Highland, IN (town) Lake County	63,750
Griffith, IN (town) Lake County	61,417
Schererville, IN (town) Lake County	56,533
Crown Point, IN (city) Lake County	54,833
Portage, IN (city) Porter County	52,391
Greenwood, IN (city) Johnson County	50,714

Argentinian
Top 10 Places Sorted by Number

Place	Dollars
No places met population threshold.	

Bolivian
Top 10 Places Sorted by Number

Place	Dollars
No places met population threshold.	

Central American
Top 10 Places Sorted by Number

Place	Dollars
Indianapolis, IN (cons. city) Marion County	41,951

Chilean
Top 10 Places Sorted by Number

Place	Dollars
No places met population threshold.	

Colombian
Top 10 Places Sorted by Number

Place	Dollars
No places met population threshold.	

Costa Rican
Top 10 Places Sorted by Number

Place	Dollars
No places met population threshold.	

Cuban
Top 10 Places Sorted by Number

Place	Dollars
Indianapolis, IN (cons. city) Marion County	38,611

Dominican
Top 10 Places Sorted by Number

Place	Dollars
No places met population threshold.	

Ecuadorian
Top 10 Places Sorted by Number

Place	Dollars
No places met population threshold.	

Guatemalan
Top 10 Places Sorted by Number

Place	Dollars
No places met population threshold.	

Honduran
Top 10 Places Sorted by Number

Place	Dollars
No places met population threshold.	

Mexican
Top 10 Places Sorted by Number

Place	Dollars
Munster, IN (town) Lake County	68,750
Dyer, IN (town) Lake County	66,010
Highland, IN (town) Lake County	61,759
Griffith, IN (town) Lake County	60,750
Schererville, IN (town) Lake County	56,541
Portage, IN (city) Porter County	54,313
Crown Point, IN (city) Lake County	49,318
Merrillville, IN (town) Lake County	49,286
Hobart, IN (city) Lake County	49,107
Warsaw, IN (city) Kosciusko County	46,042

Nicaraguan
Top 10 Places Sorted by Number

Place	Dollars
No places met population threshold.	

Panamanian
Top 10 Places Sorted by Number

Place	Dollars
No places met population threshold.	

Paraguayan
Top 10 Places Sorted by Number

Place	Dollars
No places met population threshold.	

Peruvian
Top 10 Places Sorted by Number

Place	Dollars
No places met population threshold.	

Puerto Rican
Top 10 Places Sorted by Number

Place	Dollars
Portage, IN (city) Porter County	53,958
Hobart, IN (city) Lake County	53,611
Indianapolis, IN (cons. city) Marion County	38,192
Hammond, IN (city) Lake County	37,212
Lake Station, IN (city) Lake County	36,591
Fort Wayne, IN (city) Allen County	35,625
South Bend, IN (city) Saint Joseph County	28,750
Gary, IN (city) Lake County	25,739
East Chicago, IN (city) Lake County	23,964

Salvadoran
Top 10 Places Sorted by Number

Place	Dollars
Indianapolis, IN (cons. city) Marion County	50,605

South American
Top 10 Places Sorted by Number

Place	Dollars
Indianapolis, IN (cons. city) Marion County	49,583

Spaniard
Top 10 Places Sorted by Number

Place	Dollars
No places met population threshold.	

Uruguayan
Top 10 Places Sorted by Number

Place	Dollars
No places met population threshold.	

Venezuelan
Top 10 Places Sorted by Number

Place	Dollars
No places met population threshold.	

Other Hispanic
Top 10 Places Sorted by Number

Place	Dollars
East Chicago, IN (city) Lake County	36,000
Hammond, IN (city) Lake County	33,466
Elkhart, IN (city) Elkhart County	31,875
Indianapolis, IN (cons. city) Marion County	30,679
Fort Wayne, IN (city) Allen County	27,619
South Bend, IN (city) Saint Joseph County	27,438
Lafayette, IN (city) Tippecanoe County	23,839
Gary, IN (city) Lake County	19,583

Per Capita Income

Total Population
Top 10 Places Sorted by Number

Place	Dollars
Carmel, IN (city) Hamilton County	38,906
Fishers, IN (town) Hamilton County	31,891
Munster, IN (town) Lake County	30,952
Noblesville, IN (city) Hamilton County	28,813
Schererville, IN (town) Lake County	28,528
Dyer, IN (town) Lake County	27,390
Crown Point, IN (city) Lake County	24,568
Highland, IN (town) Lake County	24,530
Greenwood, IN (city) Johnson County	23,003
Lawrence, IN (city) Marion County	22,543

Hispanic
Top 10 Places Sorted by Number

Place	Dollars
Carmel, IN (city) Hamilton County	31,906
Fishers, IN (town) Hamilton County	27,148
Munster, IN (town) Lake County	24,545
Highland, IN (town) Lake County	23,043
Griffith, IN (town) Lake County	21,408
Clarksville, IN (town) Clark County	19,526
Crown Point, IN (city) Lake County	19,220
Dyer, IN (town) Lake County	18,700
Schererville, IN (town) Lake County	18,601
Hobart, IN (city) Lake County	17,411

Argentinian
Top 10 Places Sorted by Number

Place	Dollars
No places met population threshold.	

Bolivian
Top 10 Places Sorted by Number

Place	Dollars
No places met population threshold.	

Central American
Top 10 Places Sorted by Number

Place	Dollars
Indianapolis, IN (cons. city) Marion County	13,948

Chilean
Top 10 Places Sorted by Number

Place	Dollars
No places met population threshold.	

Notes: Please refer to the User's Guide for an explanation of data; tables include places with populations > 9,999 and reflect only those areas that meet Summary File 4 population thresholds, therefore there may be less than 10 places listed

Colombian
Top 10 Places Sorted by Number

Place	Dollars
No places met population threshold.	

Costa Rican
Top 10 Places Sorted by Number

Place	Dollars
No places met population threshold.	

Cuban
Top 10 Places Sorted by Number

Place	Dollars
Indianapolis, IN (cons. city) Marion County	13,330

Dominican
Top 10 Places Sorted by Number

Place	Dollars
No places met population threshold.	

Ecuadorian
Top 10 Places Sorted by Number

Place	Dollars
No places met population threshold.	

Guatemalan
Top 10 Places Sorted by Number

Place	Dollars
No places met population threshold.	

Honduran
Top 10 Places Sorted by Number

Place	Dollars
No places met population threshold.	

Mexican
Top 10 Places Sorted by Number

Place	Dollars
Munster, IN (town) Lake County	25,952
Highland, IN (town) Lake County	25,082
Griffith, IN (town) Lake County	23,668
Dyer, IN (town) Lake County	21,234
Crown Point, IN (city) Lake County	18,685
Schererville, IN (town) Lake County	18,189
Lawrence, IN (city) Marion County	16,998
Portage, IN (city) Porter County	16,858
Clarksville, IN (town) Clark County	16,589
Gary, IN (city) Lake County	14,959

Nicaraguan
Top 10 Places Sorted by Number

Place	Dollars
No places met population threshold.	

Panamanian
Top 10 Places Sorted by Number

Place	Dollars
No places met population threshold.	

Paraguayan
Top 10 Places Sorted by Number

Place	Dollars
No places met population threshold.	

Peruvian
Top 10 Places Sorted by Number

Place	Dollars
No places met population threshold.	

Puerto Rican
Top 10 Places Sorted by Number

Place	Dollars
Hobart, IN (city) Lake County	27,509
South Bend, IN (city) Saint Joseph County	18,037
Portage, IN (city) Porter County	17,386
Indianapolis, IN (cons. city) Marion County	16,027
Lake Station, IN (city) Lake County	15,040
East Chicago, IN (city) Lake County	13,740
Fort Wayne, IN (city) Allen County	13,377
Hammond, IN (city) Lake County	12,132
Gary, IN (city) Lake County	10,598

Salvadoran
Top 10 Places Sorted by Number

Place	Dollars
Indianapolis, IN (cons. city) Marion County	15,088

South American
Top 10 Places Sorted by Number

Place	Dollars
Indianapolis, IN (cons. city) Marion County	20,279

Spaniard
Top 10 Places Sorted by Number

Place	Dollars
No places met population threshold.	

Uruguayan
Top 10 Places Sorted by Number

Place	Dollars
No places met population threshold.	

Venezuelan
Top 10 Places Sorted by Number

Place	Dollars
No places met population threshold.	

Other Hispanic
Top 10 Places Sorted by Number

Place	Dollars
Indianapolis, IN (cons. city) Marion County	15,297
Gary, IN (city) Lake County	13,191
Fort Wayne, IN (city) Allen County	11,094
Hammond, IN (city) Lake County	9,433
Lafayette, IN (city) Tippecanoe County	9,254
South Bend, IN (city) Saint Joseph County	8,558
East Chicago, IN (city) Lake County	8,317
Elkhart, IN (city) Elkhart County	8,197

Poverty Status

Total Populations with Income Below Poverty Level
Top 10 Places Sorted by Number

Place	Number
Indianapolis, IN (cons. city) Marion County	91,163
Gary, IN (city) Lake County	26,117
Fort Wayne, IN (city) Allen County	25,204
South Bend, IN (city) Saint Joseph County	17,452
Bloomington, IN (city) Monroe County	16,385
Evansville, IN (city) Vanderburgh County	16,039
Muncie, IN (city) Delaware County	14,118
Hammond, IN (city) Lake County	11,807
Terre Haute, IN (city) Vigo County	10,020

West Lafayette, IN (city) Tippecanoe County   9,099

Total Populations with Income Below Poverty Level
Top 10 Places Sorted by Percent

Place	Percent
West Lafayette, IN (city) Tippecanoe County	38.30
Bloomington, IN (city) Monroe County	29.62
Gary, IN (city) Lake County	25.79
East Chicago, IN (city) Lake County	24.37
Muncie, IN (city) Delaware County	23.09
Terre Haute, IN (city) Vigo County	19.20
Marion, IN (city) Grant County	16.93
South Bend, IN (city) Saint Joseph County	16.67
Richmond, IN (city) Wayne County	15.68
Lake Station, IN (city) Lake County	14.56

Hispanics with Income Below Poverty Level
Top 10 Places Sorted by Number

Place	Number
Indianapolis, IN (cons. city) Marion County	5,870
East Chicago, IN (city) Lake County	3,365
Hammond, IN (city) Lake County	2,791
Fort Wayne, IN (city) Allen County	2,506
South Bend, IN (city) Saint Joseph County	2,052
Elkhart, IN (city) Elkhart County	1,631
Gary, IN (city) Lake County	1,088
Goshen, IN (city) Elkhart County	1,009
Lafayette, IN (city) Tippecanoe County	985
Frankfort, IN (city) Clinton County	628

Hispanics with Income Below Poverty Level
Top 10 Places Sorted by Percent

Place	Percent
West Lafayette, IN (city) Tippecanoe County	52.77
Marion, IN (city) Grant County	41.17
Bloomington, IN (city) Monroe County	38.62
Anderson, IN (city) Madison County	35.36
Muncie, IN (city) Delaware County	34.14
Washington, IN (city) Daviess County	32.34
Frankfort, IN (city) Clinton County	27.48
Michigan City, IN (city) La Porte County	27.44
Richmond, IN (city) Wayne County	27.44
Terre Haute, IN (city) Vigo County	26.70

Argentinians with Income Below Poverty Level
Top 10 Places Sorted by Number

Place	Number
No places met population threshold.	

Argentinians with Income Below Poverty Level
Top 10 Places Sorted by Percent

Place	Percent
No places met population threshold.	

Bolivians with Income Below Poverty Level
Top 10 Places Sorted by Number

Place	Number
No places met population threshold.	

Bolivians with Income Below Poverty Level
Top 10 Places Sorted by Percent

Place	Percent
No places met population threshold.	

Central Americans with Income Below Poverty Level
Top 10 Places Sorted by Number

Place	Number
Indianapolis, IN (cons. city) Marion County	230

Notes: Please refer to the User's Guide for an explanation of data; tables include places with populations > 9,999 and reflect only those areas that meet Summary File 4 population thresholds, therefore there may be less than 10 places listed

Central Americans with Income Below Poverty Level
Top 10 Places Sorted by Percent

Place	Percent
Indianapolis, IN (cons. city) Marion County	13.56

Chileans with Income Below Poverty Level
Top 10 Places Sorted by Number

Place	Number
No places met population threshold.	

Chileans with Income Below Poverty Level
Top 10 Places Sorted by Percent

Place	Percent
No places met population threshold.	

Colombians with Income Below Poverty Level
Top 10 Places Sorted by Number

Place	Number
No places met population threshold.	

Colombians with Income Below Poverty Level
Top 10 Places Sorted by Percent

Place	Percent
No places met population threshold.	

Costa Ricans with Income Below Poverty Level
Top 10 Places Sorted by Number

Place	Number
No places met population threshold.	

Costa Ricans with Income Below Poverty Level
Top 10 Places Sorted by Percent

Place	Percent
No places met population threshold.	

Cubans with Income Below Poverty Level
Top 10 Places Sorted by Number

Place	Number
Indianapolis, IN (cons. city) Marion County	19

Cubans with Income Below Poverty Level
Top 10 Places Sorted by Percent

Place	Percent
Indianapolis, IN (cons. city) Marion County	3.63

Dominicans with Income Below Poverty Level
Top 10 Places Sorted by Number

Place	Number
No places met population threshold.	

Dominicans with Income Below Poverty Level
Top 10 Places Sorted by Percent

Place	Percent
No places met population threshold.	

Ecuadorians with Income Below Poverty Level
Top 10 Places Sorted by Number

Place	Number
No places met population threshold.	

Ecuadorians with Income Below Poverty Level
Top 10 Places Sorted by Percent

Place	Percent
No places met population threshold.	

Guatemalans with Income Below Poverty Level
Top 10 Places Sorted by Number

Place	Number
No places met population threshold.	

Guatemalans with Income Below Poverty Level
Top 10 Places Sorted by Percent

Place	Percent
No places met population threshold.	

Hondurans with Income Below Poverty Level
Top 10 Places Sorted by Number

Place	Number
No places met population threshold.	

Hondurans with Income Below Poverty Level
Top 10 Places Sorted by Percent

Place	Percent
No places met population threshold.	

Mexicans with Income Below Poverty Level
Top 10 Places Sorted by Number

Place	Number
Indianapolis, IN (cons. city) Marion County	4,604
East Chicago, IN (city) Lake County	2,268
Hammond, IN (city) Lake County	2,138
Fort Wayne, IN (city) Allen County	1,748
South Bend, IN (city) Saint Joseph County	1,621
Elkhart, IN (city) Elkhart County	1,502
Goshen, IN (city) Elkhart County	875
Lafayette, IN (city) Tippecanoe County	805
Frankfort, IN (city) Clinton County	581
Gary, IN (city) Lake County	563

Mexicans with Income Below Poverty Level
Top 10 Places Sorted by Percent

Place	Percent
Anderson, IN (city) Madison County	43.39
Marion, IN (city) Grant County	40.05
West Lafayette, IN (city) Tippecanoe County	35.71
Bloomington, IN (city) Monroe County	34.77
Muncie, IN (city) Delaware County	33.05
Washington, IN (city) Daviess County	30.17
Frankfort, IN (city) Clinton County	28.14
Lawrence, IN (city) Marion County	27.48
Michigan City, IN (city) La Porte County	27.37
Evansville, IN (city) Vanderburgh County	26.20

Nicaraguans with Income Below Poverty Level
Top 10 Places Sorted by Number

Place	Number
No places met population threshold.	

Nicaraguans with Income Below Poverty Level
Top 10 Places Sorted by Percent

Place	Percent
No places met population threshold.	

Panamanians with Income Below Poverty Level
Top 10 Places Sorted by Number

Place	Number
No places met population threshold.	

Panamanians with Income Below Poverty Level
Top 10 Places Sorted by Percent

Place	Percent
No places met population threshold.	

Paraguayans with Income Below Poverty Level
Top 10 Places Sorted by Number

Place	Number
No places met population threshold.	

Paraguayans with Income Below Poverty Level
Top 10 Places Sorted by Percent

Place	Percent
No places met population threshold.	

Peruvians with Income Below Poverty Level
Top 10 Places Sorted by Number

Place	Number
No places met population threshold.	

Peruvians with Income Below Poverty Level
Top 10 Places Sorted by Percent

Place	Percent
No places met population threshold.	

Puerto Ricans with Income Below Poverty Level
Top 10 Places Sorted by Number

Place	Number
East Chicago, IN (city) Lake County	924
Gary, IN (city) Lake County	392
Hammond, IN (city) Lake County	300
Indianapolis, IN (cons. city) Marion County	272
Lake Station, IN (city) Lake County	187
South Bend, IN (city) Saint Joseph County	174
Portage, IN (city) Porter County	114
Fort Wayne, IN (city) Allen County	111
Hobart, IN (city) Lake County	102

Puerto Ricans with Income Below Poverty Level
Top 10 Places Sorted by Percent

Place	Percent
South Bend, IN (city) Saint Joseph County	37.42
Gary, IN (city) Lake County	31.36
East Chicago, IN (city) Lake County	30.36
Lake Station, IN (city) Lake County	23.58
Hobart, IN (city) Lake County	21.52
Fort Wayne, IN (city) Allen County	18.56
Hammond, IN (city) Lake County	16.51
Indianapolis, IN (cons. city) Marion County	14.12
Portage, IN (city) Porter County	12.77

Salvadorans with Income Below Poverty Level
Top 10 Places Sorted by Number

Place	Number
Indianapolis, IN (cons. city) Marion County	88

Salvadorans with Income Below Poverty Level
Top 10 Places Sorted by Percent

Place	Percent
Indianapolis, IN (cons. city) Marion County	19.38

South Americans with Income Below Poverty Level
Top 10 Places Sorted by Number

Place	Number
Indianapolis, IN (cons. city) Marion County	85

South Americans with Income Below Poverty Level
Top 10 Places Sorted by Percent

Place	Percent
Indianapolis, IN (cons. city) Marion County	8.66

Notes: Please refer to the User's Guide for an explanation of data; tables include places with populations > 9,999 and reflect only those areas that meet Summary File 4 population thresholds, therefore there may be less than 10 places listed

Spaniards with Income Below Poverty Level
Top 10 Places Sorted by Number

Place	Number
No places met population threshold.	

Spaniards with Income Below Poverty Level
Top 10 Places Sorted by Percent

Place	Percent
No places met population threshold.	

Uruguayans with Income Below Poverty Level
Top 10 Places Sorted by Number

Place	Number
No places met population threshold.	

Uruguayans with Income Below Poverty Level
Top 10 Places Sorted by Percent

Place	Percent
No places met population threshold.	

Venezuelans with Income Below Poverty Level
Top 10 Places Sorted by Number

Place	Number
No places met population threshold.	

Venezuelans with Income Below Poverty Level
Top 10 Places Sorted by Percent

Place	Percent
No places met population threshold.	

Other Hispanics with Income Below Poverty Level
Top 10 Places Sorted by Number

Place	Number
Indianapolis, IN (cons. city) Marion County	660
Fort Wayne, IN (city) Allen County	324
Hammond, IN (city) Lake County	308
South Bend, IN (city) Saint Joseph County	199
East Chicago, IN (city) Lake County	148
Lafayette, IN (city) Tippecanoe County	72
Gary, IN (city) Lake County	56
Elkhart, IN (city) Elkhart County	17

Other Hispanics with Income Below Poverty Level
Top 10 Places Sorted by Percent

Place	Percent
Hammond, IN (city) Lake County	23.28
Fort Wayne, IN (city) Allen County	21.91
South Bend, IN (city) Saint Joseph County	20.93
Indianapolis, IN (cons. city) Marion County	19.30
Lafayette, IN (city) Tippecanoe County	18.32
East Chicago, IN (city) Lake County	13.09
Gary, IN (city) Lake County	11.38
Elkhart, IN (city) Elkhart County	2.34

Homeownership

Total Populations Who Own Their Own Homes
Top 10 Places Sorted by Number

Place	Number
Indianapolis, IN (cons. city) Marion County	190,613
Fort Wayne, IN (city) Allen County	51,316
Evansville, IN (city) Vanderburgh County	31,357
South Bend, IN (city) Saint Joseph County	26,991
Gary, IN (city) Lake County	21,360
Hammond, IN (city) Lake County	20,236
Anderson, IN (city) Madison County	16,084
Muncie, IN (city) Delaware County	15,243
Terre Haute, IN (city) Vigo County	13,542
Lafayette, IN (city) Tippecanoe County	12,650

Total Populations Who Own Their Own Homes
Top 10 Places Sorted by Percent

Place	Percent
Dyer, IN (town) Lake County	91.47
Munster, IN (town) Lake County	89.12
Hobart, IN (town) Lake County	80.25
Lake Station, IN (city) Lake County	79.03
Carmel, IN (city) Hamilton County	78.96
Highland, IN (town) Lake County	78.60
Fishers, IN (town) Hamilton County	77.93
Lawrence, IN (city) Marion County	75.47
Noblesville, IN (city) Hamilton County	75.27
Crown Point, IN (city) Lake County	74.11

Hispanics Who Own Their Own Homes
Top 10 Places Sorted by Number

Place	Number
Hammond, IN (city) Lake County	2,958
East Chicago, IN (city) Lake County	2,495
Indianapolis, IN (cons. city) Marion County	2,172
Fort Wayne, IN (city) Allen County	1,374
South Bend, IN (city) Saint Joseph County	1,257
Gary, IN (city) Lake County	976
Portage, IN (city) Porter County	675
Merrillville, IN (town) Lake County	621
Lake Station, IN (city) Lake County	567
Elkhart, IN (city) Elkhart County	557

Hispanics Who Own Their Own Homes
Top 10 Places Sorted by Percent

Place	Percent
Dyer, IN (town) Lake County	89.25
Munster, IN (town) Lake County	80.89
Highland, IN (town) Lake County	76.38
Hobart, IN (city) Lake County	74.34
Merrillville, IN (town) Lake County	74.28
Lake Station, IN (city) Lake County	73.45
Portage, IN (city) Porter County	65.85
Schererville, IN (town) Lake County	64.58
Hammond, IN (city) Lake County	63.74
Gary, IN (city) Lake County	63.25

Argentinians Who Own Their Own Homes
Top 10 Places Sorted by Number

Place	Number
No places met population threshold.	

Argentinians Who Own Their Own Homes
Top 10 Places Sorted by Percent

Place	Percent
No places met population threshold.	

Bolivians Who Own Their Own Homes
Top 10 Places Sorted by Number

Place	Number
No places met population threshold.	

Bolivians Who Own Their Own Homes
Top 10 Places Sorted by Percent

Place	Percent
No places met population threshold.	

Central Americans Who Own Their Own Homes
Top 10 Places Sorted by Number

Place	Number
Indianapolis, IN (cons. city) Marion County	125

Central Americans Who Own Their Own Homes
Top 10 Places Sorted by Percent

Place	Percent
Indianapolis, IN (cons. city) Marion County	22.94

Chileans Who Own Their Own Homes
Top 10 Places Sorted by Number

Place	Number
No places met population threshold.	

Chileans Who Own Their Own Homes
Top 10 Places Sorted by Percent

Place	Percent
No places met population threshold.	

Colombians Who Own Their Own Homes
Top 10 Places Sorted by Number

Place	Number
No places met population threshold.	

Colombians Who Own Their Own Homes
Top 10 Places Sorted by Percent

Place	Percent
No places met population threshold.	

Costa Ricans Who Own Their Own Homes
Top 10 Places Sorted by Number

Place	Number
No places met population threshold.	

Costa Ricans Who Own Their Own Homes
Top 10 Places Sorted by Percent

Place	Percent
No places met population threshold.	

Cubans Who Own Their Own Homes
Top 10 Places Sorted by Number

Place	Number
Indianapolis, IN (cons. city) Marion County	53

Cubans Who Own Their Own Homes
Top 10 Places Sorted by Percent

Place	Percent
Indianapolis, IN (cons. city) Marion County	30.81

Dominicans Who Own Their Own Homes
Top 10 Places Sorted by Number

Place	Number
No places met population threshold.	

Dominicans Who Own Their Own Homes
Top 10 Places Sorted by Percent

Place	Percent
No places met population threshold.	

Ecuadorians Who Own Their Own Homes
Top 10 Places Sorted by Number

Place	Number
No places met population threshold.	

Ecuadorians Who Own Their Own Homes
Top 10 Places Sorted by Percent

Place	Percent
No places met population threshold.	

Notes: Please refer to the User's Guide for an explanation of data; tables include places with populations > 9,999 and reflect only those areas that meet Summary File 4 population thresholds, therefore there may be less than 10 places listed

Guatemalans Who Own Their Own Homes
Top 10 Places Sorted by Number

Place	Number
No places met population threshold.	

Guatemalans Who Own Their Own Homes
Top 10 Places Sorted by Percent

Place	Percent
No places met population threshold.	

Hondurans Who Own Their Own Homes
Top 10 Places Sorted by Number

Place	Number
No places met population threshold.	

Hondurans Who Own Their Own Homes
Top 10 Places Sorted by Percent

Place	Percent
No places met population threshold.	

Mexicans Who Own Their Own Homes
Top 10 Places Sorted by Number

Place	Number
Hammond, IN (city) Lake County	2,418
East Chicago, IN (city) Lake County	1,915
Indianapolis, IN (cons. city) Marion County	1,352
South Bend, IN (city) Saint Joseph County	978
Fort Wayne, IN (city) Allen County	962
Gary, IN (city) Lake County	625
Merrillville, IN (town) Lake County	452
Portage, IN (city) Porter County	431
Elkhart, IN (city) Elkhart County	430
Goshen, IN (city) Elkhart County	391

Mexicans Who Own Their Own Homes
Top 10 Places Sorted by Percent

Place	Percent
Dyer, IN (town) Lake County	87.18
Munster, IN (town) Lake County	77.90
Merrillville, IN (town) Lake County	76.87
Hobart, IN (city) Lake County	75.90
Lake Station, IN (city) Lake County	72.58
Highland, IN (town) Lake County	72.31
Gary, IN (city) Lake County	68.31
Portage, IN (city) Porter County	66.93
Hammond, IN (city) Lake County	65.00
Marion, IN (city) Grant County	64.88

Nicaraguans Who Own Their Own Homes
Top 10 Places Sorted by Number

Place	Number
No places met population threshold.	

Nicaraguans Who Own Their Own Homes
Top 10 Places Sorted by Percent

Place	Percent
No places met population threshold.	

Panamanians Who Own Their Own Homes
Top 10 Places Sorted by Number

Place	Number
No places met population threshold.	

Panamanians Who Own Their Own Homes
Top 10 Places Sorted by Percent

Place	Percent
No places met population threshold.	

Paraguayans Who Own Their Own Homes
Top 10 Places Sorted by Number

Place	Number
No places met population threshold.	

Paraguayans Who Own Their Own Homes
Top 10 Places Sorted by Percent

Place	Percent
No places met population threshold.	

Peruvians Who Own Their Own Homes
Top 10 Places Sorted by Number

Place	Number
No places met population threshold.	

Peruvians Who Own Their Own Homes
Top 10 Places Sorted by Percent

Place	Percent
No places met population threshold.	

Puerto Ricans Who Own Their Own Homes
Top 10 Places Sorted by Number

Place	Number
East Chicago, IN (city) Lake County	453
Hammond, IN (city) Lake County	365
Gary, IN (city) Lake County	232
Lake Station, IN (city) Lake County	189
Portage, IN (city) Porter County	176
Indianapolis, IN (cons. city) Marion County	151
Hobart, IN (city) Lake County	117
Fort Wayne, IN (city) Allen County	102
South Bend, IN (city) Saint Joseph County	93

Puerto Ricans Who Own Their Own Homes
Top 10 Places Sorted by Percent

Place	Percent
South Bend, IN (city) Saint Joseph County	78.81
Lake Station, IN (city) Lake County	71.86
Hobart, IN (city) Lake County	71.78
Portage, IN (city) Porter County	63.08
Hammond, IN (city) Lake County	62.61
Fort Wayne, IN (city) Allen County	52.85
Gary, IN (city) Lake County	49.89
East Chicago, IN (city) Lake County	40.66
Indianapolis, IN (cons. city) Marion County	24.92

Salvadorans Who Own Their Own Homes
Top 10 Places Sorted by Number

Place	Number
Indianapolis, IN (cons. city) Marion County	54

Salvadorans Who Own Their Own Homes
Top 10 Places Sorted by Percent

Place	Percent
Indianapolis, IN (cons. city) Marion County	36.49

South Americans Who Own Their Own Homes
Top 10 Places Sorted by Number

Place	Number
Indianapolis, IN (cons. city) Marion County	144

South Americans Who Own Their Own Homes
Top 10 Places Sorted by Percent

Place	Percent
Indianapolis, IN (cons. city) Marion County	45.00

Spaniards Who Own Their Own Homes
Top 10 Places Sorted by Number

Place	Number
No places met population threshold.	

Spaniards Who Own Their Own Homes
Top 10 Places Sorted by Percent

Place	Percent
No places met population threshold.	

Uruguayans Who Own Their Own Homes
Top 10 Places Sorted by Number

Place	Number
No places met population threshold.	

Uruguayans Who Own Their Own Homes
Top 10 Places Sorted by Percent

Place	Percent
No places met population threshold.	

Venezuelans Who Own Their Own Homes
Top 10 Places Sorted by Number

Place	Number
No places met population threshold.	

Venezuelans Who Own Their Own Homes
Top 10 Places Sorted by Percent

Place	Percent
No places met population threshold.	

Other Hispanics Who Own Their Own Homes
Top 10 Places Sorted by Number

Place	Number
Indianapolis, IN (cons. city) Marion County	326
Fort Wayne, IN (city) Allen County	240
Hammond, IN (city) Lake County	139
South Bend, IN (city) Saint Joseph County	113
Elkhart, IN (city) Elkhart County	92
East Chicago, IN (city) Lake County	91
Gary, IN (city) Lake County	79
Lafayette, IN (city) Tippecanoe County	43

Other Hispanics Who Own Their Own Homes
Top 10 Places Sorted by Percent

Place	Percent
Gary, IN (city) Lake County	69.30
Elkhart, IN (city) Elkhart County	64.34
Fort Wayne, IN (city) Allen County	52.06
Hammond, IN (city) Lake County	50.36
East Chicago, IN (city) Lake County	47.89
South Bend, IN (city) Saint Joseph County	47.88
Indianapolis, IN (cons. city) Marion County	35.21
Lafayette, IN (city) Tippecanoe County	34.68

Median Gross Rent

All Specified Renter-Occupied Housing Units
Top 10 Places Sorted by Number

Place	Dollars/Month
Fishers, IN (town) Hamilton County	797
Munster, IN (town) Lake County	771
Carmel, IN (city) Hamilton County	748
Highland, IN (town) Lake County	711
Merrillville, IN (town) Lake County	704
Dyer, IN (town) Lake County	674
Schererville, IN (town) Lake County	656
Crown Point, IN (city) Lake County	655
Griffith, IN (town) Lake County	644
Noblesville, IN (city) Hamilton County	629

Notes: Please refer to the User's Guide for an explanation of data; tables include places with populations > 9,999 and reflect only those areas that meet Summary File 4 population thresholds, therefore there may be less than 10 places listed

Specified Housing Units Rented by Hispanics
Top 10 Places Sorted by Number

Place	Dollars/Month
Highland, IN (town) Lake County	776
Fishers, IN (town) Hamilton County	771
Carmel, IN (city) Hamilton County	748
Griffith, IN (town) Lake County	693
Munster, IN (town) Lake County	687
Dyer, IN (town) Lake County	655
Hobart, IN (city) Lake County	654
Crown Point, IN (city) Lake County	642
Merrillville, IN (town) Lake County	628
Valparaiso, IN (city) Porter County	619

Specified Housing Units Rented by Argentinians
Top 10 Places Sorted by Number

Place	Dollars/Month
No places met population threshold.	

Specified Housing Units Rented by Bolivians
Top 10 Places Sorted by Number

Place	Dollars/Month
No places met population threshold.	

Specified Housing Units Rented by Central Americans
Top 10 Places Sorted by Number

Place	Dollars/Month
Indianapolis, IN (cons. city) Marion County	563

Specified Housing Units Rented by Chileans
Top 10 Places Sorted by Number

Place	Dollars/Month
No places met population threshold.	

Specified Housing Units Rented by Colombians
Top 10 Places Sorted by Number

Place	Dollars/Month
No places met population threshold.	

Specified Housing Units Rented by Costa Ricans
Top 10 Places Sorted by Number

Place	Dollars/Month
No places met population threshold.	

Specified Housing Units Rented by Cubans
Top 10 Places Sorted by Number

Place	Dollars/Month
Indianapolis, IN (cons. city) Marion County	566

Specified Housing Units Rented by Dominicans
Top 10 Places Sorted by Number

Place	Dollars/Month
No places met population threshold.	

Specified Housing Units Rented by Ecuadorians
Top 10 Places Sorted by Number

Place	Dollars/Month
No places met population threshold.	

Specified Housing Units Rented by Guatemalans
Top 10 Places Sorted by Number

Place	Dollars/Month
No places met population threshold.	

Specified Housing Units Rented by Hondurans
Top 10 Places Sorted by Number

Place	Dollars/Month
No places met population threshold.	

Specified Housing Units Rented by Mexicans
Top 10 Places Sorted by Number

Place	Dollars/Month
Highland, IN (town) Lake County	763
Munster, IN (town) Lake County	725
Griffith, IN (town) Lake County	722
Dyer, IN (town) Lake County	655
Crown Point, IN (city) Lake County	625
Columbus, IN (city) Bartholomew County	610
Merrillville, IN (town) Lake County	607
Clarksville, IN (town) Clark County	602
Hobart, IN (city) Lake County	596
Schererville, IN (town) Lake County	595

Specified Housing Units Rented by Nicaraguans
Top 10 Places Sorted by Number

Place	Dollars/Month
No places met population threshold.	

Specified Housing Units Rented by Panamanians
Top 10 Places Sorted by Number

Place	Dollars/Month
No places met population threshold.	

Specified Housing Units Rented by Paraguayans
Top 10 Places Sorted by Number

Place	Dollars/Month
No places met population threshold.	

Specified Housing Units Rented by Peruvians
Top 10 Places Sorted by Number

Place	Dollars/Month
No places met population threshold.	

Specified Housing Units Rented by Puerto Ricans
Top 10 Places Sorted by Number

Place	Dollars/Month
South Bend, IN (city) Saint Joseph County	703
Hobart, IN (city) Lake County	683
Indianapolis, IN (cons. city) Marion County	637
Lake Station, IN (city) Lake County	596
Portage, IN (city) Porter County	590
Hammond, IN (city) Lake County	549
Gary, IN (city) Lake County	533
Fort Wayne, IN (city) Allen County	525
East Chicago, IN (city) Lake County	423

Specified Housing Units Rented by Salvadorans
Top 10 Places Sorted by Number

Place	Dollars/Month
Indianapolis, IN (cons. city) Marion County	614

Specified Housing Units Rented by South Americans
Top 10 Places Sorted by Number

Place	Dollars/Month
Indianapolis, IN (cons. city) Marion County	547

Specified Housing Units Rented by Spaniards
Top 10 Places Sorted by Number

Place	Dollars/Month
No places met population threshold.	

Specified Housing Units Rented by Uruguayans
Top 10 Places Sorted by Number

Place	Dollars/Month
No places met population threshold.	

Specified Housing Units Rented by Venezuelans
Top 10 Places Sorted by Number

Place	Dollars/Month
No places met population threshold.	

Specified Housing Units Rented by Other Hispanics
Top 10 Places Sorted by Number

Place	Dollars/Month
Hammond, IN (city) Lake County	604
Lafayette, IN (city) Tippecanoe County	557
Elkhart, IN (city) Elkhart County	533
Indianapolis, IN (cons. city) Marion County	521
South Bend, IN (city) Saint Joseph County	514
Fort Wayne, IN (city) Allen County	465
East Chicago, IN (city) Lake County	440
Gary, IN (city) Lake County	439

Median Home Value

All Specified Owner-Occupied Housing Units
Top 10 Places Sorted by Number

Place	Dollars
Carmel, IN (city) Hamilton County	205,400
Munster, IN (town) Lake County	163,800
Fishers, IN (town) Hamilton County	161,500
Schererville, IN (town) Lake County	157,900
West Lafayette, IN (city) Tippecanoe County	145,400
Noblesville, IN (city) Hamilton County	144,900
Dyer, IN (town) Lake County	141,000
Bloomington, IN (city) Monroe County	126,000
Crown Point, IN (city) Lake County	125,900
Highland, IN (town) Lake County	123,000

Specified Housing Units Owned and Occupied by Hispanics
Top 10 Places Sorted by Number

Place	Dollars
Carmel, IN (city) Hamilton County	318,300
Bloomington, IN (city) Monroe County	179,200
Dyer, IN (town) Lake County	165,200
Fishers, IN (town) Hamilton County	165,000
Munster, IN (town) Lake County	159,600
Schererville, IN (town) Lake County	156,400
Valparaiso, IN (city) Porter County	151,900
Noblesville, IN (city) Hamilton County	136,600
Highland, IN (town) Lake County	134,000
Greenwood, IN (city) Johnson County	127,200

Specified Housing Units Owned and Occupied by Argentinians
Top 10 Places Sorted by Number

Place	Dollars
No places met population threshold.	

Specified Housing Units Owned and Occupied by Bolivians
Top 10 Places Sorted by Number

Place	Dollars
No places met population threshold.	

Specified Housing Units Owned and Occupied by Central Americans
Top 10 Places Sorted by Number

Place	Dollars
Indianapolis, IN (cons. city) Marion County	71,300

Notes: Please refer to the User's Guide for an explanation of data; tables include places with populations > 9,999 and reflect only those areas that meet Summary File 4 population thresholds, therefore there may be less than 10 places listed

Specified Housing Units Owned and Occupied by Chileans
Top 10 Places Sorted by Number

Place	Dollars
No places met population threshold.	

Specified Housing Units Owned and Occupied by Colombians
Top 10 Places Sorted by Number

Place	Dollars
No places met population threshold.	

Specified Housing Units Owned and Occupied by Costa Ricans
Top 10 Places Sorted by Number

Place	Dollars
No places met population threshold.	

Specified Housing Units Owned and Occupied by Cubans
Top 10 Places Sorted by Number

Place	Dollars
Indianapolis, IN (cons. city) Marion County	59,000

Specified Housing Units Owned and Occupied by Dominicans
Top 10 Places Sorted by Number

Place	Dollars
No places met population threshold.	

Specified Housing Units Owned and Occupied by Ecuadorians
Top 10 Places Sorted by Number

Place	Dollars
No places met population threshold.	

Specified Housing Units Owned and Occupied by Guatemalans
Top 10 Places Sorted by Number

Place	Dollars
No places met population threshold.	

Specified Housing Units Owned and Occupied by Hondurans
Top 10 Places Sorted by Number

Place	Dollars
No places met population threshold.	

Specified Housing Units Owned and Occupied by Mexicans
Top 10 Places Sorted by Number

Place	Dollars
Clarksville, IN (town) Clark County	1 Mil.+
Bloomington, IN (city) Monroe County	195,800
Dyer, IN (town) Lake County	164,600
Schererville, IN (town) Lake County	151,300
Valparaiso, IN (city) Porter County	151,100
Munster, IN (town) Lake County	143,800
Highland, IN (town) Lake County	133,800
Crown Point, IN (city) Lake County	116,900
Crawfordsville, IN (city) Montgomery County	112,500
Lawrence, IN (city) Marion County	112,500

Specified Housing Units Owned and Occupied by Nicaraguans
Top 10 Places Sorted by Number

Place	Dollars
No places met population threshold.	

Specified Housing Units Owned and Occupied by Panamanians
Top 10 Places Sorted by Number

Place	Dollars
No places met population threshold.	

Specified Housing Units Owned and Occupied by Paraguayans
Top 10 Places Sorted by Number

Place	Dollars
No places met population threshold.	

Specified Housing Units Owned and Occupied by Peruvians
Top 10 Places Sorted by Number

Place	Dollars
No places met population threshold.	

Specified Housing Units Owned and Occupied by Puerto Ricans
Top 10 Places Sorted by Number

Place	Dollars
Hobart, IN (city) Lake County	121,800
Portage, IN (city) Porter County	117,700
Indianapolis, IN (cons. city) Marion County	108,000
Lake Station, IN (city) Lake County	80,200
South Bend, IN (city) Saint Joseph County	80,000
Hammond, IN (city) Lake County	77,200
East Chicago, IN (city) Lake County	75,900
Fort Wayne, IN (city) Allen County	63,800
Gary, IN (city) Lake County	42,500

Specified Housing Units Owned and Occupied by Salvadorans
Top 10 Places Sorted by Number

Place	Dollars
Indianapolis, IN (cons. city) Marion County	75,800

Specified Housing Units Owned and Occupied by South Americans
Top 10 Places Sorted by Number

Place	Dollars
Indianapolis, IN (cons. city) Marion County	109,800

Specified Housing Units Owned and Occupied by Spaniards
Top 10 Places Sorted by Number

Place	Dollars
No places met population threshold.	

Specified Housing Units Owned and Occupied by Uruguayans
Top 10 Places Sorted by Number

Place	Dollars
No places met population threshold.	

Specified Housing Units Owned and Occupied by Venezuelans
Top 10 Places Sorted by Number

Place	Dollars
No places met population threshold.	

Specified Housing Units Owned and Occupied by Other Hispanics
Top 10 Places Sorted by Number

Place	Dollars
East Chicago, IN (city) Lake County	75,000
Elkhart, IN (city) Elkhart County	71,000

Indianapolis, IN (cons. city) Marion County	69,200
Lafayette, IN (city) Tippecanoe County	62,500
Hammond, IN (city) Lake County	59,300
Fort Wayne, IN (city) Allen County	52,200
South Bend, IN (city) Saint Joseph County	52,200
Gary, IN (city) Lake County	46,800

Notes: Please refer to the User's Guide for an explanation of data; tables include places with populations > 9,999 and reflect only those areas that meet Summary File 4 population thresholds, therefore there may be less than 10 places listed

Asian Population

Population

Total Population
Top 10 Places Sorted by Number

Place	Number
Indianapolis, IN (cons. city) Marion County	782,414
Fort Wayne, IN (city) Allen County	205,941
Evansville, IN (city) Vanderburgh County	121,877
South Bend, IN (city) Saint Joseph County	107,045
Hammond, IN (city) Lake County	83,048
Bloomington, IN (city) Monroe County	69,229
Muncie, IN (city) Delaware County	67,468
Terre Haute, IN (city) Vigo County	59,563
Lafayette, IN (city) Tippecanoe County	56,244
Elkhart, IN (city) Elkhart County	51,701

Asian
Top 10 Places Sorted by Number

Place	Number
Indianapolis, IN (cons. city) Marion County	10,331
Bloomington, IN (city) Monroe County	3,458
West Lafayette, IN (city) Tippecanoe County	3,159
Fort Wayne, IN (city) Allen County	3,093
Carmel, IN (city) Hamilton County	1,636
South Bend, IN (city) Saint Joseph County	1,178
Fishers, IN (town) Hamilton County	1,153
Columbus, IN (city) Bartholomew County	1,073
Evansville, IN (city) Vanderburgh County	1,051
Munster, IN (town) Lake County	952

Asian
Top 10 Places Sorted by Percent of Total Population

Place	Percent
West Lafayette, IN (city) Tippecanoe County	10.91
Bloomington, IN (city) Monroe County	5.00
Munster, IN (town) Lake County	4.43
Carmel, IN (city) Hamilton County	4.33
Fishers, IN (town) Hamilton County	2.96
Granger, IN (cdp) Saint Joseph County	2.85
Columbus, IN (city) Bartholomew County	2.74
Schererville, IN (town) Lake County	2.11
Valparaiso, IN (city) Porter County	1.64
Lawrence, IN (city) Marion County	1.53

Native Hawaiian and Other Pacific Islander
Top 10 Places Sorted by Number

Place	Number
No places met population threshold.	

Native Hawaiian and Other Pacific Islander
Top 10 Places Sorted by Percent of Asian Population

Place	Percent
No places met population threshold.	

Native Hawaiian and Other Pacific Islander
Top 10 Places Sorted by Percent of Total Population

Place	Percent
No places met population threshold.	

Asian Indian
Top 10 Places Sorted by Number

Place	Number
Indianapolis, IN (cons. city) Marion County	3,120
West Lafayette, IN (city) Tippecanoe County	978
Bloomington, IN (city) Monroe County	572
Fort Wayne, IN (city) Allen County	530
Columbus, IN (city) Bartholomew County	426
Munster, IN (town) Lake County	419

Asian Indian
Top 10 Places Sorted by Percent of Asian Population

Place	Percent
Munster, IN (town) Lake County	44.01
Columbus, IN (city) Bartholomew County	39.70
West Lafayette, IN (city) Tippecanoe County	30.96
Indianapolis, IN (cons. city) Marion County	30.20
Fort Wayne, IN (city) Allen County	17.14
Bloomington, IN (city) Monroe County	16.54

Asian Indian
Top 10 Places Sorted by Percent of Total Population

Place	Percent
West Lafayette, IN (city) Tippecanoe County	3.38
Munster, IN (town) Lake County	1.95
Columbus, IN (city) Bartholomew County	1.09
Bloomington, IN (city) Monroe County	0.83
Indianapolis, IN (cons. city) Marion County	0.40
Fort Wayne, IN (city) Allen County	0.26

Bangladeshi
Top 10 Places Sorted by Number

Place	Number
No places met population threshold.	

Bangladeshi
Top 10 Places Sorted by Percent of Asian Population

Place	Percent
No places met population threshold.	

Bangladeshi
Top 10 Places Sorted by Percent of Total Population

Place	Percent
No places met population threshold.	

Cambodian
Top 10 Places Sorted by Number

Place	Number
No places met population threshold.	

Cambodian
Top 10 Places Sorted by Percent of Asian Population

Place	Percent
No places met population threshold.	

Cambodian
Top 10 Places Sorted by Percent of Total Population

Place	Percent
No places met population threshold.	

Chinese (except Taiwanese)
Top 10 Places Sorted by Number

Place	Number
Indianapolis, IN (cons. city) Marion County	2,054
West Lafayette, IN (city) Tippecanoe County	955
Bloomington, IN (city) Monroe County	758

Chinese (except Taiwanese)
Top 10 Places Sorted by Percent of Asian Population

Place	Percent
West Lafayette, IN (city) Tippecanoe County	30.23
Bloomington, IN (city) Monroe County	21.92
Indianapolis, IN (cons. city) Marion County	19.88

Chinese (except Taiwanese)
Top 10 Places Sorted by Percent of Total Population

Place	Percent
West Lafayette, IN (city) Tippecanoe County	3.30
Bloomington, IN (city) Monroe County	1.09

Indianapolis, IN (cons. city) Marion County	0.26

Fijian
Top 10 Places Sorted by Number

Place	Number
No places met population threshold.	

Fijian
Top 10 Places Sorted by Percent of Asian Population

Place	Percent
No places met population threshold.	

Fijian
Top 10 Places Sorted by Percent of Total Population

Place	Percent
No places met population threshold.	

Filipino
Top 10 Places Sorted by Number

Place	Number
Indianapolis, IN (cons. city) Marion County	1,369

Filipino
Top 10 Places Sorted by Percent of Asian Population

Place	Percent
Indianapolis, IN (cons. city) Marion County	13.25

Filipino
Top 10 Places Sorted by Percent of Total Population

Place	Percent
Indianapolis, IN (cons. city) Marion County	0.17

Guamanian or Chamorro
Top 10 Places Sorted by Number

Place	Number
No places met population threshold.	

Guamanian or Chamorro
Top 10 Places Sorted by Percent of Asian Population

Place	Percent
No places met population threshold.	

Guamanian or Chamorro
Top 10 Places Sorted by Percent of Total Population

Place	Percent
No places met population threshold.	

Hawaiian, Native
Top 10 Places Sorted by Number

Place	Number
No places met population threshold.	

Hawaiian, Native
Top 10 Places Sorted by Percent of Asian Population

Place	Percent
No places met population threshold.	

Hawaiian, Native
Top 10 Places Sorted by Percent of Total Population

Place	Percent
No places met population threshold.	

Hmong
Top 10 Places Sorted by Number

Place	Number
No places met population threshold.	

Notes: Please refer to the User's Guide for an explanation of data; tables reflect only those areas that meet Summary File 4 population thresholds, therefore there may be less than 10 places listed

Hmong
Top 10 Places Sorted by Percent of Asian Population

Place	Percent
No places met population threshold.	

Hmong
Top 10 Places Sorted by Percent of Total Population

Place	Percent
No places met population threshold.	

Indonesian
Top 10 Places Sorted by Number

Place	Number
No places met population threshold.	

Indonesian
Top 10 Places Sorted by Percent of Asian Population

Place	Percent
No places met population threshold.	

Indonesian
Top 10 Places Sorted by Percent of Total Population

Place	Percent
No places met population threshold.	

Japanese
Top 10 Places Sorted by Number

Place	Number
No places met population threshold.	

Japanese
Top 10 Places Sorted by Percent of Asian Population

Place	Percent
No places met population threshold.	

Japanese
Top 10 Places Sorted by Percent of Total Population

Place	Percent
No places met population threshold.	

Korean
Top 10 Places Sorted by Number

Place	Number
Indianapolis, IN (cons. city) Marion County	1,037
Bloomington, IN (city) Monroe County	971

Korean
Top 10 Places Sorted by Percent of Asian Population

Place	Percent
Bloomington, IN (city) Monroe County	28.08
Indianapolis, IN (cons. city) Marion County	10.04

Korean
Top 10 Places Sorted by Percent of Total Population

Place	Percent
Bloomington, IN (city) Monroe County	1.40
Indianapolis, IN (cons. city) Marion County	0.13

Laotian
Top 10 Places Sorted by Number

Place	Number
No places met population threshold.	

Laotian
Top 10 Places Sorted by Percent of Asian Population

Place	Percent
No places met population threshold.	

Laotian
Top 10 Places Sorted by Percent of Total Population

Place	Percent
No places met population threshold.	

Malaysian
Top 10 Places Sorted by Number

Place	Number
No places met population threshold.	

Malaysian
Top 10 Places Sorted by Percent of Asian Population

Place	Percent
No places met population threshold.	

Malaysian
Top 10 Places Sorted by Percent of Total Population

Place	Percent
No places met population threshold.	

Pakistani
Top 10 Places Sorted by Number

Place	Number
No places met population threshold.	

Pakistani
Top 10 Places Sorted by Percent of Asian Population

Place	Percent
No places met population threshold.	

Pakistani
Top 10 Places Sorted by Percent of Total Population

Place	Percent
No places met population threshold.	

Samoan
Top 10 Places Sorted by Number

Place	Number
No places met population threshold.	

Samoan
Top 10 Places Sorted by Percent of Asian Population

Place	Percent
No places met population threshold.	

Samoan
Top 10 Places Sorted by Percent of Total Population

Place	Percent
No places met population threshold.	

Sri Lankan
Top 10 Places Sorted by Number

Place	Number
No places met population threshold.	

Sri Lankan
Top 10 Places Sorted by Percent of Asian Population

Place	Percent
No places met population threshold.	

Sri Lankan
Top 10 Places Sorted by Percent of Total Population

Place	Percent
No places met population threshold.	

Taiwanese
Top 10 Places Sorted by Number

Place	Number
No places met population threshold.	

Taiwanese
Top 10 Places Sorted by Percent of Asian Population

Place	Percent
No places met population threshold.	

Taiwanese
Top 10 Places Sorted by Percent of Total Population

Place	Percent
No places met population threshold.	

Thai
Top 10 Places Sorted by Number

Place	Number
No places met population threshold.	

Thai
Top 10 Places Sorted by Percent of Asian Population

Place	Percent
No places met population threshold.	

Thai
Top 10 Places Sorted by Percent of Total Population

Place	Percent
No places met population threshold.	

Tongan
Top 10 Places Sorted by Number

Place	Number
No places met population threshold.	

Tongan
Top 10 Places Sorted by Percent of Asian Population

Place	Percent
No places met population threshold.	

Tongan
Top 10 Places Sorted by Percent of Total Population

Place	Percent
No places met population threshold.	

Vietnamese
Top 10 Places Sorted by Number

Place	Number
Indianapolis, IN (cons. city) Marion County	1,140
Fort Wayne, IN (city) Allen County	631

Vietnamese
Top 10 Places Sorted by Percent of Asian Population

Place	Percent
Fort Wayne, IN (city) Allen County	20.40
Indianapolis, IN (cons. city) Marion County	11.03

Vietnamese
Top 10 Places Sorted by Percent of Total Population

Place	Percent
Fort Wayne, IN (city) Allen County	0.31
Indianapolis, IN (cons. city) Marion County	0.15

Notes: Please refer to the User's Guide for an explanation of data; tables reflect only those areas that meet Summary File 4 population thresholds, therefore there may be less than 10 places listed

Median Age

Total Population
Top 10 Places Sorted by Number

Place	Years
Munster, IN (town) Lake County	43.0
Schererville, IN (town) Lake County	38.3
Granger, IN (cdp) Saint Joseph County	37.9
Carmel, IN (city) Hamilton County	37.3
Evansville, IN (city) Vanderburgh County	36.5
Columbus, IN (city) Bartholomew County	36.2
Hammond, IN (city) Lake County	34.1
Mishawaka, IN (city) Saint Joseph County	33.8
Indianapolis, IN (cons. city) Marion County	33.6
South Bend, IN (city) Saint Joseph County	32.9

Asian
Top 10 Places Sorted by Number

Place	Years
Hammond, IN (city) Lake County	44.5
Munster, IN (town) Lake County	42.7
Schererville, IN (town) Lake County	40.0
Granger, IN (cdp) Saint Joseph County	37.7
Lawrence, IN (city) Marion County	36.1
Carmel, IN (city) Hamilton County	34.2
Fishers, IN (town) Hamilton County	31.9
Indianapolis, IN (cons. city) Marion County	31.6
Mishawaka, IN (city) Saint Joseph County	31.5
Elkhart, IN (city) Elkhart County	31.3

Native Hawaiian and Other Pacific Islander
Top 10 Places Sorted by Number

Place	Years
No places met population threshold.	

Asian Indian
Top 10 Places Sorted by Number

Place	Years
Munster, IN (town) Lake County	36.9
Indianapolis, IN (cons. city) Marion County	30.1
Fort Wayne, IN (city) Allen County	30.0
Columbus, IN (city) Bartholomew County	28.5
Bloomington, IN (city) Monroe County	23.2
West Lafayette, IN (city) Tippecanoe County	22.4

Bangladeshi
Top 10 Places Sorted by Number

Place	Years
No places met population threshold.	

Cambodian
Top 10 Places Sorted by Number

Place	Years
No places met population threshold.	

Chinese (except Taiwanese)
Top 10 Places Sorted by Number

Place	Years
Indianapolis, IN (cons. city) Marion County	34.6
Bloomington, IN (city) Monroe County	26.3
West Lafayette, IN (city) Tippecanoe County	23.0

Fijian
Top 10 Places Sorted by Number

Place	Years
No places met population threshold.	

Filipino
Top 10 Places Sorted by Number

Place	Years
Indianapolis, IN (cons. city) Marion County	33.2

Guamanian or Chamorro
Top 10 Places Sorted by Number

Place	Years
No places met population threshold.	

Hawaiian, Native
Top 10 Places Sorted by Number

Place	Years
No places met population threshold.	

Hmong
Top 10 Places Sorted by Number

Place	Years
No places met population threshold.	

Indonesian
Top 10 Places Sorted by Number

Place	Years
No places met population threshold.	

Japanese
Top 10 Places Sorted by Number

Place	Years
No places met population threshold.	

Korean
Top 10 Places Sorted by Number

Place	Years
Indianapolis, IN (cons. city) Marion County	29.5
Bloomington, IN (city) Monroe County	26.3

Laotian
Top 10 Places Sorted by Number

Place	Years
No places met population threshold.	

Malaysian
Top 10 Places Sorted by Number

Place	Years
No places met population threshold.	

Pakistani
Top 10 Places Sorted by Number

Place	Years
No places met population threshold.	

Samoan
Top 10 Places Sorted by Number

Place	Years
No places met population threshold.	

Sri Lankan
Top 10 Places Sorted by Number

Place	Years
No places met population threshold.	

Taiwanese
Top 10 Places Sorted by Number

Place	Years
No places met population threshold.	

Thai
Top 10 Places Sorted by Number

Place	Years
No places met population threshold.	

Tongan
Top 10 Places Sorted by Number

Place	Years
No places met population threshold.	

Vietnamese
Top 10 Places Sorted by Number

Place	Years
Indianapolis, IN (cons. city) Marion County	31.2
Fort Wayne, IN (city) Allen County	30.1

Average Household Size

Total Population
Top 10 Places Sorted by Number

Place	Number
Granger, IN (cdp) Saint Joseph County	3.07
Carmel, IN (city) Hamilton County	2.72
Fishers, IN (town) Hamilton County	2.71
Lawrence, IN (city) Marion County	2.61
Munster, IN (town) Lake County	2.61
Hammond, IN (city) Lake County	2.59
Schererville, IN (town) Lake County	2.57
Elkhart, IN (city) Elkhart County	2.54
South Bend, IN (city) Saint Joseph County	2.45
Fort Wayne, IN (city) Allen County	2.41

Asian
Top 10 Places Sorted by Number

Place	Number
Granger, IN (cdp) Saint Joseph County	3.42
Munster, IN (town) Lake County	3.31
Lawrence, IN (city) Marion County	3.26
Elkhart, IN (city) Elkhart County	3.23
Carmel, IN (city) Hamilton County	3.11
Fort Wayne, IN (city) Allen County	2.81
Fishers, IN (town) Hamilton County	2.79
Valparaiso, IN (city) Porter County	2.70
Schererville, IN (town) Lake County	2.56
Indianapolis, IN (cons. city) Marion County	2.49

Native Hawaiian and Other Pacific Islander
Top 10 Places Sorted by Number

Place	Number
No places met population threshold.	

Asian Indian
Top 10 Places Sorted by Number

Place	Number
Munster, IN (town) Lake County	4.33
Fort Wayne, IN (city) Allen County	2.68
West Lafayette, IN (city) Tippecanoe County	2.52
Indianapolis, IN (cons. city) Marion County	2.45
Columbus, IN (city) Bartholomew County	2.21
Bloomington, IN (city) Monroe County	2.04

Bangladeshi
Top 10 Places Sorted by Number

Place	Number
No places met population threshold.	

Cambodian
Top 10 Places Sorted by Number

Place	Number
No places met population threshold.	

Chinese (except Taiwanese)
Top 10 Places Sorted by Number

Place	Number
Indianapolis, IN (cons. city) Marion County	2.56

Notes: Please refer to the User's Guide for an explanation of data; tables reflect only those areas that meet Summary File 4 population thresholds, therefore there may be less than 10 places listed

Place	Number
Bloomington, IN (city) Monroe County	1.86
West Lafayette, IN (city) Tippecanoe County	1.75

Fijian
Top 10 Places Sorted by Number

Place	Number
No places met population threshold.	

Filipino
Top 10 Places Sorted by Number

Place	Number
Indianapolis, IN (cons. city) Marion County	2.76

Guamanian or Chamorro
Top 10 Places Sorted by Number

Place	Number
No places met population threshold.	

Hawaiian, Native
Top 10 Places Sorted by Number

Place	Number
No places met population threshold.	

Hmong
Top 10 Places Sorted by Number

Place	Number
No places met population threshold.	

Indonesian
Top 10 Places Sorted by Number

Place	Number
No places met population threshold.	

Japanese
Top 10 Places Sorted by Number

Place	Number
No places met population threshold.	

Korean
Top 10 Places Sorted by Number

Place	Number
Indianapolis, IN (cons. city) Marion County	2.10
Bloomington, IN (city) Monroe County	1.86

Laotian
Top 10 Places Sorted by Number

Place	Number
No places met population threshold.	

Malaysian
Top 10 Places Sorted by Number

Place	Number
No places met population threshold.	

Pakistani
Top 10 Places Sorted by Number

Place	Number
No places met population threshold.	

Samoan
Top 10 Places Sorted by Number

Place	Number
No places met population threshold.	

Sri Lankan
Top 10 Places Sorted by Number

Place	Number
No places met population threshold.	

Taiwanese
Top 10 Places Sorted by Number

Place	Number
No places met population threshold.	

Thai
Top 10 Places Sorted by Number

Place	Number
No places met population threshold.	

Tongan
Top 10 Places Sorted by Number

Place	Number
No places met population threshold.	

Vietnamese
Top 10 Places Sorted by Number

Place	Number
Fort Wayne, IN (city) Allen County	3.69
Indianapolis, IN (cons. city) Marion County	2.73

Language Spoken: English Only

Total Population 5 Years and Over Who Speak English-Only at Home
Top 10 Places Sorted by Number

Place	Number
Indianapolis, IN (cons. city) Marion County	671,818
Fort Wayne, IN (city) Allen County	173,752
Evansville, IN (city) Vanderburgh County	109,760
South Bend, IN (city) Saint Joseph County	86,206
Hammond, IN (city) Lake County	62,066
Muncie, IN (city) Delaware County	60,865
Bloomington, IN (city) Monroe County	58,783
Terre Haute, IN (city) Vigo County	53,514
Lafayette, IN (city) Tippecanoe County	46,398
Mishawaka, IN (city) Saint Joseph County	40,319

Total Population 5 Years and Over Who Speak English-Only at Home
Top 10 Places Sorted by Percent

Place	Percent
Evansville, IN (city) Vanderburgh County	96.20
Muncie, IN (city) Delaware County	95.84
Terre Haute, IN (city) Vigo County	95.59
Valparaiso, IN (city) Porter County	93.62
Granger, IN (cdp) Saint Joseph County	93.27
Fishers, IN (town) Hamilton County	92.99
Mishawaka, IN (city) Saint Joseph County	92.86
Columbus, IN (city) Bartholomew County	92.84
Indianapolis, IN (cons. city) Marion County	92.70
Fort Wayne, IN (city) Allen County	91.56

Asians 5 Years and Over Who Speak English-Only at Home
Top 10 Places Sorted by Number

Place	Number
Indianapolis, IN (cons. city) Marion County	2,033
Bloomington, IN (city) Monroe County	673
Fort Wayne, IN (city) Allen County	654
West Lafayette, IN (city) Tippecanoe County	644
Carmel, IN (city) Hamilton County	290
Lafayette, IN (city) Tippecanoe County	258
Fishers, IN (town) Hamilton County	249
Evansville, IN (city) Vanderburgh County	242
South Bend, IN (city) Saint Joseph County	239

Place	Number
Munster, IN (town) Lake County	204

Asians 5 Years and Over Who Speak English-Only at Home
Top 10 Places Sorted by Percent

Place	Percent
Lafayette, IN (city) Tippecanoe County	33.99
Muncie, IN (city) Delaware County	29.59
Valparaiso, IN (city) Porter County	29.35
Fishers, IN (town) Hamilton County	24.48
Granger, IN (cdp) Saint Joseph County	24.47
Evansville, IN (city) Vanderburgh County	24.27
Hammond, IN (city) Lake County	23.24
Fort Wayne, IN (city) Allen County	22.46
Munster, IN (town) Lake County	22.25
South Bend, IN (city) Saint Joseph County	21.43

Native Hawaiian and Other Pacific Islanders 5 Years and Over Who Speak English-Only at Home
Top 10 Places Sorted by Number

Place	Number
No places met population threshold.	

Native Hawaiian and Other Pacific Islanders 5 Years and Over Who Speak English-Only at Home
Top 10 Places Sorted by Percent

Place	Percent
No places met population threshold.	

Asian Indians 5 Years and Over Who Speak English-Only at Home
Top 10 Places Sorted by Number

Place	Number
Indianapolis, IN (cons. city) Marion County	479
West Lafayette, IN (city) Tippecanoe County	158
Bloomington, IN (city) Monroe County	155
Fort Wayne, IN (city) Allen County	107
Munster, IN (town) Lake County	55
Columbus, IN (city) Bartholomew County	49

Asian Indians 5 Years and Over Who Speak English-Only at Home
Top 10 Places Sorted by Percent

Place	Percent
Bloomington, IN (city) Monroe County	27.39
Fort Wayne, IN (city) Allen County	21.70
Indianapolis, IN (cons. city) Marion County	16.69
West Lafayette, IN (city) Tippecanoe County	16.44
Munster, IN (town) Lake County	14.07
Columbus, IN (city) Bartholomew County	13.54

Bangladeshis 5 Years and Over Who Speak English-Only at Home
Top 10 Places Sorted by Number

Place	Number
No places met population threshold.	

Bangladeshis 5 Years and Over Who Speak English-Only at Home
Top 10 Places Sorted by Percent

Place	Percent
No places met population threshold.	

Cambodians 5 Years and Over Who Speak English-Only at Home
Top 10 Places Sorted by Number

Place	Number
No places met population threshold.	

Notes: Please refer to the User's Guide for an explanation of data; tables reflect only those areas that meet Summary File 4 population thresholds, therefore there may be less than 10 places listed

Cambodians 5 Years and Over Who Speak English-Only at Home
Top 10 Places Sorted by Percent

Place	Percent
No places met population threshold.	

Chinese (except Taiwanese) 5 Years and Over Who Speak English-Only at Home
Top 10 Places Sorted by Number

Place	Number
West Lafayette, IN (city) Tippecanoe County	243
Indianapolis, IN (cons. city) Marion County	237
Bloomington, IN (city) Monroe County	129

Chinese (except Taiwanese) 5 Years and Over Who Speak English-Only at Home
Top 10 Places Sorted by Percent

Place	Percent
West Lafayette, IN (city) Tippecanoe County	25.61
Bloomington, IN (city) Monroe County	17.15
Indianapolis, IN (cons. city) Marion County	12.87

Fijians 5 Years and Over Who Speak English-Only at Home
Top 10 Places Sorted by Number

Place	Number
No places met population threshold.	

Fijians 5 Years and Over Who Speak English-Only at Home
Top 10 Places Sorted by Percent

Place	Percent
No places met population threshold.	

Filipinos 5 Years and Over Who Speak English-Only at Home
Top 10 Places Sorted by Number

Place	Number
Indianapolis, IN (cons. city) Marion County	348

Filipinos 5 Years and Over Who Speak English-Only at Home
Top 10 Places Sorted by Percent

Place	Percent
Indianapolis, IN (cons. city) Marion County	26.89

Guamanians or Chamorros 5 Years and Over Who Speak English-Only at Home
Top 10 Places Sorted by Number

Place	Number
No places met population threshold.	

Guamanians or Chamorros 5 Years and Over Who Speak English-Only at Home
Top 10 Places Sorted by Percent

Place	Percent
No places met population threshold.	

Hawaiian Natives 5 Years and Over Who Speak English-Only at Home
Top 10 Places Sorted by Number

Place	Number
No places met population threshold.	

Hawaiian Natives 5 Years and Over Who Speak English-Only at Home
Top 10 Places Sorted by Percent

Place	Percent
No places met population threshold.	

Hmongs 5 Years and Over Who Speak English-Only at Home
Top 10 Places Sorted by Number

Place	Number
No places met population threshold.	

Hmongs 5 Years and Over Who Speak English-Only at Home
Top 10 Places Sorted by Percent

Place	Percent
No places met population threshold.	

Indonesians 5 Years and Over Who Speak English-Only at Home
Top 10 Places Sorted by Number

Place	Number
No places met population threshold.	

Indonesians 5 Years and Over Who Speak English-Only at Home
Top 10 Places Sorted by Percent

Place	Percent
No places met population threshold.	

Japanese 5 Years and Over Who Speak English-Only at Home
Top 10 Places Sorted by Number

Place	Number
No places met population threshold.	

Japanese 5 Years and Over Who Speak English-Only at Home
Top 10 Places Sorted by Percent

Place	Percent
No places met population threshold.	

Koreans 5 Years and Over Who Speak English-Only at Home
Top 10 Places Sorted by Number

Place	Number
Indianapolis, IN (cons. city) Marion County	365
Bloomington, IN (city) Monroe County	64

Koreans 5 Years and Over Who Speak English-Only at Home
Top 10 Places Sorted by Percent

Place	Percent
Indianapolis, IN (cons. city) Marion County	37.21
Bloomington, IN (city) Monroe County	6.98

Laotians 5 Years and Over Who Speak English-Only at Home
Top 10 Places Sorted by Number

Place	Number
No places met population threshold.	

Laotians 5 Years and Over Who Speak English-Only at Home
Top 10 Places Sorted by Percent

Place	Percent
No places met population threshold.	

Malaysians 5 Years and Over Who Speak English-Only at Home
Top 10 Places Sorted by Number

Place	Number
No places met population threshold.	

Malaysians 5 Years and Over Who Speak English-Only at Home
Top 10 Places Sorted by Percent

Place	Percent
No places met population threshold.	

Pakistanis 5 Years and Over Who Speak English-Only at Home
Top 10 Places Sorted by Number

Place	Number
No places met population threshold.	

Pakistanis 5 Years and Over Who Speak English-Only at Home
Top 10 Places Sorted by Percent

Place	Percent
No places met population threshold.	

Samoans 5 Years and Over Who Speak English-Only at Home
Top 10 Places Sorted by Number

Place	Number
No places met population threshold.	

Samoans 5 Years and Over Who Speak English-Only at Home
Top 10 Places Sorted by Percent

Place	Percent
No places met population threshold.	

Sri Lankans 5 Years and Over Who Speak English-Only at Home
Top 10 Places Sorted by Number

Place	Number
No places met population threshold.	

Sri Lankans 5 Years and Over Who Speak English-Only at Home
Top 10 Places Sorted by Percent

Place	Percent
No places met population threshold.	

Taiwanese 5 Years and Over Who Speak English-Only at Home
Top 10 Places Sorted by Number

Place	Number
No places met population threshold.	

Taiwanese 5 Years and Over Who Speak English-Only at Home
Top 10 Places Sorted by Percent

Place	Percent
No places met population threshold.	

Thais 5 Years and Over Who Speak English-Only at Home
Top 10 Places Sorted by Number

Place	Number
No places met population threshold.	

Notes: Please refer to the User's Guide for an explanation of data; tables reflect only those areas that meet Summary File 4 population thresholds, therefore there may be less than 10 places listed

Thais 5 Years and Over Who Speak English-Only at Home
Top 10 Places Sorted by Percent

Place	Percent
No places met population threshold.	

Tongans 5 Years and Over Who Speak English-Only at Home
Top 10 Places Sorted by Number

Place	Number
No places met population threshold.	

Tongans 5 Years and Over Who Speak English-Only at Home
Top 10 Places Sorted by Percent

Place	Percent
No places met population threshold.	

Vietnamese 5 Years and Over Who Speak English-Only at Home
Top 10 Places Sorted by Number

Place	Number
Indianapolis, IN (cons. city) Marion County	86
Fort Wayne, IN (city) Allen County	28

Vietnamese 5 Years and Over Who Speak English-Only at Home
Top 10 Places Sorted by Percent

Place	Percent
Indianapolis, IN (cons. city) Marion County	7.93
Fort Wayne, IN (city) Allen County	4.62

Foreign Born

Total Population
Top 10 Places Sorted by Number

Place	Number
Indianapolis, IN (cons. city) Marion County	36,067
Fort Wayne, IN (city) Allen County	10,187
South Bend, IN (city) Saint Joseph County	6,854
Hammond, IN (city) Lake County	6,034
Elkhart, IN (city) Elkhart County	5,895
Bloomington, IN (city) Monroe County	5,578
Lafayette, IN (city) Tippecanoe County	4,450
West Lafayette, IN (city) Tippecanoe County	3,851
Carmel, IN (city) Hamilton County	2,756
Columbus, IN (city) Bartholomew County	2,166

Total Population
Top 10 Places Sorted by Percent

Place	Percent
West Lafayette, IN (city) Tippecanoe County	13.30
Elkhart, IN (city) Elkhart County	11.40
Schererville, IN (town) Lake County	8.32
Bloomington, IN (city) Monroe County	8.06
Lafayette, IN (city) Tippecanoe County	7.91
Munster, IN (town) Lake County	7.90
Carmel, IN (city) Hamilton County	7.29
Hammond, IN (city) Lake County	7.27
South Bend, IN (city) Saint Joseph County	6.40
Columbus, IN (city) Bartholomew County	5.53

Asian
Top 10 Places Sorted by Number

Place	Number
Indianapolis, IN (cons. city) Marion County	7,984
Bloomington, IN (city) Monroe County	2,791
West Lafayette, IN (city) Tippecanoe County	2,430
Fort Wayne, IN (city) Allen County	2,397
Carmel, IN (city) Hamilton County	1,151
South Bend, IN (city) Saint Joseph County	917

Place	Number
Columbus, IN (city) Bartholomew County	886
Fishers, IN (town) Hamilton County	783
Evansville, IN (city) Vanderburgh County	775
Munster, IN (town) Lake County	649

Asian
Top 10 Places Sorted by Percent

Place	Percent
Elkhart, IN (city) Elkhart County	84.13
Columbus, IN (city) Bartholomew County	82.57
Bloomington, IN (city) Monroe County	80.71
Valparaiso, IN (city) Porter County	80.09
Mishawaka, IN (city) Saint Joseph County	79.77
Lawrence, IN (city) Marion County	79.40
South Bend, IN (city) Saint Joseph County	77.84
Fort Wayne, IN (city) Allen County	77.50
Indianapolis, IN (cons. city) Marion County	77.28
West Lafayette, IN (city) Tippecanoe County	76.92

Native Hawaiian and Other Pacific Islander
Top 10 Places Sorted by Number

Place	Number
No places met population threshold.	

Native Hawaiian and Other Pacific Islander
Top 10 Places Sorted by Percent

Place	Percent
No places met population threshold.	

Asian Indian
Top 10 Places Sorted by Number

Place	Number
Indianapolis, IN (cons. city) Marion County	2,386
West Lafayette, IN (city) Tippecanoe County	795
Bloomington, IN (city) Monroe County	434
Fort Wayne, IN (city) Allen County	400
Columbus, IN (city) Bartholomew County	370
Munster, IN (town) Lake County	304

Asian Indian
Top 10 Places Sorted by Percent

Place	Percent
Columbus, IN (city) Bartholomew County	86.85
West Lafayette, IN (city) Tippecanoe County	81.29
Indianapolis, IN (cons. city) Marion County	76.47
Bloomington, IN (city) Monroe County	75.87
Fort Wayne, IN (city) Allen County	75.47
Munster, IN (town) Lake County	72.55

Bangladeshi
Top 10 Places Sorted by Number

Place	Number
No places met population threshold.	

Bangladeshi
Top 10 Places Sorted by Percent

Place	Percent
No places met population threshold.	

Cambodian
Top 10 Places Sorted by Number

Place	Number
No places met population threshold.	

Cambodian
Top 10 Places Sorted by Percent

Place	Percent
No places met population threshold.	

Chinese (except Taiwanese)
Top 10 Places Sorted by Number

Place	Number
Indianapolis, IN (cons. city) Marion County	1,745
West Lafayette, IN (city) Tippecanoe County	771
Bloomington, IN (city) Monroe County	601

Chinese (except Taiwanese)
Top 10 Places Sorted by Percent

Place	Percent
Indianapolis, IN (cons. city) Marion County	84.96
West Lafayette, IN (city) Tippecanoe County	80.73
Bloomington, IN (city) Monroe County	79.29

Fijian
Top 10 Places Sorted by Number

Place	Number
No places met population threshold.	

Fijian
Top 10 Places Sorted by Percent

Place	Percent
No places met population threshold.	

Filipino
Top 10 Places Sorted by Number

Place	Number
Indianapolis, IN (cons. city) Marion County	1,013

Filipino
Top 10 Places Sorted by Percent

Place	Percent
Indianapolis, IN (cons. city) Marion County	74.00

Guamanian or Chamorro
Top 10 Places Sorted by Number

Place	Number
No places met population threshold.	

Guamanian or Chamorro
Top 10 Places Sorted by Percent

Place	Percent
No places met population threshold.	

Hawaiian, Native
Top 10 Places Sorted by Number

Place	Number
No places met population threshold.	

Hawaiian, Native
Top 10 Places Sorted by Percent

Place	Percent
No places met population threshold.	

Hmong
Top 10 Places Sorted by Number

Place	Number
No places met population threshold.	

Hmong
Top 10 Places Sorted by Percent

Place	Percent
No places met population threshold.	

Notes: Please refer to the User's Guide for an explanation of data; tables reflect only those areas that meet Summary File 4 population thresholds, therefore there may be less than 10 places listed

Indonesian
Top 10 Places Sorted by Number

Place	Number
No places met population threshold.	

Indonesian
Top 10 Places Sorted by Percent

Place	Percent
No places met population threshold.	

Japanese
Top 10 Places Sorted by Number

Place	Number
No places met population threshold.	

Japanese
Top 10 Places Sorted by Percent

Place	Percent
No places met population threshold.	

Korean
Top 10 Places Sorted by Number

Place	Number
Indianapolis, IN (cons. city) Marion County	878
Bloomington, IN (city) Monroe County	853

Korean
Top 10 Places Sorted by Percent

Place	Percent
Bloomington, IN (city) Monroe County	87.85
Indianapolis, IN (cons. city) Marion County	84.67

Laotian
Top 10 Places Sorted by Number

Place	Number
No places met population threshold.	

Laotian
Top 10 Places Sorted by Percent

Place	Percent
No places met population threshold.	

Malaysian
Top 10 Places Sorted by Number

Place	Number
No places met population threshold.	

Malaysian
Top 10 Places Sorted by Percent

Place	Percent
No places met population threshold.	

Pakistani
Top 10 Places Sorted by Number

Place	Number
No places met population threshold.	

Pakistani
Top 10 Places Sorted by Percent

Place	Percent
No places met population threshold.	

Samoan
Top 10 Places Sorted by Number

Place	Number
No places met population threshold.	

Samoan
Top 10 Places Sorted by Percent

Place	Percent
No places met population threshold.	

Sri Lankan
Top 10 Places Sorted by Number

Place	Number
No places met population threshold.	

Sri Lankan
Top 10 Places Sorted by Percent

Place	Percent
No places met population threshold.	

Taiwanese
Top 10 Places Sorted by Number

Place	Number
No places met population threshold.	

Taiwanese
Top 10 Places Sorted by Percent

Place	Percent
No places met population threshold.	

Thai
Top 10 Places Sorted by Number

Place	Number
No places met population threshold.	

Thai
Top 10 Places Sorted by Percent

Place	Percent
No places met population threshold.	

Tongan
Top 10 Places Sorted by Number

Place	Number
No places met population threshold.	

Tongan
Top 10 Places Sorted by Percent

Place	Percent
No places met population threshold.	

Vietnamese
Top 10 Places Sorted by Number

Place	Number
Indianapolis, IN (cons. city) Marion County	962
Fort Wayne, IN (city) Allen County	553

Vietnamese
Top 10 Places Sorted by Percent

Place	Percent
Fort Wayne, IN (city) Allen County	87.64
Indianapolis, IN (cons. city) Marion County	84.39

Foreign-Born Naturalized Citizens

Total Population
Top 10 Places Sorted by Number

Place	Number
Indianapolis, IN (cons. city) Marion County	12,100
Fort Wayne, IN (city) Allen County	3,332
Hammond, IN (city) Lake County	2,918
South Bend, IN (city) Saint Joseph County	2,375
Bloomington, IN (city) Monroe County	1,328
Carmel, IN (city) Hamilton County	1,251
Schererville, IN (town) Lake County	1,235
Elkhart, IN (city) Elkhart County	1,192
Munster, IN (town) Lake County	1,028
Lafayette, IN (city) Tippecanoe County	1,016

Total Population
Top 10 Places Sorted by Percent

Place	Percent
Schererville, IN (town) Lake County	4.97
Munster, IN (town) Lake County	4.78
Hammond, IN (city) Lake County	3.51
Carmel, IN (city) Hamilton County	3.31
West Lafayette, IN (city) Tippecanoe County	2.50
Elkhart, IN (city) Elkhart County	2.31
South Bend, IN (city) Saint Joseph County	2.22
Lawrence, IN (city) Marion County	2.12
Granger, IN (cdp) Saint Joseph County	2.01
Bloomington, IN (city) Monroe County	1.92

Asian
Top 10 Places Sorted by Number

Place	Number
Indianapolis, IN (cons. city) Marion County	3,423
Fort Wayne, IN (city) Allen County	942
Carmel, IN (city) Hamilton County	657
Bloomington, IN (city) Monroe County	477
Munster, IN (town) Lake County	432
Evansville, IN (city) Vanderburgh County	373
West Lafayette, IN (city) Tippecanoe County	361
Fishers, IN (town) Hamilton County	355
South Bend, IN (city) Saint Joseph County	309
Lawrence, IN (city) Marion County	295

Asian
Top 10 Places Sorted by Percent

Place	Percent
Lawrence, IN (city) Marion County	49.00
Munster, IN (town) Lake County	45.38
Schererville, IN (town) Lake County	44.19
Carmel, IN (city) Hamilton County	40.16
Hammond, IN (city) Lake County	36.57
Valparaiso, IN (city) Porter County	35.84
Evansville, IN (city) Vanderburgh County	35.49
Granger, IN (cdp) Saint Joseph County	34.29
Lafayette, IN (city) Tippecanoe County	33.50
Indianapolis, IN (cons. city) Marion County	33.13

Native Hawaiian and Other Pacific Islander
Top 10 Places Sorted by Number

Place	Number
No places met population threshold.	

Native Hawaiian and Other Pacific Islander
Top 10 Places Sorted by Percent

Place	Percent
No places met population threshold.	

Asian Indian
Top 10 Places Sorted by Number

Place	Number
Indianapolis, IN (cons. city) Marion County	851
Fort Wayne, IN (city) Allen County	160
Munster, IN (town) Lake County	155
West Lafayette, IN (city) Tippecanoe County	95
Bloomington, IN (city) Monroe County	59
Columbus, IN (city) Bartholomew County	20

Asian Indian
Top 10 Places Sorted by Percent

Place	Percent
Munster, IN (town) Lake County	36.99

Notes: Please refer to the User's Guide for an explanation of data; tables reflect only those areas that meet Summary File 4 population thresholds, therefore there may be less than 10 places listed

Place	
Fort Wayne, IN (city) Allen County	30.19
Indianapolis, IN (cons. city) Marion County	27.28
Bloomington, IN (city) Monroe County	10.31
West Lafayette, IN (city) Tippecanoe County	9.71
Columbus, IN (city) Bartholomew County	4.69

Bangladeshi
Top 10 Places Sorted by Number

Place	Number
No places met population threshold.	

Bangladeshi
Top 10 Places Sorted by Percent

Place	Percent
No places met population threshold.	

Cambodian
Top 10 Places Sorted by Number

Place	Number
No places met population threshold.	

Cambodian
Top 10 Places Sorted by Percent

Place	Percent
No places met population threshold.	

Chinese (except Taiwanese)
Top 10 Places Sorted by Number

Place	Number
Indianapolis, IN (cons. city) Marion County	457
Bloomington, IN (city) Monroe County	130
West Lafayette, IN (city) Tippecanoe County	118

Chinese (except Taiwanese)
Top 10 Places Sorted by Percent

Place	Percent
Indianapolis, IN (cons. city) Marion County	22.25
Bloomington, IN (city) Monroe County	17.15
West Lafayette, IN (city) Tippecanoe County	12.36

Fijian
Top 10 Places Sorted by Number

Place	Number
No places met population threshold.	

Fijian
Top 10 Places Sorted by Percent

Place	Percent
No places met population threshold.	

Filipino
Top 10 Places Sorted by Number

Place	Number
Indianapolis, IN (cons. city) Marion County	588

Filipino
Top 10 Places Sorted by Percent

Place	Percent
Indianapolis, IN (cons. city) Marion County	42.95

Guamanian or Chamorro
Top 10 Places Sorted by Number

Place	Number
No places met population threshold.	

Guamanian or Chamorro
Top 10 Places Sorted by Percent

Place	Percent
No places met population threshold.	

Hawaiian, Native
Top 10 Places Sorted by Number

Place	Number
No places met population threshold.	

Hawaiian, Native
Top 10 Places Sorted by Percent

Place	Percent
No places met population threshold.	

Hmong
Top 10 Places Sorted by Number

Place	Number
No places met population threshold.	

Hmong
Top 10 Places Sorted by Percent

Place	Percent
No places met population threshold.	

Indonesian
Top 10 Places Sorted by Number

Place	Number
No places met population threshold.	

Indonesian
Top 10 Places Sorted by Percent

Place	Percent
No places met population threshold.	

Japanese
Top 10 Places Sorted by Number

Place	Number
No places met population threshold.	

Japanese
Top 10 Places Sorted by Percent

Place	Percent
No places met population threshold.	

Korean
Top 10 Places Sorted by Number

Place	Number
Indianapolis, IN (cons. city) Marion County	538
Bloomington, IN (city) Monroe County	146

Korean
Top 10 Places Sorted by Percent

Place	Percent
Indianapolis, IN (cons. city) Marion County	51.88
Bloomington, IN (city) Monroe County	15.04

Laotian
Top 10 Places Sorted by Number

Place	Number
No places met population threshold.	

Laotian
Top 10 Places Sorted by Percent

Place	Percent
No places met population threshold.	

Malaysian
Top 10 Places Sorted by Number

Place	Number
No places met population threshold.	

Malaysian
Top 10 Places Sorted by Percent

Place	Percent
No places met population threshold.	

Pakistani
Top 10 Places Sorted by Number

Place	Number
No places met population threshold.	

Pakistani
Top 10 Places Sorted by Percent

Place	Percent
No places met population threshold.	

Samoan
Top 10 Places Sorted by Number

Place	Number
No places met population threshold.	

Samoan
Top 10 Places Sorted by Percent

Place	Percent
No places met population threshold.	

Sri Lankan
Top 10 Places Sorted by Number

Place	Number
No places met population threshold.	

Sri Lankan
Top 10 Places Sorted by Percent

Place	Percent
No places met population threshold.	

Taiwanese
Top 10 Places Sorted by Number

Place	Number
No places met population threshold.	

Taiwanese
Top 10 Places Sorted by Percent

Place	Percent
No places met population threshold.	

Thai
Top 10 Places Sorted by Number

Place	Number
No places met population threshold.	

Thai
Top 10 Places Sorted by Percent

Place	Percent
No places met population threshold.	

Tongan
Top 10 Places Sorted by Number

Place	Number
No places met population threshold.	

Notes: Please refer to the User's Guide for an explanation of data; tables reflect only those areas that meet Summary File 4 population thresholds, therefore there may be less than 10 places listed

Tongan
Top 10 Places Sorted by Percent

Place	Percent
No places met population threshold.	

Vietnamese
Top 10 Places Sorted by Number

Place	Number
Indianapolis, IN (cons. city) Marion County	487
Fort Wayne, IN (city) Allen County	173

Vietnamese
Top 10 Places Sorted by Percent

Place	Percent
Indianapolis, IN (cons. city) Marion County	42.72
Fort Wayne, IN (city) Allen County	27.42

High School Graduates

Total Populations 25 Years and Over Who are High School Graduates
Top 10 Places Sorted by Number

Place	Number
Indianapolis, IN (cons. city) Marion County	408,362
Fort Wayne, IN (city) Allen County	106,487
Evansville, IN (city) Vanderburgh County	64,621
South Bend, IN (city) Saint Joseph County	51,839
Hammond, IN (city) Lake County	39,524
Lafayette, IN (city) Tippecanoe County	29,342
Bloomington, IN (city) Monroe County	28,564
Muncie, IN (city) Delaware County	28,498
Terre Haute, IN (city) Vigo County	27,844
Mishawaka, IN (city) Saint Joseph County	24,299

Total Populations 25 Years and Over Who are High School Graduates
Top 10 Places Sorted by Percent

Place	Percent
Fishers, IN (town) Hamilton County	98.16
Carmel, IN (city) Hamilton County	97.02
West Lafayette, IN (city) Tippecanoe County	96.25
Granger, IN (cdp) Saint Joseph County	95.50
Munster, IN (town) Lake County	92.95
Schererville, IN (town) Lake County	92.04
Bloomington, IN (city) Monroe County	91.17
Valparaiso, IN (city) Porter County	90.63
Lawrence, IN (city) Marion County	85.56
Columbus, IN (city) Bartholomew County	84.84

Asians 25 Years and Over Who are High School Graduates
Top 10 Places Sorted by Number

Place	Number
Indianapolis, IN (cons. city) Marion County	6,068
Bloomington, IN (city) Monroe County	1,734
Fort Wayne, IN (city) Allen County	1,490
West Lafayette, IN (city) Tippecanoe County	1,238
Carmel, IN (city) Hamilton County	921
Fishers, IN (town) Hamilton County	729
Columbus, IN (city) Bartholomew County	714
South Bend, IN (city) Saint Joseph County	650
Munster, IN (town) Lake County	634
Evansville, IN (city) Vanderburgh County	580

Asians 25 Years and Over Who are High School Graduates
Top 10 Places Sorted by Percent

Place	Percent
Schererville, IN (town) Lake County	98.67
Munster, IN (town) Lake County	97.69
Bloomington, IN (city) Monroe County	97.09
West Lafayette, IN (city) Tippecanoe County	96.79
Granger, IN (cdp) Saint Joseph County	96.29
Columbus, IN (city) Bartholomew County	95.71
Carmel, IN (city) Hamilton County	92.10
Fishers, IN (town) Hamilton County	91.70
Muncie, IN (city) Delaware County	90.60
Evansville, IN (city) Vanderburgh County	89.78

Native Hawaiian and Other Pacific Islanders 25 Years and Over Who are High School Graduates
Top 10 Places Sorted by Number

Place	Number
No places met population threshold.	

Native Hawaiian and Other Pacific Islanders 25 Years and Over Who are High School Graduates
Top 10 Places Sorted by Percent

Place	Percent
No places met population threshold.	

Asian Indians 25 Years and Over Who are High School Graduates
Top 10 Places Sorted by Number

Place	Number
Indianapolis, IN (cons. city) Marion County	1,925
Fort Wayne, IN (city) Allen County	319
West Lafayette, IN (city) Tippecanoe County	296
Columbus, IN (city) Bartholomew County	277
Bloomington, IN (city) Monroe County	255
Munster, IN (town) Lake County	241

Asian Indians 25 Years and Over Who are High School Graduates
Top 10 Places Sorted by Percent

Place	Percent
Munster, IN (town) Lake County	100.00
West Lafayette, IN (city) Tippecanoe County	98.67
Columbus, IN (city) Bartholomew County	98.23
Bloomington, IN (city) Monroe County	98.08
Fort Wayne, IN (city) Allen County	93.27
Indianapolis, IN (cons. city) Marion County	89.70

Bangladeshis 25 Years and Over Who are High School Graduates
Top 10 Places Sorted by Number

Place	Number
No places met population threshold.	

Bangladeshis 25 Years and Over Who are High School Graduates
Top 10 Places Sorted by Percent

Place	Percent
No places met population threshold.	

Cambodians 25 Years and Over Who are High School Graduates
Top 10 Places Sorted by Number

Place	Number
No places met population threshold.	

Cambodians 25 Years and Over Who are High School Graduates
Top 10 Places Sorted by Percent

Place	Percent
No places met population threshold.	

Chinese (except Taiwanese) 25 Years and Over Who are High School Graduates
Top 10 Places Sorted by Number

Place	Number
Indianapolis, IN (cons. city) Marion County	1,264
Bloomington, IN (city) Monroe County	432
West Lafayette, IN (city) Tippecanoe County	395

Chinese (except Taiwanese) 25 Years and Over Who are High School Graduates
Top 10 Places Sorted by Percent

Place	Percent
West Lafayette, IN (city) Tippecanoe County	96.11
Bloomington, IN (city) Monroe County	93.91
Indianapolis, IN (cons. city) Marion County	87.11

Fijians 25 Years and Over Who are High School Graduates
Top 10 Places Sorted by Number

Place	Number
No places met population threshold.	

Fijians 25 Years and Over Who are High School Graduates
Top 10 Places Sorted by Percent

Place	Percent
No places met population threshold.	

Filipinos 25 Years and Over Who are High School Graduates
Top 10 Places Sorted by Number

Place	Number
Indianapolis, IN (cons. city) Marion County	873

Filipinos 25 Years and Over Who are High School Graduates
Top 10 Places Sorted by Percent

Place	Percent
Indianapolis, IN (cons. city) Marion County	91.61

Guamanians or Chamorros 25 Years and Over Who are High School Graduates
Top 10 Places Sorted by Number

Place	Number
No places met population threshold.	

Guamanians or Chamorros 25 Years and Over Who are High School Graduates
Top 10 Places Sorted by Percent

Place	Percent
No places met population threshold.	

Hawaiian Natives 25 Years and Over Who are High School Graduates
Top 10 Places Sorted by Number

Place	Number
No places met population threshold.	

Hawaiian Natives 25 Years and Over Who are High School Graduates
Top 10 Places Sorted by Percent

Place	Percent
No places met population threshold.	

Hmongs 25 Years and Over Who are High School Graduates
Top 10 Places Sorted by Number

Place	Number
No places met population threshold.	

Notes: Please refer to the User's Guide for an explanation of data; tables reflect only those areas that meet Summary File 4 population thresholds, therefore there may be less than 10 places listed

Hmongs 25 Years and Over Who are High School Graduates
Top 10 Places Sorted by Percent

Place	Percent
No places met population threshold.	

Indonesians 25 Years and Over Who are High School Graduates
Top 10 Places Sorted by Number

Place	Number
No places met population threshold.	

Indonesians 25 Years and Over Who are High School Graduates
Top 10 Places Sorted by Percent

Place	Percent
No places met population threshold.	

Japanese 25 Years and Over Who are High School Graduates
Top 10 Places Sorted by Number

Place	Number
No places met population threshold.	

Japanese 25 Years and Over Who are High School Graduates
Top 10 Places Sorted by Percent

Place	Percent
No places met population threshold.	

Koreans 25 Years and Over Who are High School Graduates
Top 10 Places Sorted by Number

Place	Number
Indianapolis, IN (cons. city) Marion County	548
Bloomington, IN (city) Monroe County	520

Koreans 25 Years and Over Who are High School Graduates
Top 10 Places Sorted by Percent

Place	Percent
Bloomington, IN (city) Monroe County	97.93
Indianapolis, IN (cons. city) Marion County	83.41

Laotians 25 Years and Over Who are High School Graduates
Top 10 Places Sorted by Number

Place	Number
No places met population threshold.	

Laotians 25 Years and Over Who are High School Graduates
Top 10 Places Sorted by Percent

Place	Percent
No places met population threshold.	

Malaysians 25 Years and Over Who are High School Graduates
Top 10 Places Sorted by Number

Place	Number
No places met population threshold.	

Malaysians 25 Years and Over Who are High School Graduates
Top 10 Places Sorted by Percent

Place	Percent
No places met population threshold.	

Pakistanis 25 Years and Over Who are High School Graduates
Top 10 Places Sorted by Number

Place	Number
No places met population threshold.	

Pakistanis 25 Years and Over Who are High School Graduates
Top 10 Places Sorted by Percent

Place	Percent
No places met population threshold.	

Samoans 25 Years and Over Who are High School Graduates
Top 10 Places Sorted by Number

Place	Number
No places met population threshold.	

Samoans 25 Years and Over Who are High School Graduates
Top 10 Places Sorted by Percent

Place	Percent
No places met population threshold.	

Sri Lankans 25 Years and Over Who are High School Graduates
Top 10 Places Sorted by Number

Place	Number
No places met population threshold.	

Sri Lankans 25 Years and Over Who are High School Graduates
Top 10 Places Sorted by Percent

Place	Percent
No places met population threshold.	

Taiwanese 25 Years and Over Who are High School Graduates
Top 10 Places Sorted by Number

Place	Number
No places met population threshold.	

Taiwanese 25 Years and Over Who are High School Graduates
Top 10 Places Sorted by Percent

Place	Percent
No places met population threshold.	

Thais 25 Years and Over Who are High School Graduates
Top 10 Places Sorted by Number

Place	Number
No places met population threshold.	

Thais 25 Years and Over Who are High School Graduates
Top 10 Places Sorted by Percent

Place	Percent
No places met population threshold.	

Tongans 25 Years and Over Who are High School Graduates
Top 10 Places Sorted by Number

Place	Number
No places met population threshold.	

Tongans 25 Years and Over Who are High School Graduates
Top 10 Places Sorted by Percent

Place	Percent
No places met population threshold.	

Vietnamese 25 Years and Over Who are High School Graduates
Top 10 Places Sorted by Number

Place	Number
Indianapolis, IN (cons. city) Marion County	578
Fort Wayne, IN (city) Allen County	221

Vietnamese 25 Years and Over Who are High School Graduates
Top 10 Places Sorted by Percent

Place	Percent
Indianapolis, IN (cons. city) Marion County	72.89
Fort Wayne, IN (city) Allen County	58.47

College Graduates

Total Populations 25 Years and Over Who are Four-Year College Graduates
Top 10 Places Sorted by Number

Place	Number
Indianapolis, IN (cons. city) Marion County	127,608
Fort Wayne, IN (city) Allen County	24,897
Bloomington, IN (city) Monroe County	17,174
Fishers, IN (town) Hamilton County	14,672
Carmel, IN (city) Hamilton County	14,369
South Bend, IN (city) Saint Joseph County	13,548
Evansville, IN (city) Vanderburgh County	13,402
Granger, IN (cdp) Saint Joseph County	8,812
Lafayette, IN (city) Tippecanoe County	8,377
Columbus, IN (city) Bartholomew County	7,144

Total Populations 25 Years and Over Who are Four-Year College Graduates
Top 10 Places Sorted by Percent

Place	Percent
West Lafayette, IN (city) Tippecanoe County	69.69
Fishers, IN (town) Hamilton County	60.15
Carmel, IN (city) Hamilton County	58.41
Bloomington, IN (city) Monroe County	54.82
Granger, IN (cdp) Saint Joseph County	49.46
Munster, IN (town) Lake County	39.16
Valparaiso, IN (city) Porter County	34.55
Schererville, IN (town) Lake County	29.47
Columbus, IN (city) Bartholomew County	27.61
Lawrence, IN (city) Marion County	26.83

Asians 25 Years and Over Who are Four-Year College Graduates
Top 10 Places Sorted by Number

Place	Number
Indianapolis, IN (cons. city) Marion County	4,089
Bloomington, IN (city) Monroe County	1,496
West Lafayette, IN (city) Tippecanoe County	1,163
Carmel, IN (city) Hamilton County	676
Fort Wayne, IN (city) Allen County	634
Columbus, IN (city) Bartholomew County	578
Fishers, IN (town) Hamilton County	562
Munster, IN (town) Lake County	457
South Bend, IN (city) Saint Joseph County	419
Granger, IN (cdp) Saint Joseph County	373

Asians 25 Years and Over Who are Four-Year College Graduates
Top 10 Places Sorted by Percent

Place	Percent
West Lafayette, IN (city) Tippecanoe County	90.93

Notes: Please refer to the User's Guide for an explanation of data; tables reflect only those areas that meet Summary File 4 population thresholds, therefore there may be less than 10 places listed

Place	Number
Bloomington, IN (city) Monroe County	83.76
Terre Haute, IN (city) Vigo County	77.56
Columbus, IN (city) Bartholomew County	77.48
Granger, IN (cdp) Saint Joseph County	76.91
Schererville, IN (town) Lake County	76.53
Muncie, IN (city) Delaware County	74.83
Fishers, IN (town) Hamilton County	70.69
Munster, IN (town) Lake County	70.42
Carmel, IN (city) Hamilton County	67.60

Native Hawaiian and Other Pacific Islanders 25 Years and Over Who are Four-Year College Graduates
Top 10 Places Sorted by Number

Place	Number
No places met population threshold.	

Native Hawaiian and Other Pacific Islanders 25 Years and Over Who are Four-Year College Graduates
Top 10 Places Sorted by Percent

Place	Percent
No places met population threshold.	

Asian Indians 25 Years and Over Who are Four-Year College Graduates
Top 10 Places Sorted by Number

Place	Number
Indianapolis, IN (cons. city) Marion County	1,518
West Lafayette, IN (city) Tippecanoe County	292
Columbus, IN (city) Bartholomew County	270
Fort Wayne, IN (city) Allen County	226
Bloomington, IN (city) Monroe County	223
Munster, IN (town) Lake County	198

Asian Indians 25 Years and Over Who are Four-Year College Graduates
Top 10 Places Sorted by Percent

Place	Percent
West Lafayette, IN (city) Tippecanoe County	97.33
Columbus, IN (city) Bartholomew County	95.74
Bloomington, IN (city) Monroe County	85.77
Munster, IN (town) Lake County	82.16
Indianapolis, IN (cons. city) Marion County	70.74
Fort Wayne, IN (city) Allen County	66.08

Bangladeshis 25 Years and Over Who are Four-Year College Graduates
Top 10 Places Sorted by Number

Place	Number
No places met population threshold.	

Bangladeshis 25 Years and Over Who are Four-Year College Graduates
Top 10 Places Sorted by Percent

Place	Percent
No places met population threshold.	

Cambodians 25 Years and Over Who are Four-Year College Graduates
Top 10 Places Sorted by Number

Place	Number
No places met population threshold.	

Cambodians 25 Years and Over Who are Four-Year College Graduates
Top 10 Places Sorted by Percent

Place	Percent
No places met population threshold.	

Chinese (except Taiwanese) 25 Years and Over Who are Four-Year College Graduates
Top 10 Places Sorted by Number

Place	Number
Indianapolis, IN (cons. city) Marion County	974
Bloomington, IN (city) Monroe County	385
West Lafayette, IN (city) Tippecanoe County	384

Chinese (except Taiwanese) 25 Years and Over Who are Four-Year College Graduates
Top 10 Places Sorted by Percent

Place	Percent
West Lafayette, IN (city) Tippecanoe County	93.43
Bloomington, IN (city) Monroe County	83.70
Indianapolis, IN (cons. city) Marion County	67.13

Fijians 25 Years and Over Who are Four-Year College Graduates
Top 10 Places Sorted by Number

Place	Number
No places met population threshold.	

Fijians 25 Years and Over Who are Four-Year College Graduates
Top 10 Places Sorted by Percent

Place	Percent
No places met population threshold.	

Filipinos 25 Years and Over Who are Four-Year College Graduates
Top 10 Places Sorted by Number

Place	Number
Indianapolis, IN (cons. city) Marion County	569

Filipinos 25 Years and Over Who are Four-Year College Graduates
Top 10 Places Sorted by Percent

Place	Percent
Indianapolis, IN (cons. city) Marion County	59.71

Guamanians or Chamorros 25 Years and Over are Four-Year College Graduates
Top 10 Places Sorted by Number

Place	Number
No places met population threshold.	

Guamanians or Chamorros 25 Years and Over are Four-Year College Graduates
Top 10 Places Sorted by Percent

Place	Percent
No places met population threshold.	

Hawaiian Natives 25 Years and Over Who are Four-Year College Graduates
Top 10 Places Sorted by Number

Place	Number
No places met population threshold.	

Hawaiian Natives 25 Years and Over Who are Four-Year College Graduates
Top 10 Places Sorted by Percent

Place	Percent
No places met population threshold.	

Hmongs 25 Years and Over Who are Four-Year College Graduates
Top 10 Places Sorted by Number

Place	Number
No places met population threshold.	

Hmongs 25 Years and Over Who are Four-Year College Graduates
Top 10 Places Sorted by Percent

Place	Percent
No places met population threshold.	

Indonesians 25 Years and Over Who are Four-Year College Graduates
Top 10 Places Sorted by Number

Place	Number
No places met population threshold.	

Indonesians 25 Years and Over Who are Four-Year College Graduates
Top 10 Places Sorted by Percent

Place	Percent
No places met population threshold.	

Japanese 25 Years and Over Who are Four-Year College Graduates
Top 10 Places Sorted by Number

Place	Number
No places met population threshold.	

Japanese 25 Years and Over Who are Four-Year College Graduates
Top 10 Places Sorted by Percent

Place	Percent
No places met population threshold.	

Koreans 25 Years and Over Who are Four-Year College Graduates
Top 10 Places Sorted by Number

Place	Number
Bloomington, IN (city) Monroe County	441
Indianapolis, IN (cons. city) Marion County	371

Koreans 25 Years and Over Who are Four-Year College Graduates
Top 10 Places Sorted by Percent

Place	Percent
Bloomington, IN (city) Monroe County	83.05
Indianapolis, IN (cons. city) Marion County	56.47

Laotians 25 Years and Over Who are Four-Year College Graduates
Top 10 Places Sorted by Number

Place	Number
No places met population threshold.	

Laotians 25 Years and Over Who are Four-Year College Graduates
Top 10 Places Sorted by Percent

Place	Percent
No places met population threshold.	

Malaysians 25 Years and Over Who are Four-Year College Graduates
Top 10 Places Sorted by Number

Place	Number
No places met population threshold.	

Notes: Please refer to the User's Guide for an explanation of data; tables reflect only those areas that meet Summary File 4 population thresholds, therefore there may be less than 10 places listed

Malaysians 25 Years and Over Who are Four-Year College Graduates
Top 10 Places Sorted by Percent

Place	Percent
No places met population threshold.	

Pakistanis 25 Years and Over Who are Four-Year College Graduates
Top 10 Places Sorted by Number

Place	Number
No places met population threshold.	

Pakistanis 25 Years and Over Who are Four-Year College Graduates
Top 10 Places Sorted by Percent

Place	Percent
No places met population threshold.	

Samoans 25 Years and Over Who are Four-Year College Graduates
Top 10 Places Sorted by Number

Place	Number
No places met population threshold.	

Samoans 25 Years and Over Who are Four-Year College Graduates
Top 10 Places Sorted by Percent

Place	Percent
No places met population threshold.	

Sri Lankans 25 Years and Over Who are Four-Year College Graduates
Top 10 Places Sorted by Number

Place	Number
No places met population threshold.	

Sri Lankans 25 Years and Over Who are Four-Year College Graduates
Top 10 Places Sorted by Percent

Place	Percent
No places met population threshold.	

Taiwanese 25 Years and Over Who are Four-Year College Graduates
Top 10 Places Sorted by Number

Place	Number
No places met population threshold.	

Taiwanese 25 Years and Over Who are Four-Year College Graduates
Top 10 Places Sorted by Percent

Place	Percent
No places met population threshold.	

Thais 25 Years and Over Who are Four-Year College Graduates
Top 10 Places Sorted by Number

Place	Number
No places met population threshold.	

Thais 25 Years and Over Who are Four-Year College Graduates
Top 10 Places Sorted by Percent

Place	Percent
No places met population threshold.	

Tongans 25 Years and Over Who are Four-Year College Graduates
Top 10 Places Sorted by Number

Place	Number
No places met population threshold.	

Tongans 25 Years and Over Who are Four-Year College Graduates
Top 10 Places Sorted by Percent

Place	Percent
No places met population threshold.	

Vietnamese 25 Years and Over Who are Four-Year College Graduates
Top 10 Places Sorted by Number

Place	Number
Indianapolis, IN (cons. city) Marion County	230
Fort Wayne, IN (city) Allen County	47

Vietnamese 25 Years and Over Who are Four-Year College Graduates
Top 10 Places Sorted by Percent

Place	Percent
Indianapolis, IN (cons. city) Marion County	29.00
Fort Wayne, IN (city) Allen County	12.43

Median Household Income

Total Population
Top 10 Places Sorted by Number

Place	Dollars
Carmel, IN (city) Hamilton County	81,583
Granger, IN (cdp) Saint Joseph County	80,744
Fishers, IN (town) Hamilton County	75,638
Munster, IN (town) Lake County	63,243
Schererville, IN (town) Lake County	59,243
Lawrence, IN (city) Marion County	47,838
Valparaiso, IN (city) Porter County	45,799
Columbus, IN (city) Bartholomew County	41,723
Indianapolis, IN (cons. city) Marion County	40,051
Fort Wayne, IN (city) Allen County	36,518

Asian
Top 10 Places Sorted by Number

Place	Dollars
Granger, IN (cdp) Saint Joseph County	97,358
Munster, IN (town) Lake County	95,399
Carmel, IN (city) Hamilton County	83,915
Fishers, IN (town) Hamilton County	78,295
Schererville, IN (town) Lake County	72,500
Lawrence, IN (city) Marion County	70,391
Columbus, IN (city) Bartholomew County	57,083
Hammond, IN (city) Lake County	51,429
Valparaiso, IN (city) Porter County	47,500
Elkhart, IN (city) Elkhart County	45,234

Native Hawaiian and Other Pacific Islander
Top 10 Places Sorted by Number

Place	Dollars
No places met population threshold.	

Asian Indian
Top 10 Places Sorted by Number

Place	Dollars
Munster, IN (town) Lake County	119,134
Fort Wayne, IN (city) Allen County	60,602
Columbus, IN (city) Bartholomew County	51,607
Indianapolis, IN (cons. city) Marion County	51,000
West Lafayette, IN (city) Tippecanoe County	26,200
Bloomington, IN (city) Monroe County	8,854

Bangladeshi
Top 10 Places Sorted by Number

Place	Dollars
No places met population threshold.	

Cambodian
Top 10 Places Sorted by Number

Place	Dollars
No places met population threshold.	

Chinese (except Taiwanese)
Top 10 Places Sorted by Number

Place	Dollars
Indianapolis, IN (cons. city) Marion County	36,274
Bloomington, IN (city) Monroe County	17,292
West Lafayette, IN (city) Tippecanoe County	11,528

Fijian
Top 10 Places Sorted by Number

Place	Dollars
No places met population threshold.	

Filipino
Top 10 Places Sorted by Number

Place	Dollars
Indianapolis, IN (cons. city) Marion County	57,963

Guamanian or Chamorro
Top 10 Places Sorted by Number

Place	Dollars
No places met population threshold.	

Hawaiian, Native
Top 10 Places Sorted by Number

Place	Dollars
No places met population threshold.	

Hmong
Top 10 Places Sorted by Number

Place	Dollars
No places met population threshold.	

Indonesian
Top 10 Places Sorted by Number

Place	Dollars
No places met population threshold.	

Japanese
Top 10 Places Sorted by Number

Place	Dollars
No places met population threshold.	

Korean
Top 10 Places Sorted by Number

Place	Dollars
Indianapolis, IN (cons. city) Marion County	36,000
Bloomington, IN (city) Monroe County	6,495

Laotian
Top 10 Places Sorted by Number

Place	Dollars
No places met population threshold.	

Malaysian
Top 10 Places Sorted by Number

Place	Dollars
No places met population threshold.	

Notes: Please refer to the User's Guide for an explanation of data; tables reflect only those areas that meet Summary File 4 population thresholds, therefore there may be less than 10 places listed

Pakistani
Top 10 Places Sorted by Number

Place	Dollars
No places met population threshold.	

Samoan
Top 10 Places Sorted by Number

Place	Dollars
No places met population threshold.	

Sri Lankan
Top 10 Places Sorted by Number

Place	Dollars
No places met population threshold.	

Taiwanese
Top 10 Places Sorted by Number

Place	Dollars
No places met population threshold.	

Thai
Top 10 Places Sorted by Number

Place	Dollars
No places met population threshold.	

Tongan
Top 10 Places Sorted by Number

Place	Dollars
No places met population threshold.	

Vietnamese
Top 10 Places Sorted by Number

Place	Dollars
Fort Wayne, IN (city) Allen County	46,354
Indianapolis, IN (cons. city) Marion County	36,750

Per Capita Income

Total Population
Top 10 Places Sorted by Number

Place	Dollars
Carmel, IN (city) Hamilton County	38,906
Fishers, IN (town) Hamilton County	31,891
Granger, IN (cdp) Saint Joseph County	31,367
Munster, IN (town) Lake County	30,952
Schererville, IN (town) Lake County	28,528
Lawrence, IN (city) Marion County	22,543
Valparaiso, IN (city) Porter County	22,509
Columbus, IN (city) Bartholomew County	22,055
Indianapolis, IN (cons. city) Marion County	21,640
Lafayette, IN (city) Tippecanoe County	19,217

Asian
Top 10 Places Sorted by Number

Place	Dollars
Munster, IN (town) Lake County	48,676
Schererville, IN (town) Lake County	42,244
Valparaiso, IN (city) Porter County	32,415
Granger, IN (cdp) Saint Joseph County	32,018
Carmel, IN (city) Hamilton County	30,560
Columbus, IN (city) Bartholomew County	30,263
Fishers, IN (town) Hamilton County	29,674
Lawrence, IN (city) Marion County	26,201
Indianapolis, IN (cons. city) Marion County	22,058
Evansville, IN (city) Vanderburgh County	20,210

Native Hawaiian and Other Pacific Islander
Top 10 Places Sorted by Number

Place	Dollars
No places met population threshold.	

Asian Indian
Top 10 Places Sorted by Number

Place	Dollars
Munster, IN (town) Lake County	61,671
Fort Wayne, IN (city) Allen County	30,273
Columbus, IN (city) Bartholomew County	26,204
Indianapolis, IN (cons. city) Marion County	24,645
West Lafayette, IN (city) Tippecanoe County	16,132
Bloomington, IN (city) Monroe County	14,280

Bangladeshi
Top 10 Places Sorted by Number

Place	Dollars
No places met population threshold.	

Cambodian
Top 10 Places Sorted by Number

Place	Dollars
No places met population threshold.	

Chinese (except Taiwanese)
Top 10 Places Sorted by Number

Place	Dollars
Indianapolis, IN (cons. city) Marion County	18,893
West Lafayette, IN (city) Tippecanoe County	13,138
Bloomington, IN (city) Monroe County	12,894

Fijian
Top 10 Places Sorted by Number

Place	Dollars
No places met population threshold.	

Filipino
Top 10 Places Sorted by Number

Place	Dollars
Indianapolis, IN (cons. city) Marion County	27,663

Guamanian or Chamorro
Top 10 Places Sorted by Number

Place	Dollars
No places met population threshold.	

Hawaiian, Native
Top 10 Places Sorted by Number

Place	Dollars
No places met population threshold.	

Hmong
Top 10 Places Sorted by Number

Place	Dollars
No places met population threshold.	

Indonesian
Top 10 Places Sorted by Number

Place	Dollars
No places met population threshold.	

Japanese
Top 10 Places Sorted by Number

Place	Dollars
No places met population threshold.	

Korean
Top 10 Places Sorted by Number

Place	Dollars
Indianapolis, IN (cons. city) Marion County	18,469
Bloomington, IN (city) Monroe County	6,585

Laotian
Top 10 Places Sorted by Number

Place	Dollars
No places met population threshold.	

Malaysian
Top 10 Places Sorted by Number

Place	Dollars
No places met population threshold.	

Pakistani
Top 10 Places Sorted by Number

Place	Dollars
No places met population threshold.	

Samoan
Top 10 Places Sorted by Number

Place	Dollars
No places met population threshold.	

Sri Lankan
Top 10 Places Sorted by Number

Place	Dollars
No places met population threshold.	

Taiwanese
Top 10 Places Sorted by Number

Place	Dollars
No places met population threshold.	

Thai
Top 10 Places Sorted by Number

Place	Dollars
No places met population threshold.	

Tongan
Top 10 Places Sorted by Number

Place	Dollars
No places met population threshold.	

Vietnamese
Top 10 Places Sorted by Number

Place	Dollars
Indianapolis, IN (cons. city) Marion County	18,551
Fort Wayne, IN (city) Allen County	14,784

Poverty Status

Total Populations with Income Below Poverty Level
Top 10 Places Sorted by Number

Place	Number
Indianapolis, IN (cons. city) Marion County	90,560
Fort Wayne, IN (city) Allen County	25,204
South Bend, IN (city) Saint Joseph County	17,452
Bloomington, IN (city) Monroe County	16,385
Evansville, IN (city) Vanderburgh County	16,039
Muncie, IN (city) Delaware County	14,118
Hammond, IN (city) Lake County	11,807
Terre Haute, IN (city) Vigo County	10,020
West Lafayette, IN (city) Tippecanoe County	9,099
Elkhart, IN (city) Elkhart County	6,901

Notes: Please refer to the User's Guide for an explanation of data; tables reflect only those areas that meet Summary File 4 population thresholds, therefore there may be less than 10 places listed

Total Populations with Income Below Poverty Level
Top 10 Places Sorted by Percent

Place	Percent
West Lafayette, IN (city) Tippecanoe County	38.30
Bloomington, IN (city) Monroe County	29.62
Muncie, IN (city) Delaware County	23.09
Terre Haute, IN (city) Vigo County	19.20
South Bend, IN (city) Saint Joseph County	16.67
Hammond, IN (city) Lake County	14.33
Evansville, IN (city) Vanderburgh County	13.67
Elkhart, IN (city) Elkhart County	13.56
Fort Wayne, IN (city) Allen County	12.51
Lafayette, IN (city) Tippecanoe County	12.07

Asians with Income Below Poverty Level
Top 10 Places Sorted by Number

Place	Number
Bloomington, IN (city) Monroe County	1,578
Indianapolis, IN (cons. city) Marion County	1,290
West Lafayette, IN (city) Tippecanoe County	1,205
Fort Wayne, IN (city) Allen County	367
Muncie, IN (city) Delaware County	304
South Bend, IN (city) Saint Joseph County	301
Carmel, IN (city) Hamilton County	239
Terre Haute, IN (city) Vigo County	217
Lafayette, IN (city) Tippecanoe County	212
Evansville, IN (city) Vanderburgh County	118

Asians with Income Below Poverty Level
Top 10 Places Sorted by Percent

Place	Percent
Muncie, IN (city) Delaware County	59.26
Bloomington, IN (city) Monroe County	55.08
Terre Haute, IN (city) Vigo County	52.54
West Lafayette, IN (city) Tippecanoe County	48.28
South Bend, IN (city) Saint Joseph County	26.17
Lafayette, IN (city) Tippecanoe County	25.92
Elkhart, IN (city) Elkhart County	16.39
Carmel, IN (city) Hamilton County	14.61
Indianapolis, IN (cons. city) Marion County	12.62
Valparaiso, IN (city) Porter County	12.17

Native Hawaiian and Other Pacific Islanders with Income Below Poverty Level
Top 10 Places Sorted by Number

Place	Number
No places met population threshold.	

Native Hawaiian and Other Pacific Islanders with Income Below Poverty Level
Top 10 Places Sorted by Percent

Place	Percent
No places met population threshold.	

Asian Indians with Income Below Poverty Level
Top 10 Places Sorted by Number

Place	Number
West Lafayette, IN (city) Tippecanoe County	300
Indianapolis, IN (cons. city) Marion County	225
Bloomington, IN (city) Monroe County	219
Fort Wayne, IN (city) Allen County	34
Columbus, IN (city) Bartholomew County	31
Munster, IN (town) Lake County	0

Asian Indians with Income Below Poverty Level
Top 10 Places Sorted by Percent

Place	Percent
Bloomington, IN (city) Monroe County	50.69
West Lafayette, IN (city) Tippecanoe County	39.68
Columbus, IN (city) Bartholomew County	7.28
Indianapolis, IN (cons. city) Marion County	7.25
Fort Wayne, IN (city) Allen County	6.42

| **Munster, IN** (town) Lake County | 0.00 |

Bangladeshis with Income Below Poverty Level
Top 10 Places Sorted by Number

Place	Number
No places met population threshold.	

Bangladeshis with Income Below Poverty Level
Top 10 Places Sorted by Percent

Place	Percent
No places met population threshold.	

Cambodians with Income Below Poverty Level
Top 10 Places Sorted by Number

Place	Number
No places met population threshold.	

Cambodians with Income Below Poverty Level
Top 10 Places Sorted by Percent

Place	Percent
No places met population threshold.	

Chinese (except Taiwanese) with Income Below Poverty Level
Top 10 Places Sorted by Number

Place	Number
West Lafayette, IN (city) Tippecanoe County	410
Bloomington, IN (city) Monroe County	321
Indianapolis, IN (cons. city) Marion County	318

Chinese (except Taiwanese) with Income Below Poverty Level
Top 10 Places Sorted by Percent

Place	Percent
West Lafayette, IN (city) Tippecanoe County	52.50
Bloomington, IN (city) Monroe County	49.01
Indianapolis, IN (cons. city) Marion County	15.71

Fijians with Income Below Poverty Level
Top 10 Places Sorted by Number

Place	Number
No places met population threshold.	

Fijians with Income Below Poverty Level
Top 10 Places Sorted by Percent

Place	Percent
No places met population threshold.	

Filipinos with Income Below Poverty Level
Top 10 Places Sorted by Number

Place	Number
Indianapolis, IN (cons. city) Marion County	93

Filipinos with Income Below Poverty Level
Top 10 Places Sorted by Percent

Place	Percent
Indianapolis, IN (cons. city) Marion County	6.87

Guamanians or Chamorros with Income Below Poverty Level
Top 10 Places Sorted by Number

Place	Number
No places met population threshold.	

Guamanians or Chamorros with Income Below Poverty Level
Top 10 Places Sorted by Percent

Place	Percent
No places met population threshold.	

Hawaiian Natives with Income Below Poverty Level
Top 10 Places Sorted by Number

Place	Number
No places met population threshold.	

Hawaiian Natives with Income Below Poverty Level
Top 10 Places Sorted by Percent

Place	Percent
No places met population threshold.	

Hmongs with Income Below Poverty Level
Top 10 Places Sorted by Number

Place	Number
No places met population threshold.	

Hmongs with Income Below Poverty Level
Top 10 Places Sorted by Percent

Place	Percent
No places met population threshold.	

Indonesians with Income Below Poverty Level
Top 10 Places Sorted by Number

Place	Number
No places met population threshold.	

Indonesians with Income Below Poverty Level
Top 10 Places Sorted by Percent

Place	Percent
No places met population threshold.	

Japanese with Income Below Poverty Level
Top 10 Places Sorted by Number

Place	Number
No places met population threshold.	

Japanese with Income Below Poverty Level
Top 10 Places Sorted by Percent

Place	Percent
No places met population threshold.	

Koreans with Income Below Poverty Level
Top 10 Places Sorted by Number

Place	Number
Bloomington, IN (city) Monroe County	507
Indianapolis, IN (cons. city) Marion County	206

Koreans with Income Below Poverty Level
Top 10 Places Sorted by Percent

Place	Percent
Bloomington, IN (city) Monroe County	61.60
Indianapolis, IN (cons. city) Marion County	20.38

Laotians with Income Below Poverty Level
Top 10 Places Sorted by Number

Place	Number
No places met population threshold.	

Laotians with Income Below Poverty Level
Top 10 Places Sorted by Percent

Place	Percent
No places met population threshold.	

Notes: Please refer to the User's Guide for an explanation of data; tables reflect only those areas that meet Summary File 4 population thresholds, therefore there may be less than 10 places listed

Malaysians with Income Below Poverty Level
Top 10 Places Sorted by Number

Place	Number
No places met population threshold.	

Malaysians with Income Below Poverty Level
Top 10 Places Sorted by Percent

Place	Percent
No places met population threshold.	

Pakistanis with Income Below Poverty Level
Top 10 Places Sorted by Number

Place	Number
No places met population threshold.	

Pakistanis with Income Below Poverty Level
Top 10 Places Sorted by Percent

Place	Percent
No places met population threshold.	

Samoans with Income Below Poverty Level
Top 10 Places Sorted by Number

Place	Number
No places met population threshold.	

Samoans with Income Below Poverty Level
Top 10 Places Sorted by Percent

Place	Percent
No places met population threshold.	

Sri Lankans with Income Below Poverty Level
Top 10 Places Sorted by Number

Place	Number
No places met population threshold.	

Sri Lankans with Income Below Poverty Level
Top 10 Places Sorted by Percent

Place	Percent
No places met population threshold.	

Taiwanese with Income Below Poverty Level
Top 10 Places Sorted by Number

Place	Number
No places met population threshold.	

Taiwanese with Income Below Poverty Level
Top 10 Places Sorted by Percent

Place	Percent
No places met population threshold.	

Thais with Income Below Poverty Level
Top 10 Places Sorted by Number

Place	Number
No places met population threshold.	

Thais with Income Below Poverty Level
Top 10 Places Sorted by Percent

Place	Percent
No places met population threshold.	

Tongans with Income Below Poverty Level
Top 10 Places Sorted by Number

Place	Number
No places met population threshold.	

Tongans with Income Below Poverty Level
Top 10 Places Sorted by Percent

Place	Percent
No places met population threshold.	

Vietnamese with Income Below Poverty Level
Top 10 Places Sorted by Number

Place	Number
Indianapolis, IN (cons. city) Marion County	234
Fort Wayne, IN (city) Allen County	41

Vietnamese with Income Below Poverty Level
Top 10 Places Sorted by Percent

Place	Percent
Indianapolis, IN (cons. city) Marion County	20.53
Fort Wayne, IN (city) Allen County	6.50

Homeownership

Total Populations Who Own Their Own Homes
Top 10 Places Sorted by Number

Place	Number
Indianapolis, IN (cons. city) Marion County	187,846
Fort Wayne, IN (city) Allen County	51,316
Evansville, IN (city) Vanderburgh County	31,357
South Bend, IN (city) Saint Joseph County	26,991
Hammond, IN (city) Lake County	20,236
Muncie, IN (city) Delaware County	15,243
Terre Haute, IN (city) Vigo County	13,542
Lafayette, IN (city) Tippecanoe County	12,650
Mishawaka, IN (city) Saint Joseph County	11,539
Fishers, IN (town) Hamilton County	11,259

Total Populations Who Own Their Own Homes
Top 10 Places Sorted by Percent

Place	Percent
Granger, IN (cdp) Saint Joseph County	97.52
Munster, IN (town) Lake County	89.12
Carmel, IN (city) Hamilton County	78.96
Fishers, IN (town) Hamilton County	77.93
Lawrence, IN (city) Marion County	75.47
Schererville, IN (town) Lake County	73.69
Columbus, IN (city) Bartholomew County	64.61
Hammond, IN (city) Lake County	63.19
South Bend, IN (city) Saint Joseph County	63.06
Fort Wayne, IN (city) Allen County	61.58

Asians Who Own Their Own Homes
Top 10 Places Sorted by Number

Place	Number
Indianapolis, IN (cons. city) Marion County	1,609
Fort Wayne, IN (city) Allen County	477
Carmel, IN (city) Hamilton County	386
Munster, IN (town) Lake County	279
Fishers, IN (town) Hamilton County	237
Bloomington, IN (city) Monroe County	192
Granger, IN (cdp) Saint Joseph County	190
West Lafayette, IN (city) Tippecanoe County	183
Columbus, IN (city) Bartholomew County	146
South Bend, IN (city) Saint Joseph County	140

Asians Who Own Their Own Homes
Top 10 Places Sorted by Percent

Place	Percent
Granger, IN (cdp) Saint Joseph County	85.20
Munster, IN (town) Lake County	82.54
Lawrence, IN (city) Marion County	78.29
Carmel, IN (city) Hamilton County	76.44
Schererville, IN (town) Lake County	73.91
Fishers, IN (town) Hamilton County	64.23
Hammond, IN (city) Lake County	58.68
Elkhart, IN (city) Elkhart County	50.99

Evansville, IN (city) Vanderburgh County	44.68
Fort Wayne, IN (city) Allen County	43.64

Native Hawaiian and Other Pacific Islanders Who Own Their Own Homes
Top 10 Places Sorted by Number

Place	Number
No places met population threshold.	

Native Hawaiian and Other Pacific Islanders Who Own Their Own Homes
Top 10 Places Sorted by Percent

Place	Percent
No places met population threshold.	

Asian Indians Who Own Their Own Homes
Top 10 Places Sorted by Number

Place	Number
Indianapolis, IN (cons. city) Marion County	461
Munster, IN (town) Lake County	90
West Lafayette, IN (city) Tippecanoe County	66
Fort Wayne, IN (city) Allen County	64
Bloomington, IN (city) Monroe County	29
Columbus, IN (city) Bartholomew County	24

Asian Indians Who Own Their Own Homes
Top 10 Places Sorted by Percent

Place	Percent
Munster, IN (town) Lake County	79.65
Indianapolis, IN (cons. city) Marion County	34.79
Fort Wayne, IN (city) Allen County	27.59
West Lafayette, IN (city) Tippecanoe County	21.09
Columbus, IN (city) Bartholomew County	12.00
Bloomington, IN (city) Monroe County	11.89

Bangladeshis Who Own Their Own Homes
Top 10 Places Sorted by Number

Place	Number
No places met population threshold.	

Bangladeshis Who Own Their Own Homes
Top 10 Places Sorted by Percent

Place	Percent
No places met population threshold.	

Cambodians Who Own Their Own Homes
Top 10 Places Sorted by Number

Place	Number
No places met population threshold.	

Cambodians Who Own Their Own Homes
Top 10 Places Sorted by Percent

Place	Percent
No places met population threshold.	

Chinese (except Taiwanese) Who Own Their Own Homes
Top 10 Places Sorted by Number

Place	Number
Indianapolis, IN (cons. city) Marion County	300
Bloomington, IN (city) Monroe County	83
West Lafayette, IN (city) Tippecanoe County	54

Chinese (except Taiwanese) Who Own Their Own Homes
Top 10 Places Sorted by Percent

Place	Percent
Indianapolis, IN (cons. city) Marion County	40.76
Bloomington, IN (city) Monroe County	23.58

Notes: Please refer to the User's Guide for an explanation of data; tables reflect only those areas that meet Summary File 4 population thresholds, therefore there may be less than 10 places listed

West Lafayette, IN (city) Tippecanoe County   13.99

Fijians Who Own Their Own Homes
Top 10 Places Sorted by Number

Place	Number
No places met population threshold.	

Fijians Who Own Their Own Homes
Top 10 Places Sorted by Percent

Place	Percent
No places met population threshold.	

Filipinos Who Own Their Own Homes
Top 10 Places Sorted by Number

Place	Number
Indianapolis, IN (cons. city) Marion County	205

Filipinos Who Own Their Own Homes
Top 10 Places Sorted by Percent

Place	Percent
Indianapolis, IN (cons. city) Marion County	51.00

Guamanians or Chamorros Who Own Their Own Homes
Top 10 Places Sorted by Number

Place	Number
No places met population threshold.	

Guamanians or Chamorros Who Own Their Own Homes
Top 10 Places Sorted by Percent

Place	Percent
No places met population threshold.	

Hawaiian Natives Who Own Their Own Homes
Top 10 Places Sorted by Number

Place	Number
No places met population threshold.	

Hawaiian Natives Who Own Their Own Homes
Top 10 Places Sorted by Percent

Place	Percent
No places met population threshold.	

Hmongs Who Own Their Own Homes
Top 10 Places Sorted by Number

Place	Number
No places met population threshold.	

Hmongs Who Own Their Own Homes
Top 10 Places Sorted by Percent

Place	Percent
No places met population threshold.	

Indonesians Who Own Their Own Homes
Top 10 Places Sorted by Number

Place	Number
No places met population threshold.	

Indonesians Who Own Their Own Homes
Top 10 Places Sorted by Percent

Place	Percent
No places met population threshold.	

Japanese Who Own Their Own Homes
Top 10 Places Sorted by Number

Place	Number
No places met population threshold.	

Japanese Who Own Their Own Homes
Top 10 Places Sorted by Percent

Place	Percent
No places met population threshold.	

Koreans Who Own Their Own Homes
Top 10 Places Sorted by Number

Place	Number
Indianapolis, IN (cons. city) Marion County	173
Bloomington, IN (city) Monroe County	31

Koreans Who Own Their Own Homes
Top 10 Places Sorted by Percent

Place	Percent
Indianapolis, IN (cons. city) Marion County	45.65
Bloomington, IN (city) Monroe County	7.87

Laotians Who Own Their Own Homes
Top 10 Places Sorted by Number

Place	Number
No places met population threshold.	

Laotians Who Own Their Own Homes
Top 10 Places Sorted by Percent

Place	Percent
No places met population threshold.	

Malaysians Who Own Their Own Homes
Top 10 Places Sorted by Number

Place	Number
No places met population threshold.	

Malaysians Who Own Their Own Homes
Top 10 Places Sorted by Percent

Place	Percent
No places met population threshold.	

Pakistanis Who Own Their Own Homes
Top 10 Places Sorted by Number

Place	Number
No places met population threshold.	

Pakistanis Who Own Their Own Homes
Top 10 Places Sorted by Percent

Place	Percent
No places met population threshold.	

Samoans Who Own Their Own Homes
Top 10 Places Sorted by Number

Place	Number
No places met population threshold.	

Samoans Who Own Their Own Homes
Top 10 Places Sorted by Percent

Place	Percent
No places met population threshold.	

Sri Lankans Who Own Their Own Homes
Top 10 Places Sorted by Number

Place	Number
No places met population threshold.	

Sri Lankans Who Own Their Own Homes
Top 10 Places Sorted by Percent

Place	Percent
No places met population threshold.	

Taiwanese Who Own Their Own Homes
Top 10 Places Sorted by Number

Place	Number
No places met population threshold.	

Taiwanese Who Own Their Own Homes
Top 10 Places Sorted by Percent

Place	Percent
No places met population threshold.	

Thais Who Own Their Own Homes
Top 10 Places Sorted by Number

Place	Number
No places met population threshold.	

Thais Who Own Their Own Homes
Top 10 Places Sorted by Percent

Place	Percent
No places met population threshold.	

Tongans Who Own Their Own Homes
Top 10 Places Sorted by Number

Place	Number
No places met population threshold.	

Tongans Who Own Their Own Homes
Top 10 Places Sorted by Percent

Place	Percent
No places met population threshold.	

Vietnamese Who Own Their Own Homes
Top 10 Places Sorted by Number

Place	Number
Indianapolis, IN (cons. city) Marion County	241
Fort Wayne, IN (city) Allen County	112

Vietnamese Who Own Their Own Homes
Top 10 Places Sorted by Percent

Place	Percent
Fort Wayne, IN (city) Allen County	60.87
Indianapolis, IN (cons. city) Marion County	56.84

Median Gross Rent

All Specified Renter-Occupied Housing Units
Top 10 Places Sorted by Number

Place	Dollars/Month
Granger, IN (cdp) Saint Joseph County	1,227
Fishers, IN (town) Hamilton County	797
Munster, IN (town) Lake County	771
Carmel, IN (city) Hamilton County	748
Schererville, IN (town) Lake County	656
Valparaiso, IN (city) Porter County	625
West Lafayette, IN (city) Tippecanoe County	614
Lawrence, IN (city) Marion County	590
Columbus, IN (city) Bartholomew County	579
Indianapolis, IN (cons. city) Marion County	567

Specified Housing Units Rented by Asians
Top 10 Places Sorted by Number

Place	Dollars/Month
Granger, IN (cdp) Saint Joseph County	1,875
Fishers, IN (town) Hamilton County	885

Notes: Please refer to the User's Guide for an explanation of data; tables reflect only those areas that meet Summary File 4 population thresholds, therefore there may be less than 10 places listed

Place	
Carmel, IN (city) Hamilton County	723
Columbus, IN (city) Bartholomew County	687
Munster, IN (town) Lake County	676
Hammond, IN (city) Lake County	661
Schererville, IN (town) Lake County	643
Valparaiso, IN (city) Porter County	615
Elkhart, IN (city) Elkhart County	610
West Lafayette, IN (city) Tippecanoe County	600

Specified Housing Units Rented by Native Hawaiian and Other Pacific Islanders
Top 10 Places Sorted by Number

Place	Dollars/Month
No places met population threshold.	

Specified Housing Units Rented by Asian Indians
Top 10 Places Sorted by Number

Place	Dollars/Month
Munster, IN (town) Lake County	694
West Lafayette, IN (city) Tippecanoe County	670
Columbus, IN (city) Bartholomew County	667
Indianapolis, IN (cons. city) Marion County	606
Fort Wayne, IN (city) Allen County	586
Bloomington, IN (city) Monroe County	582

Specified Housing Units Rented by Bangladeshis
Top 10 Places Sorted by Number

Place	Dollars/Month
No places met population threshold.	

Specified Housing Units Rented by Cambodians
Top 10 Places Sorted by Number

Place	Dollars/Month
No places met population threshold.	

Specified Housing Units Rented by Chinese (except Taiwanese)
Top 10 Places Sorted by Number

Place	Dollars/Month
West Lafayette, IN (city) Tippecanoe County	567
Bloomington, IN (city) Monroe County	523
Indianapolis, IN (cons. city) Marion County	502

Specified Housing Units Rented by Fijians
Top 10 Places Sorted by Number

Place	Dollars/Month
No places met population threshold.	

Specified Housing Units Rented by Filipinos
Top 10 Places Sorted by Number

Place	Dollars/Month
Indianapolis, IN (cons. city) Marion County	632

Specified Housing Units Rented by Guamanians or Chamorros
Top 10 Places Sorted by Number

Place	Dollars/Month
No places met population threshold.	

Specified Housing Units Rented by Hawaiian Natives
Top 10 Places Sorted by Number

Place	Dollars/Month
No places met population threshold.	

Specified Housing Units Rented by Hmongs
Top 10 Places Sorted by Number

Place	Dollars/Month
No places met population threshold.	

Specified Housing Units Rented by Indonesians
Top 10 Places Sorted by Number

Place	Dollars/Month
No places met population threshold.	

Specified Housing Units Rented by Japanese
Top 10 Places Sorted by Number

Place	Dollars/Month
No places met population threshold.	

Specified Housing Units Rented by Koreans
Top 10 Places Sorted by Number

Place	Dollars/Month
Indianapolis, IN (cons. city) Marion County	655
Bloomington, IN (city) Monroe County	564

Specified Housing Units Rented by Laotians
Top 10 Places Sorted by Number

Place	Dollars/Month
No places met population threshold.	

Specified Housing Units Rented by Malaysians
Top 10 Places Sorted by Number

Place	Dollars/Month
No places met population threshold.	

Specified Housing Units Rented by Pakistanis
Top 10 Places Sorted by Number

Place	Dollars/Month
No places met population threshold.	

Specified Housing Units Rented by Samoans
Top 10 Places Sorted by Number

Place	Dollars/Month
No places met population threshold.	

Specified Housing Units Rented by Sri Lankans
Top 10 Places Sorted by Number

Place	Dollars/Month
No places met population threshold.	

Specified Housing Units Rented by Taiwanese
Top 10 Places Sorted by Number

Place	Dollars/Month
No places met population threshold.	

Specified Housing Units Rented by Thais
Top 10 Places Sorted by Number

Place	Dollars/Month
No places met population threshold.	

Specified Housing Units Rented by Tongans
Top 10 Places Sorted by Number

Place	Dollars/Month
No places met population threshold.	

Specified Housing Units Rented by Vietnamese
Top 10 Places Sorted by Number

Place	Dollars/Month
Indianapolis, IN (cons. city) Marion County	631
Fort Wayne, IN (city) Allen County	413

Median Home Value

All Specified Owner-Occupied Housing Units
Top 10 Places Sorted by Number

Place	Dollars
Carmel, IN (city) Hamilton County	205,400
Munster, IN (town) Lake County	163,800
Fishers, IN (town) Hamilton County	161,500
Schererville, IN (town) Lake County	157,900
Granger, IN (cdp) Saint Joseph County	154,600
West Lafayette, IN (city) Tippecanoe County	145,400
Bloomington, IN (city) Monroe County	126,000
Valparaiso, IN (city) Porter County	121,700
Lawrence, IN (city) Marion County	116,200
Columbus, IN (city) Bartholomew County	111,900

Specified Housing Units Owned and Occupied by Asians
Top 10 Places Sorted by Number

Place	Dollars
Carmel, IN (city) Hamilton County	232,200
Schererville, IN (town) Lake County	218,800
Terre Haute, IN (city) Vigo County	217,600
Munster, IN (town) Lake County	204,100
Fishers, IN (town) Hamilton County	171,400
Valparaiso, IN (city) Porter County	166,700
West Lafayette, IN (city) Tippecanoe County	161,800
Granger, IN (cdp) Saint Joseph County	161,200
Columbus, IN (city) Bartholomew County	146,100
Lawrence, IN (city) Marion County	145,400

Specified Housing Units Owned and Occupied by Native Hawaiian and Other Pacific Islanders
Top 10 Places Sorted by Number

Place	Dollars
No places met population threshold.	

Specified Housing Units Owned and Occupied by Asian Indians
Top 10 Places Sorted by Number

Place	Dollars
Munster, IN (town) Lake County	226,700
Columbus, IN (city) Bartholomew County	195,800
Fort Wayne, IN (city) Allen County	187,500
West Lafayette, IN (city) Tippecanoe County	172,400
Bloomington, IN (city) Monroe County	132,800
Indianapolis, IN (cons. city) Marion County	125,100

Specified Housing Units Owned and Occupied by Bangladeshis
Top 10 Places Sorted by Number

Place	Dollars
No places met population threshold.	

Specified Housing Units Owned and Occupied by Cambodians
Top 10 Places Sorted by Number

Place	Dollars
No places met population threshold.	

Specified Housing Units Owned and Occupied by Chinese (except Taiwanese)
Top 10 Places Sorted by Number

Place	Dollars
West Lafayette, IN (city) Tippecanoe County	162,500
Bloomington, IN (city) Monroe County	141,500
Indianapolis, IN (cons. city) Marion County	119,400

Notes: Please refer to the User's Guide for an explanation of data; tables reflect only those areas that meet Summary File 4 population thresholds, therefore there may be less than 10 places listed

Specified Housing Units Owned and Occupied by Fijians
Top 10 Places Sorted by Number

Place	Dollars
No places met population threshold.	

Specified Housing Units Owned and Occupied by Filipinos
Top 10 Places Sorted by Number

Place	Dollars
Indianapolis, IN (cons. city) Marion County	114,200

Specified Housing Units Owned and Occupied by Guamanians or Chamorros
Top 10 Places Sorted by Number

Place	Dollars
No places met population threshold.	

Specified Housing Units Owned and Occupied by Hawaiian Natives
Top 10 Places Sorted by Number

Place	Dollars
No places met population threshold.	

Specified Housing Units Owned and Occupied by Hmongs
Top 10 Places Sorted by Number

Place	Dollars
No places met population threshold.	

Specified Housing Units Owned and Occupied by Indonesians
Top 10 Places Sorted by Number

Place	Dollars
No places met population threshold.	

Specified Housing Units Owned and Occupied by Japanese
Top 10 Places Sorted by Number

Place	Dollars
No places met population threshold.	

Specified Housing Units Owned and Occupied by Koreans
Top 10 Places Sorted by Number

Place	Dollars
Bloomington, IN (city) Monroe County	196,400
Indianapolis, IN (cons. city) Marion County	133,500

Specified Housing Units Owned and Occupied by Laotians
Top 10 Places Sorted by Number

Place	Dollars
No places met population threshold.	

Specified Housing Units Owned and Occupied by Malaysians
Top 10 Places Sorted by Number

Place	Dollars
No places met population threshold.	

Specified Housing Units Owned and Occupied by Pakistanis
Top 10 Places Sorted by Number

Place	Dollars
No places met population threshold.	

Specified Housing Units Owned and Occupied by Samoans
Top 10 Places Sorted by Number

Place	Dollars
No places met population threshold.	

Specified Housing Units Owned and Occupied by Sri Lankans
Top 10 Places Sorted by Number

Place	Dollars
No places met population threshold.	

Specified Housing Units Owned and Occupied by Taiwanese
Top 10 Places Sorted by Number

Place	Dollars
No places met population threshold.	

Specified Housing Units Owned and Occupied by Thais
Top 10 Places Sorted by Number

Place	Dollars
No places met population threshold.	

Specified Housing Units Owned and Occupied by Tongans
Top 10 Places Sorted by Number

Place	Dollars
No places met population threshold.	

Specified Housing Units Owned and Occupied by Vietnamese
Top 10 Places Sorted by Number

Place	Dollars
Indianapolis, IN (cons. city) Marion County	91,900
Fort Wayne, IN (city) Allen County	85,500

Notes: Please refer to the User's Guide for an explanation of data; tables reflect only those areas that meet Summary File 4 population thresholds, therefore there may be less than 10 places listed

Climate

INDIANA

PHYSICAL FEATURES AND GENERAL CLIMATE. Indiana has an invigorating climate of warm summers and cool winters, because of its location in the middle latitudes in the interior of a large continent. Imposed on the well-known daily and seasonal changes of temperature are changes occurring every few days as surges of polar air move southeastward or air of tropical origin moves northeastward. These outbreaks are more frequent and pronounced in the winter than in the summer. A winter may be unusually cold or a summer cool if the influence of polar air is rather continuous. Likewise, a summer may be unusually warm or a winter mild if air of tropical origin predominates. The action between these two air masses with a contrast in temperature and density fosters the development of low pressure centers which in moving generally eastward frequently pass through or near Indiana, resulting in normally abundant rain. The cyclones are least active and frequently pass north of Indiana in midsummer. Thunderstorms, often local in areal coverage, are important at such times when evaporation and loss of moisture from the soil and vegetation exceeds rainfall. Major climatological variations within the State are caused by differences of latitude, elevation, terrain, soil, and lakes.

The effect of the Great Lakes and more specifically, Lake Michigan, on the climate of northern Indiana is most pronounced just inland from the Lake Michigan shore and diminishes to insignificance in central Indiana. The result of cold air passing over the warmer lake water of Lake Michigan induces precipitation in the lee of Lake Michigan in fall and winter. Average daily minimum temperatures in the fall are higher and daily maximum temperatures in the spring are lower in northwestern Indiana than farther south. Winter precipitation, especially snowfall, is several times greater in the counties of Lake, Porter, and LaPorte as the result of this phenomena. Lake related snowfall and cloudiness often extends to central Indiana in the winter. Very local severe snowstorms have occurred just inland from Lake Michigan.

Another important variable in the composition of Indiana weather is the topography of the State. Elevations range from a little more than 300 feet at the mouth of the Wabash in the southwest corner of the State, to a little over 1,200 feet in the east-central portion (Randolph County) and northeastern section (Steuben County). Differences of terrain affect the climate considerably. South-central Indiana is unglaciated and has the most rugged relief. The Kankakee Valley in the northwest has but little slope to the west and drains what was formerly marshlands. Many small lakes abound in northeastern Indiana among numerous glacial moraines and hills. Most of the north, central, and southwest is rolling country.

TEMPERATURE. Variations of temperature and precipitation occur in short distances where terrain is hilly. On calm, clear nights the valley bottoms have lower temperatures than the slopes and tops of the surrounding hills. Mean maximum as well as mean minimum temperatures decrease from south to north with latitude and decrease from west to east with elevation. Near Lake Michigan temperatures average higher than expected for the latitude in the fall and winter, and lower than expected for the latitude in the spring and summer.

The average date of the last freezing temperature in the spring ranges from the first week of April in the Ohio River Valley of the southwest to the second week of May in the extreme northeast. The usual trend of a later date toward the north is reversed in extreme northwestern Indiana, where the average date is about April 30 near Lake Michigan. In the fall the average date of the first temperature of 32°F. or colder is from October 7 in the extreme northeast to October 26 along the Ohio River in the southwest.

Spring freezes are later in valleys and hollows and fall freezes are earlier. Longer freeze-free periods occur on ridges and hills. Southern Indiana has much of this type of terrain. The gradual slope upward from southwestern Indiana to northeastern Indiana results in lower minimum temperatures and shorter growing seasons in the east compared to the west at the same latitude. In the Kankakee Valley, peat or muck lands experience late spring and early fall frosts because of the radiative characteristic of the soil.

PRECIPITATION. Average annual rainfall ranges from 36 inches in northern Indiana to 43 inches in southern Indiana. July rainfall averages about the same in all areas. The greater precipitation in the south compared with the north comes in the winter months. Southern Indiana has the greatest rainfall in March and the least in October. The wettest month in northern and central Indiana is June and the driest is February. A drought occasionally occurs in the summer when evaporation is highest and dependence on rainfall is greatest.

Most of the state is drained by the Wabash River system. Other river basins are the Maumee in the extreme northeast, the St. Joseph (Lake Michigan) and Kankakee (Illinois River) in the north-central and northwest, and some Ohio River drainage in the extreme south and southeast. Floods occur in some part of the State nearly every year and have occurred in every month of the year. The season of greatest flood frequency is during the winter and spring months. The primary cause of floods is prolonged periods of heavy rains, although occasionally the rains falling on a snow cover and the formation of ice jams are an added factor. The most common type of flood-producing storm in the area is that having a quasi-stationary front oriented from west-southwest to east-northeast with a series of waves or perturbations moving to the east along the front.

Average annual snowfall increases from about 10 inches in southern Indiana to 40 inches in the northern portion of the State and higher in the three county areas along Lake Michigan. From year to year snowfall varies greatly, depending both on temperatures and the frequency of winter storms. At a given latitude in central and southern Indiana snowfall is greatest toward the east because of higher elevation.

OTHER CLIMATIC ELEMENTS. Cloudiness is least in the fall and greatest in the winter. The north is cloudier than the south, particularly in the winter when the Great Lakes have the greatest effect upon the weather.

Average relative humidity differs very little at night over Indiana. During the day relative humidity is usually lower in the south than in the north. This is true for all seasons. However, the simultaneous occurrence of high temperatures and high relative humidity is most frequent in the south.

Prevailing winds are from the southwest quadrant throughout most of the year. Winds from the northern quadrant occur in the winter and persist for a longer time in the north. Along the shore of Lake Michigan the sea-breeze effect is observed in the summer when winds in central United States are light or calm. Vertical currents from the heating of land during the day cause wind near the ground to flow from over water to land reducing the maximum temperature of the day. At night the breezes are in the opposite direction or from the land to water because of land cooling. These breezes are important in limiting extremely high temperatures of a summer day and account for rapid changes in short distances within a mile or so of the lake shore. Winds meet less friction passing over water so off-lake winds have a considerably higher speed than those off or over land.

Severe storms are most frequent in the spring. About one-half of the tornadoes occur between 2 p.m. and 6 p.m. and nearly three-fourths between 10 a.m. and 10 p.m. Hail falls occasionally in very local areas.

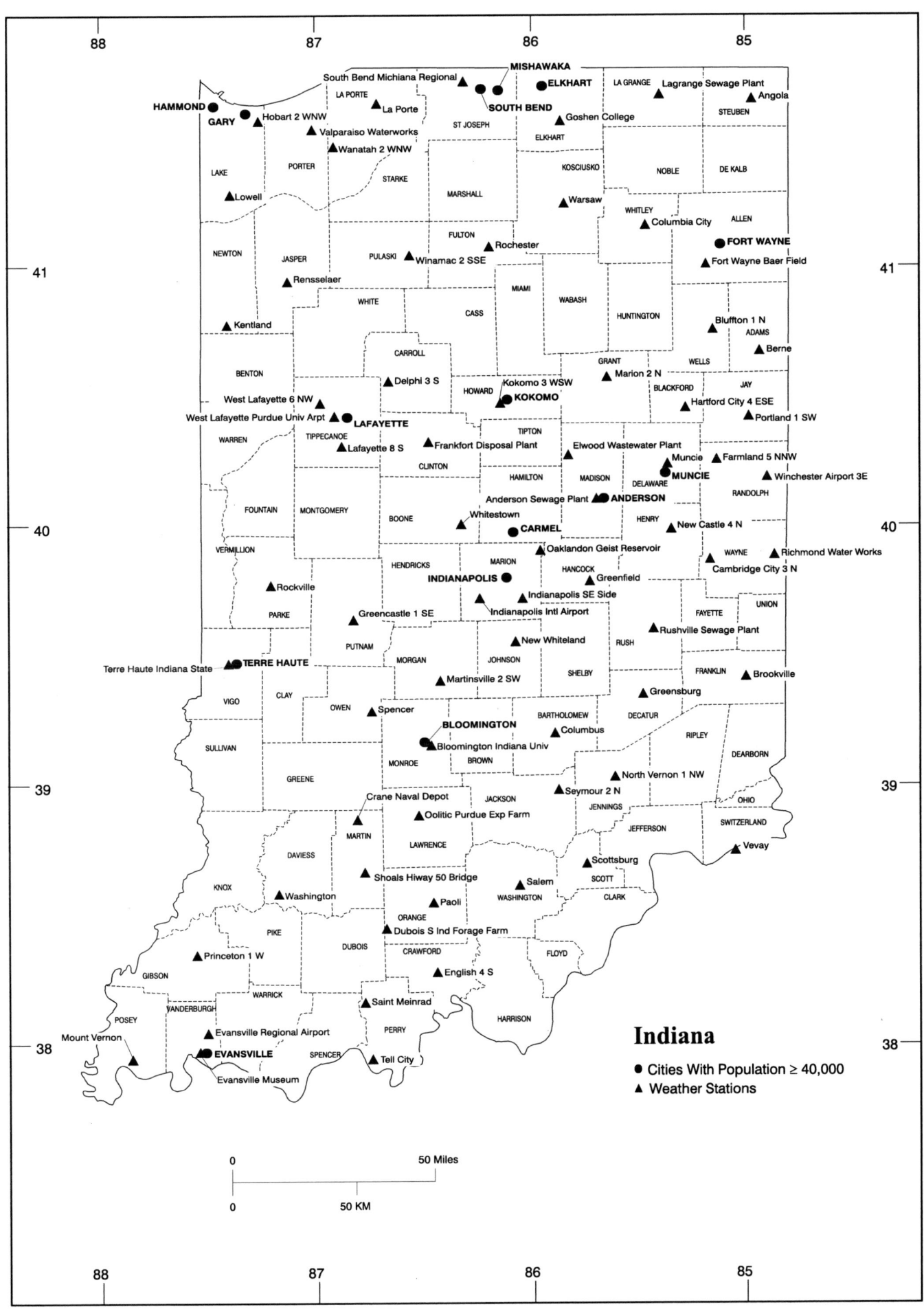

Indiana

- Cities With Population ≥ 40,000
- ▲ Weather Stations

Indiana Weather Stations by County

County	Station Name
Adams	Berne
Allen	Fort Wayne Baer Field
Bartholomew	Columbus
Blackford	Hartford City 4 ESE
Boone	Whitestown
Carroll	Delphi 3 S
Clinton	Frankfort Disposal Plant
Crawford	English 4 S
Daviess	Washington
Decatur	Greensburg
Delaware	Muncie
Dubois	Dubois S Ind. Forage Farm
Elkhart	Goshen College
Franklin	Brookville
Fulton	Rochester
Gibson	Princeton 1 W
Grant	Marion 2 N
Hancock	Greenfield
Henry	New Castle 4 N
Howard	Kokomo 3 WSW
Jackson	Seymour 2 N
Jasper	Rensselaer
Jay	Portland 1 SW
Jefferson	Madison Sewage Plant
Jennings	North Vernon 1 NW
Johnson	New Whiteland
Kosciusko	Warsaw
La Porte	La Porte
Lagrange	Lagrange Sewage Plant
Lake	Hobart 2 WNW Lowell
Lawrence	Oolitic Purdue Exp. Farm
Madison	Anderson Sewage Plant

County	Station Name
Madison (cont.)	Elwood Wastewater Plant
Marion	Indianapolis Int'l Airport Indianapolis SE Side Oaklandon Geist Reservoir
Martin	Crane Naval Depot Shoals Hiway 50 Bridge
Monroe	Bloomington Indiana Univ.
Morgan	Martinsville 2 SW
Newton	Kentland
Orange	Paoli
Owen	Spencer
Parke	Rockville
Perry	Tell City
Porter	Valparaiso Waterworks Wanatah 2 WNW
Posey	Mount Vernon
Pulaski	Winamac 2 SSE
Putnam	Greencastle 1 SE
Randolph	Farmland 5 NNW Winchester Airport 3E
Rush	Rushville Sewage Plant
Scott	Scottsburg
Spencer	Saint Meinrad
St. Joseph	South Bend Michiana Regional
Steuben	Angola
Switzerland	Vevay
Tippecanoe	Lafayette 8 S West Lafayette 6 NW West Lafayette Purdue Univ. Arpt.
Vanderburgh	Evansville Museum Evansville Regional Airport
Vigo	Terre Haute Indiana State
Washington	Salem
Wayne	Cambridge City 3 N Richmond Water Works
Wells	Bluffton 1 N
Whitley	Columbia City

Indiana Weather Stations by City

City	Station Name	Miles
Anderson	Anderson Sewage Plant	2
	Elwood Wastewater Plant	15
	Muncie	18
	New Castle 4 N	19
Bloomington	Bloomington Indiana Univ.	0
	Martinsville 2 SW	17
	Oolitic Purdue Exp. Farm	20
	Spencer	15
Carmel	Indianapolis Int'l Airport	19
	Indianapolis SE Side	18
	Oaklandon Geist Reservoir	8
	Whitestown	13
Elkhart	Goshen College	10
	South Bend Michiana Regional	19
Evansville	Evansville Museum	1
	Evansville Regional Airport	5
	Mount Vernon	19
	Henderson 7 SSW, KY	16
Fort Wayne	Columbia City	19
	Fort Wayne Baer Field	6
Gary	Chicago University, IL	19
	Park Forest, IL	18
	Hobart 2 WNW	4
	Valparaiso Waterworks	17
Hammond	Chicago University, IL	13
	Chicago Midway Airport, IL	18
	Park Forest, IL	12
	Hobart 2 WNW	11
Indianapolis	Indianapolis Int'l Airport	9
	Indianapolis SE Side	7
	New Whiteland	17
	Oaklandon Geist Reservoir	11
	Whitestown	18
Kokomo	Kokomo 3 WSW	2
Lafayette	Delphi 3 S	14
	Lafayette 8 S	8
	West Lafayette Purdue Univ. Arpt.	3
	West Lafayette 6 NW	8
Mishawaka	Goshen College	17
	South Bend Michiana Regional	9
Muncie	Anderson Sewage Plant	18
	Farmland 5 NNW	13
	Hartford City 4 ESE	18
	Muncie	3
	New Castle 4 N	15
South Bend	South Bend Michiana Regional	5
Terre Haute	Paris Waterworks, IL	20
	Terre Haute Indiana State	1

Note: Miles is the distance between the geographic center of the city and the weather station.

Indiana Weather Stations by Elevation

Feet	Station Name
1,108	Winchester Airport 3E
1,062	New Castle 4 N
1,013	Richmond Water Works
1,007	Angola
997	Cambridge City 3 N
977	Muncie
964	Farmland 5 NNW
958	Rushville Sewage Plant
941	Hartford City 4 ESE
935	Greensburg
935	Whitestown
908	Portland 1 SW
892	Lagrange Sewage Plant
872	Goshen College
862	Greenfield
859	Berne
859	Greencastle 1 SE
849	Columbia City
843	Anderson Sewage Plant
843	Indianapolis SE Side
839	Elwood Wastewater Plant
833	Frankfort Disposal Plant
830	Bloomington Indiana Univ.
823	Bluffton 1 N
816	Kokomo 3 WSW
807	La Porte
807	Warsaw
797	Salem
797	Valparaiso Waterworks
793	Oaklandon Geist Reservoir
790	Fort Wayne Baer Field
790	Indianapolis Int'l Airport
787	Marion 2 N
784	New Whiteland
770	South Bend Michiana Regional
767	Rochester
744	North Vernon 1 NW
734	Wanatah 2 WNW
731	Lafayette 8 S
728	Crane Naval Depot
702	West Lafayette 6 NW
692	Kentland
688	Dubois S Ind. Forage Farm
688	Rockville
688	Winamac 2 SSE
669	Delphi 3 S
662	Lowell
649	Oolitic Purdue Exp. Farm
649	Rensselaer
639	Hobart 2 WNW
629	Brookville
620	Columbus
606	Martinsville 2 SW
597	W. Lafayette Purdue Univ. Arpt
567	Seymour 2 N

Feet	Station Name
557	Paoli
547	Scottsburg
547	Shoals Hiway 50 Bridge
547	Spencer
524	Washington
508	English 4 S
508	Saint Meinrad
505	Terre Haute Indiana State
479	Princeton 1 W
469	Vevay
459	Madison Sewage Plant
419	Mount Vernon
396	Tell City
380	Evansville Regional Airport
377	Evansville Museum

Evansville Regional Airport

Evansville, Indiana, is located on the Ohio River. The country around Evansville ranges from level to areas of rolling terrain near the river. Dress Regional Airport, where weather observations are taken, is located in a shallow valley with low hills to the east and west which parallel the valley, but slope down to the south. There are hills five miles to the north which are about 100 feet higher than the field. The open end of the valley slopes down and south toward the city of Evansville and the Ohio River.

Prevailing wind direction is from the south-southwest. The strongest winds occur during a deep winter storm passage through the Lower Ohio Valley. Strong and cold north to northwest winds occur from late autumn to early spring, most often, in January and February, as large domes of arctic high pressure moves into the midwest.

Geographically, Evansville lies in the path of moisture-bearing low pressure formations that move from the western Gulf region, northeastward over the Mississippi and Ohio Valleys to the Great Lakes and northern Atlantic Coast. Much of the precipitation results from these storm systems, especially in the cooler part of the year.

Both temperature and precipitation are closely related to the movement of the polar front and the storms which move along the front. This is especially true in the winter and spring months. In summer and early autumn changes are less severe and periods of polar air invasions are less prolonged. There is considerable variation in seasonal and monthly temperature and precipitation from year to year as these factors depend greatly on the frequency of storm and frontal passages.

Convective thunderstorms, developing in the maritime tropical air from the Gulf of Mexico and squall line activity, combine to supply the summer rainfall. The greatest precipitation intensities for short periods of time come in the months of greatest thunderstorm frequency. The greatest intensities for 24 hours or more are confined to the winter months.

Severe storms are rather infrequent but thunderstorms cause some wind damage each year. Hail often occurs with the stronger thunderstorms. Evansville is in tornado alley with the most frequent occurrence in early spring and late fall.

Snowfall varies greatly from season to season, as do rainfall and temperature. Snowfalls of two or more inches are very infrequent, and these amounts are usually melted within a day or two.

The growing season averages 199 days, but has been as long as 250 days and as short as 169 days.

Evansville Regional Airport *Vanderburgh County*   Elevation: 380 ft.   Latitude: 38° 03' N   Longitude: 87° 32' W

	JAN	FEB	MAR	APR	MAY	JUN	JUL	AUG	SEP	OCT	NOV	DEC	YEAR
Mean Maximum Temp. (°F)	39.1	44.9	55.9	67.2	76.8	85.6	88.9	87.2	80.9	69.4	55.5	44.5	66.3
Mean Temp. (°F)	31.0	35.7	46.0	56.1	65.8	74.9	78.6	76.4	69.4	57.4	46.2	36.3	56.2
Mean Minimum Temp. (°F)	22.9	26.5	35.9	44.9	54.8	64.1	68.3	65.6	57.9	45.4	36.9	28.1	45.9
Extreme Maximum Temp. (°F)	71	77	84	91	95	102	102	102	100	91	82	77	102
Extreme Minimum Temp. (°F)	-21	-9	-6	23	32	42	51	43	34	23	10	-15	-21
Days Maximum Temp. ≥ 90°F	0	0	0	0	2	9	16	11	5	0	0	0	43
Days Maximum Temp. ≤ 32°F	9	5	1	0	0	0	0	0	0	0	0	5	20
Days Minimum Temp. ≤ 32°F	25	19	13	3	0	0	0	0	0	2	11	21	94
Days Minimum Temp. ≤ 0°F	2	1	0	0	0	0	0	0	0	0	0	1	4
Heating Degree Days (base 65°F)	1,047	820	588	287	81	5	0	1	42	255	559	883	4,568
Cooling Degree Days (base 65°F)	0	0	4	22	114	312	442	374	178	29	1	1	1,477
Mean Precipitation (in.)	2.80	2.94	4.39	4.66	5.03	4.10	3.73	3.05	2.94	2.95	4.14	3.50	44.23
Maximum Precipitation (in.)	13.5	7.3	12.8	10.3	13.5	6.9	9.7	8.4	7.0	7.9	8.5	8.2	63.1
Minimum Precipitation (in.)	0.5	0.6	1.3	1.1	0.9	0.6	0.2	0.2	0.5	trace	0.9	0.6	27.9
Maximum 24-hr. Precipitation (in.)	3.7	2.7	4.3	3.9	4.9	3.3	4.1	3.5	3.1	2.4	3.5	2.3	4.9
Days With ≥ 0.1" Precipitation	5	5	8	8	8	7	6	5	5	5	7	7	76
Days With ≥ 1.0" Precipitation	0	1	1	1	1	1	1	1	1	1	1	1	11
Mean Snowfall (in.)	4.7	4.1	2.5	0.4	trace	trace	0.0	0.0	trace	0.2	0.4	2.5	14.8
Maximum Snowfall (in.)	21	18	20	9	0	0	0	0	0	5	7	10	36
Maximum 24-hr. Snowfall (in.)	8	11	8	9	0	0	0	0	0	4	7	7	11
Days With ≥ 1.0" Snow Depth	6	6	1	0	0	0	0	0	0	0	0	2	15
Thunderstorm Days	1	1	4	5	6	7	7	5	3	2	2	1	44
Foggy Days	12	12	12	9	11	11	13	16	15	12	11	13	147
Predominant Sky Cover	OVR	OVR	OVR	OVR	OVR	OVR	SCT	CLR	CLR	CLR	OVR	OVR	OVR
Mean Relative Humidity 7am (%)	80	80	78	73	75	75	78	82	83	83	80	81	79
Mean Relative Humidity 4pm (%)	66	61	56	50	52	52	54	54	52	50	59	67	56
Mean Dewpoint (°F)	24	27	35	44	54	63	67	66	58	46	36	28	46
Prevailing Wind Direction	NW	NW	NW	SSW	S	SW	SW	SW	S	NW	S	NW	NW
Prevailing Wind Speed (mph)	12	12	12	13	9	9	8	8	8	7	10	10	10
Maximum Wind Gust (mph)	55	53	52	63	71	76	56	46	59	52	70	56	76

Fort Wayne Baer Field

Fort Wayne is located at the junction of the St. Marys, St. Joseph, and Maumee Rivers in northeastern Indiana. The surrounding area is generally level south and east of the city. Southwest and west, the terrain is somewhat rolling, while to the northwest and a few miles north from the city, it becomes quite hilly. The highest point in the general area is about 40 miles due north of Fort Wayne, near Angola, Indiana. At this point, the elevation rises to 1,060 feet above sea level.

The climate is representative of northeastern Indiana and is influenced to some extent by the Great Lakes. It does not differ greatly from the climates of other midwestern cities of the same general latitude. Temperature differences between daily highs and lows are invigorating and average about 20 degrees. The average occurrence of the last freeze in the spring is late April, and the first freeze in the fall is mid-October, making the average freeze-free period 173 days. The length of the growing season is favorable for the maturing of all crops and vegetables normally grown in the midwest.

Annual precipitation is well distributed, with somewhat larger monthly amounts falling in late spring and early summer. Damaging hailstorms occur at an average of about twice a year. One of the most notable storms caused severe damage to property, many thousands of trees, and power and telephone lines in the area. Severe flooding has also occurred in the area. Snow usually covers the ground for about 30 days during the winter months, but heavy snowstorms are not frequent.

Except for the considerable cloudiness that occurs during the winter months, Fort Wayne enjoys a good midwestern average sunshine. Heavy fog occurrence is infrequent.

Fort Wayne Baer Field *Allen County*   Elevation: 790 ft.   Latitude: 41° 00' N   Longitude: 85° 12' W

	JAN	FEB	MAR	APR	MAY	JUN	JUL	AUG	SEP	OCT	NOV	DEC	YEAR
Mean Maximum Temp. (°F)	31.0	35.3	47.0	60.0	71.8	80.9	84.6	82.1	75.7	63.1	48.8	36.6	59.7
Mean Temp. (°F)	23.6	27.4	38.0	49.3	60.7	70.2	73.9	71.6	64.6	52.7	40.9	29.8	50.2
Mean Minimum Temp. (°F)	16.2	19.4	28.9	38.7	49.6	59.4	63.2	61.0	53.4	42.1	33.0	23.0	40.6
Extreme Maximum Temp. (°F)	63	71	82	88	94	106	102	99	97	87	78	71	106
Extreme Minimum Temp. (°F)	-22	-18	-7	7	28	38	46	40	29	19	7	-18	-22
Days Maximum Temp. ≥ 90°F	0	0	0	0	1	4	7	3	1	0	0	0	16
Days Maximum Temp. ≤ 32°F	16	11	3	0	0	0	0	0	0	0	2	10	42
Days Minimum Temp. ≤ 32°F	28	24	20	8	1	0	0	0	0	5	16	26	128
Days Minimum Temp. ≤ 0°F	5	3	0	0	0	0	0	0	0	0	0	2	10
Heating Degree Days (base 65°F)	1,277	1,056	831	471	182	28	3	9	100	385	715	1,084	6,141
Cooling Degree Days (base 65°F)	0	0	1	7	55	194	295	226	90	9	0	0	877
Mean Precipitation (in.)	2.04	1.92	2.87	3.68	3.72	3.84	3.68	3.52	2.84	2.67	3.01	2.73	36.52
Maximum Precipitation (in.)	9.7	6.8	5.3	7.1	8.8	8.3	11.0	7.7	6.8	9.3	8.0	7.6	54.6
Minimum Precipitation (in.)	0.4	0.3	0.7	1.3	1.0	0.8	0.4	0.4	0.3	0.1	0.6	0.4	24.4
Maximum 24-hr. Precipitation (in.)	2.4	3.0	2.1	2.6	4.3	4.4	2.6	3.9	3.5	2.7	2.4	2.1	4.4
Days With ≥ 0.1" Precipitation	5	5	7	8	7	7	6	6	5	6	7	6	75
Days With ≥ 1.0" Precipitation	0	0	0	1	1	1	1	1	1	1	0	0	7
Mean Snowfall (in.)	9.9	7.7	4.6	1.2	trace	trace	0.0	trace	0.0	0.5	3.0	7.9	34.8
Maximum Snowfall (in.)	30	17	20	12	trace	0	0	0	0	8	14	20	62
Maximum 24-hr. Snowfall (in.)	11	8	13	6	trace	0	0	0	0	6	6	11	13
Days With ≥ 1.0" Snow Depth	16	13	4	0	0	0	0	0	0	0	2	8	43
Thunderstorm Days	< 1	1	2	4	5	7	7	6	4	2	1	< 1	39
Foggy Days	14	13	13	11	12	10	14	17	14	14	13	15	160
Predominant Sky Cover	OVR	OVR	OVR	OVR	OVR	OVR	SCT	SCT	OVR	OVR	OVR	OVR	OVR
Mean Relative Humidity 7am (%)	81	81	80	78	77	78	82	86	87	85	83	83	82
Mean Relative Humidity 4pm (%)	72	67	62	54	52	52	53	55	53	54	67	74	60
Mean Dewpoint (°F)	18	20	28	38	48	57	62	61	54	43	33	23	41
Prevailing Wind Direction	W	W	W	SW	SW	SW	SW	SW	SW	SW	SW	W	SW
Prevailing Wind Speed (mph)	14	14	14	14	12	12	9	9	10	12	13	13	12
Maximum Wind Gust (mph)	69	54	59	61	59	64	67	59	53	63	58	58	69

Indianapolis Int'l Airport

Indianapolis is located in the central part of the state and is situated on level or slightly rolling terrain. The greater part of the city lies east of the White River which flows in a general north to south direction.

The National Weather Service Forecast Office is located approximately seven miles southwest of the central part of the city at the Indianapolis International Airport. From a field elevation of 797 feet above sea level at the Indianapolis International Airport the terrain slopes gradually downward to a little below 645 feet at the White River, then upward to just over 910 feet in the northwest corner and eastern sections of the county. The street elevation at the former city office located in the Old Federal Building is 718 feet.

Indianapolis has a temperate climate, with very warm summers and without a dry season. Very cold temperatures may be produced by the invasion of continental polar air in the winter from northern latitudes. The polar air can be quite frigid with very low humidity. The arrival of maritime tropical air from the Gulf in the summer brings warm temperatures and moderate humidity. One of the longest and most severe heat waves brought temperatures of 100 degrees or more for nine consecutive days.

Precipitation is distributed fairly evenly throughout the year, and therefore there is no pronounced wet or dry season. Rainfall in the spring and summer is produced mostly by showers and thunderstorms. A rainfall of about two and a half inches in a 24-hour period can be expected about once a year. Snowfalls of three inches or more occur on an average of two or three times in the winter.

Local levees and/or channel improvements now protect some formerly flood-prone areas.

Based on the 1951-1980 period, the average first occurrence of 32 degrees Fahrenheit in the fall is October 20 and the average last occurrence in the spring is April 22.

Indianapolis Int'l Airport *Marion County*   Elevation: 790 ft.   Latitude: 39° 43' N   Longitude: 86° 16' W

	JAN	FEB	MAR	APR	MAY	JUN	JUL	AUG	SEP	OCT	NOV	DEC	YEAR
Mean Maximum Temp. (°F)	34.2	39.6	51.0	63.1	73.6	82.2	85.7	83.8	77.6	65.5	51.7	39.8	62.3
Mean Temp. (°F)	26.3	31.1	41.6	52.3	62.8	71.9	75.7	73.7	66.6	54.7	43.0	32.2	52.7
Mean Minimum Temp. (°F)	18.4	22.5	32.1	41.6	52.1	61.5	65.6	63.6	55.6	43.8	34.3	24.7	43.0
Extreme Maximum Temp. (°F)	66	75	85	89	93	102	103	102	96	88	79	74	103
Extreme Minimum Temp. (°F)	-27	-21	-7	18	30	37	48	42	32	20	7	-23	-27
Days Maximum Temp. ≥ 90°F	0	0	0	0	0	3	8	5	2	0	0	0	18
Days Maximum Temp. ≤ 32°F	13	8	2	0	0	0	0	0	0	0	1	7	31
Days Minimum Temp. ≤ 32°F	27	22	17	5	0	0	0	0	0	4	14	24	113
Days Minimum Temp. ≤ 0°F	4	2	0	0	0	0	0	0	0	0	0	1	7
Heating Degree Days (base 65°F)	1,193	952	720	385	135	14	1	3	73	328	654	1,009	5,467
Cooling Degree Days (base 65°F)	0	0	2	10	69	232	349	285	127	15	0	0	1,089
Mean Precipitation (in.)	2.45	2.38	3.46	3.70	4.27	4.04	4.47	3.73	2.80	2.78	3.60	3.01	40.69
Maximum Precipitation (in.)	12.7	5.3	10.7	8.1	9.3	7.4	11.8	8.3	8.1	7.8	8.5	7.7	55.8
Minimum Precipitation (in.)	0.4	0.4	0.9	1.0	1.1	0.4	1.2	0.7	0.2	0.2	0.8	0.4	27.9
Maximum 24-hr. Precipitation (in.)	2.8	2.5	3.0	2.6	3.1	3.8	5.1	4.5	2.9	3.9	4.1	2.1	5.1
Days With ≥ 0.1" Precipitation	6	5	7	8	8	7	7	6	5	5	7	6	77
Days With ≥ 1.0" Precipitation	0	0	1	1	1	1	1	1	1	1	1	0	9
Mean Snowfall (in.)	9.2	6.3	3.0	0.4	trace	trace	0.0	trace	0.0	0.4	1.3	5.8	26.4
Maximum Snowfall (in.)	31	18	11	4	trace	0	0	0	0	9	8	28	45
Maximum 24-hr. Snowfall (in.)	10	8	6	3	trace	0	0	0	0	8	8	10	10
Days With ≥ 1.0" Snow Depth	12	8	3	0	0	0	0	0	0	0	1	5	29
Thunderstorm Days	1	1	3	5	6	7	8	6	3	2	1	< 1	43
Foggy Days	15	13	13	11	13	12	16	18	15	13	14	15	168
Predominant Sky Cover	OVR	OVR	OVR	OVR	OVR	OVR	SCT	SCT	CLR	OVR	OVR	OVR	OVR
Mean Relative Humidity 7am (%)	81	81	79	77	80	80	84	88	87	85	83	83	82
Mean Relative Humidity 4pm (%)	69	64	59	54	53	53	56	56	53	53	63	70	59
Mean Dewpoint (°F)	20	23	31	40	51	60	65	64	56	44	34	25	43
Prevailing Wind Direction	WSW	WNW	WNW	SW	SW	SW	SW	SW	SW	SW	SW	SW	SW
Prevailing Wind Speed (mph)	12	13	14	13	10	9	8	8	9	10	12	12	10
Maximum Wind Gust (mph)	60	62	75	75	69	70	81	70	74	64	79	64	81

South Bend Michiana Regional

South Bend is located on the Saint Joseph River in the northern portion of Saint Joseph County, situated on mostly level to gently rolling terrain and some former marshland. Drainage for the area is through the Saint Joseph River and Kankakee River.

South Bend is under the climatic influence of Lake Michigan with its nearest shore 20 miles to the northwest. The lake has a moderating effect on the temperature. Temperatures of 100 degrees or higher are rare and cold waves are less severe than at many locations at the same latitude. This results in favorable conditions for orchard and vegetable growth.

Based on the 1951-1980 period, the average first occurrence of 32 degrees Fahrenheit in the fall is October 18 and the average last occurrence in the spring is May 1.

Precipitation is fairly evenly distributed throughout the year with the greatest amounts during the growing season. The predominant snow season is from November through March, although there are also generally lighter amounts in October and April.

Winter is marked by considerable cloudiness and rather high humidity along with frequent periods of snow. Heavy snowfalls, resulting from a cold northwest wind passing over Lake Michigan are not uncommon.

South Bend Michiana Regional *St. Joseph Co.*   Elevation: 770 ft.   Latitude: 41° 42' N   Longitude: 86° 20' W

	JAN	FEB	MAR	APR	MAY	JUN	JUL	AUG	SEP	OCT	NOV	DEC	YEAR
Mean Maximum Temp. (°F)	30.9	35.2	46.3	58.8	70.6	79.8	83.4	81.0	74.0	62.2	48.2	36.3	58.9
Mean Temp. (°F)	23.8	27.6	37.7	48.8	59.9	69.3	73.4	71.5	64.1	52.8	40.9	29.9	50.0
Mean Minimum Temp. (°F)	16.7	20.0	29.0	38.7	49.1	58.9	63.4	61.8	54.2	43.2	33.6	23.4	41.0
Extreme Maximum Temp. (°F)	64	72	85	89	92	104	102	103	95	86	78	70	104
Extreme Minimum Temp. (°F)	-21	-14	-2	11	28	35	44	42	32	20	5	-15	-21
Days Maximum Temp. ≥ 90°F	0	0	0	0	1	3	6	3	1	0	0	0	14
Days Maximum Temp. ≤ 32°F	17	12	4	0	0	0	0	0	0	0	2	9	44
Days Minimum Temp. ≤ 32°F	28	24	20	8	0	0	0	0	0	3	14	25	122
Days Minimum Temp. ≤ 0°F	4	3	0	0	0	0	0	0	0	0	0	1	8
Heating Degree Days (base 65°F)	1,270	1,049	842	491	207	39	5	12	109	382	715	1,082	6,203
Cooling Degree Days (base 65°F)	0	0	1	9	54	178	284	227	89	8	0	0	850
Mean Precipitation (in.)	2.23	1.95	2.92	3.67	3.46	4.07	3.77	4.04	3.86	3.32	3.41	3.08	39.78
Maximum Precipitation (in.)	5.3	4.5	8.0	6.0	6.9	10.9	7.5	8.3	9.0	9.8	6.7	5.5	55.6
Minimum Precipitation (in.)	0.7	0.5	0.5	0.5	0.8	0.5	1.2	0.3	trace	0.4	1.4	0.7	25.1
Maximum 24-hr. Precipitation (in.)	2.8	1.9	2.1	1.9	2.9	4.7	3.6	4.0	3.0	3.5	3.9	3.0	4.7
Days With ≥ 0.1" Precipitation	6	6	7	8	7	7	7	7	6	6	8	8	83
Days With ≥ 1.0" Precipitation	0	0	0	1	0	1	1	1	1	1	1	1	8
Mean Snowfall (in.)	22.9	15.5	9.2	2.0	trace	trace	trace	trace	trace	0.5	7.7	18.8	76.6
Maximum Snowfall (in.)	86	35	34	14	1	0	0	0	0	9	30	42	142
Maximum 24-hr. Snowfall (in.)	16	12	9	8	1	0	0	0	0	7	15	11	16
Days With ≥ 1.0" Snow Depth	22	16	7	1	0	0	0	0	0	0	4	14	64
Thunderstorm Days	< 1	< 1	2	4	5	8	7	6	4	2	1	< 1	39
Foggy Days	15	14	15	13	13	12	14	18	16	16	15	17	178
Predominant Sky Cover	OVR	OVR	OVR	OVR	OVR	OVR	OVR	OVR	OVR	OVR	OVR	OVR	OVR
Mean Relative Humidity 7am (%)	82	82	80	77	76	78	82	86	86	84	83	83	82
Mean Relative Humidity 4pm (%)	73	69	62	55	53	52	55	57	55	57	68	75	61
Mean Dewpoint (°F)	18	20	28	37	47	57	62	62	54	43	33	23	41
Prevailing Wind Direction	SW	SW	SW	NNW	SSW	SSW	SW	SW	SSW	SSW	SW	SW	SW
Prevailing Wind Speed (mph)	13	13	13	13	12	10	9	9	10	12	12	13	12
Maximum Wind Gust (mph)	67	58	55	66	86	71	66	59	63	59	74	69	86

Anderson Sewage Plant *Madison County*   Elevation: 843 ft.   Latitude: 40° 06' N   Longitude: 85° 43' W

	JAN	FEB	MAR	APR	MAY	JUN	JUL	AUG	SEP	OCT	NOV	DEC	YEAR
Mean Maximum Temp. (°F)	33.4	38.3	48.5	60.6	71.5	80.3	83.7	81.8	75.5	63.9	50.1	38.1	60.5
Mean Temp. (°F)	26.0	30.4	39.9	50.5	61.2	70.4	74.0	72.0	65.0	53.7	42.4	31.3	51.4
Mean Minimum Temp. (°F)	18.7	22.5	31.3	40.5	50.8	60.4	64.2	62.0	54.4	43.4	34.6	24.3	42.3
Extreme Maximum Temp. (°F)	65	73	81	87	93	101	103	101	95	88	78	75	103
Extreme Minimum Temp. (°F)	-24	-14	-7	17	27	37	47	40	31	20	10	-22	-24
Days Maximum Temp. ≥ 90°F	0	0	0	0	0	3	5	3	1	0	0	0	12
Days Maximum Temp. ≤ 32°F	14	10	3	0	0	0	0	0	0	0	1	9	37
Days Minimum Temp. ≤ 32°F	27	22	18	7	1	0	0	0	0	4	14	24	117
Days Minimum Temp. ≤ 0°F	3	2	0	0	0	0	0	0	0	0	0	1	6
Heating Degree Days (base 65°F)	1,201	971	771	435	174	25	4	9	97	358	673	1,040	5,758
Cooling Degree Days (base 65°F)	0	0	2	10	67	202	306	242	106	14	0	0	949
Mean Precipitation (in.)	2.10	2.31	3.24	3.84	4.11	4.15	4.34	3.25	2.95	2.79	3.73	2.84	39.65
Days With ≥ 0.1" Precipitation	6	5	7	9	8	7	7	6	5	6	7	7	80
Days With ≥ 1.0" Precipitation	0	0	0	1	1	1	1	1	1	0	1	0	7
Mean Snowfall (in.)	6.6	4.6	2.1	0.2	0.0	0.0	0.0	0.0	0.0	trace	0.7	3.6	17.8
Days With ≥ 1.0" Snow Depth	9	5	2	0	0	0	0	0	0	0	1	3	20

Angola *Steuben County*   Elevation: 1,007 ft.   Latitude: 41° 38' N   Longitude: 84° 59' W

	JAN	FEB	MAR	APR	MAY	JUN	JUL	AUG	SEP	OCT	NOV	DEC	YEAR
Mean Maximum Temp. (°F)	29.3	32.9	43.1	56.6	69.2	78.3	82.1	80.0	73.5	60.9	46.8	34.9	57.3
Mean Temp. (°F)	21.5	23.9	33.4	45.9	58.1	67.3	71.4	69.3	62.1	50.0	38.4	27.6	47.4
Mean Minimum Temp. (°F)	13.5	14.8	23.7	35.2	46.9	56.2	60.8	58.5	50.7	39.1	29.9	20.4	37.5
Extreme Maximum Temp. (°F)	60	70	78	85	90	101	98	97	93	89	75	69	101
Extreme Minimum Temp. (°F)	-27	-18	-13	4	25	32	40	37	27	16	8	-19	-27
Days Maximum Temp. ≥ 90°F	0	0	0	0	0	2	4	2	0	0	0	0	8
Days Maximum Temp. ≤ 32°F	19	14	6	0	0	0	0	0	0	0	3	12	54
Days Minimum Temp. ≤ 32°F	30	27	26	12	1	0	0	0	0	8	19	28	151
Days Minimum Temp. ≤ 0°F	5	5	1	0	0	0	0	0	0	0	0	2	13
Heating Degree Days (base 65°F)	1,344	1,154	973	568	246	59	14	25	143	463	792	1,152	6,933
Cooling Degree Days (base 65°F)	0	0	1	4	37	136	227	167	56	3	0	0	631
Mean Precipitation (in.)	1.96	1.75	2.68	3.46	3.98	3.71	3.91	3.89	3.39	2.74	3.15	2.67	37.29
Days With ≥ 0.1" Precipitation	5	5	6	8	7	6	7	7	6	6	7	7	77
Days With ≥ 1.0" Precipitation	0	0	0	1	1	1	1	1	1	1	1	0	8
Mean Snowfall (in.)	10.4	7.8	4.2	0.7	trace	0.0	0.0	0.0	0.0	0.3	2.2	8.0	33.6
Days With ≥ 1.0" Snow Depth	18	15	7	0	0	0	0	0	0	0	2	9	51

Berne *Adams County*   Elevation: 859 ft.   Latitude: 40° 40' N   Longitude: 84° 57' W

	JAN	FEB	MAR	APR	MAY	JUN	JUL	AUG	SEP	OCT	NOV	DEC	YEAR
Mean Maximum Temp. (°F)	32.2	37.0	48.3	60.8	72.3	81.1	84.8	82.7	76.4	63.8	49.8	37.8	60.6
Mean Temp. (°F)	24.8	28.8	39.1	50.2	61.4	70.6	74.5	72.4	65.6	53.7	41.9	30.9	51.2
Mean Minimum Temp. (°F)	17.3	20.6	29.8	39.6	50.5	60.1	64.1	62.0	54.7	43.4	34.0	23.9	41.7
Extreme Maximum Temp. (°F)	65	72	82	88	94	104	101	99	96	90	77	72	104
Extreme Minimum Temp. (°F)	-24	-14	-4	10	27	39	46	42	31	20	5	-19	-24
Days Maximum Temp. ≥ 90°F	0	0	0	0	1	4	7	4	2	0	0	0	18
Days Maximum Temp. ≤ 32°F	15	10	3	0	0	0	0	0	0	0	1	9	38
Days Minimum Temp. ≤ 32°F	28	23	20	7	0	0	0	0	0	3	14	25	120
Days Minimum Temp. ≤ 0°F	4	2	0	0	0	0	0	0	0	0	0	1	7
Heating Degree Days (base 65°F)	1,242	1,017	800	448	172	25	2	7	87	360	688	1,053	5,901
Cooling Degree Days (base 65°F)	0	0	2	9	64	205	315	250	110	14	0	0	969
Mean Precipitation (in.)	2.14	2.13	2.88	3.79	3.78	4.41	4.12	3.63	3.02	2.58	3.22	2.71	38.41
Days With ≥ 0.1" Precipitation	6	5	7	8	8	8	7	6	6	6	7	6	80
Days With ≥ 1.0" Precipitation	0	0	0	1	1	1	1	1	1	0	1	0	7
Mean Snowfall (in.)	9.4	7.2	4.4	1.1	0.0	0.0	0.0	0.0	0.0	0.4	2.1	6.1	30.7
Days With ≥ 1.0" Snow Depth	16	11	4	0	0	0	0	0	0	0	1	7	39

Bloomington Indiana Univ. *Monroe County*   Elevation: 830 ft.   Latitude: 39° 10' N   Longitude: 86° 31' W

	JAN	FEB	MAR	APR	MAY	JUN	JUL	AUG	SEP	OCT	NOV	DEC	YEAR
Mean Maximum Temp. (°F)	36.2	41.7	52.0	63.9	74.0	81.9	86.1	84.6	78.3	66.7	53.7	41.9	63.4
Mean Temp. (°F)	27.8	32.3	41.9	53.1	63.2	71.9	76.1	74.2	67.2	55.6	44.7	33.5	53.5
Mean Minimum Temp. (°F)	19.3	22.8	31.8	42.2	52.5	61.8	66.1	63.8	56.1	44.4	35.5	25.1	43.5
Extreme Maximum Temp. (°F)	69	74	82	88	93	101	104	100	97	90	80	74	104
Extreme Minimum Temp. (°F)	-21	-13	-2	18	31	41	49	44	33	23	6	-20	-21
Days Maximum Temp. ≥ 90°F	0	0	0	0	0	4	9	6	2	0	0	0	21
Days Maximum Temp. ≤ 32°F	12	7	2	0	0	0	0	0	0	0	1	6	28
Days Minimum Temp. ≤ 32°F	27	22	17	5	0	0	0	0	0	3	13	23	110
Days Minimum Temp. ≤ 0°F	3	2	0	0	0	0	0	0	0	0	0	1	6
Heating Degree Days (base 65°F)	1,146	917	712	370	129	16	1	3	67	304	605	968	5,238
Cooling Degree Days (base 65°F)	0	0	3	16	77	237	362	302	136	20	1	0	1,154
Mean Precipitation (in.)	2.60	2.62	3.70	4.46	5.07	4.08	4.32	3.94	3.52	3.12	3.95	3.34	44.72
Days With ≥ 0.1" Precipitation	6	5	7	8	8	7	7	6	6	5	7	7	79
Days With ≥ 1.0" Precipitation	0	1	1	1	2	1	1	1	1	1	1	1	12
Mean Snowfall (in.)	na	na	na	trace	0.0	0.0	0.0	0.0	0.0	0.2	trace	1.6	na
Days With ≥ 1.0" Snow Depth	na	na	1	0	0	0	0	0	0	0	0	2	na

Bluffton 1 N *Wells County*   Elevation: 823 ft.   Latitude: 40° 45' N   Longitude: 85° 10' W

	JAN	FEB	MAR	APR	MAY	JUN	JUL	AUG	SEP	OCT	NOV	DEC	YEAR
Mean Maximum Temp. (°F)	30.5	34.6	46.4	59.0	70.8	80.0	83.7	81.4	75.2	62.9	48.5	36.7	59.1
Mean Temp. (°F)	22.8	26.0	37.0	48.6	60.0	69.5	73.1	70.7	63.8	51.8	40.0	29.3	49.4
Mean Minimum Temp. (°F)	15.1	17.3	27.5	38.1	49.2	58.9	62.4	59.9	52.4	40.6	31.5	21.8	39.6
Extreme Maximum Temp. (°F)	64	72	80	87	91	100	104	99	97	88	77	70	104
Extreme Minimum Temp. (°F)	-24	-18	-7	8	22	37	41	40	27	10	5	-18	-24
Days Maximum Temp. ≥ 90°F	0	0	0	0	0	3	6	2	1	0	0	0	12
Days Maximum Temp. ≤ 32°F	17	13	4	0	0	0	0	0	0	0	2	10	46
Days Minimum Temp. ≤ 32°F	29	25	22	8	1	0	0	0	0	6	18	26	135
Days Minimum Temp. ≤ 0°F	5	4	0	0	0	0	0	0	0	0	0	2	11
Heating Degree Days (base 65°F)	1,303	1,097	863	493	202	37	6	17	117	412	742	1,100	6,389
Cooling Degree Days (base 65°F)	0	0	1	7	54	183	274	208	90	11	0	0	828
Mean Precipitation (in.)	2.06	1.81	2.64	3.33	4.07	3.82	3.98	3.62	3.02	2.53	3.07	2.65	36.60
Days With ≥ 0.1" Precipitation	6	5	7	7	8	7	6	6	6	6	7	7	78
Days With ≥ 1.0" Precipitation	0	0	0	1	1	1	1	1	1	0	1	0	7
Mean Snowfall (in.)	8.4	7.1	3.7	1.1	0.0	0.0	trace	0.0	0.0	0.2	1.8	5.6	27.9
Days With ≥ 1.0" Snow Depth	15	12	4	1	0	0	0	0	0	0	1	7	40

Brookville *Franklin County*   Elevation: 629 ft.   Latitude: 39° 25' N   Longitude: 85° 01' W

	JAN	FEB	MAR	APR	MAY	JUN	JUL	AUG	SEP	OCT	NOV	DEC	YEAR
Mean Maximum Temp. (°F)	36.3	41.2	52.2	64.2	74.6	83.0	86.9	85.2	79.1	66.5	53.7	41.8	63.7
Mean Temp. (°F)	26.8	30.4	40.5	51.2	61.5	70.4	74.6	72.8	65.7	53.2	42.9	32.7	51.9
Mean Minimum Temp. (°F)	17.2	19.7	28.6	38.2	48.4	57.7	62.3	60.4	52.4	39.8	32.1	23.5	40.0
Extreme Maximum Temp. (°F)	66	75	84	89	94	102	102	103	97	91	82	76	103
Extreme Minimum Temp. (°F)	-31	-15	-9	16	26	36	44	41	30	17	2	-20	-31
Days Maximum Temp. ≥ 90°F	0	0	0	0	1	5	10	7	3	0	0	0	26
Days Maximum Temp. ≤ 32°F	12	7	1	0	0	0	0	0	0	0	1	6	27
Days Minimum Temp. ≤ 32°F	28	24	21	9	1	0	0	0	0	8	17	24	132
Days Minimum Temp. ≤ 0°F	4	3	0	0	0	0	0	0	0	0	0	1	8
Heating Degree Days (base 65°F)	1,177	968	755	414	162	24	3	6	85	372	655	995	5,616
Cooling Degree Days (base 65°F)	0	0	2	8	60	198	320	261	109	14	0	0	972
Mean Precipitation (in.)	2.83	2.64	3.65	4.03	4.55	3.96	4.28	3.92	2.56	3.01	3.70	3.28	42.41
Days With ≥ 0.1" Precipitation	6	6	8	8	8	7	7	6	5	6	7	7	81
Days With ≥ 1.0" Precipitation	0	0	1	1	1	1	1	1	1	1	1	1	10
Mean Snowfall (in.)	na	3.8	2.3	0.3	trace	0.0	0.0	0.0	0.0	trace	1.1	2.8	na
Days With ≥ 1.0" Snow Depth	11	8	2	0	0	0	0	0	0	0	1	3	25

Cambridge City 3 N *Wayne County*   Elevation: 997 ft.   Latitude: 39° 52' N   Longitude: 85° 11' W

	JAN	FEB	MAR	APR	MAY	JUN	JUL	AUG	SEP	OCT	NOV	DEC	YEAR
Mean Maximum Temp. (°F)	32.8	37.7	48.6	60.8	71.3	79.8	83.5	81.9	76.1	64.2	50.6	38.8	60.5
Mean Temp. (°F)	24.1	27.9	38.1	48.9	59.7	68.6	72.3	70.4	63.5	51.5	40.8	30.3	49.7
Mean Minimum Temp. (°F)	15.3	18.1	27.5	37.0	48.1	57.5	61.2	58.8	50.8	38.8	30.9	21.8	38.8
Extreme Maximum Temp. (°F)	64	71	82	86	90	100	99	97	94	88	79	73	100
Extreme Minimum Temp. (°F)	-31	-19	-14	13	26	35	44	38	26	16	6	-22	-31
Days Maximum Temp. ≥ 90°F	0	0	0	0	0	2	5	2	1	0	0	0	10
Days Maximum Temp. ≤ 32°F	15	10	3	0	0	0	0	0	0	0	1	9	38
Days Minimum Temp. ≤ 32°F	29	25	22	10	1	0	0	0	0	9	18	26	140
Days Minimum Temp. ≤ 0°F	5	4	0	0	0	0	0	0	0	0	0	2	11
Heating Degree Days (base 65°F)	1,263	1,042	829	480	202	39	7	16	119	417	721	1,069	6,204
Cooling Degree Days (base 65°F)	0	0	1	4	40	153	240	186	72	7	0	0	703
Mean Precipitation (in.)	2.39	2.30	3.36	4.21	4.78	4.35	4.19	3.46	2.76	2.84	3.52	2.96	41.12
Days With ≥ 0.1" Precipitation	6	6	7	9	9	7	7	6	5	6	7	7	82
Days With ≥ 1.0" Precipitation	0	0	1	1	1	1	1	1	1	1	1	1	10
Mean Snowfall (in.)	7.2	5.4	3.5	0.5	trace	0.0	0.0	0.0	0.0	0.1	1.1	4.0	21.8
Days With ≥ 1.0" Snow Depth	12	9	4	0	0	0	0	0	0	0	1	5	31

Columbia City *Whitley County*   Elevation: 849 ft.   Latitude: 41° 09' N   Longitude: 85° 29' W

	JAN	FEB	MAR	APR	MAY	JUN	JUL	AUG	SEP	OCT	NOV	DEC	YEAR
Mean Maximum Temp. (°F)	30.5	34.9	45.9	58.6	70.6	79.5	83.3	81.2	74.9	62.3	48.4	36.2	58.9
Mean Temp. (°F)	22.4	26.1	36.2	47.7	59.1	68.4	72.2	70.1	63.1	51.1	39.9	28.7	48.7
Mean Minimum Temp. (°F)	14.3	17.1	26.5	36.7	47.6	57.2	61.1	58.9	51.3	39.8	31.3	21.1	38.6
Extreme Maximum Temp. (°F)	66	72	80	88	91	103	101	98	95	88	77	70	103
Extreme Minimum Temp. (°F)	-24	-16	-6	7	27	36	44	36	27	17	5	-22	-24
Days Maximum Temp. ≥ 90°F	0	0	0	0	0	2	5	2	1	0	0	0	10
Days Maximum Temp. ≤ 32°F	17	12	4	0	0	0	0	0	0	0	2	10	45
Days Minimum Temp. ≤ 32°F	29	25	23	10	1	0	0	0	0	7	18	27	140
Days Minimum Temp. ≤ 0°F	6	4	0	0	0	0	0	0	0	0	0	2	12
Heating Degree Days (base 65°F)	1,314	1,093	886	518	219	44	8	18	126	432	747	1,119	6,524
Cooling Degree Days (base 65°F)	0	0	1	5	40	156	246	188	73	6	0	0	715
Mean Precipitation (in.)	2.09	1.75	2.92	3.75	3.63	4.25	3.86	3.51	3.63	2.86	3.32	2.78	38.35
Days With ≥ 0.1" Precipitation	6	5	7	8	8	7	7	7	6	6	7	7	81
Days With ≥ 1.0" Precipitation	0	0	0	1	1	1	1	1	1	1	1	0	8
Mean Snowfall (in.)	9.4	7.4	4.1	1.0	trace	0.0	0.0	0.0	0.0	0.3	2.1	7.2	31.5
Days With ≥ 1.0" Snow Depth	18	13	5	1	0	0	0	0	0	0	2	9	48

Columbus *Bartholomew County* Elevation: 620 ft. Latitude: 39° 12' N Longitude: 85° 55' W

	JAN	FEB	MAR	APR	MAY	JUN	JUL	AUG	SEP	OCT	NOV	DEC	YEAR
Mean Maximum Temp. (°F)	36.2	41.3	52.0	63.8	73.8	82.1	86.0	84.5	78.5	66.6	53.3	41.8	63.3
Mean Temp. (°F)	27.4	31.6	41.4	52.3	62.6	71.5	75.4	73.5	66.5	54.3	43.5	33.3	52.8
Mean Minimum Temp. (°F)	18.6	21.8	30.8	40.8	51.4	60.9	64.9	62.4	54.5	41.9	33.7	24.7	42.2
Extreme Maximum Temp. (°F)	67	73	83	88	94	100	103	103	95	90	80	73	103
Extreme Minimum Temp. (°F)	-26	-11	-6	18	30	41	48	43	34	17	4	-20	-26
Days Maximum Temp. ≥ 90°F	0	0	0	0	0	4	8	6	2	0	0	0	20
Days Maximum Temp. ≤ 32°F	12	7	1	0	0	0	0	0	0	0	1	6	27
Days Minimum Temp. ≤ 32°F	27	23	19	6	0	0	0	0	0	5	15	24	119
Days Minimum Temp. ≤ 0°F	3	2	0	0	0	0	0	0	0	0	0	1	6
Heating Degree Days (base 65°F)	1,158	936	726	385	137	17	1	3	73	340	637	976	5,389
Cooling Degree Days (base 65°F)	0	0	2	11	70	231	348	284	122	15	0	0	1,083
Mean Precipitation (in.)	2.59	2.54	3.67	4.50	4.54	3.35	3.99	3.75	2.99	2.79	3.72	3.12	41.55
Days With ≥ 0.1" Precipitation	6	5	8	8	8	6	7	6	5	5	7	6	77
Days With ≥ 1.0" Precipitation	0	0	1	1	1	1	1	1	1	1	1	1	10
Mean Snowfall (in.)	5.1	3.5	1.9	trace	trace	0.0	0.0	0.0	0.0	trace	0.5	2.1	13.1
Days With ≥ 1.0" Snow Depth	na	na	1	0	0	0	0	0	0	0	0	3	na

Crane Naval Depot *Martin County* Elevation: 728 ft. Latitude: 38° 52' N Longitude: 86° 50' W

	JAN	FEB	MAR	APR	MAY	JUN	JUL	AUG	SEP	OCT	NOV	DEC	YEAR
Mean Maximum Temp. (°F)	38.8	44.8	55.7	67.3	76.5	84.0	87.8	86.3	80.5	69.2	55.9	44.8	66.0
Mean Temp. (°F)	30.2	35.2	45.1	55.8	65.1	73.1	77.2	75.5	69.2	57.7	46.4	36.0	55.5
Mean Minimum Temp. (°F)	21.5	25.6	34.3	44.1	53.5	62.1	66.6	64.6	57.8	46.2	36.9	27.2	45.0
Extreme Maximum Temp. (°F)	68	76	83	88	92	100	104	101	99	90	80	74	104
Extreme Minimum Temp. (°F)	-23	-12	-2	17	32	35	49	47	32	20	8	-20	-23
Days Maximum Temp. ≥ 90°F	0	0	0	0	1	5	11	8	3	0	0	0	28
Days Maximum Temp. ≤ 32°F	9	5	1	0	0	0	0	0	0	0	0	4	19
Days Minimum Temp. ≤ 32°F	25	20	14	4	0	0	0	0	0	2	11	19	95
Days Minimum Temp. ≤ 0°F	2	1	0	0	0	0	0	0	0	0	0	1	4
Heating Degree Days (base 65°F)	1,073	833	606	294	94	9	1	1	44	248	553	890	4,646
Cooling Degree Days (base 65°F)	0	0	5	22	100	262	397	336	169	30	2	0	1,323
Mean Precipitation (in.)	3.01	2.72	4.14	4.97	5.48	3.92	4.94	3.96	3.31	3.44	4.24	3.42	47.55
Days With ≥ 0.1" Precipitation	6	4	7	8	8	6	6	5	5	5	6	5	71
Days With ≥ 1.0" Precipitation	1	1	1	1	2	1	2	1	1	1	1	1	14
Mean Snowfall (in.)	na	na	1.8	trace	0.0	0.0	0.0	0.0	0.0	trace	trace	na	na
Days With ≥ 1.0" Snow Depth	na	na	0	0	0	0	0	0	0	0	0	na	na

Delphi 3 S *Carroll County* Elevation: 669 ft. Latitude: 40° 33' N Longitude: 86° 41' W

	JAN	FEB	MAR	APR	MAY	JUN	JUL	AUG	SEP	OCT	NOV	DEC	YEAR
Mean Maximum Temp. (°F)	33.0	38.4	50.5	63.5	74.4	82.9	85.8	83.5	77.9	65.5	51.3	38.7	62.1
Mean Temp. (°F)	25.0	29.7	40.7	51.7	62.3	71.2	74.5	72.3	65.9	54.1	42.7	31.3	51.8
Mean Minimum Temp. (°F)	17.0	20.9	30.8	39.8	50.2	59.6	63.2	61.1	53.8	42.6	34.1	23.7	41.4
Extreme Maximum Temp. (°F)	66	73	84	89	96	105	103	100	96	89	78	71	105
Extreme Minimum Temp. (°F)	-24	-20	0	10	26	36	42	38	27	18	6	-21	-24
Days Maximum Temp. ≥ 90°F	0	0	0	0	1	5	9	4	2	0	0	0	21
Days Maximum Temp. ≤ 32°F	14	9	2	0	0	0	0	0	0	0	1	7	33
Days Minimum Temp. ≤ 32°F	28	23	18	7	1	0	0	0	0	5	15	25	122
Days Minimum Temp. ≤ 0°F	5	3	0	0	0	0	0	0	0	0	0	1	9
Heating Degree Days (base 65°F)	1,234	991	749	405	146	19	3	6	81	345	662	1,039	5,680
Cooling Degree Days (base 65°F)	0	0	2	10	71	221	318	252	115	15	1	0	1,005
Mean Precipitation (in.)	1.94	1.90	2.99	3.64	3.92	3.90	4.23	4.05	3.01	2.69	3.12	2.67	38.06
Days With ≥ 0.1" Precipitation	5	4	6	8	7	6	6	6	5	6	6	6	71
Days With ≥ 1.0" Precipitation	0	0	1	0	1	1	1	1	1	1	1	0	8
Mean Snowfall (in.)	6.2	4.6	2.5	0.8	trace	0.0	0.0	0.0	0.0	0.2	0.9	5.3	20.5
Days With ≥ 1.0" Snow Depth	13	10	3	0	0	0	0	0	0	0	1	6	33

Dubois S Ind. Forage Farm *Dubois County* Elevation: 688 ft. Latitude: 38° 27' N Longitude: 86° 42' W

	JAN	FEB	MAR	APR	MAY	JUN	JUL	AUG	SEP	OCT	NOV	DEC	YEAR
Mean Maximum Temp. (°F)	37.3	43.0	53.4	64.6	73.9	82.1	86.0	84.9	78.7	67.2	54.4	43.2	64.1
Mean Temp. (°F)	28.6	33.0	43.1	53.9	63.1	71.7	75.7	74.2	67.6	55.6	44.8	34.3	53.8
Mean Minimum Temp. (°F)	19.8	23.0	32.7	43.1	52.3	61.3	65.5	63.5	56.4	44.0	35.2	25.4	43.5
Extreme Maximum Temp. (°F)	68	75	82	88	91	101	102	100	99	89	81	75	102
Extreme Minimum Temp. (°F)	-25	-11	-6	17	27	39	46	42	33	18	8	-20	-25
Days Maximum Temp. ≥ 90°F	0	0	0	0	0	3	8	7	2	0	0	0	20
Days Maximum Temp. ≤ 32°F	11	6	2	0	0	0	0	0	0	0	1	6	26
Days Minimum Temp. ≤ 32°F	27	22	16	5	0	0	0	0	0	4	14	22	110
Days Minimum Temp. ≤ 0°F	3	2	0	0	0	0	0	0	0	0	0	1	6
Heating Degree Days (base 65°F)	1,122	896	677	348	131	17	2	3	66	307	600	944	5,113
Cooling Degree Days (base 65°F)	0	0	5	20	82	236	362	309	148	25	1	0	1,188
Mean Precipitation (in.)	2.89	2.63	4.19	4.73	5.28	4.73	4.36	4.01	3.47	3.33	4.24	3.49	47.35
Days With ≥ 0.1" Precipitation	6	5	7	8	9	8	7	6	6	6	7	6	81
Days With ≥ 1.0" Precipitation	1	1	1	1	1	1	1	1	1	1	1	1	12
Mean Snowfall (in.)	na	na	na	trace	0.0	0.0	0.0	0.0	0.0	0.2	trace	na	na
Days With ≥ 1.0" Snow Depth	na	na	1	0	0	0	0	0	0	0	0	na	na

Elwood Wastewater Plant *Madison County*   Elevation: 839 ft.   Latitude: 40° 16' N   Longitude: 85° 51' W

	JAN	FEB	MAR	APR	MAY	JUN	JUL	AUG	SEP	OCT	NOV	DEC	YEAR
Mean Maximum Temp. (°F)	32.2	37.3	48.0	60.9	72.1	81.1	84.9	82.9	77.1	64.9	50.6	38.2	60.8
Mean Temp. (°F)	23.7	28.1	38.0	49.3	60.3	69.5	73.4	71.1	64.5	52.5	41.2	30.0	50.1
Mean Minimum Temp. (°F)	15.2	18.8	27.9	37.6	48.5	58.0	61.7	59.2	51.8	40.0	31.7	21.8	39.4
Extreme Maximum Temp. (°F)	64	74	81	88	92	102	101	99	96	89	79	72	102
Extreme Minimum Temp. (°F)	-24	-23	-8	12	27	38	46	38	29	18	5	-20	-24
Days Maximum Temp. ≥ 90°F	0	0	0	0	0	3	7	4	2	0	0	0	16
Days Maximum Temp. ≤ 32°F	15	10	3	0	0	0	0	0	0	0	1	9	38
Days Minimum Temp. ≤ 32°F	28	25	22	10	1	0	0	0	0	8	18	26	138
Days Minimum Temp. ≤ 0°F	5	3	0	0	0	0	0	0	0	0	0	2	10
Heating Degree Days (base 65°F)	1,277	1,035	832	472	192	32	4	14	105	392	709	1,078	6,142
Cooling Degree Days (base 65°F)	0	0	1	7	53	184	282	217	95	10	0	0	849
Mean Precipitation (in.)	2.28	1.91	2.99	3.77	4.05	4.32	4.49	3.91	3.22	2.68	3.61	2.95	40.18
Days With ≥ 0.1" Precipitation	6	4	7	8	8	7	7	6	6	5	7	7	78
Days With ≥ 1.0" Precipitation	0	0	0	1	1	1	1	1	1	0	1	0	7
Mean Snowfall (in.)	na	na	na	trace	0.0	0.0	0.0	0.0	0.0	trace	trace	na	na
Days With ≥ 1.0" Snow Depth	na	na	na	0	0	0	0	0	0	0	0	na	na

English 4 S *Crawford County*   Elevation: 508 ft.   Latitude: 38° 17' N   Longitude: 86° 28' W

	JAN	FEB	MAR	APR	MAY	JUN	JUL	AUG	SEP	OCT	NOV	DEC	YEAR
Mean Maximum Temp. (°F)	40.9	47.5	58.0	68.1	76.9	84.2	88.1	86.9	80.5	69.8	56.9	45.6	66.9
Mean Temp. (°F)	30.9	35.7	45.2	54.4	63.2	71.3	75.7	74.0	66.9	55.2	45.4	35.5	54.5
Mean Minimum Temp. (°F)	20.8	23.9	32.5	40.6	49.5	58.4	63.2	61.1	53.2	40.7	33.9	25.3	41.9
Extreme Maximum Temp. (°F)	72	79	85	91	97	102	104	102	98	90	84	76	104
Extreme Minimum Temp. (°F)	-31	-15	-10	15	25	36	41	35	28	14	1	-21	-31
Days Maximum Temp. ≥ 90°F	0	0	0	0	1	5	13	10	3	0	0	0	32
Days Maximum Temp. ≤ 32°F	7	4	0	0	0	0	0	0	0	0	0	4	15
Days Minimum Temp. ≤ 32°F	25	21	17	8	1	0	0	0	0	8	14	22	116
Days Minimum Temp. ≤ 0°F	3	2	0	0	0	0	0	0	0	0	0	1	6
Heating Degree Days (base 65°F)	1,052	820	606	328	120	15	1	3	66	312	581	909	4,813
Cooling Degree Days (base 65°F)	0	0	3	14	68	217	345	290	126	17	1	1	1,082
Mean Precipitation (in.)	3.49	3.22	4.90	4.95	5.11	4.85	4.15	3.82	3.48	3.31	4.28	3.99	49.55
Days With ≥ 0.1" Precipitation	7	6	9	8	8	8	6	6	6	5	8	7	84
Days With ≥ 1.0" Precipitation	1	1	1	1	1	1	1	1	1	1	1	1	12
Mean Snowfall (in.)	2.4	na	0.5	trace	0.0	0.0	0.0	0.0	0.0	trace	0.3	0.5	na
Days With ≥ 1.0" Snow Depth	7	4	1	0	0	0	0	0	0	0	0	2	14

Evansville Museum *Vanderburgh County*   Elevation: 377 ft.   Latitude: 37° 58' N   Longitude: 87° 34' W

	JAN	FEB	MAR	APR	MAY	JUN	JUL	AUG	SEP	OCT	NOV	DEC	YEAR
Mean Maximum Temp. (°F)	40.3	46.6	58.2	69.5	78.2	86.7	89.7	88.4	81.8	70.4	57.1	45.7	67.7
Mean Temp. (°F)	32.4	37.4	48.0	58.2	67.1	75.7	79.4	78.0	71.0	59.2	48.2	37.8	57.7
Mean Minimum Temp. (°F)	24.4	28.2	37.7	46.8	55.9	64.7	69.0	67.4	60.2	47.8	39.3	29.9	47.6
Extreme Maximum Temp. (°F)	71	78	86	91	94	101	102	102	98	91	83	78	102
Extreme Minimum Temp. (°F)	-17	-8	4	24	34	45	50	46	37	22	11	-15	-17
Days Maximum Temp. ≥ 90°F	0	0	0	0	2	10	17	14	6	0	0	0	49
Days Maximum Temp. ≤ 32°F	8	4	0	0	0	0	0	0	0	0	0	4	16
Days Minimum Temp. ≤ 32°F	23	18	11	2	0	0	0	0	0	1	8	18	81
Days Minimum Temp. ≤ 0°F	1	0	0	0	0	0	0	0	0	0	0	0	1
Heating Degree Days (base 65°F)	1,004	773	526	237	65	2	0	0	32	213	500	836	4,188
Cooling Degree Days (base 65°F)	0	0	6	37	140	343	472	429	216	40	3	1	1,687
Mean Precipitation (in.)	2.83	3.27	4.70	4.65	4.89	3.89	4.22	3.30	3.17	3.14	4.49	3.69	46.24
Days With ≥ 0.1" Precipitation	6	6	9	8	8	6	6	5	5	5	7	7	78
Days With ≥ 1.0" Precipitation	1	1	1	1	1	1	1	1	1	1	1	1	12
Mean Snowfall (in.)	4.9	3.5	2.6	0.5	trace	0.0	0.0	0.0	0.0	trace	0.3	2.0	13.8
Days With ≥ 1.0" Snow Depth	7	6	1	0	0	0	0	0	0	0	0	2	16

Farmland 5 NNW *Randolph County*   Elevation: 964 ft.   Latitude: 40° 15' N   Longitude: 85° 09' W

	JAN	FEB	MAR	APR	MAY	JUN	JUL	AUG	SEP	OCT	NOV	DEC	YEAR
Mean Maximum Temp. (°F)	32.0	36.6	47.4	60.1	71.4	80.4	84.2	82.2	76.4	64.1	50.0	38.2	60.2
Mean Temp. (°F)	23.7	27.3	37.5	49.0	60.3	69.5	73.2	70.8	64.1	52.1	41.0	30.1	49.9
Mean Minimum Temp. (°F)	15.4	17.9	27.4	37.9	49.0	58.7	62.3	59.5	51.8	40.1	31.9	22.0	39.5
Extreme Maximum Temp. (°F)	66	72	81	85	94	102	100	98	95	88	79	72	102
Extreme Minimum Temp. (°F)	-25	-21	-16	10	24	36	44	38	27	16	5	-21	-25
Days Maximum Temp. ≥ 90°F	0	0	0	0	0	3	6	3	1	0	0	0	13
Days Maximum Temp. ≤ 32°F	15	11	4	0	0	0	0	0	0	0	2	9	41
Days Minimum Temp. ≤ 32°F	29	25	22	9	1	0	0	0	1	7	17	26	137
Days Minimum Temp. ≤ 0°F	5	4	0	0	0	0	0	0	0	0	0	2	11
Heating Degree Days (base 65°F)	1,274	1,059	848	480	195	36	6	17	115	403	714	1,075	6,222
Cooling Degree Days (base 65°F)	0	0	1	7	55	187	282	213	95	11	0	0	851
Mean Precipitation (in.)	1.87	1.80	2.70	3.50	3.96	4.39	4.35	3.61	2.92	2.65	3.21	2.55	37.51
Days With ≥ 0.1" Precipitation	5	5	7	8	8	7	7	6	5	6	6	6	76
Days With ≥ 1.0" Precipitation	0	0	0	1	1	1	1	1	1	1	1	0	8
Mean Snowfall (in.)	8.1	6.2	4.0	0.7	trace	0.0	0.0	0.0	0.0	0.2	1.3	5.2	25.7
Days With ≥ 1.0" Snow Depth	15	11	4	0	0	0	0	0	0	0	1	6	37

Frankfort Disposal Plant *Clinton County*   Elevation: 833 ft.   Latitude: 40° 19' N   Longitude: 86° 30' W

	JAN	FEB	MAR	APR	MAY	JUN	JUL	AUG	SEP	OCT	NOV	DEC	YEAR
Mean Maximum Temp. (°F)	32.4	37.3	48.6	61.2	72.4	81.2	84.4	82.3	76.5	64.2	49.9	37.7	60.7
Mean Temp. (°F)	24.5	28.7	39.1	50.2	61.1	70.2	73.8	71.6	65.1	53.3	41.4	30.2	50.8
Mean Minimum Temp. (°F)	16.6	20.1	29.6	39.2	49.8	59.2	63.1	60.9	53.6	42.3	32.9	22.7	40.8
Extreme Maximum Temp. (°F)	64	73	83	89	92	101	105	98	95	89	78	72	105
Extreme Minimum Temp. (°F)	-25	-22	-13	14	18	36	45	38	28	18	5	-26	-26
Days Maximum Temp. ≥ 90°F	0	0	0	0	0	4	7	3	1	0	0	0	15
Days Maximum Temp. ≤ 32°F	15	10	3	0	0	0	0	0	0	0	1	9	38
Days Minimum Temp. ≤ 32°F	28	24	20	8	1	0	0	0	0	5	16	26	128
Days Minimum Temp. ≤ 0°F	4	3	0	0	0	0	0	0	0	0	0	2	9
Heating Degree Days (base 65°F)	1,250	1,018	797	443	173	26	4	10	95	368	701	1,072	5,957
Cooling Degree Days (base 65°F)	0	0	1	7	57	196	293	229	100	12	0	0	895
Mean Precipitation (in.)	1.99	1.96	3.20	3.71	4.06	4.33	4.24	3.96	3.03	2.88	3.35	2.87	39.58
Days With ≥ 0.1" Precipitation	6	5	7	8	8	7	7	6	5	6	7	7	79
Days With ≥ 1.0" Precipitation	0	0	1	1	1	1	1	1	1	0	1	0	8
Mean Snowfall (in.)	8.0	5.8	3.5	0.6	trace	0.0	0.0	0.0	0.0	0.4	1.1	6.2	25.6
Days With ≥ 1.0" Snow Depth	13	9	3	0	0	0	0	0	0	0	1	7	33

Goshen College *Elkhart County*   Elevation: 872 ft.   Latitude: 41° 33' N   Longitude: 85° 53' W

	JAN	FEB	MAR	APR	MAY	JUN	JUL	AUG	SEP	OCT	NOV	DEC	YEAR
Mean Maximum Temp. (°F)	30.9	35.4	46.8	60.0	71.6	80.7	84.1	81.6	74.9	62.5	48.3	36.2	59.4
Mean Temp. (°F)	23.8	27.5	37.8	49.4	60.4	69.7	73.5	71.3	64.4	52.6	40.7	29.8	50.1
Mean Minimum Temp. (°F)	16.6	19.5	28.8	38.8	49.1	58.7	62.9	61.0	53.7	42.6	33.2	23.3	40.7
Extreme Maximum Temp. (°F)	62	73	81	88	92	102	101	99	96	88	76	69	102
Extreme Minimum Temp. (°F)	-24	-14	-6	1	27	37	42	37	29	18	6	-18	-24
Days Maximum Temp. ≥ 90°F	0	0	0	0	1	4	6	3	1	0	0	0	15
Days Maximum Temp. ≤ 32°F	17	11	3	0	0	0	0	0	0	0	2	10	43
Days Minimum Temp. ≤ 32°F	29	24	20	8	1	0	0	0	0	5	15	26	128
Days Minimum Temp. ≤ 0°F	4	3	0	0	0	0	0	0	0	0	0	1	8
Heating Degree Days (base 65°F)	1,272	1,053	837	470	192	31	4	11	104	387	722	1,085	6,168
Cooling Degree Days (base 65°F)	0	0	1	7	56	184	284	222	88	7	0	0	849
Mean Precipitation (in.)	1.79	1.72	2.74	3.44	3.40	4.00	3.52	3.99	3.70	2.96	2.81	2.58	36.65
Days With ≥ 0.1" Precipitation	5	5	6	8	7	7	6	6	7	6	6	6	75
Days With ≥ 1.0" Precipitation	0	0	0	1	1	1	1	1	1	1	1	0	8
Mean Snowfall (in.)	10.7	8.0	5.0	1.3	trace	0.0	0.0	0.0	0.0	0.4	3.9	8.9	38.2
Days With ≥ 1.0" Snow Depth	18	14	5	0	0	0	0	0	0	0	2	10	49

Greencastle 1 SE *Putnam County*   Elevation: 859 ft.   Latitude: 39° 38' N   Longitude: 86° 51' W

	JAN	FEB	MAR	APR	MAY	JUN	JUL	AUG	SEP	OCT	NOV	DEC	YEAR
Mean Maximum Temp. (°F)	33.7	39.7	50.6	63.1	73.9	82.5	86.2	84.2	78.3	65.9	51.6	39.4	62.4
Mean Temp. (°F)	25.6	30.7	40.9	52.4	63.0	71.9	75.5	73.6	67.1	55.1	43.0	31.5	52.5
Mean Minimum Temp. (°F)	17.4	21.6	31.2	41.7	52.0	61.3	64.8	63.0	55.9	44.3	34.2	23.5	42.6
Extreme Maximum Temp. (°F)	69	72	84	90	94	103	103	102	98	90	81	74	103
Extreme Minimum Temp. (°F)	-23	-15	-3	16	30	37	47	42	32	20	5	-21	-23
Days Maximum Temp. ≥ 90°F	0	0	0	0	1	5	10	6	3	0	0	0	25
Days Maximum Temp. ≤ 32°F	14	8	3	0	0	0	0	0	0	0	1	8	34
Days Minimum Temp. ≤ 32°F	28	23	18	5	0	0	0	0	0	3	14	25	116
Days Minimum Temp. ≤ 0°F	4	2	0	0	0	0	0	0	0	0	0	2	8
Heating Degree Days (base 65°F)	1,216	963	742	388	136	19	2	5	71	321	656	1,032	5,551
Cooling Degree Days (base 65°F)	0	0	3	15	76	232	341	275	134	20	1	0	1,097
Mean Precipitation (in.)	2.40	2.45	3.66	3.84	4.73	4.24	5.18	4.18	3.15	3.12	3.93	3.07	43.95
Days With ≥ 0.1" Precipitation	6	5	7	8	8	8	7	6	5	5	7	6	78
Days With ≥ 1.0" Precipitation	0	0	1	1	1	1	2	1	1	1	1	1	11
Mean Snowfall (in.)	9.3	6.5	3.6	0.5	trace	0.0	0.0	0.0	0.0	0.2	1.5	5.7	27.3
Days With ≥ 1.0" Snow Depth	11	9	2	0	0	0	0	0	0	0	1	5	28

Greenfield *Hancock County*   Elevation: 862 ft.   Latitude: 39° 47' N   Longitude: 85° 45' W

	JAN	FEB	MAR	APR	MAY	JUN	JUL	AUG	SEP	OCT	NOV	DEC	YEAR
Mean Maximum Temp. (°F)	33.4	38.4	49.6	61.9	72.9	81.9	85.6	83.7	77.8	65.4	51.0	39.1	61.7
Mean Temp. (°F)	25.1	29.1	39.8	51.2	62.2	71.2	75.0	73.0	66.3	54.0	42.1	31.1	51.7
Mean Minimum Temp. (°F)	16.7	19.9	30.0	40.5	51.3	60.4	64.3	62.2	54.8	42.6	33.1	22.9	41.6
Extreme Maximum Temp. (°F)	65	72	84	87	93	103	102	101	95	90	79	72	103
Extreme Minimum Temp. (°F)	-29	-19	-6	16	30	39	46	41	31	19	6	-19	-29
Days Maximum Temp. ≥ 90°F	0	0	0	0	1	5	8	5	2	0	0	0	21
Days Maximum Temp. ≤ 32°F	14	9	3	0	0	0	0	0	0	0	1	8	35
Days Minimum Temp. ≤ 32°F	28	24	19	6	0	0	0	0	0	4	16	24	121
Days Minimum Temp. ≤ 0°F	4	3	0	0	0	0	0	0	0	0	0	1	8
Heating Degree Days (base 65°F)	1,233	1,005	775	418	155	24	2	6	78	349	682	1,046	5,773
Cooling Degree Days (base 65°F)	0	0	2	11	71	223	327	267	121	15	0	0	1,037
Mean Precipitation (in.)	2.45	2.35	3.34	4.06	4.74	4.36	5.01	3.97	3.05	3.10	3.90	3.08	43.41
Days With ≥ 0.1" Precipitation	6	5	7	8	9	8	7	6	6	6	7	7	82
Days With ≥ 1.0" Precipitation	0	0	1	1	1	1	2	1	1	1	1	0	10
Mean Snowfall (in.)	na	na	1.5	0.2	0.0	0.0	0.0	0.0	0.0	trace	0.7	3.0	na
Days With ≥ 1.0" Snow Depth	9	6	2	0	0	0	0	0	0	0	1	4	22

Greensburg *Decatur County*   Elevation: 935 ft.   Latitude: 39° 21' N   Longitude: 85° 30' W

	JAN	FEB	MAR	APR	MAY	JUN	JUL	AUG	SEP	OCT	NOV	DEC	YEAR
Mean Maximum Temp. (°F)	34.9	40.4	50.9	62.7	73.0	81.4	85.1	83.4	77.3	65.1	51.8	40.4	62.2
Mean Temp. (°F)	27.0	31.5	41.6	52.4	62.5	71.2	74.8	72.9	66.5	54.4	43.2	32.7	52.6
Mean Minimum Temp. (°F)	19.1	22.7	32.1	41.9	52.1	60.9	64.5	62.4	55.6	43.7	34.6	25.0	42.9
Extreme Maximum Temp. (°F)	67	75	82	86	90	101	101	101	95	87	79	73	101
Extreme Minimum Temp. (°F)	-24	-14	-12	17	24	39	44	42	32	17	6	-21	-24
Days Maximum Temp. ≥ 90°F	0	0	0	0	0	3	7	5	1	0	0	0	16
Days Maximum Temp. ≤ 32°F	13	8	2	0	0	0	0	0	0	0	1	7	31
Days Minimum Temp. ≤ 32°F	27	22	17	6	0	0	0	0	0	4	14	24	114
Days Minimum Temp. ≤ 0°F	4	2	0	0	0	0	0	0	0	0	0	1	7
Heating Degree Days (base 65°F)	1,170	938	722	387	142	19	2	6	77	337	648	995	5,443
Cooling Degree Days (base 65°F)	0	0	3	14	75	223	334	272	128	17	1	0	1,067
Mean Precipitation (in.)	2.46	2.31	3.69	4.43	4.86	4.23	4.06	4.17	3.04	3.07	3.78	3.15	43.25
Days With ≥ 0.1" Precipitation	6	5	7	9	8	7	7	6	6	6	7	7	81
Days With ≥ 1.0" Precipitation	0	0	1	1	1	1	1	1	1	1	1	1	10
Mean Snowfall (in.)	6.4	4.0	2.8	0.5	trace	0.0	0.0	0.0	0.0	0.2	0.8	3.3	18.0
Days With ≥ 1.0" Snow Depth	9	7	2	0	0	0	0	0	0	0	0	3	21

Hartford City 4 ESE *Blackford County*   Elevation: 941 ft.   Latitude: 40° 27' N   Longitude: 85° 18' W

	JAN	FEB	MAR	APR	MAY	JUN	JUL	AUG	SEP	OCT	NOV	DEC	YEAR
Mean Maximum Temp. (°F)	30.6	35.7	46.9	59.7	71.0	79.7	83.4	81.3	75.5	63.1	49.3	36.9	59.4
Mean Temp. (°F)	22.7	27.2	37.8	49.3	60.4	69.4	73.1	70.9	64.3	52.4	41.0	29.6	49.8
Mean Minimum Temp. (°F)	14.8	18.6	28.7	38.8	49.7	59.1	62.8	60.5	53.2	41.6	32.6	22.2	40.2
Extreme Maximum Temp. (°F)	64	71	82	87	90	103	99	98	95	87	77	71	103
Extreme Minimum Temp. (°F)	-26	-17	-10	8	26	37	45	39	29	19	5	-18	-26
Days Maximum Temp. ≥ 90°F	0	0	0	0	0	2	5	2	1	0	0	0	10
Days Maximum Temp. ≤ 32°F	16	12	4	0	0	0	0	0	0	0	2	10	44
Days Minimum Temp. ≤ 32°F	29	24	21	8	1	0	0	0	0	6	17	25	131
Days Minimum Temp. ≤ 0°F	6	4	0	0	0	0	0	0	0	0	0	2	12
Heating Degree Days (base 65°F)	1,305	1,062	837	472	188	33	6	14	103	393	715	1,092	6,220
Cooling Degree Days (base 65°F)	0	0	2	7	52	186	286	223	92	11	0	0	859
Mean Precipitation (in.)	1.93	2.01	2.76	3.40	3.73	4.49	4.06	4.09	2.81	2.38	3.27	2.58	37.51
Days With ≥ 0.1" Precipitation	5	5	6	7	8	8	6	6	5	5	6	7	74
Days With ≥ 1.0" Precipitation	0	0	1	1	1	1	1	1	1	0	1	0	8
Mean Snowfall (in.)	7.6	6.0	3.5	1.0	trace	0.0	0.0	0.0	0.0	0.4	1.6	5.9	26.0
Days With ≥ 1.0" Snow Depth	18	13	5	1	0	0	0	0	0	0	2	9	48

Hobart 2 WNW *Lake County*   Elevation: 639 ft.   Latitude: 41° 33' N   Longitude: 87° 17' W

	JAN	FEB	MAR	APR	MAY	JUN	JUL	AUG	SEP	OCT	NOV	DEC	YEAR
Mean Maximum Temp. (°F)	31.7	37.0	47.9	60.2	71.5	81.4	85.3	82.7	76.9	65.2	49.8	37.0	60.6
Mean Temp. (°F)	23.6	28.4	38.3	49.2	59.5	69.5	74.1	71.8	65.3	53.9	41.2	29.5	50.4
Mean Minimum Temp. (°F)	15.5	19.7	28.6	38.2	47.4	57.6	63.1	61.0	53.7	42.6	32.5	22.0	40.2
Extreme Maximum Temp. (°F)	65	71	84	90	93	105	103	102	97	90	76	69	105
Extreme Minimum Temp. (°F)	-25	-16	-1	13	27	34	42	41	29	22	4	-29	-29
Days Maximum Temp. ≥ 90°F	0	0	0	0	1	5	9	5	2	0	0	0	22
Days Maximum Temp. ≤ 32°F	15	10	2	0	0	0	0	0	0	0	1	9	37
Days Minimum Temp. ≤ 32°F	29	24	21	9	1	0	0	0	0	4	16	26	130
Days Minimum Temp. ≤ 0°F	5	3	0	0	0	0	0	0	0	0	0	2	10
Heating Degree Days (base 65°F)	1,276	1,026	821	480	220	42	6	10	94	347	710	1,092	6,124
Cooling Degree Days (base 65°F)	0	0	2	11	50	182	301	224	103	9	0	0	882
Mean Precipitation (in.)	1.88	1.55	2.68	3.63	3.88	4.39	3.48	3.73	3.70	3.02	3.47	2.41	37.82
Days With ≥ 0.1" Precipitation	5	4	6	8	7	6	6	6	6	6	7	5	72
Days With ≥ 1.0" Precipitation	0	0	0	1	1	1	1	1	1	1	1	0	8
Mean Snowfall (in.)	9.1	7.4	3.2	0.8	trace	0.0	0.0	0.0	0.0	trace	1.1	5.8	27.4
Days With ≥ 1.0" Snow Depth	17	11	4	0	0	0	0	0	0	0	1	8	41

Indianapolis SE Side *Marion County*   Elevation: 843 ft.   Latitude: 39° 43' N   Longitude: 86° 04' W

	JAN	FEB	MAR	APR	MAY	JUN	JUL	AUG	SEP	OCT	NOV	DEC	YEAR
Mean Maximum Temp. (°F)	33.8	38.8	49.6	61.8	72.8	81.4	85.1	83.3	77.3	65.2	51.4	39.6	61.7
Mean Temp. (°F)	25.9	30.1	40.1	51.4	62.2	71.3	75.2	73.2	66.3	54.3	42.7	31.7	52.0
Mean Minimum Temp. (°F)	17.9	21.3	30.6	40.9	51.6	61.1	65.3	63.0	55.3	43.3	33.9	23.8	42.3
Extreme Maximum Temp. (°F)	65	73	83	87	92	104	103	100	94	89	82	73	104
Extreme Minimum Temp. (°F)	-22	-12	0	18	29	35	49	45	30	20	3	-20	-22
Days Maximum Temp. ≥ 90°F	0	0	0	0	0	3	7	4	2	0	0	0	16
Days Maximum Temp. ≤ 32°F	14	9	3	0	0	0	0	0	0	0	1	7	34
Days Minimum Temp. ≤ 32°F	28	24	19	6	0	0	0	0	0	4	15	25	121
Days Minimum Temp. ≤ 0°F	4	2	0	0	0	0	0	0	0	0	0	1	7
Heating Degree Days (base 65°F)	1,207	980	766	413	151	22	2	5	77	339	664	1,024	5,650
Cooling Degree Days (base 65°F)	0	0	2	11	67	221	330	268	120	16	0	0	1,035
Mean Precipitation (in.)	2.02	2.02	3.09	3.82	4.55	4.05	4.91	3.58	2.51	2.83	3.66	2.77	39.81
Days With ≥ 0.1" Precipitation	5	5	7	8	8	7	7	5	5	5	6	6	74
Days With ≥ 1.0" Precipitation	0	0	1	1	1	1	1	1	1	1	1	0	8
Mean Snowfall (in.)	na	na	0.9	0.1	trace	0.0	0.0	0.0	0.0	0.2	0.2	1.4	na
Days With ≥ 1.0" Snow Depth	10	7	2	0	0	0	0	0	0	0	1	4	24

Kentland *Newton County*   Elevation: 692 ft.   Latitude: 40° 46' N   Longitude: 87° 26' W

	JAN	FEB	MAR	APR	MAY	JUN	JUL	AUG	SEP	OCT	NOV	DEC	YEAR
Mean Maximum Temp. (°F)	31.4	36.6	48.9	62.3	74.2	83.4	85.9	83.9	77.9	65.9	49.7	36.8	61.4
Mean Temp. (°F)	23.3	27.9	39.5	50.9	62.3	71.6	74.7	72.4	65.8	54.0	41.2	29.2	51.1
Mean Minimum Temp. (°F)	15.1	19.1	30.0	39.4	50.4	59.8	63.4	60.9	53.7	42.1	32.6	21.4	40.6
Extreme Maximum Temp. (°F)	61	72	85	89	94	104	103	104	98	90	78	70	104
Extreme Minimum Temp. (°F)	-25	-18	-6	3	28	37	45	44	27	17	1	-21	-25
Days Maximum Temp. ≥ 90°F	0	0	0	0	2	6	9	5	2	0	0	0	24
Days Maximum Temp. ≤ 32°F	16	10	3	0	0	0	0	0	0	0	2	9	40
Days Minimum Temp. ≤ 32°F	29	24	19	8	1	0	0	0	0	5	16	27	129
Days Minimum Temp. ≤ 0°F	5	4	0	0	0	0	0	0	0	0	0	2	11
Heating Degree Days (base 65°F)	1,286	1,043	785	428	155	19	3	8	88	350	708	1,105	5,978
Cooling Degree Days (base 65°F)	0	0	1	11	76	226	316	244	110	13	0	0	997
Mean Precipitation (in.)	1.62	1.53	2.78	3.53	4.29	4.33	4.18	3.88	3.60	2.91	3.36	2.57	38.58
Days With ≥ 0.1" Precipitation	4	4	6	8	8	7	7	6	6	6	7	6	75
Days With ≥ 1.0" Precipitation	0	0	0	1	1	1	1	1	1	1	1	1	9
Mean Snowfall (in.)	7.5	6.8	3.2	0.8	0.0	0.0	0.0	0.0	0.0	0.1	2.0	6.3	26.7
Days With ≥ 1.0" Snow Depth	14	11	4	0	0	0	0	0	0	0	2	8	39

Kokomo 3 WSW *Howard County*   Elevation: 816 ft.   Latitude: 40° 28' N   Longitude: 86° 10' W

	JAN	FEB	MAR	APR	MAY	JUN	JUL	AUG	SEP	OCT	NOV	DEC	YEAR
Mean Maximum Temp. (°F)	30.3	35.1	46.7	59.8	71.1	80.5	84.0	81.8	76.0	63.7	48.9	36.4	59.5
Mean Temp. (°F)	22.3	26.4	37.0	48.6	59.7	69.4	72.9	70.5	63.8	51.9	40.1	28.8	49.3
Mean Minimum Temp. (°F)	14.2	17.6	27.3	37.4	48.4	58.2	61.8	59.2	51.5	40.0	31.3	21.1	39.0
Extreme Maximum Temp. (°F)	62	74	82	88	93	104	102	100	95	89	81	71	104
Extreme Minimum Temp. (°F)	-26	-20	-10	8	27	34	44	37	27	17	3	-24	-26
Days Maximum Temp. ≥ 90°F	0	0	0	0	0	4	7	3	1	0	0	0	15
Days Maximum Temp. ≤ 32°F	17	12	4	0	0	0	0	0	0	0	2	11	46
Days Minimum Temp. ≤ 32°F	29	26	22	10	1	0	0	0	1	7	18	27	141
Days Minimum Temp. ≤ 0°F	6	4	0	0	0	0	0	0	0	0	0	2	12
Heating Degree Days (base 65°F)	1,320	1,085	862	493	205	38	8	19	118	410	739	1,117	6,414
Cooling Degree Days (base 65°F)	0	0	1	7	45	179	269	207	88	10	0	0	806
Mean Precipitation (in.)	2.49	2.28	3.28	3.90	4.04	3.91	4.54	4.24	3.14	3.09	3.65	3.13	41.69
Days With ≥ 0.1" Precipitation	7	6	8	8	8	7	7	6	5	6	7	8	83
Days With ≥ 1.0" Precipitation	0	0	0	1	1	1	2	1	1	1	1	1	10
Mean Snowfall (in.)	13.2	10.3	6.1	1.4	trace	0.0	0.0	0.0	0.0	0.4	2.1	9.6	43.1
Days With ≥ 1.0" Snow Depth	17	12	6	1	0	0	0	0	0	0	1	9	46

La Porte *La Porte County*   Elevation: 807 ft.   Latitude: 41° 37' N   Longitude: 86° 44' W

	JAN	FEB	MAR	APR	MAY	JUN	JUL	AUG	SEP	OCT	NOV	DEC	YEAR
Mean Maximum Temp. (°F)	29.9	34.7	45.9	58.2	70.4	79.4	83.0	80.7	73.9	61.9	47.5	35.4	58.4
Mean Temp. (°F)	22.9	27.4	37.5	48.8	60.2	69.4	73.6	71.6	64.4	52.7	40.3	29.0	49.8
Mean Minimum Temp. (°F)	15.8	20.0	29.2	39.2	50.0	59.4	64.1	62.5	54.9	43.5	33.2	22.6	41.2
Extreme Maximum Temp. (°F)	63	71	82	90	95	101	101	100	95	88	75	72	101
Extreme Minimum Temp. (°F)	-23	-16	-2	16	29	36	44	44	35	24	3	-18	-23
Days Maximum Temp. ≥ 90°F	0	0	0	0	1	3	5	2	1	0	0	0	12
Days Maximum Temp. ≤ 32°F	18	12	4	0	0	0	0	0	0	0	2	11	47
Days Minimum Temp. ≤ 32°F	29	25	21	7	0	0	0	0	0	2	15	26	125
Days Minimum Temp. ≤ 0°F	4	2	0	0	0	0	0	0	0	0	0	2	8
Heating Degree Days (base 65°F)	1,299	1,055	845	490	201	36	4	9	100	382	733	1,109	6,263
Cooling Degree Days (base 65°F)	0	0	1	8	56	175	278	225	88	7	0	0	838
Mean Precipitation (in.)	2.26	1.88	3.08	3.58	3.46	4.36	3.81	4.14	3.94	3.25	3.77	3.14	40.67
Days With ≥ 0.1" Precipitation	7	6	7	8	7	7	7	7	6	7	8	7	84
Days With ≥ 1.0" Precipitation	0	0	1	1	1	1	1	1	1	1	1	1	10
Mean Snowfall (in.)	21.6	12.6	7.1	1.4	trace	0.0	0.0	0.0	0.0	0.3	4.8	13.7	61.5
Days With ≥ 1.0" Snow Depth	20	14	6	0	0	0	0	0	0	0	2	12	54

Lafayette 8 S *Tippecanoe County*   Elevation: 731 ft.   Latitude: 40° 18' N   Longitude: 86° 54' W

	JAN	FEB	MAR	APR	MAY	JUN	JUL	AUG	SEP	OCT	NOV	DEC	YEAR
Mean Maximum Temp. (°F)	31.4	36.7	48.1	60.6	72.3	81.4	84.6	82.5	76.9	64.6	50.1	37.4	60.5
Mean Temp. (°F)	23.1	27.7	38.6	49.9	61.2	70.4	73.8	71.7	65.1	53.2	41.2	29.5	50.5
Mean Minimum Temp. (°F)	14.8	18.6	29.0	39.1	50.0	59.4	63.1	60.9	53.2	41.6	32.3	21.6	40.3
Extreme Maximum Temp. (°F)	63	73	82	89	92	104	102	98	96	90	80	71	104
Extreme Minimum Temp. (°F)	-25	-20	-8	4	26	36	43	37	26	19	5	-25	-25
Days Maximum Temp. ≥ 90°F	0	0	0	0	1	4	6	3	2	0	0	0	16
Days Maximum Temp. ≤ 32°F	16	11	3	0	0	0	0	0	0	0	1	10	41
Days Minimum Temp. ≤ 32°F	28	25	21	8	1	0	0	0	0	6	16	26	131
Days Minimum Temp. ≤ 0°F	6	4	0	0	0	0	0	0	0	0	0	2	12
Heating Degree Days (base 65°F)	1,292	1,048	814	457	177	30	6	12	100	373	707	1,093	6,109
Cooling Degree Days (base 65°F)	0	0	2	10	67	210	302	239	111	12	0	0	953
Mean Precipitation (in.)	1.83	1.67	3.02	3.52	4.14	4.15	4.04	3.68	2.79	2.50	3.02	2.52	36.88
Days With ≥ 0.1" Precipitation	5	4	7	8	7	7	6	6	5	5	6	6	72
Days With ≥ 1.0" Precipitation	0	0	0	1	1	1	1	1	1	0	1	0	7
Mean Snowfall (in.)	7.5	4.6	2.6	0.7	trace	0.0	0.0	0.0	0.0	0.5	0.8	5.1	21.8
Days With ≥ 1.0" Snow Depth	13	9	3	0	0	0	0	0	0	0	1	6	32

Lagrange Sewage Plant *Lagrange County*   Elevation: 892 ft.   Latitude: 41° 39' N   Longitude: 85° 25' W

	JAN	FEB	MAR	APR	MAY	JUN	JUL	AUG	SEP	OCT	NOV	DEC	YEAR
Mean Maximum Temp. (°F)	29.4	33.5	44.5	57.8	69.7	79.3	82.9	80.8	73.8	61.4	47.1	35.2	57.9
Mean Temp. (°F)	21.9	25.1	35.2	47.1	58.5	68.1	72.0	69.9	62.7	50.9	39.1	28.1	48.2
Mean Minimum Temp. (°F)	14.2	16.6	25.8	36.4	47.4	56.9	61.1	59.0	51.6	40.3	31.2	21.0	38.5
Extreme Maximum Temp. (°F)	61	71	79	87	93	104	101	99	95	88	75	70	104
Extreme Minimum Temp. (°F)	-22	-19	-5	8	25	32	40	38	28	18	6	-19	-22
Days Maximum Temp. ≥ 90°F	0	0	0	0	0	3	5	2	1	0	0	0	11
Days Maximum Temp. ≤ 32°F	18	14	5	0	0	0	0	0	0	0	2	11	50
Days Minimum Temp. ≤ 32°F	29	26	24	11	1	0	0	0	0	7	18	27	143
Days Minimum Temp. ≤ 0°F	5	4	0	0	0	0	0	0	0	0	0	2	11
Heating Degree Days (base 65°F)	1,330	1,121	918	537	239	52	12	22	136	438	771	1,137	6,713
Cooling Degree Days (base 65°F)	0	0	1	6	45	154	246	187	71	6	0	0	716
Mean Precipitation (in.)	1.76	1.72	2.69	3.44	3.59	4.06	3.68	3.92	3.54	2.84	2.92	2.55	36.71
Days With ≥ 0.1" Precipitation	5	5	6	8	7	7	7	7	6	6	7	7	78
Days With ≥ 1.0" Precipitation	0	0	0	1	1	1	1	1	1	0	1	0	7
Mean Snowfall (in.)	10.7	8.1	5.0	1.5	trace	0.0	0.0	0.0	0.0	0.5	3.4	9.5	38.7
Days With ≥ 1.0" Snow Depth	17	14	6	1	0	0	0	0	0	0	3	12	53

Lowell *Lake County*   Elevation: 662 ft.   Latitude: 41° 16' N   Longitude: 87° 25' W

	JAN	FEB	MAR	APR	MAY	JUN	JUL	AUG	SEP	OCT	NOV	DEC	YEAR
Mean Maximum Temp. (°F)	29.6	35.0	46.6	59.7	71.8	81.0	84.4	81.9	75.8	63.8	48.4	35.5	59.5
Mean Temp. (°F)	21.3	26.1	37.1	48.5	59.9	69.4	73.1	70.8	63.8	51.9	39.5	27.4	49.1
Mean Minimum Temp. (°F)	12.9	17.2	27.6	37.4	47.9	57.7	61.8	59.7	51.7	39.9	30.6	19.6	38.7
Extreme Maximum Temp. (°F)	65	68	84	91	93	104	101	104	98	90	76	69	104
Extreme Minimum Temp. (°F)	-28	-21	-8	7	26	33	41	38	28	18	2	-21	-28
Days Maximum Temp. ≥ 90°F	0	0	0	0	1	5	7	3	1	0	0	0	17
Days Maximum Temp. ≤ 32°F	18	12	3	0	0	0	0	0	0	0	2	11	46
Days Minimum Temp. ≤ 32°F	29	25	23	10	1	0	0	0	0	7	18	27	140
Days Minimum Temp. ≤ 0°F	7	4	0	0	0	0	0	0	0	0	0	3	14
Heating Degree Days (base 65°F)	1,350	1,092	859	496	209	39	7	15	116	409	758	1,158	6,508
Cooling Degree Days (base 65°F)	0	0	1	7	55	183	271	210	87	8	0	0	822
Mean Precipitation (in.)	1.84	1.67	2.98	4.19	4.39	4.61	3.95	3.85	3.51	3.06	3.58	2.67	40.30
Days With ≥ 0.1" Precipitation	5	4	7	8	8	8	7	6	6	6	7	6	78
Days With ≥ 1.0" Precipitation	0	0	0	1	1	1	1	1	1	1	1	1	9
Mean Snowfall (in.)	10.7	9.2	4.0	0.5	trace	0.0	0.0	0.0	0.0	0.2	1.9	6.6	33.1
Days With ≥ 1.0" Snow Depth	na	na	na	0	0	0	0	0	0	0	1	na	na

Madison Sewage Plant *Jefferson County*   Elevation: 459 ft.   Latitude: 38° 44' N   Longitude: 85° 24' W

	JAN	FEB	MAR	APR	MAY	JUN	JUL	AUG	SEP	OCT	NOV	DEC	YEAR
Mean Maximum Temp. (°F)	40.1	45.5	56.2	67.1	75.6	83.6	87.2	85.9	79.8	68.7	56.1	45.1	65.9
Mean Temp. (°F)	31.7	35.8	45.5	55.3	64.3	72.9	77.0	75.5	69.0	57.5	46.6	36.6	55.6
Mean Minimum Temp. (°F)	23.3	26.0	34.6	43.4	53.0	62.1	66.6	65.1	58.2	46.2	37.1	28.1	45.3
Extreme Maximum Temp. (°F)	68	75	84	91	93	103	103	104	97	90	84	77	104
Extreme Minimum Temp. (°F)	-17	-8	-2	19	31	40	48	43	33	23	10	-18	-18
Days Maximum Temp. ≥ 90°F	0	0	0	0	0	5	11	8	3	0	0	0	27
Days Maximum Temp. ≤ 32°F	8	4	1	0	0	0	0	0	0	0	0	4	17
Days Minimum Temp. ≤ 32°F	24	20	14	4	0	0	0	0	0	2	10	20	94
Days Minimum Temp. ≤ 0°F	1	0	0	0	0	0	0	0	0	0	0	0	1
Heating Degree Days (base 65°F)	1,025	820	601	300	102	9	0	1	43	249	546	873	4,569
Cooling Degree Days (base 65°F)	0	0	2	13	84	246	382	333	158	21	1	1	1,241
Mean Precipitation (in.)	2.95	2.82	4.27	4.28	4.94	4.33	4.30	3.98	2.90	3.28	3.83	3.61	45.49
Days With ≥ 0.1" Precipitation	6	6	8	9	9	8	7	6	5	6	7	6	83
Days With ≥ 1.0" Precipitation	1	1	1	1	1	1	1	1	1	1	1	1	12
Mean Snowfall (in.)	5.7	4.2	2.4	trace	trace	0.0	0.0	0.0	0.0	0.1	trace	2.9	15.3
Days With ≥ 1.0" Snow Depth	7	5	1	0	0	0	0	0	0	0	0	1	14

Marion 2 N *Grant County*   Elevation: 787 ft.   Latitude: 40° 34' N   Longitude: 85° 40' W

	JAN	FEB	MAR	APR	MAY	JUN	JUL	AUG	SEP	OCT	NOV	DEC	YEAR
Mean Maximum Temp. (°F)	31.6	36.3	47.5	60.2	71.7	80.9	84.5	82.3	76.4	64.1	49.8	37.6	60.2
Mean Temp. (°F)	23.8	27.6	37.7	48.9	60.1	69.7	73.7	71.4	64.7	52.7	41.2	30.0	50.1
Mean Minimum Temp. (°F)	16.0	18.7	27.9	37.5	48.5	58.5	62.8	60.4	52.9	41.2	32.6	22.5	40.0
Extreme Maximum Temp. (°F)	68	73	82	88	93	103	101	98	95	88	78	71	103
Extreme Minimum Temp. (°F)	-23	-15	-11	5	26	38	46	39	30	19	7	-20	-23
Days Maximum Temp. ≥ 90°F	0	0	0	0	0	4	7	4	1	0	0	0	16
Days Maximum Temp. ≤ 32°F	16	11	3	0	0	0	0	0	0	0	1	9	40
Days Minimum Temp. ≤ 32°F	28	25	22	10	1	0	0	0	0	6	17	26	135
Days Minimum Temp. ≤ 0°F	5	3	0	0	0	0	0	0	0	0	0	2	10
Heating Degree Days (base 65°F)	1,271	1,051	841	484	198	34	4	12	101	387	707	1,077	6,167
Cooling Degree Days (base 65°F)	0	0	1	7	52	190	291	225	98	12	0	0	876
Mean Precipitation (in.)	2.12	1.98	3.00	3.69	4.20	3.91	4.67	3.67	2.80	2.62	3.35	2.79	38.80
Days With ≥ 0.1" Precipitation	6	5	7	8	7	7	7	6	5	6	6	7	77
Days With ≥ 1.0" Precipitation	0	0	0	1	1	1	2	1	1	0	1	0	8
Mean Snowfall (in.)	7.7	6.8	3.2	1.0	0.0	0.0	0.0	0.0	0.0	0.4	1.1	6.0	26.2
Days With ≥ 1.0" Snow Depth	16	11	4	0	0	0	0	0	0	0	1	7	39

Martinsville 2 SW *Morgan County* Elevation: 606 ft.   Latitude: 39° 24' N   Longitude: 86° 27' W

	JAN	FEB	MAR	APR	MAY	JUN	JUL	AUG	SEP	OCT	NOV	DEC	YEAR
Mean Maximum Temp. (°F)	35.7	40.6	51.1	63.0	73.0	81.3	85.5	84.2	77.8	66.3	53.0	41.2	62.7
Mean Temp. (°F)	26.9	30.6	40.4	51.3	61.3	70.3	74.3	72.4	65.0	53.4	42.8	32.4	51.8
Mean Minimum Temp. (°F)	18.0	20.6	29.8	39.6	49.5	59.2	63.2	60.6	52.1	40.4	32.6	23.6	40.8
Extreme Maximum Temp. (°F)	67	74	83	88	92	101	101	100	94	88	81	75	101
Extreme Minimum Temp. (°F)	-35	-20	-15	12	27	35	45	38	28	19	9	-22	-35
Days Maximum Temp. ≥ 90°F	0	0	0	0	0	3	7	6	2	0	0	0	18
Days Maximum Temp. ≤ 32°F	12	7	2	0	0	0	0	0	0	0	1	7	29
Days Minimum Temp. ≤ 32°F	28	24	20	8	1	0	0	0	0	8	16	25	130
Days Minimum Temp. ≤ 0°F	4	3	0	0	0	0	0	0	0	0	0	2	9
Heating Degree Days (base 65°F)	1,175	965	757	414	163	26	3	8	99	366	659	1,004	5,639
Cooling Degree Days (base 65°F)	0	0	1	9	52	188	309	244	99	11	0	0	913
Mean Precipitation (in.)	2.48	2.36	3.46	4.29	4.76	3.92	4.15	3.97	3.14	2.95	3.85	3.04	42.37
Days With ≥ 0.1" Precipitation	6	5	7	8	8	7	7	6	5	5	7	7	78
Days With ≥ 1.0" Precipitation	0	0	1	1	1	1	1	1	1	1	1	1	10
Mean Snowfall (in.)	6.7	4.8	2.6	trace	0.0	0.0	0.0	0.0	0.0	0.2	0.7	2.7	17.7
Days With ≥ 1.0" Snow Depth	na	na	1	0	0	0	0	0	0	0	na	na	na

Mount Vernon *Posey County* Elevation: 419 ft.   Latitude: 37° 57' N   Longitude: 87° 53' W

	JAN	FEB	MAR	APR	MAY	JUN	JUL	AUG	SEP	OCT	NOV	DEC	YEAR
Mean Maximum Temp. (°F)	38.5	44.0	54.6	66.3	76.0	84.5	88.4	86.8	80.9	69.4	55.7	44.2	65.8
Mean Temp. (°F)	30.4	35.0	44.9	55.7	65.4	74.2	78.1	76.0	69.4	57.6	46.4	36.0	55.8
Mean Minimum Temp. (°F)	22.3	25.9	35.2	45.1	54.6	63.8	67.7	65.2	57.8	45.7	37.1	27.7	45.7
Extreme Maximum Temp. (°F)	71	76	83	90	93	101	102	103	99	91	82	77	103
Extreme Minimum Temp. (°F)	-16	-7	-3	25	35	44	50	45	35	22	10	-16	-16
Days Maximum Temp. ≥ 90°F	0	0	0	0	1	8	14	11	5	0	0	0	39
Days Maximum Temp. ≤ 32°F	10	6	1	0	0	0	0	0	0	0	0	5	22
Days Minimum Temp. ≤ 32°F	25	20	13	2	0	0	0	0	0	2	11	20	93
Days Minimum Temp. ≤ 0°F	2	1	0	0	0	0	0	0	0	0	0	1	4
Heating Degree Days (base 65°F)	1,065	841	619	298	88	7	1	1	45	253	554	893	4,665
Cooling Degree Days (base 65°F)	0	0	4	23	104	292	419	356	178	29	2	0	1,407
Mean Precipitation (in.)	3.20	3.02	4.66	4.53	5.42	3.92	4.15	3.04	2.78	3.04	4.29	3.68	45.73
Days With ≥ 0.1" Precipitation	6	6	8	8	8	7	6	5	5	5	7	7	78
Days With ≥ 1.0" Precipitation	1	1	1	1	2	1	1	1	1	1	1	1	13
Mean Snowfall (in.)	4.5	3.8	2.3	0.4	0.0	0.0	0.0	0.0	0.0	0.1	0.4	2.2	13.7
Days With ≥ 1.0" Snow Depth	7	6	1	0	0	0	0	0	0	0	0	3	17

Muncie *Delaware County* Elevation: 977 ft.   Latitude: 40° 14' N   Longitude: 85° 23' W

	JAN	FEB	MAR	APR	MAY	JUN	JUL	AUG	SEP	OCT	NOV	DEC	YEAR
Mean Maximum Temp. (°F)	32.4	37.3	48.1	61.1	72.1	81.1	85.1	82.9	76.8	64.4	50.1	38.4	60.8
Mean Temp. (°F)	24.6	28.9	38.9	50.5	61.6	70.8	74.7	72.5	65.5	53.4	41.7	30.8	51.2
Mean Minimum Temp. (°F)	16.8	20.4	29.6	39.9	51.2	60.5	64.2	62.0	54.2	42.4	33.2	23.1	41.5
Extreme Maximum Temp. (°F)	64	71	80	88	93	102	100	99	96	90	79	71	102
Extreme Minimum Temp. (°F)	-29	-13	-8	10	25	36	40	39	27	18	3	-21	-29
Days Maximum Temp. ≥ 90°F	0	0	0	0	0	3	7	4	2	0	0	0	16
Days Maximum Temp. ≤ 32°F	15	10	3	0	0	0	0	0	0	0	2	9	39
Days Minimum Temp. ≤ 32°F	28	24	20	8	1	0	0	0	0	5	16	25	127
Days Minimum Temp. ≤ 0°F	4	3	0	0	0	0	0	0	0	0	0	2	9
Heating Degree Days (base 65°F)	1,245	1,012	804	441	167	26	3	8	91	369	694	1,054	5,914
Cooling Degree Days (base 65°F)	0	0	2	9	64	201	304	240	103	13	0	0	936
Mean Precipitation (in.)	2.05	2.19	3.15	3.60	4.07	4.21	3.87	3.39	2.85	2.65	3.32	2.99	38.34
Days With ≥ 0.1" Precipitation	6	5	7	8	8	7	6	6	5	6	7	7	78
Days With ≥ 1.0" Precipitation	0	0	0	1	1	1	1	1	1	0	1	0	7
Mean Snowfall (in.)	8.4	6.0	3.0	0.5	trace	0.0	0.0	0.0	0.0	0.2	1.2	6.3	25.6
Days With ≥ 1.0" Snow Depth	13	9	3	0	0	0	0	0	0	0	1	6	32

New Castle 4 N *Henry County* Elevation: 1,062 ft.   Latitude: 39° 59' N   Longitude: 85° 22' W

	JAN	FEB	MAR	APR	MAY	JUN	JUL	AUG	SEP	OCT	NOV	DEC	YEAR
Mean Maximum Temp. (°F)	32.5	37.2	48.2	60.4	71.6	80.5	84.0	82.3	76.3	63.9	50.0	38.5	60.5
Mean Temp. (°F)	24.3	28.1	38.4	49.1	60.0	69.2	73.0	71.2	64.4	52.5	41.2	30.6	50.2
Mean Minimum Temp. (°F)	16.0	18.9	28.5	37.8	48.4	57.9	61.9	59.9	52.5	41.0	32.3	22.6	39.8
Extreme Maximum Temp. (°F)	64	71	82	87	91	103	101	100	96	88	78	72	103
Extreme Minimum Temp. (°F)	-26	-19	-9	15	26	38	45	39	29	18	8	-21	-26
Days Maximum Temp. ≥ 90°F	0	0	0	0	0	3	5	3	1	0	0	0	12
Days Maximum Temp. ≤ 32°F	15	10	3	0	0	0	0	0	0	0	2	9	39
Days Minimum Temp. ≤ 32°F	29	24	21	9	1	0	0	0	0	6	17	25	132
Days Minimum Temp. ≤ 0°F	5	3	0	0	0	0	0	0	0	0	0	2	10
Heating Degree Days (base 65°F)	1,256	1,036	819	475	198	34	5	11	106	391	709	1,061	6,101
Cooling Degree Days (base 65°F)	0	0	1	5	46	169	262	211	90	10	0	0	794
Mean Precipitation (in.)	2.22	2.22	2.98	3.97	4.62	4.57	4.65	3.54	2.81	2.99	3.63	2.78	40.98
Days With ≥ 0.1" Precipitation	5	5	7	8	8	8	7	6	5	6	7	6	78
Days With ≥ 1.0" Precipitation	0	0	0	1	1	1	1	1	1	1	1	0	8
Mean Snowfall (in.)	na	na	2.2	0.3	trace	0.0	0.0	0.0	0.0	trace	0.8	na	na
Days With ≥ 1.0" Snow Depth	na	na	1	0	0	0	0	0	0	0	0	na	na

New Whiteland *Johnson County*   Elevation: 784 ft.   Latitude: 39° 33' N   Longitude: 86° 06' W

	JAN	FEB	MAR	APR	MAY	JUN	JUL	AUG	SEP	OCT	NOV	DEC	YEAR
Mean Maximum Temp. (°F)	33.5	38.5	50.6	62.0	72.8	81.5	85.1	83.5	77.5	65.4	51.4	39.0	61.7
Mean Temp. (°F)	24.7	28.8	40.4	51.1	61.7	70.8	74.2	72.2	65.3	53.1	41.7	30.7	51.2
Mean Minimum Temp. (°F)	16.0	19.0	30.2	40.2	50.6	60.0	63.3	60.8	53.1	40.8	32.0	22.4	40.7
Extreme Maximum Temp. (°F)	65	72	82	87	95	101	100	100	97	89	80	73	101
Extreme Minimum Temp. (°F)	-36	-21	-12	18	28	37	44	38	28	17	1	-26	-36
Days Maximum Temp. ≥ 90°F	0	0	0	0	0	3	7	5	2	0	0	0	17
Days Maximum Temp. ≤ 32°F	14	9	2	0	0	0	0	0	0	0	1	8	34
Days Minimum Temp. ≤ 32°F	29	24	19	7	1	0	0	0	0	7	17	26	130
Days Minimum Temp. ≤ 0°F	5	3	0	0	0	0	0	0	0	0	0	2	10
Heating Degree Days (base 65°F)	1,241	1,017	757	420	160	22	3	10	92	373	693	1,056	5,844
Cooling Degree Days (base 65°F)	0	0	1	10	63	206	303	243	106	12	0	0	944
Mean Precipitation (in.)	2.23	2.12	3.62	4.20	4.51	4.04	4.28	3.64	2.86	2.89	4.01	3.06	41.46
Days With ≥ 0.1" Precipitation	6	na	8	9	8	7	7	6	5	5	7	6	na
Days With ≥ 1.0" Precipitation	0	0	1	1	1	1	1	1	1	1	1	0	9
Mean Snowfall (in.)	na	na	na	0.4	0.0	0.0	0.0	0.0	0.0	0.3	0.4	na	na
Days With ≥ 1.0" Snow Depth	na	na	na	0	0	0	0	0	0	0	na	na	na

North Vernon 1 NW *Jennings County*   Elevation: 744 ft.   Latitude: 39° 02' N   Longitude: 85° 38' W

	JAN	FEB	MAR	APR	MAY	JUN	JUL	AUG	SEP	OCT	NOV	DEC	YEAR
Mean Maximum Temp. (°F)	38.6	44.7	55.0	66.5	75.3	83.6	86.8	84.8	na	67.6	54.2	44.1	na
Mean Temp. (°F)	29.9	34.7	44.5	54.6	63.6	72.2	75.8	73.9	na	56.1	45.1	35.4	na
Mean Minimum Temp. (°F)	21.2	24.8	34.0	42.7	51.8	60.7	64.8	62.9	na	44.5	35.9	26.8	na
Extreme Maximum Temp. (°F)	67	76	85	87	93	101	102	103	94	90	80	74	103
Extreme Minimum Temp. (°F)	-24	-12	-6	19	29	38	45	40	33	18	3	-22	-24
Days Maximum Temp. ≥ 90°F	0	0	0	0	0	4	8	5	2	0	0	0	19
Days Maximum Temp. ≤ 32°F	9	5	1	0	0	0	0	0	0	0	0	4	19
Days Minimum Temp. ≤ 32°F	24	19	15	5	1	0	0	0	0	4	12	20	100
Days Minimum Temp. ≤ 0°F	2	1	0	0	0	0	0	0	0	0	0	1	4
Heating Degree Days (base 65°F)	1,080	847	632	322	117	12	1	2	na	290	592	911	na
Cooling Degree Days (base 65°F)	0	0	5	18	79	245	362	293	na	23	1	0	na
Mean Precipitation (in.)	2.30	2.59	3.71	4.45	4.50	3.65	4.41	4.42	2.89	3.18	3.97	3.33	43.40
Days With ≥ 0.1" Precipitation	6	5	7	8	7	6	6	6	5	6	7	6	75
Days With ≥ 1.0" Precipitation	0	1	1	1	1	1	1	1	1	1	1	1	11
Mean Snowfall (in.)	4.0	2.8	1.7	0.1	trace	0.0	0.0	0.0	0.0	0.0	0.2	na	na
Days With ≥ 1.0" Snow Depth	na	5	1	0	0	0	0	0	0	0	0	na	na

Oaklandon Geist Reservoir *Marion County*   Elevation: 793 ft.   Latitude: 39° 54' N   Longitude: 85° 59' W

	JAN	FEB	MAR	APR	MAY	JUN	JUL	AUG	SEP	OCT	NOV	DEC	YEAR
Mean Maximum Temp. (°F)	33.4	38.2	49.3	61.6	72.2	80.8	84.4	82.7	76.6	64.7	50.5	38.7	61.1
Mean Temp. (°F)	25.1	28.9	39.3	50.4	61.2	70.2	74.1	72.0	65.3	53.3	41.8	30.8	51.0
Mean Minimum Temp. (°F)	16.8	19.5	29.3	39.1	50.2	59.5	63.7	61.3	53.9	41.8	32.9	22.8	40.9
Extreme Maximum Temp. (°F)	65	72	83	86	91	102	100	99	94	89	78	72	102
Extreme Minimum Temp. (°F)	-23	-17	-8	15	27	38	46	41	32	16	6	-20	-23
Days Maximum Temp. ≥ 90°F	0	0	0	0	0	3	6	4	1	0	0	0	14
Days Maximum Temp. ≤ 32°F	15	9	3	0	0	0	0	0	0	0	1	8	36
Days Minimum Temp. ≤ 32°F	28	24	20	8	0	0	0	0	0	6	16	25	127
Days Minimum Temp. ≤ 0°F	5	3	0	0	0	0	0	0	0	0	0	2	10
Heating Degree Days (base 65°F)	1,229	1,013	788	442	169	27	3	9	91	369	691	1,055	5,886
Cooling Degree Days (base 65°F)	0	0	2	8	54	189	293	236	97	13	0	0	892
Mean Precipitation (in.)	2.28	2.32	3.36	3.97	4.84	4.10	4.72	4.02	3.35	3.08	3.90	3.15	43.09
Days With ≥ 0.1" Precipitation	5	5	7	9	9	7	7	6	6	6	7	7	81
Days With ≥ 1.0" Precipitation	0	0	0	1	1	1	1	1	1	1	1	1	9
Mean Snowfall (in.)	7.6	5.7	2.8	0.4	0.0	0.0	0.0	0.0	0.0	0.3	0.9	5.4	23.1
Days With ≥ 1.0" Snow Depth	10	8	2	0	0	0	0	0	0	0	0	5	25

Oolitic Purdue Exp. Farm *Lawrence County*   Elevation: 649 ft.   Latitude: 38° 53' N   Longitude: 86° 33' W

	JAN	FEB	MAR	APR	MAY	JUN	JUL	AUG	SEP	OCT	NOV	DEC	YEAR
Mean Maximum Temp. (°F)	36.5	42.0	52.5	63.9	73.6	81.7	85.8	84.5	78.4	66.6	53.7	42.3	63.5
Mean Temp. (°F)	27.2	31.5	41.4	52.0	61.8	70.6	74.7	73.1	65.9	53.7	43.3	32.9	52.3
Mean Minimum Temp. (°F)	17.8	20.9	30.3	40.0	50.0	59.4	63.6	61.6	53.4	40.7	32.9	23.5	41.2
Extreme Maximum Temp. (°F)	68	74	82	88	91	102	102	102	96	88	81	75	102
Extreme Minimum Temp. (°F)	-29	-14	-5	15	27	38	47	41	31	16	6	-23	-29
Days Maximum Temp. ≥ 90°F	0	0	0	0	0	3	8	6	2	0	0	0	19
Days Maximum Temp. ≤ 32°F	11	7	2	0	0	0	0	0	0	0	1	6	27
Days Minimum Temp. ≤ 32°F	28	24	19	8	1	0	0	0	0	7	16	24	127
Days Minimum Temp. ≤ 0°F	4	3	0	0	0	0	0	0	0	0	0	1	8
Heating Degree Days (base 65°F)	1,165	940	726	393	153	21	2	5	84	357	645	988	5,479
Cooling Degree Days (base 65°F)	0	0	3	10	61	205	326	271	117	13	0	0	1,006
Mean Precipitation (in.)	2.70	2.61	3.80	4.59	4.99	3.94	4.39	4.09	2.93	3.31	3.87	3.27	44.49
Days With ≥ 0.1" Precipitation	6	5	7	8	8	7	6	6	5	6	7	6	77
Days With ≥ 1.0" Precipitation	1	0	1	1	1	1	1	1	1	1	1	1	11
Mean Snowfall (in.)	5.8	3.8	2.7	trace	trace	0.0	0.0	0.0	0.0	trace	0.4	2.6	15.3
Days With ≥ 1.0" Snow Depth	9	7	2	0	0	0	0	0	0	0	0	4	22

Paoli *Orange County*　Elevation: 557 ft.　Latitude: 38° 33' N　Longitude: 86° 29' W

	JAN	FEB	MAR	APR	MAY	JUN	JUL	AUG	SEP	OCT	NOV	DEC	YEAR
Mean Maximum Temp. (°F)	39.2	45.1	55.5	66.3	76.3	83.7	87.9	86.1	79.9	68.9	55.4	44.1	65.7
Mean Temp. (°F)	29.2	33.7	43.5	53.6	63.4	71.8	76.0	74.0	66.9	55.3	44.4	34.1	53.8
Mean Minimum Temp. (°F)	19.2	22.3	31.4	40.9	50.5	59.8	64.1	61.9	54.0	41.7	33.3	24.1	41.9
Extreme Maximum Temp. (°F)	70	76	85	90	93	98	103	101	99	90	81	77	103
Extreme Minimum Temp. (°F)	-29	-15	-9	16	26	37	42	44	30	15	5	-19	-29
Days Maximum Temp. ≥ 90°F	0	0	0	0	1	6	12	9	3	0	0	0	31
Days Maximum Temp. ≤ 32°F	9	5	1	0	0	0	0	0	0	0	1	5	21
Days Minimum Temp. ≤ 32°F	27	22	17	7	1	0	0	0	0	7	15	23	119
Days Minimum Temp. ≤ 0°F	3	2	0	0	0	0	0	0	0	0	0	1	6
Heating Degree Days (base 65°F)	1,102	877	664	352	124	17	2	3	72	313	612	950	5,088
Cooling Degree Days (base 65°F)	0	0	4	16	84	236	373	301	131	22	1	0	1,168
Mean Precipitation (in.)	3.11	2.91	4.49	5.08	5.13	4.24	4.38	4.04	3.26	3.12	4.22	3.51	47.49
Days With ≥ 0.1" Precipitation	6	6	8	9	8	7	7	6	5	5	7	6	80
Days With ≥ 1.0" Precipitation	1	1	1	1	1	1	2	1	1	1	1	1	13
Mean Snowfall (in.)	na	na	1.3	0.1	0.0	0.0	0.0	0.0	0.0	0.0	0.2	2.4	na
Days With ≥ 1.0" Snow Depth	na	na	1	0	0	0	0	0	0	0	0	2	na

Portland 1 SW *Jay County*　Elevation: 908 ft.　Latitude: 40° 25' N　Longitude: 85° 00' W

	JAN	FEB	MAR	APR	MAY	JUN	JUL	AUG	SEP	OCT	NOV	DEC	YEAR
Mean Maximum Temp. (°F)	31.5	36.1	47.2	60.1	71.0	80.0	84.0	81.6	76.1	63.0	49.6	37.4	59.8
Mean Temp. (°F)	23.6	27.0	37.2	48.9	59.9	69.2	73.2	70.6	63.9	51.5	40.6	29.6	49.6
Mean Minimum Temp. (°F)	15.6	17.8	27.2	37.6	48.7	58.3	62.4	59.6	51.6	39.9	31.6	21.7	39.3
Extreme Maximum Temp. (°F)	64	72	81	87	91	102	101	100	96	86	78	72	102
Extreme Minimum Temp. (°F)	-29	-16	-13	10	27	38	45	39	28	17	4	-21	-29
Days Maximum Temp. ≥ 90°F	0	0	0	0	0	3	6	3	1	0	0	0	13
Days Maximum Temp. ≤ 32°F	16	12	4	0	0	0	0	0	0	0	2	10	44
Days Minimum Temp. ≤ 32°F	28	25	22	9	1	0	0	0	0	7	18	26	136
Days Minimum Temp. ≤ 0°F	5	4	0	0	0	0	0	0	0	0	0	2	11
Heating Degree Days (base 65°F)	1,279	1,067	856	484	204	39	6	18	115	422	726	1,092	6,308
Cooling Degree Days (base 65°F)	0	0	2	7	51	177	274	206	88	11	0	0	816
Mean Precipitation (in.)	1.88	1.90	2.63	3.64	3.87	4.09	4.45	3.90	2.66	2.60	3.06	2.45	37.13
Days With ≥ 0.1" Precipitation	5	5	6	8	8	7	7	6	5	6	6	6	75
Days With ≥ 1.0" Precipitation	0	0	0	1	1	1	2	1	1	1	1	0	9
Mean Snowfall (in.)	6.3	5.8	2.9	0.4	0.0	0.0	0.0	0.0	0.0	0.2	0.7	4.7	21.0
Days With ≥ 1.0" Snow Depth	10	7	2	0	0	0	0	0	0	0	1	5	25

Princeton 1 W *Gibson County*　Elevation: 479 ft.　Latitude: 38° 21' N　Longitude: 87° 35' W

	JAN	FEB	MAR	APR	MAY	JUN	JUL	AUG	SEP	OCT	NOV	DEC	YEAR
Mean Maximum Temp. (°F)	37.2	43.6	54.6	66.1	75.8	84.7	88.2	86.5	80.2	68.5	54.3	42.9	65.2
Mean Temp. (°F)	29.4	34.9	44.9	55.6	65.3	74.2	77.9	76.0	69.3	57.6	45.8	35.2	55.5
Mean Minimum Temp. (°F)	21.5	26.0	35.2	45.0	54.6	63.6	67.6	65.6	58.3	46.5	37.1	27.4	45.7
Extreme Maximum Temp. (°F)	69	77	83	88	95	101	102	101	98	89	81	75	102
Extreme Minimum Temp. (°F)	-19	-10	-2	21	32	44	48	47	34	20	9	-15	-19
Days Maximum Temp. ≥ 90°F	0	0	0	0	1	8	14	10	4	0	0	0	37
Days Maximum Temp. ≤ 32°F	11	6	1	0	0	0	0	0	0	0	0	6	24
Days Minimum Temp. ≤ 32°F	26	19	13	3	0	0	0	0	0	2	10	21	94
Days Minimum Temp. ≤ 0°F	2	1	0	0	0	0	0	0	0	0	0	1	4
Heating Degree Days (base 65°F)	1,098	845	619	300	93	7	0	1	47	253	573	918	4,754
Cooling Degree Days (base 65°F)	0	0	3	21	109	297	422	356	175	29	1	0	1,413
Mean Precipitation (in.)	2.71	2.79	4.33	4.71	5.14	4.00	3.98	3.81	3.10	3.41	4.44	3.59	46.01
Days With ≥ 0.1" Precipitation	6	5	8	8	8	6	6	5	5	5	7	7	76
Days With ≥ 1.0" Precipitation	0	1	1	1	2	1	1	1	1	1	1	1	12
Mean Snowfall (in.)	na	3.8	1.0	0.3	0.0	0.0	0.0	0.0	0.0	0.1	0.3	2.1	na
Days With ≥ 1.0" Snow Depth	na	na	1	0	0	0	0	0	0	0	0	1	na

Rensselaer *Jasper County*　Elevation: 649 ft.　Latitude: 40° 56' N　Longitude: 87° 09' W

	JAN	FEB	MAR	APR	MAY	JUN	JUL	AUG	SEP	OCT	NOV	DEC	YEAR
Mean Maximum Temp. (°F)	31.1	36.0	46.9	59.8	72.5	81.5	84.6	82.3	75.8	63.5	48.7	35.9	59.9
Mean Temp. (°F)	23.2	27.5	37.9	49.2	61.4	70.6	74.1	71.7	64.2	52.3	40.3	28.5	50.1
Mean Minimum Temp. (°F)	15.3	18.9	28.9	38.9	50.2	59.6	63.5	61.1	52.7	41.0	31.9	21.3	40.3
Extreme Maximum Temp. (°F)	64	78	83	90	94	103	101	104	96	90	77	67	104
Extreme Minimum Temp. (°F)	-25	-22	-5	2	28	37	42	41	30	21	2	-23	-25
Days Maximum Temp. ≥ 90°F	0	0	0	0	1	5	8	4	1	0	0	0	19
Days Maximum Temp. ≤ 32°F	16	11	4	0	0	0	0	0	0	0	2	10	43
Days Minimum Temp. ≤ 32°F	29	24	20	7	0	0	0	0	0	5	17	26	128
Days Minimum Temp. ≤ 0°F	5	3	0	0	0	0	0	0	0	0	0	2	10
Heating Degree Days (base 65°F)	1,289	1,054	835	475	175	30	6	11	110	397	733	1,125	6,240
Cooling Degree Days (base 65°F)	0	0	2	9	66	210	304	236	98	9	0	0	934
Mean Precipitation (in.)	1.99	1.67	3.16	3.53	4.27	4.36	3.84	3.51	3.45	3.10	3.24	2.68	38.80
Days With ≥ 0.1" Precipitation	5	5	7	7	7	7	6	6	6	6	6	6	74
Days With ≥ 1.0" Precipitation	0	0	0	1	1	1	1	1	1	1	1	0	8
Mean Snowfall (in.)	na	na	na	0.3	0.0	0.0	0.0	0.0	0.0	trace	0.5	na	na
Days With ≥ 1.0" Snow Depth	na	na	na	0	0	0	0	0	0	0	1	na	na

Richmond Water Works *Wayne County*   Elevation: 1,013 ft.   Latitude: 39° 53' N   Longitude: 84° 53' W

	JAN	FEB	MAR	APR	MAY	JUN	JUL	AUG	SEP	OCT	NOV	DEC	YEAR
Mean Maximum Temp. (°F)	34.1	39.0	50.2	62.0	72.6	81.0	84.7	82.9	76.6	64.3	50.9	39.6	61.5
Mean Temp. (°F)	25.6	29.7	40.0	50.5	61.0	69.6	73.5	71.6	64.7	52.8	41.9	31.6	51.0
Mean Minimum Temp. (°F)	17.1	20.3	29.7	38.9	49.3	58.1	62.3	60.3	52.8	41.2	32.8	23.5	40.5
Extreme Maximum Temp. (°F)	64	73	82	87	92	99	100	100	94	88	78	72	100
Extreme Minimum Temp. (°F)	-27	-20	-9	14	26	37	42	41	30	16	6	-22	-27
Days Maximum Temp. ≥ 90°F	0	0	0	0	0	3	6	4	1	0	0	0	14
Days Maximum Temp. ≤ 32°F	13	9	3	0	0	0	0	0	0	0	1	8	34
Days Minimum Temp. ≤ 32°F	28	24	20	8	1	0	0	0	0	6	16	25	128
Days Minimum Temp. ≤ 0°F	5	3	0	0	0	0	0	0	0	0	0	1	9
Heating Degree Days (base 65°F)	1,214	991	771	436	173	29	3	8	97	381	688	1,029	5,820
Cooling Degree Days (base 65°F)	0	0	2	6	55	181	287	227	92	11	0	0	861
Mean Precipitation (in.)	2.46	2.25	3.18	3.91	4.33	4.22	3.78	3.59	2.45	3.05	3.30	2.88	39.40
Days With ≥ 0.1" Precipitation	6	5	7	8	8	8	6	6	5	6	6	6	77
Days With ≥ 1.0" Precipitation	0	0	0	1	1	1	1	1	1	0	1	1	8
Mean Snowfall (in.)	6.7	4.7	2.4	0.7	trace	0.0	0.0	0.0	0.0	0.2	0.9	3.1	18.7
Days With ≥ 1.0" Snow Depth	10	8	2	0	0	0	0	0	0	0	0	4	24

Rochester *Fulton County*   Elevation: 767 ft.   Latitude: 41° 04' N   Longitude: 86° 13' W

	JAN	FEB	MAR	APR	MAY	JUN	JUL	AUG	SEP	OCT	NOV	DEC	YEAR
Mean Maximum Temp. (°F)	30.0	35.1	46.2	59.1	71.1	80.0	83.9	81.7	75.3	62.9	48.3	36.2	59.1
Mean Temp. (°F)	22.1	26.3	36.6	48.2	59.8	69.1	73.0	70.8	63.6	51.7	39.9	28.6	49.1
Mean Minimum Temp. (°F)	14.1	17.3	26.9	37.3	48.5	58.2	62.2	59.8	51.9	40.4	31.5	21.1	39.1
Extreme Maximum Temp. (°F)	66	72	80	89	93	102	103	101	96	90	77	70	103
Extreme Minimum Temp. (°F)	-25	-16	-7	8	27	36	42	37	29	16	1	-22	-25
Days Maximum Temp. ≥ 90°F	0	0	0	0	1	3	7	3	1	0	0	0	15
Days Maximum Temp. ≤ 32°F	17	12	4	0	0	0	0	0	0	0	2	10	45
Days Minimum Temp. ≤ 32°F	29	25	23	9	1	0	0	0	0	6	17	27	137
Days Minimum Temp. ≤ 0°F	6	4	0	0	0	0	0	0	0	0	0	2	12
Heating Degree Days (base 65°F)	1,324	1,087	875	504	208	40	7	16	123	415	748	1,120	6,467
Cooling Degree Days (base 65°F)	0	0	1	7	52	174	268	206	82	8	0	0	798
Mean Precipitation (in.)	1.99	1.71	2.71	3.90	4.12	4.01	3.87	3.63	3.54	2.92	3.42	2.66	38.48
Days With ≥ 0.1" Precipitation	5	5	6	8	8	7	7	6	6	6	7	7	78
Days With ≥ 1.0" Precipitation	0	0	0	1	1	1	1	1	1	1	1	0	8
Mean Snowfall (in.)	9.5	8.3	3.8	1.2	0.0	0.0	0.0	0.0	0.0	0.3	2.7	6.7	32.5
Days With ≥ 1.0" Snow Depth	na	na	na	0	0	0	0	0	0	0	0	na	na

Rockville *Parke County*   Elevation: 688 ft.   Latitude: 39° 46' N   Longitude: 87° 14' W

	JAN	FEB	MAR	APR	MAY	JUN	JUL	AUG	SEP	OCT	NOV	DEC	YEAR
Mean Maximum Temp. (°F)	35.5	41.7	53.1	65.7	75.8	84.3	87.4	85.1	79.2	67.6	53.2	40.8	64.1
Mean Temp. (°F)	26.8	32.1	42.6	53.8	63.7	72.5	76.1	73.8	67.4	55.9	44.0	32.7	53.4
Mean Minimum Temp. (°F)	17.9	22.5	32.0	41.9	51.6	60.7	64.8	62.4	55.5	44.1	34.9	24.5	42.7
Extreme Maximum Temp. (°F)	66	73	84	89	93	103	104	102	96	89	79	74	104
Extreme Minimum Temp. (°F)	-25	-18	-5	15	31	38	46	39	31	19	6	-21	-25
Days Maximum Temp. ≥ 90°F	0	0	0	0	1	7	11	6	3	0	0	0	28
Days Maximum Temp. ≤ 32°F	12	7	1	0	0	0	0	0	0	0	1	6	27
Days Minimum Temp. ≤ 32°F	27	22	17	6	0	0	0	0	0	4	14	24	114
Days Minimum Temp. ≤ 0°F	4	2	0	0	0	0	0	0	0	0	0	1	7
Heating Degree Days (base 65°F)	1,180	923	690	347	116	12	1	5	63	295	625	995	5,252
Cooling Degree Days (base 65°F)	0	0	3	17	84	255	364	297	138	20	1	0	1,179
Mean Precipitation (in.)	2.51	2.15	3.74	4.25	4.76	4.11	4.81	4.24	3.15	3.08	4.25	3.47	44.52
Days With ≥ 0.1" Precipitation	6	5	7	8	8	7	6	6	5	6	7	6	77
Days With ≥ 1.0" Precipitation	0	1	1	1	1	1	2	1	1	1	1	1	12
Mean Snowfall (in.)	5.0	3.3	2.2	0.2	trace	0.0	0.0	0.0	0.0	0.0	0.4	5.2	16.3
Days With ≥ 1.0" Snow Depth	11	7	2	0	0	0	0	0	0	0	0	5	25

Rushville Sewage Plant *Rush County*   Elevation: 958 ft.   Latitude: 39° 36' N   Longitude: 85° 27' W

	JAN	FEB	MAR	APR	MAY	JUN	JUL	AUG	SEP	OCT	NOV	DEC	YEAR
Mean Maximum Temp. (°F)	33.3	38.7	49.1	61.9	72.6	80.9	84.4	82.7	77.0	65.0	51.0	39.4	61.3
Mean Temp. (°F)	24.9	29.2	39.1	50.6	61.4	70.2	73.8	71.6	65.0	53.0	41.7	31.3	51.0
Mean Minimum Temp. (°F)	16.4	19.4	29.2	39.2	50.2	59.5	63.1	60.5	52.9	41.0	32.4	23.1	40.6
Extreme Maximum Temp. (°F)	64	72	83	87	92	100	100	103	93	88	78	72	103
Extreme Minimum Temp. (°F)	-28	-20	-16	16	28	38	40	41	32	17	6	-23	-28
Days Maximum Temp. ≥ 90°F	0	0	0	0	0	3	6	3	1	0	0	0	13
Days Maximum Temp. ≤ 32°F	14	10	3	0	0	0	0	0	0	0	1	8	36
Days Minimum Temp. ≤ 32°F	28	24	21	7	0	0	0	0	0	6	17	25	128
Days Minimum Temp. ≤ 0°F	5	3	0	0	0	0	0	0	0	0	0	2	10
Heating Degree Days (base 65°F)	1,240	1,006	798	435	164	26	3	9	94	376	692	1,038	5,881
Cooling Degree Days (base 65°F)	0	0	1	8	61	199	295	226	99	11	0	0	900
Mean Precipitation (in.)	2.55	2.51	3.20	4.24	4.94	4.20	4.47	3.54	2.85	2.85	3.55	3.06	41.96
Days With ≥ 0.1" Precipitation	6	5	7	8	8	7	7	6	5	5	7	6	77
Days With ≥ 1.0" Precipitation	0	0	1	1	2	1	1	1	1	1	1	1	11
Mean Snowfall (in.)	5.7	4.4	2.0	0.3	trace	0.0	0.0	0.0	0.0	0.3	0.6	2.8	16.1
Days With ≥ 1.0" Snow Depth	10	7	2	0	0	0	0	0	0	0	0	4	23

Saint Meinrad *Spencer County*   Elevation: 508 ft.   Latitude: 38° 10' N   Longitude: 86° 48' W

	JAN	FEB	MAR	APR	MAY	JUN	JUL	AUG	SEP	OCT	NOV	DEC	YEAR
Mean Maximum Temp. (°F)	40.4	46.8	57.2	68.0	76.6	84.1	87.3	86.3	80.6	69.8	56.8	45.5	66.6
Mean Temp. (°F)	31.8	36.9	46.4	56.3	65.0	73.2	76.8	75.5	69.3	57.8	47.1	36.9	56.1
Mean Minimum Temp. (°F)	23.2	27.0	35.7	44.5	53.3	62.3	66.3	64.6	57.9	45.7	37.4	28.3	45.5
Extreme Maximum Temp. (°F)	70	75	86	89	92	100	102	100	98	90	81	76	102
Extreme Minimum Temp. (°F)	-26	-10	-6	21	29	40	48	43	34	20	6	-18	-26
Days Maximum Temp. ≥ 90°F	0	0	0	0	0	5	11	9	3	0	0	0	28
Days Maximum Temp. ≤ 32°F	8	4	1	0	0	0	0	0	0	0	0	4	17
Days Minimum Temp. ≤ 32°F	24	19	14	4	0	0	0	0	0	3	11	20	95
Days Minimum Temp. ≤ 0°F	2	1	0	0	0	0	0	0	0	0	0	1	4
Heating Degree Days (base 65°F)	1,022	786	573	278	91	7	0	1	44	247	533	864	4,446
Cooling Degree Days (base 65°F)	0	0	6	22	96	262	382	336	170	31	2	1	1,308
Mean Precipitation (in.)	3.08	2.98	4.38	4.74	4.72	4.10	4.66	3.75	3.30	3.03	4.00	3.66	46.40
Days With ≥ 0.1" Precipitation	6	6	8	8	8	7	7	5	5	5	7	7	79
Days With ≥ 1.0" Precipitation	1	1	1	1	1	1	1	1	1	1	1	1	12
Mean Snowfall (in.)	3.8	2.8	1.4	trace	0.0	0.0	0.0	0.0	0.0	trace	0.1	1.6	9.7
Days With ≥ 1.0" Snow Depth	6	5	1	0	0	0	0	0	0	0	0	2	14

Salem *Washington County*   Elevation: 797 ft.   Latitude: 38° 37' N   Longitude: 86° 05' W

	JAN	FEB	MAR	APR	MAY	JUN	JUL	AUG	SEP	OCT	NOV	DEC	YEAR
Mean Maximum Temp. (°F)	39.4	45.1	55.4	66.6	75.6	83.8	87.0	85.8	80.0	68.6	55.4	44.5	65.6
Mean Temp. (°F)	30.7	34.8	44.4	54.6	63.7	72.3	76.0	74.3	68.0	56.5	45.7	35.9	54.7
Mean Minimum Temp. (°F)	22.0	24.5	33.4	42.5	51.8	60.8	64.9	62.8	56.0	44.3	35.9	27.2	43.8
Extreme Maximum Temp. (°F)	68	78	84	88	91	102	103	100	96	89	81	75	103
Extreme Minimum Temp. (°F)	-29	-15	-10	17	28	39	47	40	31	18	10	-13	-29
Days Maximum Temp. ≥ 90°F	0	0	0	0	0	4	10	8	2	0	0	0	24
Days Maximum Temp. ≤ 32°F	9	5	1	0	0	0	0	0	0	0	0	5	20
Days Minimum Temp. ≤ 32°F	25	21	16	6	0	0	0	0	0	5	12	20	105
Days Minimum Temp. ≤ 0°F	2	2	0	0	0	0	0	0	0	0	0	1	5
Heating Degree Days (base 65°F)	1,057	845	635	323	114	12	1	2	57	282	574	896	4,798
Cooling Degree Days (base 65°F)	0	0	4	17	83	234	357	301	140	23	1	0	1,160
Mean Precipitation (in.)	3.19	2.85	4.27	4.72	5.05	3.88	4.42	3.54	2.86	2.93	4.01	3.86	45.58
Days With ≥ 0.1" Precipitation	6	6	8	9	9	7	7	6	5	5	7	7	82
Days With ≥ 1.0" Precipitation	1	1	1	1	1	1	1	1	1	1	1	1	12
Mean Snowfall (in.)	5.7	5.6	3.4	0.2	0.0	0.0	0.0	0.0	0.0	0.2	0.5	2.4	18.0
Days With ≥ 1.0" Snow Depth	8	7	1	0	0	0	0	0	0	0	0	2	18

Scottsburg *Scott County*   Elevation: 547 ft.   Latitude: 38° 42' N   Longitude: 85° 46' W

	JAN	FEB	MAR	APR	MAY	JUN	JUL	AUG	SEP	OCT	NOV	DEC	YEAR
Mean Maximum Temp. (°F)	38.1	43.9	54.2	65.7	75.5	83.5	87.5	86.2	80.0	68.2	54.9	43.7	65.1
Mean Temp. (°F)	29.0	33.3	43.0	53.6	63.7	72.4	76.3	74.5	67.5	55.3	44.5	34.6	54.0
Mean Minimum Temp. (°F)	19.8	22.6	31.7	41.5	51.9	61.2	65.2	62.8	55.0	42.3	34.0	25.4	42.8
Extreme Maximum Temp. (°F)	69	75	83	89	92	101	103	103	97	91	82	76	103
Extreme Minimum Temp. (°F)	-32	-14	-9	19	29	39	47	41	31	19	6	-19	-32
Days Maximum Temp. ≥ 90°F	0	0	0	0	1	6	12	9	4	0	0	0	32
Days Maximum Temp. ≤ 32°F	10	6	1	0	0	0	0	0	0	0	0	5	22
Days Minimum Temp. ≤ 32°F	26	23	18	6	0	0	0	0	0	5	14	23	115
Days Minimum Temp. ≤ 0°F	3	2	0	0	0	0	0	0	0	0	0	1	6
Heating Degree Days (base 65°F)	1,111	890	678	352	122	14	1	3	65	315	611	937	5,099
Cooling Degree Days (base 65°F)	0	0	3	16	87	245	372	306	140	20	0	0	1,189
Mean Precipitation (in.)	2.97	2.67	4.15	4.43	4.71	4.16	4.27	4.32	3.02	3.01	3.64	3.33	44.68
Days With ≥ 0.1" Precipitation	6	6	8	8	9	7	6	7	5	6	7	7	82
Days With ≥ 1.0" Precipitation	1	1	1	1	1	1	1	1	1	1	1	1	12
Mean Snowfall (in.)	5.1	4.8	3.7	0.1	0.0	0.0	0.0	0.0	0.0	0.1	0.5	2.4	16.7
Days With ≥ 1.0" Snow Depth	7	6	2	0	0	0	0	0	0	0	0	3	18

Seymour 2 N *Jackson County*   Elevation: 567 ft.   Latitude: 38° 59' N   Longitude: 85° 54' W

	JAN	FEB	MAR	APR	MAY	JUN	JUL	AUG	SEP	OCT	NOV	DEC	YEAR
Mean Maximum Temp. (°F)	37.0	42.2	52.8	64.5	74.0	81.8	85.4	84.2	78.5	67.2	53.8	42.2	63.6
Mean Temp. (°F)	28.0	32.0	41.7	52.3	62.4	70.9	74.5	72.5	65.7	53.9	43.3	33.3	52.5
Mean Minimum Temp. (°F)	18.9	21.7	30.5	40.1	50.7	60.0	63.6	60.9	52.8	40.5	32.8	24.4	41.4
Extreme Maximum Temp. (°F)	67	74	84	88	91	101	104	102	95	92	82	75	104
Extreme Minimum Temp. (°F)	-23	-14	-10	9	29	41	47	42	29	15	8	-22	-23
Days Maximum Temp. ≥ 90°F	0	0	0	0	0	4	8	6	2	0	0	0	20
Days Maximum Temp. ≤ 32°F	11	6	1	0	0	0	0	0	0	0	1	6	25
Days Minimum Temp. ≤ 32°F	27	23	20	7	0	0	0	0	0	7	16	25	125
Days Minimum Temp. ≤ 0°F	3	2	0	0	0	0	0	0	0	0	0	1	6
Heating Degree Days (base 65°F)	1,142	925	719	386	144	20	2	6	86	353	645	975	5,403
Cooling Degree Days (base 65°F)	0	0	2	11	66	209	315	251	108	14	0	0	976
Mean Precipitation (in.)	3.05	2.70	3.79	4.73	4.94	4.04	4.41	4.33	3.00	3.30	4.00	3.35	45.64
Days With ≥ 0.1" Precipitation	7	6	8	8	9	7	7	7	6	6	7	7	86
Days With ≥ 1.0" Precipitation	1	0	1	1	1	1	1	1	1	1	1	1	11
Mean Snowfall (in.)	na	na	2.3	trace	0.0	0.0	0.0	0.0	0.0	0.2	0.6	1.9	na
Days With ≥ 1.0" Snow Depth	8	6	2	0	0	0	0	0	0	0	0	2	18

Shoals Hiway 50 Bridge *Martin County*   Elevation: 547 ft.   Latitude: 38° 40' N   Longitude: 86° 48' W

	JAN	FEB	MAR	APR	MAY	JUN	JUL	AUG	SEP	OCT	NOV	DEC	YEAR
Mean Maximum Temp. (°F)	37.5	43.4	53.9	65.6	75.3	83.2	86.8	85.4	79.4	68.0	54.6	43.1	64.7
Mean Temp. (°F)	28.2	32.7	42.5	52.9	62.5	71.2	75.2	73.6	66.8	54.9	44.2	33.9	53.2
Mean Minimum Temp. (°F)	18.9	21.9	30.9	40.2	49.7	59.3	63.6	61.7	54.2	41.8	33.9	24.6	41.7
Extreme Maximum Temp. (°F)	68	75	82	89	98	101	102	100	99	91	82	77	102
Extreme Minimum Temp. (°F)	-23	-12	-9	17	28	39	46	42	32	18	6	-20	-23
Days Maximum Temp. ≥ 90°F	0	0	0	0	1	6	10	7	3	0	0	0	27
Days Maximum Temp. ≤ 32°F	10	6	1	0	0	0	0	0	0	0	1	6	24
Days Minimum Temp. ≤ 32°F	27	22	18	8	1	0	0	0	0	7	15	23	121
Days Minimum Temp. ≤ 0°F	4	2	0	0	0	0	0	0	0	0	0	1	7
Heating Degree Days (base 65°F)	1,134	906	695	373	142	19	2	3	73	324	617	958	5,246
Cooling Degree Days (base 65°F)	0	0	4	15	70	219	338	279	128	19	1	0	1,073
Mean Precipitation (in.)	3.04	2.81	4.34	4.59	5.58	4.21	4.65	3.62	3.28	3.28	4.41	3.50	47.31
Days With ≥ 0.1" Precipitation	6	6	8	8	9	7	7	6	5	6	7	7	82
Days With ≥ 1.0" Precipitation	1	0	1	1	2	1	1	1	1	1	1	1	12
Mean Snowfall (in.)	5.7	4.0	2.8	trace	0.0	0.0	0.0	0.0	0.0	0.1	0.3	2.7	15.6
Days With ≥ 1.0" Snow Depth	10	7	2	0	0	0	0	0	0	0	0	4	23

Spencer *Owen County*   Elevation: 547 ft.   Latitude: 39° 17' N   Longitude: 86° 46' W

	JAN	FEB	MAR	APR	MAY	JUN	JUL	AUG	SEP	OCT	NOV	DEC	YEAR
Mean Maximum Temp. (°F)	35.1	40.5	51.3	63.0	73.1	81.4	85.2	83.6	77.5	65.9	52.5	40.9	62.5
Mean Temp. (°F)	25.7	30.0	40.0	50.6	60.8	69.9	73.8	72.0	64.8	52.6	42.0	31.7	51.2
Mean Minimum Temp. (°F)	16.4	19.4	28.7	38.1	48.4	58.4	62.5	60.4	52.0	39.3	31.5	22.4	39.8
Extreme Maximum Temp. (°F)	66	71	83	87	91	100	101	100	95	90	79	76	101
Extreme Minimum Temp. (°F)	-33	-19	-12	15	27	34	46	40	28	18	5	-24	-33
Days Maximum Temp. ≥ 90°F	0	0	0	0	0	3	7	4	2	0	0	0	16
Days Maximum Temp. ≤ 32°F	13	8	2	0	0	0	0	0	0	0	1	7	31
Days Minimum Temp. ≤ 32°F	28	24	21	10	1	0	0	0	0	9	18	25	136
Days Minimum Temp. ≤ 0°F	5	3	0	0	0	0	0	0	0	0	0	2	10
Heating Degree Days (base 65°F)	1,211	982	769	433	174	27	4	8	100	386	684	1,026	5,804
Cooling Degree Days (base 65°F)	0	0	1	6	43	178	283	225	90	8	0	0	834
Mean Precipitation (in.)	2.54	2.52	3.75	4.46	4.97	4.56	4.65	4.50	3.15	3.12	4.04	3.25	45.51
Days With ≥ 0.1" Precipitation	6	5	7	8	8	7	7	6	5	5	7	6	77
Days With ≥ 1.0" Precipitation	0	0	1	1	1	1	1	1	1	1	1	1	10
Mean Snowfall (in.)	5.8	5.0	2.3	0.3	0.0	0.0	0.0	0.0	0.0	trace	0.5	3.0	16.9
Days With ≥ 1.0" Snow Depth	10	7	2	0	0	0	0	0	0	0	0	4	23

Tell City *Perry County*   Elevation: 396 ft.   Latitude: 37° 57' N   Longitude: 86° 46' W

	JAN	FEB	MAR	APR	MAY	JUN	JUL	AUG	SEP	OCT	NOV	DEC	YEAR
Mean Maximum Temp. (°F)	39.5	45.0	55.3	66.6	75.9	84.0	87.8	86.8	80.8	69.1	56.1	45.1	66.0
Mean Temp. (°F)	31.4	35.6	45.1	55.3	64.8	73.6	77.7	76.3	69.7	57.5	46.7	36.9	55.9
Mean Minimum Temp. (°F)	23.3	26.3	34.9	44.0	53.6	63.1	67.6	65.7	58.6	45.9	37.3	28.5	45.7
Extreme Maximum Temp. (°F)	69	74	84	89	93	99	103	100	100	91	83	77	103
Extreme Minimum Temp. (°F)	-17	-5	-1	20	32	43	52	46	36	21	13	-14	-17
Days Maximum Temp. ≥ 90°F	0	0	0	0	1	6	13	11	4	0	0	0	35
Days Maximum Temp. ≤ 32°F	9	5	1	0	0	0	0	0	0	0	0	4	19
Days Minimum Temp. ≤ 32°F	24	20	14	3	0	0	0	0	0	2	10	20	93
Days Minimum Temp. ≤ 0°F	1	0	0	0	0	0	0	0	0	0	0	0	1
Heating Degree Days (base 65°F)	1,034	823	613	306	98	8	0	1	41	255	544	867	4,590
Cooling Degree Days (base 65°F)	0	0	4	21	97	279	418	366	185	31	1	0	1,402
Mean Precipitation (in.)	3.22	3.16	4.55	4.86	5.10	4.32	4.58	3.72	3.34	3.20	4.12	4.00	48.17
Days With ≥ 0.1" Precipitation	6	6	8	7	8	8	7	5	5	5	7	7	79
Days With ≥ 1.0" Precipitation	1	1	1	1	1	1	1	1	1	1	1	1	12
Mean Snowfall (in.)	4.4	2.6	0.7	0.1	0.0	0.0	0.0	0.0	0.0	0.0	0.4	1.0	9.2
Days With ≥ 1.0" Snow Depth	4	4	1	0	0	0	0	0	0	0	0	1	10

Terre Haute Indiana State *Vigo County*   Elevation: 505 ft.   Latitude: 39° 28' N   Longitude: 87° 25' W

	JAN	FEB	MAR	APR	MAY	JUN	JUL	AUG	SEP	OCT	NOV	DEC	YEAR
Mean Maximum Temp. (°F)	35.2	40.5	52.4	63.8	75.0	83.3	87.3	85.0	79.4	67.6	52.9	41.3	63.6
Mean Temp. (°F)	26.2	30.7	42.2	52.8	63.3	72.0	76.1	73.8	67.3	55.3	43.1	32.3	52.9
Mean Minimum Temp. (°F)	17.1	20.9	31.9	41.8	51.7	60.7	64.9	62.5	55.1	42.9	33.2	23.2	42.1
Extreme Maximum Temp. (°F)	67	73	83	86	94	102	102	98	99	90	81	74	102
Extreme Minimum Temp. (°F)	-24	-20	-7	17	29	36	41	42	30	19	5	-22	-24
Days Maximum Temp. ≥ 90°F	0	0	0	0	1	6	10	7	3	0	0	0	27
Days Maximum Temp. ≤ 32°F	13	7	1	0	0	0	0	0	0	0	1	6	28
Days Minimum Temp. ≤ 32°F	27	23	18	6	0	0	0	0	0	5	15	24	118
Days Minimum Temp. ≤ 0°F	4	2	0	0	0	0	0	0	0	0	0	1	7
Heating Degree Days (base 65°F)	1,197	962	702	373	125	15	1	3	69	314	652	1,007	5,420
Cooling Degree Days (base 65°F)	0	0	3	13	81	239	365	290	144	21	0	0	1,156
Mean Precipitation (in.)	2.15	2.52	3.68	4.19	4.40	4.02	4.36	3.80	3.02	2.84	3.72	3.05	41.75
Days With ≥ 0.1" Precipitation	6	5	7	9	8	7	7	6	5	5	7	6	78
Days With ≥ 1.0" Precipitation	0	1	1	1	1	1	1	1	1	1	1	1	11
Mean Snowfall (in.)	na	na	1.6	trace	0.0	0.0	0.0	0.0	0.0	0.0	0.5	2.2	na
Days With ≥ 1.0" Snow Depth	na	na	1	0	0	0	0	0	0	0	0	3	na

Valparaiso Waterworks *Porter County*   Elevation: 797 ft.   Latitude: 41° 31' N   Longitude: 87° 02' W

	JAN	FEB	MAR	APR	MAY	JUN	JUL	AUG	SEP	OCT	NOV	DEC	YEAR
Mean Maximum Temp. (°F)	30.5	35.8	47.0	59.8	71.4	80.1	83.3	80.9	74.6	63.3	48.6	36.1	59.3
Mean Temp. (°F)	22.9	27.7	38.0	49.2	60.1	69.1	73.1	70.9	64.3	53.2	40.8	29.3	49.9
Mean Minimum Temp. (°F)	15.3	19.5	28.9	38.5	48.7	58.1	62.8	61.0	53.9	43.0	33.0	22.5	40.4
Extreme Maximum Temp. (°F)	63	69	83	88	90	100	99	99	94	88	76	68	100
Extreme Minimum Temp. (°F)	-25	-18	-3	12	28	34	43	39	31	20	2	-20	-25
Days Maximum Temp. ≥ 90°F	0	0	0	0	0	2	4	2	1	0	0	0	9
Days Maximum Temp. ≤ 32°F	17	11	3	0	0	0	0	0	0	0	2	10	43
Days Minimum Temp. ≤ 32°F	29	24	21	8	1	0	0	0	0	4	16	26	129
Days Minimum Temp. ≤ 0°F	5	3	0	0	0	0	0	0	0	0	0	2	10
Heating Degree Days (base 65°F)	1,299	1,048	833	477	199	37	6	12	104	370	720	1,099	6,204
Cooling Degree Days (base 65°F)	0	0	2	8	53	169	271	206	90	10	0	0	809
Mean Precipitation (in.)	2.08	1.77	2.98	3.71	3.94	4.52	3.94	3.92	3.77	3.21	3.58	2.82	40.24
Days With ≥ 0.1" Precipitation	5	5	7	8	8	7	6	7	7	7	8	6	81
Days With ≥ 1.0" Precipitation	0	0	0	1	1	1	1	1	1	1	1	1	9
Mean Snowfall (in.)	11.8	9.2	5.7	1.1	trace	0.0	0.0	0.0	0.0	0.2	3.2	8.6	39.8
Days With ≥ 1.0" Snow Depth	20	13	5	0	0	0	0	0	0	0	2	11	51

Vevay *Switzerland County*   Elevation: 469 ft.   Latitude: 38° 45' N   Longitude: 85° 04' W

	JAN	FEB	MAR	APR	MAY	JUN	JUL	AUG	SEP	OCT	NOV	DEC	YEAR
Mean Maximum Temp. (°F)	40.0	45.8	56.7	68.0	77.3	85.0	88.5	86.9	80.4	68.6	55.7	45.1	66.5
Mean Temp. (°F)	31.4	35.6	45.3	55.2	64.7	73.0	77.1	75.5	68.8	56.8	46.0	36.5	55.5
Mean Minimum Temp. (°F)	22.7	25.5	33.8	42.3	52.1	61.0	65.6	64.1	57.2	44.9	36.2	27.8	44.4
Extreme Maximum Temp. (°F)	75	75	84	89	94	104	106	103	99	88	83	75	106
Extreme Minimum Temp. (°F)	-24	-11	-4	16	30	37	45	41	34	20	1	-18	-24
Days Maximum Temp. ≥ 90°F	0	0	0	0	1	7	14	10	3	0	0	0	35
Days Maximum Temp. ≤ 32°F	8	4	1	0	0	0	0	0	0	0	0	4	17
Days Minimum Temp. ≤ 32°F	24	20	15	5	0	0	0	0	0	2	11	20	97
Days Minimum Temp. ≤ 0°F	2	1	0	0	0	0	0	0	0	0	0	1	4
Heating Degree Days (base 65°F)	1,035	822	608	303	96	9	0	1	43	268	565	876	4,626
Cooling Degree Days (base 65°F)	0	0	3	16	95	264	401	347	162	23	1	0	1,312
Mean Precipitation (in.)	3.06	2.88	4.10	4.27	4.65	4.55	3.81	3.91	3.13	3.11	3.64	3.71	44.82
Days With ≥ 0.1" Precipitation	7	6	8	8	8	8	7	6	6	5	7	7	83
Days With ≥ 1.0" Precipitation	1	1	1	1	1	1	1	1	1	1	1	1	12
Mean Snowfall (in.)	6.5	5.1	3.3	0.1	trace	0.0	0.0	0.0	0.0	0.3	0.6	2.7	18.6
Days With ≥ 1.0" Snow Depth	8	6	1	0	0	0	0	0	0	0	0	3	18

Wanatah 2 WNW *Porter County*   Elevation: 734 ft.   Latitude: 41° 27' N   Longitude: 86° 56' W

	JAN	FEB	MAR	APR	MAY	JUN	JUL	AUG	SEP	OCT	NOV	DEC	YEAR
Mean Maximum Temp. (°F)	29.7	34.8	45.6	58.3	70.2	80.1	83.4	81.4	75.0	63.0	48.2	35.6	58.8
Mean Temp. (°F)	21.6	26.3	36.6	47.9	58.9	68.8	72.3	70.3	63.2	51.7	39.8	28.1	48.8
Mean Minimum Temp. (°F)	13.4	17.7	27.5	37.4	47.6	57.5	61.2	59.2	51.2	40.3	31.4	20.5	38.7
Extreme Maximum Temp. (°F)	63	71	82	90	93	105	101	101	96	89	77	70	105
Extreme Minimum Temp. (°F)	-26	-21	-6	10	26	33	42	38	27	18	2	-20	-26
Days Maximum Temp. ≥ 90°F	0	0	0	0	1	4	6	3	1	0	0	0	15
Days Maximum Temp. ≤ 32°F	18	12	4	0	0	0	0	0	0	0	2	11	47
Days Minimum Temp. ≤ 32°F	29	25	23	9	1	0	0	0	0	6	18	27	138
Days Minimum Temp. ≤ 0°F	6	4	0	0	0	0	0	0	0	0	0	3	13
Heating Degree Days (base 65°F)	1,340	1,088	876	516	235	48	13	21	129	414	751	1,138	6,569
Cooling Degree Days (base 65°F)	0	0	1	9	50	173	251	199	78	7	0	0	768
Mean Precipitation (in.)	1.63	1.56	2.78	3.63	3.74	4.27	4.15	3.68	3.77	2.91	3.41	2.48	38.01
Days With ≥ 0.1" Precipitation	4	4	6	8	7	7	6	6	7	6	7	6	74
Days With ≥ 1.0" Precipitation	0	0	0	1	1	1	1	1	1	1	1	0	8
Mean Snowfall (in.)	13.5	10.9	6.4	1.2	trace	0.0	0.0	0.0	0.0	0.3	3.3	8.9	44.5
Days With ≥ 1.0" Snow Depth	20	15	6	1	0	0	0	0	0	0	3	11	56

Warsaw *Kosciusko County*   Elevation: 807 ft.   Latitude: 41° 14' N   Longitude: 85° 52' W

	JAN	FEB	MAR	APR	MAY	JUN	JUL	AUG	SEP	OCT	NOV	DEC	YEAR
Mean Maximum Temp. (°F)	30.7	36.0	46.6	59.4	71.4	79.8	83.0	80.9	74.9	62.6	48.8	36.8	59.2
Mean Temp. (°F)	22.9	27.5	37.3	48.9	60.4	68.9	72.7	70.7	63.9	52.2	40.4	29.6	49.6
Mean Minimum Temp. (°F)	14.7	18.2	28.0	38.4	49.3	58.0	62.4	60.4	53.1	41.8	31.9	22.0	39.9
Extreme Maximum Temp. (°F)	63	73	82	87	91	102	103	98	95	86	76	69	103
Extreme Minimum Temp. (°F)	-25	-17	-9	8	28	34	42	37	29	19	3	-20	-25
Days Maximum Temp. ≥ 90°F	0	0	0	0	0	2	5	2	1	0	0	0	10
Days Maximum Temp. ≤ 32°F	17	11	3	0	0	0	0	0	0	0	2	10	43
Days Minimum Temp. ≤ 32°F	29	25	21	8	1	0	0	0	0	5	17	26	132
Days Minimum Temp. ≤ 0°F	5	3	0	0	0	0	0	0	0	0	0	2	10
Heating Degree Days (base 65°F)	1,302	1,057	854	486	193	38	8	16	112	398	733	1,092	6,289
Cooling Degree Days (base 65°F)	0	0	1	7	52	169	266	215	84	7	0	0	801
Mean Precipitation (in.)	1.81	1.39	2.08	3.46	3.75	4.43	3.99	3.96	3.21	3.25	2.93	2.51	36.77
Days With ≥ 0.1" Precipitation	5	4	5	8	7	7	7	7	6	6	6	6	74
Days With ≥ 1.0" Precipitation	0	0	0	1	1	1	1	1	1	1	1	0	8
Mean Snowfall (in.)	na	na	na	0.2	0.0	0.0	0.0	0.0	0.0	trace	na	na	na
Days With ≥ 1.0" Snow Depth	na	na	na	0	0	0	0	0	0	0	na	na	na

Washington *Daviess County*   Elevation: 524 ft.   Latitude: 38° 35' N   Longitude: 87° 12' W

	JAN	FEB	MAR	APR	MAY	JUN	JUL	AUG	SEP	OCT	NOV	DEC	YEAR
Mean Maximum Temp. (°F)	38.8	44.9	56.2	67.3	76.6	85.0	88.3	86.3	80.1	68.6	55.1	43.7	65.9
Mean Temp. (°F)	31.0	36.0	46.1	56.3	65.7	74.4	78.0	76.0	69.2	57.7	46.5	36.1	56.1
Mean Minimum Temp. (°F)	23.1	27.0	36.0	45.1	54.7	63.8	67.6	65.6	58.4	46.9	37.9	28.4	46.2
Extreme Maximum Temp. (°F)	68	76	84	88	94	101	104	101	97	89	80	75	104
Extreme Minimum Temp. (°F)	-18	-9	1	20	32	40	50	45	33	21	9	-19	-19
Days Maximum Temp. ≥ 90°F	0	0	0	0	1	7	13	9	3	0	0	0	33
Days Maximum Temp. ≤ 32°F	9	5	1	0	0	0	0	0	0	0	0	5	20
Days Minimum Temp. ≤ 32°F	24	18	13	3	0	0	0	0	0	2	10	20	90
Days Minimum Temp. ≤ 0°F	2	1	0	0	0	0	0	0	0	0	0	1	4
Heating Degree Days (base 65°F)	1,049	813	583	283	86	5	0	1	45	249	550	890	4,554
Cooling Degree Days (base 65°F)	0	0	4	25	110	297	421	356	173	31	1	0	1,418
Mean Precipitation (in.)	2.74	2.64	4.24	4.18	5.39	3.95	4.88	3.70	2.88	3.17	4.31	3.37	45.45
Days With ≥ 0.1" Precipitation	6	5	8	8	8	7	6	5	5	5	7	7	77
Days With ≥ 1.0" Precipitation	0	1	1	1	2	1	2	1	1	1	1	1	13
Mean Snowfall (in.)	4.2	3.0	1.8	trace	trace	0.0	0.0	0.0	0.0	trace	0.3	2.2	11.5
Days With ≥ 1.0" Snow Depth	6	5	1	0	0	0	0	0	0	0	0	2	14

West Lafayette 6 NW *Tippecanoe County*   Elevation: 702 ft.   Latitude: 40° 28' N   Longitude: 87° 00' W

	JAN	FEB	MAR	APR	MAY	JUN	JUL	AUG	SEP	OCT	NOV	DEC	YEAR
Mean Maximum Temp. (°F)	30.9	36.3	47.6	60.4	72.0	81.0	84.1	82.1	76.6	64.4	49.7	37.2	60.2
Mean Temp. (°F)	22.8	27.5	38.3	49.9	61.2	70.3	73.6	71.3	64.9	53.0	41.0	29.4	50.3
Mean Minimum Temp. (°F)	14.7	18.7	28.9	39.3	50.3	59.6	63.0	60.6	53.0	41.5	32.2	21.6	40.3
Extreme Maximum Temp. (°F)	64	72	82	88	93	103	100	98	96	90	78	71	103
Extreme Minimum Temp. (°F)	-24	-16	-4	7	28	35	42	38	25	19	5	-22	-24
Days Maximum Temp. ≥ 90°F	0	0	0	0	0	4	6	3	2	0	0	0	15
Days Maximum Temp. ≤ 32°F	16	11	3	0	0	0	0	0	0	0	2	10	42
Days Minimum Temp. ≤ 32°F	29	25	21	8	1	0	0	0	0	6	16	26	132
Days Minimum Temp. ≤ 0°F	6	4	0	0	0	0	0	0	0	0	0	2	12
Heating Degree Days (base 65°F)	1,301	1,053	822	457	177	30	6	13	103	380	713	1,096	6,151
Cooling Degree Days (base 65°F)	0	0	2	9	65	204	286	222	104	13	0	0	905
Mean Precipitation (in.)	1.75	1.51	2.88	3.77	4.17	4.10	3.98	3.66	3.11	2.77	3.06	2.37	37.13
Days With ≥ 0.1" Precipitation	4	3	6	8	8	7	7	6	5	5	6	6	71
Days With ≥ 1.0" Precipitation	0	0	0	1	1	1	1	1	1	1	1	0	8
Mean Snowfall (in.)	7.4	4.8	2.4	0.7	0.0	0.0	0.0	0.0	0.0	0.2	1.0	5.0	21.5
Days With ≥ 1.0" Snow Depth	14	9	4	0	0	0	0	0	0	0	1	7	35

W. Lafayette Purdue Univ. Arpt. *Tippecanoe Co.*   Elevation: 597 ft.   Latitude: 40° 25' N   Longitude: 86° 56' W

	JAN	FEB	MAR	APR	MAY	JUN	JUL	AUG	SEP	OCT	NOV	DEC	YEAR
Mean Maximum Temp. (°F)	31.7	37.0	49.4	62.1	73.5	82.8	86.2	83.9	77.4	65.1	49.9	38.3	61.4
Mean Temp. (°F)	23.9	28.7	40.2	50.9	61.7	71.2	75.3	73.3	66.1	54.1	41.7	31.0	51.5
Mean Minimum Temp. (°F)	16.0	20.4	30.8	39.7	49.9	59.7	64.3	62.6	54.6	43.0	33.5	23.8	41.5
Extreme Maximum Temp. (°F)	66	72	84	89	94	105	105	100	97	92	77	73	105
Extreme Minimum Temp. (°F)	-23	-20	-3	7	27	35	43	40	29	19	6	-16	-23
Days Maximum Temp. ≥ 90°F	0	0	0	0	1	6	10	6	2	0	0	0	25
Days Maximum Temp. ≤ 32°F	16	10	3	0	0	0	0	0	0	0	1	8	38
Days Minimum Temp. ≤ 32°F	28	23	18	7	1	0	0	0	0	5	15	24	121
Days Minimum Temp. ≤ 0°F	5	3	0	0	0	0	0	0	0	0	0	1	9
Heating Degree Days (base 65°F)	1,268	1,020	765	428	161	20	2	6	79	349	691	1,047	5,836
Cooling Degree Days (base 65°F)	0	0	1	11	59	218	334	281	116	17	0	0	1,037
Mean Precipitation (in.)	1.74	1.47	2.95	3.65	3.78	4.14	3.92	3.86	2.91	2.40	2.97	2.53	36.32
Days With ≥ 0.1" Precipitation	4	4	7	7	7	6	6	6	5	5	6	6	69
Days With ≥ 1.0" Precipitation	0	0	0	1	1	1	1	1	1	0	1	0	7
Mean Snowfall (in.)	7.2	4.8	2.1	0.6	trace	0.0	0.0	0.0	0.0	0.3	0.9	5.7	21.6
Days With ≥ 1.0" Snow Depth	13	9	3	0	0	0	0	0	0	0	1	6	32

Whitestown *Boone County*   Elevation: 935 ft.   Latitude: 40° 00' N   Longitude: 86° 21' W

	JAN	FEB	MAR	APR	MAY	JUN	JUL	AUG	SEP	OCT	NOV	DEC	YEAR
Mean Maximum Temp. (°F)	33.0	38.7	50.1	62.9	73.9	82.6	85.7	83.9	78.1	65.7	51.1	38.7	62.0
Mean Temp. (°F)	24.4	29.2	39.8	51.3	62.0	71.0	74.4	72.2	65.5	53.8	42.0	30.8	51.4
Mean Minimum Temp. (°F)	15.8	19.6	29.5	39.5	50.1	59.4	62.9	60.5	52.9	41.9	32.8	22.9	40.7
Extreme Maximum Temp. (°F)	64	73	82	88	94	104	103	100	96	90	78	73	104
Extreme Minimum Temp. (°F)	-27	-20	-10	15	27	35	44	37	28	19	5	-22	-27
Days Maximum Temp. ≥ 90°F	0	0	0	0	1	5	8	5	2	0	0	0	21
Days Maximum Temp. ≤ 32°F	14	9	2	0	0	0	0	0	0	0	1	8	34
Days Minimum Temp. ≤ 32°F	28	24	20	8	1	0	0	0	0	6	16	25	128
Days Minimum Temp. ≤ 0°F	6	4	0	0	0	0	0	0	0	0	0	2	12
Heating Degree Days (base 65°F)	1,251	1,006	777	416	156	22	3	9	89	353	684	1,052	5,818
Cooling Degree Days (base 65°F)	0	0	2	11	71	224	319	254	118	15	0	0	1,014
Mean Precipitation (in.)	2.41	2.29	3.40	3.94	4.45	4.05	4.64	3.50	2.99	2.95	3.67	3.01	41.30
Days With ≥ 0.1" Precipitation	6	5	7	9	9	7	7	6	6	5	7	7	81
Days With ≥ 1.0" Precipitation	0	0	0	1	1	1	1	1	1	1	1	0	8
Mean Snowfall (in.)	9.1	6.0	3.0	0.3	0.0	0.0	0.0	0.0	0.0	0.3	1.0	5.7	25.4
Days With ≥ 1.0" Snow Depth	13	9	3	0	0	0	0	0	0	0	1	6	32

Winamac 2 SSE *Pulaski County*   Elevation: 688 ft.   Latitude: 41° 02' N   Longitude: 86° 35' W

	JAN	FEB	MAR	APR	MAY	JUN	JUL	AUG	SEP	OCT	NOV	DEC	YEAR
Mean Maximum Temp. (°F)	31.2	36.4	47.9	61.3	72.4	80.5	83.6	81.2	74.9	63.4	49.2	36.7	59.9
Mean Temp. (°F)	22.8	27.4	38.1	50.0	61.1	69.7	73.3	71.1	64.2	52.7	40.5	29.0	50.0
Mean Minimum Temp. (°F)	14.4	18.4	28.2	38.6	49.8	58.9	62.9	60.9	53.4	41.9	31.8	21.2	40.0
Extreme Maximum Temp. (°F)	63	75	86	92	93	102	100	102	100	86	78	71	102
Extreme Minimum Temp. (°F)	-29	-20	-8	8	28	32	43	36	29	20	4	-23	-29
Days Maximum Temp. ≥ 90°F	0	0	0	0	1	3	5	2	1	0	0	0	12
Days Maximum Temp. ≤ 32°F	16	10	3	0	0	0	0	0	0	0	2	10	41
Days Minimum Temp. ≤ 32°F	29	24	22	8	1	0	0	0	0	5	17	27	133
Days Minimum Temp. ≤ 0°F	6	4	0	0	0	0	0	0	0	0	0	2	12
Heating Degree Days (base 65°F)	1,302	1,054	829	456	177	32	5	12	107	384	728	1,111	6,197
Cooling Degree Days (base 65°F)	0	0	1	10	60	186	280	218	91	9	0	0	855
Mean Precipitation (in.)	1.92	1.64	2.77	3.65	3.79	4.05	3.93	3.83	3.38	2.96	3.05	2.53	37.50
Days With ≥ 0.1" Precipitation	5	5	7	8	7	7	7	6	6	5	7	6	76
Days With ≥ 1.0" Precipitation	0	0	0	1	1	1	1	1	1	1	1	0	8
Mean Snowfall (in.)	8.5	5.3	3.2	1.2	trace	0.0	0.0	0.0	0.0	0.1	2.1	5.4	25.8
Days With ≥ 1.0" Snow Depth	16	12	4	0	0	0	0	0	0	0	1	8	41

Winchester Airport 3E *Randolph County*   Elevation: 1,108 ft.   Latitude: 40° 11' N   Longitude: 84° 55' W

	JAN	FEB	MAR	APR	MAY	JUN	JUL	AUG	SEP	OCT	NOV	DEC	YEAR
Mean Maximum Temp. (°F)	32.0	36.2	47.3	59.8	70.9	79.8	83.3	81.4	75.6	63.2	49.4	37.8	59.7
Mean Temp. (°F)	24.2	27.7	38.2	49.6	60.7	69.7	73.2	71.2	64.8	53.0	41.1	30.4	50.3
Mean Minimum Temp. (°F)	16.3	19.1	29.0	39.3	50.4	59.6	63.1	60.9	53.9	42.5	32.8	22.9	40.8
Extreme Maximum Temp. (°F)	63	72	80	85	91	101	100	97	93	88	78	71	101
Extreme Minimum Temp. (°F)	-26	-18	-11	12	27	40	48	39	29	19	6	-22	-26
Days Maximum Temp. ≥ 90°F	0	0	0	0	0	2	4	2	1	0	0	0	9
Days Maximum Temp. ≤ 32°F	16	11	4	0	0	0	0	0	0	0	2	9	42
Days Minimum Temp. ≤ 32°F	29	24	21	8	0	0	0	0	0	4	16	25	127
Days Minimum Temp. ≤ 0°F	5	3	0	0	0	0	0	0	0	0	0	2	10
Heating Degree Days (base 65°F)	1,259	1,047	826	464	182	32	5	13	100	379	710	1,066	6,083
Cooling Degree Days (base 65°F)	0	0	1	8	58	184	273	210	98	13	0	0	845
Mean Precipitation (in.)	1.79	1.60	2.87	3.69	4.05	4.33	4.29	3.53	2.69	2.66	3.23	2.75	37.48
Days With ≥ 0.1" Precipitation	4	4	6	8	8	7	7	6	5	6	7	6	74
Days With ≥ 1.0" Precipitation	1	0	0	1	1	1	1	1	1	1	1	0	9
Mean Snowfall (in.)	5.1	4.9	2.7	0.3	trace	0.0	trace	0.0	0.0	trace	0.6	2.7	16.3
Days With ≥ 1.0" Snow Depth	12	10	3	0	0	0	0	0	0	0	1	5	31

Note: See Appendix D for explanation of data.

Annual Extreme Maximum Temperature

	Highest			Lowest	
Rank	Station Name	°F	Rank	Station Name	°F
1	Fort Wayne Baer Field	106	1	Cambridge City 3 N	100
1	Vevay	106	1	Richmond Water Works	100
3	Delphi 3 S	105	1	Valparaiso Waterworks	100
3	Frankfort Disposal Plant	105	4	Angola	101
3	Hobart 2 WNW	105	4	Greensburg	101
3	Wanatah 2 WNW	105	4	La Porte	101
3	West Lafayette Purdue Univ. Arpt.	105	4	Martinsville 2 SW	101
8	Berne	104	4	New Whiteland	101
8	Bloomington Indiana Univ.	104	4	Spencer	101
8	Bluffton 1 N	104	4	Winchester Airport 3E	101
8	Crane Naval Depot	104	11	Dubois S Ind. Forage Farm	102
8	English 4 S	104	11	Elwood Wastewater Plant	102
8	Indianapolis SE Side	104	11	Evansville Museum	102
8	Kentland	104	11	Evansville Regional Airport	102
8	Kokomo 3 WSW	104	11	Farmland 5 NNW	102
8	Lafayette 8 S	104	11	Goshen College	102
8	Lagrange Sewage Plant	104	11	Muncie	102
8	Lowell	104	11	Oaklandon Geist Reservoir	102
8	Madison Sewage Plant	104	11	Oolitic Purdue Exp. Farm	102
8	Rensselaer	104	11	Portland 1 SW	102
8	Rockville	104	11	Princeton 1 W	102
8	Seymour 2 N	104	11	Saint Meinrad	102
8	South Bend Michiana Regional	104	11	Shoals Hiway 50 Bridge	102
8	Washington	104	11	Terre Haute Indiana State	102
8	Whitestown	104	11	Winamac 2 SSE	102

Annual Mean Maximum Temperature

	Highest			Lowest	
Rank	Station Name	°F	Rank	Station Name	°F
1	Evansville Museum	67.7	1	Angola	57.3
2	English 4 S	66.9	2	Lagrange Sewage Plant	57.9
3	Saint Meinrad	66.6	3	La Porte	58.4
4	Vevay	66.5	4	Wanatah 2 WNW	58.8
5	Evansville Regional Airport	66.3	5	Columbia City	58.9
6	Crane Naval Depot	66.0	5	South Bend Michiana Regional	58.9
6	Tell City	66.0	7	Bluffton 1 N	59.1
8	Madison Sewage Plant	65.9	7	Rochester	59.1
8	Washington	65.9	9	Warsaw	59.2
10	Mount Vernon	65.8	10	Valparaiso Waterworks	59.3
11	Paoli	65.7	11	Goshen College	59.4
12	Salem	65.6	11	Hartford City 4 ESE	59.4
13	Princeton 1 W	65.2	13	Kokomo 3 WSW	59.5
14	Scottsburg	65.1	13	Lowell	59.5
15	Shoals Hiway 50 Bridge	64.7	15	Fort Wayne Baer Field	59.7
16	Dubois S Ind. Forage Farm	64.1	15	Winchester Airport 3E	59.7
16	Rockville	64.1	17	Portland 1 SW	59.8
18	Brookville	63.7	18	Rensselaer	59.9
19	Seymour 2 N	63.6	18	Winamac 2 SSE	59.9
19	Terre Haute Indiana State	63.6	20	Farmland 5 NNW	60.2
21	Oolitic Purdue Exp. Farm	63.5	20	Marion 2 N	60.2
22	Bloomington Indiana Univ.	63.4	20	West Lafayette 6 NW	60.2
23	Columbus	63.3	23	Anderson Sewage Plant	60.5
24	Martinsville 2 SW	62.7	23	Cambridge City 3 N	60.5
25	Spencer	62.5	23	Lafayette 8 S	60.5

Annual Mean Temperature

	Highest			Lowest	
Rank	Station Name	°F	Rank	Station Name	°F
1	Evansville Museum	57.7	1	Angola	47.4
2	Evansville Regional Airport	56.2	2	Lagrange Sewage Plant	48.2
3	Saint Meinrad	56.1	3	Columbia City	48.7
3	Washington	56.1	4	Wanatah 2 WNW	48.8
5	Tell City	55.9	5	Lowell	49.1
6	Mount Vernon	55.8	5	Rochester	49.1
7	Madison Sewage Plant	55.6	7	Kokomo 3 WSW	49.3
8	Crane Naval Depot	55.5	8	Bluffton 1 N	49.4
8	Princeton 1 W	55.5	9	Portland 1 SW	49.6
8	Vevay	55.5	9	Warsaw	49.6
11	Salem	54.7	11	Cambridge City 3 N	49.7
12	English 4 S	54.5	12	Hartford City 4 ESE	49.8
13	Scottsburg	54.0	12	La Porte	49.8
14	Dubois S Ind. Forage Farm	53.8	14	Farmland 5 NNW	49.9
14	Paoli	53.8	14	Valparaiso Waterworks	49.9
16	Bloomington Indiana Univ.	53.5	16	South Bend Michiana Regional	50.0
17	Rockville	53.4	16	Winamac 2 SSE	50.0
18	Shoals Hiway 50 Bridge	53.2	18	Elwood Wastewater Plant	50.1
19	Terre Haute Indiana State	52.9	18	Goshen College	50.1
20	Columbus	52.8	18	Marion 2 N	50.1
21	Indianapolis Int'l Airport	52.7	18	Rensselaer	50.1
22	Greensburg	52.6	22	Fort Wayne Baer Field	50.2
23	Greencastle 1 SE	52.5	22	New Castle 4 N	50.2
23	Seymour 2 N	52.5	24	West Lafayette 6 NW	50.3
25	Oolitic Purdue Exp. Farm	52.3	24	Winchester Airport 3E	50.3

Annual Mean Minimum Temperature

	Highest			Lowest	
Rank	Station Name	°F	Rank	Station Name	°F
1	Evansville Museum	47.6	1	Angola	37.5
2	Washington	46.2	2	Lagrange Sewage Plant	38.5
3	Evansville Regional Airport	45.9	3	Columbia City	38.6
4	Mount Vernon	45.7	4	Lowell	38.7
4	Princeton 1 W	45.7	4	Wanatah 2 WNW	38.7
4	Tell City	45.7	6	Cambridge City 3 N	38.8
7	Saint Meinrad	45.5	7	Kokomo 3 WSW	39.0
8	Madison Sewage Plant	45.3	8	Rochester	39.1
9	Crane Naval Depot	45.0	9	Portland 1 SW	39.3
10	Vevay	44.4	10	Elwood Wastewater Plant	39.4
11	Salem	43.8	11	Farmland 5 NNW	39.5
12	Bloomington Indiana Univ.	43.5	12	Bluffton 1 N	39.6
12	Dubois S Ind. Forage Farm	43.5	13	New Castle 4 N	39.8
14	Indianapolis Int'l Airport	43.0	13	Spencer	39.8
15	Greensburg	42.9	15	Warsaw	39.9
16	Scottsburg	42.8	16	Brookville	40.0
17	Rockville	42.7	16	Marion 2 N	40.0
18	Greencastle 1 SE	42.6	16	Winamac 2 SSE	40.0
19	Anderson Sewage Plant	42.3	19	Hartford City 4 ESE	40.2
19	Indianapolis SE Side	42.3	19	Hobart 2 WNW	40.2
21	Columbus	42.2	21	Lafayette 8 S	40.3
22	Terre Haute Indiana State	42.1	21	Rensselaer	40.3
23	English 4 S	41.9	21	West Lafayette 6 NW	40.3
23	Paoli	41.9	24	Valparaiso Waterworks	40.4
25	Berne	41.7	25	Richmond Water Works	40.5

Annual Extreme Minimum Temperature

Highest			Lowest		
Rank	Station Name	°F	Rank	Station Name	°F
1	Mount Vernon	-16	1	New Whiteland	-36
2	Evansville Museum	-17	2	Martinsville 2 SW	-35
2	Tell City	-17	3	Spencer	-33
4	Madison Sewage Plant	-18	4	Scottsburg	-32
5	Princeton 1 W	-19	5	Brookville	-31
5	Washington	-19	5	Cambridge City 3 N	-31
7	Bloomington Indiana Univ.	-21	5	English 4 S	-31
7	Evansville Regional Airport	-21	8	Greenfield	-29
7	South Bend Michiana Regional	-21	8	Hobart 2 WNW	-29
10	Fort Wayne Baer Field	-22	8	Muncie	-29
10	Indianapolis SE Side	-22	8	Oolitic Purdue Exp. Farm	-29
10	Lagrange Sewage Plant	-22	8	Paoli	-29
13	Crane Naval Depot	-23	8	Portland 1 SW	-29
13	Greencastle 1 SE	-23	8	Salem	-29
13	La Porte	-23	8	Winamac 2 SSE	-29
13	Marion 2 N	-23	16	Lowell	-28
13	Oaklandon Geist Reservoir	-23	16	Rushville Sewage Plant	-28
13	Seymour 2 N	-23	18	Angola	-27
13	Shoals Hiway 50 Bridge	-23	18	Indianapolis Int'l Airport	-27
13	West Lafayette Purdue Univ. Arpt.	-23	18	Richmond Water Works	-27
21	Anderson Sewage Plant	-24	18	Whitestown	-27
21	Berne	-24	22	Columbus	-26
21	Bluffton 1 N	-24	22	Frankfort Disposal Plant	-26
21	Columbia City	-24	22	Hartford City 4 ESE	-26
21	Delphi 3 S	-24	22	Kokomo 3 WSW	-26

July Mean Maximum Temperature

Highest			Lowest		
Rank	Station Name	°F	Rank	Station Name	°F
1	Evansville Museum	89.7	1	Angola	82.1
2	Evansville Regional Airport	88.9	2	Lagrange Sewage Plant	82.9
3	Vevay	88.5	3	La Porte	83.0
4	Mount Vernon	88.4	3	Warsaw	83.0
5	Washington	88.3	5	Columbia City	83.3
6	Princeton 1 W	88.2	5	Valparaiso Waterworks	83.3
7	English 4 S	88.1	5	Winchester Airport 3E	83.3
8	Paoli	87.9	8	Hartford City 4 ESE	83.4
9	Crane Naval Depot	87.8	8	South Bend Michiana Regional	83.4
9	Tell City	87.8	8	Wanatah 2 WNW	83.4
11	Scottsburg	87.5	11	Cambridge City 3 N	83.5
12	Rockville	87.4	12	Winamac 2 SSE	83.6
13	Saint Meinrad	87.3	13	Anderson Sewage Plant	83.7
13	Terre Haute Indiana State	87.3	13	Bluffton 1 N	83.7
15	Madison Sewage Plant	87.2	15	Rochester	83.9
16	Salem	87.0	16	Kokomo 3 WSW	84.0
17	Brookville	86.9	16	New Castle 4 N	84.0
18	North Vernon 1 NW	86.8	16	Portland 1 SW	84.0
18	Shoals Hiway 50 Bridge	86.8	19	Goshen College	84.1
20	Greencastle 1 SE	86.2	19	West Lafayette 6 NW	84.1
20	West Lafayette Purdue Univ. Arpt.	86.2	21	Farmland 5 NNW	84.2
22	Bloomington Indiana Univ.	86.1	22	Frankfort Disposal Plant	84.4
23	Columbus	86.0	22	Lowell	84.4
23	Dubois S Ind. Forage Farm	86.0	22	Oaklandon Geist Reservoir	84.4
25	Kentland	85.9	22	Rushville Sewage Plant	84.4

January Mean Minimum Temperature

Highest			Lowest		
Rank	Station Name	°F	Rank	Station Name	°F
1	Evansville Museum	24.4	1	Lowell	12.9
2	Madison Sewage Plant	23.3	2	Wanatah 2 WNW	13.4
2	Tell City	23.3	3	Angola	13.5
4	Saint Meinrad	23.2	4	Rochester	14.1
5	Washington	23.1	5	Kokomo 3 WSW	14.2
6	Evansville Regional Airport	22.9	5	Lagrange Sewage Plant	14.2
7	Vevay	22.7	7	Columbia City	14.3
8	Mount Vernon	22.3	8	Winamac 2 SSE	14.4
9	Salem	22.0	9	Warsaw	14.7
10	Crane Naval Depot	21.5	9	West Lafayette 6 NW	14.7
10	Princeton 1 W	21.5	11	Hartford City 4 ESE	14.8
12	North Vernon 1 NW	21.2	11	Lafayette 8 S	14.8
13	English 4 S	20.8	13	Bluffton 1 N	15.1
14	Dubois S Ind. Forage Farm	19.8	13	Kentland	15.1
14	Scottsburg	19.8	15	Elwood Wastewater Plant	15.2
16	Bloomington Indiana Univ.	19.3	16	Cambridge City 3 N	15.3
17	Paoli	19.2	16	Rensselaer	15.3
18	Greensburg	19.1	16	Valparaiso Waterworks	15.3
19	Seymour 2 N	18.9	19	Farmland 5 NNW	15.4
19	Shoals Hiway 50 Bridge	18.9	20	Hobart 2 WNW	15.5
21	Anderson Sewage Plant	18.7	21	Portland 1 SW	15.6
22	Columbus	18.6	22	La Porte	15.8
23	Indianapolis Int'l Airport	18.4	22	Whitestown	15.8
24	Martinsville 2 SW	18.0	24	Marion 2 N	16.0
25	Indianapolis SE Side	17.9	24	New Castle 4 N	16.0

Number of Annual Heating Degree Days

Highest			Lowest		
Rank	Station Name	Num.	Rank	Station Name	Num.
1	Angola	6,933	1	Evansville Museum	4,188
2	Lagrange Sewage Plant	6,713	2	Saint Meinrad	4,446
3	Wanatah 2 WNW	6,569	3	Washington	4,554
4	Columbia City	6,524	4	Evansville Regional Airport	4,568
5	Lowell	6,508	5	Madison Sewage Plant	4,569
6	Rochester	6,467	6	Tell City	4,590
7	Kokomo 3 WSW	6,414	7	Vevay	4,626
8	Bluffton 1 N	6,389	8	Crane Naval Depot	4,646
9	Portland 1 SW	6,308	9	Mount Vernon	4,665
10	Warsaw	6,289	10	Princeton 1 W	4,754
11	La Porte	6,263	11	Salem	4,798
12	Rensselaer	6,240	12	English 4 S	4,813
13	Farmland 5 NNW	6,222	13	Paoli	5,088
14	Hartford City 4 ESE	6,220	14	Scottsburg	5,099
15	Cambridge City 3 N	6,204	15	Dubois S Ind. Forage Farm	5,113
15	Valparaiso Waterworks	6,204	16	Bloomington Indiana Univ.	5,238
17	South Bend Michiana Regional	6,203	17	Shoals Hiway 50 Bridge	5,246
18	Winamac 2 SSE	6,197	18	Rockville	5,252
19	Goshen College	6,168	19	Columbus	5,389
20	Marion 2 N	6,167	20	Seymour 2 N	5,403
21	West Lafayette 6 NW	6,151	21	Terre Haute Indiana State	5,420
22	Elwood Wastewater Plant	6,142	22	Greensburg	5,443
23	Fort Wayne Baer Field	6,141	23	Indianapolis Int'l Airport	5,467
24	Hobart 2 WNW	6,124	24	Oolitic Purdue Exp. Farm	5,479
25	Lafayette 8 S	6,109	25	Greencastle 1 SE	5,551

Number of Annual Cooling Degree Days

Highest			Lowest		
Rank	Station Name	Num.	Rank	Station Name	Num.
1	Evansville Museum	1,687	1	Angola	631
2	Evansville Regional Airport	1,477	2	Cambridge City 3 N	703
3	Washington	1,418	3	Columbia City	715
4	Princeton 1 W	1,413	4	Lagrange Sewage Plant	716
5	Mount Vernon	1,407	5	Wanatah 2 WNW	768
6	Tell City	1,402	6	New Castle 4 N	794
7	Crane Naval Depot	1,323	7	Rochester	798
8	Vevay	1,312	8	Warsaw	801
9	Saint Meinrad	1,308	9	Kokomo 3 WSW	806
10	Madison Sewage Plant	1,241	10	Valparaiso Waterworks	809
11	Scottsburg	1,189	11	Portland 1 SW	816
12	Dubois S Ind. Forage Farm	1,188	12	Lowell	822
13	Rockville	1,179	13	Bluffton 1 N	828
14	Paoli	1,168	14	Spencer	834
15	Salem	1,160	15	La Porte	838
16	Terre Haute Indiana State	1,156	16	Winchester Airport 3E	845
17	Bloomington Indiana Univ.	1,154	17	Elwood Wastewater Plant	849
18	Greencastle 1 SE	1,097	17	Goshen College	849
19	Indianapolis Int'l Airport	1,089	19	South Bend Michiana Regional	850
20	Columbus	1,083	20	Farmland 5 NNW	851
21	English 4 S	1,082	21	Winamac 2 SSE	855
22	Shoals Hiway 50 Bridge	1,073	22	Hartford City 4 ESE	859
23	Greensburg	1,067	23	Richmond Water Works	861
24	Greenfield	1,037	24	Marion 2 N	876
24	West Lafayette Purdue Univ. Arpt.	1,037	25	Fort Wayne Baer Field	877

Annual Precipitation

Highest			Lowest		
Rank	Station Name	Inches	Rank	Station Name	Inches
1	English 4 S	49.55	1	West Lafayette Purdue Univ. Arpt.	36.32
2	Tell City	48.17	2	Fort Wayne Baer Field	36.52
3	Crane Naval Depot	47.55	3	Bluffton 1 N	36.60
4	Paoli	47.49	4	Goshen College	36.65
5	Dubois S Ind. Forage Farm	47.35	5	Lagrange Sewage Plant	36.71
6	Shoals Hiway 50 Bridge	47.31	6	Warsaw	36.77
7	Saint Meinrad	46.40	7	Lafayette 8 S	36.88
8	Evansville Museum	46.24	8	Portland 1 SW	37.13
9	Princeton 1 W	46.01	8	West Lafayette 6 NW	37.13
10	Mount Vernon	45.73	10	Angola	37.29
11	Seymour 2 N	45.64	11	Winchester Airport 3E	37.48
12	Salem	45.58	12	Winamac 2 SSE	37.50
13	Spencer	45.51	13	Farmland 5 NNW	37.51
14	Madison Sewage Plant	45.49	13	Hartford City 4 ESE	37.51
15	Washington	45.45	15	Hobart 2 WNW	37.82
16	Vevay	44.82	16	Wanatah 2 WNW	38.01
17	Bloomington Indiana Univ.	44.72	17	Delphi 3 S	38.06
18	Scottsburg	44.68	18	Muncie	38.34
19	Rockville	44.52	19	Columbia City	38.35
20	Oolitic Purdue Exp. Farm	44.49	20	Berne	38.41
21	Evansville Regional Airport	44.23	21	Rochester	38.48
22	Greencastle 1 SE	43.95	22	Kentland	38.58
23	Greenfield	43.41	23	Marion 2 N	38.80
24	North Vernon 1 NW	43.40	23	Rensselaer	38.80
25	Greensburg	43.25	25	Richmond Water Works	39.40

Number of Days Annually With ≥ 0.1" Precipitation

	Highest			Lowest	
Rank	Station Name	Days	Rank	Station Name	Days
1	Seymour 2 N	86	1	West Lafayette Purdue Univ. Arpt.	69
2	English 4 S	84	2	Crane Naval Depot	71
2	La Porte	84	2	Delphi 3 S	71
4	Kokomo 3 WSW	83	2	West Lafayette 6 NW	71
4	Madison Sewage Plant	83	5	Hobart 2 WNW	72
4	South Bend Michiana Regional	83	5	Lafayette 8 S	72
4	Vevay	83	7	Hartford City 4 ESE	74
8	Cambridge City 3 N	82	7	Indianapolis SE Side	74
8	Greenfield	82	7	Rensselaer	74
8	Salem	82	7	Wanatah 2 WNW	74
8	Scottsburg	82	7	Warsaw	74
8	Shoals Hiway 50 Bridge	82	7	Winchester Airport 3E	74
13	Brookville	81	13	Fort Wayne Baer Field	75
13	Columbia City	81	13	Goshen College	75
13	Dubois S Ind. Forage Farm	81	13	Kentland	75
13	Greensburg	81	13	North Vernon 1 NW	75
13	Oaklandon Geist Reservoir	81	13	Portland 1 SW	75
13	Valparaiso Waterworks	81	18	Evansville Regional Airport	76
13	Whitestown	81	18	Farmland 5 NNW	76
20	Anderson Sewage Plant	80	18	Princeton 1 W	76
20	Berne	80	18	Winamac 2 SSE	76
20	Paoli	80	22	Angola	77
23	Bloomington Indiana Univ.	79	22	Columbus	77
23	Frankfort Disposal Plant	79	22	Indianapolis Int'l Airport	77
23	Saint Meinrad	79	22	Marion 2 N	77

Number of Days Annually With ≥ 1.0" Precipitation

	Highest			Lowest	
Rank	Station Name	Days	Rank	Station Name	Days
1	Crane Naval Depot	14	1	Anderson Sewage Plant	7
2	Mount Vernon	13	1	Berne	7
2	Paoli	13	1	Bluffton 1 N	7
2	Washington	13	1	Elwood Wastewater Plant	7
5	Bloomington Indiana Univ.	12	1	Fort Wayne Baer Field	7
5	Dubois S Ind. Forage Farm	12	1	Lafayette 8 S	7
5	English 4 S	12	1	Lagrange Sewage Plant	7
5	Evansville Museum	12	1	Muncie	7
5	Madison Sewage Plant	12	1	West Lafayette Purdue Univ. Arpt.	7
5	Princeton 1 W	12	10	Angola	8
5	Rockville	12	10	Columbia City	8
5	Saint Meinrad	12	10	Delphi 3 S	8
5	Salem	12	10	Farmland 5 NNW	8
5	Scottsburg	12	10	Frankfort Disposal Plant	8
5	Shoals Hiway 50 Bridge	12	10	Goshen College	8
5	Tell City	12	10	Hartford City 4 ESE	8
5	Vevay	12	10	Hobart 2 WNW	8
18	Evansville Regional Airport	11	10	Indianapolis SE Side	8
18	Greencastle 1 SE	11	10	Marion 2 N	8
18	North Vernon 1 NW	11	10	New Castle 4 N	8
18	Oolitic Purdue Exp. Farm	11	10	Rensselaer	8
18	Rushville Sewage Plant	11	10	Richmond Water Works	8
18	Seymour 2 N	11	10	Rochester	8
18	Terre Haute Indiana State	11	10	South Bend Michiana Regional	8
25	Brookville	10	10	Wanatah 2 WNW	8

Annual Snowfall

	Highest			Lowest	
Rank	**Station Name**	**Inches**	**Rank**	**Station Name**	**Inches**
1	South Bend Michiana Regional	76.6	1	Tell City	9.2
2	La Porte	61.5	2	Saint Meinrad	9.7
3	Wanatah 2 WNW	44.5	3	Washington	11.5
4	Kokomo 3 WSW	43.1	4	Columbus	13.1
5	Valparaiso Waterworks	39.8	5	Mount Vernon	13.7
6	Lagrange Sewage Plant	38.7	6	Evansville Museum	13.8
7	Goshen College	38.2	7	Evansville Regional Airport	14.8
8	Fort Wayne Baer Field	34.8	8	Madison Sewage Plant	15.3
9	Angola	33.6	8	Oolitic Purdue Exp. Farm	15.3
10	Lowell	33.1	10	Shoals Hiway 50 Bridge	15.6
11	Rochester	32.5	11	Rushville Sewage Plant	16.1
12	Columbia City	31.5	12	Rockville	16.3
13	Berne	30.7	12	Winchester Airport 3E	16.3
14	Bluffton 1 N	27.9	14	Scottsburg	16.7
15	Hobart 2 WNW	27.4	15	Spencer	16.9
16	Greencastle 1 SE	27.3	16	Martinsville 2 SW	17.7
17	Kentland	26.7	17	Anderson Sewage Plant	17.8
18	Indianapolis Int'l Airport	26.4	18	Greensburg	18.0
19	Marion 2 N	26.2	18	Salem	18.0
20	Hartford City 4 ESE	26.0	20	Vevay	18.6
21	Winamac 2 SSE	25.8	21	Richmond Water Works	18.7
22	Farmland 5 NNW	25.7	22	Delphi 3 S	20.5
23	Frankfort Disposal Plant	25.6	23	Portland 1 SW	21.0
23	Muncie	25.6	24	West Lafayette 6 NW	21.5
25	Whitestown	25.4	25	West Lafayette Purdue Univ. Arpt.	21.6

Note: See User's Guide for explanation of data.

Deadliest Storm Events in Indiana: June 1985 - May 2010

Rank	Location or County	Date	Storm Event	Fatalities	Injuries	Property Damage ($mil.)	Crop Damage ($mil.)
1	Evansville	11/6/2005	Tornado (F3)	20	200	15.0	0.0
2	Statewide	7/13/1995	Heat Wave	14	0	1.0	0.0
3	Pike County	6/2/1990	Tornado (F4)	6	60	25.0	0.0
4	Newburgh	11/6/2005	Tornado (F3)	4	30	65.0	0.0
5	Statewide	1/14/1994	Extreme Cold	3	0	5.0	0.0
6	Lafayette	4/26/1994	Tornado (F4)	3	70	5.0	0.0
7	Crawfordsville	5/13/1995	Tornado (F2)	3	5	3.5	0.0
8	South Central Indiana	1/4/2004	Flood	3	0	0.0	0.0
9	Leopold	5/25/2006	Flash Flood	3	0	0.0	0.0
10	Greenwood	6/26/2008	Tstm Wind (52 kts.)	3	2	0.0	0.0
11	Clinton County	6/3/1990	Tstm Wind	2	2	0.0	0.0
12	Seymour	4/20/1996	Tstm Wind	2	0	0.1	0.0
13	Liberty	7/19/1998	Tstm Wind (60 kts.)	2	6	0.0	0.0
14	West Fork of the Whitewater River at Alpine	1/22/1999	Flood	2	0	0.0	0.0
15	Adams, Grant, Huntington, and White Counties	1/22/1999	Flood	2	0	0.0	0.0
16	Carroll County	7/5/2003	Flash Flood	2	0	7.0	0.0
17	Lake Michigan (Beverly Shores)	7/26/2005	Rip Current	2	0	0.0	0.0
18	Rochester	1/8/2008	Flood	2	1	0.1	0.0
19	La Porte County	1/19/2008	Cold/Wind Chill	2	0	0.0	0.0
20	La Porte County	1/19/2008	Cold/Wind Chill	2	0	0.0	0.0
21	Stewartsville	1/29/2008	Tornado (F2)	2	0	0.2	0.0
22	Ogden Dunes	9/14/2008	Flash Flood	2	0	2.0	0.0
23	South Central Indiana	9/14/2008	High Wind (56 kts.)	2	0	0.0	0.0

Source: National Oceanic and Atmospheric Administration, National Environmental Satellite, Data, and Information Service, NCDC Storm Events Database

Most Destructive Storm Events in Indiana: June 1985 - May 2010

Rank	Location or County	Date	Storm Event	Fatalities	Injuries	Property Damage ($mil.)	Crop Damage ($mil.)
1	Garden	6/5/2008	Flood	0	0	150.0	150.0
2	East Columbus	6/7/2008	Flash Flood	0	0	100.0	0.0
3	Princes Lakes	6/7/2008	Flash Flood	0	0	90.0	90.0
4	Centerton	6/4/2008	Flood	0	0	80.0	100.0
5	Newburgh	11/6/2005	Tornado (F3)	4	30	65.0	0.0
6	Ohio River	3/2/1997	Flood	0	0	60.0	0.0
7	Terre Haute	6/1/2008	Flood	0	0	50.0	50.0
8	Spencer	6/4/2008	Flood	0	0	50.0	60.0
9	Bowling Green	6/4/2008	Flood	0	0	45.0	45.0
10	Central Indiana	7/5/2003	Flood	0	0	41.6	12.0
11	Southport	9/20/2002	Tornado (F2)	0	97	40.0	0.0
12	Freeman Airport	6/5/2008	Flood	0	0	30.0	30.0
13	Lawrence	5/30/2008	Tornado (F2)	0	18	29.0	0.0
14	Randolph County	3/10/1986	Tornado (F3)	0	0	25.0	0.0
15	Gibson County	4/3/1989	Tornado (F3)	0	8	25.0	0.0
16	Gibson County	6/2/1990	Tornado (F4)	0	0	25.0	0.0
17	Pike County	6/2/1990	Tornado (F4)	6	60	25.0	0.0
18	Steuben County	3/27/1991	Tornado (F3)	1	6	25.0	0.0
19	Nobel County	7/14/1992	Tornado (F2)	0	28	25.0	0.0
20	DeKalb County	7/14/1992	Tornado (F2)	0	0	25.0	0.0
21	Greenwood	9/20/2002	Tornado (F3)	0	0	25.0	0.0
22	Carroll, Howard, and Tippecanoe Counties	7/5/2003	Flood	0	0	24.0	9.0
23	Princes Lakes	6/3/2008	Tornado (F2)	0	3	23.0	0.0
24	Central Indiana	9/1/2003	Flood	0	0	22.0	0.0
25	Elliston	6/4/2008	Flood	0	0	20.0	60.0
26	Plainville	6/5/2008	Flood	0	0	20.0	30.0

Source: National Oceanic and Atmospheric Administration, National Environmental Satellite, Data, and Information Service, NCDC Storm Events Database

Demographic and Reference Maps

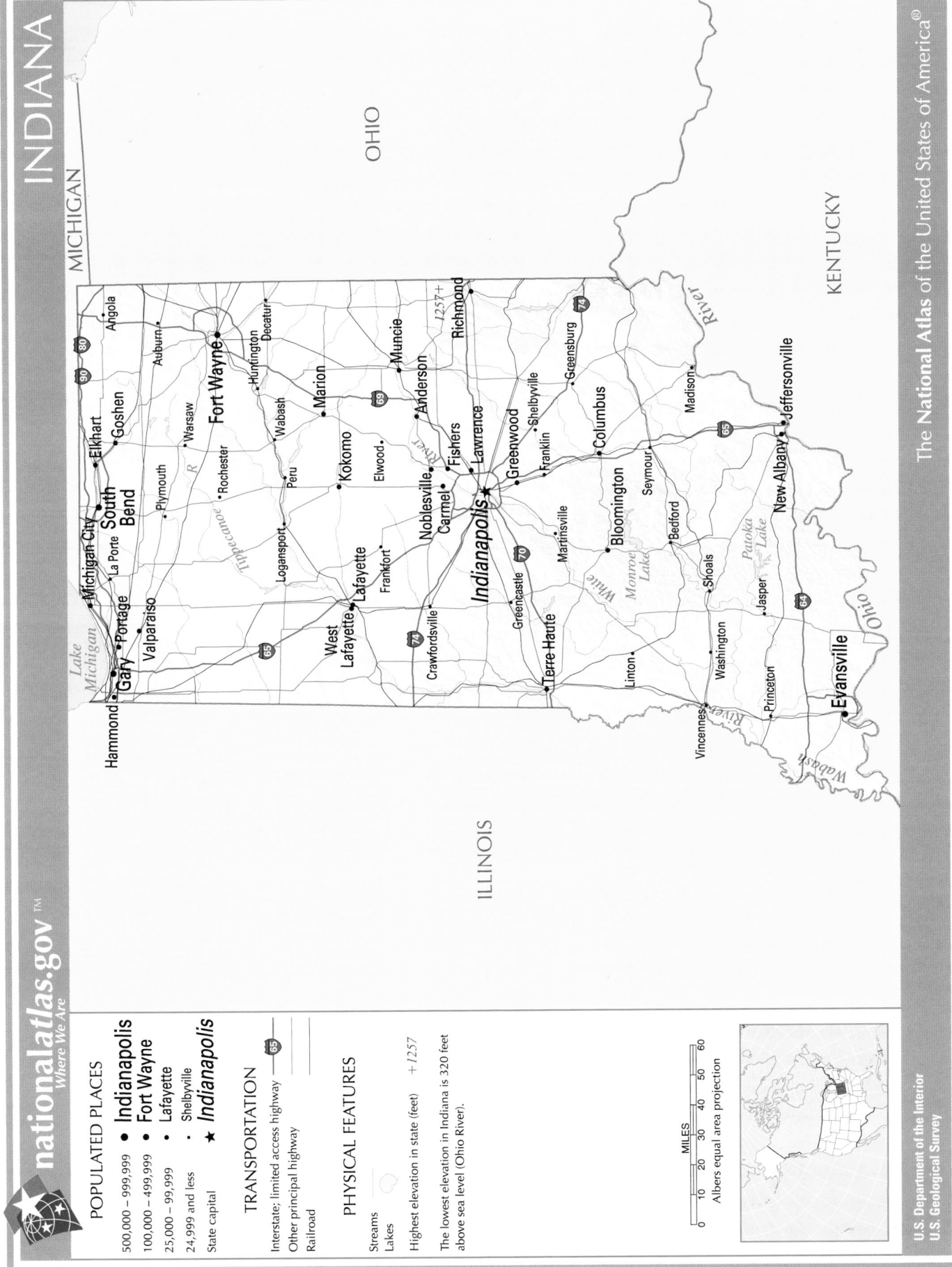

INDIANA

MICHIGAN

OHIO

ILLINOIS

KENTUCKY

The National Atlas of the United States of America®

POPULATED PLACES

500,000 – 999,999 ● Indianapolis
100,000 – 499,999 ● Fort Wayne
25,000 – 99,999 ● Lafayette
24,999 and less · Shelbyville
State capital ★ *Indianapolis*

TRANSPORTATION

Interstate; limited access highway
Other principal highway
Railroad

PHYSICAL FEATURES

Streams
Lakes
Highest elevation in state (feet) +1257

The lowest elevation in Indiana is 320 feet
above sea level (Ohio River).

MILES
0 10 20 30 40 50 60
Albers equal area projection

U.S. Department of the Interior
U.S. Geological Survey

Lake Michigan

Hammond
Gary
Portage
Valparaiso
Michigan City
La Porte
South Bend
Elkhart
Goshen
Angola
Auburn
Warsaw
Plymouth
Rochester
Fort Wayne
Huntington
Decatur
Wabash
Marion
Muncie
Richmond
1257+
Anderson
Kokomo
Peru
Logansport
Elwood
Fishers
Lawrence
Noblesville
Carmel
Greenwood
Shelbyville
Greensburg
Frankfort
Lafayette
West Lafayette
Indianapolis
Franklin
Columbus
Madison
Jeffersonville
New Albany
Crawfordsville
Greencastle
Martinsville
Bloomington
Seymour
Bedford
Shoals
Terre Haute
Linton
Washington
Vincennes
Princeton
Jasper
Patoka Lake
Evansville
Tippecanoe
White River
Wabash
Ohio River

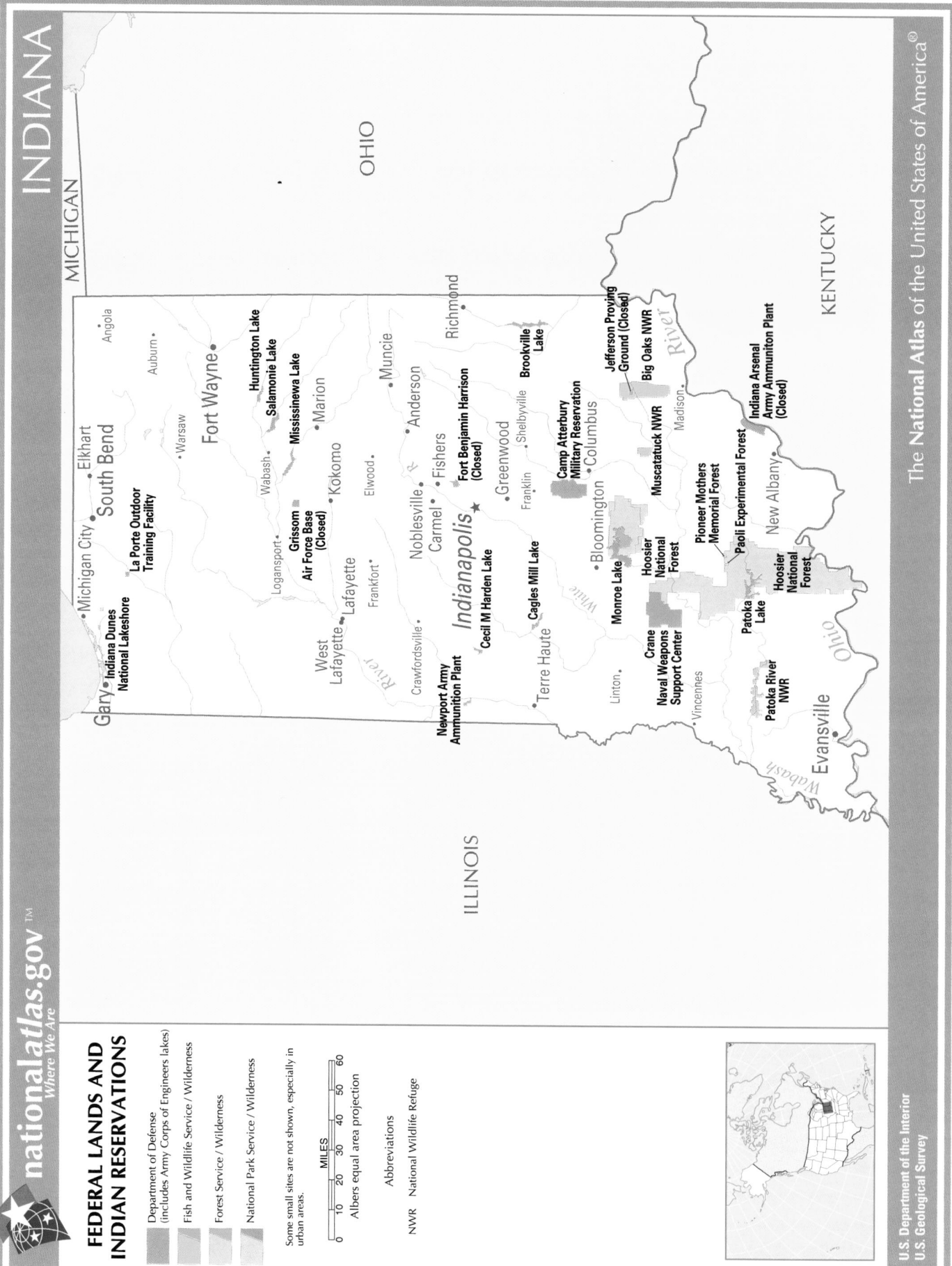

INDIANA

The **National Atlas** of the United States of America®

nationalatlas.gov ™
Where We Are

FEDERAL LANDS AND INDIAN RESERVATIONS

Department of Defense
(includes Army Corps of Engineers lakes)

Fish and Wildlife Service / Wilderness

Forest Service / Wilderness

National Park Service / Wilderness

Some small sites are not shown, especially in urban areas.

Abbreviations

NWR   National Wildlife Refuge

MILES

0   10   20   30   40   50   60

Albers equal area projection

U.S. Department of the Interior
U.S. Geological Survey

MICHIGAN

OHIO

KENTUCKY

ILLINOIS

Angola

Auburn

Fort Wayne

Elkhart

South Bend

Michigan City

Gary • Indiana Dunes
National Lakeshore

La Porte Outdoor
Training Facility

Warsaw

Huntington Lake

Salamonie Lake

Mississinewa Lake

Marion

Wabash

Logansport

Grissom
Air Force Base
(Closed)

Kokomo

Elwood

Frankfort

Lafayette

West
Lafayette

Newport Army
Ammunition Plant

Crawfordsville

Terre Haute

Linton

Vincennes

Muncie

Anderson

Noblesville   Fishers

Carmel

Indianapolis

Cecil M Harden Lake

Cagles Mill Lake

Monroe Lake

Crane
Naval Weapons
Support Center

Patoka River
NWR

Evansville

Hoosier
National
Forest

Patoka
Lake

Hoosier
National
Forest

Bloomington

Richmond

Shelbyville

Greenwood

Franklin

Columbus

Camp Atterbury
Military Reservation

Brookville
Lake

Jefferson Proving
Ground (Closed)

Big Oaks NWR

Madison

Muscatatuck NWR

Pioneer Mothers
Memorial Forest

Paoli Experimental Forest

New Albany

Indiana Arsenal
Army Ammuniton Plant
(Closed)

Fort Benjamin Harrison
(Closed)

River

White

Wabash

Ohio

River

INDIANA - Core Based Statistical Areas and Counties

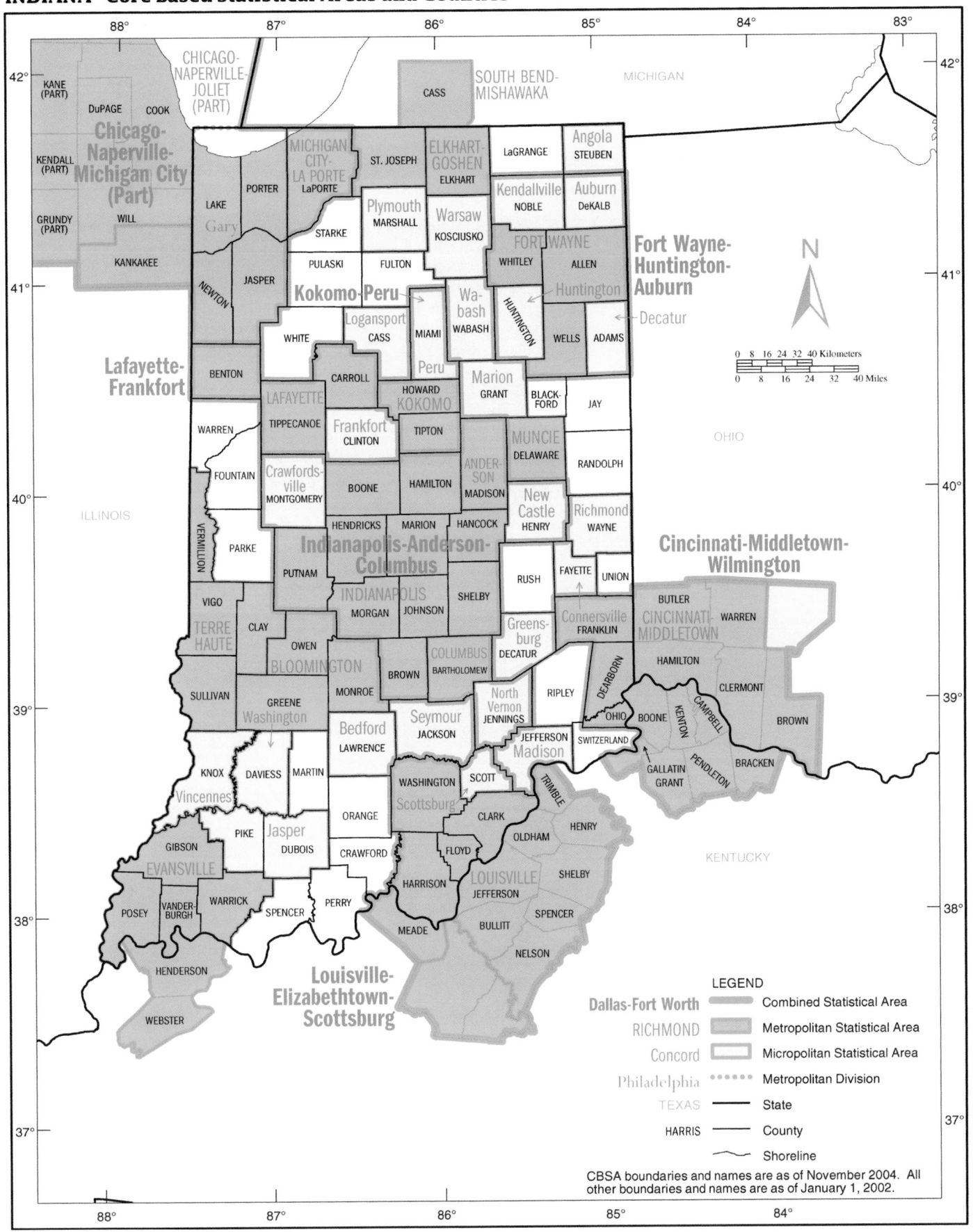

LEGEND

Dallas-Fort Worth	Combined Statistical Area
RICHMOND	Metropolitan Statistical Area
Concord	Micropolitan Statistical Area
Philadelphia	Metropolitan Division
TEXAS	State
HARRIS	County
	Shoreline

CBSA boundaries and names are as of November 2004. All other boundaries and names are as of January 1, 2002.

INDIANA

MICHIGAN

OHIO

KENTUCKY

ILLINOIS

nationalatlas.gov ™
Where We Are

CONGRESSIONAL DISTRICTS
110th Congress (January 2006 - January 2008)

The Constitution prescribes Congressional apportionment based on decennial census population data. Each state has at least one Representative, no matter how small its population. Since 1941, distribution of Representatives has been based on total U.S. population, so that the average population per Representative has the least possible variation between one state and any other. Congress fixes the number of voting Representatives at each apportionment. States delineate the district boundaries. The first House of Representatives in 1789 had 65 members; currently there are 435. There are non-voting delegates from American Samoa, the District of Columbia, Guam, Puerto Rico, and the Virgin Islands.

1
2
3
4
5
6
7
8
9

MILES
0   10   20   30   40   50   60
Albers equal area projection

U.S. Department of the Interior
U.S. Geological Survey

The **National Atlas** of the United States of America®

Lake Michigan

Gary
Michigan City
South Bend
Elkhart
Fort Wayne
Angola
DeKalb
Auburn
Allen
Steuben
LaGrange
Noble
Whitley
Warsaw
Koscuisko
Marshall
St Joseph
LaPorte
Starke
Pulaski
Fulton
Miami
Wabash
Huntington
Wells
Adams
Jay
Blackford
Grant
Marion
Muncie
Randolph
Delaware
Anderson
Madison
Elwood
Henry
Wayne
Richmond
Fayette
Union
Franklin
Kokomo
Tipton
Hamilton
Noblesville
Fishers
Carmel
Indianapolis
Marion
Hancock
Rush
Shelbyville
Greenwood
Shelby
Johnson
Decatur
Columbus
Bartholomew
Brown
Jennings
Ripley
Dearborn
Ohio
Switzerland
Jefferson
Madison
Scott
Clark
New Albany
Floyd
Harrison
Washington
Jackson
Lawrence
Orange
Crawford
Perry
Spencer
Evansville
Vanderburgh
Warrick
Gibson
Posey
Dubois
Pike
Knox
Vincennes
Daviess
Martin
Greene
Monroe
Bloomington
Owen
Clay
Terre Haute
Vigo
Sullivan
Linton
Parke
Vermillion
Warren
Fountain
Montgomery
Crawfordsville
Boone
Clinton
Frankfort
Tippecanoe
Lafayette
West Lafayette
Carroll
White
Benton
Newton
Jasper
Porter
Lake
Logansport
Cass
Putnam
Hendricks
Morgan
Brown

1
2
3
4
5
6
7
8
9

Economic Losses from Hazard Events, 1960-2005

State of Indiana

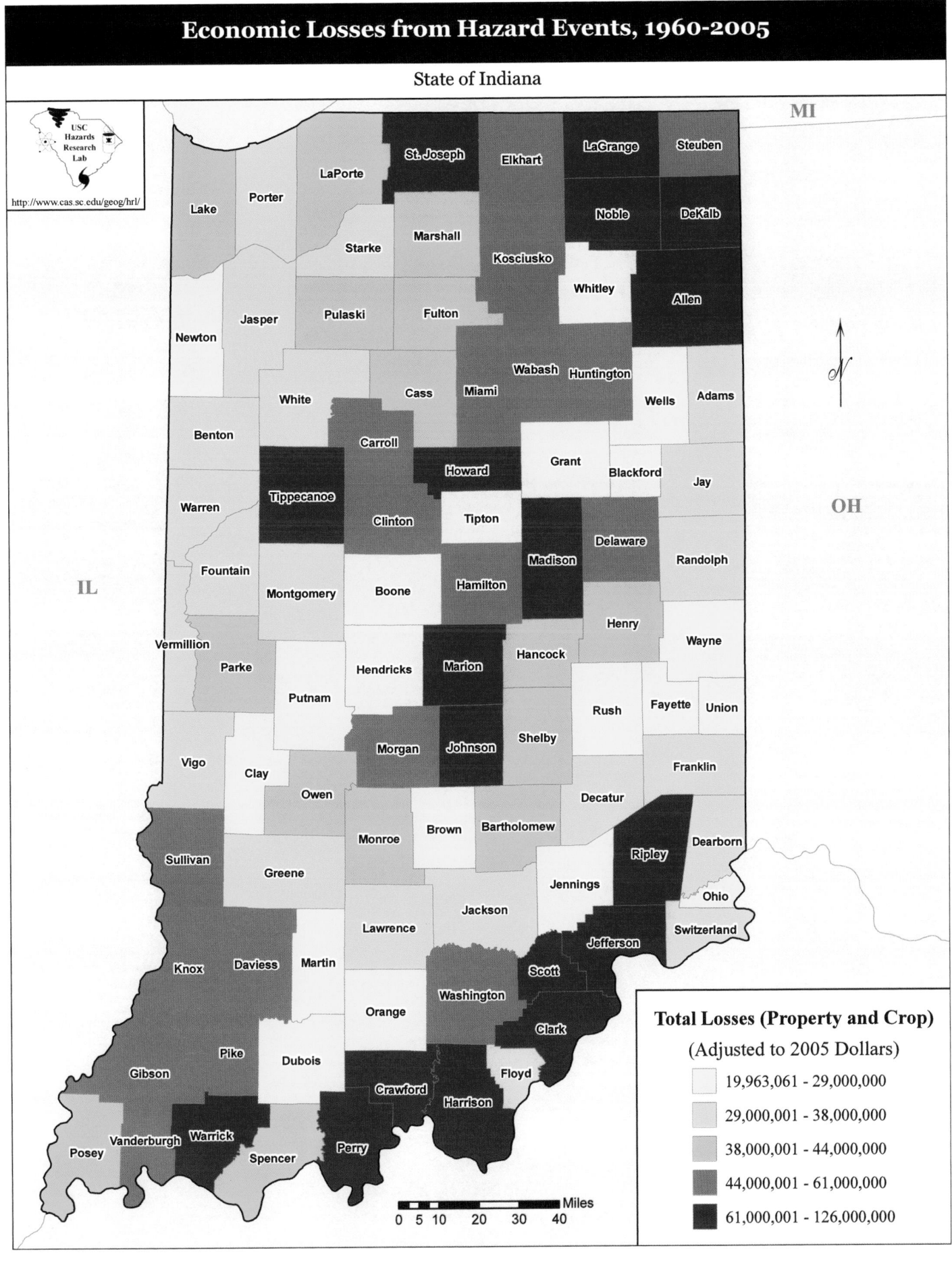

Total Losses (Property and Crop)

(Adjusted to 2005 Dollars)

- 19,963,061 - 29,000,000
- 29,000,001 - 38,000,000
- 38,000,001 - 44,000,000
- 44,000,001 - 61,000,000
- 61,000,001 - 126,000,000

Population (2010)

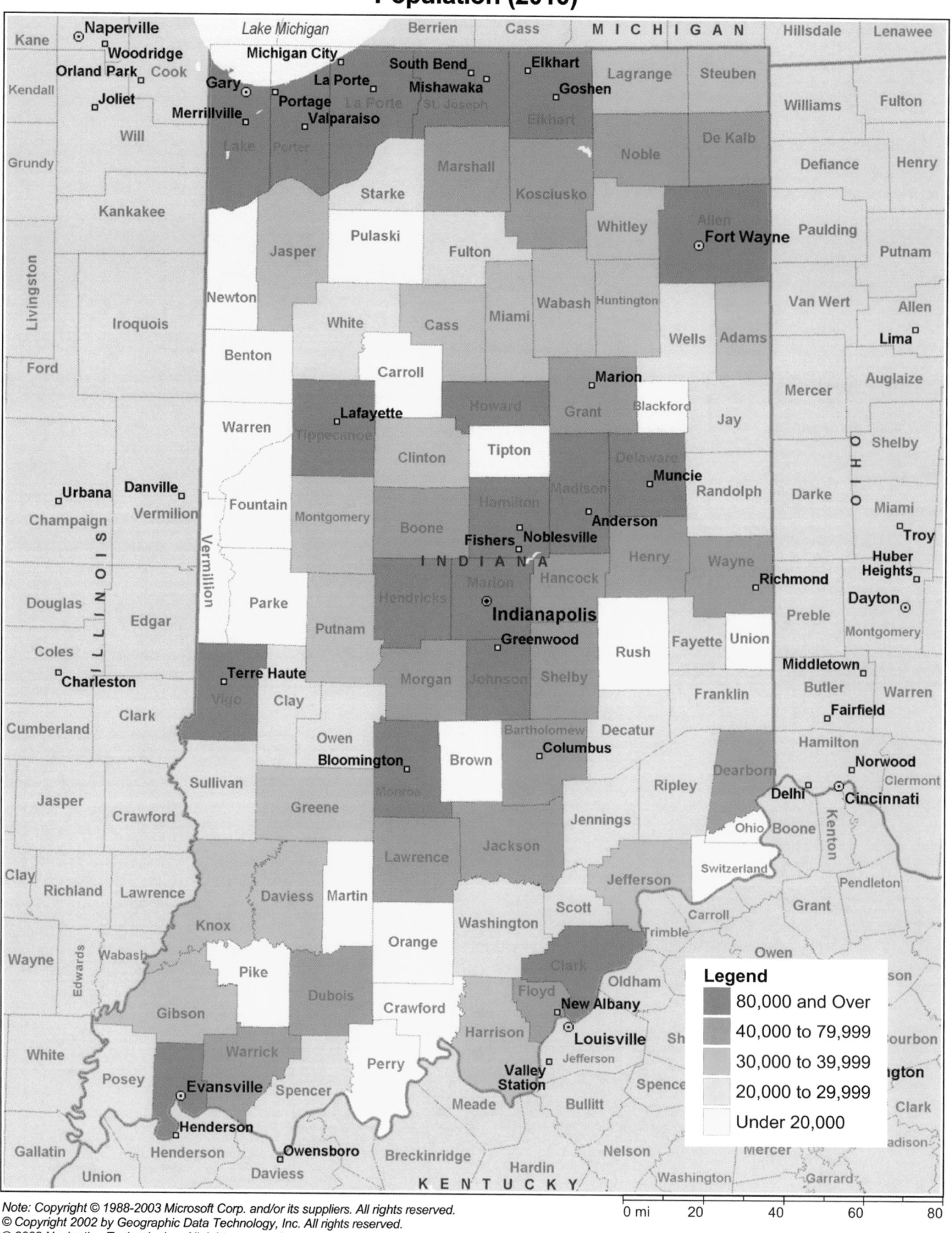

Legend

■	80,000 and Over
■	40,000 to 79,999
■	30,000 to 39,999
■	20,000 to 29,999
□	Under 20,000

0 mi   20   40   60   80

Percent White (2010)

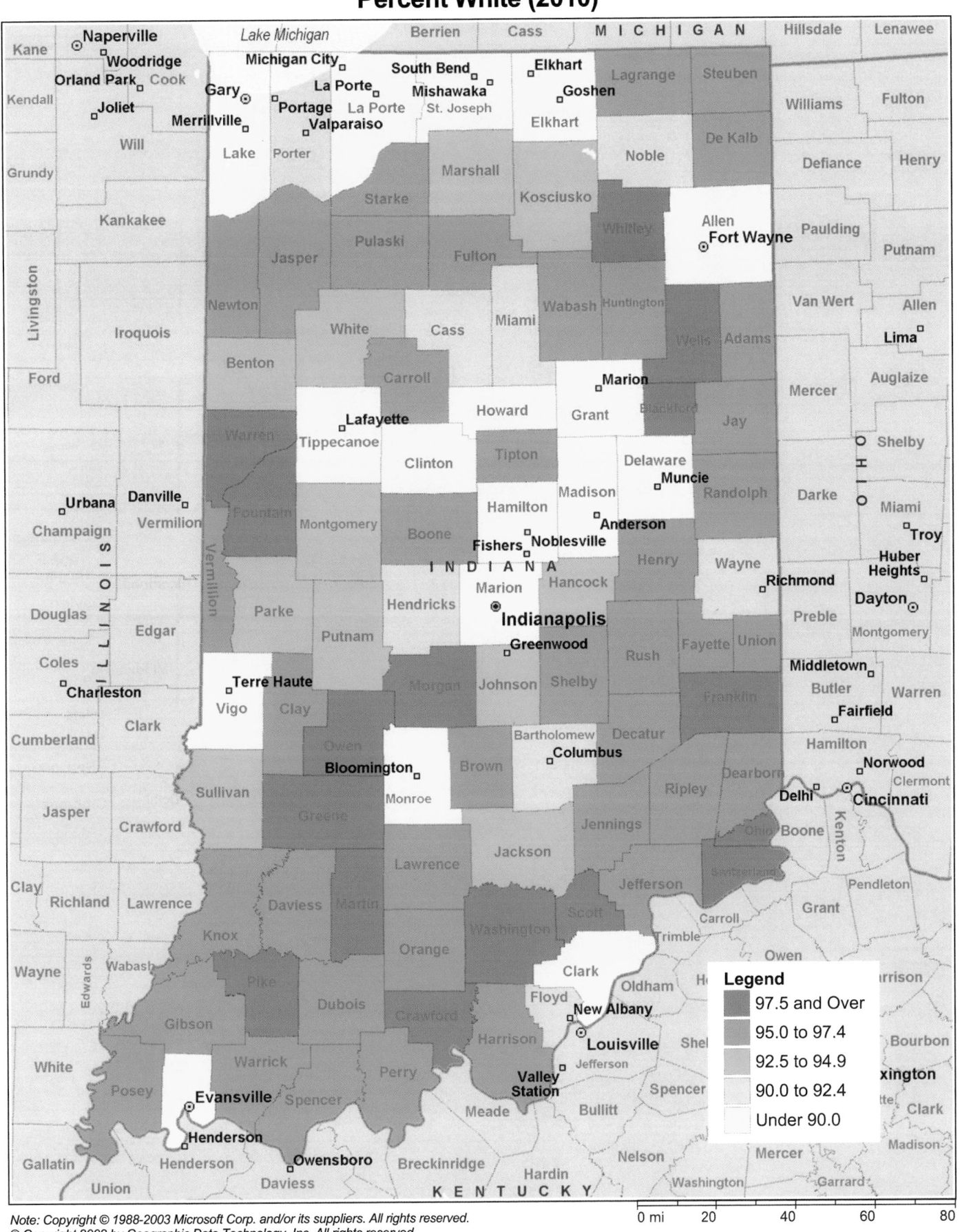

Legend

	97.5 and Over
	95.0 to 97.4
	92.5 to 94.9
	90.0 to 92.4
	Under 90.0

0 mi   20   40   60   80

Percent Black (2010)

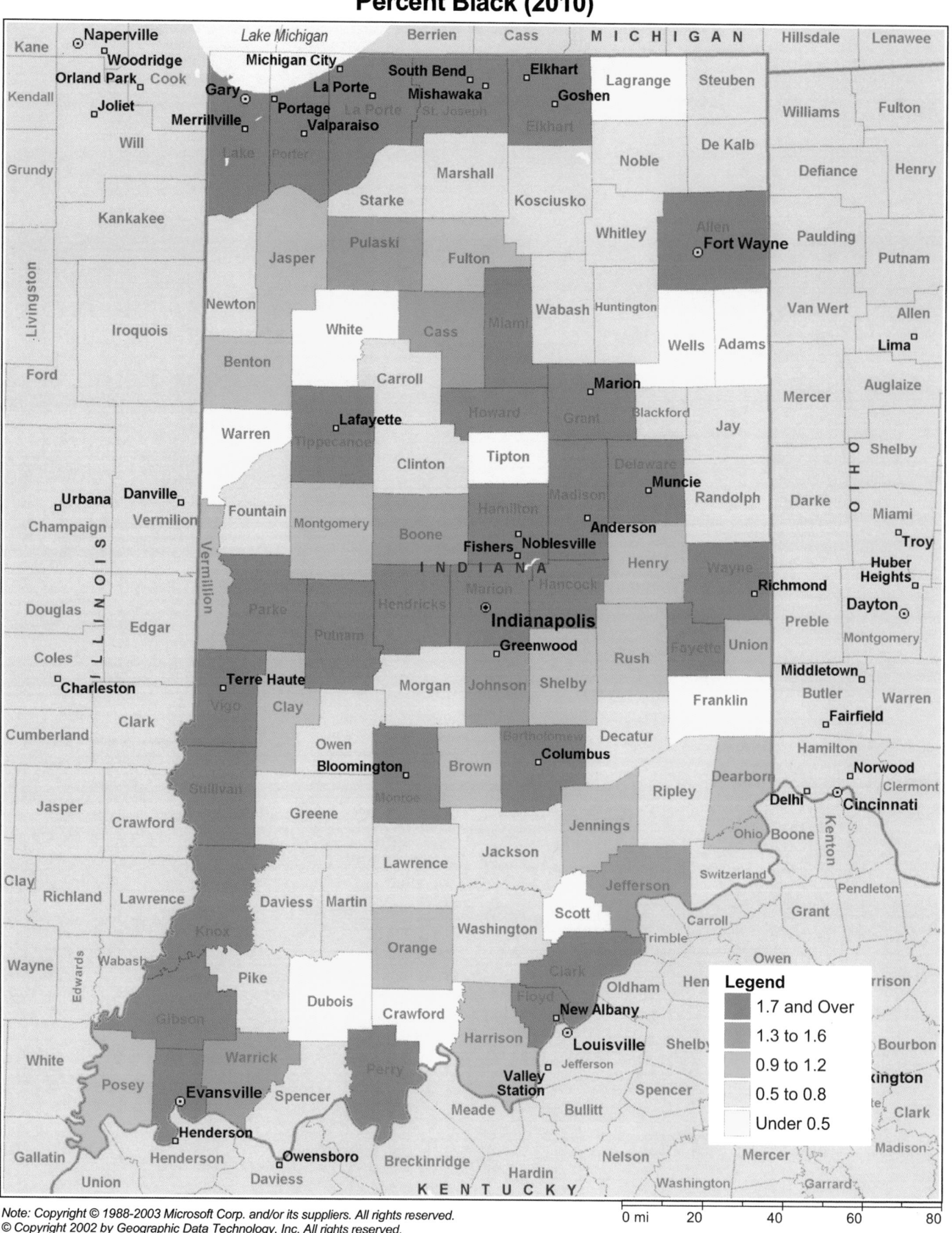

Legend

■	1.7 and Over
■	1.3 to 1.6
■	0.9 to 1.2
■	0.5 to 0.8
□	Under 0.5

0 mi   20   40   60   80

Percent Asian (2010)

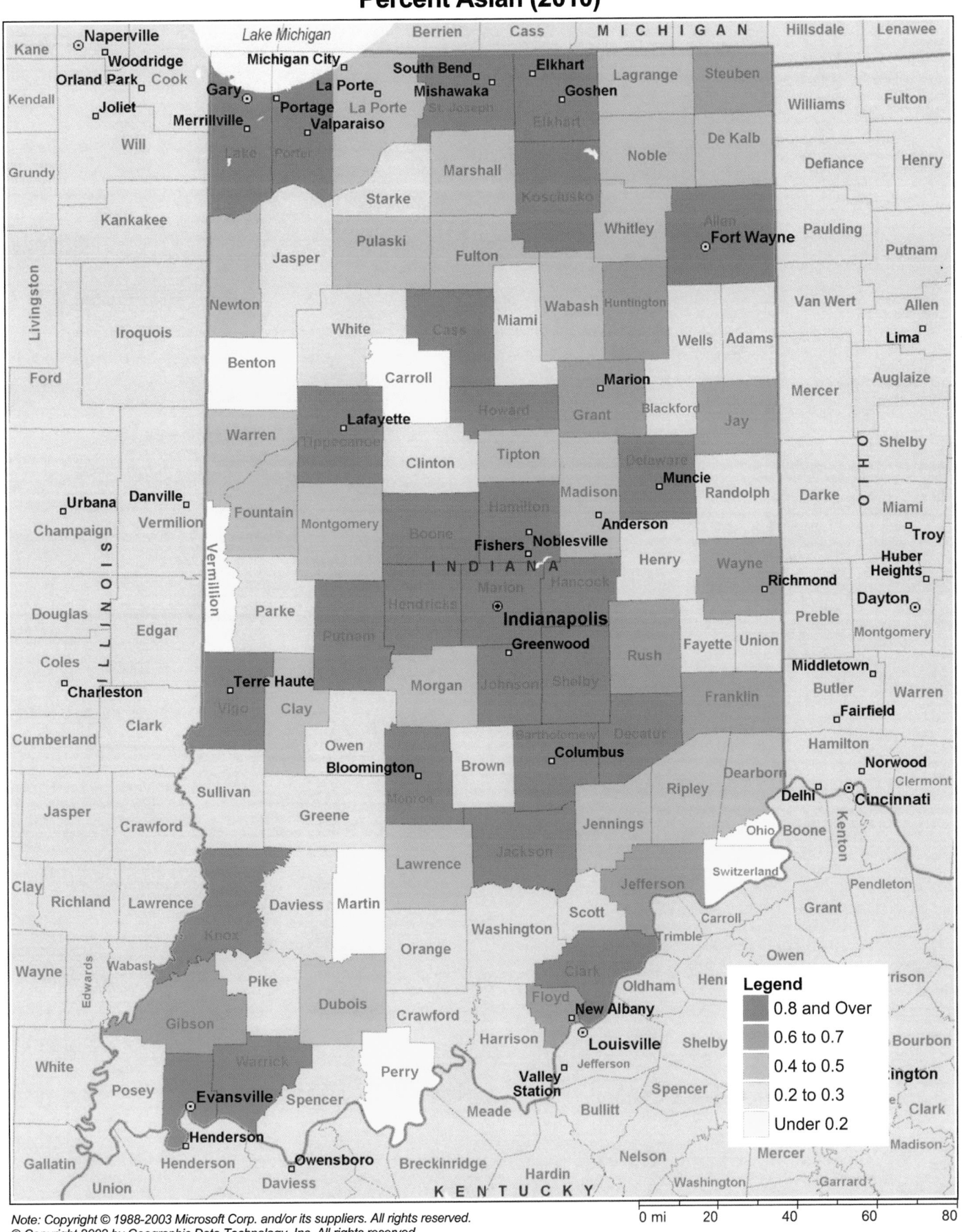

Legend

▓	0.8 and Over
▒	0.6 to 0.7
░	0.4 to 0.5
	0.2 to 0.3
	Under 0.2

0 mi   20   40   60   80

Percent Hispanic (2010)

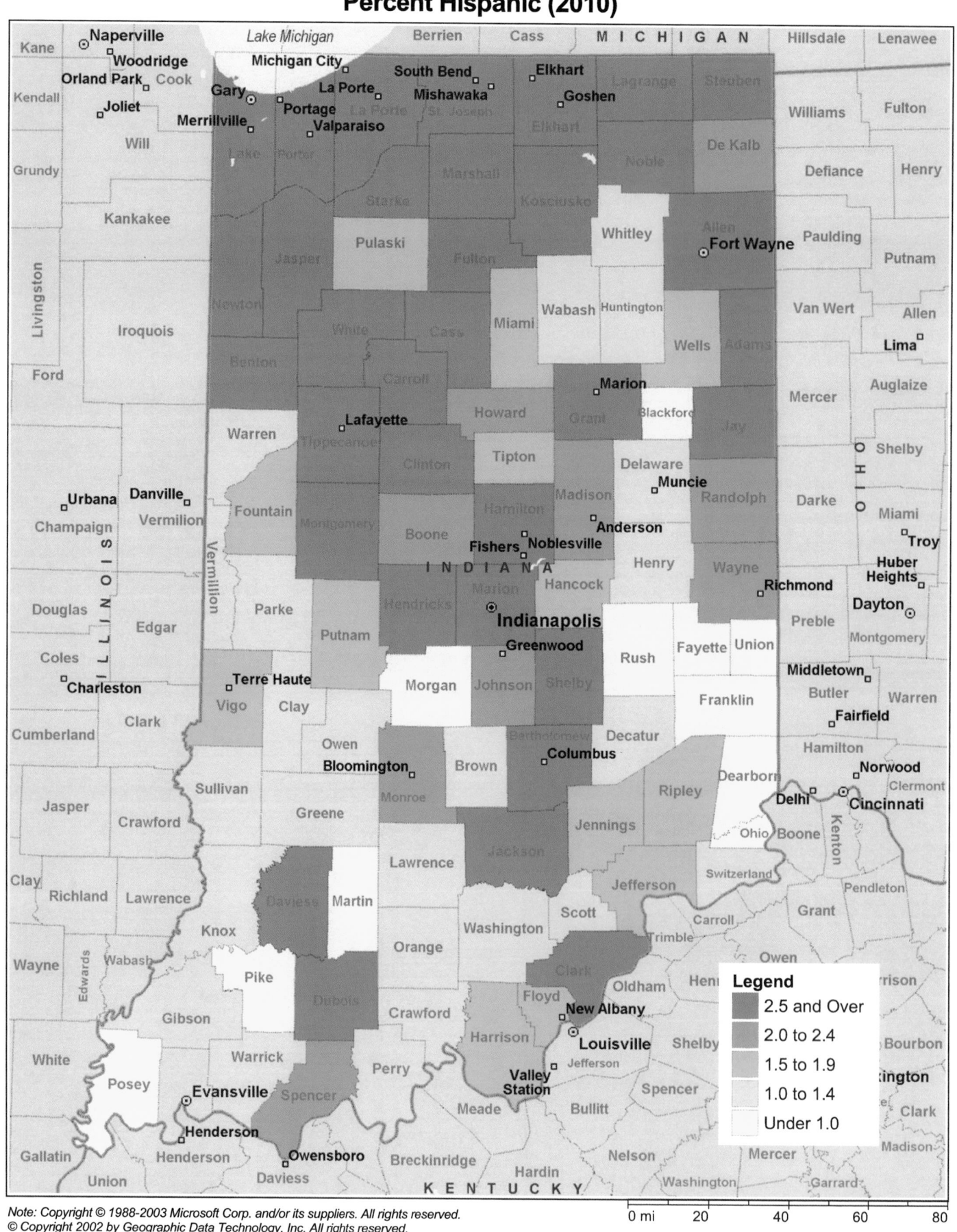

Legend

- 2.5 and Over
- 2.0 to 2.4
- 1.5 to 1.9
- 1.0 to 1.4
- Under 1.0

0 mi   20   40   60   80

Median Age (2010)

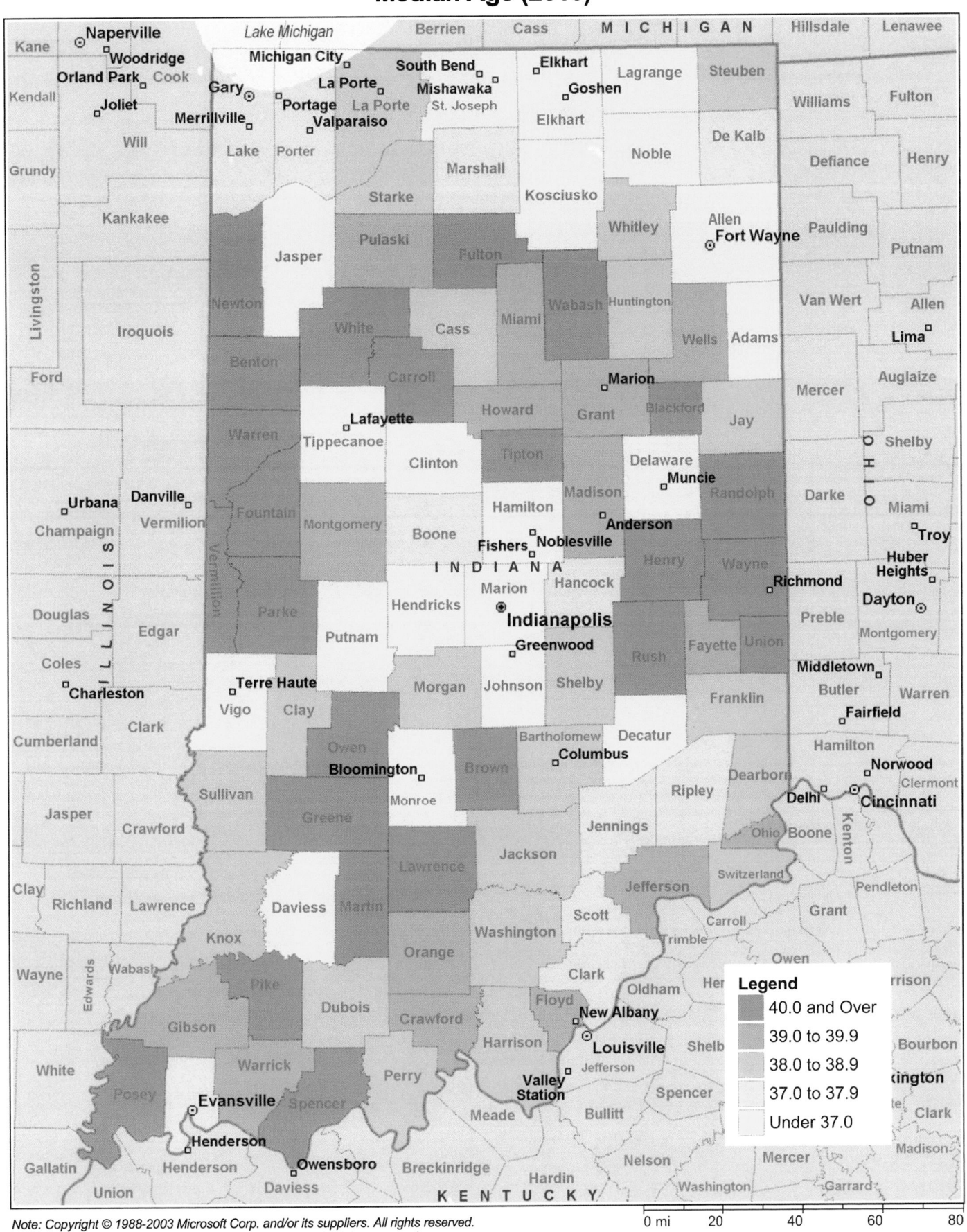

Legend

	40.0 and Over
	39.0 to 39.9
	38.0 to 38.9
	37.0 to 37.9
	Under 37.0

0 mi   20   40   60   80

Median Household Income (2010)

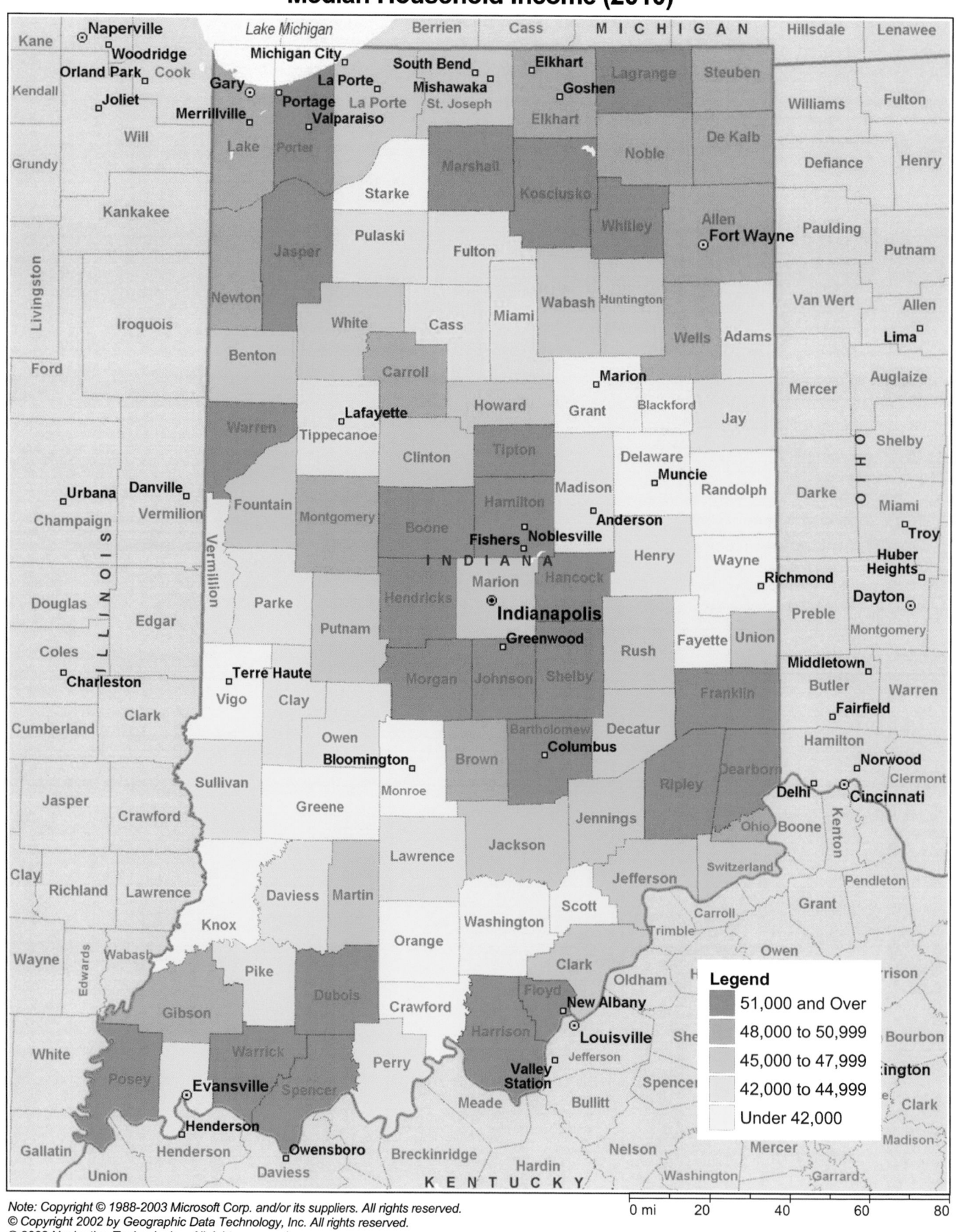

Legend
- 51,000 and Over
- 48,000 to 50,999
- 45,000 to 47,999
- 42,000 to 44,999
- Under 42,000

0 mi   20   40   60   80

Median Home Value (2010)

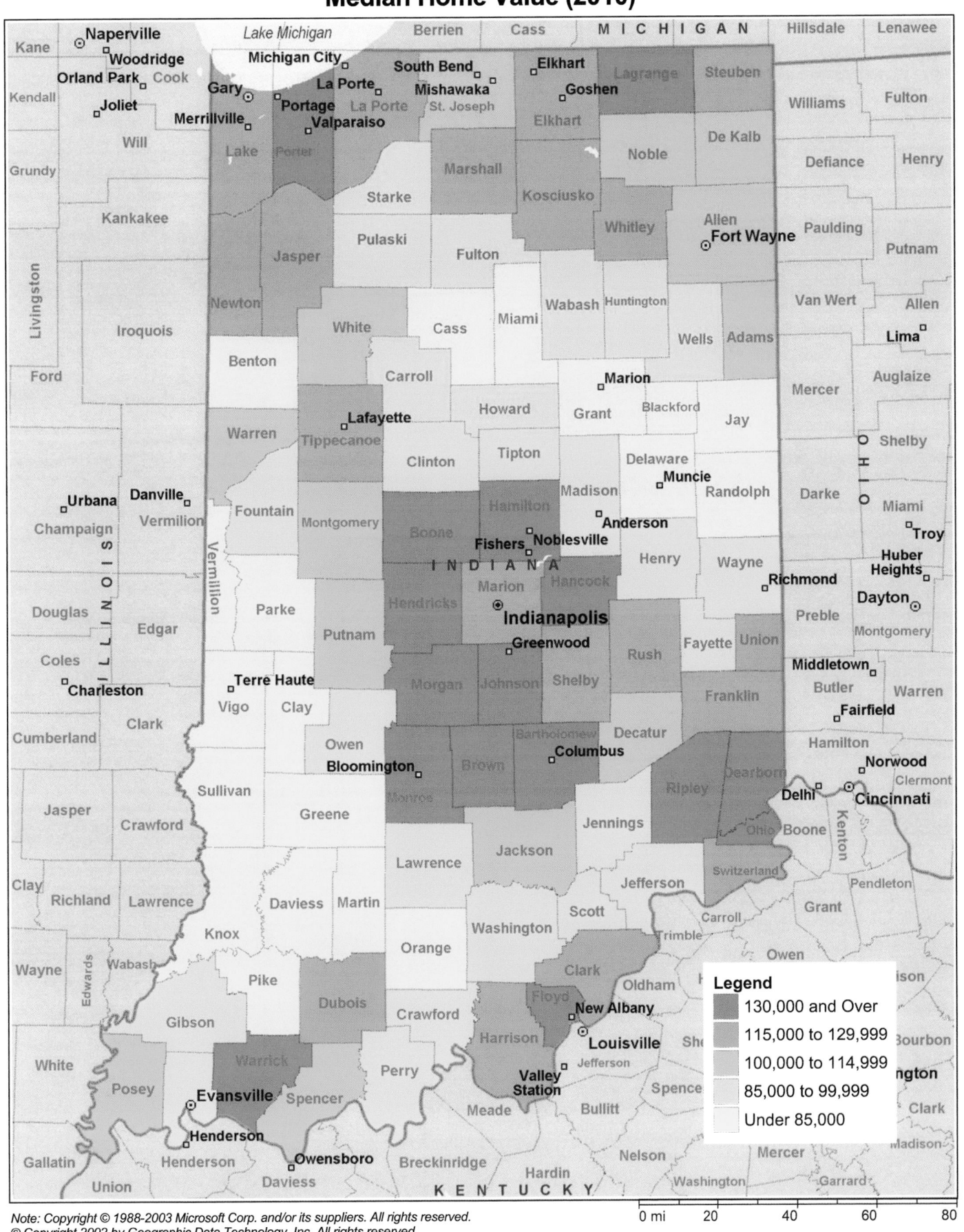

Legend
- 130,000 and Over
- 115,000 to 129,999
- 100,000 to 114,999
- 85,000 to 99,999
- Under 85,000

0 mi   20   40   60   80

High School Graduates* (2010)

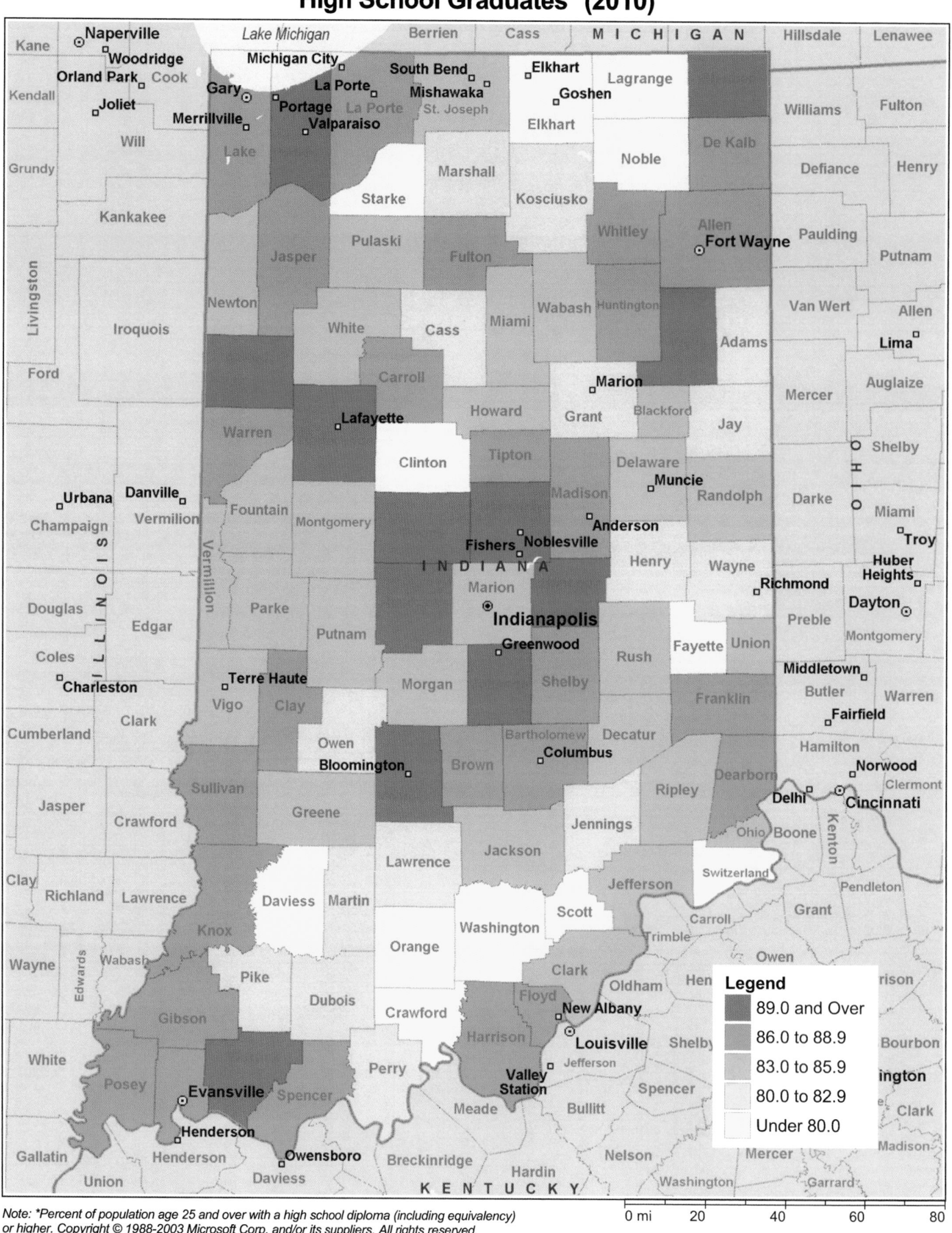

Legend

■	89.0 and Over
■	86.0 to 88.9
■	83.0 to 85.9
□	80.0 to 82.9
□	Under 80.0

*Note: *Percent of population age 25 and over with a high school diploma (including equivalency) or higher. Copyright © 1988-2003 Microsoft Corp. and/or its suppliers. All rights reserved.*
© Copyright 2002 by Geographic Data Technology, Inc. All rights reserved.
© 2002 Navigation Technologies. All rights reserved.*

0 mi   20   40   60   80

College Graduates* (2010)

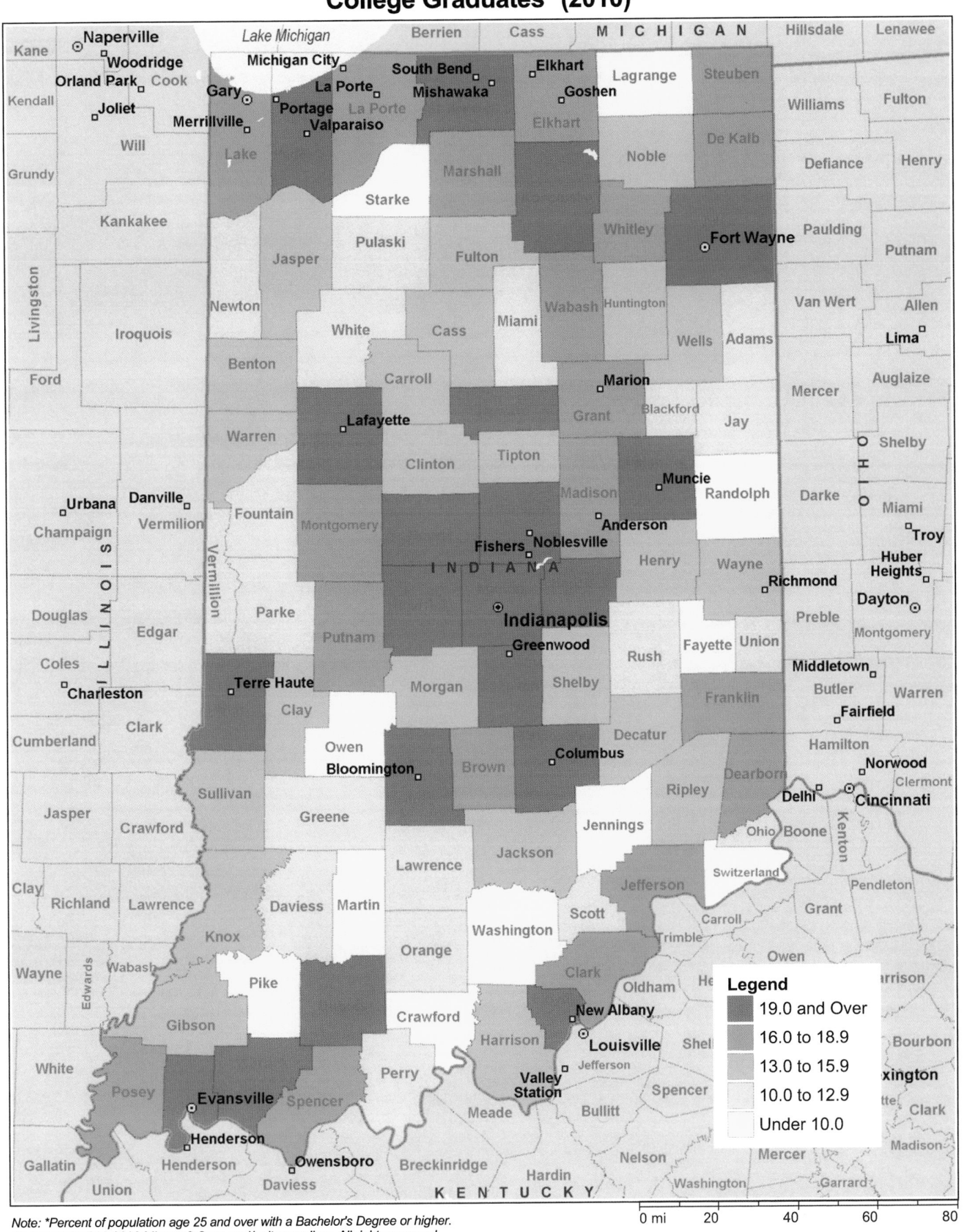

Legend

	19.0 and Over
	16.0 to 18.9
	13.0 to 15.9
	10.0 to 12.9
	Under 10.0

0 mi   20   40   60   80

*Note: *Percent of population age 25 and over with a Bachelor's Degree or higher.*
Copyright © 1988-2003 Microsoft Corp. and/or its suppliers. All rights reserved.
© Copyright 2002 by Geographic Data Technology, Inc. All rights reserved.
© 2002 Navigation Technologies. All rights reserved.

Percent of Population Who Voted for Barack Obama in 2008

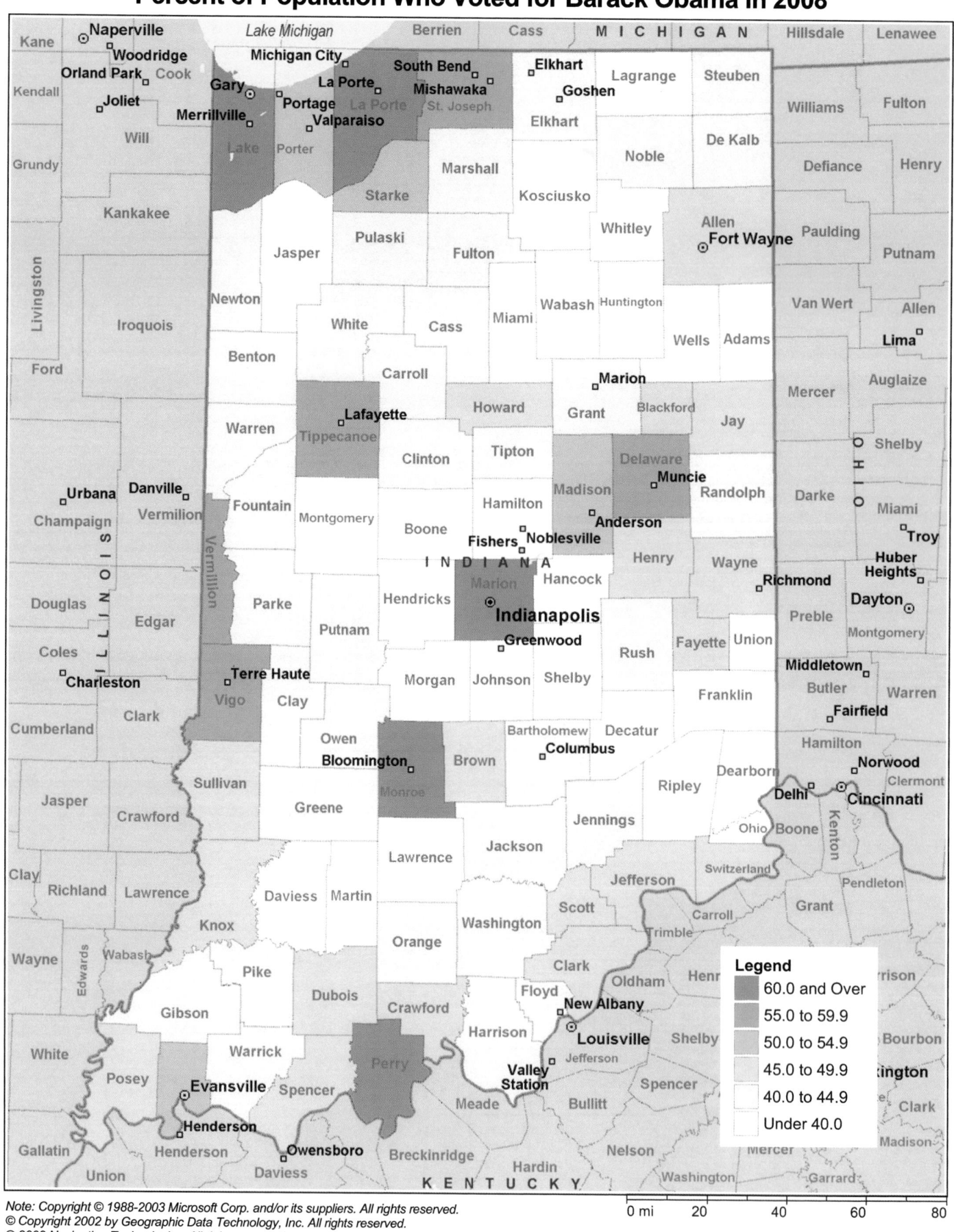

Legend

- 60.0 and Over
- 55.0 to 59.9
- 50.0 to 54.9
- 45.0 to 49.9
- 40.0 to 44.9
- Under 40.0

0 mi   20   40   60   80

Grey House Publishing
2010 Title List
Visit **www.greyhouse.com** for Product Information, Table of Contents and Sample Pages

General Reference
American Environmental Leaders: From Colonial Times to the Present
An African Biographical Dictionary
Encyclopedia of African-American Writing
Encyclopedia of American Industries
Encyclopedia of Emerging Industries
Encyclopedia of Global Industries
Encyclopedia of Gun Control & Gun Rights
Encyclopedia of Invasions & Conquests
Encyclopedia of Prisoners of War & Internment
Encyclopedia of Religion & Law in America
Encyclopedia of Rural America
Encyclopedia of the United States Cabinet, 1789-2010
Encyclopedia of Warrior Peoples & Fighting Groups
Environmental Resource Handbook
From Suffrage to the Senate: America's Political Women
Global Terror & Political Risk Assessment
Historical Dictionary of War Journalism
Human Rights in the United States
Nations of the World
Political Corruption in America
Speakers of the House of Representatives, 1789-2009
The Environmental Debate: A Documentary History
The Evolution Wars: A Guide to the Debates
The Religious Right: A Reference Handbook
The Value of a Dollar: 1860-2009
The Value of a Dollar: Colonial Era
University & College Museums, Galleries & Related Facilities
Weather America
World Cultural Leaders of the 20th & 21st Centuries
Working Americans 1880-1999 Vol. I: The Working Class
Working Americans 1880-1999 Vol. II: The Middle Class
Working Americans 1880-1999 Vol. III: The Upper Class
Working Americans 1880-1999 Vol. IV: Their Children
Working Americans 1880-2003 Vol. V: At War
Working Americans 1880-2005 Vol. VI: Women at Work
Working Americans 1880-2006 Vol. VII: Social Movements
Working Americans 1880-2007 Vol. VIII: Immigrants
Working Americans 1770-1869 Vol. IX: Revol. War to the Civil War
Working Americans 1880-2009 Vol. X: Sports & Recreation
Working Americans 1880-2010 Vol. XI: Entrepreneurs & Inventors

Bowker's Books In Print®Titles
Books In Print®
Books In Print® Supplement
American Book Publishing Record® Annual
American Book Publishing Record® Monthly
Books Out Loud™
Bowker's Complete Video Directory™
Children's Books In Print®
El-Hi Textbooks & Serials In Print®
Forthcoming Books®
Large Print Books & Serials™
Law Books & Serials In Print™
Medical & Health Care Books In Print™
Publishers, Distributors & Wholesalers of the US™
Subject Guide to Books In Print®
Subject Guide to Children's Books In Print®

Business Information
Directory of Business Information Resources
Directory of Mail Order Catalogs
Directory of Venture Capital & Private Equity Firms
Food & Beverage Market Place
Grey House Homeland Security Directory
Grey House Performing Arts Directory
Hudson's Washington News Media Contacts Directory
New York State Directory
Sports Market Place Directory
The Rauch Guides – Industry Market Research Reports

Statistics & Demographics
America's Top-Rated Cities
America's Top-Rated Small Towns & Cities
America's Top-Rated Smaller Cities
Comparative Guide to American Suburbs
Comparative Guide to Health in America
Profiles of... Series – State Handbooks

Health Information
Comparative Guide to American Hospitals
Comparative Guide to Health in America
Complete Directory for Pediatric Disorders
Complete Directory for People with Chronic Illness
Complete Directory for People with Disabilities
Complete Mental Health Directory
Directory of Health Care Group Purchasing Organizations
Directory of Hospital Personnel
HMO/PPO Directory
Medical Device Register
Older Americans Information Directory

Education Information
Charter School Movement
Comparative Guide to American Elementary & Secondary Schools
Complete Learning Disabilities Directory
Educators Resource Directory
Special Education

TheStreet.com Ratings Guides
TheStreet.com Ratings Consumer Box Set
TheStreet.com Ratings Guide to Bank Fees & Service Charges
TheStreet.com Ratings Guide to Banks & Thrifts
TheStreet.com Ratings Guide to Bond & Money Market Mutual Funds
TheStreet.com Ratings Guide to Common Stocks
TheStreet.com Ratings Guide to Credit Unions
TheStreet.com Ratings Guide to Exchange-Traded Funds
TheStreet.com Ratings Guide to Health Insurers
TheStreet.com Ratings Guide to Life & Annuity Insurers
TheStreet.com Ratings Guide to Property & Casualty Insurers
TheStreet.com Ratings Guide to Stock Mutual Funds
TheStreet.com Ratings Ultimate Guided Tour of Stock Investing

Canadian General Reference
Associations Canada
Canadian Almanac & Directory
Canadian Environmental Resource Guide
Canadian Parliamentary Guide
Financial Services Canada
History of Canada
Libraries Canada

Grey House Publishing
4919 Route 22, PO Box 56, Amenia NY 12501-0056 | (800) 562-2139 | www.greyhouse.com | books@greyhouse.com